/*Younger Than Jesus*/ Artist Directory

The essential handbook to a new generation of artists

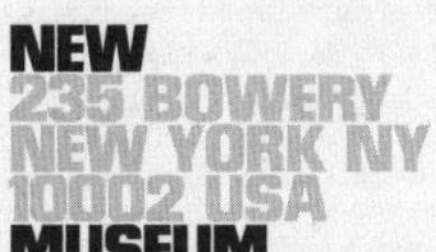

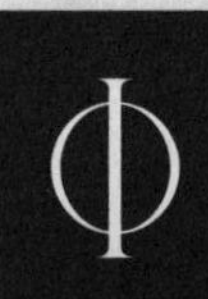

Phaidon Press Limited
Regent's Wharf
All Saints Street
London N1 9PA

Phaidon Press Inc.
180 Varick Street
New York, NY 10014

www.phaidon.com

First published 2009
©2009 Phaidon Press Limited
All works are © the artists

ISBN: 9 780 7148 4981 2

A CIP catalogue record of this book
is available from the British Library

All rights reserved. No part of
this publication may be reproduced,
stored in a retrieval system or
transmitted in any form or by any
means, electronic, mechanical,
photocopying, recording
or otherwise, without the written
permission of Phaidon Press Ltd.

Designed by Sonya Dyakova
with Karishma Rafferty

Typeset in Bell Centennial, designed
by Mathew Carter for AT&T.

Printed in China

Picture credits

Works of art in this book have been provided in most cases by the artists or their representatives. Every effort has been made to secure all permissions, and we apologize for any inadvertent errors or omissions.

Abbas Artium and Green Cardamom, London
Abney Neumann Family Collection; Rubell Family Collection; Mr. and Mrs. Arnold Lehman Collection; Schorr Family Collection Kravets/Wehby Gallery, New York
Acevedo Velarde Galeria Leme, São Paulo
Arakawa Reena Spaulings Fine Art, New York
Arcangel Team Gallery, New York
Armstrong Michael Lett, Auckland
Assaël Galleria Zero..., Milan
Bader Rivington Arms, New York
Baker Foxy Production, New York
Barateiro Galeria Pedro Cera, Lisbon
Basualdo Esteban Tedesco Collection; Bienal De Pontevedra, Spain, 2006
Beckett T293, Naples; Lüttgenmeijer, Berlin; Bürofriedrich, Berlin Germany
Bell-Smith Foxy Production, New York
Bestue and Vives Galeria Estrany-de La Mota, Barcelona; Maribel López Gallery, Berlin
Blightman Hotel, London
Bonil La Central Gallery Collection, Bogotá
Bonillas Galeria OMR, Mexico City
Bopape De Ateliers, Amsterdam
Bruce High Quality Foundation Collection of Francisco Pellizzi; Francisco Clemente Collection; Collection of Phil and Shelley Aarons
Canell Mother's Tankstation, Dublin
Cao Fei Lombard-Freid Projects, New York
Carr Michael Lett, Auckland
Carron Praz-Delavallade, Paris; Eva Presenhuber, Zurich
Chambaud Collection Fond National D'art Contemporain, France
Chong Vitamin Creative Space, Beijing
Conte Van Horn, Düsseldorf; image © Daniela Steinfeld, Düsseldorf
Danz original Photo By Andrea Huyoff
Darbyshire Ibid Projects, London
Davis, N. Roberts & Tilton, Culver City, Los Angeles
Davis, P. Seventeen Gallery, London
De Magalhaes Studio Museum In Harlem, New York
De Serio Guido Costa Projects, Turin
De Soto Marta Paz; Indymedia Estrecho Hackitectura.net; Tcsextremadura Laboral, Asturias, Spain
Denny Michael Lett, Auckland
Dudeck Pari Nadimi Gallery, Toronto
Edwards Limoncello, London
Egan Mary Mary, Glasgow
Entwistle Lux Artists Film and Video, London
Ewan Ancient & Modern, London
Faitakis The Breeder, Athens
Ferris Sunday L.E.S., New York
Fowler, L. The Modern Institute/Toby Webster Ltd., Glasgow
Frazier Collections of Harvard University Fogg Art Museum, Center for Photography at Woodstock, and Samuel Dorsky Museum of Art at SUNY New Paltz; Collection of Jane U. Harris
Frei Balice Hertling, Paris
Galhotra Collection Swapan Seth and The Devi Foundation; Collection Renu Modi
Gallo Broadway 1602, New York
Gatsas James Fuentes LLC, New York
Ghani Lemmons Contemporary, New York
Greenwood Susanne Vielmetter Los Angeles Projects
Grubanov Loock, Berlin
Gupta Galleryske, Bangalore
Gusmão Instituto das Artes, Ministério da Cultura, ZDB, Lisbon
Hansdottir Collection National Gallery of Iceland
Heinz Galerie Sandra Bürgel, Berlin
Henda Sindika Dokolo Collection
Herrero Sies + Höke Galerie, Düsseldorf
Hetherington Mary Mary, Glasgow
Hung Postmasters Gallery, New York
Johne Galerie Christian Nagel, Cologne/Berlin
Johnson, S. Julie Saul Gallery, New York
Jones, J. Project Art Centre Dublin Ballymun, Dublin
Kadan Luigi Pecci Centre, Prato, Italy; FAIT Gallery, Krakow
Kaneuji Kodama Gallery, Tokyo and Osaka
Karmakar Galerie Mirchandani + Steinrueke, Mumbai
Kessler Lombard-Freid Projects, New York
Kirschner Hollybush Gardens, London
Koh Peres Projects, Berlin/Los Angeles
Komad Gallery Krinzinger, Vienna
Letelier Citypulse Collection
Liang Yuanwei Collection Ulli Sigg, Switzerland; White Rabbit Collection, Sydney
Liden Reena Spaulings Fine Art, New York
Linares Trápaga Hackett Collection
Lieske Galerie Daniel Buchholz, Cologne/Berlin
López, J. La Fábrica, Madrid
López, M. Galeria Casas Riegner, Bogotá
Lorrenzen Project Gentili, Prato, Italy
Macari Workplace Gallery, Gateshead, Uk
Madani Lombard-Freid Projects, New York
Magdy Newman Popiashvili Gallery, New York
Maire Hollybush Gardens; Cortex Athletico, Bordeaux
McKenzie Redcat Gallery, Los Angeles
Meise Greene Naftali, New York
Milan Taxter & Spengemann, New York
Mntambo Michael Stevenson, Cape Town
Møller Harris Lieberman, New York; Galerie Kamm, Berlin
Moris Collection Femsa, Mexico
Mosquito We Are Here! Films
Moulton Broadway 1602, New York
Muresan Kontainer Gallery, Los Angeles; Plan B Gallery, Cluj-Napoca, Romania
Nenflidio A Gentil Carioca, Rio de Janeiro
Nilthamrong Rijksakademie van Beeldende Kunsten, Amsterdam
Nuur Martin van Zomeren
Panayiotou Rodeo Gallery, Istanbul
Pendleton Jan Shaw and Sig Heller Collection; Performa, New York
Pijnappel Galerie Juliette Jongma, Amsterdam
Pisano Ellen De Bruijne Projects, Amsterdam; Balice Hertling, Paris; Hollybush Gardens, London
Premnath Collection Devi Art Foundation, New Delhi
Prieto Nogueras Blanchard, Barcelona
Raeder Collecion Jumex, Mexico City
Rees T293, Naples
Rhodes Overduin and Kite, Los Angeles
Richardot Balice Hertling, Paris
Roach Sies + Höke, Düsseldorf
Rozendaal Collection Sebastien de Ganay
Ruiz Otis Collection Museum of Contemporary Art San Diego
Saldamando Cheech Marin Collection
Sanchez, L. Galeria Casas Riegner
Sastre Gallerie Filles du Calvaire, Paris
Satorre Galerie Xippas, Paris and Athens
Schmidt Galerie Andreas Huber, Vienna
Schroeren Galerie Sandra Bürgel, Berlin
Šedá Franco Soffiantino Arte Contemporanea, Turin
Shaw Rennie Collection, Vancouver
Singh Monitor Gallery, Rome; Ballroom, Marfa, Texas
Skála Vit Havranek
Smith, J. Luhring Augustine, New York
Smith, M. Store, London; Western Bridge, Seattle
Stricker Clages, Cologne
Tadiello T293, Naples
Thomas Jack Shainman Gallery, New York
Tirtiaux Galerie Martin Janda, Vienna
Tóthová Federico Bianchi Contemporary Art, Milan; City of Vienna
Trevisani Galerie Mehdi Chouakri, Berlin
Trushevsky Moscow House of Photography Collection, Moscow; Stella Art Foundation Collection, Moscow; Marat Guelman; Gallery Collection, Moscow
Vaerslev T293, Naples
Valentine Lisa Cooley Fine Art, New York
Van Yetter Josef Dalle Nogare Collection, Italy; Gregory Papadimitrion Collection, Greece; Galerie Micky Schubert, Berlin
Veleko Goodman Gallery, Johannesburg
Vogel Galerie Martin Janda, Vienna
Vonna-Michell Studio A © Berlin Biennial for Contemporary Art, Uwe Walter, 2008
Walker Angels, Barcelona
Randall-Weeks Collection Juan Carlos Verme
Wrinkle Collection Raymond Pettibon
Wu Ingrid Tsang Redcat Studio Series, Los Angeles
Youngblood Margo Leavin Gallery, Los Angeles
Yun Chu Uli Sigg Collection, Switzerland; The Guy & Myriam Ullens Foundation Collection
Zhilyaev Collection Moscow Modern Art Museum, Moscow
Zin Arario Gallery, Beijing, Seoul, New York
Zlomovitz Micky Schubert, Berlin

This book, published in conjunction with "The Generational: Younger Than Jesus," brings together the work of more than 500 artists – a vast pool of submissions gathered from the suggestions of curators, critics, and artists from all continents. The curators refer to it modestly as a "sourcebook," but it is in fact a concise picture (albeit in collage form) of the state of the best of emerging contemporary art in our world today.

This project has been envisioned by the curatorial team of Lauren Cornell, Massimiliano Gioni, and Laura Hoptman. They have conceived not only a book and an exhibition, but also the beginning of a new network of artists, a consolidation of art resources, and a research methodology, all inspired by the technologies that seem to drive the way members of this newest generation communicate with one another and with the world. The curators created a flexible, inclusive, and innovative structure for gathering information about young artists everywhere. The three curators called on more than 150 colleagues, who submitted material or just names of artists born after 1975 who were working in a notable manner.

Vast bodies of information are the stock in trade of our wired world, but books like this can be created only with the help of expert voices. The artists born after 1975 whose work is represented here are numerous but exemplary, because they have been carefully chosen by a group of peers who know the artistic production not only in their communities but also in the field at large. The variety is mind-boggling and includes painting, sculpture, drawing, video, film, animation, installation, performance, dance and countless hybrids of these mediums. There has been talk of late of a kind of "international Esperanto" of a style that is detectable in large international group exhibitions, but this book belies this observation, proving that although there are discernable strands of affinities among artists, there are no stylistic groupings across continents that emerge strongly enough to be called a universal trend.

This book and the accompanying exhibition inaugurate a new Triennial at the New Museum that will focus on innovative contemporary art created by the newest voices all over the world. Our time is replete with international exhibitions tied to cities, countries, or boards of curators. The New Museum Triennial is the only international show of its kind in New York and the only one dedicated to an emerging generation and a look to the future.

This project, begun barely a year ago, has been a massive challenge that the staff at the New Museum has wholeheartedly embraced. Massimiliano Gioni, Director of Special Exhibitions, has led a team that includes Lauren Cornell, Executive Director of Rhizome and Adjunct Curator at the New Museum, and Laura Hoptman, Kraus Family Senior Curator. Jarrett Gregory, Curatorial Assistant, has orchestrated the artists' materials, managing a team of dedicated researchers including Anna Clifford, Martha Kirszenbaum, and Cloé Perrone. Interns Lukas Baden and Marion Ritter were vital and got the process up and running. Karen Wong, Director of External Affairs, and Karen Hansgen, Head of Publications, organized a team of talented writers and researchers, including Rebecca Brown, Jean Dykstra, Michael Femia, Elizabeth Van Meter, Chris Wiley, and Michael Wilson; Sarah Valdez edited the whole publication.

I want to extend my deepest gratitude to the Andy Warhol Foundation for the Visual Arts, who provided an extraordinary grant to support this exhibition. A special thank you also goes to our remarkable Friends of the Generational – a group of passionate supporters who share an interest in supporting artists who are shaping the next wave – co-chaired by Maja Hoffman and Dakis Joannou. We also greatly appreciate the significant support of the Leadership Council of the New Museum, the Fundación Almine Y Bernard Ruiz-Picasso Para El Arte, the J. McSweeney and G. Mills Publications Fund, the Toby Devan Lewis Emerging Artists Exhibitions Fund, and The Robert Mapplethorpe Photography Fund.

The book would not have been possible without the partnership of Phaidon Press, to whom we owe our thanks, especially Craig Garrett, Commissioning Editor for Contemporary Art, and Lupe Núñez-Fernández, Project Editor. Finally, the New Museum salutes all the contributors and all of the participating artists for creating a book that will no doubt be an eye-opening must-read for everyone who cares about the future of contemporary art.

Lisa Phillips
Toby Devan Lewis Director
New Museum

Younger Than Jesus: Artist Directory brings together materials on over 500 artists born after 1975. This publication, an unsystematic attempt to compile the first census of a new generation, was assembled through a collective effort: more than 150 critics, curators, artists, and friends were asked to recommend younger artists whose work appears to mark a generational shift.

Based on the conviction that some of the most radical gestures in art history have been carried out by artists in the early stages of their careers, this compendium intends to amplify the signals of an emerging generation of individuals now in their twenties and early thirties.

The best artworks can seem to be written in a foreign language; it is a similar, momentary fissure between radical unfamiliarity and recognition that also characterizes generational conflicts. It is a truism that each new generation appears strange to those that came before it. Kids these days don't abide by established rules and codes: their attitudes, vocabularies, tastes, sexualities, and political leanings are threatening, complex, and, of course, fascinating to those outside of their generation. Other times, generations are less preoccupied with broadening the gap that separates them from their predecessors; they try instead to assimilate traditions and repossess them quietly, succumbing to the anxiety of influence.

As German sociologist Karl Mannheim wrote in his classic text "The Problem of Generations" (1928), it is through the incessant ebb and flow of generations that societies learn not to remember but to forget – to wash away the debris of history and write new narratives for the future.[1]

As in a rite of passage, **Younger Than Jesus: Artist Directory** marks the coming of age of a generation that sociologists, journalists, and marketing experts have been frantically trying to label.

In current demographic studies, the so-called Generation Y – also known as the iGeneration or simply as the Millennials – is considered to begin around 1980. People belonging to this generation are the first natives of a digital world; they have experienced first-hand the birth of the Internet, with its impact on every aspect of our lives. They have witnessed the collapse of the myth of peaceful globalization and the return of international conflict and localized violence. For some, this political deterioration has been a distant experience, with the media blitz surrounding the fall of the Berlin Wall or CNN real-time coverage of the Gulf War providing some of their first engagements with global politics. For others, the divisive shattering of regions along ethnic lines is a daily, polarizing reality. These extreme differences of experience are why generations have often been understood to grow at different speeds across different nations and continents. One underlying question in our research has been whether the impact of new technologies has been able to forge similarities between contemporaries living in geographically distant places. This is a generation for which technology is pervasive, totally connective, highly personalized, and always on shuffle. In a landscape of proliferating commercial platforms that seek to shape social exchanges, like Facebook, YouTube, or Twitter, this generation has found ways to innovate and to produce genuinely creative gestures within these readymade frames. Concomitantly, they have also found that these platforms can become defaults, limiting rather than expanding creativity, and thus have used them critically, or moved beyond them.

Like the spread of Gen X mania, this newest generation is attracting enormous attention in popular culture, politics, and economics. As with Gen X, the curiosity surrounding the Millennials has to do with the need to predict their behaviors as consumers. But there is evidence that this generation might enact a significant change beyond the prophecies of marketing experts and trend spotters.

With a population of roughly 95 million in the United States alone, the Millennials comprise the largest generation since the baby boomers. By 2016 they will make up a third of the voting population, and statistics show their opinions differ from their elders. Strong majorities of young Americans, for example, advocate greatly increased support of issues surrounding sexuality, immigration, and gay rights.[2]

Whether such changes in generational outlook may find an equivalent in the field of visual art is the question this publication raises. Part yearbook, part search engine, in its very structure **Younger Than Jesus: Artist Directory** relies on a participatory model that resonates with contemporary communication tools. Assembled with the help of twenty correspondents active in different nations and contexts and with the support of a group of more than 150 informal advisors, this book could be described both as a plebiscite and a social network. Pure information overload, **Younger Than Jesus** is an idiosyncratic lexicon rather than an encyclopedia. It is excessive, inclusive, and nonhierarchical – more personal and emotional than systematic.

In its extreme diversity, this large collection of works gives credence to what Karl Mannheim described nearly a century ago: that generations create within themselves multiple, often contradictory tensions, sharing common practices and beliefs, but also points of divergence and radical differences. This group might be a choir, but it is a dissonant one. Or, as Martin Heidegger wrote, "the inescapable fate of living in and with one's generation completes the full drama of individual human existence."[3]

Lauren Cornell, Massimiliano Gioni, and Laura Hoptman
New Museum

1. Karl Mannheim, "The Problem of Generations" in Essays on the Sociology of Knowledge, Routledge, New York, 1928/1952 and 1957

2. PEW Research Center, "A Portrait of 'Generation Next': How Young People View Their Lives, Futures and Politics," 9 January, 2007, http://people-press.org/report/300/a-portrait-of-generation-next

3. Martin Heidegger, Being and Time, trans. John Macquarrie and Edward Robinson, SCM Press, London, 1962

The curatorial team asked each of these 150 curators, teachers, critics and artists, known for their work with and knowledge of emerging artists, to recommend three young artists who they felt represented a generational shift in contemporary art. Ten correspondents were asked for more focused and extensive research, each one suggesting up to twenty artists.

Ateqqa Ali
Assistant Professor, Department of Communication and Cultural Studies, National College of Art, Lahore, Pakistan

Markus Andresson
curator and filmmaker, Reykjavik

Nadja Argyropoulou
Curator, 2009 Athens Biennial

Negar Azimi (correspondent)
Senior Editor, Bidoun Magazine, New York

Sonia Becce
curator; member of Advisory Committee of CIFO, Buenos Aires

Tobias Berger
critic and curator, Hong Kong

Daniel Birnbaum
critic and curator; Principal at the Städelschule, Frankfurt; Director, 2009 Venice Biennale

Rob Blackson
Curator, Reg Vardy Gallery, Sunderland, UK

Francesco Bonami
Manilow Curator at Large, Museum of Contemporary Art Chicago; Curator, 2010 Whitney Biennial

Iara Boubnova
curator; Founding Director, Institute of Contemporary Art, Sofia

Nicolas Bourriaud
writer and curator, Paris; Curator, Tate Triennial 2009

AA Bronson
artist, New York

Guillermo E. Brown
jazz musician, New York

Cecilia Brunson (correspondent)
Curator, InCubo, Santiago, Chile

Rashida Bumbray
Assistant Curator, The Kitchen, New York

Rosina Cazali
critic and curator, Guatemala

Elizabeth Cerejido
artist, Miami

Luca Cerizza
art historian and curator, Berlin

Howie Chen (correspondent)
artist; Co-Founder, Dispatch, New York

Colin Chinnery
curator, artist and writer, London and Beijing

Doryun Chong (correspondent)
Associate Curator, Visual Arts, Walker Art Center, Minneapolis

Carolyn Christov-Bakargiev
Chief Curator, Castello di Rivoli, Turin; Artistic Director, Documenta 13 (2012)

Stuart Comer
Curator of Film and Events, Tate Modern, London

Sarah Cook
Curator and Co-Founder, CRUMB, Newcastle, UK

Daniell Cornell
Curator of American Art and Director of Contemporary Art Projects, Fine Arts Museums of San Francisco

Silvia Karman Cubiñá
Director and Chief Curator, Bass Museum of Art, Miami Beach

Dean Daderko
Curator, Founder and Director, Parlour Projects, Brooklyn

Régine Debatty
blogger, we-make-money-not-art.com, Italy

Ann Demeester
Director, de Appel, Amsterdam

Nikola Dietrich
Curator, MGK Basil, Frankfurt and Berlin

Corinne Diserens
curator; artistic advisor, Association Carta Blanca Editions, Marseille

Aleksandra Domanovic
Internet artist, Berlin

Abdul Dube
photographer and designer; founding member of MOPP, Cape Town

Yvette Dunn
curator, Cape Town

Yilmaz Dziewior
curator; Chair at the Hochschule fur Bildende Kunst, Hamburg

Christine Eyene (correspondent)
curator; Publishing Director, Africultures

Jacob Fabricius
curator, publisher and writer, Copenhagen

Michele Faguet (correspondent)
Founder and Director, Espacio La Rebeca, Bogotá

Cecilia Fajardo-Hill
curator and art historian, Miami

Hu Fang
Artistic Director, Vitamin Creative Space, Guangzhou

Annie Fletcher
curator, Amsterdam

Richard Flood
Chief Curator, New Museum, New York

Anna-Catharina Gebbers
curator, Berlin

Julieta González
curator, San Juan

Katerina Gregos
curator and critic, Mechelen, Germany

Ulrike Groos
writer and curator; Director, Kunsthalle Düsseldorf

Andrea Grover
curator; founding Director of Aurora Picture Show, Houston

Inti Guerrero
Curator in Residence at Capacete Entretenimentos, Rio de Janeiro

Bruce Hainley
critic and writer, Los Angeles; Contributing Editor, Artforum

Ed Halter
critic and curator; Co-Founder, Light Industry, New York

Hou Hanru
Director of Exhibitions and Public Programs and Chair of the Exhibitions and Museum Studies Program, San Francisco Art Institute

Geir Haraldseth
curator, Berlin

Vít Havránek
curator; Head, Tranzit Display Gallery, Prague

Jörg Heiser
critic; Associate Editor, Frieze, Berlin

Sirje Helme
curator and writer, Estonia

Sofia Hernández Chong Cuy
curator, New York and Paris

Jennifer Higgie
critic; Co-Editor, Frieze, London

Matthew Higgs
artist and writer; Curator and Director, White Columns, New York

Jens Hoffmann
curator and writer; Director, CCA Wattis Institute for Contemporary Arts, San Francisco

Michael Ned Holte
critic and curator, Los Angeles

Henriette Huldisch
writer and curator, Berlin; Co-Curator, 2008 Whitney Biennial

Suhjung Hur
curator and writer, Seoul

C. Krydz Ikwuemesi
painter, writer and curator, Nigeria

Gregor Jansen
art historian; Head, ZMK, Karlsruhe, Germany

Kathrin Jentjens
curator, Cologne

Gianni Jetzer
Director, Swiss Institute Contemporary Art, New York

Paddy Johnson
blogger, artfagcity.com, Brooklyn

Caitlin Jones
curator and writer, Brooklyn

Eungie Joo (correspondent)
Director and Curator of education and public programs, New Museum, New York

Aylin Kalem
curator, writer and lecturer; Co-Founder, boDig, Istanbul

Stefan Kalmár
Director, Kunstverein Munich

Xenia Kalpaktsoglou
curator; Artistic Director, XYZ, Athens

Mami Kataoka
Curator, Hayward Gallery, London; Senior Curator, Mori Art Museum, Tokyo

Inés Katzenstein
curator, critic and writer; Curator, Buenos Aires Museum of Latin American Art

Eva Khachatrian
curator; Co-Director, Department of Fine Arts at the Armenian Center for Contemporary Experimental Art, Yerevan

Heejin Kim
Curator, Insa Art Space, Seoul

Udo Kittelmann
Director, Nationalgalerie, Berlin

Guillermo Kuitca
artist, Buenos Aires

Lisette Lagnado
curator and writer, São Paulo

Thomas Lawson
Dean, California Institute of Arts, Valencia

Olia Lialina
Internet artist, theorist, and curator, Stuttgart

Arshiya Lokhandwala
curator and critic, Founder of Lakeeren Contemporary Art Gallery, Mumbai

Raimundas Malasauskas
Curator, Artists Space, New York

Francesco Manacorda
Curator, Barbican Art Gallery, London

Chus Martínez
Curator, MACBA, Barcelona

Midori Matsui
curator and art historian, Tokyo

Gerald Matt
Director, Kunsthalle Wien

Gene McHugh
Editorial Fellow, Rhizome, New York

Mariangela Méndez
critic and curator, Bogotá

Mihnea Mircan
Curator, National Museum of Contemporary Art, Bucharest

Viktor Misiano
curator and art historian; Editor in Chief, Moscow Magazine

Akiko Miyake
writer and curator; Co-Founder and Programme director, Center for Contemporary Art, Kitakyushu, Japan

Naeem Mohaiemen
artist and writer, Dhaka and New York

Stephanie Moisdon
critic and curator; Co-Founder BDV (Bureau des vidéos); Chief Editor, Frog Magazine; lecturer, University of Lausanne, Switzerland

Jessica Morgan
Curator of Contemporary Art, Tate Modern, London

Tom Morton
Curator, Hayward Gallery, London; Contributing Editor, Frieze Magazine

Tumelo Mosaka
Associate Curator of Exhibitions, Brooklyn Museum

Gerardo Mosquera
curator, critic and art historian, Havana; Adjunct Curator, New Museum, New York

Ceci Moss
writer, musician, DJ, and curator; Senior Editor, Rhizome, New York

Hanne Mugaas
curator and writer, New York

Edi Muka
curator, Tirana and Stockholm; Co-Founder and Co-Director, Tirana Biennale; Lecturer, Academy of Fine Arts, Tirana

Jorge Munguía Matute
Curator of Education, Museo Tamayo Art Contemporaneo, Mexico City

Will Munro
artist, Toronto

Joanna Mytkowska
Director, Warsaw Museum of Modern Art

Deeksha Nath (correspondent)
art historian, critic and curator, New Delhi

Hans Ulrich Obrist
curator and writer; Co-Director of Exhibitions and Programme and Director of International Projects, Serpentine Gallery, London

Marisa Olson
artist and critic, New York

Tobias Ostrander
Contemporary Curator, Museo Tamayo, Mexico City

Sean O'Toole
journalist and writer, Johannesburg; Editor, Art South Africa

Yevgeny Palamarchuk
poet, musician, curator and video-artist, Kaliningrad, Russia

Dan Perjovschi
artist and writer, Bucharest

Lisa Phillips
Toby Devan Lewis Director, New Museum, New York

Jenelle Porter
Associate Curator, Institute of Contemporary Art, Philadelphia

Alisa Prudnikova
Director, National Centre for Contemporary Arts, Ekaterinburg, Russia

Daria Pyrkina (correspondent)
Founder and Director, Moscow International Biennial of Young Art

Loyiso Qanya
Curator, Cape Africa Platform, Cape Town

Edwin Ramoran
Director of Exhibitions and Programs, Aljira, Newark

Gabriela Rangel
Director of Visual Arts, The Americas Society, New York

Yasmil Raymond
Curator, Walker Art Center, Minneapolis, Minnesota

Prerana Reddy
Director of Public Events, Queens Museum of Art, New York

Billy Rennekamp
artist, New York

Kathrin Rhomberg
curator, Vienna; Artistic Director, 2010 Berlin Biennial

Ana Riaboshenko
artist and curator, Tbilisi

José Ignacio Roca
Head of Temporary Exhibitions, Angel Arango Library, Bogotá

Astrida Rogule
Head of the Collections Department, Contemporary Art Museum, Riga

Beatrix Ruf
Director and Curator, Kunsthalle Zürich

Adrienne Samos
editor, critic and curator, Panama City

Ingrid Schaffner
Senior Curator, Institute of Contemporary Art, Philadelphia

Joe Scotland
Curator, Studio Voltaire, London

Bernhard Serexhe
Lecturer in Digital Media and Culture, Istanbul Bilgi University

Oksana Shatalova
artist, Kazakhstan

Erin Sickler
writer and curator, New York

Bisi Silva
Artistic Director, Centre for Contemporary Art, Lagos

Franklin Sirmans
Curator of Modern and Contemporary Art, Menil Collection, Houston

Paul Slocum
artist; Director and Co-Founder, And/Or Gallery, Dallas

Polly Staple (correspondent)
Director, Chisenhale Gallery, London

Ali Subotnick
writer; Adjunct Curator, Hammer Museum, Los Angeles

Astria Suparak
Director, Miller Gallery, Carnegie Mellon University, Pittsburgh

Adam Szymczyk
Director, Kunsthalle Basel

Lanka Tattersall
curator, New York

Nato Thompson
Curator and Producer, Creative Time, New York

Philip Tinari
writer and curator; Director, Office for Discourse Engineering, Bejing; Contributing Editor, Artforum

Rirkrit Tiravanija
artist and curator, New York and Thailand

Elena Tsvetaeva
Director, National Centre for Contemporary Arts, Kaliningrad, Russia

Ijeoma Loren Uche-Okeke
artist and curator, Johannesburg

Marc-Olivier Wahler
curator and writer; Director, Palais de Tokyo, Paris

William Wells
Founder and Director, Townhouse Gallery, Cairo, Egypt

Matt Wolf
filmmaker, New York

Rein Wolfs
Artistic Director, Kunsthalle Fridericianum, Kassel, Germany

Andrew Jeffrey Wright
Founding Member, Philadelphia's Space 1026

Elena Yaichnikova
curator, Moscow and Paris

Wendy Yao
artist; owner, book/zine store Ooga Booga, Los Angeles

What, How & For Whom (WHW)
Curatorial collective, Zagreb, Croatia; Curators, 2009 Istanbul Biennial

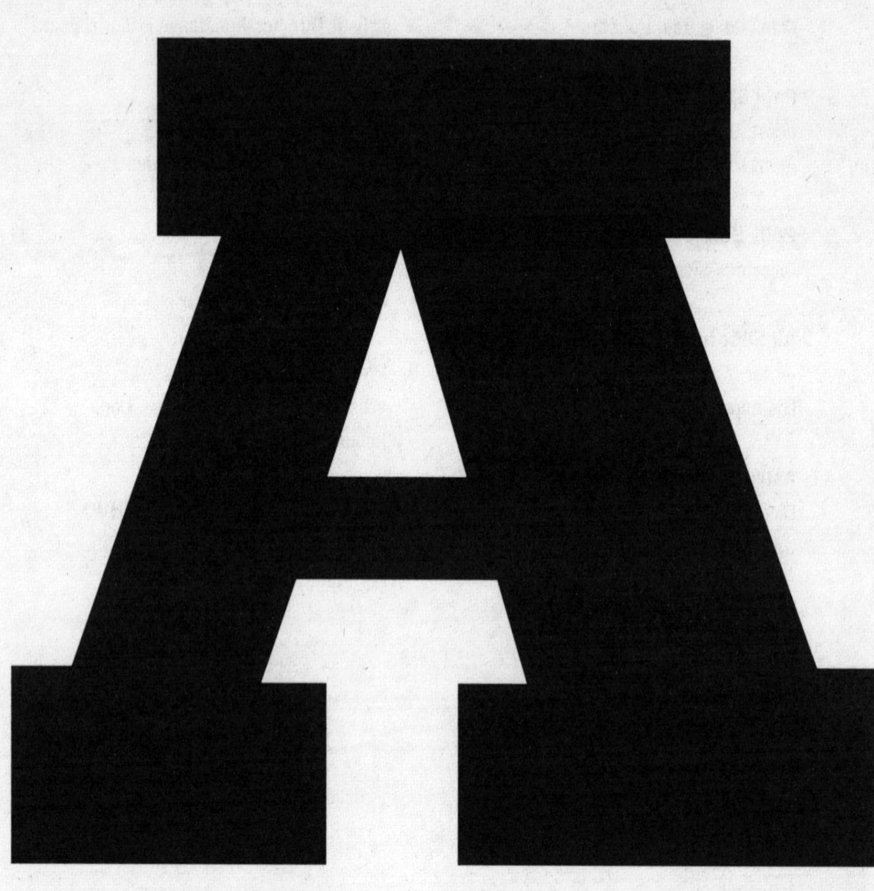

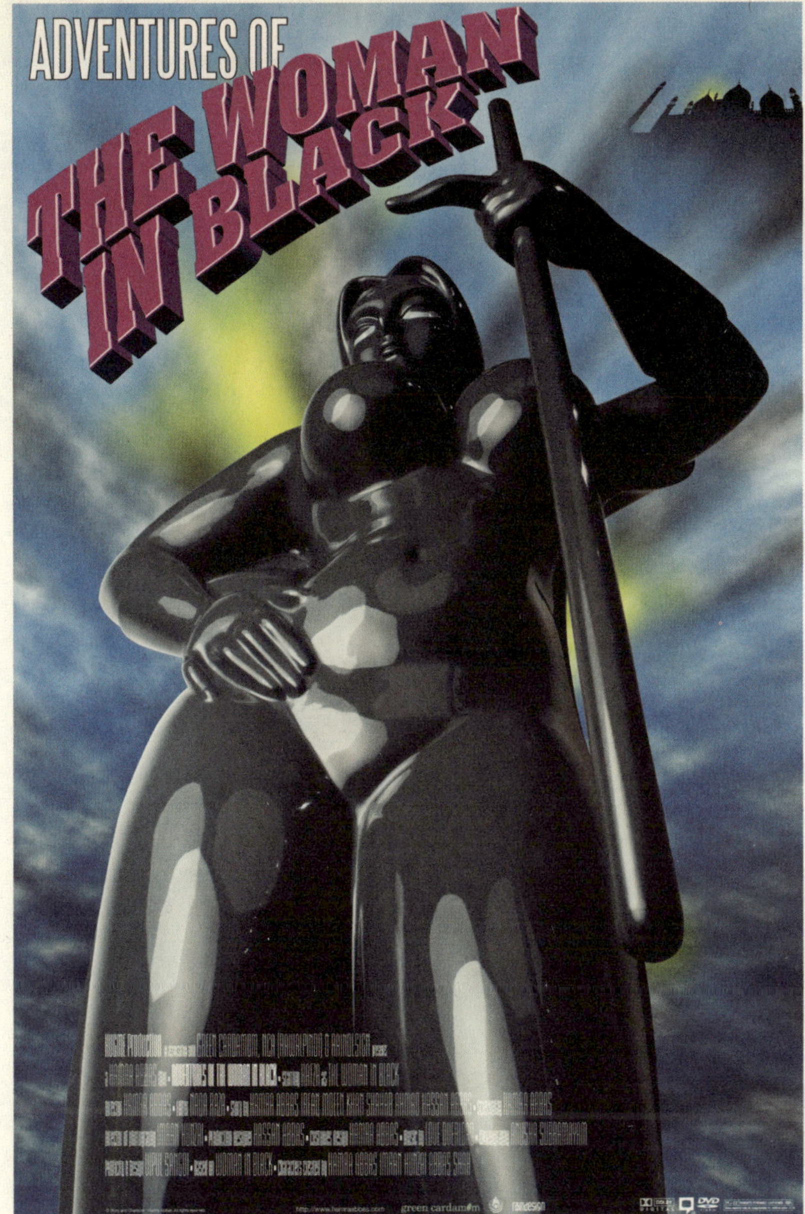

1.

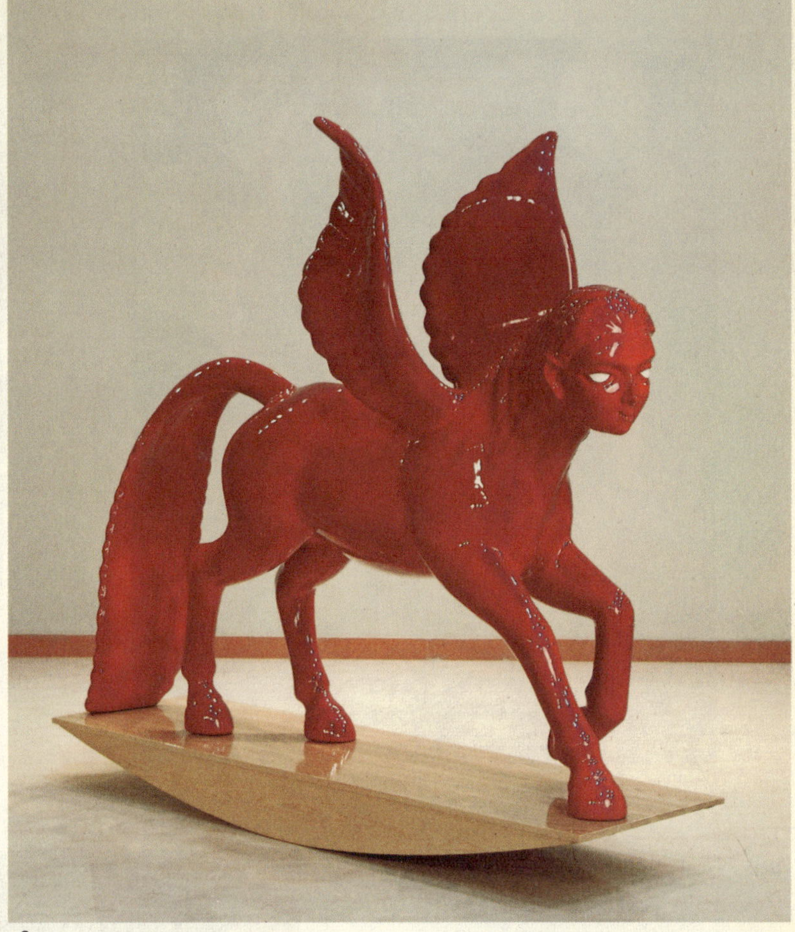
2.

Hamra Abbas studied at the National College of Arts, Lahore, and the Universität der Künste, Berlin. Based in Islamabad, Pakistan, she fuses religious and cultural traditions of the East and West in sculpture, installation, and animation. The series **Lessons on Love**, shown at the 10th Istanbul Biennial in 2007, reimagines figures from Persian miniature paintings as plasticine sculptures making love while armed with weapons.

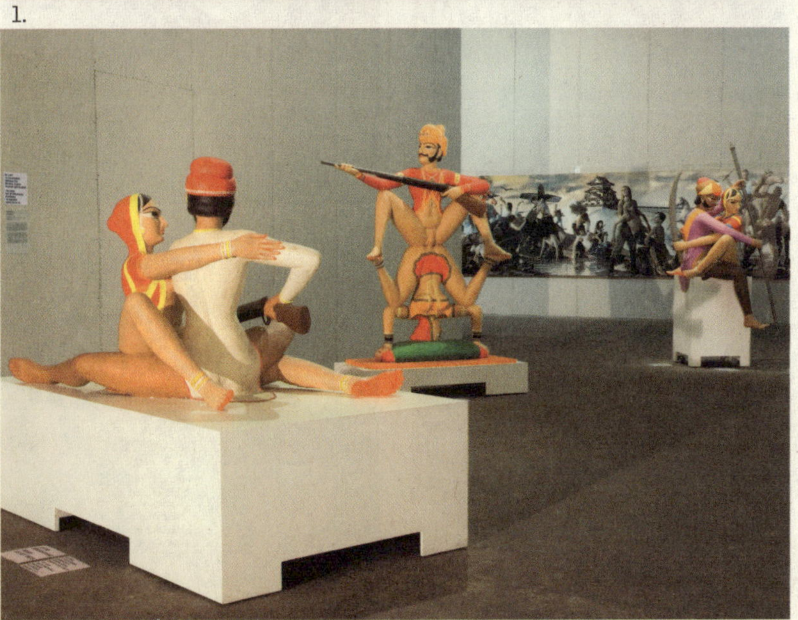
3.

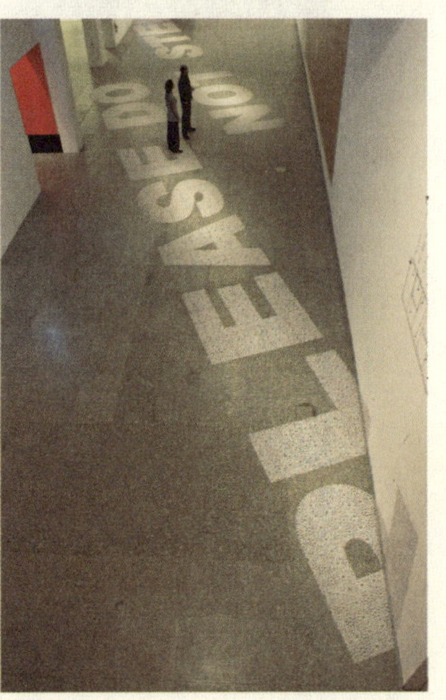

4.

1. **Woman in Black**
2008, chromogenic print, 60 × 36 in (152 × 91cm)

2. **Ride**
2008, painted fiberglass, 80 × 93 × 32 in (203 × 236 × 81 cm)

3. **Lessons on Love**
2007, plasticine, dimensions variable

4. **Please Do Not Step 2**
2008, collage, length approx 100 ft (31 m)

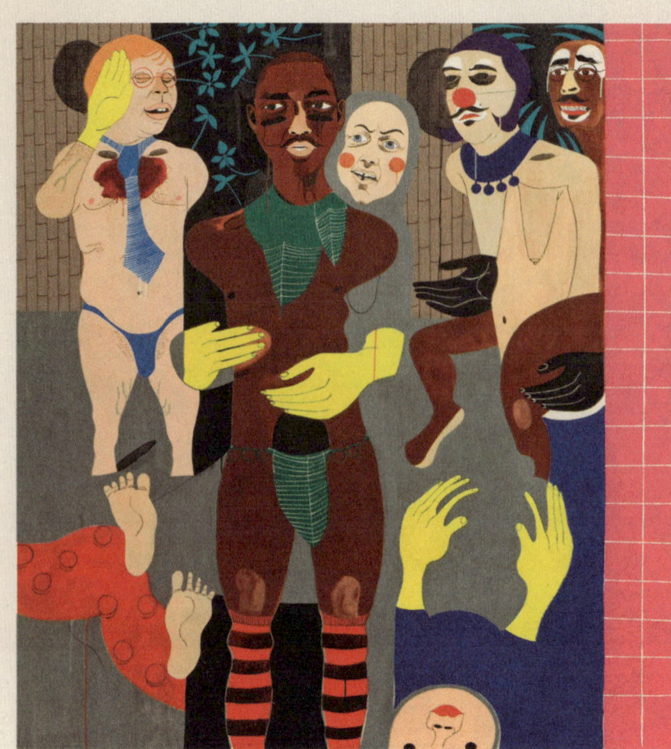
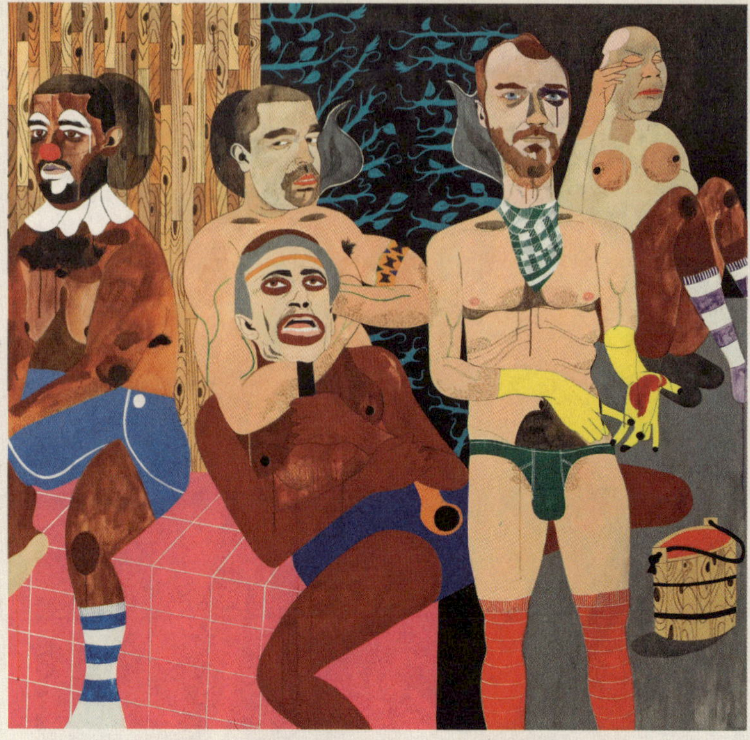

1.

Nina Chanel Abney earned her MFA from Parsons: The New School for Design in New York, where she continues to live. Often using friends and family as models, she paints explosive figurative scenes that refer to history painting and political caricature. Contemporary race relations and stereotypes were among the primary themes of her debut exhibition in 2008.

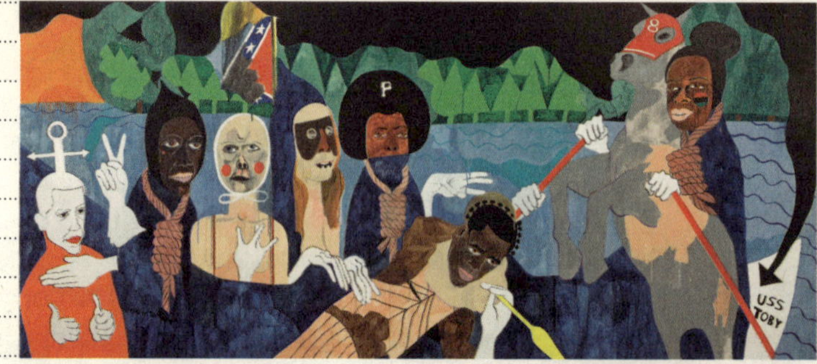

2.

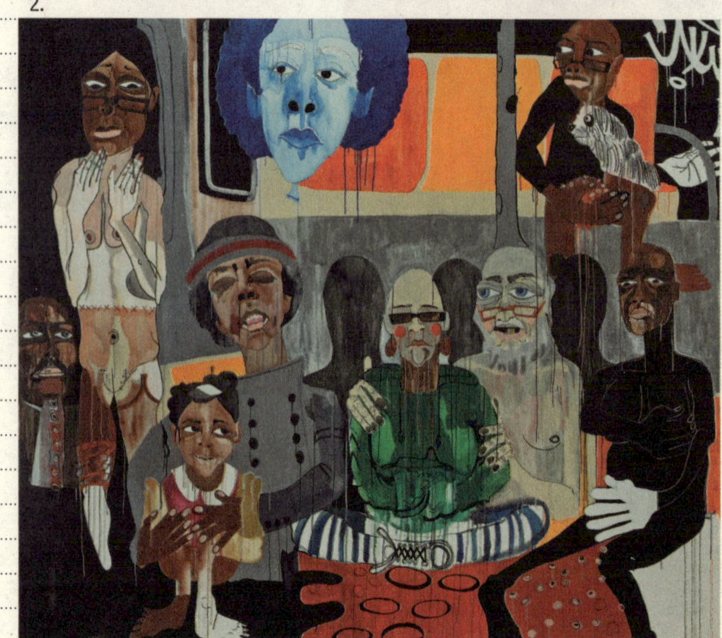

4.

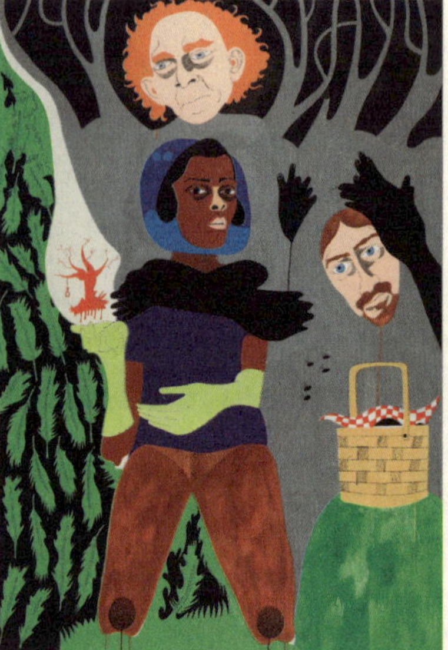

3.

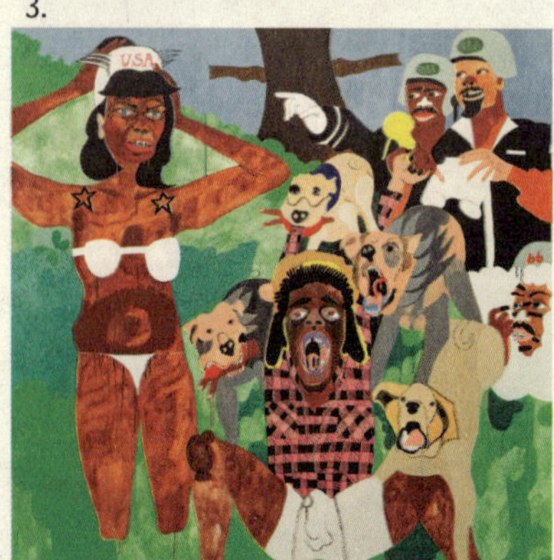

5.

1. The Boardroom
2008, acrylic on canvas, 2 panels, overall dimensions 77 × 153 ½ in (196 × 390 cm)

2. The Takeover
2008, acrylic on canvas, 66 × 154 in (168 × 391 cm)

3. The Money Tree
2008, acrylic on canvas, 78 ¼ × 56 in (199 × 142 cm)

4. Four Stops
2007, acrylic on canvas, 108 × 126 in (274 × 320 cm)

5. Randaleeza
2008, acrylic on canvas, 90 × 92 in (229 × 234 cm)

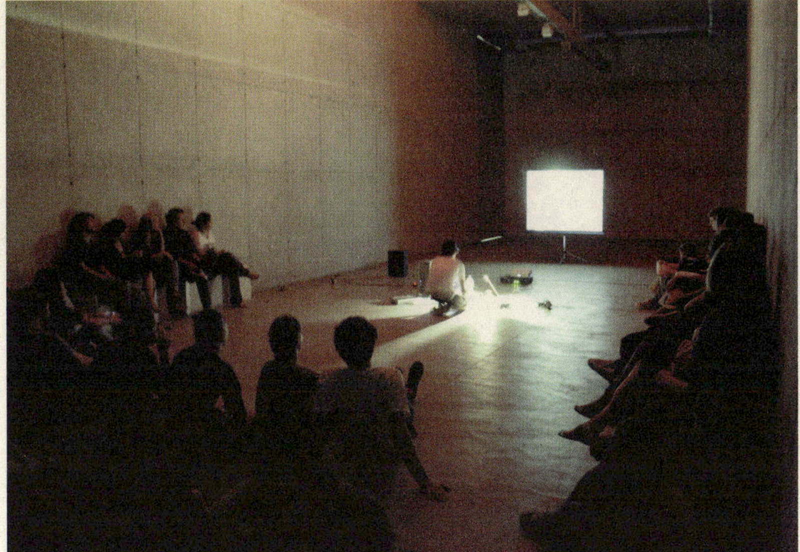

1.

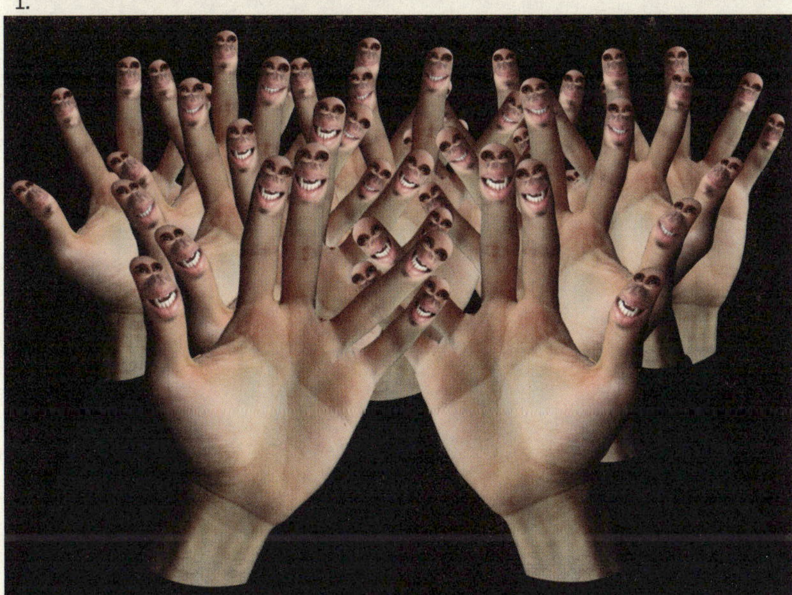

2.

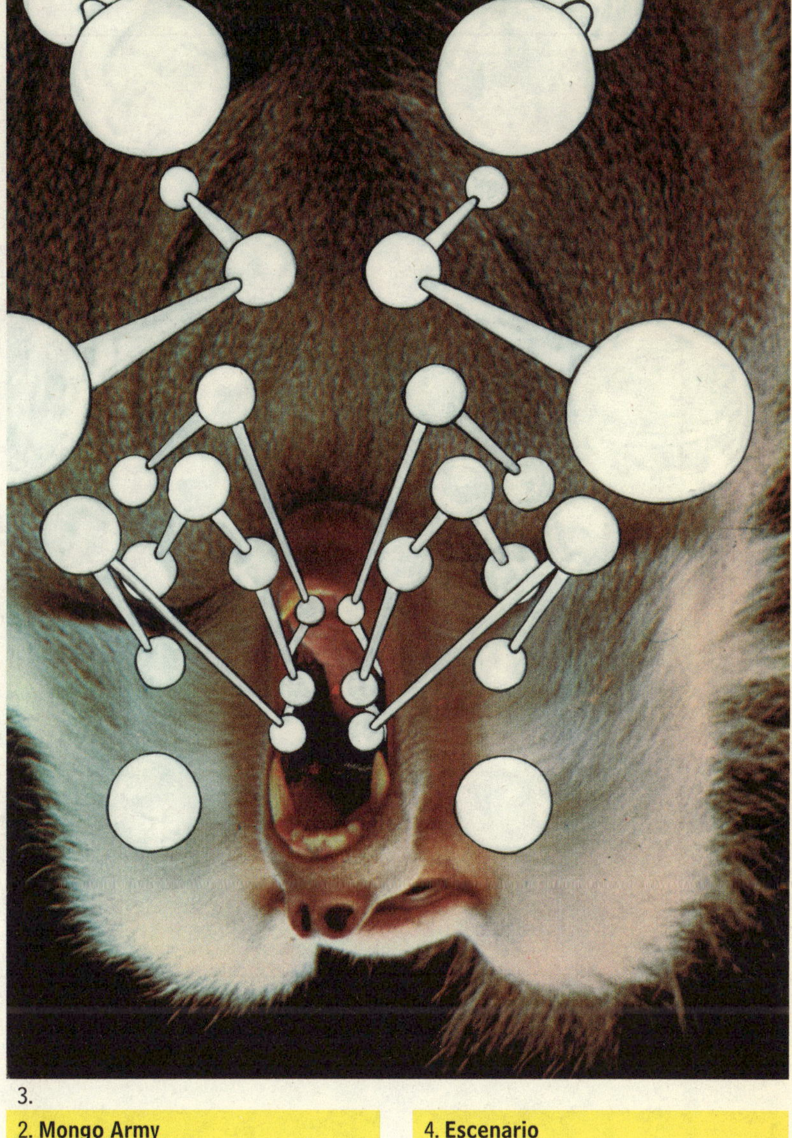

3.

Gabriel Acevedo Velarde received his BA in fine arts from Universidad de las Américas, Puebla, Mexico, and also studied in the photography department at the Instituto Gaudí in Lima. He currently lives in Mexico City and São Paulo. Using drawn animation in film and video installations, he creates parables that explore human psychology and contemporary life. Works often include an element of performance, such as live editing.

1. **Marathon 1**
2008, performance with portable screen, video projection, sound system, computer, and audio loop station, 49 min

2. **Mongo Army**
2008, animation, 3 min 20 sec

3. **Tartamudo**
2006, pen and gouache on magazine paper, 10 × 7 in (25 × 17 cm)

4. **Escenario**
2004, animation, 3 min

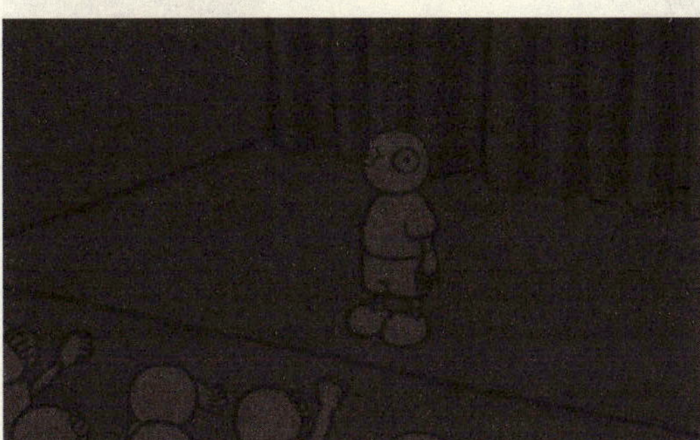

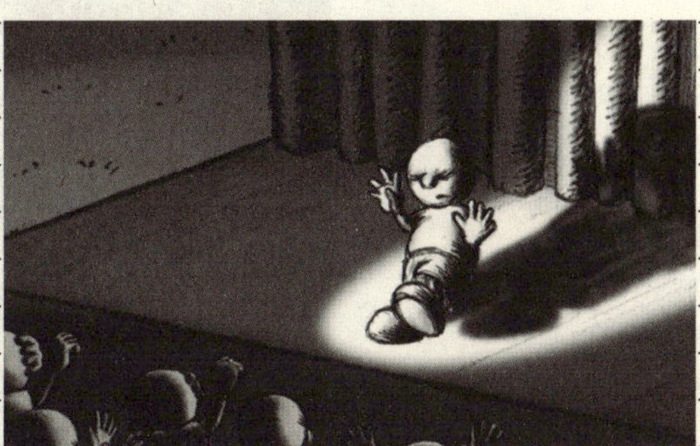

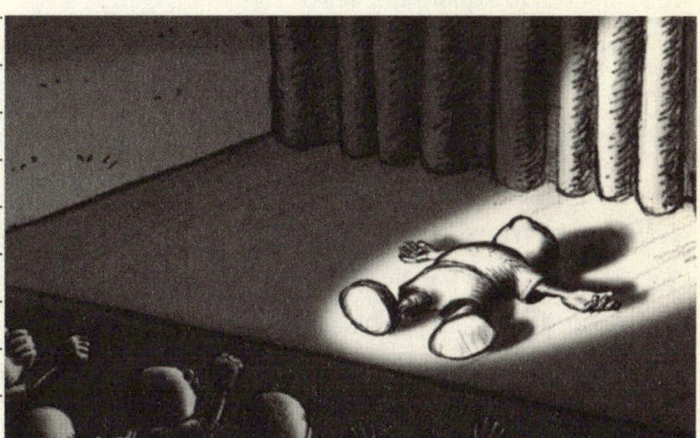

4.

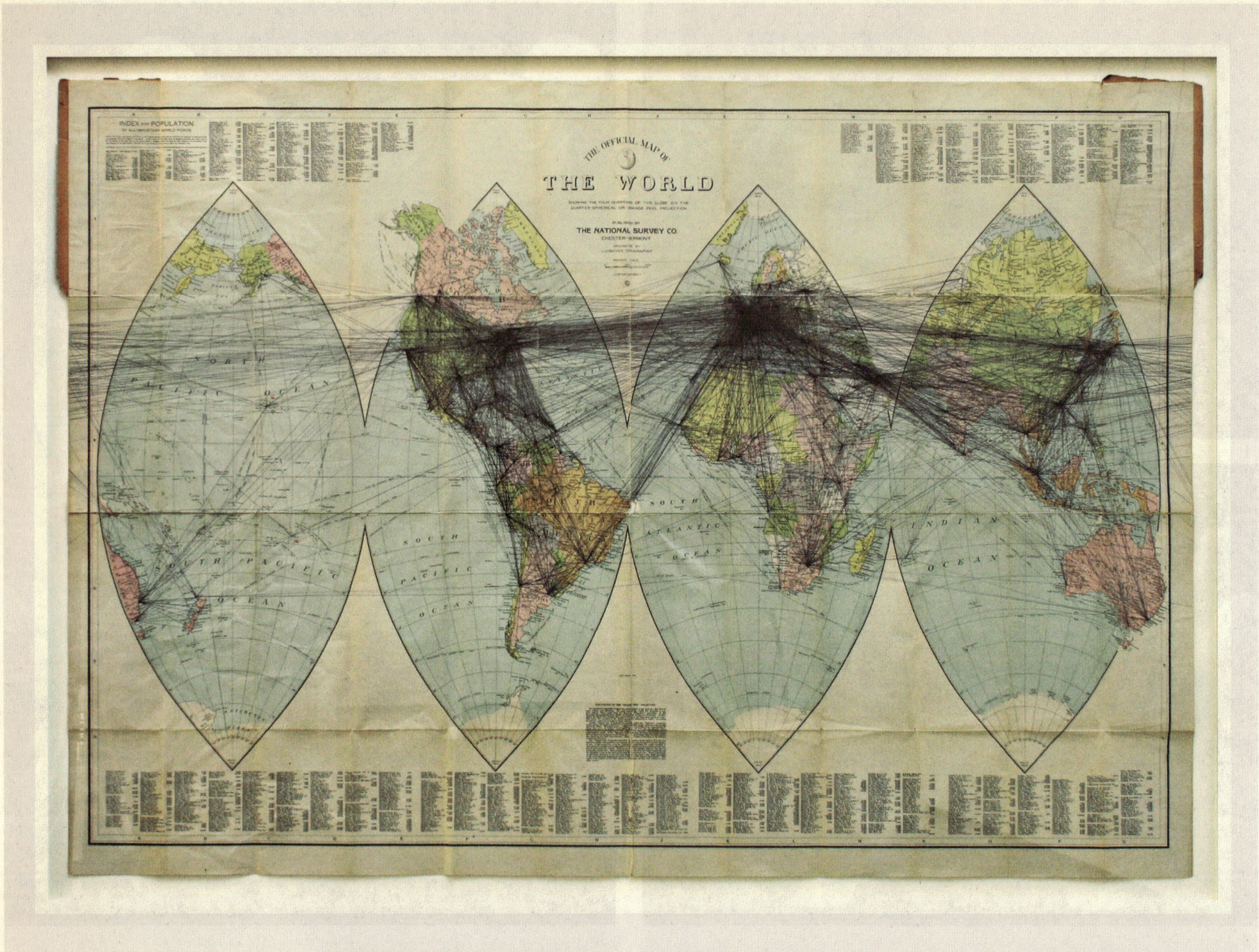

1.

Stian Ådlandsvik attended the National Academy of Fine Arts in Oslo, where he continues to live and work. A kind of artist-archaeologist, he creates drawings, photographs, and sculptures that transform and reinterpret history. Real events, objects, and images are reconfigured to explore themes of Norwegian national identity – such as the effects of Norway's massive oil resources on its people – in a global context.

1. Vision of transit from two pasts

2008, Fisher Space Pen on world map from 1920, 36 1/2 × 54 3/4 in (93 × 139 cm)

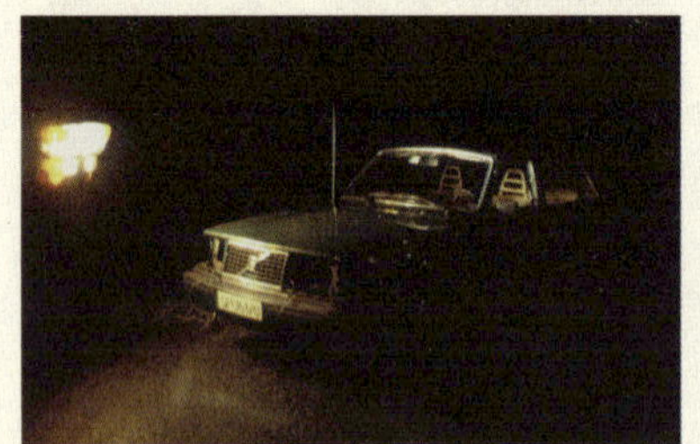

2.

2. Suddenly clear-sighted

2006, reassembled 1979 Volvo 244DL car and cables, dimensions variable

3. Illuminated transition

2008, found fabrics from Beijing construction sites, 32 1/2 × 23 × 23 in (83 × 58 × 58 cm)

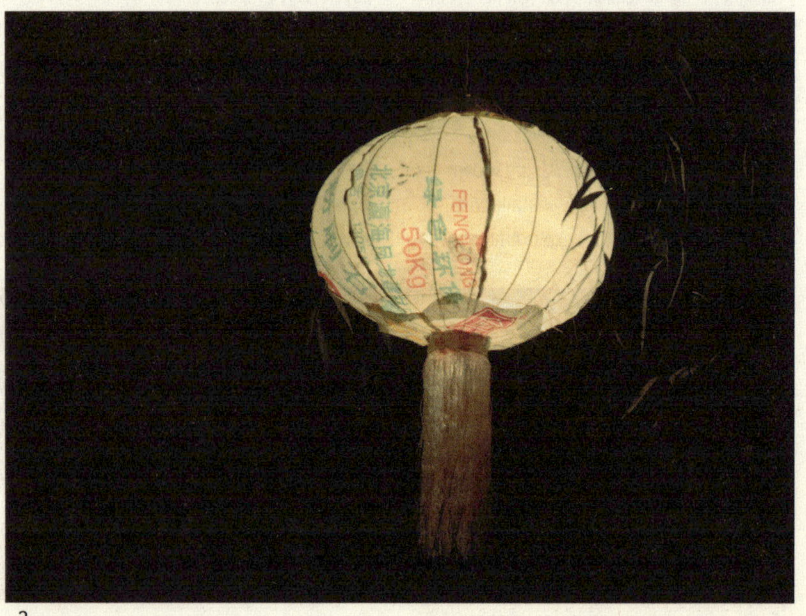

3.

AIDS-3D is a two-person artistic team consisting of Daniel Keller and Nik Kosmas. They received their BFA degrees from the School of the Art Institute of Chicago and currently live and work in Berlin. After meeting in an art therapy class for troubled youths, they joined forces to explore communication technologies and social activism. They produce objects, performance events, and also digital work, accessible through their website, AIDS-3D.com.

1. **Discarded Mask**
2008, latex fetish mask and EL panel, 11 ¾ × 11 ¾ in (30 × 30cm)

2. **OMG Obelisk**
2007, Styrofoam, wire, tape, acrylic, and fire, 118 × 19 ¾ × 19 ¾ in (300 × 50 × 50 cm)

3. **Bluetooth Hotspot**
2008, balsa wood and fire, 78 ¾ × 15 ¾ in (200 × 40 cm)

4. **Expulsion 2.0**
2008, EL wire and hot glue, 157 ½ × 74 in (400 × 190cm)

5. **The Last Cyborg**
2008, insulation foam, paint, cement dust, LEDs, and velum, 23 ½ × 47 ¼ in (60 × 120cm)

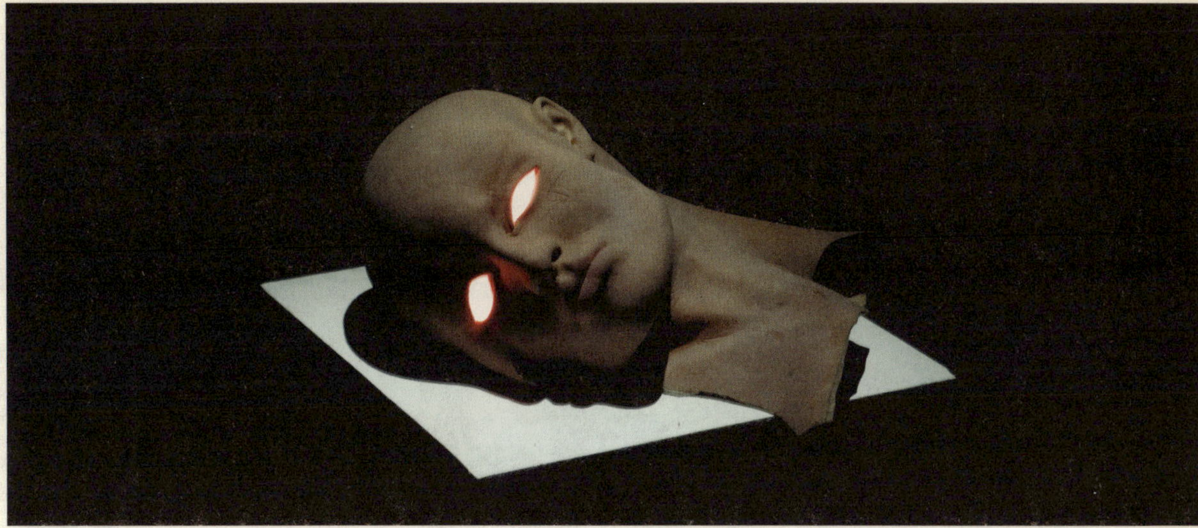

1.

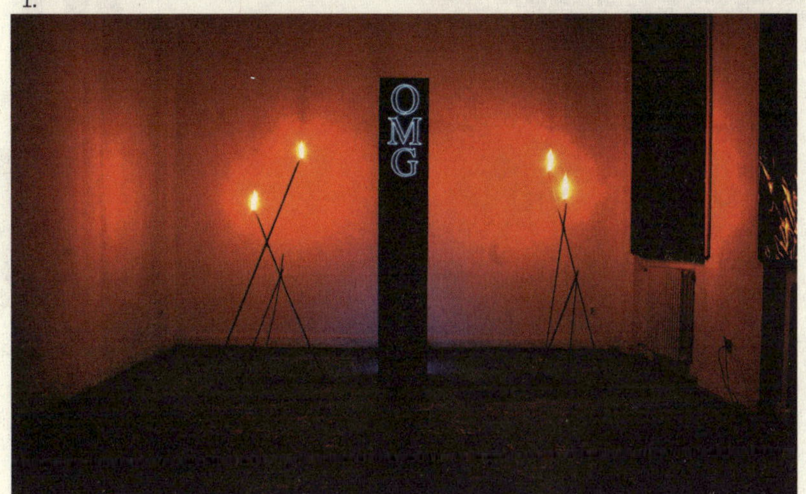

2.

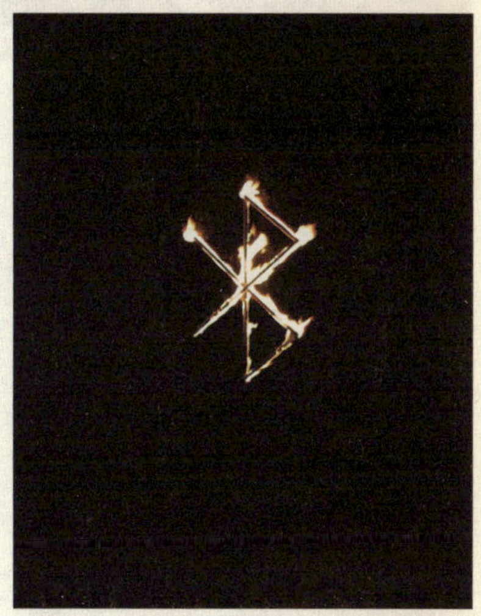

3.

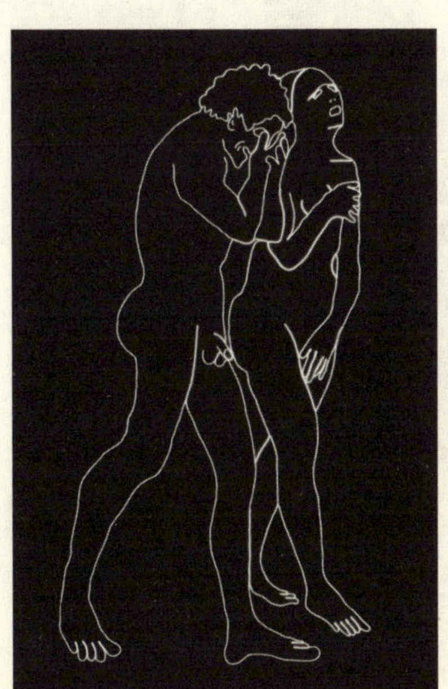

4.

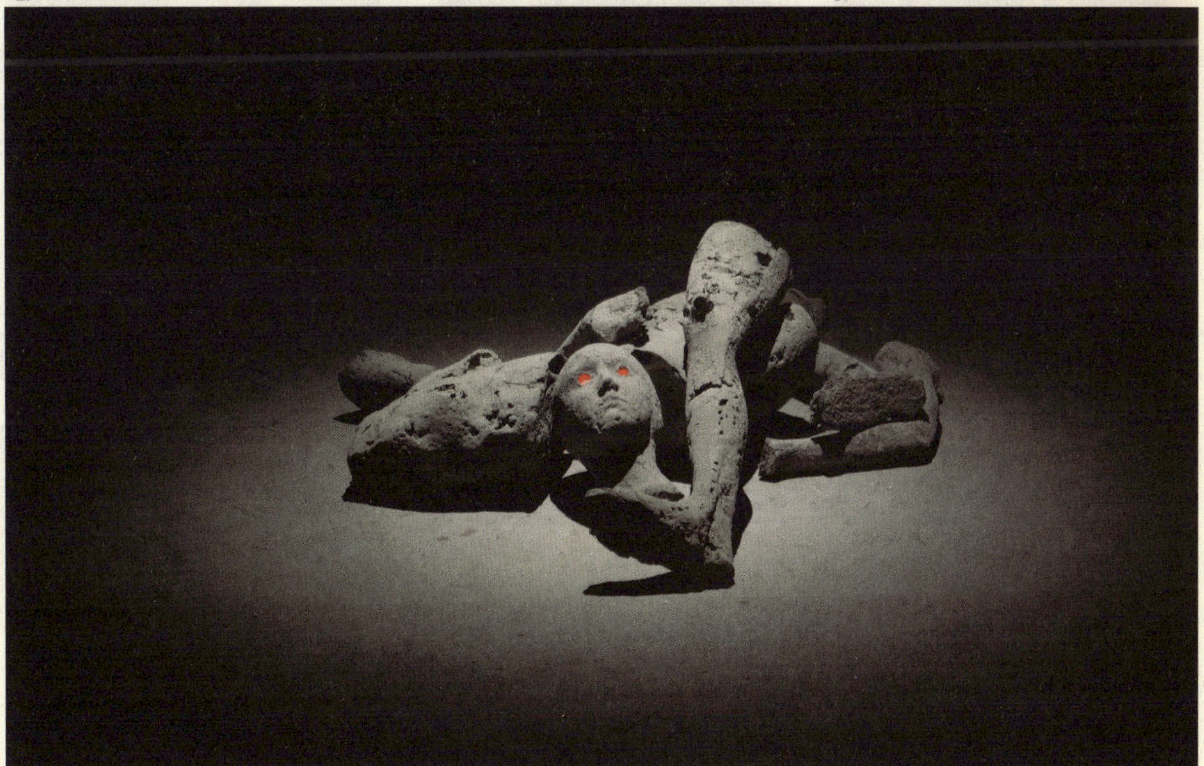

5.

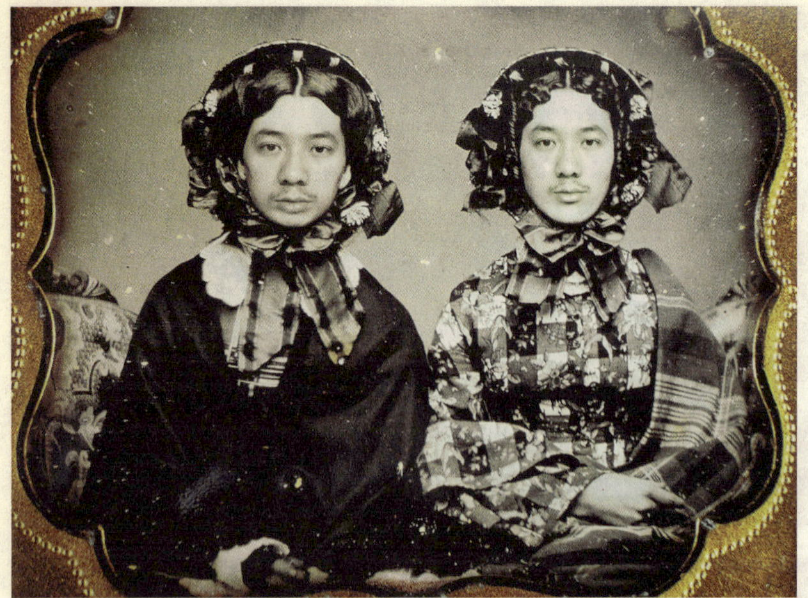

1.

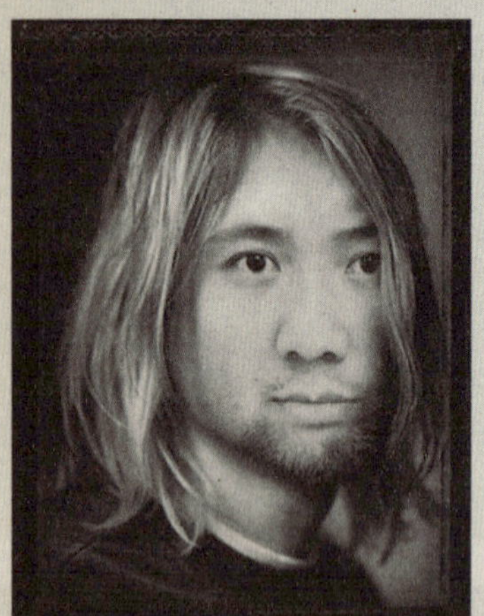

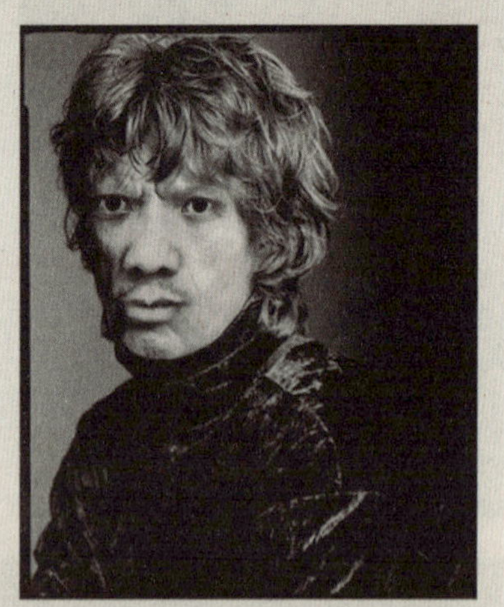

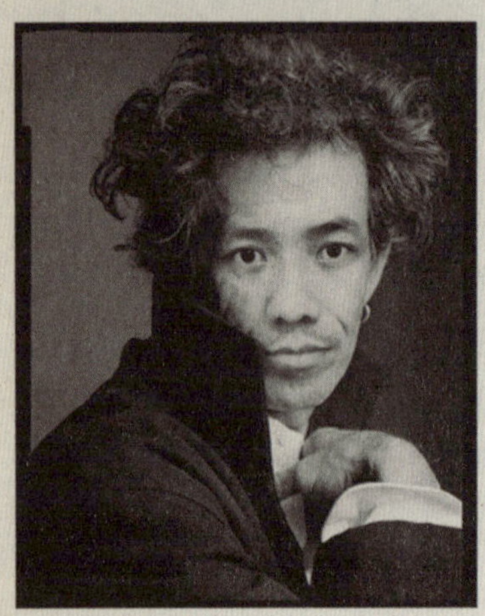

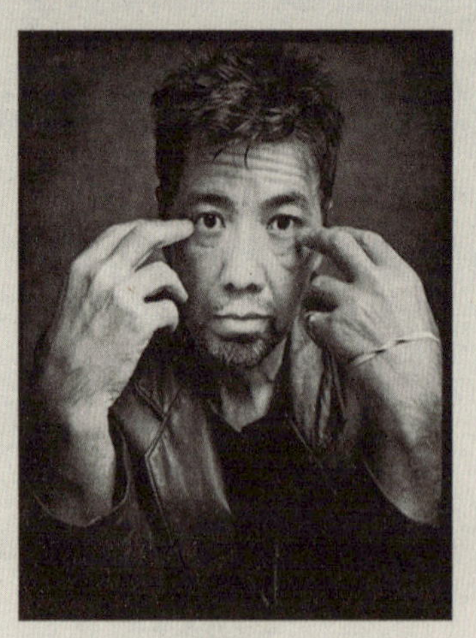

2.

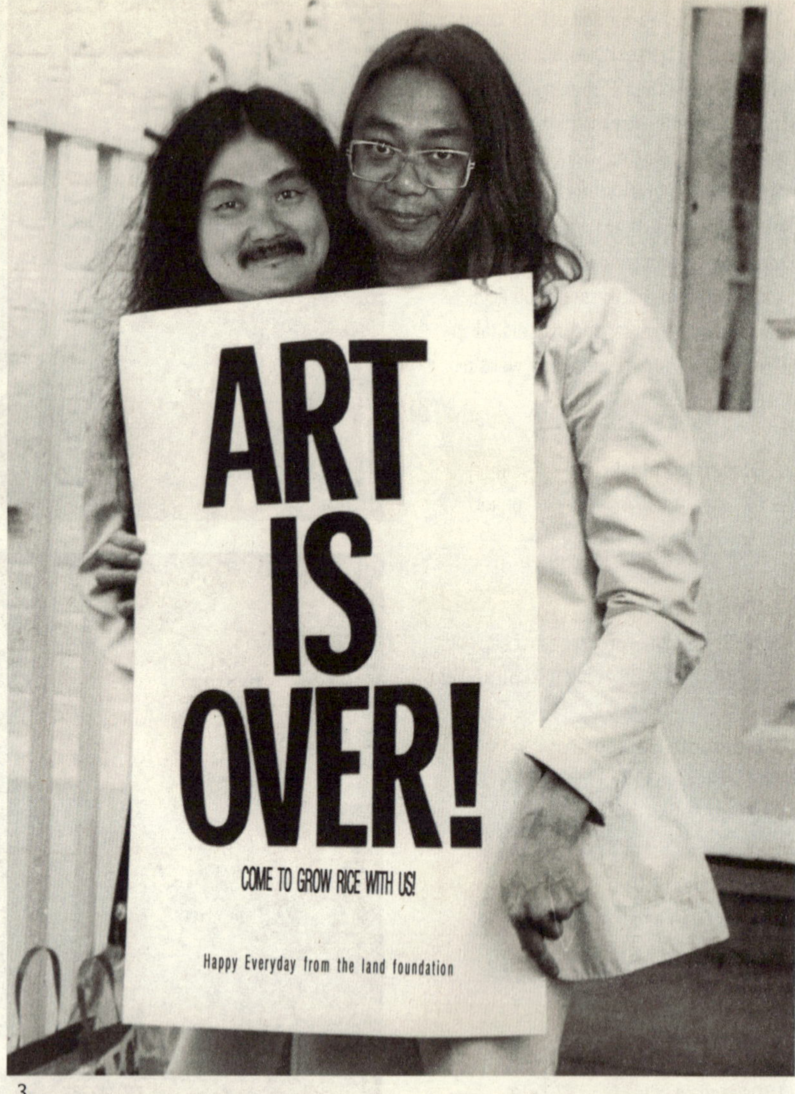

3.

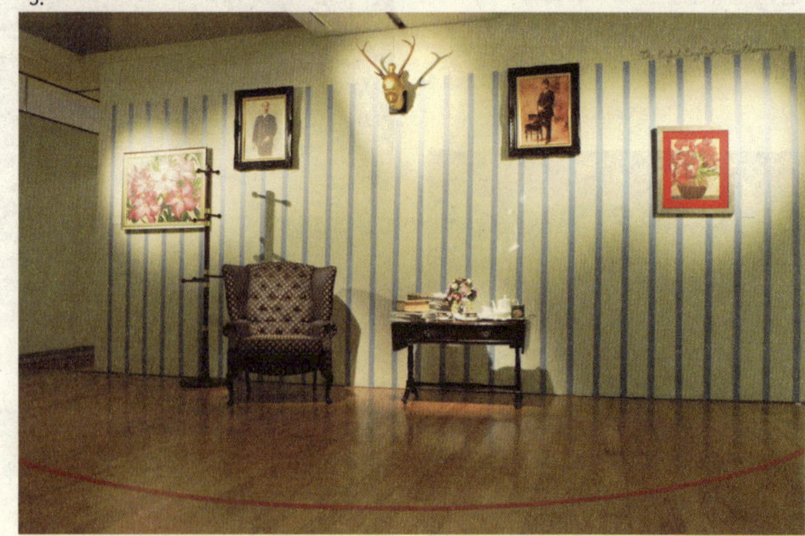

4.

Angkrit Ajchariyasophon earned his MFA in media arts and design from Chiang Mai University and currently lives in Chiang Rai, Thailand. He uses photography, installation, and performance to explore meetings of Eastern and Western cultures.

Many works portray satiric assimilation with the West, such as **The Perfect English Gentleman** (2006), which documents the artist's personal transformation into this particular Western identity.

1 & 2. **Westernized**
2008, digital images, dimensions variable

3. **Art is Over**
2007, digital image, 27 × 20 in (60 × 50 cm)

4. **The Perfect English Gentleman**
2006, mixed media, dimensions variable, installation view at "Platform," the Queens Gallery, Bangkok

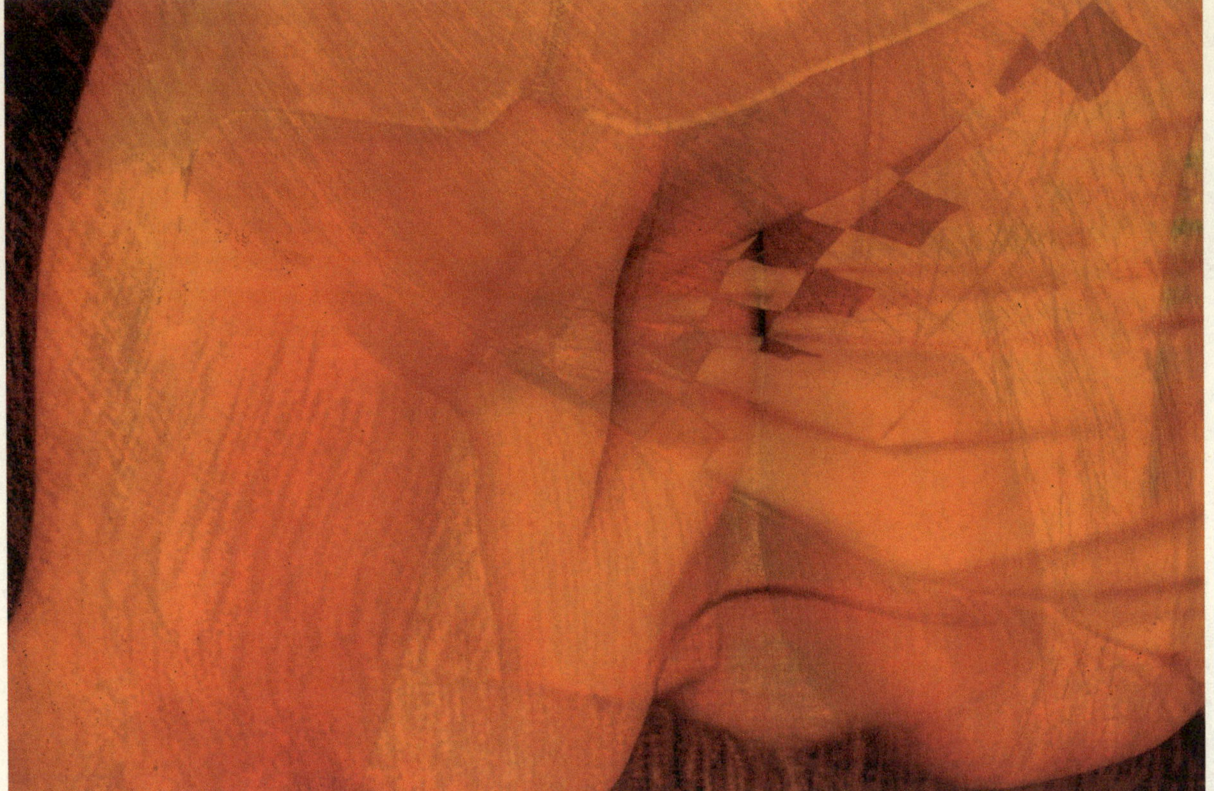

1.

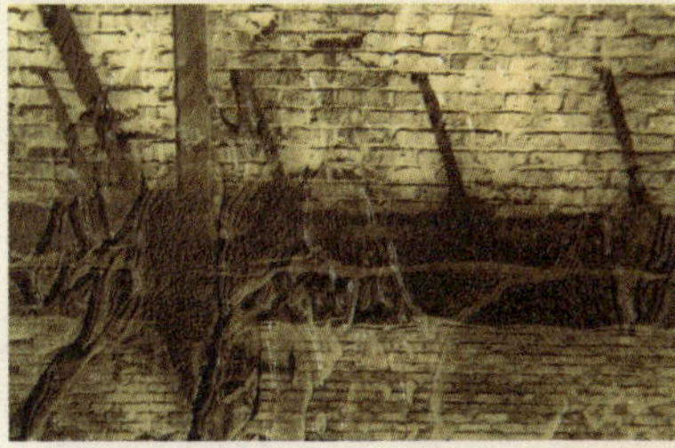

2.

Ahmet Atif Akin lives and works in Istanbul. His photographs, videos, and sculptural installations often reflect his training in industrial design, depending on techniques developed in the context of, for example, engineering or graphics. Akin has produced work as an individual artist, and as a member of xurban_collective.

1. Crash
2007, chromogenic print, 12 × 8 in (30 × 20 cm)

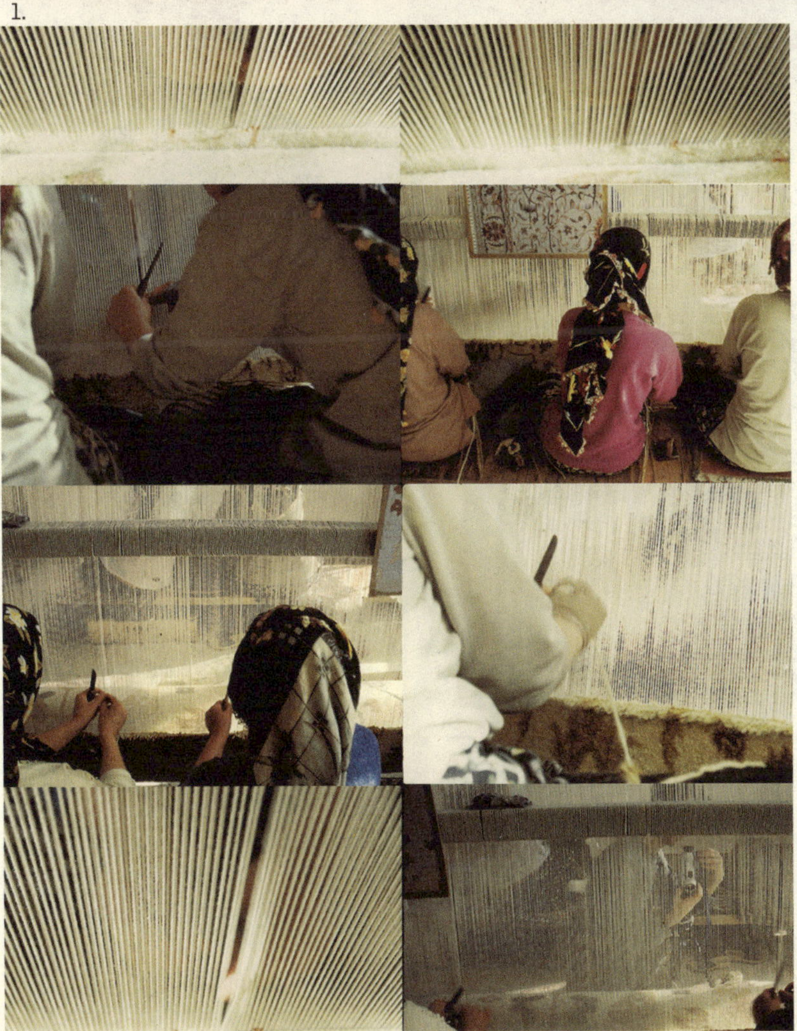

3.

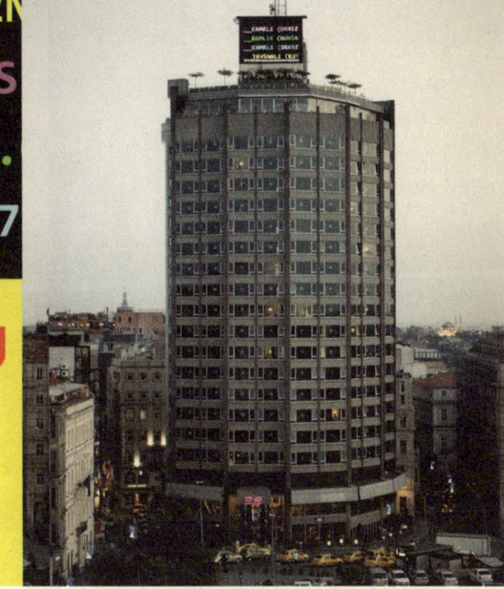

4.

2. Chemistry of Photography
2003, photo emulsion on glass, $3\frac{1}{2} \times 4 \times \frac{1}{4}$ in (9 × 10 × 1 cm)

3. Knit++
2003, film, 2 min 38 sec

4. Evacuate Istanbul
2008, urban screen, $47\frac{1}{2} \times 63$ in (120 × 160 cm)

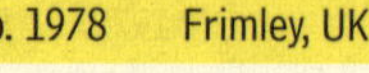

Laura Aldridge received her BA in fine art from Wimbledon School of Art, London, and her MFA from the Glasgow School of Art. She continues to live and work in Glasgow. Her sculptures feel at once natural and artificial – like the glossy but biomorphic shapes of houseplants. Emphasizing display and presentation, she creates a theaterlike "object garden" in the gallery space.

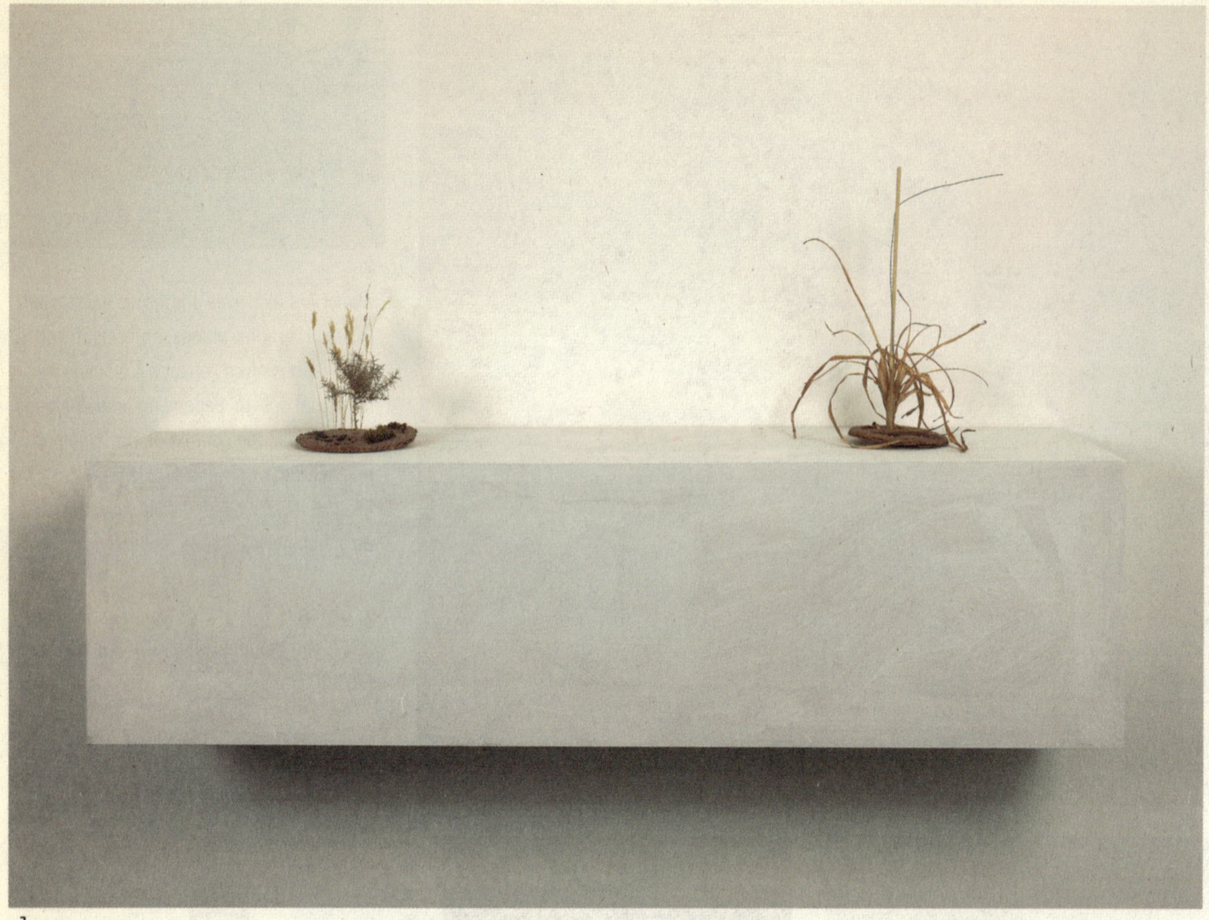

1.

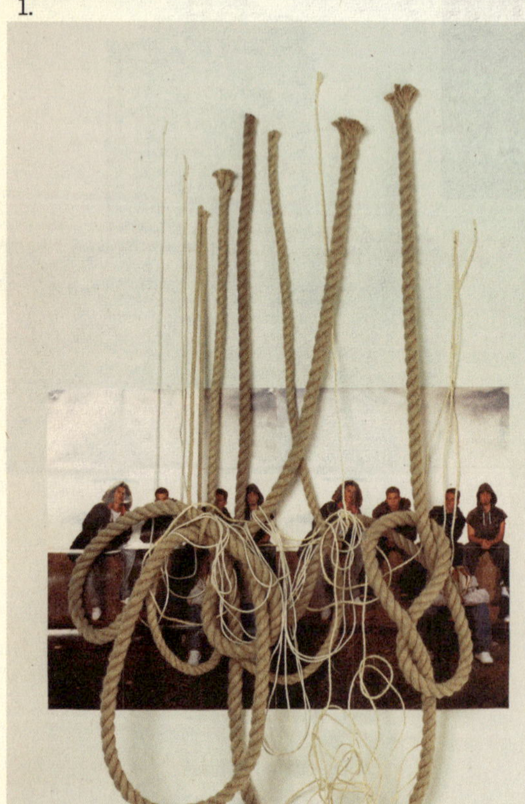

2.

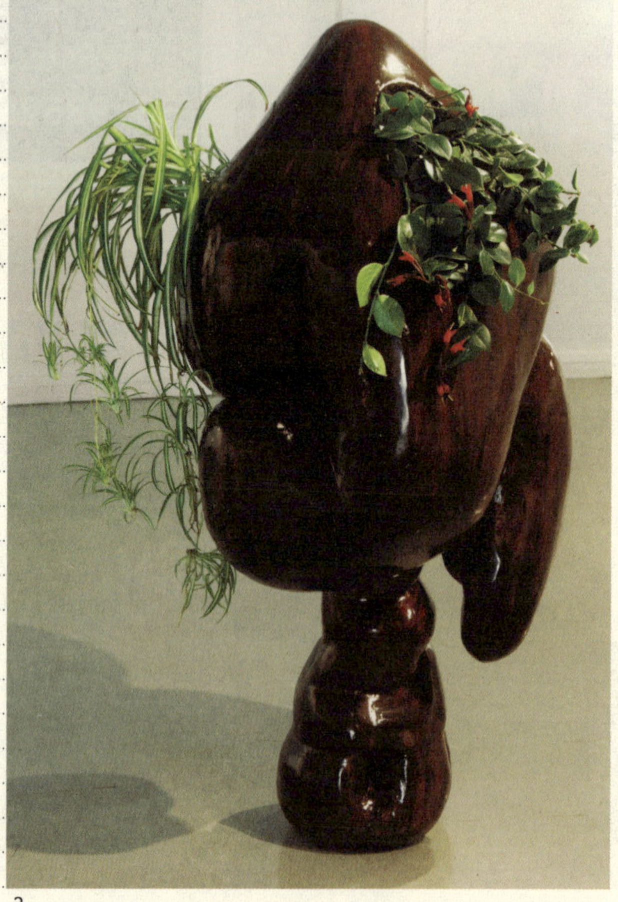

3.

4.

1. Plants will grow to please

2008, clay, cardboard, moss, charcoal, grass, stones, cloves, and tea, 27 1/2 × 55 × 15 3/4 in (70 × 140 × 40 cm)

2. We have done so much with so little for so long

2007, wire, rope, string, and CD inserts, 39 1/2 × 31 1/2 in (100 × 80 cm)

3. Holders

2008, mixed media and houseplants, 47 × 29 1/2 × 31 1/2 in (120 × 75 × 80 cm)

4. Blows and Bombs

2008, poster print, dimensions variable

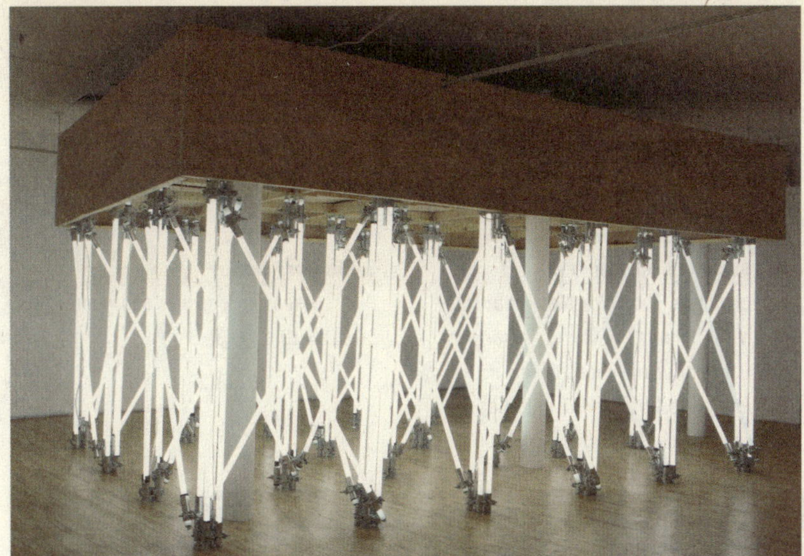
1.

Alejandro Almanza Pereda graduated with a BFA from the University of Texas at El Paso in 2005. He currently lives and works in New York, where he had a solo exhibition at Art in General in 2007. His sometimes perilous and fragile installations use various discarded objects and are influenced by urban landscapes and his childhood in Mexico City.

1. Andamio (Temporary Frameworks)
2007, fluorescent light tubes, steel clamps, ballast, and wood, 12 × 20 × 13 ft (365 × 600 × 400 cm)

2. Just empty cups
2008, fish tank, table, water, cups, tray, tabletop, and air, dimensions variable

3. Untitled (Wardrobe)
2006, wardrobe, fluorescent light tubes, fish tanks, bricks, plant, and sheets, dimensions variable

4. Untitled (Chest of drawers)
2006, lumber, chest of drawers, table, fish tanks, water, doily, carpet, cinder blocks, electrical cable, lamp, bed sheets, vase, and plant, dimensions variable

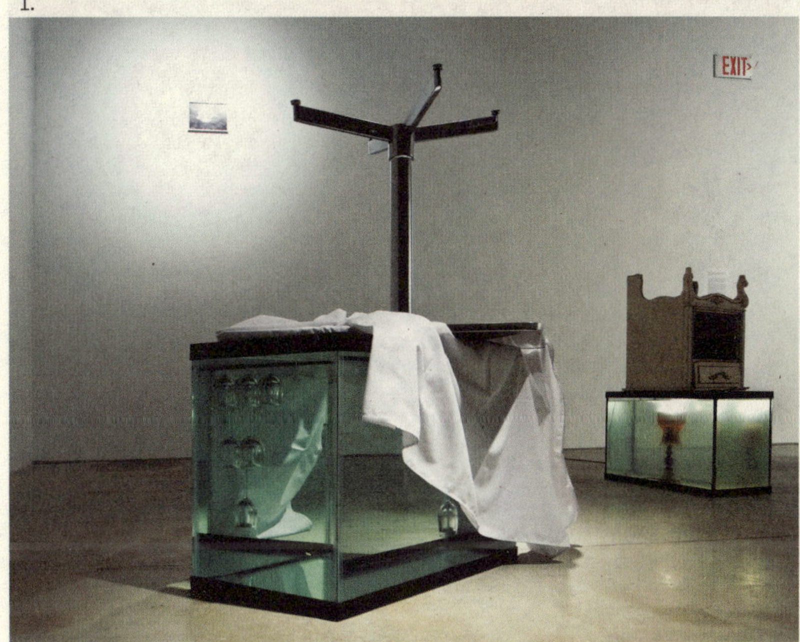

2.

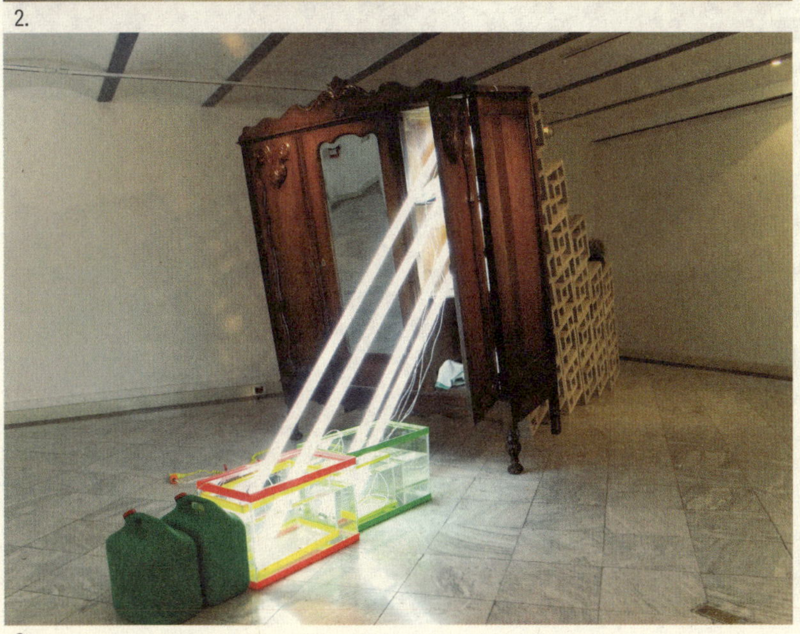
3.

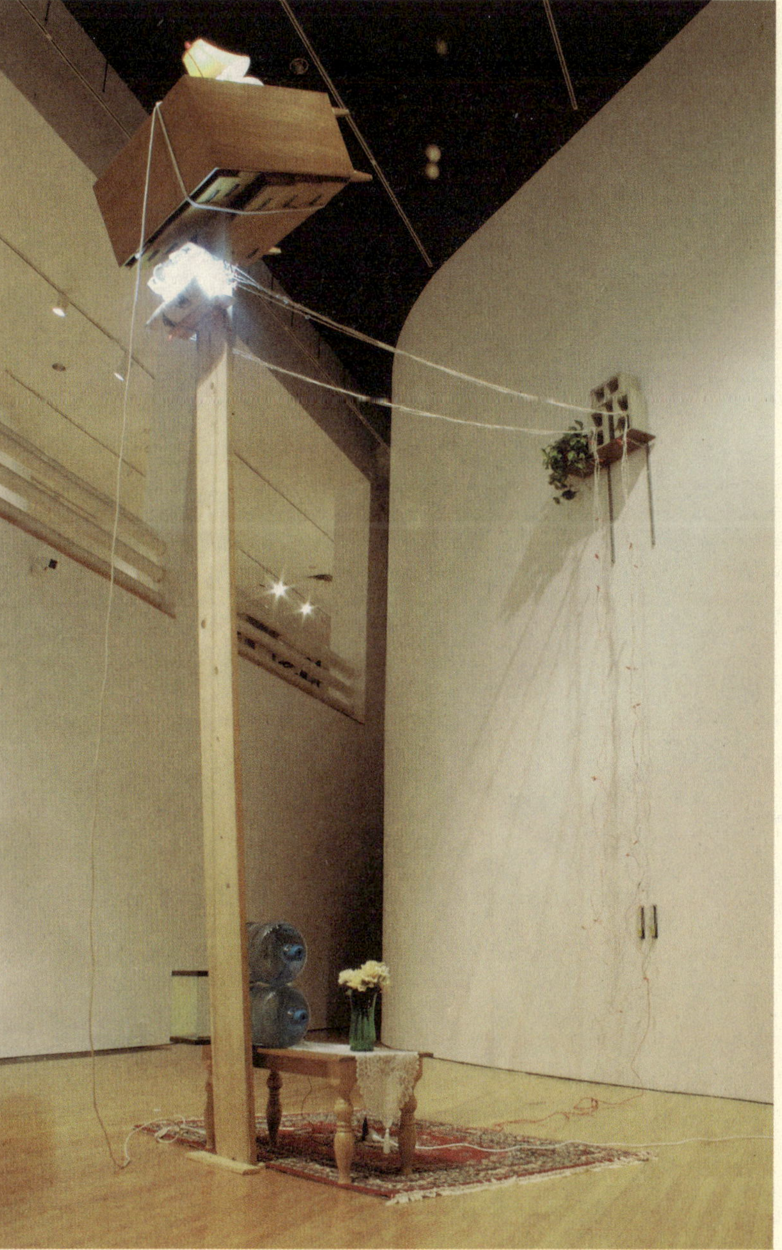
4.

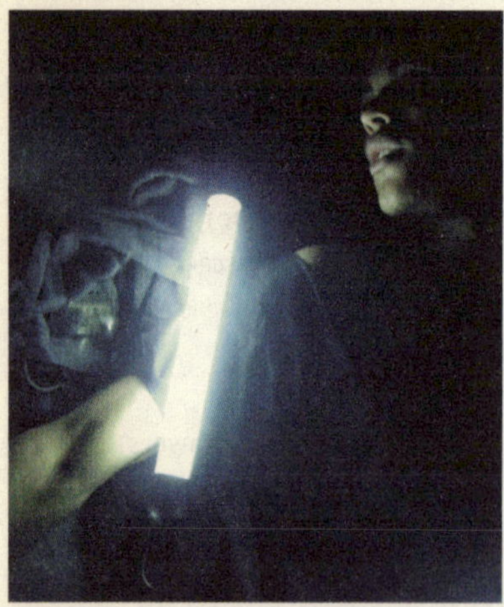

1.

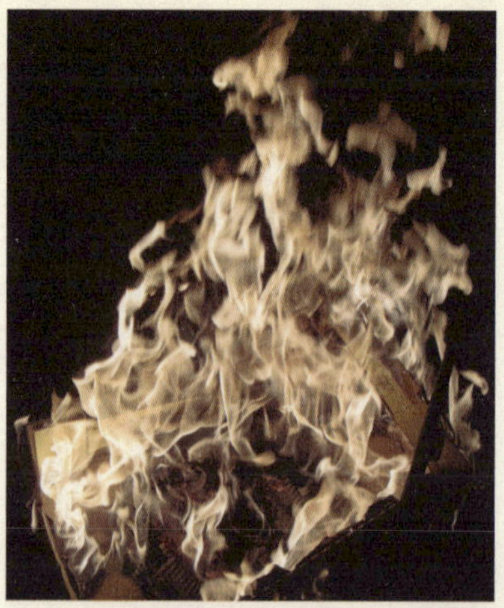

2.

Joël Andrianomearisoa attended the Ecole Spéciale d'Architecture, Paris, and currently lives in Paris and Antananarivo, Madagascar. With a diverse background in fashion and architecture, he currently works in media ranging from textiles, collage, and sculpture to video and performance. The color black features prominently in many works, in various forms of paper or pieces of fabric assembled to form an inhabitable structure, as in **Memory Box** (2007).

1. **IRY** (detail)
2006, digital print on polyester, 39 ½ × 39 ½ in (100 cm × 100 cm)

2. **L'etranger (The Stranger)**
2007, video, 6 min 40 sec

3. **Memory Box**
2007, mixed black textiles and wood, 10 × 10 × 10 ft (3 × 3 × 3 m)

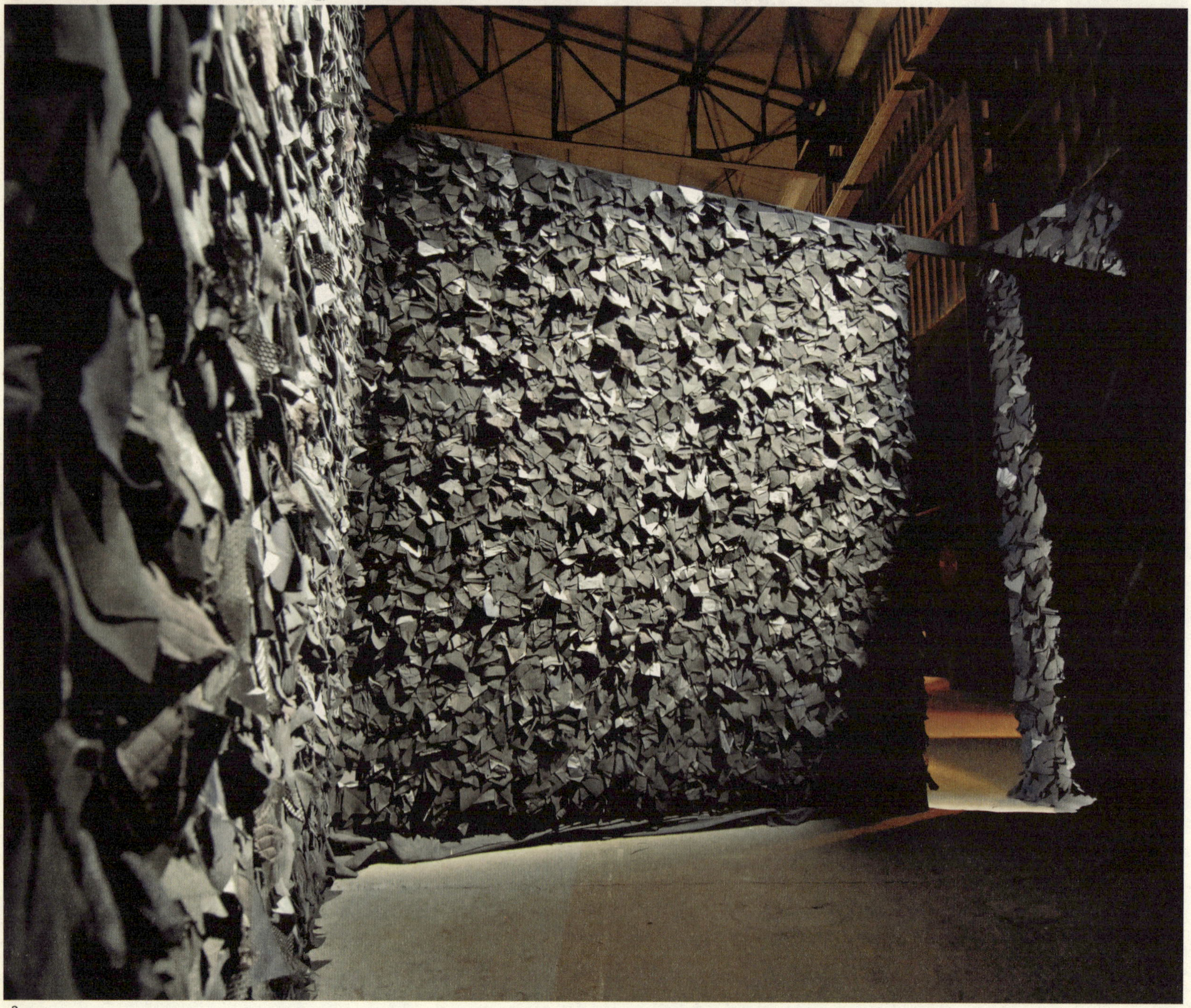

3.

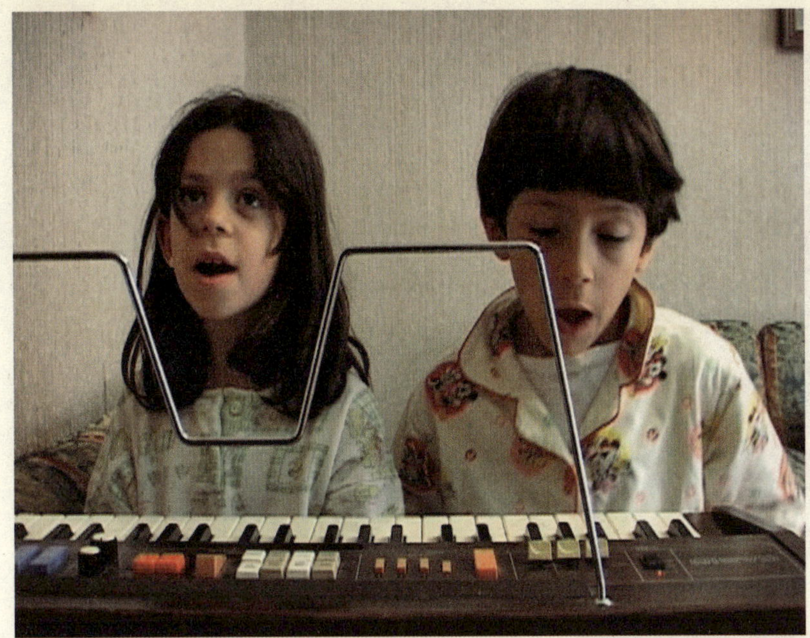

1.

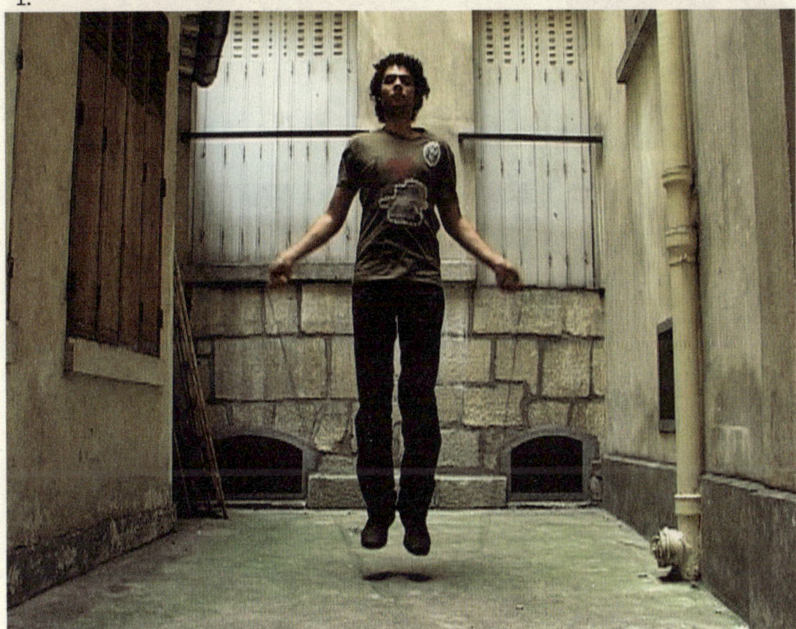

2.

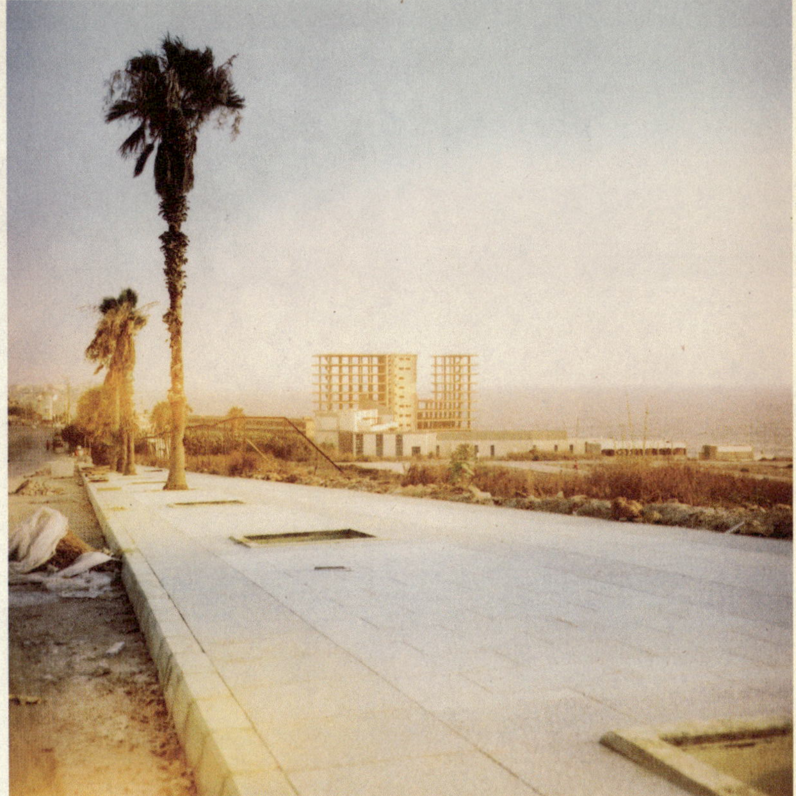

3.

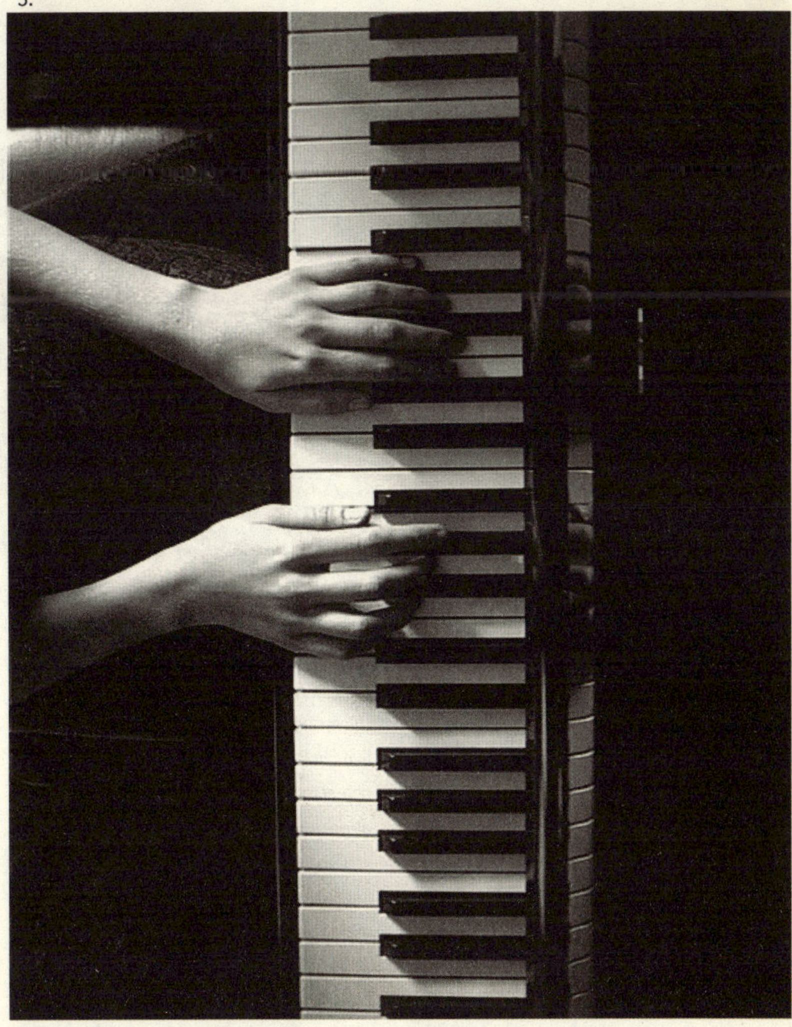

4.

Ziad Antar grew up during the war in Lebanon, studied agricultural engineering at the American University of Beirut, and currently lives in Saida and Paris. In 2002 he began making video and photographs addressing the country's conflicts directly and indirectly. Videos often document a specific action using a single shot, as in **WA** (2004), which shows two children singing along to a synthesizer drum beat.

1. **WA**
with Nathalie and Mohamed Bsat
2004, video, 3 min

3. **La corde**
with Ayman Abdel Hafez
2007, video, 3 min

2. **Coral Beach**
with Rasha Salti
from the series **Beirut Bereft**
2007, chromogenic print, 48 ½ × 48 ½ in
(123 × 123 cm)

4. **La Marche Turque**
with Matea Marras
2006, video, 3 min

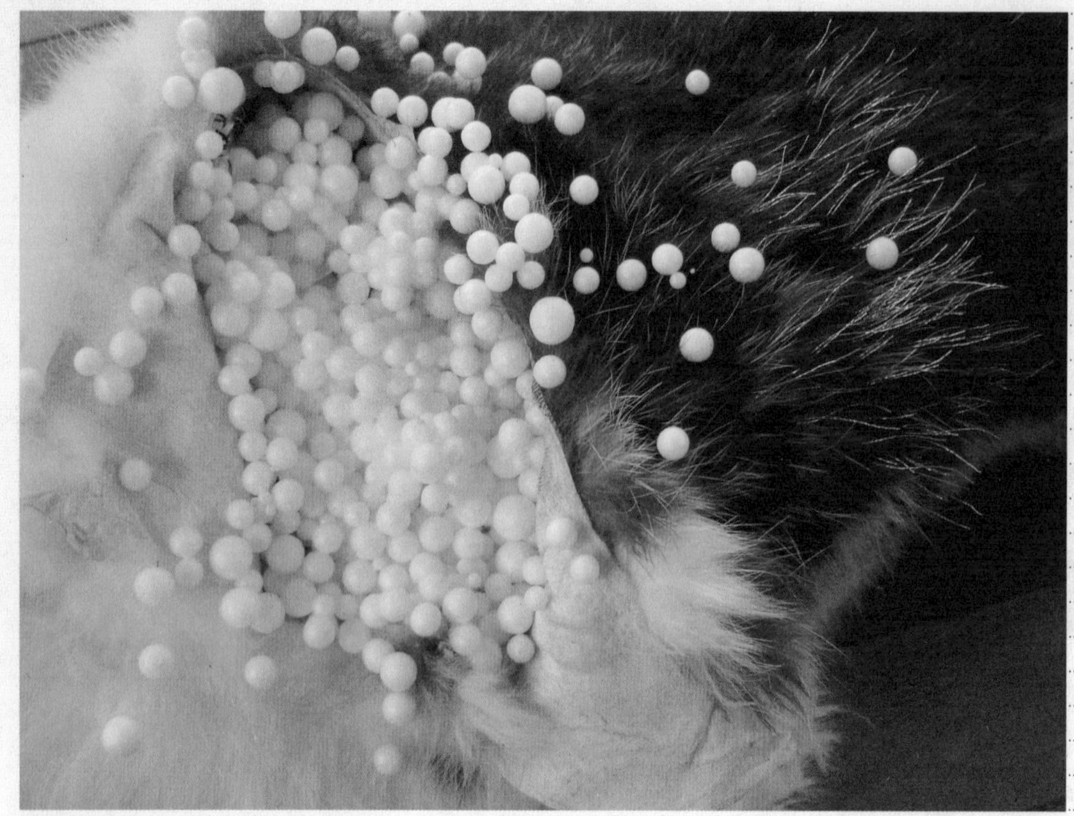

1.

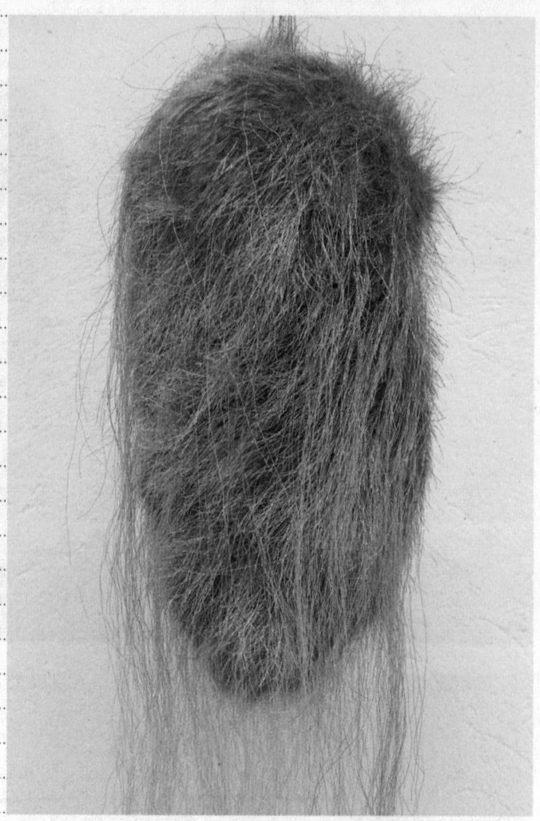

2.

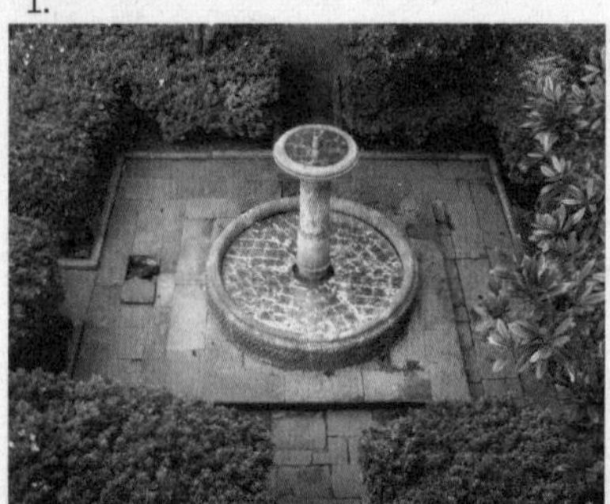

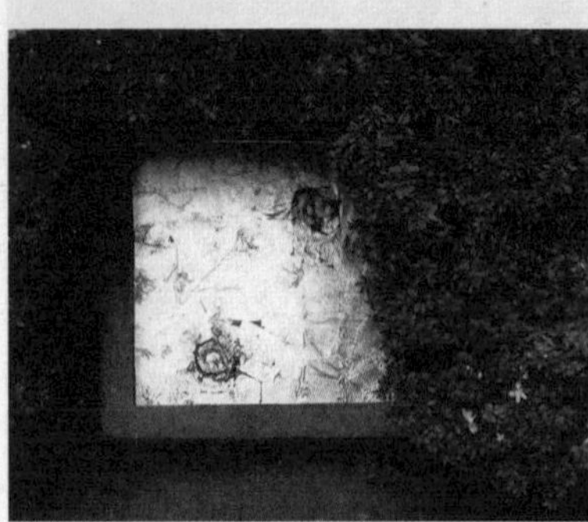

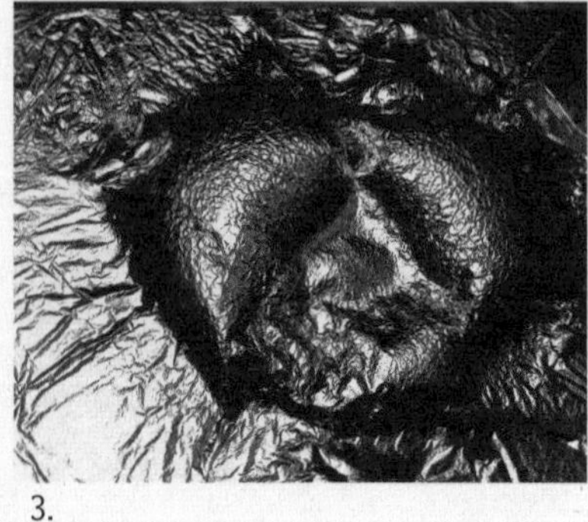

3.

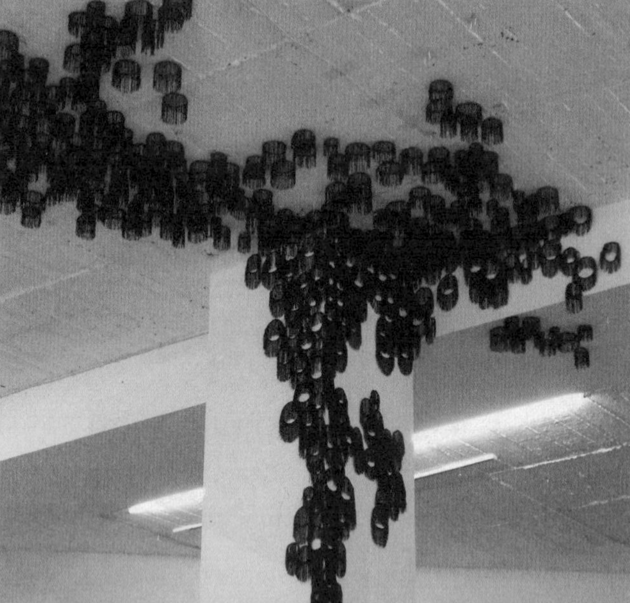

4.

5.

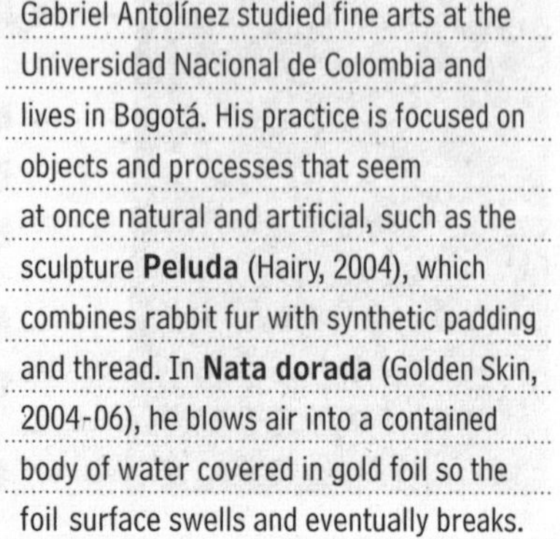

Gabriel Antolínez studied fine arts at the Universidad Nacional de Colombia and lives in Bogotá. His practice is focused on objects and processes that seem at once natural and artificial, such as the sculpture **Peluda** (Hairy, 2004), which combines rabbit fur with synthetic padding and thread. In **Nata dorada** (Golden Skin, 2004-06), he blows air into a contained body of water covered in gold foil so the foil surface swells and eventually breaks.

1. **Bolsa de pieles** (Fur bag) (detail)
2004, rabbit fur, golden thread, and Styrofoam balls, $6\frac{3}{4} \times 31\frac{1}{2} \times 8$ in (17 × 80 × 20 cm)

2. **Peluda** (Hairy)
2004, rabbit fur, synthetic padding, and golden thread, core size $12 \times 5\frac{1}{2} \times 5\frac{1}{2}$ in (30 × 14 × 14 cm)

3. **Nata dorada** (Golden skin)
2004-06, water, golden foil, air pumps, hose, and DVD, dimensions variable

4 & 5. **Discos y flecos** (Discs and fringes)
2005, fringe, cardboard, glue, and adhesive tape, disc diameters vary from $1\frac{1}{4}$ to 3 in (3-7 cm)

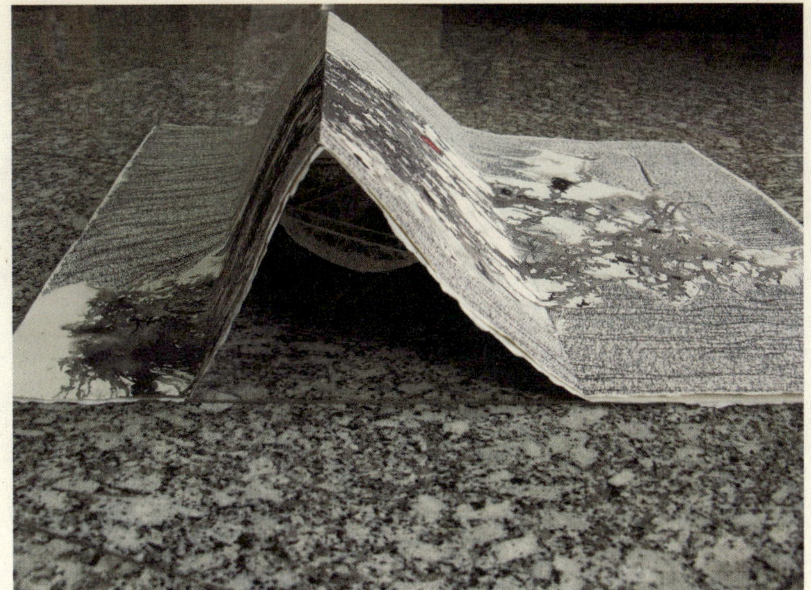
1.

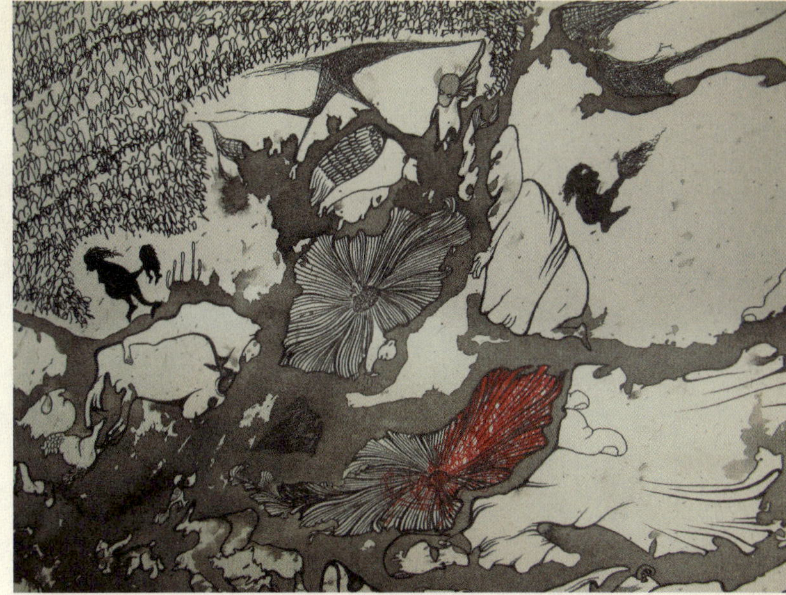
2.

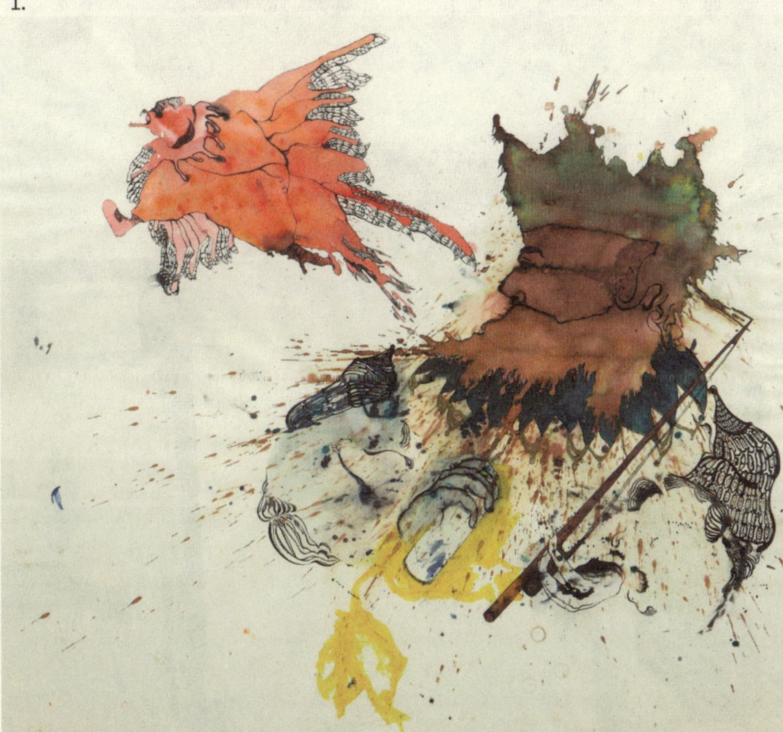
3.

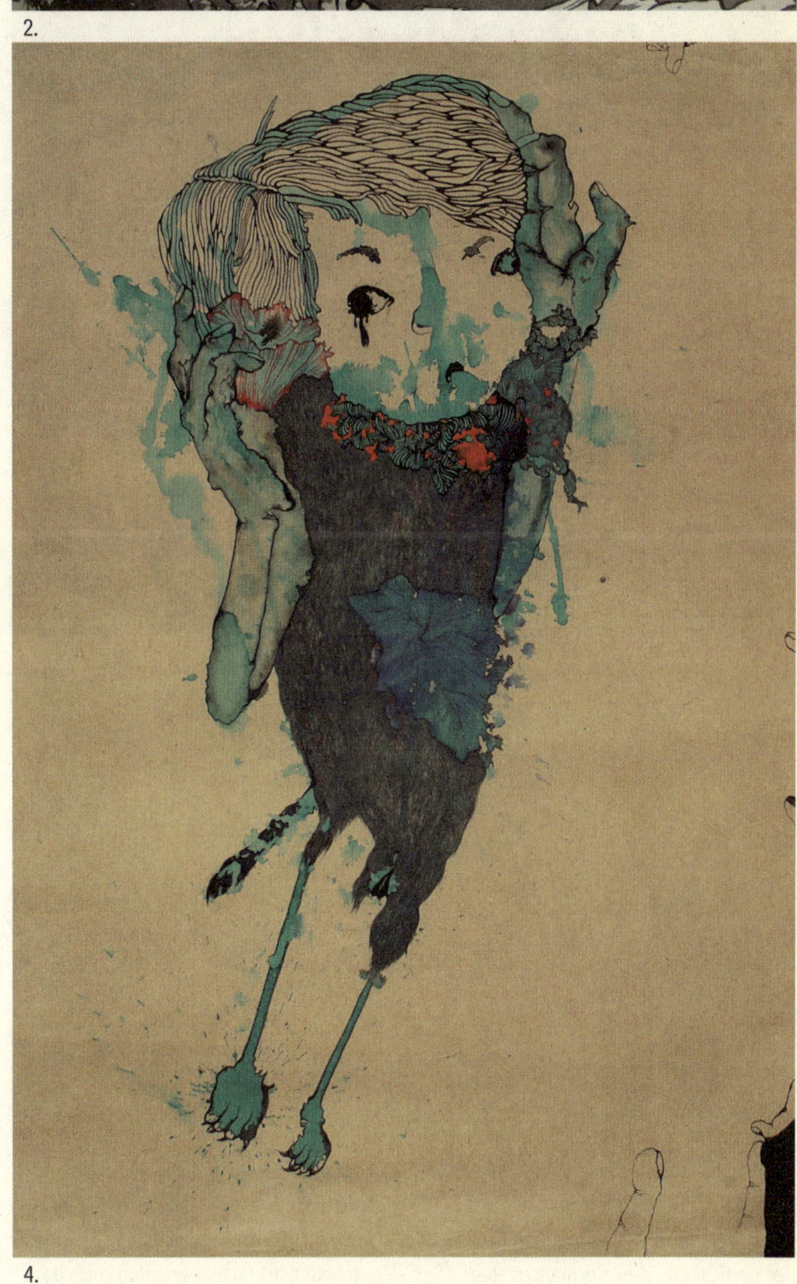
4.

Minam Apang earned her MFA from the Sir J. J. School of Art, Mumbai, and currently lives in Bangalore. Inspired by fables and mythology from northeast India, she uses acrylic, watercolor, and ink on paper to create intricate works that mix abstraction with dreamlike figuration. As a student, she cofounded the Lazy Rebels collective, organizing public lectures and films on contemporary Western art practices.

1 & 2. **Untitled**
2008, ink on paper, glue, cotton thread, and granite, 25 × 30 in (64 × 76 cm)

3. **Jester King**
2007, acrylic and ink on paper, 54 × 58 1/2 in (137 × 149 cm)

4. **Untitled**
2007, ink on paper, 33 × 22 in (84 × 56 cm)

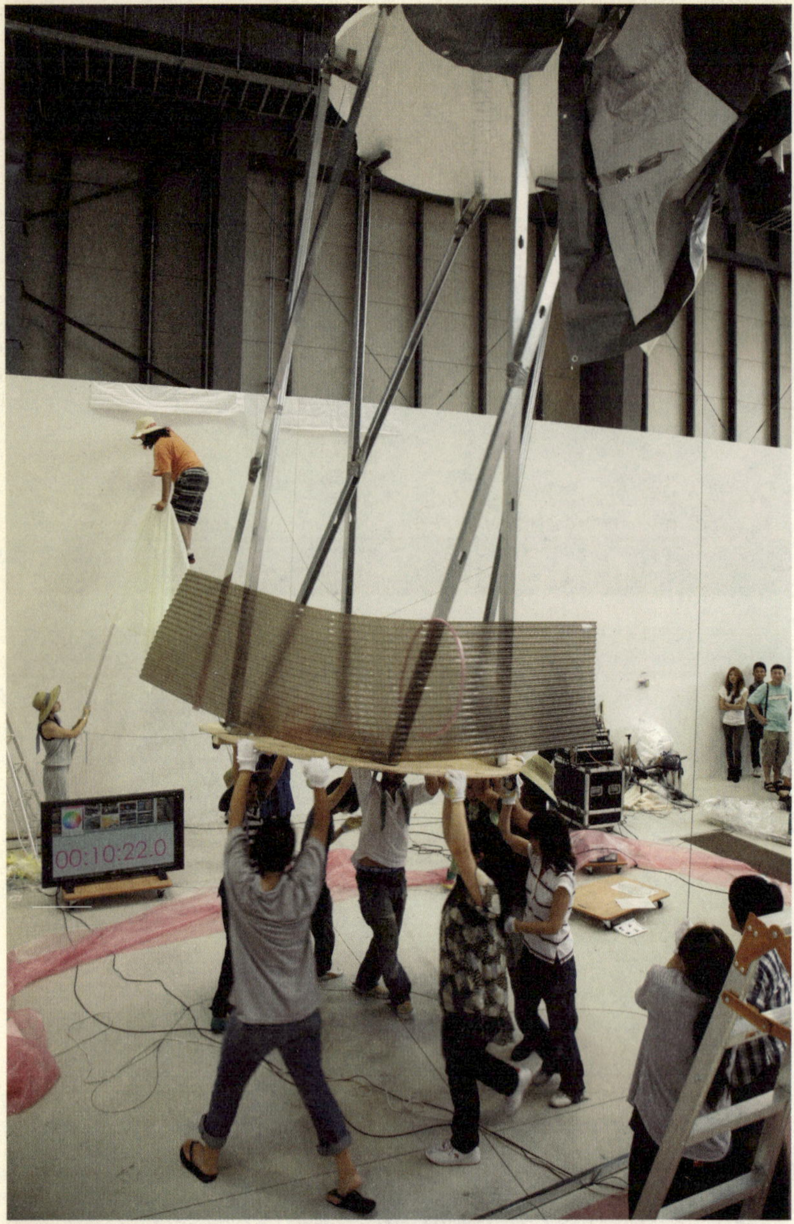

1.

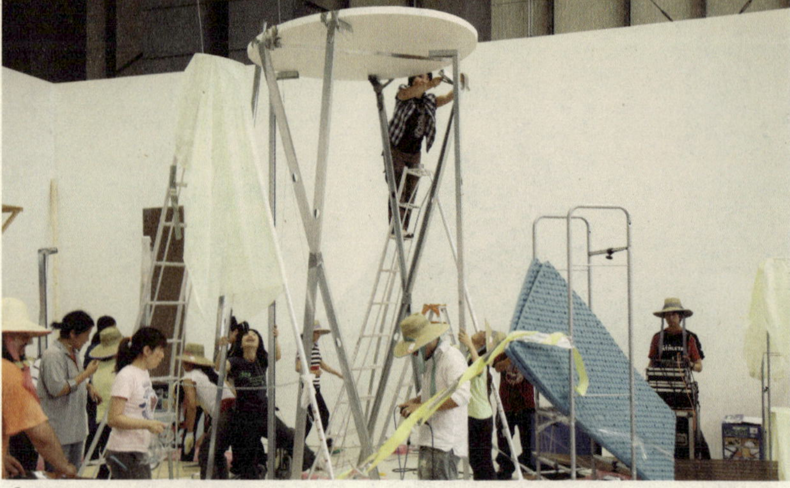

2.

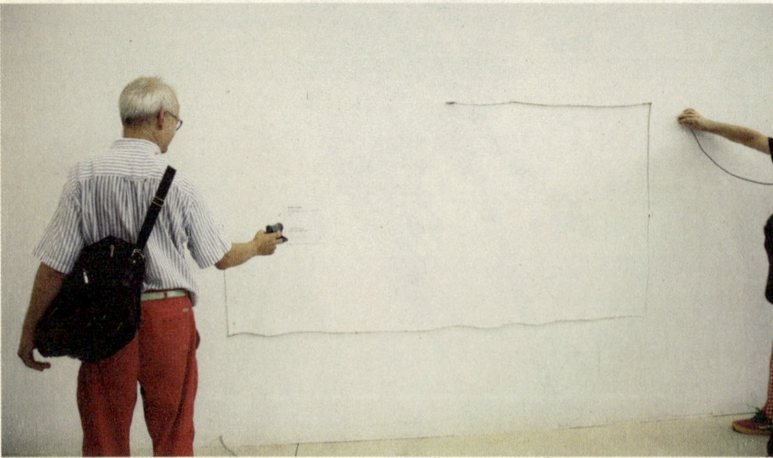

3.

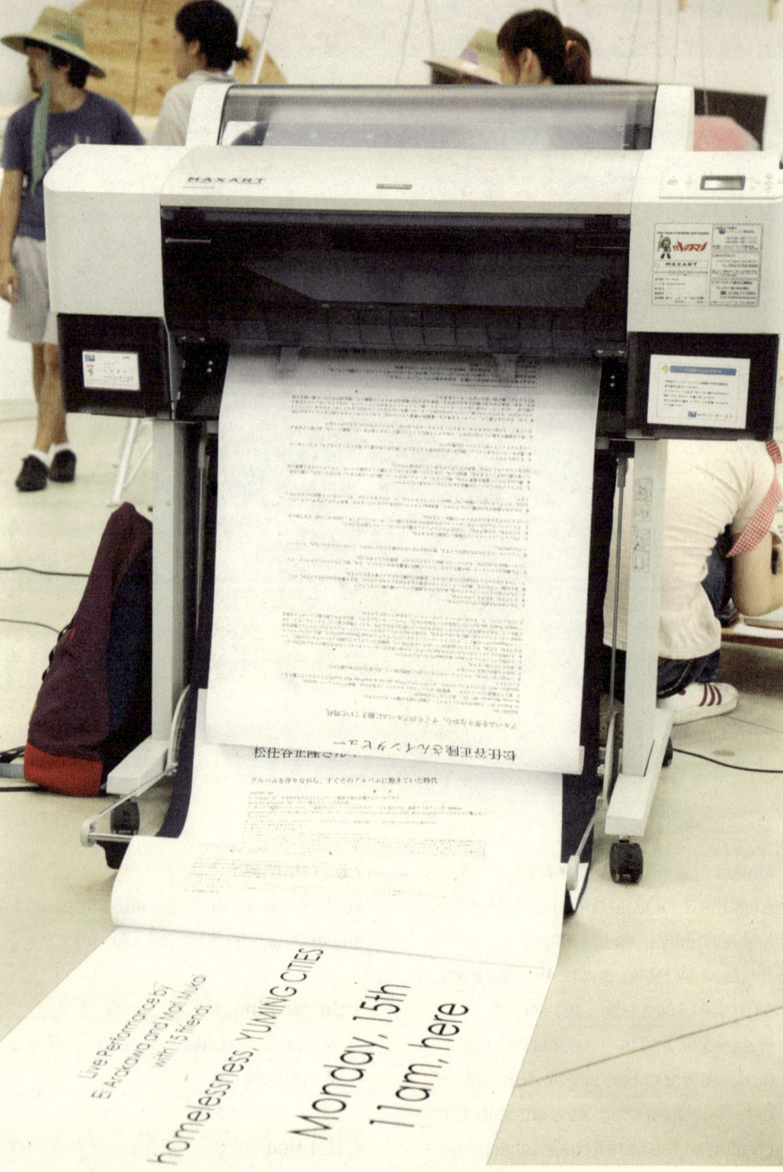

4.

Ei Arakawa earned his MFA in film and video from Bard College and currently lives in New York. He organizes groups of participants in performances that are partly choreographed and partly spontaneous action. They include the rapid building and unbuilding of a stage; a manned art factory creating replicas of On Kawara paintings; and a calisthenics class in homage to the action art of the Japanese Gutai group.

1, 2, 3 & 4. **homelessness, YUMING CITIES**
with Mari Mukai
2008, mixed media performance

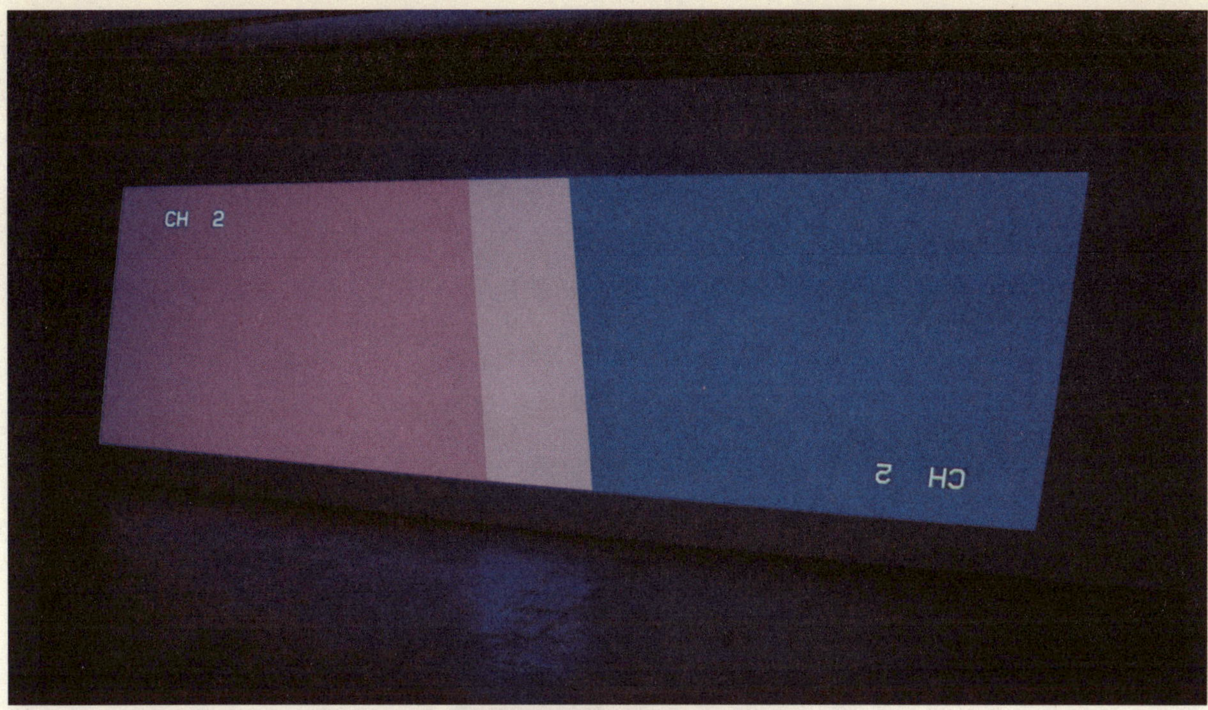

1.

Cory Arcangel attended the Oberlin Conservatory of Music in Ohio and currently lives in Brooklyn. He is an artist, electronic musician, and founding member of the record label and computer-programming ensemble Beige. His process often involves reconfiguring obsolete computer and video game systems, as in **Super Mario Clouds** (2002-05), in which all but the clouds have been erased from the famous 1980s video game interface.

1. **Two Keystoned Projectors (one upside down)**
2007, 2 projectors and VCR

2. **Untitled (After Lucier)**
2006, digital work on Mac Mini support

3. **Apple GarageBand Auto Tune Demonstration**
2007, projection from a digital source

4. **Sweet 16**
2006, projection from a digital source

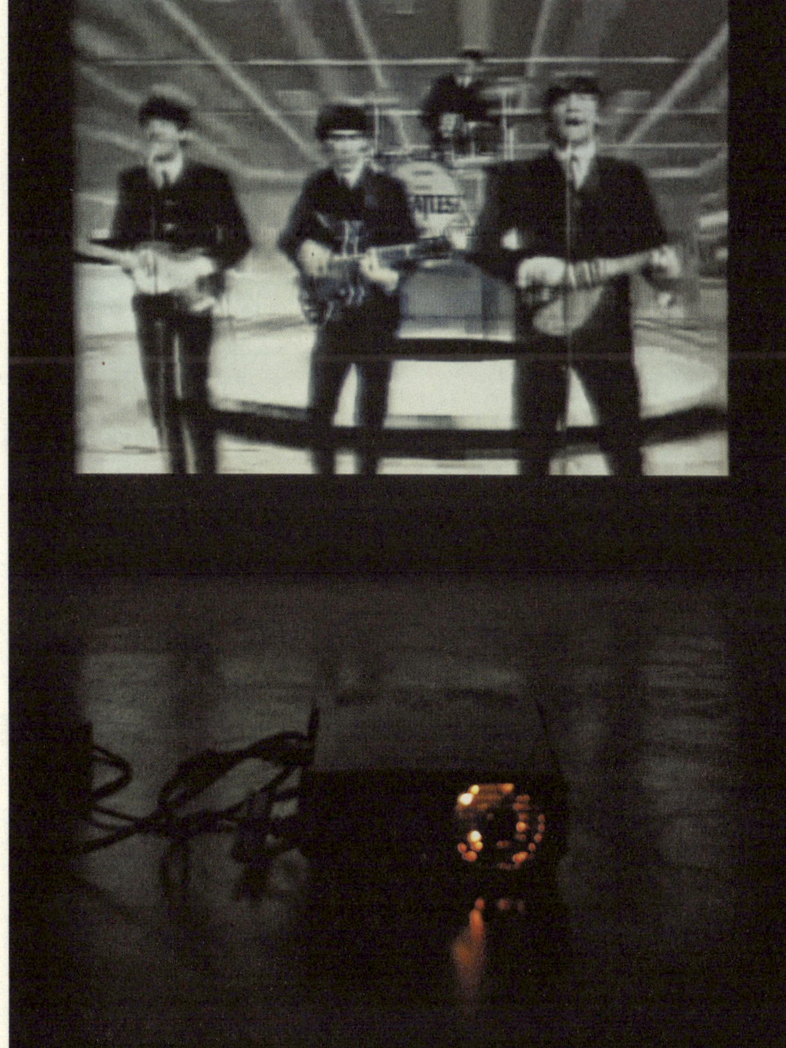
2.

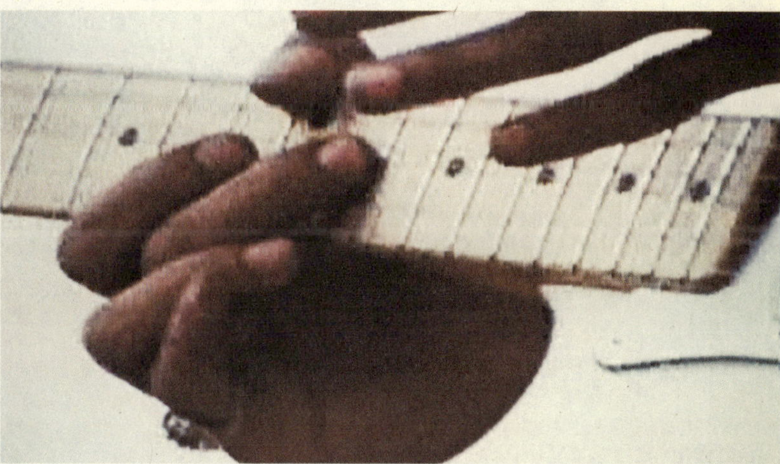
3.

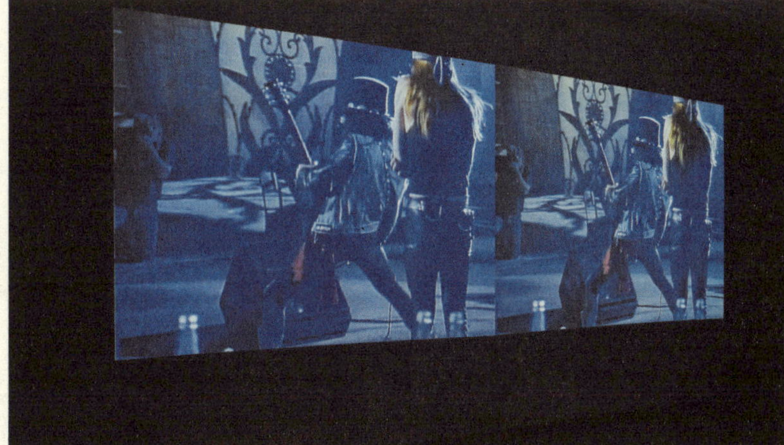
4.

Quentin Amand studied at l'École supérieure d'art, Grenoble, and has since participated in group exhibitions including "Hardcore" at the Palais de Tokyo, Paris (2003), and "Holiday In" at Gasworks, London (2007). He works with found objects and everyday situations, and stages small fractures and interventions into the ordinary. For "Hardcore," Armand asked the security guards of the Palais de Tokyo to wear jackets inscribed with the word "sérénité" (serenity), challenging and subverting their role within the gallery.

1. Untitled
2007, mixed media, dimensions variable

2. Please become a stone
2008, used notebooks, papers, drawings, cord, plastic wheels, and hat, 50 3/4 × 13 3/4 × 13 3/4 in (129 × 35 × 35 cm)

3. Chess
2006, steel and stickers, 11 × 25 1/2 × 25 1/2 in (28 × 65 × 65 cm)

4. 100% bottle of beer
2008, tire and bottles, 35 × 35 × 17 3/4 in (89 × 89 × 45 cm)

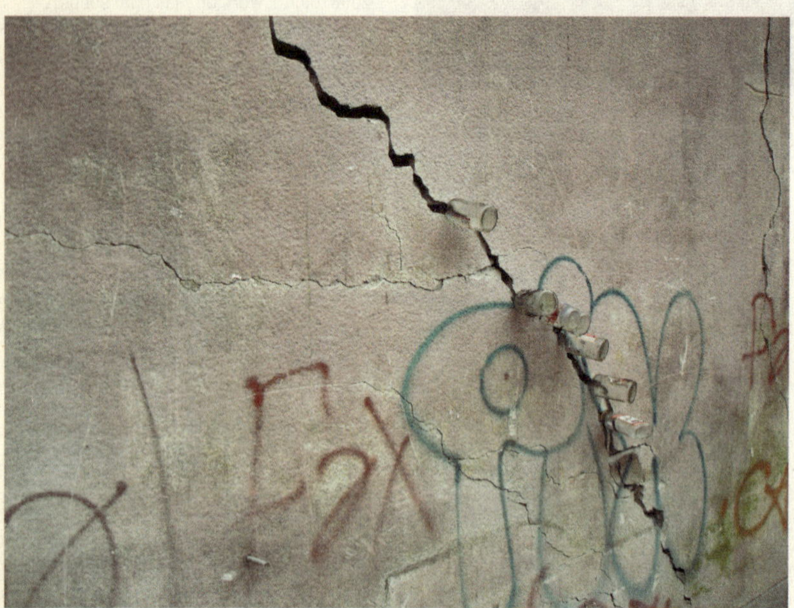

1.

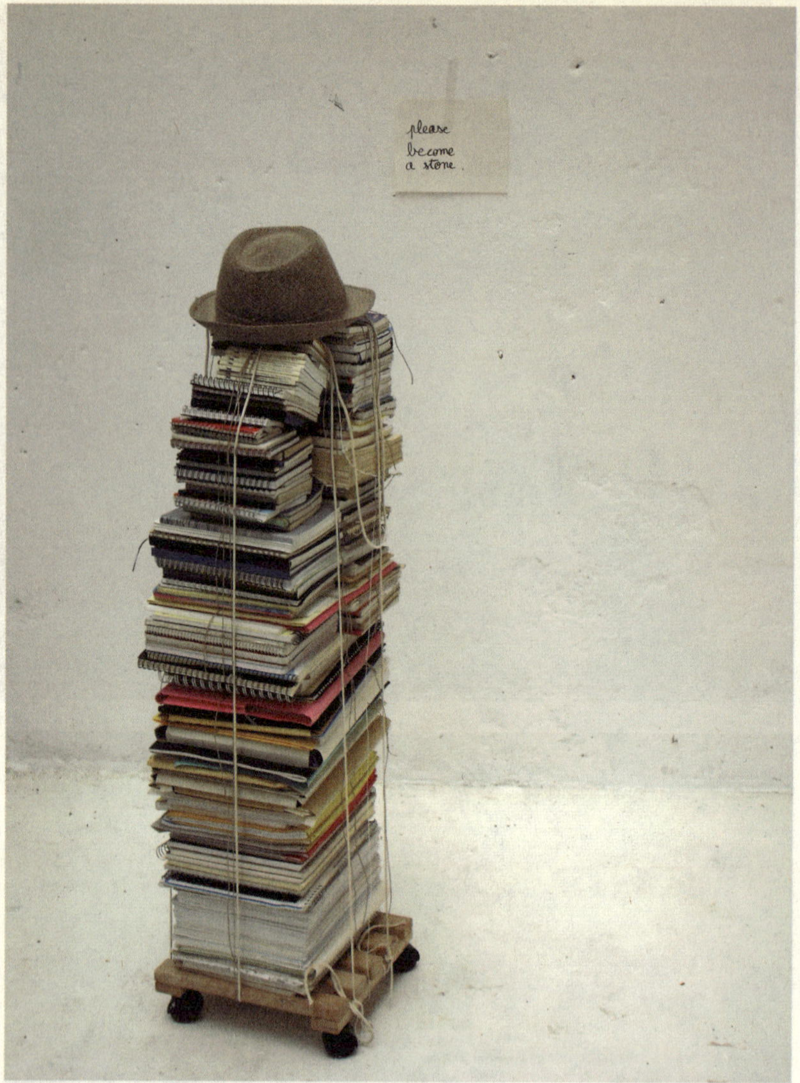

2.

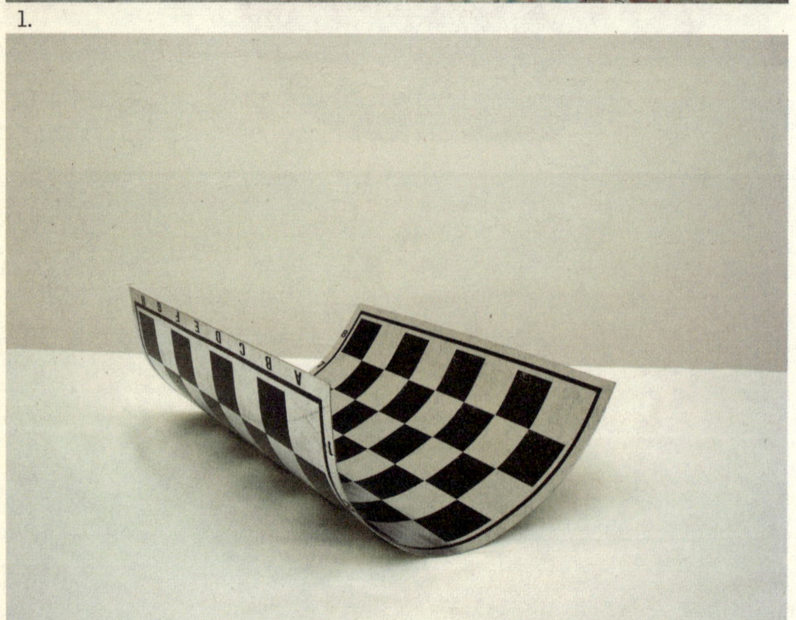

3.

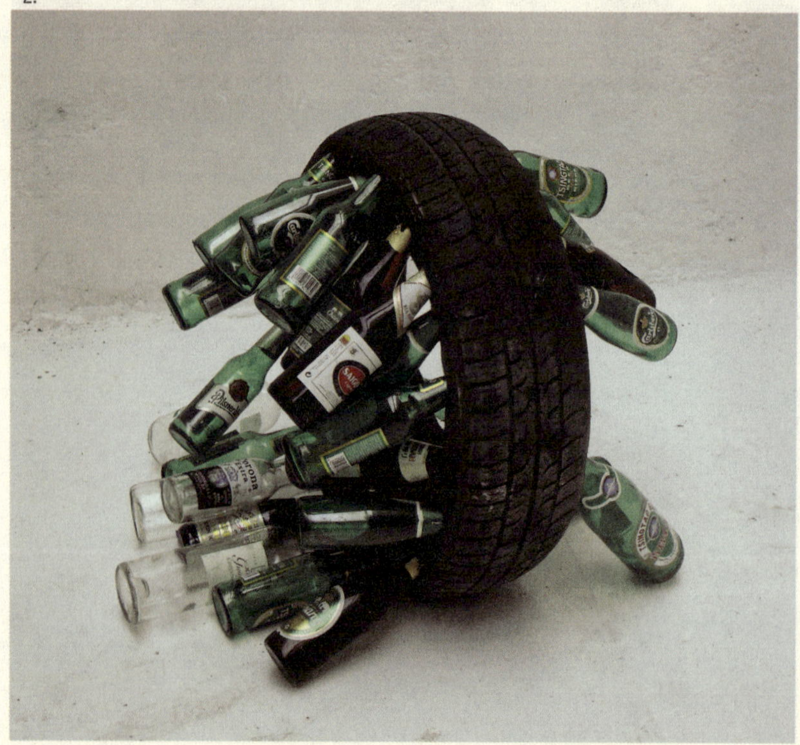

4.

Eve Armstrong earned her BFA from the Elam School of Fine Arts, University of Auckland, and continues to live in Auckland. She identifies her practice as the making of "adaptable support structures" in the form of objects, installations, and social interactions. Whether assembling urban scraps with packing tape or creating a trading table for the exchange of objects, skills, ideas, and information, she reimagines the form, function, and value of material and disused things.

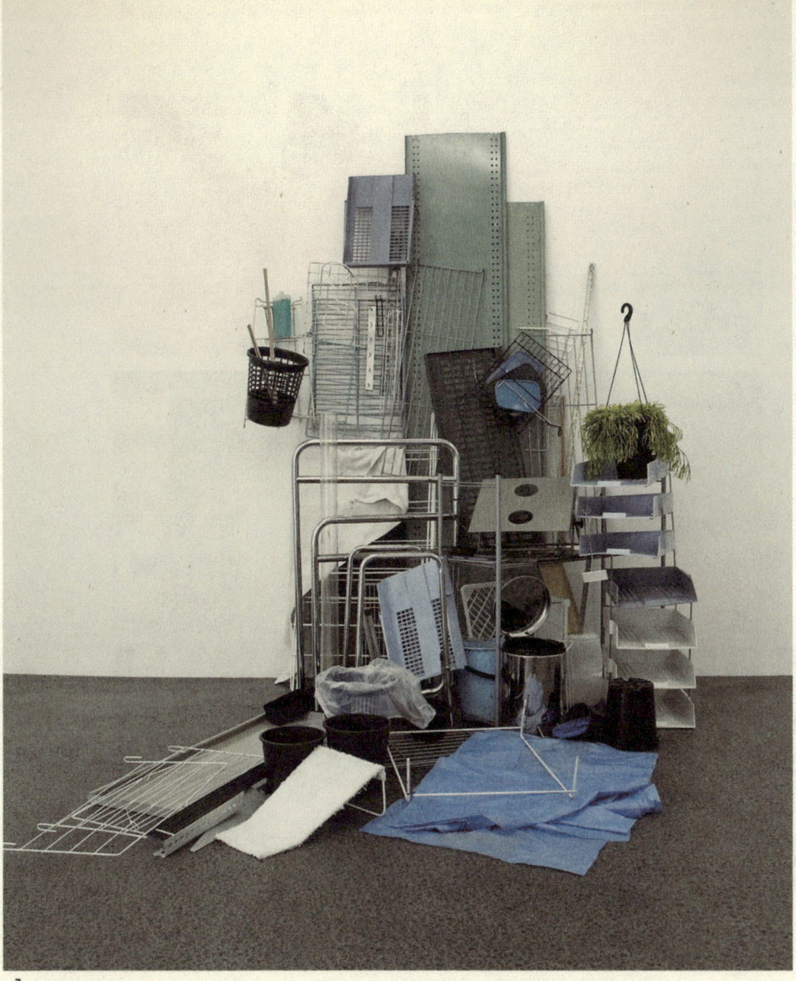

1.

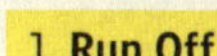

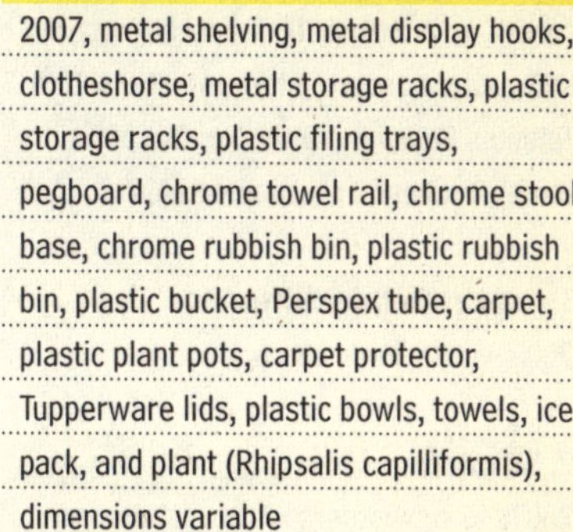

2.

1. Run Off

2007, metal shelving, metal display hooks, clotheshorse, metal storage racks, plastic storage racks, plastic filing trays, pegboard, chrome towel rail, chrome stool base, chrome rubbish bin, plastic rubbish bin, plastic bucket, Perspex tube, carpet, plastic plant pots, carpet protector, Tupperware lids, plastic bowls, towels, ice pack, and plant (Rhipsalis capilliformis), dimensions variable

2. Clearout

2007, trash bag, air, and storage rack, approx 47 1/4 × 19 1/2 in (120 × 50 cm)

3. In and Out

2007, photographs on adhesive vinyl, packing tape, and chairs, 8 × 13 ft (250 × 400 cm), installation view at Te Tuhi, Centre for the Arts, Auckland

4. Trading Table

2003-present, mixed media, dimensions variable

5. Arrangement: Pick Up (detail)

2007, color photographs and packing tape on found metal shelves, 12 3/4 × 23 × 17 3/4 in (31 × 58 × 45 cm)

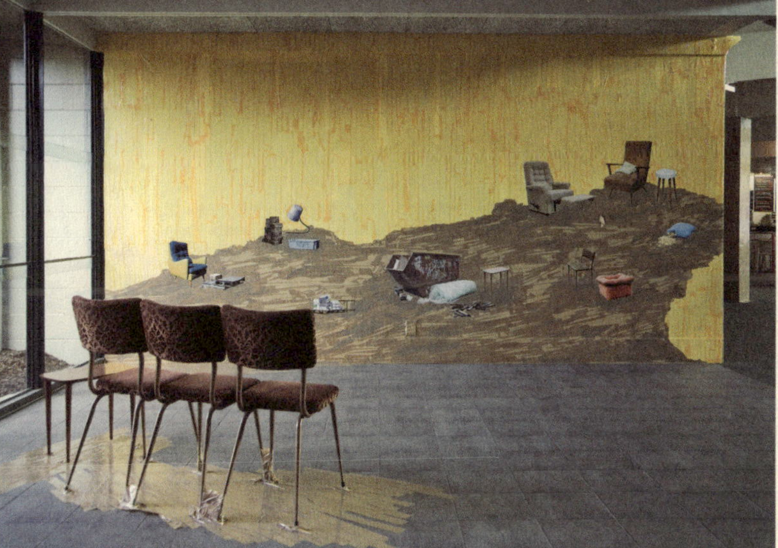

3.

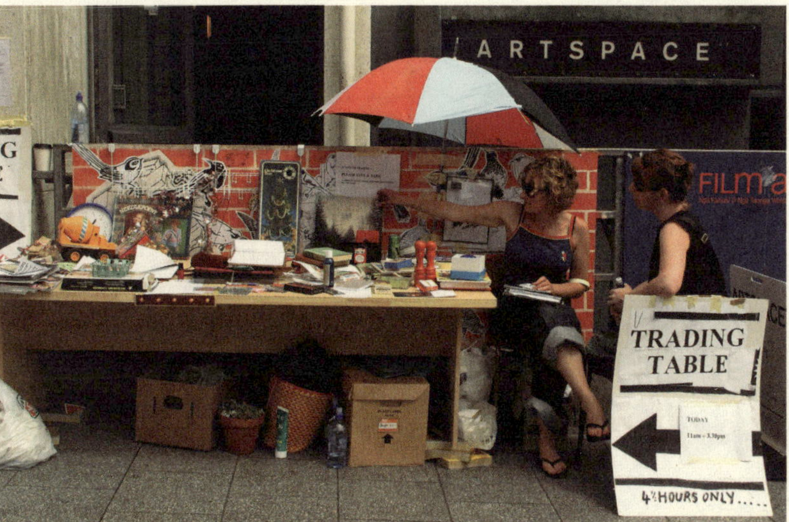

4.

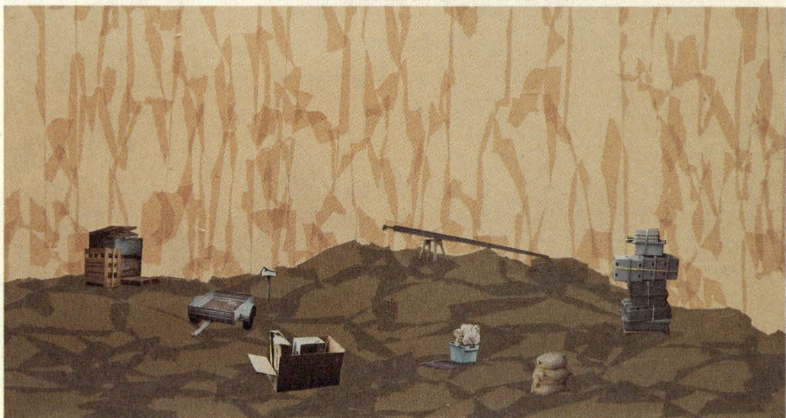

5.

Selçuk Artut earned his PhD in media and communications from the European Graduate School in Switzerland. He holds an MA in sonic arts and a degree in mathematics, and he teaches sound, interactivity, art, and design at Sabanci University in Istanbul, where he currently lives. Sound performance and installation are among his primary activities; his recent work **Substairs** features forty-six subwoofers under a staircase at the 10th Istanbul Biennial (2007). He also plays in the experimental rock band Replikas.

1. youcanttellthedifference
2005, video, 2 min 13 sec

2. Substairs
2007, 46 subwoofers under a staircase, dimensions variable, installation view at the 10th Istanbul Biennial

3. Abstract for Substairs
2007, digital image

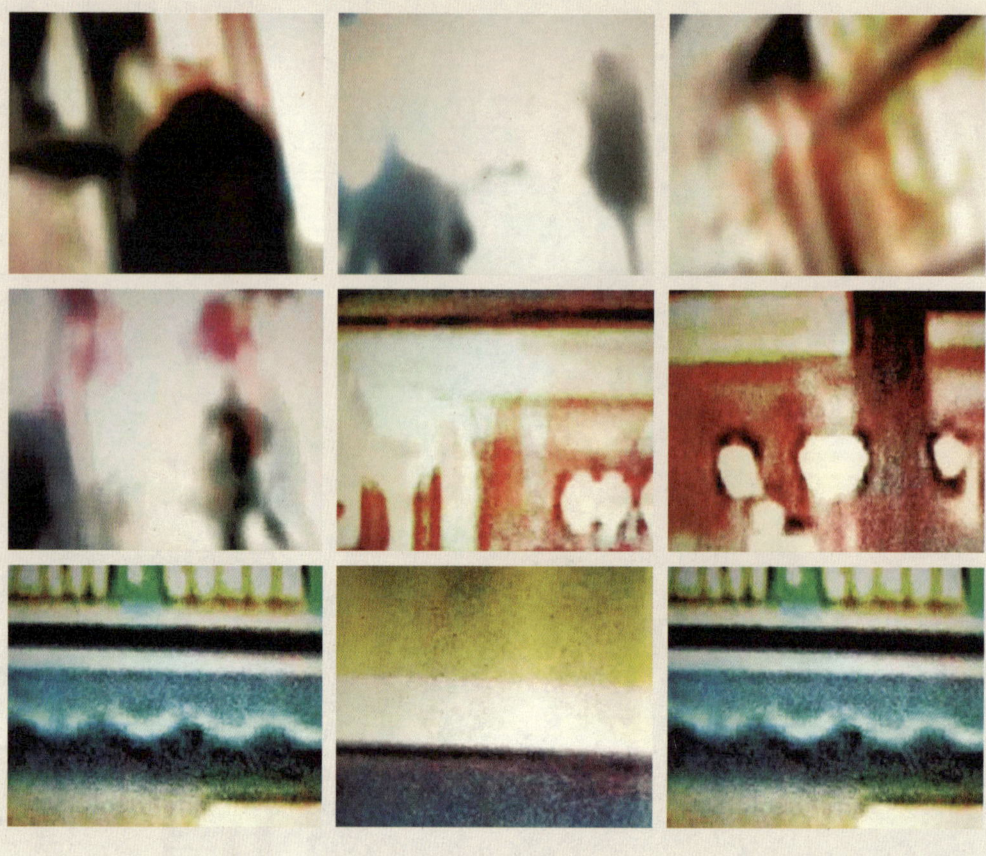

1.

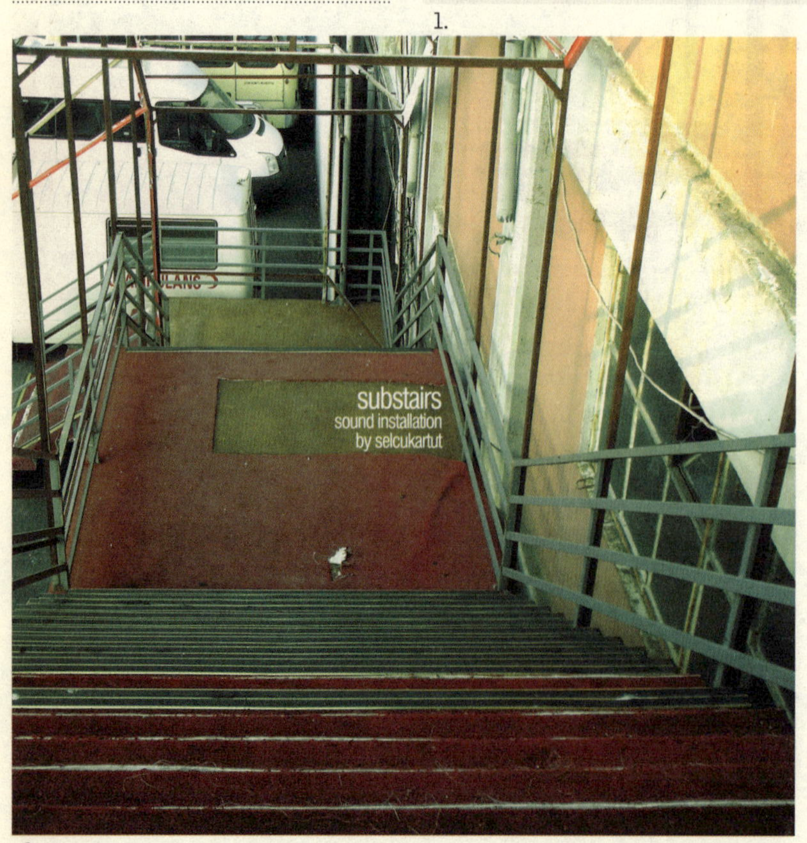

2.

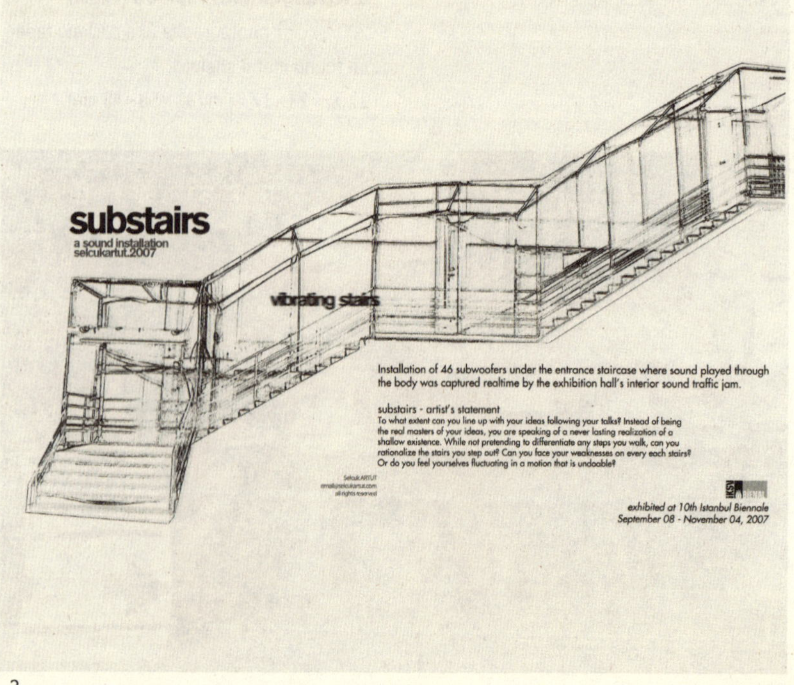

3.

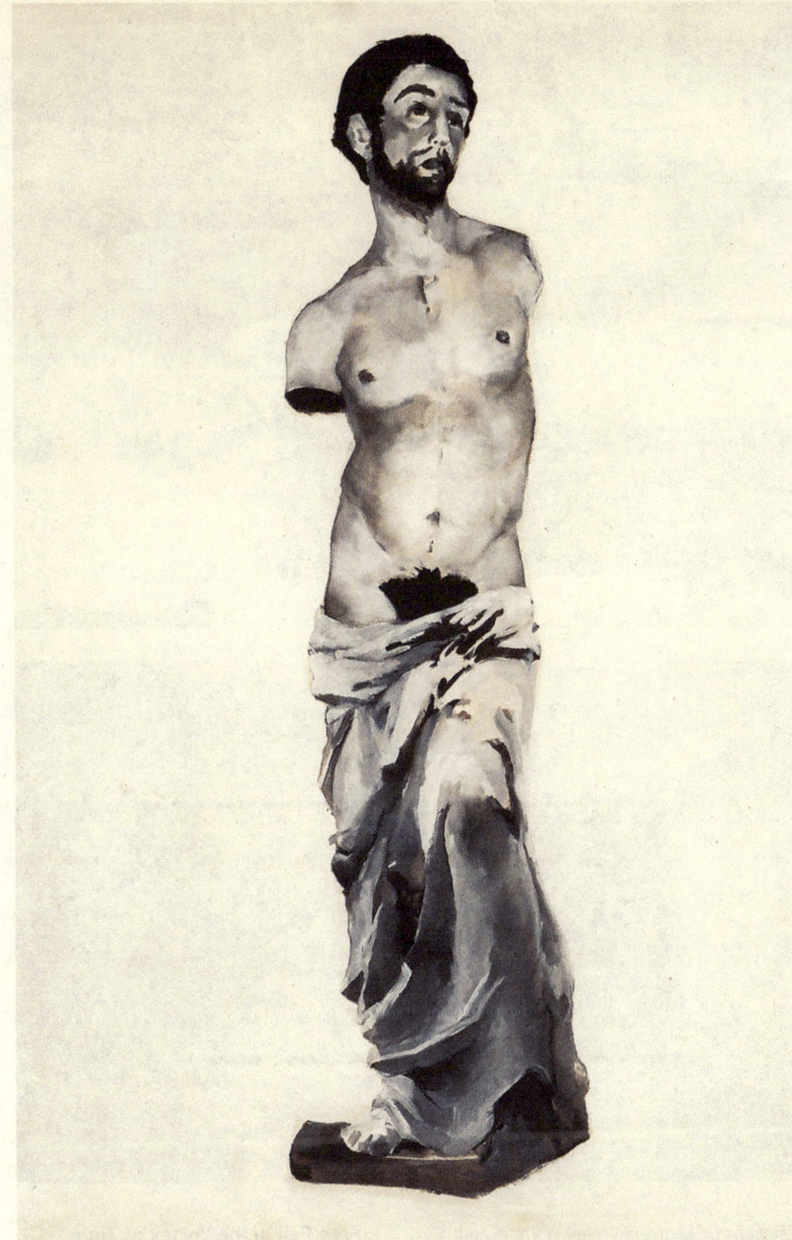

1.

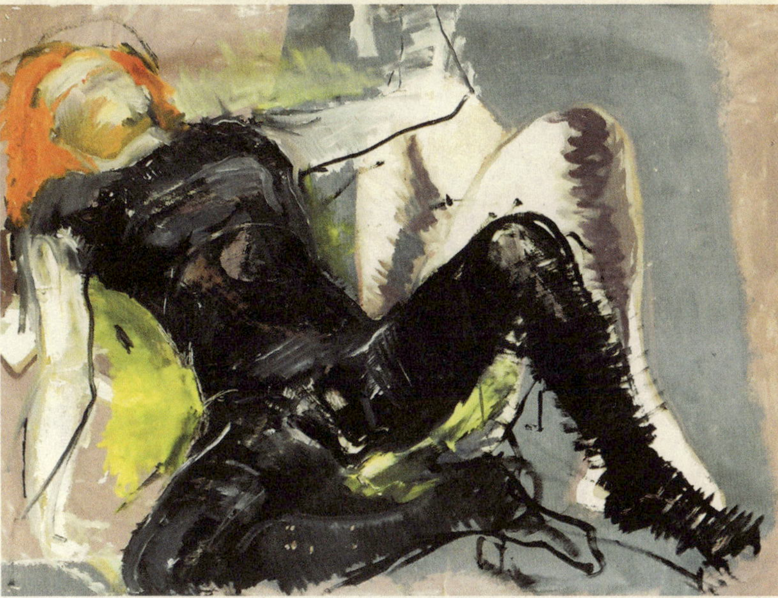

3.

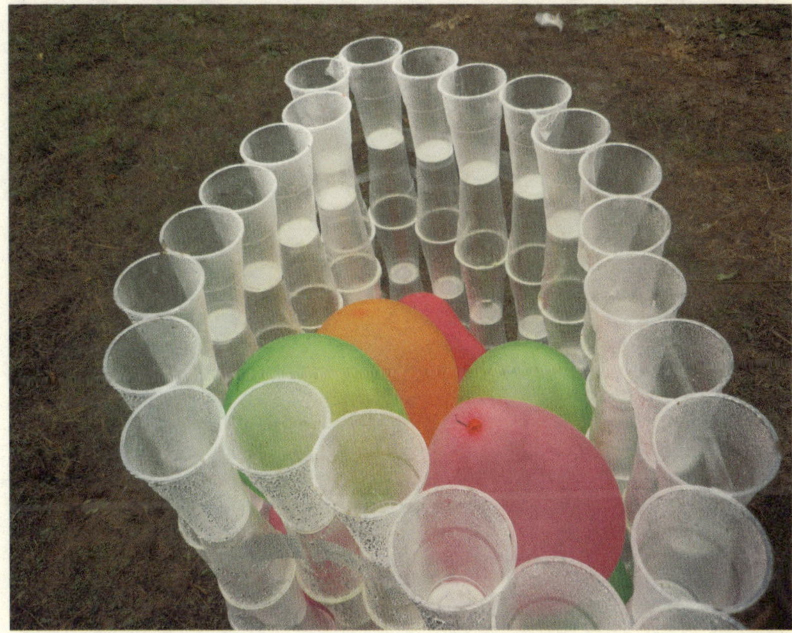

4.

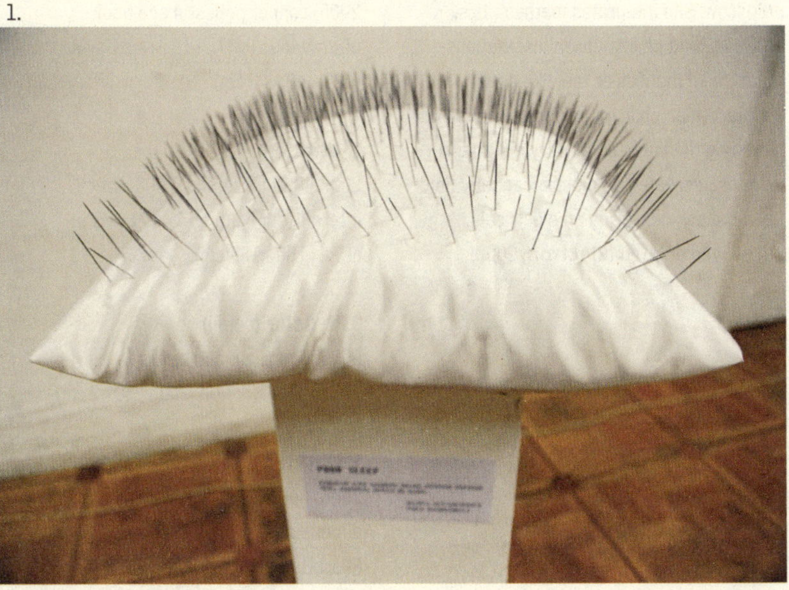

2.

Tekla Aslanishvili studied at the Tbilisi State Academy of Art and has produced works dealing with contemporary anomie, insomnia, and individual isolation. She is currently working on a series of text-based paintings that deal with creative frustration in the face of theories on the end of originality. Her work was included in "Untitled" at the Georgian Art Academy, Tbilisi (2007), and she produced a sculptural work in collaboration with Dato Kuxalashvili and Levan Cubinidze for the inauguration of the Tbilisi Center for Contemporary Art (TCCA) in Shindisi, Georgia, in 2008.

1. **Venus De Milo**
2007, oil on canvas, 35 ½ × 23 ½ in (90 × 60 cm)

2. **Poor Sleep**
2007, wool, satin, and needles, dimensions variable

3. **Lying Women Figure**
2007, oil on paper, 27 ½ × 39 ½ in (70 × 100 cm)

4. **Balloon Sculpture**
2007, plastic, glass, balloons, and lamp, dimensions variable

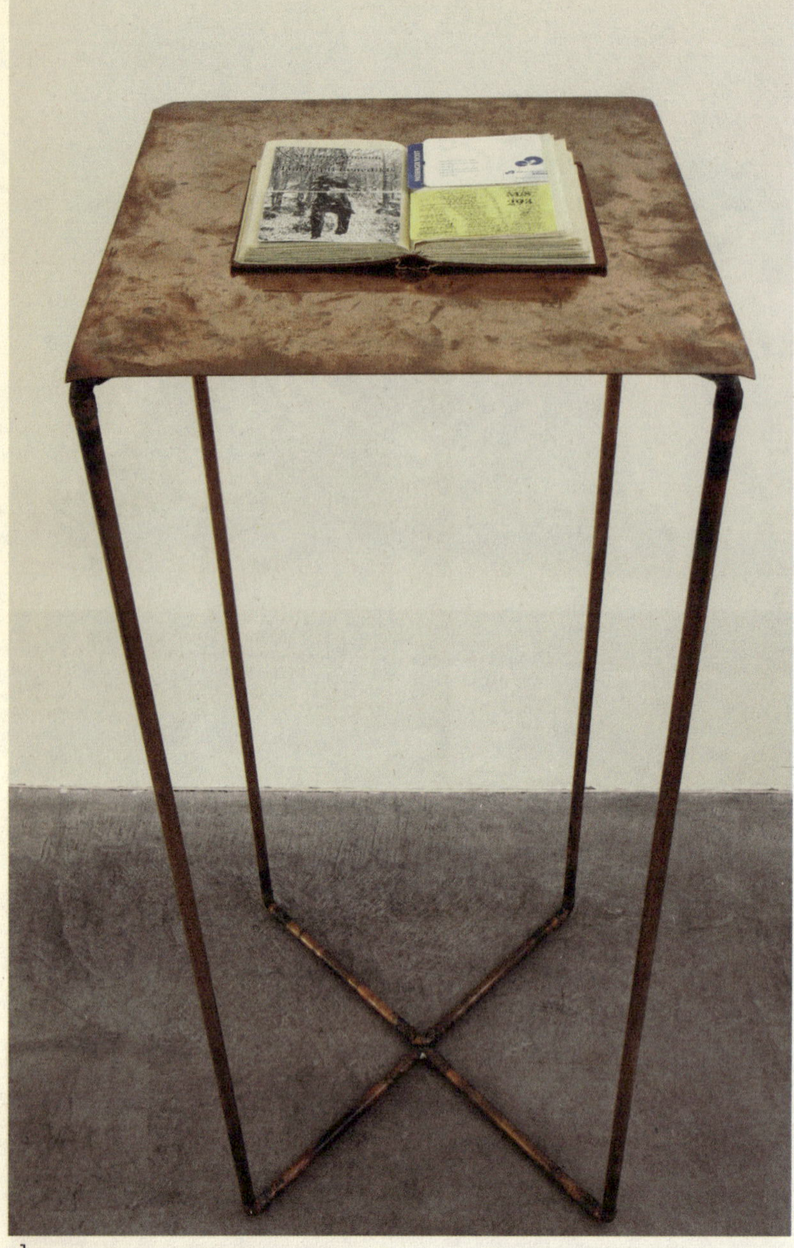

1.

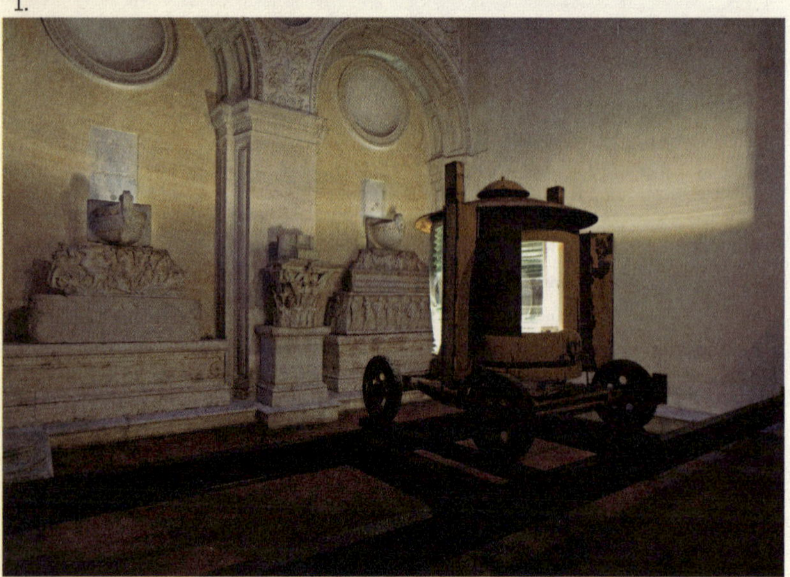

2.

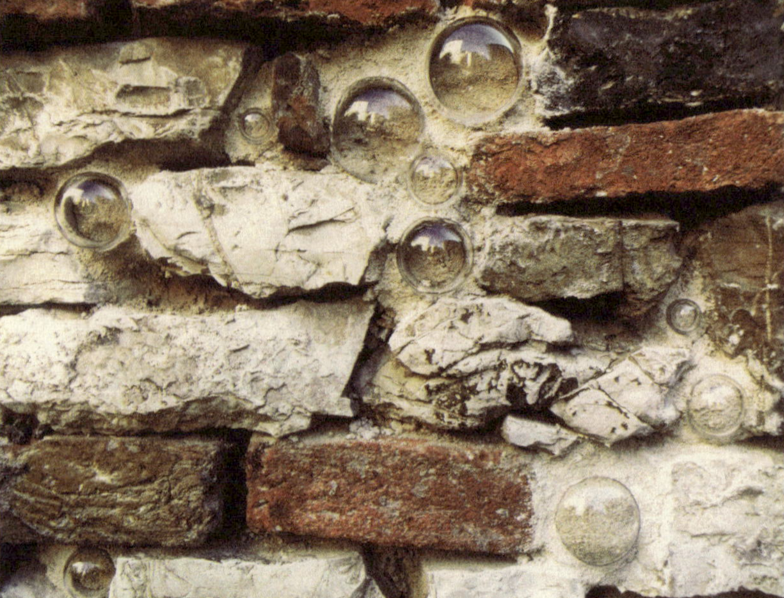

3.

4.

Micol Assaël currently lives in Rome and Moscow. She integrates mathematics, physics, and philosophy in installations that make the viewer feel like a test subject in an obscure science experiment. Pushing the limits of sensory experience, she once created an electromagnetic field in a gallery, delivering an electrical charge to all who entered (**Electron**, 2007).

1. **Free Fall in the Vortex of Time**
2005, copper pedestal and book of drawings, 47 ¼ × 15 ¾ × 15 ¾ in (120 × 40 × 40 cm)

2. **Untitled**
2007, lighthouse and 2,000-watt intermittent light, 60 ½ × 71 × 73 in (154 × 180 × 185 cm)

3. **Nydalur** (detail)
2000, glass, air, and bricks, 275 ½ × 98 ½ × ¾ in (700 × 250 × 2 cm)

4. **Untitled**
2003, floor removal and ringing phone, dimensions variable, installation view at Fuori Uso, Ferrotel, Pescara, Italy

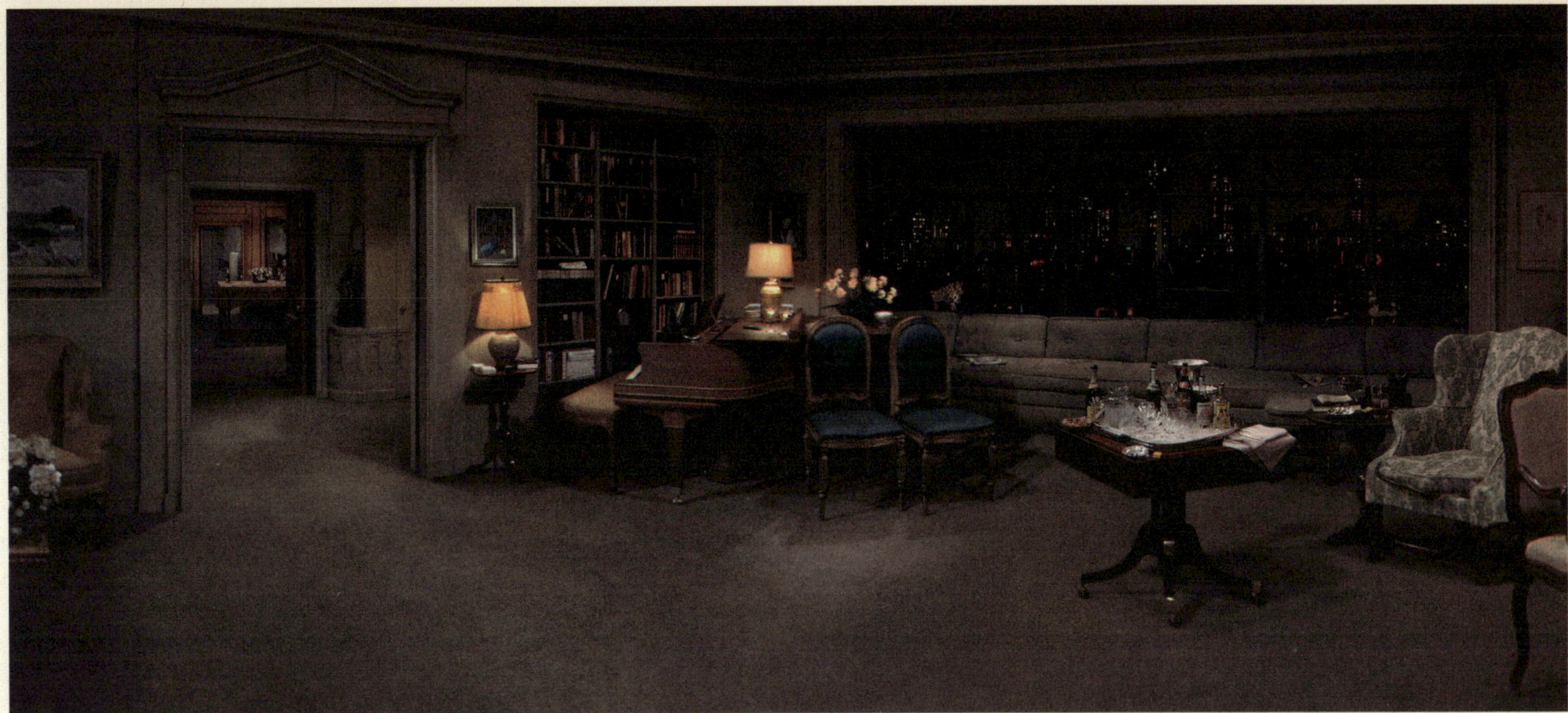

1.

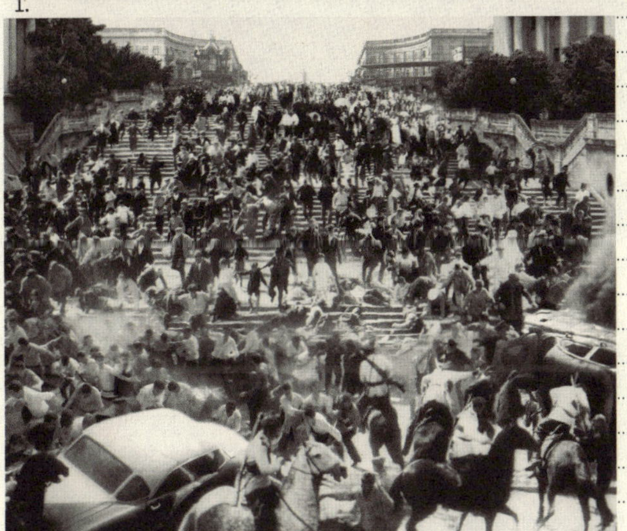

2.

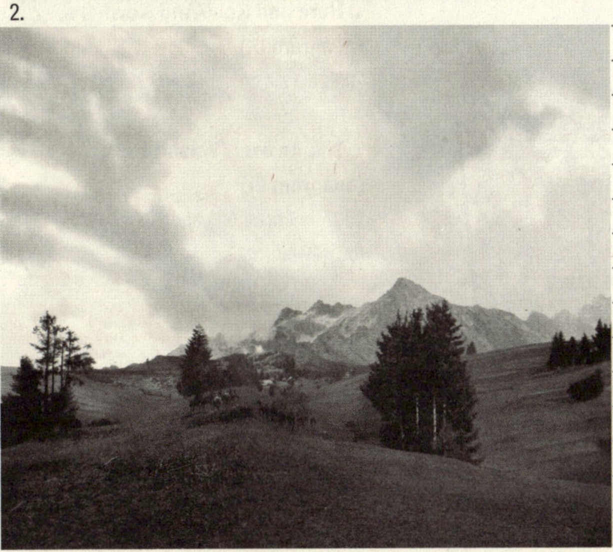

3.

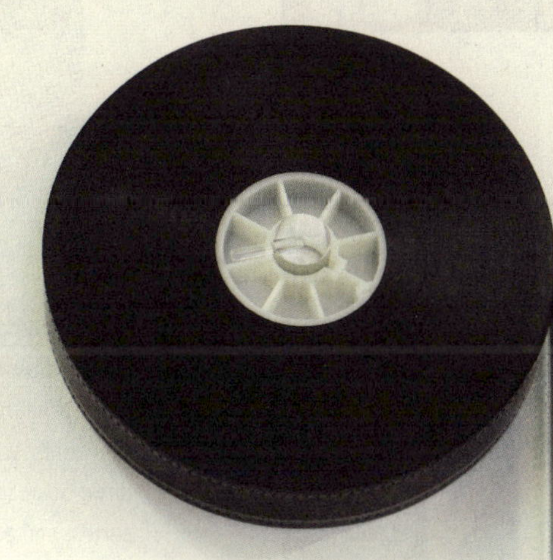

4.

Julien Audebert studied art at the Université Toulouse and currently lives in Paris. His process begins with preexisting images, films, and texts that are modified to generate new meanings. In **Odyssey (adaptation)** (2007) he transfers Homer's entire text onto 35 mm film and displays it on a reel.

1. **Studio**
2006, Diasec-mounted Lambda print, plywood, and aluminum, 35 × 75 in (89 × 191 cm)

2. **1925-1964**
2008, Diasec-mounted Lambda print, plywood, and aluminum, 48 × 56 in (122 × 142 cm)

3. **Landschaft**
2005, Diasec-mounted barite print, plywood, and aluminum, 47 × 57 in (119 × 145 cm)

4. **Odyssey (adaptation)**
2007, 35 mm film and Plexiglas, dimensions variable

1.

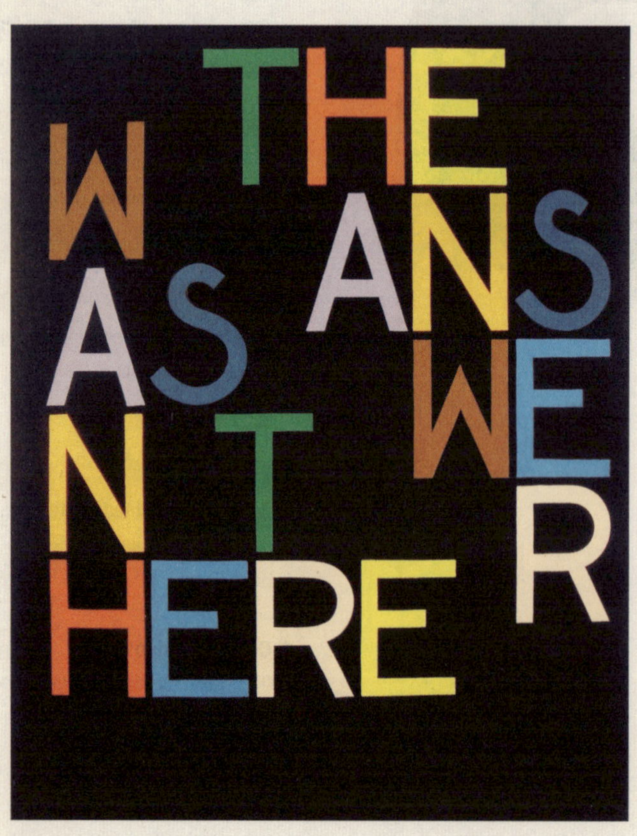

2.

3.

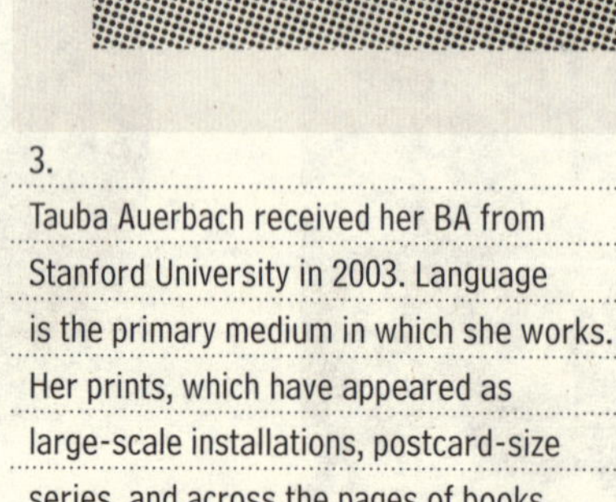

Tauba Auerbach received her BA from Stanford University in 2003. Language is the primary medium in which she works. Her prints, which have appeared as large-scale installations, postcard-size series, and across the pages of books, render letters in new ways, confusing their phonetic logic, breaking them into fragments, and laying them out in space in unexpected and seemingly unnatural structures.

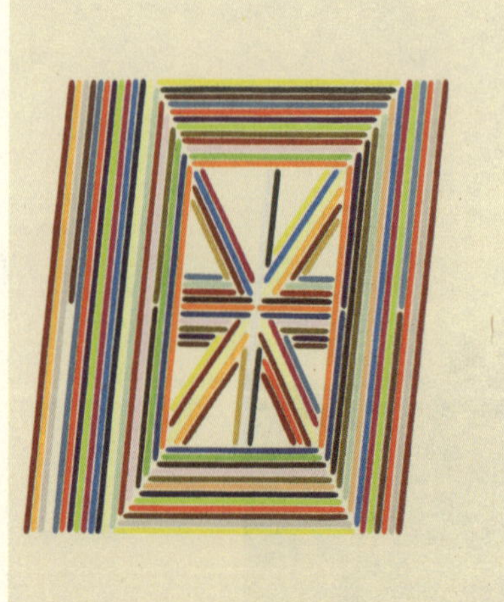

4.

1. **Here and Now/And Nowhere (anagram IX)**
2008, acrylic on panel, 40 × 32 in (102 × 81 cm)

2. **The Answer/Wasn't Here (anagram III)**
2007, gouache on paper, 24 1⁄4 × 19 1⁄4 in (62 × 49 cm)

3. **Crumple I**
2008, acrylic on canvas, 80 × 60 in (203 × 152 cm)

4. **The Whole Alphabet, From the Center Out, Digital V**
2006, gouache on paper on panel, 30 × 22 in (76.2 × 55.9 cm)

B

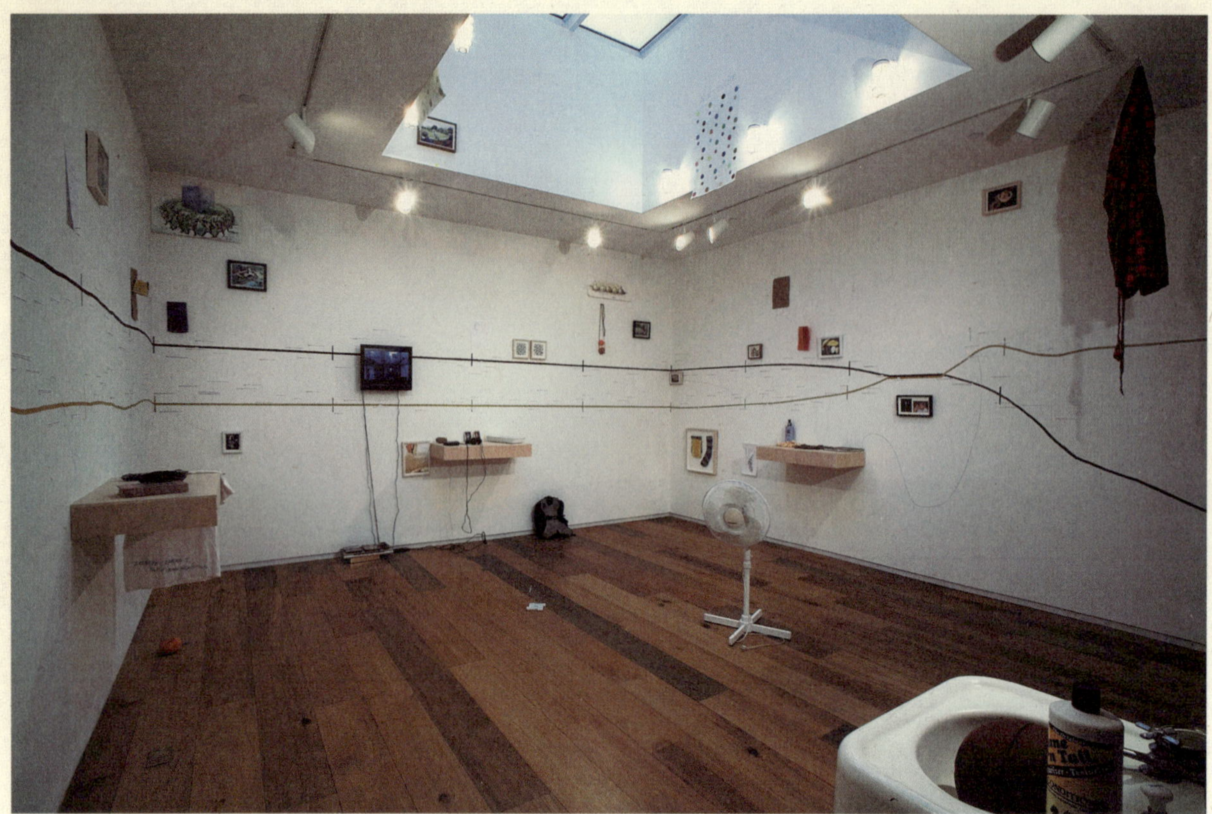
1.

Darren Bader earned his BFA from New York University and continues to live in New York as an artist, writer, and curator. His free-associative landscapes of objects, images, and text refer to all levels of culture in a tone that is at once slapstick and sharply incisive. His books **James Earl Scones** (2005) and **Pulturebook** (2008) enact a similarly twisted and far-reaching form of institutional critique.

1, 2 & 3. **as = poaching the poachers**
2007, mixed media, installation view at Rivington Arms, New York

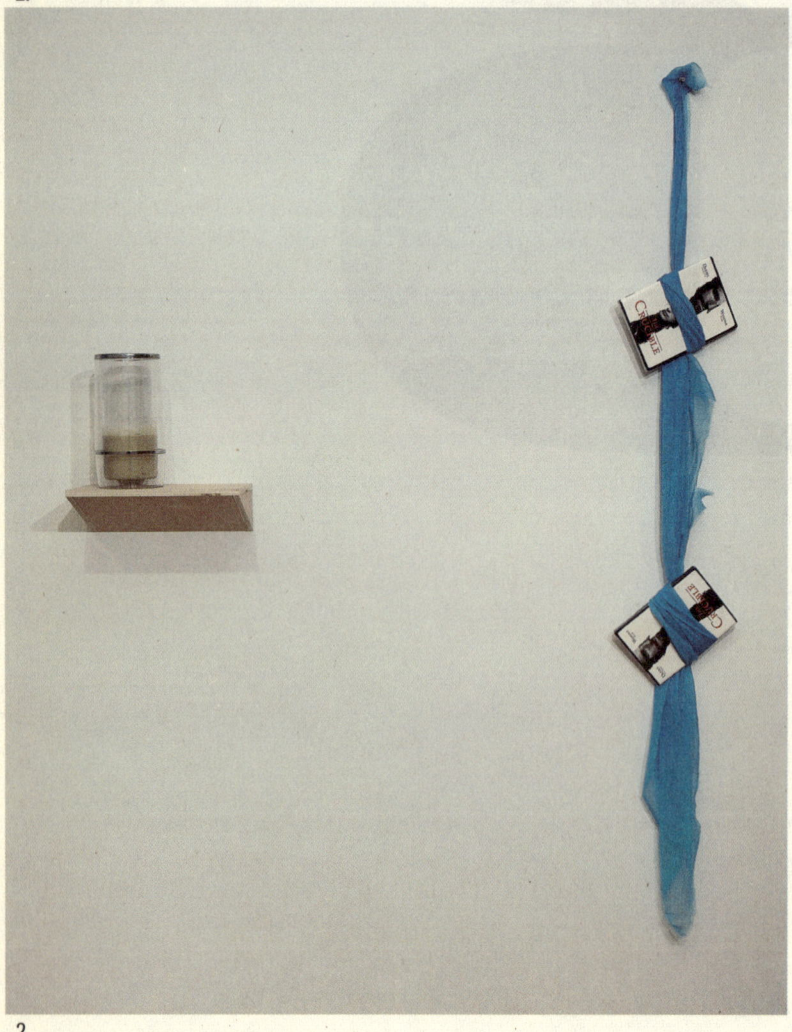
2.

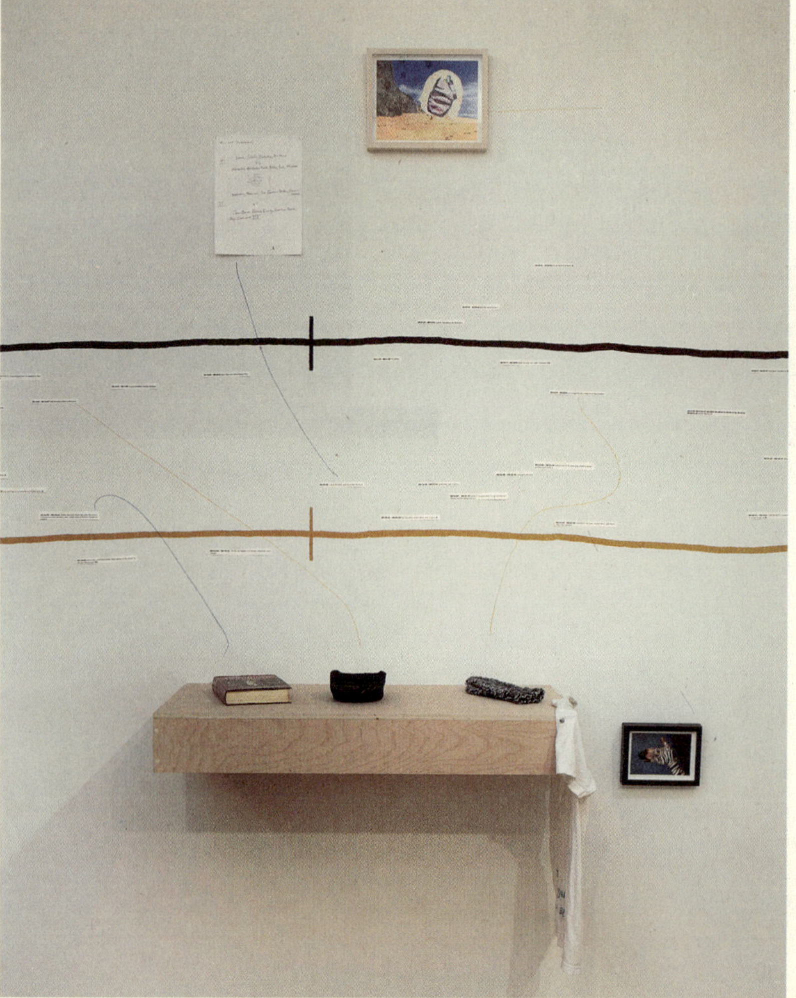
3.

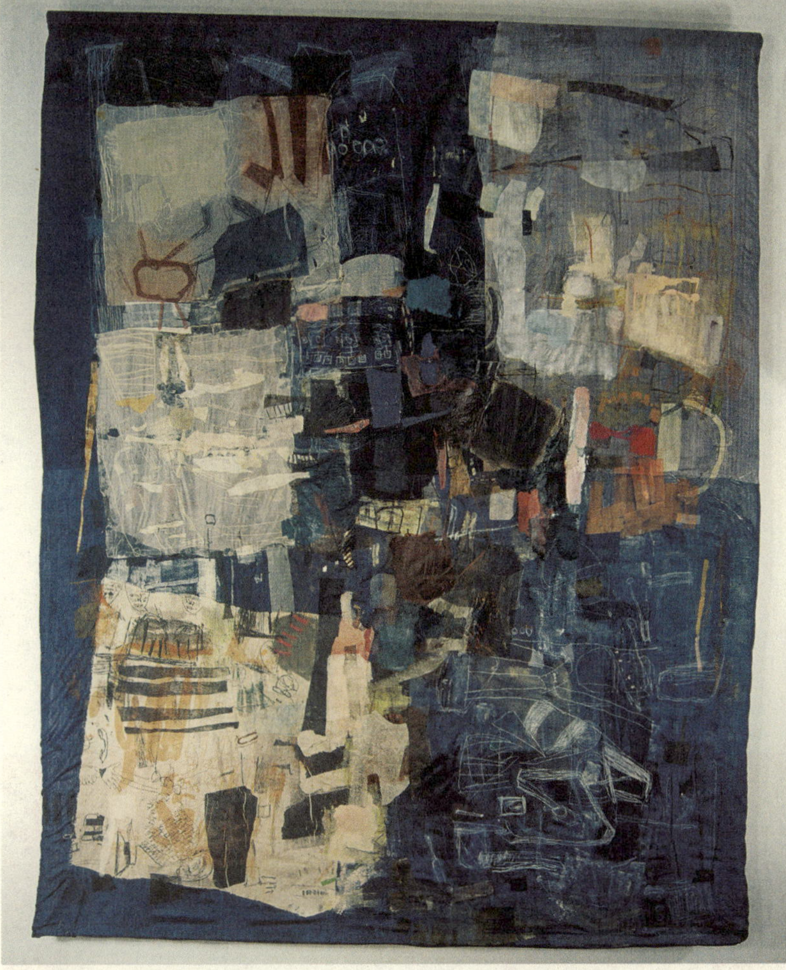

1.

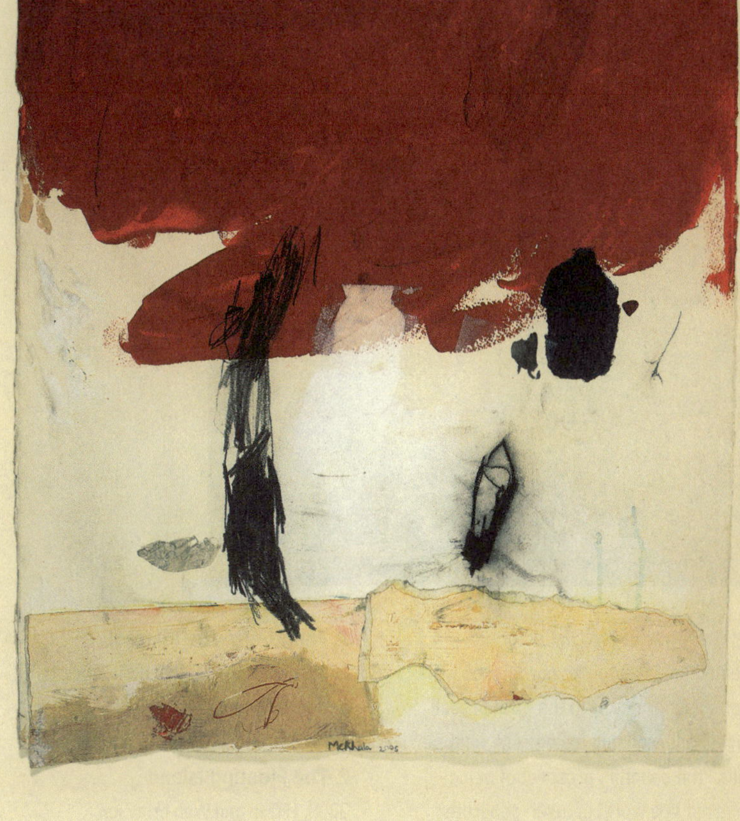

2.

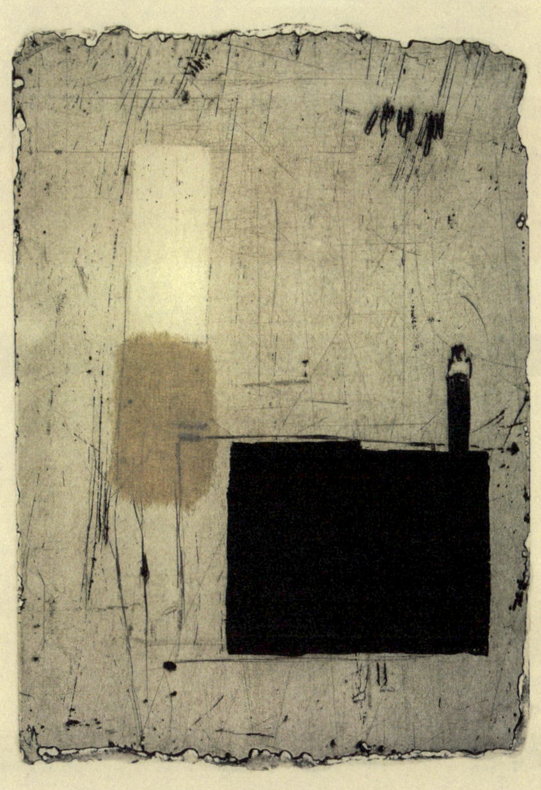

3.

Mekhala Bahl earned her BFA in printmaking from the Rhode Island School of Design and currently lives in Delhi. She combines materials from acrylic and ink to collage, lithography, etching, and blockprint – often within a single work. Titling an exhibition "Anecdote" (2008), she relates her vocabulary of abstract mark-making to dreams, memories, moments, and short stories. She has experimented with quilting as well as sculpture and installation with candy floss, silk, and blown glass, in a constant effort to push the limits of material and color.

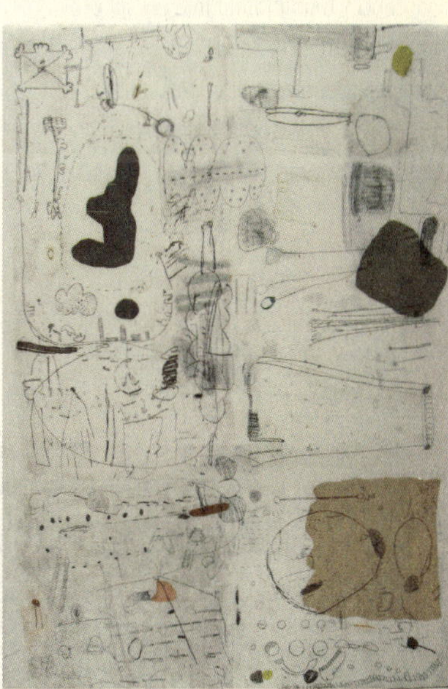

4.

1. Saamnay
2003, lithography, etching, blockprint, and chine-collé on quilted silk, 79 × 57 in (200 × 145 cm)

2. Fire-Sky
2005, acrylic, charcoal, and pencil on paper, 25 × 22 in (63.5 × 56 cm)

3. Pink Under This
2002, etching with chine-collé on paper, 8 × 5 ½ in (20 × 14 cm)

4. Saw-war
2008, mixed media on quilted silk, 42 × 58 in (107 × 147 cm)

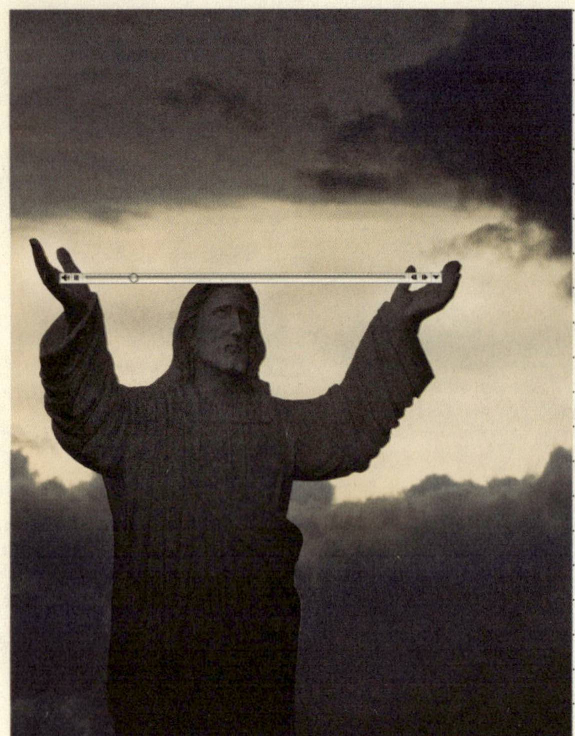

1.

2.

Jeff Baij lives in Venice, California. Trained as a painter, he now makes work that exists primarily in the form of Web pages, allowing him to confront what he calls "the daunting prospect of being an artist in a world of 'user-generated content.'" Using found images, photo-editing software, and HTML programming, his work reflects and contributes to a visual world built on increasingly unstable ground.

1. **The King / The Pharaoh**
2008, found image, found MP3 file, HTML, and Web browser

2. **The Floating Island**
2008, HTML and Web browser

3. **Diamond Cutter**
2007, HTML and Web browser

4. **Sliced Artery Triptych**
2008, found digital video, HTML, Photoshop, and Web browser

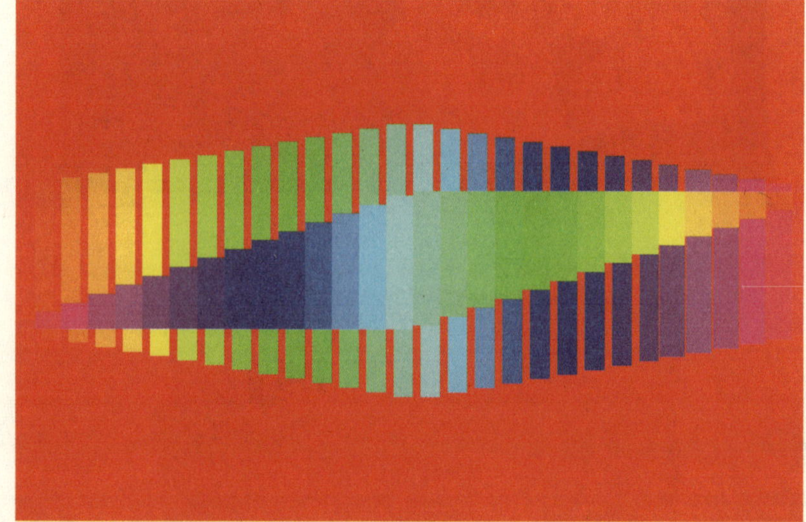

3.

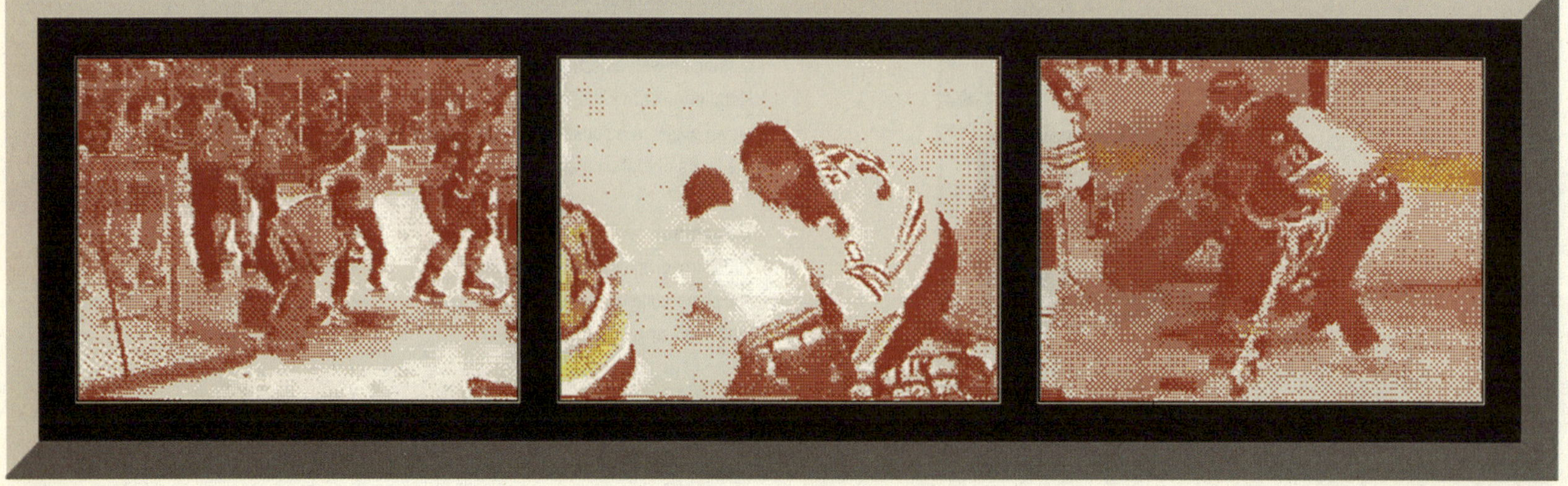

4.

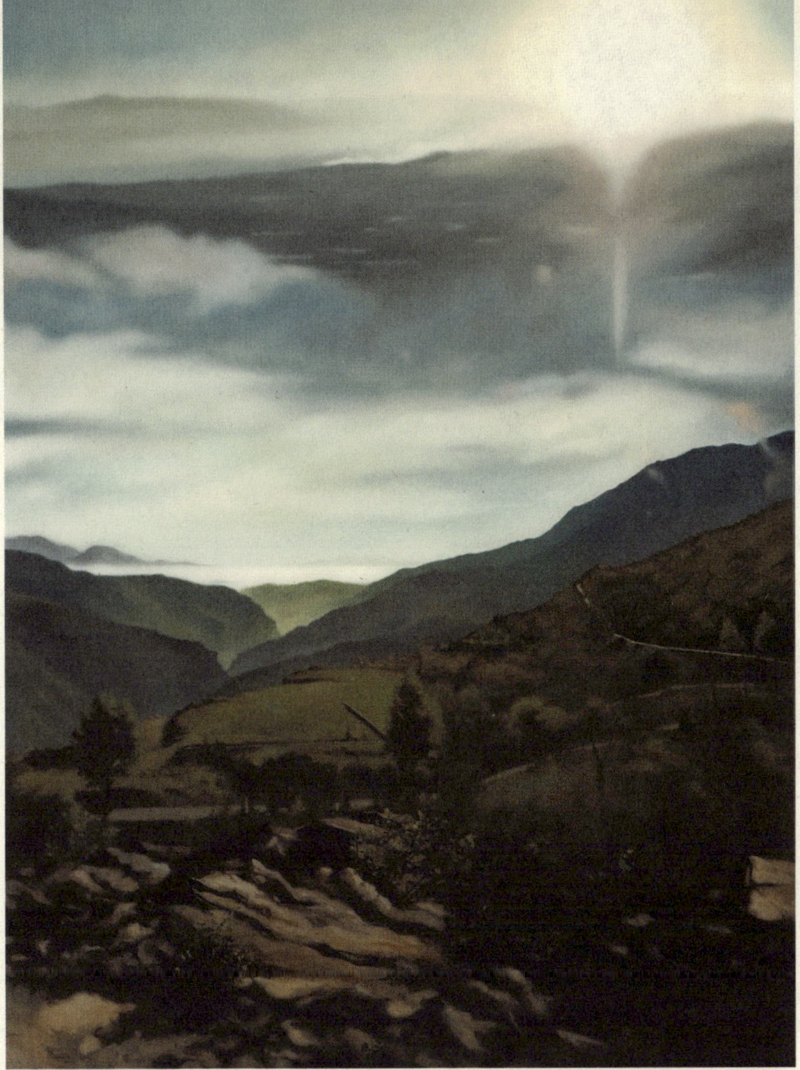

1.

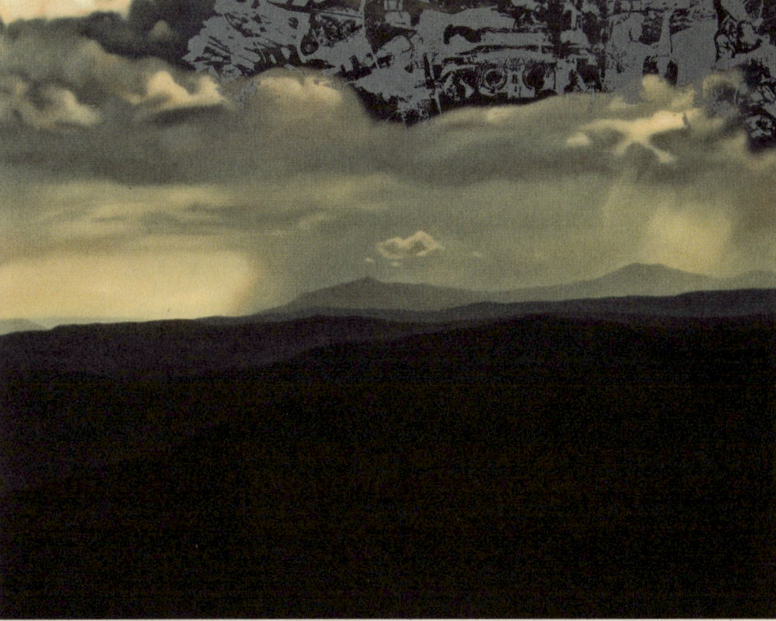

2.

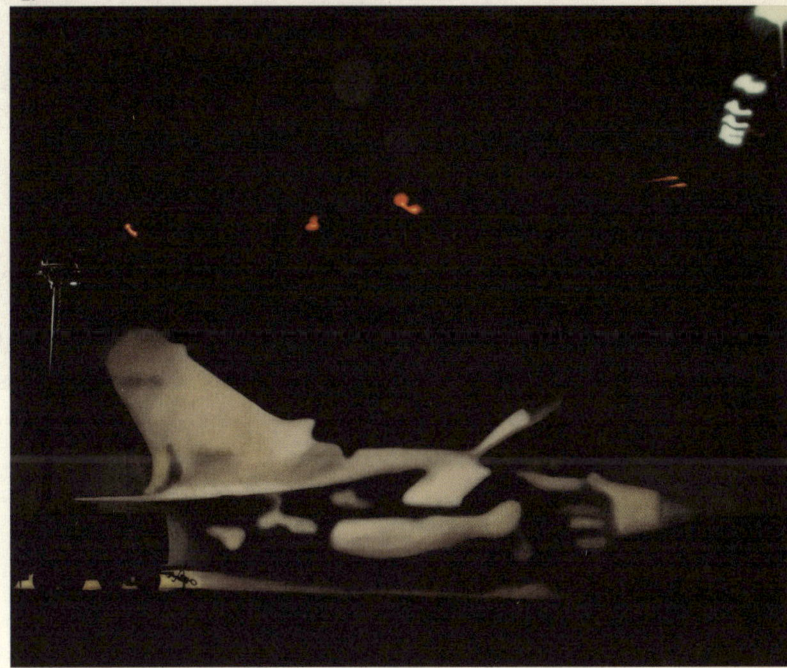

4.

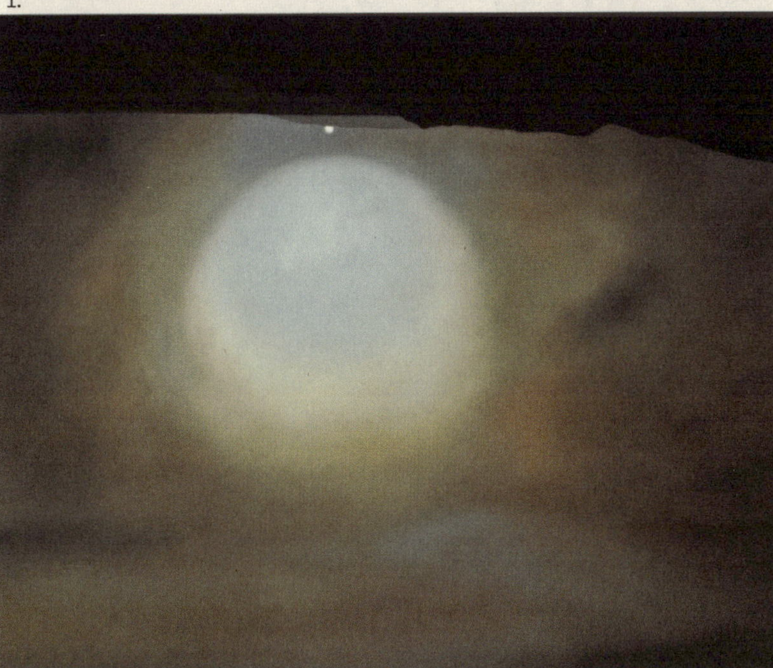

3.

Jimmy Baker earned his MFA from the University of Cincinnati and continues to live in the city. His paintings integrate traditions of the past (from Rembrandt to Turner to Photo-Realism) with ominous emblems of the present and future: iPods, jet planes, and fluorescent-lit hooded figures. Installations often include other objects, like a cell phone showing a looped video of Saddam Hussein's execution.

1. **Kunar Twilight (Catskills)**
2008, oil and resin on canvas, 32 × 24 in (81 × 61 cm)

2. **Into the Void**
2008, oil, resin, and screenprint on panel, 31 × 38 in (79 × 97 cm)

3. **Dust Storm**
2008, oil and resin on canvas, 30 × 38 in (76 × 97 cm)

4. **A Stillness**
2008, oil and resin on canvas, 36 × 46 in (91 × 117 cm)

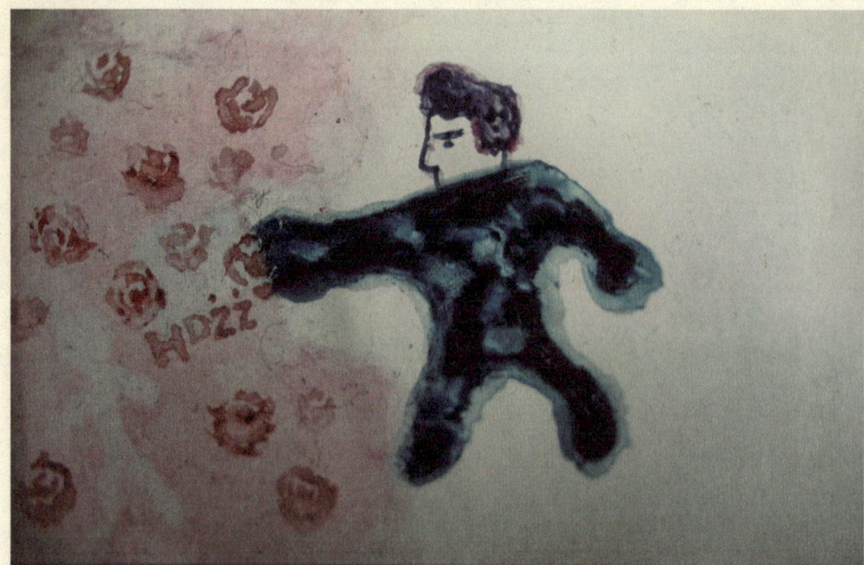

1.

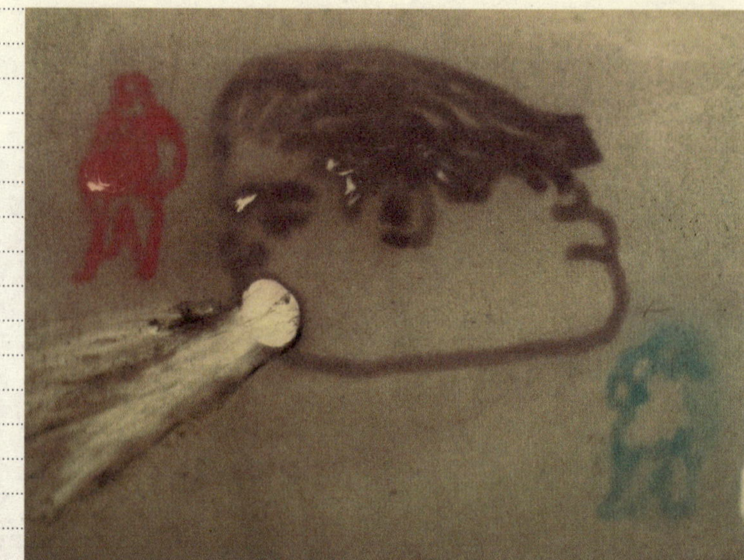

2.

Wojciech Bąkowski attended the Academy of Fine Arts in Poznań, Poland. The primary elements of his practice are poetry, drawing, and animation. He uses humor and satire to build narratives in which a naive, childlike impulse collides with the sublime or the tragic. He often combines mediums – such as drawing on film with a pen – and has also produced music, performances, and radio plays.

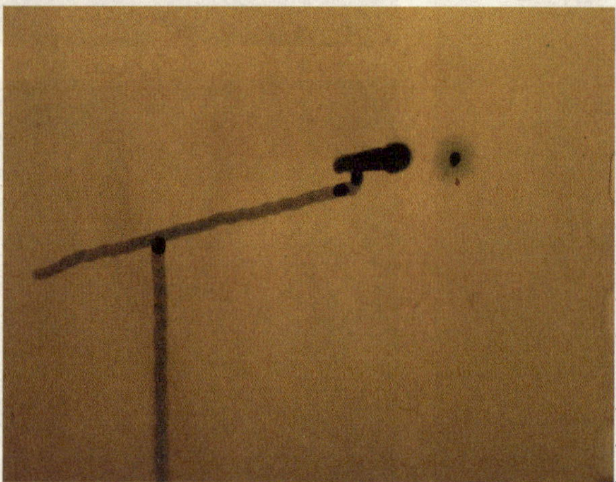

3.

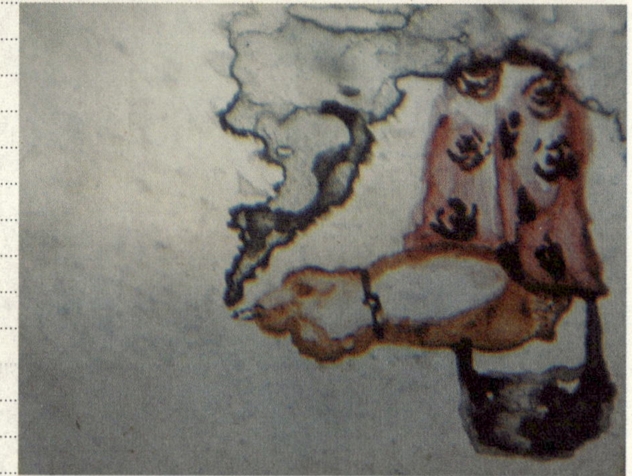

4.

5.

6.

1. I will charm you with flowers
2007, drawing on film tape, $1 \times 1\frac{1}{2}$ in (3 × 4 cm)

2. Spoken movie 3
2008, animation frame, 720 × 576 pixels

3. Bark you mongrel raise hell my pearl!
2006, animation frame, 720 × 576 pixels

4. Spoken movie 1
2007, animation frame, 720 × 576 pixels

5 & 6. I'm going to school
2008, drawing on film tape, $1 \times 1\frac{1}{2}$ in (3 × 4 cm); printed in the book **Warm dog,** $7 \times 8\frac{1}{2}$ in (18 × 22 cm)

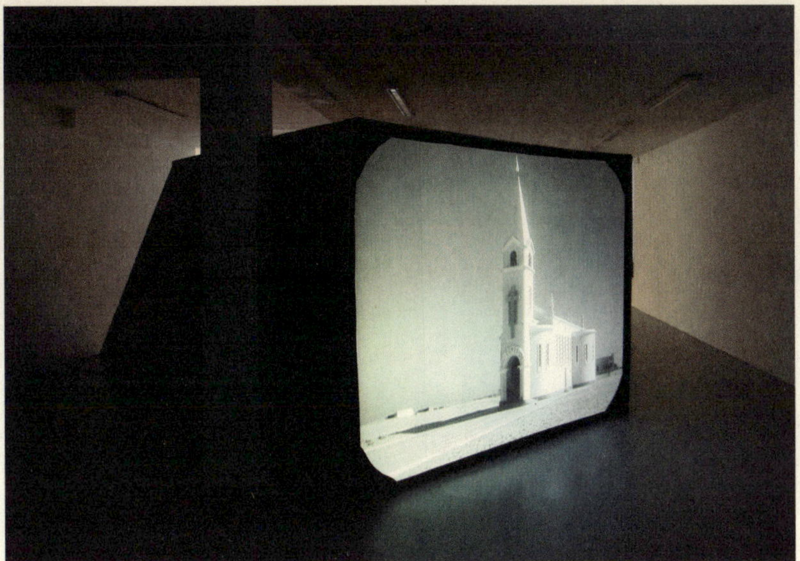

1.

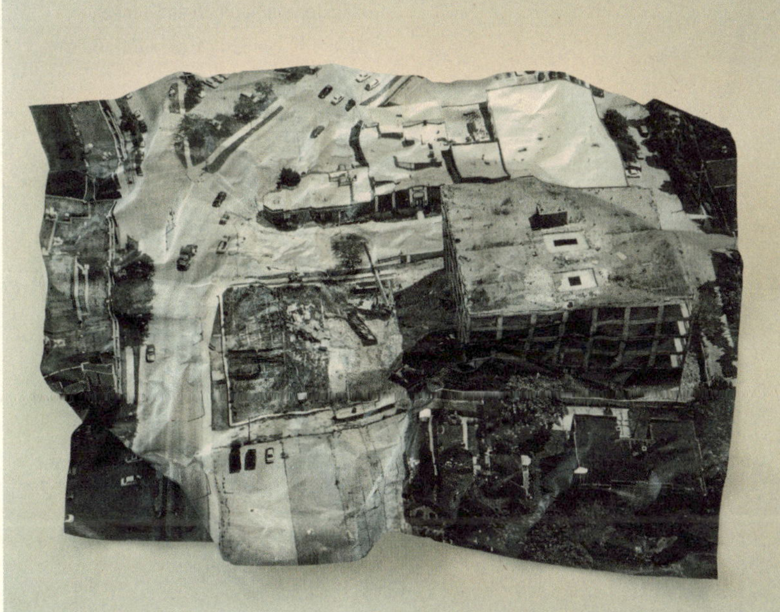

2.

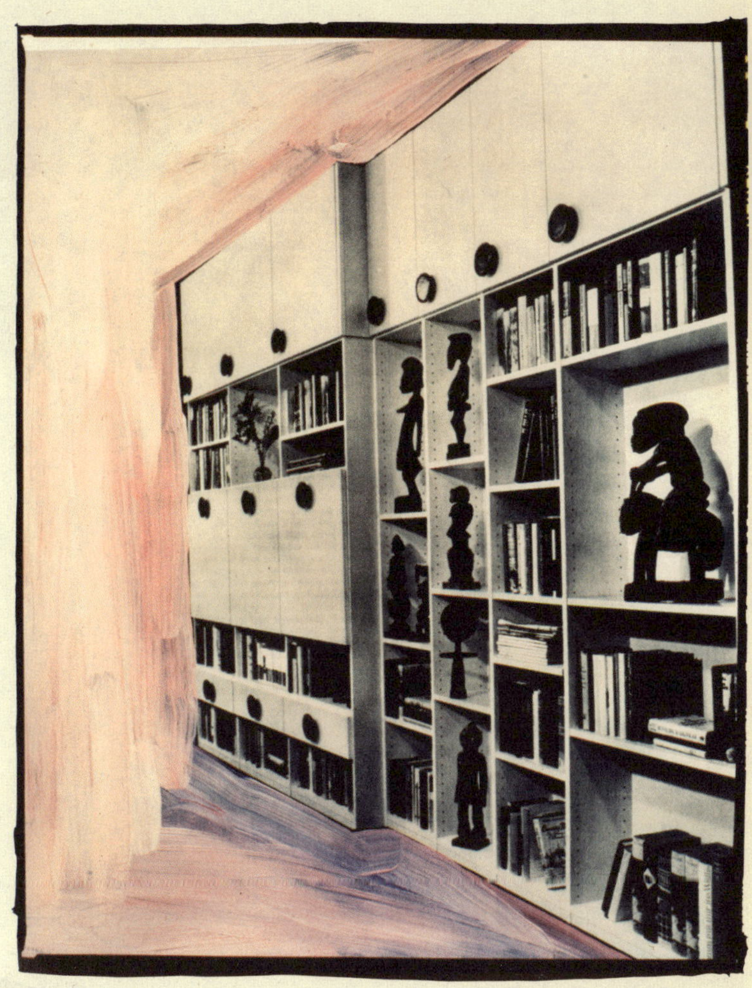

3.

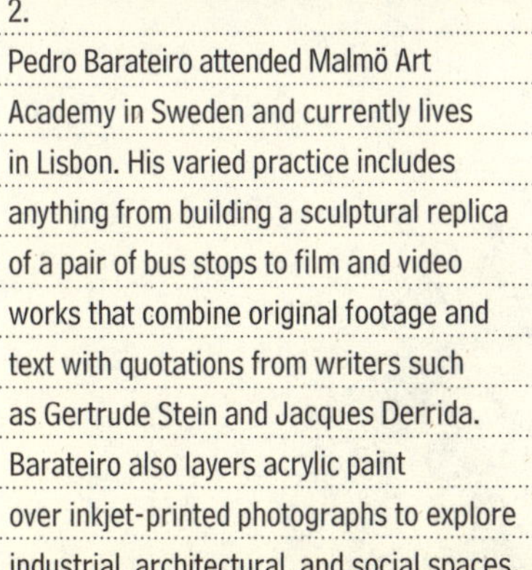

Pedro Barateiro attended Malmö Art Academy in Sweden and currently lives in Lisbon. His varied practice includes anything from building a sculptural replica of a pair of bus stops to film and video works that combine original footage and text with quotations from writers such as Gertrude Stein and Jacques Derrida. Barateiro also layers acrylic paint over inkjet-printed photographs to explore industrial, architectural, and social spaces.

1. **Travelogue**
2006, 16 mm black and white film transferred to DVD, rear projection screen, wood, video projector, and DVD player, 5 min 16 sec

2. **Psychogeographic Map I**
2006, RA-4 process photograph, 72 × 84 in (183 × 220 cm)

3. **Escultura de Casa**
2008, RA-4 process photograph, 62 ¼ × 50 in (158 × 127 cm)

4. **The Naked City**
2008, sculptural replica of two bus stops in mixed media, 19 ½ × 8 × 10 ½ ft (600 × 250 × 320 cm) and 19 ½ × 13 × 11 ½ ft (600 × 400 × 350 cm), vinyl prints, and booklets, installation view at the Berlin Biennial

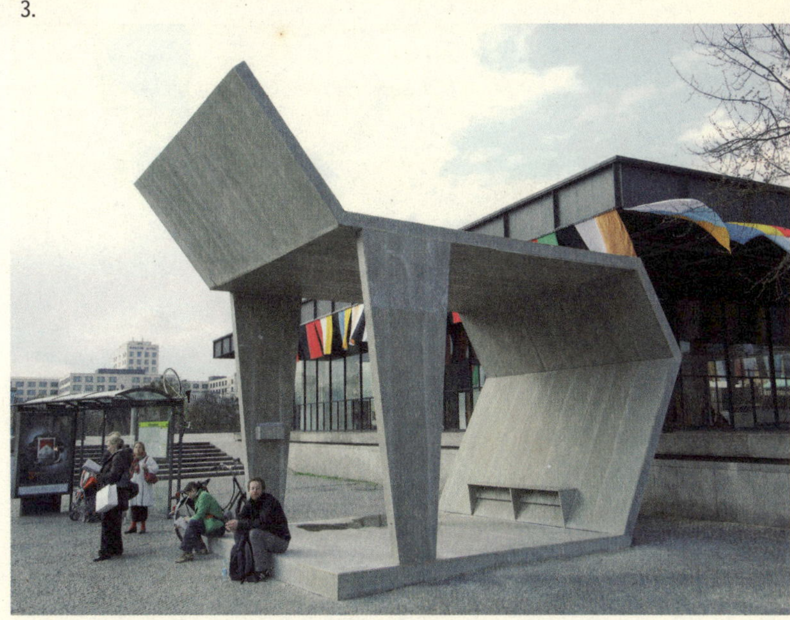

4.

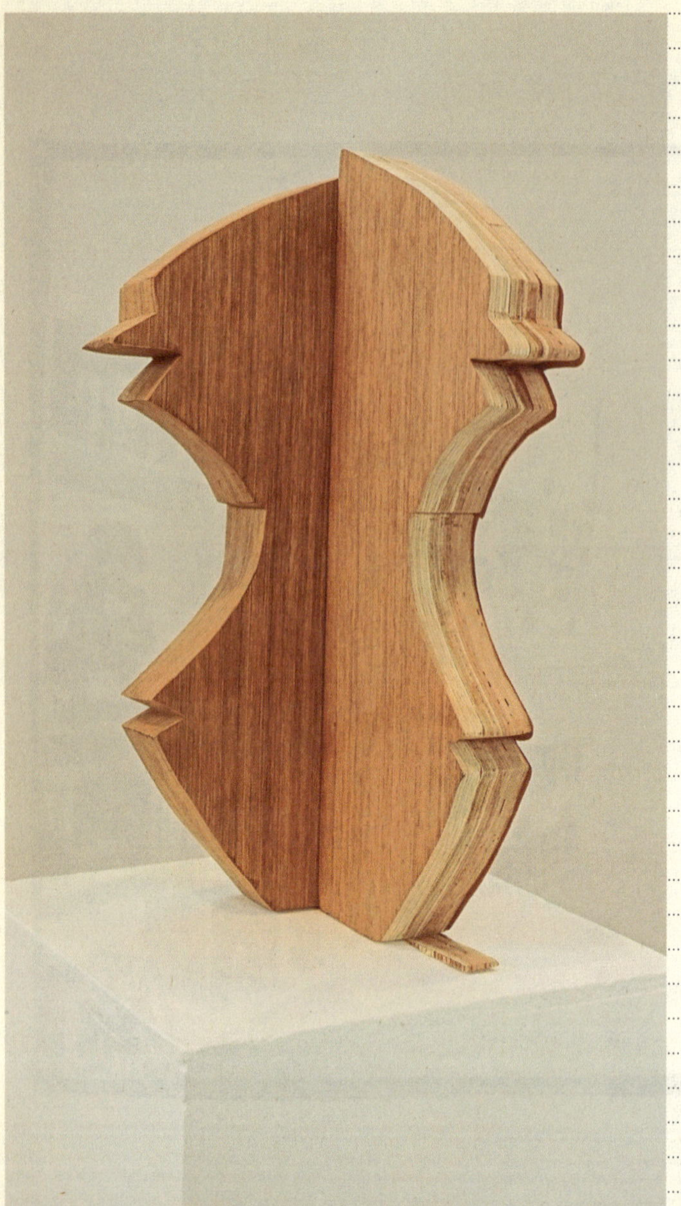

1.

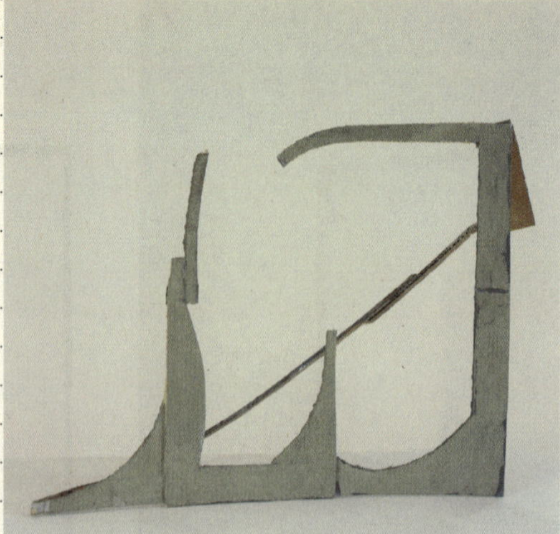

2.

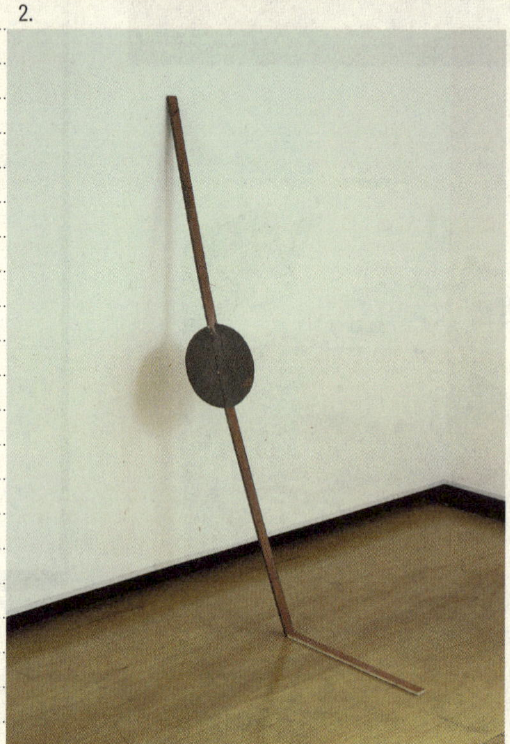

3.

Sara Barker earned her BA in painting from the Glasgow School of Art and continues to live in Glasgow. She assembles industrial material in sculptures that hover between Romantic Expressionism and Minimalist objectivity. Concrete and cement are combined with cheap plywood and cardboard in objects that divide, delineate, and frame space instead of simply inhabiting it.

1. Falling Abbey
2007, cardboard, cement, acrylic paint, wood filler, and wood plinth, 23 ½ × 18 × 10 in (60 × 46 × 25 cm)

2. Sand Clock
2005, plywood plinth and veneer, 31 ½ × 39 ½ × 31 ½ in (80 × 100 × 80 cm)

3. Martha's Act
2007, cement and plywood, 52 ¾ × 8 ½ × 18 in (134 × 22 × 46 cm)

4. Bracket
2007, cardboard, cement, acrylic paint, and wood filler, 11 ½ × 13 ¼ × 1 ½ in (29 × 34 × 4 cm)

5. C is for couple
2006, metal plinth, veneer, and mortar, 98 ½ × 12 × 5 in (250 × 31 × 13 cm)

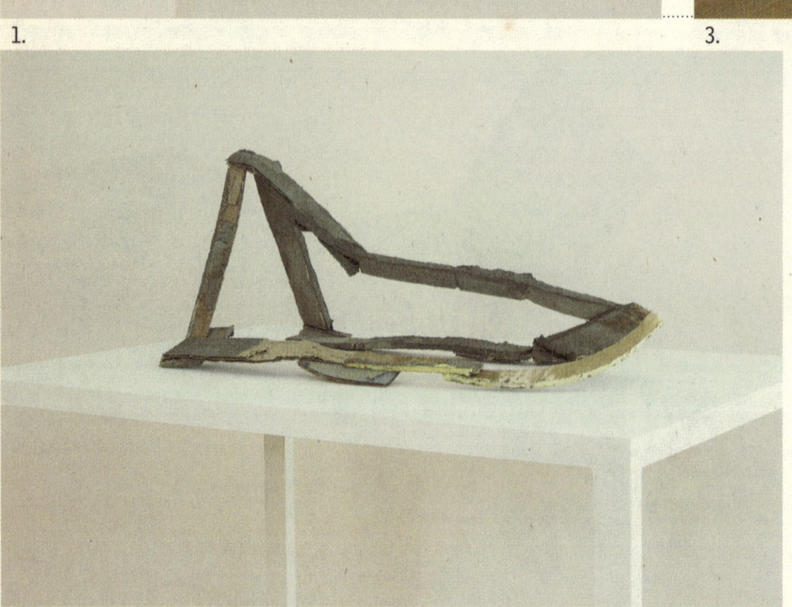

4.

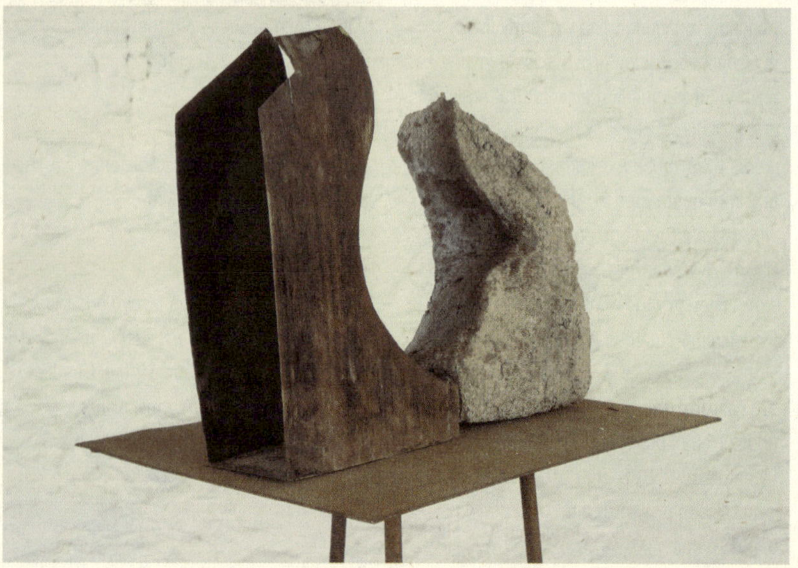

5.

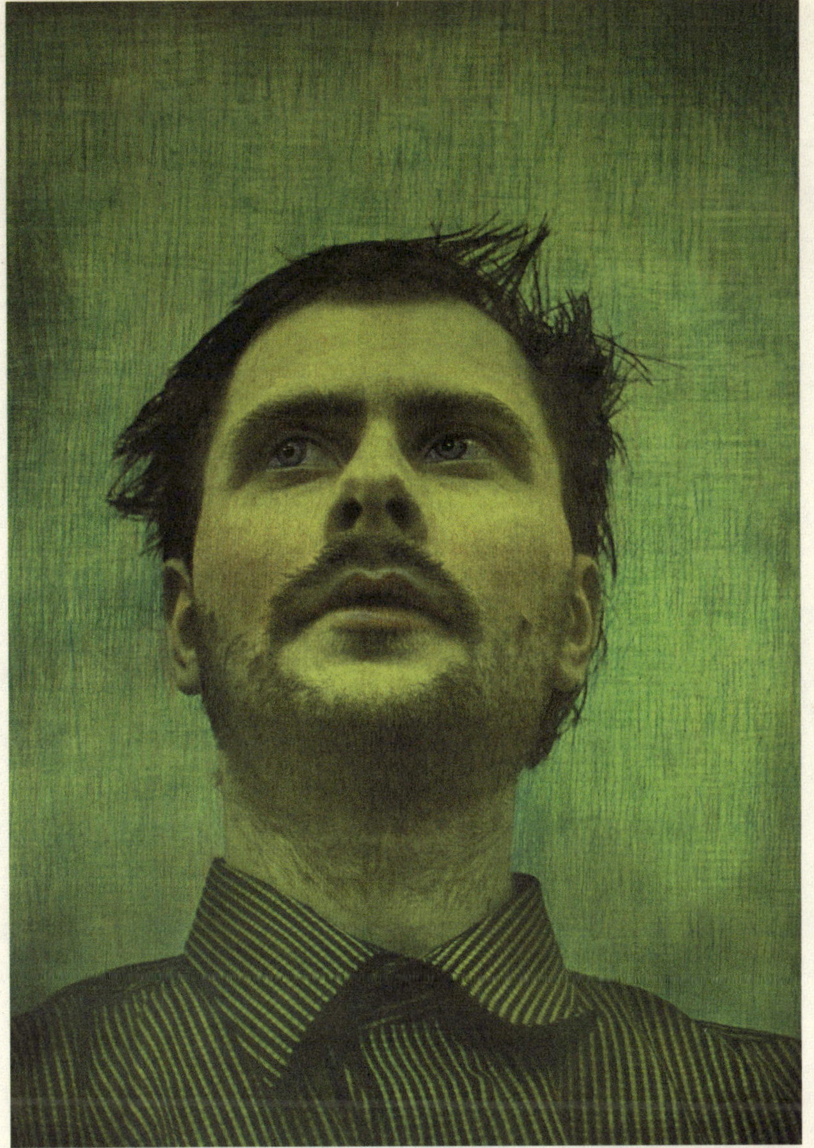

1.

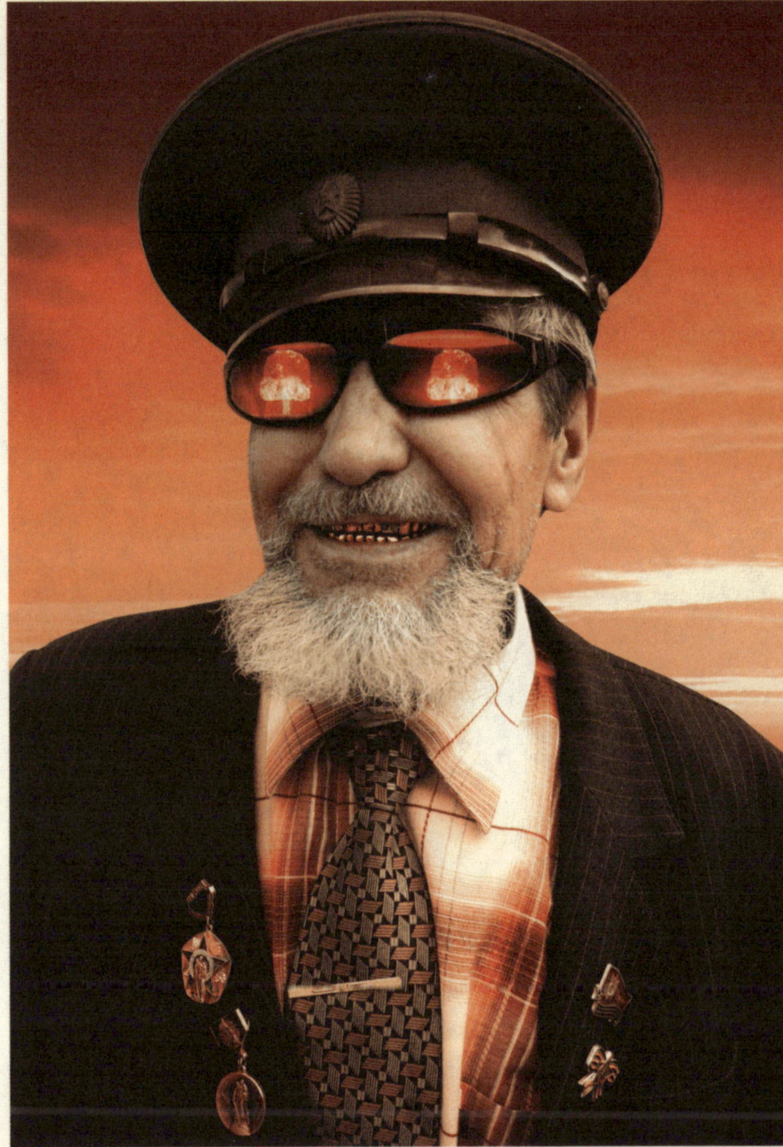

2.

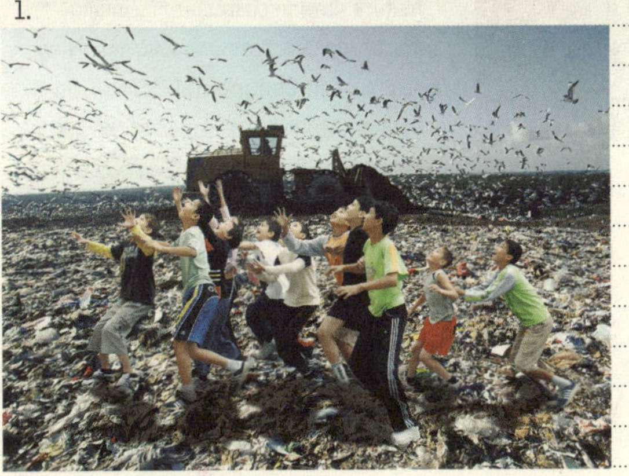

3.

4.

5.

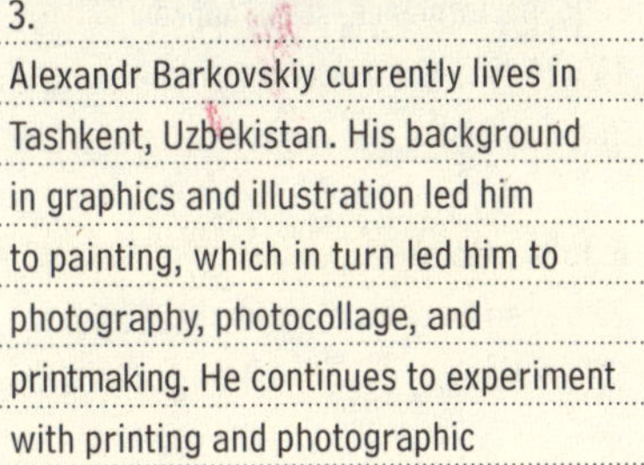

Alexandr Barkovskiy currently lives in Tashkent, Uzbekistan. His background in graphics and illustration led him to painting, which in turn led him to photography, photocollage, and printmaking. He continues to experiment with printing and photographic technologies while making images that bring a surreal, otherworldly element to portraiture, narrative, and landscape.

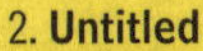

1. Schizophrenic Portrait
2008, photocollage, 16 ½ × 12 in (42 × 30 cm)

2. Untitled
2008, photocollage, 23 ½ × 12 in (60 × 30 cm)

3. All the Best for Children
2006, photocollage, 11 × 17 ¾ in (30 × 45 cm)

4. Sweet Fairy-tales of Childhood
2008, photocollage, 12 × 16 ½ in (30 × 42 cm)

5. Mein Kampf
2006, photocollage, 19 ½ × 27 ½ in (50 × 70 cm)

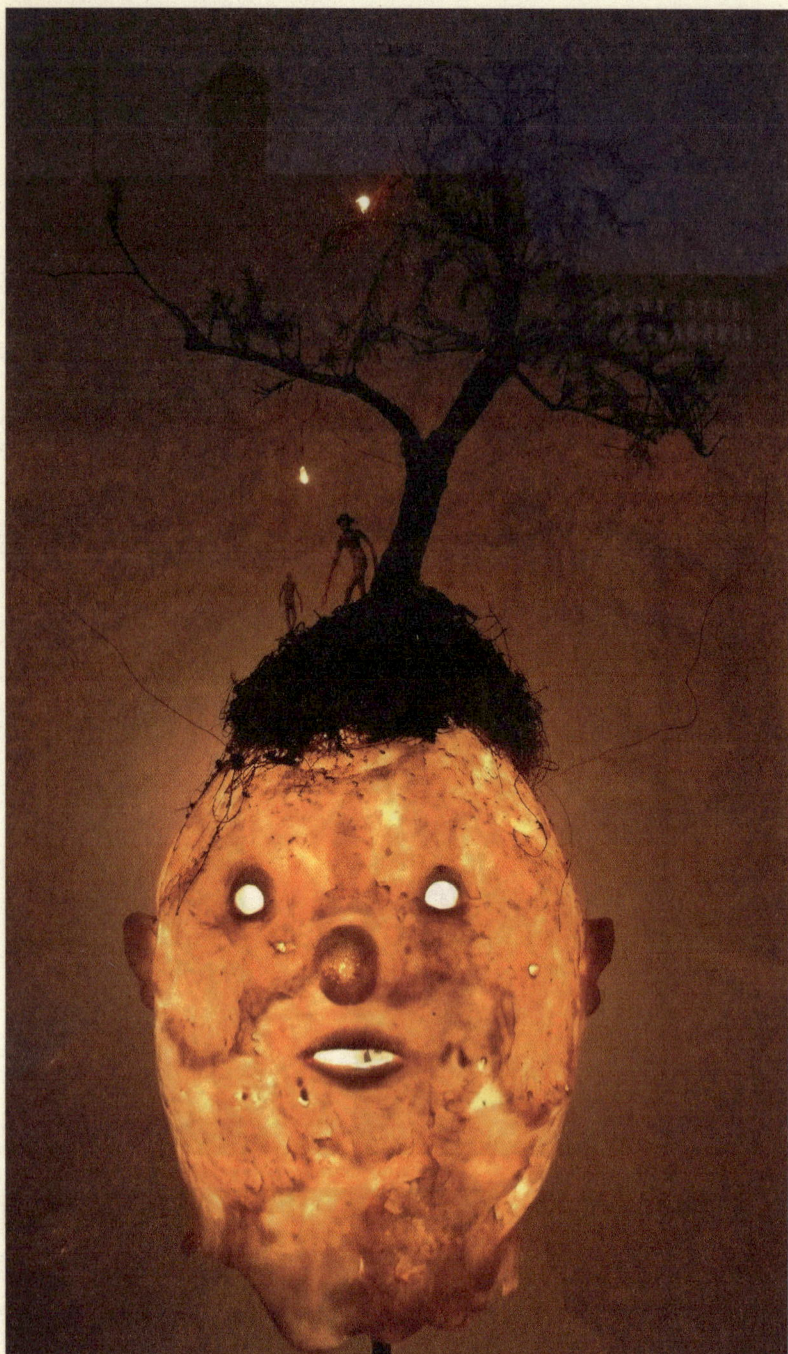
1.

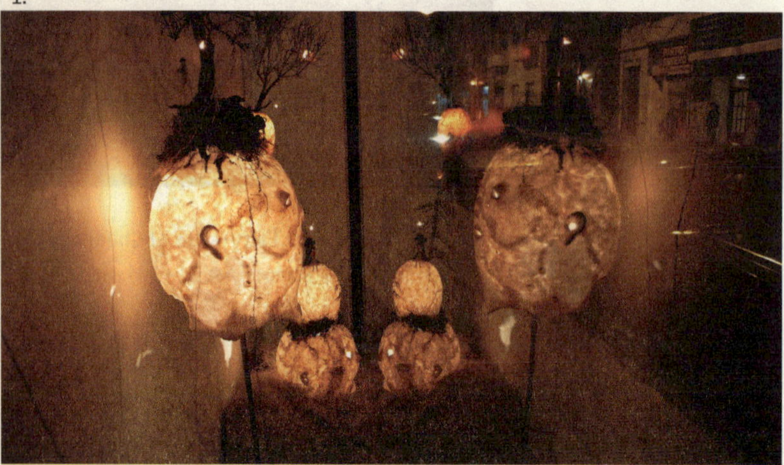
2.

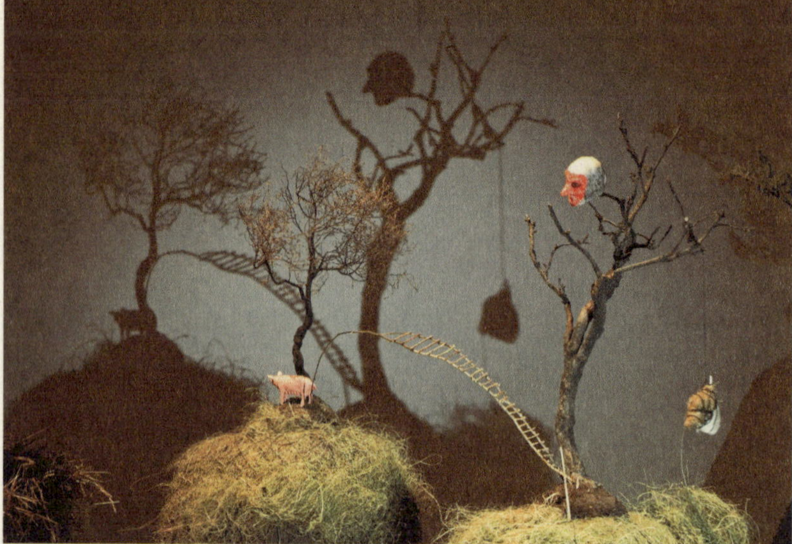
3.

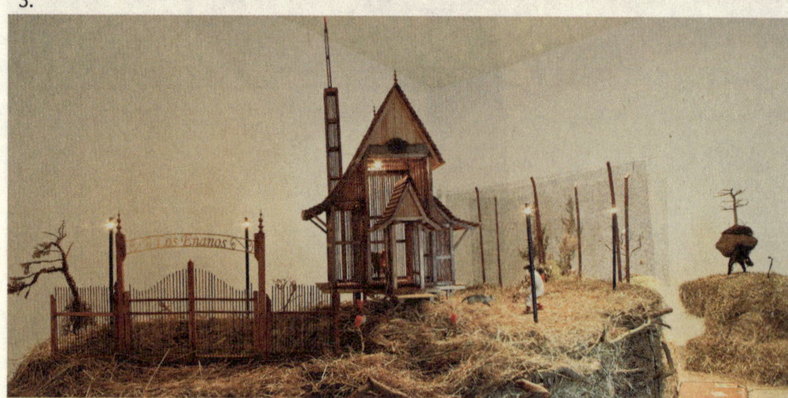
4.

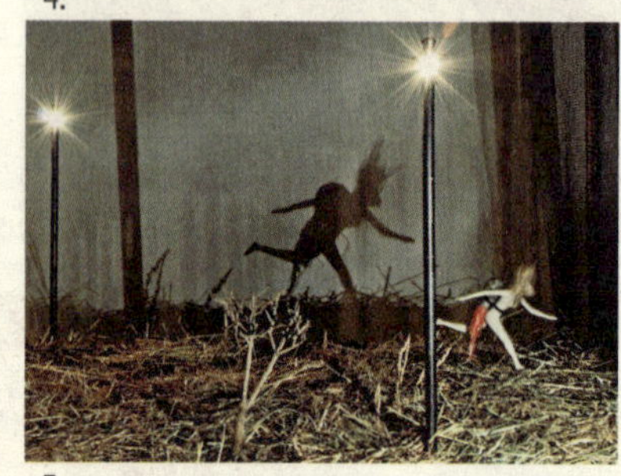
5.

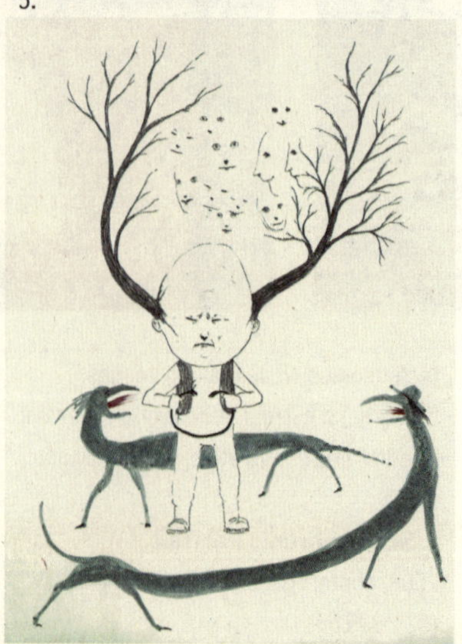
6.

Eduardo Tomás Basualdo weaves mythological narratives through drawing, sculpture, and performance. Merging fantasy and reality, his imaginary worlds feature diverse characters including mutant figures, tree-animals, and living shadows. **El Camino del Zorro** (The Path of the Fox), performed at the 2006 Pontevedra Biennial in Spain, is concerned with concepts and experiences of exile.

1 & 2. **Azotado por el viento**
2007, mixed media, approx $78\frac{3}{4} \times 39\frac{1}{2}$ in (200×100 cm)

3, 4 & 5. **El Camino del Zorro**
2006, performance, stage approx $13 \times 19\frac{1}{2}$ ft (4×6 m), Pontevedra Biennial, Spain

6. **Intersticio**
2007, pen on canvas, approx. $10\frac{1}{2} \times 8$ in (27×20 cm)

BEAL, JUSTIN

b. 1978 Boston, Massachusetts, USA

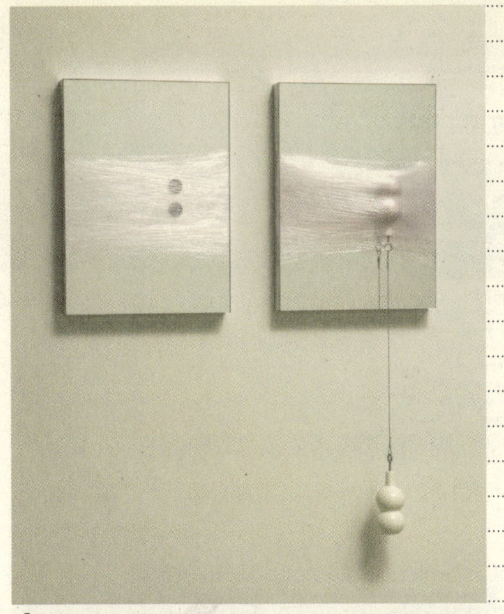

1.

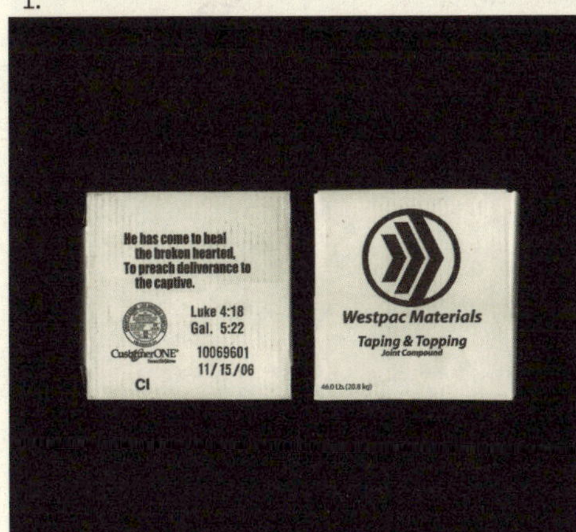

2.

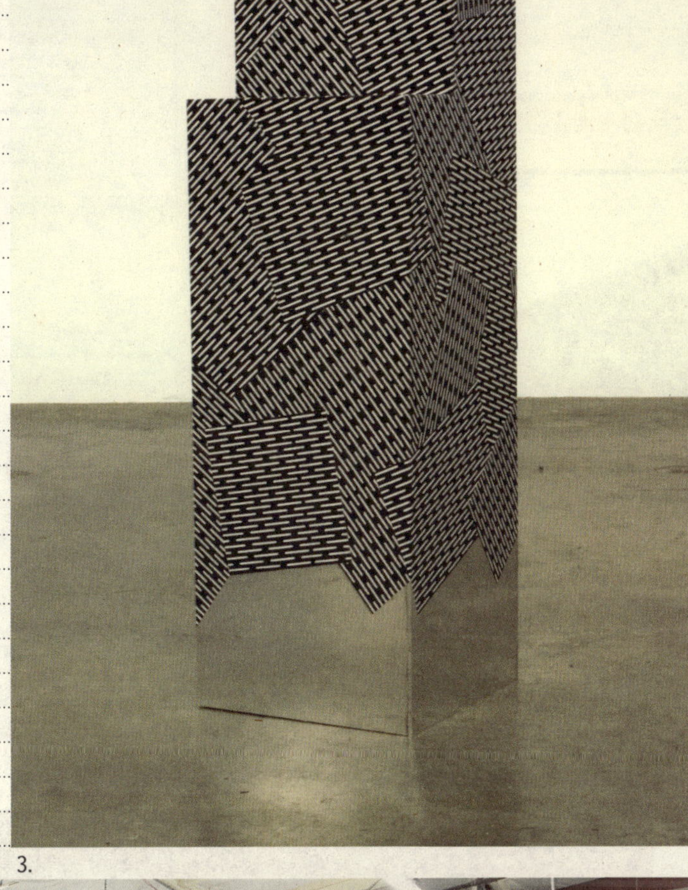

3.

Justin Beal received his MFA from the University of Southern California in Los Angeles, where he lives and works. Many of his sculptures, photography, and text-based works are engaged with aesthetic and theoretical aspects of architecture and design, which he studied as an undergraduate at Yale. Beal has also made a series of constructions featuring casts of Pom juice bottles that function both as design icon and psychosexual signifiers.

1. **POM 4: Quadruplex**
2008, mirror, aluminum, stretch wrap, plaster, and hardware, 72 × 36 × 5 in (183 × 91 × 13 cm)

2. **Westpac**
2007, Lightjet print in frame, 30 × 40 in (76 × 101 cm)

3. **Lamiera**
2006, MDF, aluminum, and stickers, 42 × 14 × 14 in (107 × 36 × 36 cm)

4. (left) **"Thesis Show 2007"**
2007, animation on monitor, 2 min

4. (right) **Untitled**
2007, drywall, plywood, aluminum studs, and paint, 6 × 16 × 10 ft (2 × 3 × 5 m)

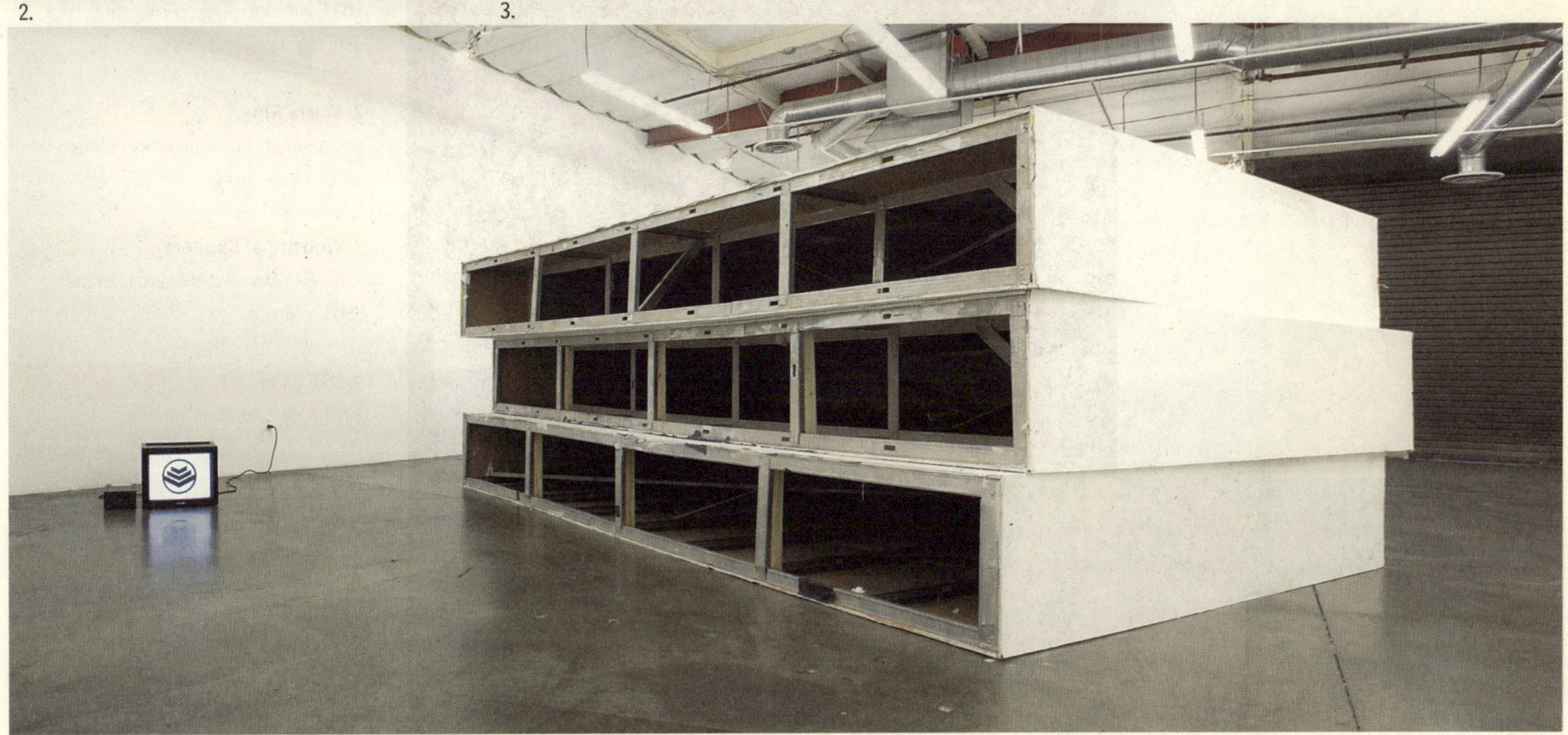

4.

Jona Bechtolt dropped out of high school to play in his brother's band, and he continues to channel his abundant energy into a variety of punk projects. The Portland-based artist makes little distinction between his music, dancing, performances, and online interventions; they are all facets of a single life-project that operates on humor and adrenaline.

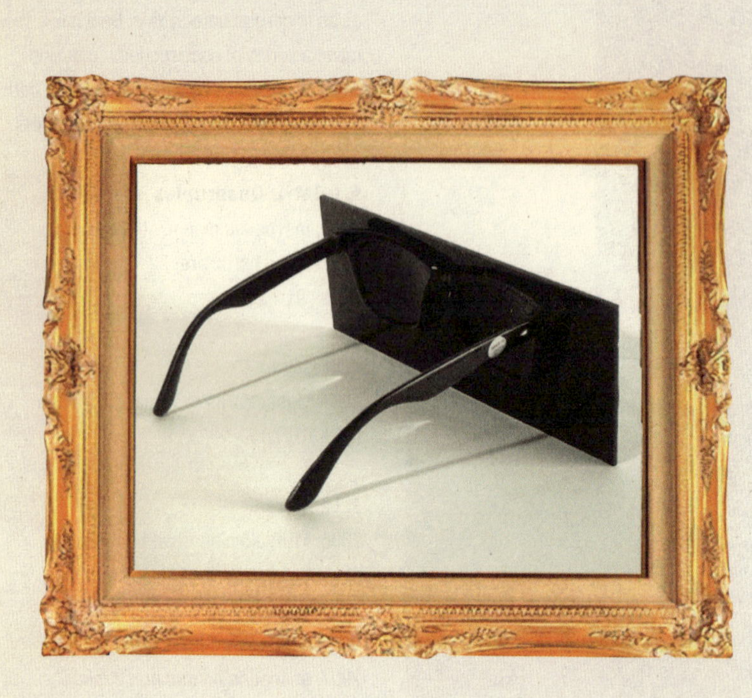

1.

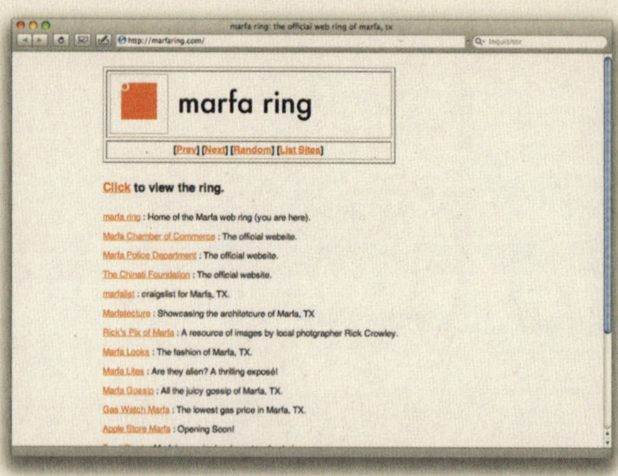

2.

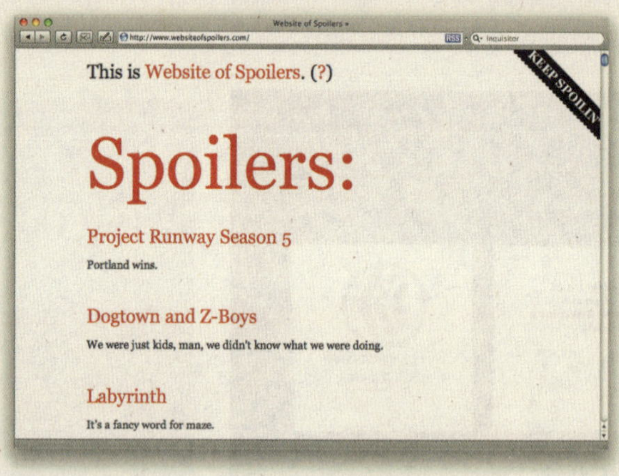

3.

4.

1. Flickrblockrs
2007, website, video, certificate of authenticity, and invoice

2. Marfa Ring
with Claire L. Evans and Flint Jamison
2008, 14 websites

3. Website of Spoilers
with Mike Merrill and Claire L. Evans
2008, website

4. NTSC-Ya
2008, video, duration variable

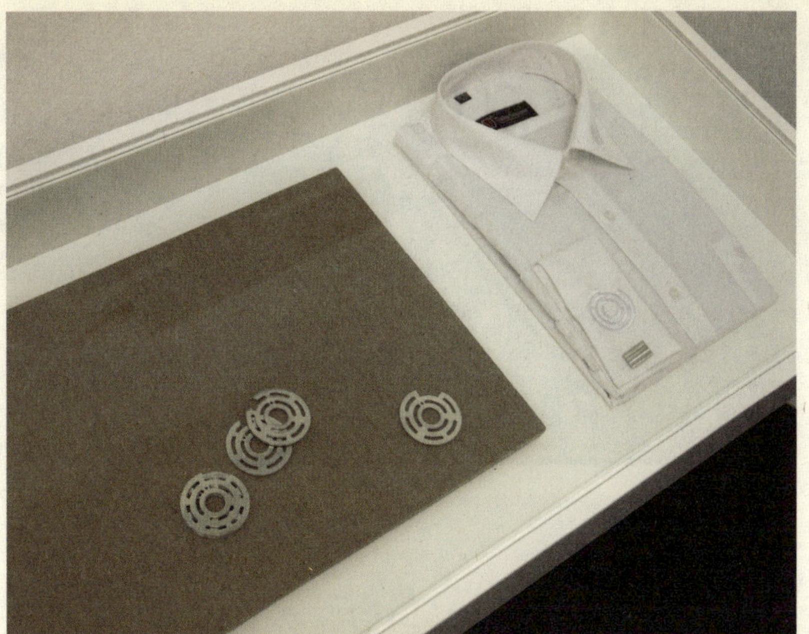

1.

James Beckett attended the Rijksakademie in Amsterdam, where he continues to live and work. His sculpture, installation, live performance, and sound works explore pathways between history, science, and music. Projects include a concert for percussion on 150 trophies (2006), a printer that translates the vibrations of passing trains into punched holes in paper (2006), and a temporary interactive radio show in Besengue City, Cameroon, Africa (2002).

1. **Valves**
2008, stainless steel on canvas, embroidered shirt, and vitrine, 17 ¾ × 59 × 8 in (45 × 150 × 20 cm)

2. **Mill-1**
2008, milled dual-layer Plexiglas following found model, dimensions variable, smallest 4 ¼ × 3 × 6 ¼ in (11 × 8 × 16 cm)

3. **Punch-Printers**
2006, electronics, mechanics, and paper, each 86 ½ × 55 × 13 ¼ in (220 × 140 × 34 cm)

4. **N.L.13 – Tribune per teatro all'aperto – Castello Sfprzesco, Milano**
2008, India ink, gouache, and white pencil on paper, 23 ½ × 31 ½ in (60 × 80 cm)

5. **Beckett-Beaumont**
2007, self-registered tartan, shown as neckties, 17 ¾ × 2 ¾ in (45 × 7 cm)

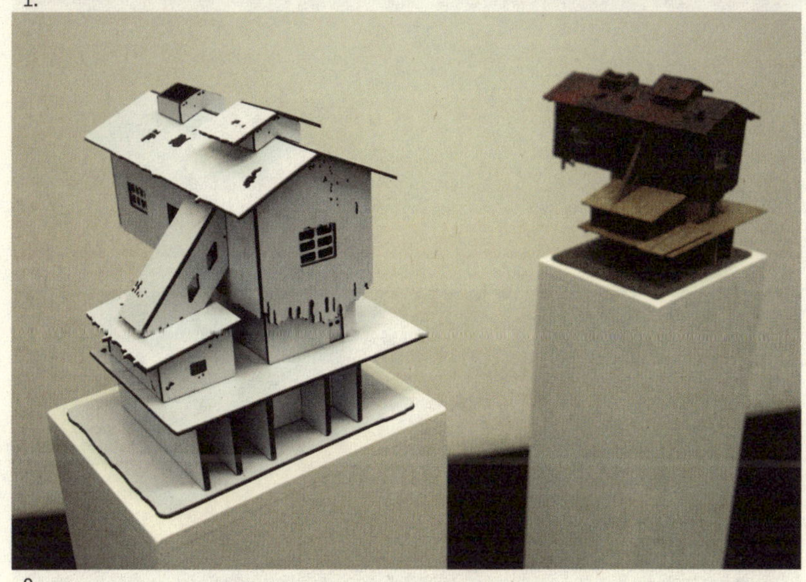

2.

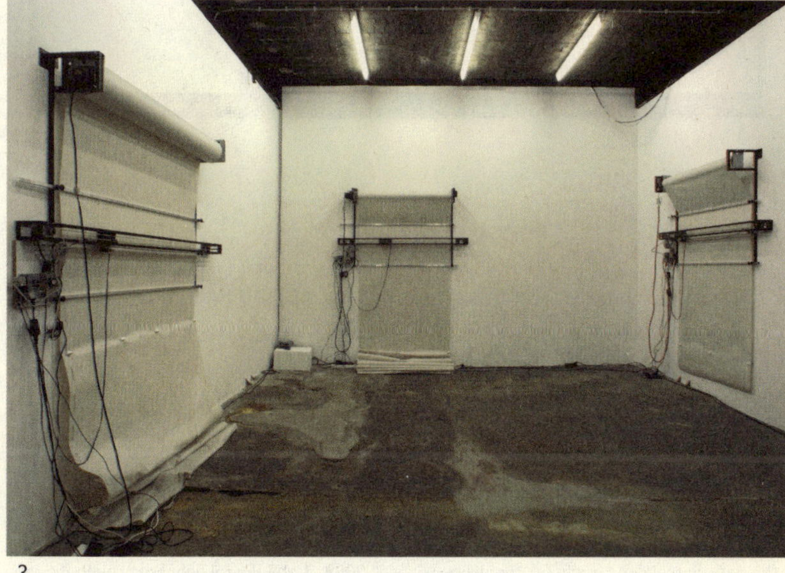

3.

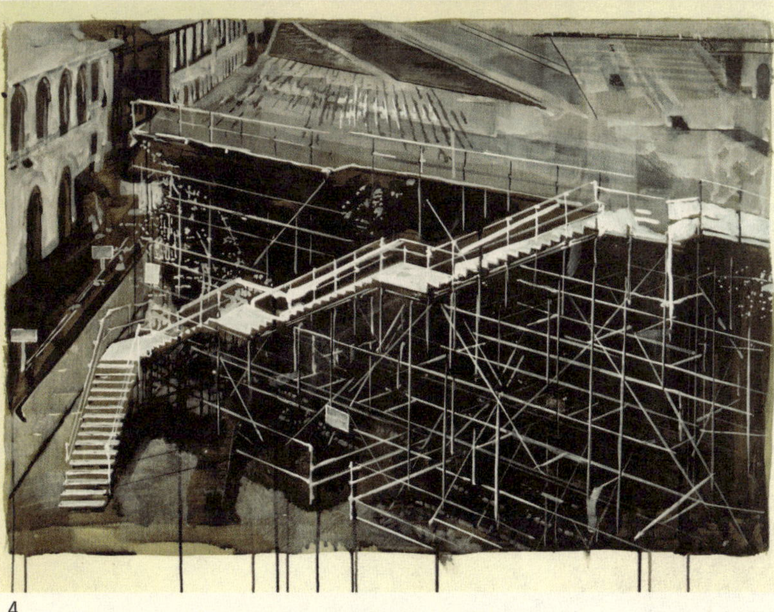

4.

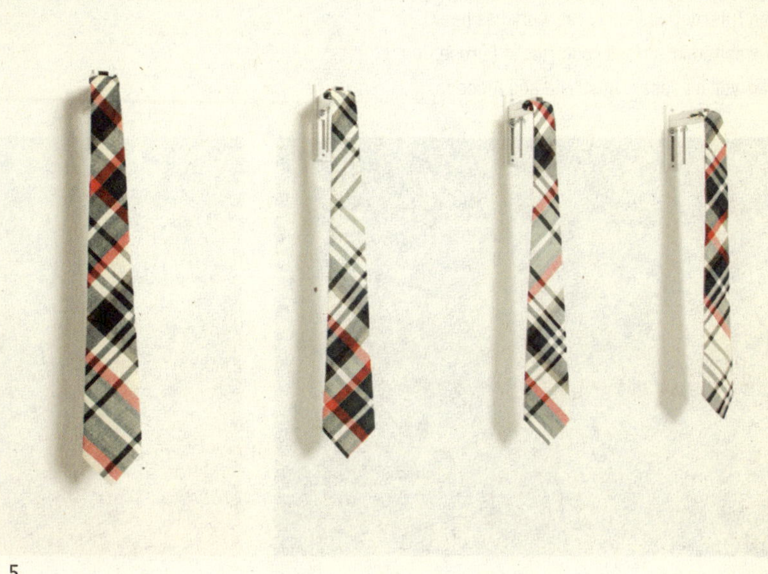

5.

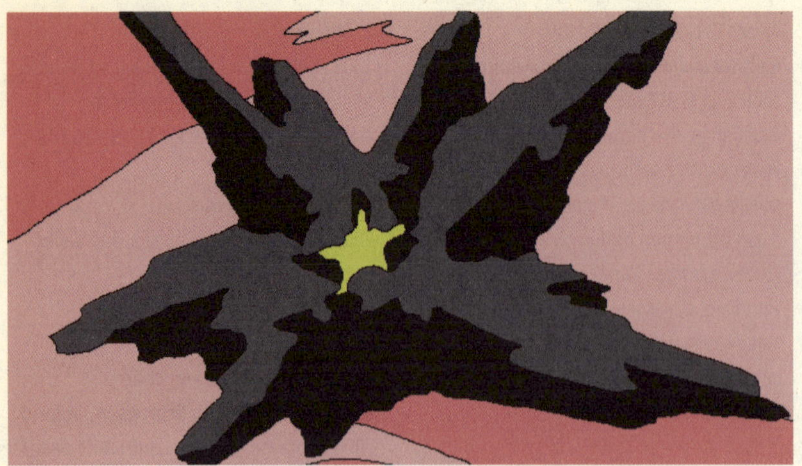
1.

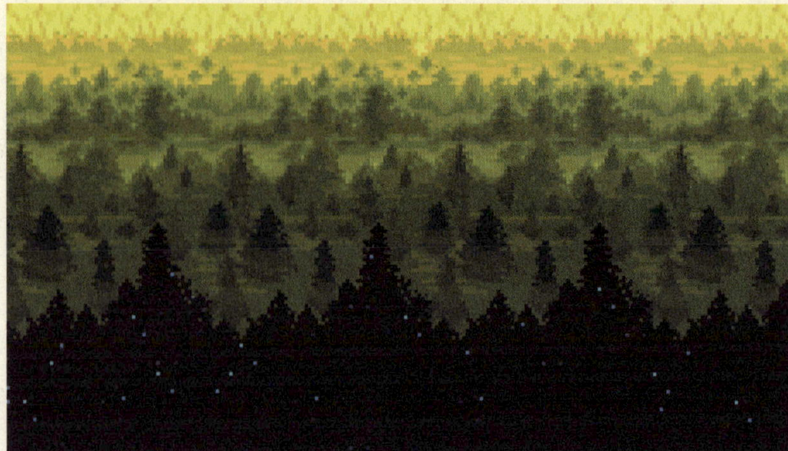
3.

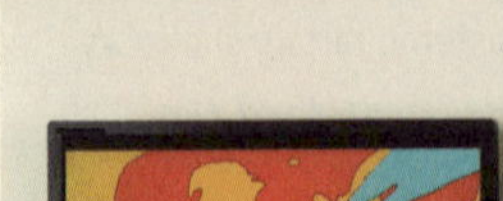
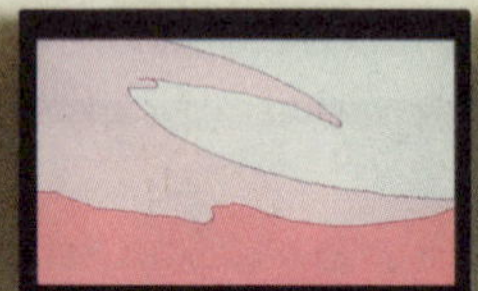
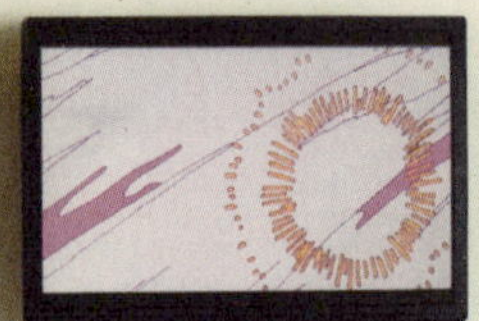
2.

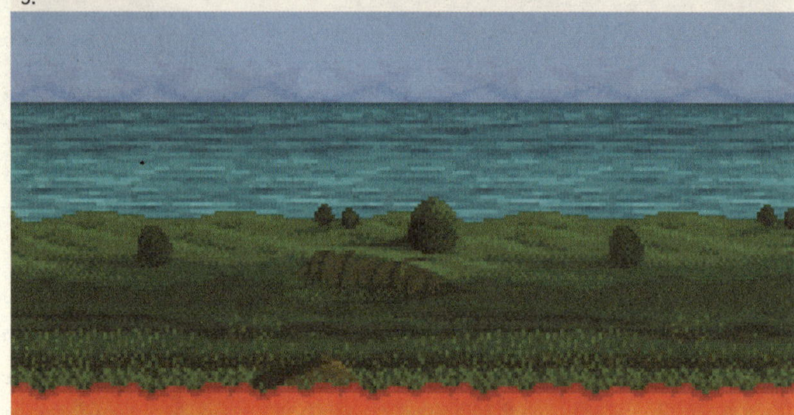
4.

Michael Bell-Smith studied semiotics at Brown University in Providence. His work examines the relationship between popular technologies and contemporary visual culture, frequently referencing the aesthetics of commonly used computer programs. Bell-Smith's work ranges from screen-based works intended for the gallery to videos made for theatrical screenings and digital art created for an Internet audience. His work has been exhibited in various countries in Europe, as well as Japan, Australia and America.

1 & 2. **ACTION HACK (PLATINUM)**
2006, video, 11 sec

3, 4 & 5. **UP AND AWAY**
2006, video, 6 min 40 sec

6, 7 & 8. **MOVING, ENDLESS (SAMPLES)**
2008, 3 of 5 digital light boxes with digital files, each 15 × 18 in (38 × 46 cm)

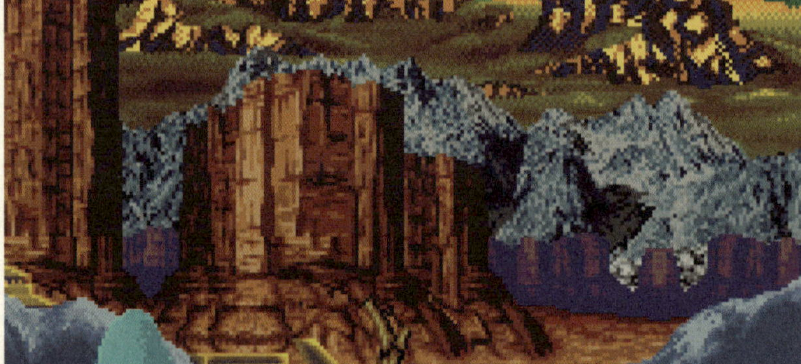
5.

6. 7. 8.

Caitlin Berrigan is currently pursuing her master's degree in visual studies at MIT and lives in Cambridge, Massachusetts. She works in edible sculpture and interactive performance to explore our evolving relationships with our bodies. Themes of disease, consumption, and the form and function of parts themselves recur in her work, including a five-foot marzipan tampon and chocolates cast as the hepatitis C virus (**Viral Confections**, 2006).

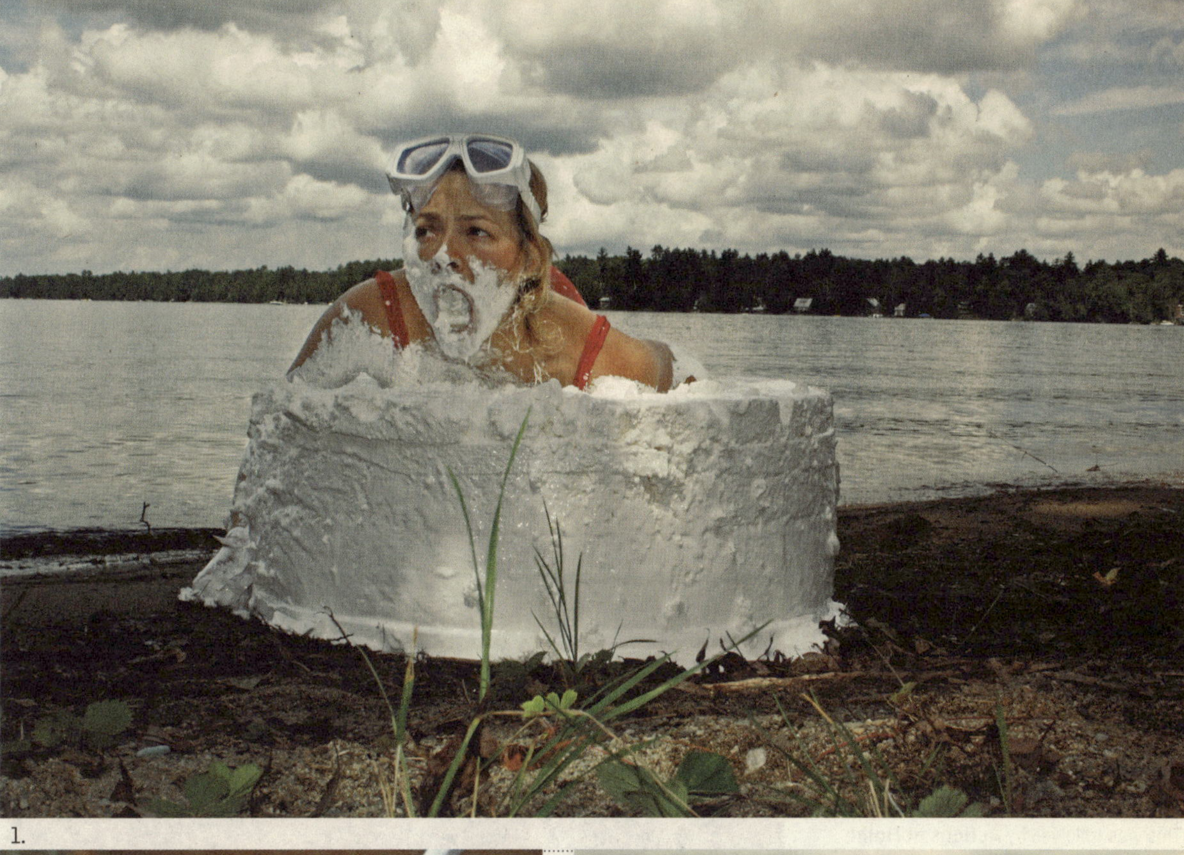

1.

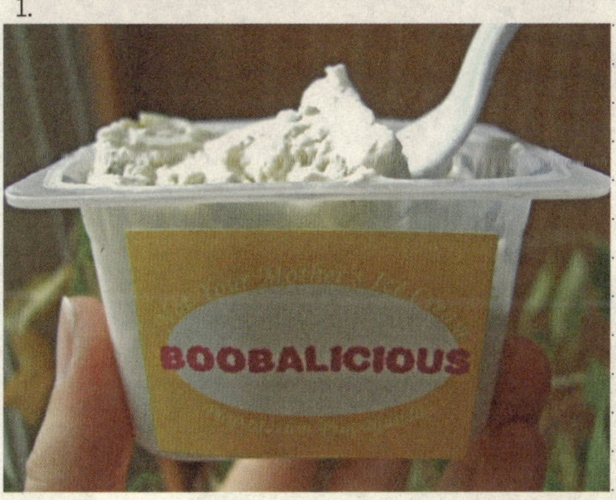

2.

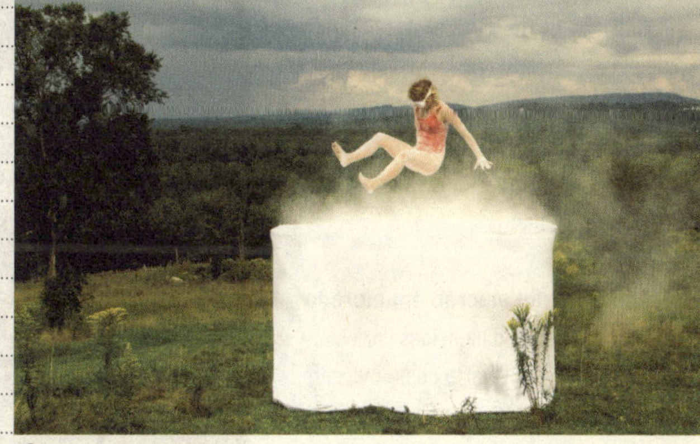

3.

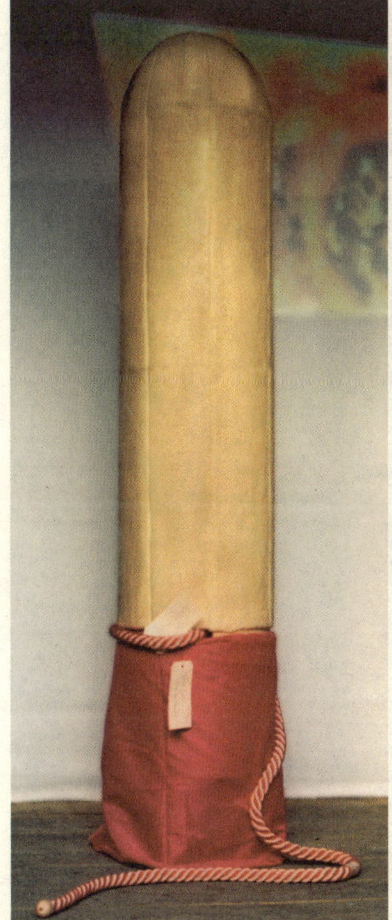

4.

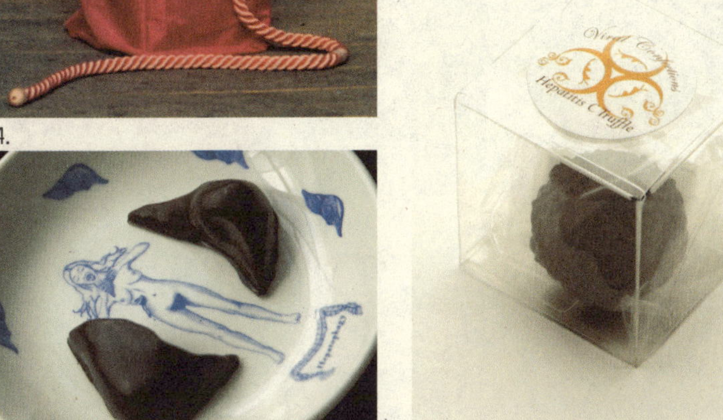

5.

6.

1. Marshmallow Suicide
2008, video, 9 min

2. Boobalicious
2008, public ice cream social with kulfi-flavored ice cream made with human breast milk

3. Marshmallow Crash
2008, video, 8 min, with modified trampoline, Lycra, and cornstarch, 5 × 8 ft (152 × 244 cm)

4. The Giant Tampon
2003, marzipan, polystyrene foam, and cord, 60 × 18 × 18 in (152 × 46 × 46 cm)

5. Hepatophagy
2008, porcelain with ceramic decal and cast chocolate, diameter 4 ¼ in (10 cm)

6. Viral Confections (detail)
2006, handmade cast chocolate and packaging, 2 × 2 × 2 in (5 × 5 × 5 cm)

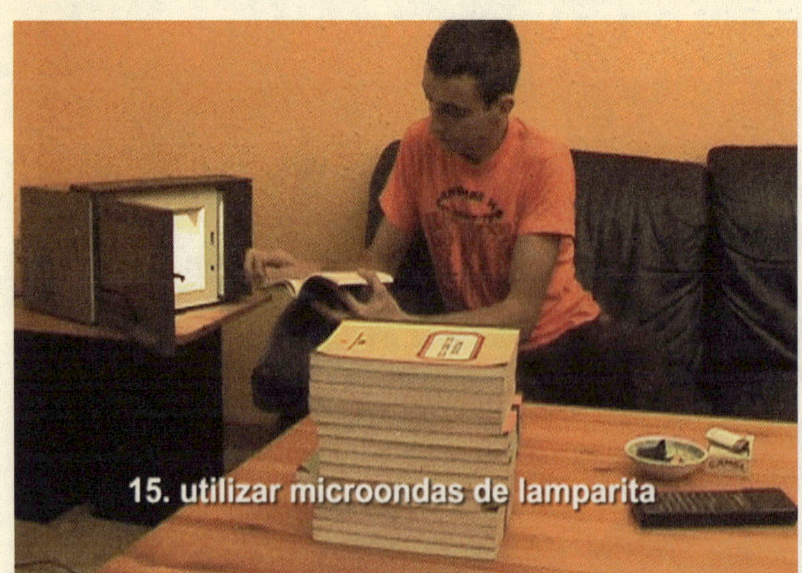

1.

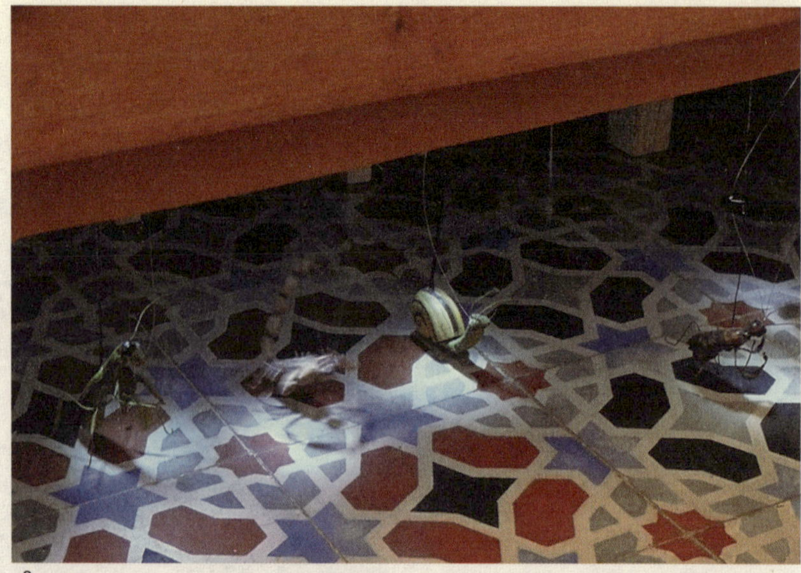

2.

David Bestué and Marc Vives graduated from the University of Barcelona with degrees in fine arts. They initiated the collaborative "Actions" cycle in 2002 with the book **Actions in Mataró** documenting forty-six public interventions that took place in a small Catalan town. This was followed by **Actions at Home** (2005), **Actions in the Body** (2006), and **Actions in the Universe** (2008), taking the respective forms of video, performance, and an installation.

1. **Actions at home**
2005, video, 33 min

2. **La historia del alacrán enamorado**
2007, mixed media, dimensions variable, installation view at Huerta de San Vicente, Fundación Federico García Lorca, Granada

3. **Actions in the body**
2006, video, 48 min

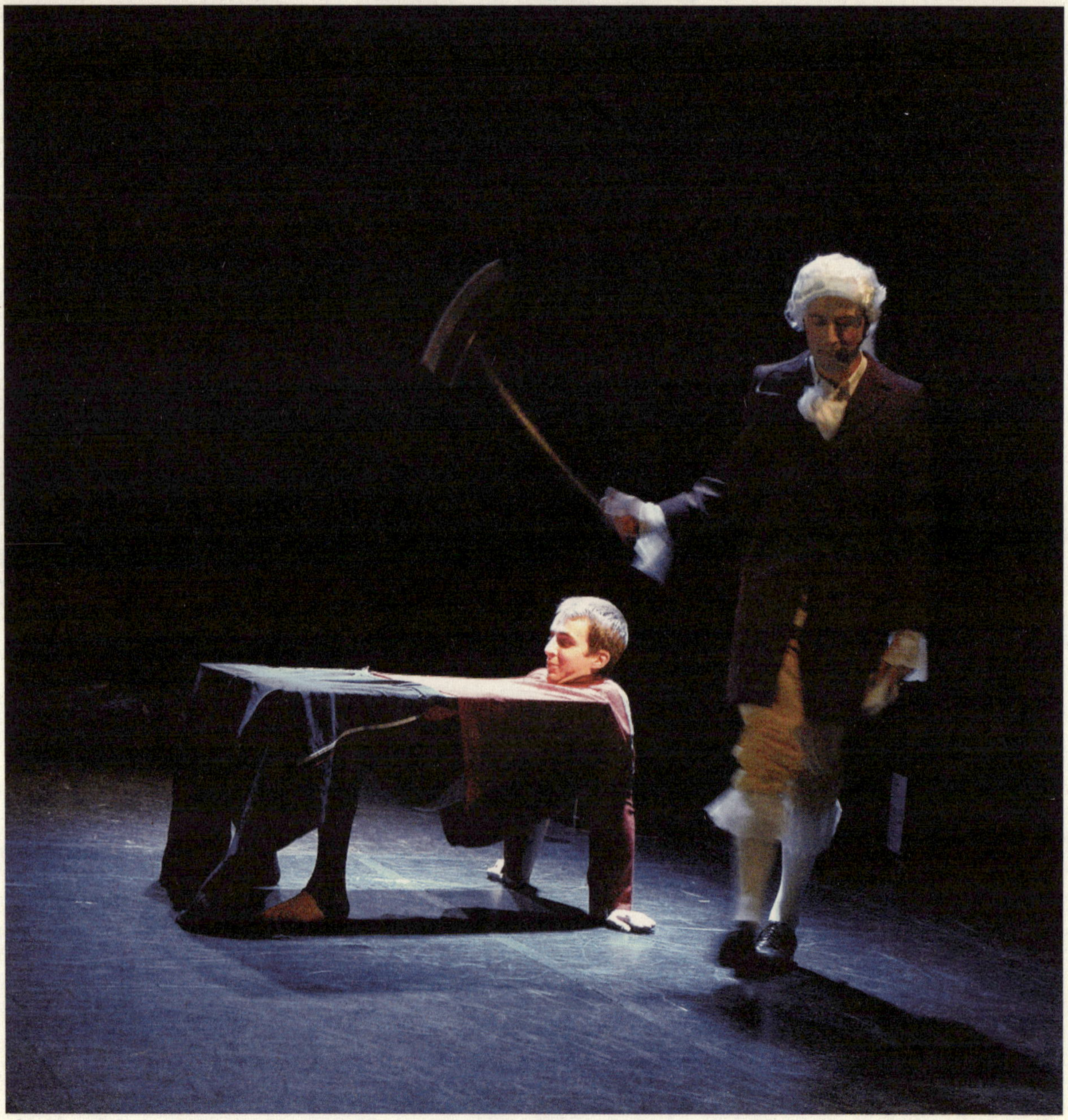

3.

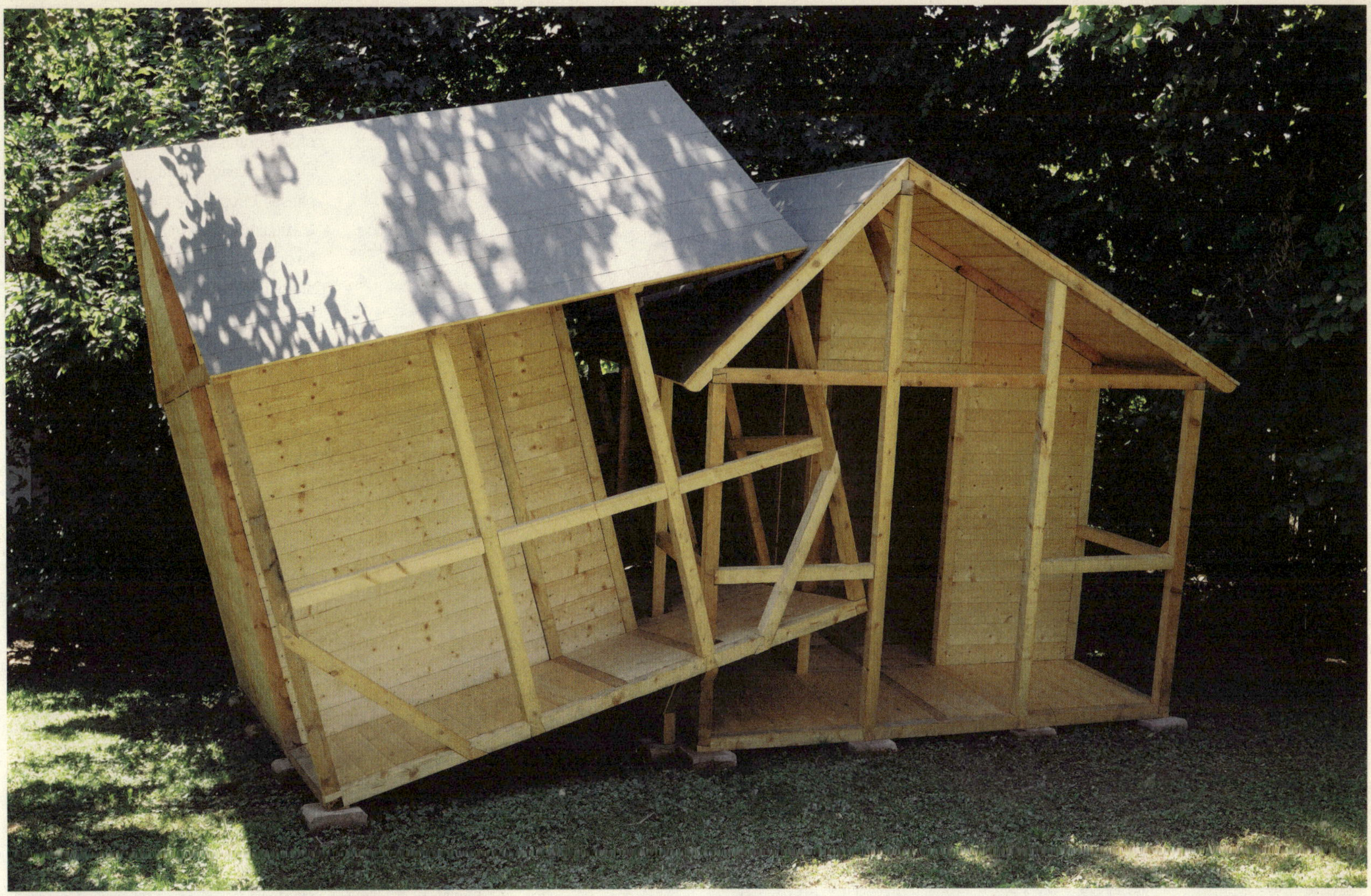

1.

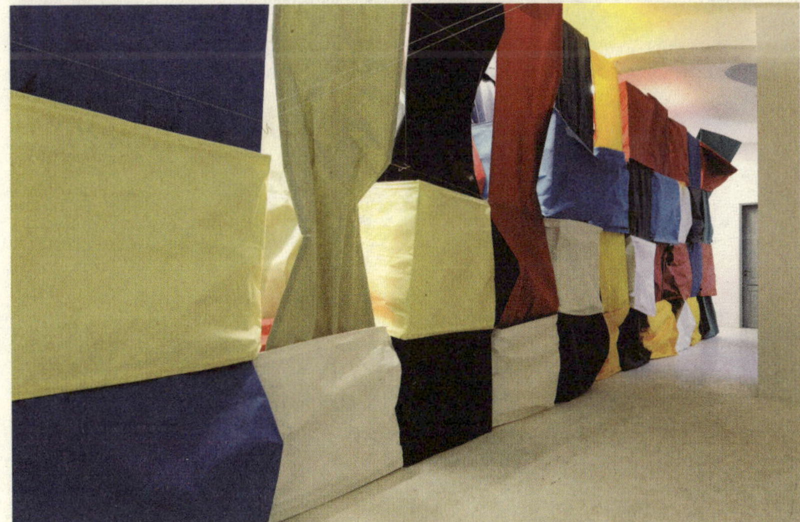

2.

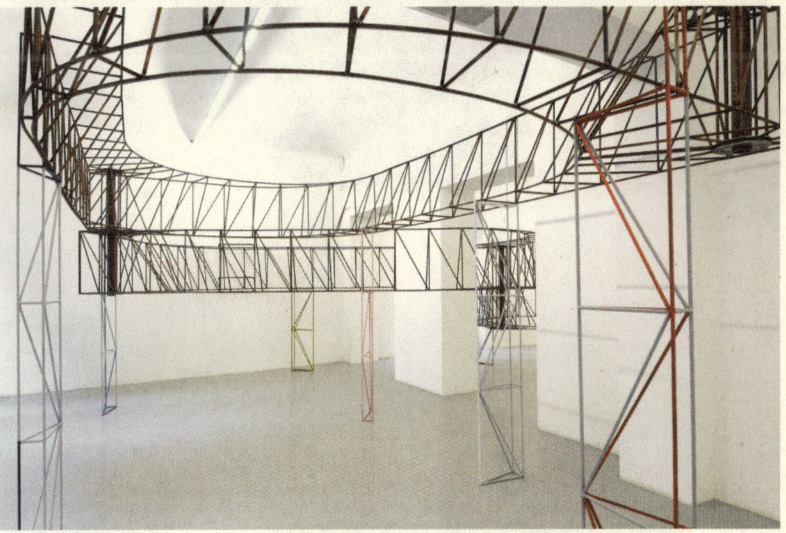

3.

Michael Beutler earned his MFA from the Glasgow School of Art and currently lives and works in Berlin. He creates site-specific installations that relate directly to the spaces they occupy. These may be accompanied by machines that perform the tasks Beutler requires – corrugating paper, stretching plastic, etc. – revealing the process at work in constructing space as we know it.

1. **Cufflink**
2005, wood, $19\frac{1}{2} \times 9\frac{3}{4} \times 9\frac{3}{4}$ ft ($6 \times 3 \times 3$ m)

2. **Sotto**
2008, paper, wood, glue, and reed, dimensions variable

3. **Sopra**
2008, rebar, wire, and paint, dimensions variable

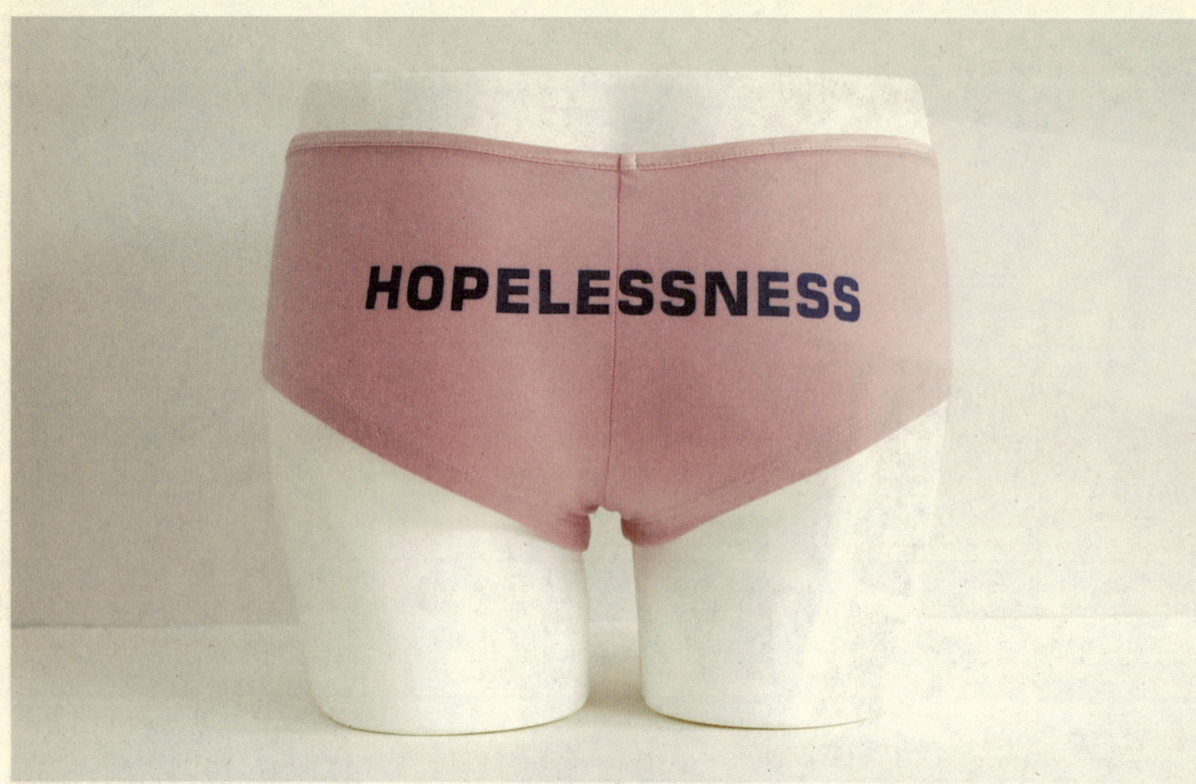

1.

Kevin Bewersdorf earned his BFA from the Rhode Island School of Design and currently "lives and works online." His art practice involves various forms of self-branding, modeled after companies like Fox, Wendy's, and Toyota. Marketing himself through the corporate identity of Maximum Sorrow (maximumsorrow.com), he produces photographs, logos, promotional objects, and performances.

1. **Maximum Sorrow Merchandise**
2007, mixed media, dimensions variable

2. **Life Mug # 1**
2007, ceramic mug ordered on the Internet, 4 × 3 ½ × 3 in (11 × 9 × 8 cm)

3. **Self-Portrait in CD**
2008, digital photograph, dimensions variable

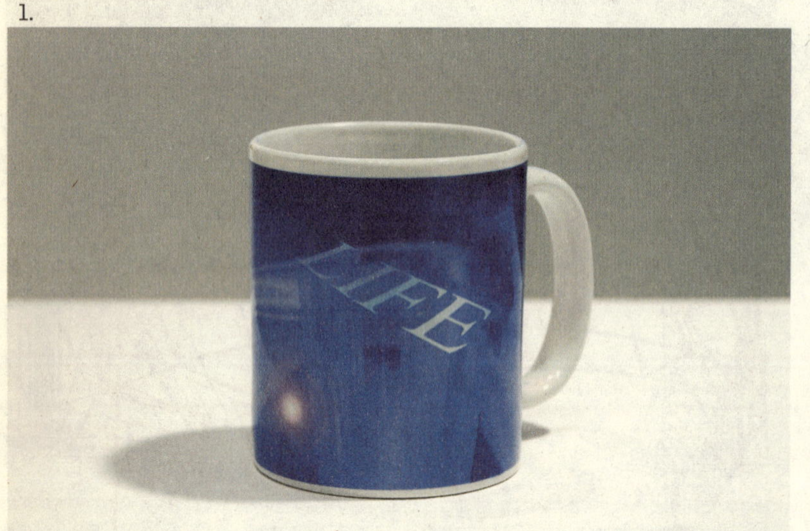

2.

3.

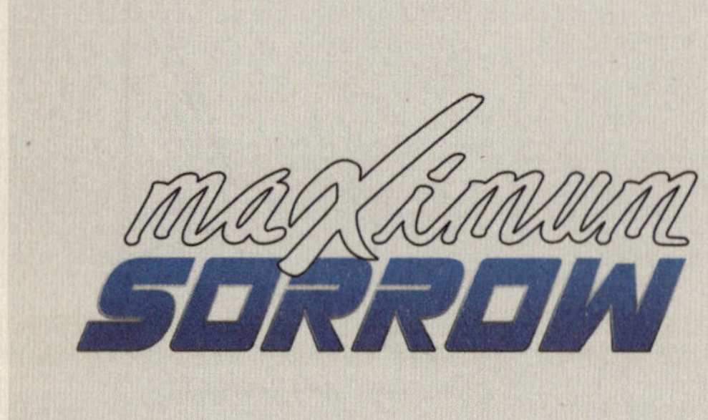

4.

5.

4. **Maximum Sorrow Logo**
2007, digital file, dimensions variable

5. **Maximum Sorrow Merchandise**
2007, mixed media, dimensions variable

Ashutosh Bhardwaj earned his MFA from Maharaja Sayajirao University in Baroda, where he continues to live. He works in painting and video installation to integrate stylized figures and animals with the language of graphic design – bold-colored geometry, patterns, and symbols. These imaginary worlds reveal forces of power and violence in contemporary life.

1. **Sleepwalker**
2008, video projection, 1 min 30 sec; 2-channel video, 1 min 30 sec; iron, wood, printed flex, radium stickers on laminated board, LED lights, bricks, and gravel on tar sheets, dimensions variable, minimum size 40 × 25 × 10 ft (12 × 8 × 3 m)

2. **God Has Alzheimer's**
2007-08, oil, acrylic, and pen on canvas, 84 × 60 in (213 × 152 cm)

3 & 4. **Matrix – We Love America, America Loves Us**
2004, video projection, 6 min; ladder, lights, ropes, digital print, painting on wall, newspaper, and collage, dimensions variable

5. **Induced Epidemic**
2007-08, oil, acrylic, and pen on canvas, 3 parts, overall dimensions 8 × 15 ft (244 × 457 cm)

6. **Dance of Democracy**
2008, oil, acrylic, and pen on canvas, 3 parts, overall dimensions 8 × 15 ft (244 × 457 cm)

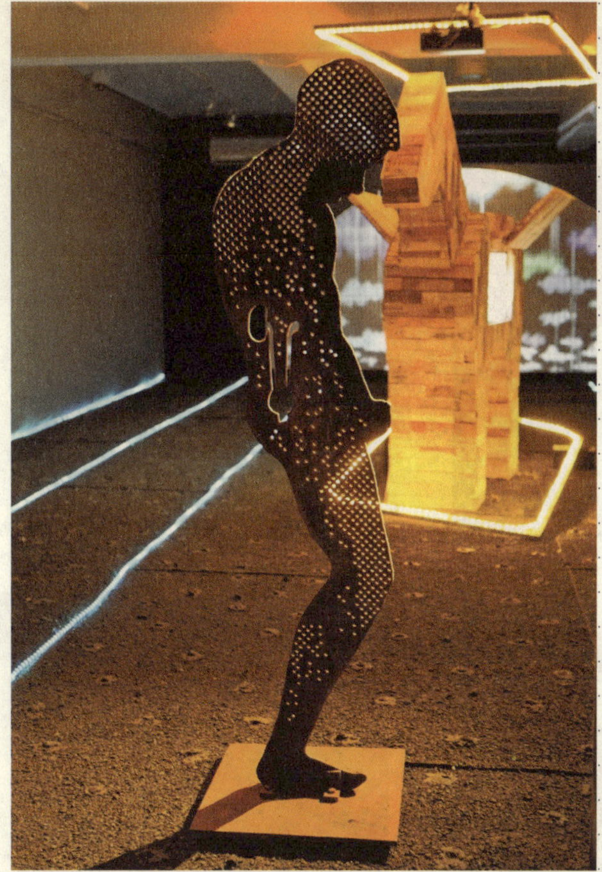
1.

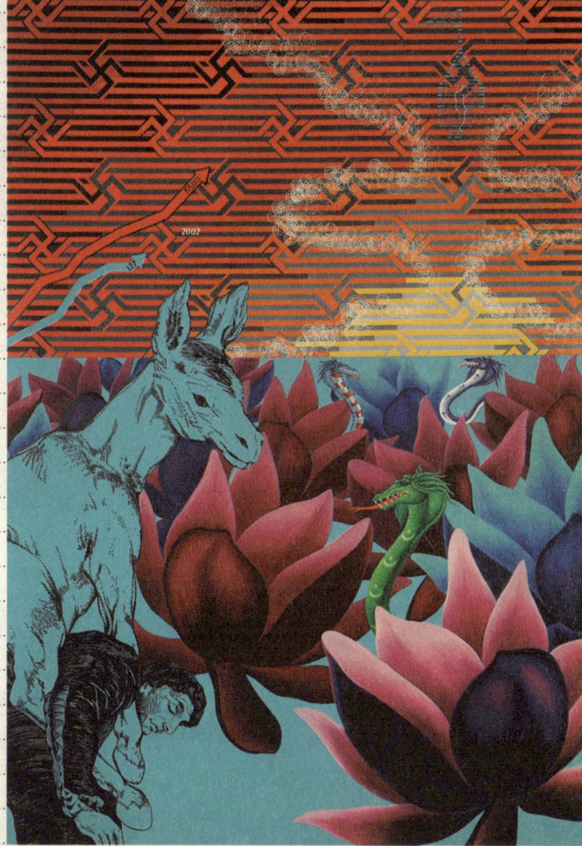
2.

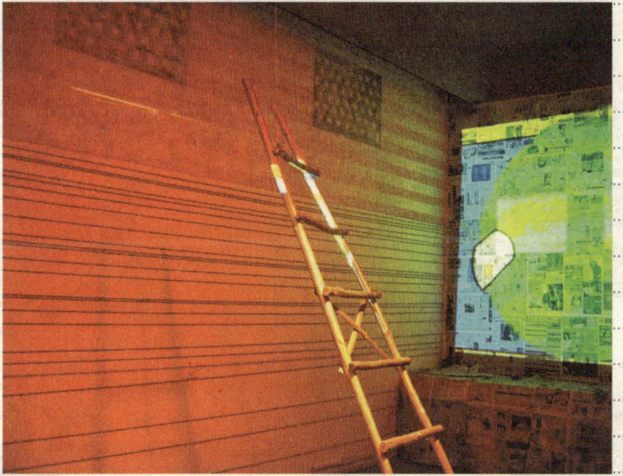
3.

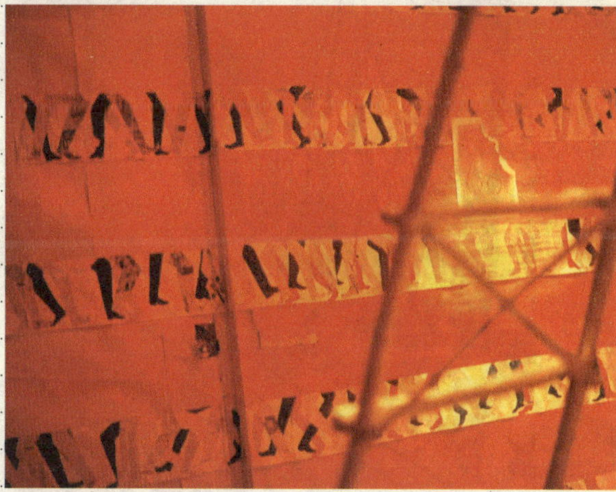
4.

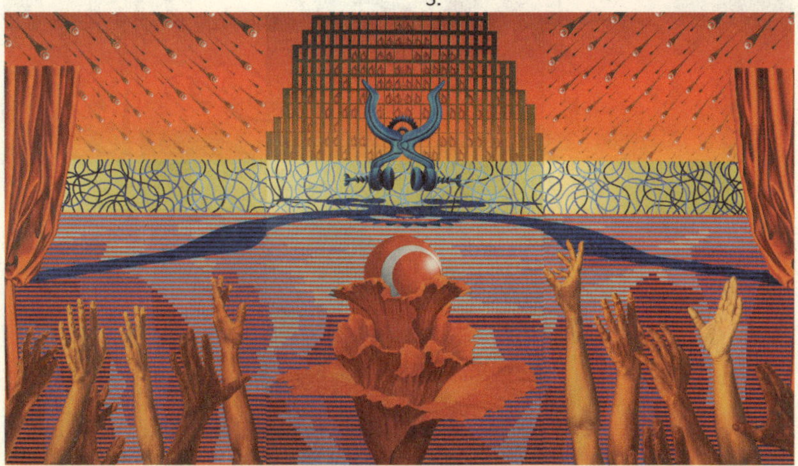
5.

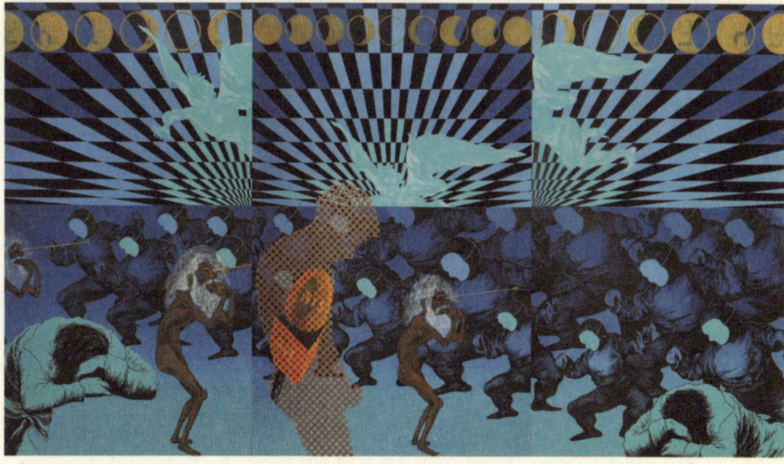
6.

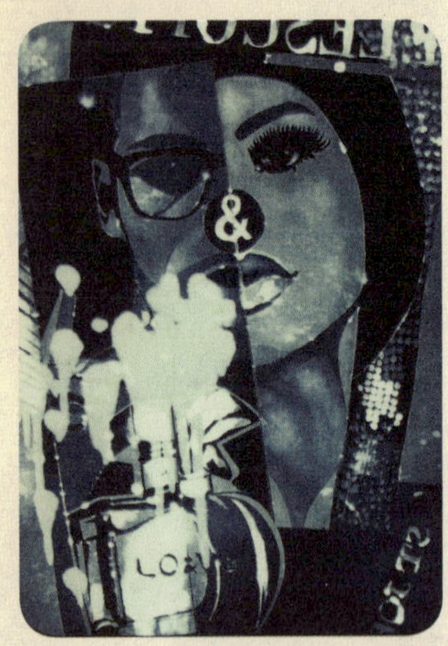

1.

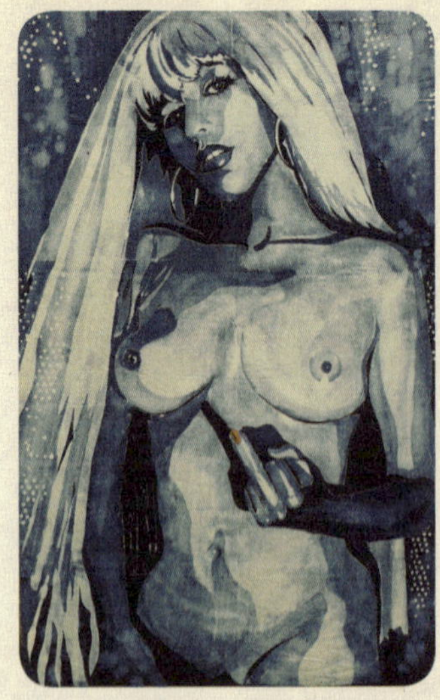

2.

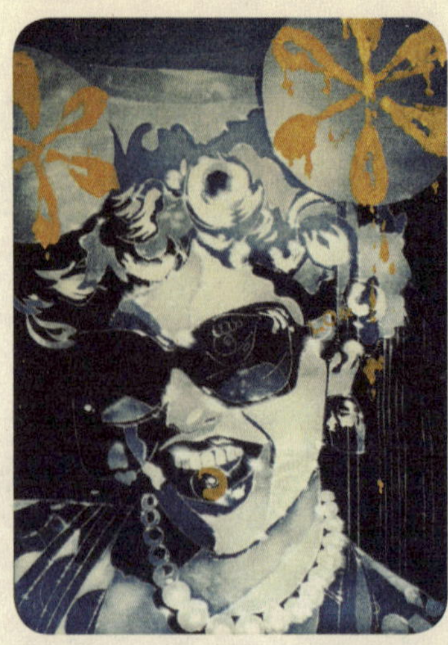

3.

2. SnowWhite & Co
2007, paint on denim, $86\frac{1}{2} \times 55$ in
(220 × 140 cm)

3. MOUSEgirl
2007, paint on denim, $49\frac{1}{4} \times 35\frac{1}{2}$ in
(125 × 90 cm)

4. FLYpark
2007, paint on denim, $49\frac{1}{4} \times 35\frac{1}{2}$ in
(125 × 90 cm)

5. Anti-Pop
2007, paint on denim, $86\frac{1}{2} \times 55$ in
(220 × 140 cm)

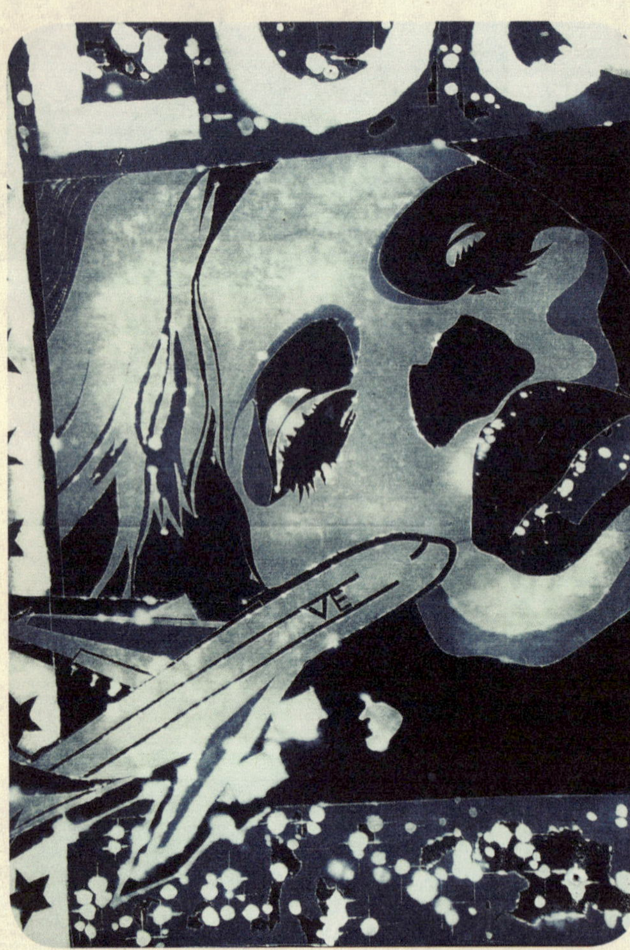

4.

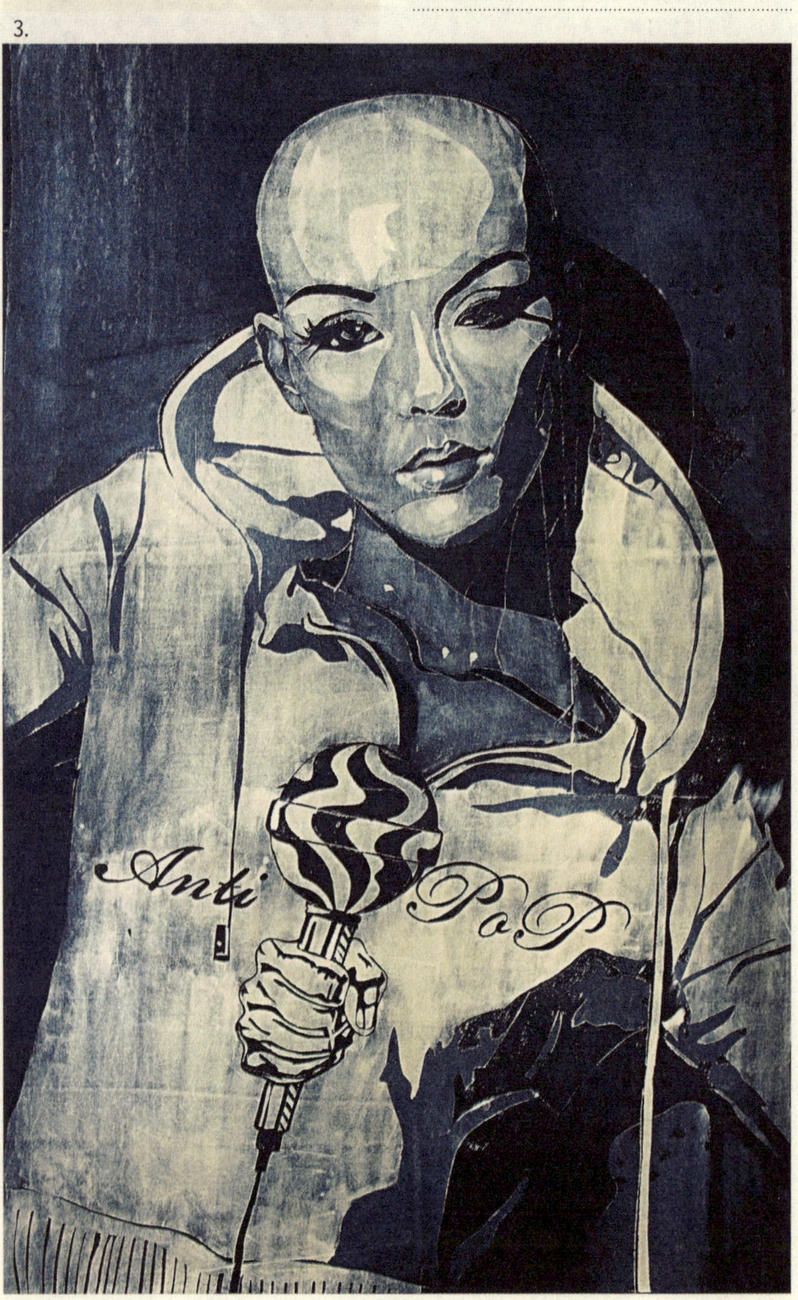

5.

Auce Biele graduated from the Visual Communications department at the Latvian Academy of Art, and currently lives and works in Riga. She identifies herself as a contemporary Pop artist, making paintings inspired by advertising, fashion, and MTV. She has embraced the technique of painting on denim instead of canvas as a way to directly integrate material culture into her work.

1. Woman
2007, paint on denim, $49\frac{1}{4} \times 35\frac{1}{2}$ in
(125 × 90 cm)

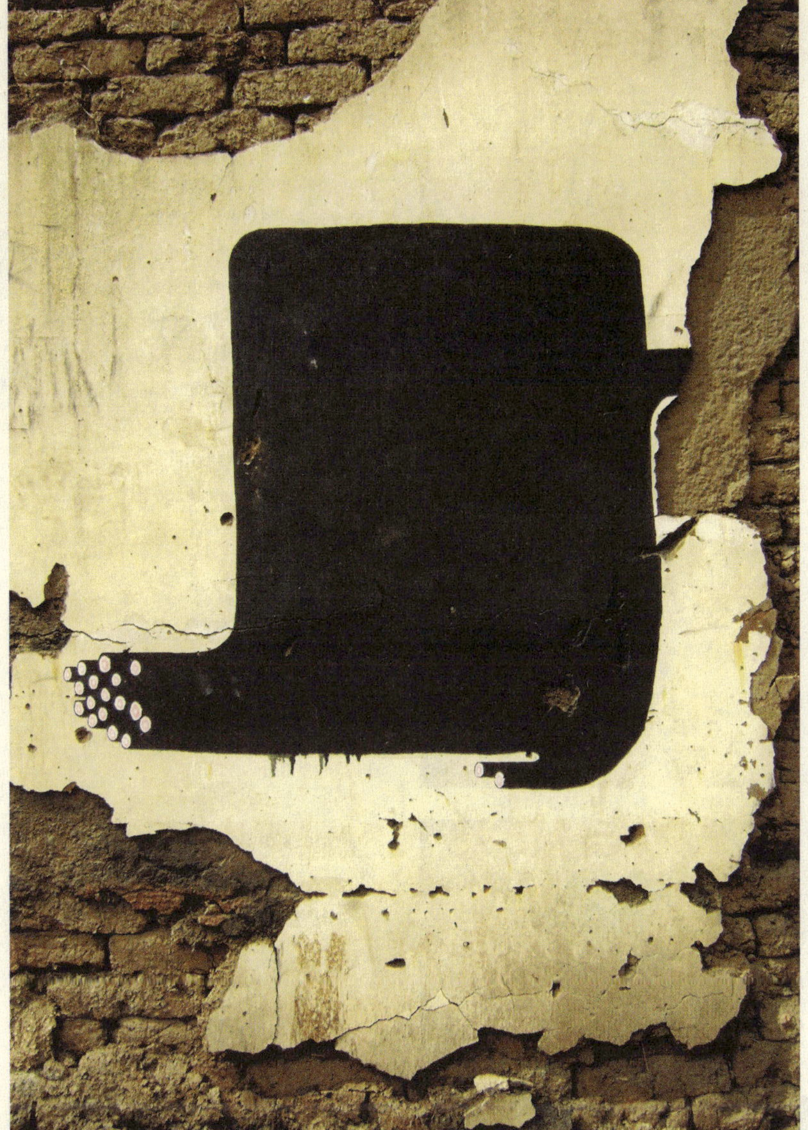

1.

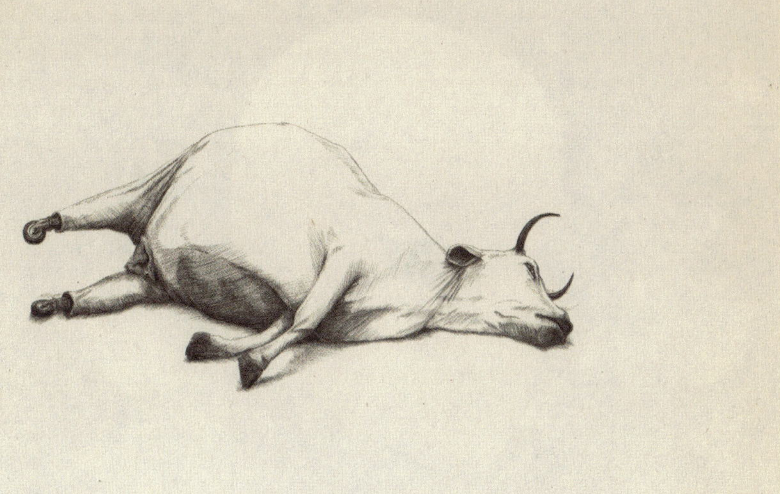

2.

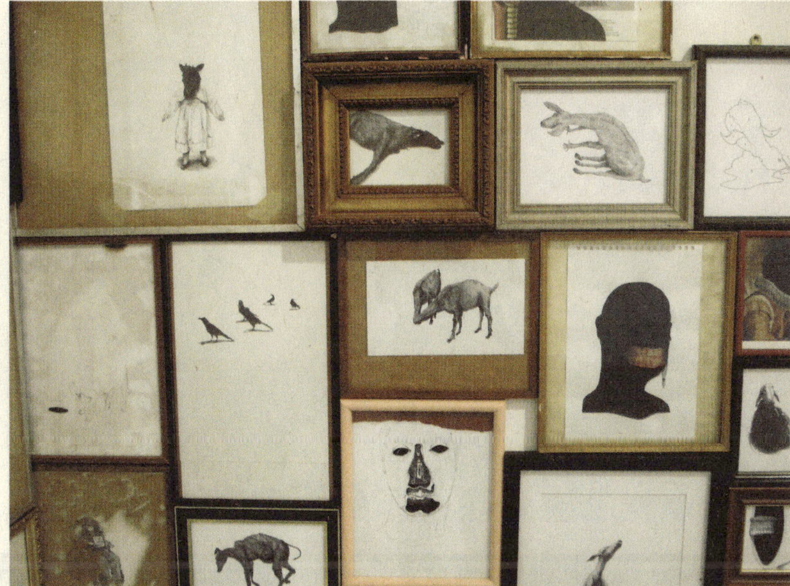

3.

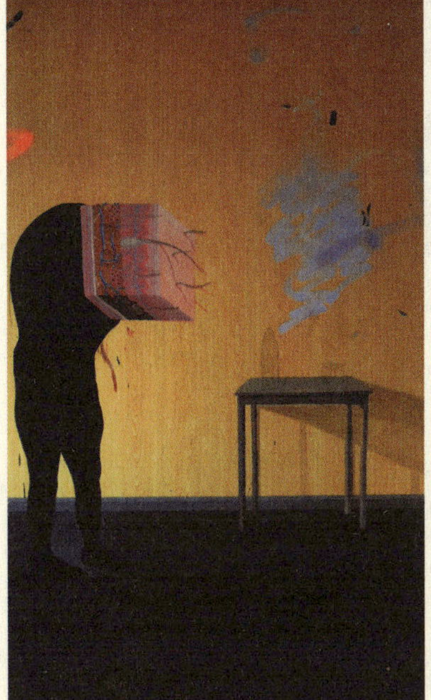

4.

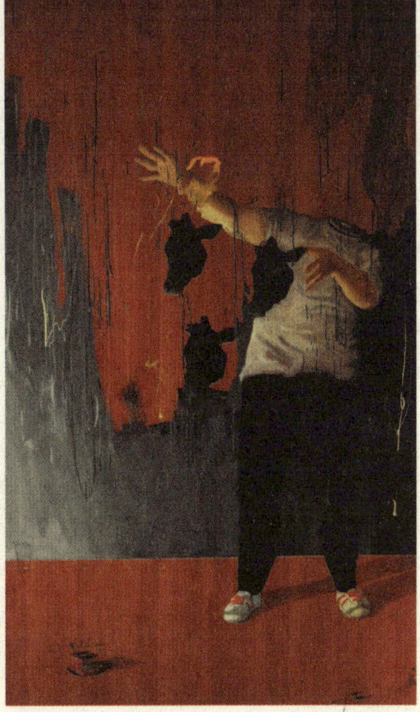

5.

Adolfo Bimer studied visual arts at the University of Chile and currently lives in Santiago. He uses pencil, tempera, pastels, and other tools in a rigorous drawing practice that explores real and imagined organic systems. Disembodied teeth, veins, and hair follicles populate images presented individually, in closely packed groups, or integrated with other objects in installations.

1. **Fragment 4**
2008, latex on wall, approx 78 3/4 × 63 in (200 × 160 cm)

2. **Smile from the streets you hold**
2008, pencil on paper, 8 1/2 × 11 in (22 × 28 cm)

3. **Untitled** (detail)
2008, 54 drawings, collages, and pictures in frames, dimensions variable

4. **Untitled and Hommage to the Teiker in the Back**
2008, oil, enamel, spray paint, and varnishes on plywood, 96 × 60 in (244 × 152 cm)

5. **Untitled (0:25 a.m.)**
2008, oil, enamel, spray paint, and varnishes on plywood, 96 × 60 in (244 × 152 cm)

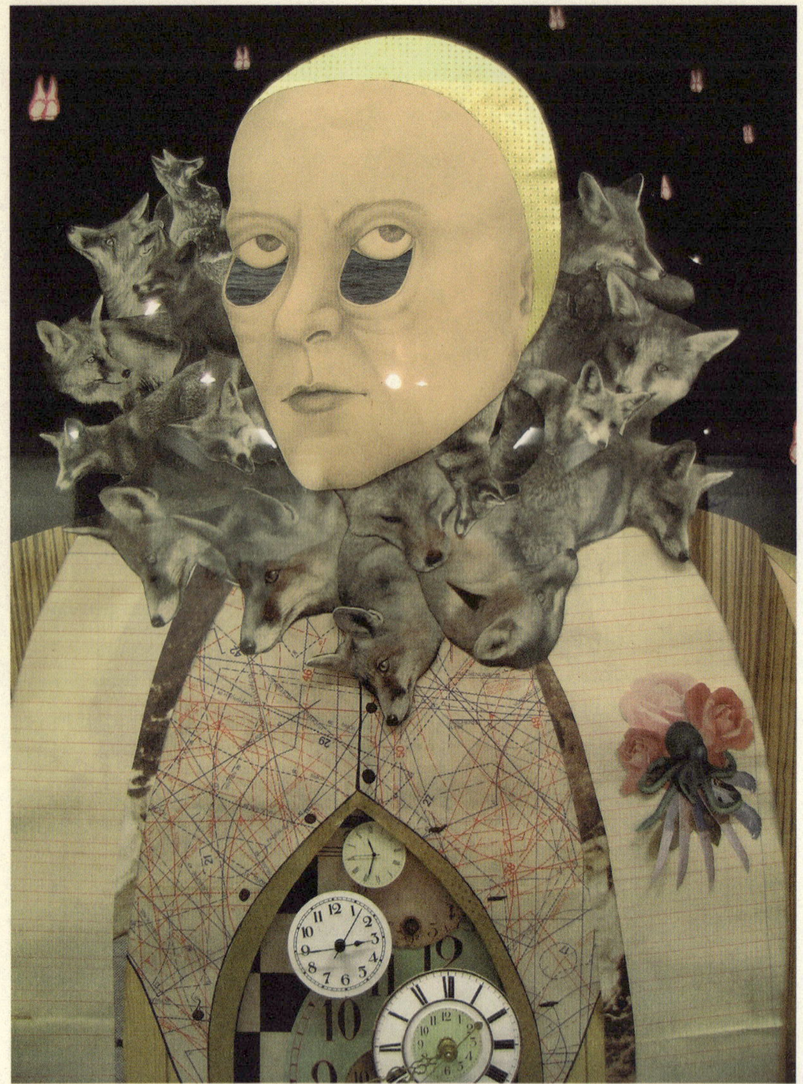

1.

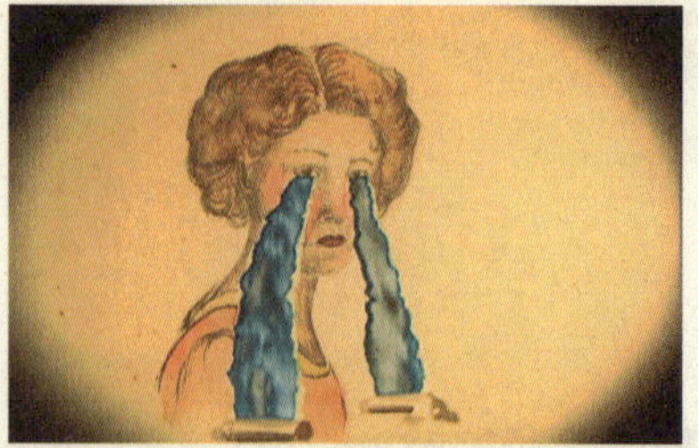

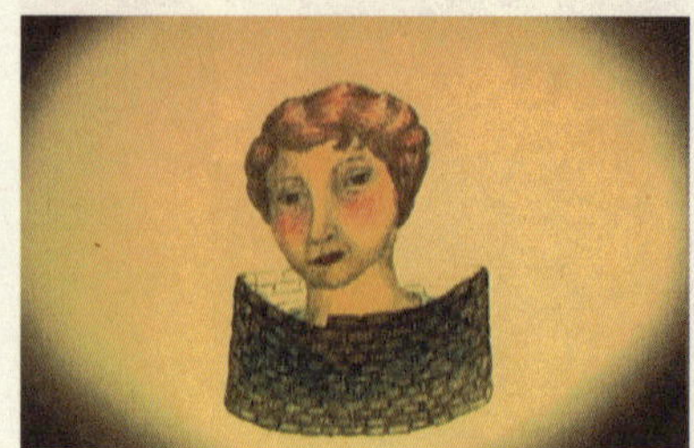

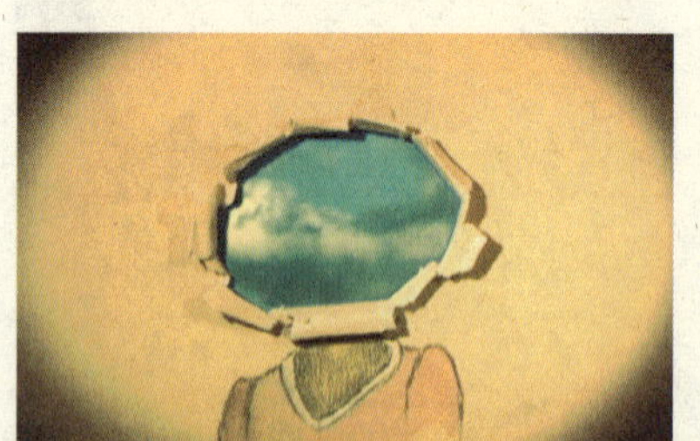

2.

Ingibjörg Birgisdóttir attended the Iceland Academy of Arts and currently lives in Reykjavík. She makes intricate video animations using hundreds of drawings, old book pages, newspapers, and postcards. In **Seven Sisters**, she weaves a dreamlike narrative through multilayered collage and drawing. She is also a member of the indie-folk band Seabear, currently recording its second album, and makes music videos, album covers, posters, and book illustrations.

1. **Lord Monday** (detail)
2006, drawing and collage, 106 × 79 in (270 × 200 cm); video

2. **Seven Sisters**
2008, animation, 3 min 23 sec

3 & 4. **No title**
2005, paper birds and string, height 118 in (300 cm)

5. **Princes of Royal Blood**
2008, drawing and collage, 11 × 8 ¼ in (28 × 21 cm)

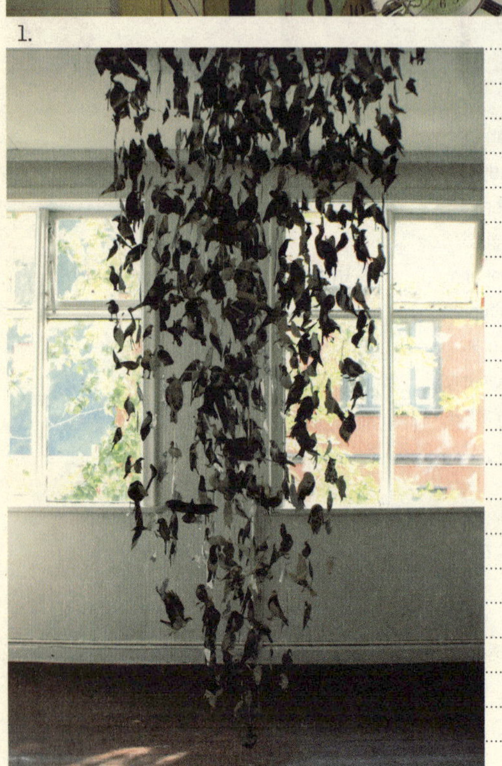

3.

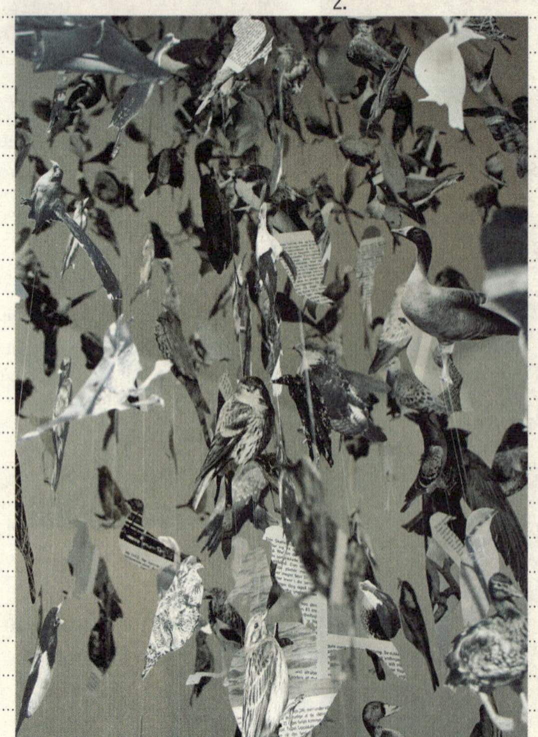

4.

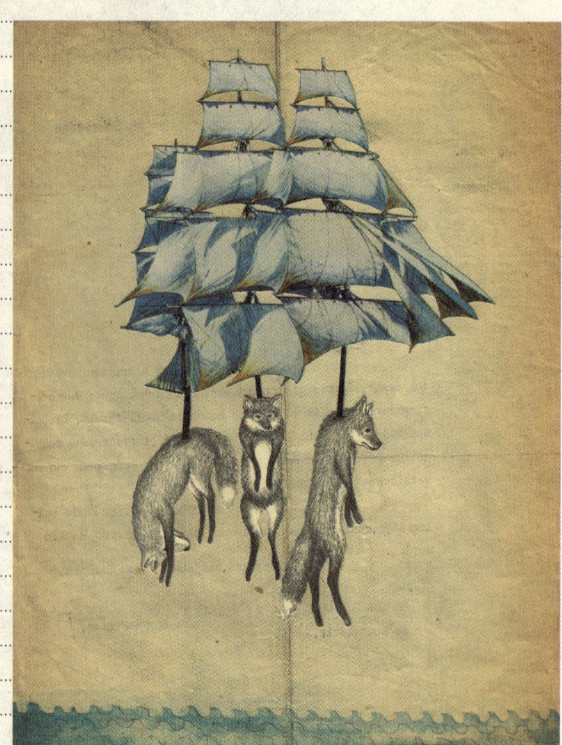

5.

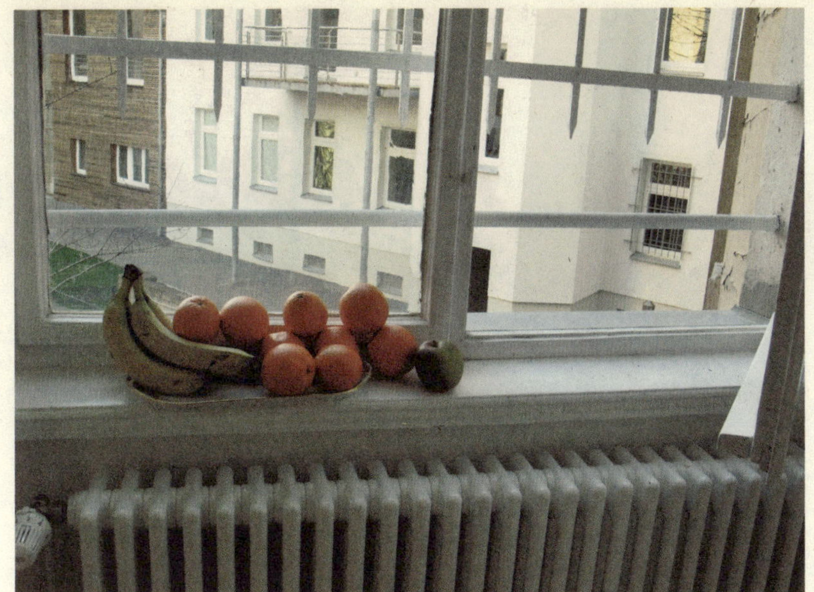

1.

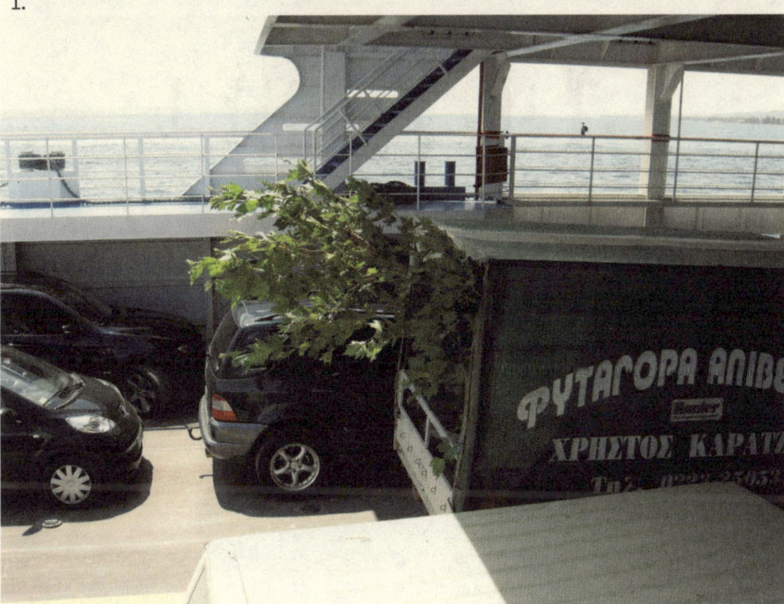

2.

Juliette Blightman earned her MA from the Byam Shaw School of Art, in London, where she currently lives. In single, three-minute shots (the duration of 100 feet of 16 millimeter film stock), she documents sparse actions to mark and measure the passing of time. Her 2008 exhibition "Please Water the Plant and Feed the Fish" at London's ICA consisted of her brother coming to the gallery daily at 3 p.m. to perform the tasks stated in the show's title.

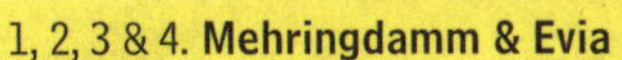

1, 2, 3 & 4. **Mehringdamm & Evia**

2008, digital image

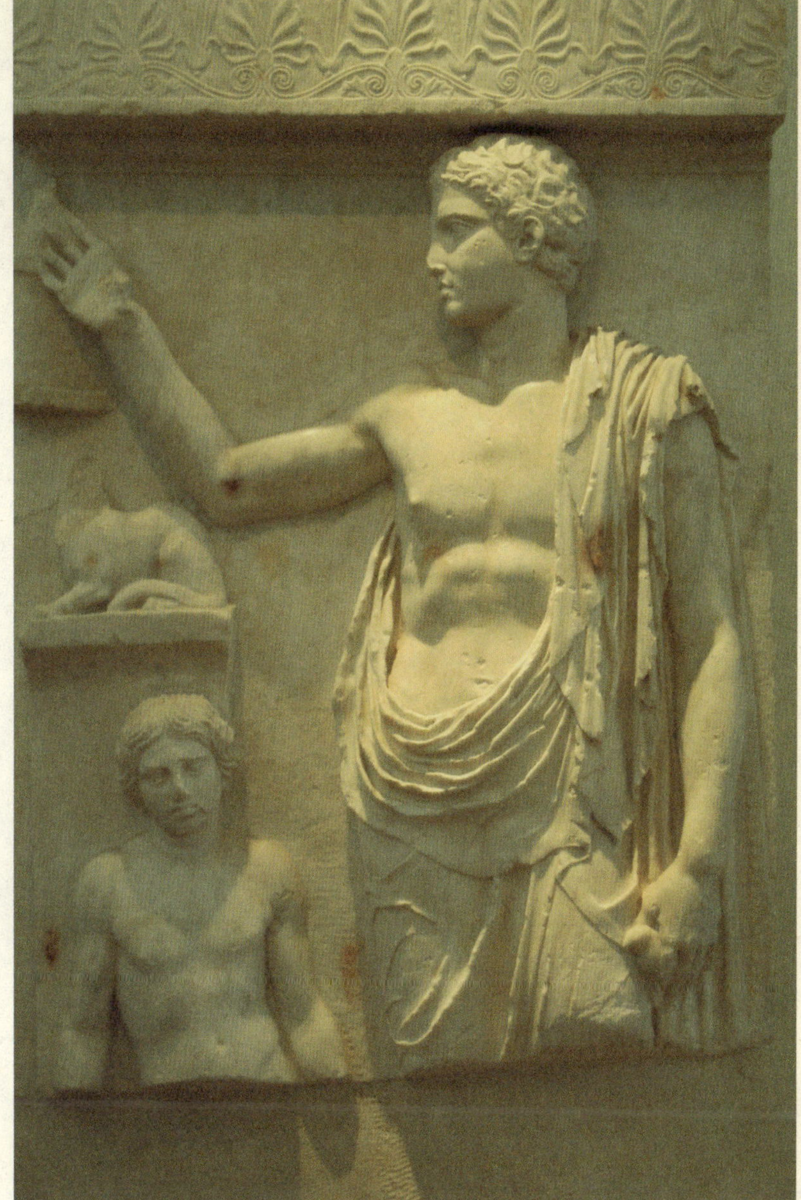

3.

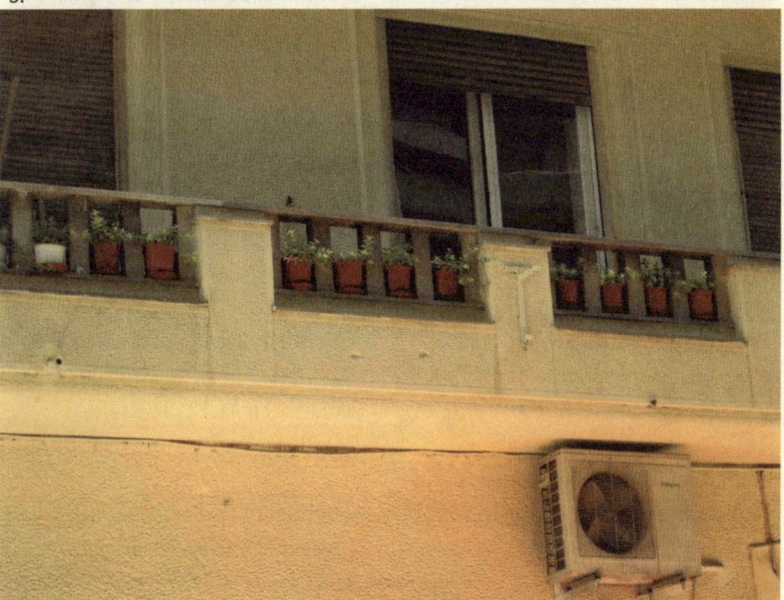

4.

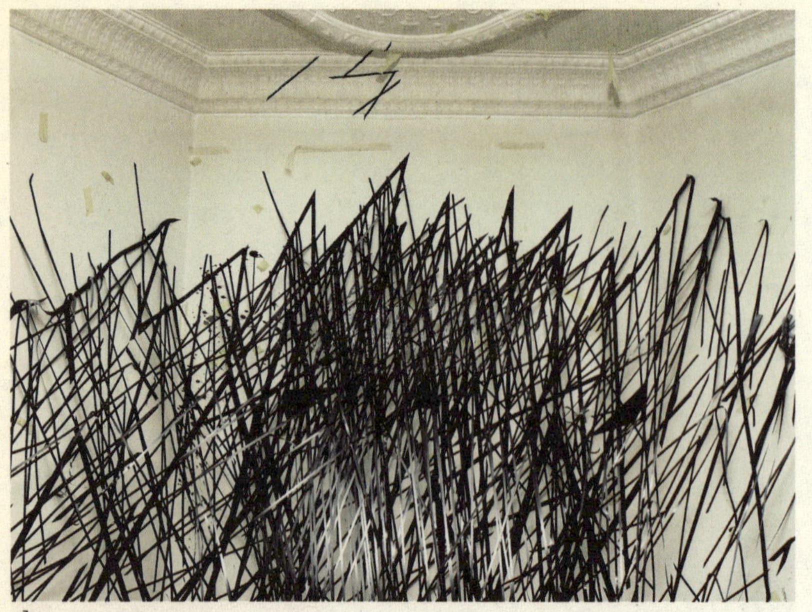
1.

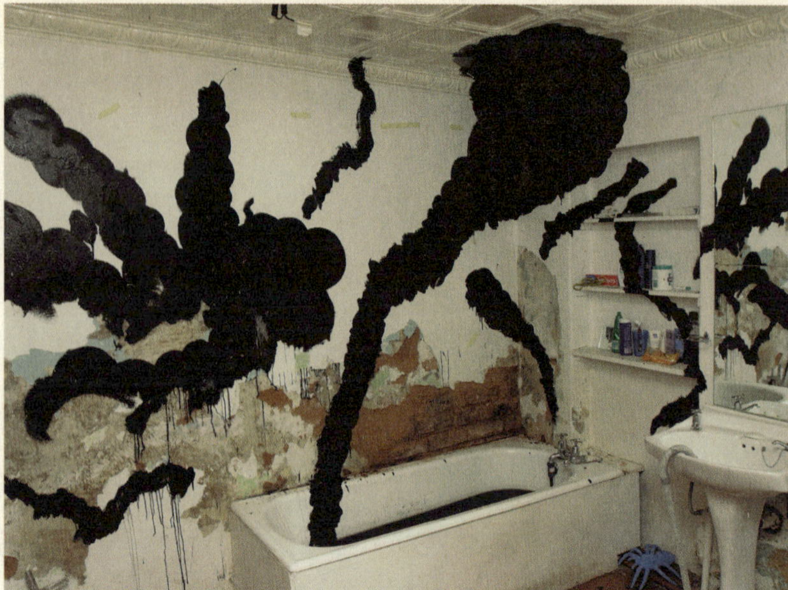
2.

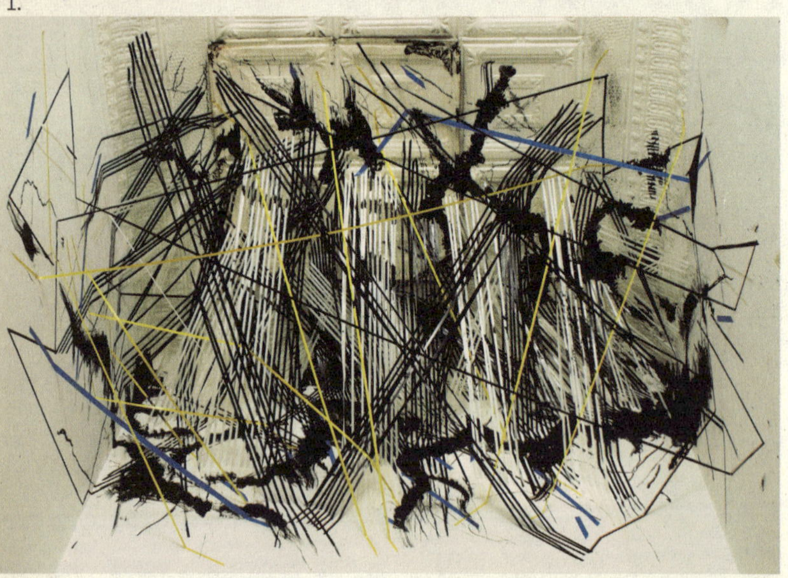
3.

4.

Zander Blom currently lives in Johannesburg. He works in painting, drawing, assemblage, sculpture, and photography to explore the development of modernism in Africa. Projects often include a site-specific installation that is photographed and then destroyed. Blom prints images in editions of one to mimic the originality of painting and sculpture. His book **The Drain of Progress – A Catalogue Raisonné** was published in 2007 to accompany his first "retrospective" exhibition.

1. **Untitled, Bedroom 1, Corner 3, 8.07 p.m., Thursday, 29 March 2007**
2007, inkjet print, 22 × 31 ¾ in (56 × 81 cm)

2. **Untitled, Bathroom, 2.01 a.m., Wednesday, 23 May 2007**
2007, inkjet print, 22 × 31 ¾ in (56 × 81 cm)

3. **Untitled, or The Boulevard, Bedroom 1, Corner 2, 5.11 p.m., Friday, 1 June 2007**
2007, inkjet print, 29 ¾ × 43 ¼ in (76 × 110 cm)

4. **Untitled, Corridor, Corners 2 & 3, 2.29 p.m., Friday, 18 May 2007**
2007, inkjet print, 22 × 31 ¾ in (56 × 81 cm)

5. **Untitled, Bedroom 1, Corner 3, 2.36 p.m., Sunday, 20 May 2007**
2007, inkjet print, 22 × 31 ¾ in (56 × 81 cm)

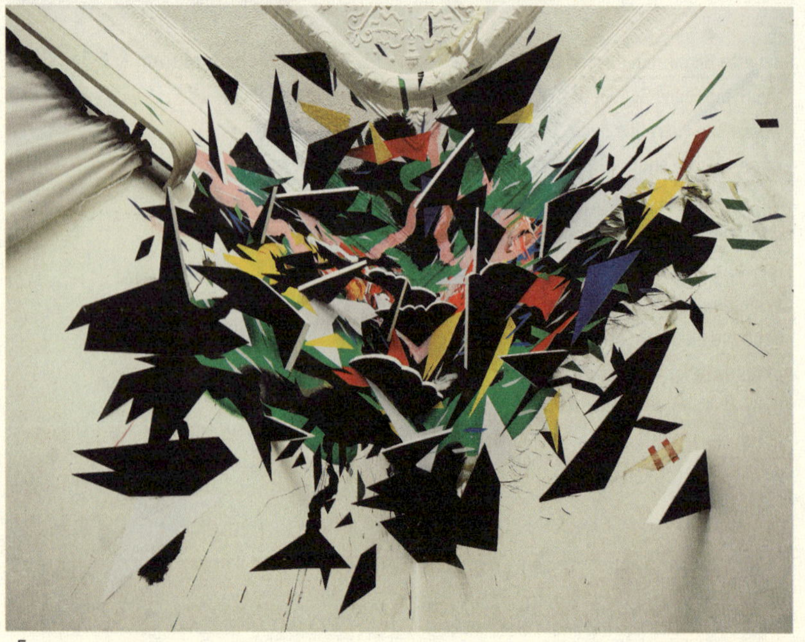
5.

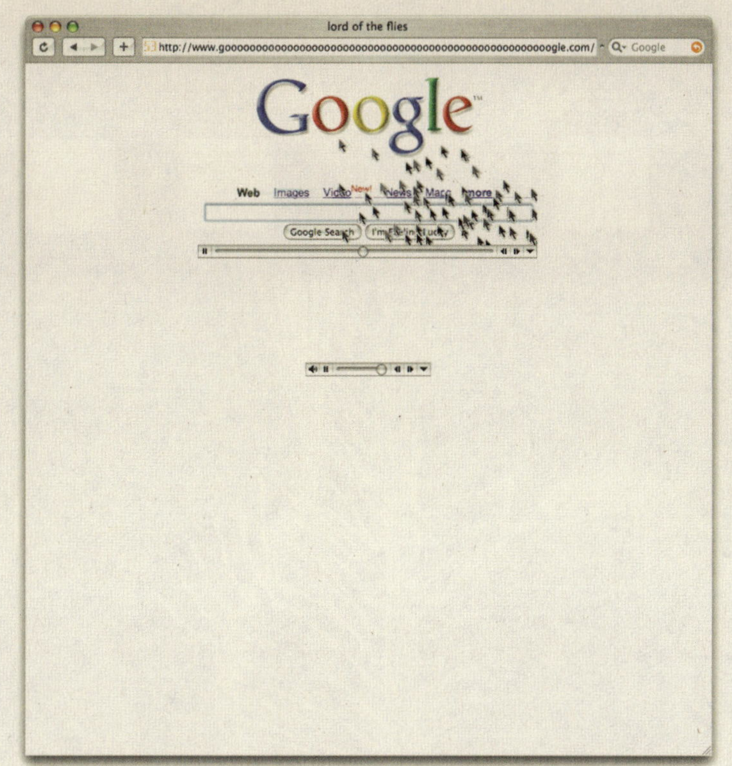

1.

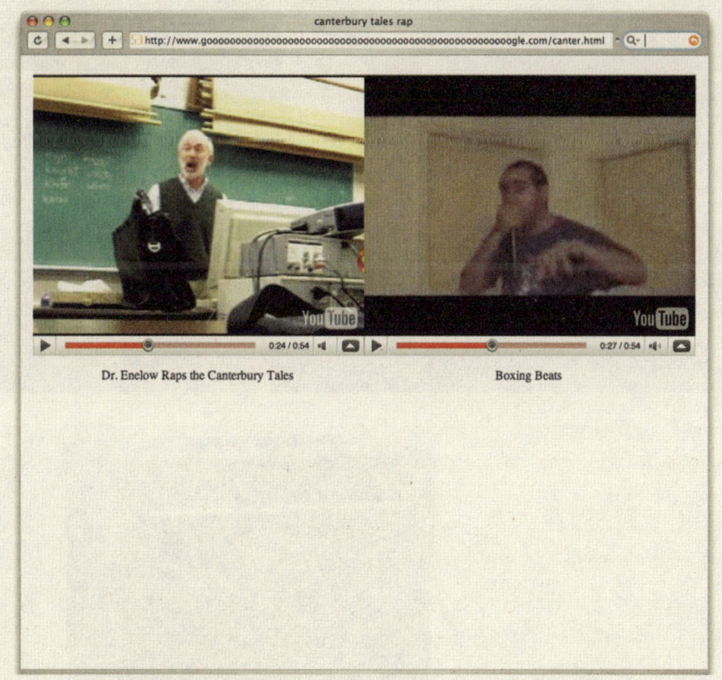

2.

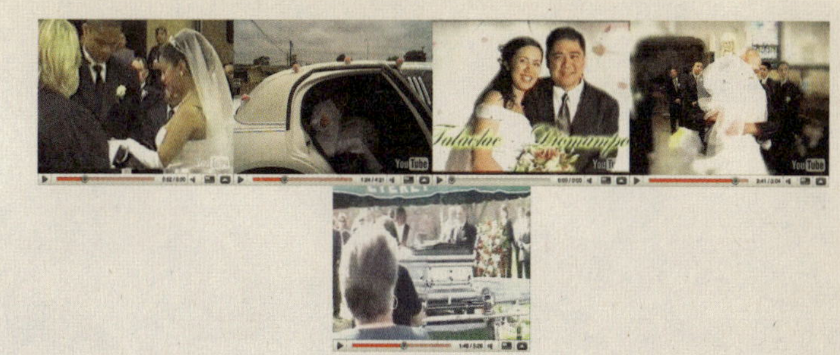

3.

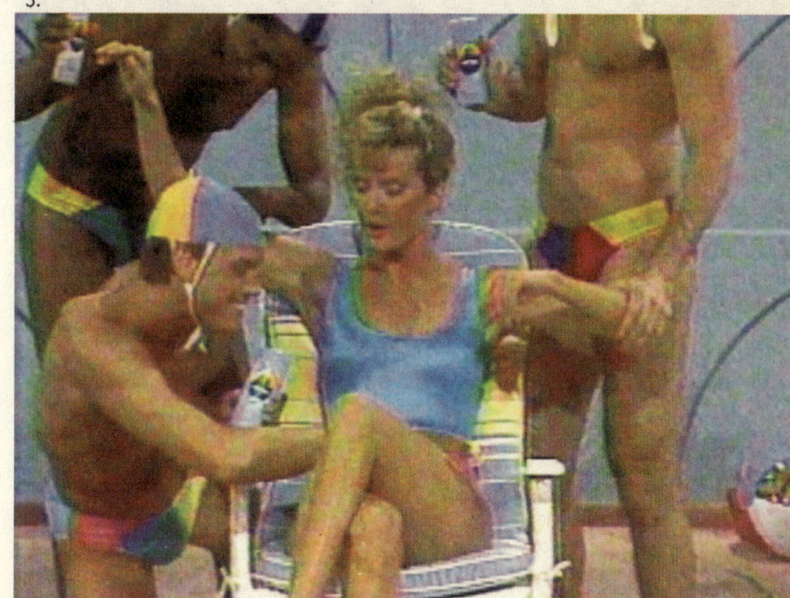

4.

5.

John Michael Boling earned his BFA in digital media from the University of Georgia in Athens, where he lives. He makes video and Internet art in various forms, including video mash-ups using found Internet footage from the 1980s.

He is creator of the website www.goooooooooooooooooooooooooooooooooooooooooooooooooooooogle.com ("53 o's") and a founding member of the Internet surfing club Nasty Nets.

1. Lord of the Flies
2006, video, infinite loop

2. Canterbury Tales Rap
2007, video, 54 sec

3. Four Weddings and a Funeral
2006, video, infinite loop

4. Body Magic
with Javier Morales
2006, video, 2 min 25 sec

5. Blood Fantasy
with Javier Morales
2007, video, 5 min

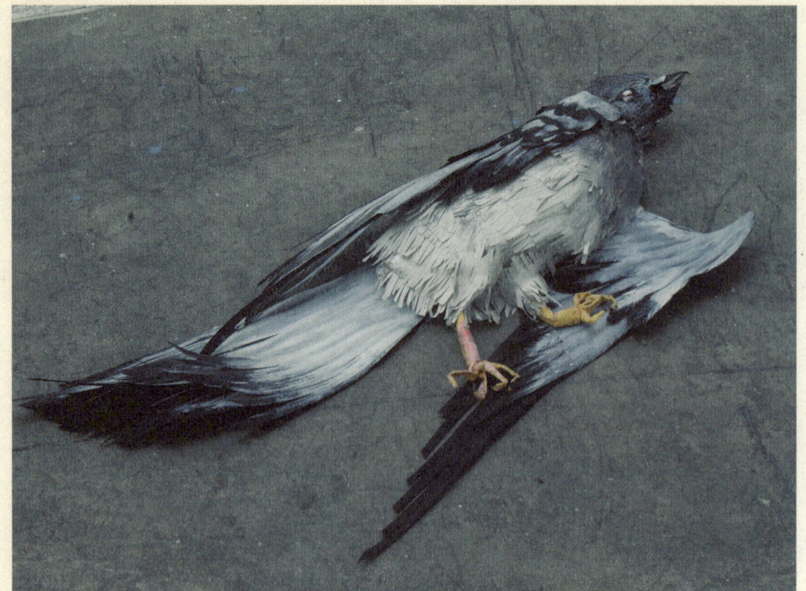

1.

Carlos Bonil was educated at the Universidad Nacional de Colombia, Bogotá. He is an interdisciplinary practitioner who has worked as a sculptor, video artist, curator, and musician. His wry, meticulous sculptures are created using repurposed technological waste and detritus. He is also the front man of Mugre, an experimental hardcore band in which he performs alongside his brother Germán, and for which he creates new instruments and unusual sounds using outdated electronic equipment, household appliances, and other cast-off materials.

1. Dead Dove
2007, paper, glue, and watercolors, 11 × 8 × 2 in (28 × 20 × 5 cm)

2. Fish
2007, plastic spoons, knives, forks, and toy bucket; fish, 59 × $31\frac{1}{2}$ × $15\frac{3}{4}$ in (150 × 80 × 40 cm); bucket, $\frac{3}{4}$ × $\frac{3}{4}$ × $1\frac{1}{2}$ in (2 × 2 × 4 cm)

3. Mugre
2005–present, band utilizing homemade instruments, old keyboards, bass, and voice

4. Drums
2007, mixed media, 8 × 8 × 6 in (20 × 20 × 15 cm)

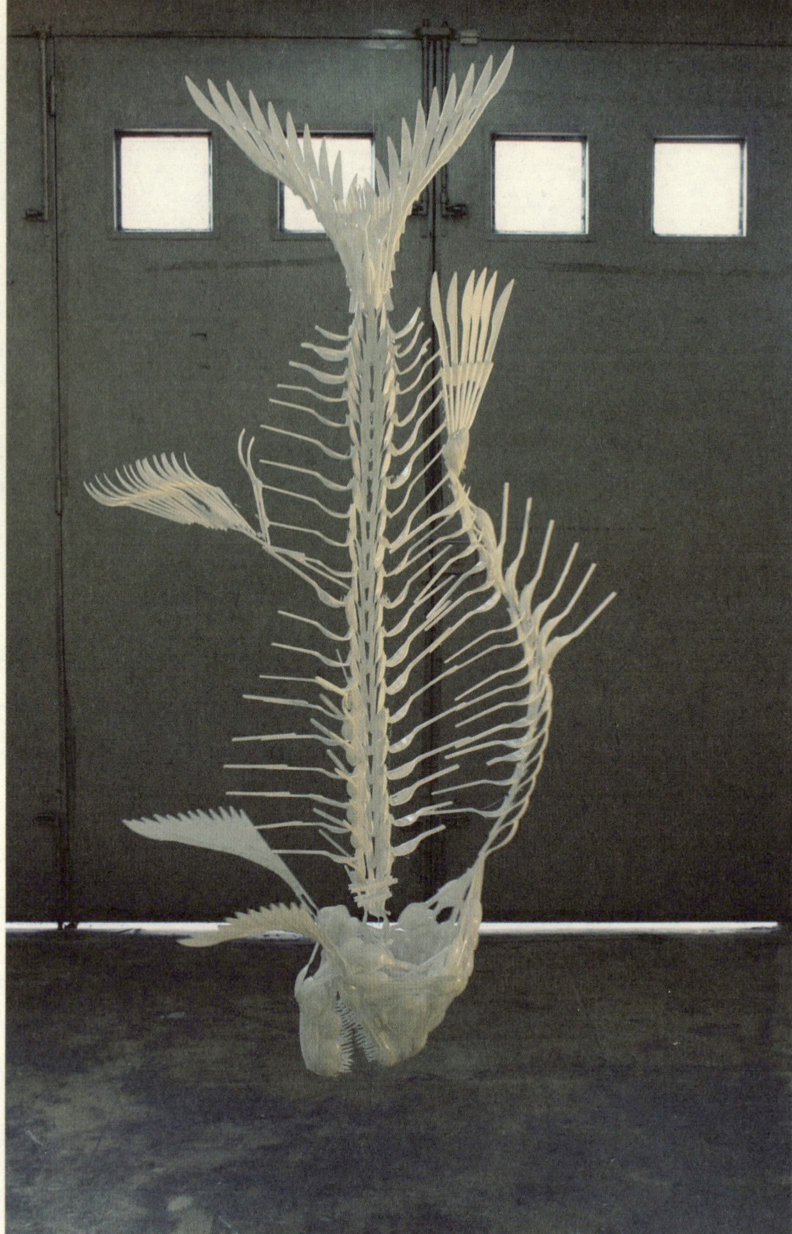

2.

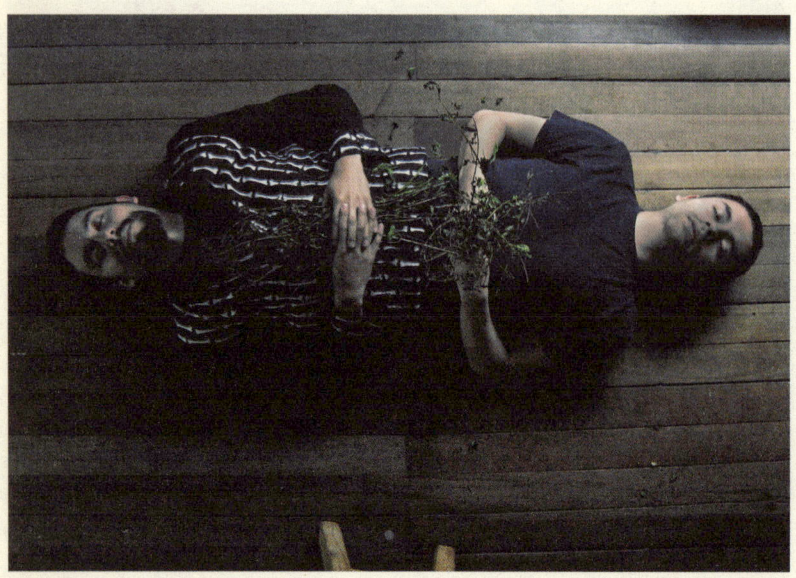

3.

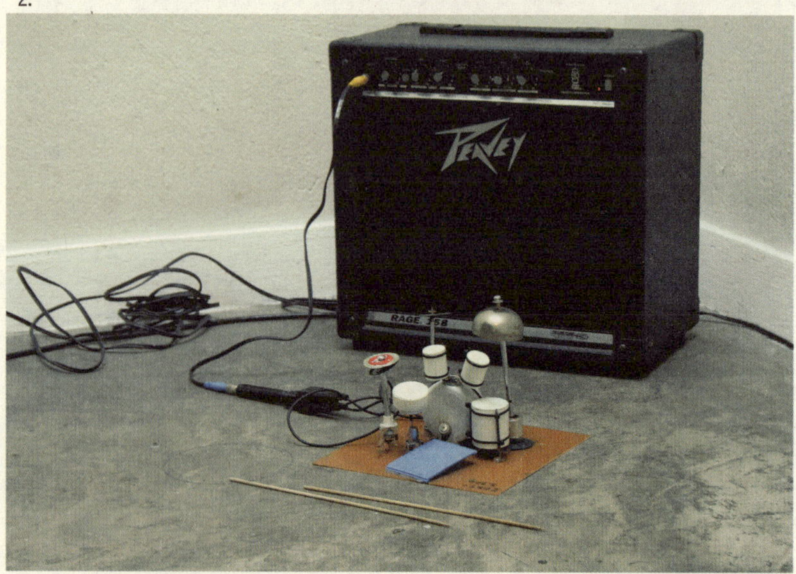

4.

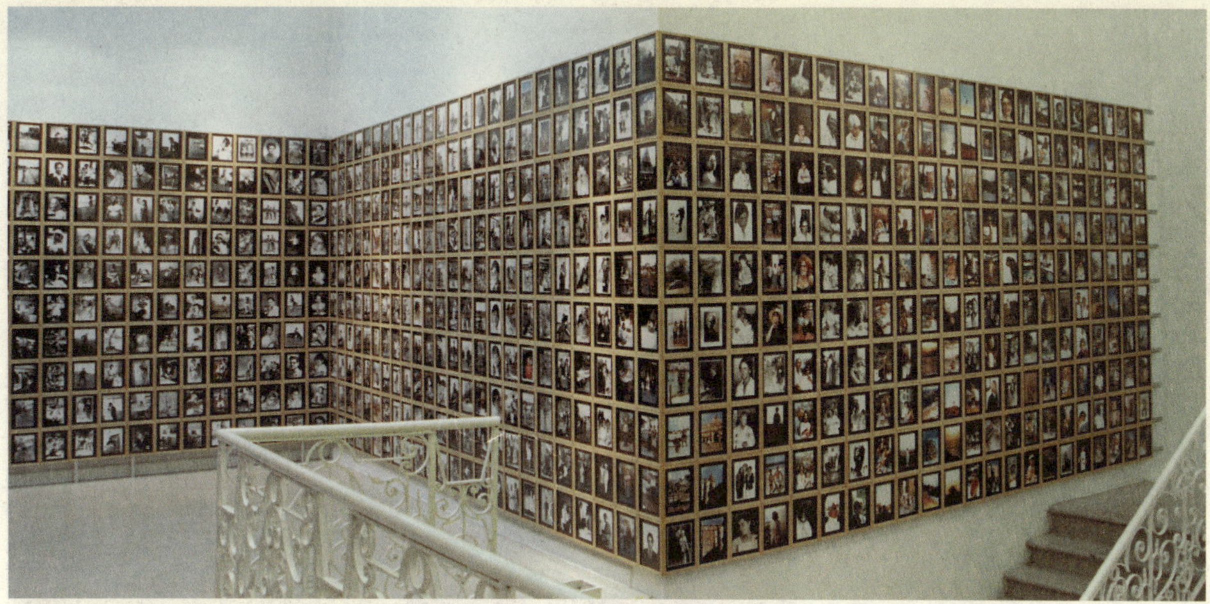

Iñaki Bonillas lives in Mexico City. His Conceptual practice is focused on experiments with the medium of photography, such as a series of works presenting the photographic archive of his grandfather in different contexts and formats. His installation, sound, and book works explore spatial dynamics and uses of light. He was included in "Utopia Station" at the 2003 Venice Biennale.

1.

1. **Todas las fotografías verticales de los archivos de J.R. Plaza, documentadas fotográficamente** (All of the vertical photographs from the archive of J.R. Plaza, photographically documented)
2004, 990 pictures in wood frames, each 11 × 8 in (28 × 23 cm); overall 90 3/4 × 78 ft (28 × 24 m)

2. **Naufragio en silencio** (Shipwreck in silence)
2007, chalk line reel on white cotton paper, each 12 × 25 in (31 × 63 cm)

3. **Espectador del naufragio** (Shipwreck's spectator)
2007, light boxes with 2 plaques of 4 × 5 in (negative and positive), each 9 × 16 1/2 × 4 in (23 × 42 × 11 cm)

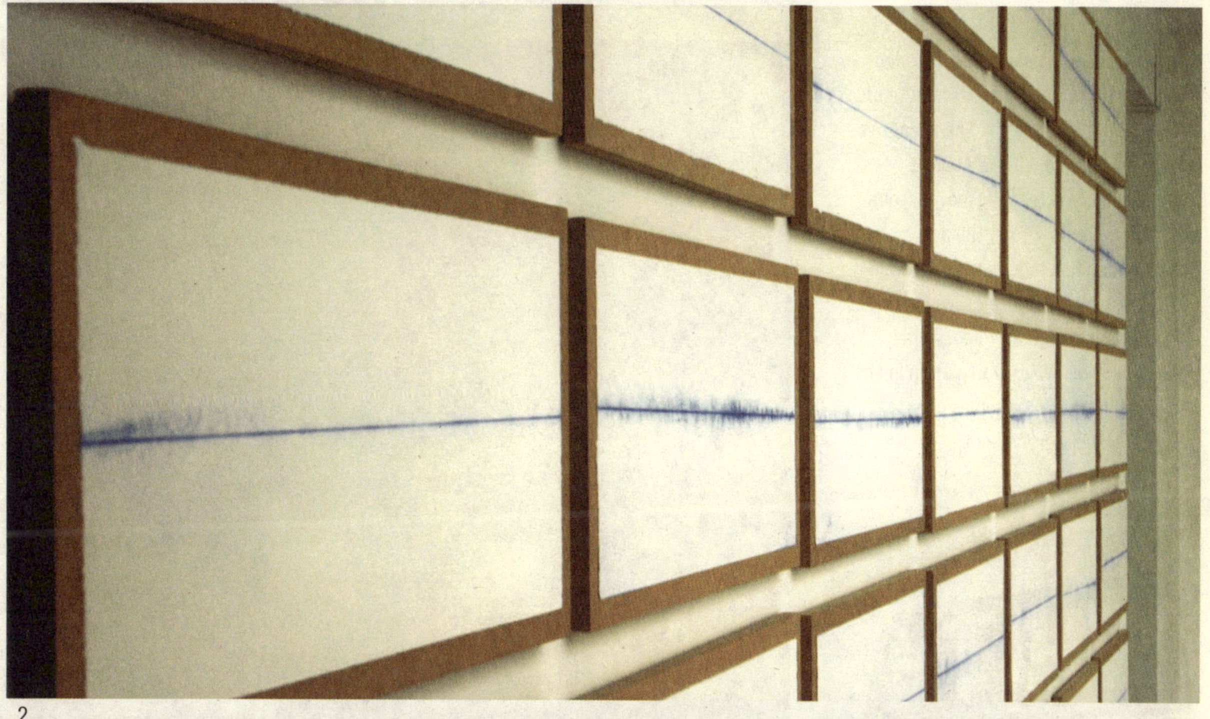

2.

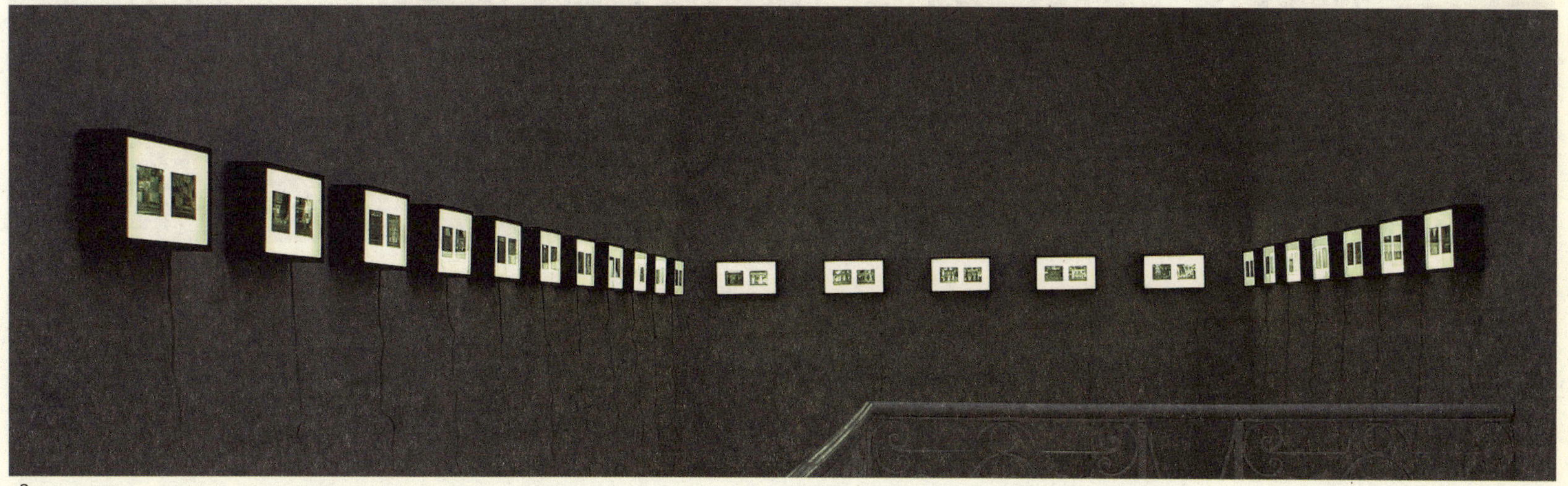

3.

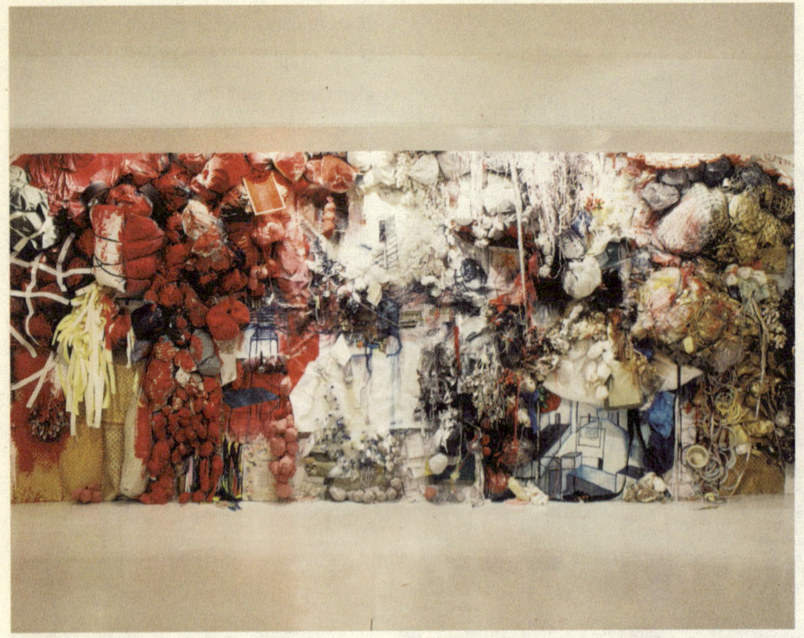

1.

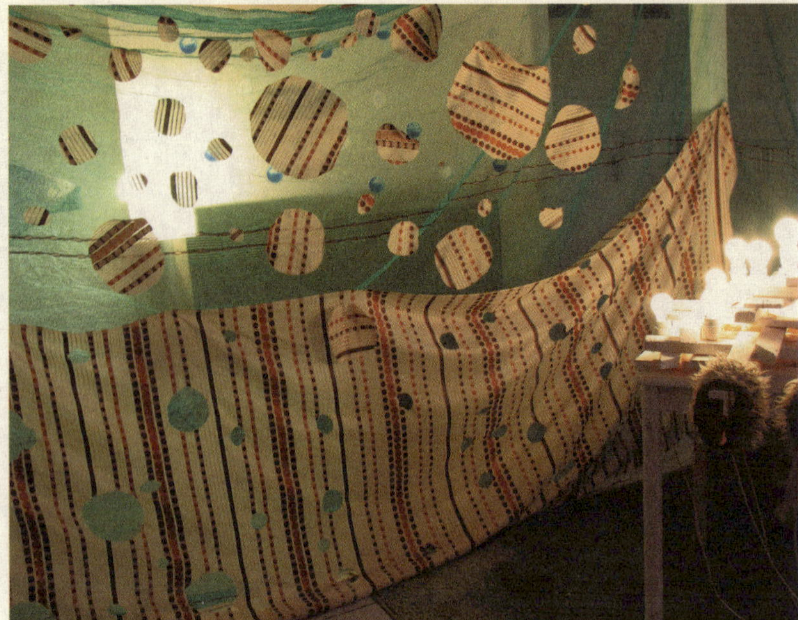

2.

Dineo Seshee Bopape earned her degree in fine art from the Durban Institute of Technology, South Africa. She spent two years as a resident at De Ateliers, Amsterdam, and recently moved from Cape Town to New York. The act of collecting ties together her diverse practice, which includes drawing, sculpture, installation, video, sound, and slide shows. Her works often inject sexual impulses into themes of race, gender, and cultural identity.

3.

4.

1. Growing everyday

2005, mixed media, 106 1/4 × 238 × 49 in (270 × 605 × 124 cm)

2. Displaced light

2007, pinned fabric, net, and light, dimensions variable

3. White noise

2007, paint on board, dimensions variable

4. (left) **itchy fairy**

2007, wood, lights, fabric sacks, fake fur, and green carpet, dimensions variable

4. (right) **you are portable**

2007, photograph

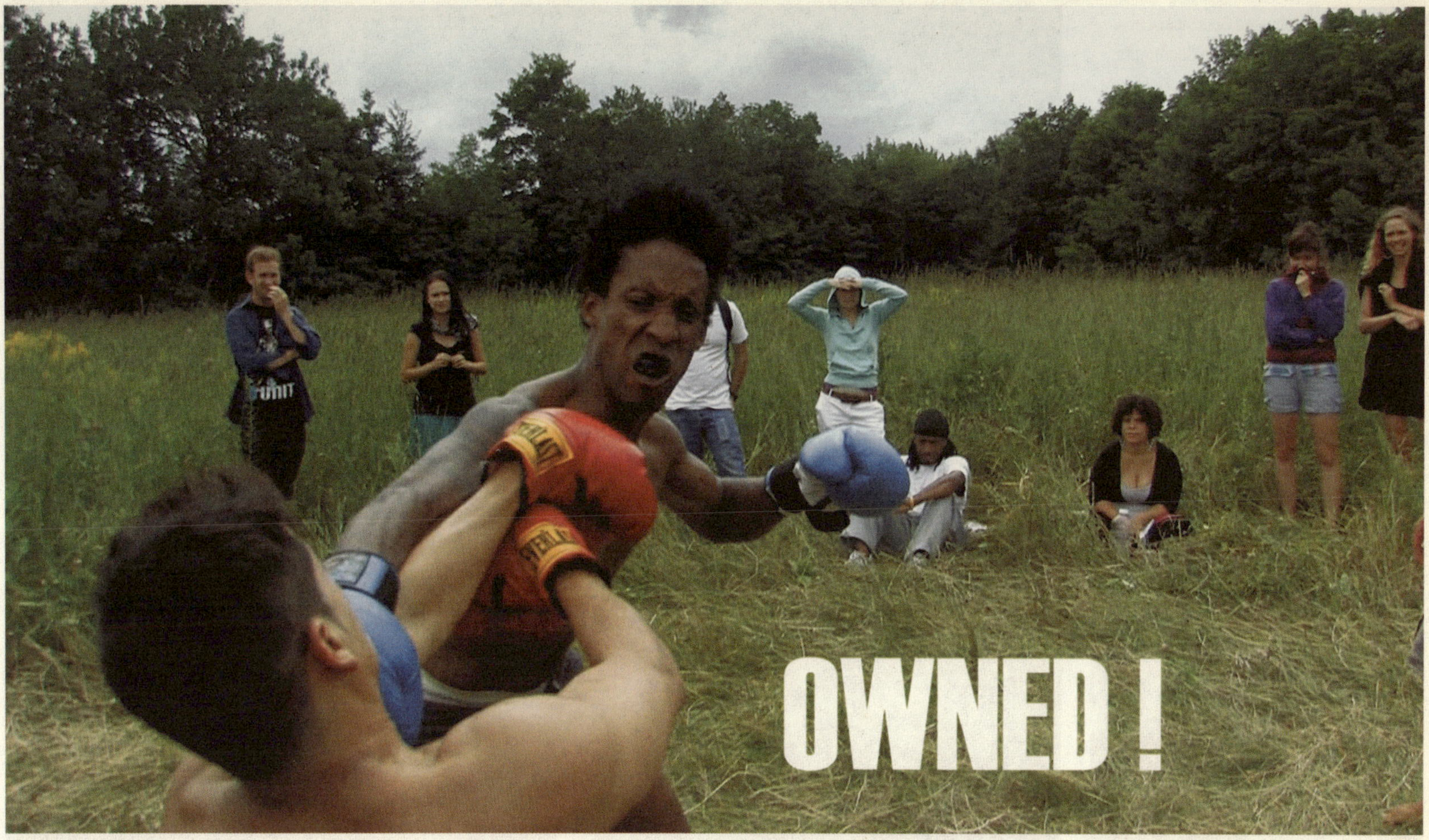

1.

Javier Bosques specialized in video and sculpture at the Cooper Union, New York. After graduating in 2008, he was awarded an artist's residency at the Skowhegan School for Painting and Sculpture in Maine. Bosques's autobiographical videos explore the nature of oral traditions and the transmission of knowledge across generations. In performances, such as **Vid.A (Video Art)** (2006), Bosques investigates the different ways in which people perform their identities in domestic and public situations. He currently lives and works in Brooklyn.

1. Spectacle
2008, video, 9 min

2. Celebración
2008, digital print, 15 × 20 in (38 × 51 cm)

3. Transeúnte
2008, digital print, 15 × 20 in (38 × 51 cm)

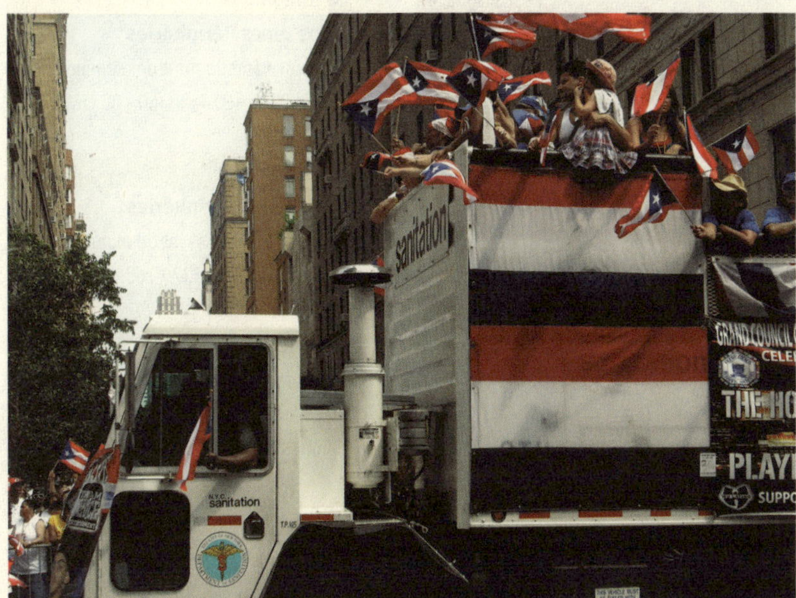

2.

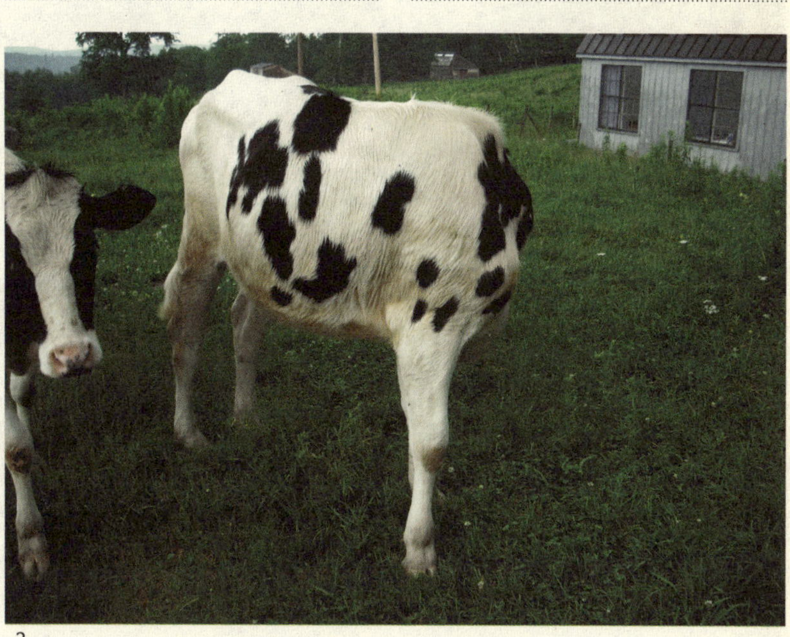

3.

Photographer Mohamed Bourouissa attended the Ecole Nationale Supérieure des Arts Décoratifs in Paris, where he lives. He photographs staged scenes in some of France's ghettolike suburbs, focusing on power dynamics within groups. He is most interested in "that very fleeting tenth of a second when the tension is at its most extreme ... when the tension seems more violent than the confrontation with the other."

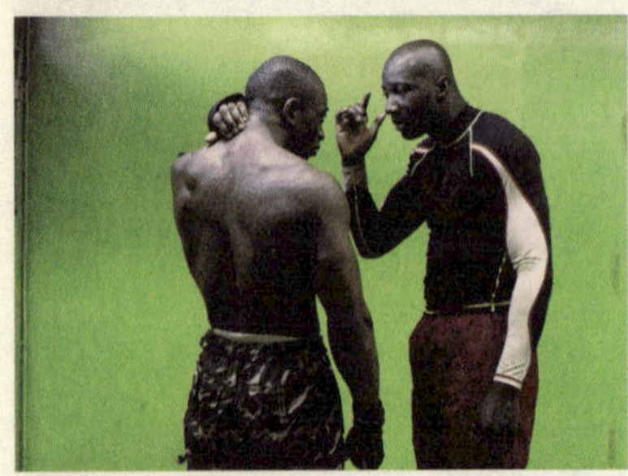

1.

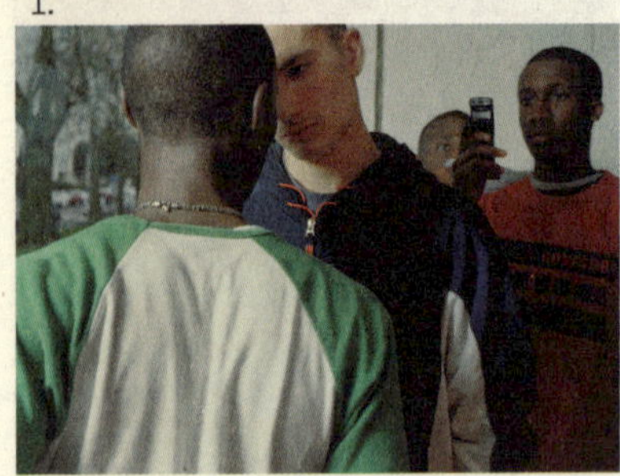

2.

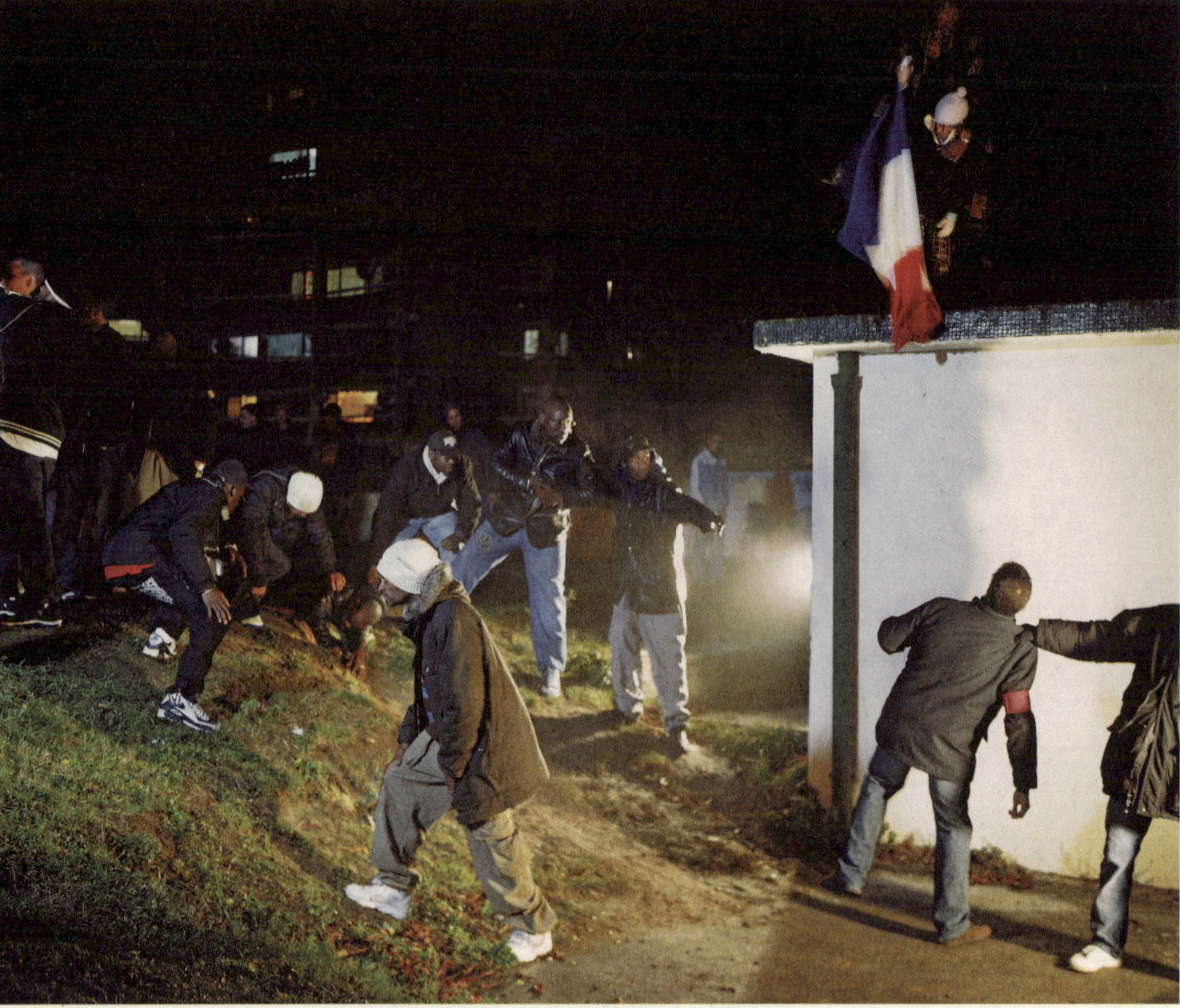

3.

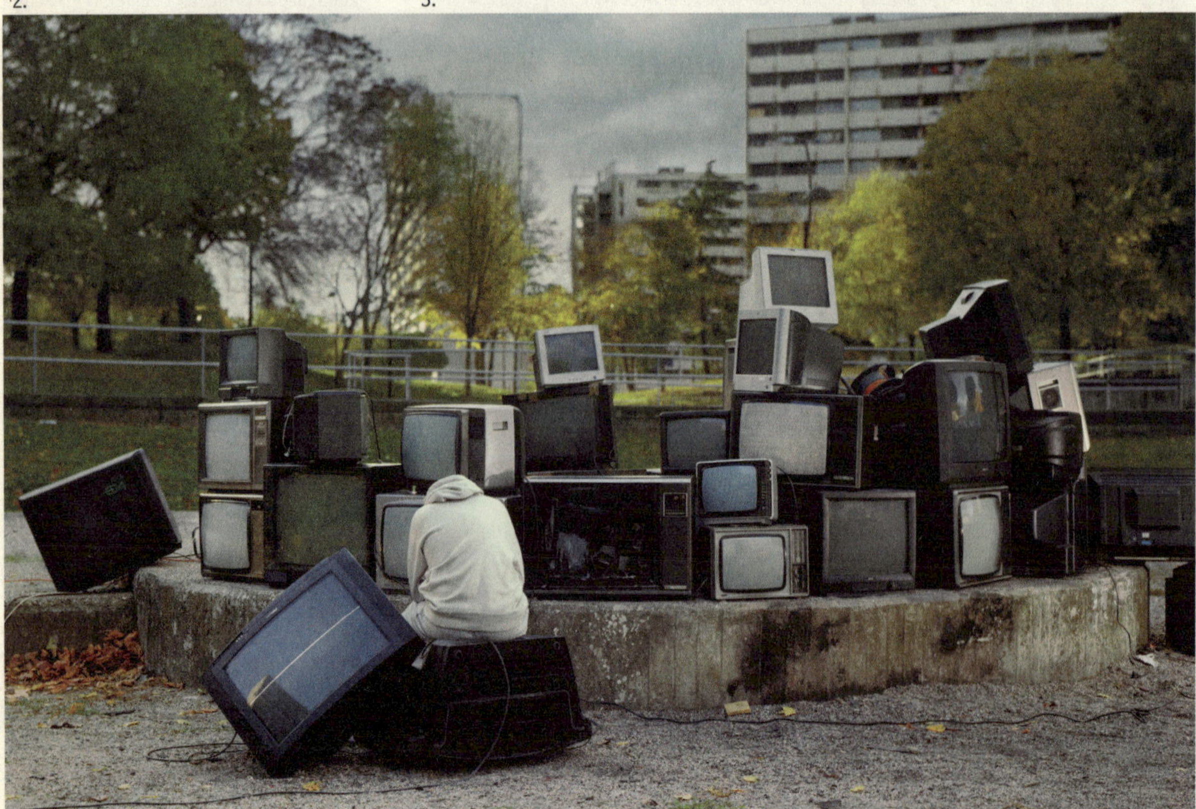

4.

1. **La fenêtre**
from the series **Périphéries**
2005, color Lambda print on aluminum
in frame, 23 ½ × 31 ½ in (60 × 80 cm)

2. **Le telephone**
from the series **Périphéries**
2006, color Lambda print on aluminum
in frame, 23 ½ × 31 ½ in (60 × 80 cm)

3. **La République**
from the series **Périphéries**
2006, color Lambda print on aluminum
in frame, 54 × 65 in (137 × 165 cm)

4. **Le reflet**
from the series **Périphéries**
2007, color Lambda print on aluminum
in frame, 37 × 63 in (95 × 160 cm)

Sarah Bowker-Jones earned her MFA in painting from the Slade School of Fine Art in London, where she currently lives. She sees the act of drawing at the core of her practice, whether working in two or three dimensions. Using a process based simultaneously in system and in play, she combines material from plaster to cat litter in works that hover between painting and sculpture.

1 & 3. **Pomme pom (with polka dots), LOOKING IN**
2008, air, yoga ball, plastic, foam, muslin, PVA, pigment, foam-coat paint, glitter paint, carpet, aluminum, steel, and transparent film, 13 × 4 ¾ × 13 ft (4 × 2 × 4 m)

2. **Spiked** (detail)
2008, paper, acrylic paint, brass paper fasteners, staples, and bronze, 27 ½ × 23 ½ × 23 ½ in (70 × 60 × 60 cm)

4. **Tight Sbends**
2008, aluminum, Sculptamold, acrylic, and glitter glue, 10 × 10 × 10 in (25 × 25 × 25 cm)

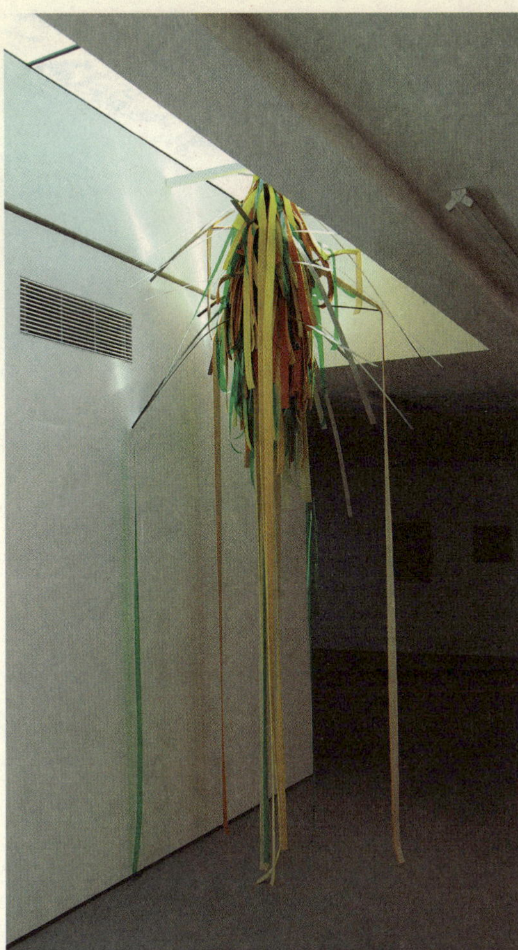
1.

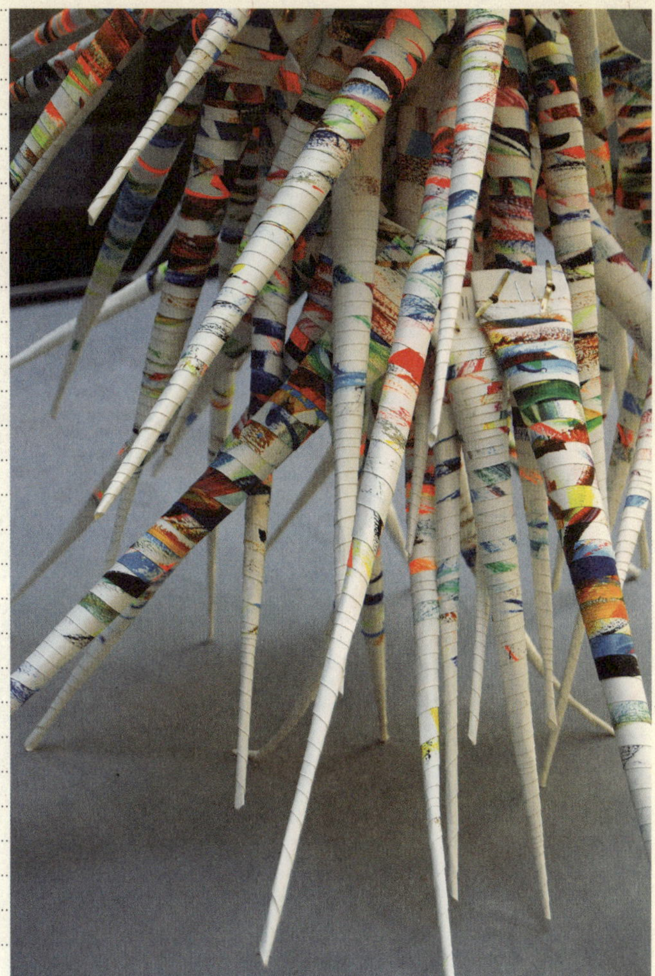
2.

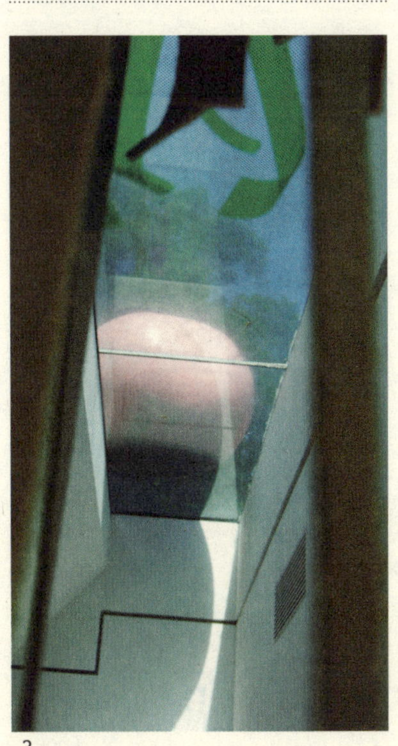
3.

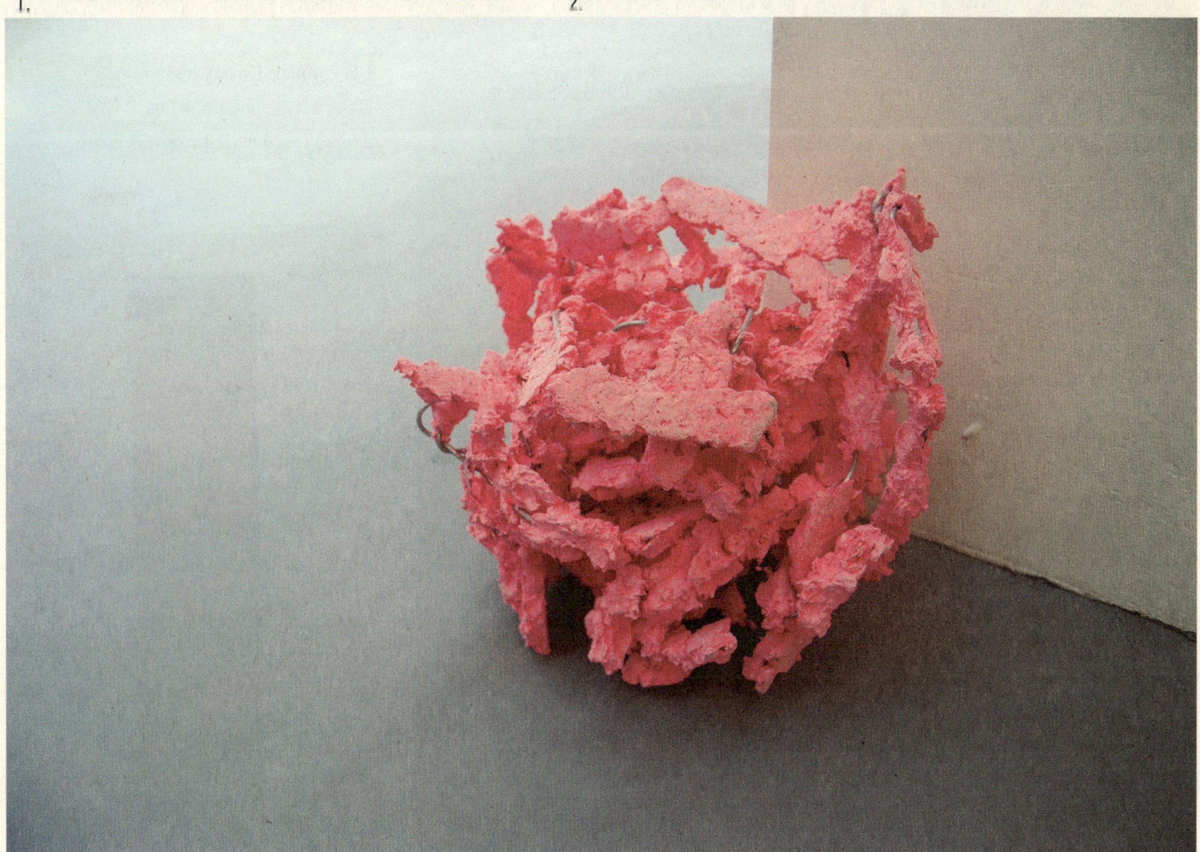
4.

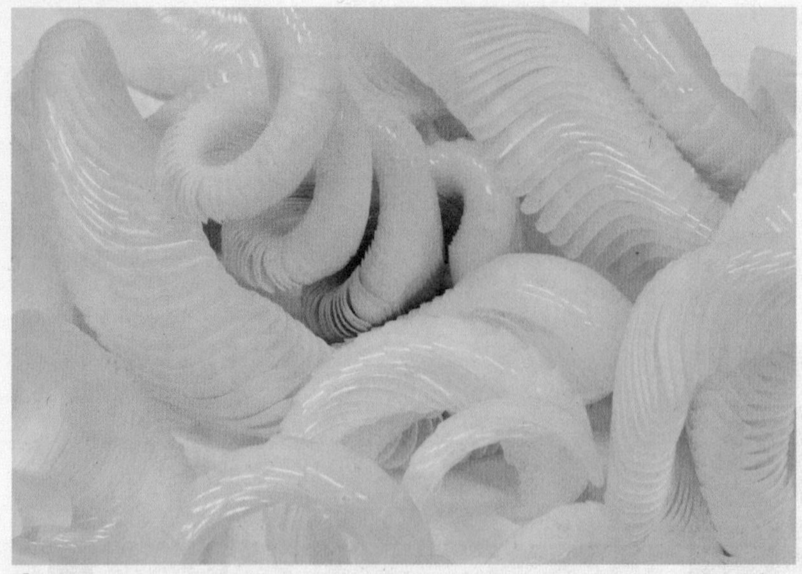
1.

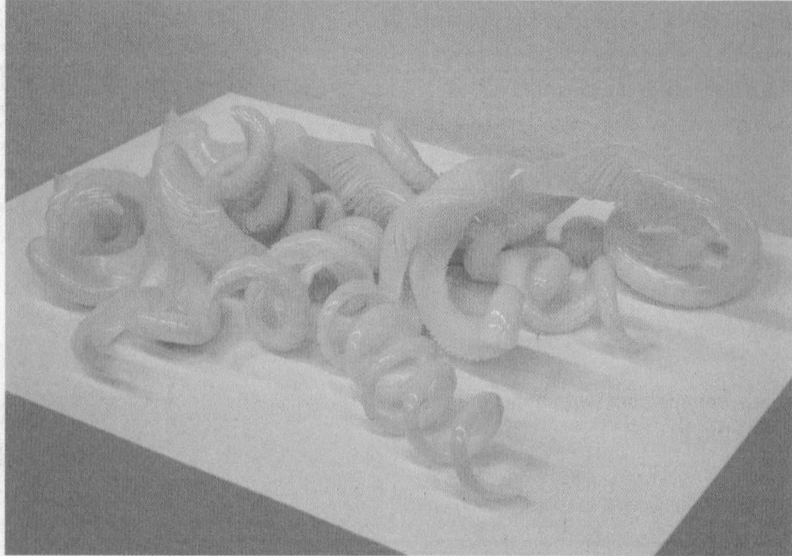
2.

Los Angeles-based David Brady makes objects, installations, and sound works using a range of materials and processes. These include growing crystals from his own tears, manipulations of bulletproof glass or acrylic fingernail tips, and computer programming applications. His **The Origin of the World Wallpaper** (2007) extends the legacy of Gustave Courbet's 1866 painting by fracturing pornographic images into decorative, kaleidoscopic patterns.

1 & 2. **False Cavity** (detail)
2008, acrylic fingernail tips, 3 ½ × 11 × 14 in (8.9 × 28 × 35.6 cm)

3. **Fragile x**
2008, 200 linear ft of zinc-plated GR30 ½ inch steel tow chain, 32 × 32 × 23 in (81 × 81 × 58 cm)

4. **Knowledge of Self**
2008, bulletproof glass, 72 × 18 × 2 in (183 × 46 × 5 cm)

5. **Everything Doesn't Not Have an Opposite**
2008, painted wood, 84 × 28 × 9 in (213 × 71 × 23 cm)

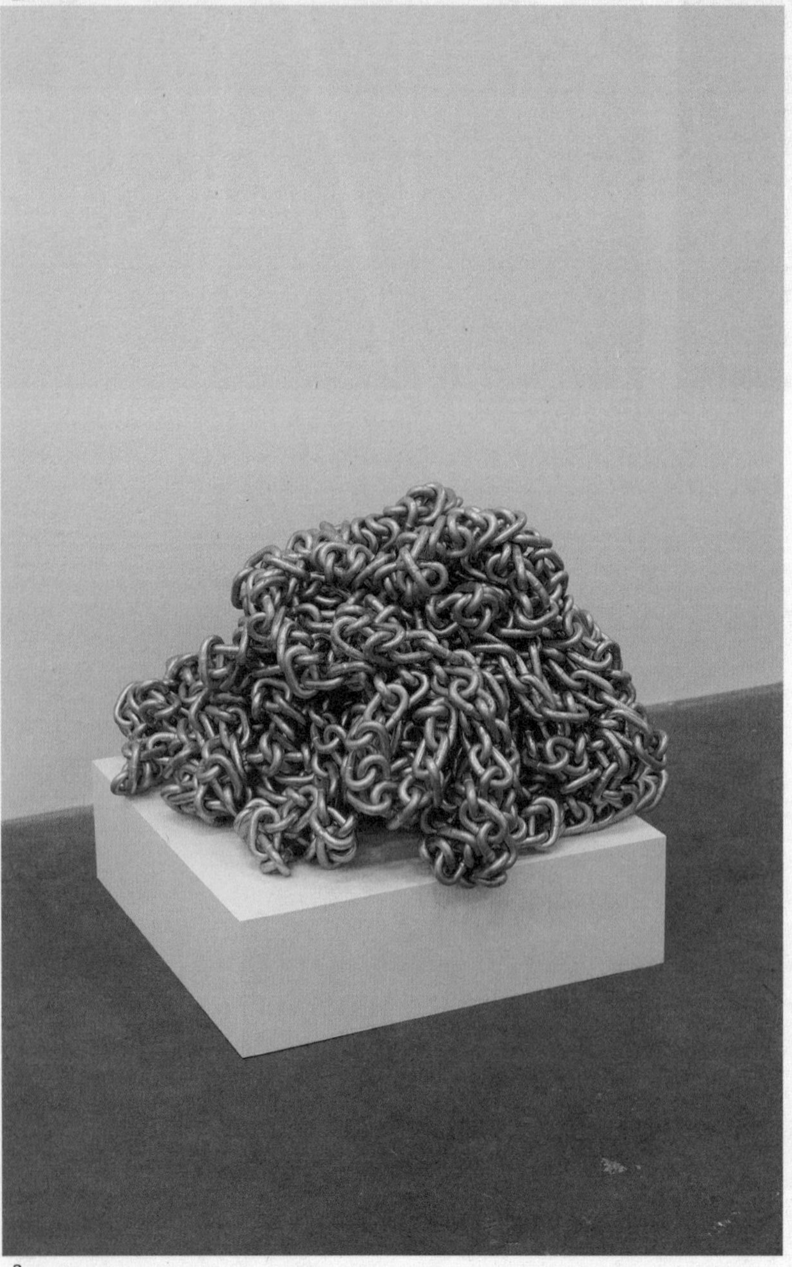
3.

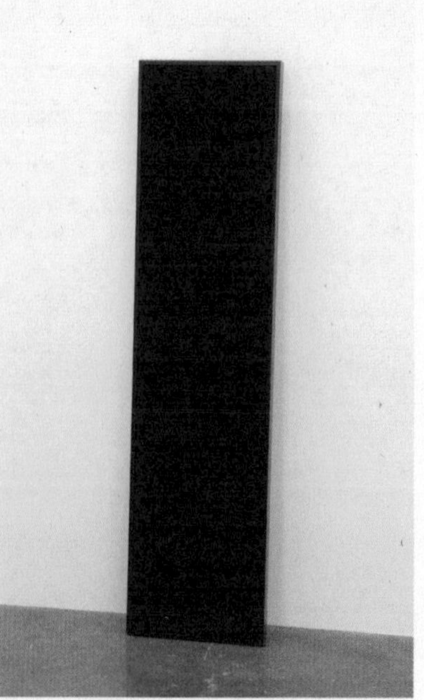

4.

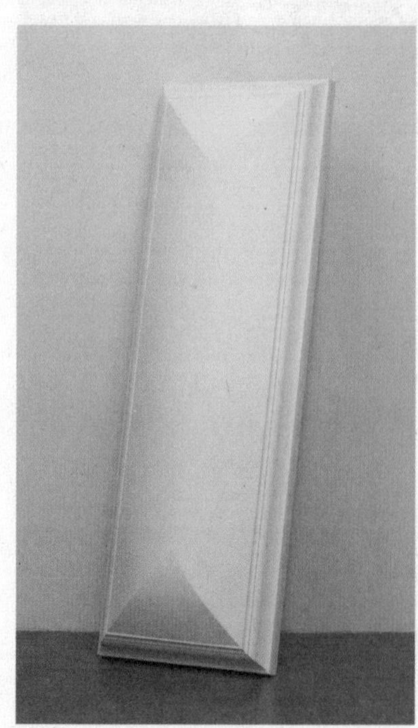
5.

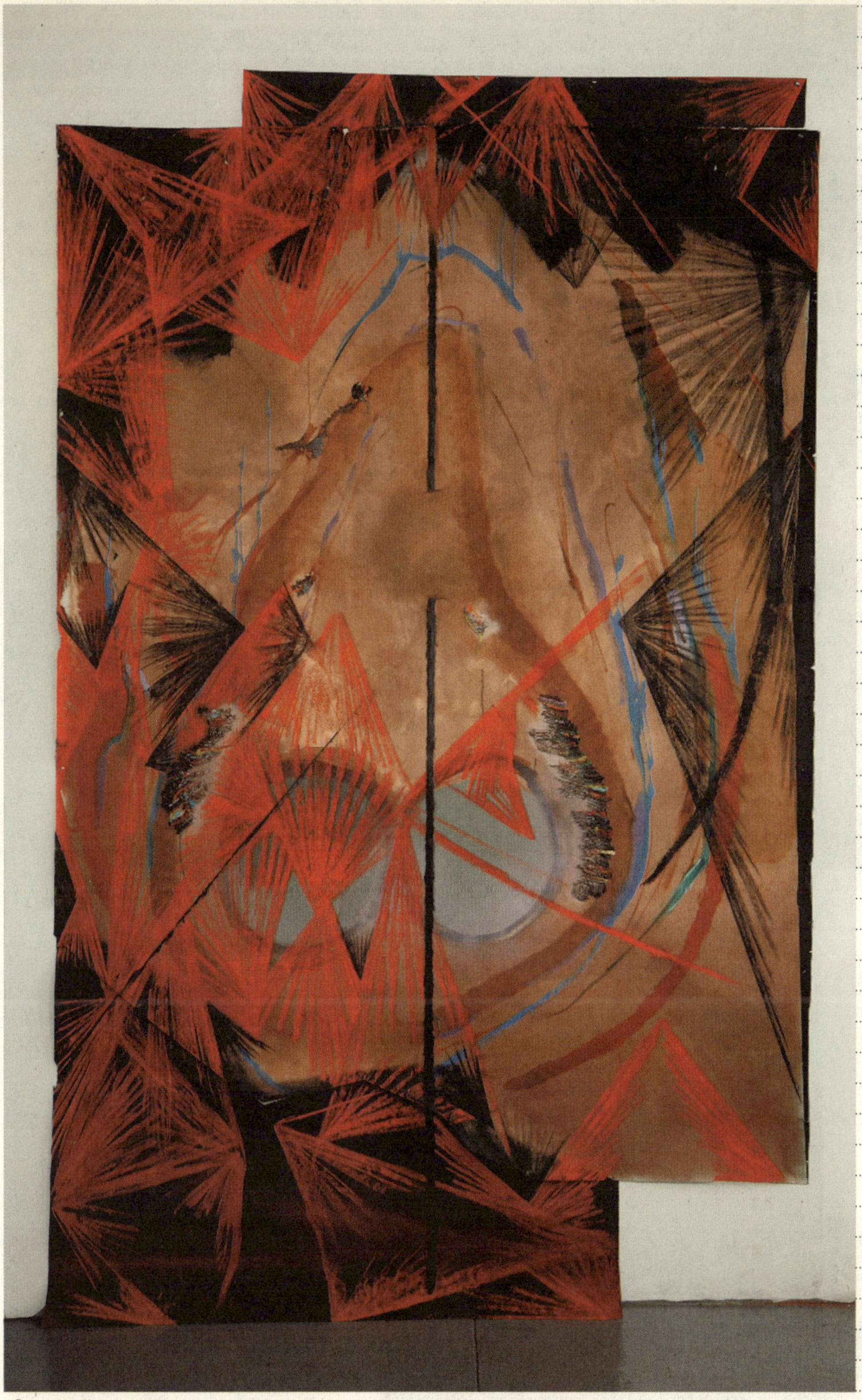

1.

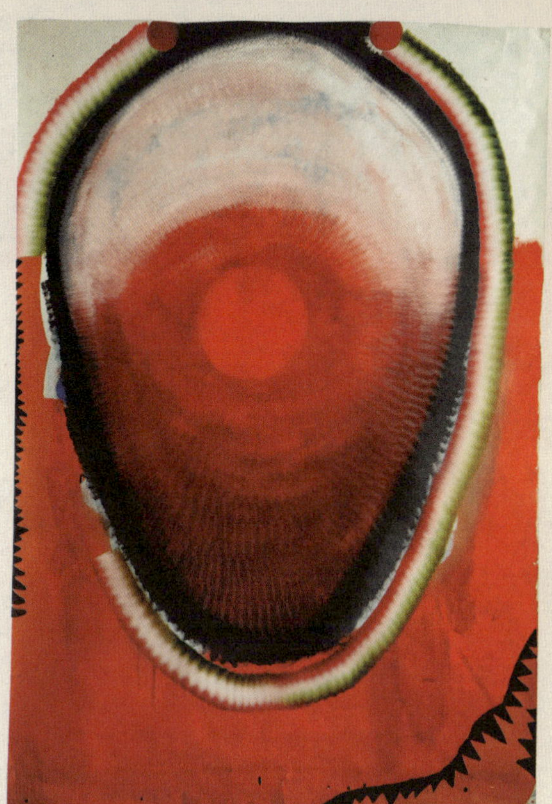

2.

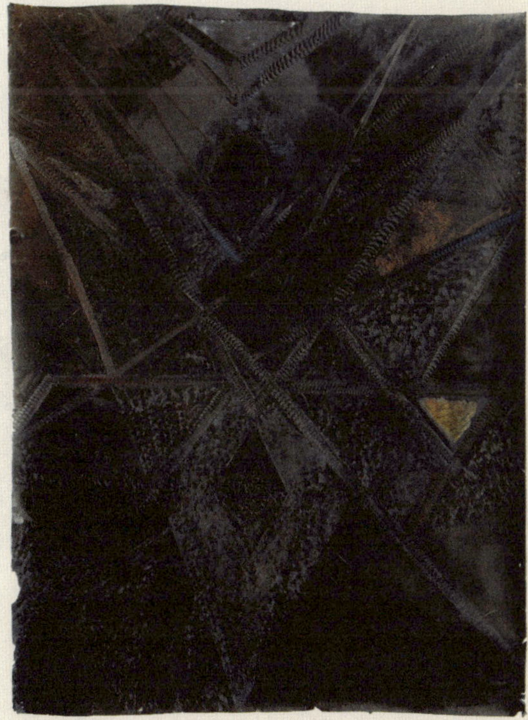

3.

Kerstin Brätsch earned her MFA from Columbia University and currently lives in New York and Berlin. She makes large paintings on paper that often symbolize psychics and spirit guides. She has also made several works experimenting with the process of photocopying—reproducing images until they are illegible. She has also used photocopied sheets as wallpaper on which to mount paintings.

1, 2 & 3. **Untitled**
from the series **Psychic**
2008, paint on paper, each 98 ½ × 69 in
(250 × 175 cm)

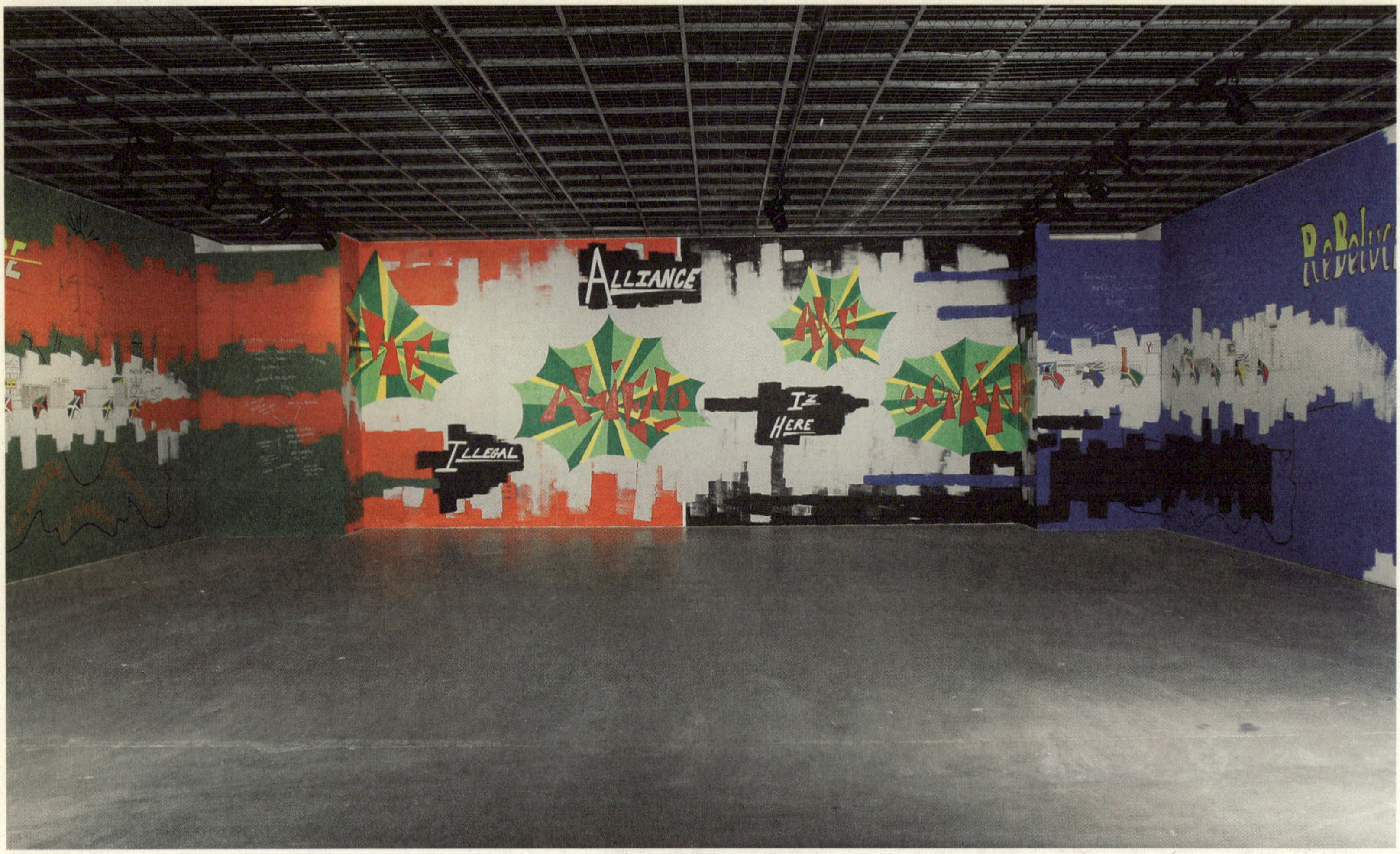

1.

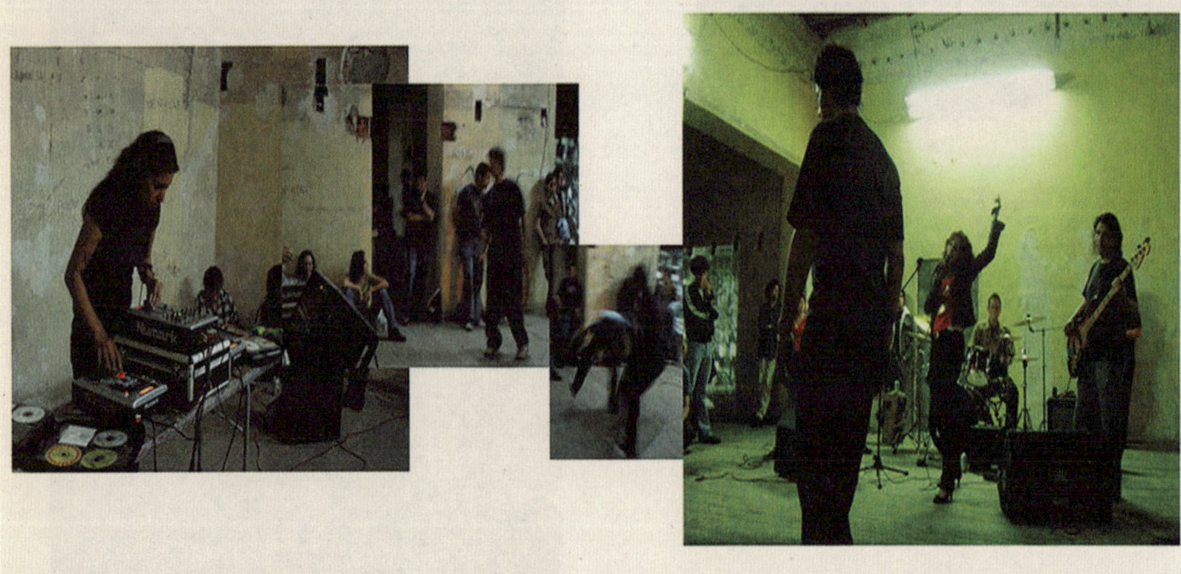

2.

Cindy Santos Bravo received her MFA from the California Institute of the Arts in Valencia, California. Her installations, performances, and videos investigate the mutability and hybridity of sociocultural identity historically and within contemporary urban culture. Her investigations are largely focused on jazz music, both as a literal engine of social transformation and exchange and as a metaphoric signifier for the innovative power of improvisation. Her work was included in the first MexiCali Biennial (2006) and shown at the California African American Museum, Los Angeles (2008).

1. **Rebelución**
2006, acrylic paint, acrylic markers, chalk, and found objects, 10 × 109 ft (3 × 33 m)

2. **Ejercicio del Diálogo: DJ Santos vs Venereas Edecanes**
2006, performance with DJ and live band, 60 min

1. Fowl
2006, oil on canvas, 39 ½ × 39 ½ in (100 × 100 cm)

2. Lana
2007, oil on canvas, 39 ½ × 59 in (100 × 150 cm)

3. Bitch
2007, acrylic and oil on canvas, 43 ½ × 39 ½ in (110 × 150 cm)

4. Dove
2007, oil on canvas, 35 ½ × 25 ½ in (90 × 65 cm)

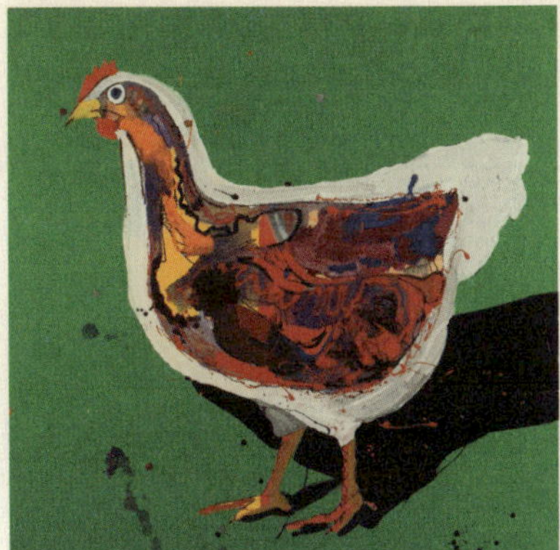

1.

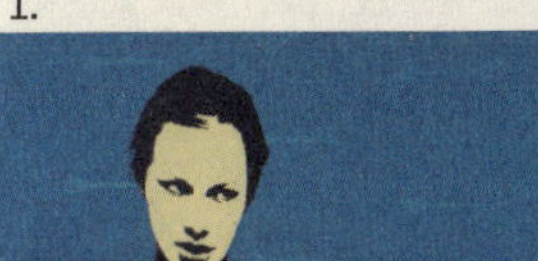

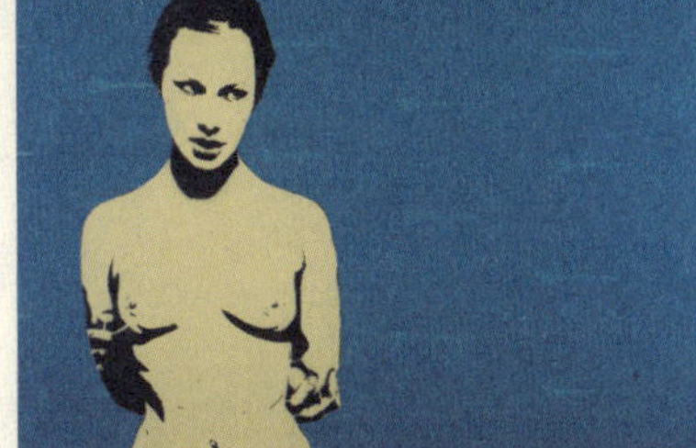

2.

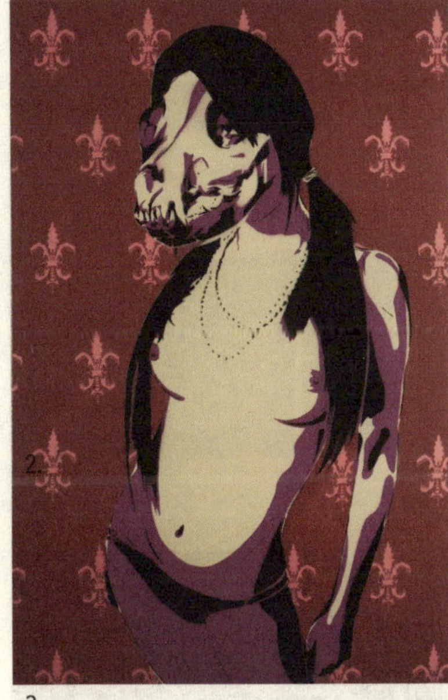

3.

Kristians Brekte attended the Latvian Academy of Art in the department of stage design and currently lives in Riga. He uses the media of painting, stencil, and sculpture to create bold, colorful images of people and animals. His paintings draw from Pop art, while his sculptures – such as a series of toy animals submerged in glasses of water – add a layer of surreal conceptualism.

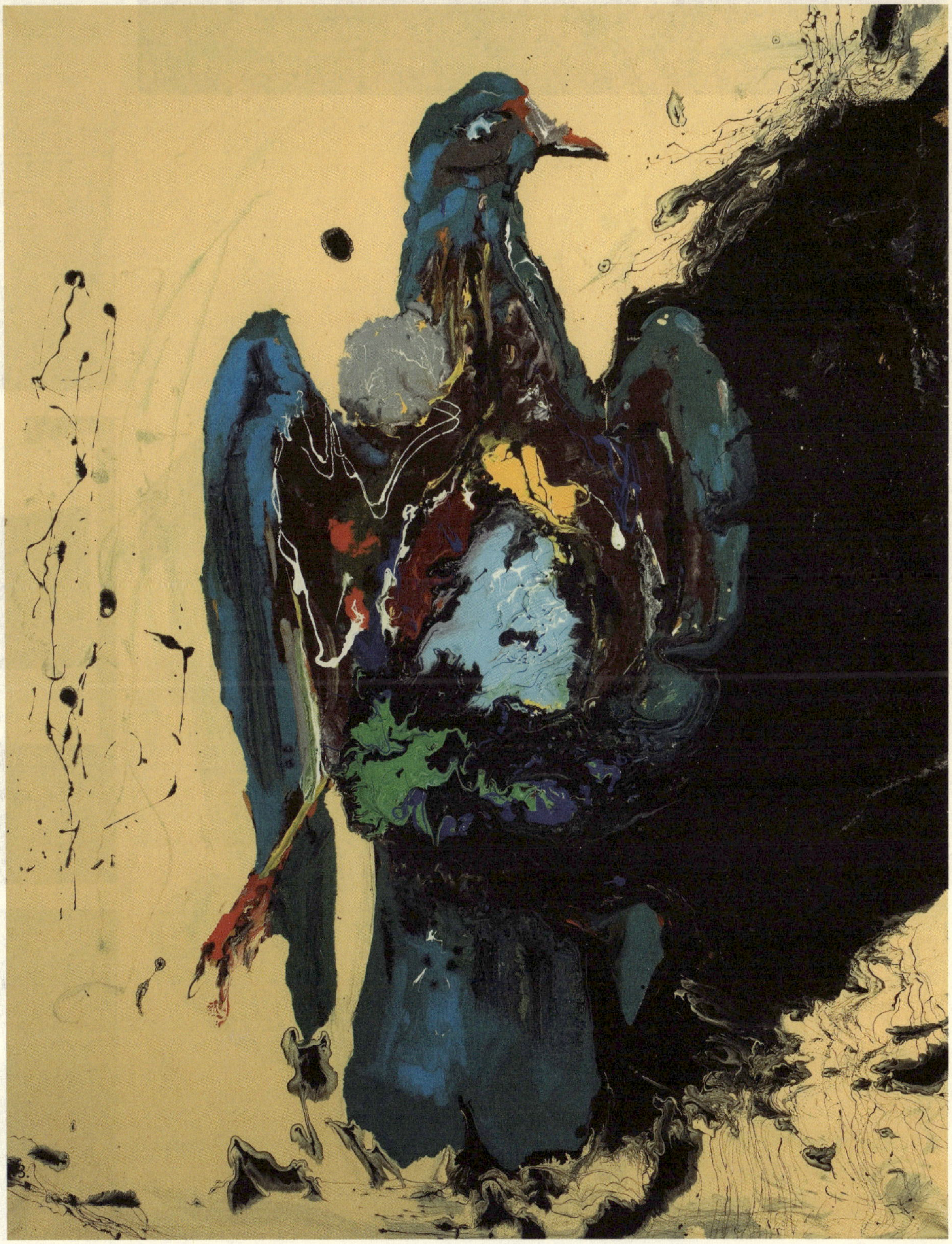

4.

1.

2.

Charles Broskoski earned his BFA in design and technology from Parsons: The New School of Design and currently lives in Brooklyn. He has created a range of Internet-based works, including the 2008 project **Computer Skills**, a 400-day performance in which he read 356 online books on technology and programming instruction. In addition to his own website, since 2001 he has run supercentral.org, a website that houses content that is updated daily by a number of users.

1. New Flag
2008, digital image

2. Computer Skills (XML Hacks)
2008, documentation of performance

3. Two Terminators
2008, computer, code, and XML subtitle files

4. Regular Expression
2008, digital image

5. MySpace Biennale
2006, MySpace servers, code, and computers

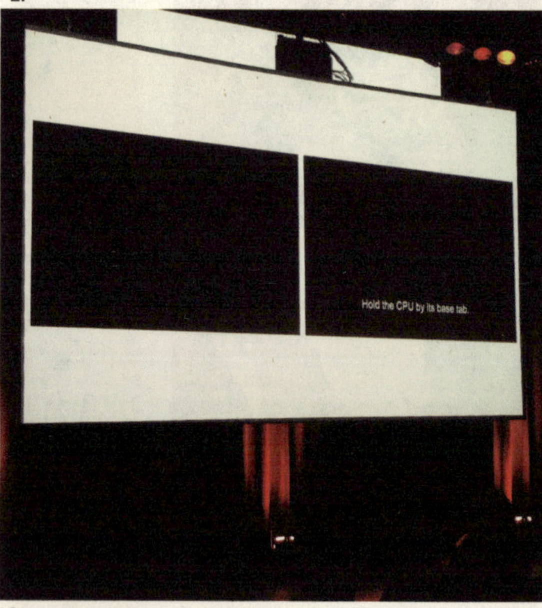

3.

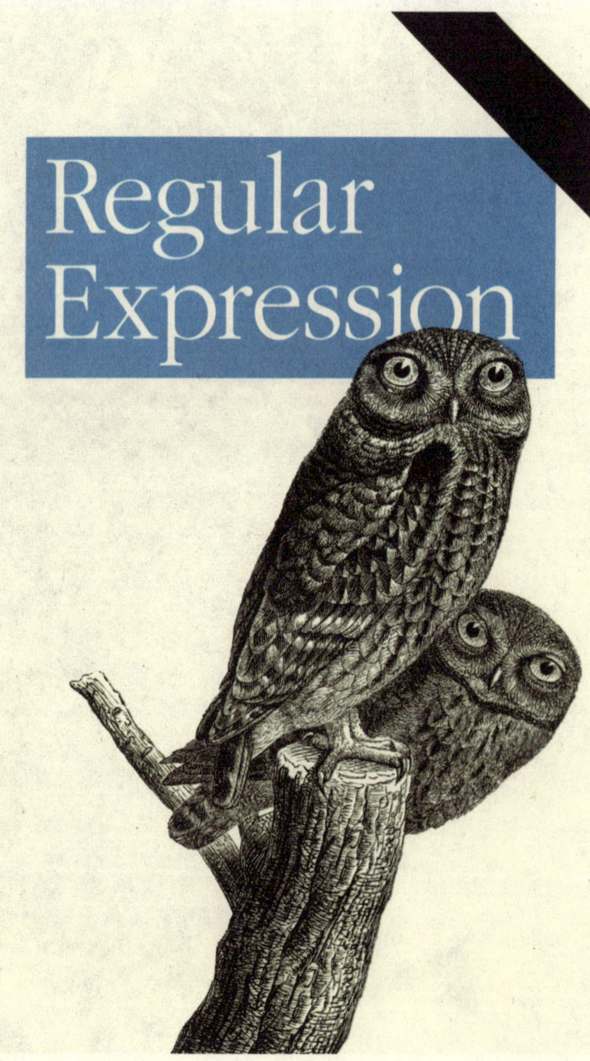

4.

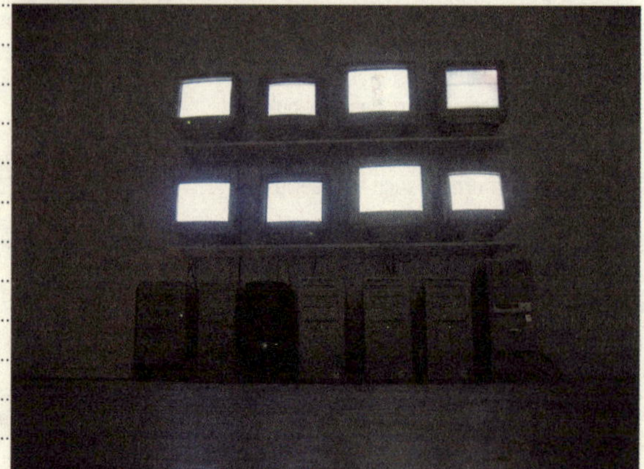

5.

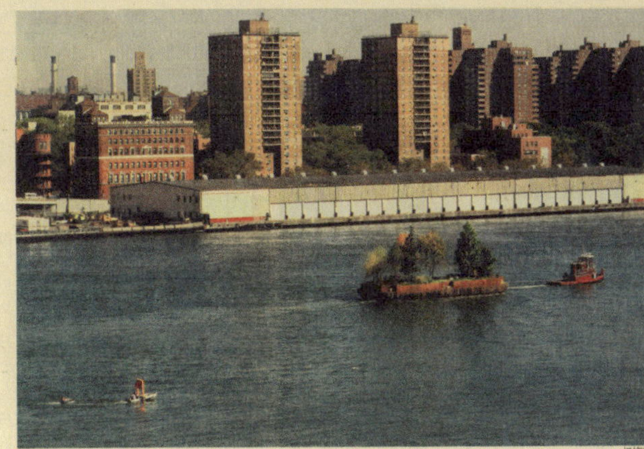

THE Arts B9

SATURDAY, SEPTEMBER 24, 2005

The New York Times

A Miniature Gate in Hot Pursuit of a Miniature Central Park

1.

Formed in the aftermath of 9/11, The Bruce High Quality Foundation is dedicated to the preservation of the legacy of the late social sculptor Bruce High Quality. In the spirit of his life, they "aspire to invest the experience of public space with wonder; to resurrect art history from the bowels of despair; and to impregnate institutions of art with the joy of man's desiring."

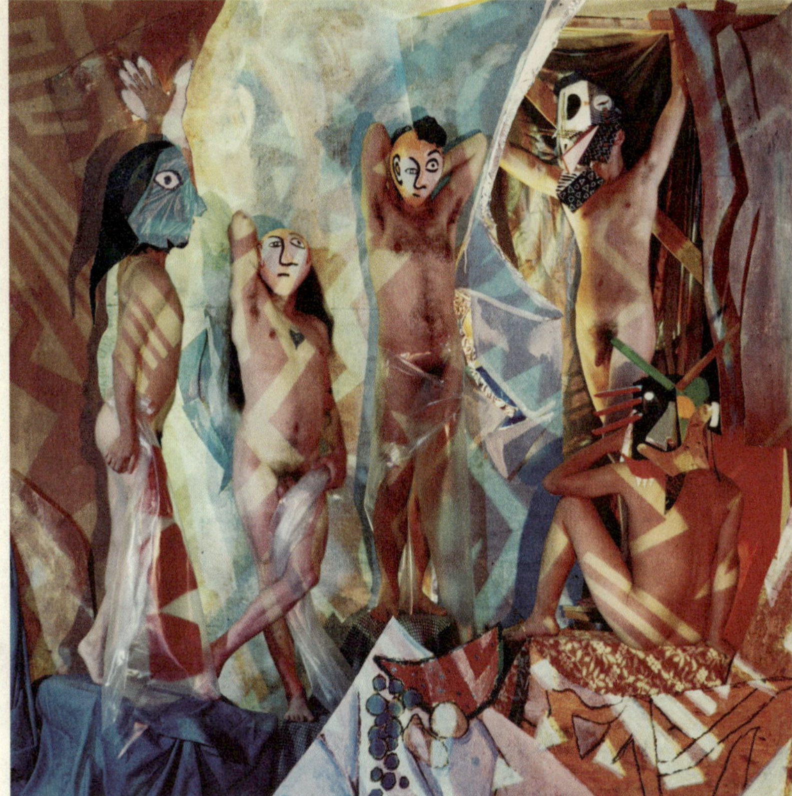

2.

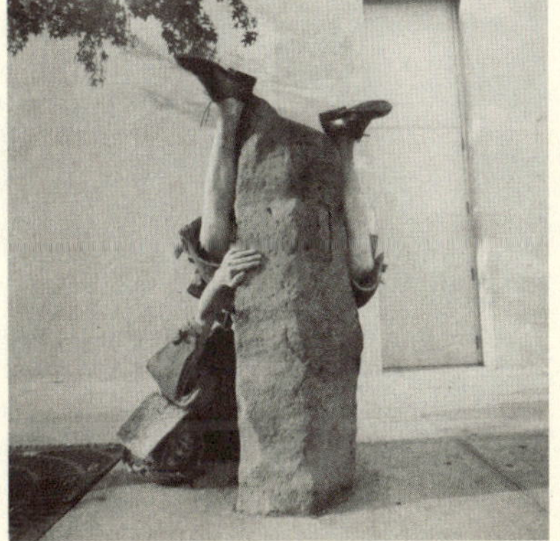

3.

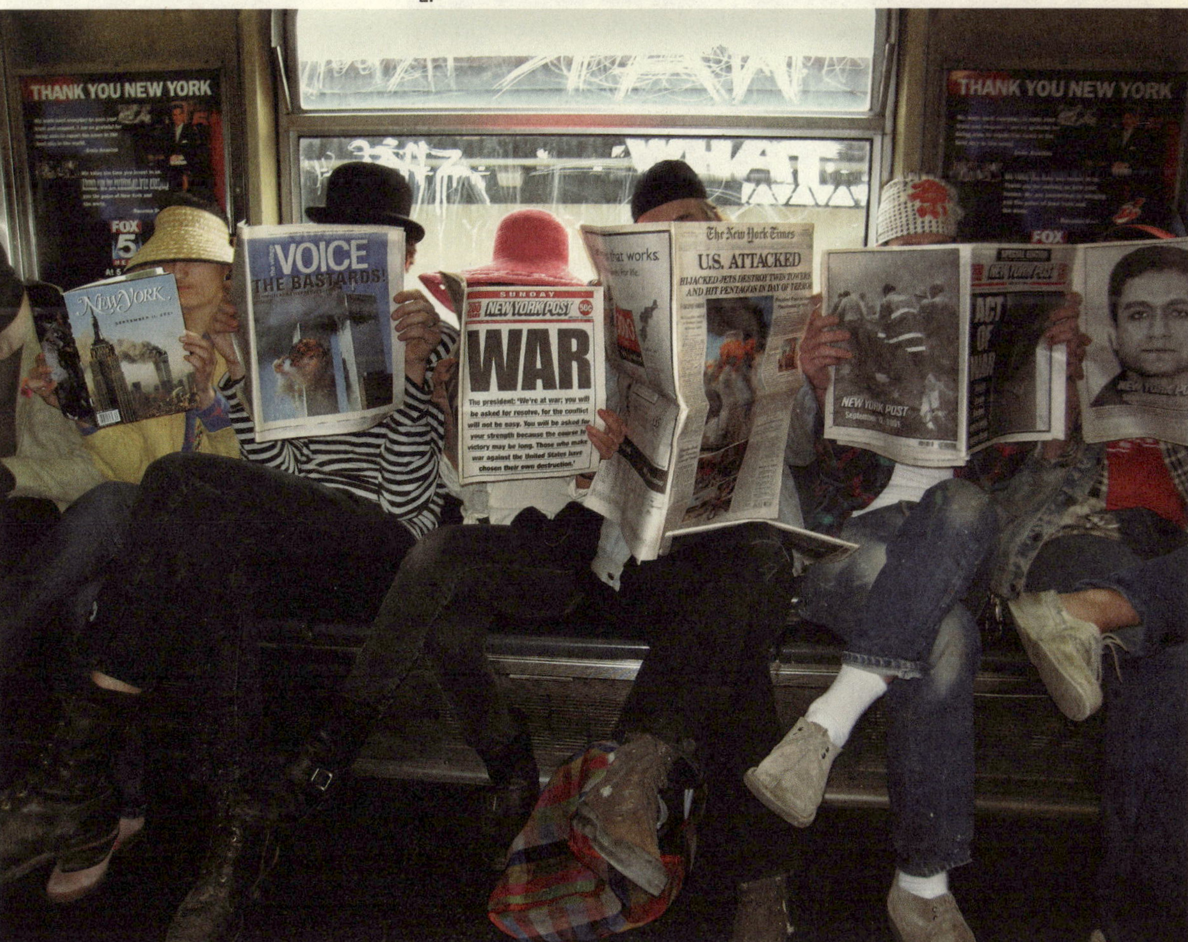

4.

1. The Gate: Not the Idea of the Thing But the Thing Itself
2006, inkjet print, 40 × 60 in (101 × 152 cm)

2. The Bachelors of Avignon
2004, chromogenic print, 48 × 48 in (122 × 122 cm)

3. Sculpture Tackle (Beuys)
2007, gelatin silver print, 15 × 15 in (38 × 38 cm)

4. Thank You New York
2008, inkjet print, 24 × 36 in (61 × 91 cm)

BRYANT III, ERNEST ARTHUR

b. 1978 Minneapolis, Minnesota, USA

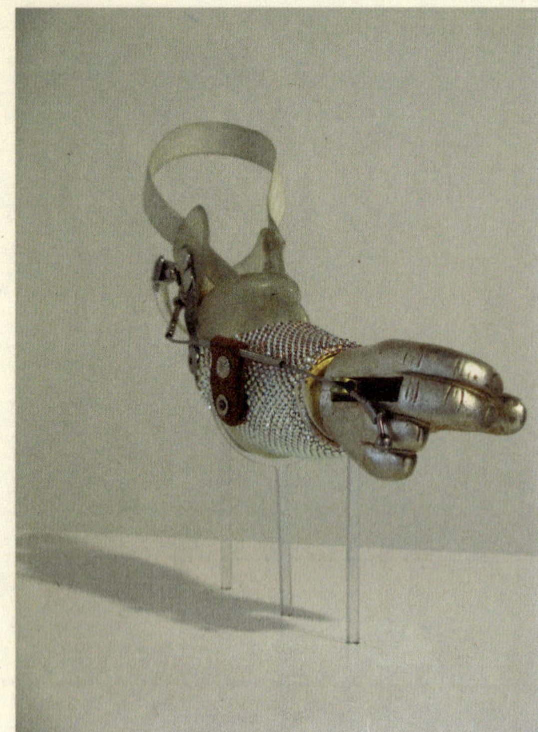

1.

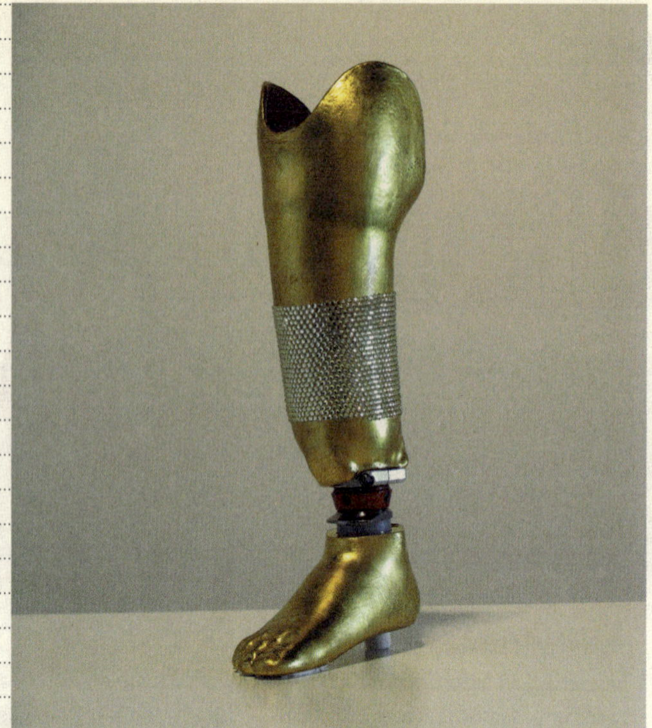

2.

Ernest Arthur Bryant III earned his BFA from the Minneapolis College of Art & Design and continues to live in Minneapolis. His assemblage works incorporate a range of material from textile fragments to military medals and prosthetic body parts. He has hosted the series of events **Chicken Party Flight Jacket Potlatch** (2007-08), in which he serves free barbecue chicken to participants with plans to make jackets from the accumulated bones.

1. Untitled
2007, prosthetic arm, silver, gold, and Swarovski rhinestones, 20 × 2 × 2 in (51 × 5 × 5 cm)

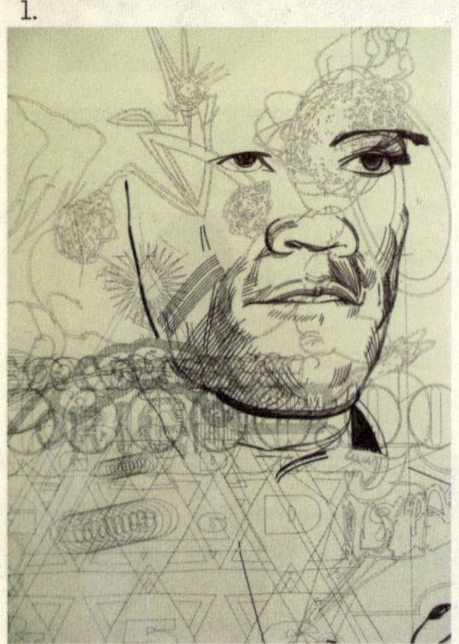

3.

4.

2. Untitled
2006, prosthetic leg, gold, and Swarovski rhinestones, 24 × 3 × 4 in (61 × 8 × 10 cm)

3. Untitled (detail)
2007, ballpoint pen on paper, 23 × 35 in (58 × 89 cm)

4. Untitled (detail)
2008, ballpoint pen and marker on paper, 23 × 35 in (58 × 89 cm)

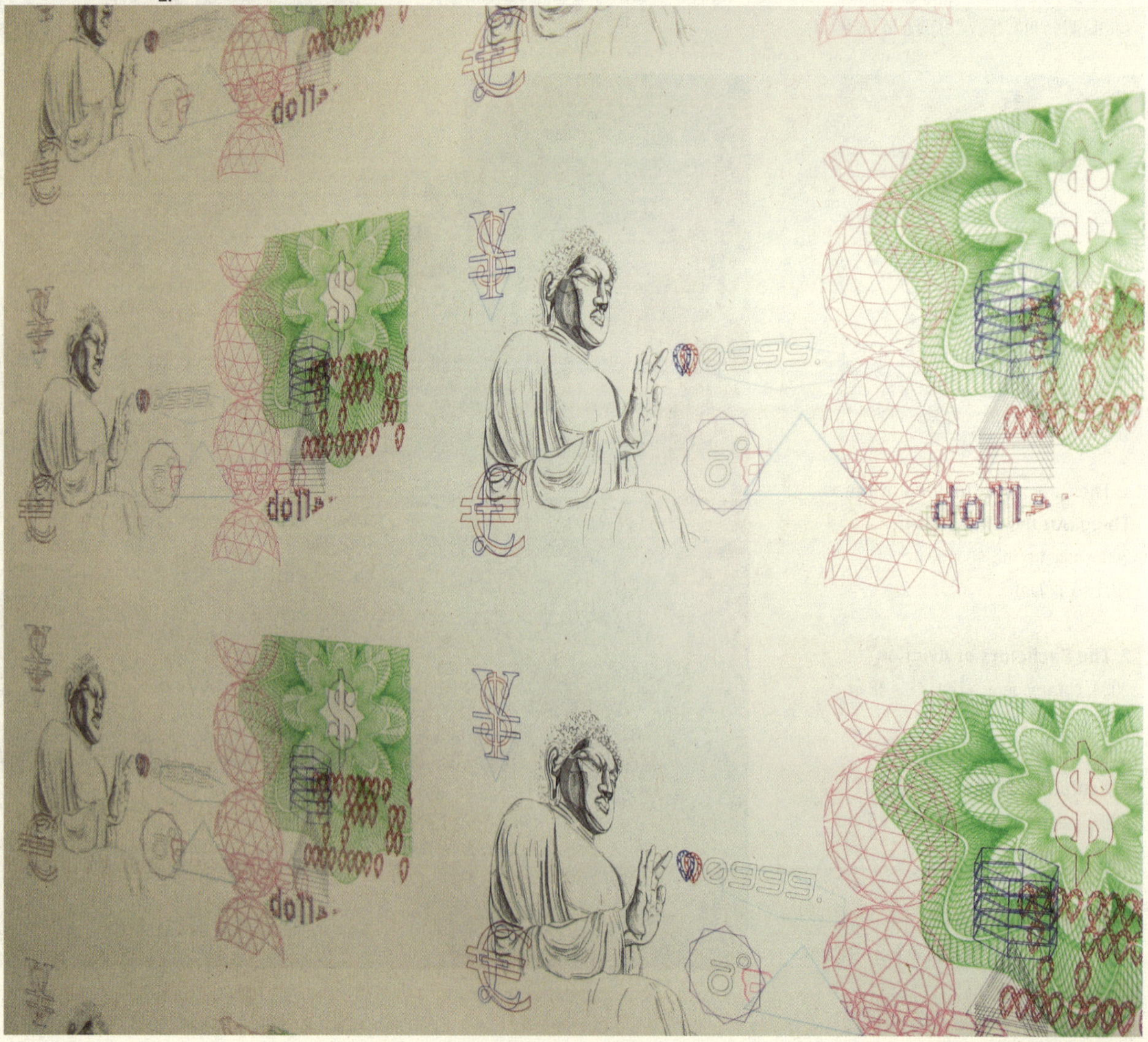

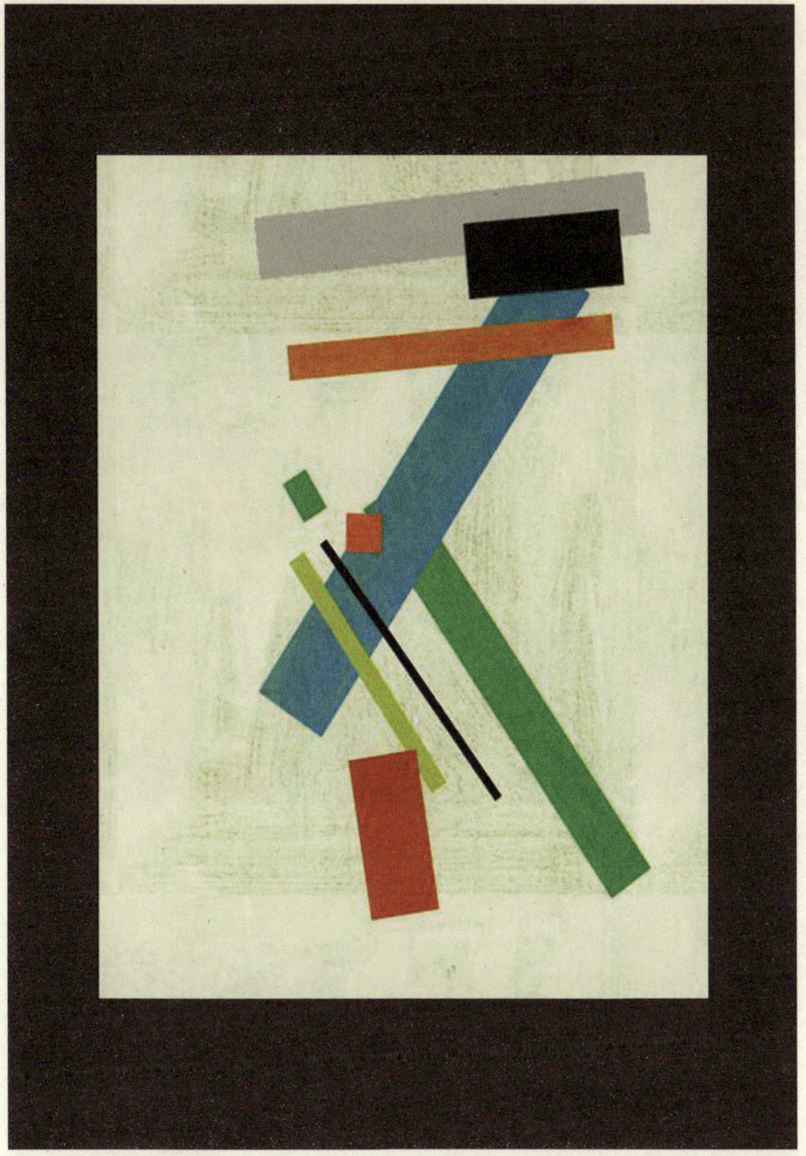

1.

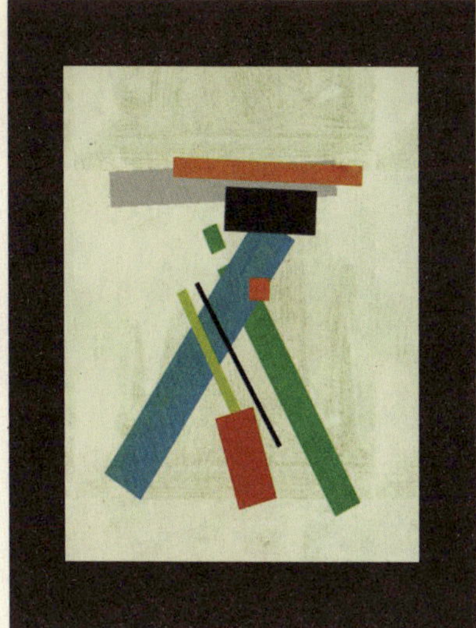

2.

Moscow-based Alex Buldakov makes witty comments on contemporary life, technology, and Russian art history using painting, video, and animation. One series animates the shapes of classic works by Kasimir Malevich and El Lissitzky so that it appears they are engaged in sexual activity, producing a kind of Suprematist porn.

1, 2 & 3. **xxx malevich**
2008, video, 5 min 22 sec

4 & 5. **mute**
2008, video, 6 min 16 sec

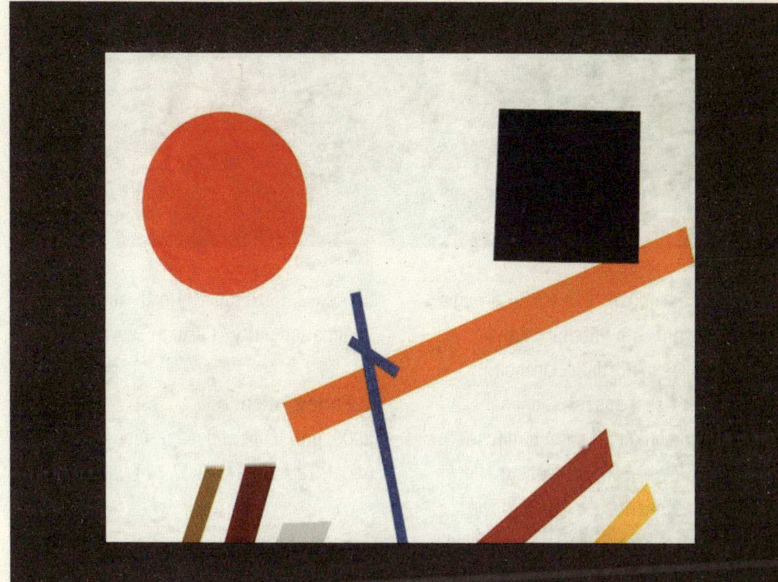

3.

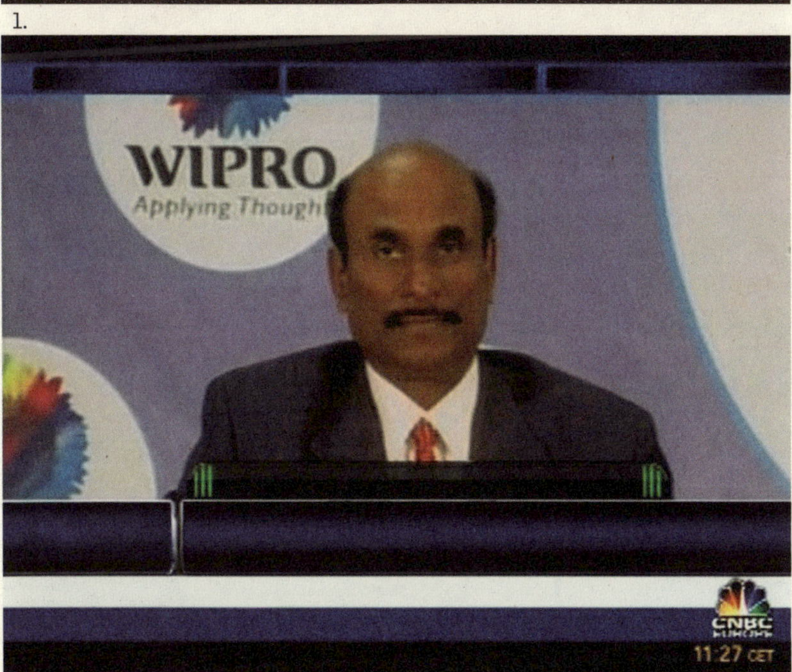

4.

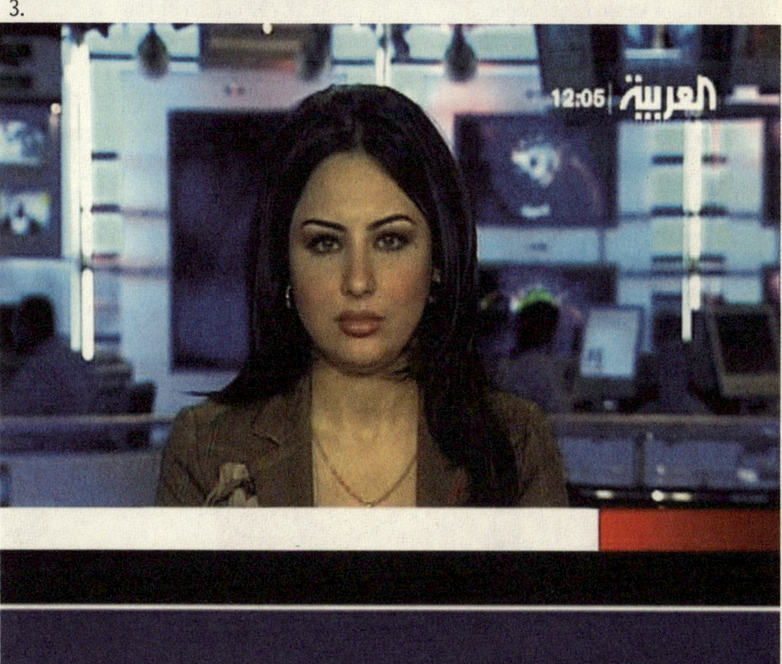

5.

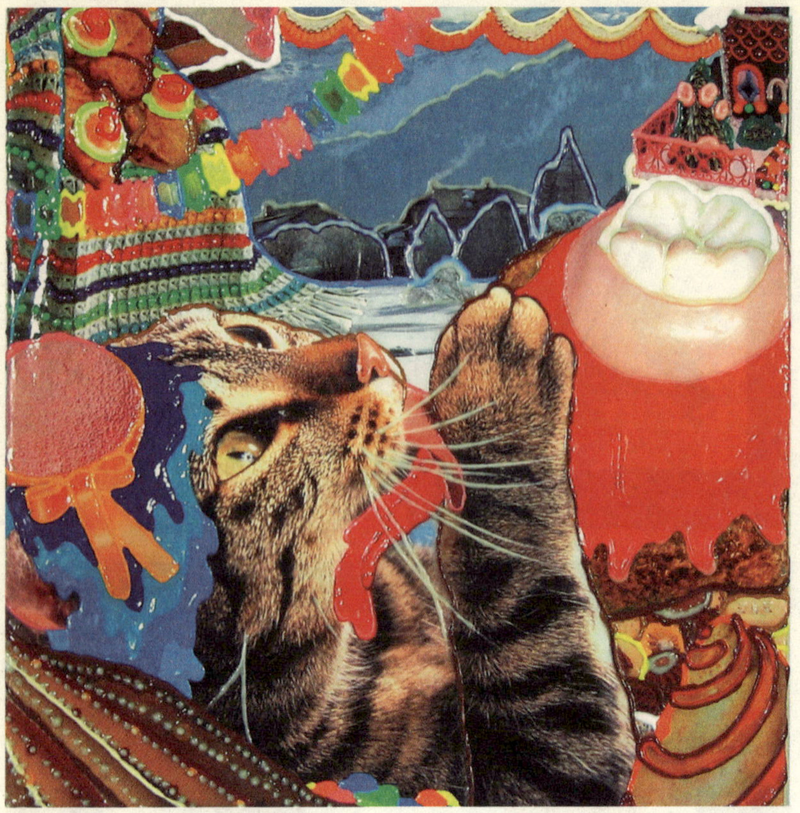

1.

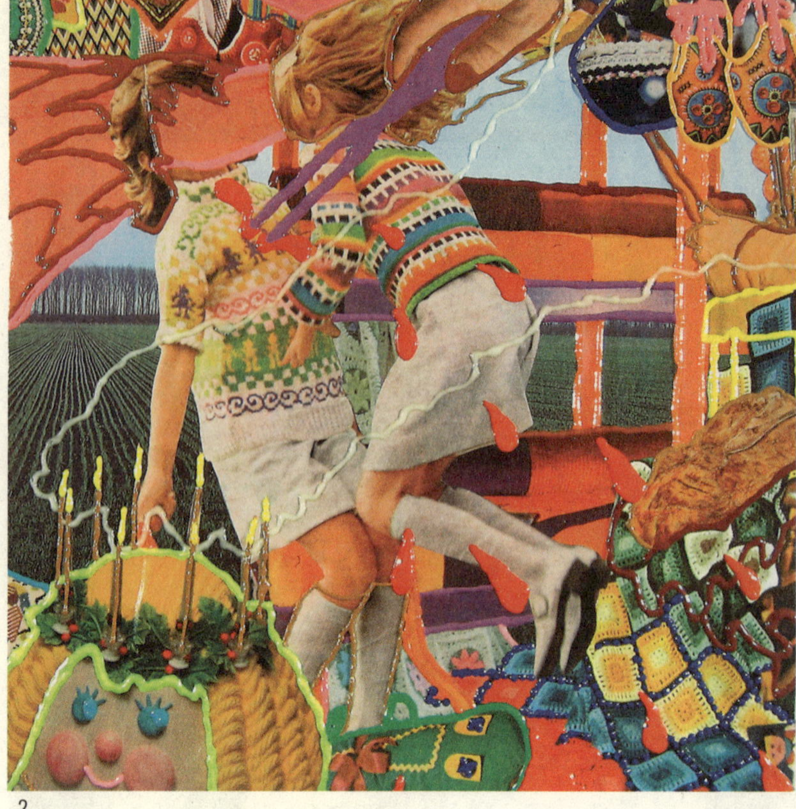

2.

Peter Burr earned his BFA from Carnegie Mellon University in Pittsburgh and currently lives in Portland, Oregon. His collages use magazines, animal trading cards, and puff paint to infuse wholesome Americana with absurd and sexual elements. He is half of the traveling performance duo Hooliganship, with Christopher Doulgeris, a group that combines kaleidoscopic video art, animation, live music, and dance. Since 2006 they have toured North America with "animation party" Cartune Exprez.

1. Fancy Feast
2006, puff paint and magazines on wood panel, 12 × 12 in (31 × 31 cm)

2. Front Massage
2005, puff paint and magazines on wood panel, 12 × 12 in (31 × 31 cm)

3. Sklly Attk
2006, puff paint, stickers, and magazines on calendar paper, 15 × 23 in (31 × 59 cm)

4 & 5. Realer
2007, performance

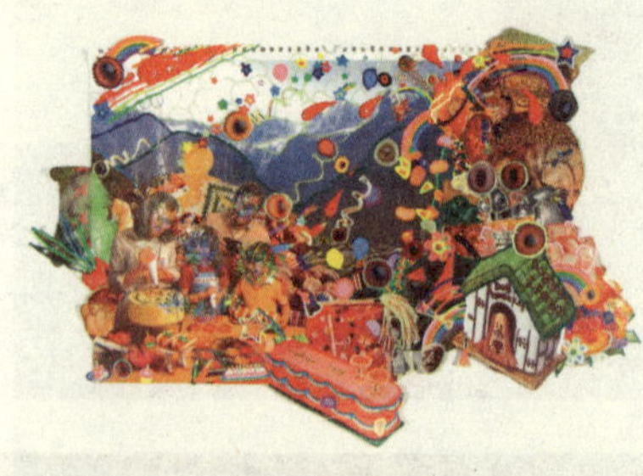

3.

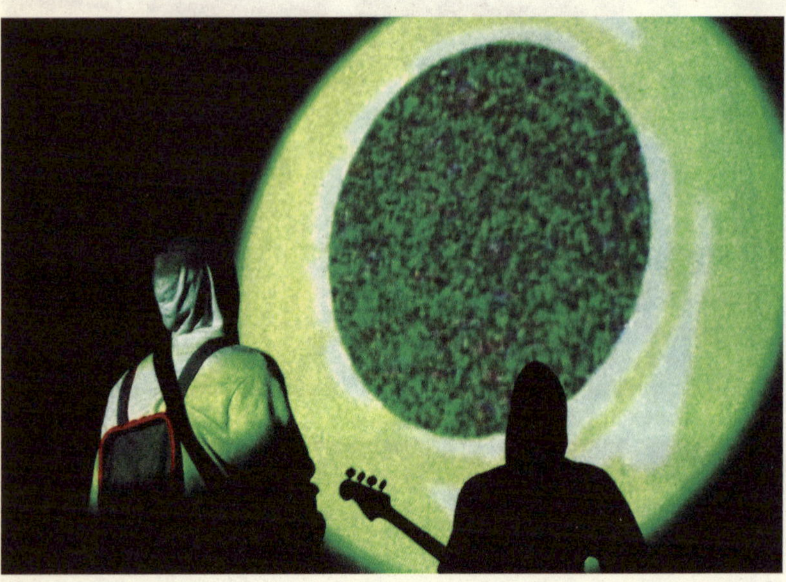

4.

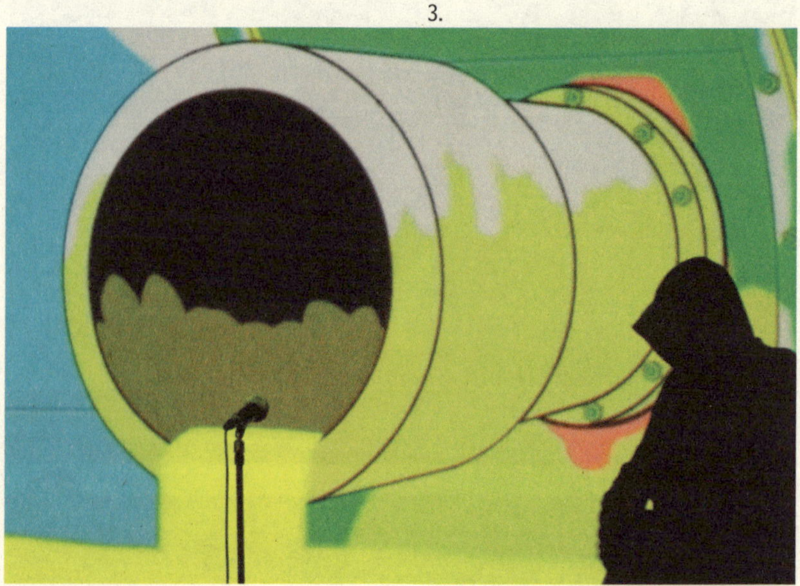

5.

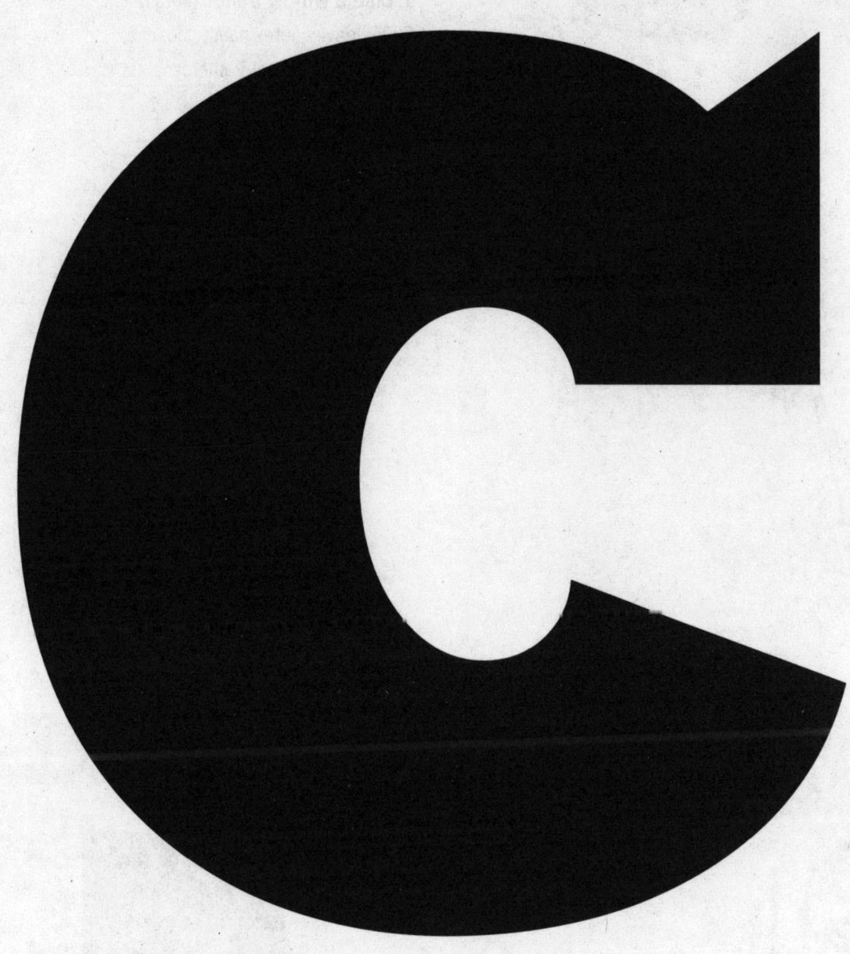

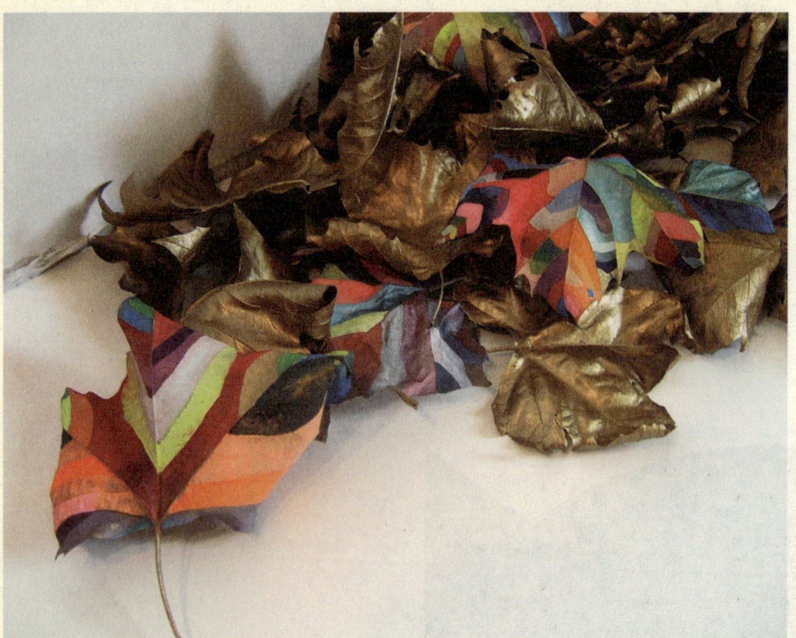

1.

Sarah Cain earned her MFA from the University of California at Berkeley and currently lives in Los Angeles. She uses latex, gouache, acrylic, ink, and spray paint to make bold-colored abstractions in two and three dimensions. A winner of the 2006 SECA Award at the San Francisco Museum of Modern Art, she builds layers of material to connect the practice of painting to sculpture and architecture.

1. **Like a willow bends** (detail)
2006, leaves, latex paint, gouache, watercolor, and color photocopies, dimensions variable

2. **We push ourselves into the mountain until we explode into the sky**
2007, latex paint, spray paint, gouache, acrylic, ink, tree branch, paper, and thread, dimensions variable

3. **Untitled (Zurich work on site)**
2008, tie-dyed silk scarf, beads, spray paint, latex, tape, and gouache on wall and floor, 134 × 95 × 67 in (340 × 241 × 170 cm)

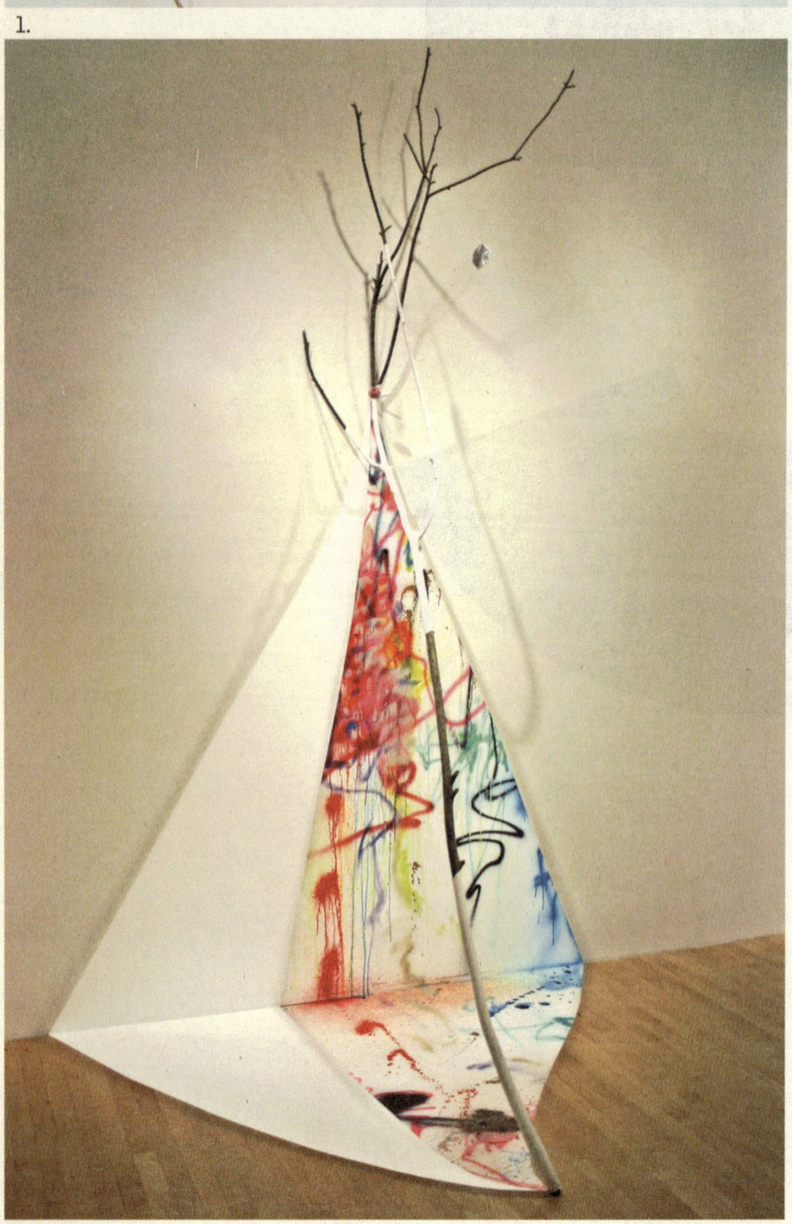

2.

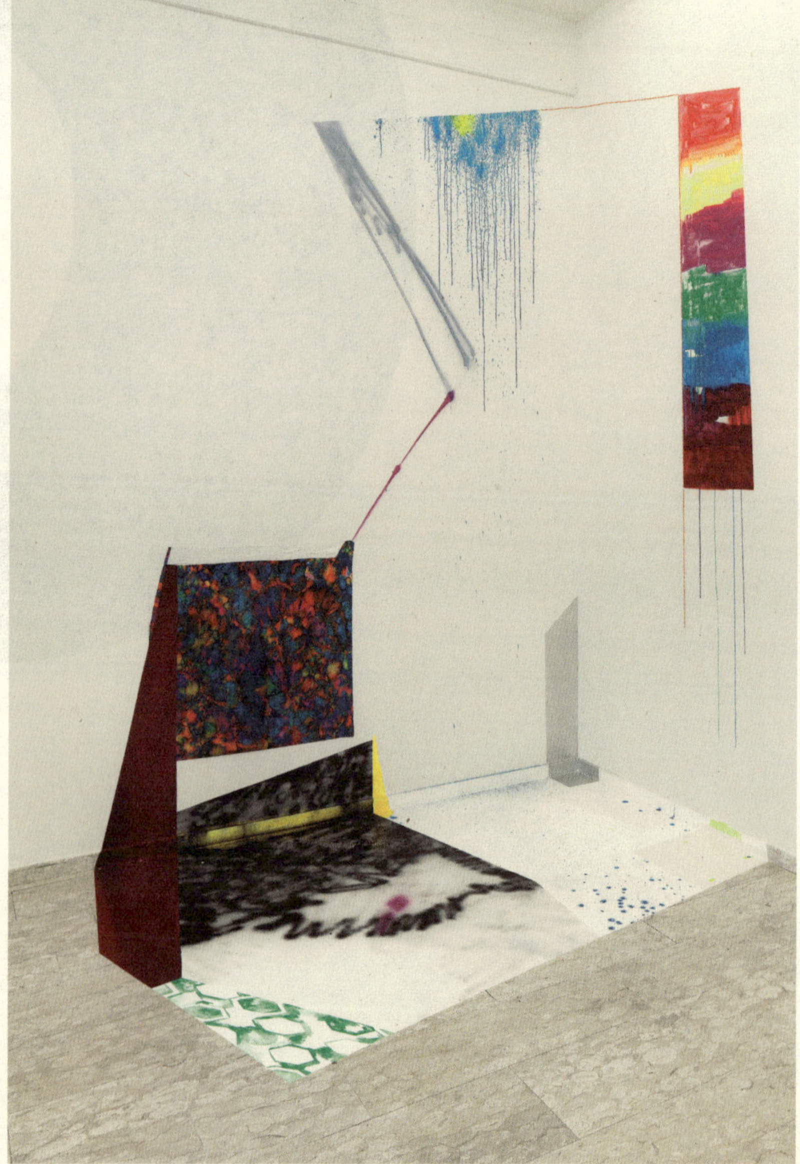

3.

Nina Canell attended Dun Laoghaire Institute of Art, Design, and Technology, Ireland, and currently lives in Dublin. She integrates buckets, funnels, neon lights, tree branches, electrical equipment, and other materials in sculpture and installation works that reevaluate the function and hierarchy of objects. With collaborator Robin Watkins, she has also produced film and video, musical recordings, and live performance events.

1. **Ventilate the Bright White Light**
2008, electric fan organ, window blinds, microphone, amplifier, cable, and timer, 35 ½ × 12 × 19 ½ in (90 × 30 × 50 cm)

2. **"Slight Heat of the Eyelid"**
exhibition view at mother's tankstation, Dublin (2008)

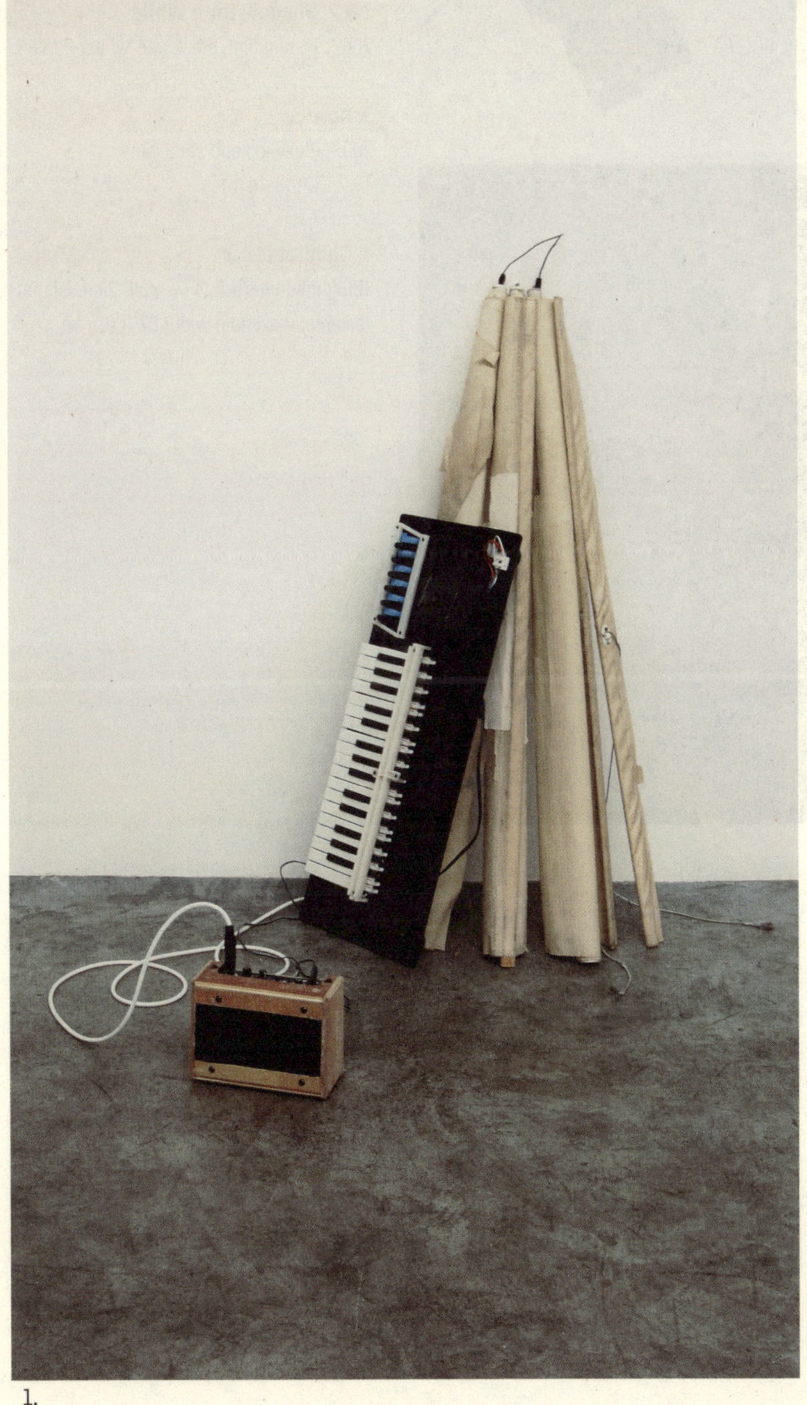

1.

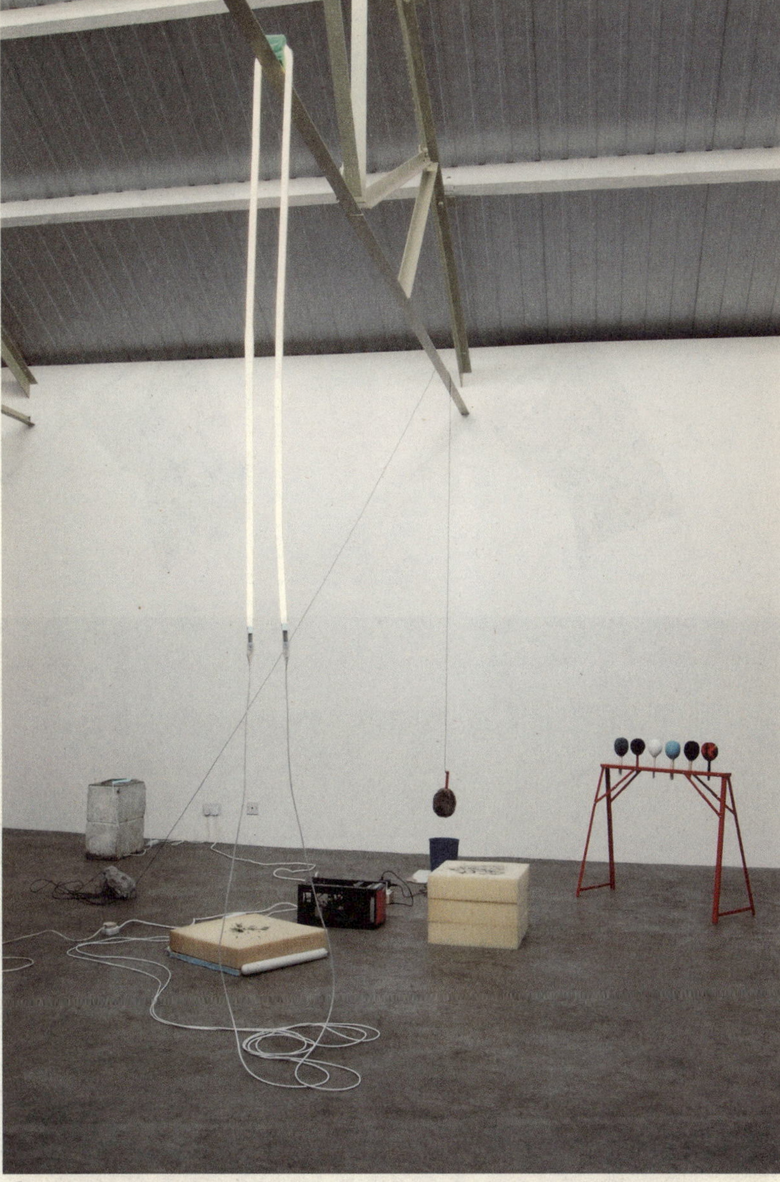

2.

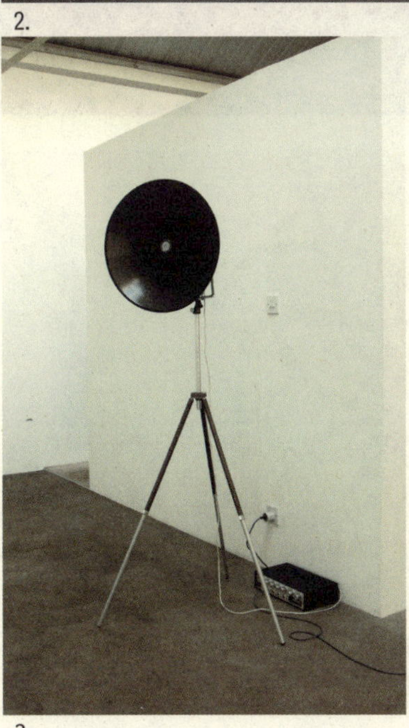

3.

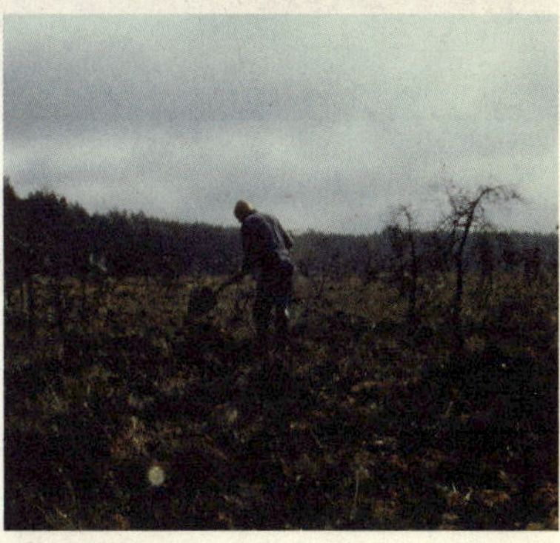

4.

3 & 4. **Digging a Hole**
with Robin Watkins
2008, electric megaphone, stand, electric cable, dimensions variable; 16 mm film, 2 min 18 sec

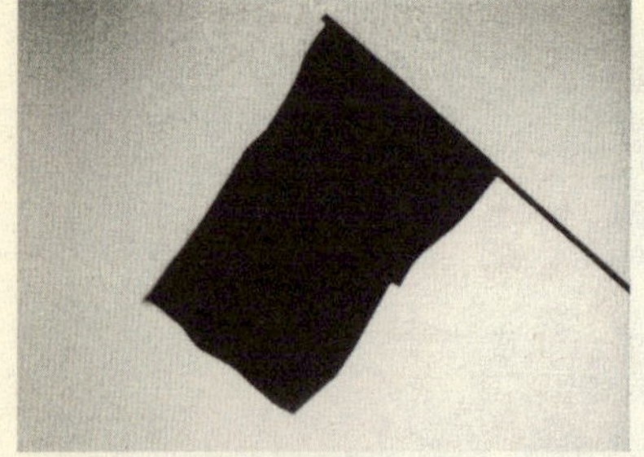
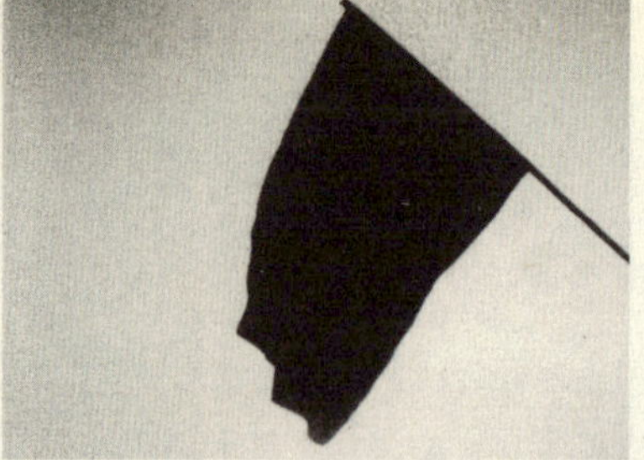
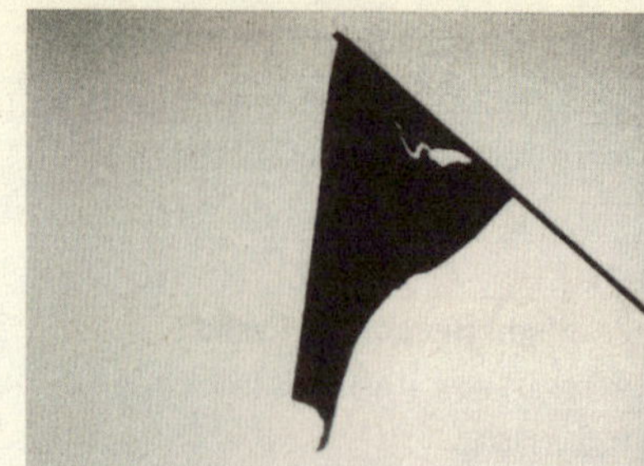
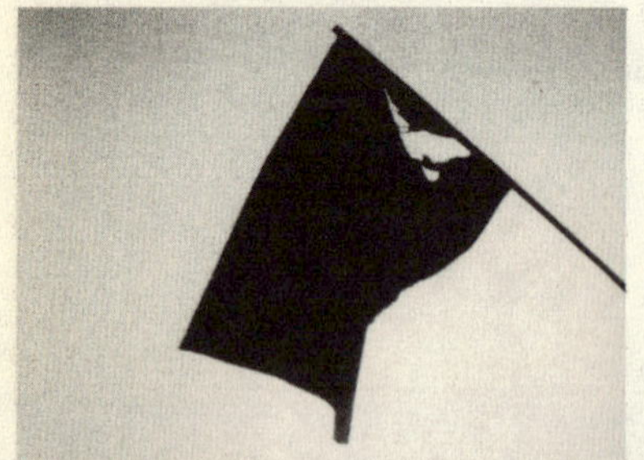
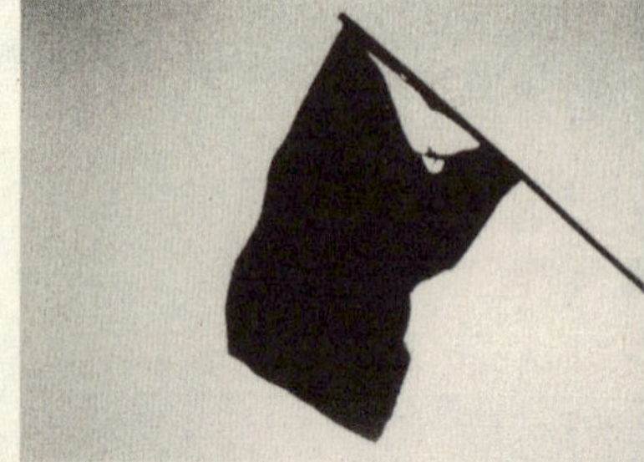
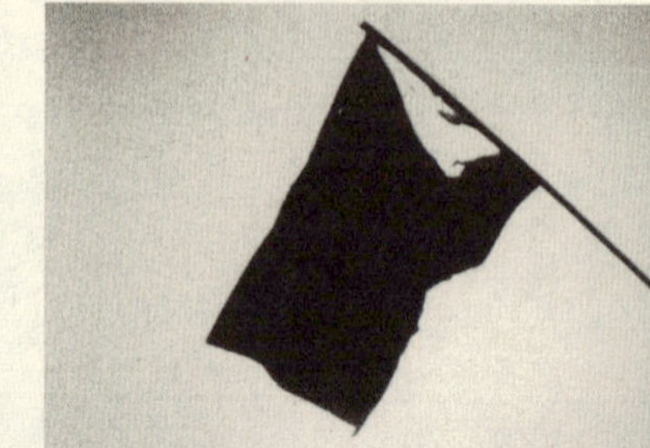

1.

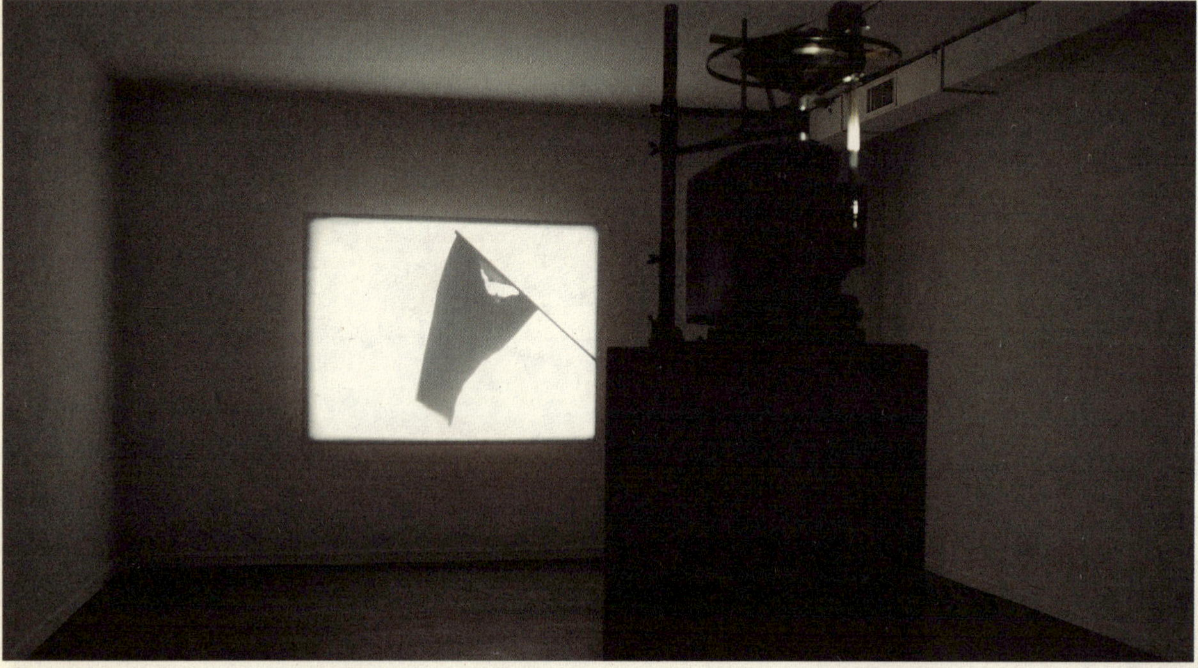

2.

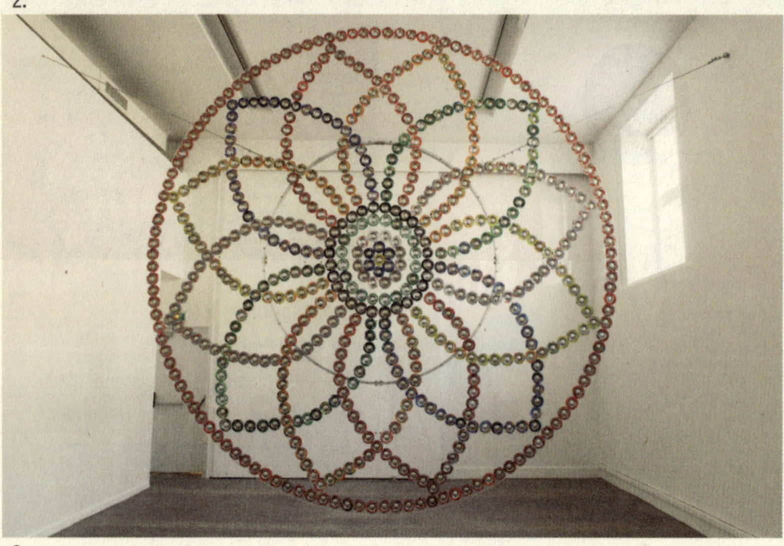

3.

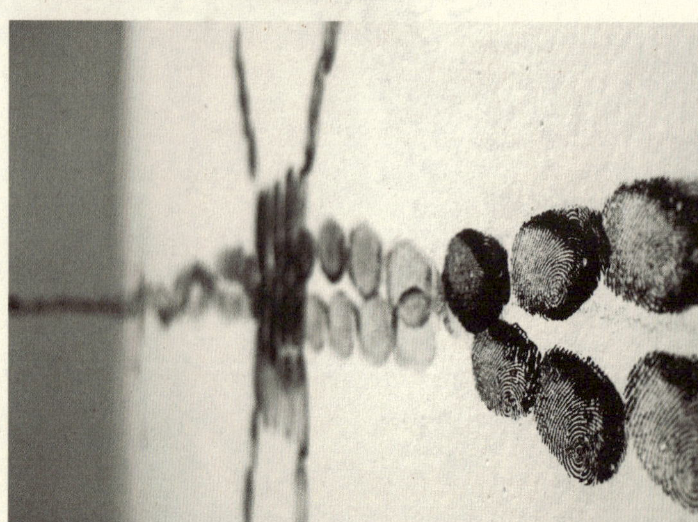

4.

Mircea Cantor grew up in Romania during the communist era and currently lives in Paris and Cluj-Napoca, Romania. He first gained attention for his 2005 video **Deeparture**, which documents the tense meeting between a deer and a wolf in a pristine gallery space. Using diverse media, his work continues to investigate issues of national identity, immigration, displacement, and difference. He is also cofounder and coeditor of the artist-run magazine **VERSION**.

1 & 2. **Shadow for a While**
2007, 16 mm film, black and white, 2 min

3. **Rosace**
2007, Plexiglas and soda cans, 13 × 13 ft (4 × 4 m)

4. **Chaplet** (detail)
2007, ink fingerprints on wall, dimensions variable, maximum width 82 ft (25 m)

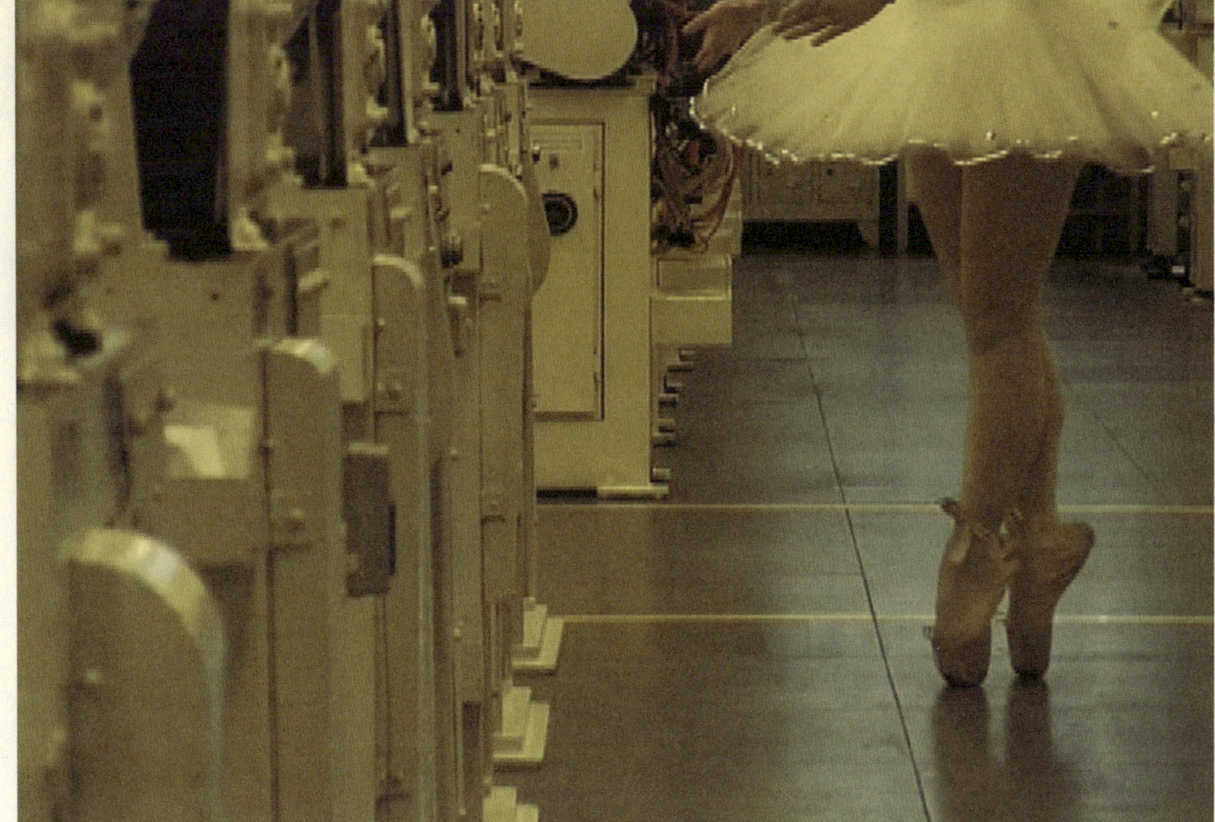

1.

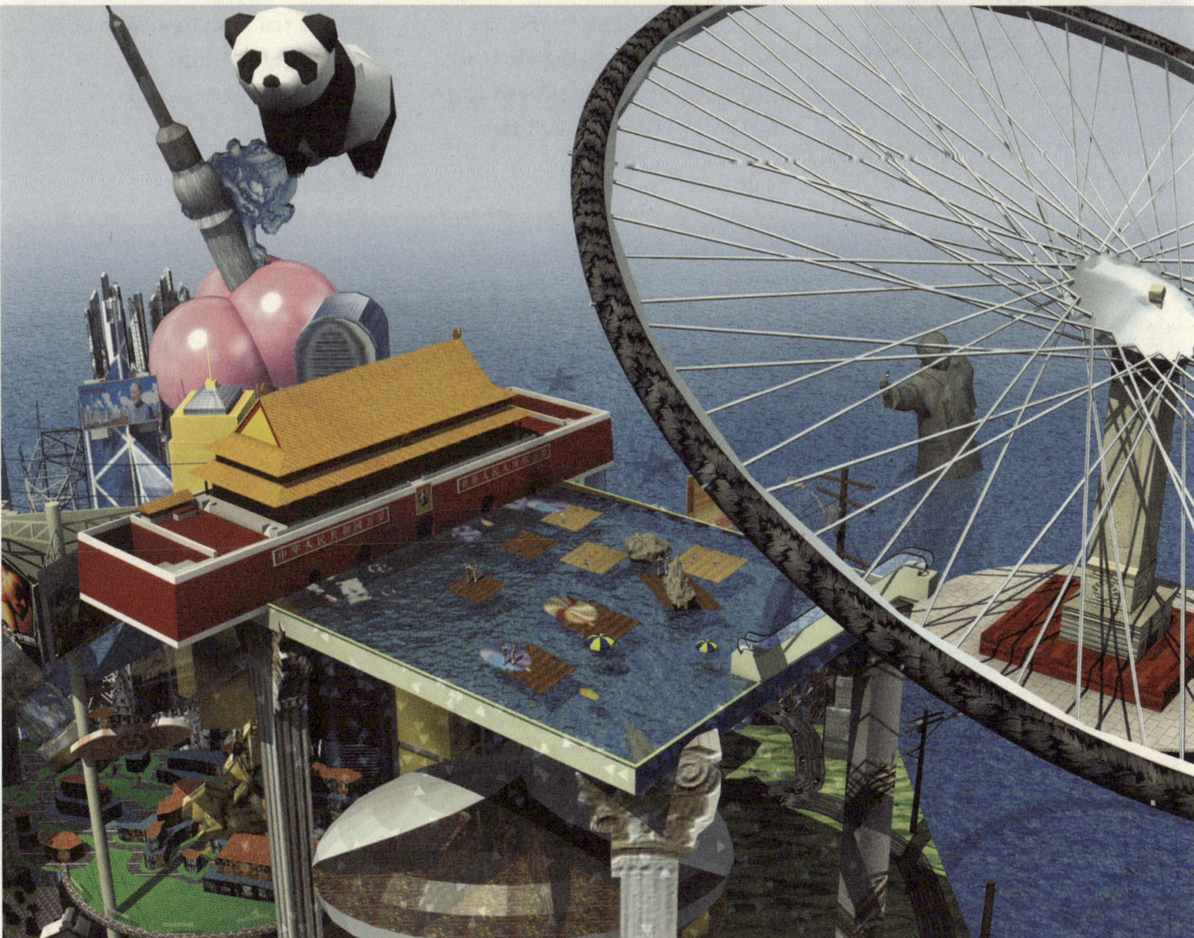

2.

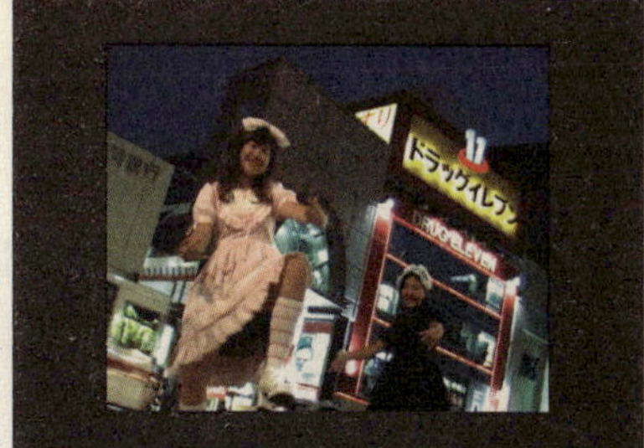

3.

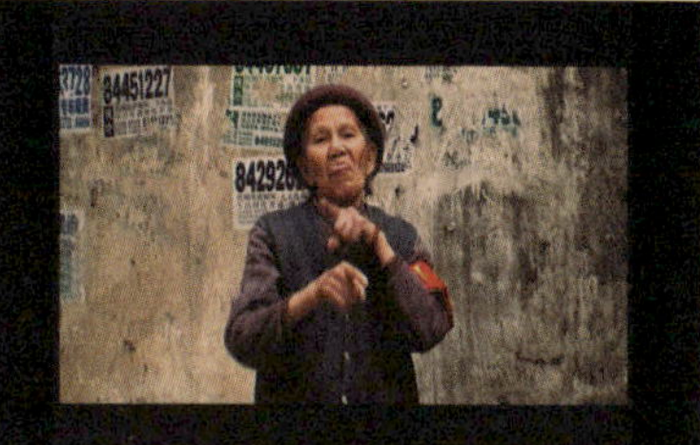

4.

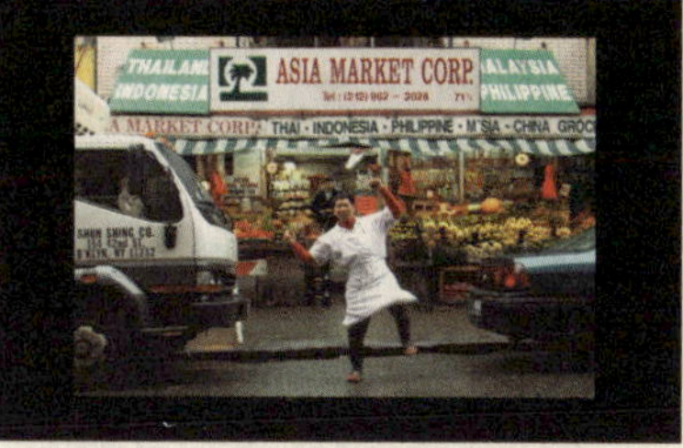

5.

Cao Fei earned her BFA from Guangzhou Academy of Fine Arts and currently lives in Beijing. She works in photography, video, and installation to merge fantasy worlds with realities of working life in China. Her "documentary" **i.Mirror**, created entirely in the online game Second Life, which allows participants to create complex virtual identities, was presented at the Venice Biennale in 2007.

1. **Whose Utopia**
2006, video, 20 min

2. **RMB CITY 8**
2007, digital chromogenic print, 47 1/4 × 63 in (120 × 160 cm)

3. **Hip Hop Fukuoka**
2005, video, 7 min

4. **Hip Hop Guangzhou**
2003, video, 3 min

5. **Hip Hop New York**
2006, video, 5 min 10 sec

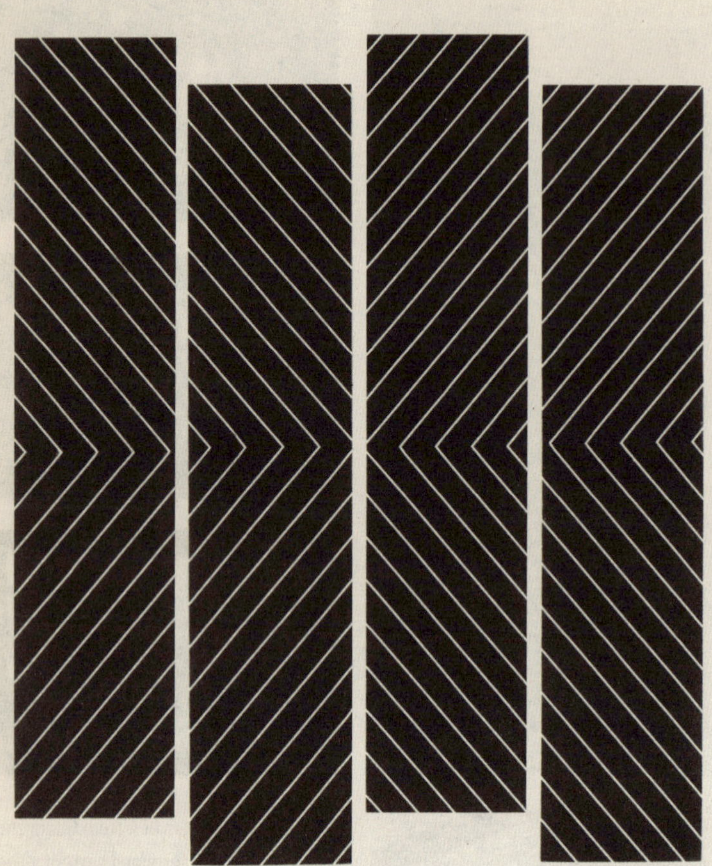

1.

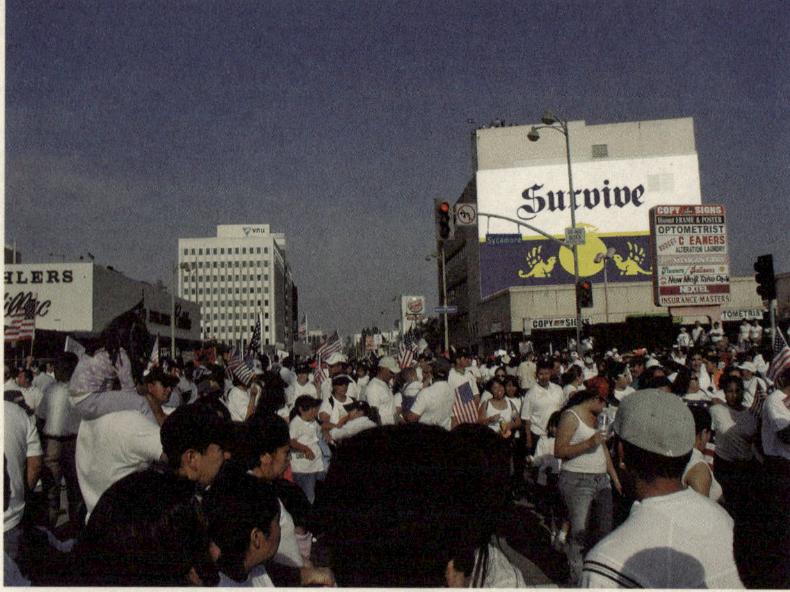

2.

Juan Capistran earned his MFA from the University of California, Irvine, and currently lives in Los Angeles. He formulates social and political critique through prints, photography, sculpture, installation, and video. **The Breaks** (2000), included in "Phantom Sightings: Art after the Chicano Movement" at the Los Angeles County Museum of Art (2008), shows Capistran break-dancing on LACMA's own Carl Andre lead floor.

1. **white minority**
2005, acrylic and flocking on canvas, 4 panels, each 90 × 19 in (229 × 48 cm)

2. **What Makes A Man Start Fires?**
2007, mural proposal

3. 1. **Do You Want New Wave or Do You Want The Truth?**
2007, print on paper, 10 × $13\frac{1}{2}$ ft (305 × 412 cm)

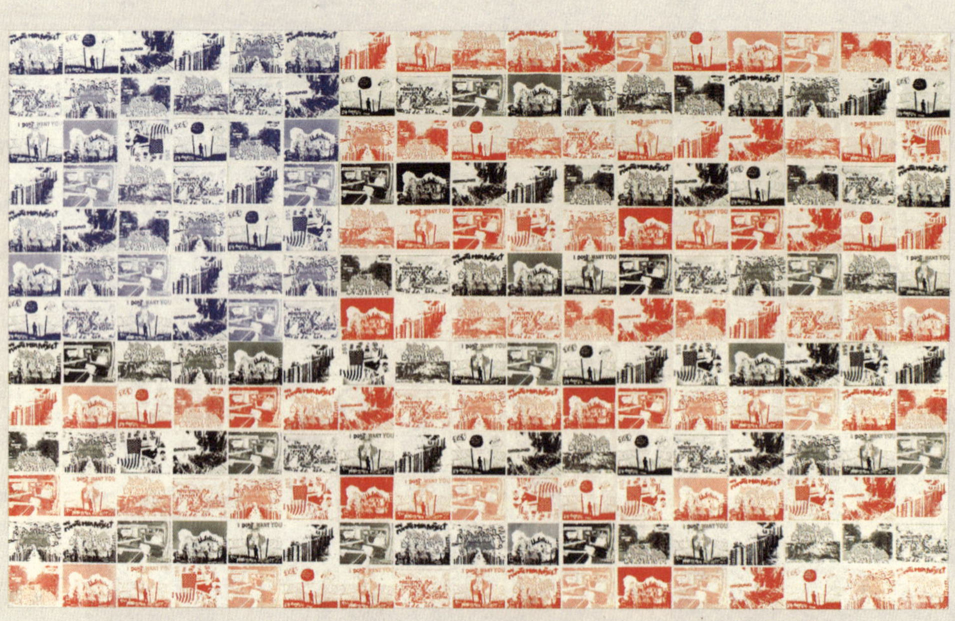

3.

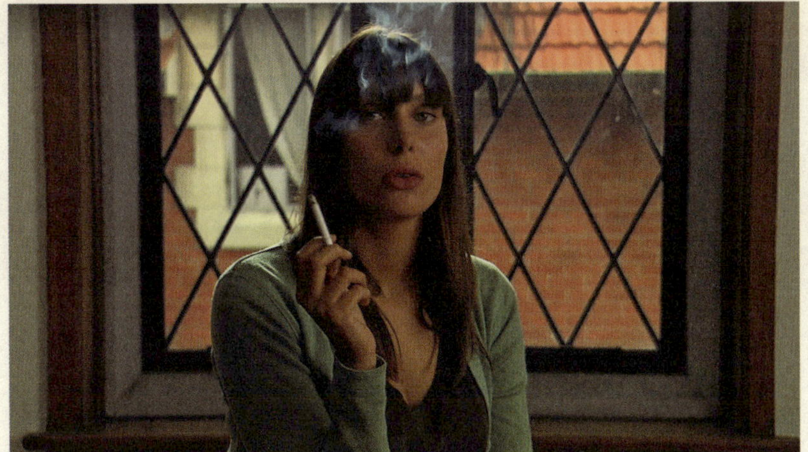
1.

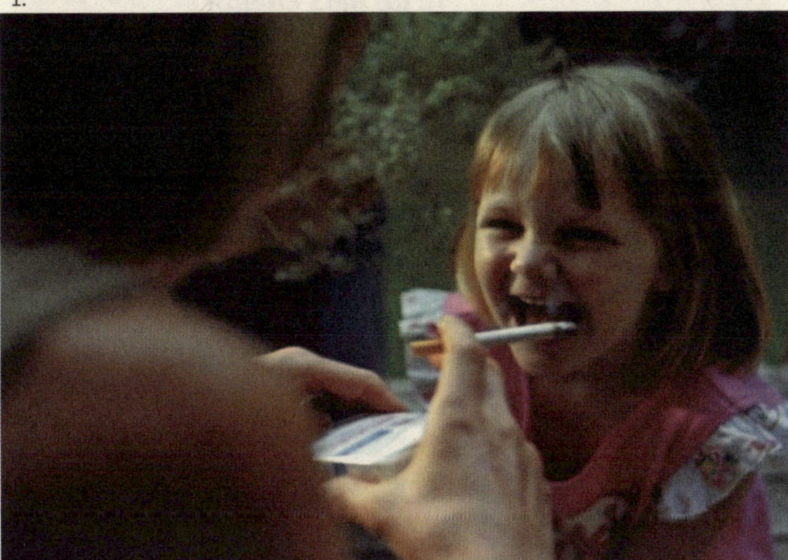
2.

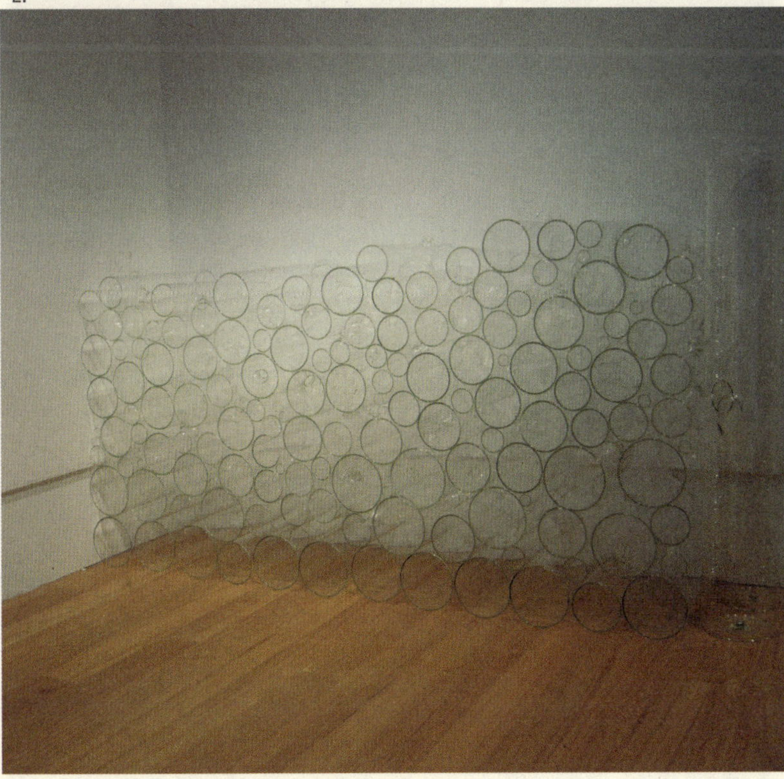
3.

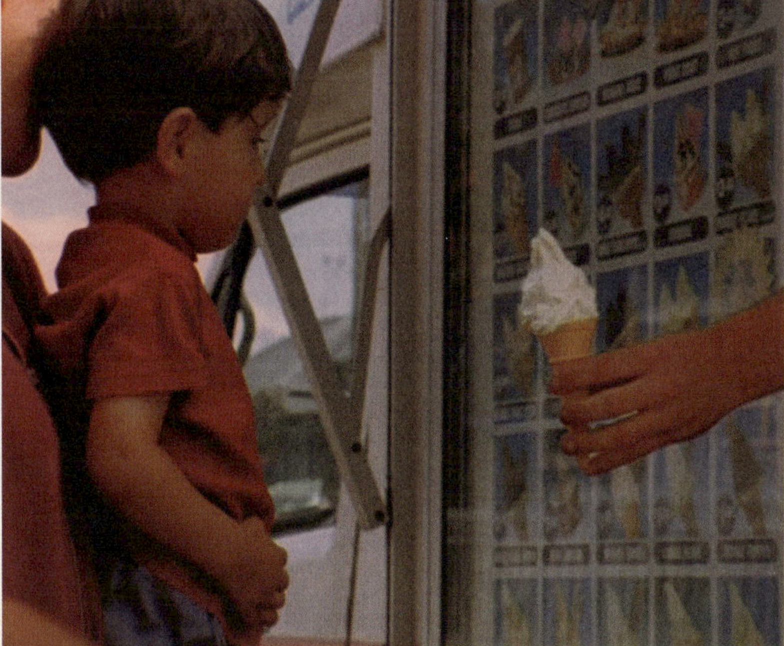
4.

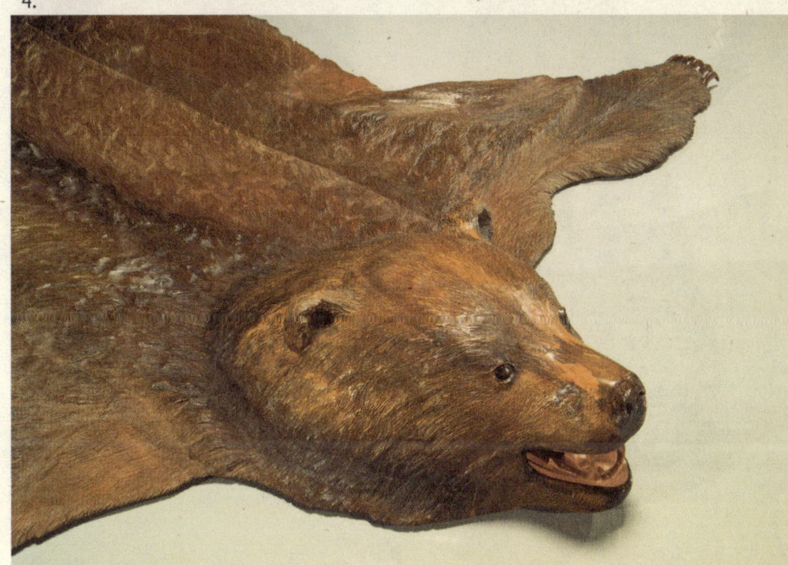
5.

Steve Carr earned his MFA from the Elam School of Fine Arts, University of Auckland, and continues to live in Auckland. He infuses elements of humor, sexuality, and childlike play into film, sculpture, and photography. He often performs in his own works, including **Cowboys and Indians** (2002), in which he is the only adult participating in the children's dress-up game. He is also cofounder of the nonprofit Blue Oyster Gallery in Dunedin.

1. **Annabel**
2007, video, 70 min

2. **Smoke Train**
2007, 35 mm film, loop

3. **Log Stack**
2006, glass, 35 $^{1}{}_{2}$ × 63 × 12 in (90 × 160 × 30 cm)

4. **Mr Whippy**
2002, 16 mm film, 1 min 58 sec

5. **Bear Rug**
2008, stained kauri wood and acrylic, 12 × 78 $^{3}{}_{4}$ × 78 $^{3}{}_{4}$ in (30 × 200 × 200 cm)

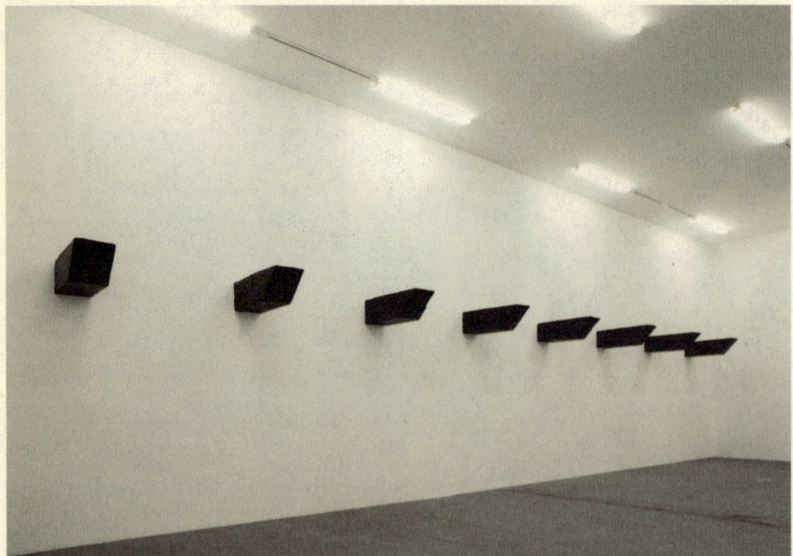
1.

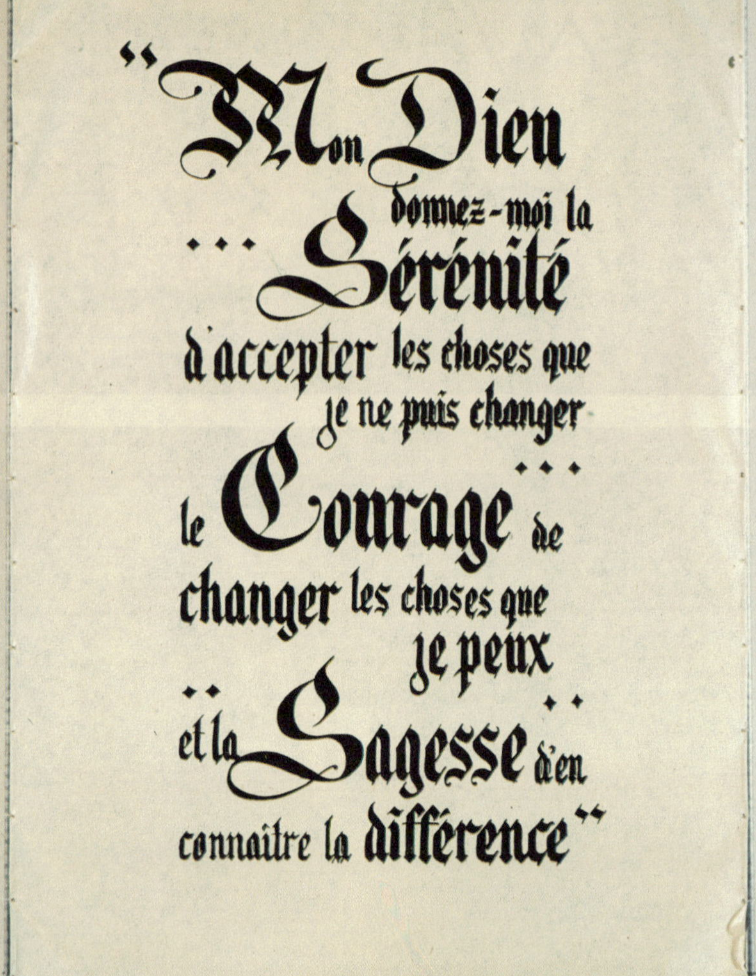

2.

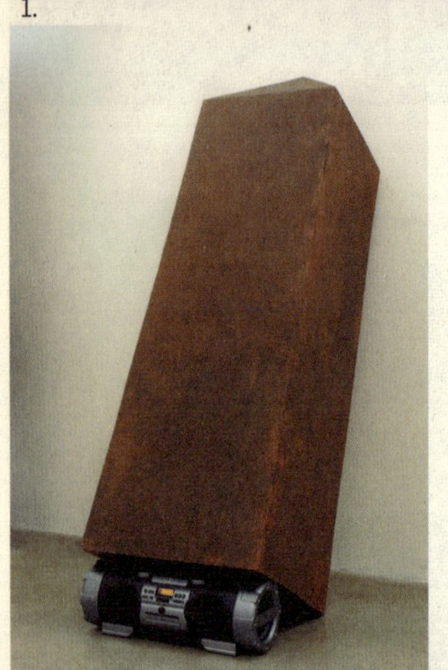
3.

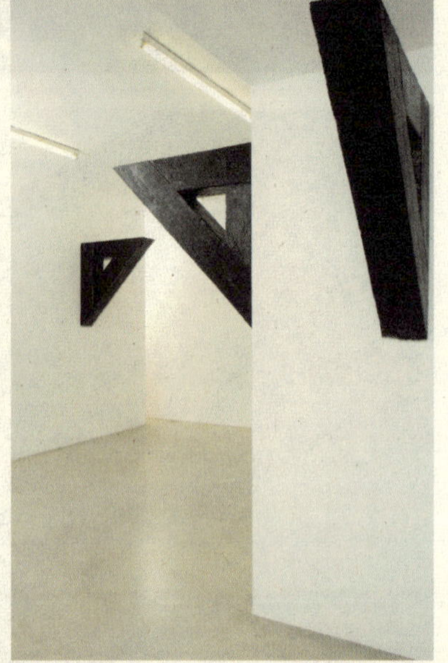
4.

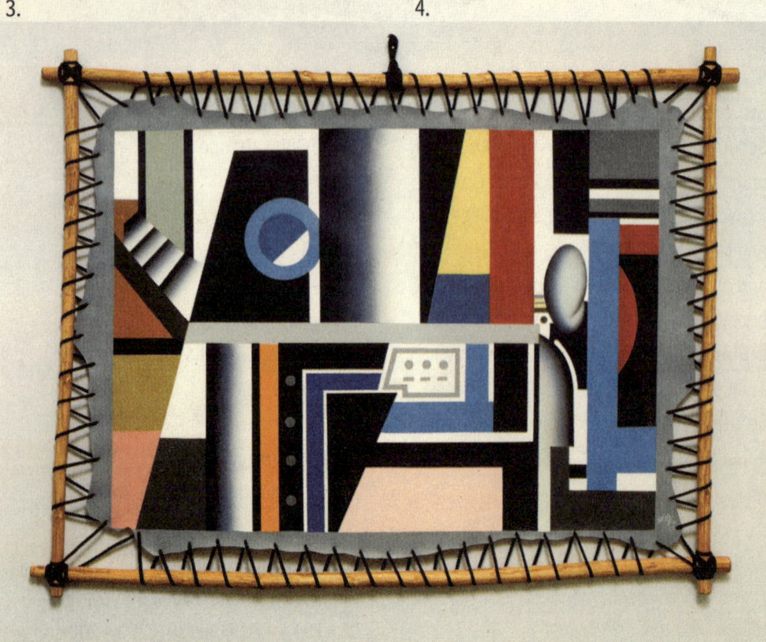
5.

Valentin Carron lives and works in Fully, Switzerland. He creates sculptures and installations that reflect on the iconography of Swiss culture (wine, chalets, the work of Alberto Giacometti), using his local perspective to address realities of globalization. He often reproduces objects and monuments that are historically and politically ambiguous, such as a cannon from the reign of Louis XVI.

1. (left to right) **Poison Infiltration; After the Sepulture; Macabre Operetta; Blood Ritual; With the Gleam of the Torches; Bestial Devotion; Defensive Personalities; Until the Chaos**
2005, polystyrene, fiberglass, synthetic resin, acrylic, 8 parts, each 12 × 12 × 39 in (30 × 30 × 100 cm)

2. **Untitled**
2006, Tiflex on tarpaulin and galvanized steel, 94 × 71 in (240 × 180 cm)

3. **Untitled**
2003, polystyrene, fiberglass, synthetic resin, acrylic, boom box, sound, $90\frac{1}{2} \times 27\frac{1}{2} \times 27\frac{1}{2}$ in (230 × 70 × 70 cm)

4. (left to right) **Caecilia; Wasted Again; Punish Yourself**
from the series **collection jaune souffre**
2007, Styrofoam, fiberglass, resin, acrylic paint, each 100 x 100 x 20 cm

5. **Untitled**
2005, painting on calfskin and wood, $41 \times 55\frac{1}{2}$ in (107 × 141 cm)

Marcos Castro attended Escuela Nacional de Pintura, Escultura y Grabado, La Esmeralda, and currently lives in Mexico City. He brings cartoonlike imagery to fables and fairy tales using drawing, painting, photography, and animation. The delicate and the grotesque coexist as he places animals and human beings in natural and supernatural worlds.

1. Despues de Caravaggio (El Descendimiento)
2005, chromogenic print, 7 1/4 × 10 in (19 × 25 cm)

2. Despues de Caravaggio (San Gerónimo En Su Estudio)
2005, chromogenic print, 10 × 7 1/4 in (25 × 19 cm)

3. Marcos y el Lobo
2008, oil on canvas, 5 3/4 × 9 3/4 ft (180 × 300 cm)

4. Miedo a la Obscuridad
2008, oil on canvas, 9 3/4 × 6 1/2 ft (300 × 200 cm)

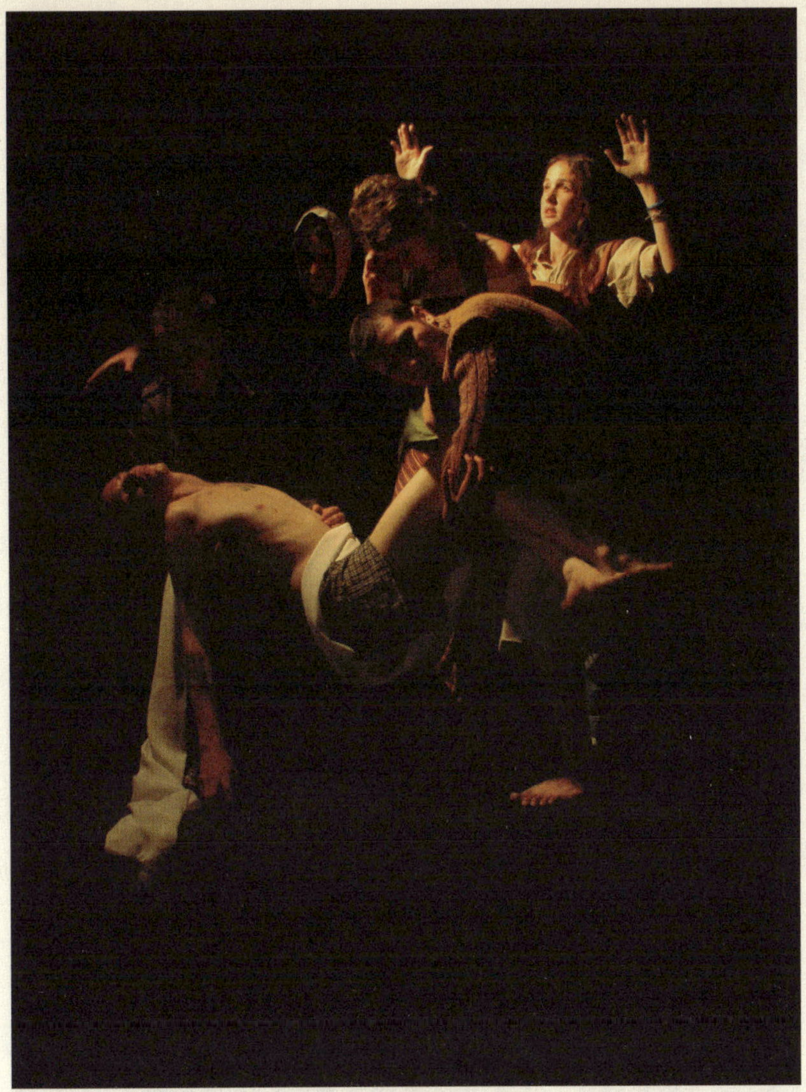
1.

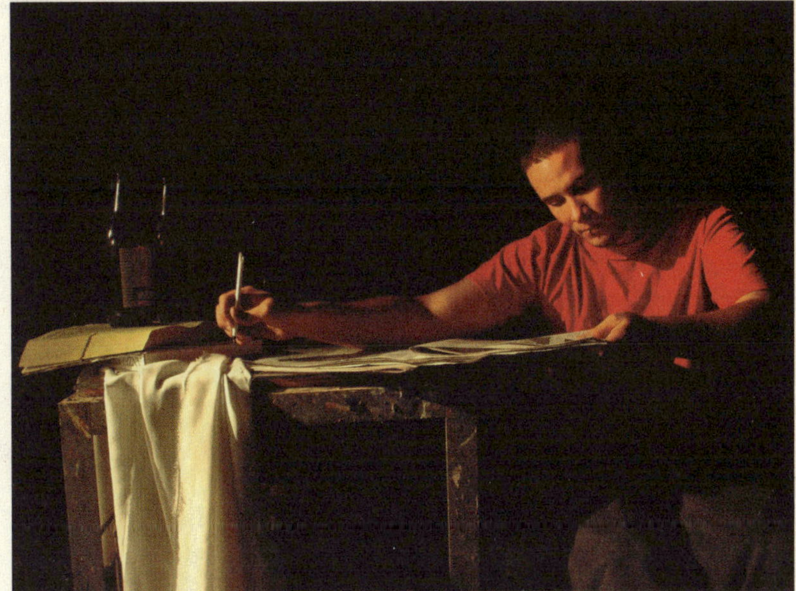
2.

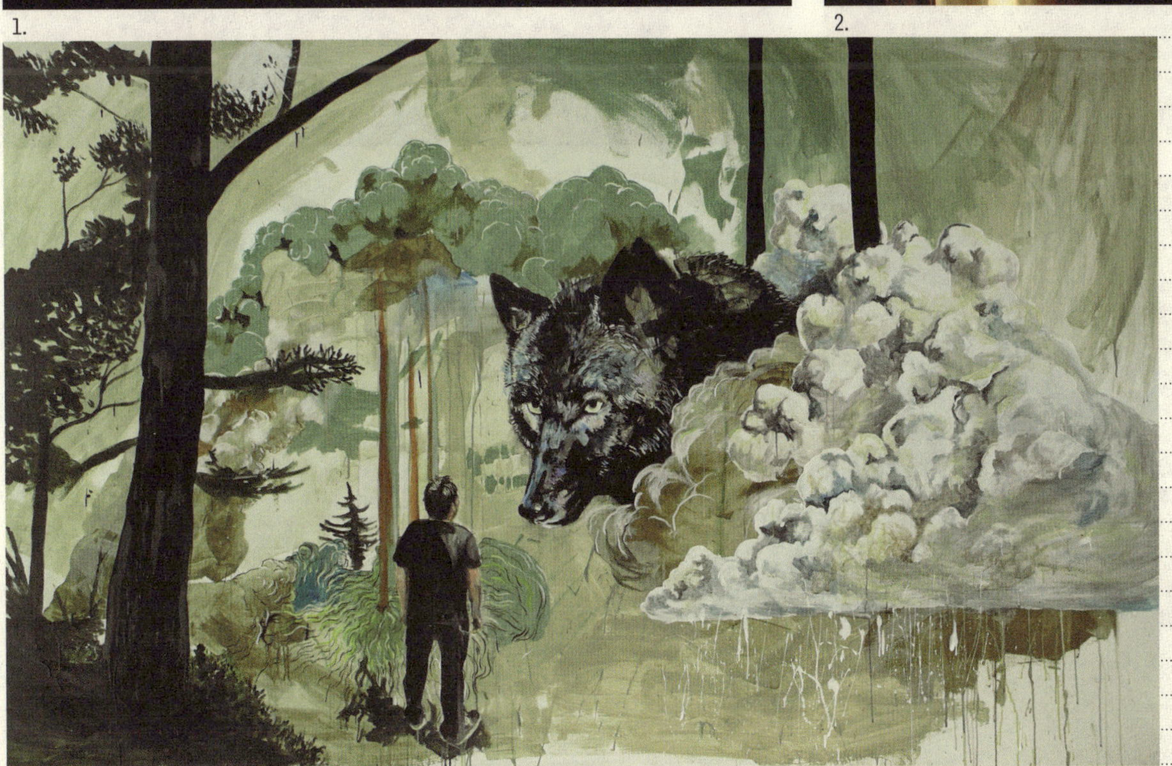
3.

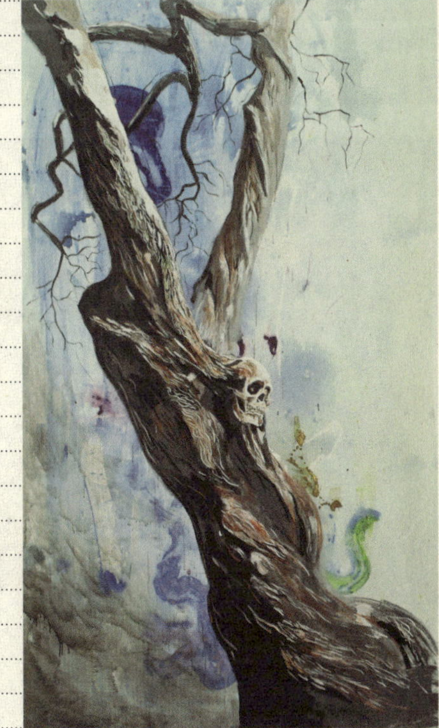
4.

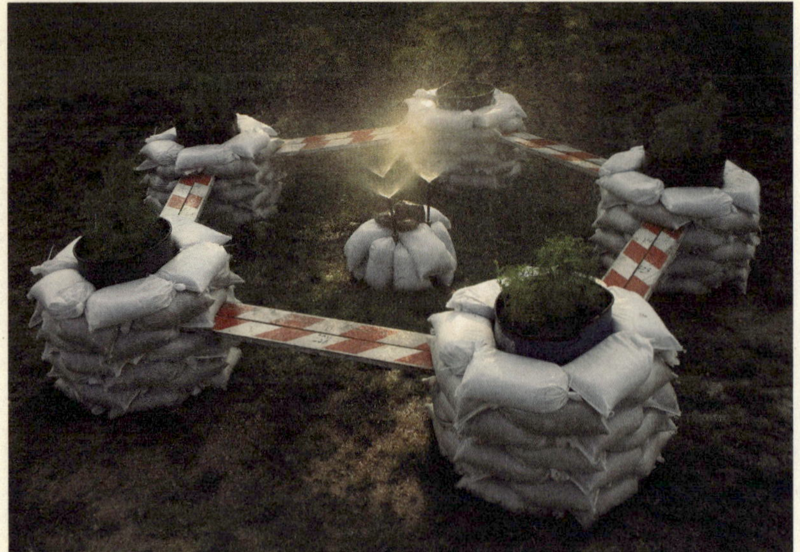

1.

Michael Cataldi earned his BFA from the Maryland Institute College of Art and currently lives in Brooklyn. He explores dynamics of public and private space with site-specific architectural interventions. Works include growing gardens in unfilled Baltimore potholes, tire swings created from every discarded tire found in an urban area, and a public "plaza" made of sandbags, oil drums, chain-link fencing, and weeds at the Socrates Sculpture Park, New York in 2006.

1. **Urban Plaza Equivalent** (detail)
2006, mixed media, dimensions variable

2. **Prop**
2007, steel, wood, fabric, dirt, and turf, 4 × 15 × 15 ft (121 × 457 × 457 cm)

3. **Pavilion**
2004, mixed media, dimensions variable

4. **Tire Swings** (detail)
2004, rope, found rubber tires, dimensions variable

5. **Flower-Pot-Hole**
2004, potting soil, plants, dimensions variable

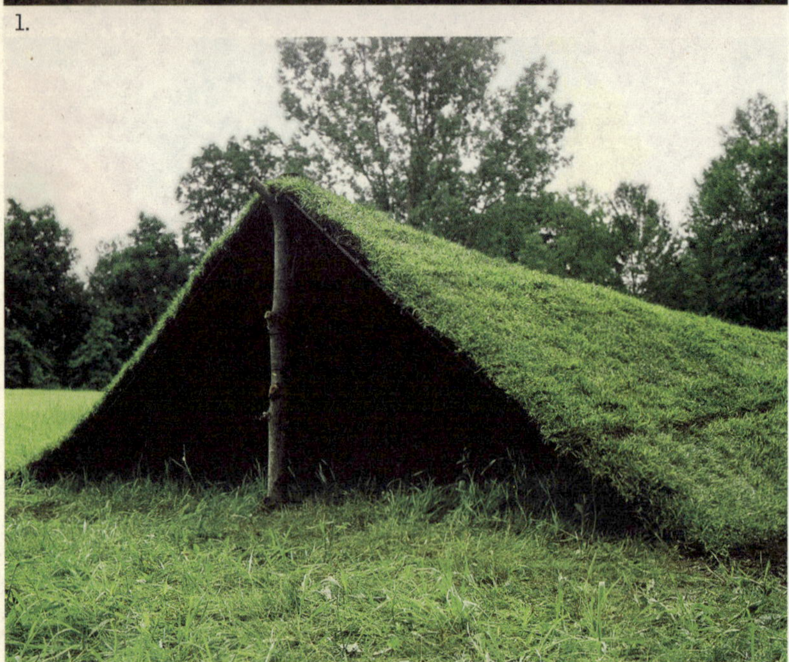

2.

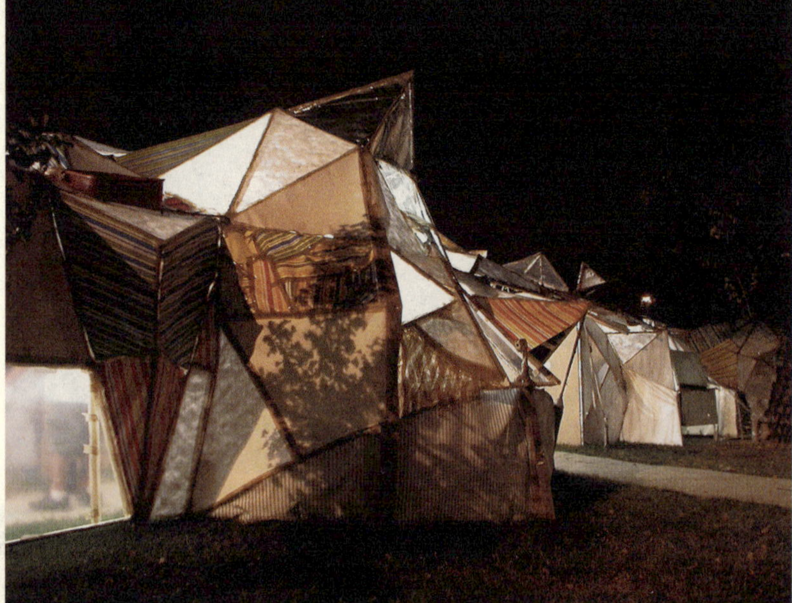

3.

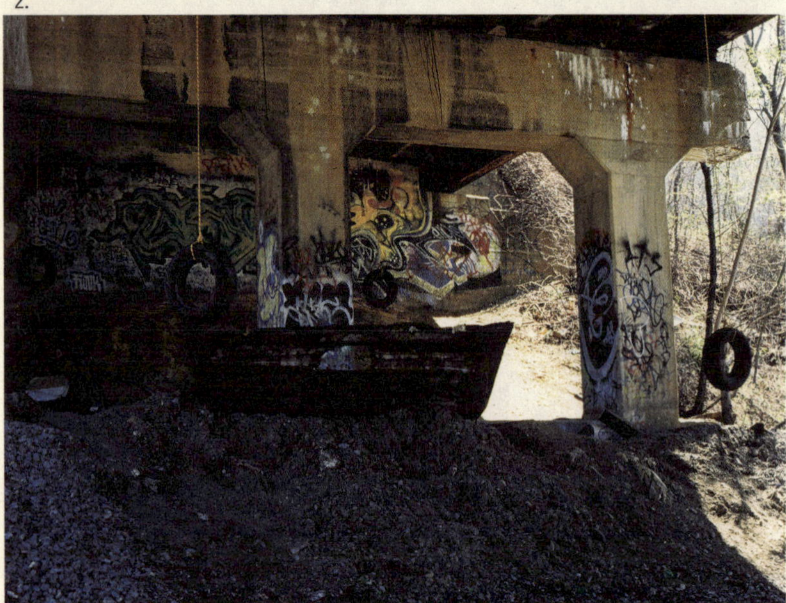

4.

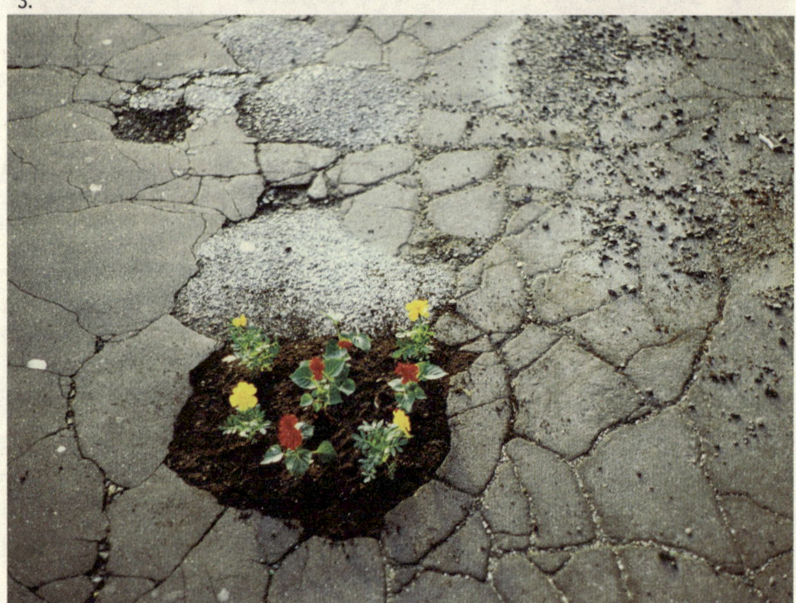

5.

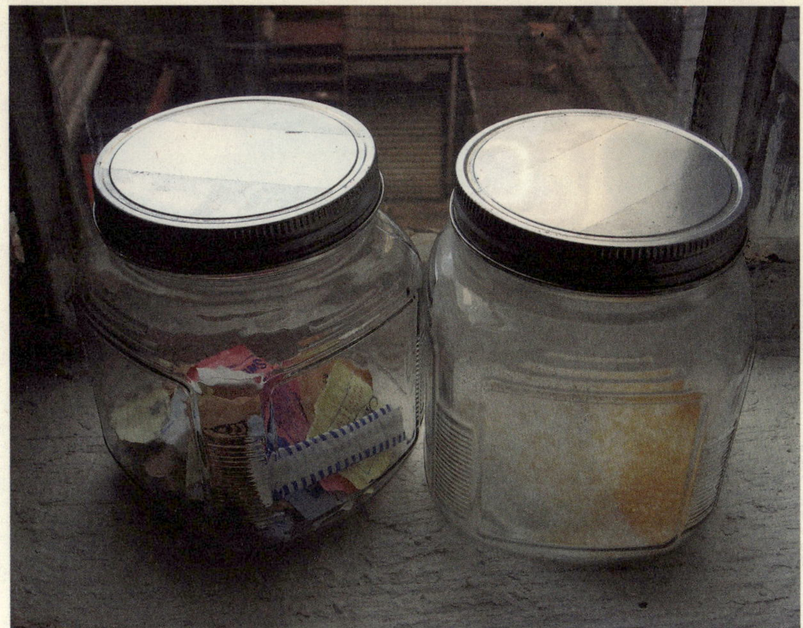

1.

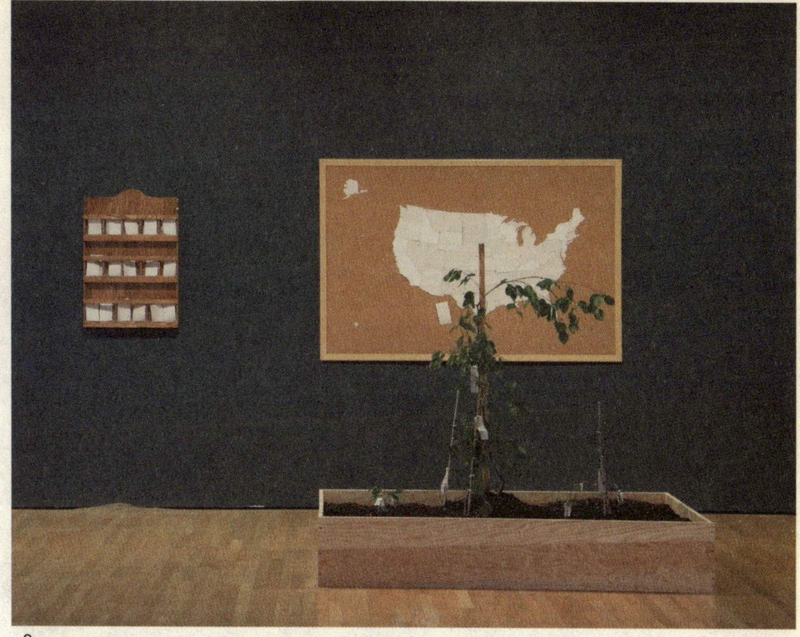

2.

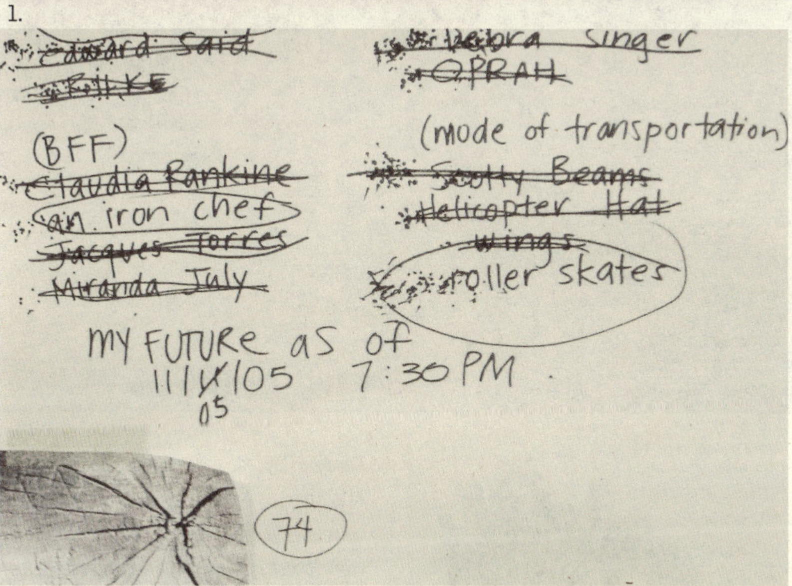

3.

We are infront of some kindof door wer waiting 4 wires so wecan hav light inside
From. Dad Ph
1:00am 6/15/06

Hi I'm on my way2 Langihan petron. Helping out this week anay here – we start monday on d project kay some of our people worked on other jobs2 get by. Ho
w r things? I'm so in a hurry2 get this done. Luv n miss u all much
From: Dad Ph
7:31am 9/14/06

Its 5am getting up early 2day cos we head back2 gingoog 2day. its d 1st day wer goin bak2 work with dcomplete crew n we got a new pump too. Wer all in a hurry hope we finish in3 wks. How r things? Luv u n miss u all. Dad
From: Dad Ph
5:06pm 9/17/06

Its a collection of poems and short stories to u. Just edit it. I'll write a couple more just 2 keep bz.
From: Dad Ph
12:24am 10/10/06

Hi ur txt just 2me. On my way bak2 gingoog now. I'll probably just mail whatever it is i can finish hy friday daw ka diutay pa man. Just go over it. Gadu la-dula signal "sending failed" msgs. 3x na cos were by d mountain i'll try when we get2d coast
From: Dad Ph
8:05pm 10/22/06

My tkt is confrmed dec 7 but i hope 2get it done way b4 then. Meanwhile im still writing just 2have somthin 2do
From: Dad Ph
2:18am 10/23/06

Just got 2 cebu n going2d airport now 2take dplane 2 ilo2x at 1pm. Accdg 2 t2eds last txt ur lolo is already partly conscious n d operation went well
From: Dad Ph
5:06pm 11/8/06

Getting off d ship now. Its like a circus out there
From: Dad Ph
5:18pm 11/8/06

4.

Emmy Catedral was raised in Queens, New York, and currently lives in Manhattan. She creates multipart conceptual works that include actions, objects, and documentation. In **Germinalia** (2008), she reproduces the first weeping beech tree planted in Queens in homage to the Flushing Remonstrance, an early document of religious freedom in America written and signed by Queens residents.

1. Sugar
2006-present, 2 glass jars, various sugar packets, dimensions variable

2. Germinalia
2008, raised garden bed, weeping beech saplings, paper made from discarded religious pamphlets, dimensions variable

3. uncertainties: a M.A.S.H. project with the help of city trees (detail)
2005-present, 2-channel video of performance and permanent marker on paper, dimensions variable

4. Unfinished Portrait of My Father In Search of Buried Treasure
2006, digital collage of text-message screen shots

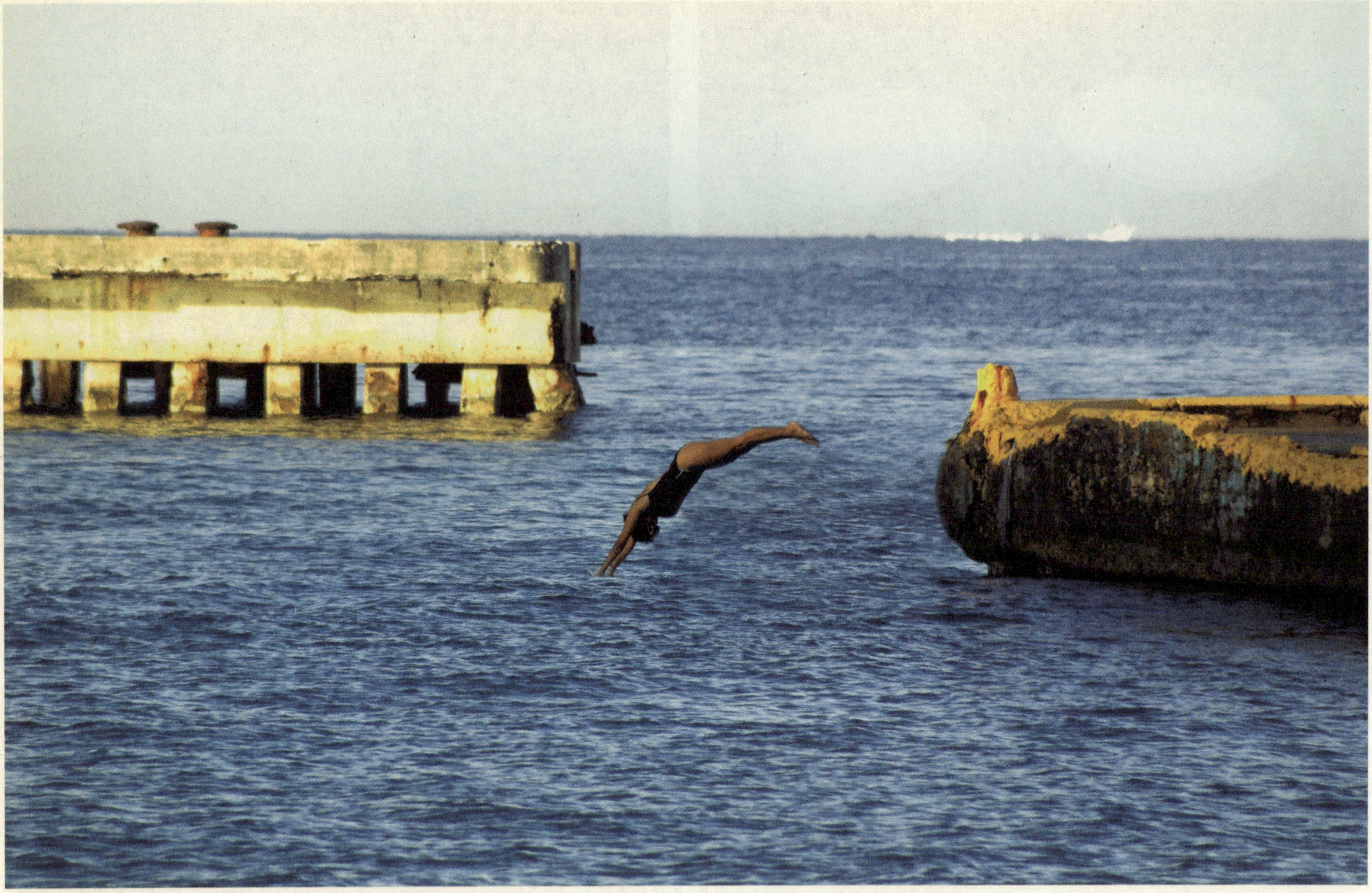

1.

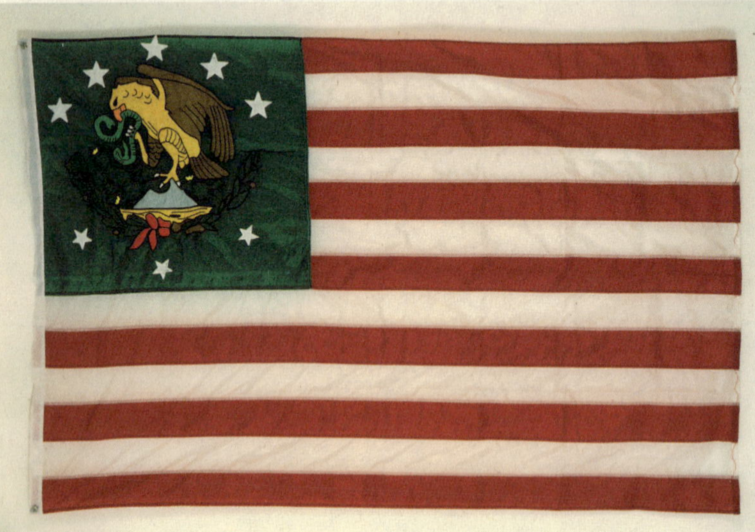

2.

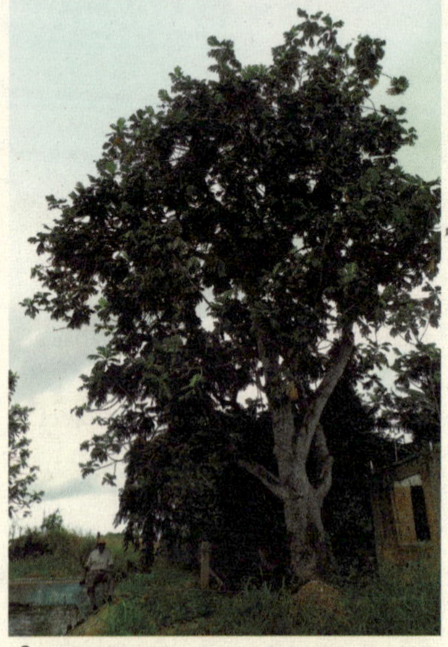

3.

Carolina Caycedo earned her BA in Fine Arts from Los Andes University, Bogotá, and currently lives in Isabela, Puerto Rico. Her work focuses on interaction and exchange between people of different backgrounds, including a march for immigrants in London and a Reggaeton dance competition in Puerto Rico. **DAYTODAY**, presented in the 2006 Whitney Biennial, is an interactive project Caycedo carried out both in her van and on a website, allowing her to arrange exchanges of anything from food to companionship and from babysitting to haircutting.

1. Planté Bandera Entrance
2007, color digital print, 2 parts, each 20 × 26 ½ in (51 × 67 cm)

2. Mexicamerican Flag
2007, hand-sewn nylon flag, 60 × 96 in (152 × 244 cm)

3. Don Paco y Su Pana
2008, giclée print, 30 × 22 ½ in (76 × 57 cm)

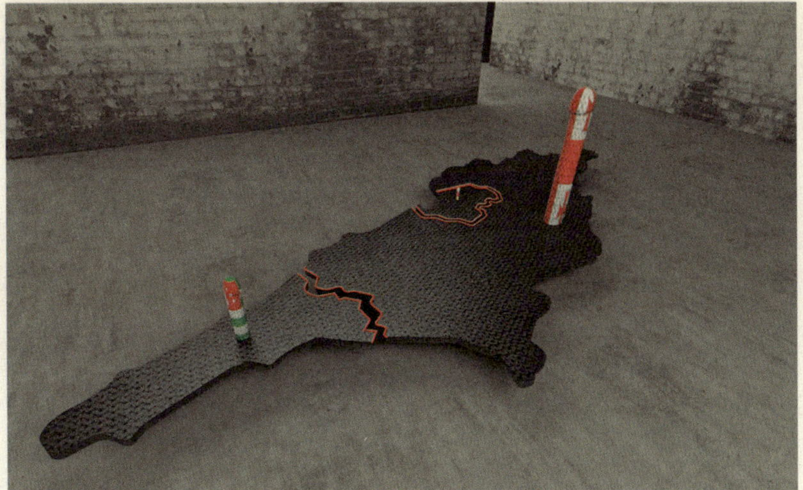
1.

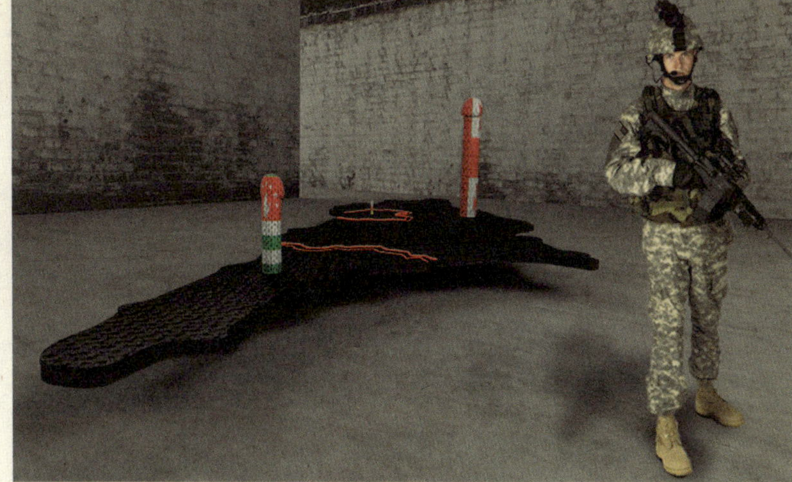
2.

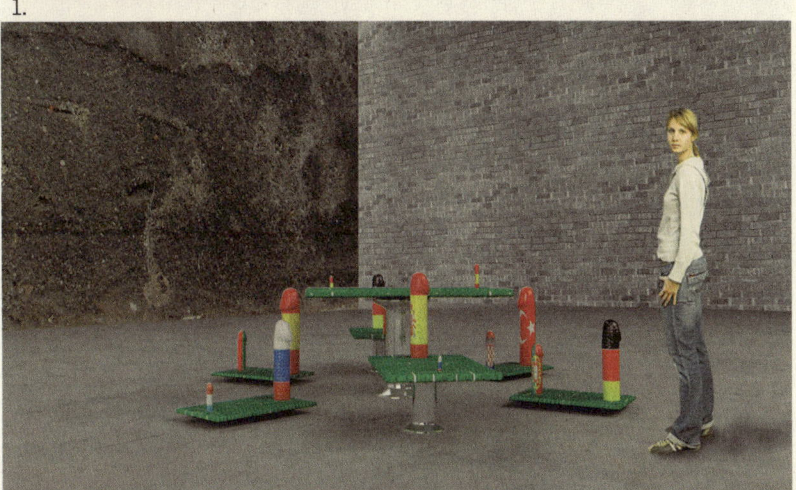
3.

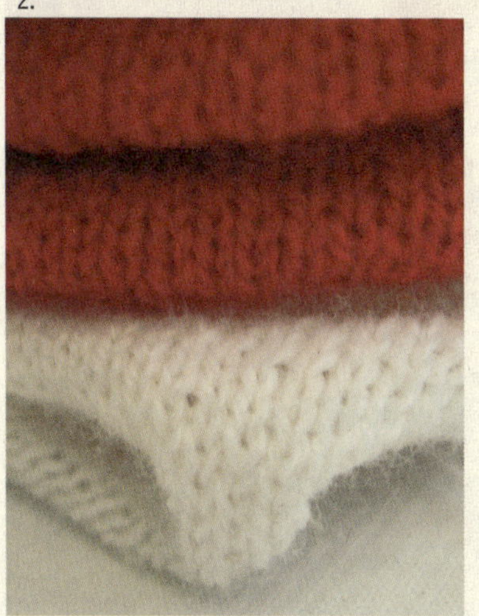
4.

Bella Chagall attended the Academy of Arts, Berlin, and currently lives in Berlin and Eze, France. Her installations combine knitted elements with other construction materials to address gender dynamics in global politics. **G8** (2008) represents each country with a knitted penis proportional to its population size.

1 & 2. Caucasus – The Eternal Conflict
2008, wool yarn, synthetic cotton, and plywood, 4 × 10 ft (120 × 300 cm)

3. Evro 2008
2008, wool yarn, synthetic cotton, and plywood, 9 ¾ x 13 ft (3 x 4 m)

4, 5 & 6. G8
2008, wool yarn, synthetic cotton, and plywood, 9 × 11 ½ ft (280 × 350 cm)

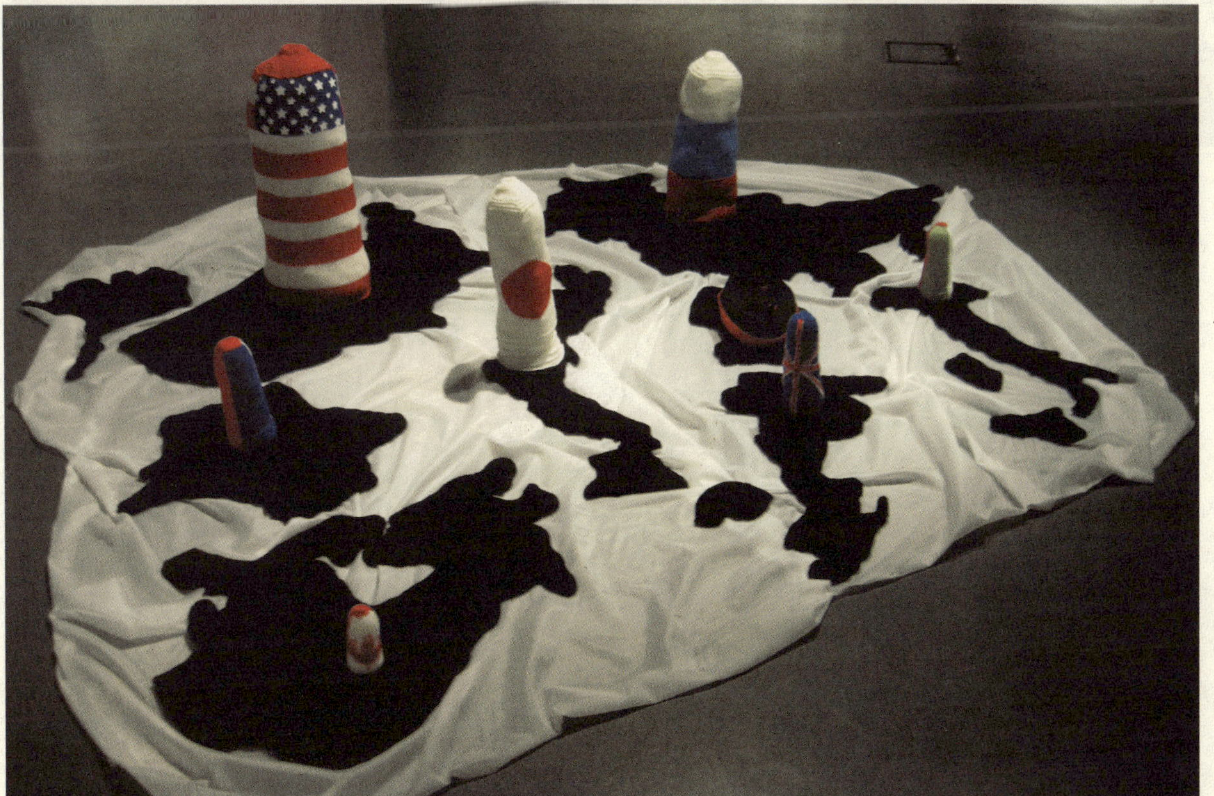
5.

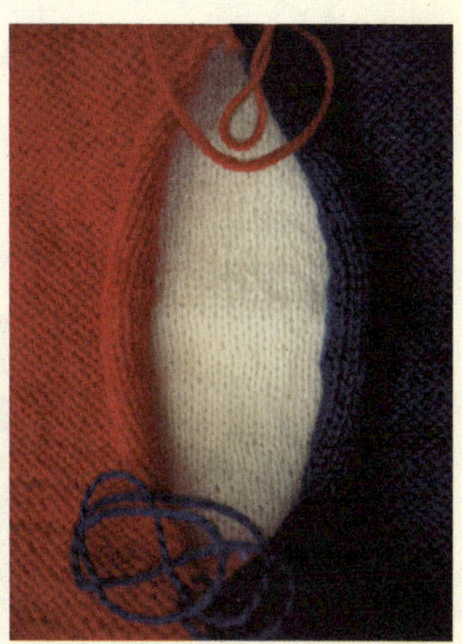
6.

Lia Chaia currently lives in São Paulo and works in performance, video, photography, and installation. She often uses her own body as a vessel through which to investigate her environment – urban or natural. In one piece, she consumes and regurgitates images of buildings along the controversial Minhocão ("huge worm"), an elevated roadway connecting two neighborhoods in São Paulo.

1. **Coluna**
2003, color photograph, 33 × 22 in (84 × 58 cm)

2. **Presa Predador**
2008, collage, 51 × 71 in (130 × 180 cm)

3. **Pelos Tubos** (detail)
2007-08, mixed media, dimensions variable, installation view at Galeria Vermelho, São Paulo

4. **Folíngua M**
2003, color photograph, 26 × 26 in (66 × 66 cm)

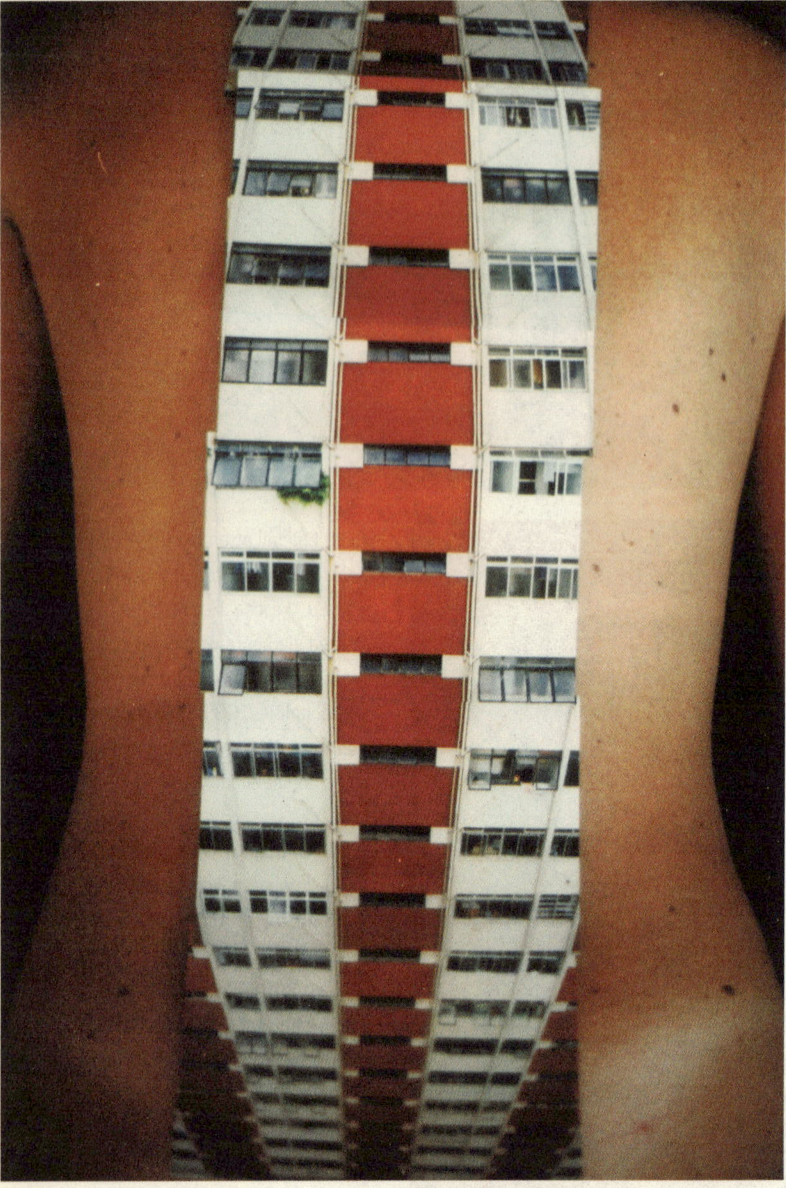

1.

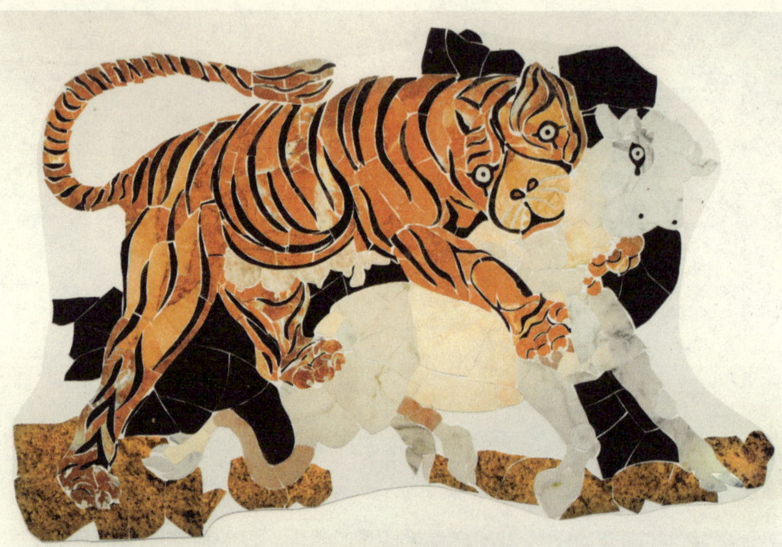

2.

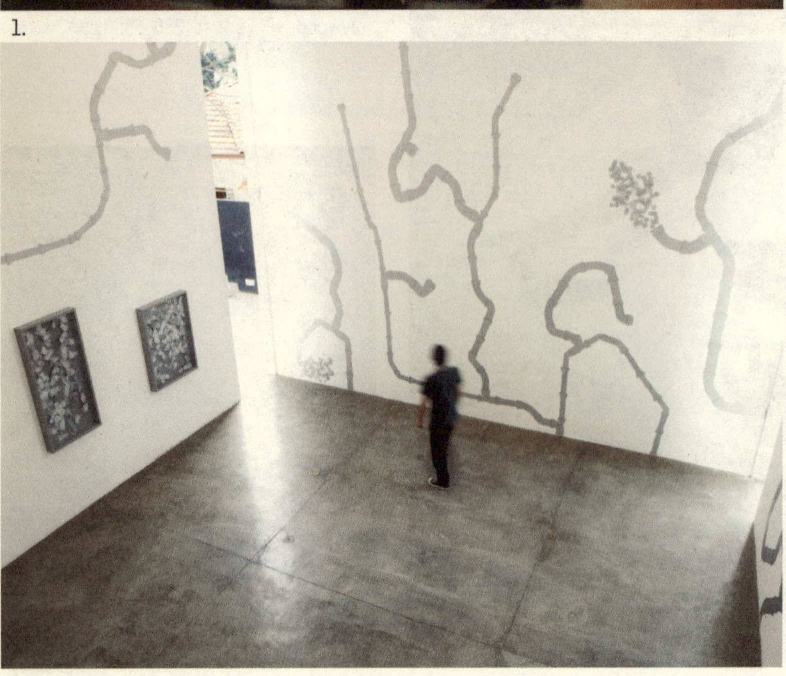

3.

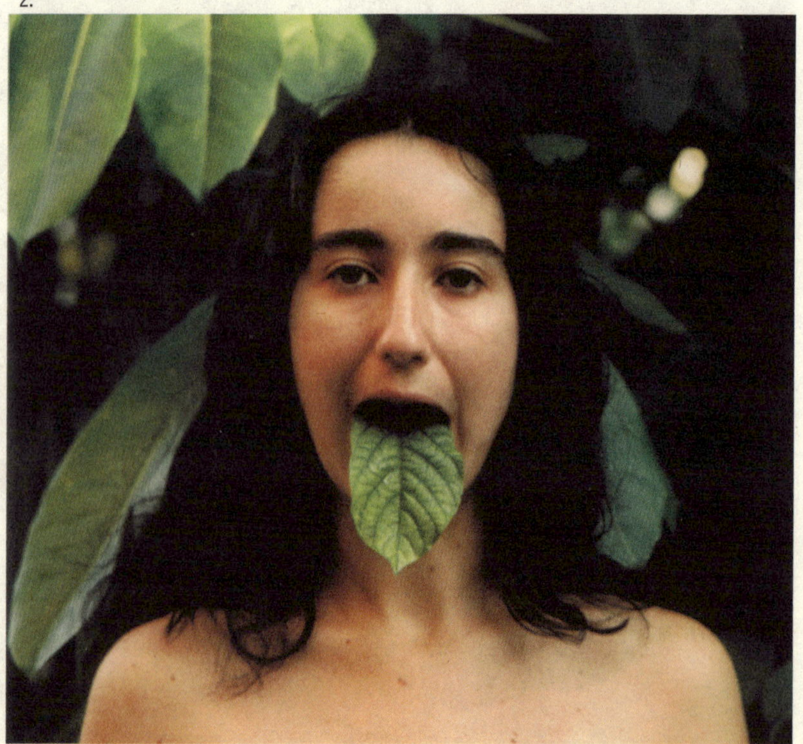

4.

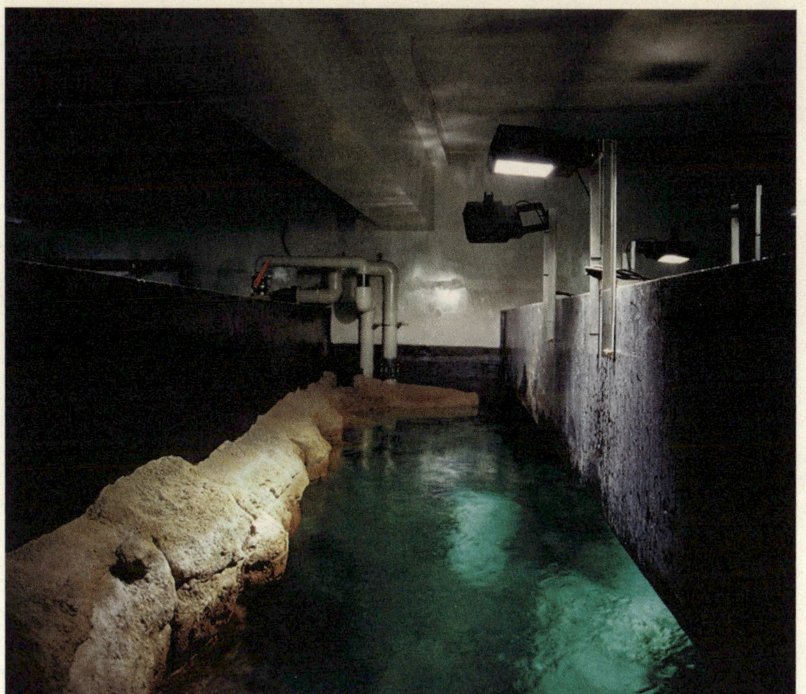

1.

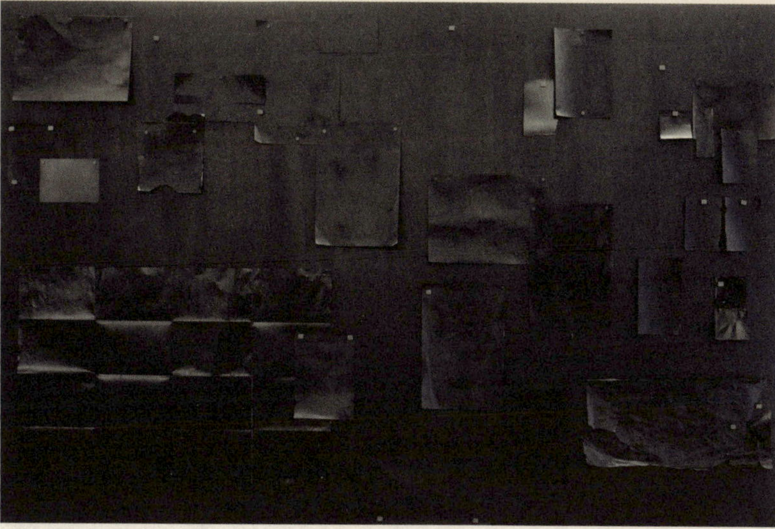

2.

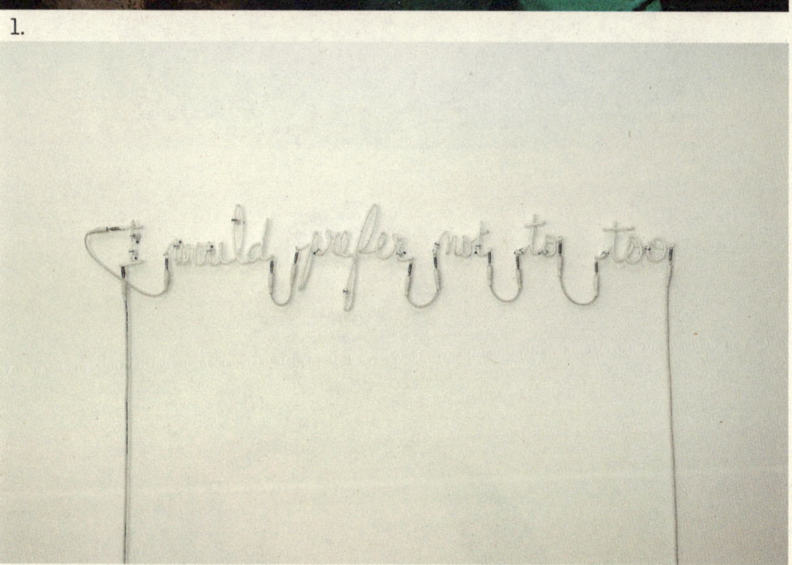

3.

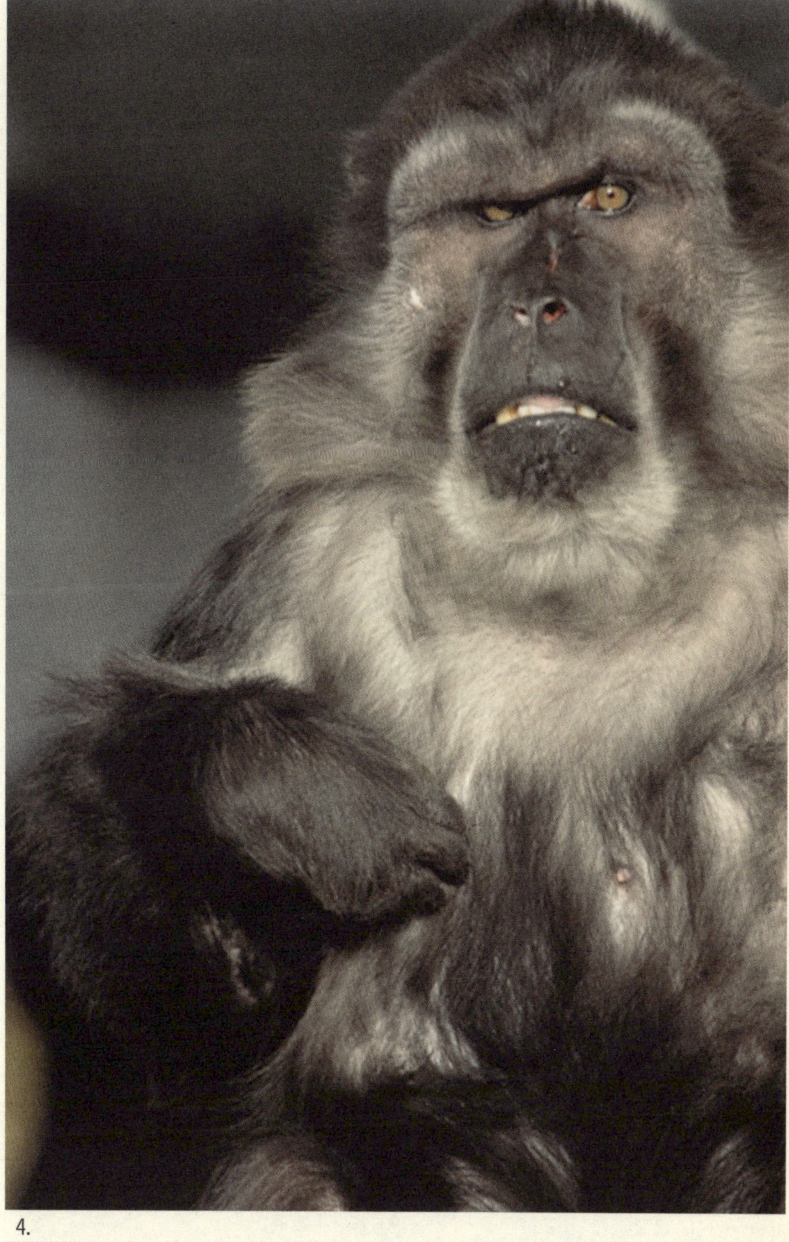

4.

Etienne Chambaud attended the Ecole des Beaux-Arts in Lyon and currently lives in Paris. His first solo exhibition, "The Abyss" (2007), combined objects, collages, photographs, and lighting fixtures to access in-between spaces, passageways, gaps, and boundaries. Participatory projects include his 2007 reenactment of The Blind Man, the extinct Dada magazine to which contributions were submitted by readers, and which was published only twice.

1. **Satire de l'Abîme**
(Satire of the Abyss)
2007, framed color photograph, $19\frac{3}{4} \times 23\frac{1}{2}$ in (50×60 cm)

2. **Le Comble**
2007, acrylic and magnetic paint on canvas, spray-painted paper, and magnets, $51 \times 78\frac{3}{4}$ in (130×200 cm)

3. **Disclaimer**
2007, unlit neon, $10 \times 71 \times 2$ in ($25 \times 180 \times 5$ cm)

4. **Le Troupeau du Dehors**
(The Outside Herd)
2004, aluminum, surveillance camera, streaming video system, dimensions variable

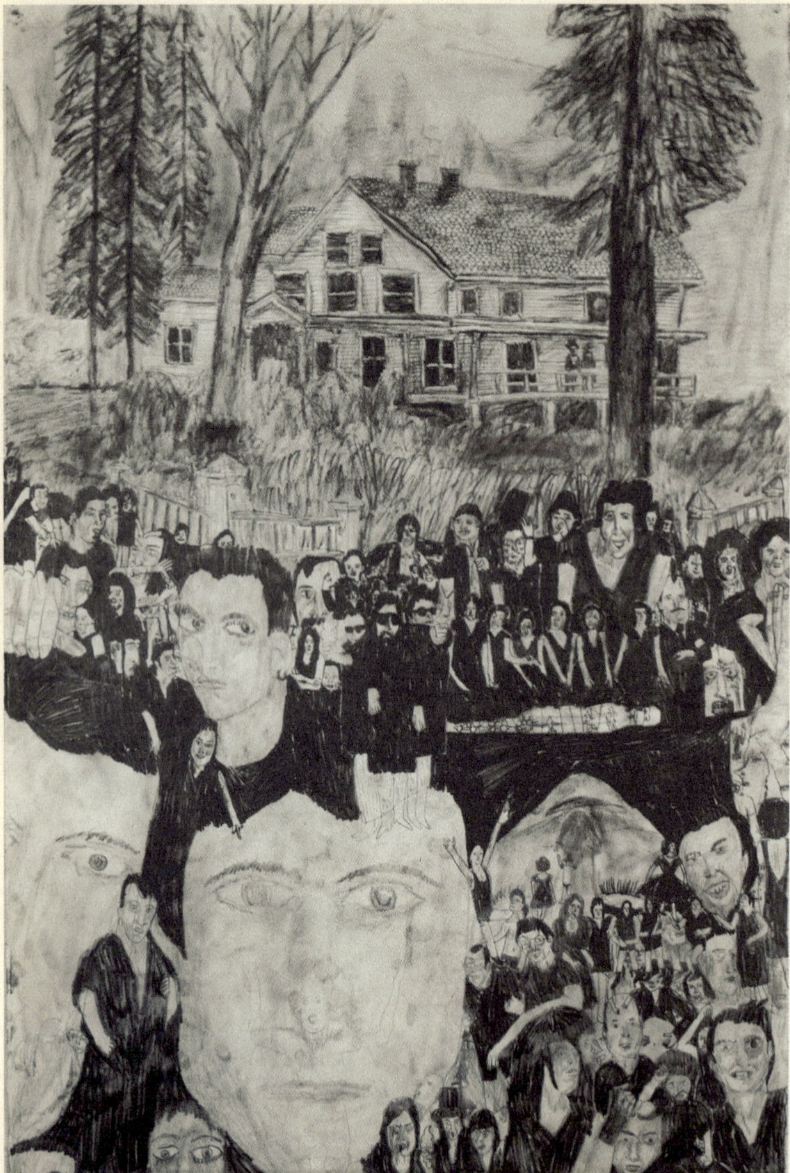

1.

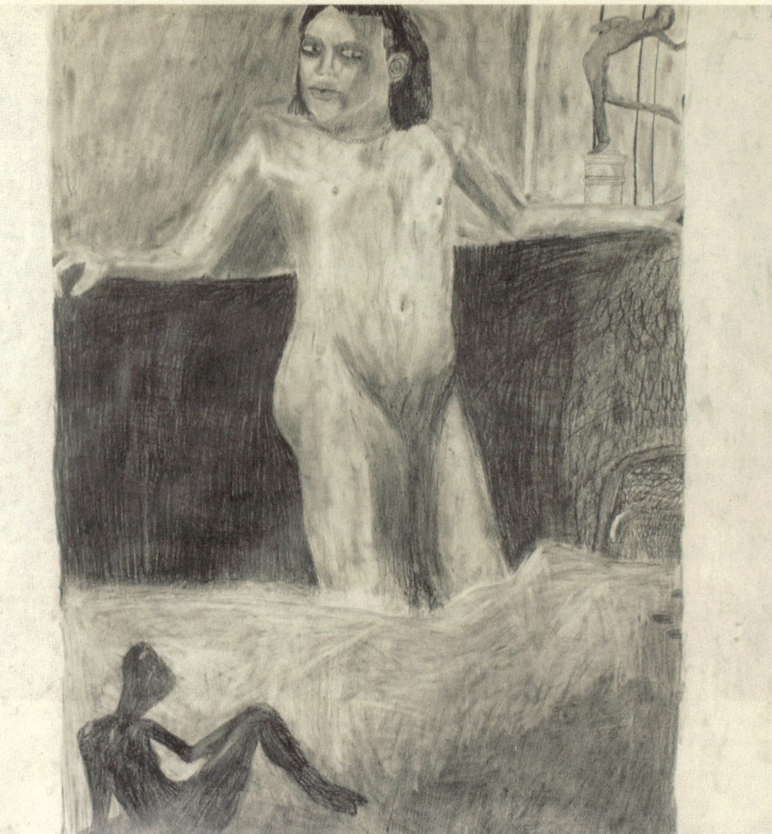

2.

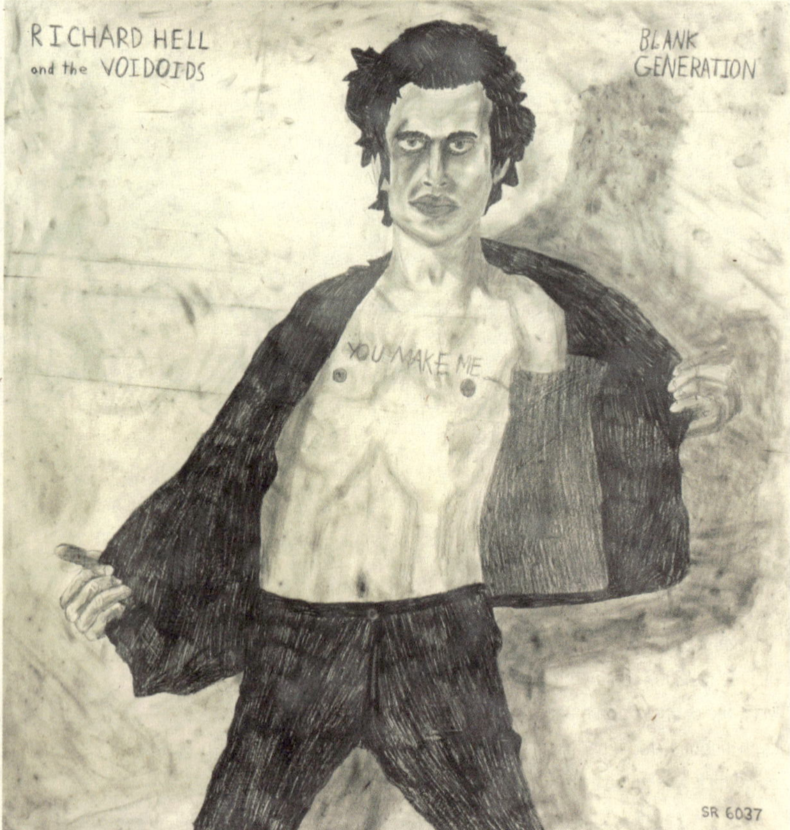

3.

Matthew Chambers received his MFA from the Art Center in Los Angeles, where he continues to live and work. His dark and naive drawings, paintings, sculptures, and installations draw their inspiration from a hodgepodge of cultural sources, from Richard Hell and Bela Tarr to Groucho Marx and Jan van Eyck. Chambers occasionally operates under the pseudonym TRUDI, which he originally adopted to avoid the strictures of producing work under a single "brand name." He has since opened a small gallery space in Los Angeles that shares his alter ego's name.

1. **About Town (Sometimes A Great Notion)**
2008, pencil on paper, 44 × 30 in (112 × 76 cm)

2. **Some Untitled Shit 1983 (Brooke)**
2007, pencil on paper, 42 × 42 in (107 × 107 cm)

3. **Some Untitled Shit 1977 (Richard Hell)**
2007, pencil on paper, 42 × 42 in (107 × 107 cm)

b. 1982 Taipei, Taiwan

CHANG, MICHAEL HJ

Michael HJ Chang earned his MFA from California Institute of the Arts in Los Angeles, where he lives. Chang questions the forces and systems that structure our lives through objects, actions, and performances. Often inspired by his favorite modernist author, Donald Barthelme, he has documented the slightly extraordinary activities of a Los Angeles couple (himself and another artist), attempted to integrate his dog Bacon into human life, and copied the paintings of an MFA classmate.

1. **Composition for Fanfare, Megan Sant's Works Copied by Mike HJ Chang**
2008, acrylic on canvas and papier-mâché, dimensions variable

2. **Horizon, or Do Fish Drink Water**
2008, video, 61 min

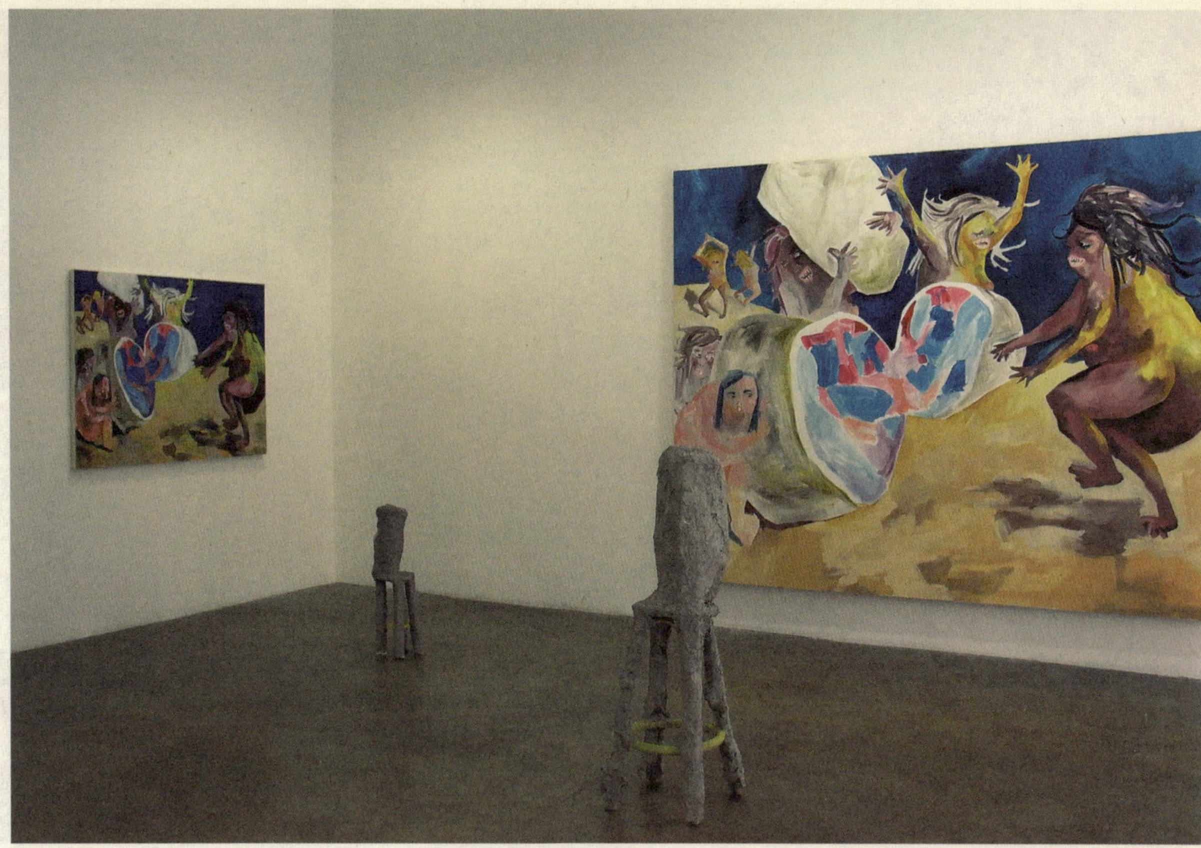

1.

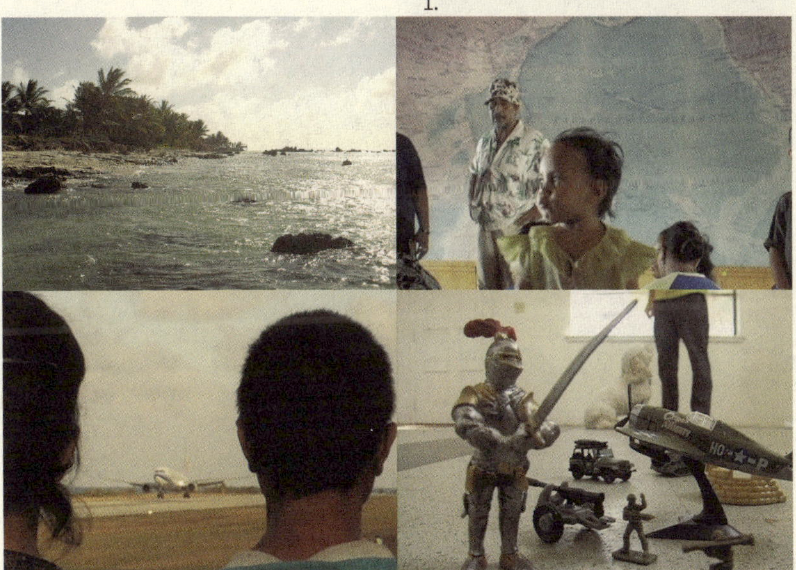

2.

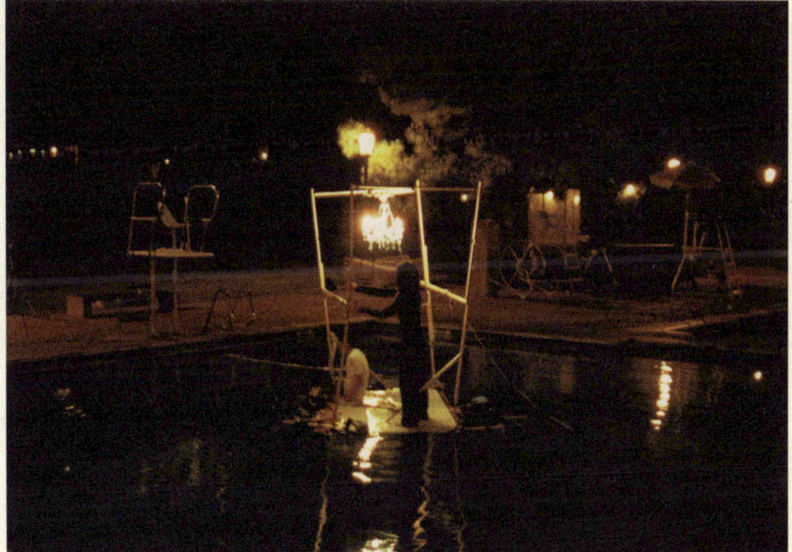

3.

3. **Light House**
with Juka Araikawa
2005, video, 11 min

4. **Skip Me**
2008, digital print

skip me

a gift made of a rock and white-out painting of a dog for a girl who i really liked but she doesn't want me and i vaguely remembered that i taught her how to skip stone somewhere in mexico this is for her to keep or not

4.

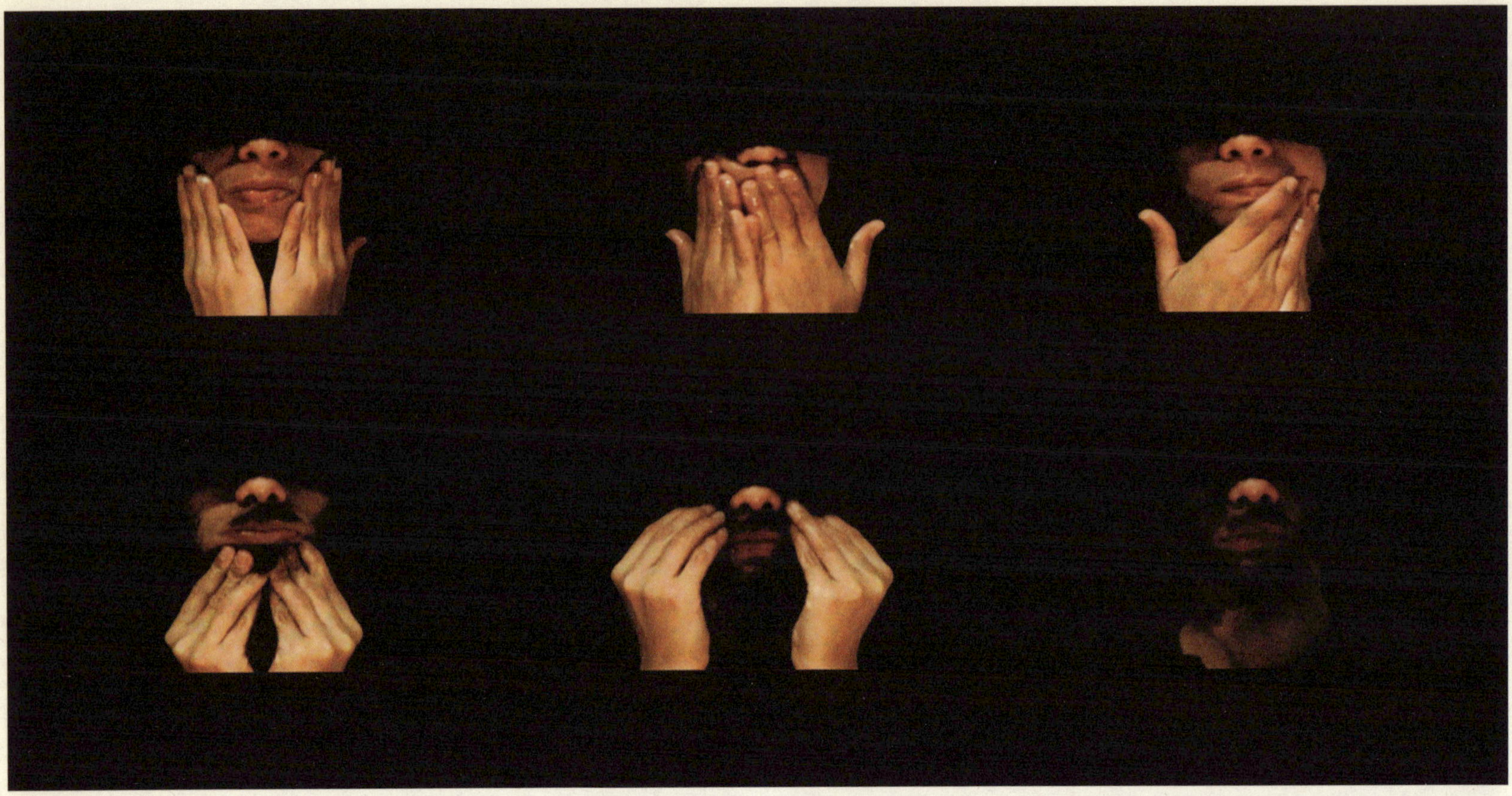

1.

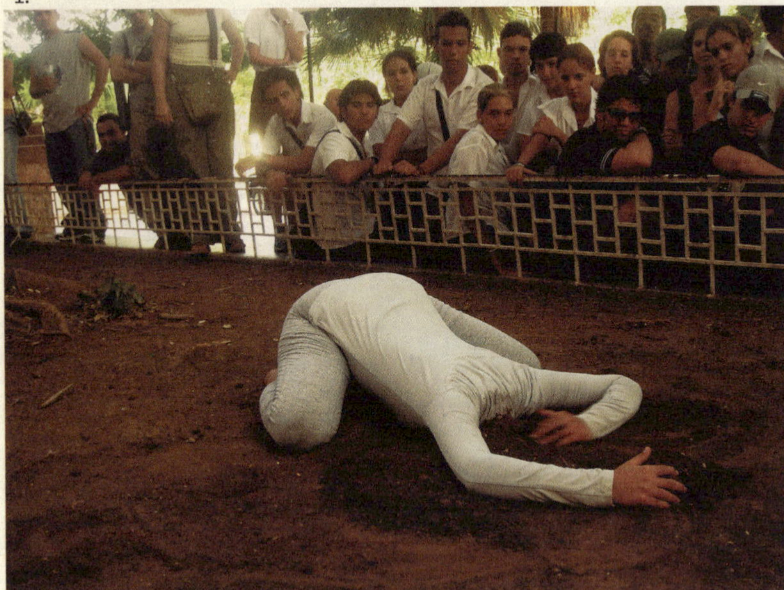

2.

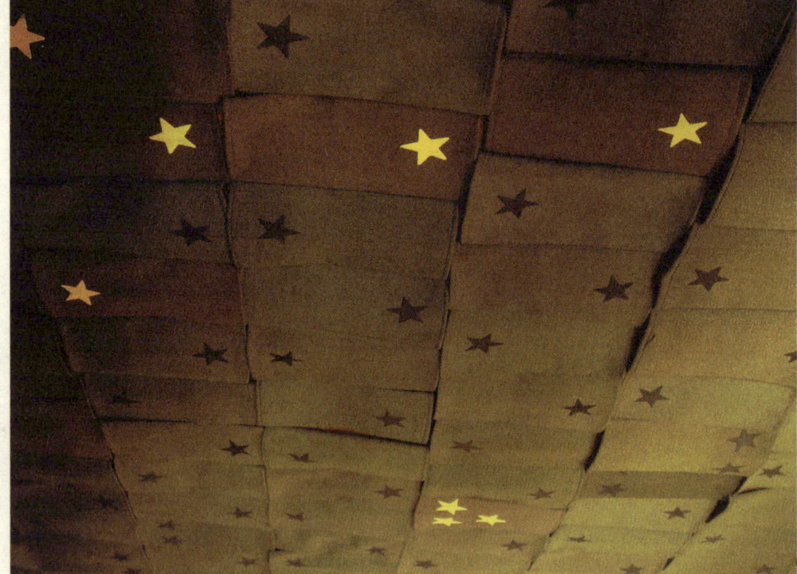

3.

Jeanette Chavez is currently studying at the Instituto Superior de Arte (ISA) in Havana. Much of her work – in video, installation, performance, and photography – is concerned with conditions of life in contemporary Cuba. In her 2006 video **Self-Censorship**, she ties string around her tongue until it turns blue and then black, ultimately closing her mouth to hide her silence.

1. **Ánimus**
2007, video, 3 min 59 sec

2. **Ostrich**
2005-06, performance at the Primer Encuentro de Arte Público, Ciego de Ávila, Cuba (2005)

3. **Change of state**
2006, military epaulettes mounted to gallery ceiling, dimensions variable

4. **Self-Censorship**
2006, video, 2 min 52 sec

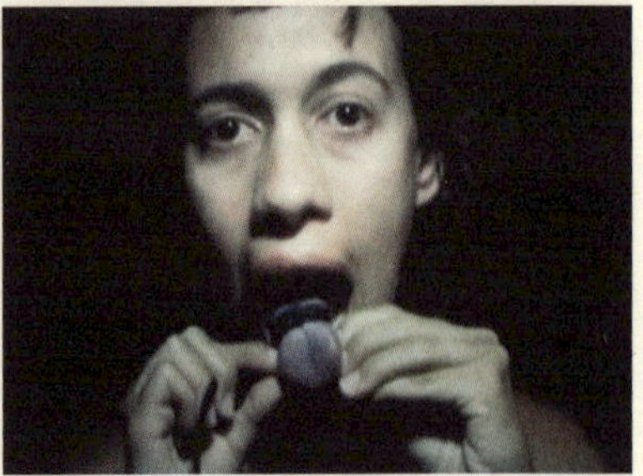

4.

Kudzanai Chiurai was the first black student to study fine art at the University of Pretoria in South Africa, where he was named "Most Promising Art Student" in 2003. A member of what has been dubbed the "Born Free" generation (born after Great Britain granted Zimbabwe independence in 1980), Chiurai makes work focused on the social, economic, and political turmoil of his homeland. He has made bodies of work that address the brutality and corruption of President Robert Mugabe, as well as Zimbabwe's HIV/AIDS crisis.

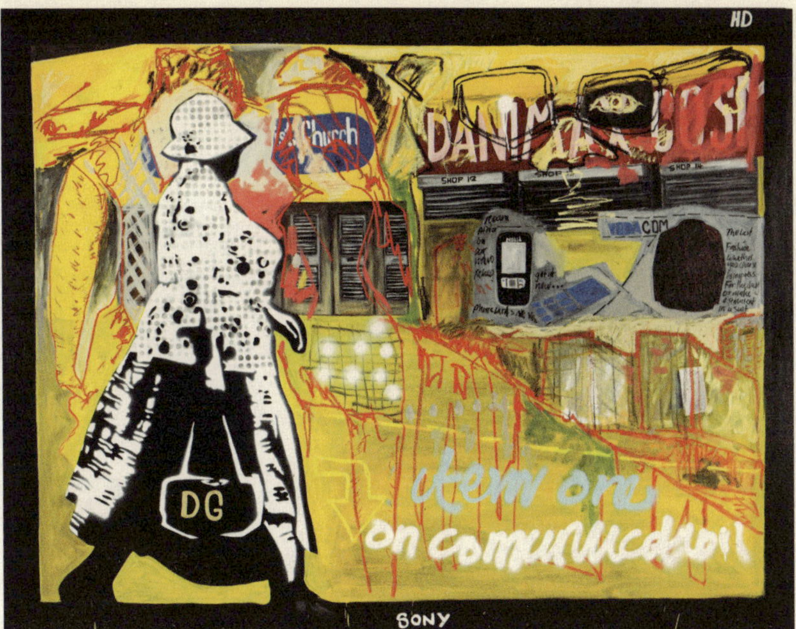

1.

1. Item One on Communication
2008, mixed media, 67 × 86 ½ in
(170 × 220 cm)

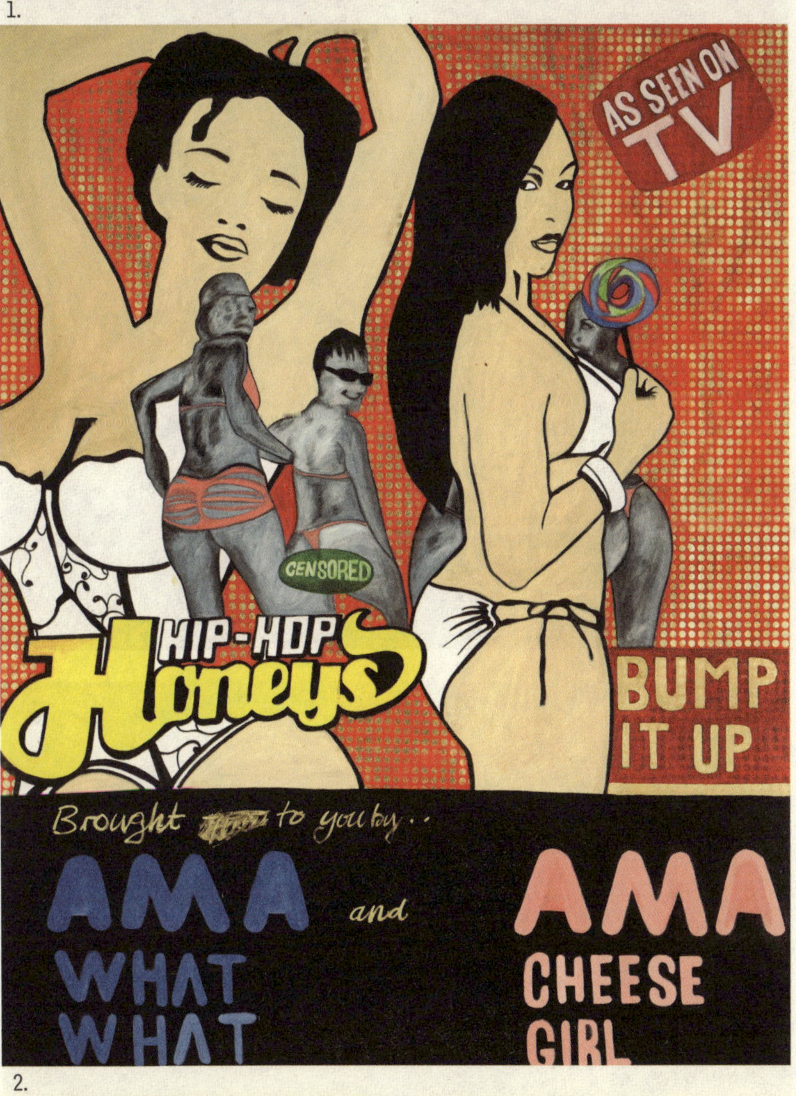

2.

2. As Seen on TV
2008, mixed media, 86 ½ × 67 in
(220 × 170 cm)

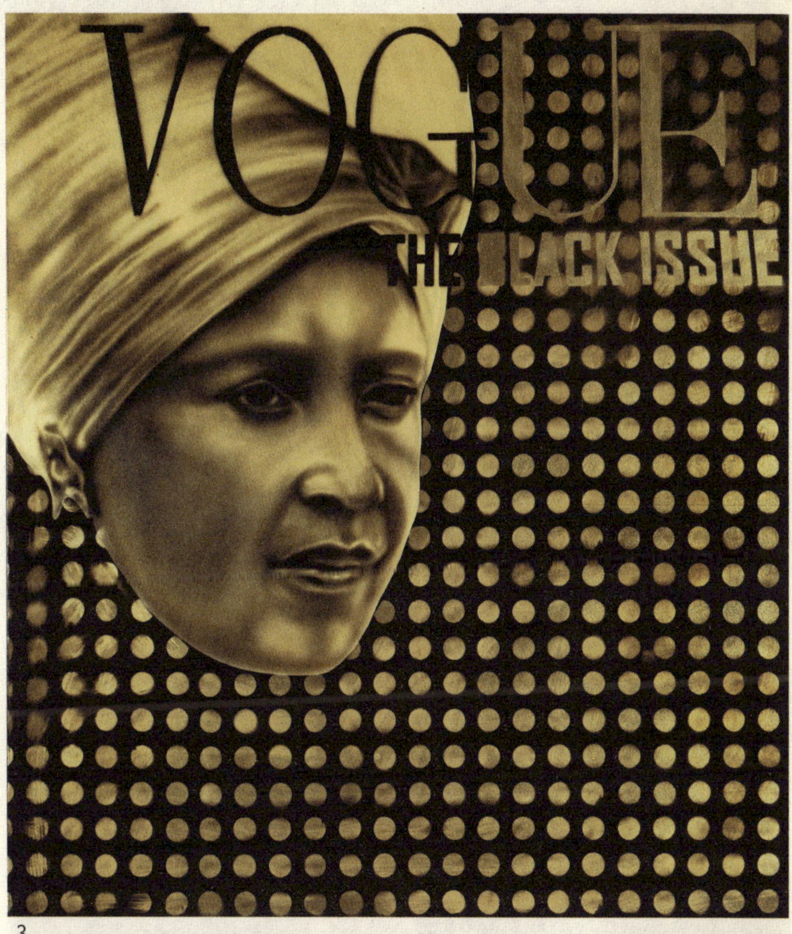

3.

3. The Black Issue
2008, mixed media, 78 ¾ × 71 in
(200 × 180 cm)

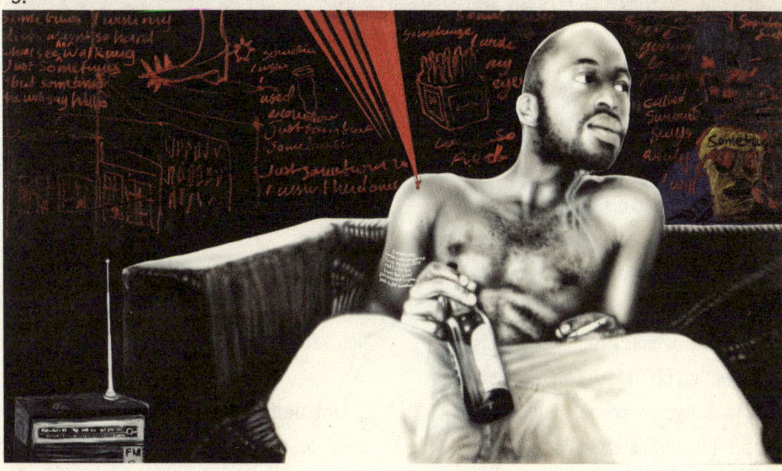

4.

4. Sometimes
2008, mixed media, 47 ¼ × 86 ¼ in
(120 × 220 cm)

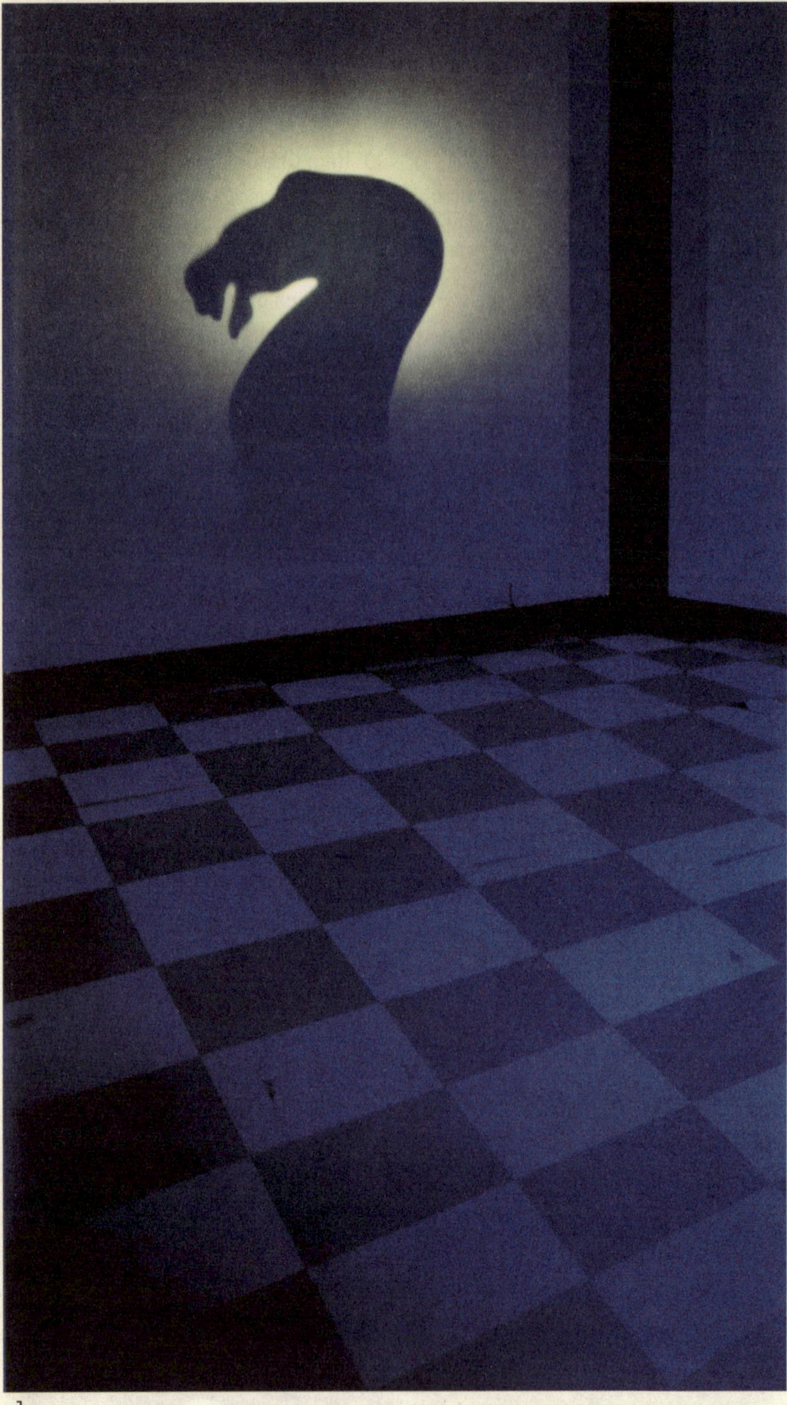

1.

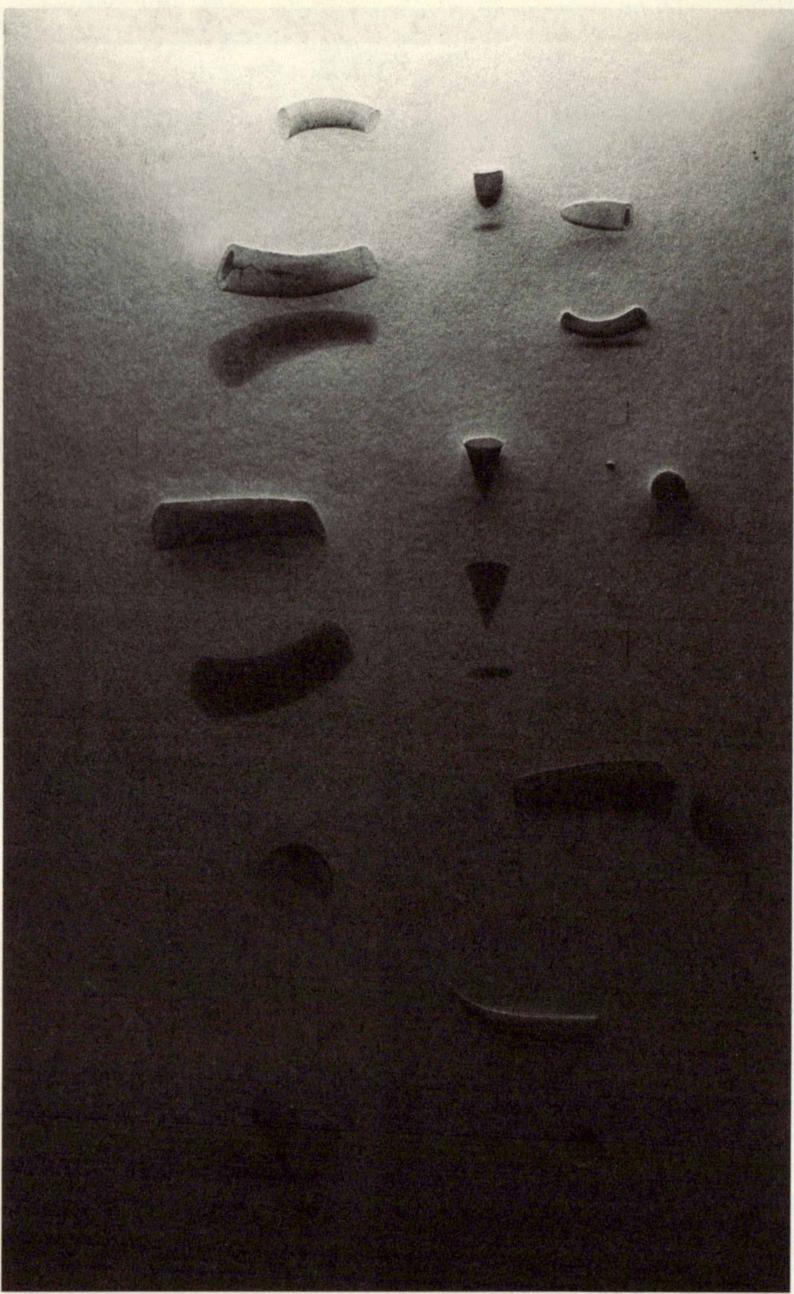

2.

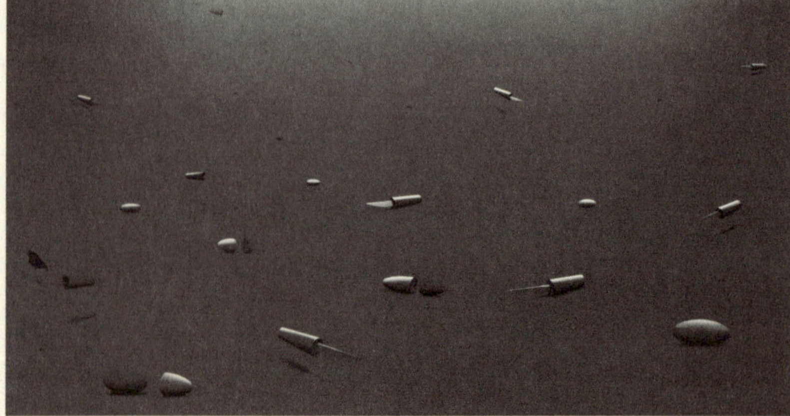

3.

Dilip Chobisa earned his MFA from Maharaja Sayajirao University in Baroda, where he continues to live. Rooted in sculpture, his practice includes photography and experimentation with light and optics, as well as works on paper. Using materials from graphite, acrylic, ink, and watercolor to X-ray film and glass marker, he depicts groups of objects or scenes that often focus on a window. His works draw connections between the observation of inner and outer worlds.

1. **Corner Û**
2008, graphite on paper, watercolor, glass marker, fluorescent light, acrylic sheet, and colored wood, 84 × 48 × 4 in (213 × 122 × 10 cm)

2. **Visibility**
2005, graphite on paper and fluorescent light, 36 × 24 in (91 × 61 cm)

3. **Untitled**
2007, graphite on paper and fluorescent light, 48 × 72 in (122 × 183 cm)

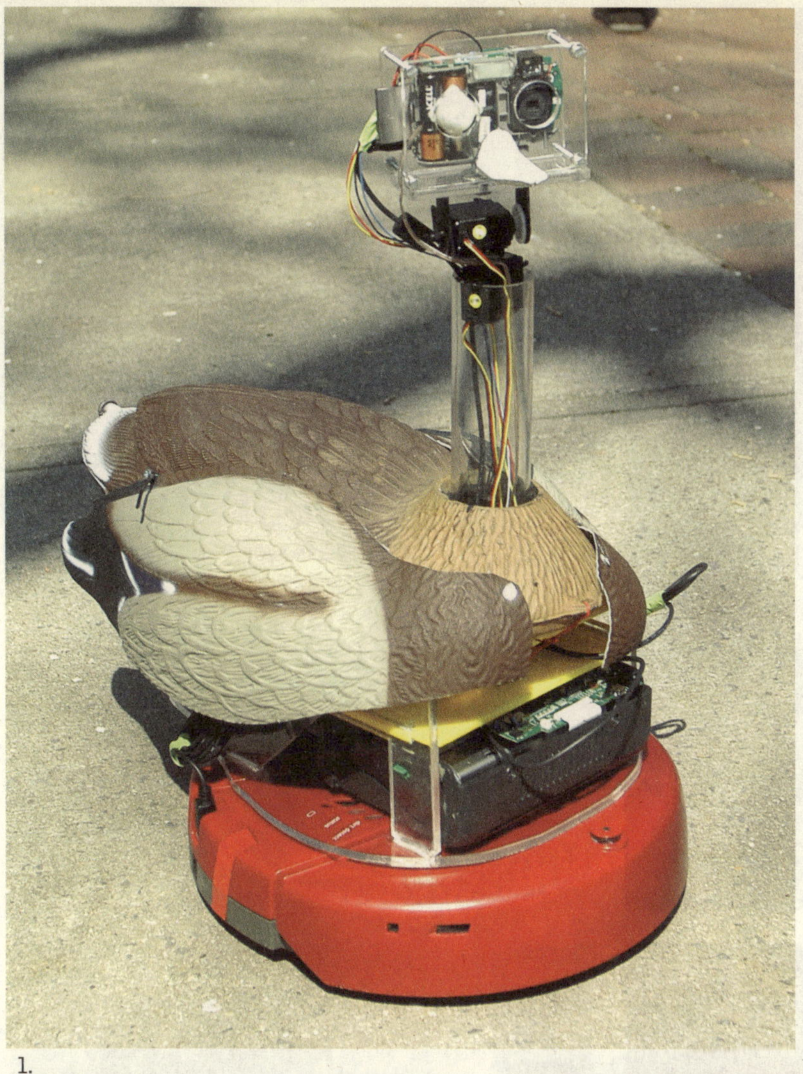

1.

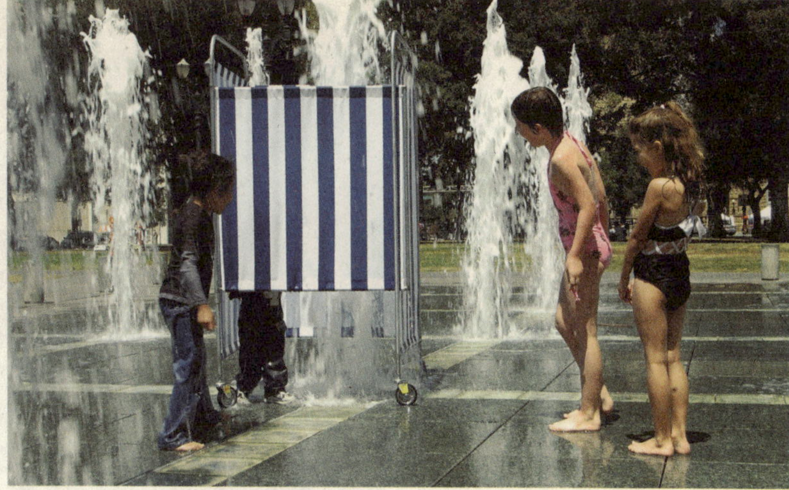

2.

Taeyoon Choi earned his BFA from the School of the Art Institute of Chicago, and his MS at the Korea Advanced Institute of Science and Technology. He is a performance and digital media artist based in Seoul, and a 2008 commissioned resident at the Eyebeam Center for Art and Technology, New York City. Many works include interaction and intervention in communities and public space, such as **Camerautomata Charlie** (2008), a robotic duck that takes pictures, prints them, and posts them on the Internet.

1. Camerautomata Charlie
2008, hacked electronic objects, digital camera, printer, and robotic vacuum, 17 × 21 × 12 in (43 × 53 × 31 cm)

2. Moveable Types and Instant Spaces
2006, public installation, 36 × 36 × 84 in (91 × 91 × 213 cm)

3. Object of Desire
2005, performance, 20 min

4. Shoot Me If You Can
2005, mobile game with camera phone, 5 min

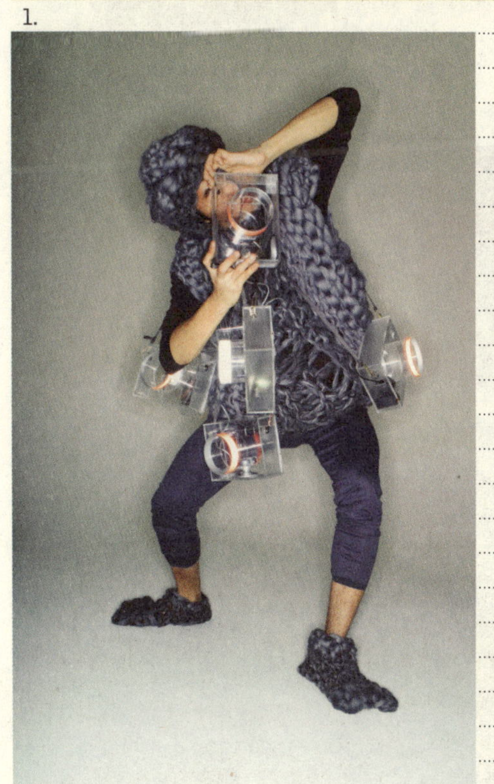

3.

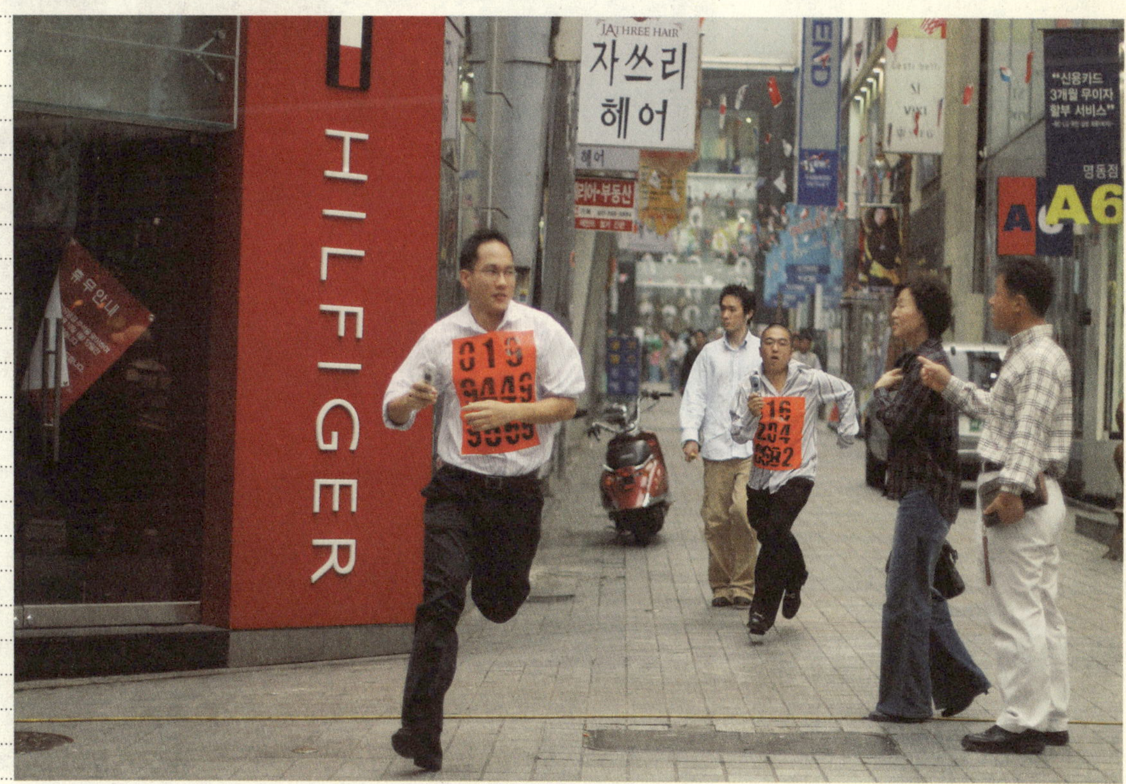

4.

Raised in Singapore, Heman Chong earned his MA in communication art and design from the Royal College of Art, London, and currently lives in Berlin and Singapore. He investigates philosophies, reasons, and methods of individuals and communities imagining the future. This research is translated into objects, images, installations, events, texts, and collaborations, including the science fiction novel **Philip** (2007), cowritten by eight art professionals during a seven-day workshop. Chong was one of three artists representing Singapore at the 50th Venice Biennale in 2003.

1. **Teardrop (Inversed)**
2008, offset print on 3,000 self-adhesive stickers, dimensions variable

2. **Everyday life in the modern world, What is the artist role today? Protest and Intimacy**
2005, 4 books and 4 perfume bottles

3. **Philip**
concept by Heman Chong, collectively written by Mark Aerial Waller, Cosmin Costinas, Rosemary Heather, Francis McKee, David Reinfurt, Steve Rushton, Heman Chong, and Leif Magne Tangen
2007, novel

4. **ONE HUNDRED YEARS OF SOLITUDE**
2008, aluminum on outdoor wall fixture, 23 x 32 3/4 ft (7 x 10 m)

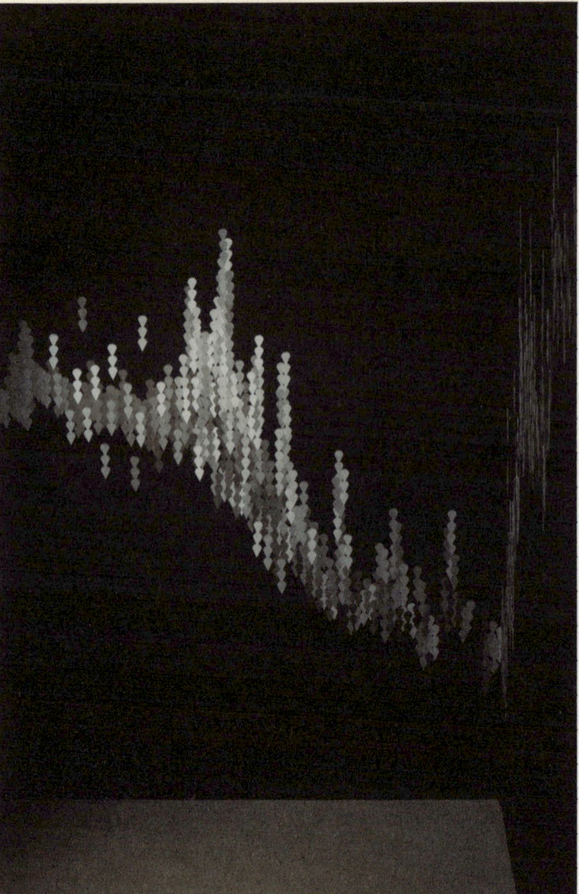

1.

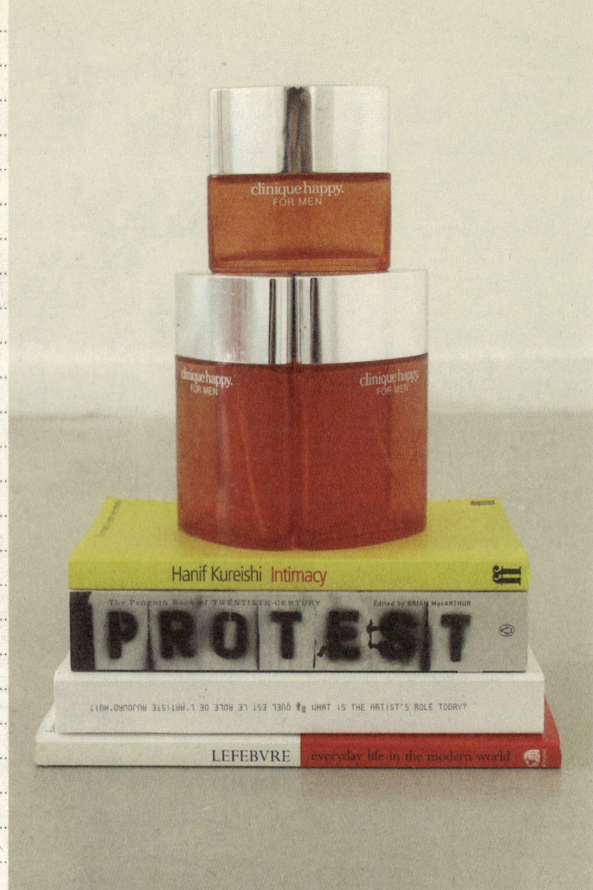

2.

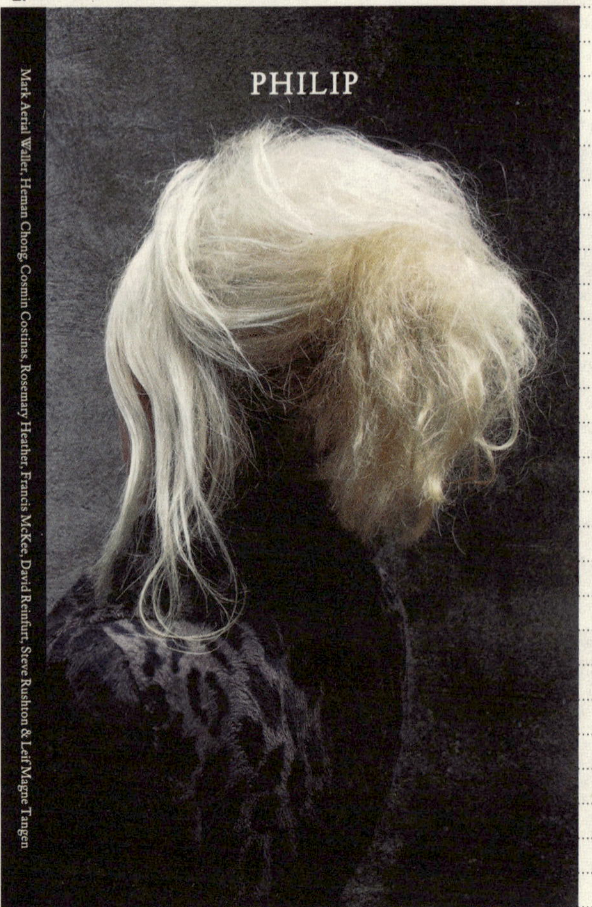

3.

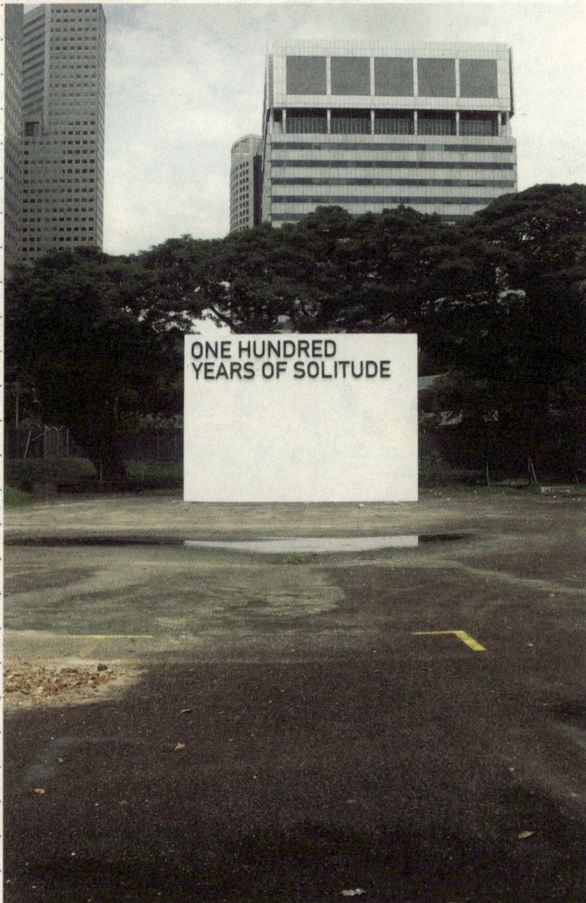

4.

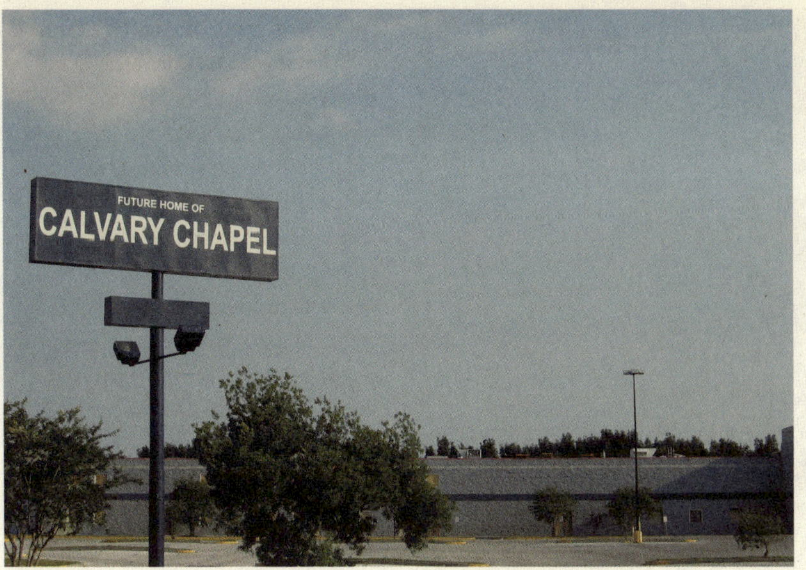

1.

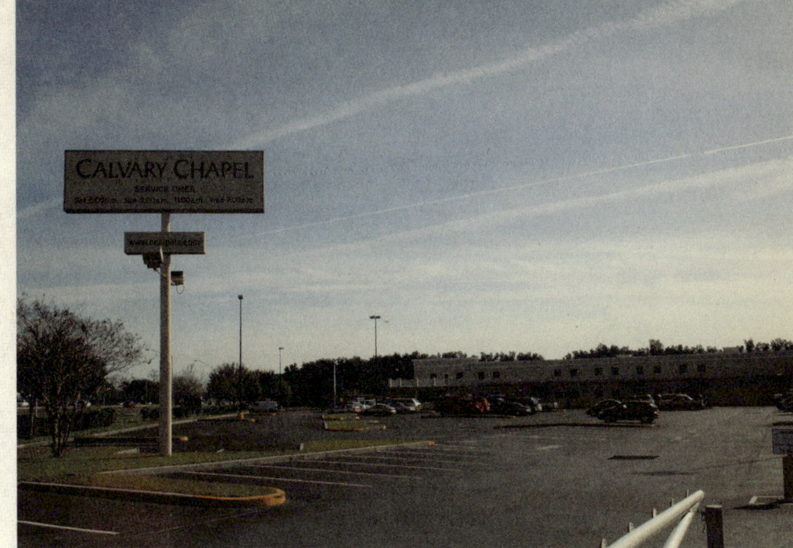

2.

Julia Christensen earned her MFA in integrated electronic arts from Rensselaer Polytechnic Institute, Troy, New York. She currently teaches at Oberlin College, Ohio, in the Studio Arts and TIMARA (Technology in Music and Related Arts) departments. Working at the intersection between art and research, she has been traveling the country since 2003 for the project **Big Box Reuse**, a book (MIT Press, 2008) and a website exploring the transformation of abandoned big box stores across America into cultural sites.

1. Big Box Reuse: Future Home of Calvary Chapel, abandoned Wal-Mart Building, Pinellas Park, FL
2004, digital photograph

2. Big Box Reuse: Calvary Chapel, Renovated Wal-Mart Building, Pinellas Park, FL
2007, digital photograph

3. The UnBox
2008, regionally sourced wood, reused security mirrors, muslin, and reused cord, dimensions variable

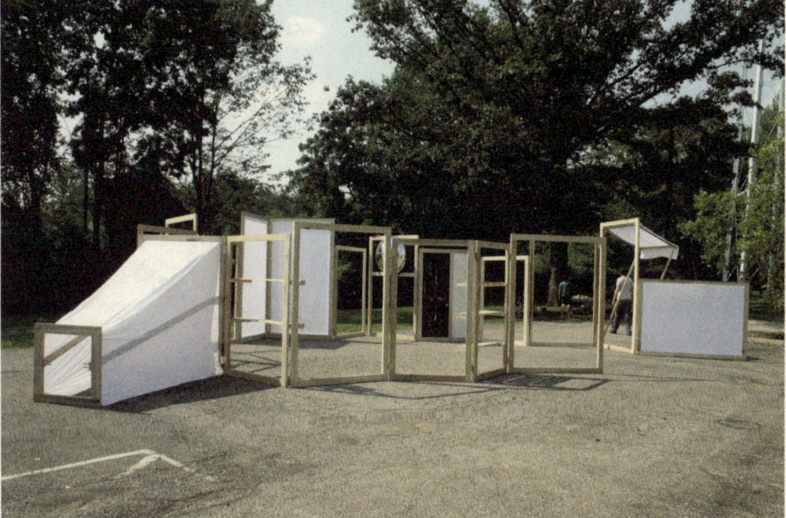

3.

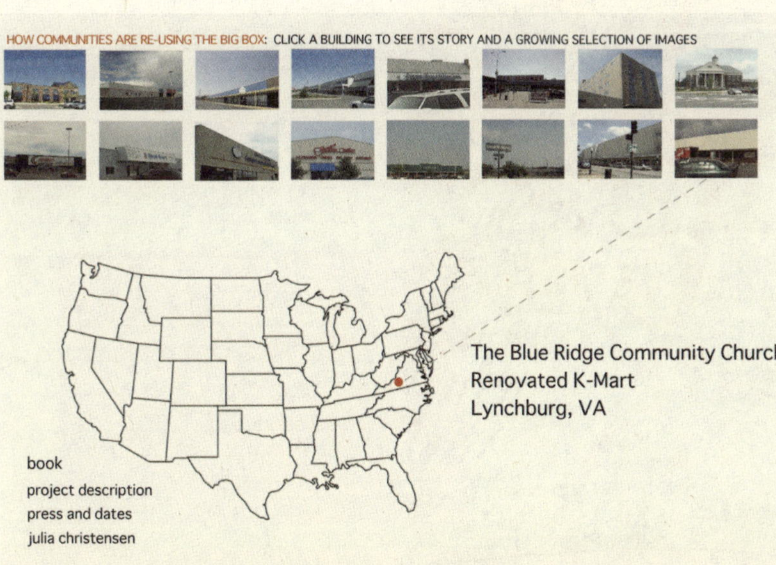

4.

LAKE PONTCHARTRAIN
LAKE BORGNE
NEW ORLEANS
NEW ORLEANS, LA

I cross the bridge over the
Inner Harbor Navigational Canal
from St. Bernard to the Ninth Ward.
The trains are suspicious.
Everything is suspicious.
Something about these trains
makes everything feel exposed.
New Orleans re-emerges as a machine
with a defined function.
I put the car in park, and slip off my sandals.
I dangle my microphone out the open window.

click here to stop sounds

(go back)

5.

4. Big Box Reuse
2004, interactive website
http://bigboxreuse.com/

5. Rust Belt / Bayou
2007, interactive website
http://transition.turbulence.org/works/rustbelt_bayou/

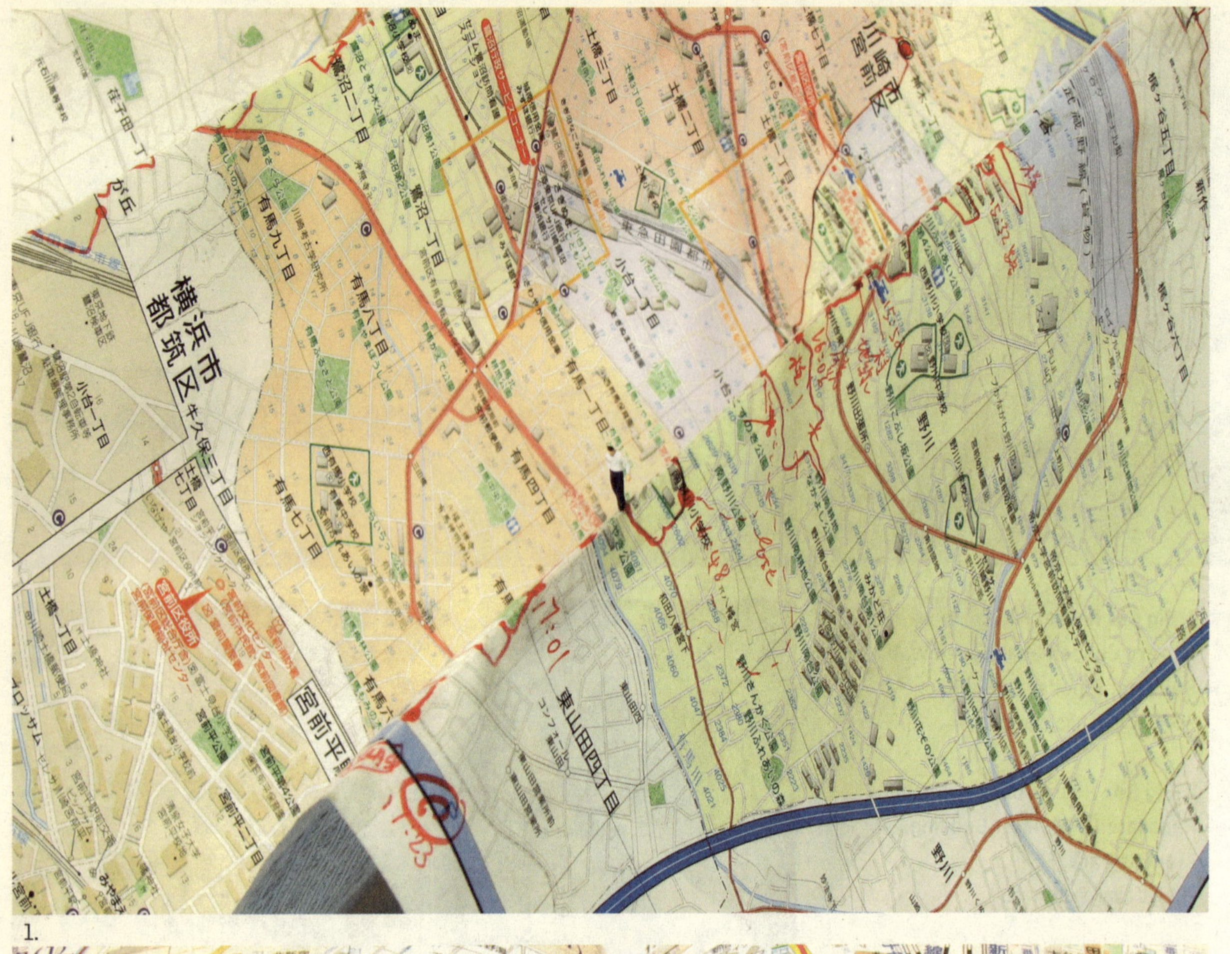

1.

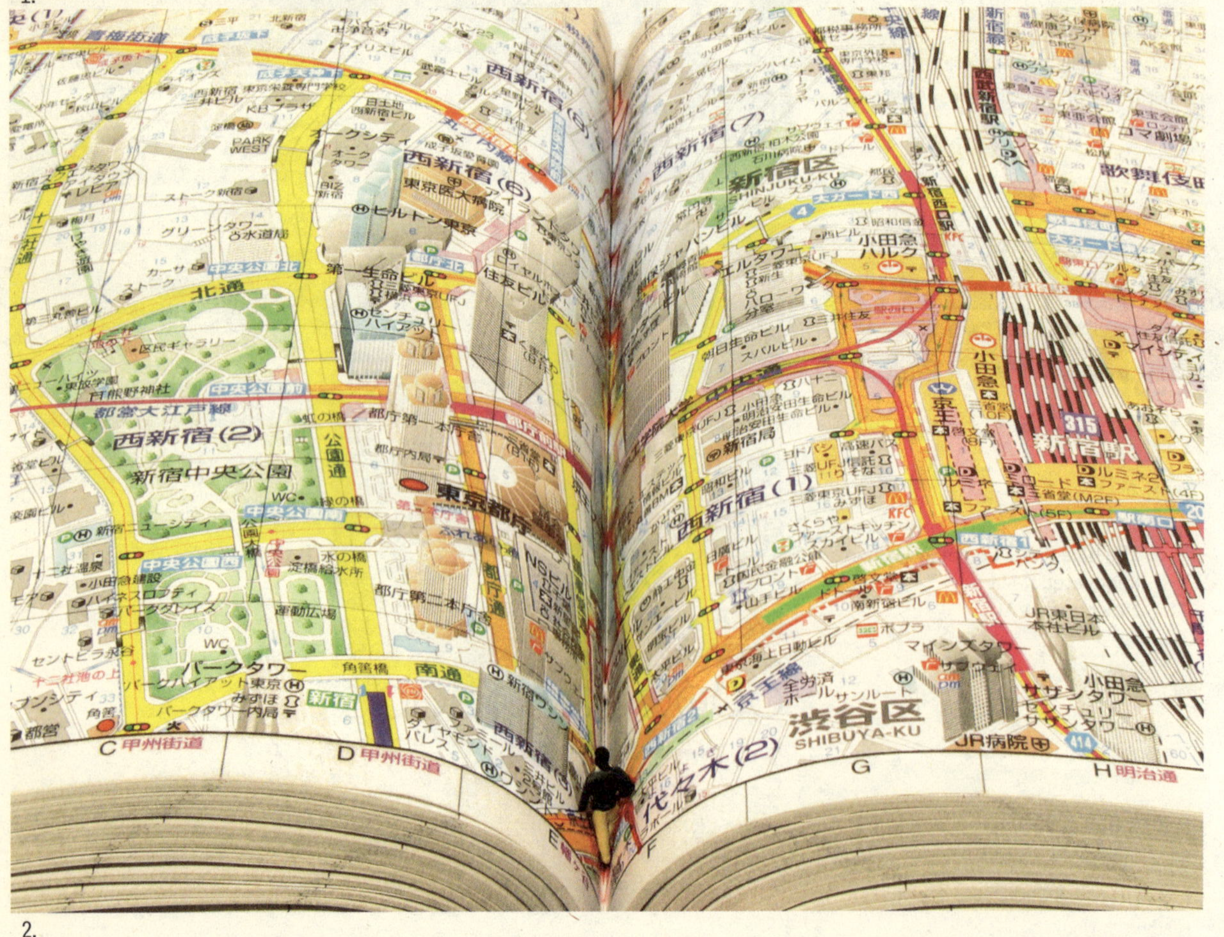

2.

Pak Sheung Chuen received his BA in fine arts from the Chinese University of Hong Kong, and currently lives in Hong Kong and Beijing. His conceptual projects call attention to everyday phenomena through action or performance. In **Breathing House** (2006), he captures air from each of his breaths in a plastic bag until he fills the entire space of his home with filled bags. He also contributes a weekly project to the local newspaper Ming Pao in a further effort to permeate everyday life.

1. **Mountains Trip / Tokyo / I walked along all the folds of a map. / 4 days**
2007, mixed media, dimensions variable

2. **Valleys Trip / Tokyo / I walked along all the gaps in a map book, from the south Tokyo to the north. / 5 days**
2007, mixed media, dimensions variable

Jay Chung and Q Takeki Maeda attended the Städelschule in Frankfurt and live in Berlin, where they have worked together since 2001. Their conceptual practice takes the form of action, performance, installation, and descriptive narrative. Works include the guided **Nickel Tour** (2005), commissioned by the Frieze Art Fair in London, and **Modus Tollens** (2003), which stages the fake, confidential, and repeated departure of Maeda for Japan.

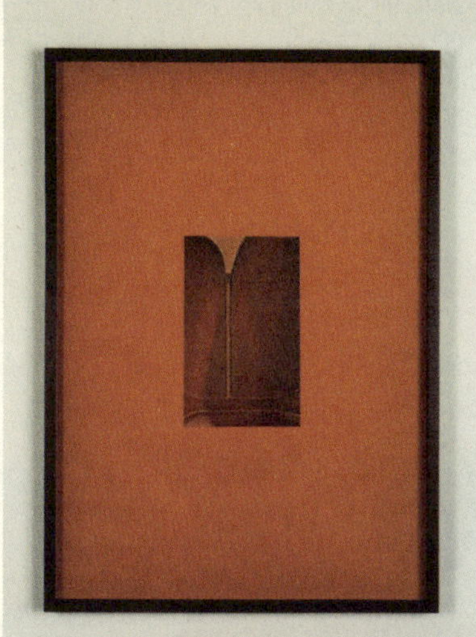

1.

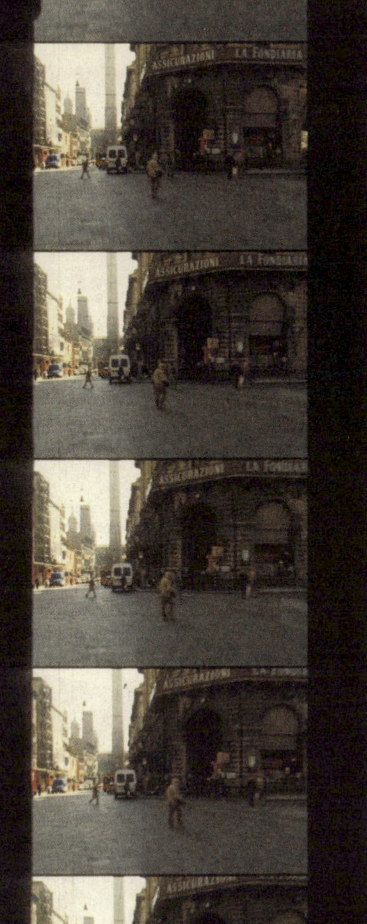

2.

3.

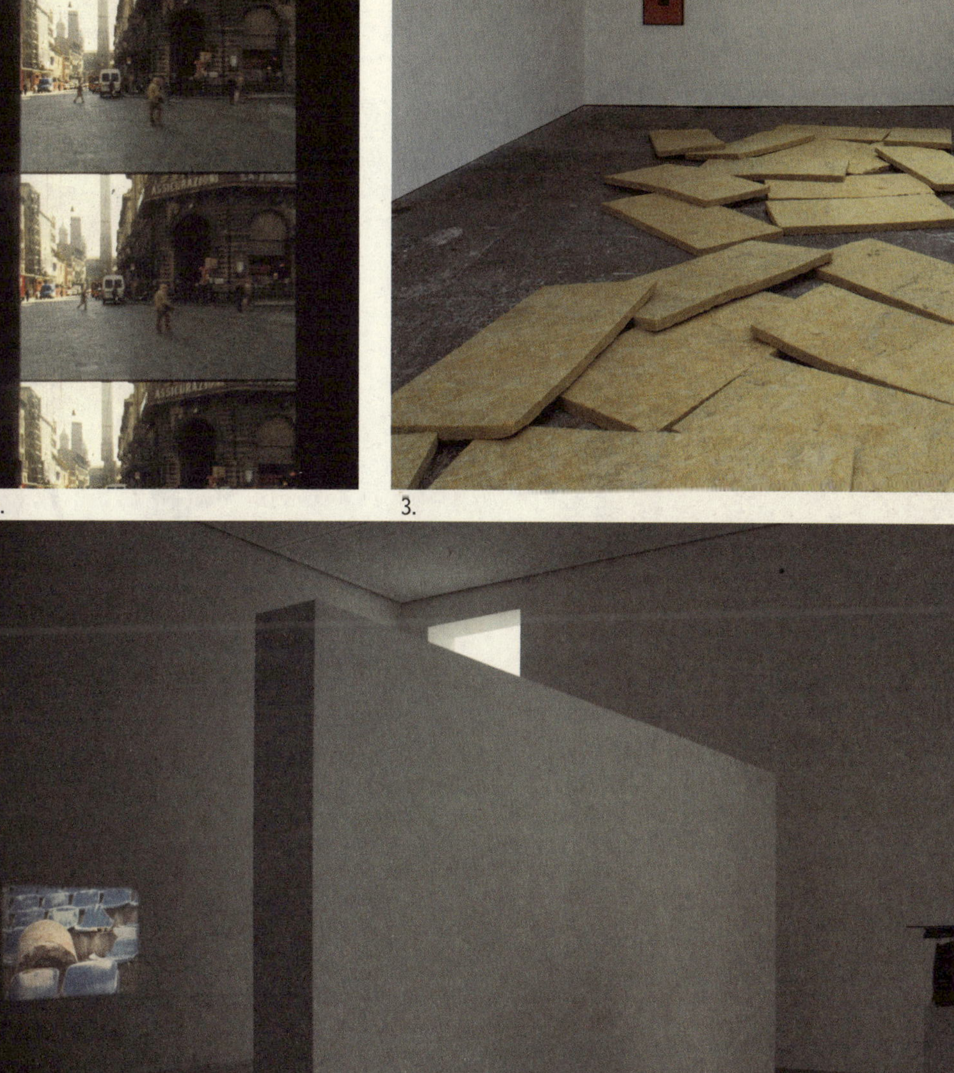

4.

1 & 3. Hardy Boys and Gilmore Girls
2008, insulation, high-fidelity speakers, and framed drawing, dimensions variable, installation view at Cubitt, London

2 & 4. (right) Caducean City
2006, 16 mm film, 22 min

4. (left) Artxanda
2005, video, 3 min

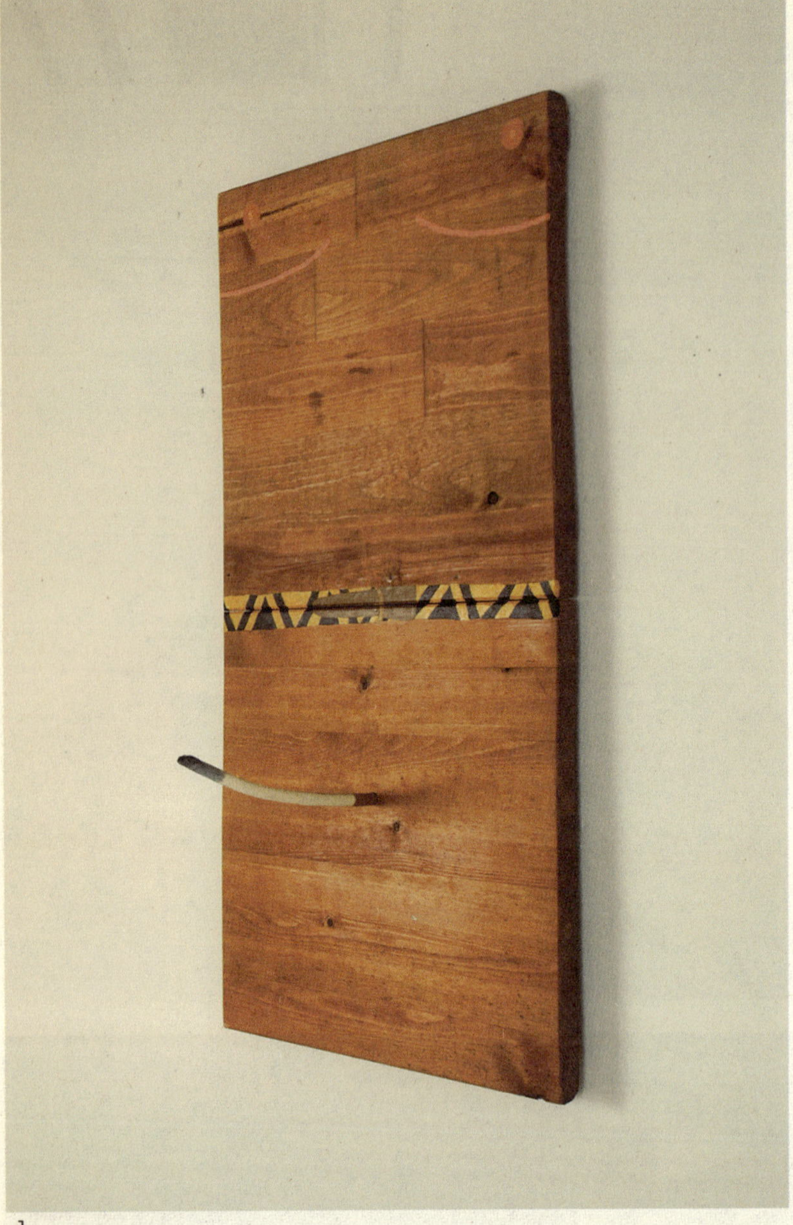
1.

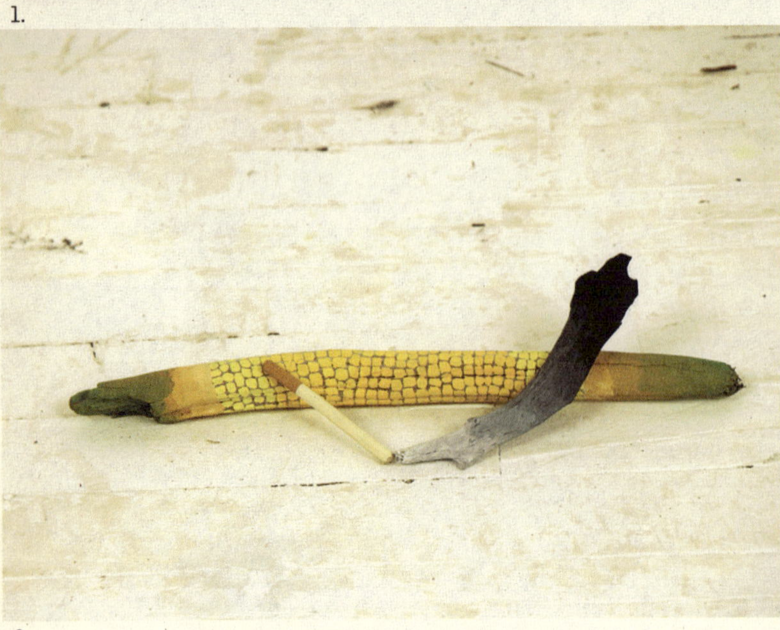
2.

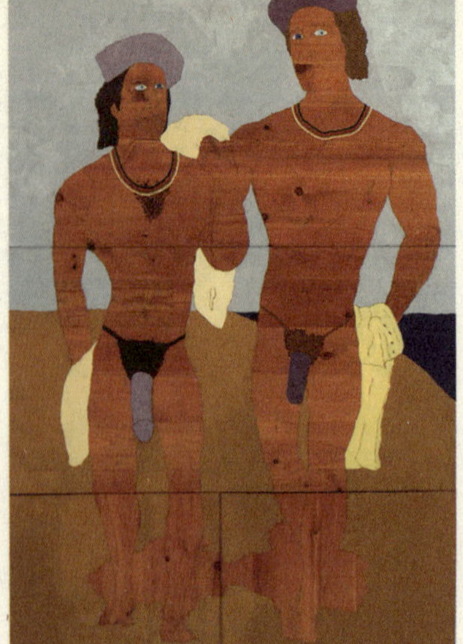
3.

Leidy Churchman is an MFA candidate at Columbia University and currently lives in Brooklyn. With the aim of making "transgender pictures," his practice of painting is informed by transitions, the humor of uncertainty, and the relationships of supposed opposites. He uses an illustrative style to infuse familiar objects, environments, and human interactions with absurd or sexual dimensions.

1. **Outfit**
2007, oil on wood, 23 ½ × 12 × 5 ½ in (57 × 31 × 14 cm)

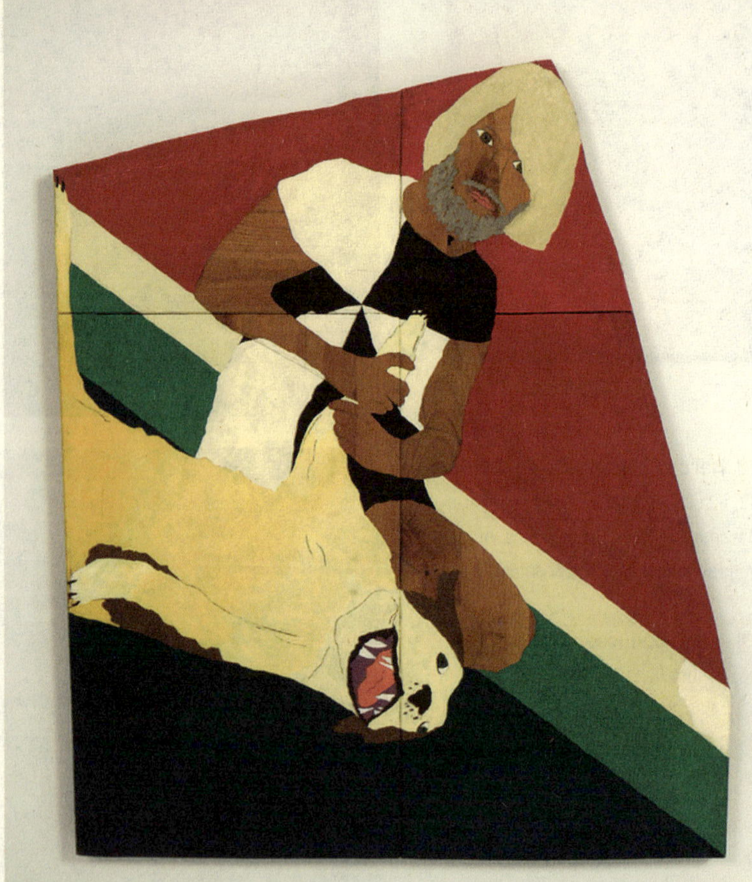
4.

2. **Corn and Cig!**
2007, acrylic gouache on wood, 4 × 12 ½ × 3 in (10 × 32 × 8 cm)

3. **Purple Pals**
2007, oil on wood, 31 ½ × 23 ½ in (80 × 60 cm)

4. **Dutch**
2007, oil on wood, 28 × 23 ½ in (71 × 57 cm)

Rob Churm earned his BA from the Glasgow School of Art and continues to live in Glasgow. He makes drawings using felt-tip and ballpoint pen and India ink on paper, combining surreal characters, gestural marks, dense cross-hatching, and references to Japanese illustration. He is also the front man of No Wave band Park Attack and designs posters and T-shirts.

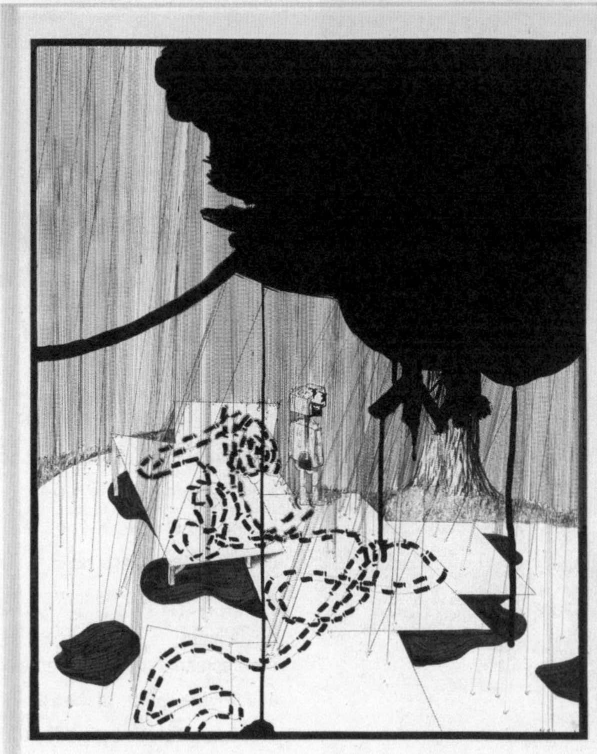

1.

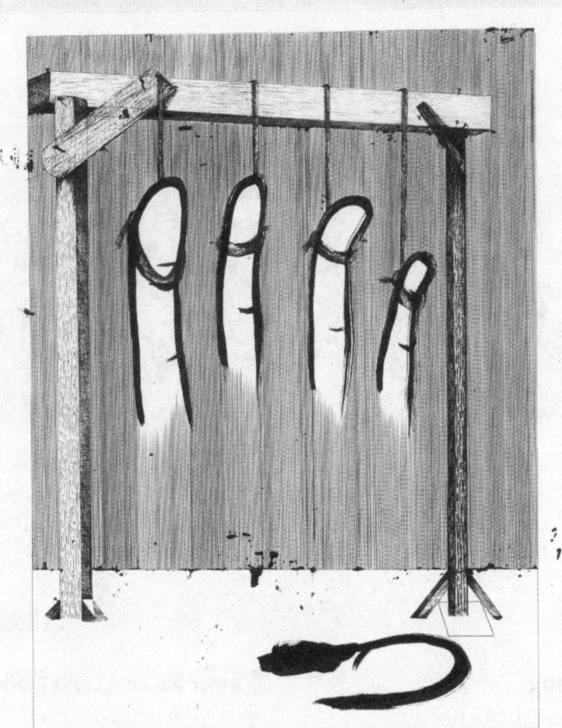

2.

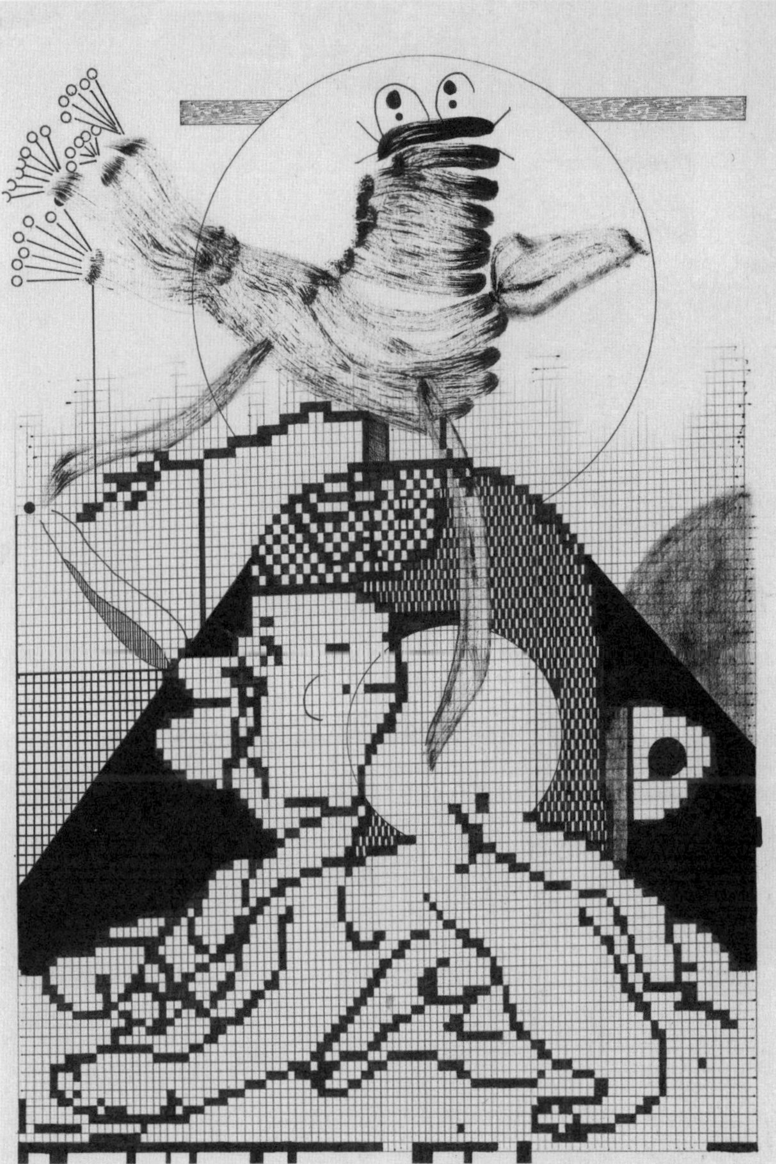

3.

1. more in the way of failure
2007, felt-tip pen, India ink, and ballpoint on paper in frame, 29 × 24 ½ in (74 × 62 cm)

2. this is my hand I can move it
2007, India ink, ballpoint, and felt-tip pen on paper, 24 ¼ × 20 ½ in (64 × 52 cm)

3. the tweeter
2008, felt-tip pen, India ink, and ballpoint on paper in frame, 16 ½ × 12 in (42 × 30 cm)

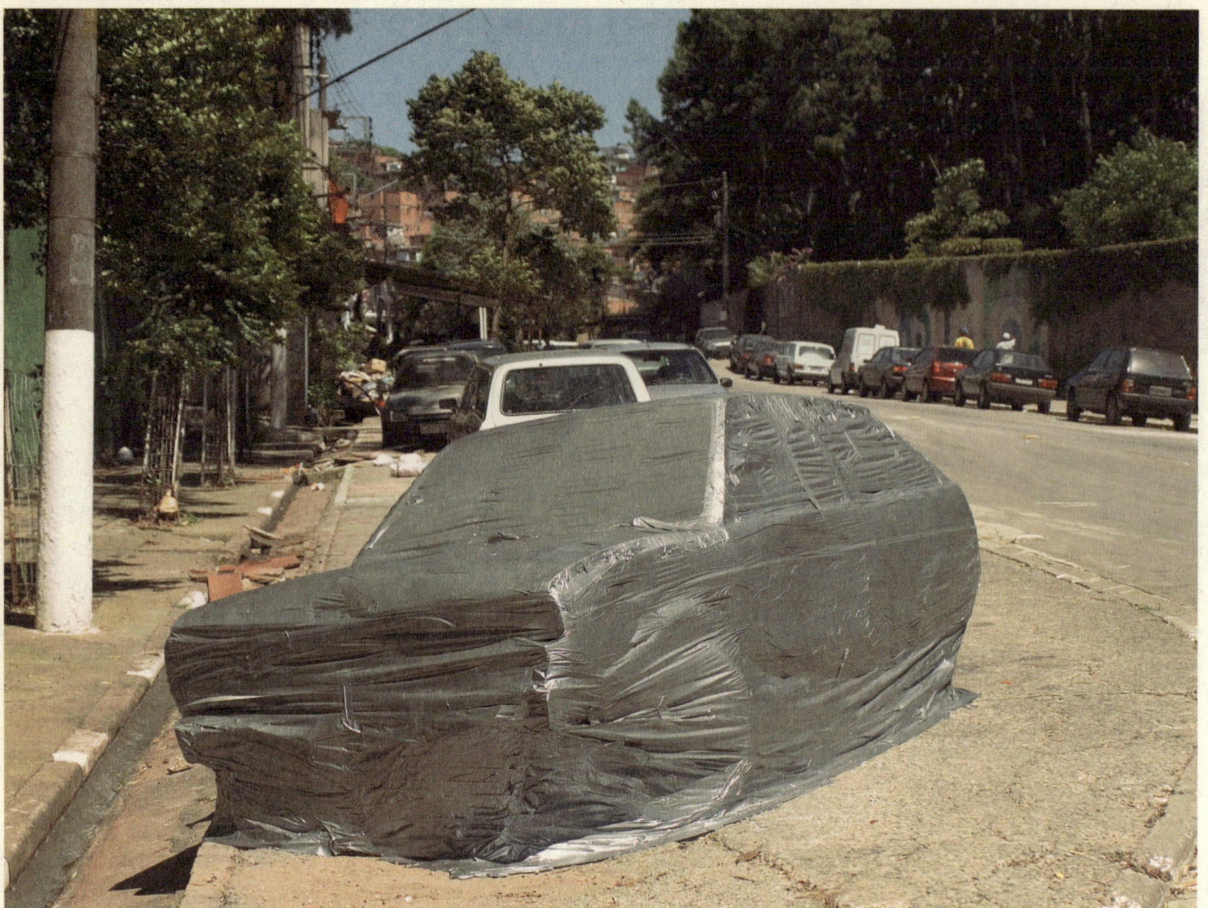

1.

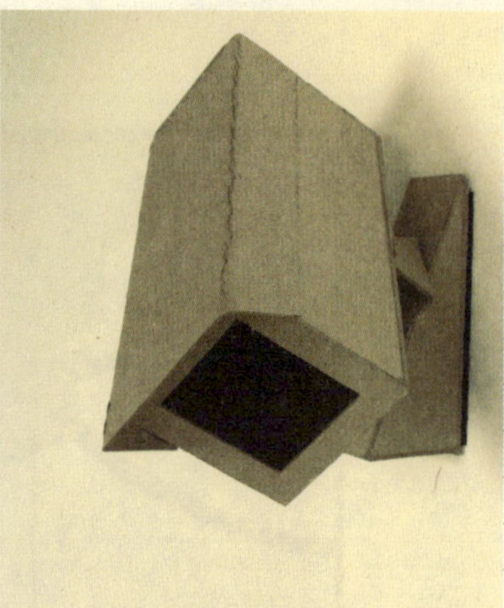

2.

A background as a graffiti artist has led Marcelo Cidade to his current practice, linking street culture with the language of contemporary art. His installation, performance, and video works take up themes of risk, surveillance, urban development, and the dynamics of public and private space. In the 2006 installation **Transestatal**, he built a fountain in the gallery space from a massive accumulation of debris found in the streets of São Paulo.

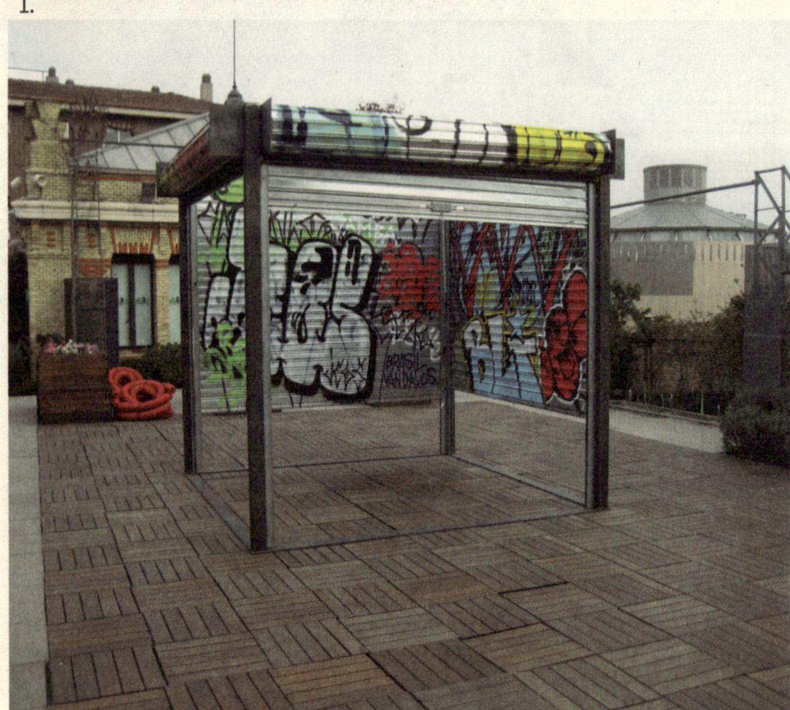

3.

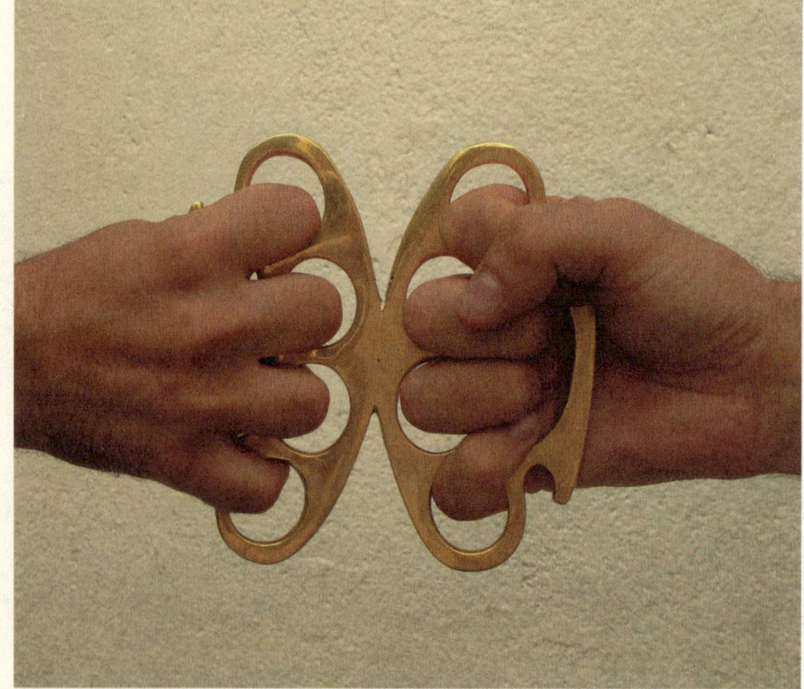

4.

1. Eu preciso estar seguro de você 2
2006, color photograph, $15\frac{3}{4} \times 23\frac{1}{2}$ in (40 × 60 cm)

2. Direito de Imagem
2004, cardboard, $10\frac{1}{2} \times 10\frac{1}{2} \times 9$ in (27 × 27 × 23 cm)

3. Espaço Entre
2008, mixed media, 10 × 10 × 10 ft (3 × 3 × 3 m)

4. Amor e ódio á Lygia Clark
2006, brass, $5\frac{3}{4} \times 5 \times \frac{1}{4}$ in (15 × 13 × 1 cm)

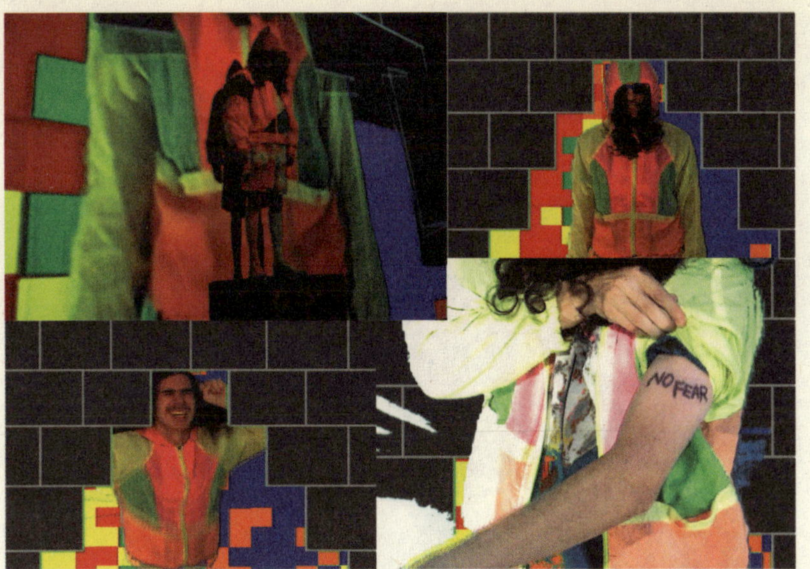

1.

Jacob Ciocci earned his BA in computer science and art from Oberlin College and currently lives in Pittsburgh. With Ben Jones and sister Jessica Ciocci, he is a founding member of the collective Paper Rad, which injects cultural critique into fun-loving, playful celebration. Digital collage and montage are central motifs in his video, animation, performance, sound, book, and Internet-based works.

1. **No Fear**
2004, live performance with video, 4 min 30 sec

2. **Umbrella Zombie Datamosh Mistake**
with Paul Davis
2007, hacked video, sound, 1 min 30 sec

3. **Extreme Animals The Movie Part 1**
with Paper Rad and Matthew Ryan Barton
2005, animatronic road kill, thrift-store animals, and 3-channel video, 96 × 96 in (244 × 244 cm)

4 & 5. **Don't Worry Be Happy**
2006, video and animation, sound, 3 min 30 sec

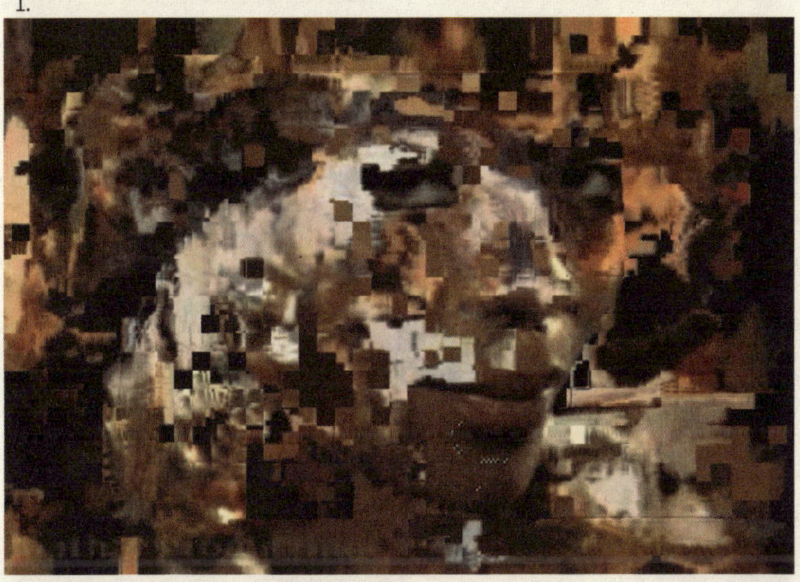
2.

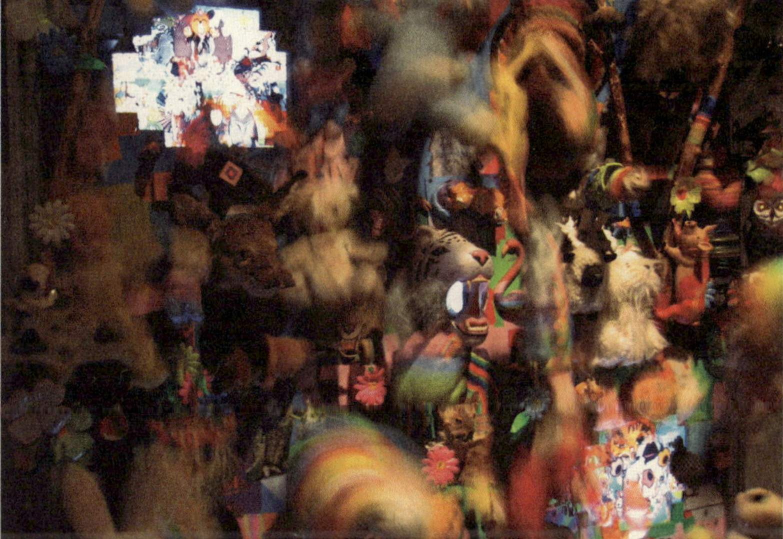
3.

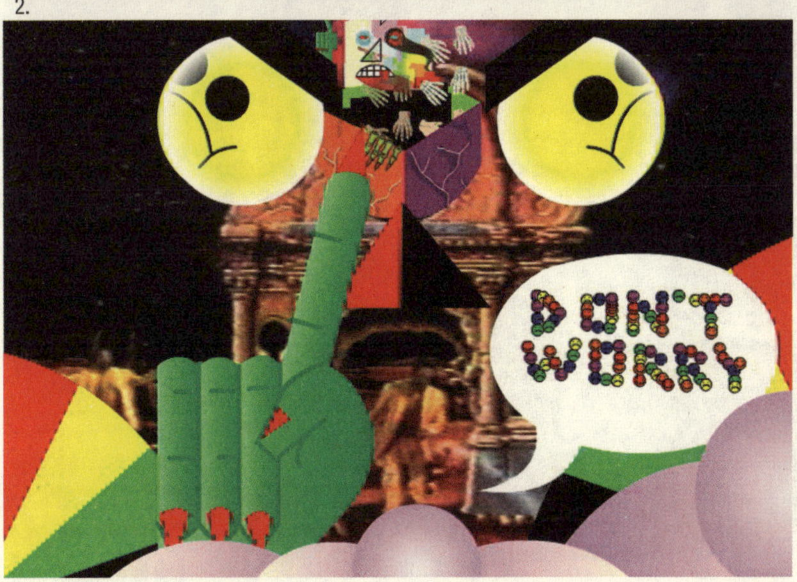

4.

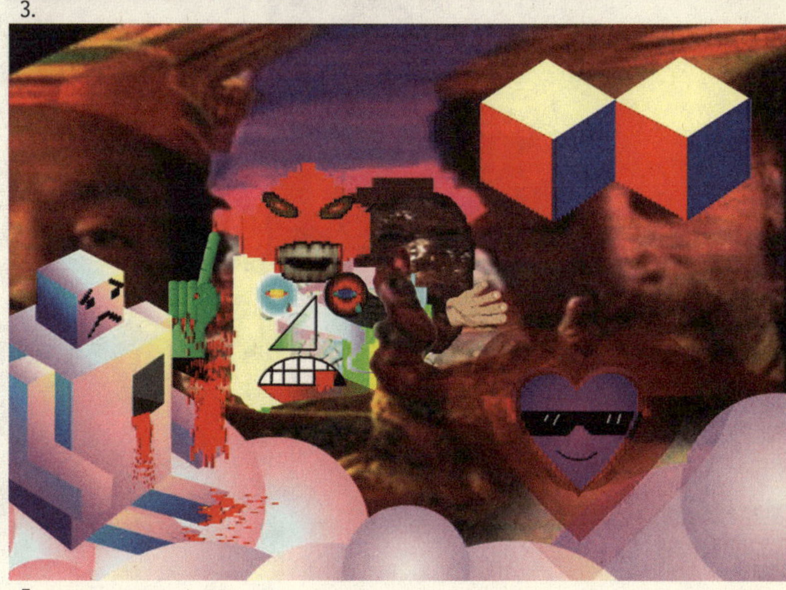
5.

CIRIO, PAOLO

b. 1979 Turin, Italy

Paolo Cirio earned a degree from the University of Turin in 2005, where his dissertation on performance in information spaces drew on his experience as a media activist. He was awarded a Rhizome Commission in 2006 for **Google Will Eat Itself**, a collaboration in which artists used money made from Google ads to buy the company's shares. He has organized urban interventions in several cities, with illegal exhibitions that blocked off streets. Cirio's installations for more conventional venues make common settings and visuals unfamiliar, like airport security checkpoints and corporate logos, to heighten awareness of the limits imposed by power structures

1 & 2. **Check Check Reality**
with Nina Roth
2007, mixed media, 12 × 12 × 12 in
(31 × 31 × 31 cm)

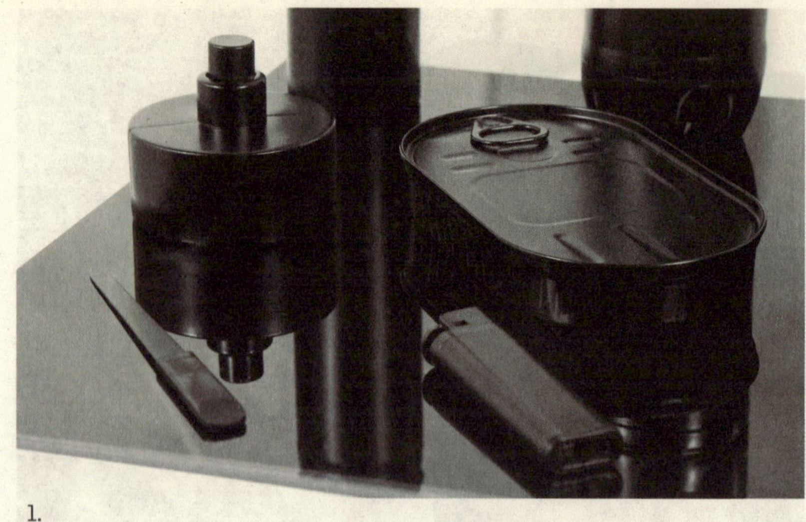

1.

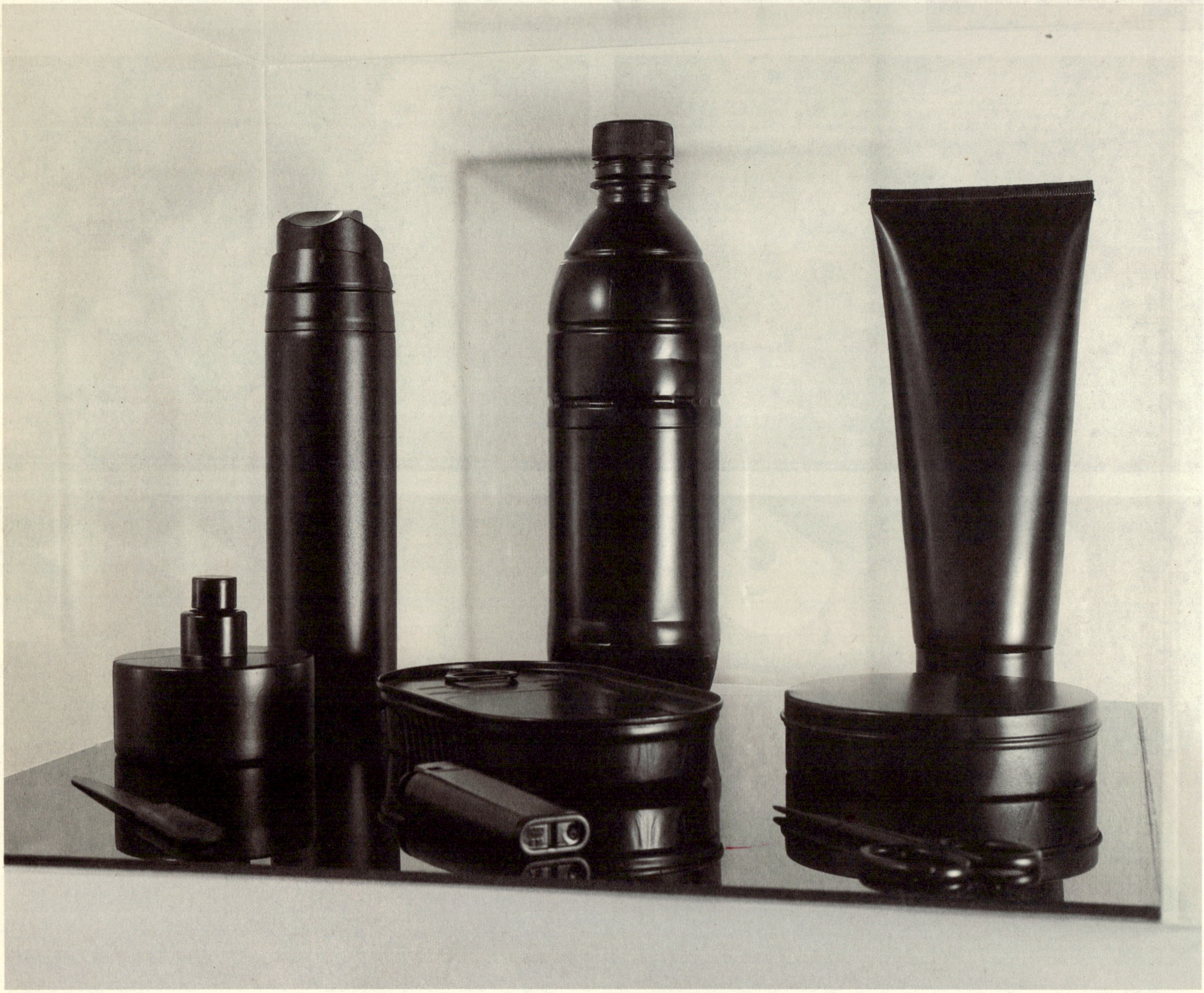

2.

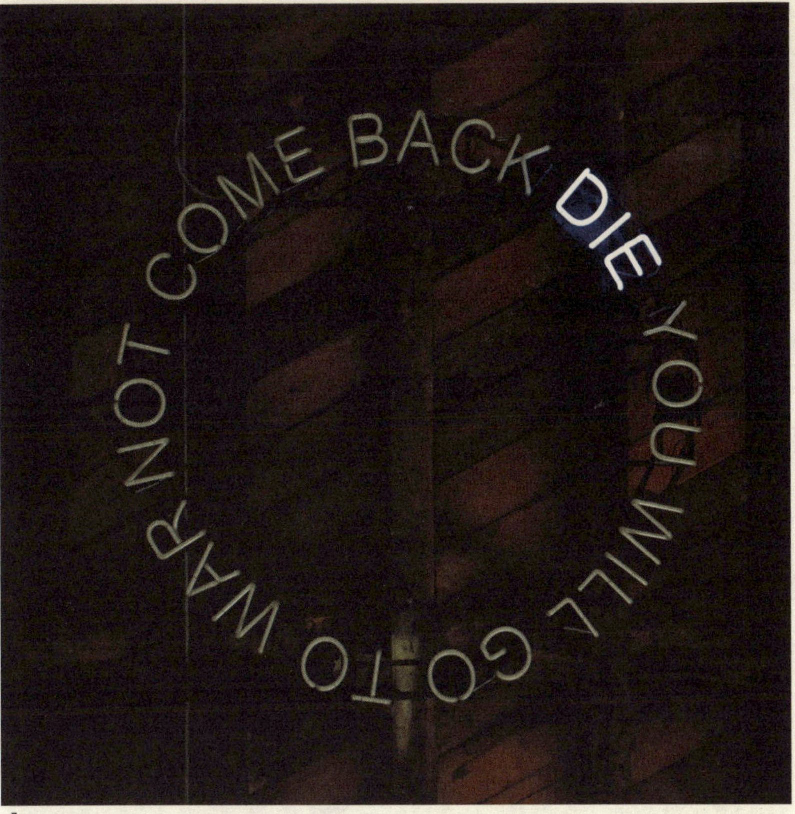

1.

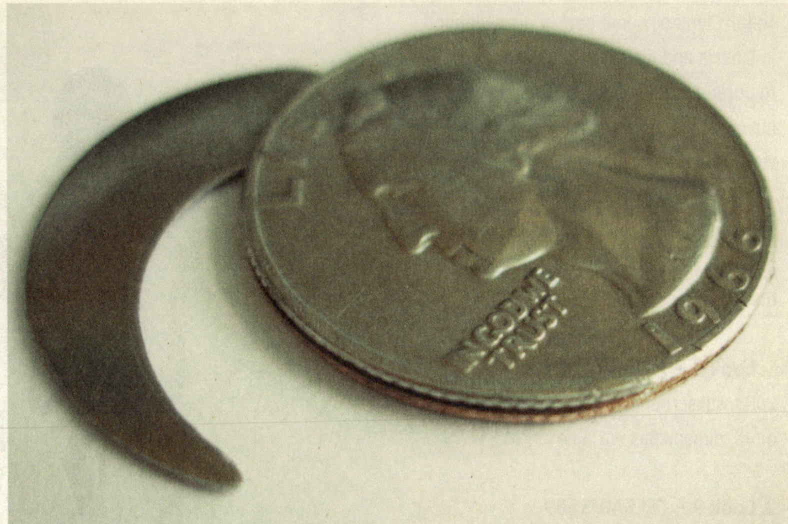

2.

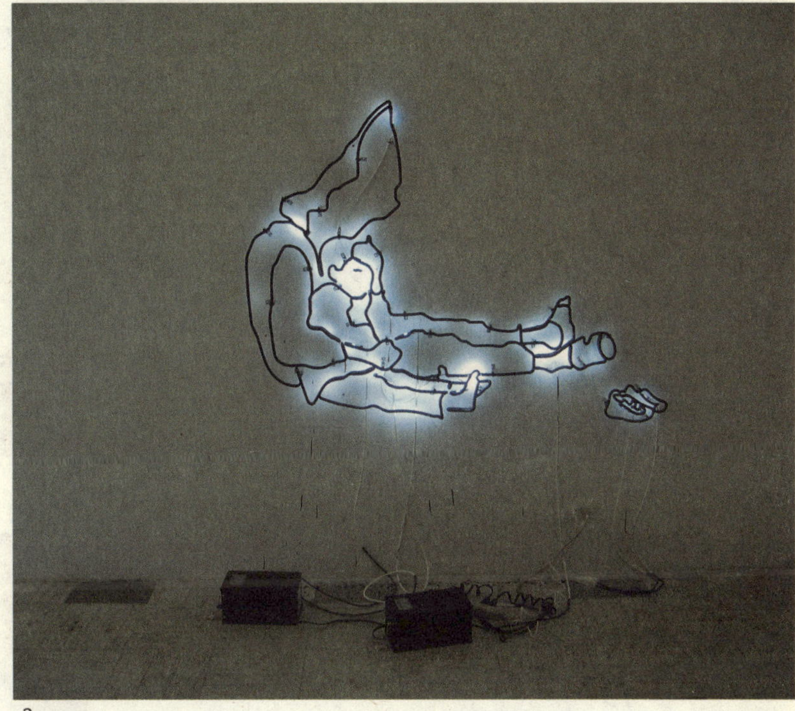

3.

Claire Fontaine is a collective based in Paris whose name is lifted from a popular brand of French school supplies. Identified by the singular feminine subject, she is a self-declared "readymade" artist forming a practice of and around political impotence.

1. **Ibis redibis non morieris in bello**
2006, neon, electronic programmer, cabling, framework, 9 lampfittings, and lamps, dimensions variable

2. **In God They Trust**
2005, coin, steel box-cutter blade, solder, and rivet, diameter 1 in (3 cm)

3. **Father and Son (Prisoner with child)**
2005, neon, oil-based paint, cabling, transformers, 59 × $31\frac{1}{2}$ in (150 × 80 cm)

4. **371 Grand**
2006, alloy, 2 × 4 in (5 × 10 cm)

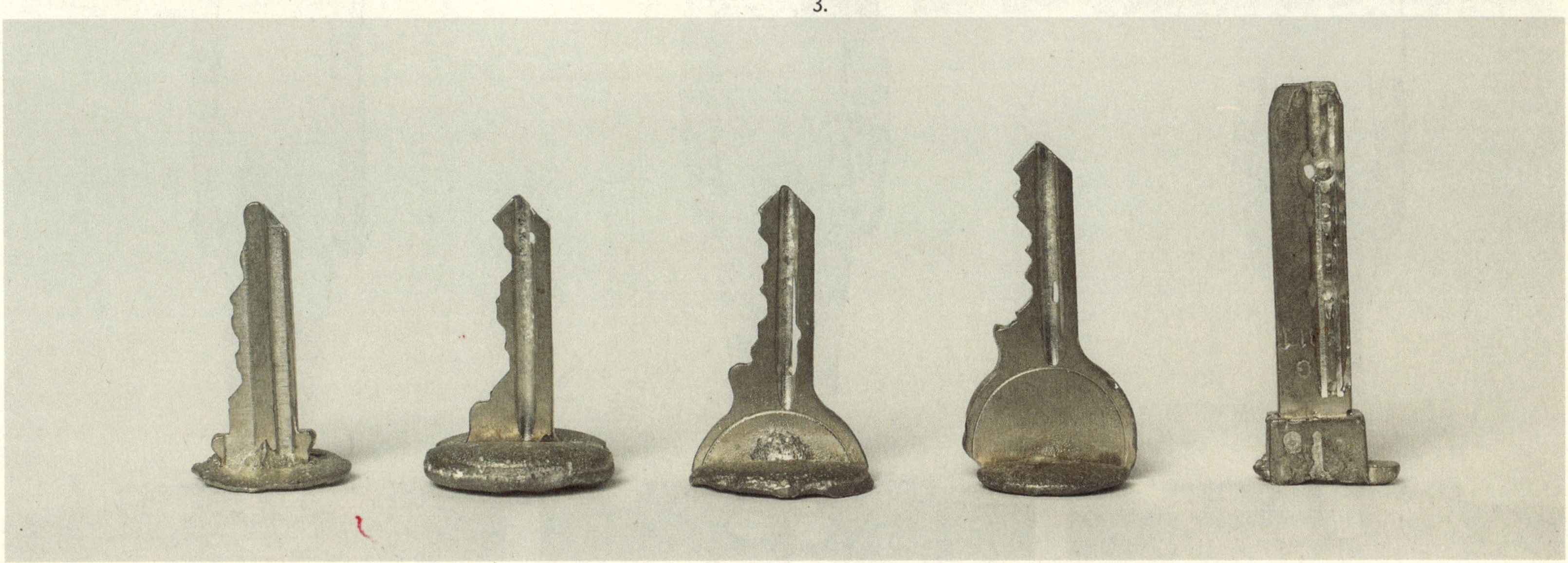

4.

Telfar Clemens spent part of his childhood in Liberia and moved to New York in 2002 to pursue modeling. He began designing his own fashion collection by reassembling vintage clothing and launched his label TELFAR in 2004. His current designs for men and women are based on his principle of "simplexity" and often include unique color, draping, and material.

1. **Look 3 – TELFAR**
2008, silkscreened tank dress with bicycle motif, dimensions variable

2. **Look 9 – TELFAR SS09**
2008, unisex mesh tank dress with matching backpack, dimensions variable

3. **Look 10 – TELFAR SS09**
2008, sport-inspired menswear, dimensions variable

4. **Look 16 – TELFAR**
2008, denim collection with attached jumpsuit, dimensions variable

5. **Look 19 – TELFAR SS09**
2008, menswear denim and sport collection, dimensions variable

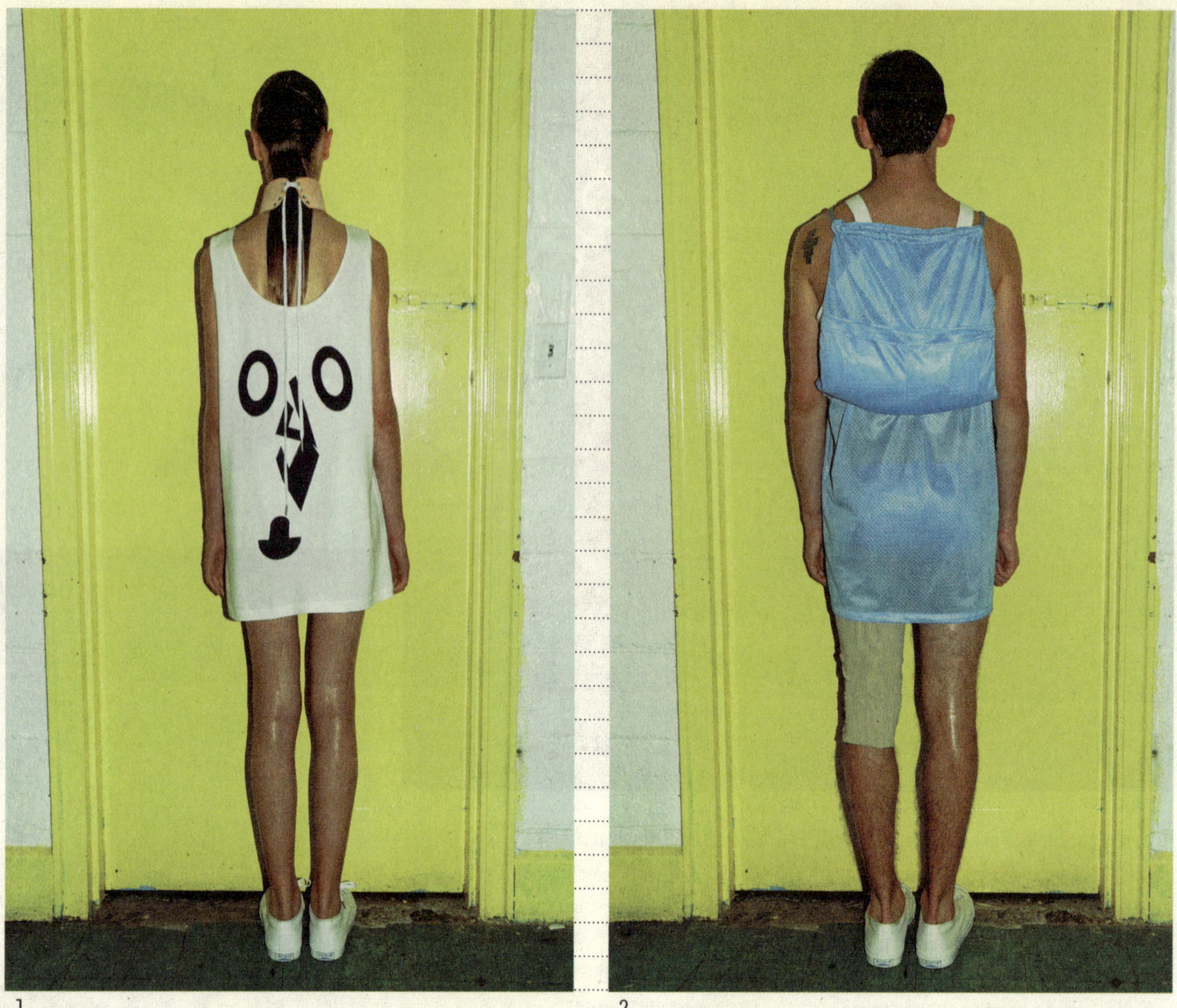

1. 2.

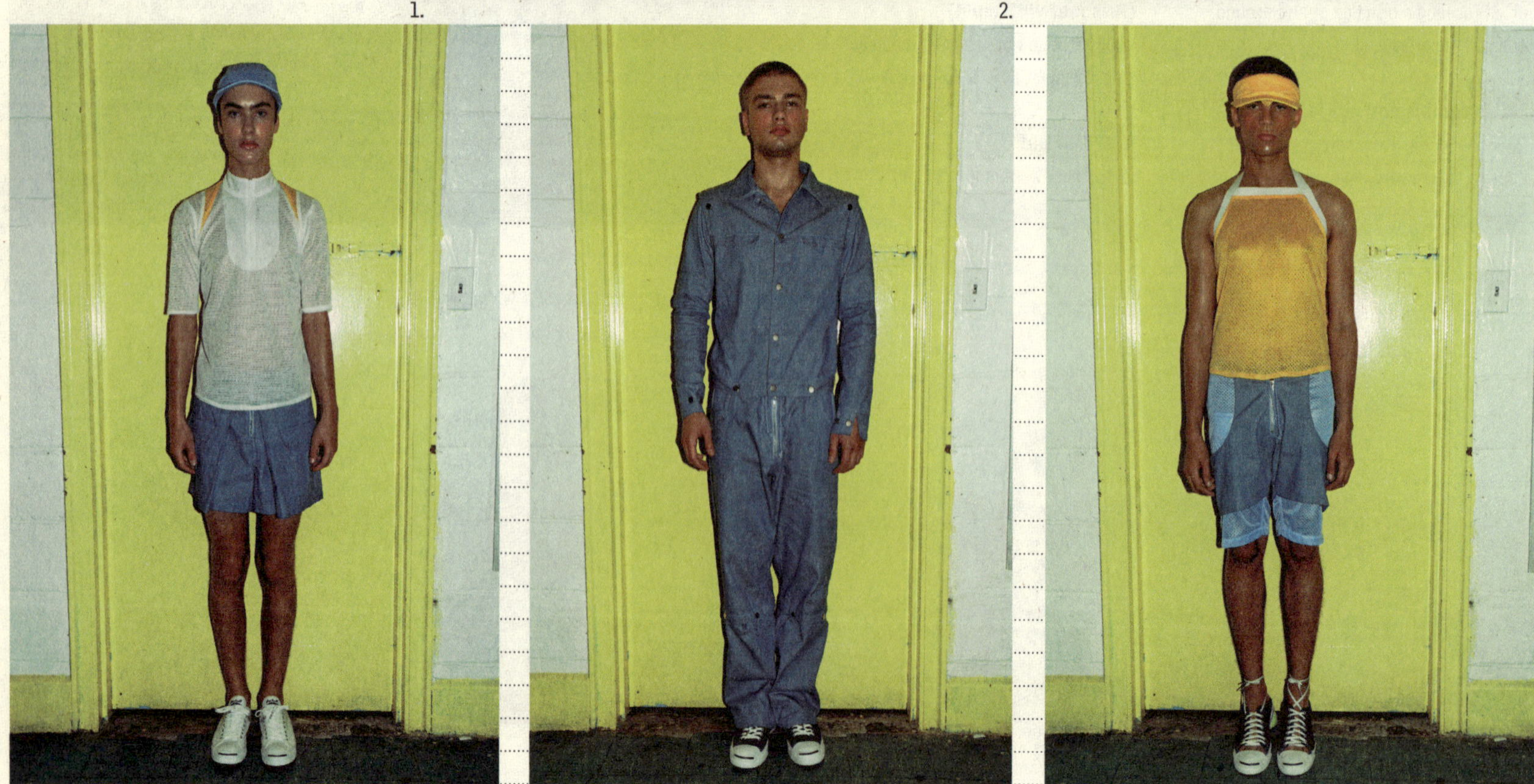

3. 4. 5.

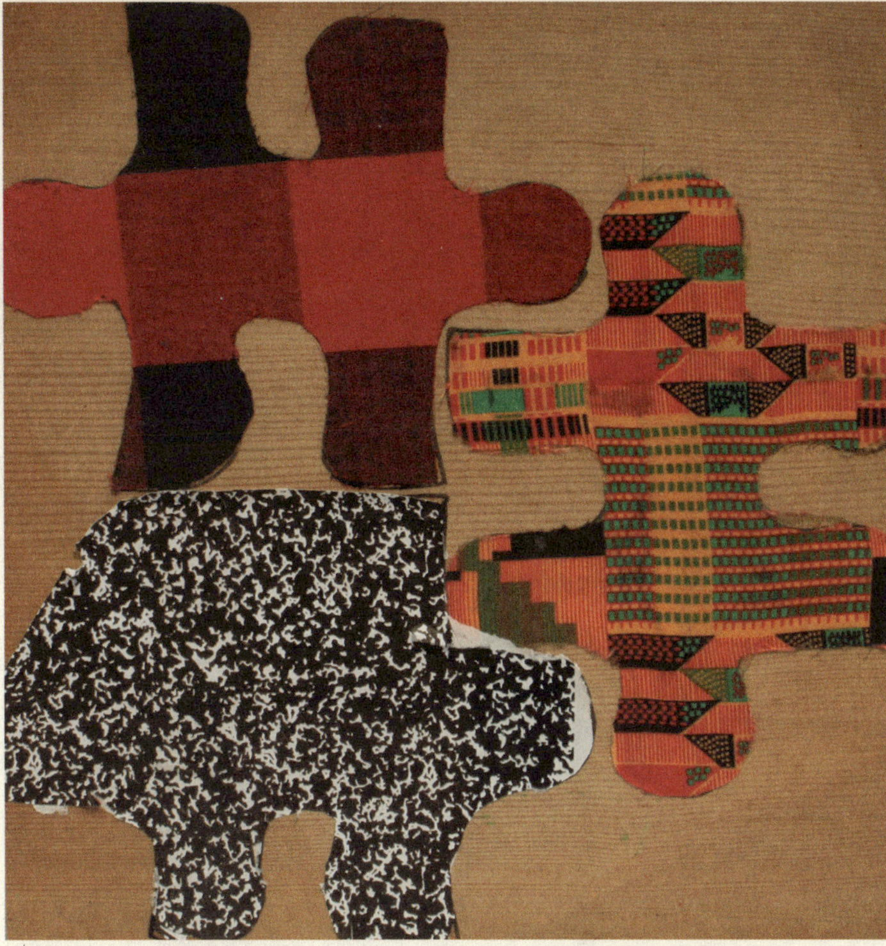

1.

2.

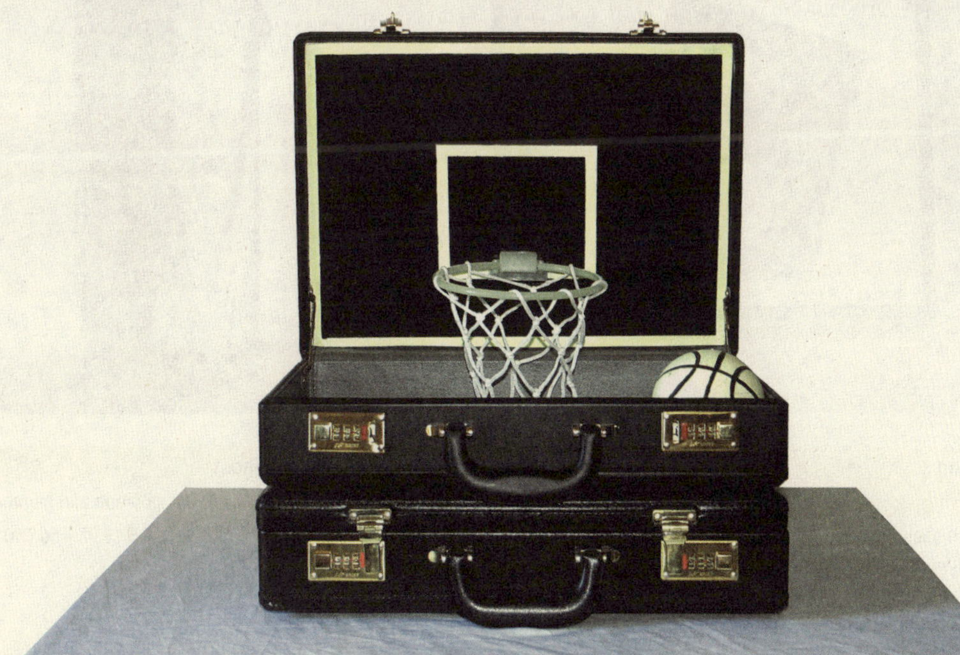

3.

Sara Clendening earned a MFA from the Mountain School of Arts in Los Angeles, where she currently lives and works. Her sculptures and installations operate on unlikely manipulations of familiar objects – a scattering of puzzle pieces with incompatible shapes and patterns; a can of soda on a pedestal under a glass box sprayed with liquid, as if the beverage exploded inside; a reworking of the office toy that illustrates principles of Newtonian mechanics, for which the artist replaced ball bearings with model cars. By introducing elements of conflict and violence to harmless objects, Clendening suggests that chaos is always near.

1. Untitled
2007, wood, fabric, and paper, 20 × 20 in (51 × 51 cm)

2. Fun Sponge
2007, tie-dyed canvas and sponge, 24 × 18 in (61 × 46 cm)

3. Night Court
2008, briefcases, basketball nets, basketball, and glow paint, 18 × 22 in (46 × 56 cm)

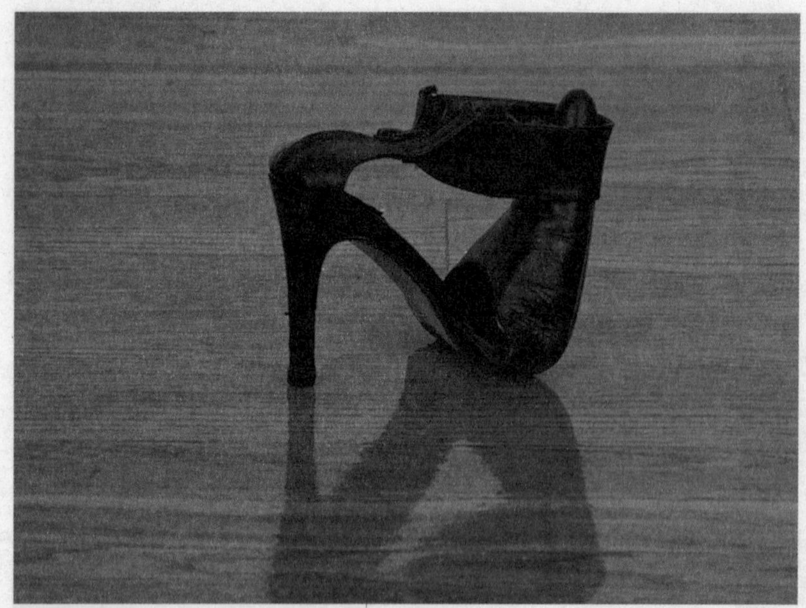
1.

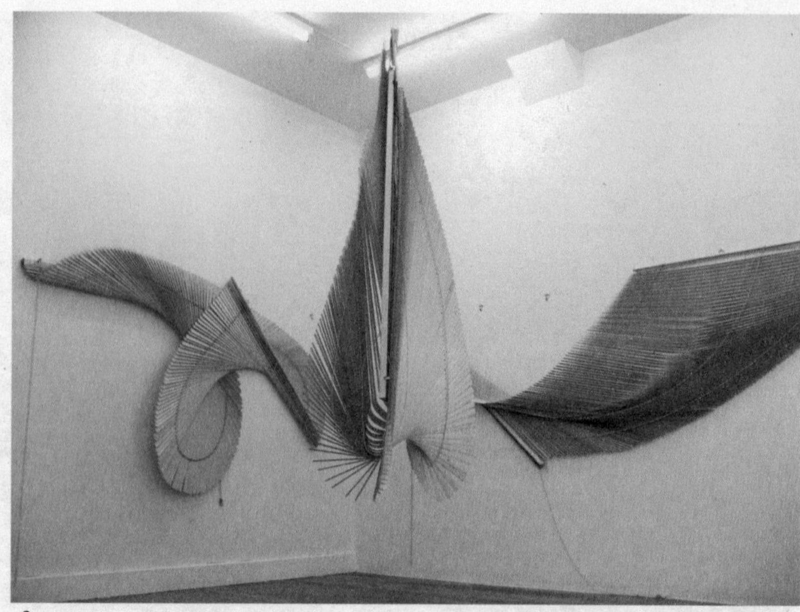
2.

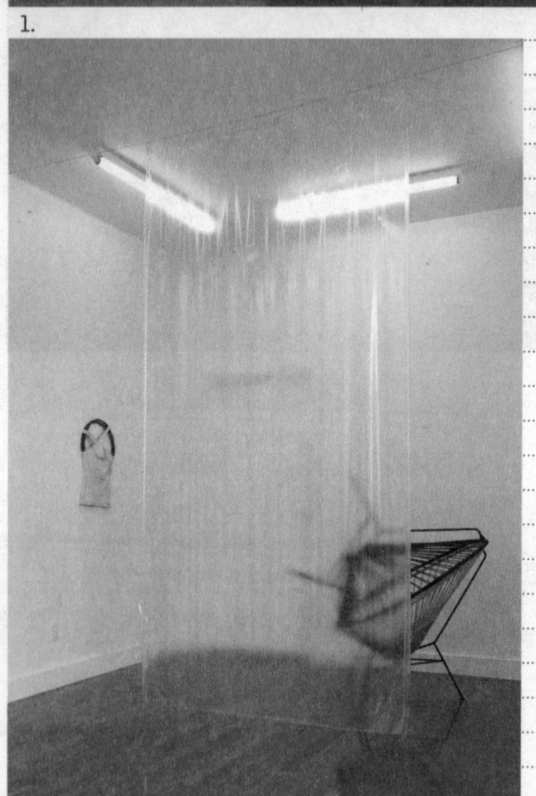
3.

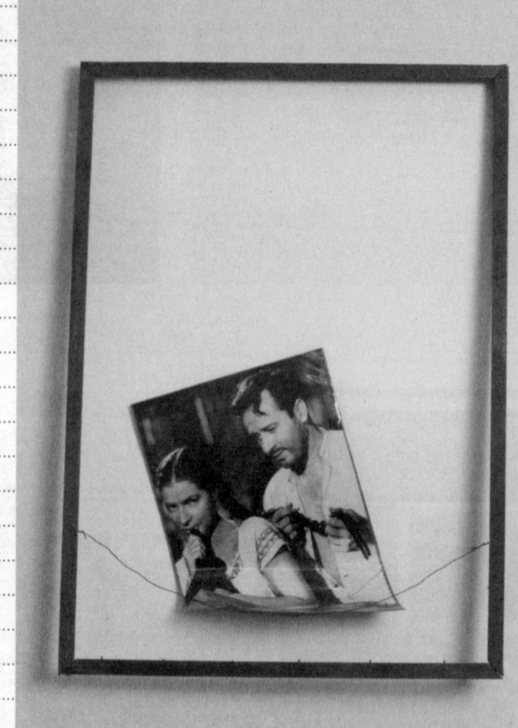
4.

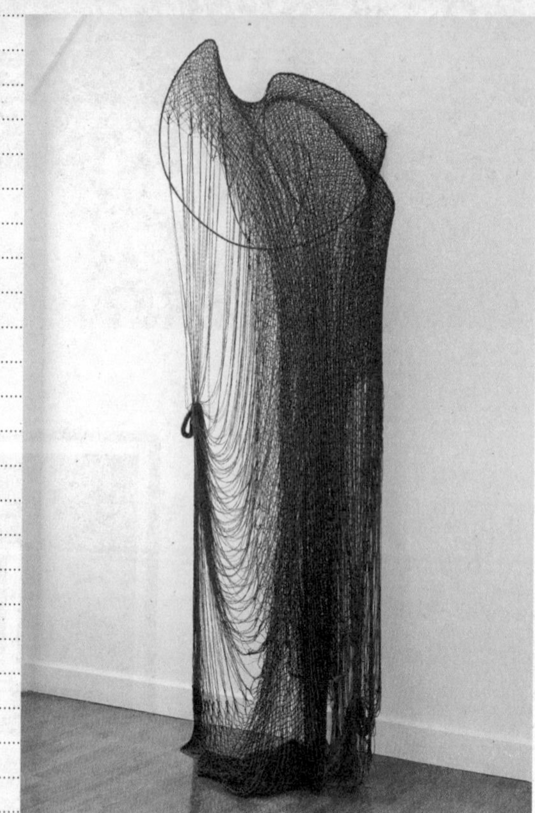
5.

Mexico City-based sculptor Martin Soto Climent combines ordinary, recognizable objects like beer bottles, high heels, and bicycle parts in tenuous sculptures. Through simple transformations, he examines the values of, and relationships between, objects – as seen in his set of Venetian blinds twisted into birdlike form.

1. **Paseo Detenido** (Arrested Walk)
2008, vintage high-heeled shoe, $6\frac{1}{4} \times 4\frac{1}{4} \times 4\frac{1}{4}$ in (16 × 11 × 11 cm)

2. **Paraboloide de Polvo** (Parabolic Dust)
2007, 6 gray Venetian office blinds, each 90 × 54 in (228 × 137 cm), total dimensions variable

3. **Espacio Nebuloso** (Blurry Space)
2008, vinyl, body imprint, and wire, 106 × 60 in (270 × 153 cm)

4. **Couple**
2008, vintage frame and black and white photograph (poster by Pedro Infante), $31\frac{1}{2} \times 23\frac{1}{2} \times 8$ in (80 × 60 × 20 cm)

5. **Ghost**
2008, wire composition and hammock, 100 × 38 × 22 in (257 × 97 × 56 cm)

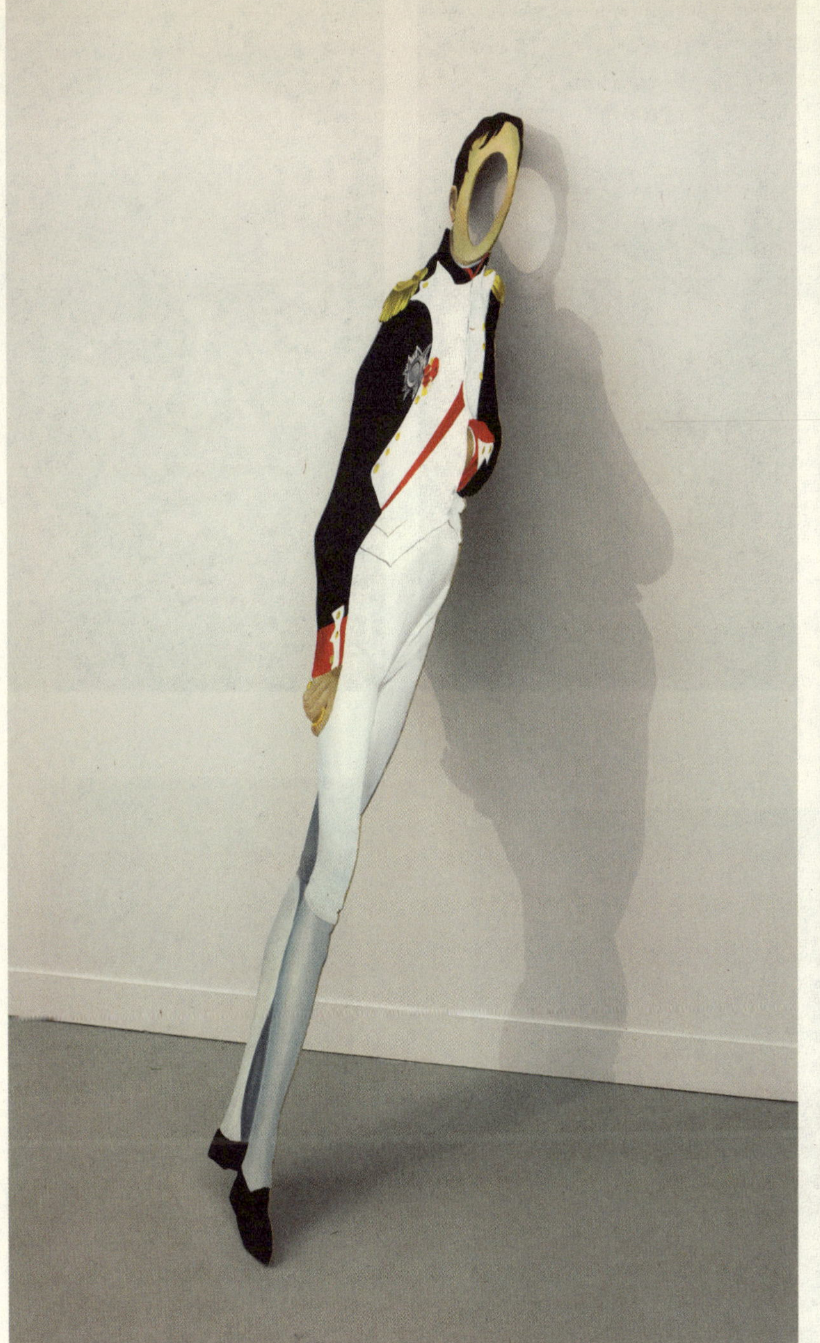

1.

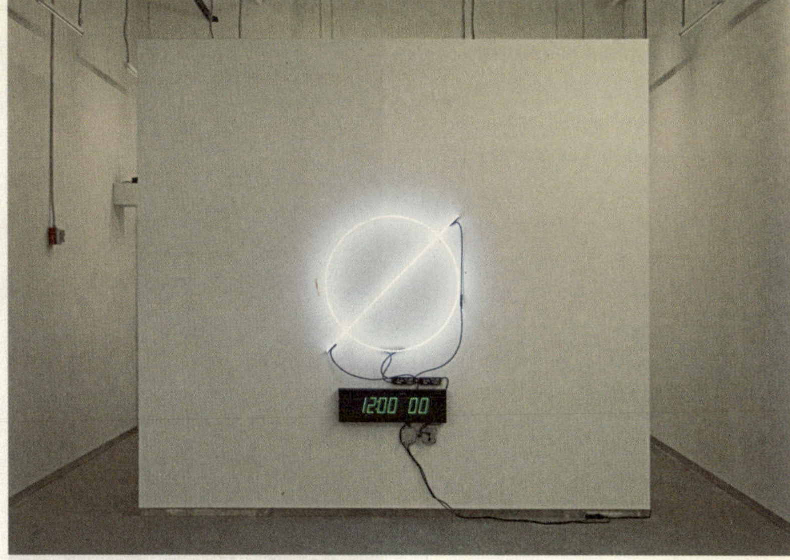

2.

3.

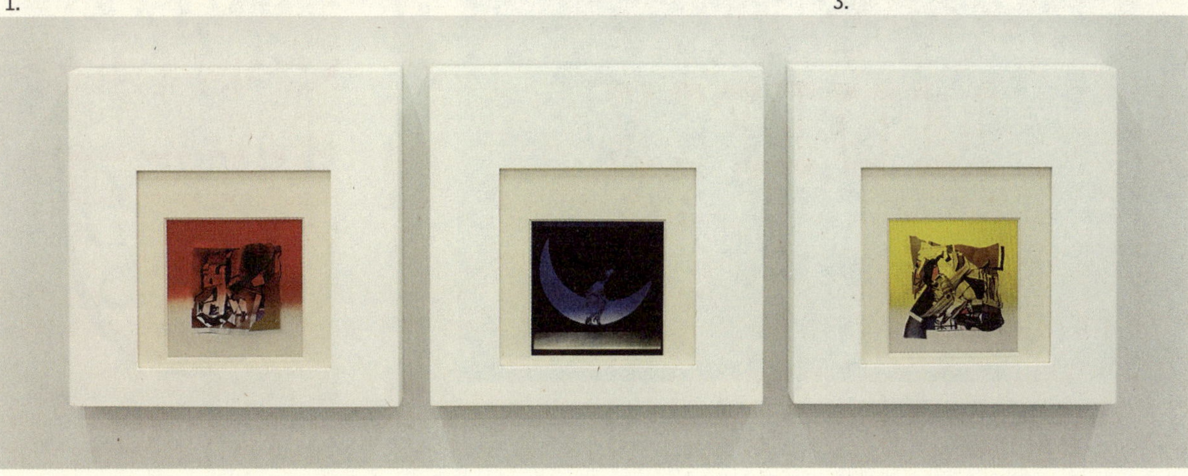

4.

Tyler Coburn received his BA from Yale University in 2006 and currently lives in New York. His conceptual practice explores conditions of image-making and storytelling in a world of accelerating technologies. Producing actions, objects, photographs, and videos, he frequently collaborates with other artists and also writes regularly on art for several publications and blogs.

1. **5' 2"**
2007, acrylic on Masonite, spotlight, and shadow, 62 × 18 in (158 × 46 cm)

2. **Twice Over**
with Benjamin Farnsworth
2008, digital clock and neon, dimensions variable

3. *****
2007, laminated digital chromogenic print on Sintra, 67 × 32 in (170 × 81 cm)

4. **Homage to Red, Homage to Blue, Homage to Yellow**
2008, three archival pigment prints, frames, and mats, each 11 × 11 in (28 × 28 cm)

London-based Lucy Coggle has degrees in English literature and fine art. Her practice begins with traditions of figure drawing and portraiture reimagined through unpredictable juxtapositions of text. Narrative fragments, non sequiturs, and quirky aphorisms are presented alongside images like advertising slogans to open a discourse on gender, culture, and communication.

1. Babes of the Month
2006, acrylic on paper, each 26 × 14 ½ in (66 × 37 cm)

2. Posters (muffin)
2006, pencil, spray paint, and acrylic on paper, 51 × 38 ½ in (130 × 98 cm)

3. Posters (walkway)
2006, pencil, spray paint, and acrylic on paper, 51 × 38 ½ in (130 × 98 cm)

4. Posters (Seems, Madam?)
2006, pencil, spray paint, and acrylic on paper, 51 × 38 ½ in (130 × 98 cm)

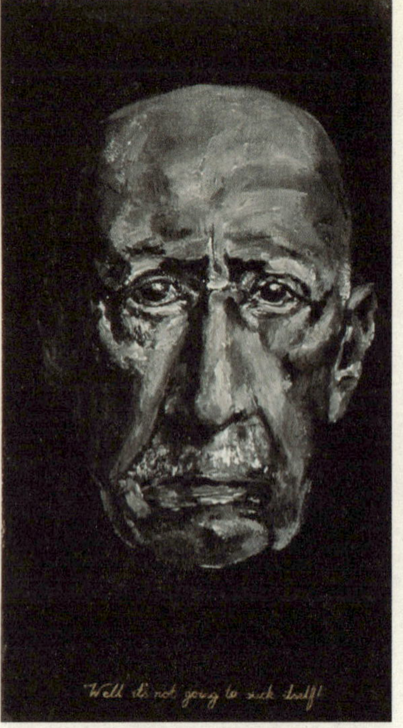
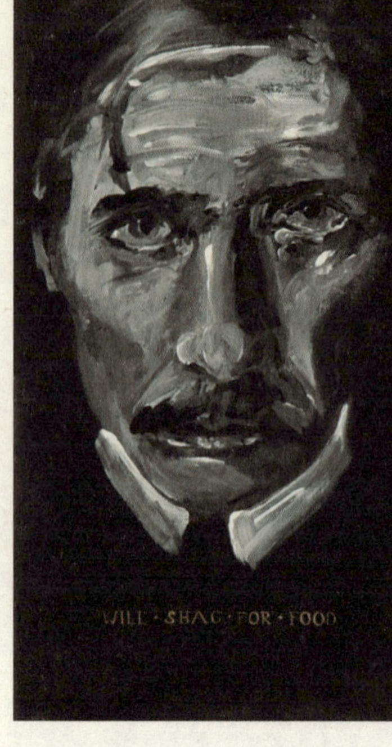

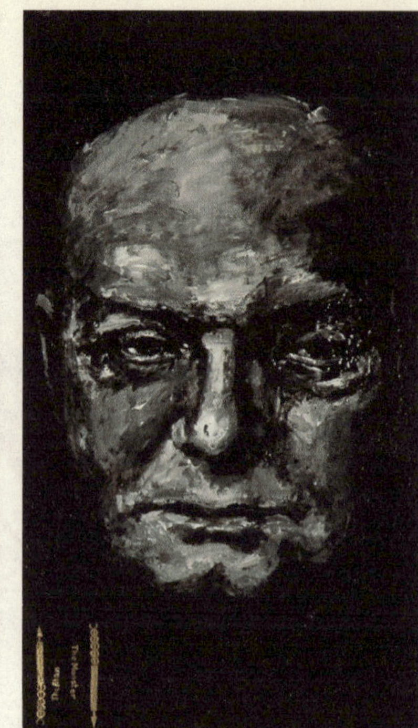
1.

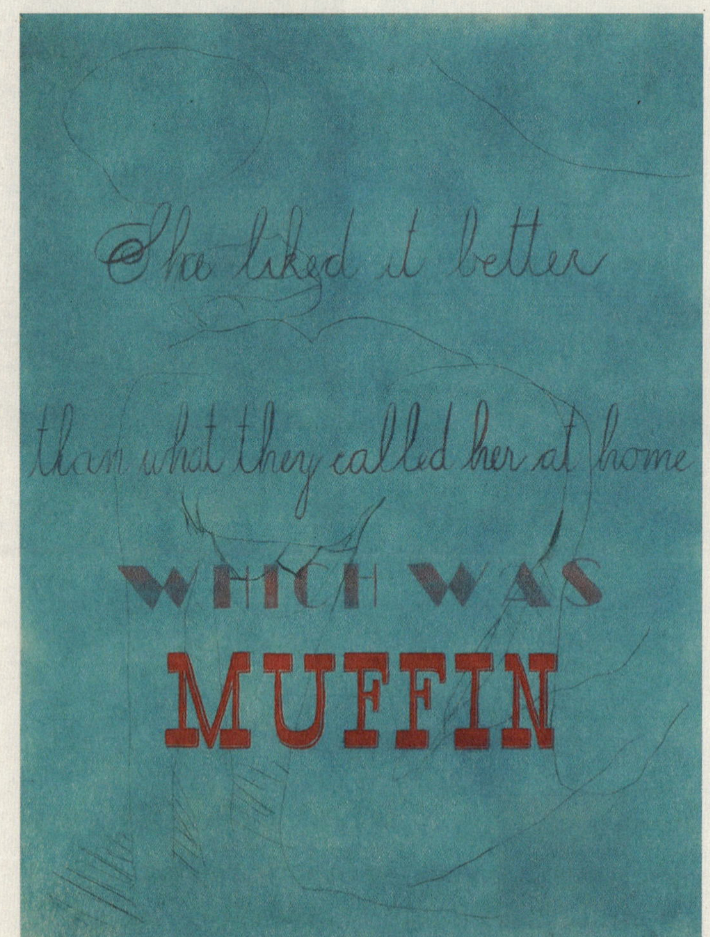

2.

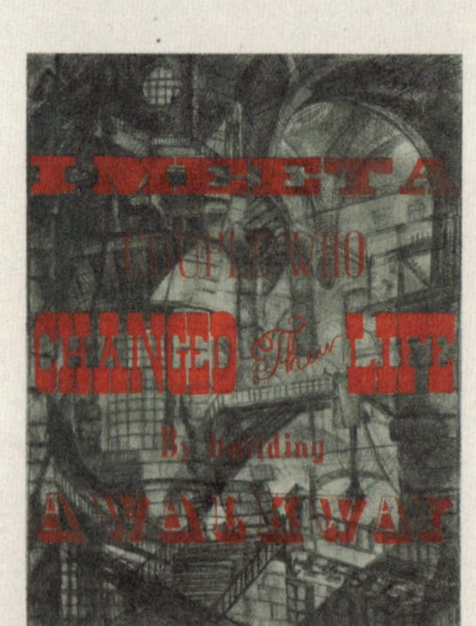

3.

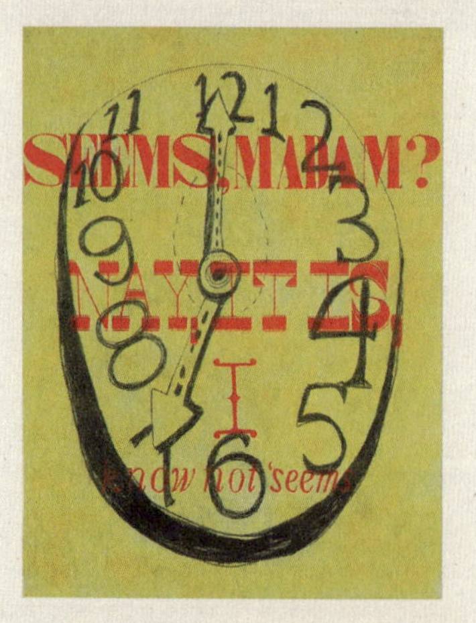

4.

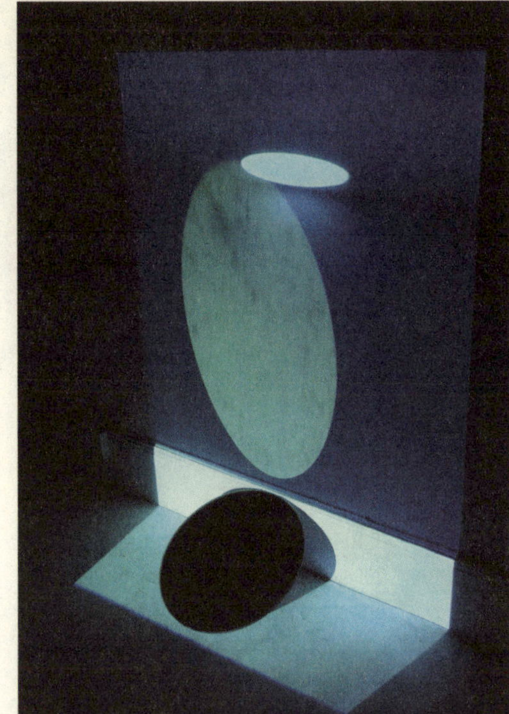

1.

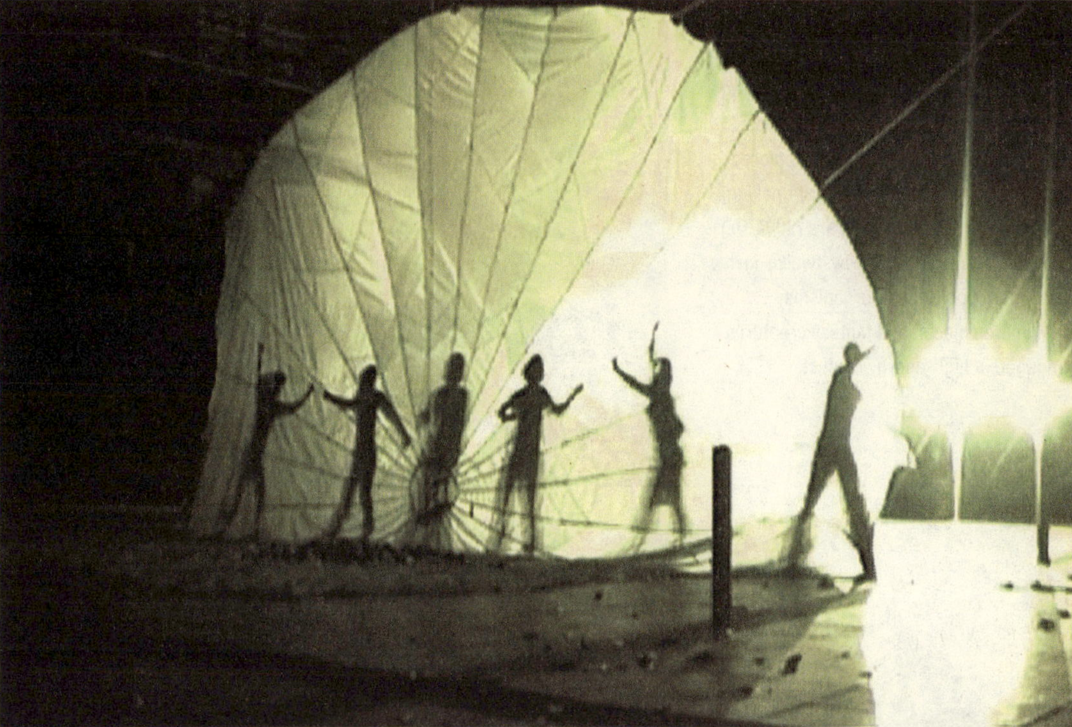

2.

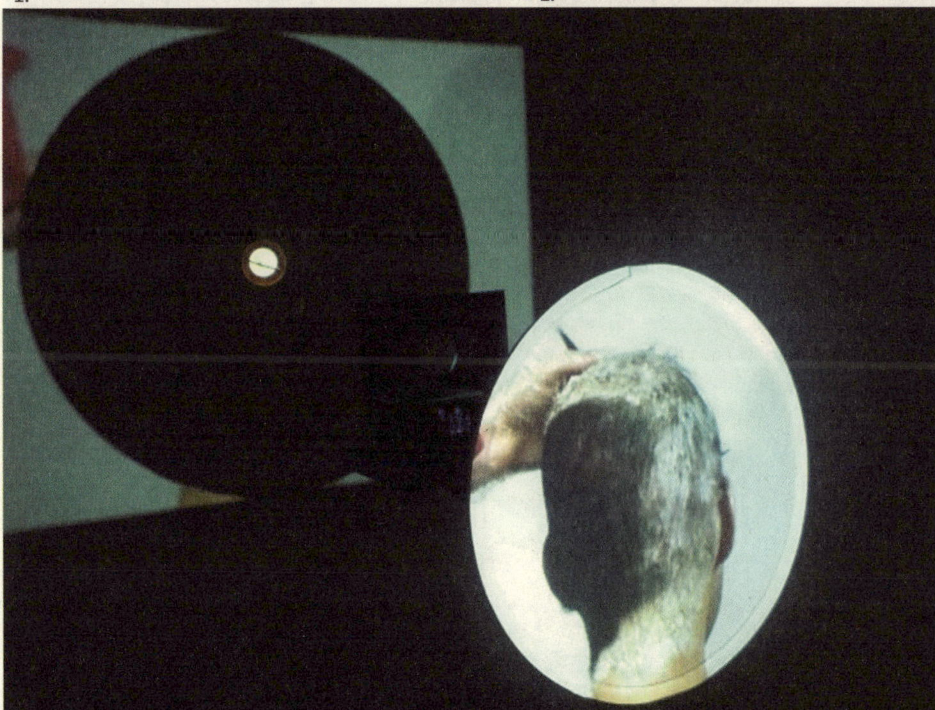

3.

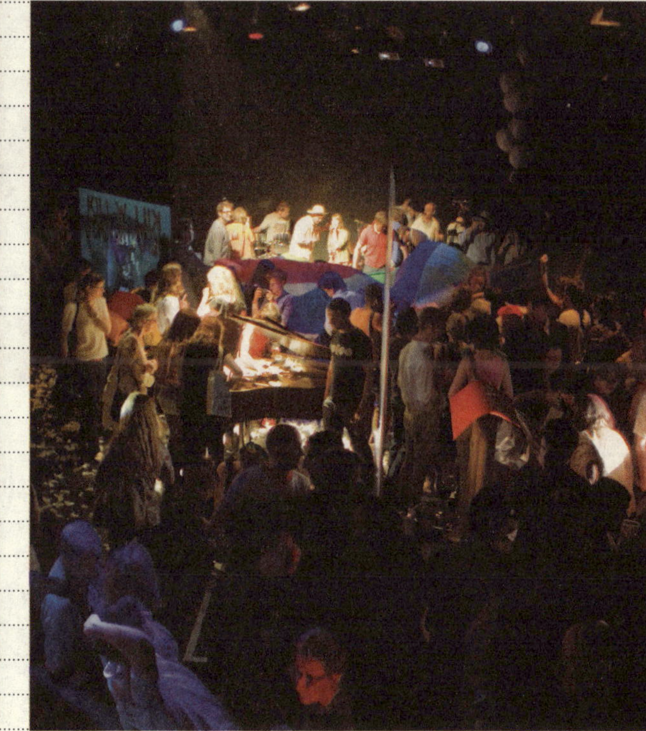

4.

Kim Coleman and Jenny Hogarth describe their collaboration as "a discussion about creativity and making art as well as a model of teamwork and friendship." Both attended Edinburgh College of Art and continue to live in the UK (Coleman in London, and Hogarth in Glasgow and Edinburgh). Their work ranges from performance and participation – like their restaging of the 1965 Boyle Family happening **Oh What a Lovely Whore** – to recent experiments with video and light works.

1. Reflect
2008, data projector, C-stand, and mirror, $59 \times 78\ ^3\!/_4 \times 157\ ^1\!/_2$ in (150 × 200 × 400 cm); video, 3 min

2. Demonstration
2003, performance, army parachute, metallic and glow-in-the-dark giant confetti, live band, and theatrical lighting, 15 min

3. Affect
2008, 2 data projectors, $6\ ^1\!/_2 \times 6\ ^1\!/_2 \times 16\ ^1\!/_2$ ft (2 × 2 × 5 m); 2 videos, 20 min

4. Oh What a Lovely Whore
with the Boyle Family
2008, performance at the ICA, London

Ernest Concepcion earned his BFA from the University of the Philippines, Diliman, and currently lives in Brooklyn. Beginning with ink drawing on paper, his practice has expanded to include work in colored pencil, oil and acrylic paints, printmaking, and sculpture. **The Line Wars** (2004-07) consists of over 100 nine-by-twelve-inch drawings representing organisms, inanimate objects, and fantasy creatures engaged in high-energy conflict.

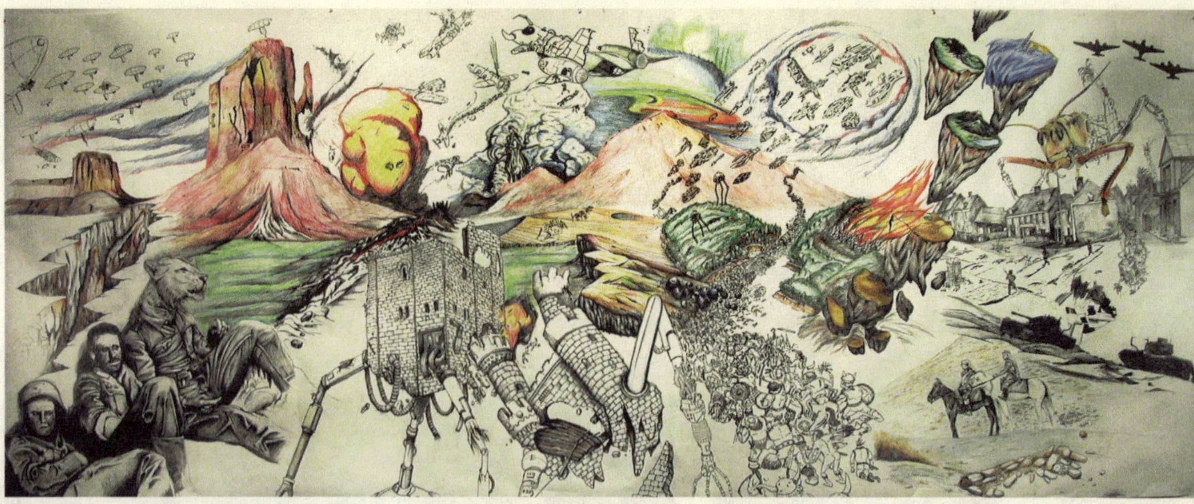

1.

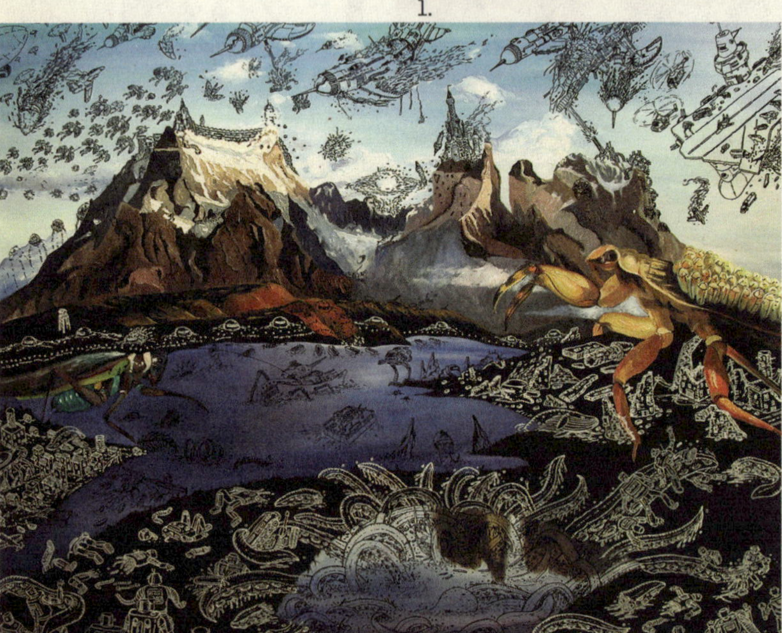

2.

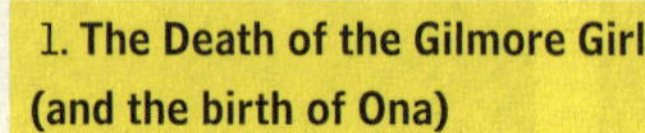

1. The Death of the Gilmore Girl (and the birth of Ona)
2006, ink, graphite, and colored pencil on paper, approx 6 × 12 ft (2 × 4 m)

2. An Introduction of Sorts (or how it affected my concerns regarding land invasion)
2006, oil and ink on canvas, 36 × 48 in (91 × 122 cm)

3. Rise Line Wars Rise (Putangina!)
2008, oil, colored pencil, enamel, and ink on paperboard, 30 × 20 in (76 × 51 cm)

4. I Saw Night & Syd (and the Tuber Attack)
2007, screenprint on paper, 34 × 25 in (86 × 64 cm)

5. Torpedo Bomber vs. Wasps
2006, oil on canvas, 48 × 48 in (122 × 122 cm)

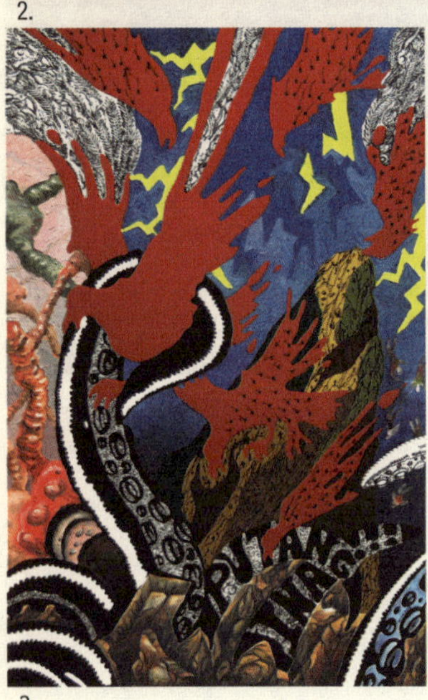

3.

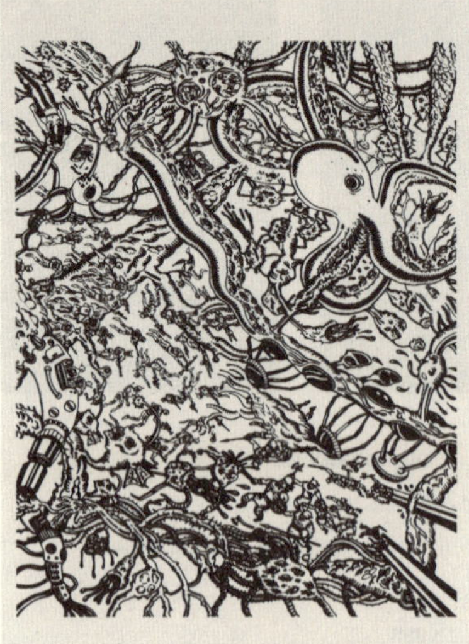

4.

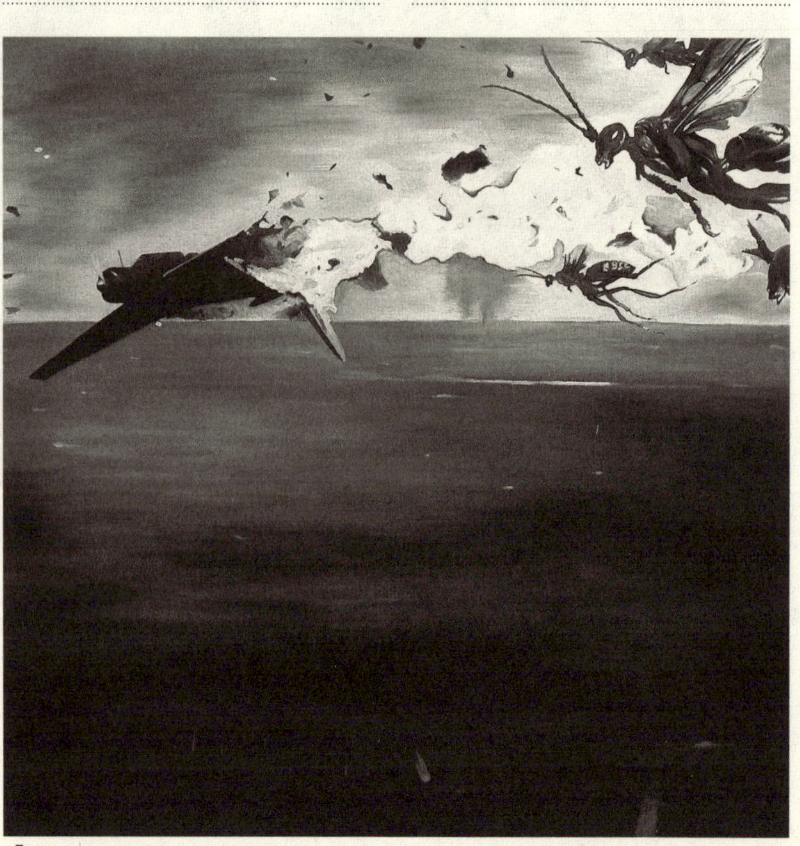

5.

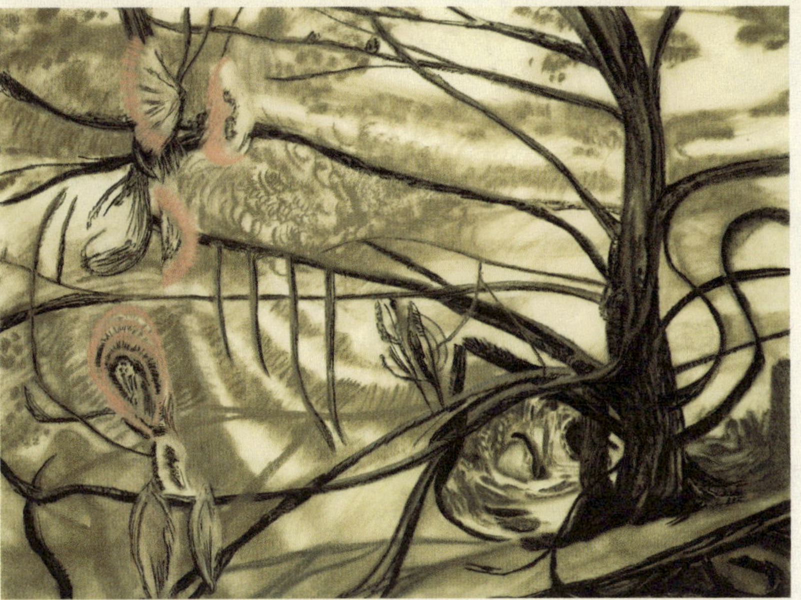
1.

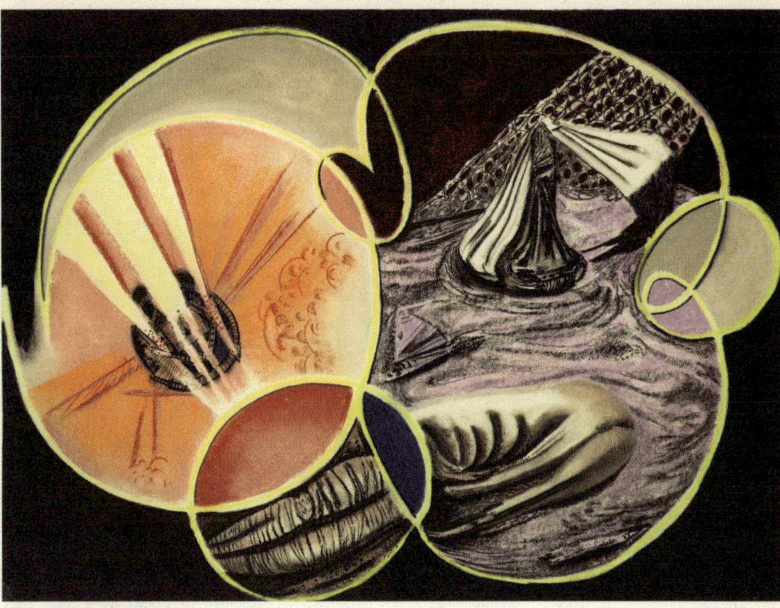
2.

Vanessa Conte earned her MFA from the University of California, Los Angeles, and currently lives in Düsseldorf, Germany. Her paintings and drawings weave organic forms, fantasy creatures, and references to landscape and the cosmos into abstract compositions. These works in paint, pastel, and charcoal suggest links between interior and exterior worlds.

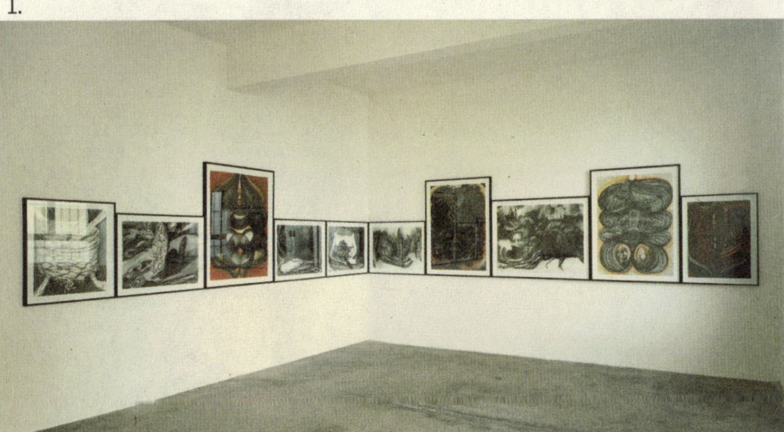
3.

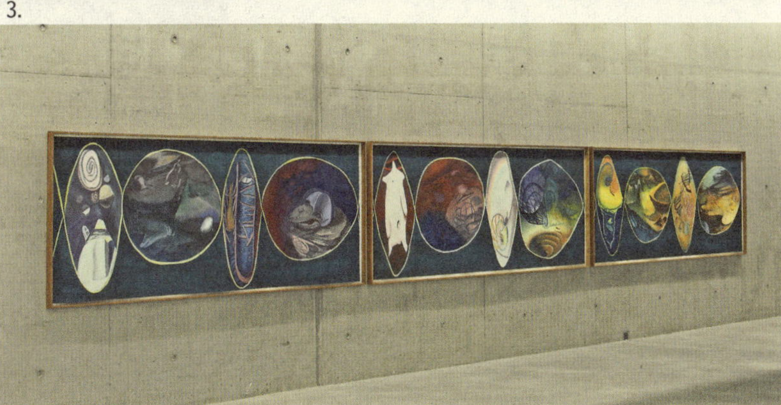
4.

1. Tired lids over tired eyes
2006, pastel on paper, 31 × 42 ½ in (79 × 108 cm)

2. Infinity Knot 1
2006, pastel on paper, 31 × 42 ½ in (79 × 108 cm)

3. "In The Moonlight"
exhibition view at Van Horn, Düsseldorf (2005-06)

4. Die Geschichte des Lebens erzählt von einer Molluske
2007, pastel on paper, 3 panels, each 59 × 118 in (150 × 300 cm)

5. Dorothea
2008, oil on canvas, 31 ½ × 24 in (80 × 61 cm)

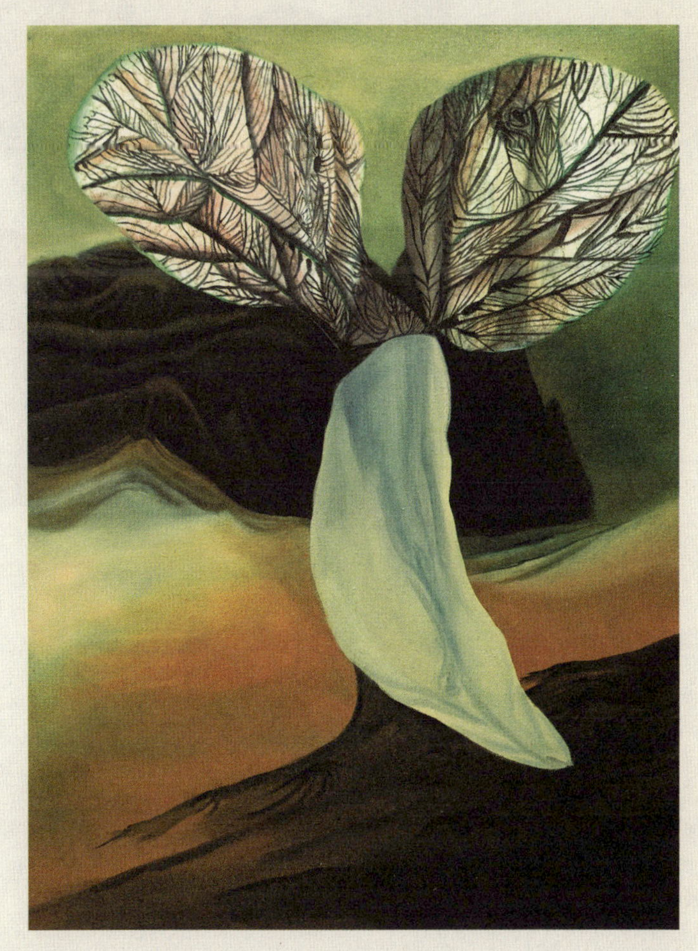
5.

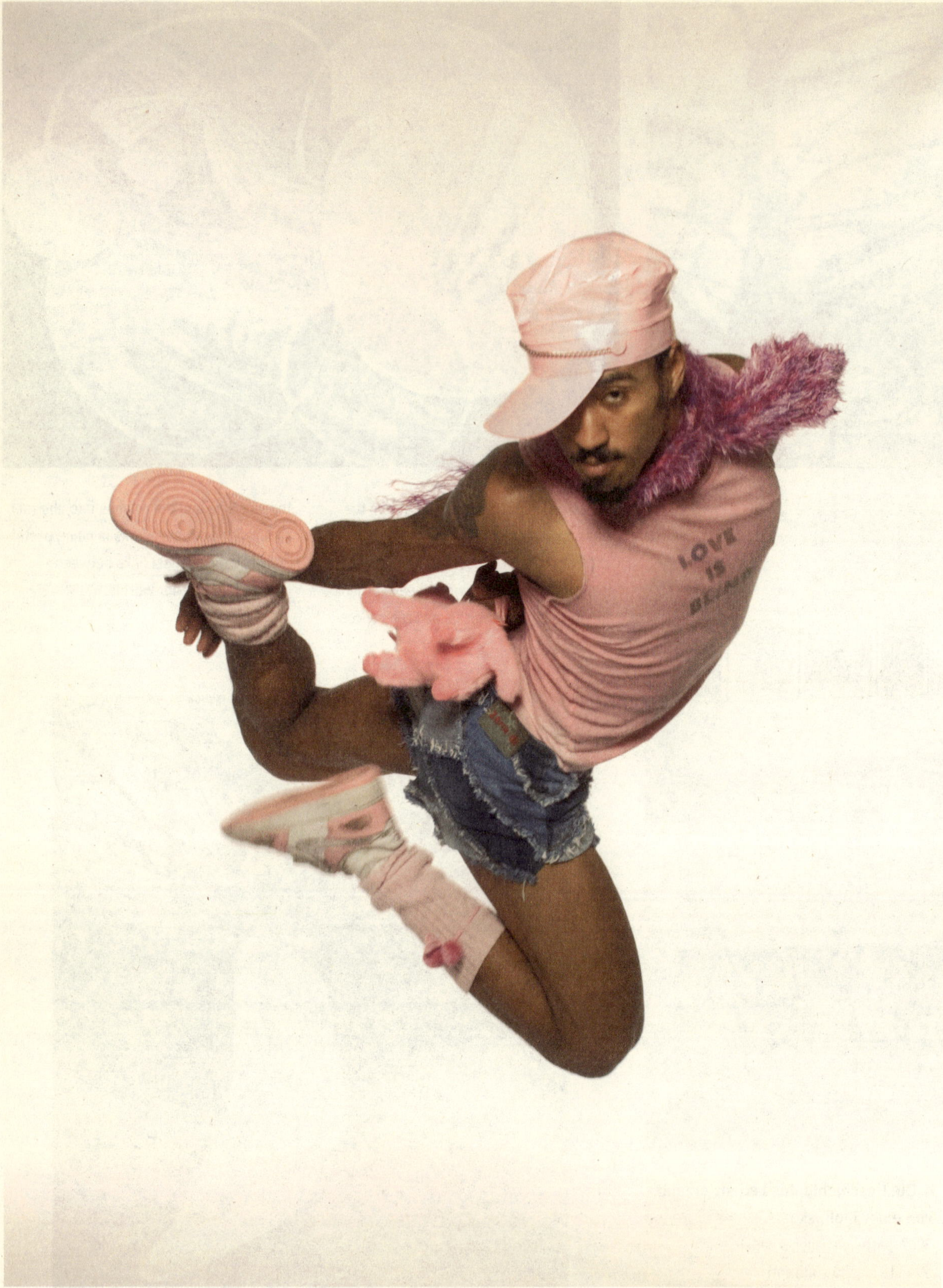

1.

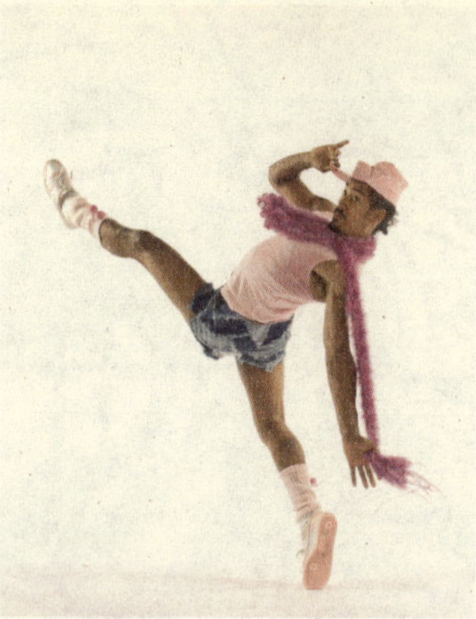

2.

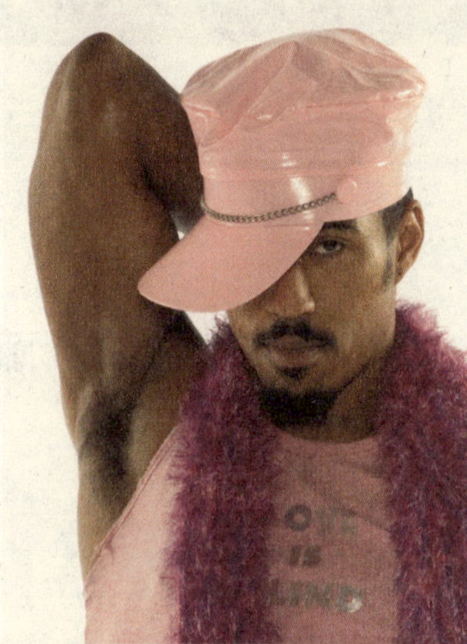

3.

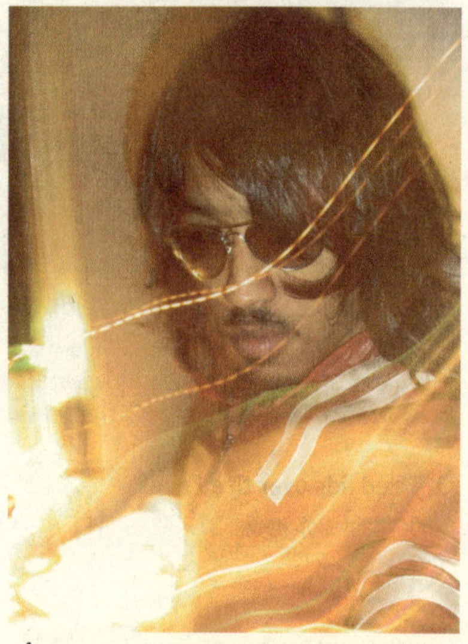

4.

Wendell Cooper received his BA in dance and religion from George Washington University, Washington, D.C., and currently lives in Brooklyn. He is a dance artist integrating urban forms (house, break dance, vogue, etc.) with African and Native American traditions as well as contemporary modern dance. Performances often include live choreography, music, and video elements.

1, 2 & 3. **Ms. Oops**
2008, digital photographs

4. **Progress Reports**
2005, digital photograph from color video

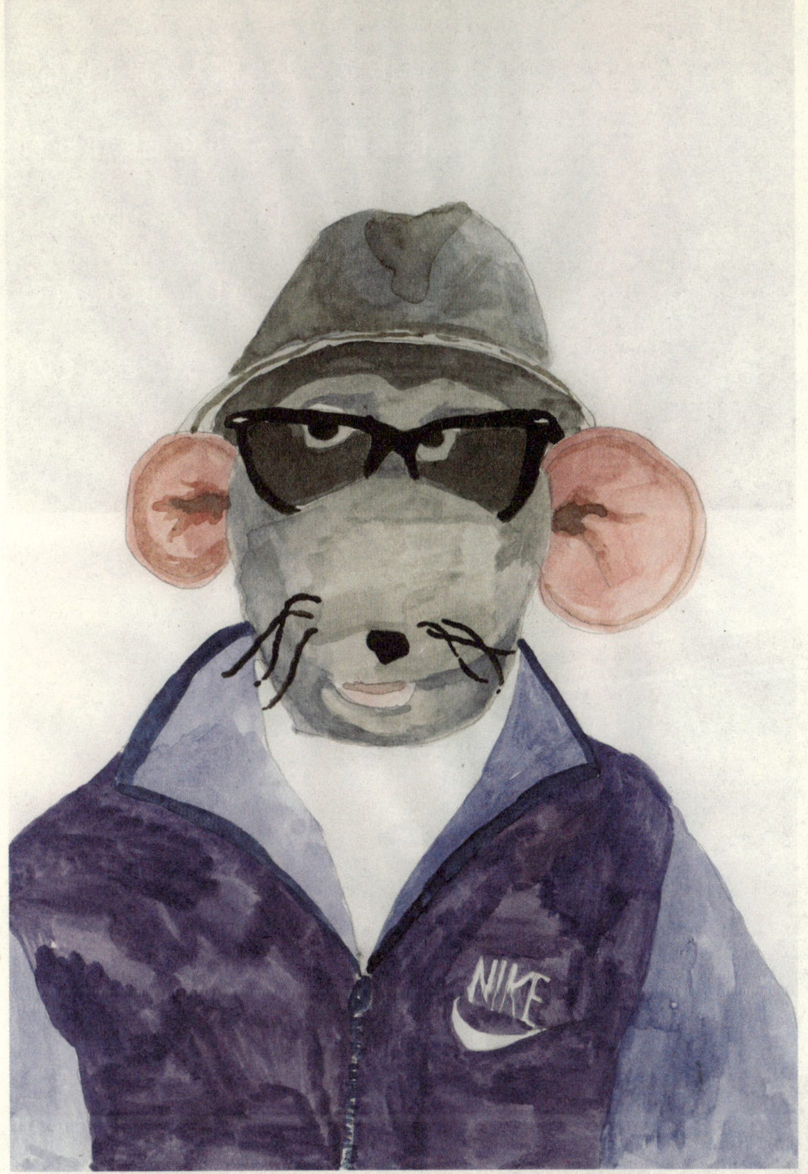

1.

2.

After earning his BA from the Bristol School of Art, Media and Design, Rhys Coren was selected for "New Contemporaries," an annual exhibition of young British artists. His works feature deliberately clumsy drawing and copious text in which scrawled letters are the vehicle for a joking, at times barely literate voice. His subject matter is often self-consciously self-centered, like CDs or sneakers he has owned. By turns obnoxious and candid, Coren's art is a fresh expression for the truism that punk exteriors are affected to conceal vulnerability.

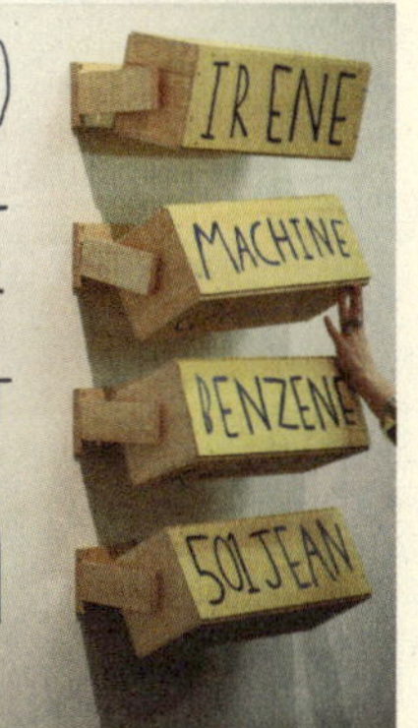

3.

1. Roland Rat
from the series **Male Role Models**
2008, watercolor on paper, 8 × 6 in
(20 × 15 cm)

2 & 3. cats protection poem (detail)
2008, enamel, acrylic, plywood, and steel,
100 × 117 in (250 × 300 cm)

4 & 5. Trainers (all of them)
2008, acrylic on wood,
dimensions variable

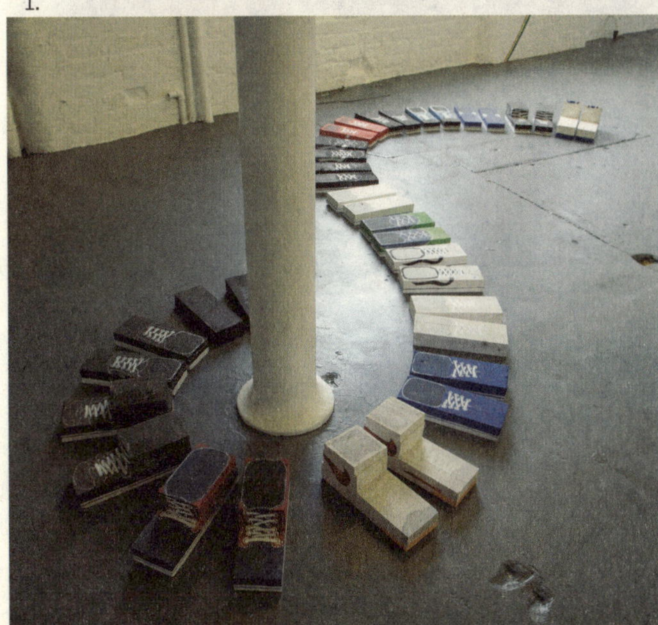

4.

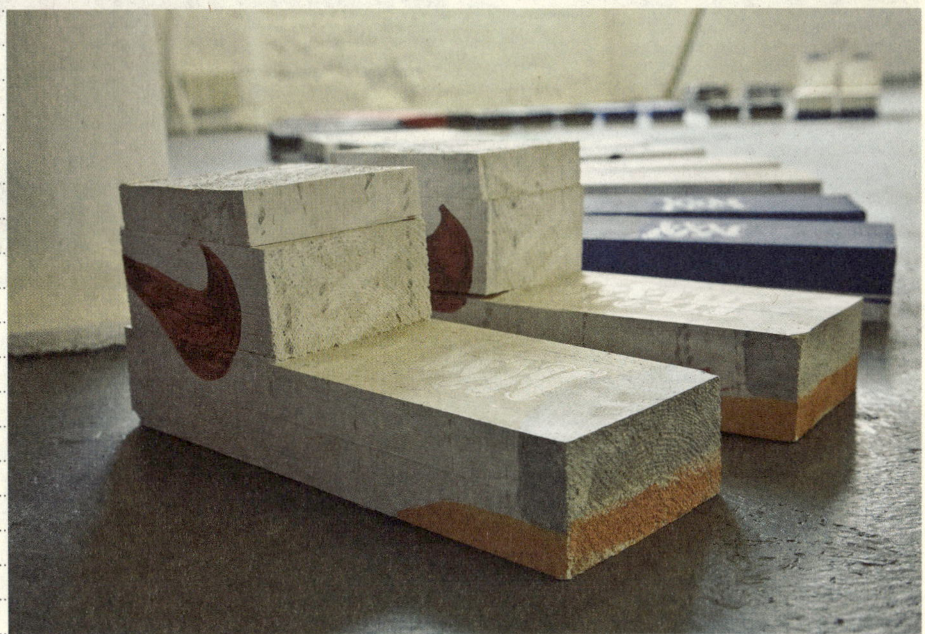

5.

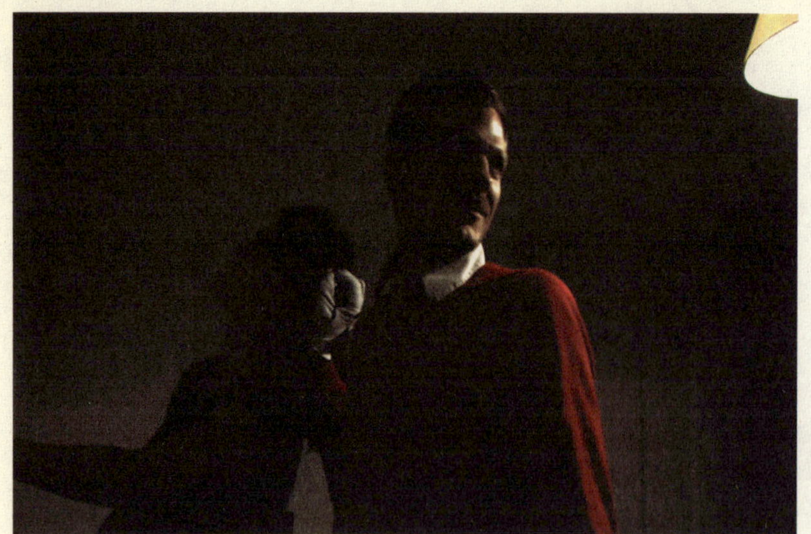

1.

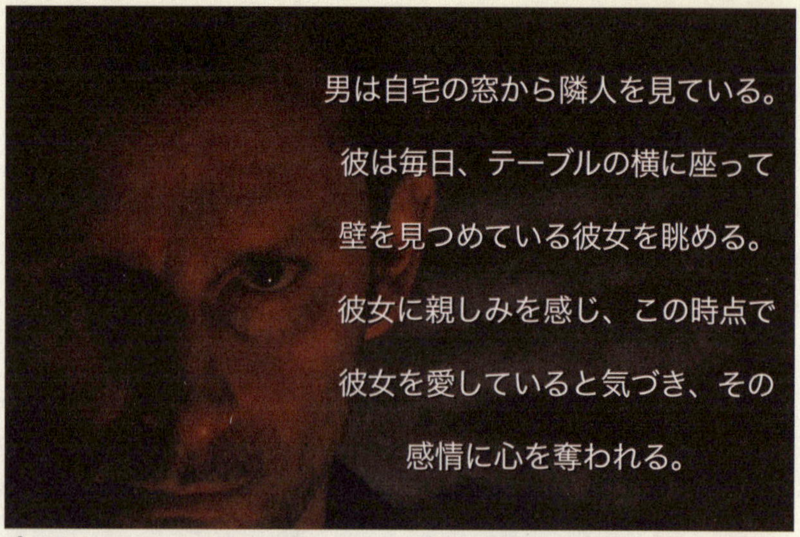

男は自宅の窓から隣人を見ている。
彼は毎日、テーブルの横に座って
壁を見つめている彼女を眺める。
彼女に親しみを感じ、この時点で
彼女を愛していると気づき、その
感情に心を奪われる。

2.

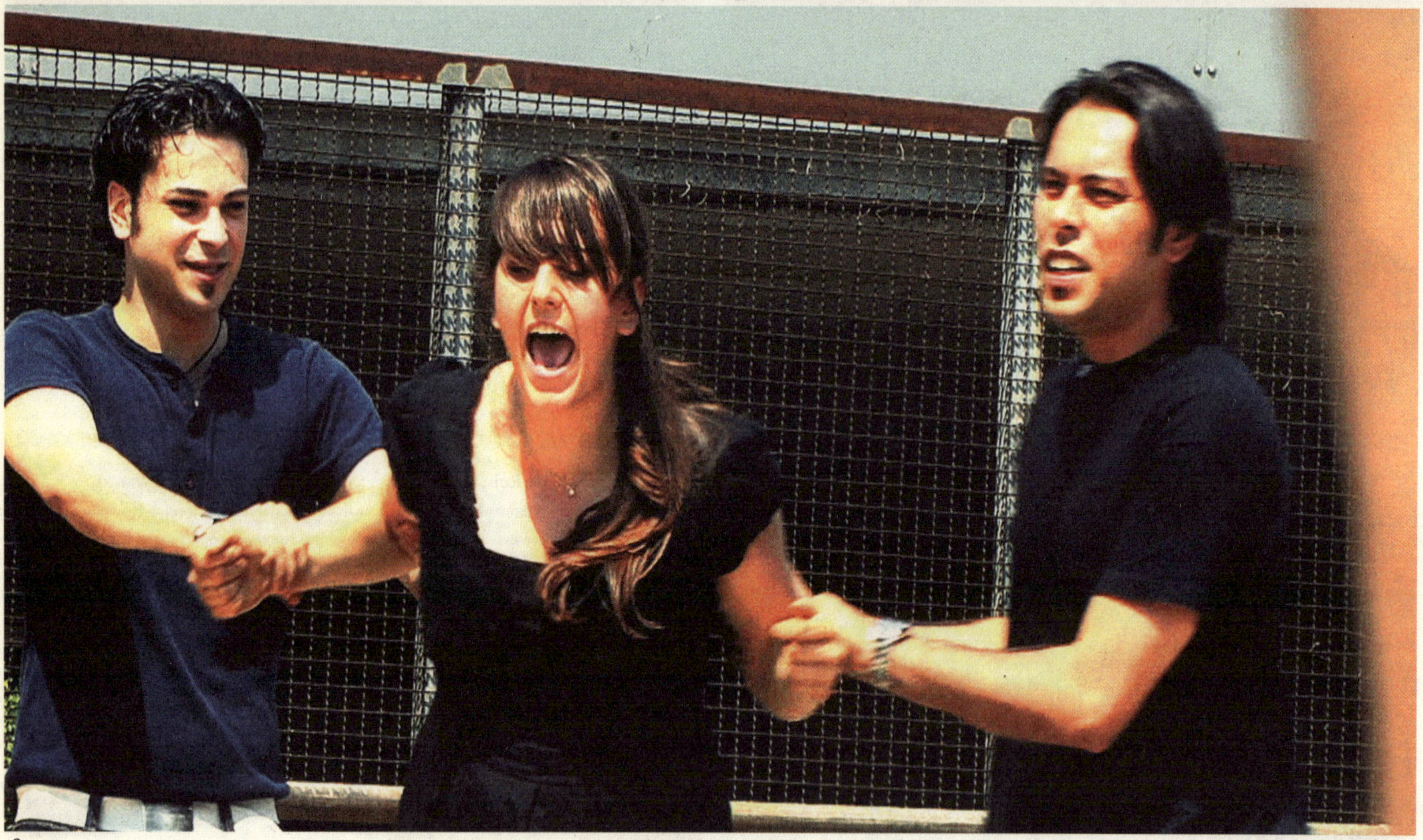

3.

Keren Cytter attended the the Avni Institute, Tel Aviv, and currently lives in Berlin. She makes videos that combine bookish, unrealistic language with soap-operatic content to emphasize the artificiality of documentary narration. Her scripted scenes combine influences from reality television to Dogme and the French New Wave. She was awarded the Baloise Art Prize at Art Basel in 2006.

1 & 2. **G for Murder**
2008, digital video, 7 min

3. **In search for brothers**
2008, digital video, 7 min

4. **Force from the past**
2008, digital video, 7 min

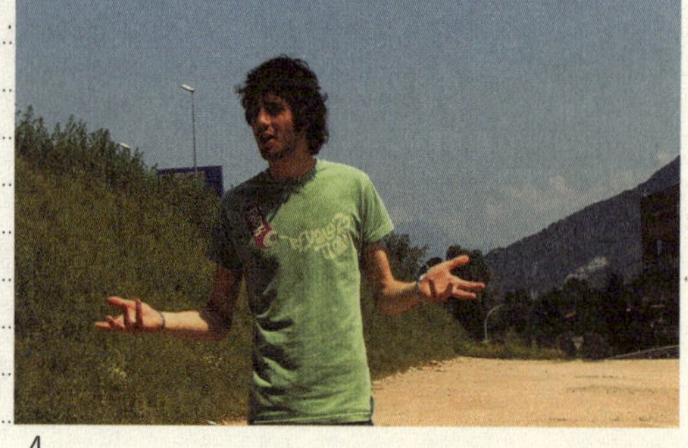

4.

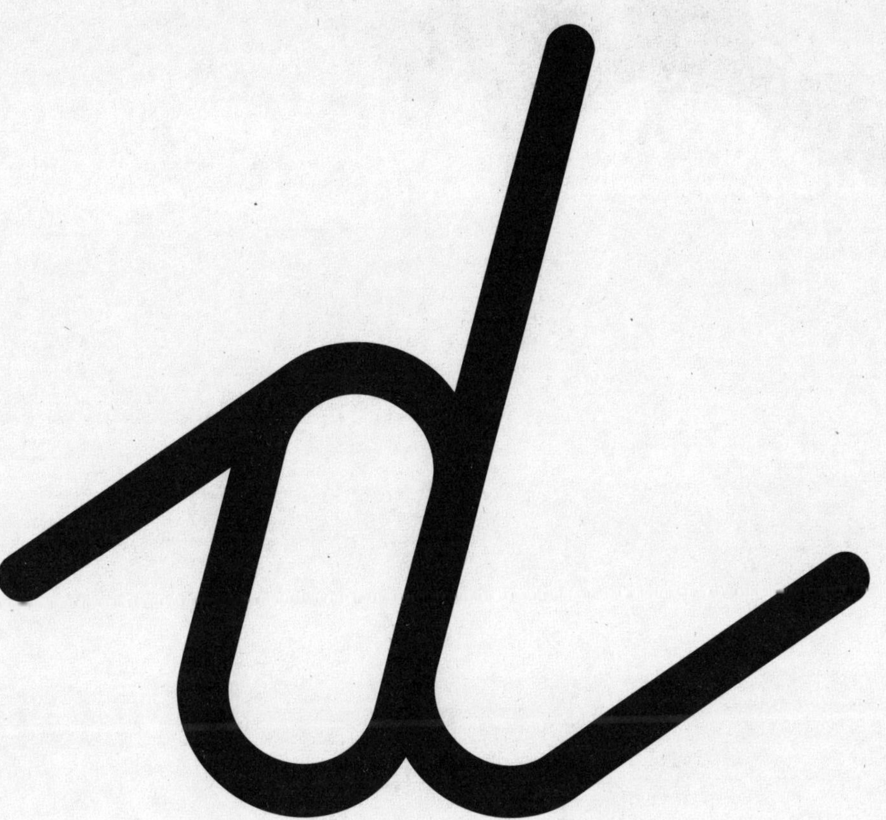

DA CORTE, ALEX

b. 1980 Camden, New Jersey, USA

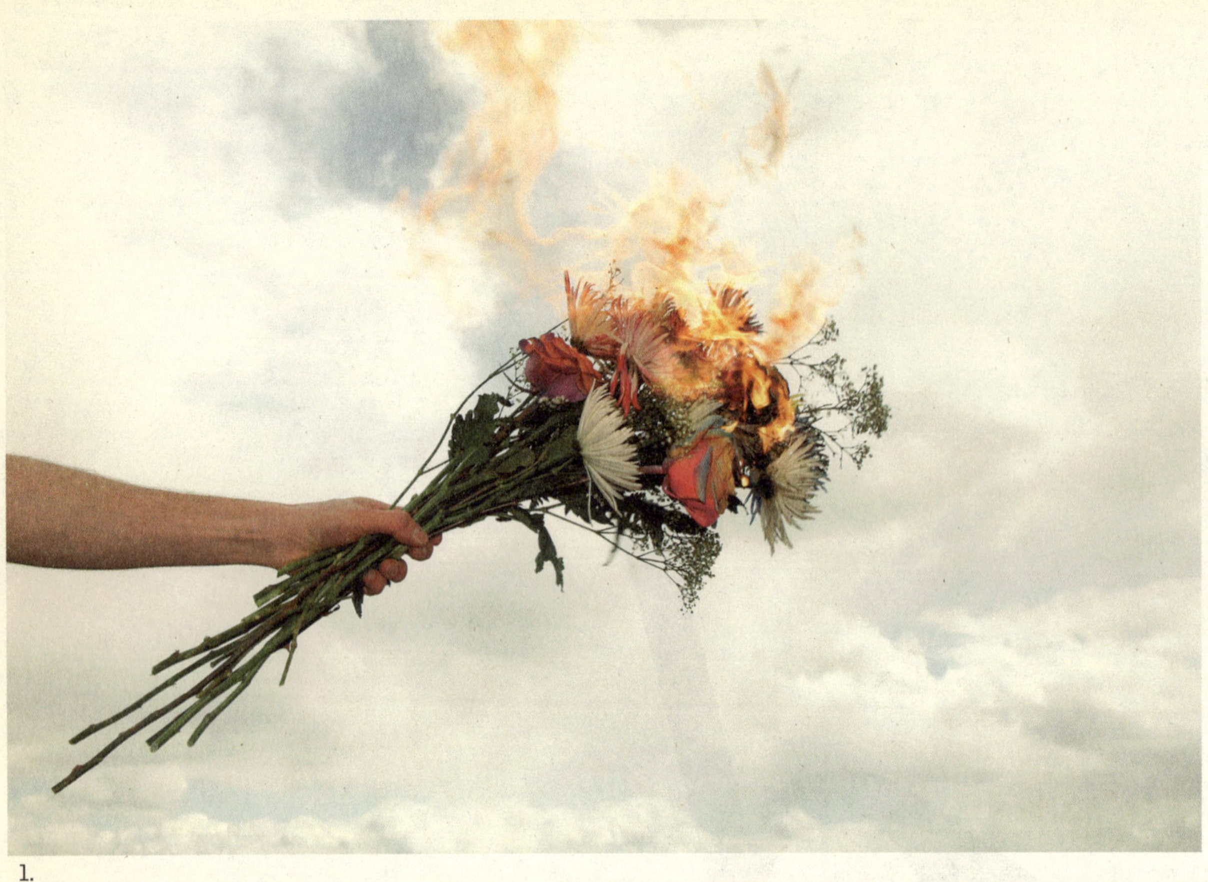

1.

Alex Da Corte received his BFA from the University of the Arts, Philadelphia, and is currently pursuing his MFA degree at Yale University. An apprenticeship at the Fabric Workshop and Museum in Philadelphia led him to integrate eclectic fabrics into sculptures that combine diverse materials: stuffed snakelike forms, toy soldiers, floral wallpaper, and fake Christmas trees, to name a few. His practice also includes performance and photographic works that investigate fantasy, vulnerability, and human interaction.

1. **Miracle**

2007, archival pigment print on Museo Silver Rag, 44 × 66 in (112 × 168 cm)

2. **Forever and Ever**

2007, paper, enamel, epoxy resin, and brass fasteners, 20 × 64 in (51 × 163 cm)

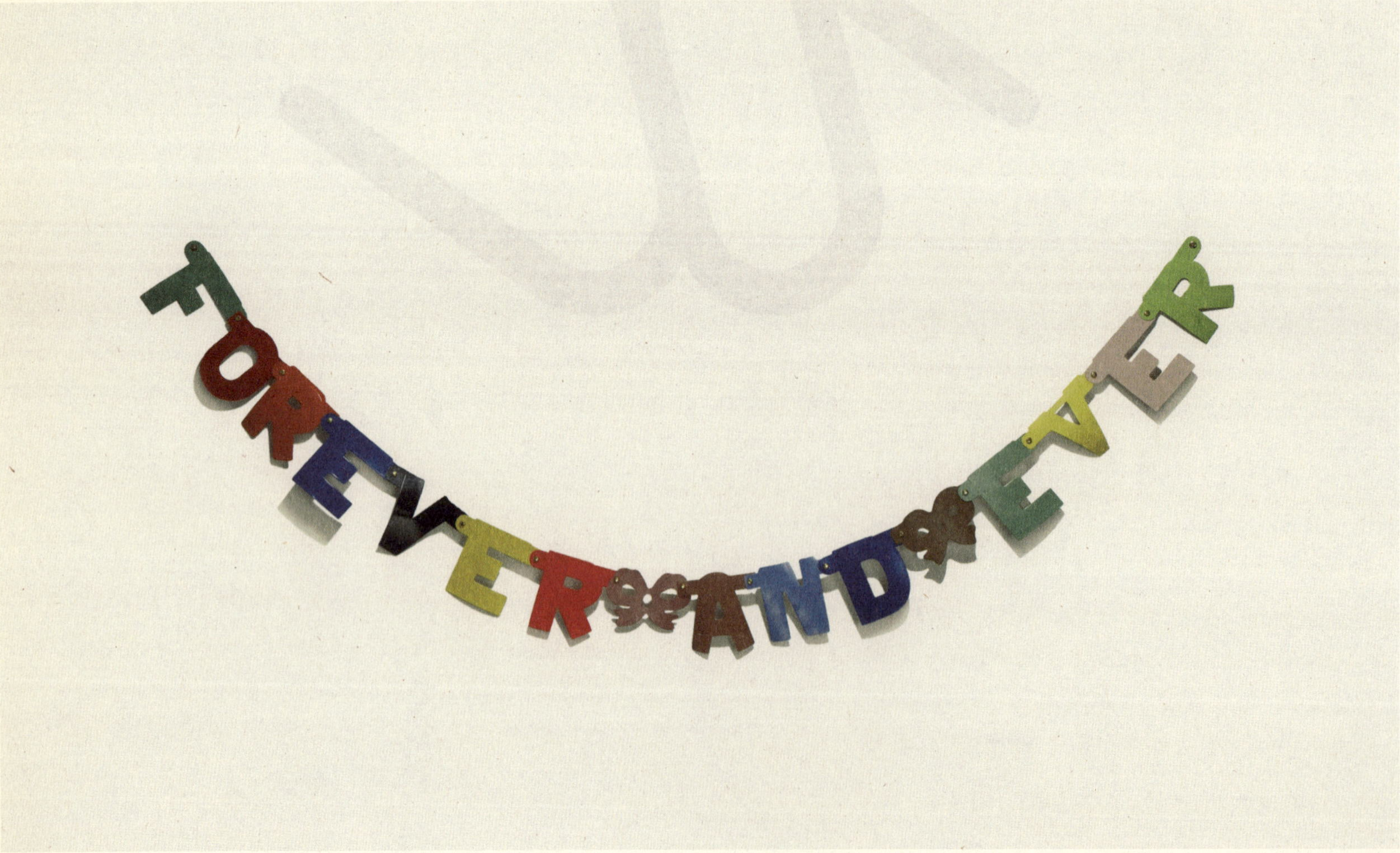

2.

Flavia Da Rin studied at the National University Institute of Art (IUNA) in Buenos Aires, where she lives. Her manipulated digital photographs integrate references that range from Renaissance painting to the films of David Lynch. For **Eyes Wide Open**, commissioned by the Speed Art Museum in 2007, she created ten large-scale billboard images to be installed across Louisville, Kentucky.

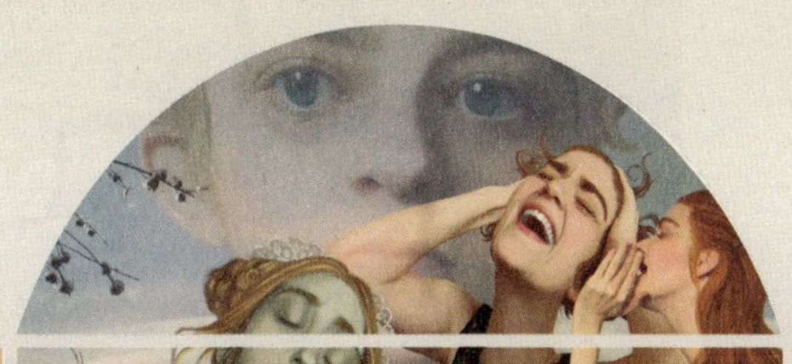
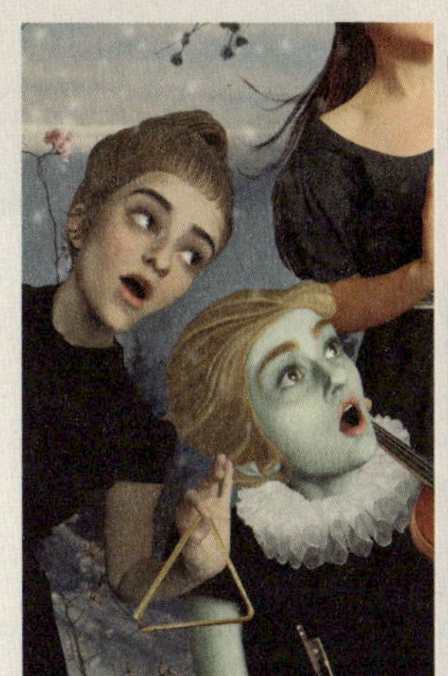
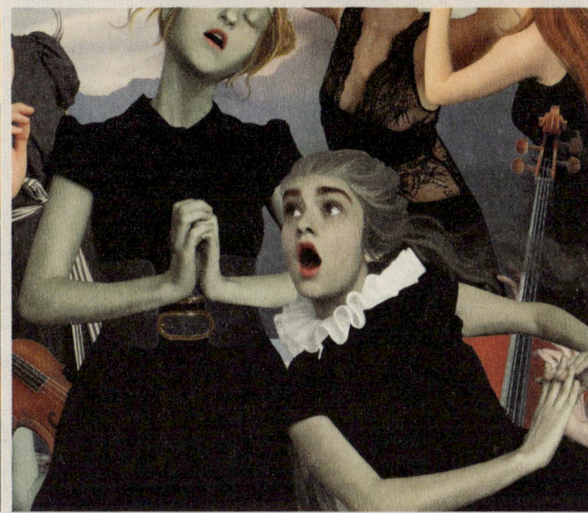
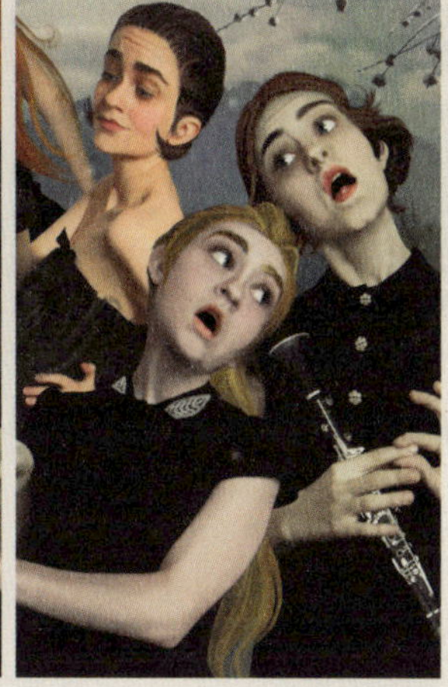

1.

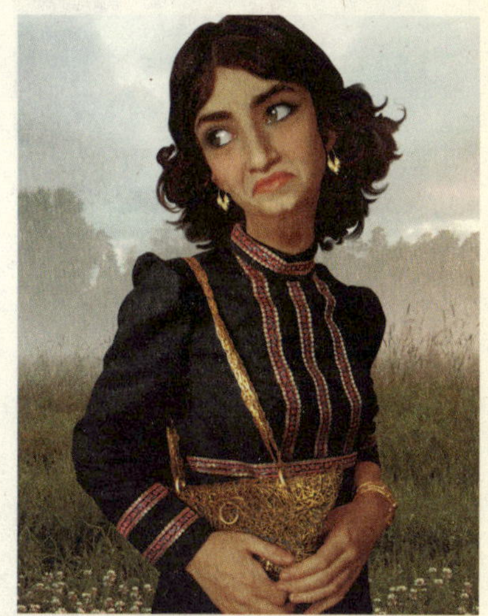

3.

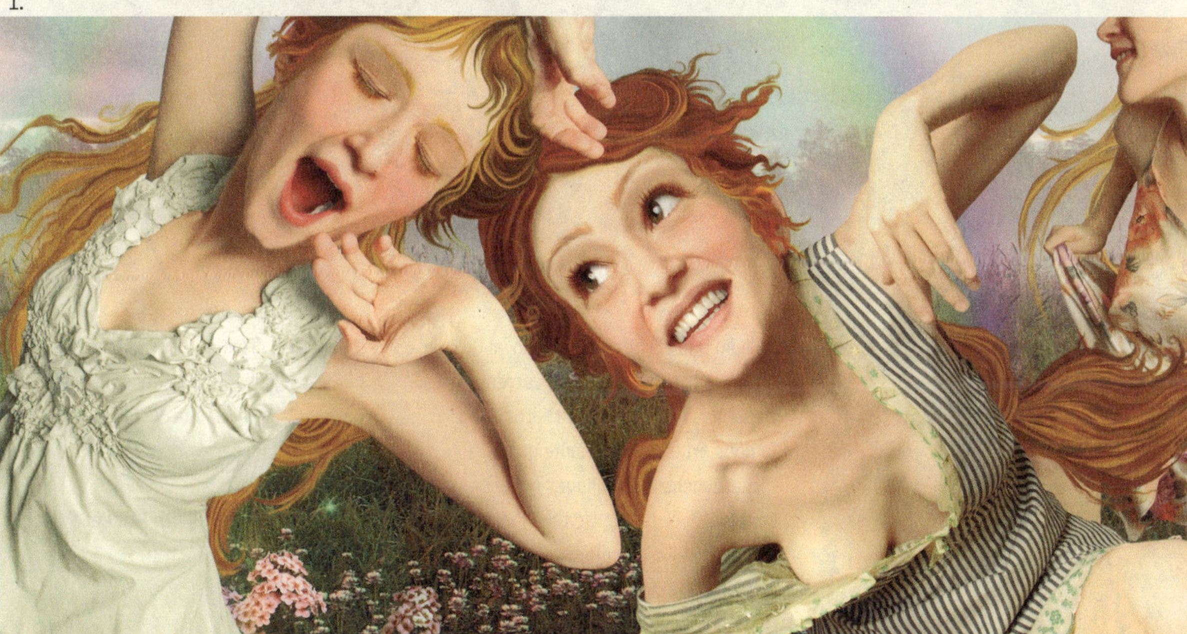

2.

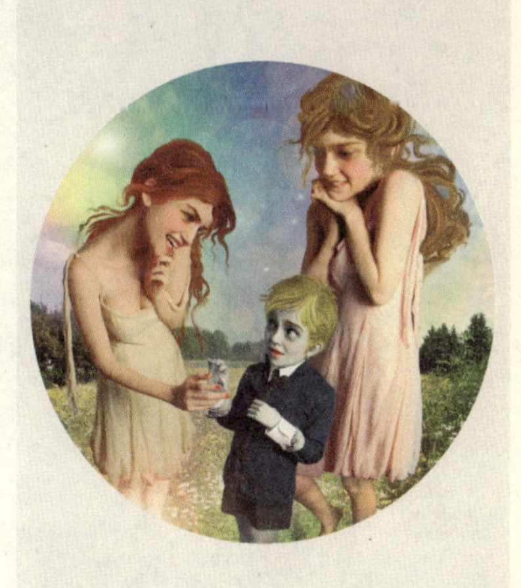

4.

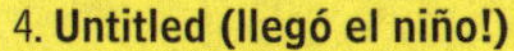
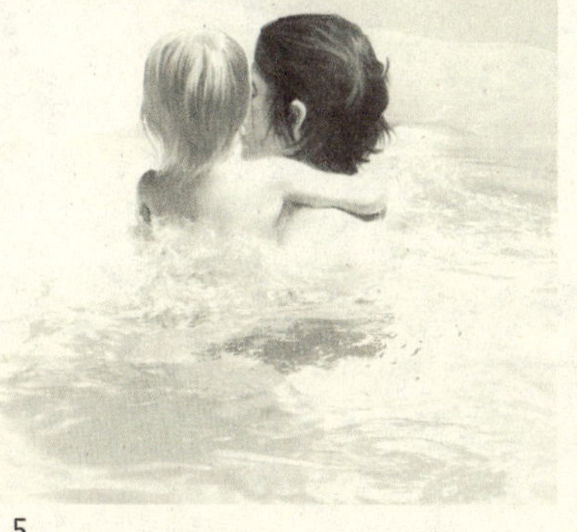

5.

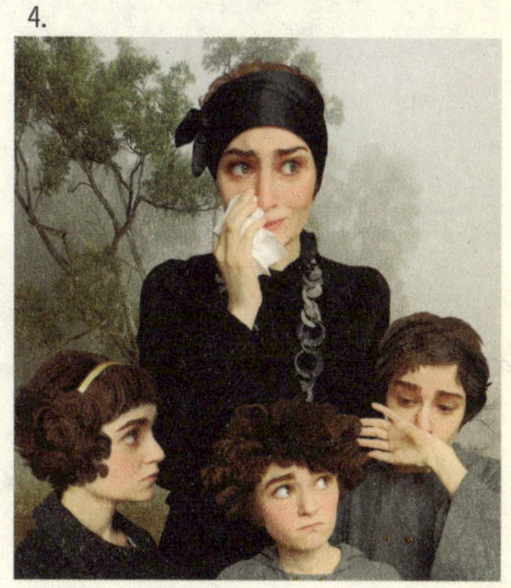

6.

1. Untitled (hadas negras polyptich)
2008, chromogenic print, 59 × 100 in (150 × 254 cm)

2. Untitled (díptico ninfas 1)
2008, chromogenic print, $39\frac{1}{2} \times 76\frac{3}{4}$ in (100 × 195 cm)

3. Untitled (maestra)
2008, chromogenic print, 50 × 40 in (127 × 102 cm)

4. Untitled (llegó el niño!)
2008, chromogenic print, diameter $15\frac{3}{4}$ in (40 cm)

5. Untitled (nadando)
2008, gelatin silver print, $12 \times 12\frac{1}{2}$ in (30 × 32 cm)

6. Untitled (luto)
2008, chromogenic print, $50 \times 47\frac{1}{4}$ in (127 × 120 cm)

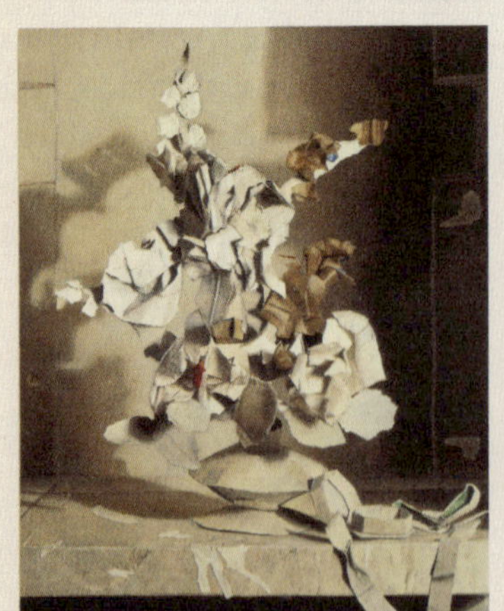
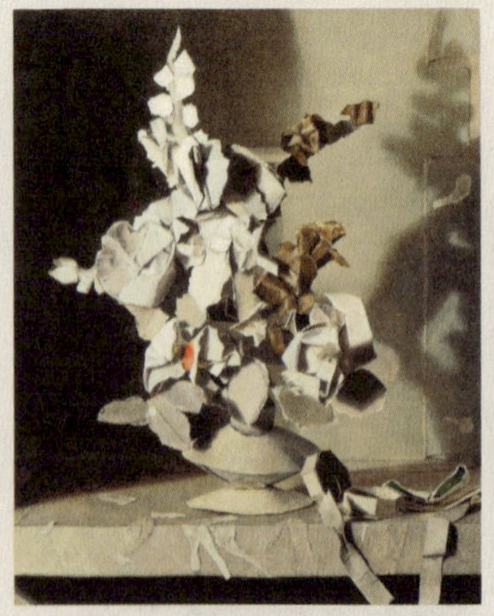

1.

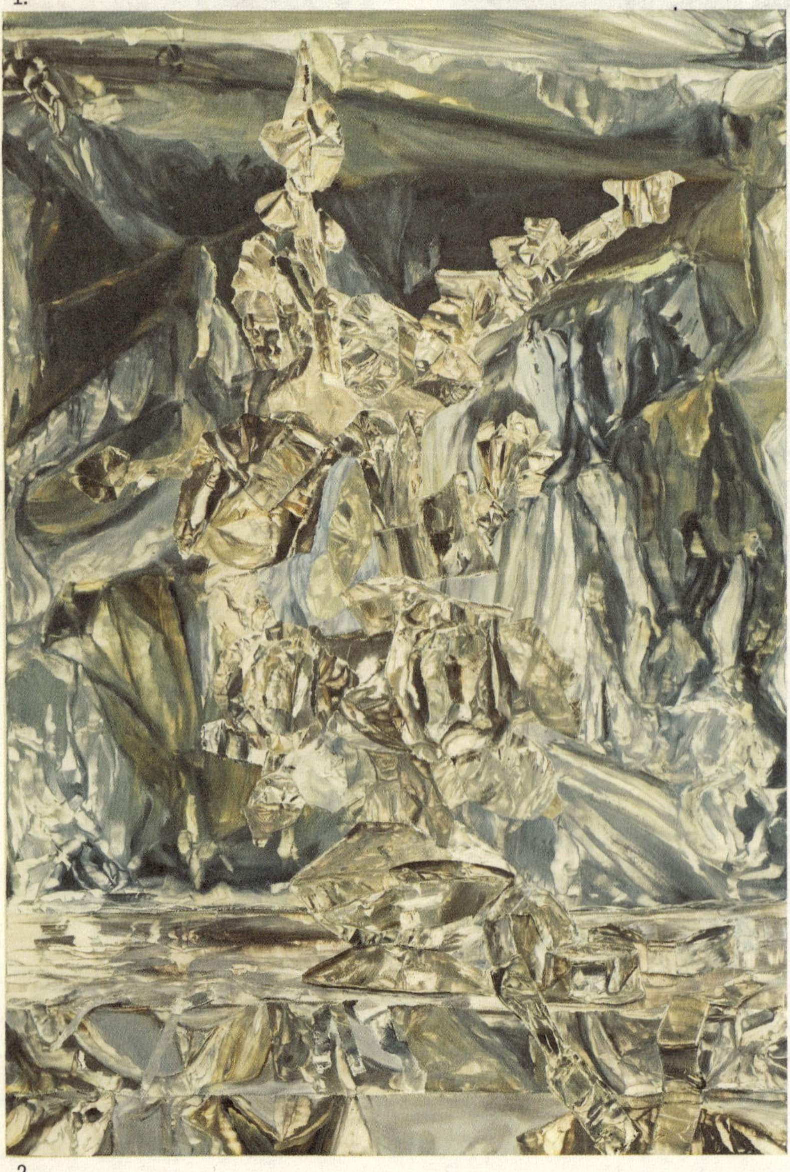

2.

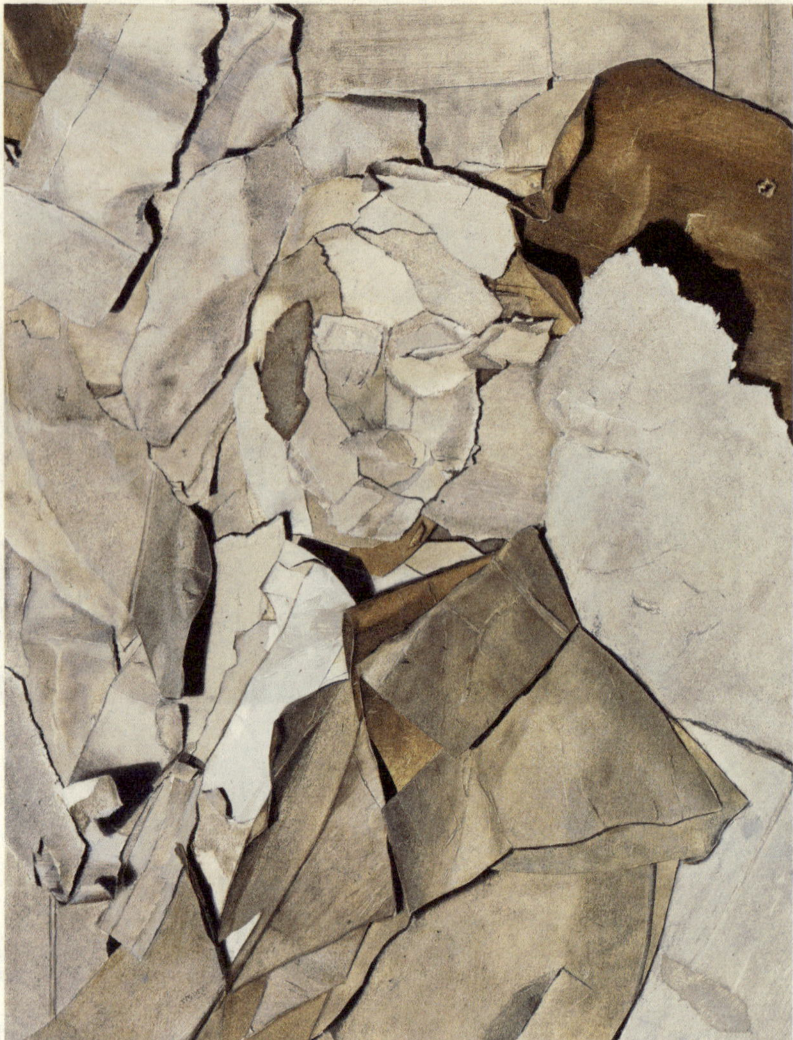

3.

William Daniels attended the Royal College of Art in London, where he currently lives. He begins his process by reproducing famous art historical paintings as three-dimensional collages in paper, cardboard, or tinfoil. He then makes trompe-l'oeil oil paintings of these maquettes, creating new adaptations of Caravaggio's Incredulity of St Thomas, Cézanne's Mont Sainte-Victoire series, and other familiar works.

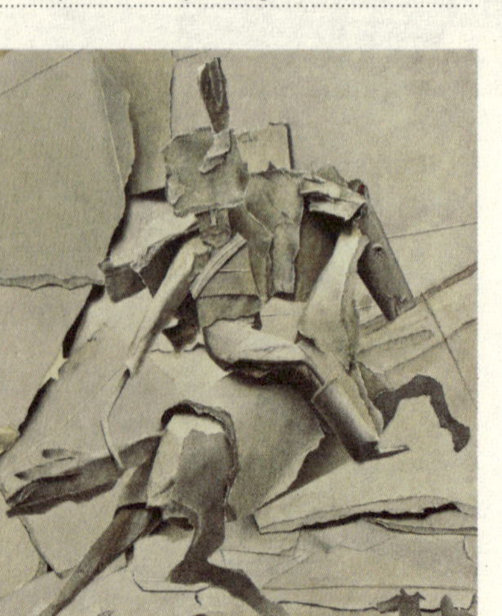

4.

1. Vase of Flowers with Pocket Watch
2005, oil on wood, each 14 ½ × 12 in (37 × 30 cm)

2. Vase of Flowers with Pocket Watch
2007, oil on wood, 16 × 11 ½ in (41 × 29 cm)

3. Jacques-Luis David
2006, oil on board, 13 × 10 ¼ in (33 × 26 cm)

4. Charging Chasseur
2006, oil on wood, 12 ½ × 10 ¼ in (32 × 26 cm)

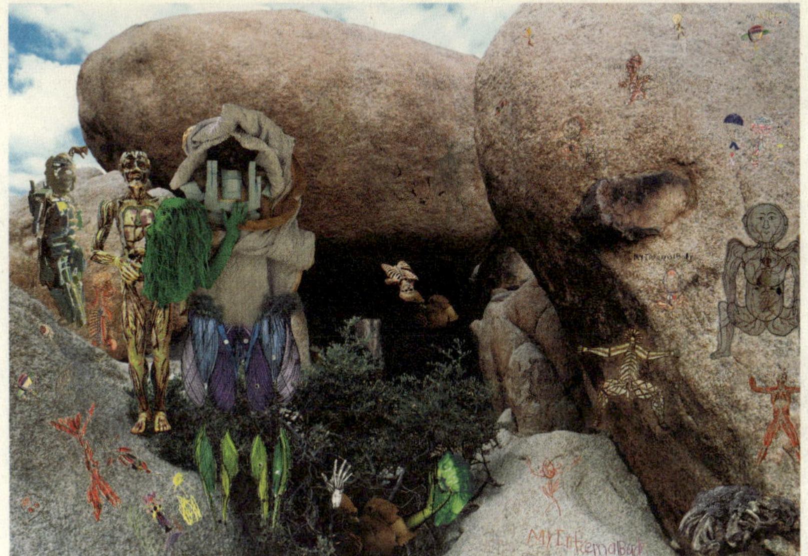

1.

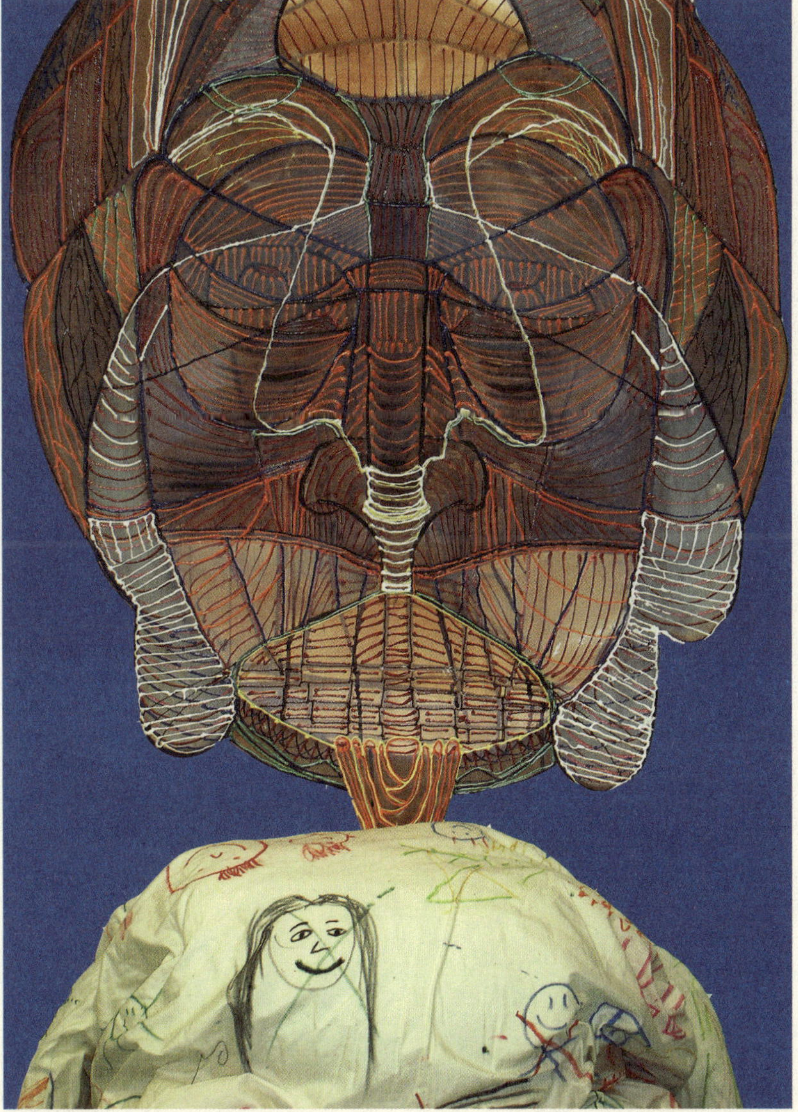

3.

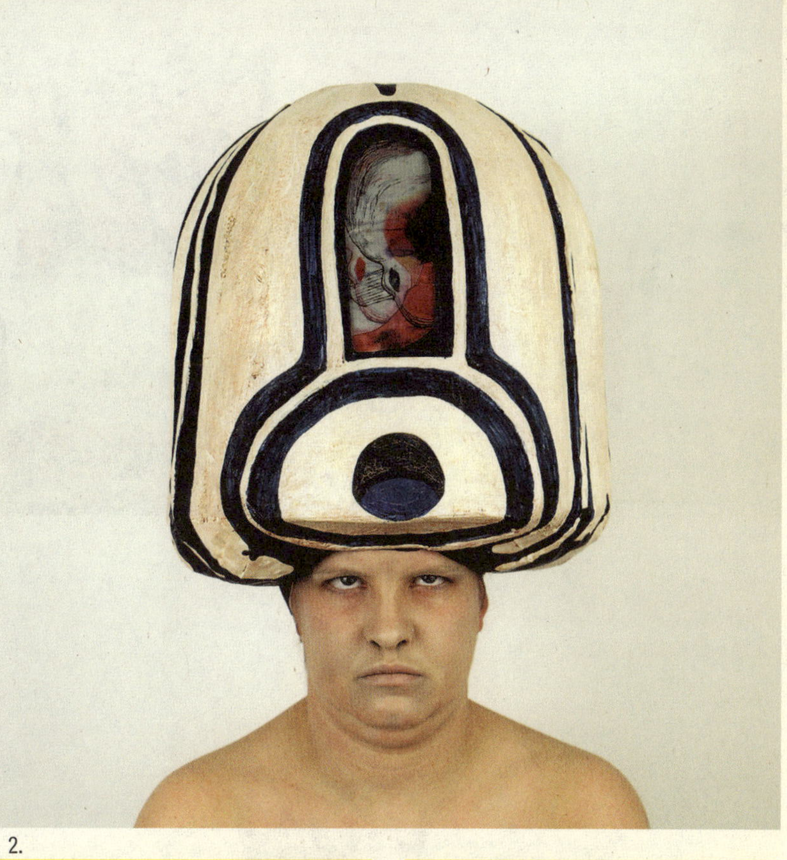

2.

1. Fossilizing the Body Border Disorder
2008, digital print, 98×146 in (250×370 cm)

2. YE (Pilzschiel)
2006, color photograph mounted on aluminum, $55 \times 39\frac{1}{2}$ in (140×100 cm)

3. untitled/maskpuff
2008, collage with puffpaint on paper, $43\frac{1}{4} \times 35\frac{1}{2}$ in (110×90 cm); children's drawings on costume, dimensions variable

4. Gospel of Bully
2007, digital photograph of performance, dimensions variable

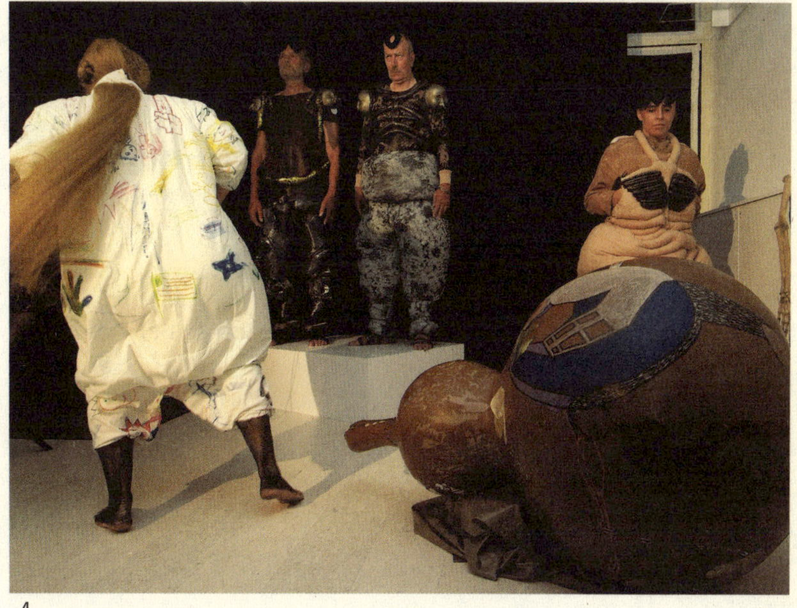

4.

Mariechen Danz earned her MFA in art and integrated media from California Institute of the Arts and currently lives in Los Angeles. She stages performances that reference religious ceremony, cult ritual, and the gendered body. Her process includes the production of costumes, masks, props, scenery, choreography, and drawings.

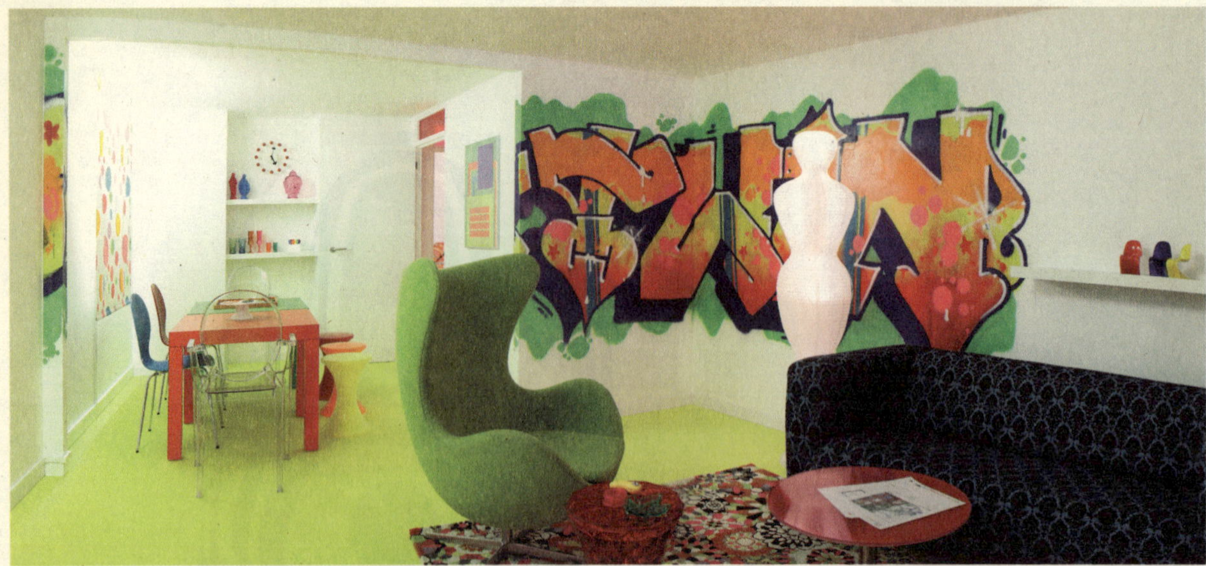

1.

Matthew Darbyshire attended the Royal Academy Schools in London, where he continues to live and work. He creates installations that explore the nonspecificity of today's design language, and its implications in terms of class, background, and other social barriers. In "Blades House," his 2008 exhibition at Gasworks in London, he replicated the domestic interior of a fictitious middle-class professional in his mid-thirties.

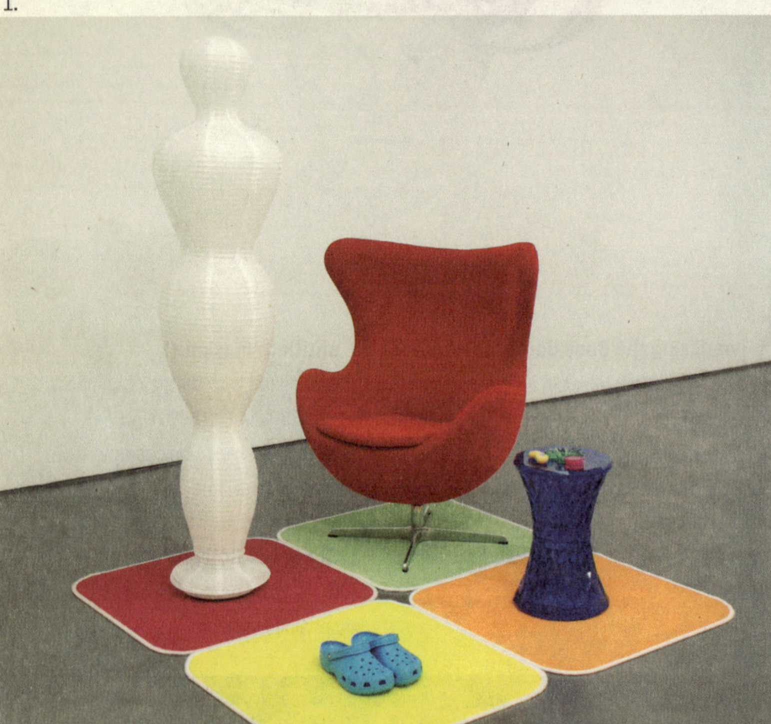

2.

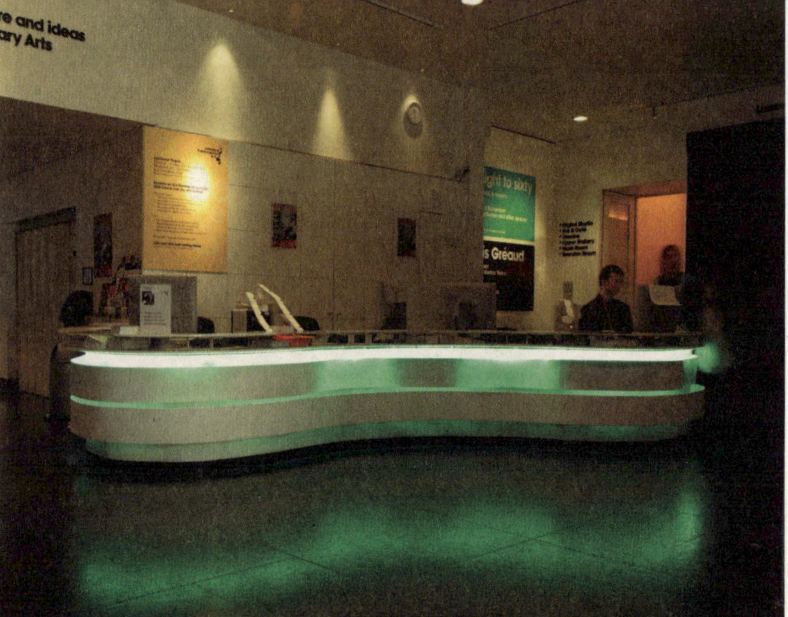

3.

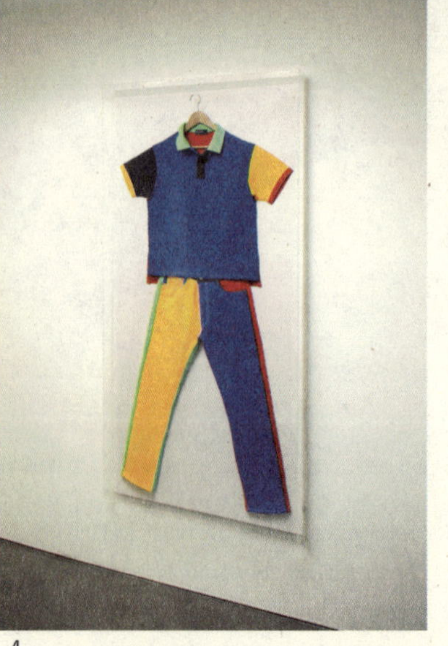

4.

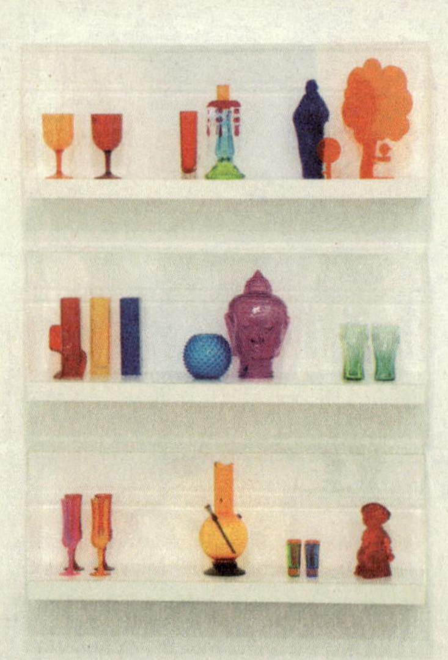

5.

1. "Blades House"
2008, exhibition view at Gasworks, London

2. **Untitled (Furniture Island)**
2008, carpet, stool, lamp, shoes, replica egg chair, weed grinder, ashtray, and lighter, 67 × 63 × 63 in (170 × 160 × 160 cm)

3. **BP p.l.c. Headquarters (reception), 1 St James's Square, London SW1**
2008, colored lighting, mixed media, dimensions variable, installation view at ICA, London

4. **Homage to Henri Matisse No. 2**
2006, dyed Ralph Lauren polo shirt, dyed Levis 501s, and Plexiglas, 76 × 38 × $4\frac{3}{4}$ in (193 × 96 × 12 cm)

5. **Untitled (Shelves 1-3)**
2008, Perspex, glass, and found objects, $58\frac{1}{2}$ × $43\frac{1}{4}$ × $10\frac{1}{2}$ in (149 × 110 × 27 cm)

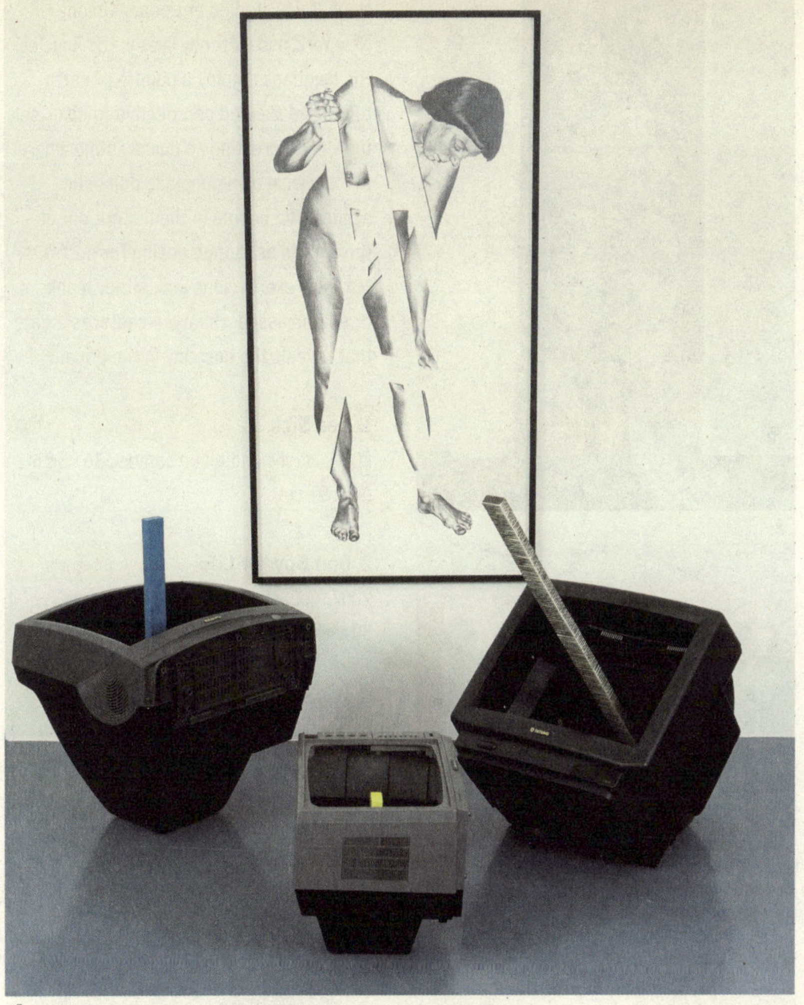

1.

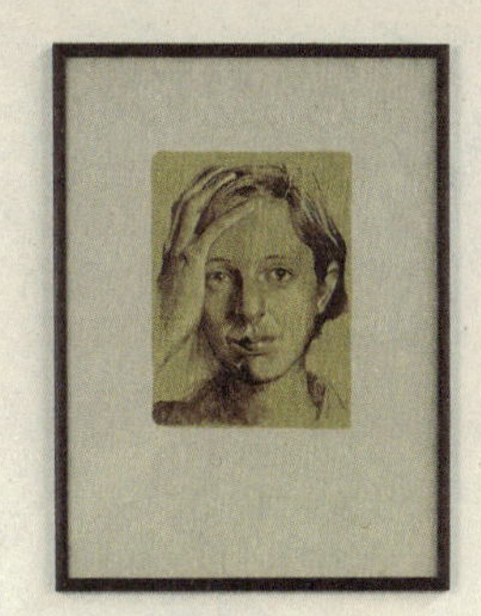

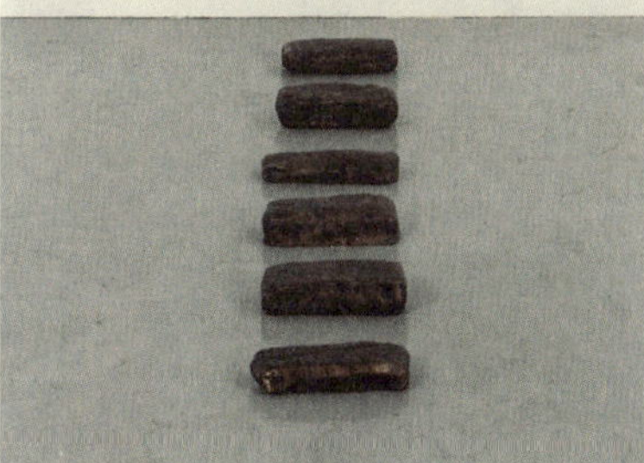

2.

Kate Davis attended the Glasgow School of Art and continues to live in Glasgow. She combines pencil drawings with photographs, collages, and sculptural elements to create surrealistic narrative installations. The body is her most prevalent reference, whether drawn directly, distorted and fragmented, or suggested through anthropomorphic objects.

1. (top) **Waiting in 1972;** (bottom) **What About 2007?**
2007, pencil on paper in frame 53 × 27 ½ in (135 × 70 cm);
2007, ceramic batons and televisions, three parts, 19 ½ × 18 ½ × 37 ½ in (50 × 47 × 95 cm), 15 ½ × 12 ¼ × 13 ½ in (39 × 35 × 70 cm) and 16 × 12 × 13 in (40 × 31 × 34 cm)

2. **I Want to Function in The Present Time (Self-Portrait II and Bricks)**
2006, framed drawing and print on paper and bronze bricks, 18 × 8 × 4 ½ in (46 × 20 × 11 cm)

3. **Your Body is a Battleground Still (poster) 1**
2007, graphite on paper in frame, 39 ½ × 29 ½ in (100 × 75 cm)

4. **Who is a Woman Now? (2)**
2008, silkscreen print and pencil on paper in frame, 67 × 51 in (170 × 130 cm)

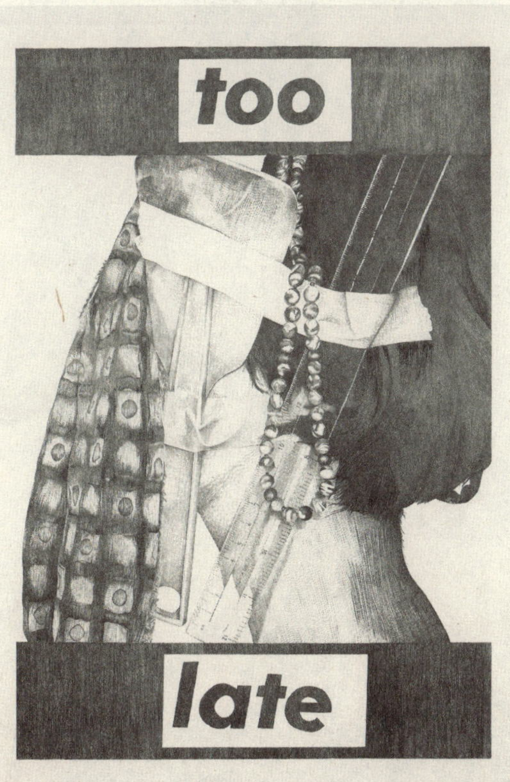

3.

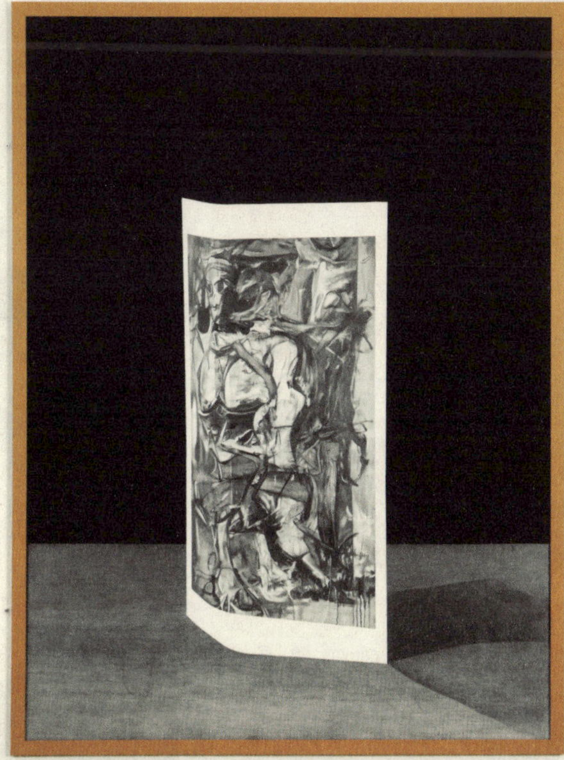

4.

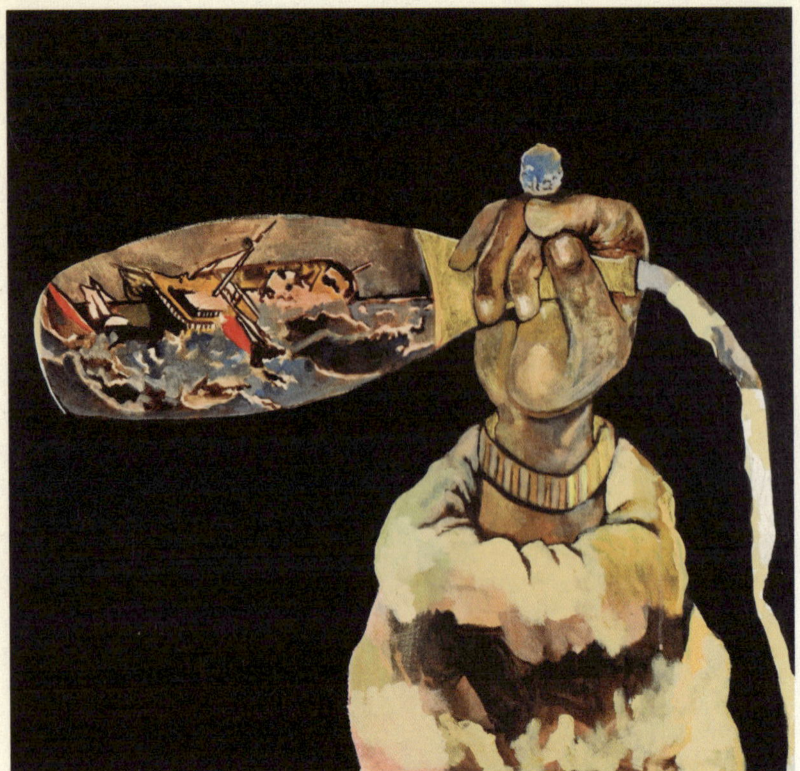
1.

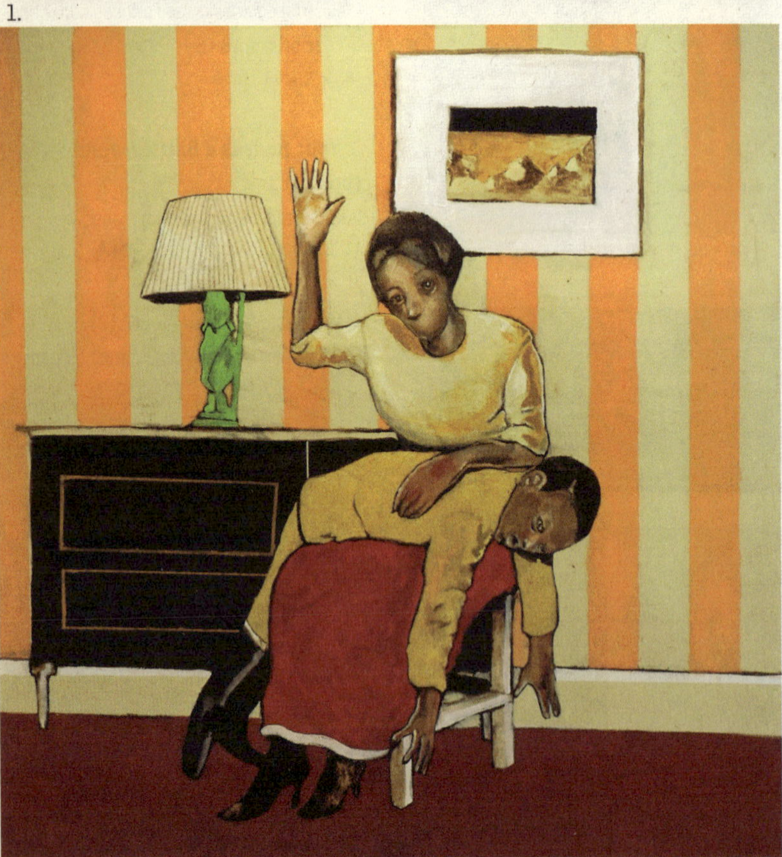
2.

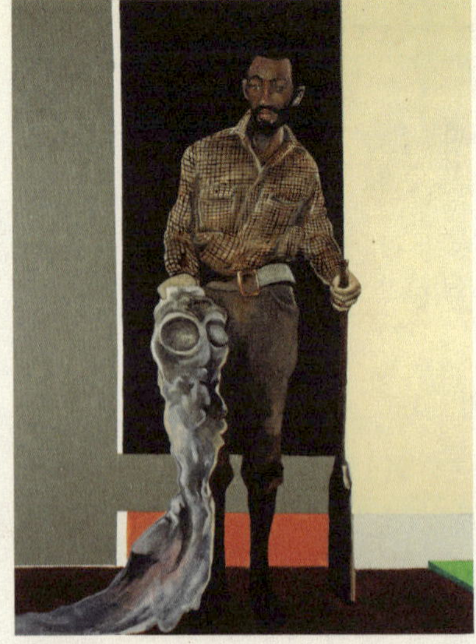
3.

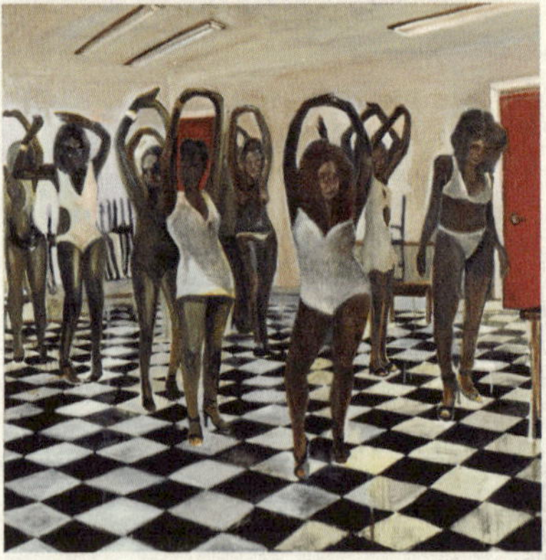
4.

Noah Davis studied at Cooper Union, New York, and currently lives in Los Angeles. His paintings employ a palette of earth tones and skewed perspective to disorient the viewer, creating an uneasy atmosphere in otherwise commonplace domestic scenes. The people in them stare out of the canvas as though posing for portraits, but their expressions look either blank or embarrassed. His work captures a gaze that reveals the uncanny in the banal.

1. **Sea Sick**
2007, acrylic and oil on canvas, 36 × 36 in (91 × 91 cm)

2. **Bad Boy for Life**
2007, gouache and acrylic on canvas, 30 × 30 in (76 × 76 cm)

3. **Man with Shotgun and Alien**
2008, acrylic and oil on canvas, 54 × 42 in (137 × 107 cm)

5.

4. **Casting Call**
2008, oil and acrylic on canvas, 60 × 62 in (152 × 158 cm)

5. **Richard's Reply**
2008, oil and acrylic on canvas, 62 × 60 in (158 × 152 cm)

Paul Davis studied studio art and technology at the School of the Art Institute of Chicago, and earned his PhD in fine art from Central St. Martins in London, where he continues to live. He is an artist, composer, and cofounder of the record label and computer programming ensemble Beige. A pioneer of the hacked Nintendo game cartridge as an artistic medium, he wrote in 2007, "I am obsessed with computers and I make art that helps me understand how they work."

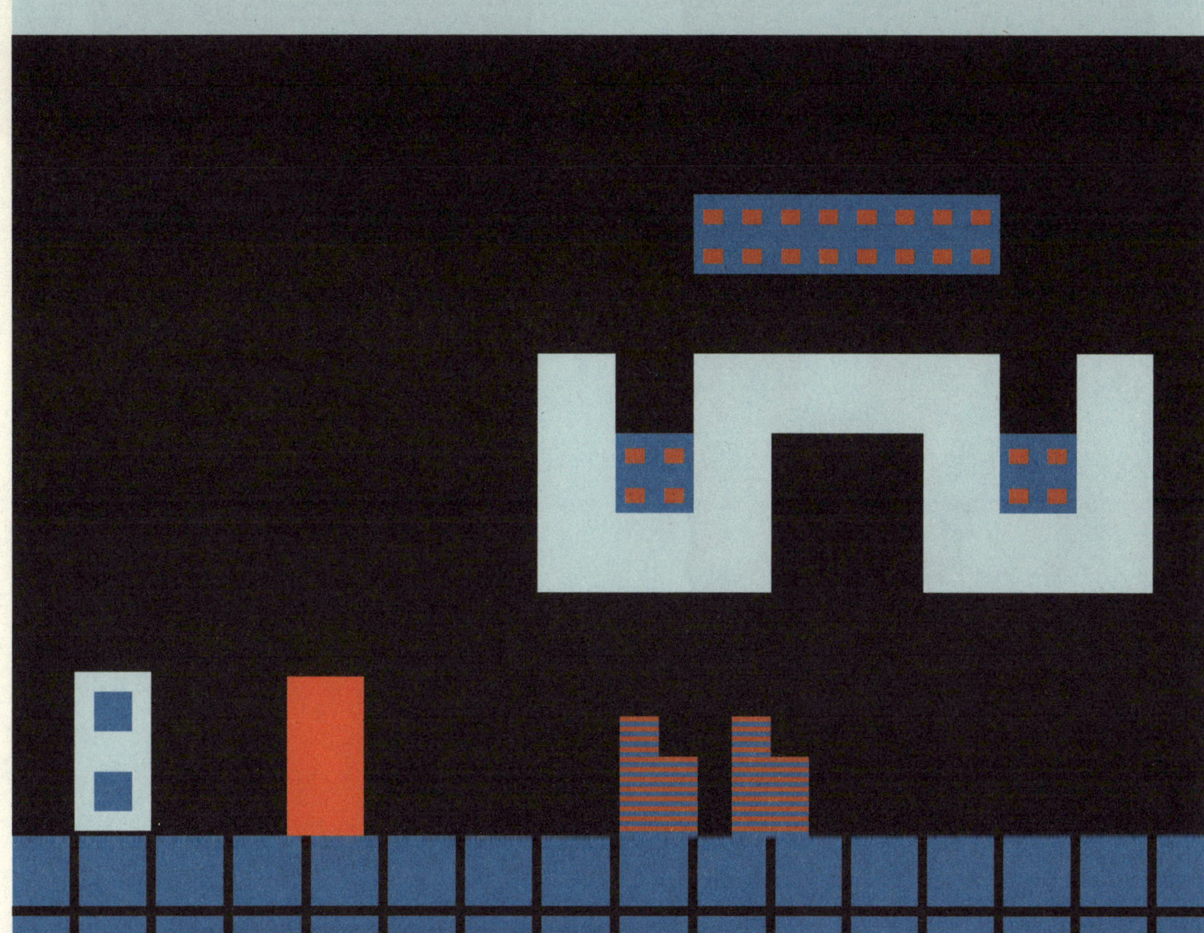

1.

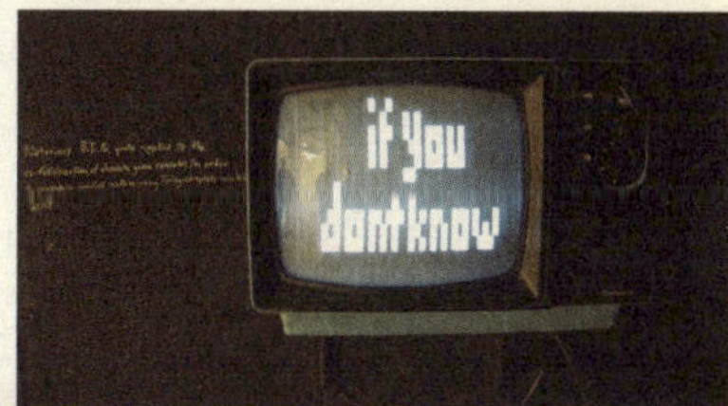

2.

NoS (No operating System) v0.1
his work is, and is about, the execution of instructions. NoS is an interventi
into the boot process of a Windows PC. It exists to control a contemporary co
uter system and can only display the text you are now reading, providing conte
and content both for itself and the work in this space. My intention is to ha
instructions run on a machine without any mediation, Microsoft or otherwise,
ke they do with my game hack pieces. Now the $20 throwaway console and the $20
laptop, each using all their computing power to do nothing but draw text on a
creen, are visually equivalent in the same way they already were computational
equivalent. Parts of my practice are built on conceptual models that propose
ys to manipulate a given system and are then carried out step by step regardle
of the final output. However, machine instructions are tied to a formalism th
limits their scope, more so than natural languages or "ideas". So other parts
f my practice are built on giving very specific instructions to machines where
know exactly what will be seen. In these cases it's often more important what
not seen; the workings of the system and how an intention is expressed by it.
erhaps it's an important difference between my work and the instruction based
rk which came out of the conceptual art movement in the 1960s and 1970s: that
rk was often a reaction to formalism whereas my hacked game consoles and MPEG
deos and PC's are tied to the formalism of logic and digital information. Howe
r, instead of creating meaning through the subversion of symbols and semantics
create meaning through subversion of assumptions about processes of logic. Ar
those assumptions also only semantic? They could be. But I'm trying to see if
's possible for the semantic interpretation of a formal symbol system be made
trinsic to the system, rather than just parasitic on the meanings in our heads

3.

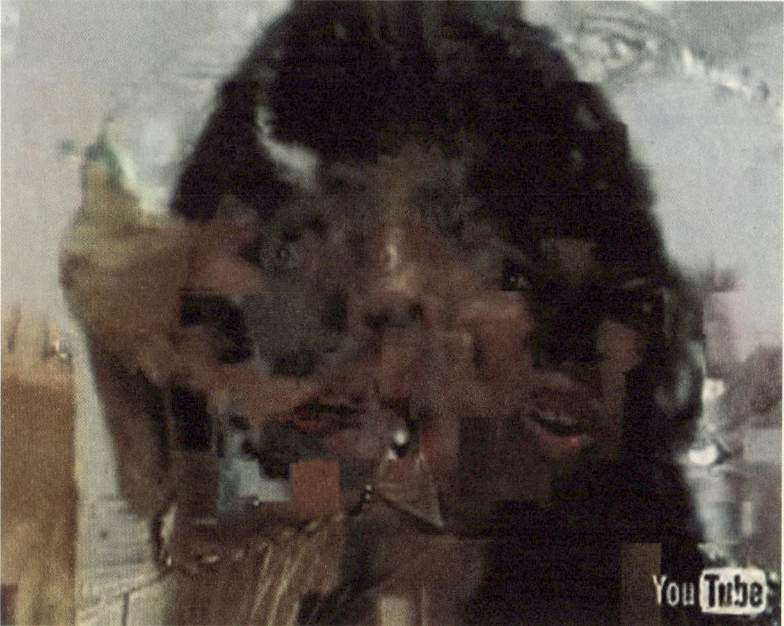

4.

1. **Super Abstract**
2000, hacked Nintendo NES video game cartridge

2. **Notorious B.I.G. quote applied to the de-fetishization of obsolete game consoles in order to propose a unified medium among Turing-complete machines**
2008, Atari 2600, Nintendo NES, Atari 5800, hacked video game cartridges, and 3 televisions, dimensions variable

3. **N.O.S. (No Operating System)**
2008, assembly boot code and computer

4. **Superfreaks (Compression Study #3)**
2007, digital projection, dimensions variable

Nzuji De Magalhaes earned her MFA from the University of Southern California and currently lives in Costa Mesa, California. Drawing on the early influence of Angolan folklore and mythology, she uses material from yarn, sand, glitter, and beads to chalk, acrylic, and oil paint. Her work explores the exchange between African and American cultures, bringing forward issues of gender, child labor, and the experience of minority communities in the United States and abroad.

1. Souvenir: Soldier Killing Woman
2001-05, yarn, sand, glitter, beads, and oil paint, 8 × 6 in (20 × 15 cm)

2. Souvenir: Young Girl
2001-05, yarn, sand, glitter, beads, and oil paint, 7 × 5 in (18 × 13 cm)

3. Souvenir: Model
2001-05, yarn, sand, glitter, beads, and oil paint, 8 × 6 in (20 × 15 cm)

4. Souvenir: Soldiers
2001-05, yarn, sand, glitter, beads, and oil paint, 7 × 5 in (18 × 13 cm)

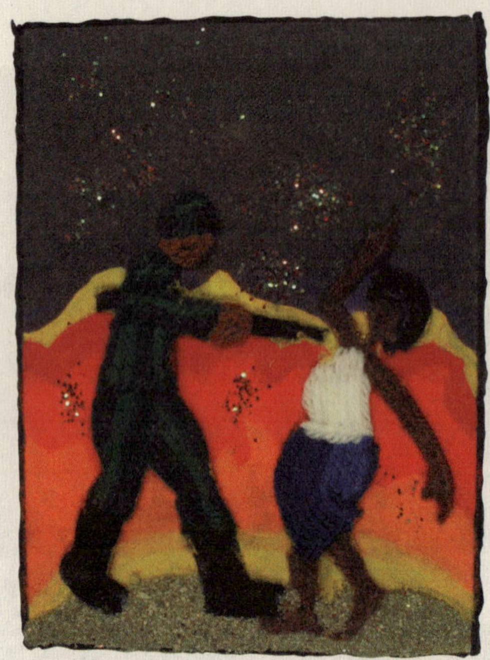
1.

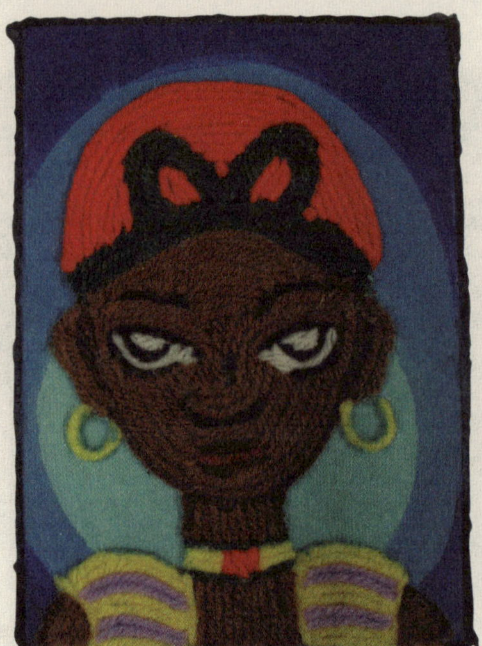
2.

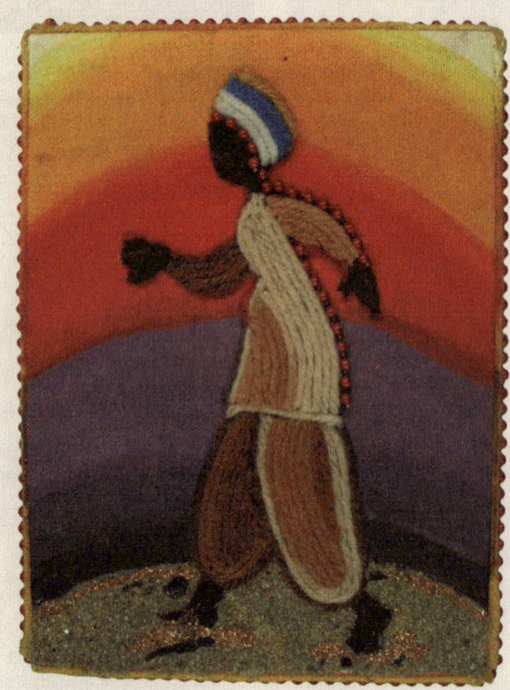
3.

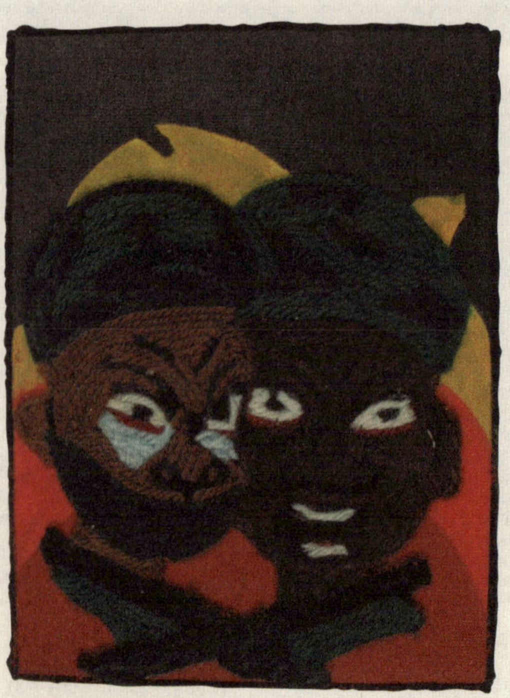
4.

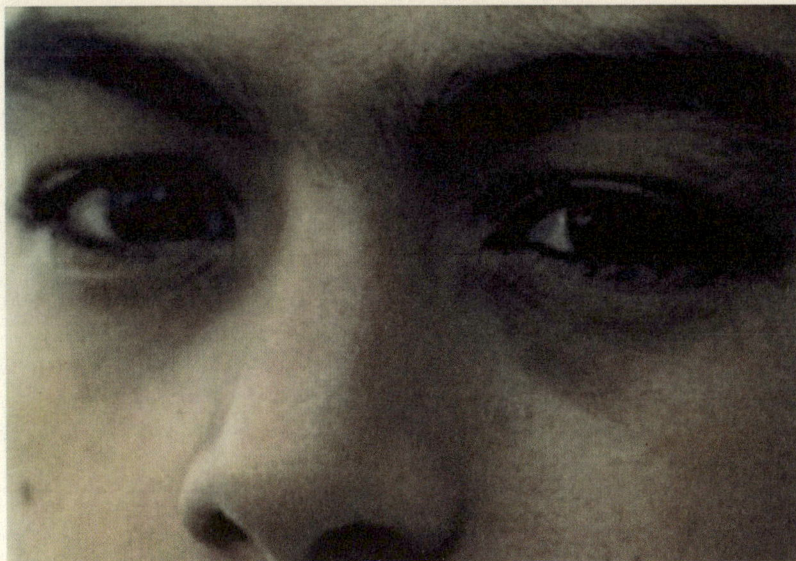

1.

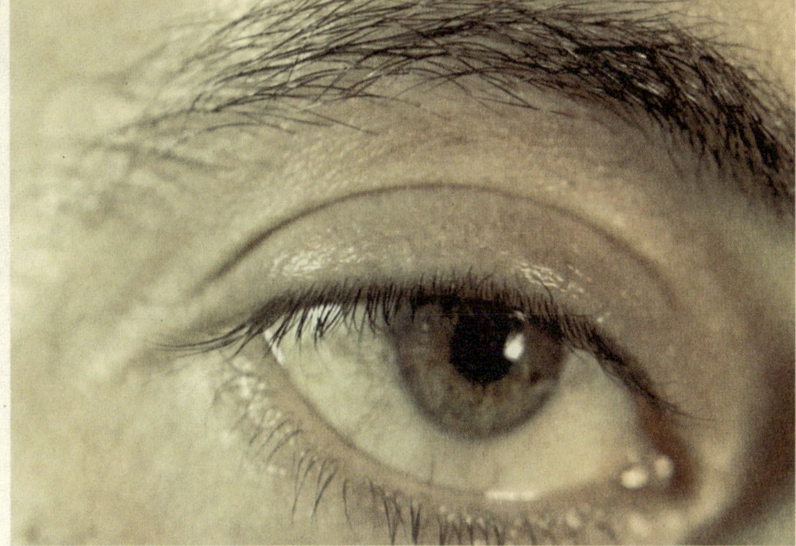

2.

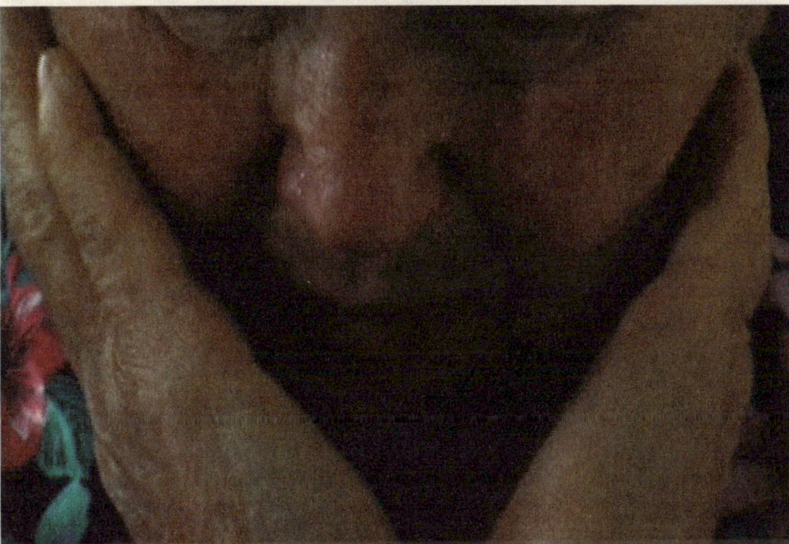

3.

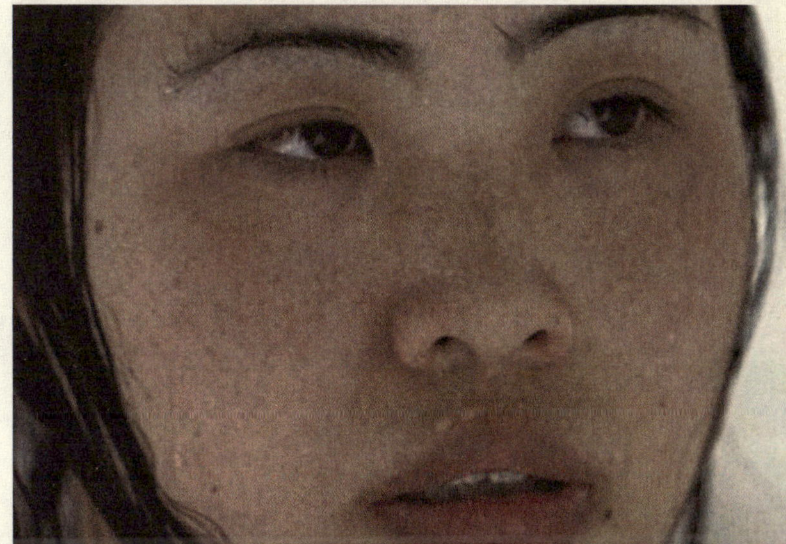

4.

Combining backgrounds in art history, technology, and cinema, Gianluca and Massimiliano De Serio have been working collaboratively since 1999 and currently live in Turin. Their films address immigrant culture, mixed identities, and the general climate of global politics by representing experience through intersections between reality, memory, and fiction.

1. **Lezioni di arabo**
2005, 35 mm cinemascope film, color, 14 min

2. **Salvatore/A Star Love**
2008, 2-channel video projection, 7 min

3. **Tanatologia, 14 maggio 1958**
2007, video, 11 min

4. **Mio fratello Yang**
2004, 35 mm film, color, 15 min

5. **Maria Jesus**
2003, 35 mm film, color, 13 min

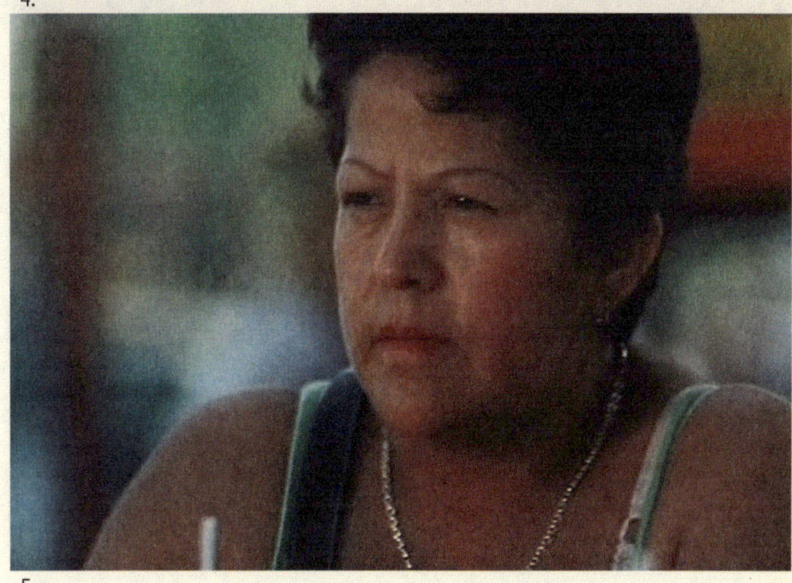

5.

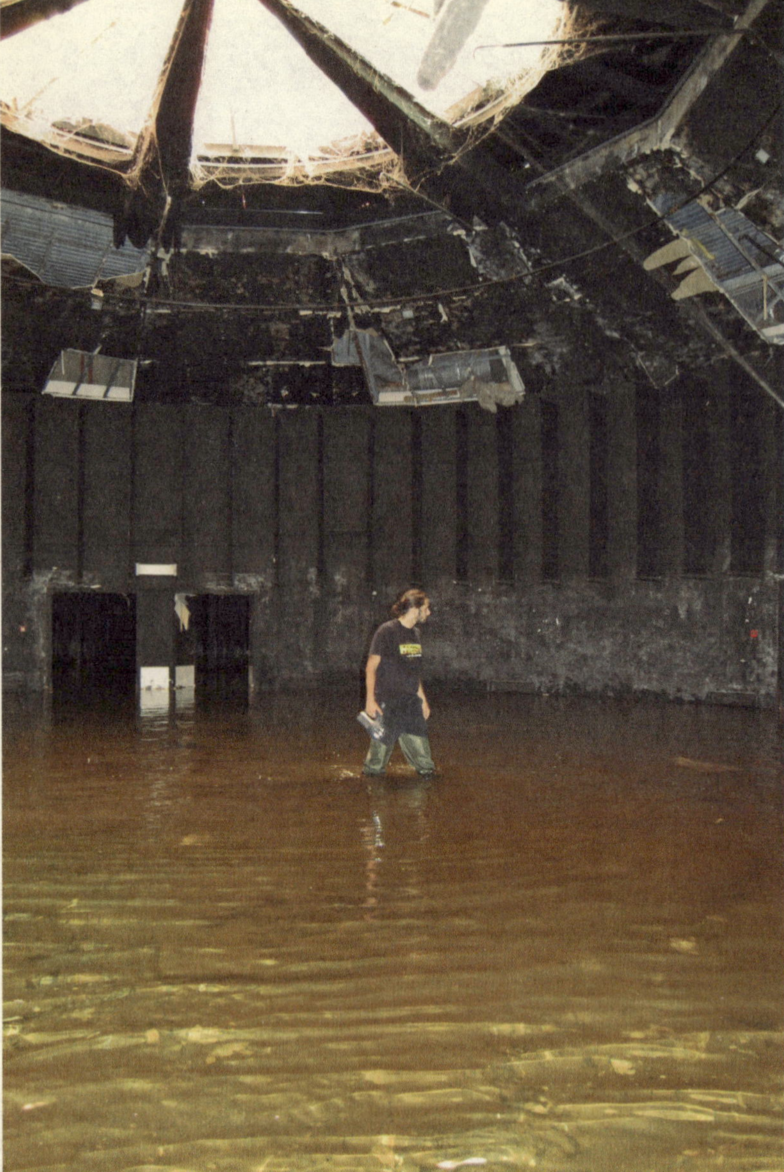

1.

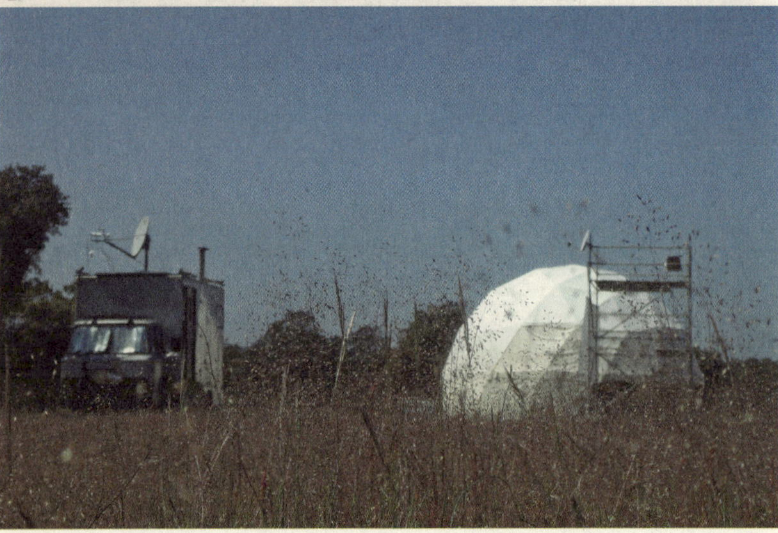

2.

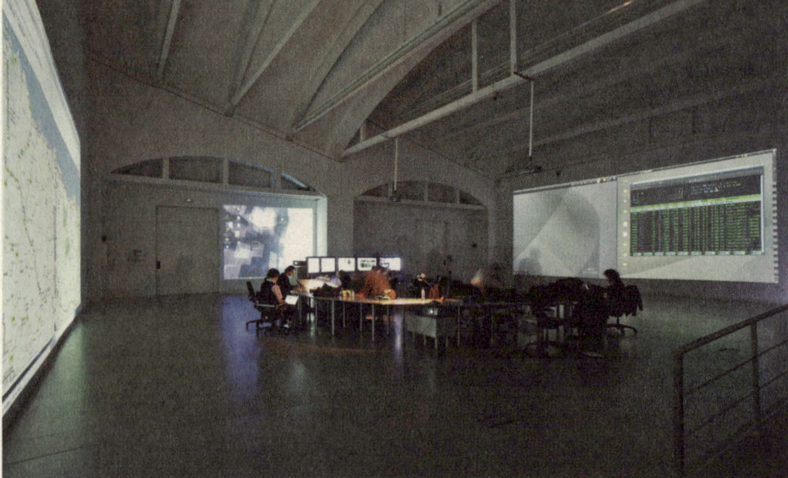

3.

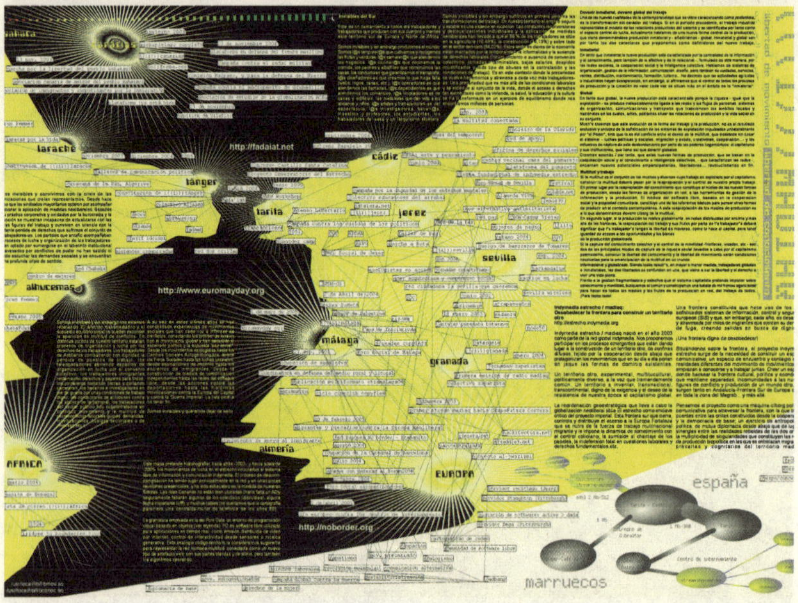

4.

Pablo de Soto earned his MA in architecture from the KTH Royal Institute of Technology in Stockholm. He is a founding member of hackitectura.net, a "posse of architects, hackers, and social activists experimenting in the emerging territories of recombining spatial cyborgs composed by physical spaces, ICT networks, and bodies." A pioneer of "information arts," he conceived the experiment-simulation **Situation Room** (2008) as a forum for experts in various fields to share knowledge.

1. **Water 4 Bits**
with José Pérez de Lama/hackitectura.net
2008, synchronized installation in physical and digital space, installation view at Europe Pavilion, Cartuja 93, BIACS3, Seville

2. **Emergent Geolab**
2007, temporary outdoor media lab at Valdecaballeros abandoned nuclear plant, Spain, dimensions variable

3. **Situation Room**
with José Pérez de Lama
2008, prototype of a citizen's control room, dimensions variable, installation view at LABoral Centro de Arte, Gijón, Spain

4. **Tactical Cartography of the Strait of Gibraltar**
2004, map, 33 × 47 in (84 × 119 cm)

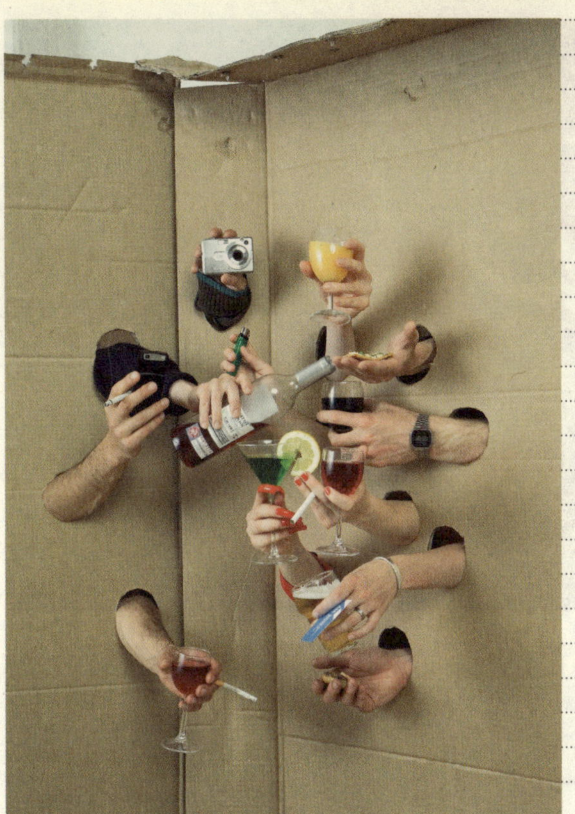
1.

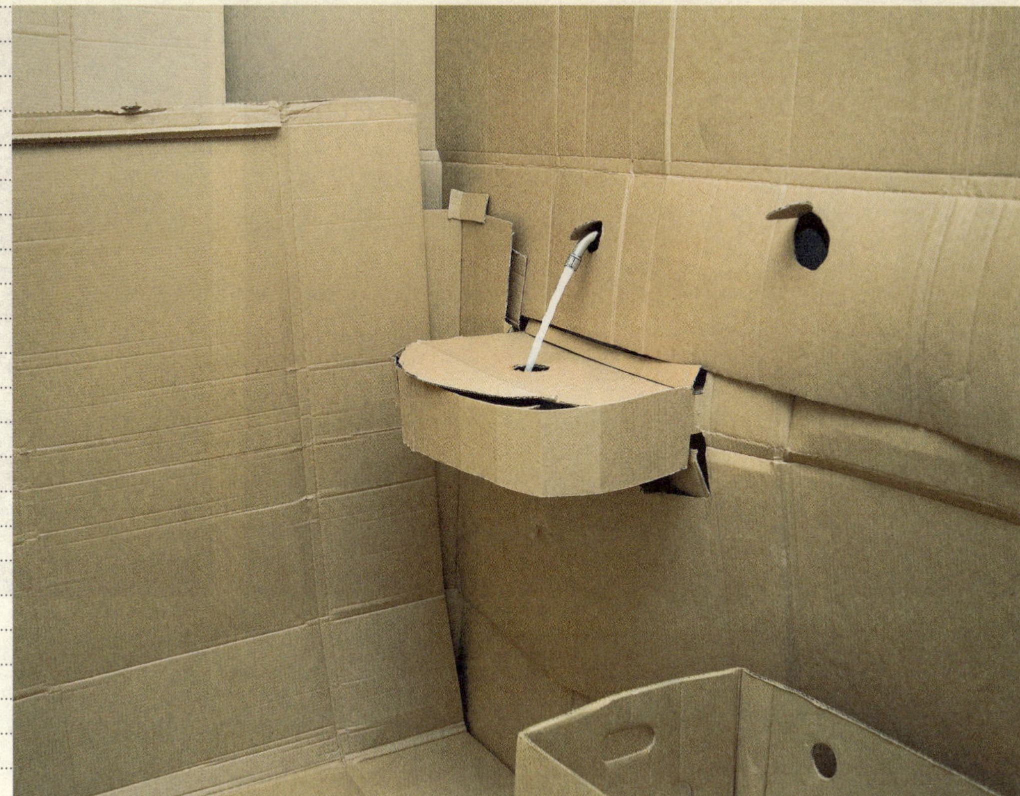
2.

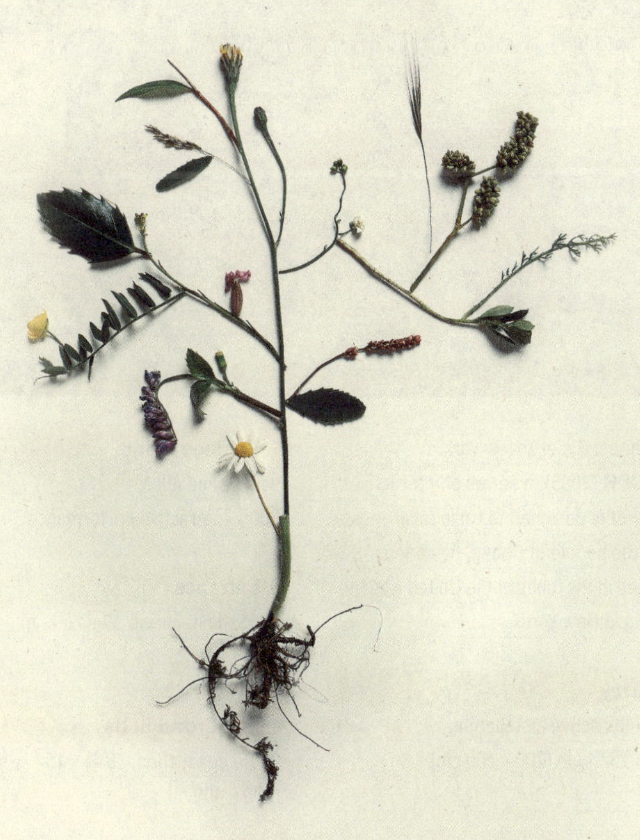
3.

Anne de Vries attended Gerrit Rietveld Academie, Amsterdam, and currently lives in Amsterdam and Berlin. Her color photographs show staged scenes that bring absurd, comic, and sexual dimensions to ordinary situations. Her practice also includes video, installation, performance, and collaborative projects, as well as work related to fashion, advertising, and graphic design.

1. My private cardboard party
2007, chromogenic print on Dibond with DuraSec, 56½ × 38½ in (144 cm × 98 cm)

2. You can't erase the stream
2007, chromogenic print on Dibond with DuraSec, 56½ × 80¼ in (144 × 204 cm)

3. Plan
2005, chromogenic print in frame, 23 × 12¾ in (58 × 45 cm)

4. Perform your duty
2003, chromogenic print in frame, 12¾ × 23 in (45 × 58 cm)

5. Dead darling
2007, chromogenic print on Dibond with DuraSec, 27½ × 12¾ in (70 × 45 cm)

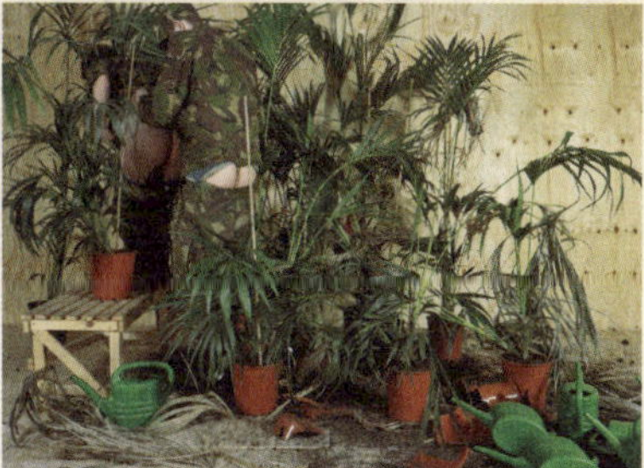
4.

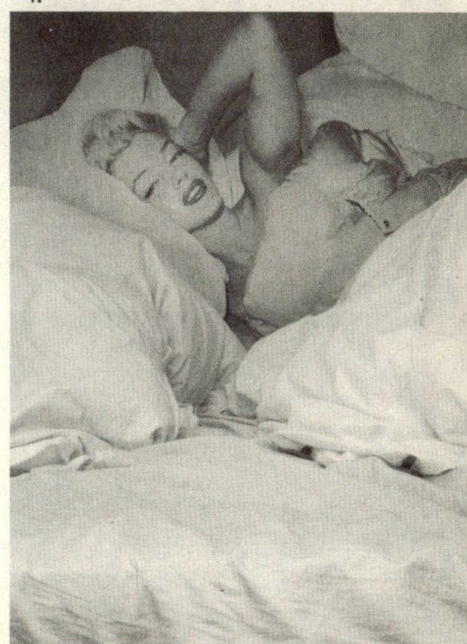
5.

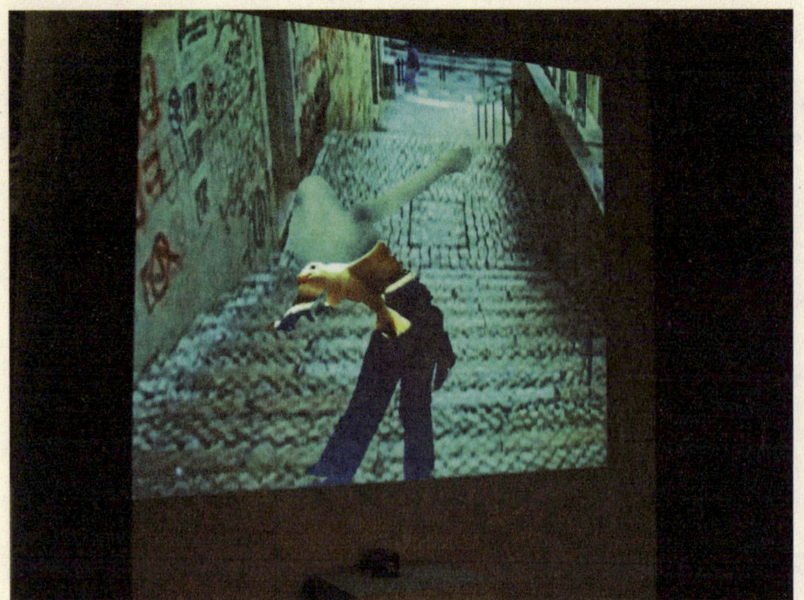

1.

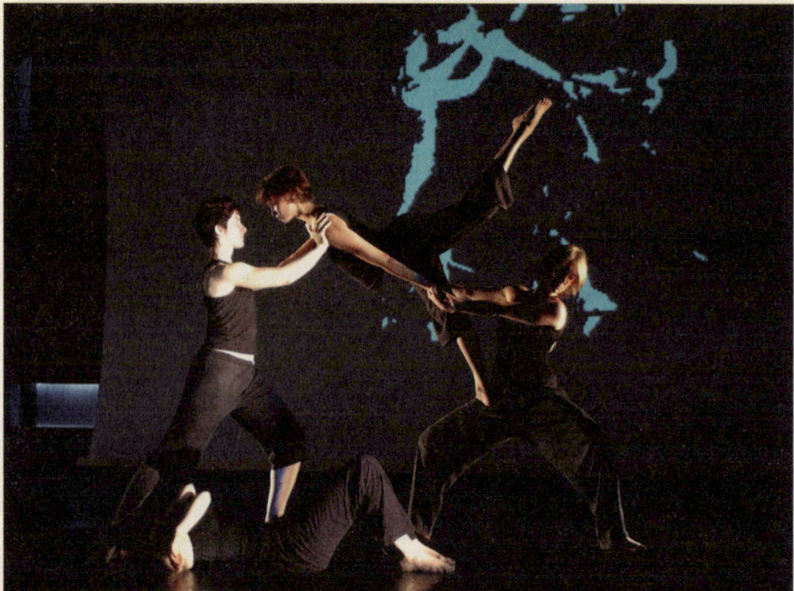

2.

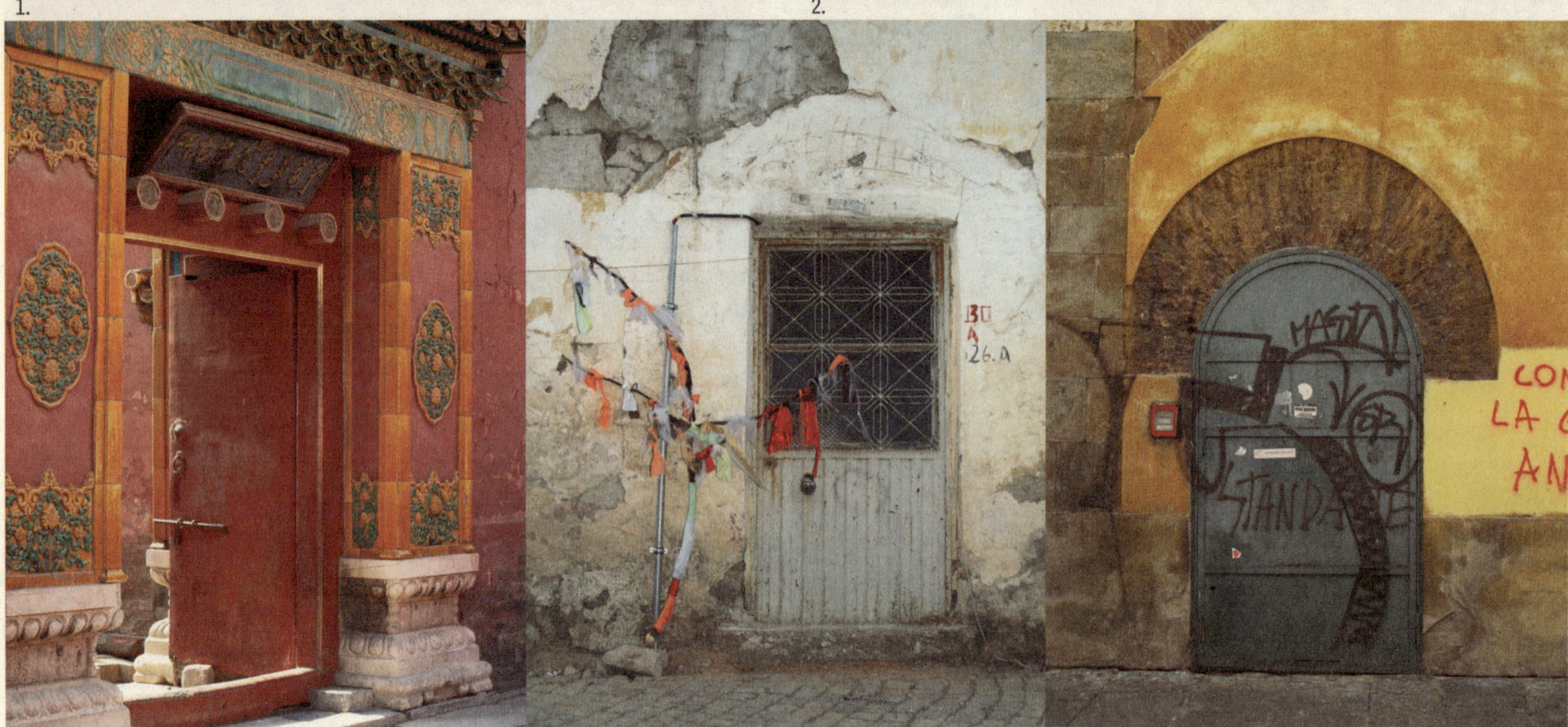

3.

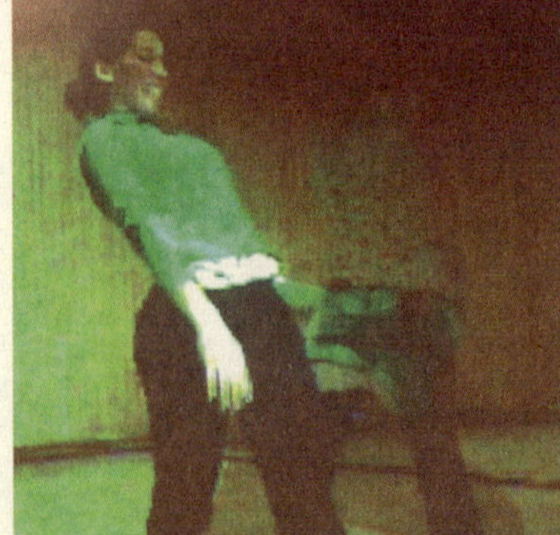

4.

Beliz Demircioglu is a choreographer and new media artist who received her MPS in interactive telecommunications from New York University's Tisch School of the Arts. Her work links live performance with various forms of responsive digital media, creating a feedback loop between the real and the virtual. Her multimedia dance project **Vantage Point** (2005), created in collaboration with Jamie Allen, was realized with a Baryshnikov Arts Center Fellowship and was performed at Eyebeam Gallery, New York. **INTOUCH** (2005), a series of interactive video works designed to raise awareness about the people of Ghana, has been exhibited in the lobby of the United Nations Building in New York.

1. **Icyuzey**
2007, interactive installation, 78 ¾ × 157 ½ in (200 × 400 cm)

2. **Vantage Point**
with Jamie Allen
2005, interactive performance

3. **Entrance**
2006, digital print, 59 × 26 ¼ in (150 × 67 cm)

4. **The Crowd in Us**
2005, installation, 78 ¾ × 157 ½ in (200 × 400 m)

Simon Denny attended the Städelschule, Staatliche Hochschule für Bildende Künste, Frankfurt, and currently lives in Auckland and Frankfurt. He makes site-specific installations that call attention to relationships between found and made objects. His work was included in the 2008 Brussels Biennial and he is a founding member of the artist-run initiative Gambia Castle in Auckland.

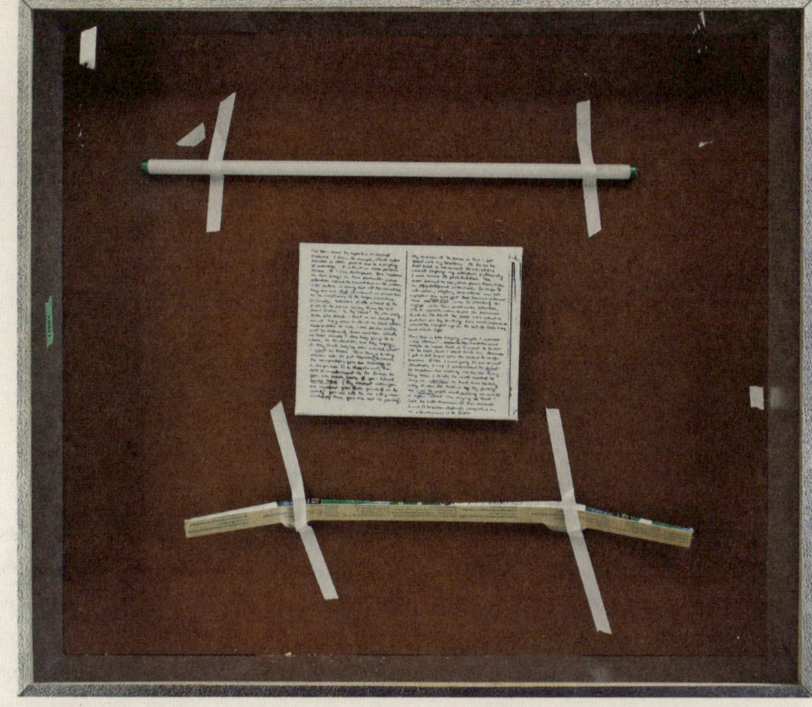

1.

2.

1. Performance Video
2008, custom textured aluminum frame, cardboard, silkscreen on canvas, description of Peter Roche performance by Wystan Curnow, masking tape, and packaged fluorescent lightbulbs, 43 ½ × 51 ¼ × 8 in (110 × 130 × 20 cm)

2. Two Boats
2008, photographic prints, conservation tape, and packaged fluorescent tube in textured aluminum frame, 27 ½ × 35 ½ × 8 in (70 × 90 × 20 cm)

DESPONT, LOUISE

b. 1983 New York, New York, USA

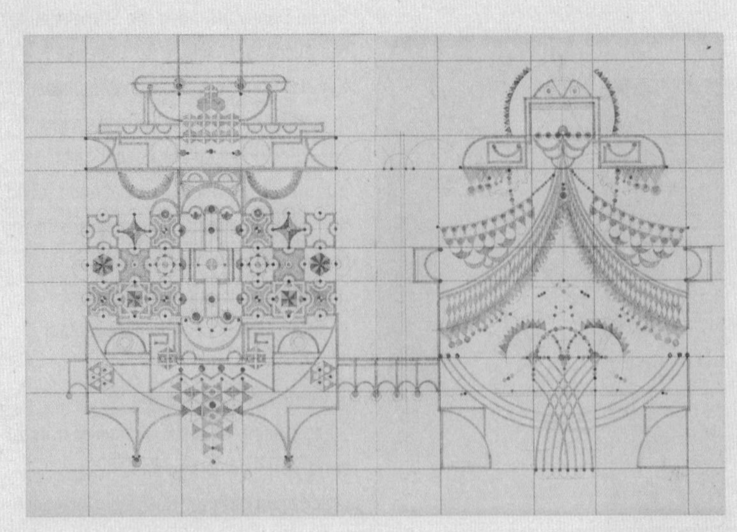

1.

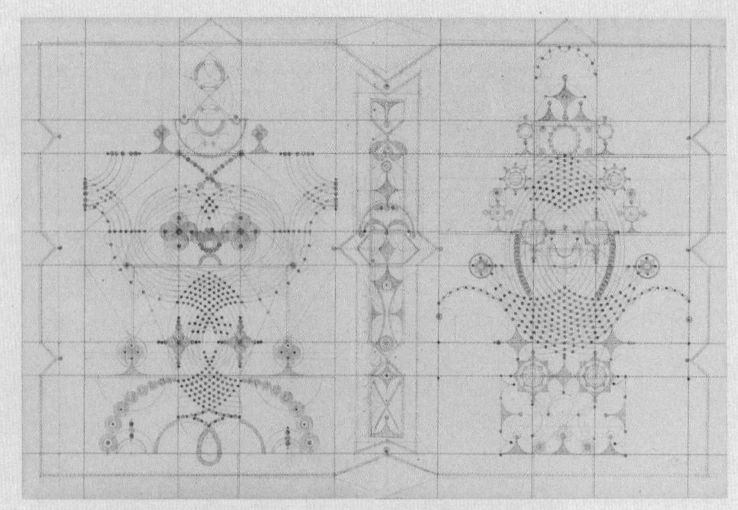

2.

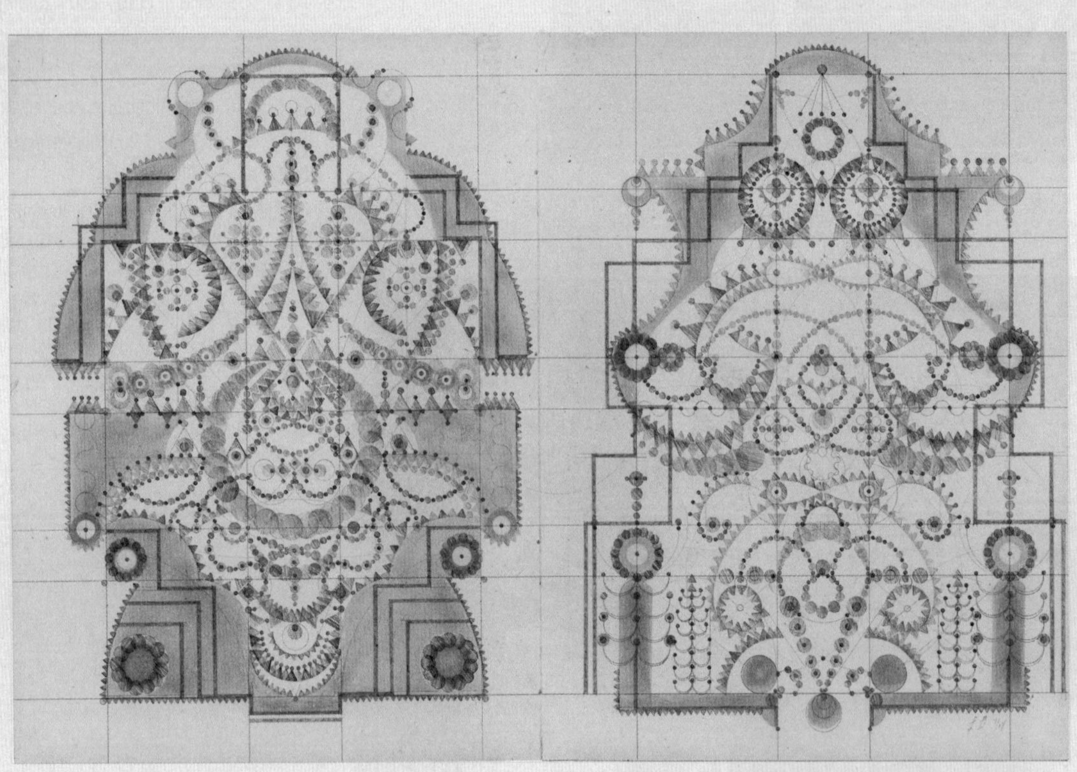

3.

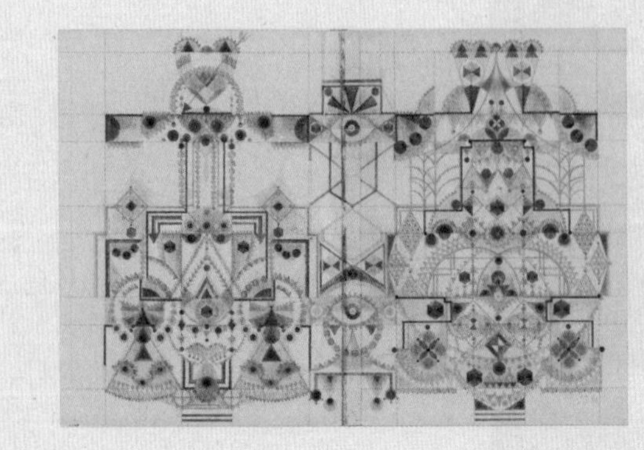

4.

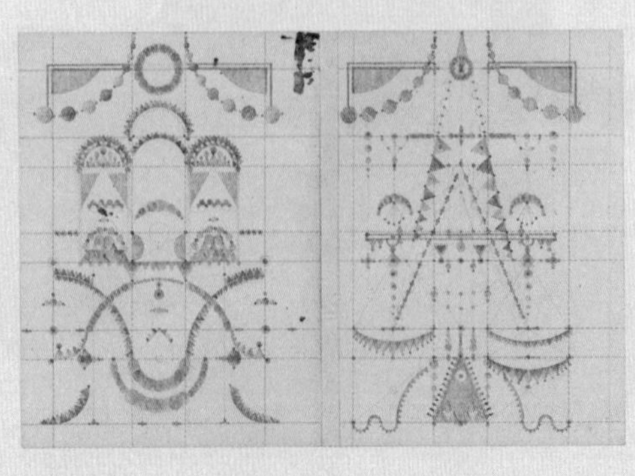

5.

Louise Despont earned her BA in art semiotics from Brown University and currently lives in New York. She makes drawings on the pages of antique ledger books, as well as stop-motion animation films where her vocabulary of pattern, symbol, and symmetry is taken apart and reassembled. According to the artist, both bodies of work are about "the passage of time and the possibility of the imperfect becoming whole through series."

1. **Bridge Organ**
2008, graphite and ink on antique ledger book pages, 15 ½ × 23 in (39 × 58 cm)

2. **Anagrams of Vision No. 3**
2008, graphite and ink on antique ledger book pages, 15 ½ × 23 in (39 × 58 cm)

3. **The Tomb in the Garden**
2008, graphite and ink on antique ledger book pages, 15 ½ × 23 in (39 × 58 cm)

4. **Writing Letters to the Shades**
2008, graphite and ink on antique ledger book pages, 15 ½ × 23 in (39 × 58 cm)

5. **The Door, The Scale, The Hymn**
2008, graphite and ink on antique ledger book pages, 15 ½ × 23 in (39 × 58 cm)

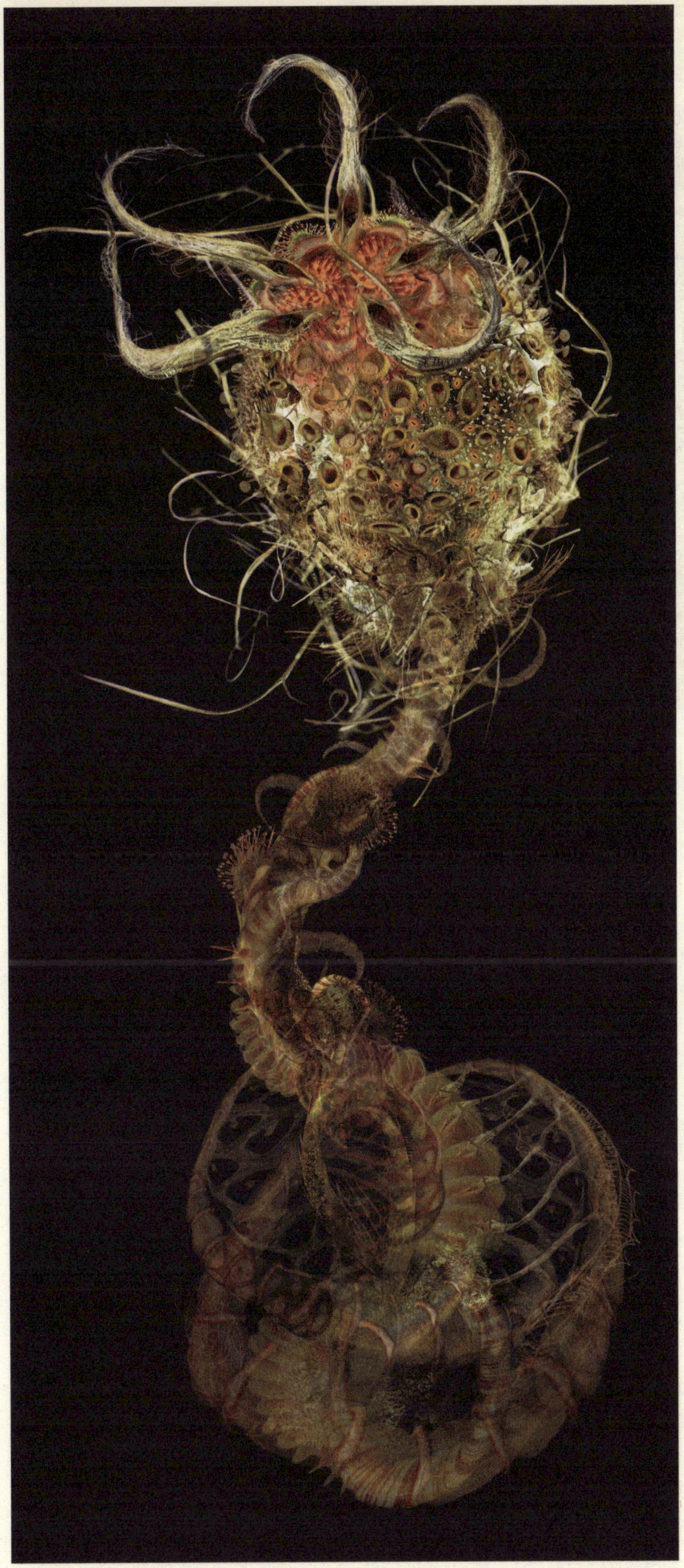

Rohini Devasher earned her MA in printmaking from the Winchester School of Art, UK, and currently lives in New Delhi. She draws elements from different forms of printmaking – the continuous line of woodcut, the multiple, and the repeated image – to create layered, weblike compositions. Her process is based on "principles of growth" inspired by the natural world, and often involves digital printing, drawing, and mural-size works.

1. **Archetype I**
2007, digital print and drawing on archival photo rag paper, 106 × 42 in (269 × 107 cm)

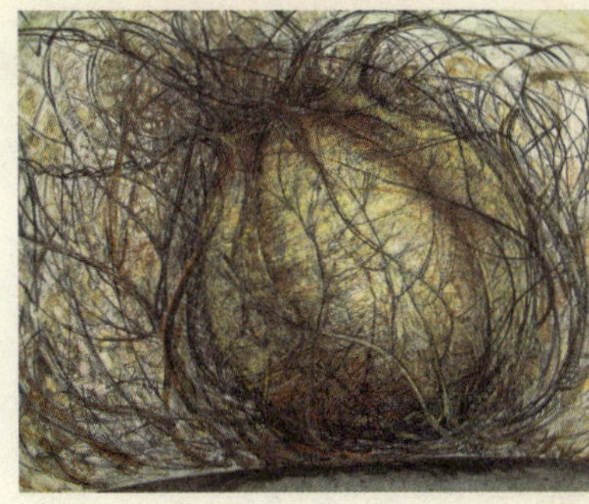

2.

2. **Untitled Wall Drawing**
2004, mixed media on wall, 96 × 180 in (244 × 457 cm)

3. **Untitled Wall Drawing** (detail)
2008, mixed media on wall, 108 × 132 in (274 × 335 cm)

1.

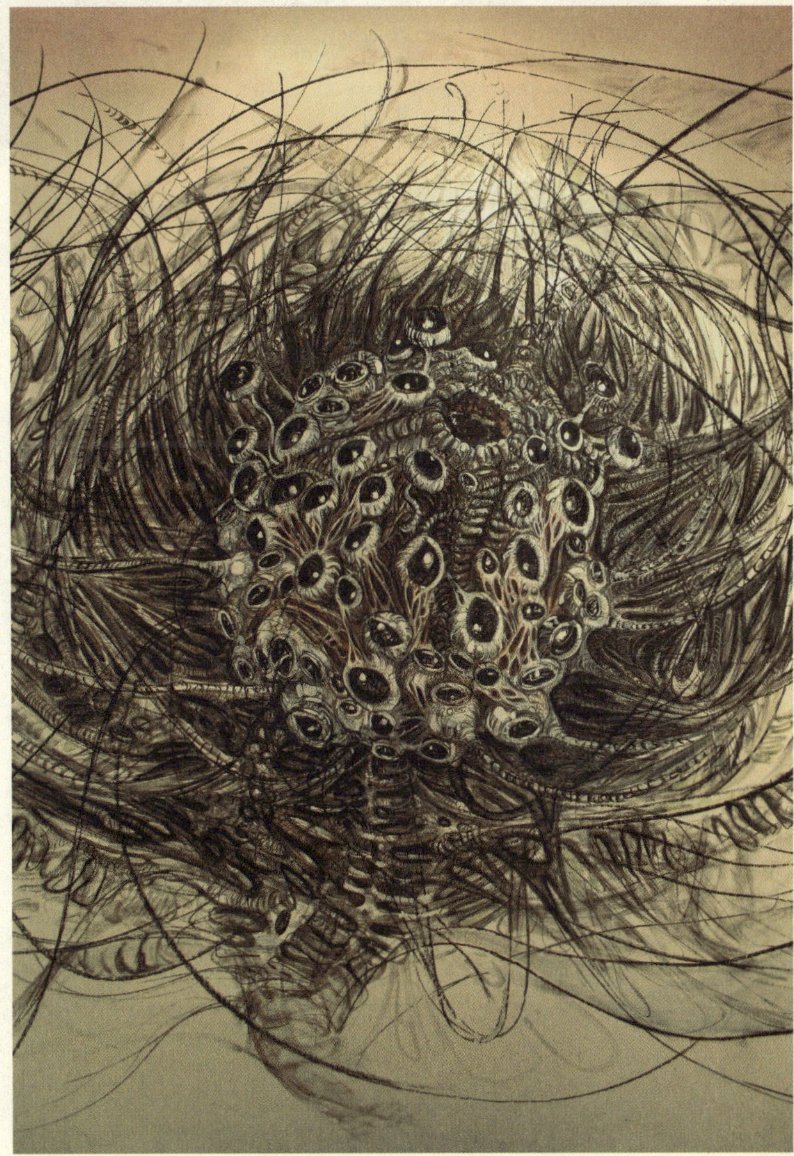

3.

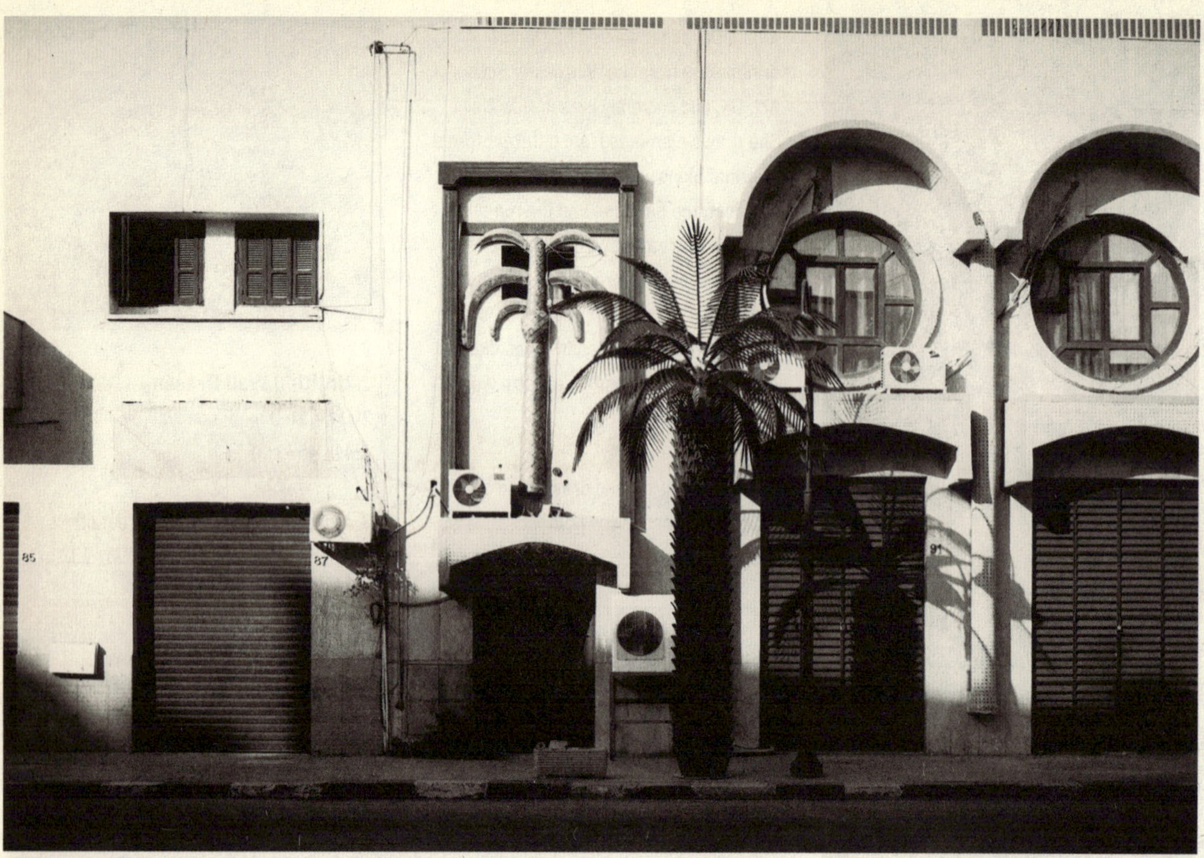
1.

Patrizio di Massimo is currently pursuing his MA degree at the Slade School of Fine Art in London. Using photography, video, installation, and performance, he draws connections between the present and various pasts: his own family history, art history, and Italy's cultural and political history. His video **Pelo & Contropelo** (2007) traces the life and work of Pino Pascali, pioneer of the Arte Povera movement.

1. Oae
2008, black and white photograph, 11 3/4 × 16 1/2 in (30 × 42 cm)

2. Untitled
2008, charcoal on canvas and tissue paper, 39 1/2 × 27 1/2 in (100 × 70 cm)

3. Untitled (my father emulating me)
2007, color photograph from 1970s, 7 × 5 in (18 × 13 cm)

4. Never Real and Yet Always True
2005, color photograph, 53 × 75 in (135 × 190 cm)

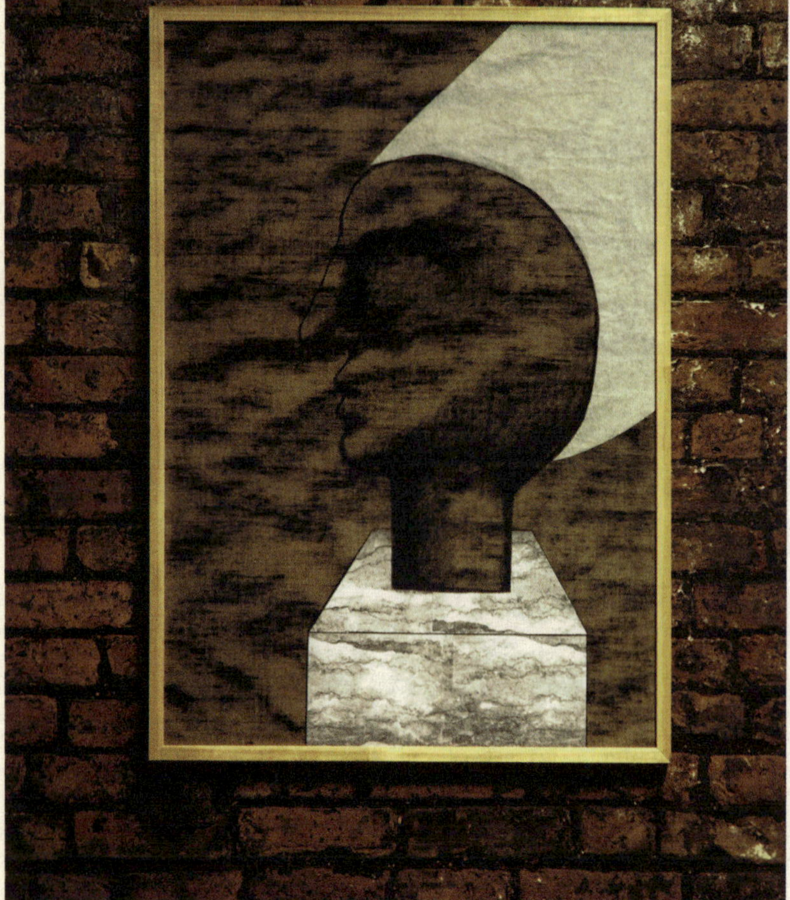
2.

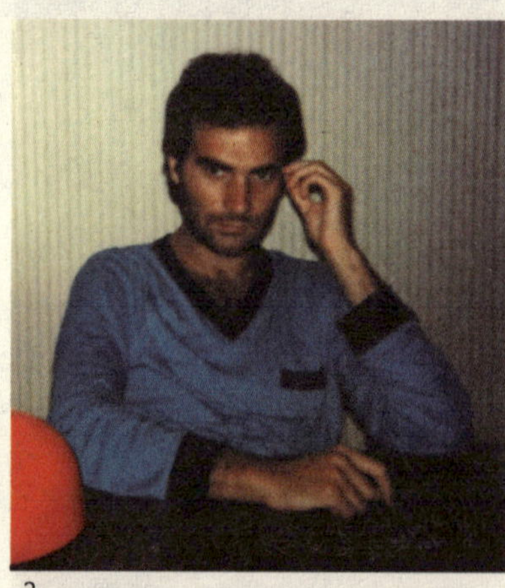
3.

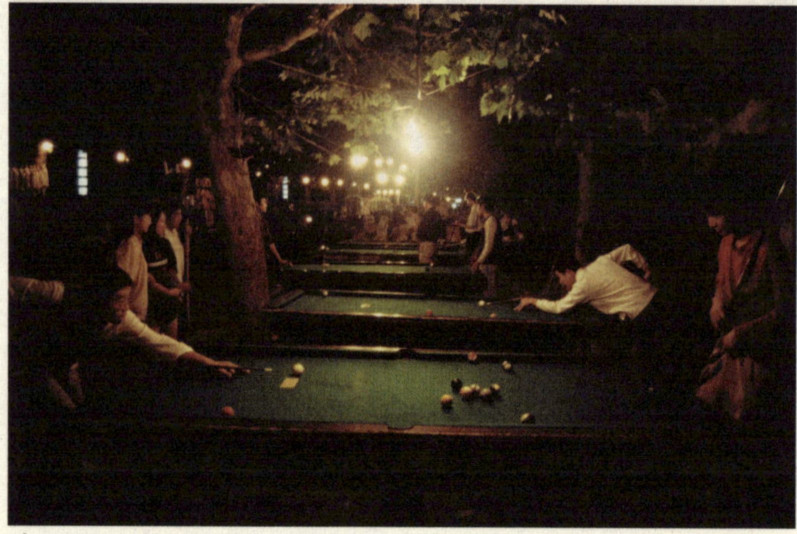
4.

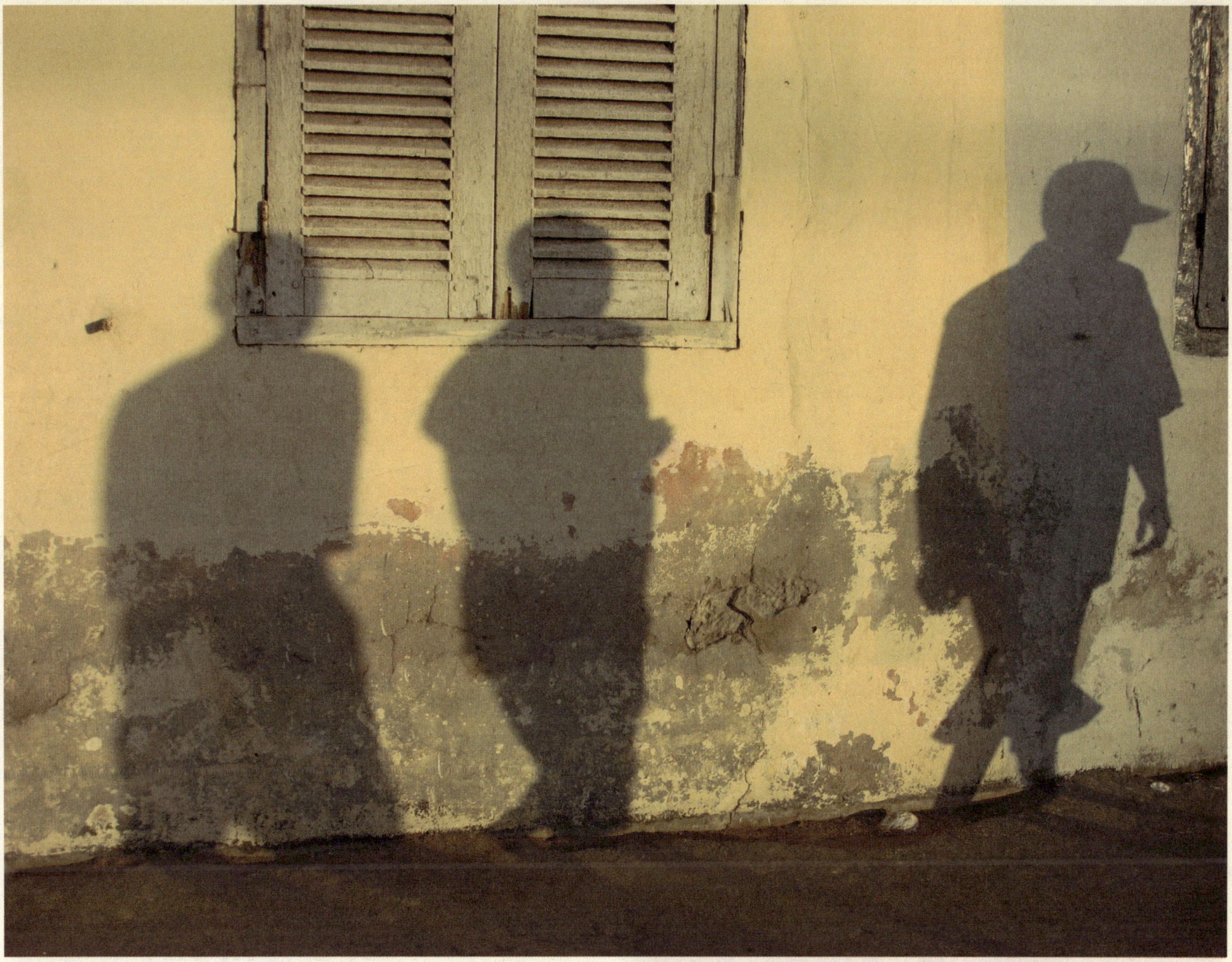

1.

As a child shepherd in his village, Saïdou Dicko began drawing the shadows of lambs on soil. Now based in Dakar, Senegal, he takes photographs that tell stories through shadows of people and animals on the exteriors of houses, shops, and vehicles. His book **Le Voleur d'Ombres** (The Shadow Thief) was published in 2008 by Africalia. He also presented photographs and paintings at Dak'Art 2008, the 8th biennial of contemporary African art.

1. **Pantalon sauté** (Trousers jumped)
2006, digital print, $31\frac{1}{2} \times 39\frac{1}{2}$ in (80 × 100 cm)

2. **Le container** (The container)
2006, digital print, $31\frac{1}{2} \times 39\frac{1}{2}$ in (80 × 100 cm)

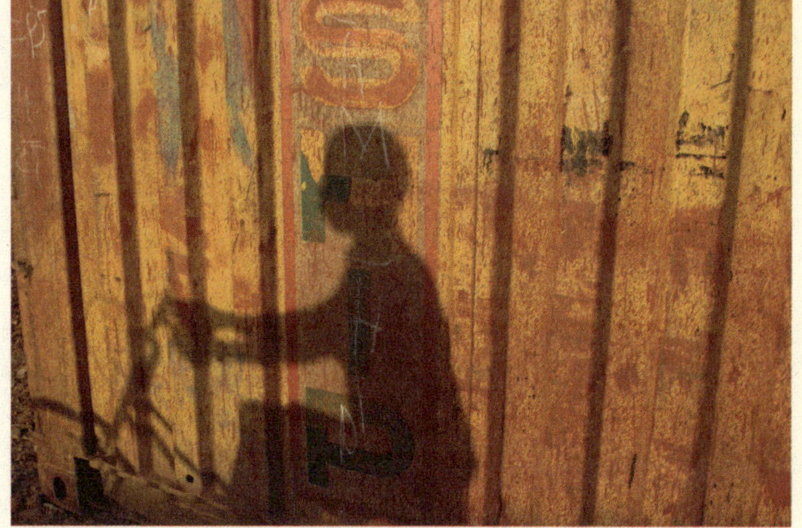

2.

Gintaras Didžiapetris attended the Vilnius Academy of Art and continues to live in Vilnius. Rooted in the conceptual tradition, his practice includes the presentation of objects, actions, sound, text, postcards, photographs, and slide projections. **Konceptas** (2006) uses photographs, sound, booklets, and a hand-drawn map to document the Lithuanian village whose name translates to "Concept" in English.

1. **Untitled** (detail)
2007, 1 of 2 offset printed postcards in frame, dimensions variable

2. **Untitled**
2007, production still, dimensions variable

3. **Gerard Byrne's 1984 and Beyond at The Art Exhibition Hall, Vilnius**
2008, chromogenic print, 12 1/4 × 13 1/2 in (31 × 34 cm)

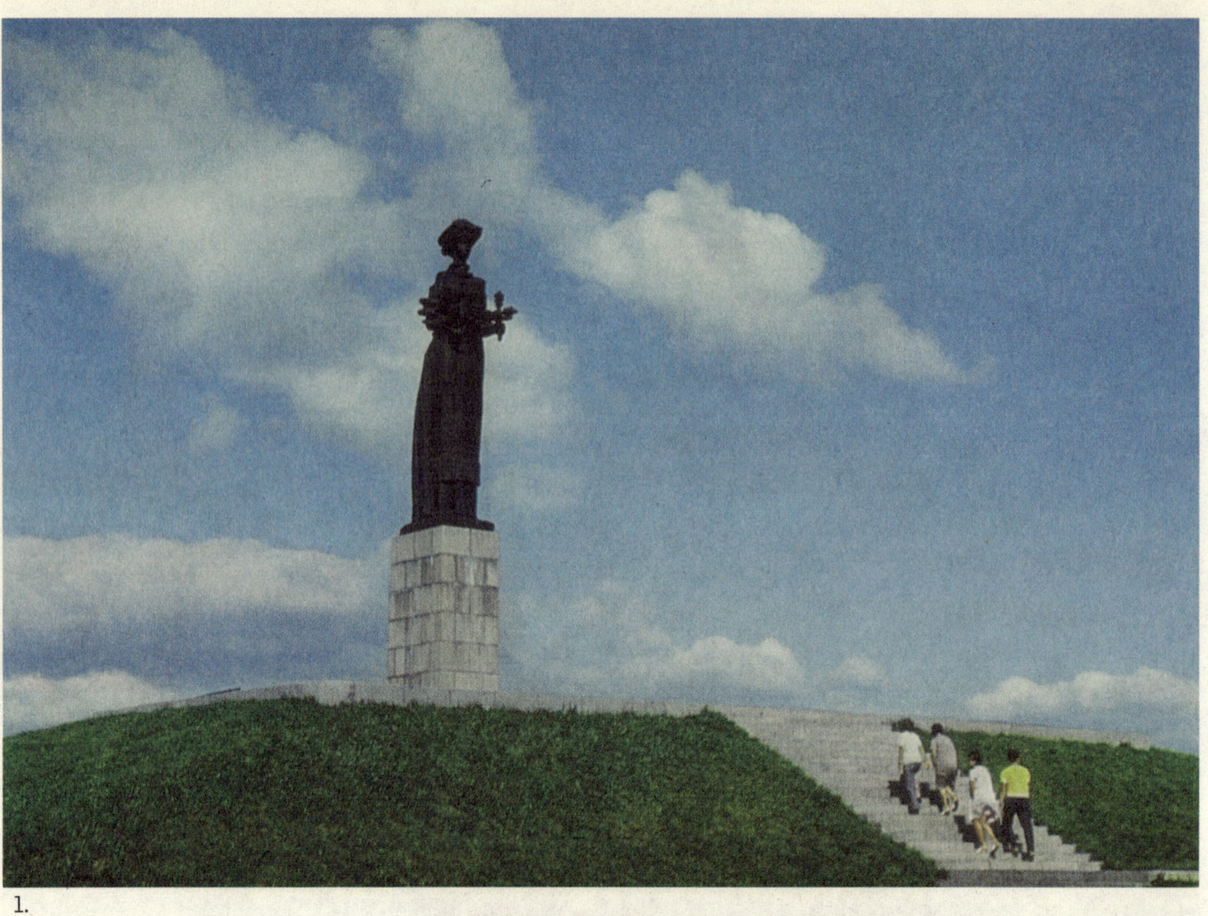

1.

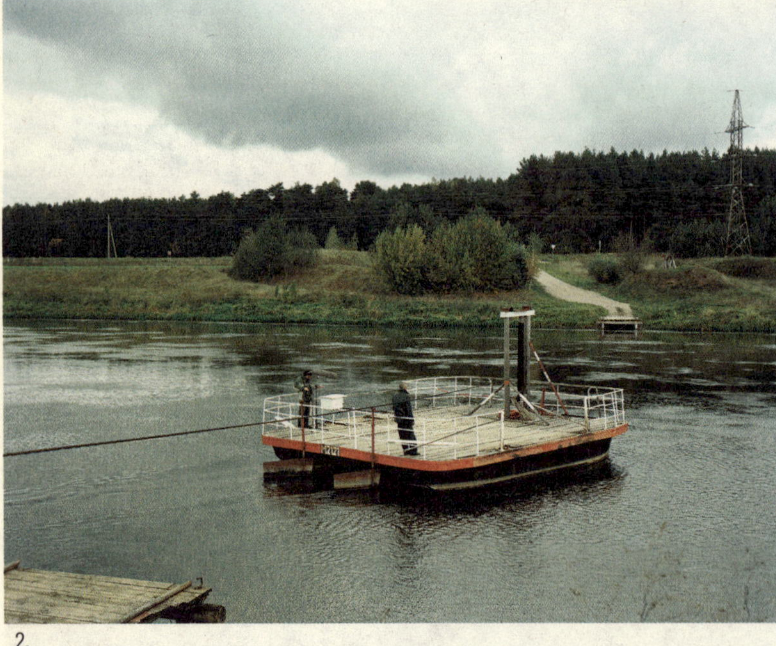

2.

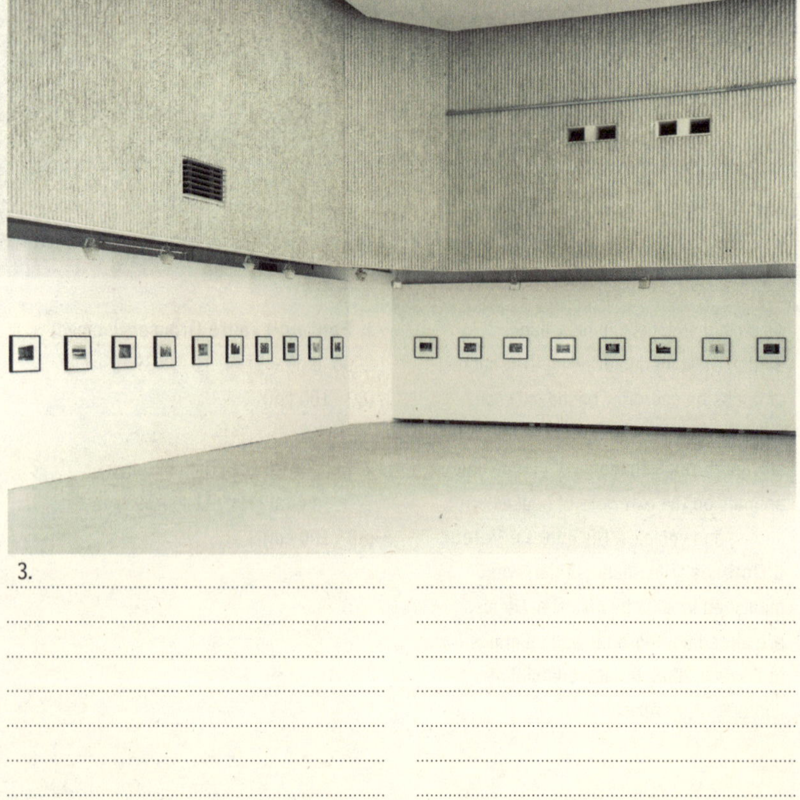

3.

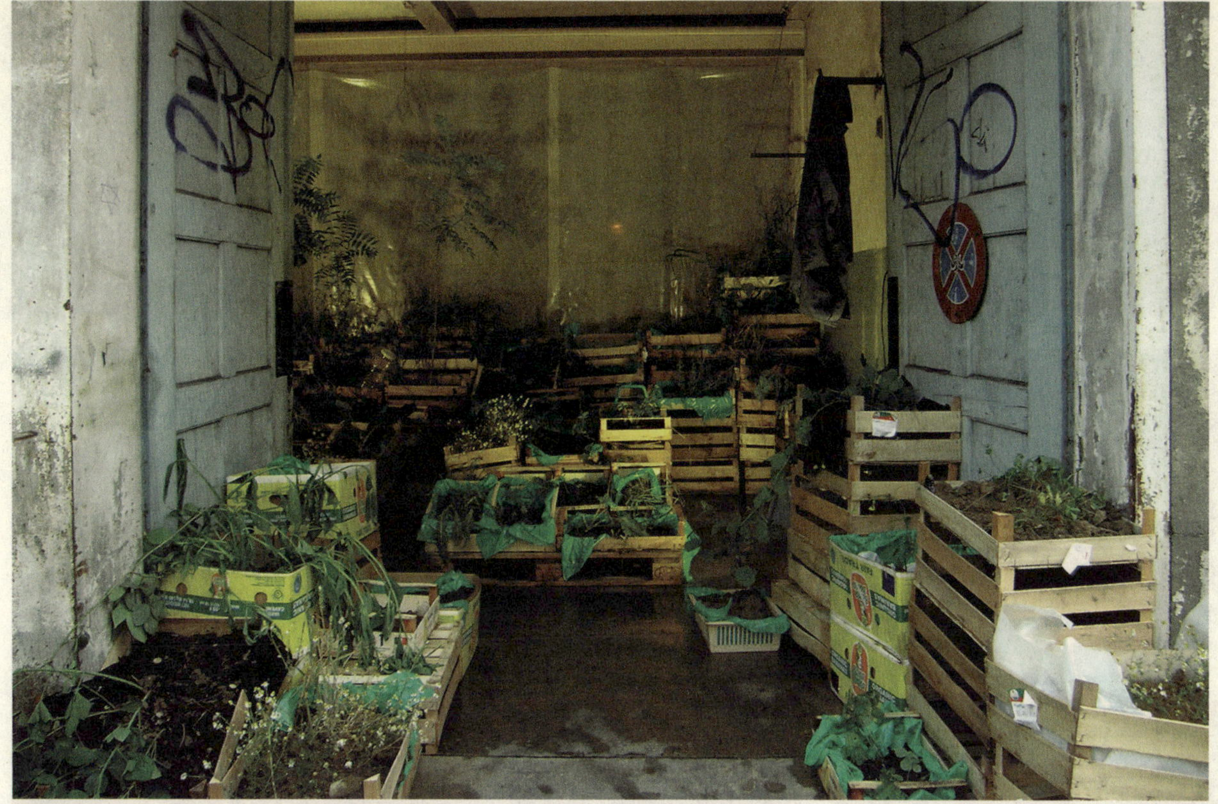
1.

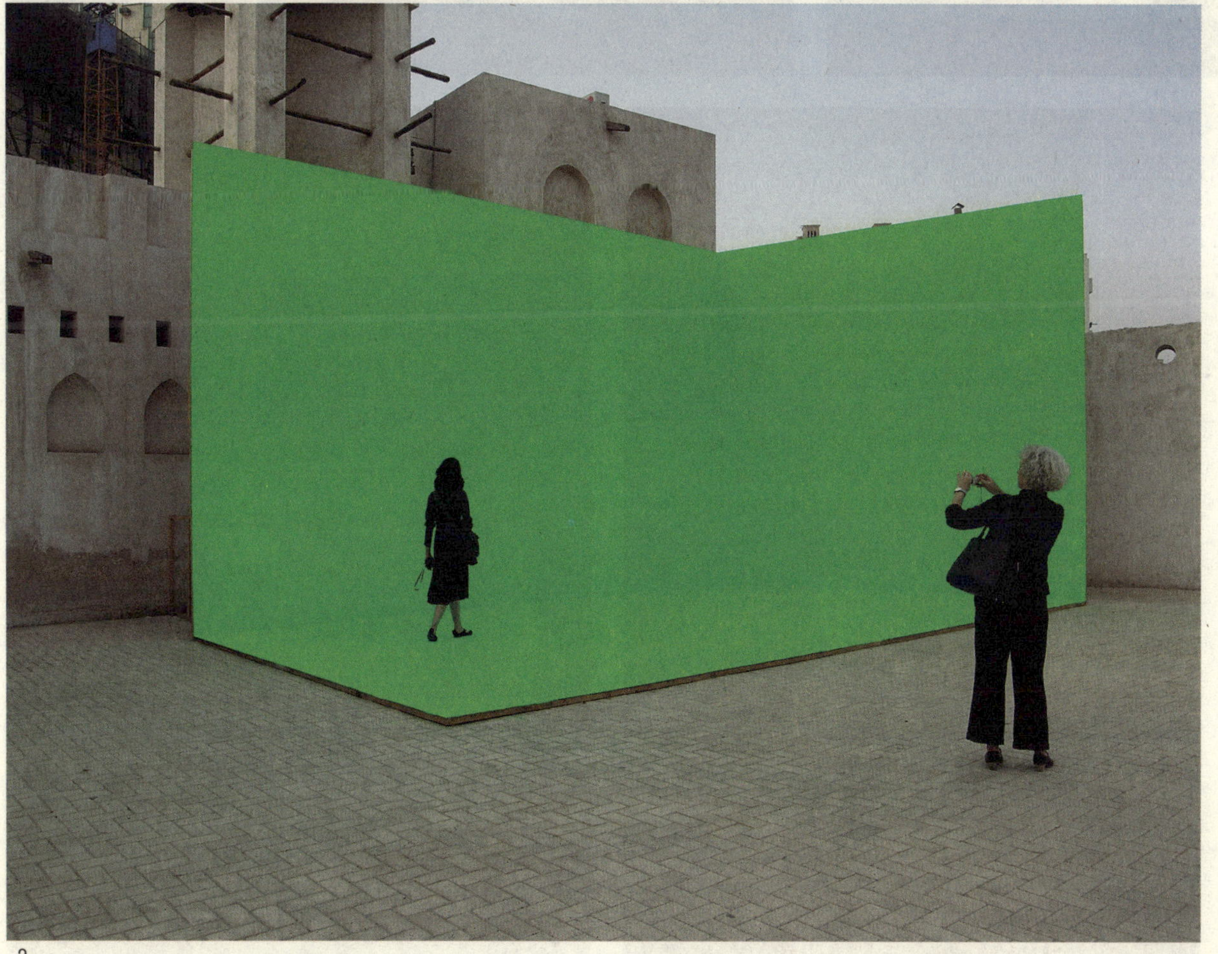
2.

Marjolijn Dijkman studied in the fine art department at Jan van Eyck Academy in Maastricht, Netherlands, and currently lives in Rotterdam. Her practice ranges from worldwide research projects to site-specific interventions. **Theatrum Orbis Terrarum** (2005-present), named after the first modern atlas, is a photographic archive divided into "Gestures," "References," and "Speculations." Dijkman is also cofounder of Enough Room for Space, an artist-run organization challenging the barriers between disciplines of art, science, and activism.

1. Cityfood
2005, vegetable plants, wooden crates, and soil, dimensions variable, installation view at "Enough Room For Space," Filiale, Basel

2. Wandering through the Future
2007, video, 60 min

Margarita Dittborn Valle studied photography at the ARCOS Professional Institute in Santiago, where she continues to live. Her practice of digital photography is rooted in traditions of painting, particularly Baroque and Renaissance. One series uses distortions of scale and fantastic content – like a human head with bunny ears – to inject Surrealism into still lifes reminiscent of Chardin.

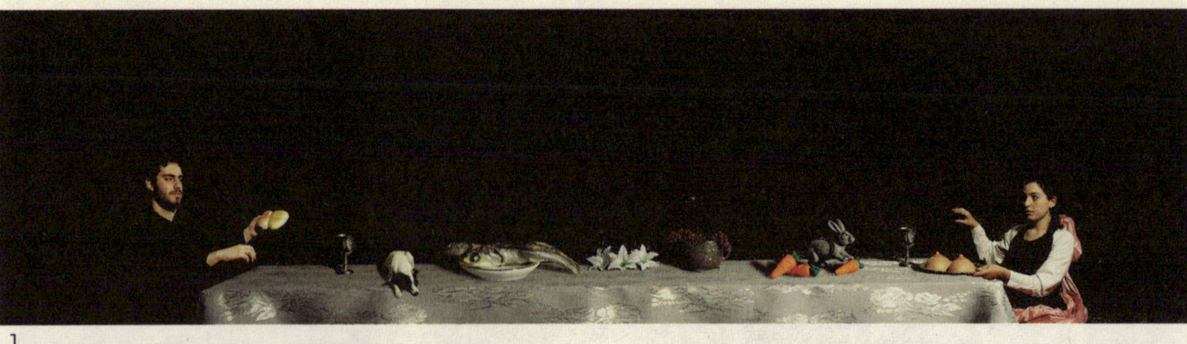

1.

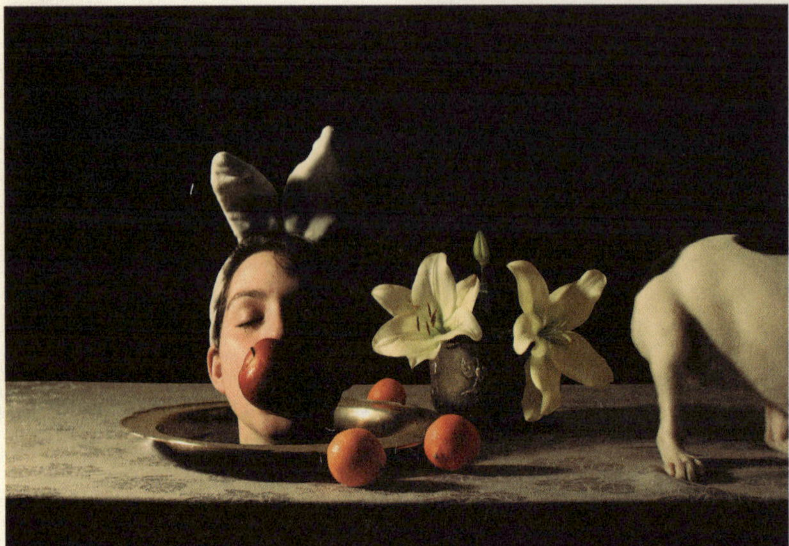

2.

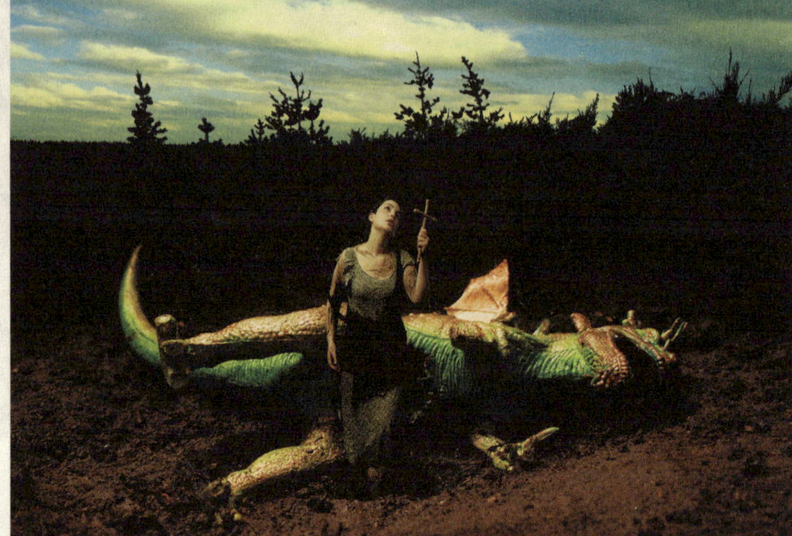

3.

1. Invented dinner between Saint Roch of Montpellier and Saint Angueda of Sicilia
2007, color photograph, 12 × 39 1/2 in (30 × 100 cm)

2. Still Life I
2006, color photograph, 24 1/2 × 36 1/2 in (62 × 93 cm)

3. Saint Margarita from Antioch
2006, color photograph, 24 1/2 × 36 1/2 in (62 × 93 cm)

4. Cooking Scene
2008, color photograph, 38 × 24 1/2 in (97 × 62 cm)

5. Lovesick woman IV
2008, color photograph, 71 × 47 1/4 in (180 × 120 cm)

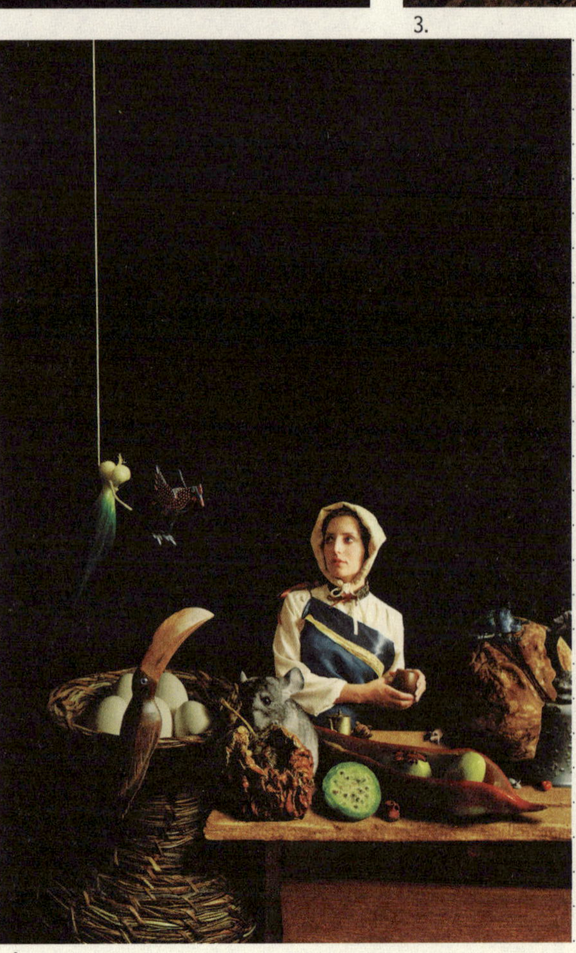

4.

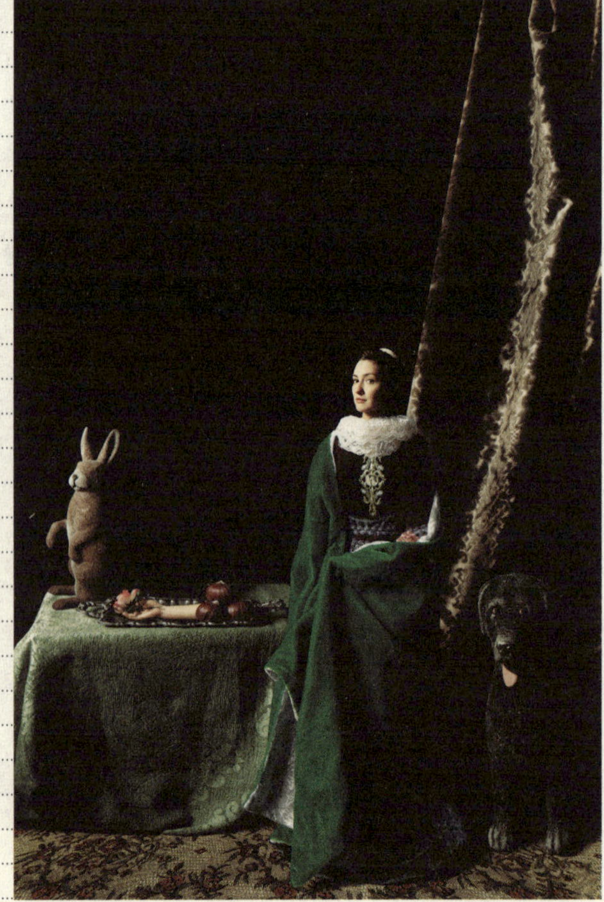

5.

Aleksandra Domanović studied architecture and graphic design and currently lives in Berlin and Ljubljana, Slovenia. She creates videos and other Internet-based work by collecting and reassembling existing information, such as the website **HottestToColdest.com**, a constantly updated list of the world's national capitals according to their current air temperature. She also co-runs the blog **VVORK.com**, a daily compendium for new art online.

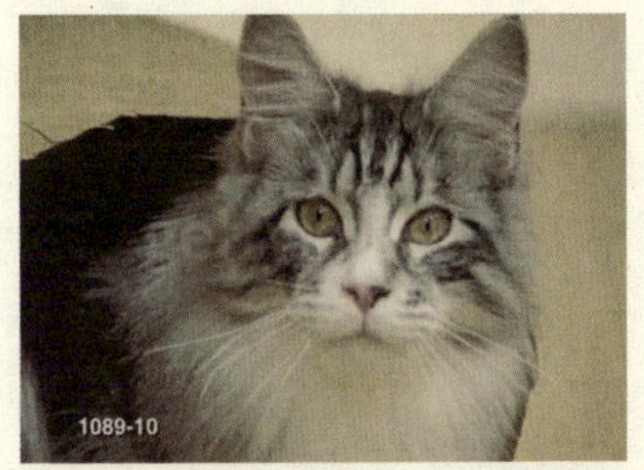

1.

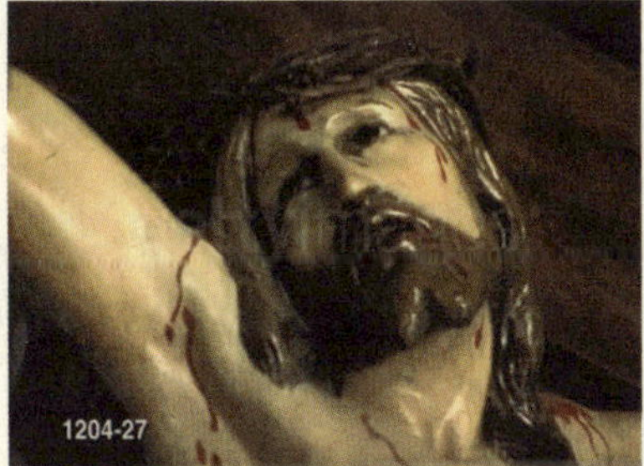

2.

3.

1 & 2. Anhedonia
2007, video, 90 min

3. DEGA
2007, video, 1 min 16 sec

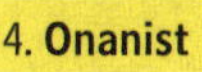

4. Onanist
2004, chromogenic print, 27 ½ × 39 ½ in (70 × 100 cm)

5. New Me
2006, video, 5 min

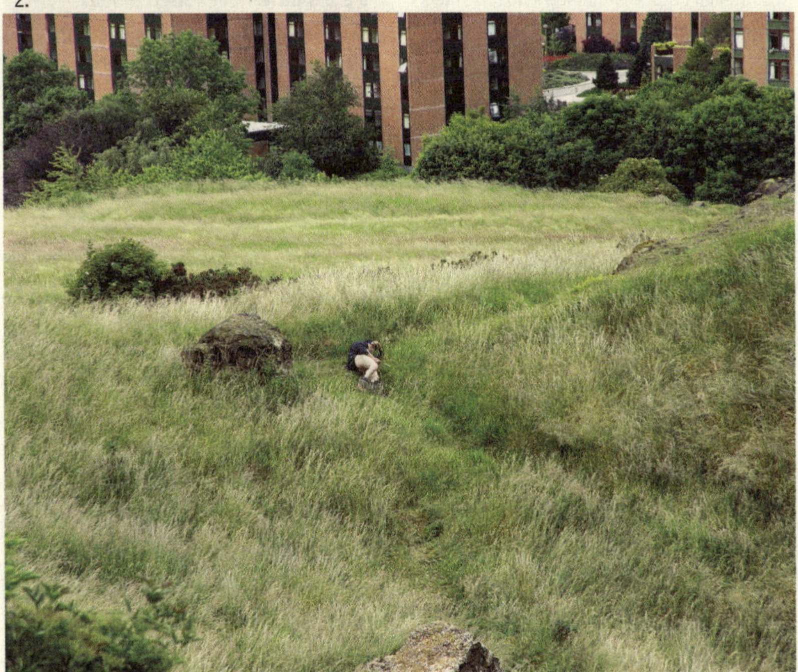
4.

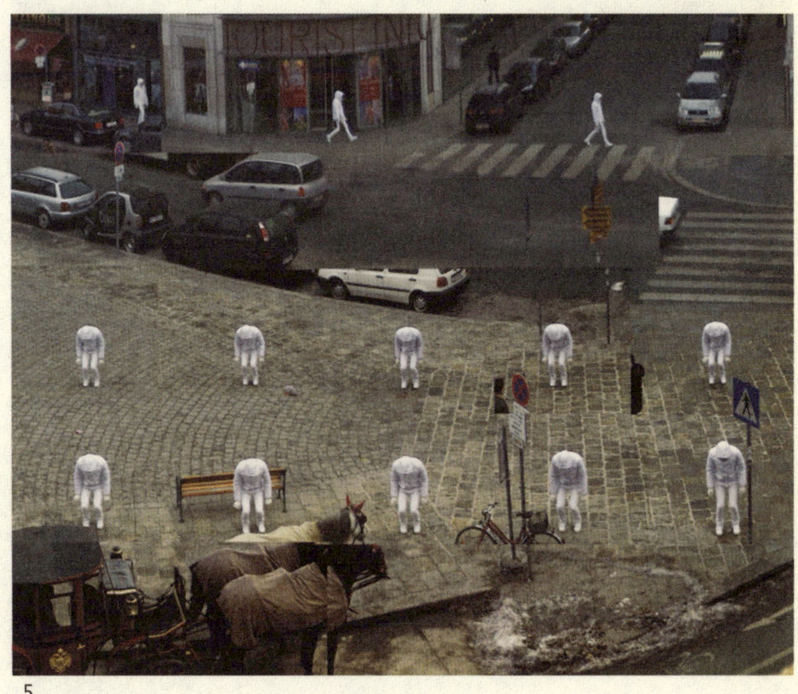
5.

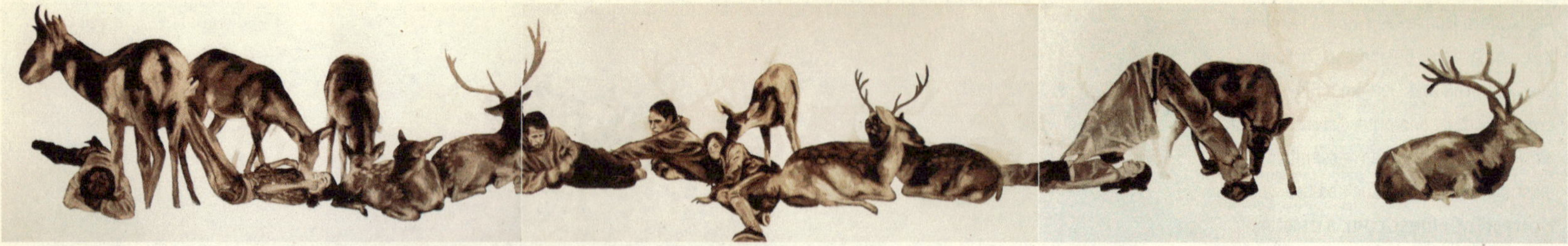

1.

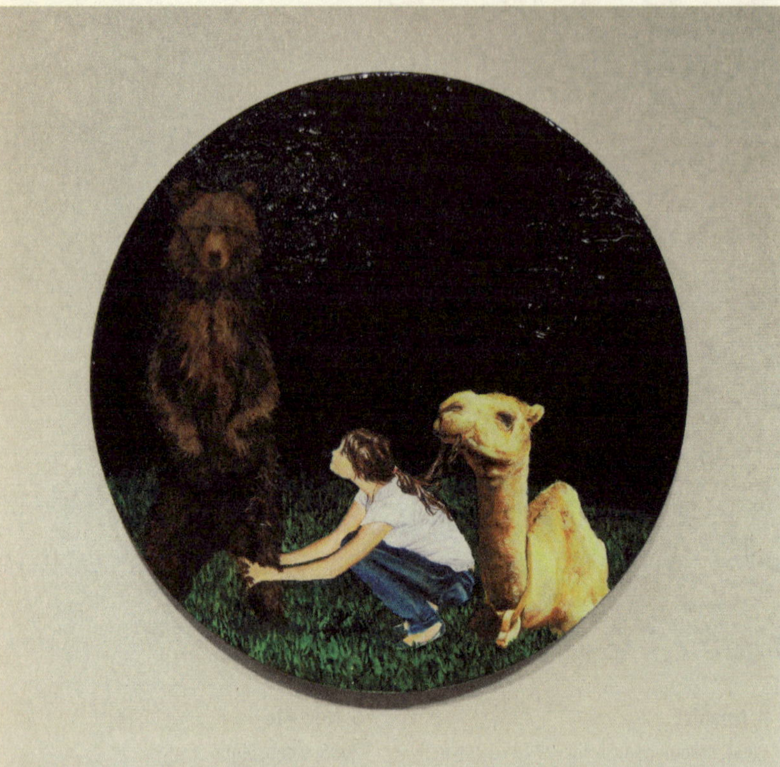

2.

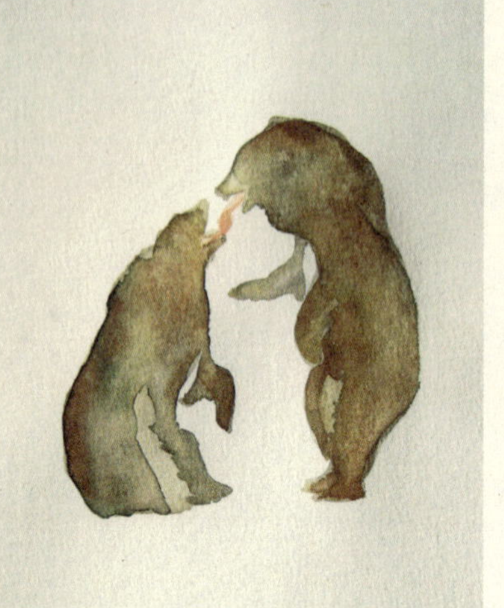

3.

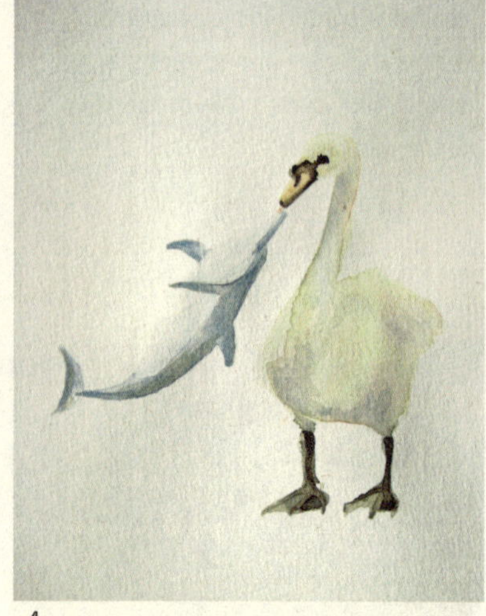

4.

Patricia Domínguez attended the Catholic University School of Art in Santiago, where she continues to live. Though she has never seen a live deer, the animal figures prominently in her paintings, as a result of her collection and observation of media images. As the Internet provides source material on plants and animals, it becomes an alternative "ecosystem" that she documents in the same way traditional naturalist painters documented living ecosystems.

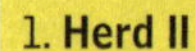

1. **Herd II**
2007, oil and synthetic paint, 35 × 236 in (89 × 599 cm)

2. **Night Study**
2008, oil and Venetian turpentine, diameter 12 in (31 cm)

3. **Study for chains (I)**
2008, watercolor, 9 × 6 in (23 × 15 ¼ cm)

4. **Study for chains (II)**
2008, watercolor, 9 × 6 in (23 × 15 ¼ cm)

5 & 6. **I have never seen a deer**
2007, oil, industrial pigment, lacquer and resin, diameters vary from 35 to 59 in (89 to 150 cm)

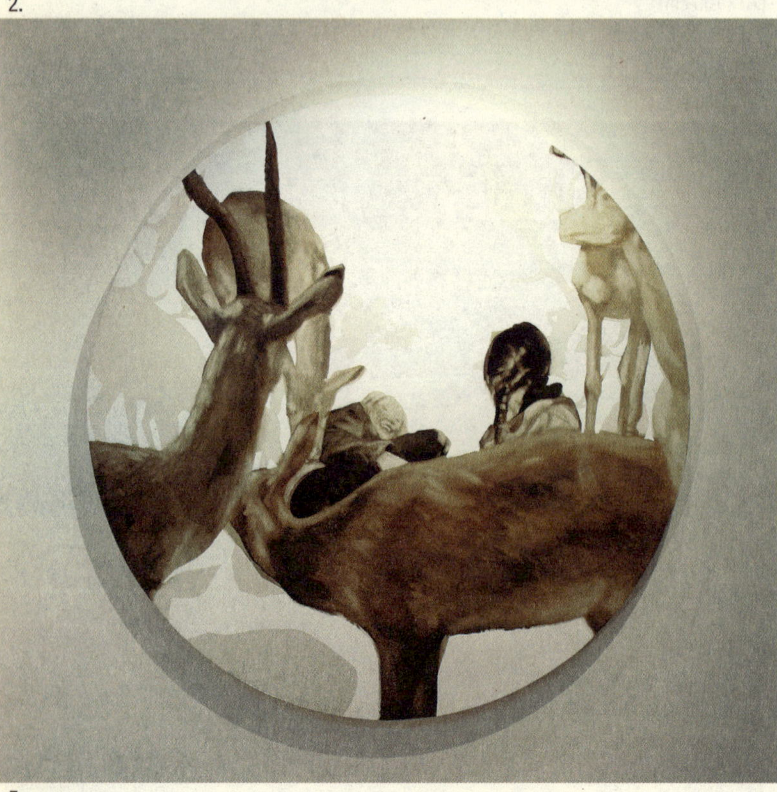

5.

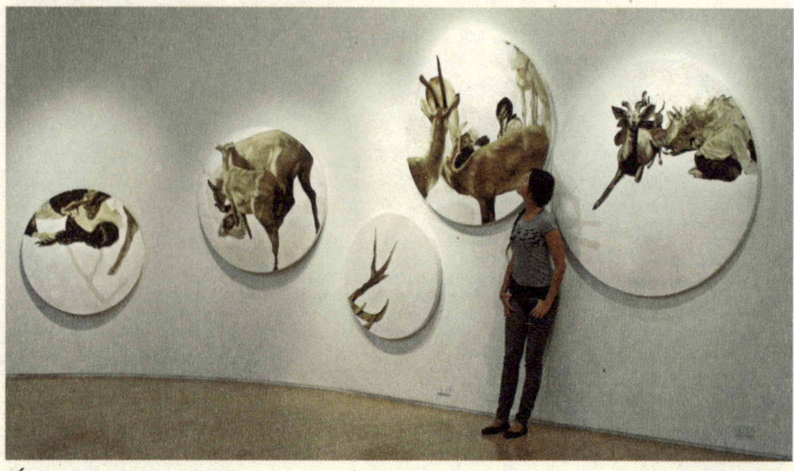

6.

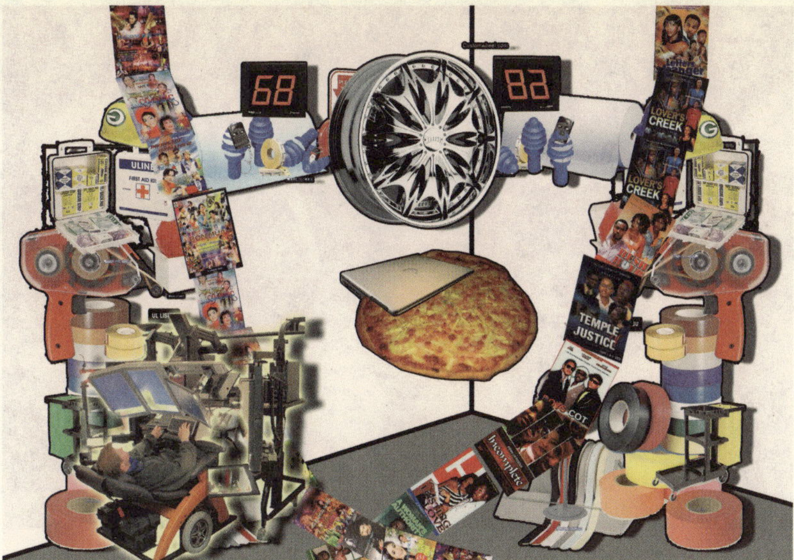

1.

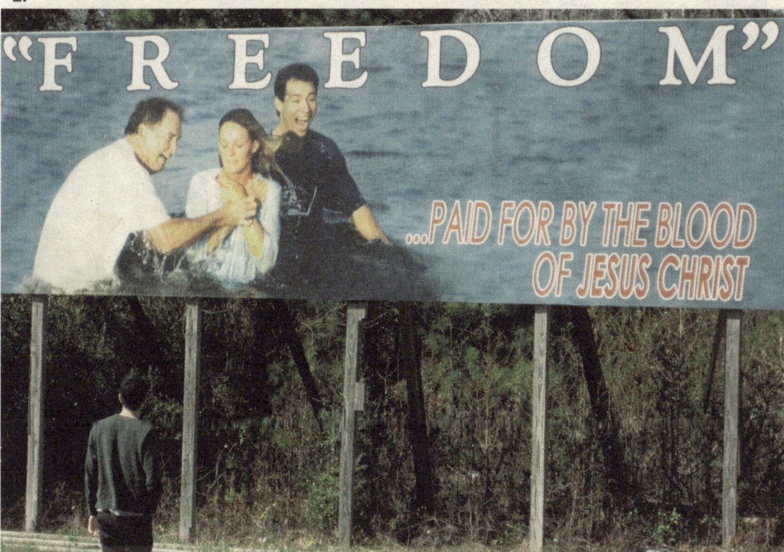

2.

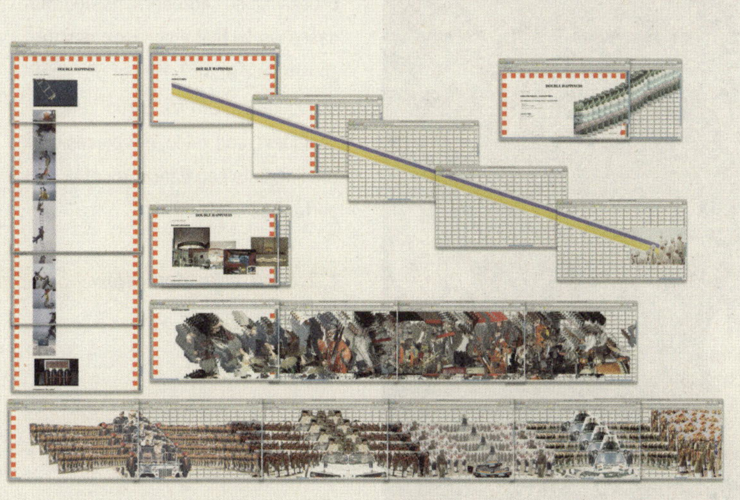

4.

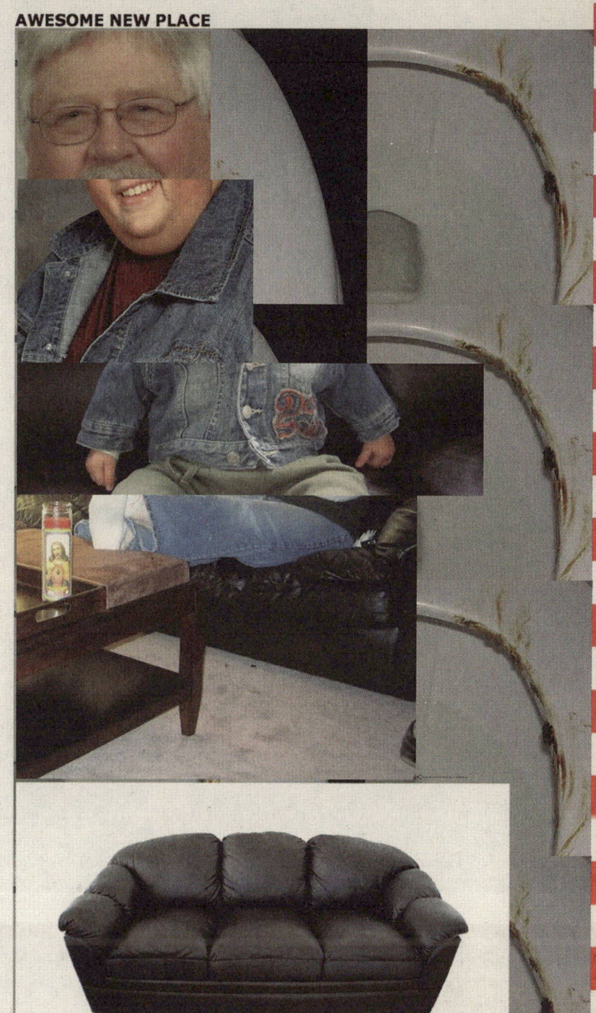

3.

Double Happiness is an Internet art collective composed of Eric Laska, Evan Roth, Borna Sammak, Jeff Sisson, and Bennett Williamson. The collective, who take their name from a common Chinese character, create frenetic collages of Internet content that seem to surge toward a catastrophic information overload. Their website, an over-the-top mélange of competing video loops, sound files, and appropriated images, is decidedly not user-friendly. This is, of course, by design. As member Borna Sammak declares, "I pride myself in having the worst website on the Internet."

1. **Sketch of sculpture for vertexList "New Blood" exhibition**
2008, digital image, dimensions variable

2. **Divine Sponsorship**
2008, digital image, dimensions variable

3. **Awesome New Place**
2008, website, dimensions variable

4. **Bat Ladder, Power Stripe, Endless Pools, Deluxe Upcharge, GROITS BIG BAND, Troops**
2008, website collage, dimensions variable

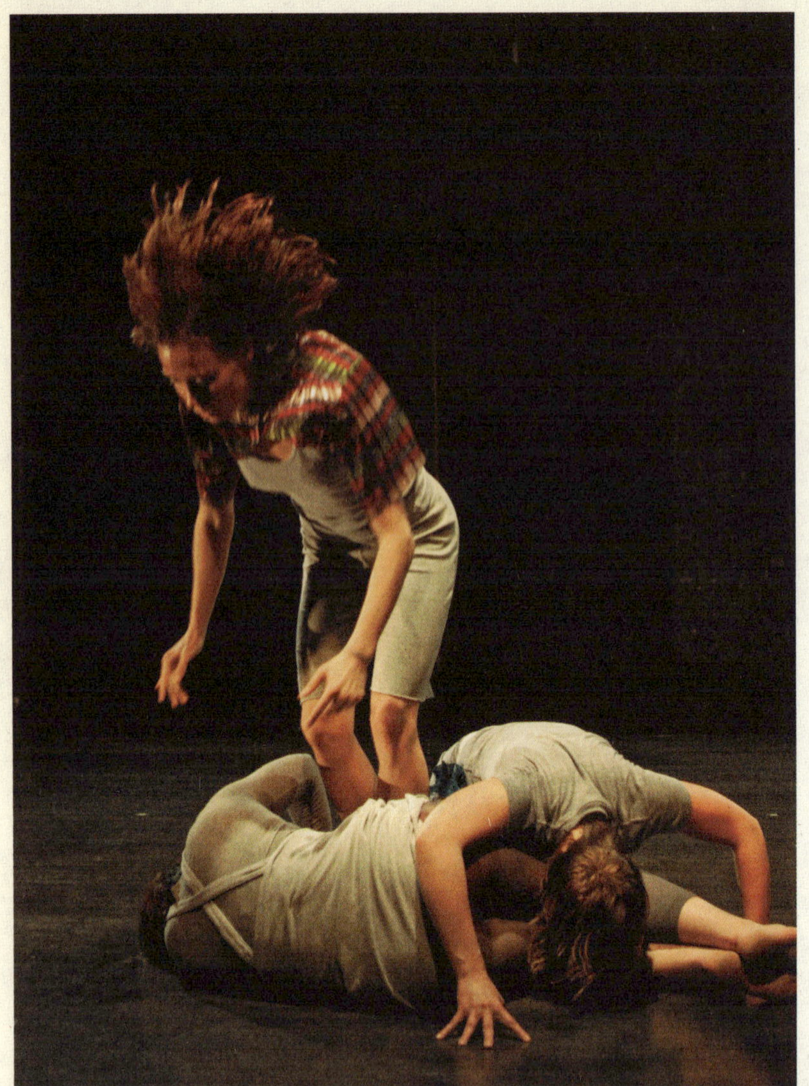
1.

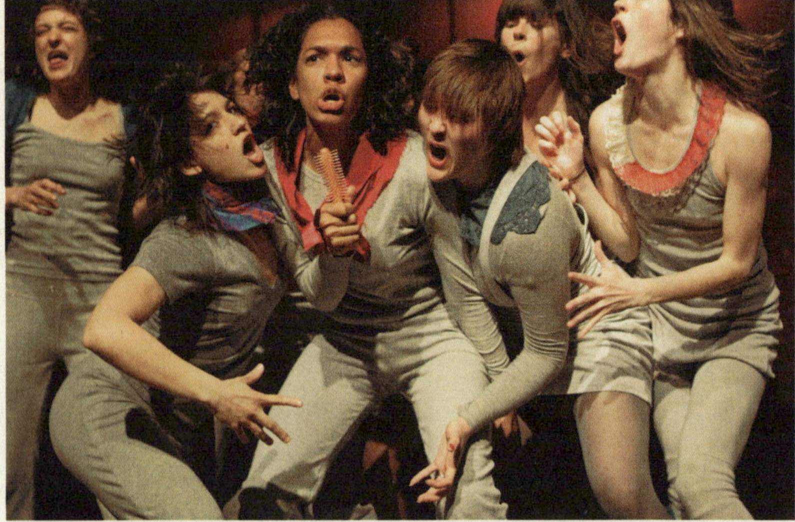
2.

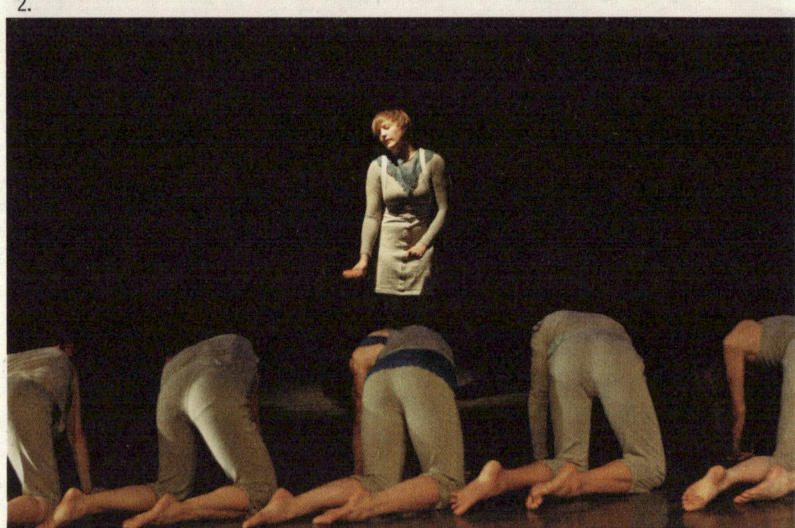
3.

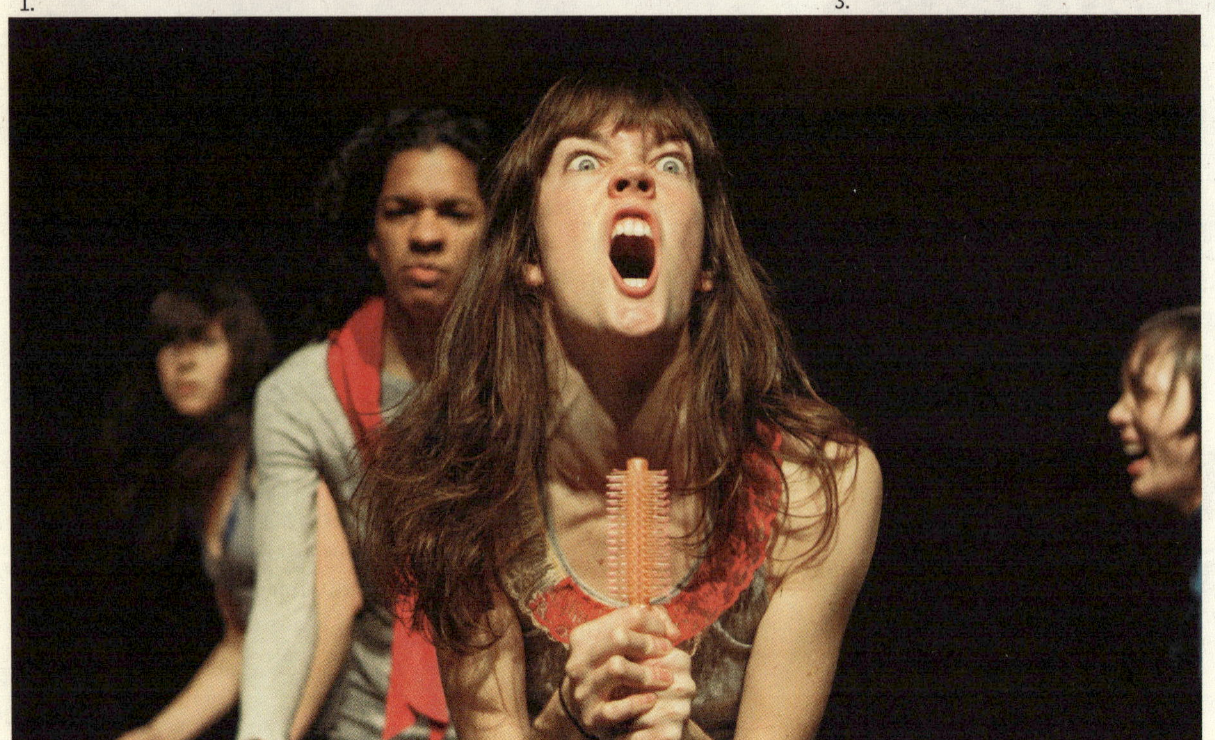
4.

Faye Driscoll earned her BFA in Dance from New York University's Tisch School for the Arts and currently lives in Brooklyn. She choreographs rigorous dance works that emphasize gesture, spasm, and other forms of physical manipulation. Often incorporating song, text, and video, her pieces walk the line between dance, theater, and performance art.

1, 2, 3 & 4. **Wow Mom, Wow**
2007, performance

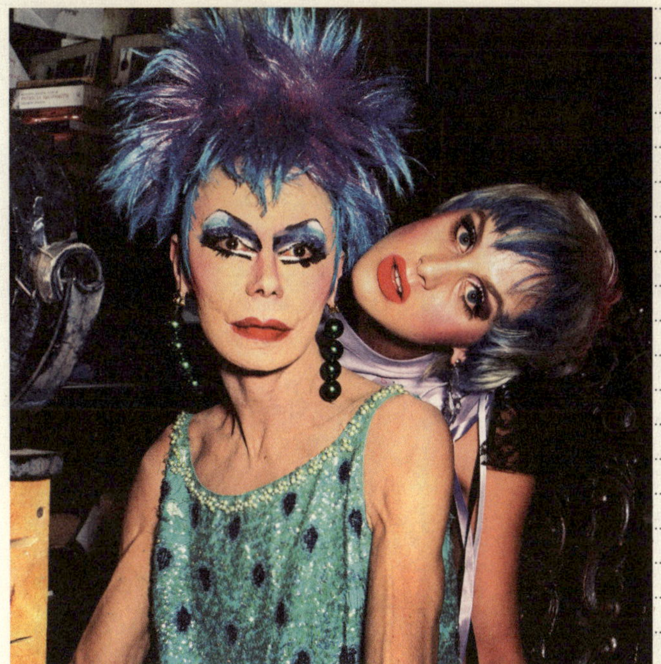
1.

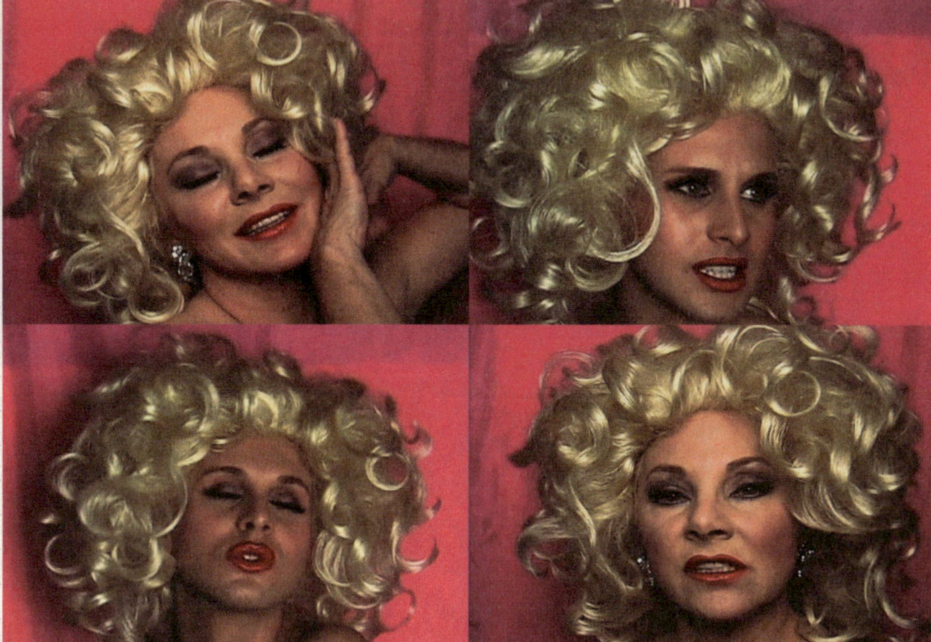
2.

Zackary Drucker received his MFA from the California Institute of the Arts in Valencia, California. A self-described "limp-wristed, gender-queer, freaky, fierce, faggot-tranny-queen," he makeswork that is primarily based in photography and deals with issues of gender identity and the representation of queer culture. For his MFA thesis show, titled "5 East 73rd Street" (2007), Drucker presented a series of still-life and portrait photographs made in the apartment of Mother Flawless Sabrina, a legendary drag queen, more informally known as "Jack," who began performing in the late 1950s.

1. 5 East 73rd Street
2005, Cibachrome print, 30 × 30 in (76 × 76 cm)

2. FISH: A Matrilineage of Cunty White-Woman Realness
2008, digital video, 2 min

3. Kyky Love
2008, performance, 7 min

4. The Inability to Be Looked At and The Horror of Nothing To See
2008, performance, 12 min

5. Psychopathia Transexualis
2008, limited edition artist's book and digital print, 4 × 6 in (10 × 15 cm)

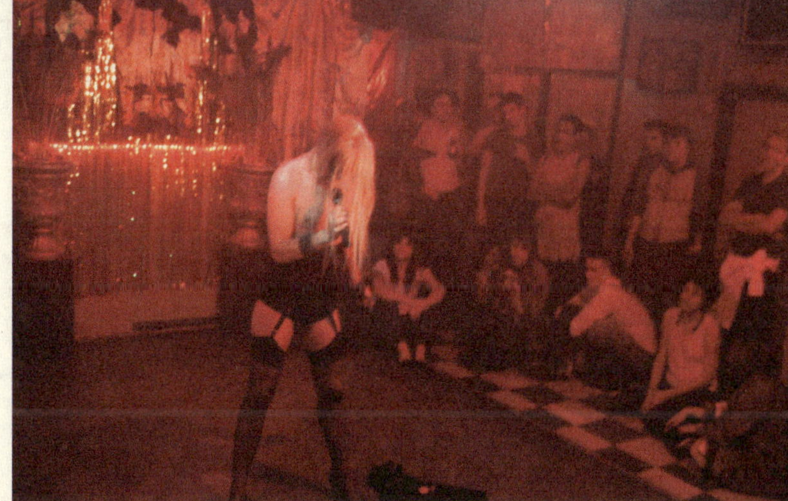
3.

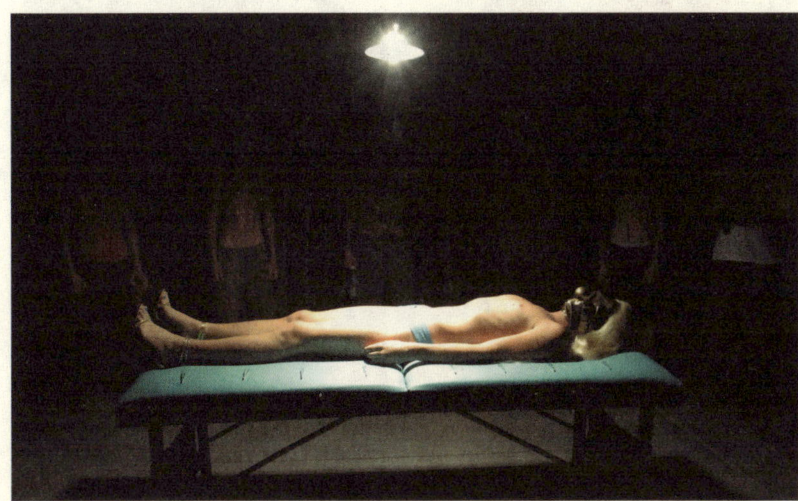
4.

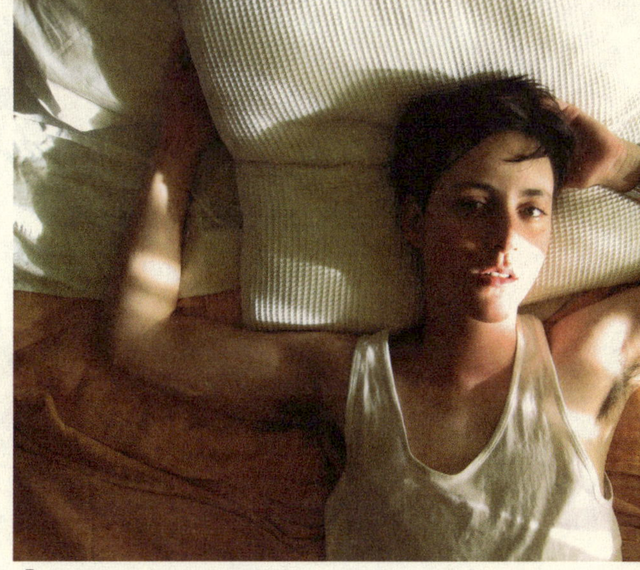
5.

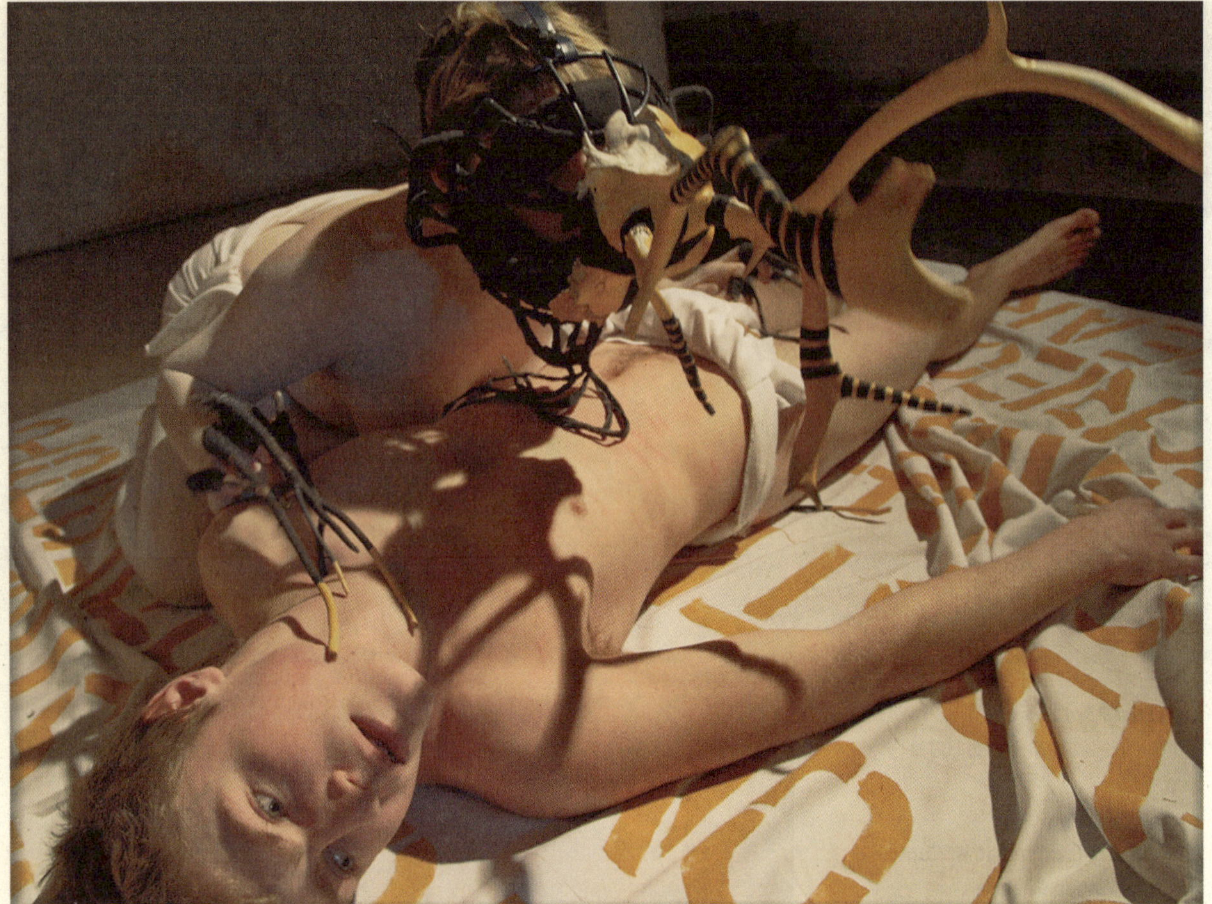

1.

Michael Dudeck earned his BFA from the University of Manitoba School of Art and currently lives in Winnipeg. His various self-declared identities include Performance Artist, Witch Doctor, Trans-disciplinary Nomad, and Countercultural Avatar. He moves between diverse mediums to explore themes of religion, science, sexuality, binary distinctions, and alternative belief systems.

1. **Only One Who Draws the Knife Gets Isaac**
2008, video installation, dimensions variable

2. **Embryo (Halo of an Effigy)** (detail)
2008, graphite, ink, and spray paint on paper, 20 × 20 in (51 × 51 cm)

3. **Effigy I (to trudge through the enormity)**
2008, graphite, ink, watercolor, and hockey tape on paper, 81 × 38 in (205 × 96 cm)

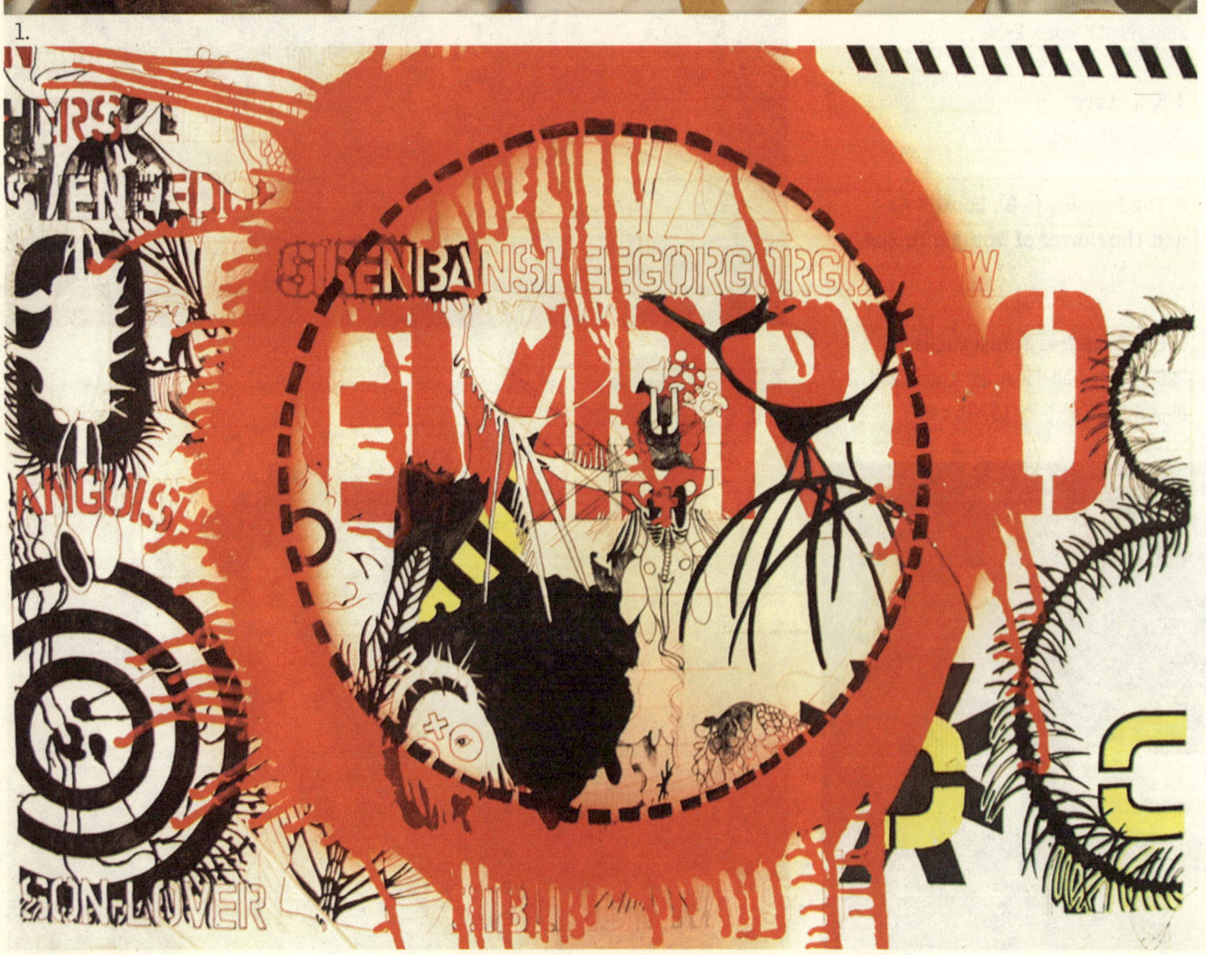

2.

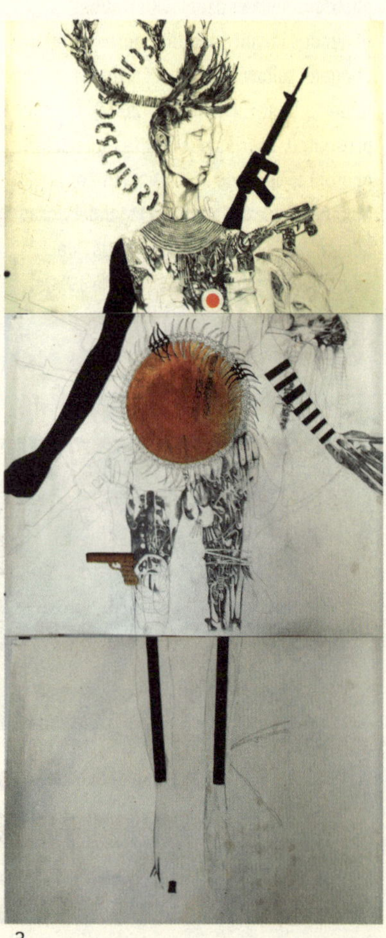

3.

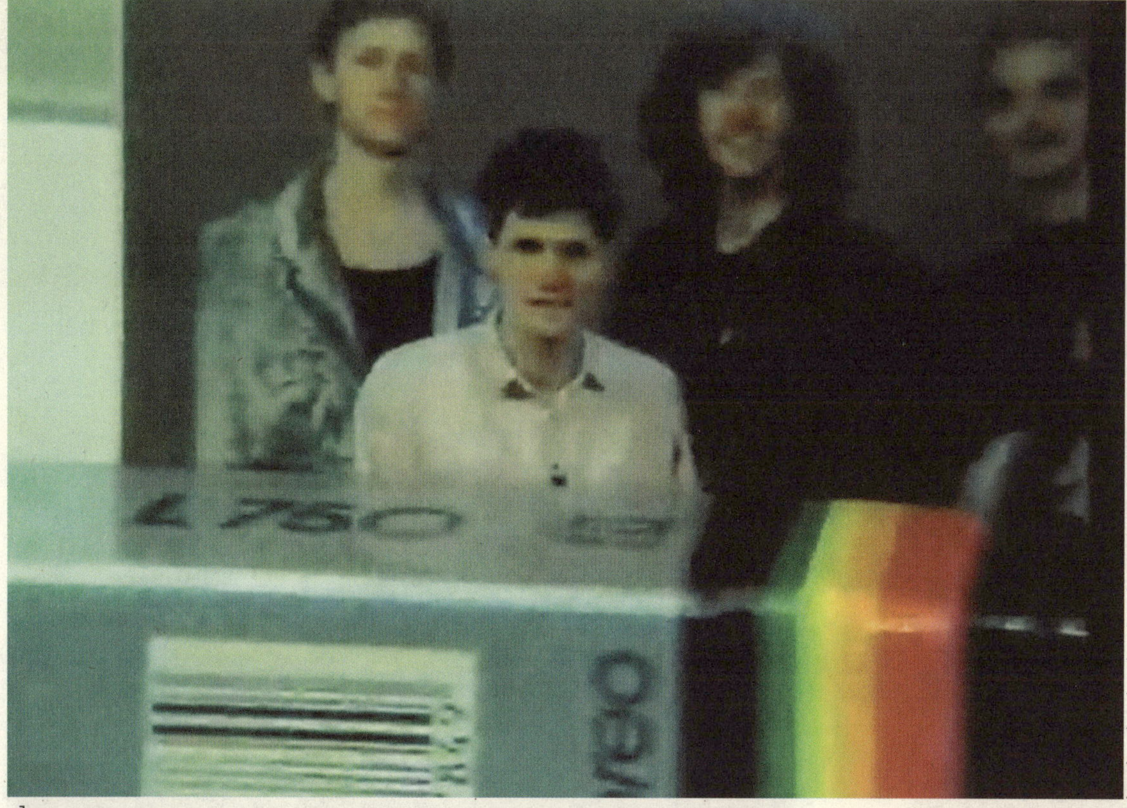

1.

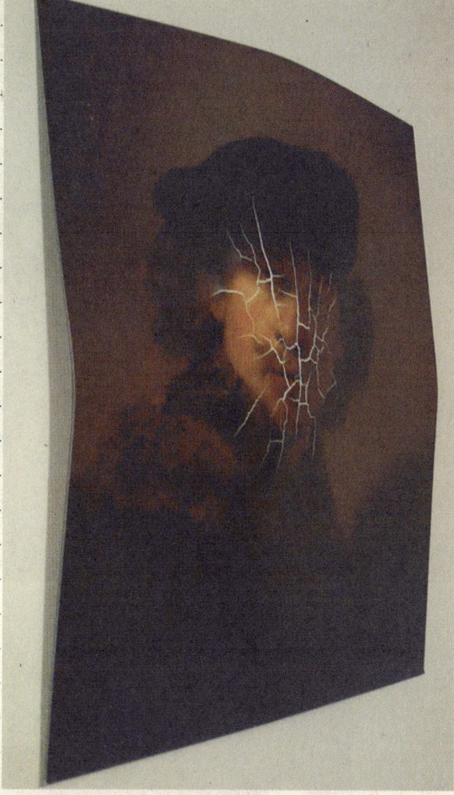

2.

3.

4.

5.

Constant Dullaart attended the Gerrit Rietveld Academie in Amsterdam, where he continues to live. He sold his video camera in 2007 in order to collect, examine, and manipulate existing material: news programs, talk shows, Hollywood cinema, and amateur footage found on the Internet. His **Blown Up** series shows digital images at twenty times their original size, including Antonioni's Blow Up in its entirety (blownupblowup.com).

1. **Effect tests found on VHS tapes still 2** (detail)
2008, chromogenic print in wooden frame, 12 × 15 ¾ in (30 × 40 cm)

2. **My Rembrandt**
2006, chromogenic print on aluminum, 23 ½ × 15 ¾ in (60 × 40 cm)

3 & 4. **blownupblowup.com**
2008, chromogenic prints on aluminum, each 8 × 12 in (20 × 30 cm)

5. **Andy Warhol**
2008, chromogenic print in wooden frame, 12 × 15 ¾ in (30 × 40 cm)

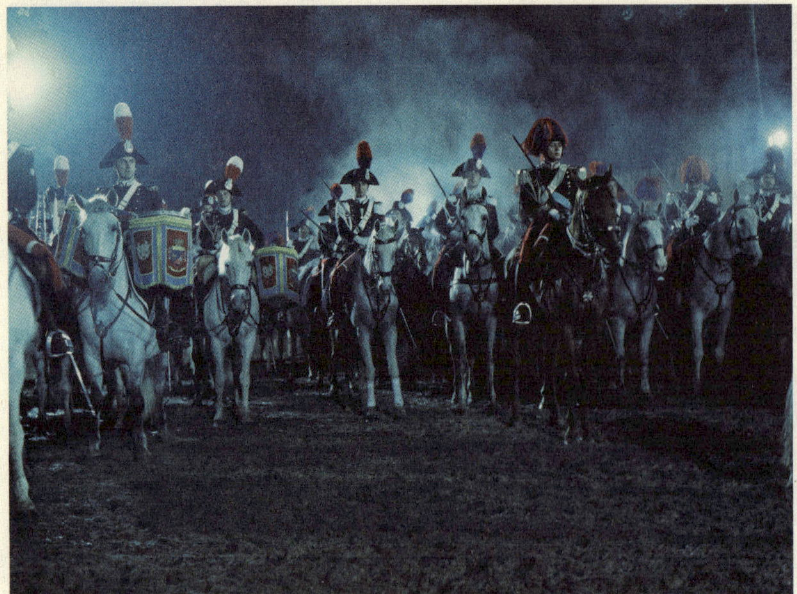

1.

Charlotte Dumas was a resident at the Rijksakademie in Amsterdam, and currently lives in Amsterdam and New York City. Her interest in photographing animals began with police dogs in 2000, and now includes horses, wolves, and tigers. Her portraits are the products of long-term observation and interaction with her subjects, usually in a sanctuary or some form of captivity.

1. Untitled (2004/1)
2004, chromogenic print, $35\frac{1}{2} \times 47\frac{1}{4}$ in (90 × 120 cm)

2. Untitled (2004/8)
2004, chromogenic print, $45\frac{1}{4} \times 60\frac{1}{2}$ in (115 × 154 cm)

3. Untitled (Eerie)
2005, chromogenic print, $29 \times 37\frac{1}{2}$ in (74 × 95 cm)

4. Untitled (Zeus)
2007, chromogenic print, $39\frac{3}{4} \times 53$ in (101 × 135 cm)

5. Untitled (Sam)
2007, chromogenic print, $39\frac{3}{4} \times 53$ in (101 × 135 cm)

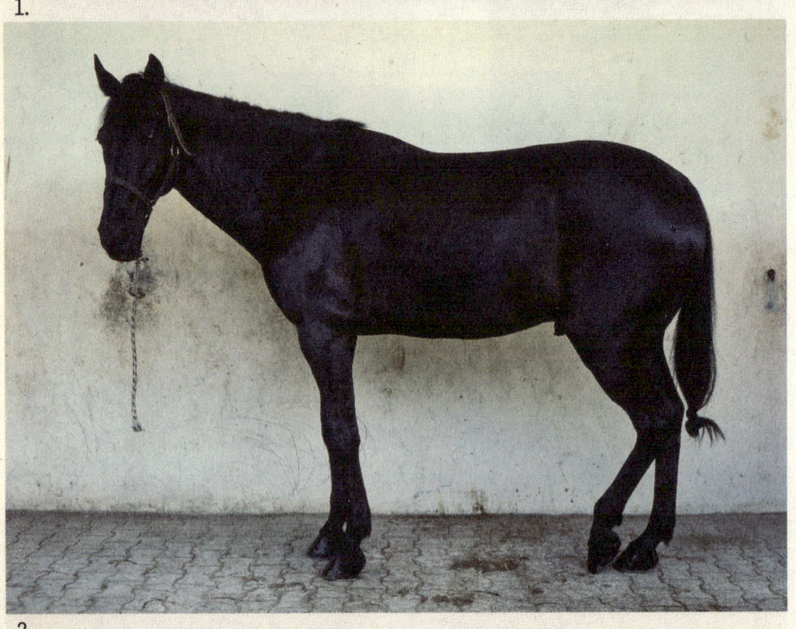

2.

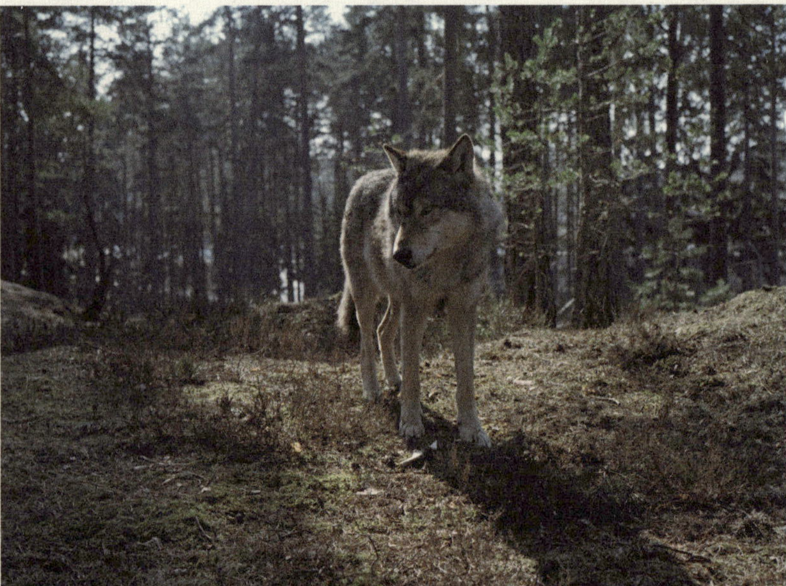

3.

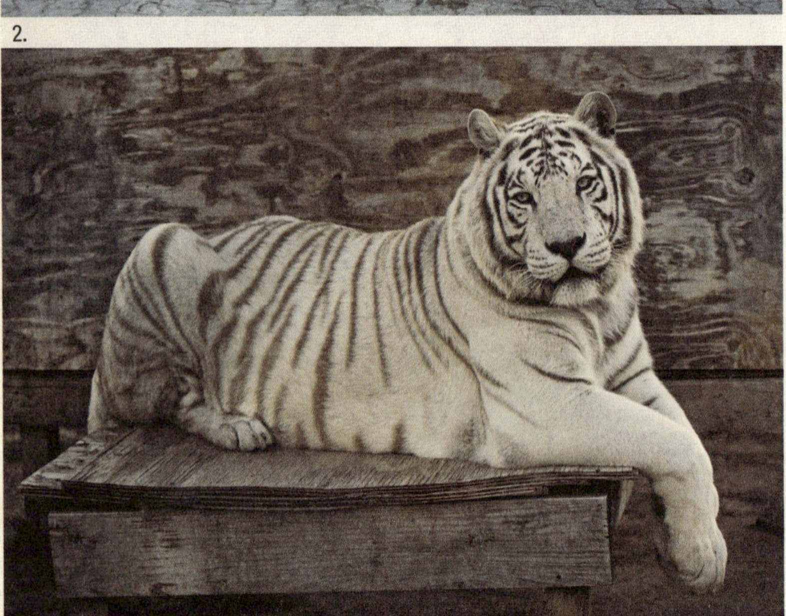

4.

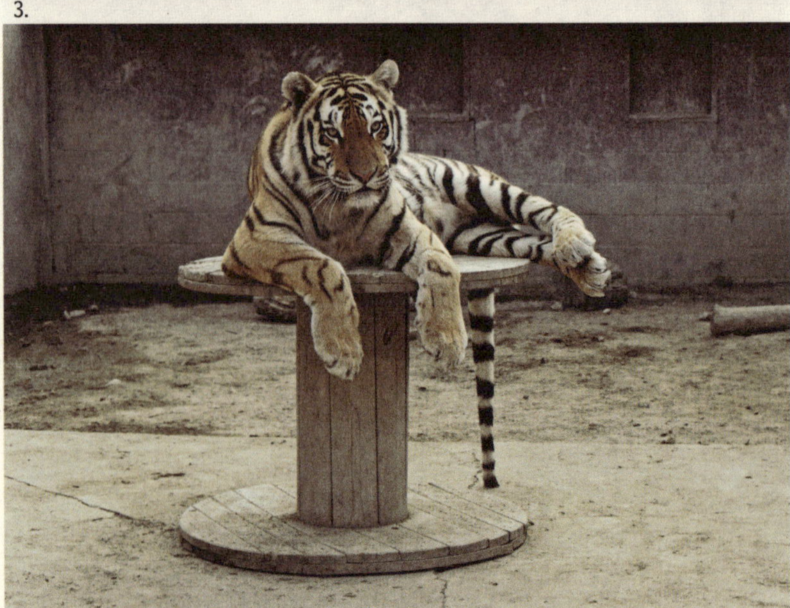

5.

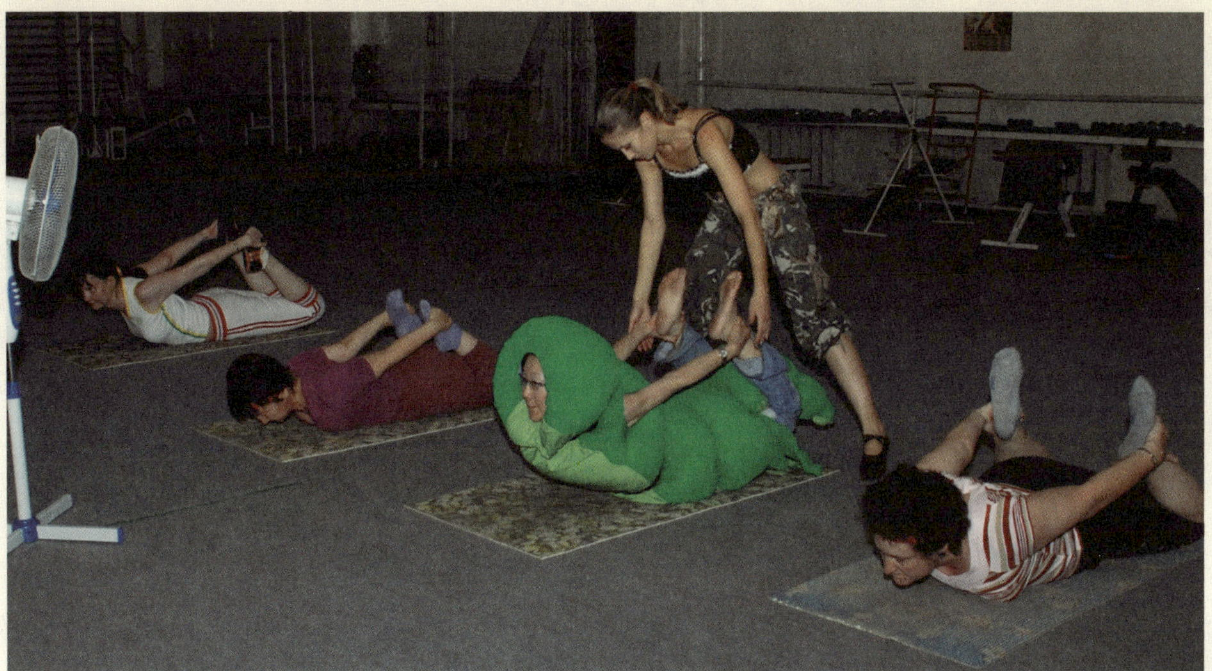

1.

Natalya Dyu studied fine art at the Buketov Karaganda State University in Karaganda, Kazakhstan, and currently lives in Almaty. Her video and animation works link personal narrative with cultural references from the East and West. In **I Love Naomi, Naomi Loves Fruit** (2001), she imagines the ideal life of supermodel Naomi Campbell merging with her own as she sits on a toilet.

1 & 2. **The Caterpillar**
2008, digital photographs, dimensions variable

3, 4 & 5. **The Caterpillar**
2008, video, 10 min

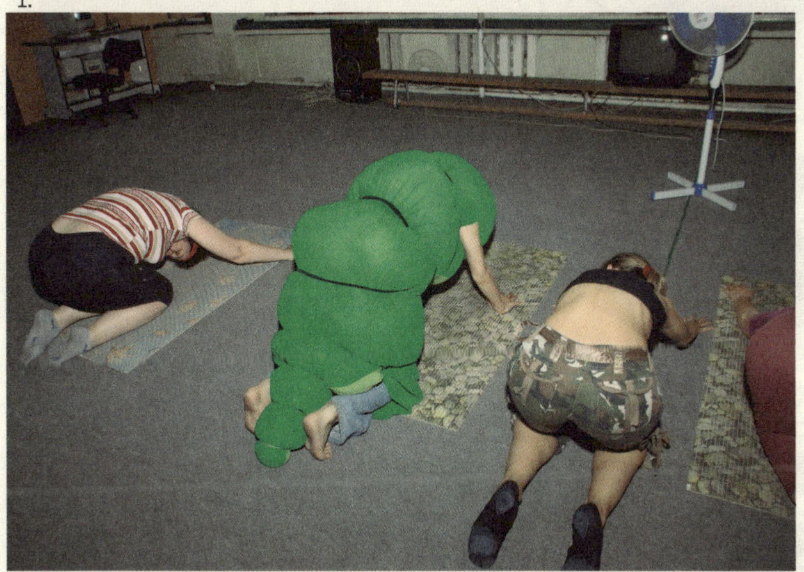

2.

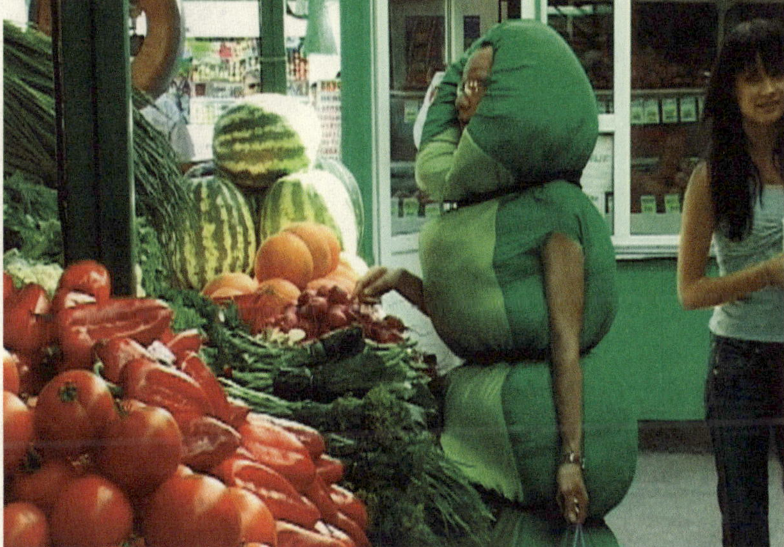

3.

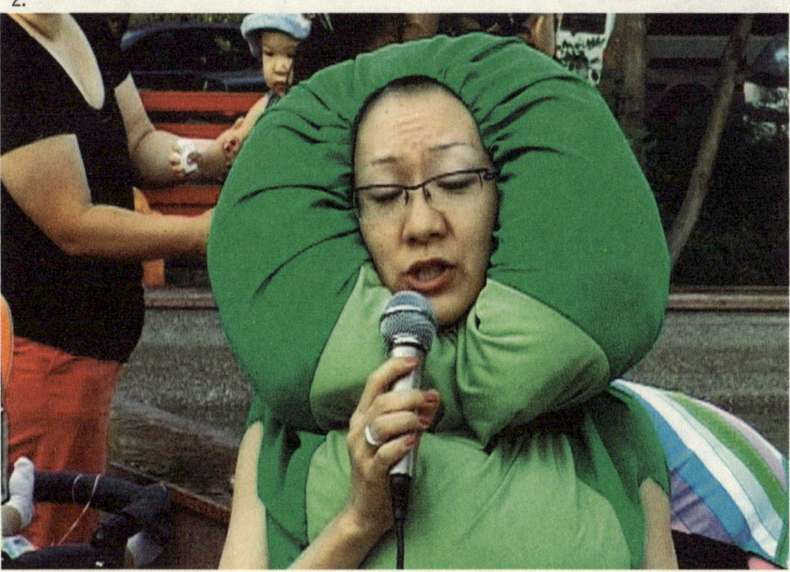

4.

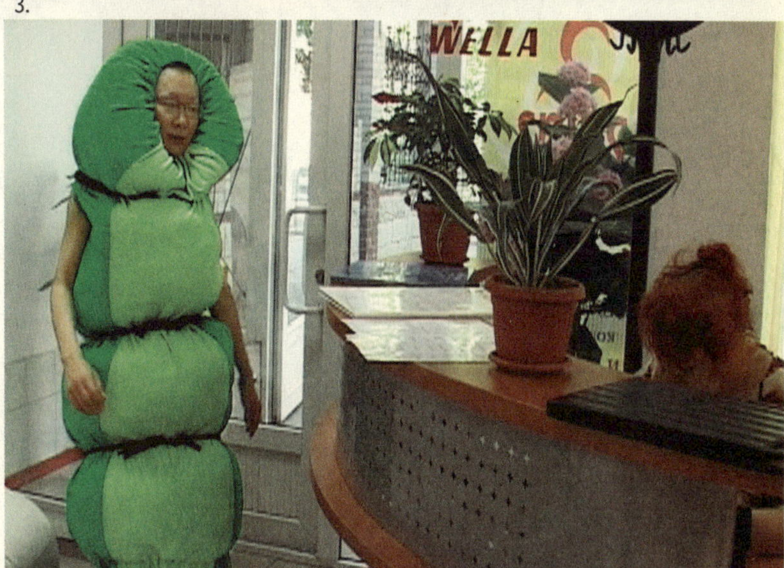

5.

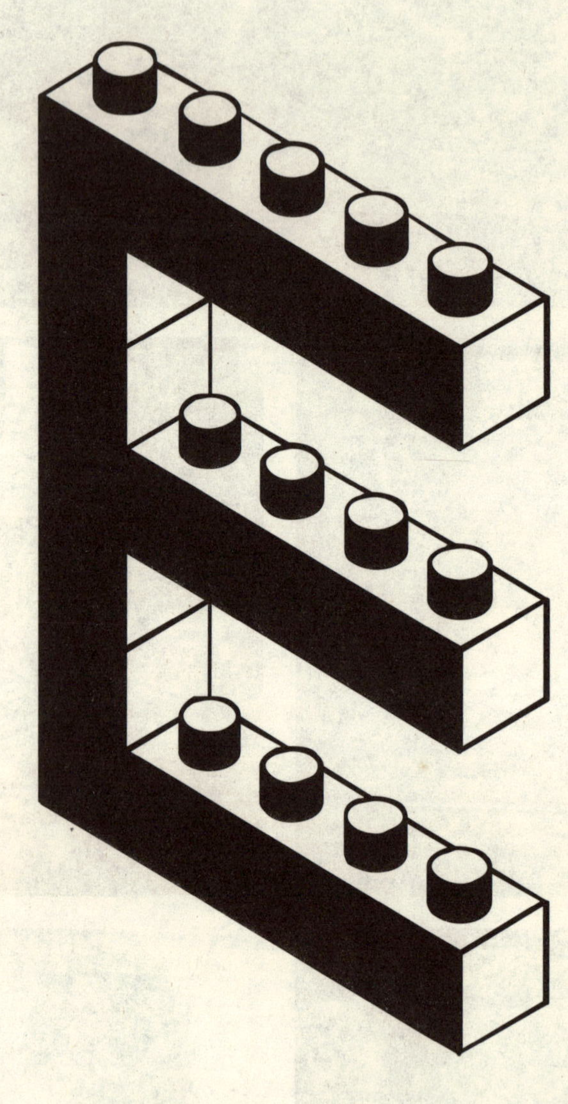

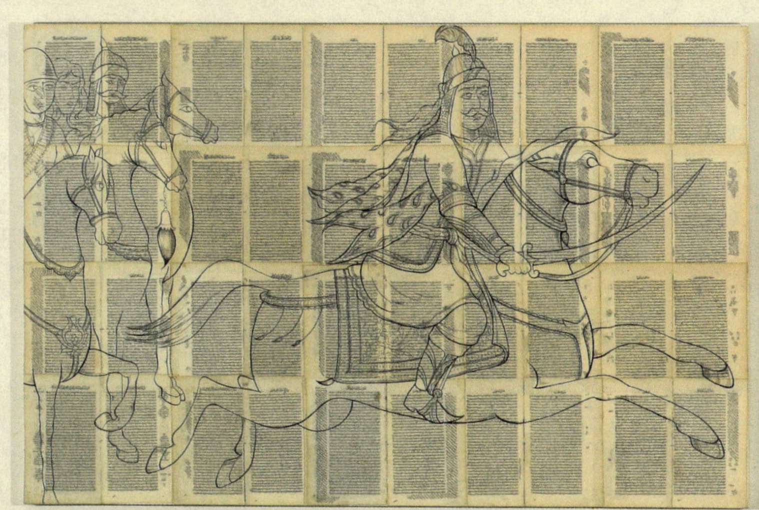

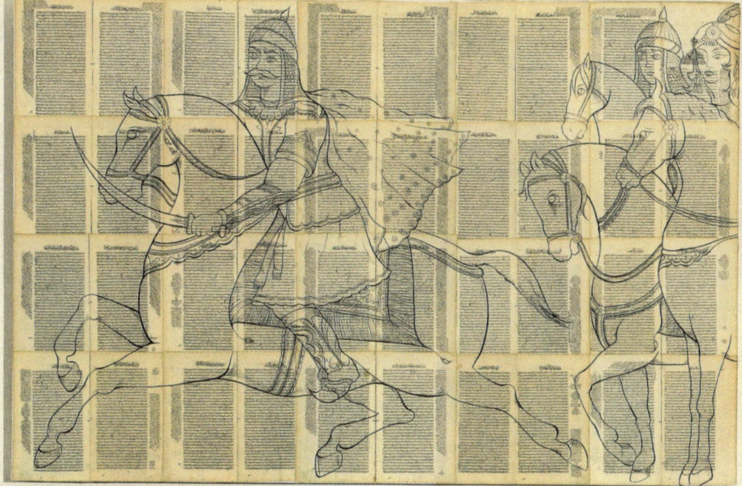

1.

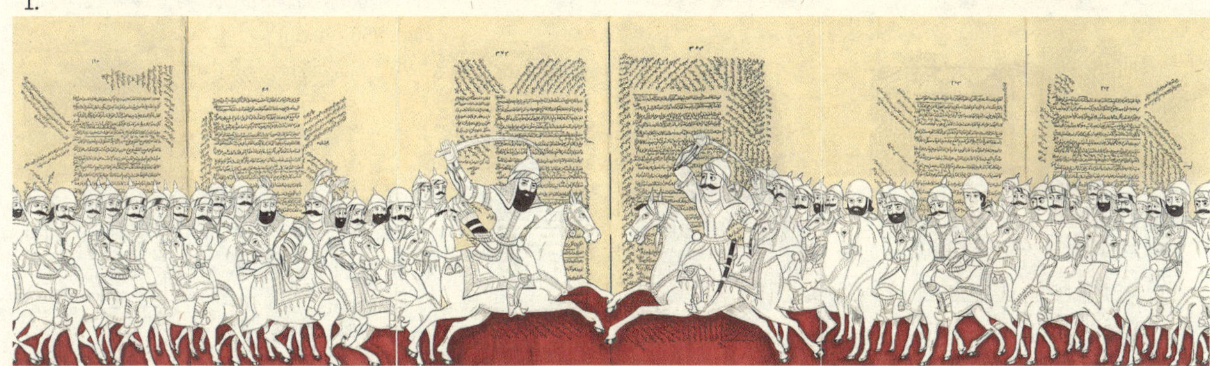

2.

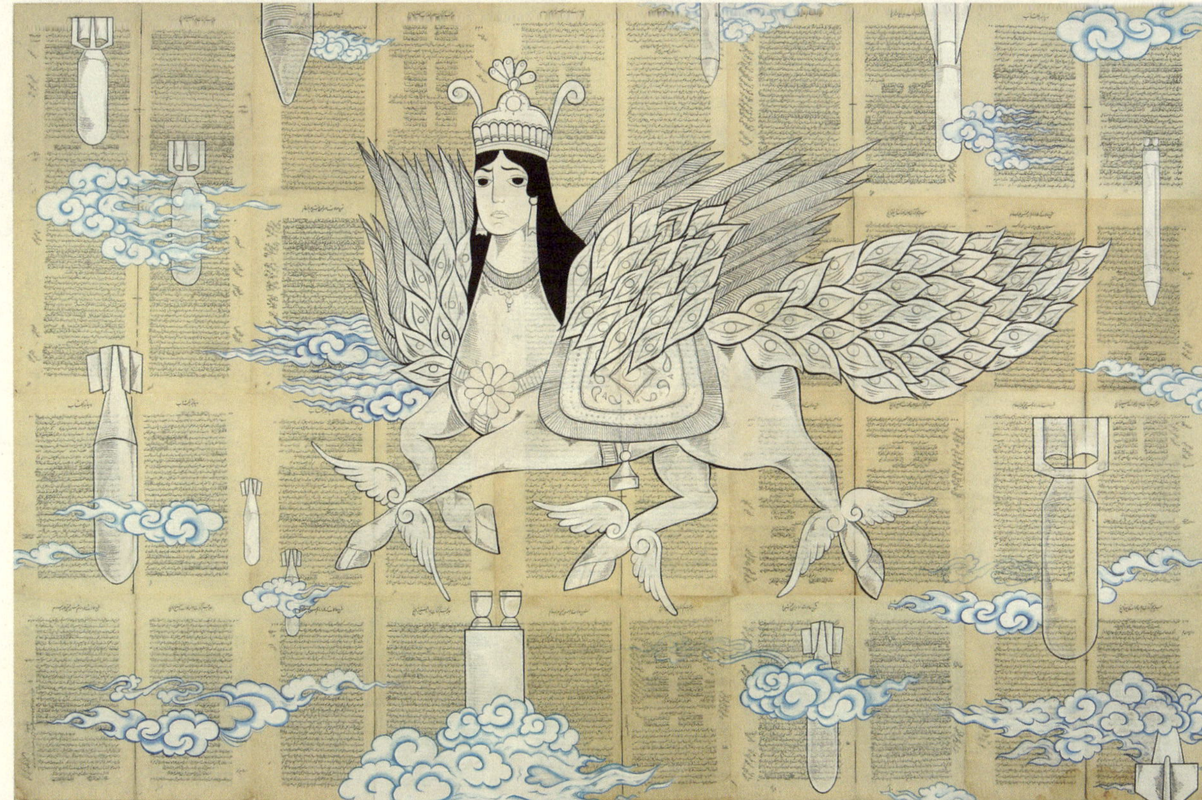

3.

Ala Ebtekar earned his MFA from Stanford University and currently lives in Palo Alto, California. His drawings, prints, and installations explore contrasts and similarities between traditional Iranian and contemporary hip-hop cultures. Growing up in the Bay Area with activist Iranian parents in exile, he developed a unique identity, leading to works like the 2004 installation **Elemental**, a model Iranian coffeehouse that also contains boomboxes, sneakers, and other hip-hop paraphernalia.

1. **Serenity**
2007, ink over charcoal underdrawing on book pages mounted on canvas, two parts, each 51 1/2 × 81 in (131 × 206 cm)

2. **The Invisible Fold**
2002, ink and watercolor on book pages, 17 1/2 × 54 3/4 in (45 × 139 cm)

3. **Ascension**
2007, acrylic and ink on book pages mounted on canvas, 51 1/2 × 81 in (131 × 206 cm)

Juan Pablo Echeverri studied art at the Pontificia Universidad Javeriana in Bogotá, where he continues to live and work. He uses photography and video to explore personal identity, expression, and gender roles. Portraiture, primarily of himself, is his focus. In one artwork, he took daily self-portraits in a photo booth, documenting the mutability of a single person's appearance from day to day, and over time.

1. MUTILady
2003, chromogenic prints, each 25 ¼ × 25 ¼ in (64 × 64 cm)

2. soMos
2007, Lambda prints, each 19 ¾ × 27 ½ in (50 × 70 cm)

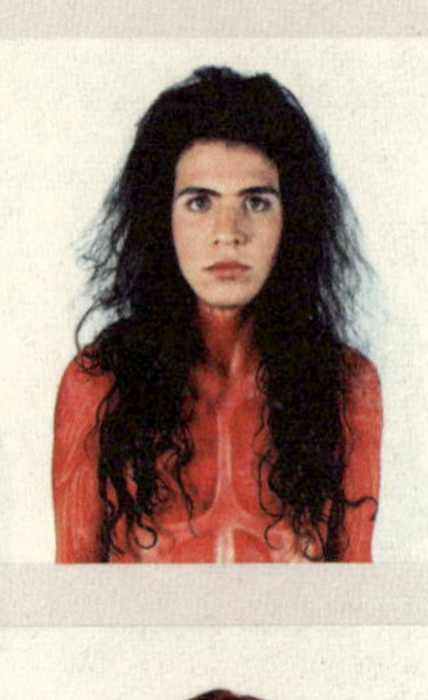
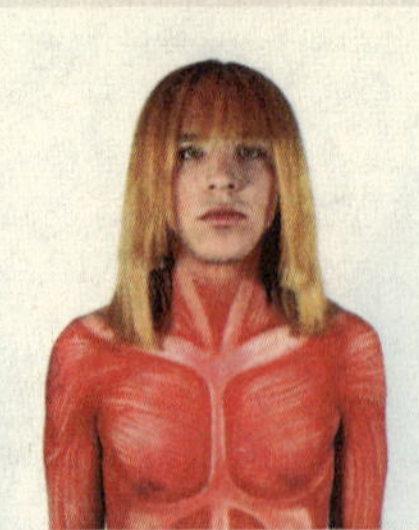
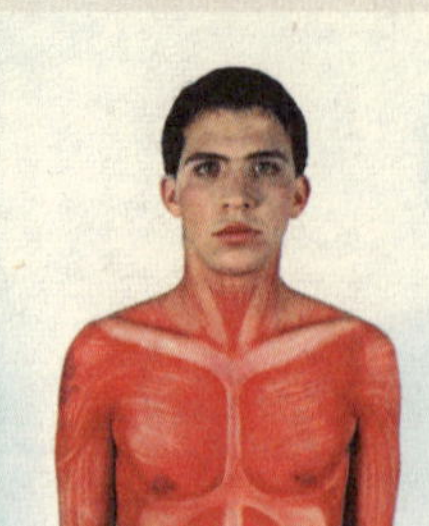
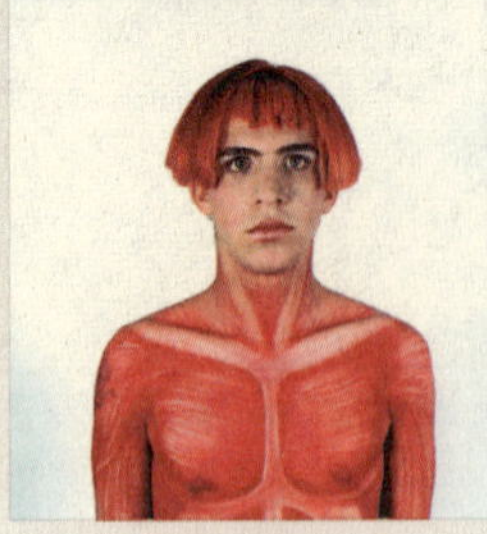
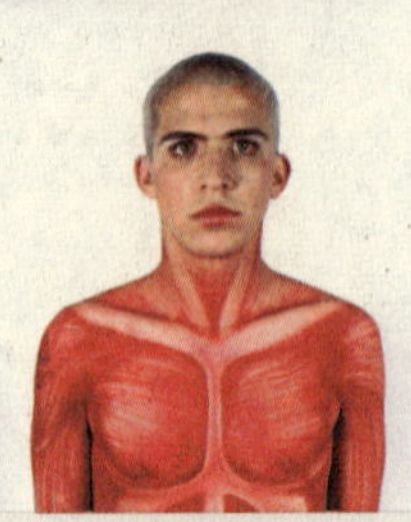
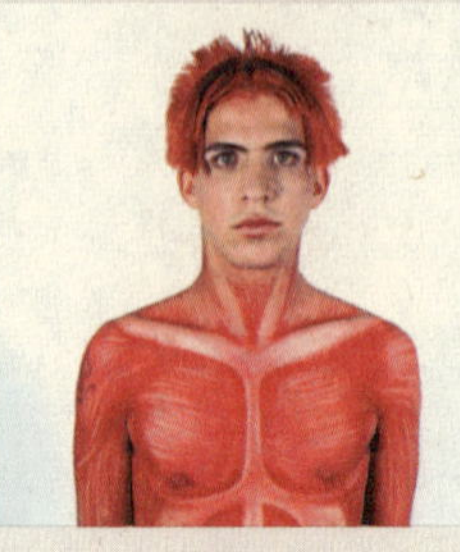
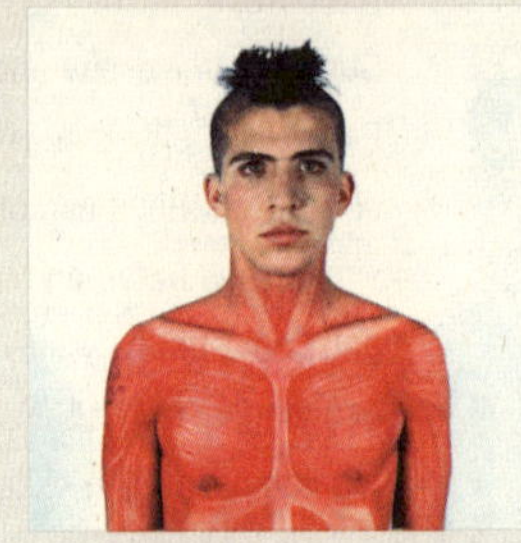
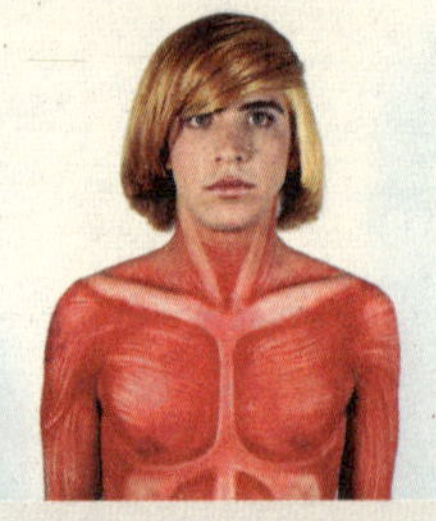
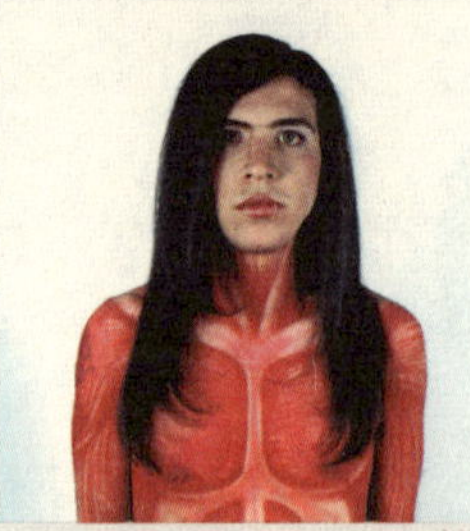

1.

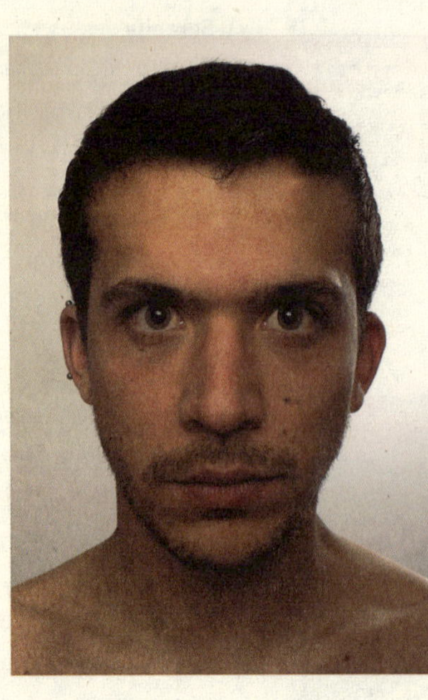
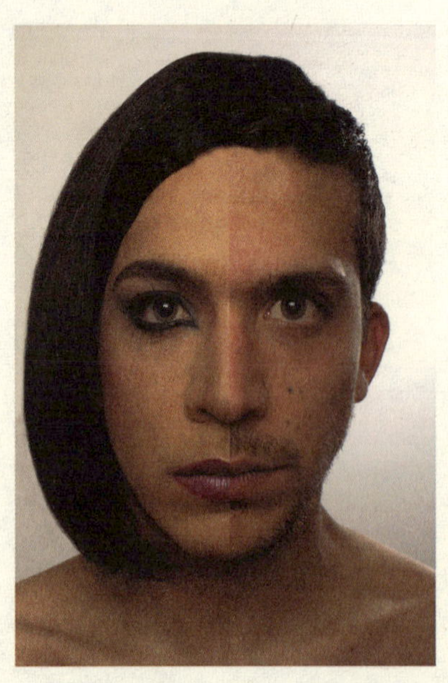
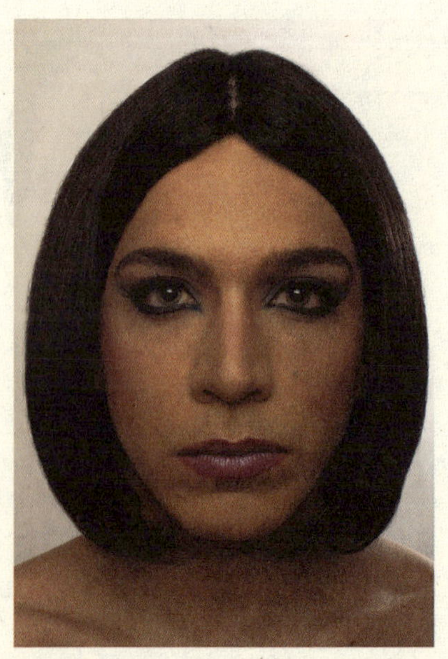

2.

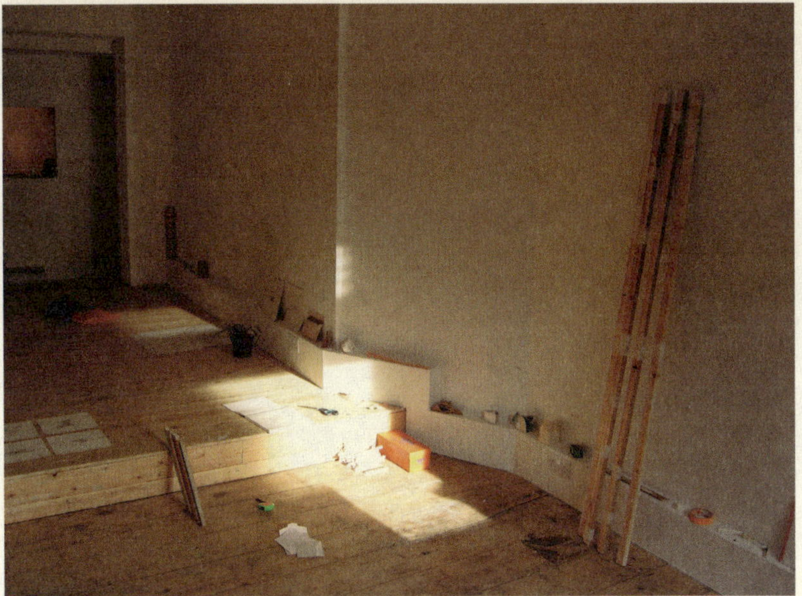

1.

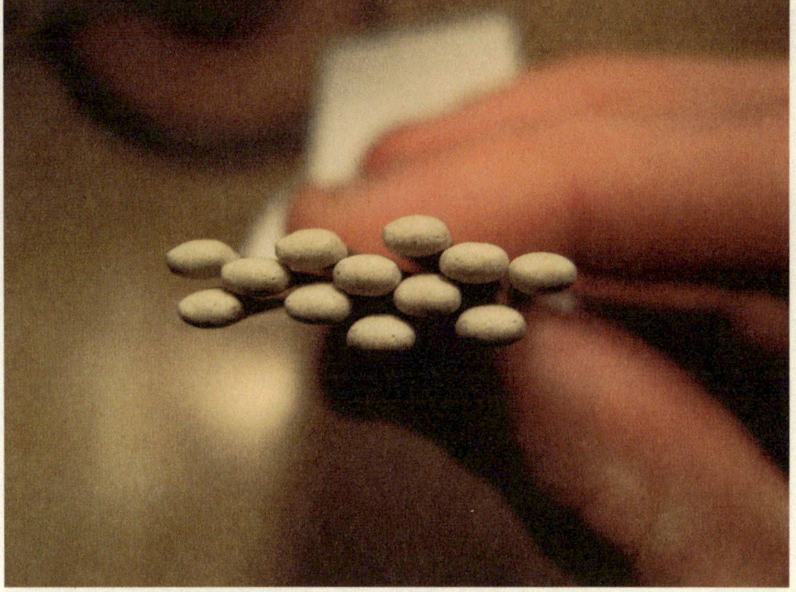

2.

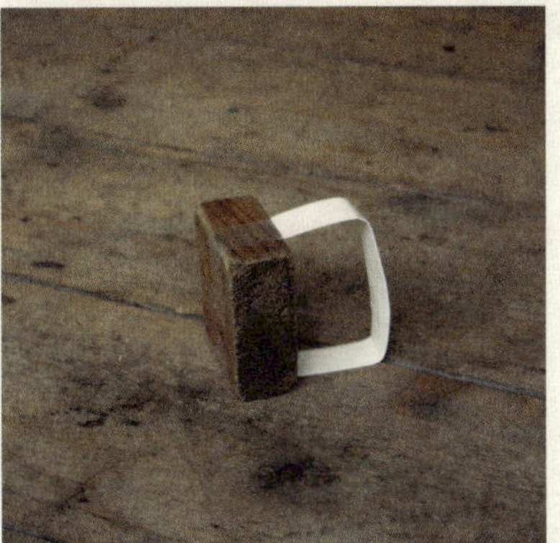

3.

Sean Edwards earned his MA in Fine Art from the Slade School of Fine Art, London, and currently lives in Abergavenny, Wales. Working with sculpture, installation, video, and the readymade, he investigates the form and function of ordinary mass-produced objects, such as wooden dowels, newspapers, and plastic bags. In one piece, he stacked photocopies of a pencil to create a facsimile while sanding away the original.

1. **Maybe something like the way it should have been**
2007, digital print, 6 × 8 ¼ in (15 × 21 cm)

2. **Snowing like a Checkerboard**
2008, chromogenic print in frame, 9 × 12 ¼ in (23 × 31 cm)

3. **Untitled**
2008, found driftwood, plastic, and tape, 3 ½ × 4 × 3 in (9 × 10 × 8 cm)

4. **Untitled (Chipboard Sticks)**
2007, chipboard and gouache, 6 × 19 ¼ × ¾ in (15 × 49 × 2 cm)

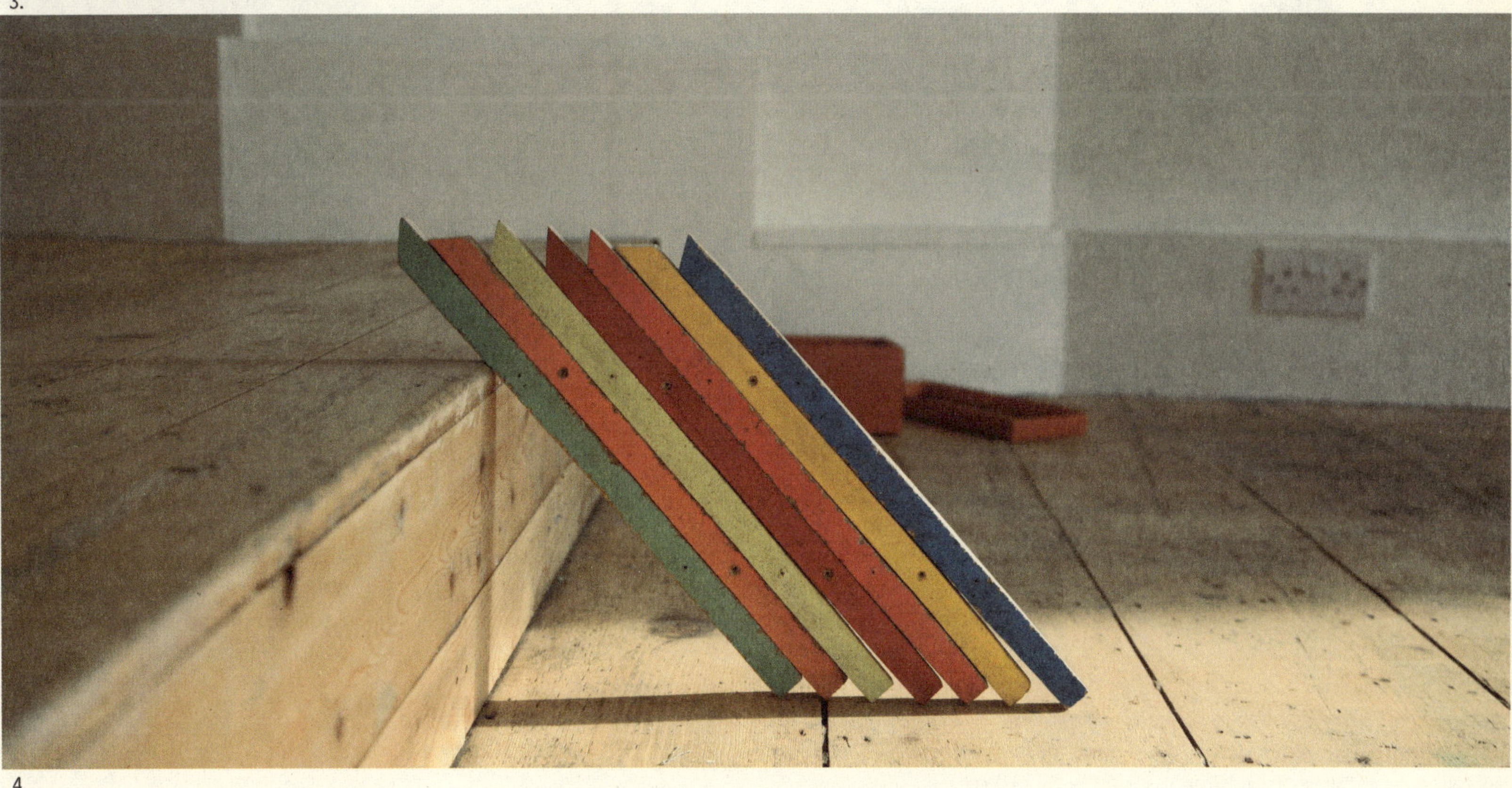

4.

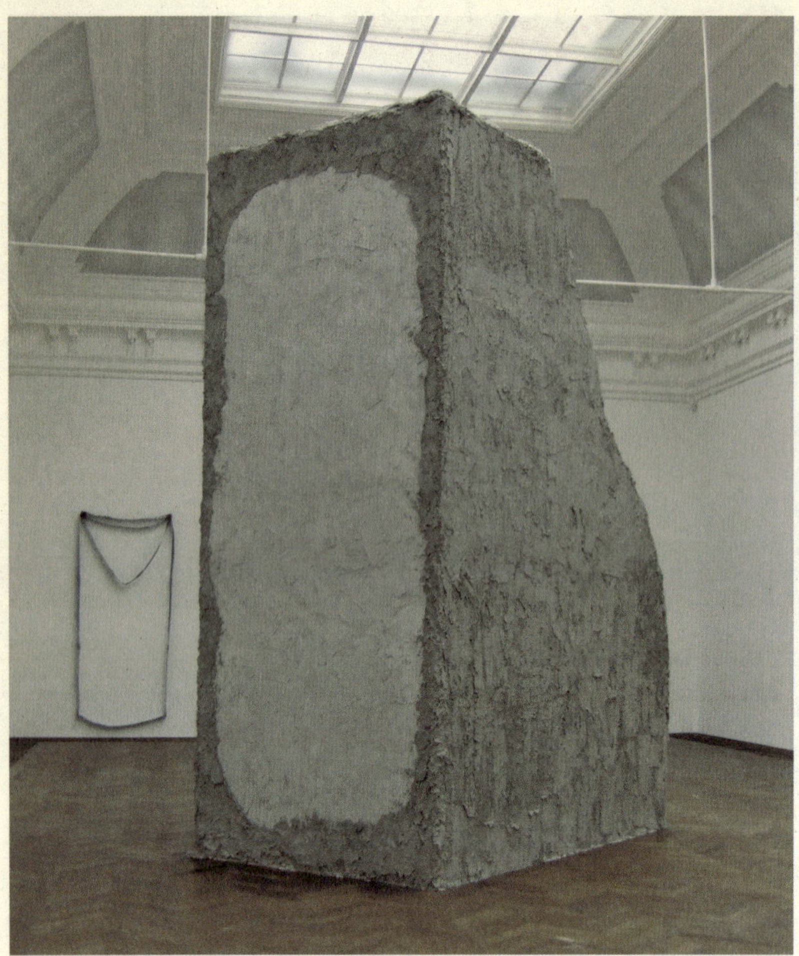

1.

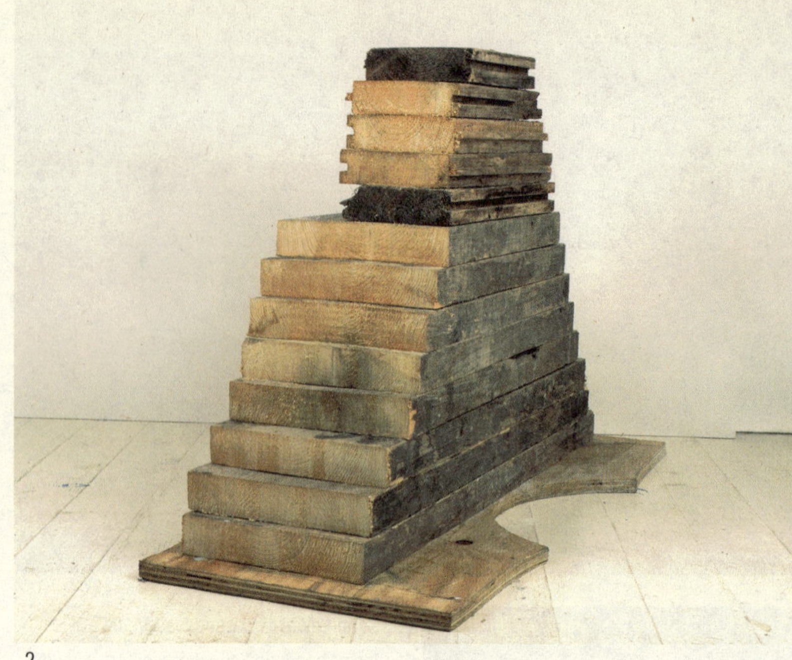

2.

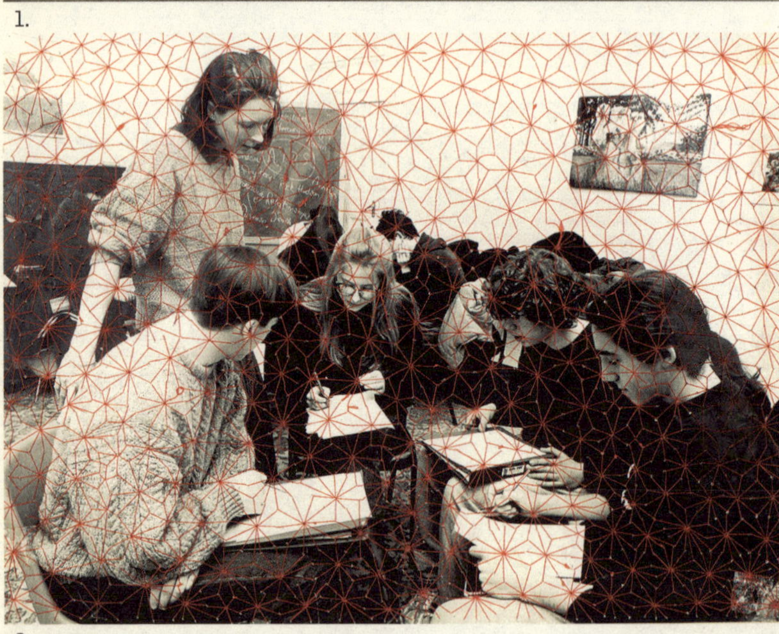

3.

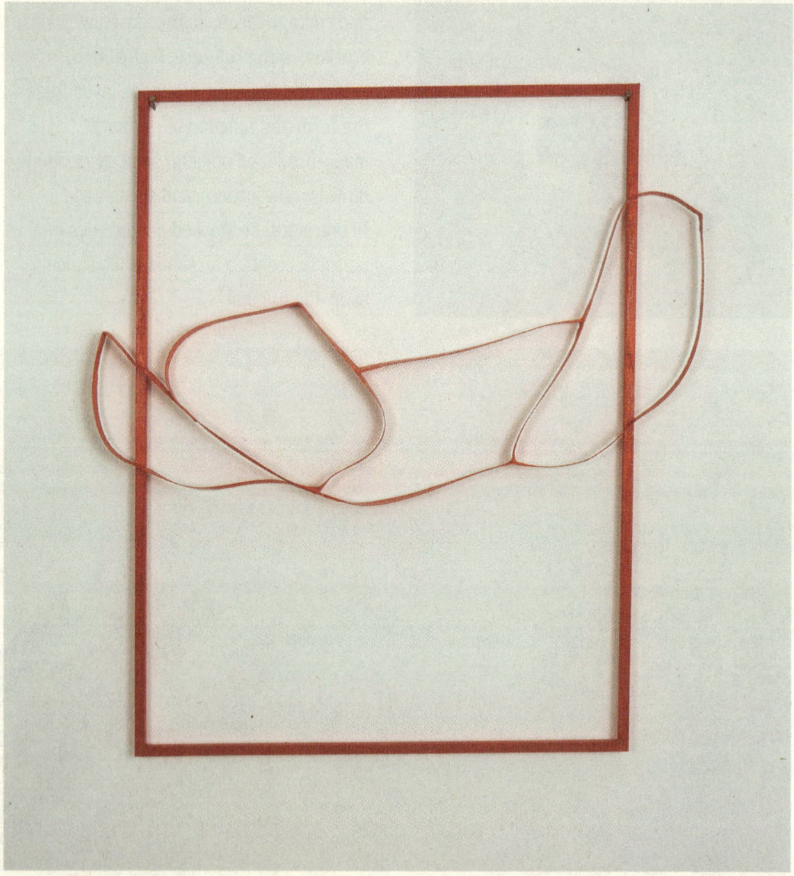

4.

Aleana Egan earned her BA from the Glasgow School of Art and currently lives in Dublin and Berlin. Her works in sculpture, collage, and drawing perform subtle manipulations on industrial materials. Her 2008 exhibition at the Kunsthalle Basel, "We sat down where we had sat before," draws its title from The Sea, The Sea by Iris Murdoch, echoing the novel's conflation of human psychology and a rugged coastline.

1. **Stage of Concern**
2008, bonding, cement, plaster, paint, wood, and foam, 200 ¾ × 59 × 132 ½ in (510 × 150 × 337 cm)

2. **Untitled (Villenueve Loubet)**
2004-06, wood, 36 × 22 ½ × 9 in (91 × 57 × 23 cm)

3. **Health-ed class**
2004, black and white photograph and red thread, 14 ½ × 19 ½ in (37 × 50 cm)

4. **Blue lines**
2006, wood, card, tape, paint, copper nails, and polyvinyl-acetate glue, 30 × 23 ¼ × 1 in (77 × 59 × 3 cm)

Ida Ekblad received her BA and MA from the National Academy of Art in Oslo, where she continues to live and work. An artist and curator, she co-runs the space Willy Wonka Inc. in Oslo, which hosts exhibitions, performances, concerts, and screenings. Her own work draws on popular culture – from Jessica Simpson to McDonald's – and takes the form of photographs, collages, posters, and sculptures.

1. **Political Song for Jessica Simpson to Sing**
2008, screenprint and chewing gum, 63 × 35 ½ in (160 × 90 cm)

2. **Air Jordan #2**
2008, gelatin silver print and pigment print mounted on aluminum, 80 × 65 in (203 × 165 cm)

3. **Ghost Bucksters**
2008, stamped, black-dyed dollar bills

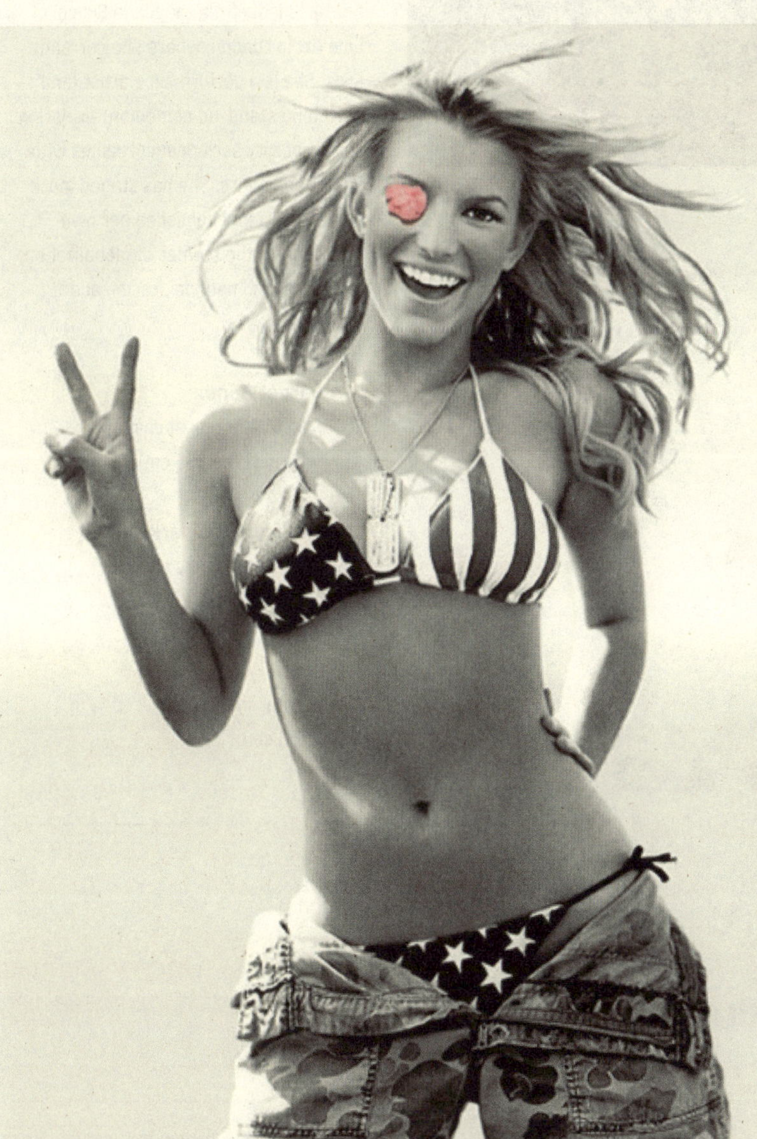
1.

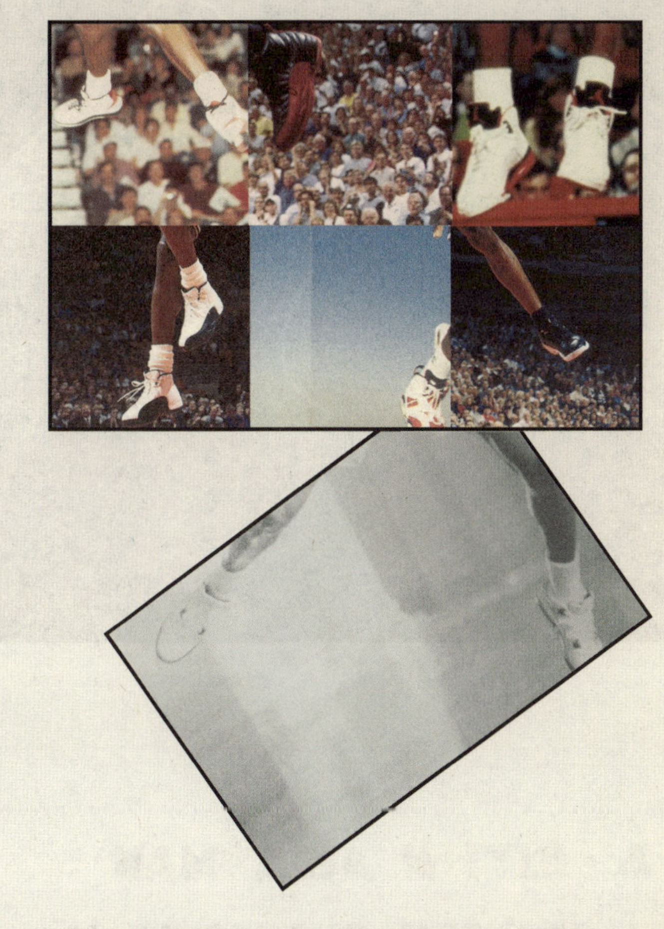
2.

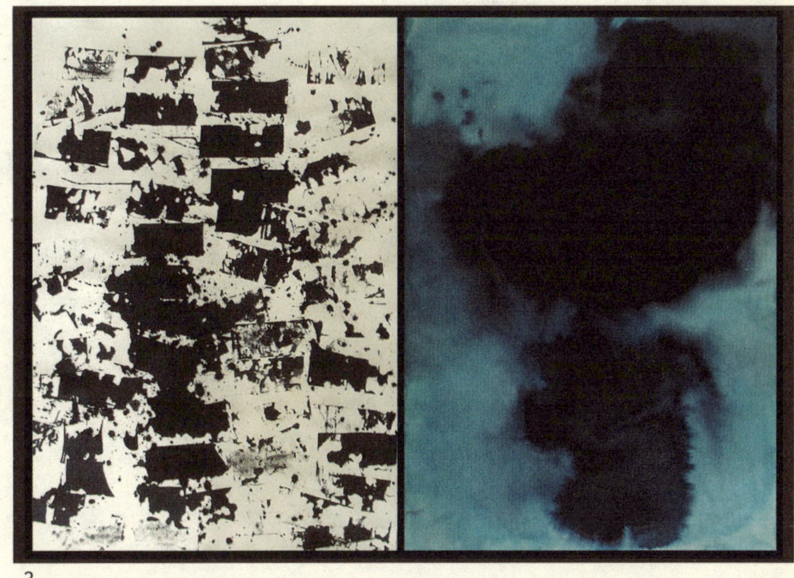
3.

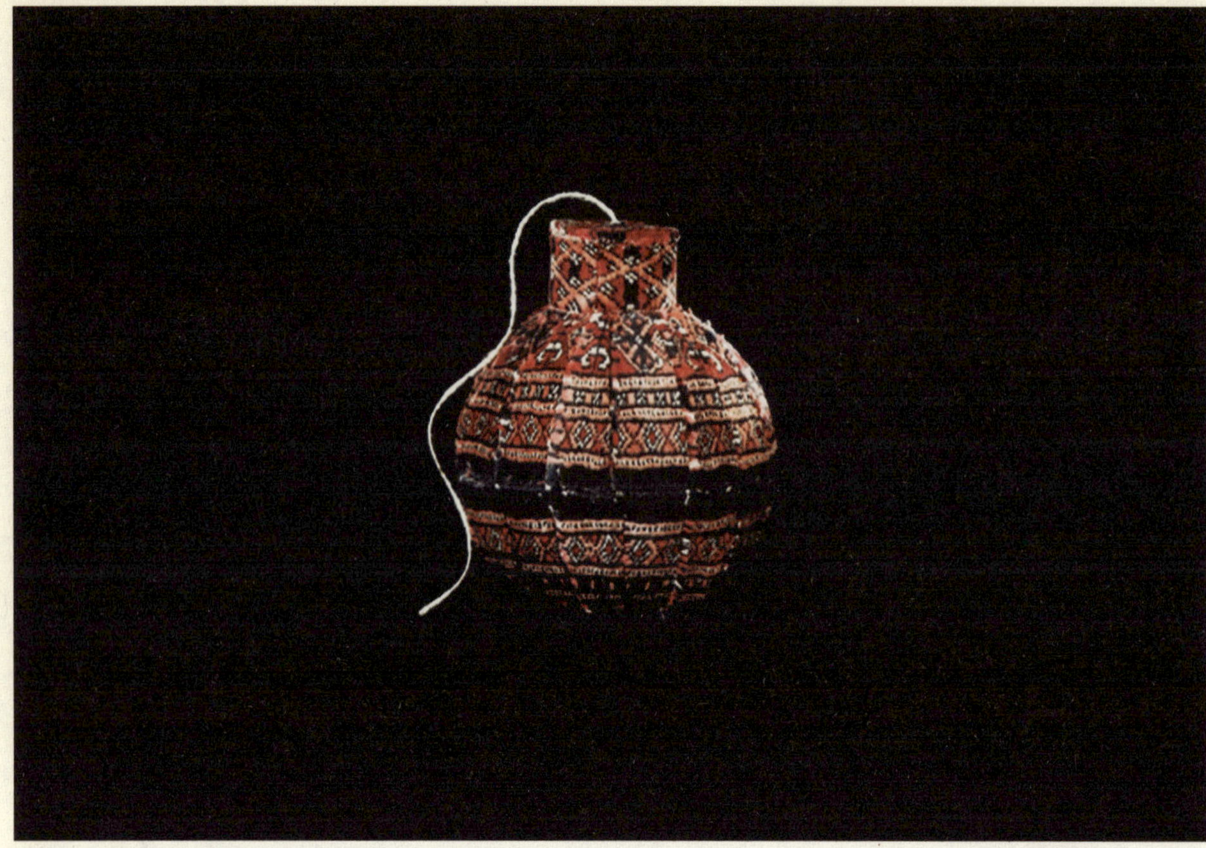

1.

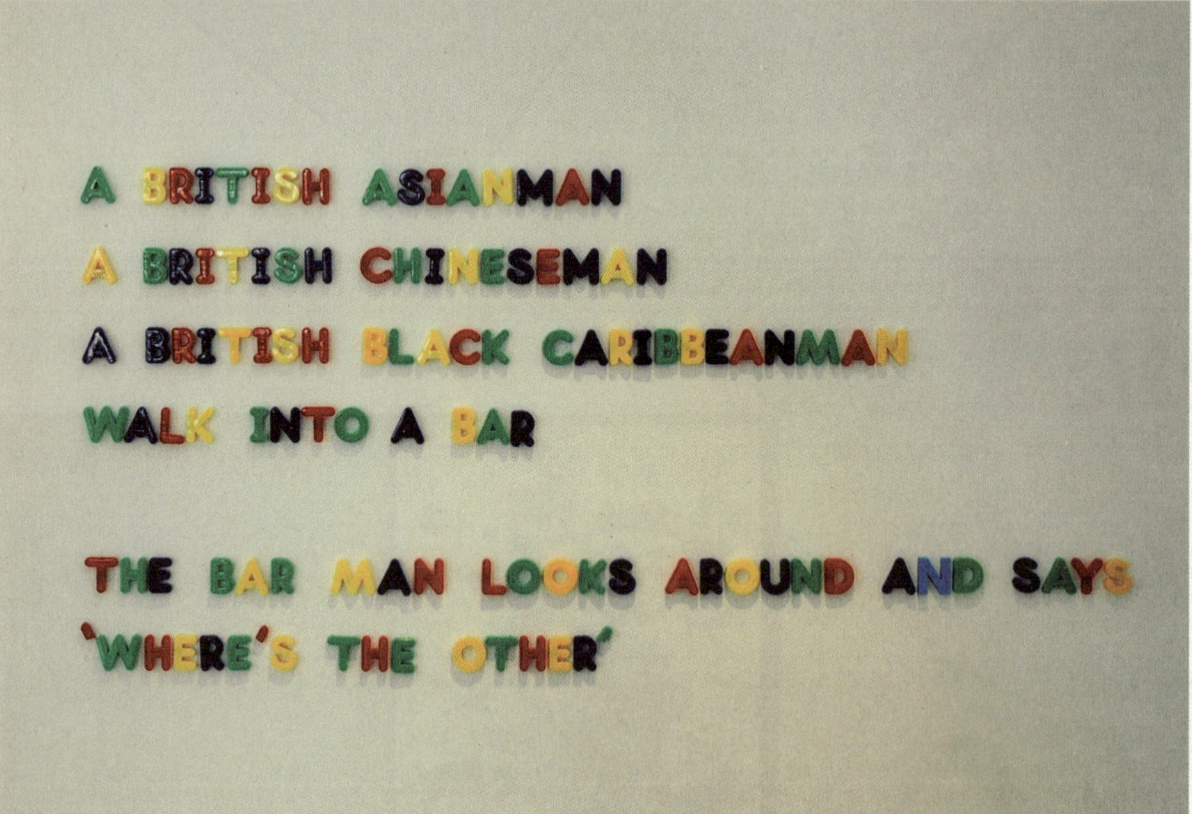

2.

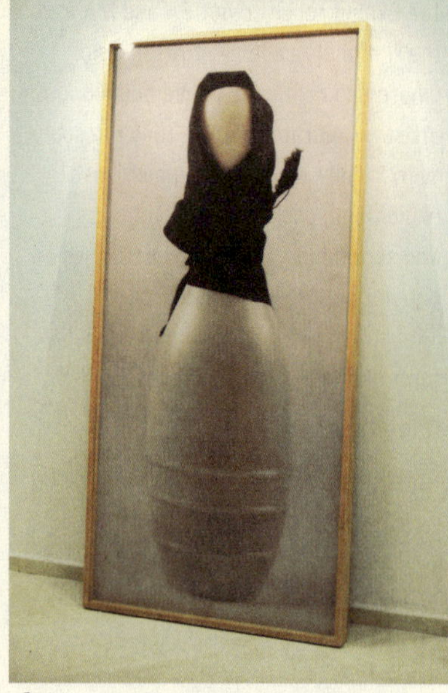

3.

Yara El-Sherbini received her MA in fine-art media from the Slade School of Fine Art in London, where she currently lives. She is a performance artist (and part-time stand-up comedian) exploring contemporary sociopolitical issues with humor and satire. She has staged mock game shows and published her own joke book on the themes of globalization, terrorism, and national, racial, and ethnic identity.

1. **A Carpet Bomb**
2005, digital print on aluminum, 43 ½ × 73 in (110 × 185 cm)

2. **Jokes from the dark side III**
2007, plastic magnetic letters, dimensions variable

3. **Skit**
2006, digital image, 39 ½ × 60 ¼ in (100 × 153 cm)

Redmond Entwistle currently lives in London and New York. He injects formal and technical experimentation into documentary filmmaking, from the images and sound on-screen to the space of the auditorium itself. **Paterson – Lódz** (2006) explores the cities in New Jersey and Poland, respectively, with a ten-channel computer-based sound track consisting of ambient sound and recorded interviews, played at random in different sequences each time the film is shown.

1, 2, 3, 4 & 5. **Paterson – Lodz**
2006, 16 mm film, color, with variable 10-channel computer-based sound track, 60 min

6, 7, 8 & 9. **Social Visions**
2000, 16 mm film, black and white, 15 min

1.

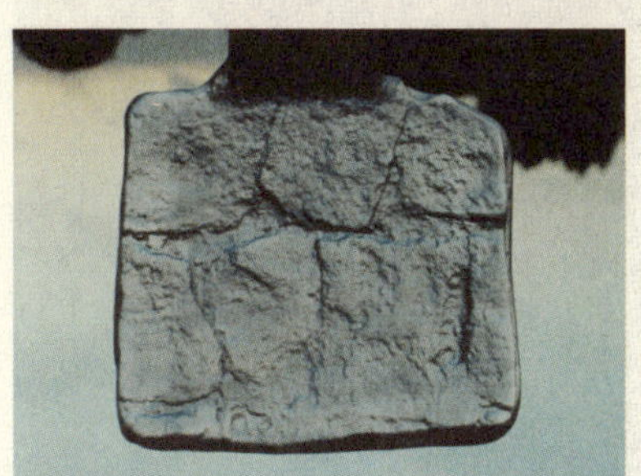
2.

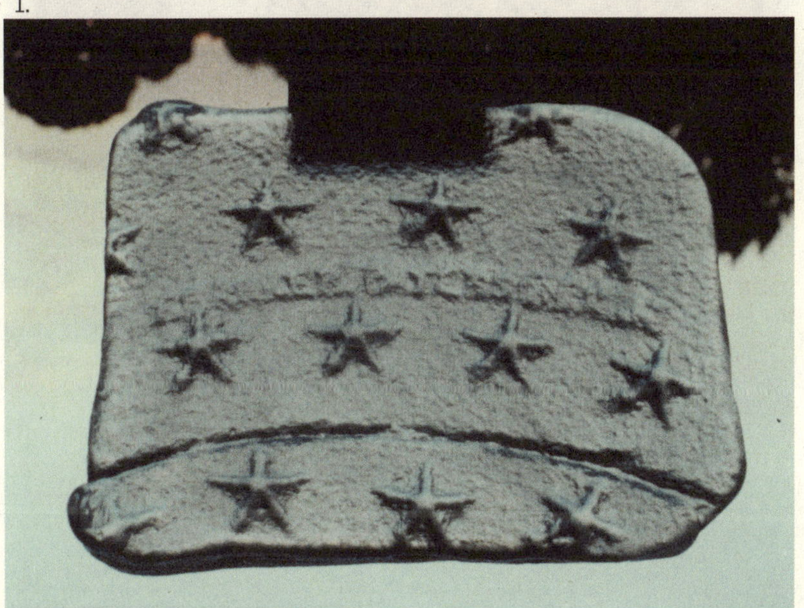
3.

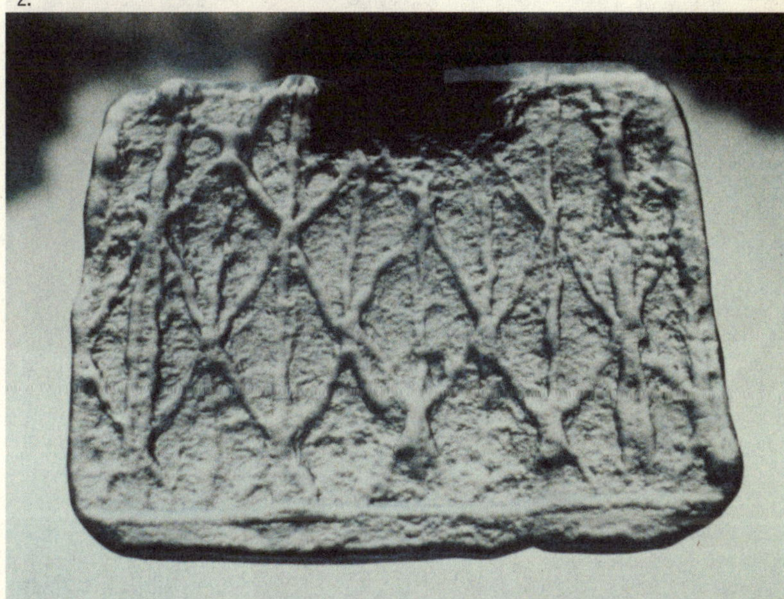
4.

5.

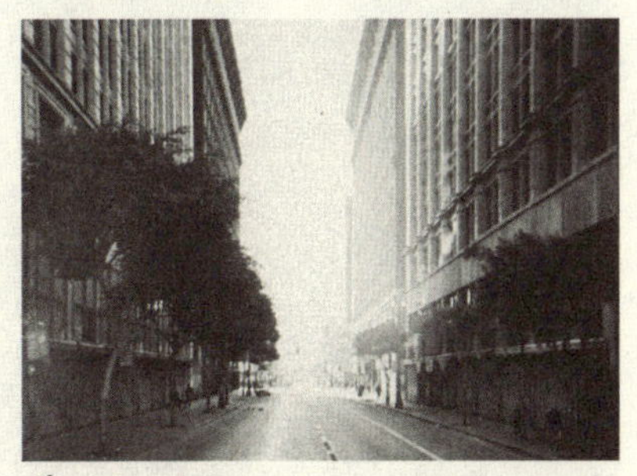
6.

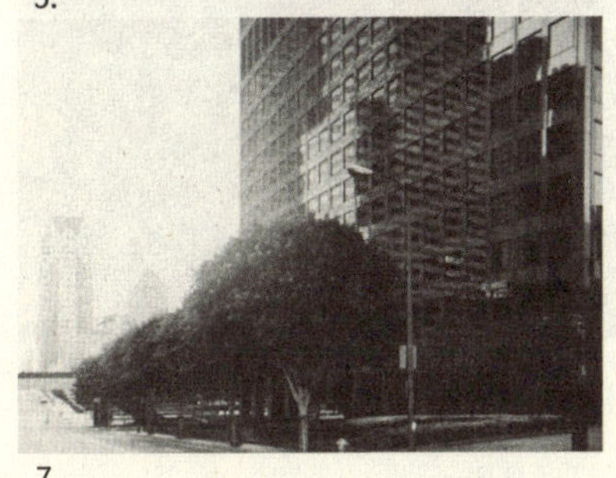
7.

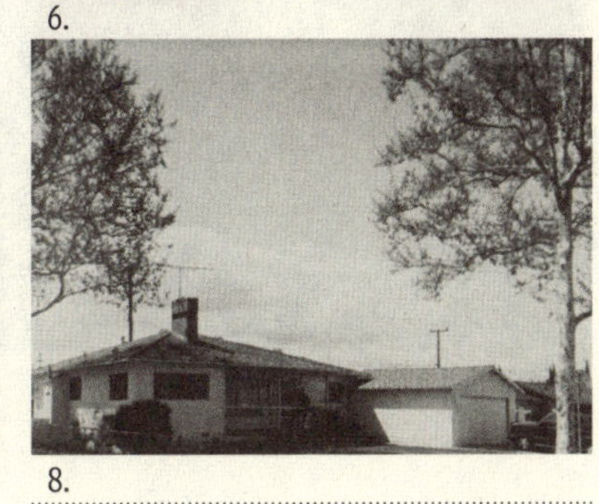
8.

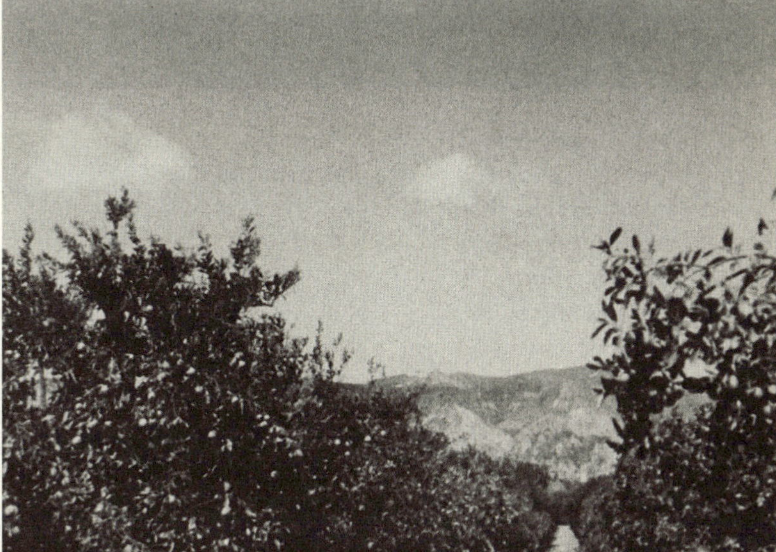
9.

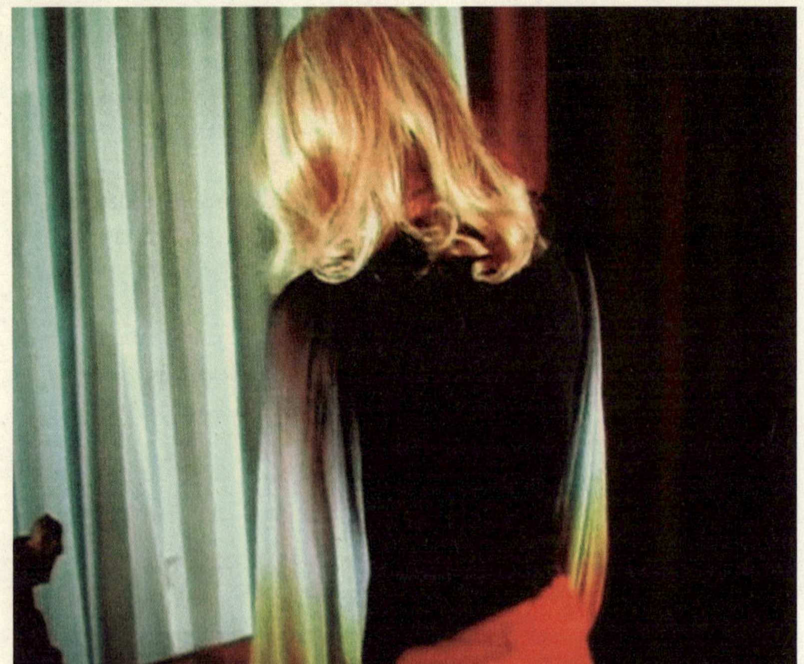

1.

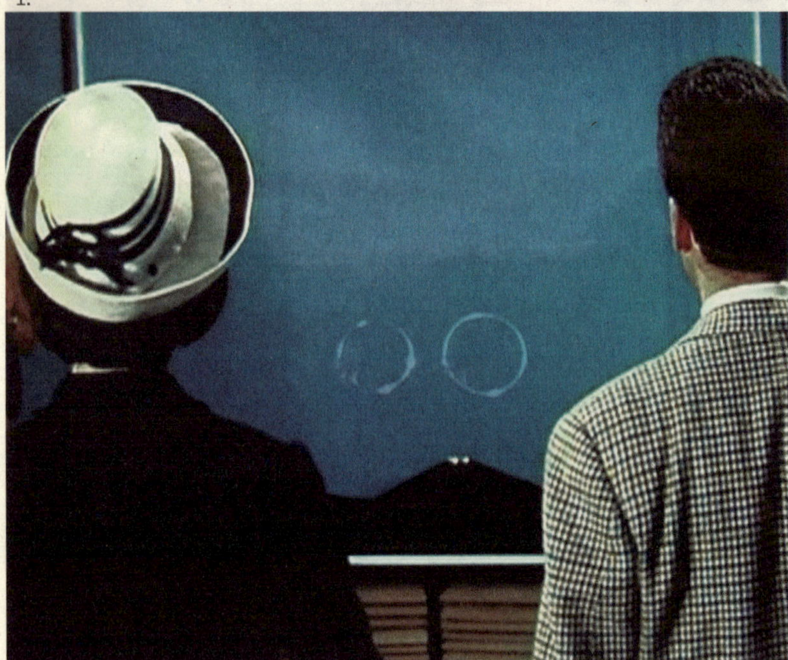

2.

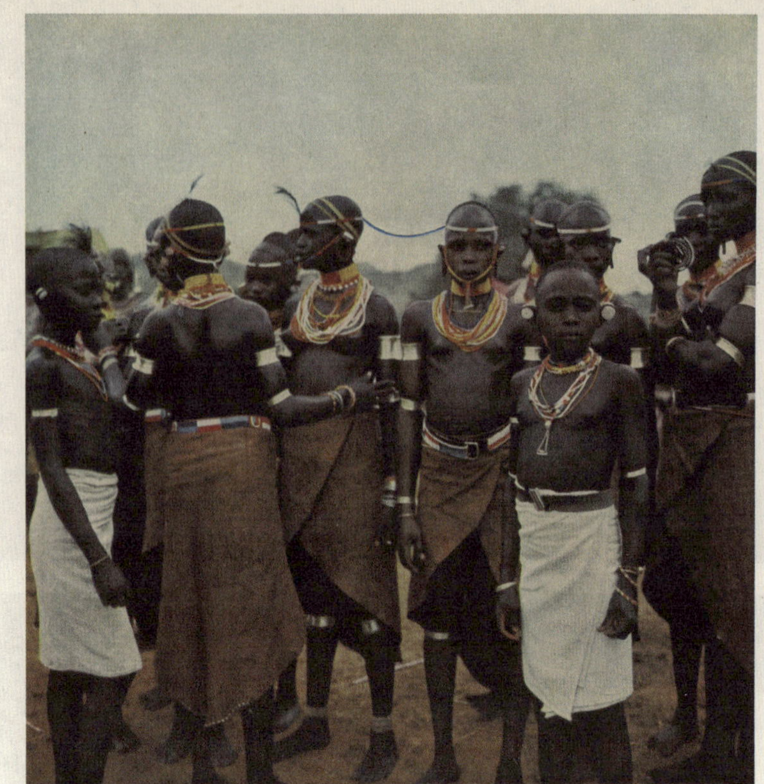

3.

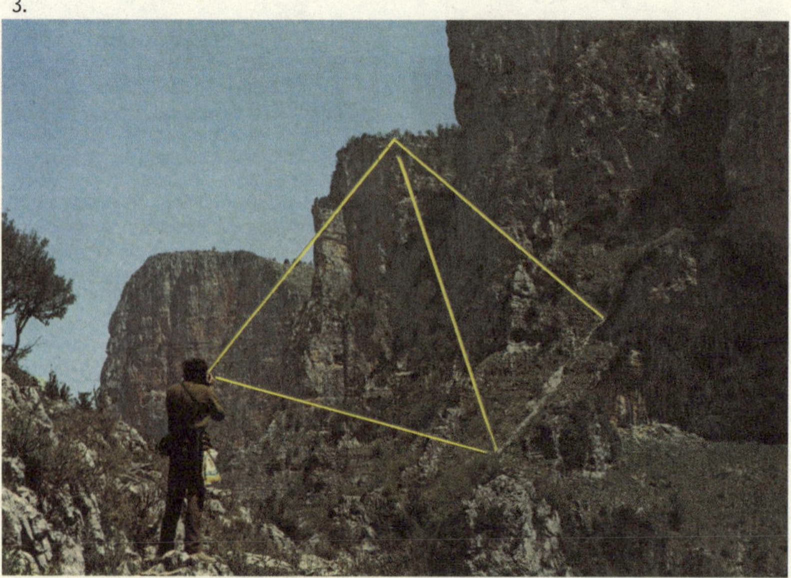

4.

Haris Epaminonda attended the Royal College of Art in London and currently lives in Berlin. She makes collages and videos by collecting and reassembling images from a variety of sources, including 1960s snapshots, interiors from French magazines, and Egyptian soap operas. Co-representing Cyprus at the 2007 Venice Biennale, she created poetic juxtapositions and delicate times, places, and bodies.

1. 'Tarahi IIII'
2007, video, 1 min 27 sec

2. 'Tarahi V'
2007, video, 3 min 11 sec

3. Untitled 03c/a
2007, paper collage, 9 3/4 × 7 in (25 × 18 cm)

4. Untitled 009c/g
2007, paper collage, 4 1/2 × 7 in (12 × 18 cm)

Berlin-based Köken Ergun has a degree in classics from King's College, London, and an MA in visual communication design from Bilgi University, Istanbul. He works in video and performance to explore Turkish nationalism through religious, military, and cultural traditions. One series documents ceremonies performed in large stadiums during state-controlled national holidays.

1. WEDDING
2007-08, 3-channel video, 13 min

2. untitled
2004, video, 7 min

3. the flag
2006, 2-channel video, 9 min

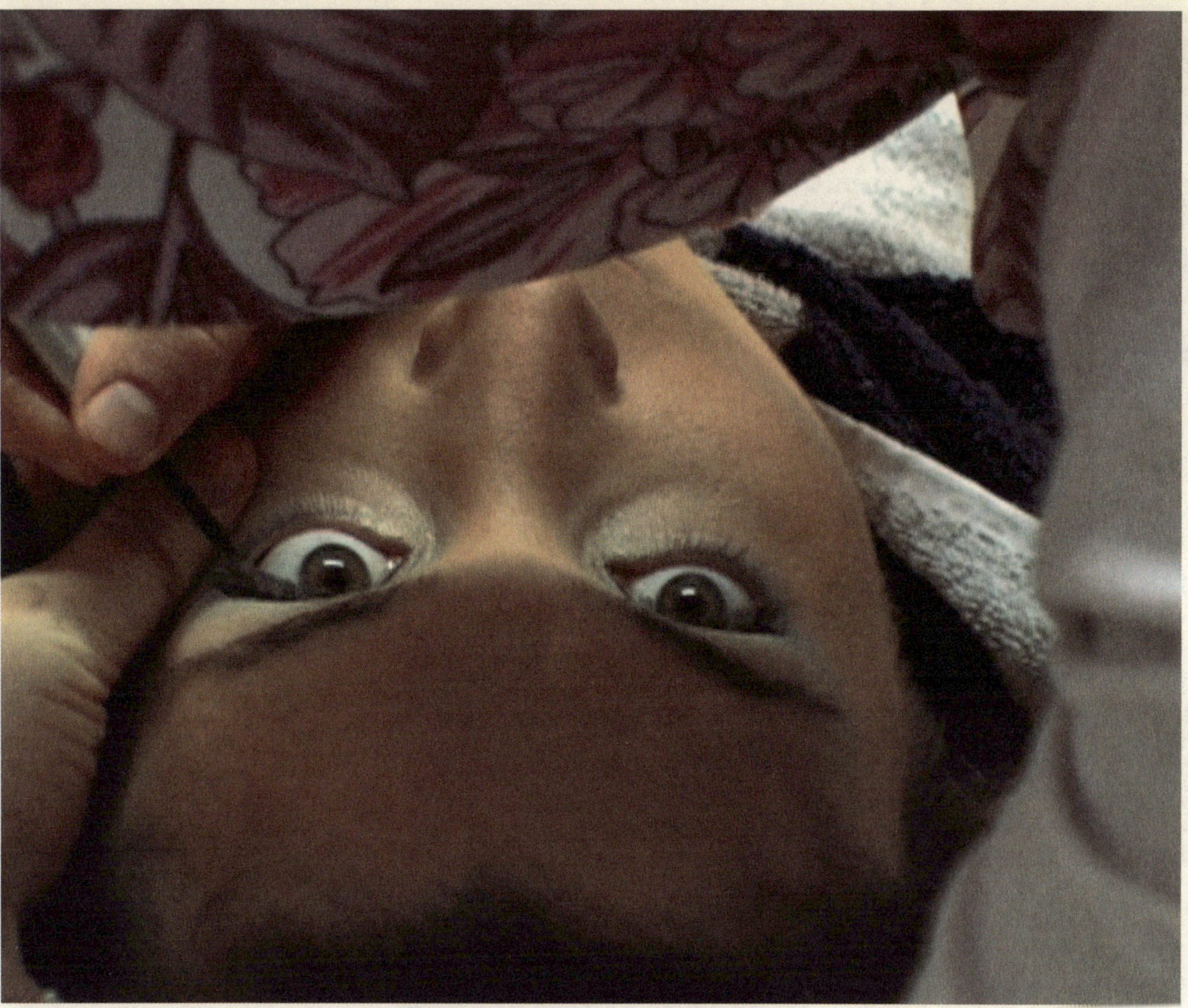

1.

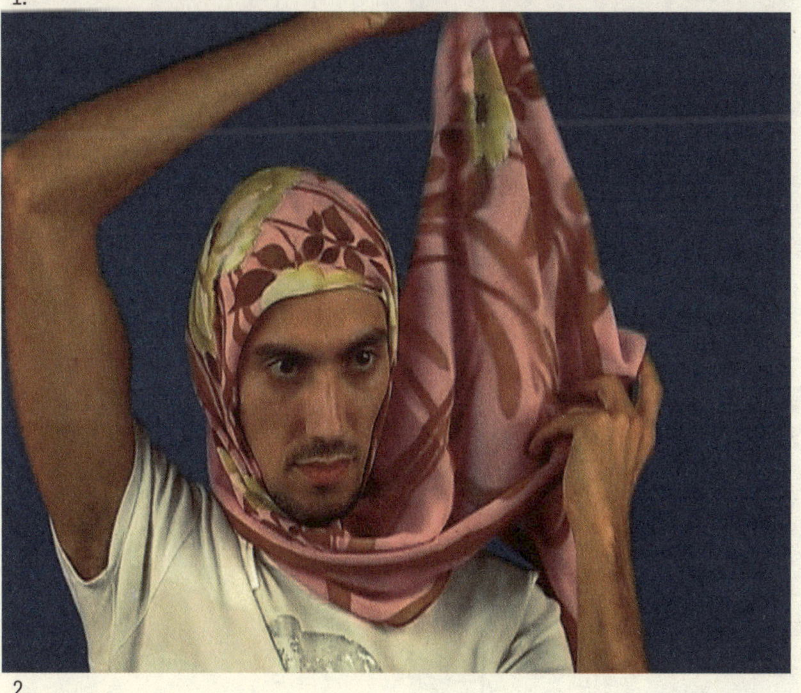

2.

3.

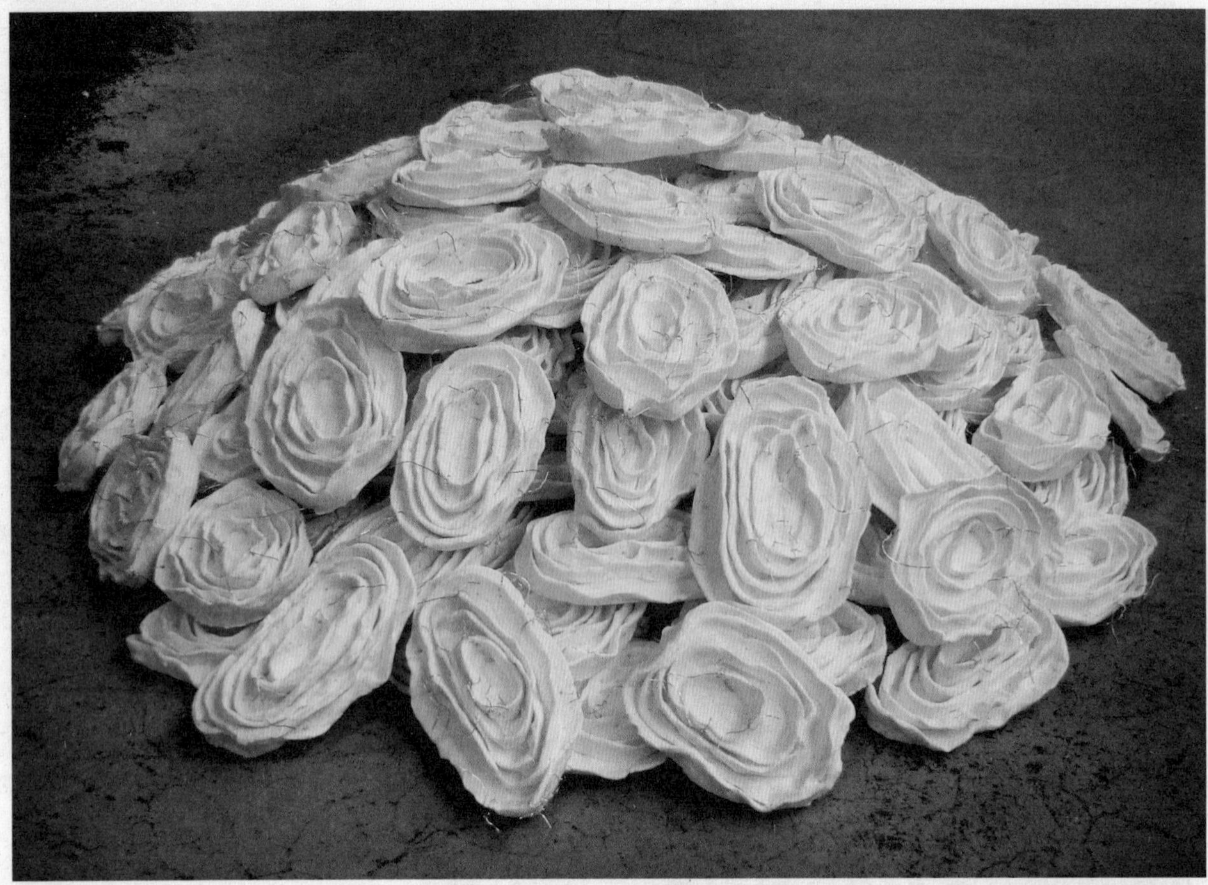

1.

2.

Safaa Erruas attended l'Institut National des Beaux-Arts in Tétouan, where she continues to live. She reclaims materials associated with the tradition of Moroccan dressmaking in sculptures, installations, and public works. Cotton, gauze, tissue paper, pins, and razors are assembled and reconfigured in abstractions that are at once threatening and delicately meditative. She is a member of the Collectif 212 group of contemporary Moroccan artists.

1. **Le bouquet romantique**
2006, porcelain and metal threads, diameter 19 ¾ in (50 cm)

2. **Couteaux**
2006, knives and porcelain, dimensions variable

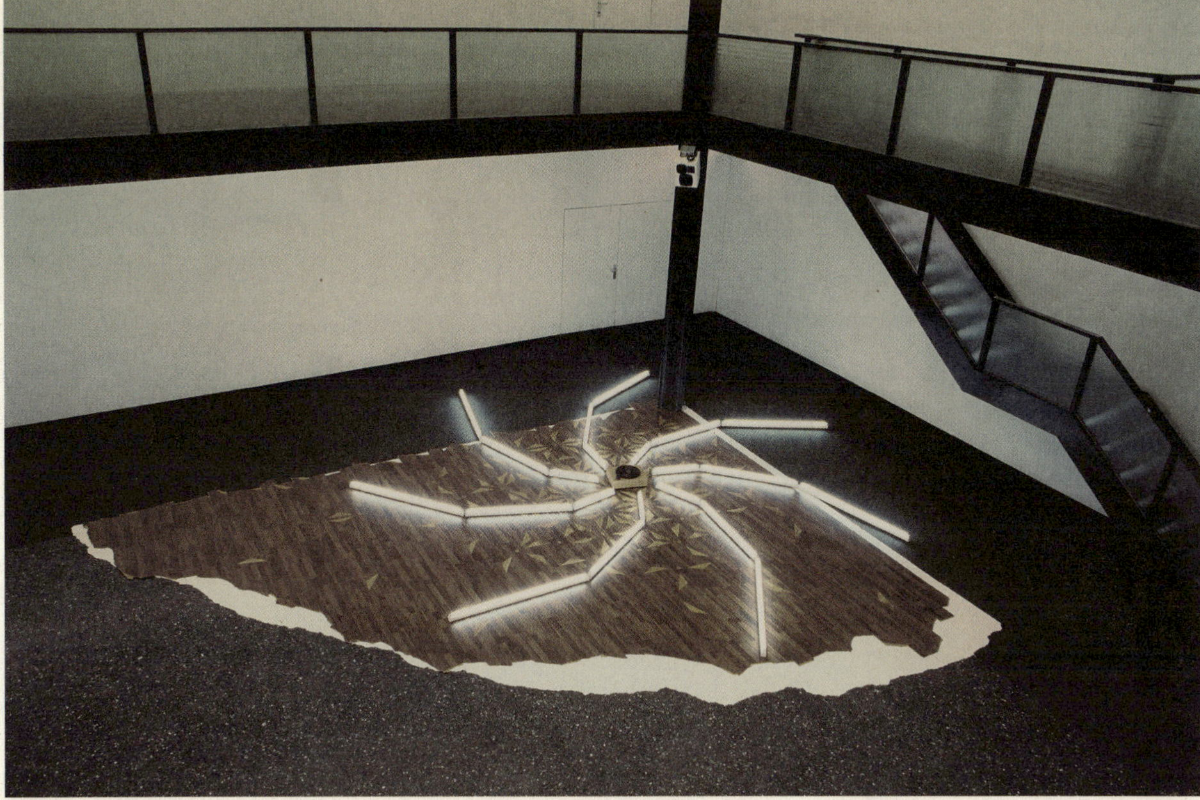

1.

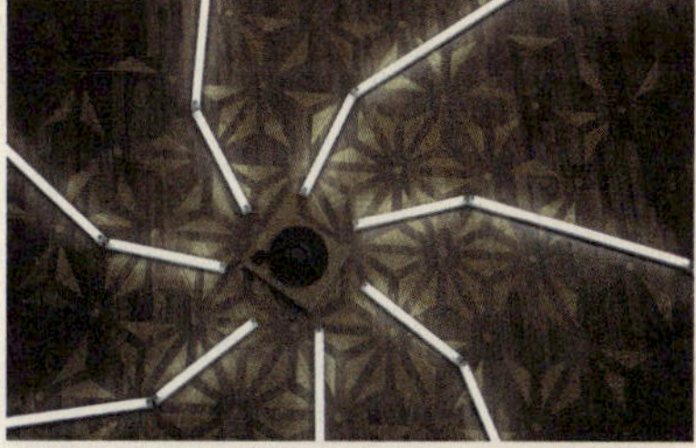

2.

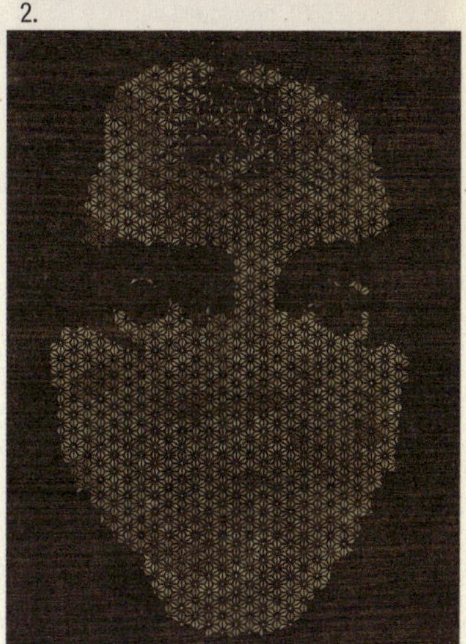

3.

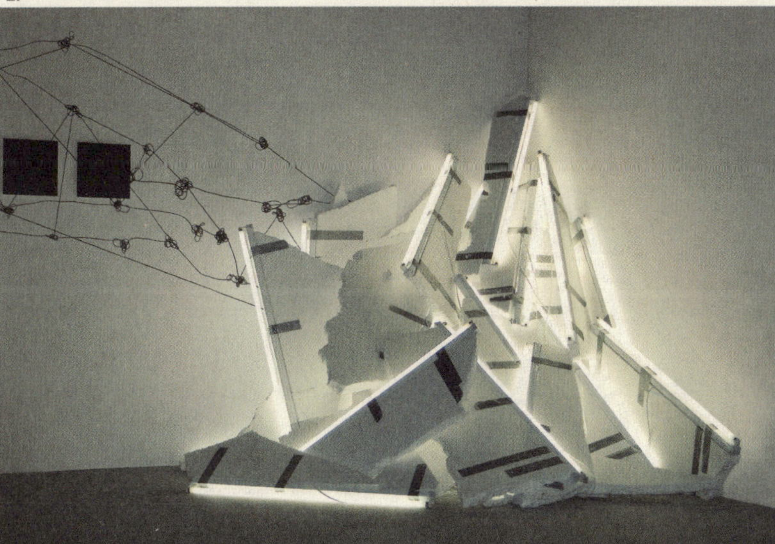

4.

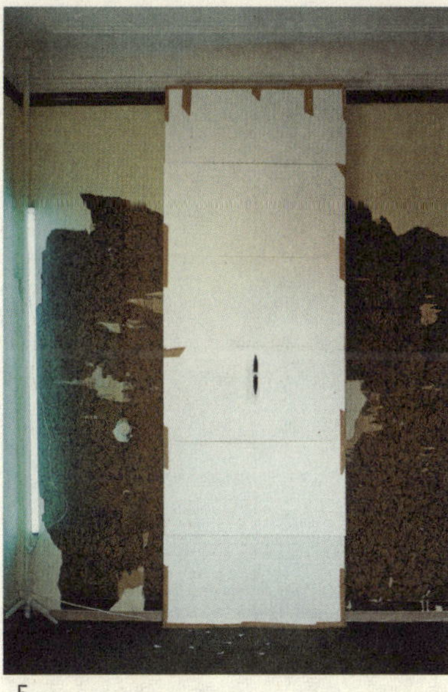

5.

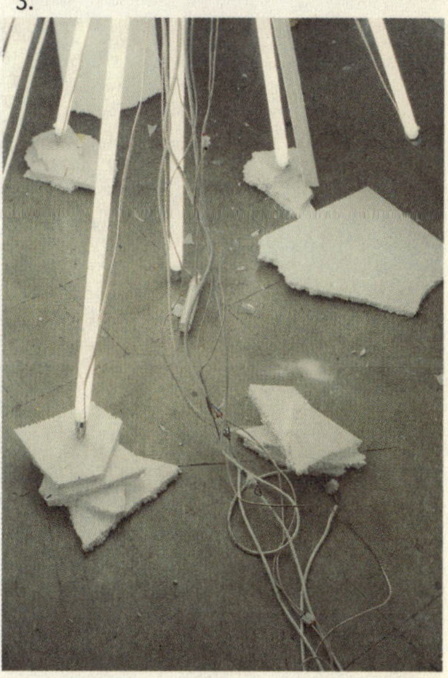

6.

Christian Ertel is an installation artist living in Karlsruhe. Fluorescent light tubes, Styrofoam, and gaffer tape are among the industrial materials that he assembles and disassembles in his melancholy environments. Works often feature traces of the organic, such as skulls, dissected butterfly wings, or elements of motorized action, including a Black Sabbath album spinning on a record player.

1 & 2. **Whenever, Whatever, Keep Going**
2008, Styrofoam, fluorescent tubes, laminate, PVC, MDF, record, record player, and speaker, approximately 20 × 26 ft (6 × 8 m)

3. **Untitled (Self Portrait I)**
2007, chromogenic print mounted on Alu-Dibond, 23 × 16 $\frac{1}{2}$ in (58 × 42 cm)

4. **The Ascension of Obduracy**
2007, fluorescent tubes, Styrofoam, gaffer tape, wallpaper, and laser prints on Alu-Dibond, dimensions variable

5. **Tris**
2006, alabaster miniature, drawings, wire, wood, magnets, gaffer tape, PVC, Styrofoam, and ultraviolet fluorescent tube, dimensions variable

6. **Untitled (Twww4y)** (detail)
2007, fluorescent tubes, Styrofoam, polyethylene foam, and mixed media, approx 59 × 59 in × 59 in (150 × 150 × 150 cm)

Andrew Esiebo is a photographer based in Ibadan, Nigeria. He documents various aspects of Nigerian life, including hugely attended Pentecostal and Evangelical services, and soccer games in different contexts across the country. The project **Eyes from South to West** (2008), developed during a residency at Gasworks, London, in conjunction with Africa Beyond, the BBC Web portal celebrating African arts and music in the UK, explores the lives of Nigerian immigrants in Europe through photography and audio interviews.

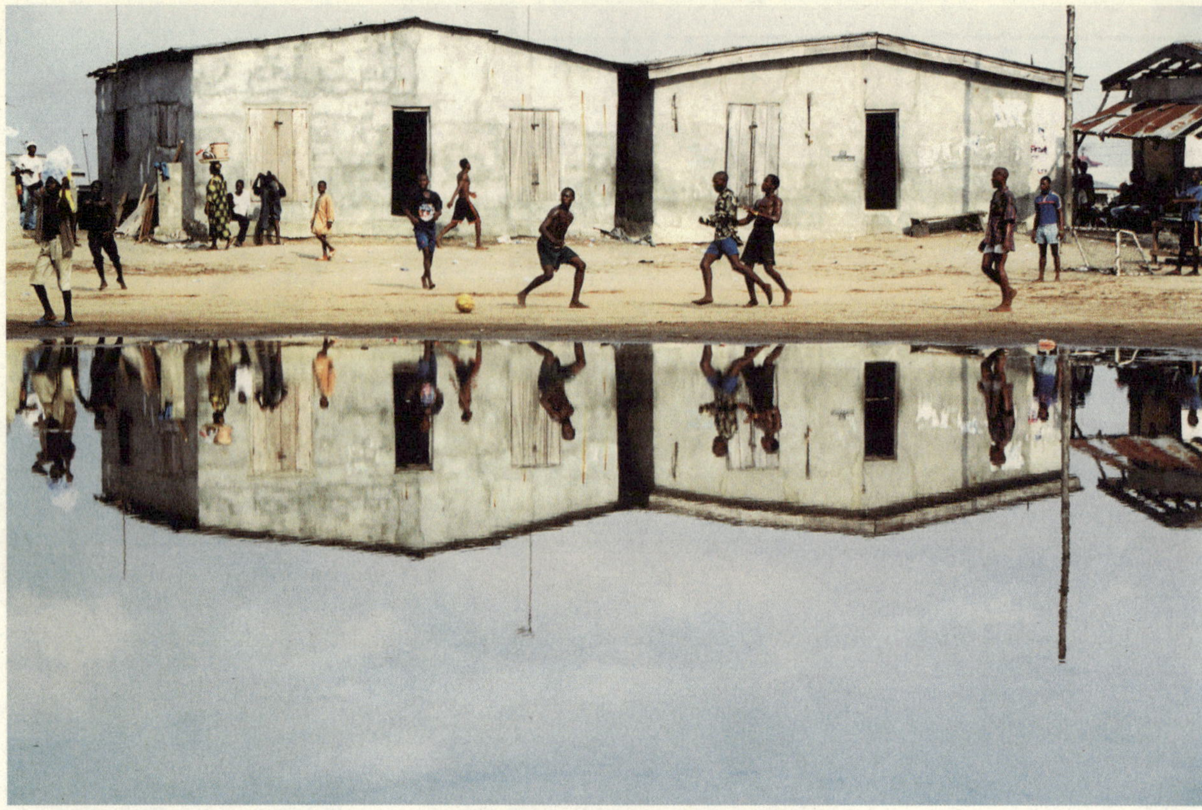

1.

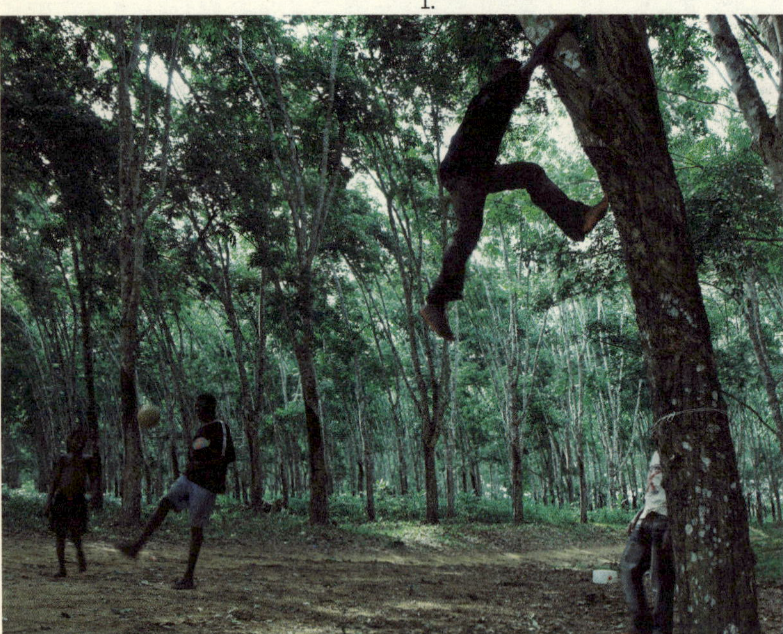

2.

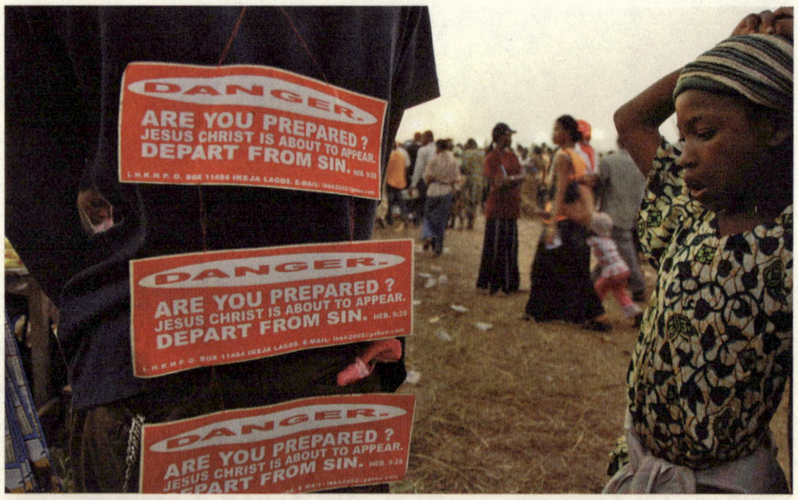

3.

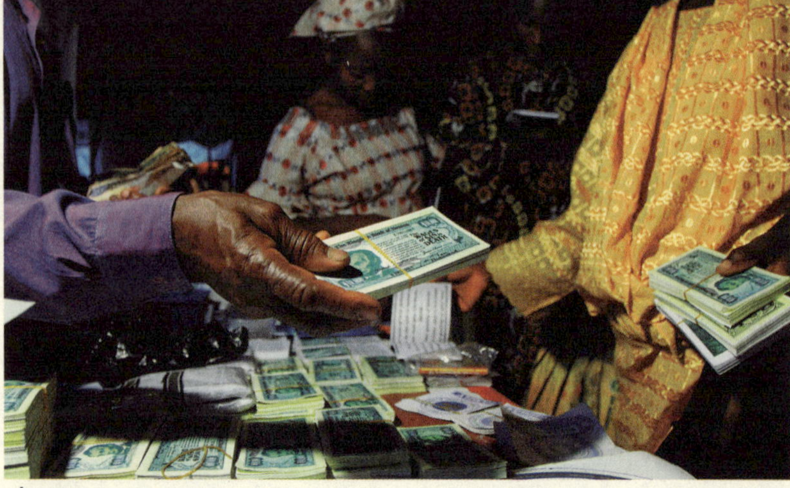

4.

1 & 2. **Soccer World**
from the series **Soccer World**
2006-07, color photographs,
dimensions variable

3 & 4. **God is Alive**
from the series **God is Alive**
2007, color photographs,
dimensions variable

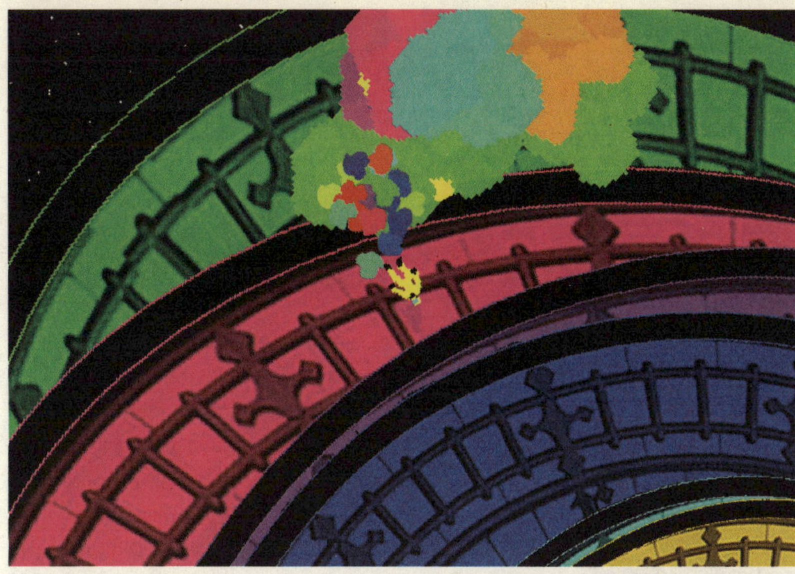

1.

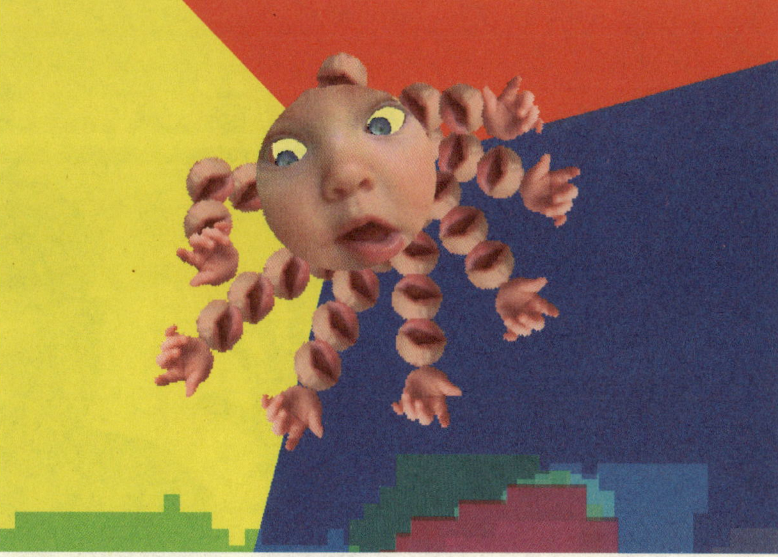

2.

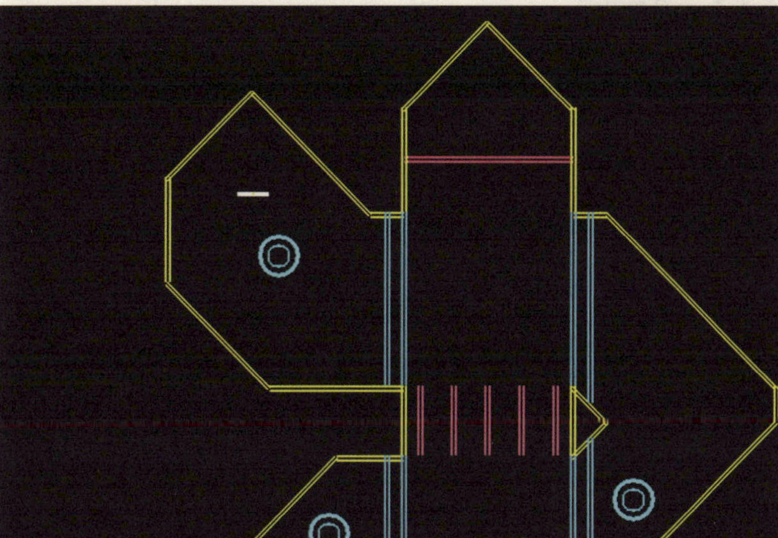

3.

Mark Essen, aka Messhof, attended Bard College in Annandale-on-Hudson, New York, and currently lives in Brooklyn. He is an art-game designer who combines psychedelic visuals, elements of avant-garde cinema, and electronic sound tracks in games like the complex and challenging **Randy Balma: Municipal Abortionist** (2008). His game portfolio is free to download from his website, messhof.com.

1 & 2. **Randy Balma: Municipal Abortionist**
2008, Windows EXE file

3. **Flywrench**
2007, Windows EXE file

4. **Punishment: The Punishing**
2007, Windows EXE file

5. **Cowboyana**
2008, Windows EXE file with two controllers

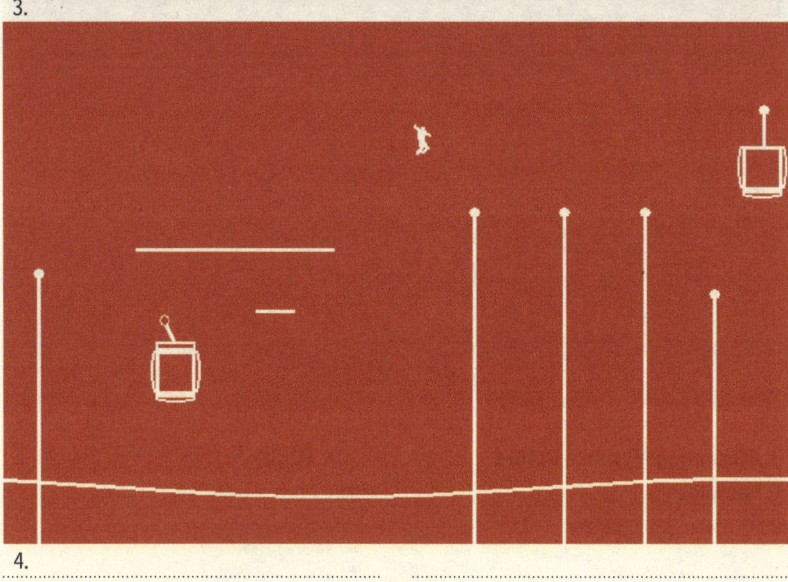

4.

5.

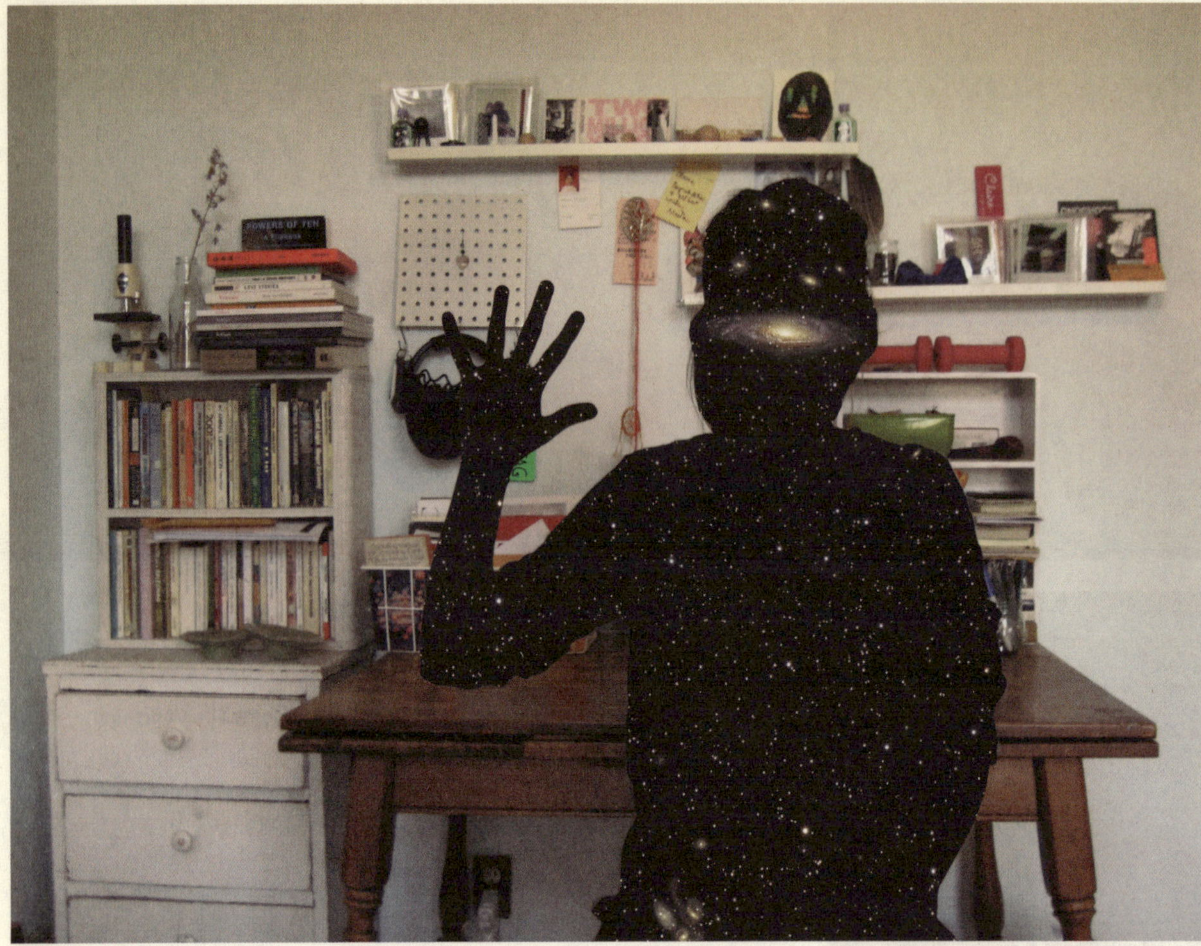

1.

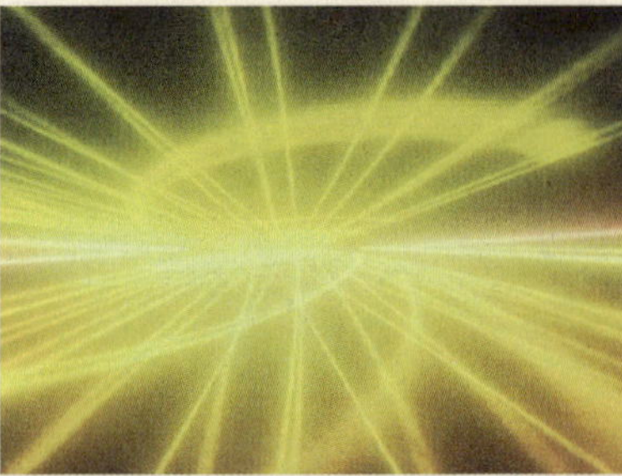

2.

Claire Evans attended Occidental College in Los Angeles and currently works in Portland, Oregon, as an artist and writer. Taking technology as a medium and a subject, she creates video and live performance works drawing source material from the Internet. **Digital Decay** (2007) traces the decomposition of an image as it loses quality over time.

1. Self-Portrait of Claire L. Evans
from the **Starstuff** series
2008, digital photograph,
dimensions variable

2. Digital Decay
2007, video, 2 min 47 sec

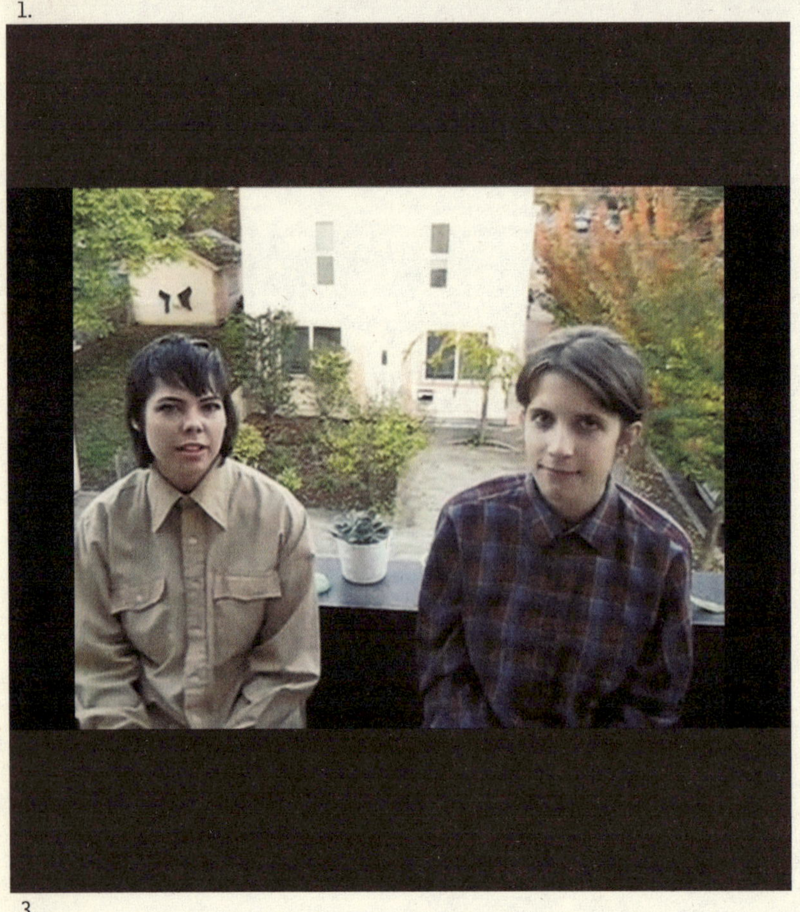

3.

Digital bits, compatible at last to the new generation of tools that see, hear, speak, and compute, march in precise, soldierly fashion, one figure after another.
This means that any video, audio, or photographic work of art can be endlessly reproduced, without degradation, always the same, always perfect.

4.

3. Evacuating Myspace Before It Recycles
2007, video, 3 min 56 sec

4. OK TO GO
2008, video, 4 min 8 sec

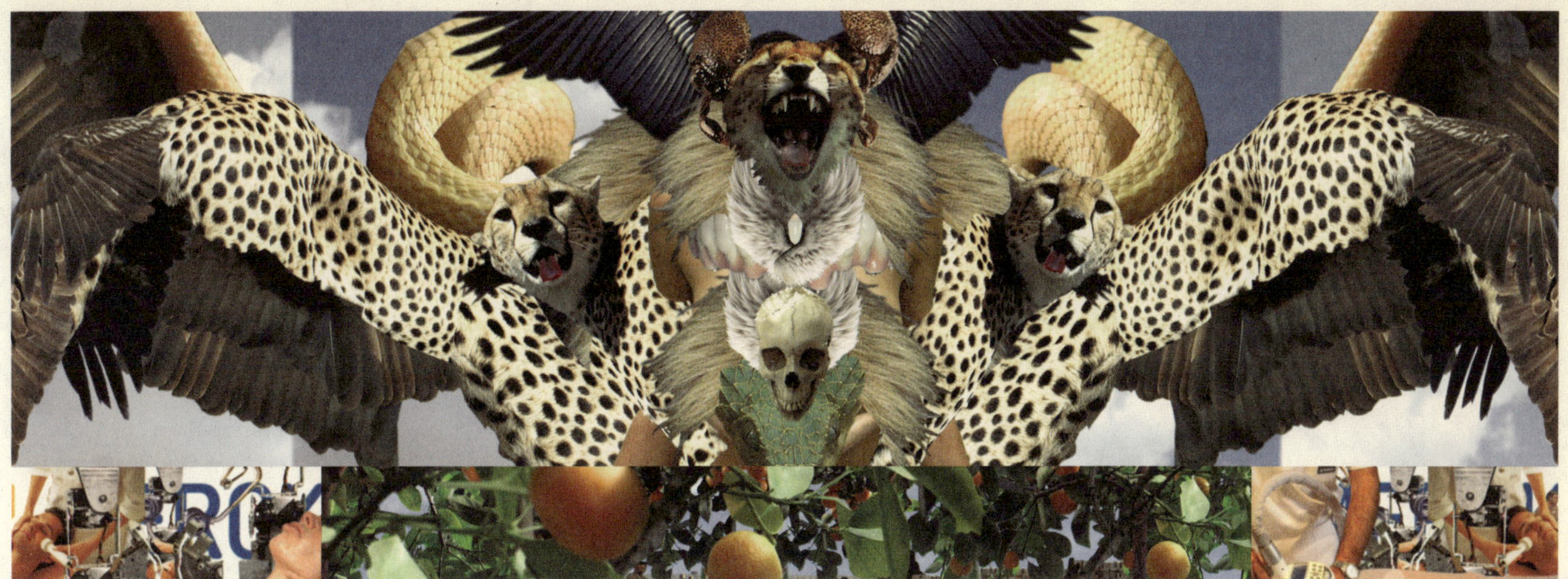

1.

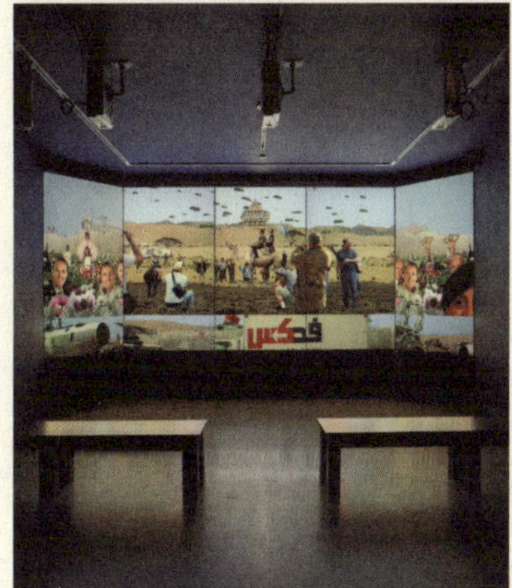

2.

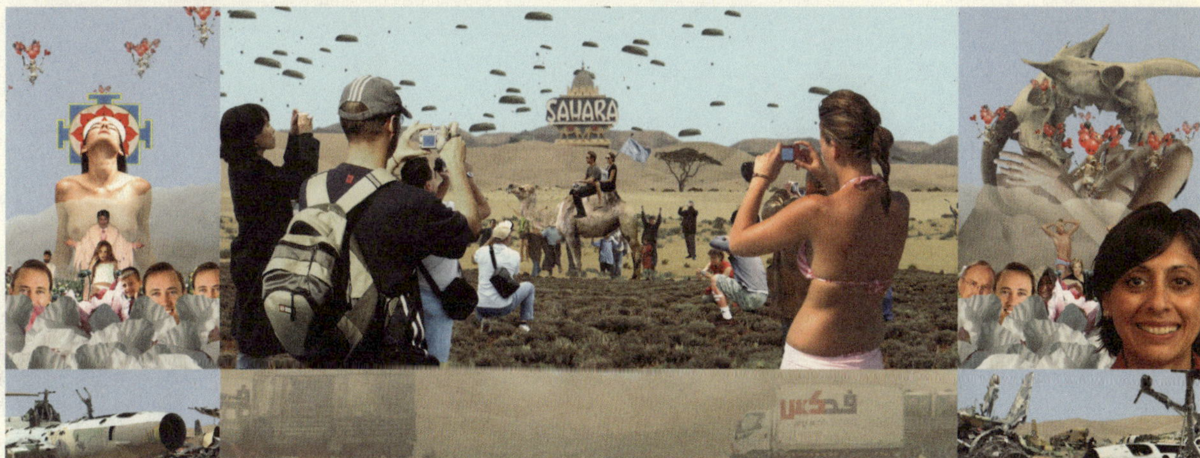

3.

Cliff Evans was raised in Texas, attended the School of the Museum of Fine Arts, Boston, and currently lives in Brooklyn. He creates multichannel video animations addressing global politics and pop culture. Using images drawn from governmental, corporate, military, commercial, and entertainment websites, he builds sequences of moving photomontage with devout energy reminiscent of Hieronymus Bosch.

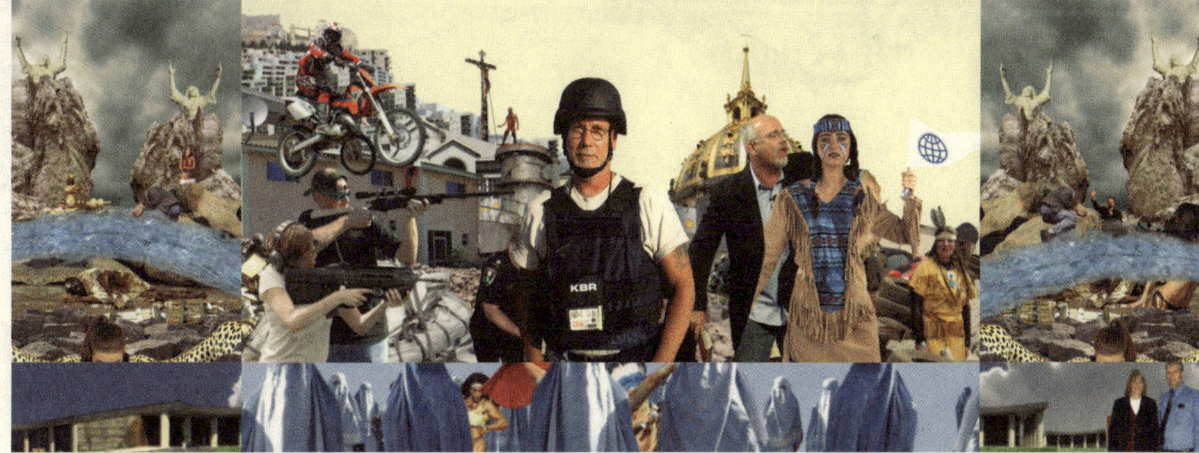

4.

1, 2, 3 & 4. **Empyrean**
2007, 5-channel video projection, stereo sound, and computer playback, 6 min 33 sec

5. **The Road to Mount Weather**
2006, 3-channel HD digital video projection, stereo sound and computer playback, 14 min 46 sec

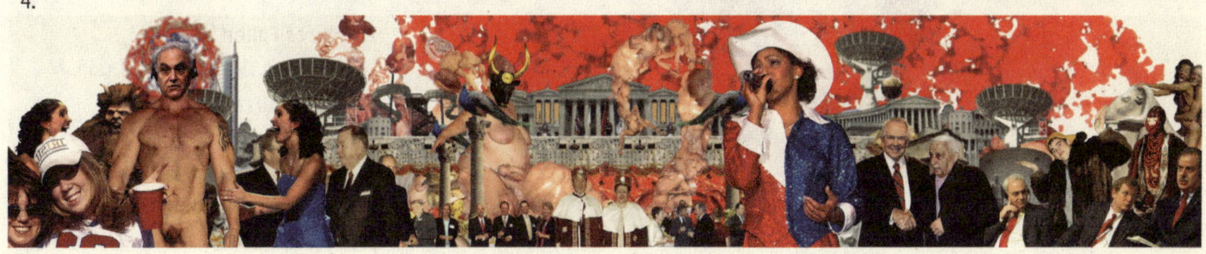

5.

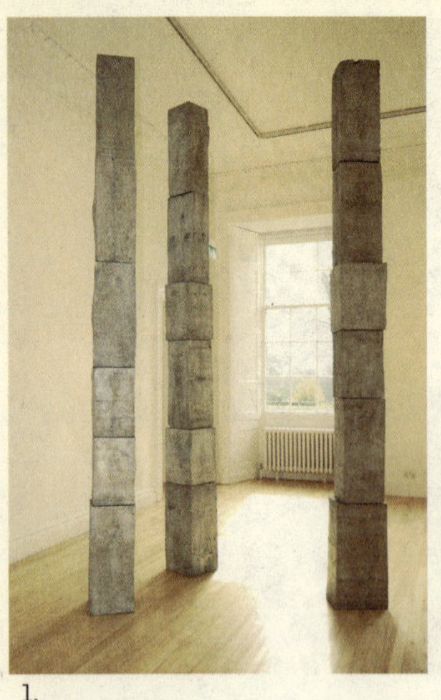

1.

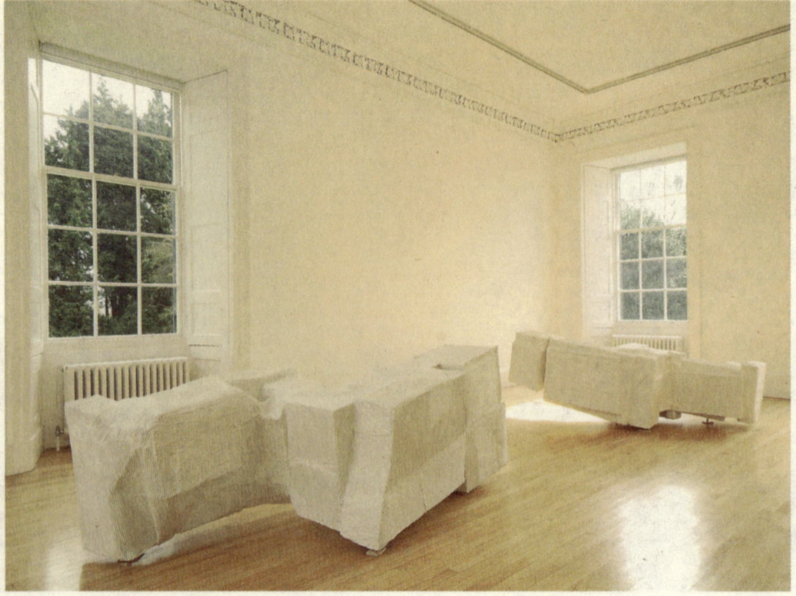

2.

Nick Evans earned his BA in sculpture and environmental art from the Glasgow School of Art, and continues to live in Glasgow. He uses materials such as cast and assembled resin, poured aluminum, and hand-built ceramics, often painting over the final assemblage. Sculptures combine abstract and figurative elements, with references from Cubism and Abstract Expressionism to graffiti and Pop art.

1. **Figures Standing**
2008, sand-cast aluminum,
130 × 11 3/4 × 11 3/4 in (330 × 30 × 30 cm)

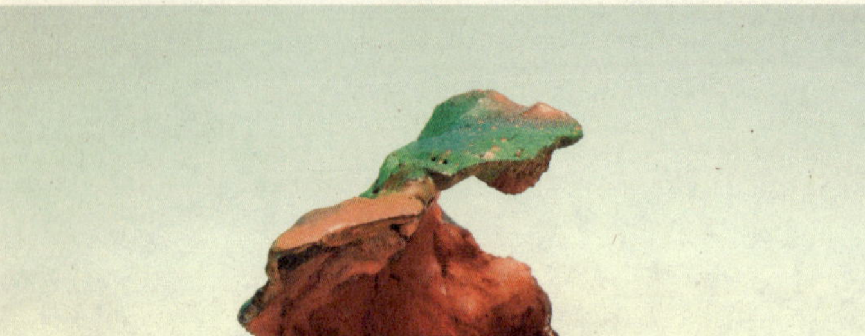

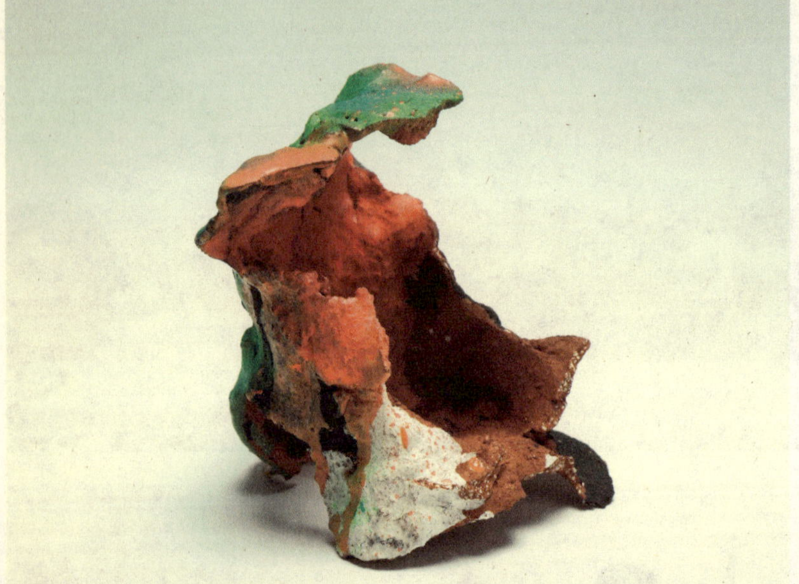

3.

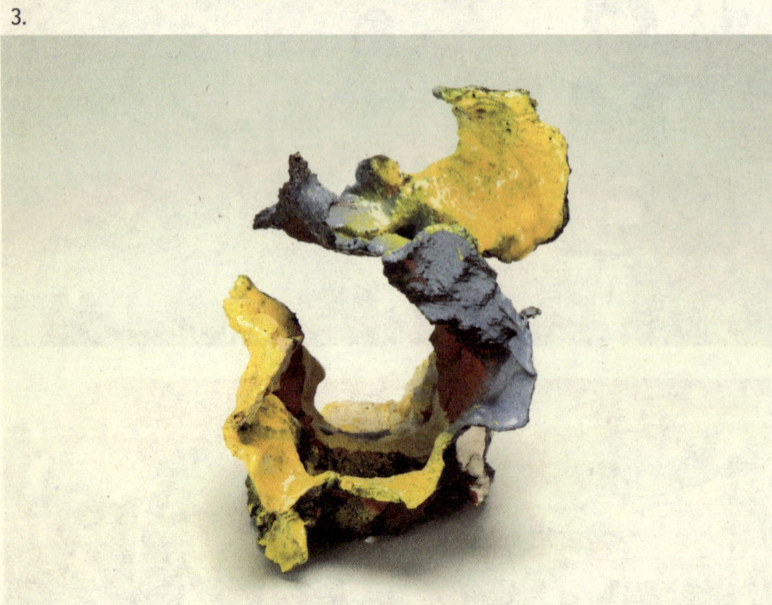

4.

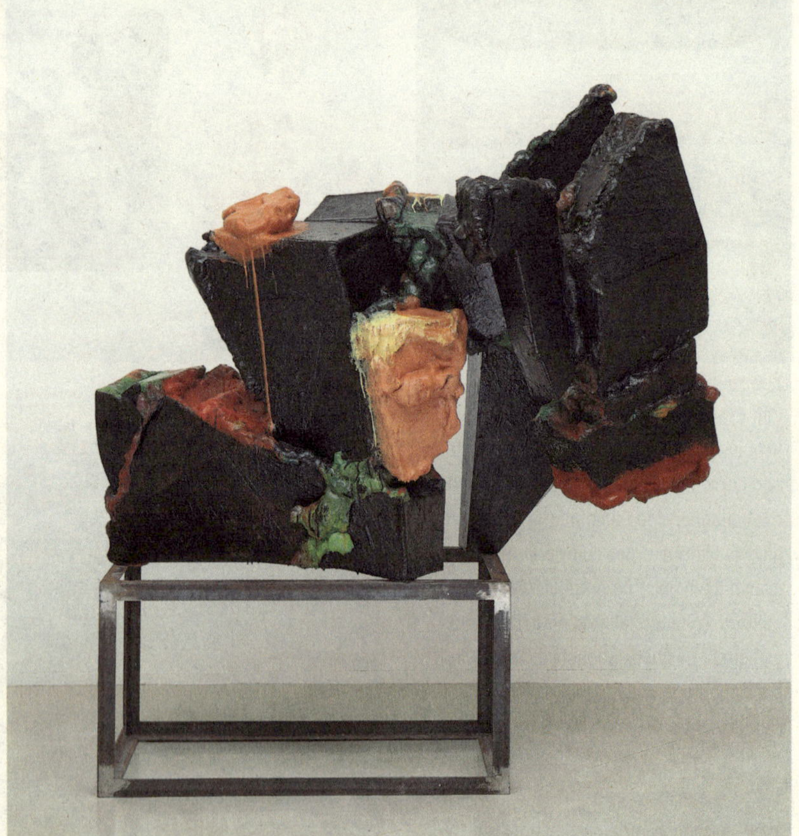

5.

2. **Figures Fallen**
2008, plaster, 31 1/4 × 98 1/2 × 43 1/4 in (80 × 250 × 110 cm)

3 & 4. **Models B-J** (detail)
2006, glazed and painted terra-cotta, 9 parts, each maximum height 10 in (25 cm)

5. **Figure Y**
2006, colored polyester resin and fiberglass on metal stand,
82 1/2 × 78 3/4 × 47 1/4 in (210 × 200 × 120 cm)

GET OFF YOUR KNEES!

1.

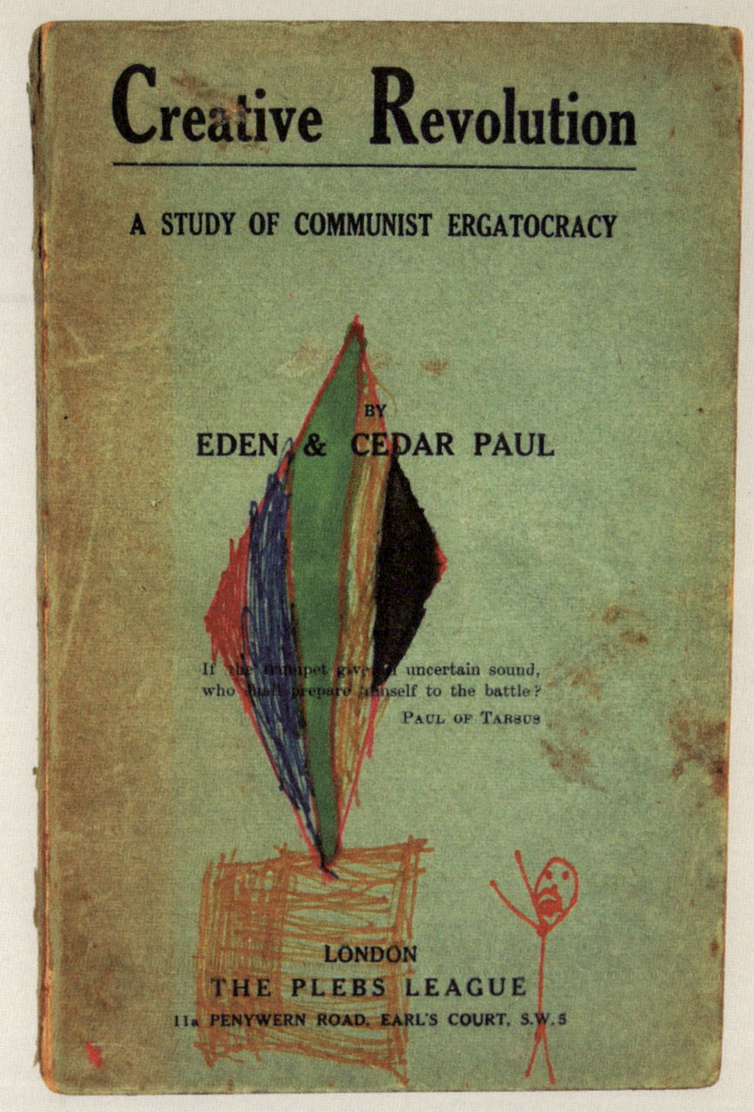

2.

Ruth Ewan earned her BA from Edinburgh College of Art and currently lives in London. Many of her works suggest contemporary applications of socialist and utopian histories. Her practice often includes a large degree of community organizing. For **Did You Kiss The Foot That Kicked You?** (2007), for example, she placed 100 buskers around the city of London, instructing them to perform the protest song "Ballad of Accounting" every ten minutes for one week.

1. **Get off your Knees! (copied by Jamie Barker aged 13)**
2006, ink on paper, $11 \times 8\frac{1}{4}$ in (28×21 cm)

2. **Creative Evolution** (detail)
2007, ink on book, $24\frac{1}{2} \times 13\frac{3}{4}$ in (57×35 cm)

3. **Unrecorded future, tell us what broods there**
2008, performance

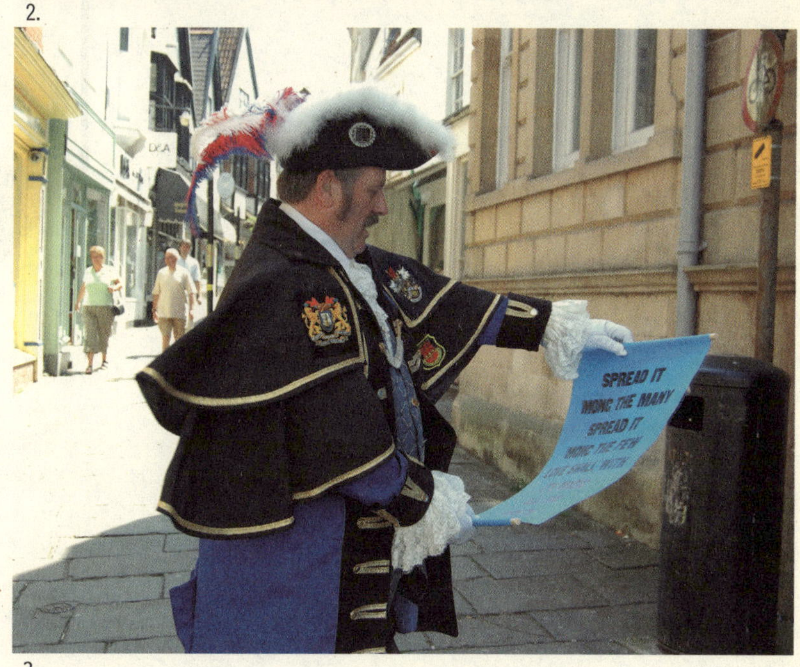

3.

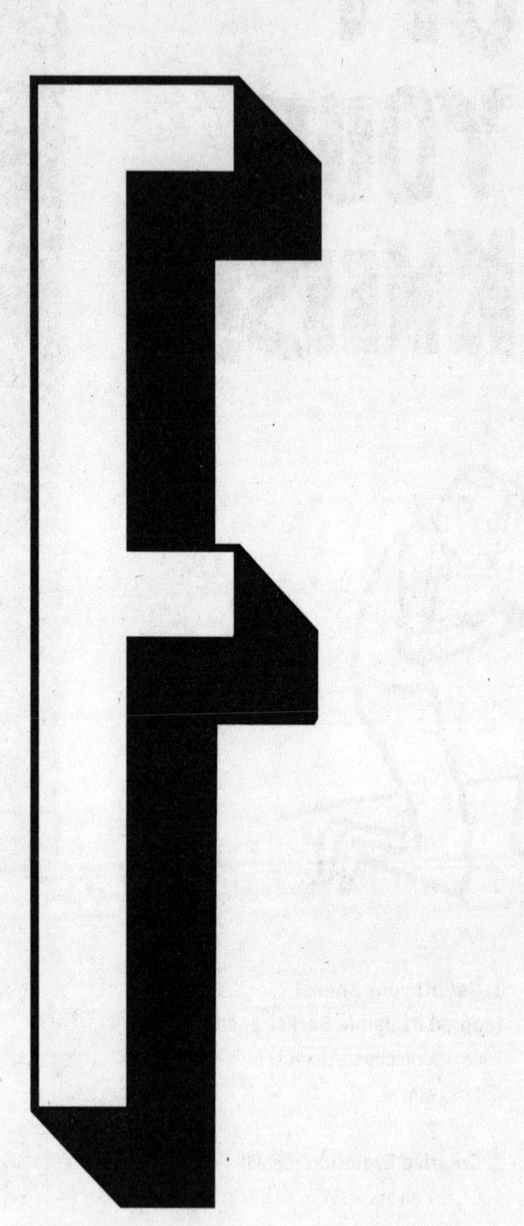

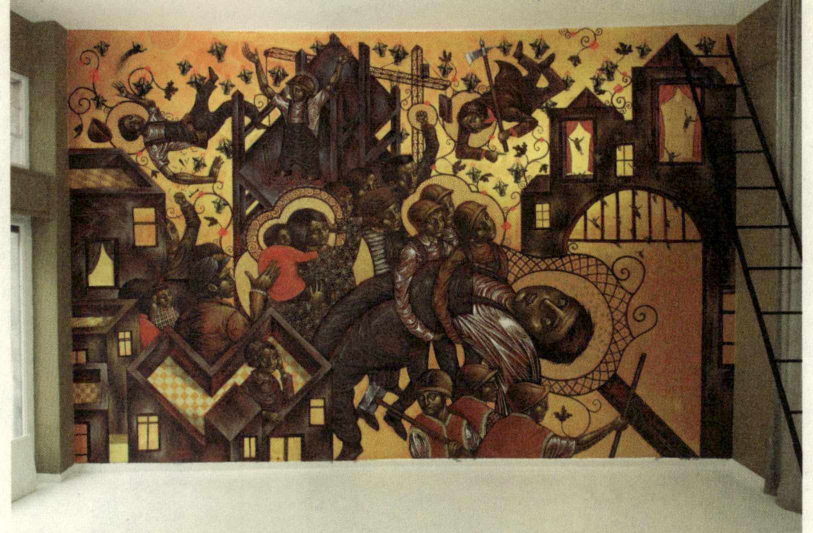
1.

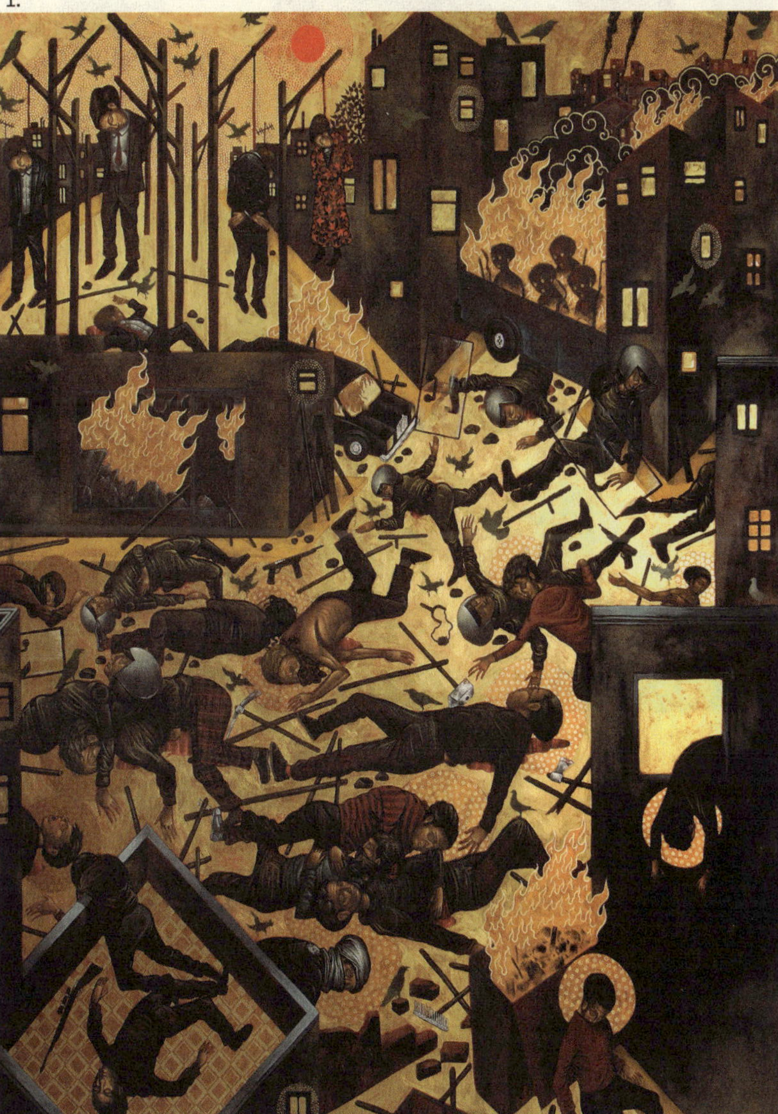
2.

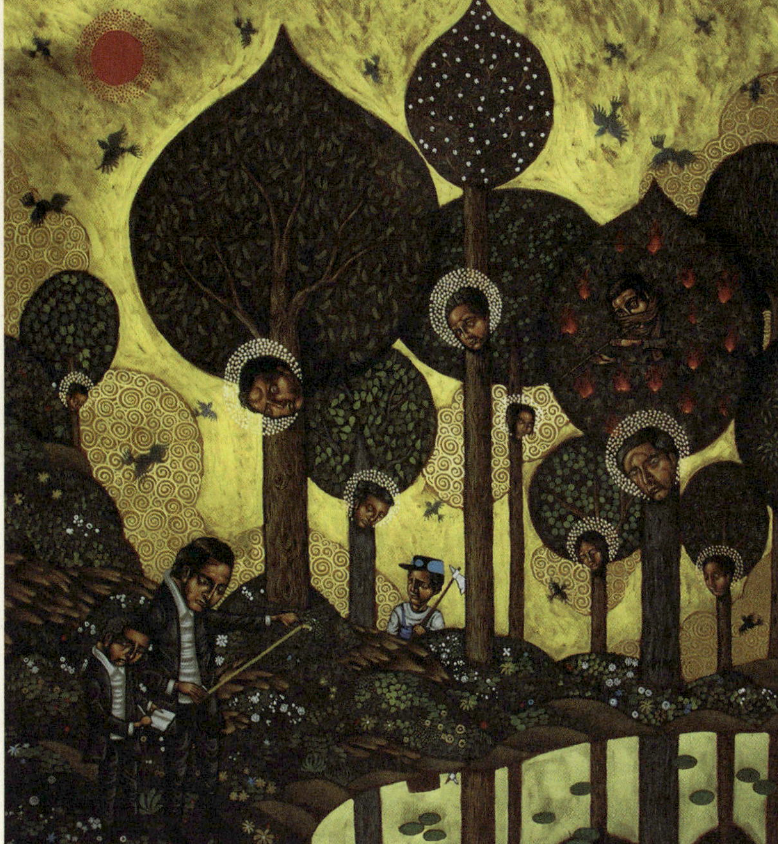
3.

Stelios Faitakis attended the Athens School of Fine Arts and lives in Athens. His large-scale paintings combine references to graffiti and street art, Mexican Muralism, Italian and Dutch painting from the 14th and 15th centuries, and Byzantine religious iconography. Drawing connections between conflicts over time and across the map, he presented the mural **Socrates Drinks the Conium** at the first Athens Biennial in 2007.

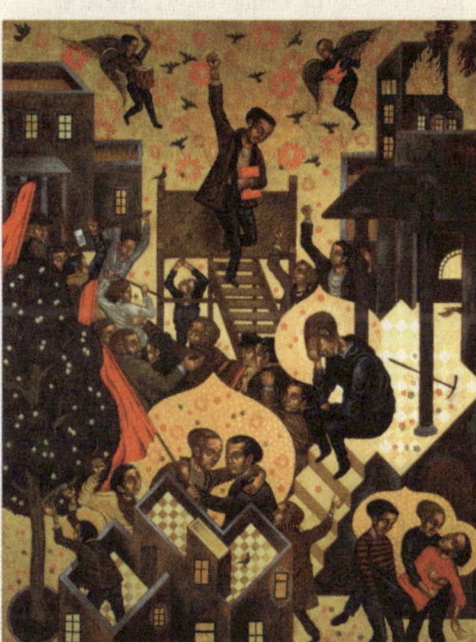
4.

1. Occupational Hazard
2008, oil, acrylic, latex, metallic paint, and spray paint, 13 × 16 ½ ft (4 × 6 m)

2. Landscape
2008, oil, acrylic, latex, egg tempera, metallic paint, and spray paint on canvas, 94 ½ × 75 in (240 × 190 cm)

3. I'm Not The One To Blame
2007, spray paint, latex, acrylic, metallic paint, and egg tempera, 31 ½ × 27 in (80 × 69 cm)

4. Dream
2008, oil, acrylic, latex, egg tempera, metallic paint, and spray paint on canvas, 94 ½ × 75 in (240 × 190 cm)

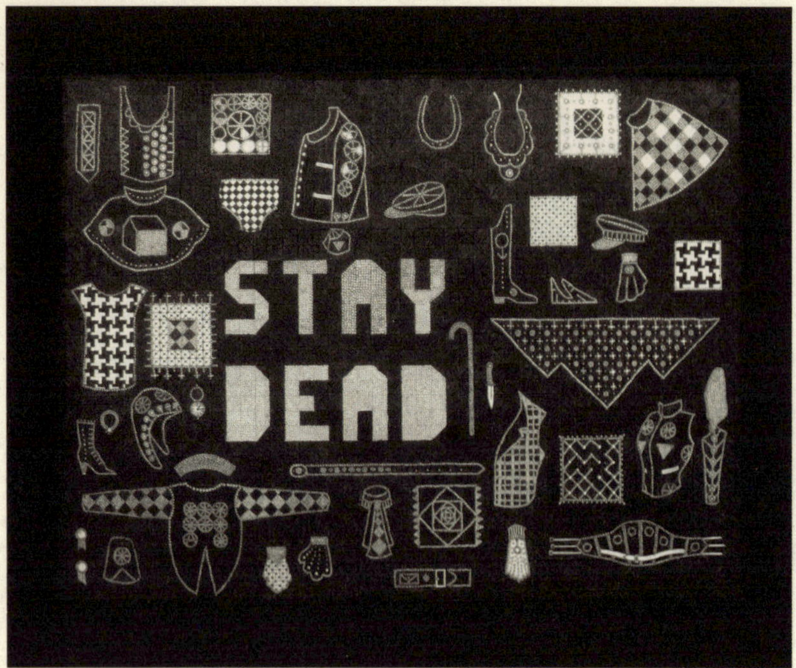

1.

Edie Fake earned his BFA from the Rhode Island School of Design. He currently lives in San Francisco, where he is an apprentice at the Black and Blue Tattoo Shop. The act of "fighting for a Gay Utopia" is at the center of his practice, which includes books, zines, comics, drawings, and tattoos as well as video, installation and performance.

1. Stay Dead
2007, ink on paper, 18 × 24 in (46 × 61 cm)

2. Feminist
2007, ink and collage on paper, 12 × 9 in (31 × 23 cm)

3. The PeaceCore ZineTour
2006, performance, Edie Fake (left) and Dewayne Slightweight (right)

4. Gay Gene
2005, ink and gouache on paper, 17 × 22 in (43 × 56 cm)

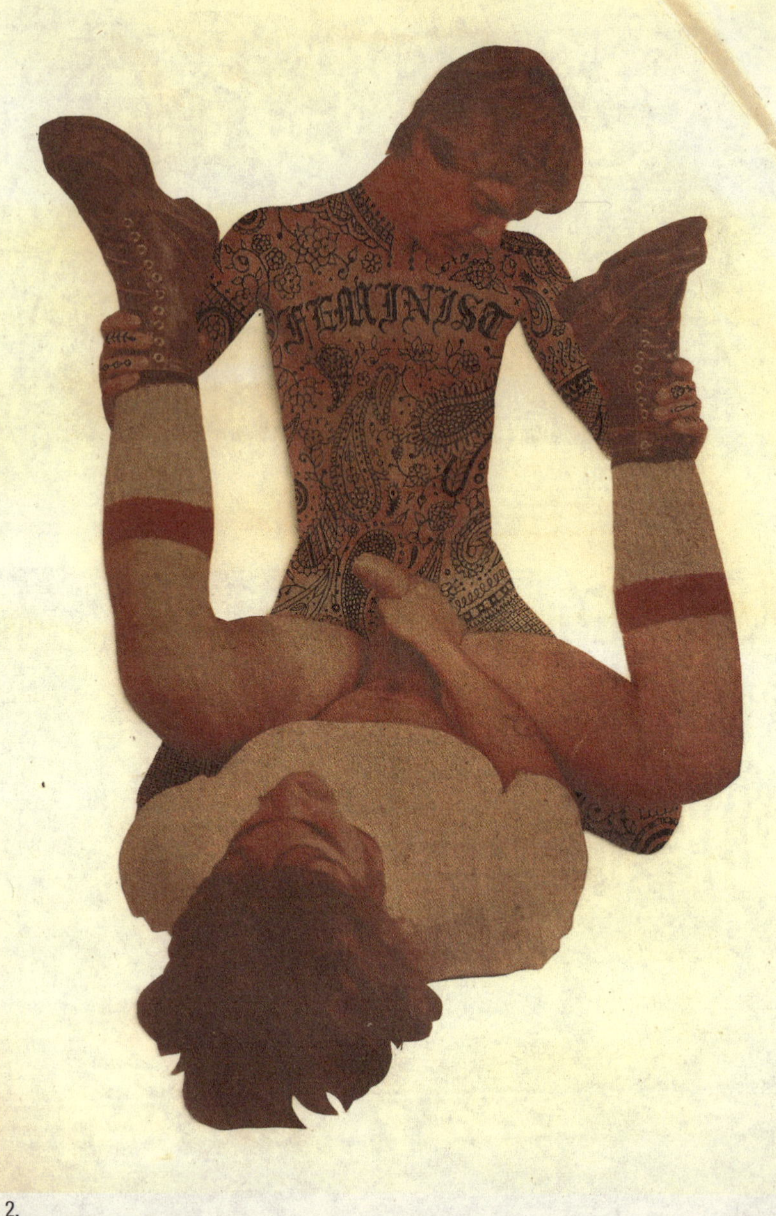

2.

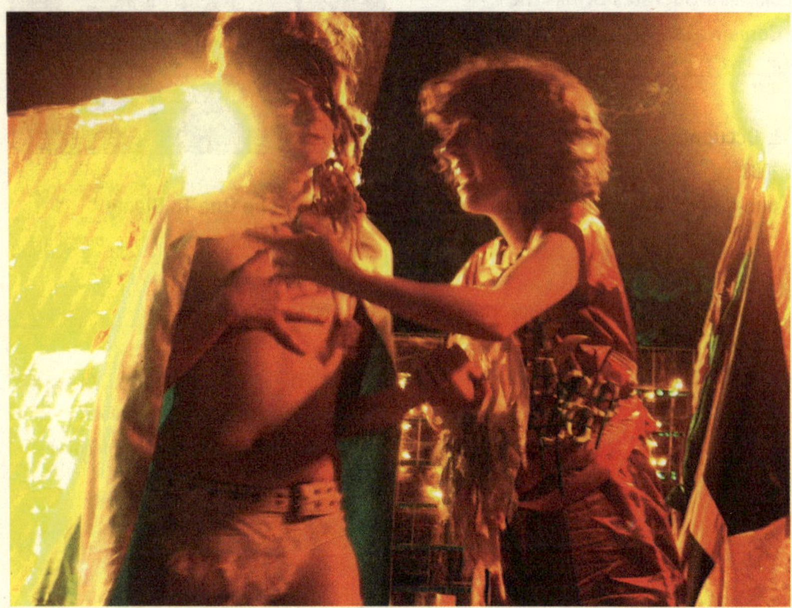

3.

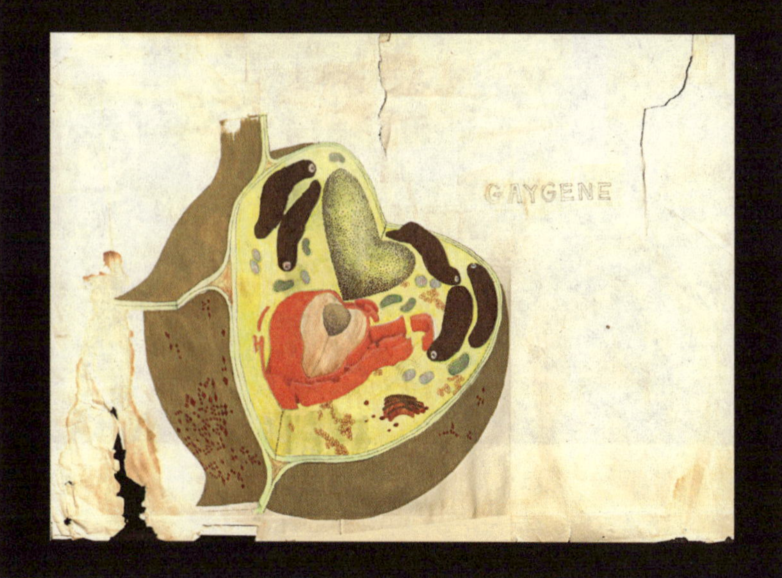

4.

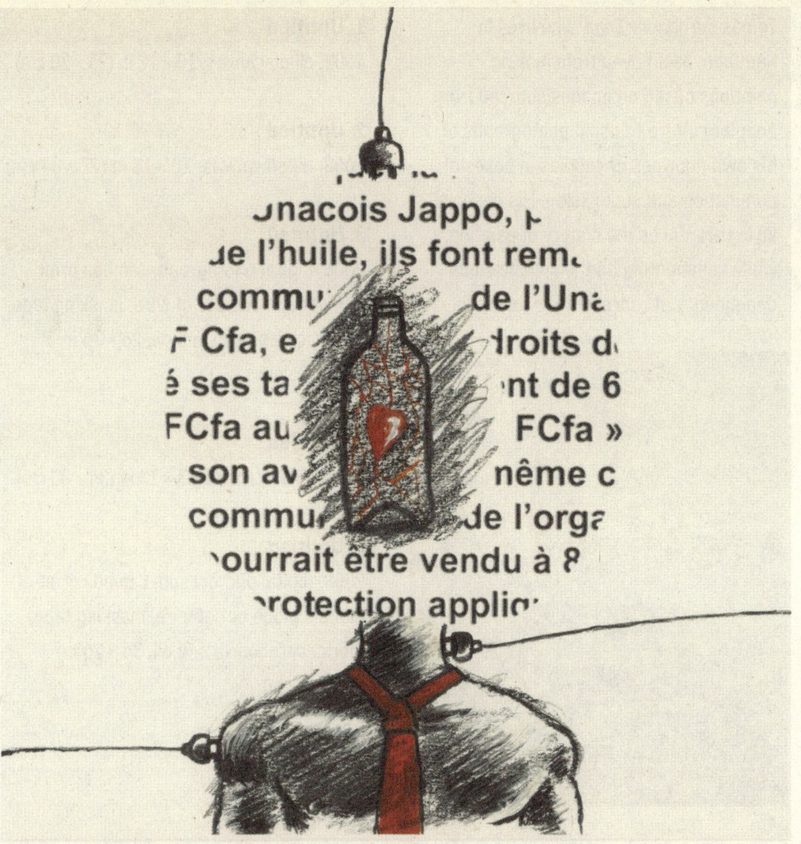

1.

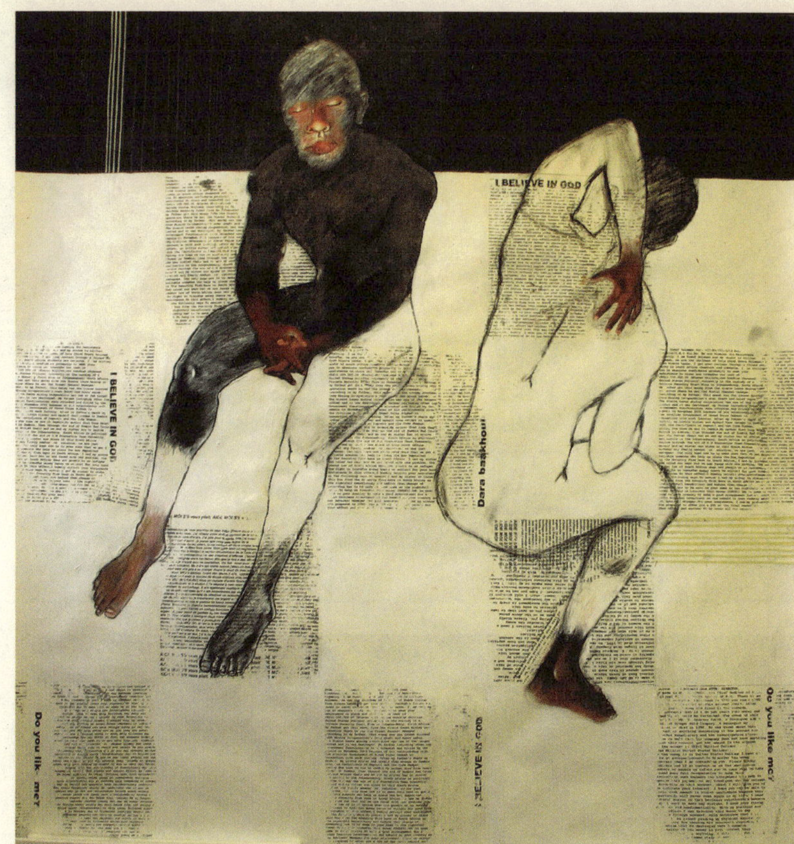

2.

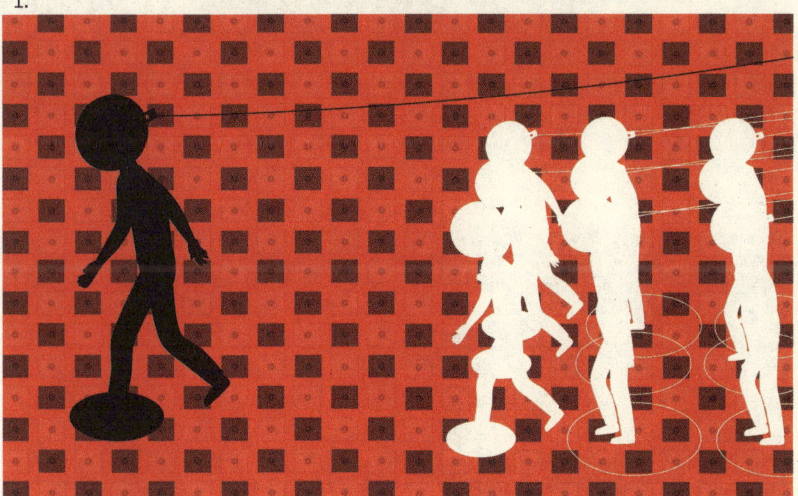

3.

4.

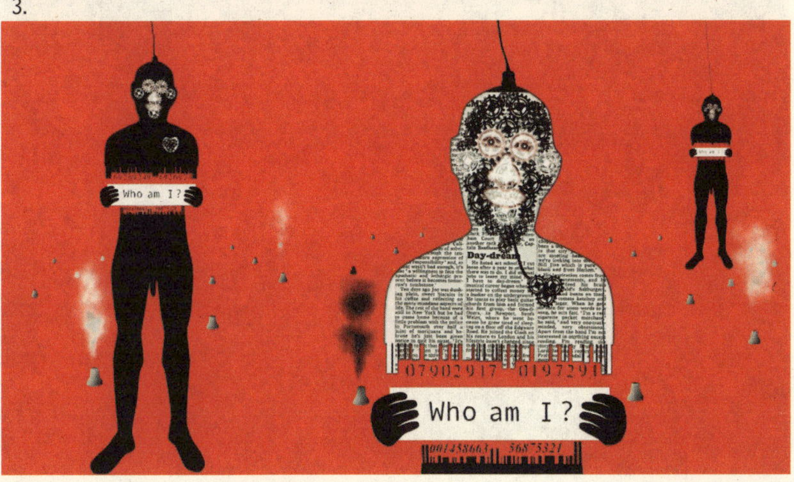

5.

After studying animation in Dakar, Samba Fall attended the Médiefabrikken in Oslo, Norway, where he continues to live. The animated film **Consumania** (2007), presented at Dak'Art 2008, explores acts of overconsumption pervading all races and cultures. In 1999 he started the group Art Express, which organizes exhibitions and workshops for young artists.

1. Photo d'identit
2008, charcoal, chalk, and graphite on paper, 10 × 10 in (25 × 25 cm)

2. I Believe in God
2006, mixed media, 59 × 59 in (150 × 150 cm)

3, 4 & 5. Consomania
2007, animation, 4 min 41 sec

Tomás Fernandez Diaz, who lives in Santiago, has moved from making paintings based on images sourced from popular culture to using photographs of his own figurines of couples in poses of domination and submission. His gestural style references the history of painting, while commenting on the complex interdependency of representational media.

1. Untitled
2008, oil on canvas, 10 × 12 in (25 × 30 cm)

2. Untitled
2008, oil on canvas, 10 × 13 in (27 × 34 cm)

3. Untitled
2008, digital photograph, Lambda print of models made out of wire, masking tape, fabric, cardboard, and oil, 26 × 36 in (65 × 92 cm)

4. Untitled
2008, oil on canvas, 13 × 12 in (34 × 30 cm)

5. Untitled
2008, digital photograph, Lambda print of models made out of wire, masking tape, fabric, cardboard, and oil, 36 × 26 in (92 × 65 cm)

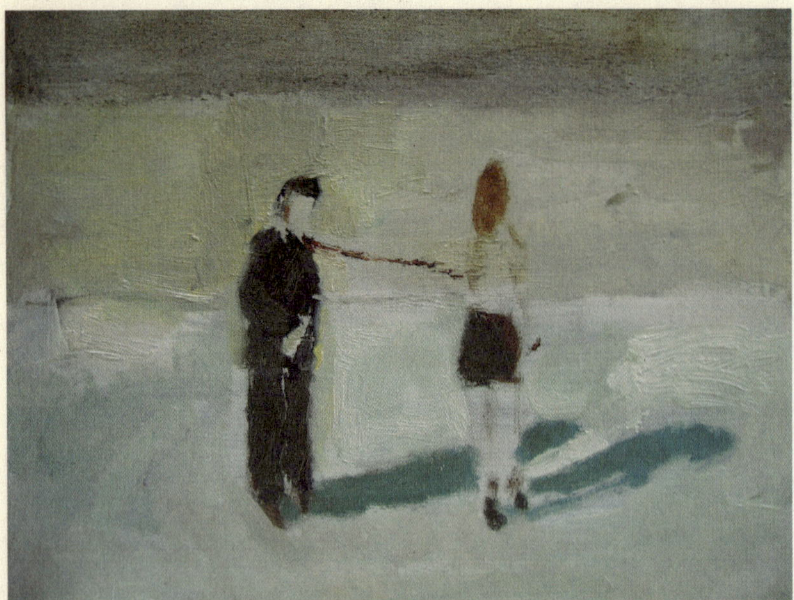
1.

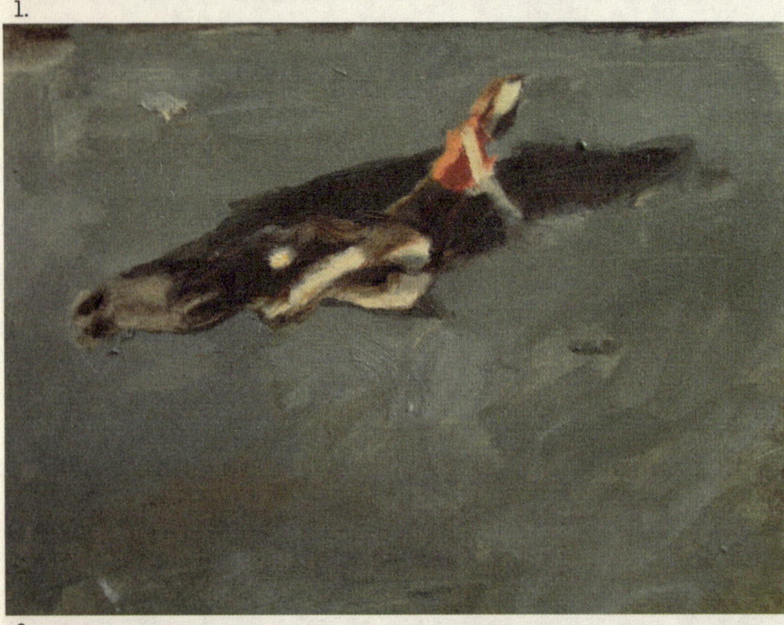
2.

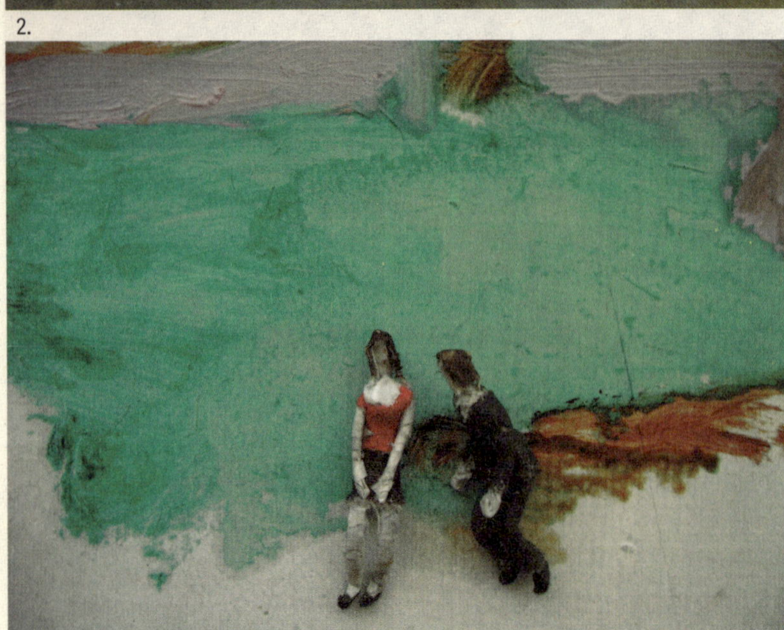
3.

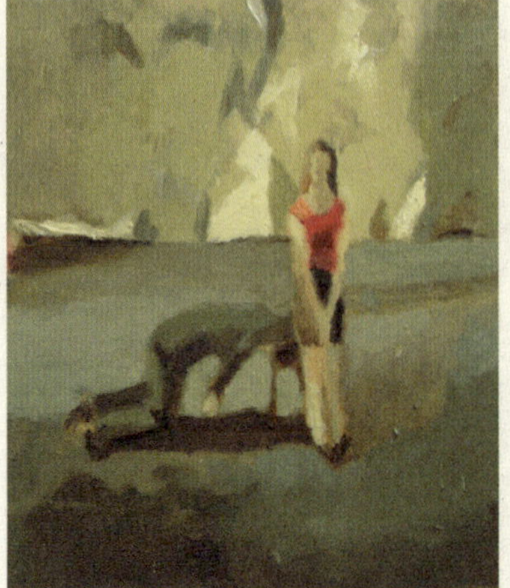
4.

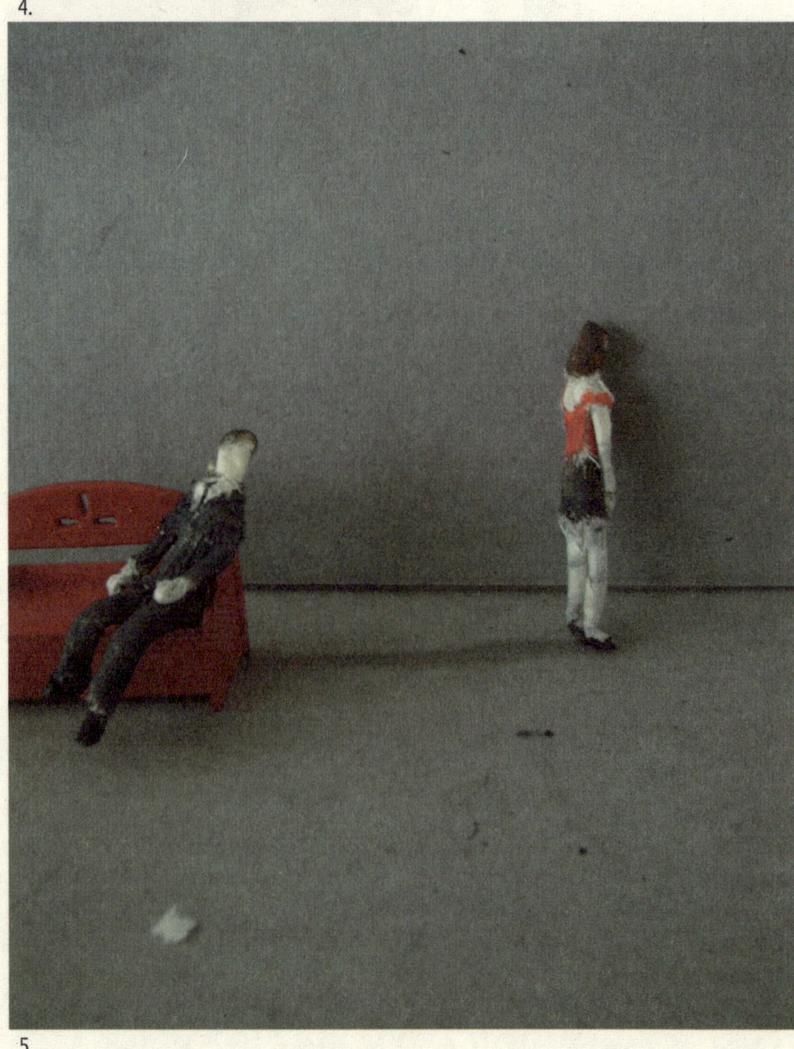
5.

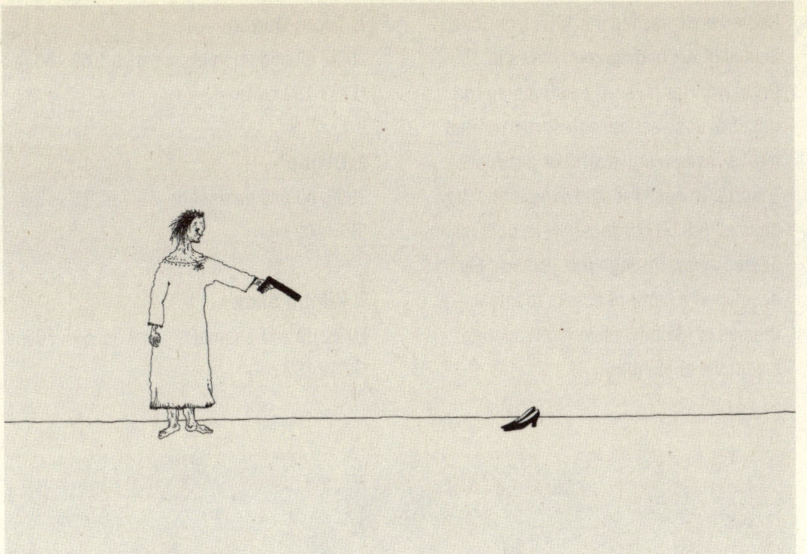

1.

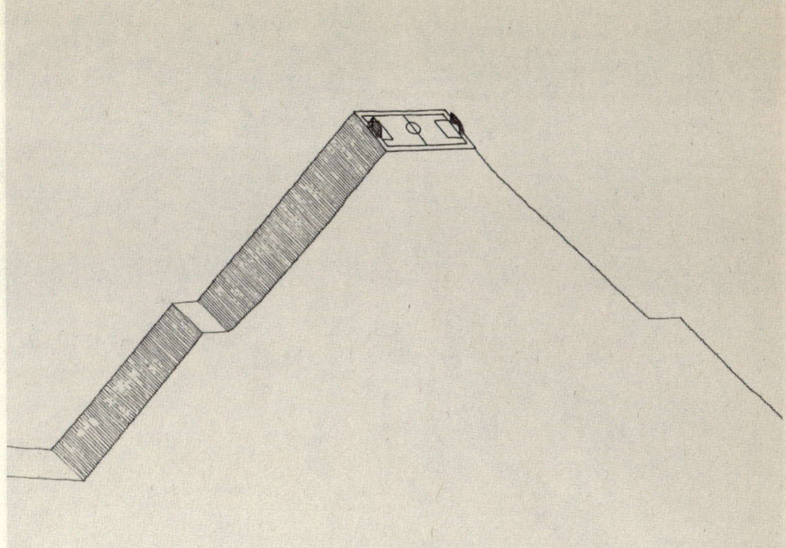

2.

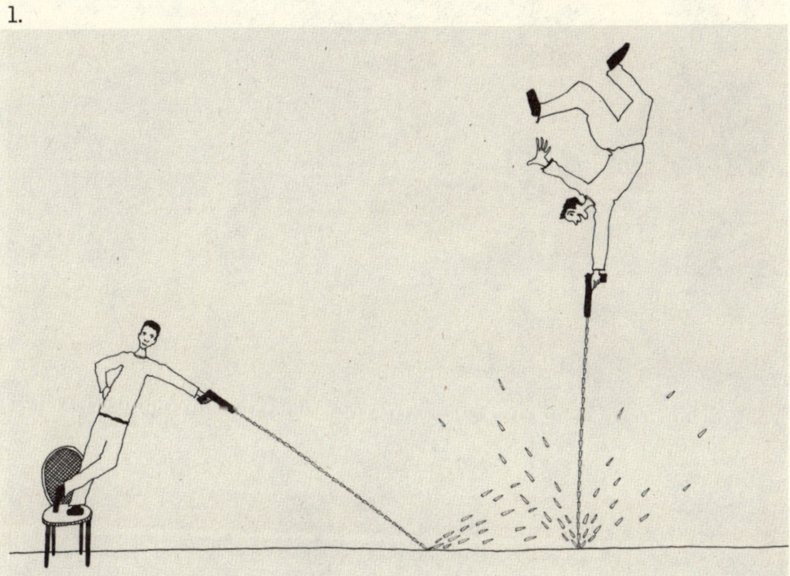

3.

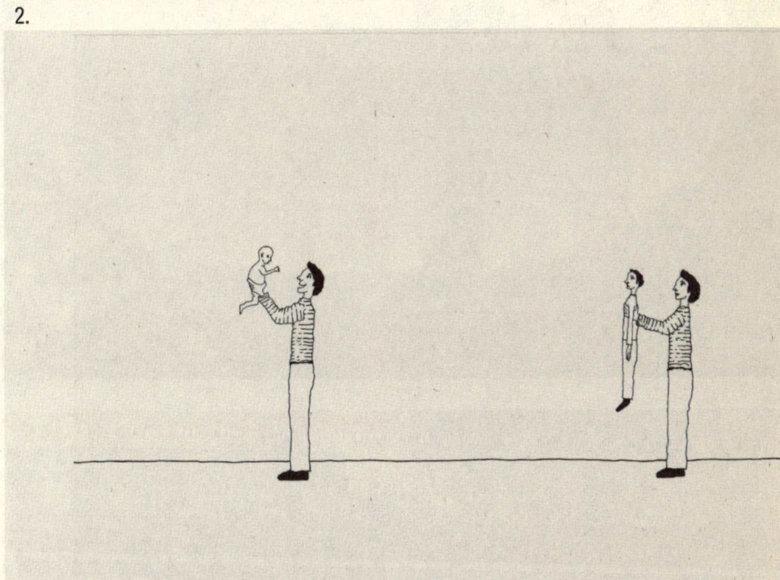

4.

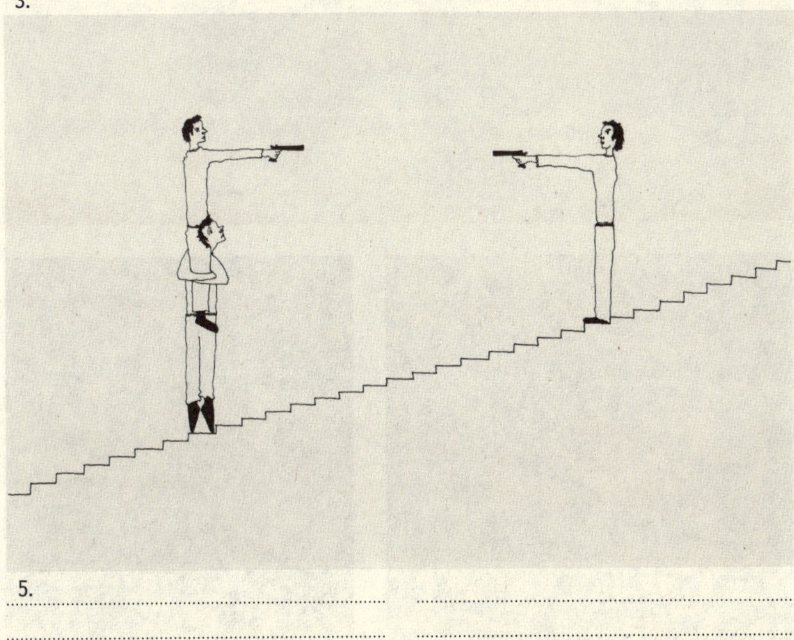

5.

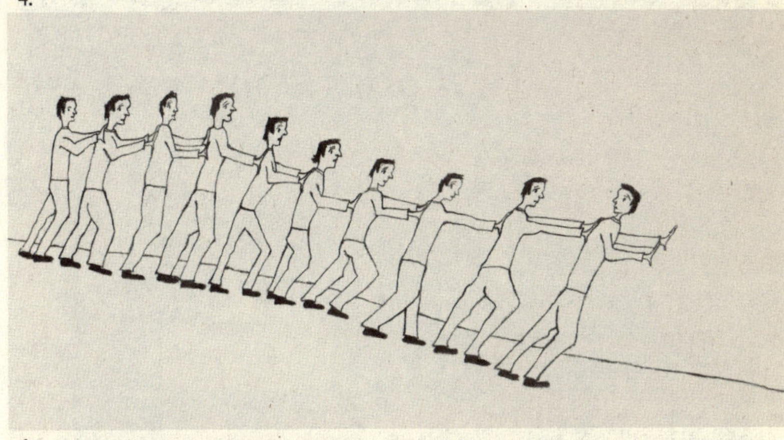

6.

Jakup Ferri lives and works in Prishtina. Questioning Kosovo's perceived cultural "lateness" – that everything worthwhile has been done before (and elsewhere) – he makes videos and drawings that present new takes on existing works and recontextualize received ideas and methods, revealing their inherent absurdity.

1, 2, 3, 4, 5 & 6. **Untitled**
2006, 6 of 7 drawings, ink on paper, each 12 × 16 $\frac{1}{2}$ in (30 × 42 cm)

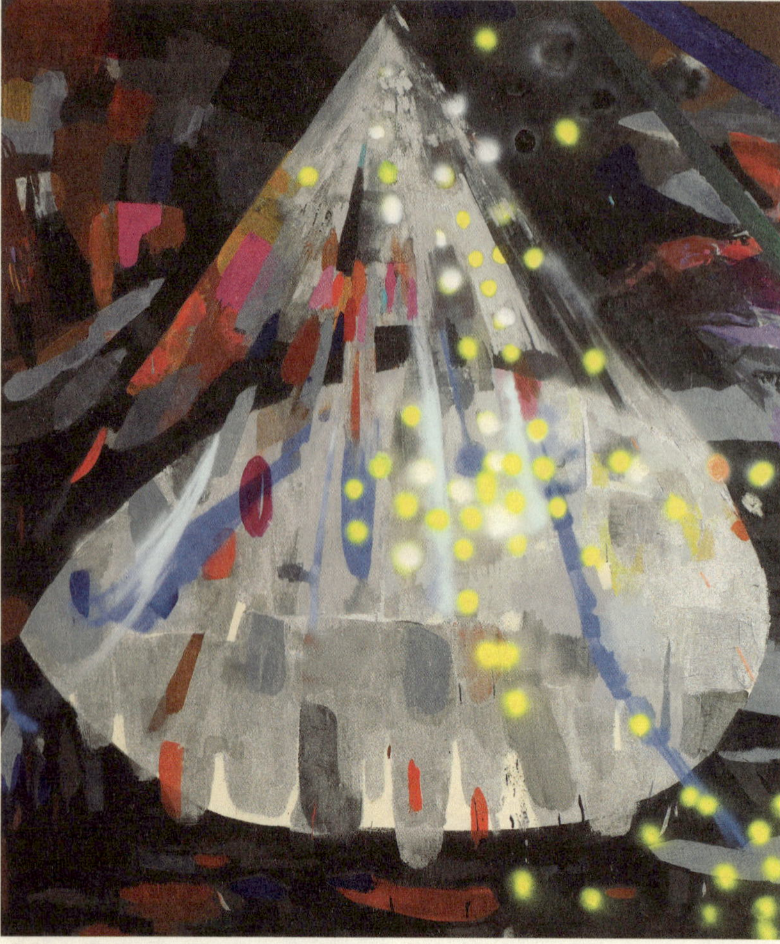

1.

Keltie Ferris earned her MFA from Yale School of Art and currently lives in Brooklyn. Her layered paintings merge gestural abstraction with spray-painted marks resembling graffiti or airbrushed T-shirts. In her first solo exhibition, "boy genius" (2007), surfaces were built up and peeled away. Through this process Ferris developed a motif of masks to engage themes of identity while interrogating traditions of painting.

1. **Team Queen**
2008, oil and enamel on canvas, 69 × 60 in (175 × 152 cm)

2. **D'vine**
2008, oil and enamel on canvas, 35 × 40 in (89 × 102 cm)

3. **Kimbo Slice**
2008, oil and enamel on canvas, 69 × 60 in (175 × 152 cm)

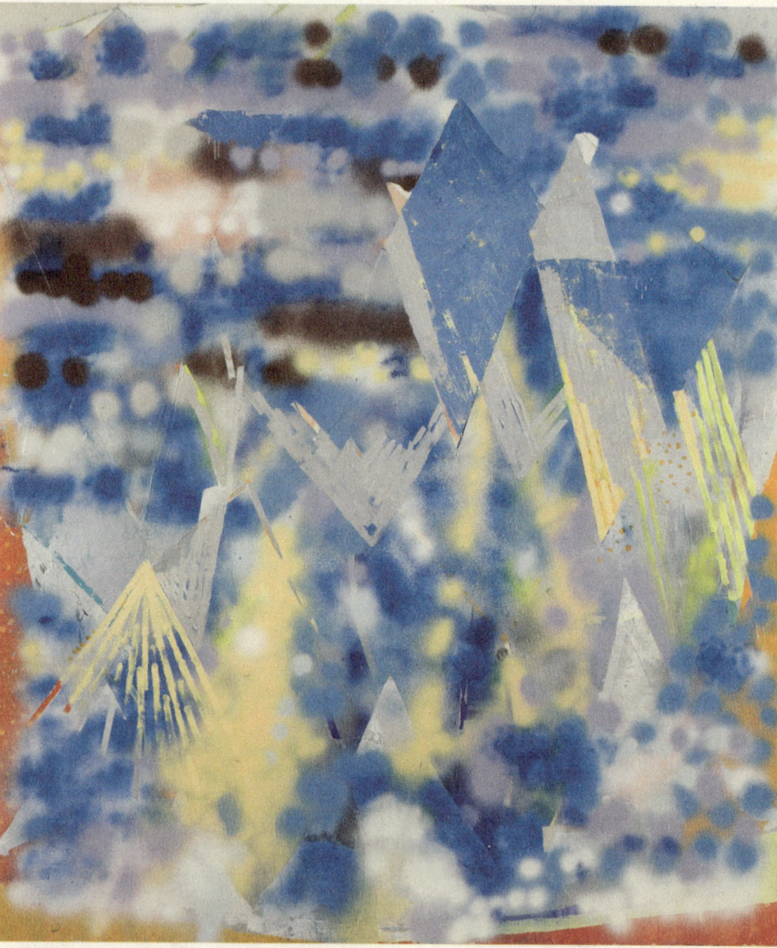

3.

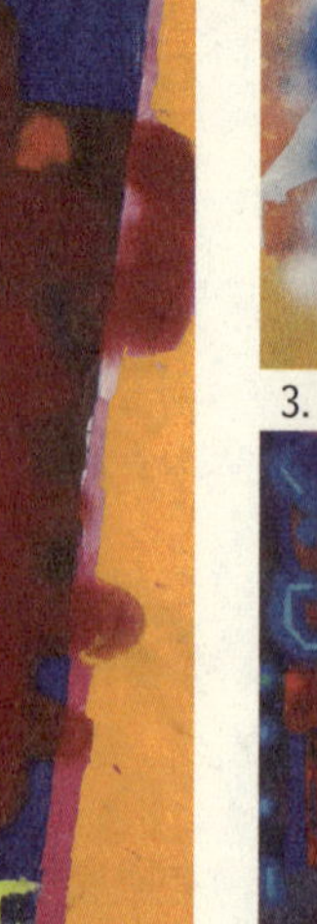

2.

4. **Stritch**
2008, oil and enamel on canvas, 54 × 54 in (137 × 137 cm)

5. **Magicum**
2008, oil and enamel on canvas, 54 × 54 in (137 × 137 cm)

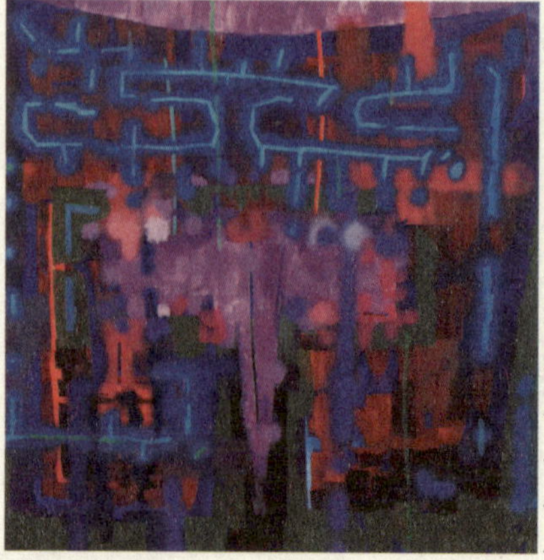

4.

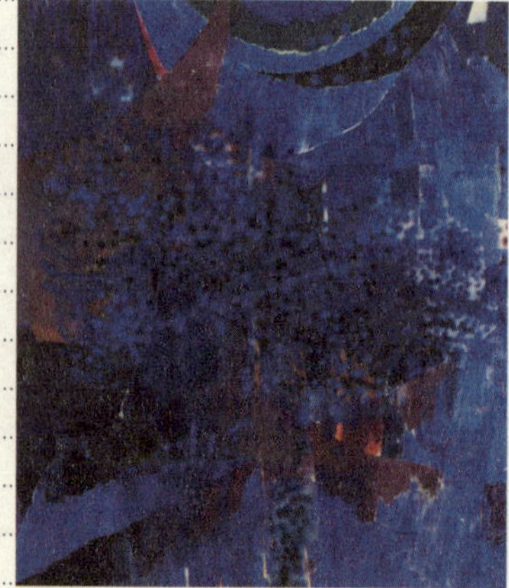

5.

Tehran-based Shahab Fotouhi works with video and photography. In his videos, he merges the playful and the serious, presenting a series of inconclusive arguments and counterarguments. In his photographs, he depicts local interiors, found objects, and portraits, emphasizing the strangeness of the everyday with the help of carefully staged composition.

1 & 2. **Internal Affairs**
2006, digital prints, dimensions variable

3. **Census**
2003, mixed media, dimensions variable

4. **Study for Nuclear Bomb Shelter (no. 136)**
2005, mirror, wood, and lightbulbs, dimensions variable

5. **Toward Salvation (in Commemoration of Epic 11th September)**
2004, digital print, dimensions variable

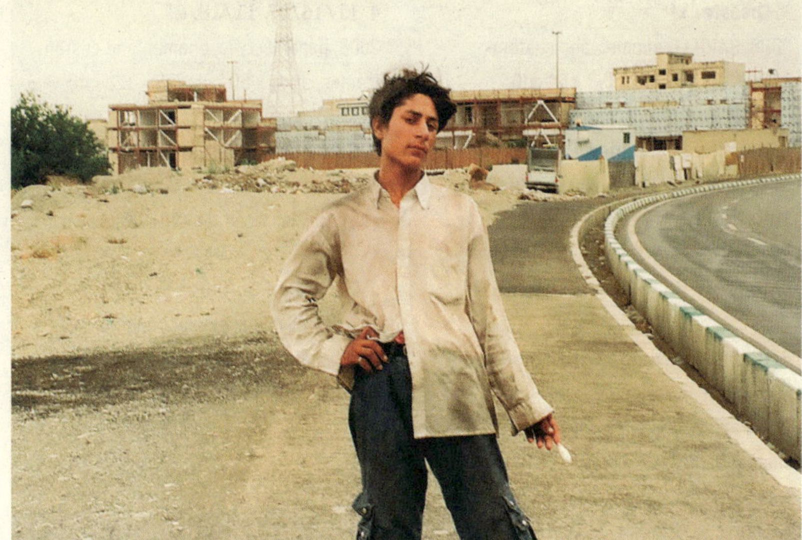

1.

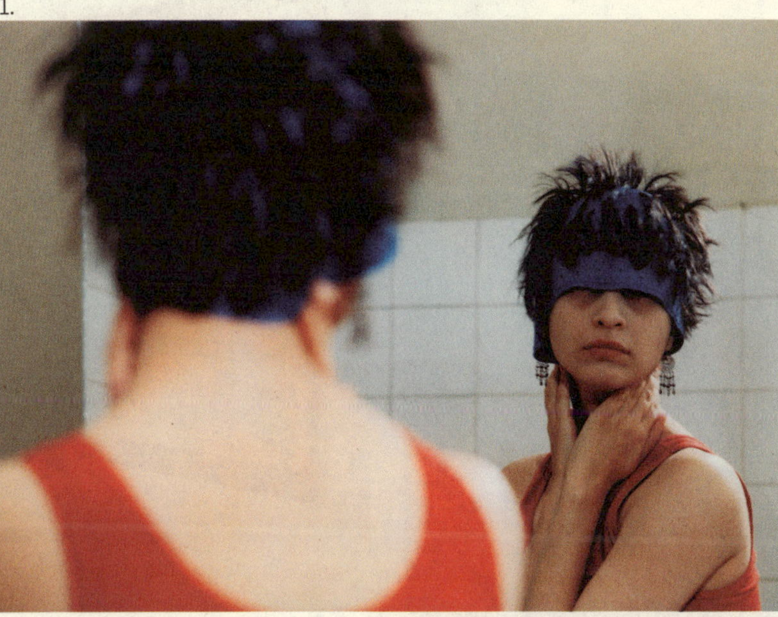

2.

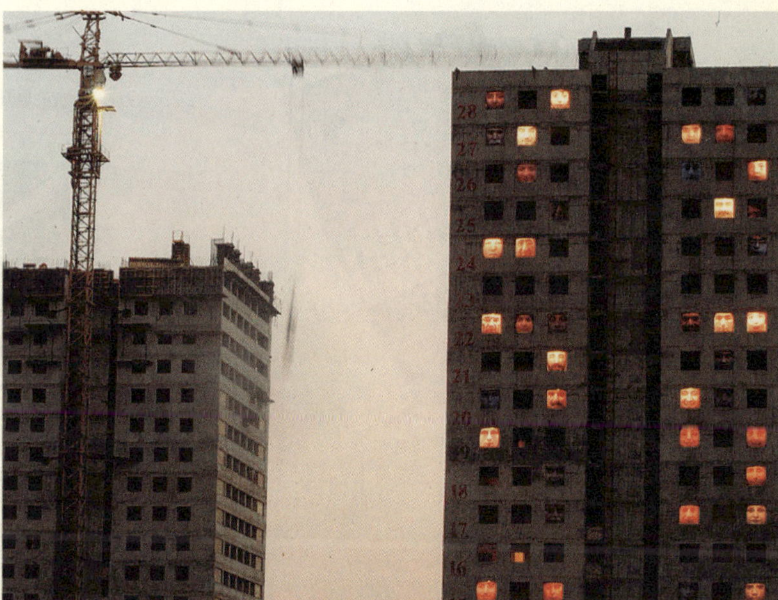

3.

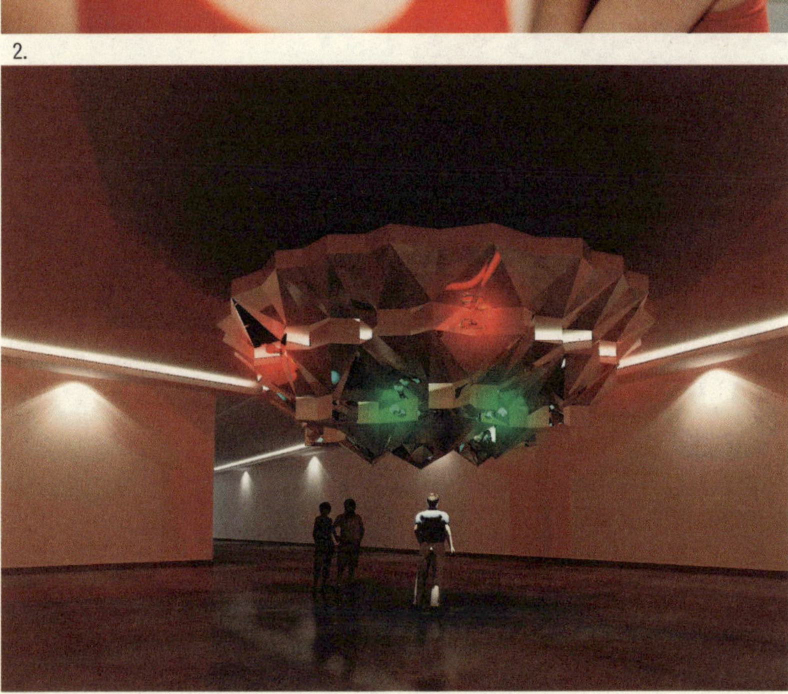

4.

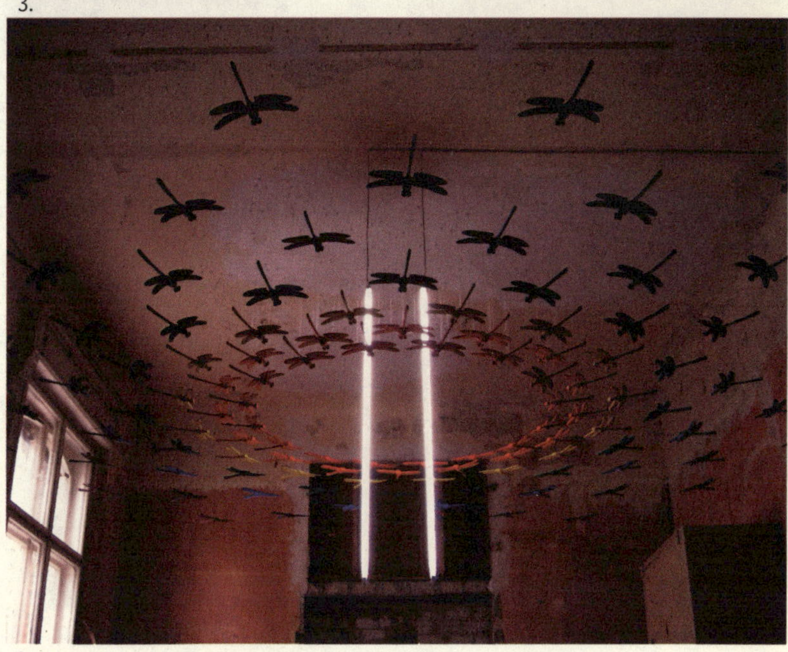

5.

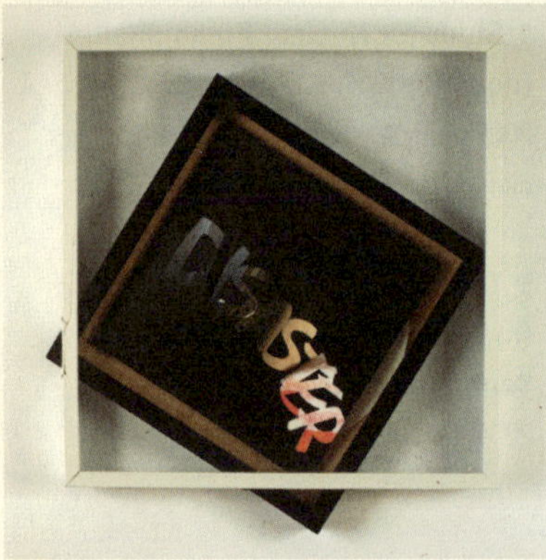

1.

Brendan Fowler earned his BFA from Sarah Lawrence College and currently lives in Los Angeles. He is an artist, musician, and coeditor of the free arts magazine **ANP Quarterly**. As BARR, his "one-person public speaking band," he writes songs, plays concerts, and records albums around reflective, often self-deprecating themes. The more recent performance project **Disaster** begins as an assessment of its own name in relation to the tones and implications of other band names.

1. **Disaster LP**
2008, BARR LP, enamel, and custom frames, 23 × $21\frac{1}{2}$ in (58 × 54 cm)

2. **Untitled (Cancelled Barr/Soiled Mattress and The Springs Summer Tour 2008)**
2008, cover of "Body And Record" and photograph, 30 × 52 in (76 × 132 cm)

3. **Poster for Dialog with The Band Aids Wolf**
2008, acrylic and photocopy on paper in custom frame, 41 × 27 in (104 × 68 cm)

4. **11/16/07, 11/18/07**
2008, paper, acrylic, enamel, and custom frames, $30\frac{1}{2}$ × $50\frac{1}{4}$ in (78 × 128 cm)

5. **Cancelled Summer Tour #1**
2008, inkjet print, enamel, glass, UV Plexiglas, and wood, 24 × 20 in (61 × 51 cm)

6. **Cancelled Summer Tour #2**
2008, archival inkjet print, enamel, glass, UV Plexiglas, and aluminum, 18 × 12 in (46 × 31 cm)

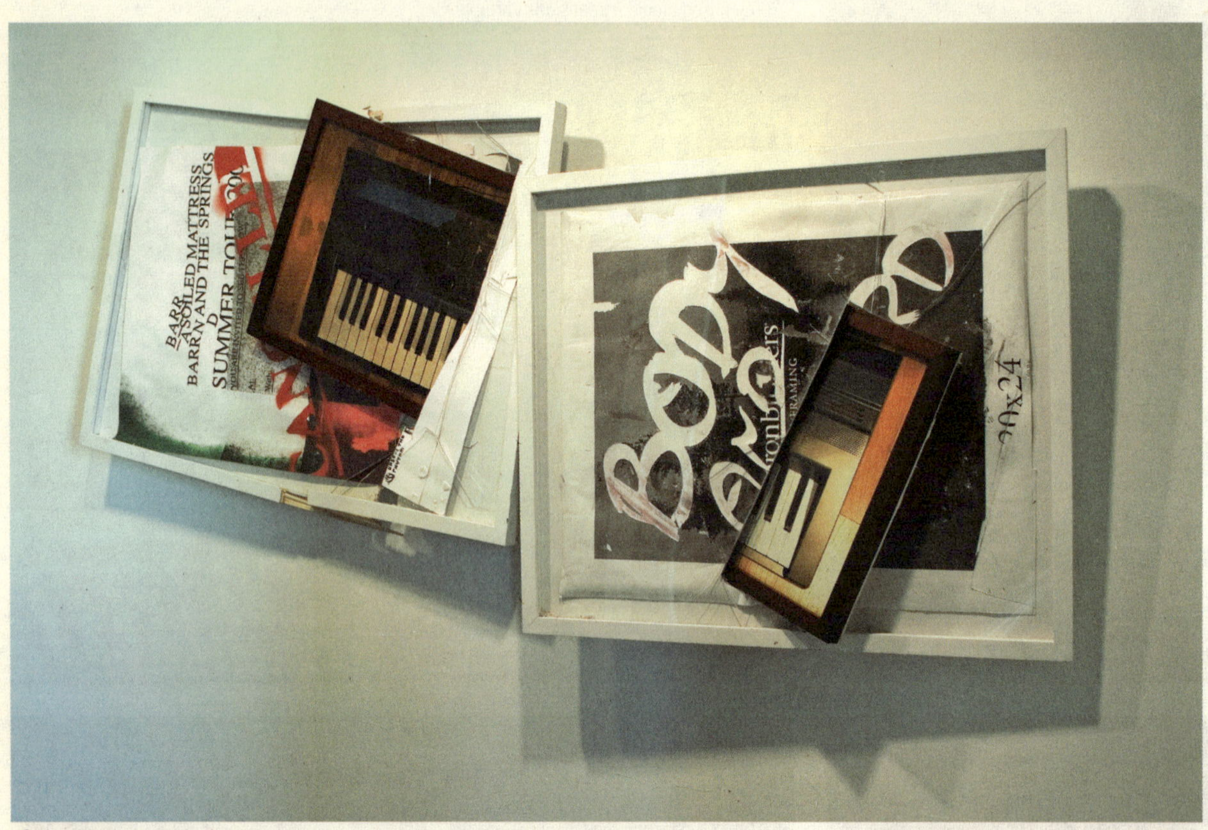

2.

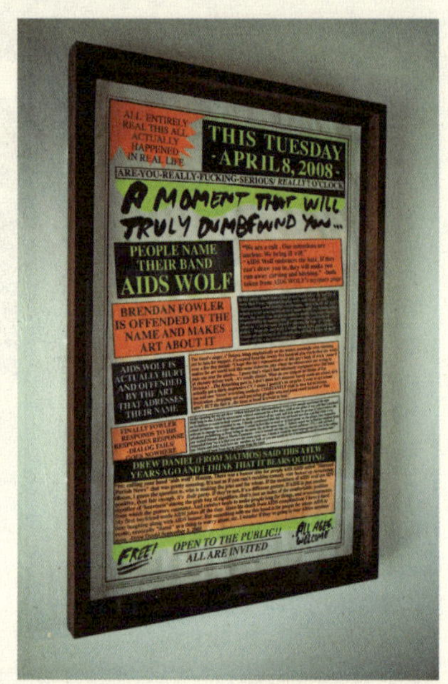

3.

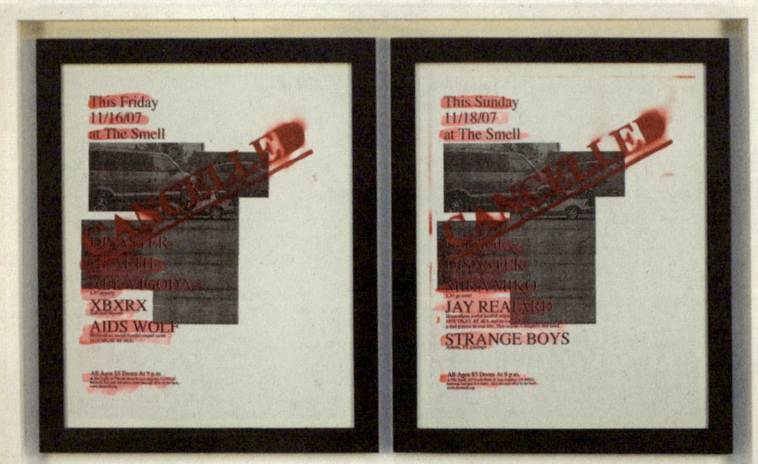

4.

5.

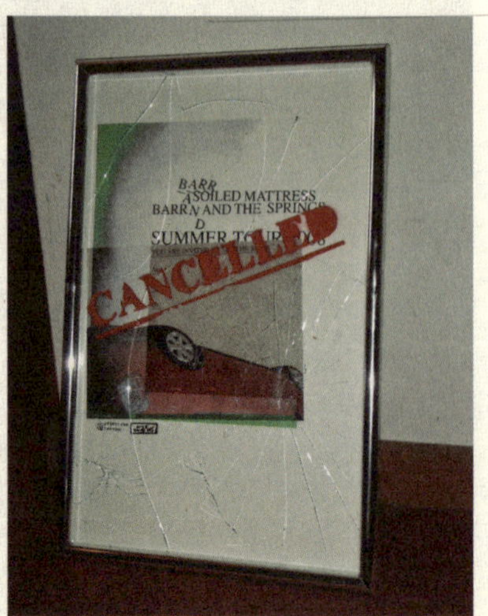

6.

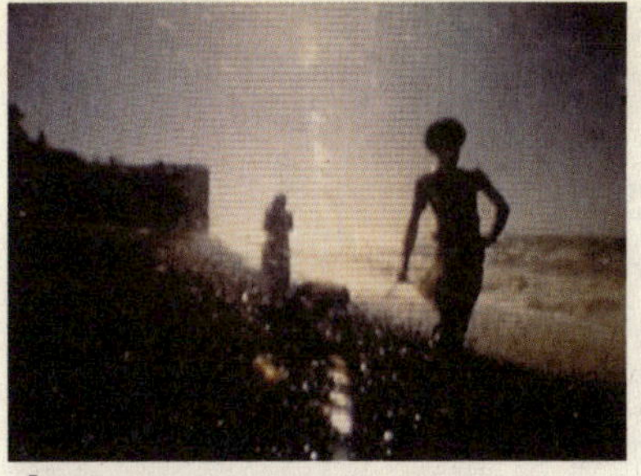
1.

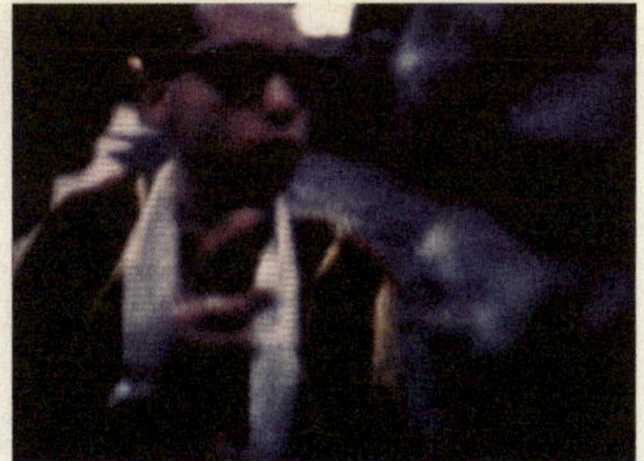
2.

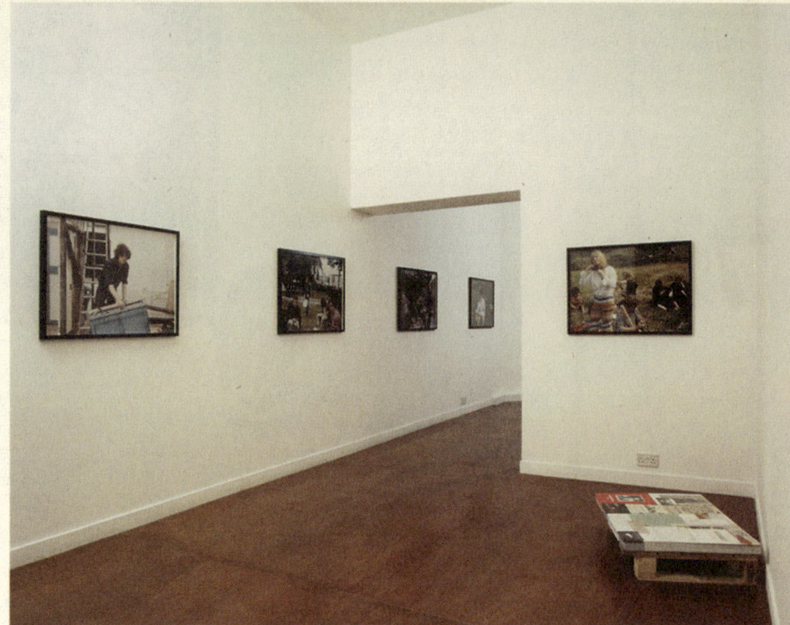
4.

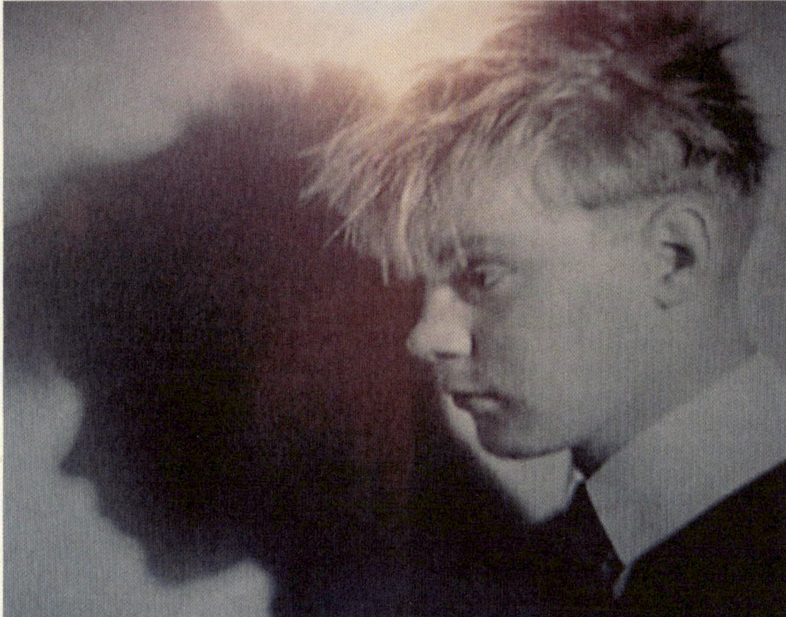
3.

village concert

SCRATCH ORCHESTRA

2/-

PLACE

DATE

TIME

SCRATCH MUSIC

CLASSICS

IMPROVISATIONS

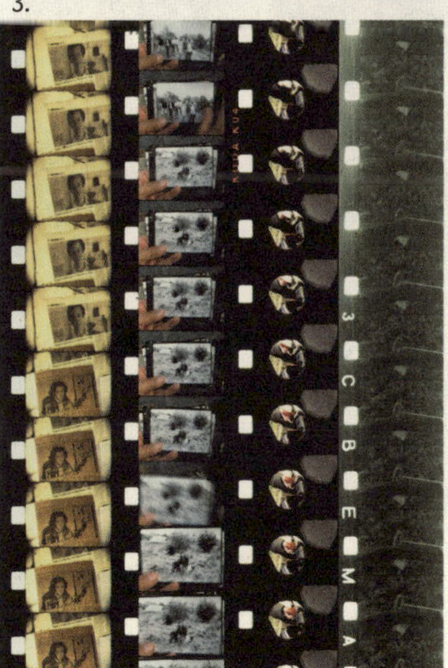
5.

Artist, filmmaker, and musician Luke Fowler earned his BA from Duncan of Jordanstone College of Art, Dundee, and currently lives in Glasgow. He makes film portraits of social and creative experiments that favor a poetic, impressionistic account over a documentary style. Subjects include composer Cornelius Cardew's Scratch Orchestra and psychoanalyst R. D. Laing's Kingsley Hall community.

1, 2 & 3. **The Way Out**
2003, video, 33 min 10 sec

4. "Pilgrimage From Scattered Points"
exhibition view at The Modern Institute/ Toby Webster Ltd., Glasgow (2006)

5. **Pilgrimage From Scattered Points**
2006, video, 45 min

6. **Village Concert**
2006, silkscreen print of poster designed by Keith Rowe (1970), 44 × 30 ¼ in (112 × 77 cm)

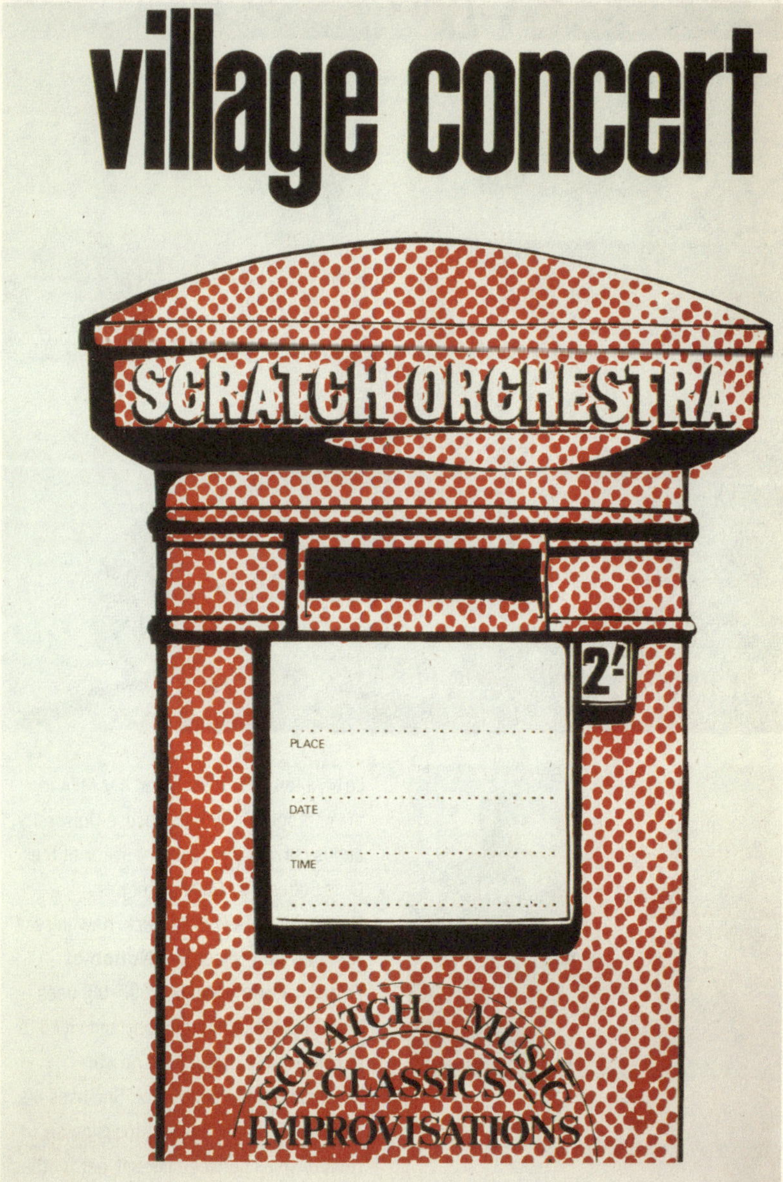

6.

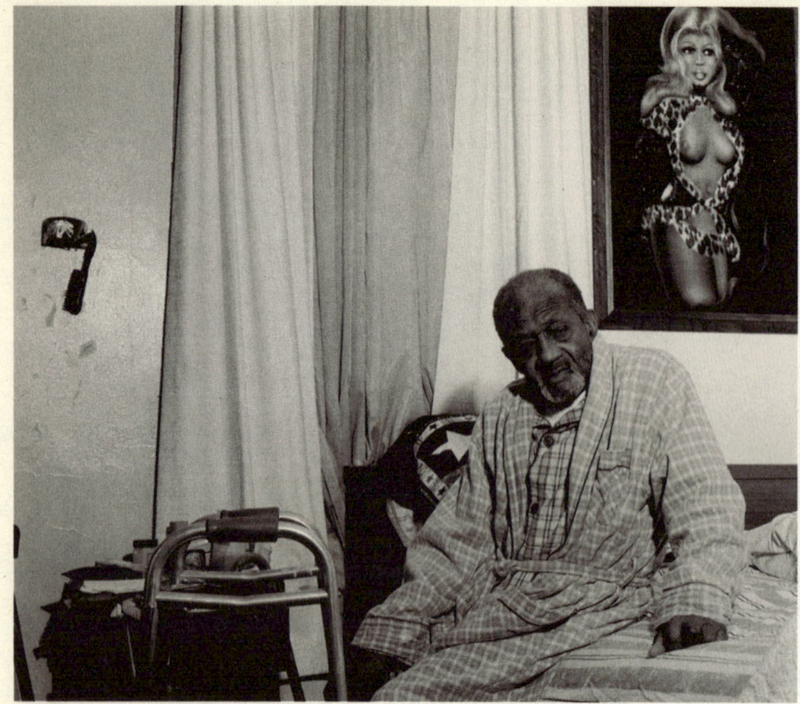
1.

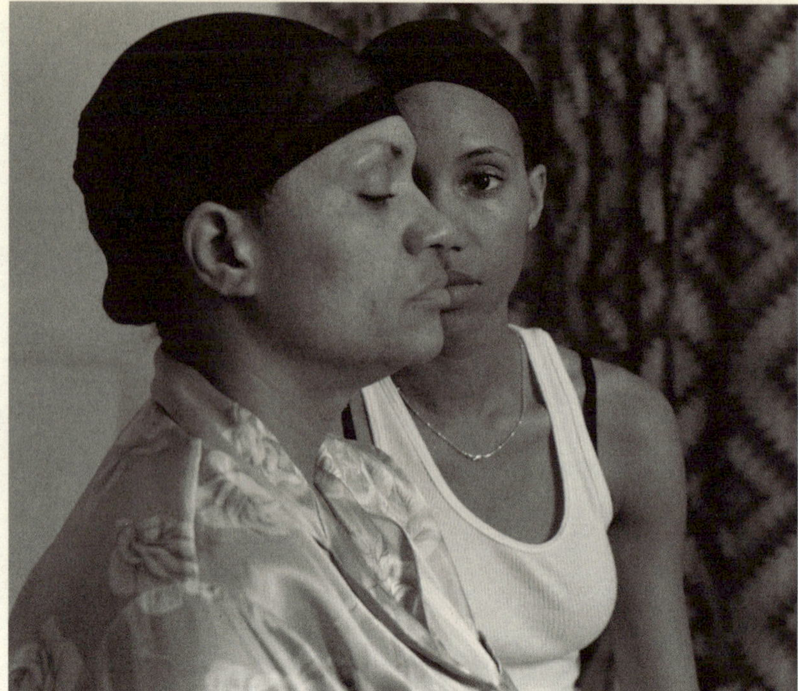
2.

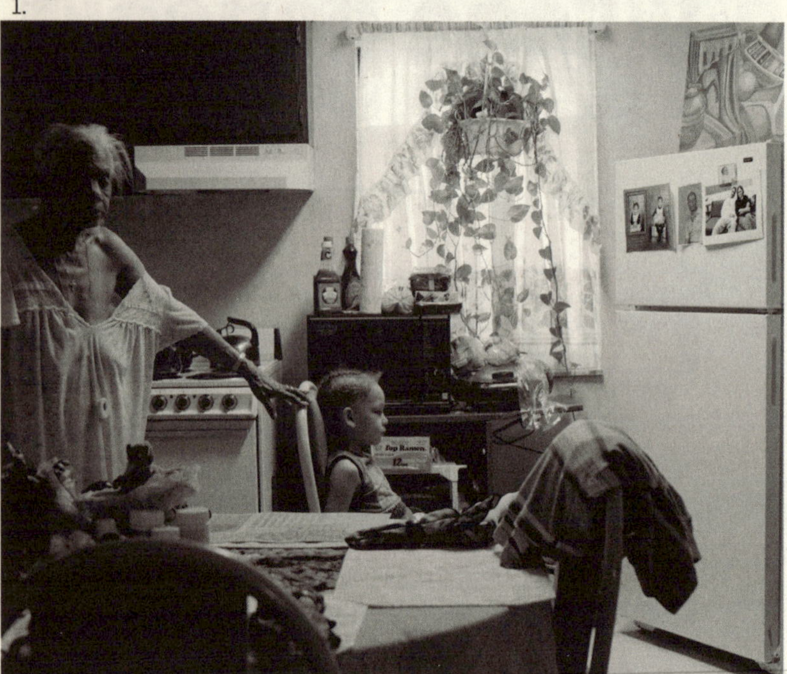
3.

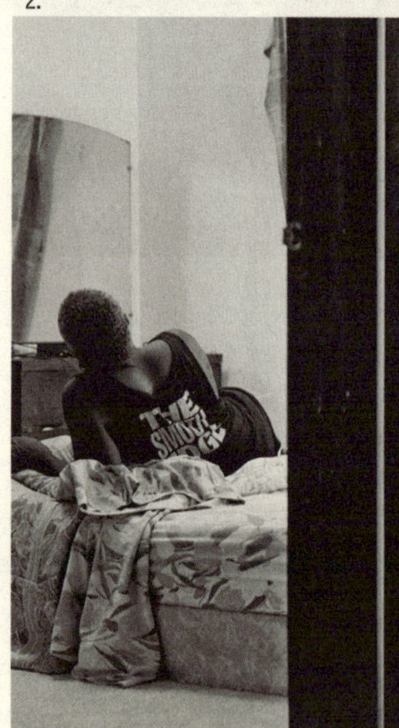
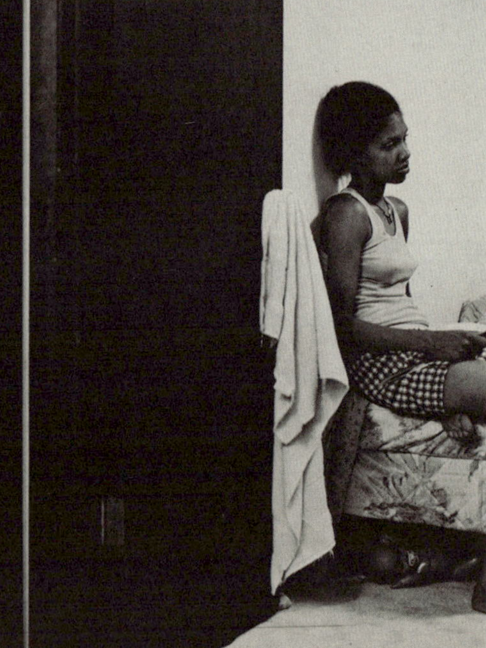
4.

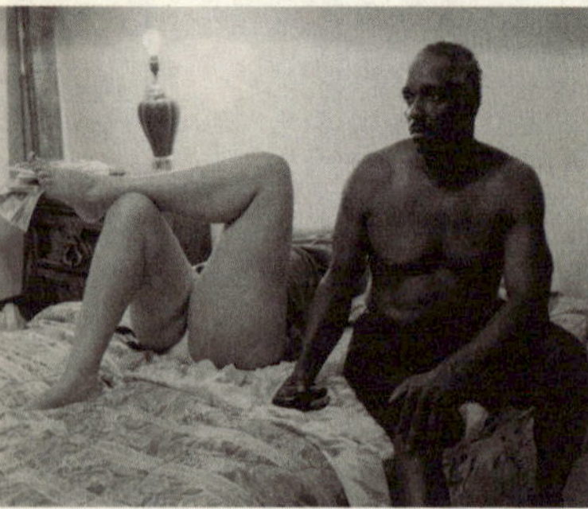
5.

LaToya Ruby Frazier earned her MFA in art photography from Syracuse University and is currently associate curator at the Civic Square Art Gallery, Rutgers University, in New Brunswick, New Jersey. Her six-year project **The Notion of Family: Family Work** (2002-08) uses black and white photography and video to document and explore the African-American family experience. She uses her own family as her subject, focusing on relationships between herself, her mother, and her grandmother.

1. Gramps in his bedroom
2003, gelatin silver print, 16 × 20 in (41 × 51 cm)

2. Momme
2008, gelatin silver print, 16 × 20 in (41 × 51 cm)

3. Grandma, JC and me
2006, gelatin silver print, 16 × 20 in (41 × 51 cm)

4. Me and Mom's Boyfriend Mr. Art
2005, gelatin silver print, 16 × 20 in (41 × 51 cm)

5. Mom and her Boyfriend Mr. Art
2005, gelatin silver print, 16 × 20 in (41 × 51 cm)

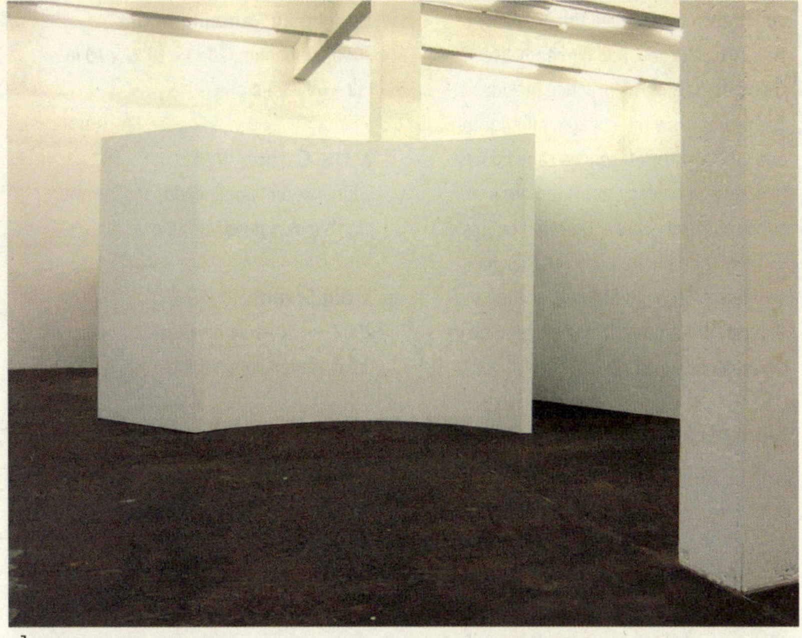

1.

2.

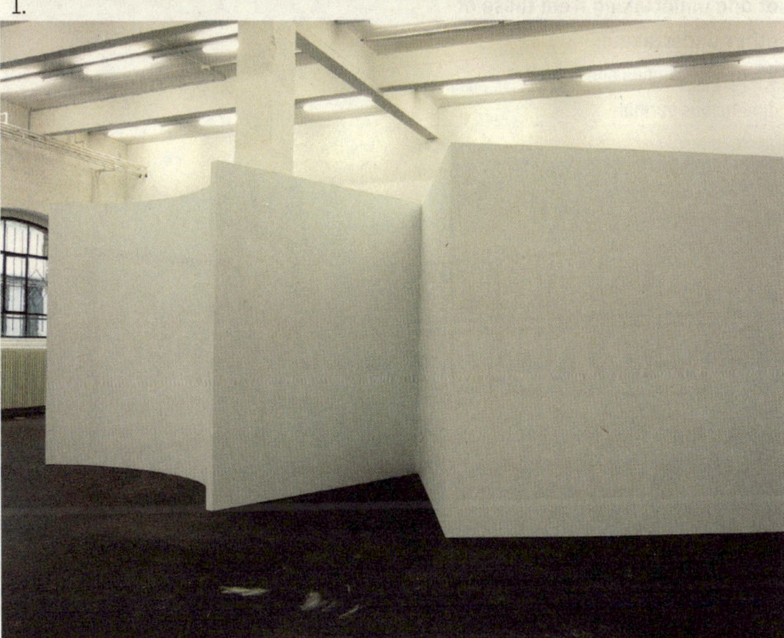

3.

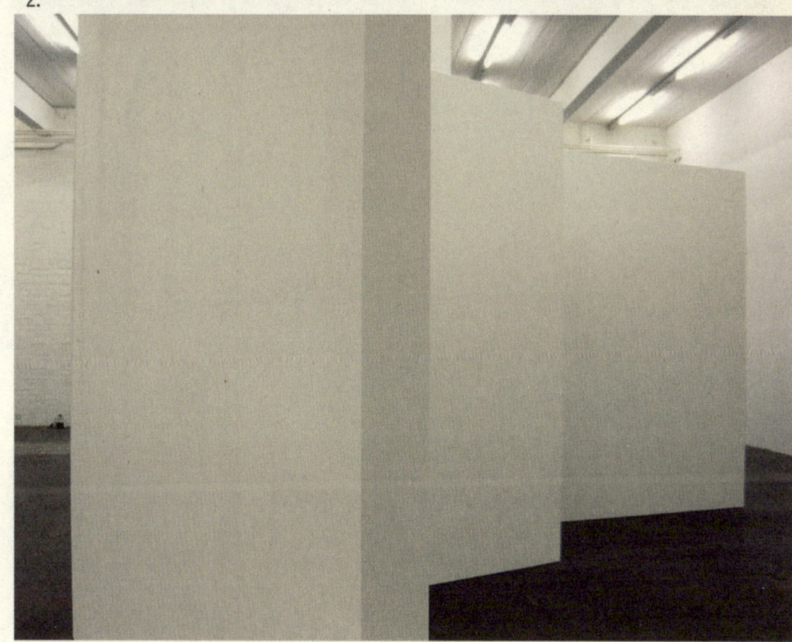

4.

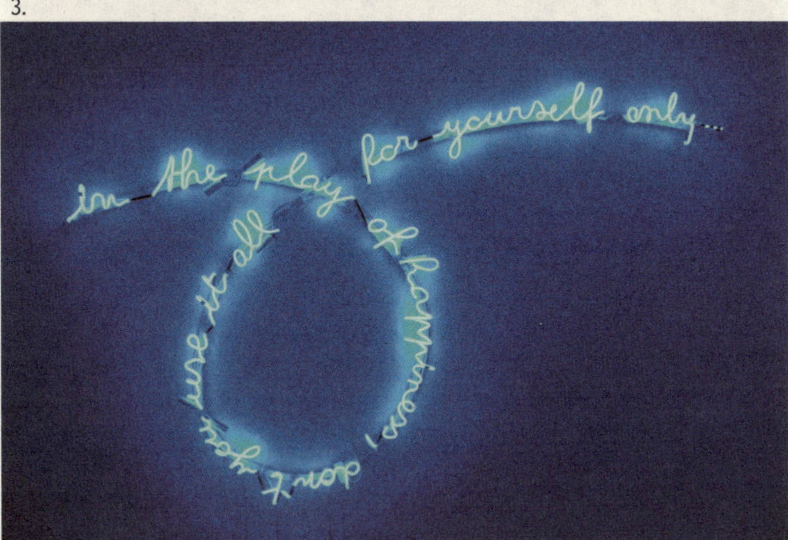

5.

Luca Frei earned his MFA from Malmö Art Academy, Sweden, and continues to live in Malmö. He works around themes of education, language, architecture, and utopian visions to produce sculpture, installation, and interactive environments. In 2004 he founded Gruppo Parole e Immagini, a public reading group with the mission of communicating free appropriation and elaboration, and of distributing textual and visual materials.

1, 2, 3 & 4. **brilliant corners**
2008, painted MDF, 23 × 8 × 13 ft
(700 × 245 × 400 cm)

5. **Untitled**
(from the last letter of Nicola Sacco)
2008, neon light tubes, width 75 in
(190 cm)

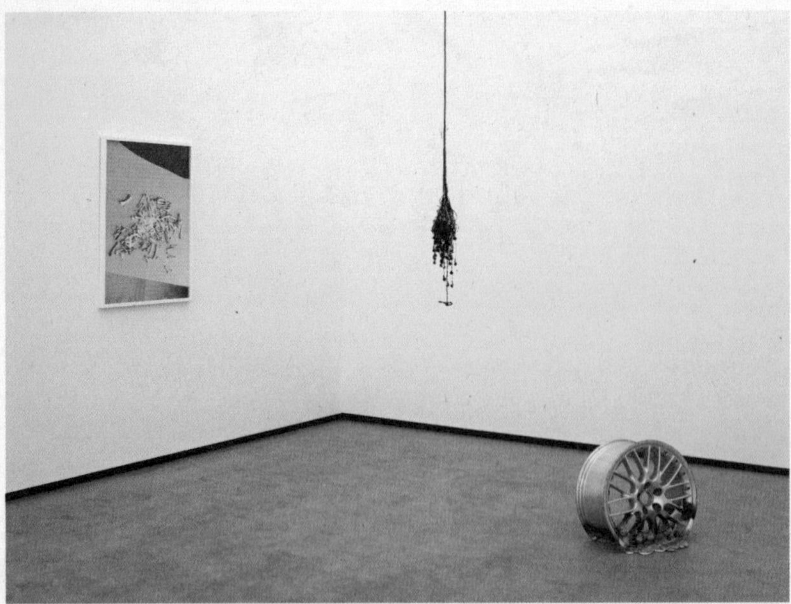

1.

Jan Freuchen attended the Academy of Fine Arts, Bergen, and currently lives in Oslo and Berlin. His practice includes sculpture, drawing, collage, photography, and video, with references ranging from biology and geology to art history and contemporary culture. He often begins with existing phenomena (Ed Ruscha's Twentysix Gasoline Stations or the Capgras syndrome) to trace evolution or deterioration over time.

1. (left) **Chicken Wings (500g)**
2006, digital print, 37 ½ × 27 ½ in
(95 × 70 cm)

1. (middle) **Any sign (...) capable of distinguishing the goods or services of one undertaking from those of other undertakings**
2006, headphones and sound, dimensions variable

1. (right) **20" aluminum rim**
2006, aluminum, 20 ½ × 19 ¼ × 10 in
(52 × 49 × 25 cm)

2. **The Carbon Web**
2006, ink on paper, wood, and burned plant, dimensions variable

3. **Big Stealth**
2007, wood, drywall, plaster, and acrylic paint, dimensions variable

4. **Letters of Resignation**
2007, oil on wood, 39 ½ × 147 ¼ in
(100 × 374 cm)

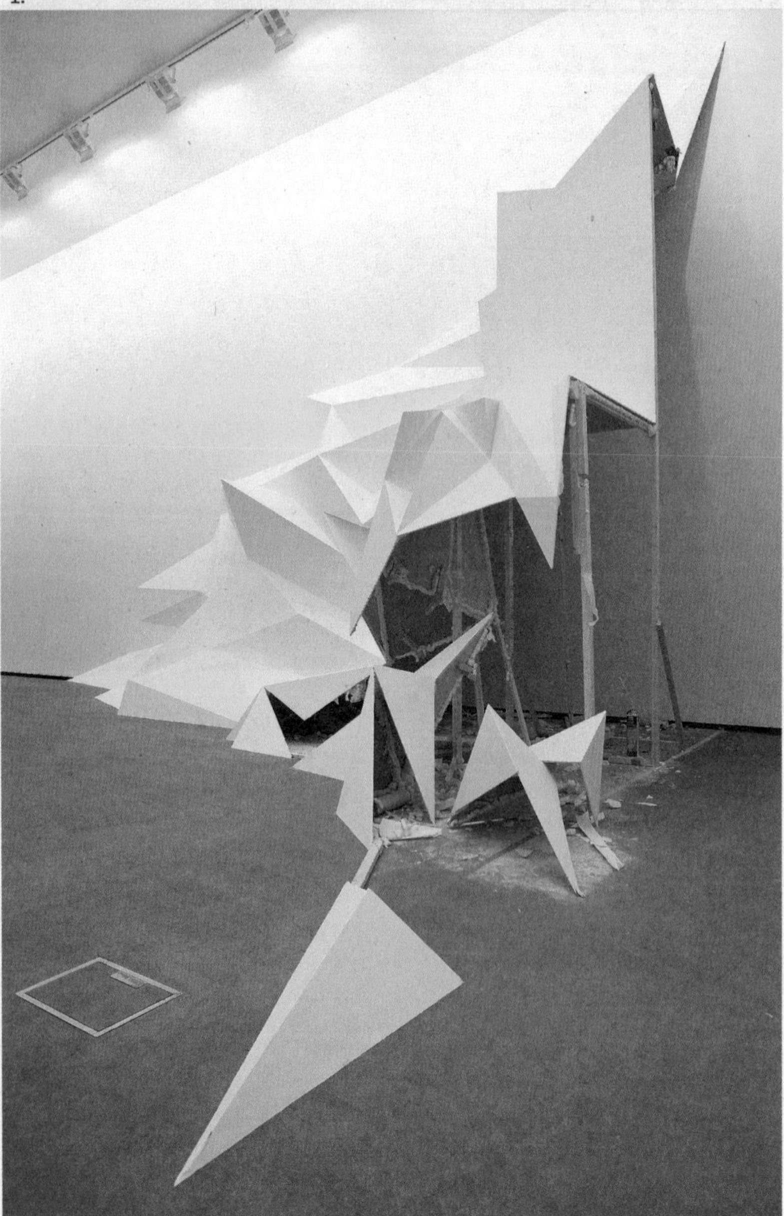

3.

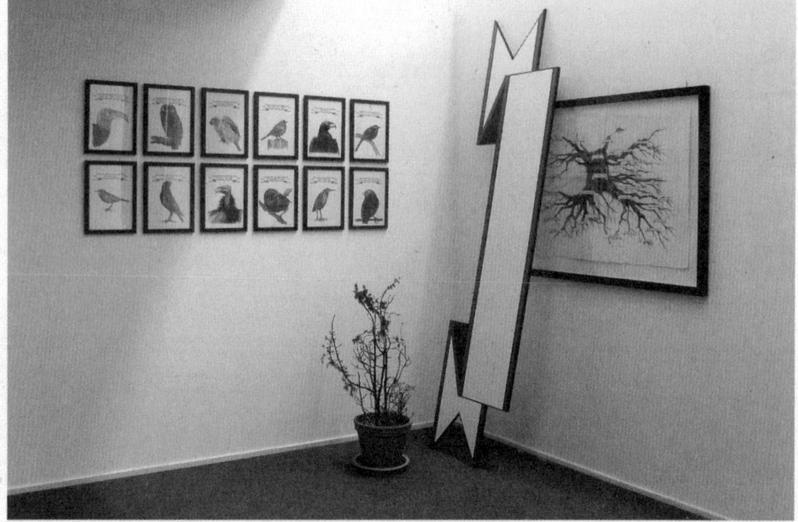

2.

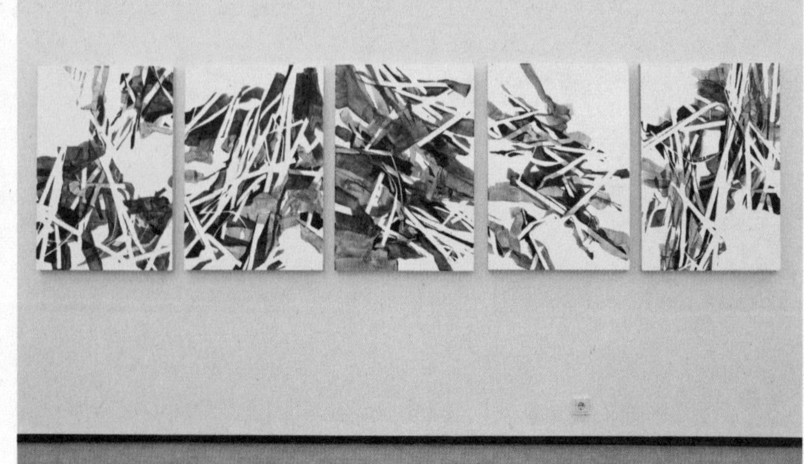

4.

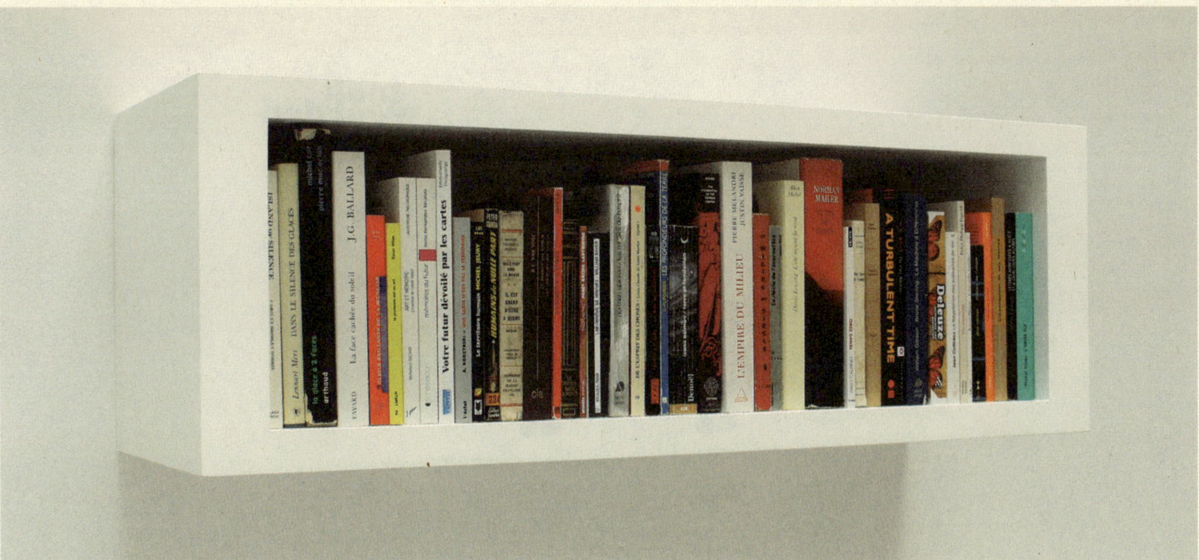

1.

Aurélien Froment attended the École Régionale des Beaux Arts, Nantes, and currently works as a film projectionist in Paris. Much of his practice addresses the experience and implications of film as a medium, particularly as it affects our relationship to time. Works include objects, actions, installations, drawings, and the film **The Apse, the Bell and the Antelope** (2005), made at Arcosanti, the experimental town founded by architect Paolo Soleri in the Arizona desert.

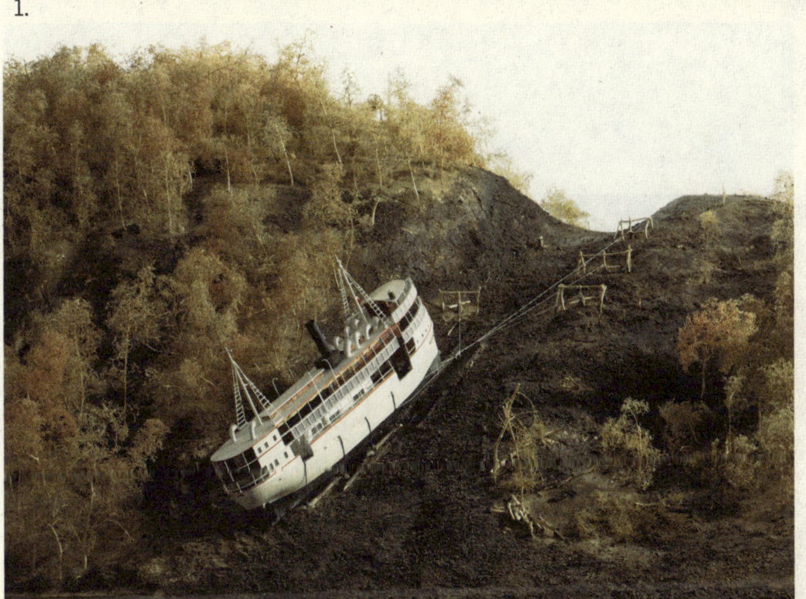

2.

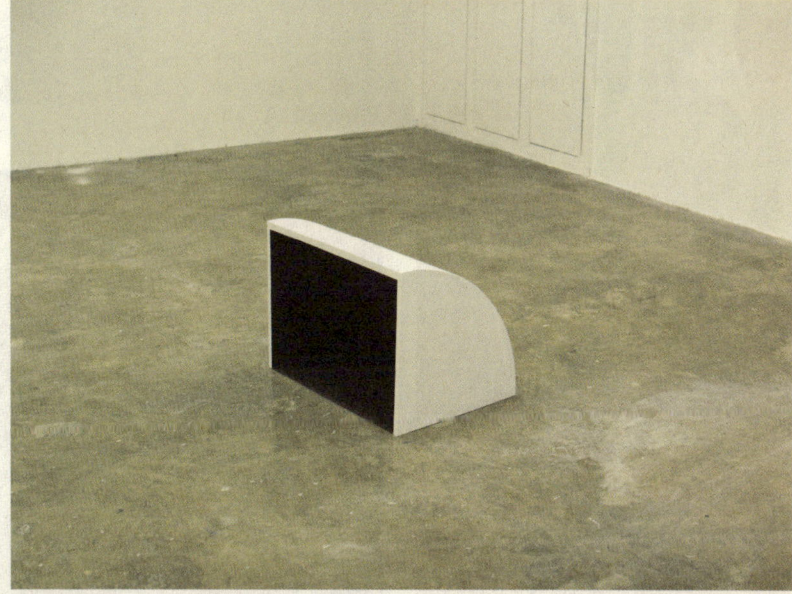

3.

1. De L'île à hélice à Ellis Island
2005, 44 books on a wooden shelf,
12 × 35 ½ × 12 in (30 × 90 × 30 cm)

2. Werner Herzog (detail)
2002, dried vegetation, plaster, plastic, and wood (1:100 scale model),
55 × 78 ¾ × 78 ¾ in (140 × 200 × 200 cm)

3. The Prompter's Box
2007, wood, 15 ¾ × 31 ½ × 13 ¾ in
(40 × 80 × 35 cm)

4. Théâtre de poche
with music by Erwan Corré
2007, video, 12 min

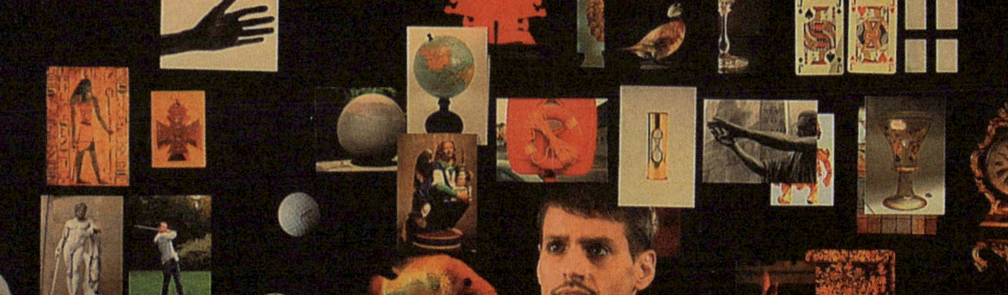

4.

Alistair Frost earned his MA in painting from the Royal College of Art, London, and currently lives in London and Amsterdam. He uses painting to build layered groupings of related signs and symbols. These include pieces of text (often the word "look"), abstract marks, and recognizable objects with multiple references – such as a pair of martini glasses that double as the eyes on a face.

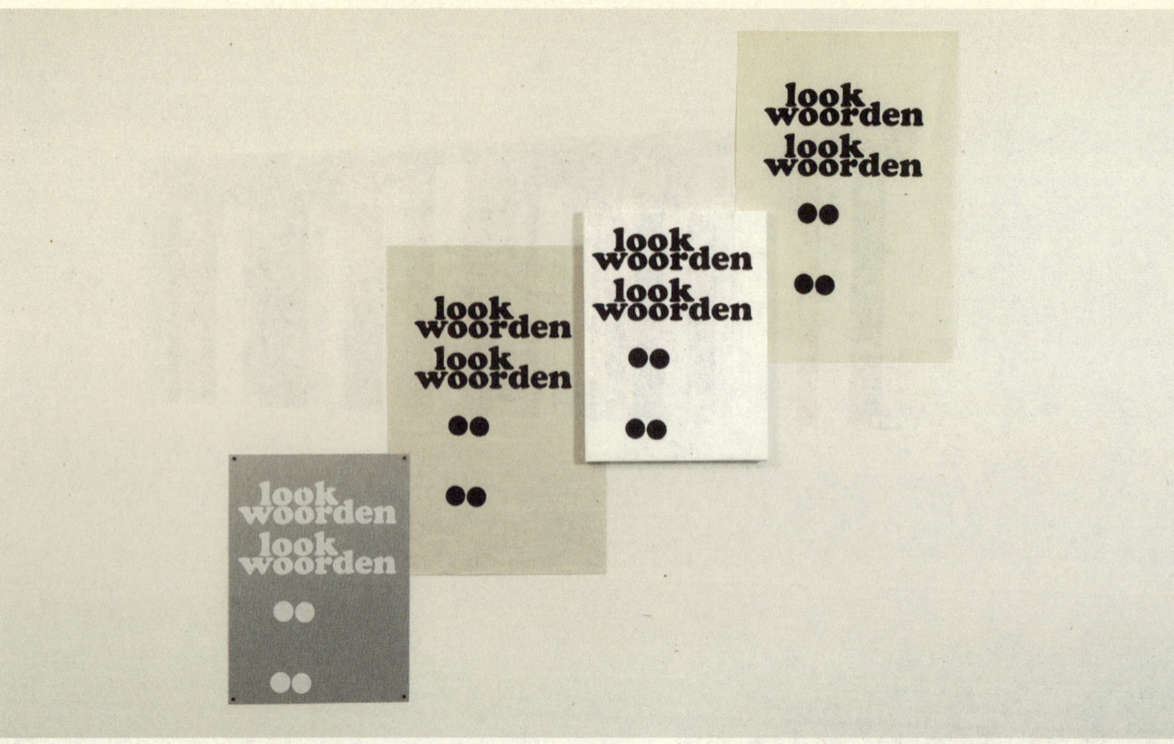

1.

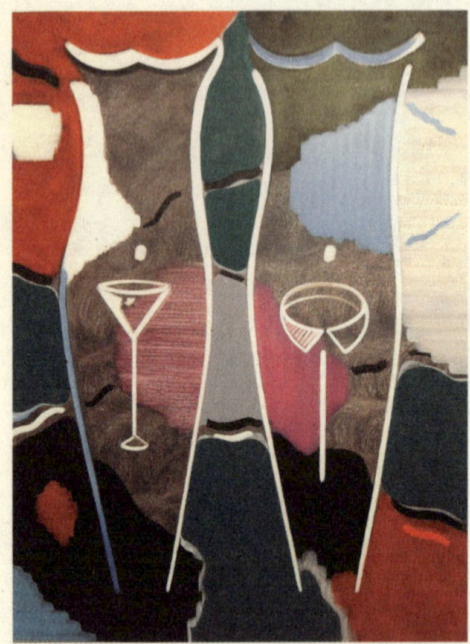

2.

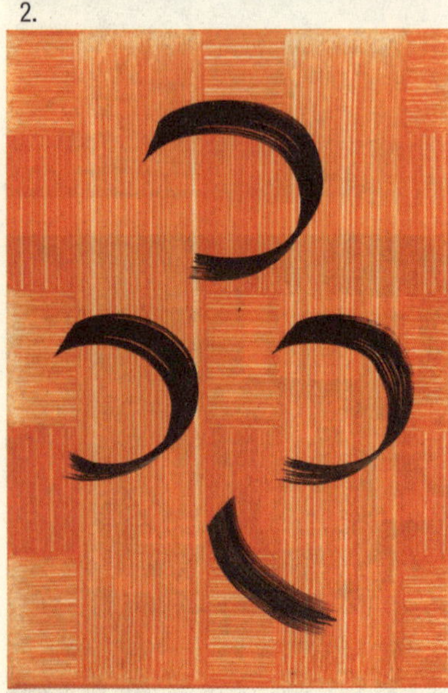

3.

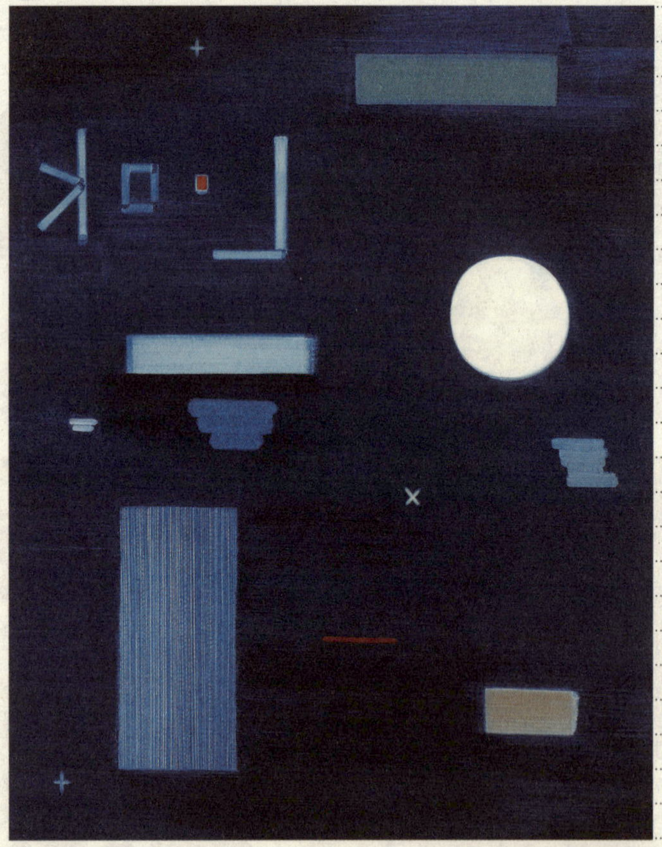

4.

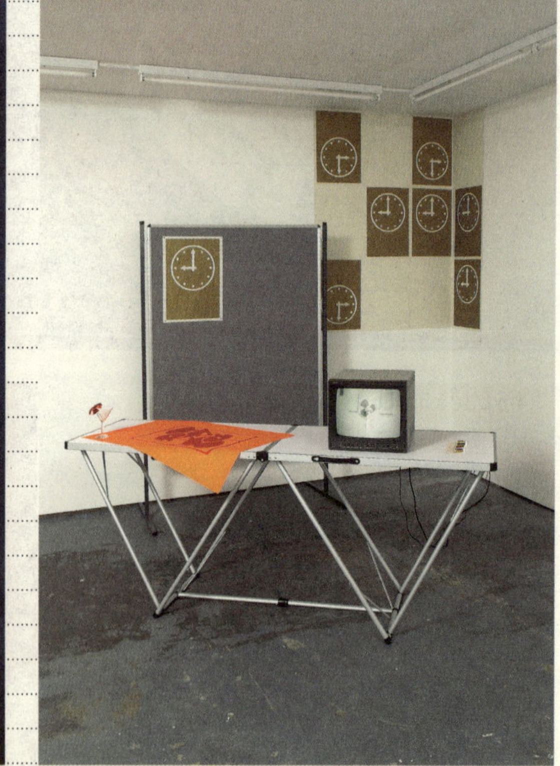

5.

1. look/woorden
2008, 4 parts, from left: screenprint on aluminum, screenprint on newsprint, screenprint on canvas, and screenprint on newsprint, dimensions variable

2. Color/Repeat
2007, oil on canvas, 59 × 45 ½ in (150 × 116 cm)

3. BAR/Saloon
2008, oil on canvas, 11 ¾ × 8 in (30 × 20 cm)

4. one/word/look<>k
2008, oil on canvas, 59 × 47 ¼ in (150 × 120 cm)

5. one/word/look<>look woorden
2008, folding table, martini glass, cocktail umbrellas, CRT video monitor, free-standing pinboard, and screenprints on paper, dimensions variable

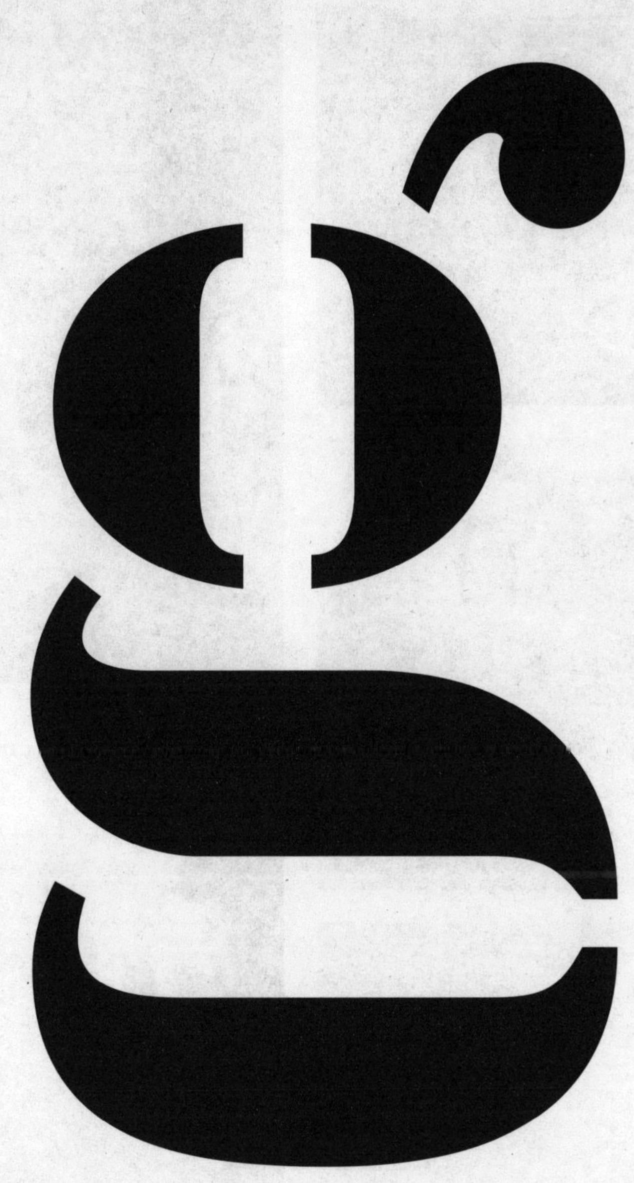

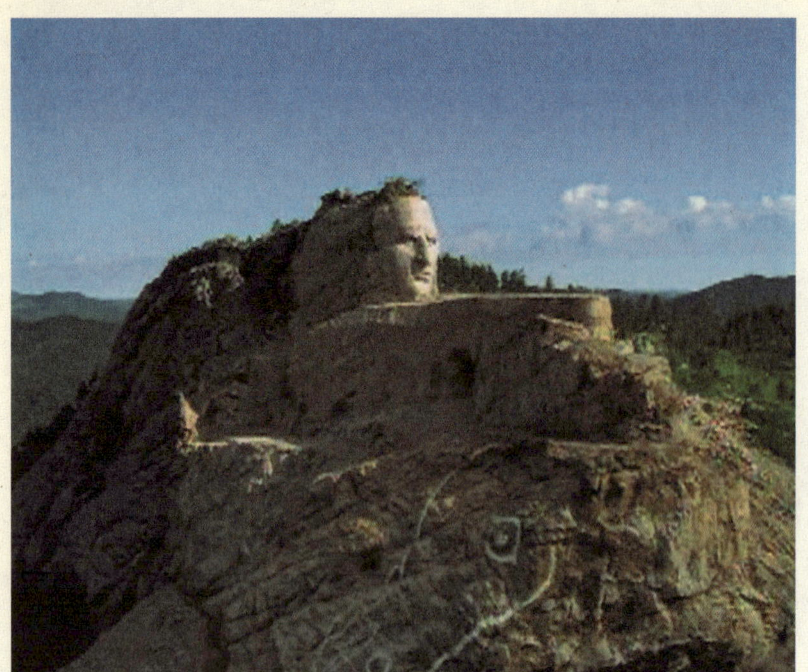

1.

Cyprien Gaillard attended l'Ecole Cantonale d'Art, Lausanne, and currently lives in Paris. His film, video, photography, and installation projects offer historical analysis of landscape, architecture, and notions of vandalism and destruction. Works often emphasize the contrasts between utopian ideals and contemporary realities, as in the video **Desniansky Raion** (2007), which juxtaposes suburban landscapes of St. Petersburg, Paris, and Kiev.

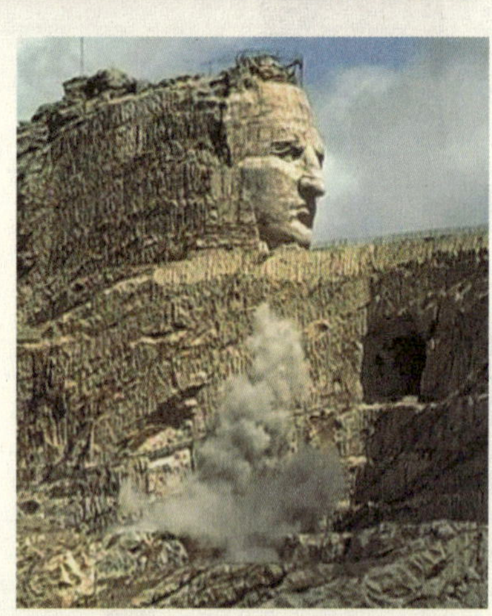

2.

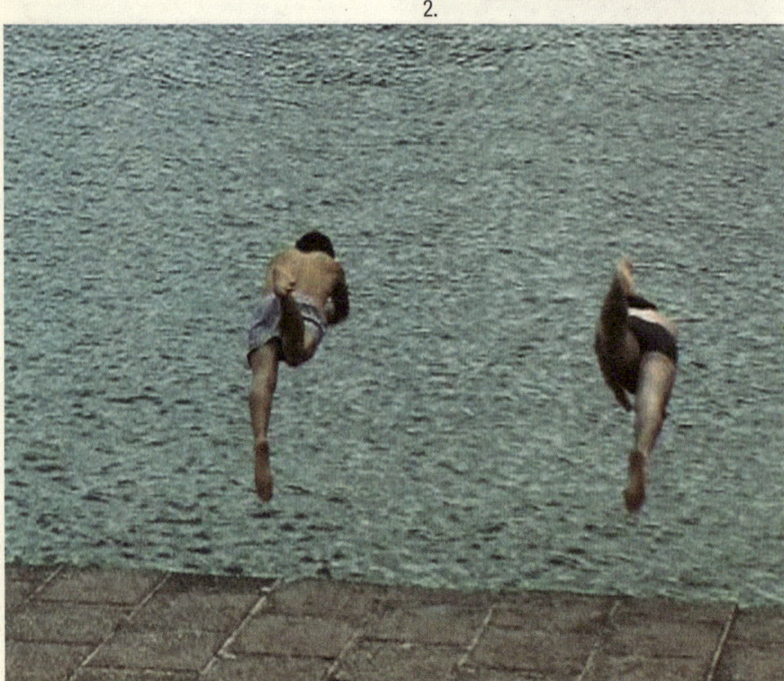

4.

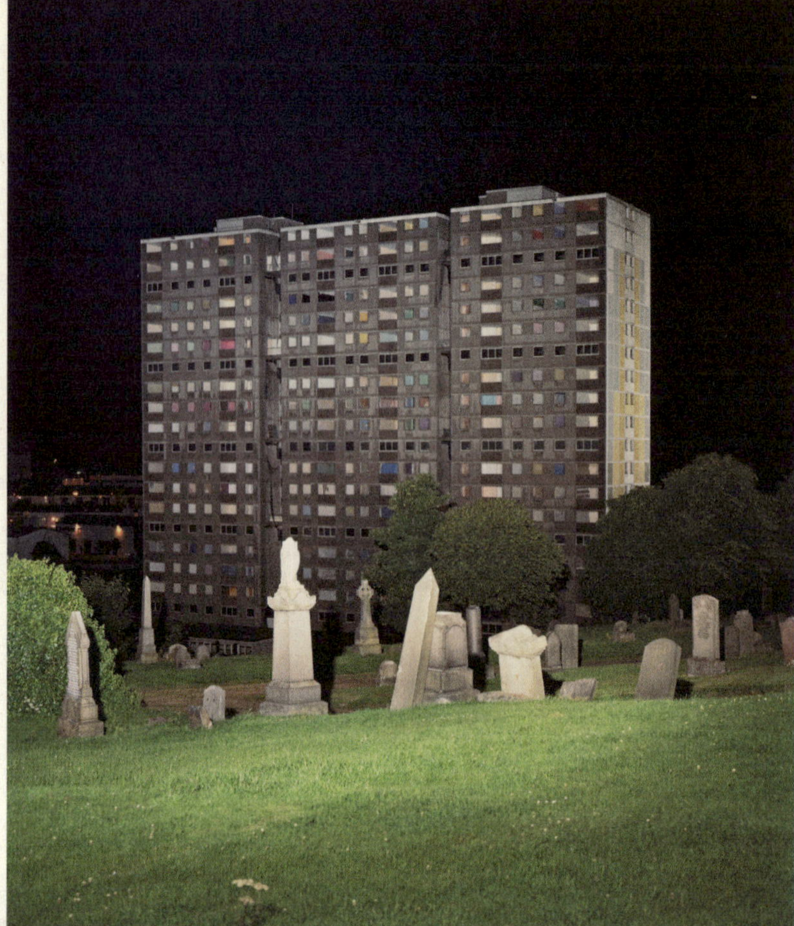

3.

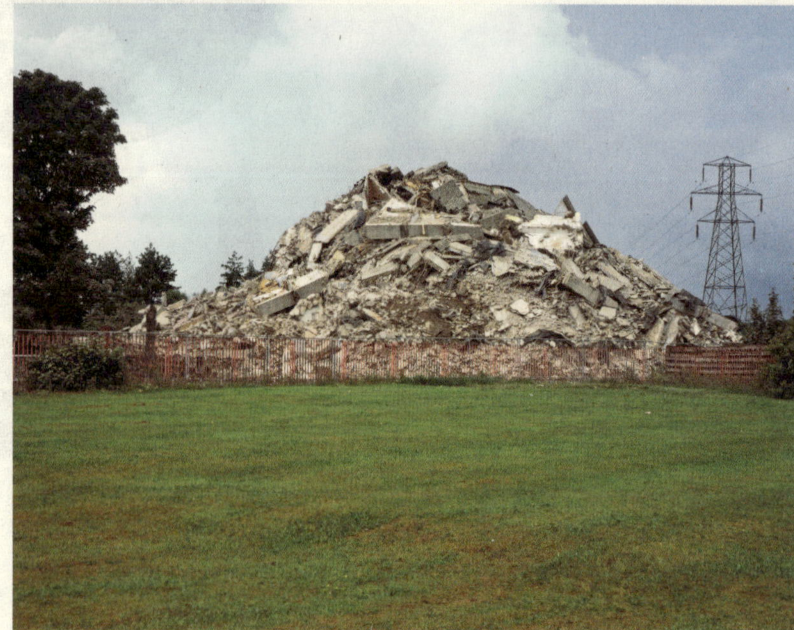

5.

1 & 2. **Crazy Horse**
with music by KOUDLAM
2008, video, 24 min

3. **Untitled (Sitehill)**
2008, chromogenic print, 83 in × 67 in (211 × 170 cm)

4. **The Lake Arches**
2007, video, 1 min 43 sec

5. **Millerfield, Dalmarnock, 1965–2007**
2007, chromogenic print, 59 × 88 ½ in (150 × 225 cm)

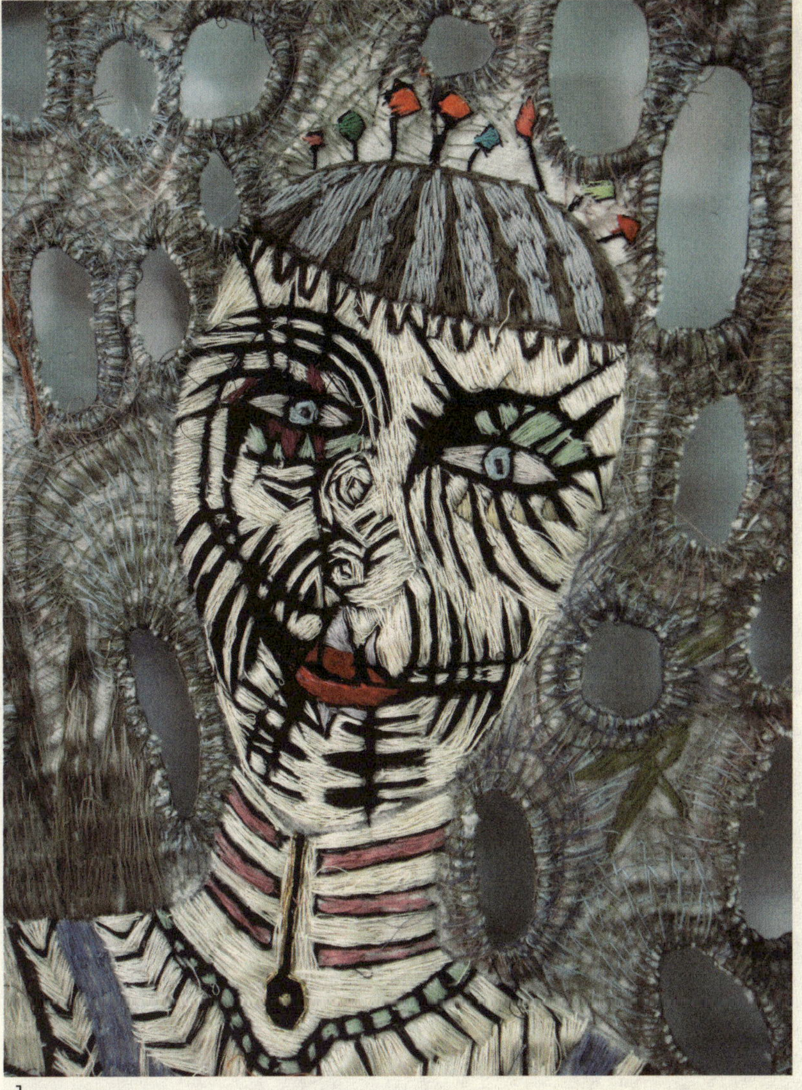

1.

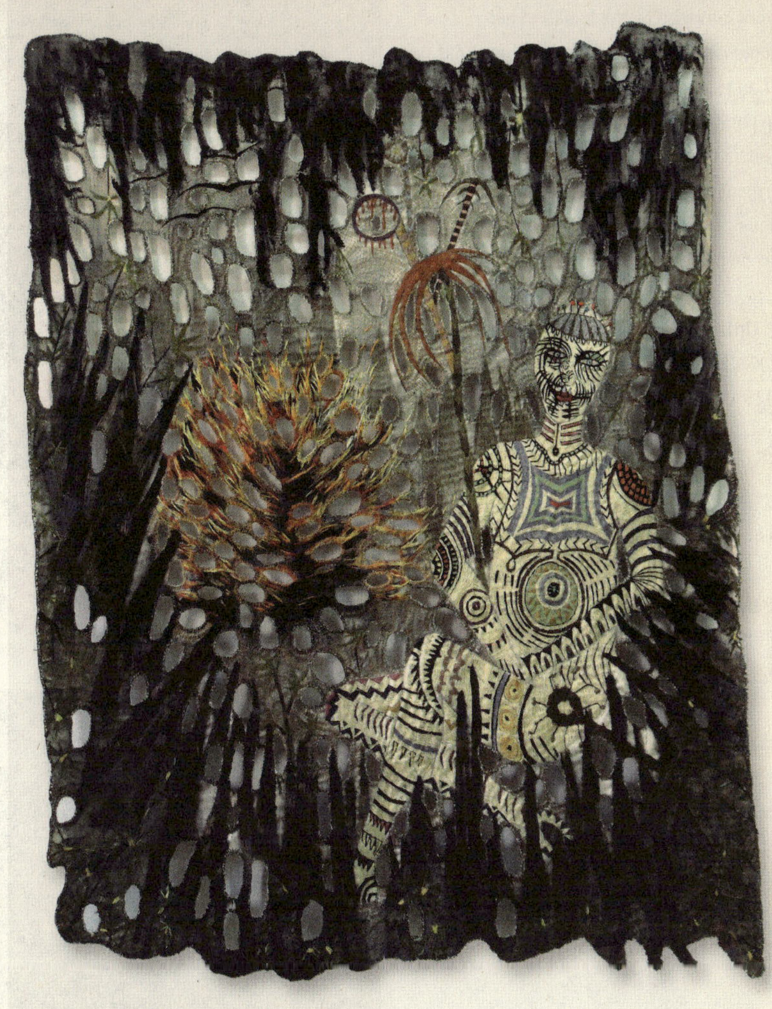

2.

Zoi Gaitanidou attended the Athens School of Fine Arts, Greece, and currently lives in Berlin. She weaves dreamlike narratives using drawing and embroidery. Merging traditional craft with contemporary and futuristic content, one series represents the life of a fictional tribe haunted by the symbol of a spaceship.

1 & 2. Untitled
2008, acrylic and thread on canvas, 67 × 51 in (170 × 130 cm)

3. Baal 2 (detail)
2007, ink, plastic color, and thread on canvas, 61 × 63 in (155 × 160 cm)

4. Untitled
2007, ink on handmade Nepalese paper, 27 ½ × 19 ½ in (70 × 50 cm)

5. Inflourence
2007, acrylic and thread on canvas, 86 ½ × 55 in (220 × 140 cm)

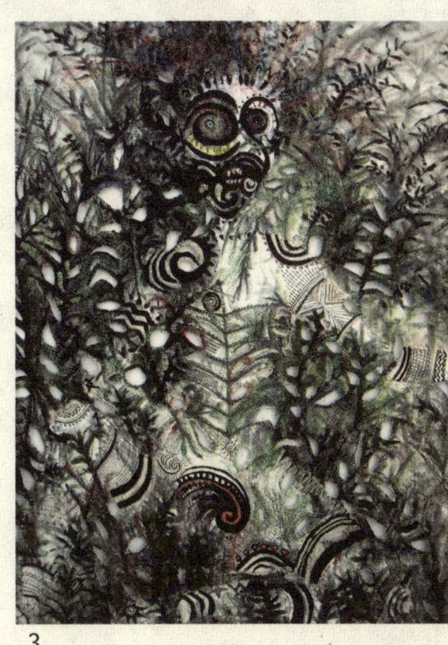

3.

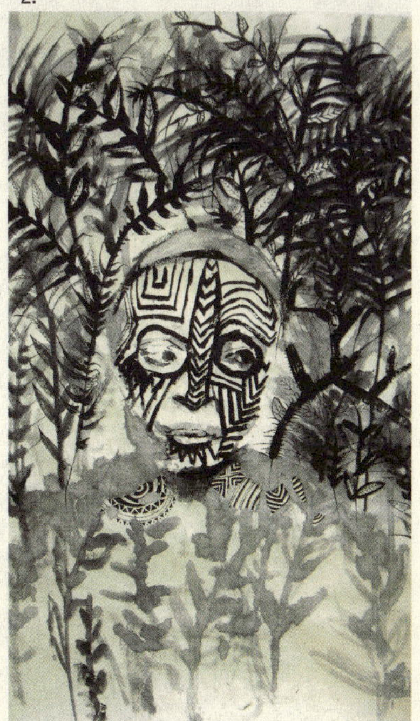

4.

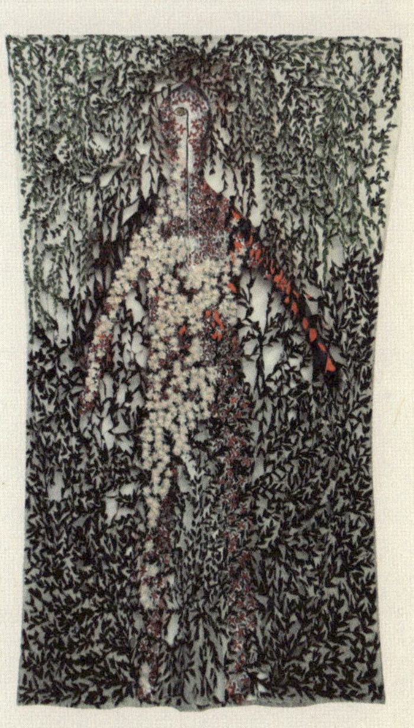

5.

New Delhi-based Vibha Galhotra makes work informed by the tumult of her home city, which is currently in the midst of an extensive construction program. In paintings, photographs, sculptures, and installations, Galhotra offers a critique of the governmental bureaucracy and depletion of natural resources that accompany such initiatives.

1. **Untitled**
2007, brass trinkets, 47 × 84 × 36 in (119 × 213 × 91 cm)

2. **Work in Progress**
2007, hollow cast brass, dimensions variable

3. **Inconvenience Regretted**
2008, brass, 22 × 61 × 5 in (55 × 154 × 13 cm)

4. **Missing**
2007, copper wire and steel, 84 × 33 × 18 in (213 × 84 × 46 cm)

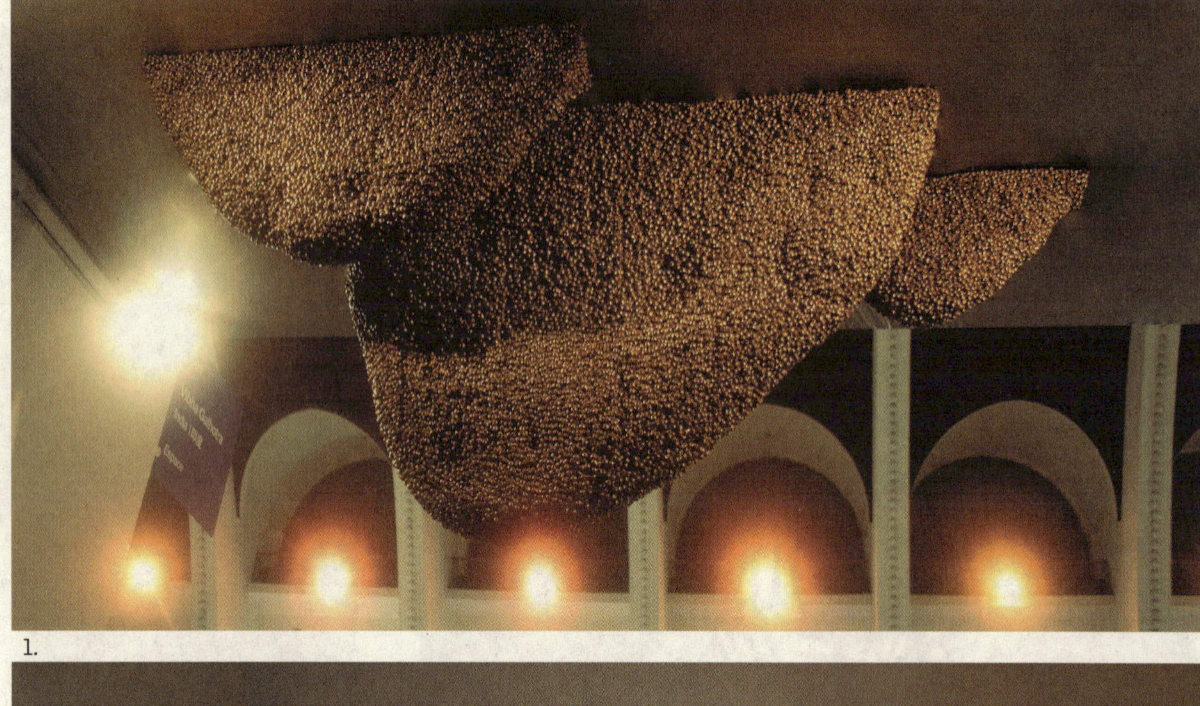

1.

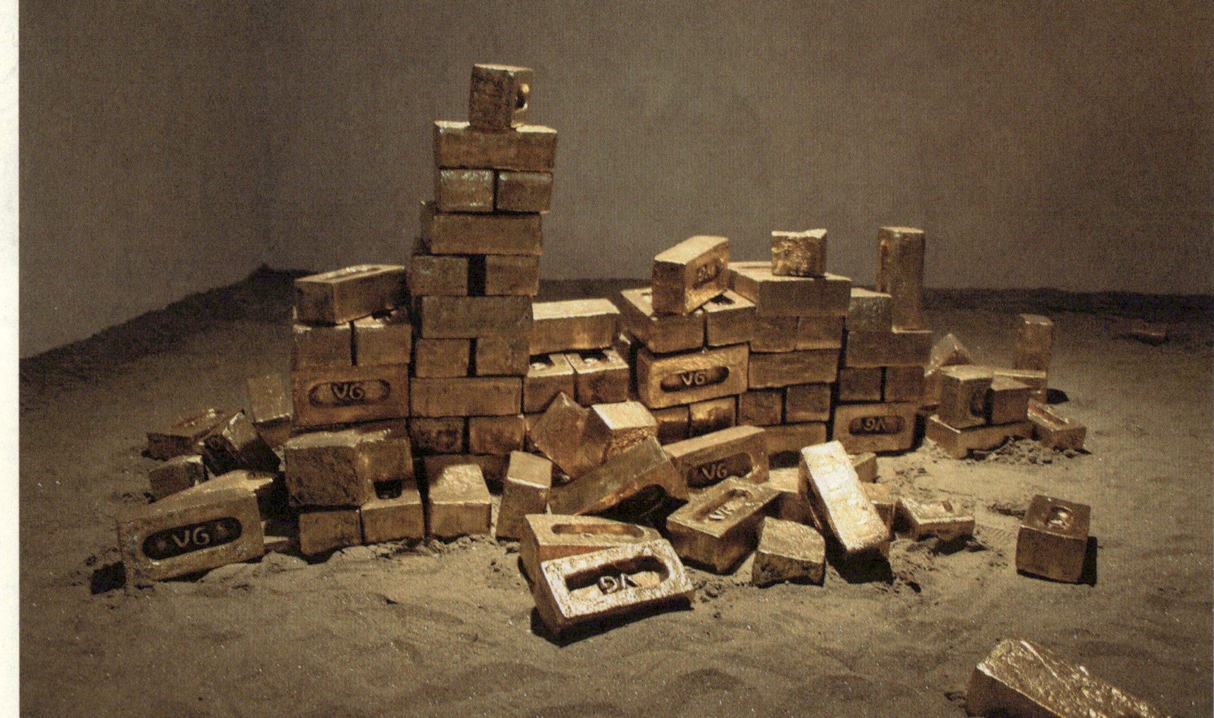

2.

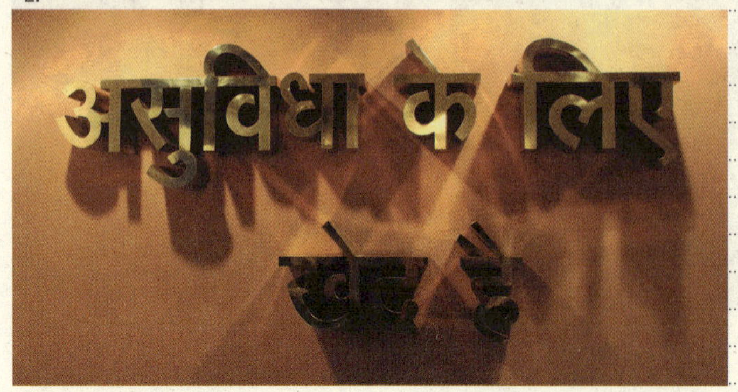

3.

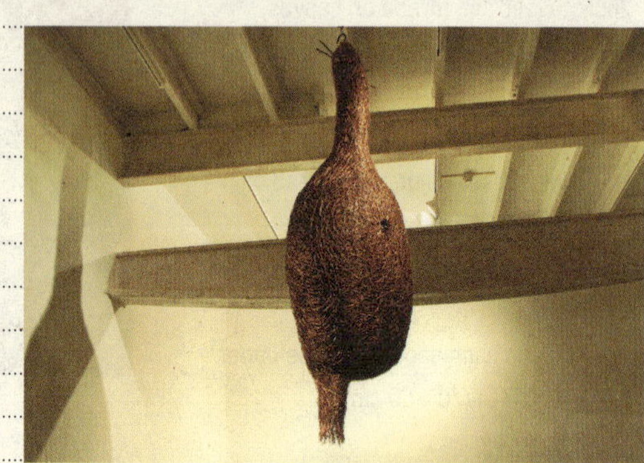

4.

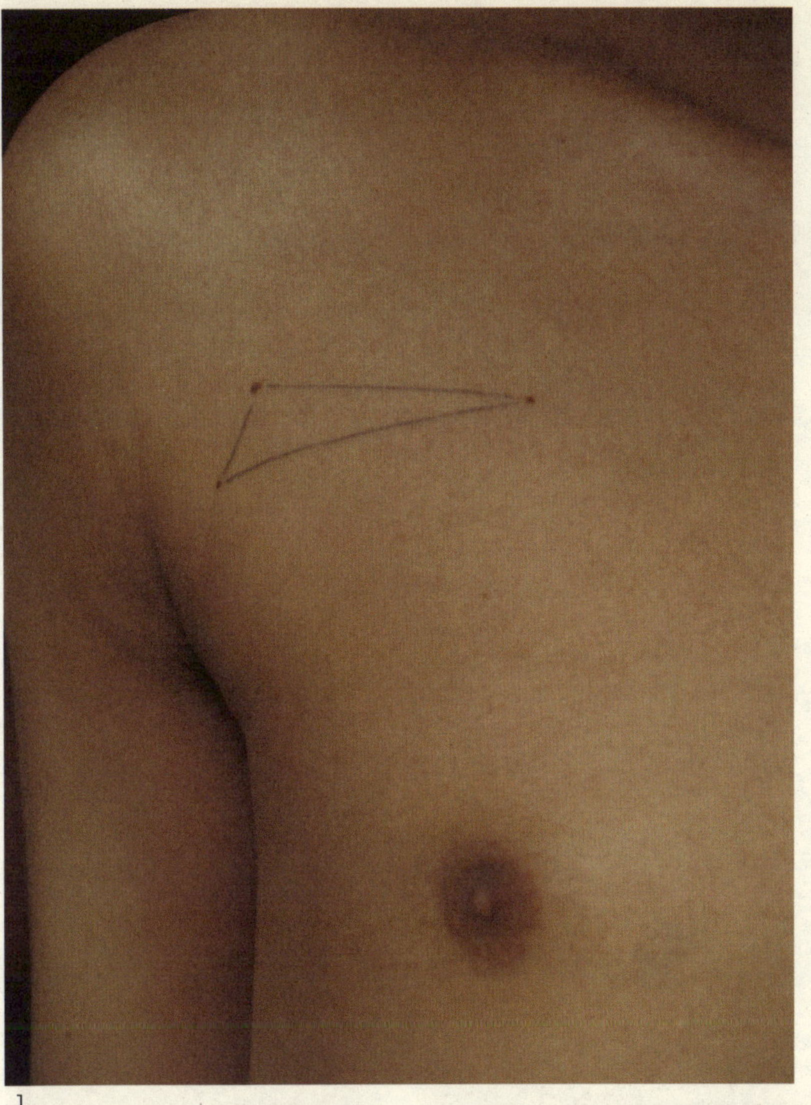

1.

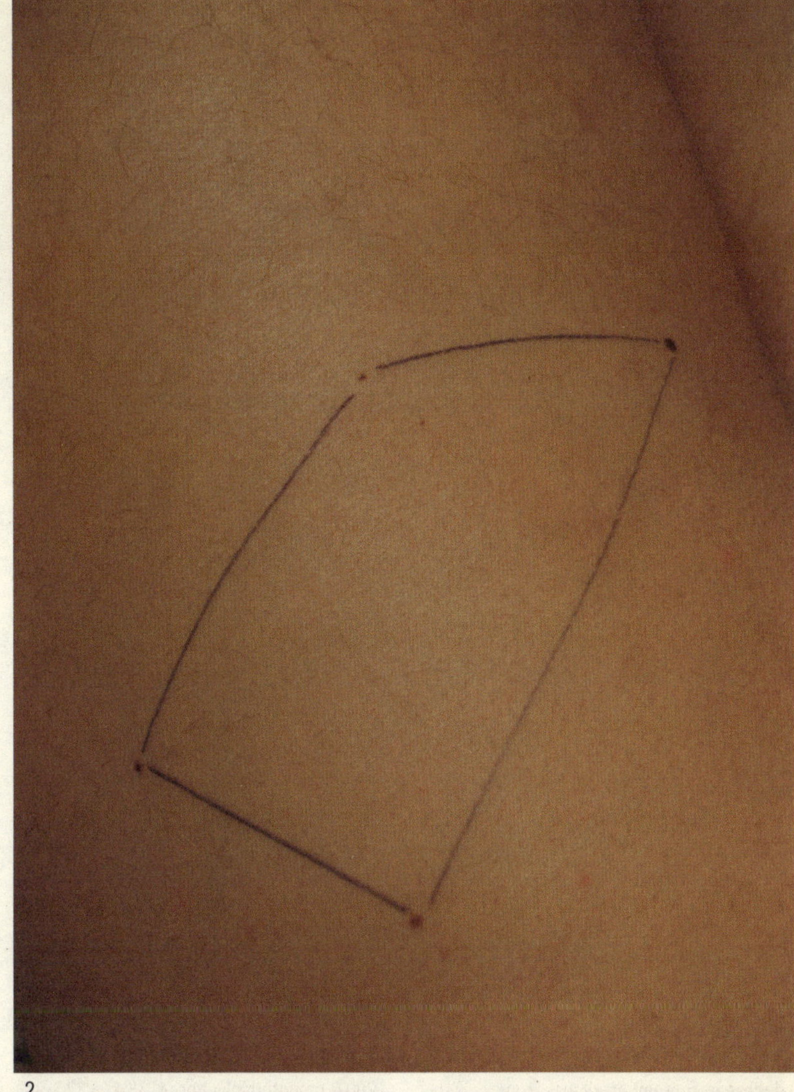

2.

3.

4.

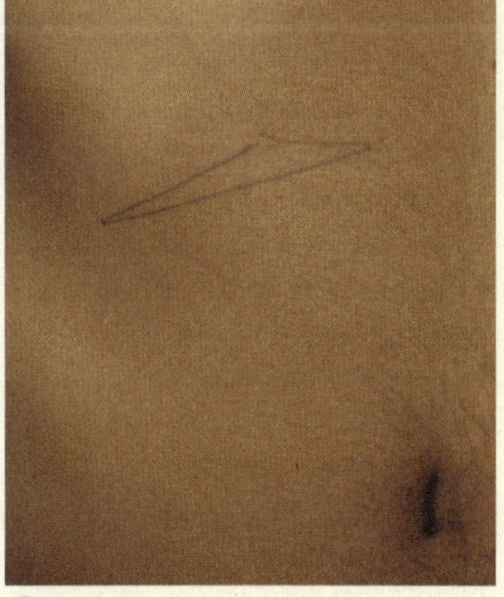

5.

Moscow-based Alexandra Galkina participated in the School of Contemporary Art directed by Avdey Ter Oganjan and the Radek Community. Her works in public intervention, graffiti, video, and photography investigate Russian national identity through the lens of its complex cultural, political, and art historical past.

1. **Constellation1**
2006-08, color photograph,
$23\frac{1}{2} \times 15\frac{3}{4}$ in (60 × 40 cm)

2. **Constellation2**
2006-08, color photograph,
$23\frac{1}{2} \times 15\frac{3}{4}$ in (60 × 40 cm)

3. **Constellation3** (detail)
2006-08, color photograph,
$23\frac{1}{2} \times 15\frac{3}{4}$ in (60 × 40 cm)

4. **Constellation4** (detail)
2006-08, color photograph,
$15\frac{3}{4} \times 23\frac{1}{2}$ in (40 × 60 cm)

5. **Constellation5** (detail)
2006-08, color photograph,
$23\frac{1}{2} \times 15\frac{3}{4}$ in (60 × 40 cm)

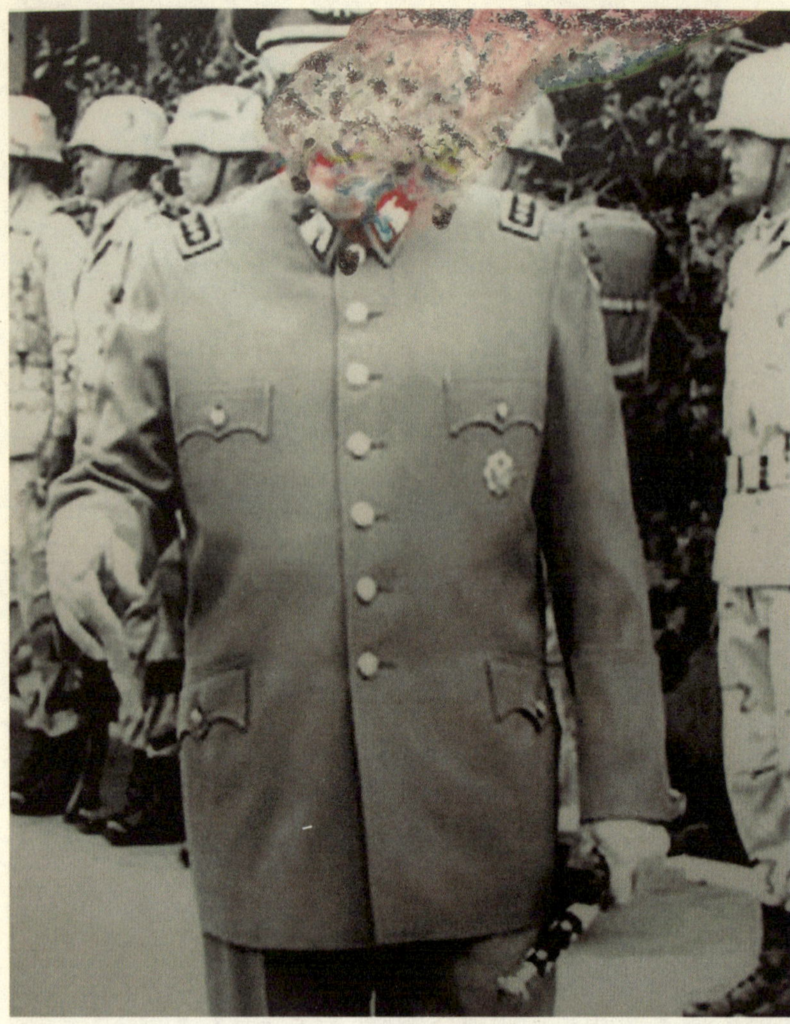

1.

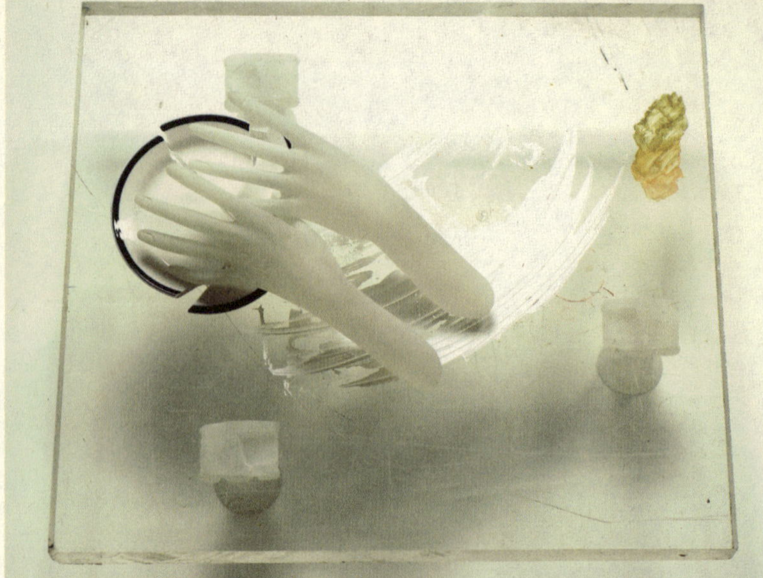

2.

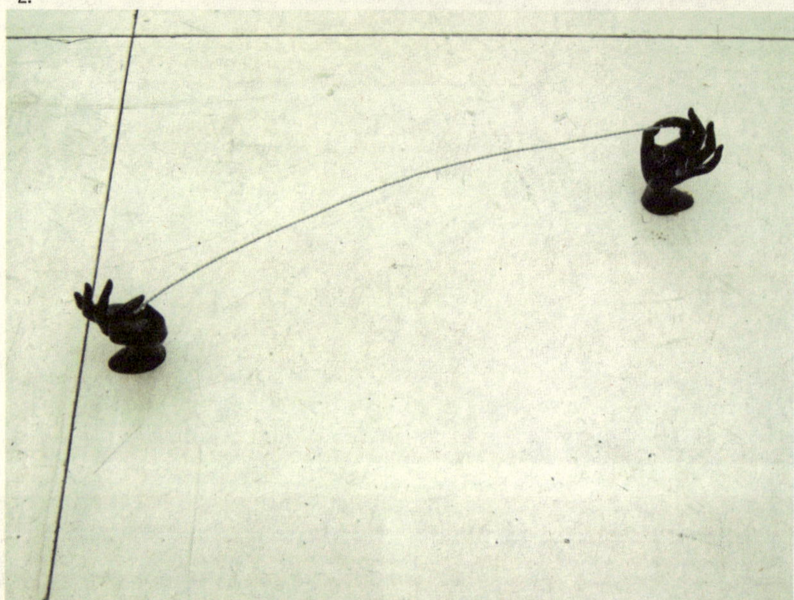

3.

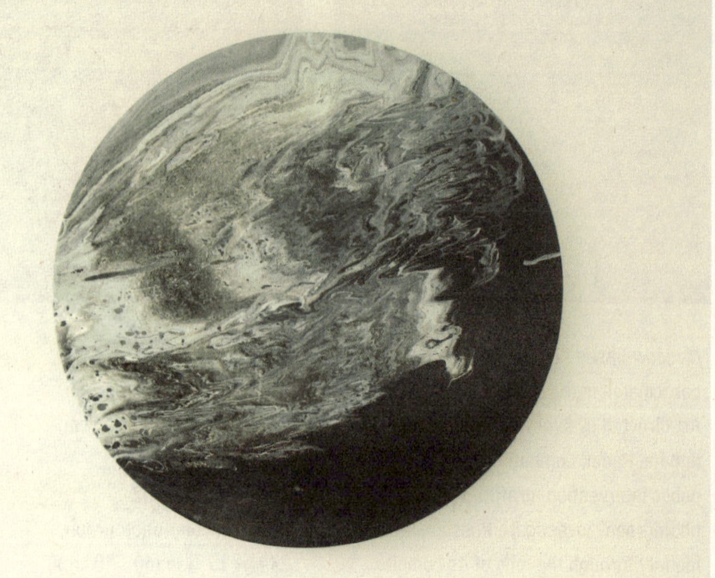

4.

Manuela Viera Gallo holds a postgraduate degree in contemporary arts from the Universidad Católica de Chile. She was born in Rome while her parents were living in political exile; her family returned to their home city of Santiago in 1984, while the country was still controlled by military dictator Augusto Pinochet. She is thus a member of the "post-dictatorship generation of 2000," and much of her work is profoundly influenced by both her personal experience and the historical legacy of the Pinochet era. She currently lives and works in New York.

1. **Portrait of a Dictator**
2007, mounted inkjet print, 38 3/4 × 32 3/4 in (98 × 83 cm)

2. **Primitive Hard**
2007, glass, ceramic, and paint, 18 × 18 × 8 in (46 × 46 × 20 cm)

3. **DOWN HILL**
2006, plastic, enamel, and metal cord, 7 in × 112 in (18 × 285 cm)

4. **Lapsus**
2005, enamel on canvas, diameter 32 in (81 cm)

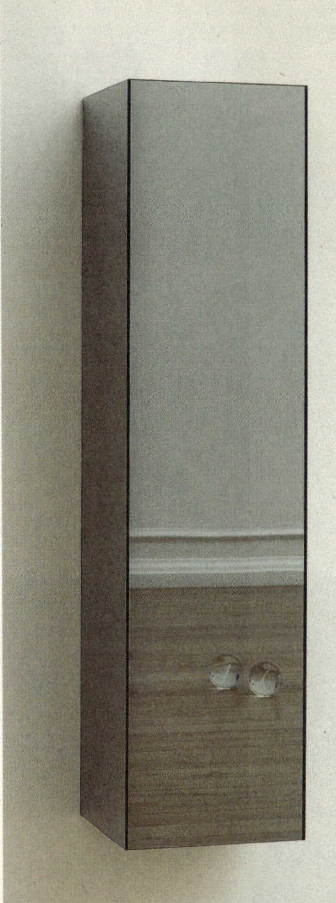

1.

1. She Spoke in Images Like Some New Language (Alchemy Box No. 3)
2008, one-way mirrored glass with objects from artist's collection, 47 1/4 × 12 × 12 in (120 × 30 × 30 cm)

2. A sheet of paper on which I was about to draw, as it slipped from my table and fell to the floor
2008, 3 of 100 crystal balls, each containing a suspended laser-etched 3D picture of a sheet of paper, each diameter 6 in (15 cm), overall dimensions variable

3. Felix provides a stage (Eleven sketches for 'A sheet of paper on which I was about to draw, as it slipped from my table and fell to the floor')
2008, digital photograph, dimensions variable

4. Is this guilt in you too (Study of a car in a field)
2005, video, sound, and white-carpet installation, dimensions variable

5. Man on a Bridge (a study of David Lange)
2008, 16 mm film

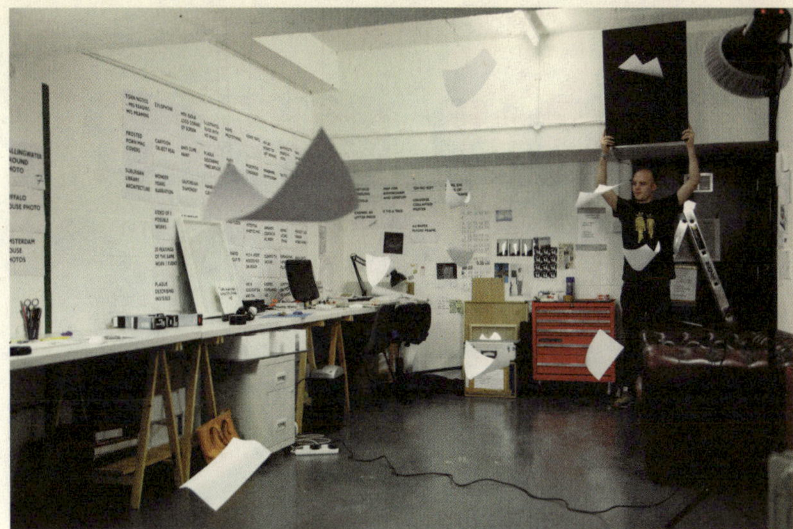

3.

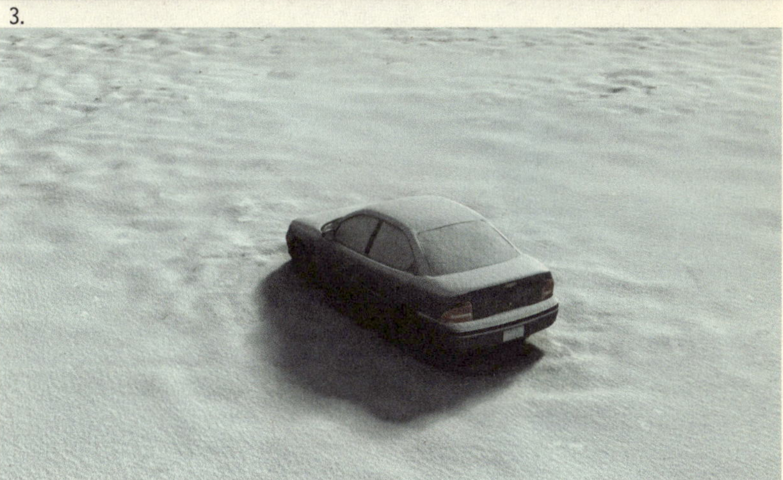

4.

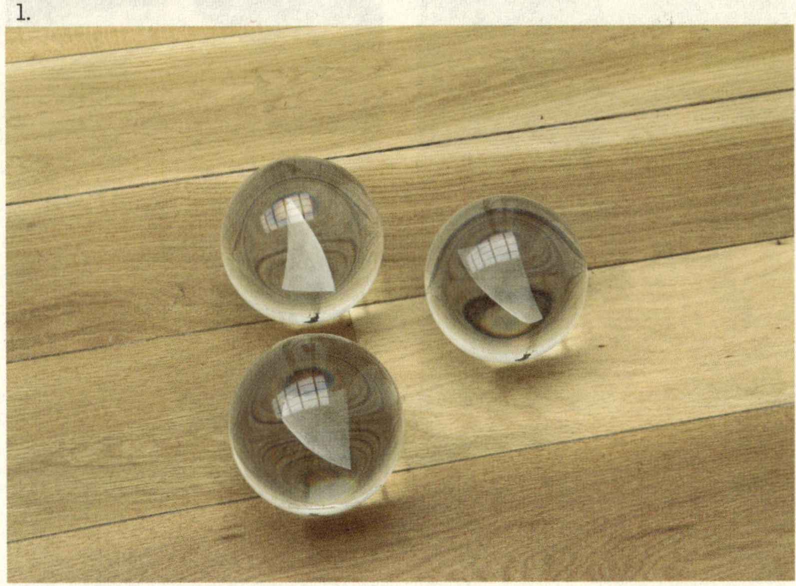

2.

Ryan Gander was a resident at the Rijksakademie in Amsterdam after attending Jan van Eyck Akademie, Maastricht. He currently lives in London. From sculpture, video, and installation to printed books and lectures, his practice often demands detective work over simple viewing. **A sheet of paper on which I was about to draw, as it slipped from my table and fell to the floor** (2008) consists of 100 crystal balls, each etched with the image of a falling sheet of paper.

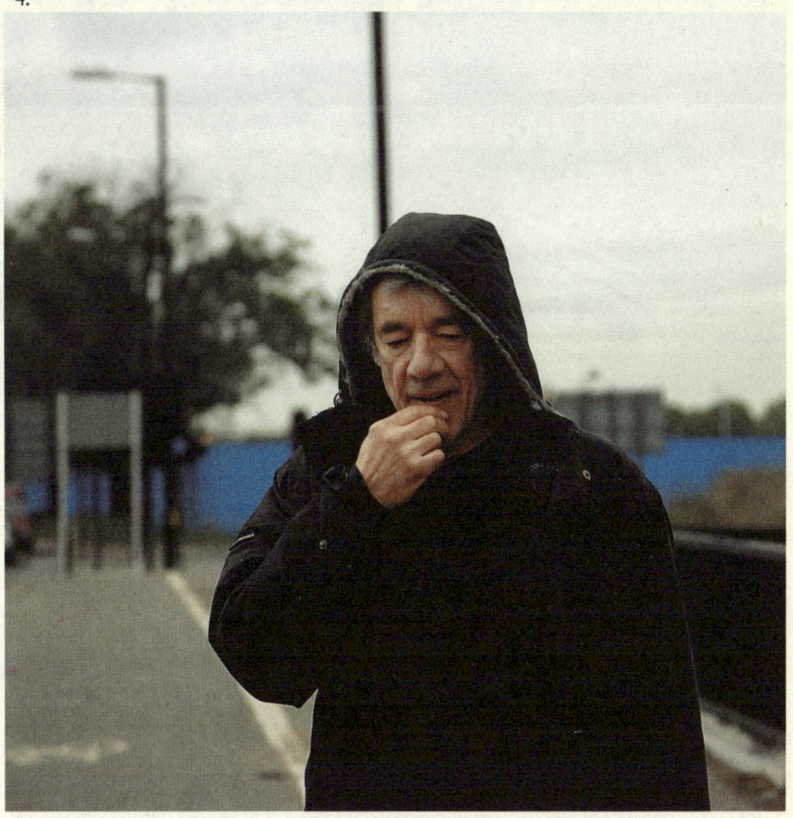

5.

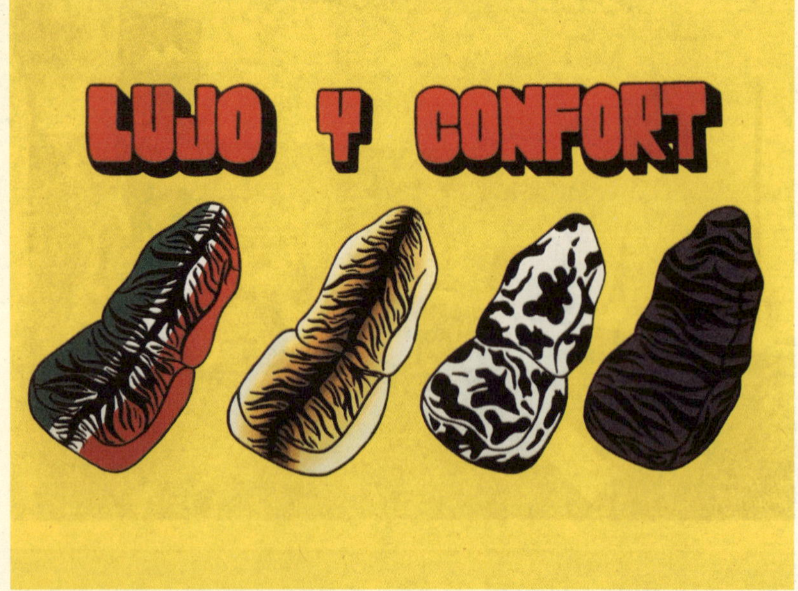

1.

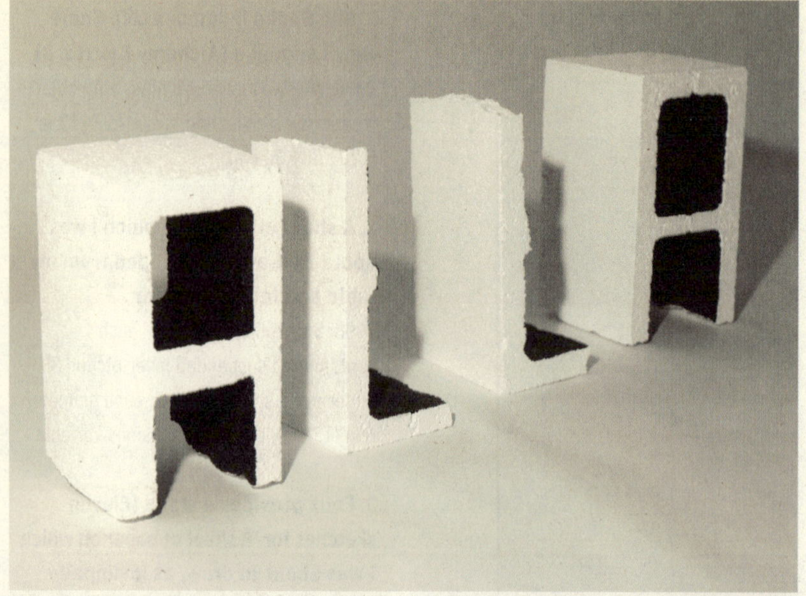

2.

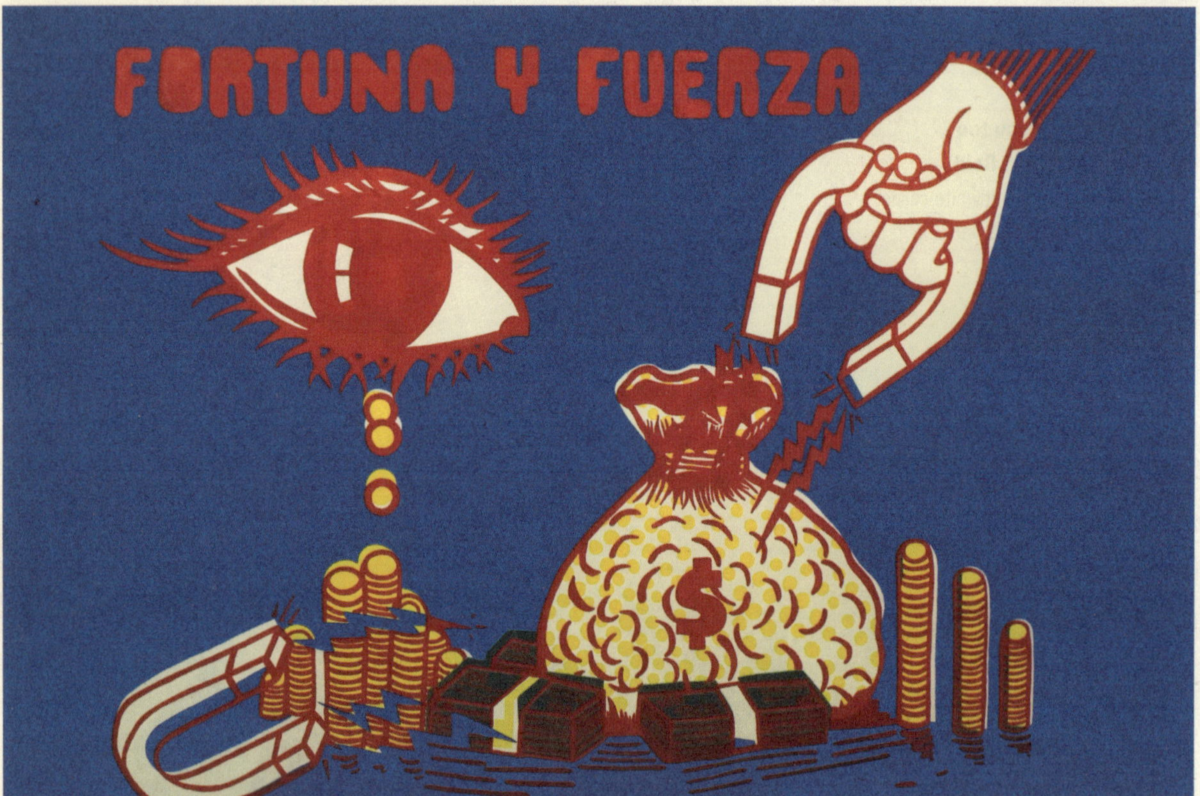

3.

4.

5.

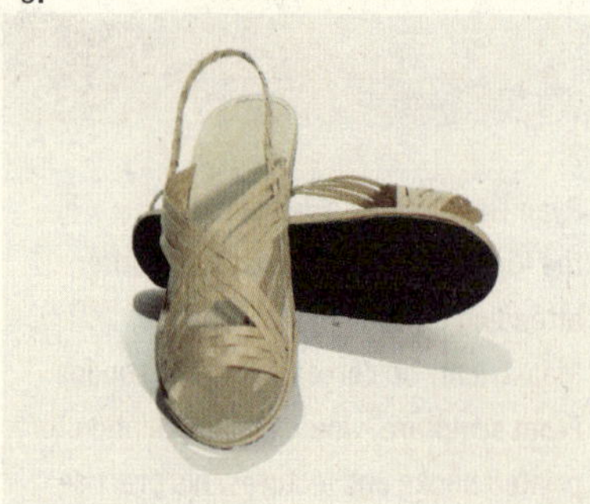

6.

Gary Garay earned his BFA from the Art Center College of Design in Pasadena and currently lives in Los Angeles. Sometimes known as Alla ("over there" in Spanish), he defines himself as a first-generation Mexican born in the United States. His paintings, sculptures, and installations draw on street advertising, murals, and other cross-cultural icons to explore the identities and experiences of Mexicans living in Los Angeles.

1. Lujo y Confort
2008, acrylic and flocking (rayon fibers) on wood, 36 × 48 in (91 × 122 cm)

2. Cinder Block Alla
2008, acrylic on cinder block, 14 × 44 × 7 1/2 in (36 × 112 × 19 cm)

3. Fortuna y Fuerza
2008, acrylic and flocking (rayon fibers) on wood, 34 × 52 in (86 × 132 cm)

4. Westside Pop
2004, mango juice and wood, 6 3/4 × 2 3/4 × 3/4 in (17 × 7 × 2 cm)

5. Cortez Classics – Black
2005, acrylic on cardboard, 5 × 10 × 3 3/4 in (13 × 25 × 10 cm)

6. Huaraches
2007, cardboard, thread, and bicycle tire, 3 × 10 3/4 × 4 in (8 × 27 × 10 cm)

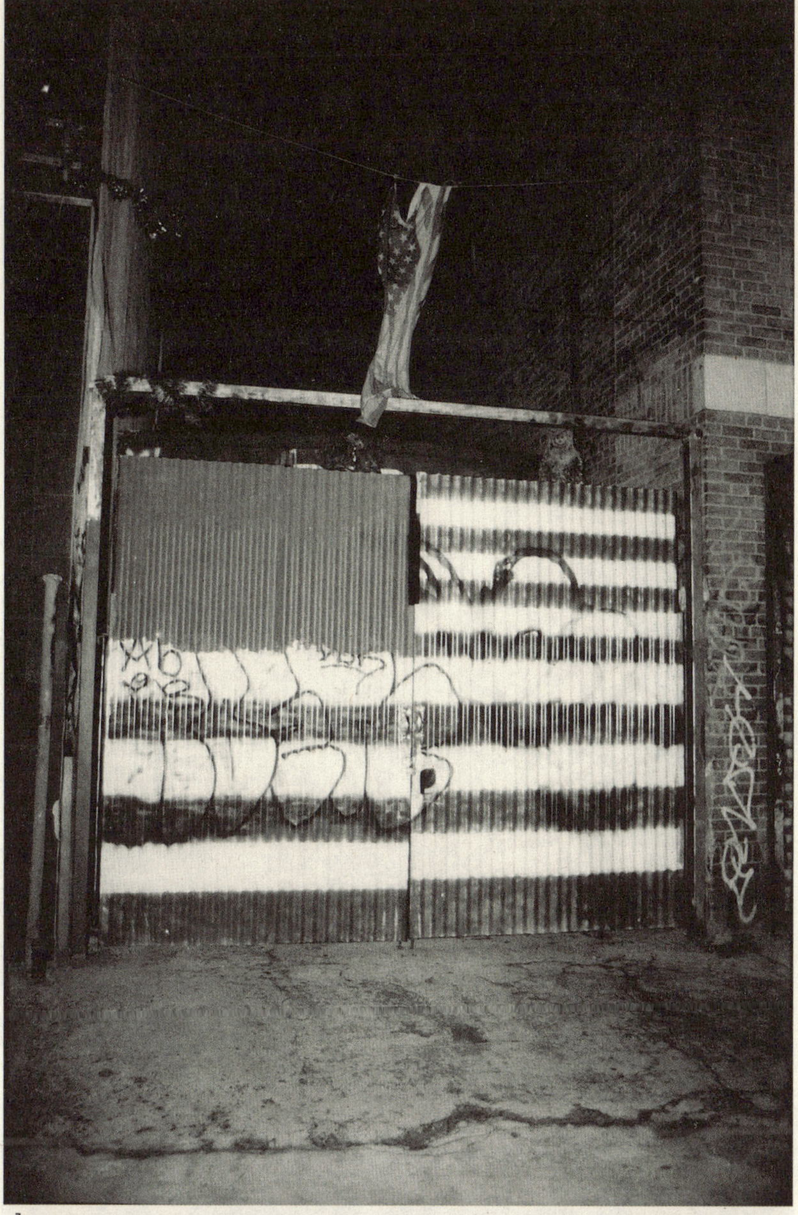
1.

Georg Gatsas currently lives in Switzerland and New York, and is interested in documenting what he calls a "global avant-garde." His photographs of artists and musicians are often exhibited with the works of his subjects themselves, creating a multidimensional portrait of an individual or community. His most recent exhibition, "Five Points," traces remnants of a creative scene in the changing landscape of downtown Manhattan.

1. **American Flag**
2007, Cibachrome print on aluminum,
53 × 35 in (135 × 89 cm)

2. **Brian DeGraw (paired with Brian DeGraw's Wall)**
2007, Cibachrome print on aluminum,
35 × 24 in (89 × 61 cm)

3. **Rita Ackermann**
2007, Cibachrome print on aluminum,
53 × 35 in (135 × 89 cm)

4. **Empty Birdhouse**
2007, Cibachrome print on aluminum,
24 × 35 in (61 × 89 cm)

5. **Sunflower on Eldridge Street**
2007, Cibachrome print on aluminum,
24 × 35 in (61 × 89 cm)

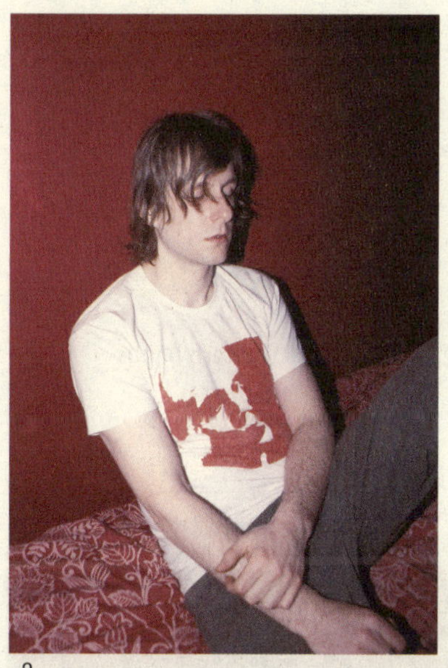
2.

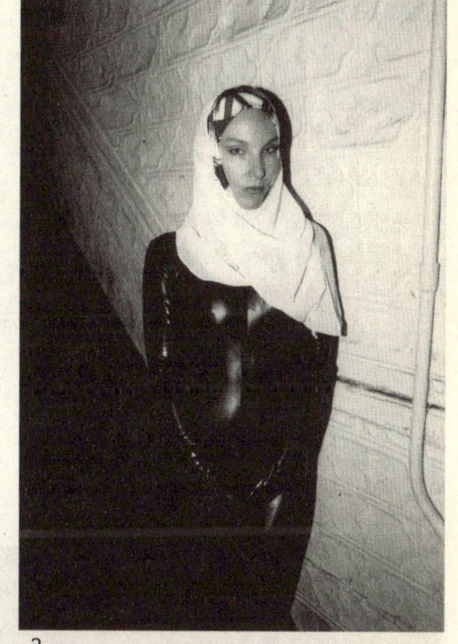
3.

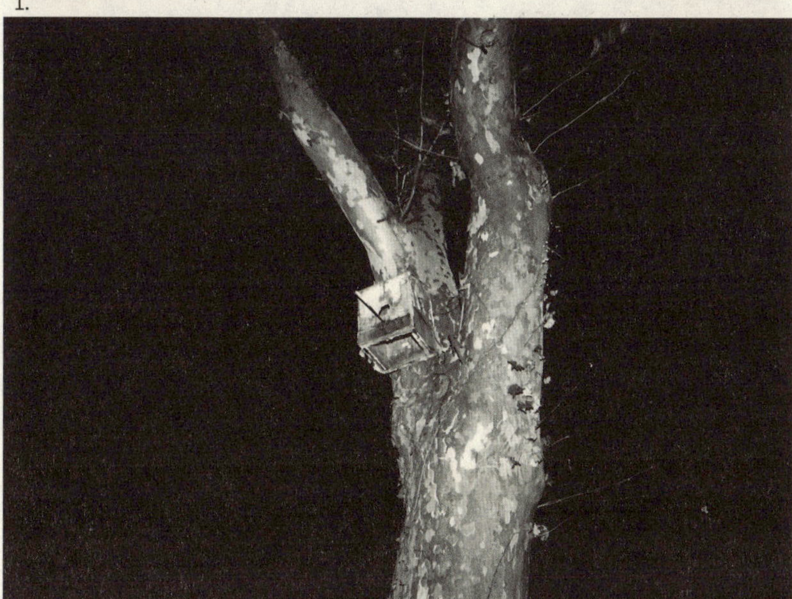
4.

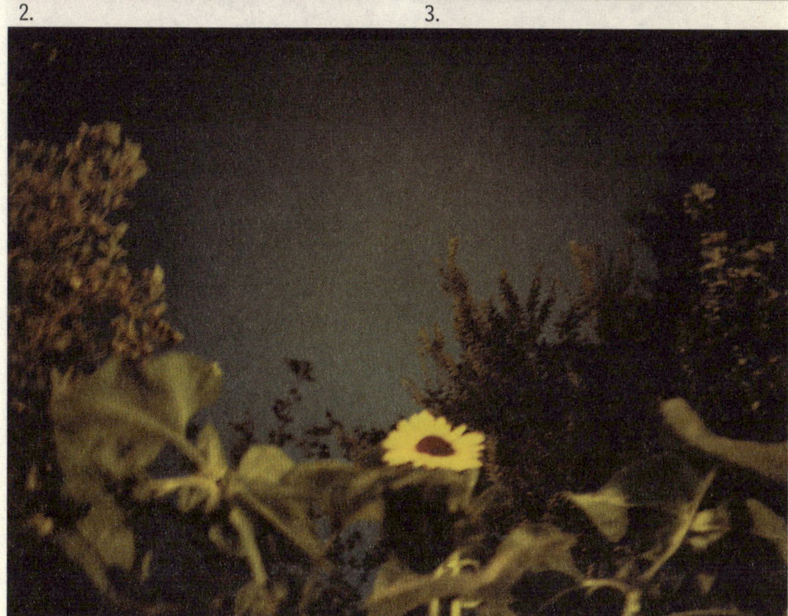
5.

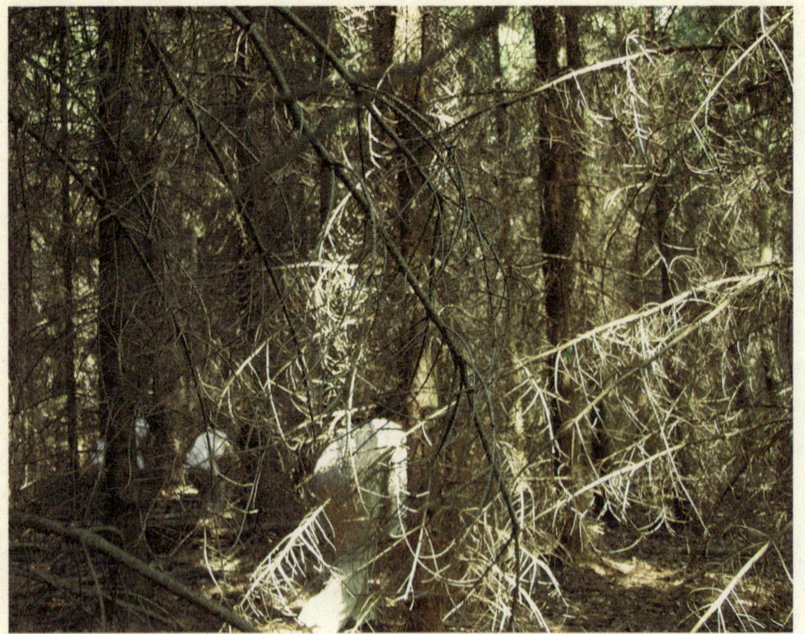

1.

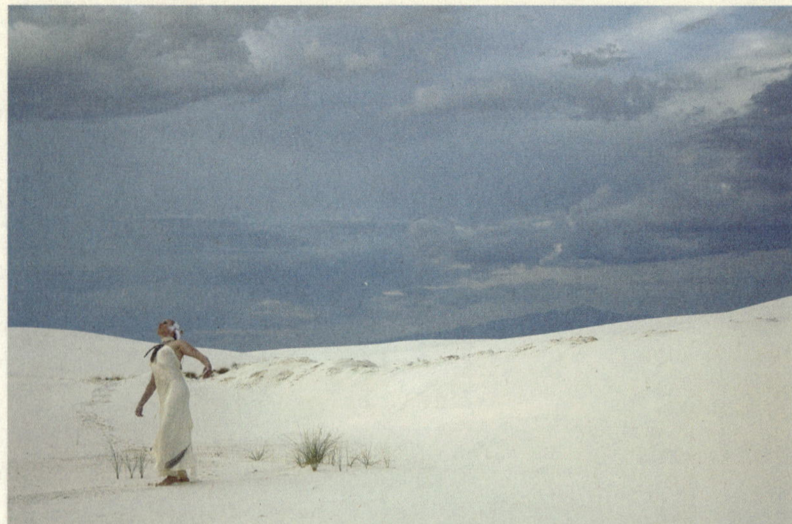

2.

Mariam Ghani earned her BA in comparative literature from New York University and her MFA in photography, video, and related media from the School of Visual Arts. She is an artist, writer, and community organizer based in Brooklyn. Works include video, installation, new media, photography, performance, and public dialogue, such as the interactive documentary **Kabul: Reconstructions** (2003-present), which explores the city at one-year intervals in the aftermath of political and military conflict.

1. **Fugitive Refrains III**
with Erin Ellen Kelly
from the video **Fugitive Refrains**
2006-07, chromogenic print,
16 × 20 in (41 × 51 cm)

2. **Pioneer #1**
with Erin Ellen Kelly
from the video **Western Myths**
2008, chromogenic print,
20 × 30 in (51 × 76 cm)

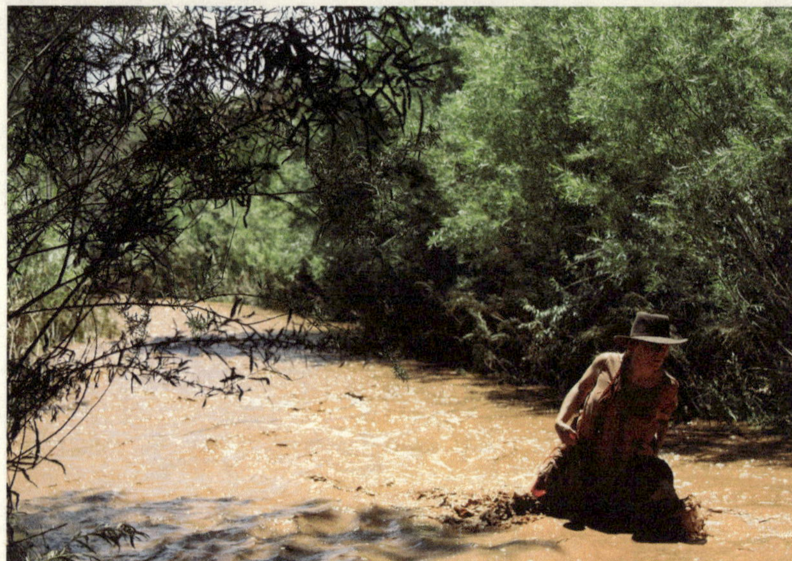

3.

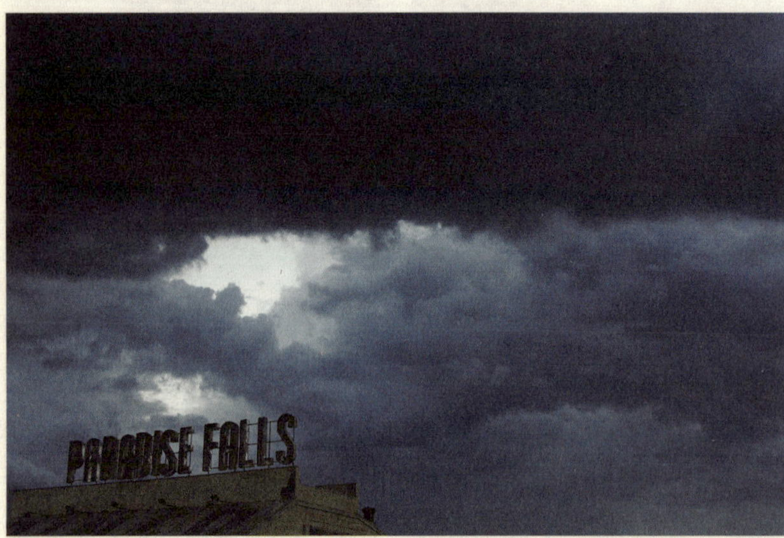

4.

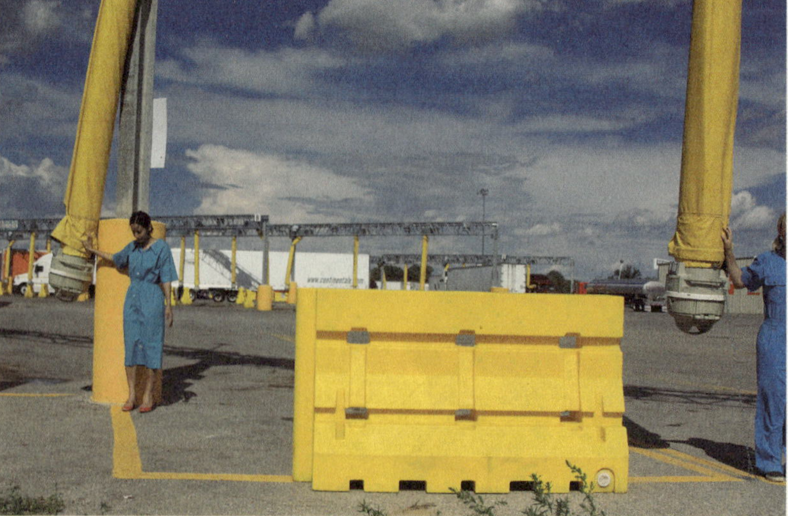

5.

3. **Pioneer #2**
with Erin Ellen Kelly
from the video **Western Myths**
2008, chromogenic print,
20 × 30 in (51 × 76 cm)

4. **Paradise Falls #1**
with Erin Ellen Kelly
from the video **Western Myths**
2008, chromogenic print,
20 × 30 in (51 × 76 cm)

5. **Route 66 #1**
with Erin Ellen Kelly
from the video **Western Myths**
2008, chromogenic print,
20 × 30 in (51 × 76 cm)

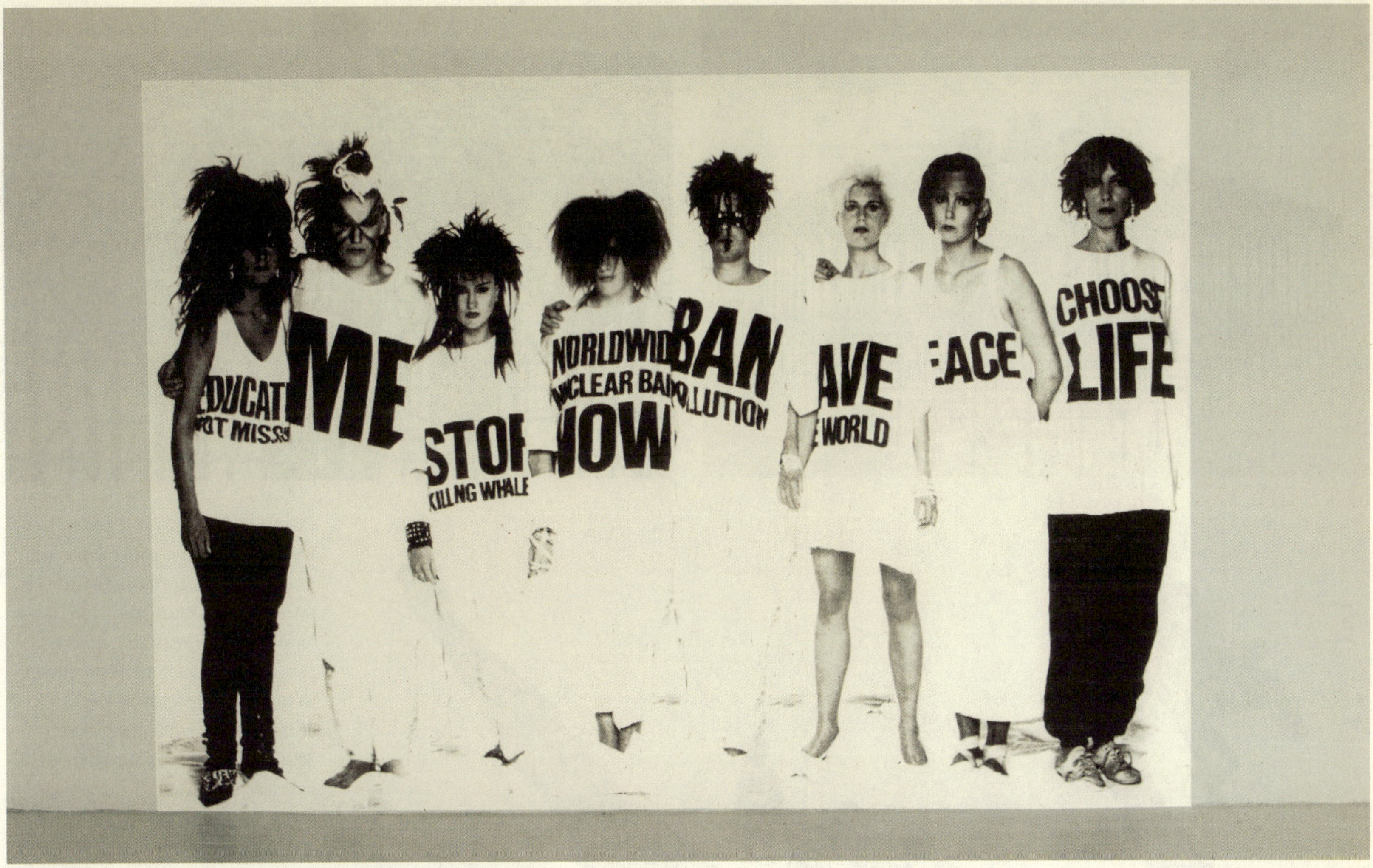

1.

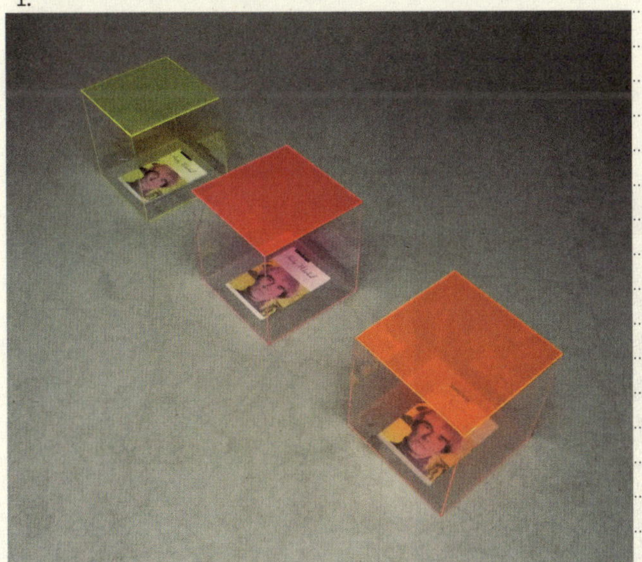

2.

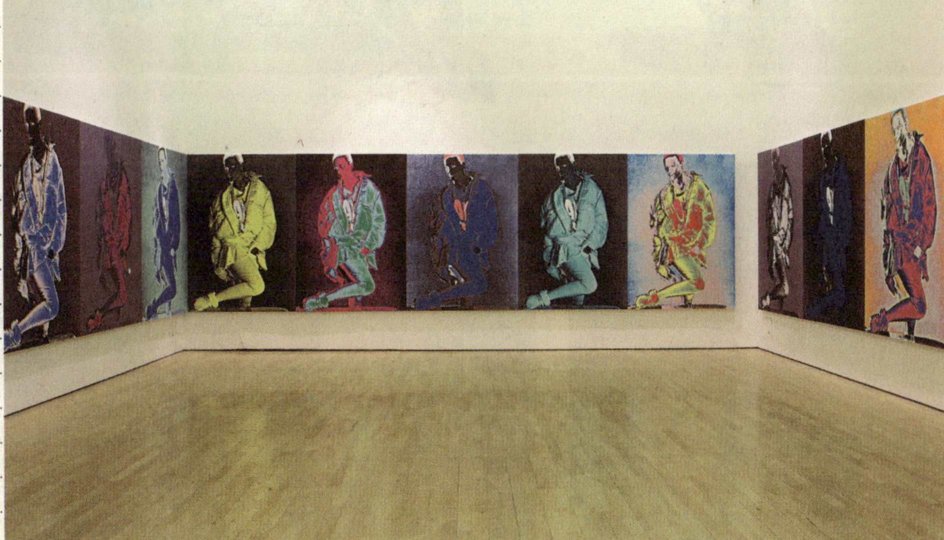

3.

Babak Ghazi earned his MA from Chelsea College of Art and Design in London, where he lives. He draws on cultural icons of the 1980s – music, fashion, and advertising – to examine the production of meaning in consumer society. Informed by Pop art's simultaneous affirmation and critique of such material, in one case he makes direct reference to Andy Warhol's painting series Shadows with **Model** (2008), Ghazi's repeated image of a posing fashion model.

1. **Katherine Hamnett 1983**
2008, billboard posters, 80 × 120 in (203 × 305 cm)

2. **Andy Warhol In His Own Words**
2008, Perspex and books, each cube $12\frac{1}{2} \times 12\frac{1}{2} \times 12\frac{1}{2}$ in (32 × 32 × 32 cm)

3. **Model**
2008, digital prints on canvas, dimensions variable

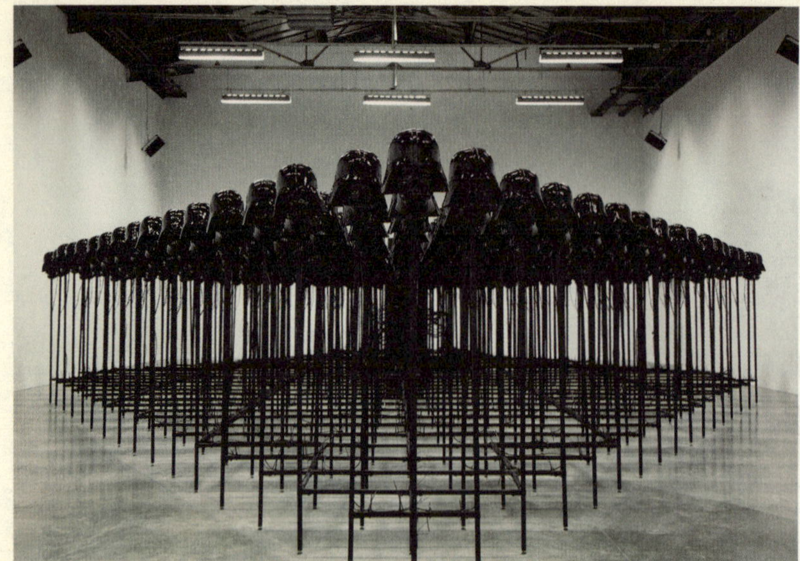

1.

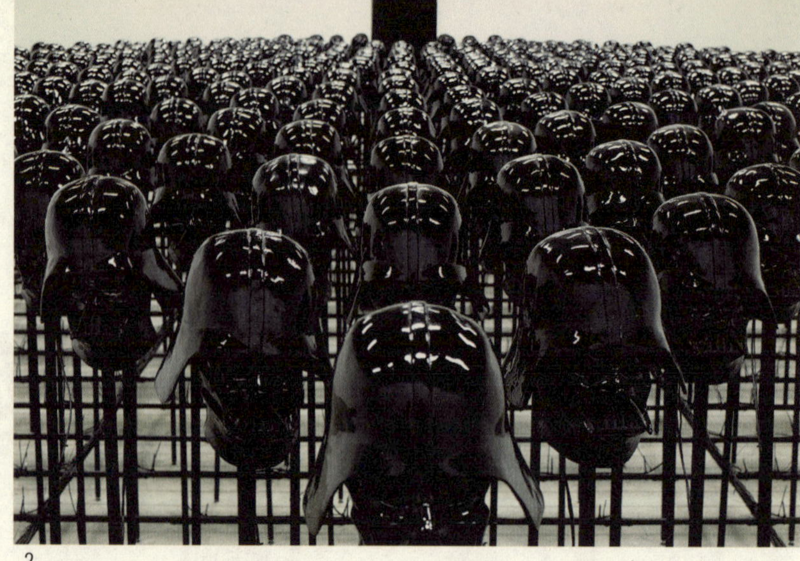

2.

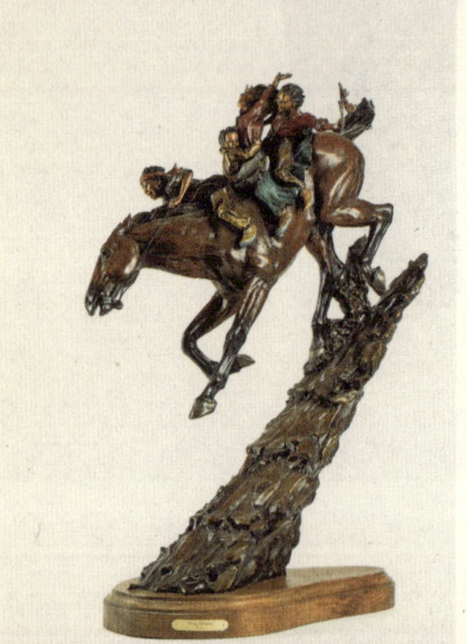

3.

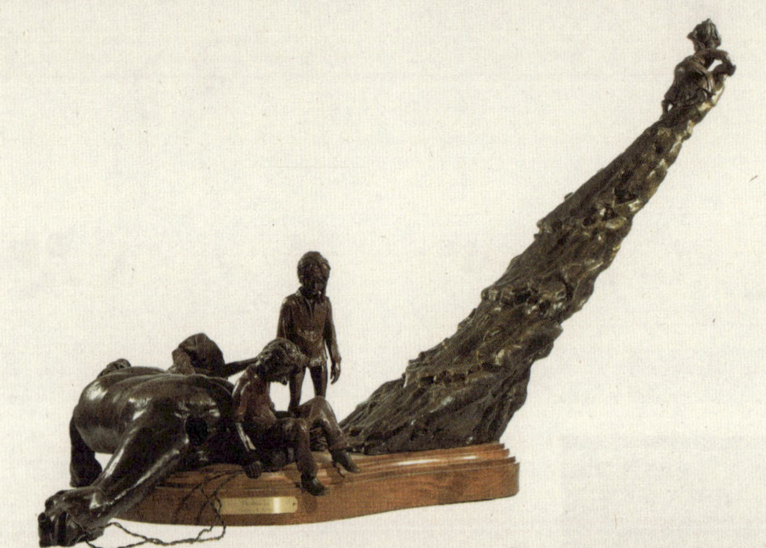

4.

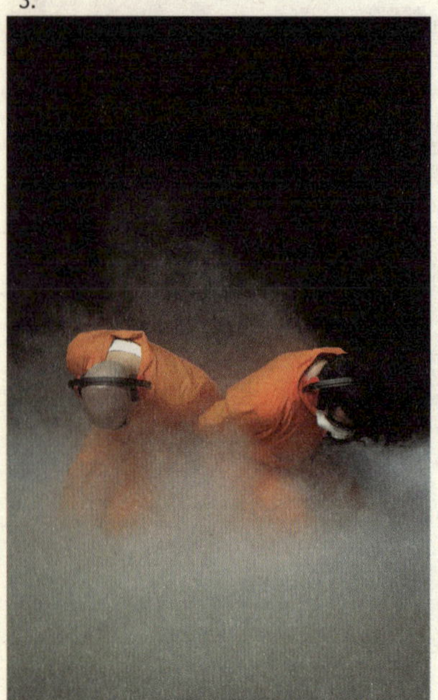

5.

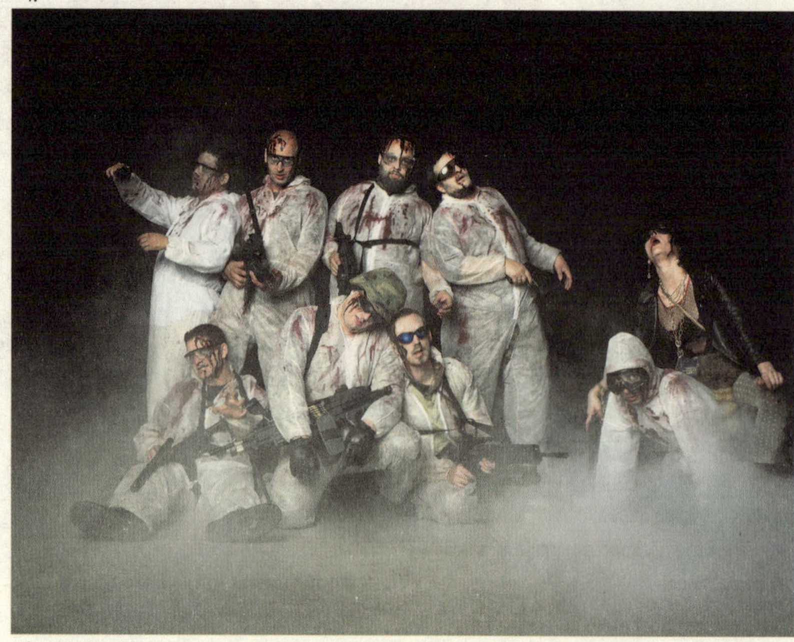

6.

Fabien Giraud and Raphael Siboni currently live in Paris and have been collaborating since 2007. They are interested in belief systems around which human subcultures form – from Star Wars enthusiasts to punk rock devotees. **Last Manoeuvres in the Dark**, shown at the Palais de Tokyo, Paris, in 2008, consisted of 300 Darth Vader masks aligned in military formation, programmed by a computer server to compose and play the ultimate song of the Dark Side.

1 & 2. **Last Manoeuvres in the Dark**
2008, terra-cotta, black enamel, steel, and artificial intelligence, dimensions variable

3. **The Abduction**
2008, bronze sculpture after Ed Natiya's Abduction

4. **The Abduction**
2008, bronze sculpture by Ed Natiya before abduction

5. **Friendly Fire, Guantanamo Team**
2007, video, 13 min; chromogenic print, 39 ½ × 31 ½ in (100 × 80 cm)

6. **Friendly Fire, Zombie Team**
2007, video, 13 min; chromogenic print, 31 ½ × 39 ½ in (80 × 100 cm)

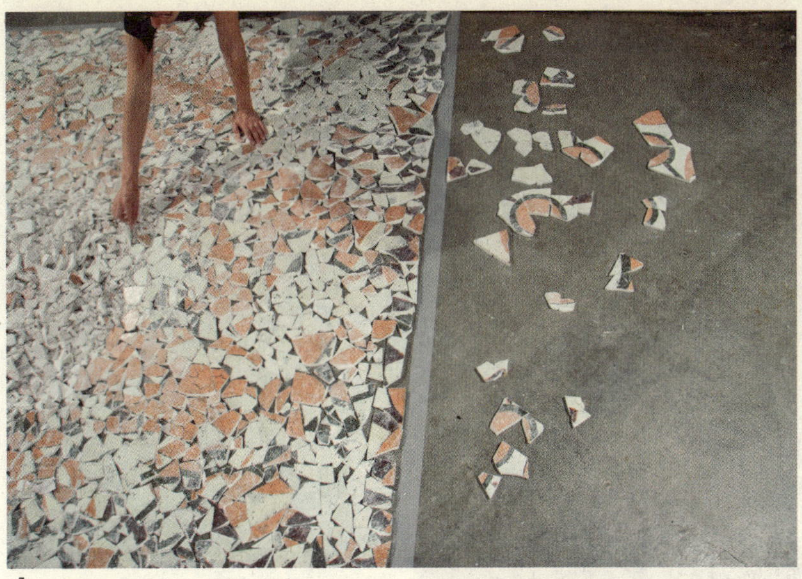

1.

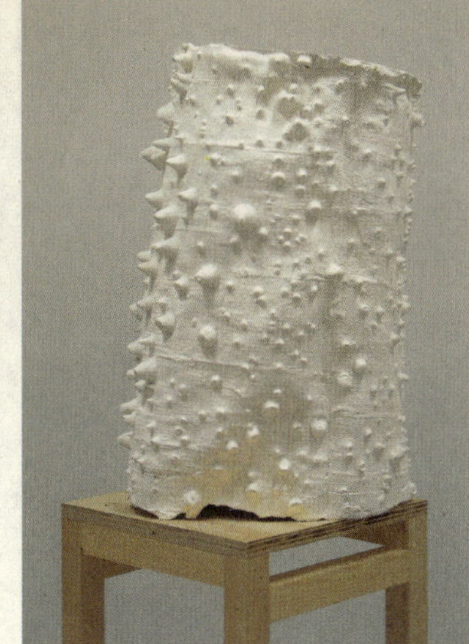

2.

Los Angeles–based Liz Glynn earned her BA in visual and environmental studies from Harvard and her MFA in art and integrated media from CalArts in Los Angeles. Her participatory performance works include **The 24 Hour Roman Reconstruction Project, or Building Rome in a Day** (2008), in which she led a group of volunteers in a re-creation of the architectural history of the ancient capital, from 753 BC to its sacking in AD 410.

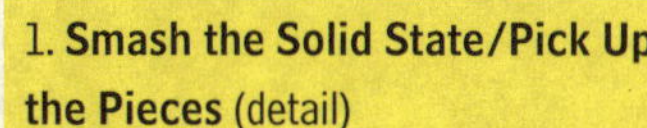

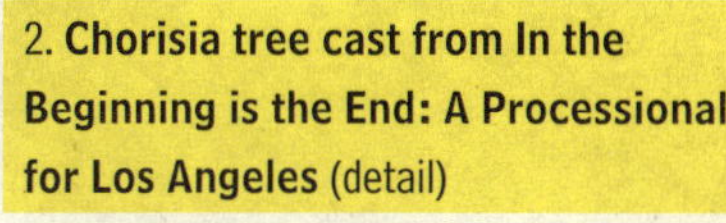

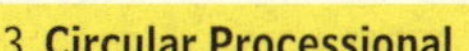

3.

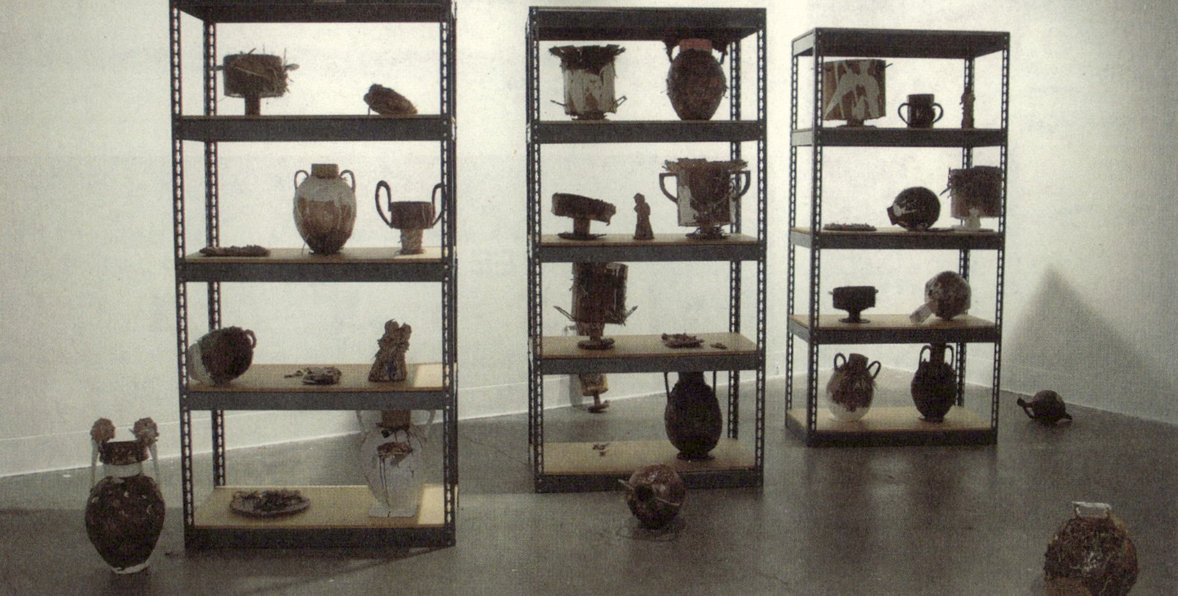

4.

1. Smash the Solid State/Pick Up the Pieces (detail)
2008, cast plaster floor, 120 × 120 in (305 × 305 cm), production photograph

2. Chorisia tree cast from In the Beginning is the End: A Processional for Los Angeles (detail)
2008, cast plaster, linen banners, botanical matter, California surrogates, and wood, overall installation approx 72 × 96 × 96 in (183 × 244 × 244 cm)

3. Circular Processional
2008, 6 of 20 color slides, projection 48 × 72 in (122 × 183 cm)

4 & 5. California Surrogates for the Getty
2008, California yard waste, trash, plaster, and Victory wax, overall installation approx 72 × 132 × 48 in (183 × 335 × 122 cm)

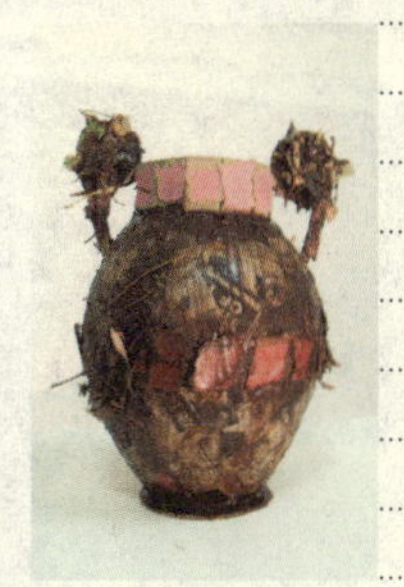

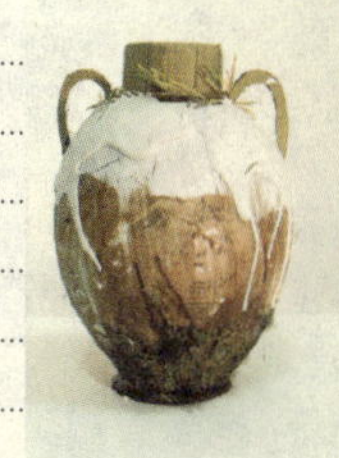

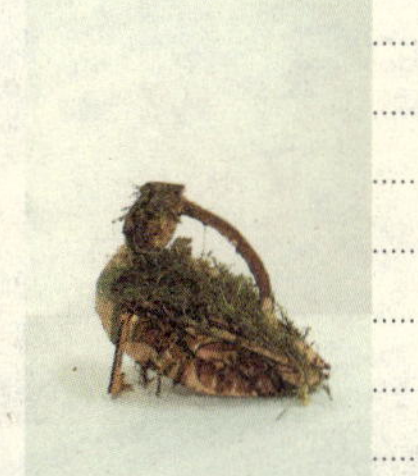

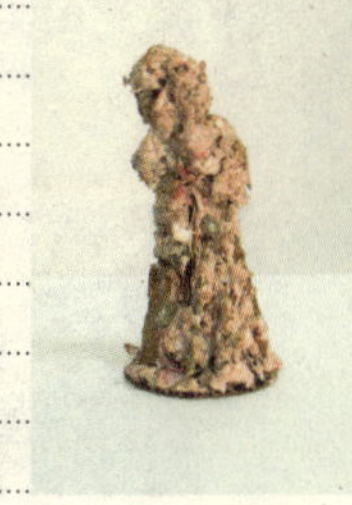

5.

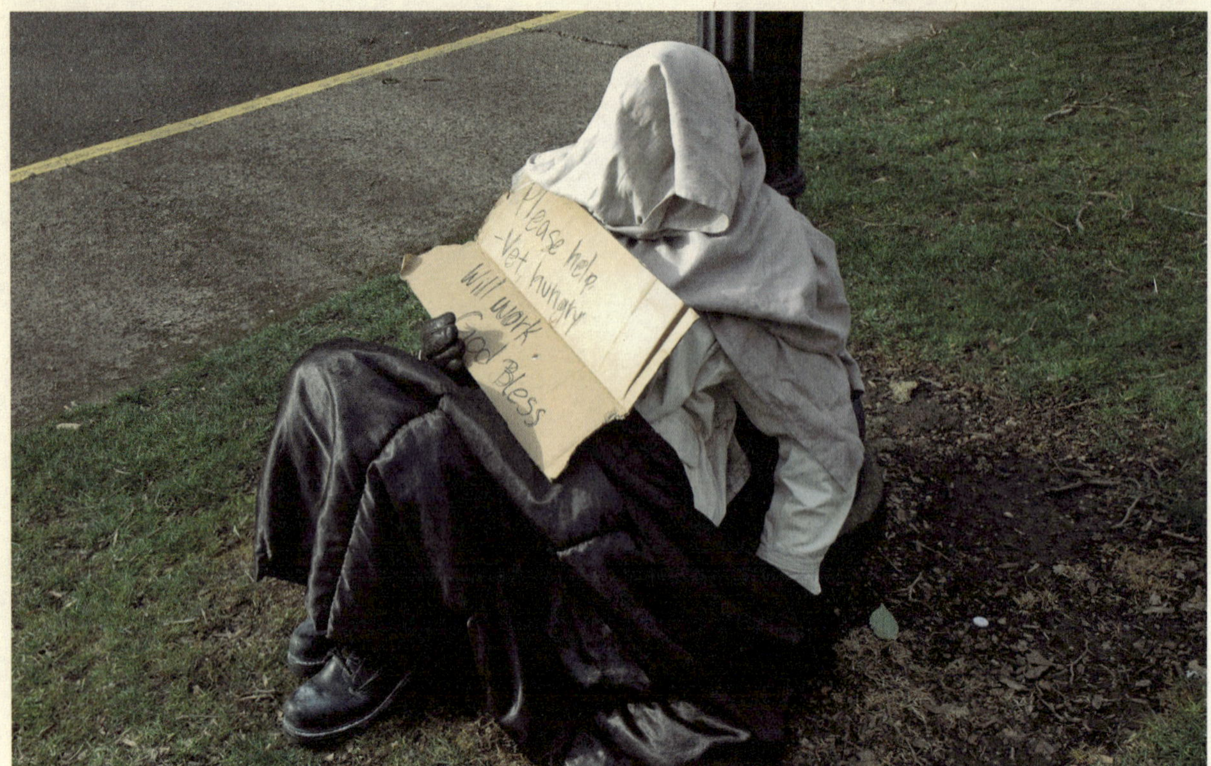

1.

Goldbricker Society is a collective "dedicated to addressing the contradiction inherent in the American dream." Bradford Duffy, Pepper Fajans, Stevie Foner, and Hans Maharawal joined forces at Sarah Lawrence College and are currently based in the Bronx, New York. Their methods are propaganda, performance, and protest, including signs, T-shirts, public installations, and collaborations with other artists and community members.

1. **Pedro of the Unentitled**
2006, mixed media, dimensions variable

2. **Goldbricks 2006!**
2006, plaster, paint, insulation, asphalt, wood, tar, and utility trailer, 8 × 12 × 7 ½ ft (244 × 366 × 229 cm)

3. **Righteous Kill**
2008, screenprint and adhesive on paper, 24 × 24 in (61 × 61 cm)

4. **Free Love Now**
2006, screenprint and adhesive on paper, 48 × 108 in (122 × 274 cm)

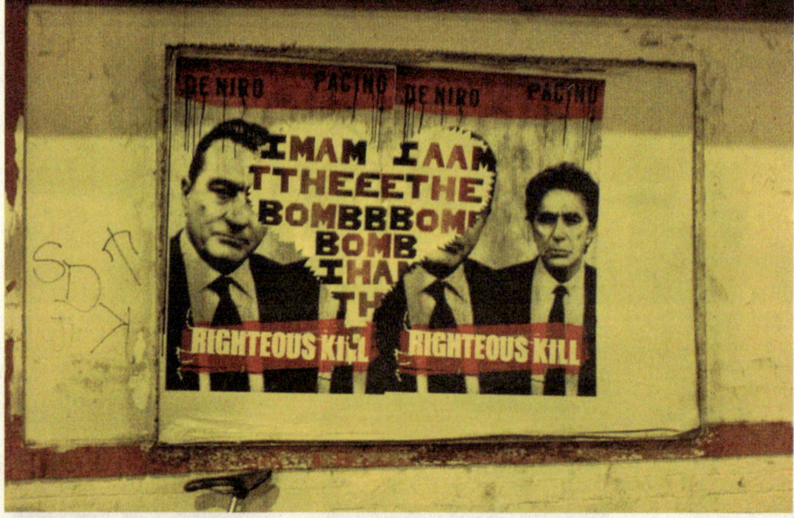

3.

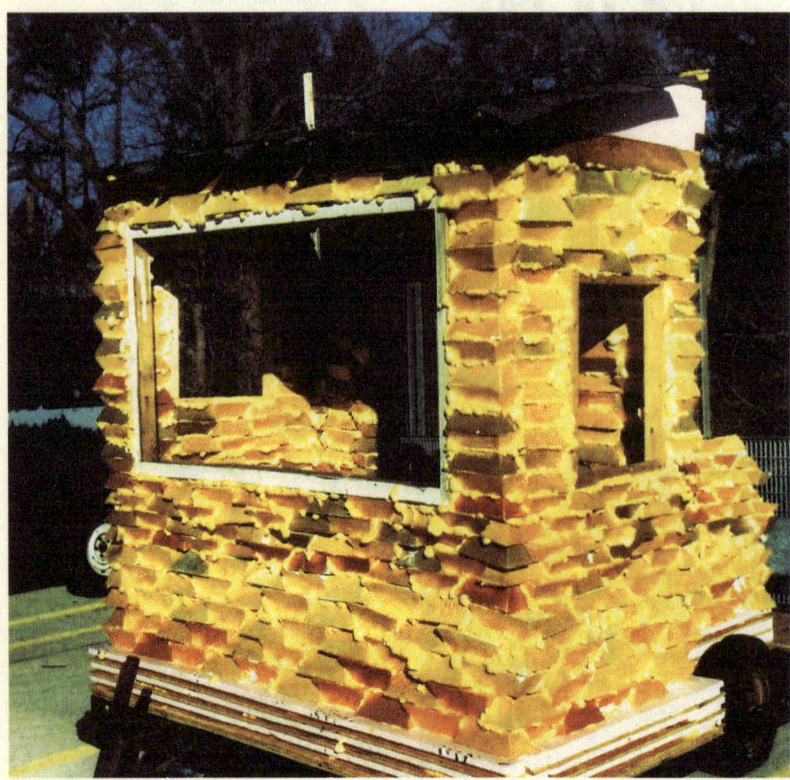

2.

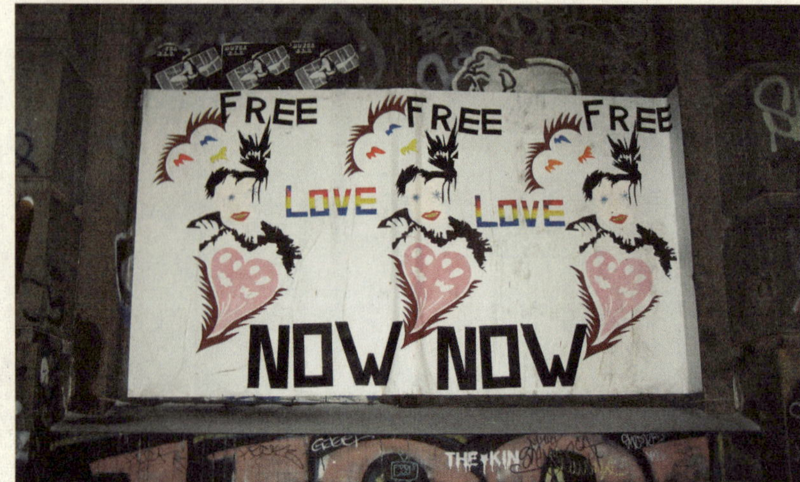

4.

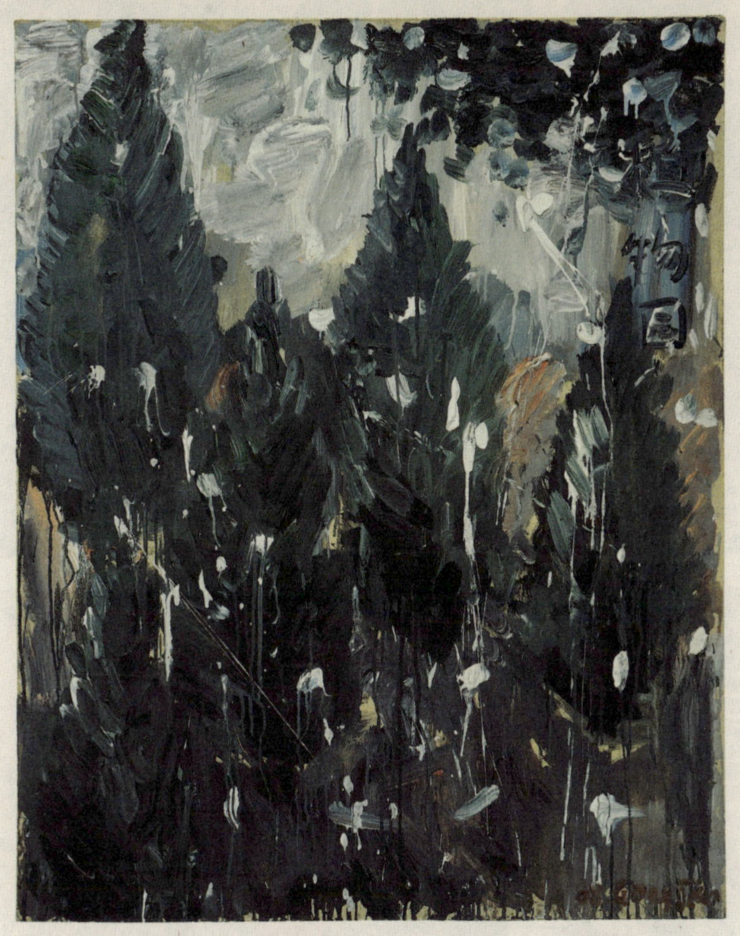

1.

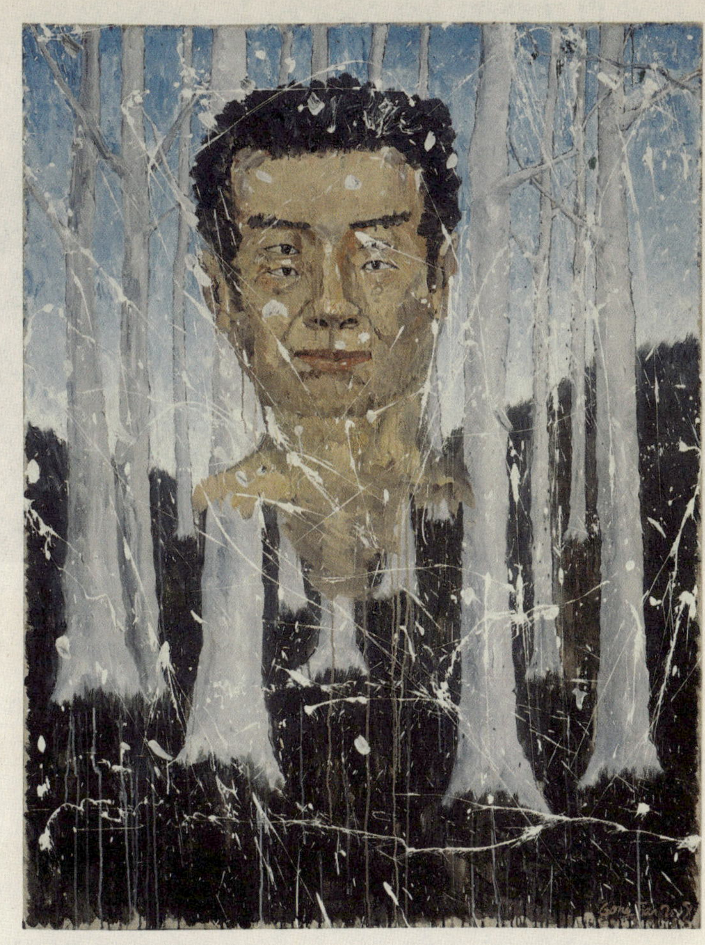

2.

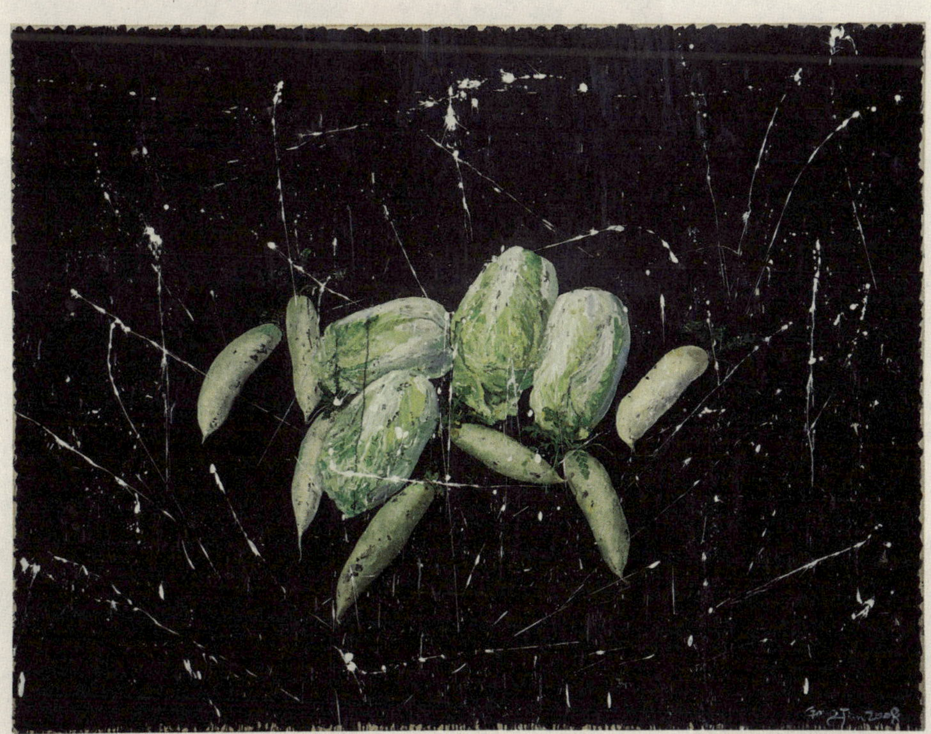

3.

Gong Jian graduated from the Institute of Fine Art in Hubei, China, where he continues to live and work. In his paintings, installations, and works in other media, he experiments with perceived degrees of authenticity by playing with the relationship between style and content.

1. Arboretum
2008, acrylic on canvas, 47 1/4 × 38 1/4 in (120 × 97 cm)

2. Dizzy No.3
2008, acrylic on canvas, 67 × 51 1/4 in (170 × 130 cm)

3. Cabbage and turnip
2008, acrylic on canvas, 65 × 87 in (165 × 220 cm)

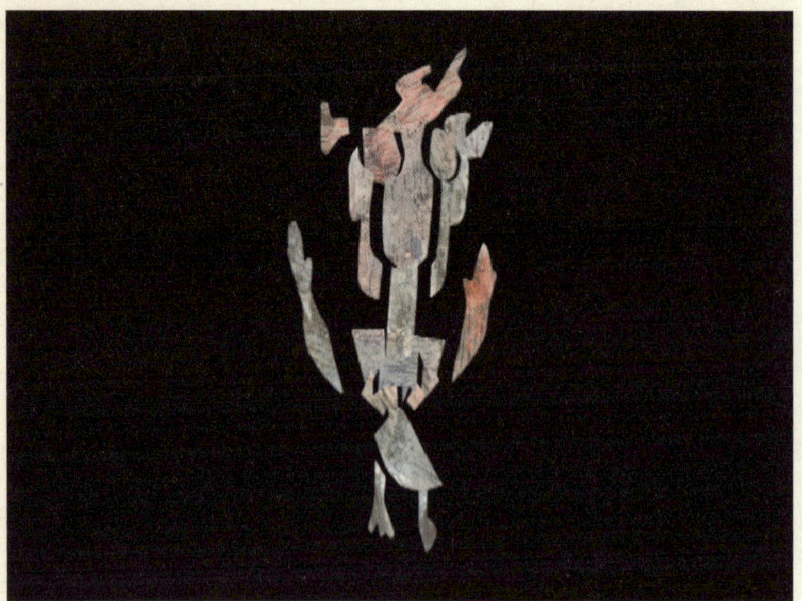

1.

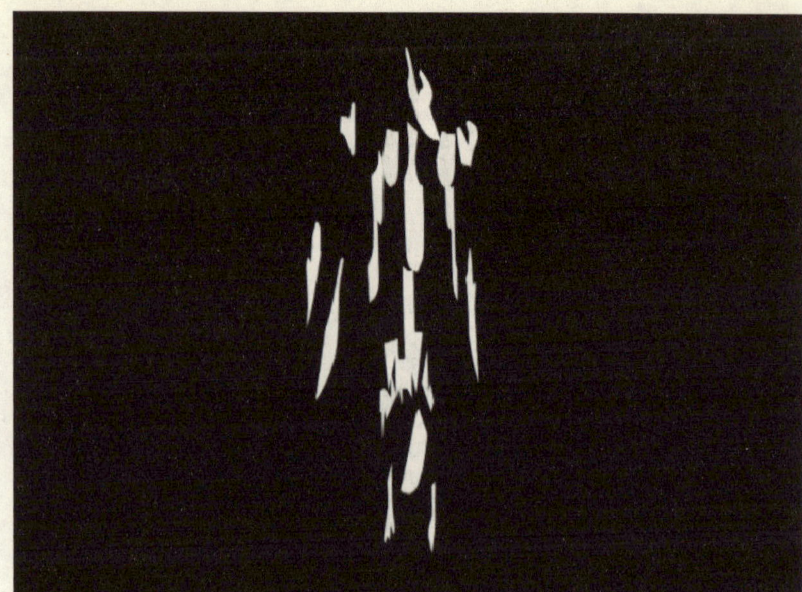

2.

Julia Gouin studied fine arts at La Sorbonne in Paris and Chelsea College and Goldsmiths College in London. Using a variety of media, she explores the way her identity and her work interact through malleable, organic processes. In 2007 she won the Graham Thomas Fine Art Award, and in 2008 she participated in a group show at Galeria 13, Mexico.

1 & 2. **Untitled (janusing the Aangelus Nnovus)**
2008, animation

3 & 4. **Untitled (medivalmedieval)**
2008, video

5. **Untitled (medieval)**
2008, video

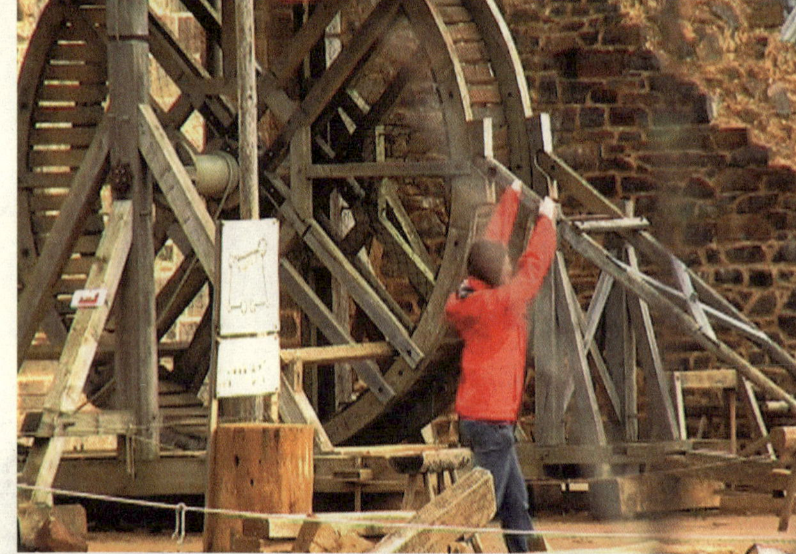

3.

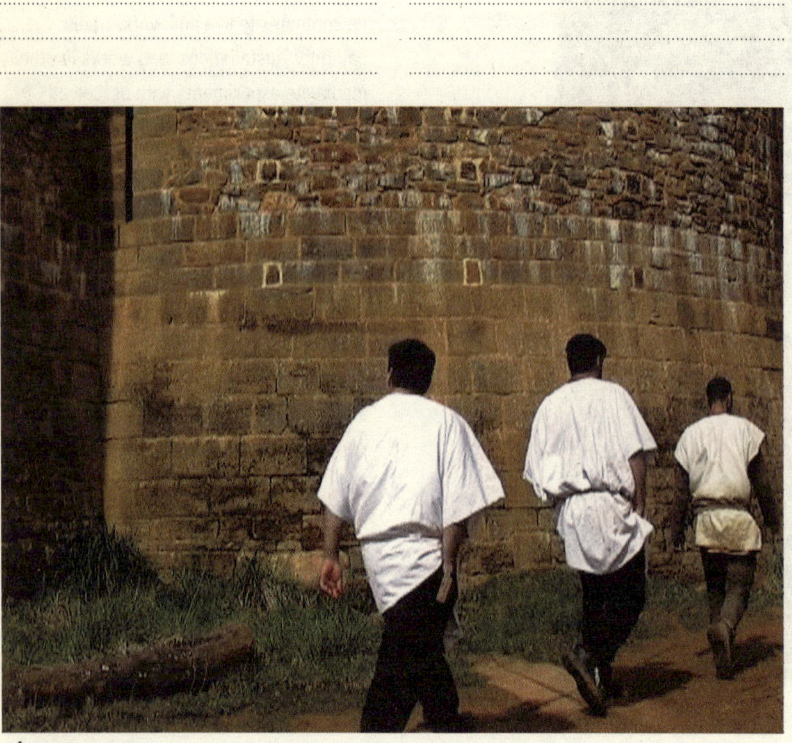

4.

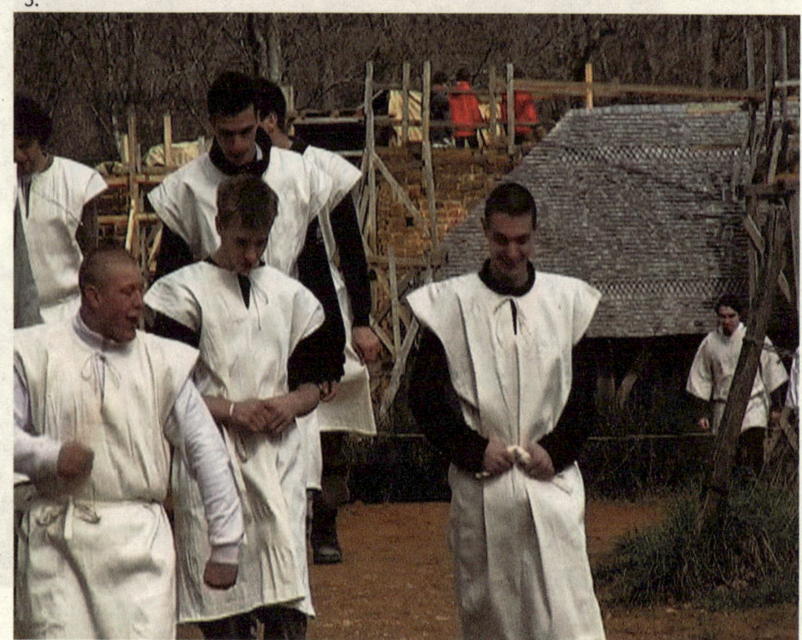

5.

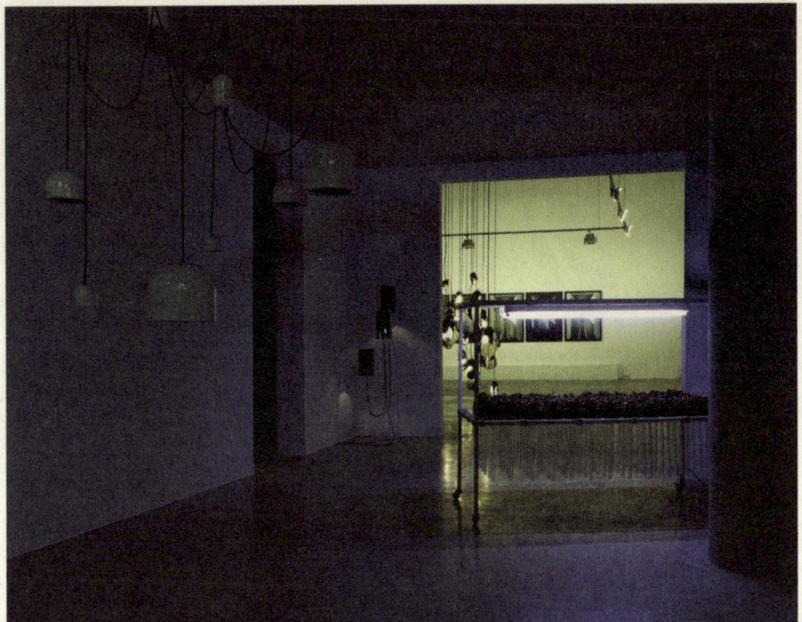
1.

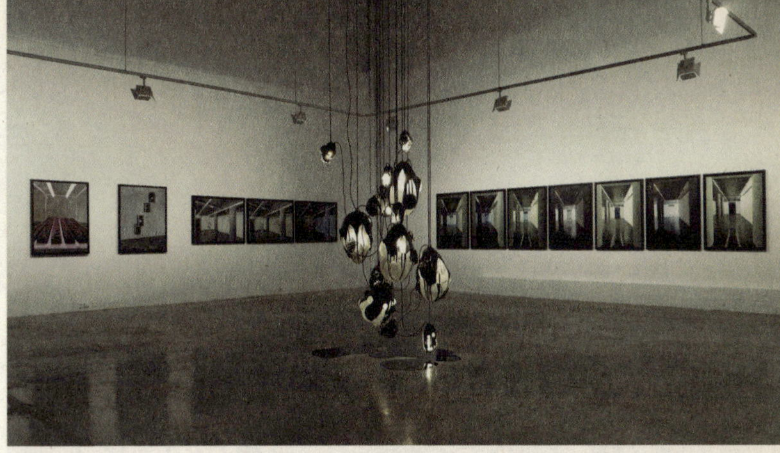
5.

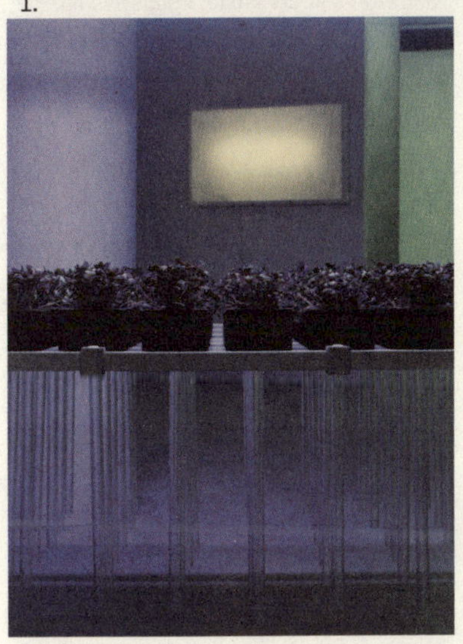
2.

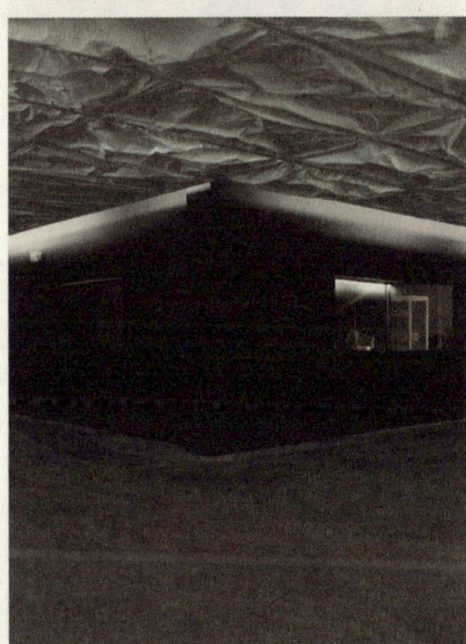
3.

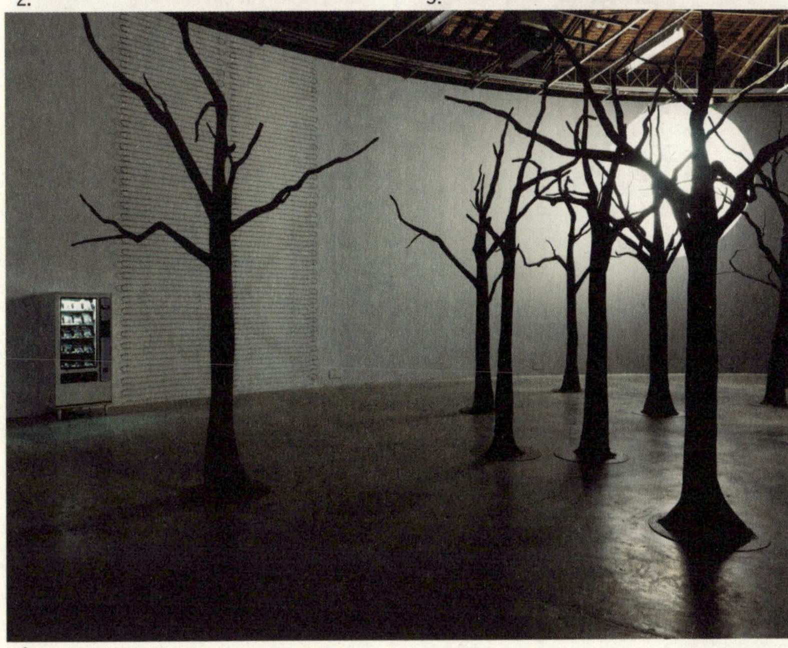
4.

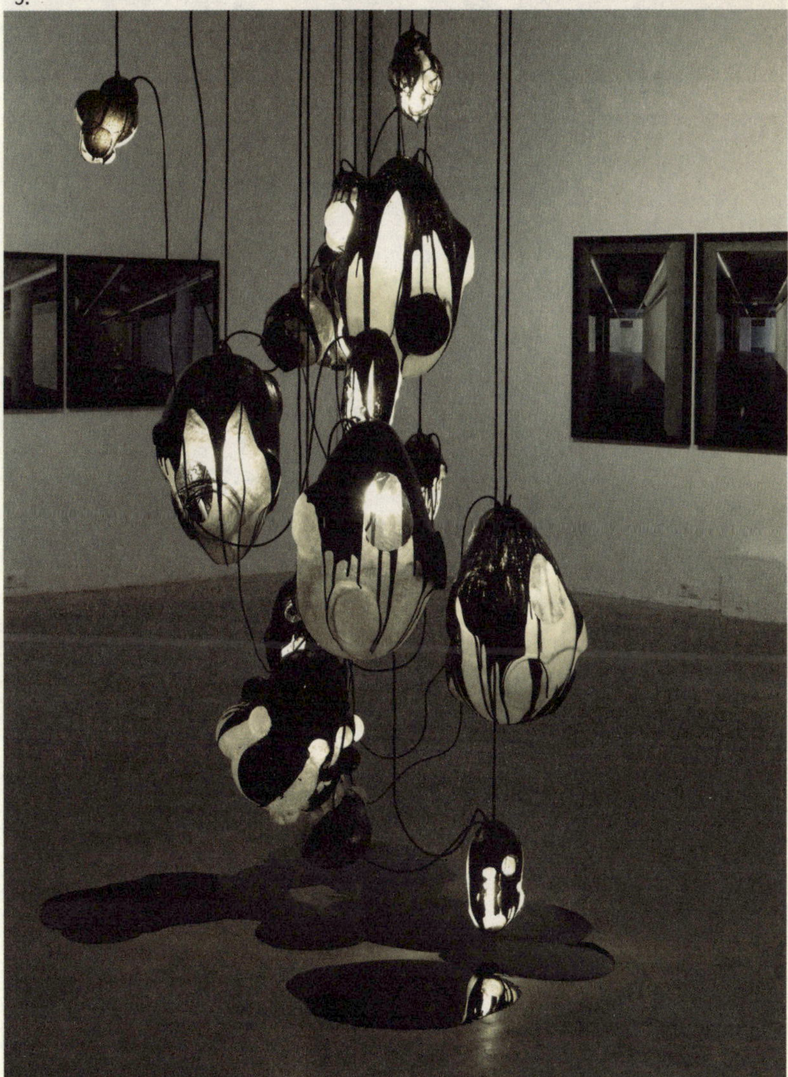
6.

Loris Gréaud was expelled from a music conservatory at age fourteen for forming his own studio of "musical unlearning." He currently lives in Paris and Ho Chi Minh City. His exhibition "Cellar Door" (2008), a "paradise of conceptual art" filling the entire Palais de Tokyo and extending outward, included edible candies with no flavor, tree sculptures coated in gunpowder, and plastic bottles releasing the imagined smell of Mars.

1-6. "Cellar Door" exhibition views at Palais de Tokyo, Paris (2008)

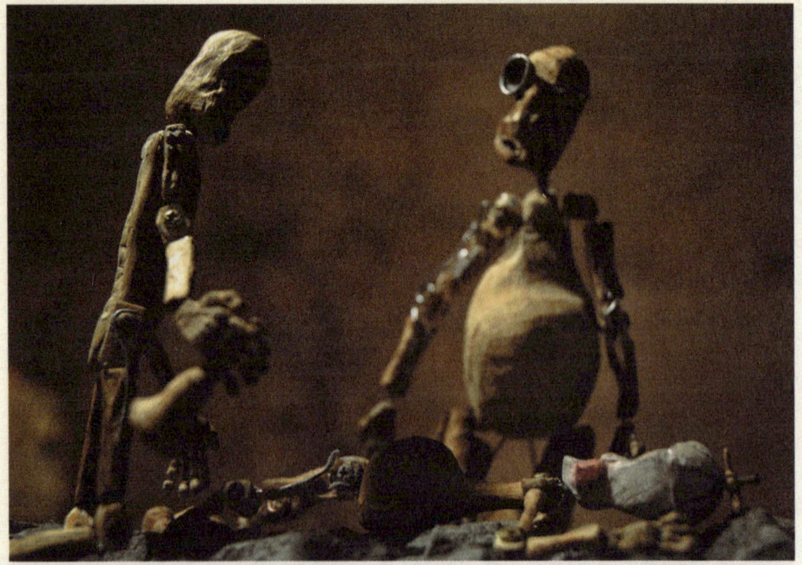
1.

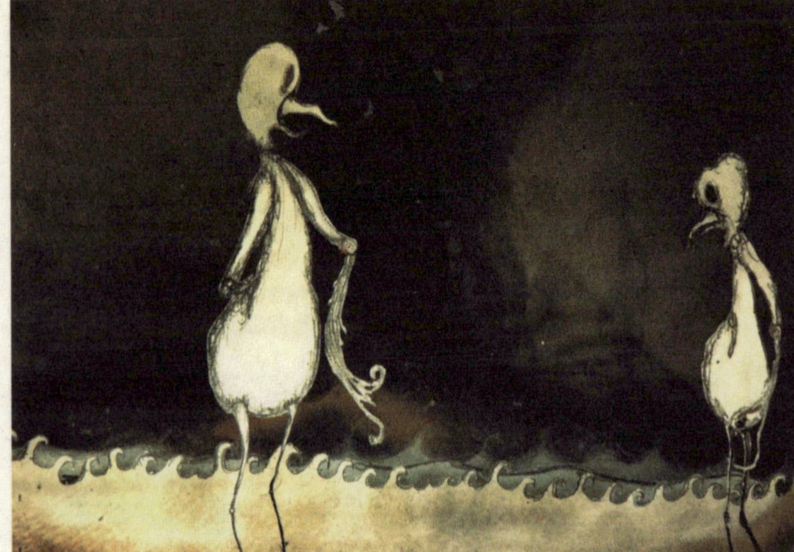
2.

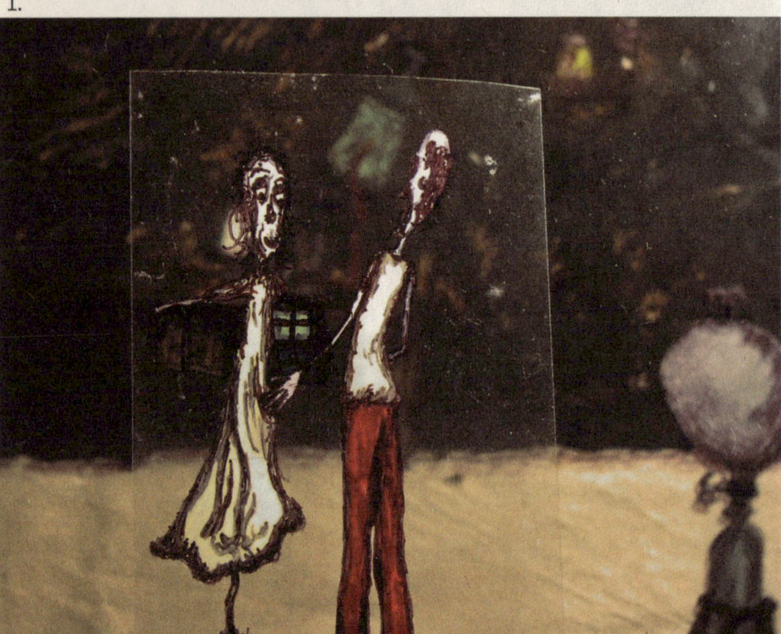
3.

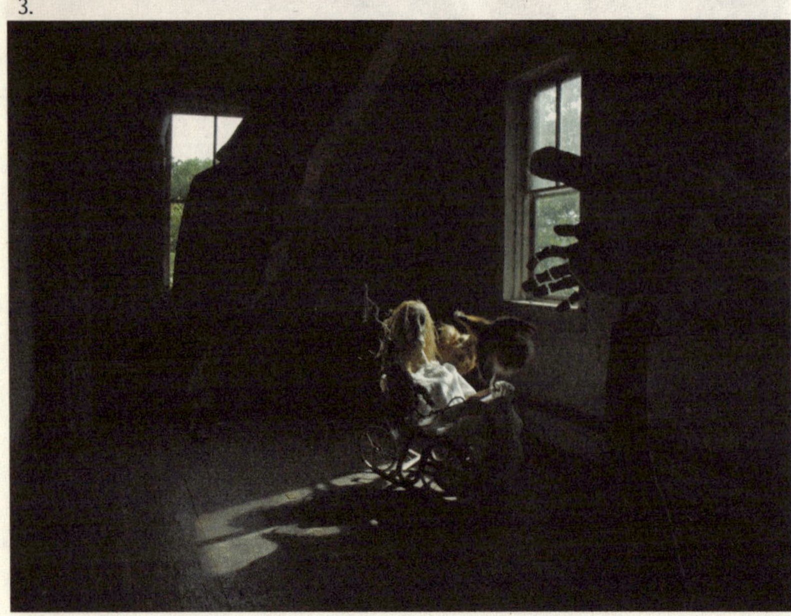
4.

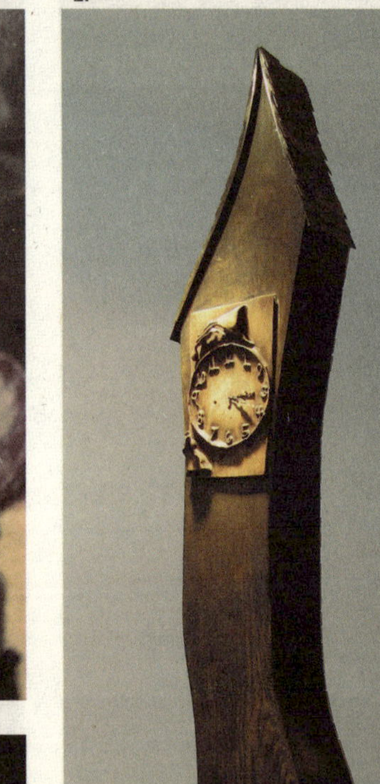
5.

Self-taught animator Brent Green lives and works in Cressona, Pennsylvania. His films include stop-motion using carved wooden figures, small sculptures, found props, drawings, and exposed Scotch tape. They are often shown with live narration by Green and music played by well-known indie-rock musicians. **Paulina Hollers** (2006) tells the story of a pious mother who follows her disturbed son to hell.

1. **Paulina Hollers**
2006, animation with Sharpie marker on glass, 20 min

2. **Walt Whitman's Brain**
2007, paper cut-out animation, 3 min 30 sec

3. **Hadacol Christmas**
2005, animation with Sharpie marker on glass, 11 min 6 sec

4. **Carlin**
2006, video, 7 min 30 sec

5. **Grandfather Clock**
2006, hand-carved wood and metal clock, 114 × 14 × 9 in (290 × 36 × 23 cm); hand-drawn animated film, 43 sec

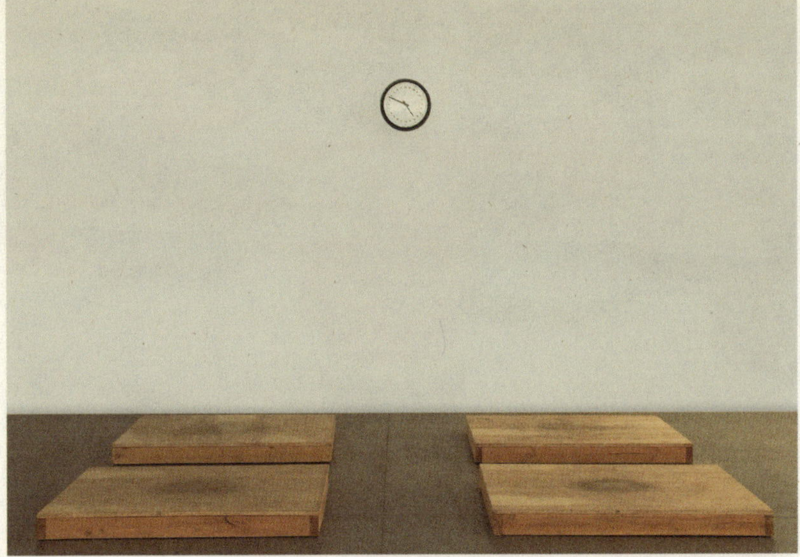

1.

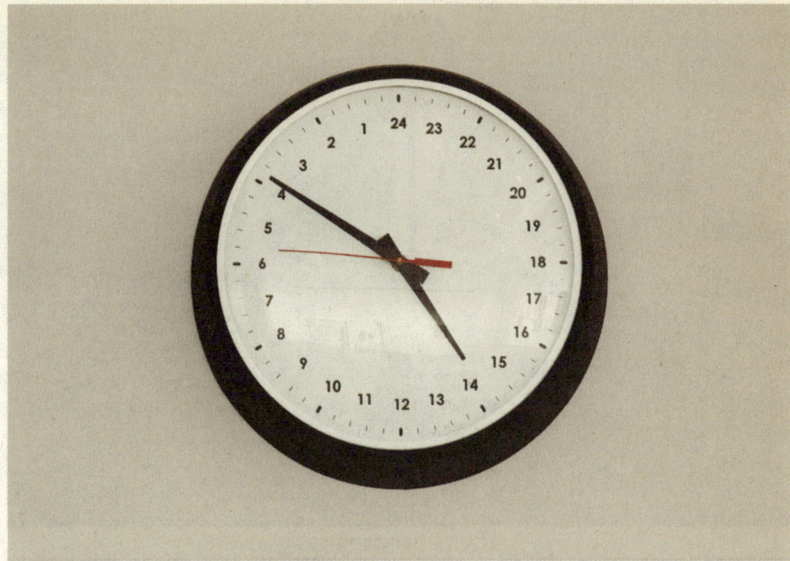

2.

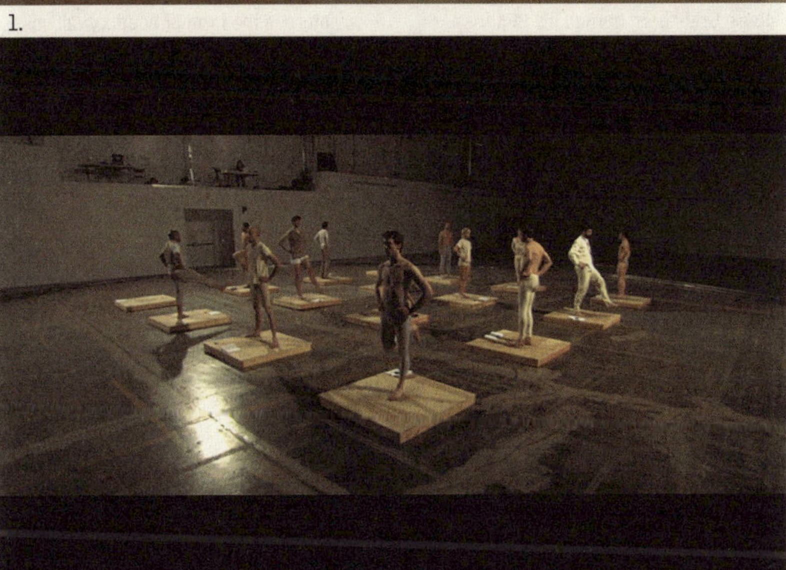

3.

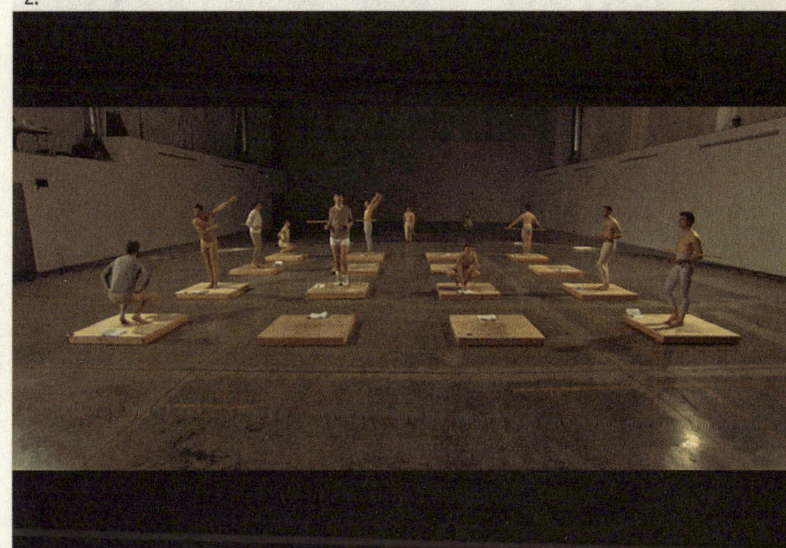

4.

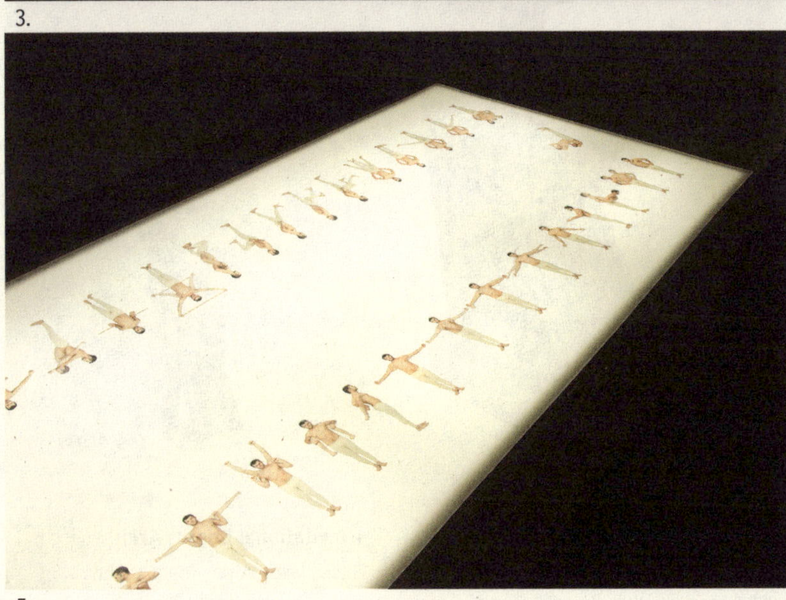

5.

Los Angeles–based artist Jesse Aron Green earned his BA from Harvard University in visual and environmental studies, and his MFA from UCLA in interdisciplinary studio art. His **Ärztliche Zimmergymnastik** (Medical Indoor Gymnastics, 2008) is an eighty-minute video of a performance using the 1855 book by German physican Daniel Gottlob Moritz Schreber as its score. Forty-five body exercises are performed in association with procedures and structures borrowed from high Conceptualism.

1 & 2. **The Future of My Nervous Illness (after Felix Gonzalez-Torres)**
2008, 24-hour backwards-motion clock, diameter 14 in (36 cm)

3 & 4. **Ärztliche Zimmergymnastik**
2008, video projection, 80 min

5. **Illustration and Description of the Medico-Gymnastic Exercises**
2008, pigment inkjet print on plywood lightbox table, 36 × 96 × 48 in (92 × 244 × 122 cm)

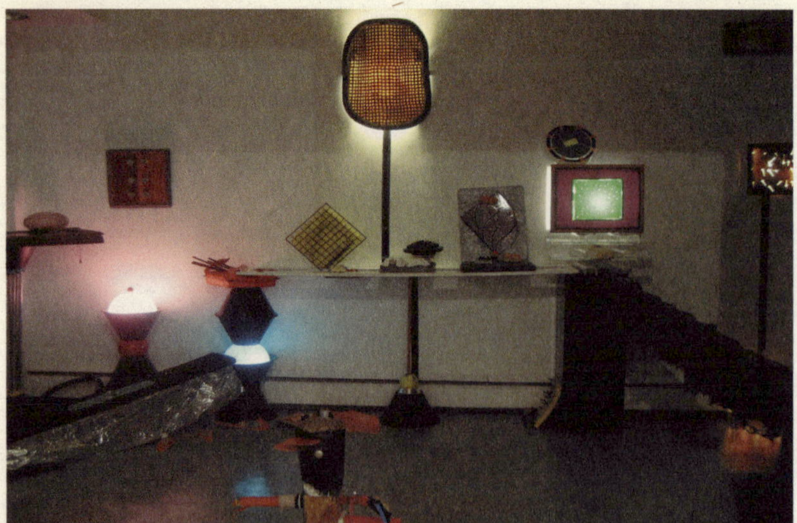

1.

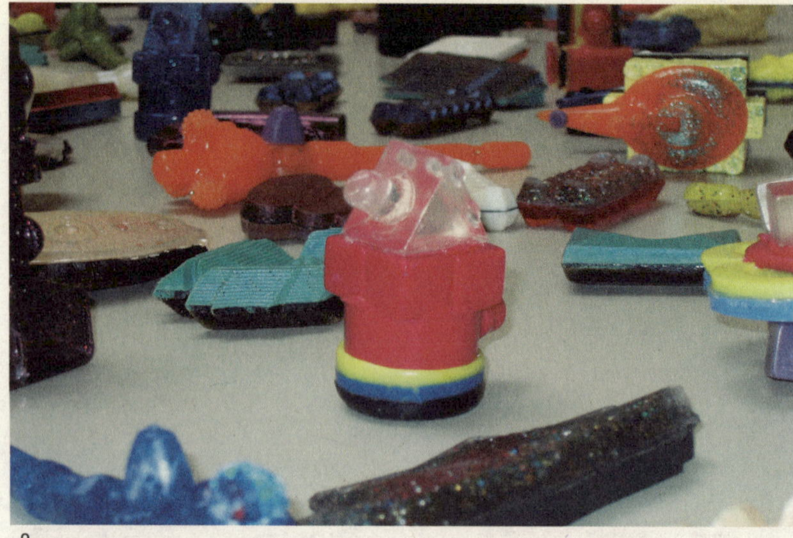

2.

Jesse Greenberg earned his BFA from the Rhode Island School of Design and currently lives in Philadelphia. Using material scavenged from the street or purchased for 10 cents per pound from scrap dealers, he creates interactive sculpture in the form of booths, wall units, and entire rooms. Each **MegaBinx** work becomes a stage on which viewers can act and be participants in what Greenberg calls "a completely plastic experience."

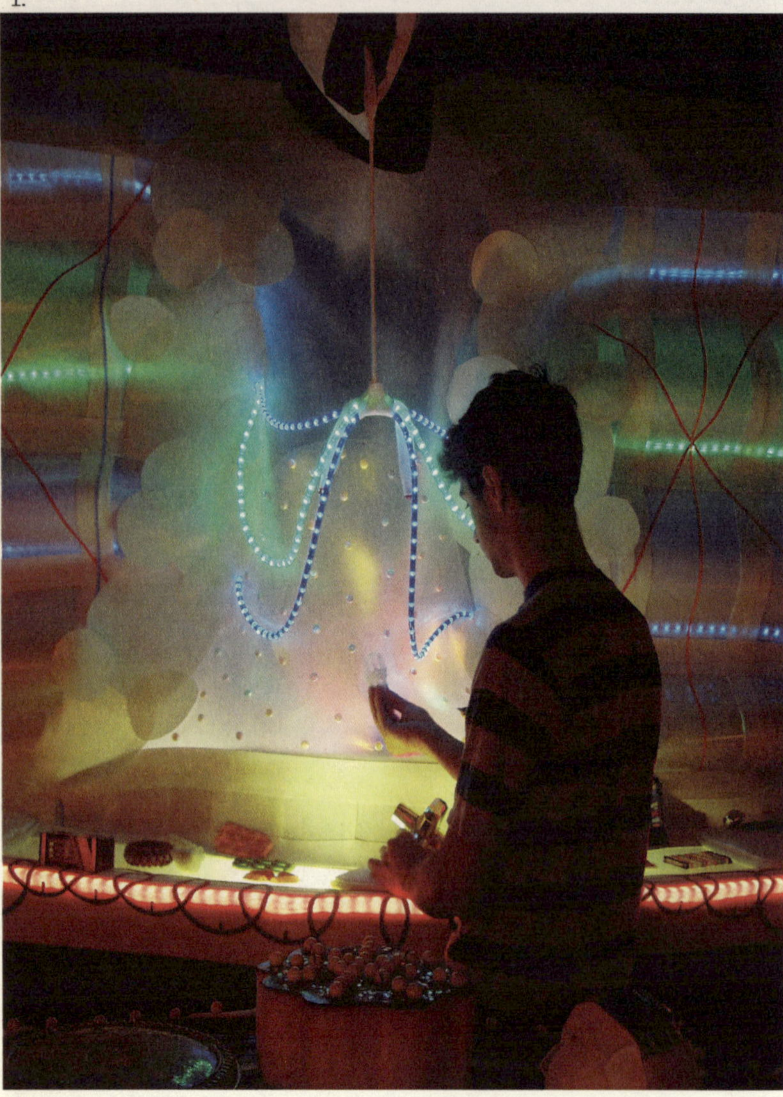

3.

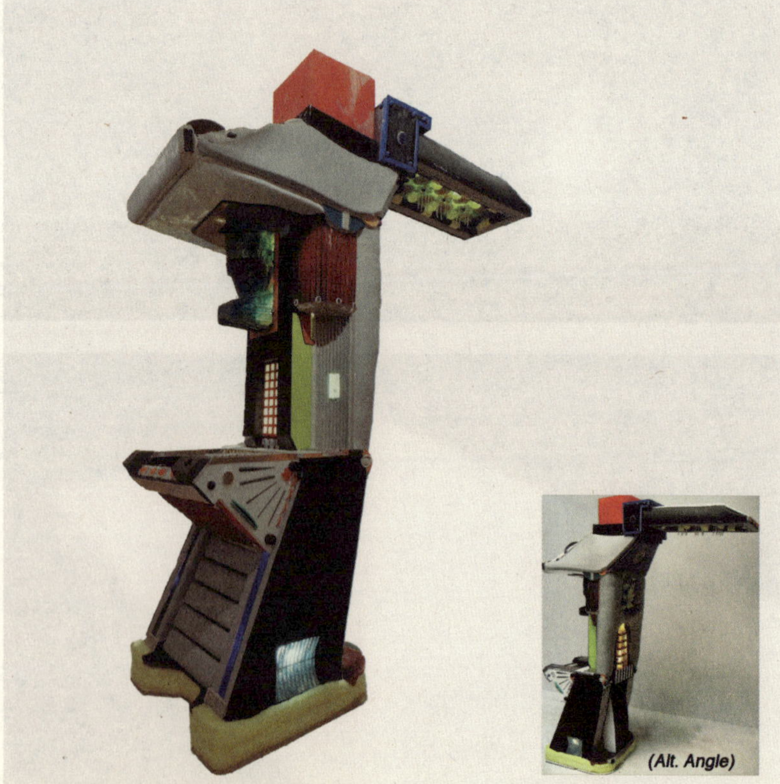

4.

1. Networked Bridge of Binx
2007, plastic, foam, rubber, Mylar, urethane, styrene, acrylic, Plexiglas, wood, fabric, enamel paint, aluminum, steel, flocking, and fluorescent illumination, 14 × 8 × 10 ft (427 × 244 × 305 cm)

2. Touchables and Hand Helds
from the series **MegaBinx**
2006, plastic, rubber, and foam, dimensions variable

3. MegaBinx 2 (Fully Interactive Environment) (detail)
2004, plastic, rubber, foam, fabric, wood, Plexiglas, glitter, metal, Mylar, video projections, performers, sound, and food, 700 sq ft (65 m^2)

4. Invitational Booth; Arch
2006, plastic, Mylar, foam, rubber, acrylic, urethane, silicon, electric lighting, vinyl, and fabric, 90 × 72 × 30 in (229 × 183 × 76 cm)

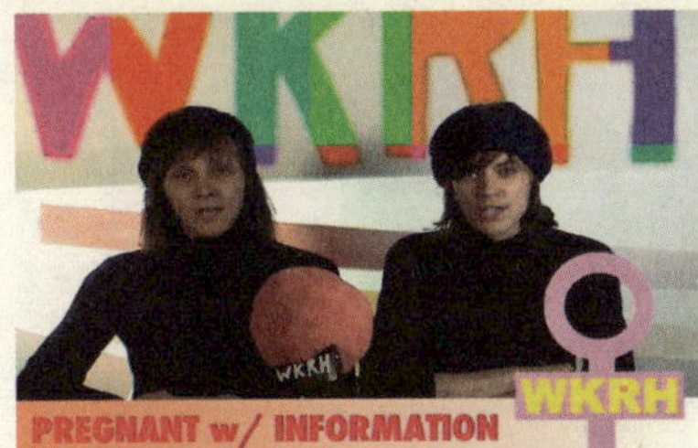

1.

Wynne Greenwood is a Seattle-based artist who completed the Whitney Independent Study Program and received an MFA from Bard in 2004. She first garnered attention with Tracy + the Plastics, a trio in which she played Tracy live as well as two instrumentalists/back-up singers who appear on video. The band broke up in 2006, but Greenwood's subsequent projects, video, sculpture, and photography have elaborated on its messy overlap of identities. Her work explores lesbian and feminist identity with a playful treatment of language that leaves wide gaps between tone and content.

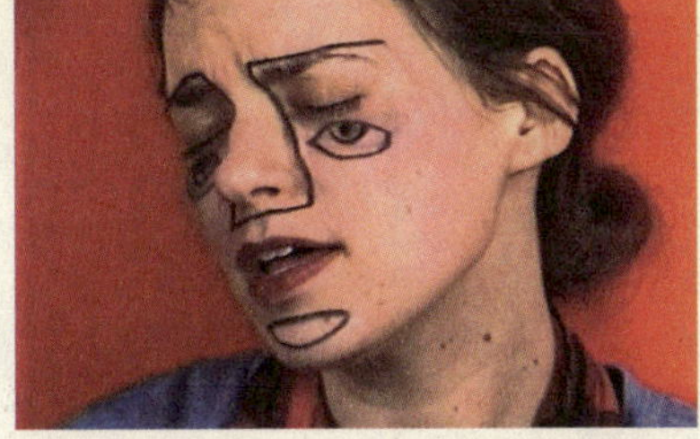

2.

1. New Report
2005, video, 12 min

2. Big Candy
2008, video, 3 min 5 sec

3. Other Looking (detail)
2006, chromogenic print mounted on black Sintra, 18 × 24 in (45 × 60 cm)

4. "Face It"
2008, exhibition view at Susanne Vielmetter Projects, Los Angeles

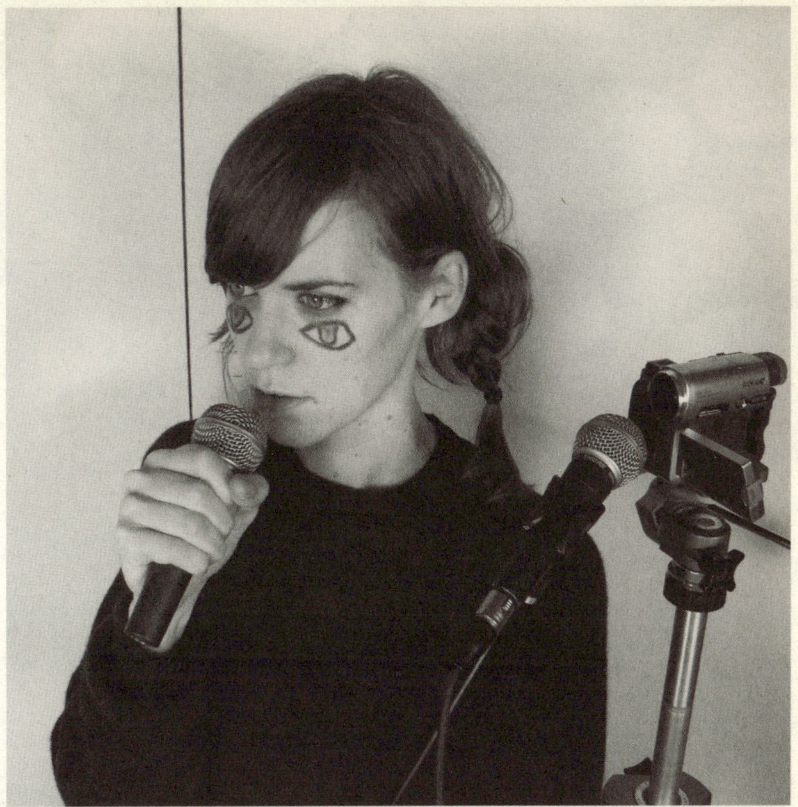

3.

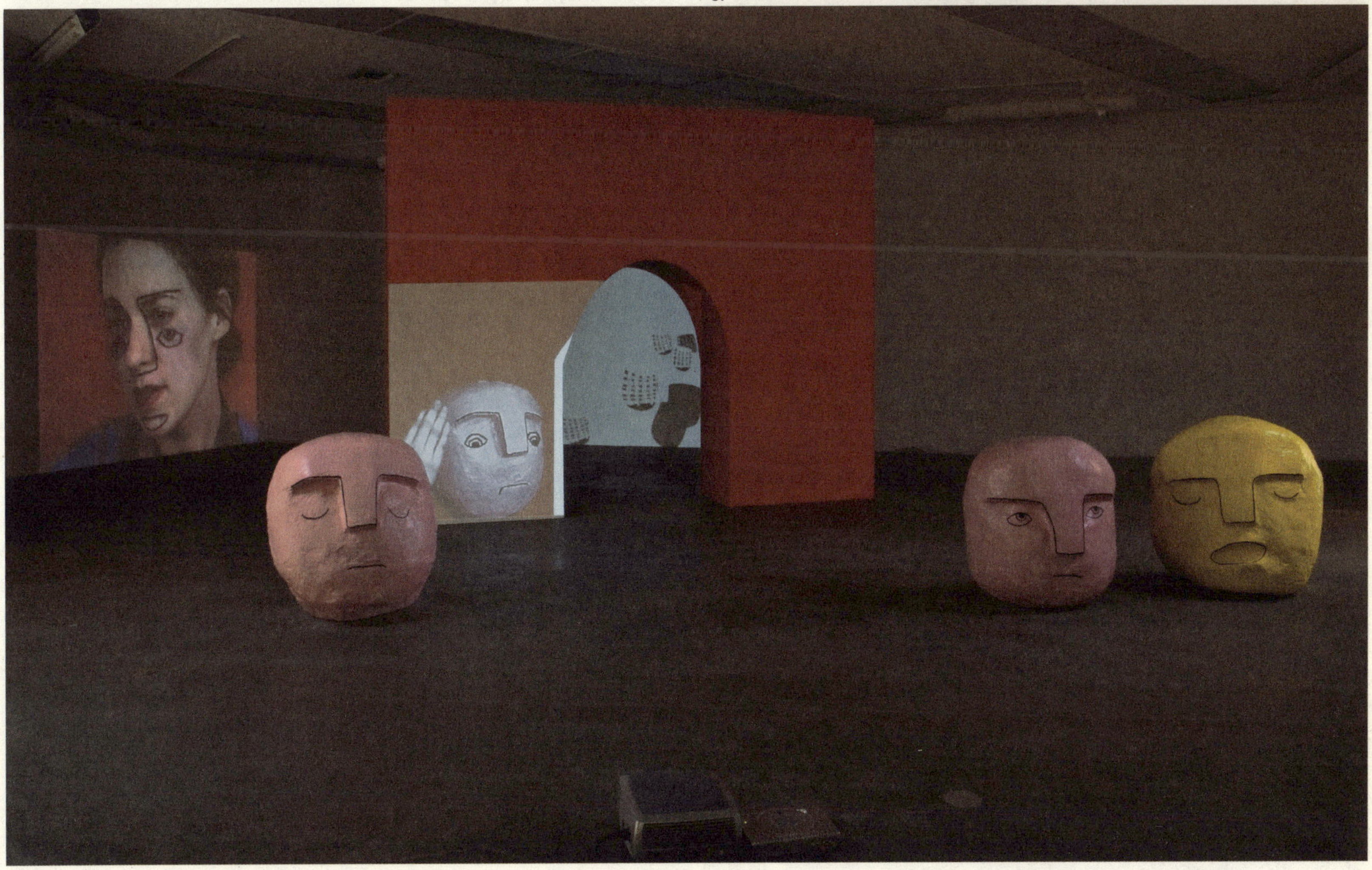

4.

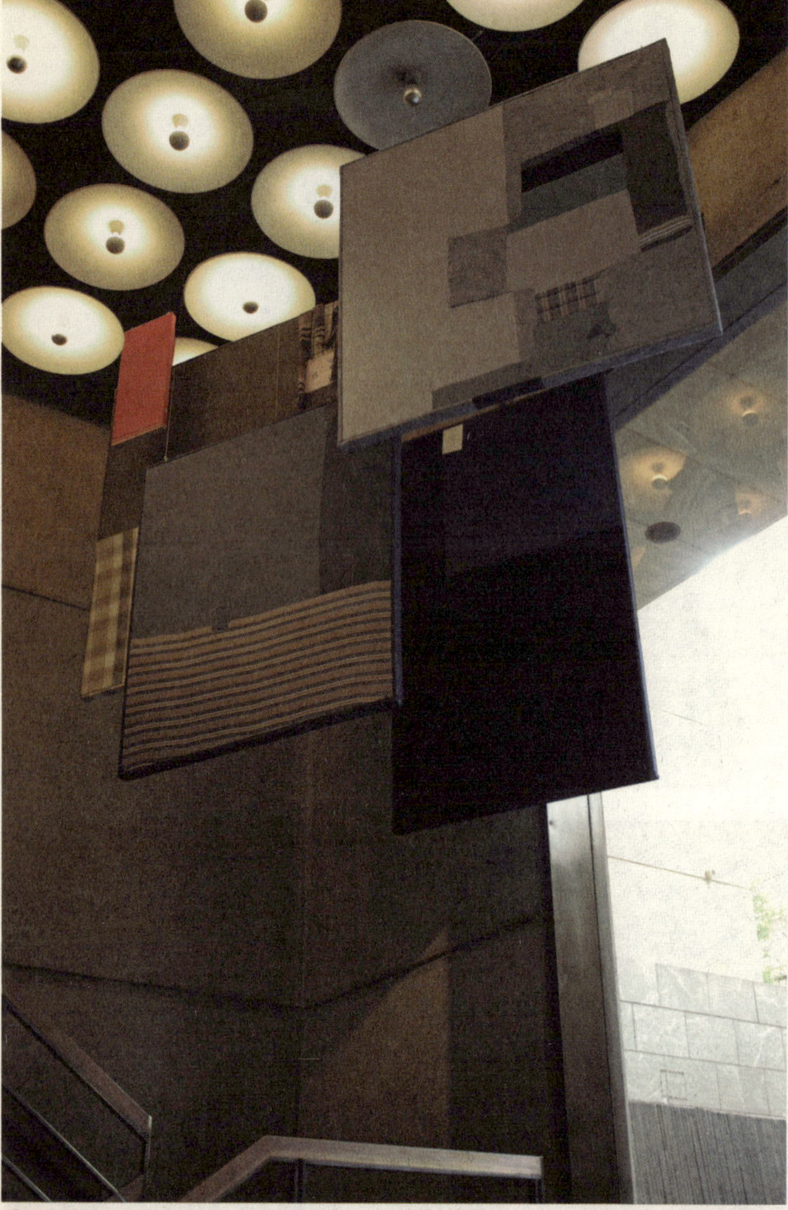

1.

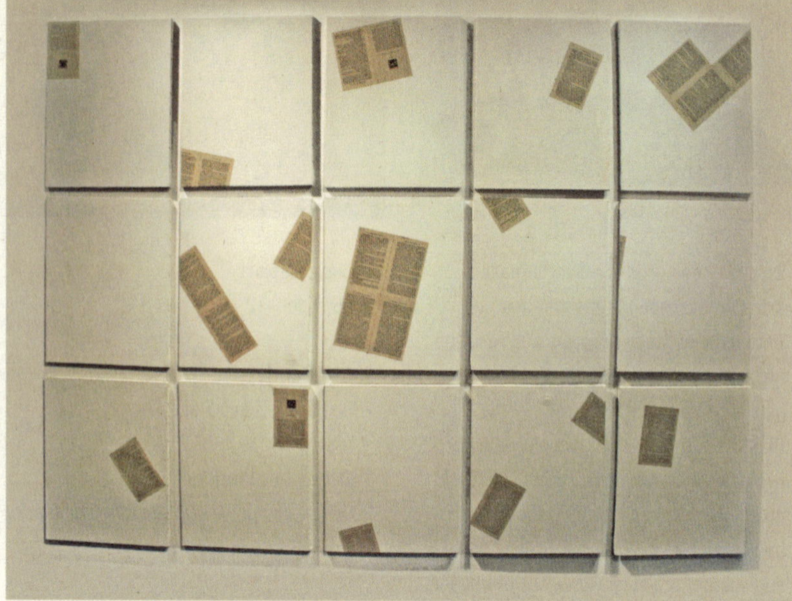

2.

Rashawn Griffin received his MFA from Yale University and currently lives and works in New York. His moody, nostalgic, and often somber paintings and assemblages spring from a poetic investigation of social space and personal memory. His work utilizes evocative everyday detritus and materials culled from his personal life, as well as wistful and romantic-utopian literary sources such as Marcel Proust's Swann's Way and Ursula K. LeGuin's Wizard of Earthsea. His work was included in the 2008 Whitney Biennial.

1. Algernon
2008, fabric, wool, foam, pockets, and scarf, dimensions variable, installation view at the Whitney Museum of American Art, New York

2. GED
2008, pages on canvas, each 20 × 16 in (51 × 41 cm)

3. To Bring Love/Terrible Things
2004, video, 2 min 48 sec

4. The Mysterious Disappearance of Jonathan Appleseed
2008, fabric, denim, wood, and foam, 82 × 83 × 12 in (208 × 208 × 31 cm)

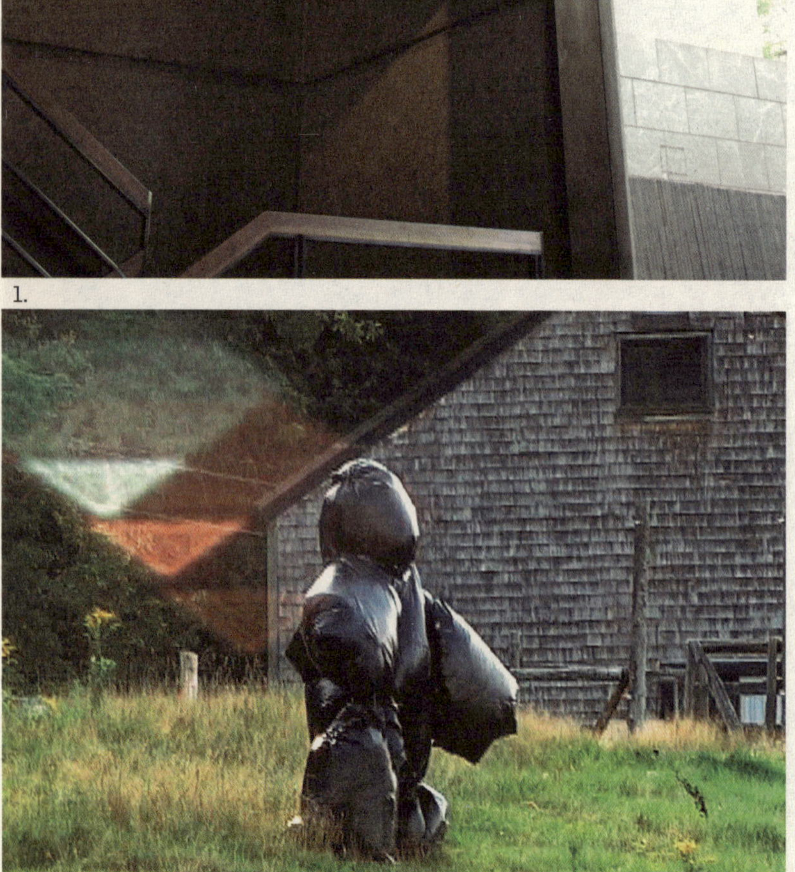

3.

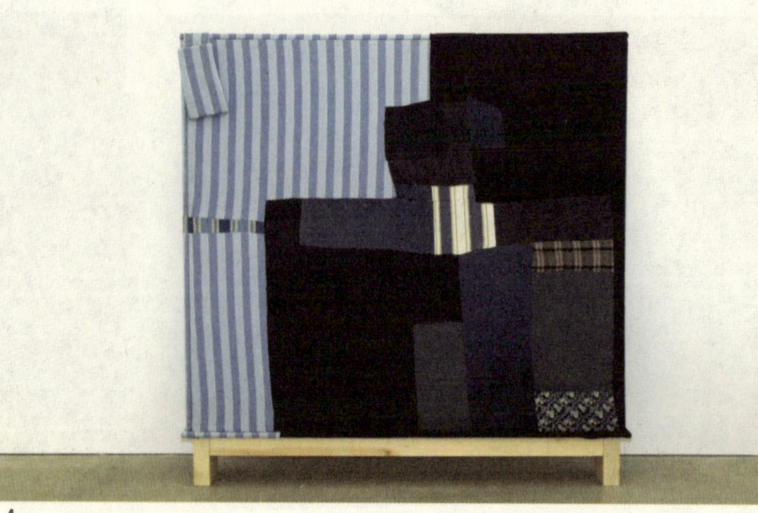

4.

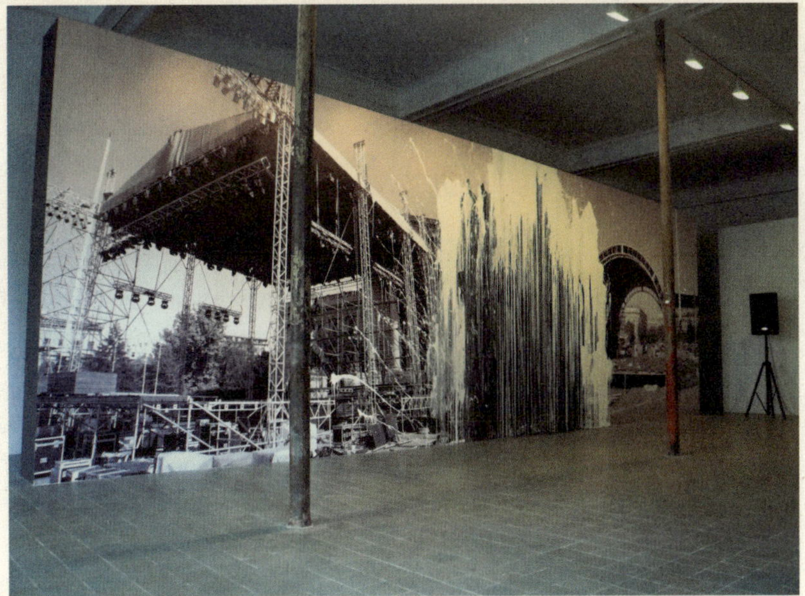
1.

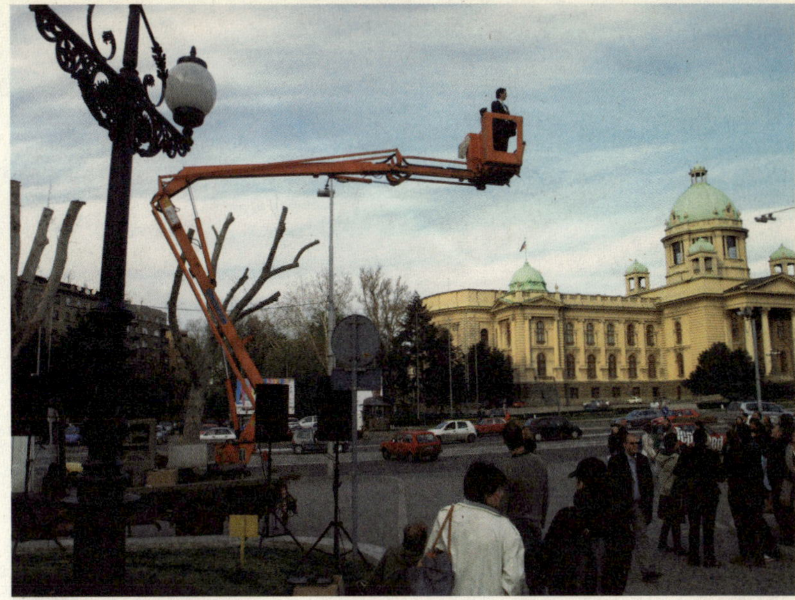
2.

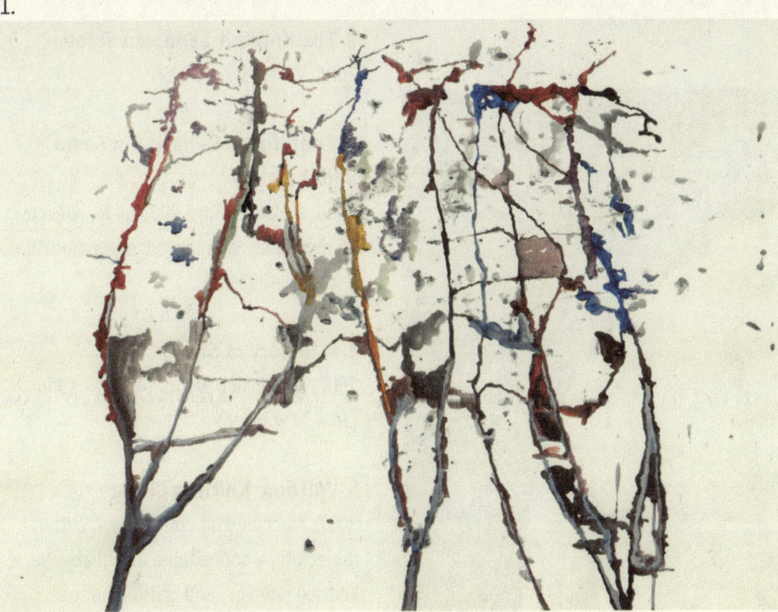
3.

Ivan Grubanov graduated with a degree in painting from the Academy of Fine Arts in Belgrade. He moved to Amsterdam in 2002 for a residency at the Rijksakademie and currently lives in London and Belgrade. He works in a range of media, from painting, drawing, and comics to installation, performance, and video. Many projects are concerned with the means of memory – documenting and reinterpreting the past – particularly relating to the political events that shaped his upbringing in Serbia.

1. **Non-Institutional**
2007, mixed media, dimensions variable

2. **Speech in Front of the National Parliament**
2006, performance

3. **Powerbush**
2008, watercolor on paper, 27 ½ × 39 ½ in (70 × 100 cm)

4. **Wall of Ideology**
2008, 100 black and white posters, overall 98 ½ × 197 × 20 in (250 × 500 × 50 cm)

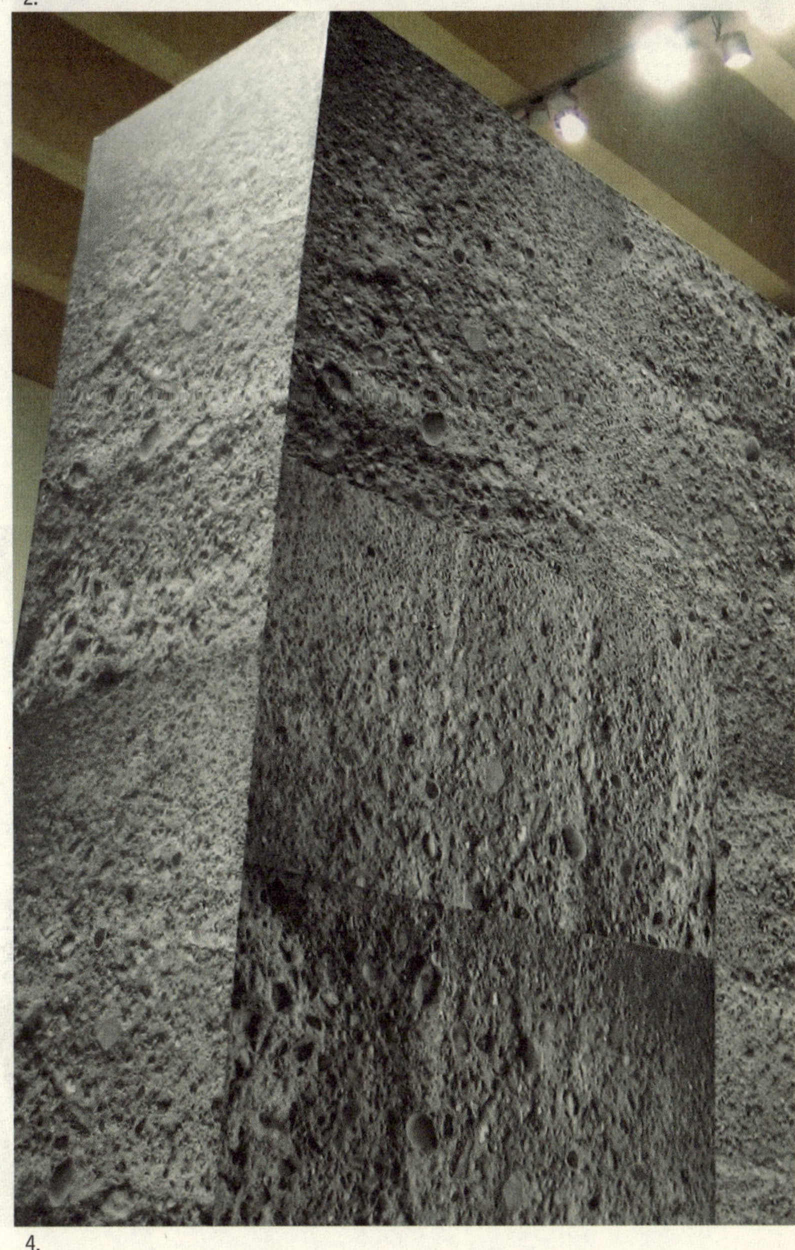
4.

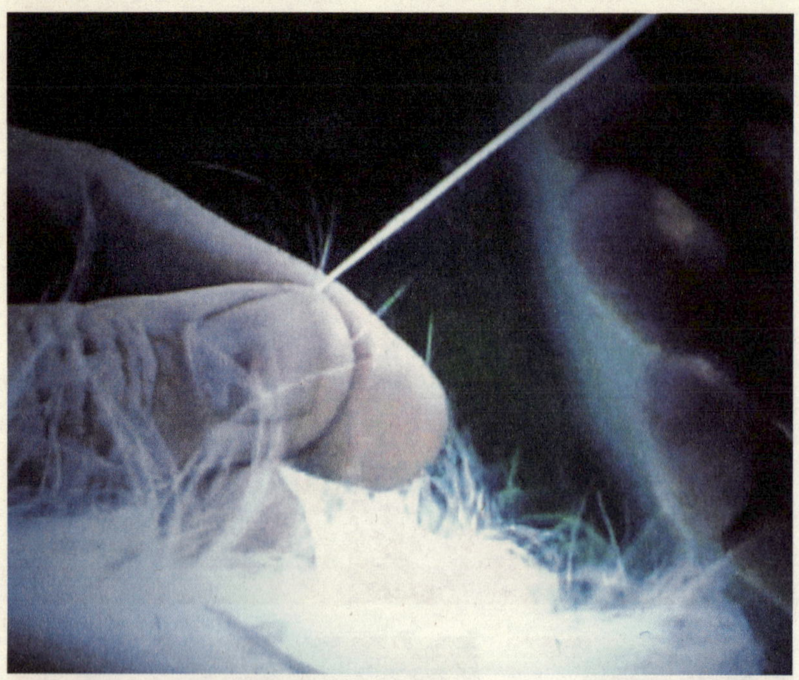
1.

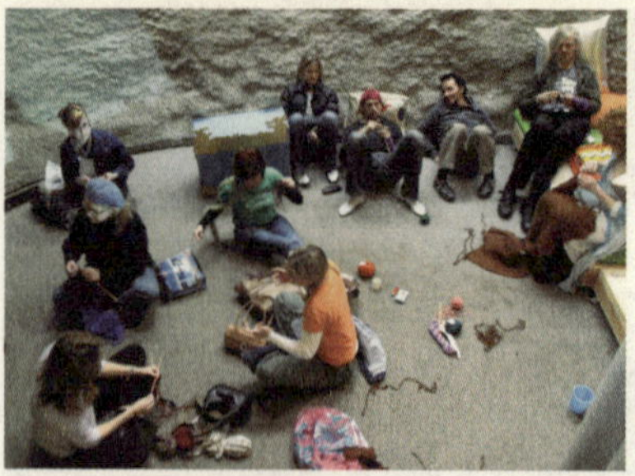
2.

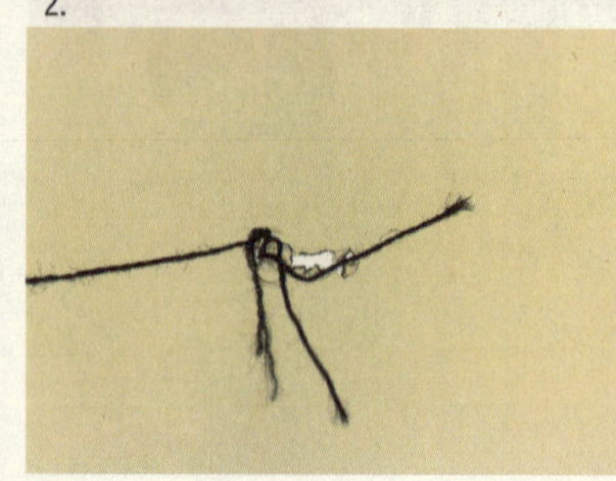
3.

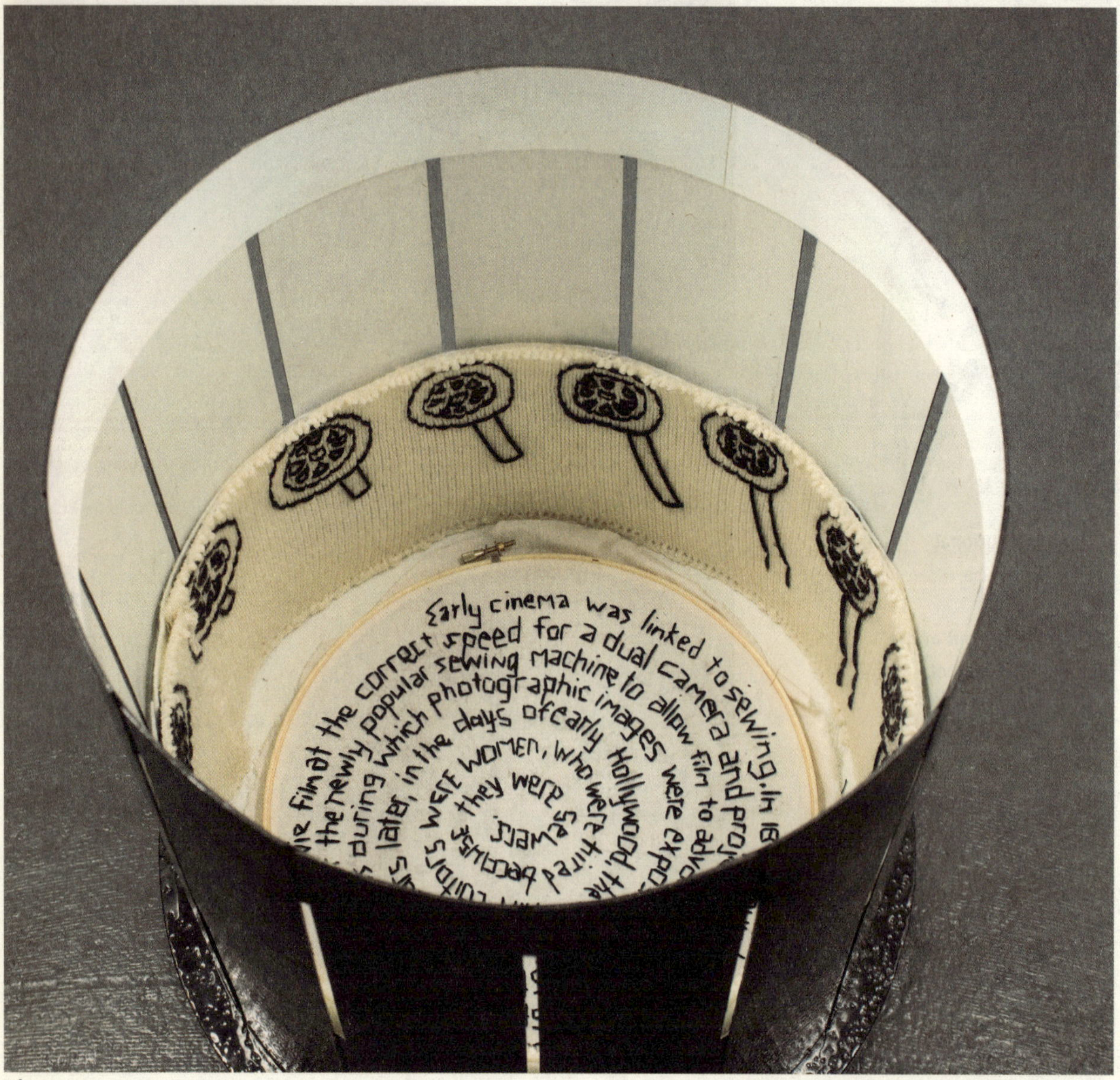

4.

Sabrina Gschwandtner earned her BA from Brown University and her MFA from Bard College. She is a New York City-based artist and writer working in textiles, film, video, and installation. With the belief that knitting can take the diverse forms of "graffiti, gift, clothing, protest, performance, and sculpture," she founded **KnitKnit** in 2002, a limited-edition journal dedicated to the intersection of traditional craft and contemporary art. Her book **KnitKnit: Profiles and Projects from Knitting's New Wave** was published in 2007.

1. **A History of String**
2007, video

2. **The KnitKnit Sundown Salon**
2004, video, 6 min 36 sec

3. **Phototactic Behavior in Sewn Slides** (detail)
2004, Kodak Ektapro 9000 slide projector, 35 mm slides, and thread, projection 10 × 8 ft (244 × 305 cm)

4. **A History of String**
2007, plastic and wood, 14 × 13 × 13 in (36 × 33 × 33 cm).

5. **Wartime Knitting Circle**
2007, machine-knit cotton wool, cotton tablecloth, wooden table and chairs, yarn, knitting needles, and knitting notions, dimensions variable

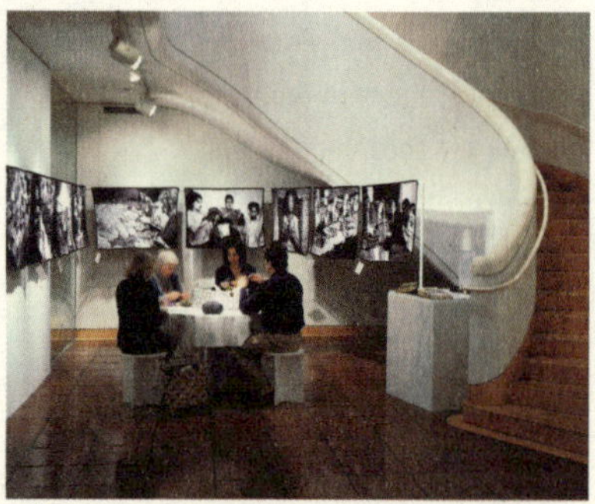
5.

Guan Rong's paintings and installations focus on notions of impermanence and absence. **Untitled**, a work from 2005, features three paintings, increasing in size, with a pink ground and a black area in the center where there would be a face in a portrait.

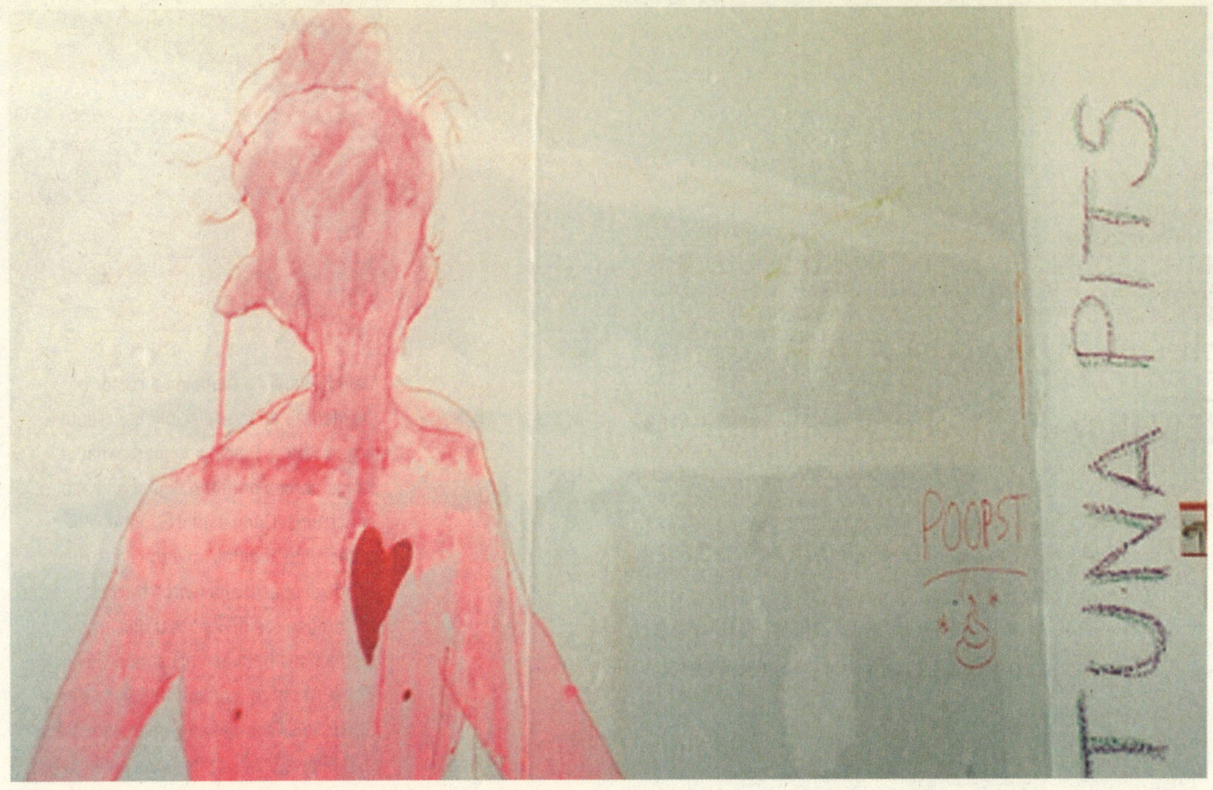

1.

Nomad Post Scool
Anyone Anywhere
Anytime AnySubject

2.

10-101-110 South
exit Olympic
Turn Right at Blaine st.
Turn left at W Olympic
" " Fedora.

3.

Miss

4.

1. I had a fun time with you
2005, performance

2. Untitled
2008, rubber stamp, 1 ½ x ½ in (4 × 1 cm)

3. One Way to Fedora Street in Los Angeles
2007, marker on paper, approx 8 × 6 in (20.3 × 15.2 cm)

4. September 17th 2008, 0:41am
2008, marker on paper

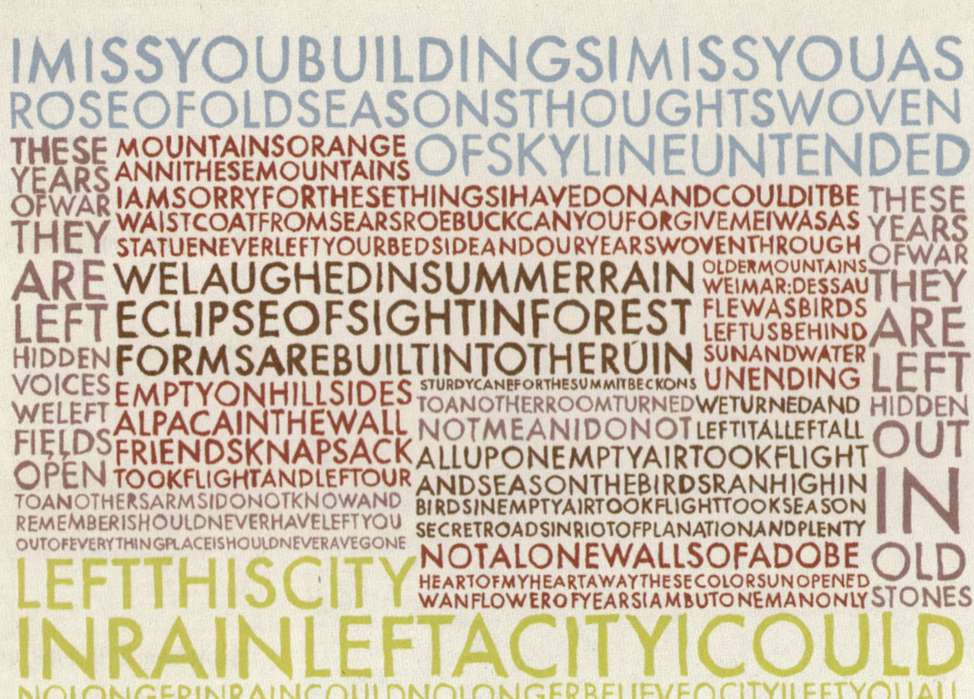

1.

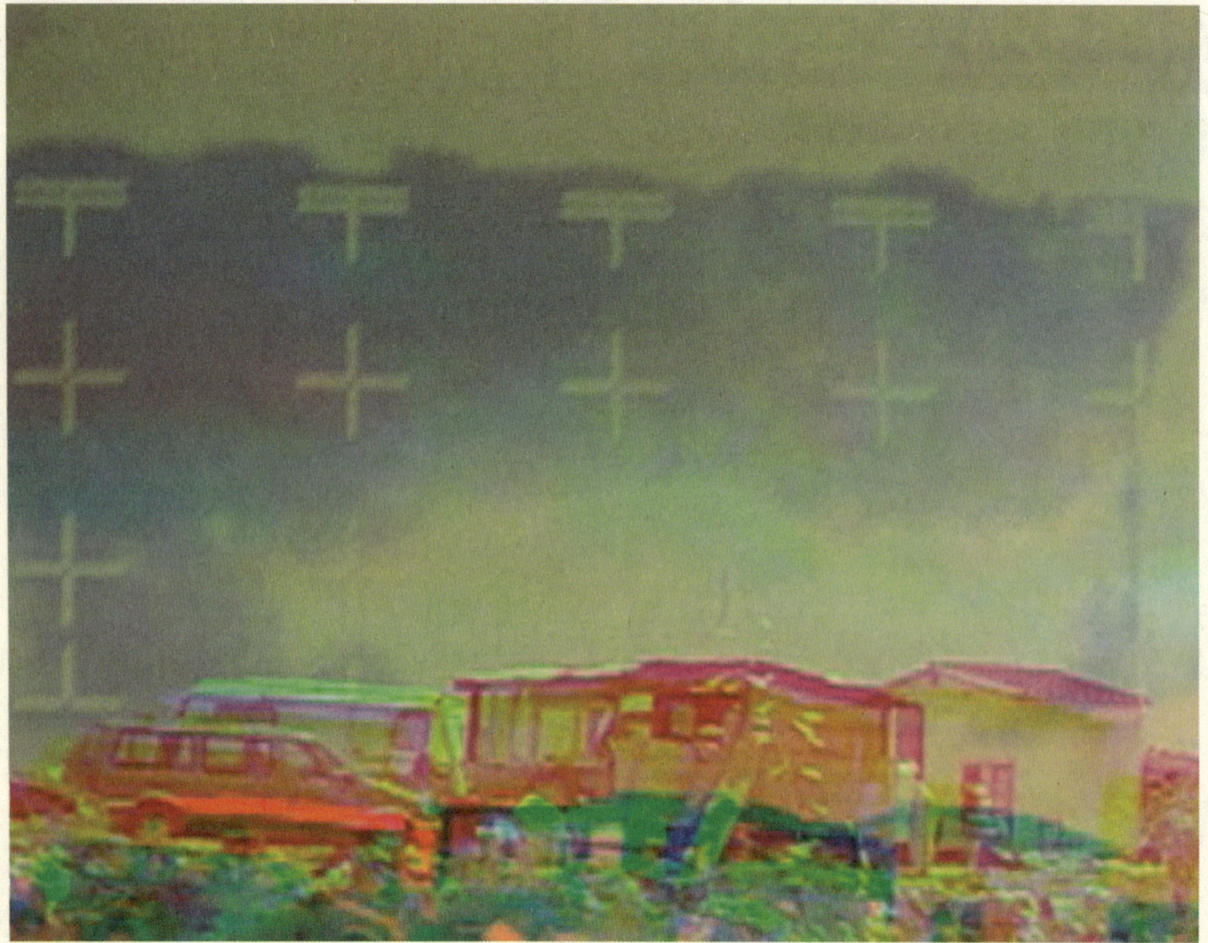

3.

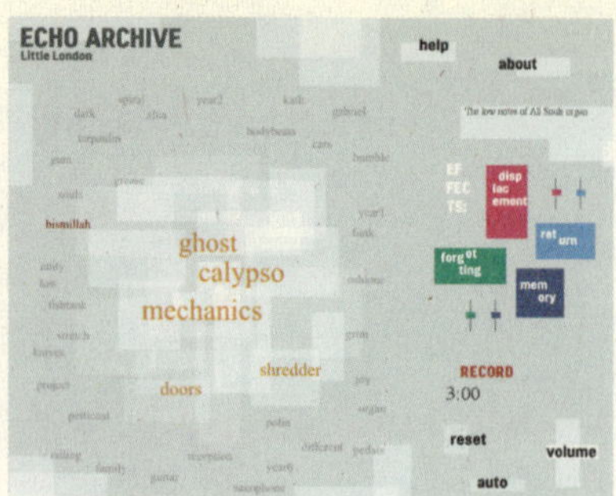

2.

David Gunn is a founding director of Incidental, an interdisciplinary creative organization. Employing media that range across both the digital and analog spectrums, Gunn explores notions of authorship, identity, and the construction of social space, and works to create forms of "diffuse creativity" that blur traditional distinctions between artist and viewer. His **Echo Archive**, commissioned by Opera North, is a Web-based compositional tool that allows users to create a sonic portrait of the fast-disappearing Little London area of Leeds, using sounds gathered by Gunn in collaboration with local residents.

1. **To Mitla, 1940**
from the series **Josef Albers**
2008, digital print, 6 × 4 in (15 × 10 cm)

2. **Echo Archive**
with ObjectiveSubject
2008, digital instrument commissioned by Opera North and made possible by the support of Paul Hamlyn Foundation

3 & 4. **Open Cities / Waste**
with Guillermo E. Brown
2008, performance

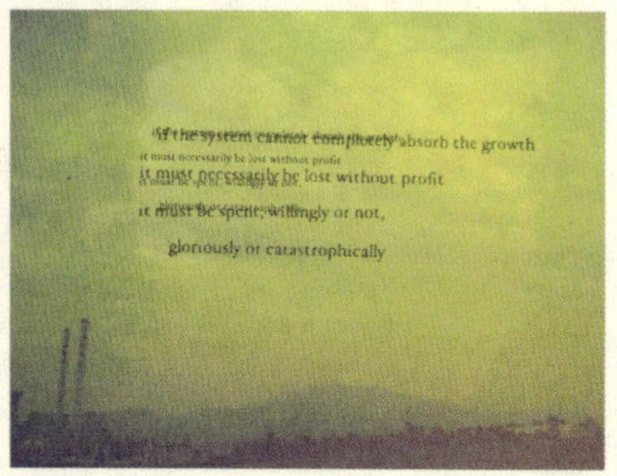

4.

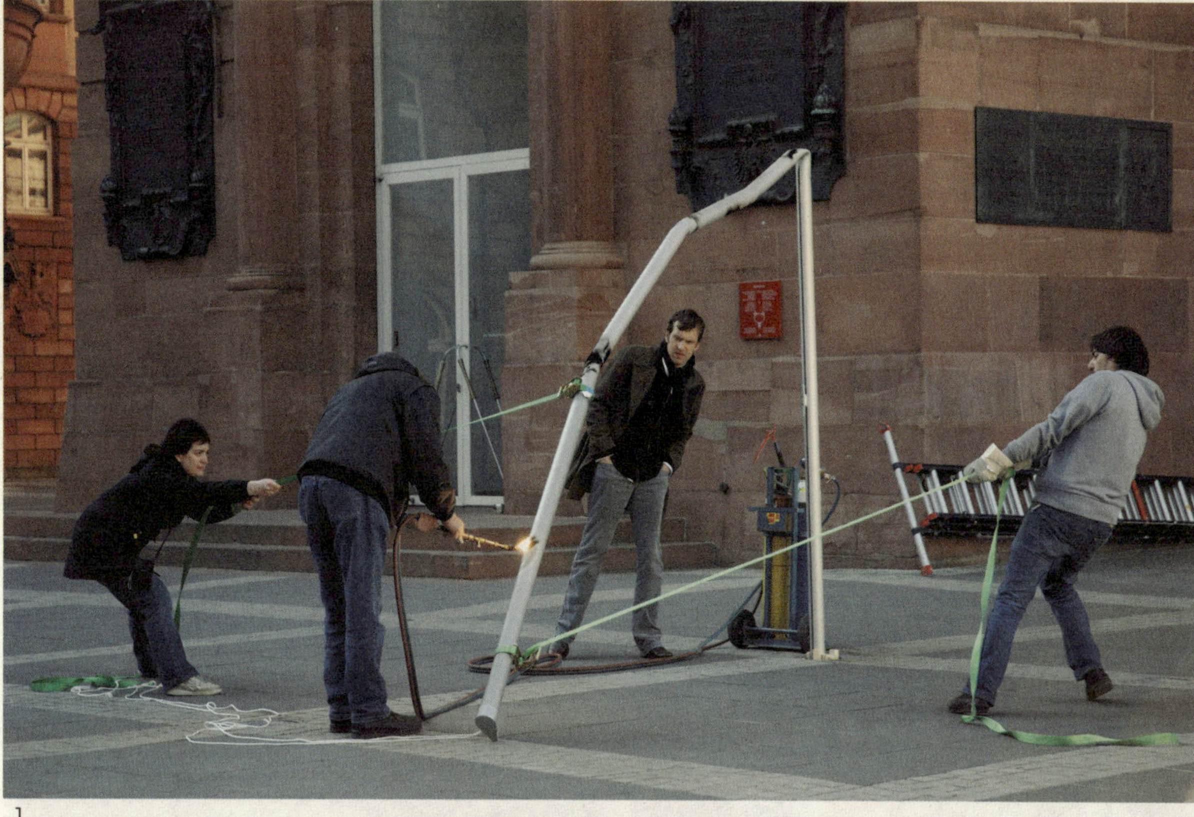
1.

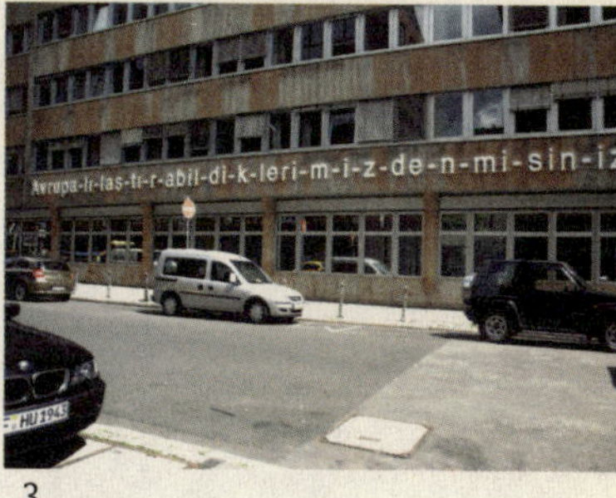
3.

In formally heterogeneous practices, Frankfurt-based Özlem Günyol and Mustafa Kunt question and dismantle images of collective and individual identity. They are interested in the mass media and other communicative forms, in particular as they pertain to the construction of cultural and national belonging.

1. Flagpole
2007, video, 21 min

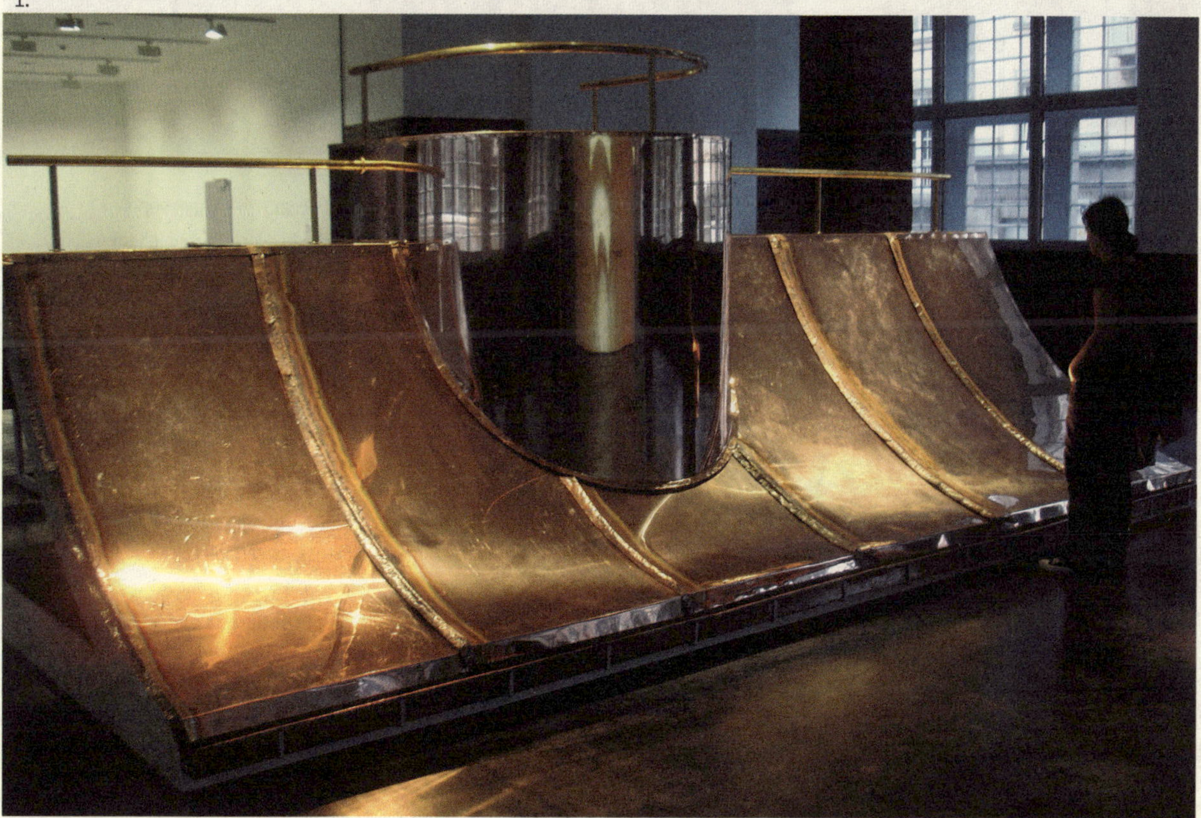
2.

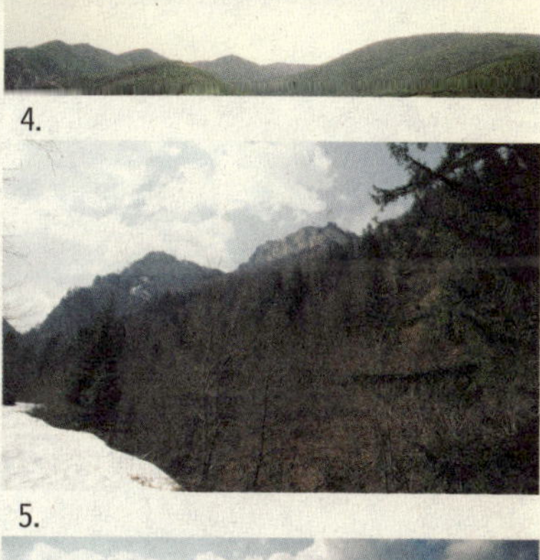
4.

5.

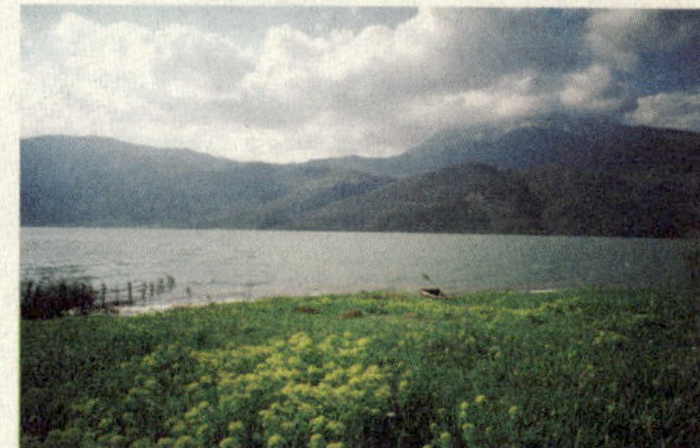
6.

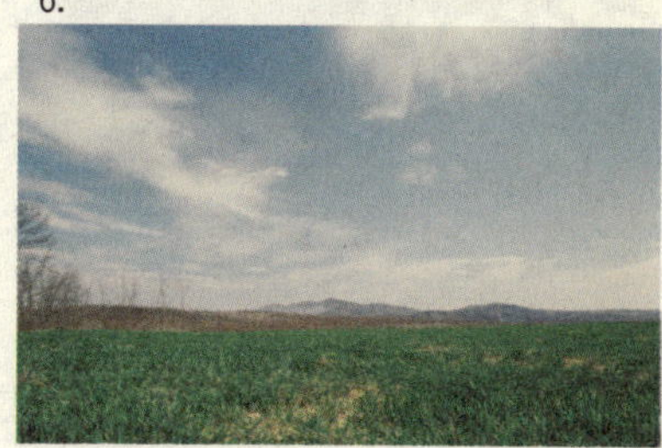
7.

2. Balkon
2008, brass, copper, wood, pebbles, iron, $7\frac{1}{2} \times 18\frac{1}{2} \times 16\frac{1}{2}$ ft (230 × 570 × 503 cm); video, 15 min 26 sec

3. Avrupalilastirabildiklerimizdenmisiniz
2006, aluminum, white paint on polystyrene, and adhesive letters, dimensions variable

4, 5, 6 & 7. Scenes
2005, chromogenic prints, each $39\frac{1}{2} \times 59$ in (100 × 150 cm)

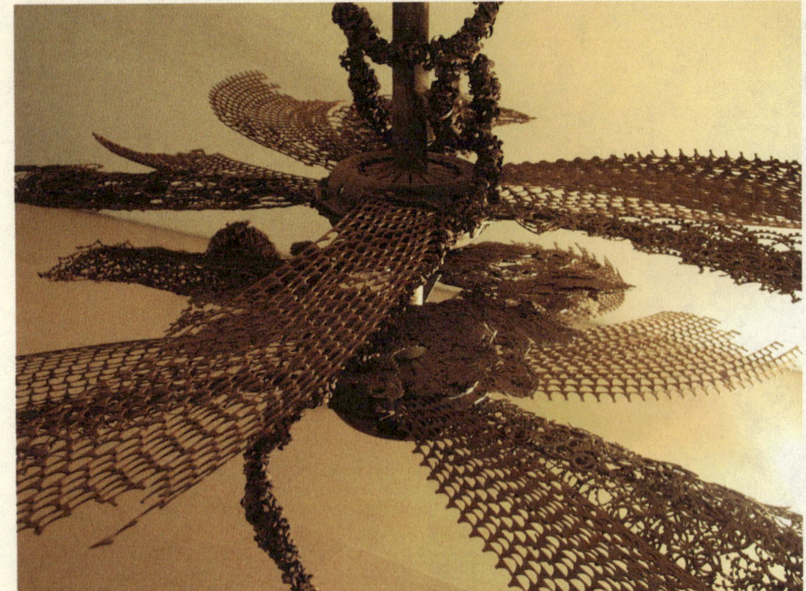
1.

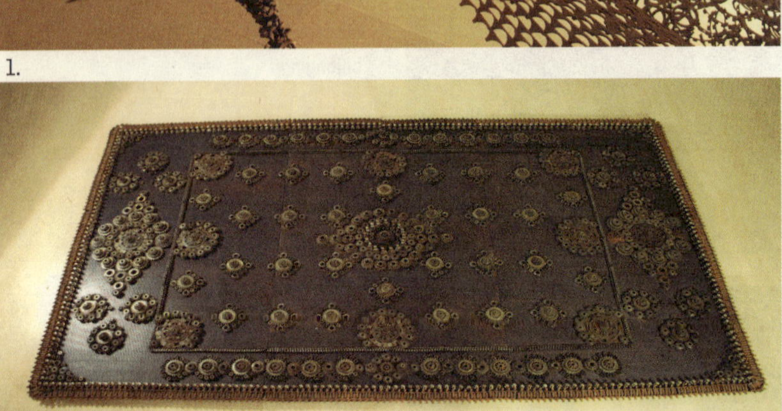
2.

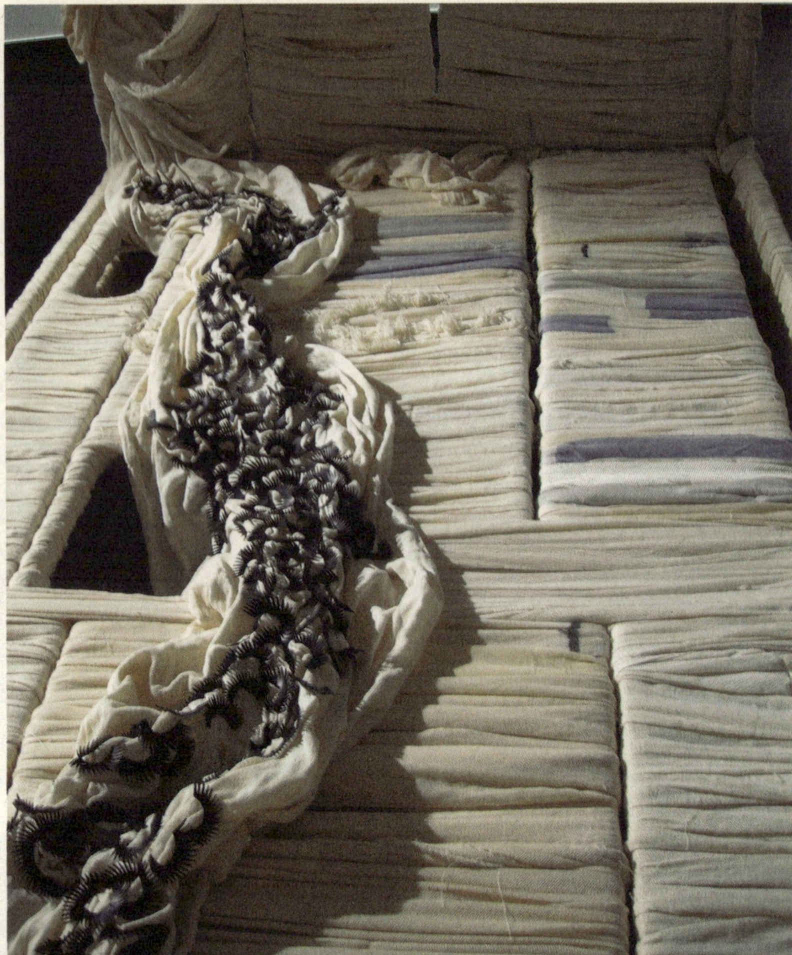
4.

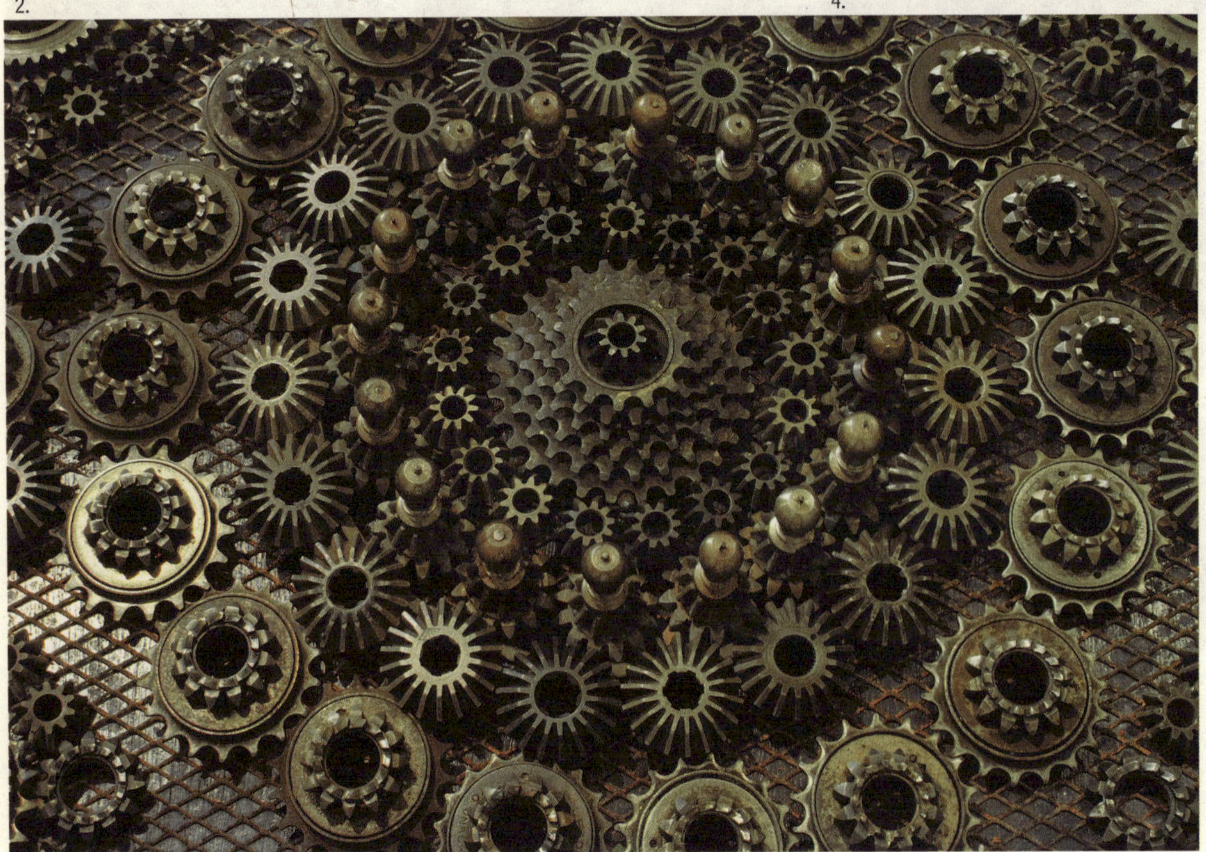
3.

Sakshi Gupta lives and works in New Delhi. His work, which thrives on real-world contradictions and complexities, has involved the sculptural reinterpretation of everyday objects. Often working in direct response to a particular site, he also strives to use local materials.

1. **Some Beast**
2008, scrap iron, soldering material, dimensions variable.

2 & 3. **Freedom is everything**
2007, plywood, metal scrap, 84 × 144 in (213 × 366 cm).

4. **Untitled**
2007, fabric, leather, and wood, 79 × 54 × 46 in (201 × 137 × 117 cm)

CERTIFICATE

21 GUN SALUTE FOR THE DEATH OF A COLLECTOR

A: PERSONAL AND STATISTICAL PARTICULARS OF THE COLLECTOR		
Surname:	First name:	Middle name:
Date of Birth: (dd/mm/yyyy)	Place of Birth:	
Nationality:	Gender:	Race:
ADDRESS Street:	City:	
State / Province:	Country	
Next of Kin:		
B: PARTICULARS OF THE DEATH OF THE COLLECTOR		
Place of Death:	Date: (dd/mm/yyyy)	Time:
C: PERSONAL AND STATISTICAL PARTICULARS OF THE ARTIST		
Surname:	First name:	Middle name:
Date of Birth: (dd/mm/yyyy)	Place of Birth:	
Nationality:	Gender:	Race:
ADDRESS Street:	City:	
State / Province:	Country	
D: SIGNATURES		
Collector:	Artist:	
Witness:	Witness:	
Date: (dd/mm/yyyy)	Date: (dd/mm/yyyy)	

CERTIFICATE

21 GUN SALUTE FOR THE DEATH OF A COLLECTOR

Conditions

21 Gun Salute for the Death of a Collector

- Upon purchase of the artwork, 21 Gun Salute for the Death of a Collector, the collector agrees to the staging of a 21 gun salute at his/her funeral.
- Upon the purchase of the artwork, the collector must complete section A of the certificate, Personal and Statistical Particulars of the Collector, and sign the certificate. This binds the collector to the work.
- The executor of the collector's will must complete section B, Particulars of the Death of the Collector, at the time of the collector's death.
- After the purchase of 21 Gun Salute for the Death of a Collector, neither the collector nor any member of his/her family may refuse the staging of the artwork.
- A portion of the sale of the artwork shall be placed in a trust fund which will be made available to the executor of the collector's will expressly for the purpose of the 21 Gun Salute.
- The artwork, including this certificate, may not be sold or transferred to anyone before the completion of the 21 gun salute at the funeral of the collector.
- This certificate will remain as the only document of the artwork after the staging of the 21 gun salute and may be sold by the estate of the collector as such.

1.

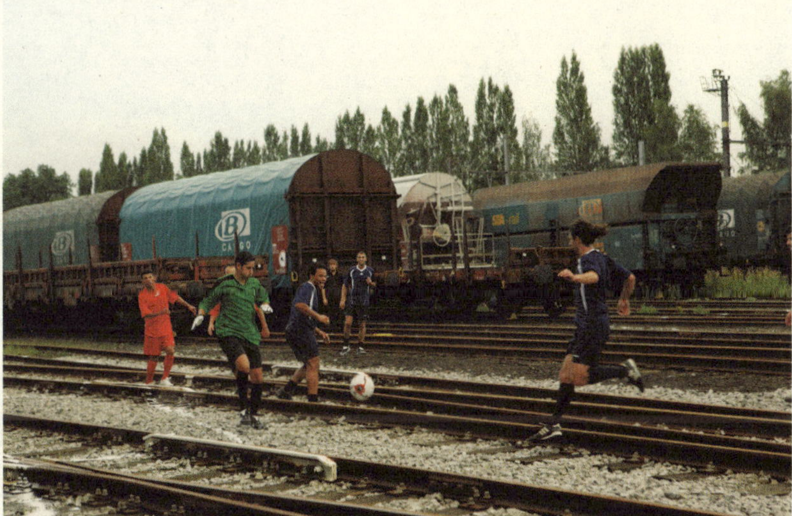

2.

Simon Gush earned his BA in Fine Art from the University of the Witwatersrand, Johannesburg, and is currently attending the Higher Institute for Fine Arts in Ghent, Belgium. His conceptual practice uses sculpture, installation, video, and performance to comment on contemporary social and political issues, from immigration in Ghent to gentrification in Johannesburg. He founded the Parking Gallery in 2007 to create an alternative space for Johannesburg artists lacking representation.

1. **21 Gun Salute for the Death of a Collector**
2007, action

2. **In the Company Of**
2008, video and 10-channel audio

3. **Moving House**
2006, site-specific action

4. **Serenade**
2008, performance

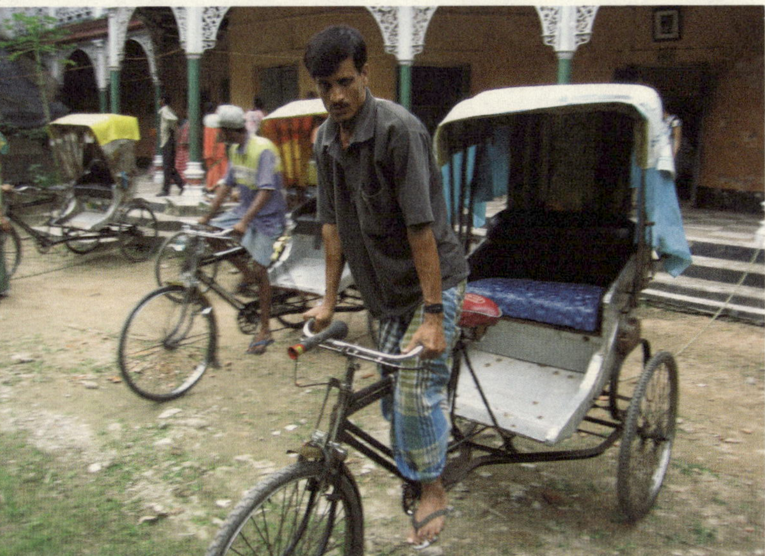

3.

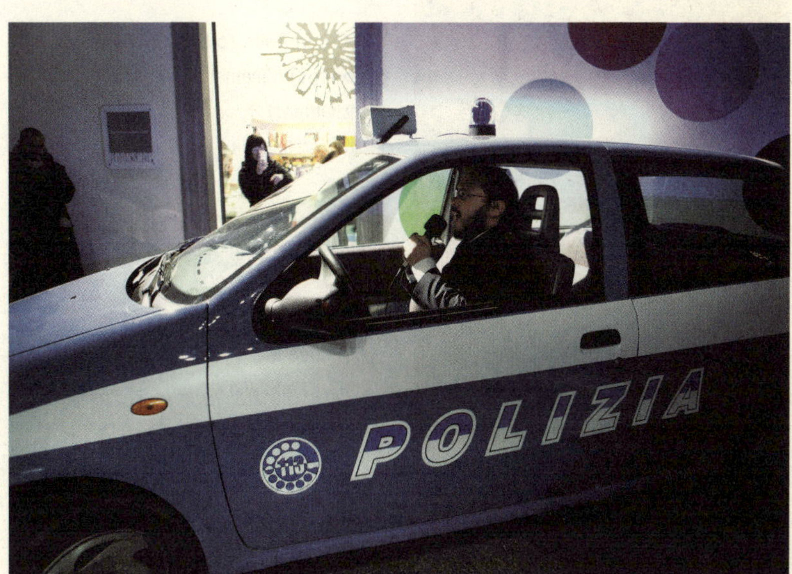

4.

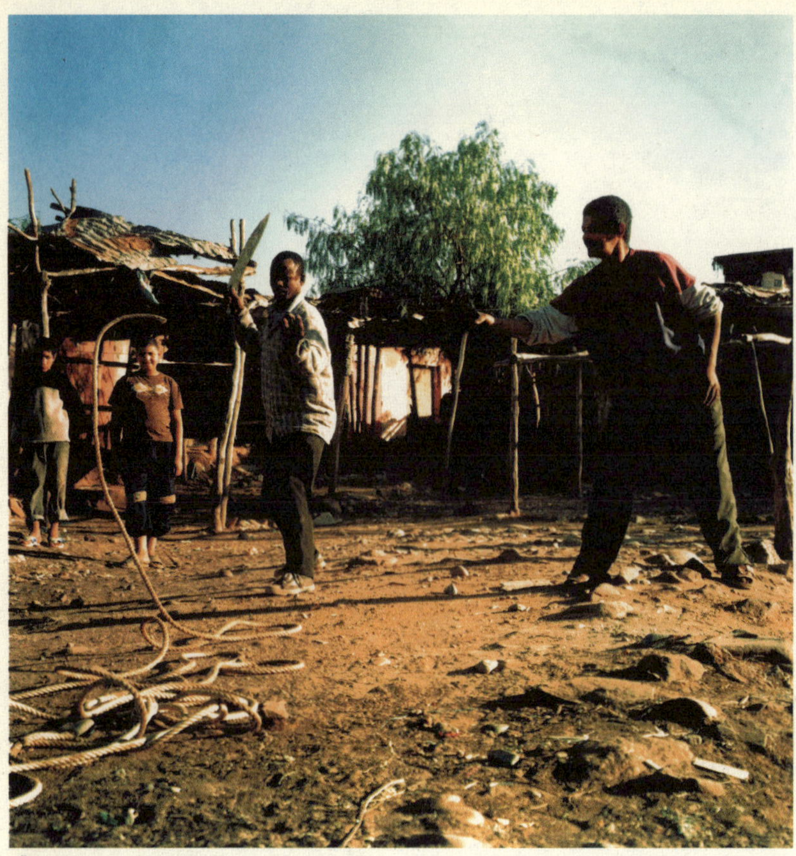

1.

Drawing inspiration from philosophical literature and science fiction, João Maria Gusmão and Pedro Paiva are best known for the short, silent 16 mm films that they have been developing together since 2004. In works such as **O Oculto** (The Occult; 2007), the Lisbon-based artists construct humorous, enigmatic narratives that challenge the viewer to question their perceptions of the world and notions of individuality. Their work has been exhibited in solo and group shows in Europe, America, and Asia.

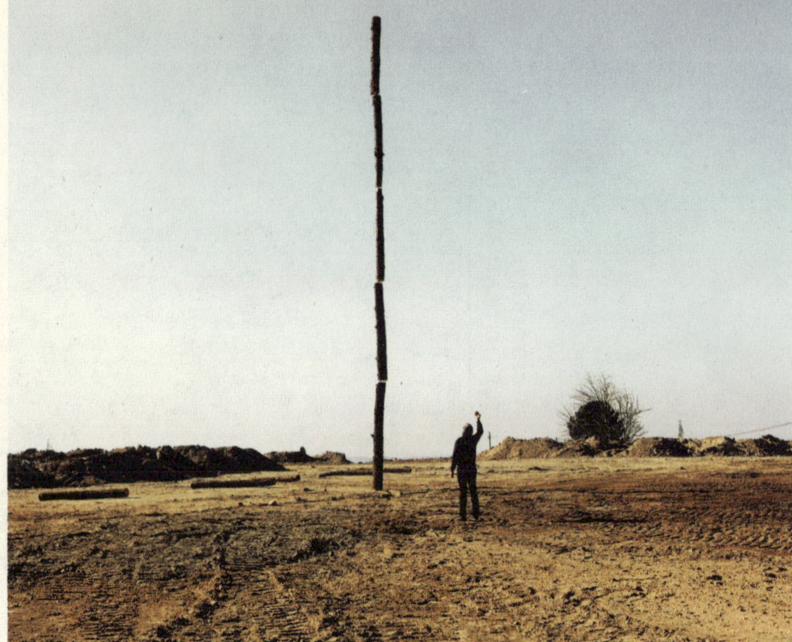

2.

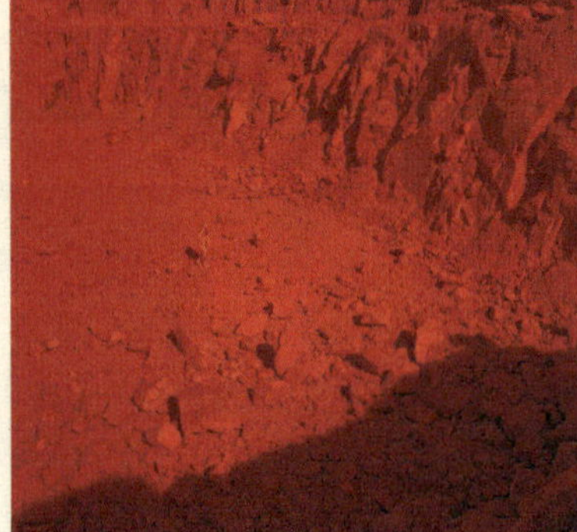

3.

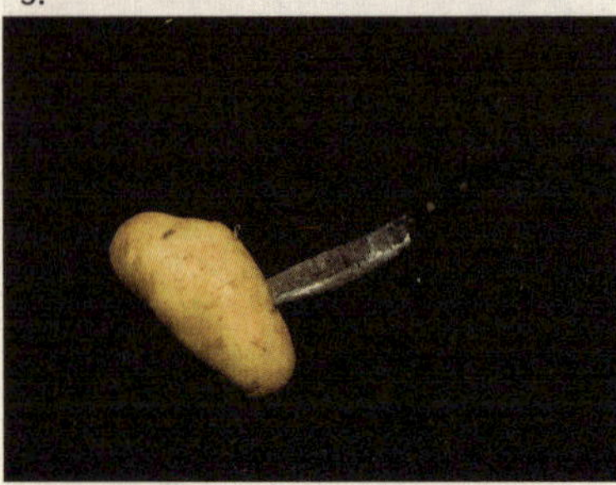

4.

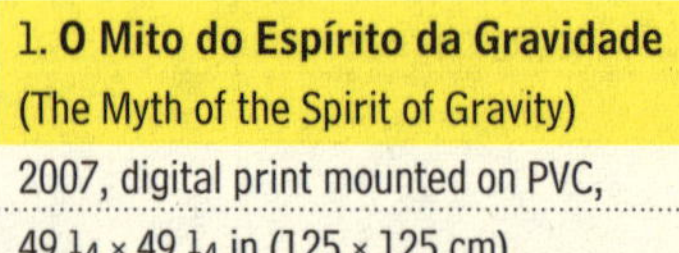

1. **O Mito do Espírito da Gravidade** (The Myth of the Spirit of Gravity)
2007, digital print mounted on PVC, 49 1/4 × 49 1/4 in (125 × 125 cm)

2. **Cinemática (o hipnotizador de troncos)** (Cinematics [or the log enchanter])
2006, 16 mm film, 1 min 50 sec

3. **A Intrusão** (The Intrusion)
2007, digital print mounted on PVC, 49 1/4 × 49 1/4 in (125 × 125 cm)

4. **A Faca Meteórica** (The Meteoric Knife)
2008, potato and knife, 8 × 12 × 2 in (20 × 30 × 5 cm)

5. **Encapuçado** (The Hooded Man)
2008, painted bronze, 10 1/2 × 5 1/2 × 9 in (27 × 14 × 22 cm)

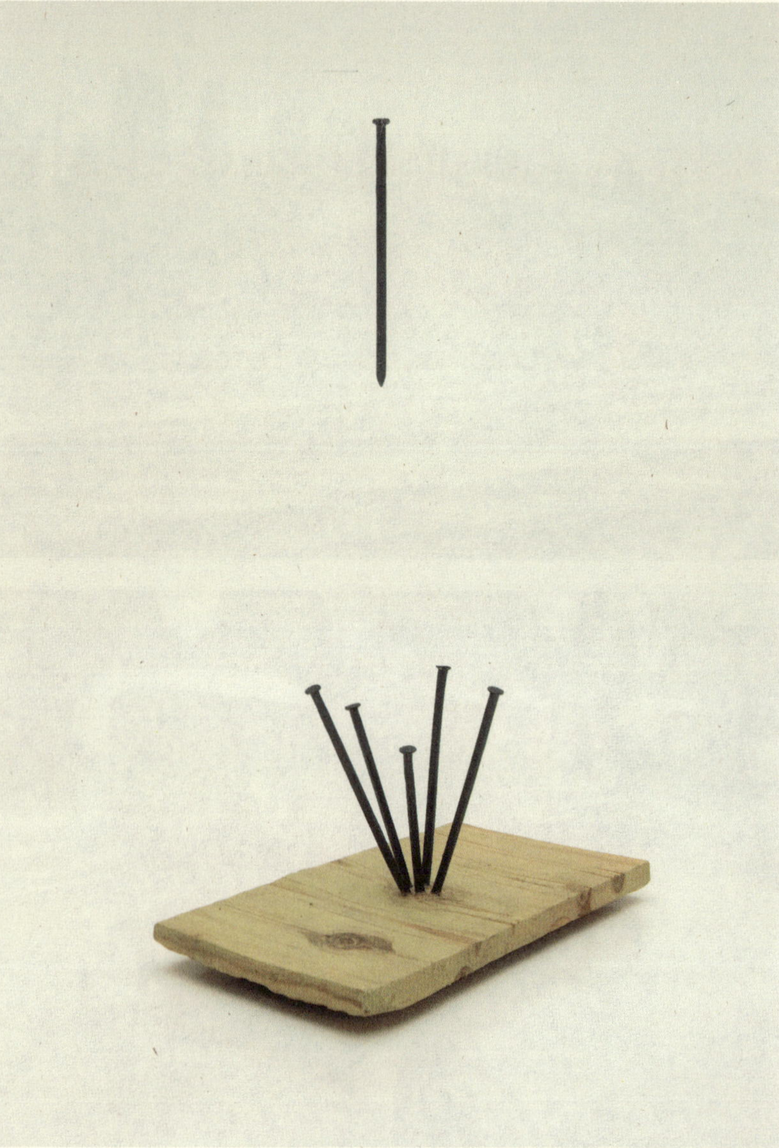

5.

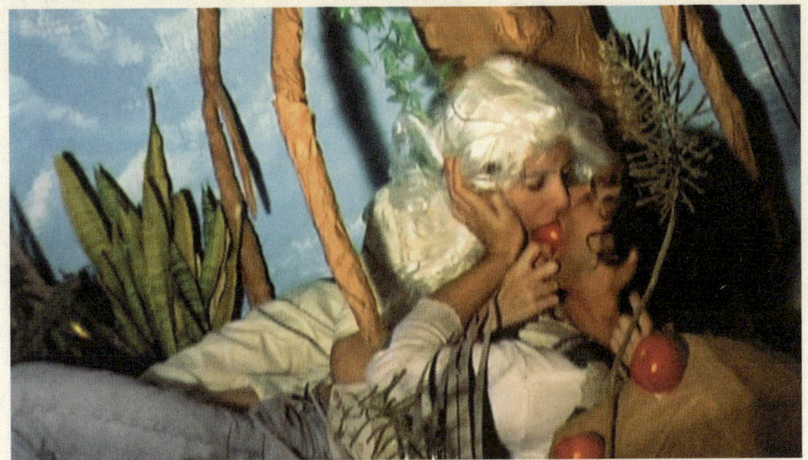

1.

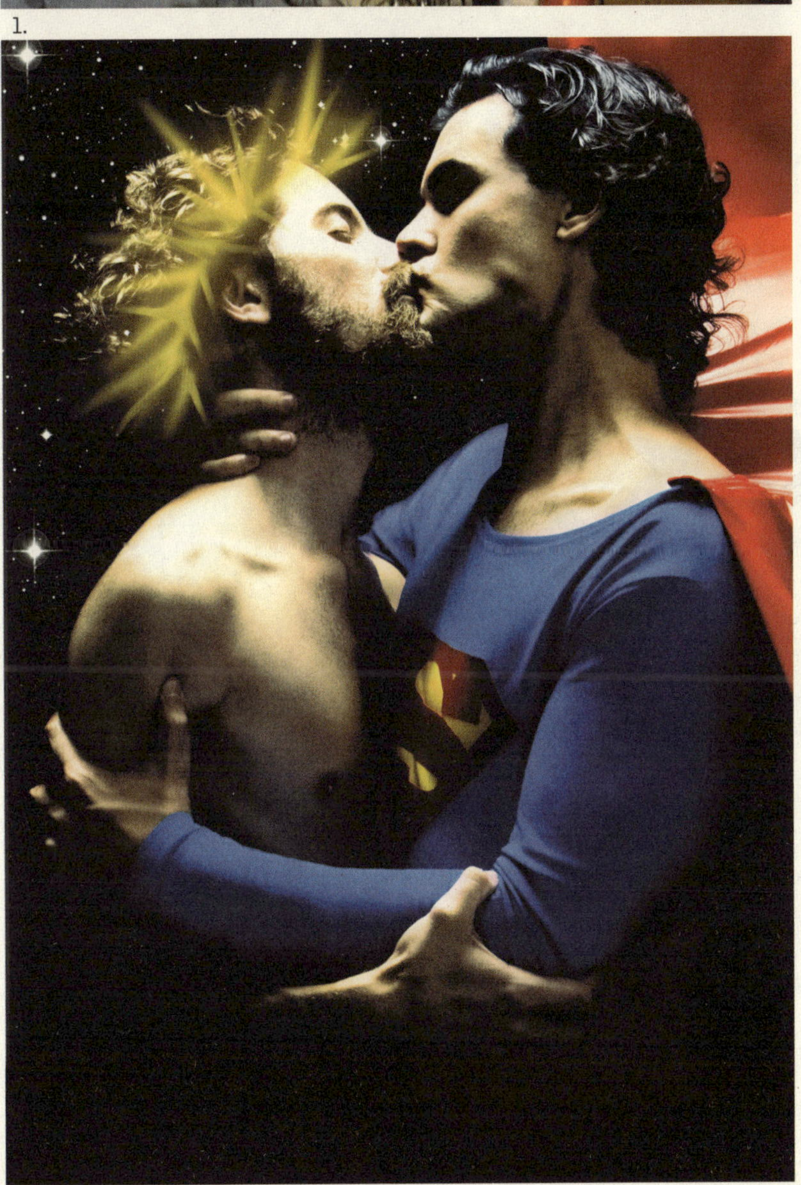

2.

Rosario-based Mauro Guzmán is an artist, actor, and director who produces film, theater, photographs, and installations. His satiric films draw on different cinematic traditions, including Hollywood B-movies and Argentinean films of the mid-1970s. The project **Linda Bler, artista poseída** (Linda Blair, artist possessed) creates an imaginary picture of horror hero Linda Blair through remakes of The Exorcist, Carrie, and Rosemary's Baby.

1. **Nazareno Cruz y el arte**
2008, video, 27 min 40 sec

2. **La historia de amor más grande más bella y más heroica de todos los tiempos** (The greatest, most beautiful, and most heroic history of love of all time)
2007-08, graphic novel

3. **Rosemaría's baby**
2008, video, 18 min 45 sec

4. **Carrie, the power of the mind**
2007, video, 14 min 15 sec

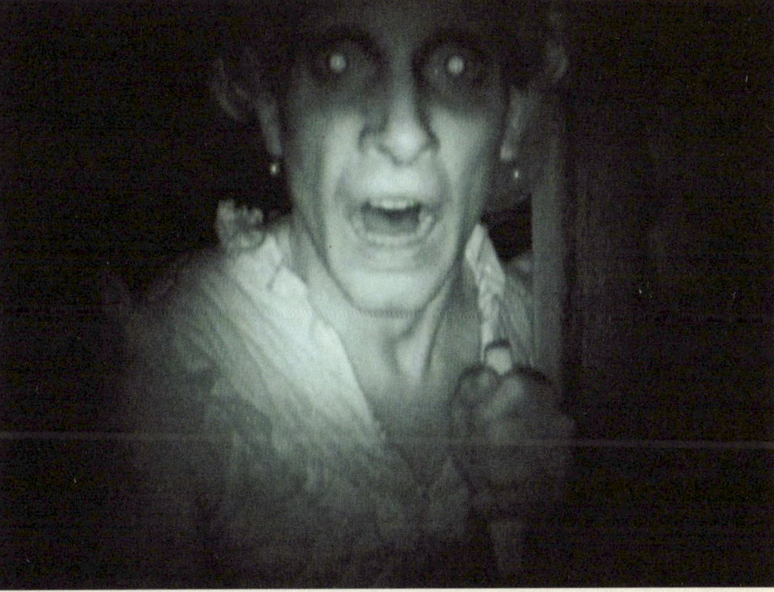

3.

4.

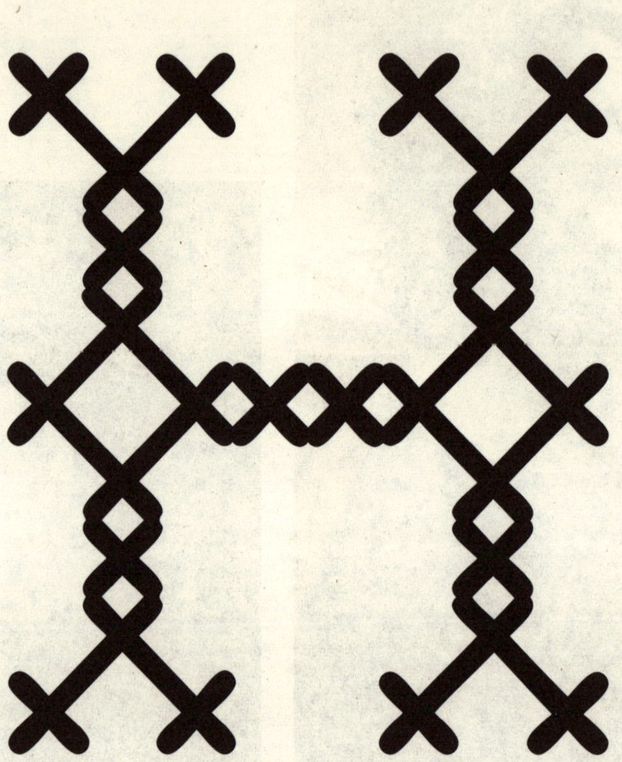

Grit Hachmeister studied photography at the Academy of Fine Arts in Leipzig, where she continues to live. Thought to represent a "second wave" of the Leipzig School, she works in drawing, painting, collage, and photography, often combining these elements in installations. Motifs of childhood collide with adult themes, tied together by a warped, often abstract treatment of the figure.

1. **Gulliver**
2007, digital print, 39 ½ × 59 in (100 × 150 cm)

2. **Das schaf** (The Sheep)
2006, ink and watercolor on paper, 12 × 8 in (30 × 20 cm)

3. **coolcoolcool**
2008, pencil on paper, 15 ¾ × 12 in (40 × 30 cm)

4. **Selbstporträt als tier** (Self-Portrait as an Animal)
2005, chromogenic print, 27 ½ × 17 ¾ in (70 × 45 cm)

5. **Boxer**
2007, chromogenic print, 55 × 36 ¼ in (140 × 92 cm)

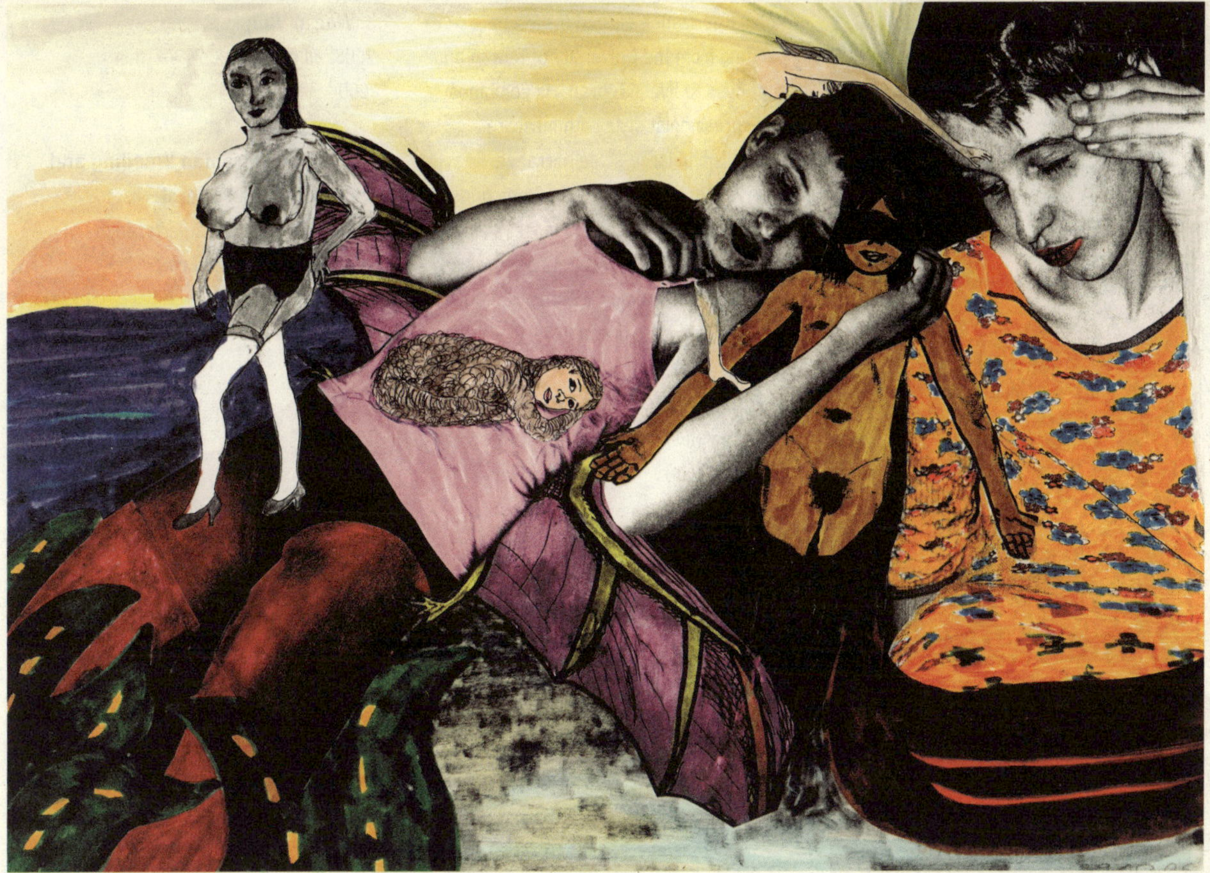

1.

2.

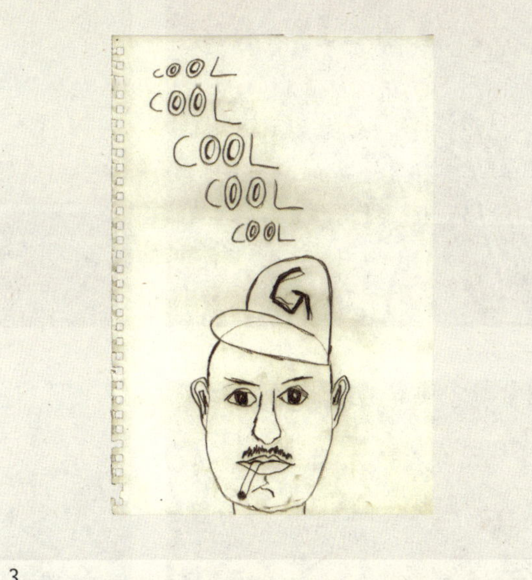

3.

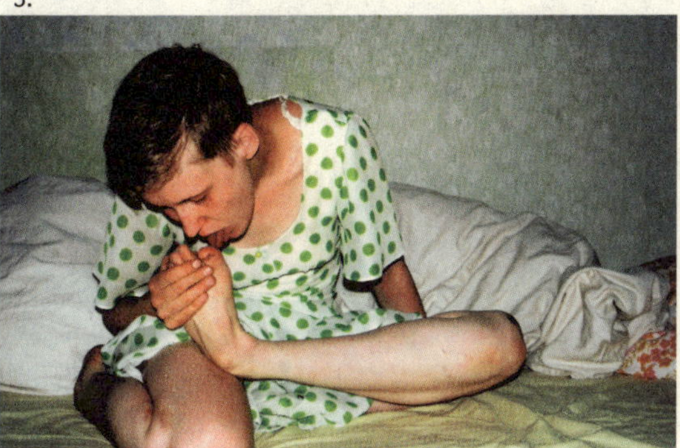

4.

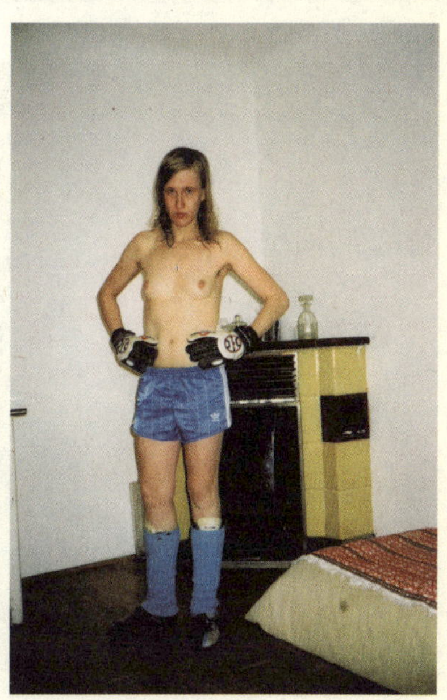

5.

Rokni Haerizadeh earned his MA in painting from the University of Tehran and continues to live in Tehran. He combines an Expressionist style with intricate symbolism in large-scale narrative paintings of daily life in Iran. Depictions of weddings, funerals, and street scenes are integrated with elements of Persian history and mythology, Islamic traditions, and contemporary pop culture.

1. Tuesday Afternoon – Pahlavi Street
2008, oil and acrylic on canvas, 79 × 98 in (200 × 250 cm)

2. The 30th Anniversary of the Islamic Republic Revolution
2008, oil on canvas, 79 × 118 in (200 × 300 cm)

3. War in Vain
2008, oil on canvas, 79 × 118 in (200 × 300 cm)

4 & 5. Typical Iranian Wedding and Typical Iranian Funeral
2008, oil on canvas, 2 parts, each 79 × 118 in (200 × 300 cm)

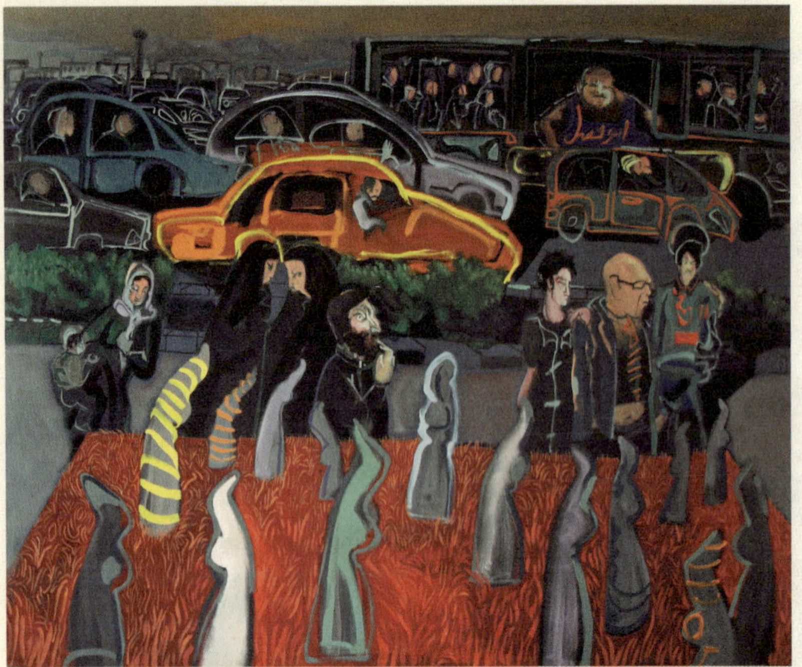

1.

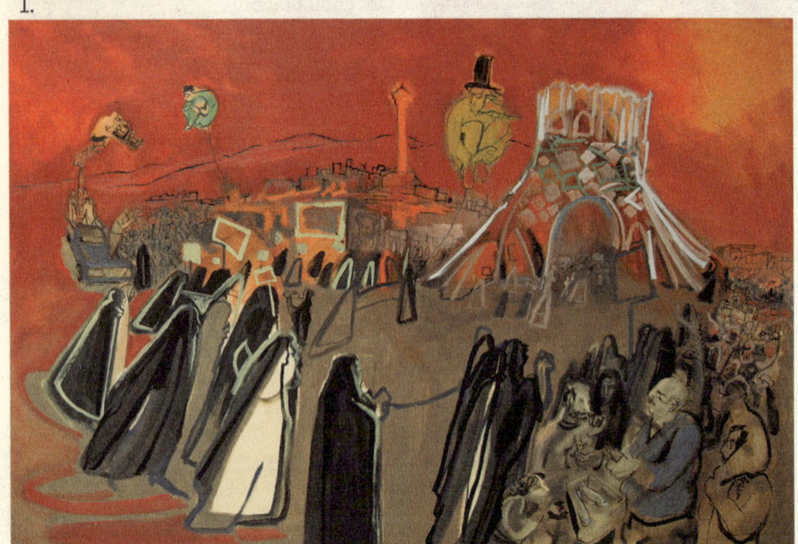

2.

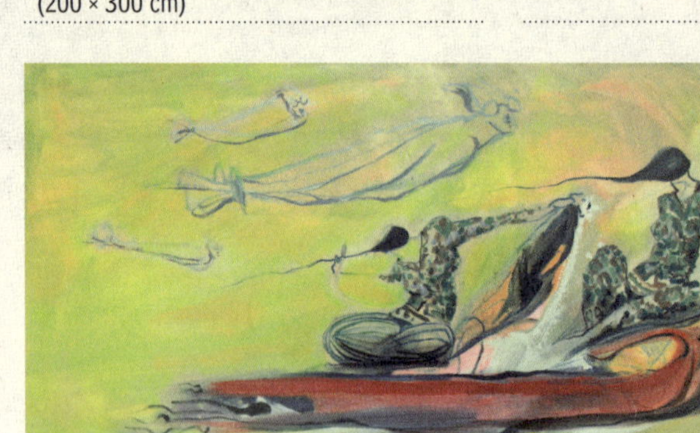

3.

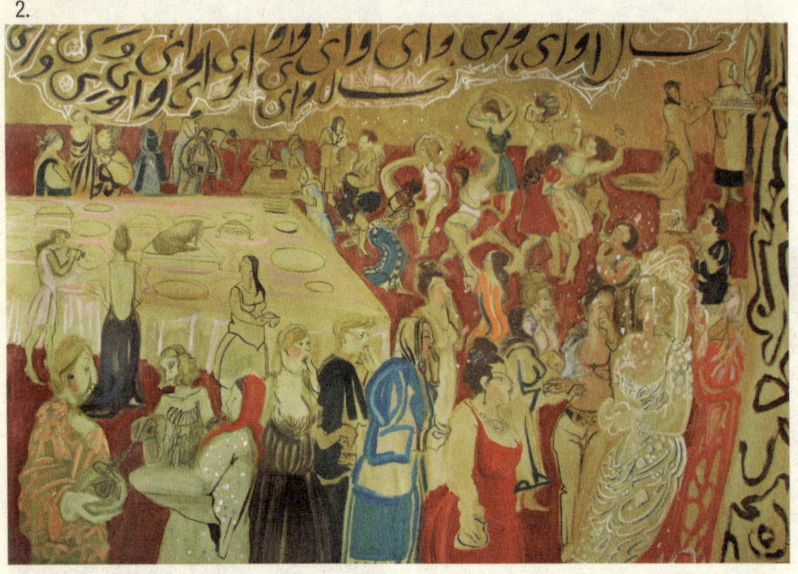

4.

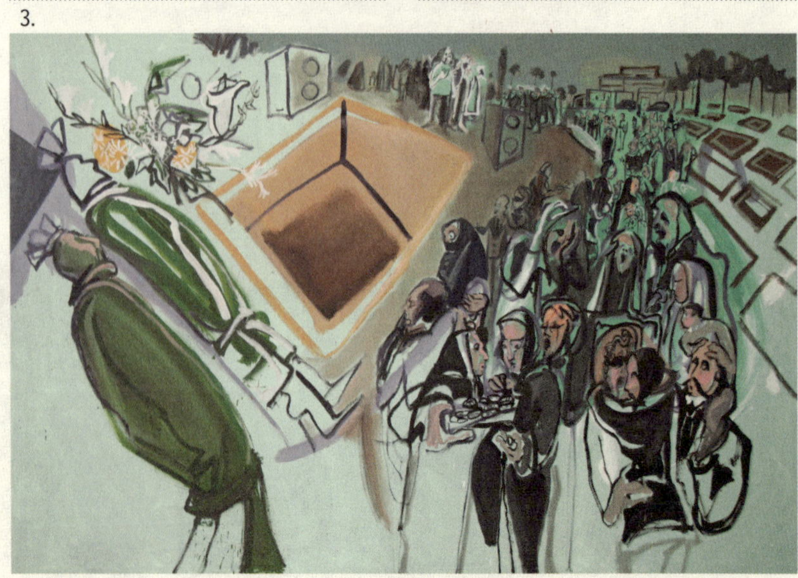

5.

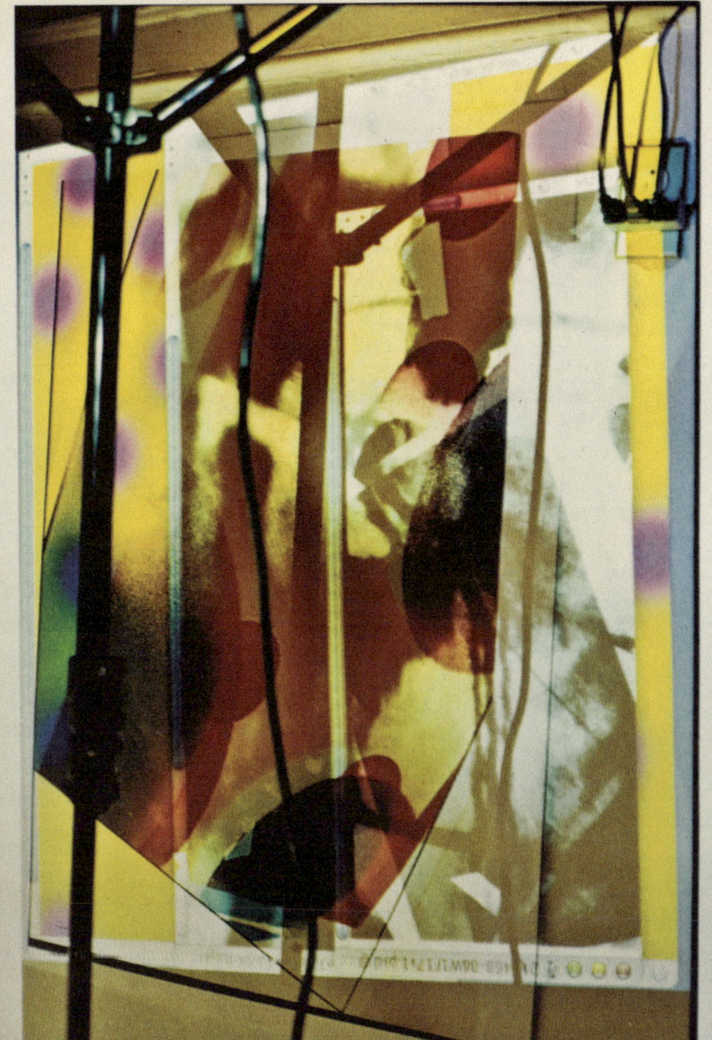

1.

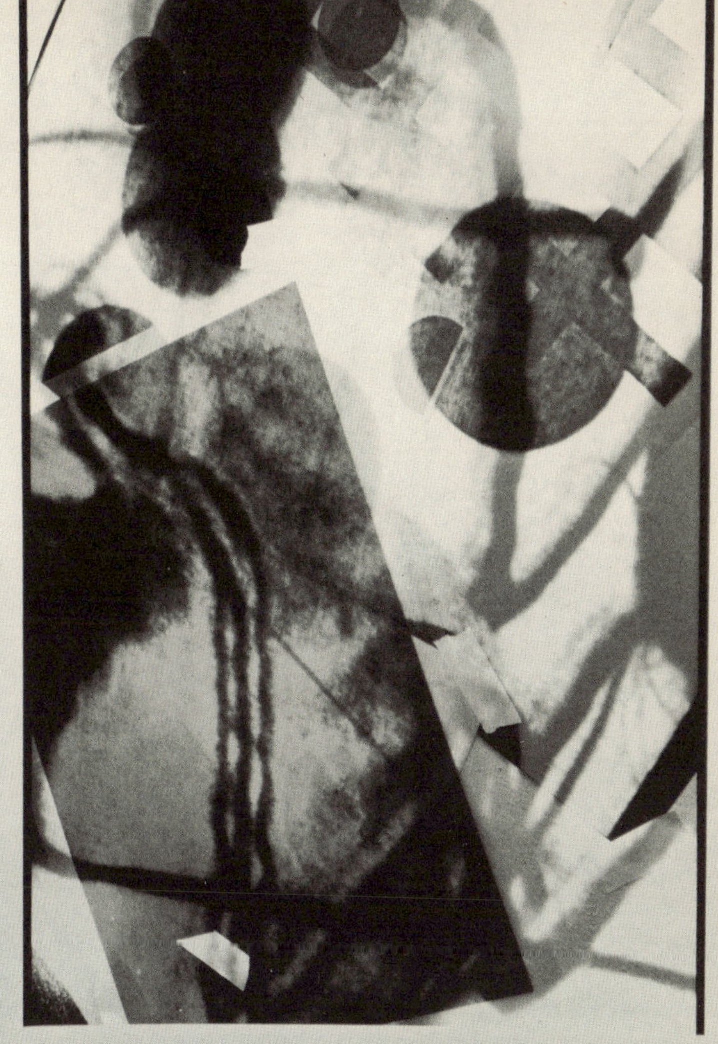

2.

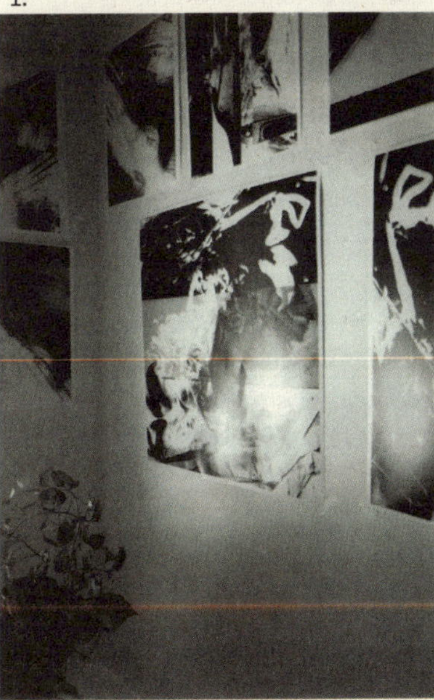

3.

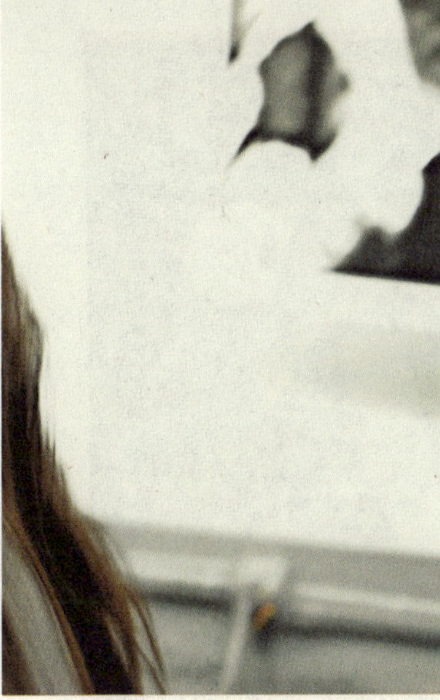

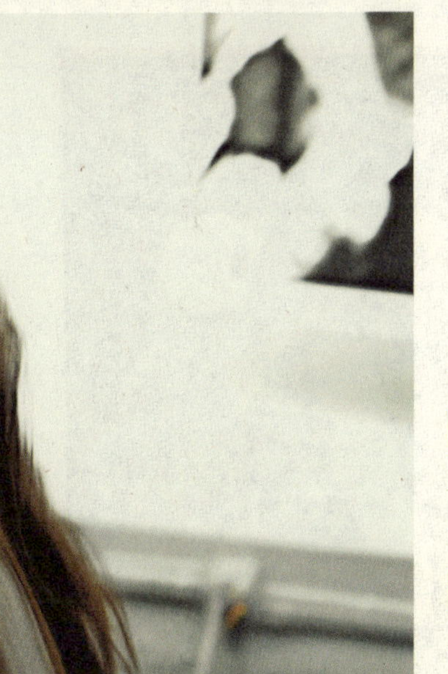

4.

Tamar Halpern earned her MFA from Columbia University in New York, where she continues to live. She uses a range of photographic processes to explore and assess the legacies of modernist abstraction. Her layered images are produced through multiple iterations of photography, digital manipulation, scanning, and printing.

1. **FLORIDA**
2008, chromogenic print, 40 × 30 in (102 × 76 cm)

2. **NEBRASKA**
2008, gelatin silver print, 40 × 30 in (102 × 76 cm)

3. **STUDIO 2007**
2008, inkjet print, 24 × 18 in (61 × 46 cm)

4. **JUNKO**
2008, digital chromogenic print, 40 × 30 in (102 × 76 cm), installation view

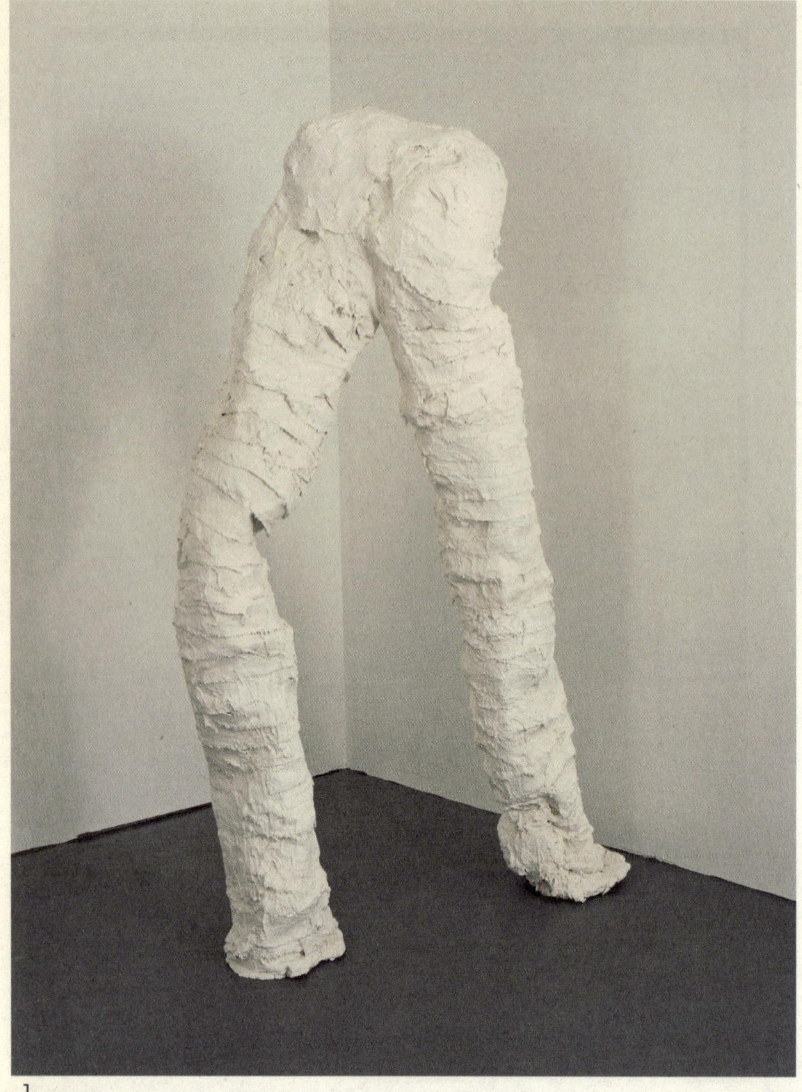

1.

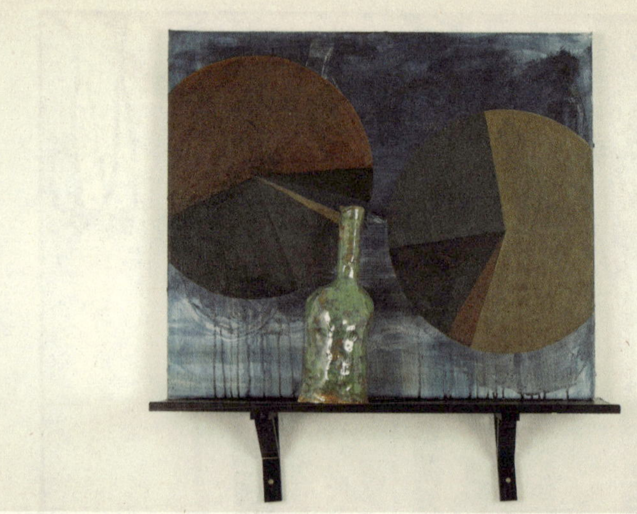

2.

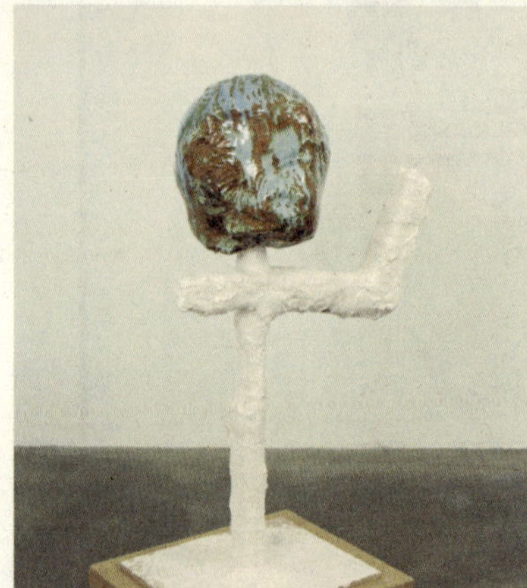

3.

Charlie Hammond earned his BA from the Glasgow School of Art and continues to live in Glasgow. He uses painting and sculpture to mine the territory between sophisticated and naive mark-making, forming a clever critique of the "modern primitive" style. One of his methods involves attaching brushes to a power drill to generate spirals across surfaces.

1. Untitled

2006, plaster, chicken wire, and foam filler, 67 × 15 $\frac{3}{4}$ × 43 $\frac{1}{4}$ in (170 × 40 × 110 cm)

2. Conversation Over Bottle of New World

2008, oil on canvas and stoneware ceramic, 20 $\frac{1}{2}$ × 24 × 6 in (52 × 61 × 15 cm)

3. Small Statue with Virtual Reality Helmet

2008, plaster, wood, polystyrene, and stoneware ceramic, 44 × 29 × 18 in (112 × 74 × 46 cm)

4. After Eating Bad Horsemeat

2006, oil on canvas in frame, 20 $\frac{1}{2}$ × 16 $\frac{1}{2}$ in (52 × 42 cm)

5. Mouldy Bread Man (Macaroni Style)

2007, oil and stoneware ceramic on canvas in frame, 20 $\frac{1}{2}$ × 2 $\frac{3}{4}$ × 20 $\frac{1}{2}$ in (52 × 7 × 52 cm)

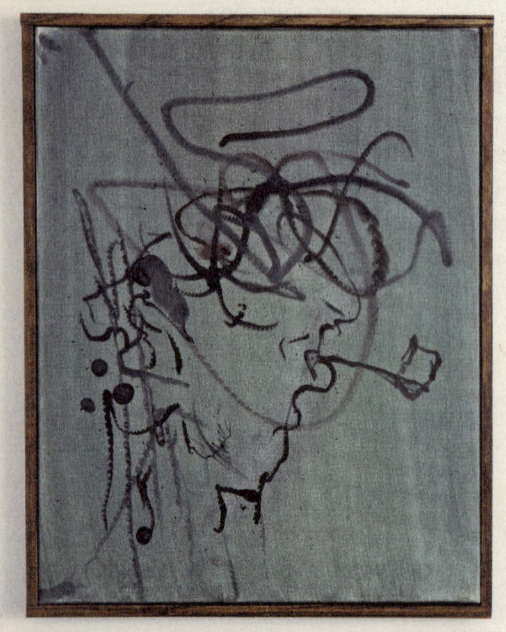

4.

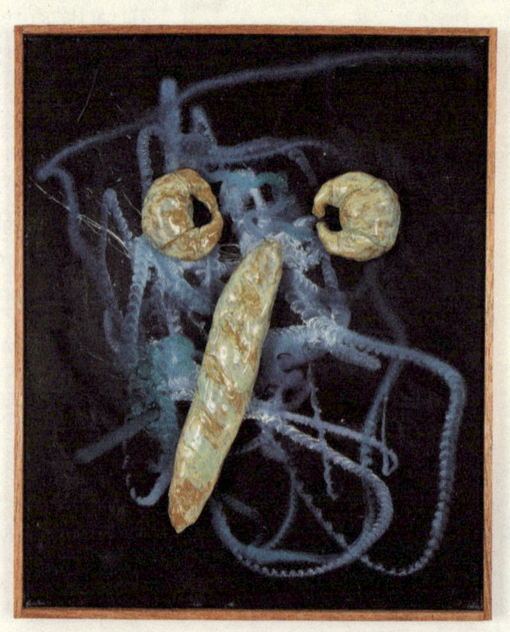

5.

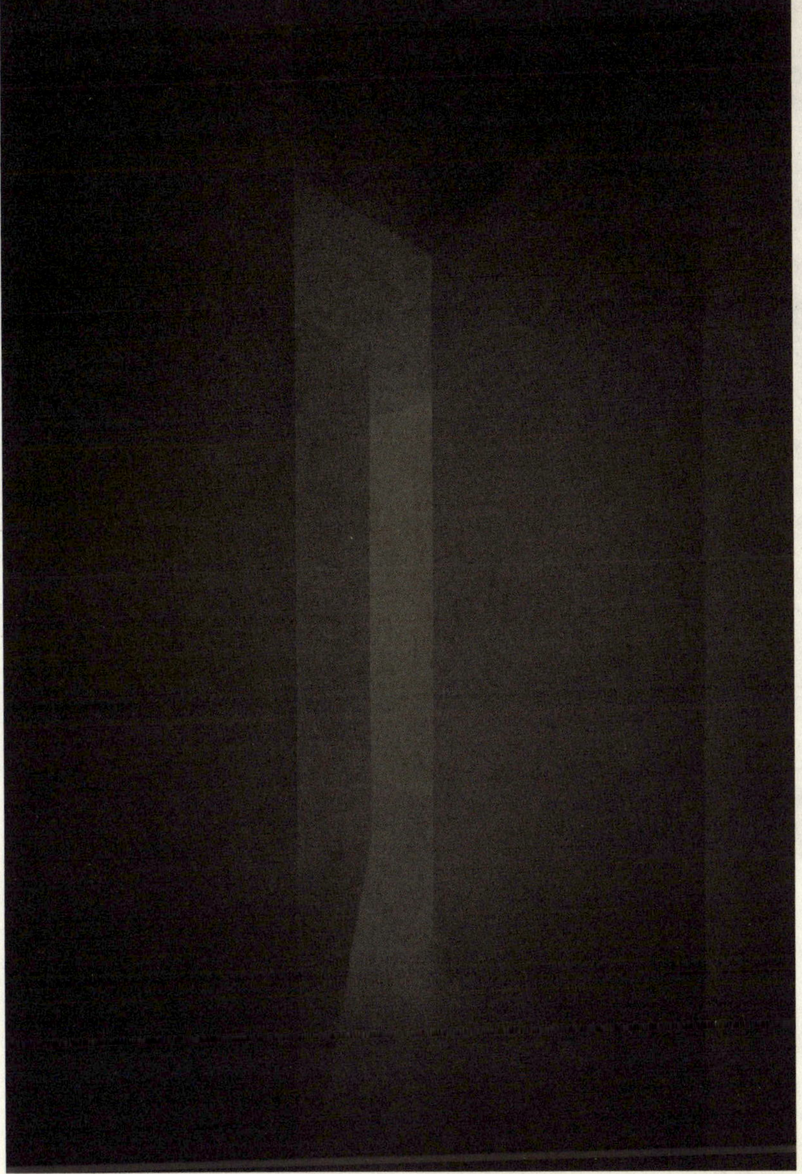

1.

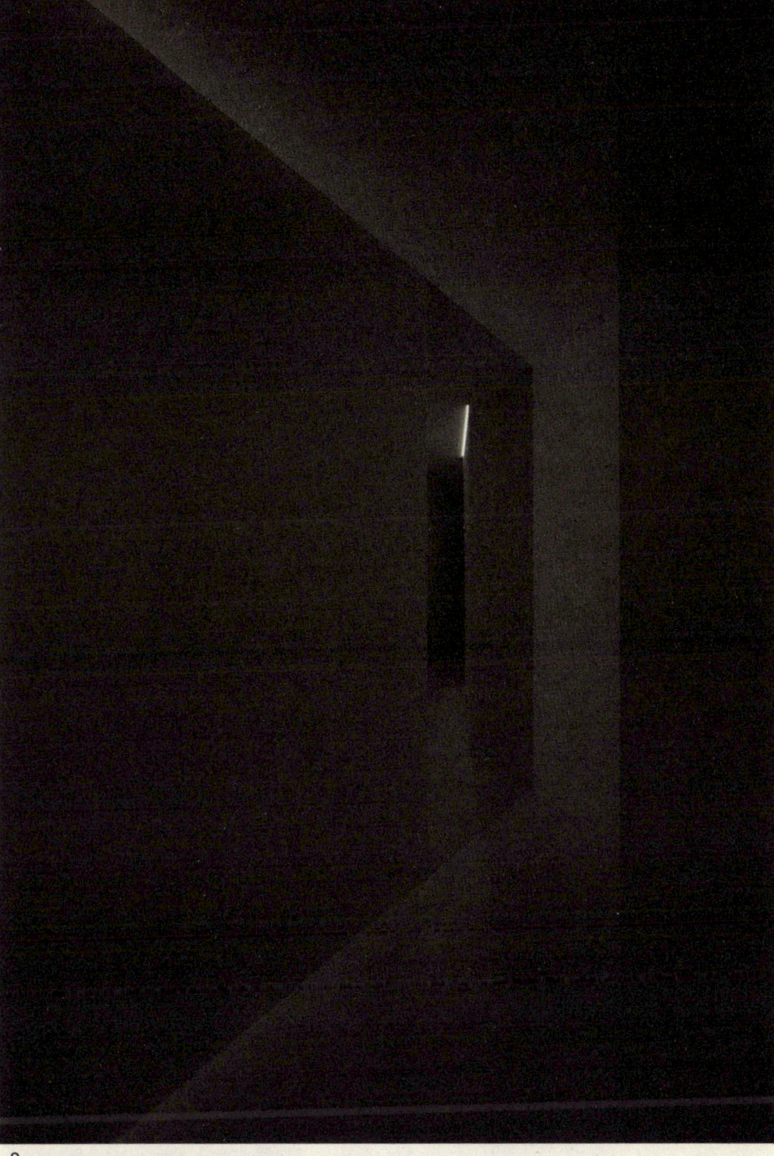

2.

Elin Hansdóttir attended the School of Art and Design in Berlin, where she continues to live. Her site-specific installations use architecture, light, and sound to heighten the viewer's awareness of space, often with disorienting results. **Path** (2008) turns a room into a white maze with sharp corners and irregular light, so that one easily mistakes shadows and light for walls, and walls for space.

1 & 2. **Path**
with sound by Úlfur Hansson
2008, mixed media, dimensions variable

3. **Untitled (Nafnlaust)**
with Anne Kockelkorn, Neulant van Exel, and Darri Lorenzen
2005, mixed media, dimensions variable

4. **Peripheral**
2007, mixed media, dimensions variable

3.

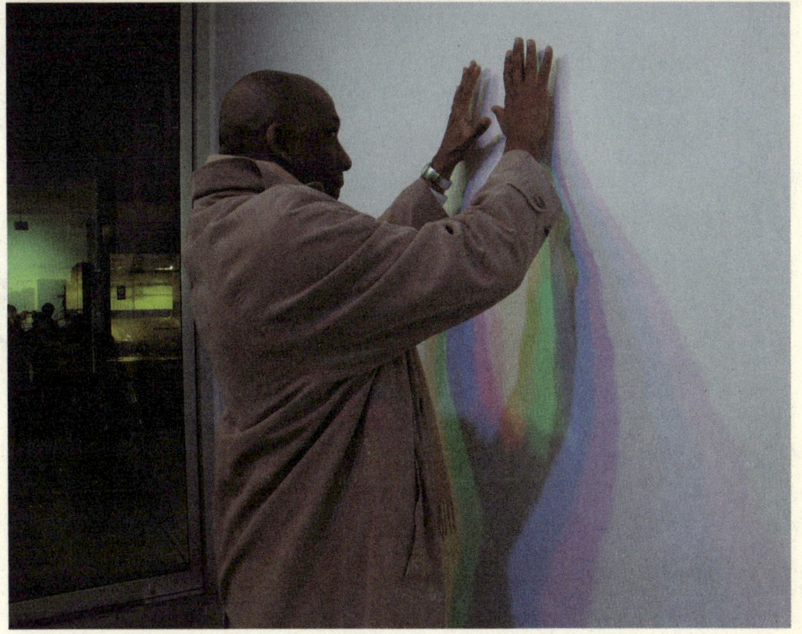

4.

1.

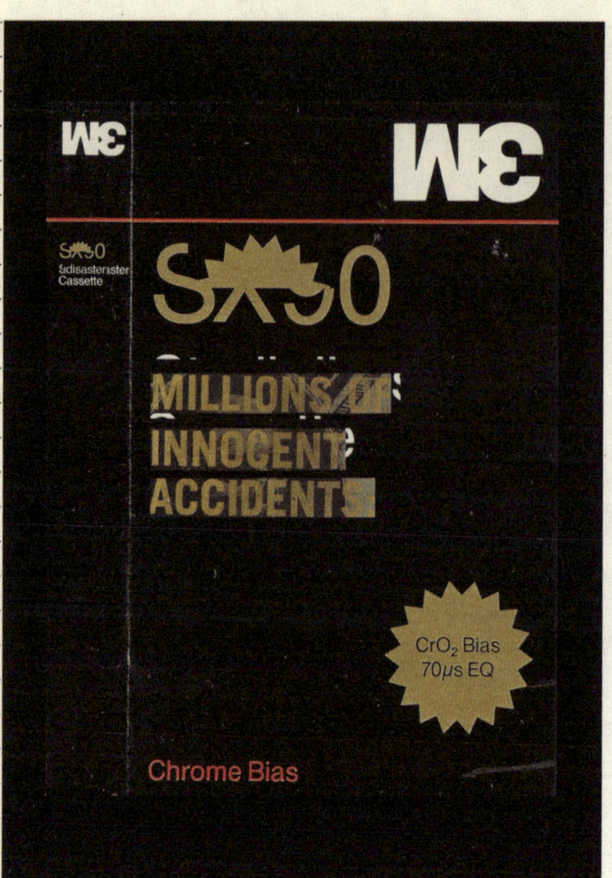

2.

Aaron Anderson (b. 1981), Eric Carlson (b. 1984), and Crystal Quinn (b. 1983) combined their backgrounds in art, animation, and graphic design to form the Minneapolis-based collective Hardland/Heartland. They produce performance, installation, painting, drawing, books, and fashion with references to popular and digital culture, Robert Rauschenberg, and contemporary science fiction.

1. **War is Over**
2008, poster, 22 × 14 in (56 × 36 cm)

2. **Millions of Innocent Accidents (WE)**
2008, exhibition postcard, Minneapolis Institute of the Arts

3. **Us Doves**
2008, printing spreads for Van Abbe Museum's Heartland magazine, mixed media, each 5 × 7 ½ in (13 × 19 cm)

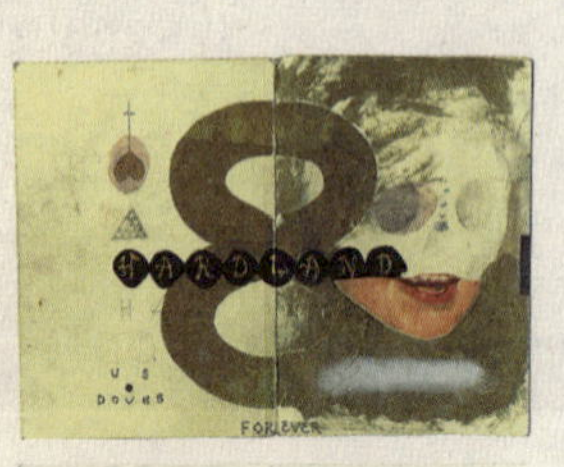
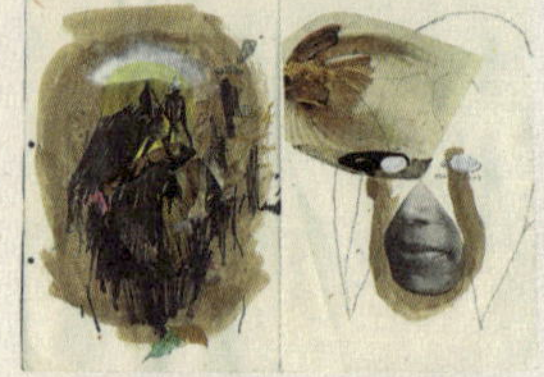
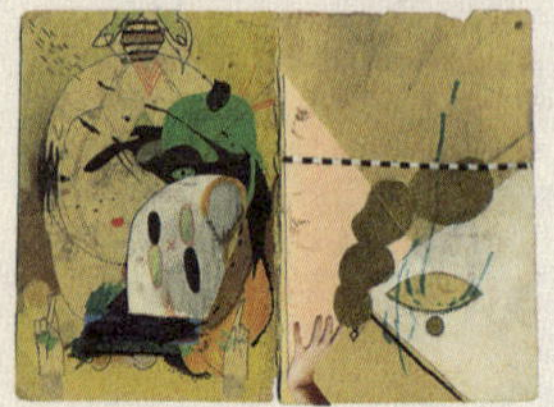
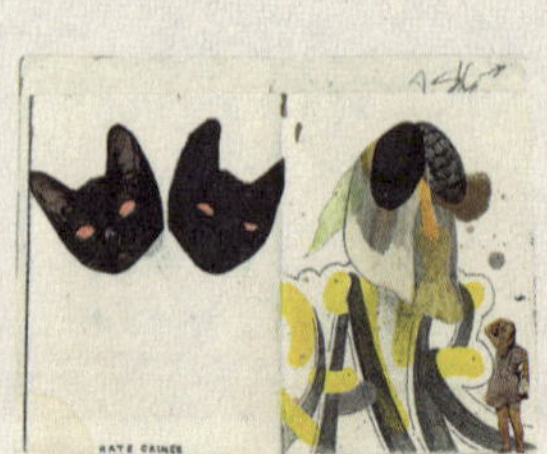
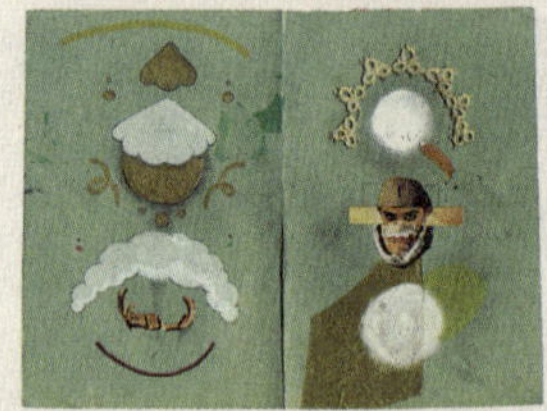
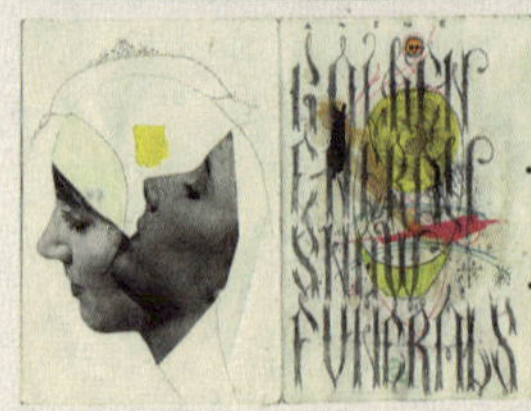
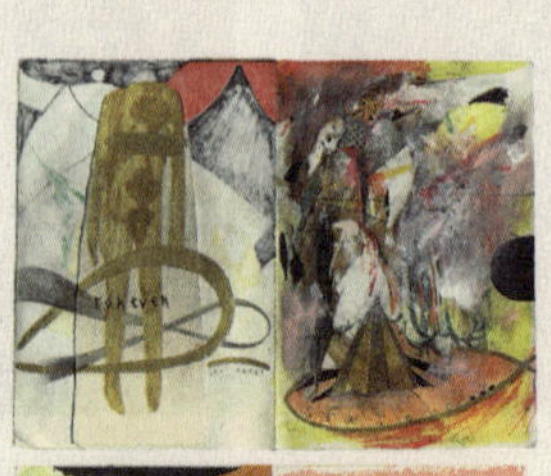
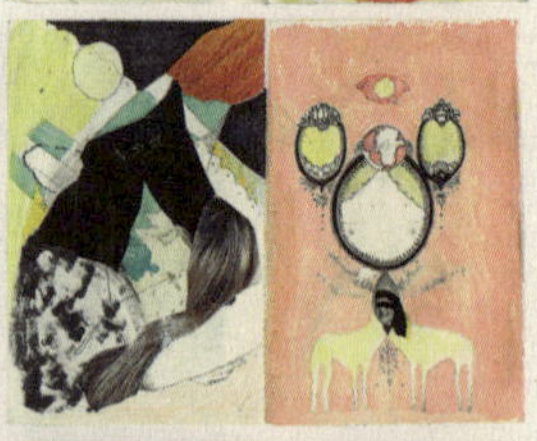
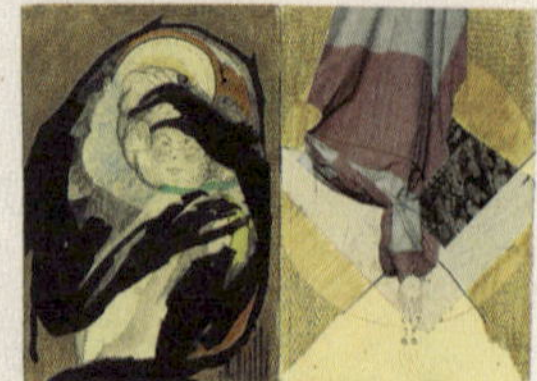

3.

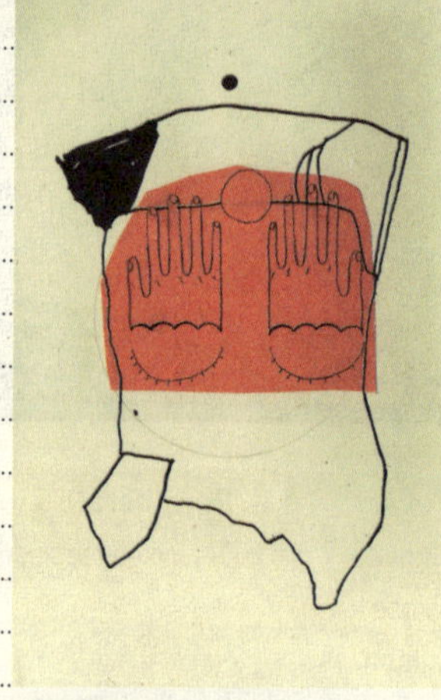
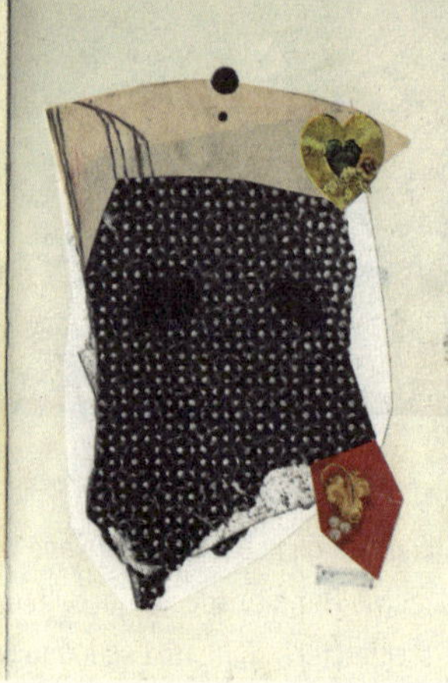

4.

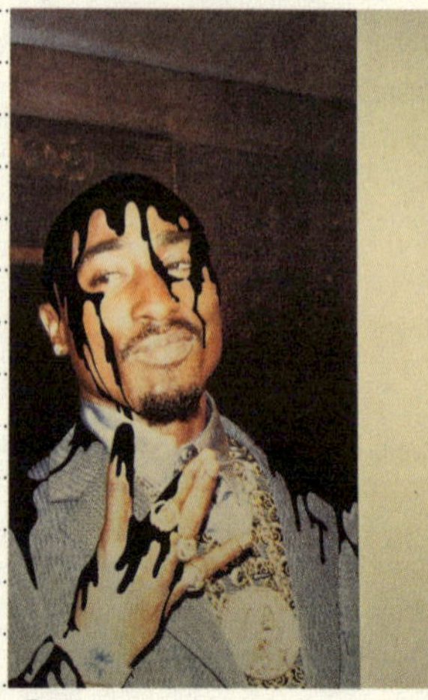
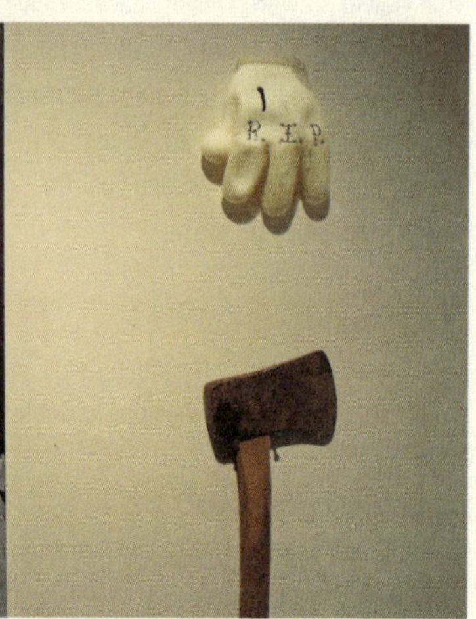

5.

4. **Befoul'd**
2007, mixed media, 5 × 7 ½ in (13 × 19 cm)

5. **"Serious Art"**
exhibition view at First Amendment Gallery, Minneapolis, Minnesota (2008)

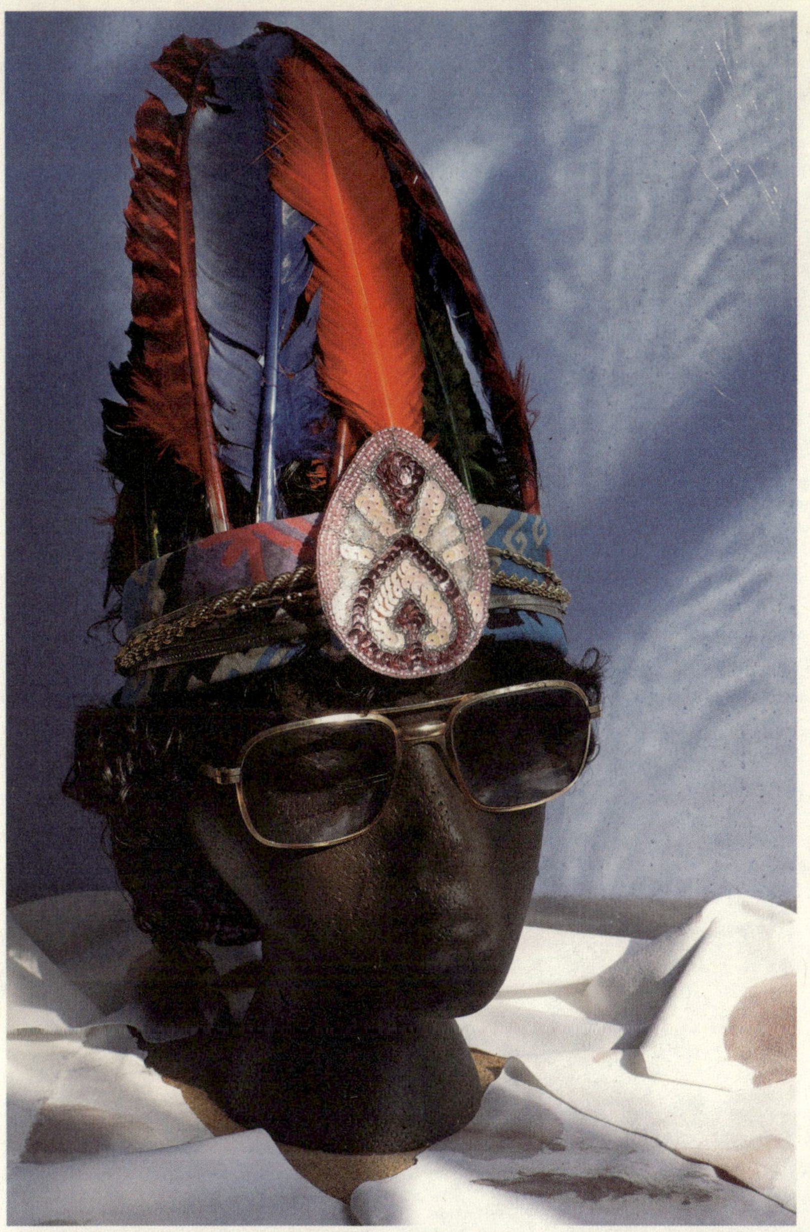

1.

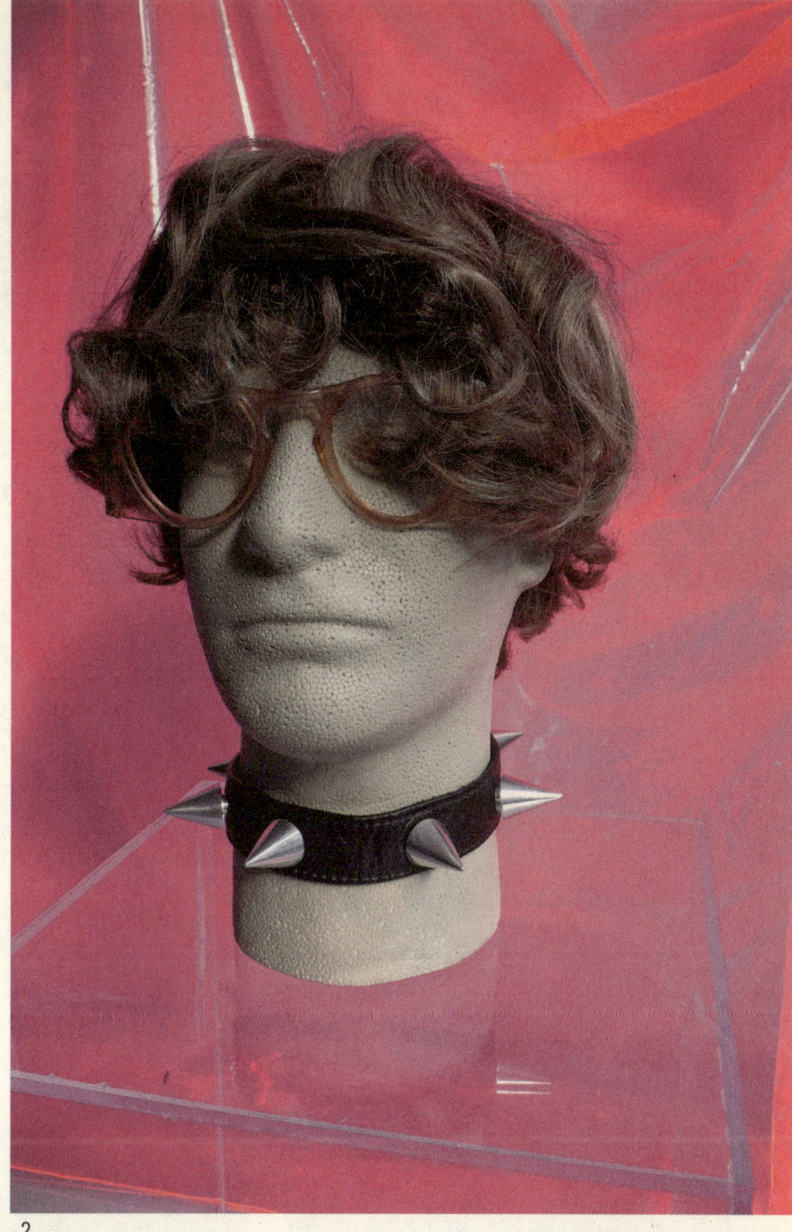

2.

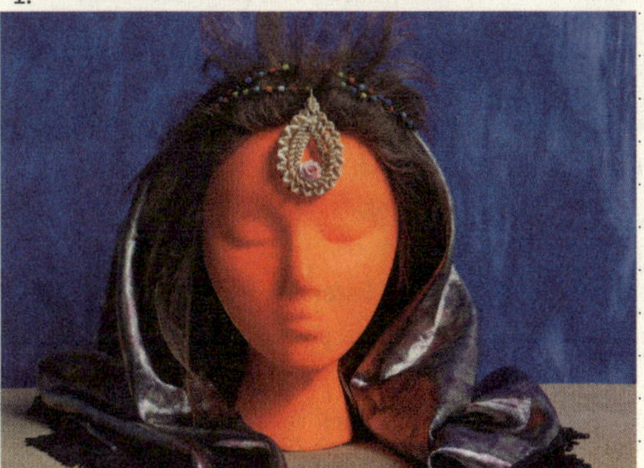

3.

4.

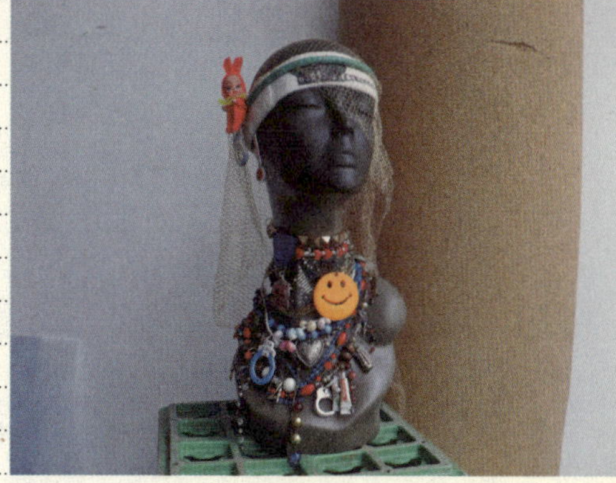

5.

K8 Hardy adopted the alternative, skater-inflected spelling of her first name as a teenager, when she was producing zines. Now she applies the same punk attitude to feminist critical theory in videos, photographs, performances, and texts. Hardy was active in Portland for several years before she relocated to New York City. She attended the Whitney Independent Study Program and Bard College. Hardy's early interest in collaborative publication continues in the journal **LTTR**, a political and aesthetic platform for the artists involved in its production.

1-5. **Untitled**
from the series **Polyamorous Relationship Style**
2008, mixed media, dimensions variable

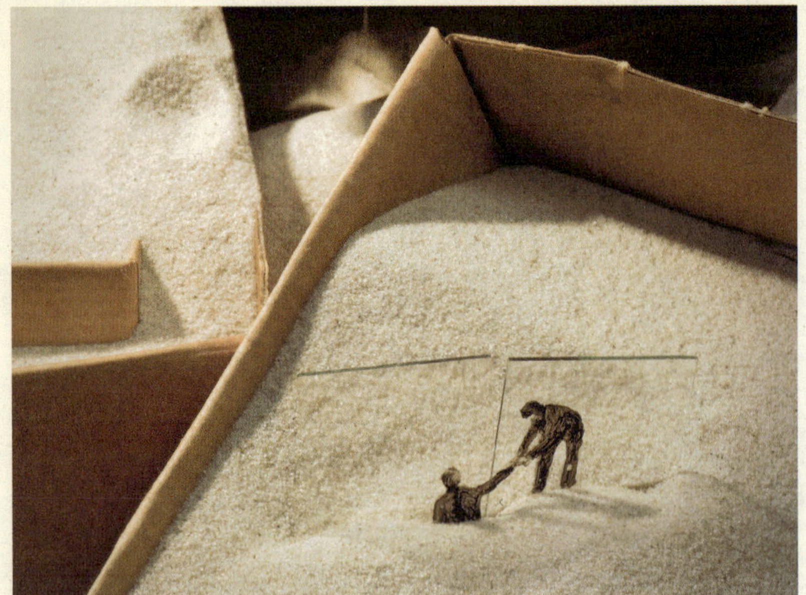
1.

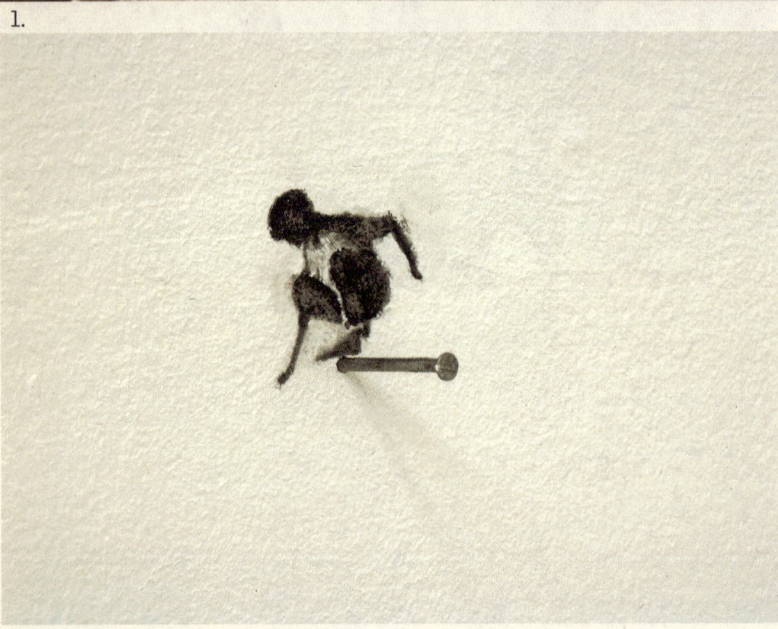
2.

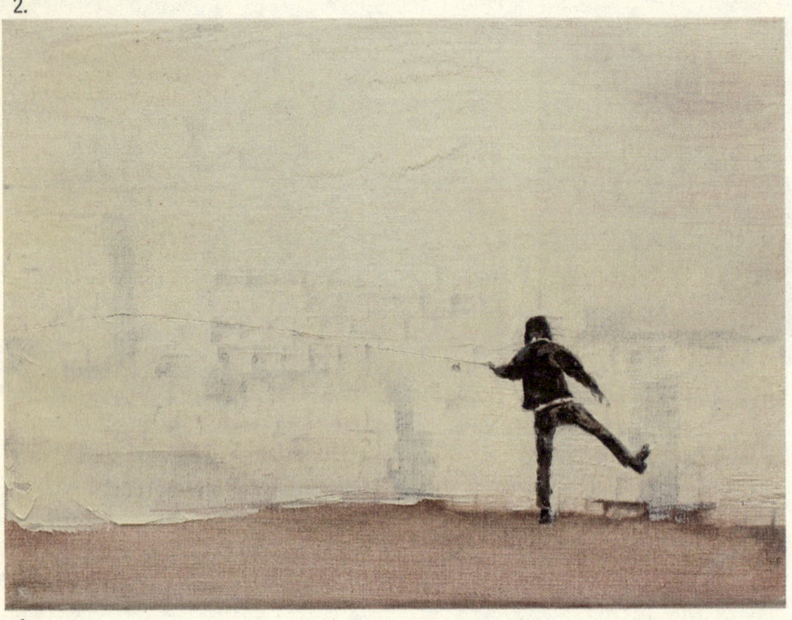
4.

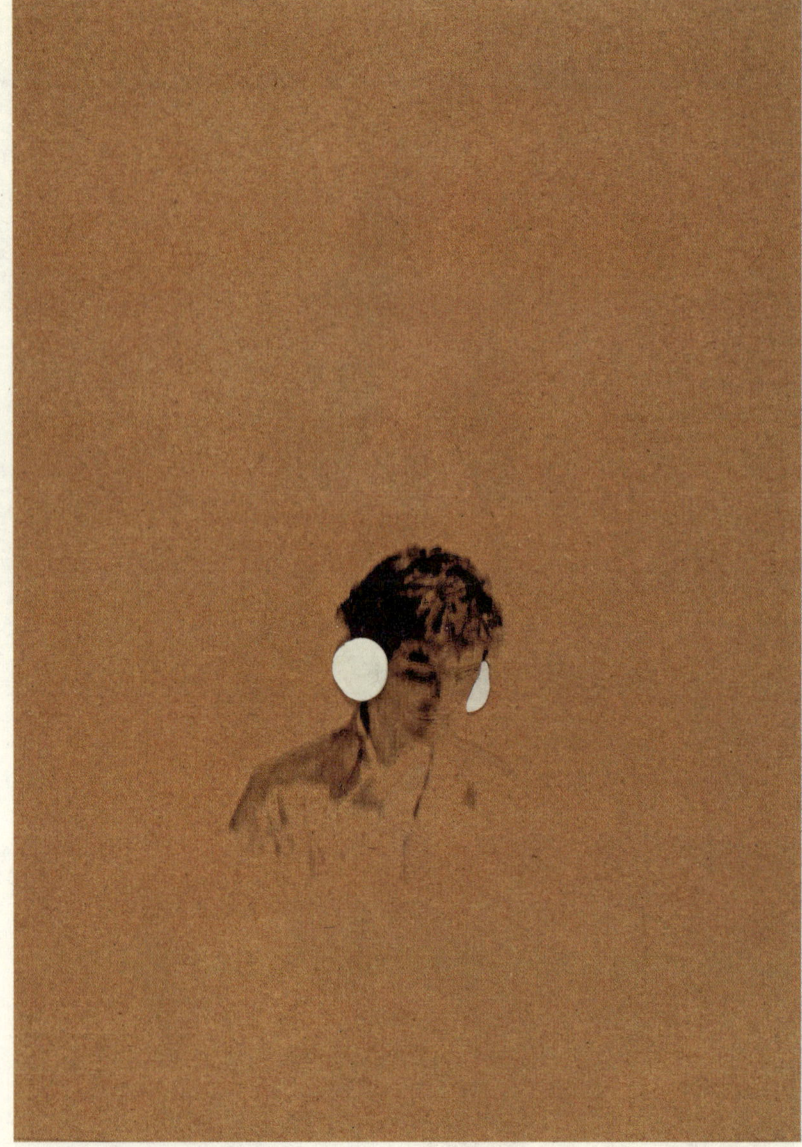
3.

Claire Harvey attended the Chelsea College of Art in London and currently lives in Amsterdam. She works in a figurative language that is at once intimate and anonymous. Appearing on unconventional surfaces like Post-it notes, transparencies, and glass slides, in addition to canvas, her characters perform ordinary and extraordinary tasks in delicate vignettes that often include three-dimensional elements.

1. **Swept Away** (detail)
2007, oil on glass, cardboard boxes, and sand, dimensions variable

2. **The man on the nail**
2004-05, oil paint and nail, dimensions variable

3. **The listener**
2007, transparent sheet, oil paint, cardboard, and sticky tack, 12 × 8 1/4 in (30 × 21 cm)

4. **Fishing Chris**
2004, oil on canvas, 10 × 13 3/4 in (25 × 35 cm)

Abhishek Hazra studied graphic design at Srishti School of Art, Design and Technology in Bangalore, India, where he continues to live and work. He makes videos that explore Bengali identity as well as India's relationship to Western thought and culture. Among his artworks is a study of the collaboration between Albert Einstein and the Indian physicist S. N. Bose, and an eBay auction of a handwritten translation of the Communist Manifesto in Bengali.

1. www.ebayaday.com
2008, mixed media, including eBay.com, handwritten manuscripts, and video, dimensions variable

2. Shouting Needham from Rooftops
2008, video projection with sound, 7 min 58 sec

3. Laughing in a Sine Curve
2008, video projection

4. Summation [pH]n1 to [pH]n2
2007, video projection, 4 monitors, sound

5. Bose Einstein Chapters: Part 01 Distribution
2007, video projection, 6 min 42 sec

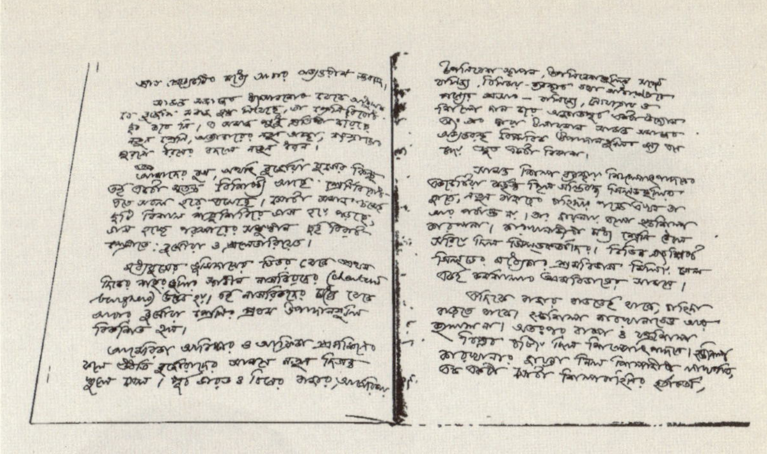

1.

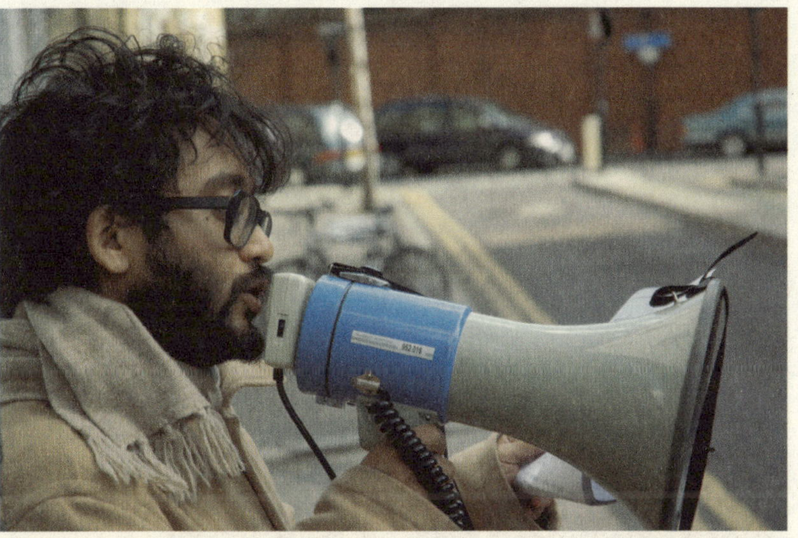

2.

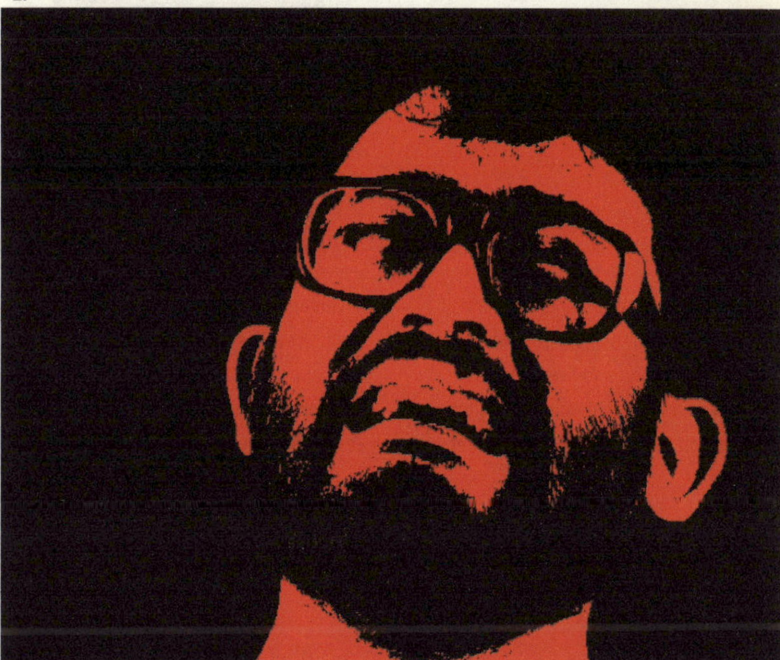

3.

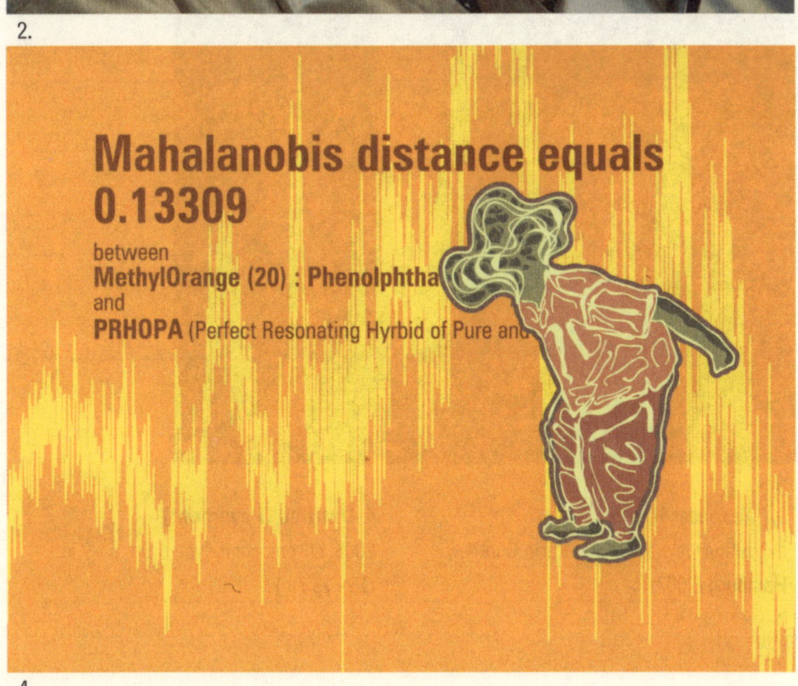

4.

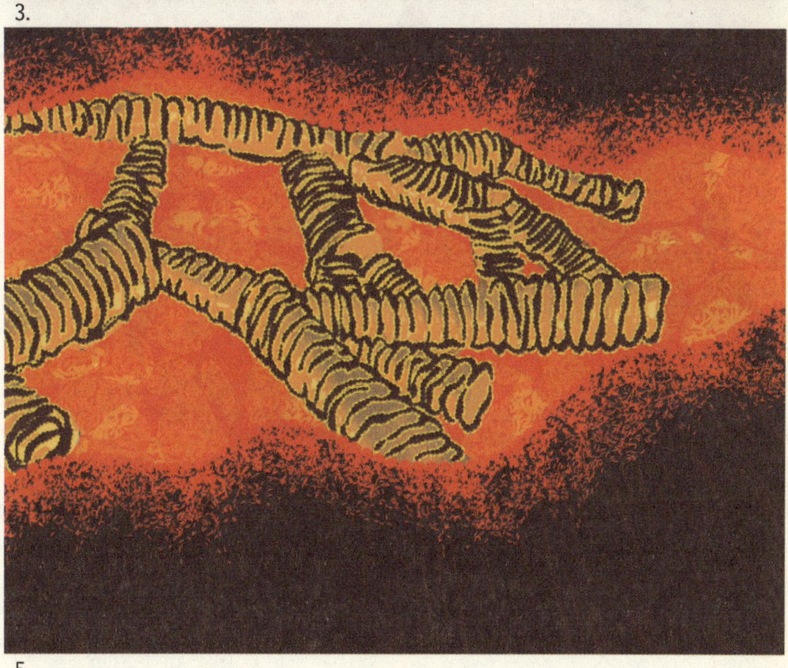

5.

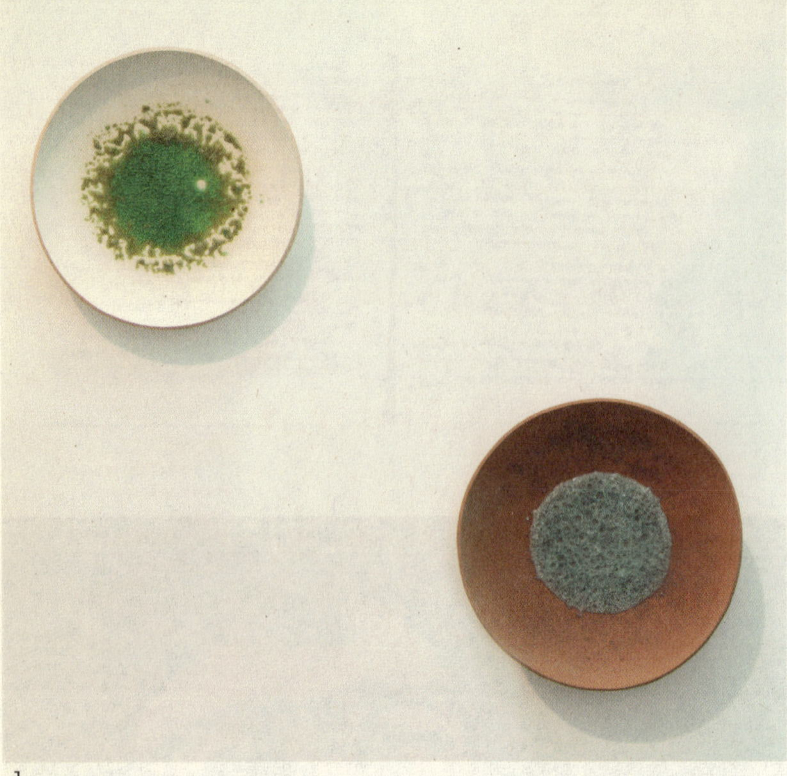

1.

Alexander Heim earned his MA in fine art from Goldsmiths College in London, where he continues to live and work. He makes a variety of objects, including ceramic plates, photographs of street pavement, and clifflike papier-mâché sculptures. His video work often explores the behavior of animals, for example pigeons or stray dogs, in an urban environment.

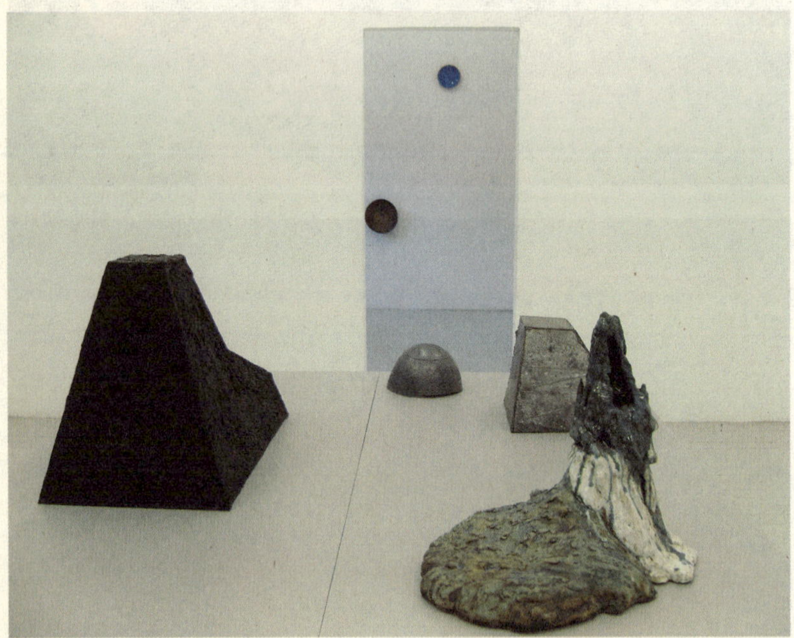

3.

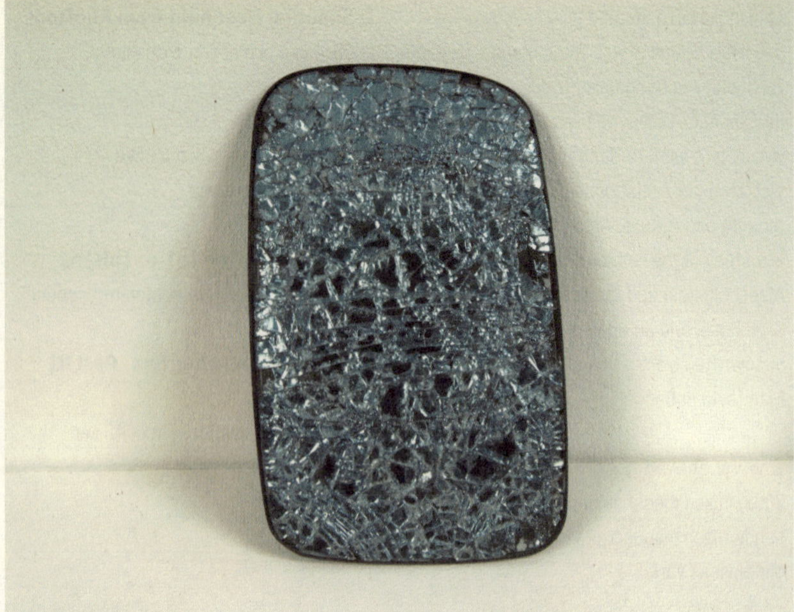

2.

4.

1. **gis and cis**
2007, stoneware, green glass, earthenware, and white glass, two parts, diameter each 15 3⁄4 in (40 cm)

2. **Untitled (Five found wing mirrors from Rotherhithe Tunnel)** (detail)
2006, plinth and found mirrors, 47 1⁄4 × 51 1⁄4 × 4 3⁄4 in (120 × 130 × 12 cm)

3. "Alexander Heim"
exhibition view at Galerie Karin Günther, Hamburg (2007)

4. **Untitled (Pavement)**
2008, chromogenic-type print, 6 × 9 in (15 × 23 cm)

Martina Heinz attended the Staatliche Akademie der Bildenden Künste in Karlsruhe, and currently lives in Berlin. Rooted in painting, her practice has evolved into drawing with a limited range of tools – pencil, chalk, ballpoint pen. She creates intimate studies in figuration, from the real to the supernatural.

1. **Untitled (Eros)**
2006, ballpoint pen on paper, $11 \frac{1}{2} \times 8$ in (30 × 20 cm)

2. **Horror Vacui** (detail)
2006, pencil on paper, 3 parts, each $11 \frac{3}{4} \times 9 \frac{1}{2}$ in (30 × 24 cm)

3. **Untitled (Self)** (detail)
2006, ballpoint pen and oil on paper, $8 \times 5 \frac{3}{4}$ in (20 × 15 cm)

4. **Untitled (Horse)**
2008, black chalk and graphite on paper, 63 × 118 in (160 × 300 cm)

5. **Agonie** (detail)
2006, oil on canvas, $55 \frac{1}{2} \times 35 \frac{1}{2}$ in (140 × 90 cm)

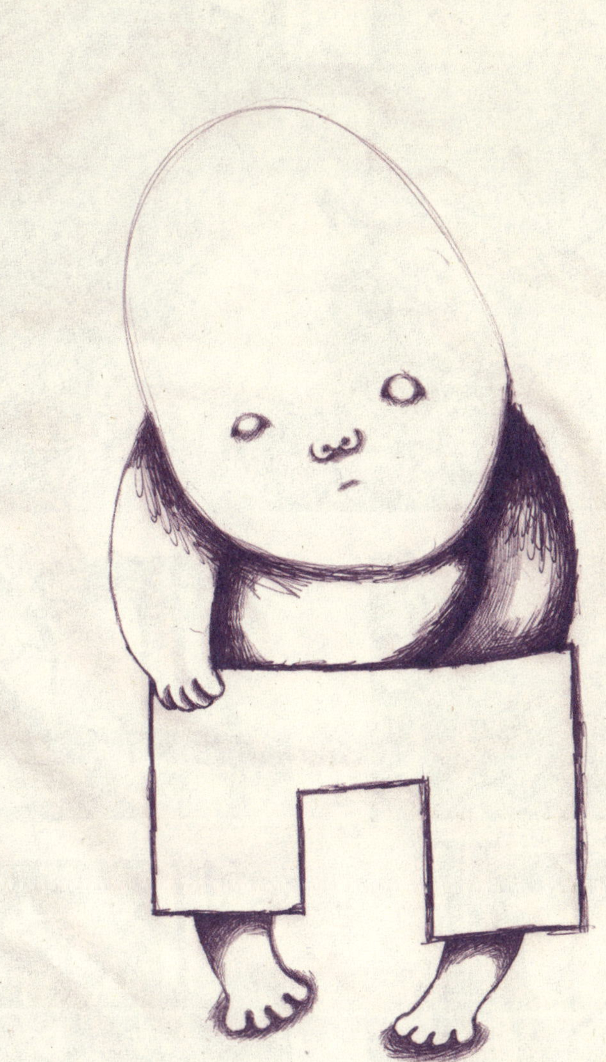

1.

4.

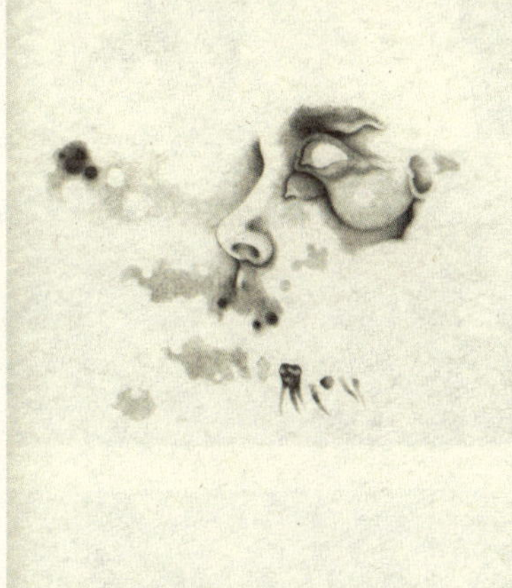

2.

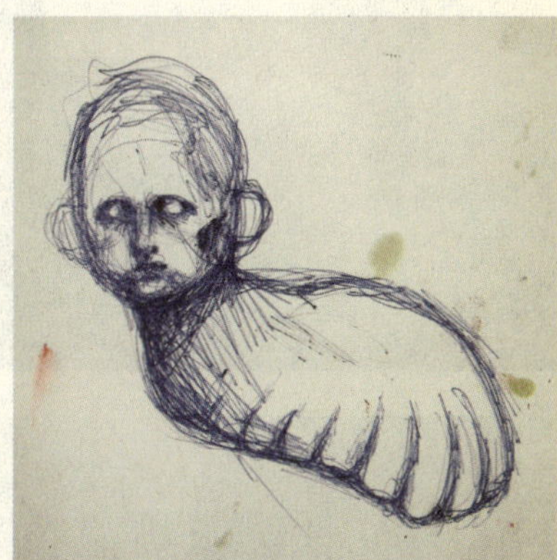

3.

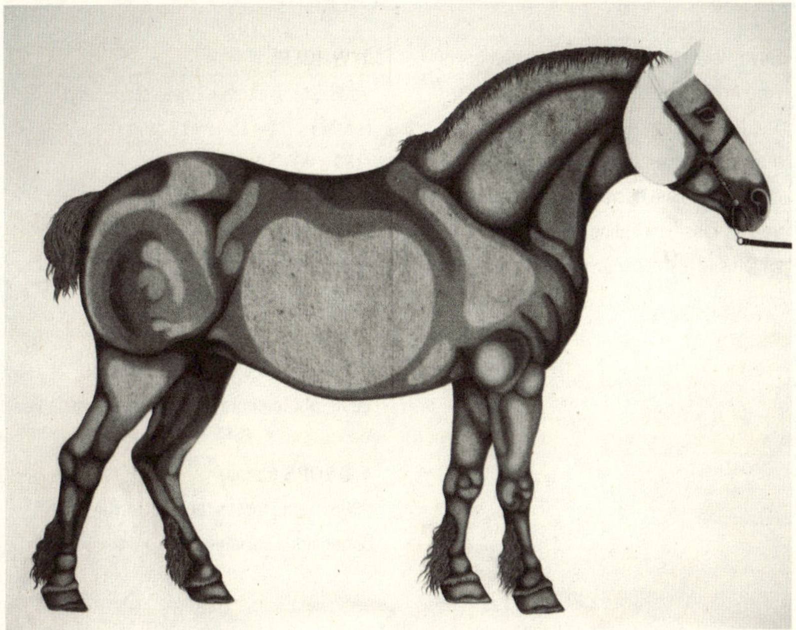

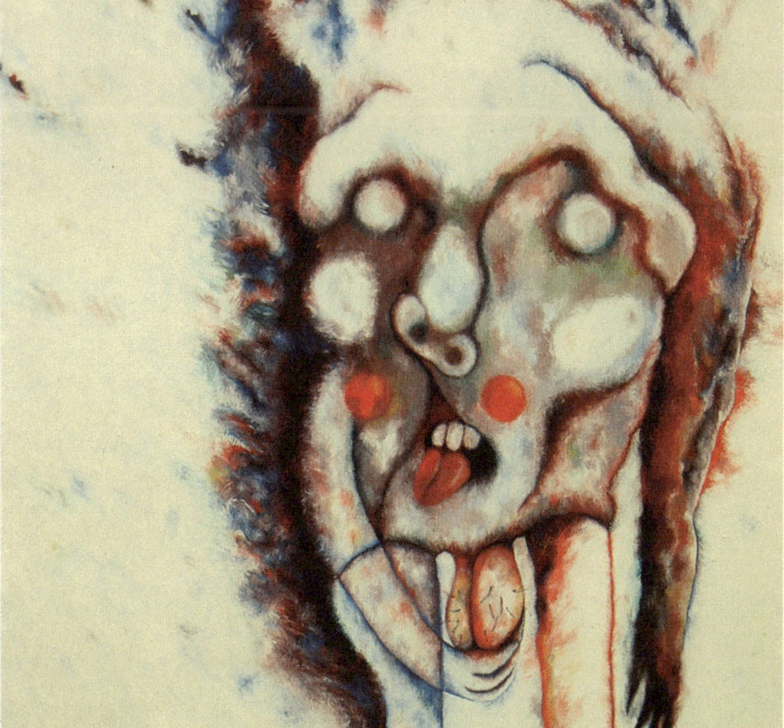

5.

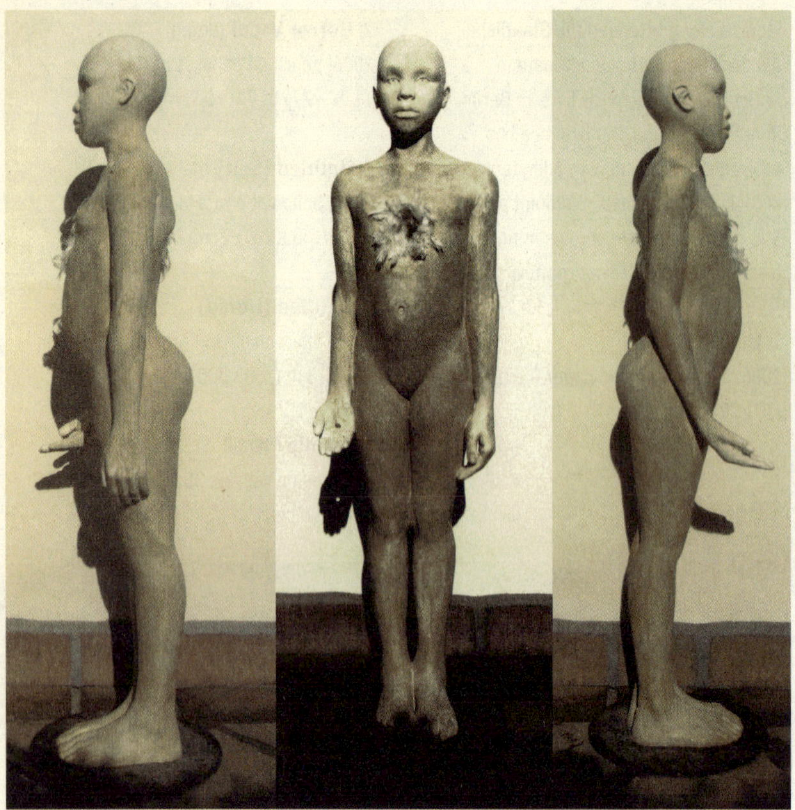

1.

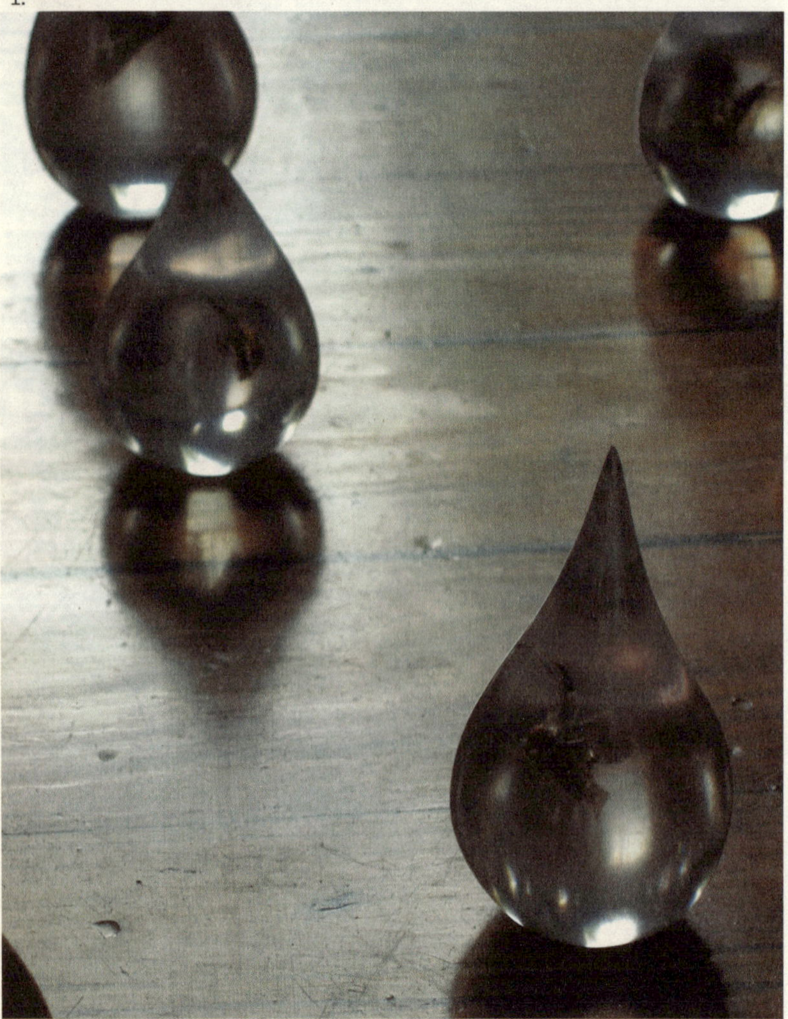

3.

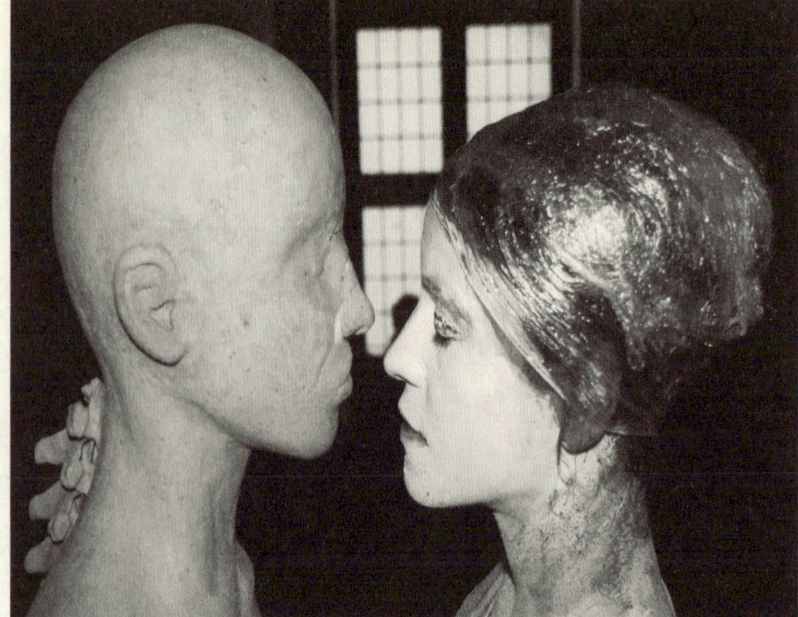

2.

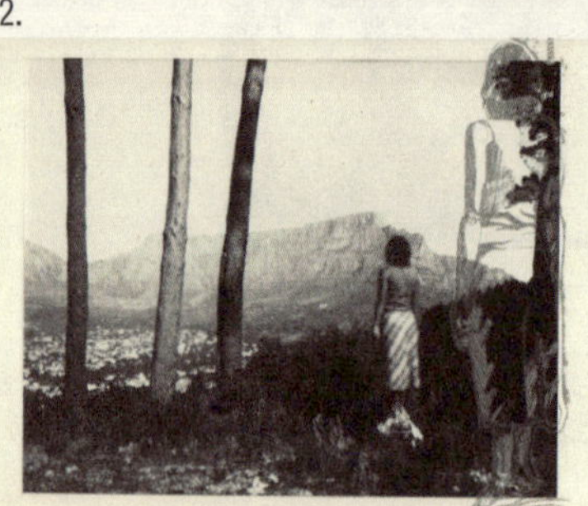

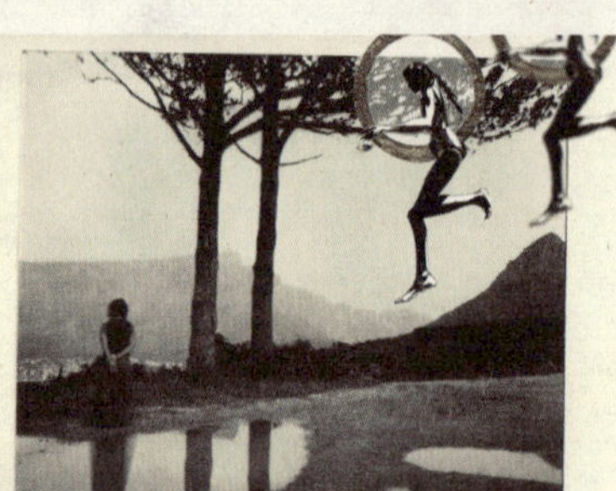

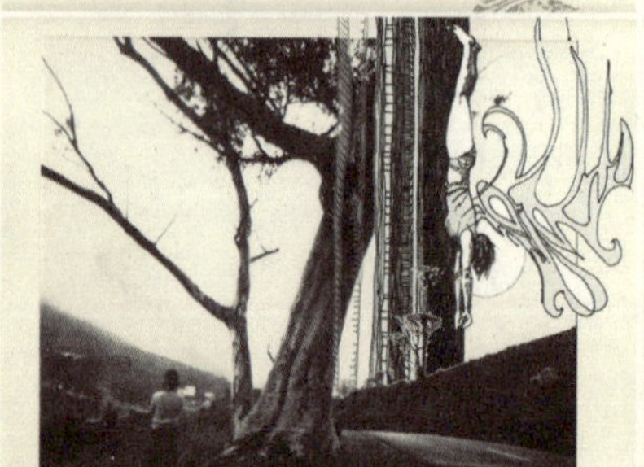

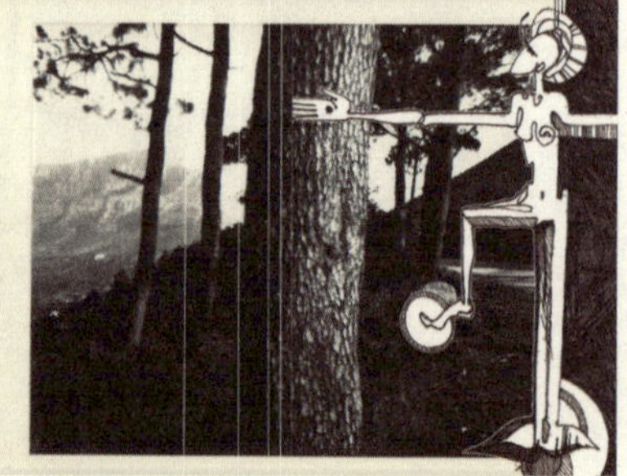

4

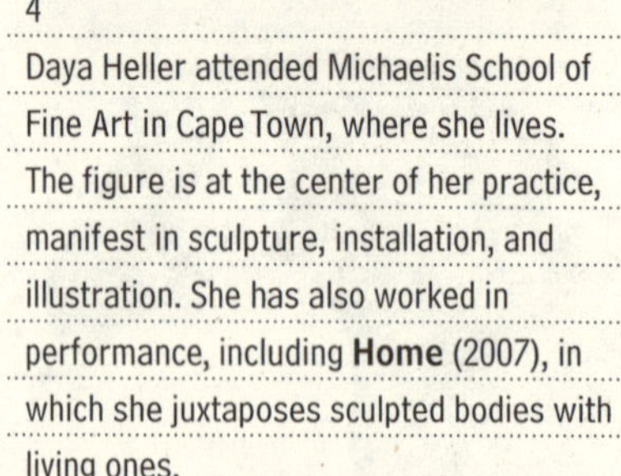

Daya Heller attended Michaelis School of Fine Art in Cape Town, where she lives. The figure is at the center of her practice, manifest in sculpture, installation, and illustration. She has also worked in performance, including **Home** (2007), in which she juxtaposes sculpted bodies with living ones.

1. **WHOLE**
2008, steel, plaster, Crete stone, and feathers, 71 × 15 ¾ × 19 ¾ in (180 × 40 × 50 cm)

2. **JOURNEY**
2007, performance

3. **Untitled**
from the series **CITY BOWL GIRL**
2008, photomontage, dimensions variable

4. **DROPS** (detail)
2006, resin, moths, and butterflies, dimensions variable

Kiluanji Kia Henda's practice is focused on photography, from documentary images of contemporary African life to conceptual projects like **Icarus 13** (2006), which tells the story of a spaceship constructed and launched from Africa to explore the sun. He has also worked in music and theater production, and was included in "Check List Luanda Pop" at the 52nd Venice Biennale (2007), and in the first Luanda Triennial, Angola (2007).

1. **Baby Lonia**
2007, color photograph on aluminum,
$39\frac{1}{2} \times 59$ in (100 × 150 cm)

2. **Kixima Remix**
2008, color photograph on matte paper,
$31\frac{1}{2} \times 47\frac{1}{4}$ in (80 × 120 cm)

3. **Some say we are in Africa** (detail)
2008, color photograph on matte paper,
$63 \times 47\frac{1}{4}$ in (160 × 120 cm)

4. **Placenta**
2005, color photograph on aluminum,
$31\frac{1}{2} \times 47\frac{1}{4}$ in (80 × 120 cm)

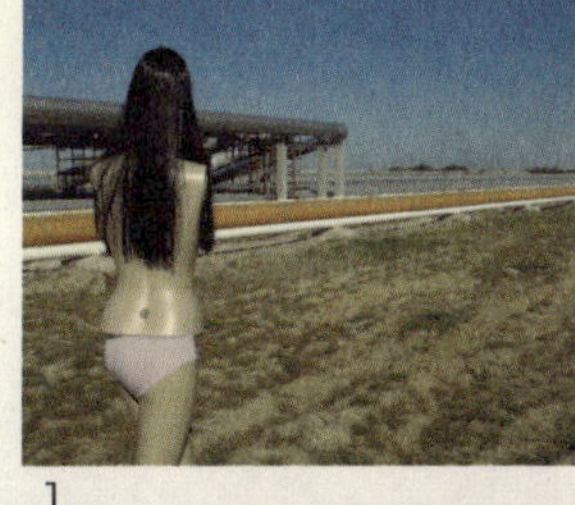

1.

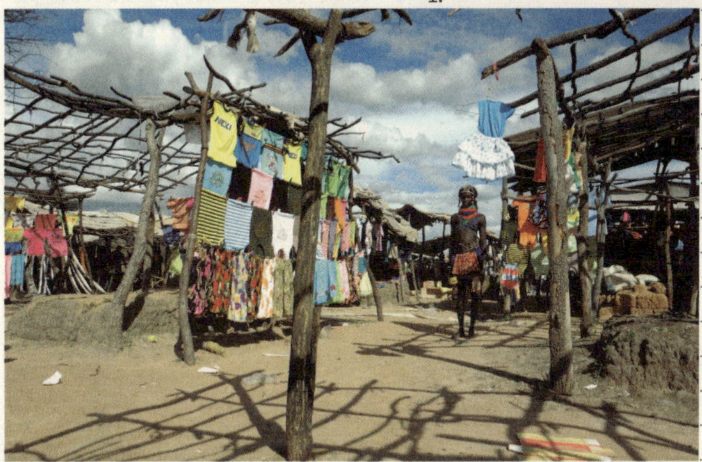

2.

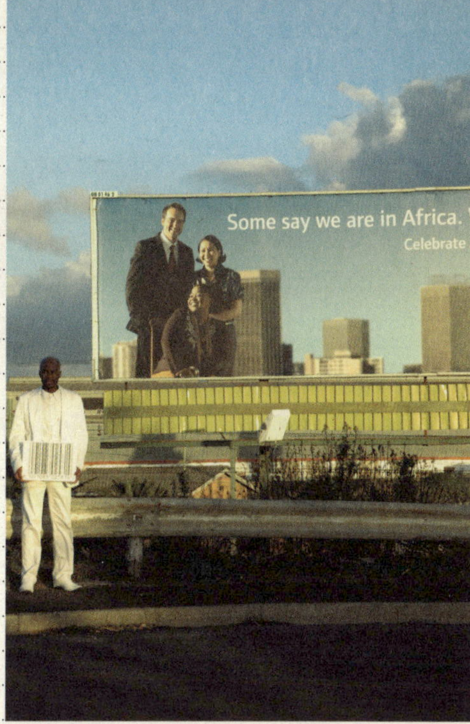

3.

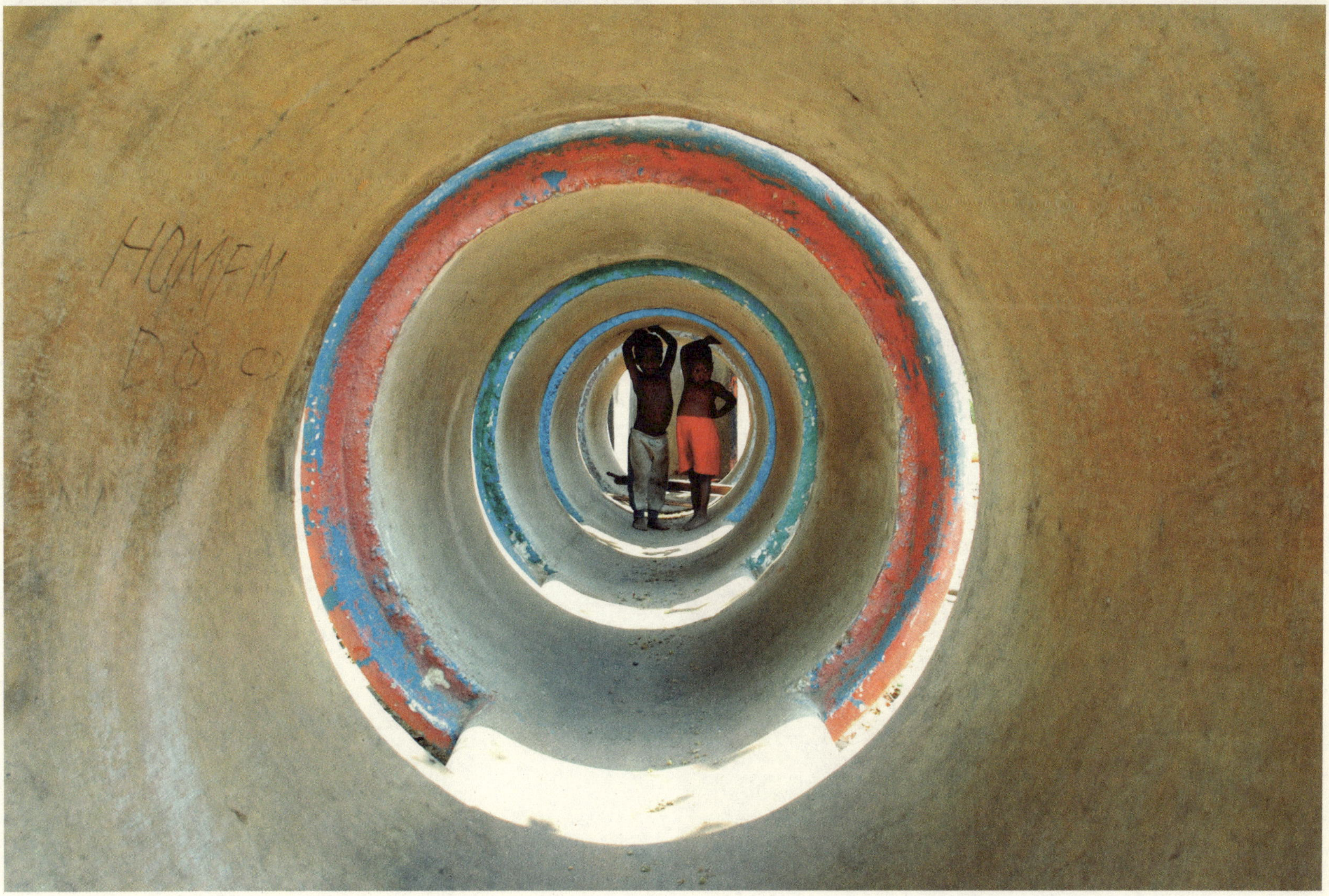

4.

Inti Hernandez completed a residency at the Rijksakademie in Amsterdam, and currently lives in Amsterdam and Havana. He works in performance, sculpture, and public installation to explore social and political dynamics, particularly as they contrast between his two homes. Many works focus on shifting notions of public and private space.

1. **Encounter Place (a presence)**
2007, ink on paper and etching, $13\frac{3}{4} \times 17\frac{1}{2}$ in (35 × 44 cm)

2. **Encounter Place 3/8 (model I & II)**
2006-07, wood, plywood, balsa wood, and mirror; model I: $8 \times 12 \times 27\frac{1}{2}$ in (20 × 30 × 70 cm); model II: $15\frac{3}{4} \times 23\frac{1}{2} \times 16$ in (40 × 60 × 140 cm)

3. **Encounter Place (variations)**
2006, balsa wood, plywood, metal, and mirror, $27\frac{1}{2} \times 27\frac{1}{2} \times 27\frac{1}{2}$ in (70 × 70 × 70 cm)

4. **Shared experience (Amsterdam)**,
2005, performance and Epson archival print, $39\frac{1}{2} \times 27\frac{1}{2}$ in (100 × 70 cm)

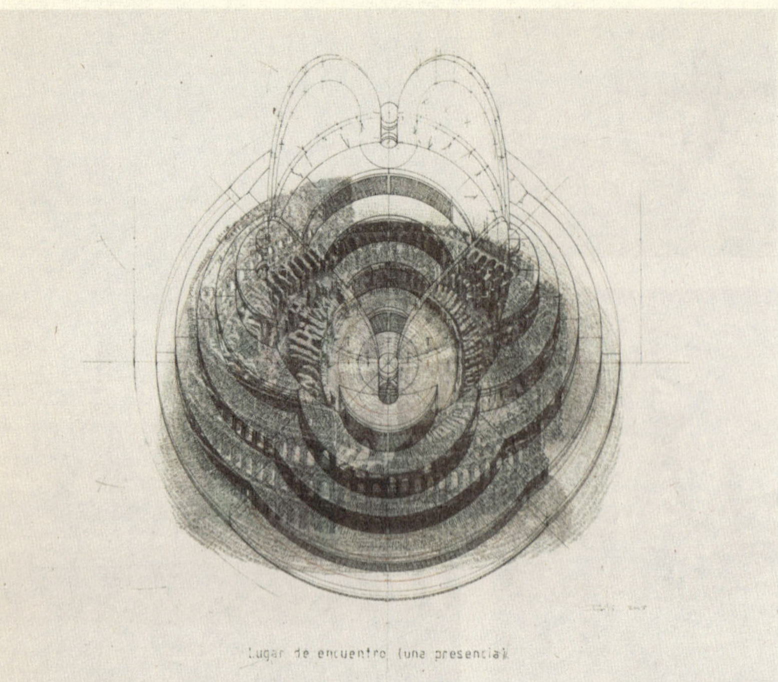

1.

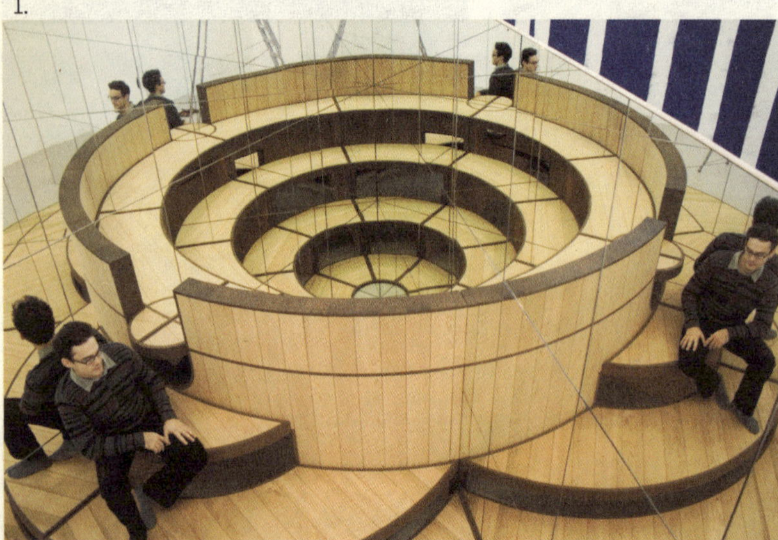
2.

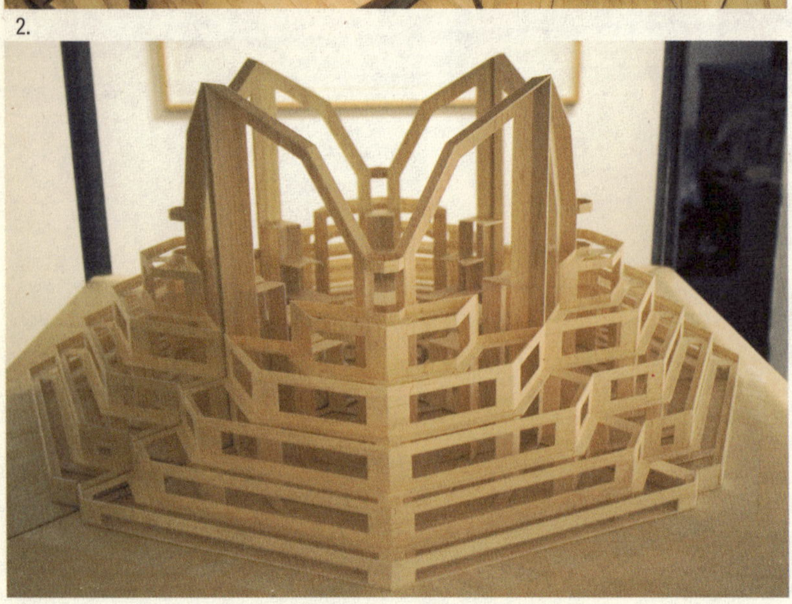
3.

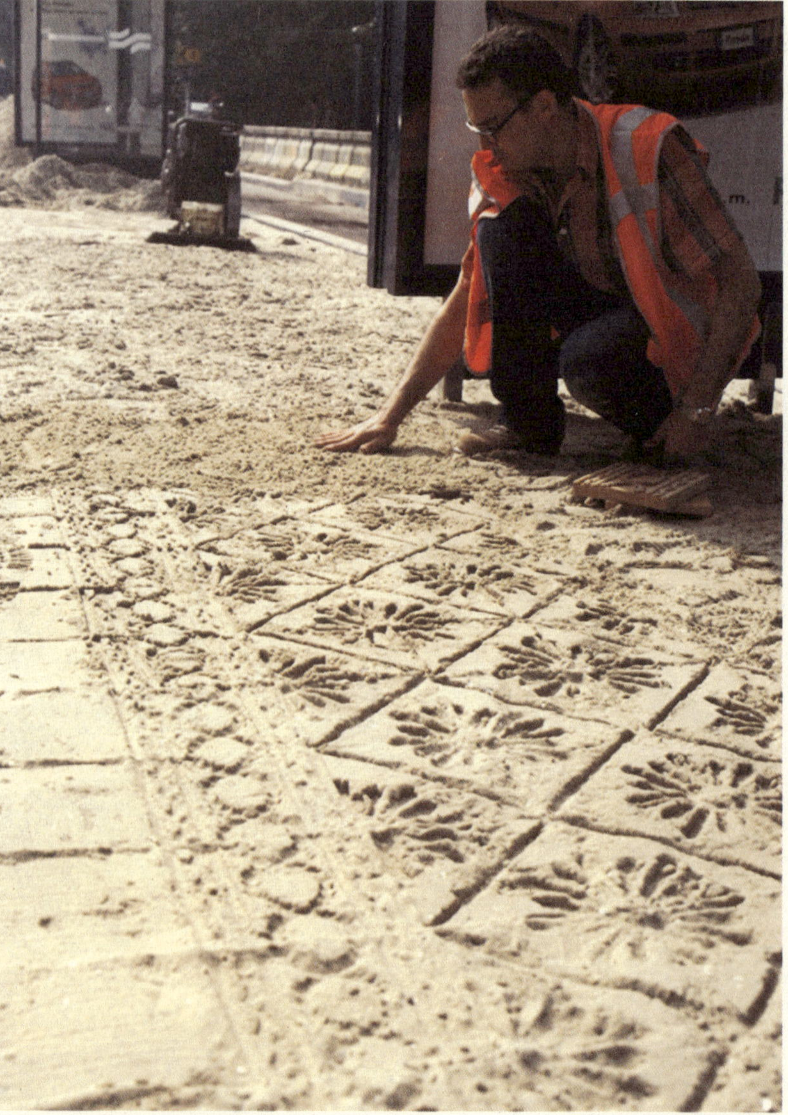
4.

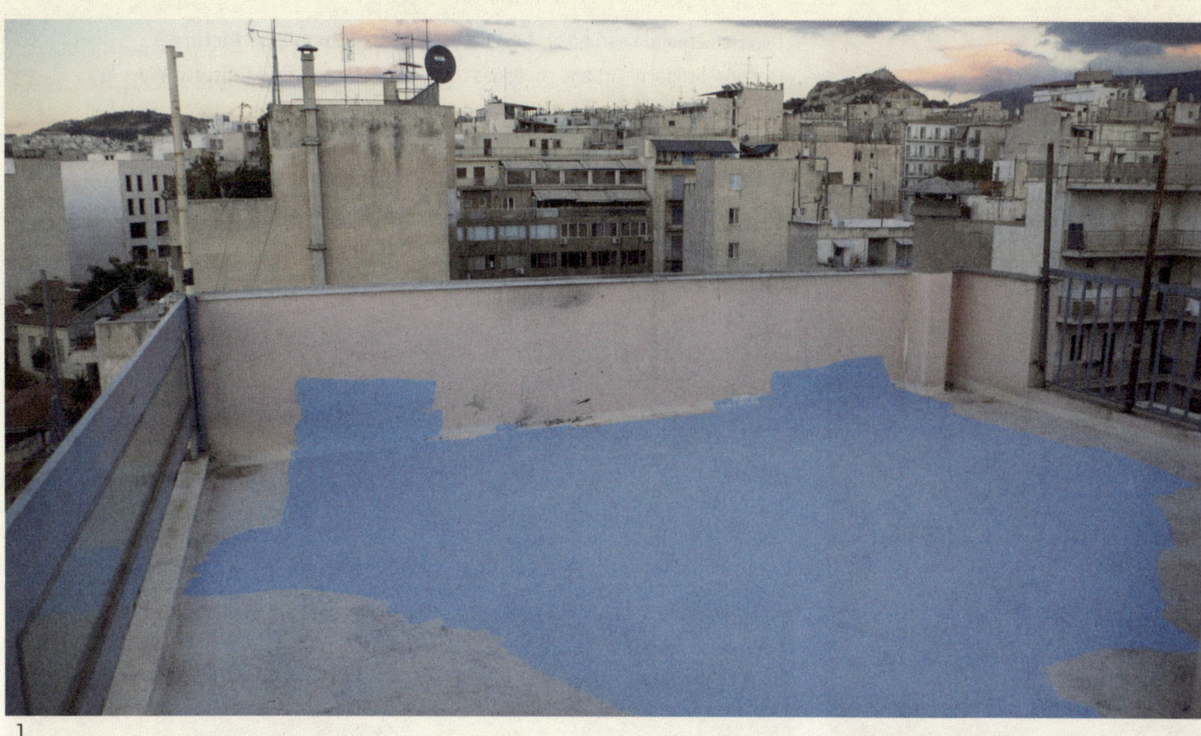

1.

Federico Herrero studied painting at the Pratt Institute, New York, and currently lives in San José, Costa Rica. He translates the diverse shapes and colors of San José streets and the surrounding tropical landscape into paintings that exist inside and outside the gallery. Surfaces have included buses, swimming pools, parking garages, building facades, and freeway underpasses. In 2001 he was awarded the Golden Lion for best artist under 35 at the 49th Venice Biennale.

1. Rooftop

2007, mixed media painting, dimensions variable, installation view in Athens

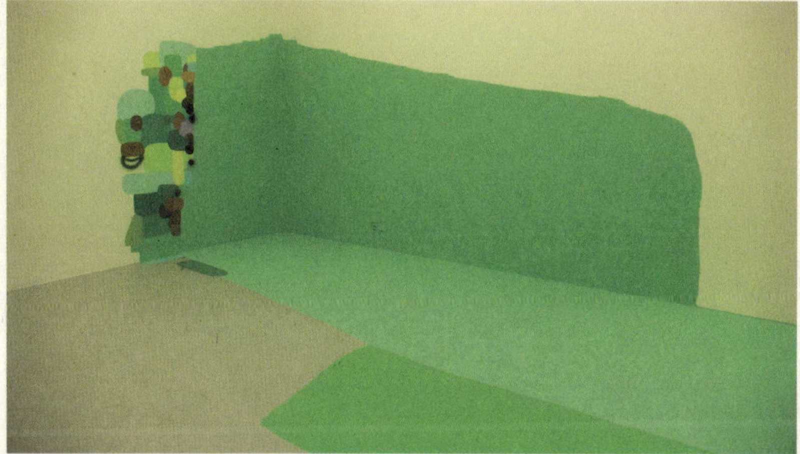

2.

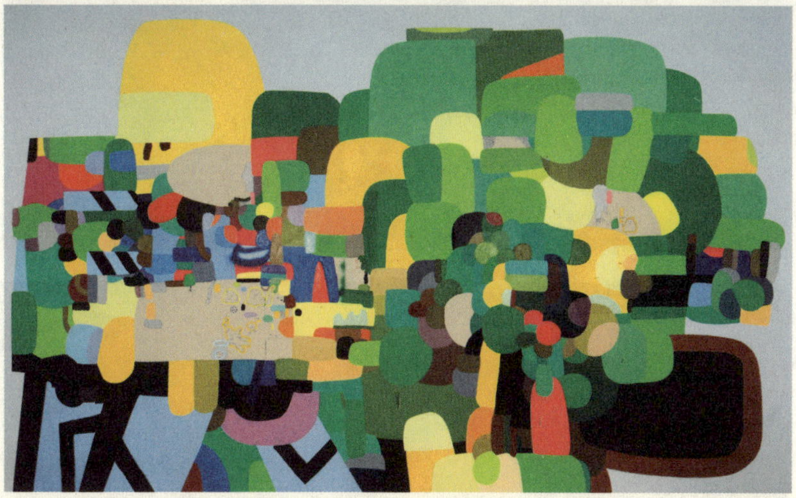

3.

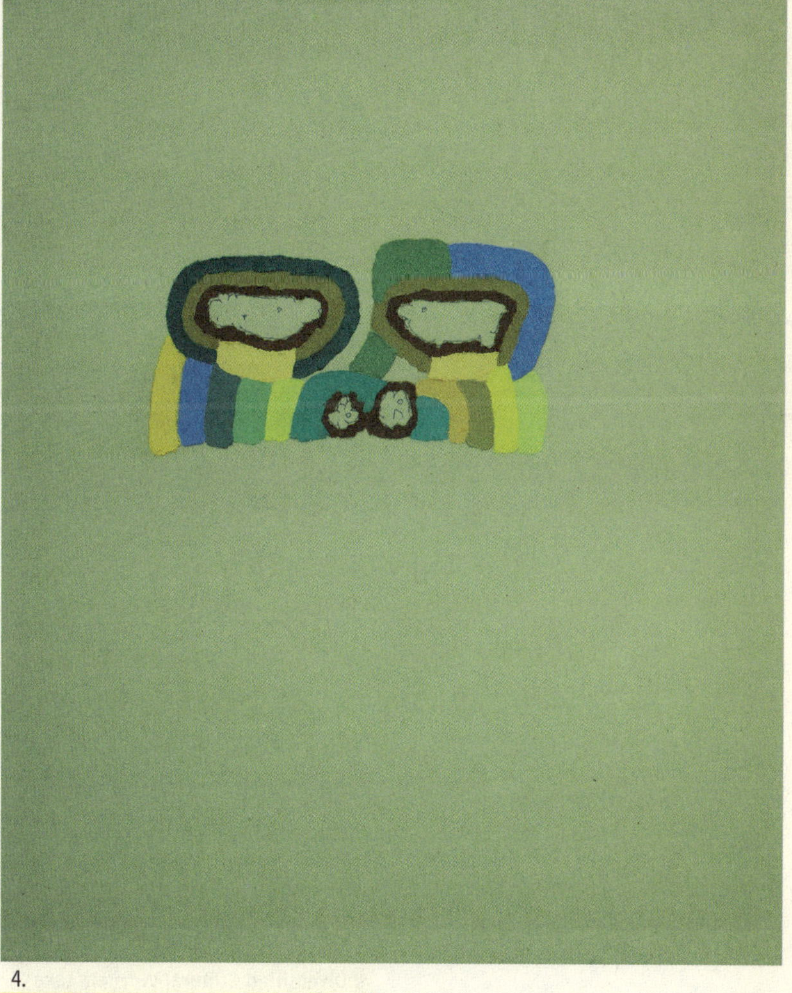

4.

2. UNTITLED (green corner)

2008, mixed media painting, dimensions variable, installation view at Kunstverein Freiburg, Germany

3. CARACOLA

2008, mixed media on canvas, $10 \times 16\frac{1}{2}$ ft (3×5 m)

4. Mask

2008, oil on canvas, $31\frac{1}{2} \times 27\frac{1}{2}$ in (80×70 cm)

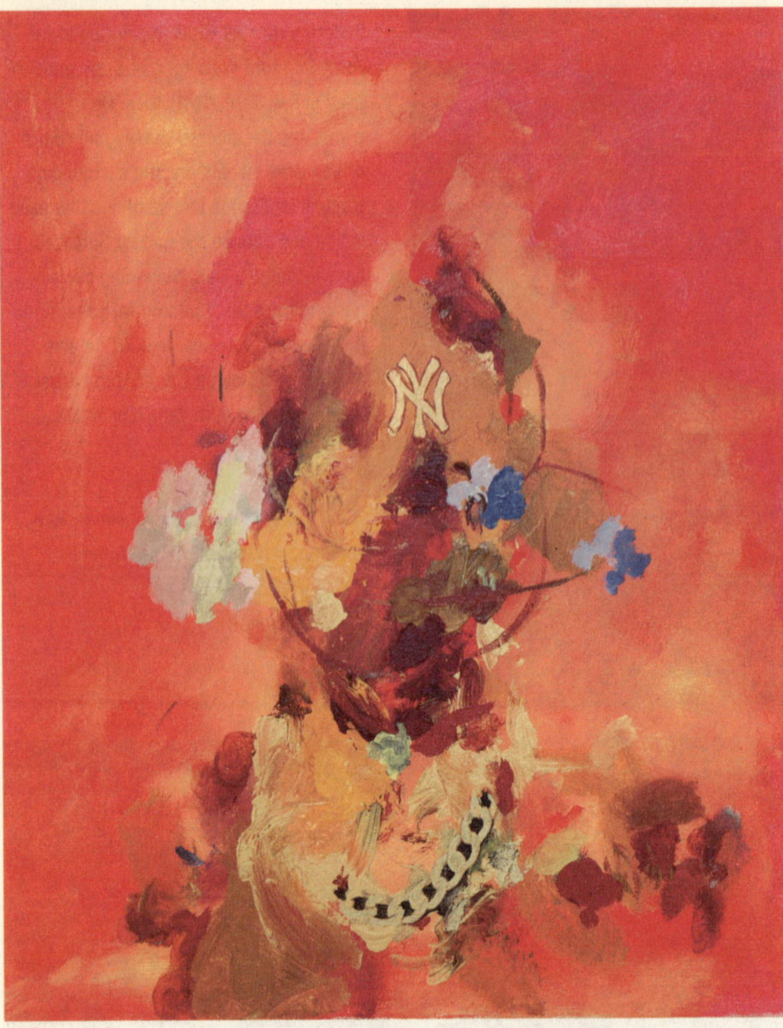

1.

Iain Hetherington earned his MFA from Glasgow School of Art and continues to live in Glasgow. His satirical portraits, including those in the recent series **Diversified Cultural Workers** (2007–08), shown at the Institute of Contemporary Arts in London, emphasize accessories over physical features: baseball caps and gold chains, for instance, are rendered with photorealistic precision while faces are reduced to abstract smears of paint.

1. **Composite Picture 3 (Diversified Cultural Worker)**
2008, acrylic on canvas, 22 × 18 in (56 × 46 cm)

2. **Group engaged in what looks like Action**
2007, acrylic on canvas, 59 × 78 3/4 in (150 × 200 cm)

3. **Composite Picture 1 (Diversified Cultural Worker)**
2008, oil on canvas, 30 × 28 in (76 × 71 cm)

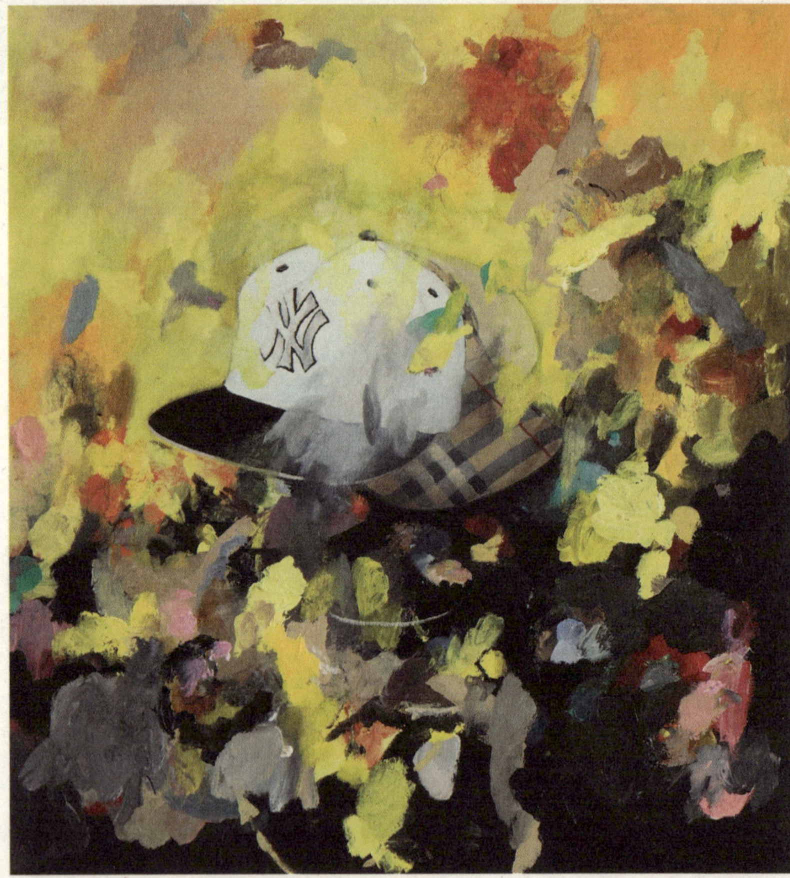

3.

2.

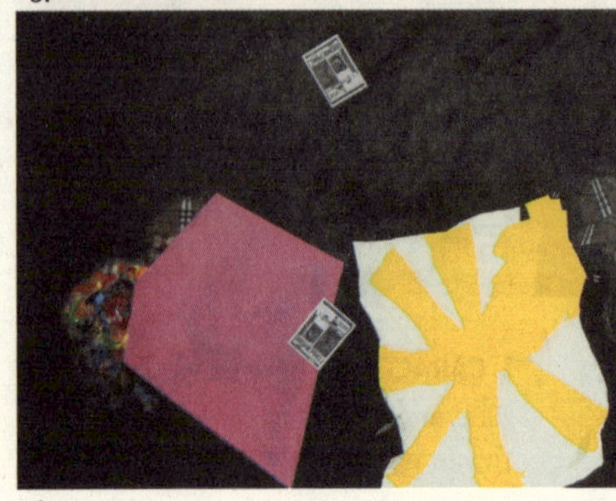

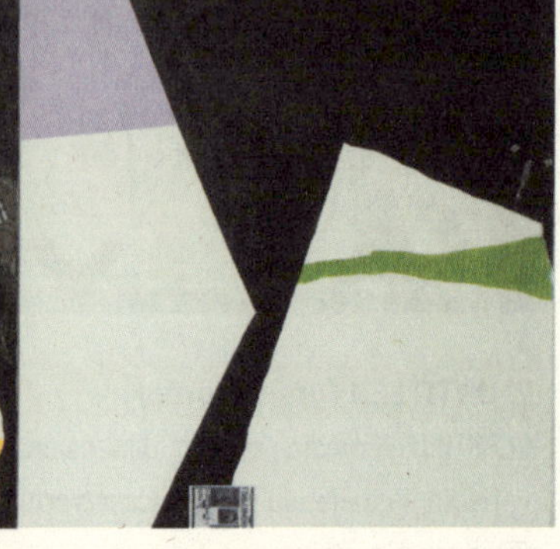

4.

4. **Diversified Cultural Workers take shelter behind brightly coloured forms**
2007, acrylic on canvas, 59 × 137 3/4 in (150 × 350 cm)

Leslie Hewitt earned her MFA from Yale University and currently lives in Saint Albans, New York. She makes photographs and photo-based installations that explore relationships between history and memory. Combining found images and objects – family snapshots, books, letters, ephemera – she builds narrative through specific layering, juxtaposition, framing, and reframing. Her works address subjects from civil rights activism to the legitimacy of photography as a record of the past.

1, 2, 3 & 4. **Riffs on Real Time (7 of 10)**
2002-05, chromogenic prints, each
30 × 24 in (76 × 61 cm)

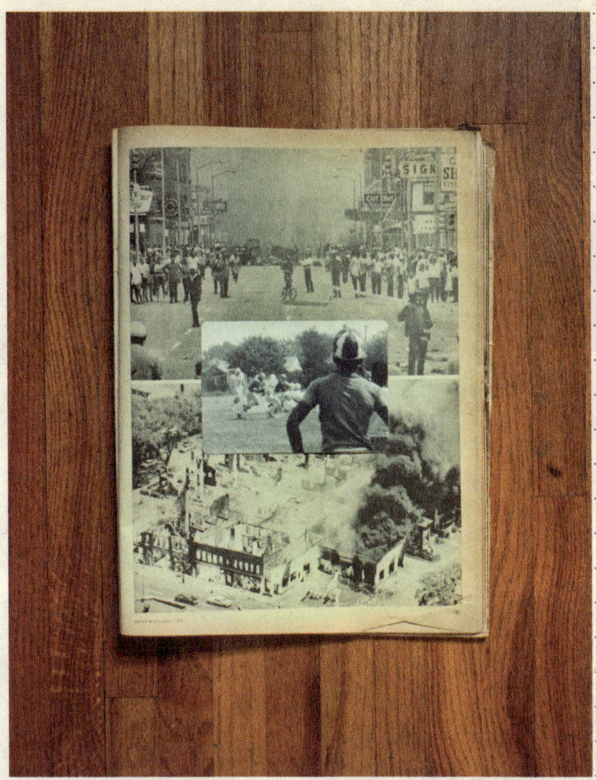

1.

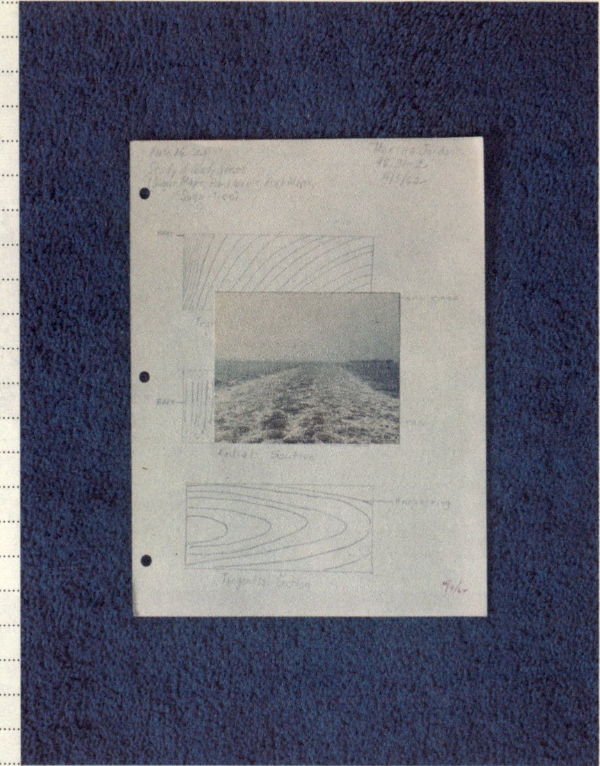

2.

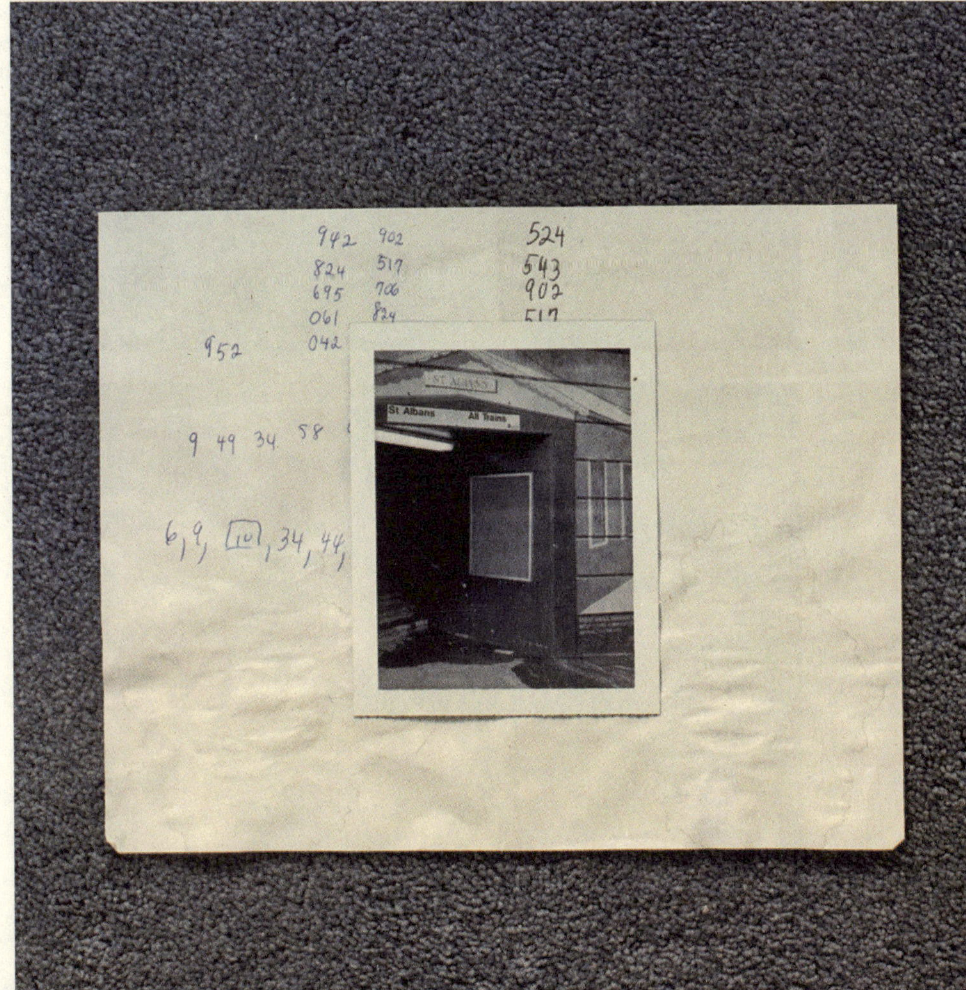

3.

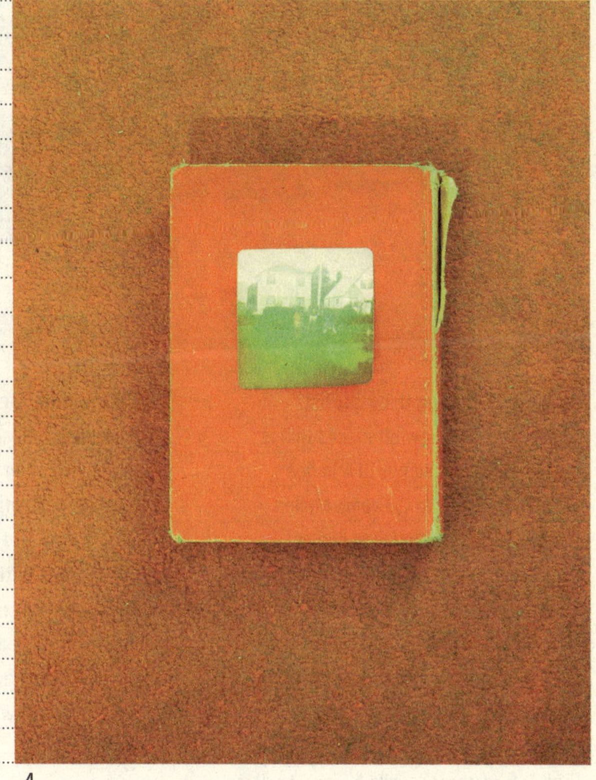

4.

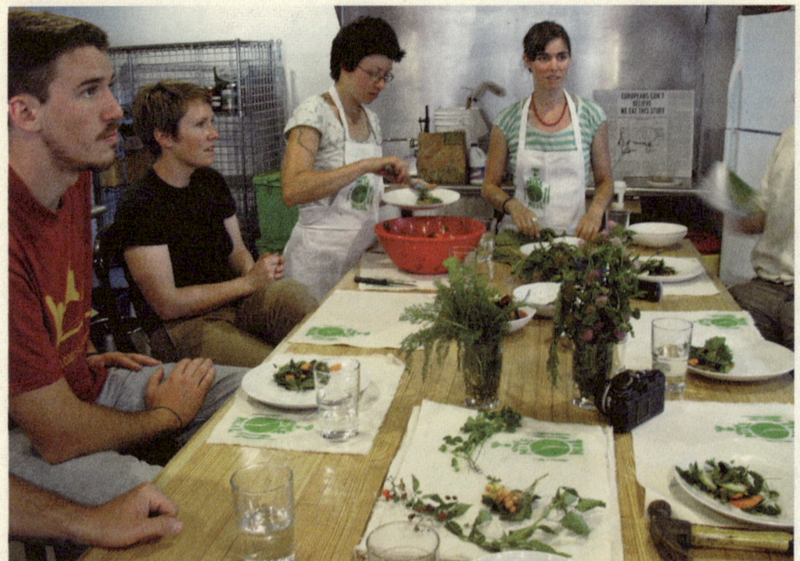
1.

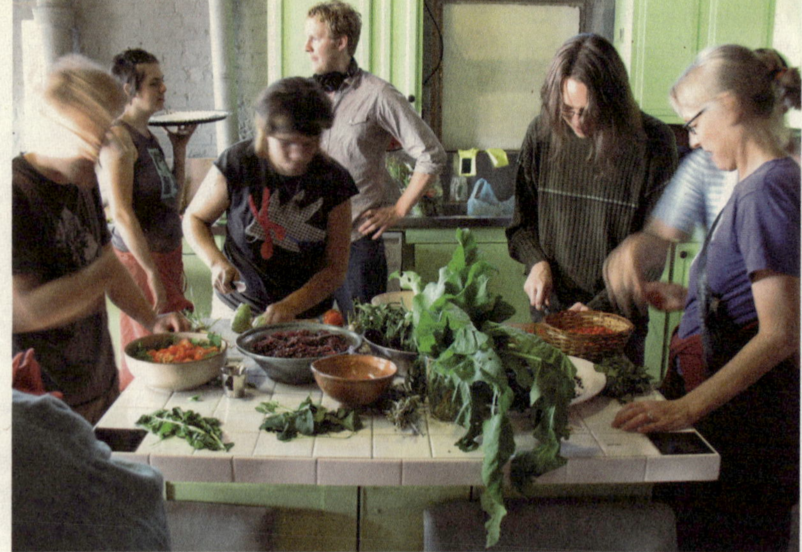
2.

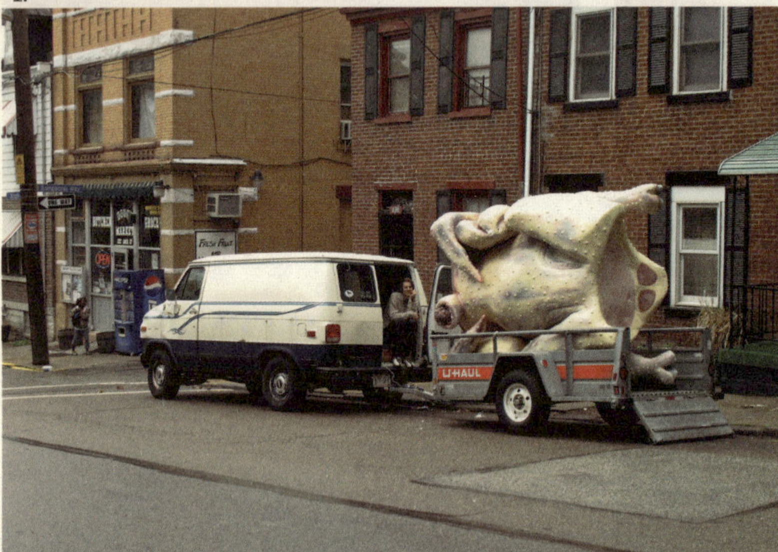

3.

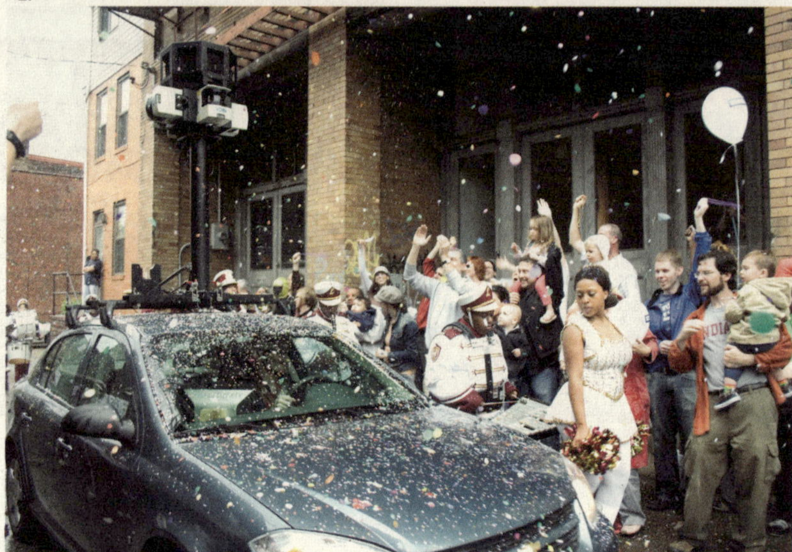
4.

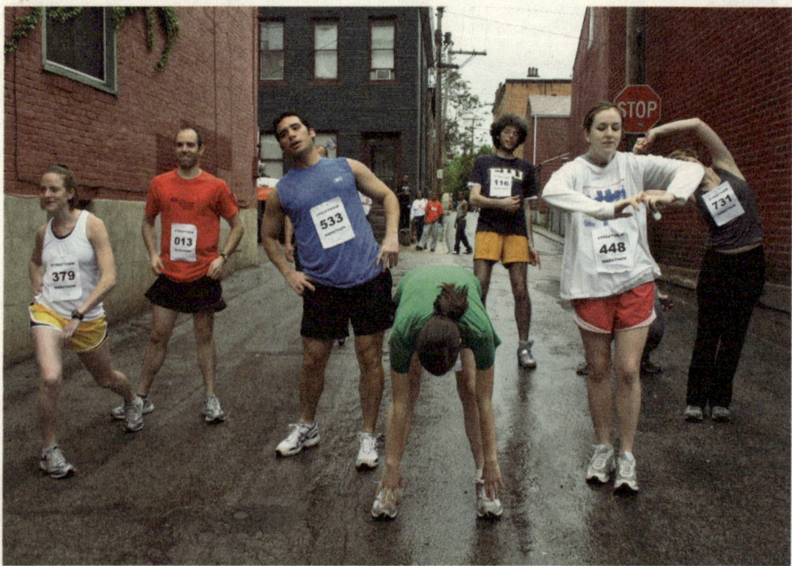

5.

Rather than making things, artist/organizer Robin Hewlett makes things happen. She earned her BFA in fine art and drama from Carnegie Mellon University and continues to live in Pittsburgh. Her ongoing project **ReTool** investigates alternative economies through interviews, sound installations, workshops, and a website. In **One Mile Meal** (2007-present), she and a partner prepare a meal with a community using local food gathered while biking. Hewlett also runs Spare Room, an informal exhibition space and residency program in her home.

1 & 2. **One Mile Meal**
2007-present, research and performance expedition exploring local community and sustainable food initiatives

3, 4 & 5. **Street with a View**
2008, 150 performers staged fictional events photographed by Google Inc. technicians, and images were uploaded to Google's Street View mapping platform

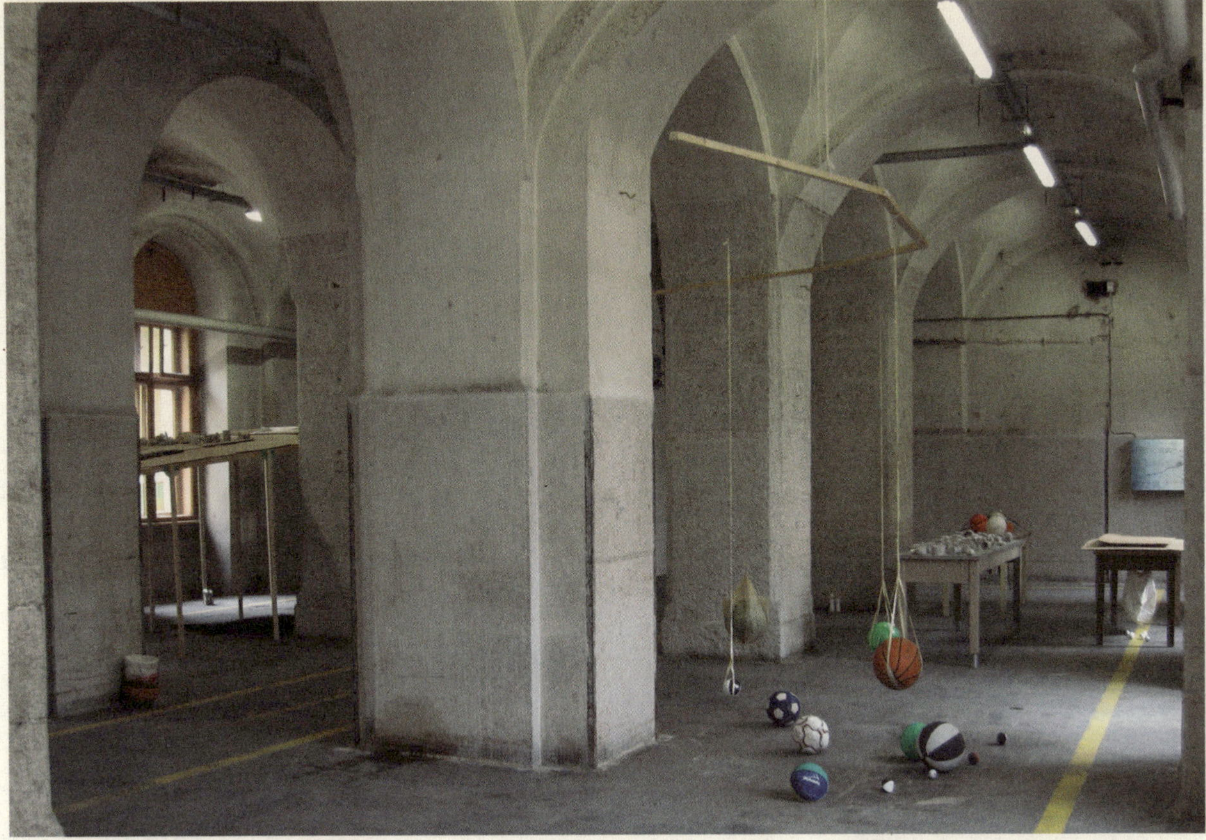

1.

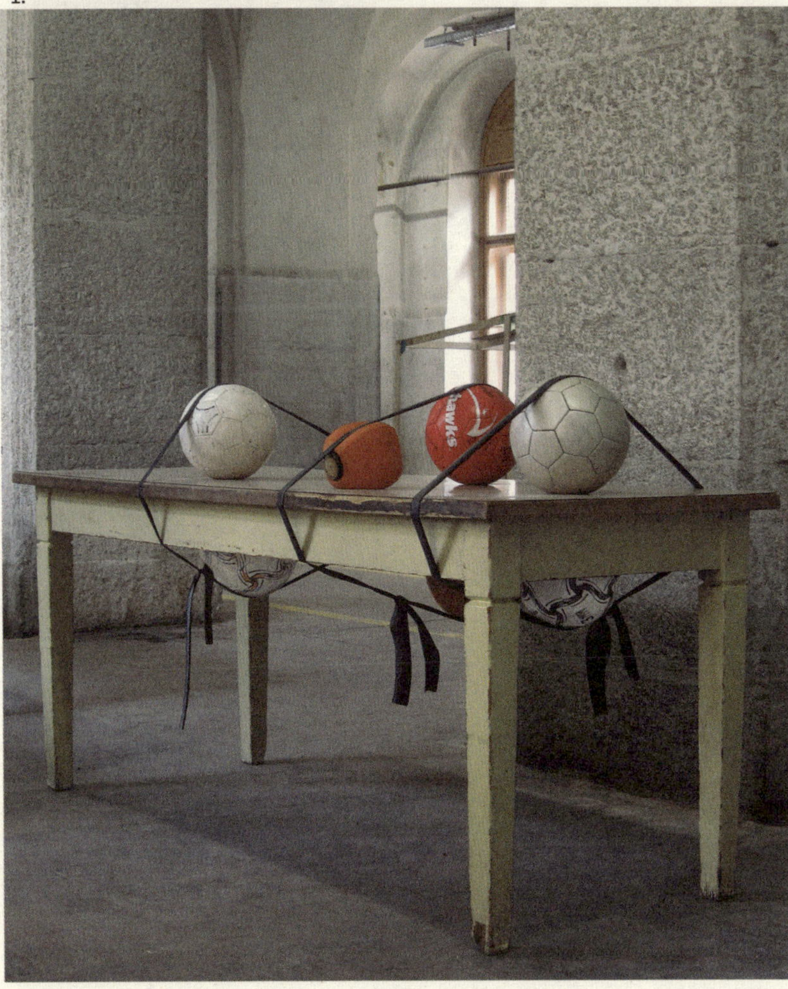

2.

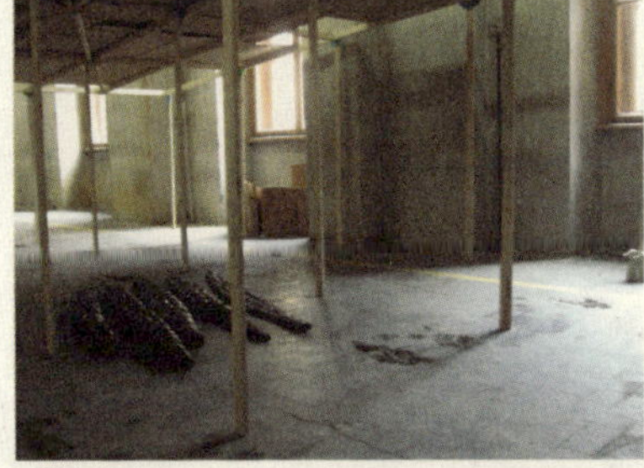

3.

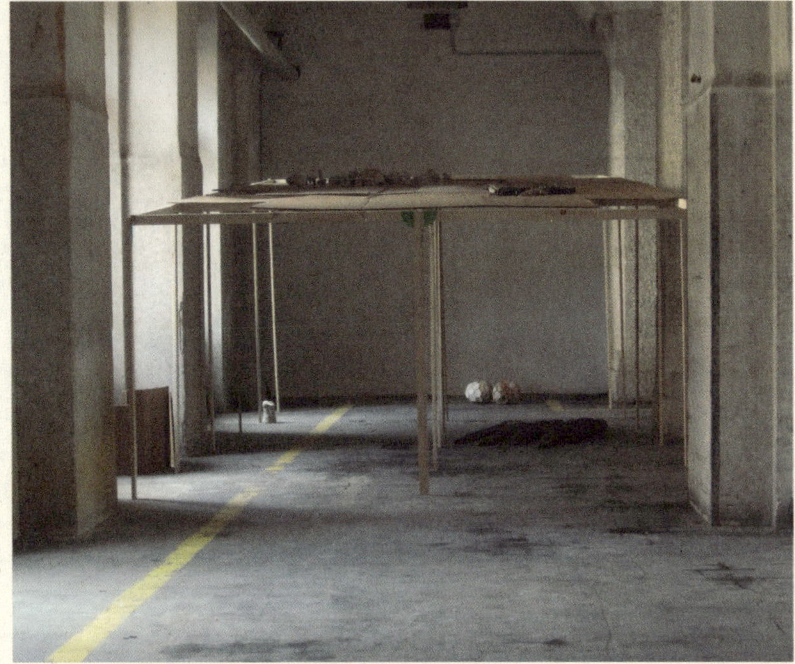

4.

Heide Hinrichs attended the Academy of Fine Arts in Dresden and currently lives in Oldenburg, Germany, and Seattle, Washington. Her installations convey fantasized narratives through found, sculpted, and manipulated objects. **The Expected Obedience of Your Thoughts**, shown at Manifesta 7 in 2008, combines clay birds, inner tubes, and soccer balls in a kind of Wunderkammer.

1. **The Expected Obedience of Your Thoughts** (detail)
2006-08, mixed media installation, dimensions variable

2. **The Expected Obedience of Your Thoughts** (detail)
2006-08, inner tubes and balls, dimensions variable

3 & 4. **The Expected Obedience of Your Thoughts** (detail)
2006-08, wood, cardboard, and plastic, $6\frac{1}{2} \times 9\frac{3}{4} \times 19\frac{1}{2}$ ft (2 × 3 × 6 cm)

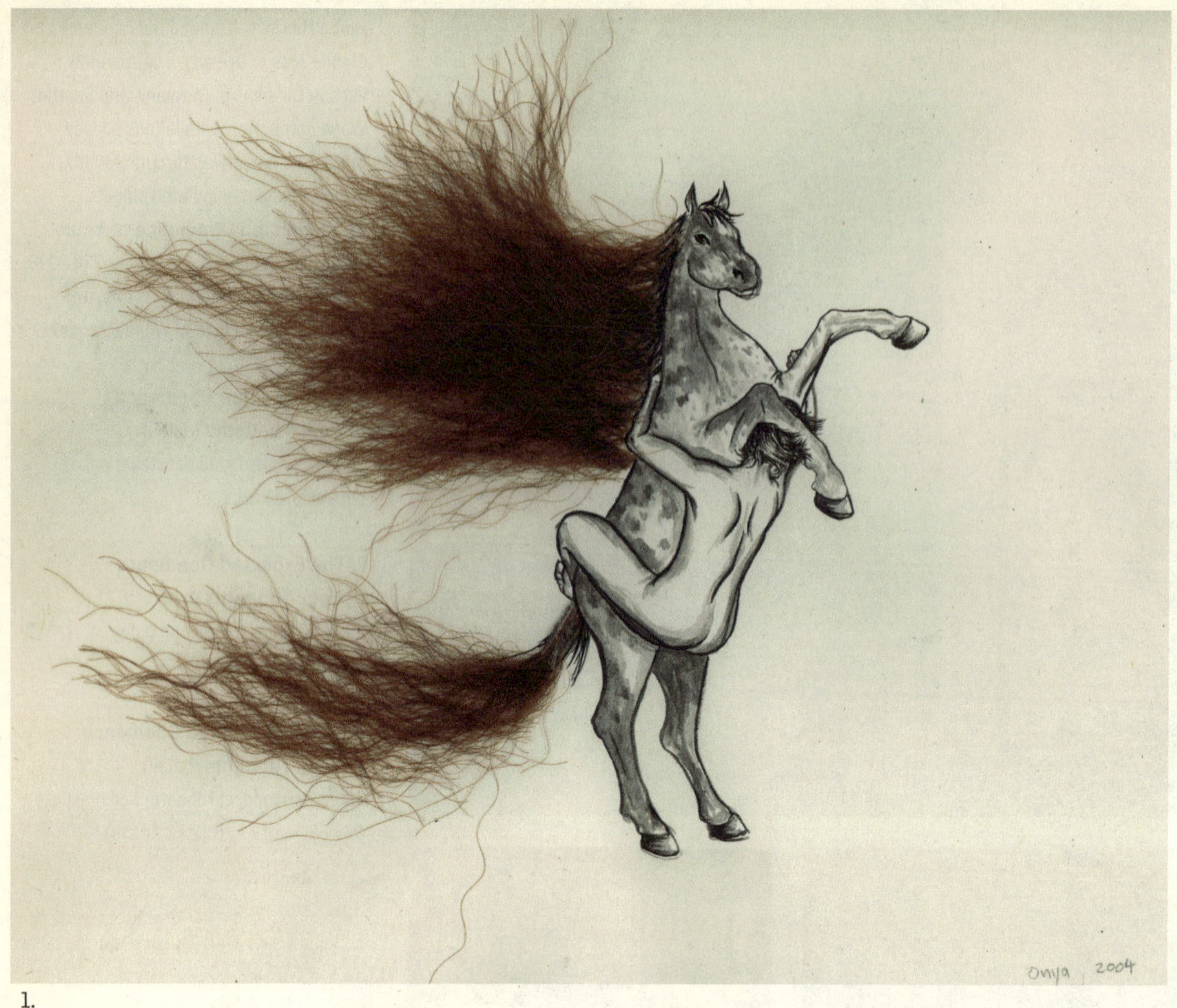

1.

Onya Hogan-Finlay earned her BFA in studio arts from Concordia University in Montreal, where she currently lives. Informed by feminist methodologies and queer theory, she is an artist and curator linking a practice of drawing to activism, community work, and academics. She is cofounder of the **BOOKMOBILE** project, a touring collection of artist books, zines, and independent publications in a vintage Airstream trailer.

1. **Rider**
2005, ink on paper, 8 × 11 in (20 × 28 cm)

2. **Skaters**
2005, silkscreen print on paper, 6 × 4 in (15 × 10 cm)

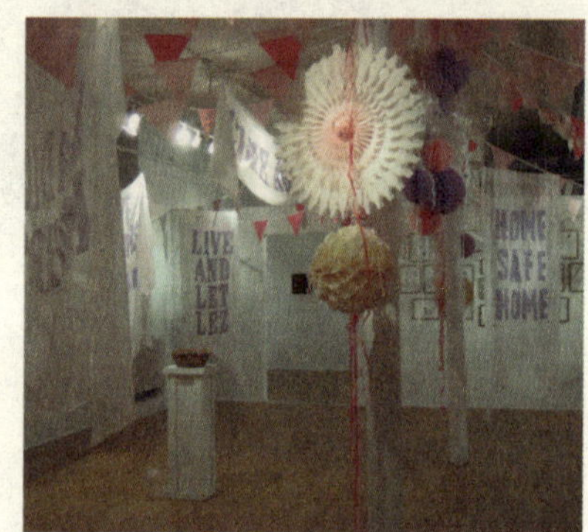

3.

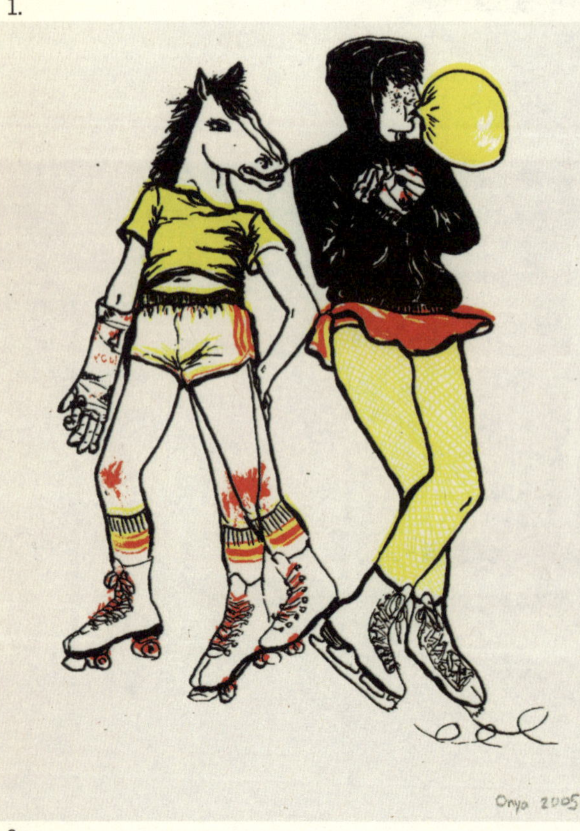

2.

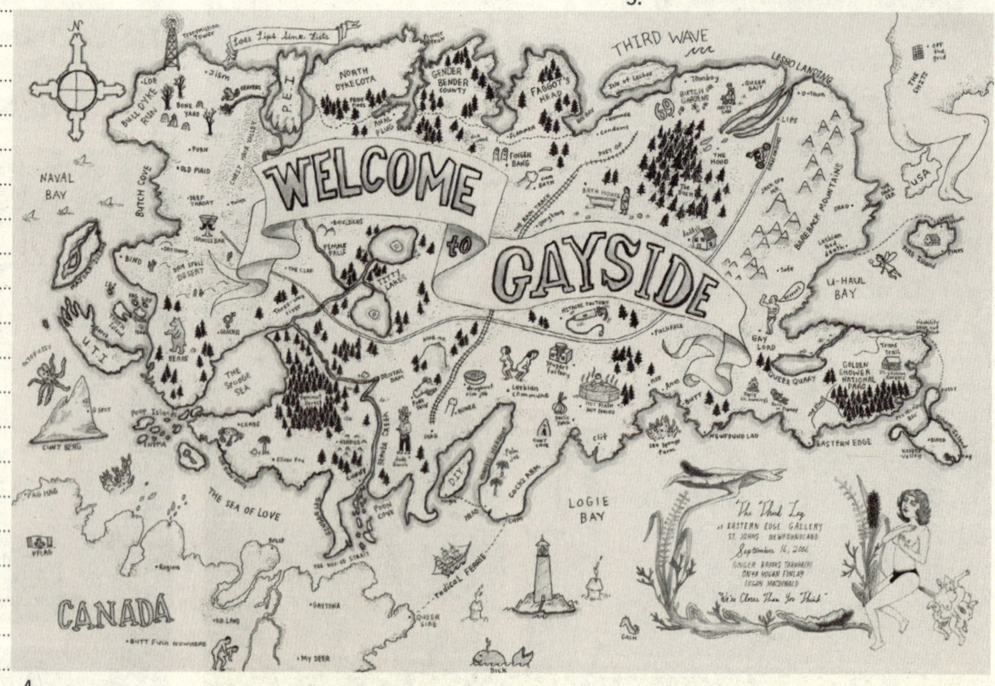

4.

3. **"Welcome to Gayside"**
exhibition view at Eastern Edge Gallery, St. John's, Newfoundland, Canada (2006)

4. **Welcome to Gayside**
2006, double-sided offset printed poster, 15 × 22 in (38 × 56 cm)

Lars "The Contemporary Future" Holdhus attended the Gerrit Rietveld Academie in Amsterdam. His practice integrates photography, video, and public intervention. Works include **New Market Resources** (2007), a wooden stall selling original New Kids On The Block merchandise outside a remote town in the former East Germany, and **Shimmns** (2008), a collaborative documentary about traveling by freight train in Europe.

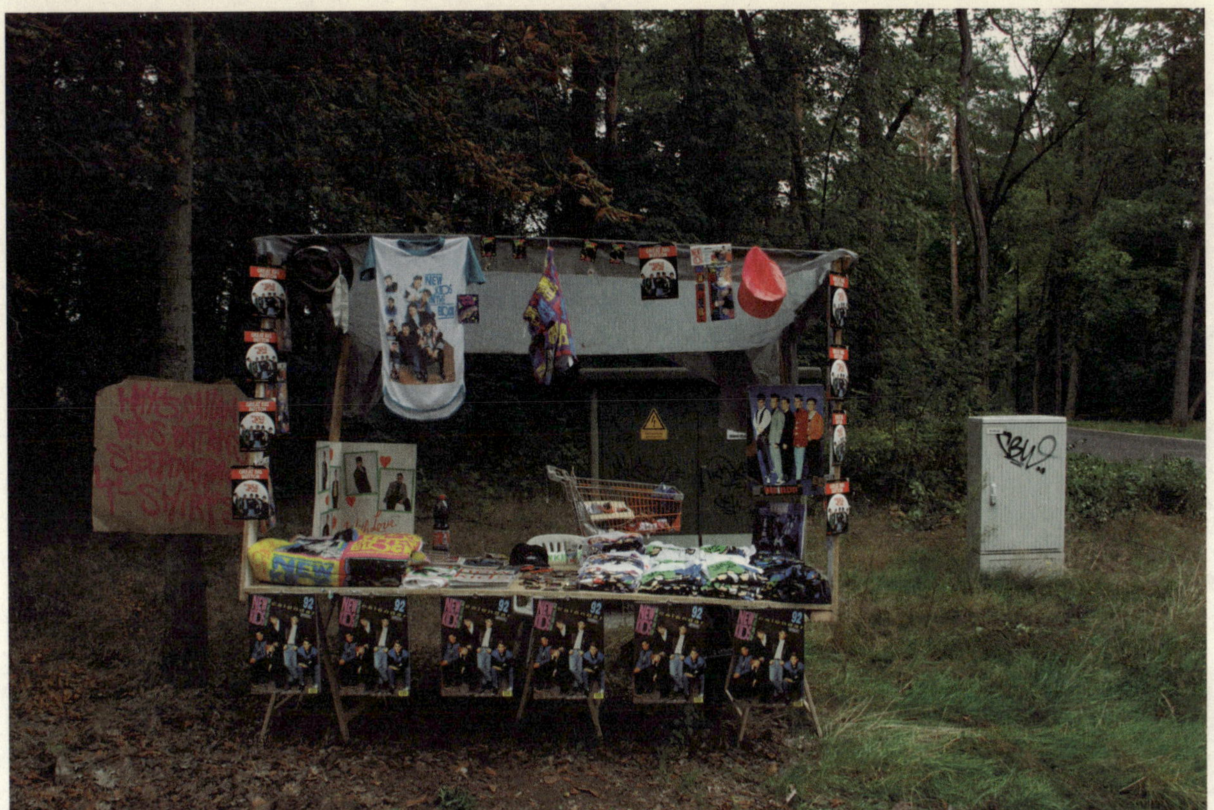

1.

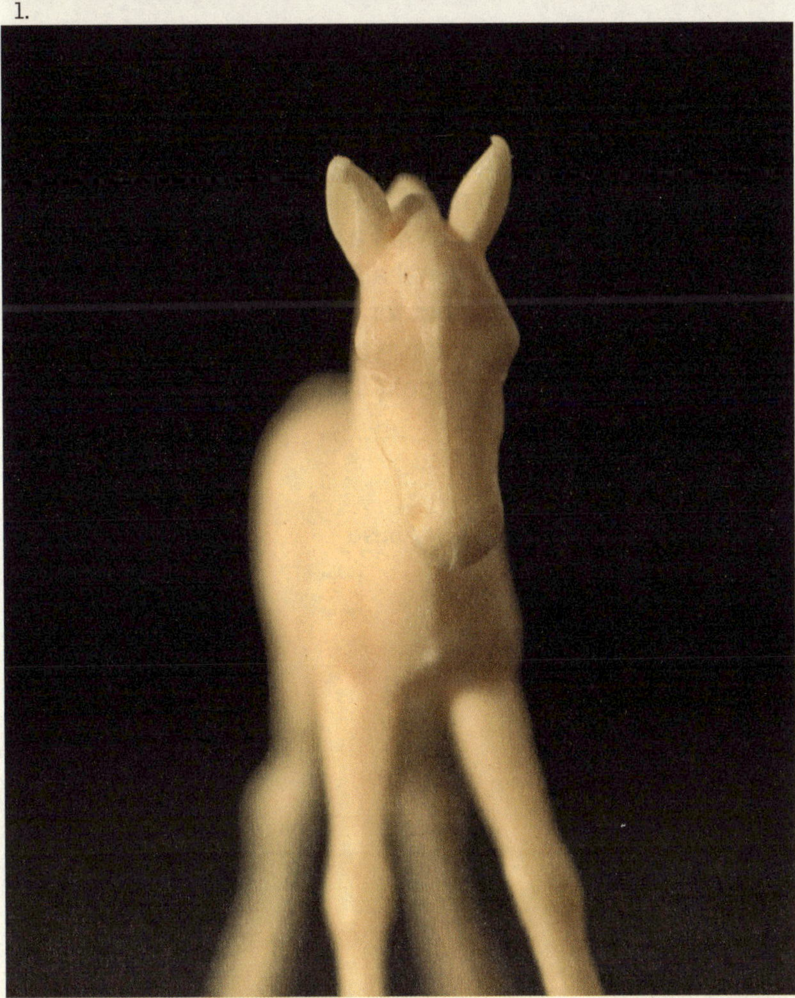

2.

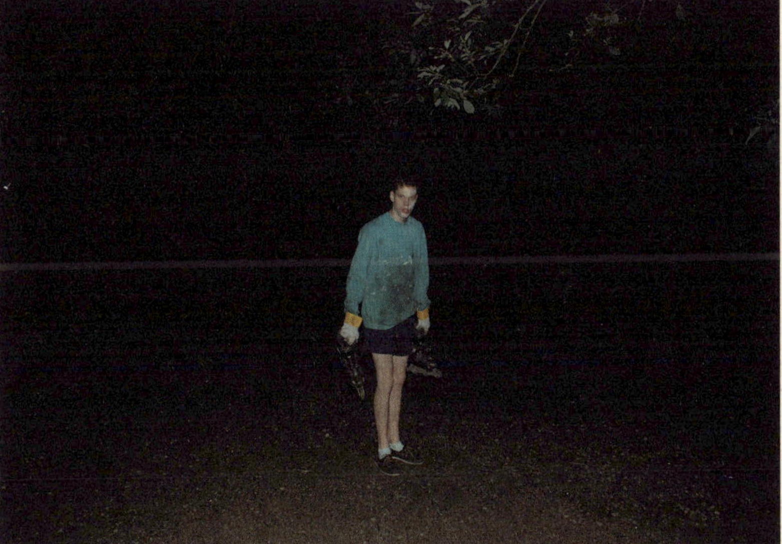

3.

1. New Market Resources
2007, site-specific installation with wooden stall and New Kids On The Block merchandise for sale, dimensions variable

2. Untitled
from the series **Horse Collection**
ongoing, digital photographs, dimensions variable

3. Untitled
from the series **Did You Like My Dancing?**
ongoing, digital photograph, dimensions variable

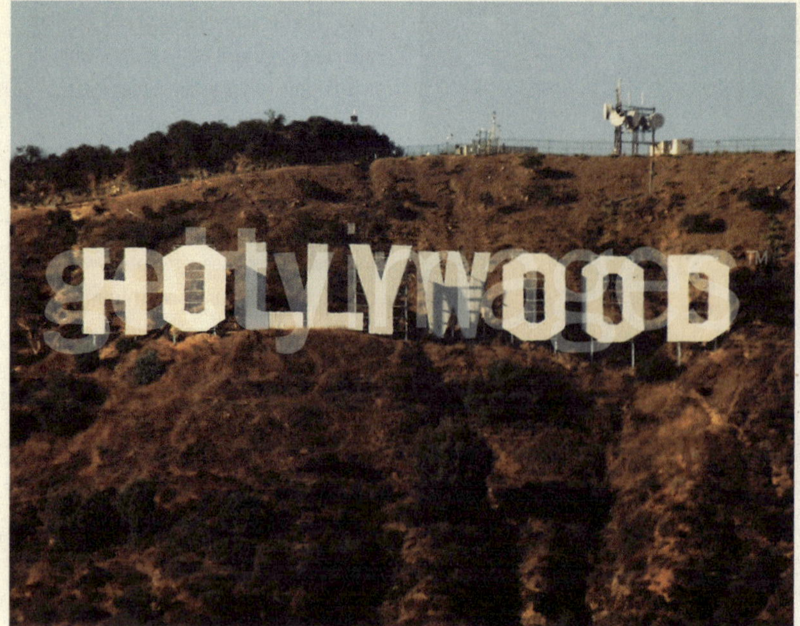

1.

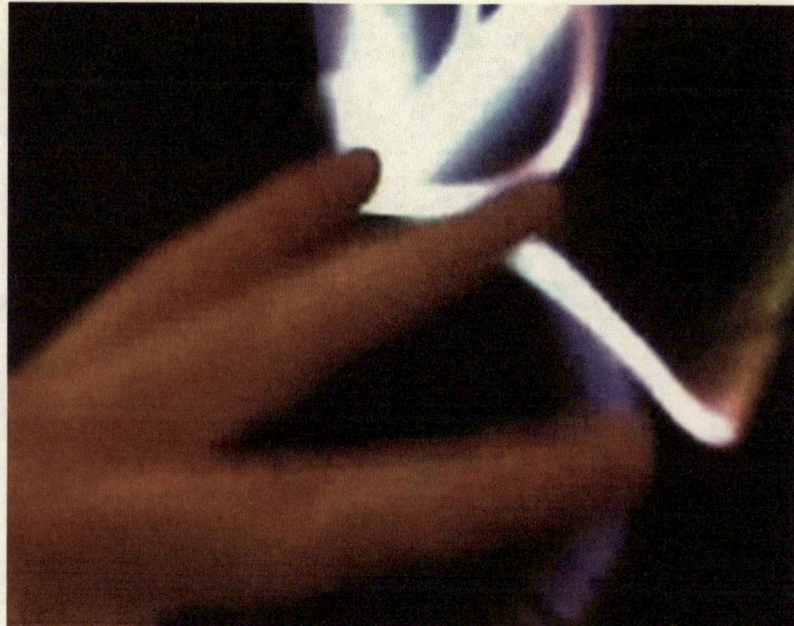

2.

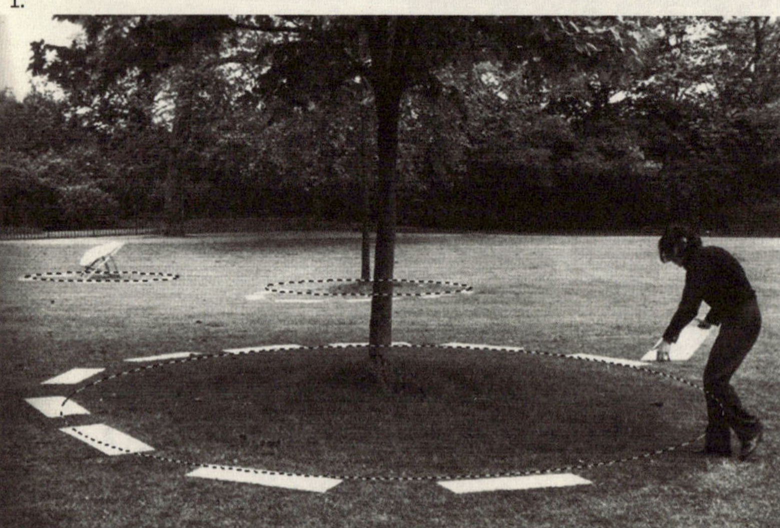

3.

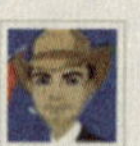

dms47

Best Answer - Chosen by Asker

Happens all the time, sometimes I don't want to lug the camera bag and tripod around with me. One time I got home from work and there was a chipmunk, squirrel, robin and cardinal all eating bread that someone put out for them and no camera! But then I think maybe that scene was meant just for me! (Thank you, God, I need that!)

3 months ago

1 0 Report Abuse

4.

slam p

slam poetry Suggestions

5.

Joel Holmberg earned his BFA from Virginia Commonwealth University and currently lives in Berlin. He combines and manipulates existing material (the Michael Keaton film My Life and the text of A Thousand Plateaus by Deleuze and Guattari, for example) to make witty and evocative works in a variety of media. He also creates sculpture, video, books, and Web-based projects, including an archive of responses to questions on Yahoo! Answers (yahoo.answers.com), and is a founding member of the Internet surfing club Nasty Nets.

1. **Getty Images Hollywood Sign (Phony)**
2007, archival inkjet print, 20 × 35 in (51 × 89 cm)

2. **Hand Flurry**
2008, video, 1 min

3. **Demarcating David Lamelas Demarcating Three Objects, 1968**
2008, animation, duration variable

4. **My Role as an Artist on Yahoo! Answers is Analogous with my Role as an Artist**
2008-present, archive of responses elicited by the artist's questions on Yahoo! Answers

5. **Suggestion Slam**
2008, video, 30 sec

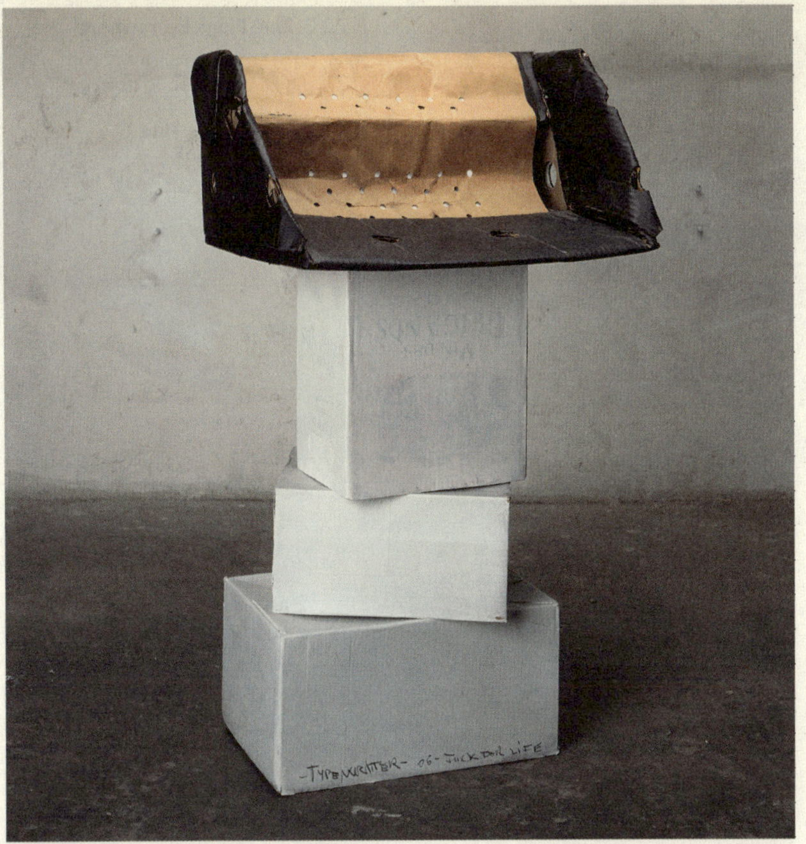

1.

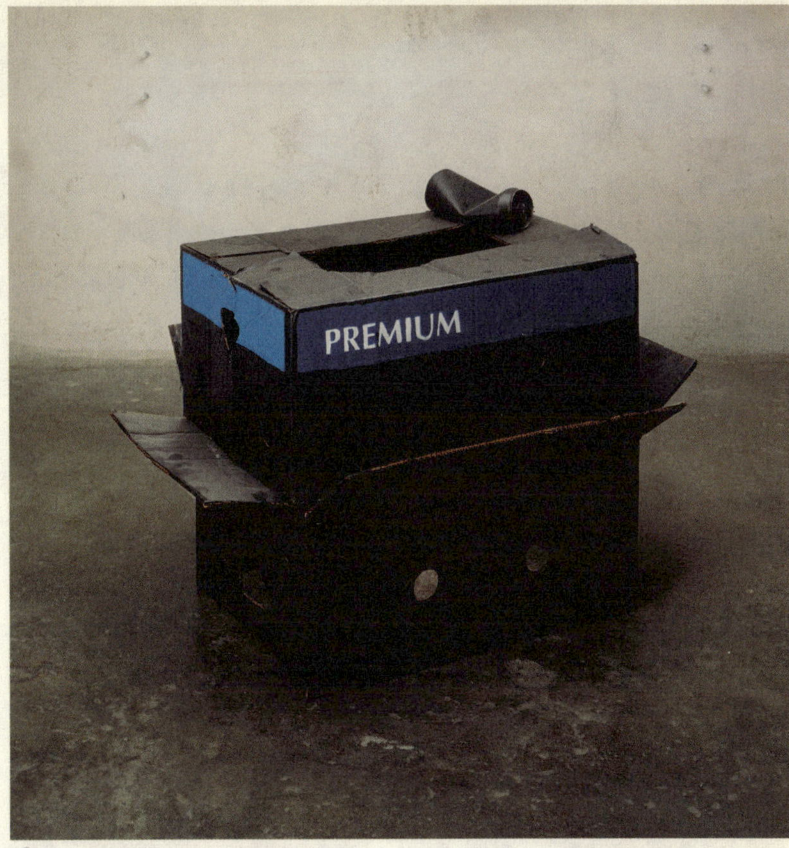

2.

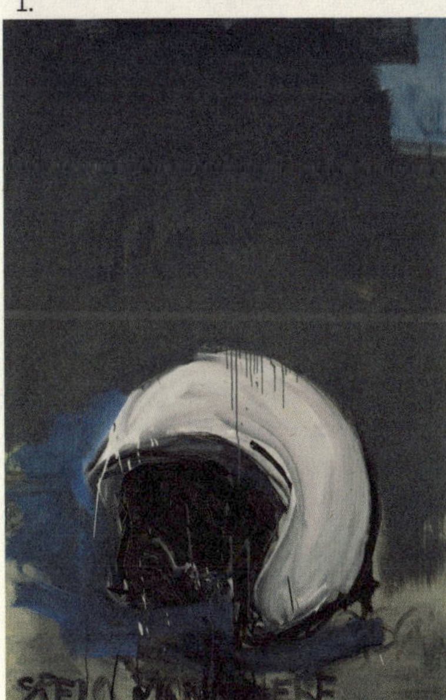

3.

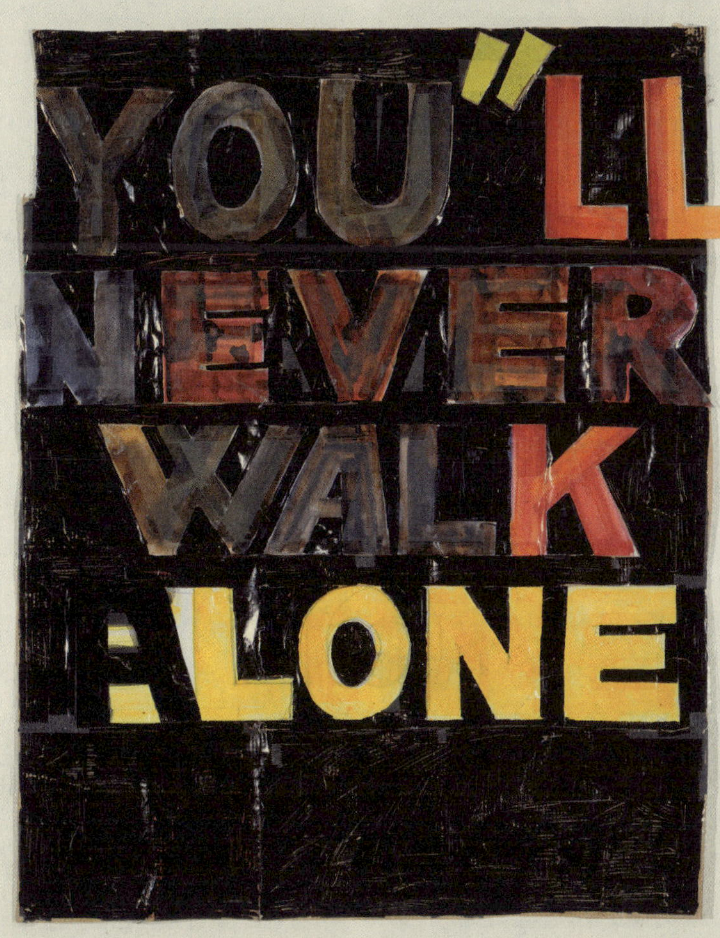

4.

David Hominal currently lives in Lausanne, Switzerland. He makes paintings, drawings, collages, and simply crafted sculptures in cardboard that explore and interrogate the tradition of painting. Walking the line between sincerity and irreverence, his vocabulary includes crosses, skulls, abstract gestures, and painted text – from "BULLSHIT" to the names Goya, Velázquez, and Hominal.

1. Typewriter
2006, acrylic on cardboard and paper, 36 ¼ × 21 ½ × 15 in (92 × 55 × 38 cm)

2. XeroX
2006, acrylic on cardboard and aluminum can, 23 ¼ × 29 ½ × 21 ¼ in (59 × 75 × 54cm)

3. Still Life 1
2002, oil on canvas, 59 × 39 ½ in (150 × 100 cm)

4. You'll Never Walk Alone
2005, watercolor, Scotch tape, and marker on paper, 21 × 16 in (53 × 41 cm)

南亭村第三届村民委员会选举满18周岁
选民名单：
西叁队

1.

Hu Xiangqian lives and works in Guangzhou. His work engages with the social and political structures of his childhood town of Nanting. He ran for mayor of Nanting at the age of 22, though he was not registered to run, and the video **Flying Blue Flag** (2005) documents his experience in local politics. In his video **Trend Blindly** (2005), he placed a group of models of buildings on the Zhujiang River, commenting on the precarious social situation created by economic growth in China.

1, 2 & 3. **Blue Flags Everywhere**
2006, video of performance, 20 min

4 & 5. **Drift with the Tide**
2005, video, 4 min

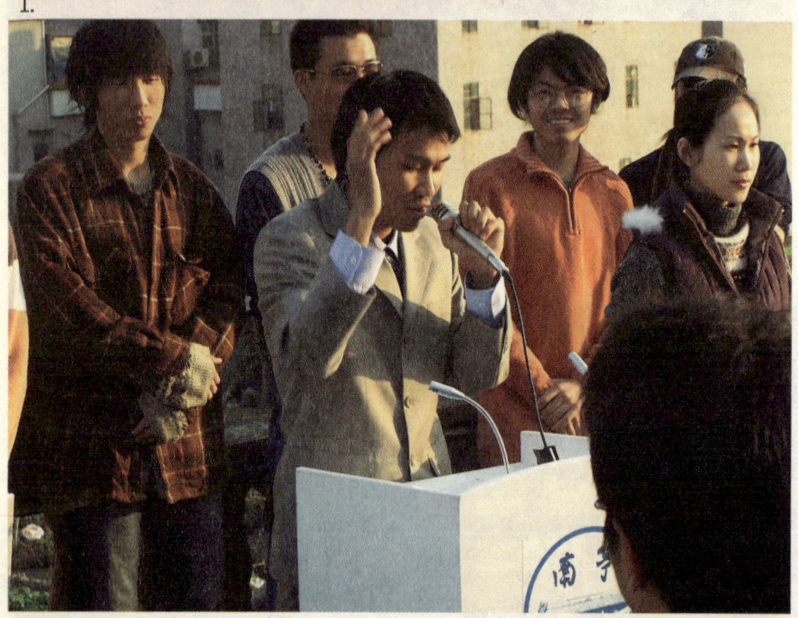

2.

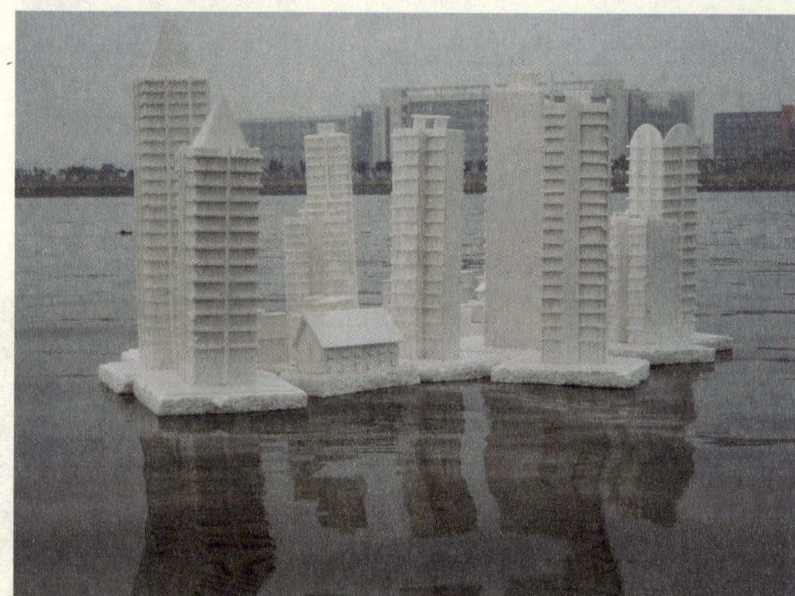

4.

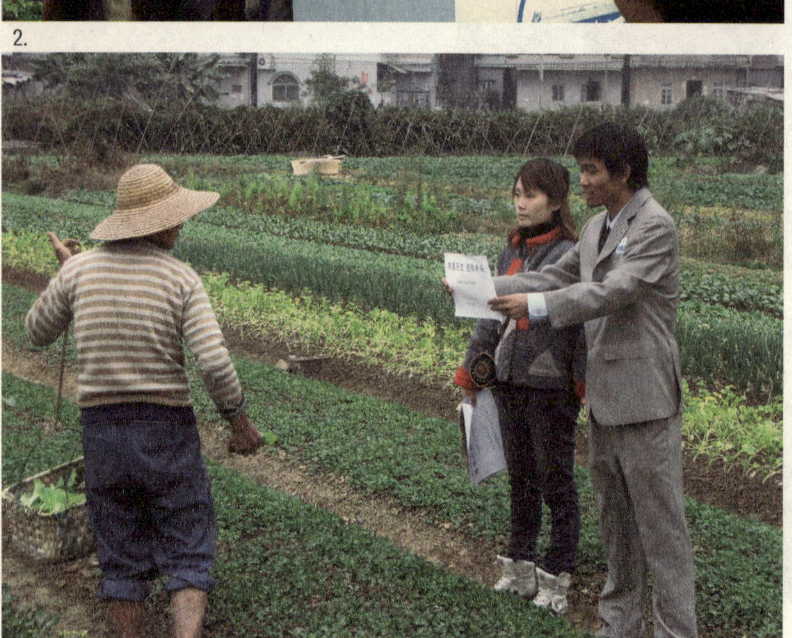

3.

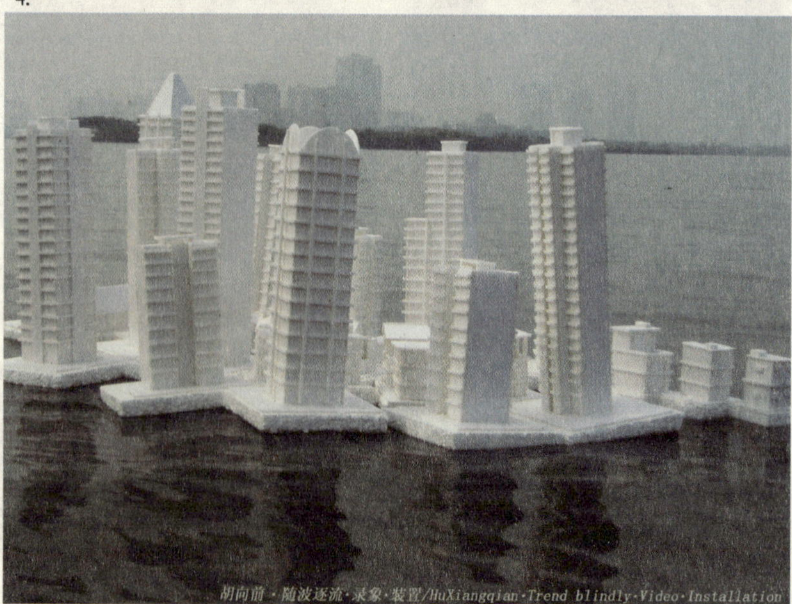

5.

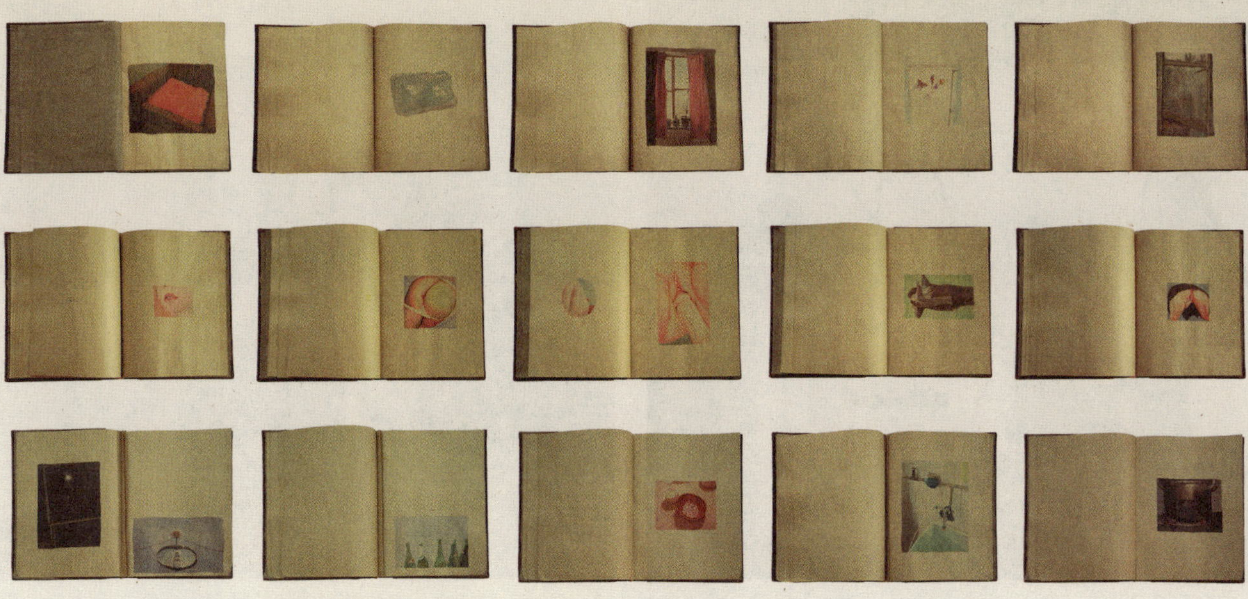

1.

Hu Xiaoyuan graduated from the Central Academy of Fine Arts in Beijing, where she currently lives and works. Her artworks, made with personal, intimate objects and materials, have included **Mine**, 2006, watercolor paintings on the pages of Braille Bibles, and **A Keepsake I Cannot Give Away** (2004-05), needlepoint scenes of traditional Chinese stories made with her own hair.

1. Mine
2004, Braille Bible and watercolor, each book $12\frac{1}{2} \times 9\frac{1}{2}$ in (32 × 25 cm)

2. Mute
2008, watercolor, silk, mechanical clock, iron loudspeaker, and tone arm, dimensions variable

3. San Yi Liu Wu
2008, wood, thin silk, traditional Chinese painting pigment, clothing, and graveclothes, dimensions variable

4. A Keepsake I Cannot Give Away (detail)
2005-06, artist's hair, white twill-weave silk, old embroidery frames, dimensions variable

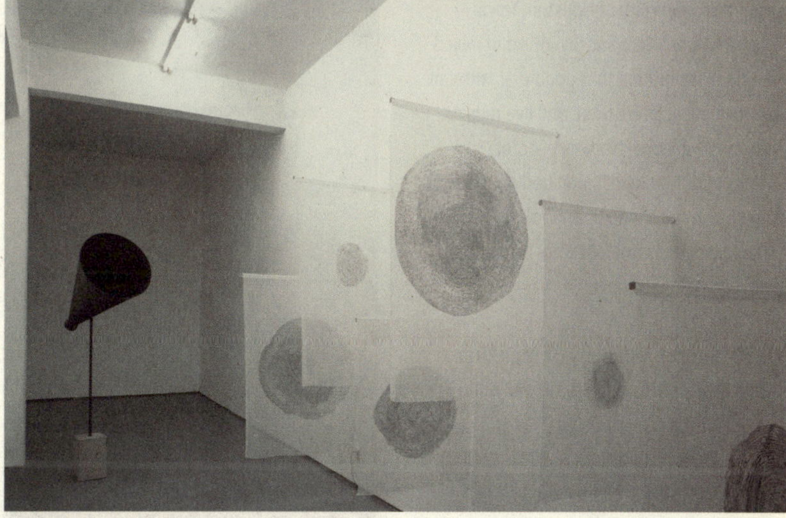

2.

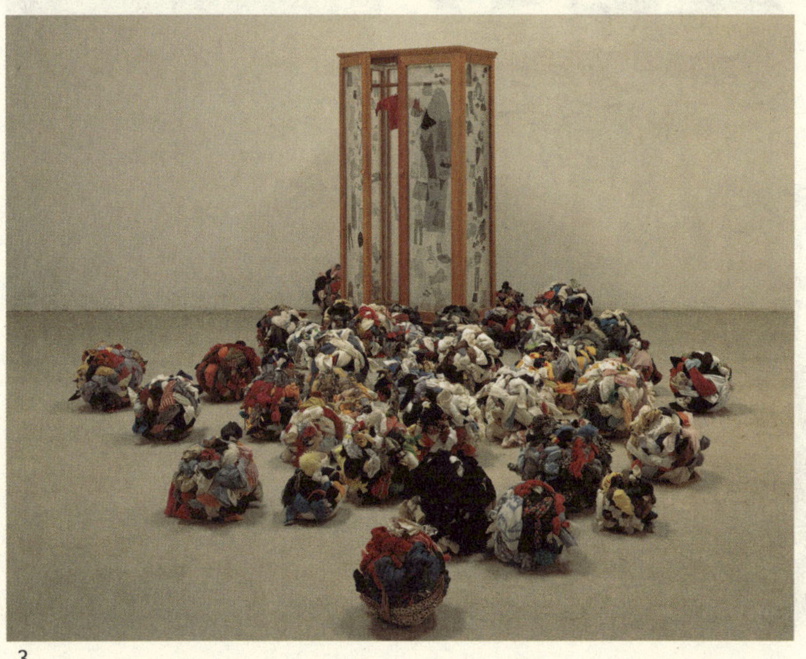

3.

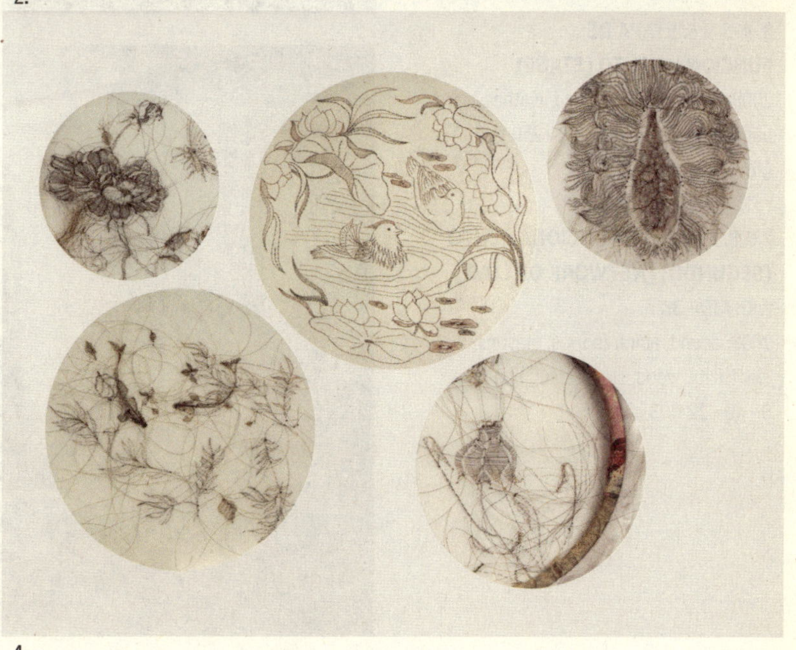

4.

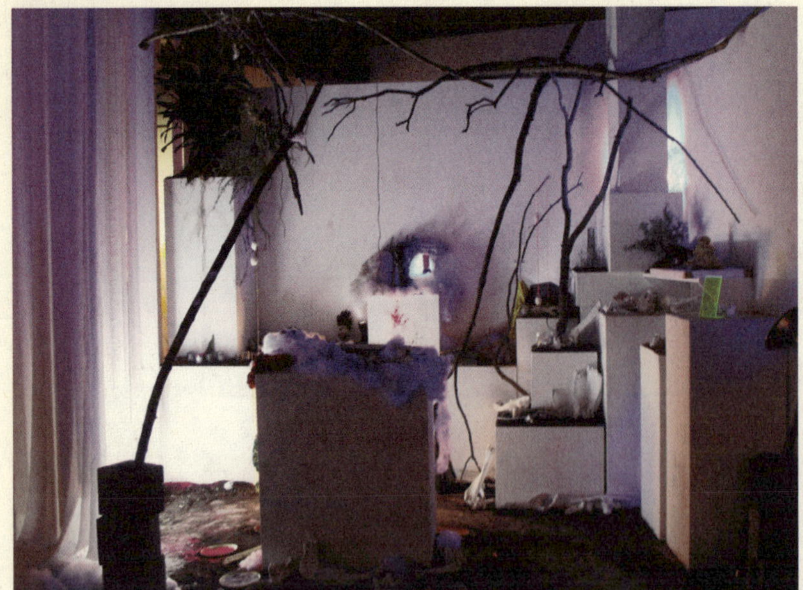
1.

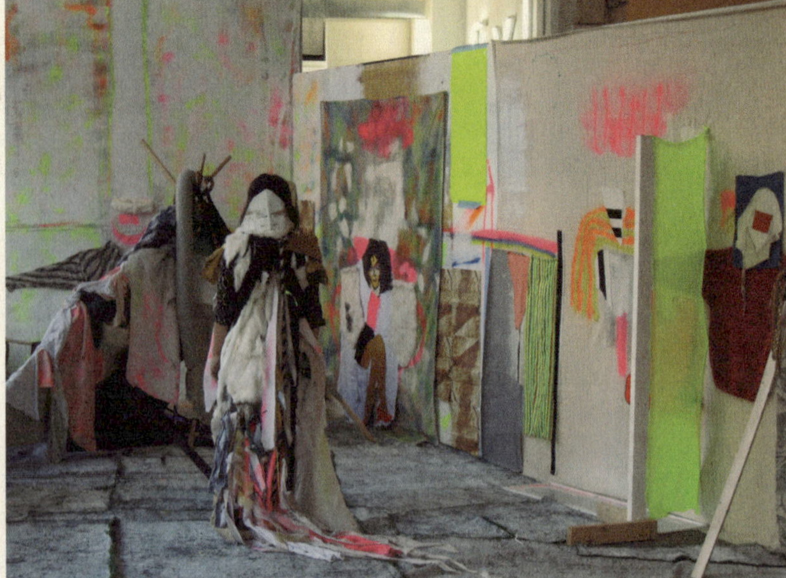
3.

Donna Huanca received her BFA in 2004 from the University of Houston, Texas. She layers painting and sculpture in mixed media installations that double as sites of performance, interaction, and live music. Her most recent exhibition, "Secret Museum of Mankind," included puppets, eggshells, toilet paper, and fake bones in a psychedelic autobiography tracing her family's Bolivian roots.

1 & 2. Secret Museum Of Mankind
2008, performance, light, digital video, wood, clothes, fog machine, lasers, eggs, bones, and drums, 2,500 × 2,500 ft (762 × 762 m), installation views

3, 4, 5 & 6. ETAPA DE FUNCIONAMIENTO (STAGE)
2008, performance, sound, clothes, spray paint, wood, and bed, 250 × 250 ft (76 × 76 m)

7 & 8. ETAPA DE FUNCIONAMENTO (SEGUNDO) (NETWORK OF LOVE)
with AIDS-3D
2008, sound, paint, fabrics, plastics, electricity, wood, clothes, fur, and tape, 8 × 40 × 22 ft (3 × 12 × 7 m)

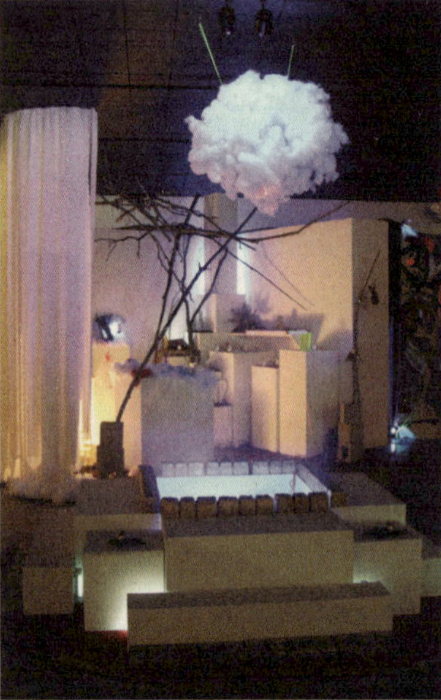

2.

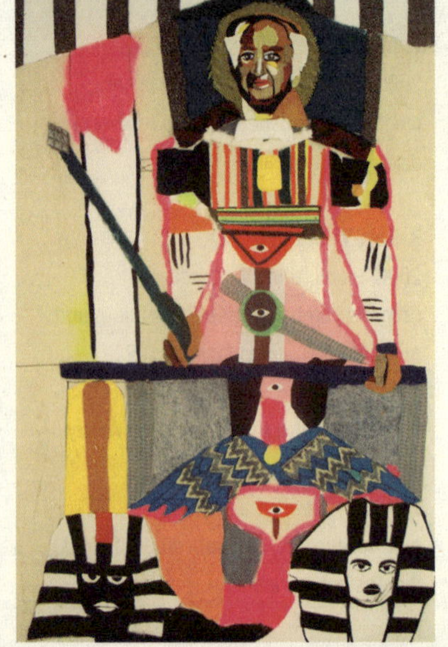
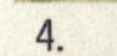
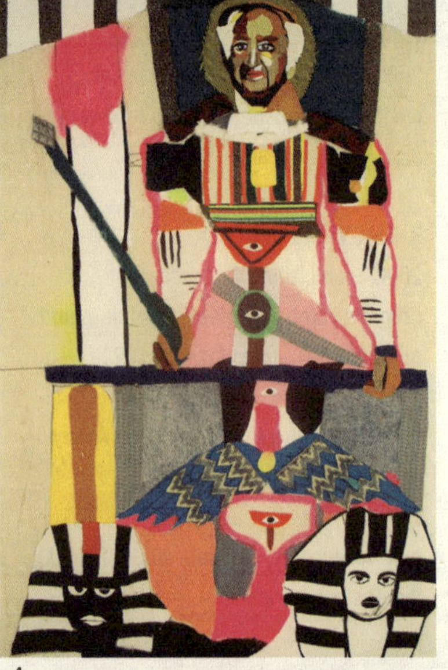

4.

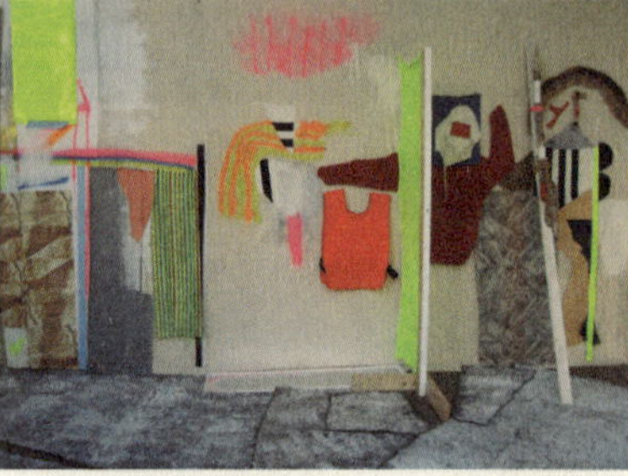
5.

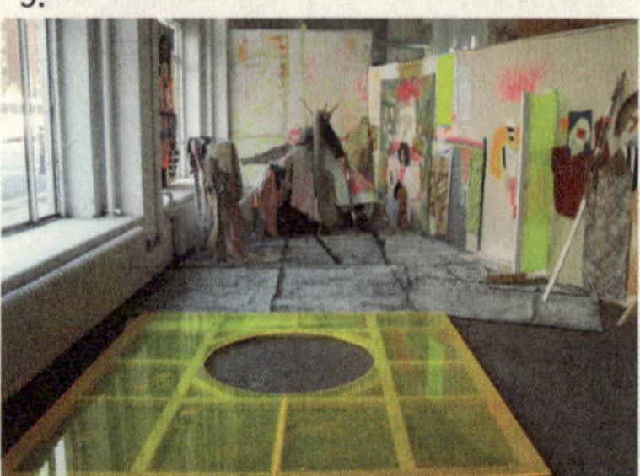
6.

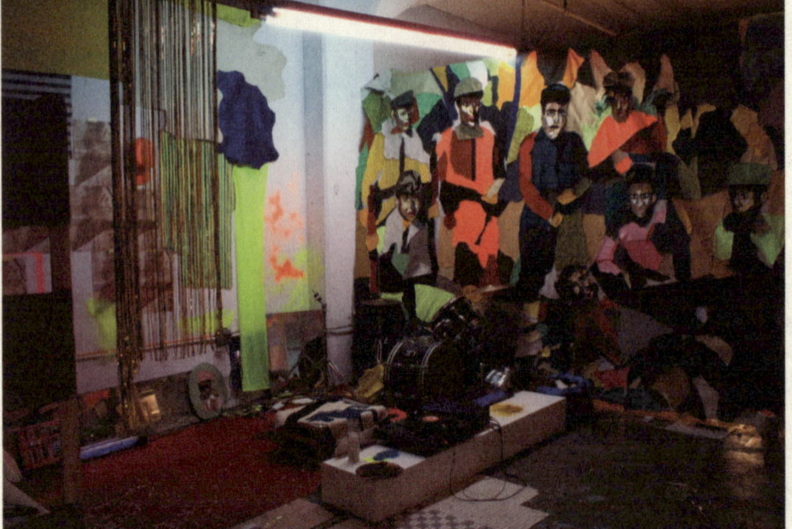

7.

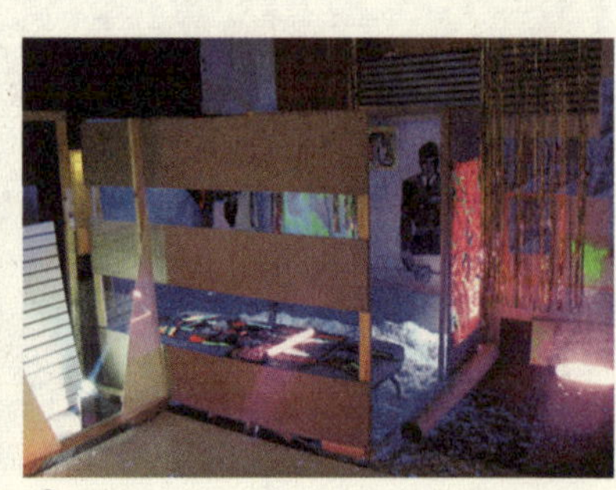
8.

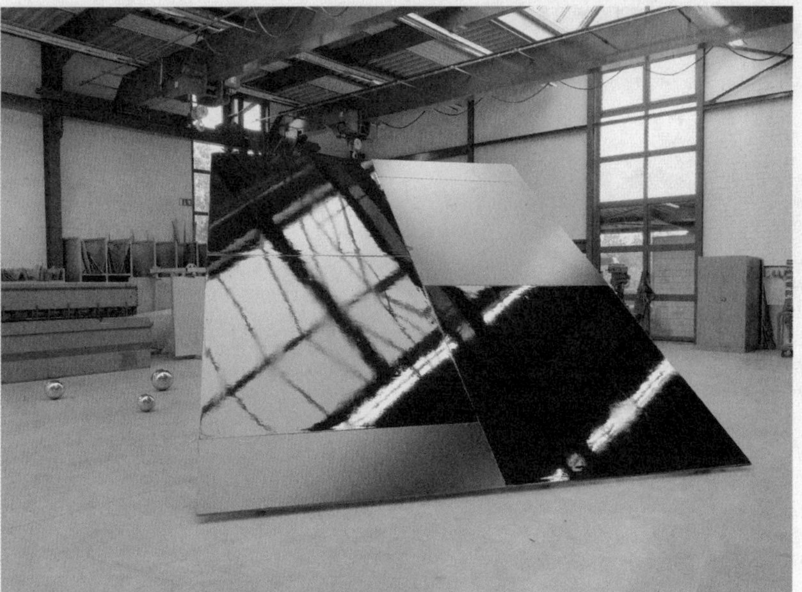

1.

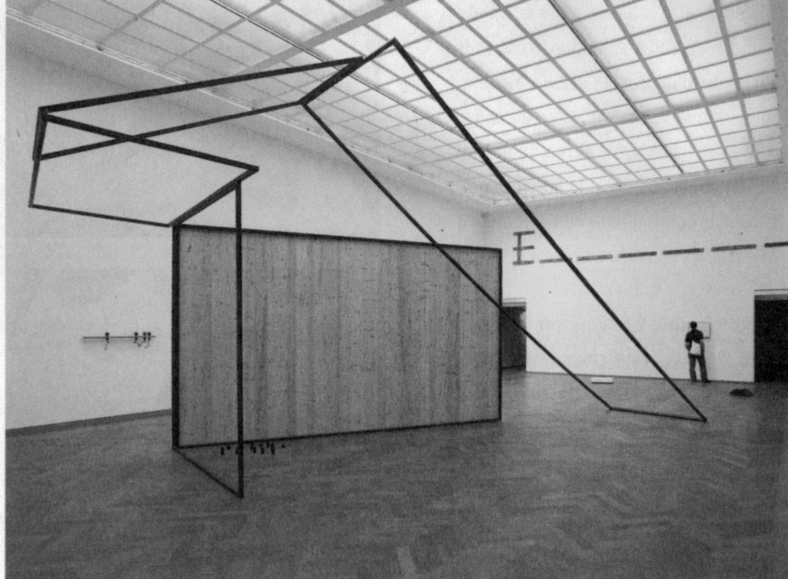

2.

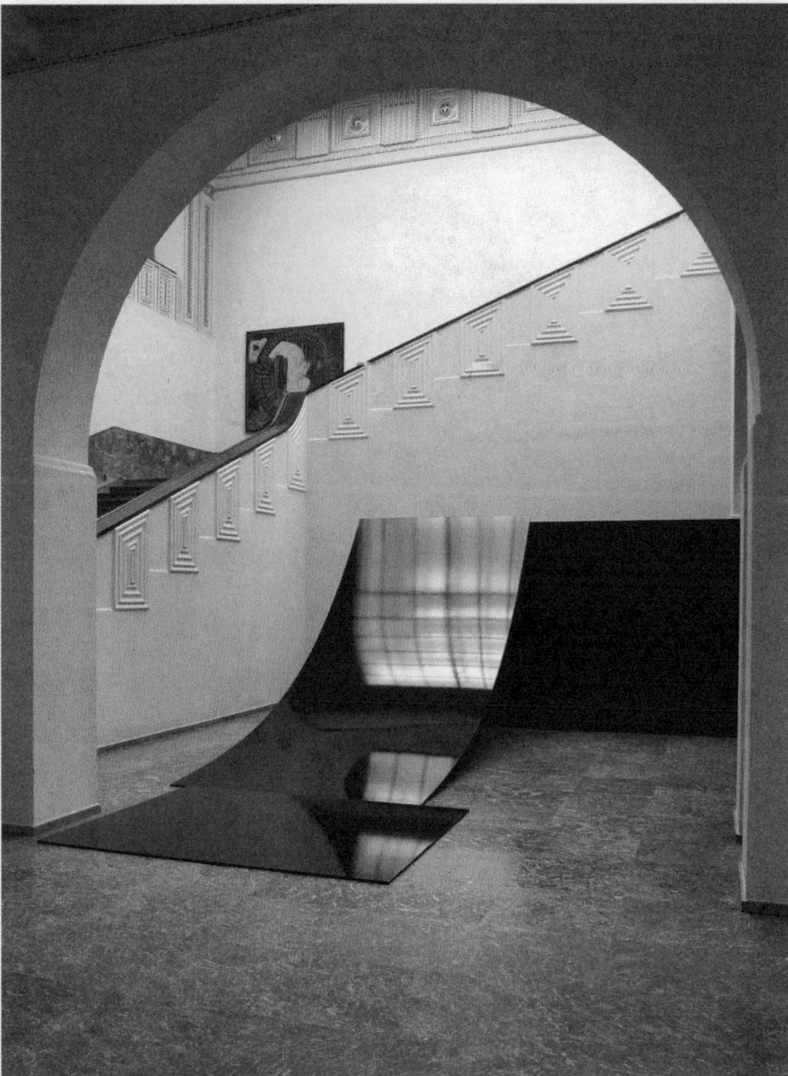

3.

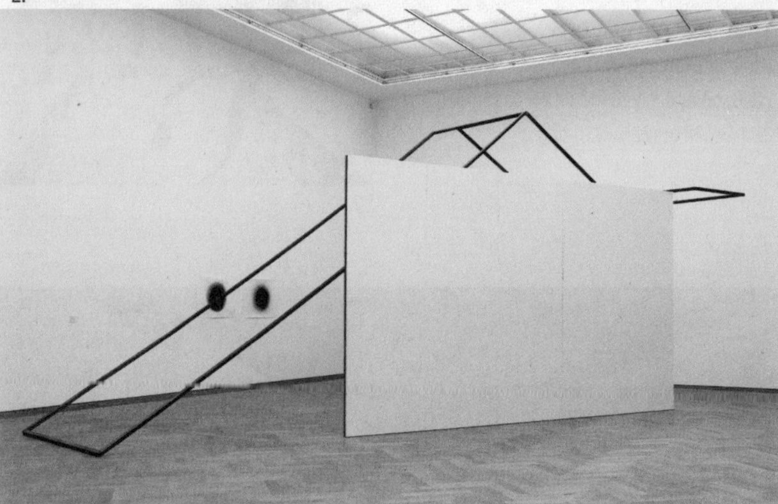

4.

5.

Karin Hueber attended the University of Art and Design in Basel, and currently lives in Basel and Rotterdam. She makes site-specific architectural installations using elements of the gallery's physical structure, such as the floor plan or the entryway, as a reference. Industrial materials like wood, chipboard, and mirrors are folded and contorted to alter the viewer's sense of perspective and orientation in space.

1. **Silent surroundings**
2006, wooden stilts, recycled wooden plates, black varnish, and steel balls, 13 1/2 × 23 × 10 1/2 in (420 × 700 × 320 cm)

2. **Ausläfer II**
2008, MDF plates, varnish, mirror, and hinges, dimensions variable

3. **lonesomeness**
2008, MDF plates, varnish, and wooden stilts, approx 26 1/4 × 23 × 7 1/2 (8 × 7 × 2 m)

4. **Schwankender Boden**
2007, metal, recycled wooden plates, white varnish, 26 1/4 × 16 1/4 × 13 1/2 ft (8 × 5 × 4 m)

5. **Untitled**
2007, carbon sticks, dimensions variable

Volker Hueller is a Berlin-based painter, printmaker, and installation artist with a background in graphic design. He often combines woven fabric, silk, fur, and paper cutouts in paintings that merge abstraction and figuration. Inherent to his work are questions of ornamentation and decoration as elements of a fine art practice.

1. **This is how we walk on the moon**
2008, etching, watercolor, and shellac on paper, 15 $\frac{1}{2}$ × 11 $\frac{1}{2}$ in (40 × 30 cm)

2. **Stechschritt im Garten**
(Goose step in the garden)
2008, mixed media on canvas, 80 $\frac{1}{4}$ × 125 $\frac{1}{4}$ in (204 × 318 cm)

3. **Nur Himmel und Dreck**
(Only heaven and dirt)
2008, oil and mixed media on paper, 88 $\frac{1}{2}$ × 122 in (225 × 310 cm)

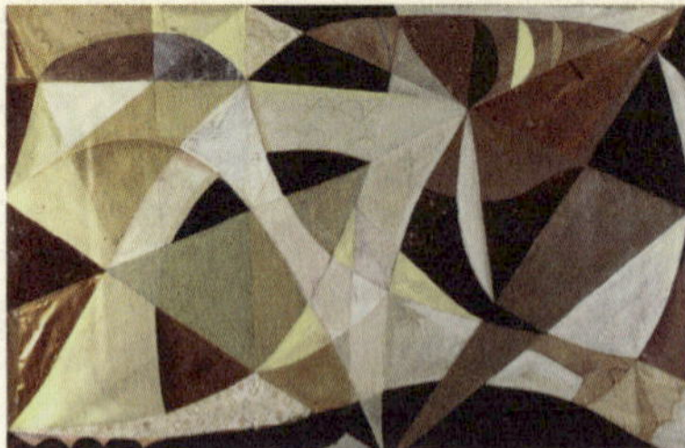

1.

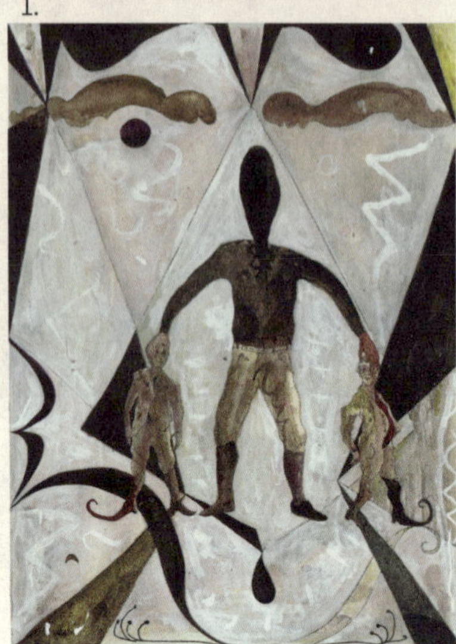

2.

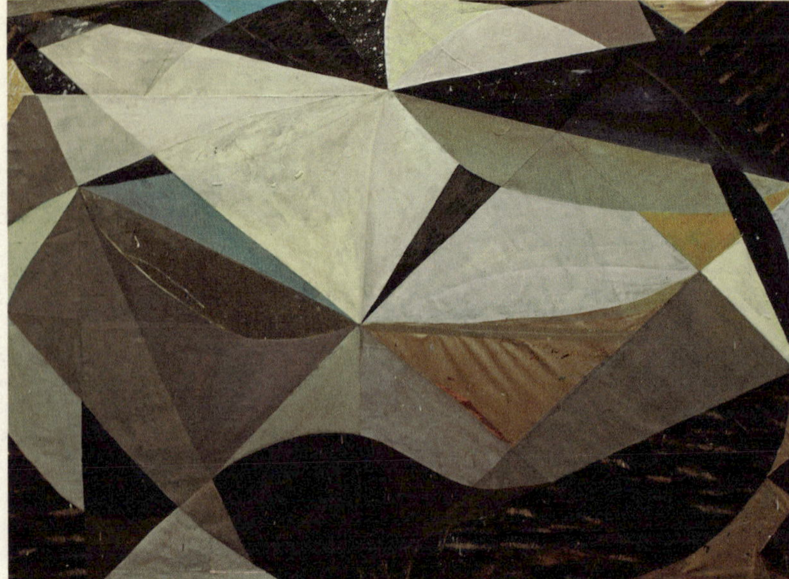

3.

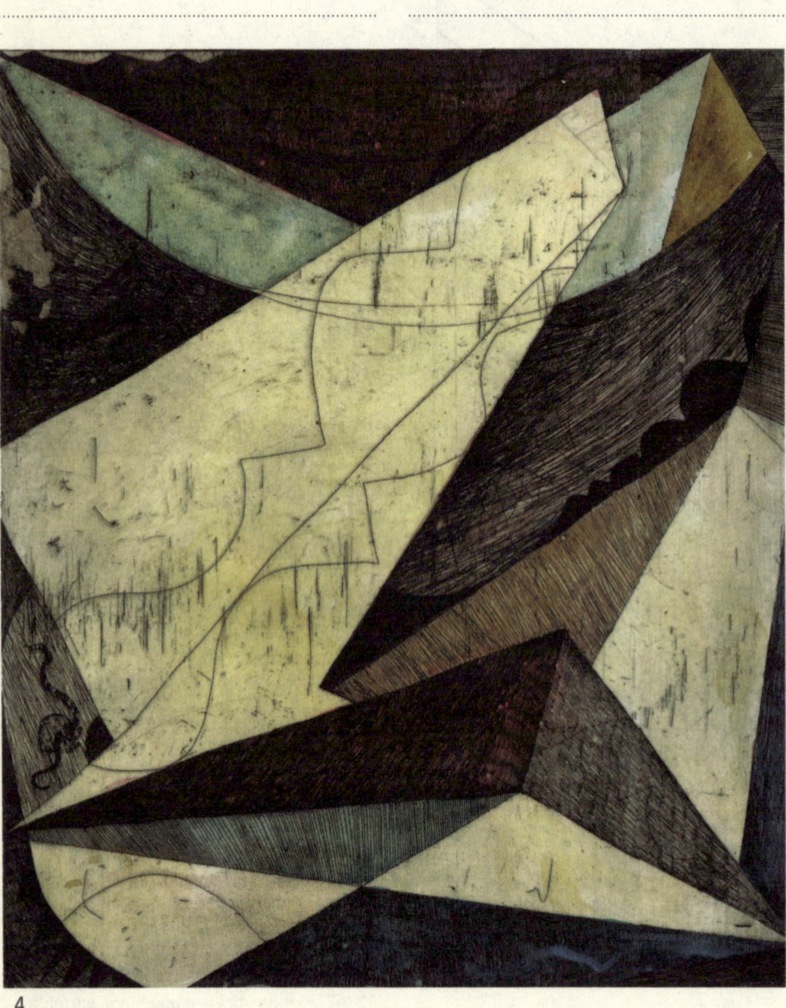

4.

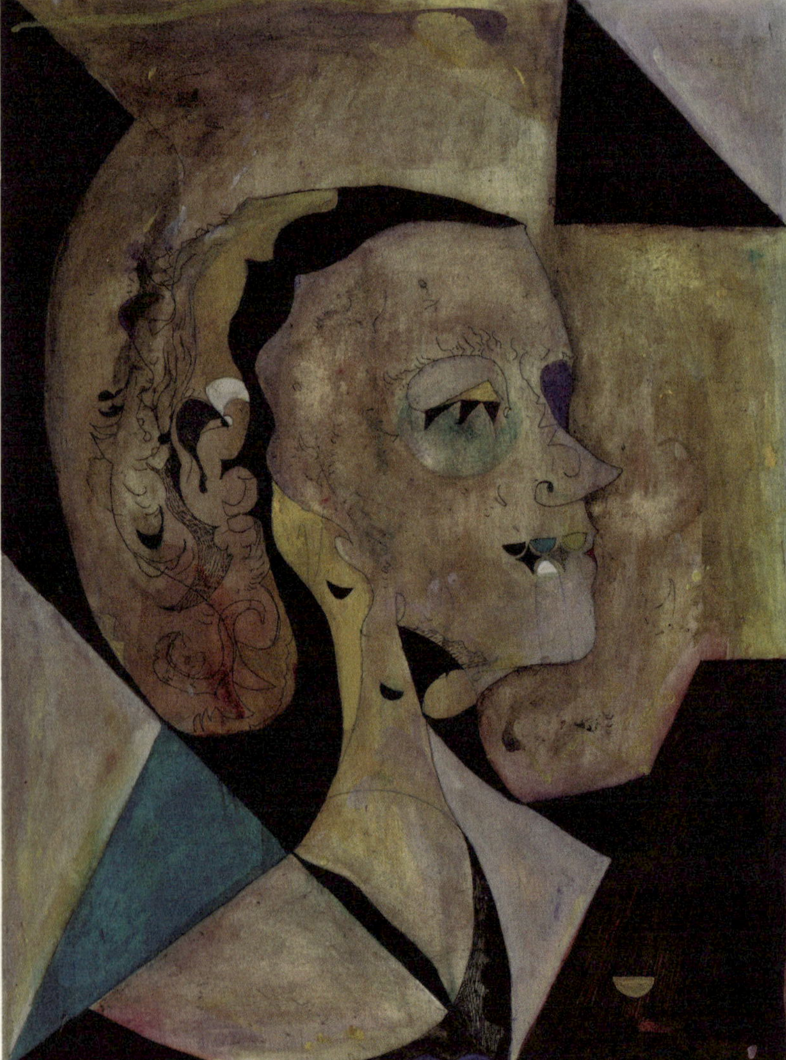

5.

4. **Gomorrha II**
2007, etching on paper with watercolor and shellac, 19 $\frac{3}{4}$ × 15 $\frac{1}{2}$ in (50 × 40 cm)

5. **Selbst als krankes Madchen**
(Self as sick girl)
2007, etching, watercolor, and shellac on paper, 15 $\frac{3}{4}$ × 12 in (40 × 30 cm)

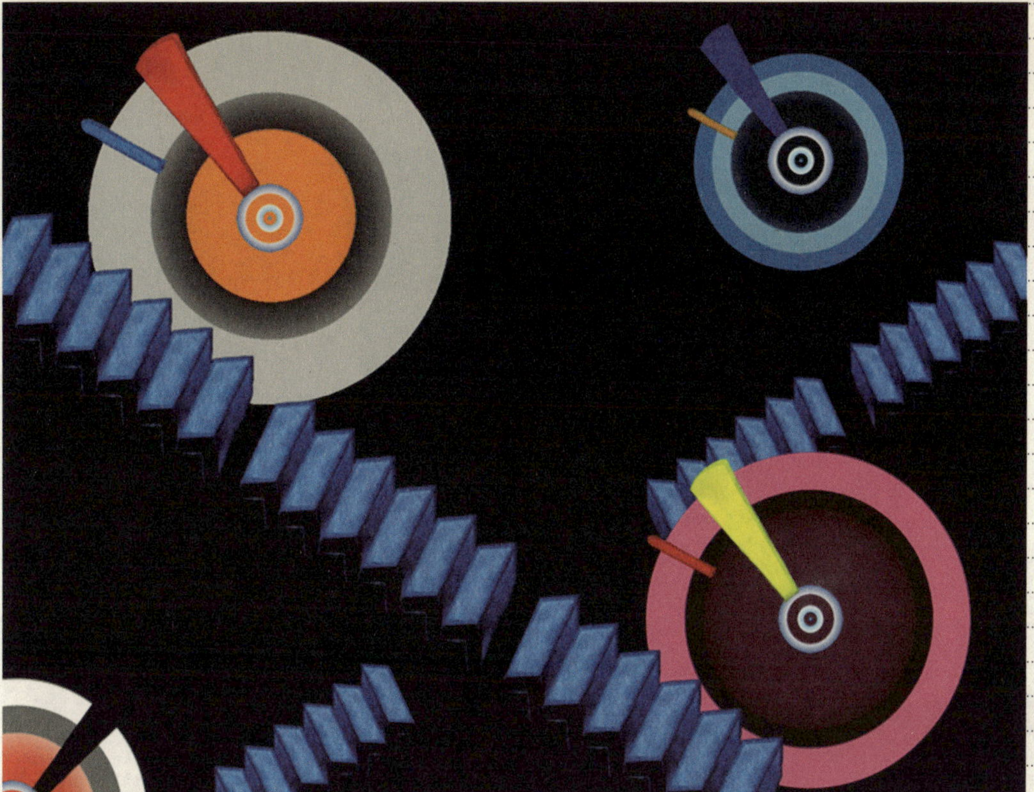

1.

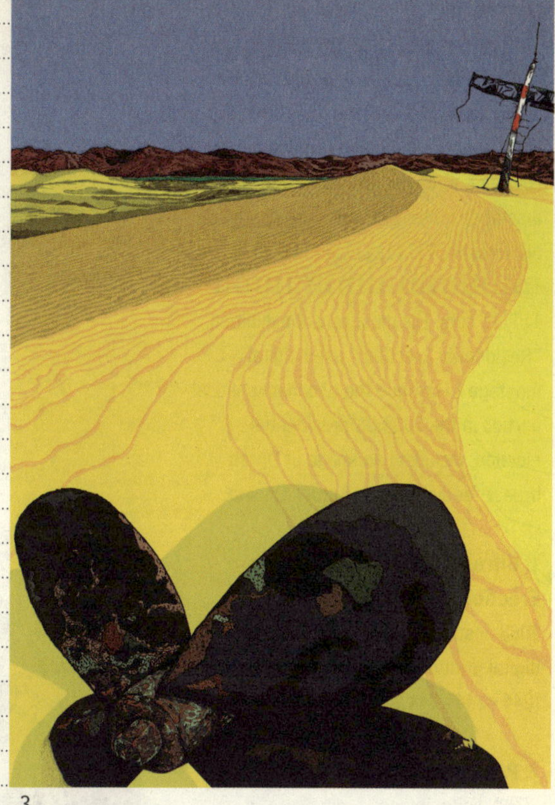

3.

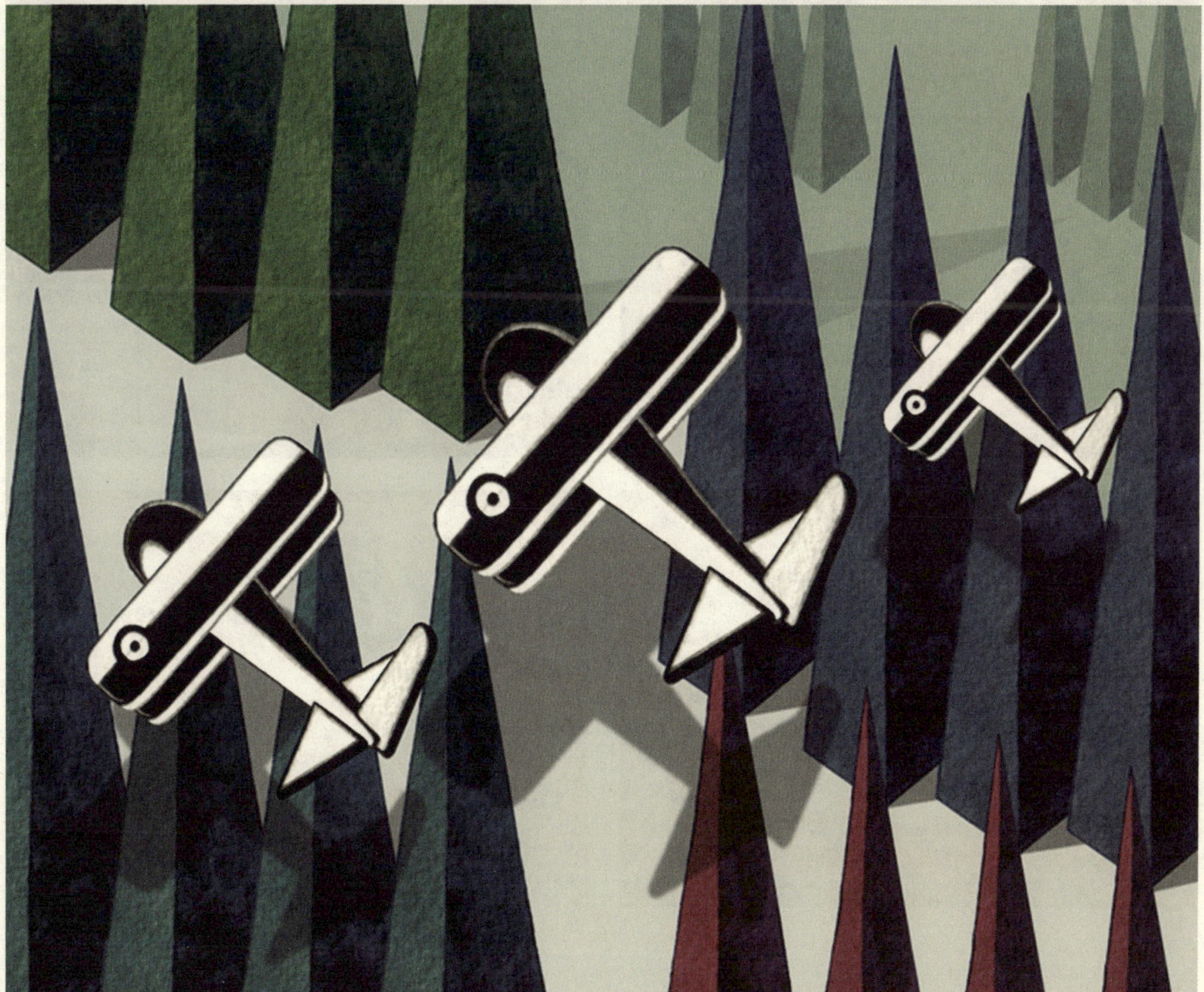

2.

Emre Hüner was educated at the Brera Academy of Fine Arts in Milan. His work deals with man's relationship to nature, ecological devastation, and the dialectical tension between technological progress and technologically abetted ruin. In his animated video **Panoptikon** (2005) he conjures a lush alternate universe inhabited by monstrous creatures and obscure technologies, while his spare, poignant film **Boumont** (2006) gives the viewer a glimpse of a postapocalyptic world beyond hope. Hüner's work was included in the 10th Istanbul Biennial (2007).

1 & 2. **Total Realm**
2008, animation, duration variable

3. **Desert**
2005, print on paper, 8 1/4 × 6 in (21 × 15 cm)

Kenneth Tin-Kin Hung received his BA in art from San Francisco State University, and currently lives in New York City. He performs a unique brand of psychedelic political satire mediated through neon-colored pop-up constructions and video animations, many of which are posted on his website, 1111111111111111111111111111111111111111111111111111111111111111.com. His most recent exhibition, "Residential Erection," used digital montage to critique the two main political parties in the 2008 US presidential election, including an image of Oprah breast-feeding a baby Barack Obama.

1. Ultra Donkey (Residential Erection: Pop-up Democrats)
2008, installation view, wood, foam, and digital print on paper, 8 × 8 × 8 ft (244 × 244 × 244 cm)

2. P.A.C.M.A.O.++++++
2002, digital image

3. Shamnesty Straight Talk Express (Residential Erection: Video)
2008, video, 5 min

4. Sexxxy Tony Thatcher plays with your wicked wanker!
2006, digital image

5. MeccaDonald's Happy Meal! I'm Lovin' it! (Because Washington is Hollywood for Ugly People)
2007, video, 7 min 38 sec

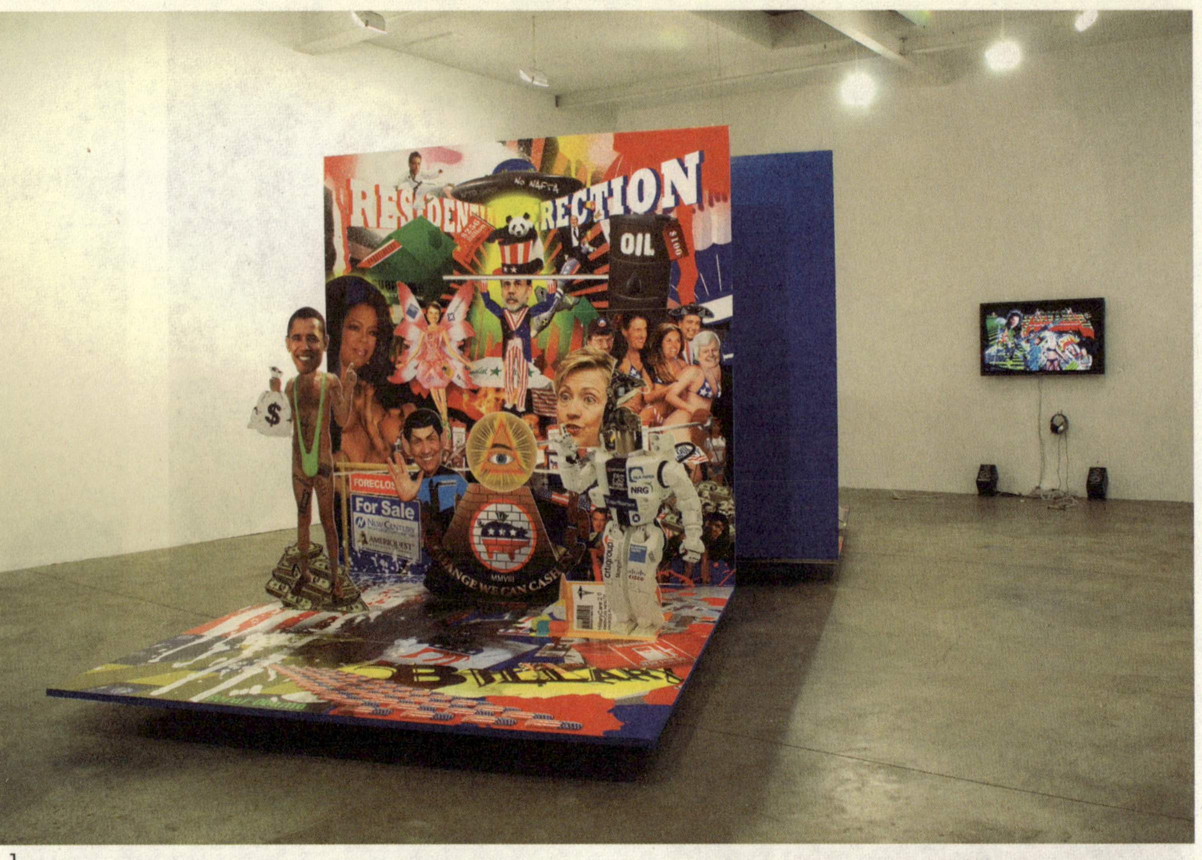

1.

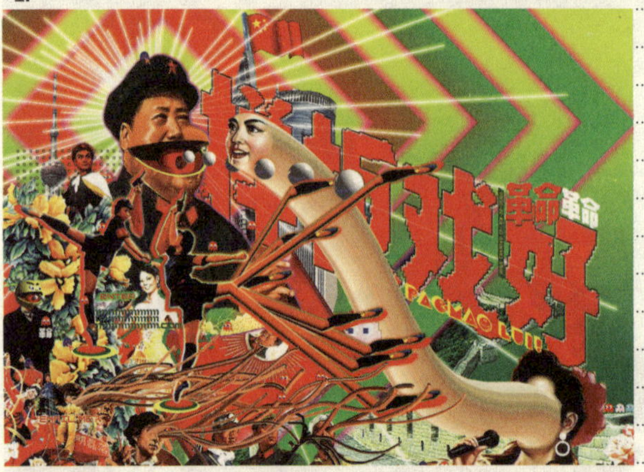

2.

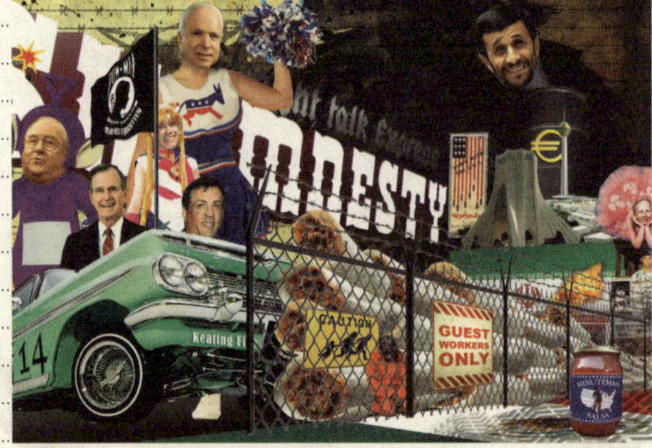

3.

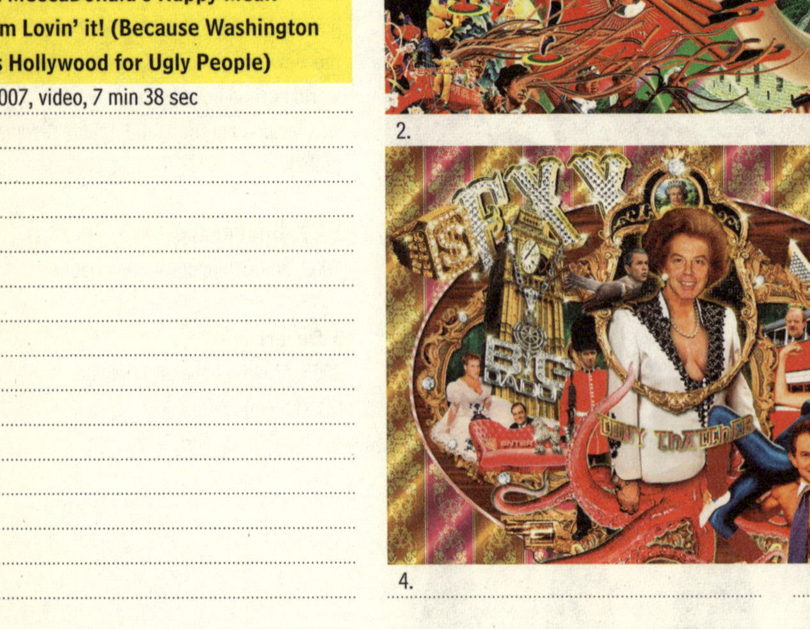

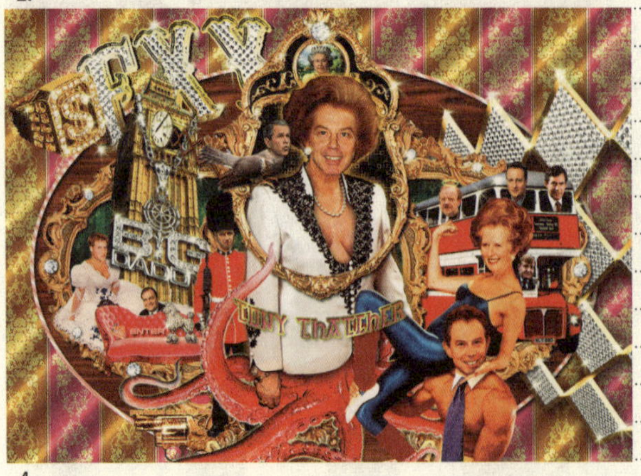

4.

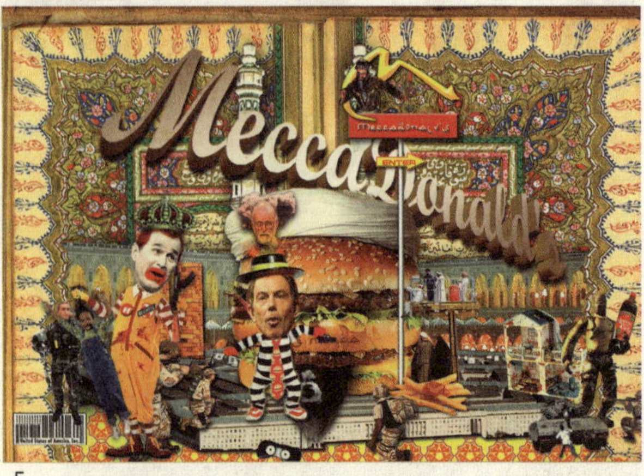

5.

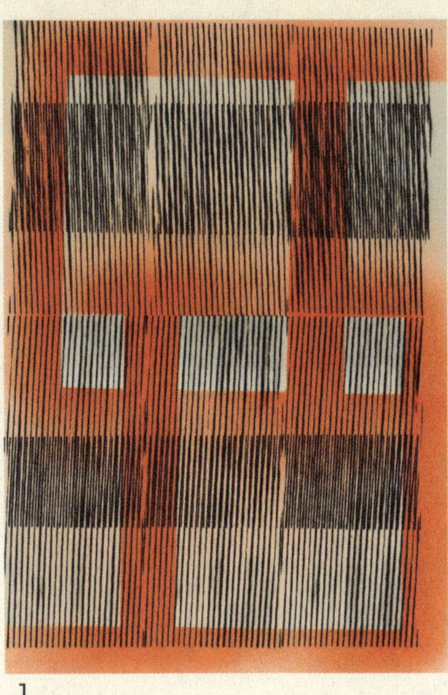
1.

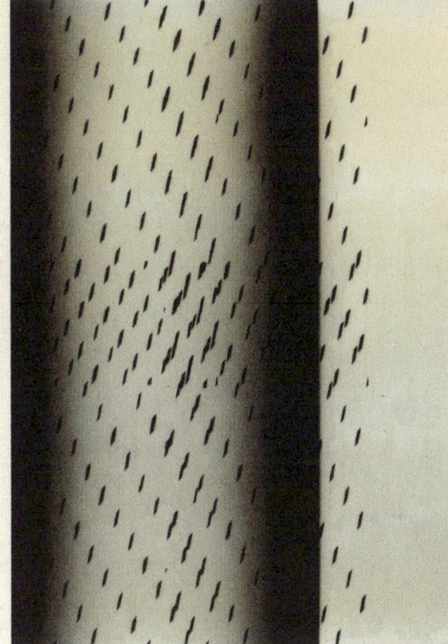
2.

Nathan Hylden earned his MFA from Art Center College of Design in Pasadena, California, and currently lives in Los Angeles. He creates paintings, installations, and works on paper using screen print, collage, acrylic, and spray paint. Works often juxtapose a simple painted pattern with a similar pattern occurring in a found image – connecting the language of Minimalism with Pop representation.

1. Untitled
2008, acrylic on linen, 94 × 67 ½ in (239 × 172 cm)

2. Untitled
2008, acrylic on linen, 67 ½ × 47 in (172 × 119 cm)

3. Untitled
2008, acrylic on linen, 67 ½ × 47 in (172 × 119 cm)

4. Untitled
2008, acrylic on linen, 67 ½ × 47 in (172 × 119 cm)

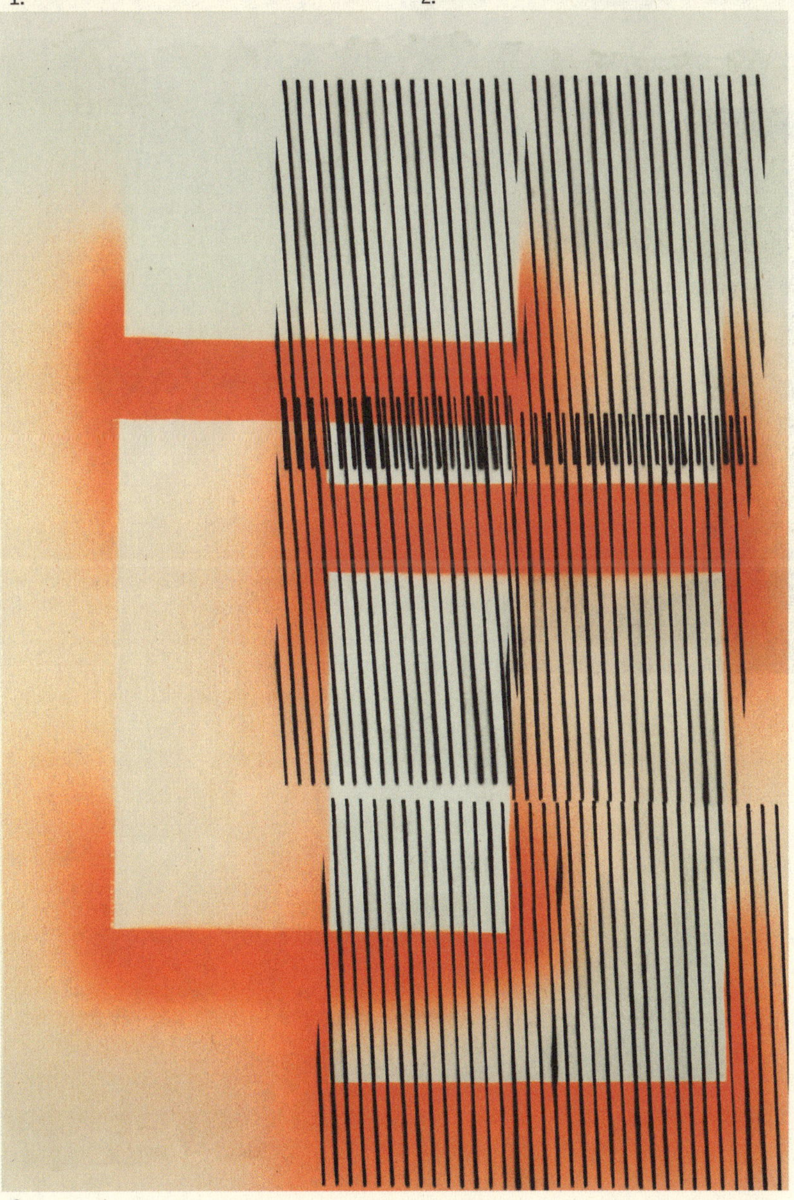
3.

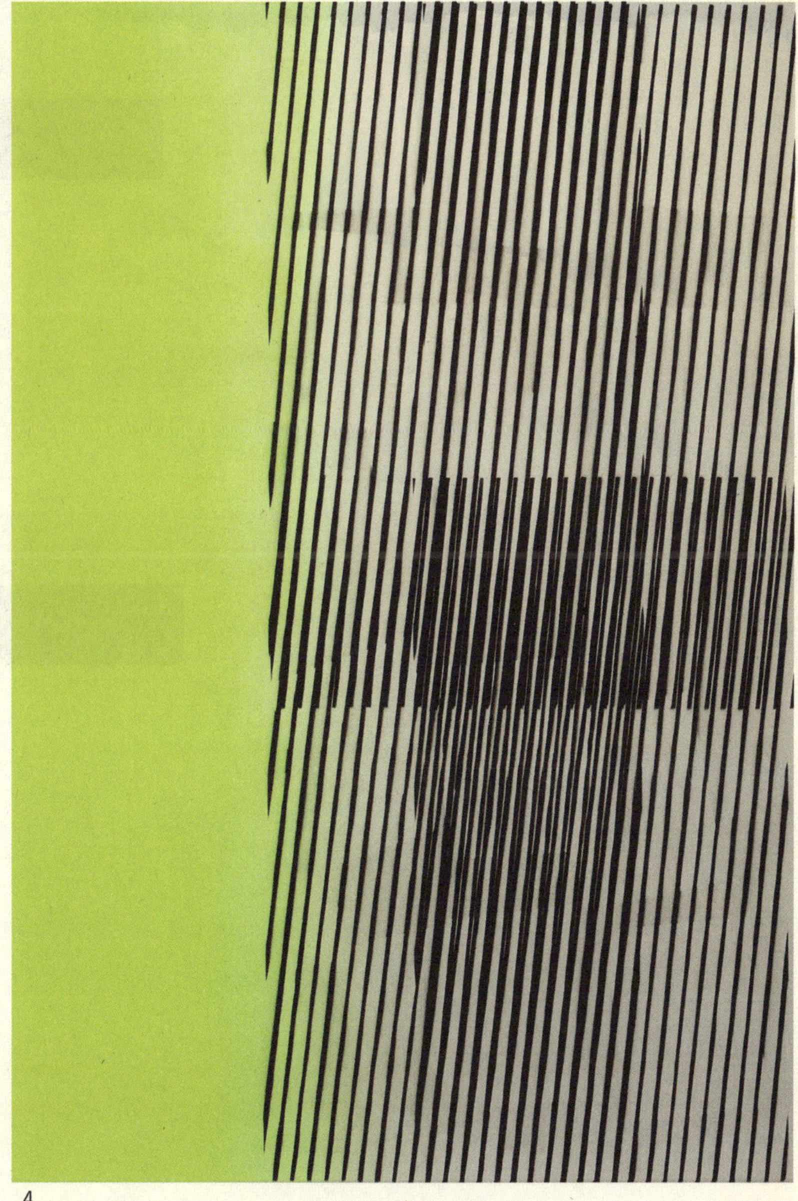
4.

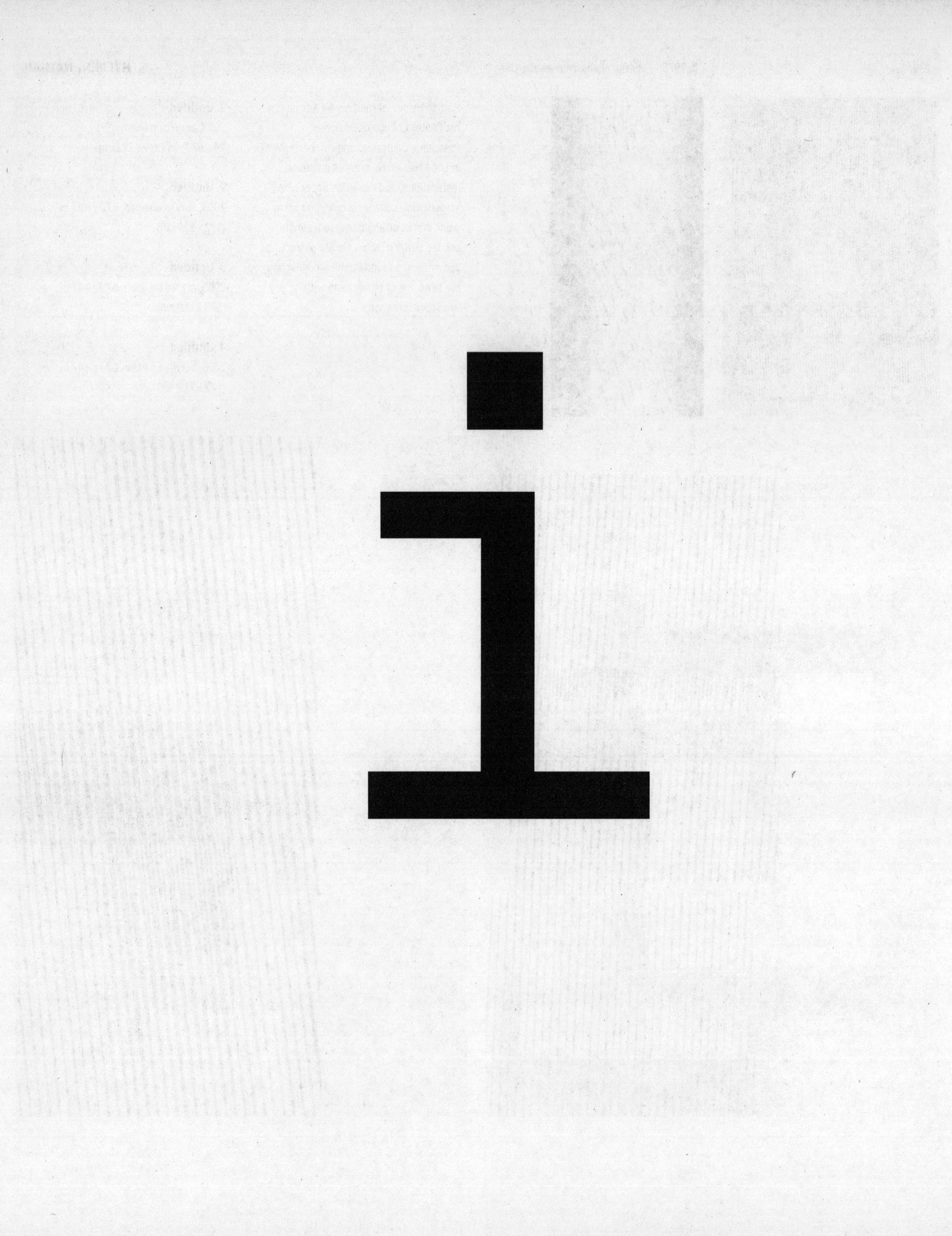

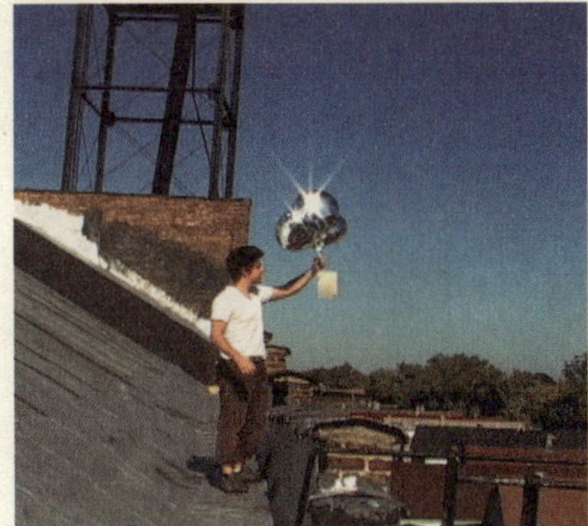

1.

InCUBATE (the Institute for Community Understanding Between Art and The Everyday), founded by Bruce Dwyer, Roman Petruniak, Abigail Satinsk, and Ben Schaafsma, is a Chicago-based research and residency program dedicated to challenging established notions of artistic production, funding, and administration. InCUBATE exhibits, curates, speaks, publishes, disseminates, and organizes, seeing every facet of its practice as creative.

1. **Welcome to the InCUBATE Correspondence Network**
2007, video, 4 min

2. **Sunday Soup Grant Program**
2008, guest chefs, soup, grant applications

3. "Other Options"
traveling exhibition in Chicago; Grand Rapids, Michigan; Syracuse, New York; Pittsburgh; and New York City (2008)

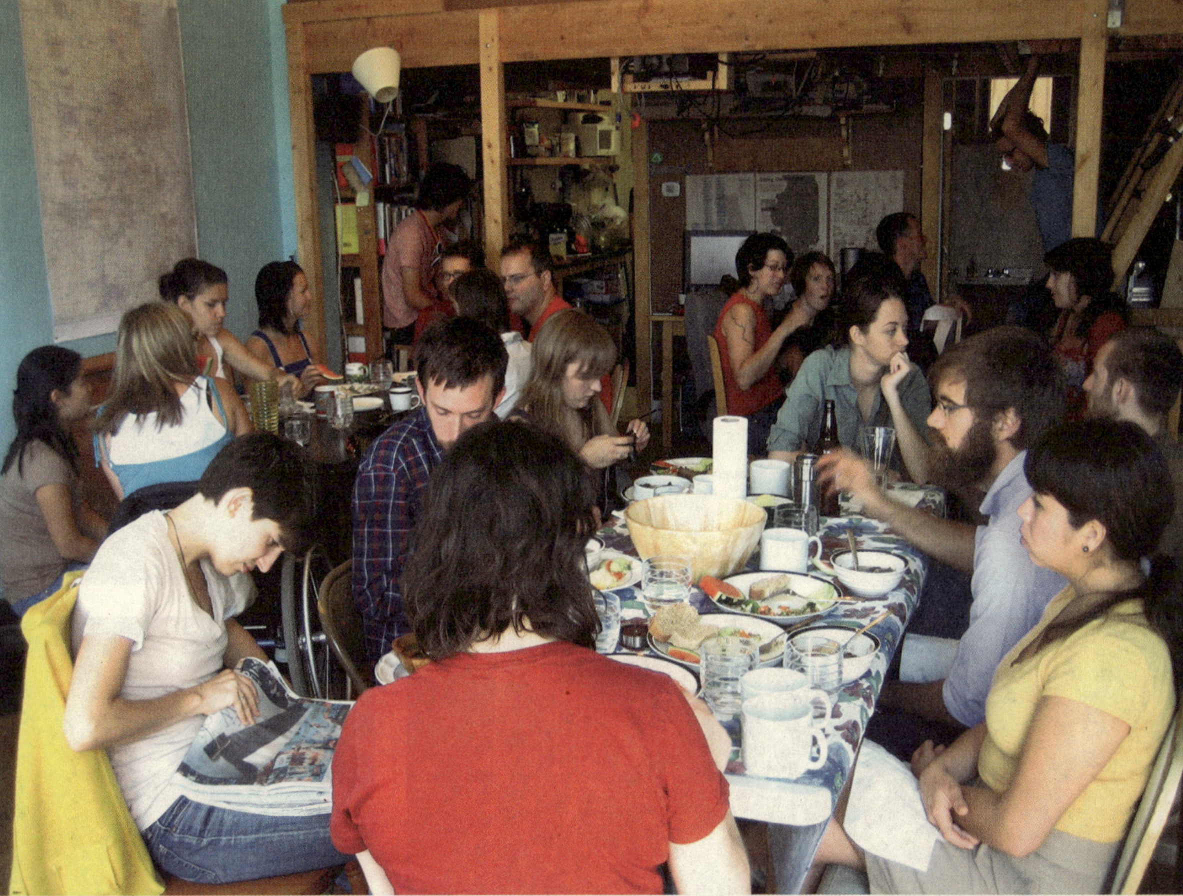

2.

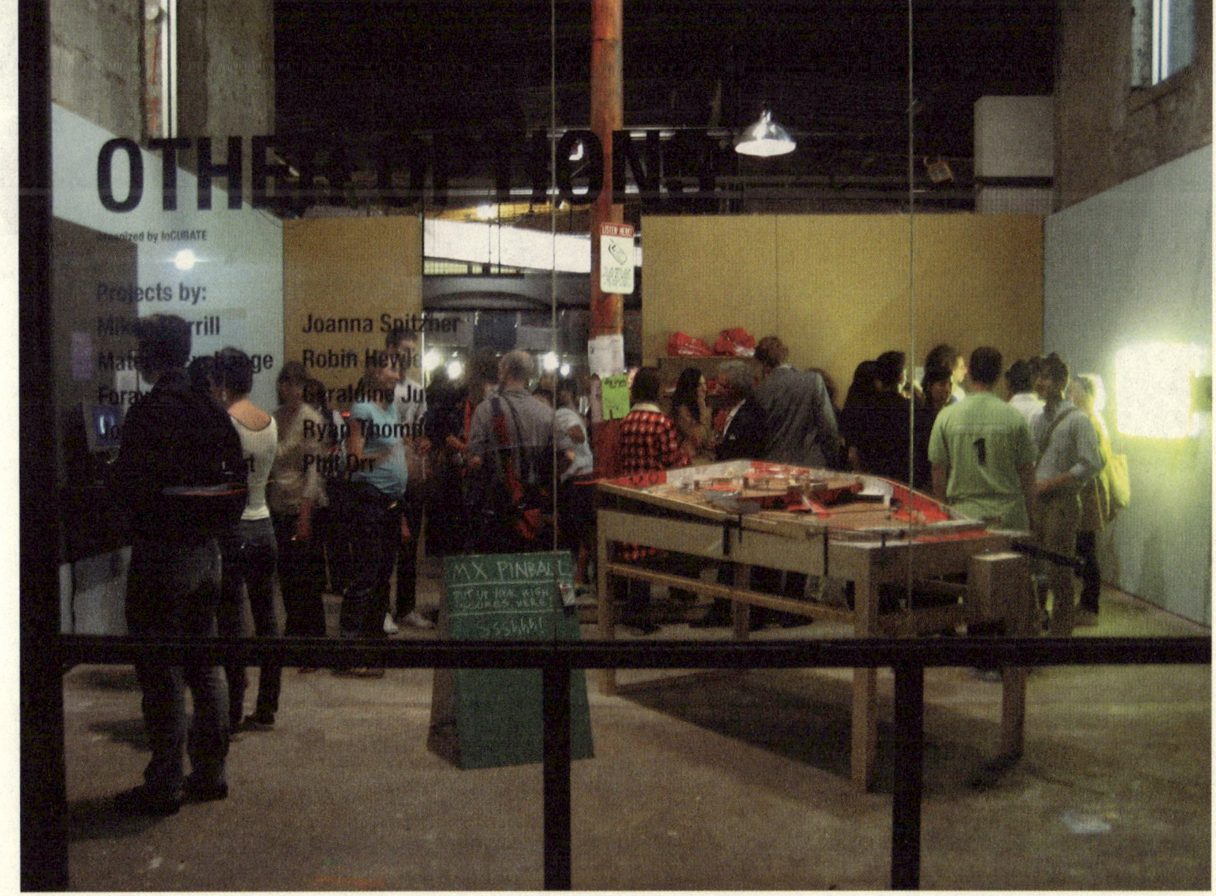

3.

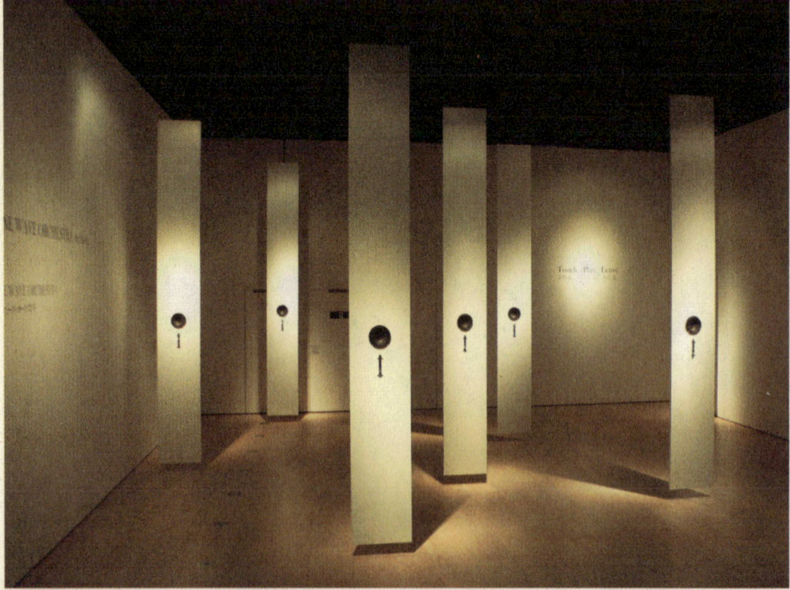

1.

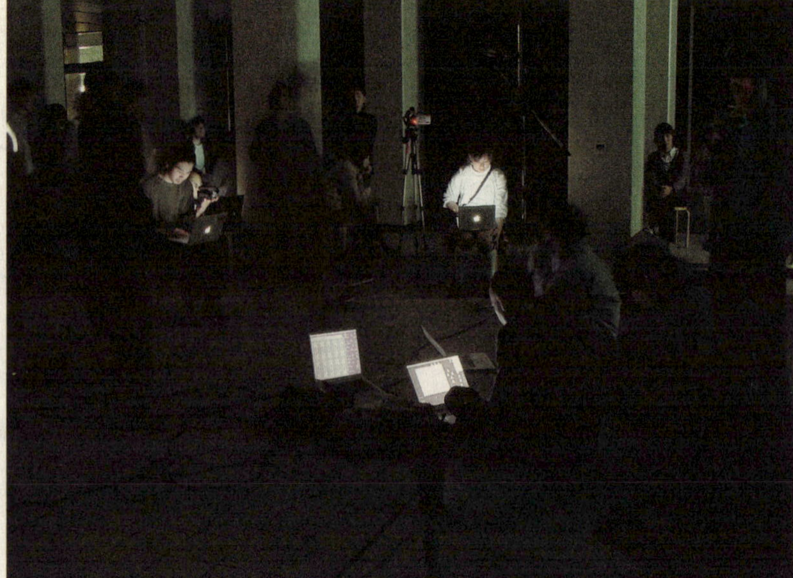

2.

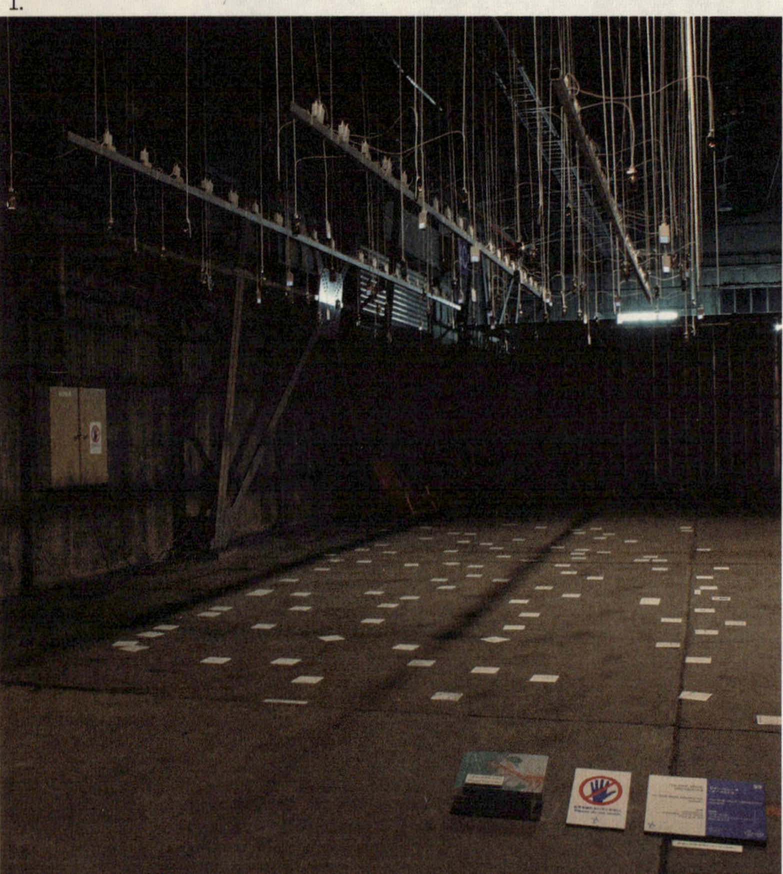

3.

4.

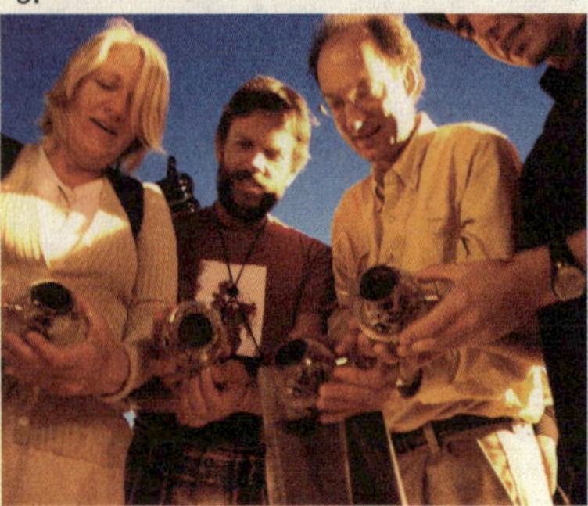

5.

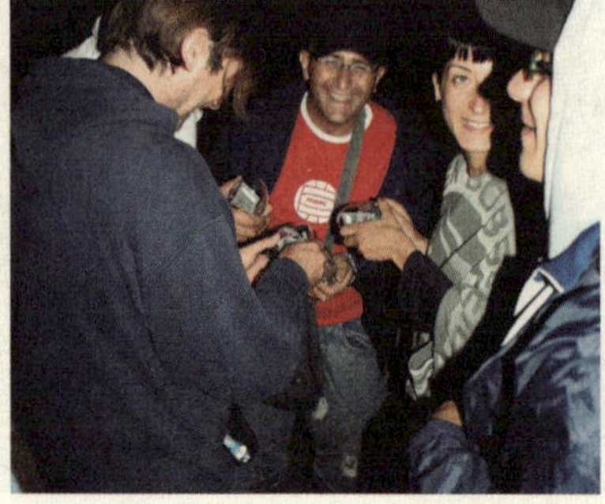

6.

Daisuke Ishida lives and works in Berlin. He is interested in the realization of synthetic sound space, achieved through the production of computer-generated music in conjunction with work in other electronic media. He is a founding member of the Sine Wave Orchestra, a participatory experiment in the formation of collective aural environments.

1. **The "Sine Wave Orchestra" Mediate**
2006, mixed media installation, dimensions variable

2. **Sine Wave Orchestra**
2003, performance

3. **The "Sine Wave Orchestra" Nomadic**
2005, 120 Apple iPods, 120 small iPod speakers, 120 iPod power supplies, metal bar, string, and 120 ceramic tiles, dimensions variable

4. **The Stairway of the "Sine Wave Orchestra"**
2004, semi-public space, 50 self-made sine wave devices with light sensors, 8 lights with DMX controllers, and 200 participants, $33 \times 98\frac{1}{2} \times 33$ ft ($1000 \times 3000 \times 1000$ cm), approx 60 min

5 & 6. **The "Sine Wave Orchestra" tour**
2006, public space, at least 100 participants, and 50 self-made sine wave devices, approx 60 min

Iman Issa lives and works in Cairo and New York. In her videos, photographs, and sculptural installations, she presents incongruent combinations of form and function as the results of specific physical and ideological situations. Focusing in particular on the grandiose and monumental, she throws familiar forms off balance in the search for new meaning.

1. **Bucket**
from the series **Making Places**
2008, chromogenic print, $18\frac{1}{4} \times 27\frac{1}{2}$ in (47 × 70 cm)

2. **Building**
2003, wood and scrap mirrors, $165\frac{1}{2} \times 35\frac{1}{2}$ in (420 × 90 cm)

3. **Golden House**
2003, wood and glitter, 79 × 98 × 79 in (200 × 250 × 200 cm), installation view in Nuweiba, Egypt

4. **Car Wash**
2006, single-channel video, 13 min 21 sec

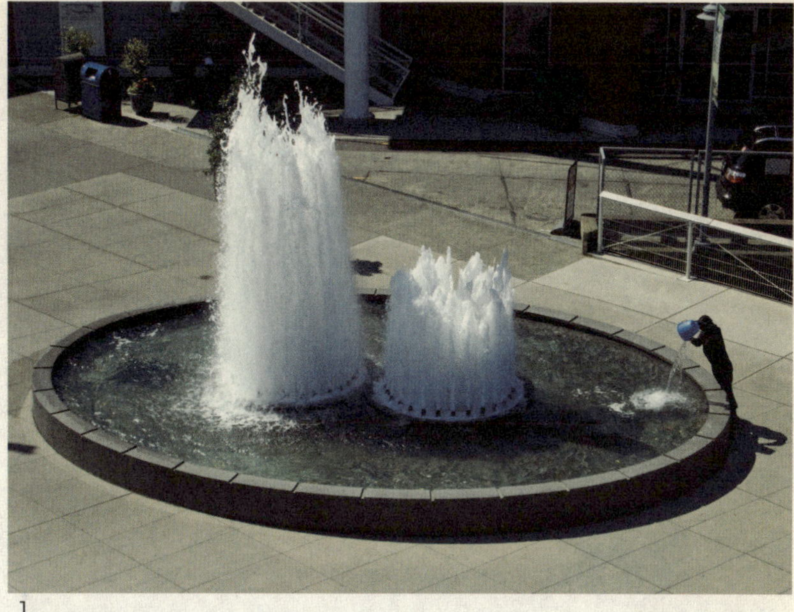
1.

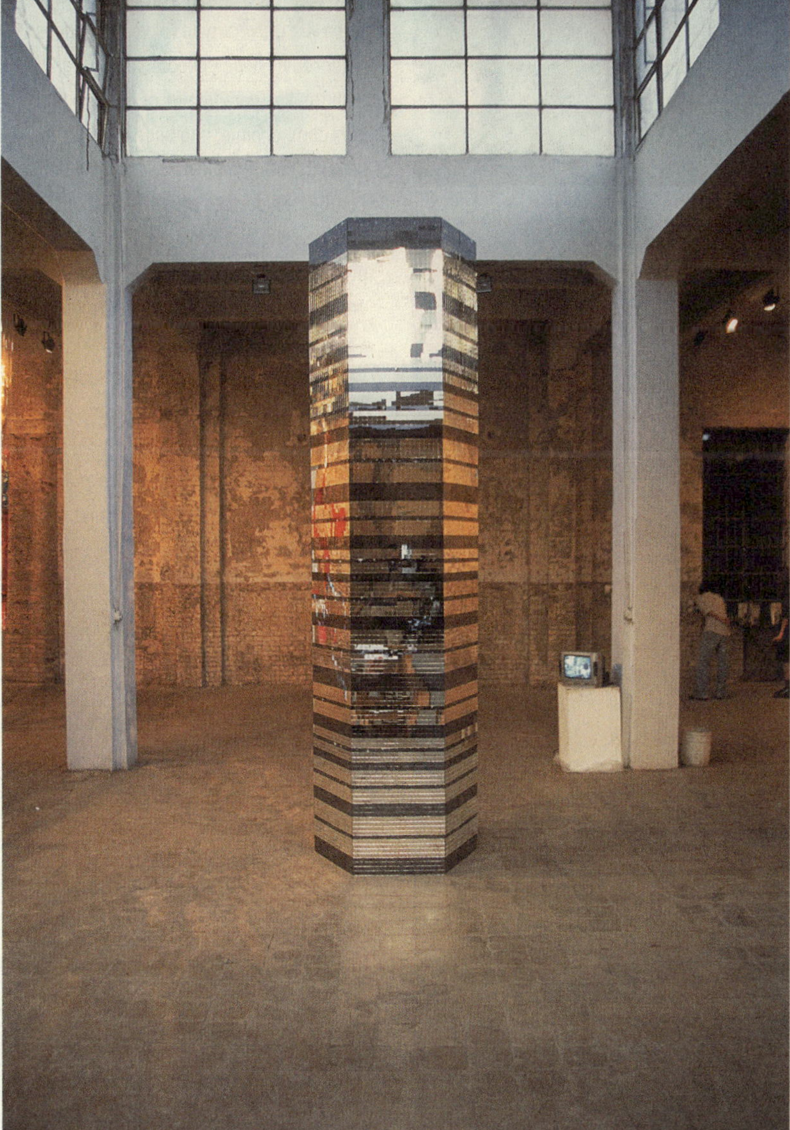
2.

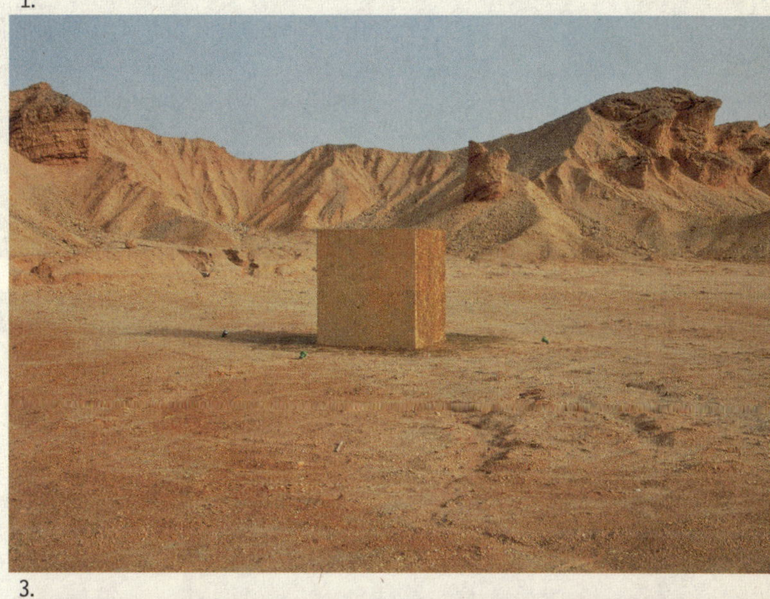
3.

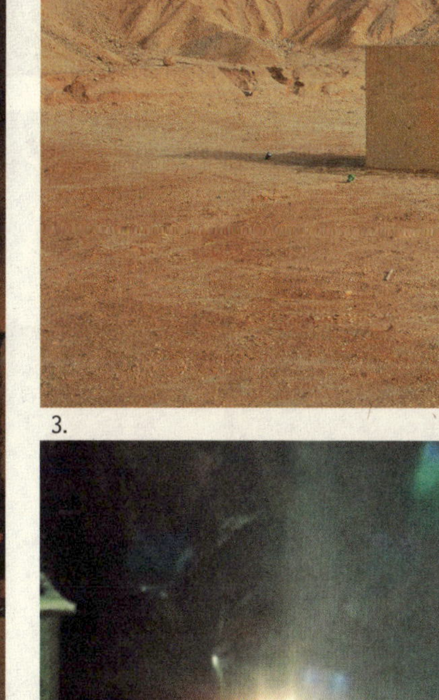

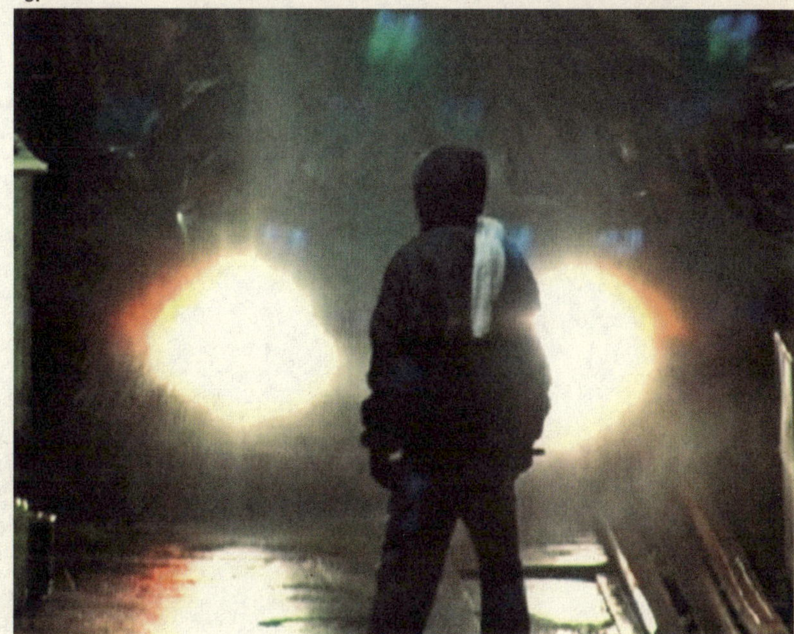
4.

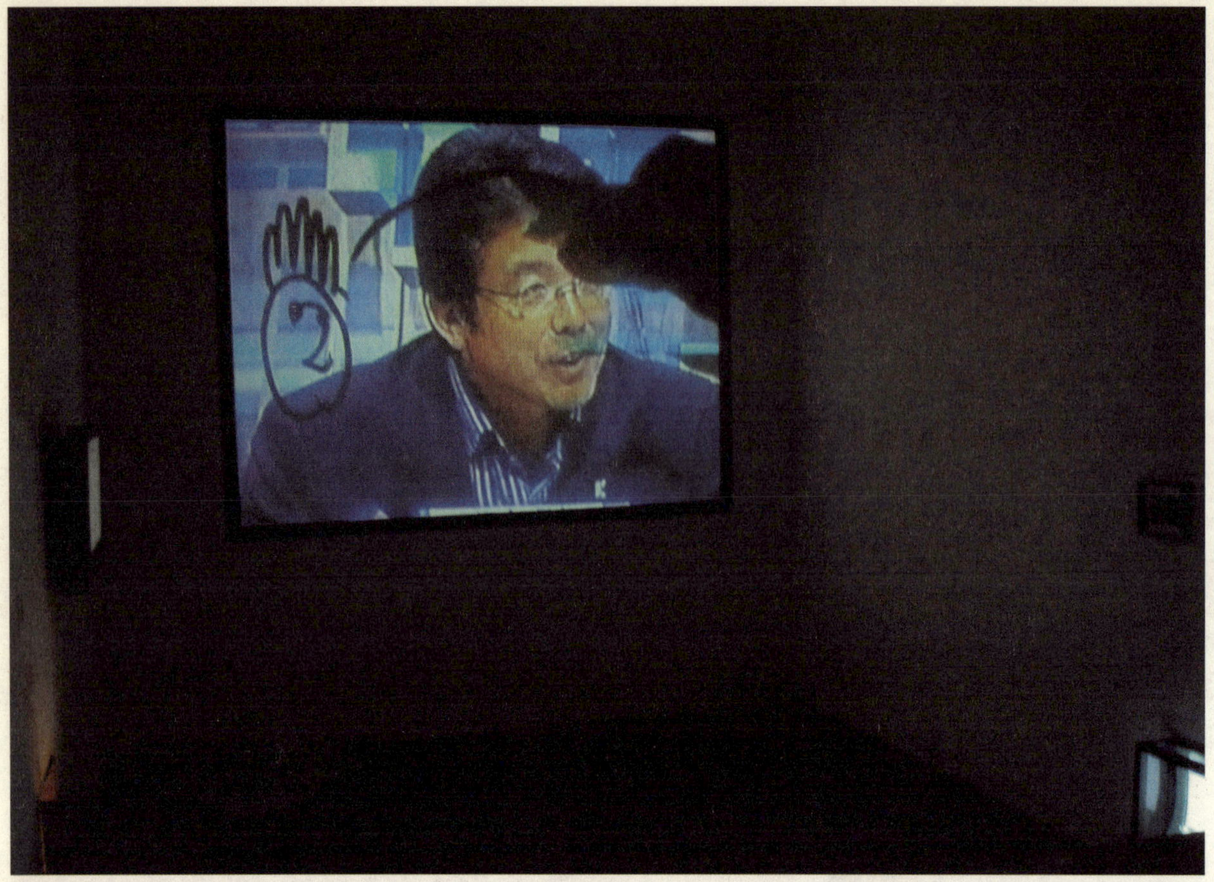

1.

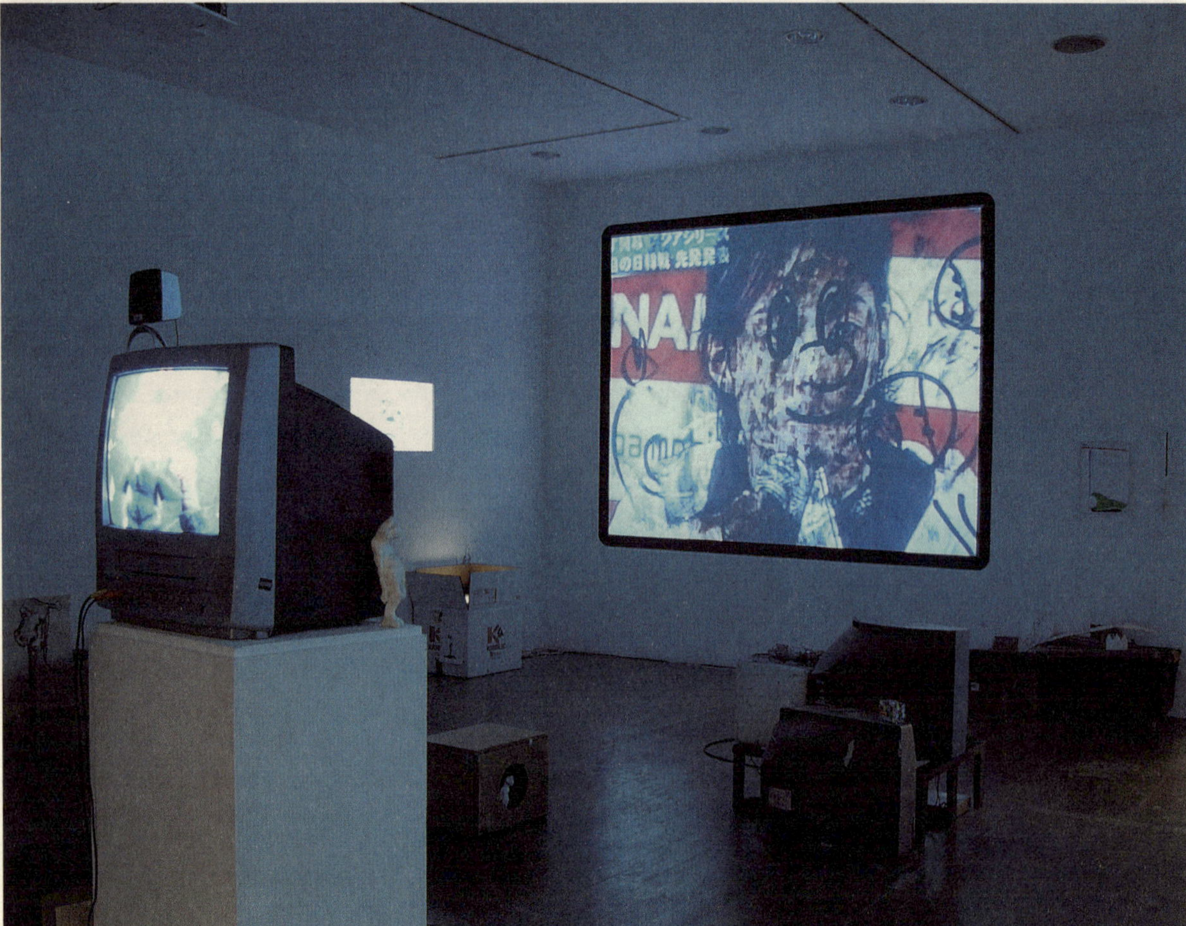

2.

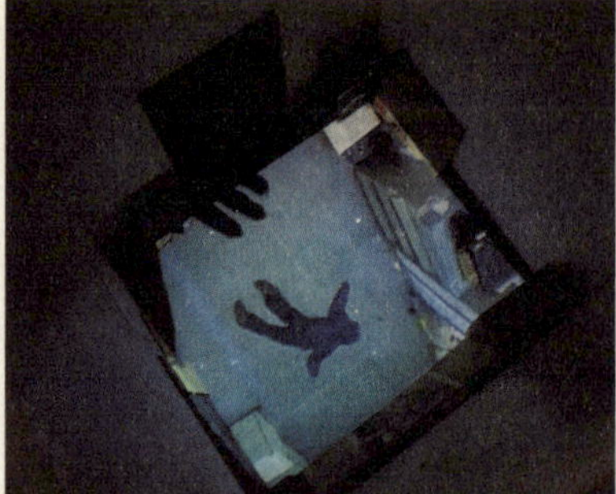

3.

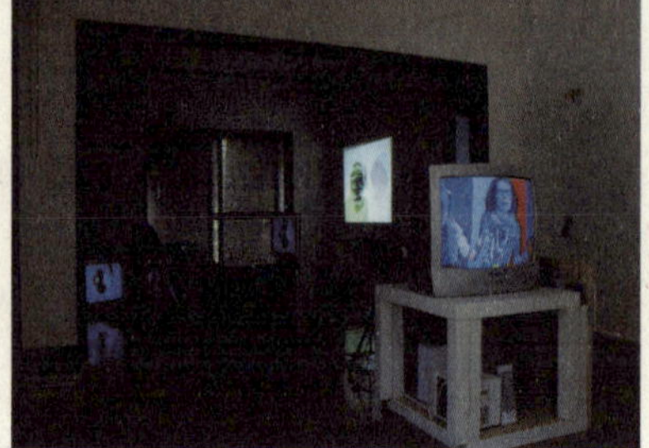

4.

Taro Izumi received his MFA from the Tama Art University in Tokyo. His videos humorously depict people struggling with the key pathologies of modern life: boredom, anomie, and alienation. In keeping with the playful air of his videos, Izumi often devises creative methods for installing his work, employing nontraditional projection techniques and sculptural supports to create media-saturated environments. His work has been included in shows at BankART 1929 in Yokohama (2008), Daelim Contemporary Art Museum in Seoul (2007), and the Museum of Contemporary Art in Los Angeles (2007). He lives and works in Tokyo.

1 & 2. **Curos Cave**
2005, video, 7 min

3. **Lime at the Bottom of the Lake**
2006, video, 1 min 30 sec

4. **Untitled**
2008, video, 45 sec, installation view in "Jungle Book" exhibition, Gallery Stump Kamakura, Tokyo

J

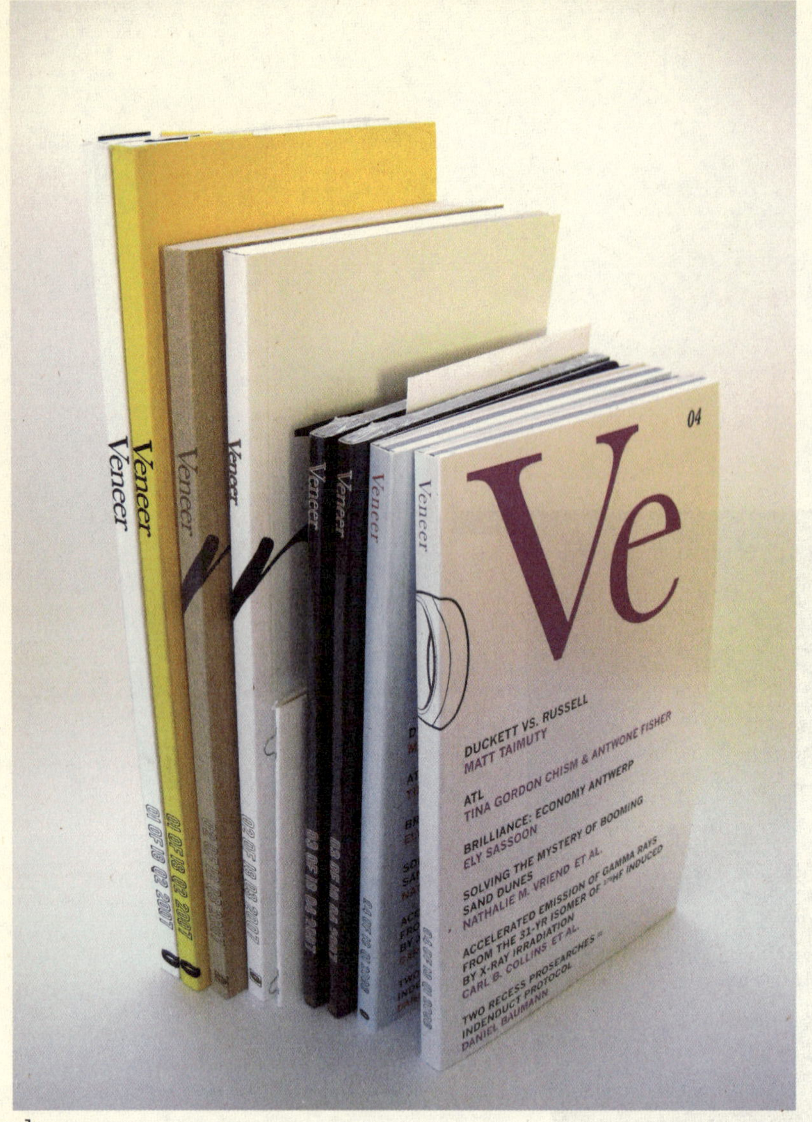

1.

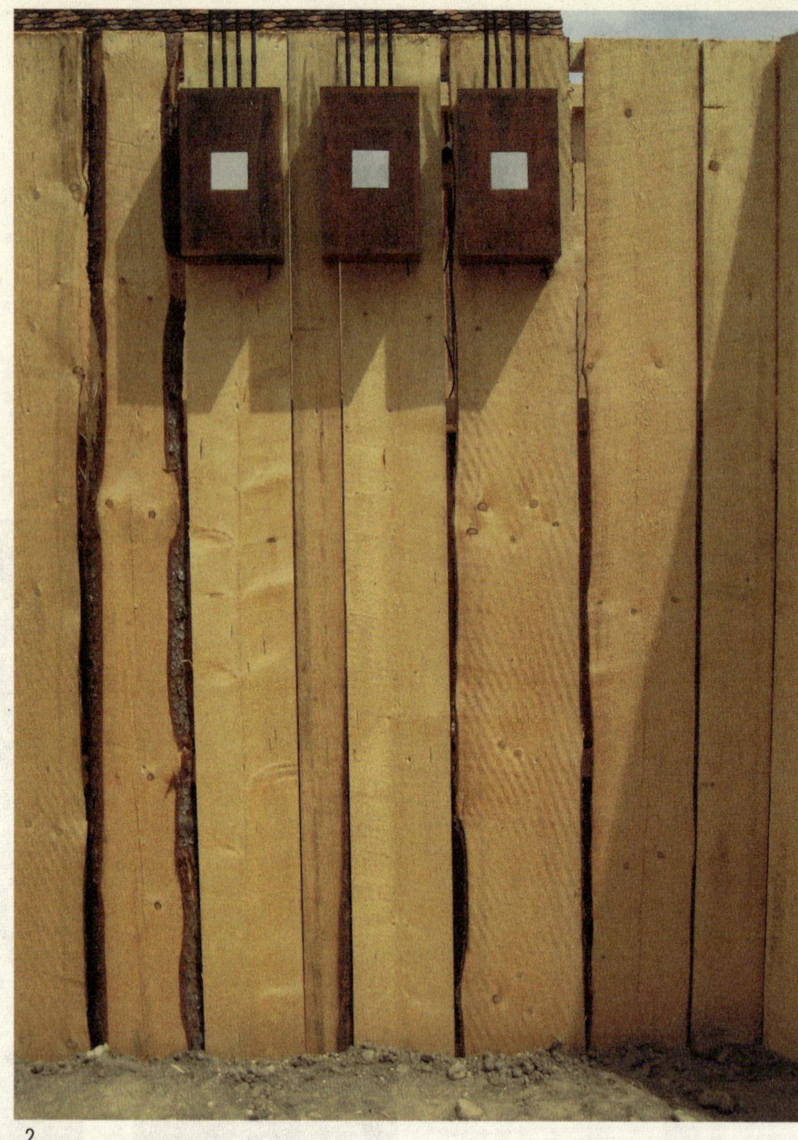

2.

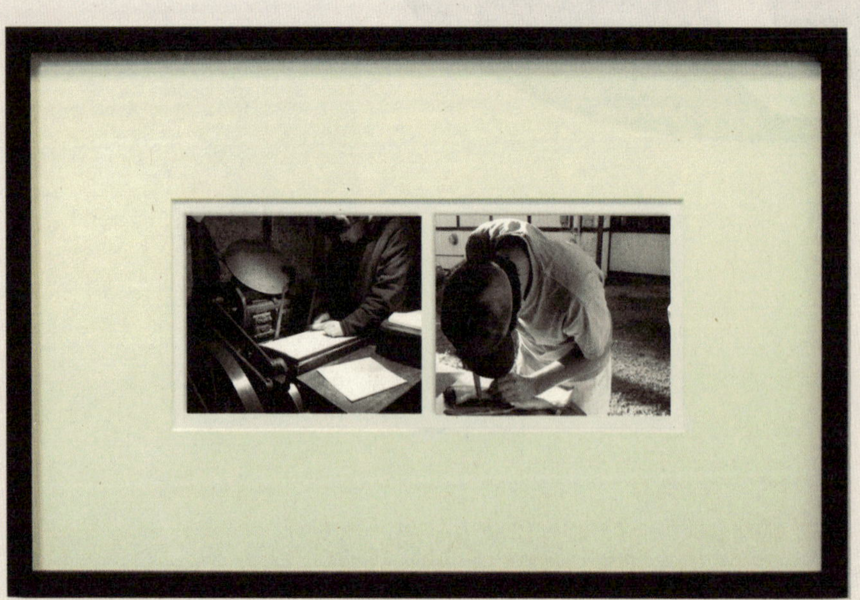

3.

Aaron Flint Jamison currently lives and works in San Francisco. He has written computer and Bluetooth viruses, rewired electronic devices, and made photographs, sculptures, and sound works. He also cofounded the artist-run community center Department of Safety.

1. Veneer Magazine (01-14/18)
2007-08, mixed media,
dimensions variable

2. The Shield, Jammer, or **Untitled**
2008, wood, titanium, various electronics in aluminum heat sink, and antennae, each $26 \times 14 \times 5$ in ($66 \times 36 \times 13$ cm)

3. Untitled
2006, gelatin silver print, two parts, overall dimensions 4×11 in (10×28 cm)

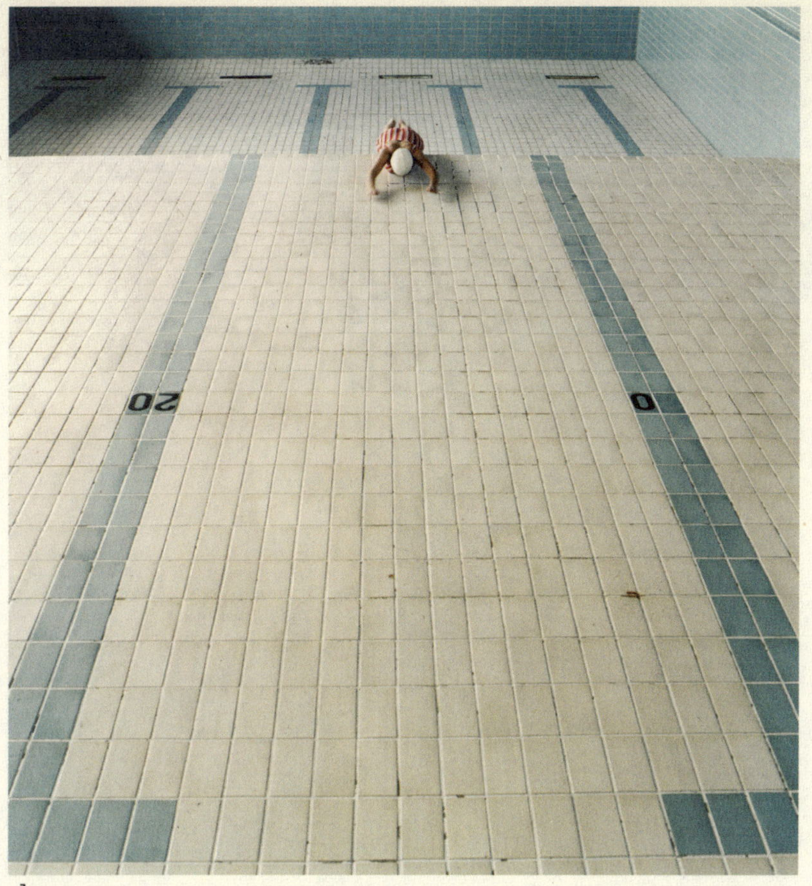

1.

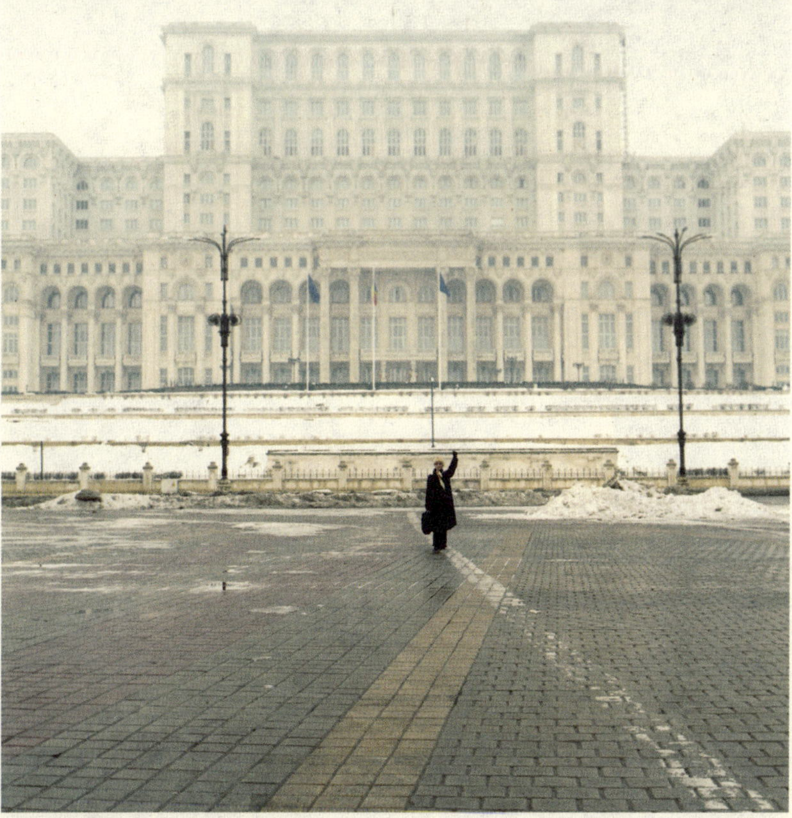

2.

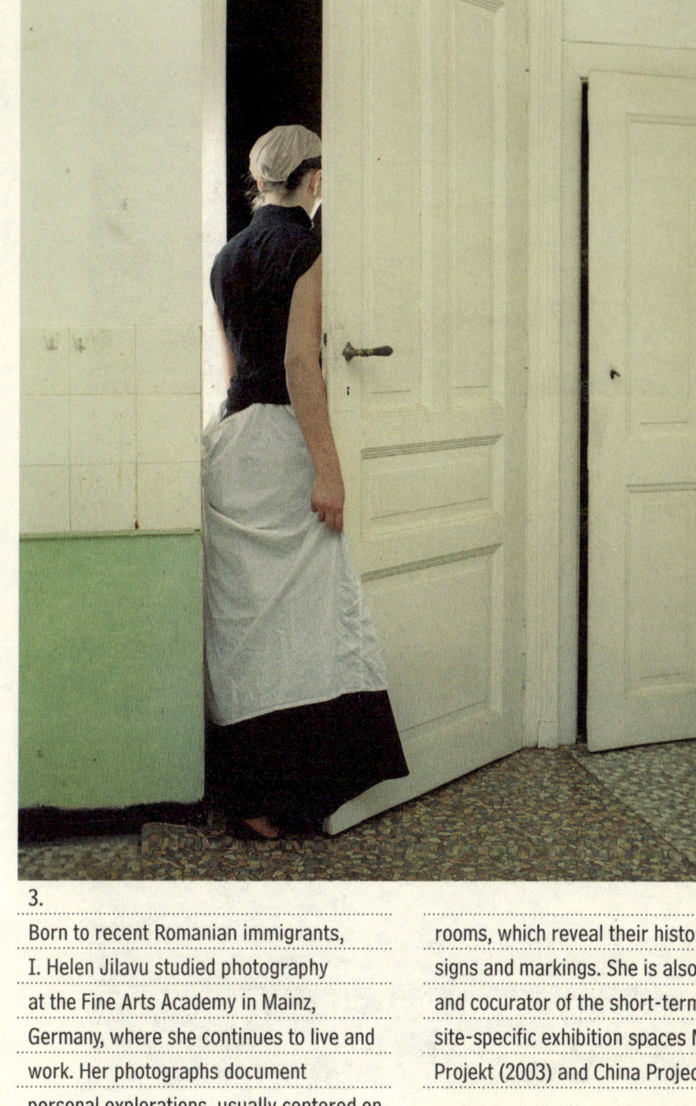

3.

Born to recent Romanian immigrants, I. Helen Jilavu studied photography at the Fine Arts Academy in Mainz, Germany, where she continues to live and work. Her photographs document personal explorations, usually centered on her own figure. In one body of work, she is pictured in a series of abandoned rooms, which reveal their histories through signs and markings. She is also cofounder and cocurator of the short-term, site-specific exhibition spaces Moguntia Projekt (2003) and China Project (2006).

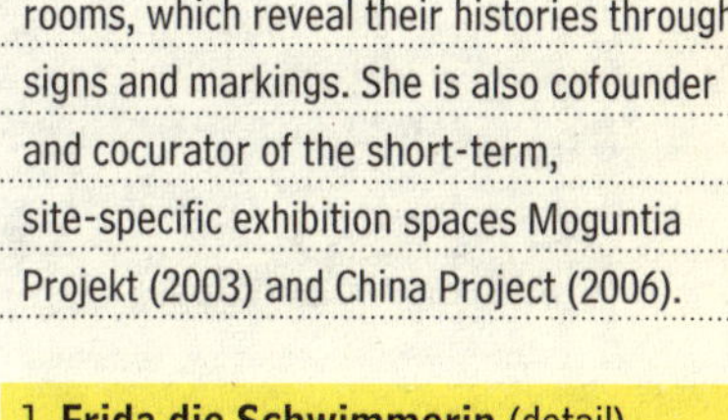

4.

1. **Frida die Schwimmerin** (detail)
2004, color photograph, 23 ½ × 23 ½ in (60 × 60 cm)

2. **Palatul Poporului** (detail)
2005, color photograph, 23 ½ × 23 ½ in (60 × 60 cm)

3. **Untitled**
2003, color photograph, 19 ½ × 15 ¾ in (50 × 40 cm)

4. **Sedna**
2005, color photograph, 47 ¼ × 43 ¼ in (120 × 110 cm)

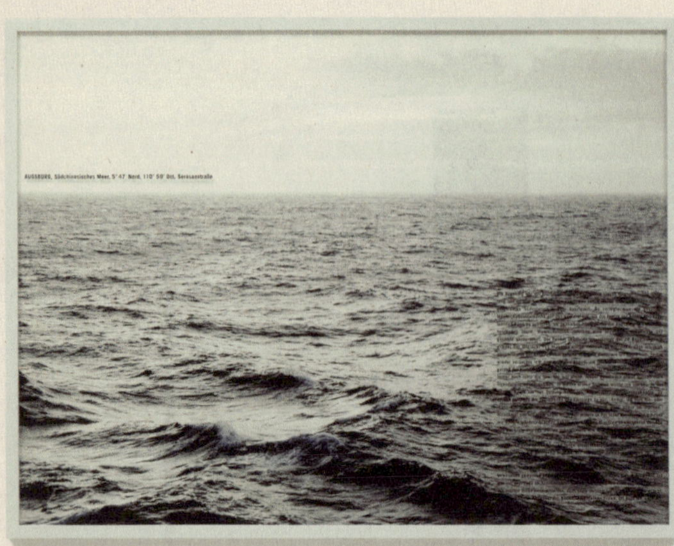

1.

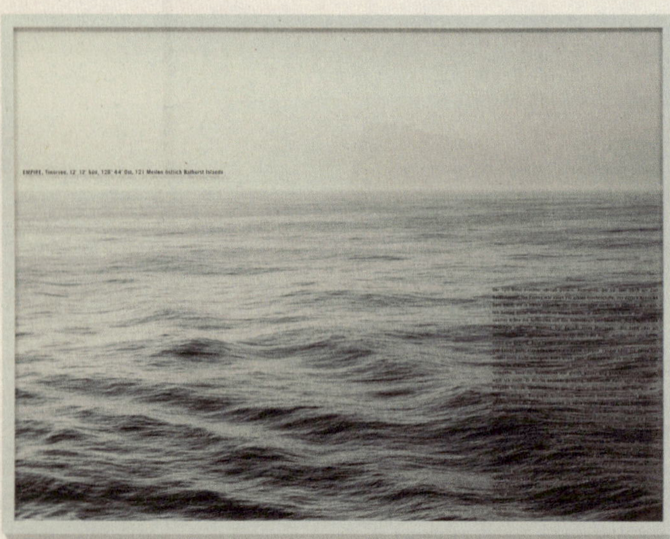

2.

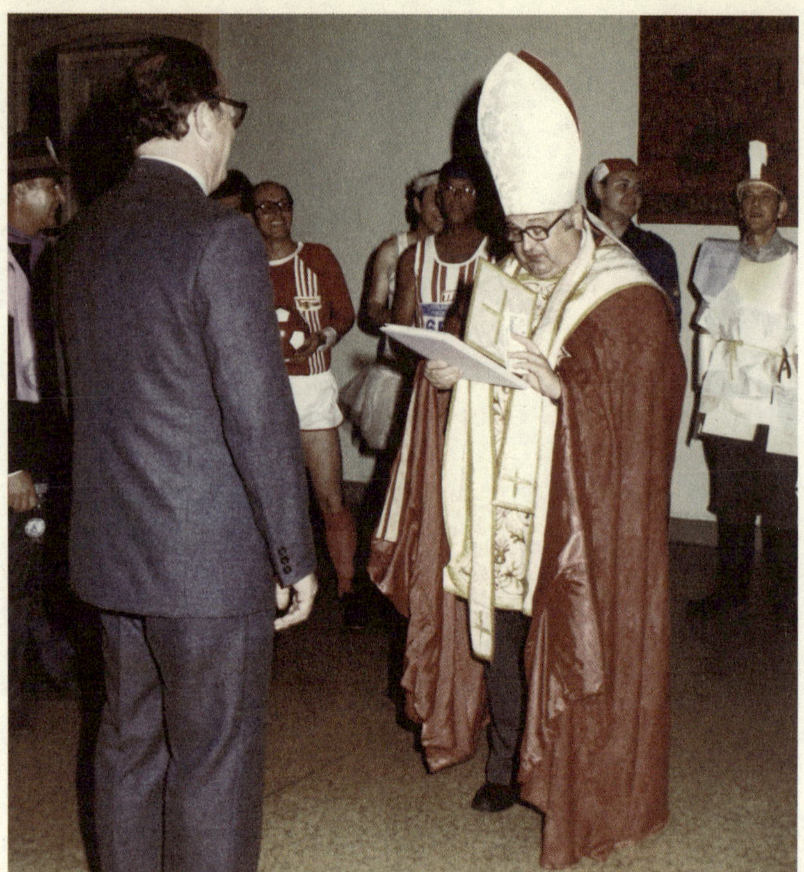

3.

4.

Sven Johne studied photography at the Academy of Visual Arts in Leipzig, where he continues to live and work. He uses photographs and text to form a documentary-style narrative that is part fact, part fiction. By revisiting sites and subjects of past crises – the forest path where killer wolves may have trodden, the birthday party of a Stasi official – he reveals the changing, often layered, identities of people and places.

1. Augsburg
from series **Ship Cancellation**
2004, Lambda print and silkscreen on glass, 43 ½ × 59 in (110 × 150 cm)

2. Empire
from series **Ship Cancellation**
2004, Lambda print and silkscreen on glass, 43 ½ × 59 in (110 × 150 cm)

3 & 4. Carnival
2008, 2 chromogenic Diasec prints of found photographs, 2 panels, each 63 × 51 ½ in (160 × 130 cm)

Winnipeg-based Sarah Anne Johnson uses a variety of media to investigate the intersection of social and ideological structures in the context of environmentalism. Her photographic installation **Tree Planting** (2005), for example, documents reforesting in Canada by juxtaposing photographs from life with others depicting miniature sculptural tableaux.

1. **The Birds**
2005, chromogenic print, dimensions variable

2, 3 & 4. **The House**
2005, wood, paint, and polymer clay

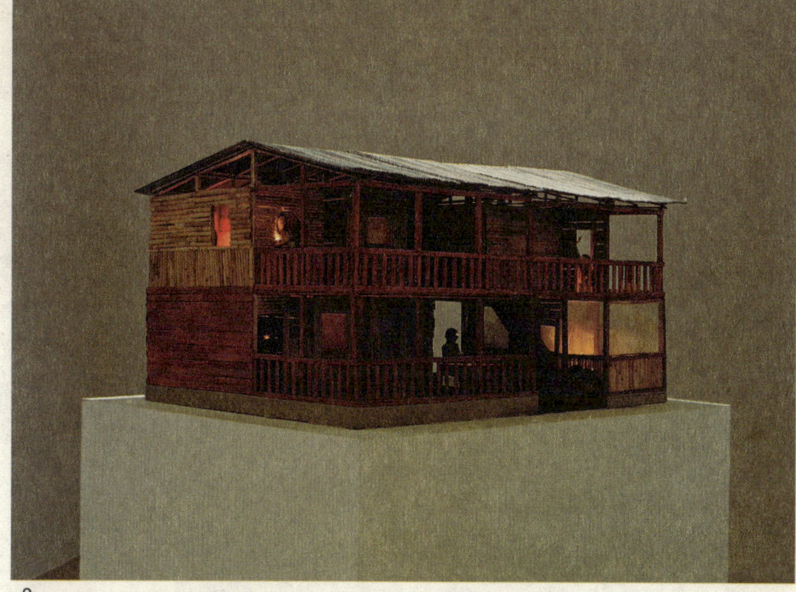

2.

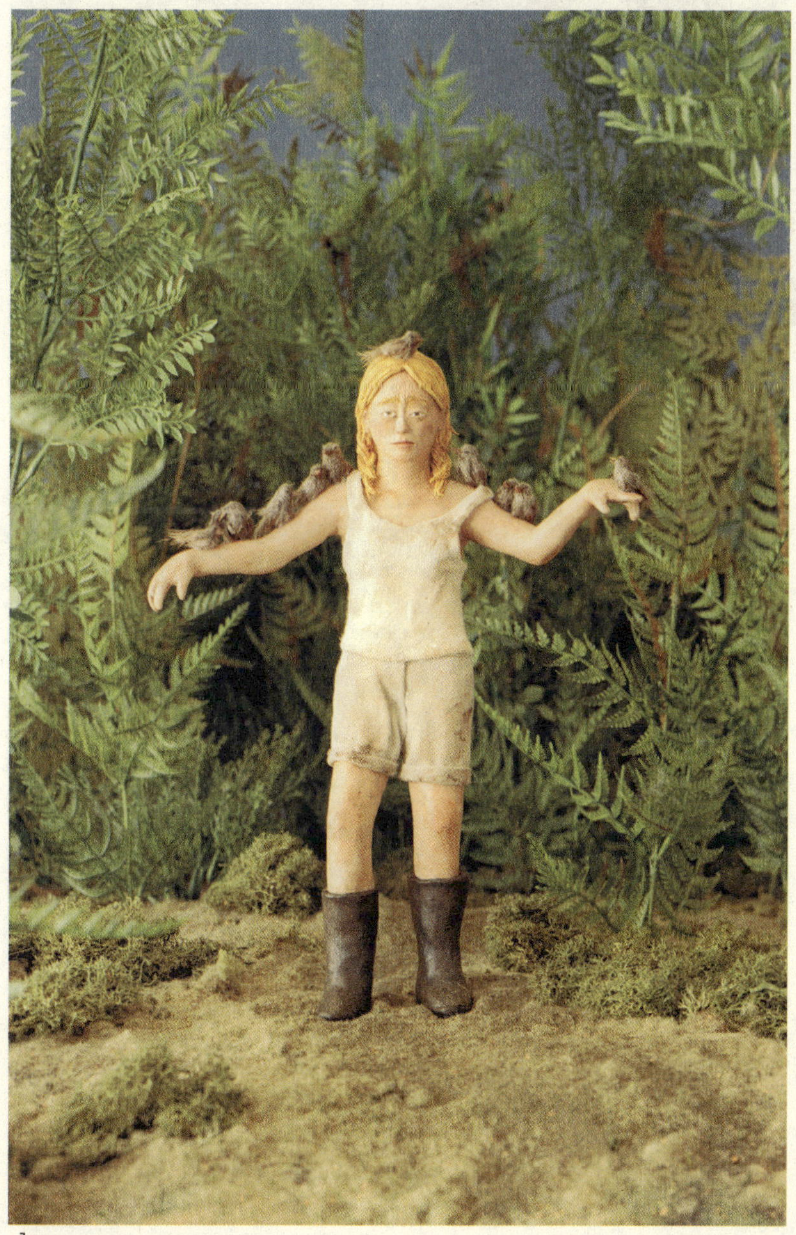

1.

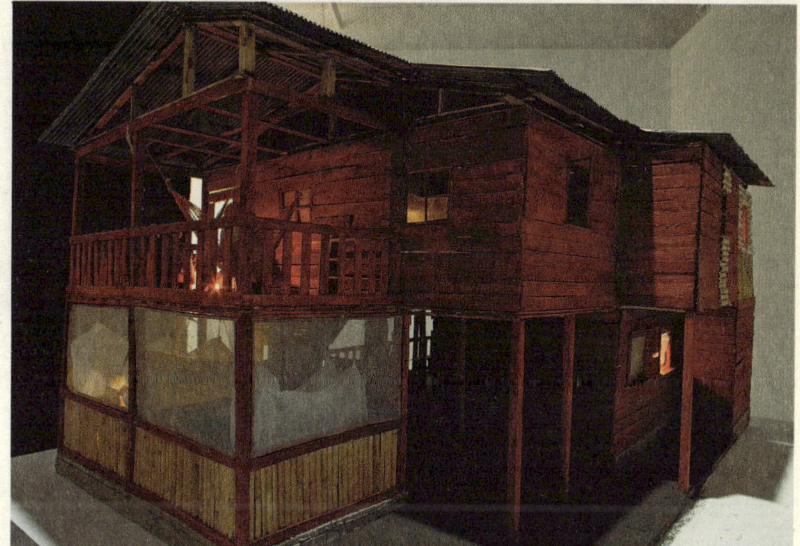

3.

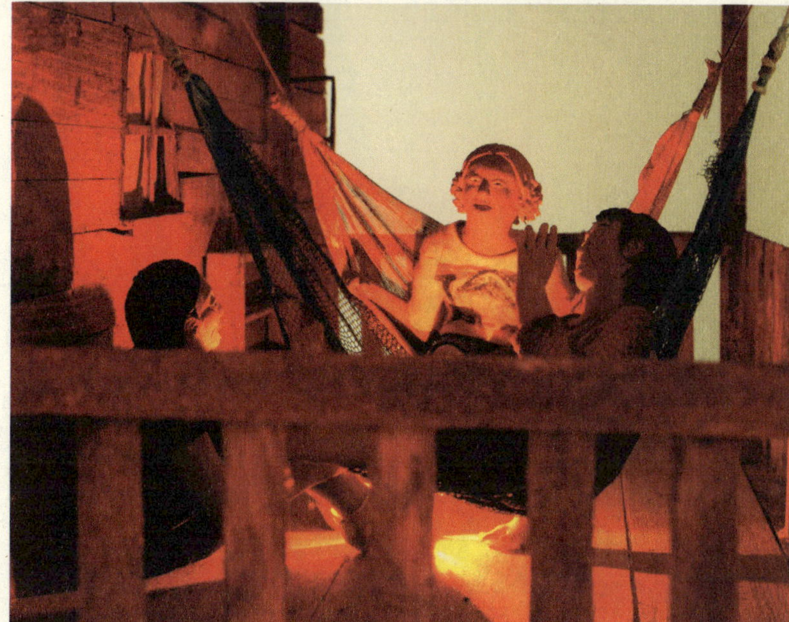

4.

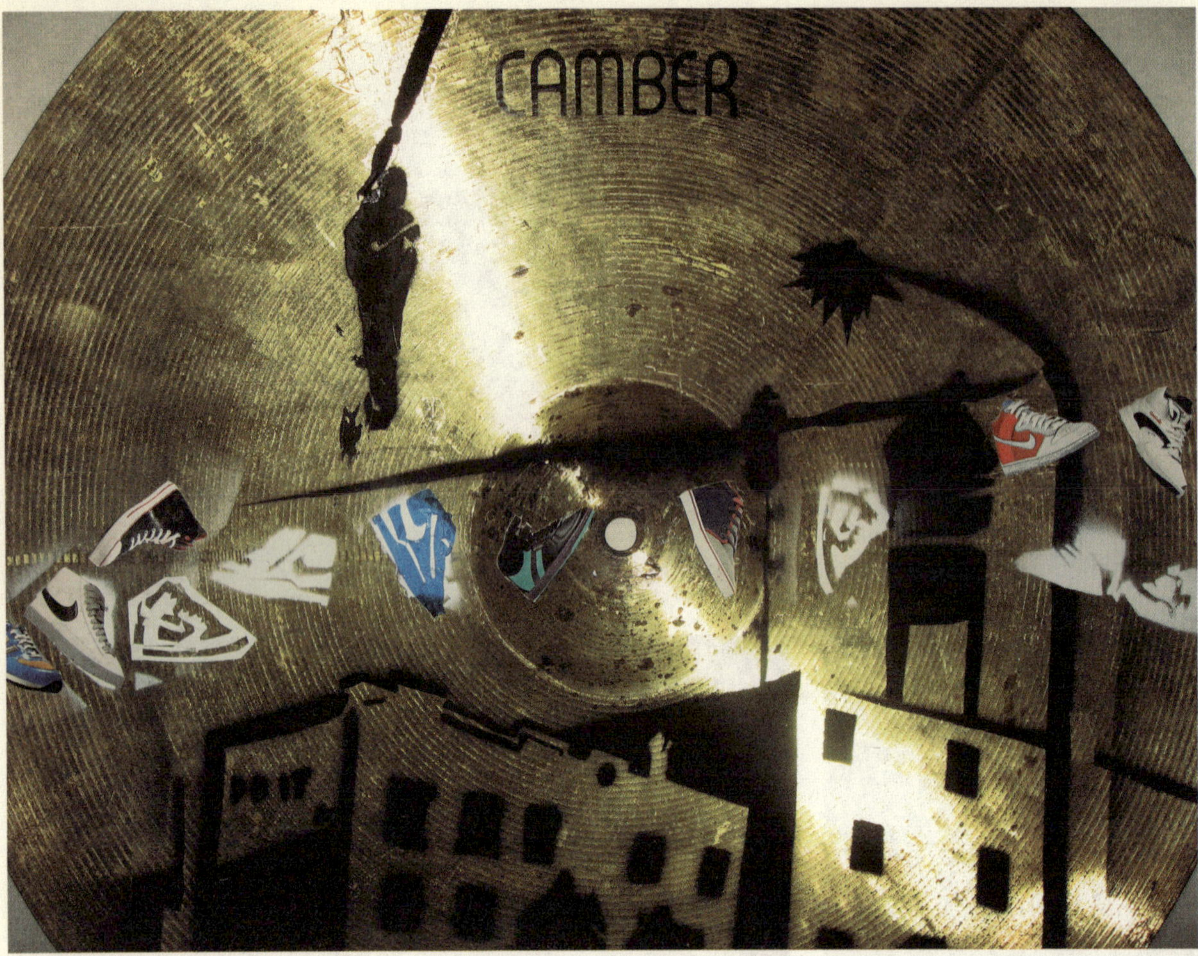

1.

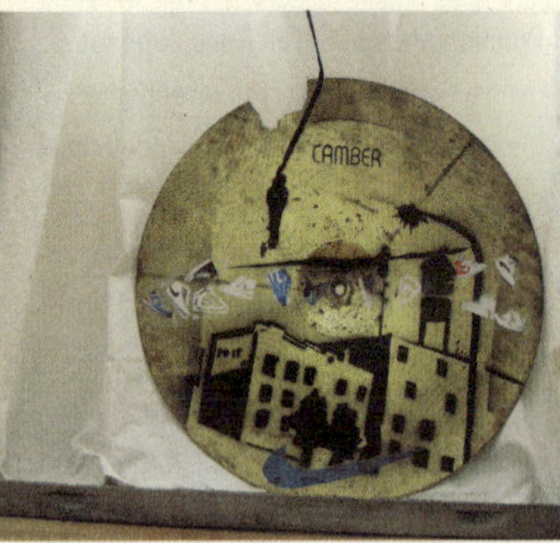

2.

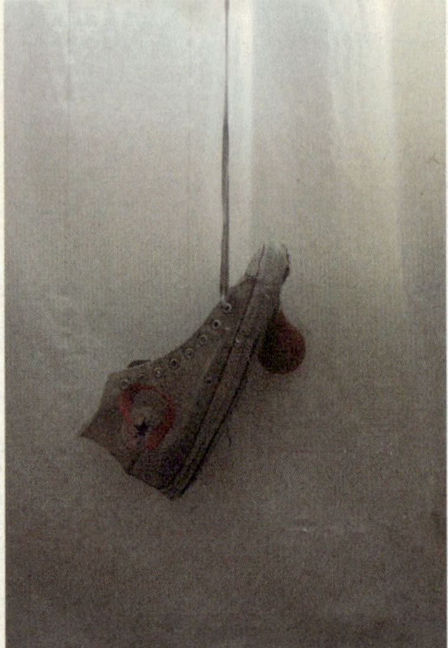

3.

Brooklyn-based William Johnson draws on his musical knowledge to produce sculptures that incorporate sound. Commenting on possible readings of the term "intellectual property," he incorporates sampled audio into painted found objects that relate, in part, to rap lyrics. Juxtaposing past and present, seen and heard, Johnson creates communal spaces framed by cultural reference.

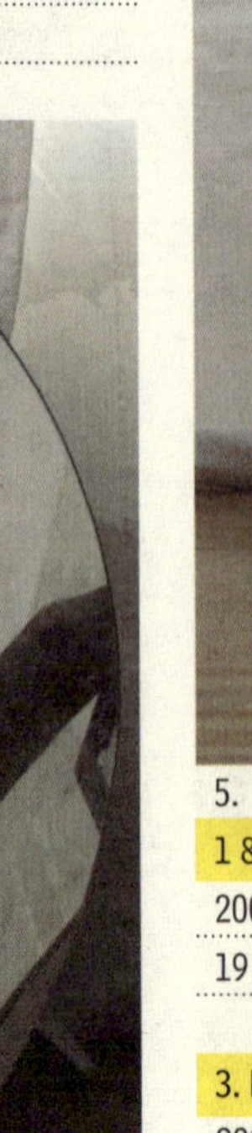

4.

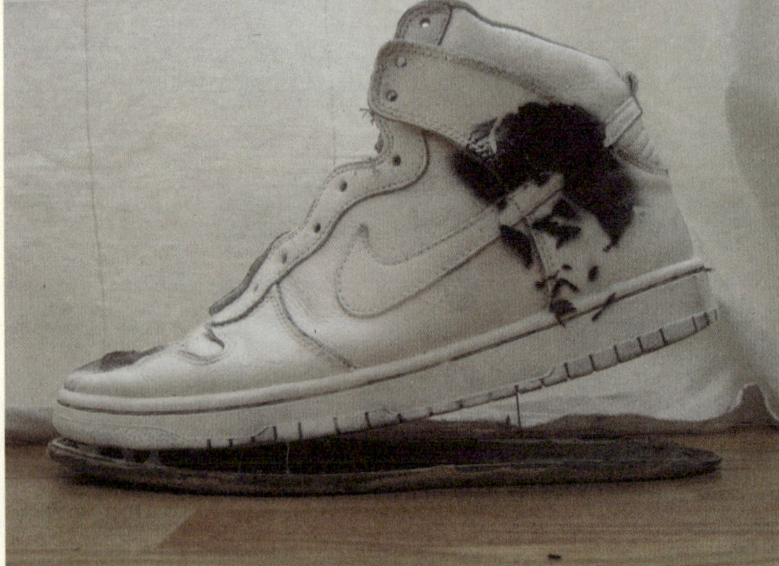

5.

1 & 2. Symbol 1
2008, spray paint on metal, diameter 19 in (48 cm)

3. Rip-Off
2008, plastic, canvas, glass, and spray paint, 30 × 19 × 3 in (76 × 48 × 8 cm)

4. Saving Face
2008, spray paint on glass, 24 × 28 in (61 × 71 cm)

5. Rubber Sole
2008, spray paint on leather sneaker, 7 × 10 × 4 in (18 × 25 × 10 cm)

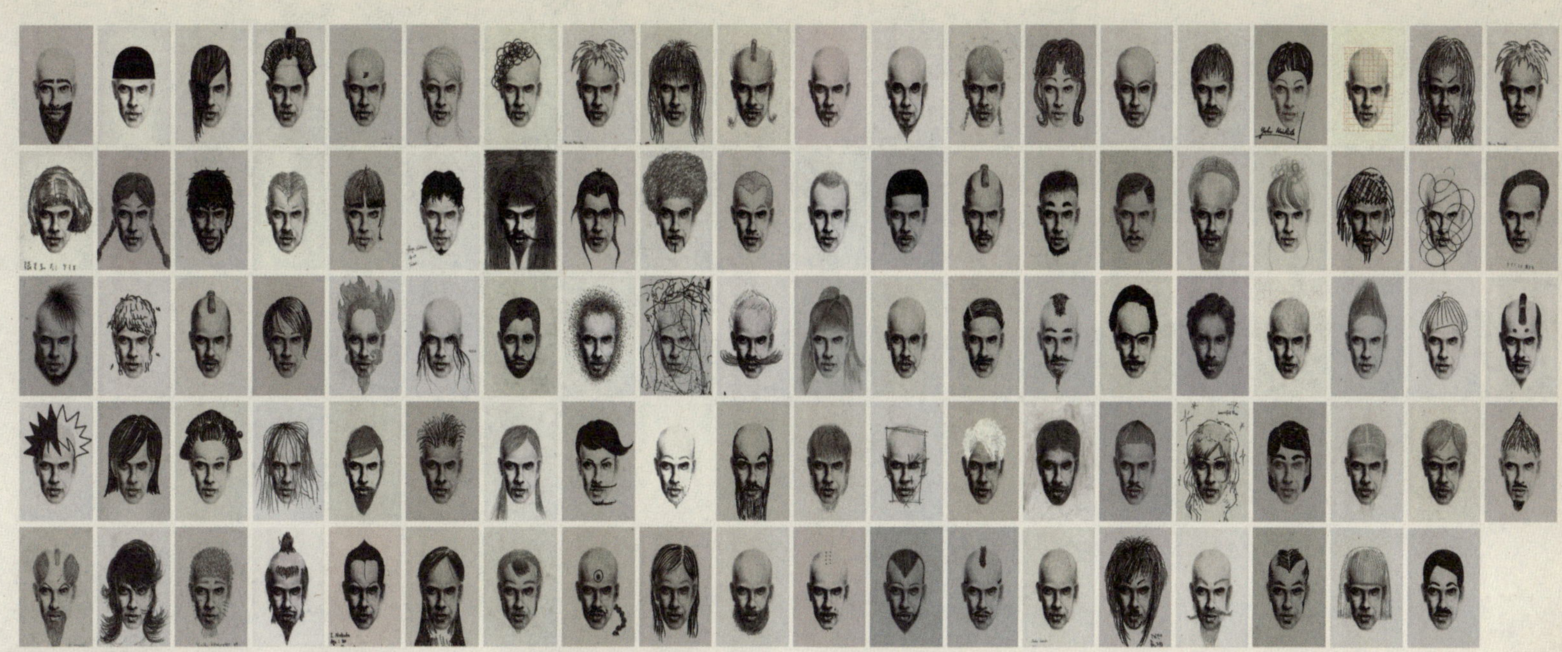

1.

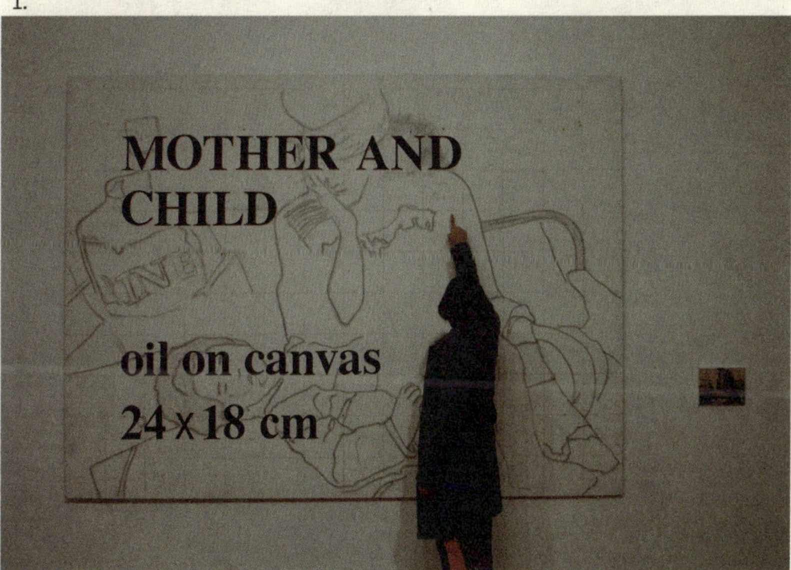

2.

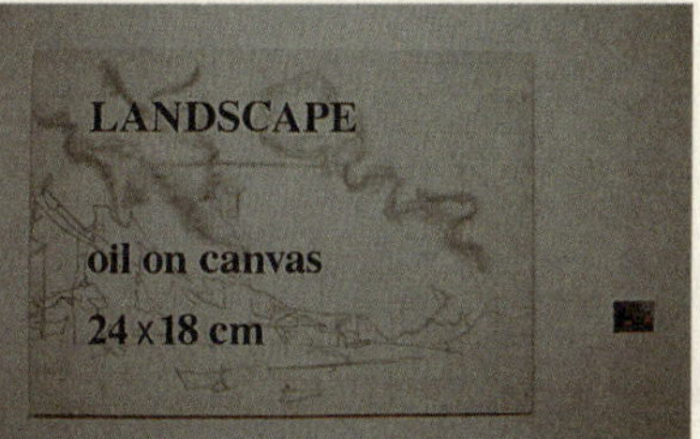

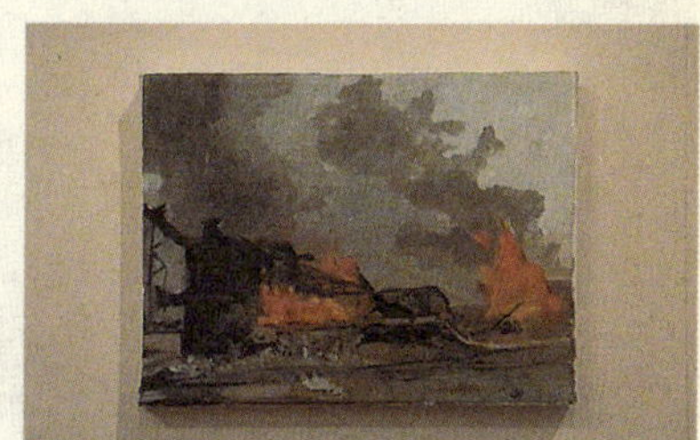

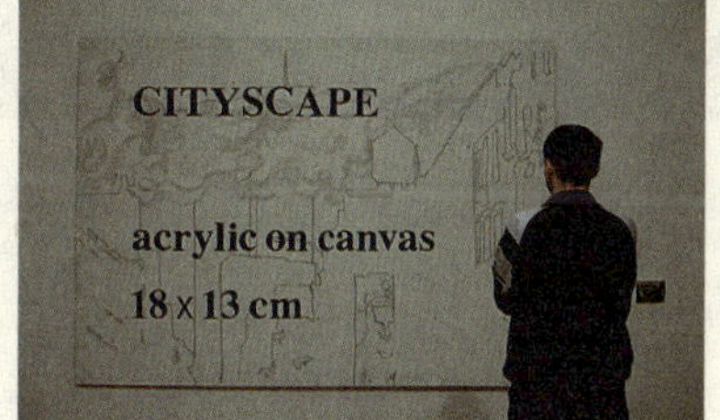

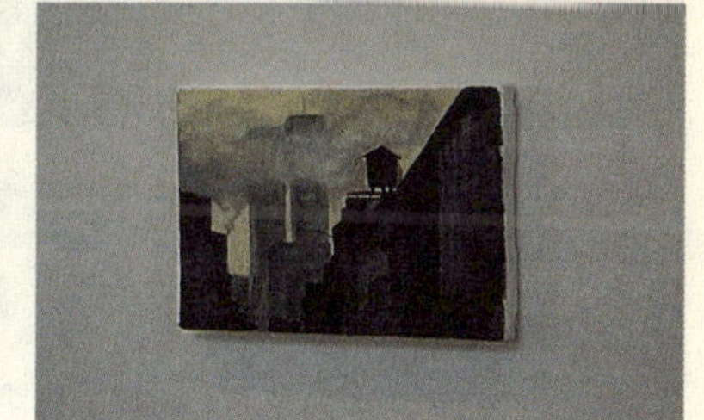

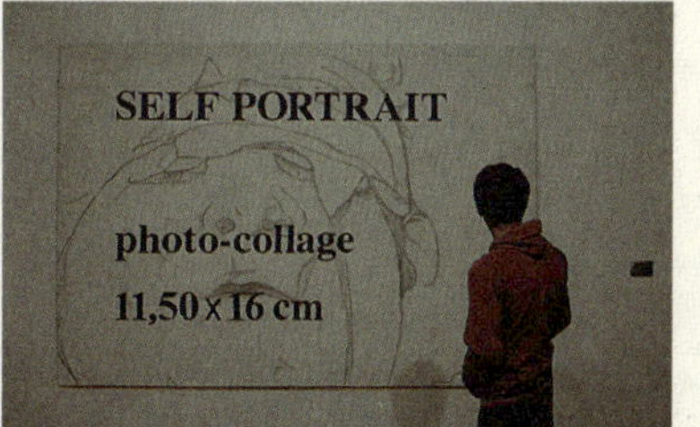

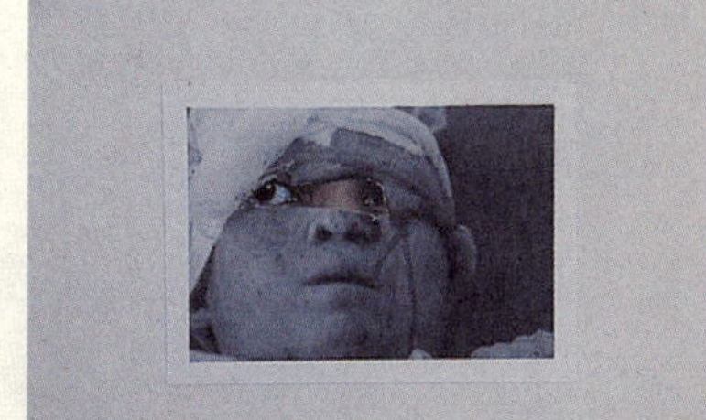

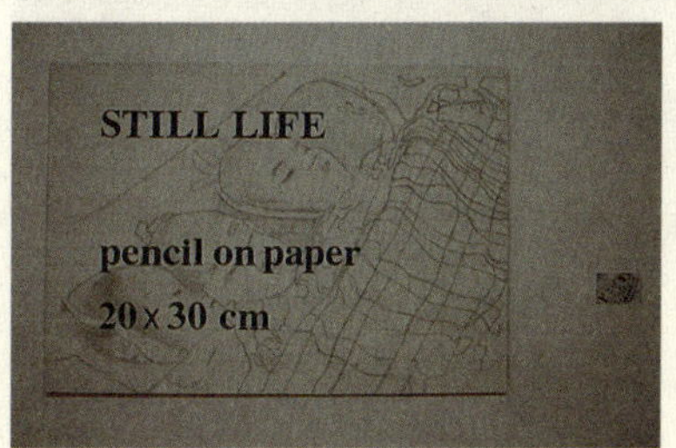

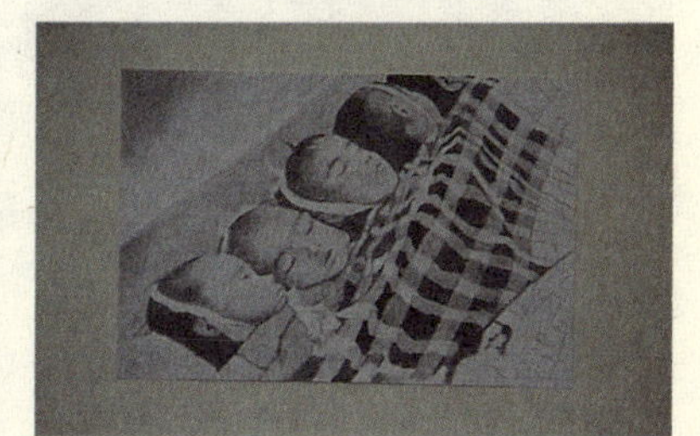

3.

Ayaz Jokhio lives and works in Lahore, and was a poet before turning to visual art. He dissects the grammar of images with a certain intellectual logic. Jokhio uses drawing, painting, and text to pose questions about the ways in which we regard and represent our world, often also commenting on the conventions of gallery display.

1. Self-Portraits (Portraits)
2005, 100 prints of a self-portrait desecrated by different people in various black and white media, mounted on wood, each 11 × 8 1/4 in (28 × 21 cm)

2. Mother and Child
from the series **Titled**
2001, left: gesso, graphite, and paper collage on boards, 6 3/4 × 9 ft (207 × 280 cm); right: oil on canvas, 7 × 9 1/2 in (18 × 24 cm)

3. Untitled
from the series **Titled**
2001, mixed media, dimensions variable

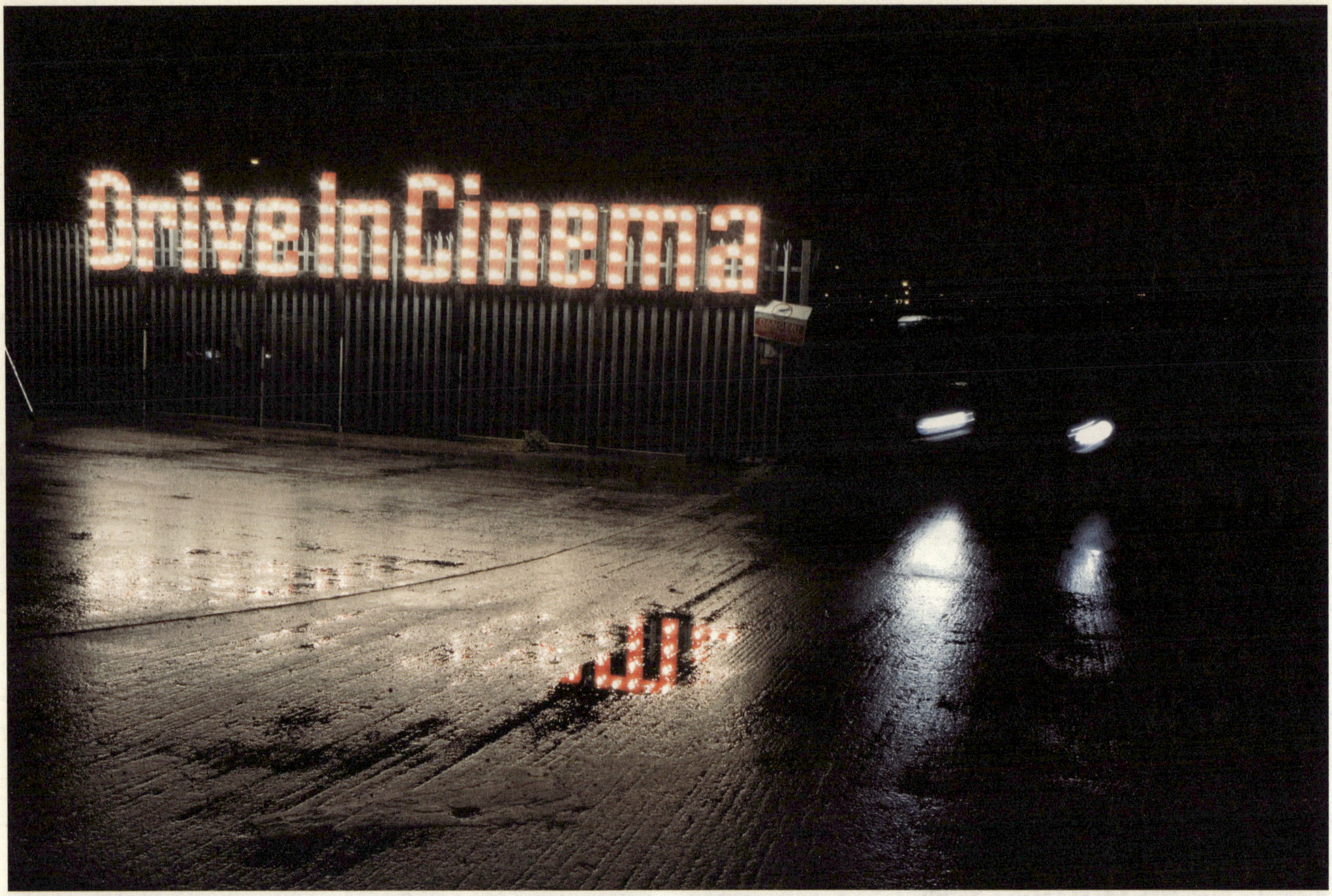

1.

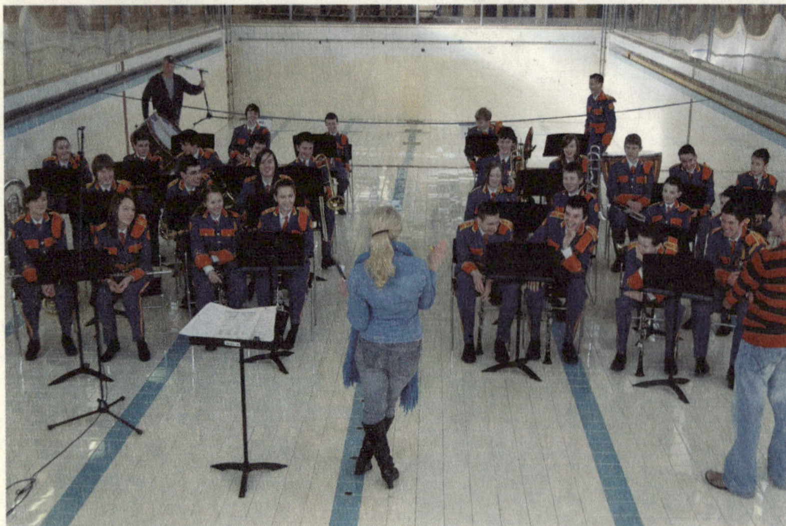

2.

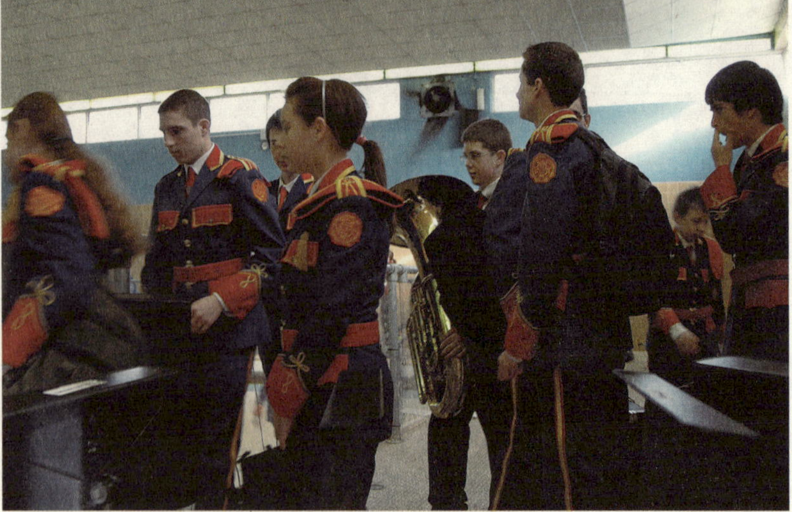

3.

Dublin-based Jesse Jones makes videos and stages events that focus on moments when previously hidden political and social histories rise to the surface of everyday life. She often borrows from popular culture, engineering situations in which her work and its site engage in a critical interaction with one another. For example, as part of one project, she organized a drive-in screening of films blacklisted during the 1950s.

1. **12 Angry Films**
2006, collaborative artist project in Dublin

2 & 3. **Zarathustra**
2008, 16 mm film, 4 min 46 sec, production still

k

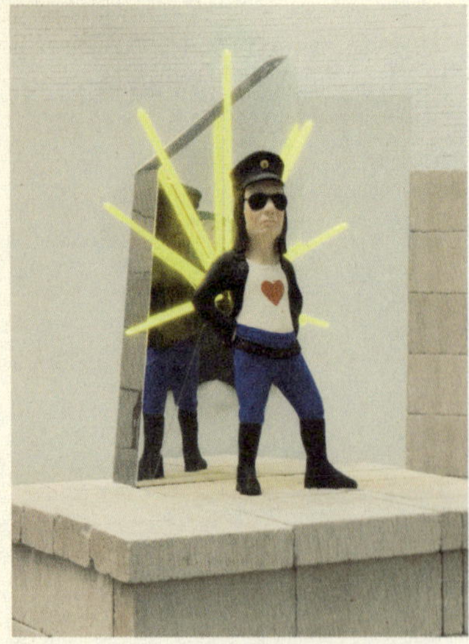

1.

Heike Kabisch was educated at the Glasgow School of Art in Scotland and at the Kunstakademie Münster in Germany. His wry, occasionally disturbing sculptures, often featuring subtly grotesque figures in various states of contemplation, confront themes of isolation, frustration, power, and interdependency. His work has been included in Bloomberg New Contemporaries 2007 in London, Manchester, and Birmingham, and in "Kunstsalon" in Berlin (2006).

1. **GOOD MAN, THE LAST WAVE BY, CRYING HOW BRIGHT** (detail)
2008, mixed media, $87\frac{1}{2} \times 197 \times 98\frac{1}{2}$ in (210 × 500 × 250 cm)

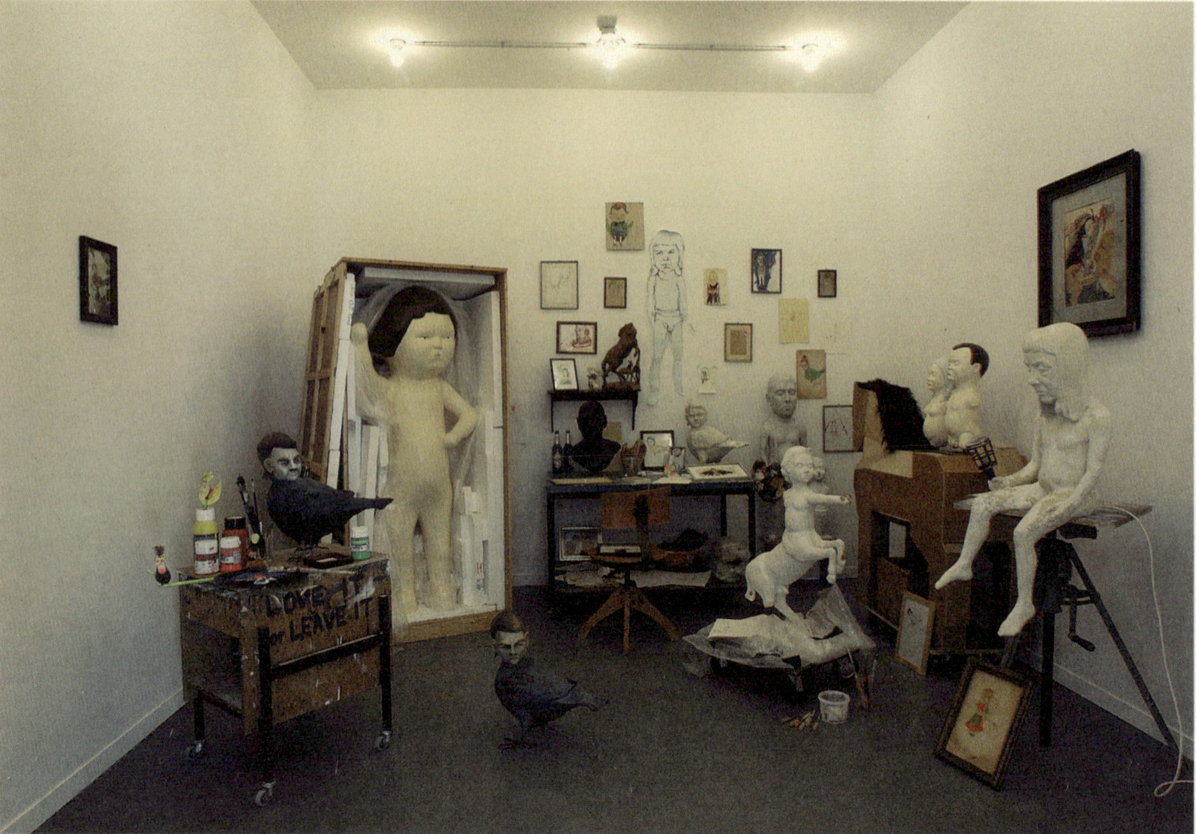

2.

2. **Untitled**
2006, mixed media, dimensions variable

3. **OH MY LORD, I AM SO BORED**
2008, mixed media, $130 \times 157\frac{1}{2} \times 137\frac{3}{4}$ in (330 × 400 × 350 cm)

4. **RUCKE DI GUCK** (detail)
2007, mixed media, 118 × 118 in (300 × 300 cm)

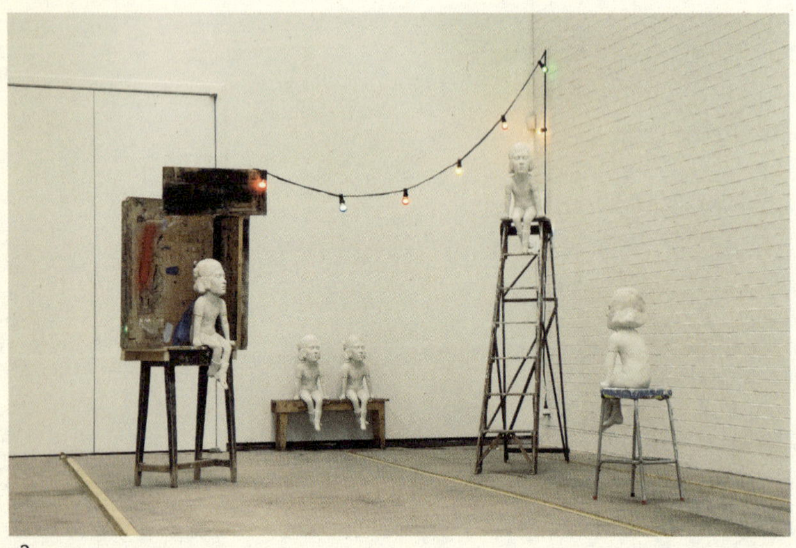

3.

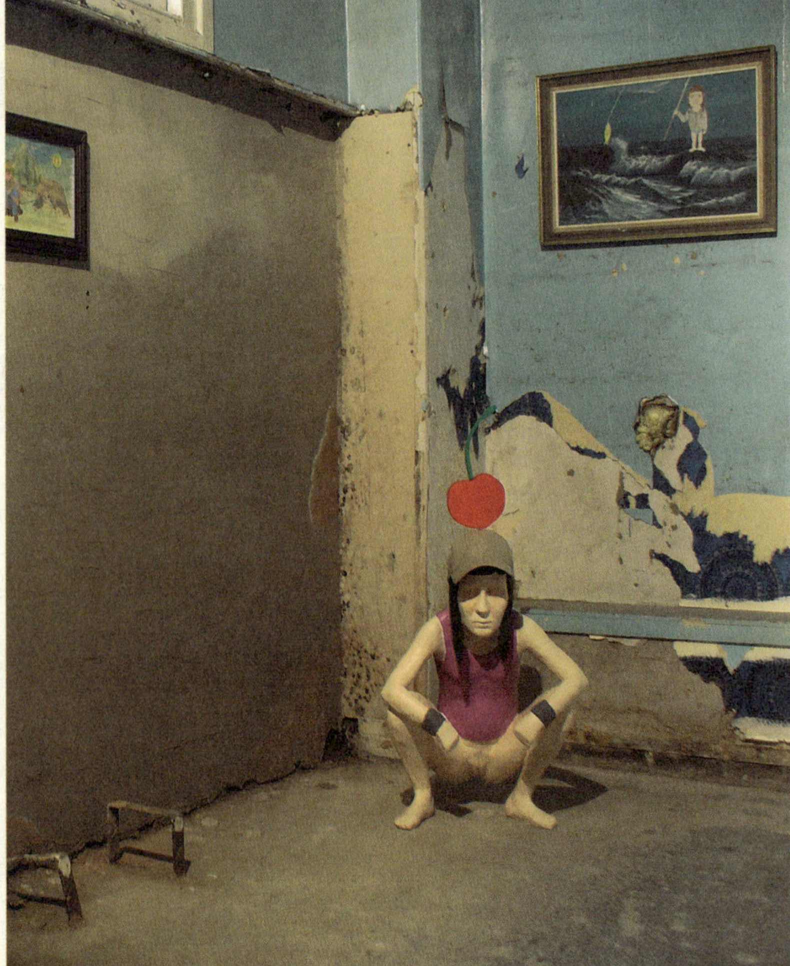

4.

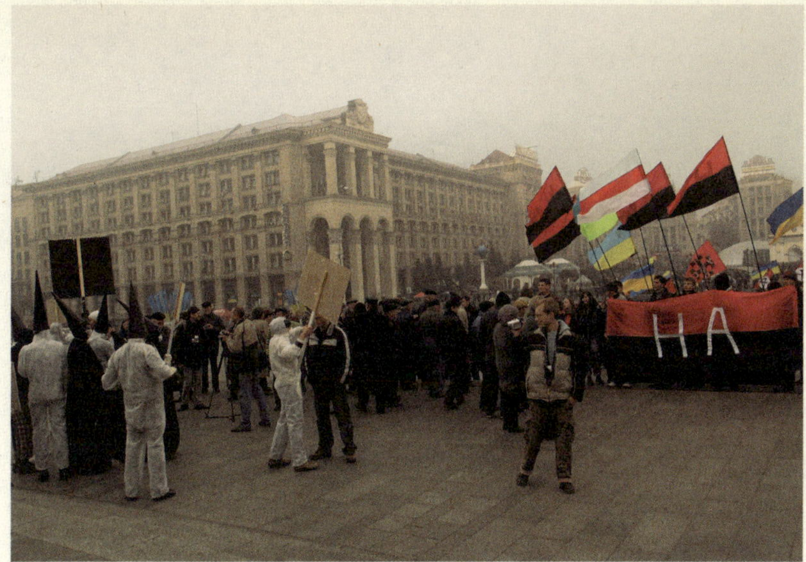

1.

Nikita Kadan graduated from the National Academy of Fine Art and Architecture in Kiev, and has been a member of the R.E.P. (Revolutionary Experimental Space) collective since 2004. R.E.P. stage interventionist performances and paint murals on public buildings as ways to question ideological rhetoric. Kadan's work with the group offers a critique of collective memory as mediated by political context, stressing the importance of genuine community.

1. **We will R.E.P. you**
2005, action in Kiev

2. **Patriotism Checkpoint**
2008, mixed media mural drawing, dimensions variable

3. **Patriotism**
2008, mixed media mural, dimensions variable

4. **Untitled action**
2005, action in a field near Kiev

5. **Patriotism. Hymn**
2006, mixed media mural, dimensions variable

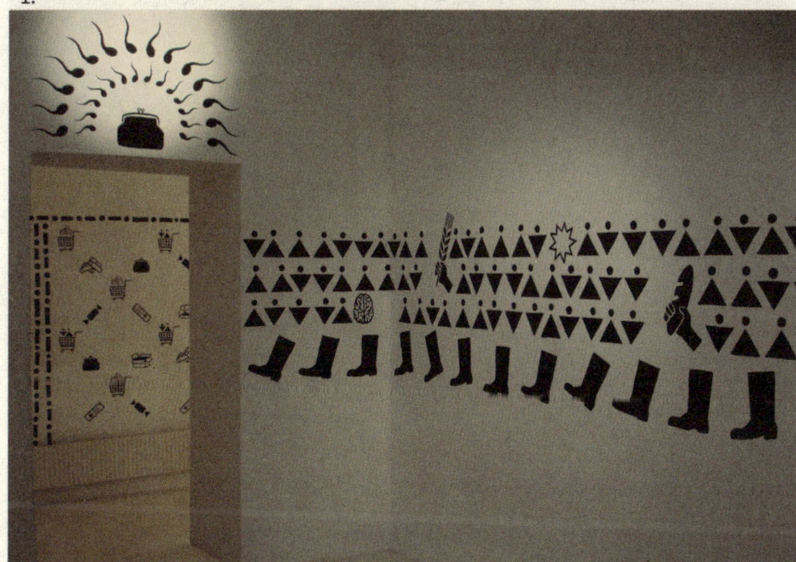
2.

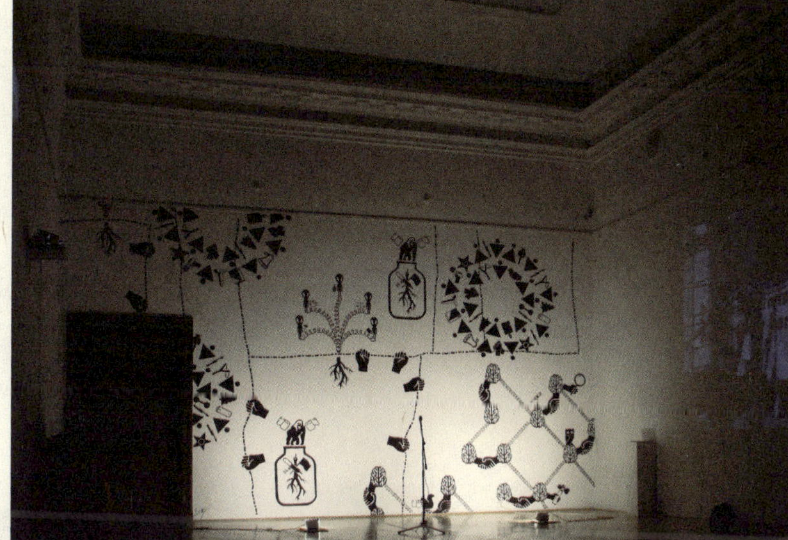
3.

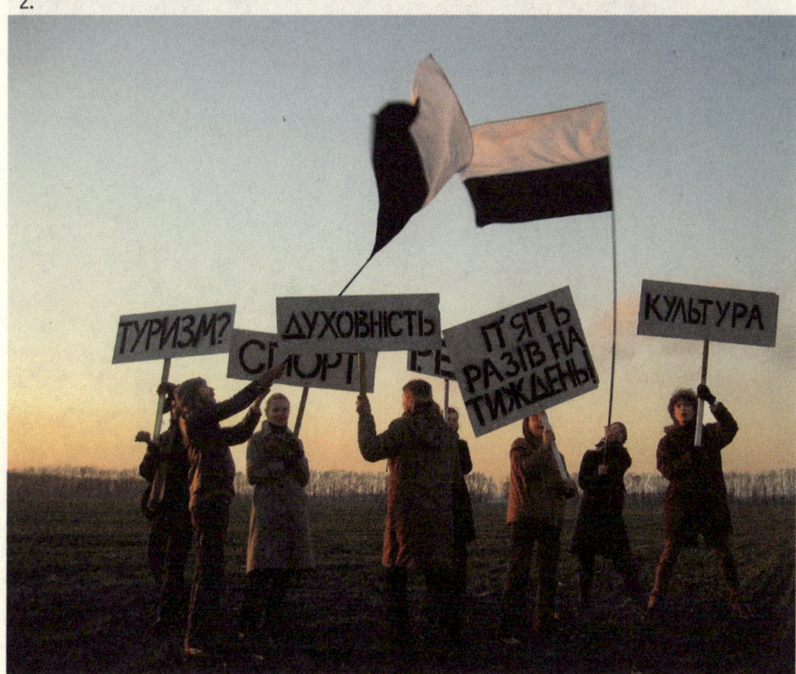

4.

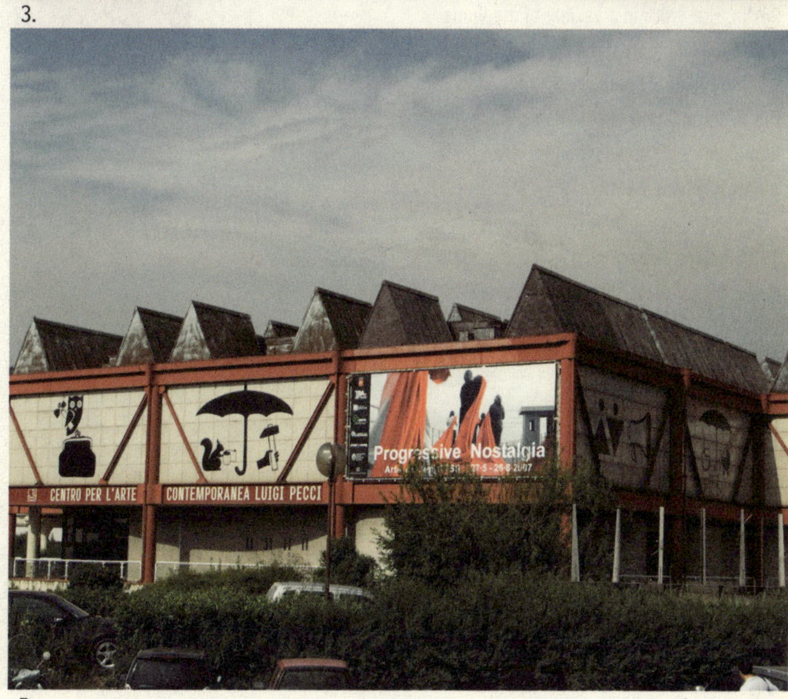

5.

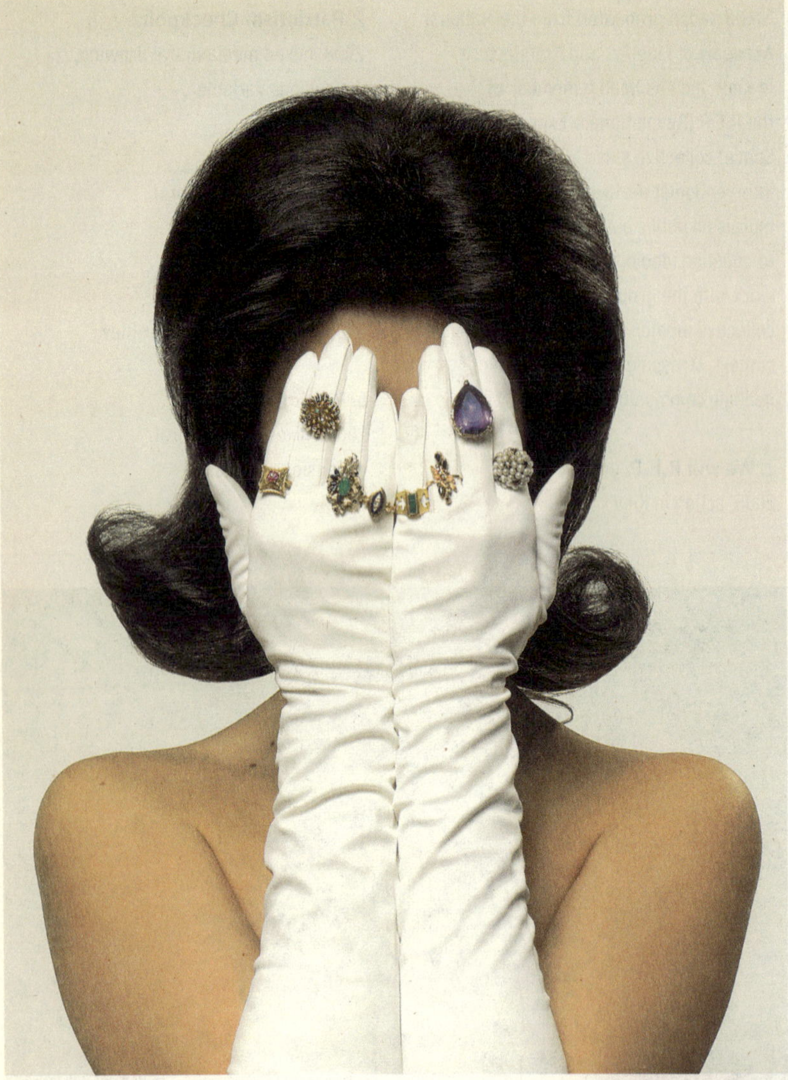

1.

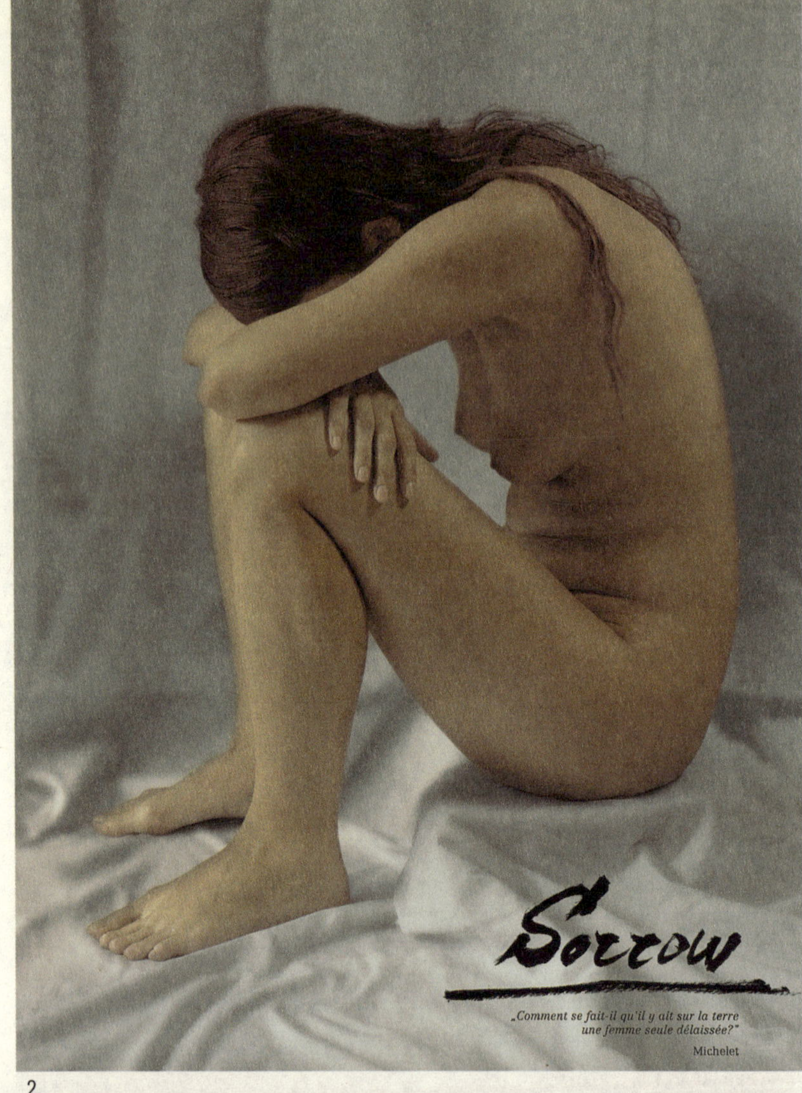

2.

Šejla Kamerić is based in Sarajevo and Berlin. Her work in a variety of mediums accentuates a perceived conflict between local and global traditions to reflect on the disintegration of communism in her homeland and the subsequent search for a new national identity.

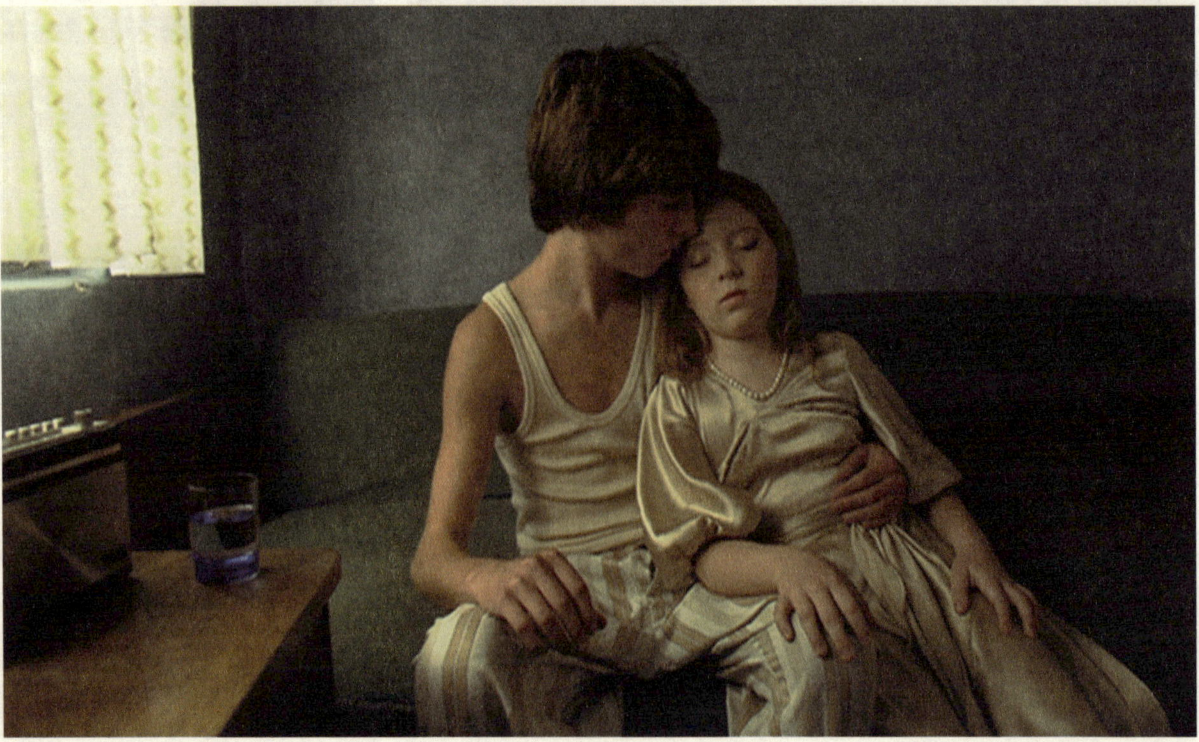

3.

1. 30 Years After
2006, digital print, dimensions variable

2. Sorrow
2005, digital print and lightbox,
69 ½ × 52 ½ in (177 × 133 cm)

3. What do I know
2007, 35 mm film, 15 min

Kaneuji Teppei earned an MA in sculpture from the Kyoto City University of Arts and currently lives and works in Kyoto. In his sculptures and installations, he takes such objects as maps, toys, action figures, and bottles, then deconstructs and reassembles them with other elements to suggest organic forms. In a piece from his **White Discharge** series, for example, indiscernible objects and structures are covered with white resin, the drippings left to harden where they fall.

1. **teenage fun club**
2006, plastic figure and hot-melt adhesive, 9¾ × 4¾ × 14½ in (25 × 12 × 37 cm)

2. **small animals and great flood (nude)**
2006, felt tip pen and ink bleed on paper, 25½ × 35¾ in (65 × 91 cm)

3. **splash and flake**
2008, wood, mirrors and magnifying glasses, 20¼ × 22½ × 8¾ ft (6 × 7 × 3 m)

4. **muddy stream from mug #7**
2006, wood, plastic, hot-melt adhesive, and cutouts of coffee-stained paper, 31½ × 29½ × 35¾ in (83 × 75 × 91 cm)

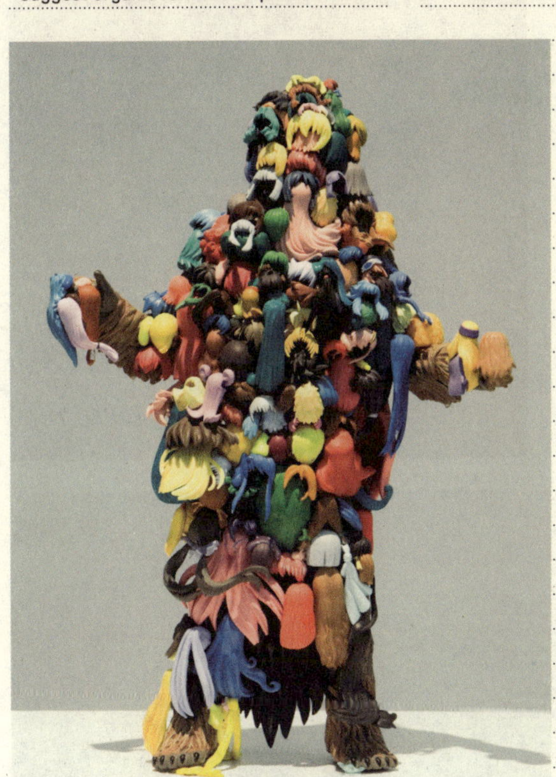

1.

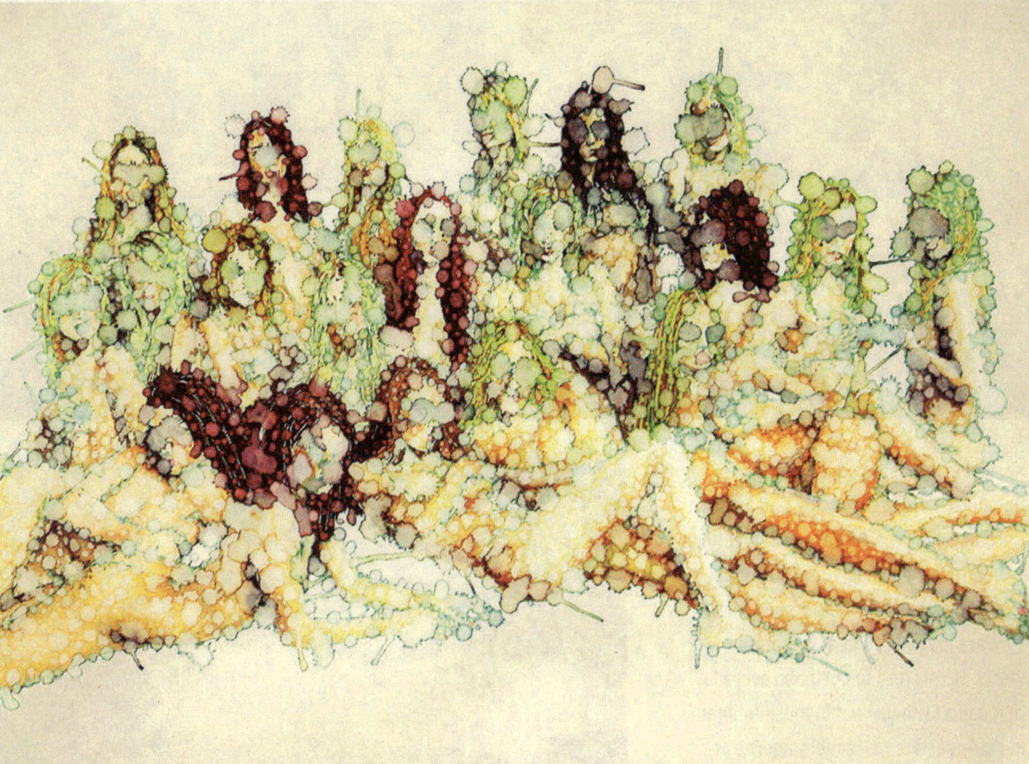

2.

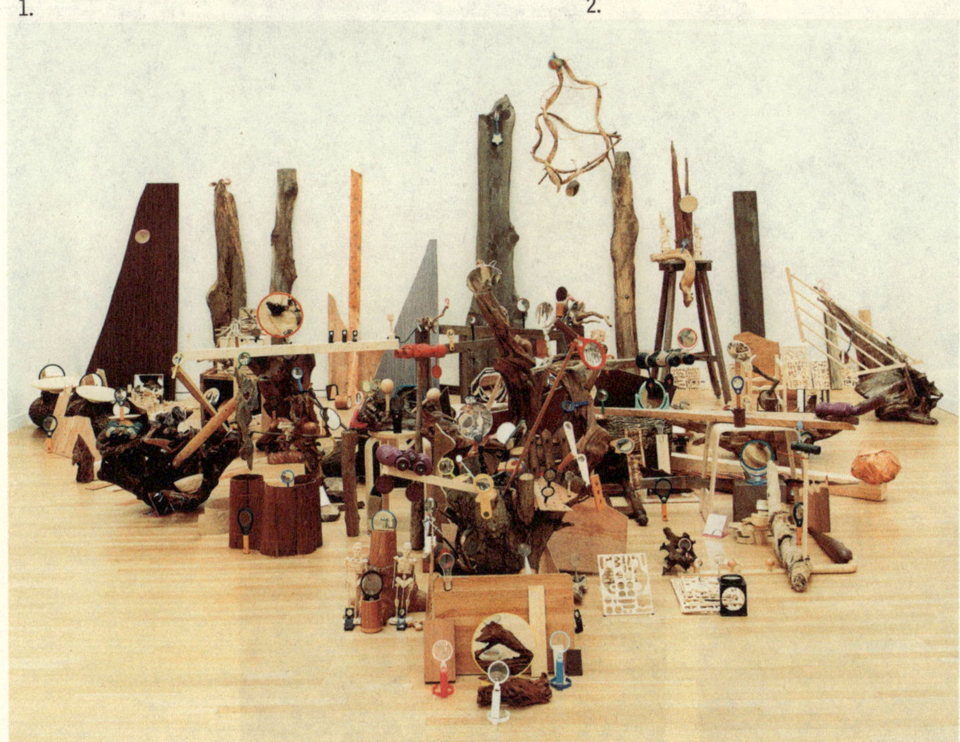

3.

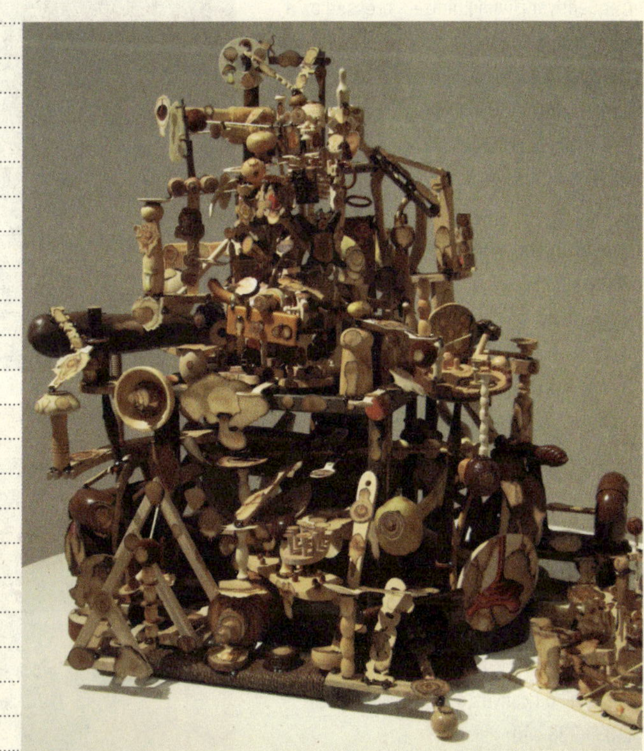

4.

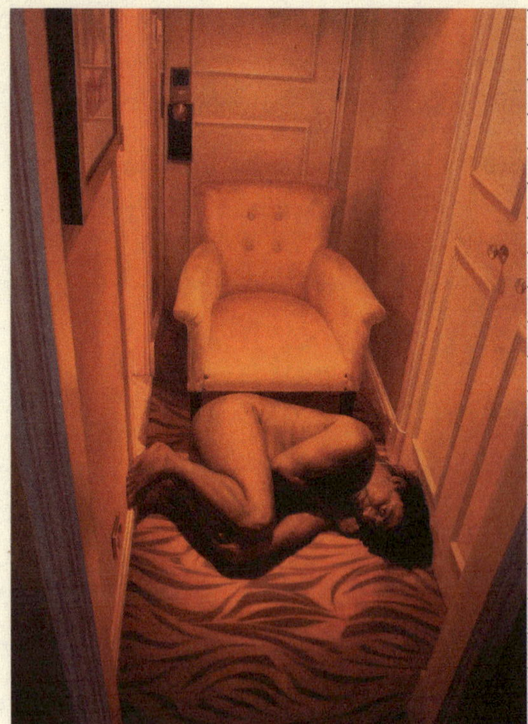
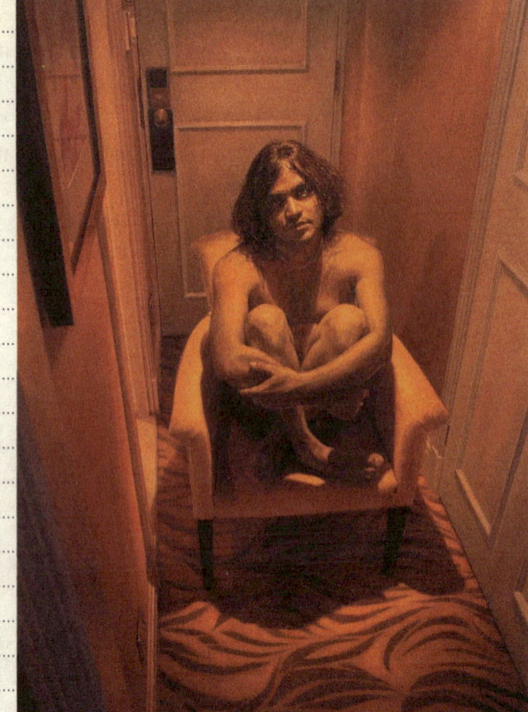
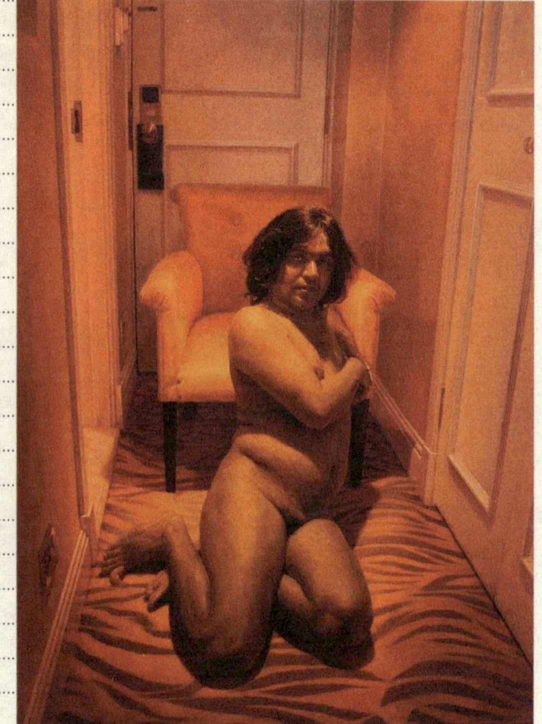

1.

Karmakar Abir studied painting at Rabindra Bharati University and lives in Baroda, India. His confessional paintings – with their beguilingly realistic detail, easily mistaken for photographs – lure viewers into a secluded, homoerotic world. He prefers to compose everyday domestic settings, and in these intimate indoor quarters he renders figures, frequently including himself, dressed as a woman and a man, as his way of exploring the male-female duality within all humans as well as the concept of Ardhanarishwara (a principal and hermaphroditic form of the Hindu deity Shiva).

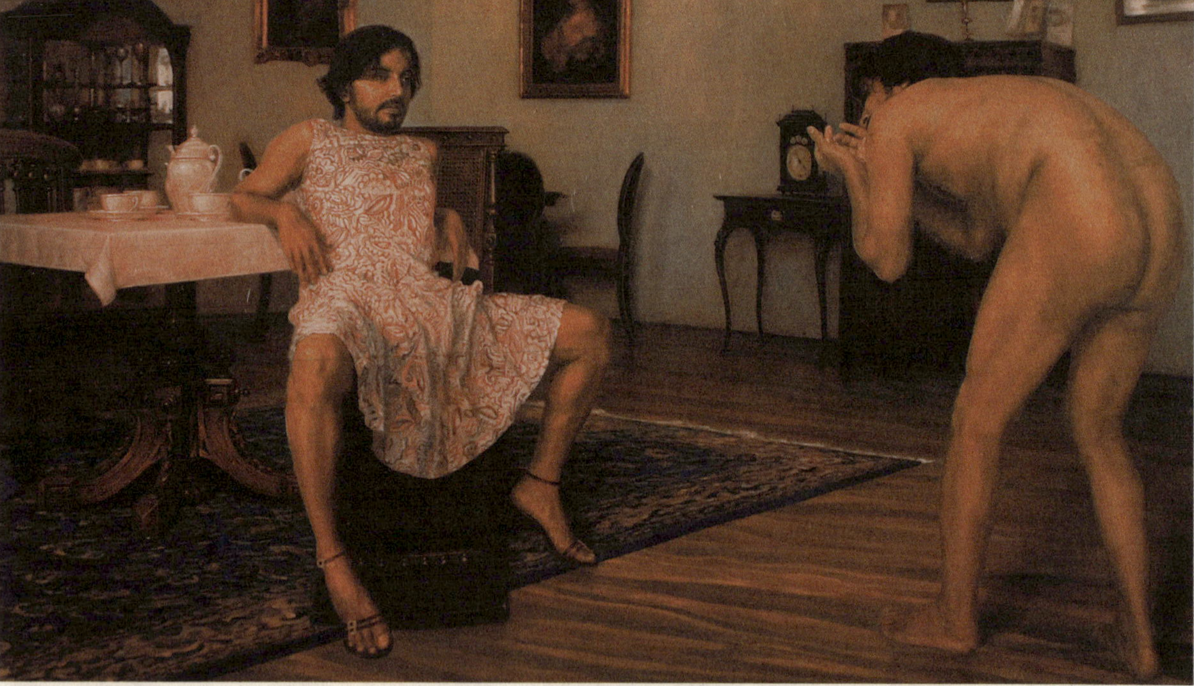

2.

1. Within the Walls I
2008, oil on canvas, 3 panels, overall dimensions 72 × 144 in (183 × 366 cm)

2. Within the Walls II
2008, oil on canvas, 72 × 132 in (183 × 336 cm)

3. Within the Walls III
2008, oil on canvas, 72 × 108 in (183 × 275 cm)

4. Within the Walls IV
2008, oil on canvas, 72 × 90 in (183 × 228 cm)

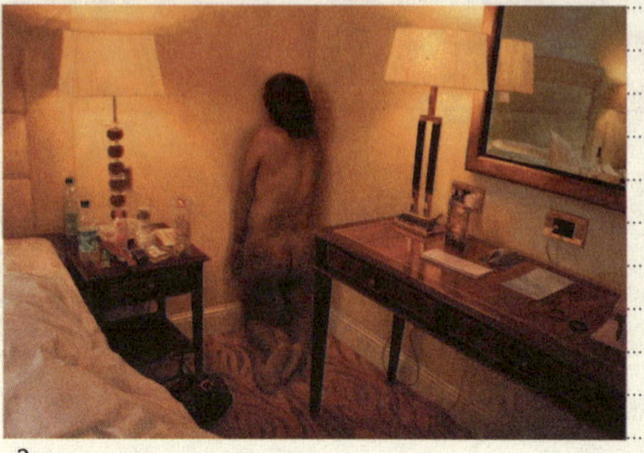

3.

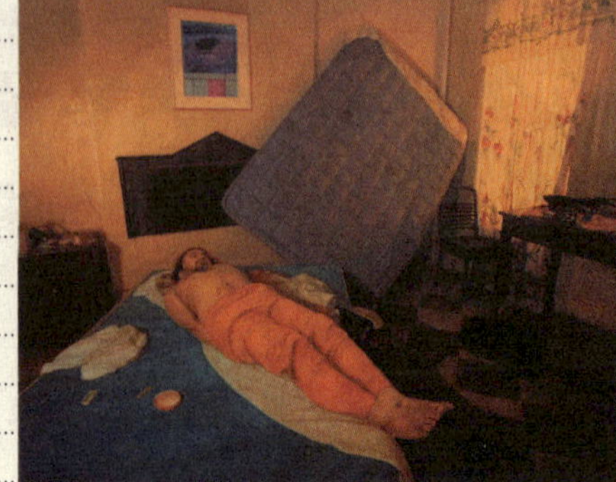

4.

Lana Kataeva's recent work often challenges the viewer to interact, wittily interrogating the multiple meanings of exchange. She has given away pumpkin plants and poppy seeds to gallery visitors, distributed postcards covered with loose charcoal, documented computer users' physiological reactions to mouse clicks on their onscreen photographs, and explored the use of food as a sculptural material.

1 & 2. Artificial Landscapes
2006-08, plastic containers, cotton, and pumpkin sprouts, $11\frac{1}{2} \times 9\frac{3}{4}$ ft (4×3 m)

3. First Second Third
2006-08, digital video, color, 1 min 20 sec

4. Action Artificial Landscapes 2 (detail)
2006-08, cotton and poppy sprouts, $59 \times 47\frac{1}{4}$ in (150×120 cm)

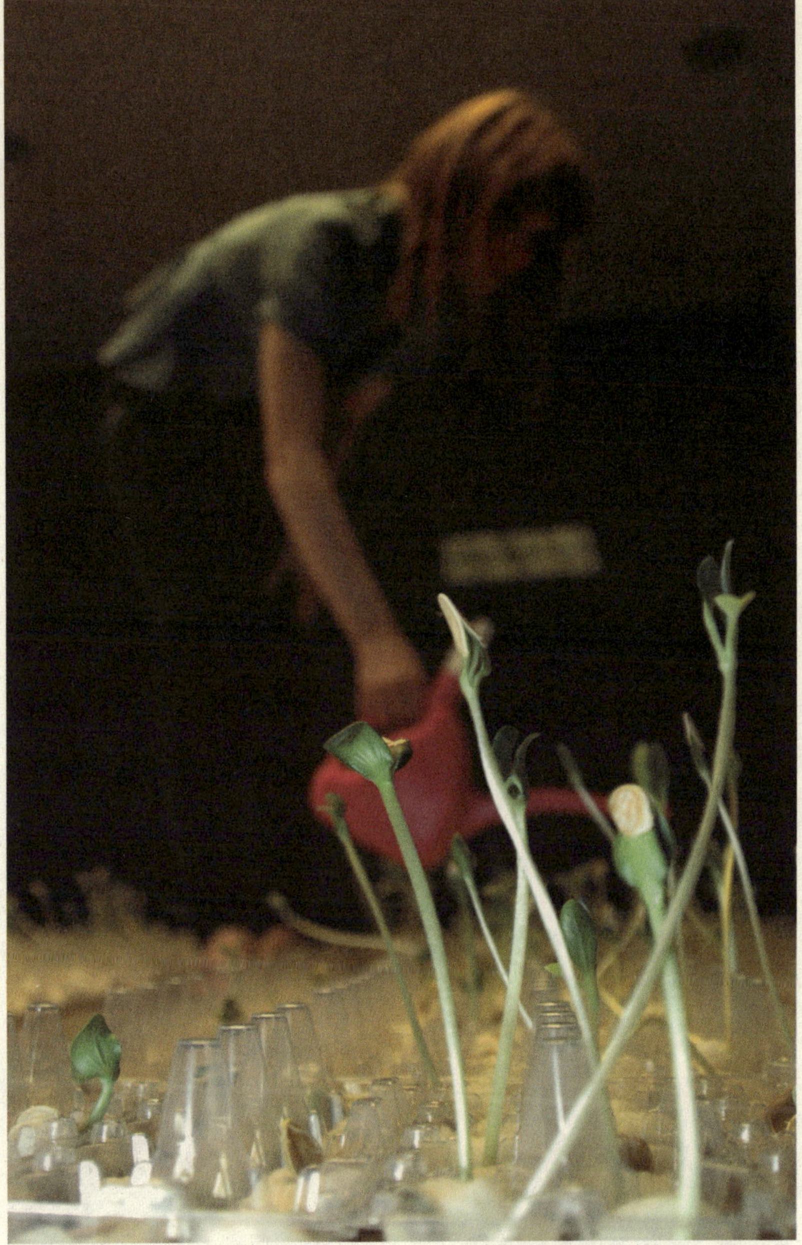

1.

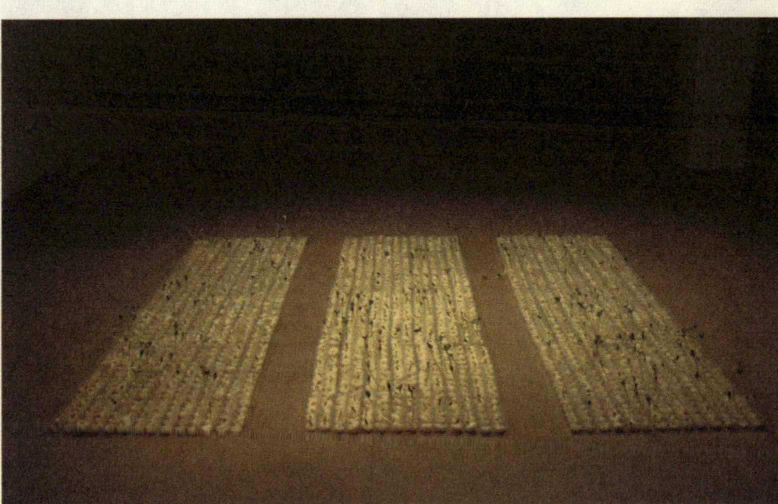

2.

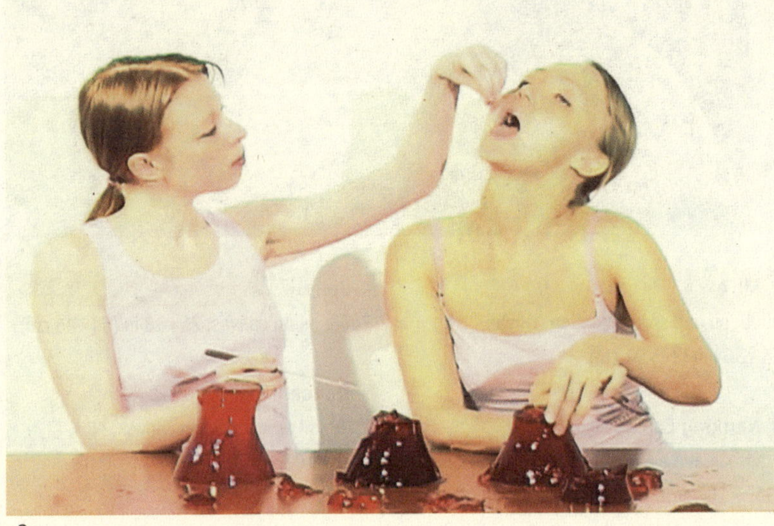

3.

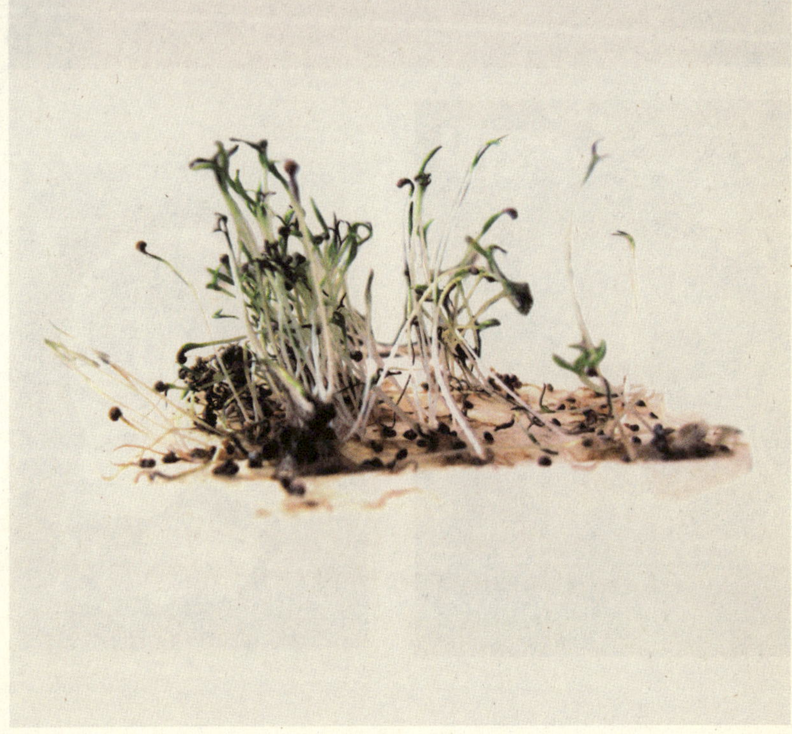

4.

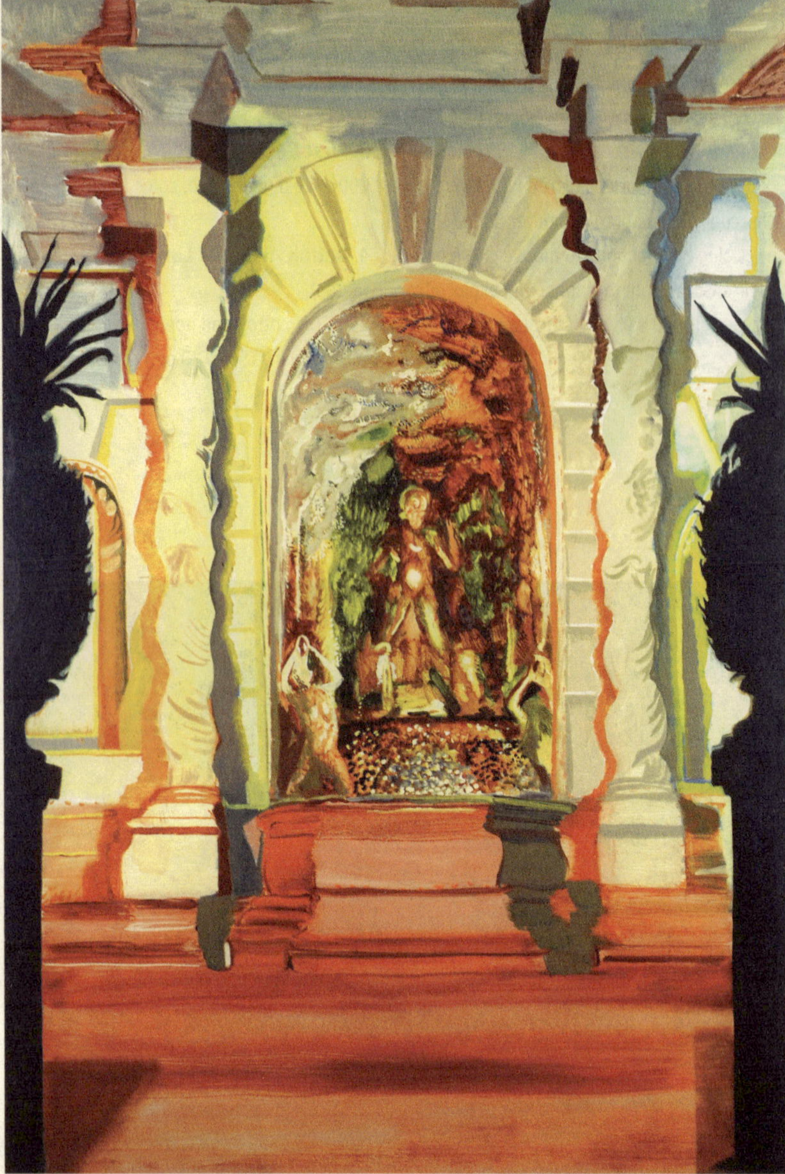
1.

Alison Katz holds a BFA from Concordia University in Montreal and now lives in New York, where she completed an MFA at Columbia University in 2008. She works in oil, occasionally employing spray paint and splashes of turpentine for effects of soft distortion. Gardens, parks, and fountains are often the setting for Katz's fanciful paintings, in which indistinct drawing causes her figures to appear to float. These works suggest that painting's role today is as a vehicle for lyrical reflection.

1. Fountain of Proserpine
2007, oil on canvas, 60 × 42 in (152 × 107 cm)

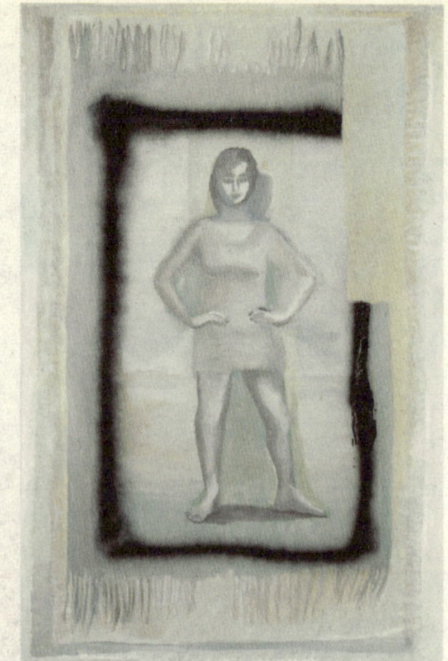
2.

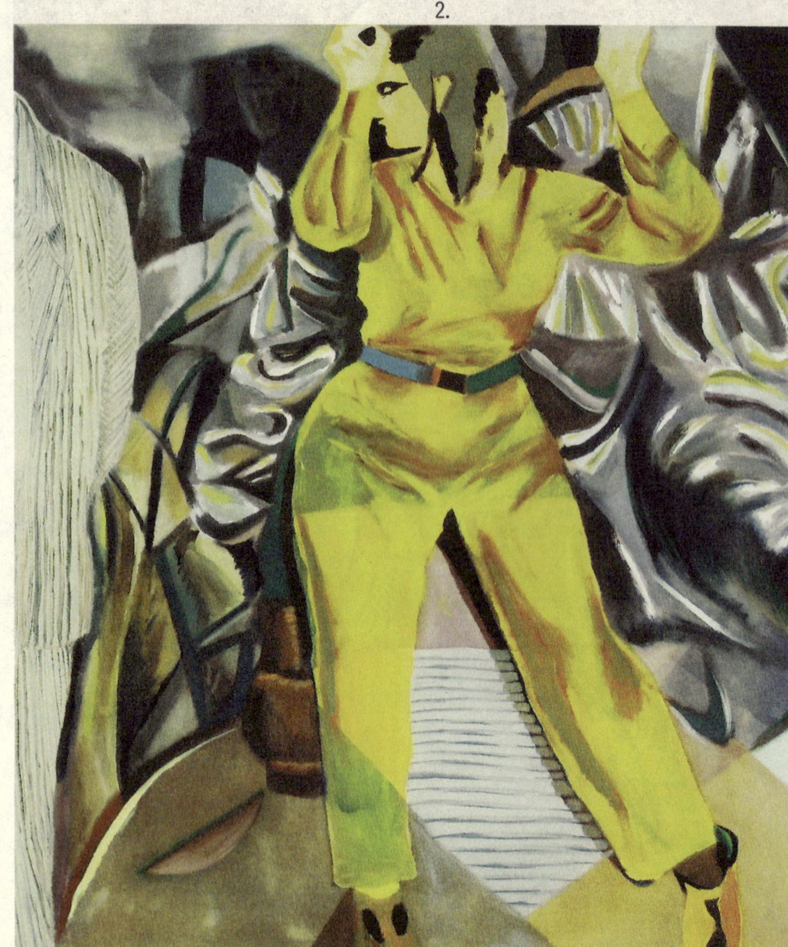
5.

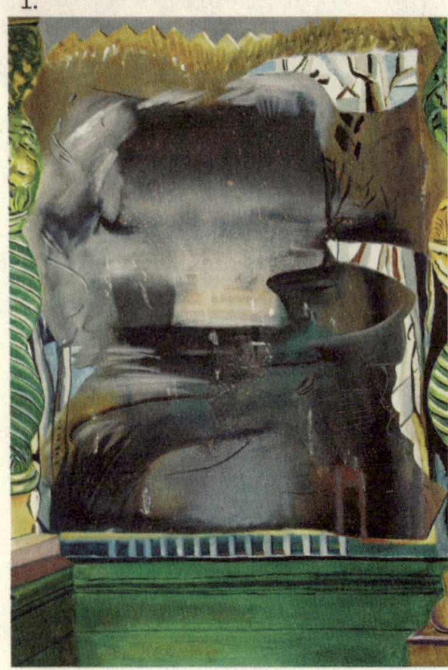
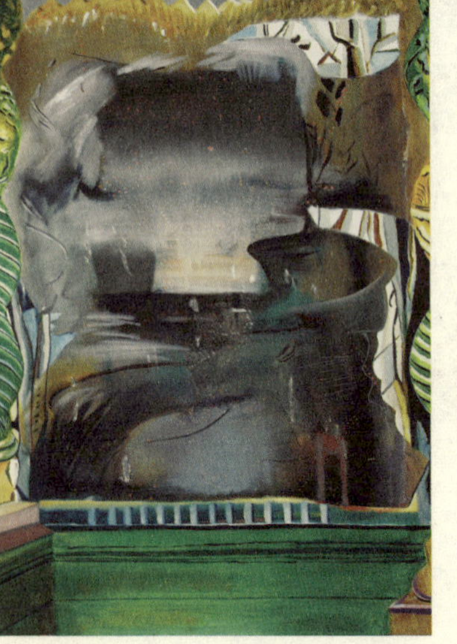
3.

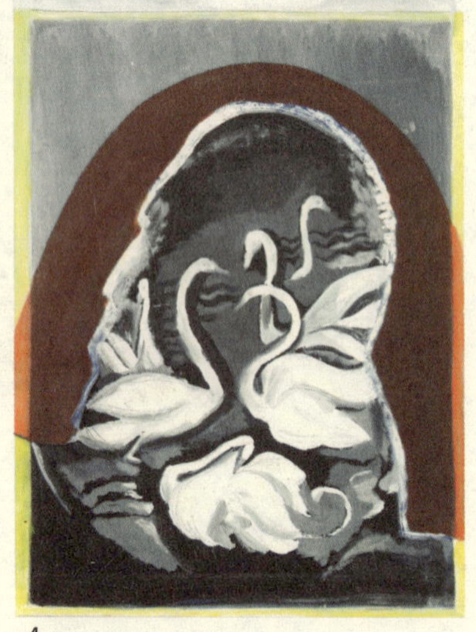
4.

2. Mire
2008, oil and spray paint on canvas, 54 × 36 in (137 × 91 cm)

3. Nanking Bricks
2008, oil and acrylic on canvas, 60 × 42 in (152 × 107 cm)

4. Jelly
2008, oil on canvas, 25 × 18 in (64 × 46 cm)

5. Dancer
2008, oil and acrylic on canvas, 48 × 42 in (122 × 107 cm)

Matt Keegan received an MFA from Columbia University in New York, where he lives. His diverse practice includes photography, collage, sculpture, and text-based works, but also extends into publishing (as the cofounder of North Drive Press) and curatorial projects (as an independent curator and the cofounder of Public-Holiday Projects, an artist-run curatorial initiative). Much of his artistic practice investigates the simultaneously banal and destabilizing force of repetition, using both text and photographic images.

1 & 2. "Now's The Time"
exhibition view at Anna Helwing Gallery, Los Angeles (2008)

3. **You, Me, I, We**
2007, silkscreen, 30 × 25 in (76 × 64 cm)

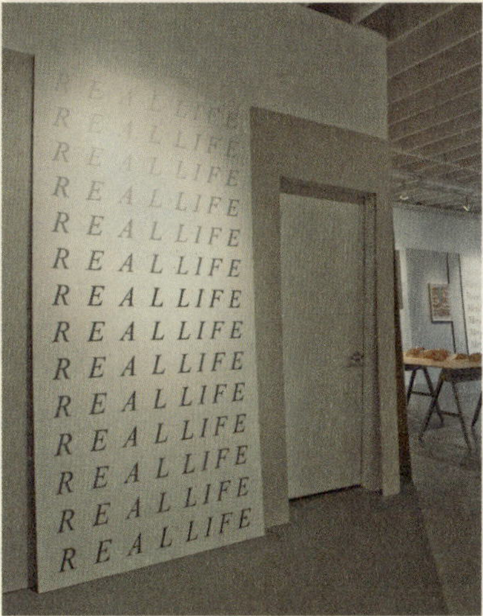

1.

4. **Without touch, we can't connect. Without skin, we can't touch**
2008, silkscreen on paper, 27 3/4 × 23 in (71 × 58 cm)

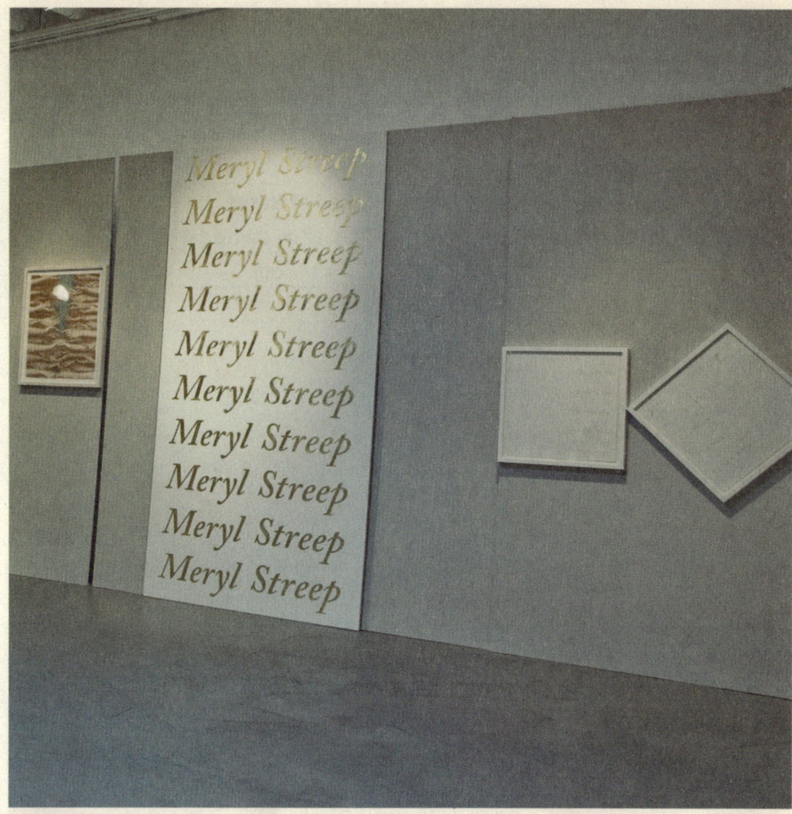

2.

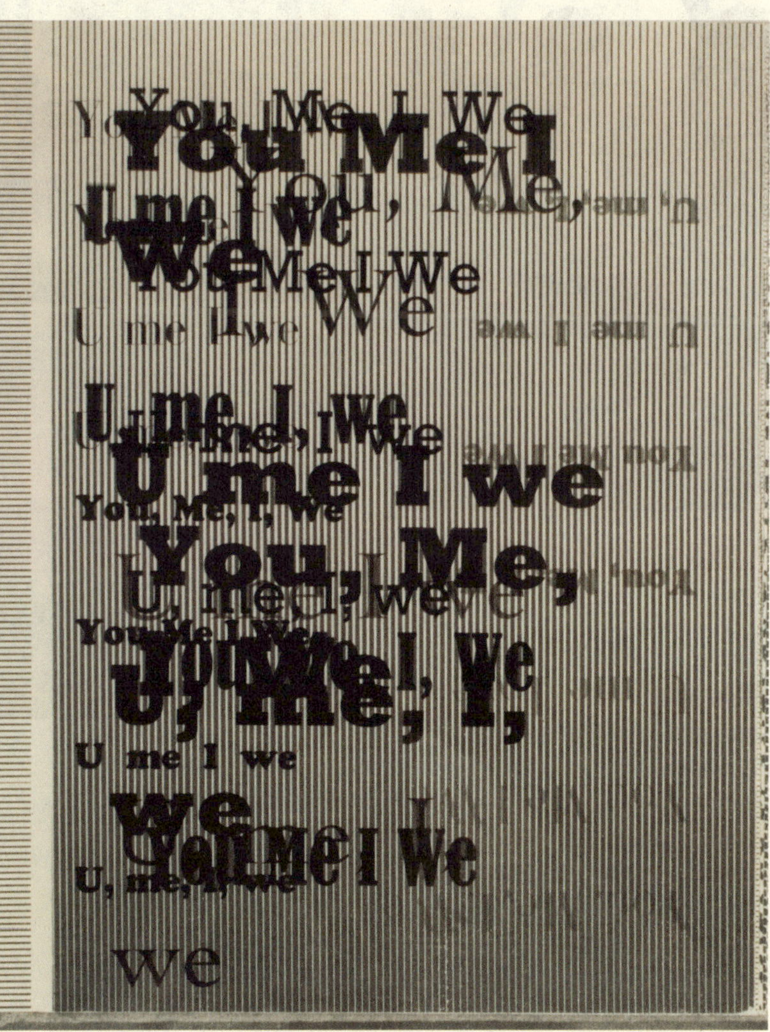

3.

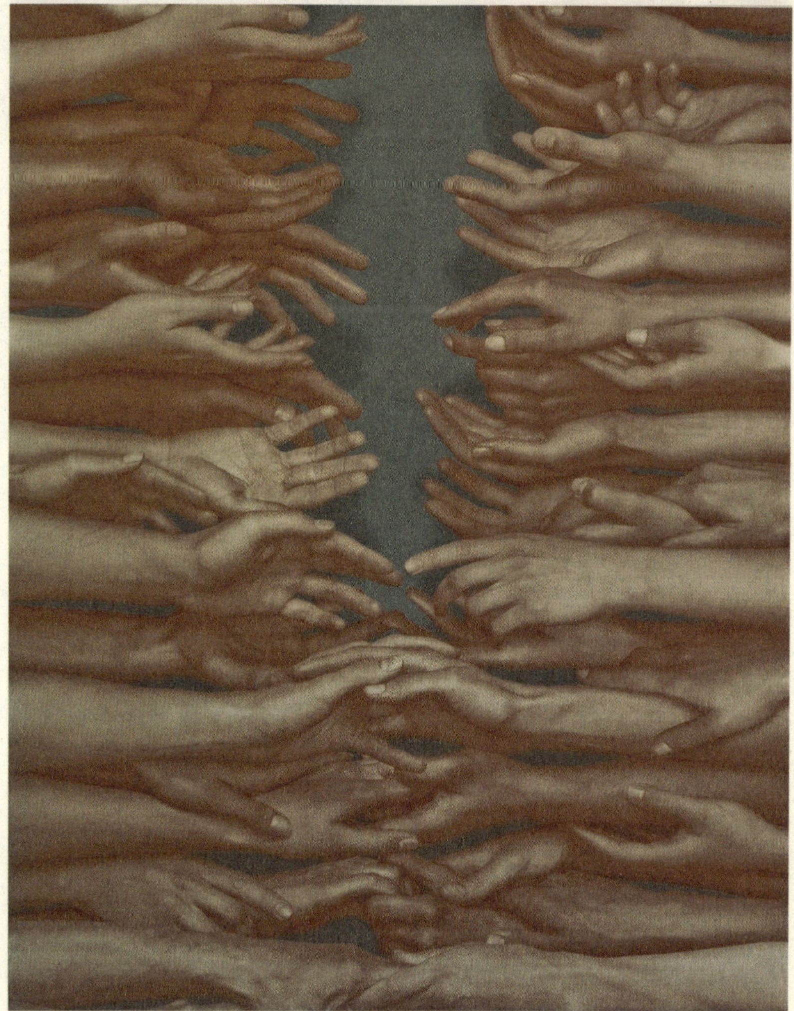

4.

Khalif Kelly holds a BFA in painting from the School of the Art Institute of Chicago and is currently enrolled in the MFA program at Yale University. His paintings use a vivid palette and cartoonish figuration – simultaneously evoking storybook illustration and racial caricature – to depict children whose playtime is disrupted by acts of malice.

In Kelly's scathing vision, greed and cruelty crystallize in the early stages of life; his canvases are elliptical narratives of childhood trauma.

1. Bed of Noses
2008, oil on canvas, 54 × 58 in (137 × 147 cm)

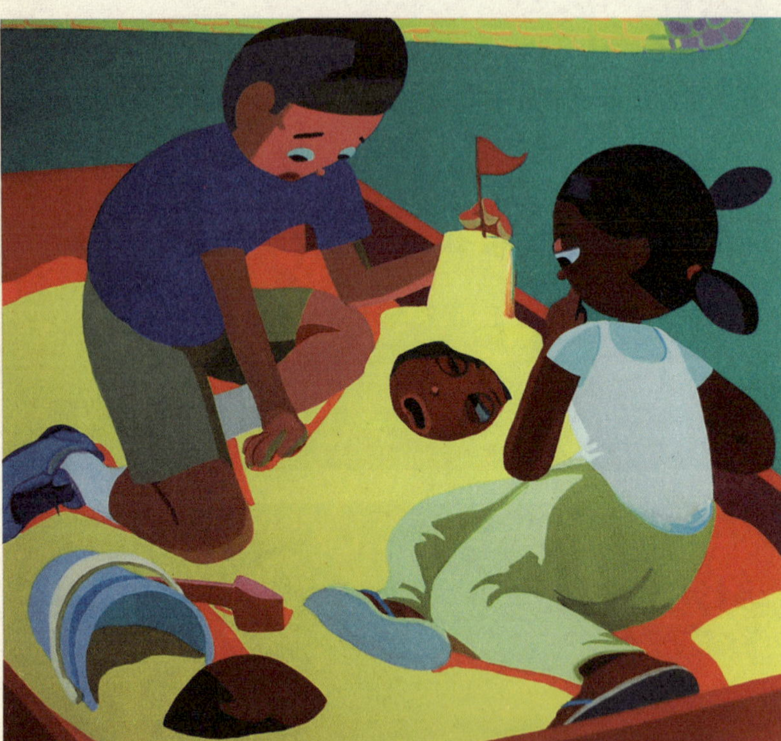
1.

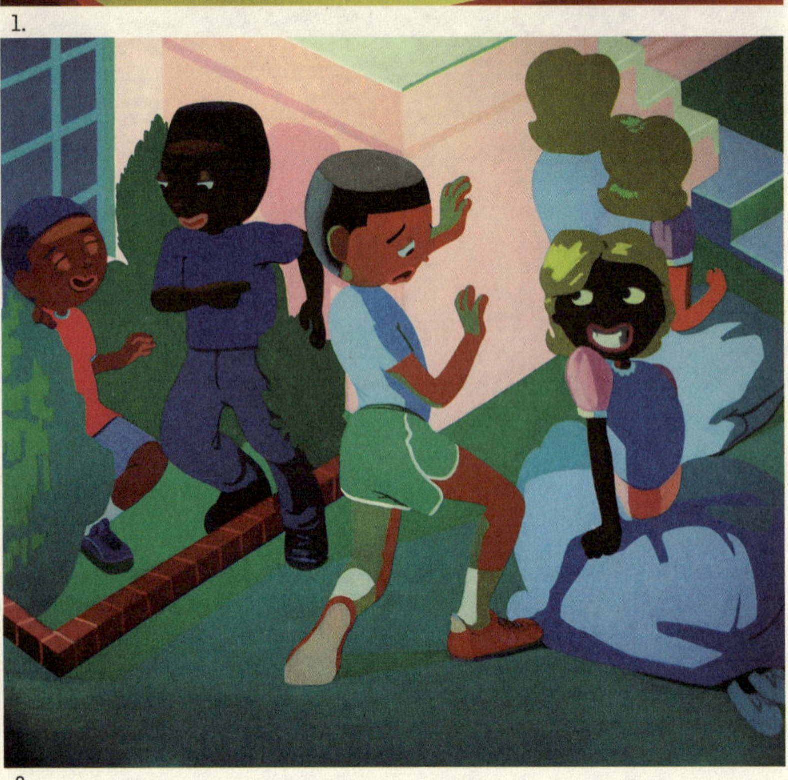
2.

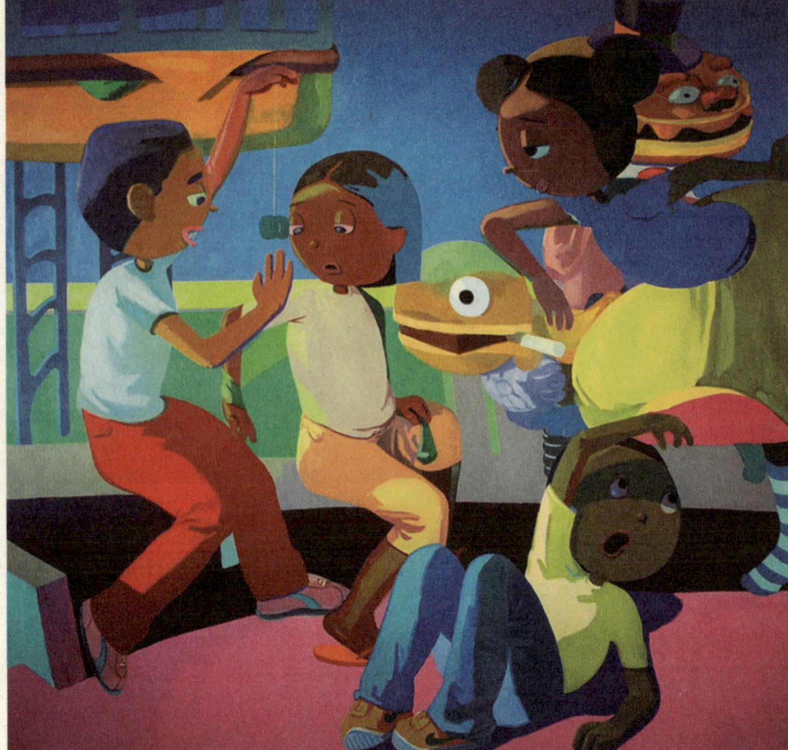
3.

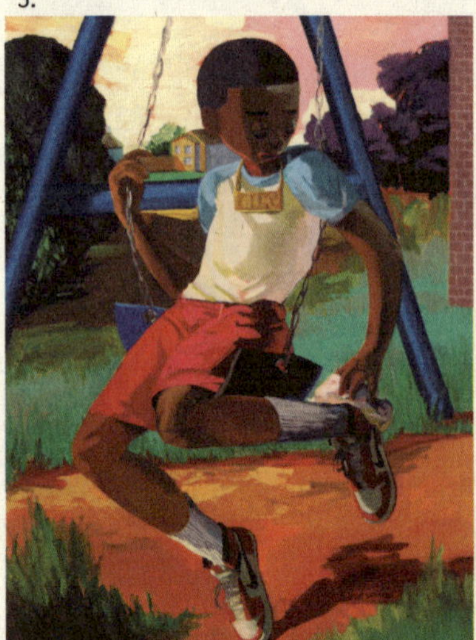
4.

2. Cruel Joke
2008, oil on canvas, 78 × 90 in (198 × 229 cm)

3. Playland
2008, oil on canvas, 90 × 96 in (229 × 244 cm)

4. Boy on Swing
2007, oil on canvas, 63 × 47 in (160 × 119 cm)

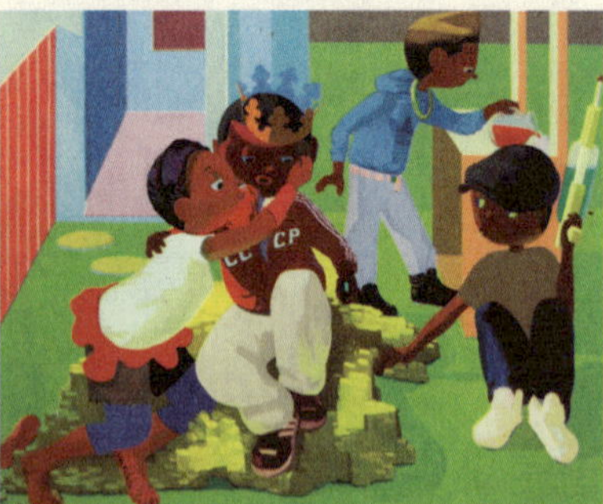
5.

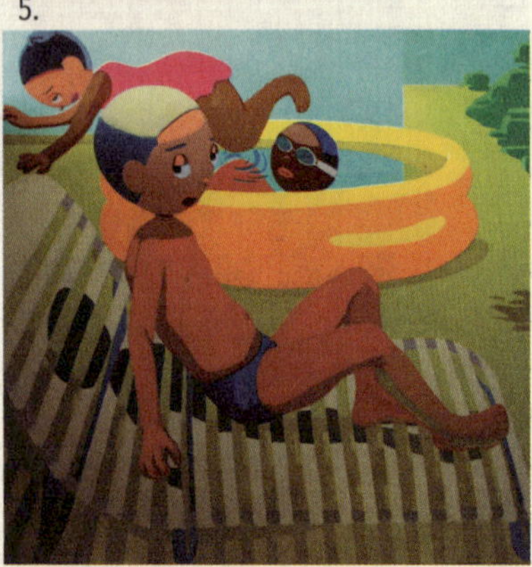
6.

5. Kool-Aid Stand
2008, oil on canvas, approx 84 × 108 in (211 × 272 cm)

6. Poolside
2008, oil on canvas, 64 × 68 in (163 × 173 cm)

Yuree Kensaku lives and works in her native city of Bangkok. While the cute, cartoonish figures, gaudy color combinations, and allusions to traditional styles in her work may be typical of pan-Asian Pop art, the gummy, rough textures are not. Kensaku sometimes plays with formal norms and traditional narratives, as in the gender-bending version of the Japanese tale of Momotaro, produced during her 2007 residency at the Yokohama Museum of Art. By thickening and obscuring surfaces of stereotypical imagery and cheaply produced, souvenir-like objects, Kensaku questions the ways in which a culture presents and represents itself.

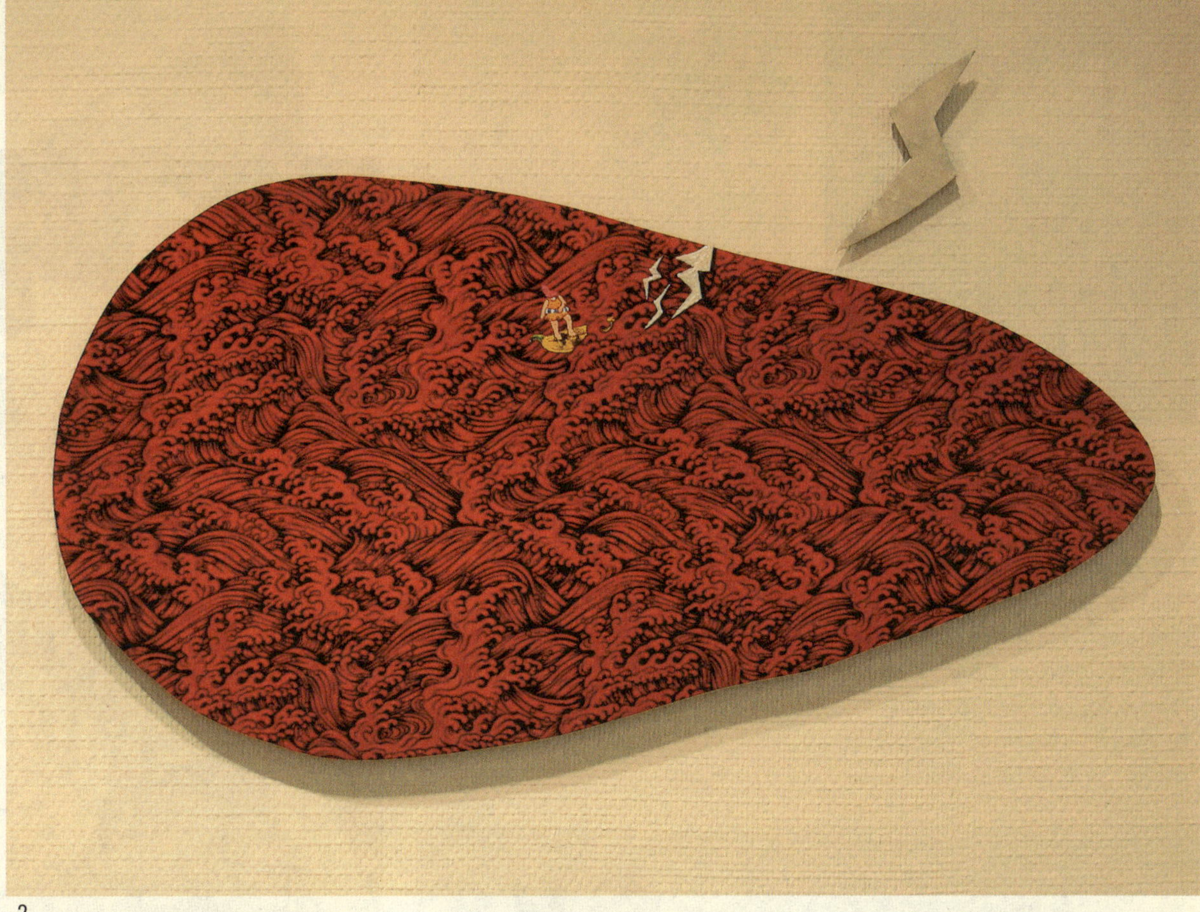

2.

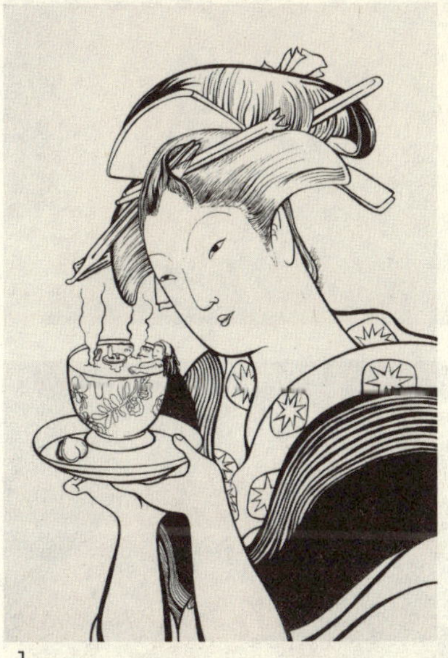

1.

1. the adventure of momotaro girl (detail)

2007, pen, pastel, oil pastel, acrylic, and paper, 23 1/2 × 16 1/2 in (60 × 42 cm)

2. crazy wave

2007, acrylic, Japanese paper, aluminum, and wood, 17 3/4 × 26 3/4 × 3/4 in (45 × 68 × 2 cm)

3. momotaro boy and girl

2007, pen, acrylic, gouache, and Japanese paper, 6 × 14 1/2 in (16 × 37 cm)

4. 109 hands

2007, spray paint, acrylic, sticker, doll hands, and stainless tray, 5 3/4 × 12 1/2 × 3/4 in (14 × 32 × 2 cm)

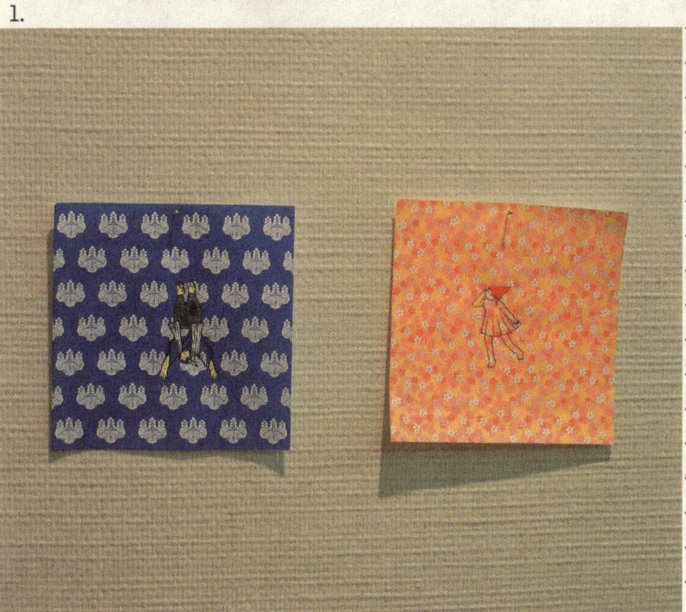

3.

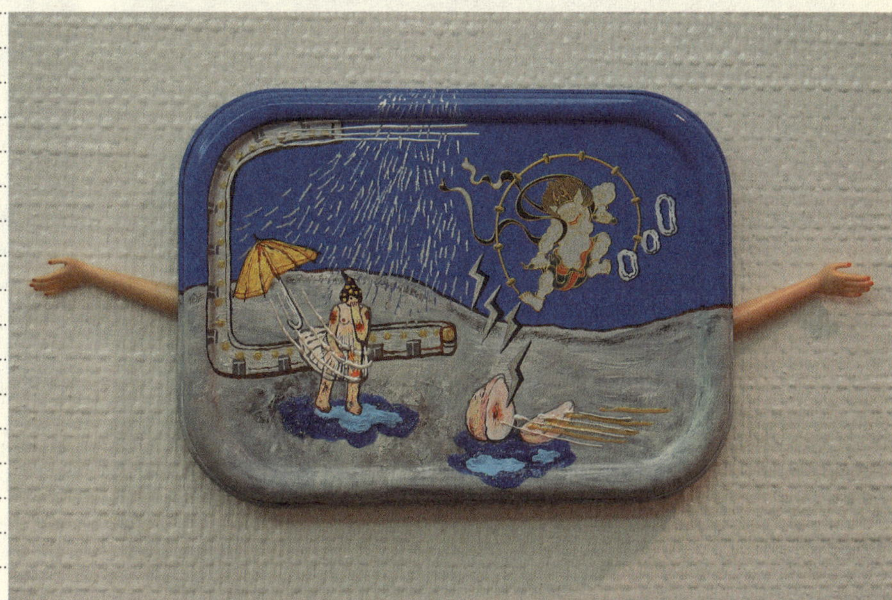

4

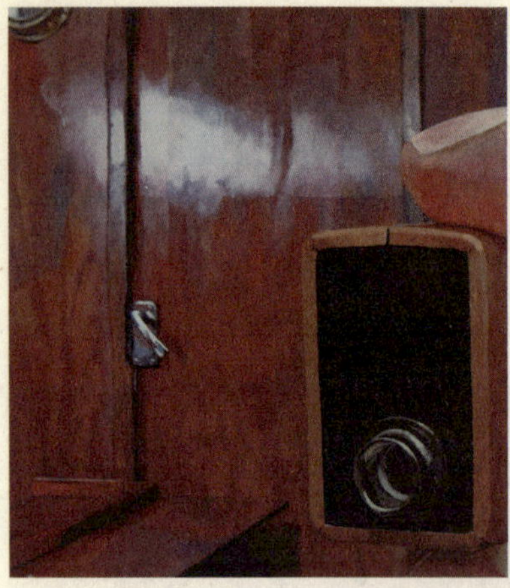

1.

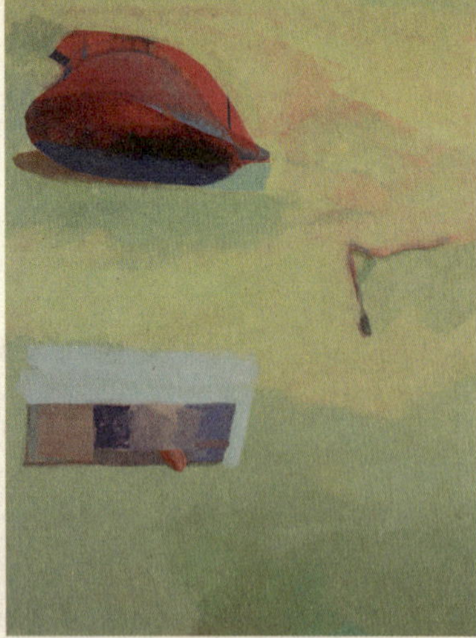

2.

Andrew Kerr is based in Glasgow. Moving from rough-and-ready found-material-based sculpture to painting and back again, he remains interested in exploring parallels between figuration and abstraction, the apparent subject of an image and the facts of its material composition.

1. Battery
2006, acrylic on canvas, 44 × 40 in (112 × 102 cm)

2. Three Articles
2007, acrylic on canvas, 50 × 38 in (127 × 97 cm)

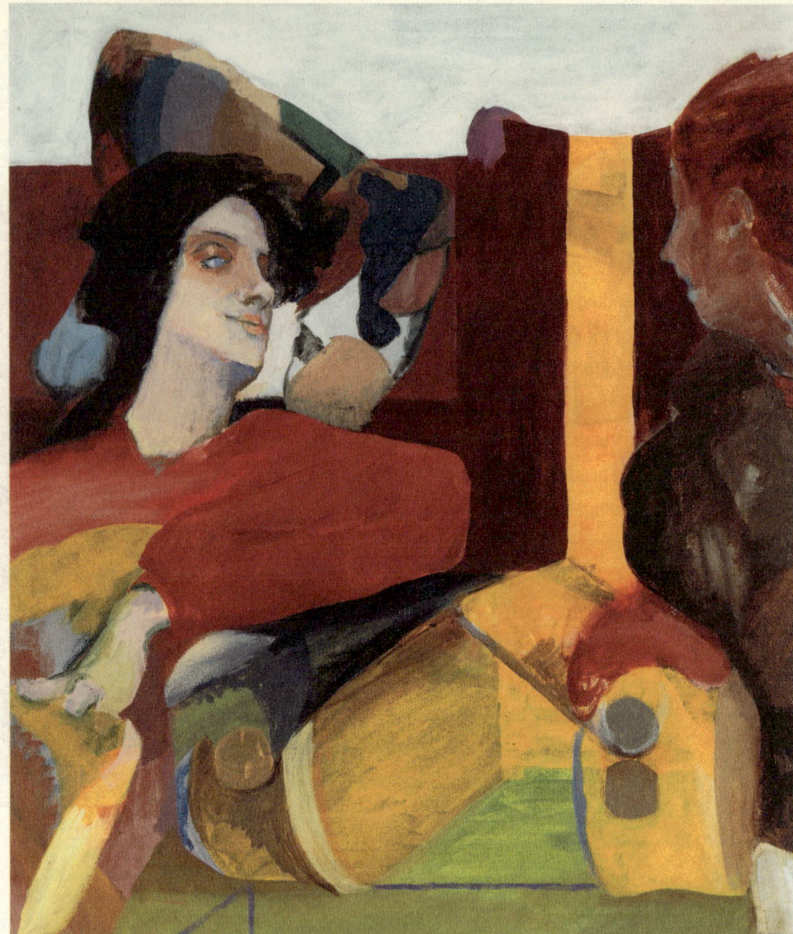

4.

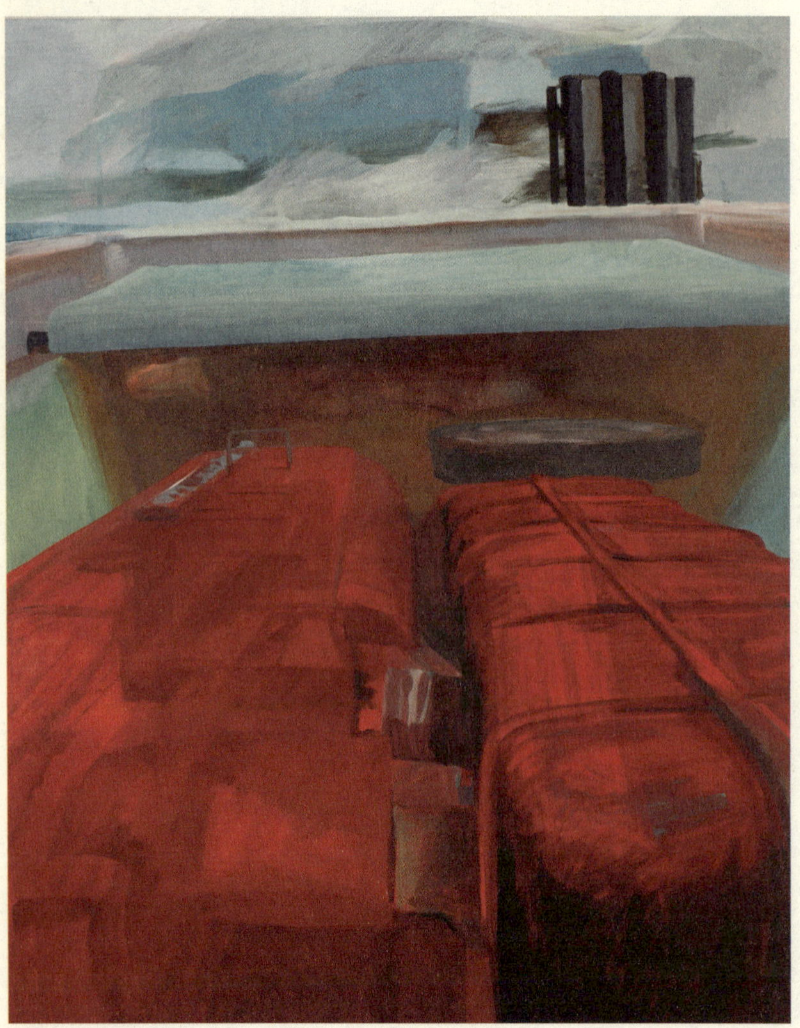

3.

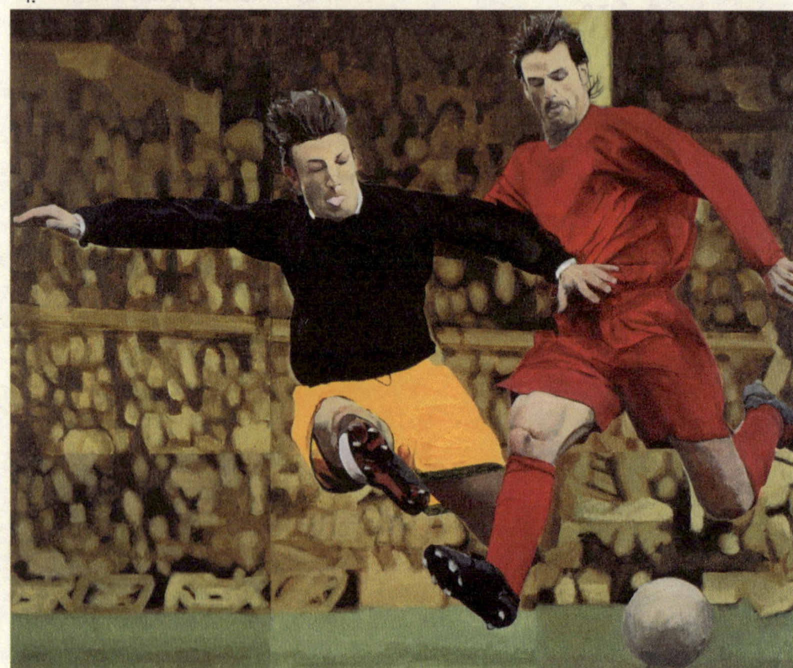

5.

3. Untitled
2007, acrylic on canvas, 65 3/4 × 54 in (167 × 137 cm)

4. Untitled
2007, acrylic on canvas, 32 × 28 in (69 × 82 cm)

5. Untitled
2005, acrylic on board, 27 × 33 in (69 × 84 cm)

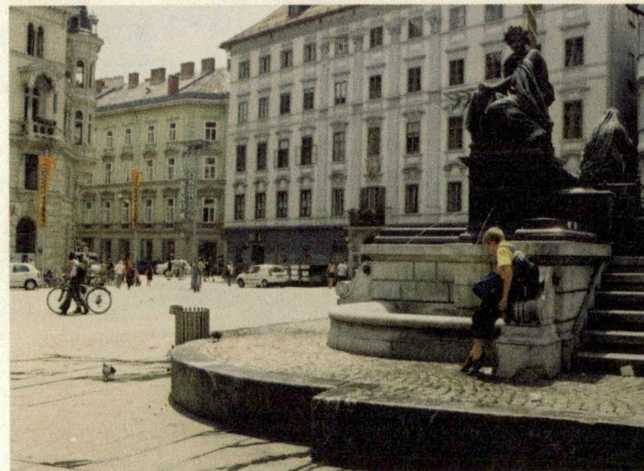

1.

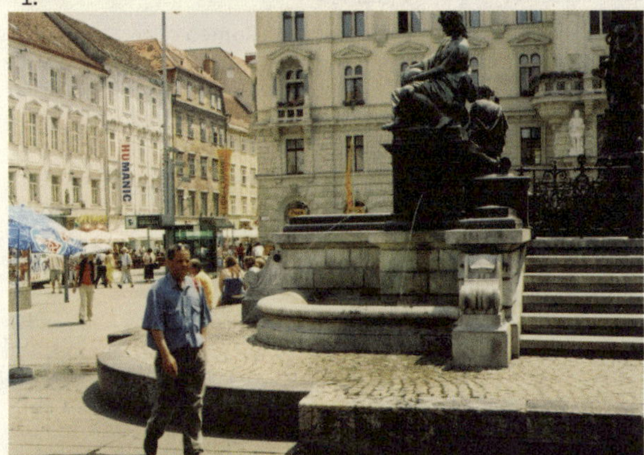

2.

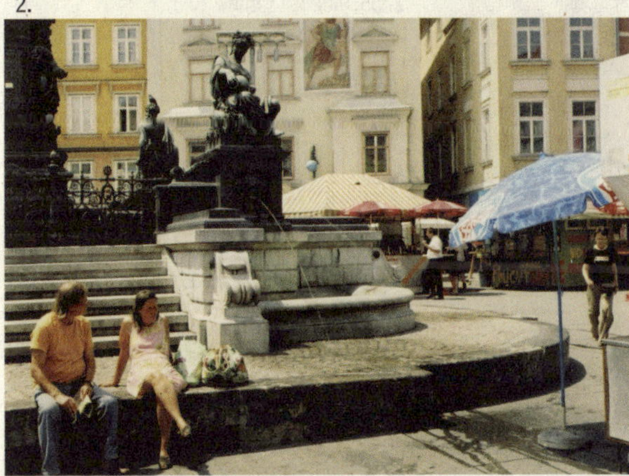

3.

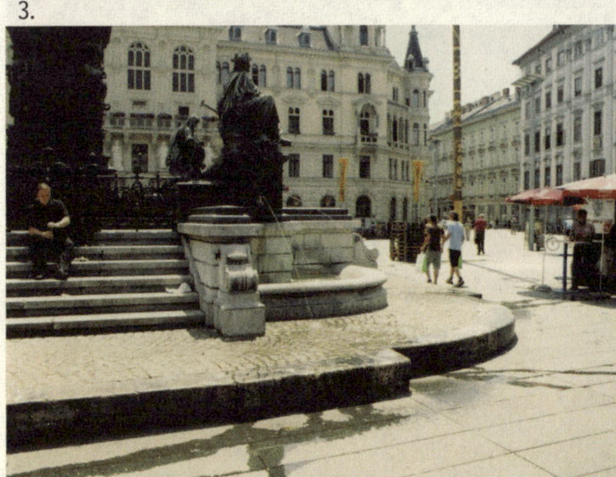

4.

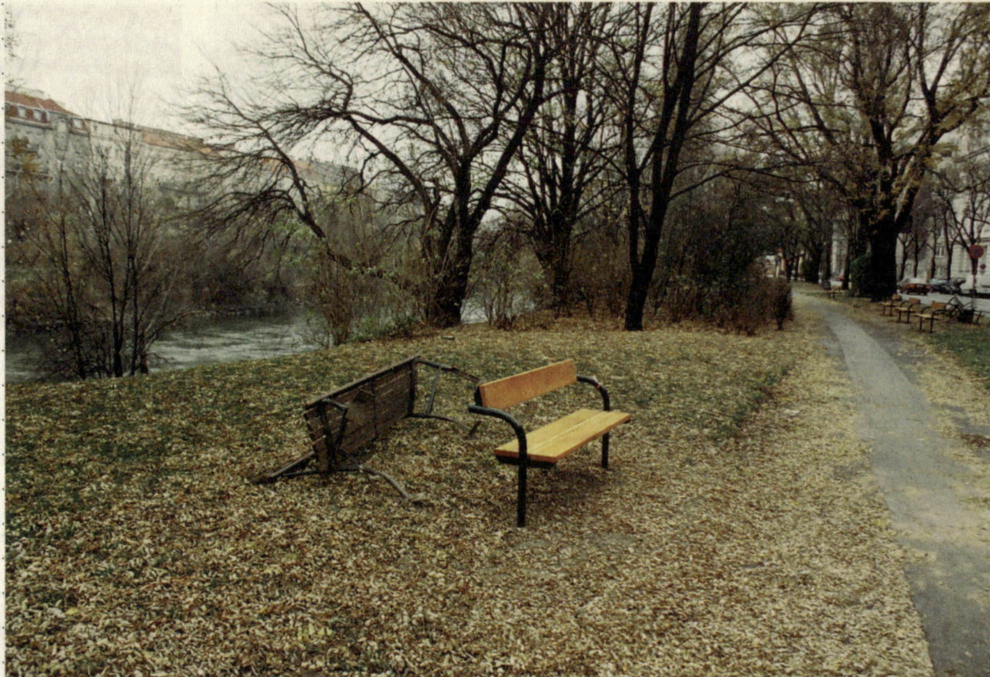

5.

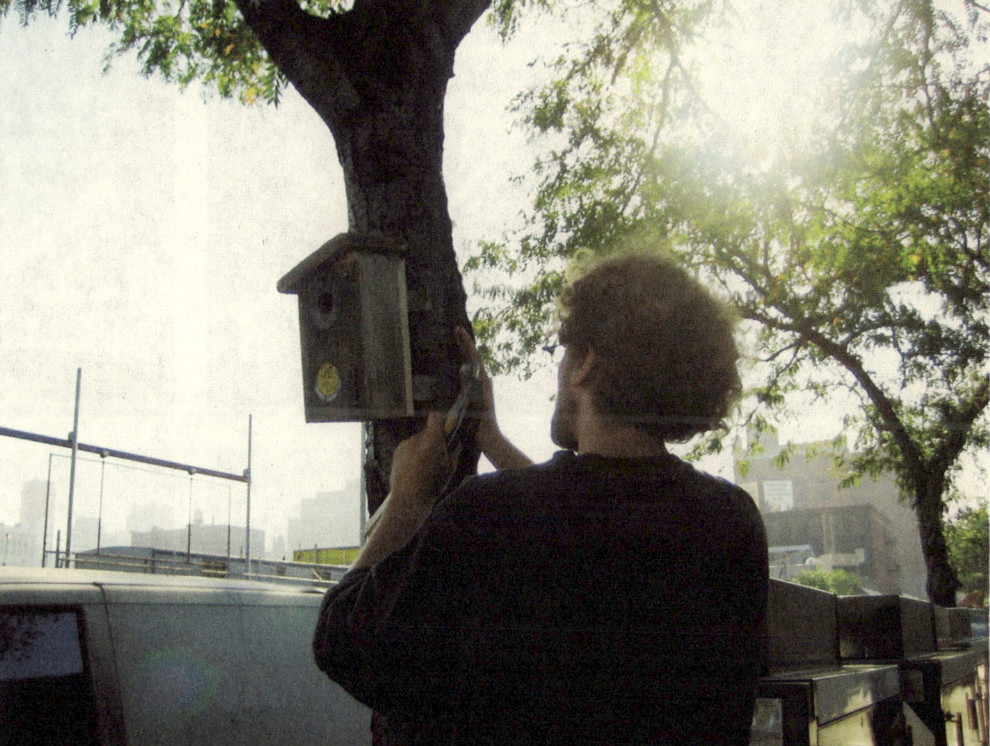

6.

Leopold Kessler lives and works in Vienna. He makes videos and photographs that document covert public interventions. For Kessler, art becomes a kind of offbeat social service, exploiting the creative opportunities that result from gaps in the organization of urban social space.

1, 2, 3 & 4. **Rotana Fountain**
2007, 2-channel video, 6 min 50 sec

5. **Replaced Bench**
2007, photograph of found situation, dimensions variable

6. **Birdhouses/NYC**
2005, video, 8 min

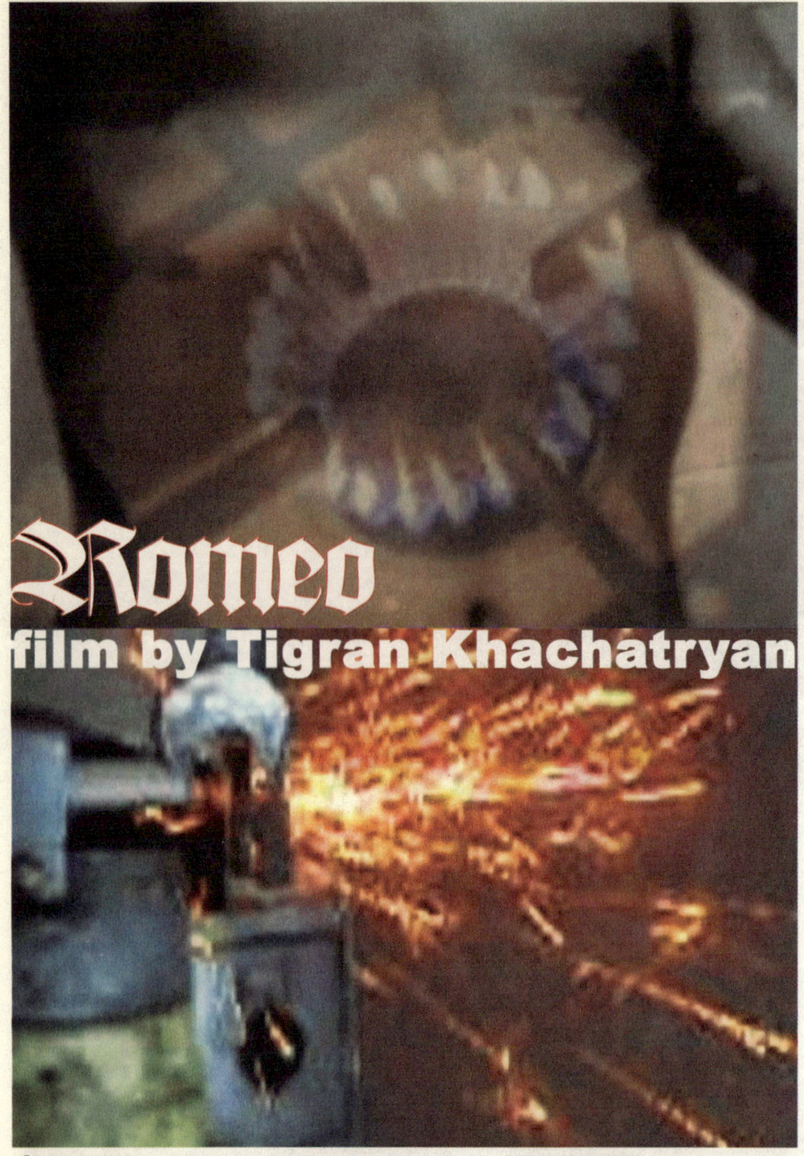

1.

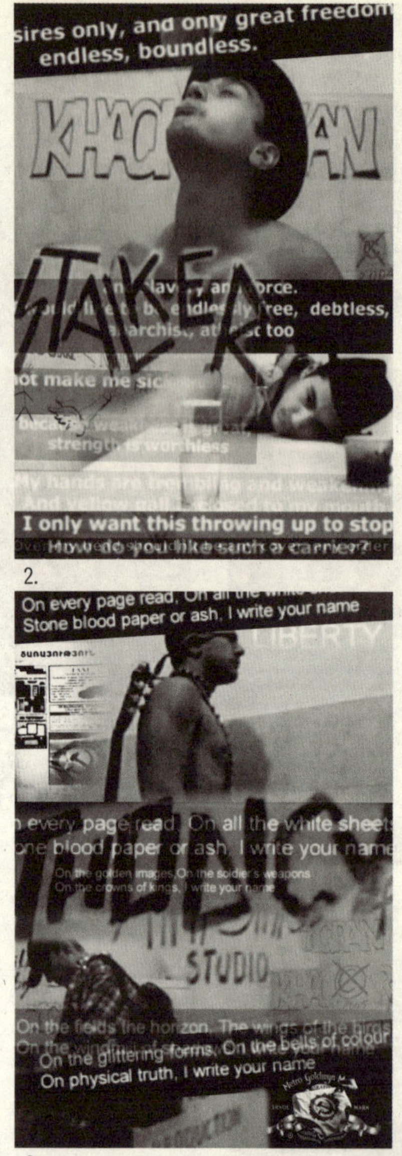

2.

3.

Since 2000, Tigran Khachatryan has been working on a series of filmic reinterpretations of classic movies. His **Garage Videos** are edited with the intention of liberating the originals from the stylistic inhibitions of their makers, investing them with new personal and political meanings. Khachatryan focuses on images that are multilayered, emphasizing their embodiment of ideological contrast and conflict.

1. **Romeo**
2003, poster for **Romeo** video, 27 ½ × 21 in (70 × 53 cm)

2. **Stalker**
2003, poster for **Stalker** video, 27 ½ × 21 in (70 × 53 cm)

3. **Thodicy**
2005, poster for **Thodicy** video, 27 ½ × 21 in (70 × 53 cm)

4. **Brother of La Chinoise**
2005, video, 11 min 7 sec

5. **Stalker**
2004, video, 12 min 33 sec

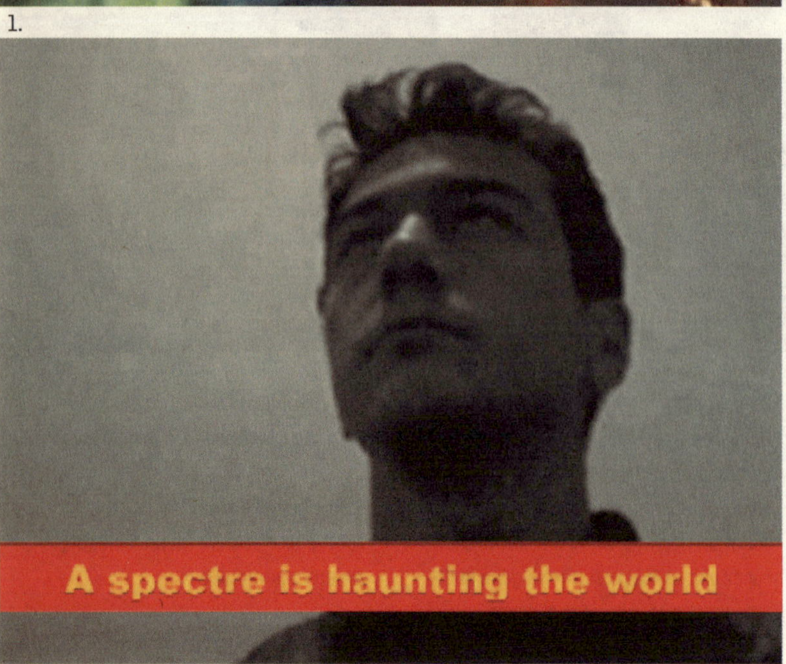

4.

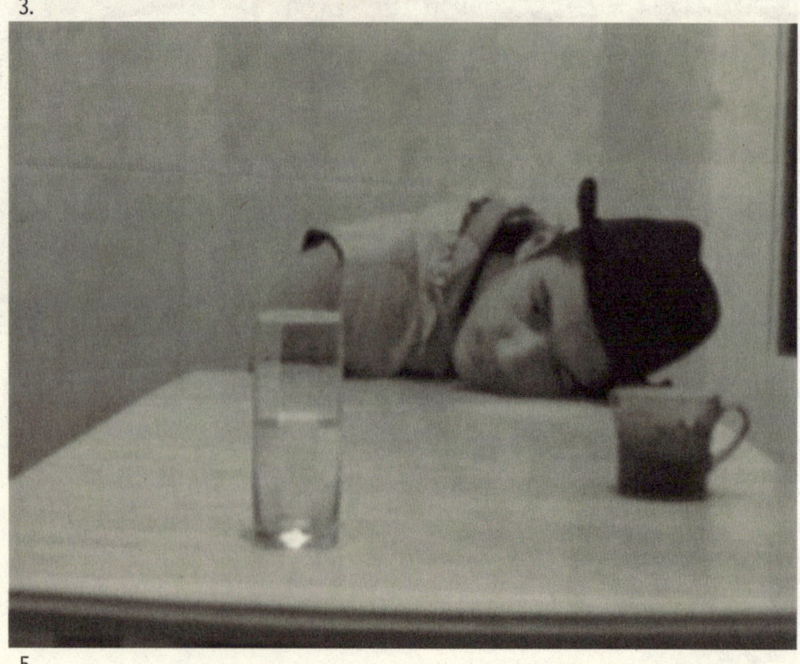

5.

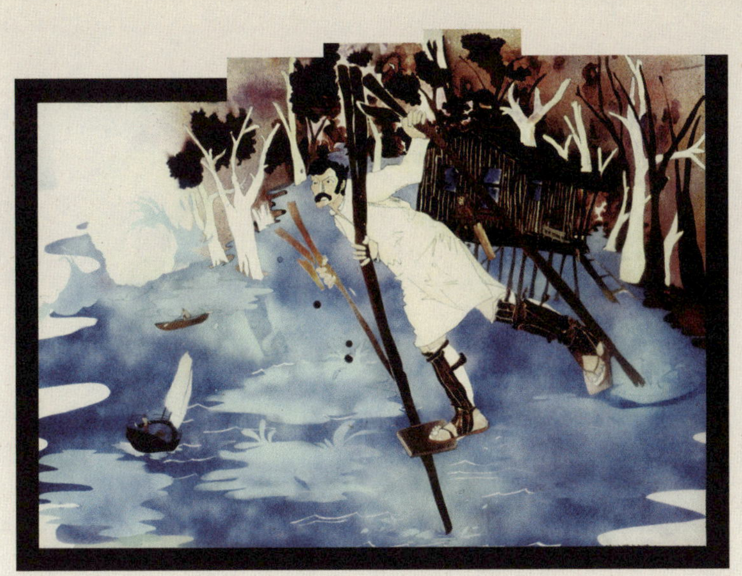

1.

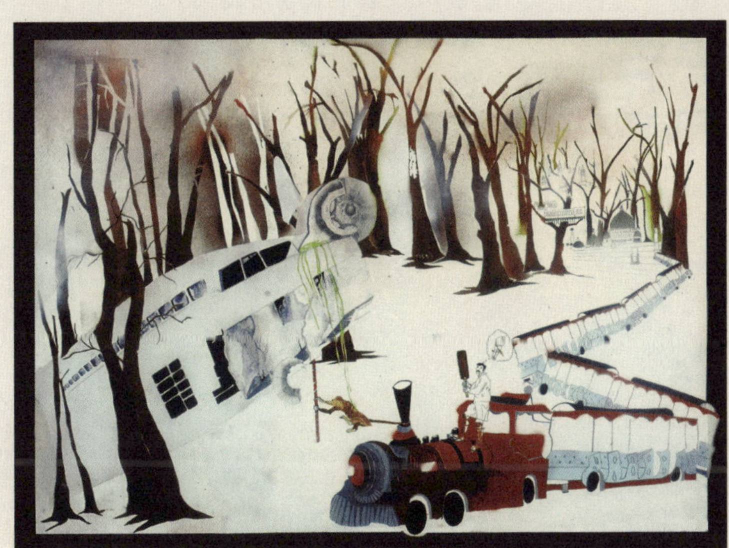

2.

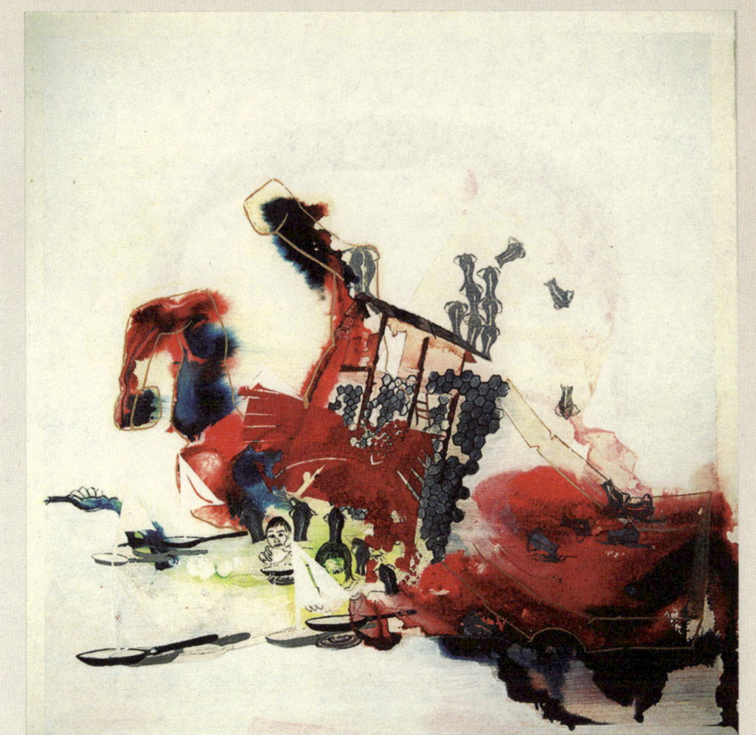

3.

Baseera Khan was born of Indian parents in Texas but now lives and works in Brooklyn. She makes richly allusive paintings on paper in which layered images and juxtaposed spatial orientations evoke the subtleties of diverse but coexistent cultural and personal perspectives.

1. Learning to Swim
2006, acrylic, ink, enamel, and spray paint on paper, 40 × 50 in (102 × 127 cm)

2. Training Saag
2007, acrylic, ink, and enamel spray paint on paper, 38 × 52 in (97 × 132)

3. Horse and Carriage
2008, acrylic, ink, enamel, and spray paint on paper, 23 × 23 in (58 × 58 cm)

4. Descending Stare
2005, acrylic, ink, enamel, spray paint, and paper collage on paper, 20 × 30 in (51× 76 cm)

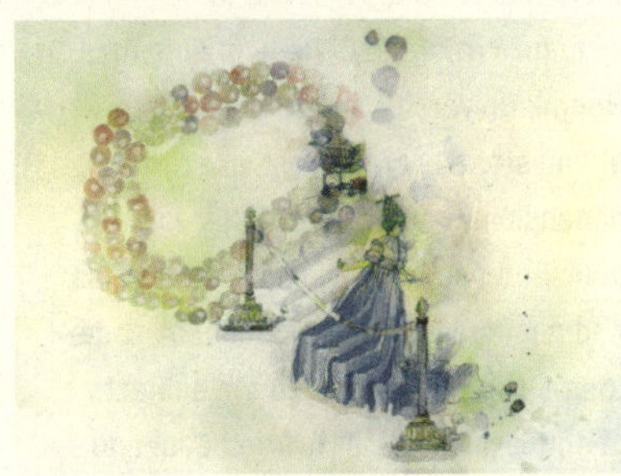

4.

5. Financial Fiasco
2008, acrylic and ink on paper, 23 × 23 in (58 × 58 cm)

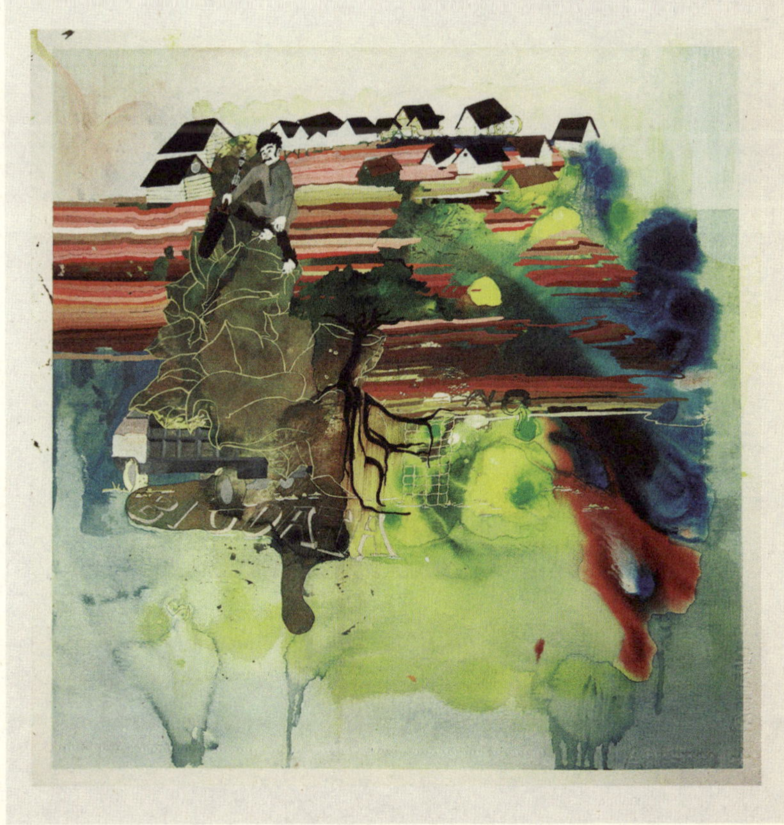

5.

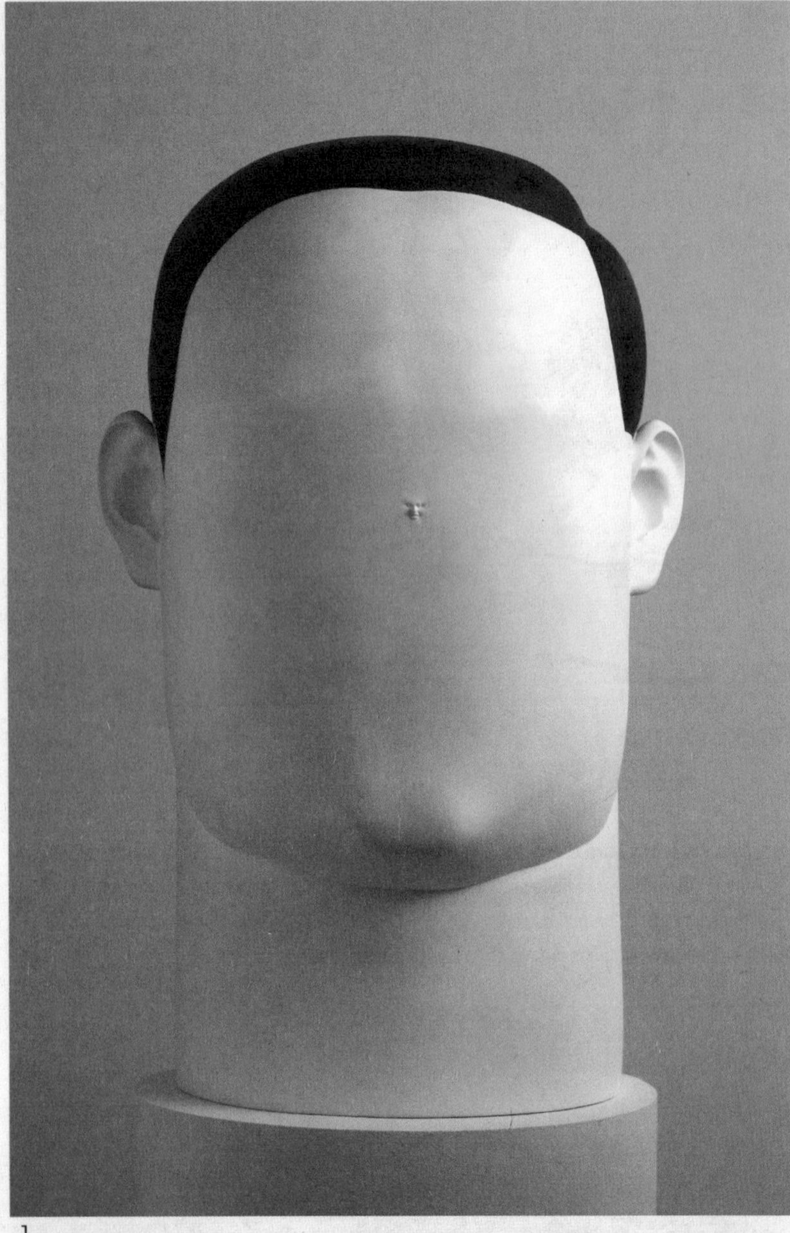

1.

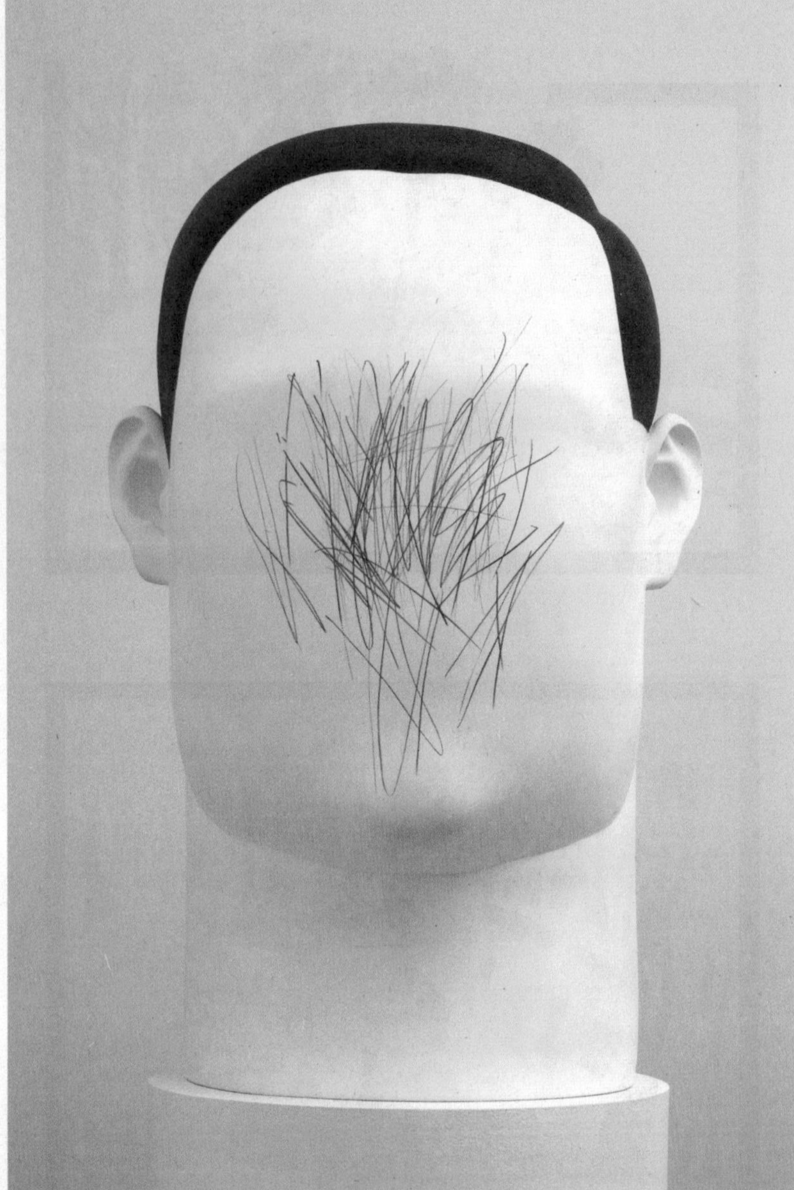

2.

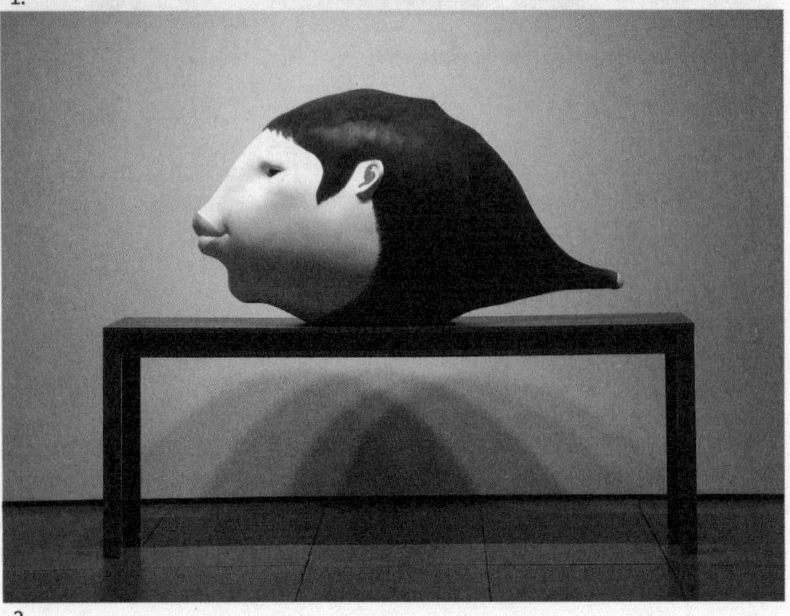

3.

Inbai Kim received his MFA in sculpture from the College of Fine Arts, Hongik University, Seoul. His sculptures of "mysterious creatures" are three-dimensional realizations of his surreal pencil-on-paper drawings – the dreams and nightmares of his sketchbook come to life. His work has been the subject of solo exhibitions at Arario Seoul and Gallery Skape in Seoul.

1. **Deller hon Dainy**
2007, plaster and pencil,
31 ½ × 19 ½ × 17 ¾ in (80 × 50 × 45 cm)

2. **Deller hon Dainy**
2007, plaster and pencil,
31 ½ × 19 ½ × 17 ¾ in (80 × 50 × 45 cm)

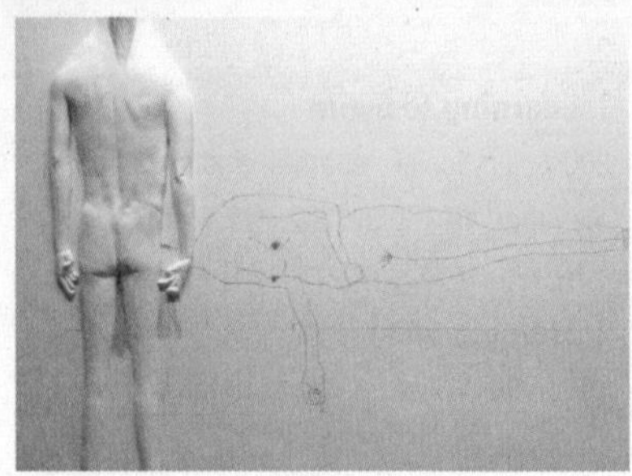

4.

3. **Shamoralta Shamoratha**
2007, plastic and pencil,
35 ½ × 59 × 21 ½ in (90 × 150 × 55 cm)

4. **Magic** (detail)
2007, plastic and pencil,
dimensions variable

Anja Kirschner moved to the UK in 1995 and is currently based in London. She works with film, painting, and drawing to explore themes of criminality, rebellion, and social transformation. Her films combine documentary elements with literary and historical references in the context of popular narrative genres. Kirschner has also released music as part of the band Antifamily and the electronic duo Asja Auf Capri.

1. **Trail of the Spider**
2006, video, 54 min, poster

2. **Untitled – Outlaw Series**
2007, pencil on paper, 23 ½ × 16 ½ in (59 × 42 cm)

3. **POLLY II**
2006, video, 30 min, production photograph

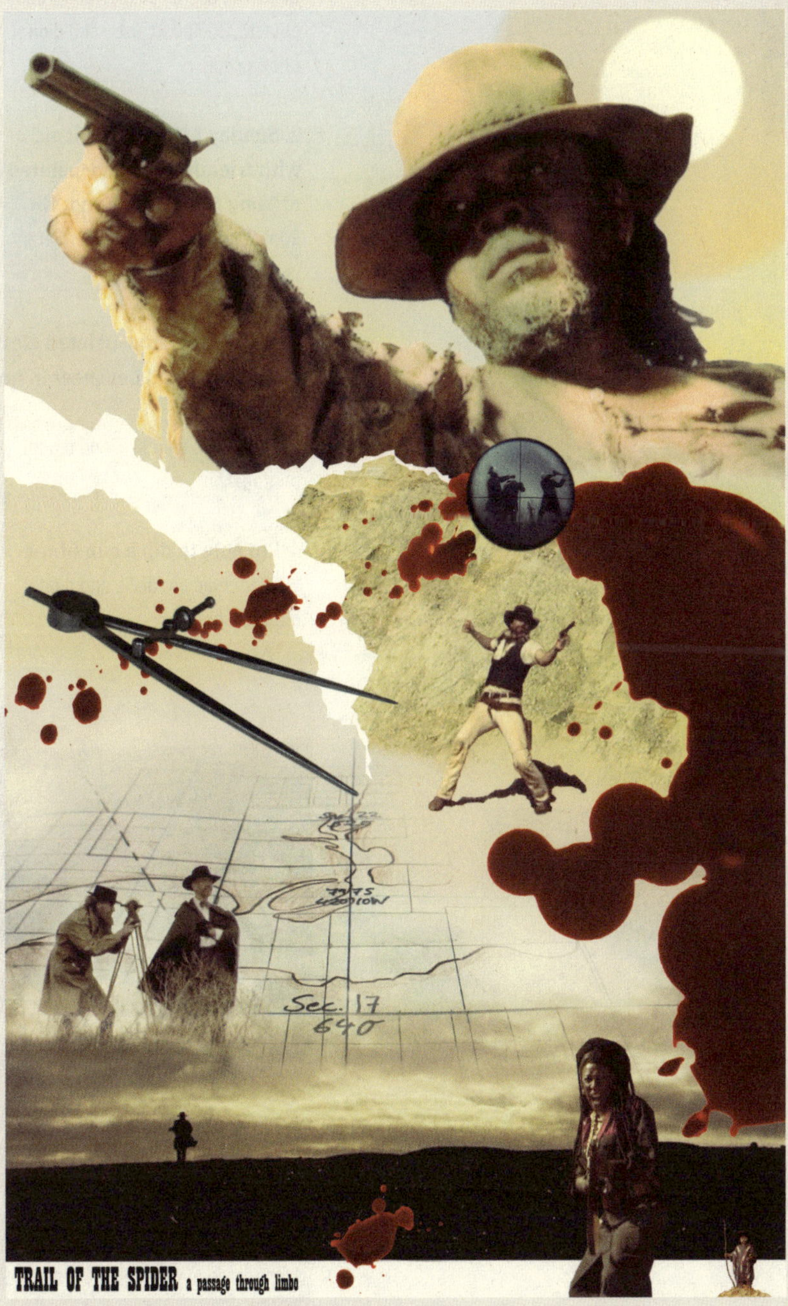

1.

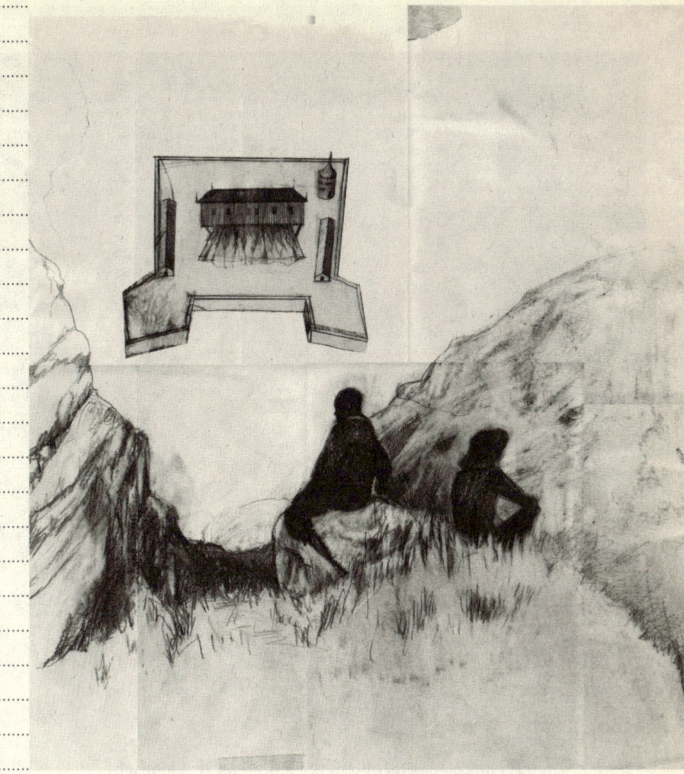

2.

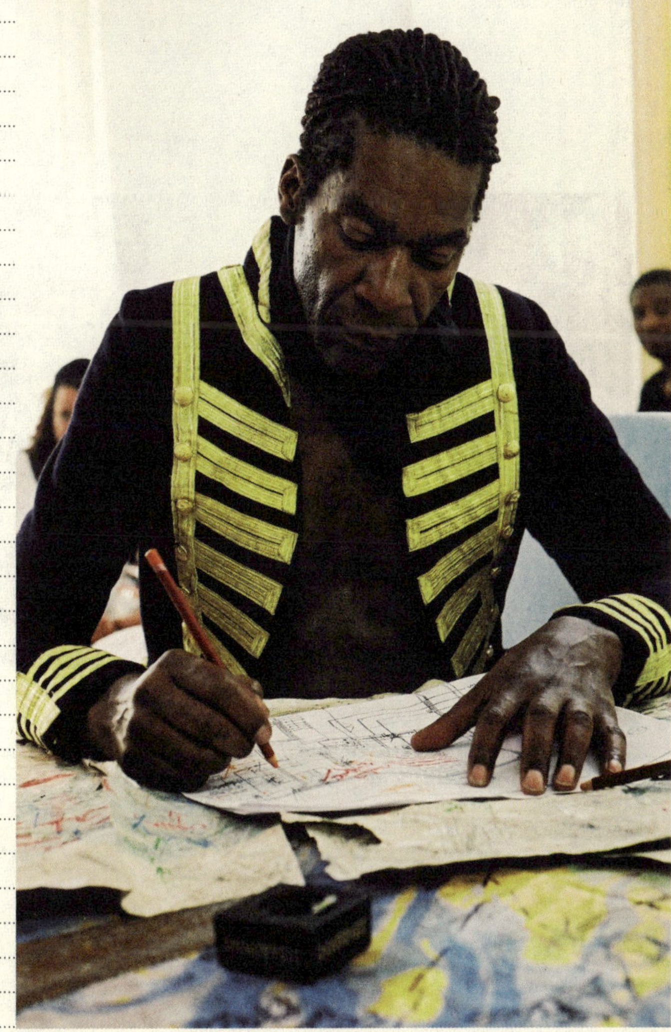

3.

Hong Kong-based painter Lee Kit has gradually moved from conventional abstraction to more objective examinations of the medium of paint, abandoning the stretched panel altogether in favor of loose sheets of painted fabric. By introducing these sheets into everyday settings – as tablecloths, for example – he meditates on the nature of creativity and the possibility of intimacy within communal space.

1. Scratching the table surface
2006-08, acrylic on plywood, readymade objects, 300 postcards, and digital photograph

2. Sunday Afternoon: Picnic with friends and hand-painted cloth at Yung Shu O, Sai Kung, HK
2003, acrylic on fabric and digital photograph

3. A holiday: Hand-painted cloth as picnic cloth and bedsheet in hotel in Singapore
2005, acrylic on fabric and digital photograph

4. I'm able to dip a cup of tea
2007, acrylic on fabric and digital photograph

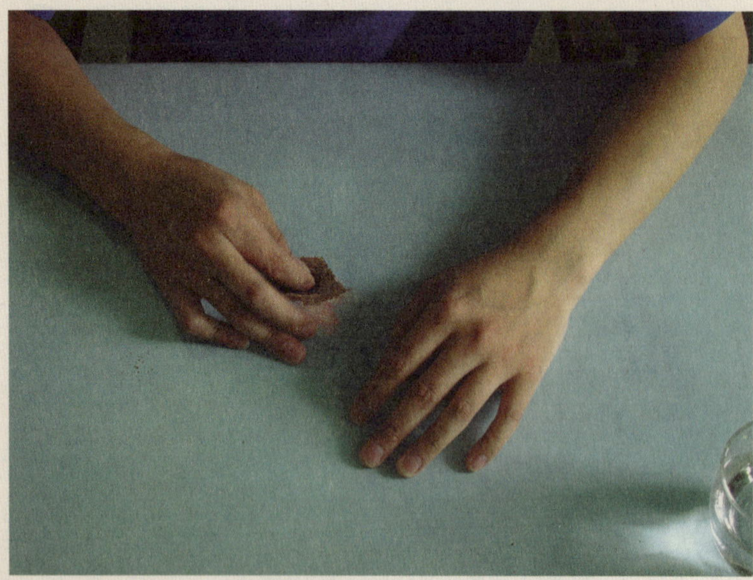

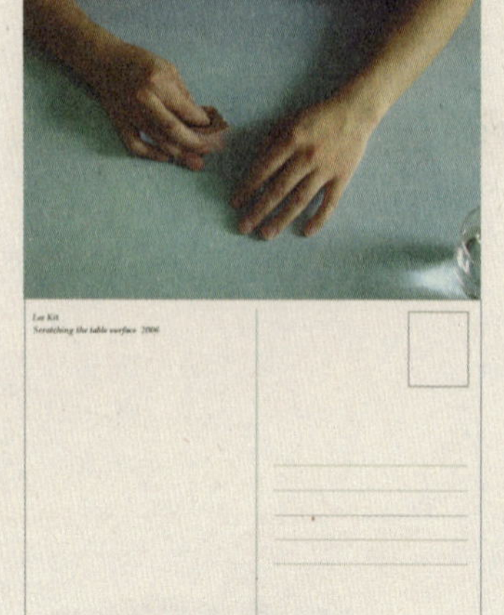

Scratching the table surface. 2006-08
Acrylic on plywood, readymade objects, 300postcards and photo document

I keep scratching a table surface to make a hole on it. Meanwhile, I will send 300 postcards to my friends to tell them I'm scratching the table surface.

1.

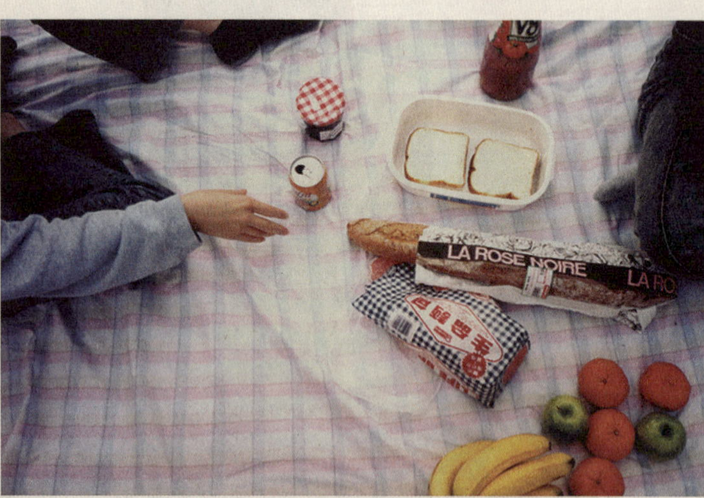

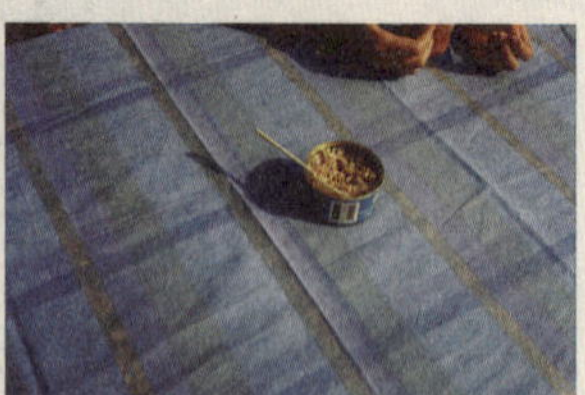

Sunday Afternoon: Picnic with friends and hand-painted cloth at Yung Shu O, Sai Kung, HK. 2003

Acrylic on fabric, photo document

2.

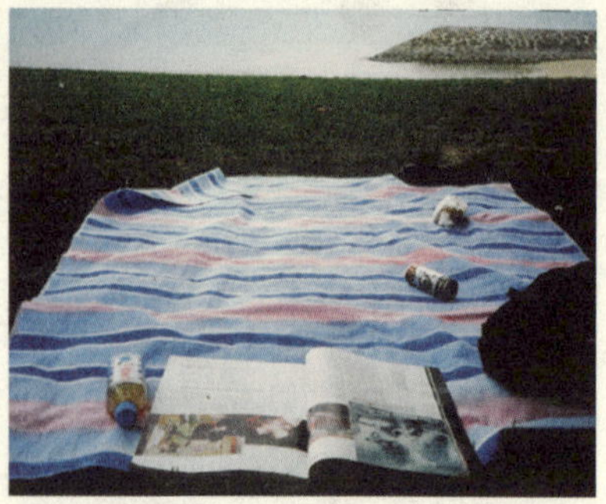

3.

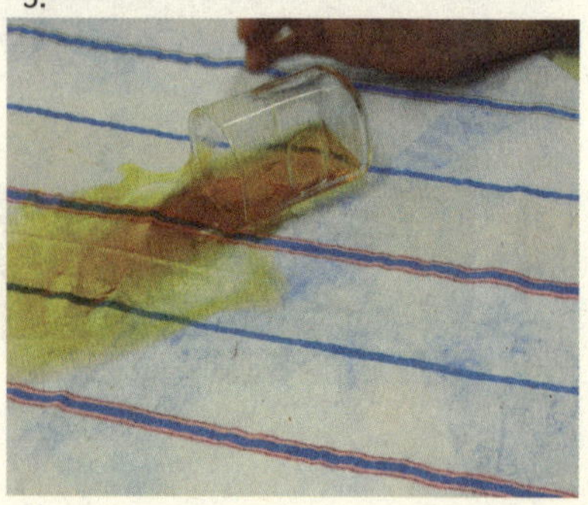

4.

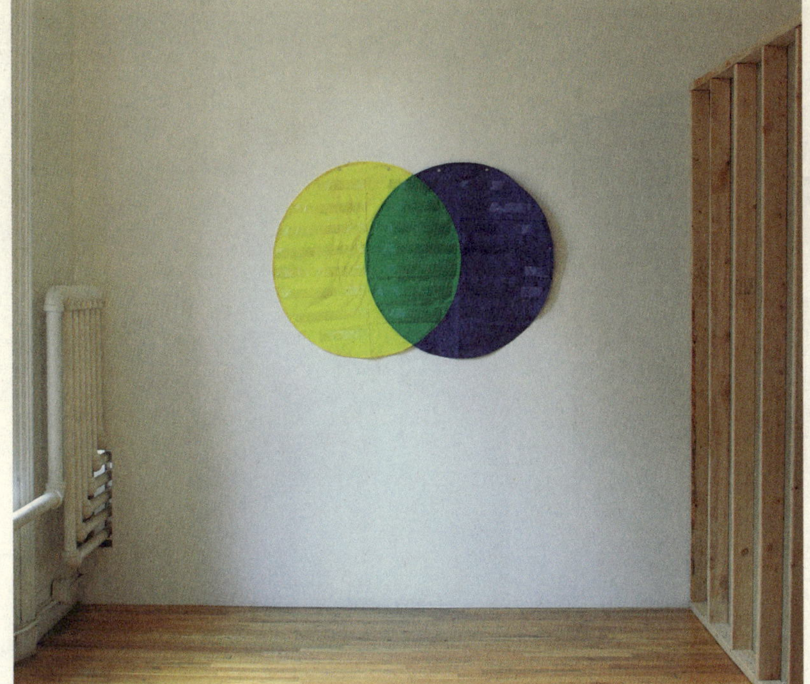

1.

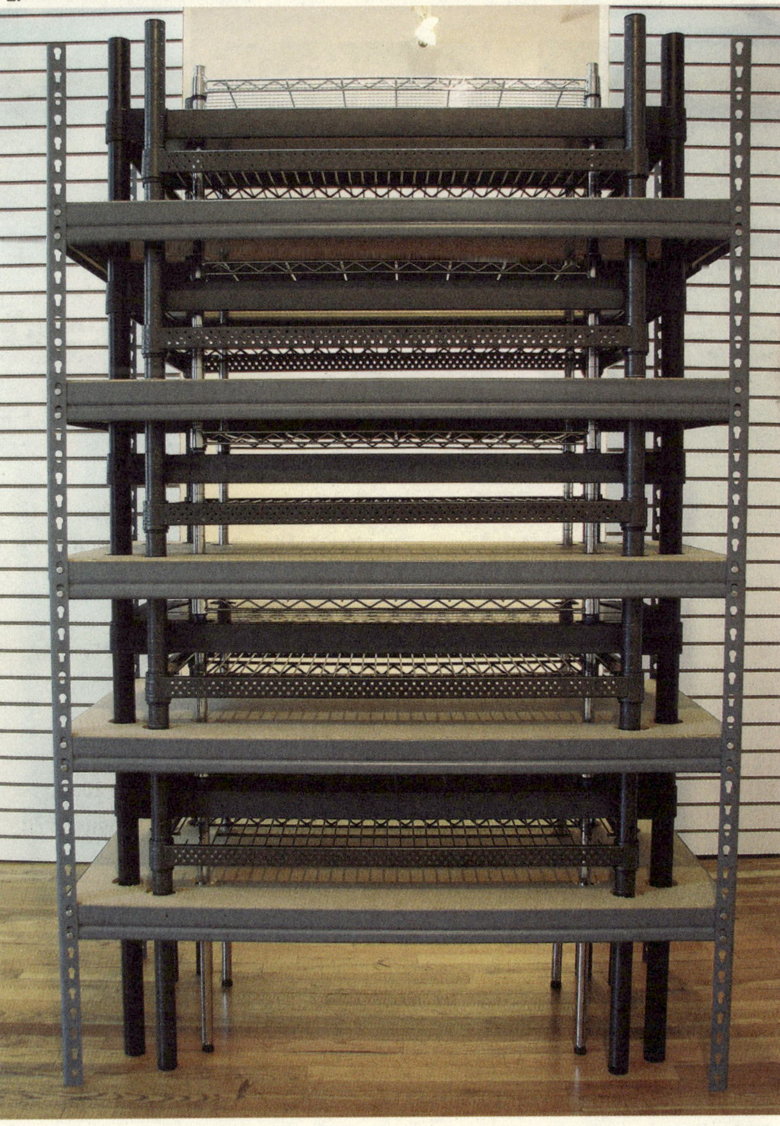

3.

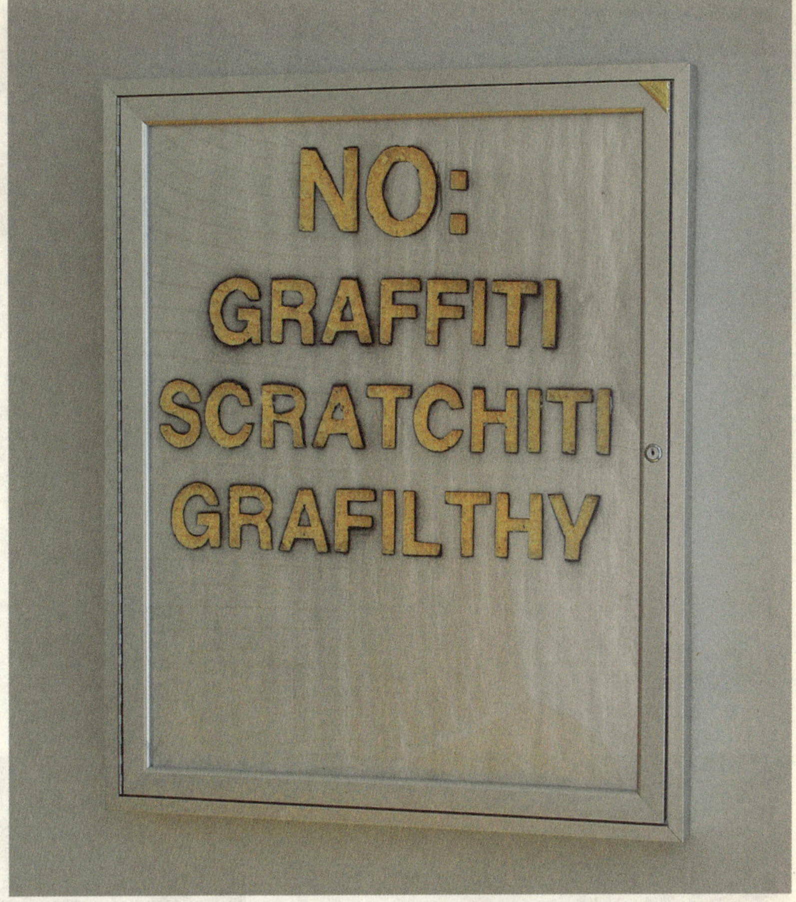

2.

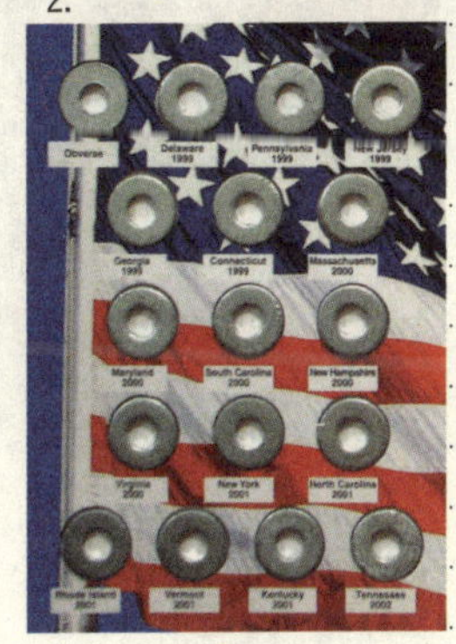

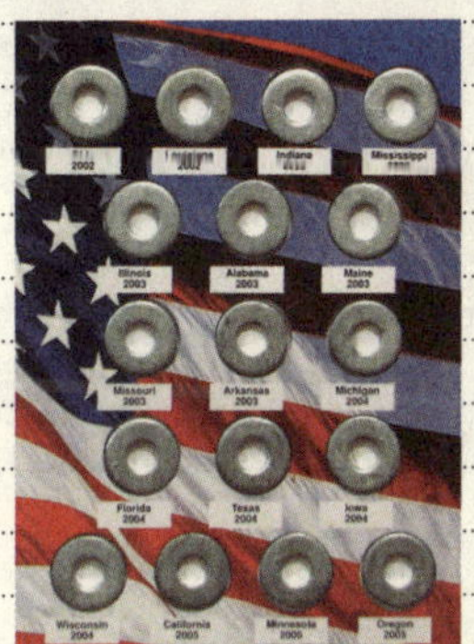

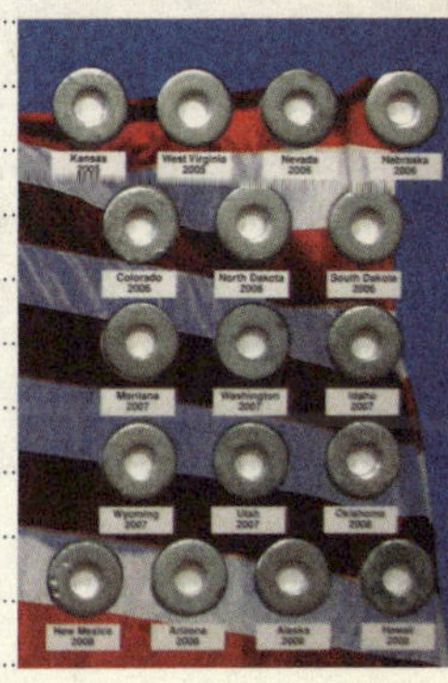

4.

Zak Kitnik studied at Bard College and currently lives and works in Brooklyn. His work is concerned with the processing and presentation of information, often employing mass-produced objects and images in sculptural and photographic tableaux that explore the complex cultural associations of the functional and the decorative.

1. **If Nothing Else, Proof that Fusion is Possible**
2008, nylon and vinyl, 36 × 48 in (91 × 122 cm)

2. **No Stuff**
2008, insulation foam and aluminum frame, 36 × 30 in (91 × 76 cm)

3. **Zuhandenheit**
2008, industrial shelving units, 72 × 48 × 24 in (183 × 122 × 61 cm)

4. **Slugs**
2007, 50-state quarter collection case and washers, 8 × 18 in (20 × 46 cm)

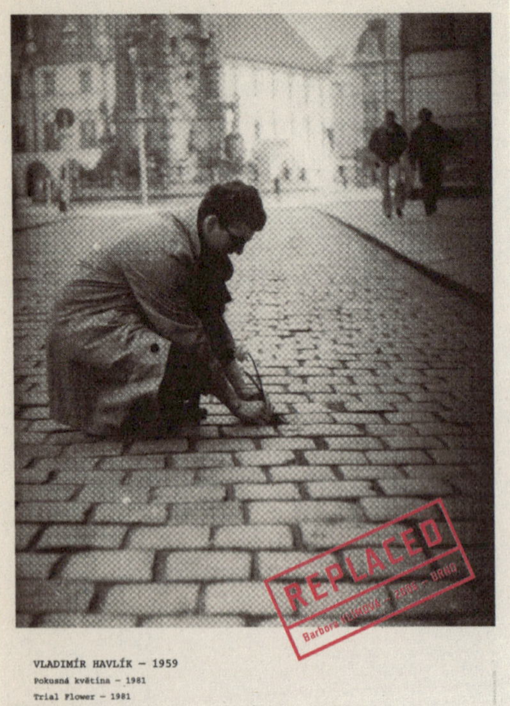

1.

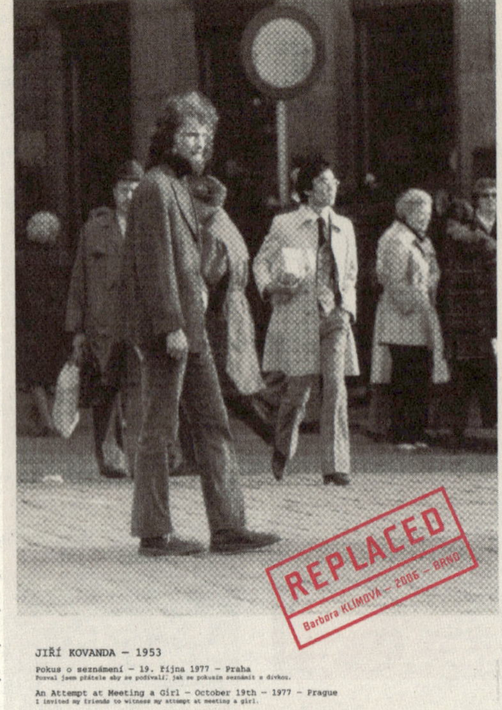

2.

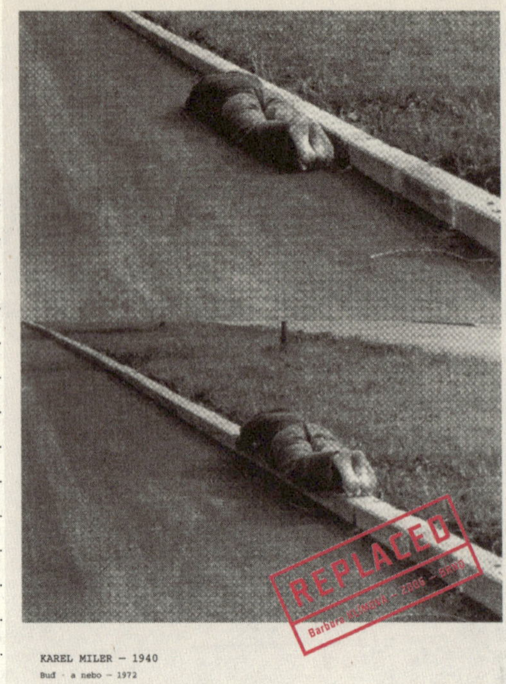

3.

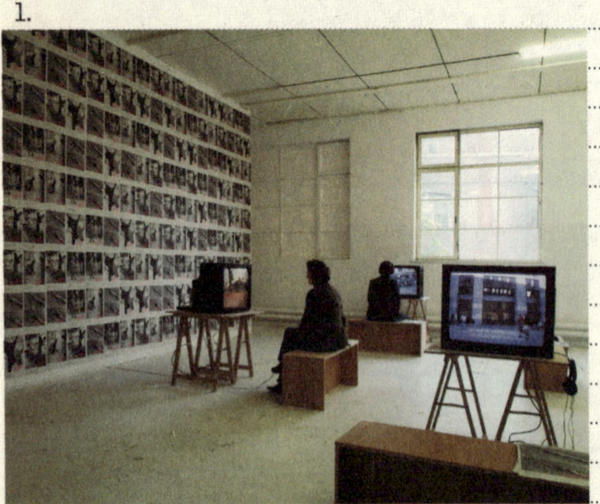

4.

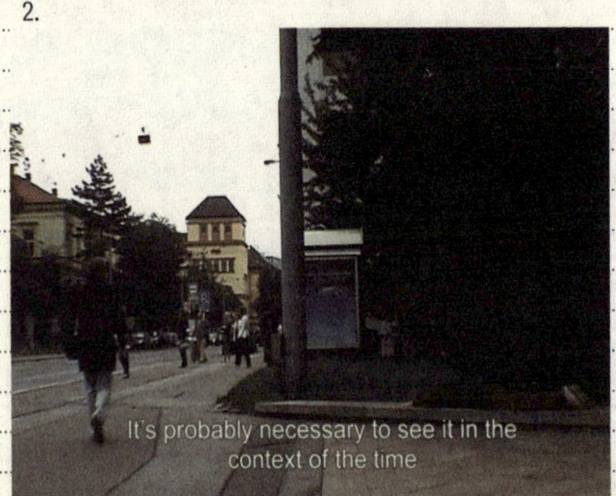

5.

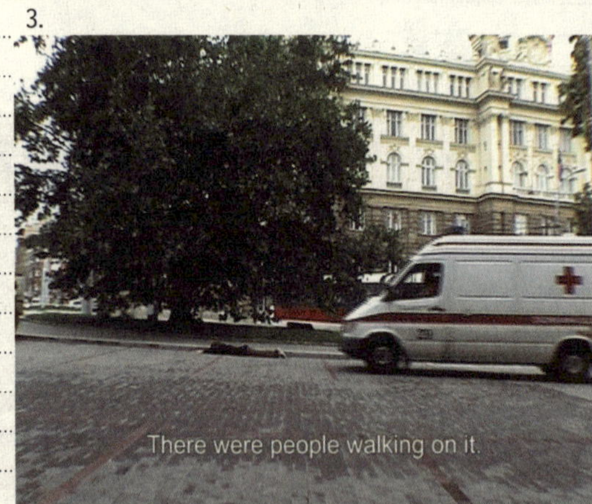

6.

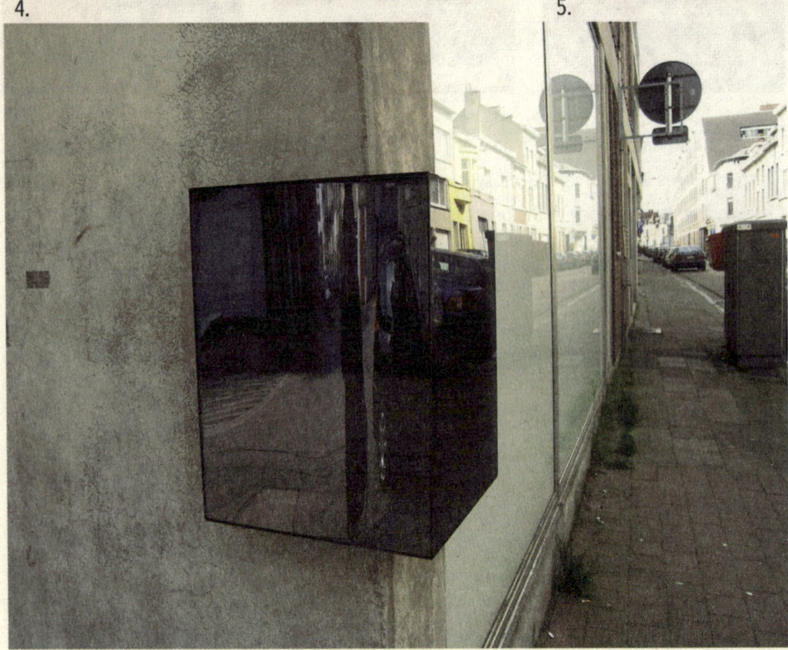

7.

Barbora Klímová lives and works in Sobotovice in the Czech Republic. Her performances, texts, and subtle site-responsive interventions rely on appropriation, allusion, and mimicry to create unexpected rifts in the everyday reality of public space, and suggest research into her homeland's recent political history.

1. **REPLACED – BRNO – 2006. Vladimír Havlík, Trial Flower, Olomouc 1981**
2006, poster, dimensions variable

2. **REPLACED – BRNO – 2006. Jirí Kovanda, An Attempt at Meeting a Girl, Prague 19th October 1977**
2006, poster, dimensions variable

3. **REPLACED – BRNO – 2006. Karel Miler, Either-Or, Prague 1972**
2006, poster, dimensions variable

4. **REPLACED – BRNO – 2006.**
2006, 5-channel video installation and posters on paper, dimensions variable

5 & 6. **REPLACED – BRNO – 2006. Karel Miler, Either-Or, Prague 1972**
2006, video, 4 min 31 sec

7. **Object for looking around a corner**
2006, plastic, $4\frac{3}{4} \times 19\frac{3}{4} \times 27\frac{1}{2}$ in (12 × 50 × 70 cm), installation view

Terence Koh earned his BA from the Emily Carr Institute of Art and Design in Vancouver, where he was raised, and currently lives in New York City. He first became known for his website and zine **asianpunkboy** and now works primarily in photography, sculpture, and installation. Much of his work investigates race, gender, sexuality, and queer culture.

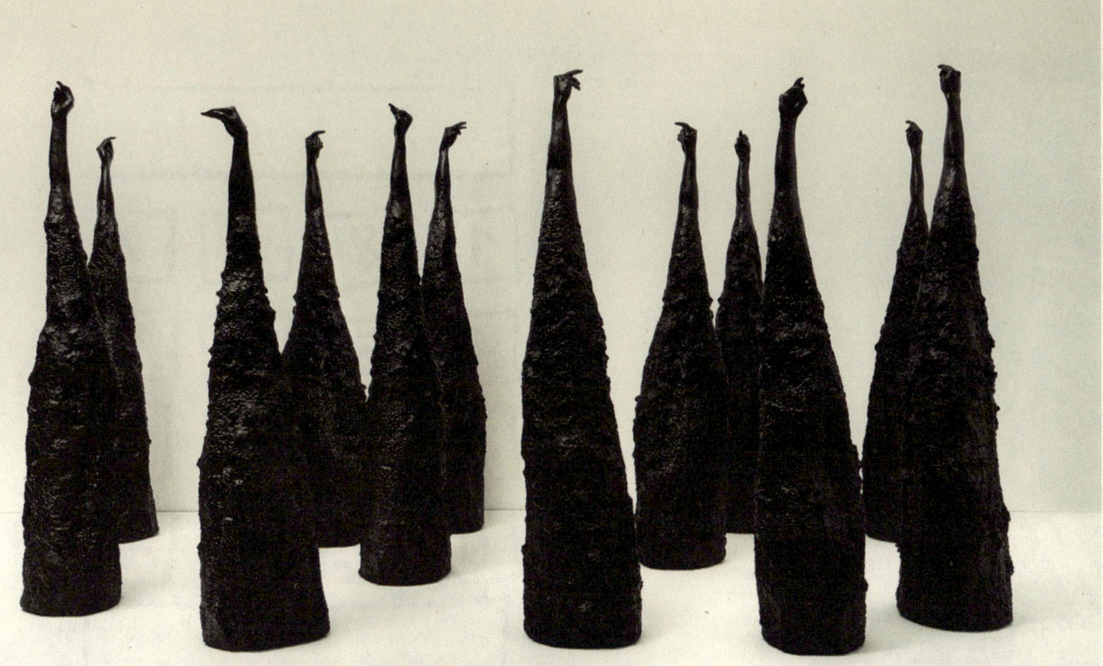

1.

1. My Path to Heaven, You Blind Bastard God
2007, wax, Styrofoam, plaster, paint, remnants of incense sticks, mineral oil, and Eau d'Orange Verte by Hermès, dimensions variable

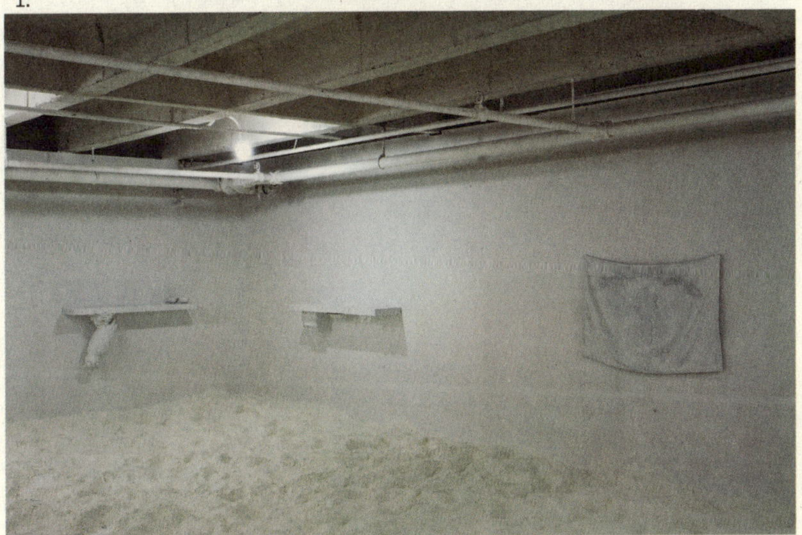

2.

2. The Whole Family
2008, bronze, aluminum, steel, magnesium, and automotive paint, dimensions variable

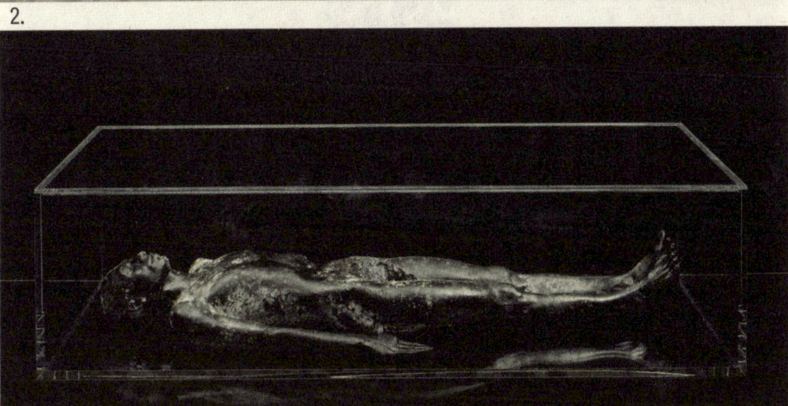

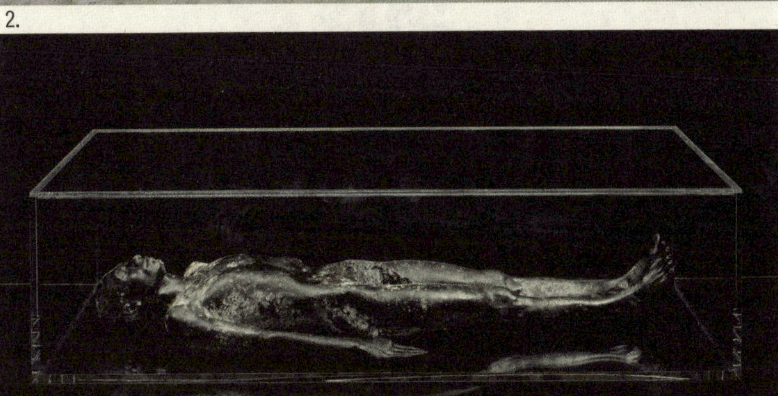

3.

3. Snow Black 1
2007, plaster cast of artist's body, nylon, wax, paint, hermetically sealed Plexiglas box, crushed ants, and mold, 21 × 78 ¾ × 30 in (54 × 200 × 71 cm)

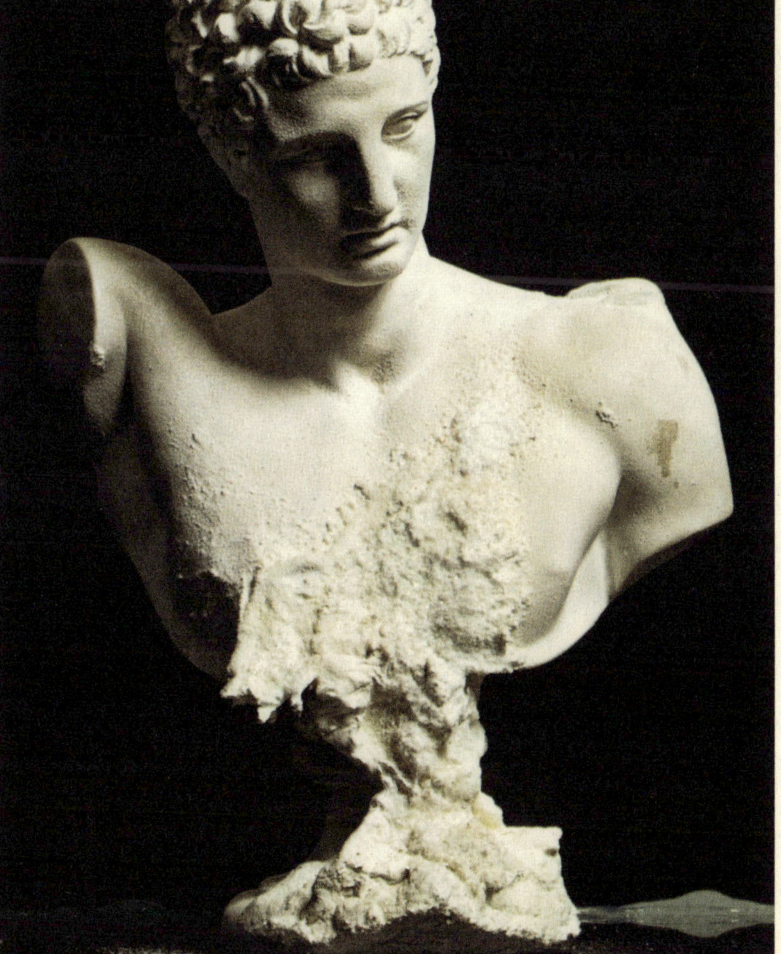

4.

4. Cokehead
2006, diamond dust, sugar, paint, and plaster sculpture enclosed in glass vitrine, 23 ¾ × 13 ¾ × 13 ¾ in (60 × 35 × 35 cm)

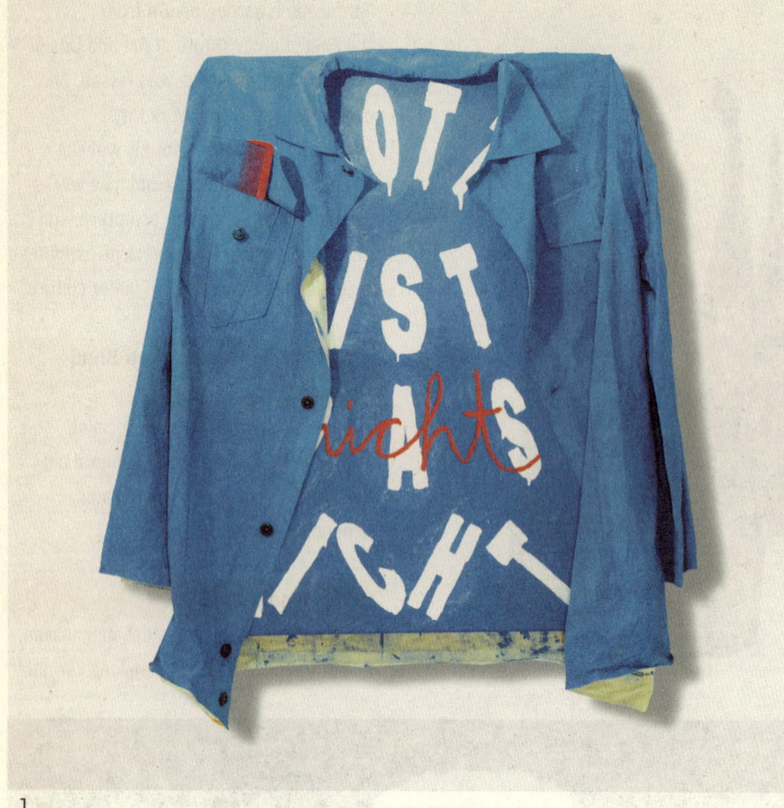

1.

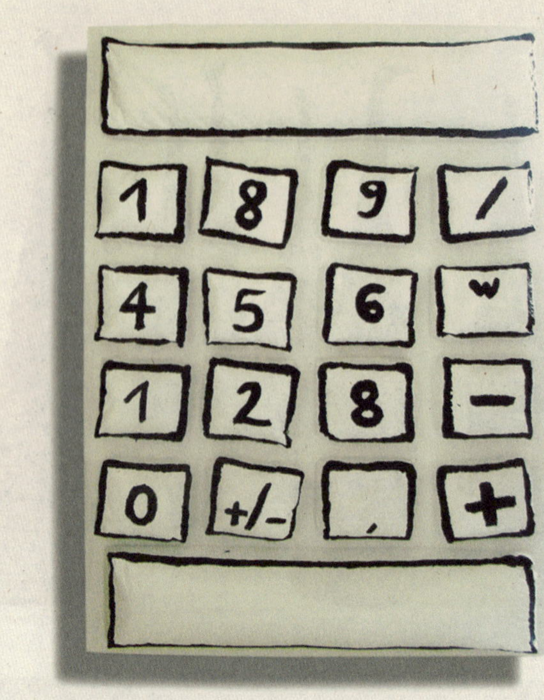

2.

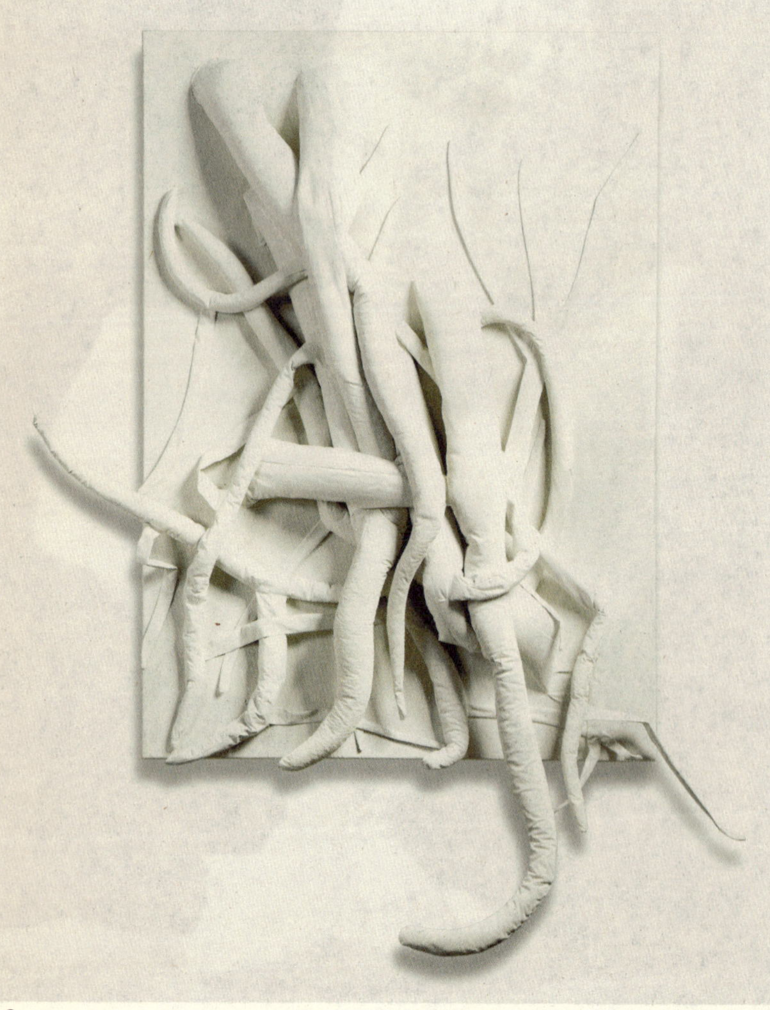

3.

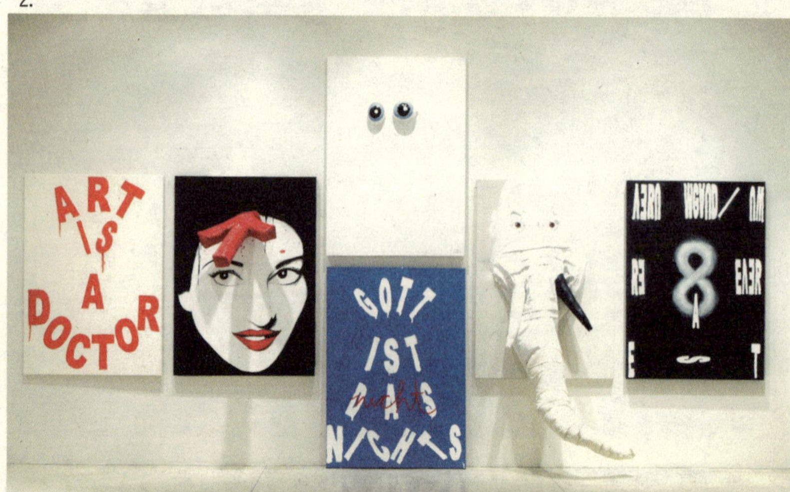

4.

Vienna-based Zenita Komad works in installation, painting, "sculptural painting," film, and even opera. Her practice evidences a panoramic range of influences, combining the "sincere irony" of Pop art with the heartfelt theatricality of the Viennese Actionists in an ongoing investigation of spirituality and desire.

1. god in jeans jacket
2005-08, mixed media and acrylic on canvas, 63 × 43 1/2 × 4 in (160 × 110 × 10 cm)

2. aus göttlicher quelle hilfreiche kraft
2008, mixed media and acrylic on canvas, 59 × 43 1/2 × 4 in (150 × 110 × 10 cm)

3. Weisse Wurzel
2006, mixed media and oil on canvas, 71 × 51 1/4 × 12 in (180 × 130 × 30 cm)

4. "Zenita Komad"
exhibition view at Galerie Krinzinger, Vienna (2006)

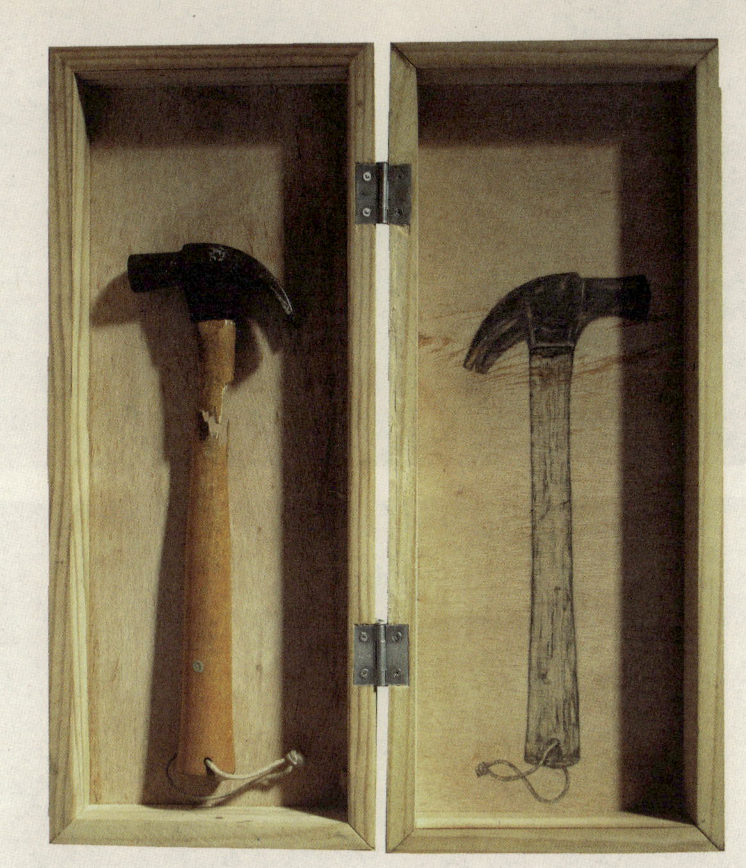

1.

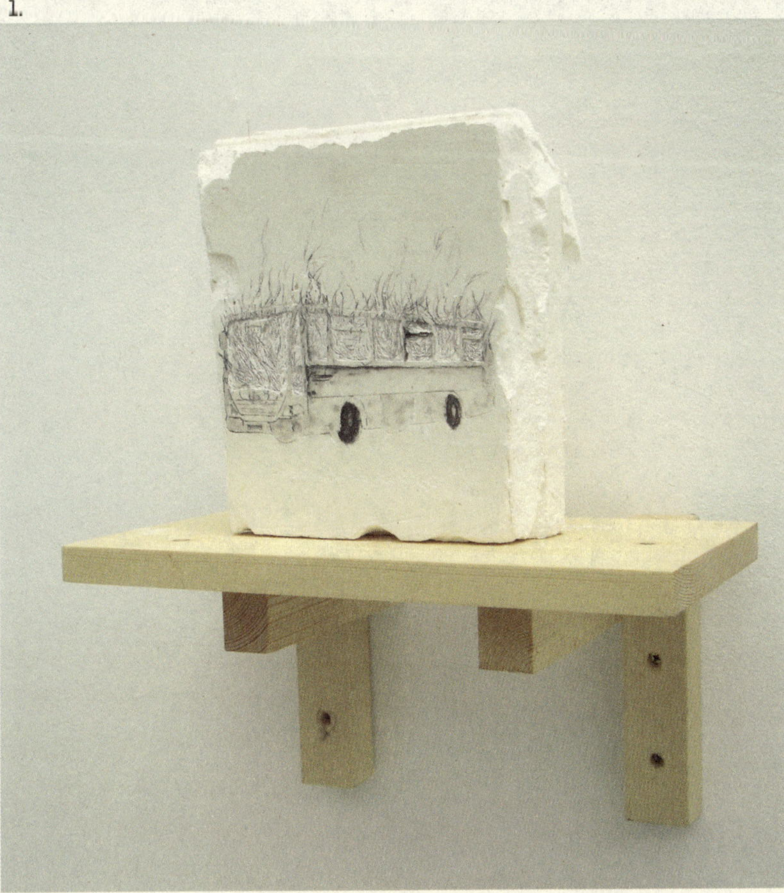

2.

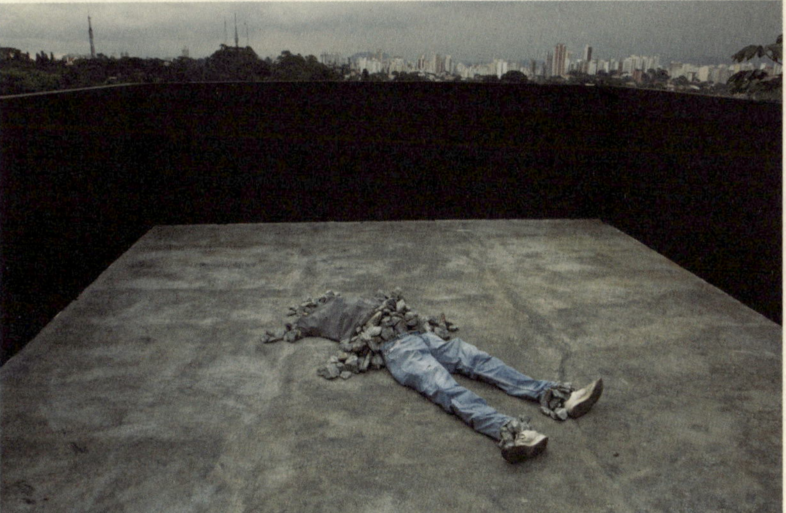

3.

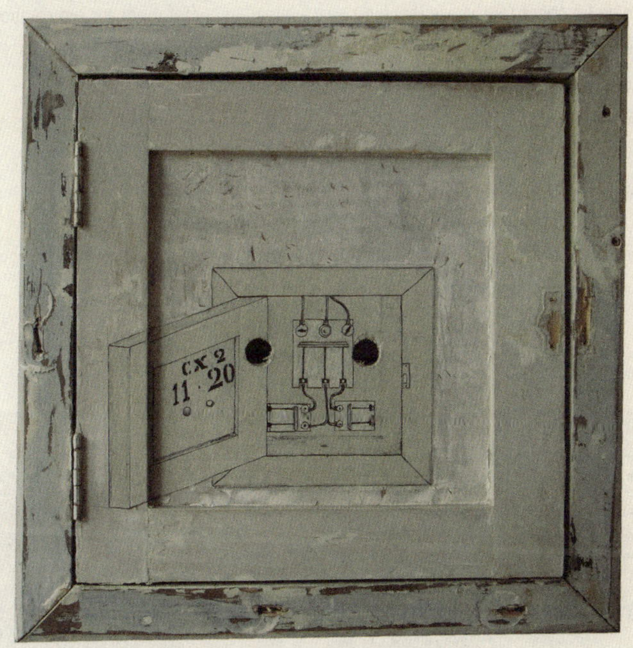

4.

André Komatsu creates drawings, sculptures, videos, and installations that address the construction and destruction of urban space. In **West or Until Where the Sun Can Reach**, a video work from 2006, he navigates São Paulo using a compass, taking the most direct possible path west, regardless of physical or legal obstacles. Alternately, his sculpture **Concrete Dissemination** (2006) consists of his discarded clothes stuffed with rubble from building sites in the city. In this way he draws a parallel between the city and the body, both impermanent and subject to disintegration.

1. **Suspension**
2005, wood, graphite, and hammer,
20 ½ × 17 ½ × 4 in (52 × 44 × 10 cm)

2. **Um Dia de Glória II**
from the series **Refluzo Sazonal**
2008, plaster fragment and wood,
10 ¼ × 18 ¼ × 4 ¾ in (26 × 46 × 12 cm)

3. **Concrete Dissemination**
2006, installation, dimensions variable

4. **Power Box**
from the series **Inserted**
2005, drawing on wood,
15 ¾ × 15 ¾ × 1 ¼ in (40 × 40 × 3 cm)

KONATÉ, MOHAMED

b. 1978 Bamako, Mali

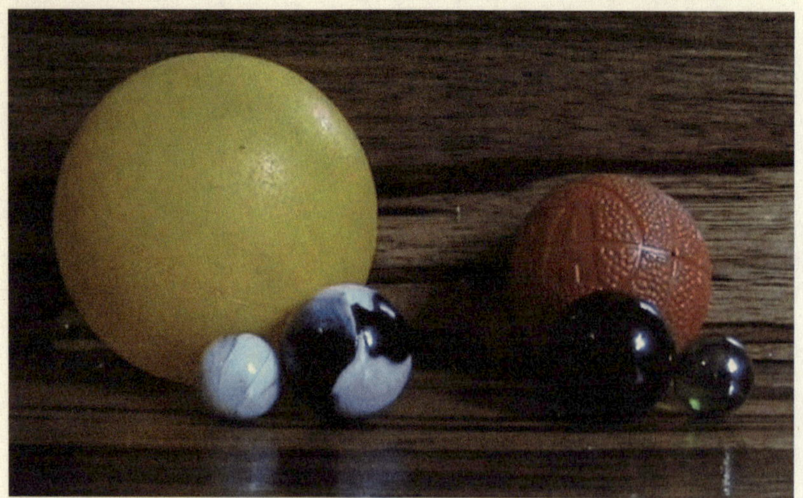

1.

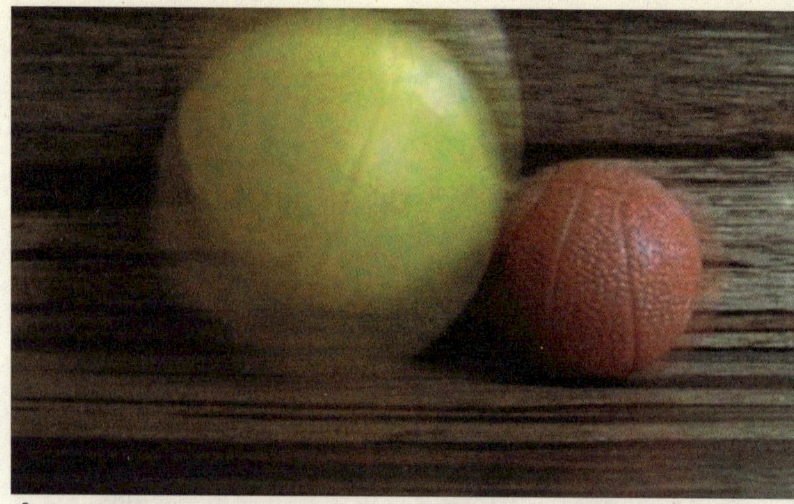

2.

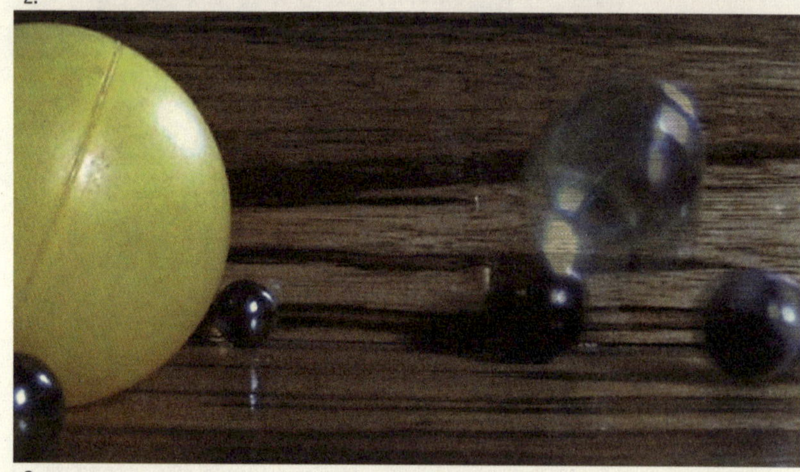

3.

Mohamed Konaté studied fine arts at the National Institute of Arts in Bamako, after which he spent four years teaching fine arts at the Teacher Training Institute in Gao, Mali. In 2005 he attended Balla Fasseke Kouyate Conservatoire of Arts and Crafts, studying multimedia. Konaté's videos, paintings, and photographs celebrate the nuances of everyday materials, focusing on minute details and small accidents. In work such as **Attraction** he analyzes the chance encounter between marbles and a balloon, used as a metaphor for the relationships that regulate society.

1, 2 & 3. **Attraction**

2008, video, 2 min 30 sec

4. **Djé** (Union)

2008, video, 1 min 8 sec

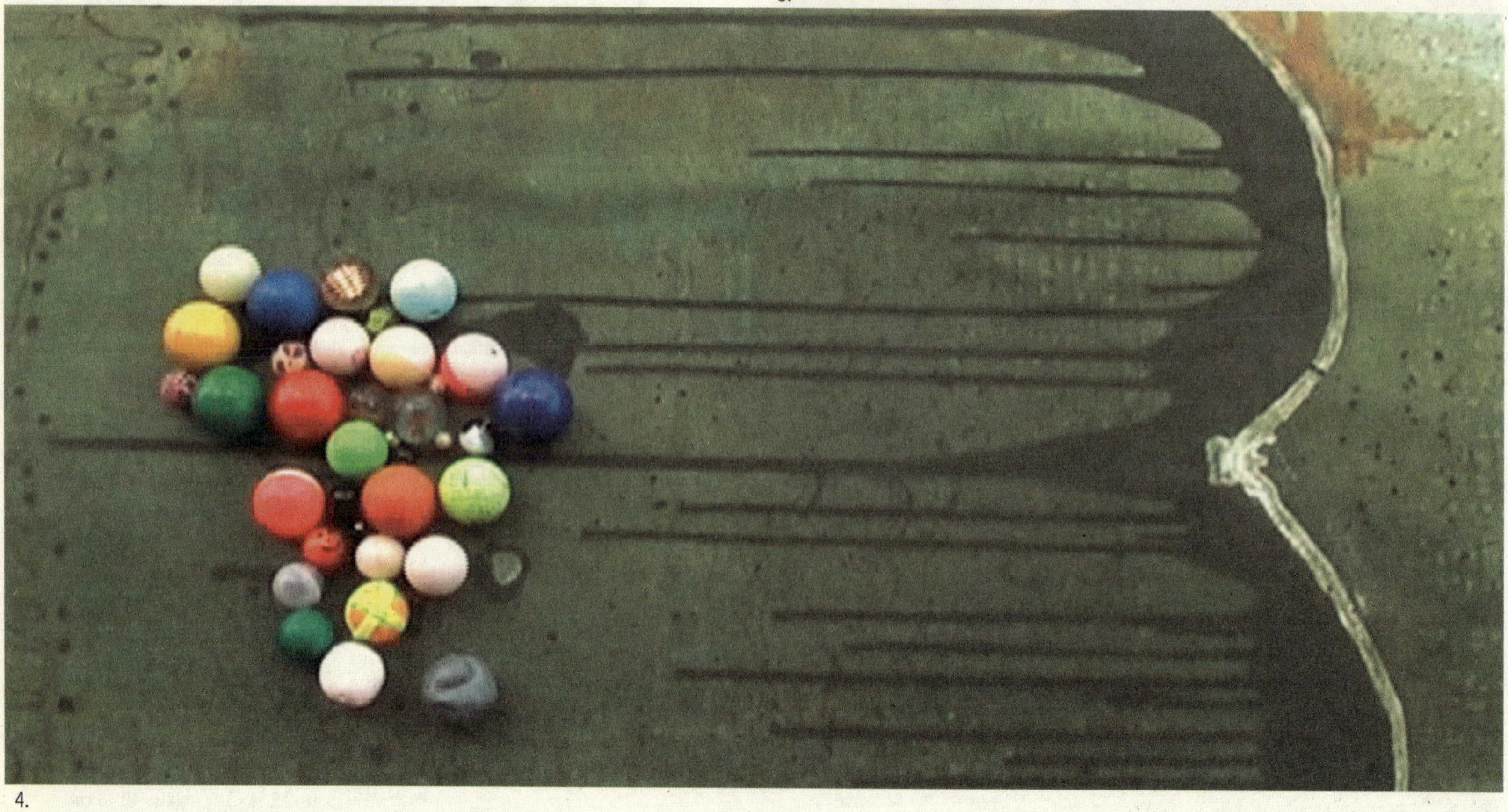

4.

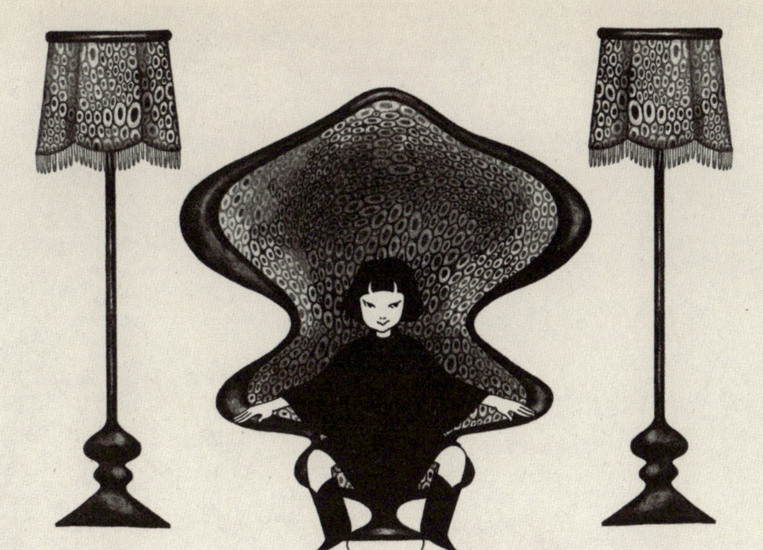

1.

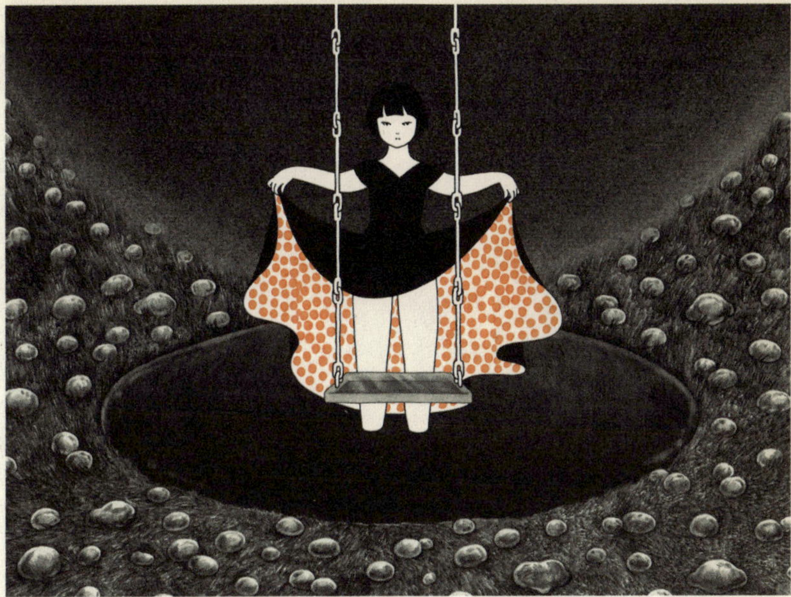

2.

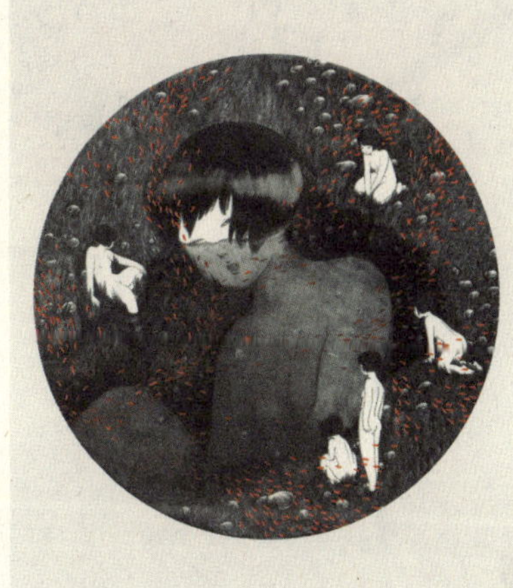

3.

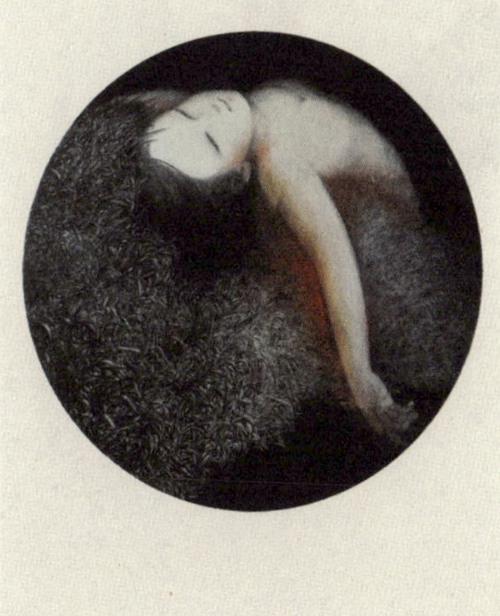

4.

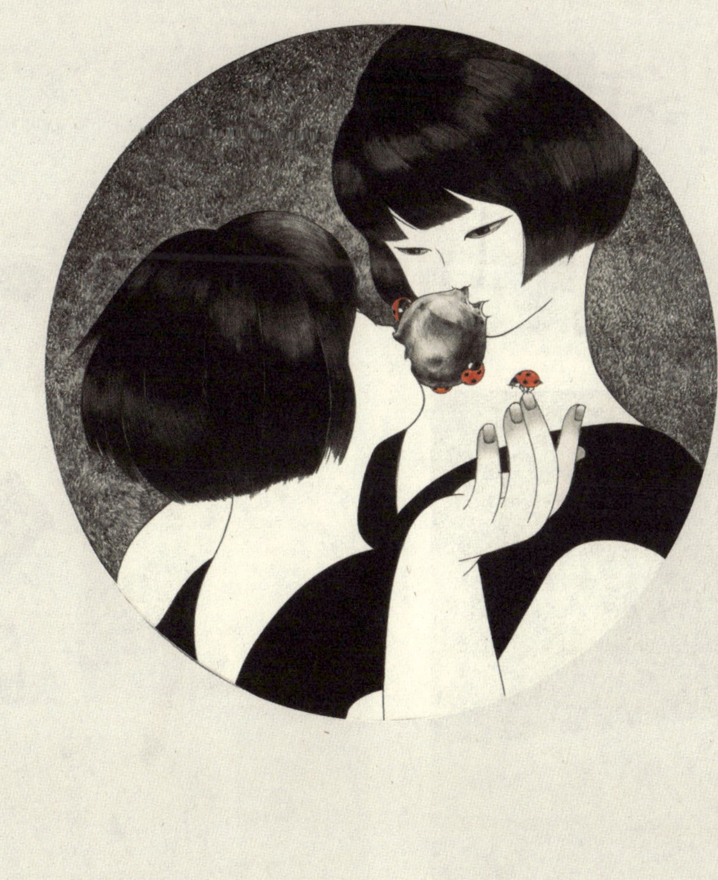

5.

During high school, Kondoh Akino produced a comic book called **Memoirs of a High School Girl**. She now works in various mediums, including acrylic, pastel, and graphite, using delicate lines and sultry color to create figurative drawings whose cuteness is deftly undercut by their quirkiness. Akino also combines her illustrations in Photoshop and adds motion with After Effects to make videos. **Ladybirds' Requiem** is a graphic-driven, non-narrative, pattern-heavy video in which a girl encounters a cat, ladybugs, buttons, clover, and ribbons in a phantasmagorical sequence of events, set to music by Tokashi Chiku, former member of the band Tama.

1. **The Evening Traveling**
2001-02, video, 3 min 56 sec

2. **Ladybirds' Requiem**
2005-06, video, 5 min 38 sec

3. **I hear the beat of the night vol.2**
2005, acrylic and pencil on gesso mounted on board, diameter 10 in (25 cm)

4. **Extra Scene from Ladybirds' Requiem**
2007, graphite, pastel, and acrylic on gesso mounted on canvas, diameter 27 ½ in (70 cm)

5. **Ladybirds' Requiem 2-10-02**
2006, graphite and acrylic on gesso mounted on board, diameter 10 in (25 cm)

KOSCHMIEDER, ANDREI

b. 1980 Frankfurt, Germany

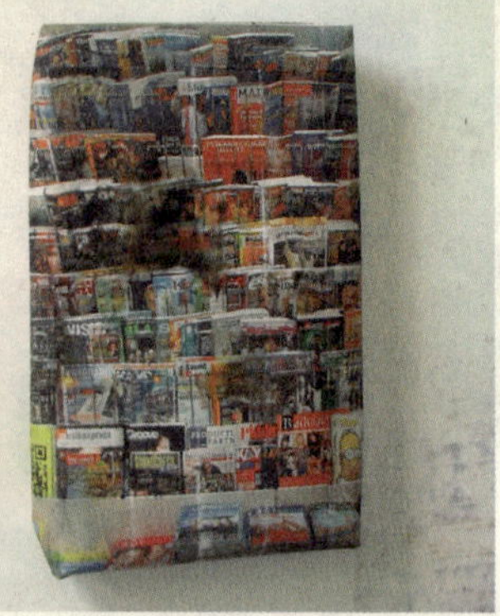

1.

Andrei Koschmieder studied at the Academy of Arts in Frankfurt. His work has been exhibited in group shows throughout Germany and in London. In 2006 he received the city of Rüsselsheim scholarship and in 2008 he won the Ermenegildo Zegna travel scholarship. He primarily works with photographs, layering drawings and graffiti on top of images, and using words and symbols to alter the meaning of the original sources.

1. Mattress

2008, inkjet print on cardboard,
61 × 41 ½ × 10 in (155 × 105 × 25 cm)

2, 3 & 4. **Untitled**

2008, inkjet print on found image,
8 × 12 in (20 × 30 cm)

5. **In My Pocket**

2008, inkjet print on silk scarf,
35 ½ × 35 ½ in (90 × 90 cm)

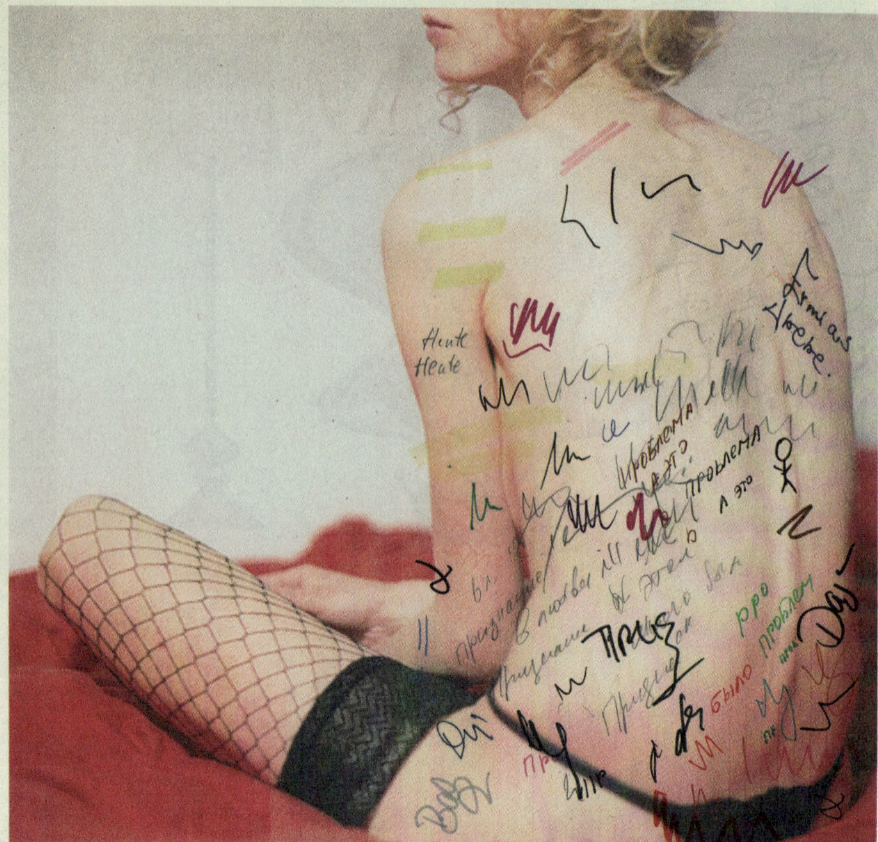

2.

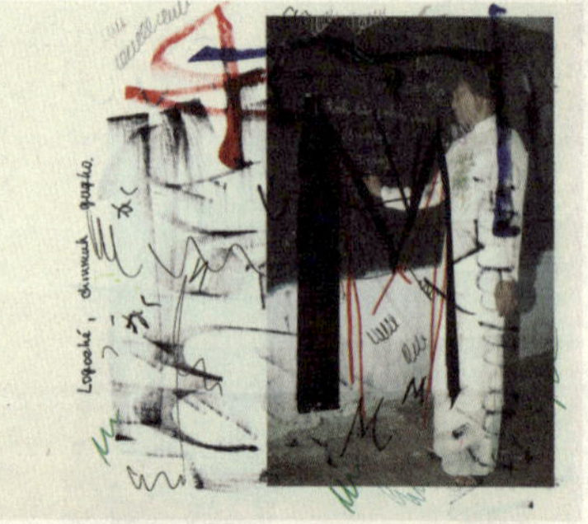

3.

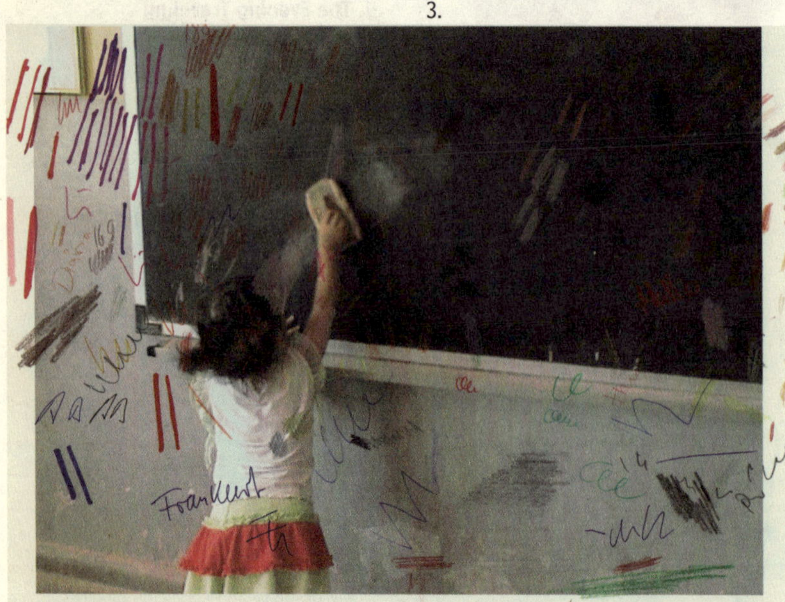

4.

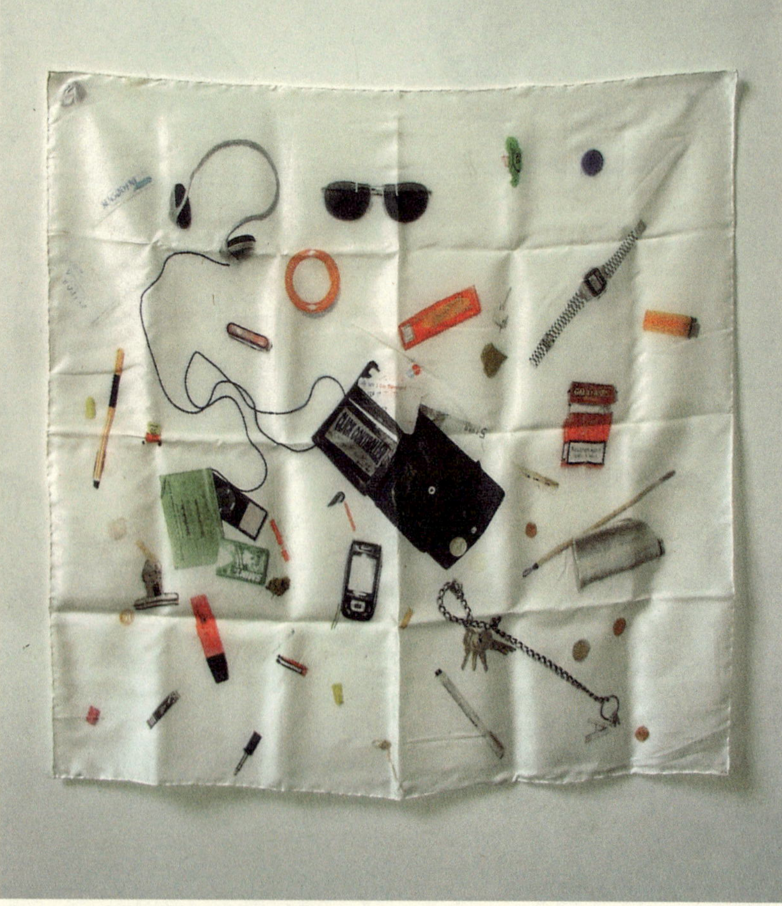

5.

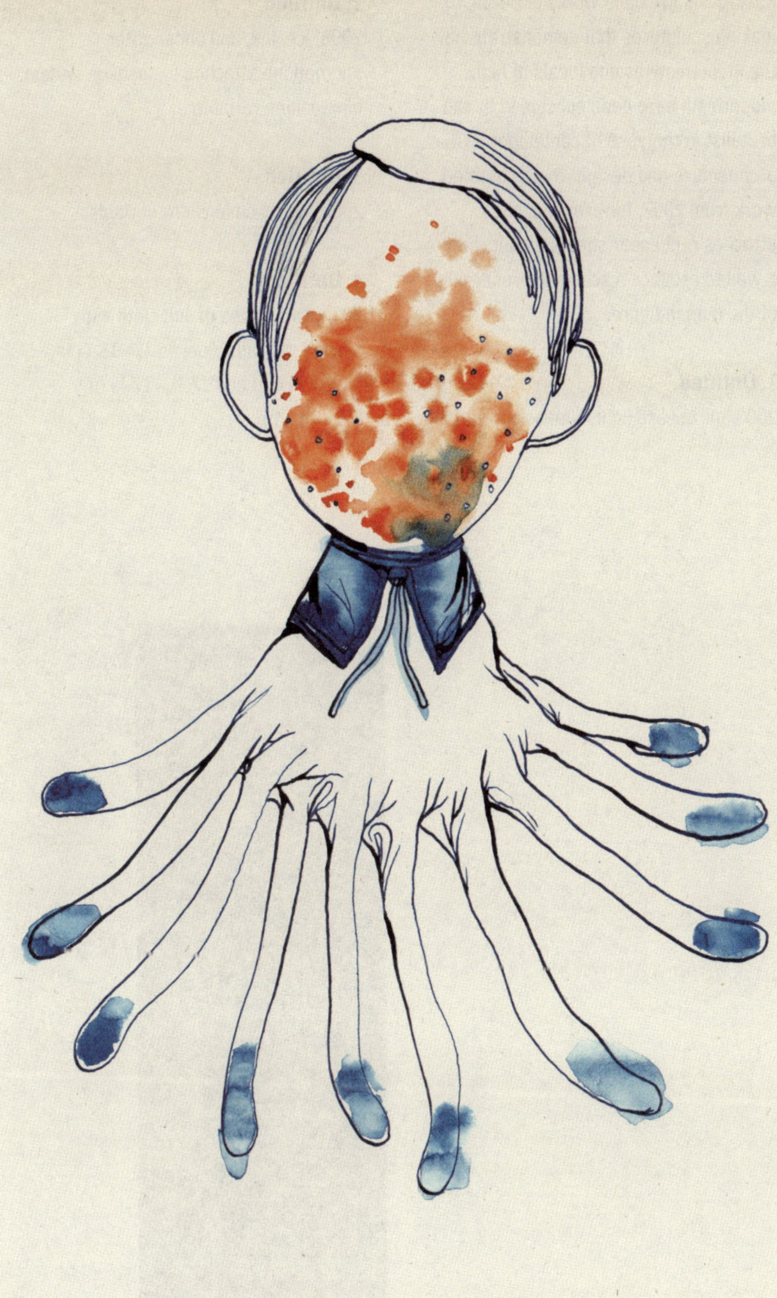

1.

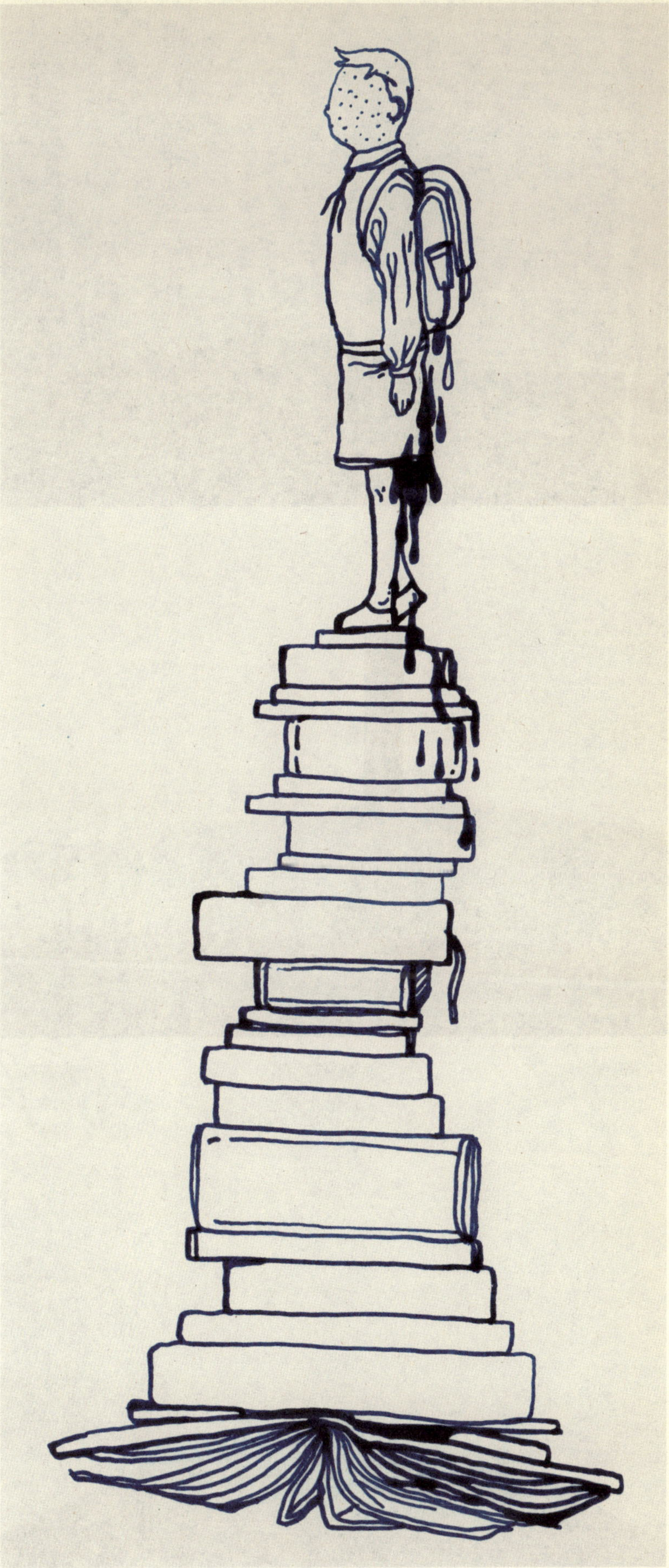

Eva Kotátková was educated at the Academy of Fine Arts and the Academy of Applied Arts in Prague as well as the San Francisco Art Institute. Her installations, drawings, sculptures, and performances interrogate the mechanisms, rituals, and objects of everyday life. Her series of **Set-Ups** (2006-07), for instance, recontextualize common household items to create unexpected sculptural arrangements. Kotátková's work is also frequently endurance-based, as in her video **1 Hour Without Movement** (2006), in which she glued herself to the middle of a sidewalk and functioned as a "life obstacle" for an hour.

1. **Untitled**
from the series **Walk to School**
2008, pen and ink on paper, collage, watercolor, 16 1/2 x 12 in (42 × 30 cm)

2. **Untitled**
from the series **Walk to School**
2008, pen and ink on paper, collage, watercolor, 16 1/2 × 12 in (42 × 30 cm)

2.

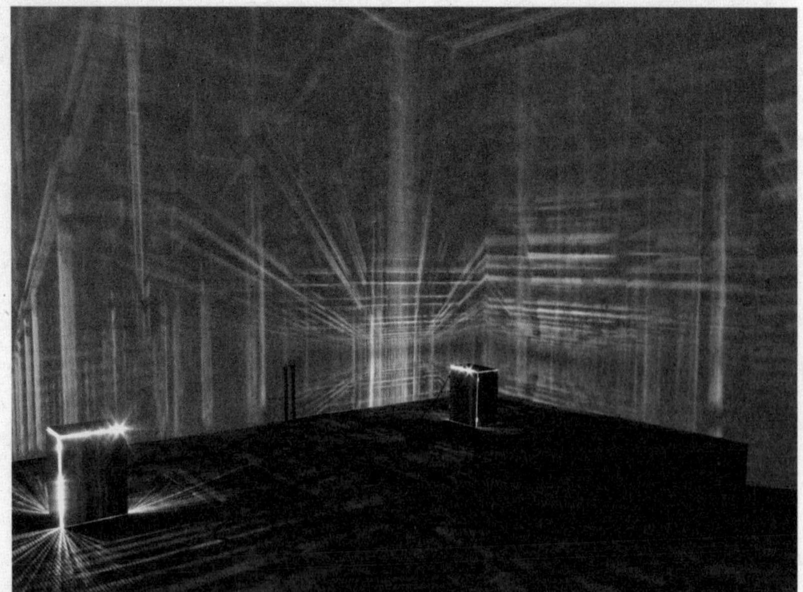
1.

Kitty Kraus lives and works in Berlin, making sculptures that demonstrate how the utopian myths and ideals of high modernism have been subsumed by the brutalist archetypes of contemporary architecture and design. In one untitled work from 2007, for example, she attaches rectilinear sheets of suit cloth to a wall to produce a schematic rendering of the human figure.

1. **Untitled**
2008, mirror and light, dimensions variable

2. **Untitled**
2008, ice, ink, and underwater microphone attached to speaker system, dimensions variable

3. **Untitled**
2008, glass, dimensions variable

4. **Untitled**
2007, two pieces of suit cloth with black 9 mm pinstripe, $46\frac{1}{2} \times 13\frac{1}{4}$ in (119 × 34 cm) and $27\frac{3}{4} \times 17\frac{1}{4}$ in (70 × 44 cm)

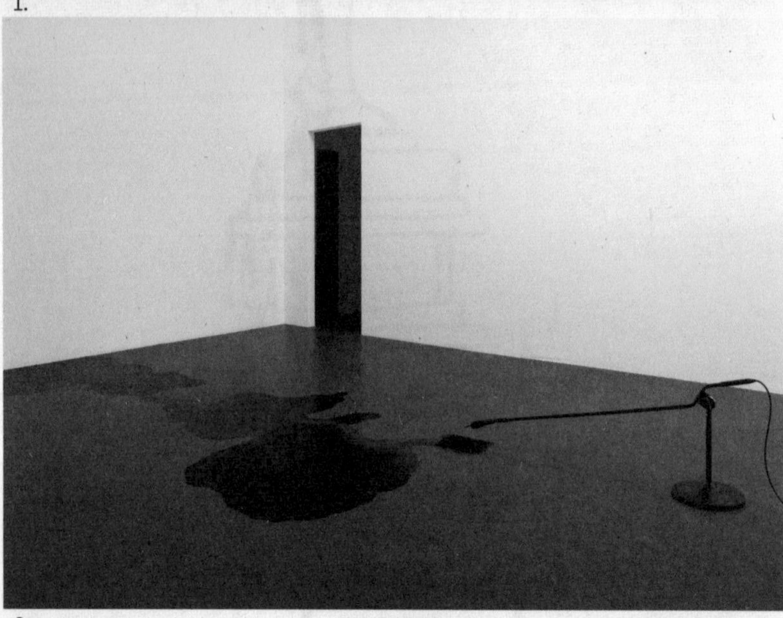
2.

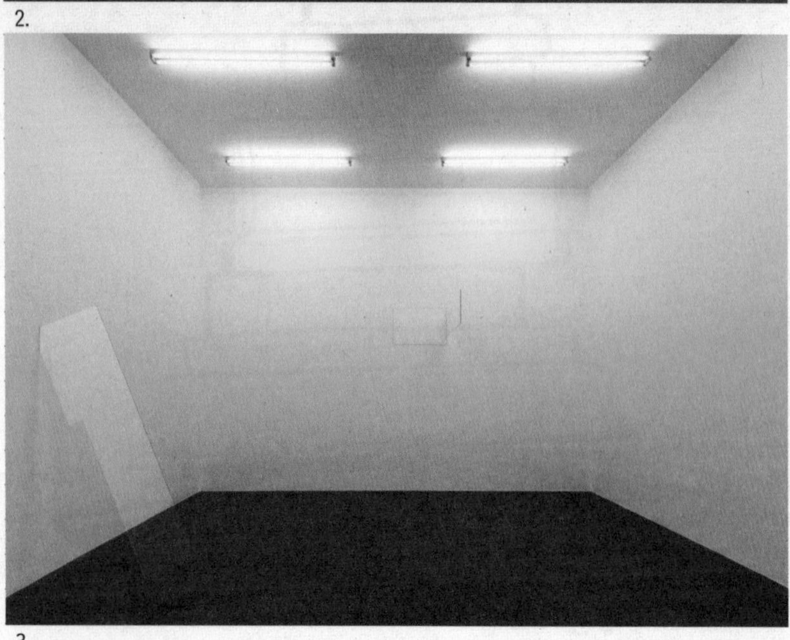
3.

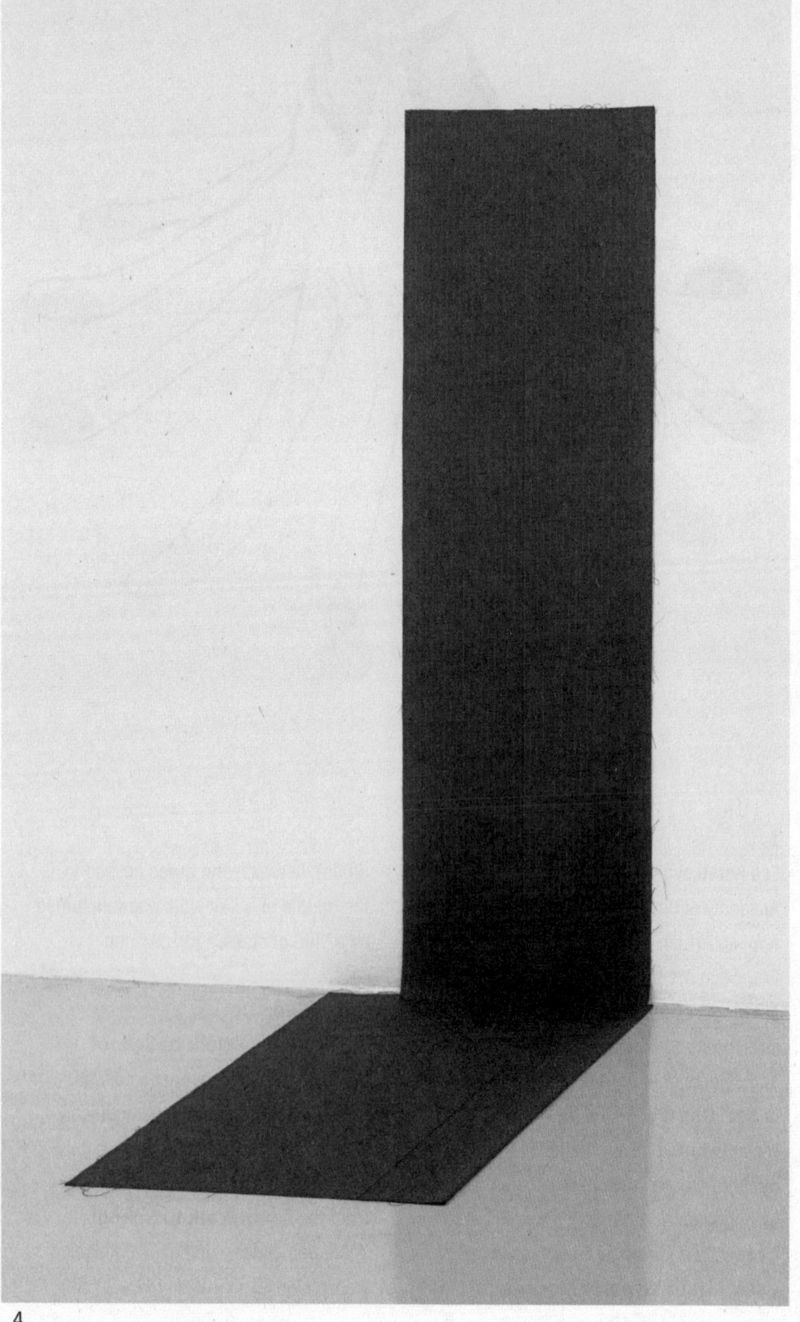
4.

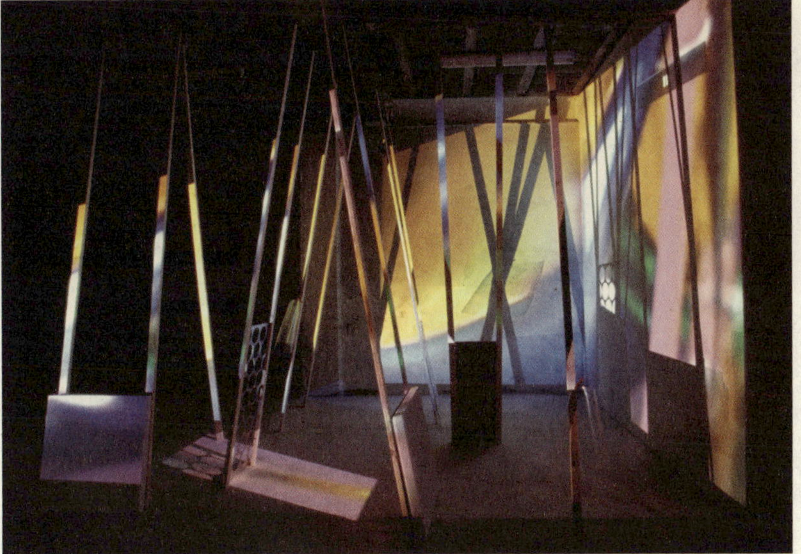
1.

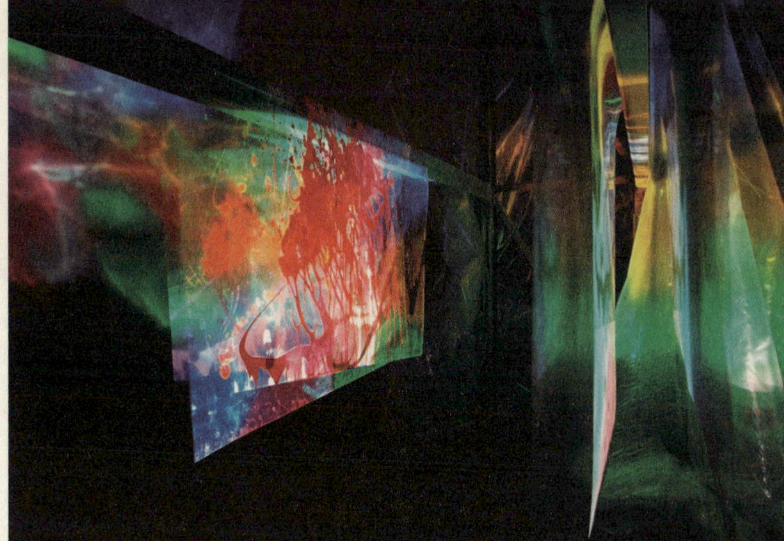
2.

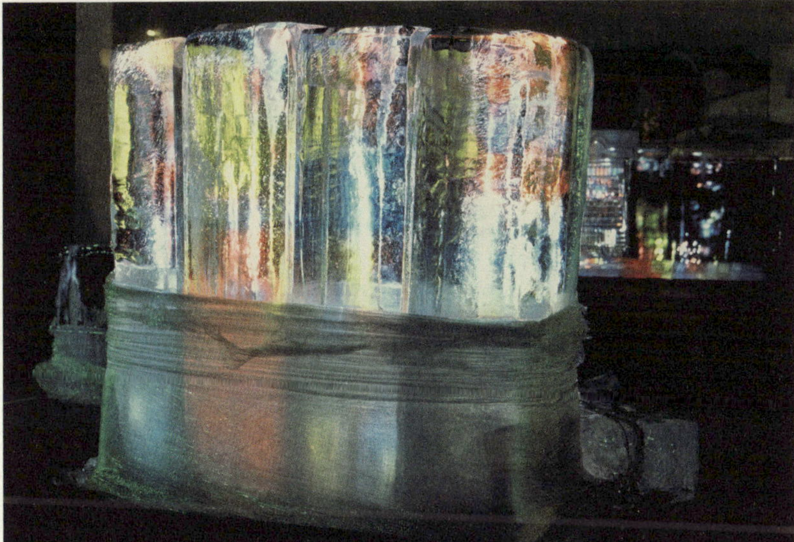
3.

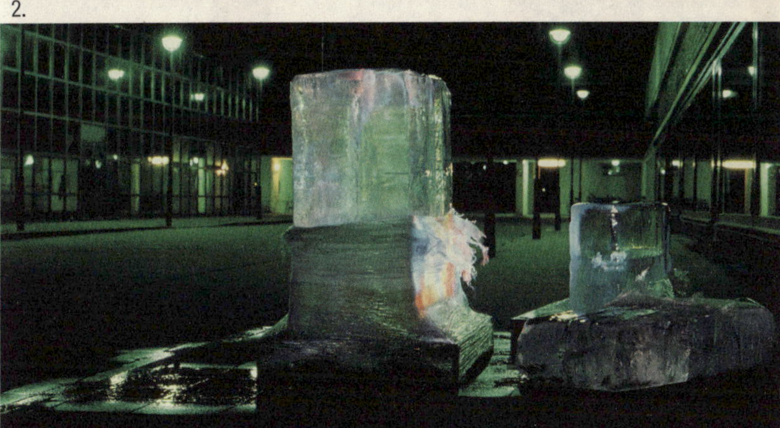
4.

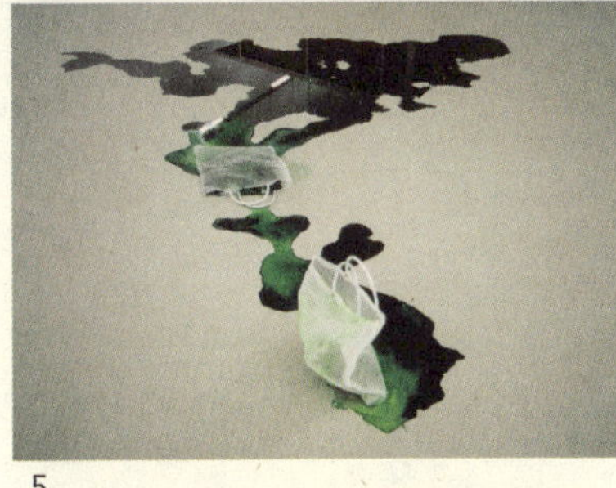
5.

Schirin Kretschmann lives and works in Berlin and has studied fine arts at Staatliche Akademie der Bildenden Künste Karlsruhe and the Universität Basel. Her practice explores the contemporary discourse of painting as it pertains to the moving image, three-dimensional space, and time; her works are mainly abstract, formally defined sculptural in situ installations built into public and institutional spaces, in which her artworks are understood as ephemeral occurrences that depend on spectators' subjective points of view. For **Solo hoy (mañana tambien)** (2007), for instance, Kretschmann filled several bags with colored ice that, as it melted, spread across the gallery floor, and eventually dried.

1. **Pink**
2006, video, projector, roof battens, and mixed media, dimensions variable

2. **Movil**
2005, video, projector, and mixed media, dimensions variable

3 & 4. **Lauro**
2006, video, projector, ice blocks, and polyethylene foil, dimensions variable

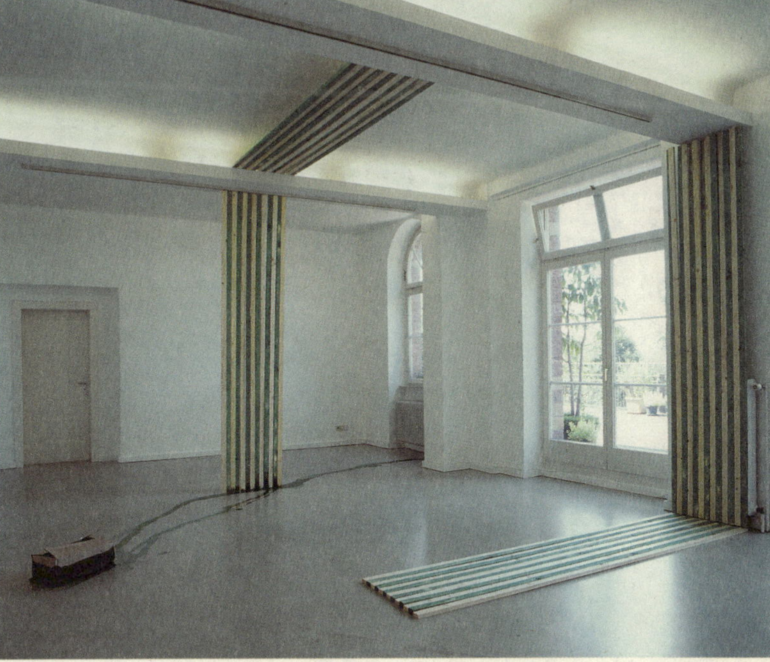
6.

5. **Solo hoy (mañana tambien)**
2007, colored ice and woven plastic bags, dimensions variable

6. **Alameda**
2007, untreated and green impregnated wooden roof battens, cardboard box, and colored ice, dimensions variable

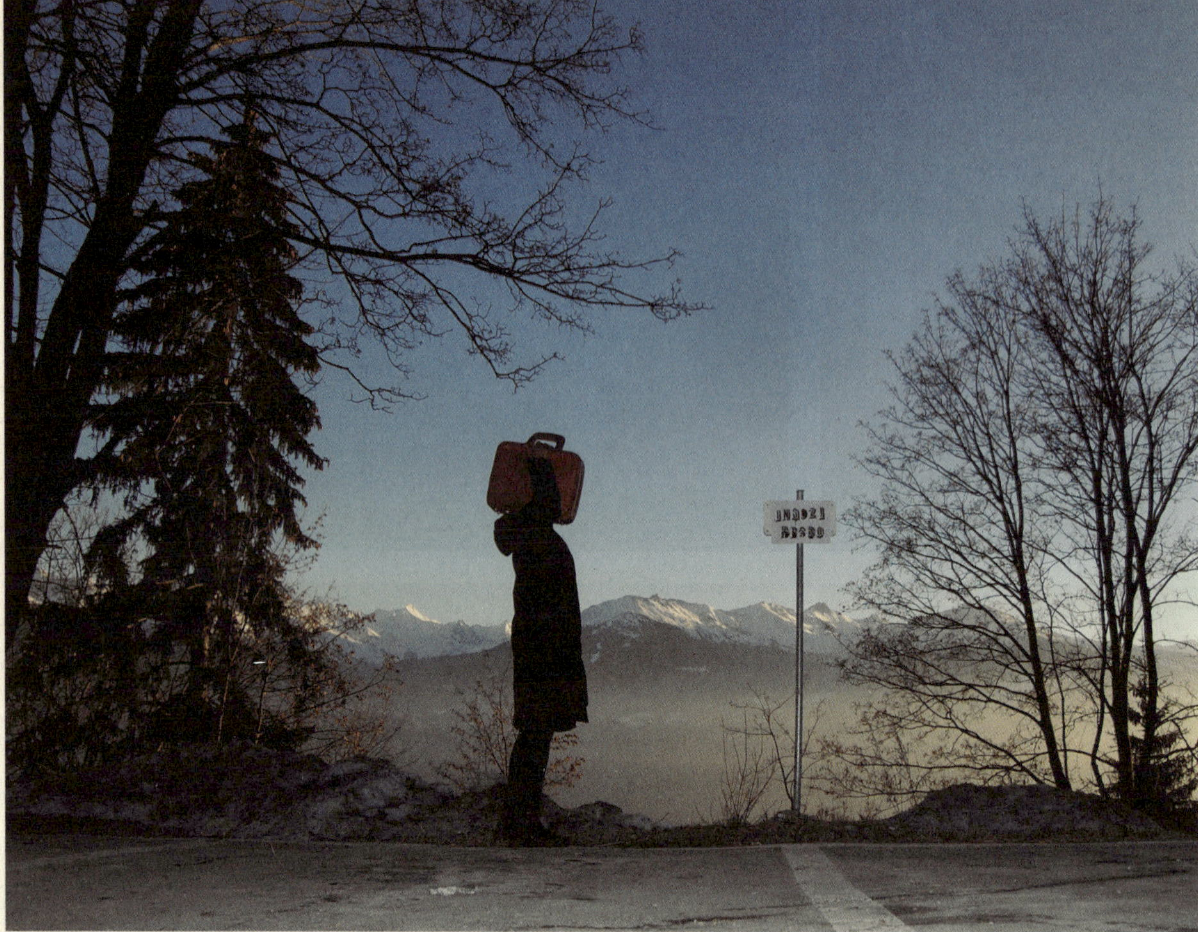

1.

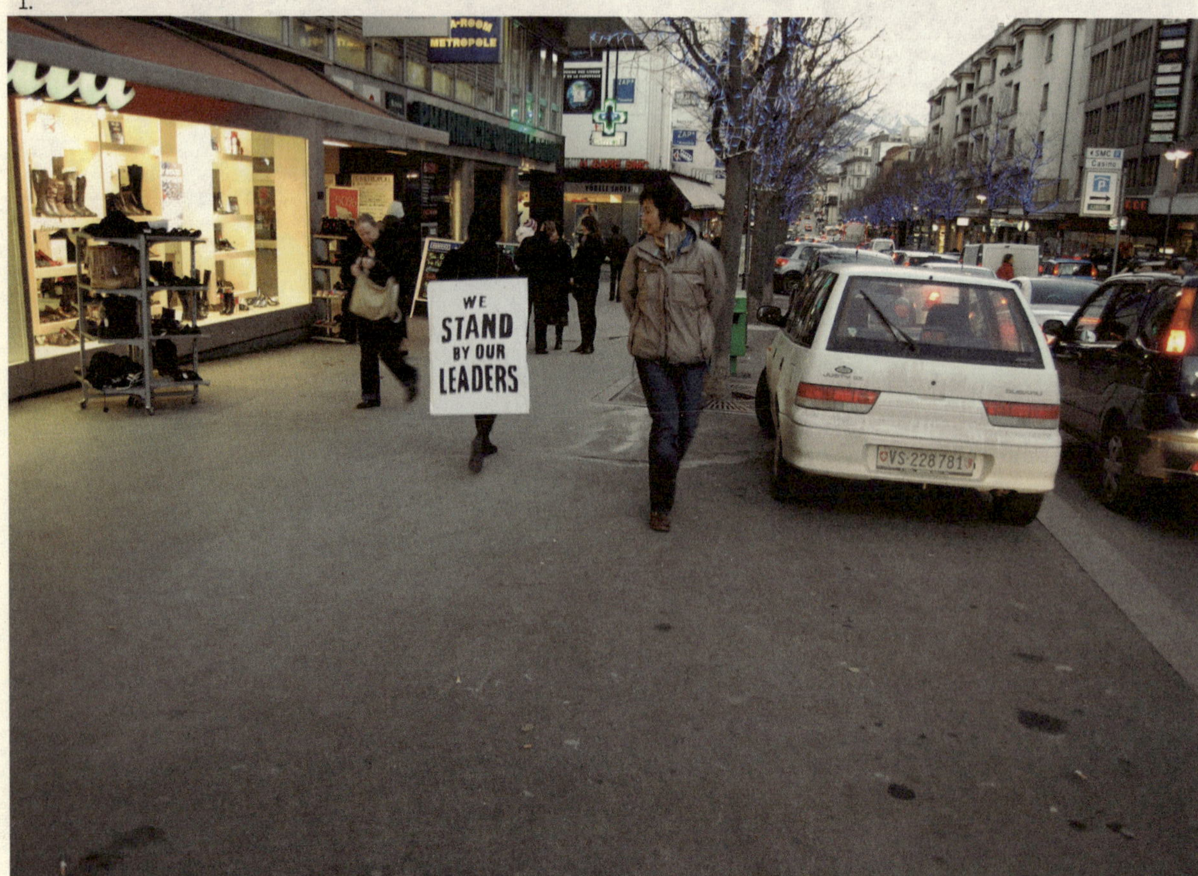

2.

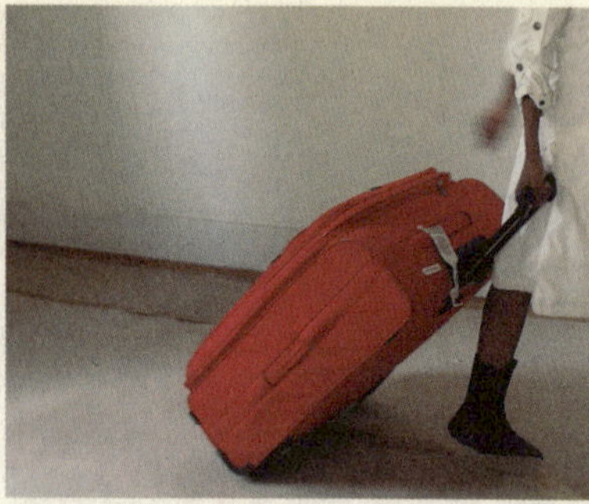

3.

Donna Kukama is based in Pretoria, South Africa. Her work is derived from an interest in everyday rituals, specifically their potential for transformation through displacement. In her provocative performances, Kukama adopts a variety of identities in order to investigate the power relations existing between artist and audience.

1. **The Red Ingozi Briefcase**
2007, magazine spread and pinup poster, $35\frac{1}{2} \times 47\frac{1}{4}$ in (90 × 120 cm)

2. **Treason 2 (We Stand by our Leaders)**
2007, performance

3. **The Red Suitcase**
2006, performance

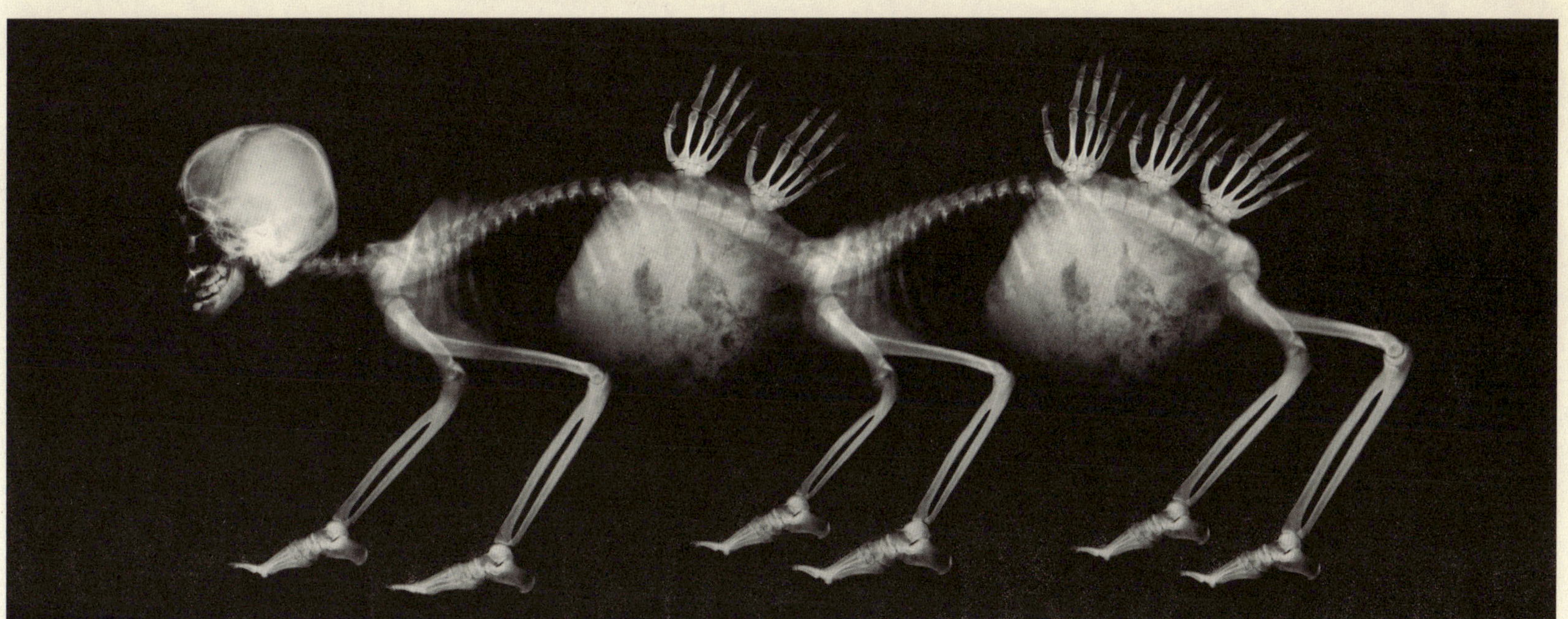

1.

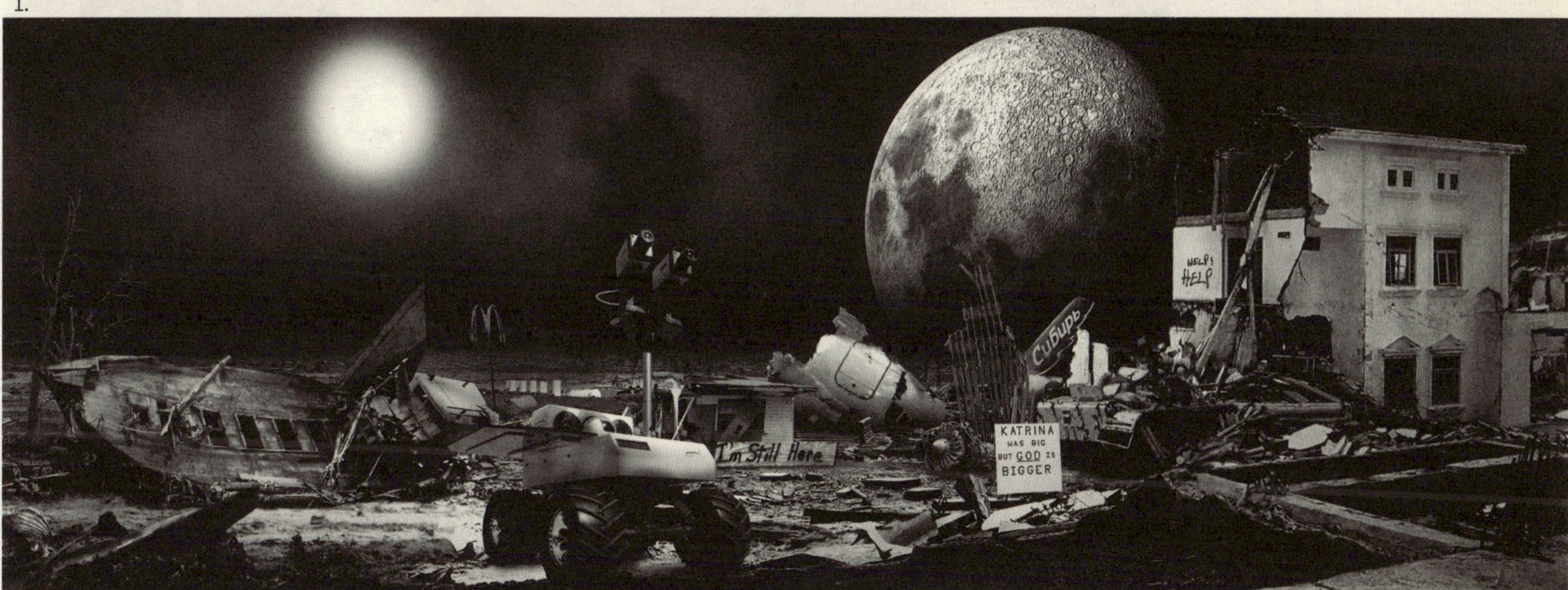

2.

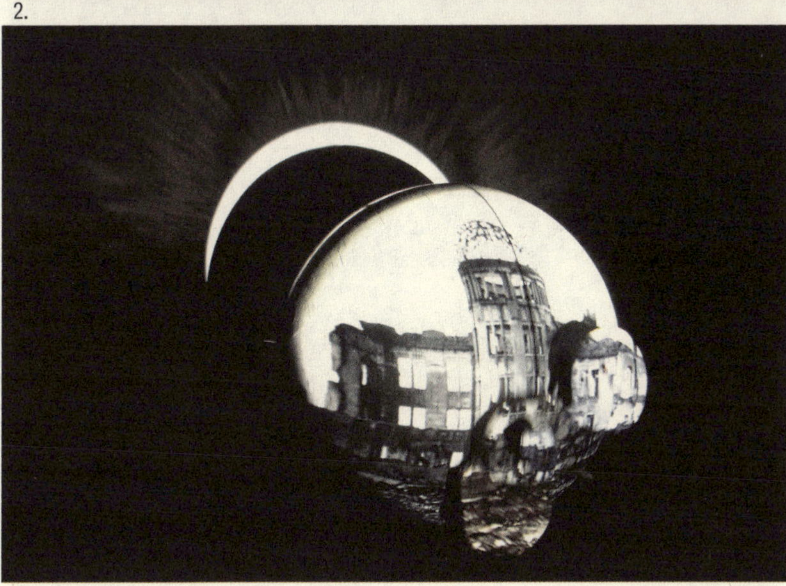

3.

Kuo I-Chen attended the Graduate School of Art and Technology at Taipei National University of Art and continues to live in Taipei. He employs sophisticated technology to create timely and poetic works in video, installation, and performance. In **Lost Contact**, he attaches surveillance cameras to helium balloons released into the air above Taipei. The image transmitted by wireless device widens as the balloons rise, and ultimately fades as the distance exceeds the device's range.

1. **Survivor Project, X**
2007, digital print and light box, 31 ½ × 78 ¾ in (80 × 200 cm)

2. **Survivor Project, 41°N, 74°W**
2007, digital print, 34 ¼ × 94 ½ in (87 × 240 cm)

3. **Survivor Project, Eclipses the Dream**
2007, multimedia installation, 12 × 19 ¾ × 8 in (30 × 50 × 20 cm)

Toru Kuwakubo received his BFA from Tama Art University, Japan, and currently lives in Tokyo. An oil painter who cites Impressionism as his inspiration, he depicts sea, sky, and landscape with hints of Surrealism, including floating objects, misplaced figures, and mysterious dashes of color.

1. Atelier
2008, oil on canvas, 76 1/2 × 102 in
(194 × 259 cm)

2. Twenty Flowers of Hole in the Sand
2004, oil on canvas, 36 × 45 3/4 in
(91 × 117 cm)

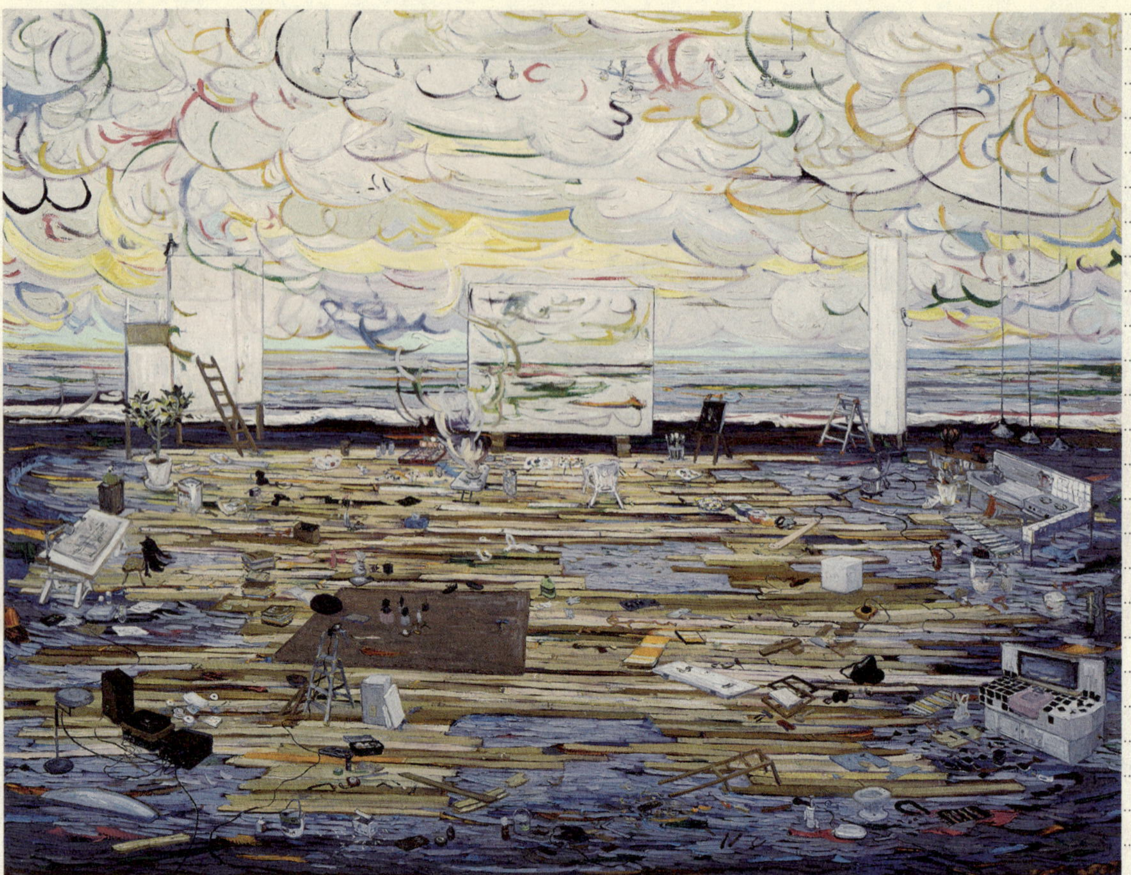

1.

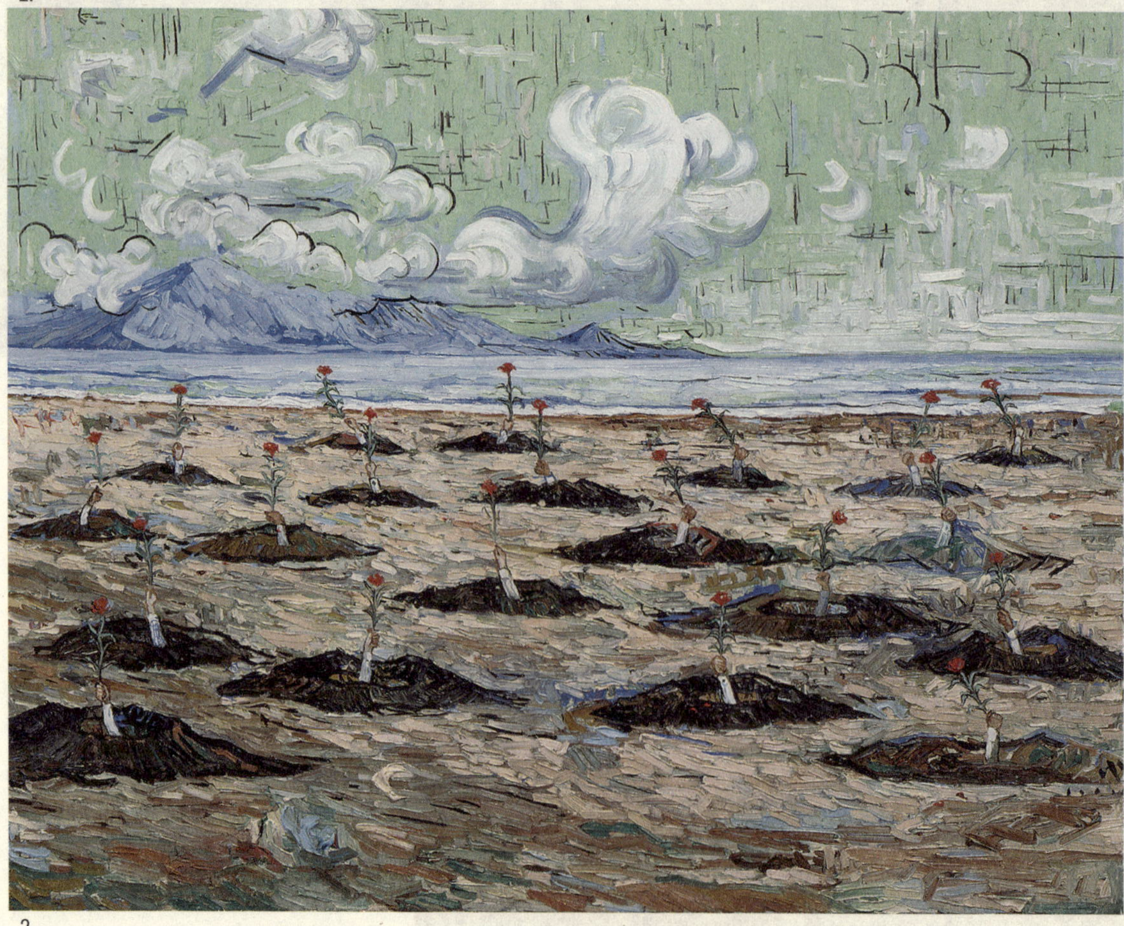

2.

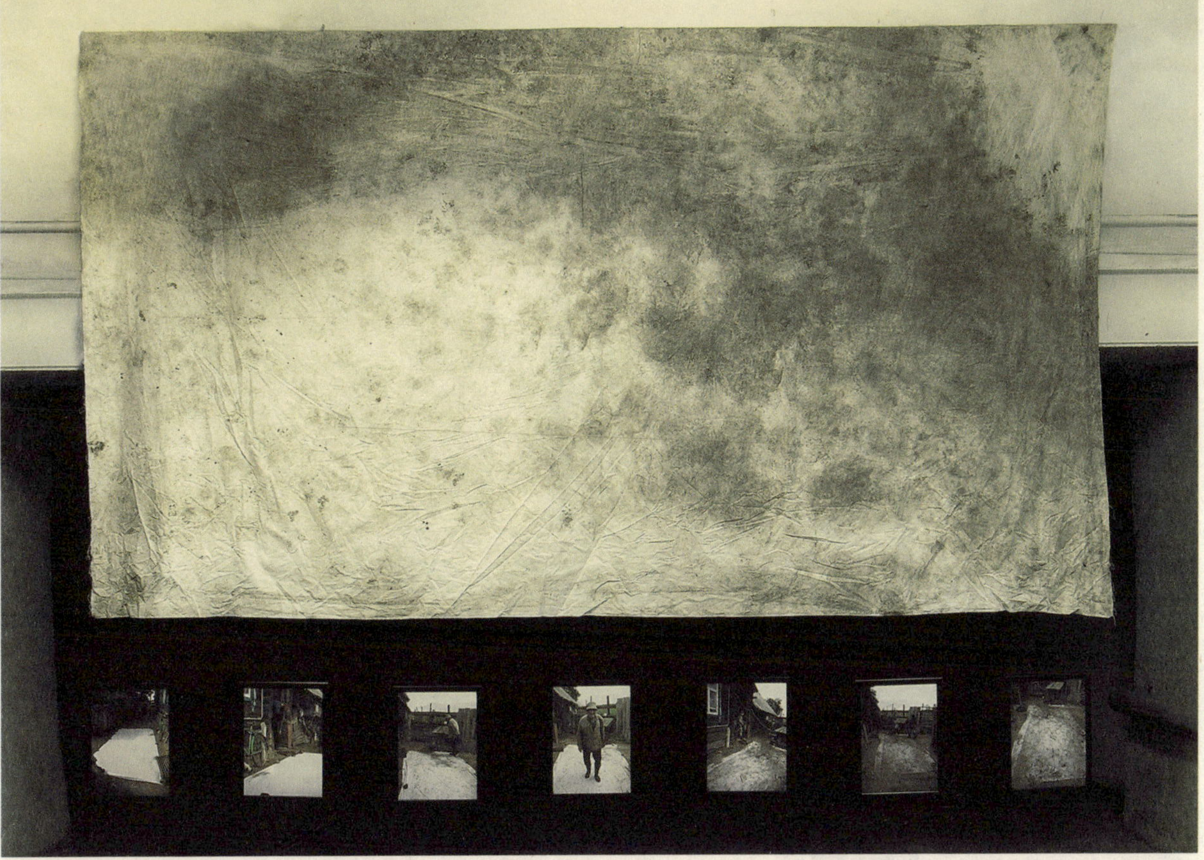

1.

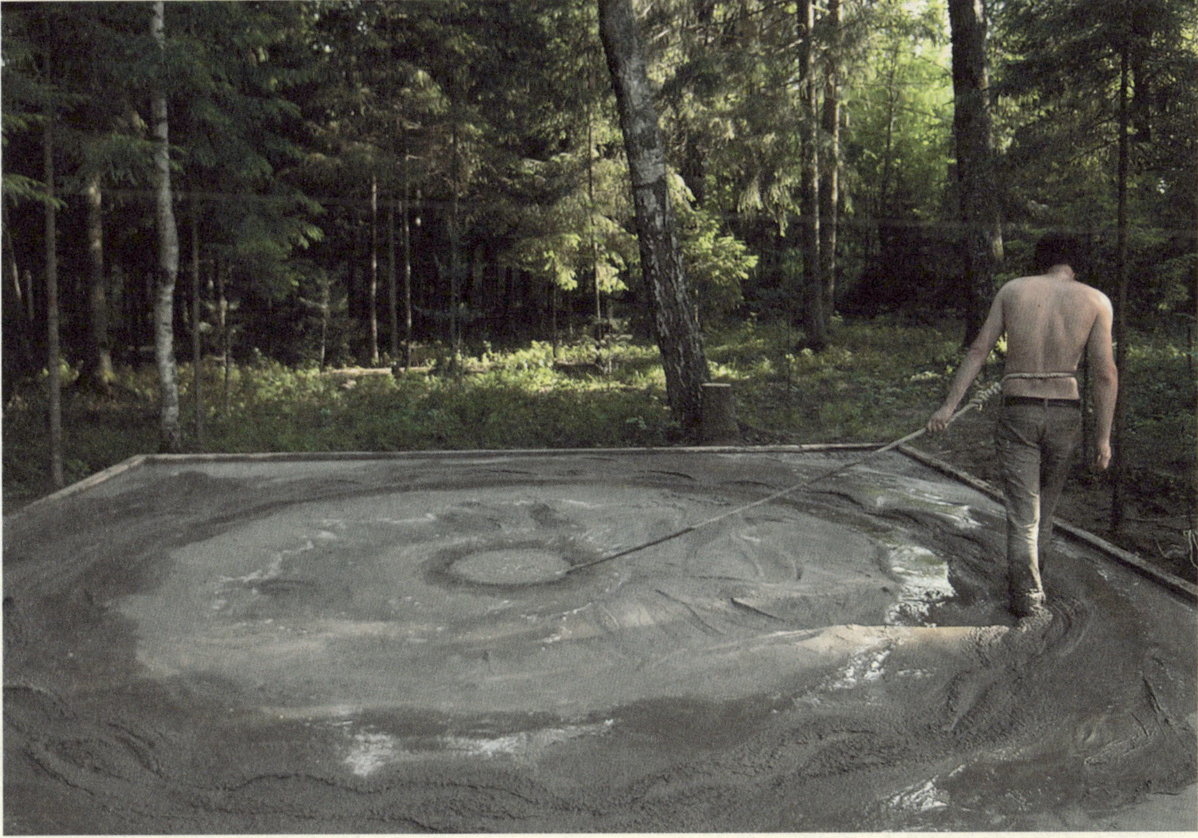

2.

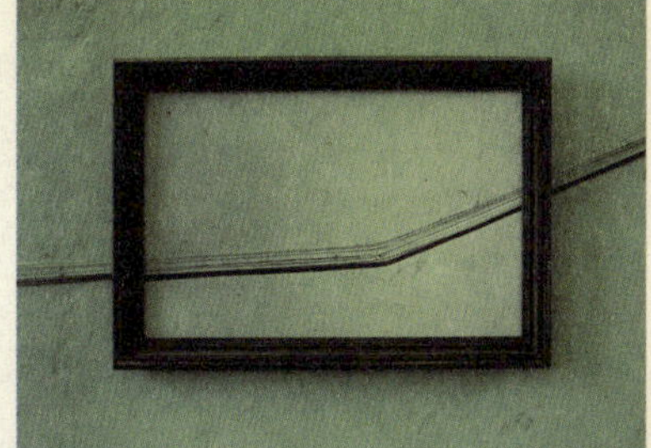

3.

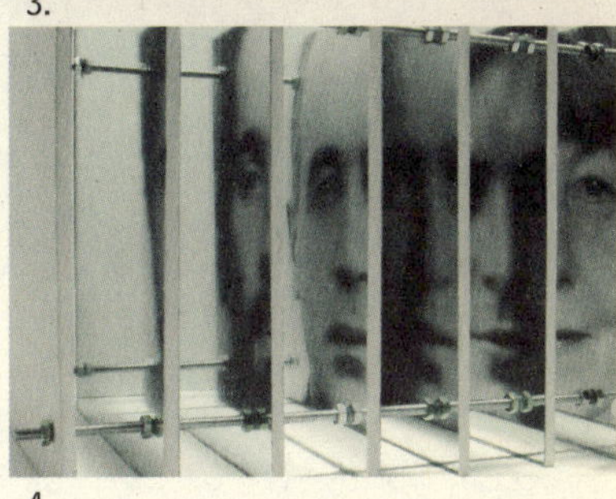

4.

Andrey Kuzkin lives and works in Moscow. In performances, sculptures, and installations, he uses visual and verbal language to wittily destabilize viewers' assumptions about the origins, histories, and functions of objects and sites. In **The Other Bank** (2008), for example, giant wooden letters placed in an empty field beside a river promise "IT'S MUCH BETTER HERE."

1. Traces
2006, stretched canvas and color photographs, 118 × 158 in (300 × 400 cm)

2. In a Circle
2008, performance

3. La condition humaine
2007, photographic installation, dimensions variable

4. Relatives (detail)
mirrors, metal rods, and black and white photographs, each panel 78 ½ × 78 ½ in (200 × 200 cm)

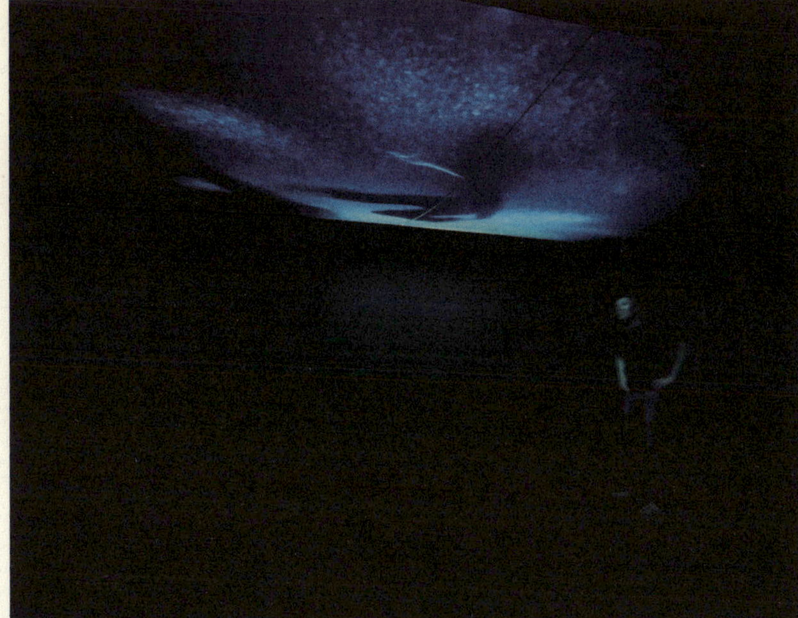
1.

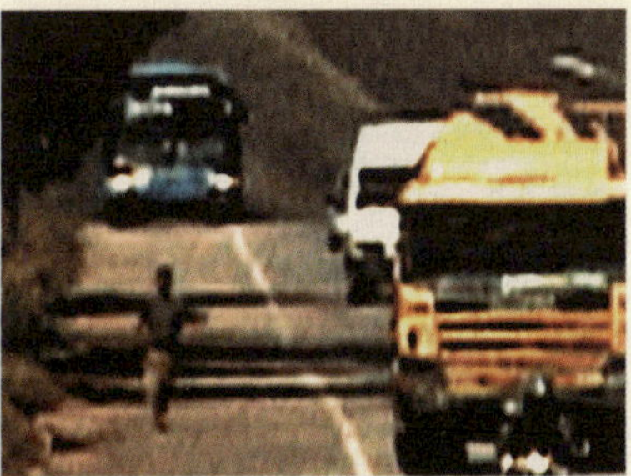
4.

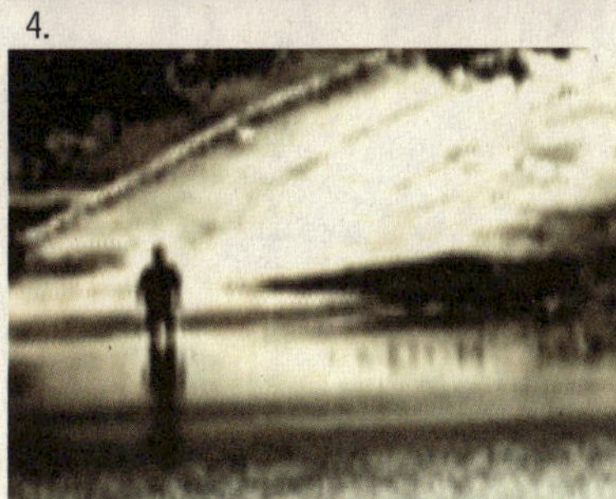
5.

Video installation artist Marcellvs L. lives and works in Berlin and has exhibited at biennials in São Paulo, Havana, and Santiago. Focusing on commonplace objects and overlooked events, his works heighten our perception of ephemeral detail and the passage of time.

1. **Overground**
with sound by M. L. and Djodjo (pexbaA)
2008, video, 13 min 36 sec

2. **spree**
2007, video and 4-channel sound system, 7 min 6 sec

3. **52°30'50.13" N 13°22'42.05" E**
2007, 5-channel video transferred to Blu-ray disc, duration variable

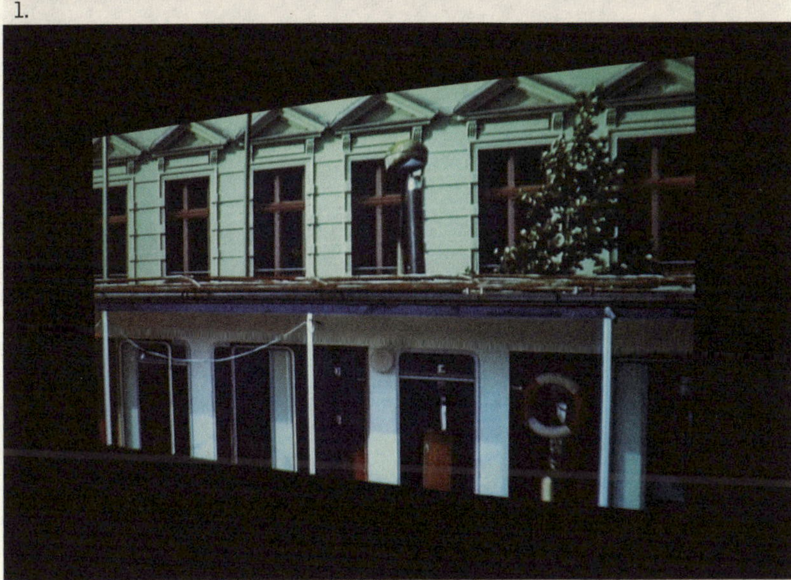
2.

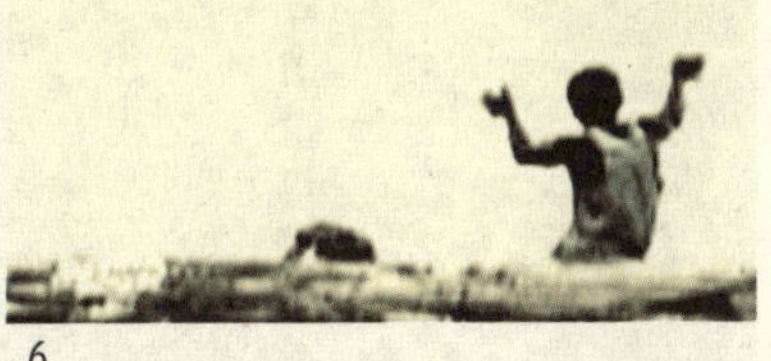
6.

4. **0667**
2003, video, 9 min 21 sec

5. **0778**
2004, video, 9 min 27 sec

6. **3195**
2005, video, 12 min 21 sec

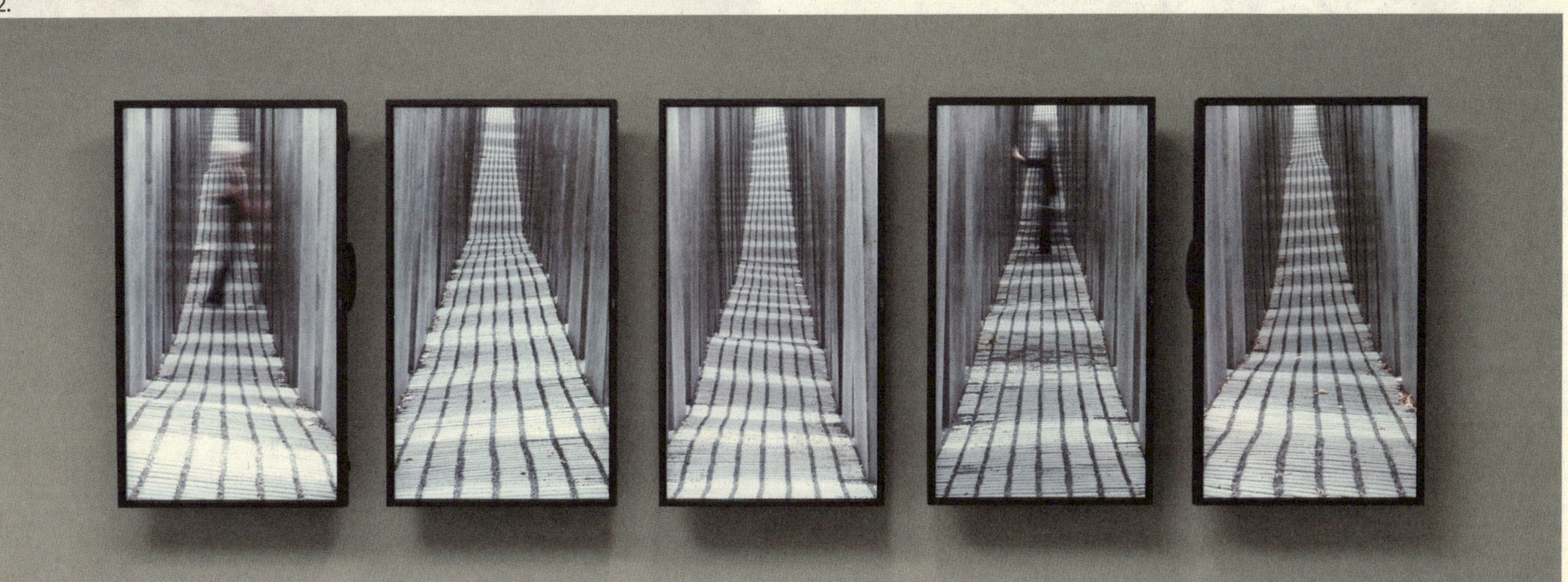
3.

Luciana Lamothe attended the Prilidiano Pueyrredon National School in Buenos Aires, where she continues to live and work. Her anarchic sculptures, videos, and urban interventions skirt the line between construction and destruction, mixing conceptual strategies with the aesthetics of vandalism. Her installation **Steelkill** (2008) was exhibited as part of the 5th Berlin Biennial and explored the social and architectural implications of the demolition of the Palast der Republik, the former seat of the East German parliament.

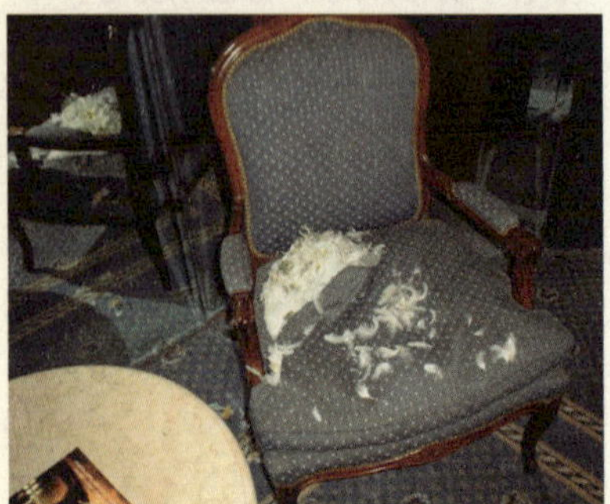

1.

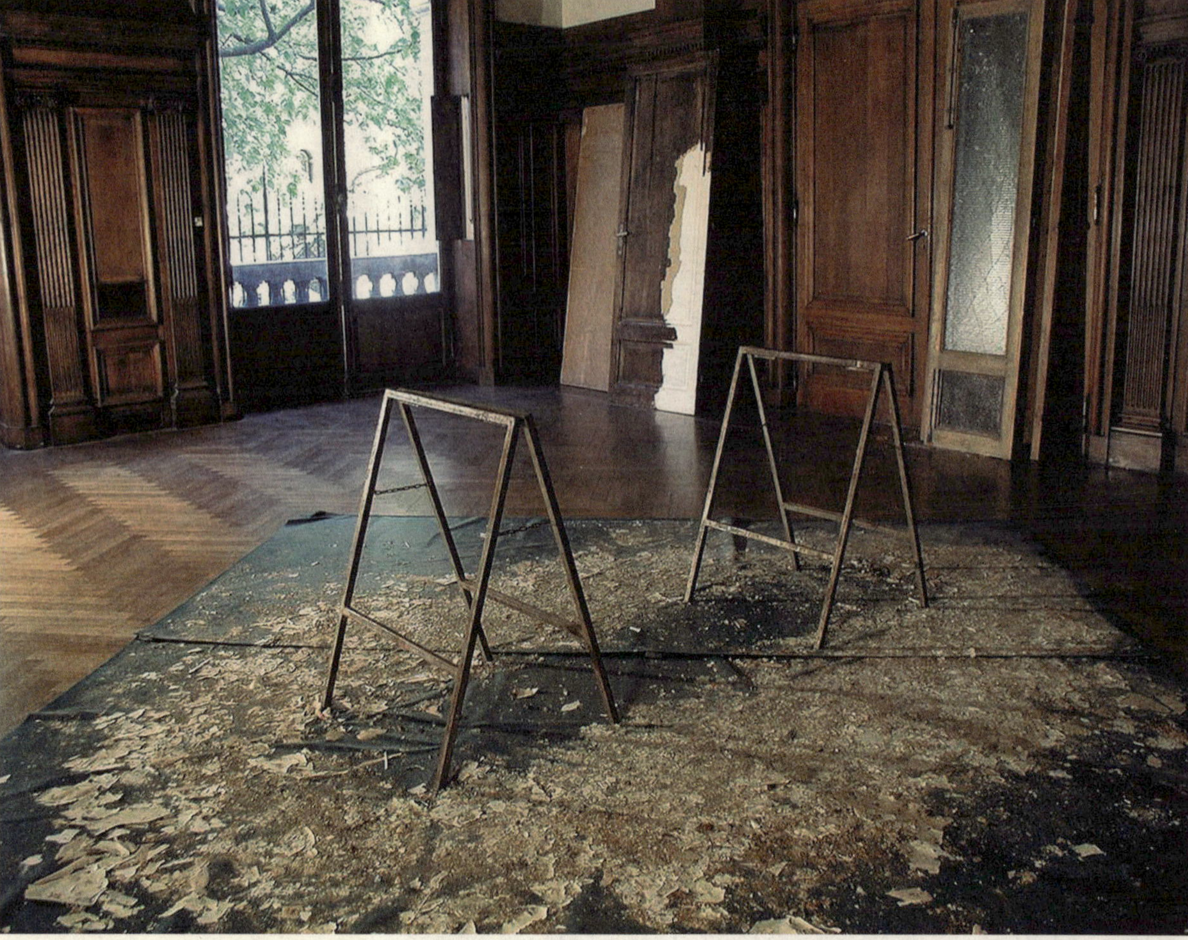

2.

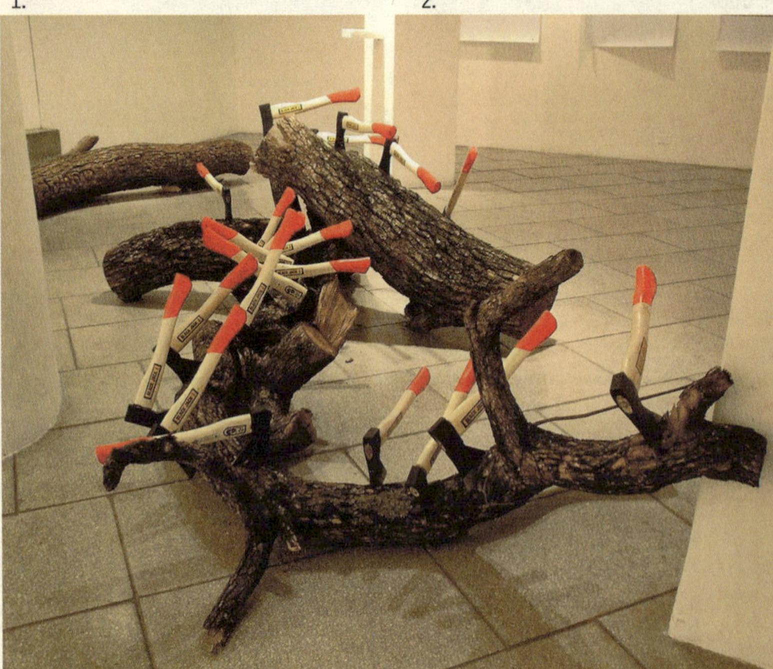

3.

4.

1. **Untitled (Sillon)**
2004, documentation of intervention, dimensions variable

2. **Untitled (Metro)**
2004, site-specific installation, 32 ¾ × 49 ¼ ft (10 × 15 m)

3. **Wood Love Steel (Hachas)**
2007, wood and axes, approx 10 × 10 × 3 ft (300 × 300 × 90 cm)

4. **SteelKill**
2008, mixed media, 23 × 18 × 10 ft (7 × 6 × 3 m)

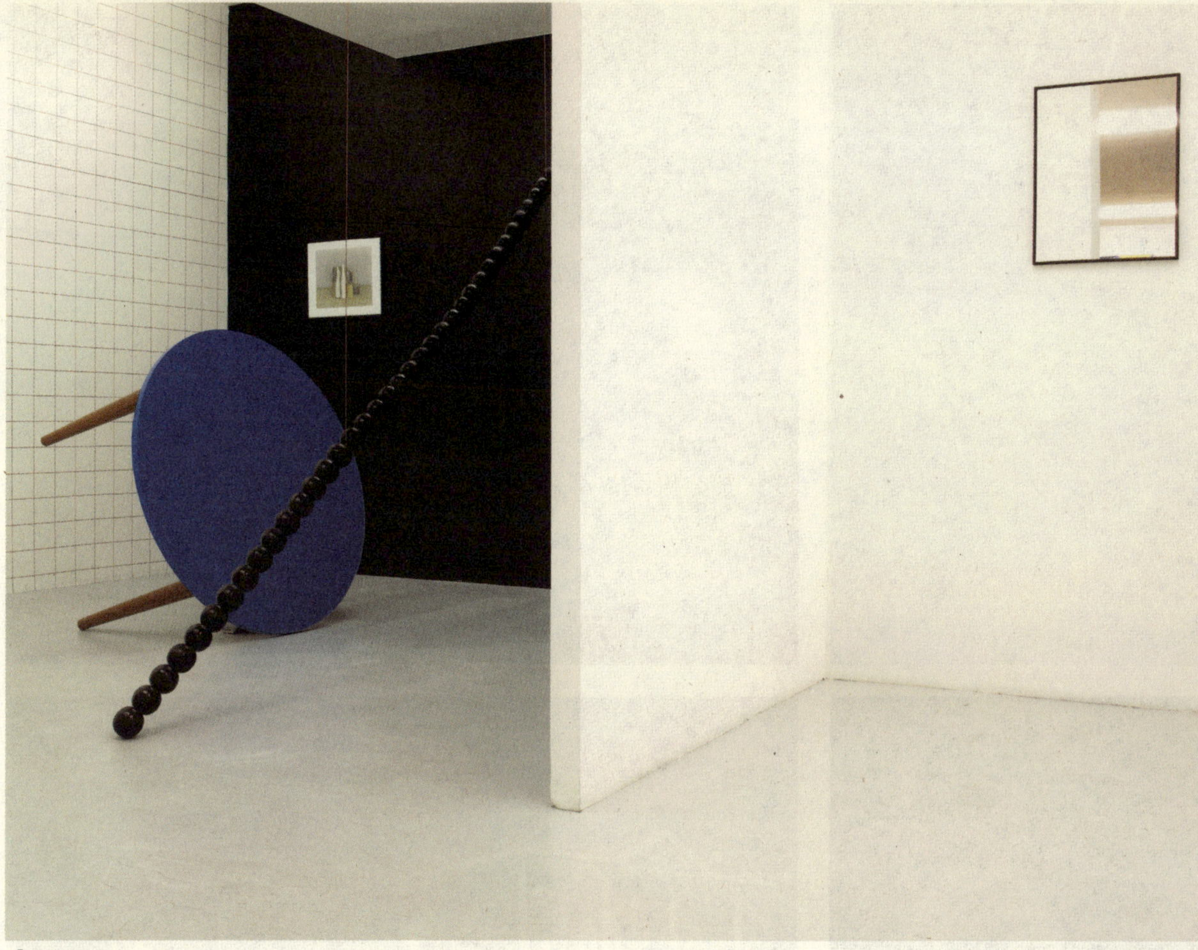

1.

Adriana Lara lives in Mexico City. Her work is concerned with systems, and she makes use of a wide variety of media to visualize the results of her research. Her projects have charted social and conceptual networks; one example involved mapping the apparent global movement of ideas from artist to artist.

1. **"A problem has occurred"**
exhibition view at Galerie Air de Paris, Paris (2007)

2. **Caracoles/Shells**
2008, mixed media, dimensions variable

3. **Unidentified (working title)** (detail)
2007, from a series of 22 spherical sculptures, mixed media, dimensions variable

4. **Art Film 1: Ever present yet ignored**
2006, 16 mm film, black and white, Italian with English and Spanish subtitles, 7 min 30 sec

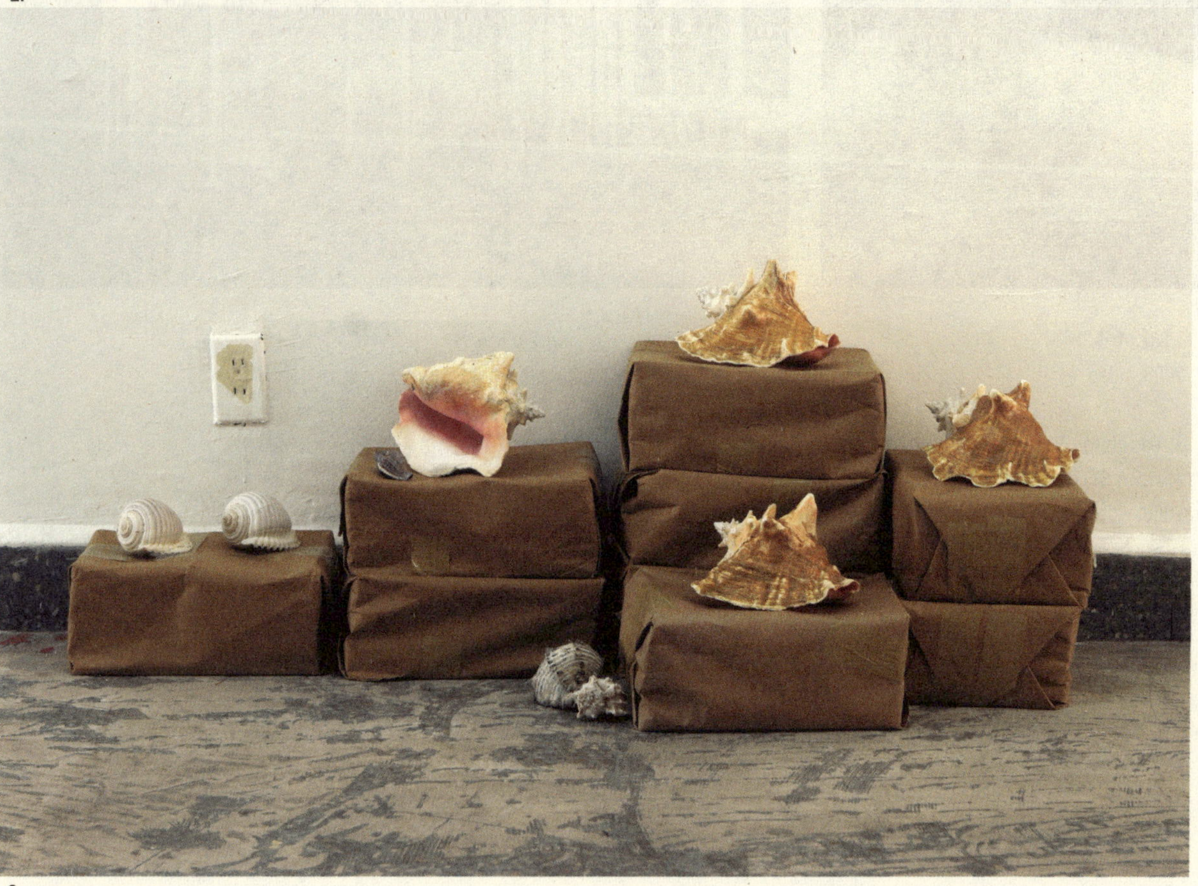

2.

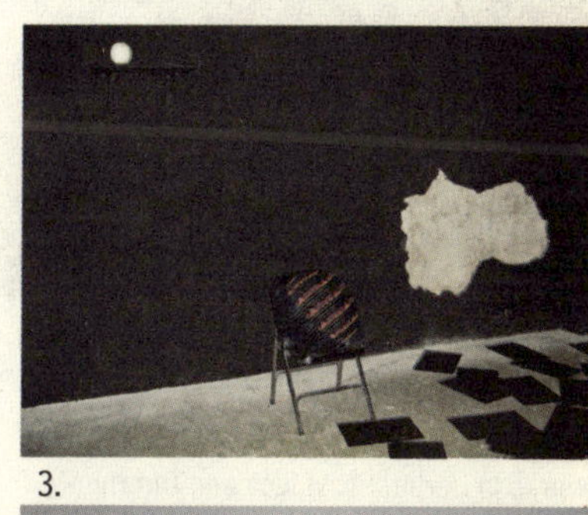

3.

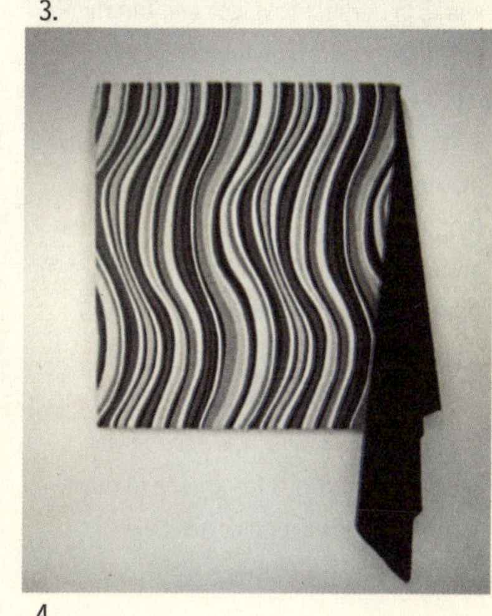

4.

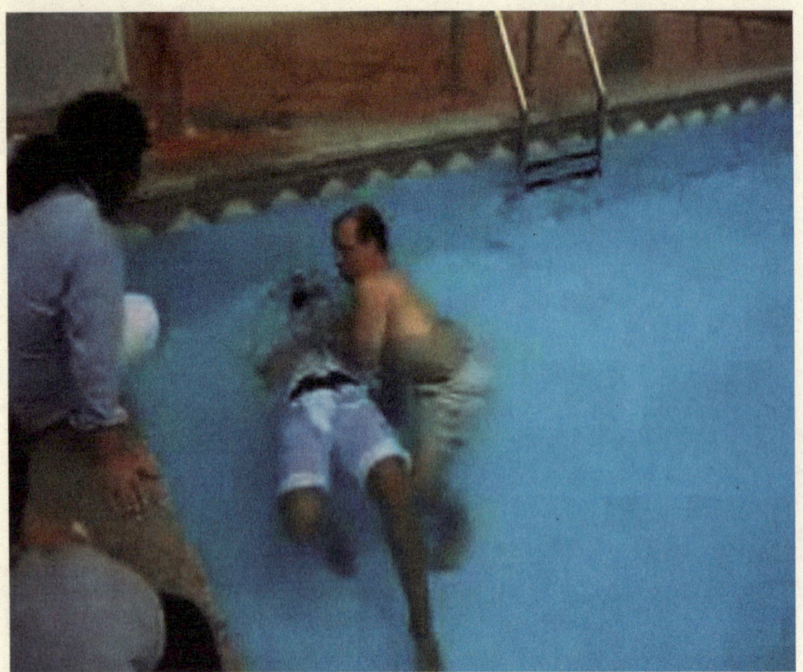

1.

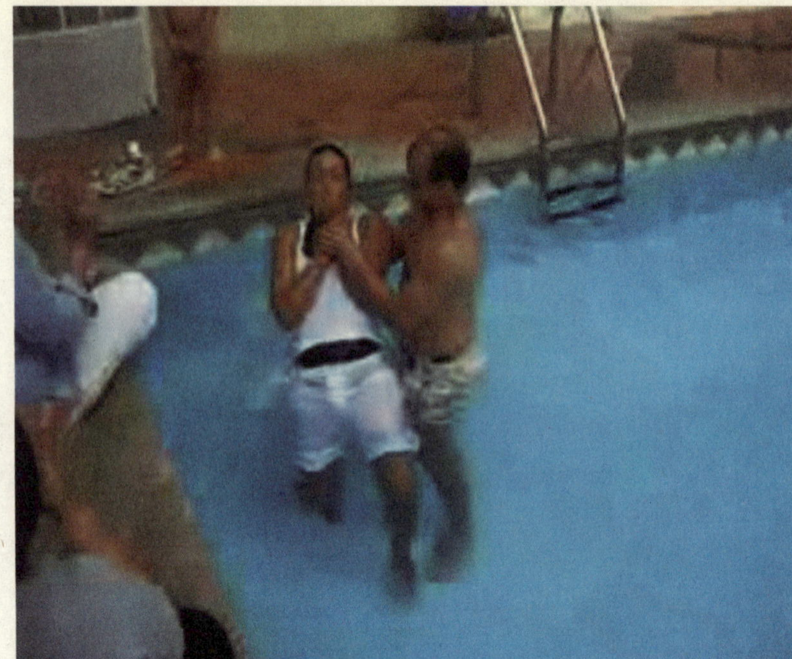

2.

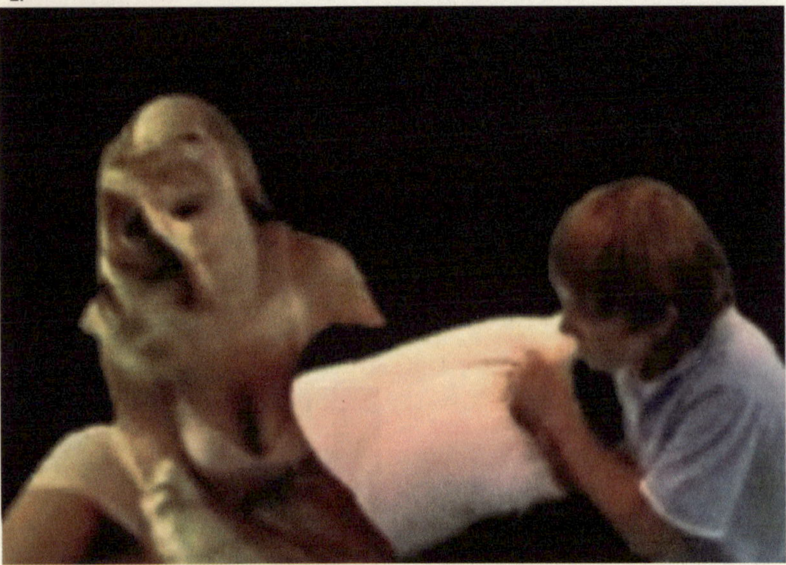

3.

4.

Oliver Laric attended the University of Applied Arts in Vienna and now lives and works in Berlin. His videos and Internet-based works draw on found footage, mostly scoured from the Web, that he edits to generate new meaning. Often his individual works function like templates that, once released online, become used and remade. With **Touch My Body (Green Screen Version)**, Laric used a green-screen filter to block out all content in pop star Mariah Carey's "Touch My Body" video. This new version was then put on YouTube for anyone to remix by layering new graphics and thus creating new narratives.

1 & 2. ↑↓
2008, video

3. **Touch My Body (Green Screen Version)**
2008, video

4. **Our House by Crosby, Stills, Nash & Young (1970)**
from the series **Songs Translated To Buildings**
2008, digital chromogenic print on Diasec, 16 ½ × 11 in (42 × 28 cm)

5. **Masking Variations**
2008, video

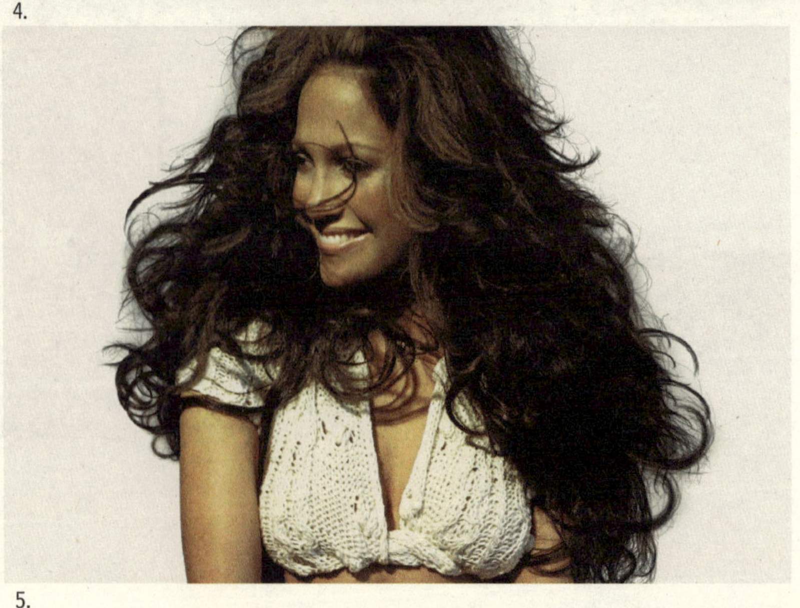

5.

Mexico City-based Paulina Lasa expresses an interest in naïveté and optimism through her interventions and performances. Since 2004 she has been part of the Bordermates collective, with whom she produces events in public spaces and collaborates with emerging artists.

1. **Preacher**
2006, performance

2. **Paulina vs. The Machine (Homage to Nicolas Bourriaud)**
2006, performance

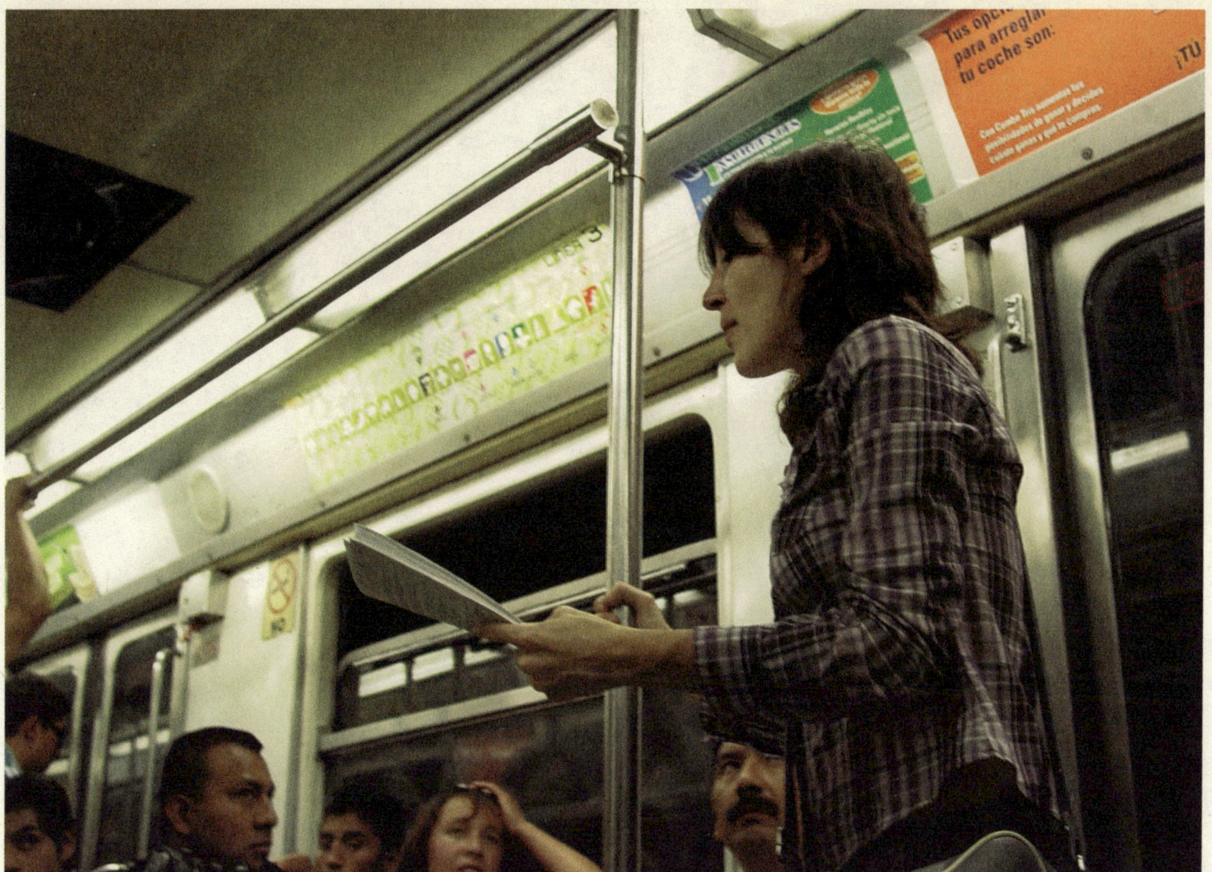

1.

2.

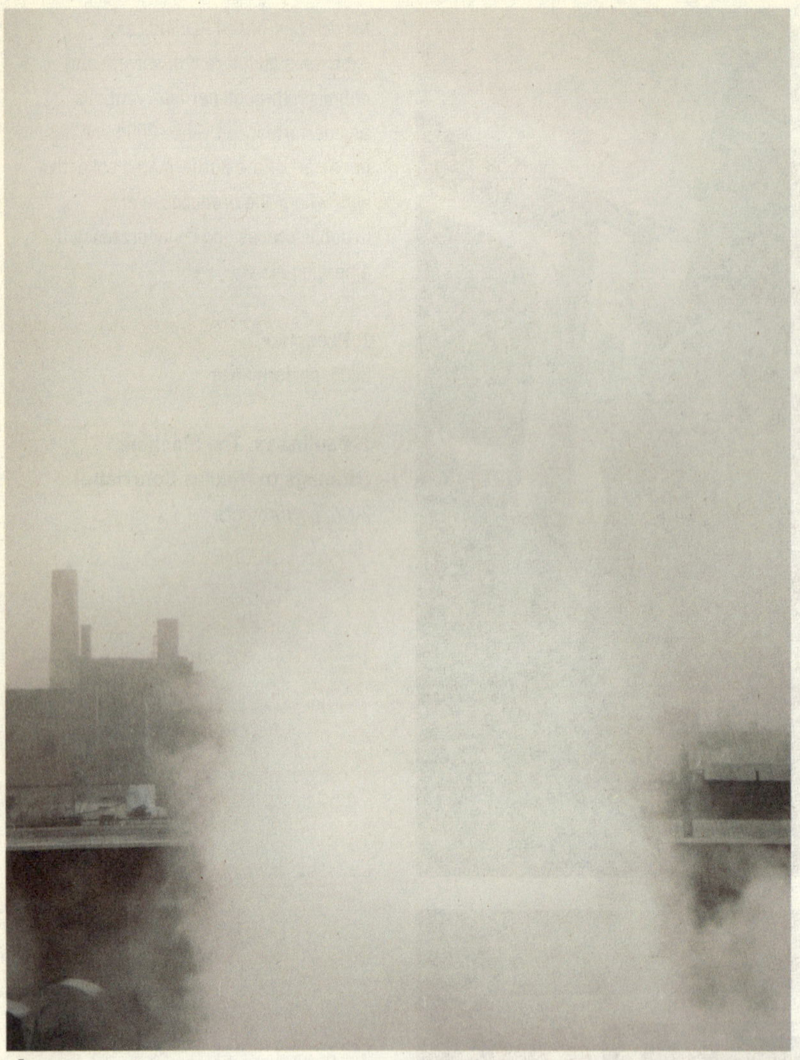
1.

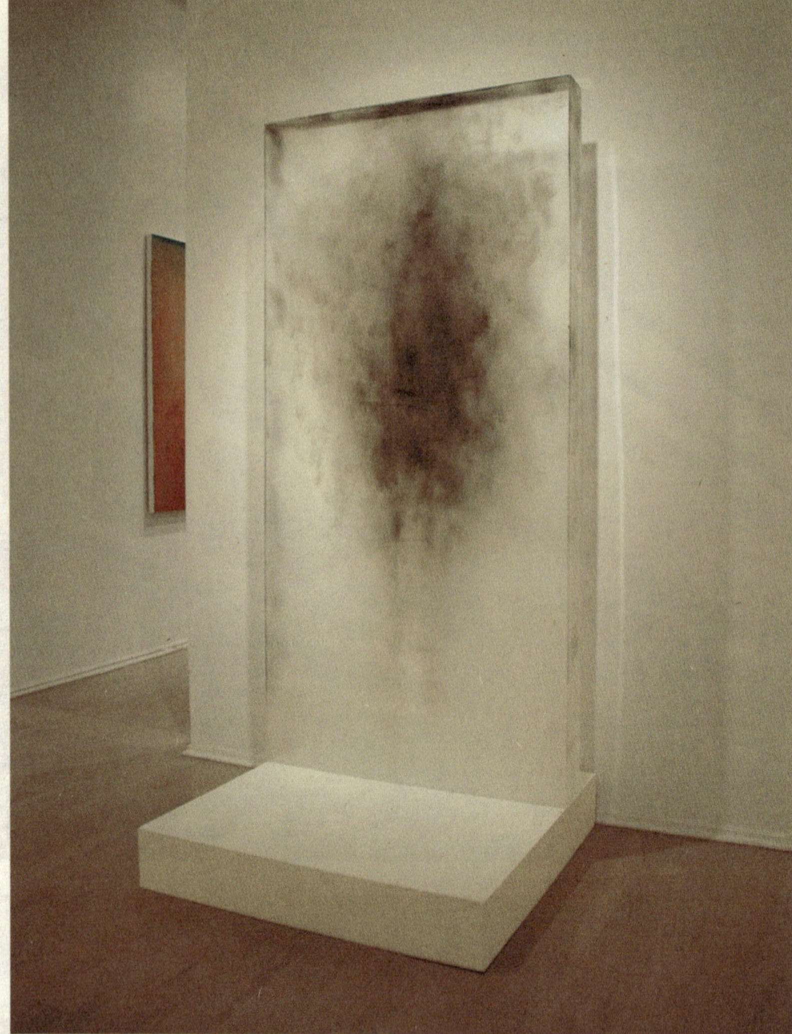
2.

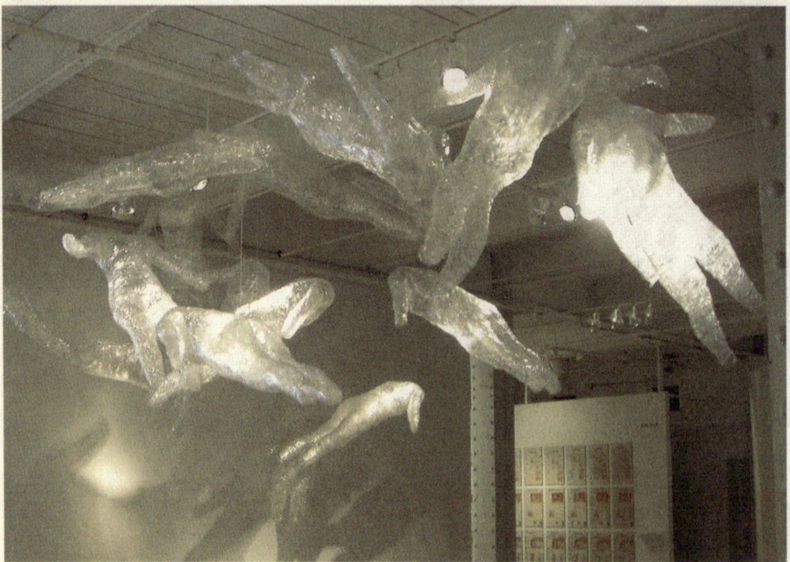
3.

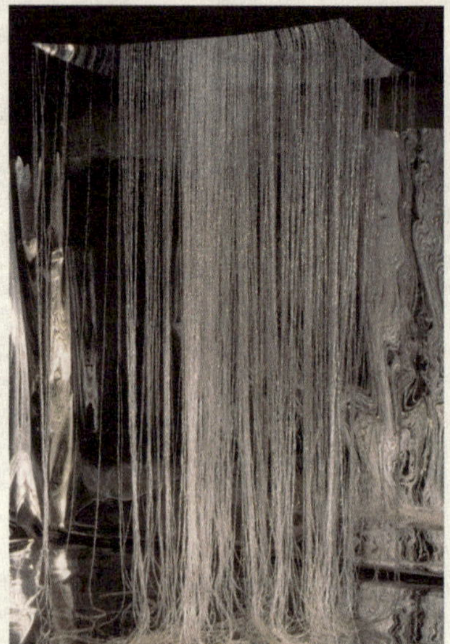
4.

Sungmi Lee earned her MFA in sculpture from Maryland Institute College of Art, Baltimore, and currently lives in Brooklyn. She describes the process of layering and repetition in her work as an act of personal ritual akin to Buddhist meditation. Her sculptures and installations collect ordinary materials in large quantities – found glass, white plastic ties, drips from a hot-glue gun – to transcend their original functions and produce new forms.

1. white air 2
from the series **white air**
2006-08, chromogenic print on aluminum, 14 × 11 in (36 × 28 cm)

2. Untitled #600
2006, incense smoke on Plexiglas, 72 × 36 × 5 in (183 × 91 × 13 cm)

3. Healing I
2005, 19 clear tape castings of artist's body, each approx 54 × 24 × 24 in (137 × 61 × 61 cm)

4. Infinitive memory
2004, reflective Plexiglas, Mylar, hot glue, and fishing wire, approx 96 × 48 × 36 in (244 × 122 × 91 cm)

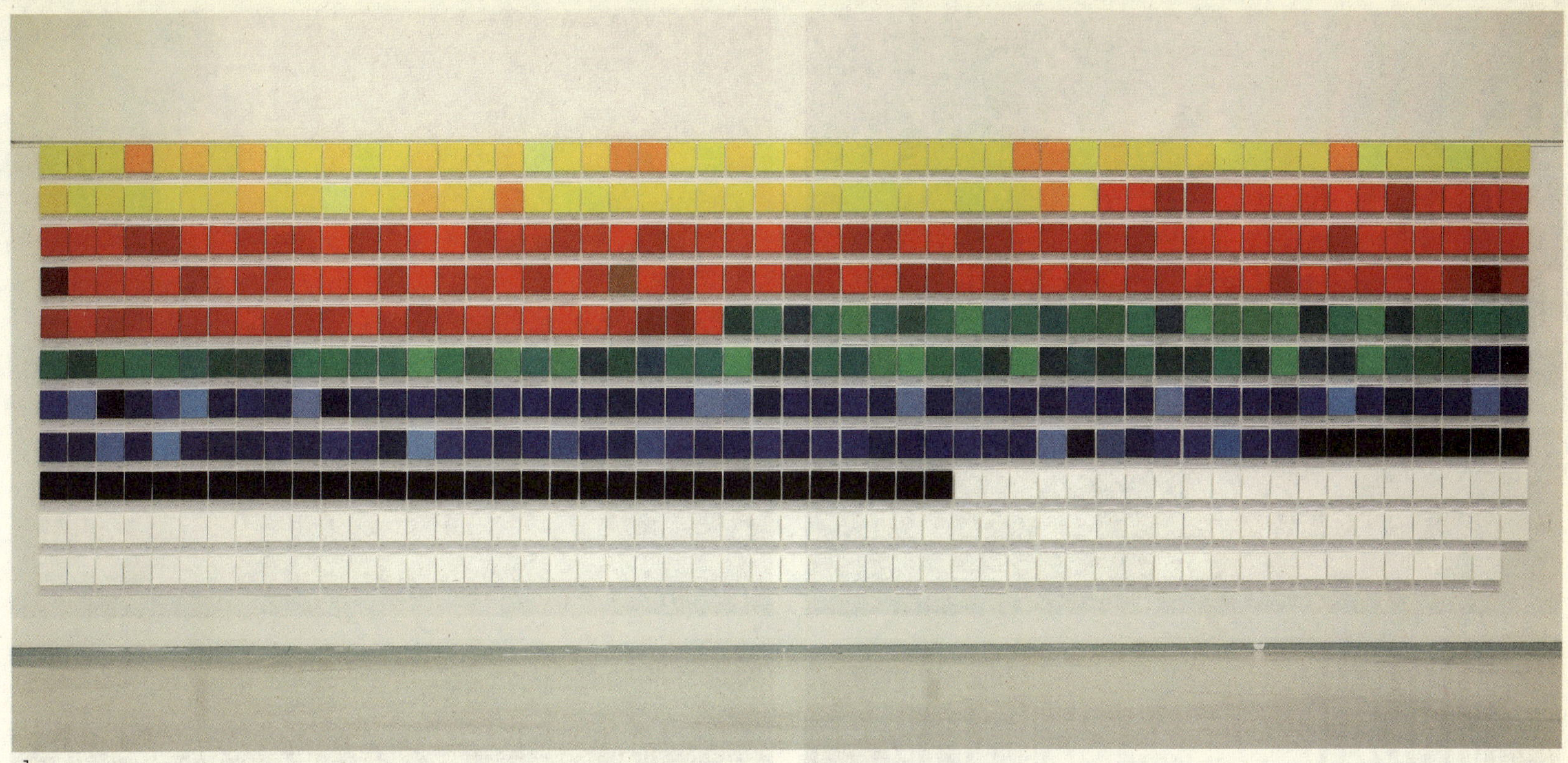

1.

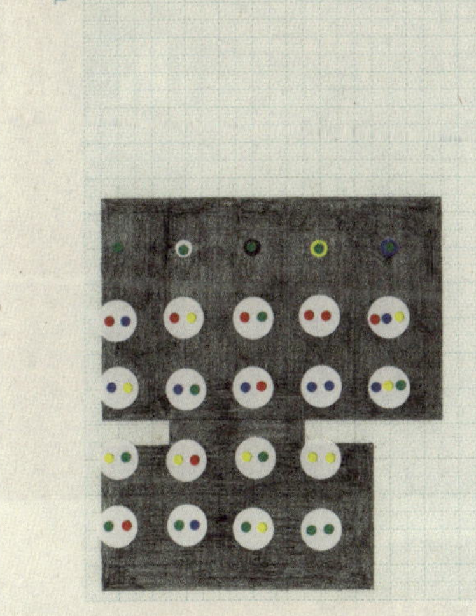

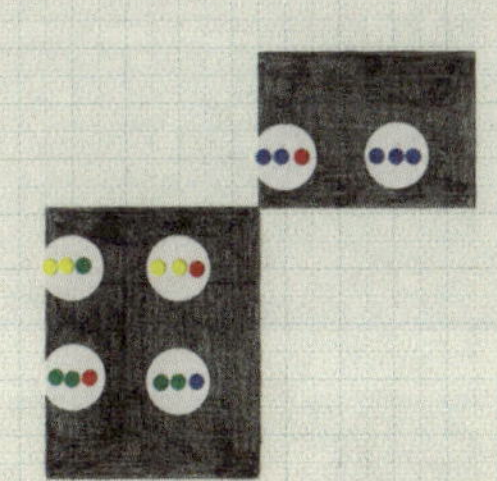

2.

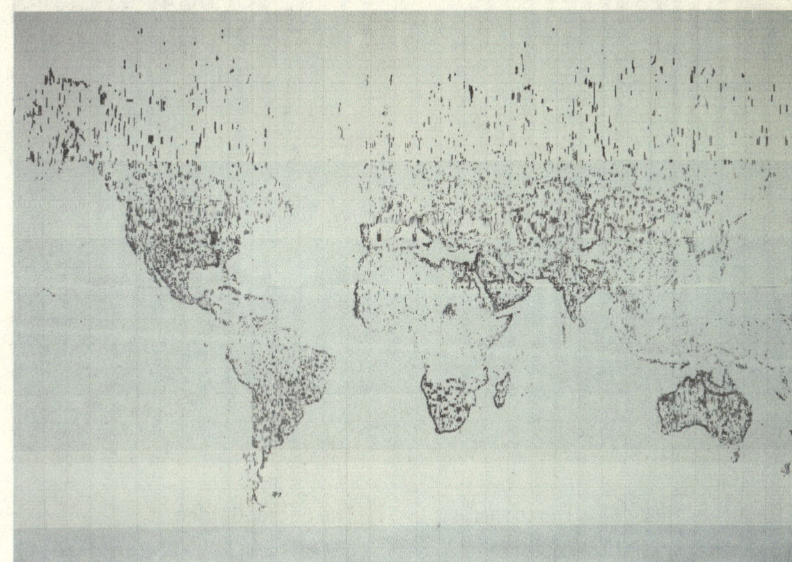

3.

Eunu Lee received her MFA from the School of Visual Arts, Korea National University of Arts in Seoul. Her conceptually based practice is concerned with systems of categorization and classification, particularly the way in which these systems influence and are influenced by their social, political, and historical contexts. In 2007 she was awarded the 29th Joongang fine arts Prize by the Joongang Daily in Seoul.

1. **International Colors**
2007, oil on canvas, 33 × 10 ft (10 × 3 m)

2. **0011111224339485567** (detail)
2008, pencil and stickers on plotting paper, dimensions variable

3. **Google Landscape 2006**
2006, vinyl on wall, pencil on paper, $7\frac{1}{2} \times 11\frac{3}{4}$ ft (2 × 4 m)

4. **Untitled**
2004-05, digital print, $3\frac{1}{2} \times 13$ ft (1 × 4 m)

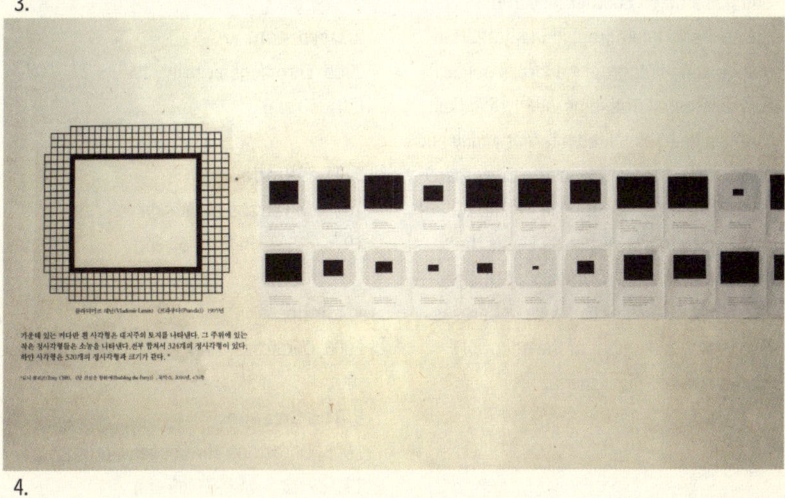

4.

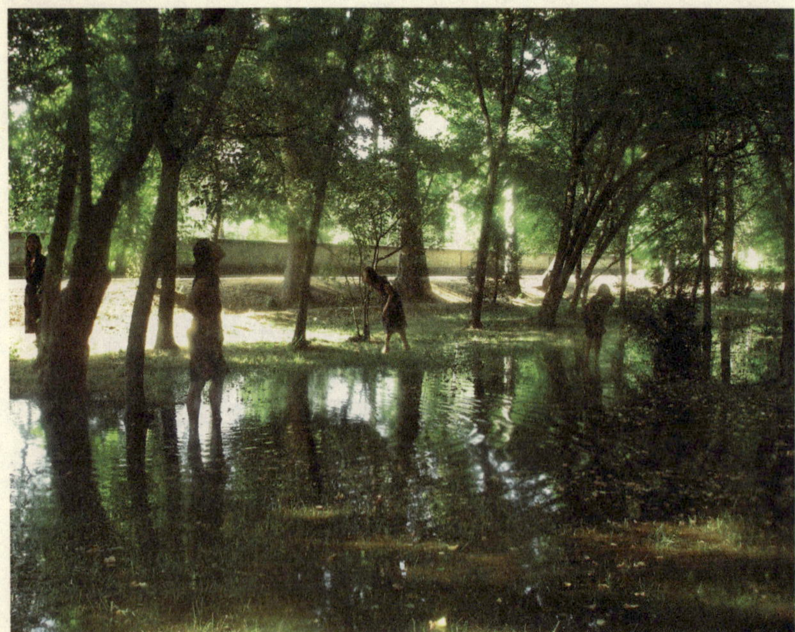

1.

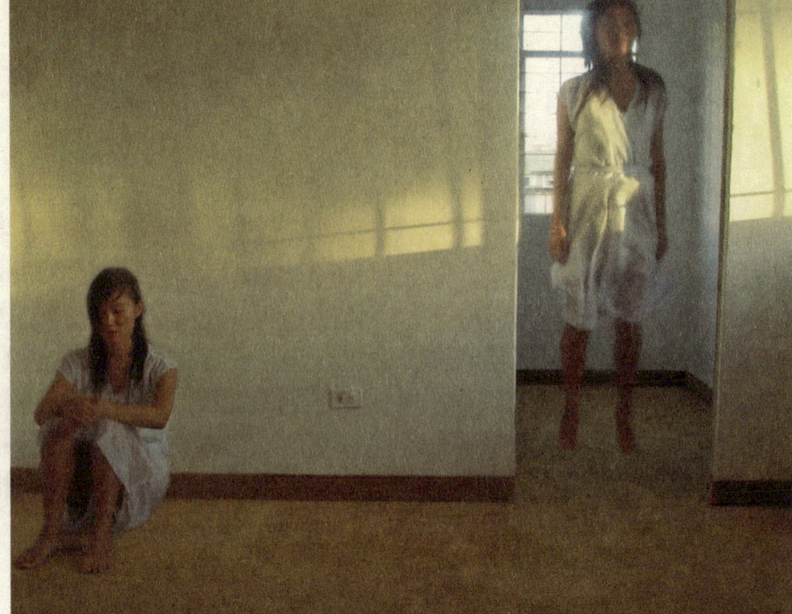

2.

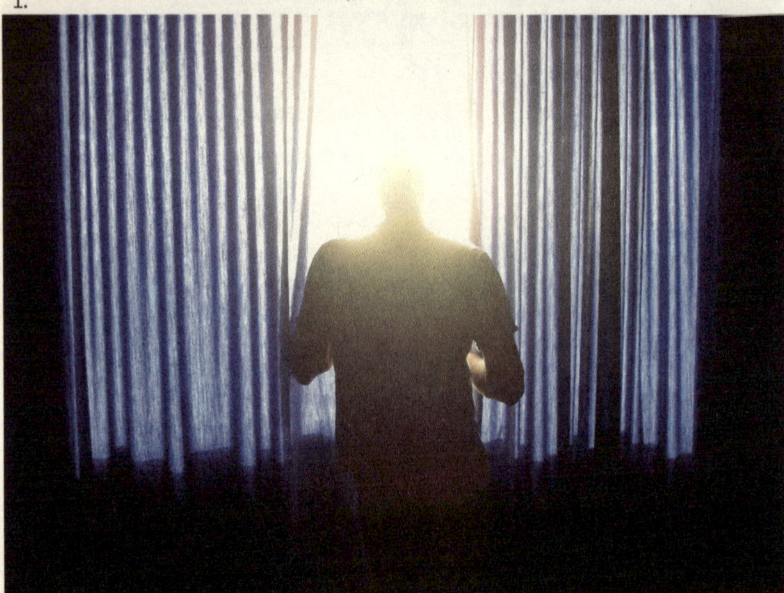

3.

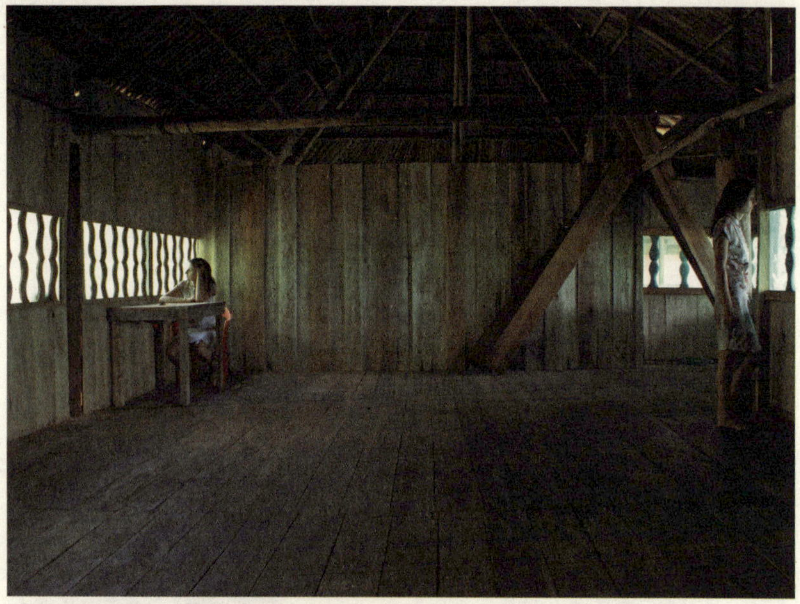

4.

Suwon Lee holds a BA in French studies from the American University of Paris and has studied photography at the Spéos-Paris Photographic Institute. Her videos and photographs address political and existential problems with lyrical flair. She has been exhibited internationally and has received a grant from the Cisneros Fontanals Art Foundation in Miami. In addition to her art practice, Lee is the cofounder, with Luis Romero, of Oficina #1, the only artist-run space in Caracas. She is also a member of the editorial committee of Pulgar magazine.

1. **The Secret Garden**
2006, Duratrans, 19 ¾ × 23 ¾ in (50 × 60 cm)

2. **Daydream**
2006, chromogenic print, 19 ¾ × 23 ¾ in (50 × 60 cm)

3. **The Window**
2006, Duratrans chromogenic print, 19 ¾ × 23 ¾ in (50 × 60 cm)

4. **Limbo**
2006, Duratrans, 19 ¾ × 23 ¾ in (50 × 60 cm)

5. **The Stranger**
2006, Duratrans chromogenic print, 19 ¾ × 23 ¾ in (50 × 60 cm)

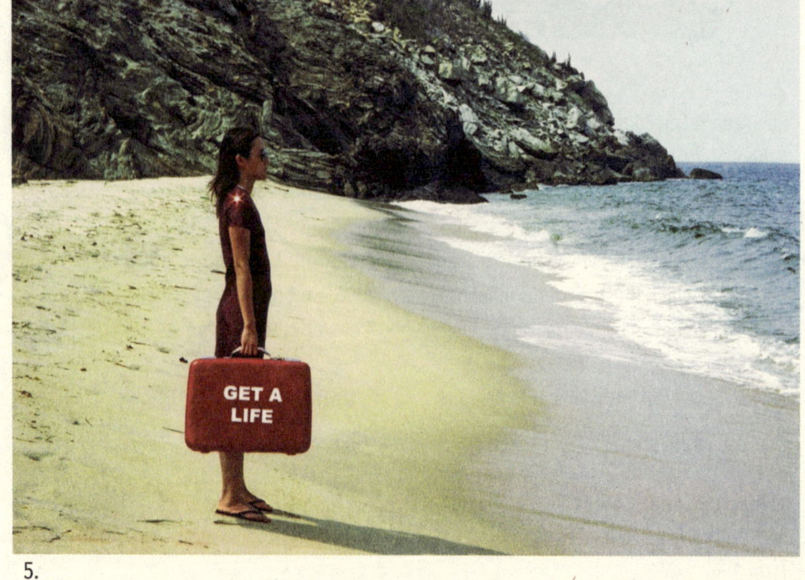

5.

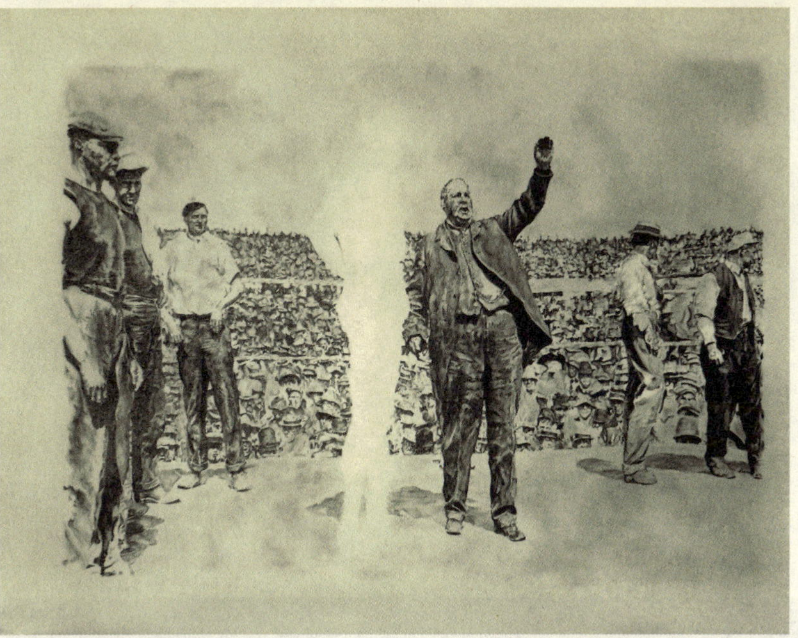

1.

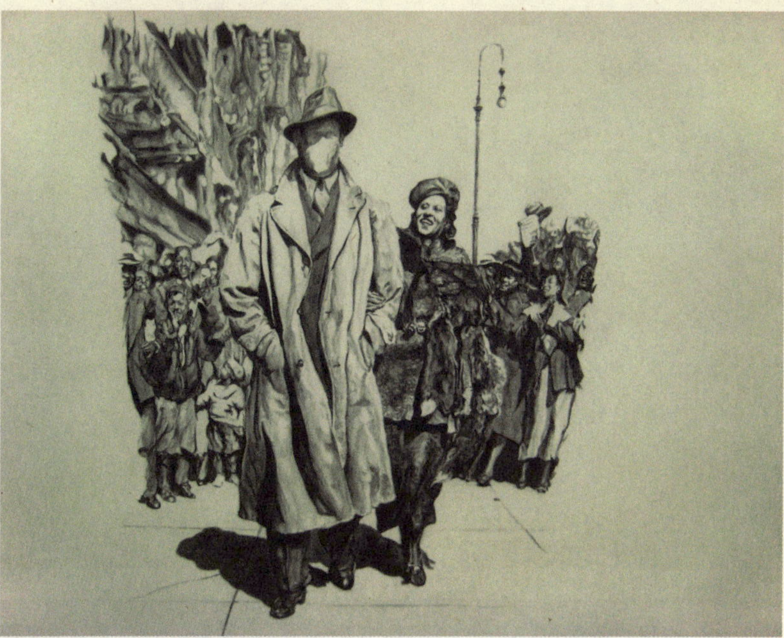

2.

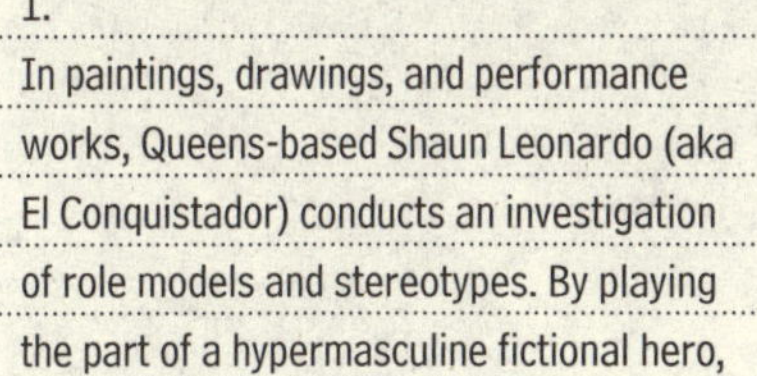

In paintings, drawings, and performance works, Queens-based Shaun Leonardo (aka El Conquistador) conducts an investigation of role models and stereotypes. By playing the part of a hypermasculine fictional hero, he manifests a tension between physical vulnerability, cultural exclusion, and the representation or embodiment of virility.

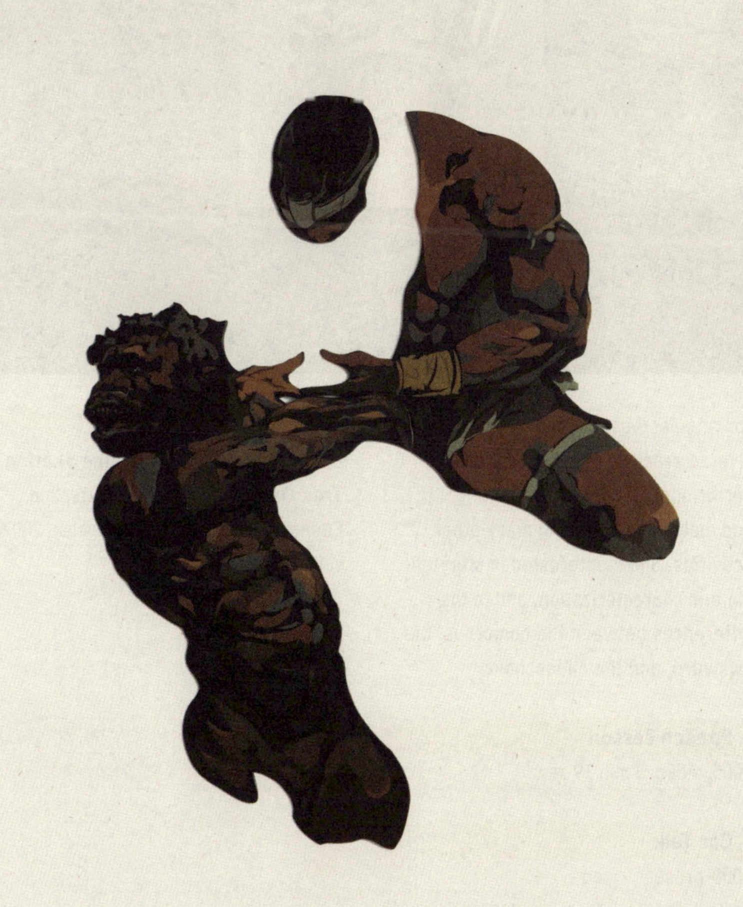

3.

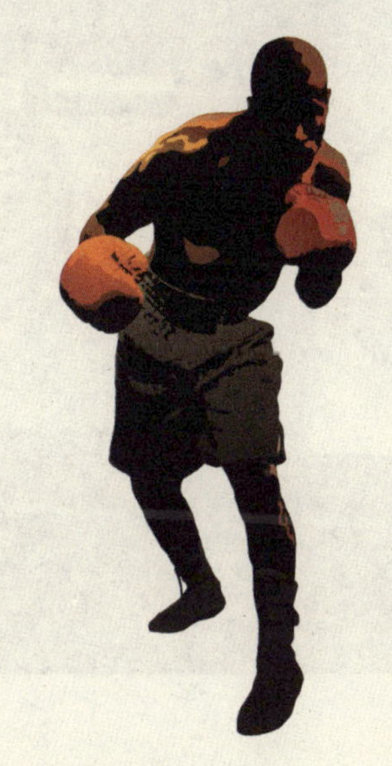

4.

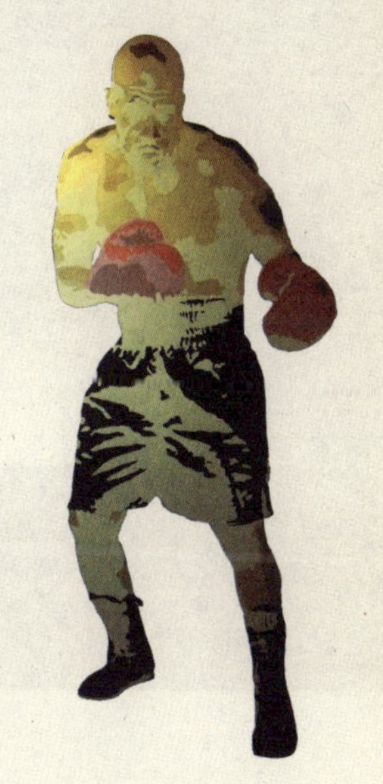

5.

1. Self-Portrait Fight (drawing 5)
2007, graphite on paper, 24 × 32 in (61 × 81 cm)

2. Self-Portrait Fight (drawing 2)
2007, graphite on paper, 24 x 32 in (61 x 81 cm)

3. Self-Portrait Icon (painting 1)
2006, sign enamel on plywood cutout, 108 × 108 in (274 × 274 cm)

4. Self-Portrait Fight (painting 1)
2007, sign enamel and metallic enamel on plywood cutout, 84 × 48 in (213 × 122 cm)

5. Self-Portrait Fight (painting 2)
2008, sign enamel and metallic enamel on plywood cutout, 90 × 36 in (229 × 91 cm)

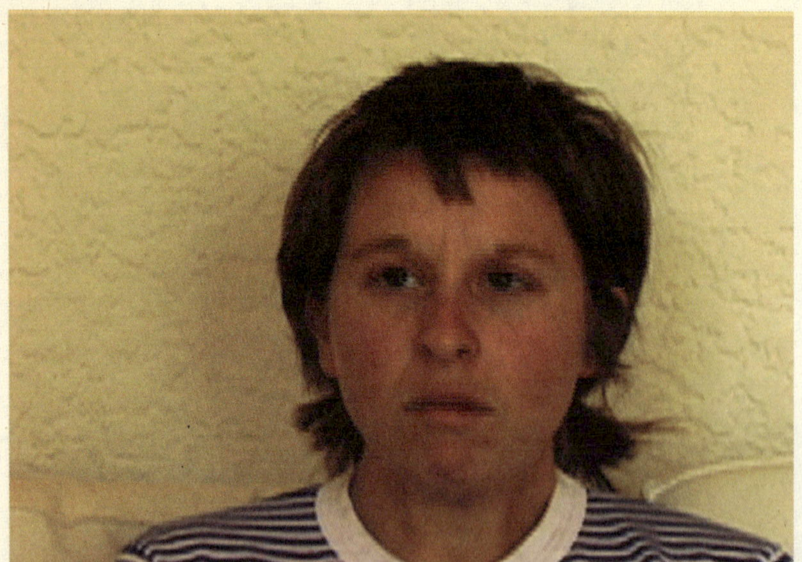

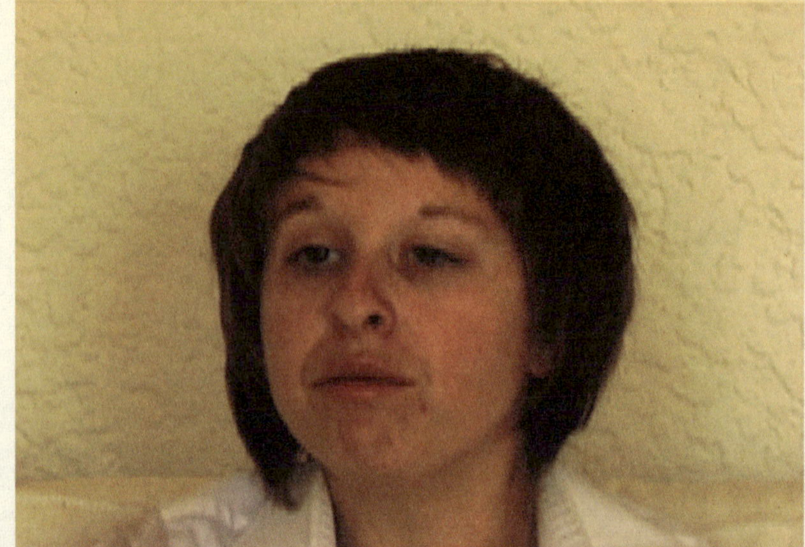

1.

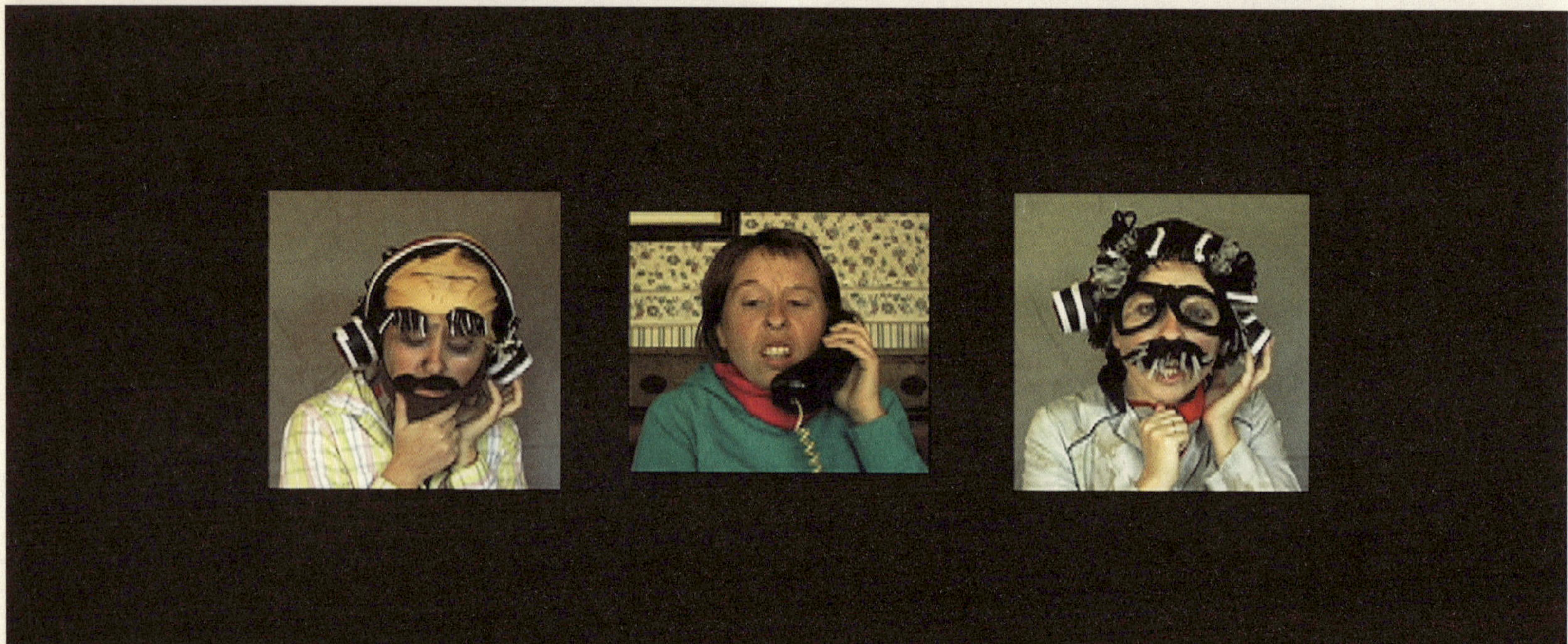

2.

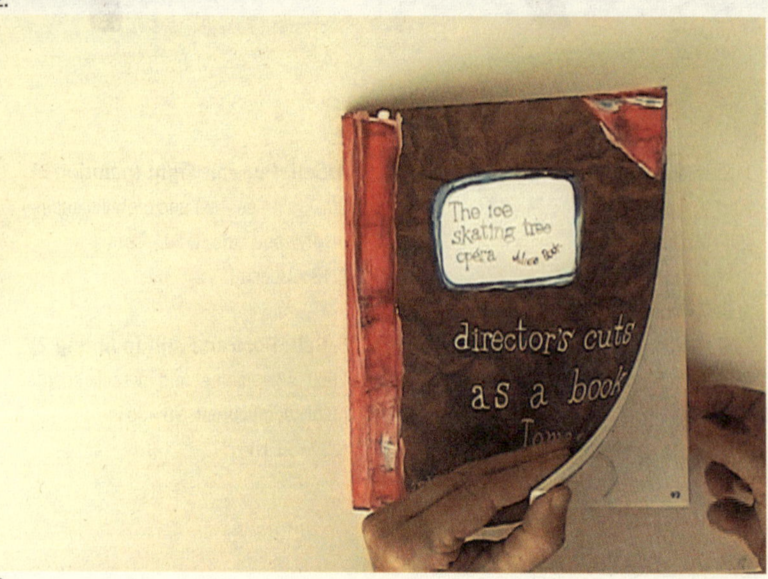

3.

Los Angeles-based Julie Lequin's diverse practice encompasses video, performance, watercolor painting, and making lists, among many other activities. She is interested in storytelling and characterization, and in the differences between the humorous, the awkward, and the melancholic.

1. **Speech Lesson**
2005, video, 5 min 19 sec

2. **Car Talk**
2008-present, video

3. **Gossip Videos**
from the book/DVD project **Ice Skating Tree Opera – Director's Cuts**, 2nd Cannons Publications, Los Angeles, 2007, video, 6 min 40 sec

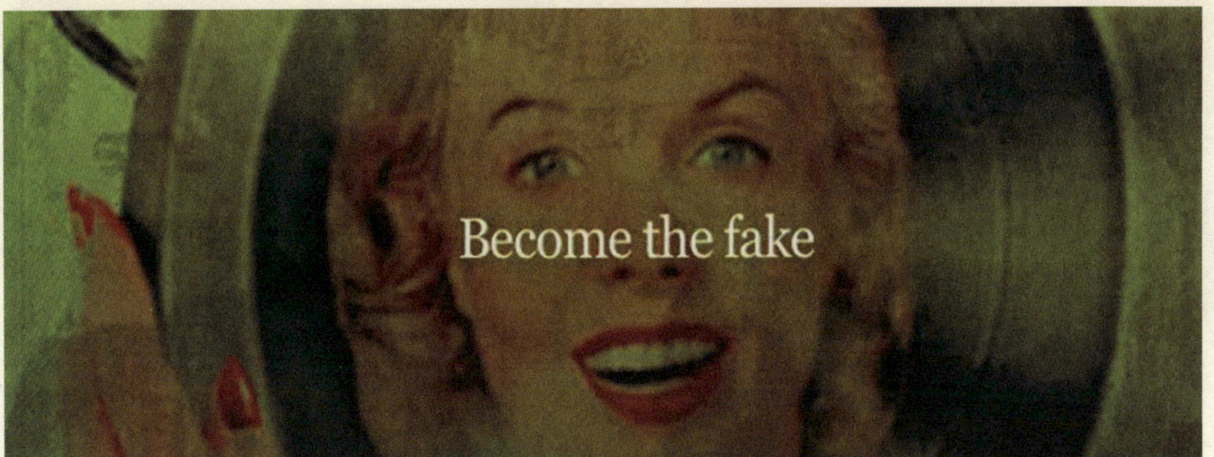

1.

2.

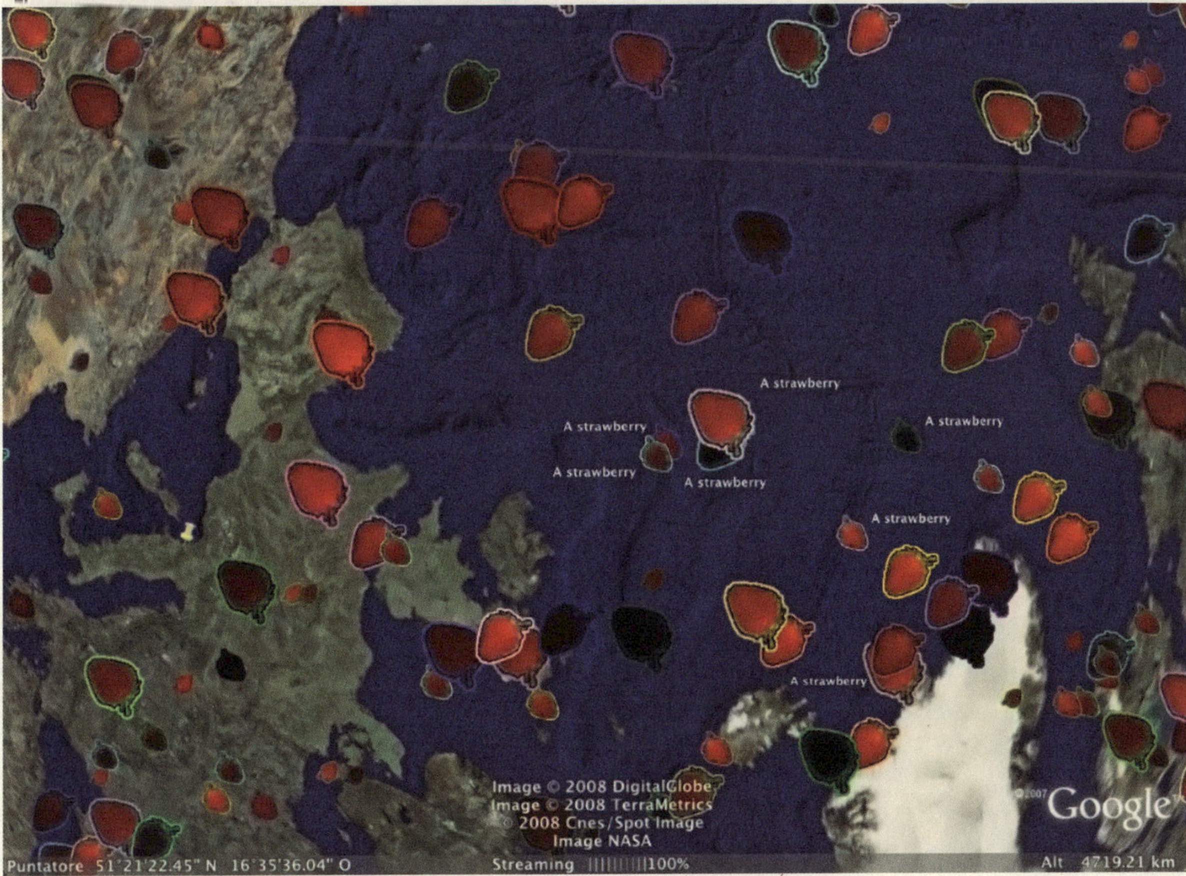

3.

Les Liens Invisibles is an "imaginary art-group" from Italy comprised of media artists Clemente Pestelli (b. 1979, Florence) and Gionatan Quintini (b. 1980, Florence). Their work is based on "the invisible links between the info sphere, neural synapses, and real life." It revolves around the subversive strategies of Situationist-style détournement offered by user-generated websites, as well as participatory democratic models. Offline, they have participated in shows at the Villa Borbone, Lucca, Italy (2008), and the Edith-Ruß-Haus für Medienkunst in Oldenburg, Germany (2007), among others.

1. A Fake is a Fake. Anyway
2008, website, fake.isafake.org

2. Peking2008.com
2008, fake website, peking2008.com

3. Google Is Not The Map
2008, website, google.isnotthemap.net

Michelle Letelier investigates the impact of mining industries – and of their collapse – on social history, primarily in a six-year documentation of the closing of a copper-mining camp in her native Chile.
Since moving to Berlin in 2007, Letelier has shifted her focus to the German coal industry. By superimposing text on documentary photographs and video and presenting them alongside found objects, Letelier evokes the connection between rocky, rugged landscapes and the people whose livelihood depends on them.

1 & 2. **DESARME**
with sound by Andrés Bucci
2004-07, video, 2 min 19 sec

3 & 4. **Erase**
from series **Erase**
2002, black and white photograph, dimensions variable

5. **ZERFRESSEN**
2008, 3-channel video, 1 min

6. **Elsewhere**
with sound by Andrés Bucci
2008, series of 5 videos, 3 min

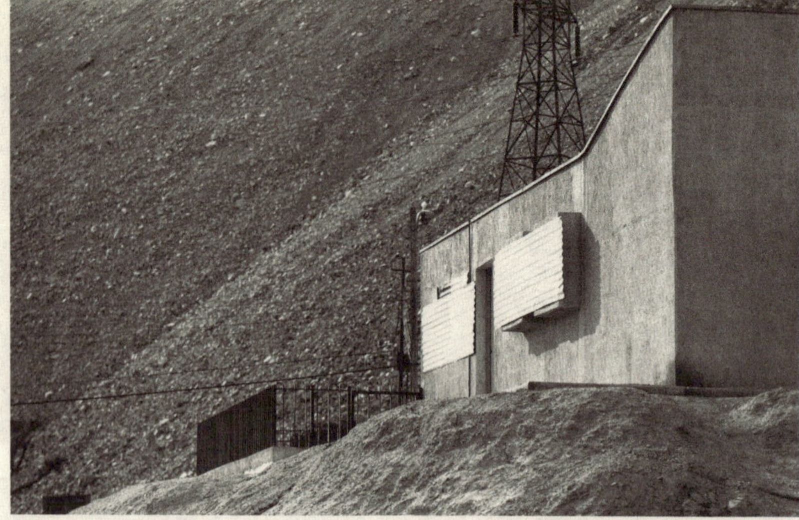
3.

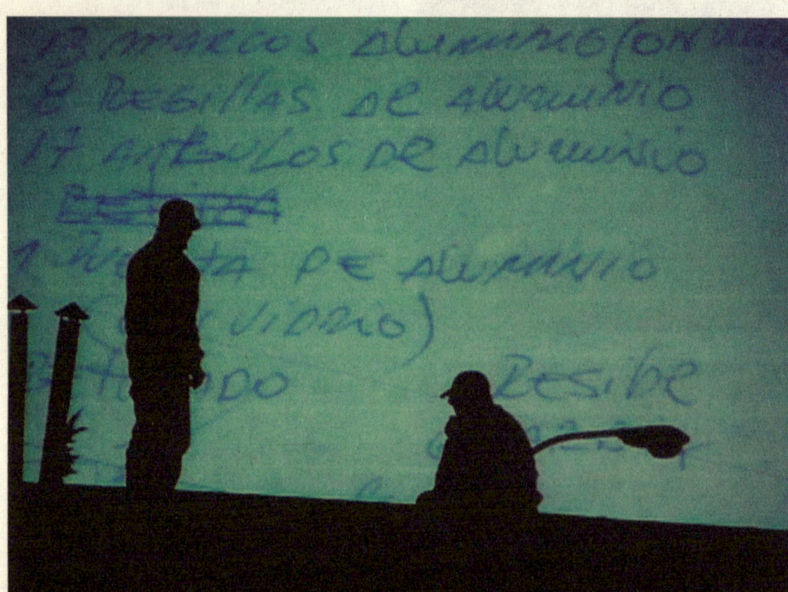
1.

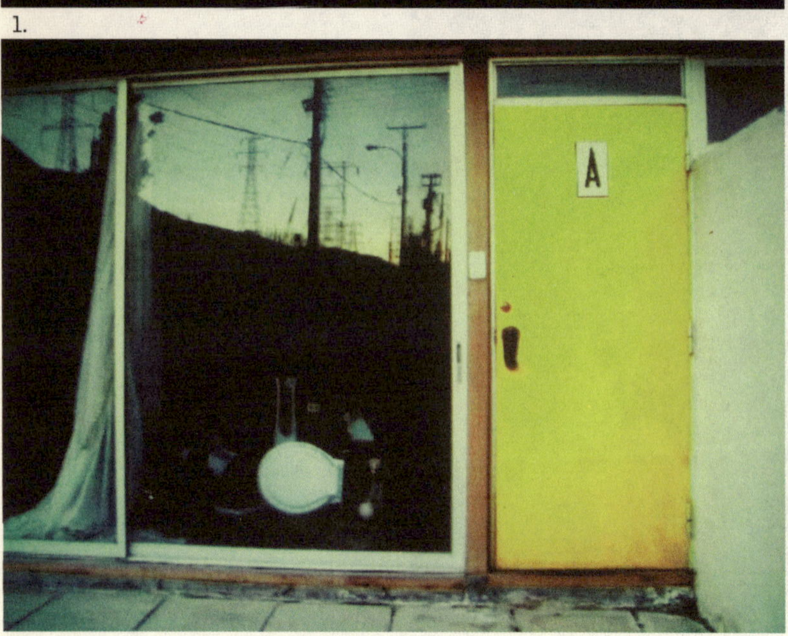

2.

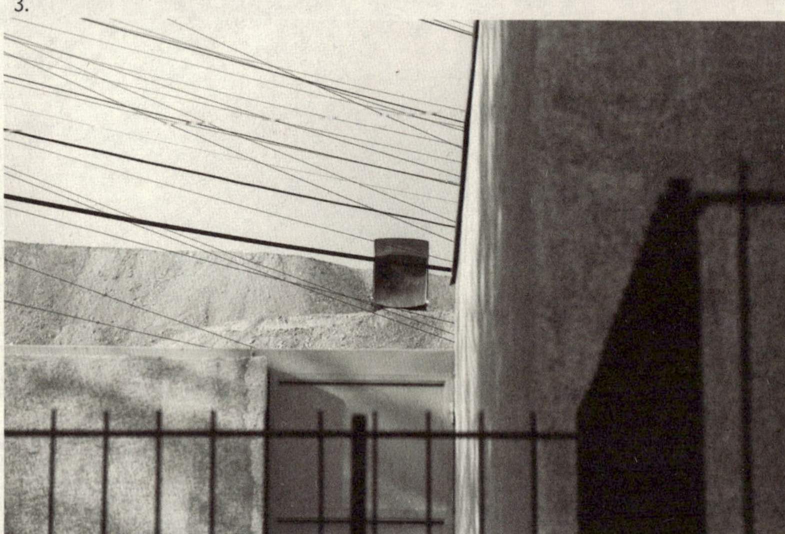
4.

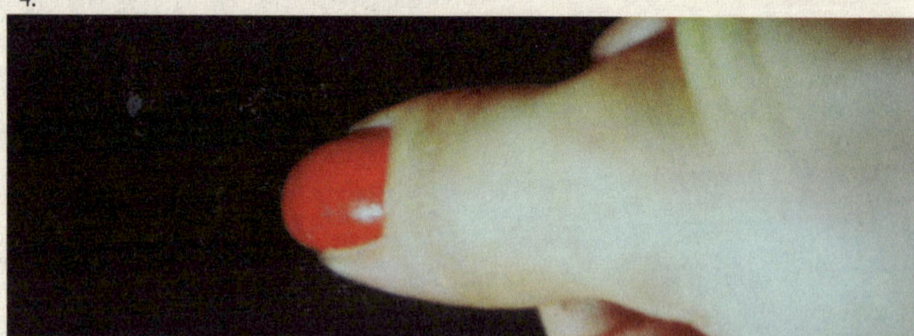
5.

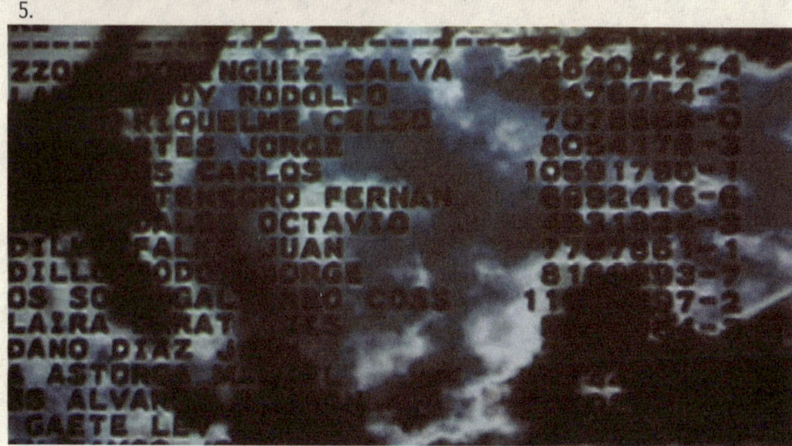
6.

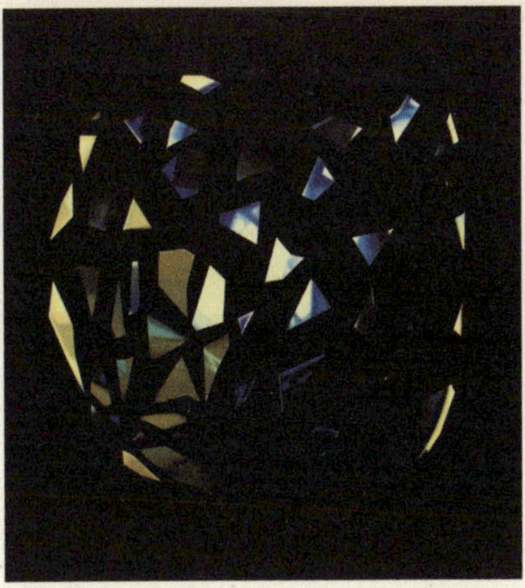

1.

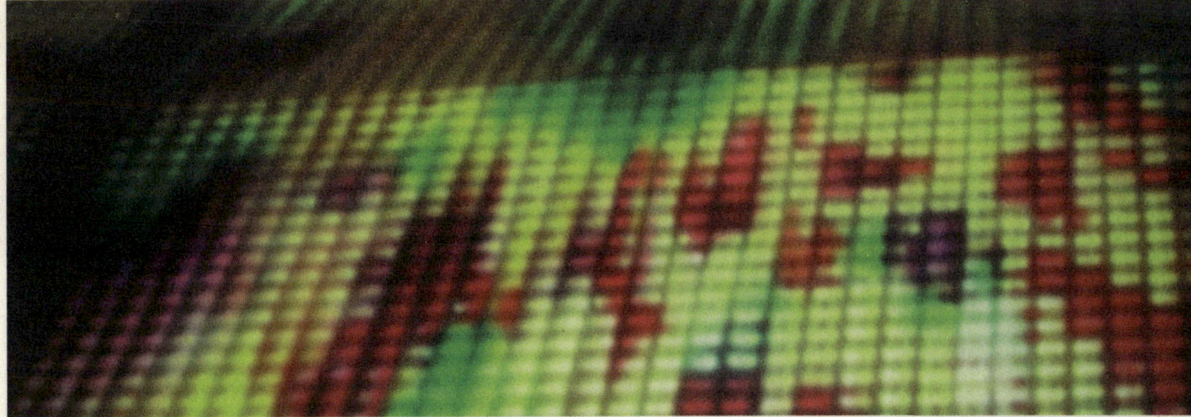

2.

Li Shurui graduated from the Sichuan Fine Arts Institute and now lives and works in Beijing. She makes large-scale abstract airbrush acrylic paintings from photography of music club interiors. **Untitled Lights** (2007-08) depicts kaleidoscopic images that suggest her fascination with synthetic light.

1. Another kind of light No 3
2008, acrylic on canvas, 6 ¾ × 6 ¾ ft (2 × 2 m)

2. Lights No. 20
2006, acrylic on canvas, 39 ½ × 118 ¼ in (1 × 3 m)

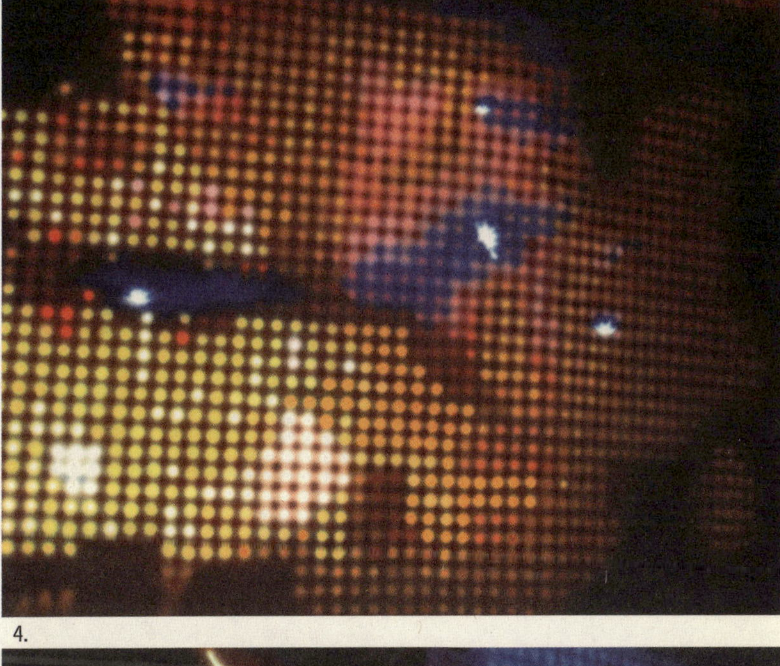

4.

3.

5.

3. Room Named Elevator
2008, elevator and daylight lamp, dimensions variable

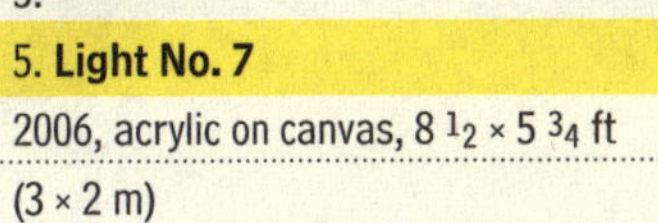

4. Light No. 9
2006, acrylic on canvas, 8 ½ × 5 ¾ ft (3 × 2 m)

5. Light No. 7
2006, acrylic on canvas, 8 ½ × 5 ¾ ft (3 × 2 m)

1.

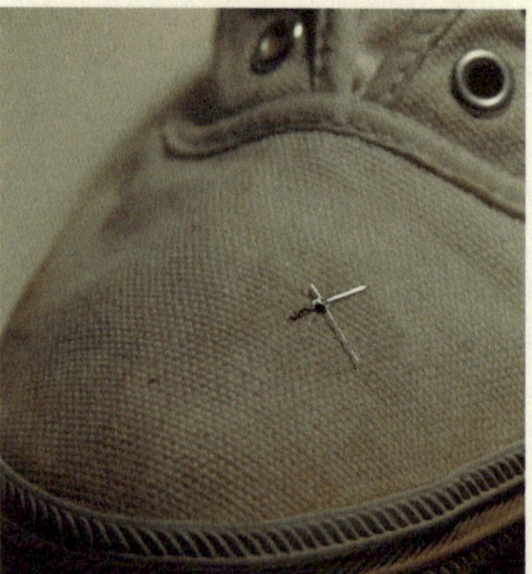

2.

Liang Yuanwei graduated with a BA and an MA from the China Central Academy of Fine Art. She lives and works in Beijing. The rigorous oil paintings from her 2008 **Pieces of Life** series were inspired by fabrics and prints from her own clothing. Her thickly painted surfaces suggest textures and patterns, focusing on the meticulous process of their production. As a member of the N12 group, she has also organized exhibitions of other emerging artists.

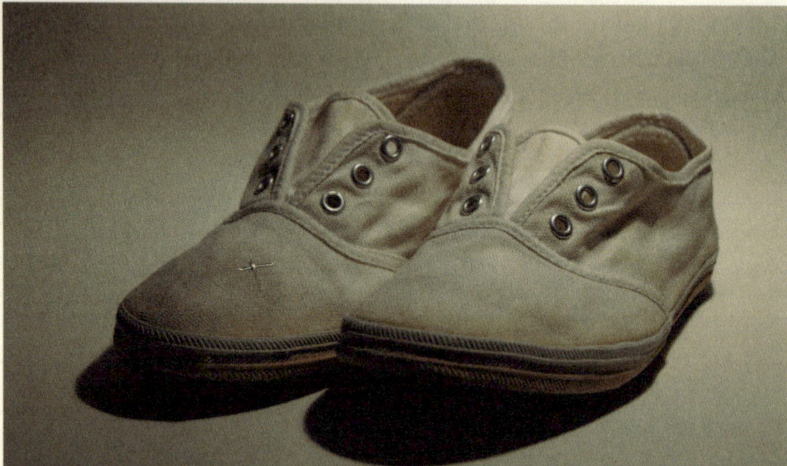

3.

1. **Piece of life No.12**
2007, oil on canvas, 47 ¼ × 55 ¼ in (120 × 140 cm)

2 & 3. **Salt** (details)
2006, cores of quartz watches and mixed media, dimensions variable

4. **Day & Night** (detail)
2008, 100 inkjet prints transferred to wall with water, dimensions variable

5. **umustbestrong**
2004-07, performance with typewriter and toilet paper, approx 12 × 12 × 8 in (30 × 30 × 20 cm)

4.

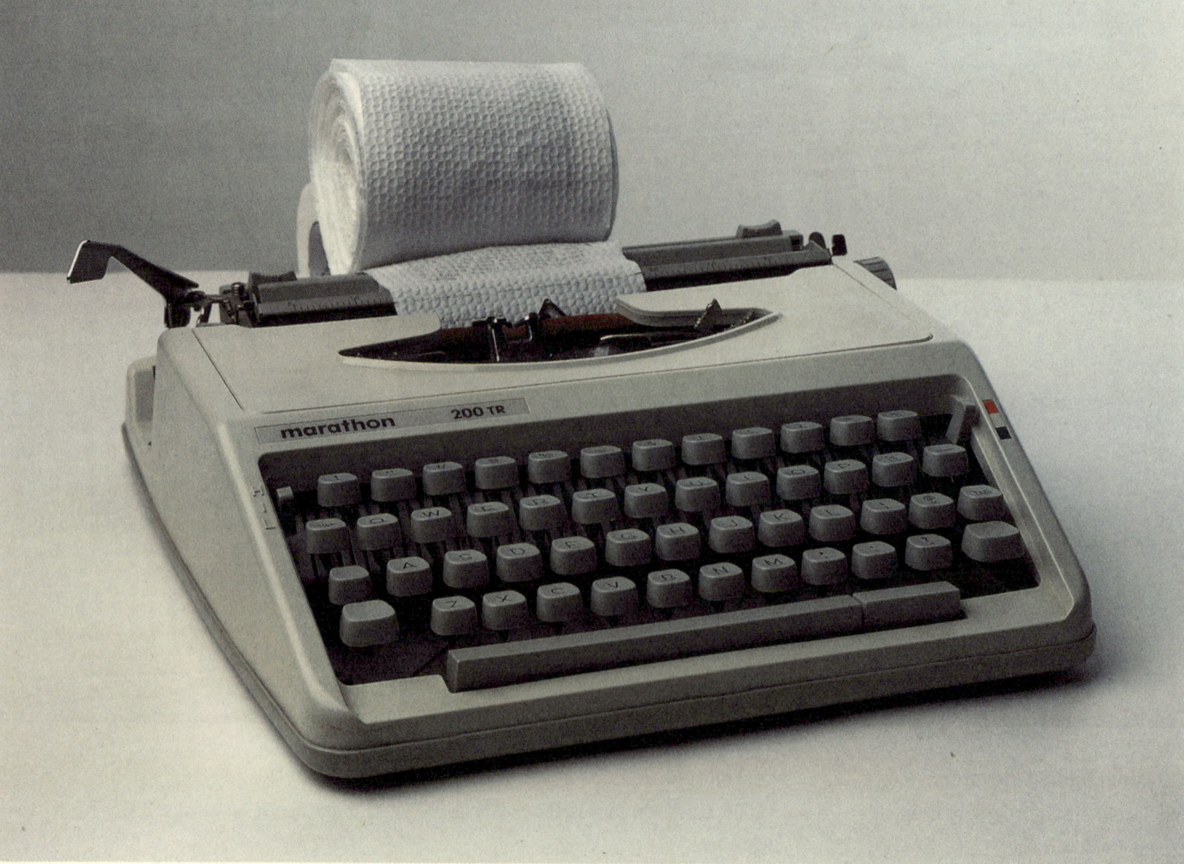

5.

Klara Liden was educated at the School of Architecture, Royal School of Technology, Stockholm, and University College of Arts Crafts and Design, Konstfack, Stockholm. She is recognized for her disquieting video work and her architectural interventions and assemblages. For her exhibition at Reena Spaulings Fine Art, "Elda för kråkorna" (2008), she reconstituted the gallery space as partial habitat for the local pigeon population, bringing a slice of urban bedlam inside the white cube. She currently lives and works in Berlin.

1. **Slide Show (Handicap)**
2006, carousel with handmade slides (inkjet on paper), dimensions variable

2. **Moonwalk**
2008, video, 5 min

3. **Bodies of Society**
2006, video, 4 min

4. **Benign**
2004, cardboard, steel pipes, framed photos, and stepladder, dimensions variable, installation view, Reena Spaulings Fine Art, New York

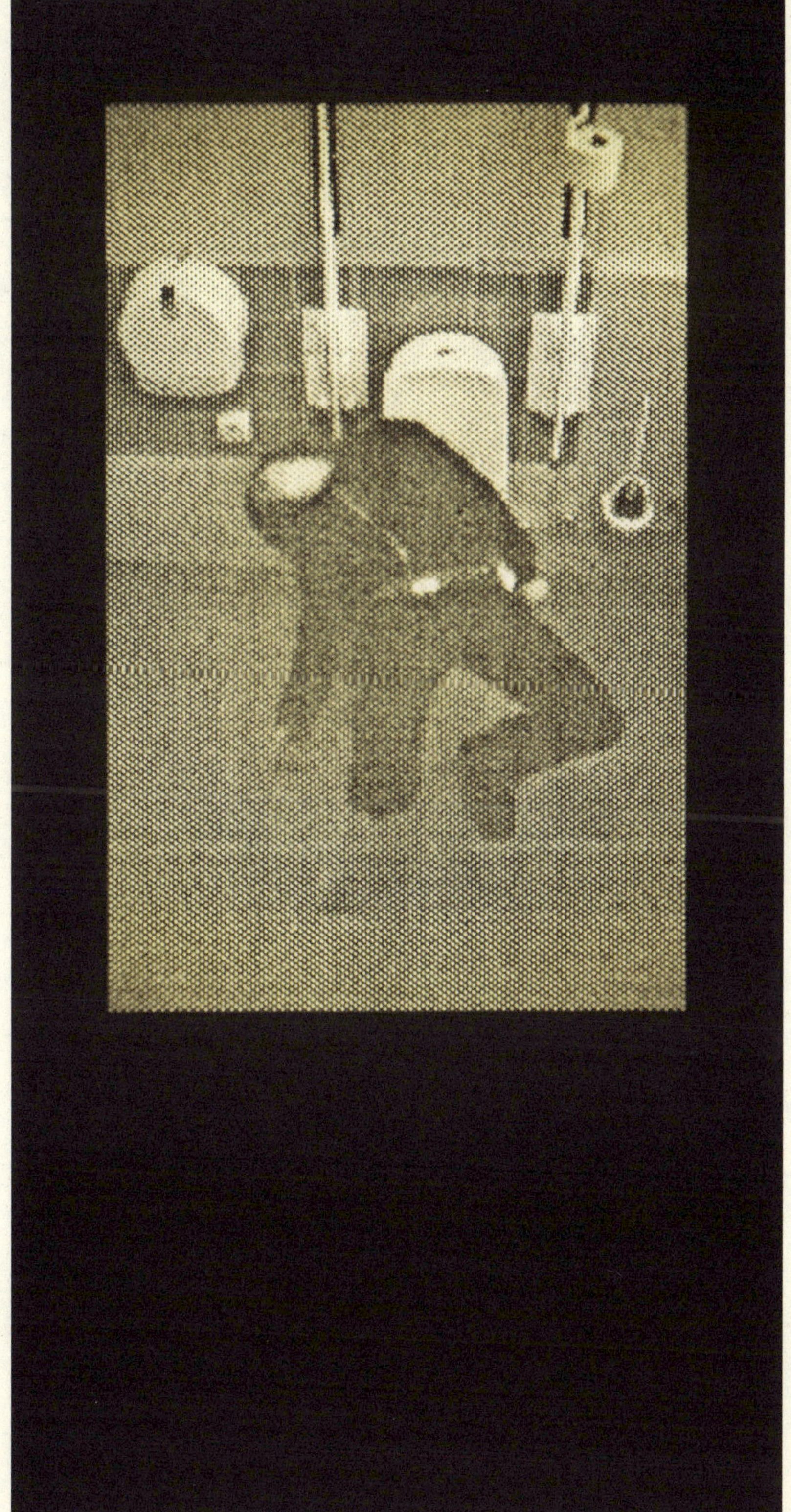

1.

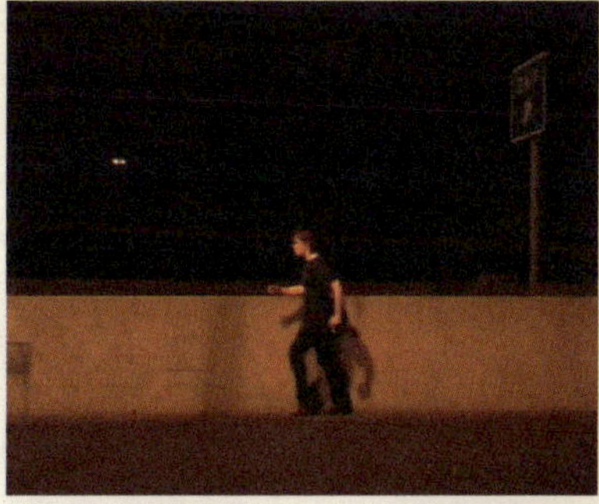

2.

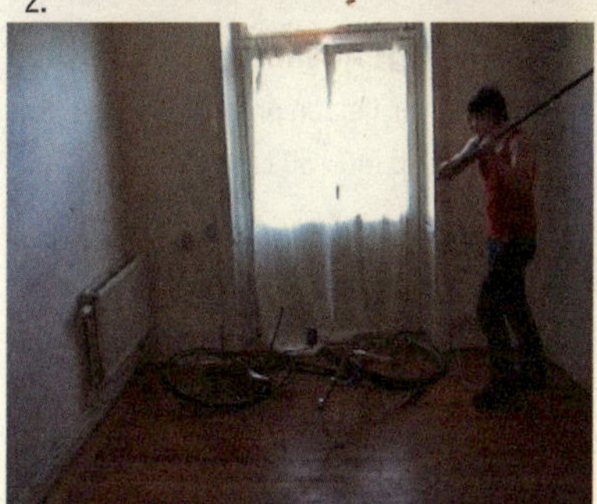

3.

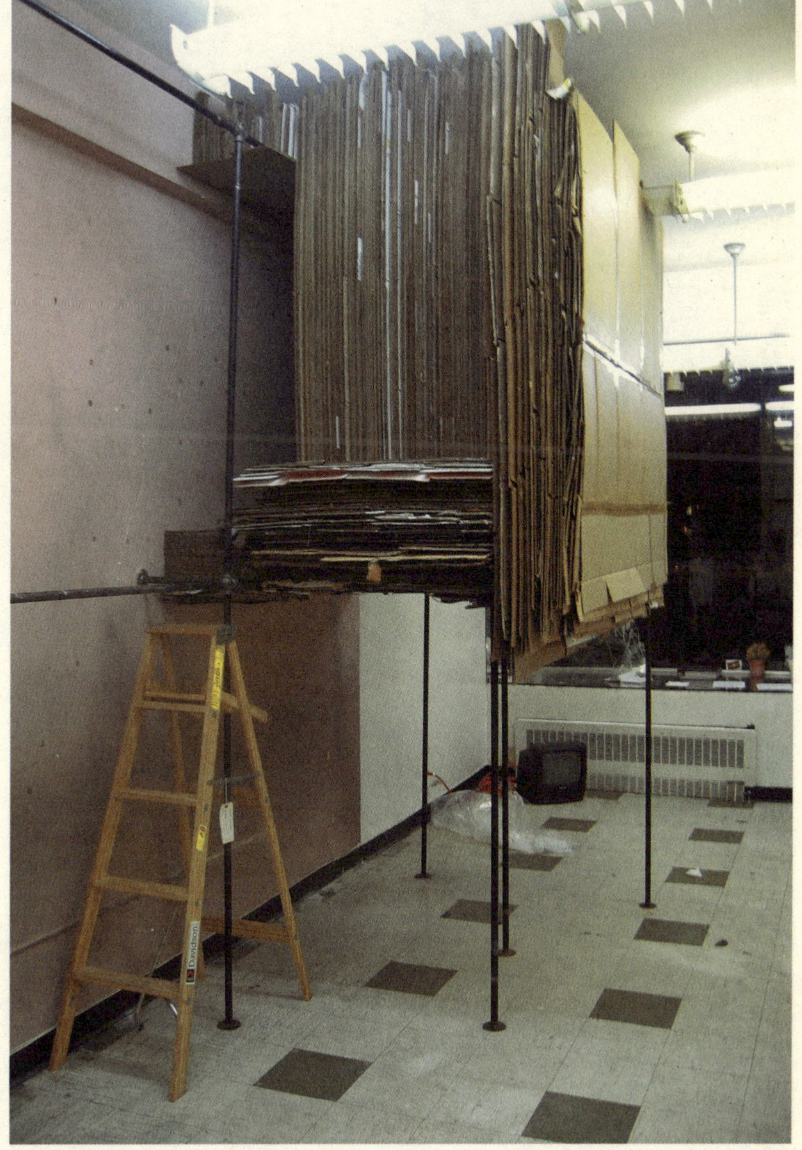

4.

David Lieske is currently based in Berlin. Drawing on a diverse range of materials, methods, and references (from the classical to the contemporary), he examines the possibilities of production, presentation, and context. Lieske habitually exploits misunderstanding, coincidence, and self-reference, allowing happenstance to lead him from one idea to the next.

1. **(Imagining) Atlantis 1-15**
2006, 15 silver gelatin prints, each 15 ½ × 11 ¾ in (40 × 30 cm)

2. **The Atlantis Dialogue** (detail)
2006, Plato bust, paint, and text, dimensions variable

3. **Atlantis (Indeterminated Jump)**
2006, plots, framed, each 23 ½ × 33 in (60 × 84 cm); bricks, wood, and paint, 32 × 38 ¼ × 23 in (81 × 97 × 58 cm)

4. **Case Arse**
2004, obstacle bars, obstacle pillars, and metal brackets, approx 6 ft × 9 ¾ × 9 ¾ ft (180 × 300 × 300 cm); framed prints, each 21 ¼ × 18 ½ in (54 × 47 cm)

1.

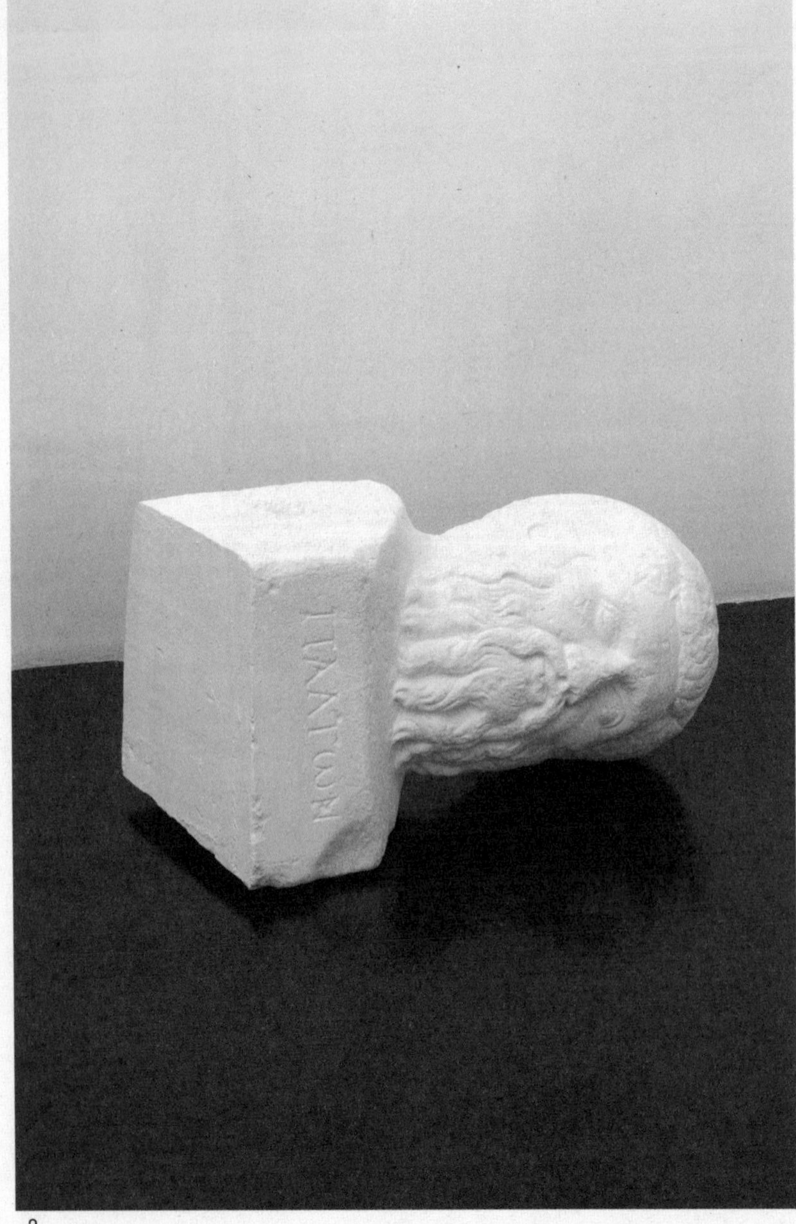
2.

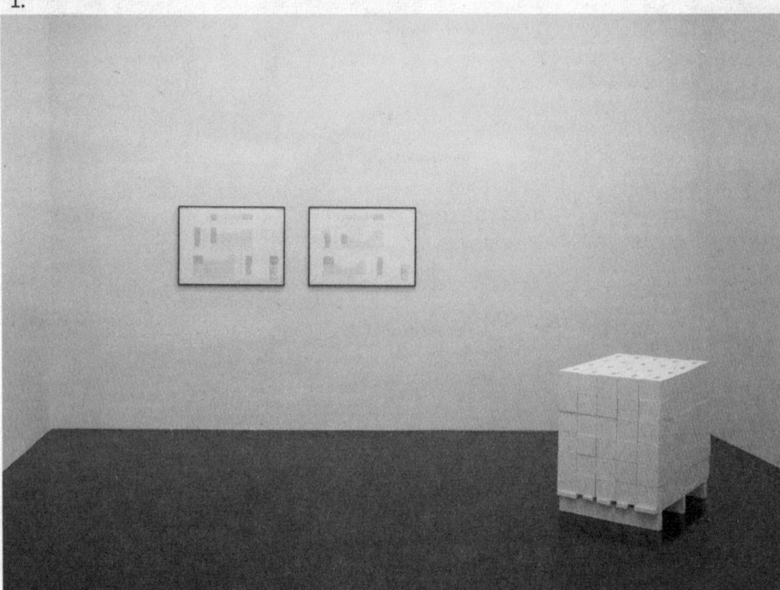
3.

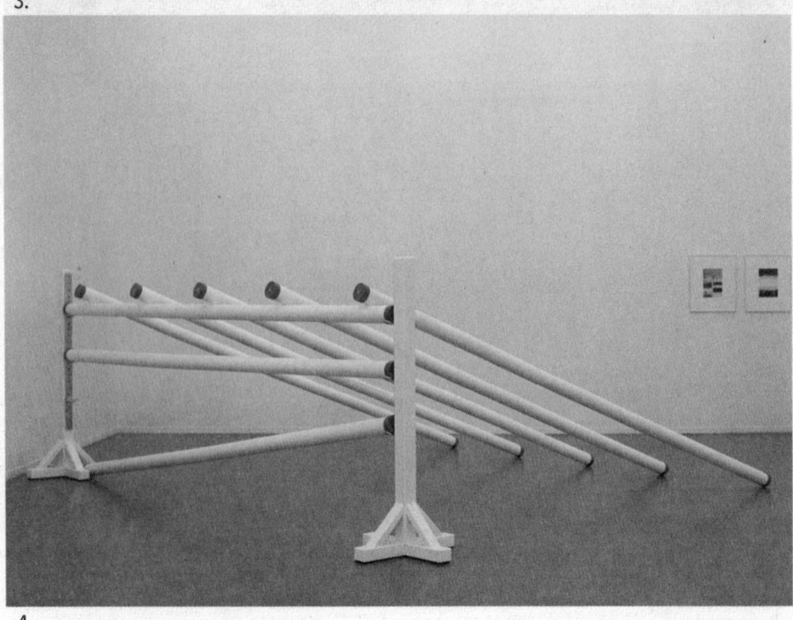
4.

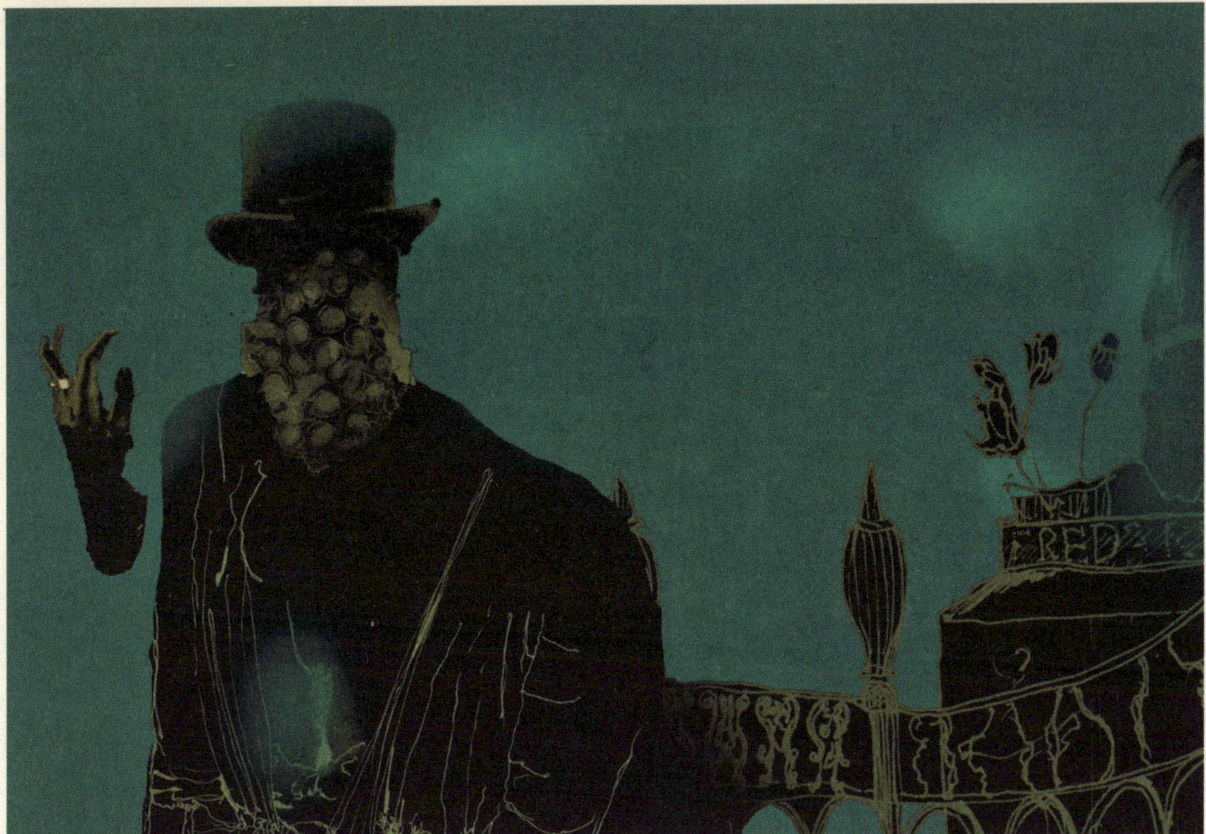

1.

Geoff Lillemon is based in Amsterdam. His Surrealist-inspired electronic paintings fuse new and traditional mediums, while his Oculart website (oculart.com) accompanies animated imagery with music and poetry, often to hallucinatory effect.

1. **Une Vieillardes**
2007, digital image

2. **Silk Field**
2008, digital image

3. **Tomorrow**
2006, digital image

4. **Hey Death**
2006, digital image

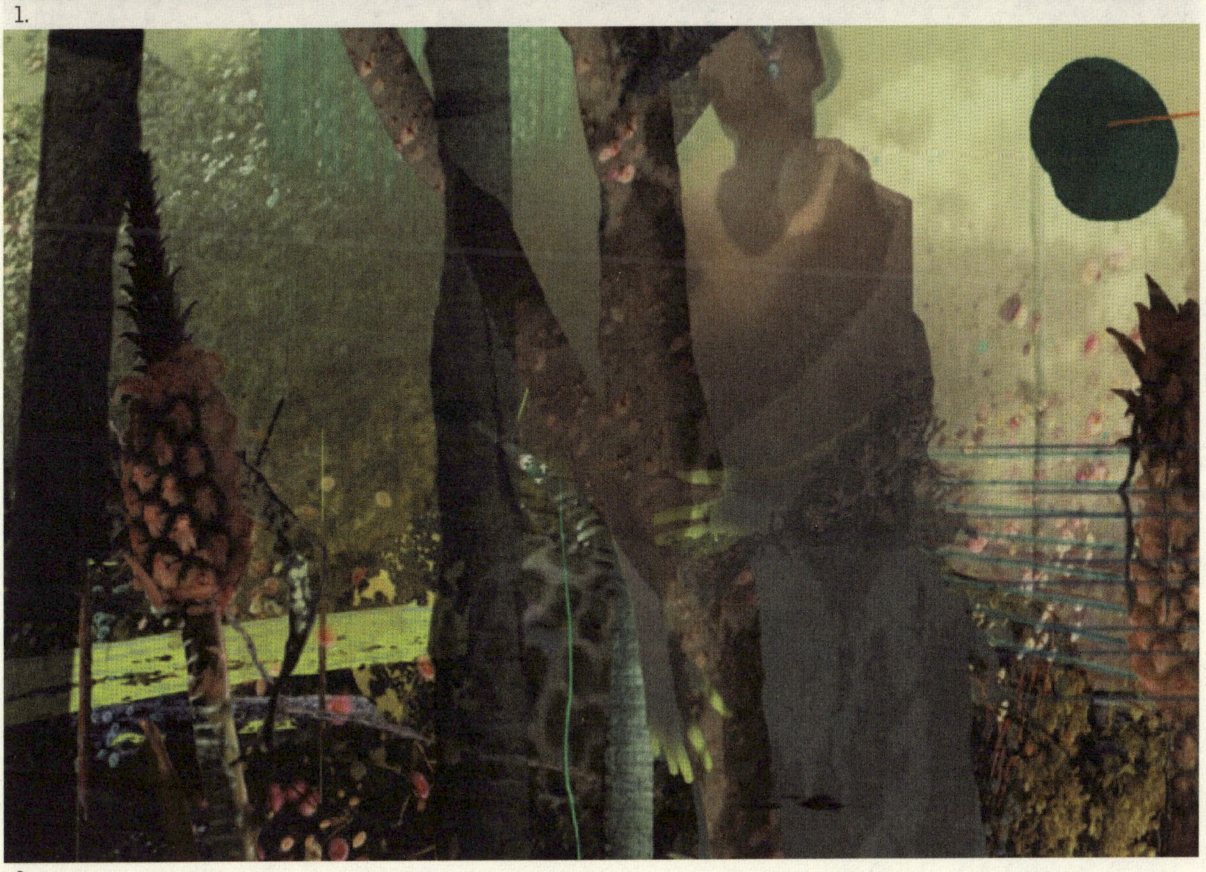

2.

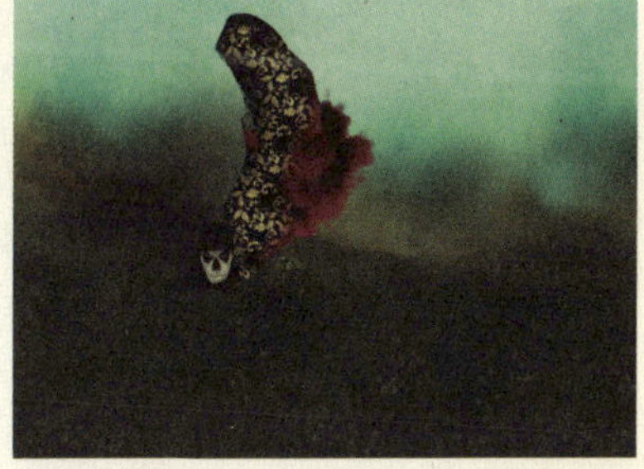

3.

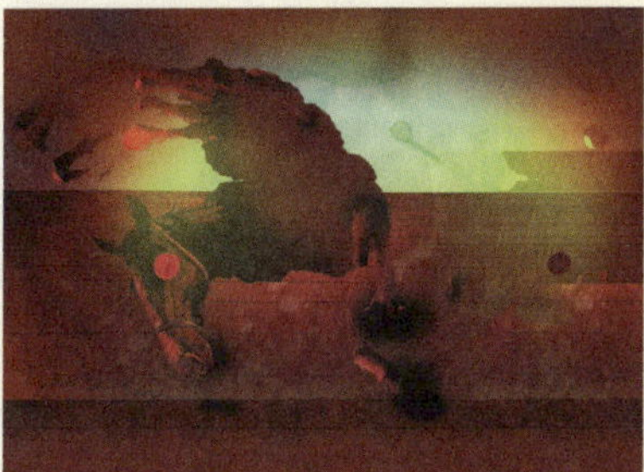

4.

Michael D. Linares is an artist born and based in San Juan, Puerto Rico. His works take a variety of paths to directly address his audience. Whether in the form of adlike slogans, visual riddles, or social spaces, Linares's art demands the presence and response of the viewer to reach completion.

1. **Untitled** (detail)
2006, acrylic on canvas, 72 × 72 in (183 × 183 cm)

2. **On, Chris, Daniel**
from the series **Affordable (Paintings)**
2008, acrylic on canvas, 3 parts, each 16 × 20 in (41 × 51 cm)

1.

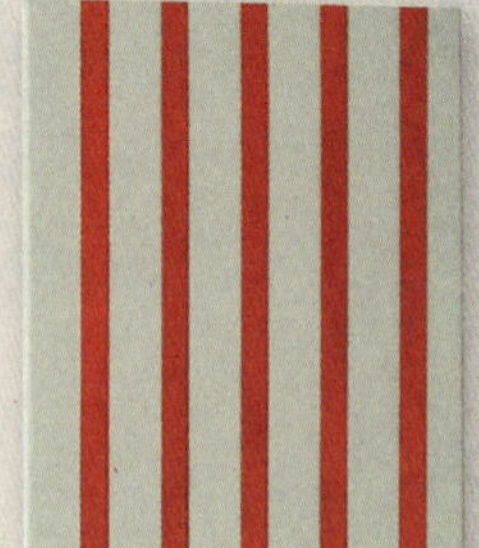

2.

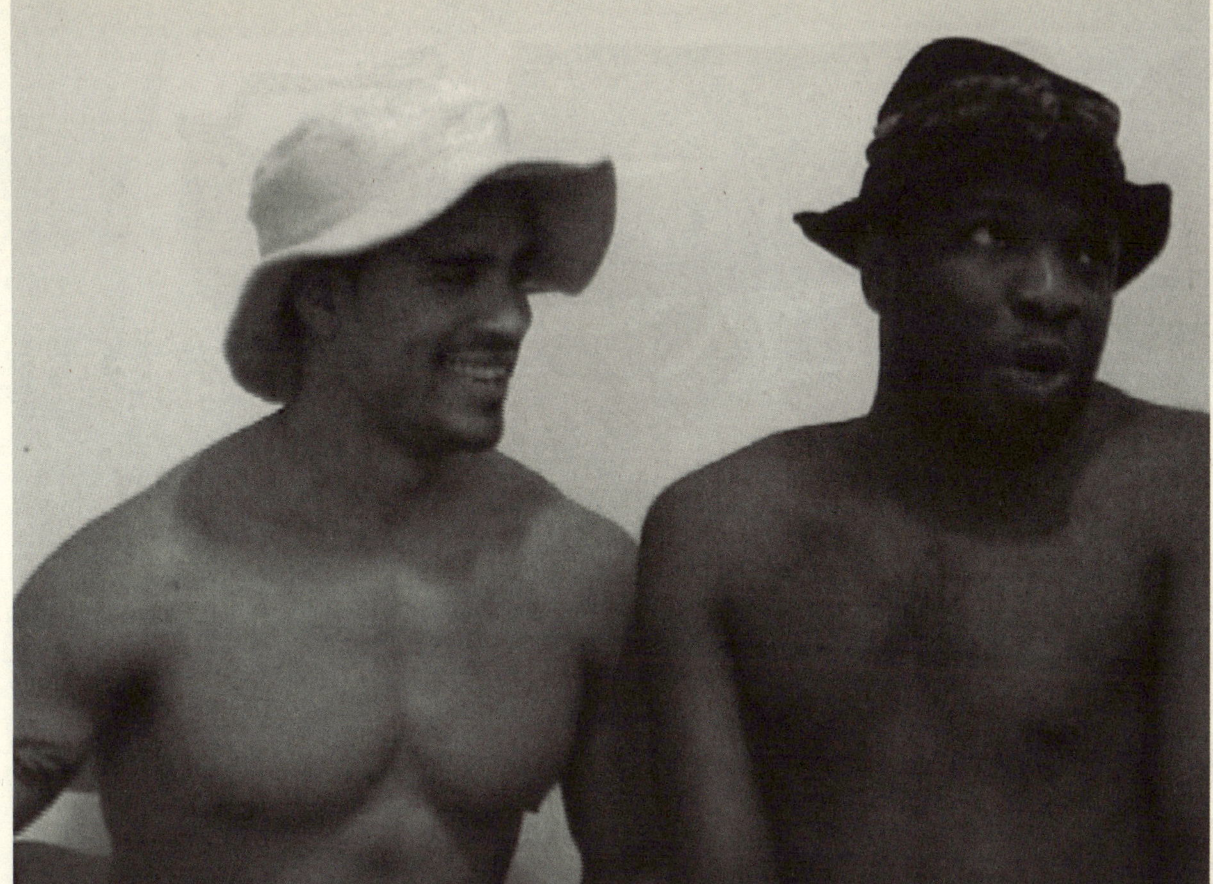

1.

Kalup Linzy graduated from the University of South Florida and is currently based in Brooklyn. In his campy performances and videos, he often satirizes television soap operas, playing many of the characters – male and female – en route to a witty deconstruction of racial and gender stereotypes.

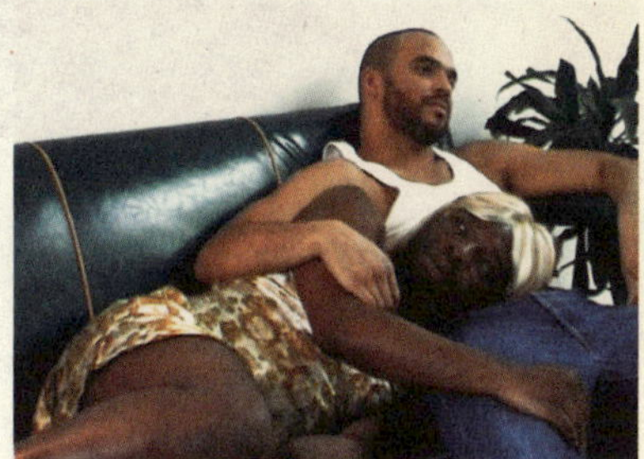

3.

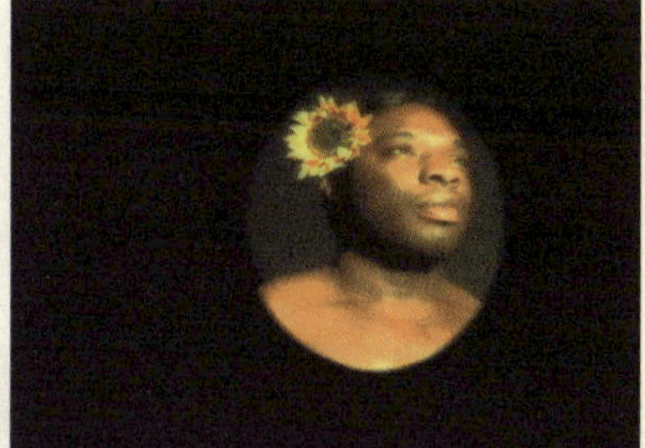

4.

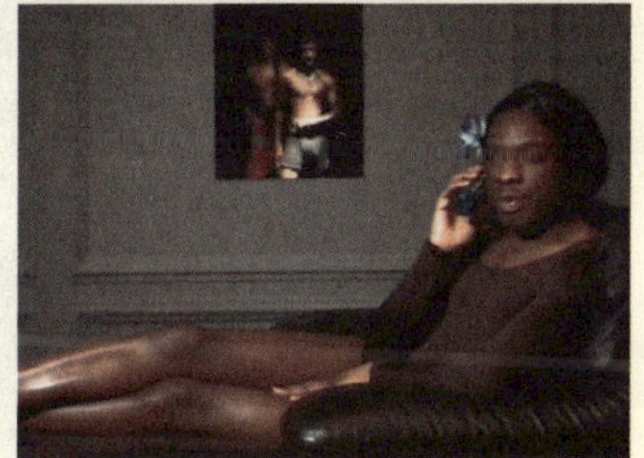

5.

2.

1. **Lollypop**
2006, video, 3 min 24 sec

2. **Melody Set Me Free**
2007, video, 15 min 19 sec

3. **Conversation Wit De Churen V: As Da Art World Might Turn**
2006, video, 12 min 9 sec

4. **Sweet Berry Sonnet**
2008, video, 37 min 54 sec

5. **Conversations wit de Churen III: Da Young and Da Mess**
2005, video, 16 min 56 sec

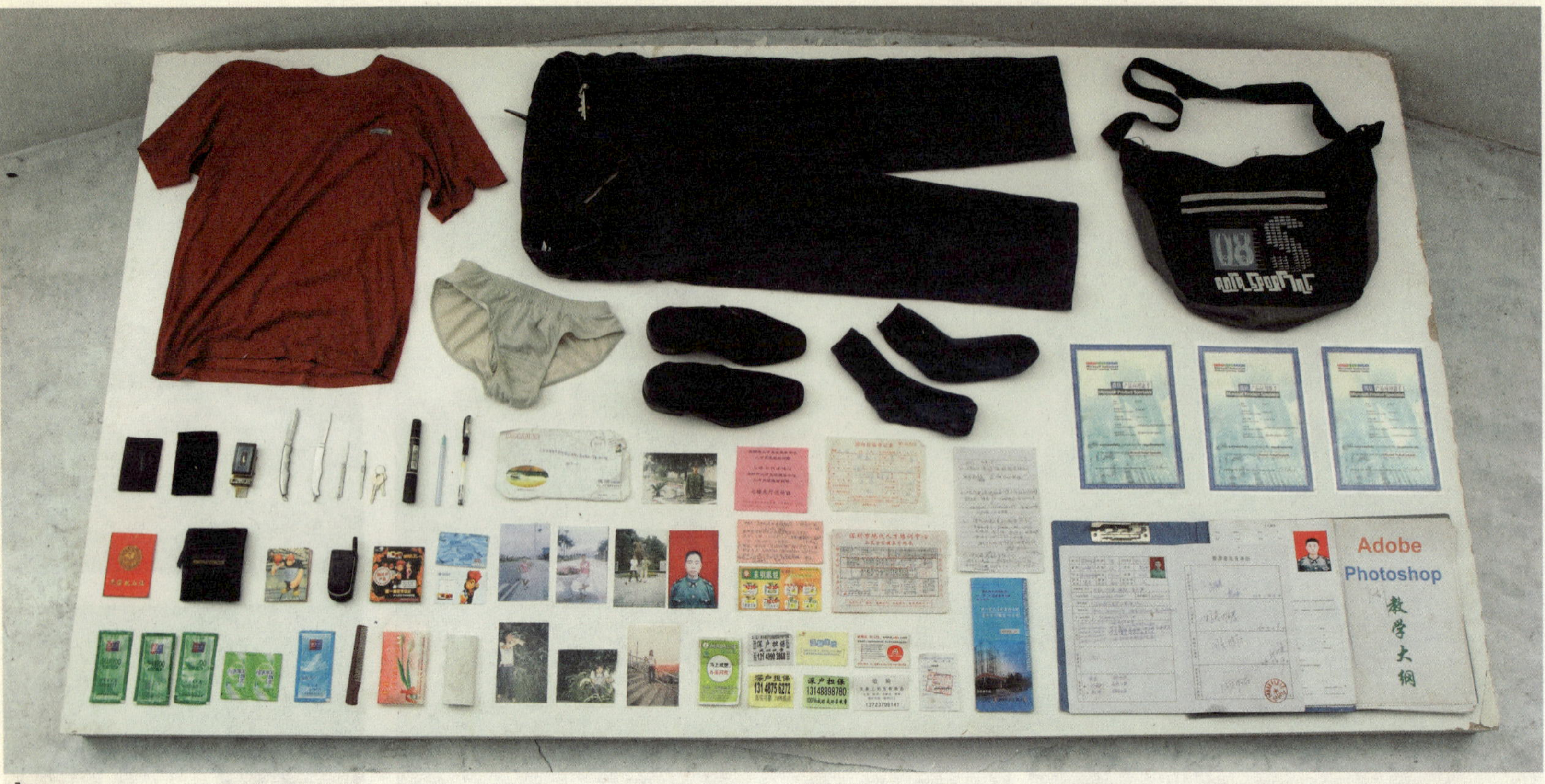

1.

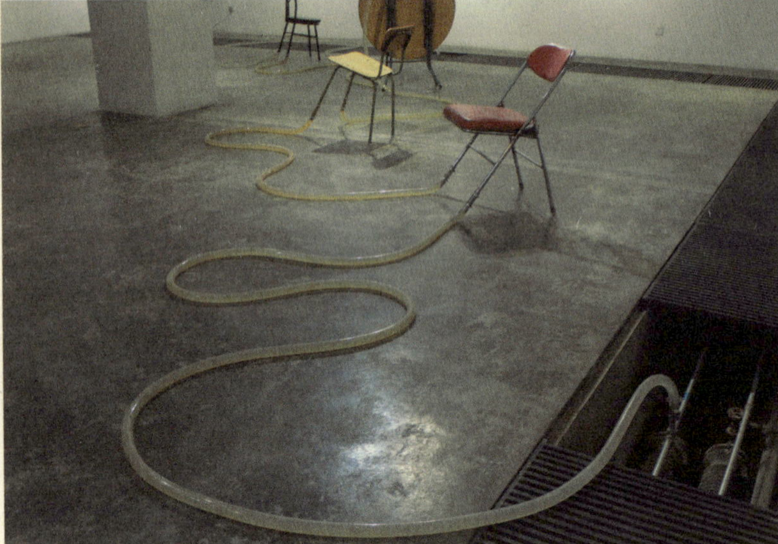

2.

Liu Chuang attended the Hubei Fine Arts Academy and currently lives in Beijing. His practice is often concerned with highlighting specific actions or characteristics of urban life in China. Sculptural installations include **Untitled (Unknown River) II** (2008), which channels the city's tap water in tubes running through chair frames, and **Split Landscape** (2005), which reproduces the steel cages on many Chinese windows.

1. Buying Everything On You (Zhou Shuping)
2006, mixed media, 94½ × 47¼ × 8 in (240 × 120 × 20 cm)

2. Untitled (Unknown River) II
2008, water pipe, chair, table, dimensions variable

3. Untitled (History of sweat)
2007, air-conditioning system, dimensions variable

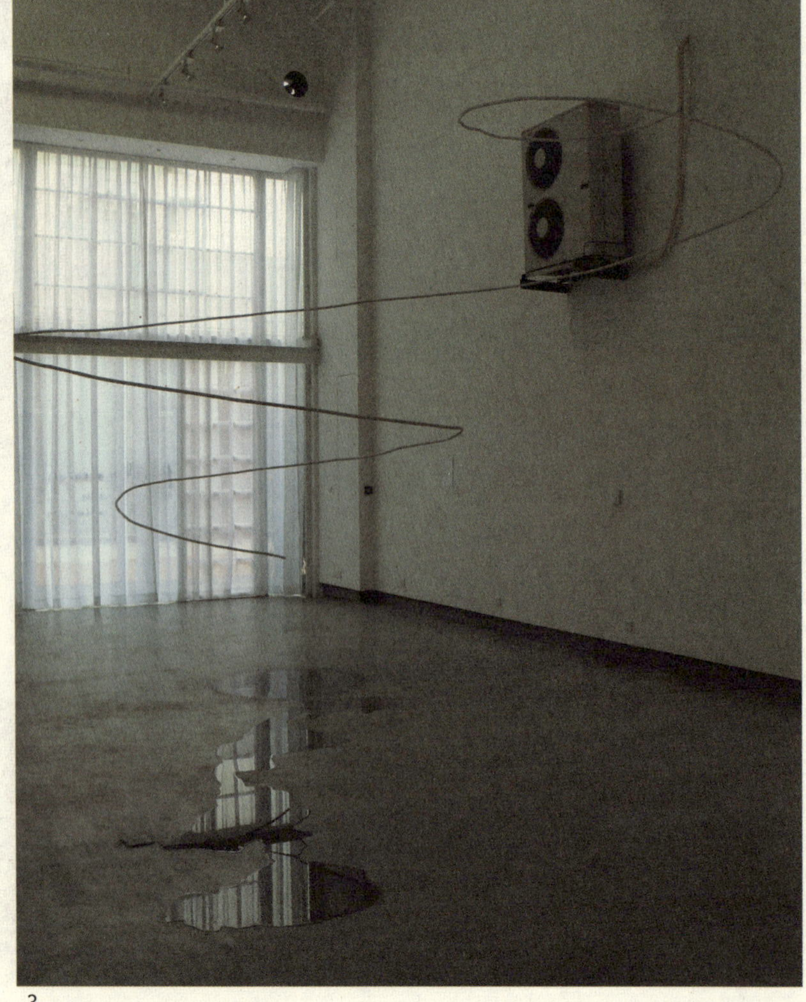

3.

Lindsay Ljungkull received an MFA from the University of Southern California, and continues to work in Los Angeles. Her works take a wry, skeptical attitude toward the power and mythology of film. Ljungkull showcases the conventions and artifice of film with deliberate flaws, like grainy textures, and elements that highlight the medium's reliance on time.

1. American Record Player

2006, chromogenic print, 40 × 30 in (102 × 76 cm)

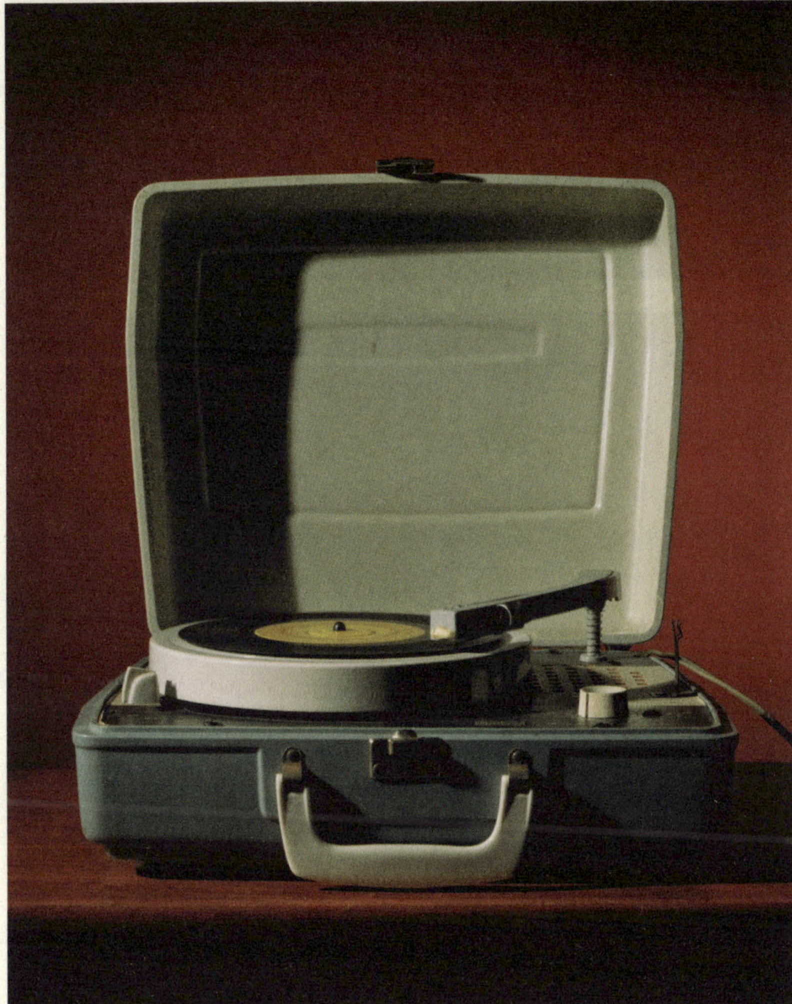

1.

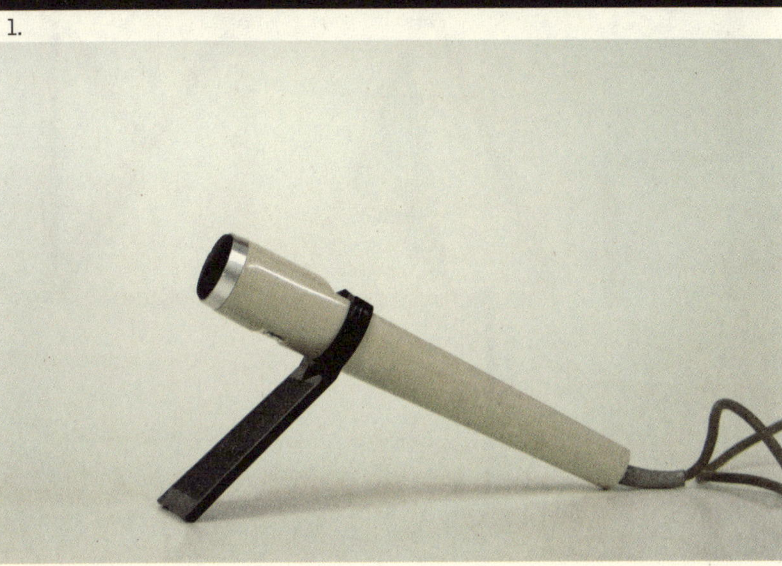

2.

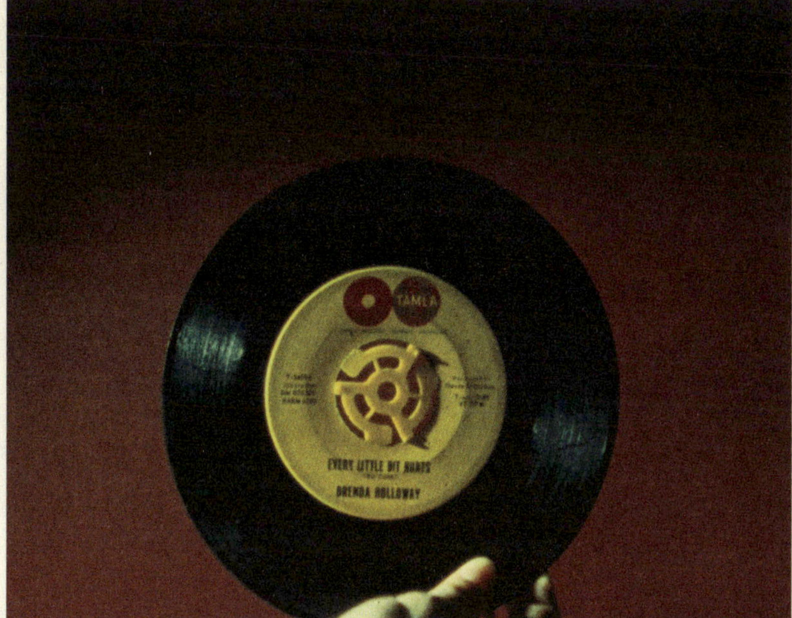

3.

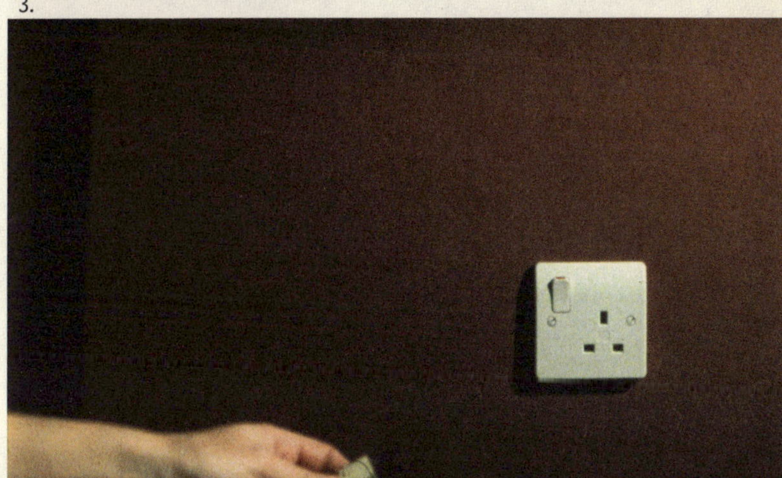

4.

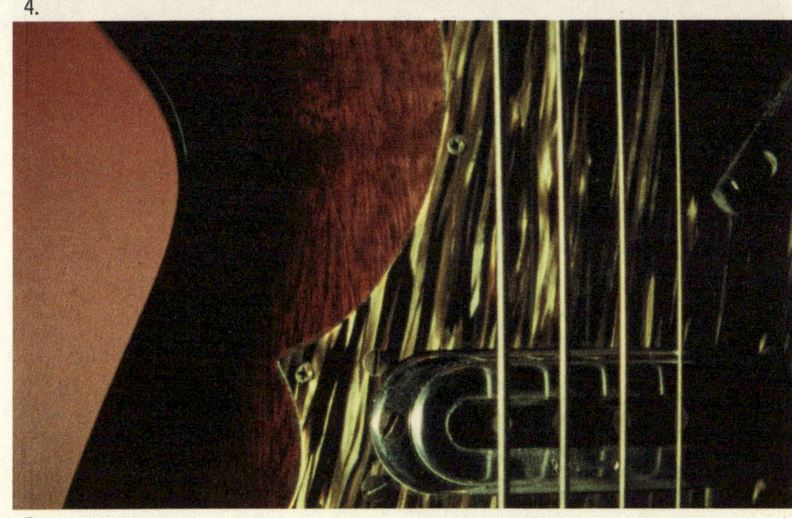

5.

2. Microphone

2006, chromogenic print, 4 × 6 in (10 × 15 cm)

3, 4 & 5. Darkness Silence Touch

2006, 16 mm film, 5 min

Maria Loboda was trained in the Interdiciplinary Fine Art Studies program at the Hochschule für Bildende Künste, Städelschule in Frankfurt, Germany. Her work is concerned with alternative registers of knowledge and agency, such as divination, magic, and the occult. Loboda explores how these practices relate to the modernist understanding of creativity, and the now-anachronistic notion of the art object as spiritual catalyst and perceptual transformer. Her work has been included in shows at the Frankfurter Kunstverein and the Auckland Art Gallery in New Zealand.

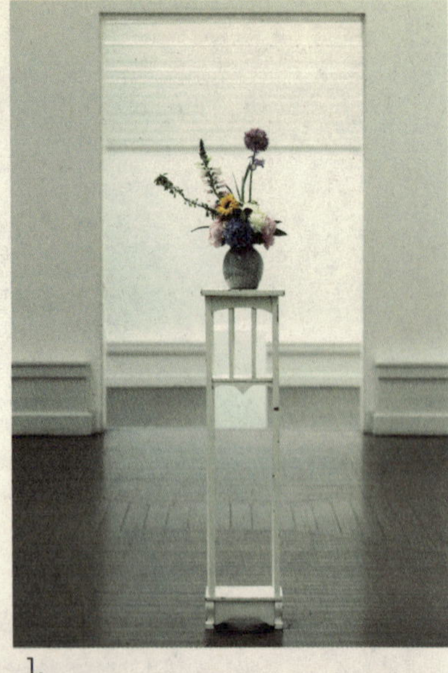

1.

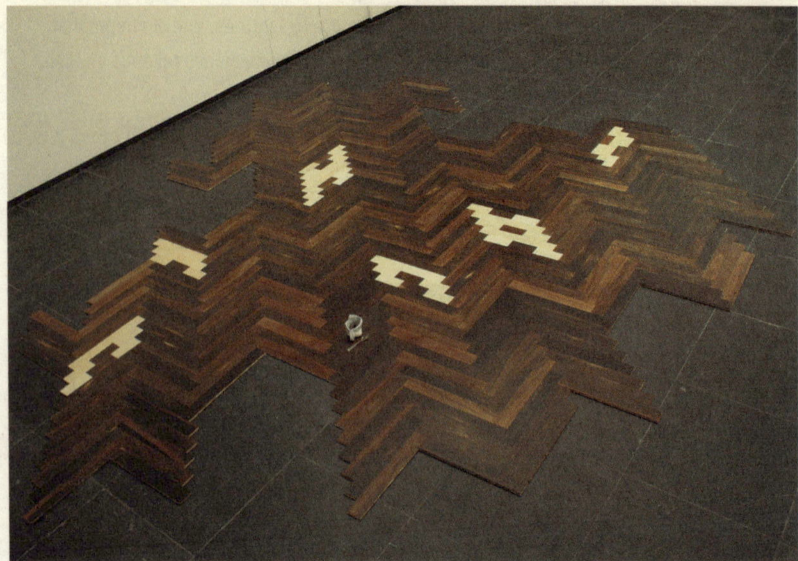

2.

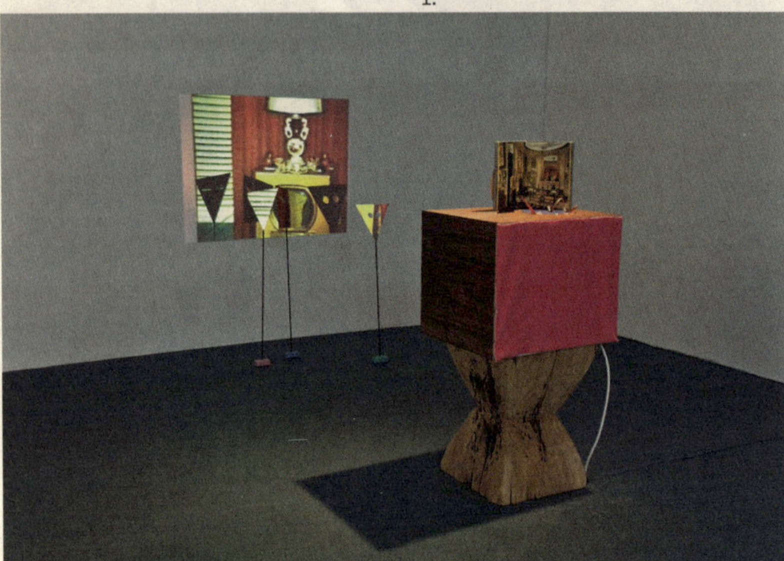

3.

4.

1. A GUIDE TO INSULTS AND MISANTHROPY

2004-08, flowers, herbs, vase, pedestal, dimensions variable

2. WHAT WILL HAPPEN?

2007, oak and maple parquet floor, dimensions variable

3. THREE TRAGEDIES AND A SATYR PLAY

2008, mixed media, dimensions variable

4. FOUR OR FIVE MANIFESTATIONS OF A NIGHTMARE

2008, mixed media, dimensions variable

5. SPHERE, CONE, SCREW, ROD, CRYSTALLINE FORM, PLATE, STRIP

2008, wood, glass, book page, construction paper, aluminum, quartz crystal, marmor paper, and Led Zeppelin T-shirt, 27 ½ × 55 ¼ in (70 × 140 cm)

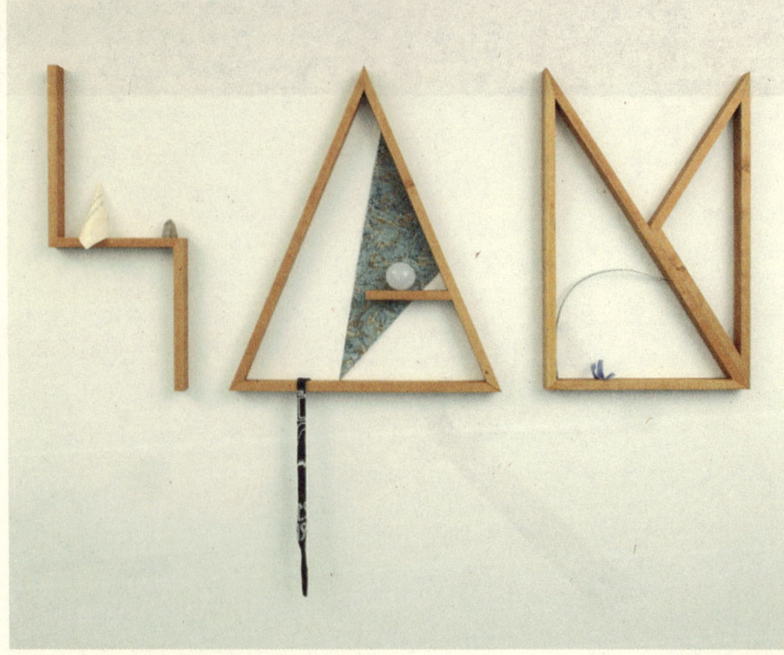

5.

b. 1980 Samara, Russia

LOGUTOV, VLADIMIR

1.

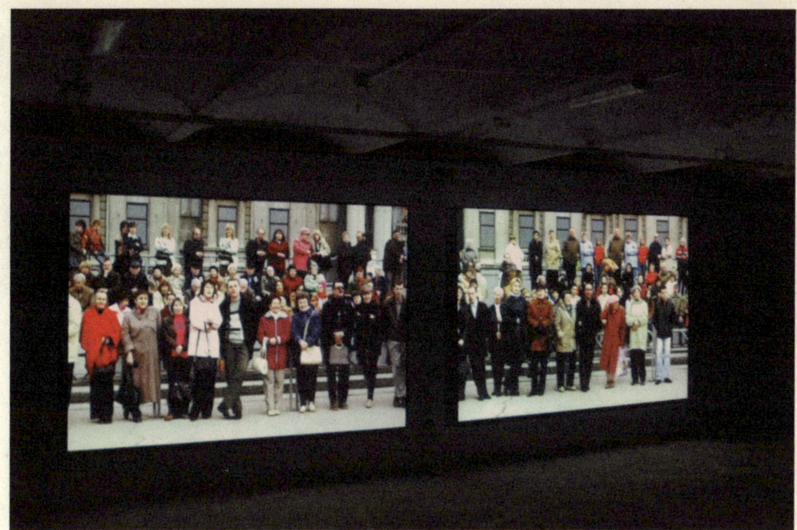

3.

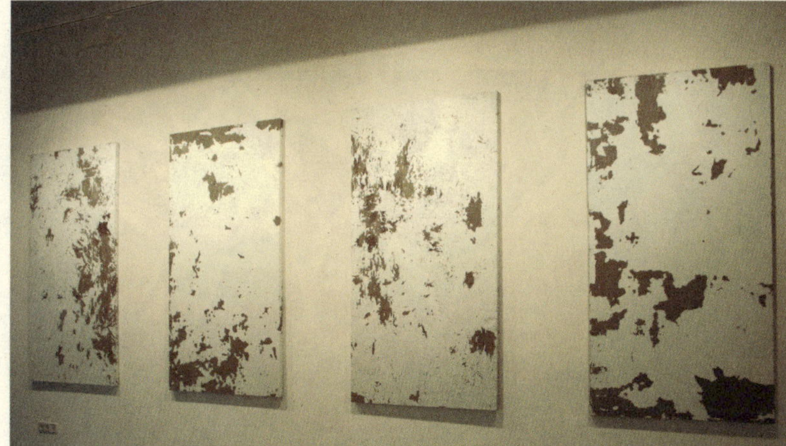

4.

2.

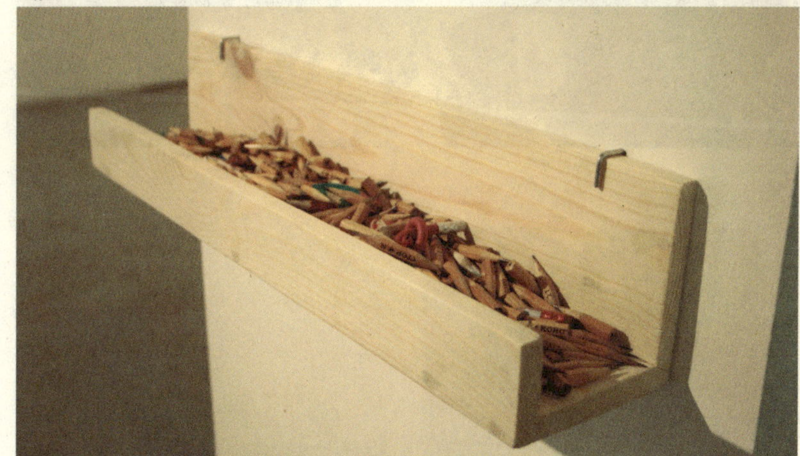

5.

Vladimir Logutov was educated at Samara Art College and Samara State Pedagogical University in Russia. His disconcerting video works use digital technology to disturb and dislocate urban space, rendering the commonplace strange and the strange commonplace. His video **Twilight** (2005), for instance, shows an ordinary street scene that, upon close inspection, reveals itself to be impossible – pedestrians walk around without heads, and red traffic lights are reflected in puddles as green. His work has been included in shows at the Moscow Museum of Modern Art (2007) and M'ARS Contemporary Art Centre in Moscow (2007).

1. **Crossword**
2007, acrylic on canvas, $37\frac{1}{2} \times 37\frac{1}{2}$ in (95 × 95 cm)

2. **Untitled**
from the series **Shadows**
2007, acrylic on cardboard, $37\frac{1}{2} \times 41\frac{1}{2}$ in (95 × 105 cm)

3. **Expectation**
2006, 2-channel video, 60 min

4. **Spoilage**
2007, acrylic on canvas, $71\frac{1}{2} \times 39\frac{1}{2}$ in (180 × 100 cm)

5. **Remnants**
2007, mixed media, $4 \times 19\frac{3}{4} \times 43\frac{1}{4}$ in (10 × 50 × 8 cm)

The work of Los Angeles-based Guthrie Lonergan addresses home computing as a key contemporary manifestation of pop culture. Critiquing the supposed democracy and creative potential of this forum from the viewpoint of a non-specialist user, he highlights the Internet's peculiarities and bizarre possibilities.

1. **2001<<<>>>2006**
2007, video, approx 3 min

2. **Bricks video**
2006, video, 1 min 12 sec

3. **Floor Warp 2**
2008, video on seamless loop, 20 sec loop

4. **Artist Looking At Camera**
2006, video, 3 min

5. **Myspace Intro Playlist**
2006, 2-channel video, approx 15 min

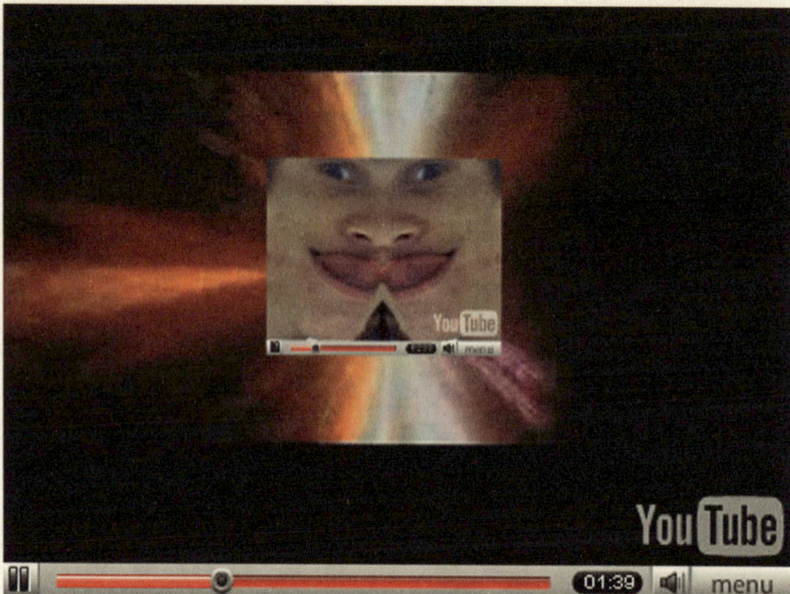

1.

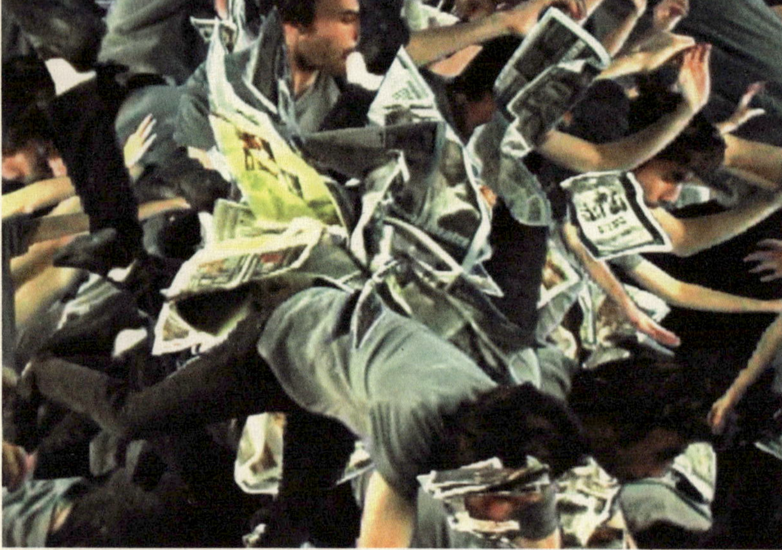

2.

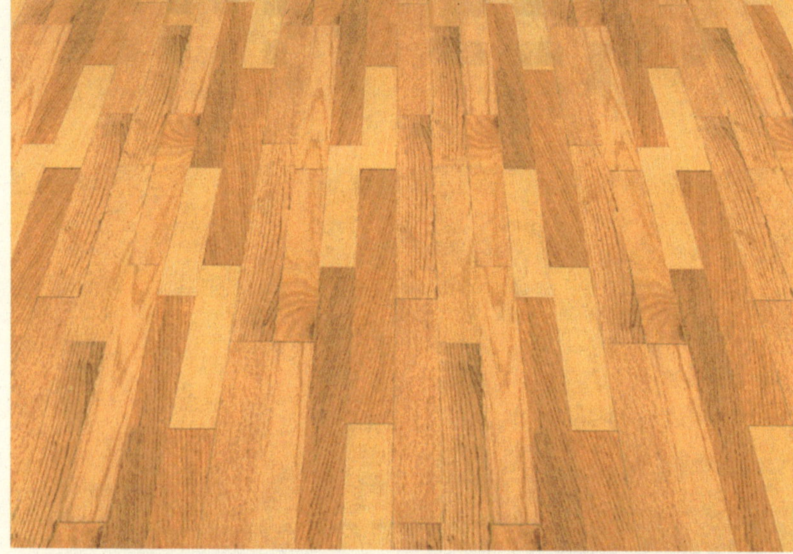

3.

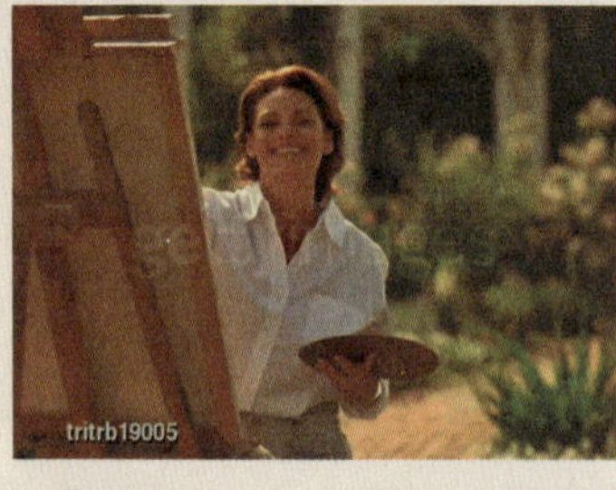

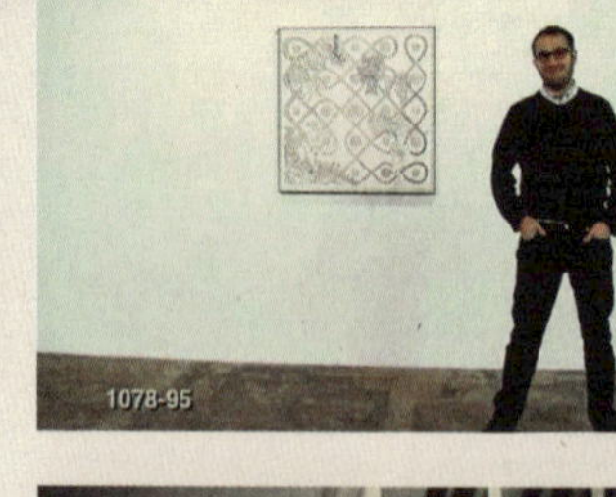

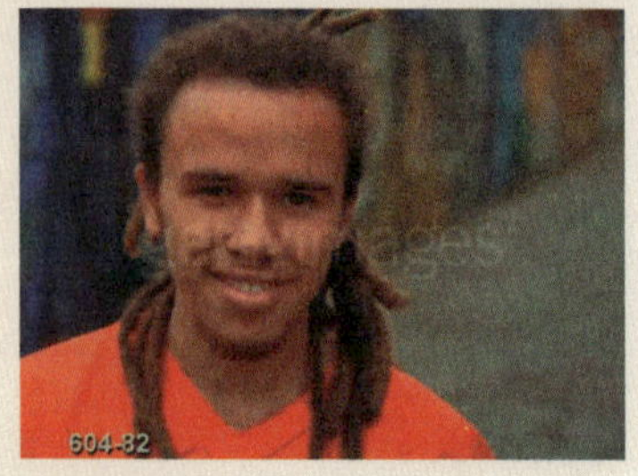

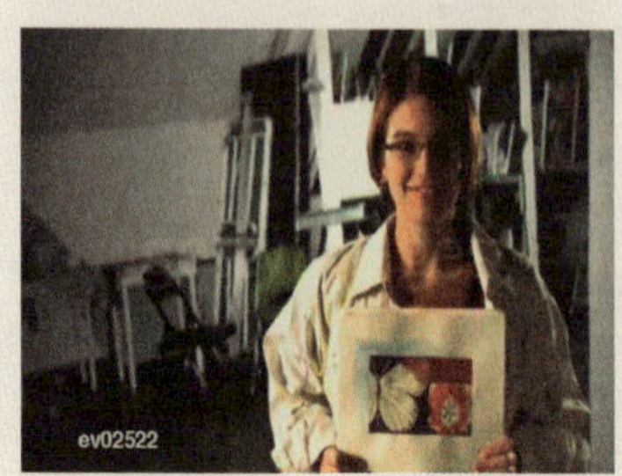

4.

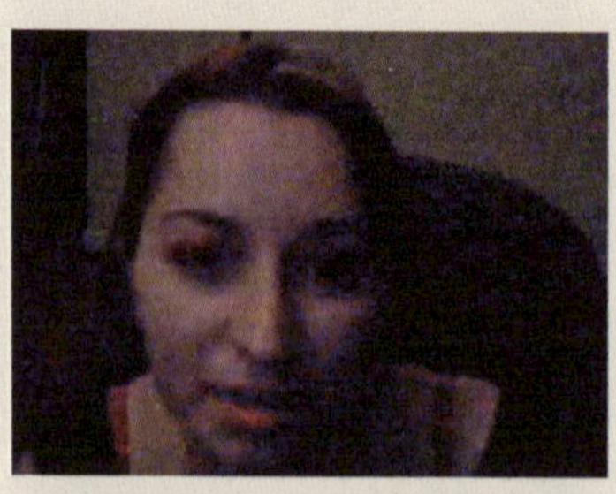

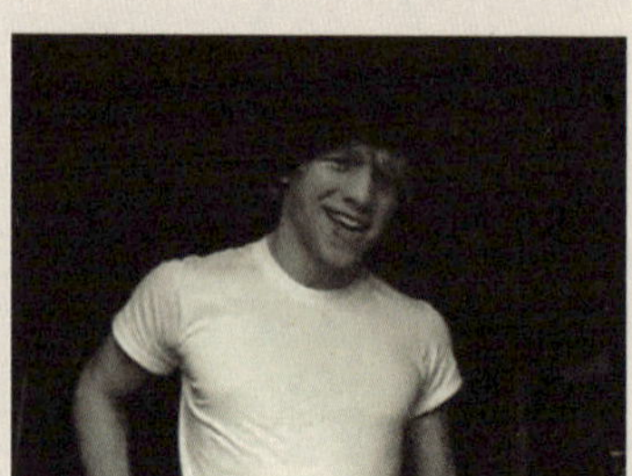

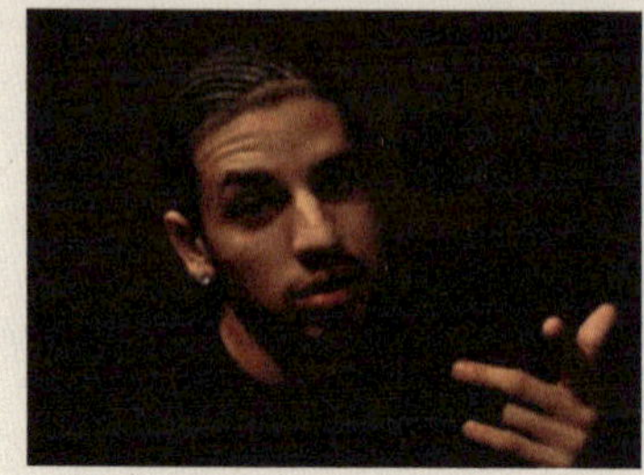

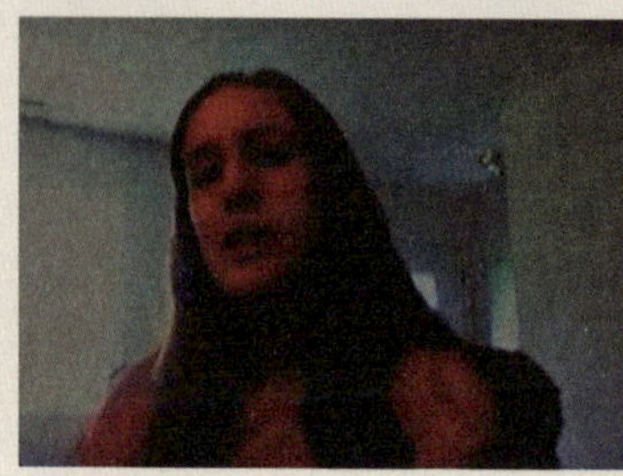

5.

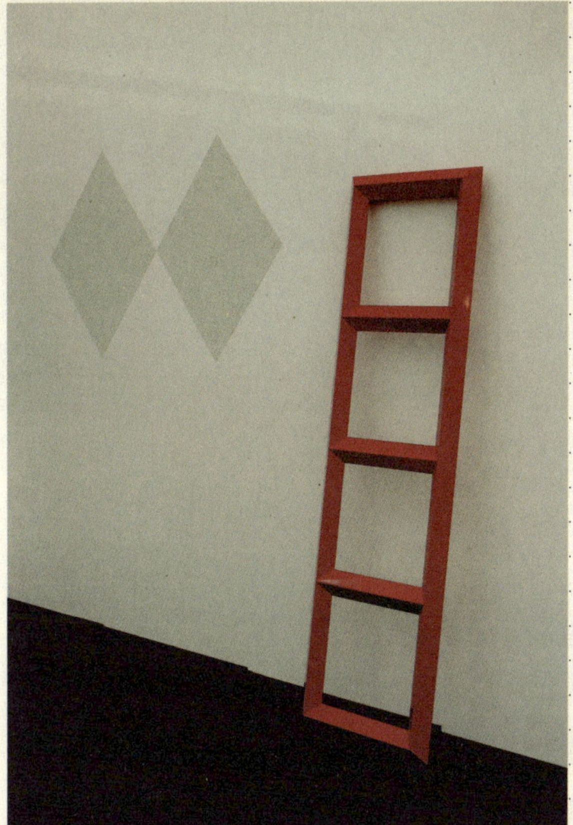

1.

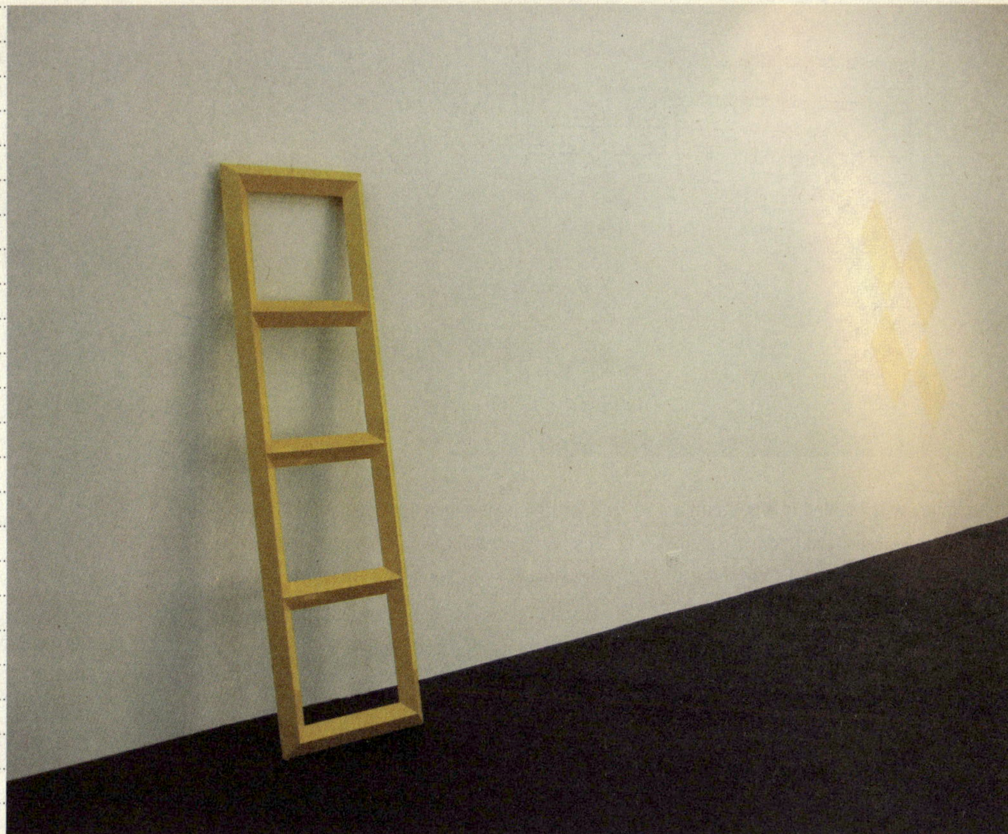

2.

London-based George Henry Longly investigates the ways we perceive objects when their use value has been stripped away, and the effects these forms have on the spaces in which they are located. His sculptures and installations question whether our responses to materials and structures are learned or innate.

1. escalade/red
2007, laminated solid-wood frame; 80 $\frac{3}{4}$ × 23 × 4 in (205 × 58 × 10 cm)

2. escalade/yellow
2007, laminated solid-wood frame; 31 × 19 × 2 $\frac{1}{2}$ in (79 × 48 × 6 cm)

3. Local Vignette
2008, TriLite truss sections and gloss paint, dimensions variable

4. "Mass Damper"
exhibition view at S1 Artspace, Sheffield (2007)

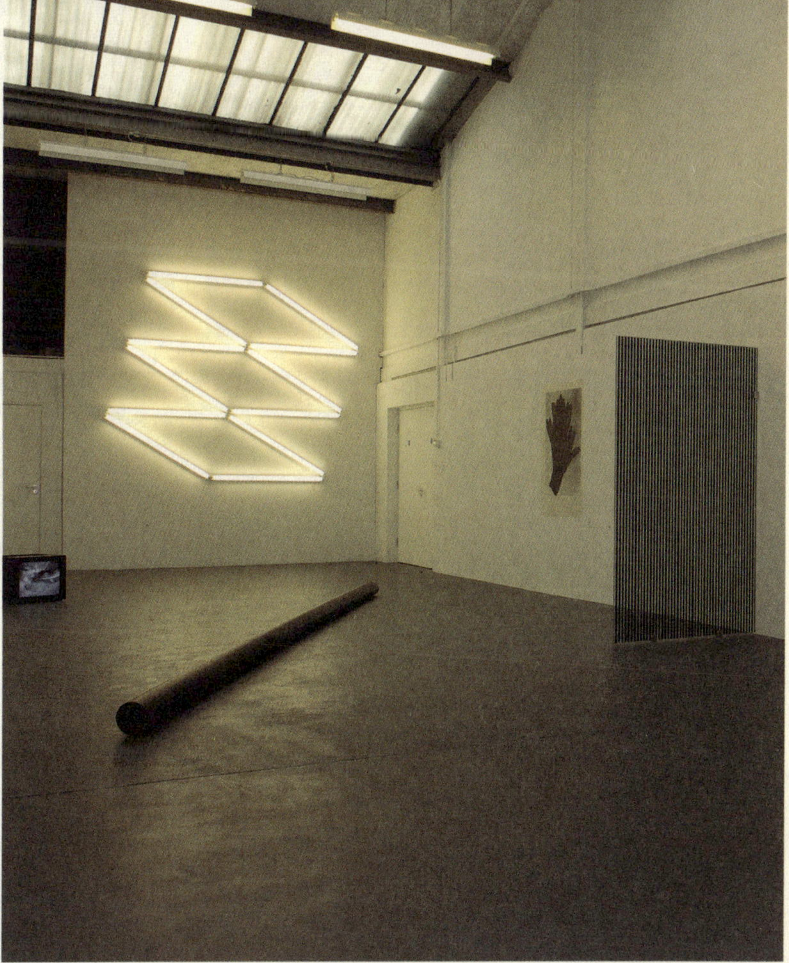

4.

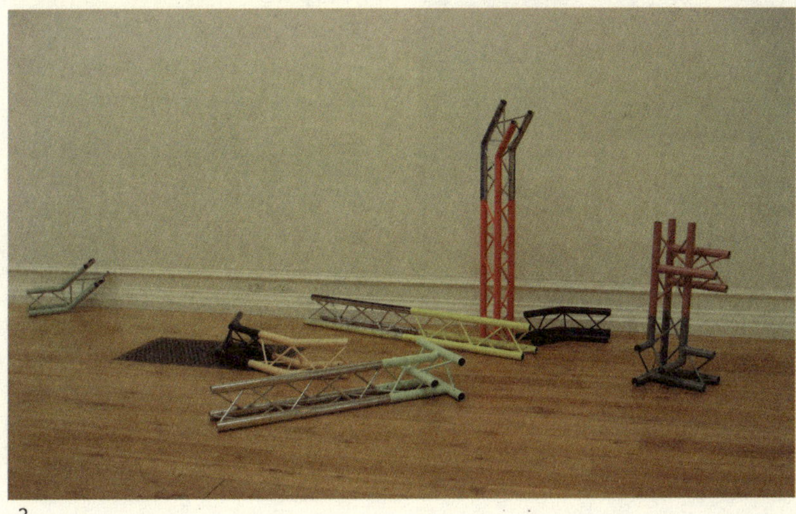

3.

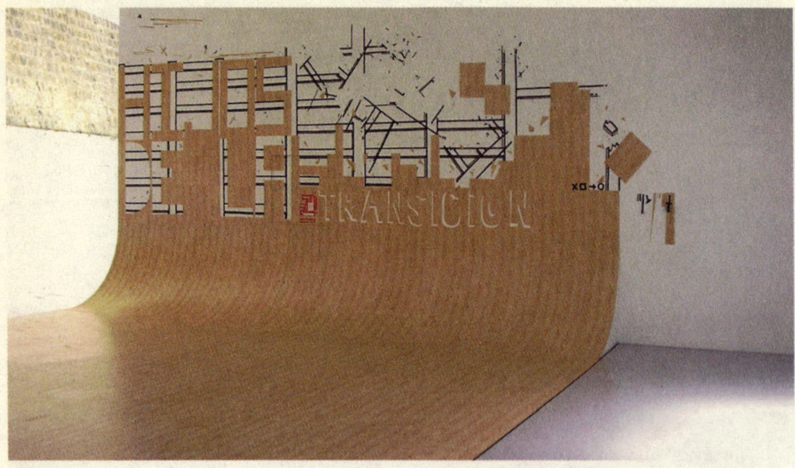

1.

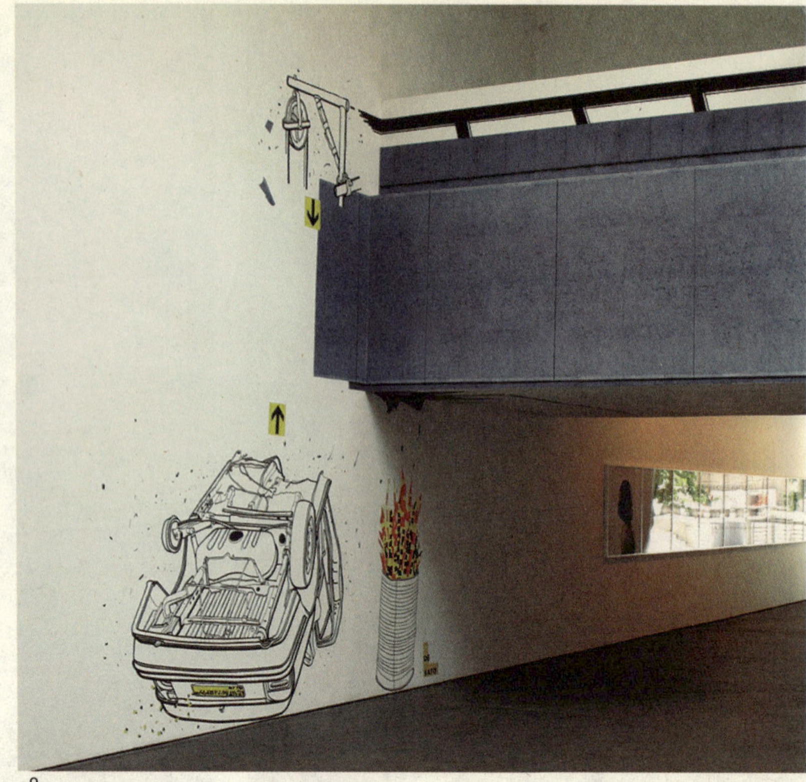

2.

Juan López was trained at the Castilla La Mancha University in Cuenca, Spain. His large-scale installations are heavily influenced by graphic design and combine emblems of urban space in flux (construction equipment, temporary road signs, flaming oil drums) rendered in adhesive vinyl with video projections to create multimedia environments. His outdoor works, similarly rendered in adhesive vinyl, or simply cut from existing billboards with a knife, broadcast cryptic messages such as "All is Impossible." His work was included in PHOTOEspaña 2008 in Madrid.

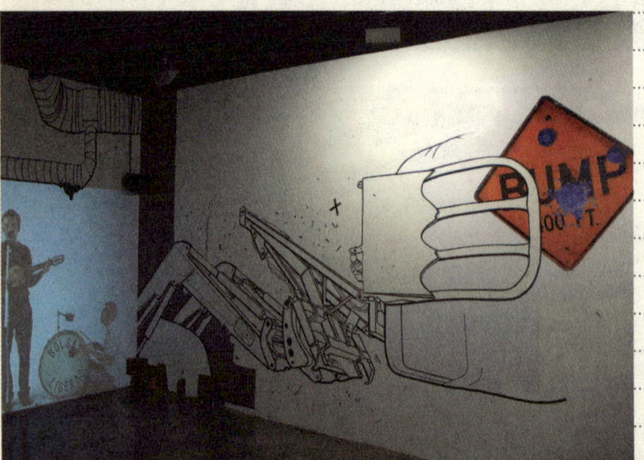

3.

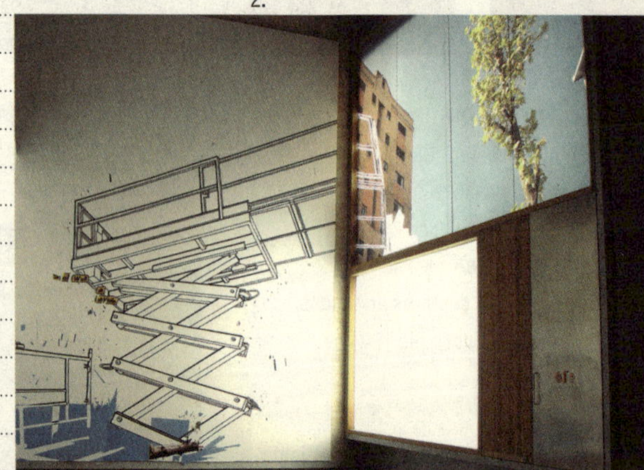

4.

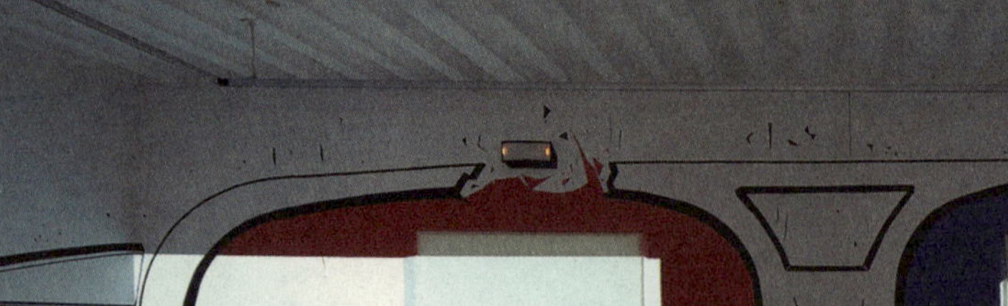

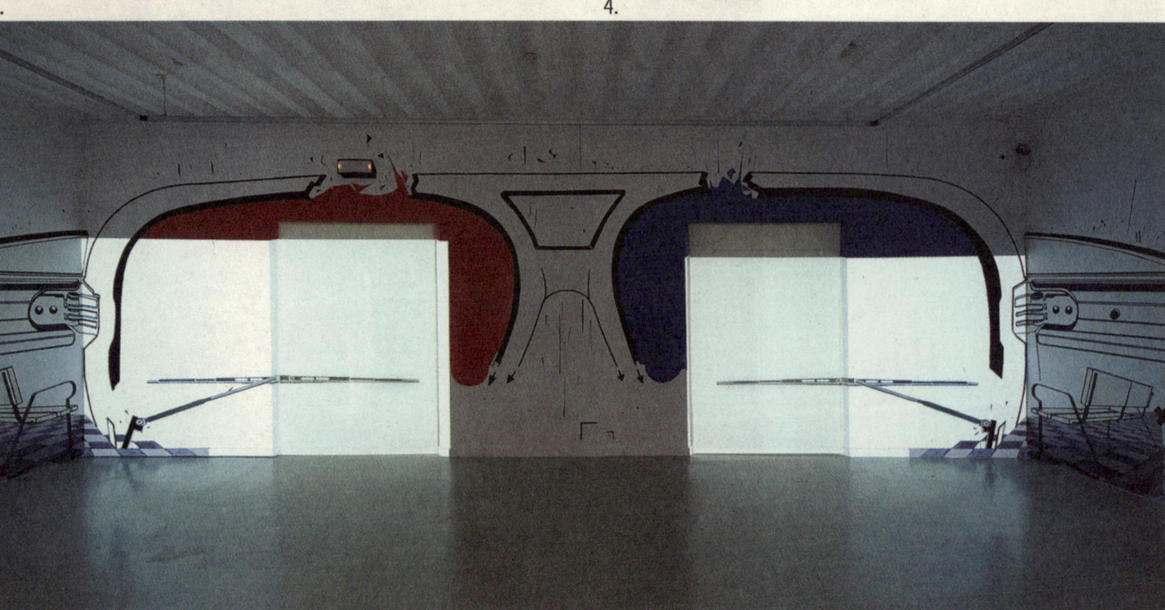

5.

1. **Hijos de la transición**
2007, vinyl, insulating tape, and wood, 14 3/4 × 26 1/4 × 46 ft (5 × 8 × 14 m), installation view at "Planes futuros," Sala del Baluarte de Pamplona, Spain

2. **Juan Lopéz Cigars II**
2007, vinyl and insulating tape, 23 × 13 1/4 ft (7 × 4 m), installation view at Galería Salvador Díaz, Madrid

3. **Muta ó GR**
2008, vinyl, insulating tape, and video, 10 × 42 1/2 ft (3 × 13 m)

4. **Desgrava**
2006, vinyl, insulating tape, and video, 16 3/4 × 65 1/2 ft (5 × 20 m), installation view at MUSAC, León, Spain

5. **Buenan!**
2008, vinyl, insulating tape, and video, 10 1/2 × 46 ft (3 × 14 m)

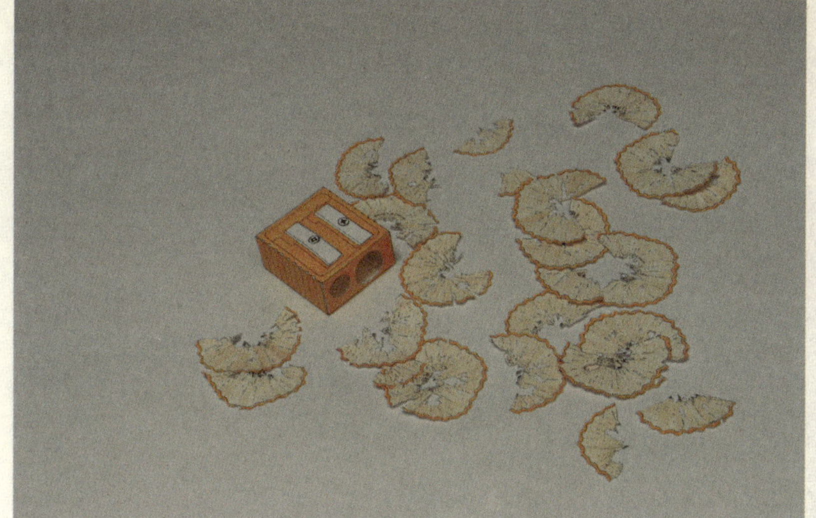

1.

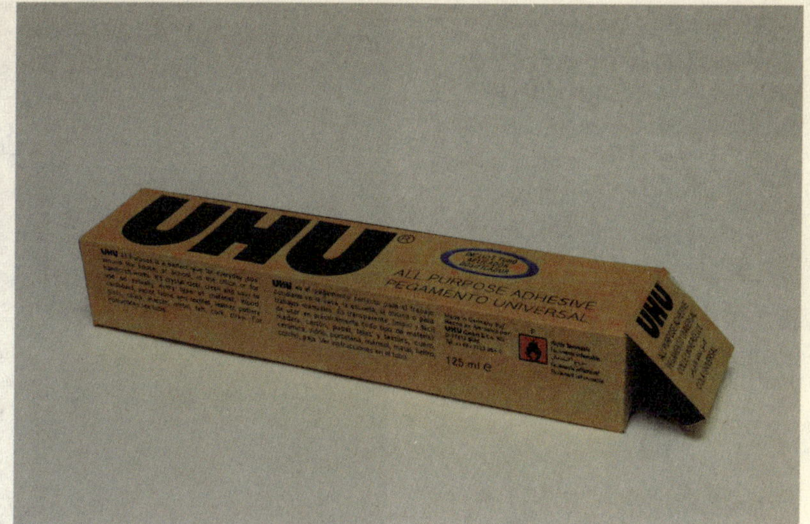

2.

3.

Mateo López Parra studied art at Universidad de Los Andes in Bogotá, where he continues to live and work. He cuts, folds, and manipulates paper, pushing the boundaries of drawing in order to explore objects and environments. His first solo exhibition was a month-long performance in which he replicated every object in his studio on pieces of paper, ultimately replicating the studio itself in the gallery space.

1. **Pencil Sharpener**
2006, color pencil on paper, dimensions variable

2. **Caja de Uhu!** (Uhu! Box)
2006, ink on paper, 2 × 8 $\frac{1}{2}$ × 1 $\frac{1}{2}$ in (5 × 22 × 4 cm)

3. **Topografía Anecdótica** (Anecdotal Topography)
2007, mixed media, dimensions variable

4. **Avion Mariposa** (Butterfly Airplane) (detail)
2008, mixed media, dimensions variable

5. **Calle 53** (53rd Street) (detail)
2004-05, ink on paper, 19 $\frac{3}{4}$ × 19 $\frac{3}{4}$ in (50 × 50 cm)

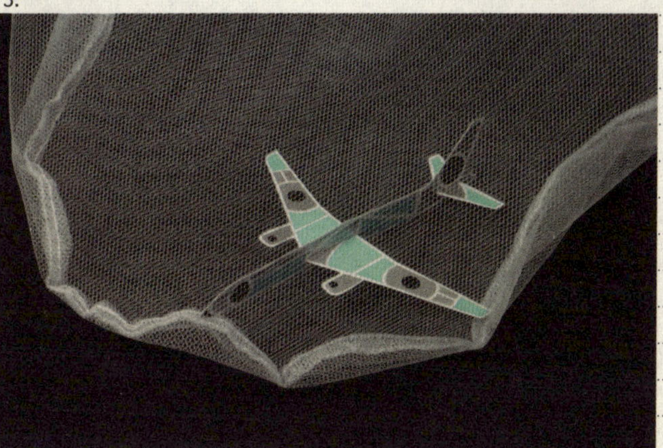

4.

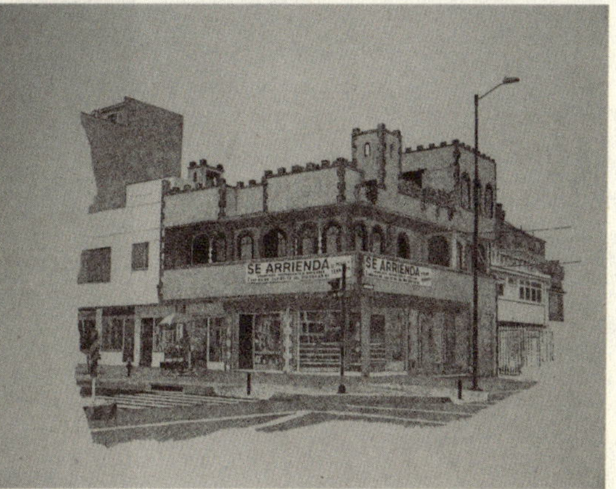

5.

Darri Lorenzen is based in Reykjavik and Berlin. Working in a variety of media including sound and photography, he exploits the specific qualities of exhibition spaces to disorient the viewer. Introducing unexpected reflections and echoes, silences and amplifications, he exercises a striking influence over the viewer's movements and perceptions.

1. **THROUGH OUT**
2006, 13-channel video and 13 MDF boxes, dimensions variable

2. **Site Scene**
with Elin Hansdóttir
2005, site-specific installation, dimensions variable, installation view at "New Icelandic Art II," National Gallery of Iceland

3. **Genuflect**
2007, chromogenic print, 43 ¼ × 55 ¼ in (110 × 140 cm)

4. **Round Here**
2007, site-specific photographs, glass, and circling lightbulb, dimensions variable

5. **Altostratus Suite**
with Orn Helgason, Egill Kalevi Karlsson, and Thor Sigurthorsson
2006, installation with video and sound, dimensions variable

1.

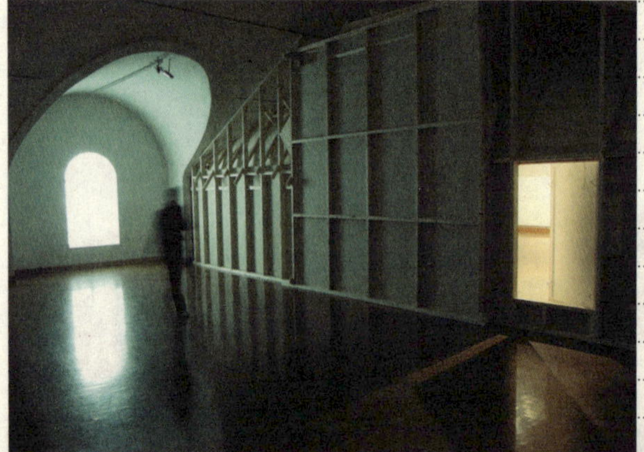
2.

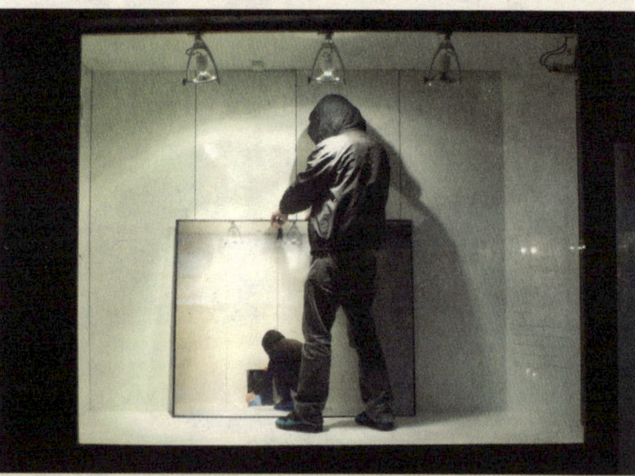
3.

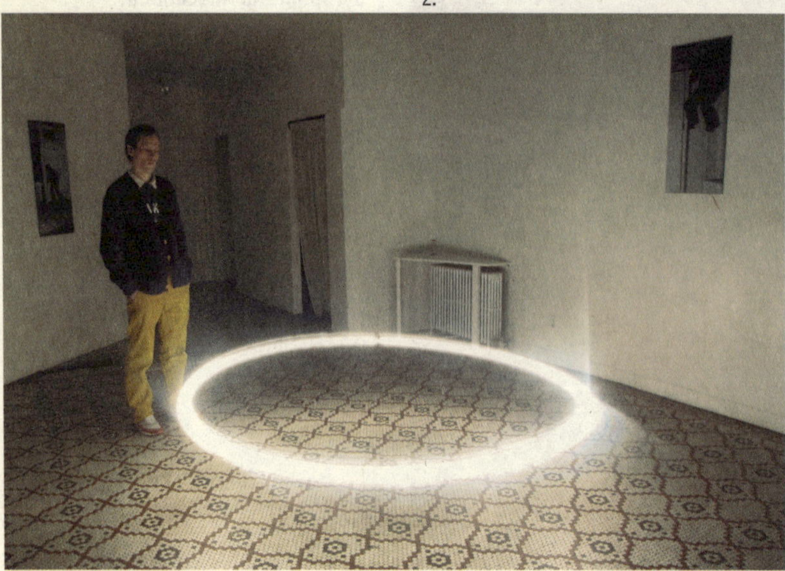
4.

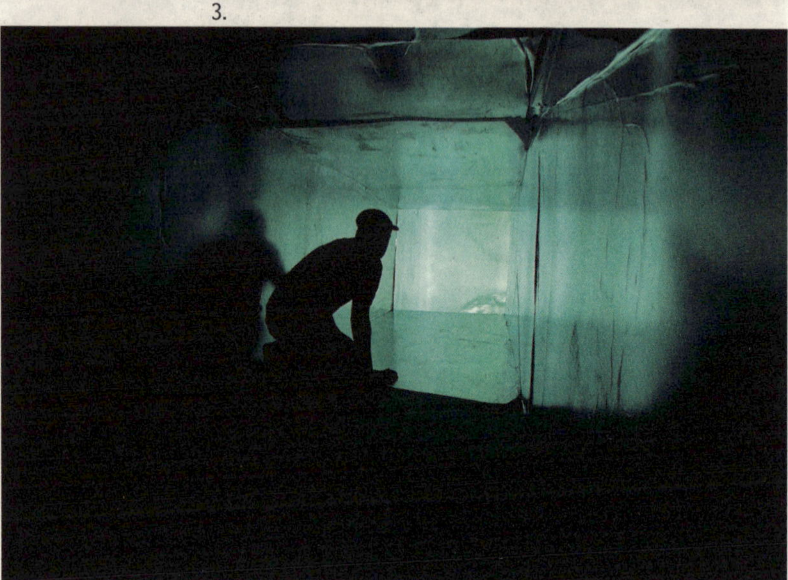
5.

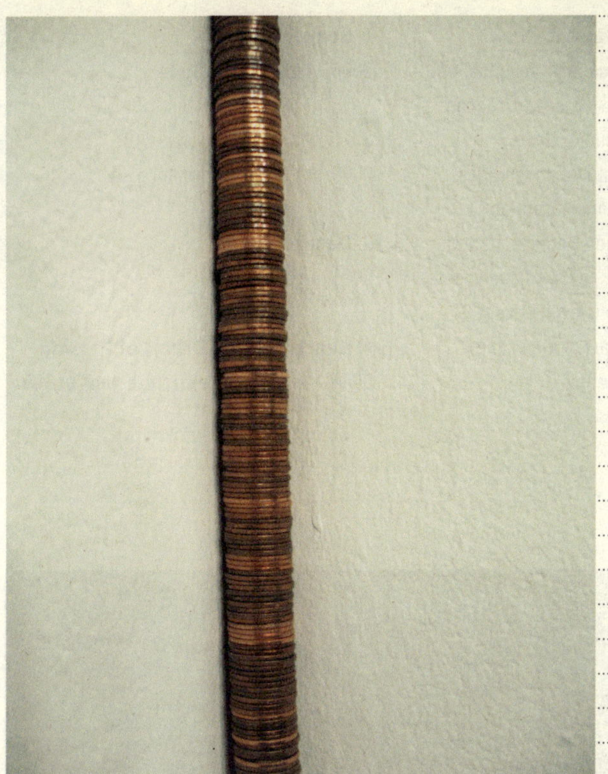

1.

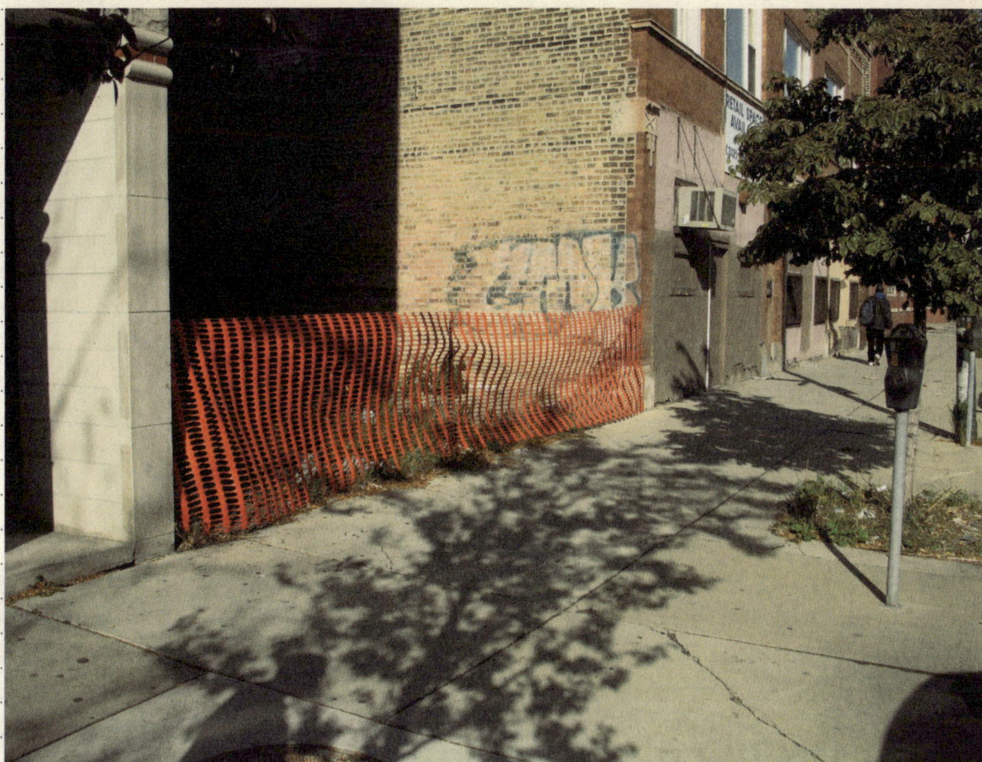

2.

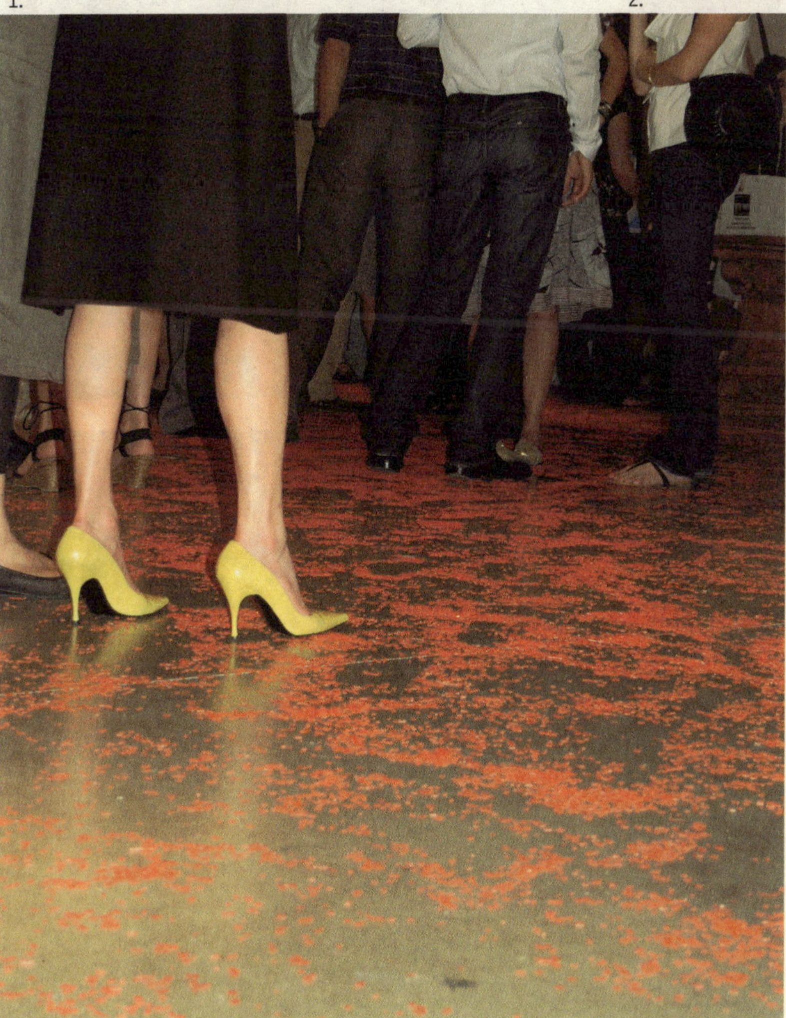

3.

Chicago-based Tim Louis makes sculptural interventions that occupy a space between presence and absence, questioning the relationship between weakness and strength. In **Fence** (2007), he stretched a plastic utility fence across a space and gradually cut it to pieces. The buildup of plastic fragments constituted the finished work.

1. **Formal IV** (detail)
2007, pennies and rod, 9 ½ ft (3 m)

2 & 3. **Untitled (fence)**
2008, utility fence cut down, collected, and dispersed, dimensions variable

4. **Empire Up**
2006, hollow aluminum foil casts of a single brick, dimensions variable

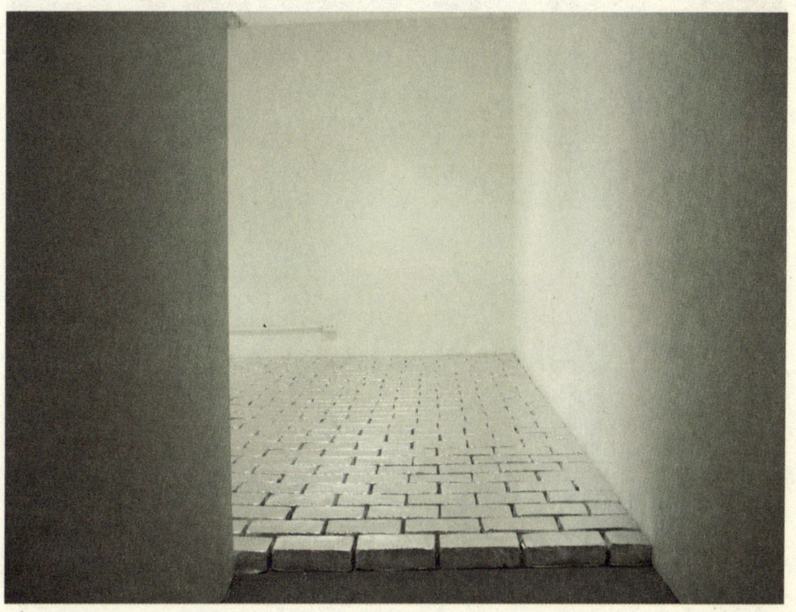

4.

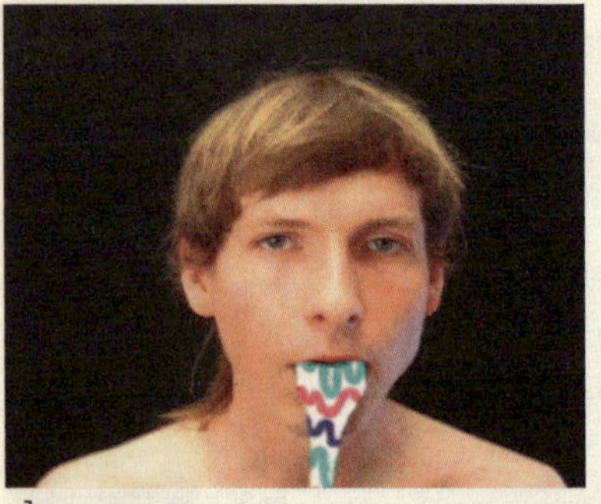

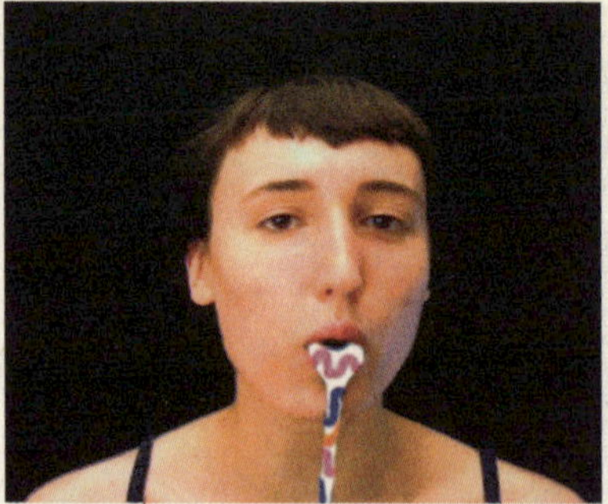

1.

Luke Fischbeck and Sarah Rara, aka Lucky Dragons and Sumi Ink Club, are based in Los Angeles. As Lucky Dragons, they collaborate on audio, video, performance, and installation work; as Sumi Ink Club, they concentrate on painting, drawing, and sculpture. In both incarnations, the pair relies on audience participation and publishes low-cost multiples. "At the heart of it all," they write, "is playing together."

1. Sexy Proposal
2006, video, 3 min 45 sec

2 & 5. Make a Baby
2005-present, performance

3. Desert Walkers
2006, performance

4. Heartstopping Drums of Passion
2006, gouache on cassette, edition of 100

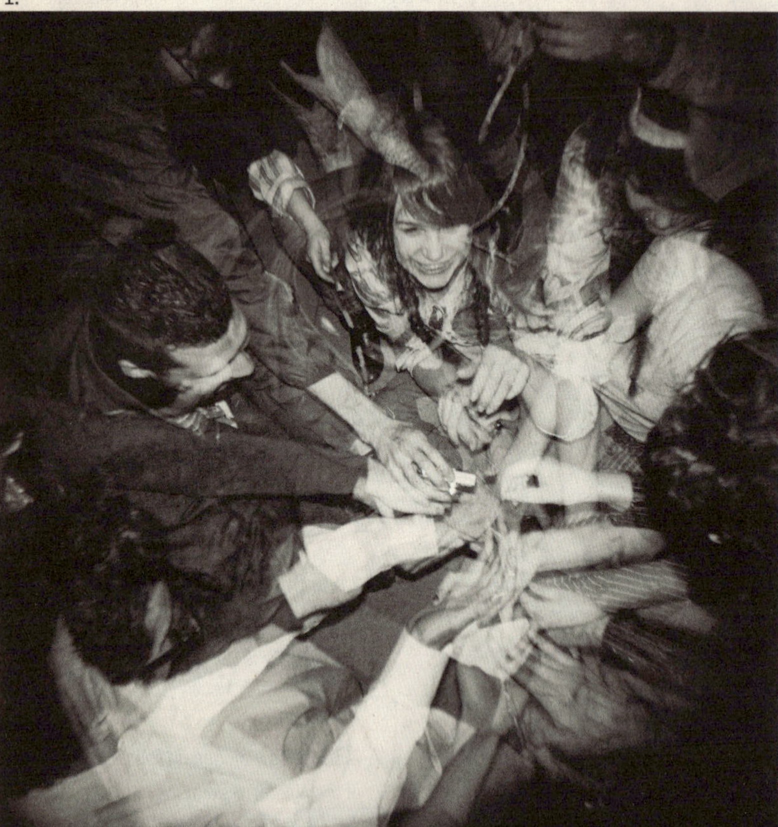

2.

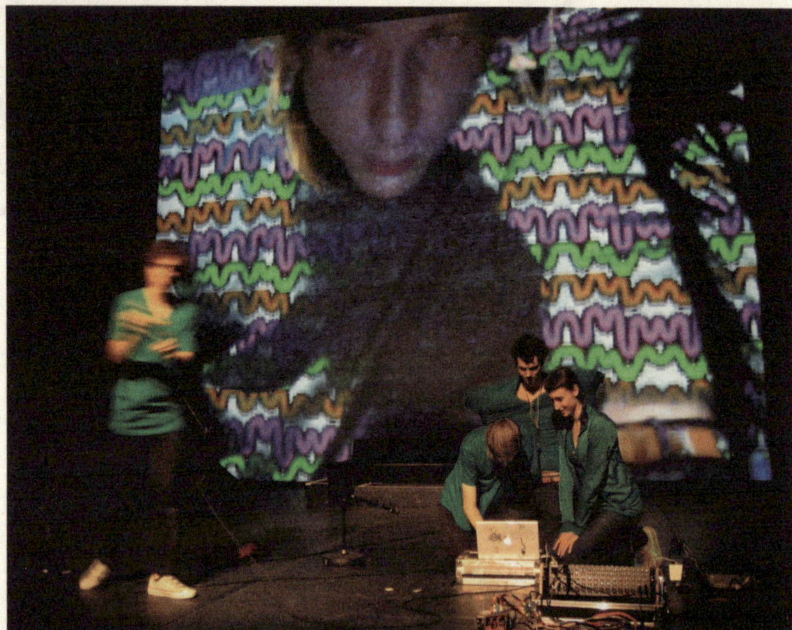

3.

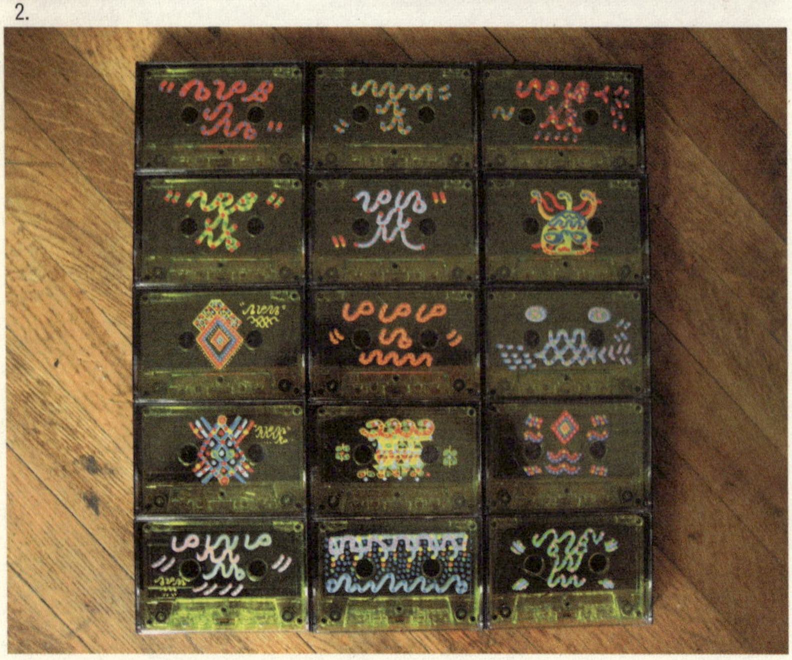

4.

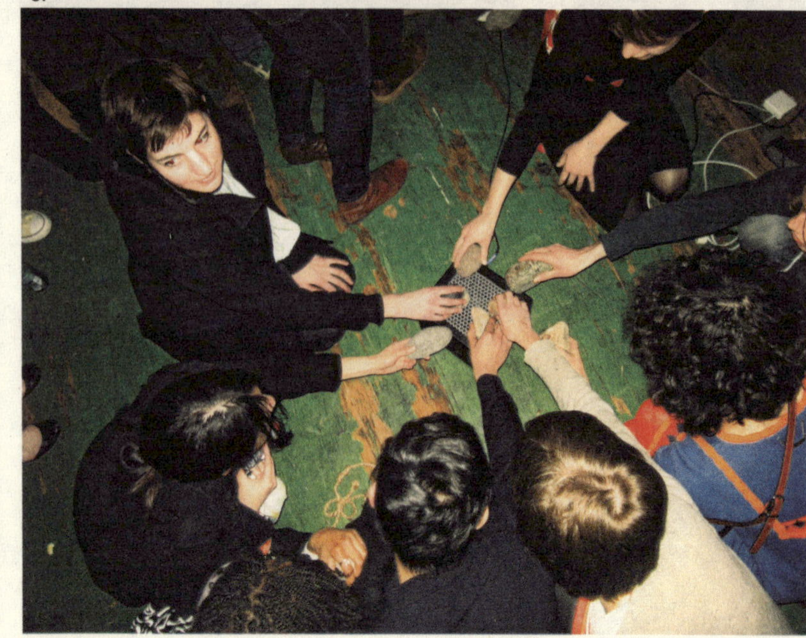

5.

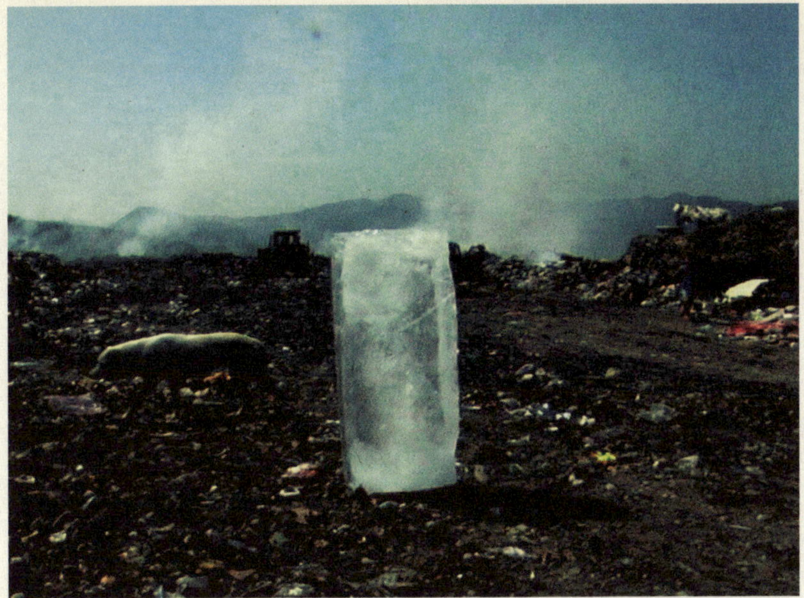

1.

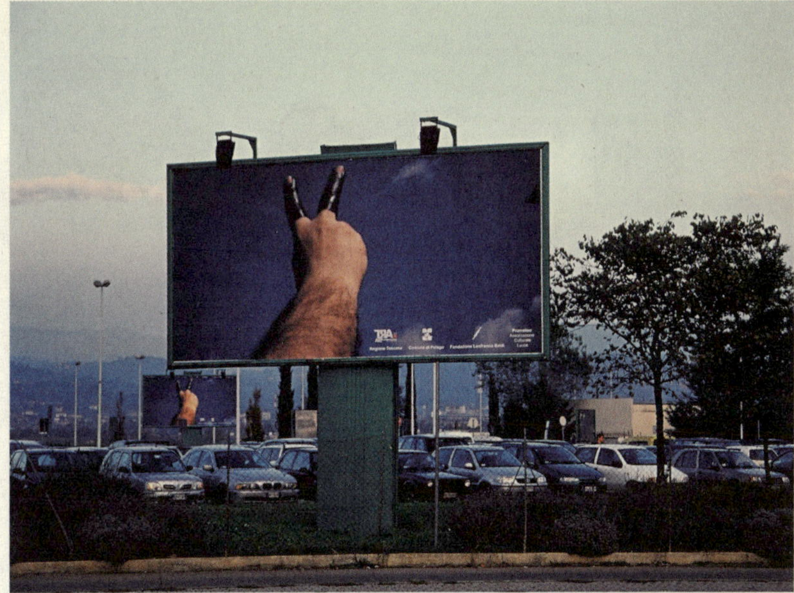

2.

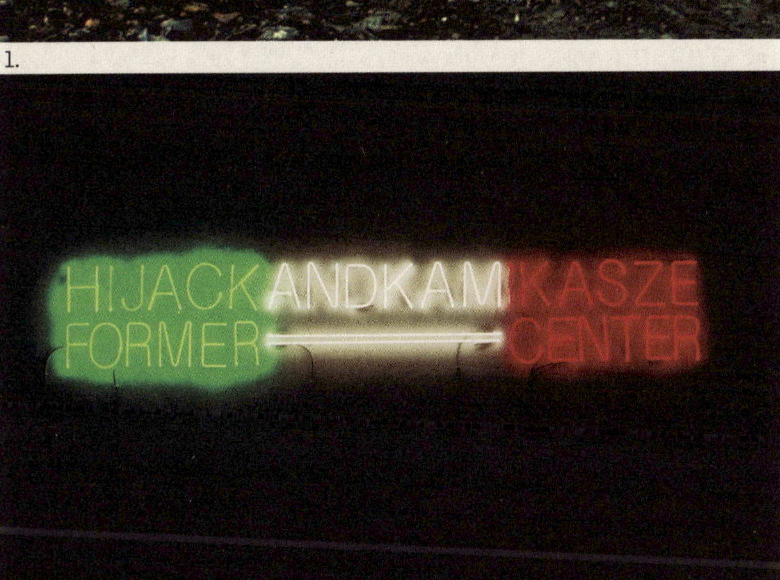

3.

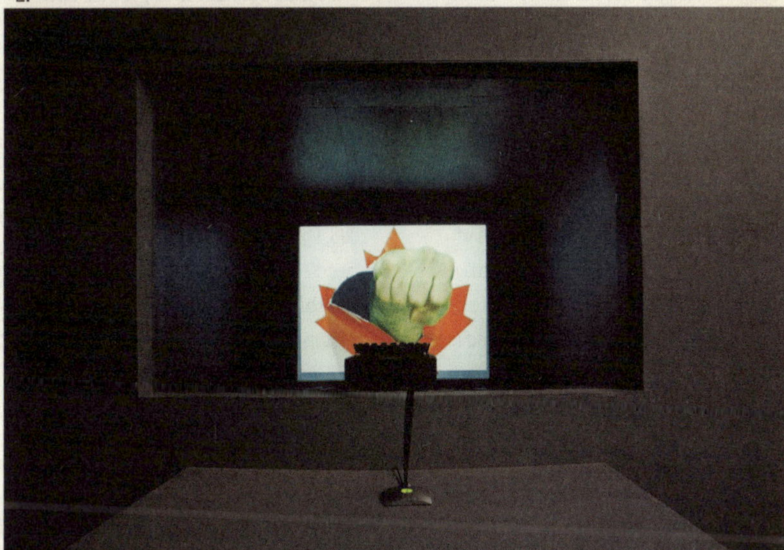

4.

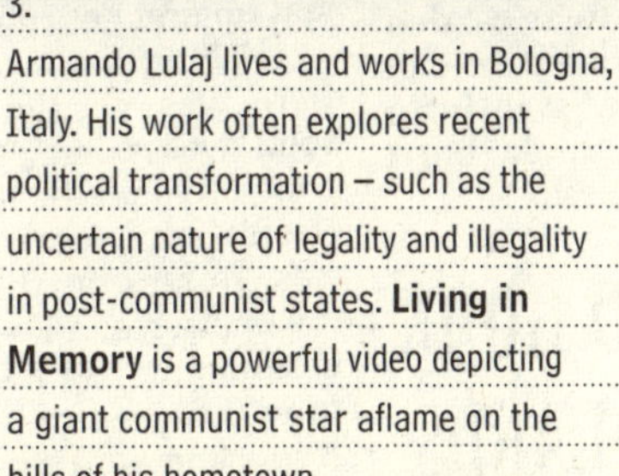

Armando Lulaj lives and works in Bologna, Italy. His work often explores recent political transformation – such as the uncertain nature of legality and illegality in post-communist states. **Living in Memory** is a powerful video depicting a giant communist star aflame on the hills of his hometown.

1. Time Out of Joint
2006, two-channel video projection, 15 min 39 sec

2. Playcracy
2002, billboard, dimensions variable, installation view at Amerigo Vespucci Airport, Florence

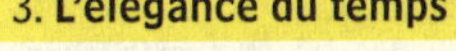

3. L'elegance du temps
2004, neon, 15 ¾ × 118 ¼ in (40 × 300 cm)

4. DeepEst Sound/Common Assembly, Act 1
2007, site-specific installation with video projection, recording studio, and miniature replica of the conference table at the United Nations Security Council, dimensions variable

5. Living in Memory
2004, video, 5 min 20 sec

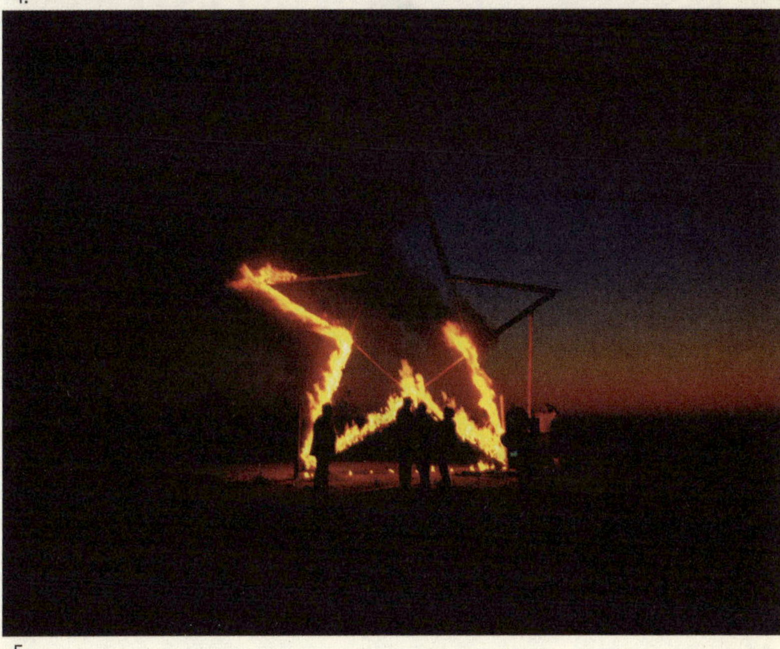

5.

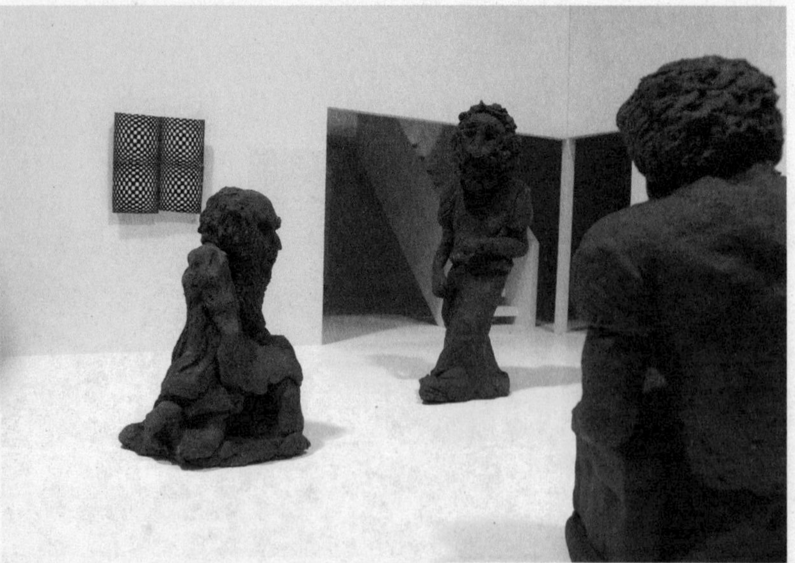

1.

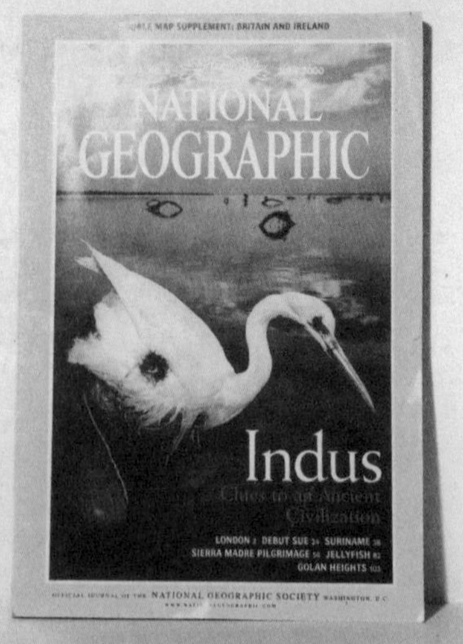

2.

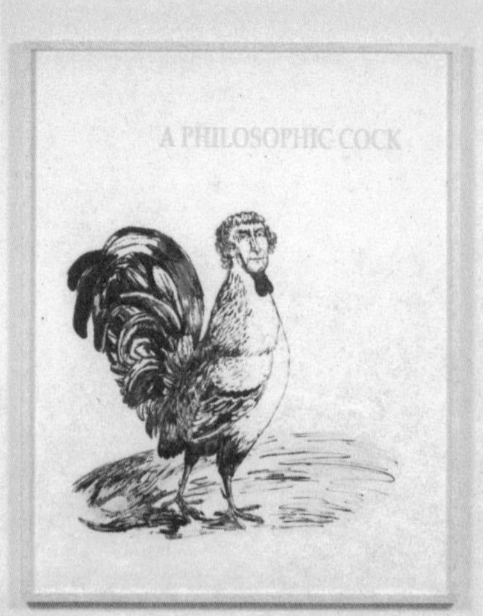

3.

Shana Lutker earned her MFA from the UCLA School of Arts and Architecture, and continues to live in Los Angeles. Her interdisciplinary practice includes drawing, sculpture, and photography, and often results in large, multi-part installations. Much of her work is informed by psychoanalysis, including the series of sculptures **Art That I Dreamt That I Made** and **Dream Book**, in which she prints her dreams as newspaper headlines.

1. **Art that I dream that I made with House (1986-1996)** with **Art That I Dreamt That I Made** (detail)
2005-07, mixed media, dimensions variable

2. **Indus, Industry, In Us.**
2008, lightjet print, 50 × 40 in (127 × 102 cm)

3. **A Philosophic Cock (Thomas Jefferson's head on bird body)**
2008, ink and gouache on paper with yellow frame and etched glass, 50 × 40 in (127 × 102 cm)

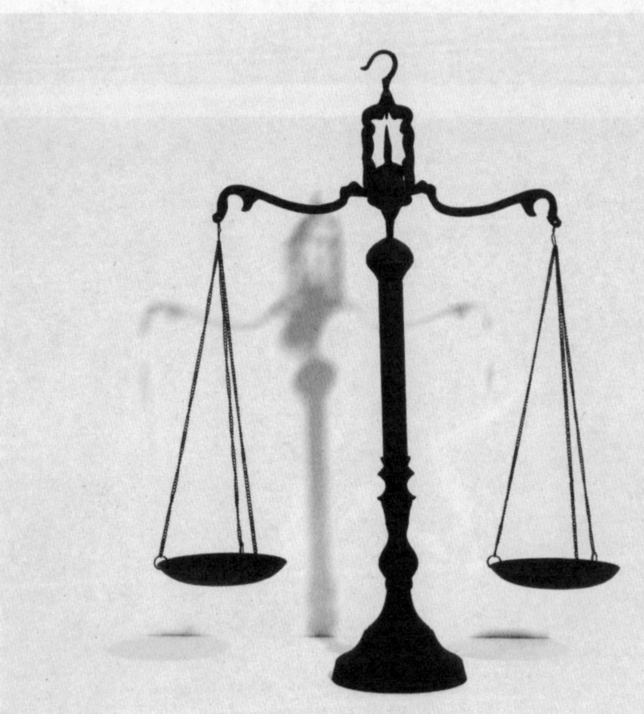

4.

ETS STOPPED AT THE DOOR

Club Refuses Entry

was doing research on ers, for some art proj- drove to this strip joint knew about, it had a dirt g lot and was not very d in the middle of the en I was there.

walked in and it was ight, there was some f waiting area, very s like. The walls were ht antiseptic yellow re was nothing but d of weird empty of- way. I looked for the the bar or a person, lly found a partially window, behind was a large office, a it tickets and prices. was sitting there, at w, like a doctor's of- as surly. I was read- gn and he popped sliding chair. He of annoyed that I He asked what he or me, young lady. s just checking on s. He asked to see id I didn't think I now. He said that question. I handed He said I was very and young-look- oked remarkably He scanned my ID e and handed it

friend had to go to a quick meeting with the Chinese management, so she handed over the guestlist to me for a minute. There was a long line and all of these people started coming up to me, asking me if they could be number one on the list, or telling me that so and so had told them that they were number one on the list.

DANCETROOP COMES TO TOWN AND TAKES OVER

There was a dancetroop in town. Damian might have been in it. they took over. I was reluctant at first, but then I gave in. They wanted me to be in this main act, but I was too inexperienced and I didn't know how to be carried over the audience and hold in my stomach. I was wearing a white leotard, I think, but I could not see myself.

WHERE TO GO IN FORIEGN LANDS

Hatoum Sculpture Described Improperly

Then, we were in a foreign country and I was tell-

CAR COMM MOUS GUY NEEDING R

Hooligans Carve Wires; Stomach Or

I had left my ca in a lot, so it was t both the day and th There were constru per signs on all of that had been there and into the night if you leave your ca and into the night heat up and get ruin

When I got to there was no sign hood was open. T a lot of space in th wasn't sure for a was looking at the the engine. and I wa if someone had tak gine. I turned on th it worked, so I figu okay.

I was getting go and then this f was outside of my came over to talk knew Damian and a poster of him o

5.

4. **Scales of Justice**
2007, lightjet print, 40 × 50 in (102 × 127 cm)

5. **Dream Book 2003** (detail)
2005, 365 inkjet prints on newsprint, hardbound with box, dimensions variable

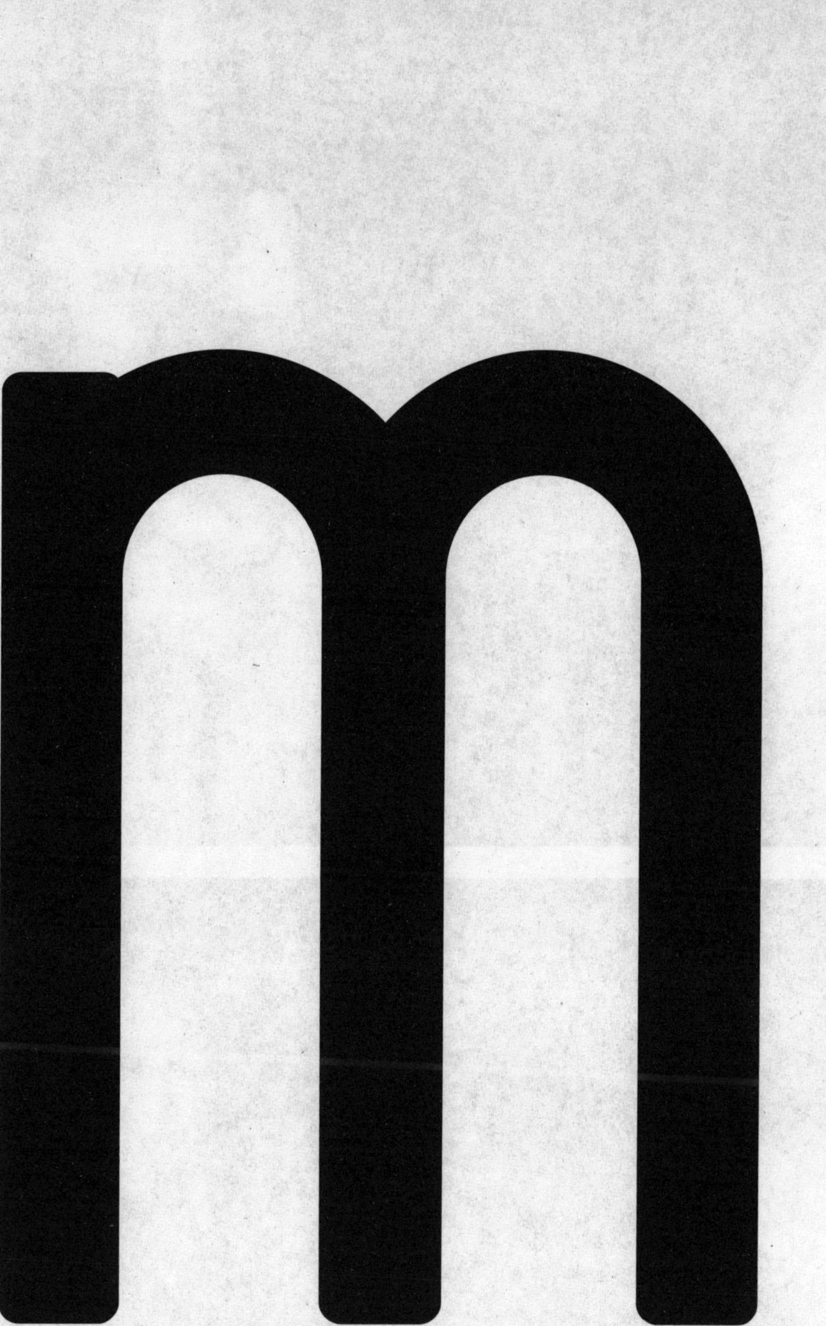

MAAZOUZ, FOUAD

b. 1977 Casablanca, Morocco

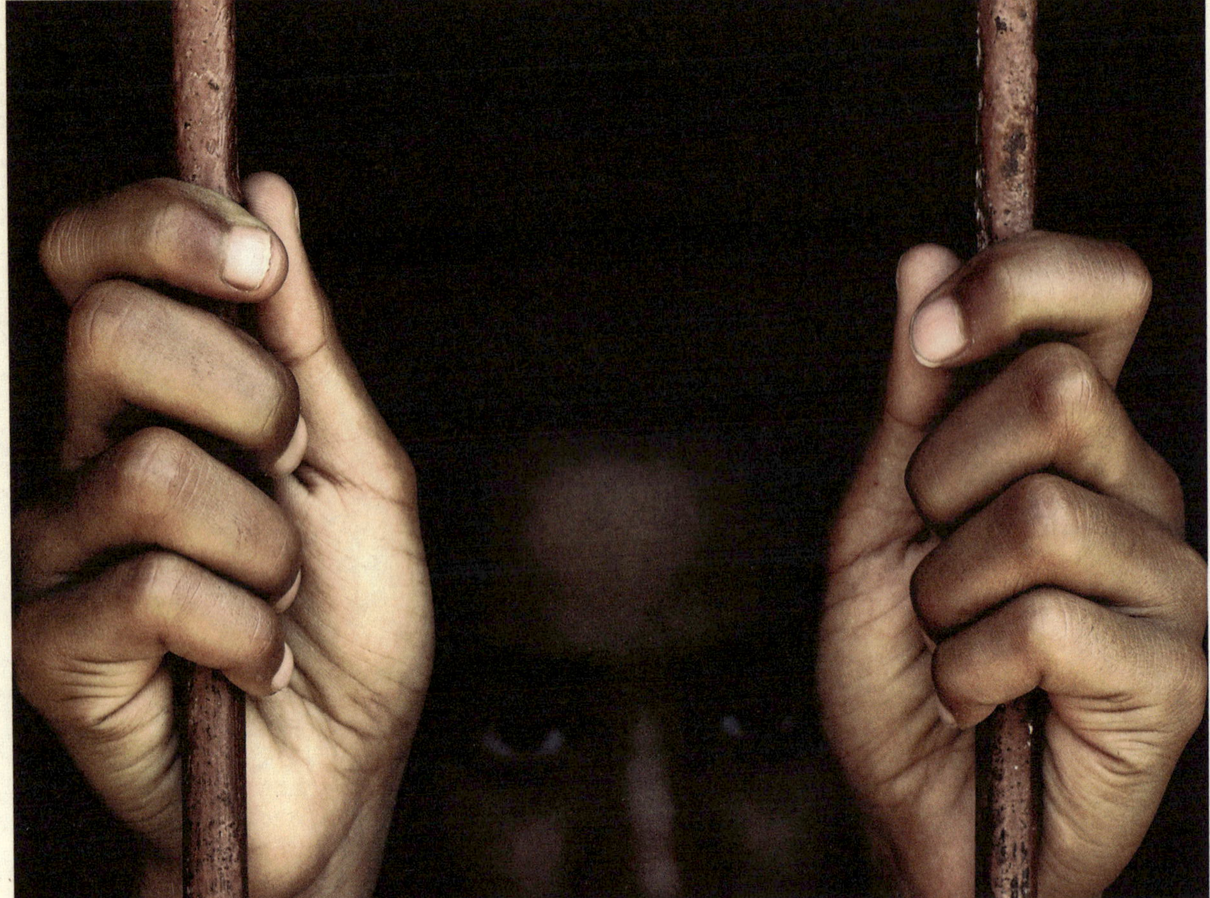

1.

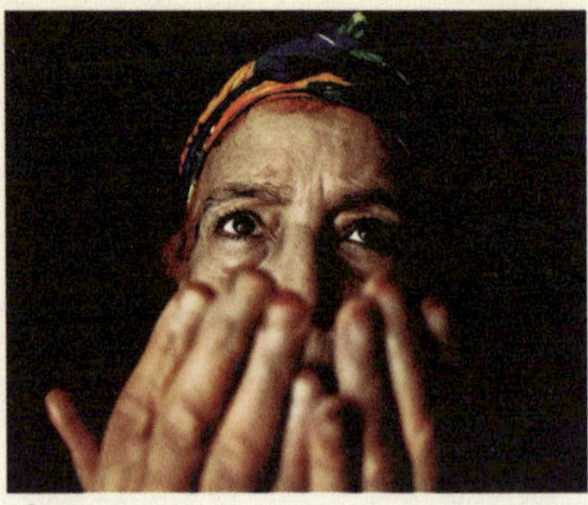

2.

While studying graphic design in his early twenties, Fouad Maazouz discovered photography, specifically its ability to immortalize a moment in time or a human subject. His work, mainly conducted in North Africa, documents everyday life in lushly produced, highly detailed chromogenic prints, including a poignant photograph of a Moroccan market captured at night, when humans take on wraithlike qualities. His work has been included in exhibitions in Morocco as well as Europe, Africa, and the Middle East, and has won him several international awards.

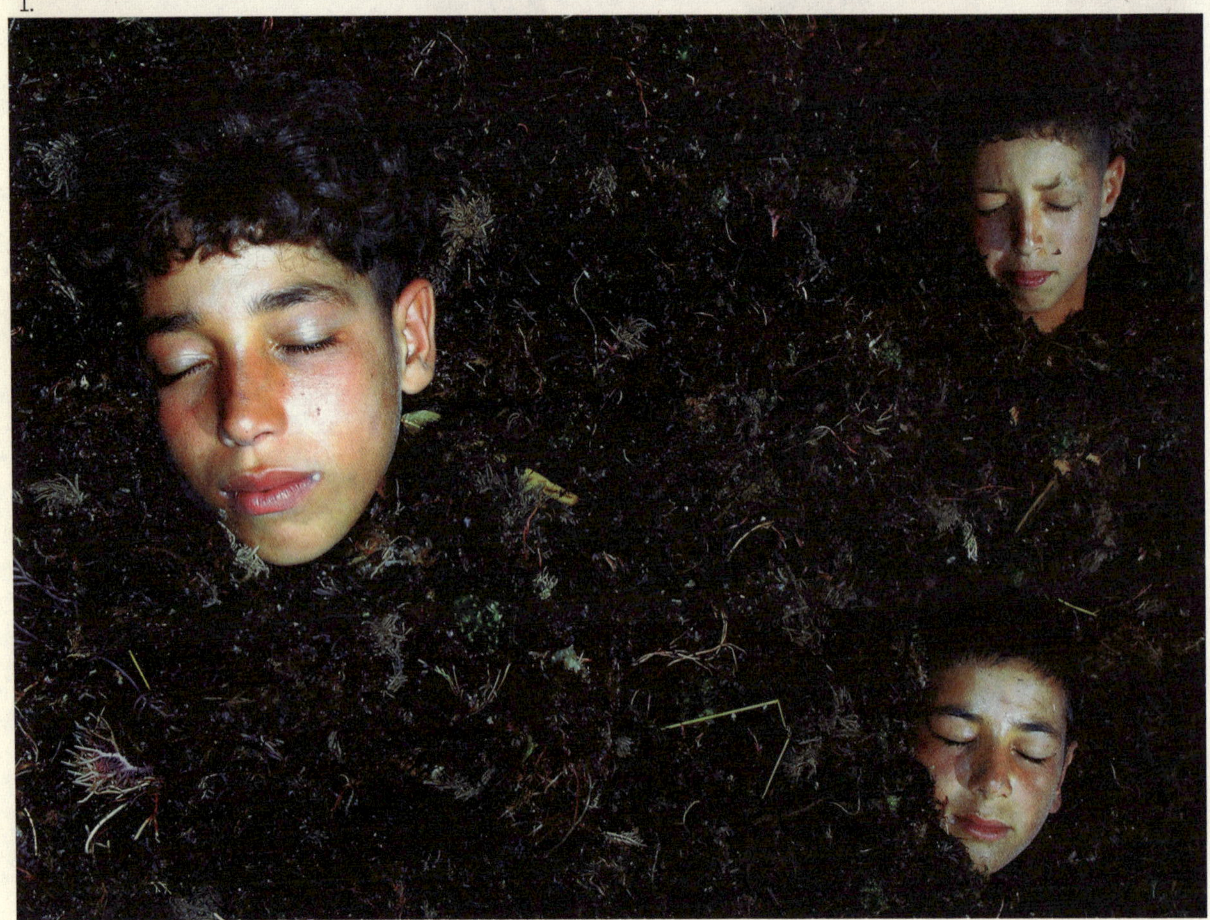

3.

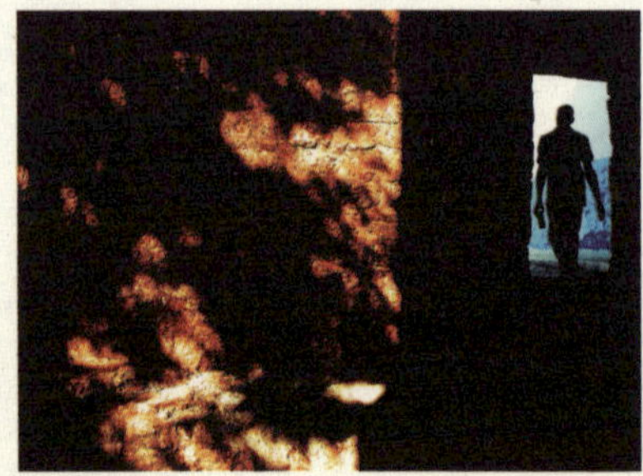

4.

1. l'enfant
2006, digital photograph, 19 ¾ × 27 ½ cm (50 × 70 cm)

2. Jadati
2007, digital photograph, 19 ¾ × 27 ½ cm (50 × 70 cm)

3. Dream land
2006, digital photograph, 19 ¾ × 27 ½ cm (50 × 70 cm)

4. Dark side of the moon
2004, digital photograph, 19 ¾ × 27 ½ in (50 × 70 cm)

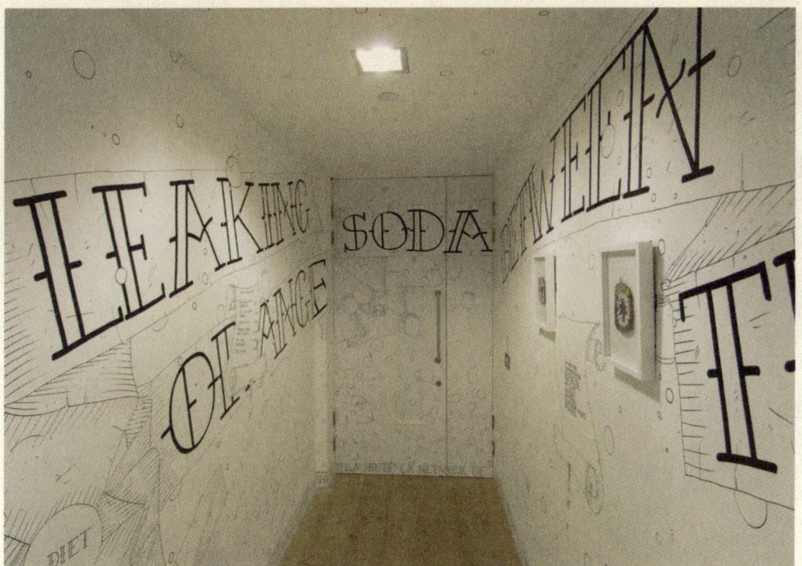

1.

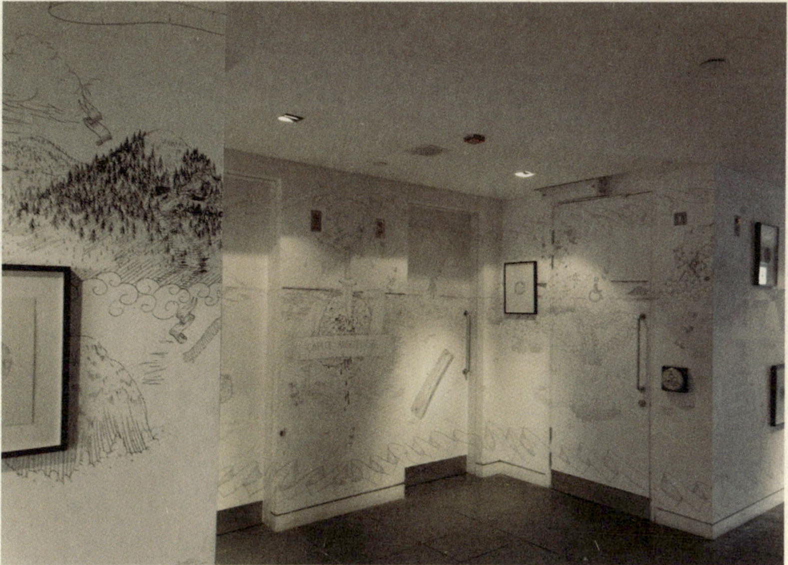

2.

Ant Macari, who had a solo exhibition at the Baltic CCA in Gateshead in 2007, lives in Newcastle. His work, based around drawing and writing, makes reference to street and tattoo art, heraldry, and myth. Through the recombination of sources and genres – often in the context of interventions in galleries and public spaces – Macari encourages a close reading of the cultures he references.

1. **The Plight of Colamon pt III: The Battle for Hearts and Minds**
2007, site-specific drawing, installation view at Baltic Centre for Contemporary Art, Gateshead, UK

2. **Caput Mortuum (Fresh As Tomorrow)**
2007, site-specific drawing, installation view at Baltic Centre for Contemporary Art, Gateshead, UK

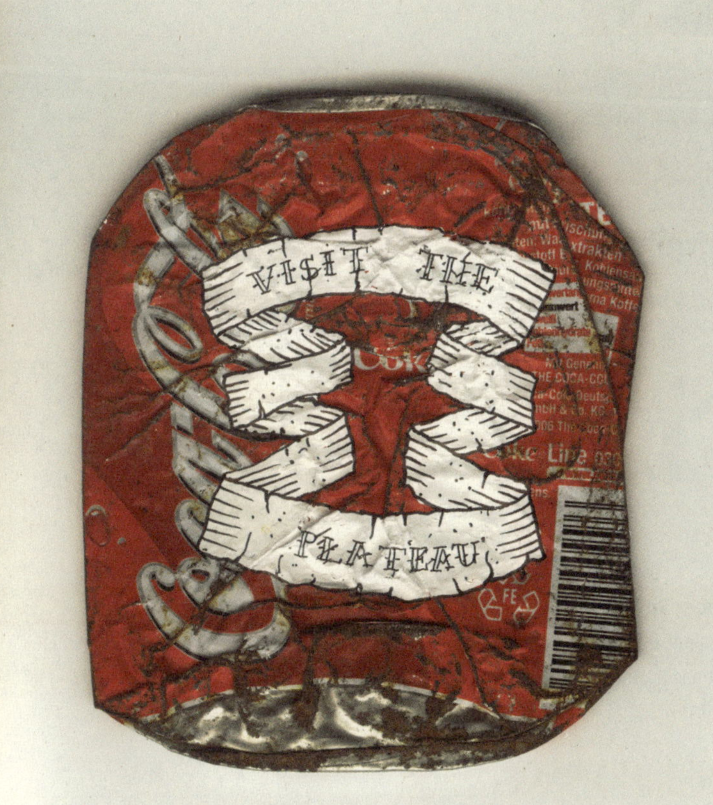

3.

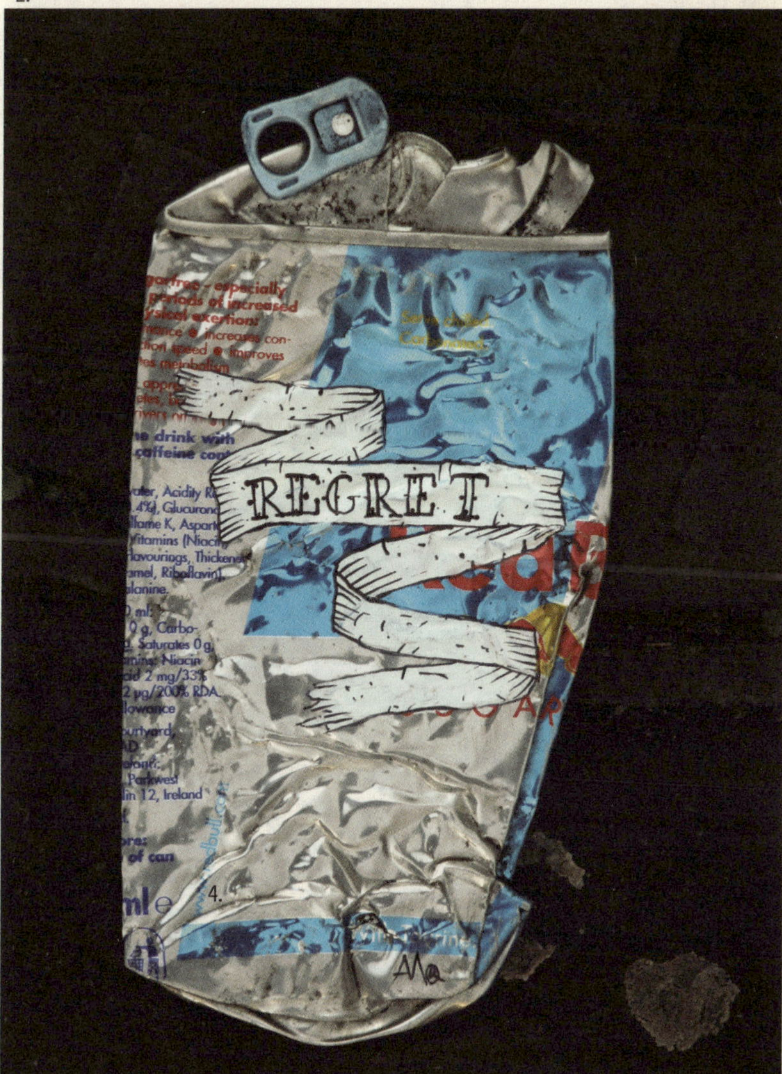

4.

3. **Untitled (Visit The...)**
2006, correction fluid and India ink on found aluminum can, 5 ¼ × 4 in (13 × 10 cm)

4. **Untitled (Regret...)**
from the series **Navel Lint**
2006, correction fluid and India ink on found aluminum can, 6 × 3 in (15 × 8 cm)

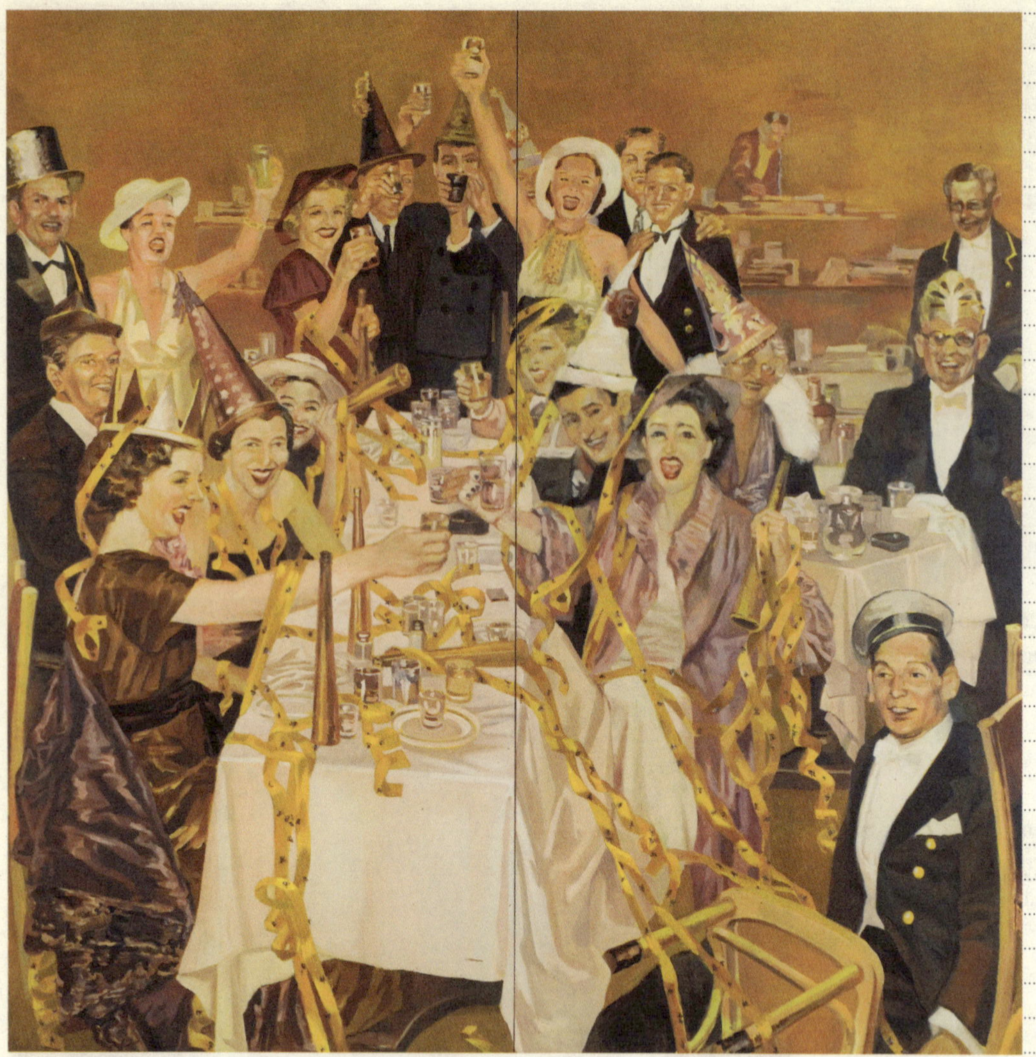

1.

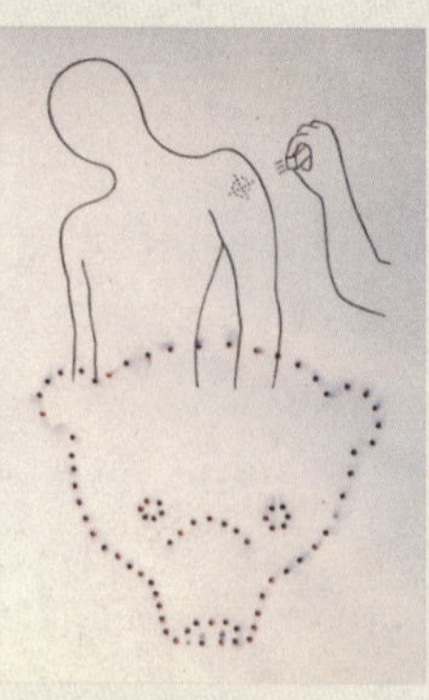
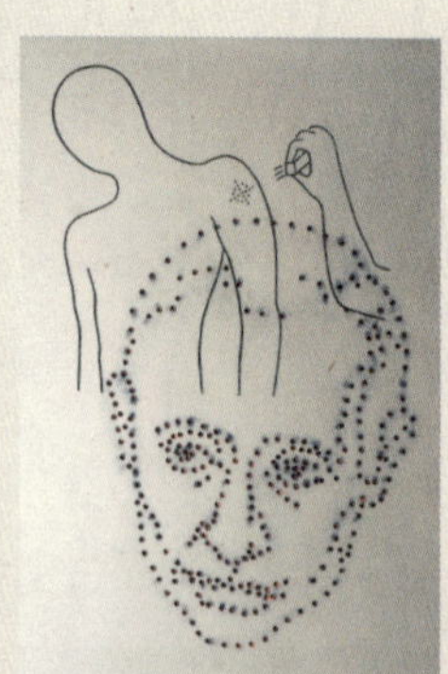
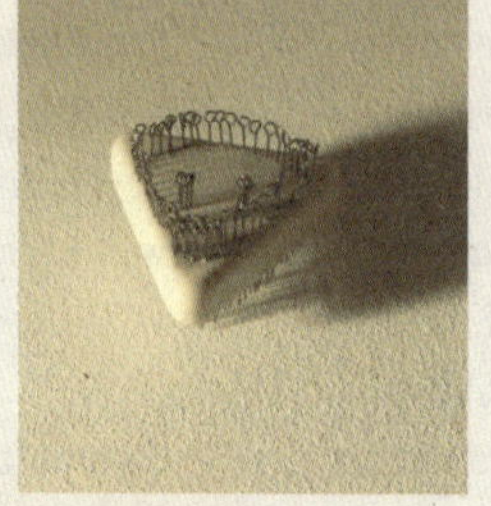
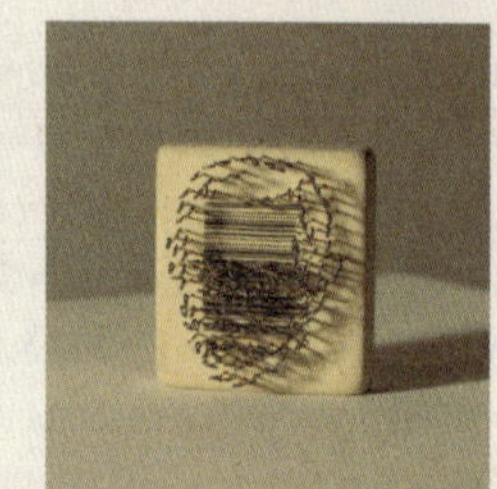

2.

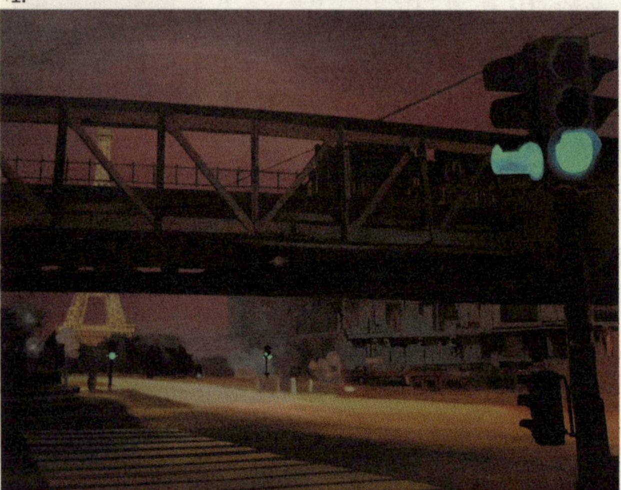

3.

4.

Diana Machulina lives and works in Moscow. Exploiting unexpected events and contradictory juxtapositions, her objects and paintings expose the hidden and often highly politicized meanings of everyday objects and images. In the series **A Farewell to Arms** (2008), for example, she renders items confiscated by airport security as classically styled still-life paintings.

1. Birthday
from the series **Old New**
2007, oil on canvas, 110 × 110 in (280 × 280 cm)

2. Rubber Soul (detail)
2008, paper, ink, rubber erasers, and metal needles, each approx 4 × 4 in (10 × 10 cm)

3. Paris
from the series **Green Light** 2007, oil on canvas, $52\frac{1}{2} \times 78\frac{3}{4}$ in (133 × 200 cm)

4. Eternal Life
2008, metal, human skull, carbon dust, and electric saw, $17\frac{3}{4} \times 51\frac{1}{4} \times 53\frac{1}{4}$ in (45 × 130 × 135 cm)

Lorna Macintyre received her MFA in 2007 from the Glasgow School of Art, and continues to live and work in Glasgow. Her delicate sculptures, installations, and photographs often take their inspiration from literary figures like Jorge Luis Borges and Fernando Pessoa. She was the subject of a solo show at the Institute of Contemporary Arts in London in 2008.

1. Pisces (for CL)
2005, copper, wood, ink, and enamel on found image, painted pine cone, and stone, 56 ¾ × 22 ½ × 10 ¾ in (144 × 57 × 27 cm)

2. Specular Composition 1
2006, black and white digital print and wood, 14 ¼ × 24 ½ × 1 ¼ in (36 × 62 × 3 cm)

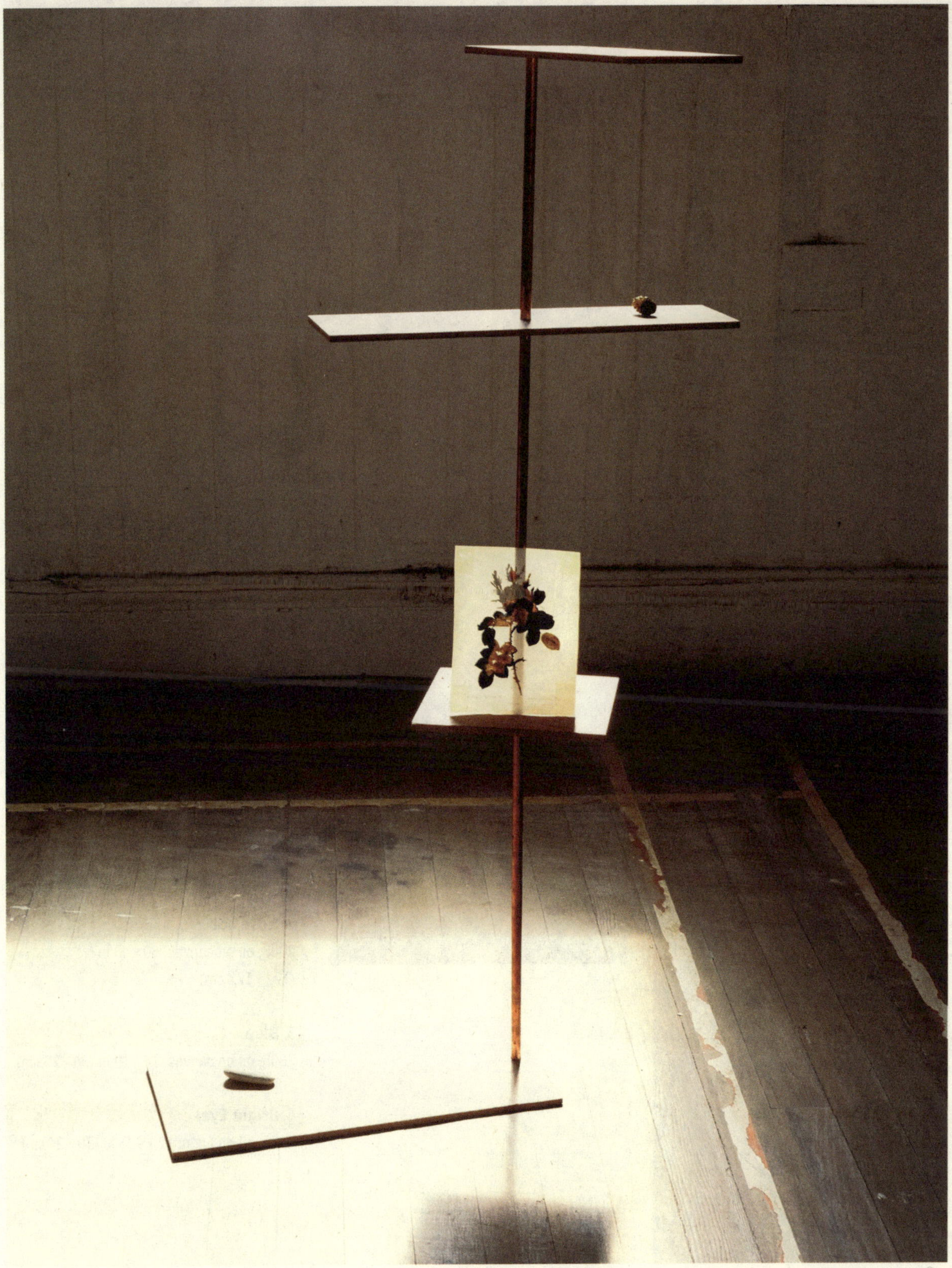

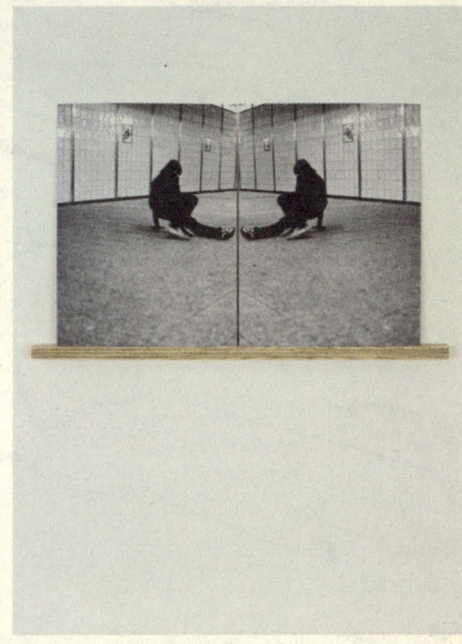

2.

3. Untitled (detail)
2008, 4 wooden columns, each 55 ¼ × 11 ¾ × 11 ¾ in (140 × 30 × 30 cm); silver crystals and folded copper, each 10 × 10 × 8 in (25 × 25 × 20 cm)

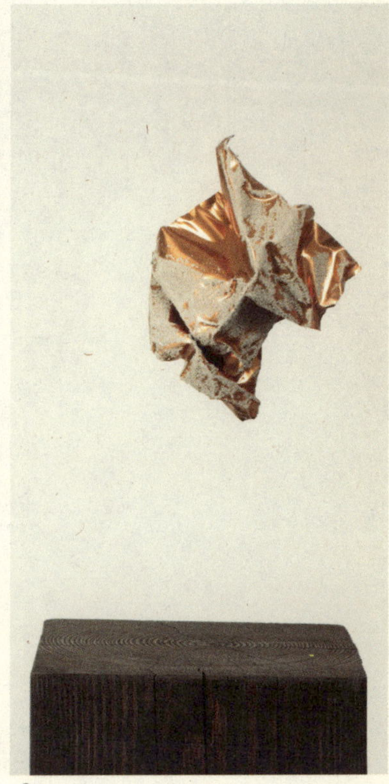

3.

1.

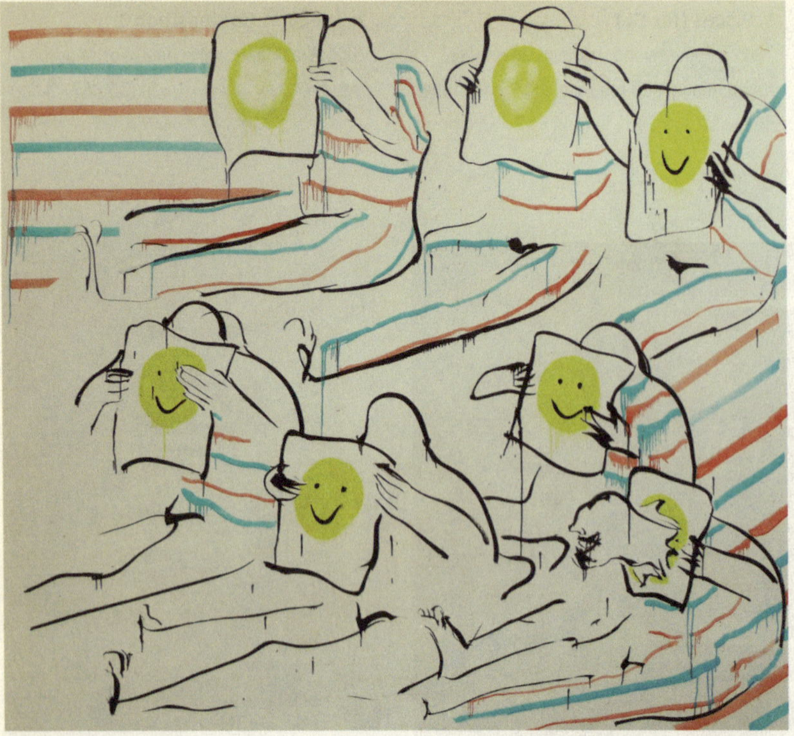
1.

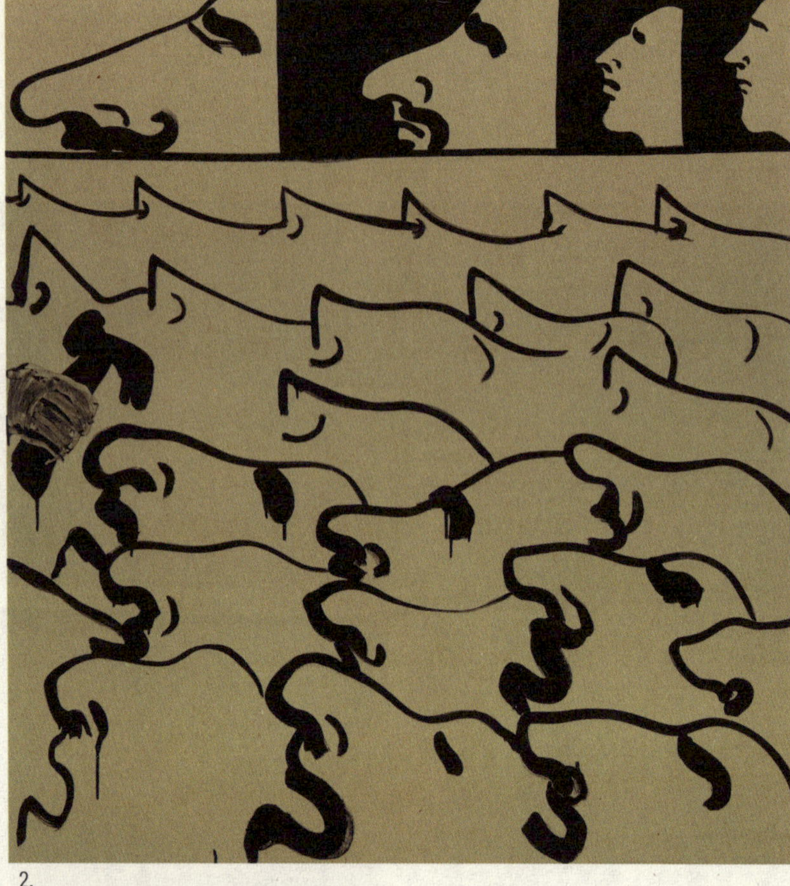
2.

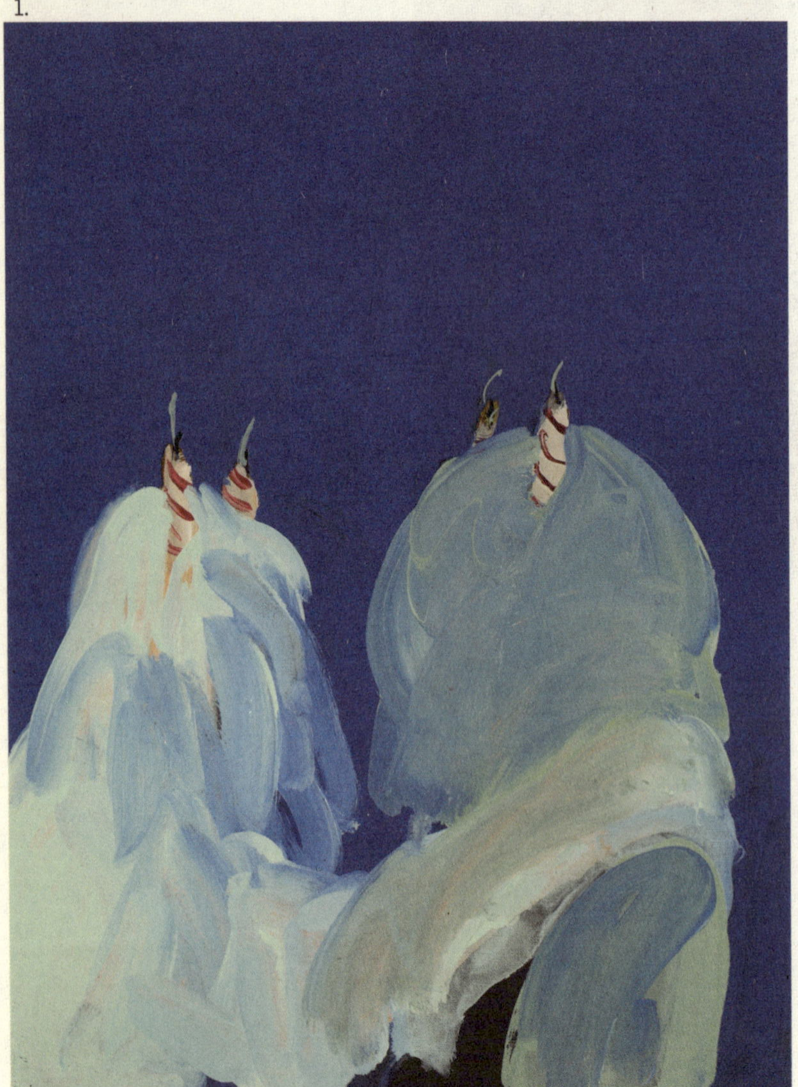
3.

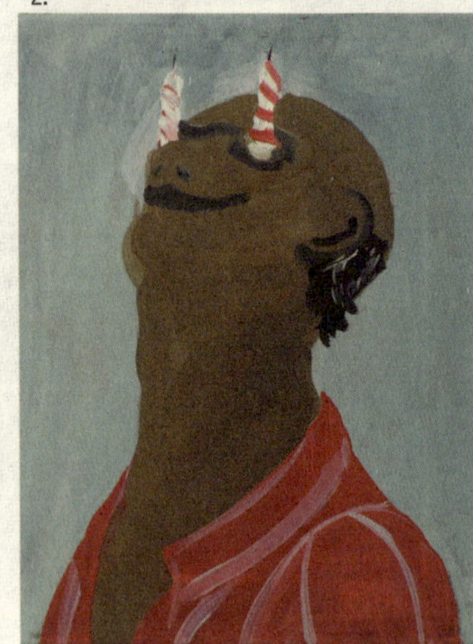
4.

Tala Madani lives and works in Amsterdam, but her work continues to reference Iran. Madani's small and often crude, richly exuberant paintings are witty fusions of the political and the personal that evoke, in their mixing of formal and narrative styles, Abstract Expressionism, political cartooning, and Persian miniatures.

1. Smiley
2008, oil on linen, 75 × 82 3/4 in (190 × 210 cm)

2. Nose Job
2008, oil on canvas, 50 × 48 in (127 × 122 cm)

3. Blue
2008, oil on canvas, 14 × 10 in (36 × 25 cm)

4. Bright Eyes
2007, oil on linen, 12 × 9 1/2 in (30 × 24 cm)

Gaisha Madanova lives and works in Almaty, Kazakhstan. In multi-part photographic installations, she has contrasted the internal realm of the artist's studio and daily working practice with the urban construction boom in her post-socialist homeland. She has documented her experience of Paris and its inhabitants as observed through a pair of binoculars in her ongoing work **Documentation of Space**.

1, 2 & 3. **Documentation of Space**
2007-present, digital photographs

4 & 5. **Transformation of Space**
2007, digital photographs

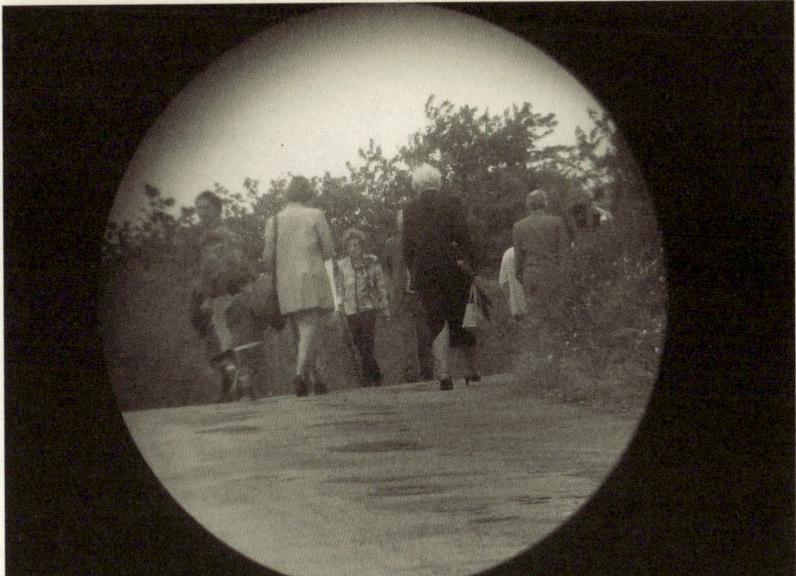
1.

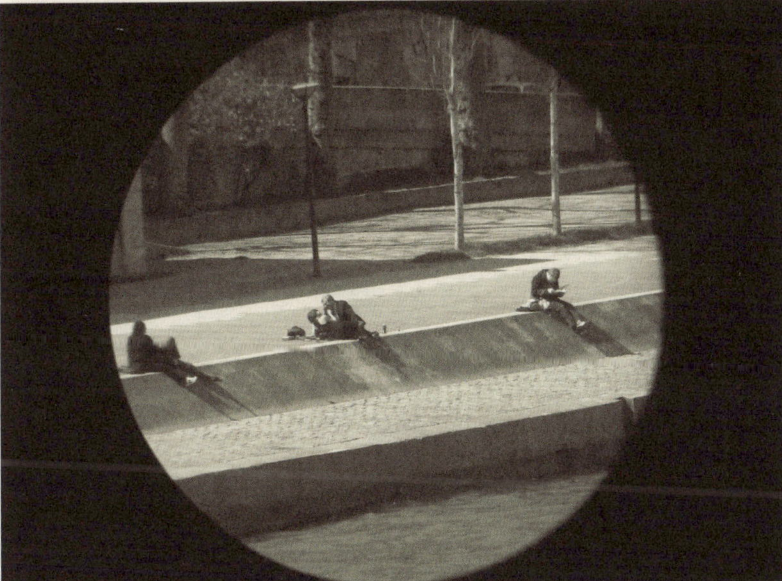
2.

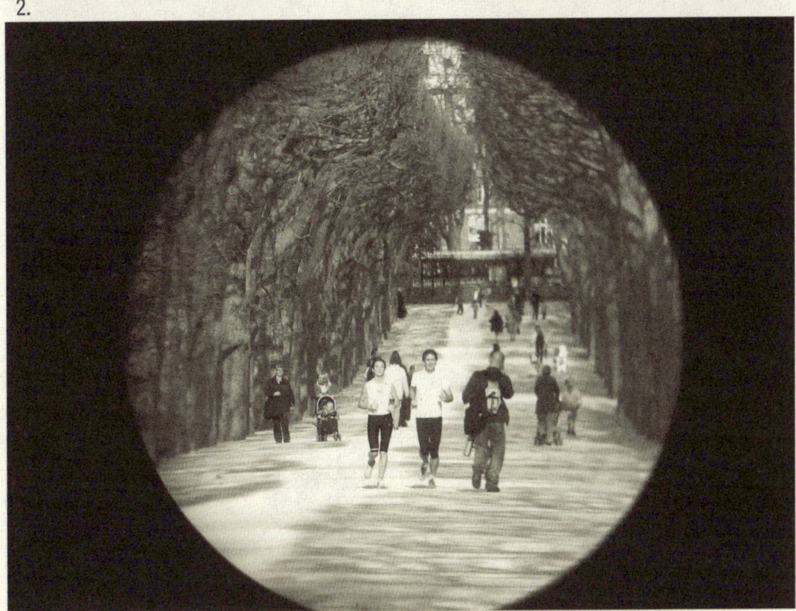
3.

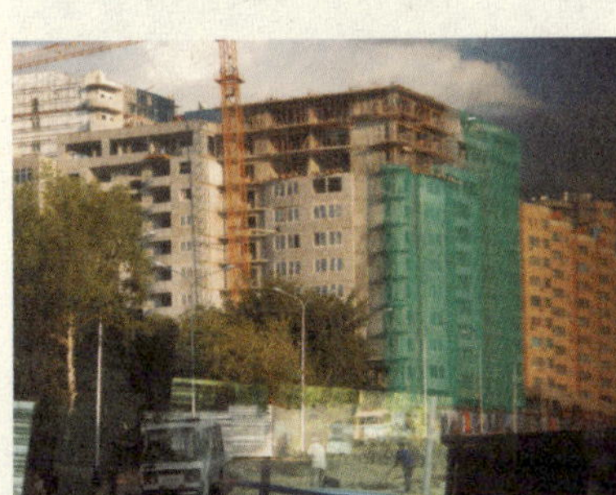
4.

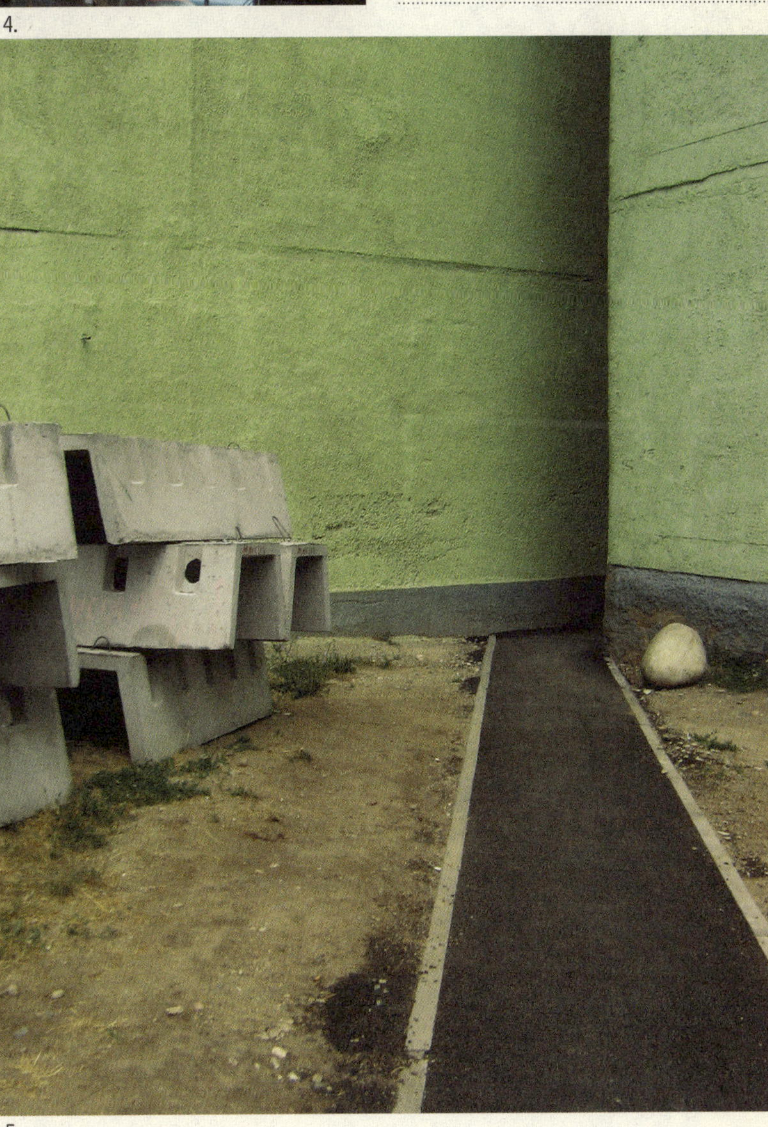
5.

1.

Basim Magdy is currently based in Cairo, Egypt, and Basel, Switzerland. He employs a wide variety of materials and methods including painting, drawing, and video to reflect on the continual recycling and reinterpretation of ideas and information perpetuated by popular media. He often concentrates on dubious heroes and disputed histories; a recent installation at Austin's Okay Mountain explored the story of the ongoing search for Bigfoot.

1. Untitled
2006, chromogenic print, 6 × 4 in (15 × 10 cm)

2. In the grave of intergalactic utopia
2006, mixed media, dimensions variable, installation view at Newman Popiashvili Gallery, New York

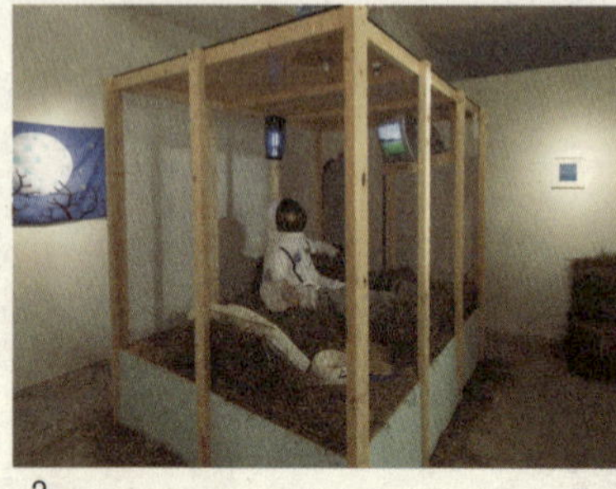

2.

3. The future of your head
2008, mirrored glass, wood, Christmas lights, and electric wiring, 84 ½ × 98 ½ × 31 ½ in (215 × 250 × 80 cm)

4. Victory is mine
2006, spray paint and gouache on paper, 9 ½ × 13 ½ in (24 × 34 cm)

5. A contracted excavation of extinct secret societies
2008, acrylic, oil, and enamel on paper, 19 ½ × 27 ½ in (50 × 70 cm)

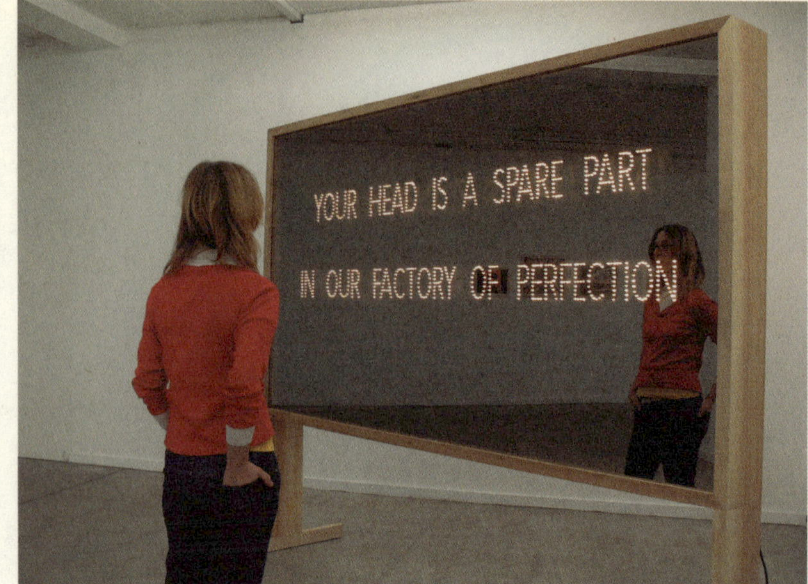

3.

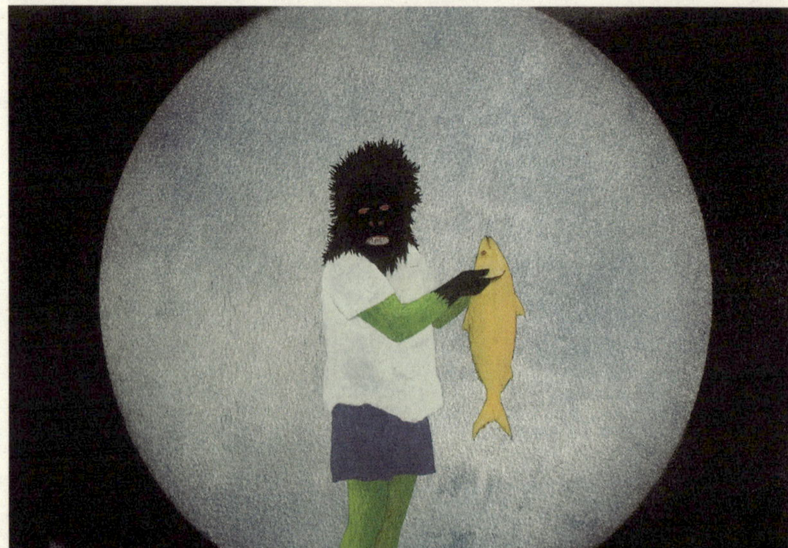

4.

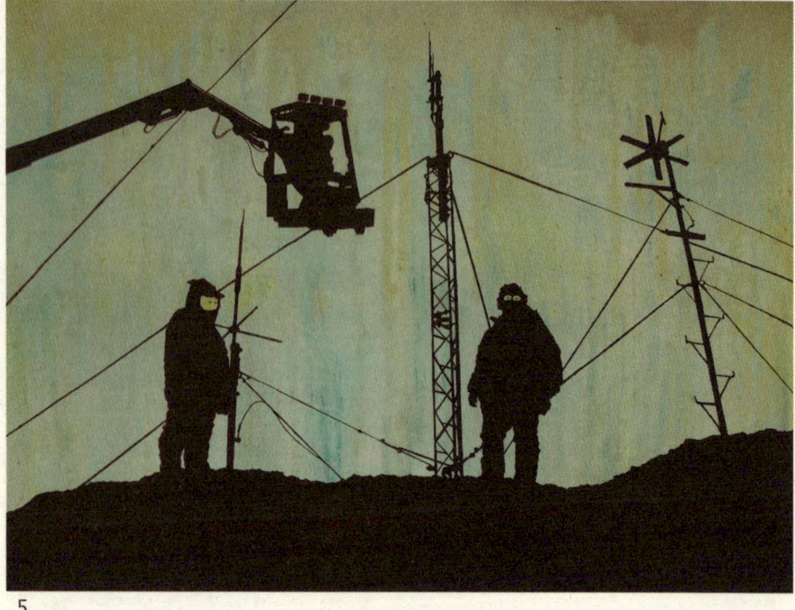

5.

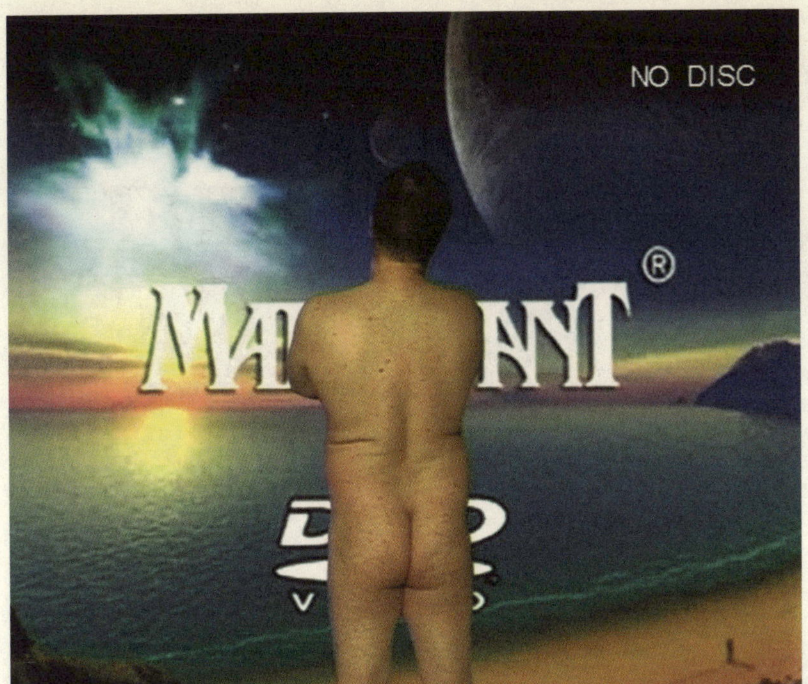

1.

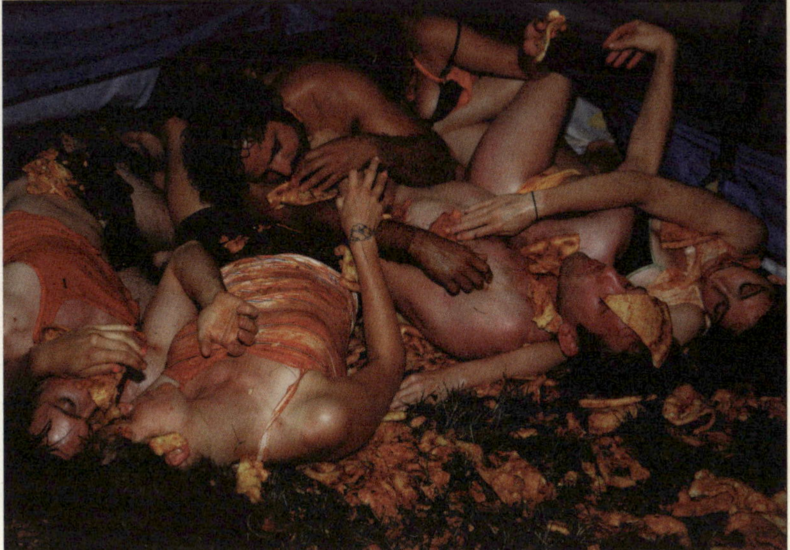

2.

1. Seeking Adam

2007, video, loop

2. Delivery

with Liz Magic, Laser, and Ben Fain

2008, video, 5 min 50 sec

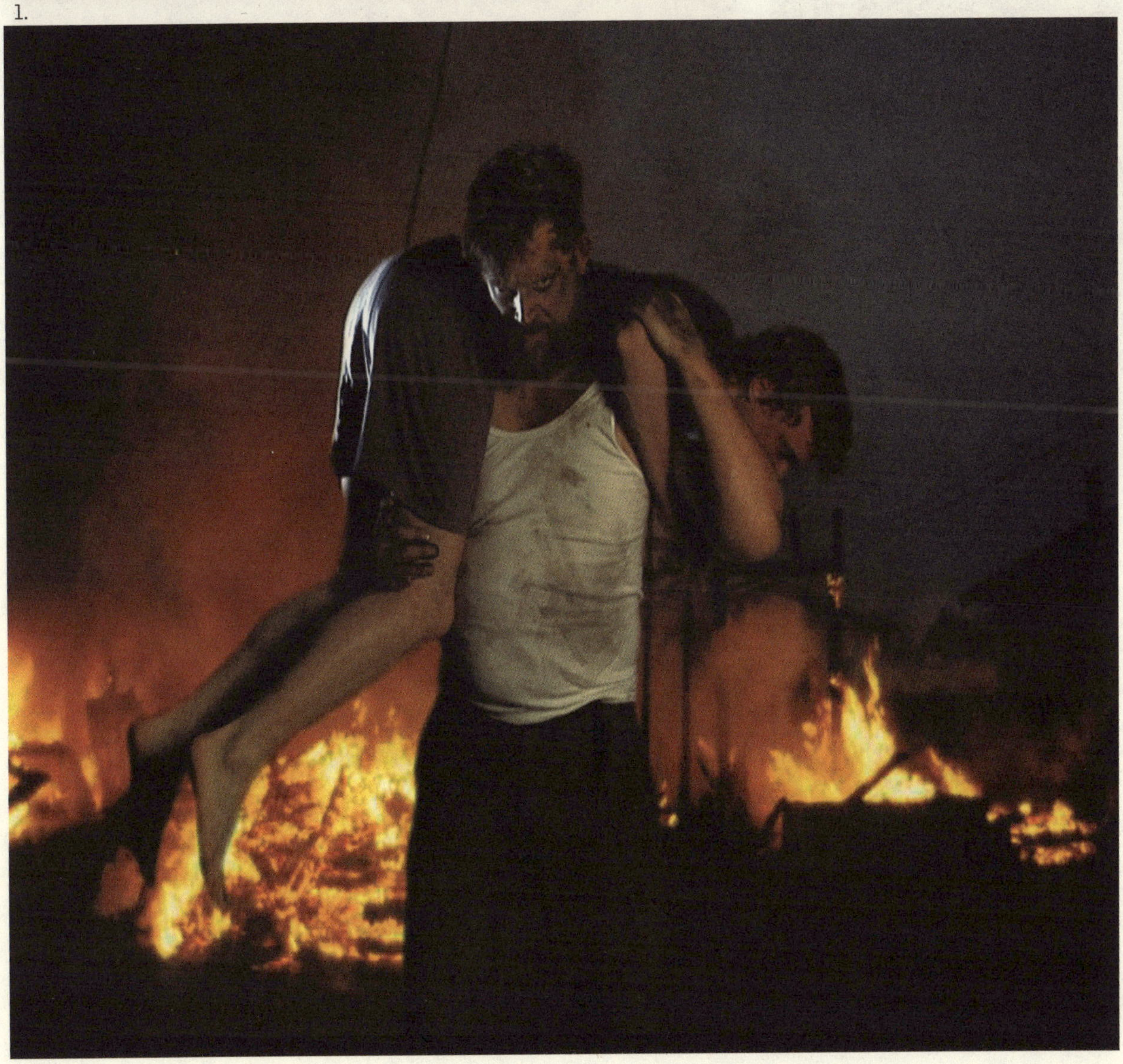

3.

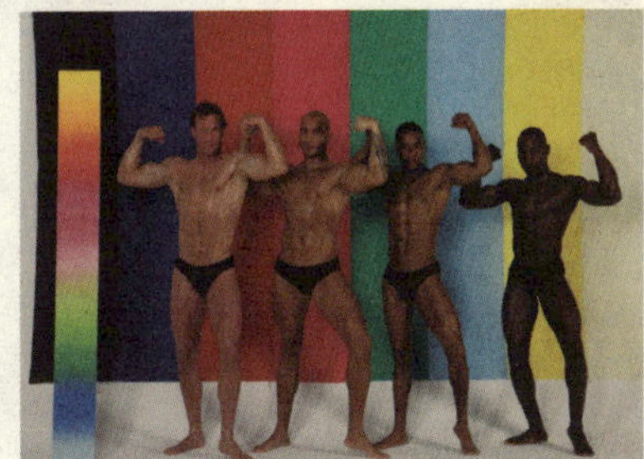

4.

Dafna Maimon currently lives and works in Amsterdam. Using humor as a tool for cultural critique, she makes works that overturn viewers' expectations. In the video **After All** (2007) she reflects on the filmic presentation of tragic romance by adopting the role of Scarlett O'Hara, while in the performance **I Work Here** (2007) she replaces the single gallery receptionist with ten people.

3. Disaster

2007, video, loop

4. Amateur Body Builder Gradient

2008, chromogenic print, 39 1/2 × 59 × in (150 × 100 cm)

Benoît Maire makes richly discursive objects that make gently allude to philosophical discourse around repetition, reflection, and artistic-curatorial convention. In the video **Meeting Sébastian Planchard** (2006), for example, the artist meets and interviews a fictional character from his own book.

1. **the tears**
2007, wood and inkjet print,
23 ½ × 12 × 8 in (60 × 30 × 20 cm)

2. **histoire de la géométrie #5 (étude de l'industrie)**
2008, wood, plastic, found images,
15 ¾ × 23 ½ in (40 × 60 cm)

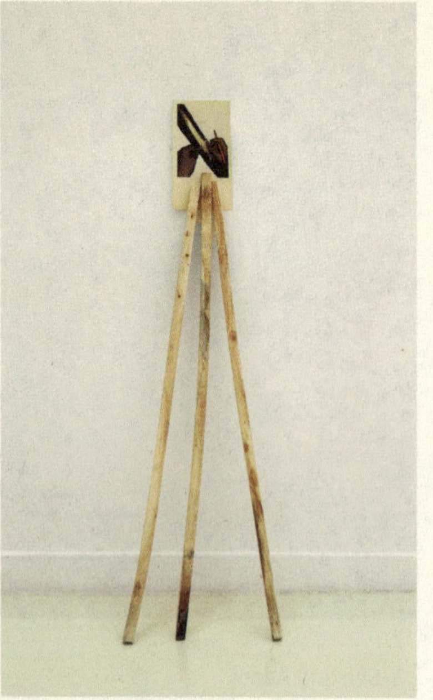

1.

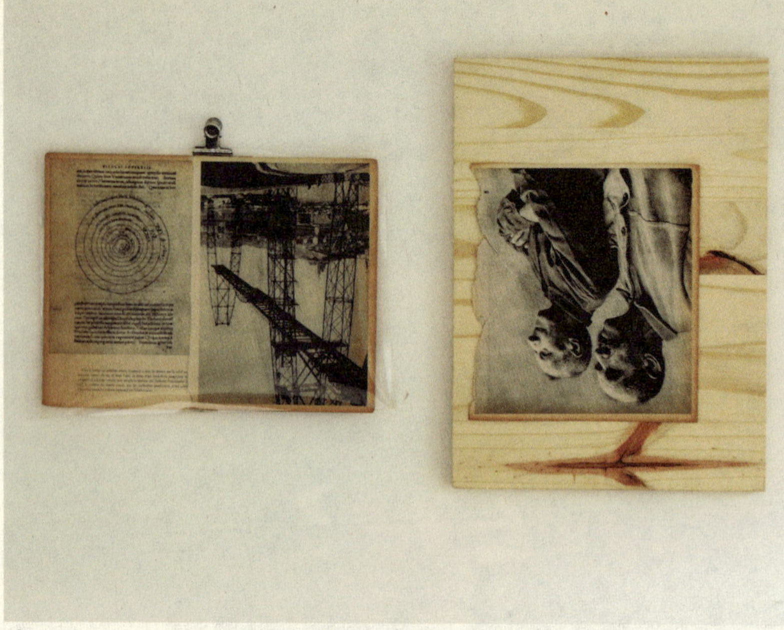

2.

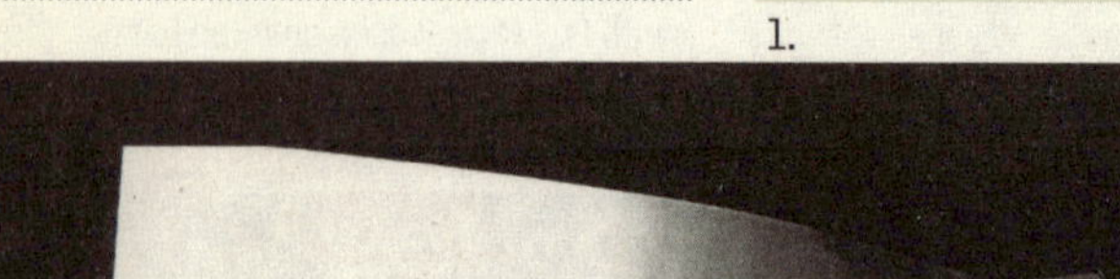

Aesthetics of the Conference of Aesthetics

« c'est assez dire : abîme et satire de l'abime »
Jacques Derrida, la vérité en peinture, Flammarion, Paris, 1978
« We screw it all up »
Easy Rider, 1969
« Art is the definition of art »
Joseph Kosuth, Art after philosophy, 1969

This short text aims at questioning the nature of the space-time experienced by an audience attending a conference of aesthetics. To question the *quality of nature* means to insist not on the concepts the conference produces, but rather on the space-time it generates for an audience, and on the spectacular which is at stake. The situation is as follows: There is a face-to-face, someone addresses an audience about – or in the name of?[1] – art, and there is an absent object – during the conference, art is not directly and immediately present, it is at best represented by means of slides – and there is a discourse.

Does this discourse frame its object? Is it situated between the inside and the outside? *Is it in short* a *parergon* with respect to its object? If this question was crucial in 1978, it no longer is the case today, since we consider that the conference of aesthetics is a format of contemporary art and is thus *totally inherent to it* – the categories of art and philosophy dissolved in 1969, as we will see in a moment. So, *without even mentioning* frames, what can be said about the relationship between an audience and the sonic sculpture made by an aesthetician speaker? This is a new question, which can arise through questioning the relationship between art and truth in post-fictional statements.

a—on post-fiction
After the stage of post-modern fiction as emergence of authoritative discourses after the era of narratives[2] – the first stage of a theoretical fiction tainted with a nihilism linked to the notion of crisis and the collapse of reference points –, the idea of truth returns in aesthetics in a conceptual aspect. Truth returns, though not like a ghost returns to the place it haunts; it is not the idea of truth which returns, but its new embodiment; truth returns to its concept and is thought as a philosophical category. Alain Badiou: "Which can be said as well: art itself is a truth-procedure. Or: the philosophical identification of art belongs to the category of truth"[3]. Therefore this new fact, the coming of truth as a concept and not as an *ideality*, happens in theoretical post-fiction. Indeed, it appears that the break with postmodernity (in its aftermath, its "post-", its "square post-", or its "modernist-alternativity"), is being elaborated or plotted[4] in contemporary aesthetic thought, under its various possible names ("post-post-…", "after", "alter-"…) which can also be thought as theories of post-fiction. But in such a *break with*, can there be an agreement on a category of truth and how can it be elaborated in the artistic space?

b—on performative statements
There is this recent fact: the importance of a direct communication unmediated by screens, that is, the re-assessment – in recent artworks – of performativity: the only traces of an artistic event lie in it being told by word of mouth, by a person to another, by connoisseurs to their friends. Can we speak here of a sonic sculpture whose supporting element is the very body of an audience absent during the original performative event? Does this open up a liberated relationship

[1] See Thierry De Duve, *Kant after Duchamp* (Cambridge, Mass.: MIT Press, 1998).
[2] What is called 'narratives' after Lyotard is not fiction in terms of their proper historical efficacy; rather they become fiction retroactively from the perspective of postmodernity which no longer believes in them. Since postmodernity treats past ideologies as narratives, it talks about its own relationship with ideology – a relationship with fiction.
[3] Alain Badiou, *Petit Manuel d'inesthétique* (Paris: Editions du Seuil, 2000, p. 21).
[4] The *plot* is a form of conceptual elaboration.

3.

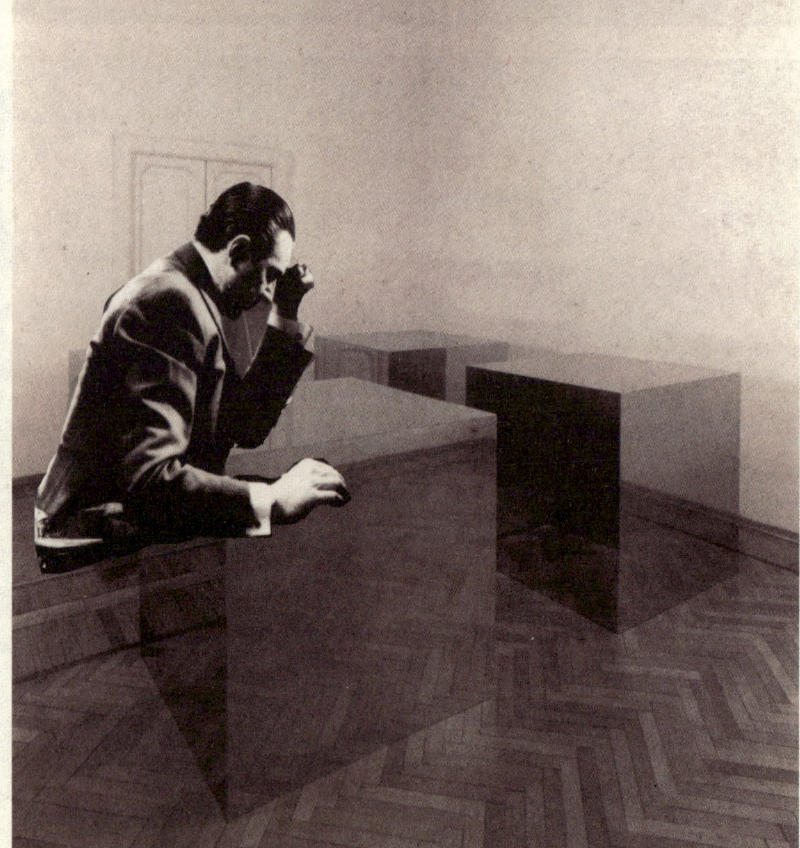

4.

3. **Aesthetics of the Conference of Aesthetics**
2006, printed text, unlimited edition,
11 ¾ × 8 ¼ in (30 × 21 cm)

4. **histoire de la géométrie #1**
2007, collage on Lambda print,
23 ½ × 23 ½ in (60 × 60 cm)

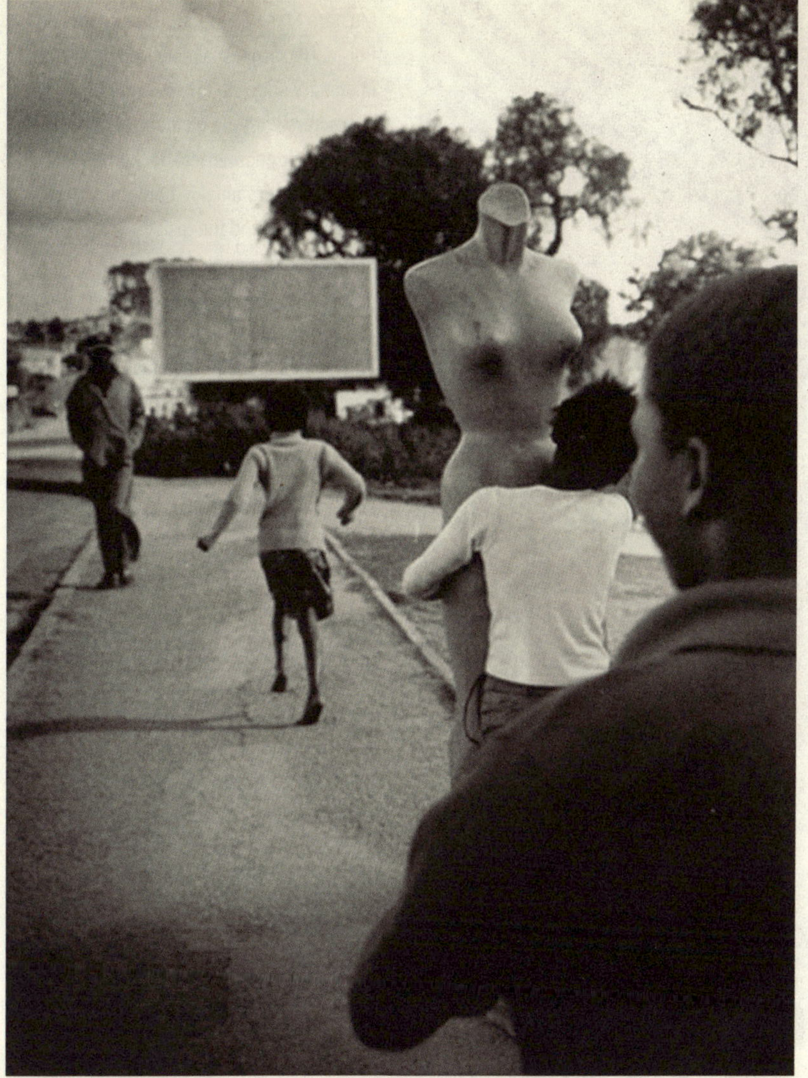

1.

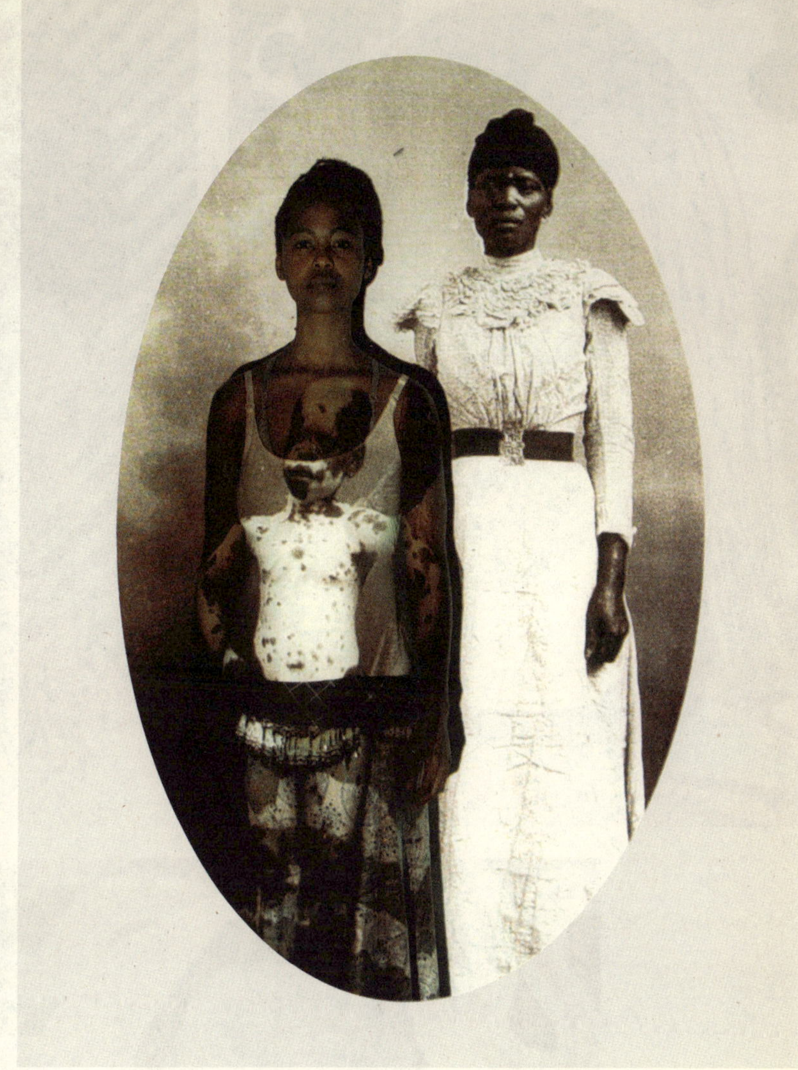

2.

3.

Nomusa Makhubu received a BFA and an MA in art history from Rhodes University in Grahamstown, South Africa. Her work investigates the construction of identity and the historical objectification and oppression of African bodies by colonial interlopers. She has created a large body of work utilizing anthropological photographs originally made for use in pseudo-scientific enterprises such as physiognomy. By projecting these images digitally onto her own body, she provokes a tension between contemporary and historical notions of otherness and representation.

1. **...or so we dreamt**
2005, digital print on archival paper, 15 ¾ × 12 in (40 × 30 cm)

2. **Umasifanisane** (detail)
2007, digital print on archival paper, 1 of 2 parts, each 31 ½ × 23 ½ in (80 × 60 cm)

3. **Silently** (detail)
2006, digital print on archival paper, 3 parts, each 15 ¾ × 19 ½ in (40 × 50 cm)

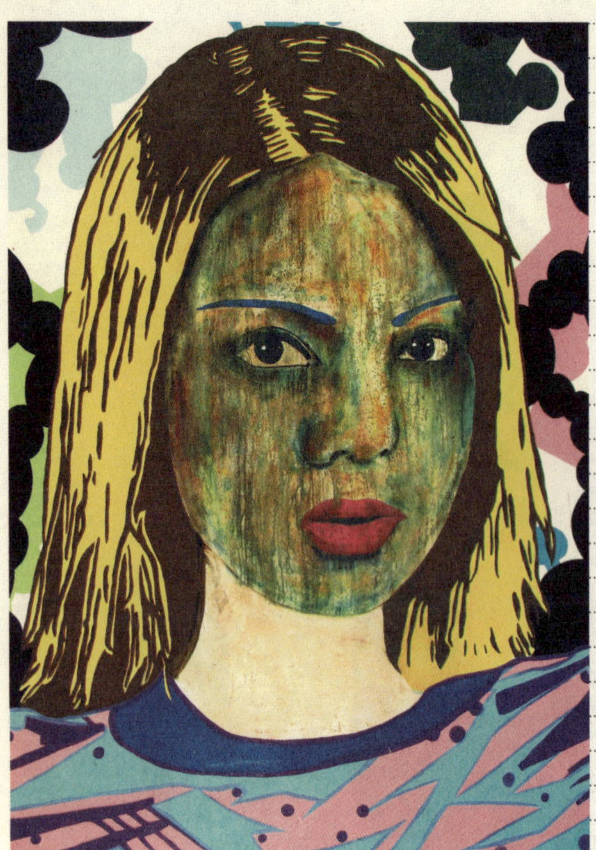

1.

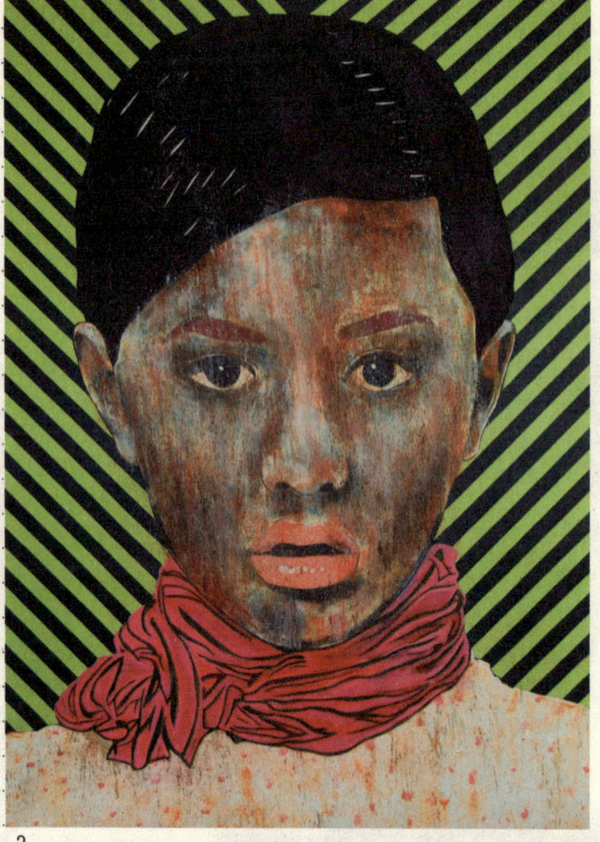

2.

Mustafa Maluka lives in Amsterdam and Berlin. His large-scale stylized portraits of imaginary subjects invest youthful characters with the glamour of celebrities. The vibrant geometrical backdrops that Maluka prefers amplify both the sitters' personalities and the artist's immersion in borderless pop culture.

1. I can't make you love me if you don't
2007, oil and acrylic on canvas,
72 × 52 1/2 in (183 × 133 cm)

2. I can't believe you think that of me
2007, oil and acrylic on canvas,
72 × 52 1/2 in (183 × 133 cm)

3. Don't stand me down
2006, oil and acrylic on canvas,
72 × 52 1/2 in (183 × 133 cm)

4. No more keeping my feet on the ground
2007, oil on canvas, 72 × 52 1/2 in
(183 × 133 cm)

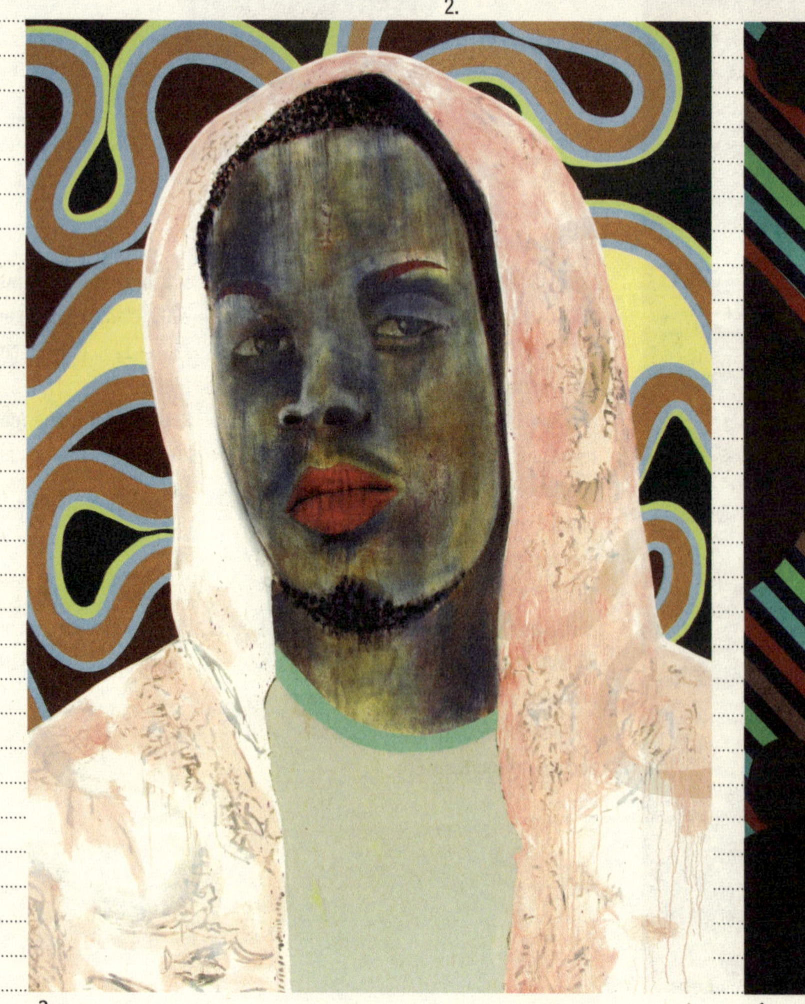

3.

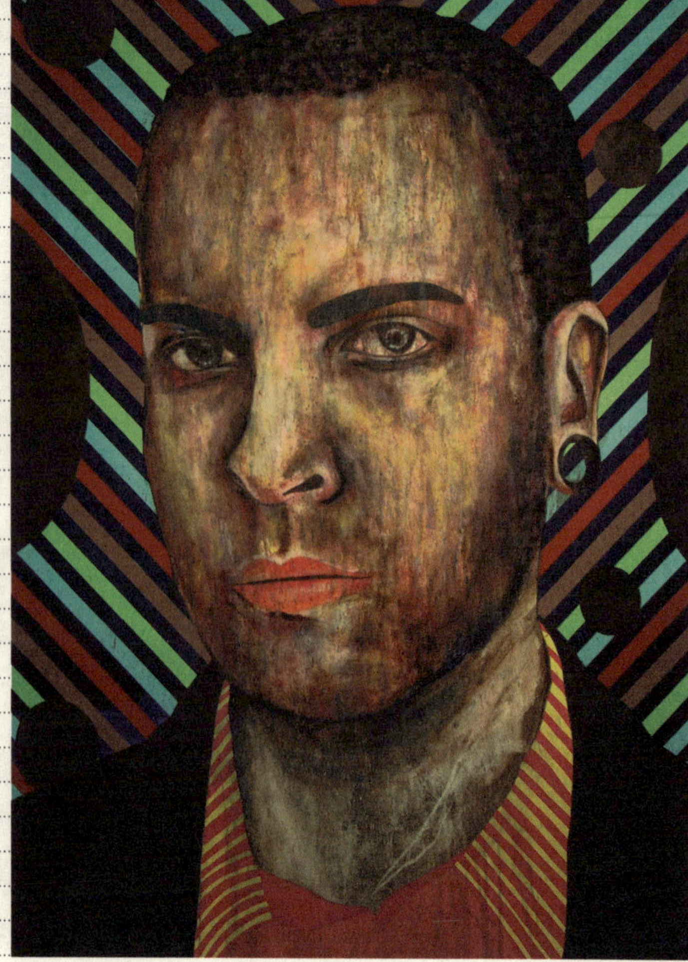

4.

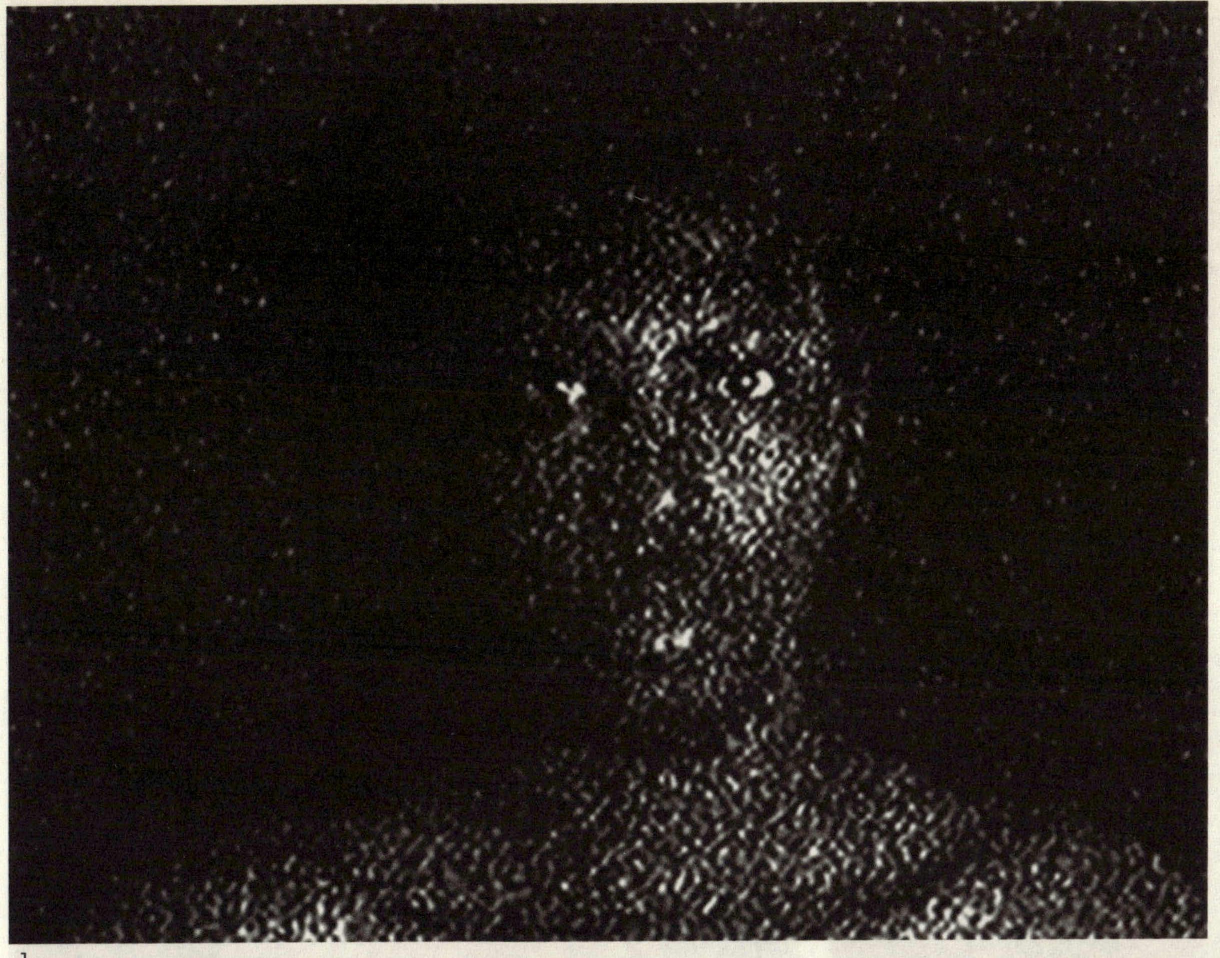

1.

Thando Mama studied printmaking and photography at a the Technikon Natal, in Durban, South Africa, where he is currently based. Mama was introduced to video in 2000, and since then he has utilized the medium to explore social and political themes against the background of postcolonial, postapartheid South Africa. Mama's videos analyze the ways in which the South African male identity is constructed, as well as the myths and half-truths that are passed down between generations to inform notions of self. In 2005, Mama was awarded a fellowship to the Sally and Don Lucas Artists Programmes, California. He is a founding member of the South African artists collective Third Eye Vision.

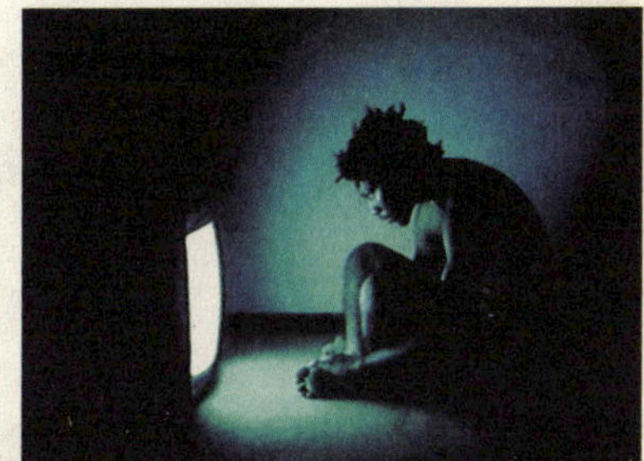

2.

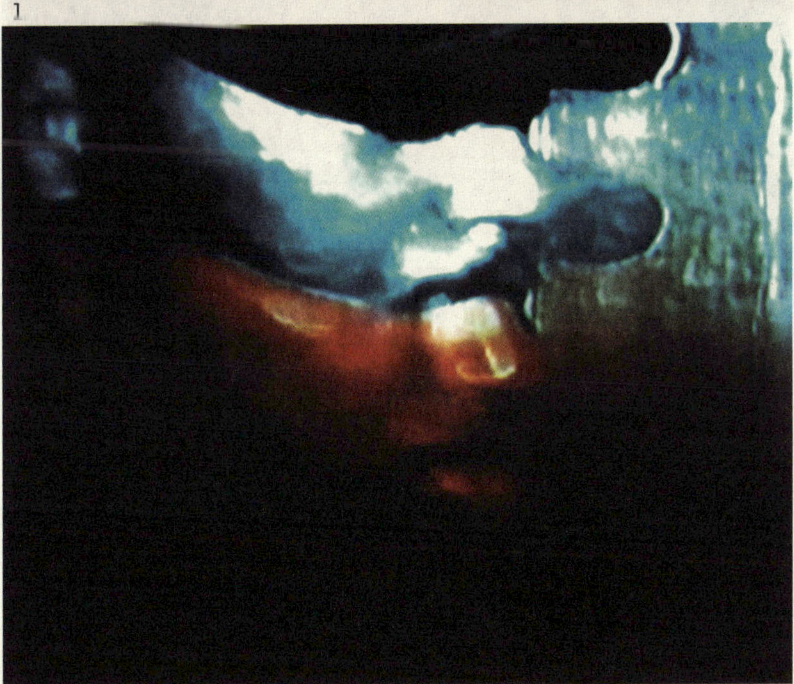

3.

4.

1. We Are Afraid

2003, archival print, $17\frac{3}{4} \times 23\frac{1}{2}$ in (45×60 cm); video, 4 min

2. Back to Me

2003, archival print, $17\frac{3}{4} \times 35\frac{1}{2}$ in (60×90 cm); 2-channel video, 3 min 30 sec

3. Revolution now III

2008, archival print, $17\frac{3}{4} \times 23\frac{1}{2}$ in (45×60 cm); 3-channel video, 1 min, 3 min, and 7 min

4. Mind-space

2004, archival print, $17\frac{3}{4} \times 23\frac{1}{2}$ in (45×60 cm); video, 3 min

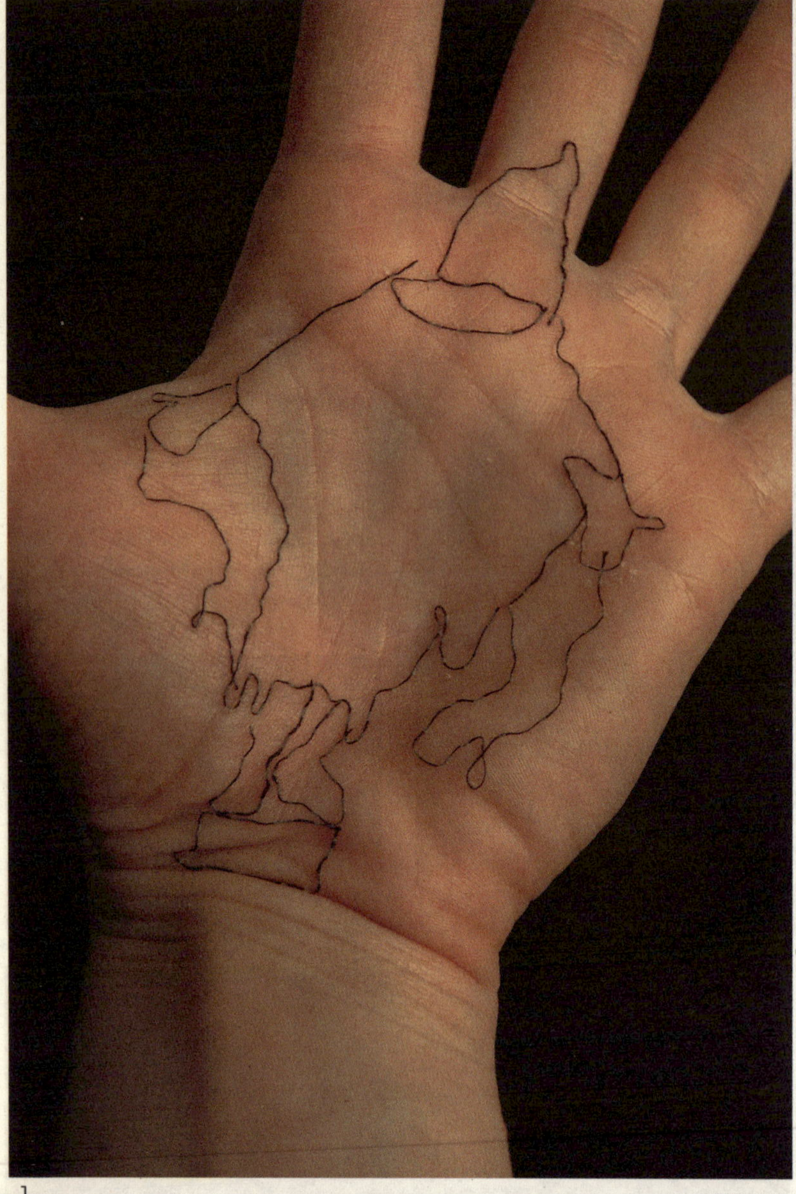

1.

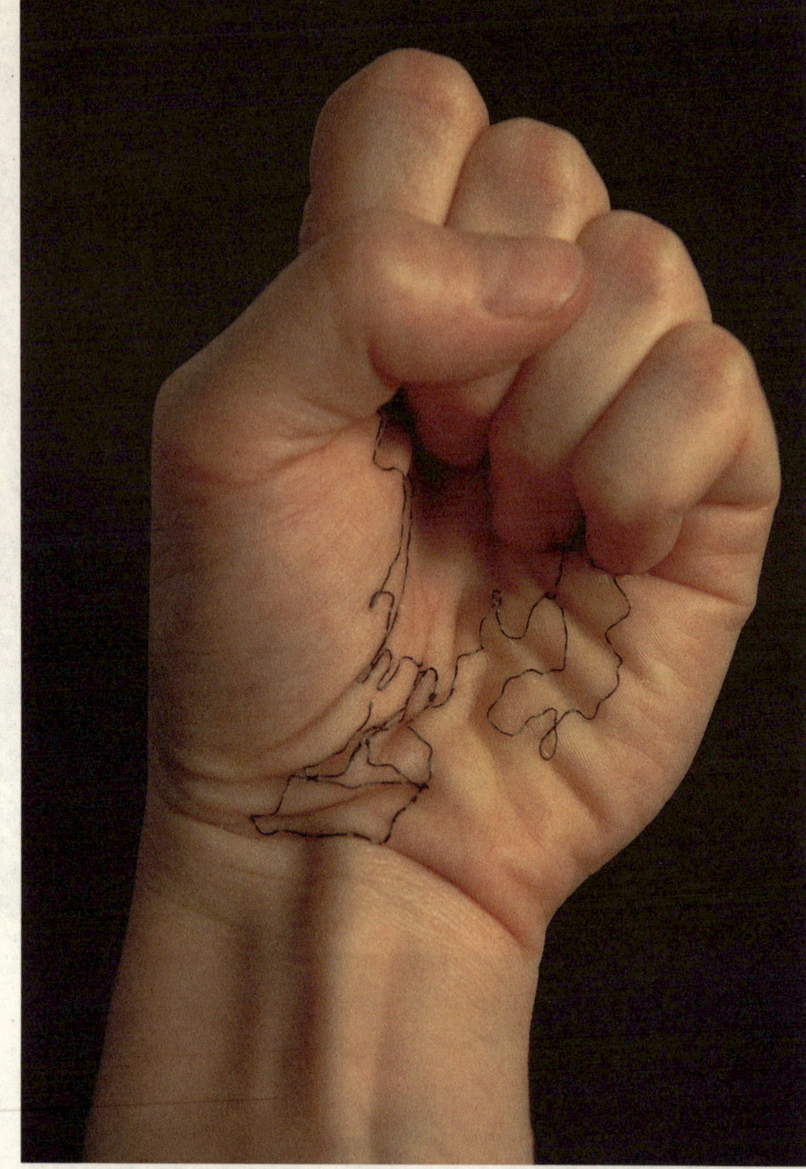

2.

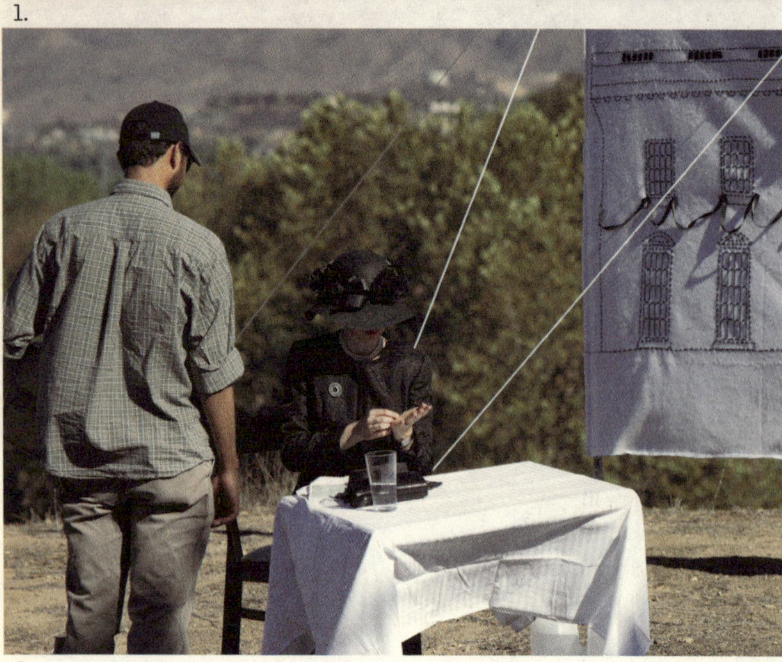

3.

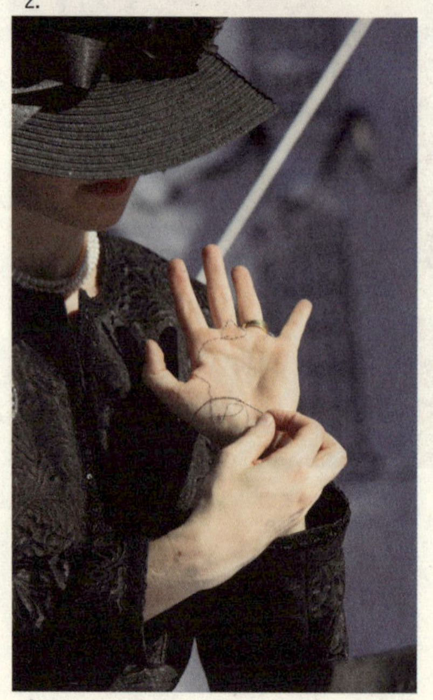

4.

Elana Mann received her MFA from the California Institute of the Arts in Valencia, California. Her interdisciplinary work investigates the theatrics of everyday life and the breakdown of social spaces through performance, video, installation, and curatorial projects, which often involve elements of participation, collaboration, and exchange. Recently, her work has focused on aspects of the war in Iraq, particularly the abuse of prisoners held at Abu Ghraib.

1 & 2. **Evidence: Embroid, Embroil**
2008, digital prints, 2 parts, each 20 × 13 in (51 × 33 cm)

3 & 4. **Embroid, Embroil**
2007, performance, 90 min

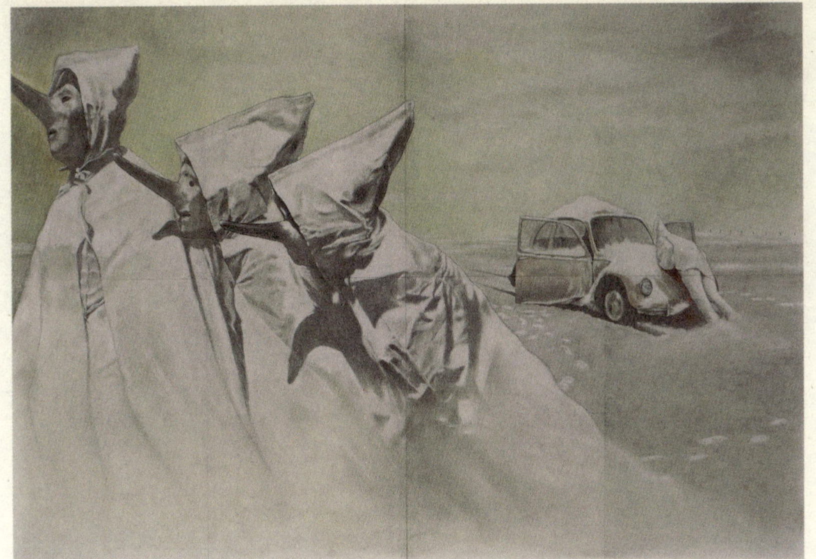
1.

Duncan Marquiss lives and works in London. His paintings, drawings, and videos explore human conceptualizations of nature through a cultural history of the ecstatic, the uncanny, the animalistic, and the sublime. Borrowing imagery from folk tales and subjects from horror and sci-fi cinema, he comments on our fascination with the unknown.

1 Snowblindness
2008, pencil and chalk on paper, $31\frac{1}{2} \times 47\frac{1}{4}$ in (80 × 120 cm)

2 & 3. **A Nothing With A Vengeance**
2006, video projection with sound, 5 min

4. **The Curving Murals**
2006, pencil on paper, 26 × 19 in (66 × 48 cm)

5. **Hello**
2006, pencil on paper, $17\frac{3}{4} \times 13$ in (45 × 33 cm)

6. **Gemeinschaft**
2006, watercolor on paper, $17\frac{1}{2} \times 22$ in (44 × 56 cm)

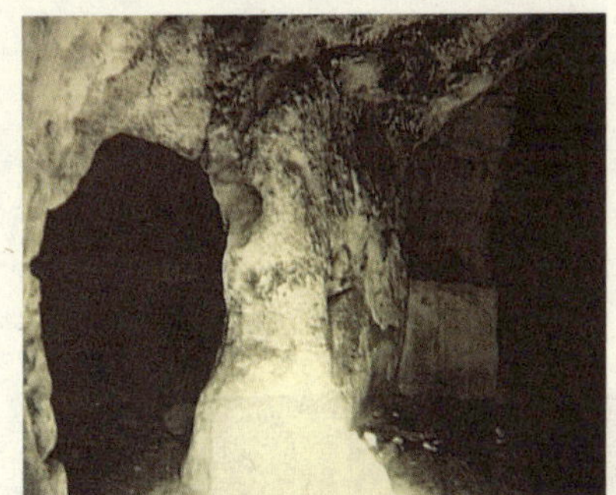
2.

3.

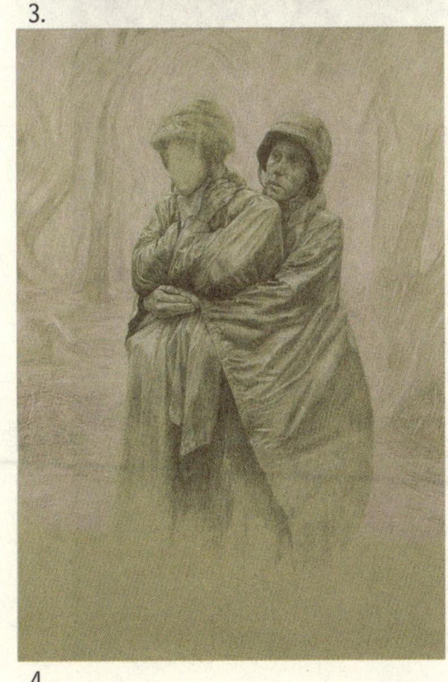
4.

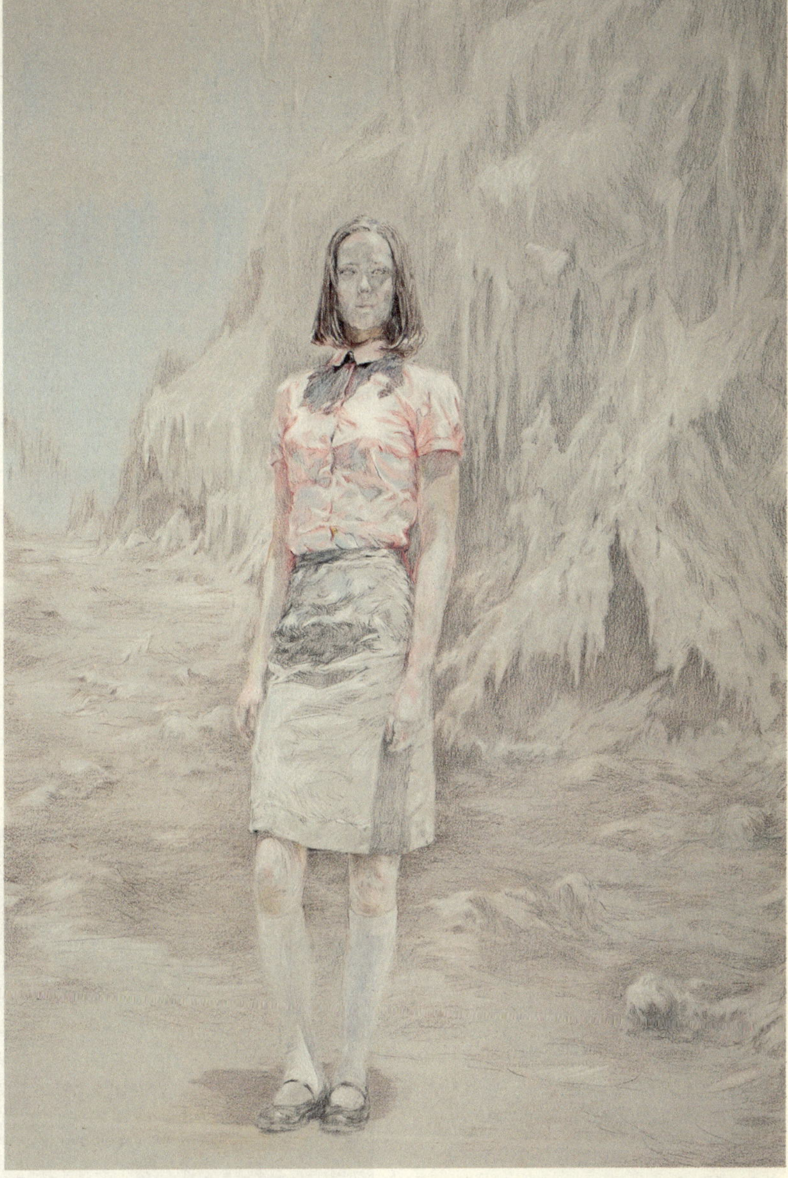
5.

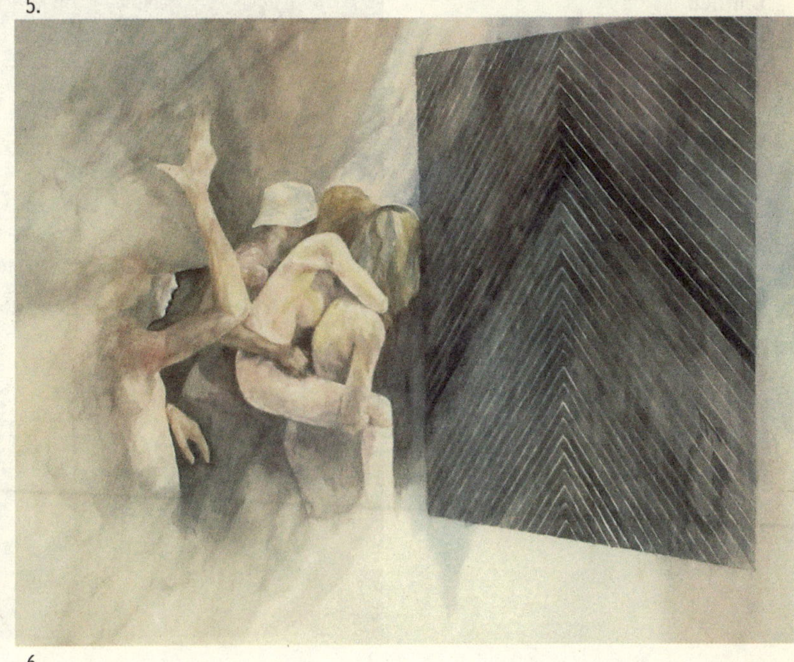
6.

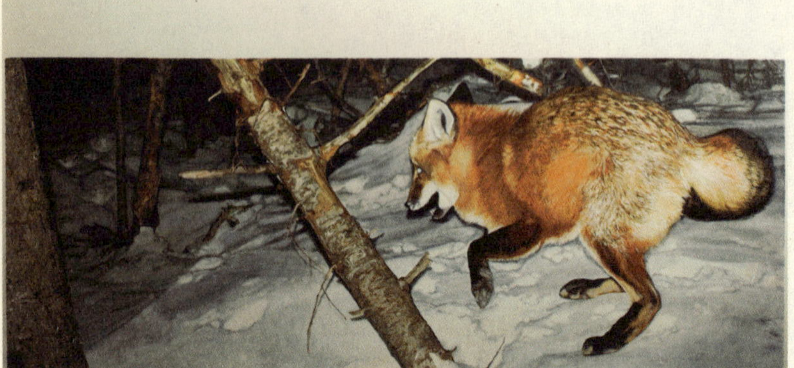

1.

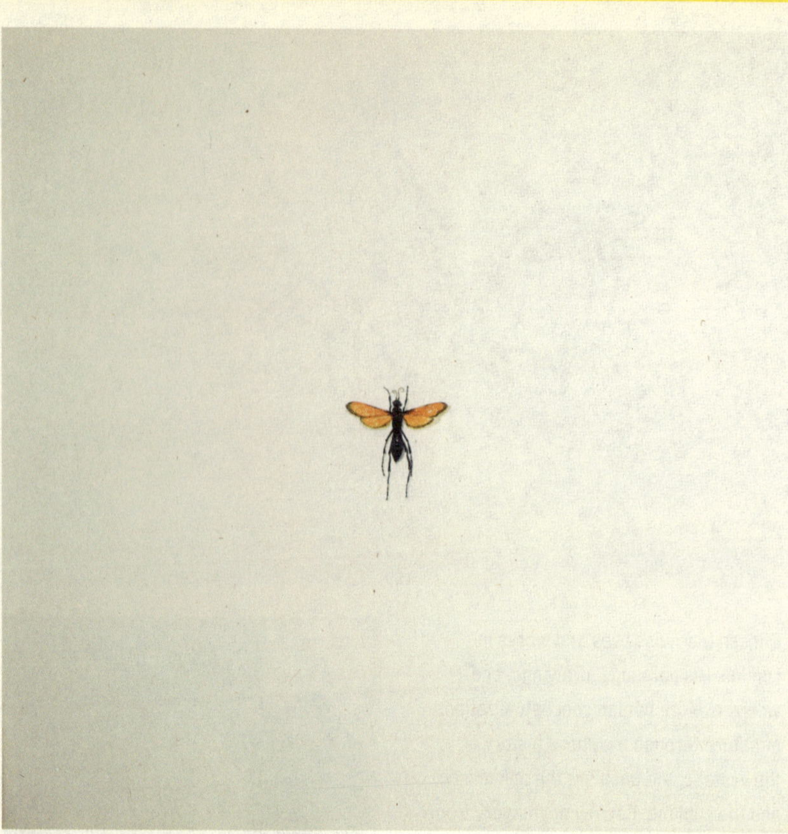

2.

Diego Martinez is based in Santiago, Chile. Beginning with photographs (either his own shots or, more often, samples from online archives), he makes naturalistic oil paintings that reflect on the classification of visual data. The artist's recent search for images tagged with his own name was the source material for a hundred-panel suite.

1. Untitled
2008, oil on canvas, 59 × 47 $\frac{1}{4}$ in (150 × 120 cm)

2. Untitled
from the series **Insectos**
2008, oil on canvas, 23 $\frac{1}{2}$ × 23 $\frac{1}{2}$ in (60 × 60 cm)

3. Untitled
2008, oil on canvas, 59 × 47 $\frac{1}{4}$ in (150 × 120 cm)

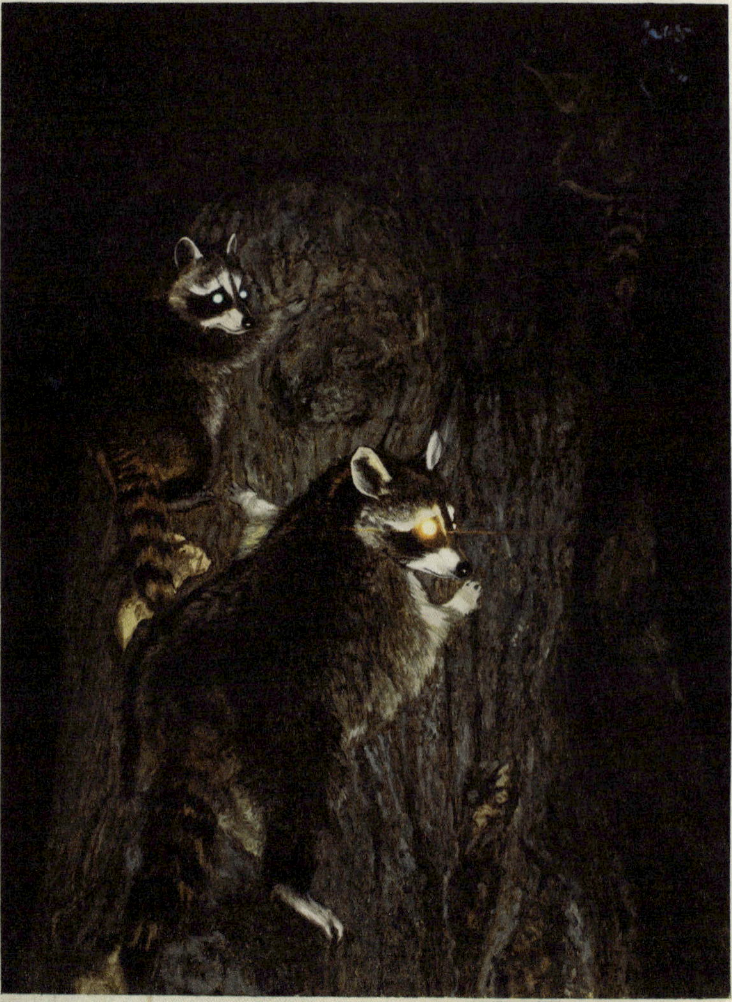

3.

Brooklyn-based Rachel Mason filters the archetypal forms of political art – the bust, the anthem, the portrait – through an expressionistic physicality. Using video, drawing, and handcrafted sculpture, she investigates political, scientific, and historical power relations, often highlighting their latent absurdity.

1. Mobutu Sese Seko
2007, performance with audio from "The Ambassadors Volume I," lyrics by Emory Holmes II, and music by the artist

2. Saddam Hussein
2008, performance with audio from "The Ambassadors Volume II" and music by the artist, performance view at Eighteen-Thirty, Los Angeles

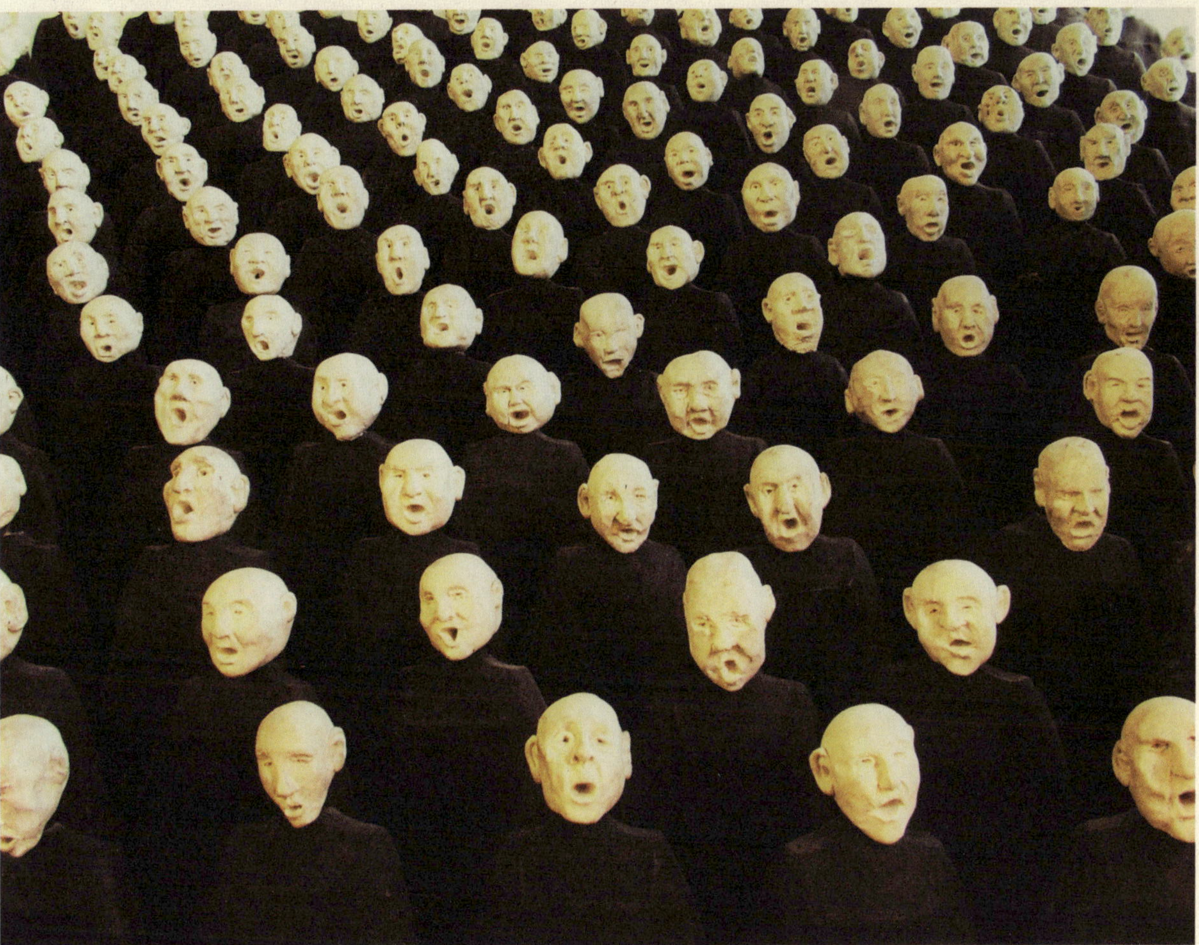

3.

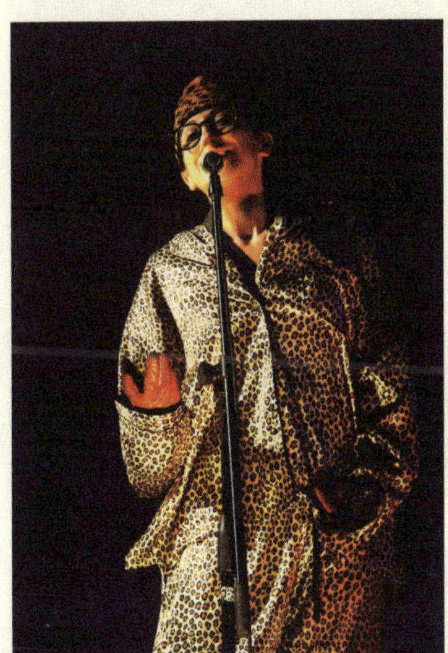

1.

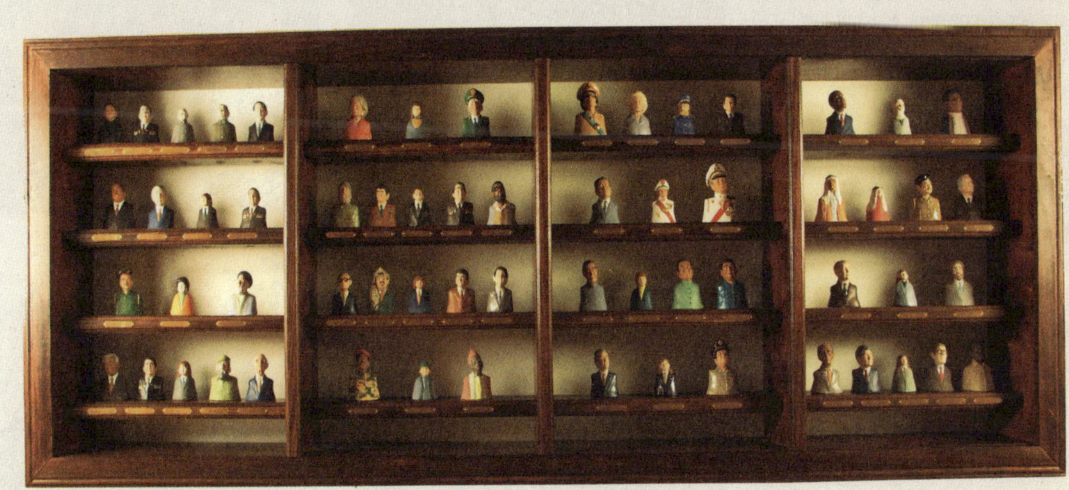

4.

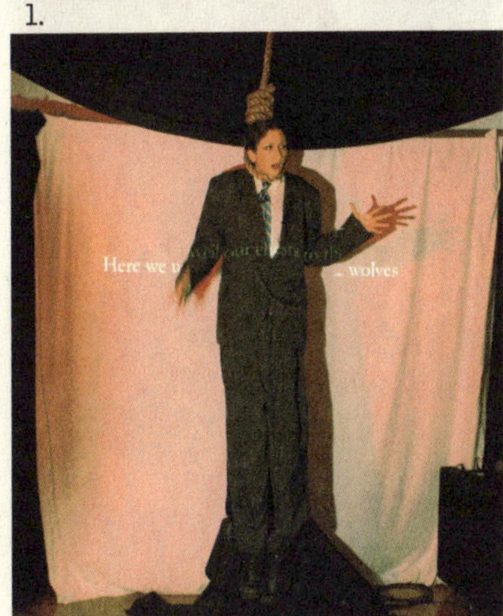

2.

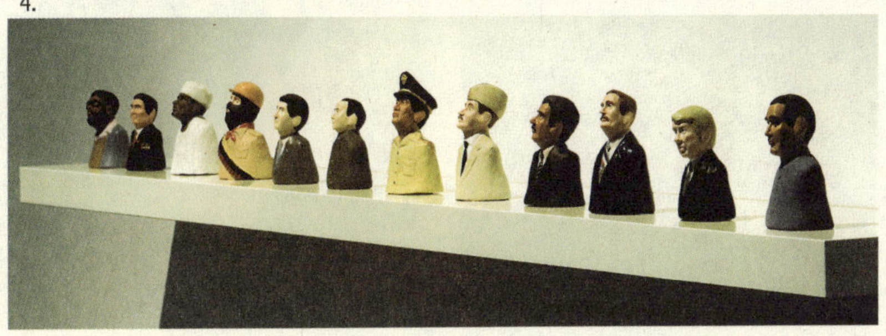

5.

3. Chiefs of State
2002-04, polymer clay, plaster, wood, and paint, 6 × 5 ½ × 5 ft (182 × 168 × 152 cm)

4 & 5. My Cabinet
2004-present, wood, porcelain, paper, glass, 6 ½ × 16 × ¾ ft (198 × 488 × 25 cm)

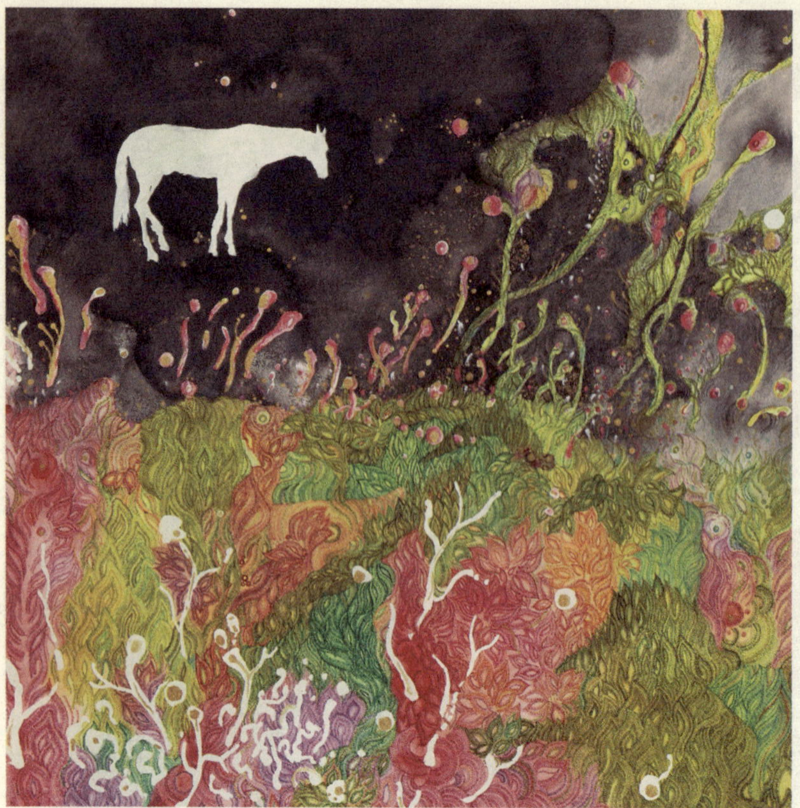

1.

Yoshino Masui earned her BFA from Tama Art University in Tokyo, where she lives. With watercolor on paper, she creates abstract landscapes that reference mythological narrative alongside traditions of pattern and decoration. Most of her compositions include a single animal moving through imaginary environments.

1. planned site
2007, watercolor, ink, gilt, pastel, and paper mounted on paper, 16 × 16 in (41 × 41 cm)

2. Sunset, Border
2007, watercolor and ink on paper on panel, 9 × 7 in (23 × 18 cm)

3. Sunset, Site
2007, watercolor, ink, and gilt on paper mounted on paper, 20 ¾ × 11 ½ in (53 × 30 cm)

4. Eclipse
2005, watercolor on paper, 14 ½ × 20 ¼ in (37 × 51 cm)

5. Sunset, red horse of solitary
2007, watercolor and ink on paper mounted on paper, 8 ¼ × 9 ¾ in (21 × 30 cm)

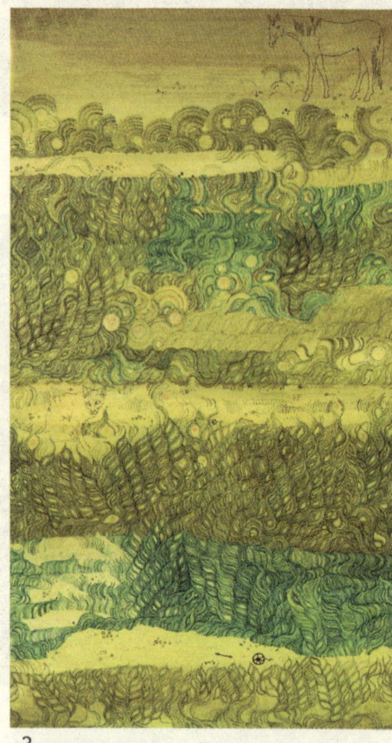

3.

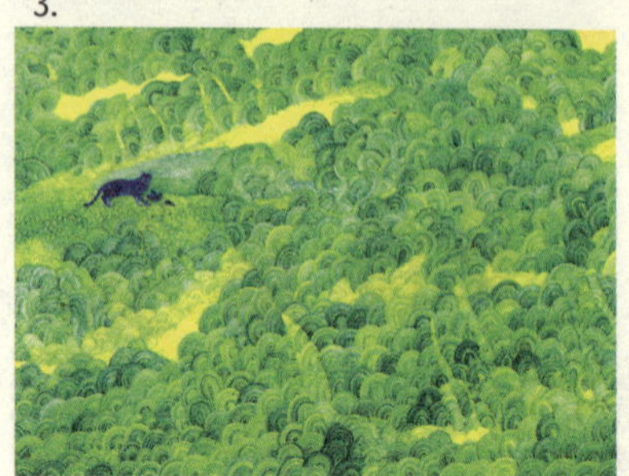

4.

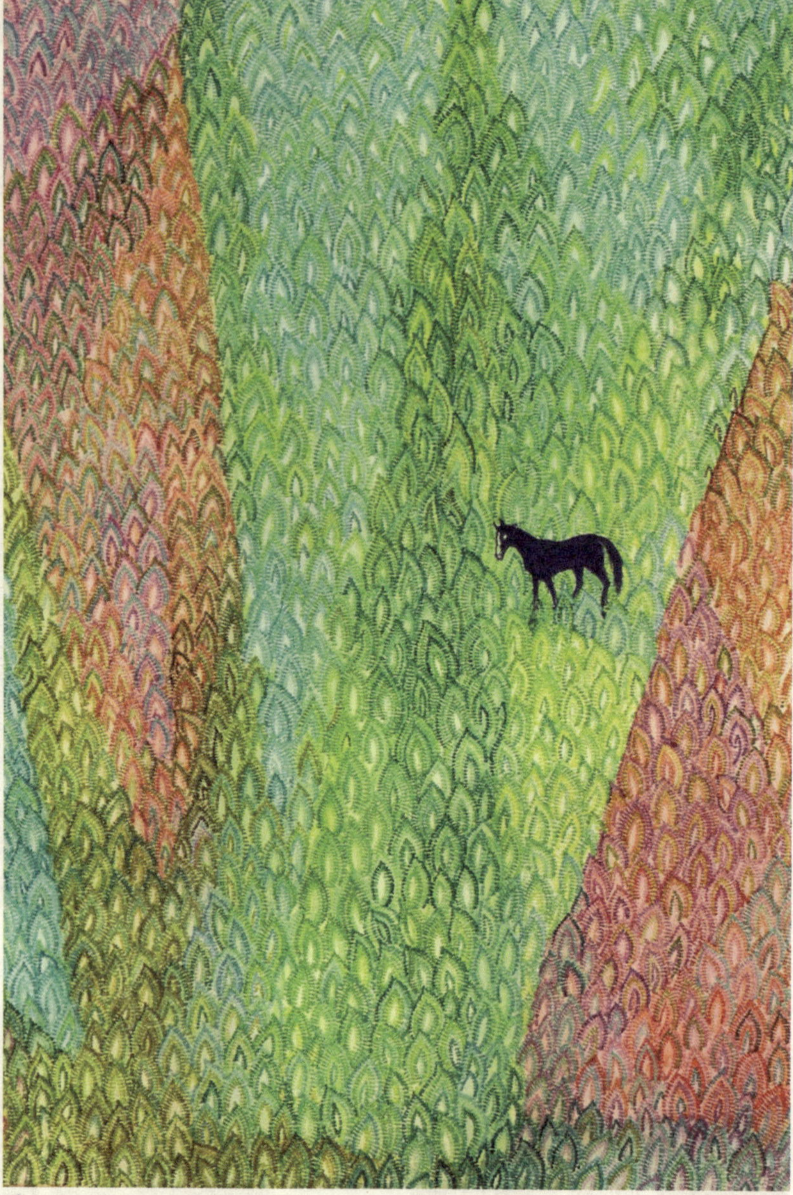

2.

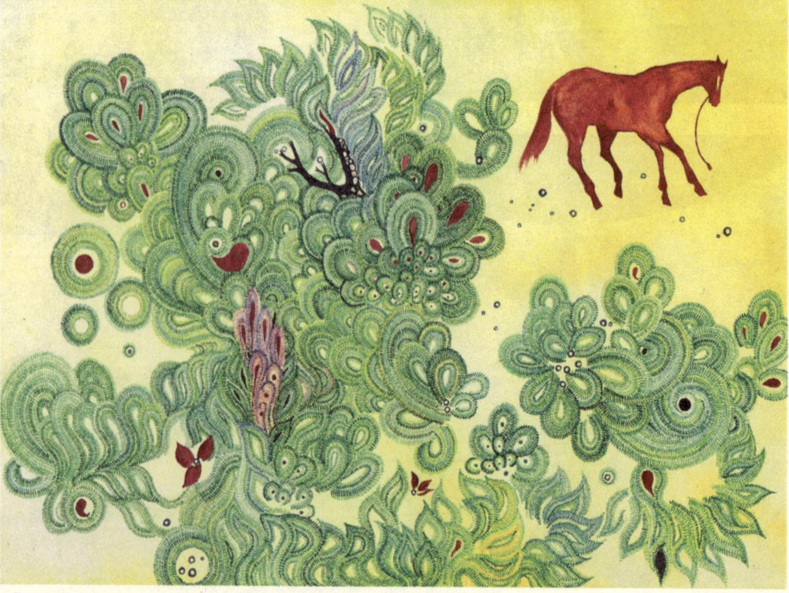

5.

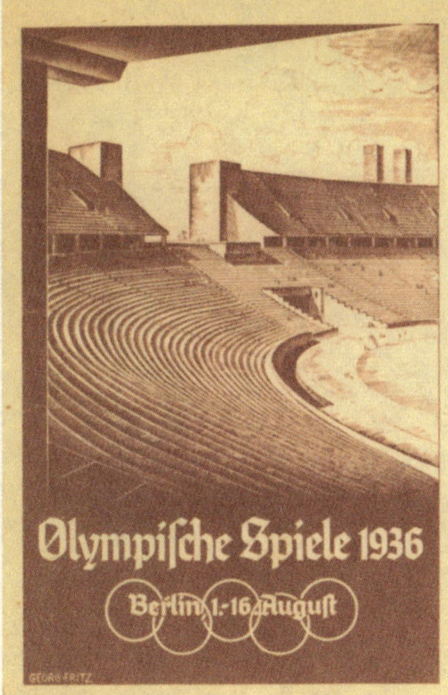

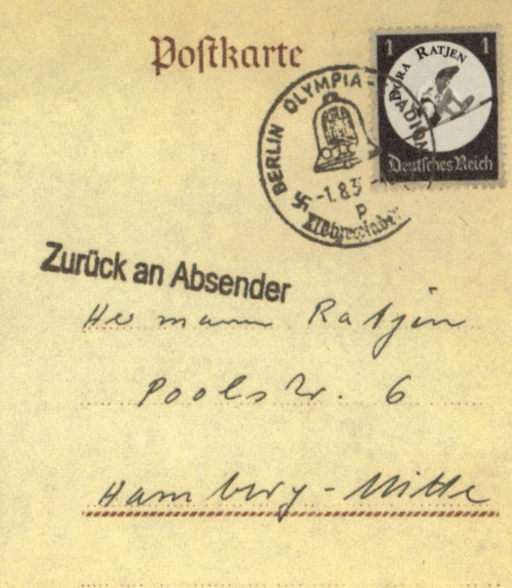

1.

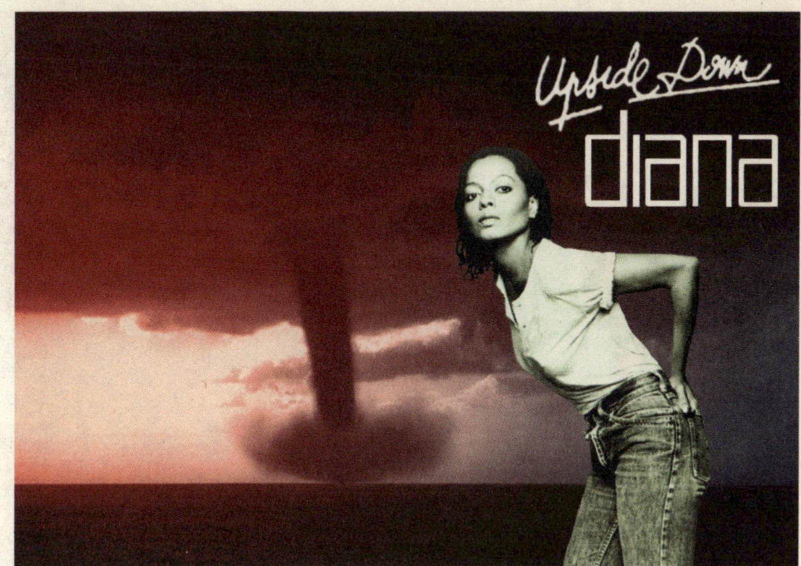

2.

3.

Artist and activist Tara Mateik is based in New York and exhibits internationally. He works in performance and video, casting himself as transvestite characters from pop music, competitive sport, and exploratory science. In 2002, he founded the Society of Biological Insurgents (SBI), an organization aimed at the overthrow of sexual norms.

1. **Zurück an Absender**
(Return to Sender)
2005, altered postcard from 1936 Olympics with commemorative stamp, 4 × 6 in (10 × 15 cm)

2. **Upside Down**
from the series **Men with Missing Parts** (formerly **Man Behind the Curtain**)
2008, album cover, 7 × 7 in (18 × 18 cm)

3. **Case 133: Psychosexual Metamorphosis**
2005-08, zoetrope assembled from a Victor talking machine, mixed media, and looping MP3 audio recordings, 16 ½ × 15 ¼ × 20 ¼ in (42 × 39 × 51 cm)

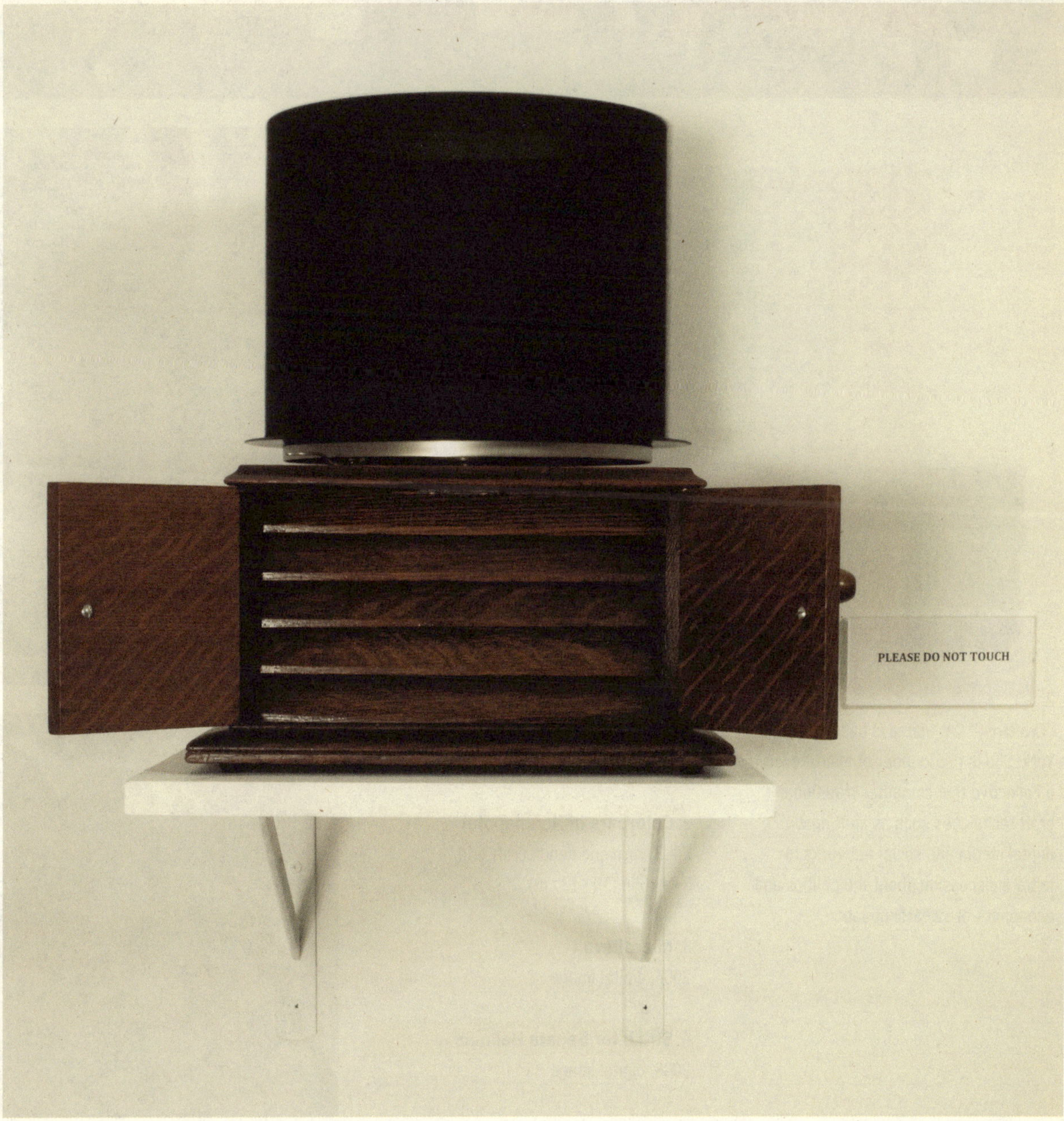

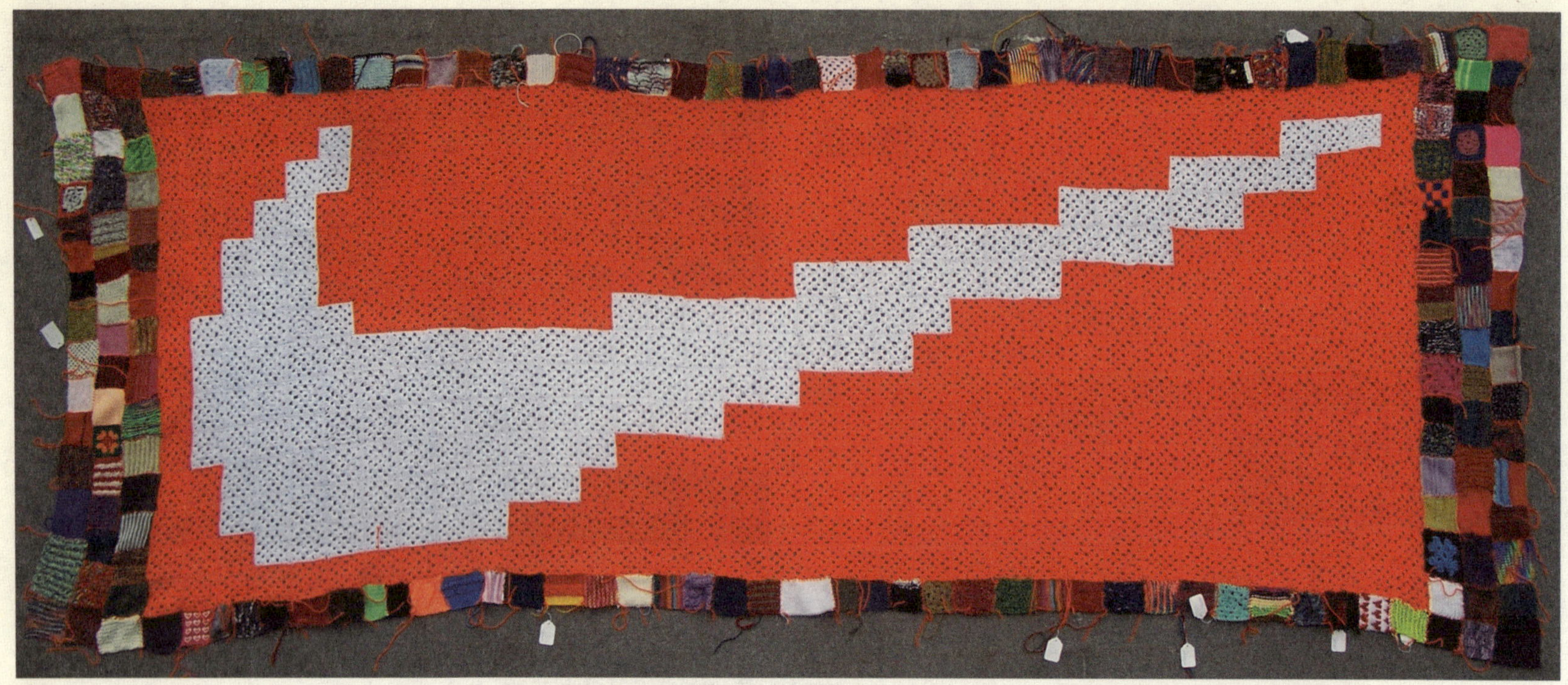

1.

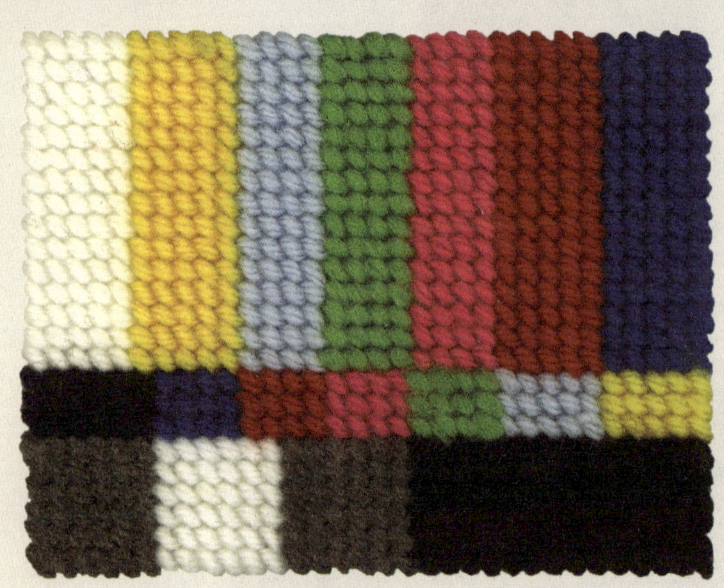

2.

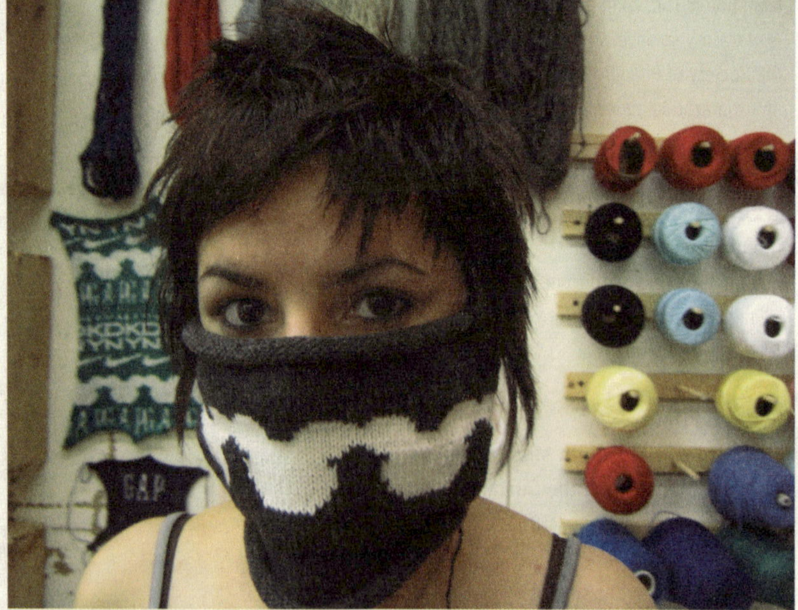

3.

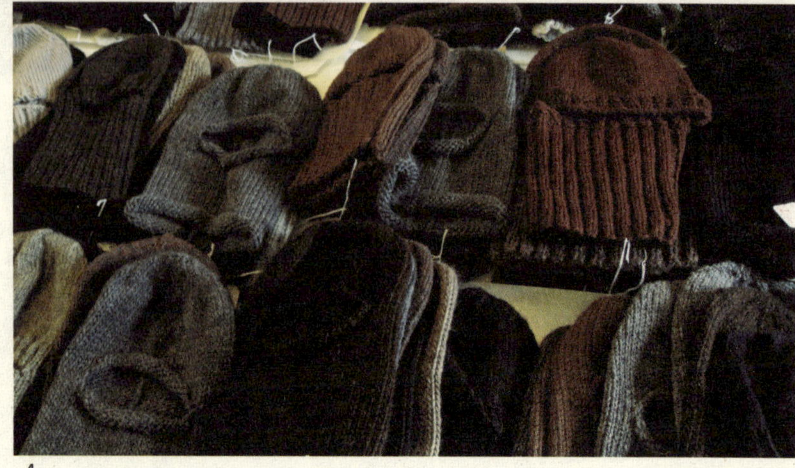

4.

"Craftivist" Cat Mazza is based in New York. She is the founder of microRevolt, a collective that combines traditional craft techniques such as knitting with digital media and social networks to initiate discussion about the politics and economics of sweatshop labor.

1. Nike Blanket Petition
2003-08, yarn, 14 × 6 ft (4 × 2 m)

2. Colorbars in Needlepoint
2003, yarn and needlecraft grid, 3 3/4 × 5 in (10 × 13 cm)

3. MicroRevolt
2006, digital image

4. Stitch for Senate Helmets
2008, digital image

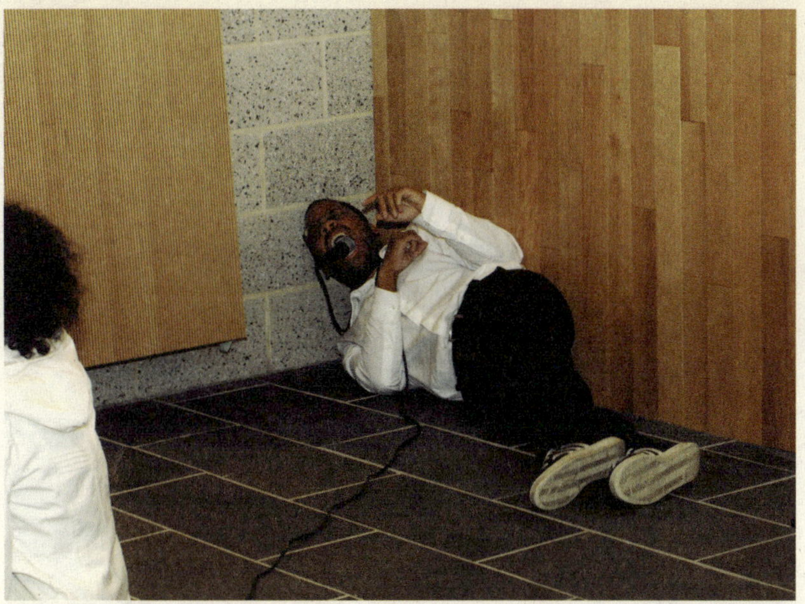

1.

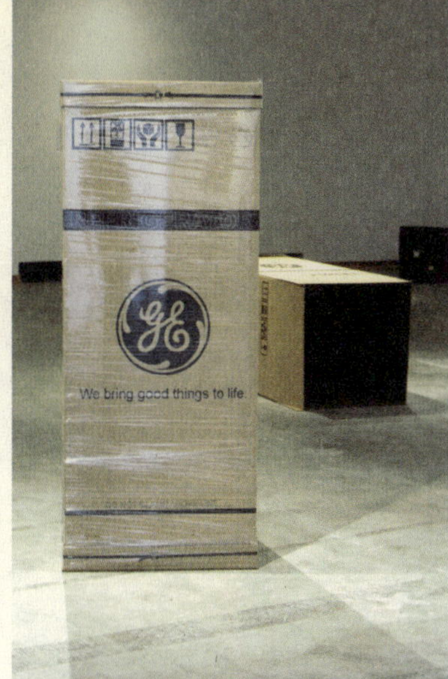

2.

David McKenzie received his BFA from the University of the Arts in Philadelphia. In his largely performance-based work, he explores the mutability of identity and the difficulty, or impossibility, of communication. His work often uses celebrity, or the notion of a commodified public persona, to investigate the larger concept of the self as performance. His series of four performances **All Together Now**, which took place in and around the Studio Museum in Harlem, was included as a part of Performa 07. He currently lives and works in New York.

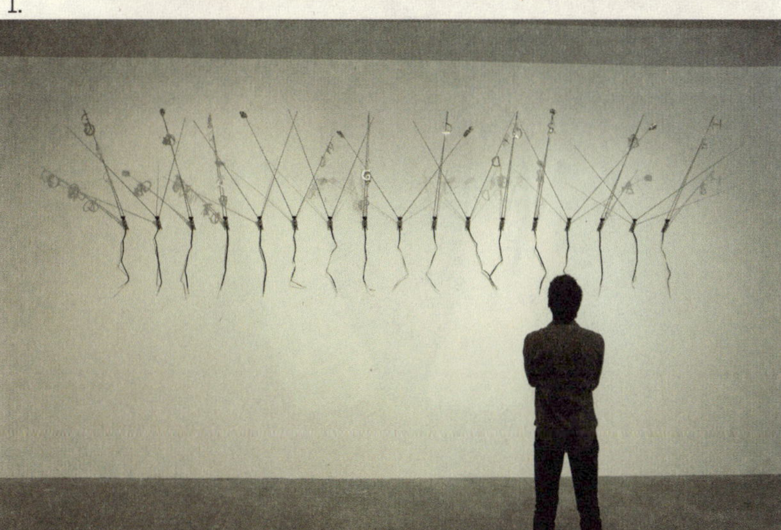

3.

1. **Babel**
2000-06, performance

2. **Keep On Pushing** (detail)
2008, video, cardboard, paint, plastic, stereo, and MP3 player, dimensions variable

3. **Good Looking Out**
2008, television antennas, aluminum, and plastic, dimensions variable

4. **BING**
2008, acrylic, spray paint, wood, and fake brick, dimensions variable

5. **Private Dancer**
2007, performance at "You & Me, Sometimes…," Lehmann Maupin, New York

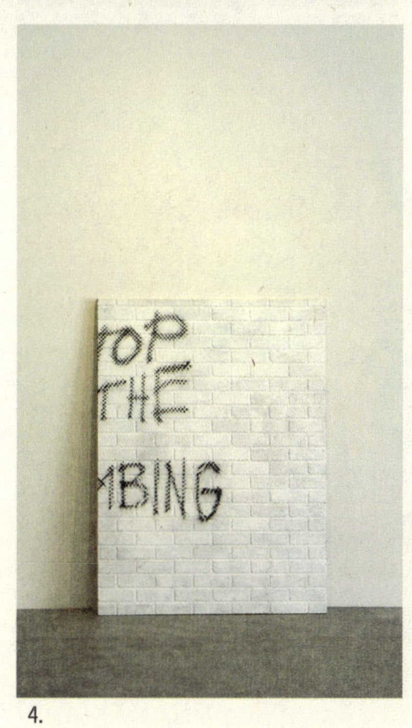

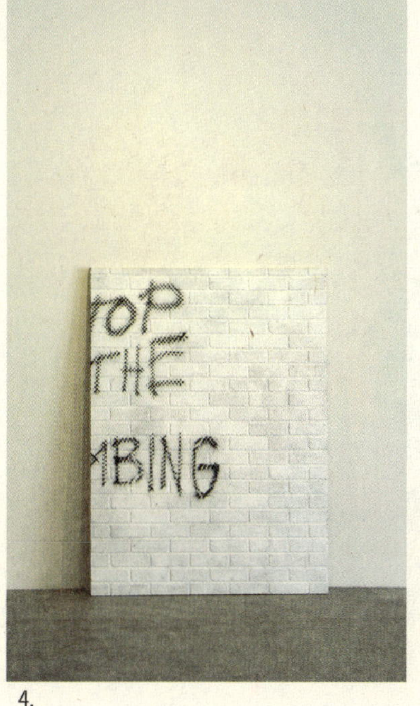

4.

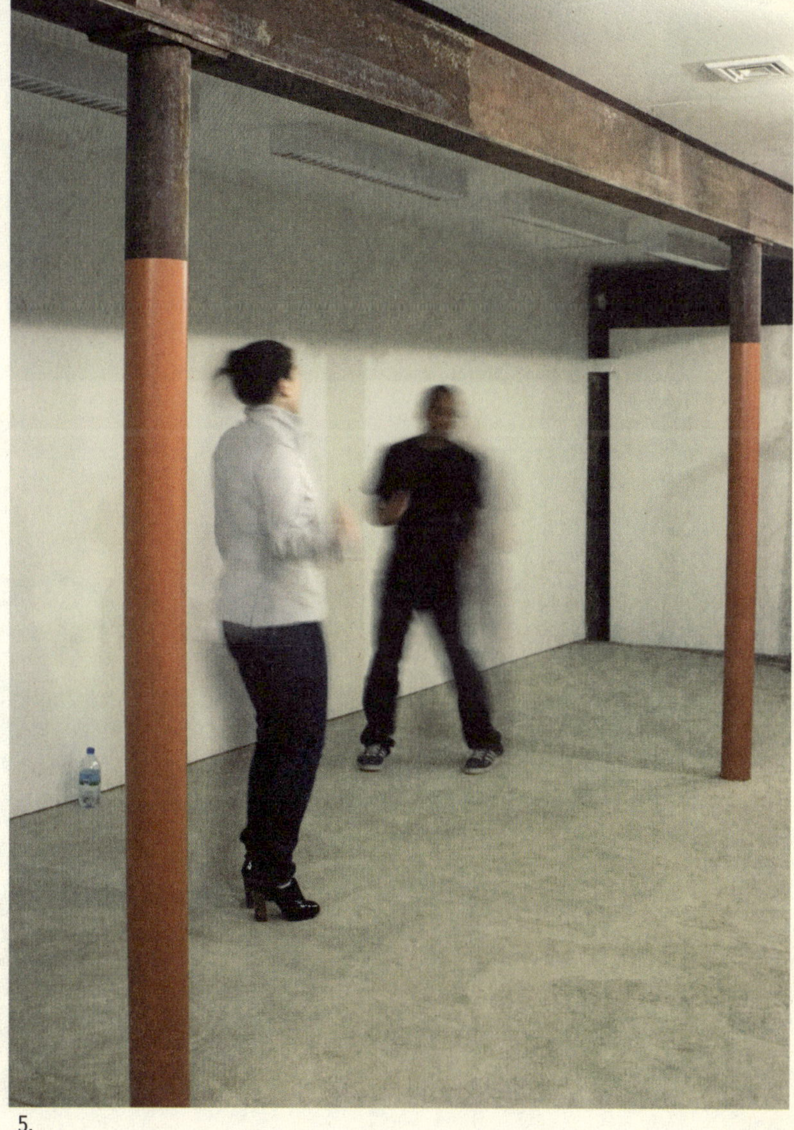

5.

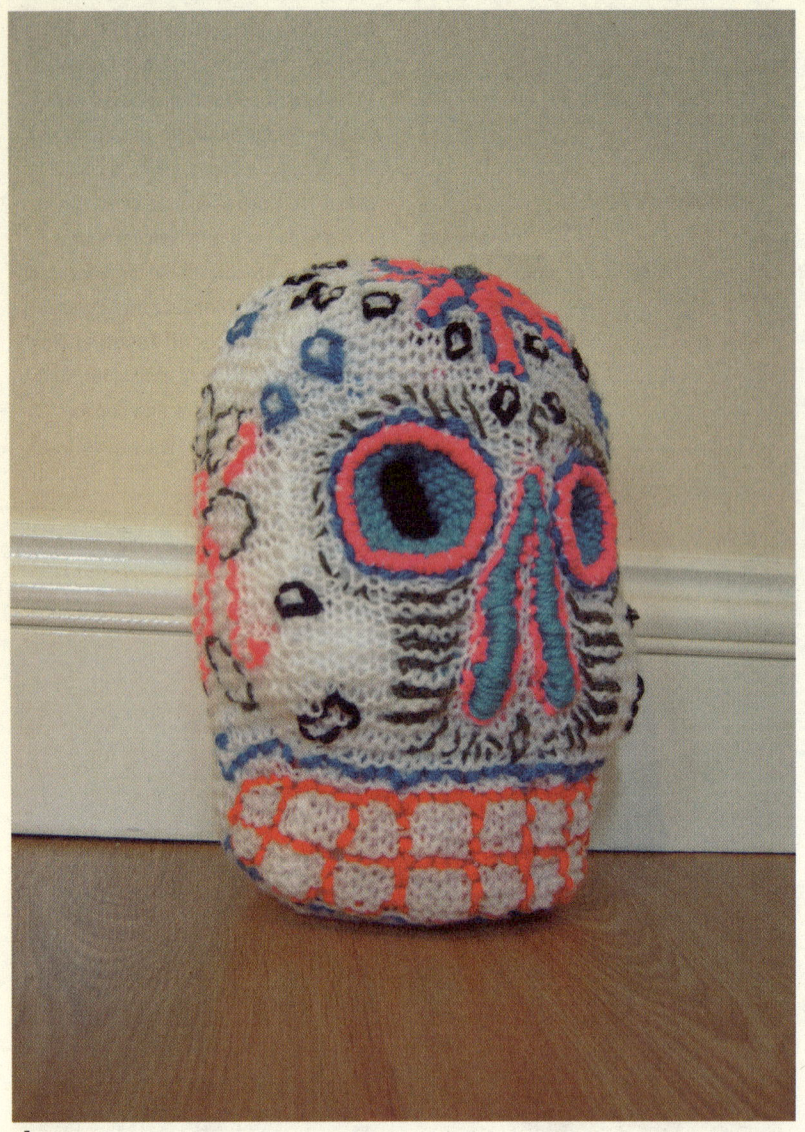

1.

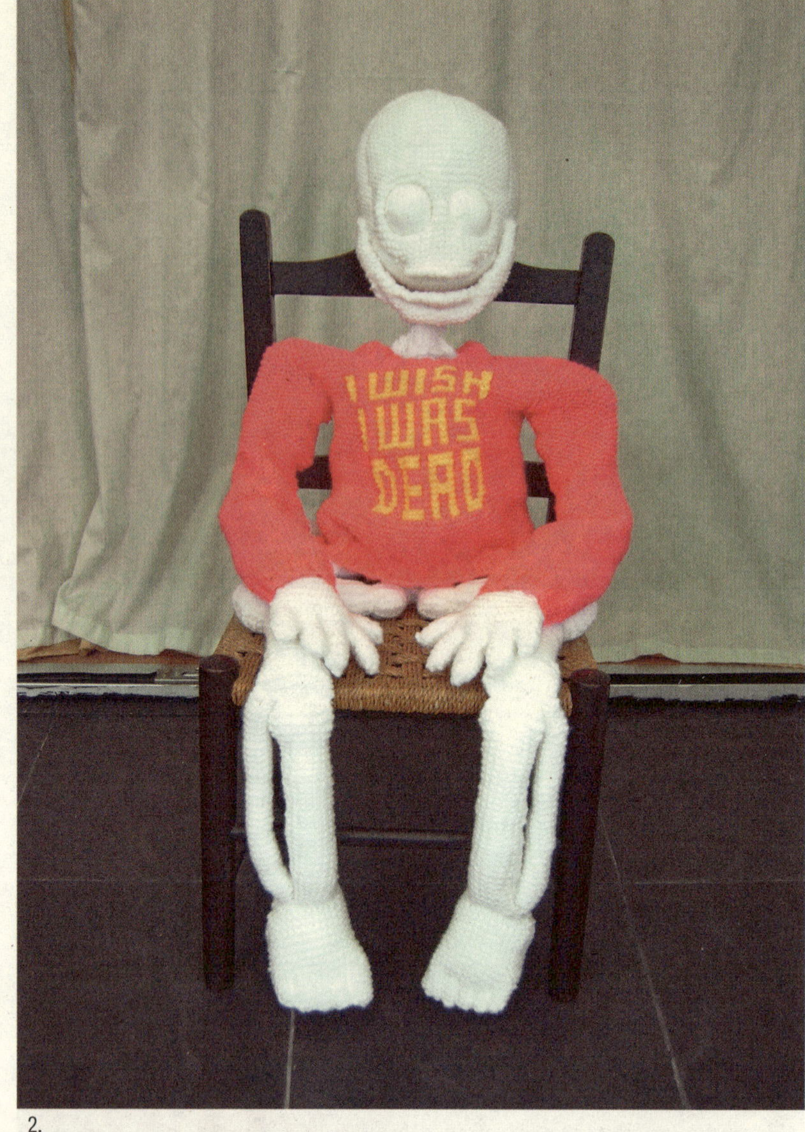

2.

3.

Janine McLellan uses humble, low-tech materials to construct a darkly comic sculptural universe. Her series of knitted figures depicting former pop star and convicted sexual offender Gary Glitter, for example, reflects on the intersection of "retro cool" with darker realities.

1. Skull
2007, wool, 11 × 8 × 8 in (28 × 20 × 20 cm)

2. I Wish I Was Dead
2008, mixed media, 27 $\frac{1}{2}$ × 16 $\frac{1}{2}$ × 12 $\frac{1}{4}$ in (70 × 42 × 31 cm)

3. Cats
2007, wool and plastic, 8 × 4 × 6 $\frac{3}{4}$ in (20 × 10 × 17 cm)

After graduating from Cooper Union in New York, Mores McWreath received an MFA from UCLA in 2008. He lives and works in New York and studied at the Whitney Independent Study Program. His videos and mixed-media installations draw on experimental cinema, movie trailers, vaudeville, and YouTube, as well as the plays of Samuel Beckett, to address the complexity of consumer culture.

1. **The Right Place is Everywhere**
2008, digital print, 17 × 56 in (43 × 142 cm)

2. **Airlock**
2008, lightjet print, 17 × 56 in (43 × 142 cm), installation view

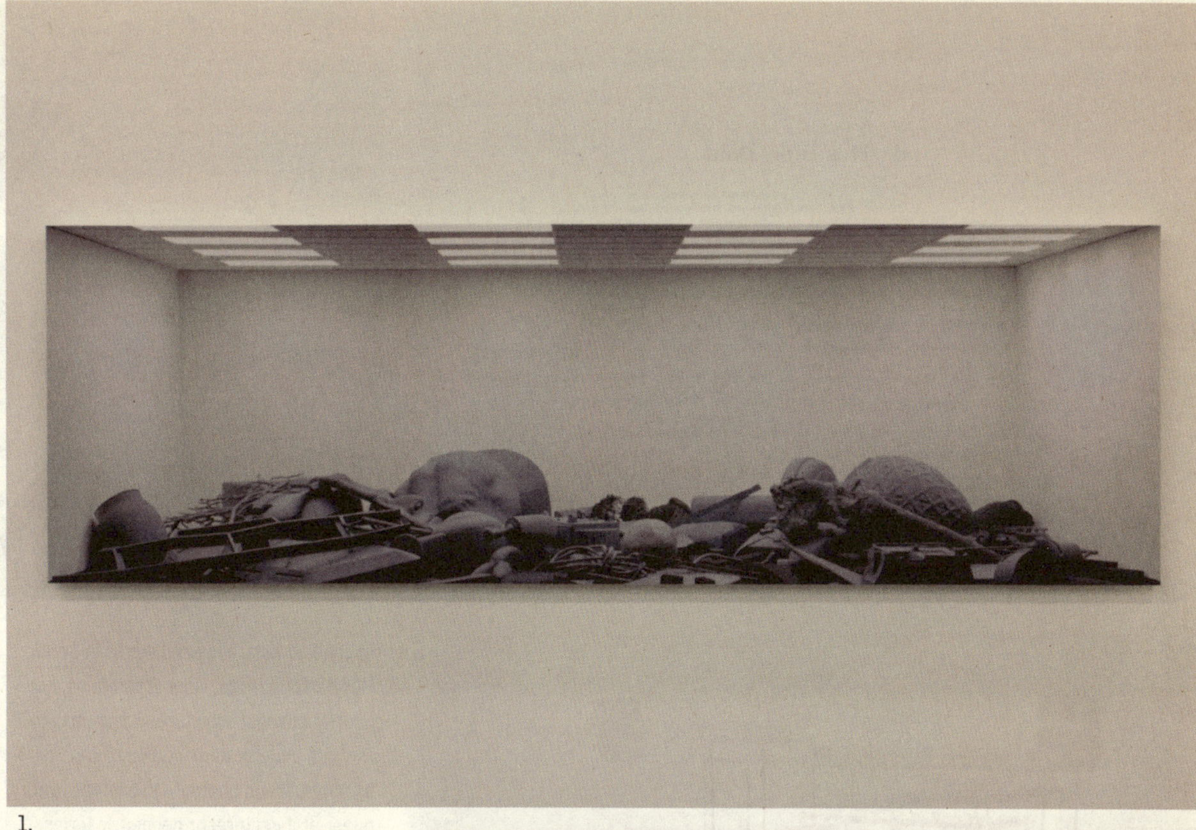

1.

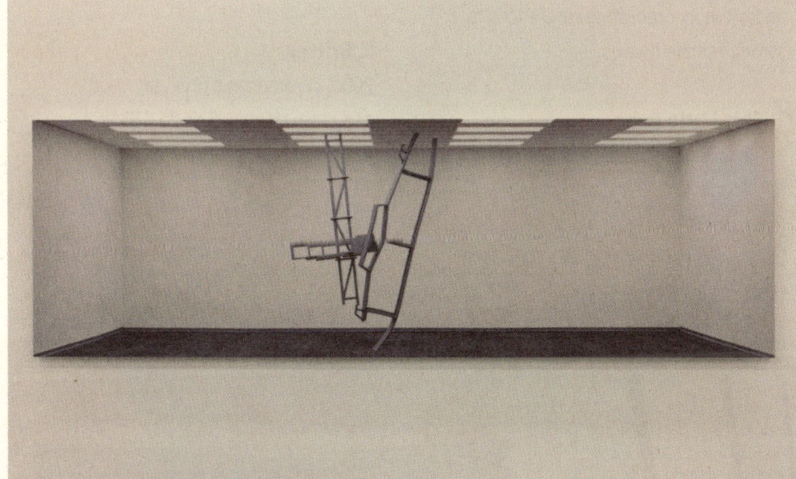

2.

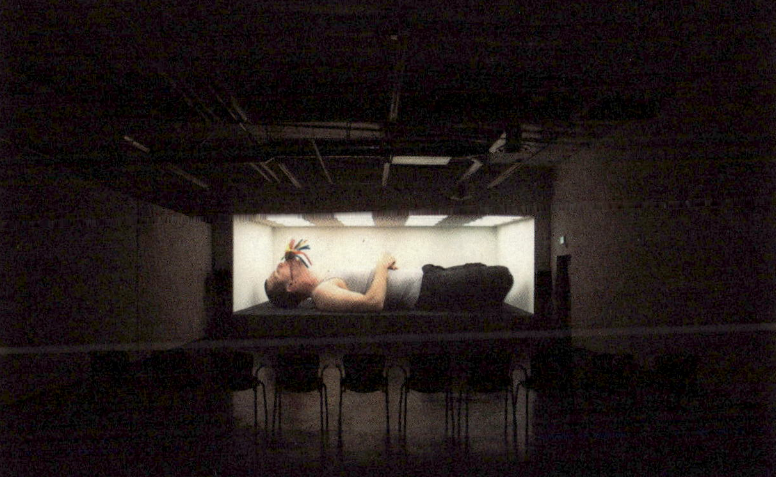

4.

3.

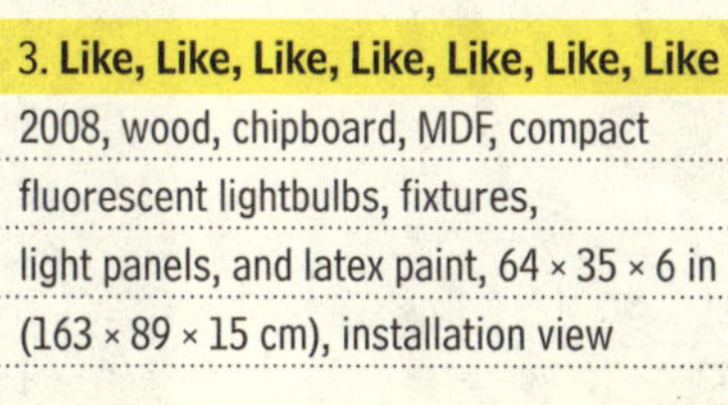

3. **Like, Like, Like, Like, Like, Like, Like**
2008, wood, chipboard, MDF, compact fluorescent lightbulbs, fixtures, light panels, and latex paint, 64 × 35 × 6 in (163 × 89 × 15 cm), installation view

4 & 5. **The Bud, the Seed, the Egg**
2008, video, 20 min

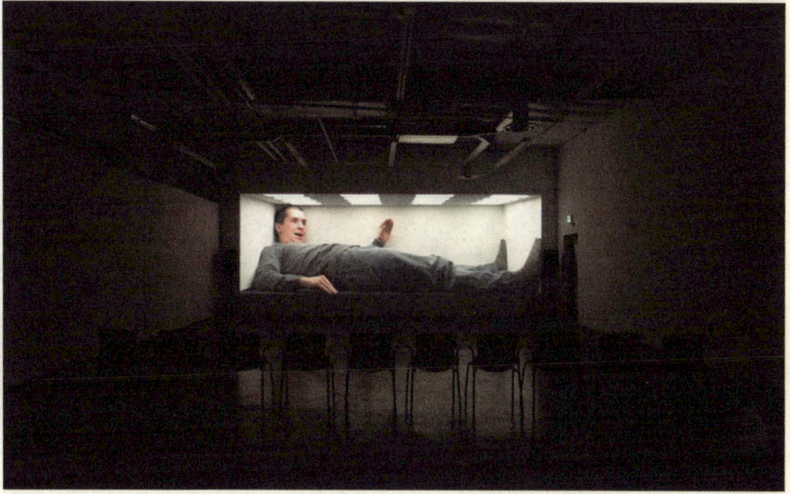

5.

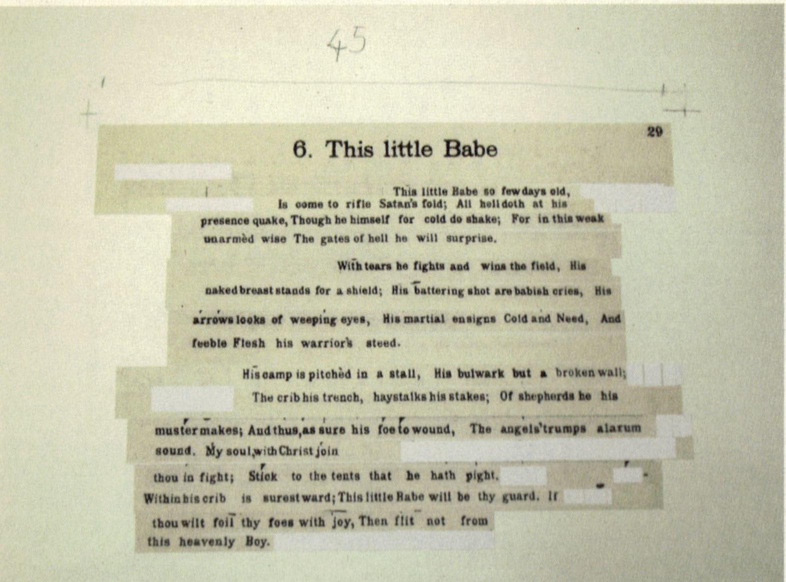

45

29

6. This little Babe

This little Babe so few days old,
Is come to rifle Satan's fold; All hell doth at his
presence quake, Though he himself for cold do shake; For in this weak
unarmèd wise The gates of hell he will surprise.

With tears he fights and wins the field, His
naked breast stands for a shield; His battering shot are babish cries, His
arrows looks of weeping eyes, His martial ensigns Cold and Need, And
feeble Flesh his warrior's steed.

His camp is pitchèd in a stall, His bulwark but a broken wall;
The crib his trench, haystalks his stakes; Of shepherds he his
muster makes; And thus, as sure his foe to wound, The angels' trumps alarum
sound. My soul, with Christ join
thou in fight; Stick to the tents that he hath pight.
Within his crib is surest ward; This little Babe will be thy guard. If
thou wilt foil thy foes with joy, Then flit not from
this heavenly Boy.

1.

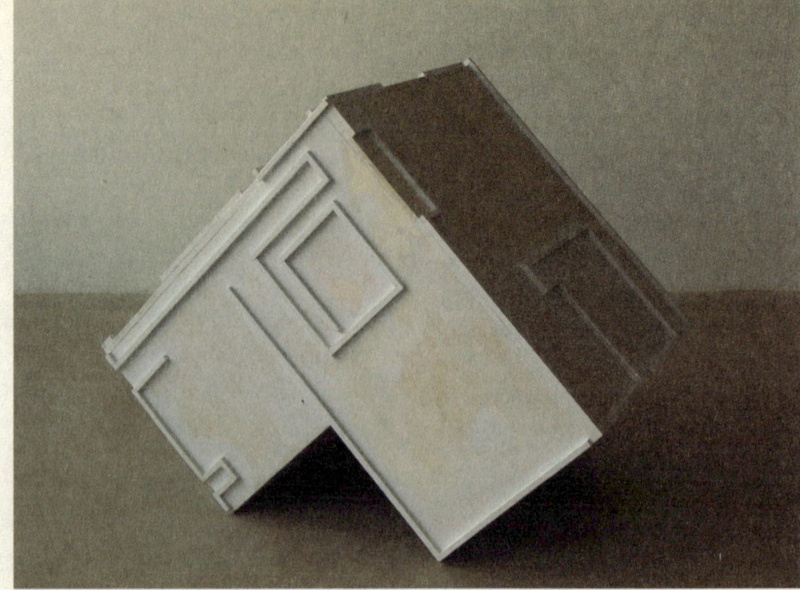

2.

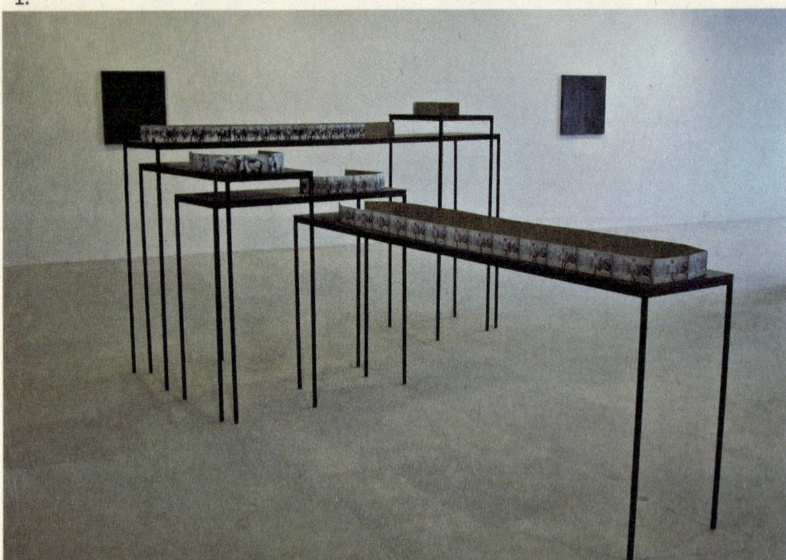

3.

Michaela Meise lives and works in Berlin. Her performances, videos, paintings, and post-Minimalist sculptures communicate through understatement, combining, for example, found photographic images with quasi-architectural or geometric forms, and often incorporating references to strong female figures.

1. **This Little Babe**
2006, mixed media, dimensions variable

2. **Brain 1**
2007, wood and acrylic, 39 × 50 × 33 in (100 × 128 × 84 cm)

3. "Ceremony of Carols"
exhibition view at Greene Naftali, New York (2006)

4. **Hair** (detail),
2006, mixed media, dimensions variable

5. **Britten**
2006, chromogenic print, plywood, and resin lacquer, 37 × 24 × 35 in (96 × 62 × 90 cm)

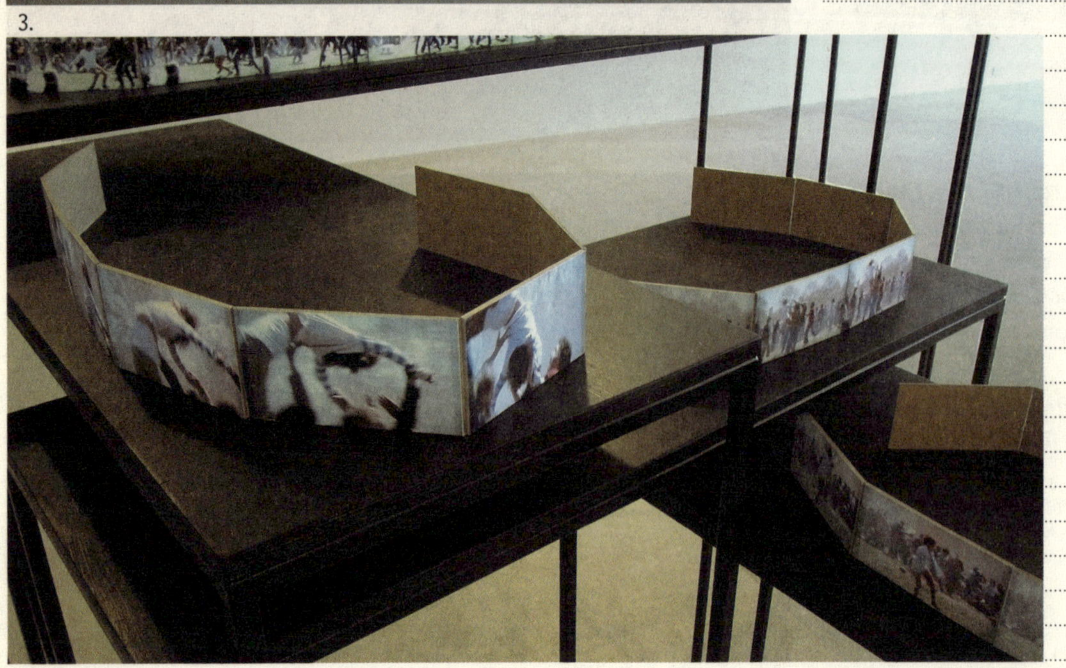

4.

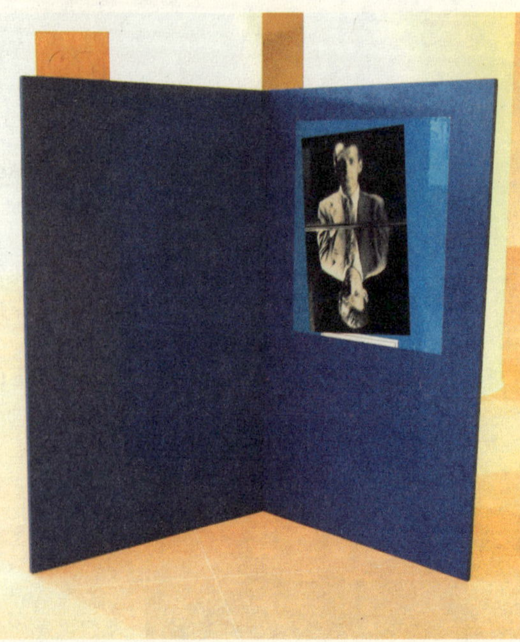

5.

Wardell Milan lives and works in New York and was an artist in residence at the Studio Museum in Harlem in 2006. His work confronts issues of racial and sexual identity, using large-scale drawings of male figures and photographs of elaborate dioramas to conjure alternative historical narratives around the making and remaking of black America.

1. The Re-Birth of Venus Hottentot and the Death of Cupids (Love Lost Pt. 5)
2005, digital chromogenic print on aluminum, 33 ½ × 49 ¼ in (85 × 125 cm)

2. The Fights No. 3
2008, mixed media on paper, 51 ½ × 45 in (131 × 114 cm)

3. Battle Royale No. 18
2007, paper collage, 10 × 8 ¾ in (25 × 22 cm)

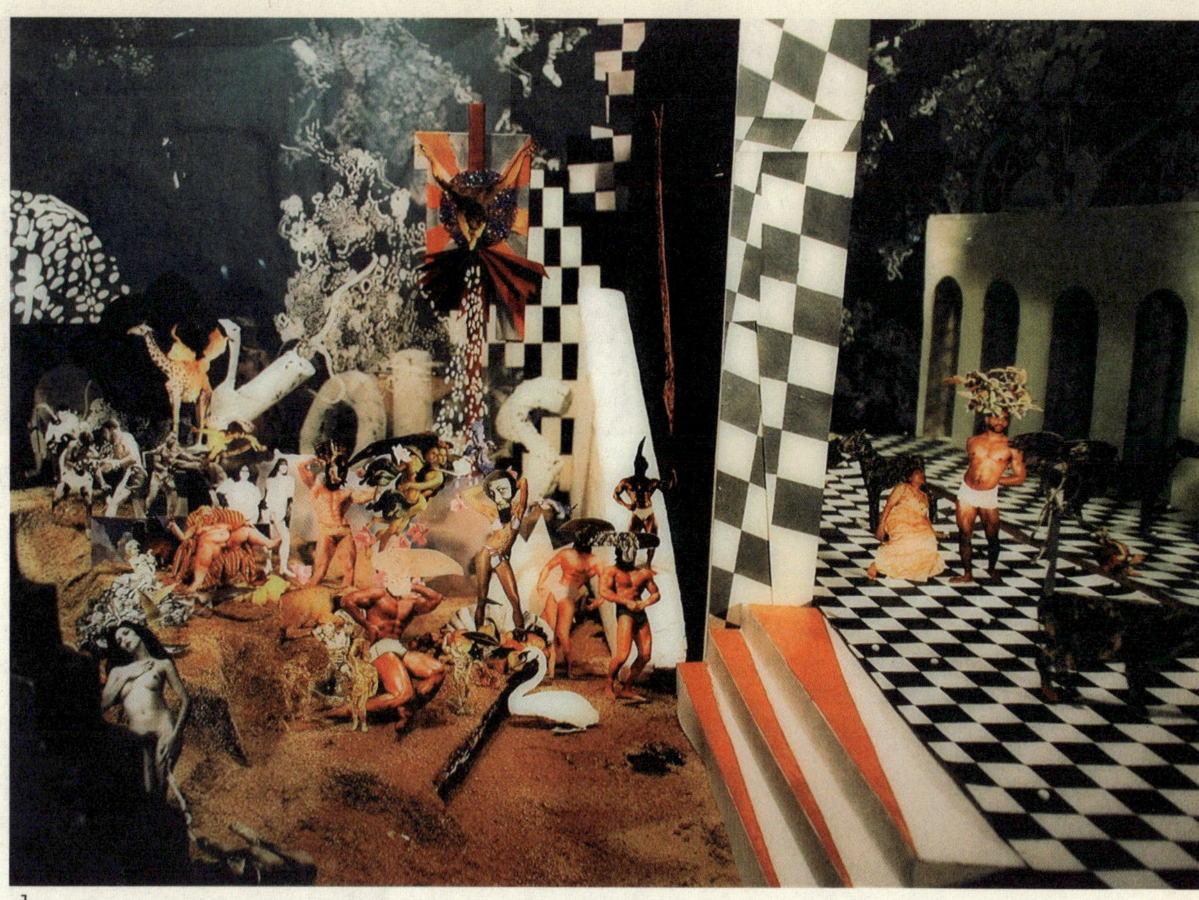
1.

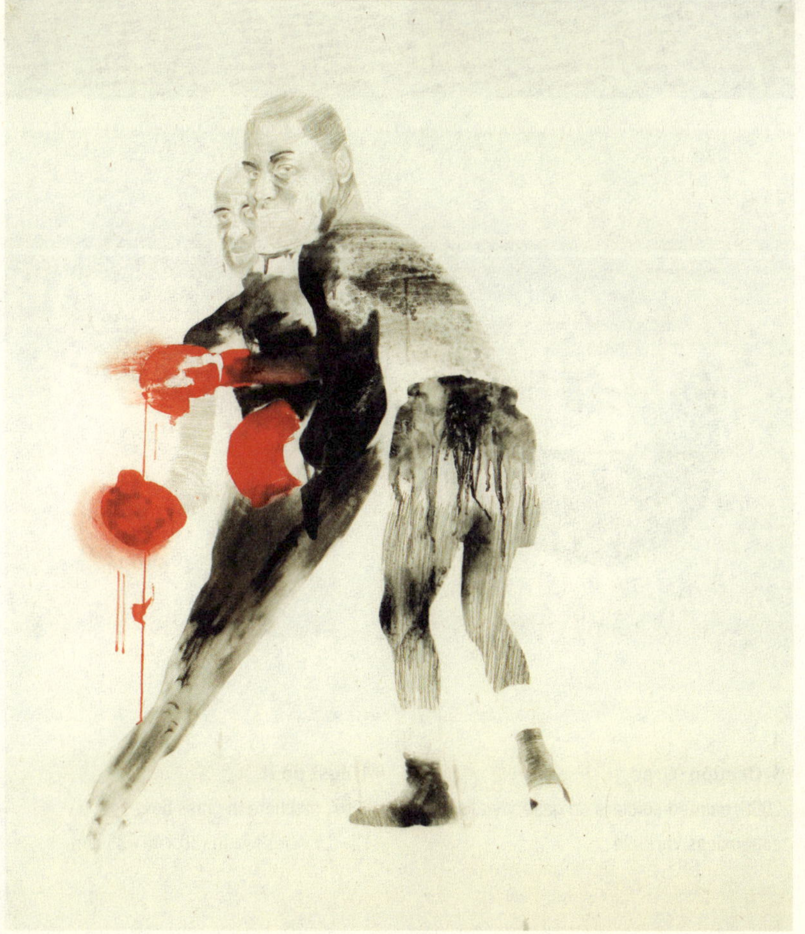
2.

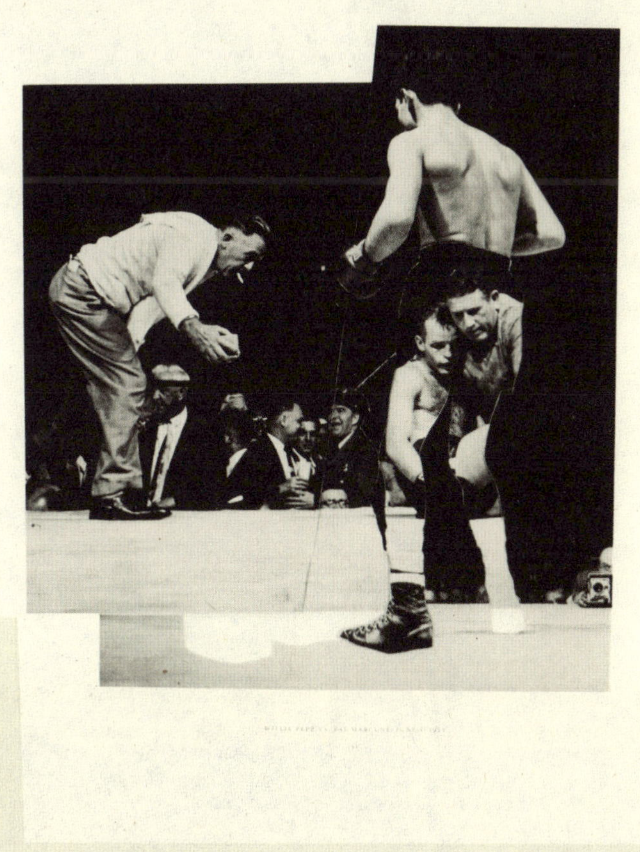
3.

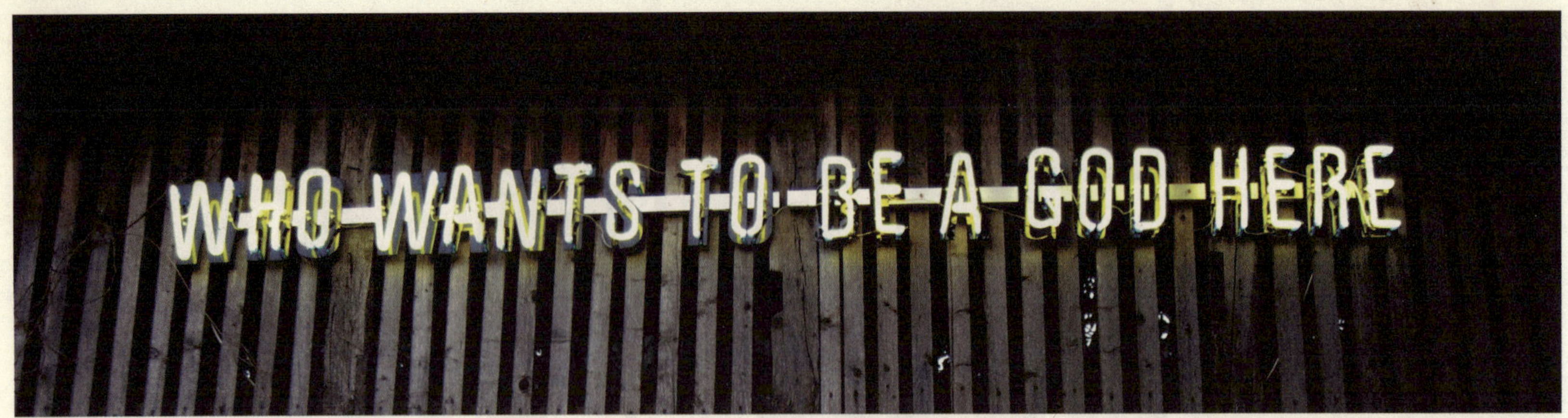

1.

Mladen Miljanovic is based in Banja Luka, Bosnia and Herzegovina. His work pictures some of the ways in which repressive governments attempt to rewrite history according to their own agendas. In **My Shiny Disco War** (2008) he projects images of soldiers and weaponry onto a spinning disco ball.

1. Who wants to be a god here
2008, neon lights, 10 × 118 in (25 × 300 cm)

2. Welcome to my country
2006, chair and rope, dimensions variable

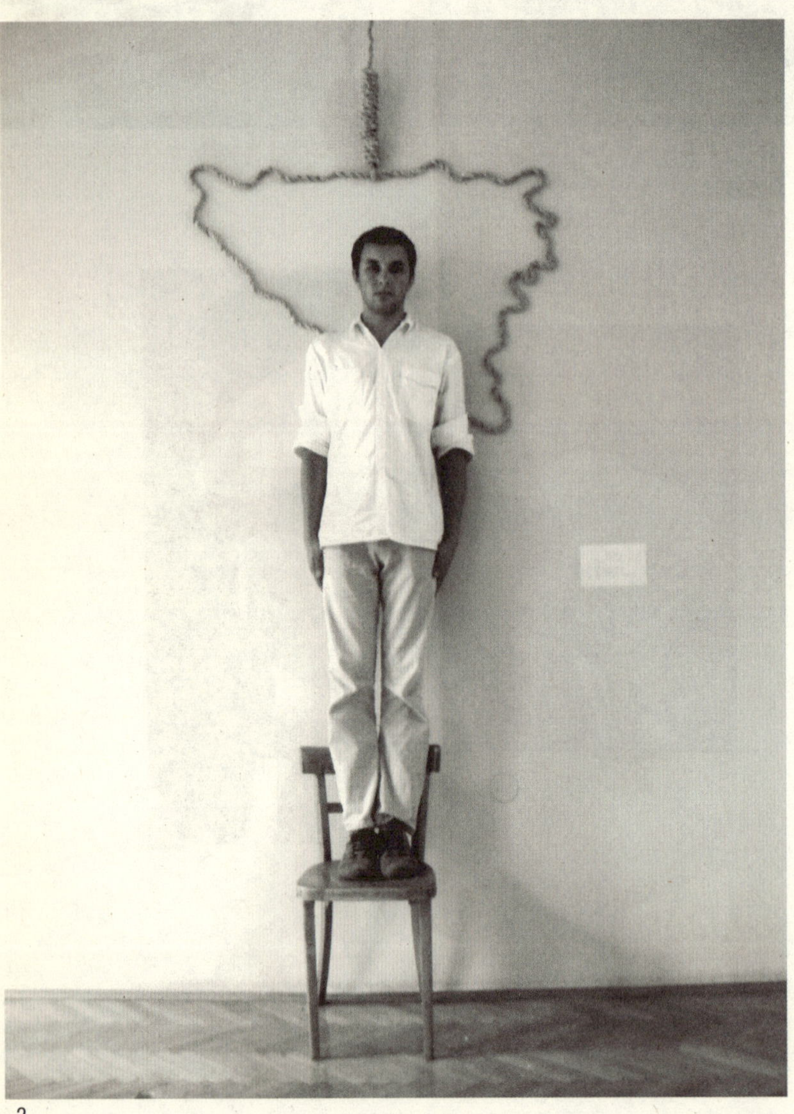

2.

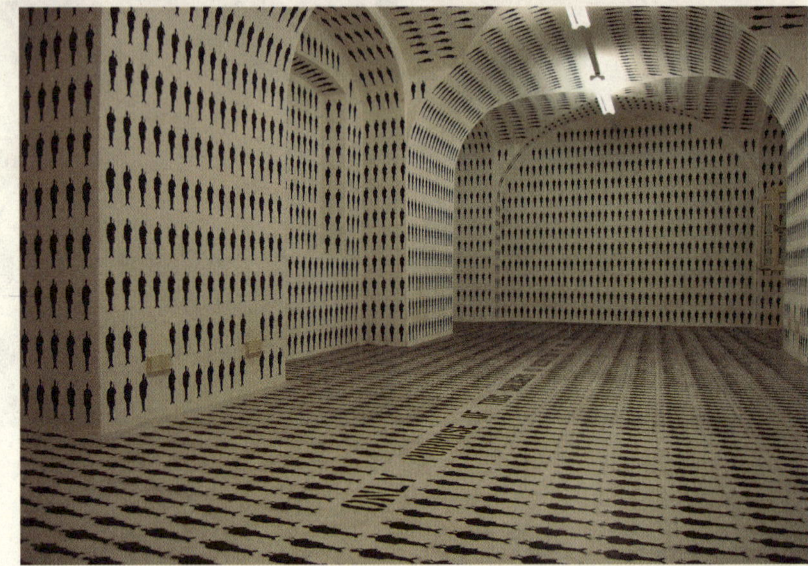

3.

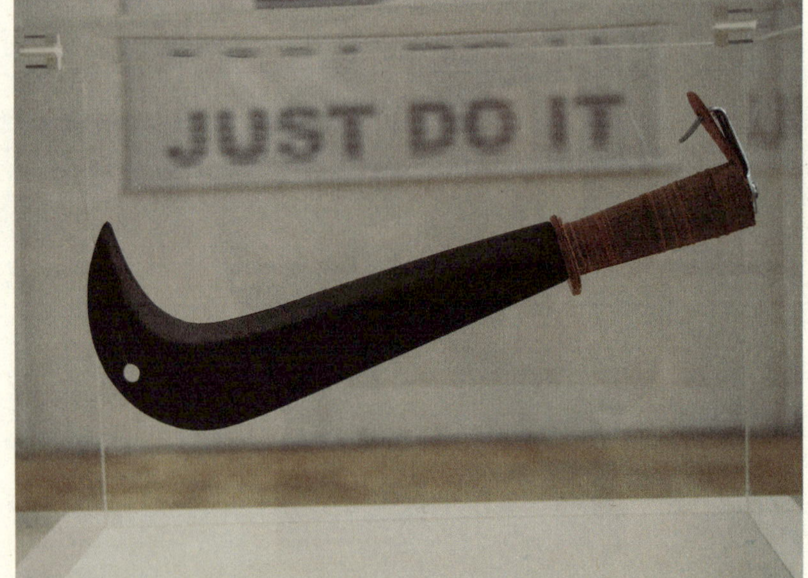

4.

3. Occupo-Grac
2008, painted soldiers on gallery walls, dimensions variable

4. Just do it
2007, machete in glass box, 12 × 15 ¾ × 13 ¾ in (30 × 40 × 35 cm)

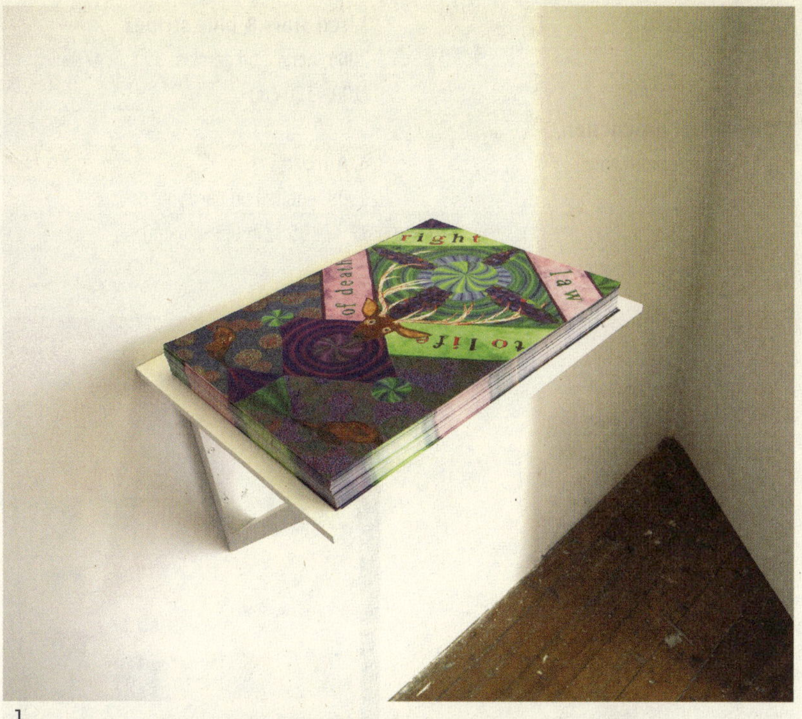

1.

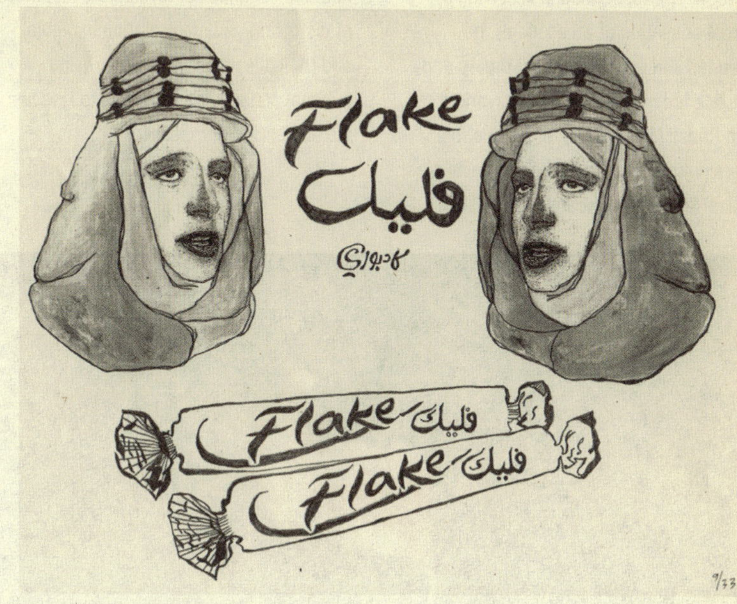

3.

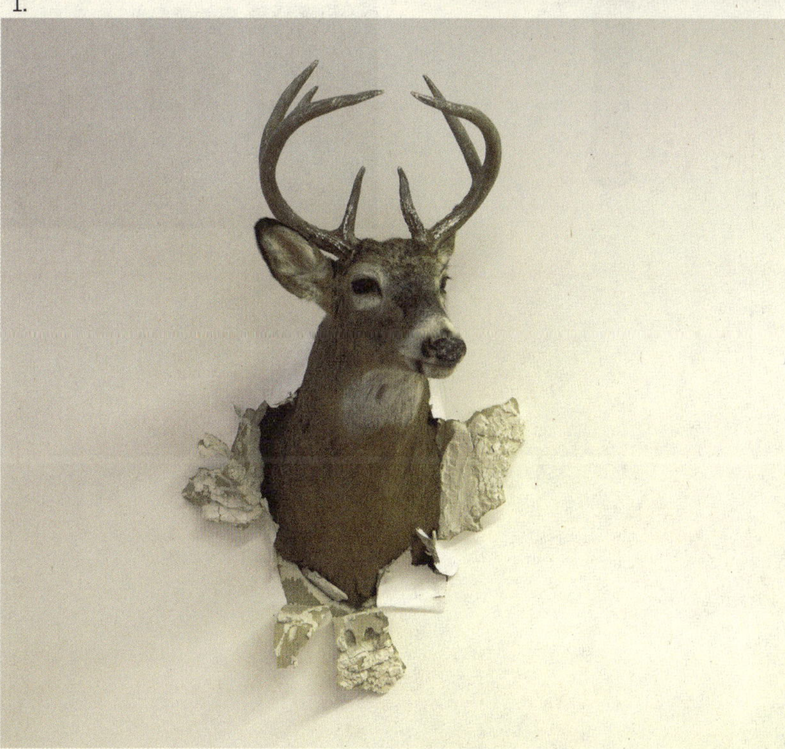

2.

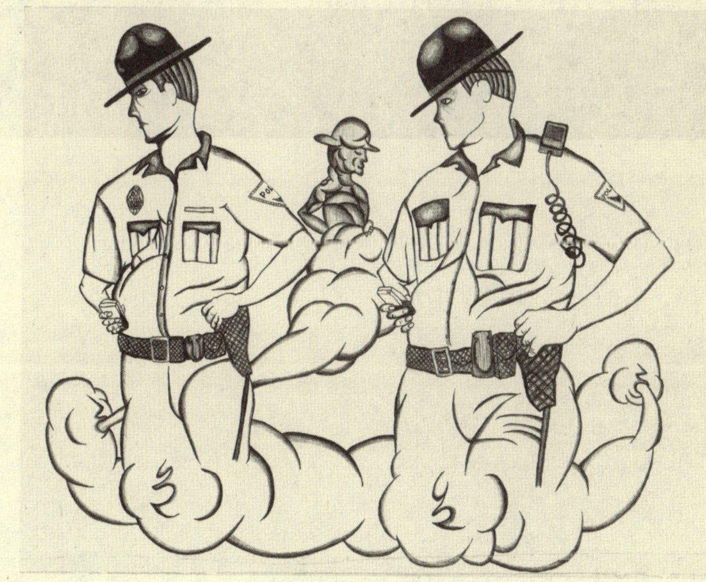

4.

Jarrett Mitchell, an award winner at EAST International in 2006, lives in Portland, Oregon. In drawings, paintings, and sculptures, he investigates the use of force in human relationships. He has used the image of the Appaloosa horse as a metaphor for government brutality toward indigenous peoples and animals. A series is based on observation of public servants tending to their private lives.

1. **The Dawn of the Birth of the Battle of the Right to Life vs. the Law of Death**
2006, printed posters

2. **The Dawn of the Birth of the Battle of the Right to Life vs. the Law of Death**
2006, taxidermied deer

3. **Le Bubba, Issue One** (back cover)
2007, photocopy on paper, 8½ × 11 in (22 × 28 cm)

4. **Cop with Text Message: Cloud Control**
2008, pencil on paper, 13 × 17 in (33 × 43 cm)

Pavel Mitenko lives and works in Moscow, where, instead of receiving a formal education at an academy, he attended seminars on critical theory and practice led by artists. He also worked with Radek (1997-2005), a group of his peers who shared an interest in reviving radical leftist thought amid the consumerism of post-Soviet society. Mitenko continues to investigate instances of distortion and manipulation in media and the collective imagination, using minimal actions and materials to refocus his audience's perspective.

1. **Burning flag**
2007, video

2. **means of production**
2008, hammer and nails

3. **red stars & blue stripes**
2006, acrylic on canvas, $39\frac{1}{2} \times 47\frac{1}{4}$ in (100×120 cm)

4. **Aurora**
2008, enamel on cardboard, $17\frac{3}{4} \times 35\frac{1}{2}$ in (45×90 cm)

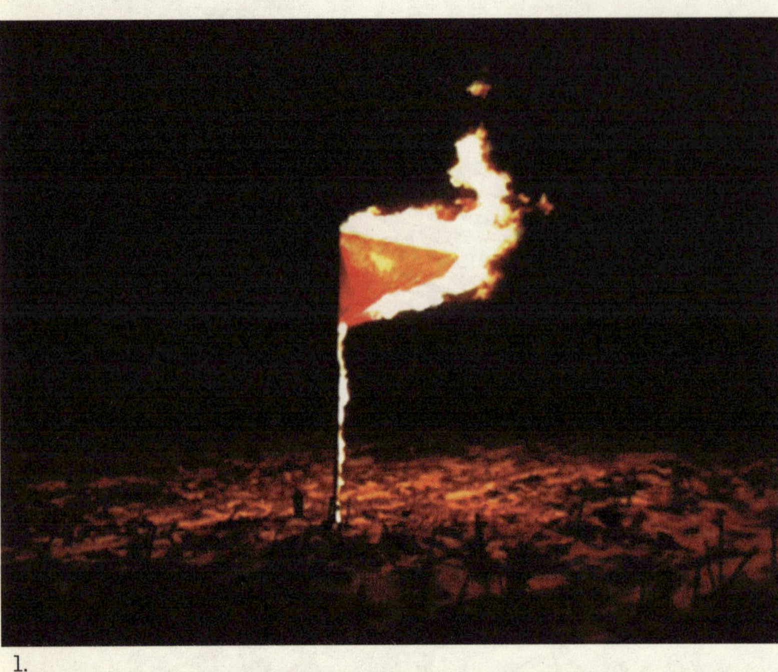
1.

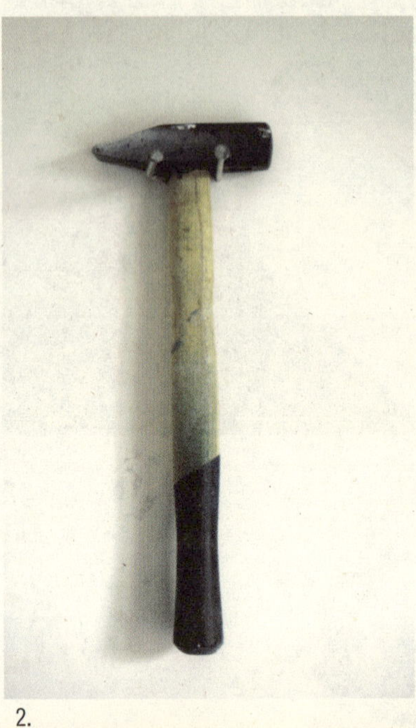
2.

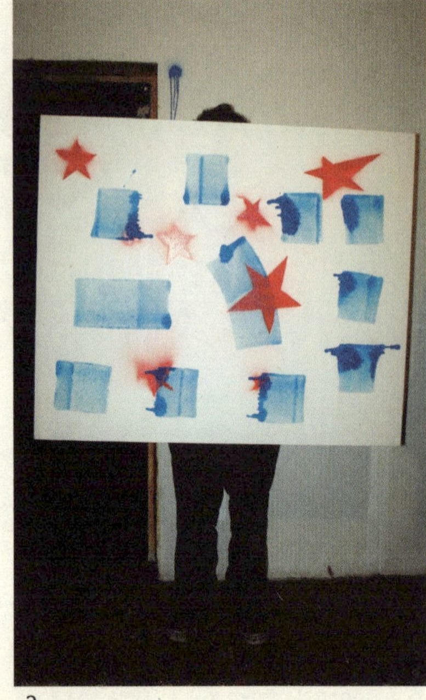
3.

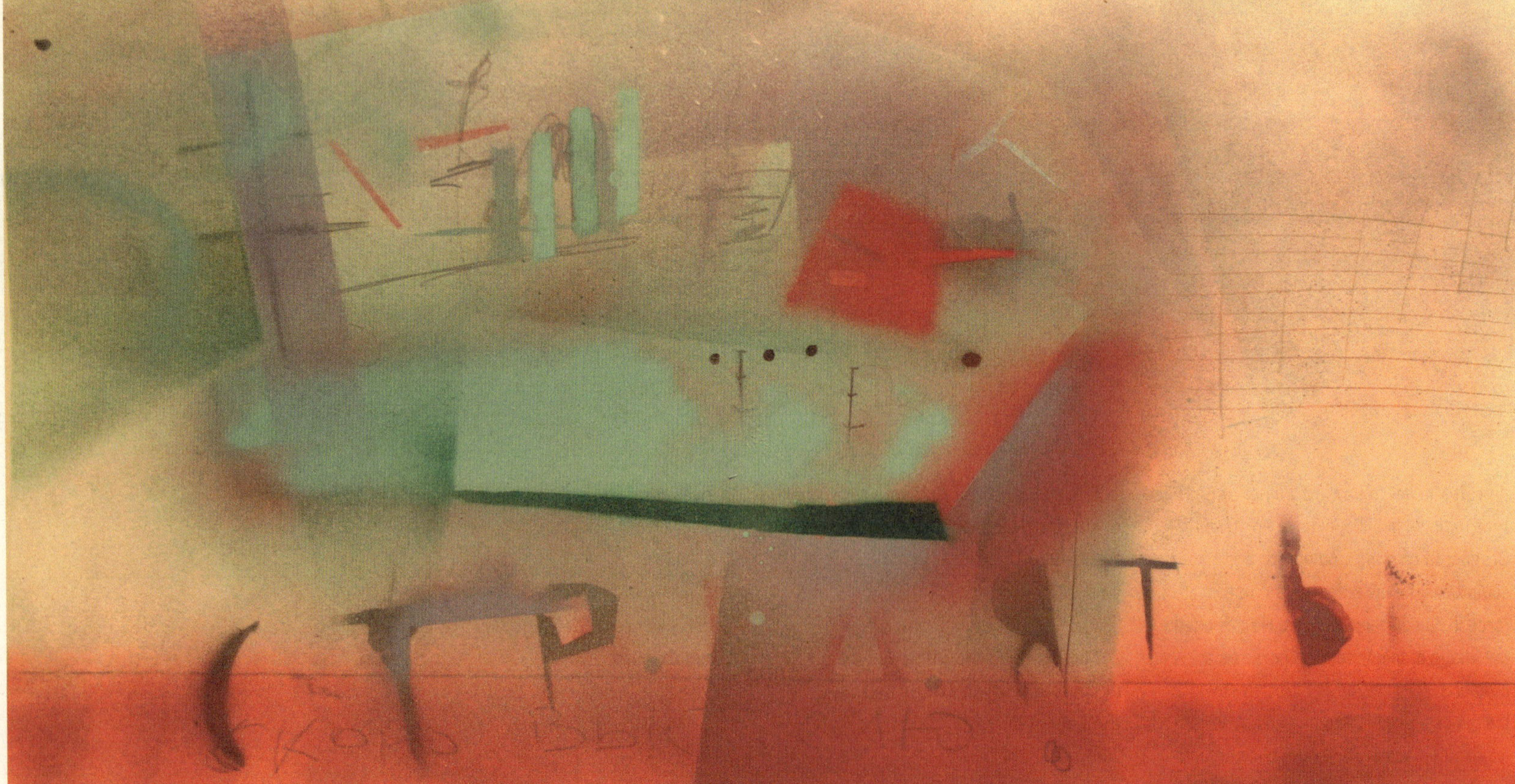
4.

Nandipha Mntambo uses cowhide to make casts, often of her own body, aiming to "challenge and subvert preconceptions regarding representation of the female body," and to "disrupt perceptions of attraction and repulsion."

1 & 2. Mlwa ne Nkunzi
2008, color photograph on cotton rag paper, 2 parts, each 44 × 32 ¼ in (112 × 84.5 cm)

3. The Fighters
2006, cowhide, resin, polyester mesh, waxed cord, dimensions variable

4. Indlovukati
2007, cowhide, resin, polyester mesh, waxed cord, 60 ¼ × 35 × 27 ½ in (153 × 89 × 70 cm)

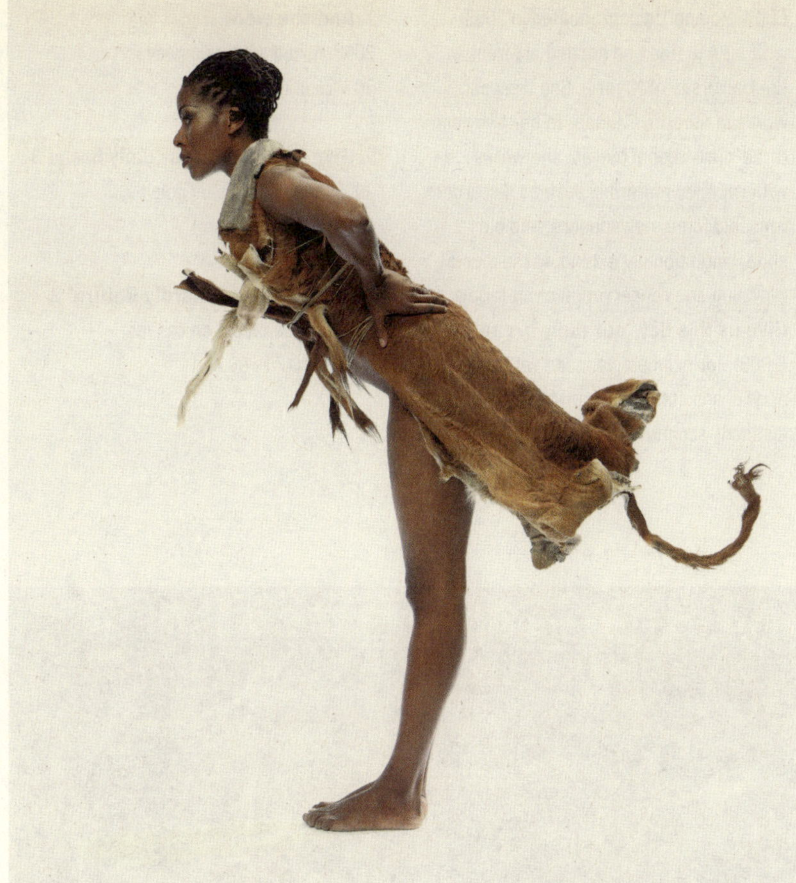
1.

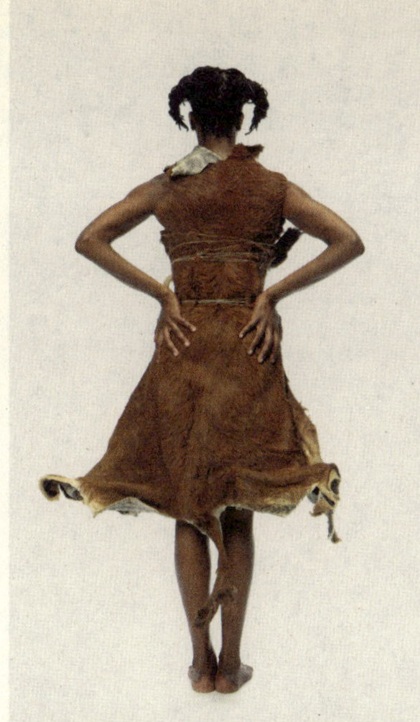
2.

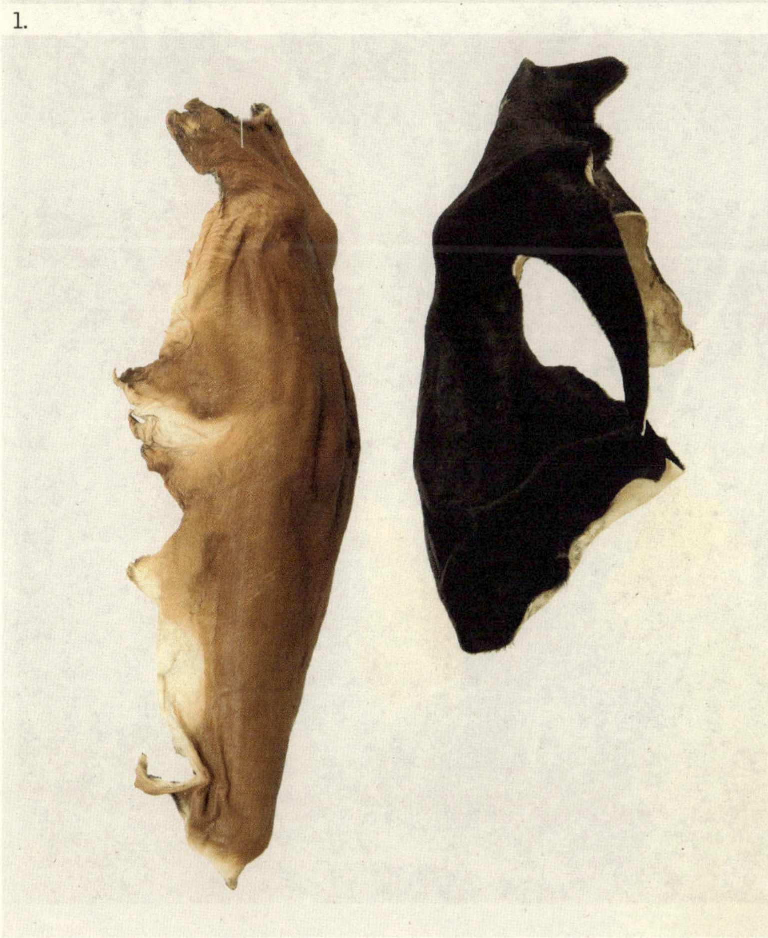
3.

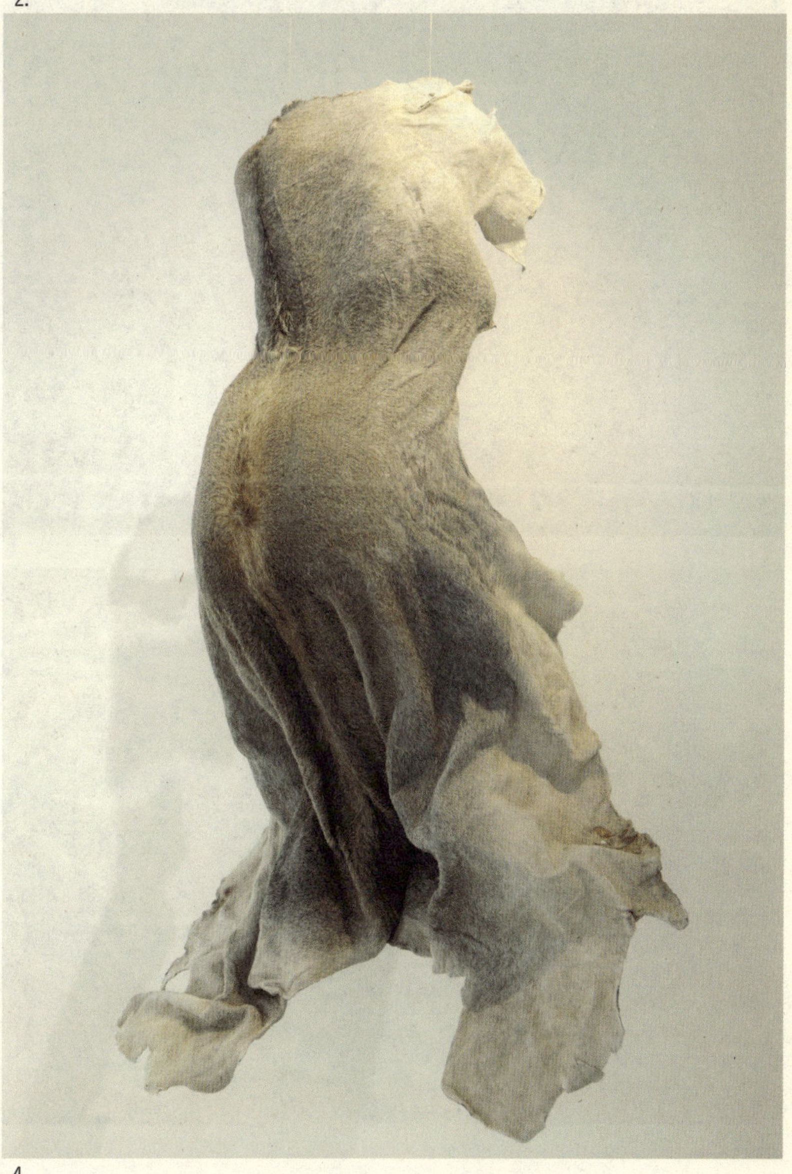
4.

Chika Modum-Udok graduated in 2003 with a BA in fine and applied art from the University of Nigeria. She lives and works in Alberta, Canada. In her two- and three-dimensional pieces, she works with recycled materials such as discarded rags, old foam, newspapers, and old shoes, intentionally extending the idea of recycling and conservation of materials. **Give us this day, our daily bread** (2008), for example, is made with rags, acrylic, and cutlery on canvas, yet has a distinctly sculptural quality.

1. And she went...
2008, mixed media on canvas,
20 × 16 in (51 × 41 cm)

2. Give us this day, our daily bread 3
2008, mixed media on canvas,
20 × 24 in (51 × 61 cm)

3. A place called 'Hardly Return' 2
2008, mixed media on canvas,
30 × 24 in (76 × 61 cm)

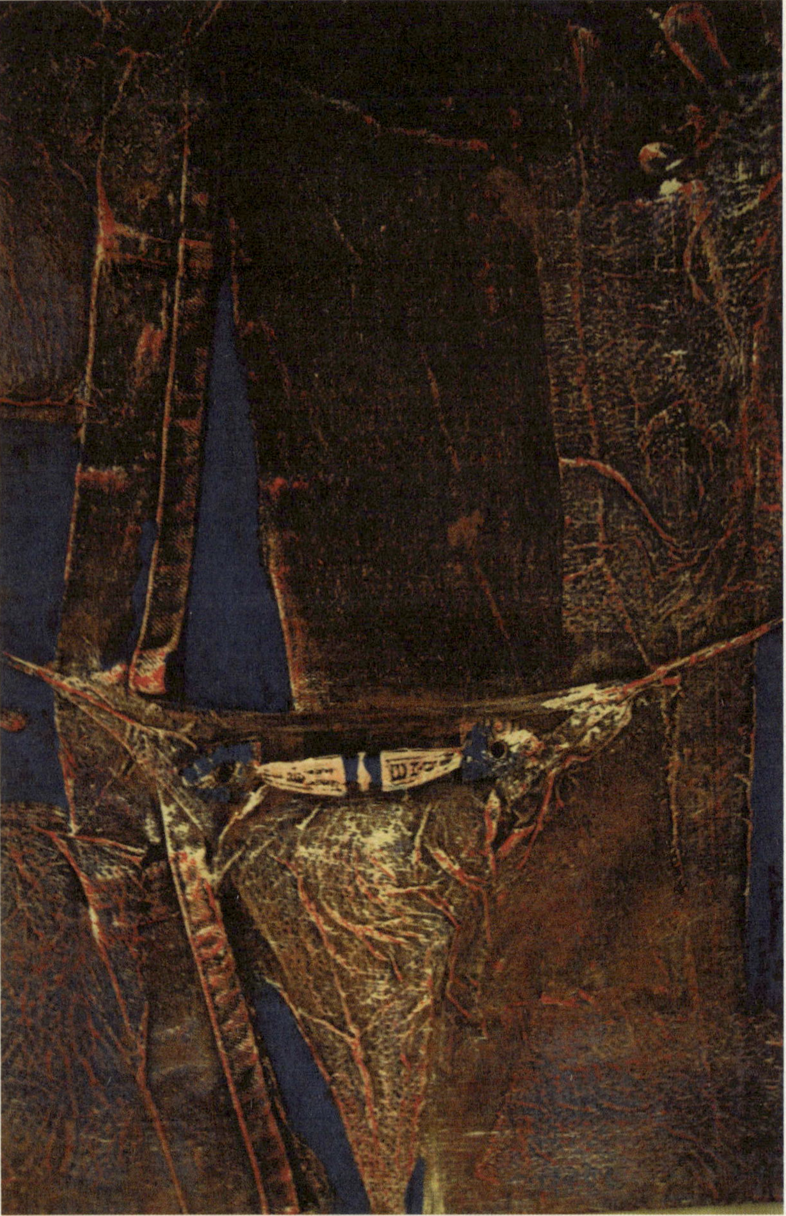

1.

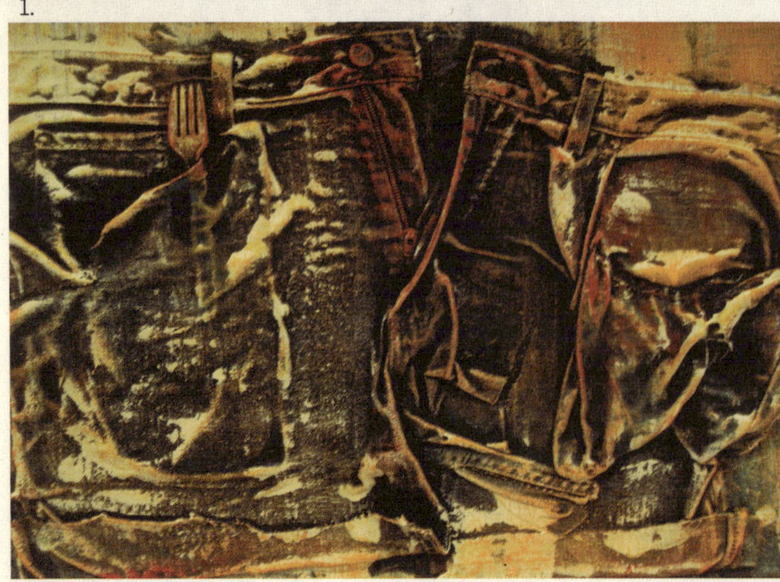

2.

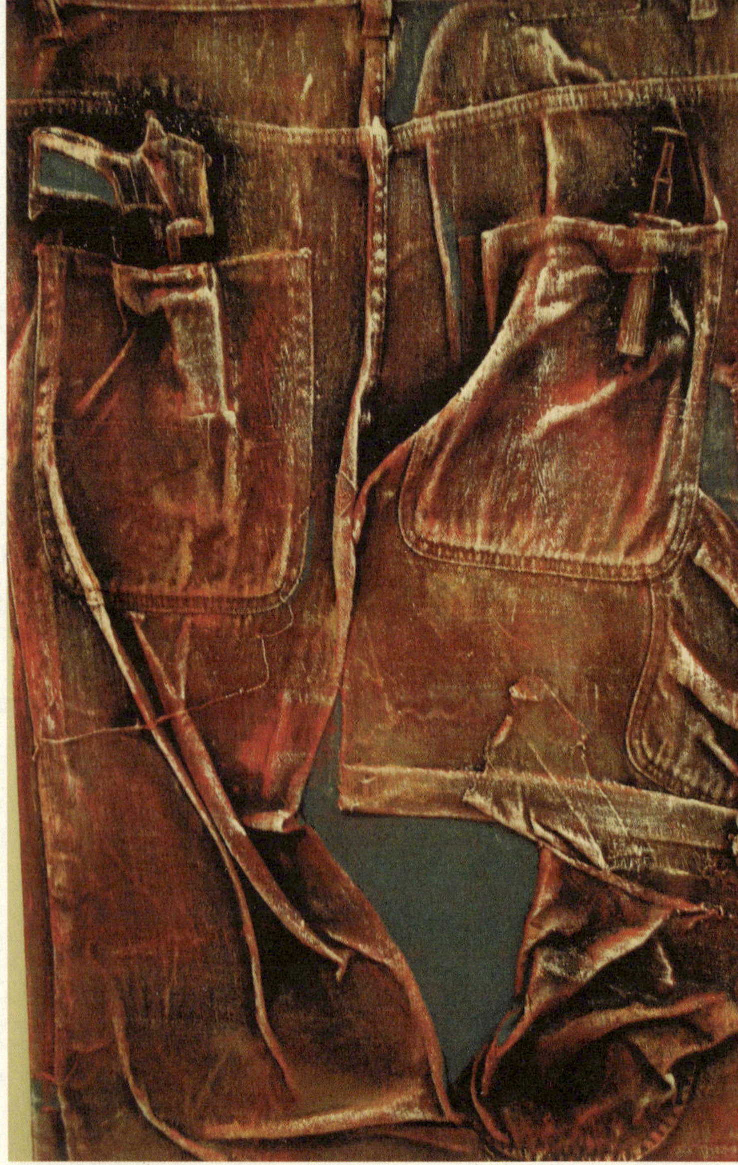

3.

Simon Dybbroe Møller attended the Staatliche Hochschule für Bildende Künste Städelschule, Frankfurt, and currently lives in Frankfurt and New York. His conceptual practice mines various art historical, literary, and cultural pasts, from using works by Bruce Nauman and Dan Flavin as points of departure to a literal merging of texts by August Strindberg and Sol LeWitt.

1. **Curtain for Neue National Galerie (no more Moore)**
2008, mixed media, dimensions variable

2. **Letter From The New World to The Old World**
2006, mixed media, dimensions variable, installation view at Künstlerhaus Bremen, Germany

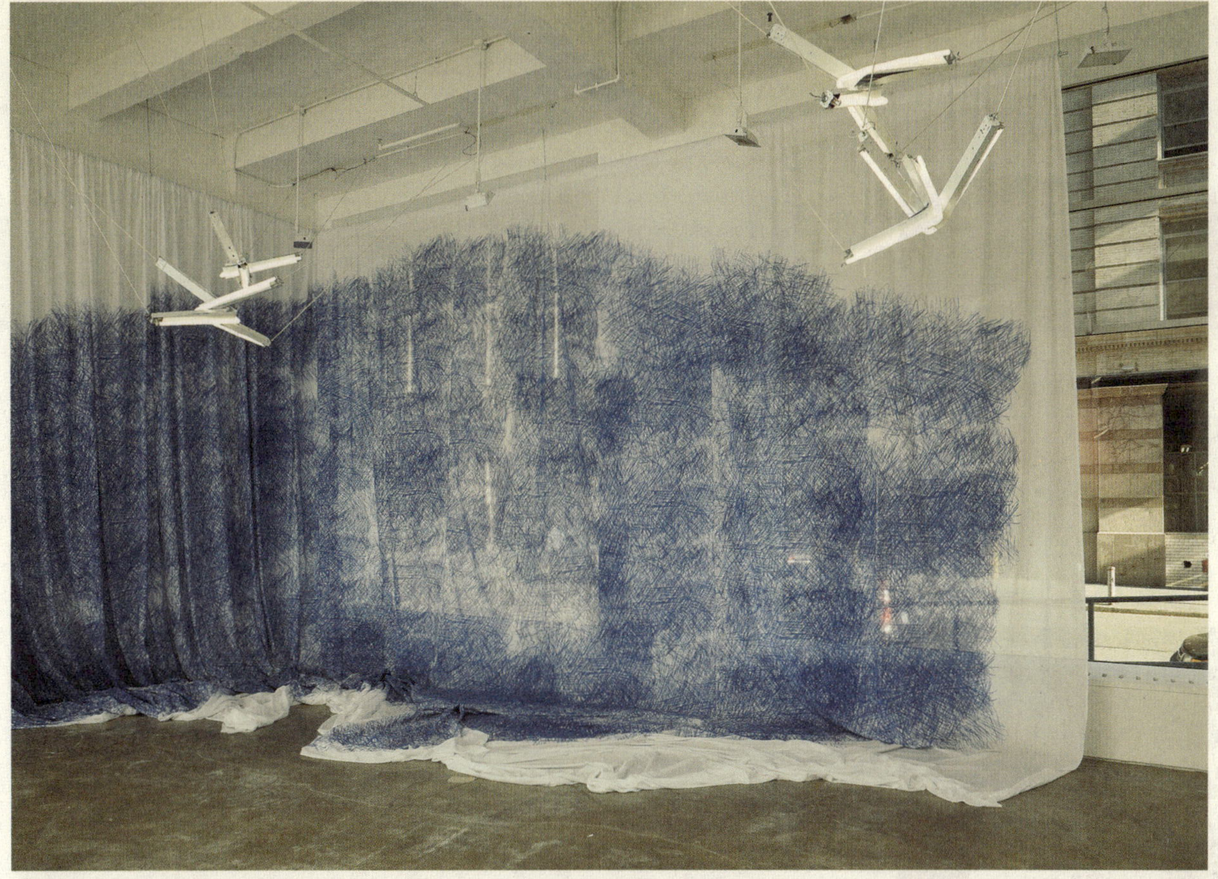

1.

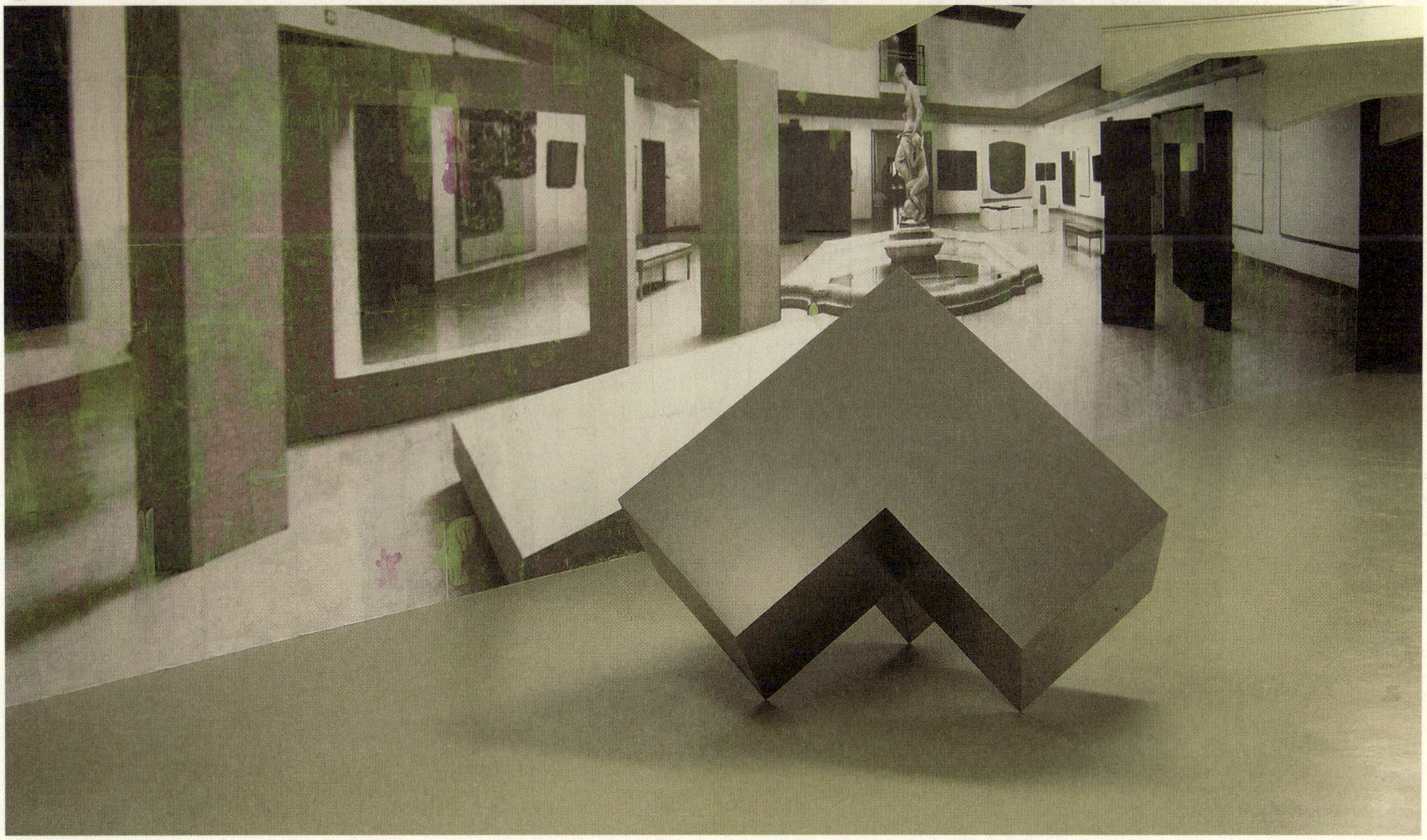

2.

Anna Möller lives and works in Hamburg. Her selective appropriations of image, text, and event often deliberately negate expectations of practical use or art-historically bolstered "meaning." She is especially interested in subverting the allusions of Minimalism and Conceptual art to a functionalist aesthetic, creating narratives without conclusion and situations that deliberately frustrate.

1. **Untitled (Action)**
2007, inkjet print on paper,
32 1/4 × 16 1/2 in (82 × 42 cm)

2. **Was können die von der sonne beschienen dinge dafür dass sie uns in den augen wehtun** (Don't blame things sweetly illuminated by the sun for hurting your eyes)
2007, ink on paper, plywood, lacquer, and screws, 78 3/4 × 78 3/4 × 59 in (200 × 200 × 150 cm)

3. **Mapping 1-5 (#3)**
2004, inkjet print on paper, 11 3/4 × 8 1/4 in (30 × 21 cm)

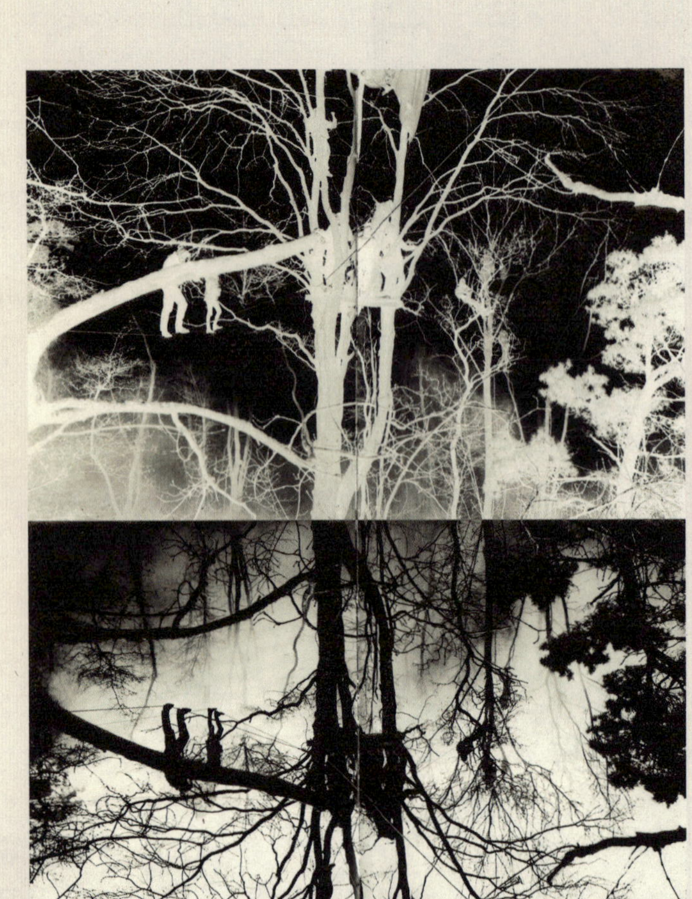

1.

2.

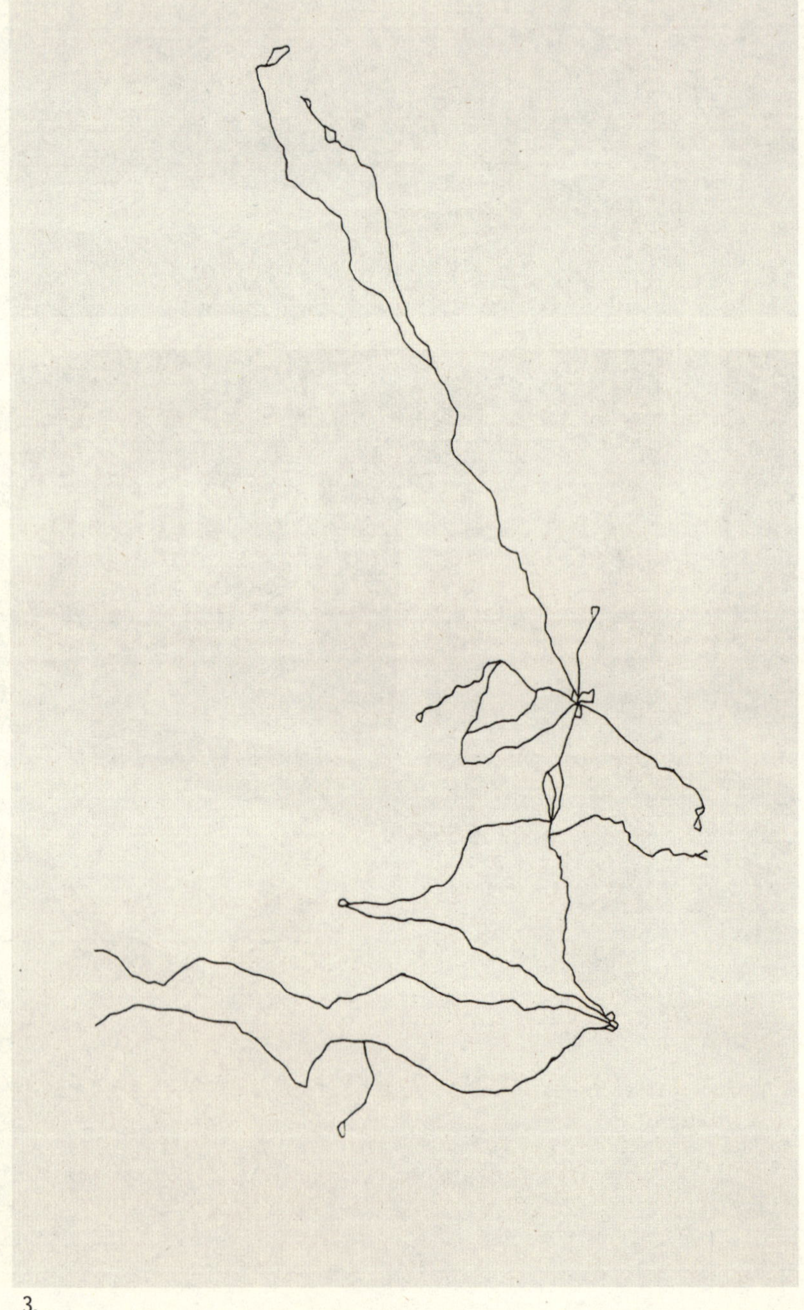

3.

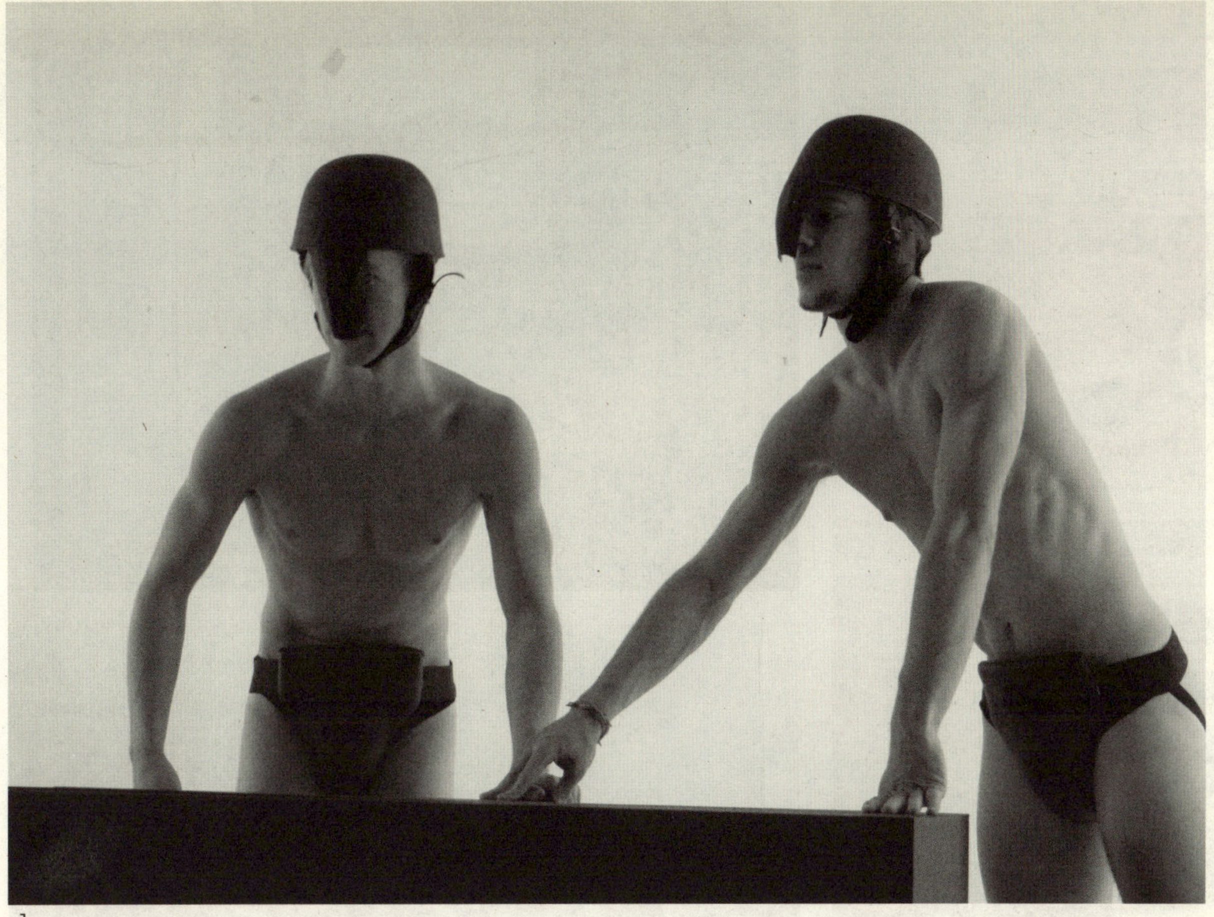

1.

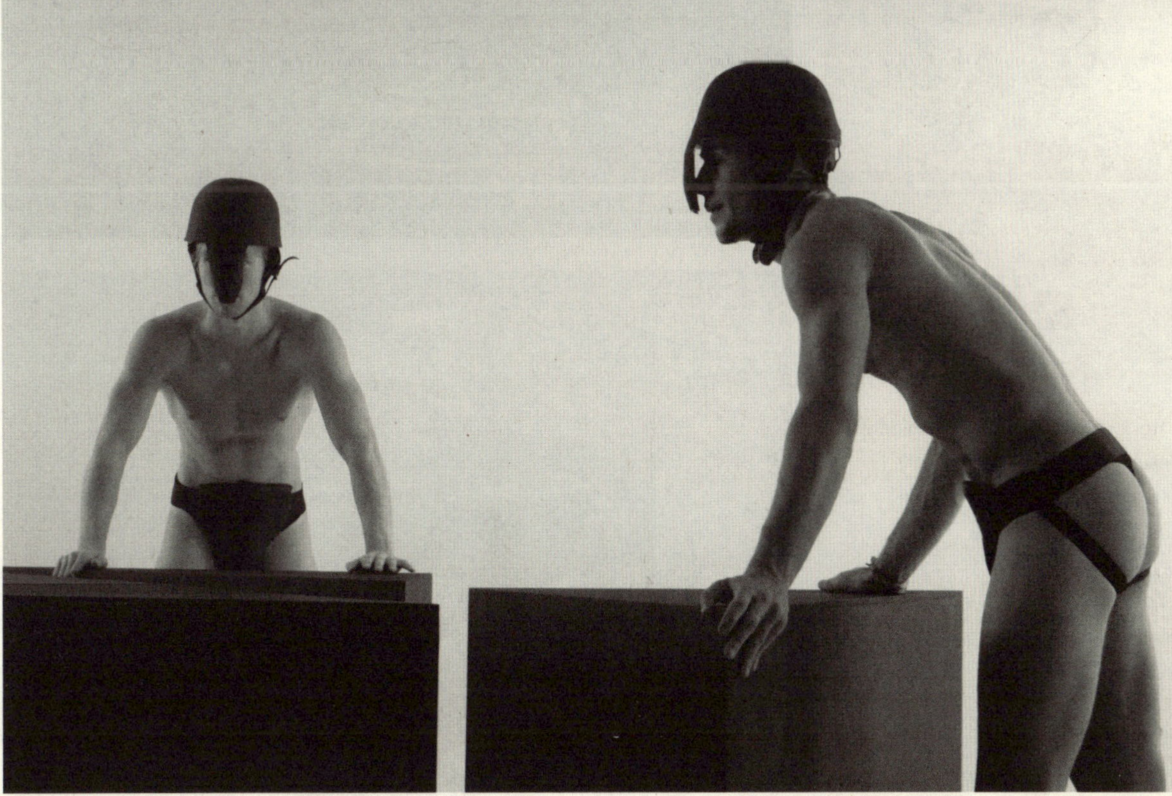

2.

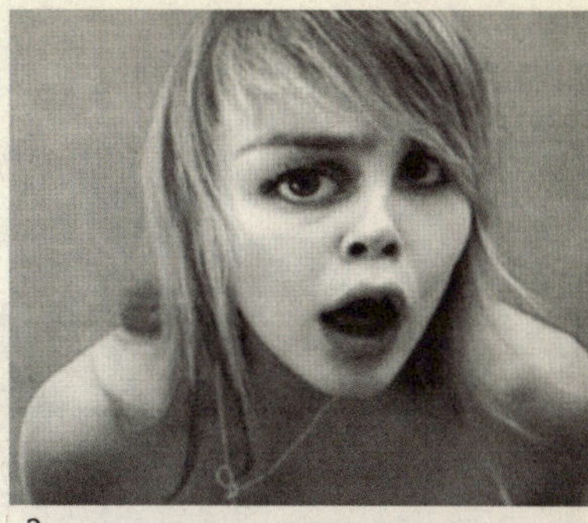

3.

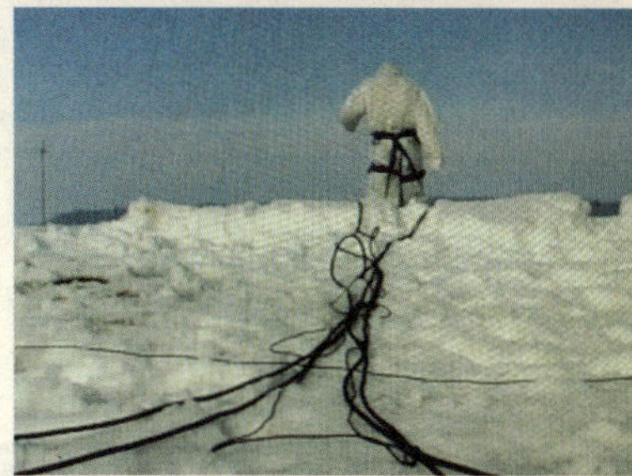

4.

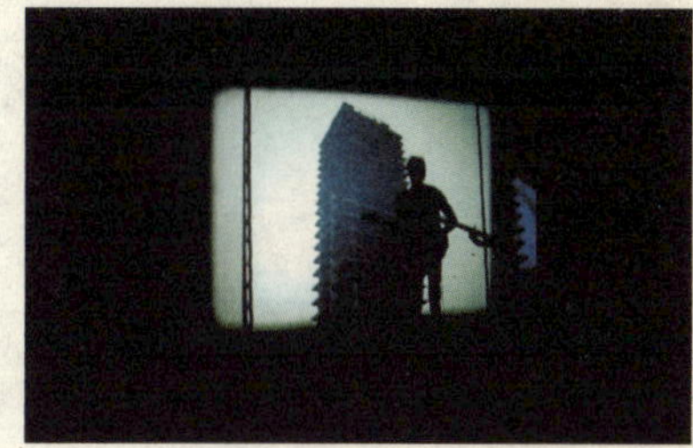

5.

In the work of Warsaw-based Anna Molska, as the artist points out, "nothing is what it seems." She is interested in the intersection of the abstract or idealized with tangible reality, and her films document the conceptual dissonance that results. In **Tanagram** (2006-07), for example, two Russian-speaking models are shown arranging geometrically shaped puzzle pieces in a wry allusion to Suprematism.

1 & 2. **Tanagram**
2006-07, video, 5 min 10 sec

3. **Jesus Loves Me**
2005, video, 2 min 43 sec

4. **Perspective**
2006, video, 1 min 30 sec

5. **Improvised Szkieletor Soundtrack (Attempt #5)**
2007, mixed media, dimensions variable

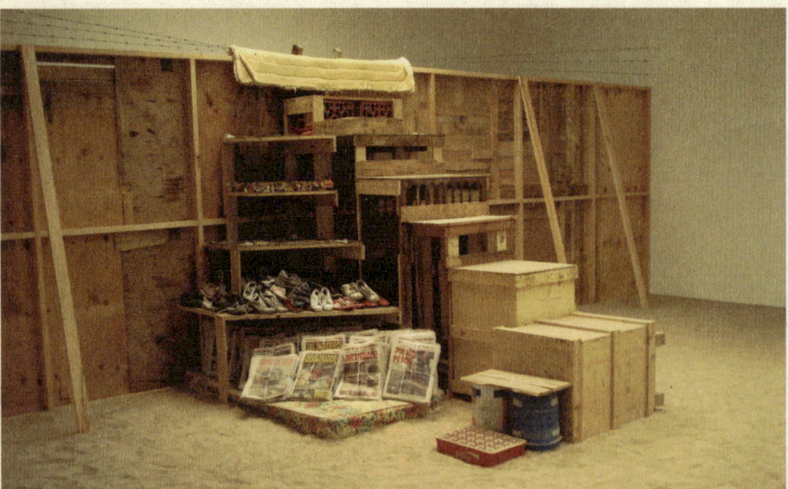

1.

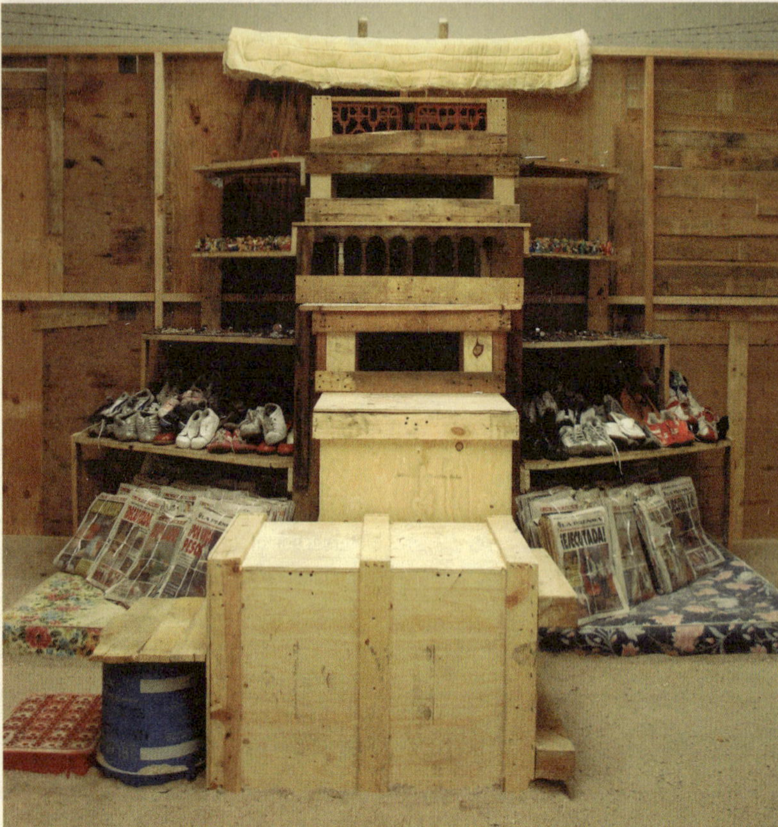

2.

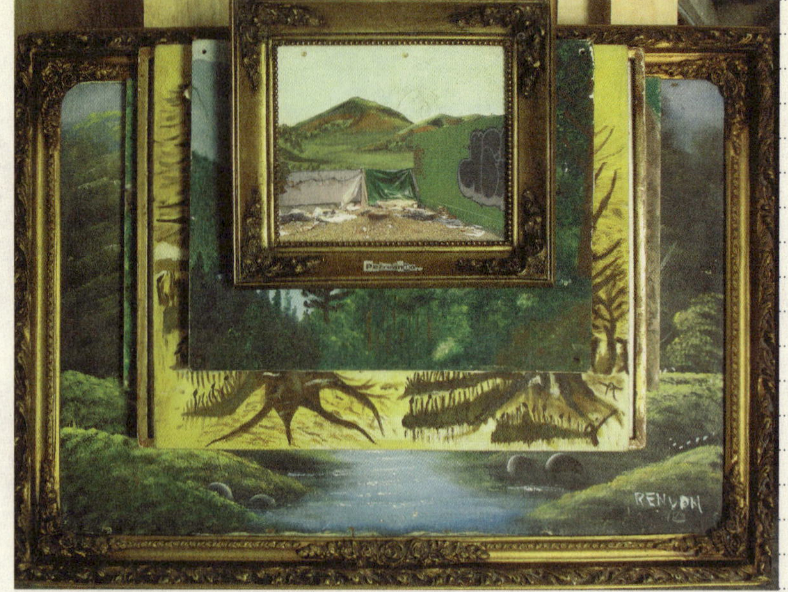

3.

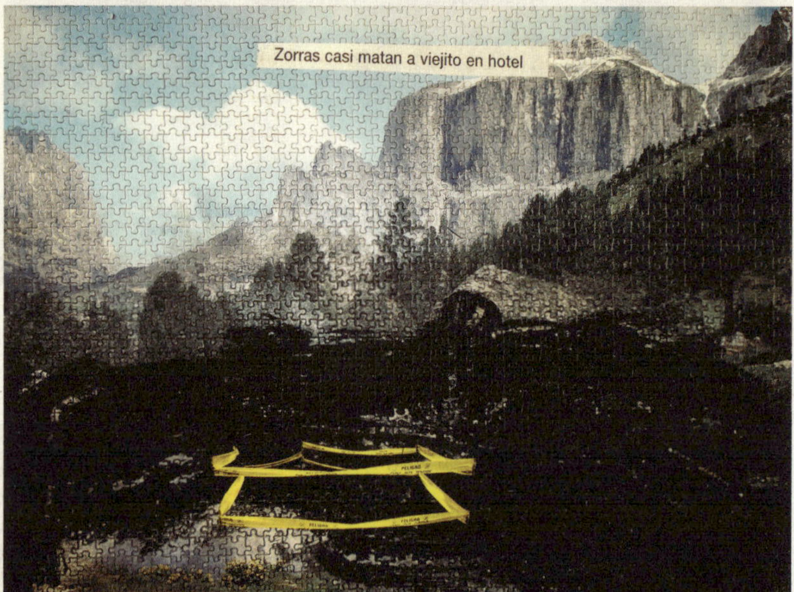

4.

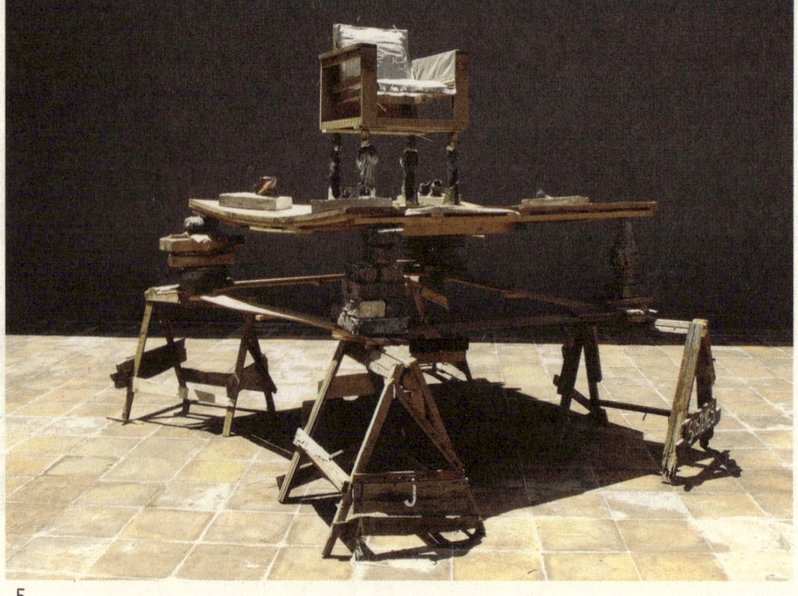

5.

Mexico City-based Israel Meza Moreno, aka Moris, imports the stuff of slum living – old mattresses and bits of wood, newspapers and animal hides, rubber tires and metal sheeting – into gallery settings, refashioning them according to his own peculiar version of makeshift shantytown architecture.

1 & 2. **Hermoso paisaje 4, "El baldio"** (Beautiful andscape 4, "Empty lot")
2008, mixed media, dimensions variable

3. **Hermoso paisaje 6, "Perreando"** (Beautiful landscape 6, "Dogging")
2008, mixed media, 39 ½ × 31 ½ in (100 × 80 cm)

4. **Zorras casi matan a viejito en hotel** (Foxes almost kill an old man in a hotel)
2008, mixed media, 39 ½ × 31 ½ in (100 × 80 cm)

5. **Que tan leal es un perro hambriento** (How loyal is a hungry dog)
2008, mixed media, 157 ½ × 157 ½ × 157 ½ in (400 × 400 × 400 cm)

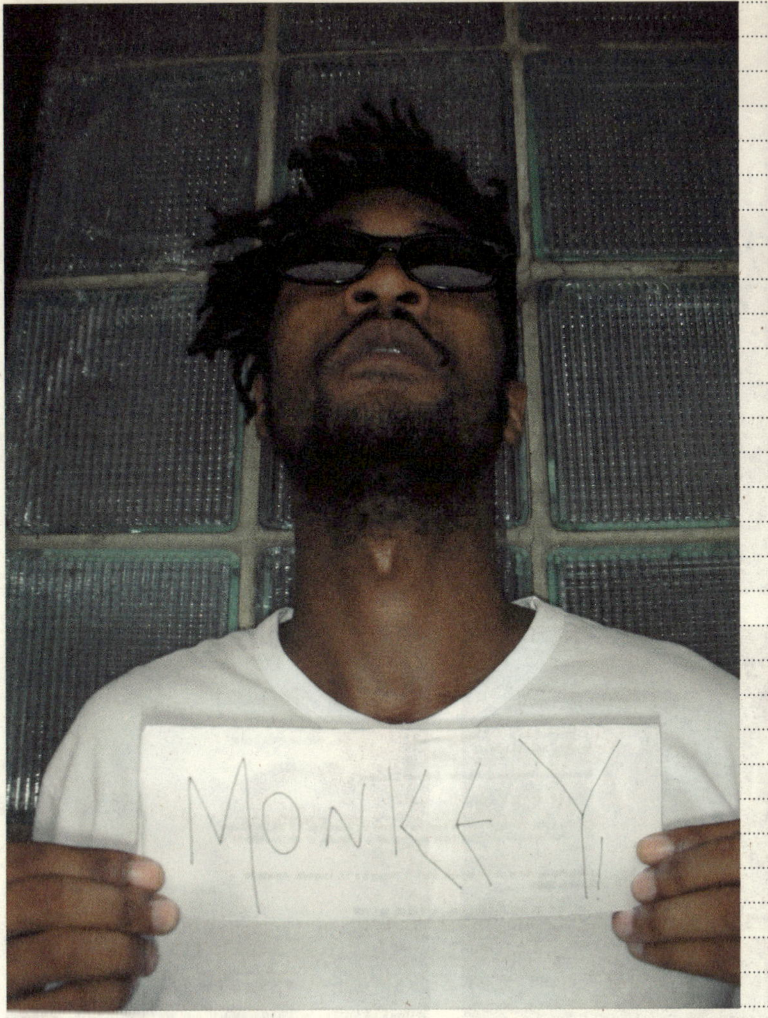

1.

2.

3.

Nástio Mosquito is a poet, performance artist, actor, and filmmaker. His disillusionment with his early work as a television presenter and documentary filmmaker for Angola public television led him to live performance and various video projects. His work often deals with issues pertaining to the elemental human needs for food and sex, but his excavations of his personal identity occasionally touch on his nationality, as in his hilarious and viciously tongue-in-cheek **Fuck Africa**. His work was included in the African Pavilion of the 52nd Venice Biennial (2007), and as part of the 12th Poetry Africa Festival (2008).

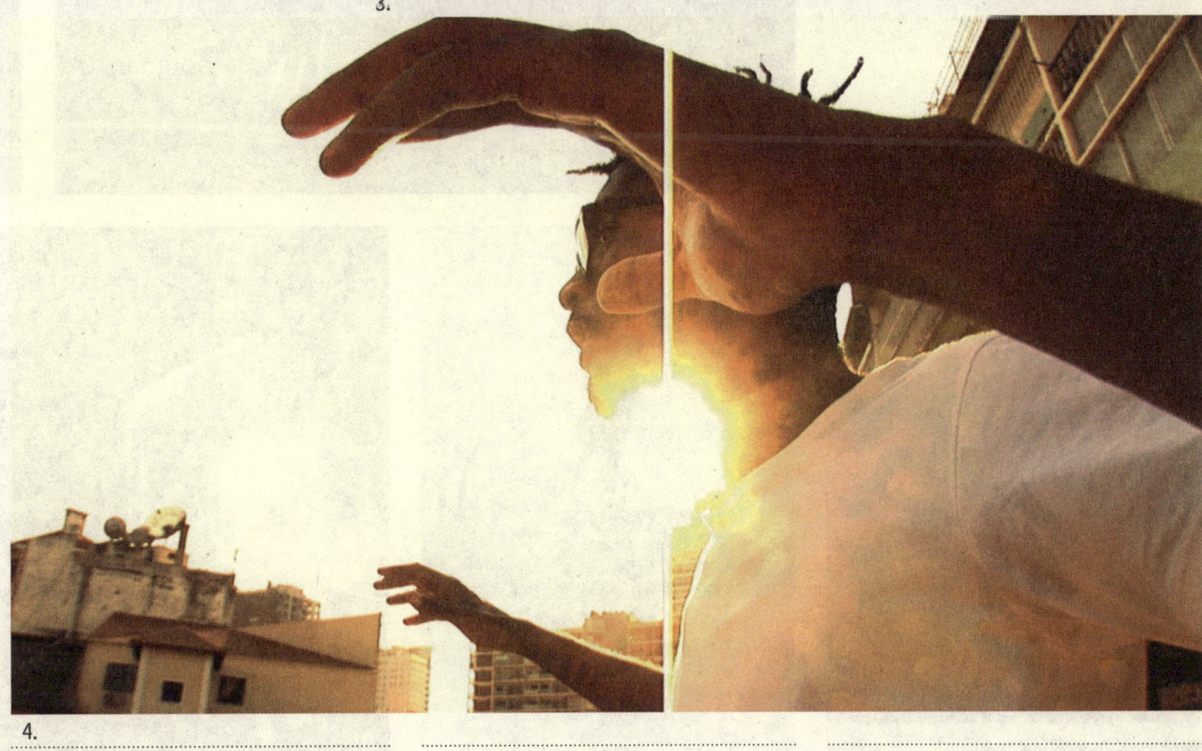

4.

1. **Self-Portrait**
2007, digital photograph

2 & 3. **Nastia's Manifesto**
2008, video

4. **Africalls?**
2007, video

Carlos Motta lives and works in New York and was the subject of a solo exhibition at the ICA, Philadelphia, in 2008. He works in photography, video, and installation, applying modes of address borrowed from documentary filmmaking and sociological study to interrogate the implications of modern governmental structure and the repercussions of political events.

1. **SOA: Black & White Tales**
2005-06, mixed media, dimensions variable

2. **Untitled**
2007, blade cuts on black paper over windows, dimensions variable

3. **Pesca Milagrosa**
(Miraculous Fishing) (detail)
2002-04, inkjet prints, 25 × 13 in (76 × 40 cm)

4, 5 & 6. **Leningrad Trilogy**
2006, 3-channel video and photographs, dimensions variable

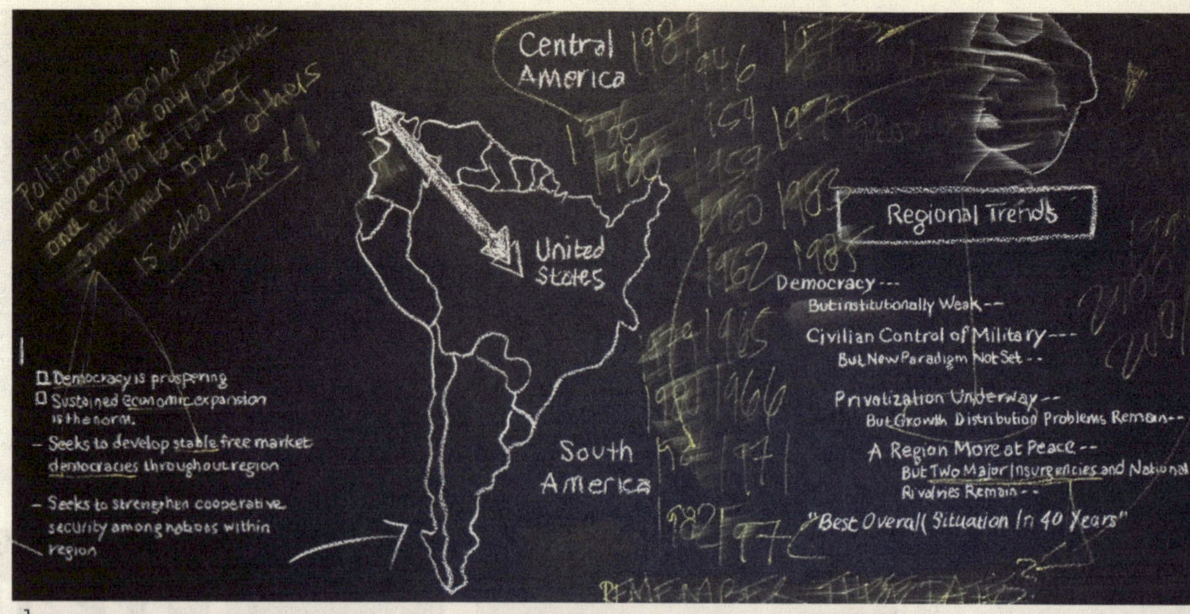

1.

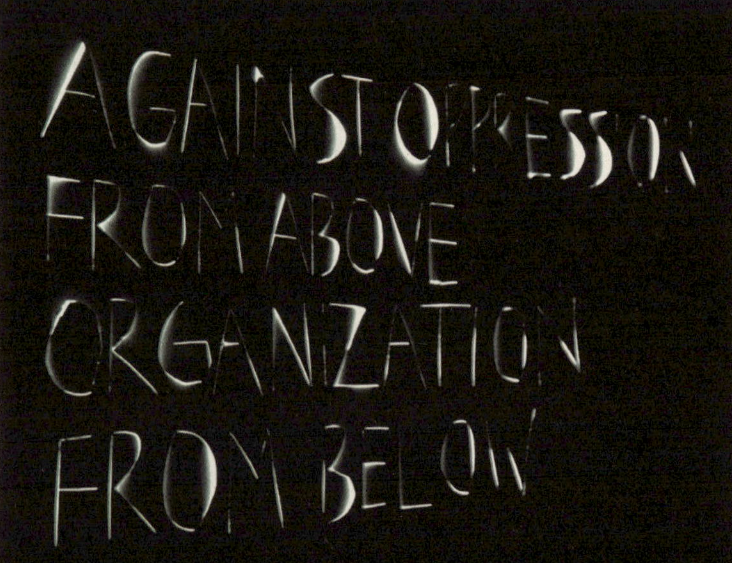

2.

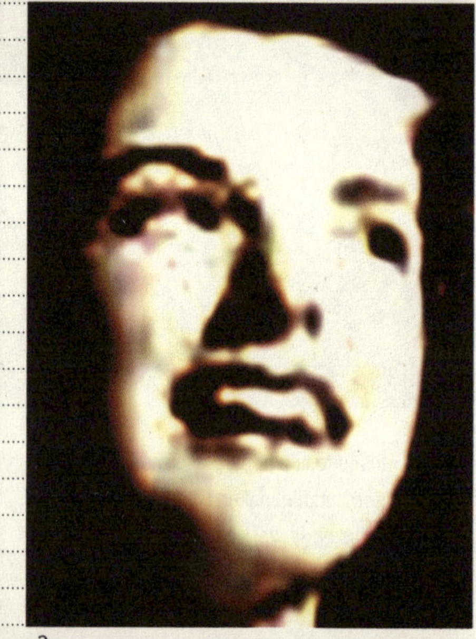

3.

4.

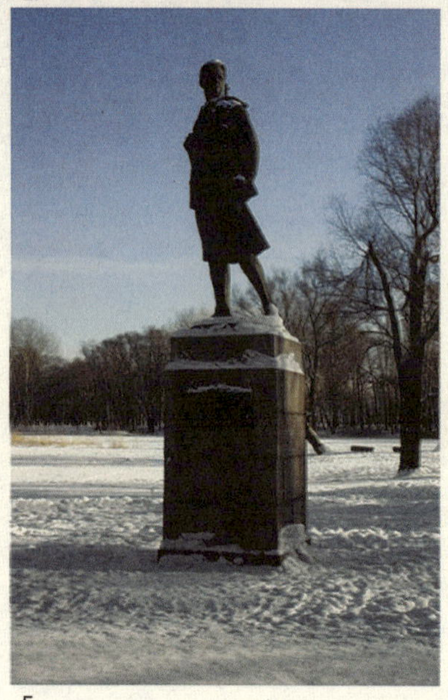

5.

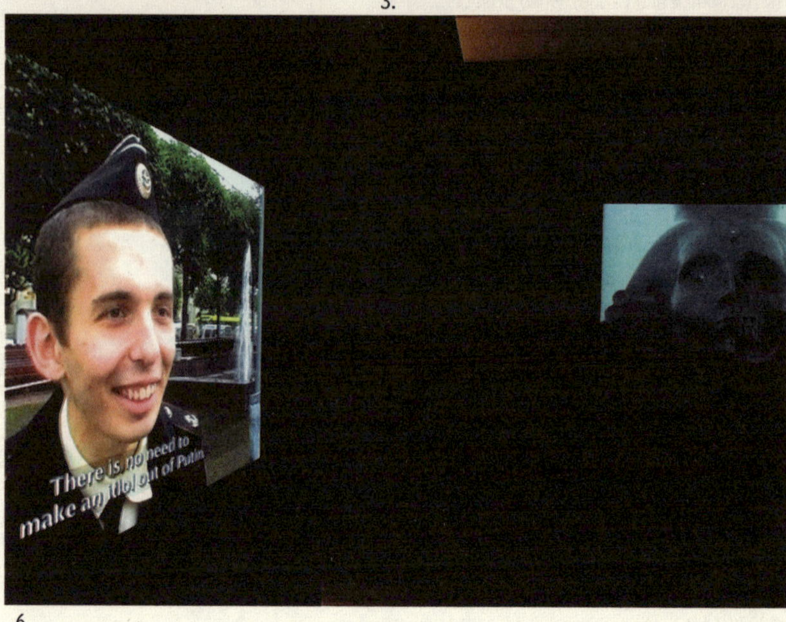

6.

Chris Moukarbel lives and works in New York. His videos and installations explore ideas around time, memory, and the ways in which objects may act as cultural talismans. He is particularly interested in the political implications of memorials, and in the supplanting of one idea (sometimes embodied in a stylistic trope) by another.

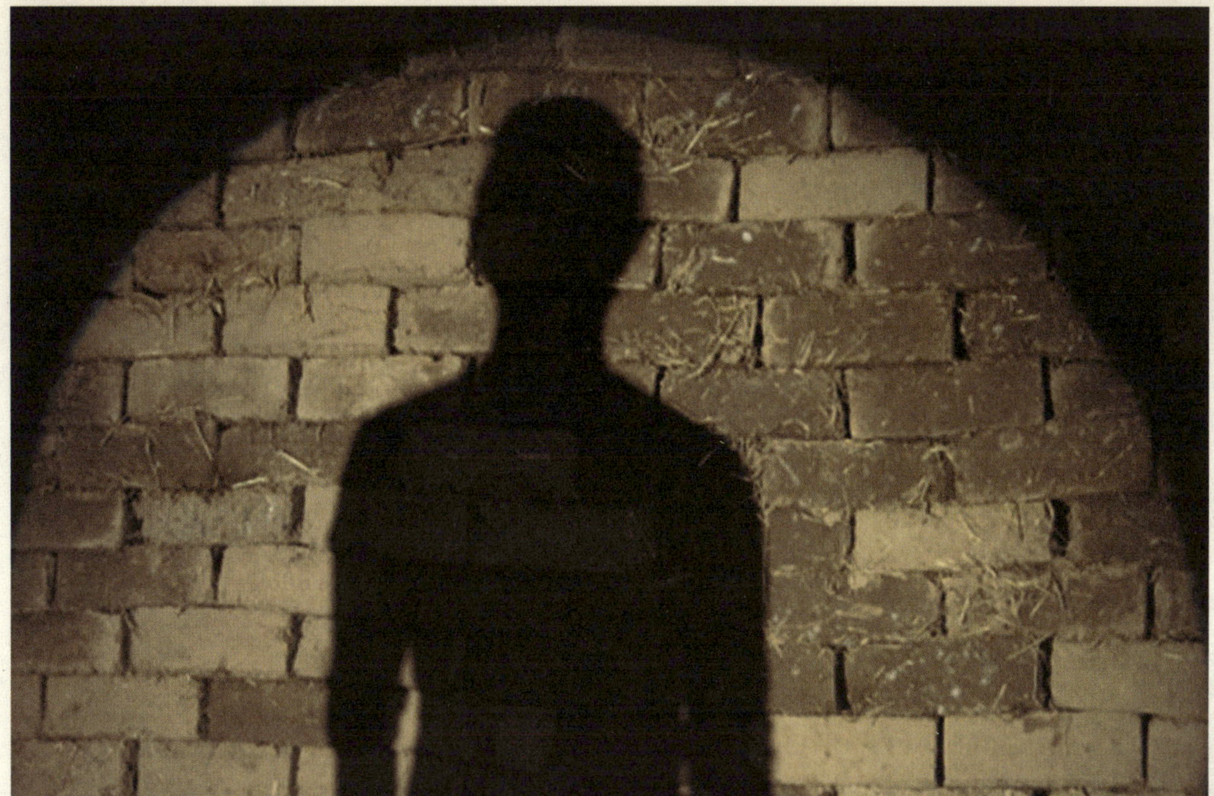

1.

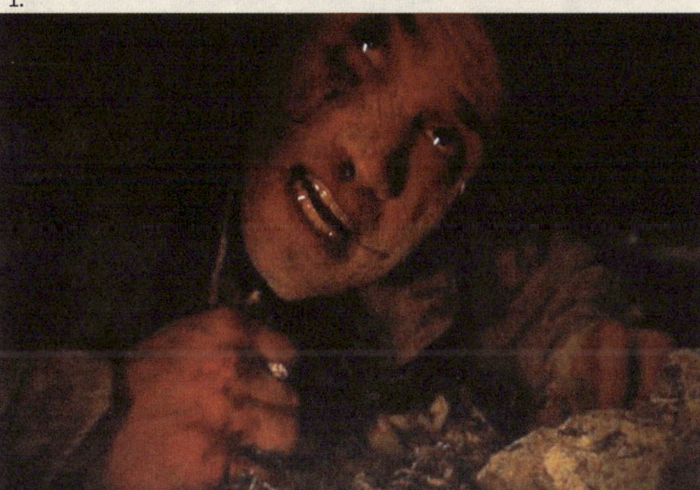

2.

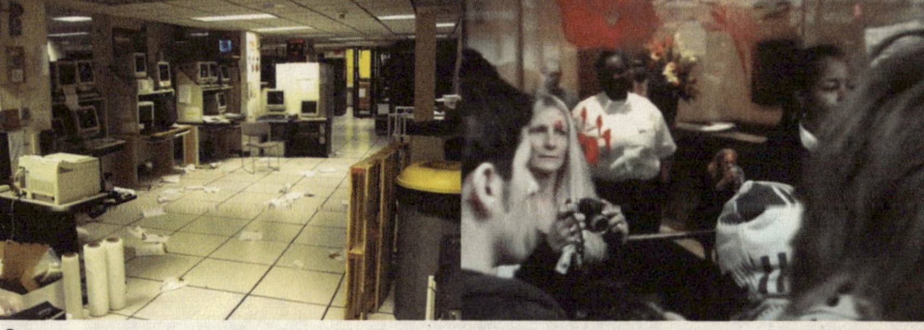

3.

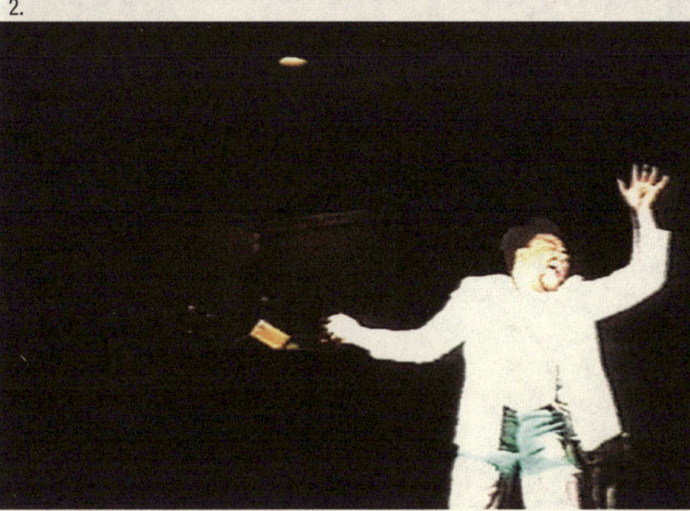

4.

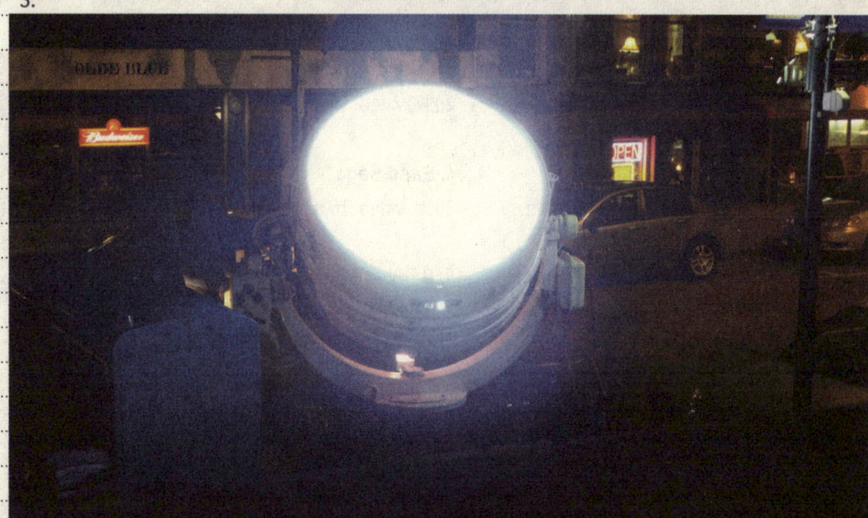

5.

1. IN/OUT
2006, bricks, brick molds, buckets, and mixed media, dimensions variable

2. World Trade Center 2006
2006, video

3. NYT/WDC
2008, chromogenic print, 30 × 80 in (76 × 203 cm)

4. AJ Turner
2005, video still, dimensions variable

5. World Trade Center 2006, Followspot
2006, digital image

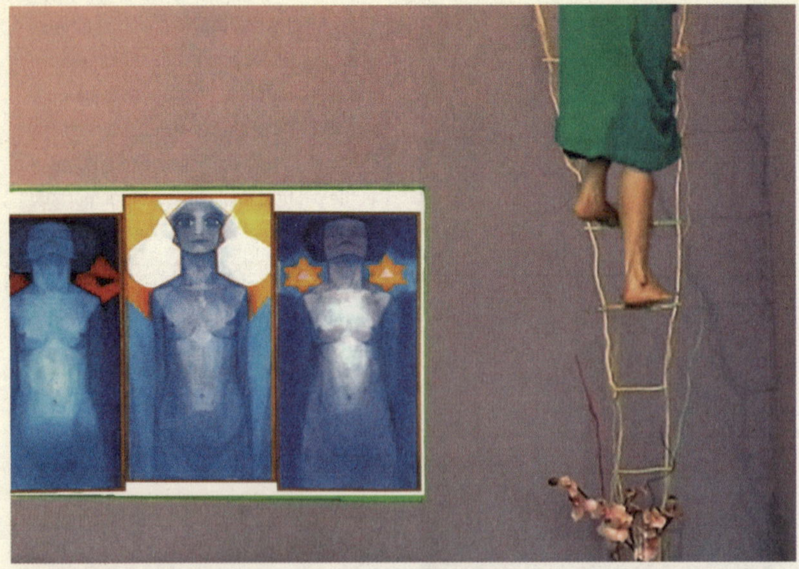
1.

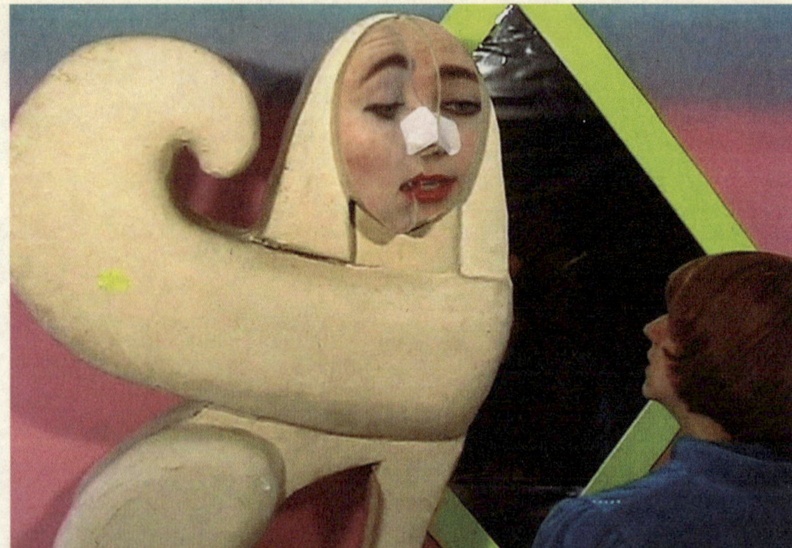
2.

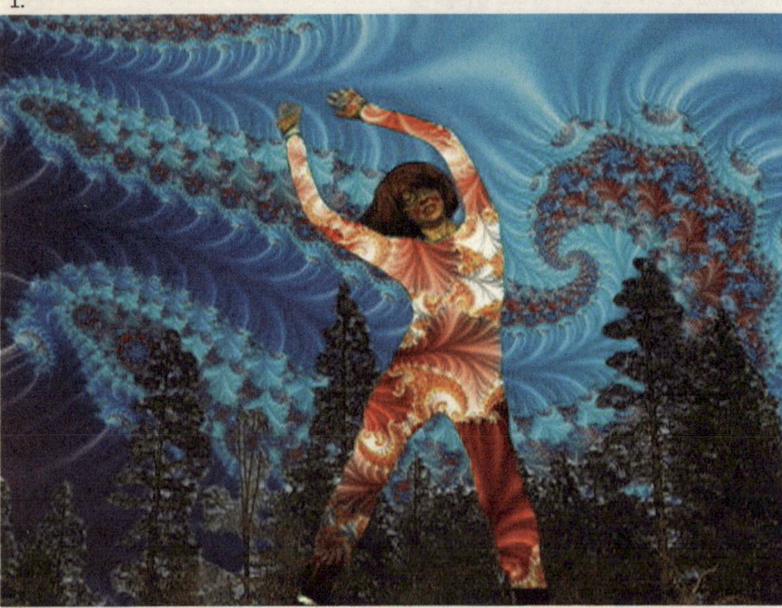
3.

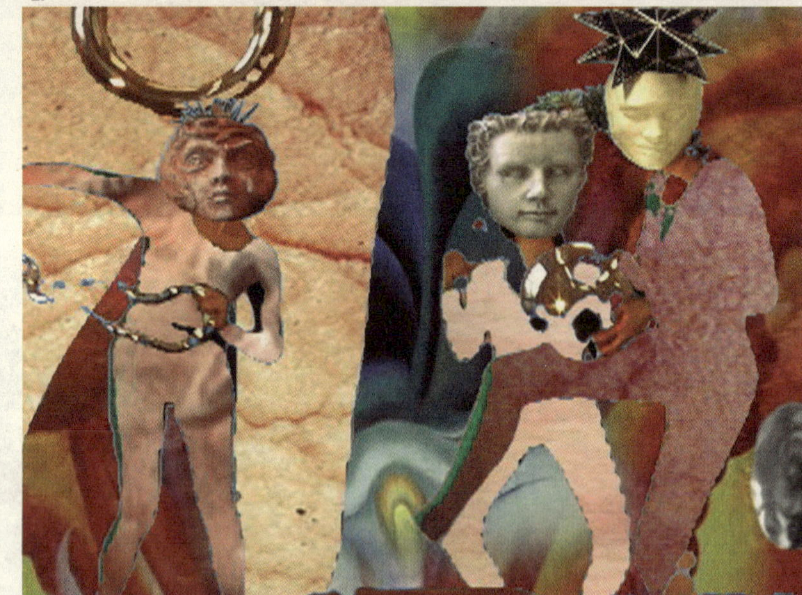
4.

Shana Moulton studied at the University of California, Berkeley, and Carnegie Mellon University, Pittsburgh. She currently lives and works in Brooklyn, producing videos and performances that combine wry humor with a low-tech Pop aesthetic. Her use of simple video effects and animation invests the domestic settings with an otherworldly quality.

1. Whispering Pines 8
2006, video, 7 min 34 sec

2. Whispering Pines 7
2006, video, 4 min 43 sec

3. Whispering Pines 4
2007, video, 11 min 34 sec

4. Sand Saga
2008, video, 10 min 29 sec

5. Body ÷ Mind + 7 = Spirit
2008, performance and 2-channel video projection, 15 min

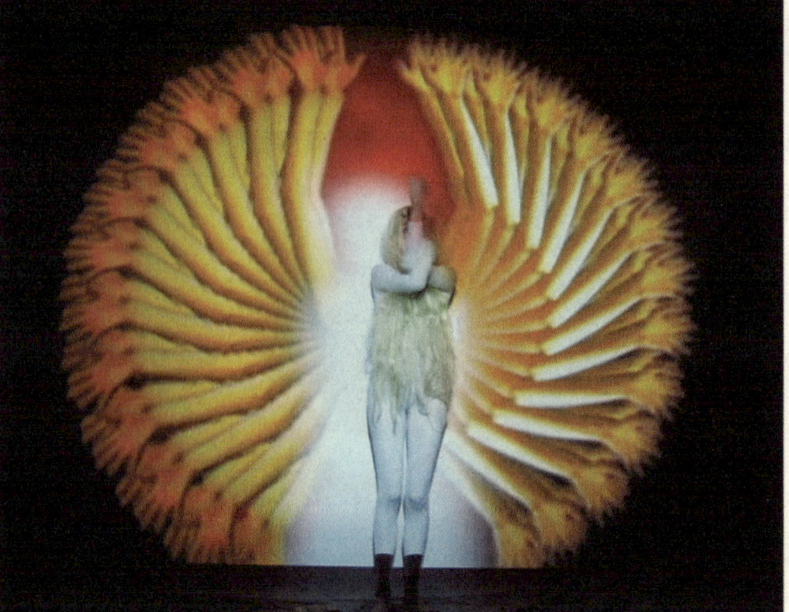
5.

Ciprian Muresan lives and works in Cluj, Romania. His videos, drawings, installations, photographs, and paintings explore history, religion, and the intersection of art and everyday life.

Frequently alluding to the turbulence of his country's recent past, Muresan uses situational humor as the most effective response to shattering events.

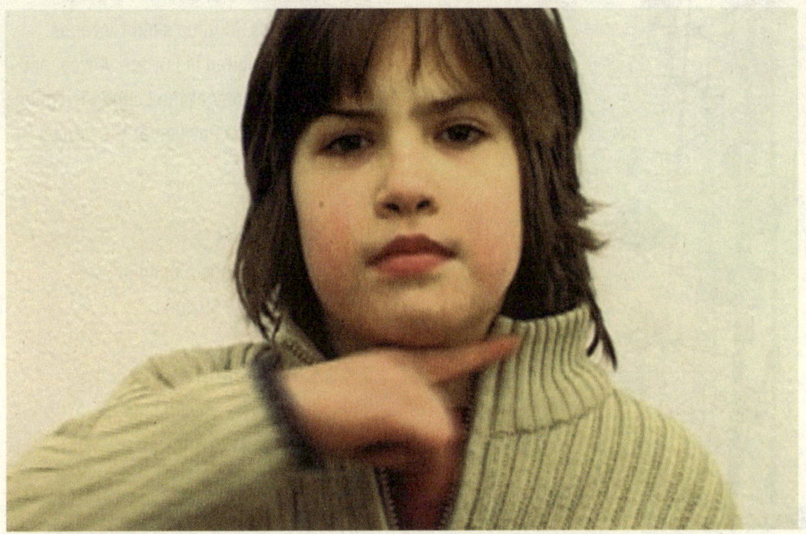

1.

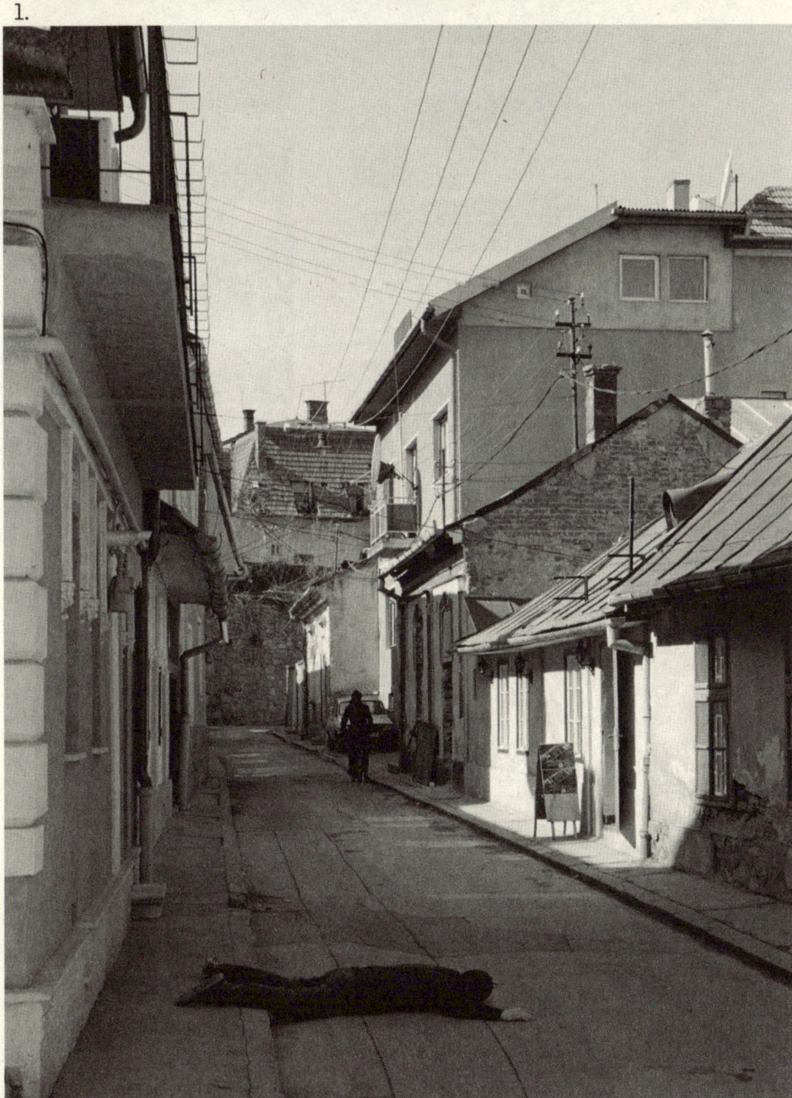

3.

communism
never
happened

2.

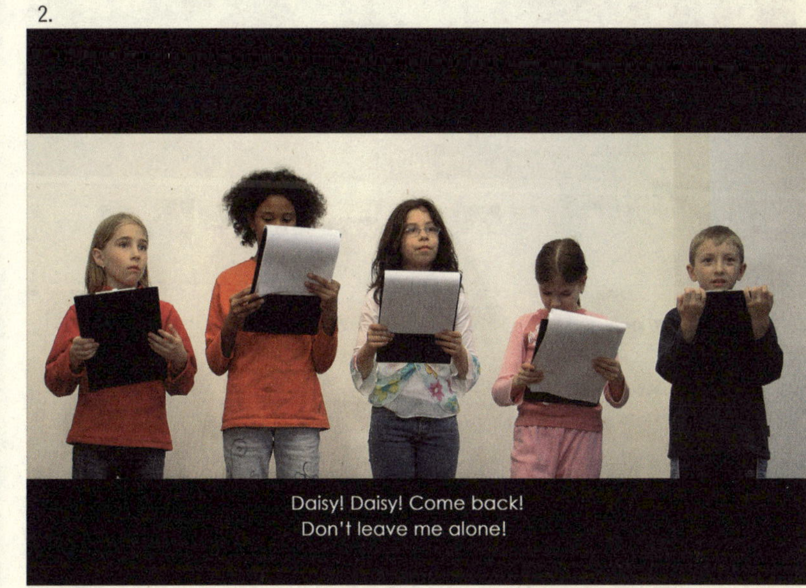

4.

1. Stanca
2006, video, 17 sec

2. Communism Never Happened
2006, letters cut from vinyl records, dimensions variable

3. Leap into the Void, after 3 seconds
2004, black and white print, $39\frac{1}{2} \times 27\frac{1}{2}$ in (100 × 70 cm)

4. Rhinoceros
2006, video, 25 min

1.

2.

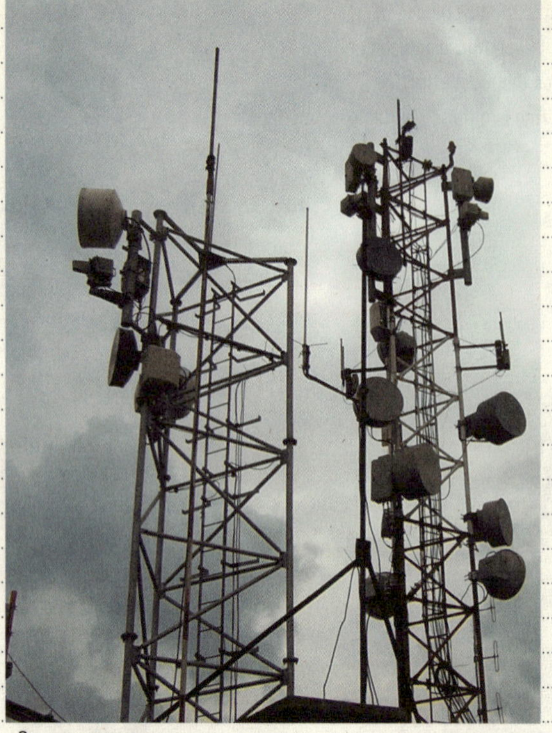
3.

Ndilo Mutima's photography depicts the recovery of a country only recently freed from almost three decades of civil war. Appropriating scenes from the everyday, he uses sparsely populated landscapes and muted colors to offer insight into themes of loss. Mutima's photographs have been exhibited in Europe, Africa, and Asia, most recently at the Luanda Triennial and in the African Pavilion at the Venice Biennale in 2007.

1 & 2. **Manbarras**
2006, digital print on aluminum,
15 × 19 ¾ in (38 × 50 cm)

3, 4 & 5. **Red Line**
2004, digital print on aluminum,
47 ¼ × 35 ½ in (120 × 90 cm)

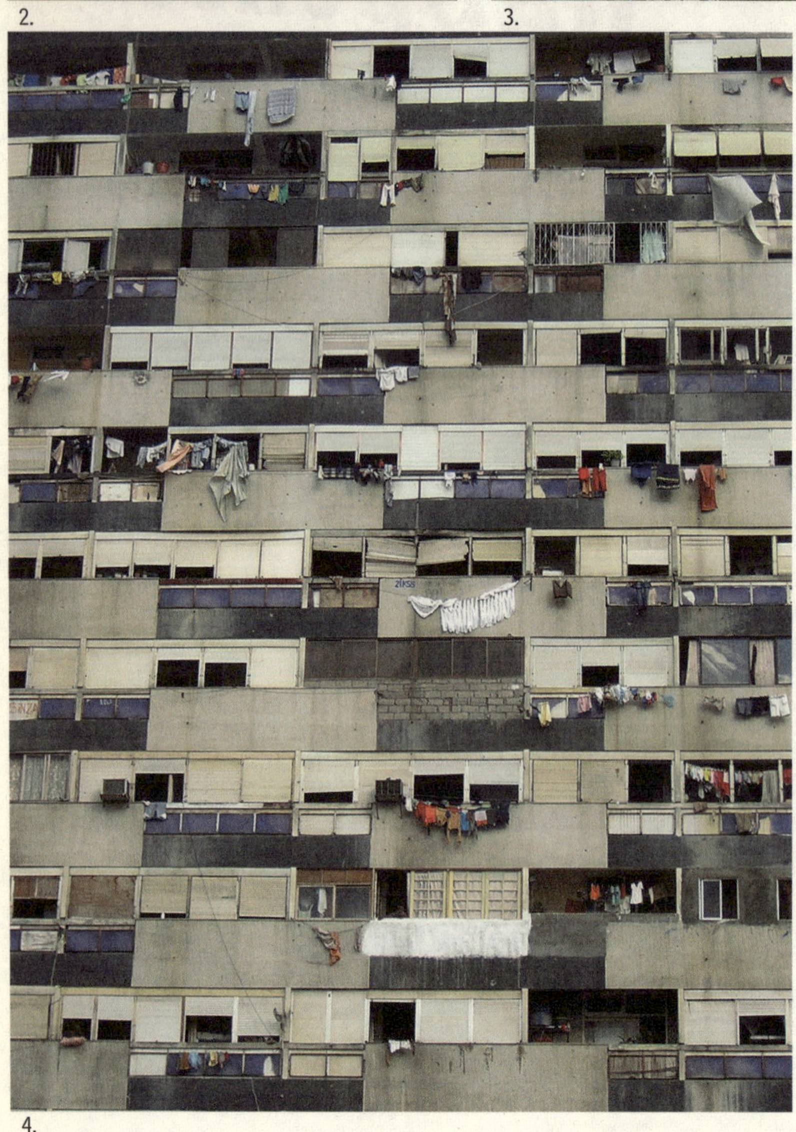
4.

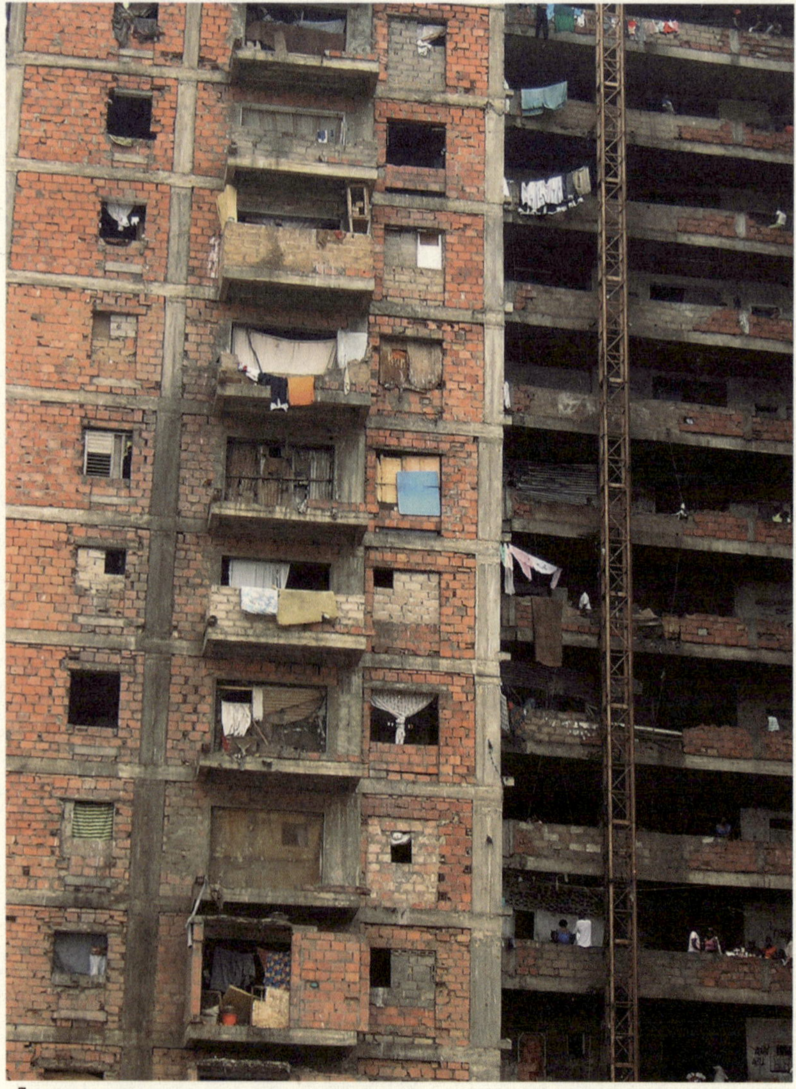
5.

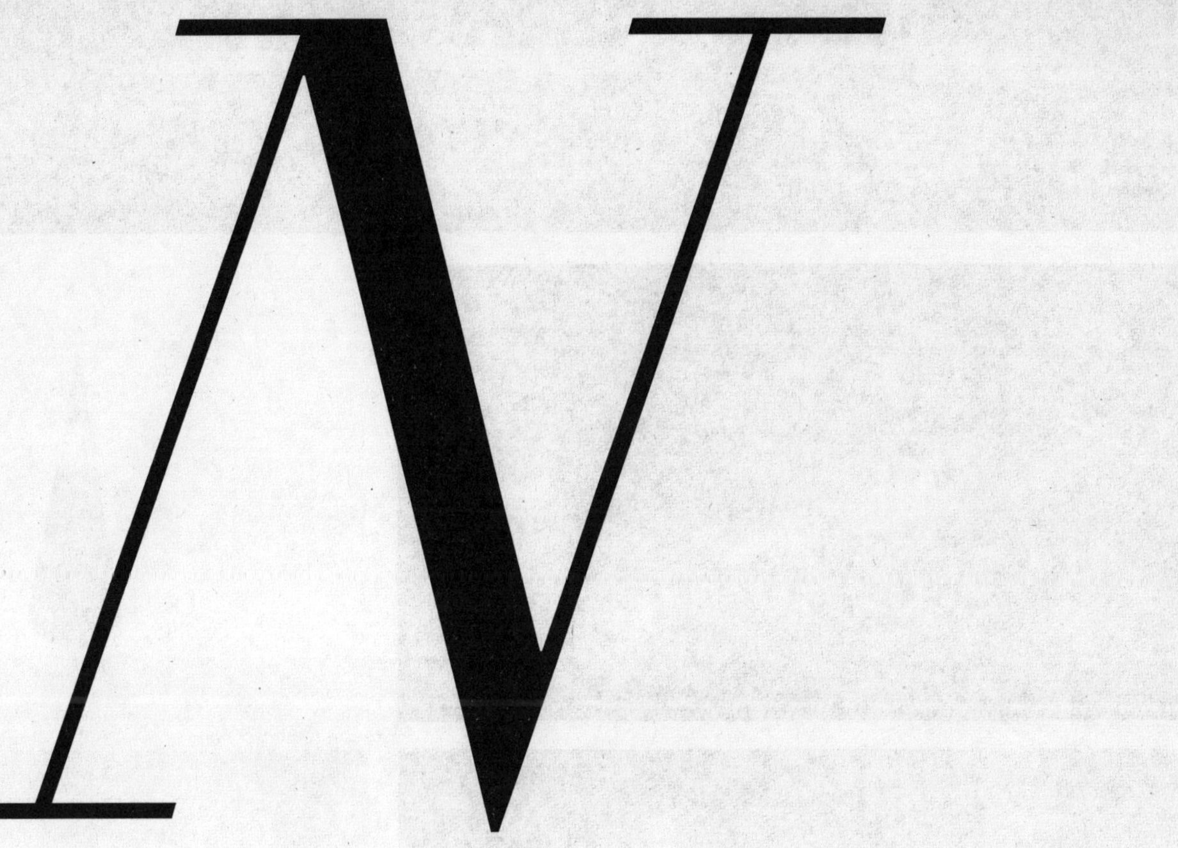

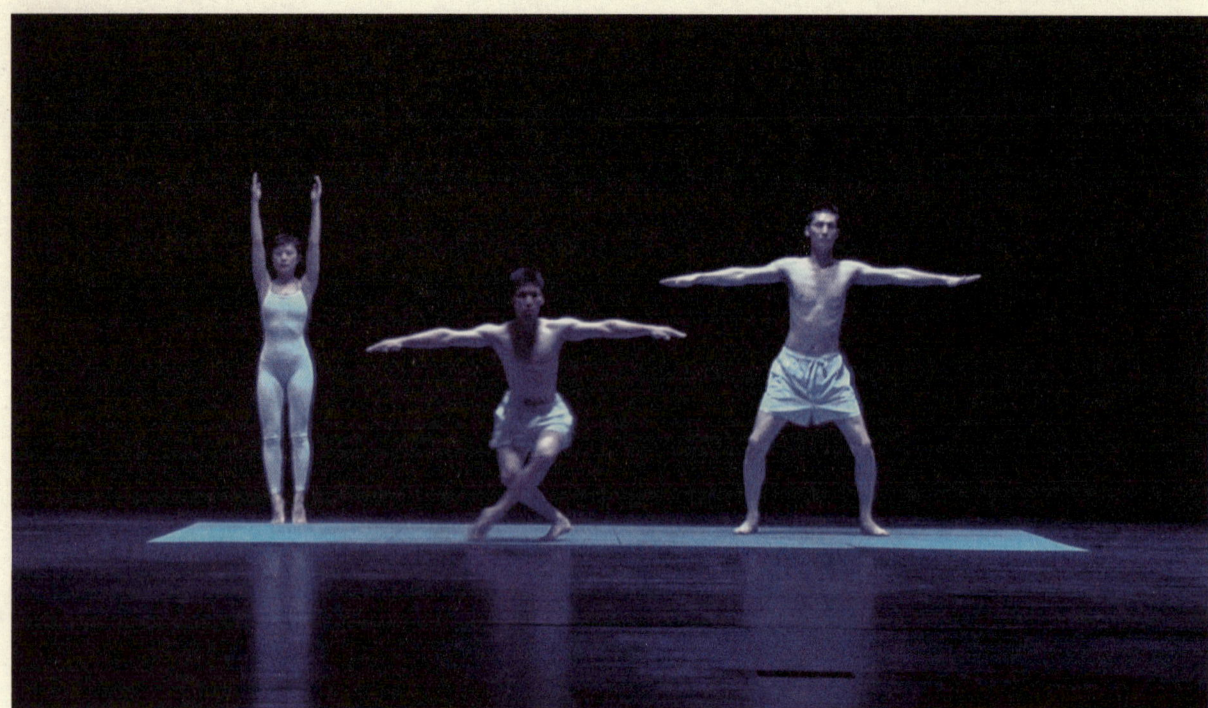
1.

Hwayeon Nam earned her MFA from Korea National University of Arts and lives in Seoul. Working in media ranging from scripted video to drawing, she infuses the political with personal, meditative narratives. One series of drawings imagines secret military facilities (control towers, surveillance cameras) hidden in ordinary urban facades. Her work was in the 7th Gwangju Biennial, Korea (2008).

1 & 2. **Delusion Beach**
2008, 3-channel video, 15 min

3. **Design for a control tower**
2006, drawing on paper, $15\frac{1}{2} \times 21\frac{1}{4}$ in (39 × 54 cm)

4 & 5. **I Give You My Knife**
2008, video, 6 min 20 sec

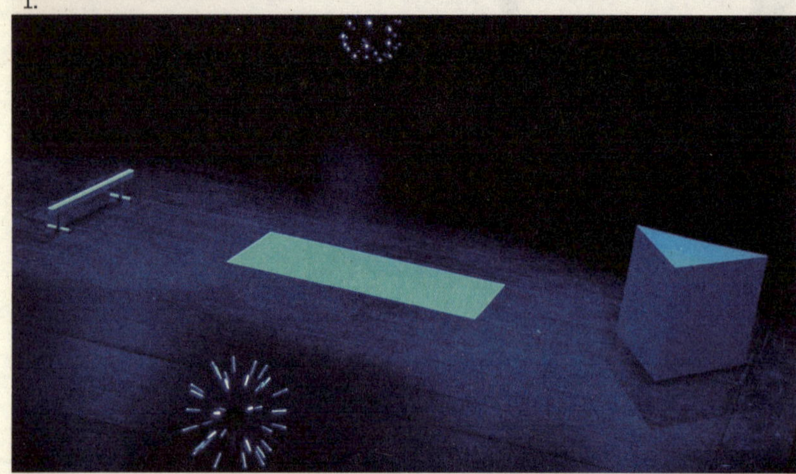
2.

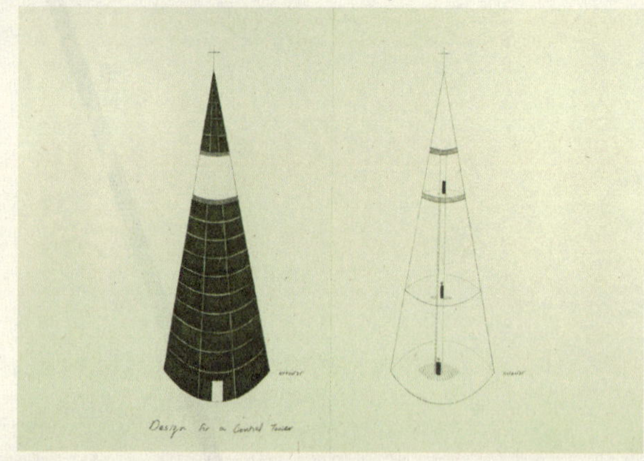
3.

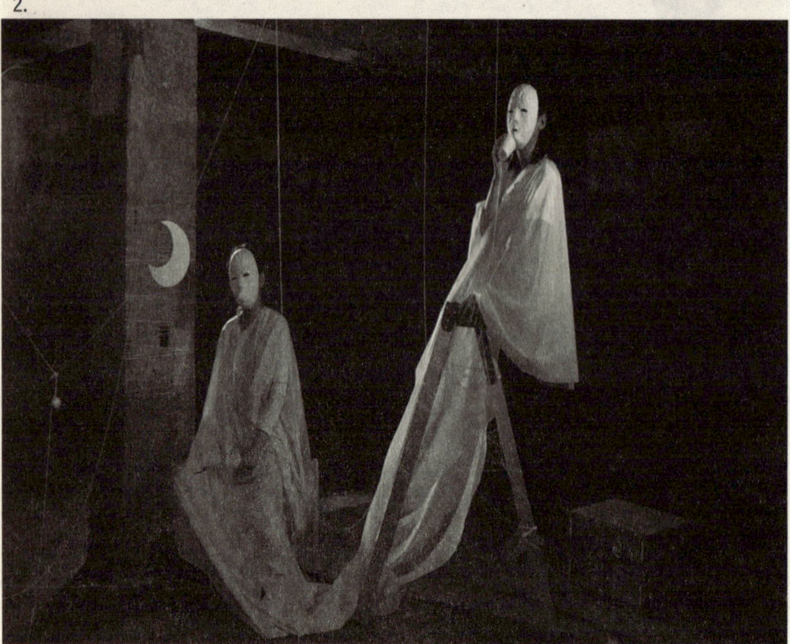
4.

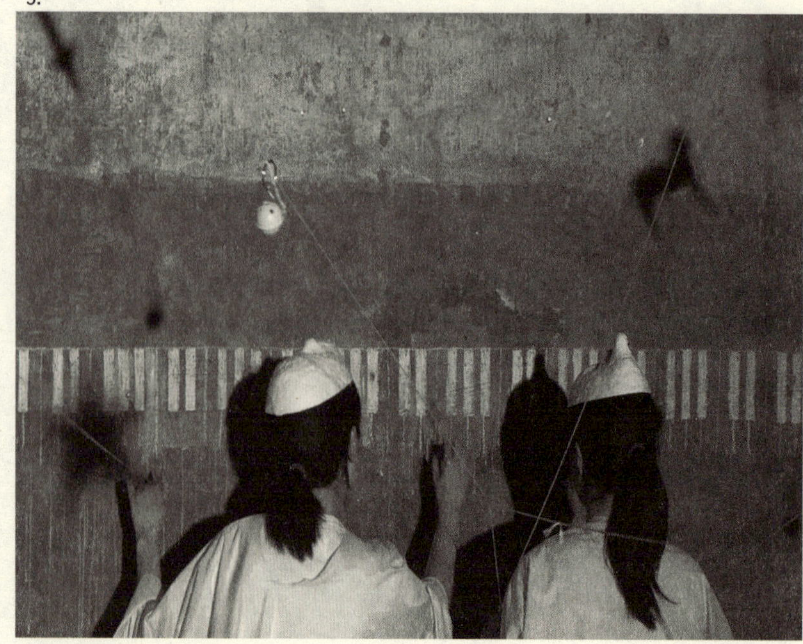
5.

Marina Naprushkina lives and works in Minsk. Her work is based around a sustained critical examination of the totalitarian regime in her native Belarus headed by Alexander Lukashenko. Working in a wide variety of mediums, Neprushkina appropriates, recontextualizes, and subverts Lukashenko's propaganda, commenting on the continued power of images to influence popular opinion.

1. Belarus today
2008, video, 4 min

2. Spasi i soxrani...
2006, oil on canvas, 51 × 67 in (130 × 170 cm)

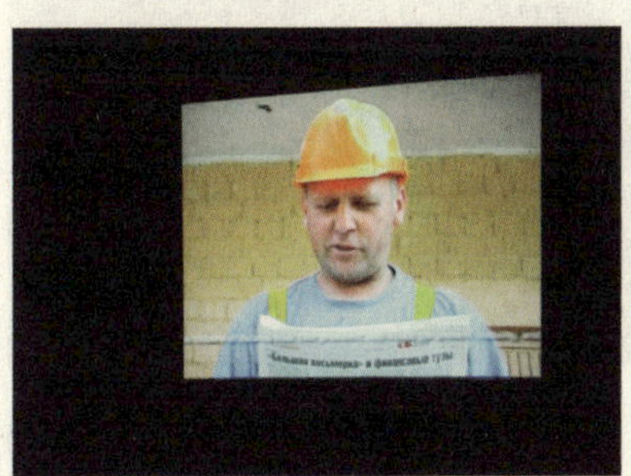

1.

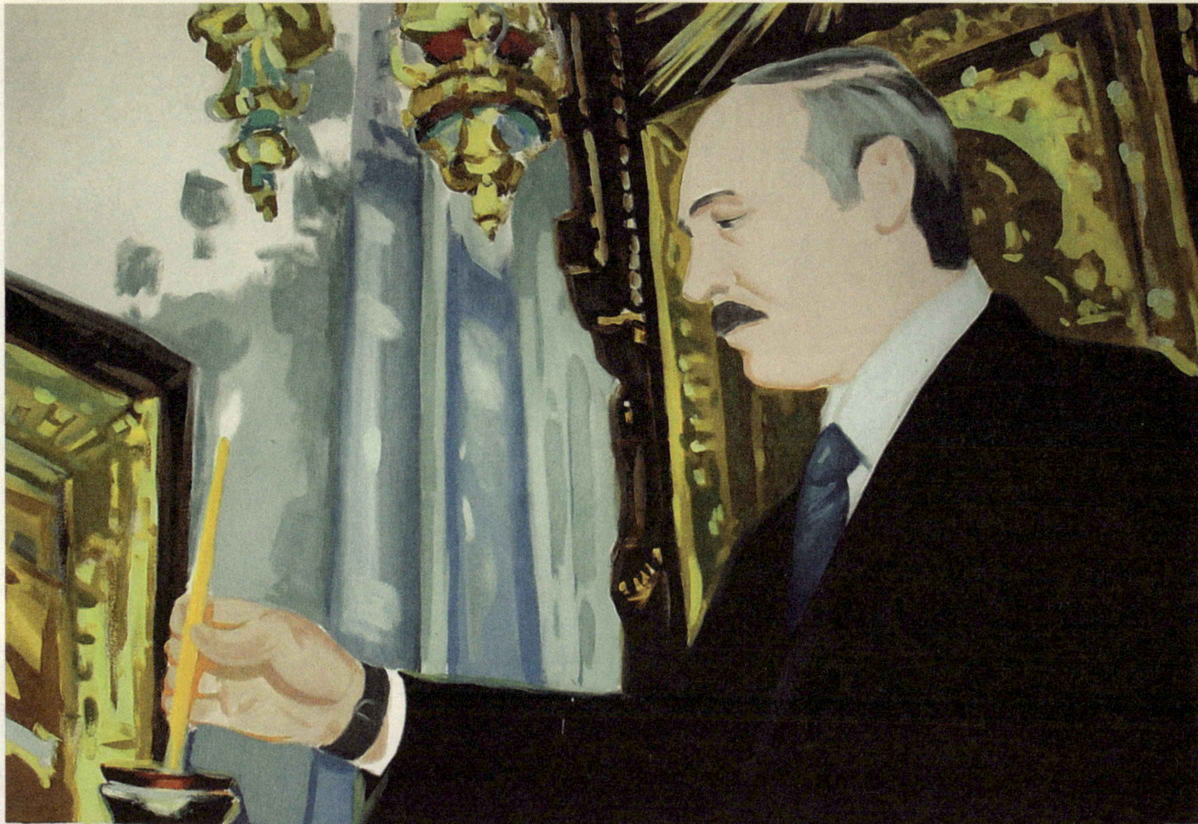

2.

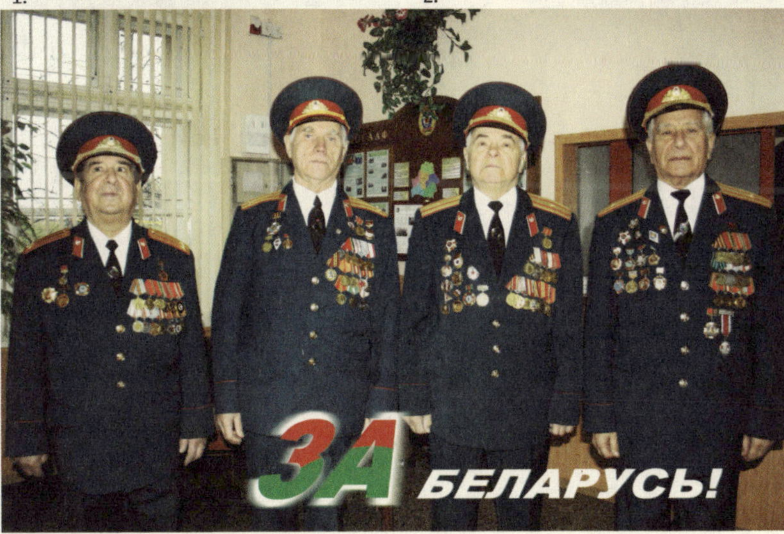

3.

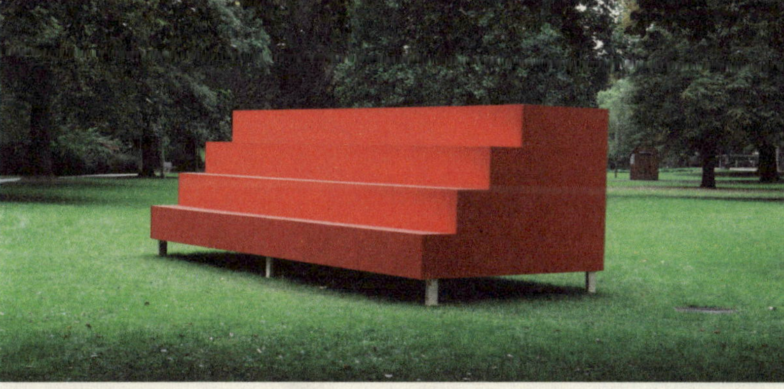

4.

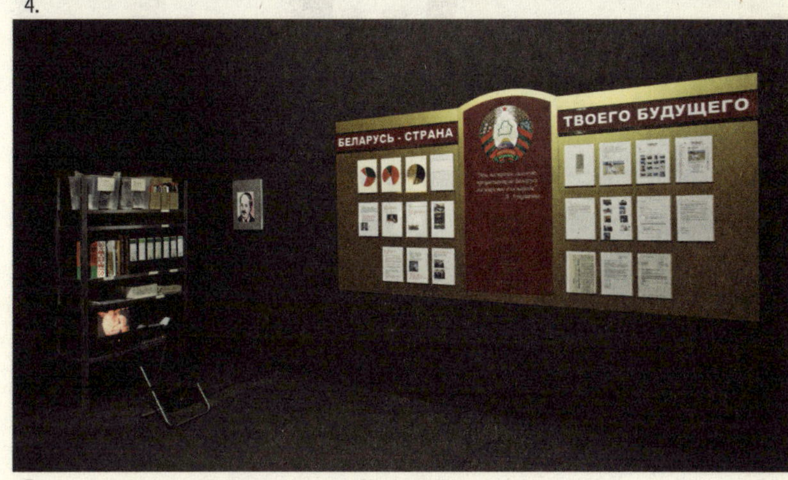

5.

3. We are Belarus!
2007, print, $8\frac{1}{4} \times 11\frac{1}{2}$ ft (20 × 35 m)

4. The president's platform
2007, mixed media, $9\frac{3}{4} \times 22\frac{3}{4} \times 6\frac{1}{2}$ in (30 × 70 × 20 cm)

5. Office for Anti-Propaganda
2004-08, mixed media, dimensions variable

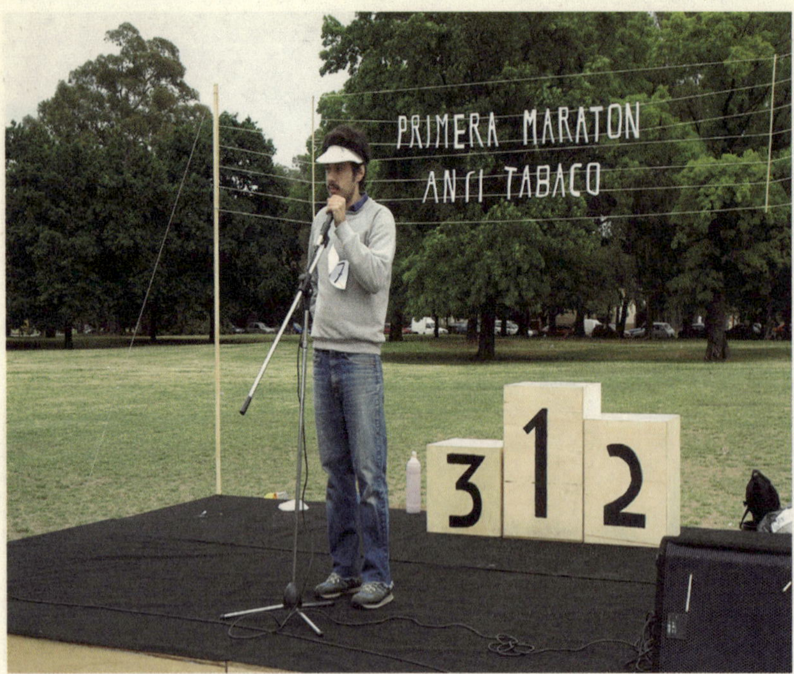

1.

Making use of his architectural training, Eduardo Navarro constructs or repurposes buildings in order to generate creative and developmental opportunities that he shares with specific social groups, such as Mormons or former prisoners, whose self-image may be at odds with their popular identity. Navarro, who lives and works in Buenos Aires, also maintains a prolific improvisational drawing practice.

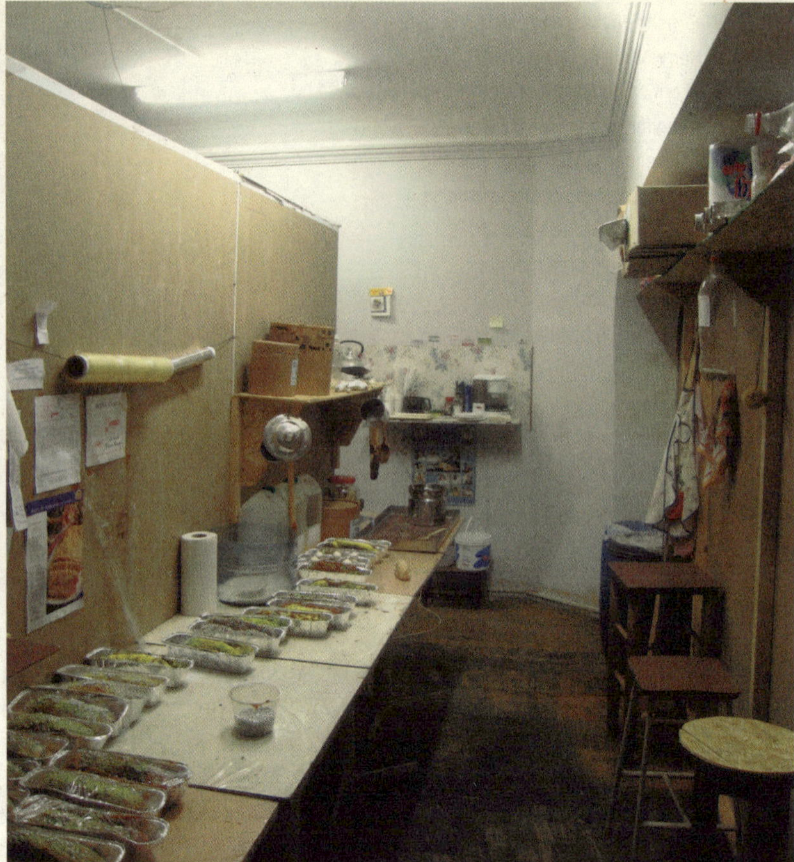

2.

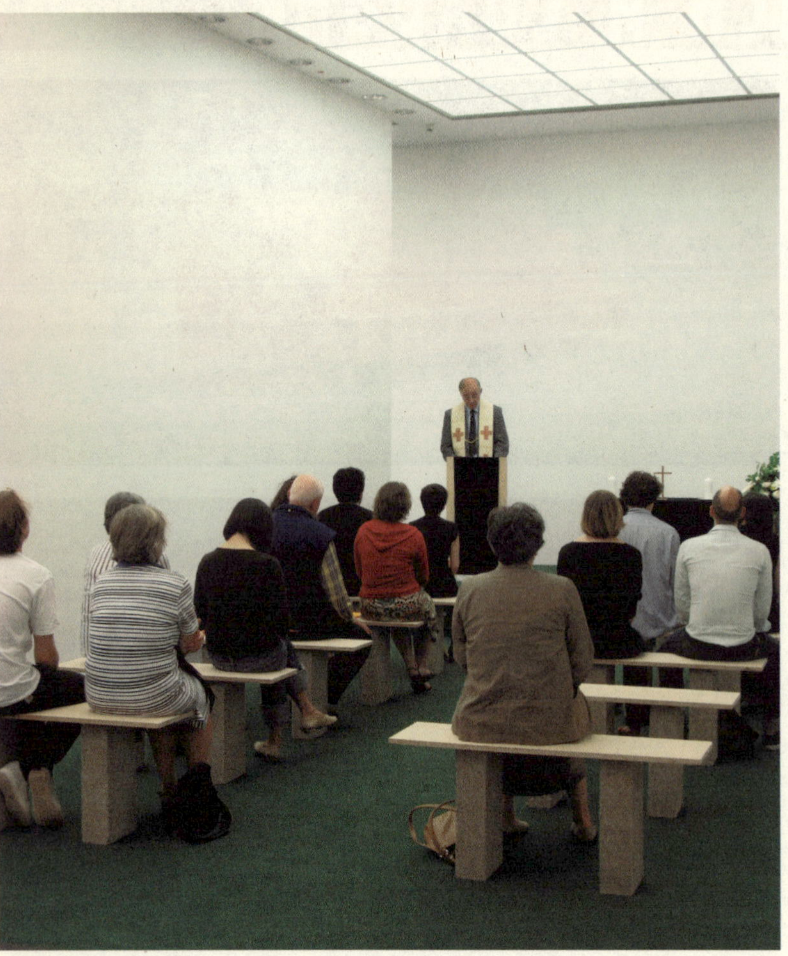

3.

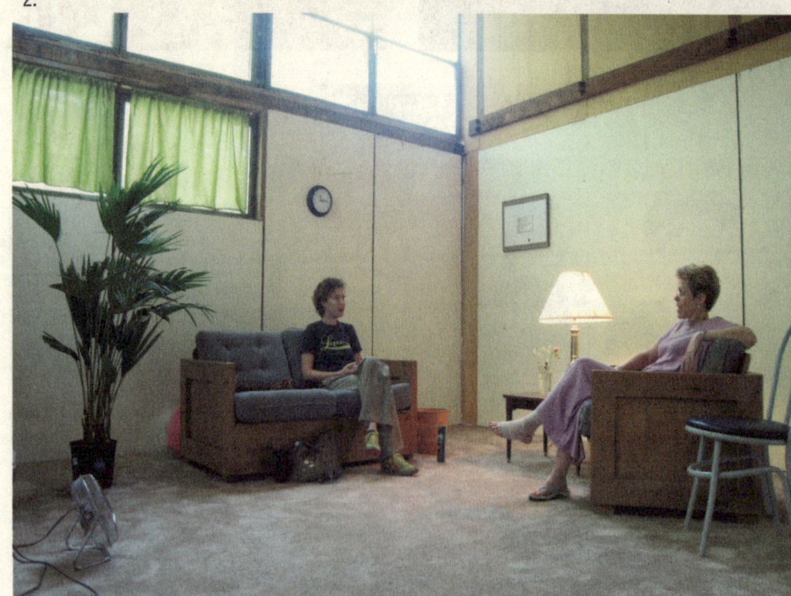

4.

1. Primer Maraton Antitabaco (detail)
2005, stage, helium balloons, red cross, two 12-foot cigarettes, 400 water bottles, and sound PA

2. Fabricantes Unidos
2008, decoration and packaging area of Clandestine Pudding Factory, 150 × 150 ft (14 × 14 m), installed on first floor of a black-market shopping mall

3. Art Center Chapel
2008, carpet, bricks, altar, candles, cross, flowers, and fabric, 30 × 9 ft (914 × 274 cm)

4. Colleagues
2006, artist's studio converted to counseling office, student's therapy sessions paid for with artwork

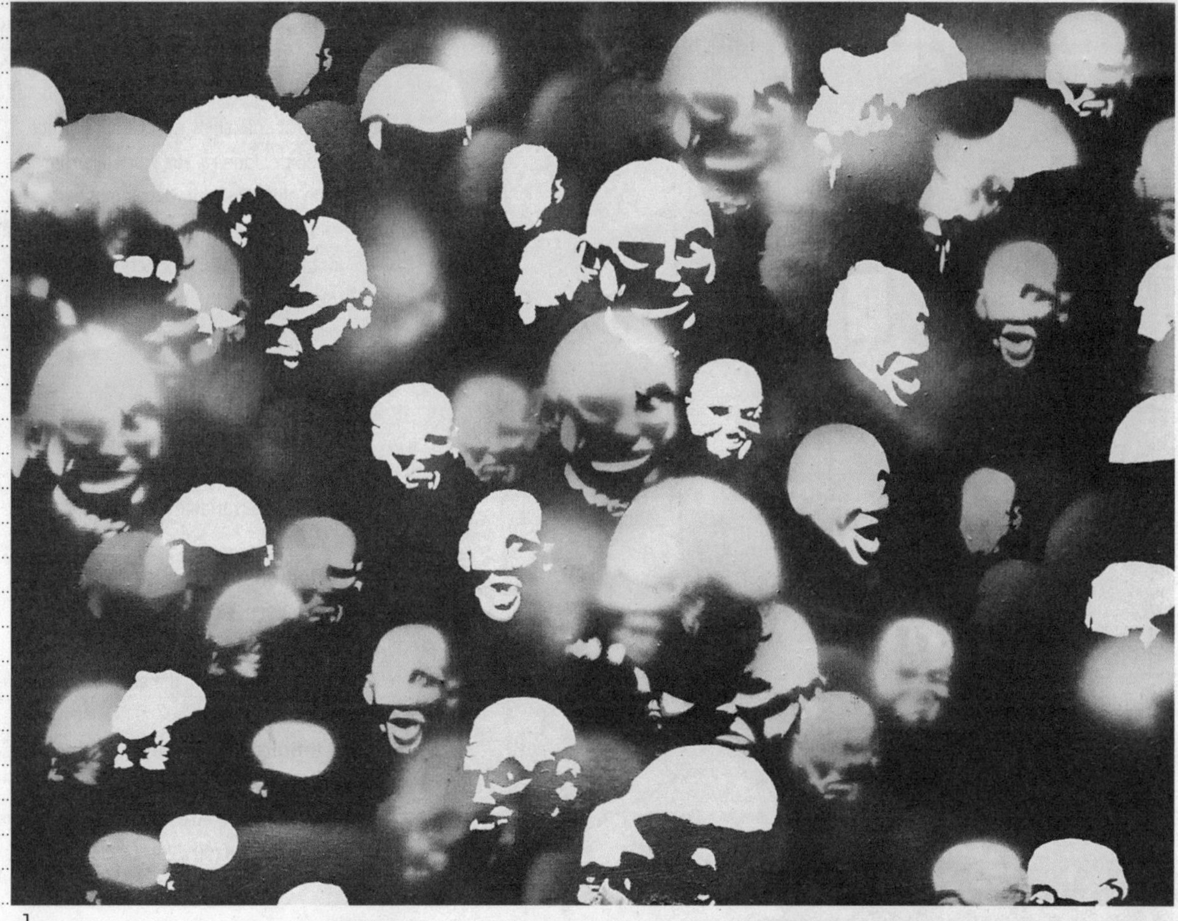

1.

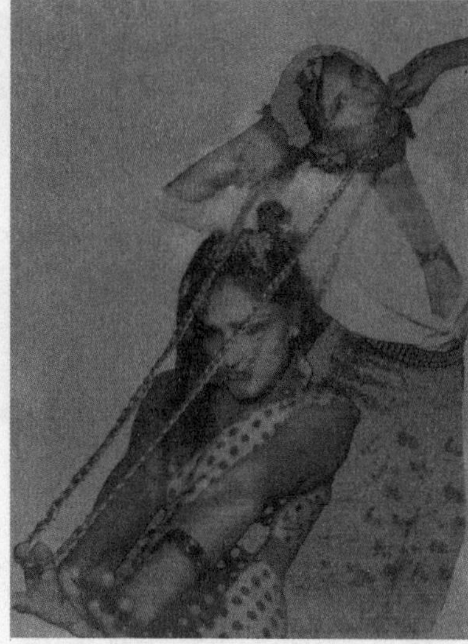

2.

In her performances and images, Natalie Nebieridze presents strong, complex images of women. She is also interested in remaking iconic works by other artists, giving them a slant that both refreshes their original intent and reflects her own interests and attitudes. Restaging Oleg Kulik's infamous animal imitation, for example, she played the part of a studio cat instead of Kulik's snarling dog.

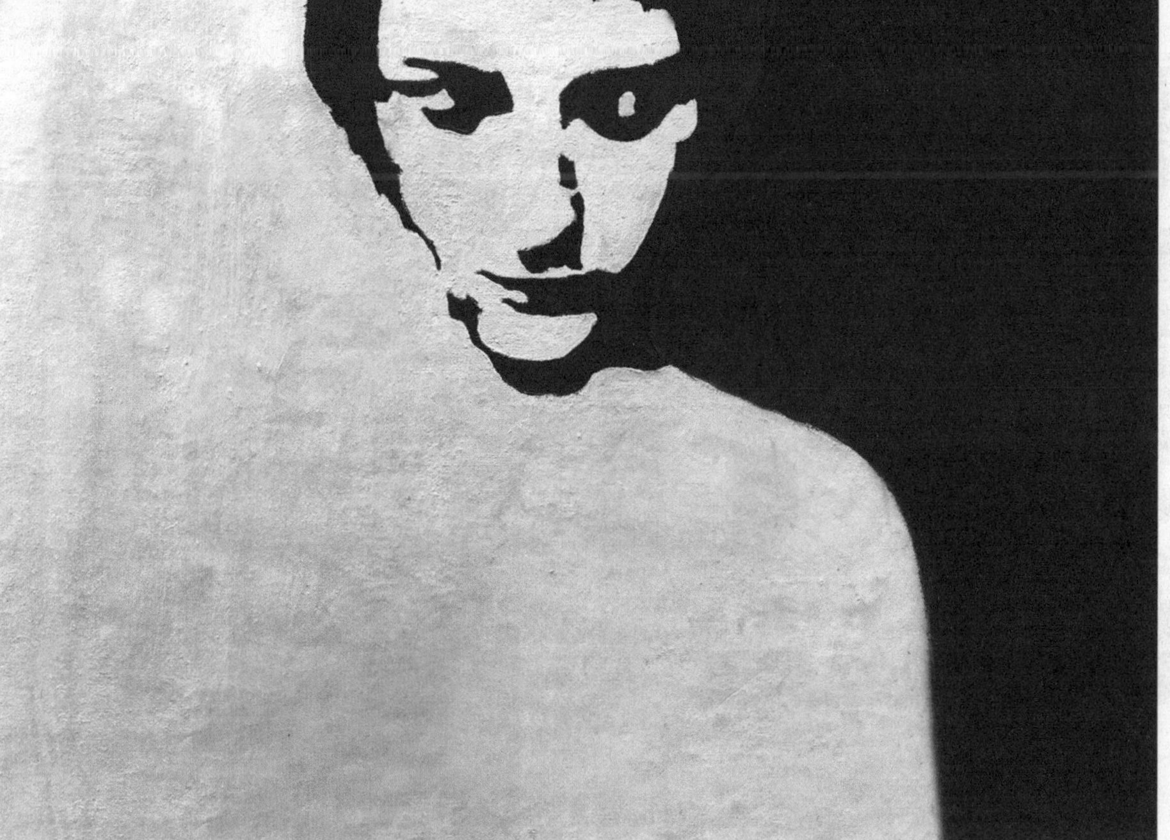
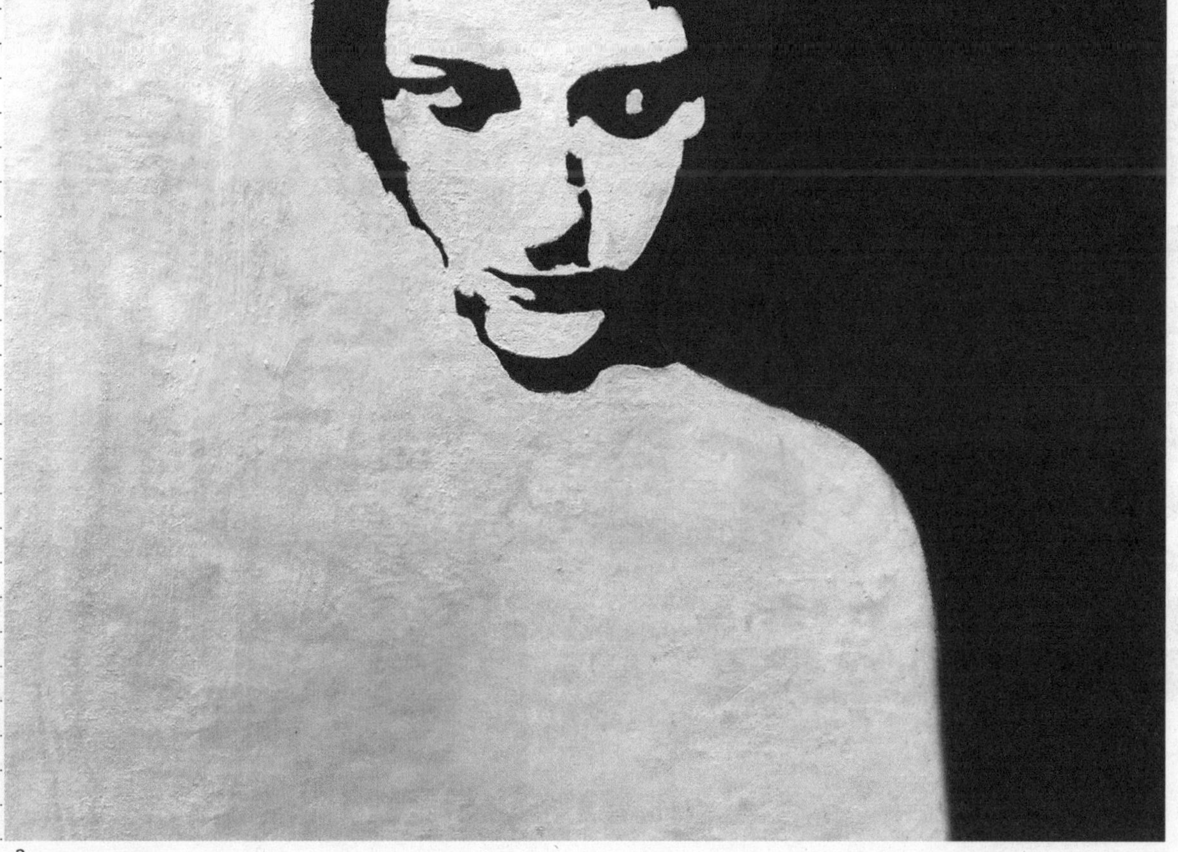

3.

1. **Snow White**
2008, oil on canvas, 23 ½ × 31 ½ in
(60 × 80 cm)

2. **Icon**
2008, print on paper, 11 × 8 ¼ in
(28 × 21 cm)

3. **Self-Portrait**
2008, oil on canvas, 17 ¾ × 23 ½ in
(45 × 60 cm)

NENFLIDIO, PAULO

b. 1976 San Bernardo do Campo, Brazil

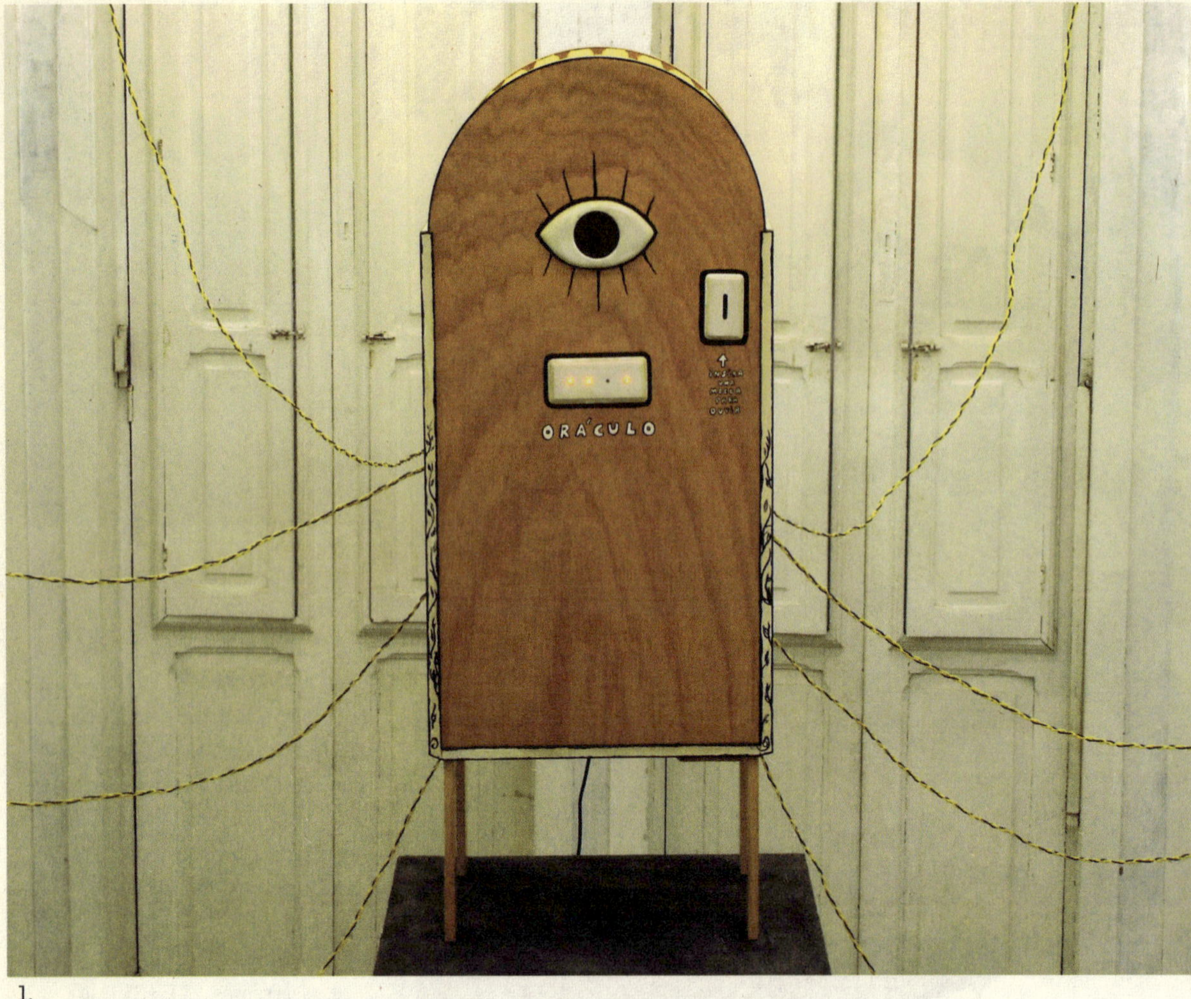

1.

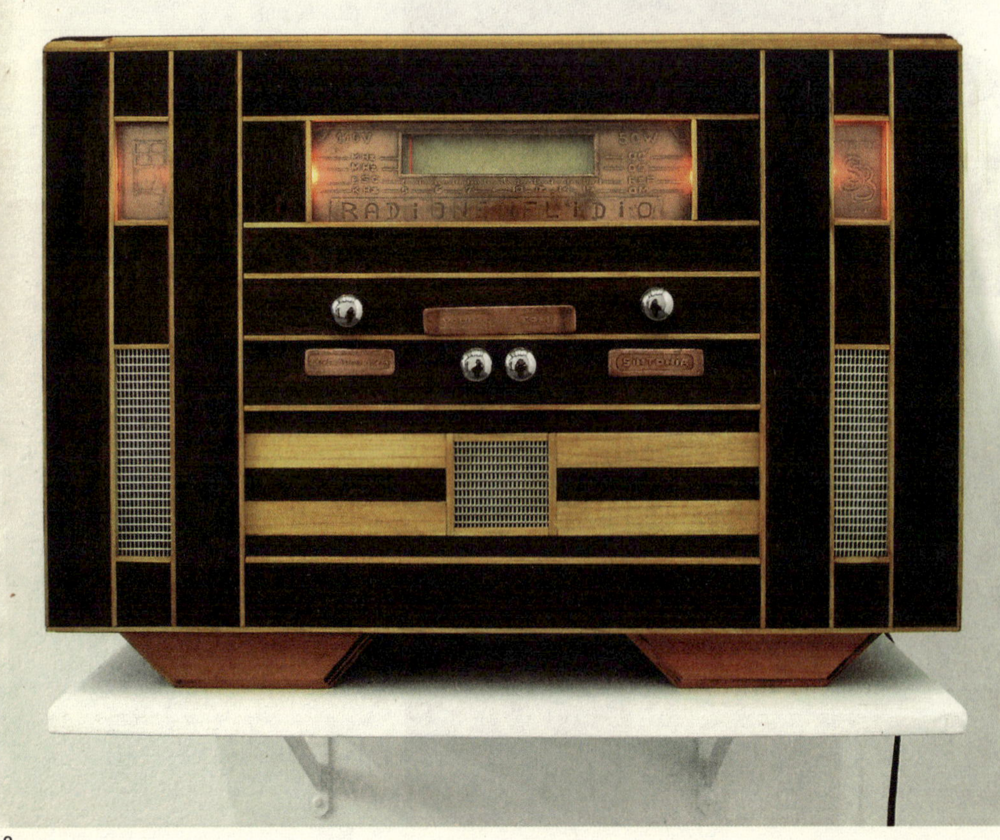

2.

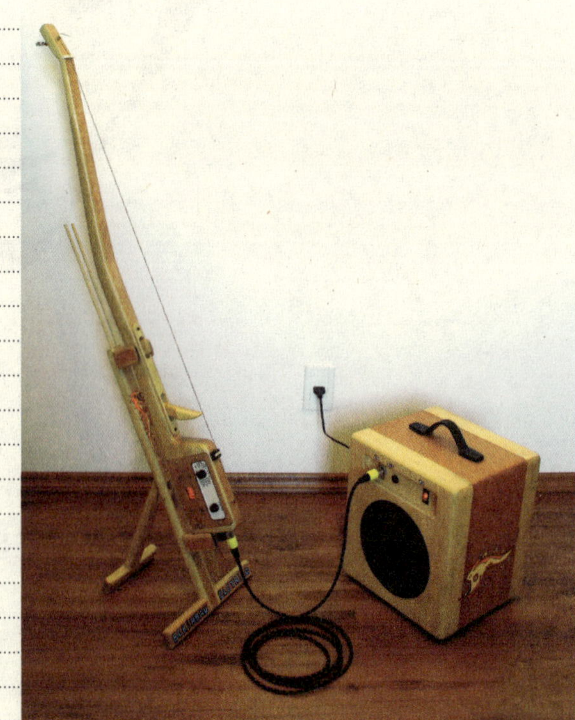

3.

Paulo Nenflidio is a sound artist who also works in sculpture and drawing. In 2005, he won the Sergio Motta Award and had his first solo show at A Gentil Carioca in Rio de Janeiro. His work incorporates such objects as bicycles, amplifiers, and radios, transforming them into sculptural installations. His "gadgets," as he calls them, explore the relationships between art, music, and technology.

1. **Oraculo**
2007, wood, speaker wire, electronic circuits, and MP3 audio players, dimensions variable

2. **Radionenflidio**
2005, wood, electronic circuits, copper board, lightbulbs, CD/MP3 player, MP3 files, and amplifier, dimensions variable

3. **Infinite Monochord** (detail)
2008, wood, electronic circuits, steel rope, bobbin, eletromagnet, and cloth, 35 ½ × 7 × 6 in (90 × 20 × 15 cm)

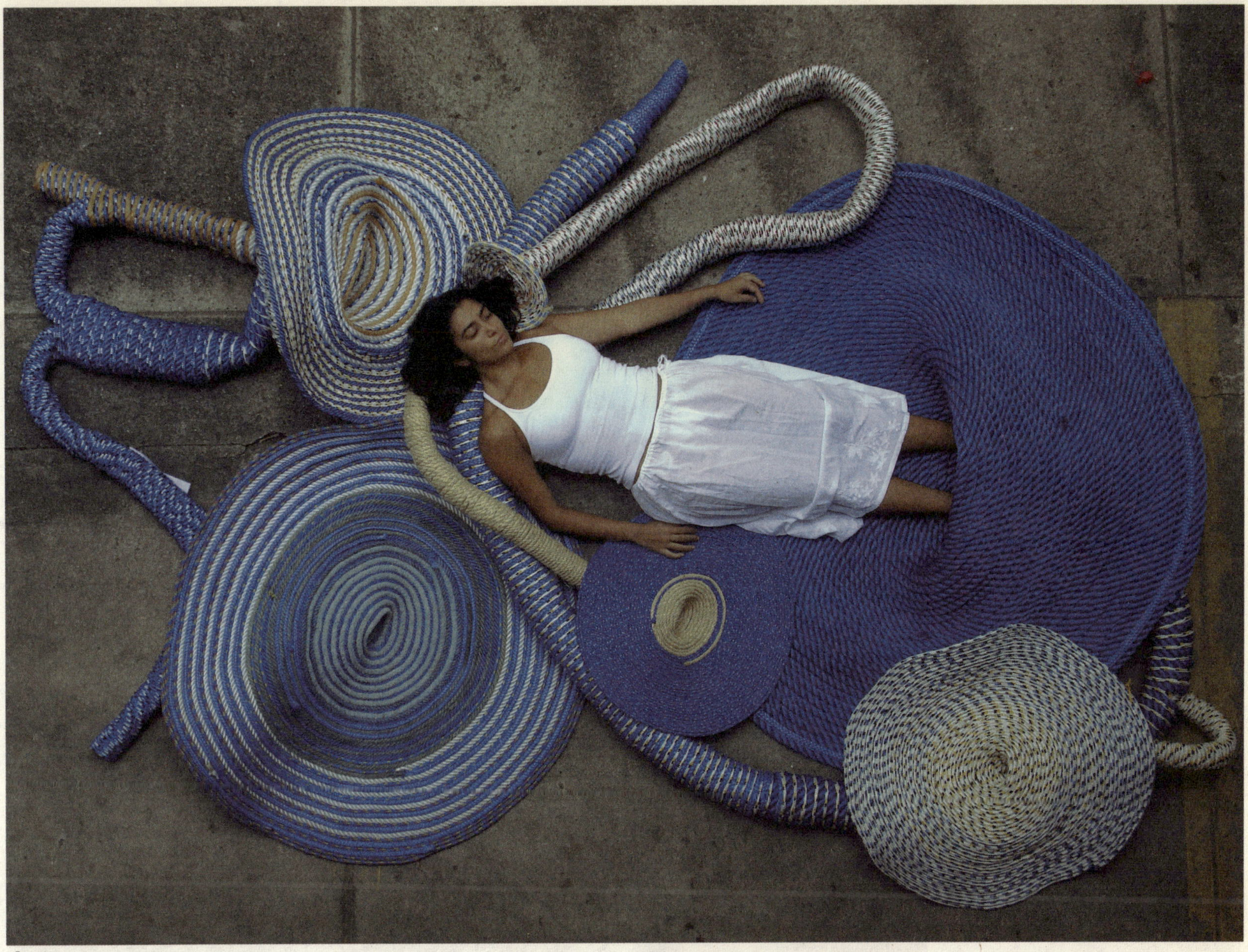

1.

Maria Nepomuceno was educated at the Parque Laje School of Visual Arts, the Faculdade da Cidade, and the Universidade do Rio de Janeiro, Brazil. Her biomorphic sculptures are rooted strongly in the crafts tradition and are painstakingly constructed from rope, beads, and, more recently, braided straw. She describes them as "primitive organisms that suck in air and emit vibrations that expand into the great imaginary sound of Ohm, the sound of the universe." She was the subject of a solo show at the Paço das Artes in São Paulo, Brazil.

1. **Superflux 2**
2007, sewn ropes, $101\frac{1}{2} \times 62\frac{1}{2}$ ft (31 × 19 m)

2. **Untitled** (detail)
2007, sewn ropes, dimensions variable

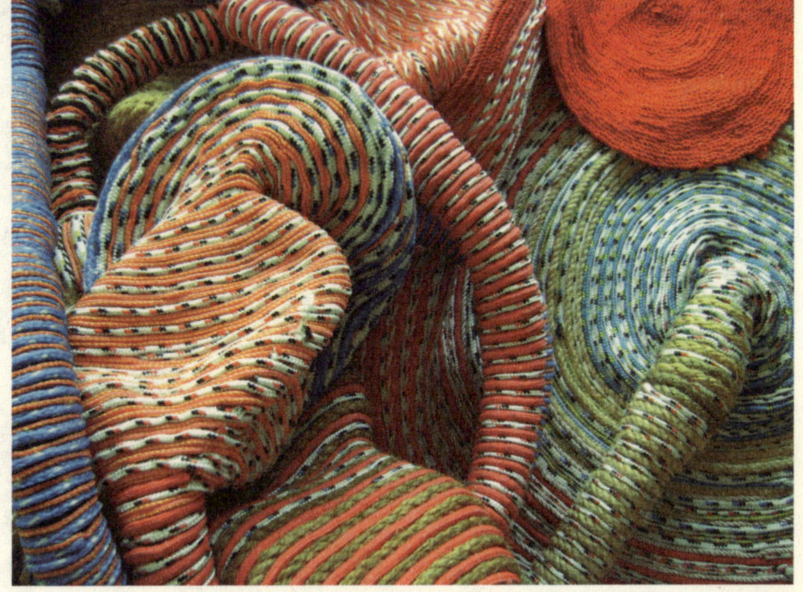

2.

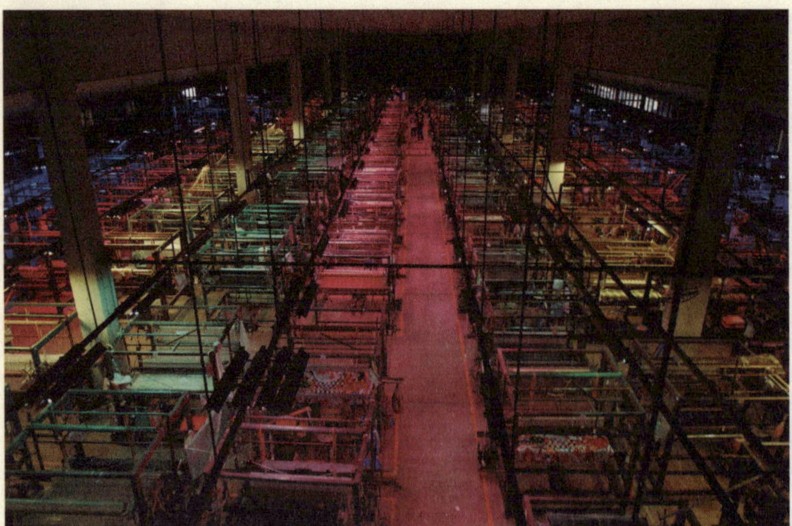
1.

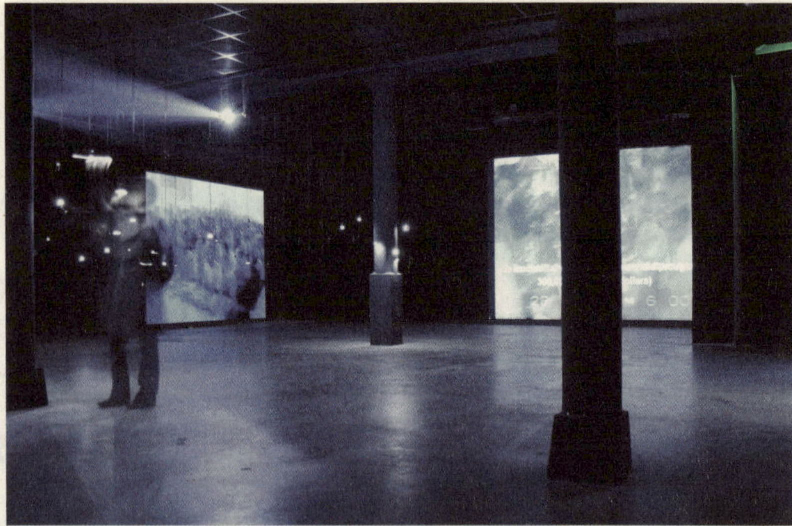
2.

Jakrawal Nilthamrong was educated at Silpakorn University in Bangkok, Thailand, and the Pratt Institute in New York, and he holds an MFA from the School of the Art Institute of Chicago. He has exhibited his films in both art galleries and film festivals since 2002. His video **Dripping** (2004) won a prize at the 10th Thai Short Film and Video Festival in Bangkok (2006), and in 2007 he was selected to be an artist in residence at the Rijksakademie in Amsterdam.

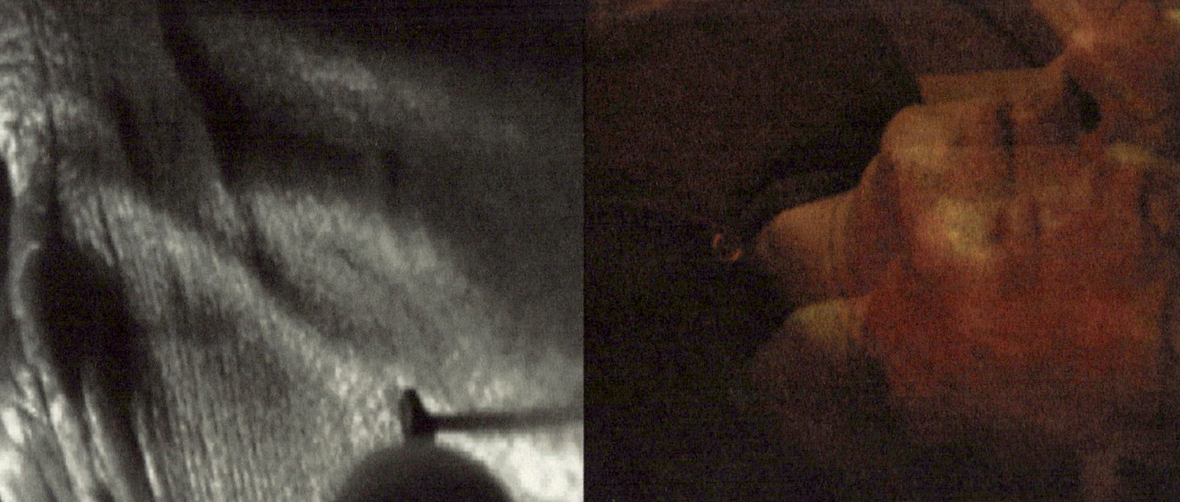
3.

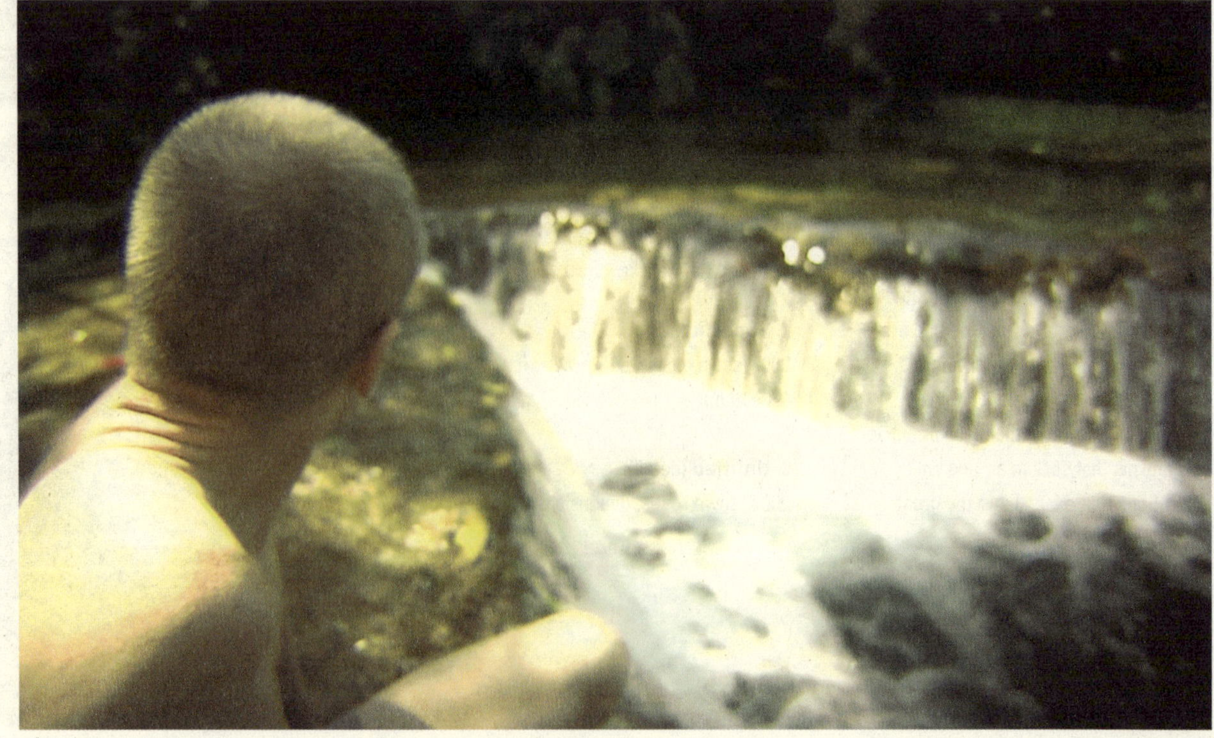
4.

1. **Orchestra**
2008, video, 30 min

2. **Pimpaka Towira, Akritchalerm Kalayanamitr and Koichi Shimizu, Black Air**
2007, interactive 6-channel video projection with control buttons

3. **Dripping**
2004, video, 8 min

4. **A Voyage of Foreteller (Pilot'07)**
2007, video, 7 min

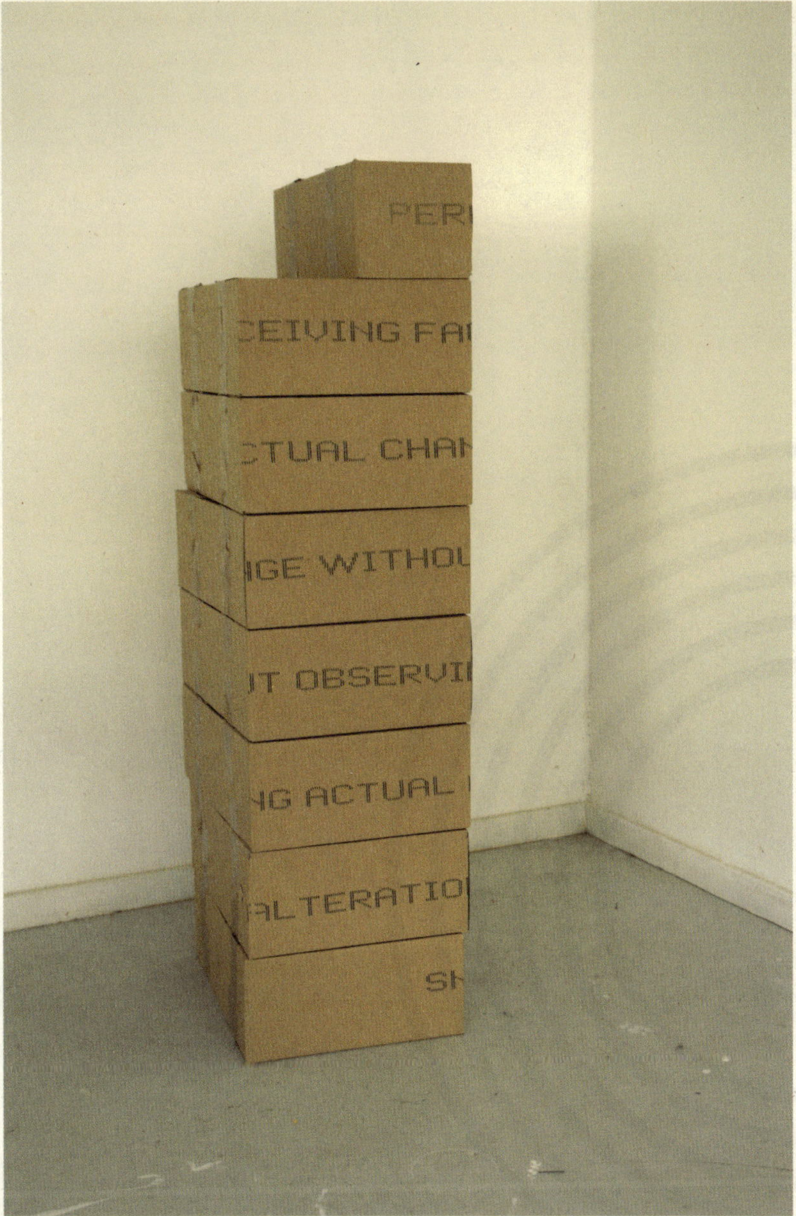

1.

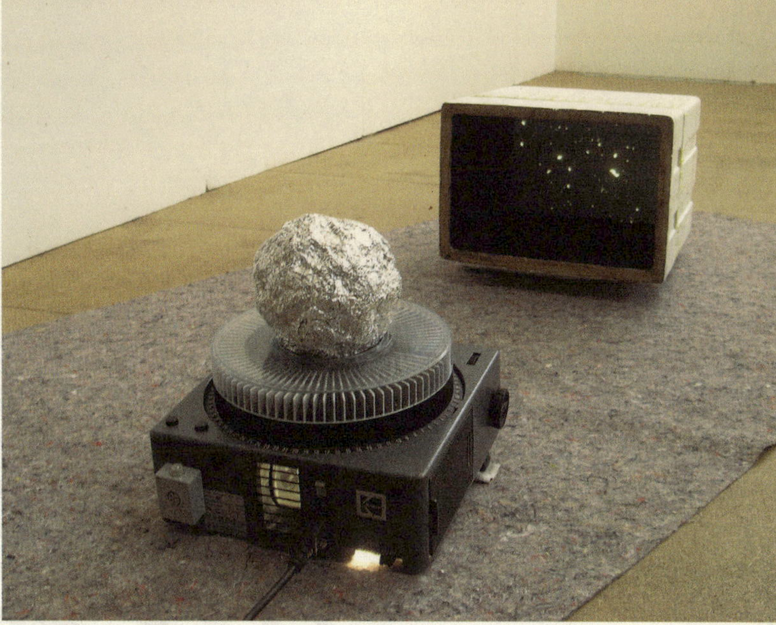

3.

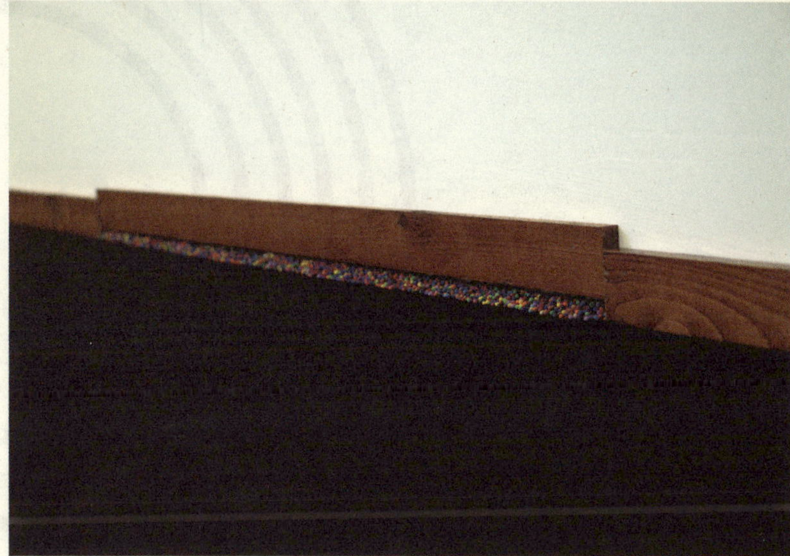

4.

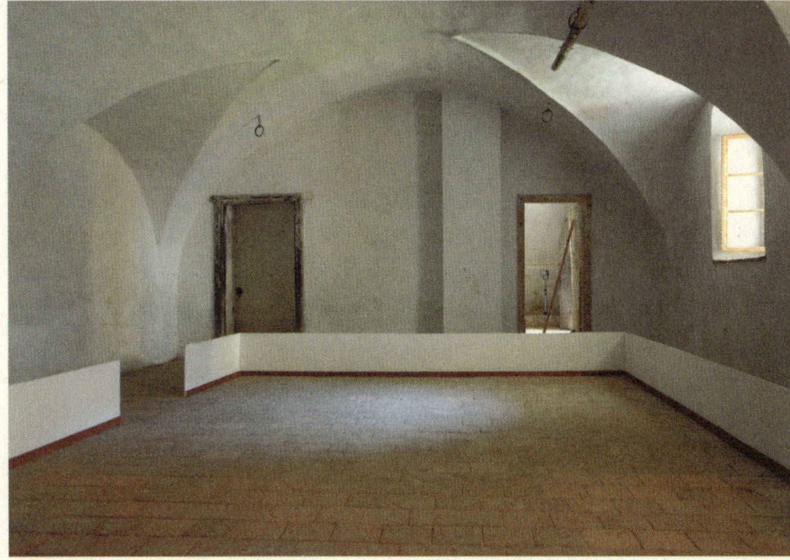

2.

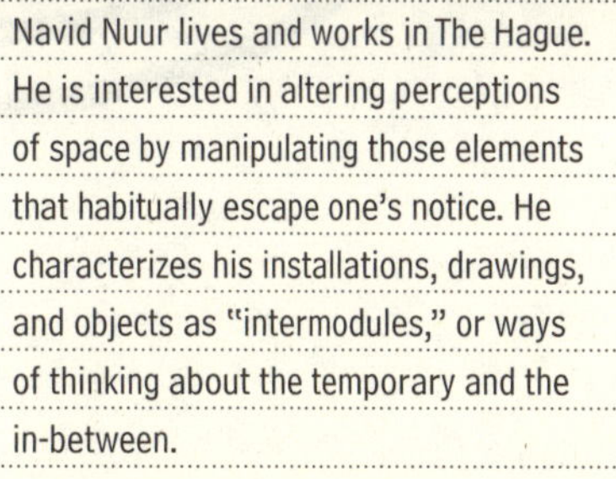

Navid Nuur lives and works in The Hague. He is interested in altering perceptions of space by manipulating those elements that habitually escape one's notice. He characterizes his installations, drawings, and objects as "intermodules," or ways of thinking about the temporary and the in-between.

1. Untitled

2007, custom-printed cardboard boxes and tape, 55 × 31 × 19 in (140 × 80 × 50 cm)

2. Room for Retreat

2005-08, baseboard and plaster, dimensions variable

3. Insidee

2008, aluminum foil, slide carousel, slides, wooden box, and carpet, 63 × 40 × 19 in (160 cm × 100 cm × 50 cm)

4. A black dark ridge found under a baseboard, stuffed with the absorbed colors, which make the ridge turn black in the first place

2005-08, baked Fimo clay, dimensions variable

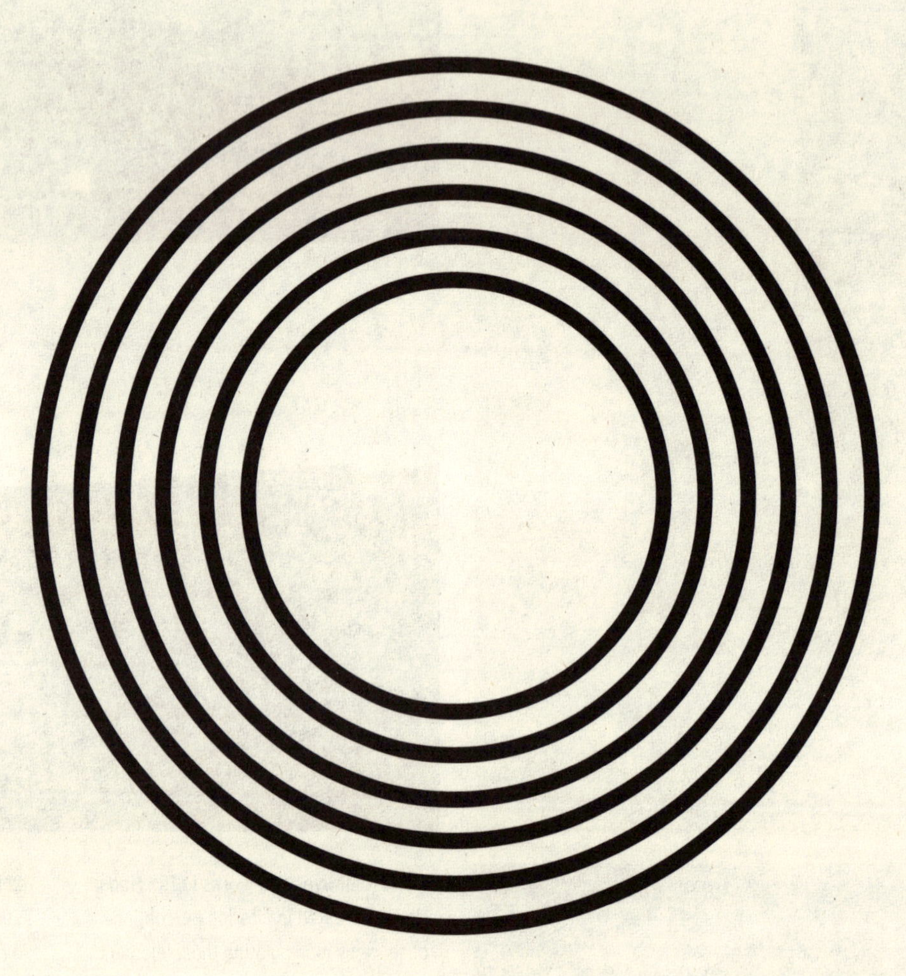

Ahmet Öğüt lives and works in Amsterdam, where he coedits the contemporary art publication **muhtelif**. He graduated with an MA in art and design from Yildiz Teknik University in Istanbul. His video and performance work evolves out of an interest in the sense of community that forms around play, and the way communities deal with conflict.

1. **Three Spots**
2007, video, 3 min 17 sec

2. **Ground Control**
2008, wall-to-wall asphalt, dimensions variable, installation at 5th Berlin Biennial

3 & 4. **Somebody Else's Car**
2005, slide projection, dimensions variable

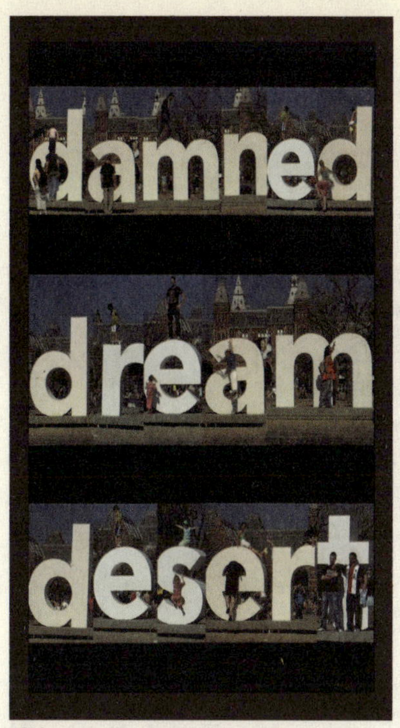

1.

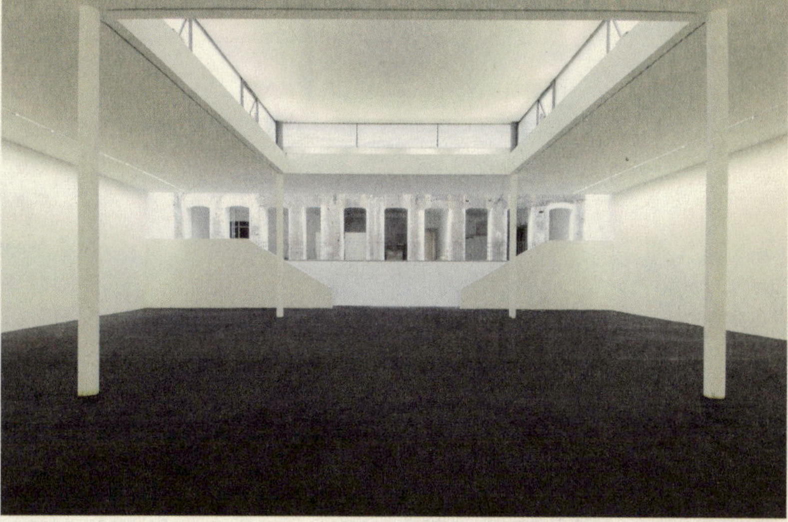
2.

5. **Light Armoured,**
2006, animation, 1 min

6. **Mutual Issues, Inventive Acts: School Memories**
2008, chromogenic print, 55 × 39 ½ in (140 × 100 cm)

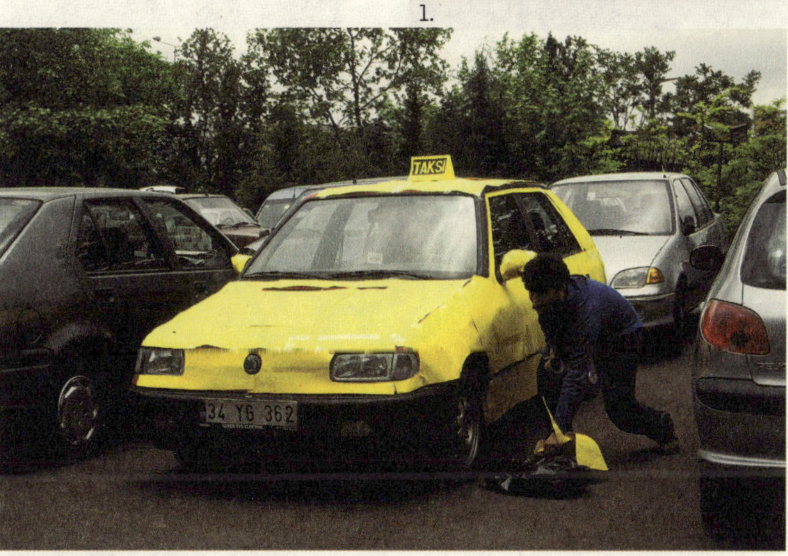

3.

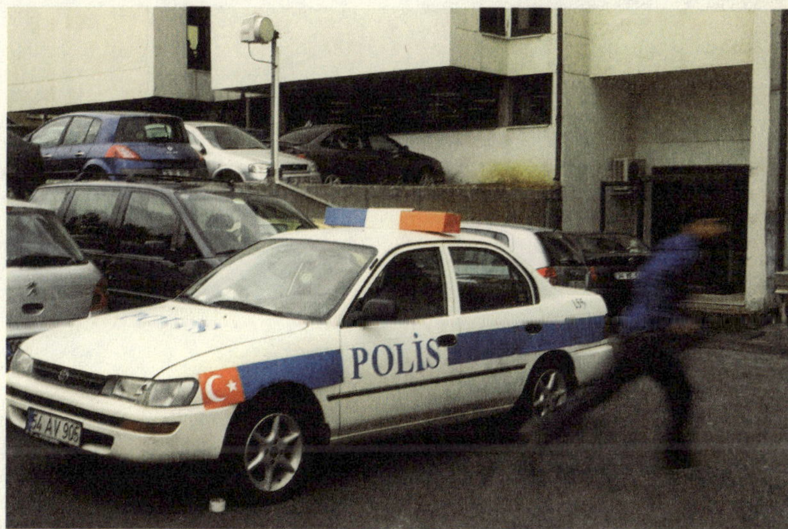

4.

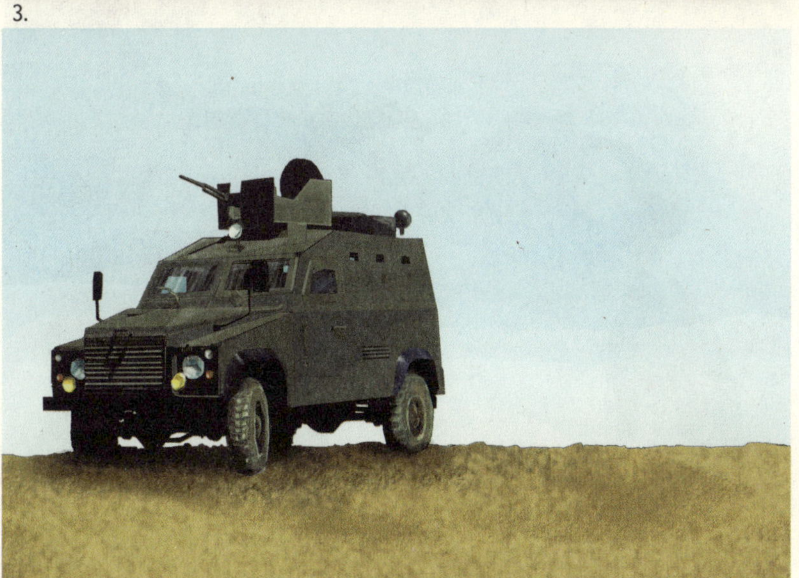
5.

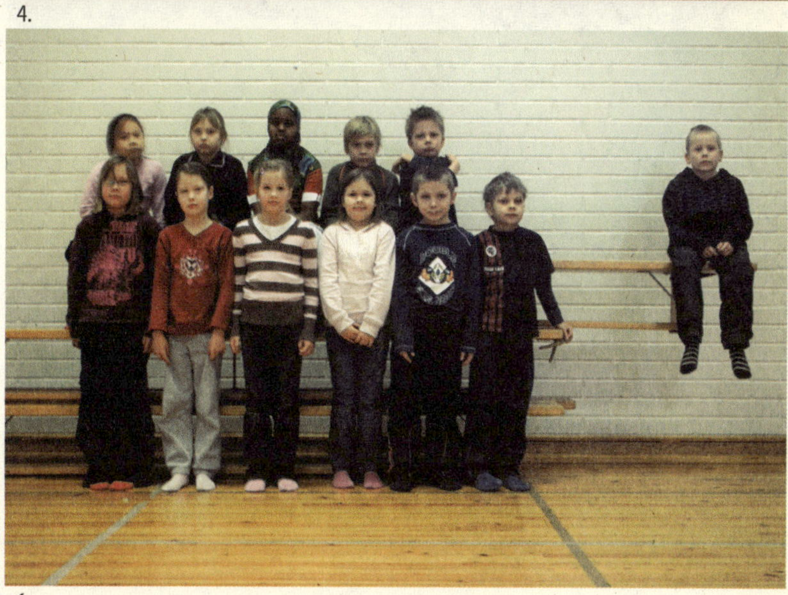
6.

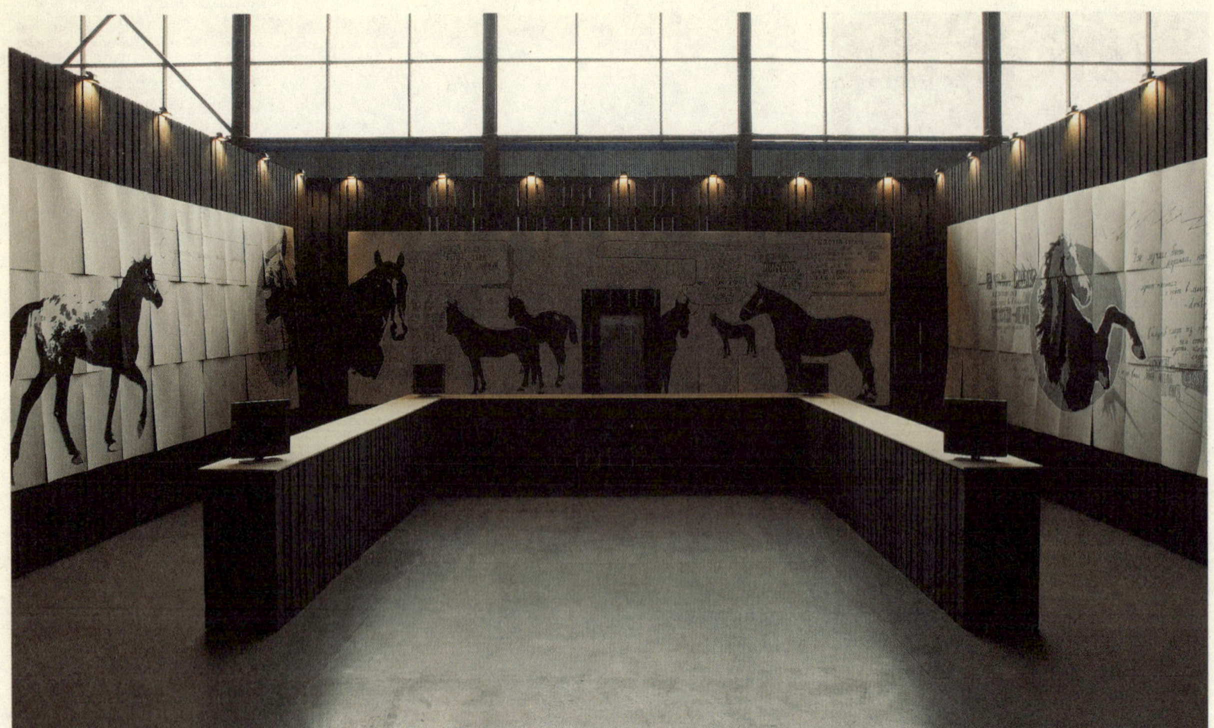

1.

In his murals and works on paper, Moscow-based Nikolay Oleynikov employs a heightened form of social realism to examine the intersection of culture and state. Employing a narrative system inspired by comic strips, Oleynikov involves viewers in an ongoing negotiation of personal and political identities.

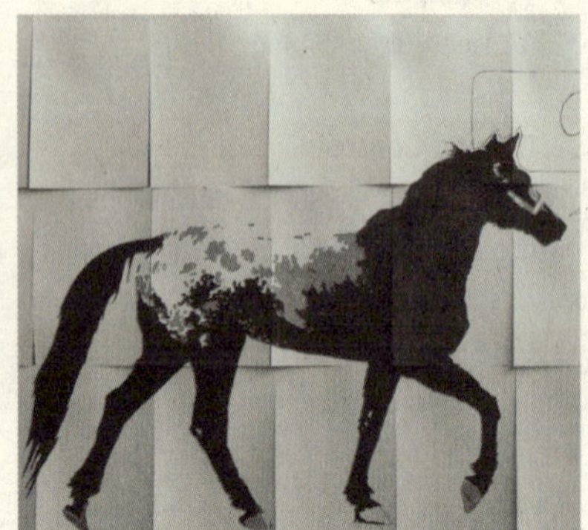

2.

3.

4.

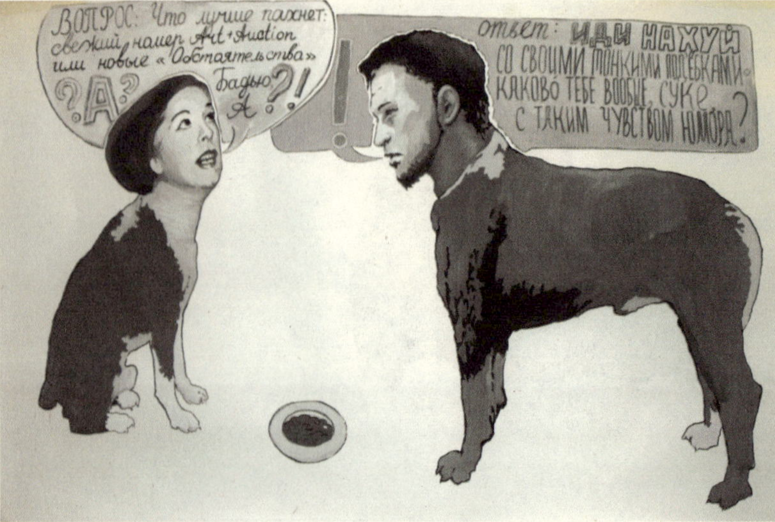

5.

1 & 2. STALL

2008, gouache on 108 sheets of cardboard, each 39 ½ × 27 ½ in (100 × 70 cm); overall dimensions 10 × 92 ft (3 × 28 m)

3. MANIFESTATION album (detail)

2007, pencil on paper, 12 × 15 ¾ in (30 × 40 cm)

4 & 5. Untitled

from the series **NOFUCKINFUNNY**

2008, gouache on paper, dimensions variable

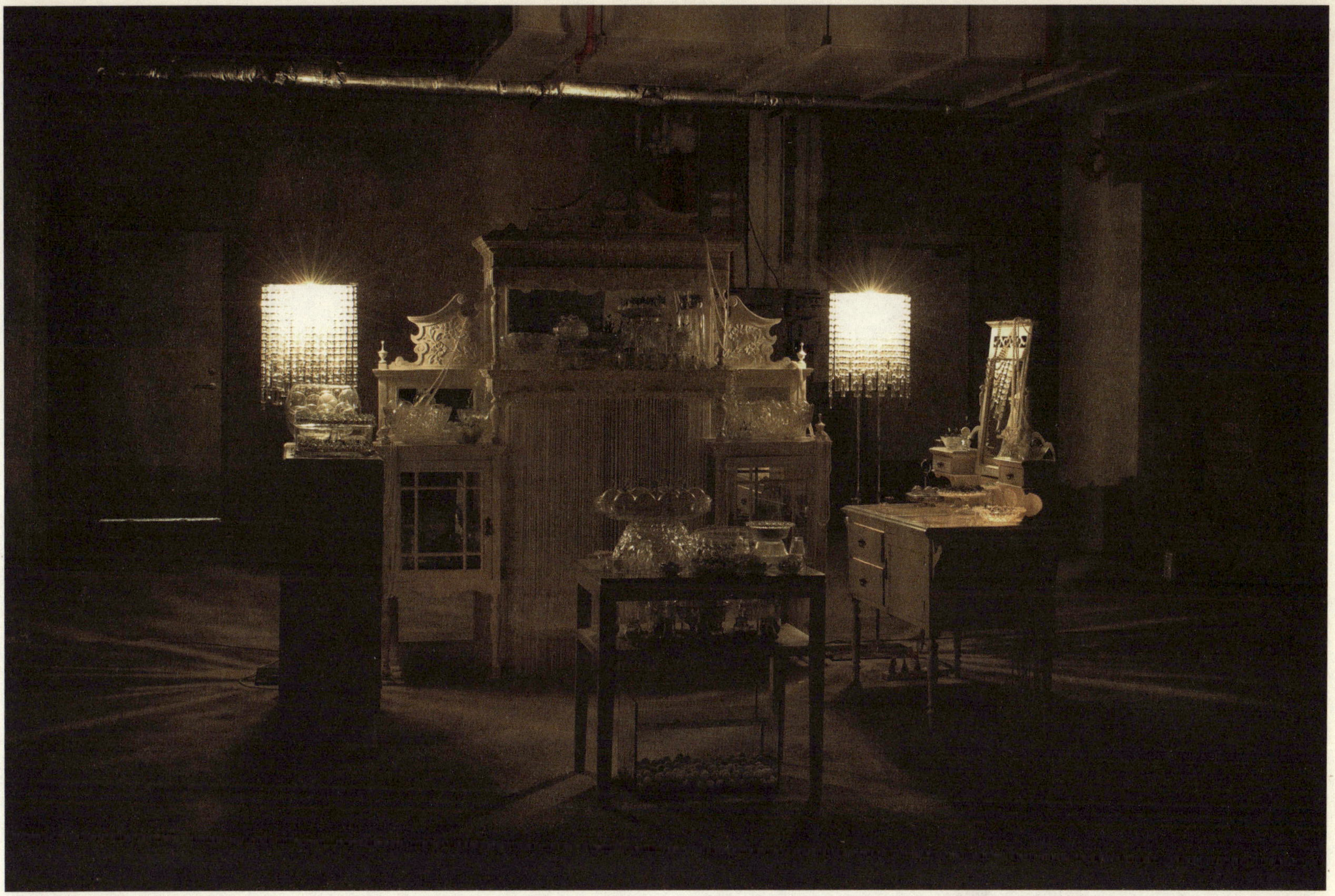

1.

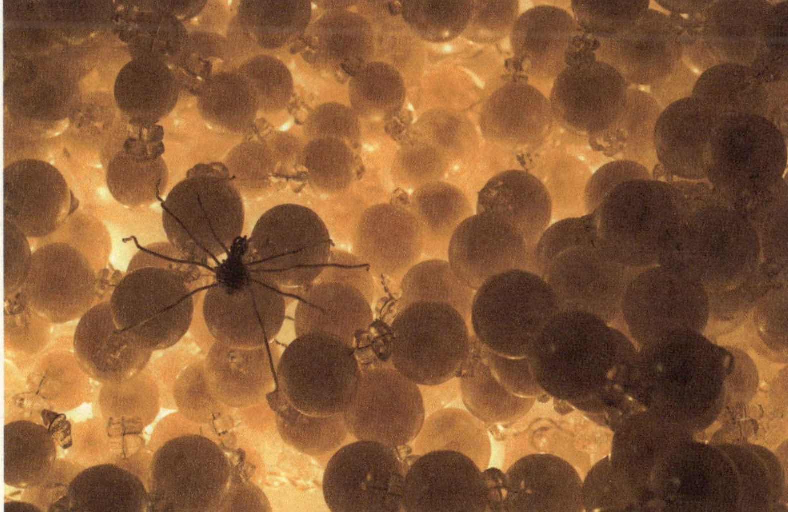

2.

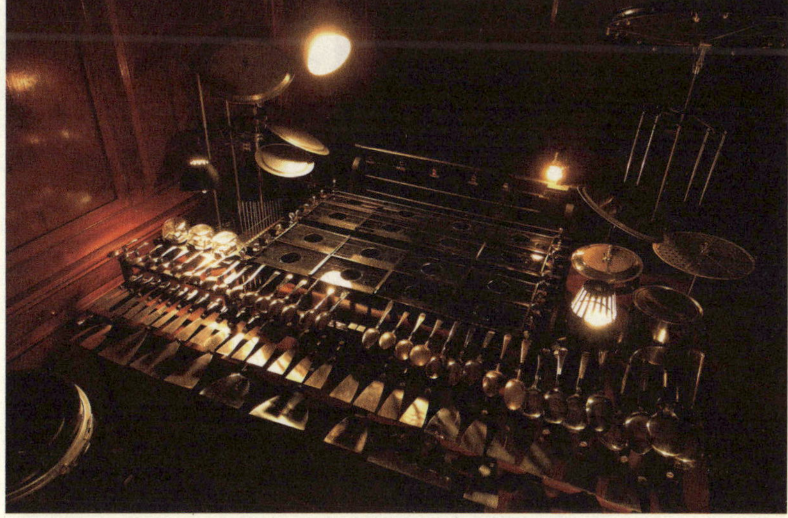

3.

Donna Ong is based in Singapore. In her elaborate sculptural installations, everyday objects are recontextualized in a reflection on the persistent nature of childhood fantasy.

1 & 2. **The Third Day** (detail)
2008, mixed media installation, dimensions variable

3. **Secret, Interiors: Chrysalis** (detail)
2006, mixed media installation, dimensions variable

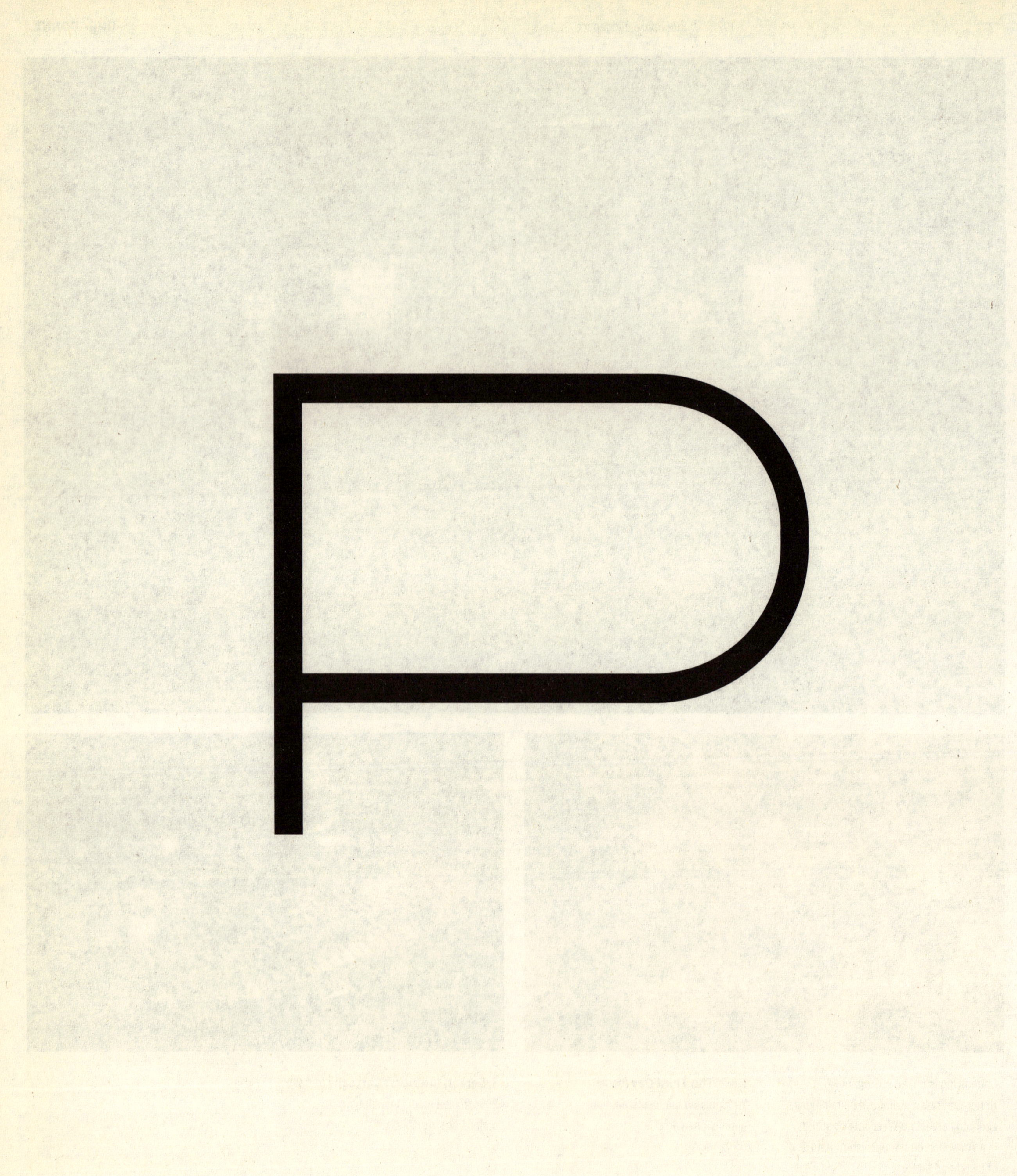

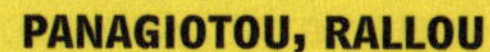

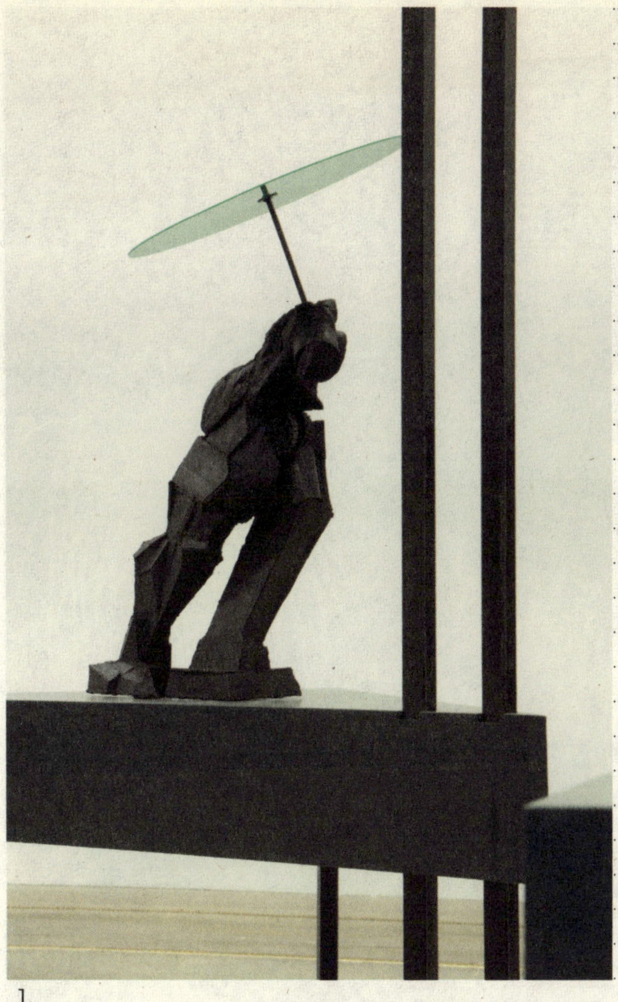

1.

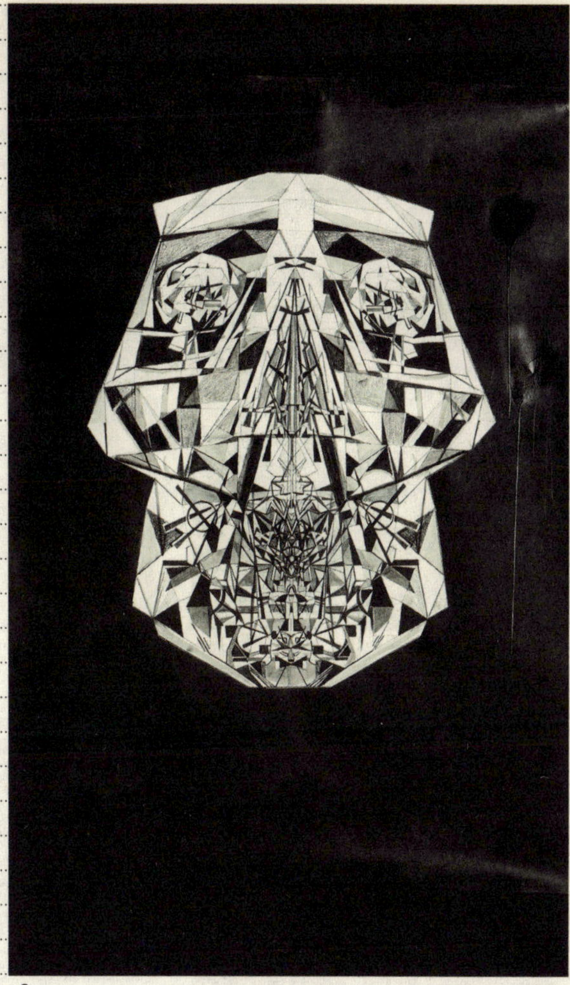

2.

Rallou Panagiotou received his MFA from the Glasgow School of Art. His sculptures and installations are explorations of psychological and historical tension. Using references as diverse as Hieronymus Bosch, Italian Futurism, and Bruce Weber, mixed with subtle injections of history and memory, Panagiotou tries to strike a balance between the past and the present, the personal and the historical. His work has been included in exhibitions at the Deste Foundation in Athens (2007) and the Glasgow School of Art (2008).

1. **KTIMA**
2008, jesmonite, wood, metal, Plexiglas, and porcelain, $101\frac{3}{4}$ × 59 × 48 in (258 ×148 × 122 cm)

2. **Death mask I**
2007, pencil and spray paint on paper, 71 × 59 in (180 × 150 cm)

3. (back wall) **Vampiring Again,** (foreground, left and center) **KTIMA,** (foreground, right) **We Will Fall**
2008, mixed media installation, dimensions variable

4. **The Isle of the Dead (after Arnold Boecklin)** (detail)
2007, wax, wood, paint, and framed photocopy, 70 × 52 × 52 in (170 × 133 × 133 cm)

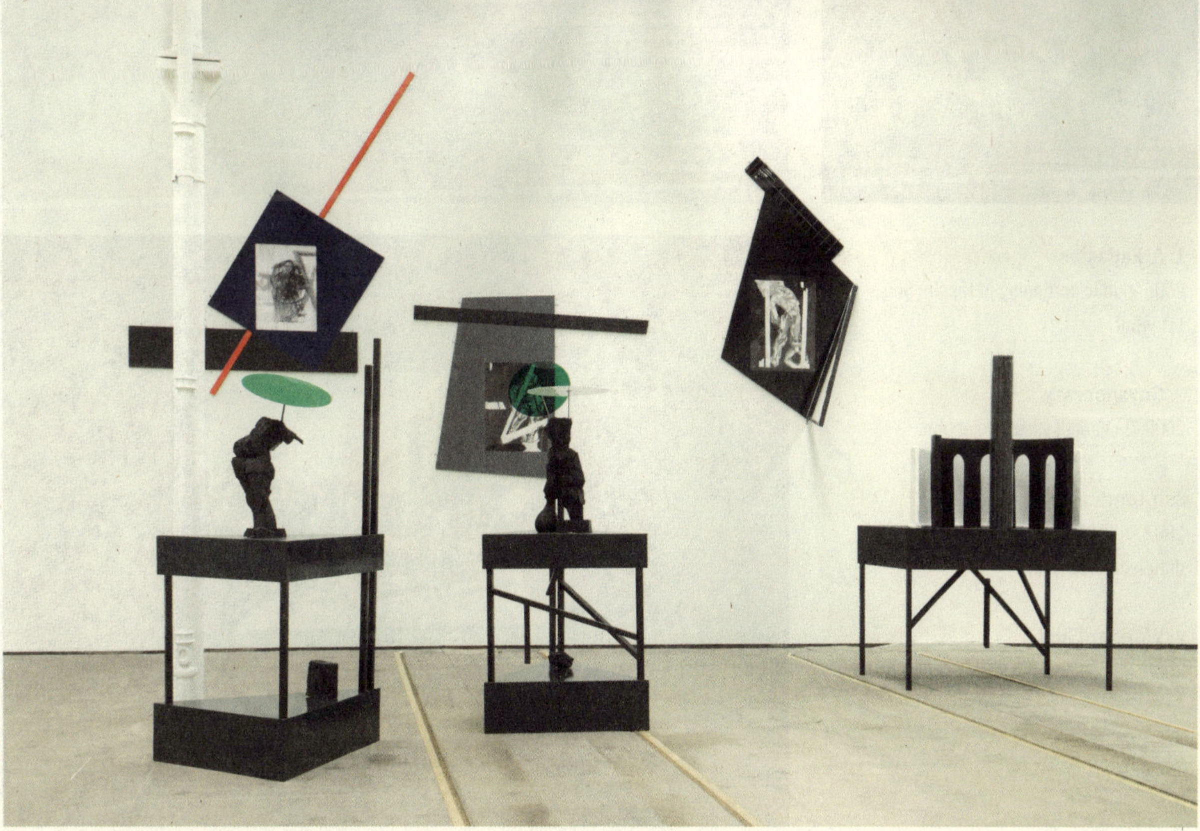

3.

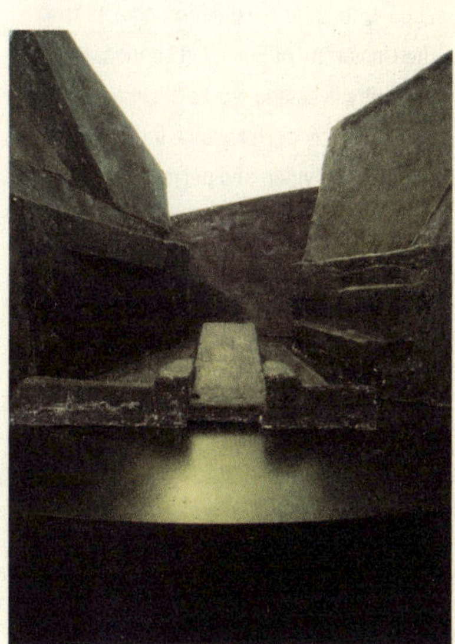

4.

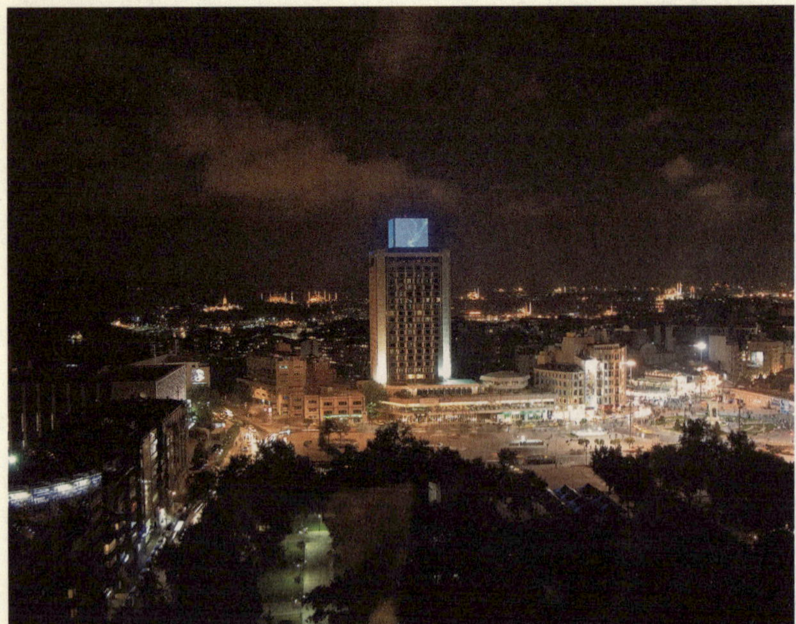

1.

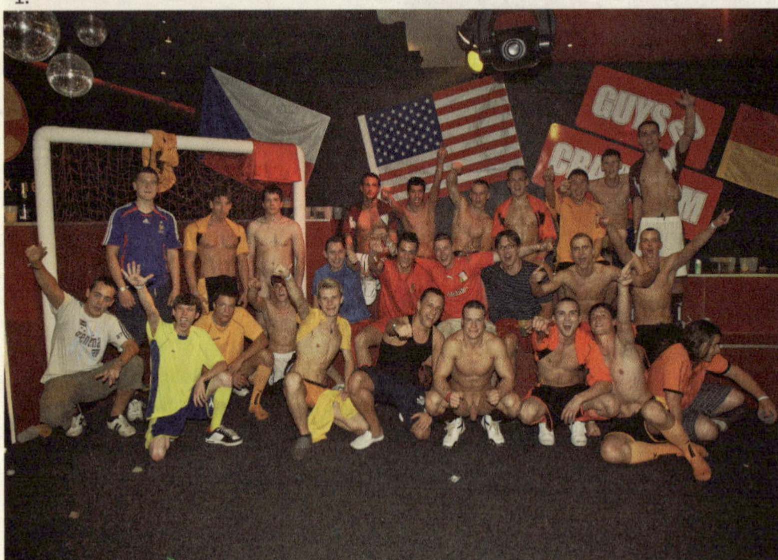

2.

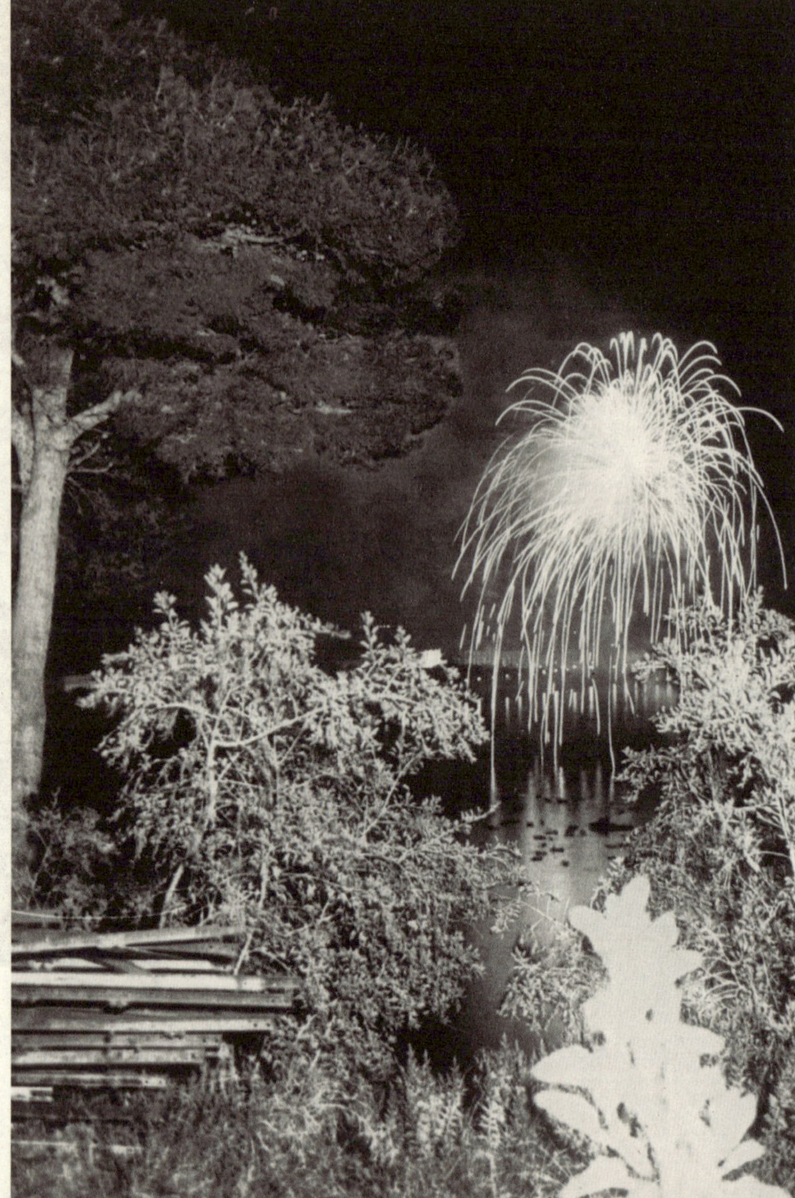

3.

Christodoulos Panayiotou graduated in 2003 with an MA in performing arts from the University of Surrey in London. He currently lives and works in Limassol. All of his work is performance based. In the ongoing video and performance **Slow Dance Marathon**, a group of people, alternating partners, dance together to well-known love songs for a full day and night, provoking a consideration of the way the participants relate to each other. Panayiotou had a solo show at the Museum of Modern Art in Oxford in 2006.

1. **Arkadaşlar**
2006, public screening in Taksim Square, Istanbul

2. **Guysgocrazy**
2008, 2-channel video projection

3. **if tomorrow never comes**
2007, 1 of 27 black and white slides, dimensions variable

4. **Wonder Land**
2008, 80 color slides, dimensions variable

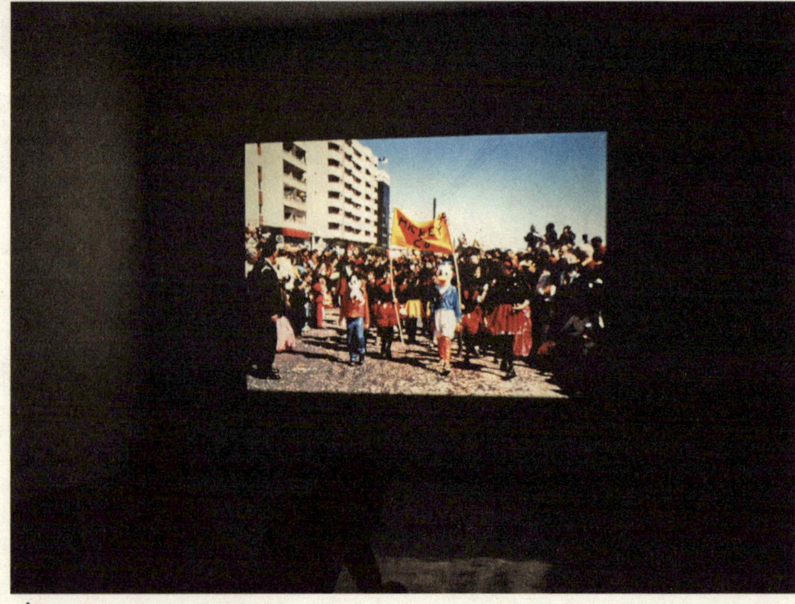

4.

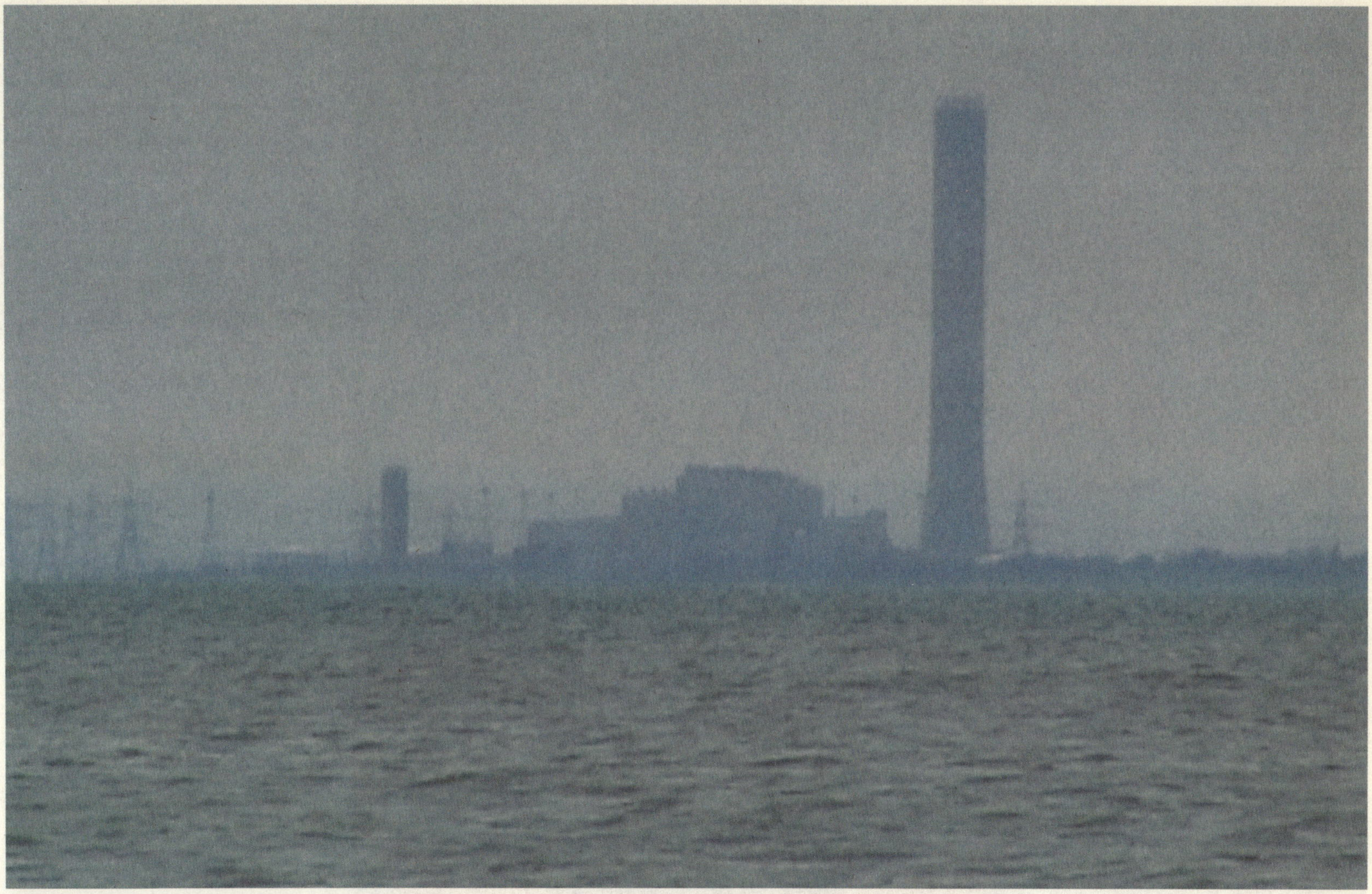

1.

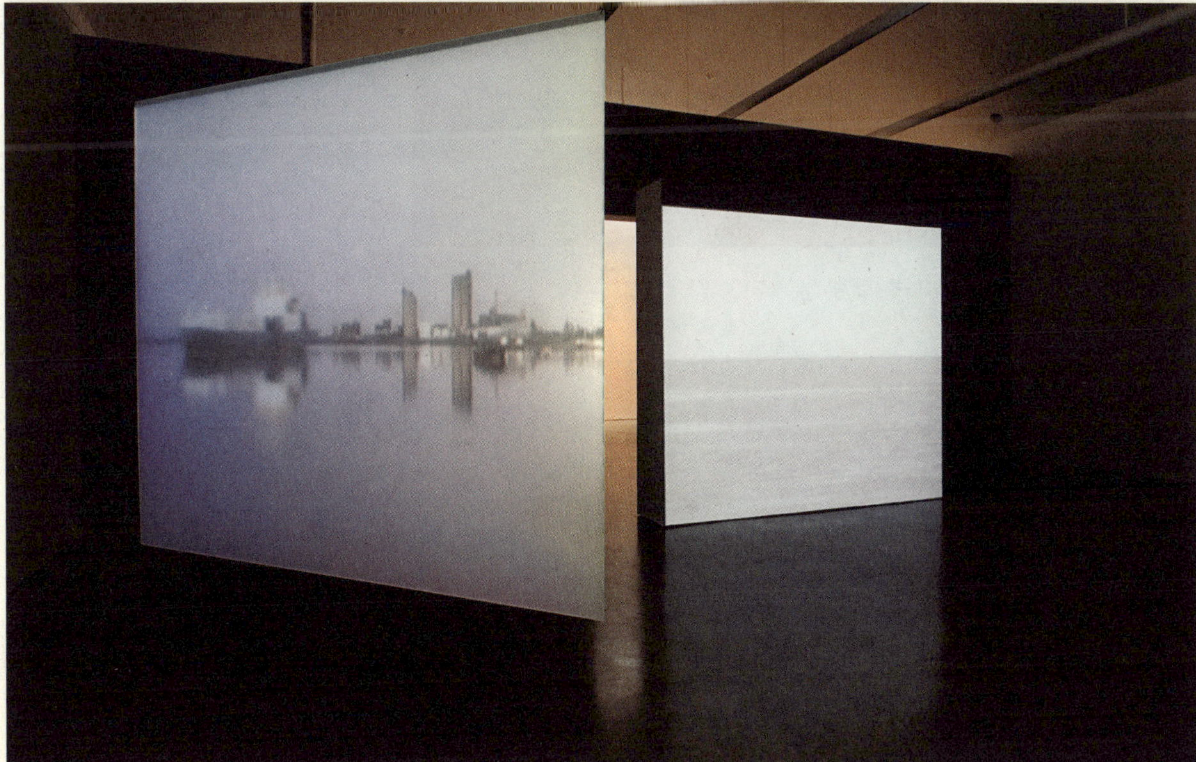

2.

Gemma Pardo received her MA in fine art from the Byam Shaw School of Art at St. Martins College, London. Her meditative, enigmatic video works treat time as a nonlinear construct, conflating historical periods in ways that problematize traditional notions of progress. Her video **Congo 1880** (2007), a slowly metamorphosing panorama of an almost featureless landscape that culminates in a view of a spectral industrial site, was selected for the Bloomberg New Contemporaries exhibition in 2007.

1 & 2 (left). **Congo 1880**
2007, video, 6 min

2. (right) **Untitled 1900**
2007, video projection, 6 min, 12 min

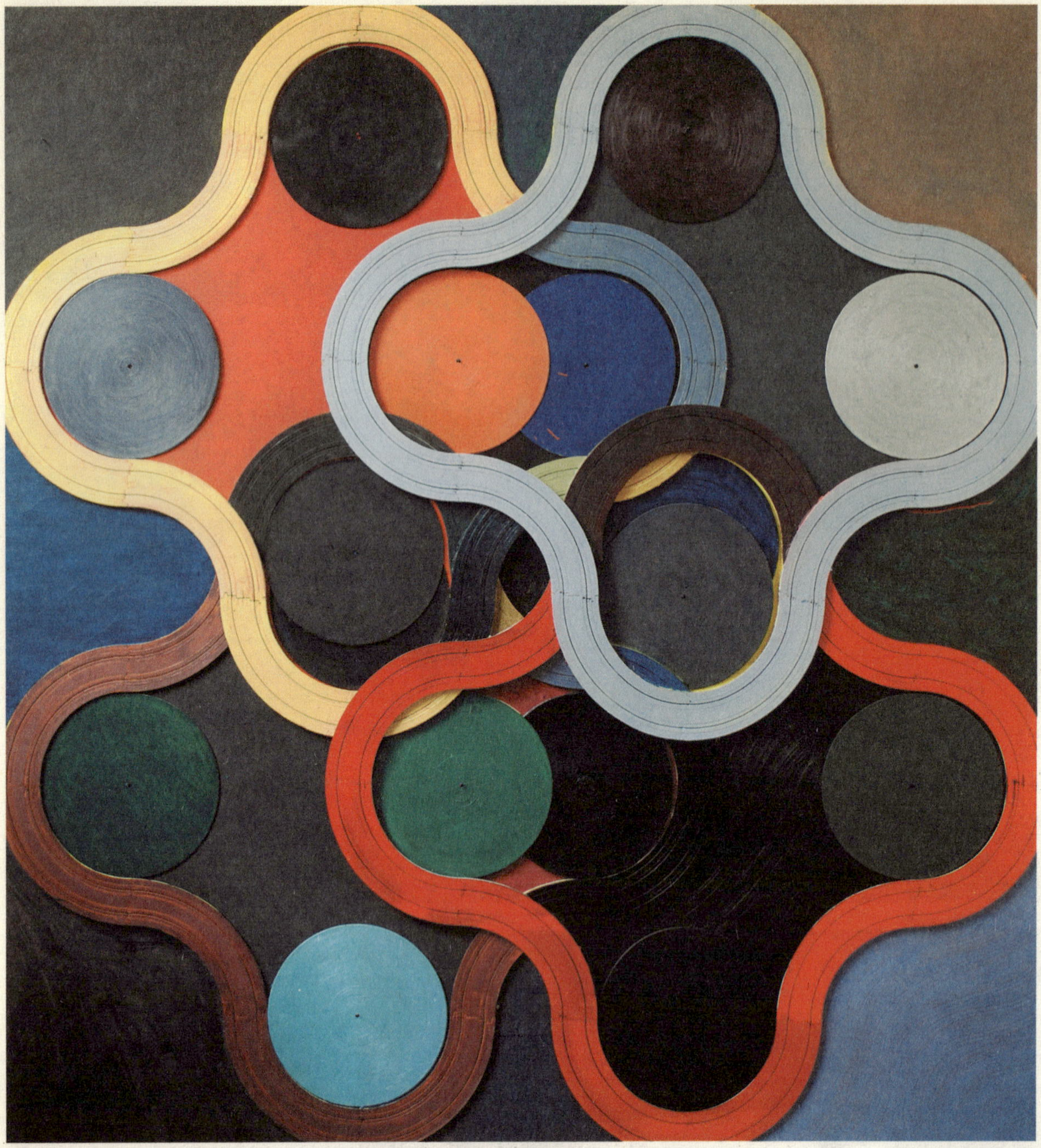

Daniel Pasteiner lives and works in London, where he earned his BA at the Camberwell School of Art and his MA in fine art at the Royal College of Art. While at Camberwell, he and several other students founded Students for Stuckism, which they described as "the only emerging force against Brit Art and stagnant Conceptualism." His paintings allude to pop culture and science fiction. **Love builds up**, a 2008 painting, incorporates oil paint as well as vinyl records and pieces of track used for racing Tyco toy cars.

1. **love builds up**
2008, oil on vinyl records and Tyco track on MDF, 74 ½ in × 70 in (189 × 178 cm)

2. **0000 Children of telepathic experience**
2008, oil and spray paint on linen mounted on MDF, 74 in × 70 in (187 × 180 cm)

3. **paintings of colour**
2008, mixed media, dimensions variable

4. **use flesh that rots away**
2006, hollowed-out television set, foam board, and light source, 25 ¼ × 32 ¾ × 15 ¾ in (64 × 83 × 40 cm)

1.

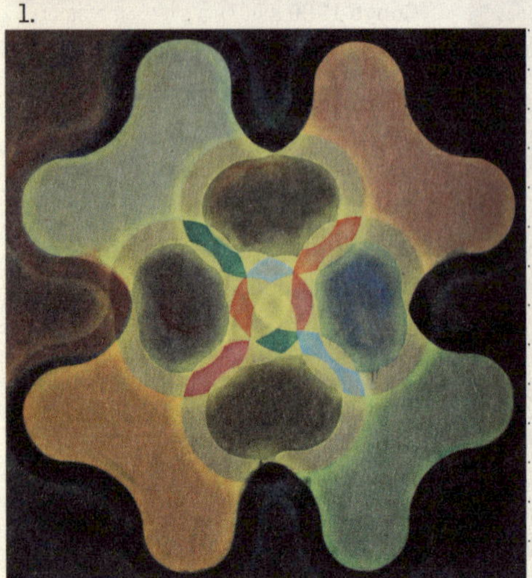

2.

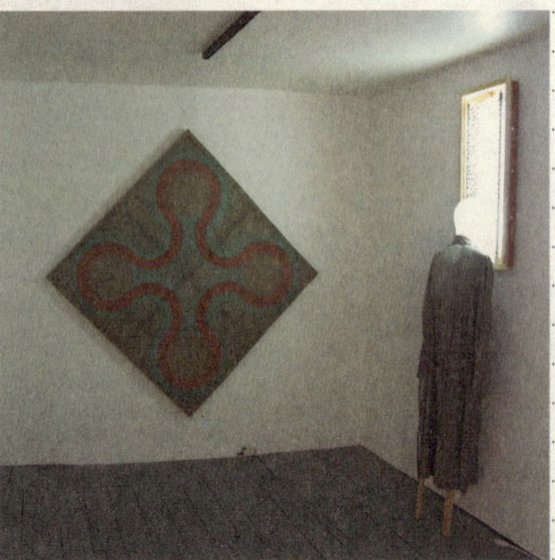

3.

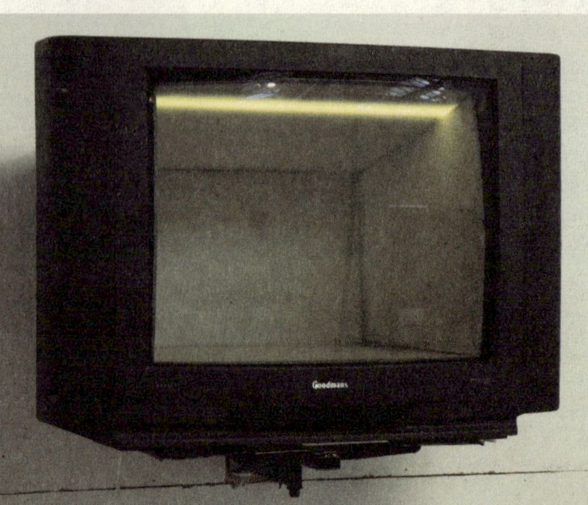

4.

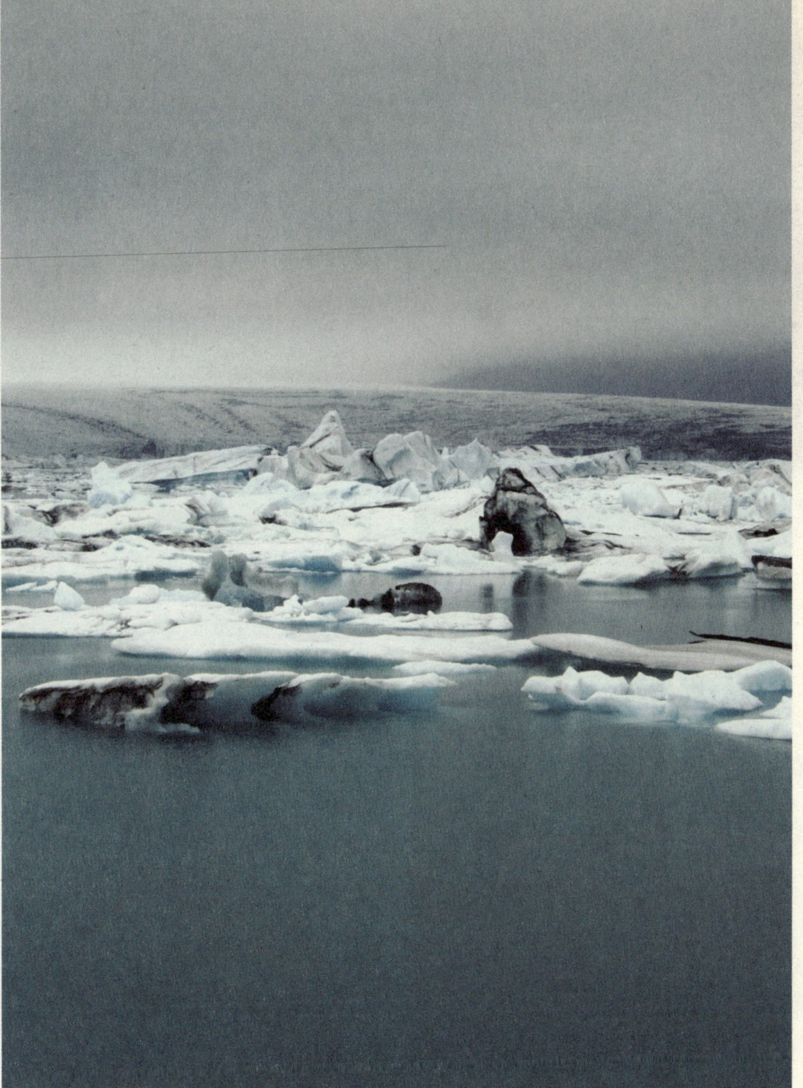
1.

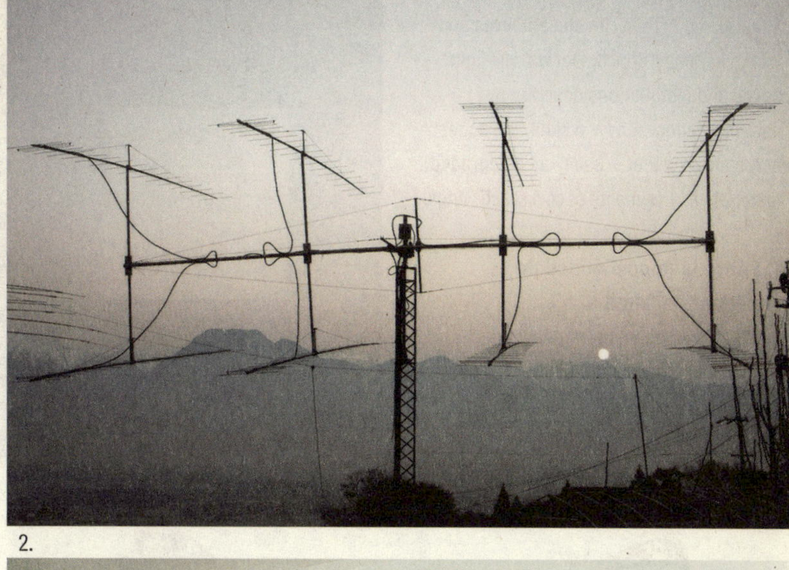
2.

3

4.

5.

Katie Paterson lives and works in London, where she graduated with an MFA from the Slade School of Fine Art. Among her sound installations and editions, which reference the conceptual art practices of such artists as John Cage and Christian Marclay, is a live phone line connected to an Icelandic glacier, from which listeners can hear the sound of the melting ice.

1. **Vatnajökull (the sound of)**
2007-08, color photograph

2. **Earth-Moon-Earth (Moonlight Sonata Reflected from the Surface of the Moon)**
2007-08, color photograph

3. (left) **Vatnajökull (the sound of)**;
2007-08, DE500, hydrophone, mobile phone, and white neon, 68 in × 12 ¼ in (172 × 31 cm)

3. (right) **Earth-Moon-Earth**
2007-08, E.M.E transmitter/receiver, Yamaha Disklavier piano, 47 ¼ × 39 ½ × 39 ½ in (120 × 100 × 100 cm)

4 & 5. **Earth-Moon-Earth (Moonlight Sonata Reflected from the Surface of the Moon)**
2007-08, documents showing Morse code as sent to the moon and received on earth

Fabián Peña graduated from the Instituto Superior de Arte in Havana and lives and works in Miami Beach, Florida. His light boxes and installations describe a personal topography – a skull, the bones of a hand or a foot – using such degraded materials as fragments of cockroach wings.

1. **Sobre la imposibilidad de almacenar el alma II**
2007, cockroach wing fragments on translucent paper and 3 light boxes

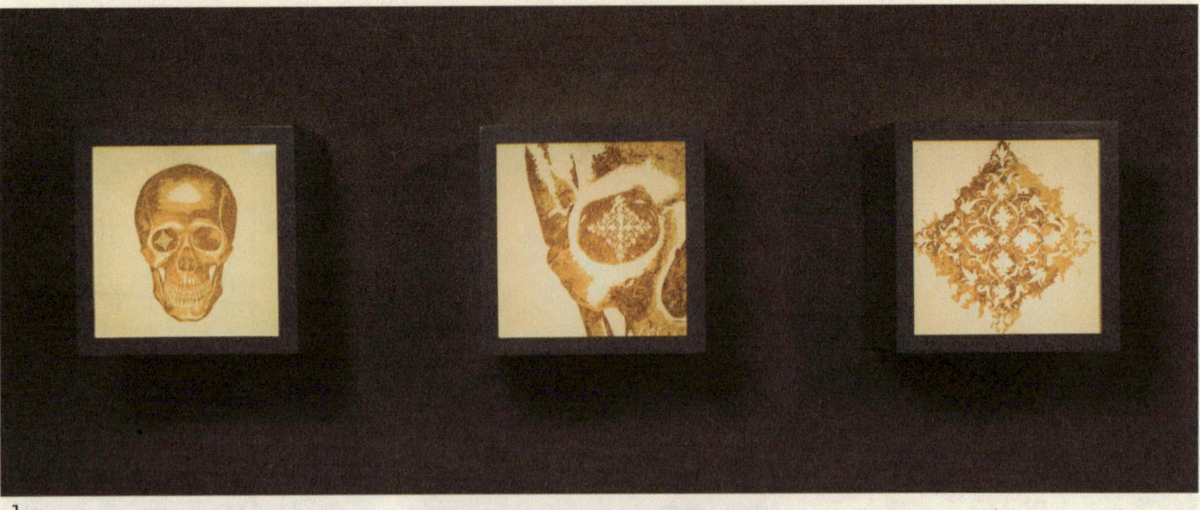

1.

2.

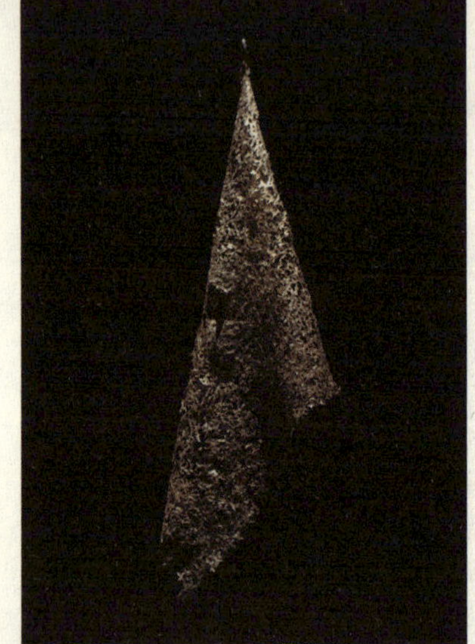

3.

2. **Prosthesis**
2006, cockroach wing fragments, cockroach antennae, and butterfly wings on canvas, 16 × 20 in (41 × 51 cm)

3. **Frozen Flight** (detail)
2008, fabric made of fly wings, dimensions variable

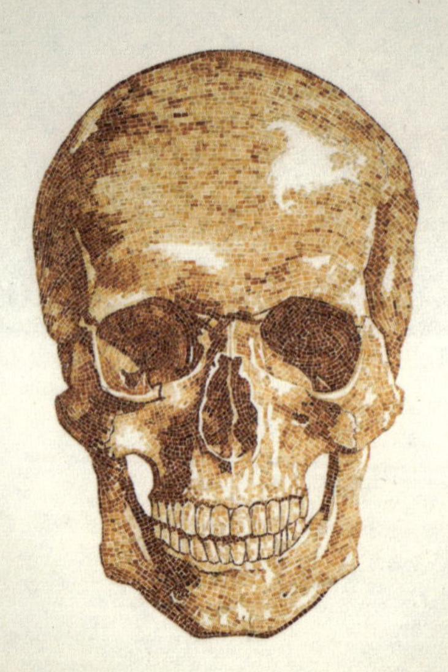

5.

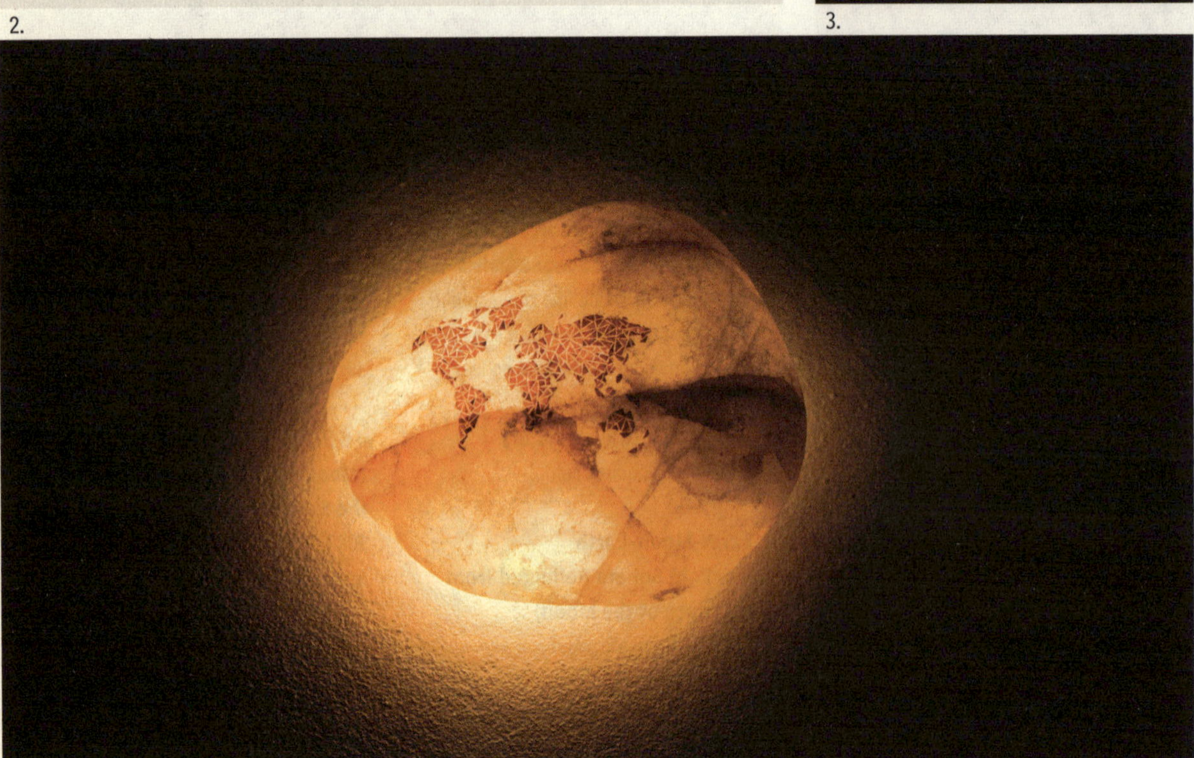

4.

4. **Fossil** (detail)
2008, cockroach wing fragments on semi-transparent stone, light, and pedestal, 36 × 18 × 18 in (91 × 46 × 46 cm)

5. **Sobre la imposibilidad de almacenar el alma I (Self-Portrait)** (detail)
2007, cockroach wing fragments and light boxes

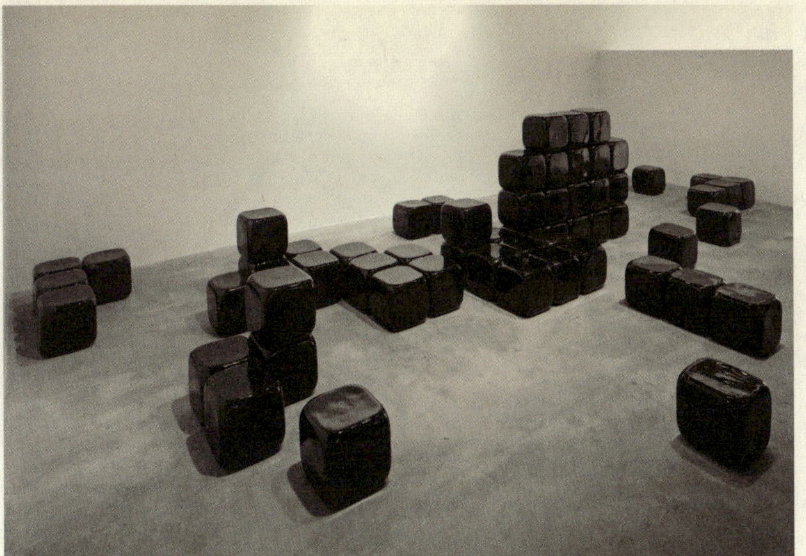

1.

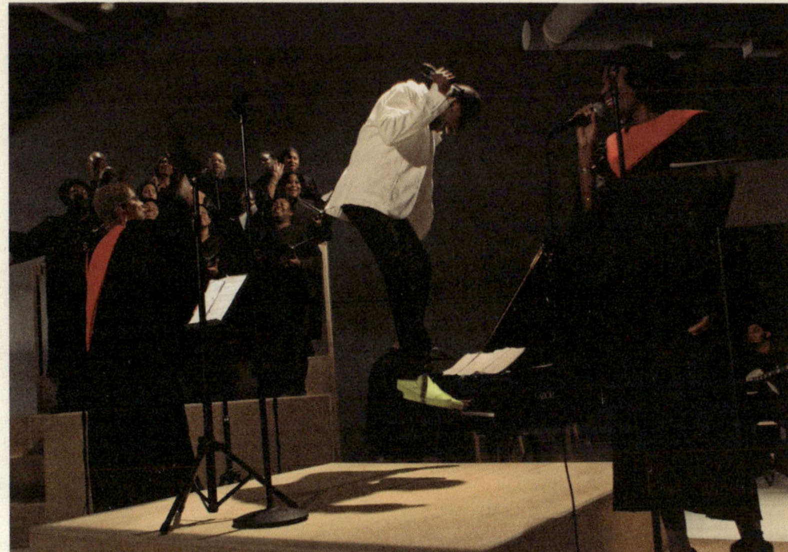

2.

Adam Pendleton was educated in the Artspace Independent Study Program in Pietrasanta, Italy. His practice ranges across disciplines, often utilizing politicized texts and images as source material. His performance **The Revival** (2007) was included as part of Performa07 and saw Pendleton take on the role of a gospel preacher, delivering a sermon of spliced-together quotations about racism, family, marriage, and AIDS. He currently lives and works in Brooklyn.

1. **Rendered in Black**
2007, 65 glazed 10-inch ceramic black cubes, 41 × 228 × 135 in (104 × 579 × 343 cm)

2. **The Revival**
2007, performance

3. (left) **Black Dada (LK/DDA)**, (right) **Black Dada (LC/AK/AA)**
2008, silkscreen on canvas, 2 panels, each 47 ¾ × 74 in (121 × 188 cm); overall dimensions 95 ½ × 74 in (243 × 188 cm)

3.

Rakhi Peswani received her MFA in sculpture from the Maharaja Sayajirao University of Baroda, India. Her often surrealistic sculptures are largely composed using needlepoint and other traditional, craft-based practices, an aesthetic choice that provides a self-conscious counterpoint to the rapidly modernizing landscape of postcolonial metropolitan India. In 2007 she received the Emerging Artist Award from the Foundation for Indian Contemporary Art (FICA), Vadehra Art Gallery, New Delhi.

1. **Here and there – I**
from the series **Attempts at locating location**, 2006, hand embroidery on cotton fabric, 14 1/4 × 20 1/2 in (36 × 52 cm)

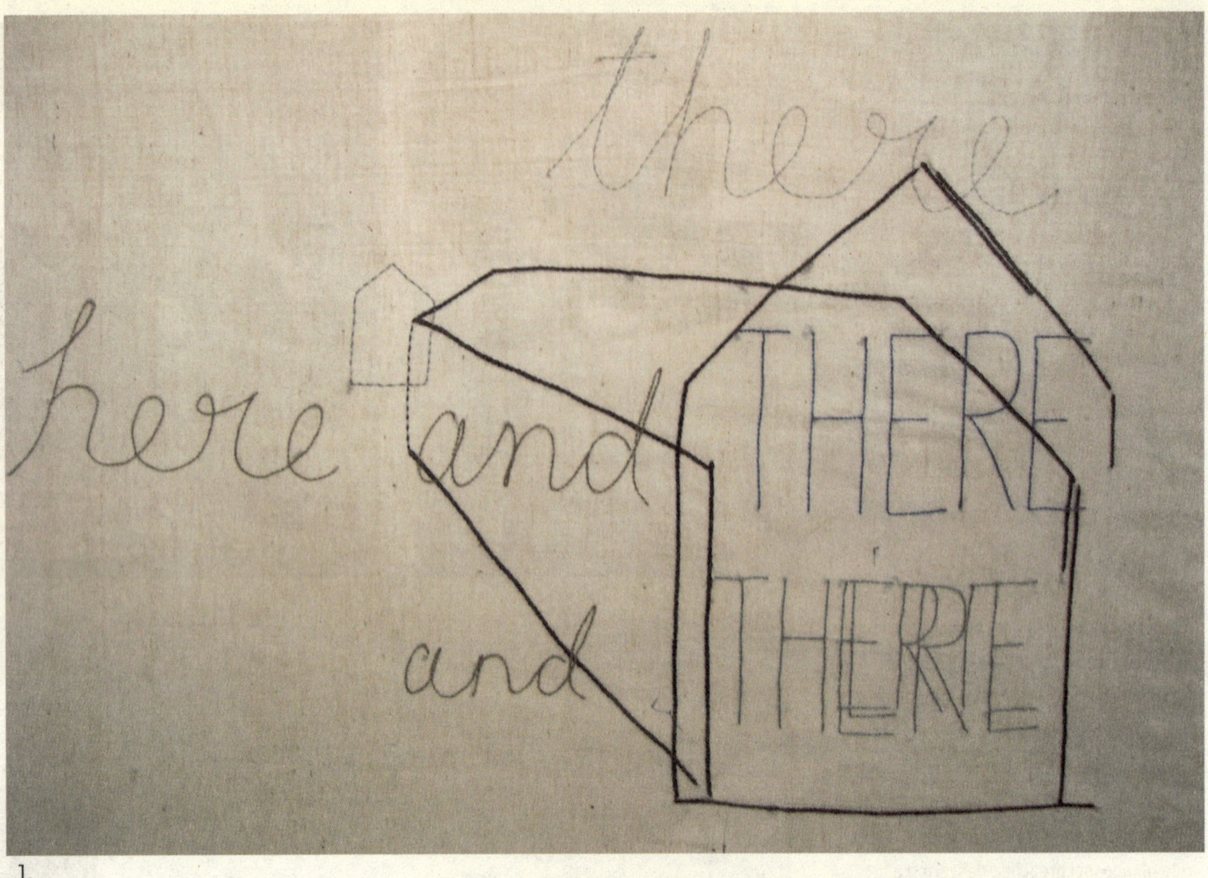

1.

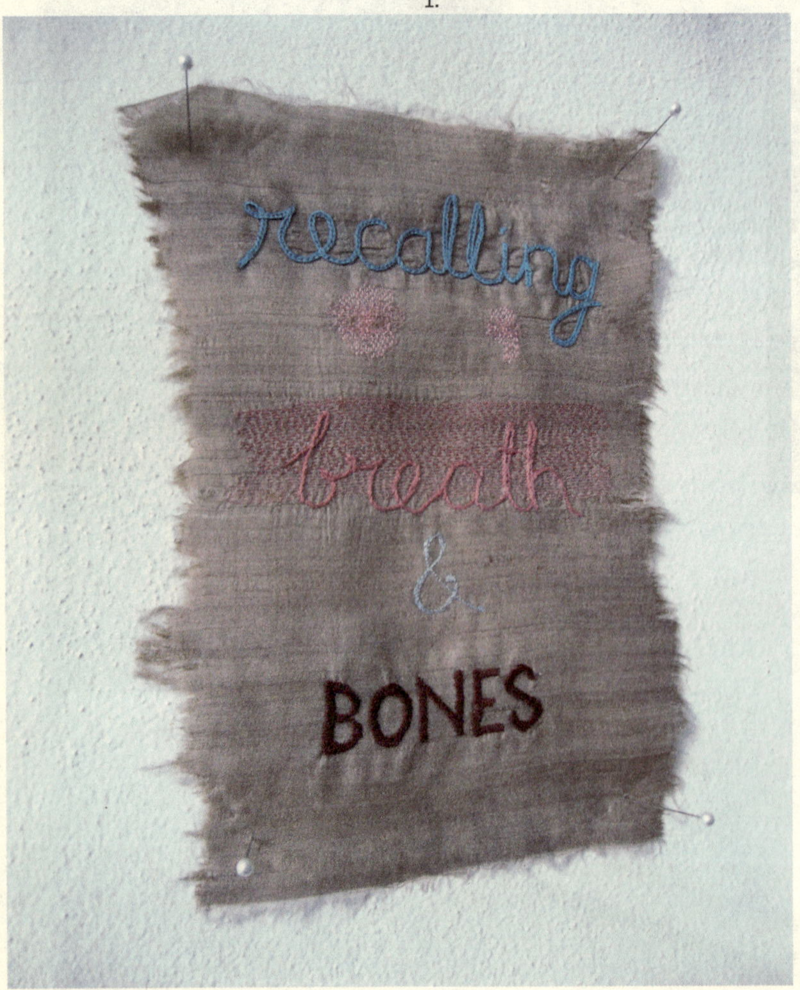

2.

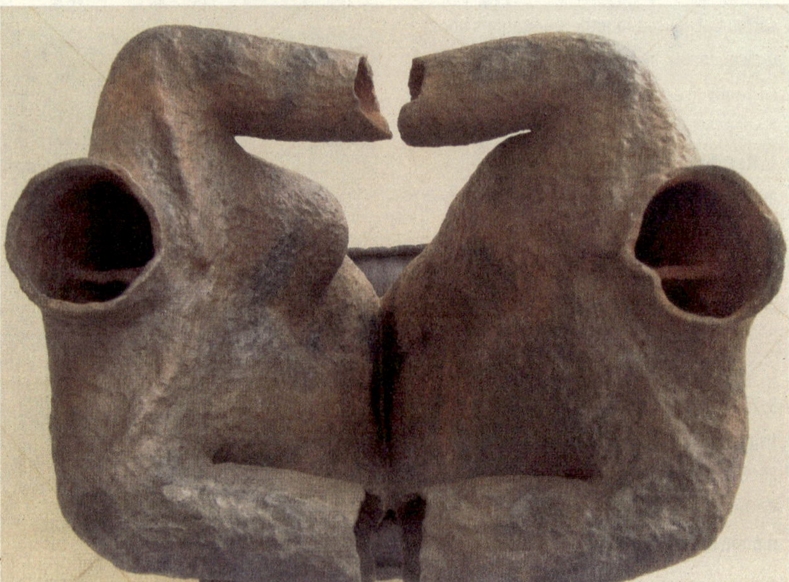

3.

2. **Living – Language** (detail)
2006, hand-embroidered text on worn silk, approx 10 × 7 in (25 × 18 cm)

3. **Requiem for Strangers**
2004, smoke-fired terra-cotta, scratched and tinted with iron oxide and manganese dioxide, and satin cushion, 64 × 45 × 31 in (163 × 118 × 78 cm)

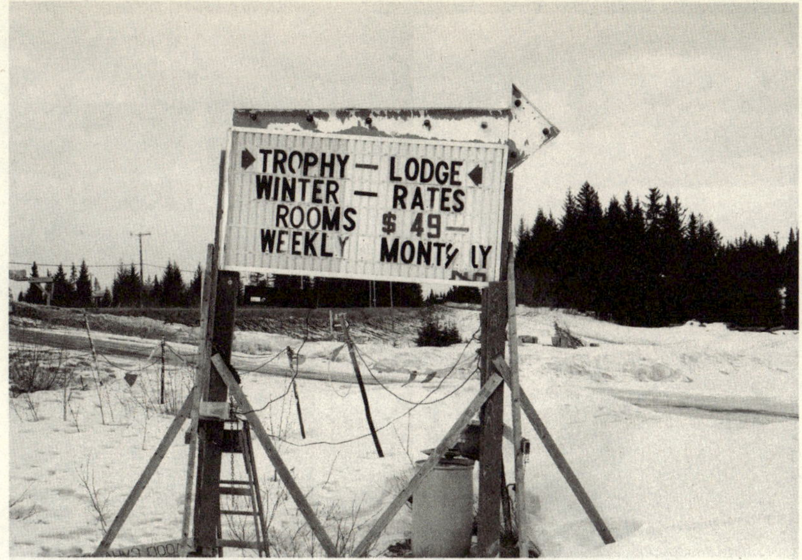

1.

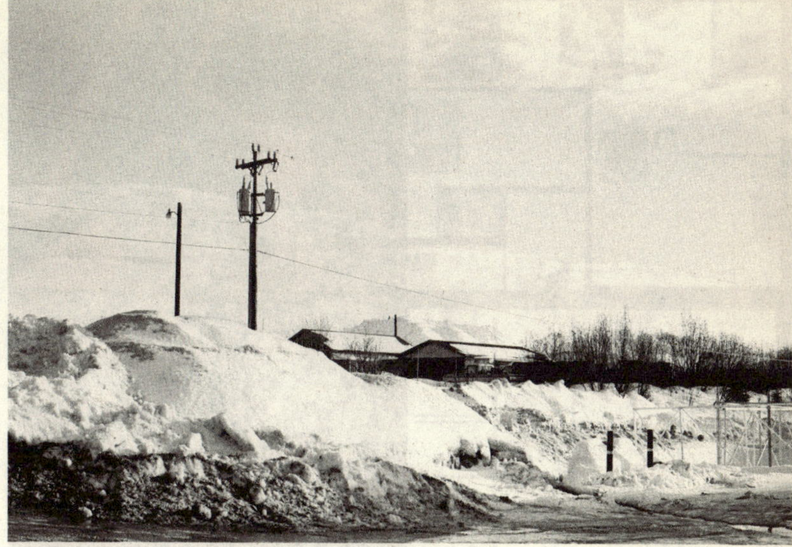

2.

Brazilian artist Pablo Pijnappel graduated from the Rijksakademie van Beeldende Kunsten in Amsterdam, where he currently lives and works. The films and videos of this cosmopolitan artist are explorations of narrative that draw on his own biography and consider the way identity is shaped.

1, 2 & 3. **Homer**
2008, 3 synchronized slide projectors and sound

4, 5 & 6. **Walderedo**
2007, 16 mm film, color, 16 min

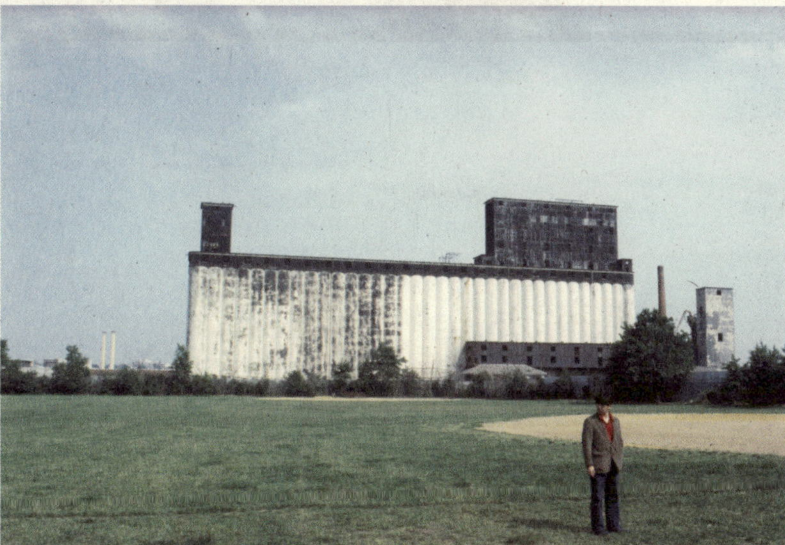

3.

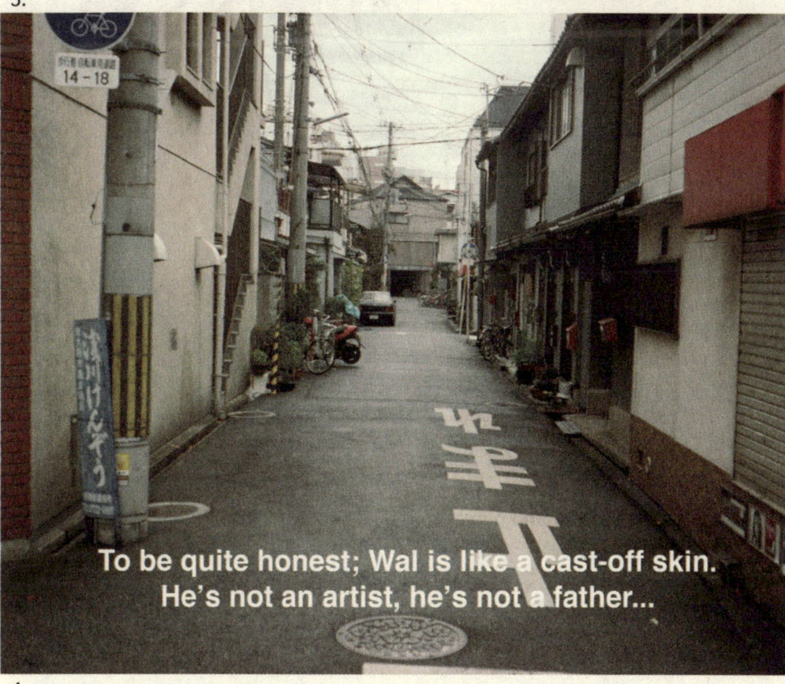

4.

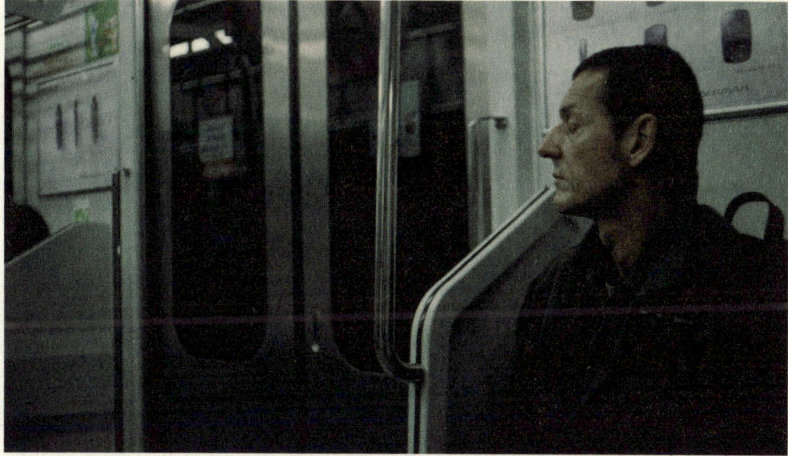

5.

6.

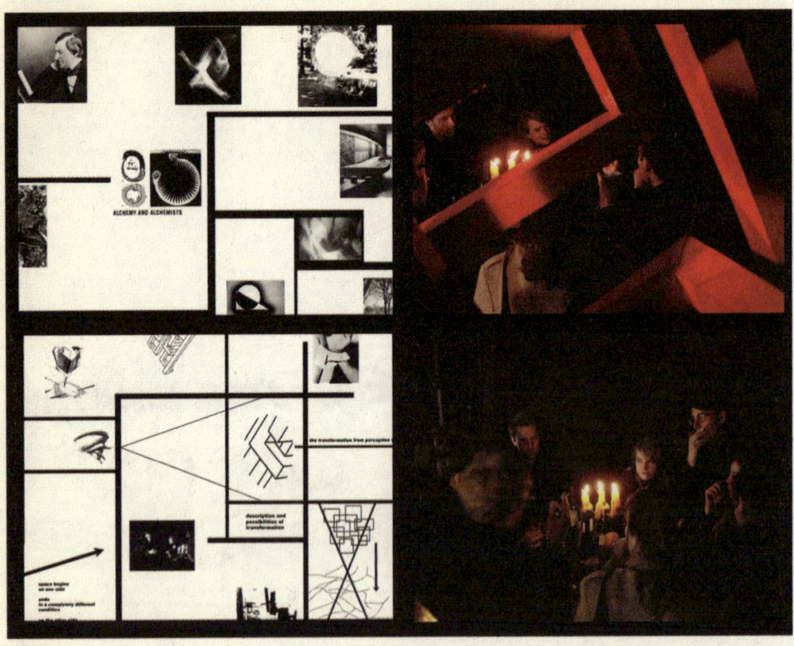

1.

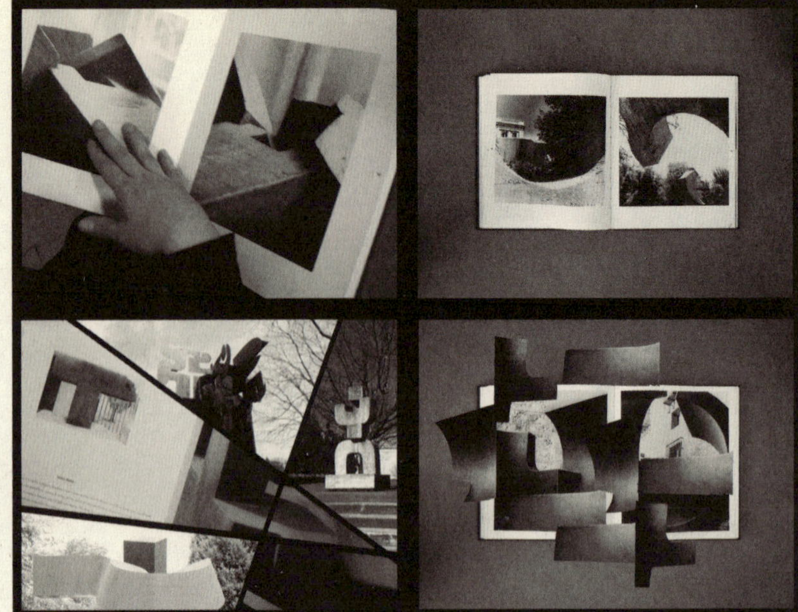

2.

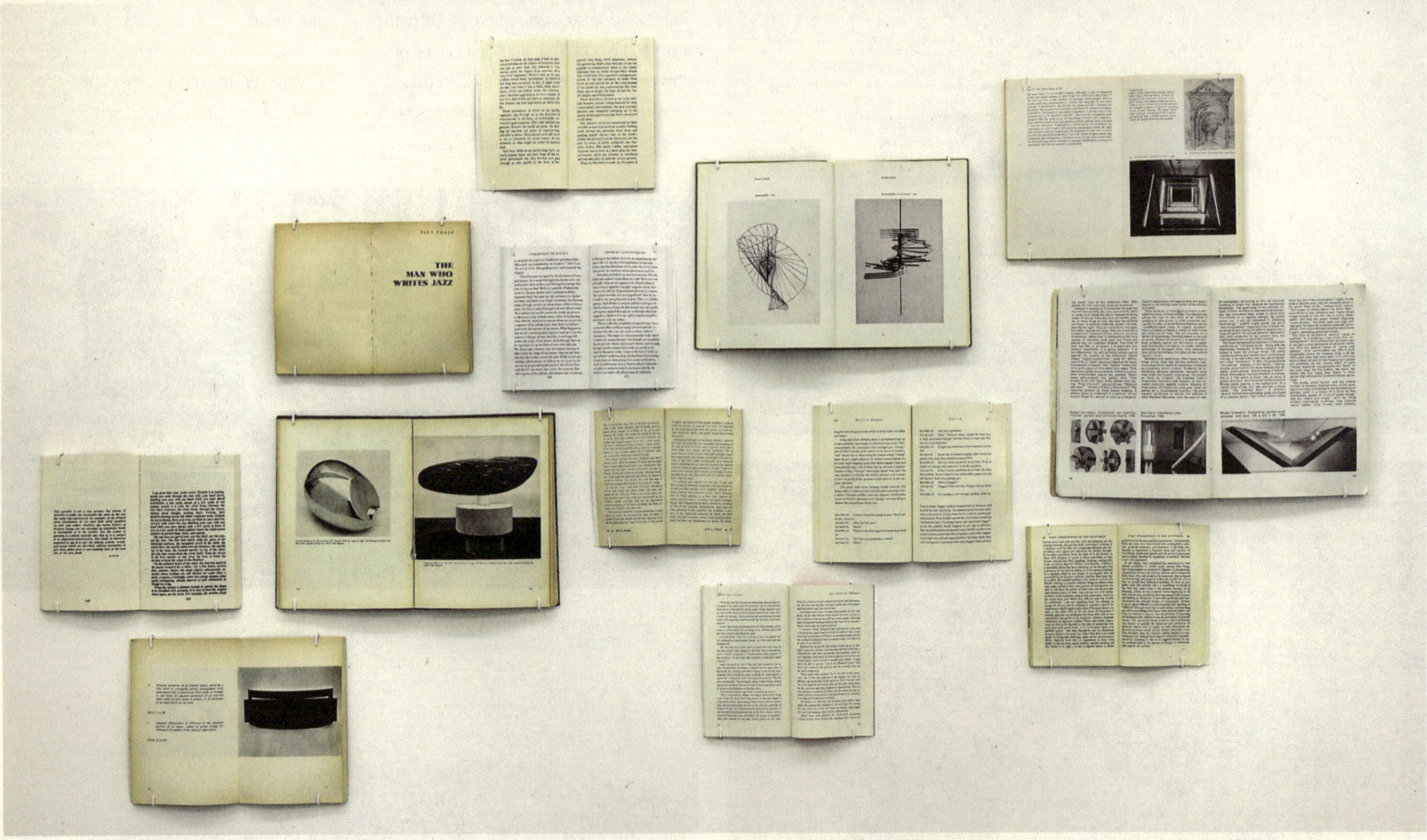

3.

Falke Pisano studied at the Jan van Eyck Academie in Maastrict, Netherlands. Much of her work takes the form of lectures, or videos of lectures, in which art historical categories are discussed and questioned. Her lecture **Concrete Abstractions**, for example, examines the history and theory of abstract public sculpture, with particular attention paid to the problem of viewing these works as autonomous objects, and to the development of new forms of abstraction. In 2008 her work was included in an exhibition at the Kunsthalle Basel.

1. **A Sculpture turning into a Conversation, part zero and part one**
2006, 2-channel video installation, 25 min

2. **Chillida (Forms & Feelings)**
2006, 2 videos, 14 min

3. **Object Construction #1: Reflective Abstraction (Mishima)**
2007, wall installation with 13 books, dimensions variable

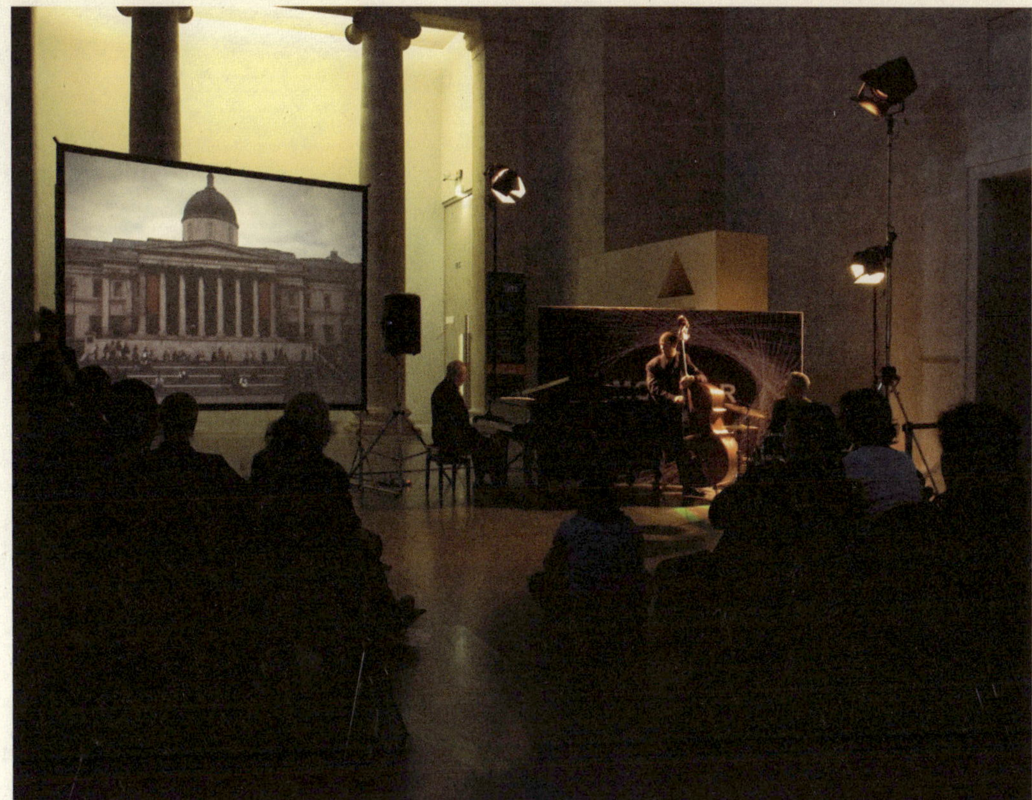

1.

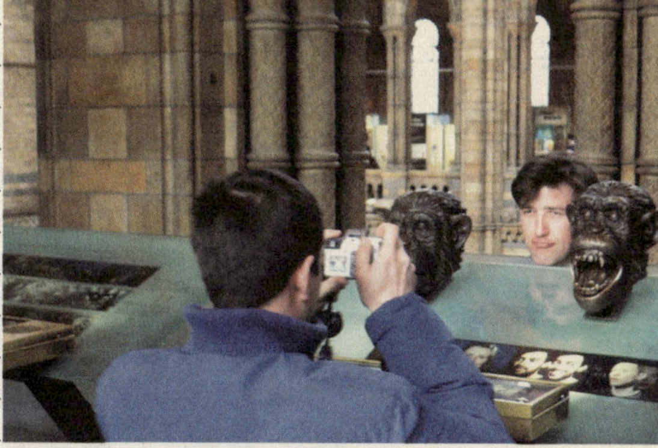

2.

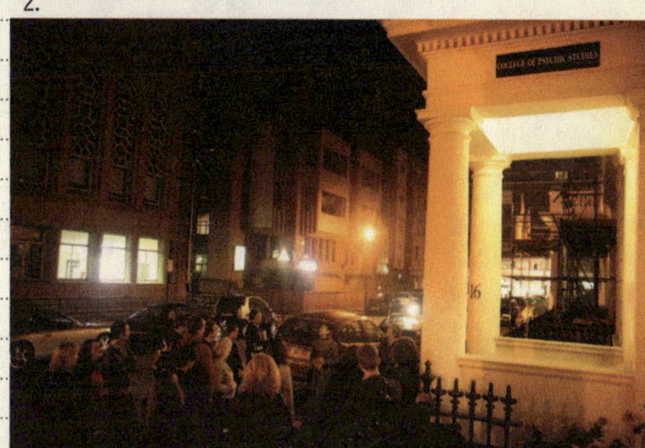

3.

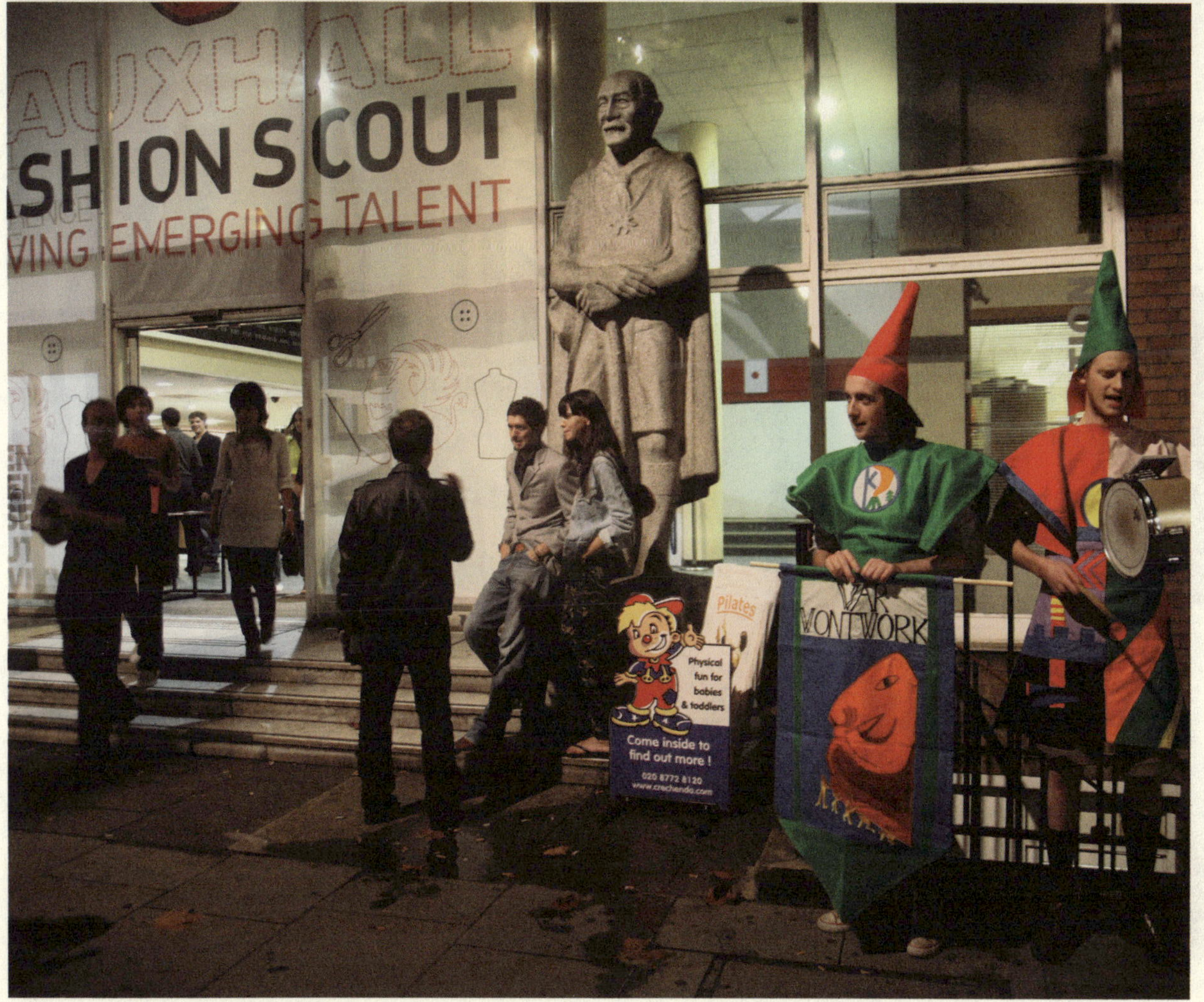

4.

Olivia Plender, an artist as well as co-editor of the art magazine **Untitled**, lives and works in London. She graduated from St. Martins College in in 1998. Her drawings reflect an interest in magazines, comic strips, and pulp fiction book cover illustrations. Recent works include fictional posters mimicking twentieth-century advertisements and **The Masterpiece**, a comic book about an imaginary artistic genius living in London in the 1950s.

1 & 2. **Monitor**
2006, performance at Tate Triennial, Tate Britain, London

3 & 4. **In Search of the New Republic (or the tables turned) – A Walking Tour**
2006, performance in London

Megan Plunkett lives and works in Brooklyn, where she received her BFA from Pratt Institute in 2008. Her work incorporates found materials, such as digital prints of found images, screenprints, and altered book covers.

1. Untitled (Being Here)
2008, altered found book cover, 8 × 6 in (20 × 15 cm)

2. Untitled (The World Is Everywhere)
2008, found image and digital print, 7 × 6 in (18 × 15 cm)

3. Untitled (Fortune)
2008, found image and digital print, 17 × 12 in (43 × 301 cm)

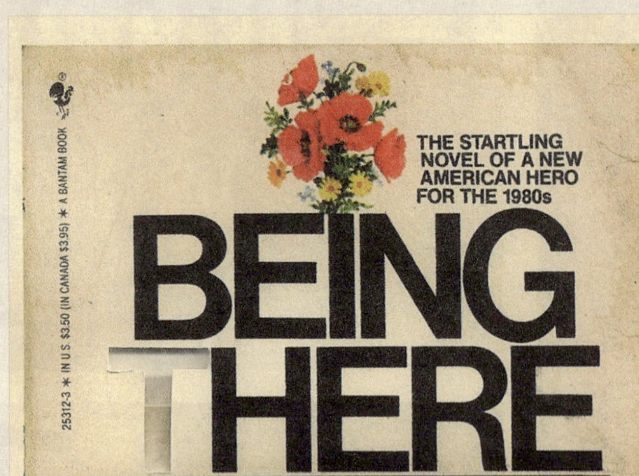

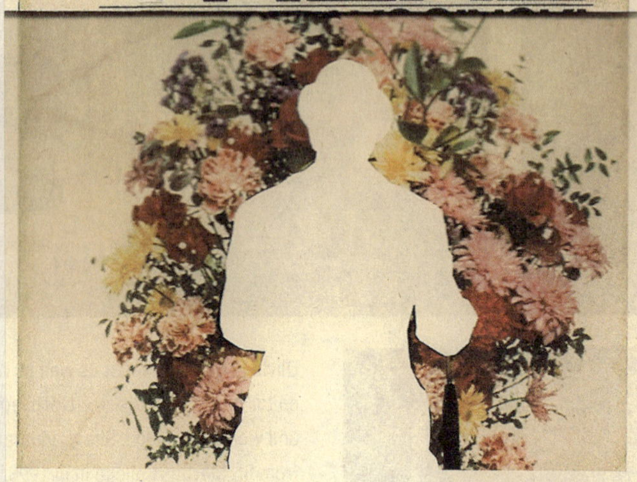

1.

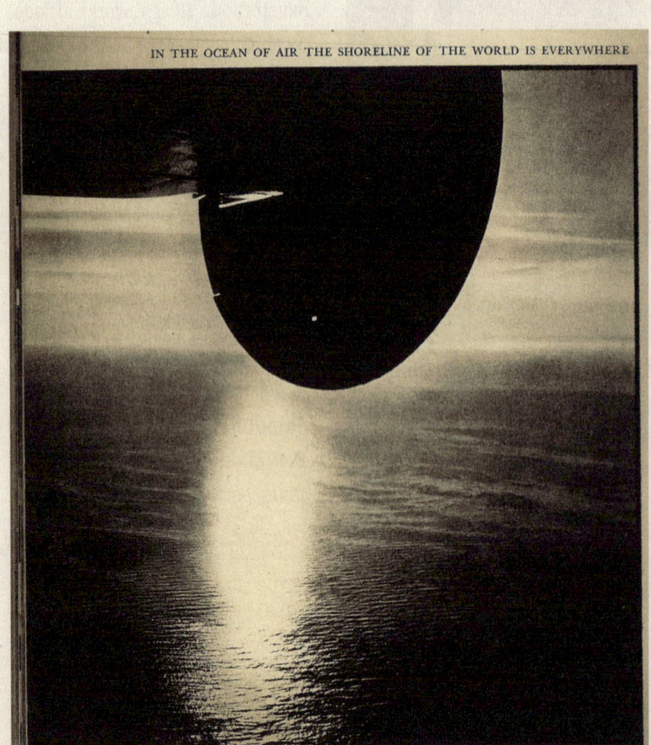

2.

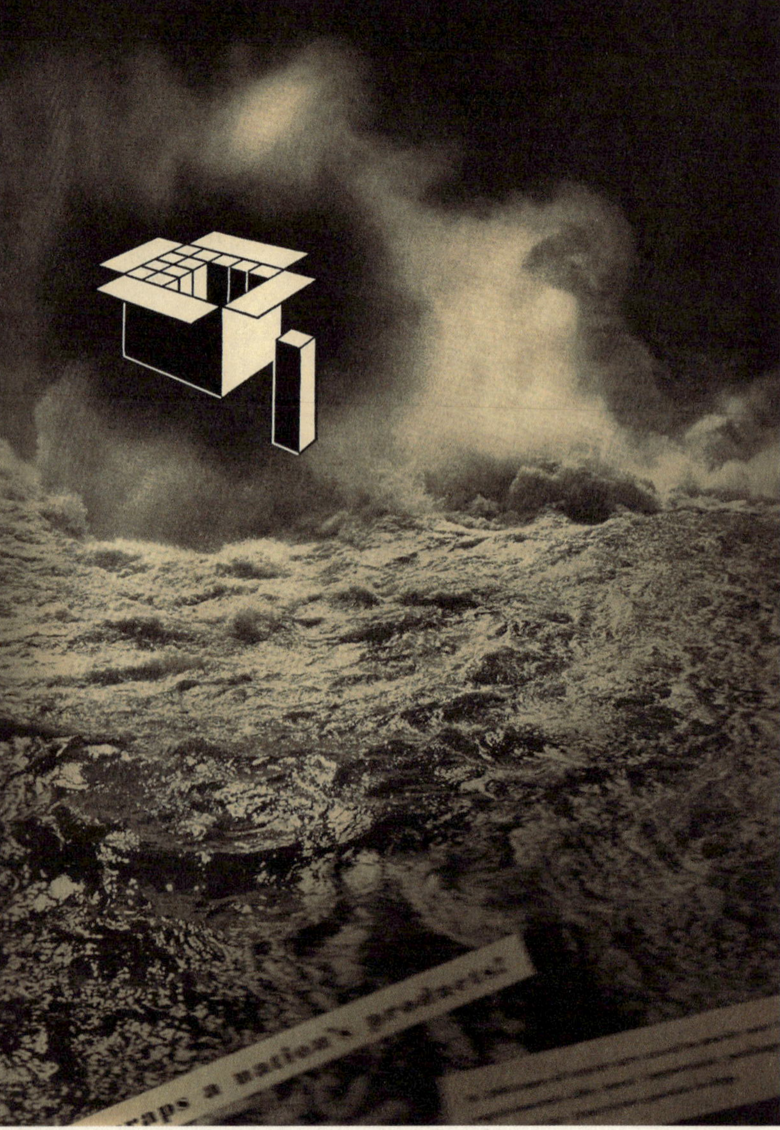

3.

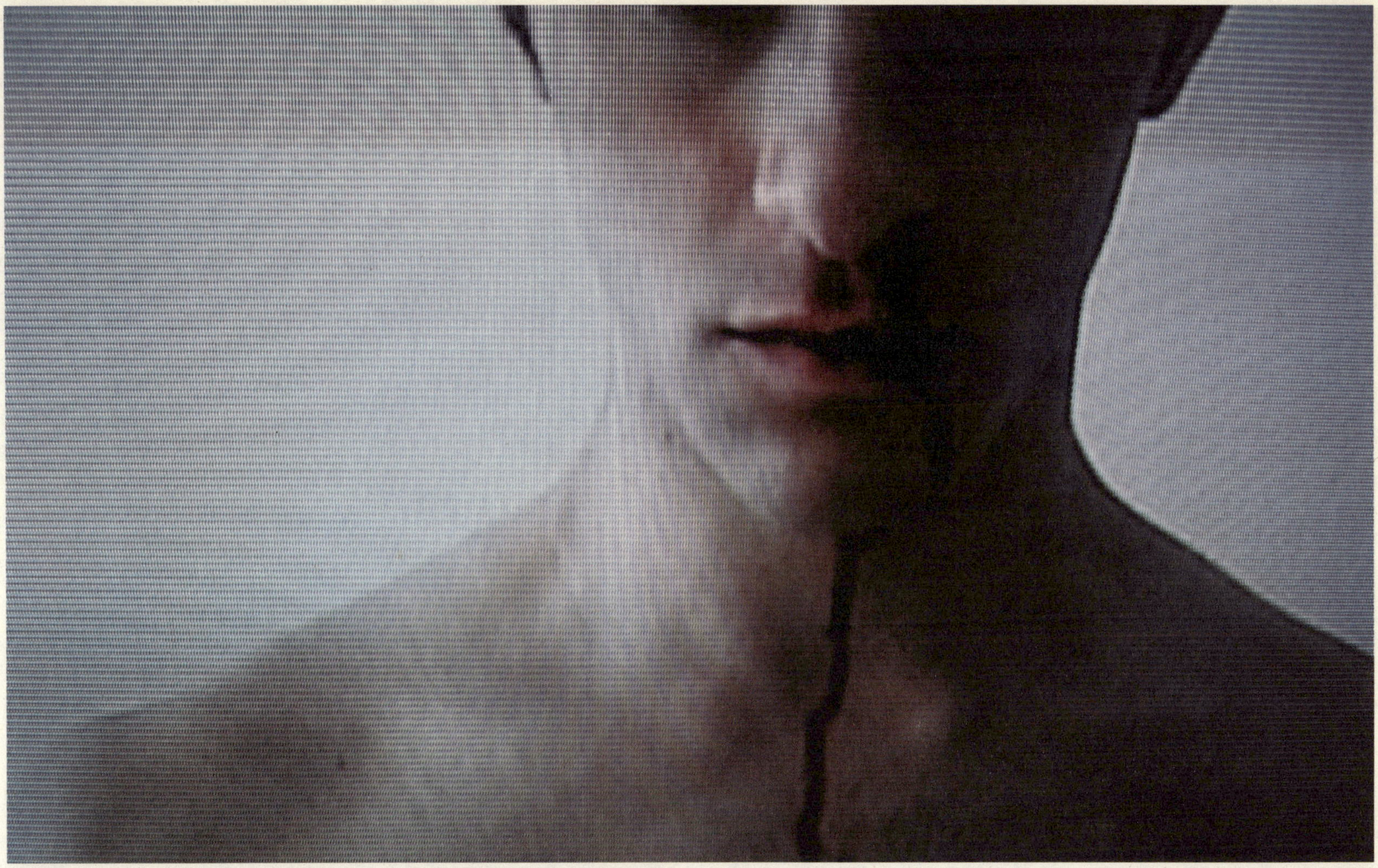

2.

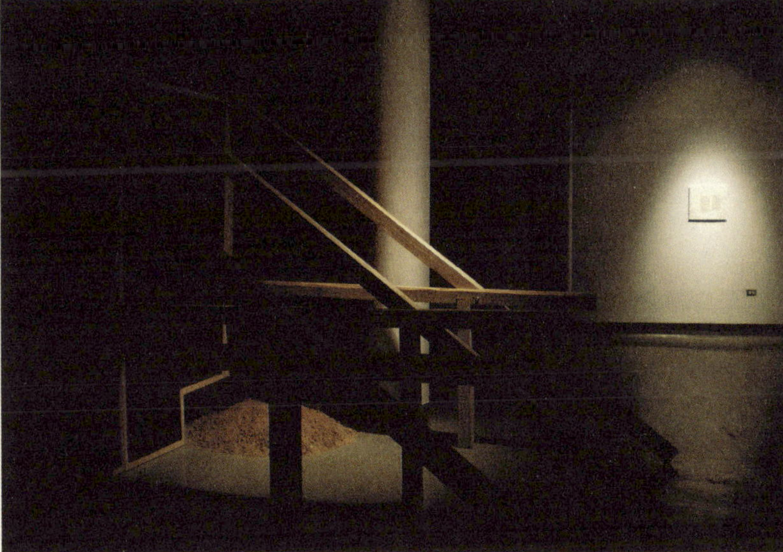

1.

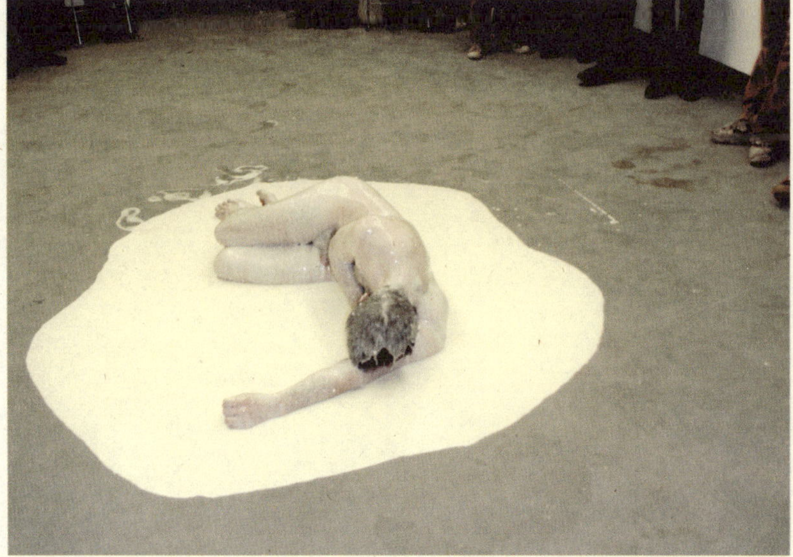

3.

Brooklyn-based Cyrus Saint Amand Poliakoff studied at Deep Springs College in California and at the Cooper Union School of Art, New York. He incorporates sculpture, video, sound, and text in multi-part performance works that explore relationships between individual bodies and a collective, political body. **Picture a Coalition** (2008) positions two viewers side by side looking at a reflective black screen on which fragments of Gregg Bordowitz's 1987 AIDS activist text appear and disappear.

1. **Earkiss**
2007-08, performance, wood, felt, hardware, fermenting rice bran, letterpress print, and headphones, 3 min 30 sec

2. **Concentration**
2006, 2-channel video installation, 30 min

3. **Mochi**
2006, performance using 25 gallons of mochi (Japanese sweet rice paste), 27 min

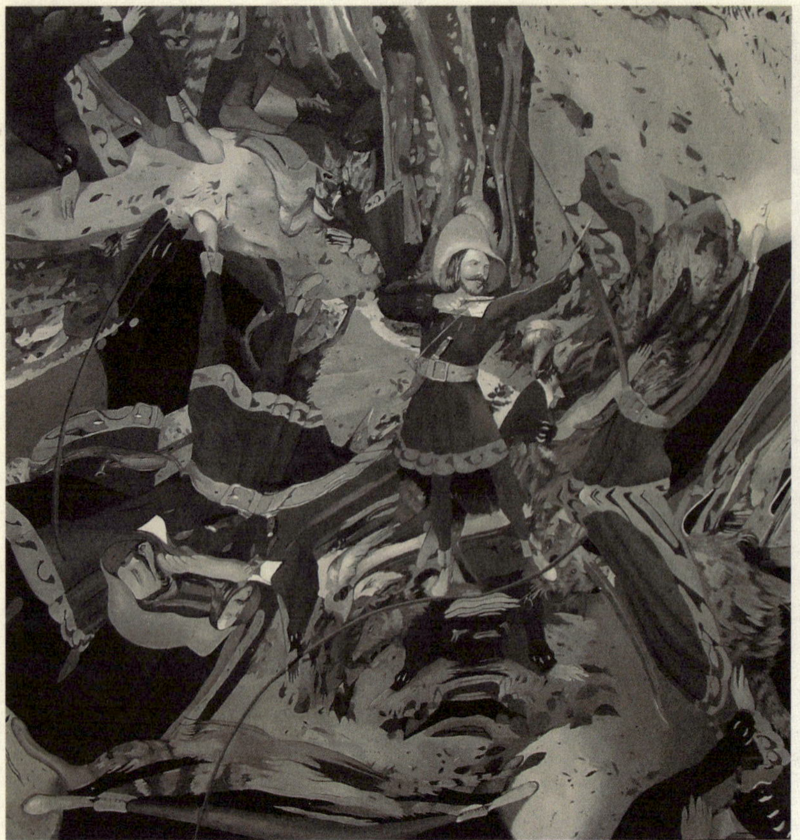

1.

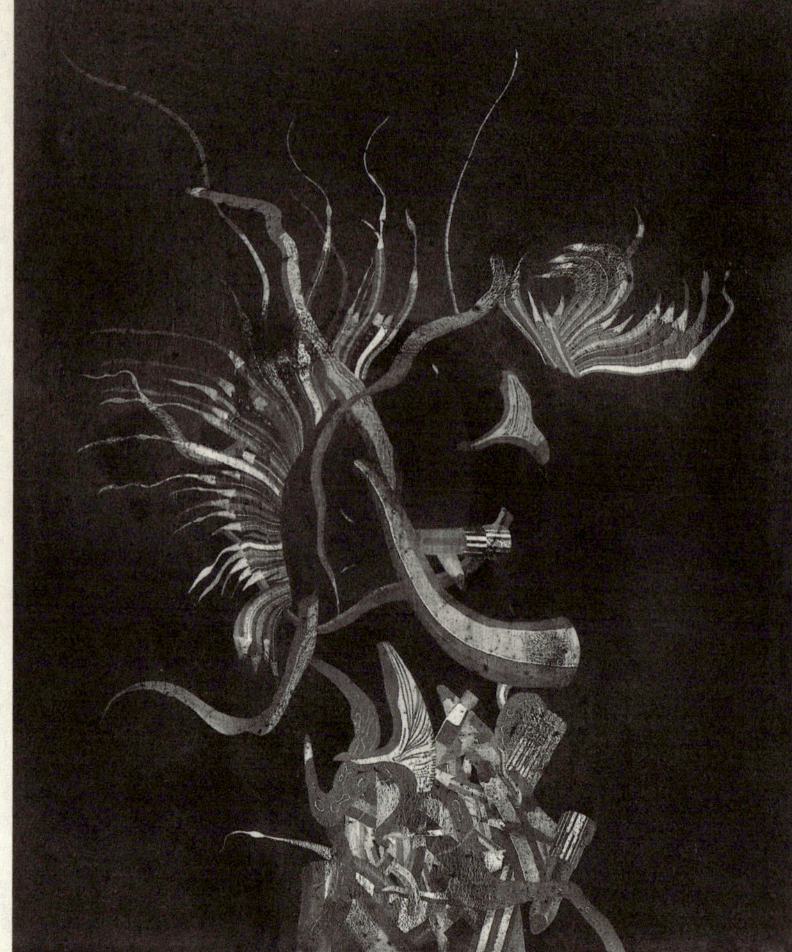

2.

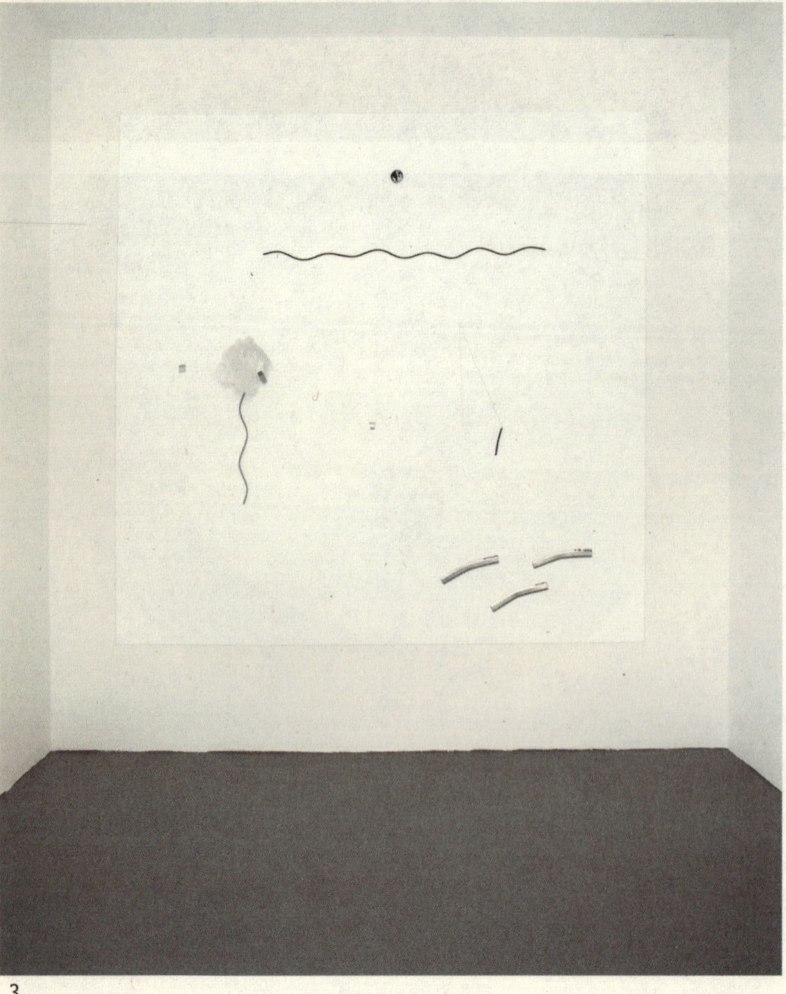

3.

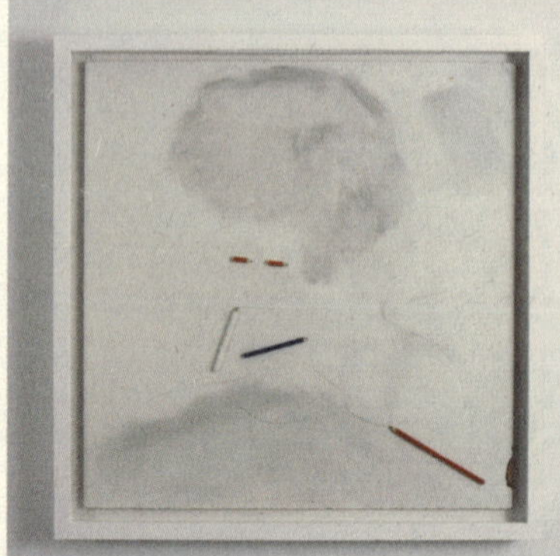

4.

Alex Pollard lives and works in Glasgow. He creates sculptures, paintings, and drawings that seem to be made of scrap materials though often involve more staid mediums such as bronze and plaster. Out of pencils and compasses (dipped in bronze and then covered with paint), for example, Pollard has fashioned sculptures of gangly birds, bony hands, dinosaurs, and elderly humans. Among the works on view in his 2007 exhibition "Nightscape" was the **Romo's Getting Ready** series of collage drawings, in which broken pencils blend with the semi-abstract images drawn by them, as well as a wall drawing evocative of a landscape, made of black lipstick and resin pencils.

1. Hunting for inanimacy
2008, oil on canvas, 55 × 55 in (140 × 140 cm)

2. Profile
2007, oil on canvas, 35 × 30 in (89 × 76 cm)

3. Landscape from a Nonsense Poem
2006, acrylic, jesmonite, and graphite on wall, dimensions variable

4. Portrait
from the series **Young Men**
2006, framed acrylic and jesmonite on conte board, 29 1⁄4 × 29 1⁄4 in (74 × 74 cm)

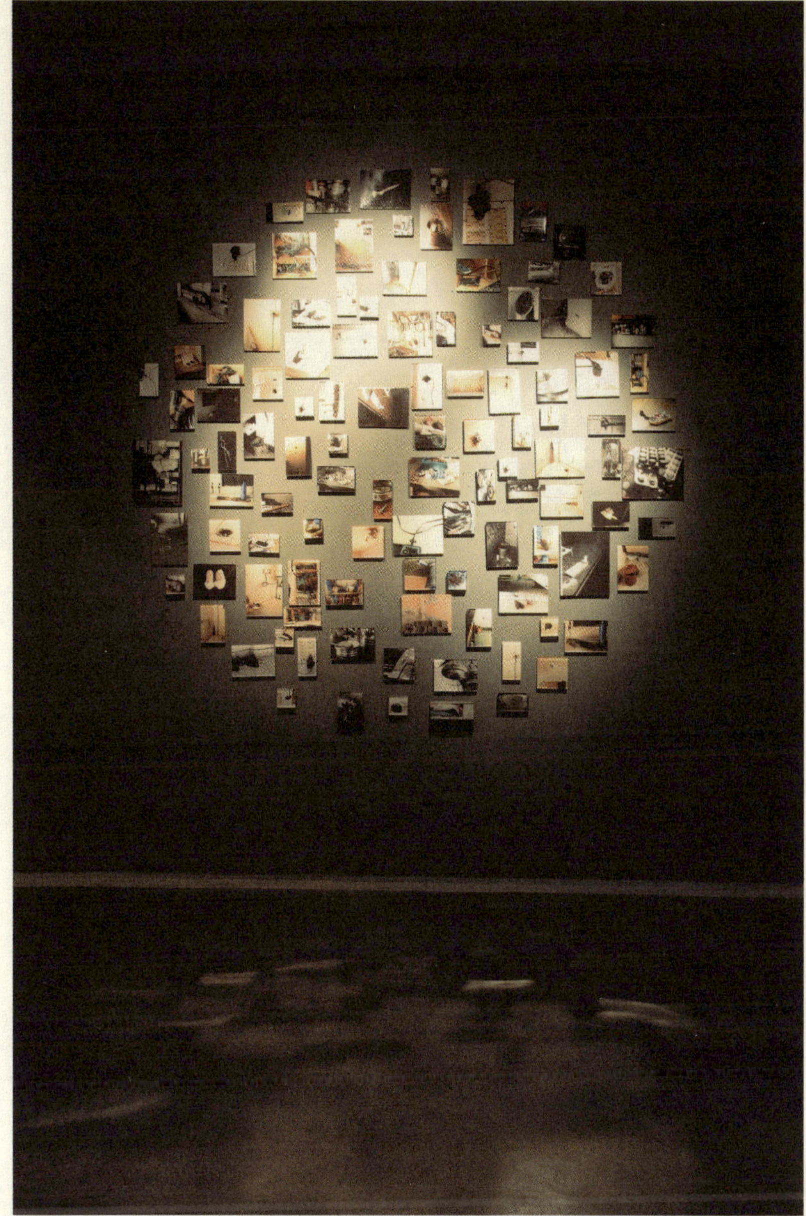

1.

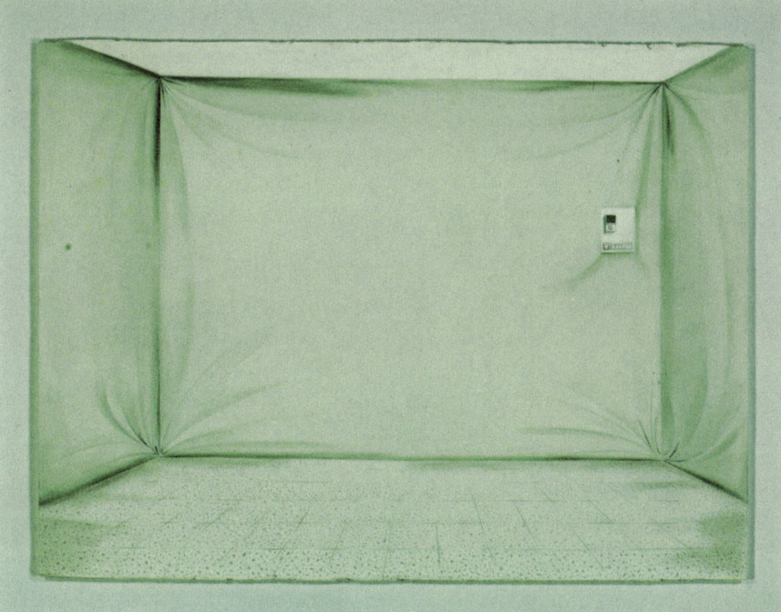

2.

Prajakta Potnis Ponmany received her MFA in Painting from Sir J. J. School of Arts, Mumbai, and has since expanded her practice to include sculpture, photography, and installation. Her often unnerving and surrealistic works investigate the landscape and objects of everyday life. For a recent series of sculptures, Ponmany adorned household objects such as shoes, lightbulbs, and toothbrushes with tumorous masses of tiny beads, lending these quotidian objects an air of the horrible. In 2005 the National Gallery of Modern Art, Mumbai, named her Artist of the Year.

1. **Untitled**
2008, Plexiglas, 109 frames, and 109 photographs, dimensions variable

2. **Porous Walls**
2008, acrylic and dry pastel on paper, 30 × 40 in (76 × 102 cm)

3 & 4. **Porous Walls**
2008, electrical bulb, plastic beads, tea strainer, mustard seeds, drainage sink, shoe, and granite stone on metal stand, 23 × 44 × 30 in (58 × 112 × 76 cm)

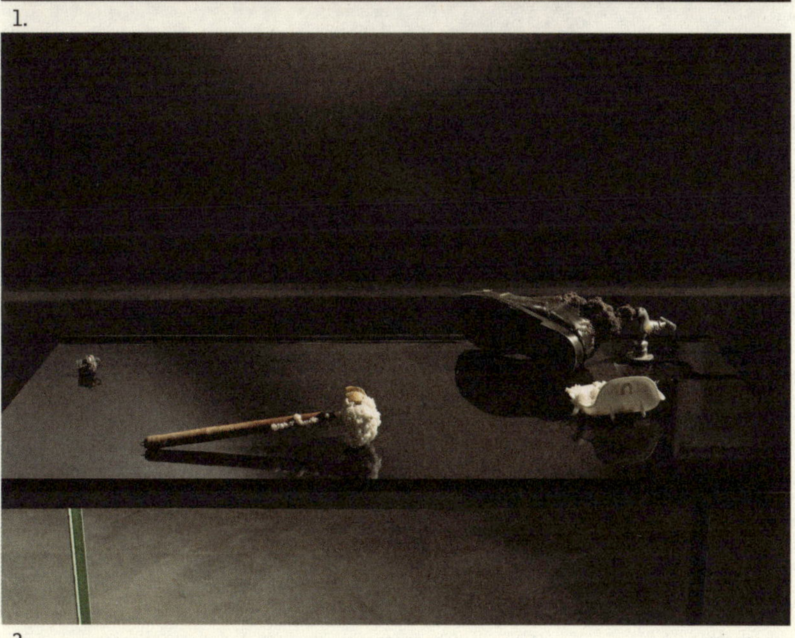

3.

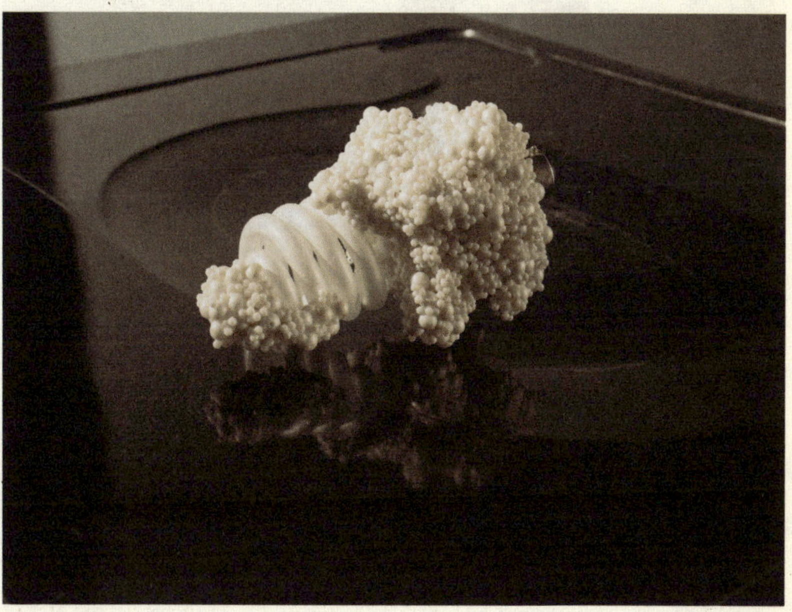

4.

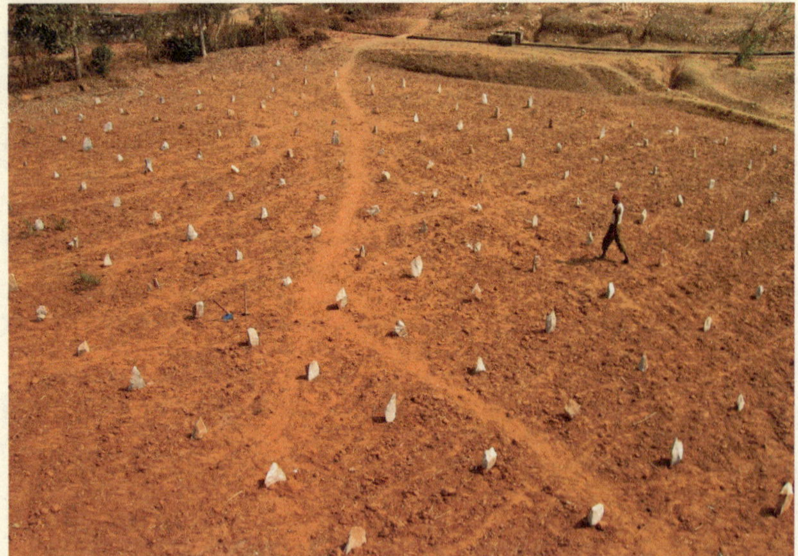

1.

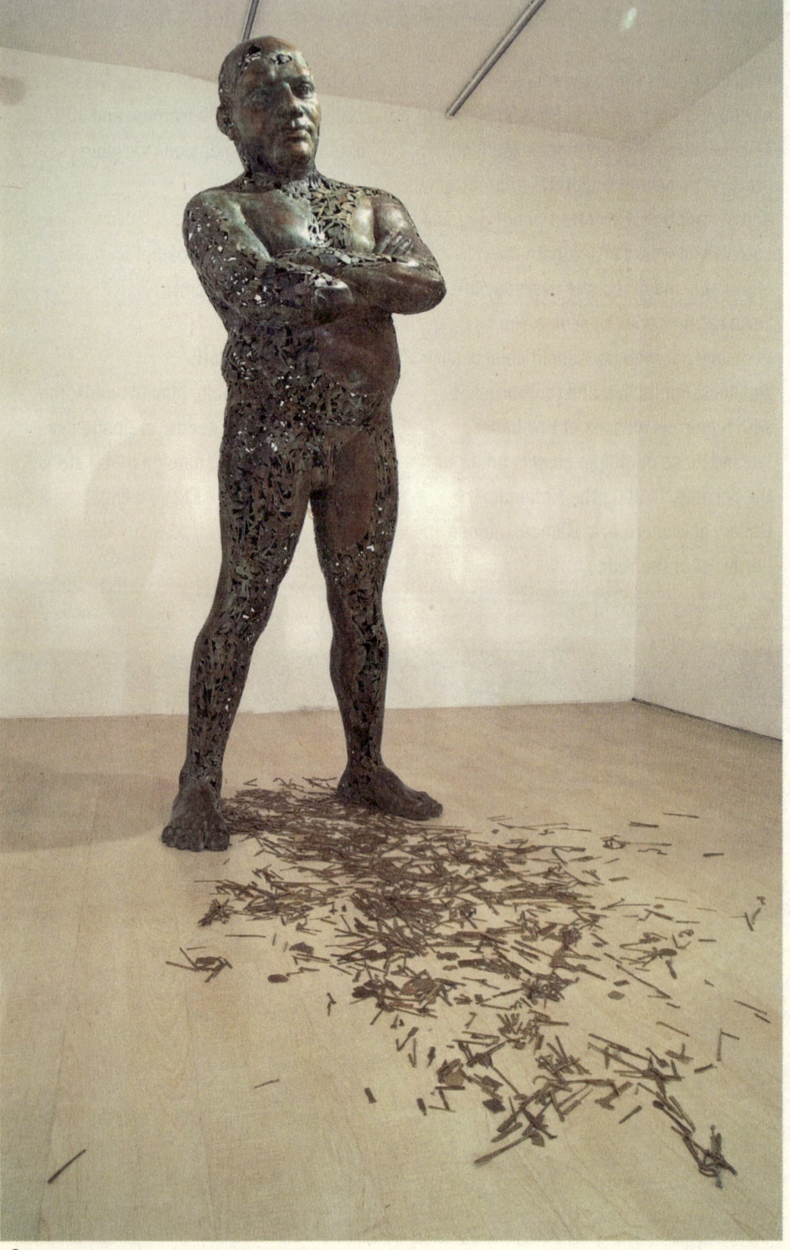

2.

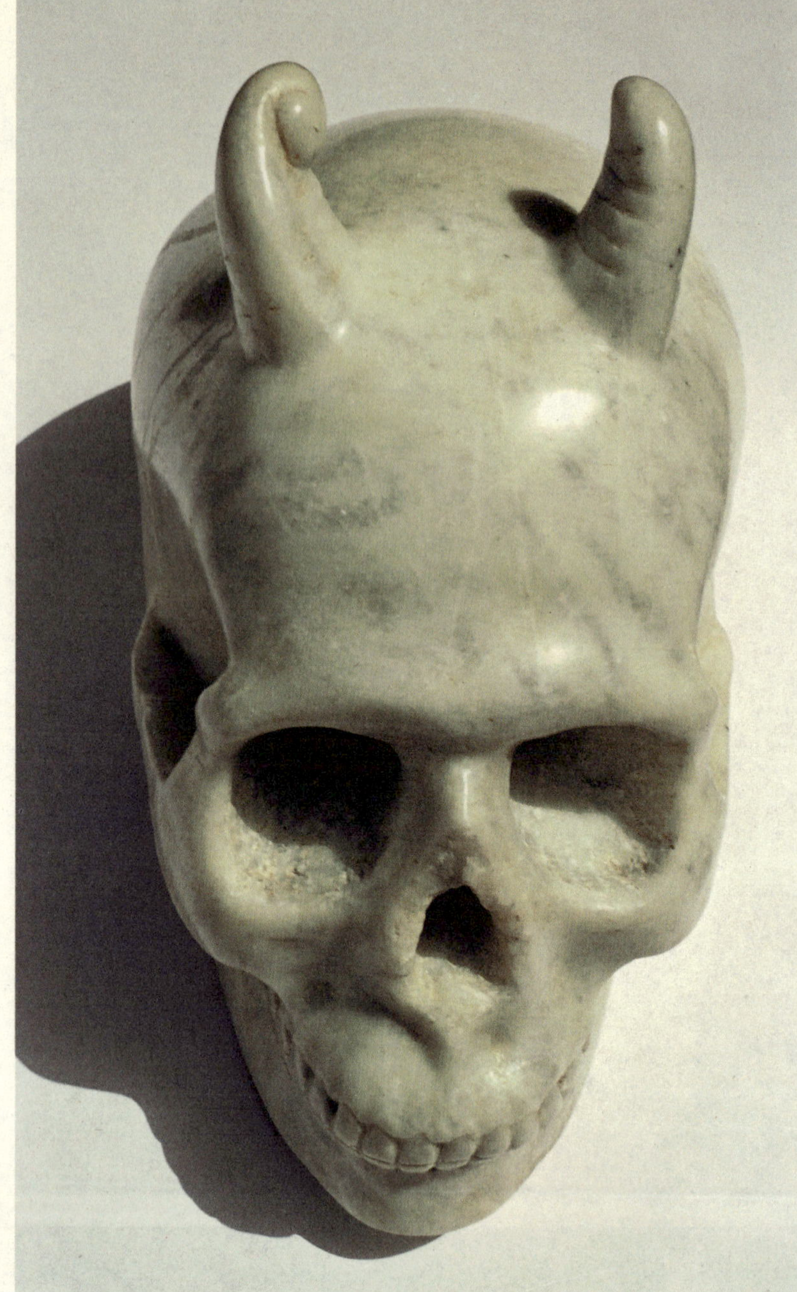

3.

Chinmoy Pramanick received his MFA from the Maharaja Sayajirao University of Baroda, West Bengal. An artist whose primary focus is sculpture, Pramanick utilizes a rotating group of metaphorically charged objects to explore a wide range of themes, from the problems inherent in knowledge transmission and interpersonal communication to the psychic and spiritual costs of unbridled materialism. In 2006 he received the Promising Artist Award, from Art India and IHC.

1. **I Came and Kept My Word / Looking for Another One**

2006, site-specific installation with earth and stone, dimensions variable

2. **Untitled**

2002, marble, 17 × 14 × 9 in (43 × 36 × 23 cm)

3. **Untitled**

2007, patinated brass, 85 × 34 $\frac{1}{2}$ × 23 in (216 × 88 × 57 cm)

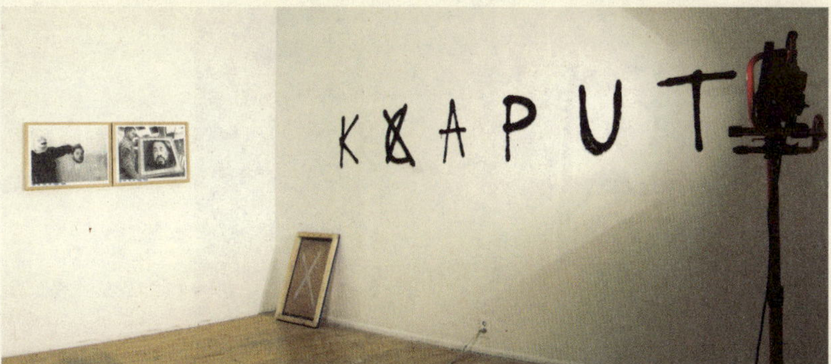

1.

Sreshta Premnath received his MFA from Bard College in 2006 and was a studio fellow at the Whitney Independent Study program in 2008. His work explores how otherness is constituted through complex matrices of knowledge, power, subjugation, and mediation. His installation **Contraband**, for instance, is comprised of three steel trunks containing indigenous medicinal plant species from which American pharmaceutical corporations have patented isolated genes for commercial use, drawing our attention to the ways in which systems of knowledge can be colonized. Premnath lives and works in New York.

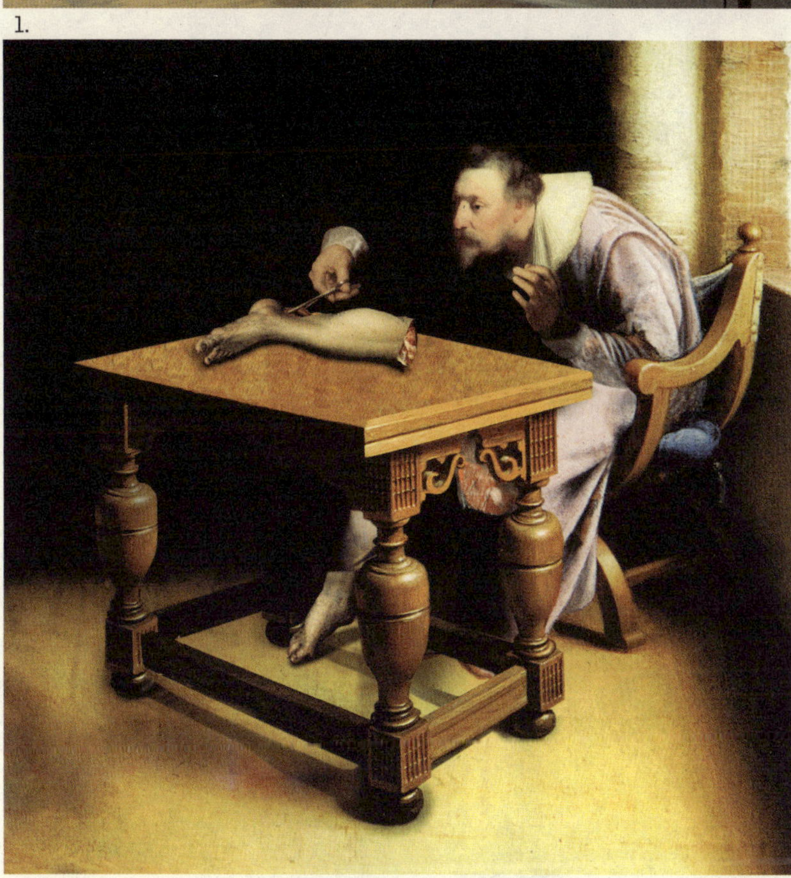
2.

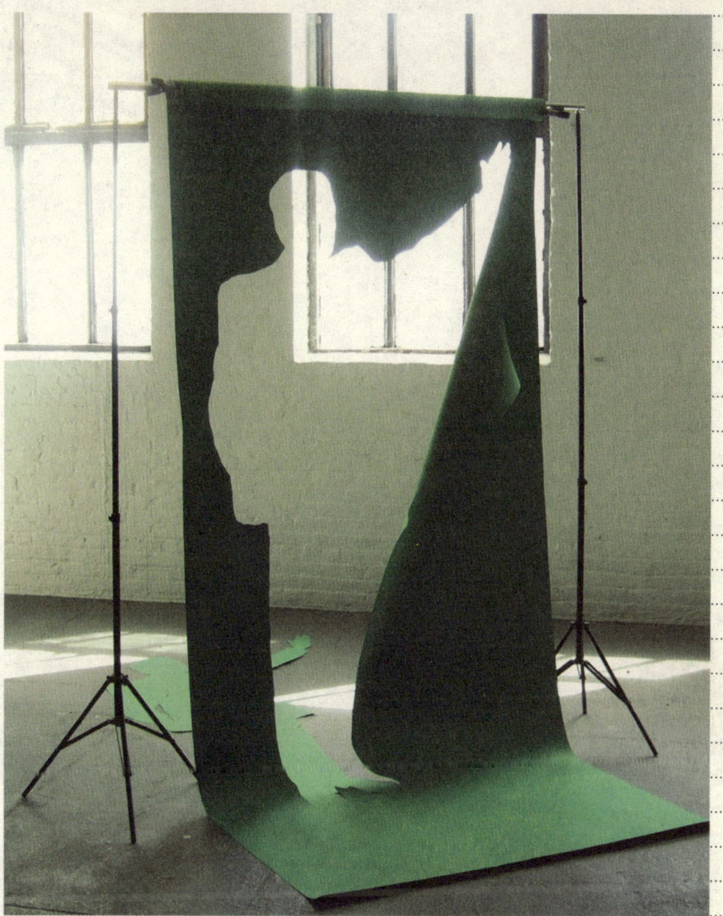
3.

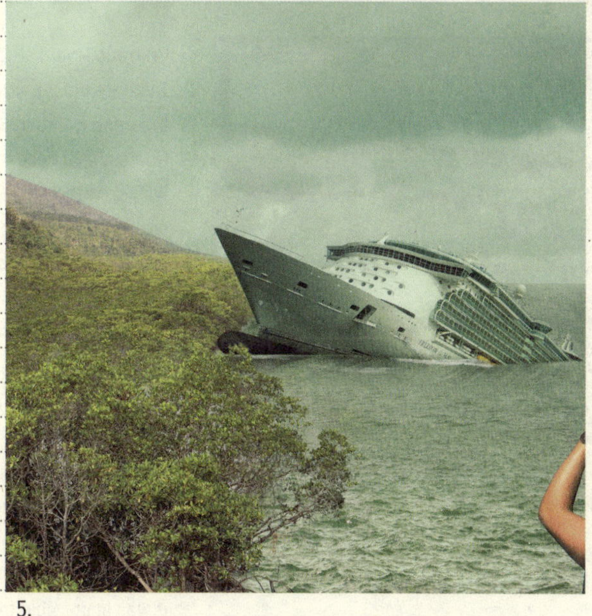
4. 5.

1. KXAPUT
2006, mixed media, dimensions variable

2. Philip Verheyen dissects his amputated leg
2006, digital image

3. Green Screen
2008, chroma key green backdrop paper and support, 7 × 7 × 8 ft (2 × 2 × 2.5 m)

4 & 5. Duty Free
from the series **Freedom of the Seas**
2008, digital composite chromogenic print, 2 parts, each 28 × 28 in (71 × 71 cm)

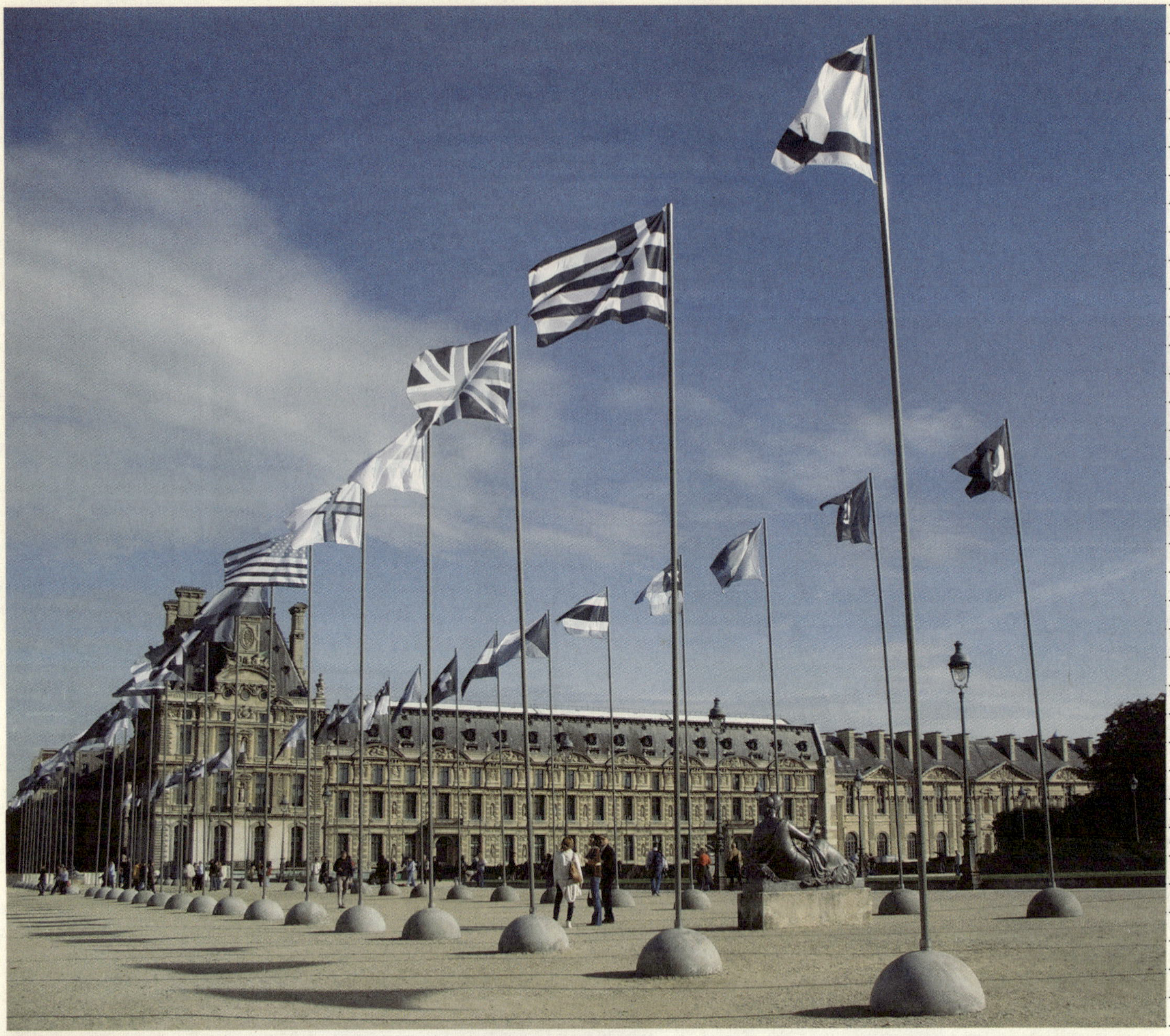

1.

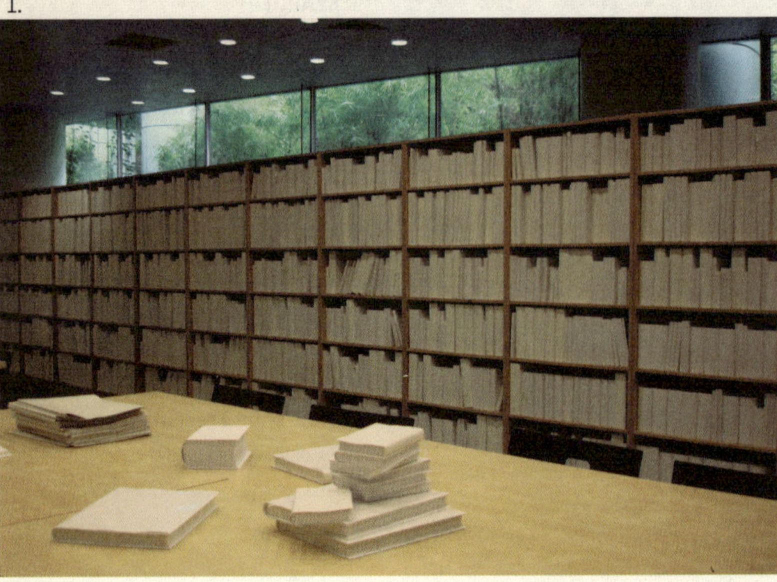

2.

Wilfredo Prieto studied at the Higher Institute of Fine Arts in Havana. He lives and works in Barcelona. He was a Guggenheim Fellow in 2006 and the 2008 winner of the Cartier Award. His work draws on such post-Conceptual artists as Gabriel Orozco, but also on earlier traditions of narrative and performance. For his 2006 work **Mute**, for example, he transformed a gallery into a disco dance floor, with spinning and flashing colored lights – but with no music. For the 2008 Frieze Art Fair, Prieto created a site specific piece: a red carpet that traced a route throughout the fair, but ultimately led up to the top of a tall flagpole, where it was impossible to follow.

1. **Apolitical**
2001, black, gray, and white flags from every country, dimensions variable, installation view at the Louvre, Paris (2006)

2. **Untitled (white library)**
2004, white books, shelves, tables, and chairs, dimensions variable, installation view at 1st Singapore Biennial, Singapore (2006)

Ana Prvacki is the founder and CEO of Ananatural Production, a semi-fictional innovation and lifestyle consultancy firm that provides solutions for our everyday worries, fears, and conundrums. She has provided papaya facials at the ARCO art fair in Madrid (2006), invited viewers at the 2006 Singapore Biennial to take a **Leap of Faith** (2006) onto a minimalist grid of Velcro while wearing a specially designed Velcro vest, and wiped currency clean in **At the tips of your fingertips** (2008). She lives and works in New York and Singapore.

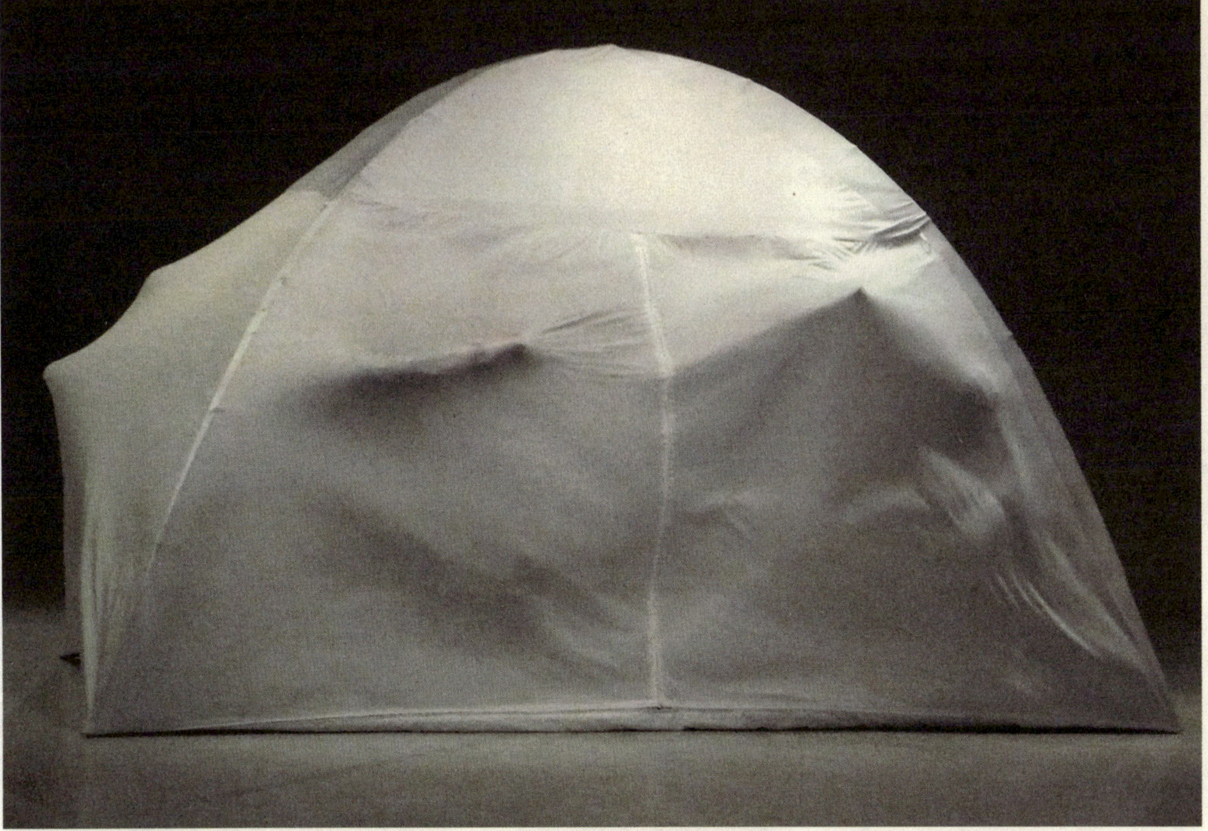

1.

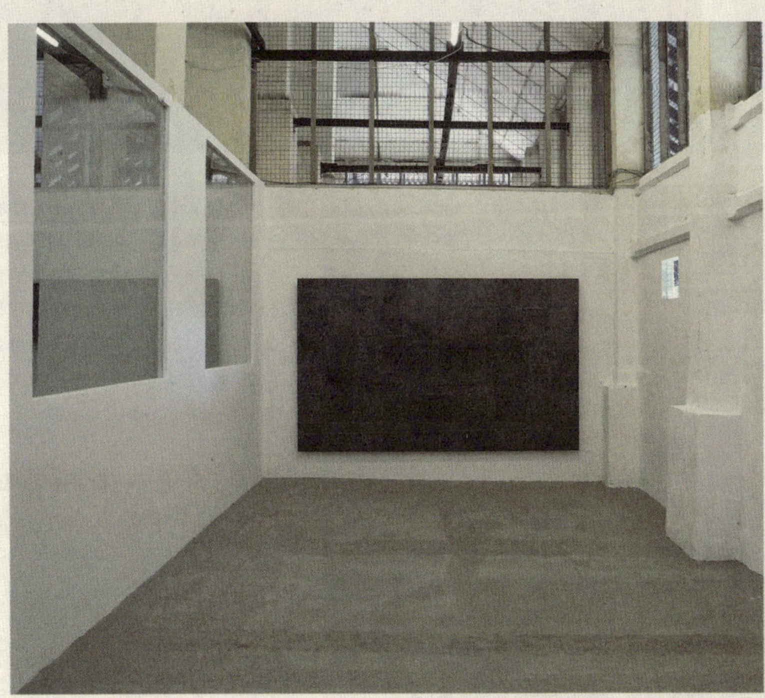

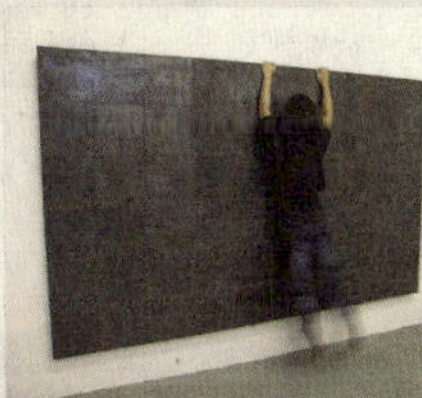

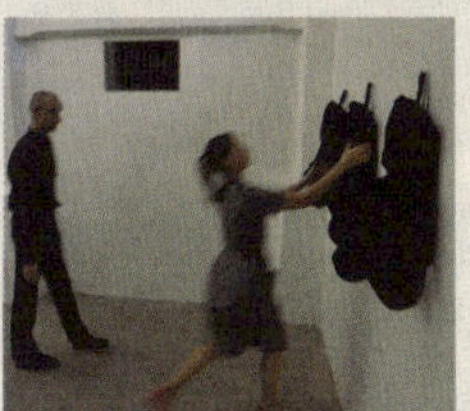

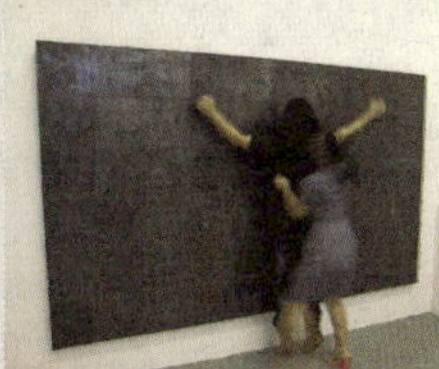

2.

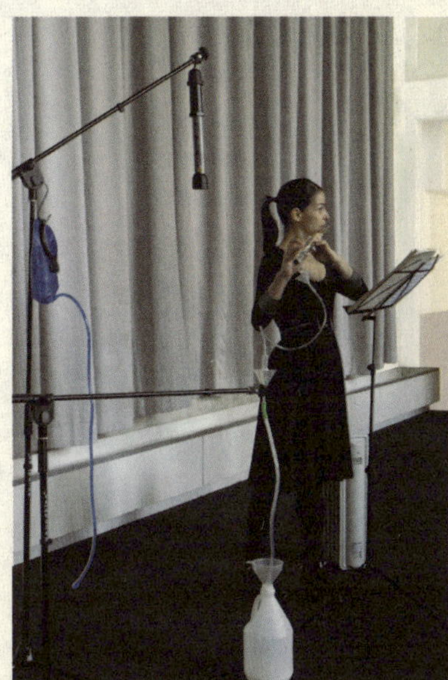

3.

1. Tent, Quartet, Bows and Elbows
2007, video and performance

2. Leap of Faith
2006, video, mixed media, and service, installation view at the Singapore Biennial

3. Music derived pain killer
2008, product and performance at Sydney Biennial

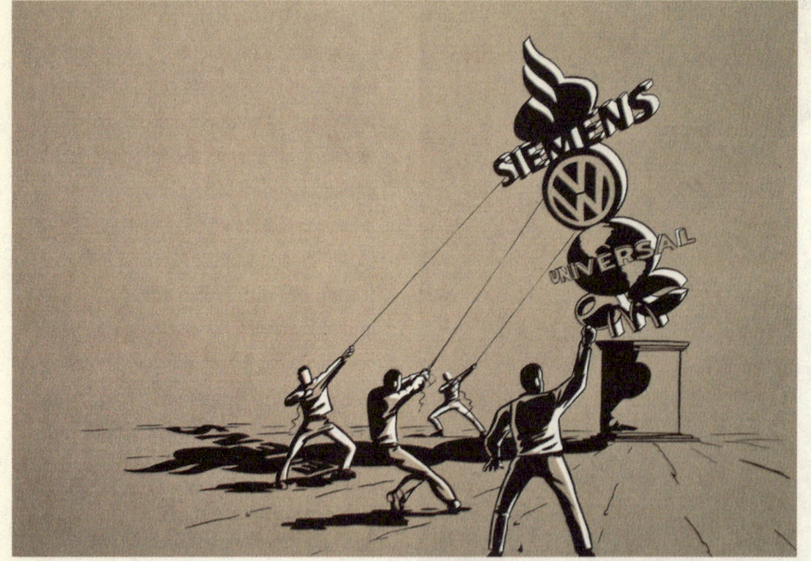

1.

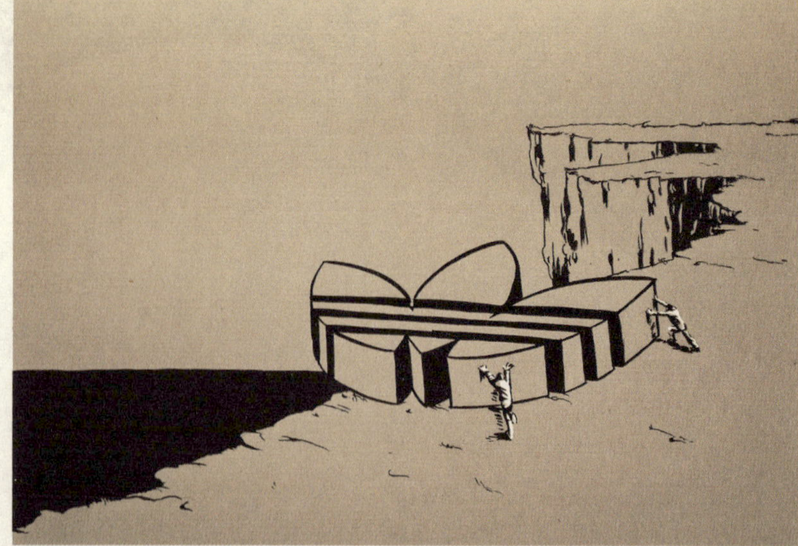
2.

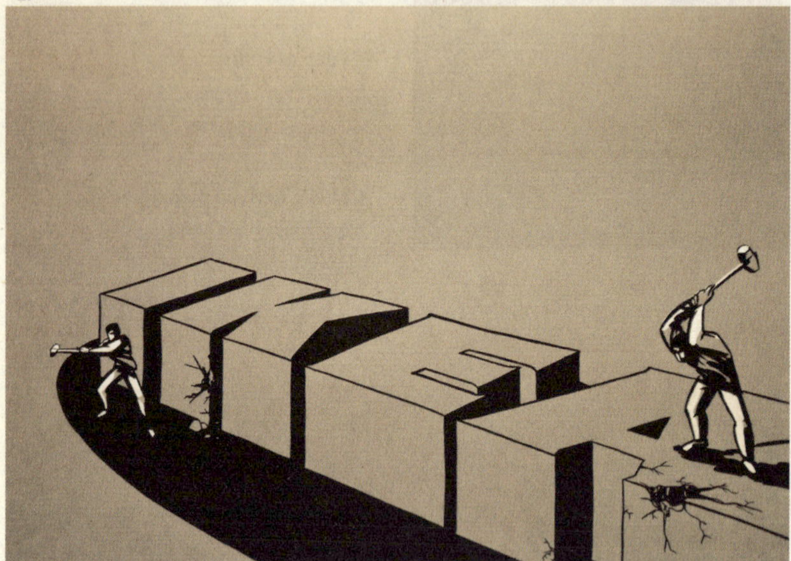
3.

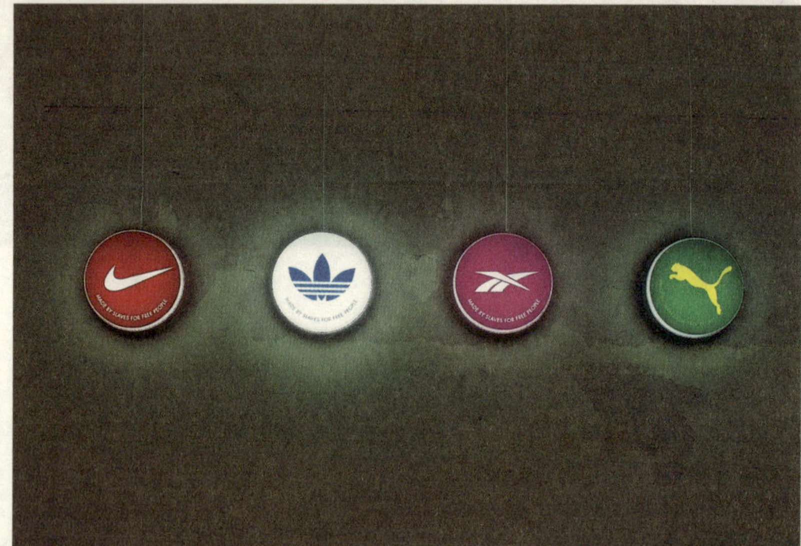
4.

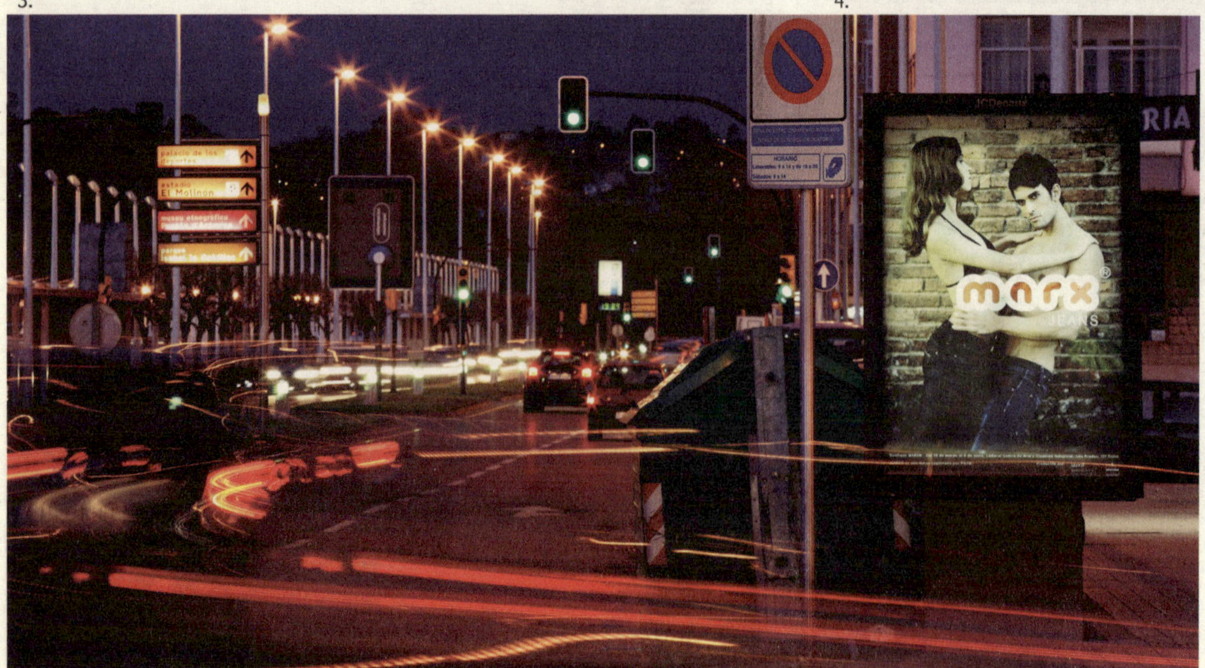

5.

Berlin-based duo PSJM make use of strategies associated with marketing to explore the connection between art and commerce. One of their projects involved creating a range of Marx logo products. Another used light boxes to take a dig at sportswear manufacturers.

1, 2 & 3. **Struggle (Brand Totem), (Adidas), (Ikea)**
2007, ink and acrylic on paper, 3 drawings, each 14 × 19 in (35 × 50 cm)

4. **Asia Project**
2008, 4 light boxes, 6 × 17 in (15 × 45 cm)

5. **Marx® (outside campaign)**
2008, advertisements, installation view, dimensions variable

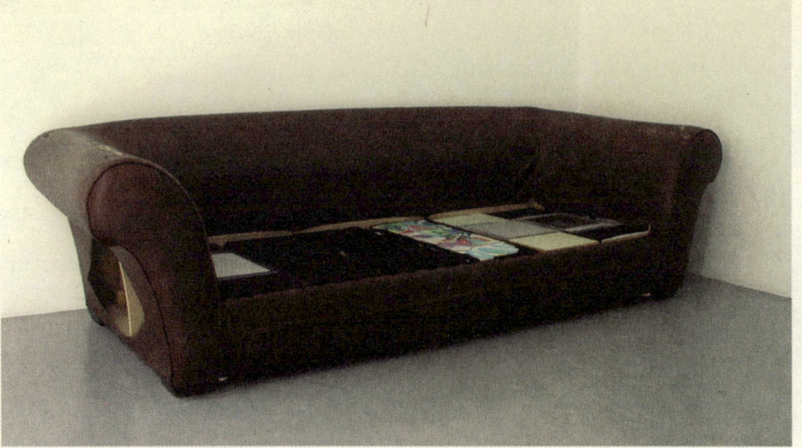

1.

Reto Pulfer is a self-taught artist who lives and works in Berlin and Basel. His enigmatic sculptures, installations, and musical performances are rough-hewn and provisional, utilizing made-up language, self-made instruments, mysticism, and magic to create deeply personal and idiosyncratic hermeneutic systems. His work has been the subject of solo exhibitions at Galerie Balice Hertling, Paris (2008), Galerie Montgomery, Berlin (2008), and D21, Leipzig (2006), among others.

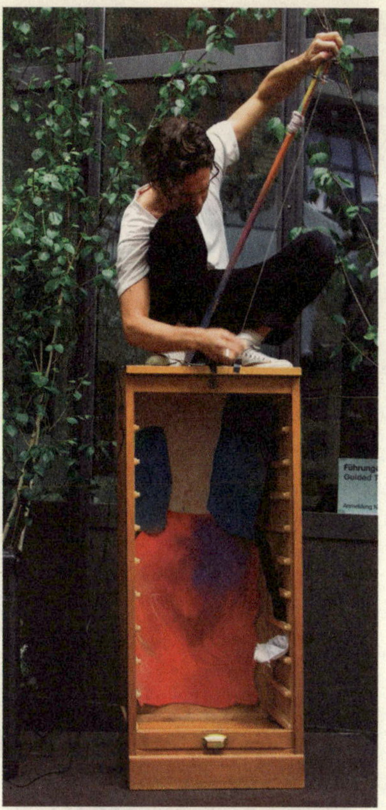

2.

1. **Ofaz 1442**
2007-08, sofa, velvet, black and white photograph, pencil drawing on wood, amplifier, and guitar string, 37 ½ × 94 ½ × 25 ½ in (95 × 240 × 65 cm)

2. **Ognams**
2008, performance

3. **Chlopf-Taefu-Liecht Schacht**
2008, microphones, fabric, pastel on wood, pencil on wood, and guitar string, dimensions variable

4. **Hermetisch**
2008, wood, ceramic, pen on paper and cloth, mercury, plumb, and audio, dimensions variable

5. **ZR Potzwaus**
2008, pastel on paper, fabric, zipper, thread, and framed printed text, 126 × 96 ½ in (320 × 245 cm)

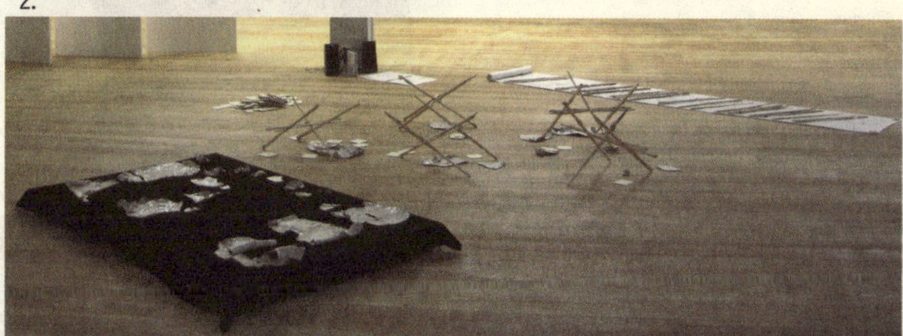

4.

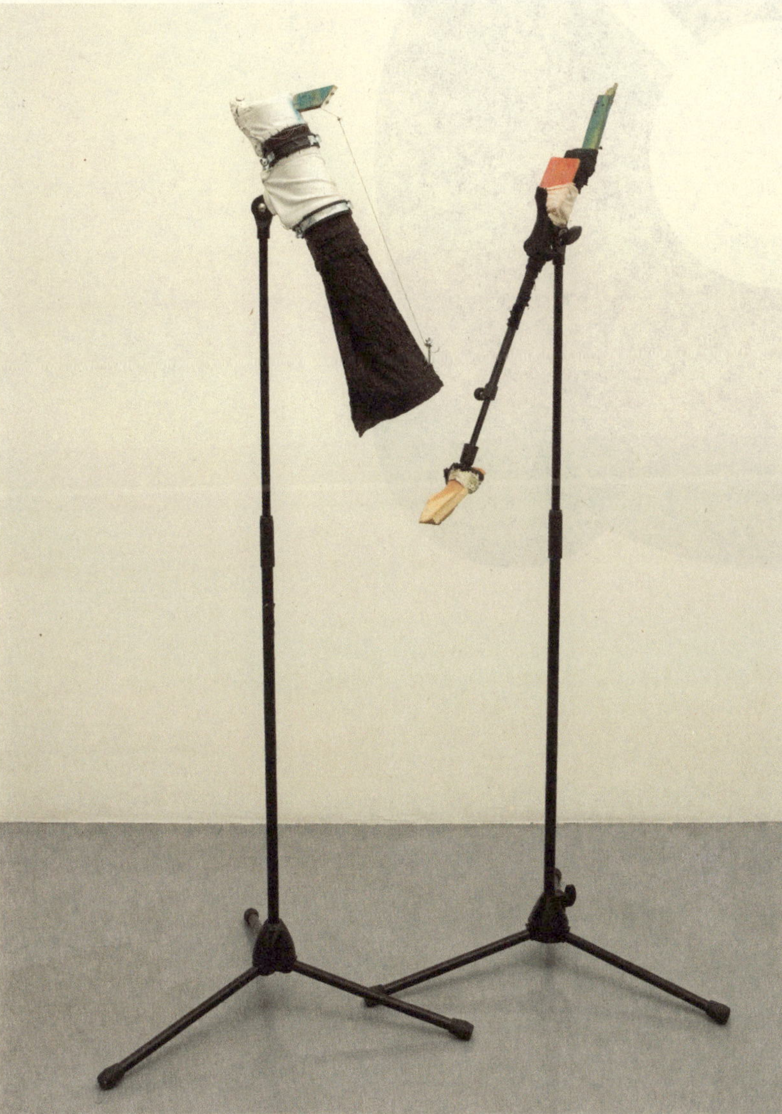

3.

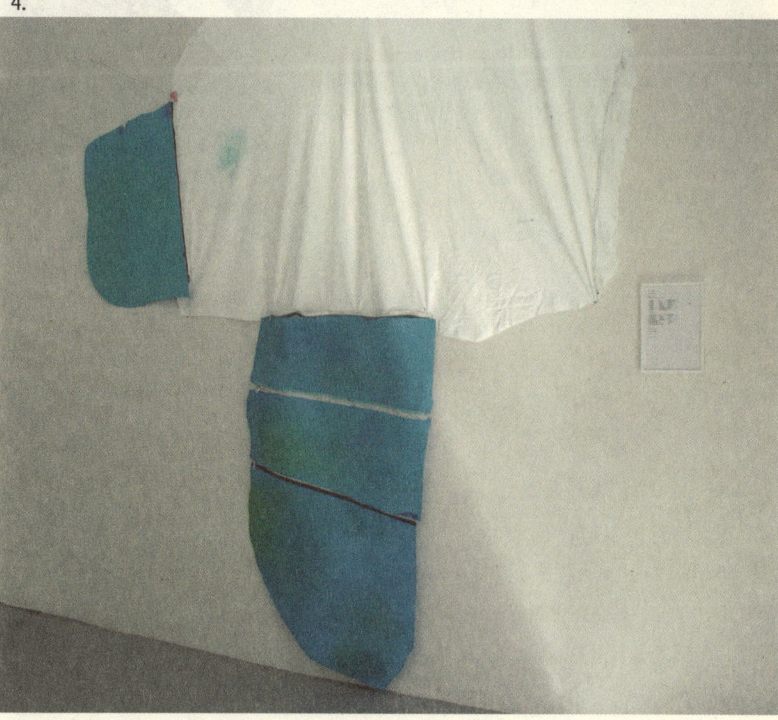

5.

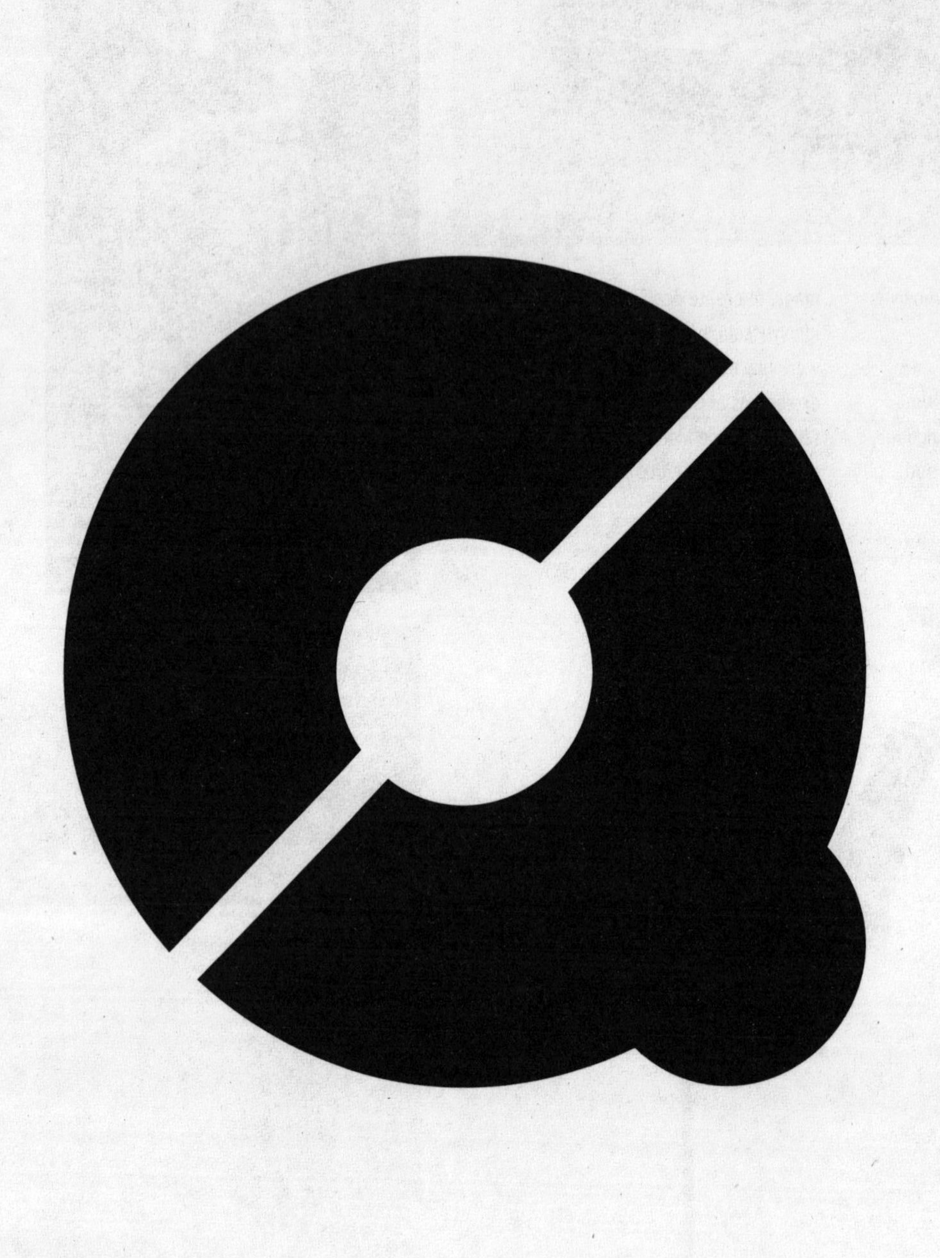

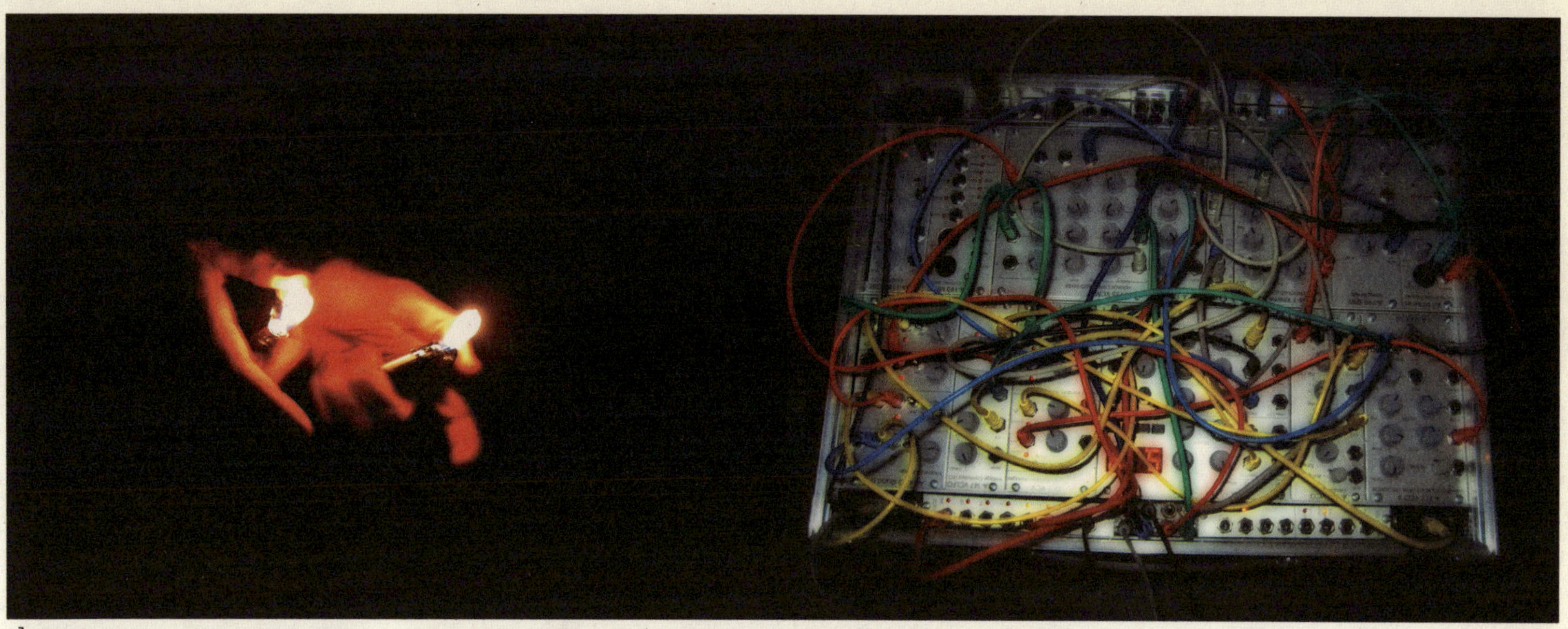

1.

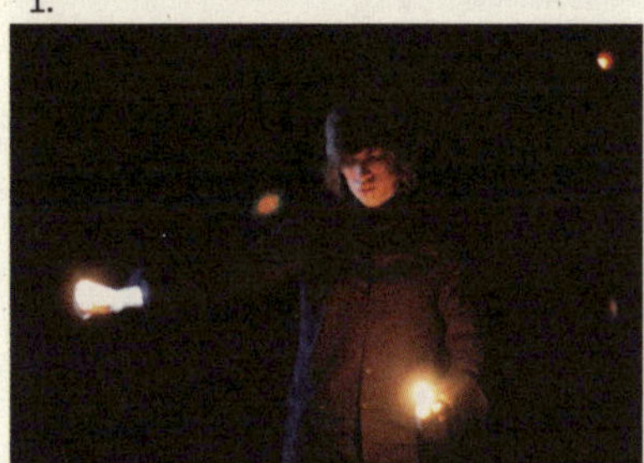

2.

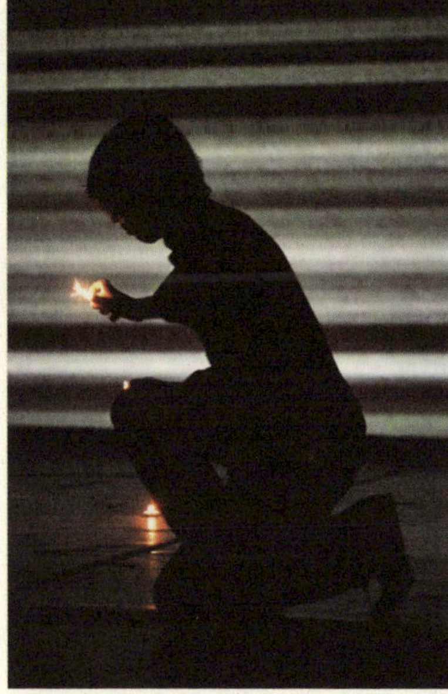

3.

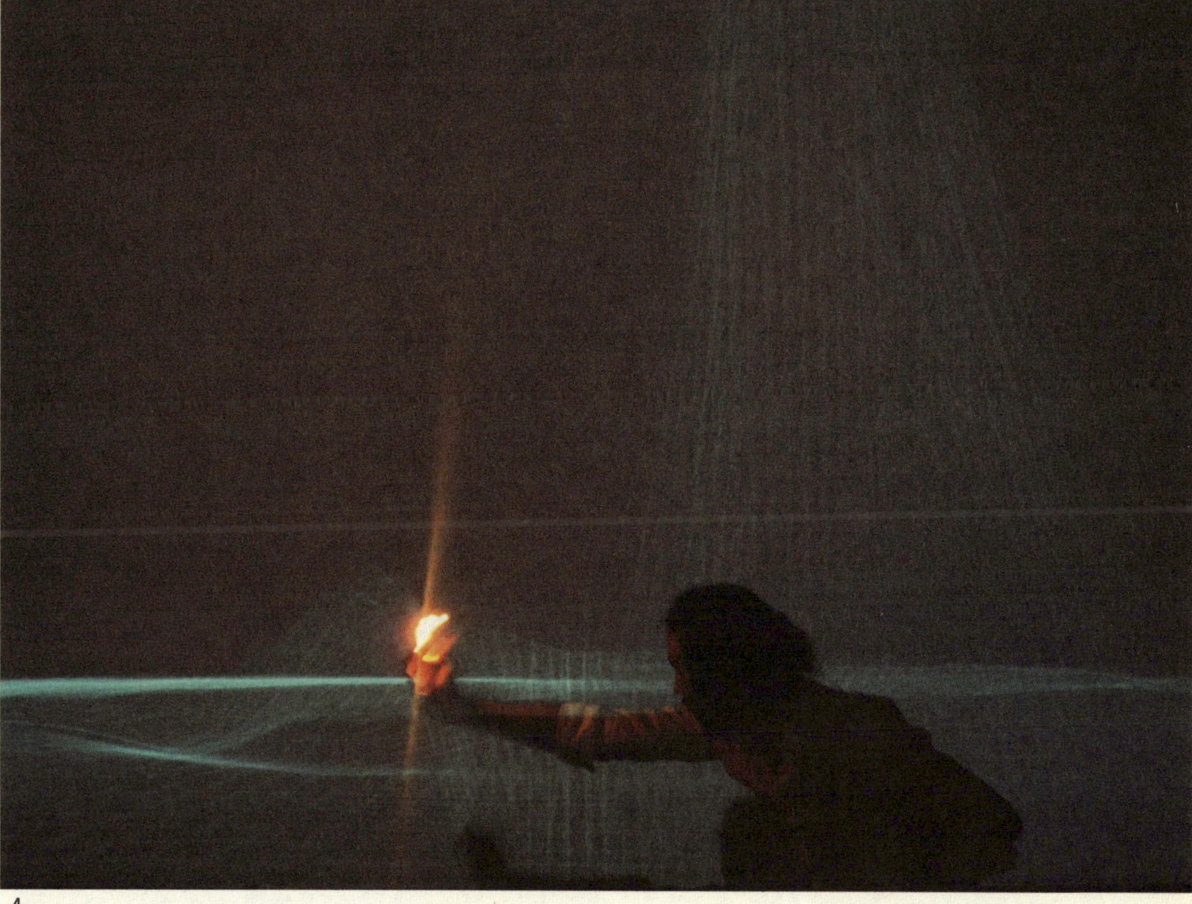

4.

Lisbon-based Rudolfo Quintas studied computer graphics engineering and virtual environments at the School of Engineering, Minho University, Portugal. He creates interactive performance, installation, and sound works combining art and software design. In 2005 he cofounded the research and development collective Swap-Project, which focuses on performance art and new technologies.

1, 2 & 3. **Burning The Sound**
2007, custom interactive software application

4. **Burning The Sound: Inversed Metaphors**
2008, custom interactive software application

R

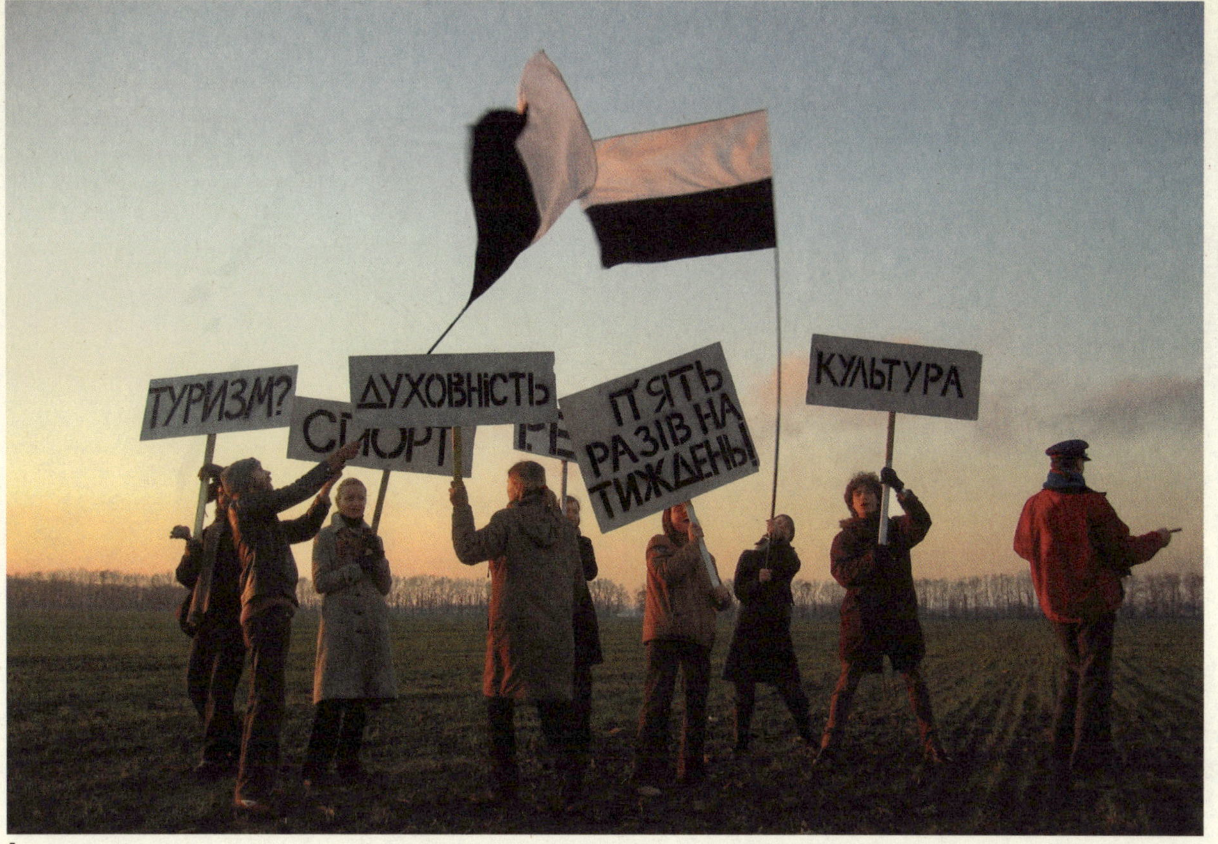

1.

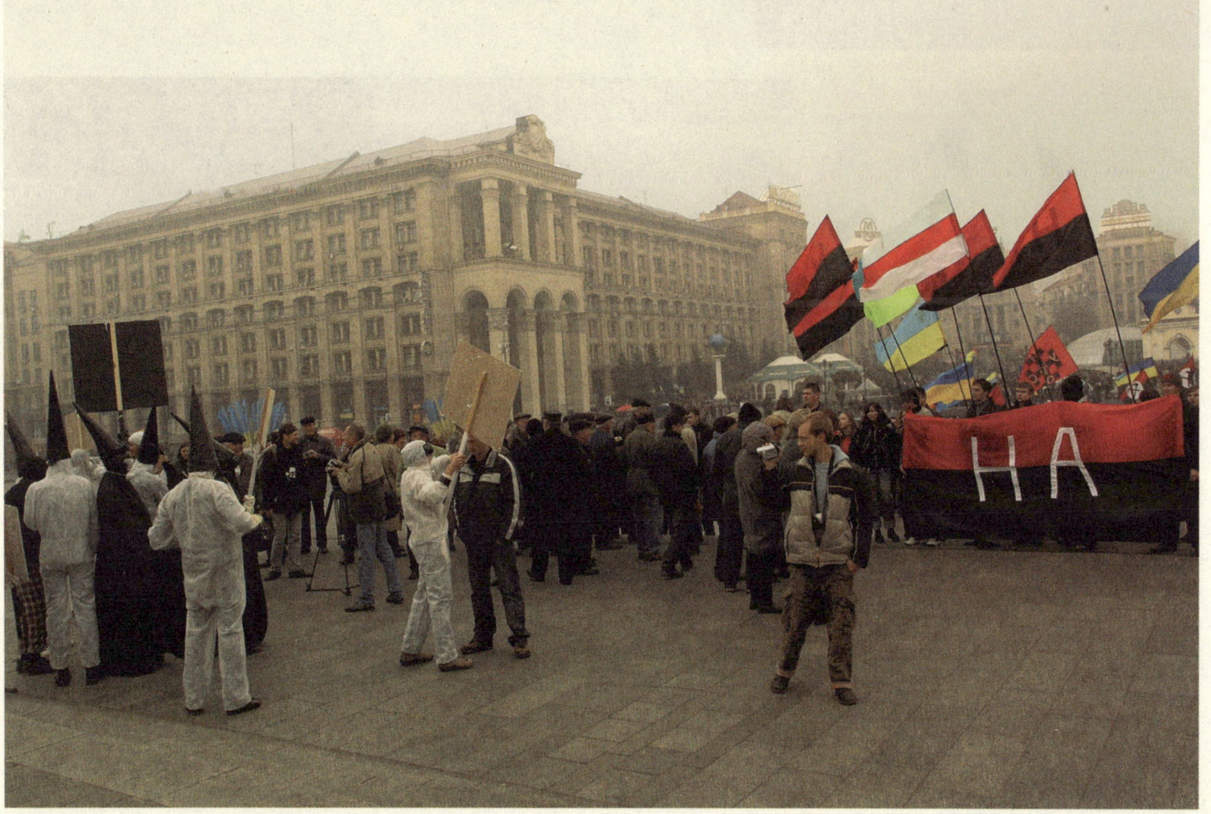

2.

The Revolutionary Experimental Space group was founded in 2004 during the Ukranian "Orange Revolution" as a large group of young artists working collectively to produce public art projects and organize themselves in protest groups. The Centre for Contemporary Art at the Kiev-Molyla Academy gave the group space for a residency. Since 2006, the group has been made up of six artists: Lada Nakonechka, Lesia Khomenko, Nikita Kadan, Zhanna Kadyrova, Ksenia Gnylytska, and Volodymyr Kuznetsov. Their ongoing **Patriotism** project involves creating a visual lexicon of various terms (power, friendship, equal rights) and creating installations and narratives using these signs.

1. **Untitled Action**
2005, performance

2. **We will R.E.P. you**
2005, performance

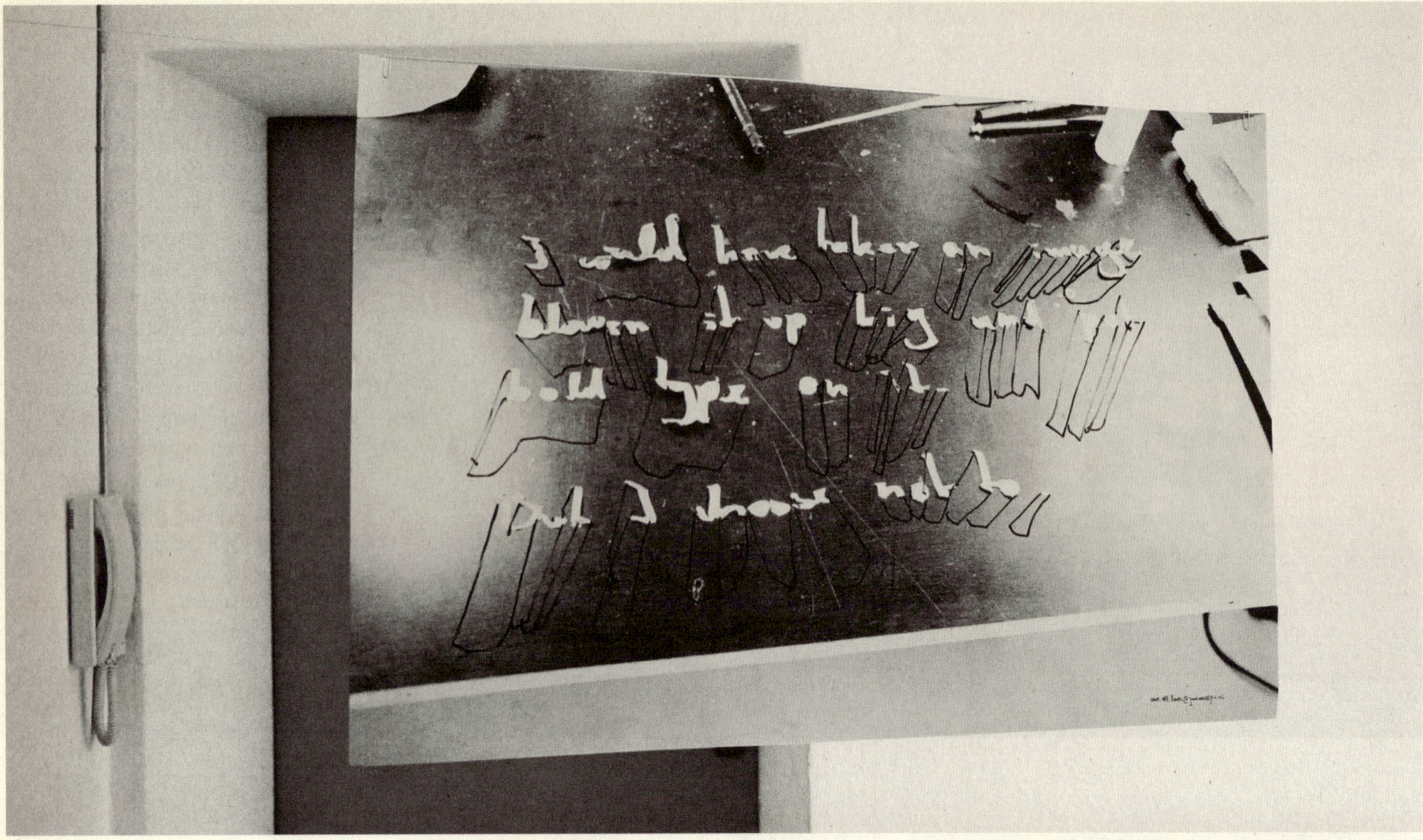

1.

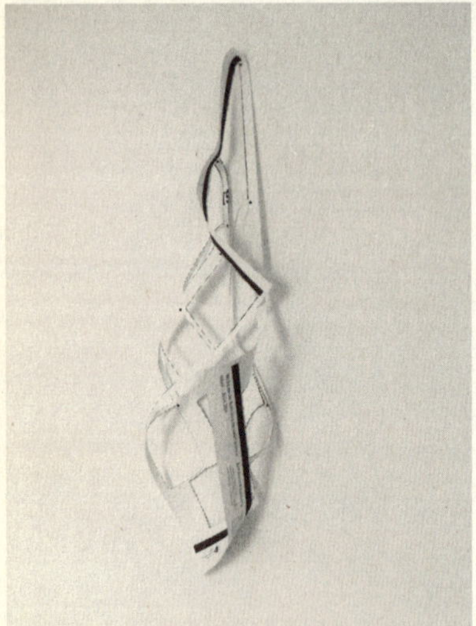

2.

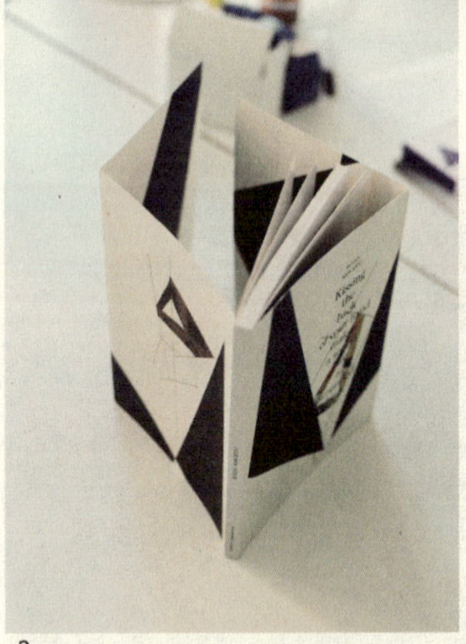

3.

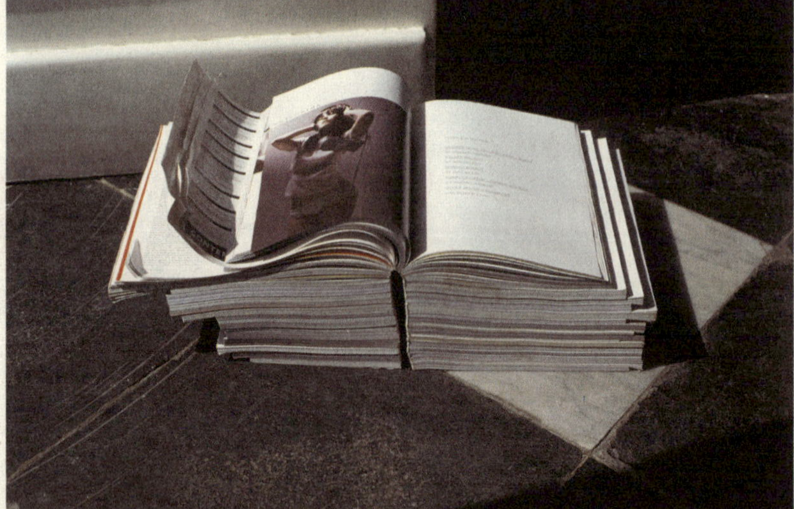

4.

Manuel Raeder studied at the London College of Printing and completed a postgraduate degree at the Jan van Eyck Akademie in Maastricht. He lives and works in Berlin. He has collaborated with other artists, designers, curators, and musicians to design, among other things, a typeface based on complex polygon shapes, a font developed by stretching chewing gum onto a flatbed scanner, furniture, exhibitions, clothing, and a 2007 limited-edition day planner that functions as an organizer and a way to investigate how people manage their time.

1. **I could have taken an image blown it up big and put bold type on it. But I choose not to**
2001, offset printed paper, $23\frac{1}{2} \times 33$ in (59 × 84 cm)

2. **I Have Never Seen It So Far Away**
2007, offset printed paper, dimensions variable

3. **Wounded Bird**
2007, book and shapes, dimensions variable

4. **Doorstopper**
2003, magazines and door, dimensions variable

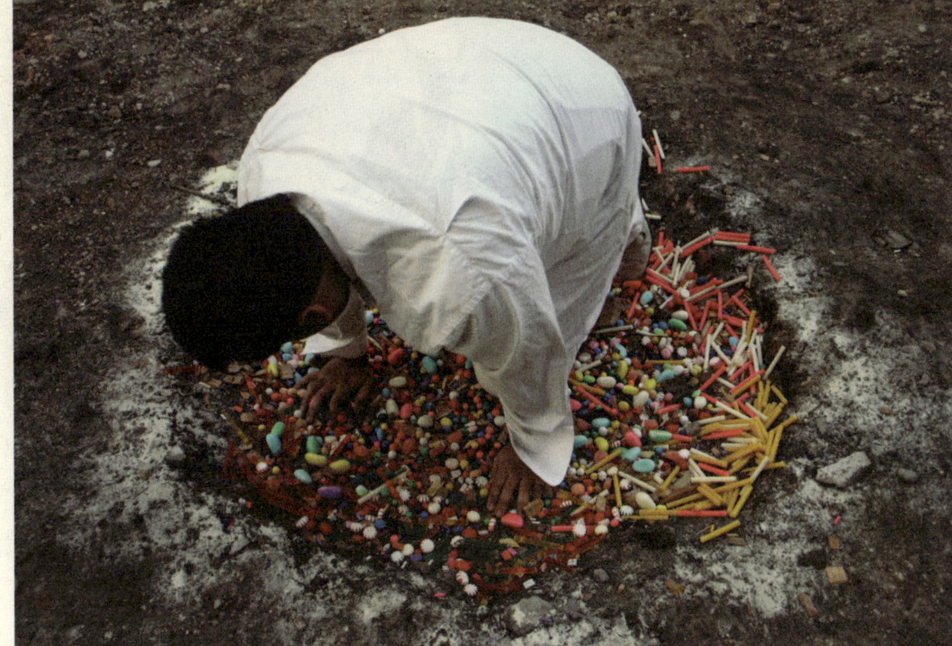

1.

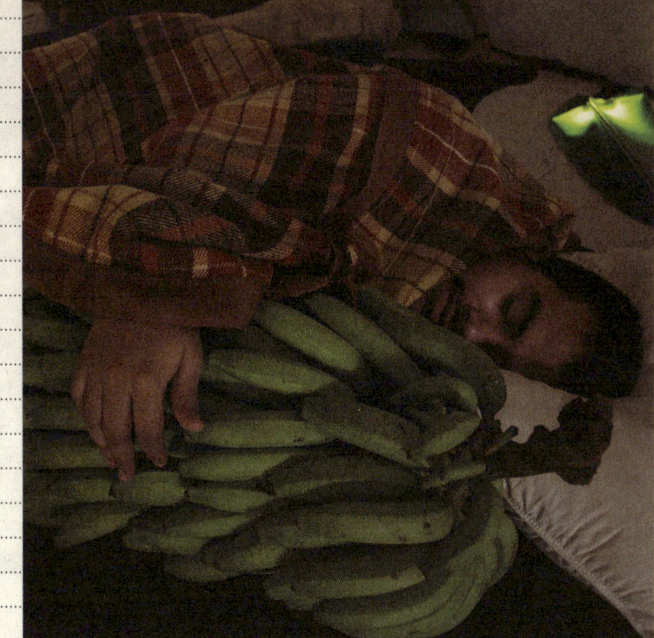

2.

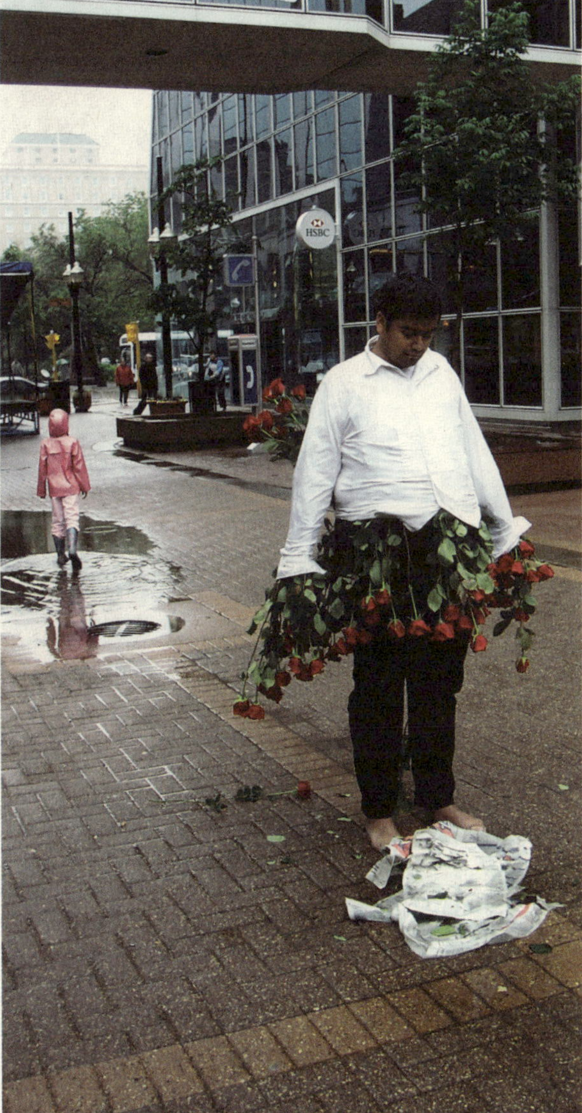

3.

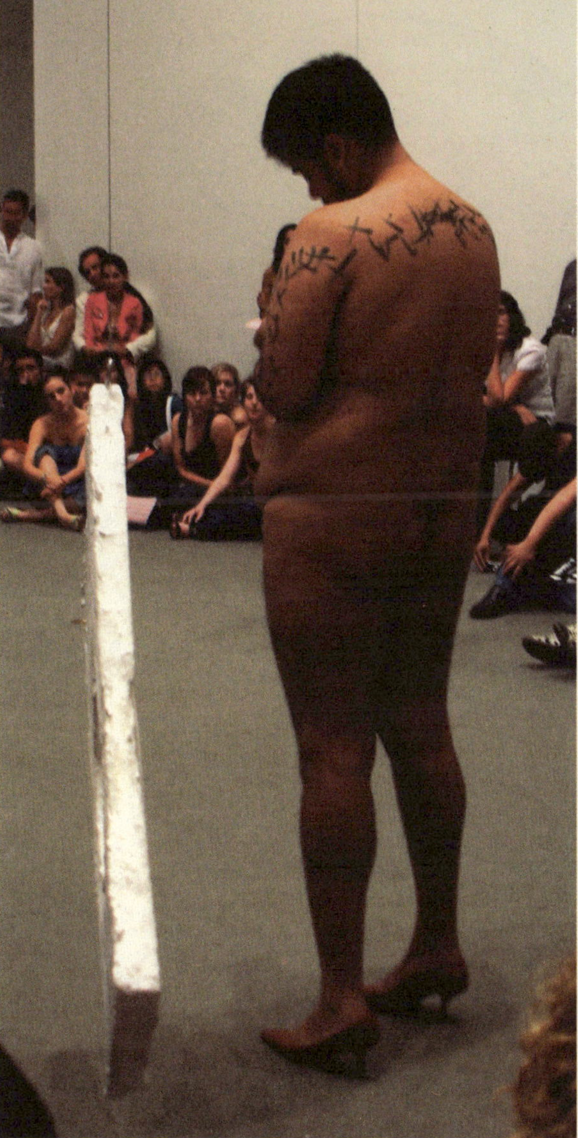

4.

Naufús Ramírez-Figueroa received an MFA from the School of the Art Institute of Chicago in 2007 and currently lives in Flores, Guatemala. His video works, installations, and performances address issues related to his Guatemalan identity, such as the country's civil war and ensuing diaspora, or the survival of ancient ritual practices in contemporary mass culture. Ramírez-Figueroa often uses perishable materials (bananas, fireworks) that transform over the course of his videos or performances. This heightens the viewer's awareness of the present moment even as the content alludes to the past, reflecting the artist's understanding of his own relation to history.

1. **Muxux Uleu**
2006-07, performance and ephemeral installation

2. **Para Ti El Banano Madura Al Peso De Tu Dulce Amor**
2008, performance and ephemeral installation

3. **Written Sorrows**
2006, performance

4. **Color is Emptiness**
2005, performance

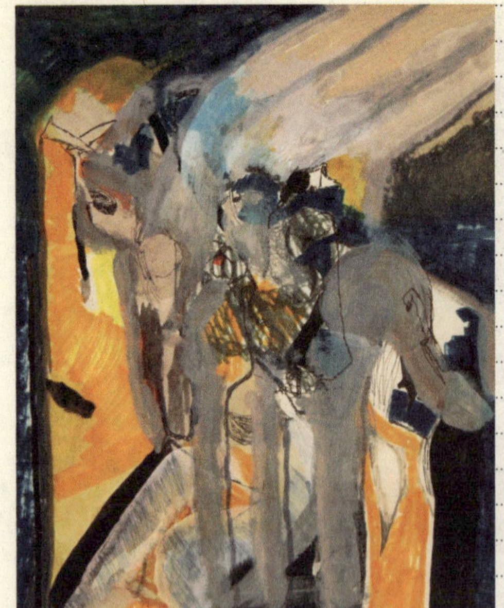

1.

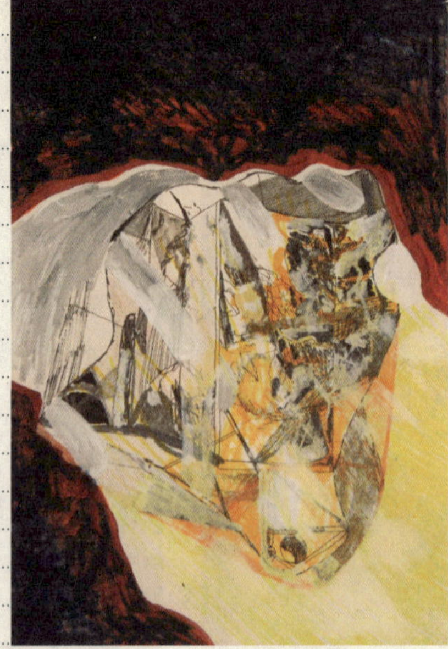

2.

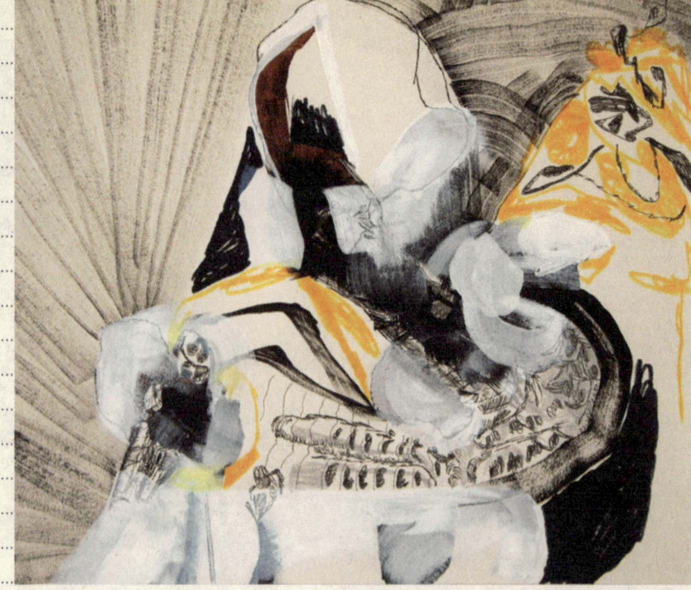

3.

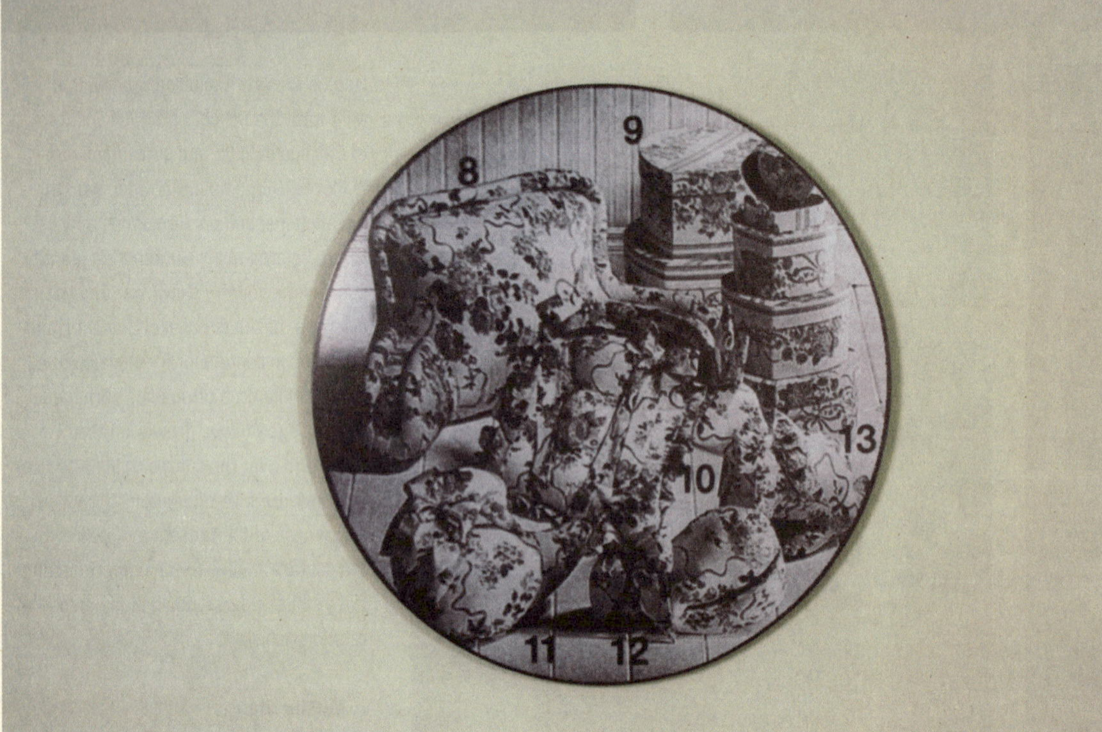

4.

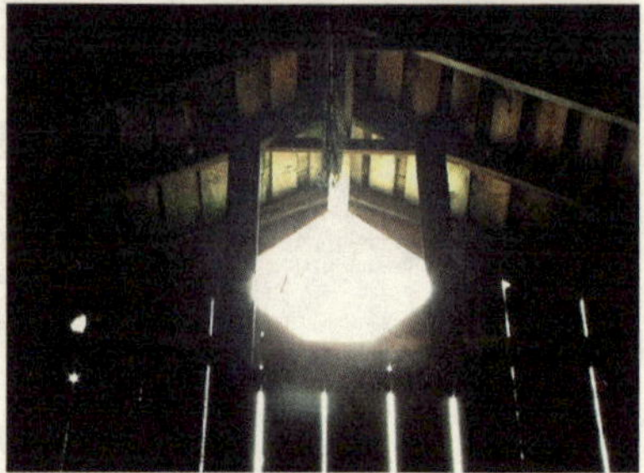

5.

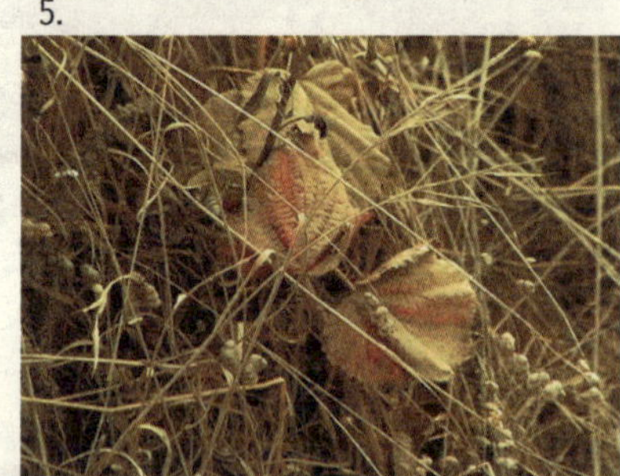

6.

7.

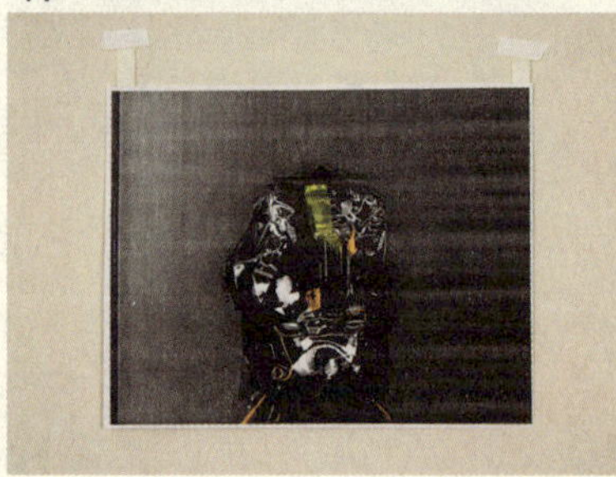

8.

Chadwick Rantanen received his BFA from the Minneapolis College of Art and Design and attended the Skowhegan School of Painting and Sculpture. He lives and works in San Francisco. His paintings on paper, sculptures, and videos draw on his upbringing as a Jehovah's Witness, but his work also addresses gallery space itself. An untitled 2007 video made from hand-drawn and painted vignettes depicts what the Artist Space Gallery in New York looks like after hours.

1. **CRCTSWUND**
2008, pen, gouache, marker, pencil, and colored pencil, 8 × 7 in (20 × 18 cm)

2. **RKBLST**
2008, pen, gouache, marker, pencil, and colored pencil, 11 × 8½ in (28 × 22 cm)

3. **MTLSPN**
2008, pen, gouache, marker, ink, pencil, and colored pencil, 15 × 17 in (38 × 43 cm)

4. **Untitled** (detail)
2006, circular color photographs, 1 of 3 parts

5, 6 & 7. **Absorber I**
2006, video, 3 min 30 sec

8. **HD**
2008, collage with photocopy, whiteout, and marker, 8½ × 11 in (22 × 28 cm)

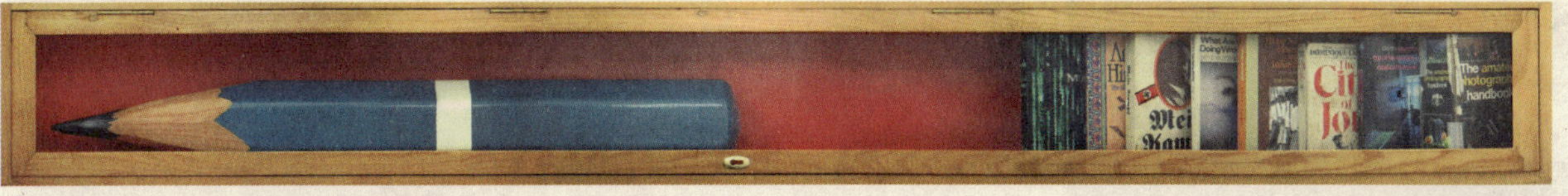
1.

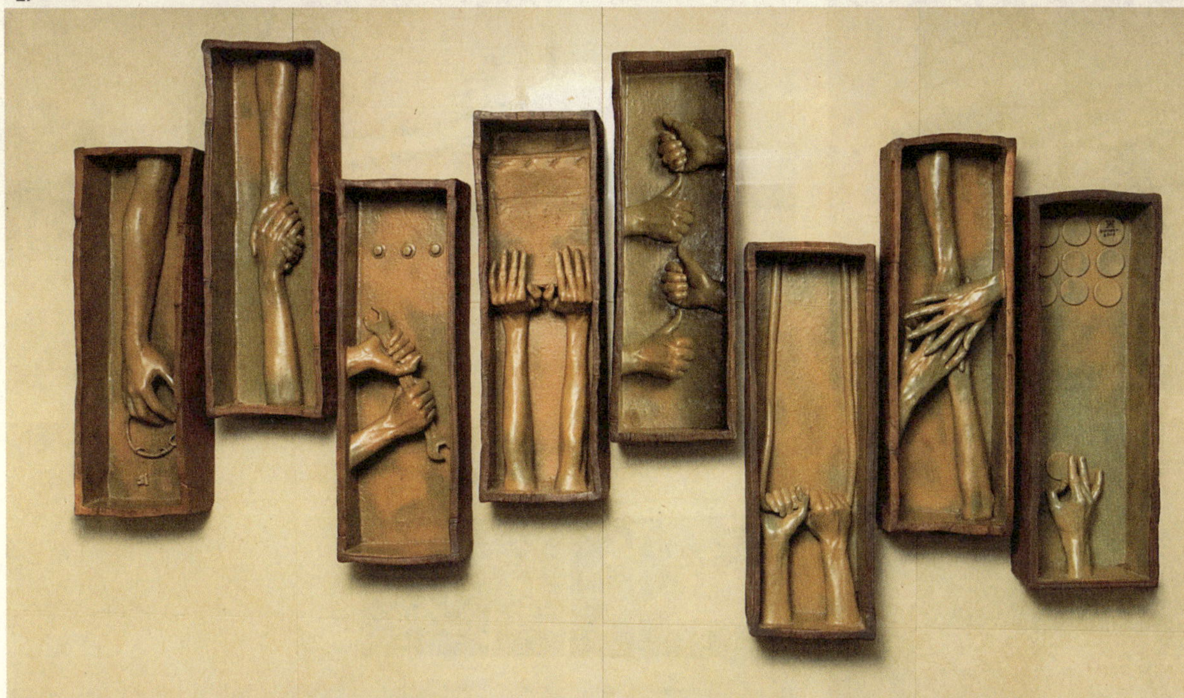
2.

Sukhdev Rathod studied painting, pottery, and ceramics at M.S. University of Baroda, India. He lives and works in Pratapgunj, India. Drawing on an interest in Surrealist art, he creates three-dimensional works that mimic the painted backdrops and spaces that one would see on a proscenium stage.

1. **Living in Baroda – 1**
2006, mixed media, 10 × 89 × 5 ½ in (25 × 226 × 14 cm)

2. **Abhivykti**
2003, stoneware ceramic, 48 × 96 × 6 in (122 × 244 × 14 cm)

3. **contradiction between eye and mind – 12**
2007, watercolor on paper, 18 × 24 in (46 × 61 cm)

4. **Untitled** (prototype)
2006, stoneware ceramic, 192 × 66 × 66 in (488 × 167 × 167 cm)

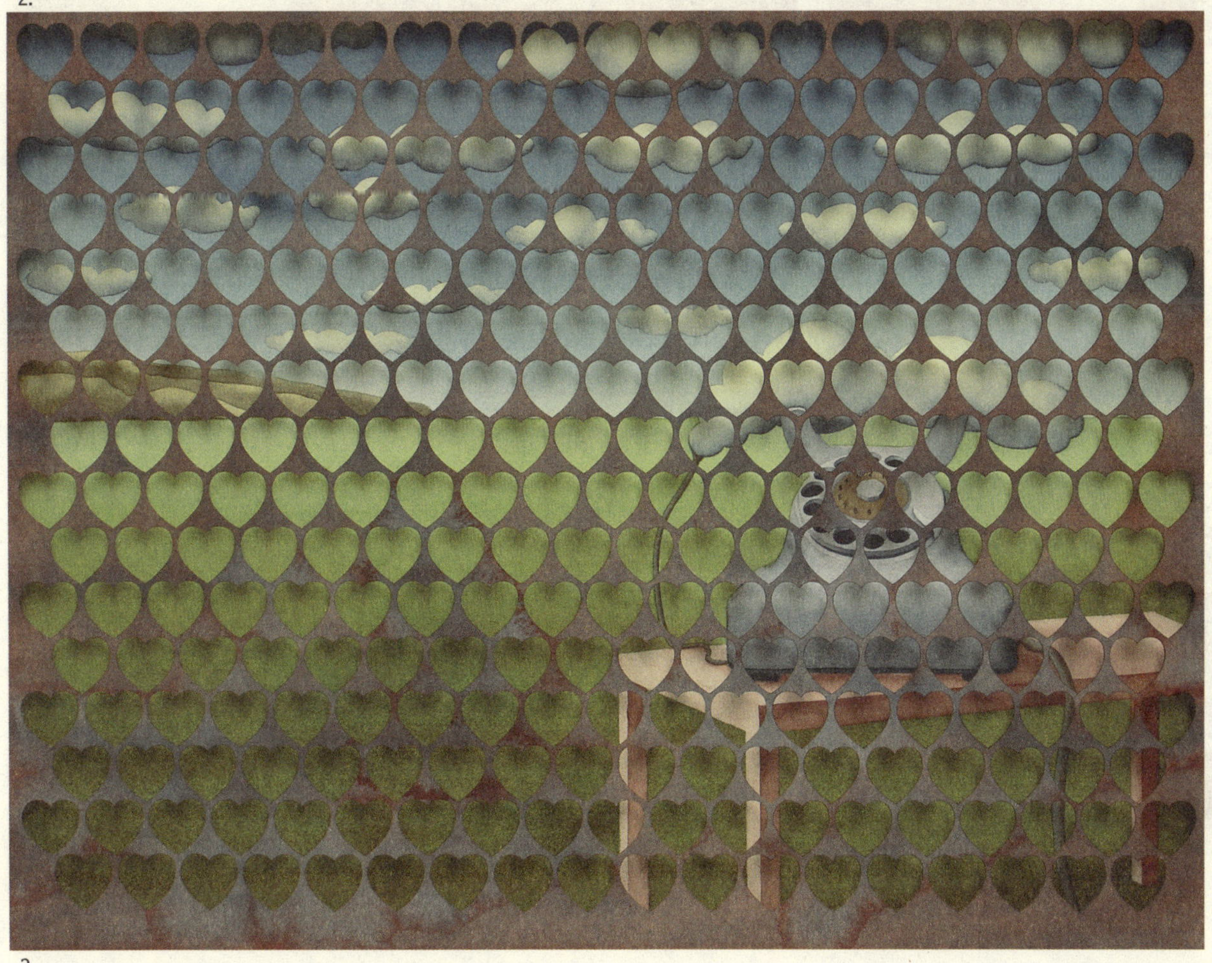
3.

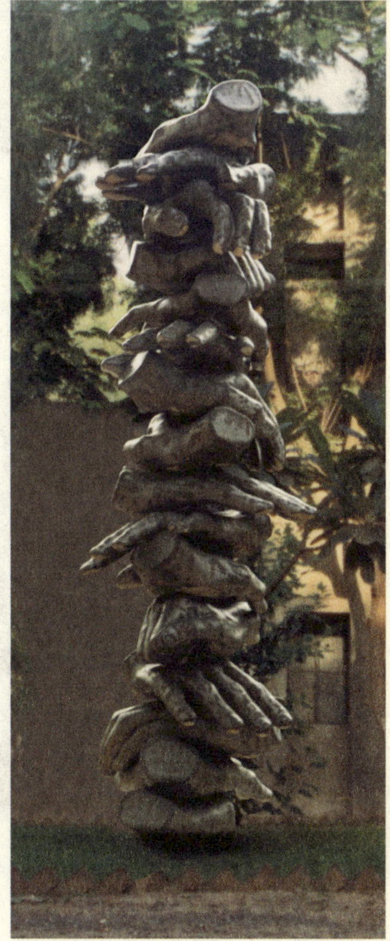
4.

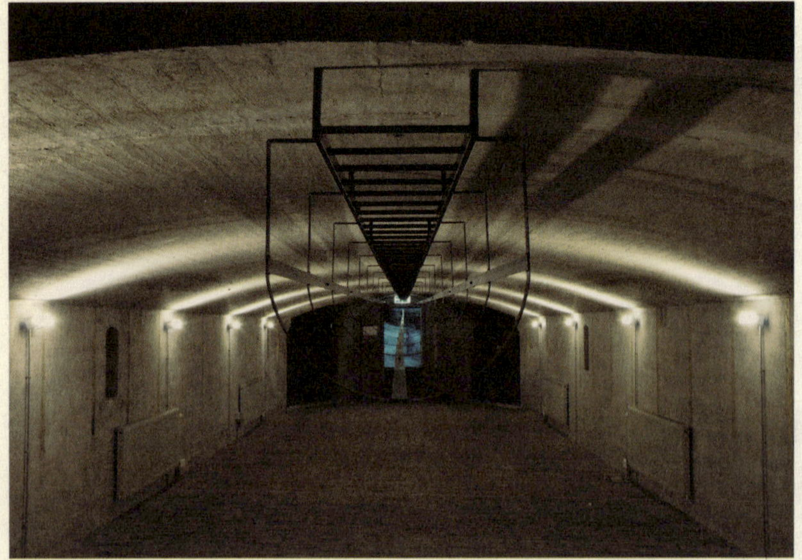

1.

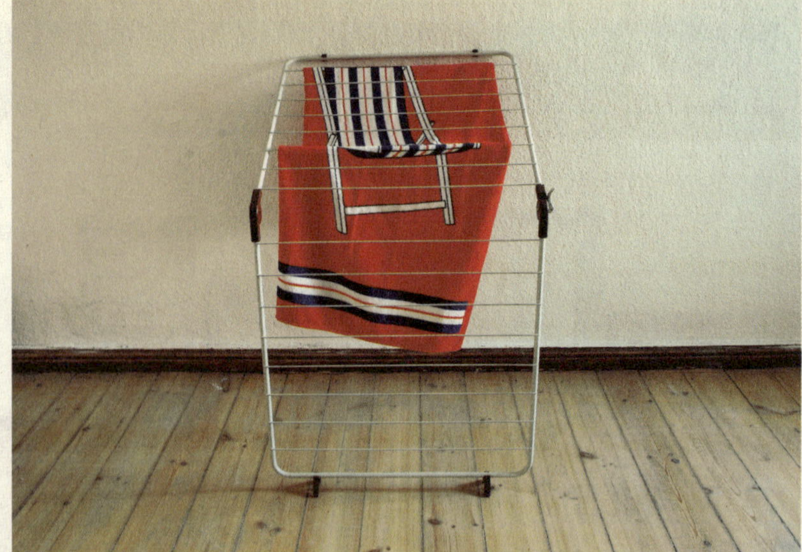

2.

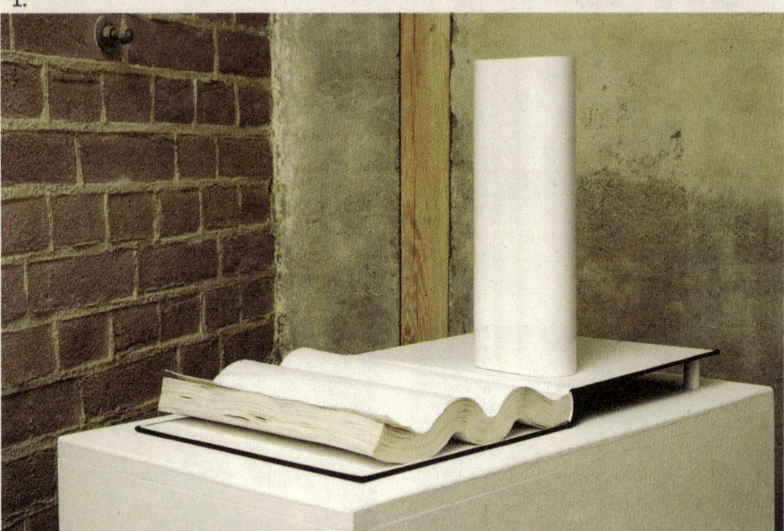

3.

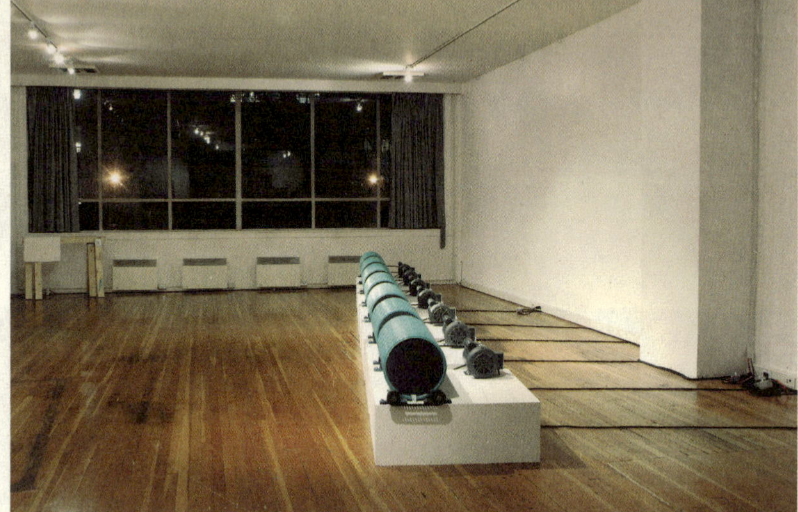

4.

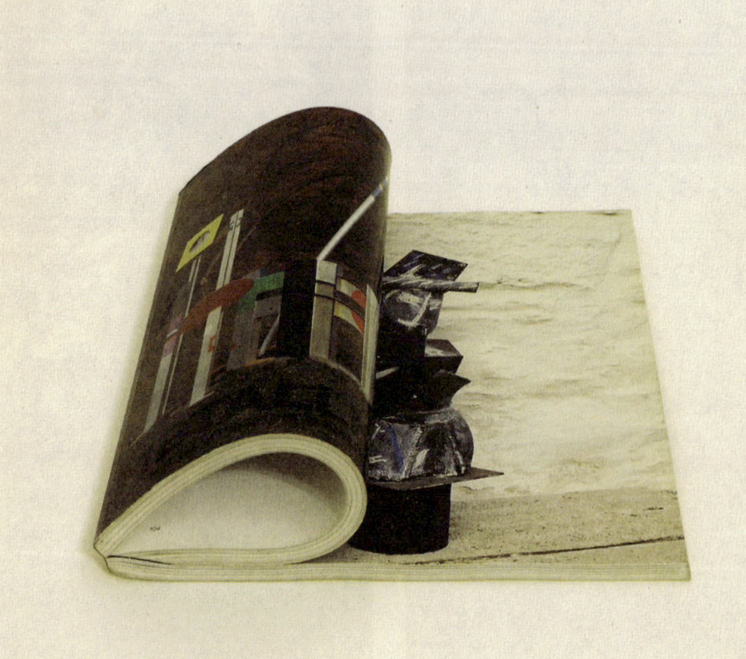

5.

Nicole Raufeisen and Ryan Witt, a collaborative artist couple, received BAs in visual art from Simon Fraser University in British Columbia in 2004 and are based in Berlin. In their site-specific installations, they are interested in uncovering the language of the particular materials they use in their artworks, and in the political contexts in which their work is presented. **Rainbow Mall** (2008) consists of seven abstract paintings they made to donate to a hospital charity thrift store after it was evicted from a local mall.

1. Blackbird
2007, steel and paint, length 56 ft (17 m)

2. Untitled (Classic)
2008, towel and drying rack, 24 × 35 × 28 in (61 × 89 × 71 cm)

3. Wet process
2007, water-damaged book (Grain Elevators by the Bechers), 13 × 21 × 12 in (33 × 53 × 30 cm)

4. Drowning the drowning
2007, 7 homemade tumblers, pea gravel, grit (silicone carbide, cerium oxide), and water, dimensions variable

5. Metallkunst (1989)
2008, book (Metallkunst aus der DDR), 9 ½ × 12 in (24 × 31 cm)

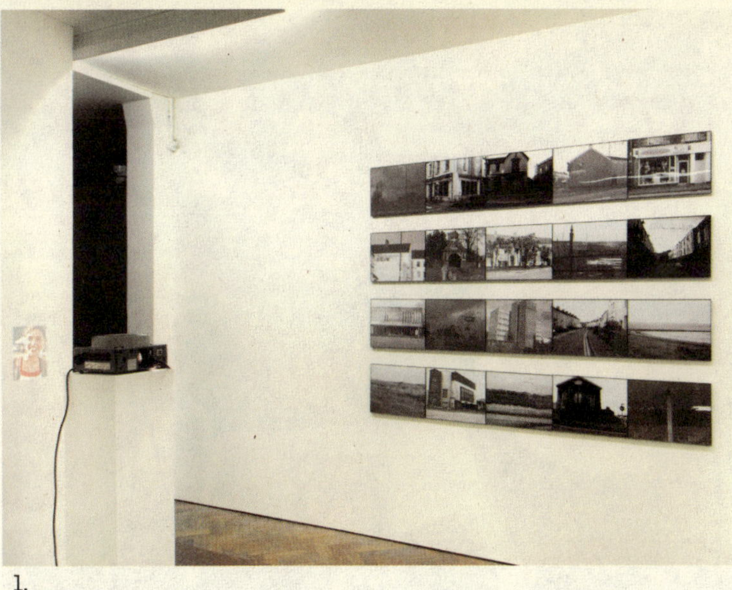

1.

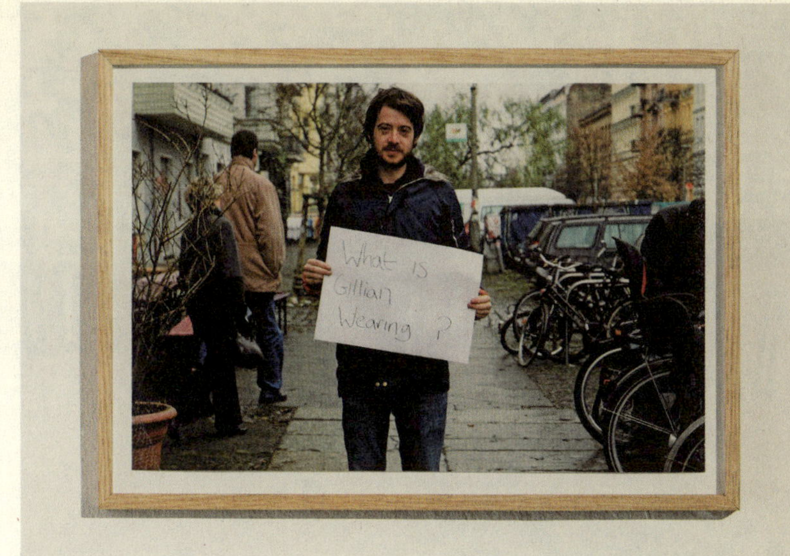

2.

Dan Rees lives and works in Berlin and London. His photographs and videos draw on the idea of communication and conversations with art history and established artists: **Variable Peace** (2006-present) comprises videos of Rees playing table tennis while talking with Conceptual artists a generation older than himself (including Jonathan Monk and Simon Starling). Another nod to Conceptual art traditions is Rees's slide projection **80 Girlfriends in 2007** (2007), a reference to Ed Ruscha's Five 1955 Girlfriends.

1. **One Afternoon and Evening in Llanelli; An ode to Cerith Wyn Evans**
2006, 20 photographs and frames, each 11×14 in (28×36 cm)

2. **What is Gillian Wearing?**
2005, color photograph and frame, $17\frac{3}{4} \times 25\frac{1}{2}$ in (45×65 cm)

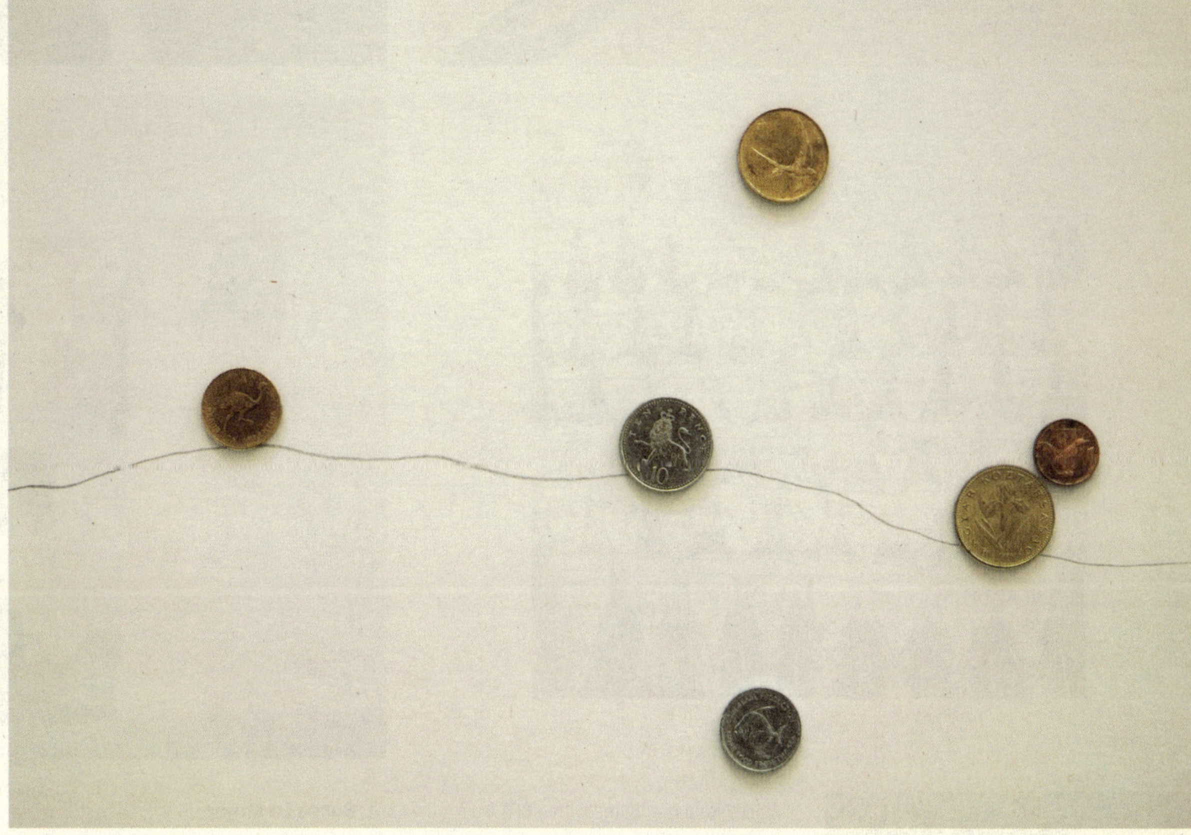

3.

4.

3. **Holiday Money**
2006, coins on paper, $8\frac{1}{4} \times 12$ in (21×30 cm)

4. **The Postman's Decision Is Final**
2006, postcards, glue, and wood shelf, dimensions variable, minimum duration of one year

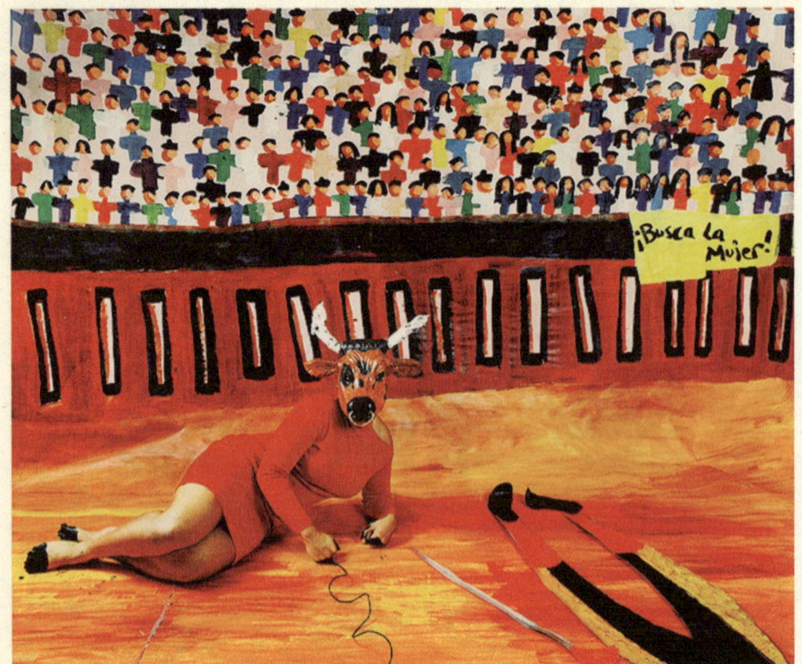

1.

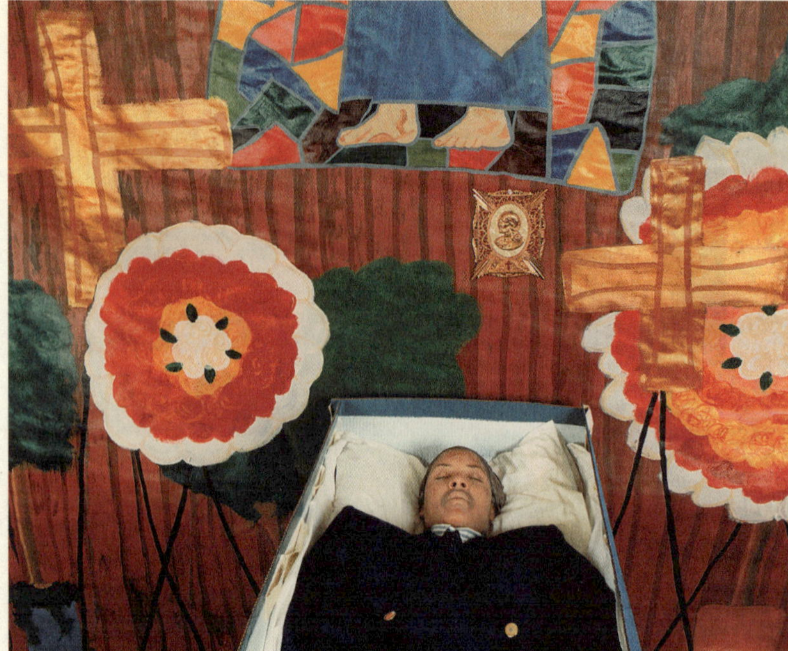

2.

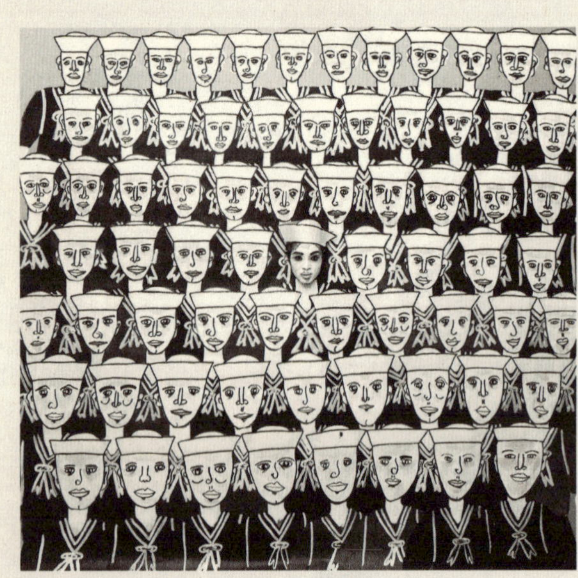

3.

4.

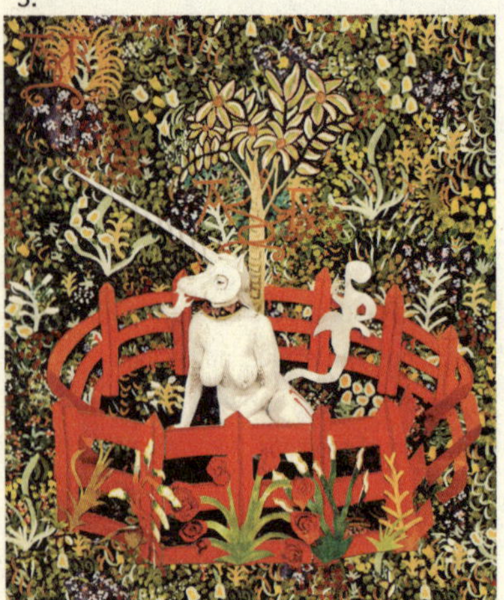

5.

Ashley Reid graduated with a BFA from the School of Visual Arts in New York, where she lives and works. Her large-scale, staged, photo-based works are fictions drawn on events in her own life. **Imitation of Life** (2008) drew on a time when she was a child and lived with her grandparents. The title is based on the Douglas Sirk film in which a black woman passes for white. Race is a theme in much of Reid's work, including **Don't Be a Paleface** (2007), in which the artist stands in for the suntanned child from the Coppertone sunscreen ad campaign.

1. **Busca La Mujer**
2006, collaged paper and acrylic on digital chromogenic print mounted on aluminum, 30 × 40 in (76 × 102 cm)

2. **Papa's Funeral**
2008, collaged paper and acrylic on digital chromogenic print mounted on aluminum, 30 × 40 in (76 × 102 cm)

3. **All for One** (detail)
2007, collaged paper and acrylic on digital chromogenic print mounted on aluminum, 30 × 40 in (76 × 102 cm)

4. **Papa's Closet**
2007, collaged paper and acrylic on digital chromogenic print mounted on aluminum, 30 × 40 in (76 × 102 cm)

5. **Captivity**
2007, collaged paper, cardboard, and acrylic on digital chromogenic print mounted on aluminum, 40 × 30 in (102 × 76 cm)

Isaac Resnikoff graduated with a BFA from the Cooper Union in 2002 and plans to finish his MFA at UCLA in 2009. He lives and works in Los Angeles. Resnikoff's practice draws on American folk art traditions as well as fine art conventions in sculpture and drawing that lampoon and celebrate American history and ideology. His sculptures of coffeepots, candles, and bars of soap, for instance, are whittled out of wood and represent American thought from the Revolutionary War to the present, questioning what it means to be American, and how objects attain mythic status.

1. **The Complete History of the U.S.A. Versions I & II** (detail)
2006, acrylic on carved pine and plywood, $96 \times 14\frac{1}{2} \times 14\frac{1}{2}$ in ($244 \times 37 \times 37$ cm)

2. **Oh, Liberia!**
2006, carved wood, $27 \times 36 \times 19$ in ($69 \times 91 \times 48$ cm)

3. **Death of the Sunshine Patriot**
2006, carved wood, $45 \times 72 \times 55\frac{3}{4}$ in ($114 \times 183 \times 142$ cm)

4. **We Run Out of Continent**
2005, carved pine, carpet, and rope, $25 \times 36 \times 36$ in ($64 \times 91 \times 91$ cm)

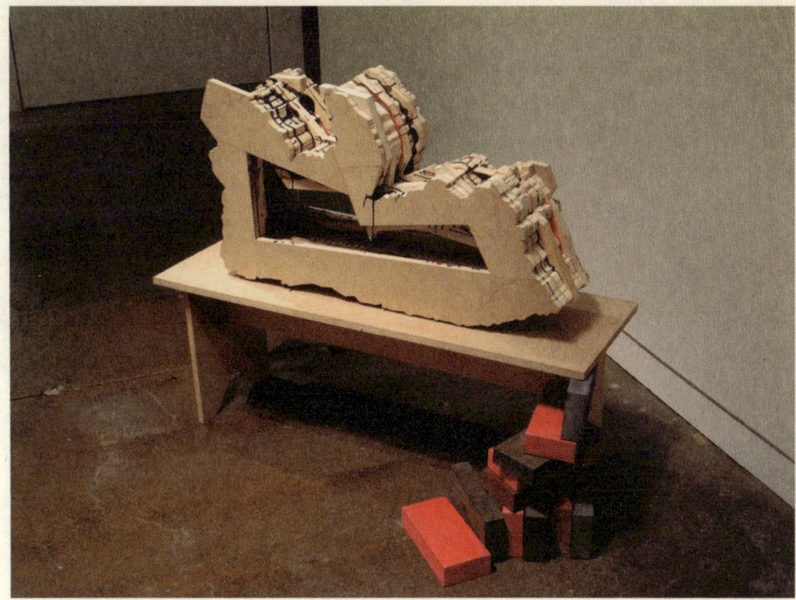

2.

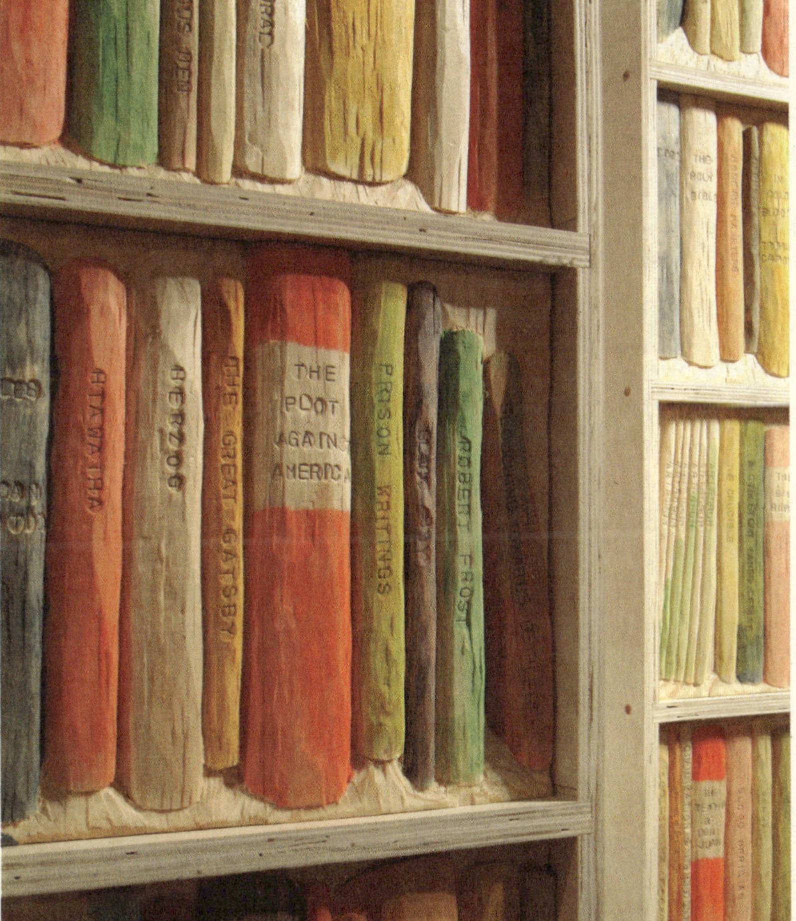

1.

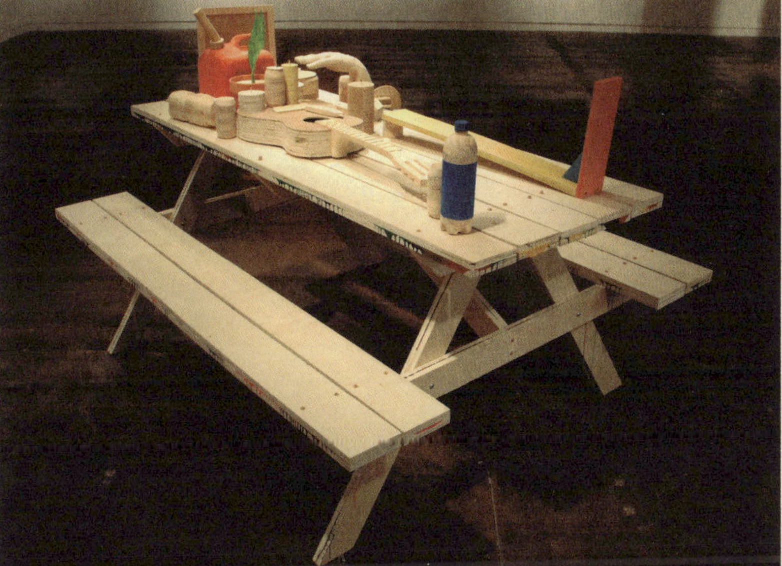

3.

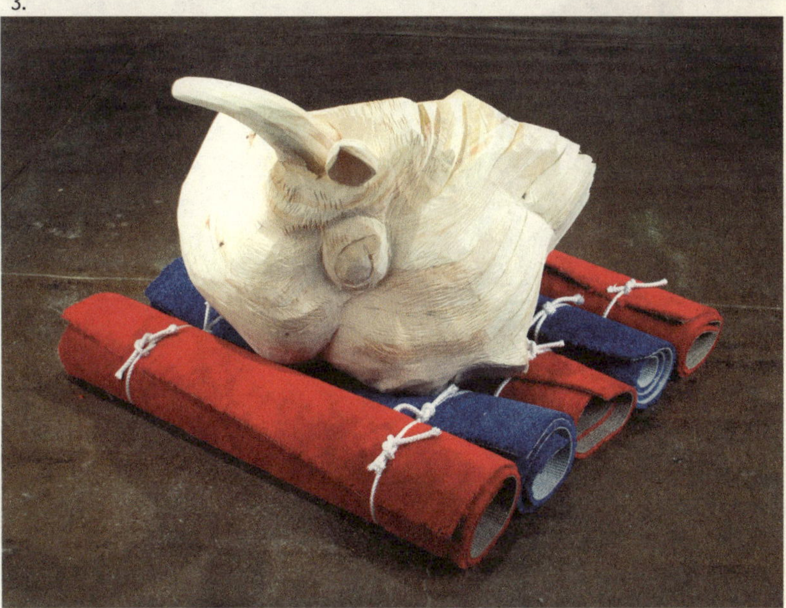

4.

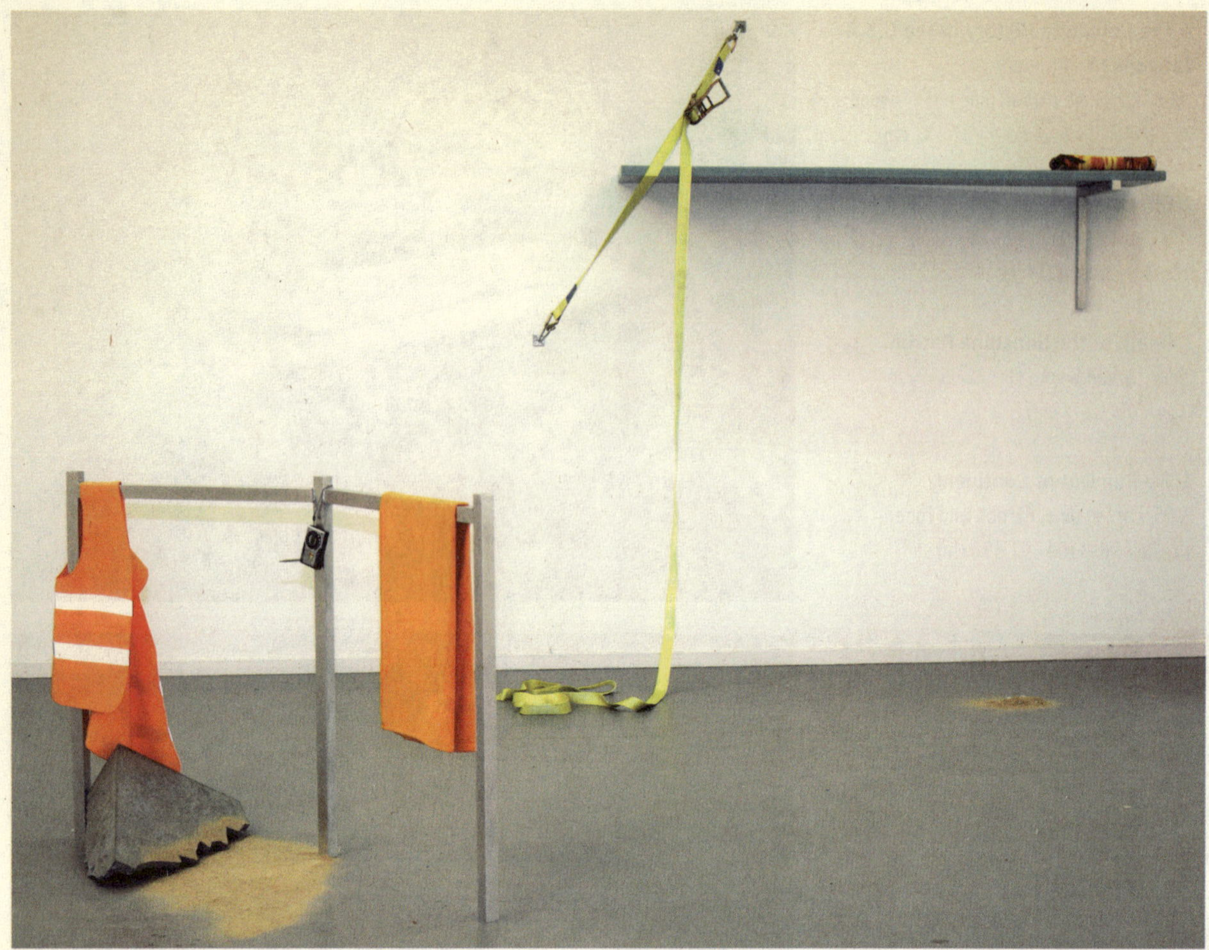

1.

Magali Reus graduated with a BFA and an MFA from Goldsmiths College in London and currently lives and works in London. Recent sculptures and video works, which incorporate beach towels, sunglasses, and lifejackets, reference her interest in Land Art, and in the media attention surrounding the fires in Malibu, California, in 2007. **Fire Storms**, for example, is made up of multicolored lenses taken from cheap sunglasses hung on a silver chain. More recently, her minimal installations reflect an interest in work and leisure environments.

1. Synthetics

2008, aluminum, concrete, MDF sawdust, beach towel, nylon, radio, and sound, 63 ¾ × 43 ½ × 27 ½ in (162 × 110 × 70 cm)

2. Export Forecast Bright

2008, fiberglass, polyester resin, and beach towels, dimensions variable

3. Fire Storms

2007, sunglass lenses, ballchain, and screw, 11 ½ × 3 in (29 × 8 cm)

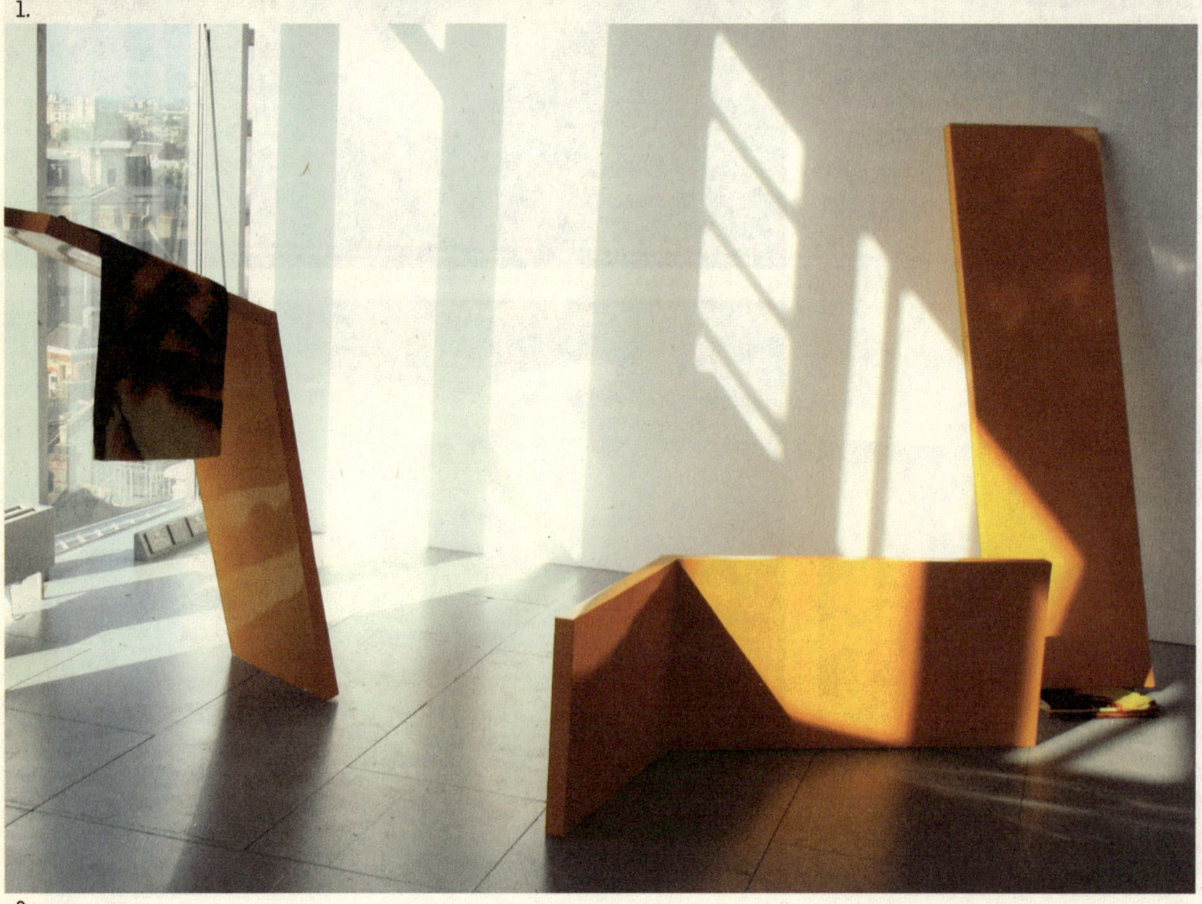

2.

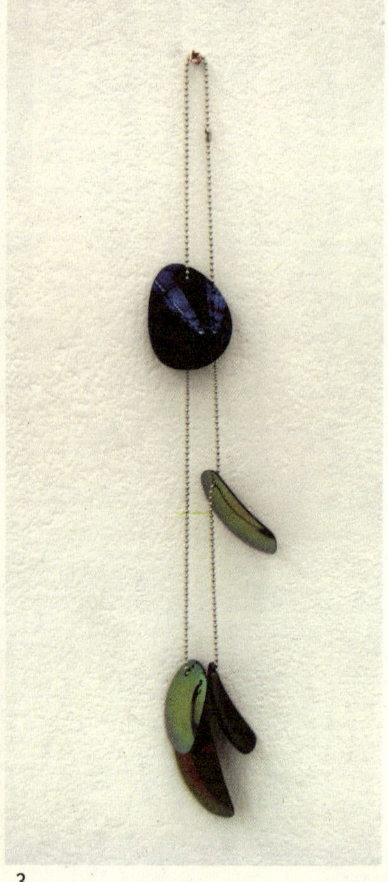

3.

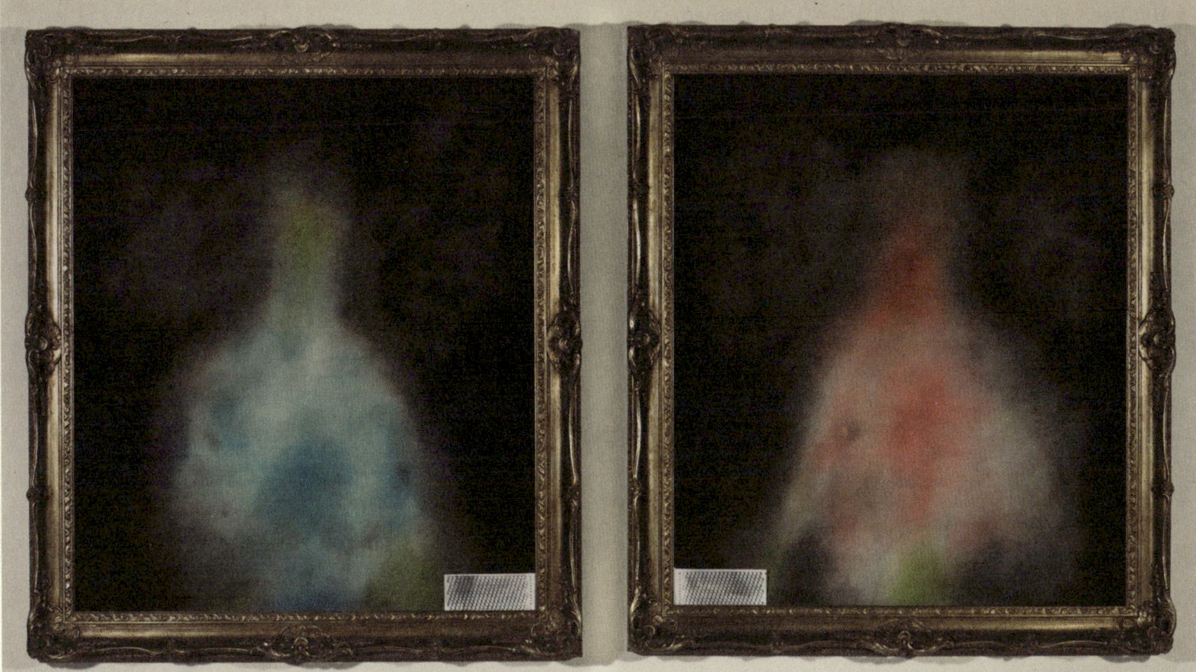

1.

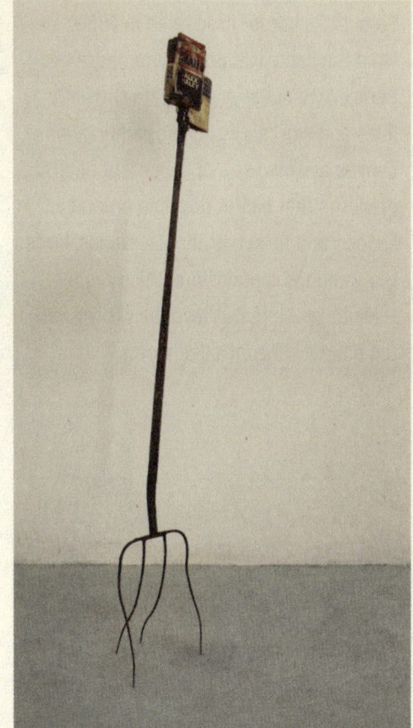

2.

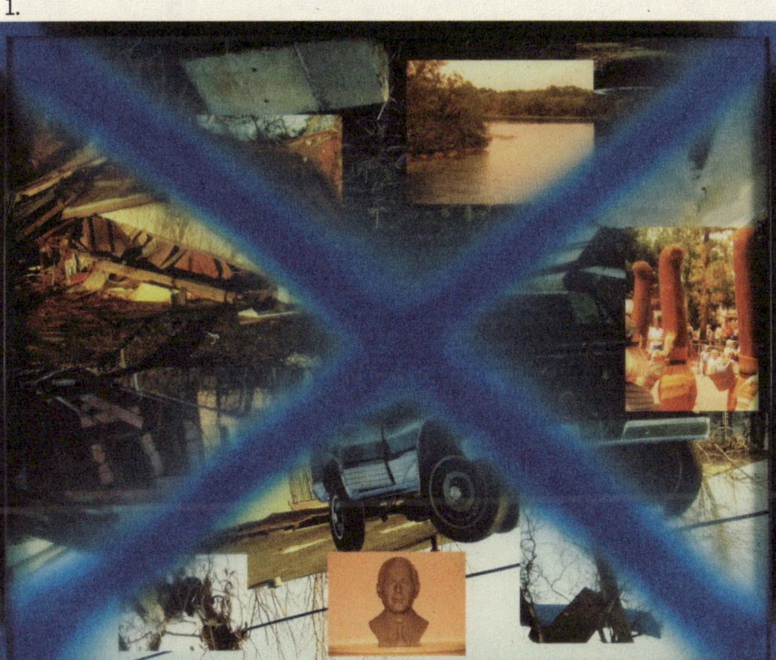

3.

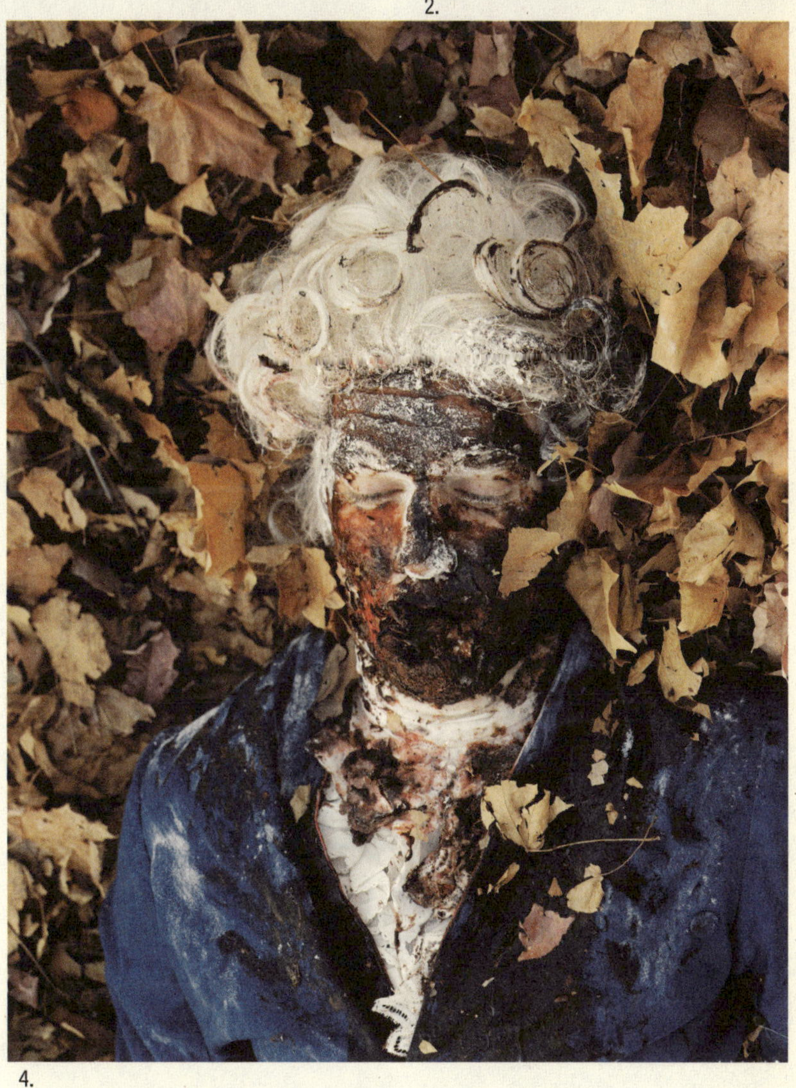

4.

Stephen G. Rhodes earned an MFA from the Art Center College of Design in Pasadena in 2005 and currently lives in Los Angeles. His installations are chaotic collision points for several mediums; they include totemic sculptural pieces alongside collages of new photographs and found snapshots. The result is a tangled web of associations that all tangentially skirt an archetypal narrative.

1. Vacant Portraits (Red & Blue)
2008, oil and collage on canvas, 2 parts, framed, each 45 × 40 in (114 × 102 cm)

2. Broken Continuum
2008, mixed media, 82 × 12 × 12 in (208 × 31 × 31 cm)

3. Excerpt (Bush Brooms)
2007, framed chromogenic print with paint, 24 × 30 in (61 × 76 cm)

4. Your shit is in my mouth
2001, chromogenic print, 30 × 24 in (76 × 61 cm)

Samuel Richardot graduated in 2006 from the Ecole Nationale Supérieure des Beaux-Arts in Paris, where he currently lives and works. His acrylic paintings on canvas are made up of exuberant abstract gestures that hint at possible organic shapes and forms: branches, clouds, birds. His paintings contain "breathing room" – white space that draws the viewer into the playful yet controlled works.

1. Untitled
2008, acrylic paint and tape on canvas,
6 ½ × 8 ¼ ft (200 × 250 cm)

2. Untitled
2007, acrylic paint and tape on canvas,
6 ½ × 8 ¼ ft (200 × 250 cm).

3. Untitled
2007, acrylic paint on canvas,
6 ½ × 8 ¼ ft (200 × 250 cm)

4. Untitled
2008, acrylic paint on burned canvas,
6 ½ × 8 ¼ ft (200 × 250 cm)

1.

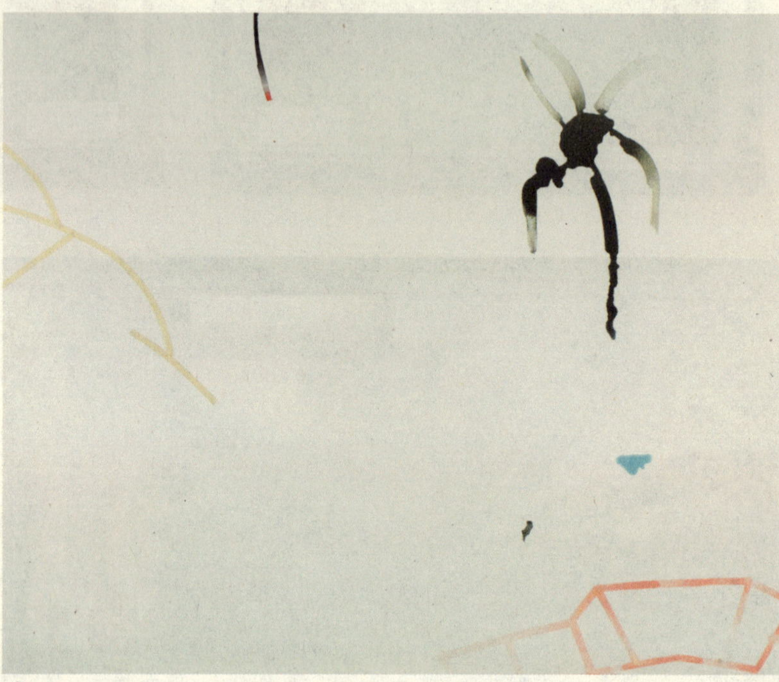

2.

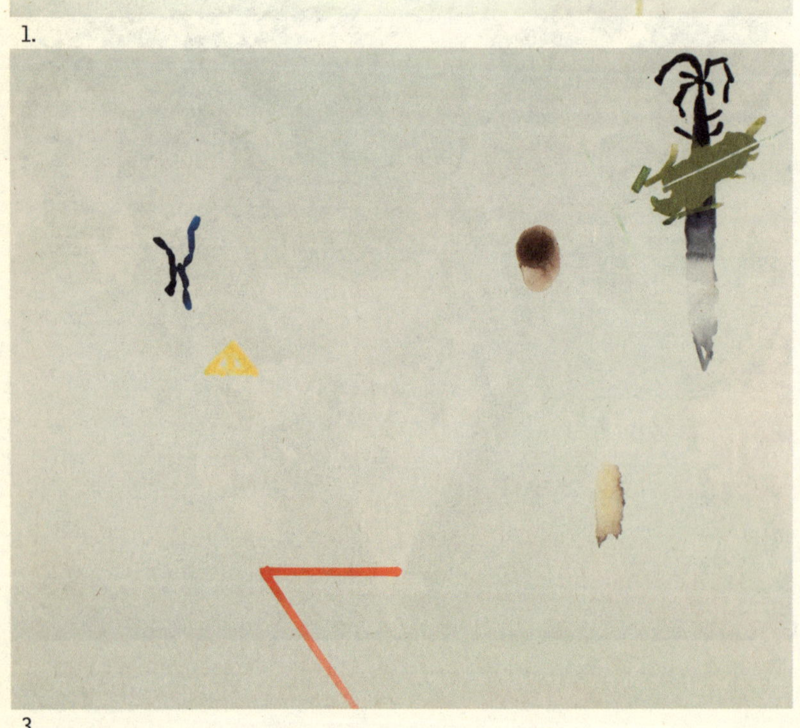

3.

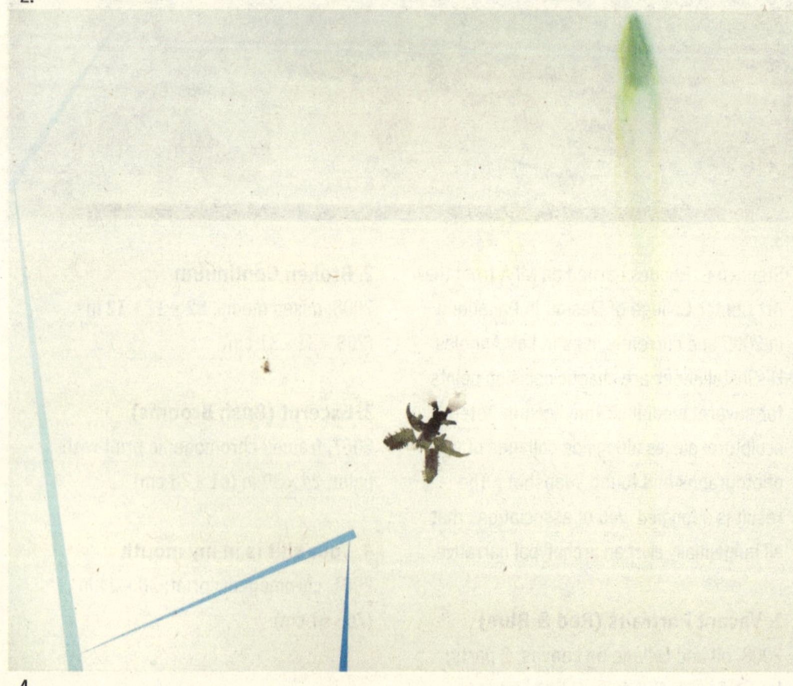

4.

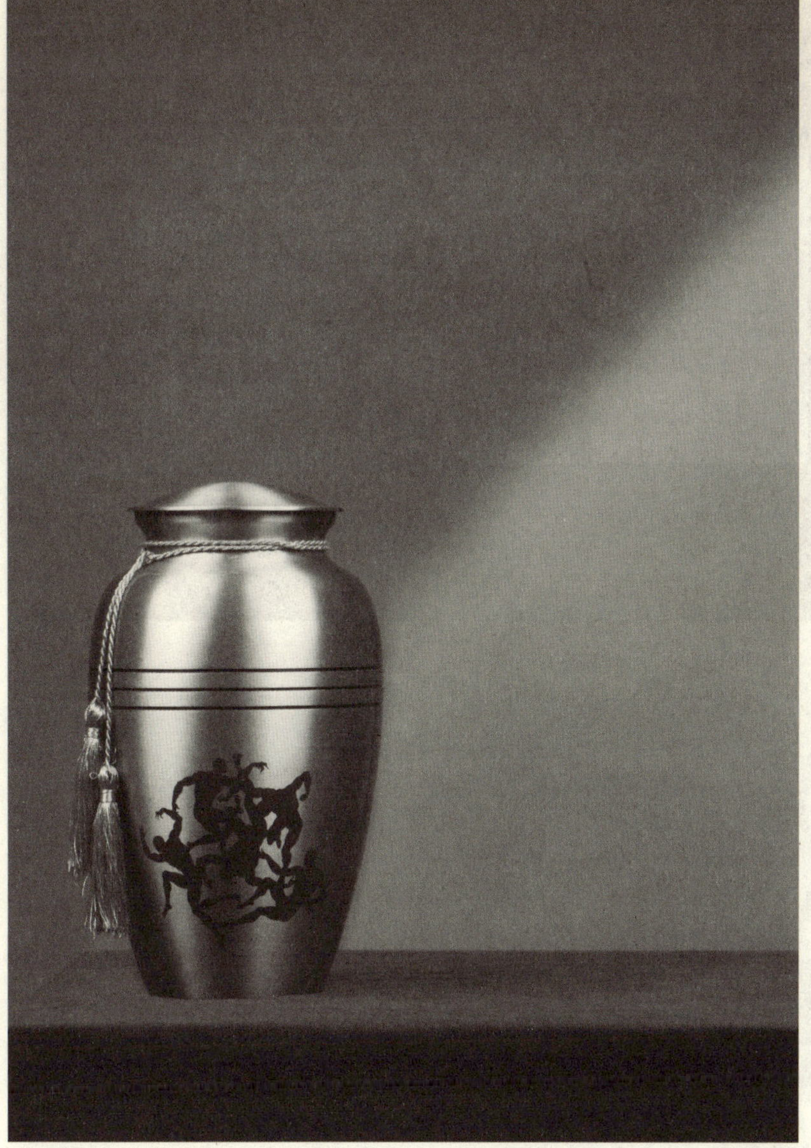

1.

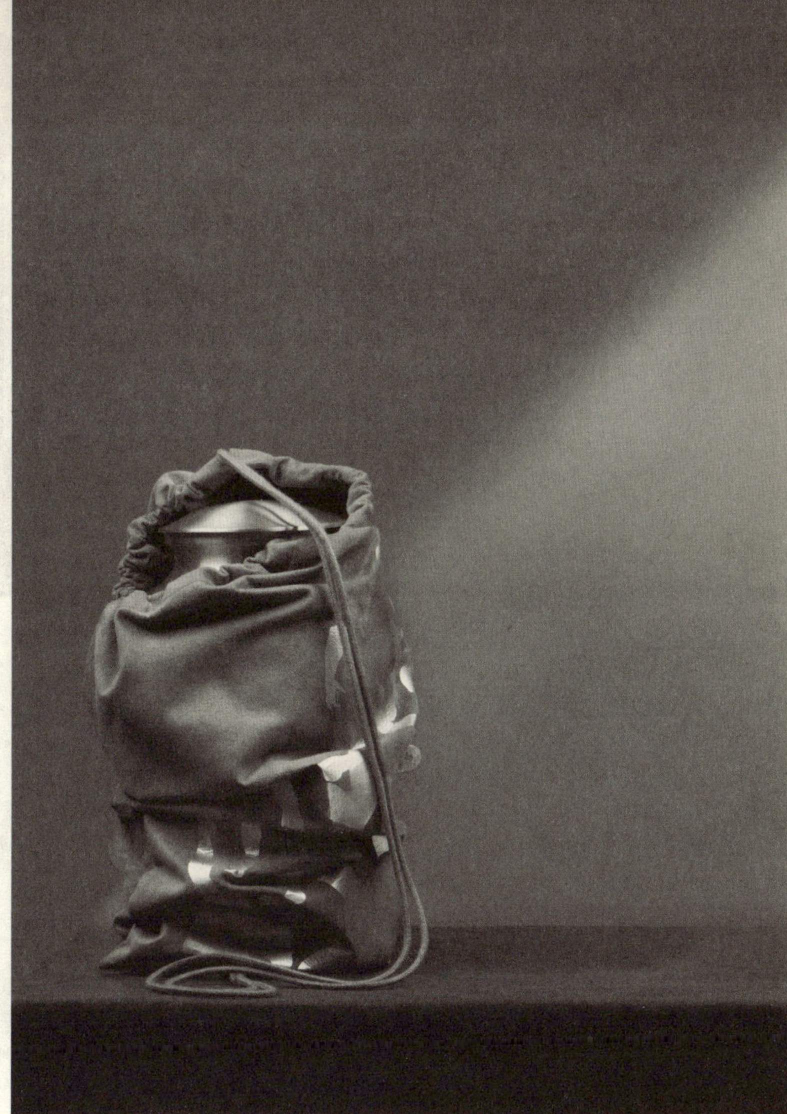

2.

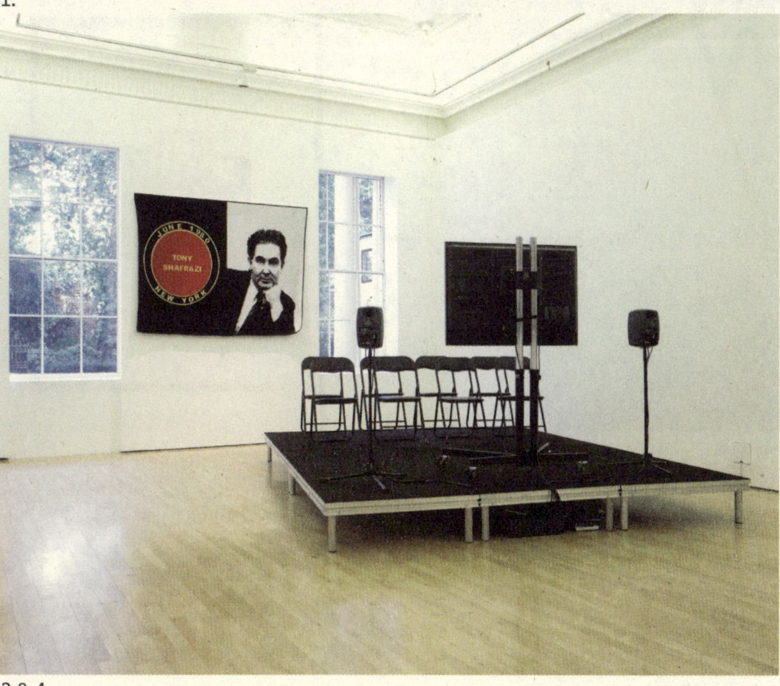

3 & 4.

Based in London, James Richards graduated in 2006 from Chelsea School of Art and Design and completed a 16 mm/ Super 8 residency at the no.w.here lab in London. His film and video work is assembled from original footage as well as material sourced from the Web. Richards draws on conventions of public screenings as well as the mores of private mix tapes by re-editing VHS footage, exploring the possibilities of distortion and repetition. His installation **Untitled Merchandise (Lovers and Dealers)** (2007) shows images of lovers and dealers of the artist Keith Haring, with Haring himself cropped out of the image.

1 & 2. **Untitled Merchandise (Trade Urn)**
2008, laser etched pewter urn with fake suede sports bag, dimensions variable

3. (foreground) **Active Negative Programme**
2008, digital video and mixed media, dimensions variable

4. (background) **Untitled Merchandise (Lovers and Dealers)**
2007, 1 of 6 nylon knitted blankets, dimensions variable, installation view at the ICA, London (2008)

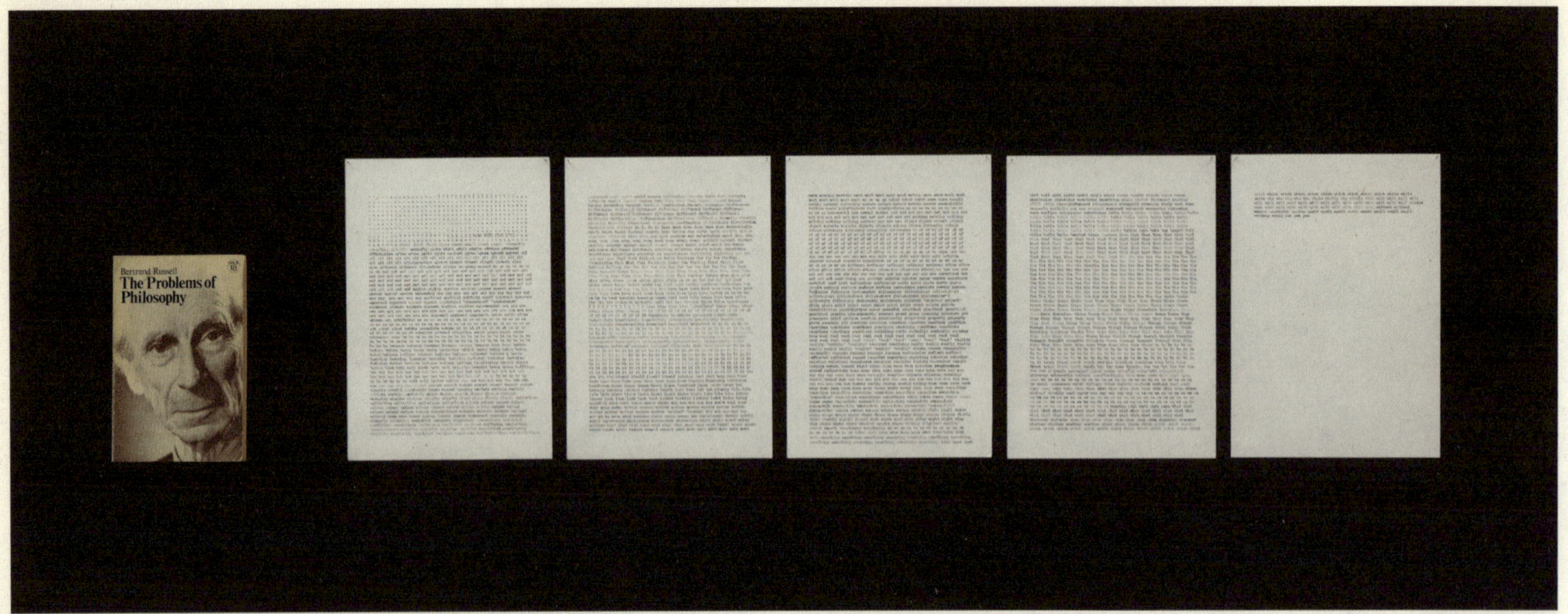

1.

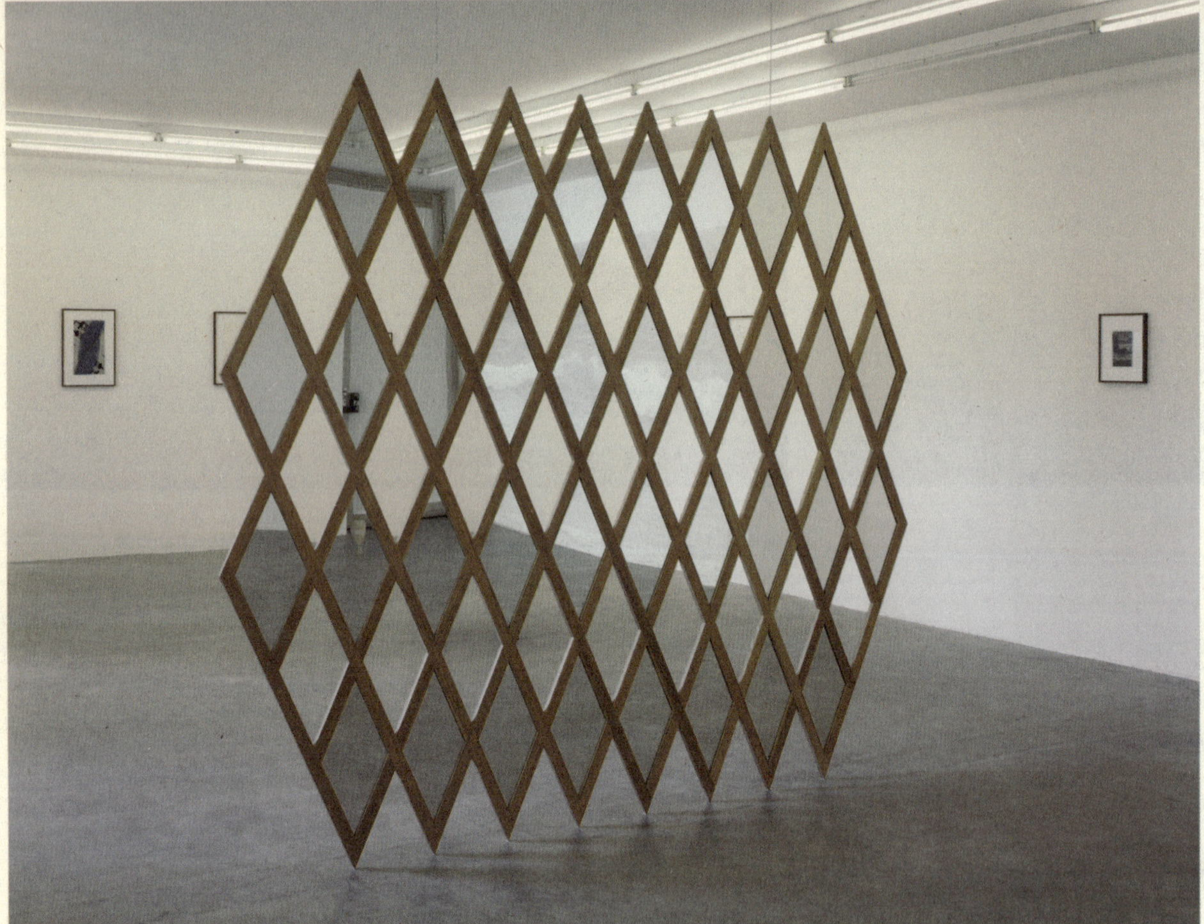

2.

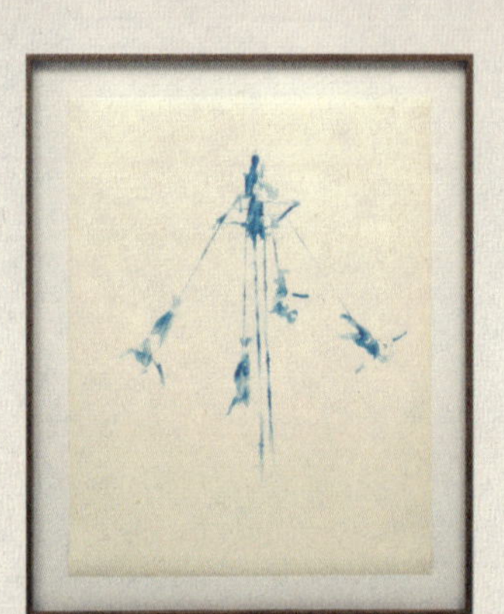

3.

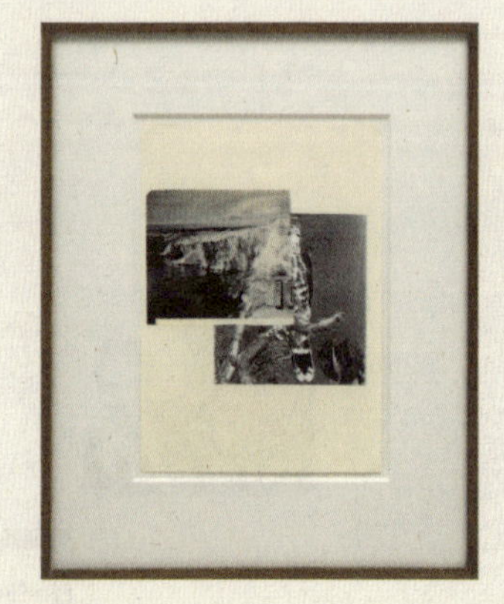

4.

Damien Roach graduated with a MA in painting from the Royal College of Art, London, where he lives and works. He incorporates video, painting, sculpture, installation, and audio into his artworks, which are often made using mundane found objects. His work has explored the idea of escape through altered perception, as in **Eidolon** (2005), in which the tea stains on an overturned table become palm trees, or **Kaleidoscope** (2004), in which he painted old pieces of plywood or old chairs and then etched delicate landscapes onto their surfaces.

1. Chapter 1: Appearance and reality
2007, typewritten paper and book, 24 1/4 × 66 × 3 in (62 × 167 × 8 cm)

2. Field
2007, mirrored structure, 94 × 102 in (230 × 260 cm)

3. Untitled
2007, watercolor on paper, 28 1/4 × 21 3/4 in (72 × 56 cm)

4. Untitled (melt)
2007, collage, 11 3/4 × 8 in (30 × 20 cm)

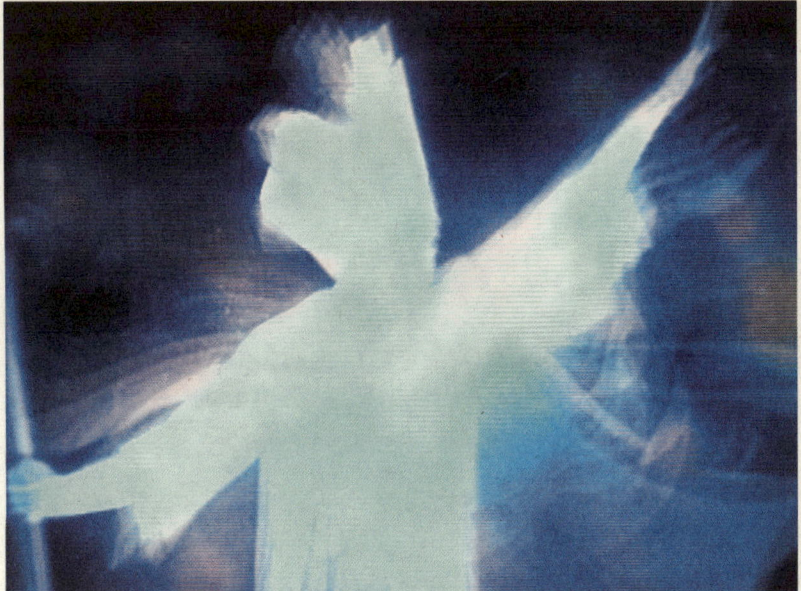
1.

Michael B. Robinson received his BFA in film, photography, and visual art from Ithaca College and his MFA from the University of Illinois, Chicago, where he lives and works. Robinson combines pop sound tracks with footage from video games and old films. **And We All Shine On** (2007) conjures a postapocalyptic landscape, including a night shot of trees blowing in the wind and other landscapes appropriated from video games, while karaoke is overheard on the sound track.

1. **All Through The Night**
2008, video, 4 min 30 sec

2. **Light Is Waiting**
2007, video, 11 min

3. **Victory Over the Sun**
2007, 16 mm film, 12 min 30 sec

4. **The General Returns From One Place to Another**
2006, 16 mm film, 11 min

5. **And We All Shine On**
2006, 16 mm film, 7 min

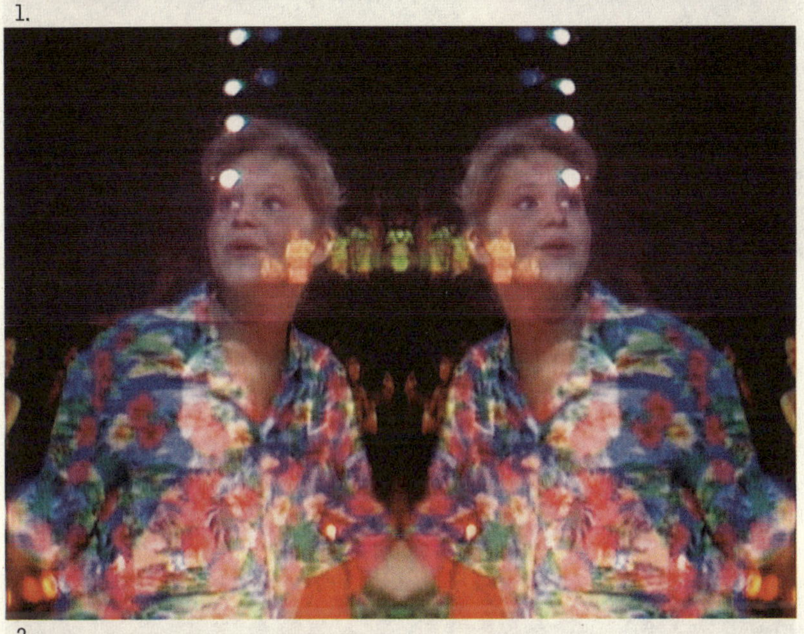
2.

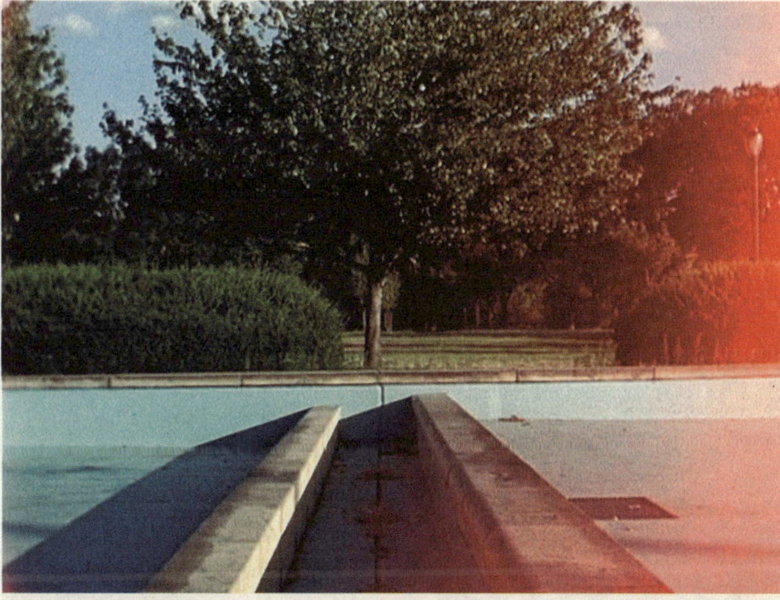
3.

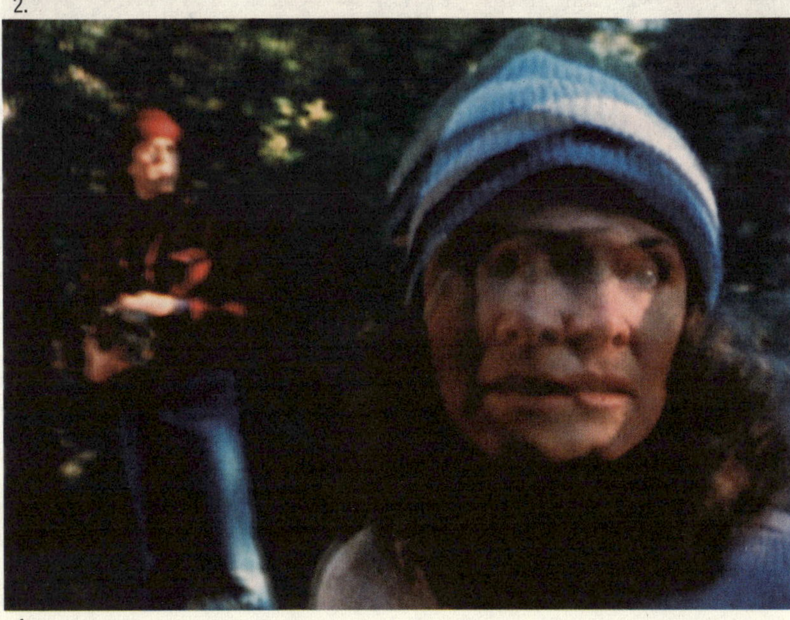
4.

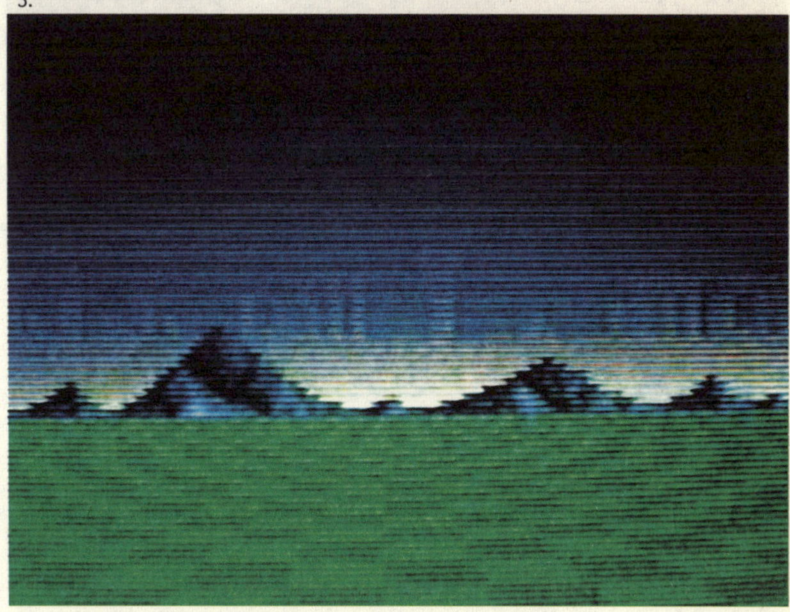
5.

Rio de Janeiro-based Thiago Rocha Pitta explores representations of nature through video, installation, photography, and performance. Caught between J. M. W. Turner's vision of the Sublime and today's demystified and often destructive experience of nature, works include recurring motifs of boats, fires, cliff sides, and bodies of water in surreal or ominous conditions.

1. Requiem
2006, salt crystals on embers, dimensions variable

2. The secret sharer
2008, photograph, 19 × 29 in (50 × 75 cm)

3. Youth
2006, saltwater on stainless-steel boat on charcoal, dimensions variable

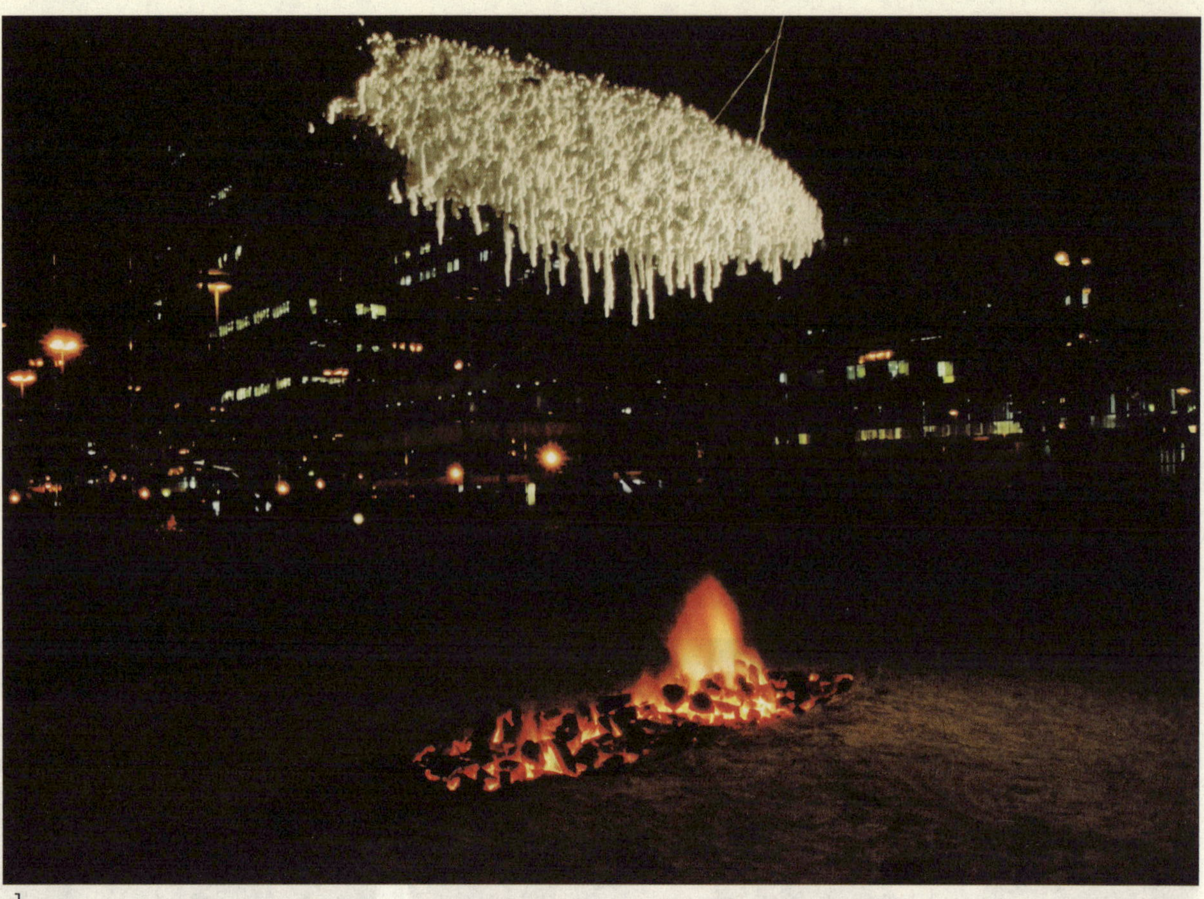

1.

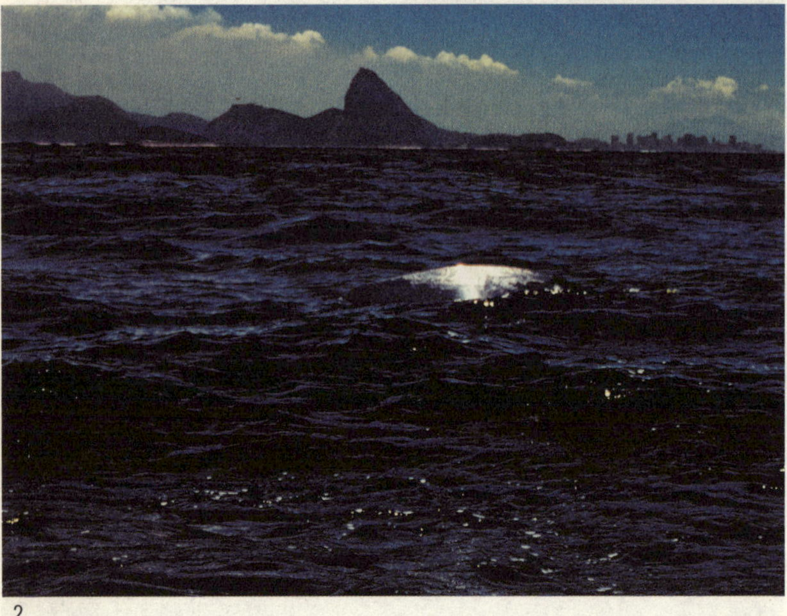

2.

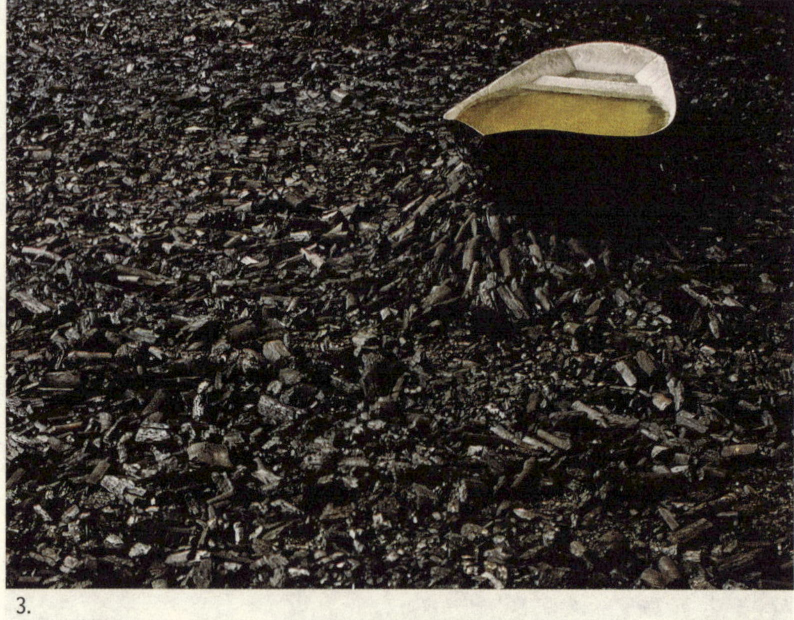

3.

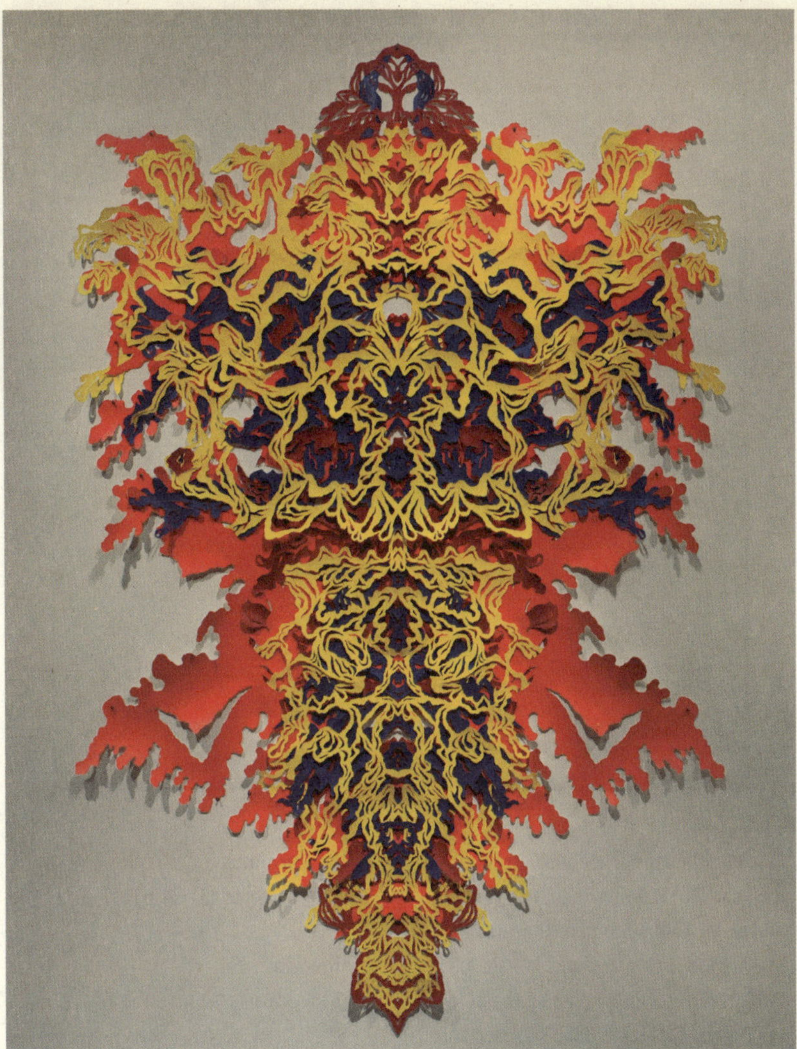

1.

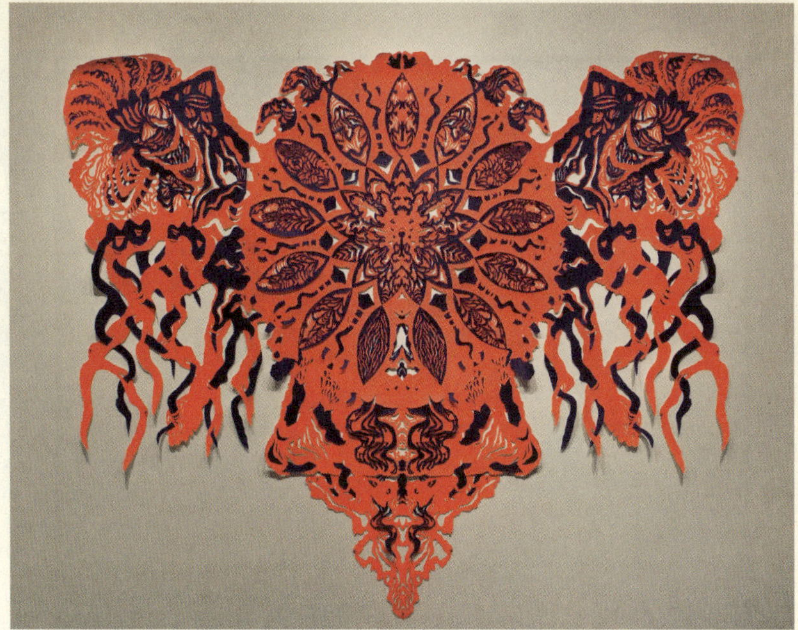

2.

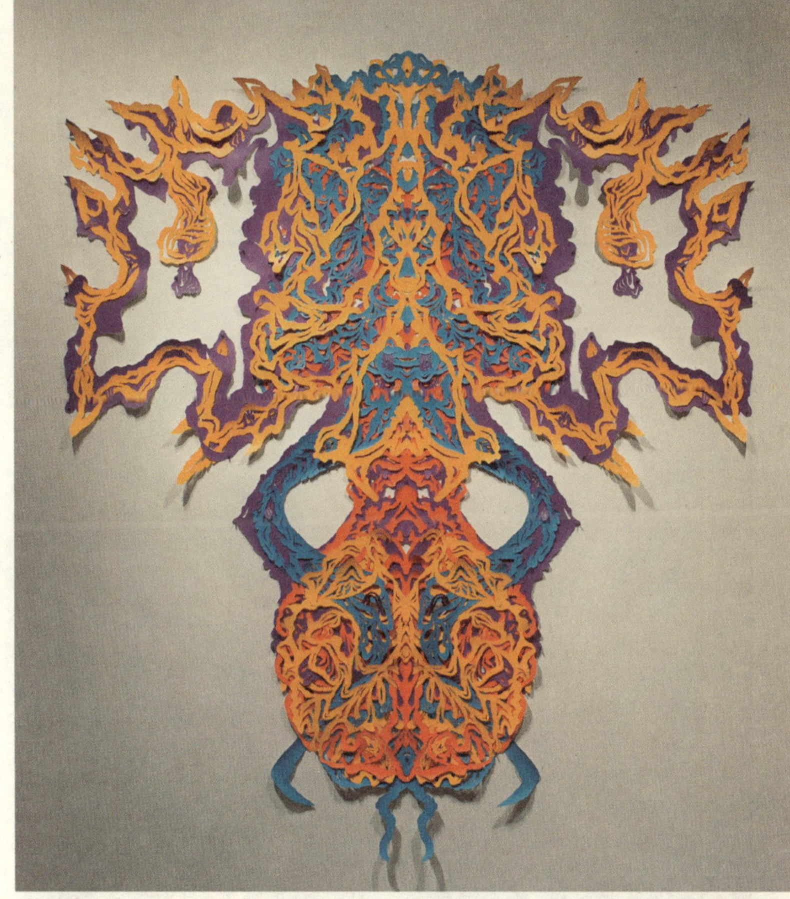

3.

Jimmy Joe Roche graduated with a BFA from the Film Conservatory of SUNY Purchase College and an MFA from the Mt. Royal School of Art at the Maryland Institute College of Art in Baltimore. He is a longtime collaborator with the Baltimore-based musician Dan Deacon; together they made the 2007 work **Ultimate Reality**, comprised of clips from Arnold Schwarzenegger movies, slowed down and saturated with color. Roche had a solo exhibition, "Totems," in 2008 at the RARE Gallery in New York, which included monumental hand-cut and painted paperworks.

1. **New Power**
2008, acrylic on cotton rag paper, 114 × 78 in (292 × 198 cm)

2. **Old Growth**
2008, acrylic and Day-Glo acrylic latex on cotton rag paper, 104 × 132 in (264 × 335 cm)

3. **Little Faith**
2008, acrylic on cotton rag paper, 114 × 78 in (269 × 198 cm)

4. **Ultimate Reality**
2007, video

5. **Gather 'Round**
2008, video

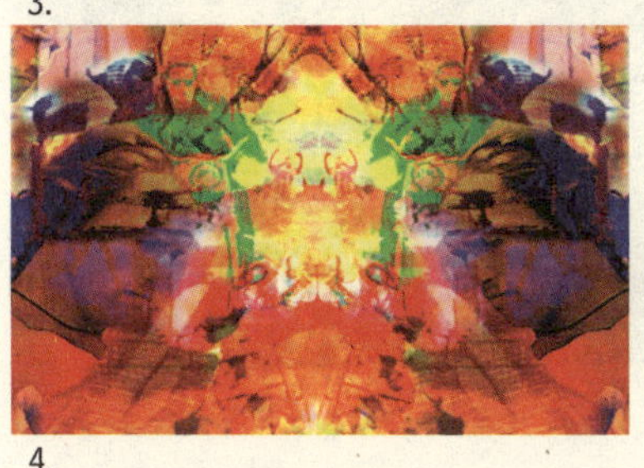

4.

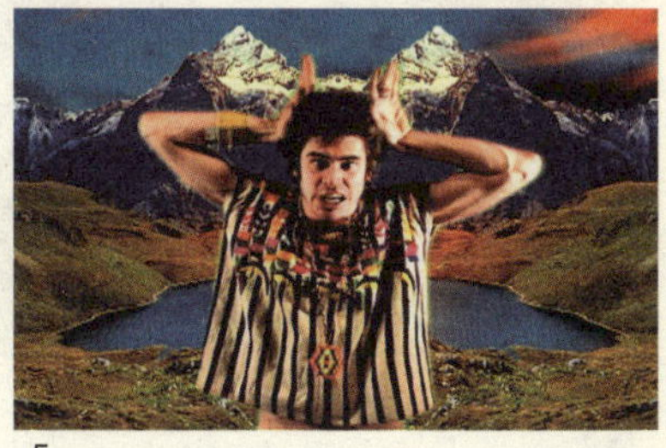

5.

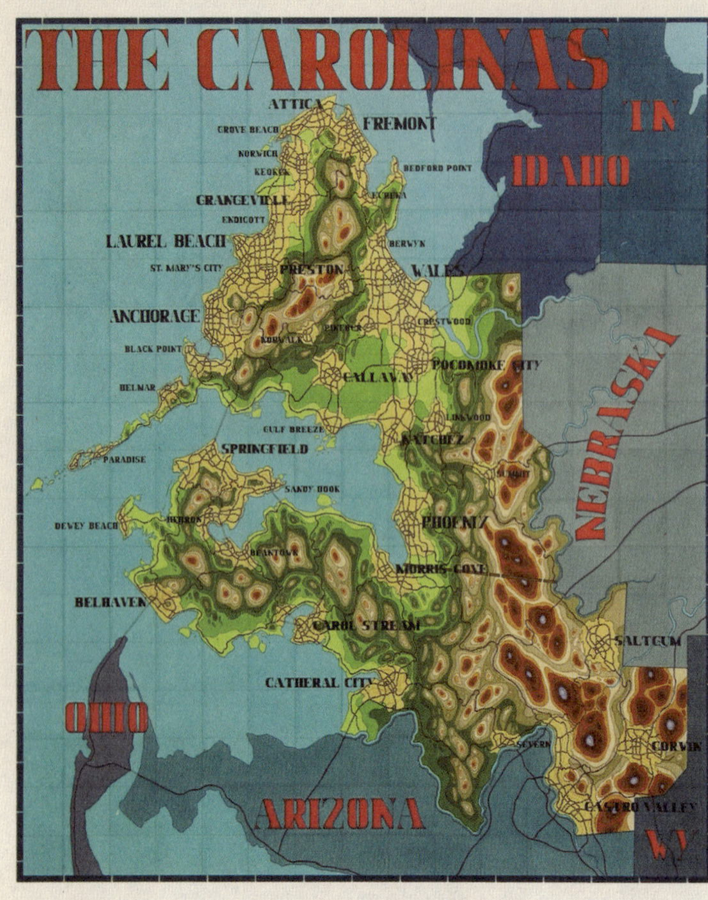

1.

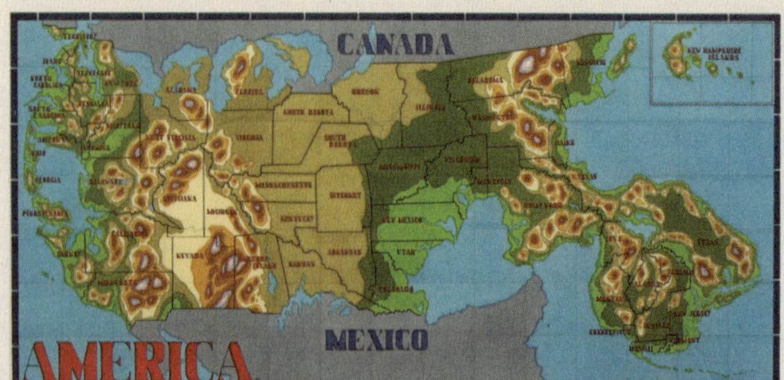

2.

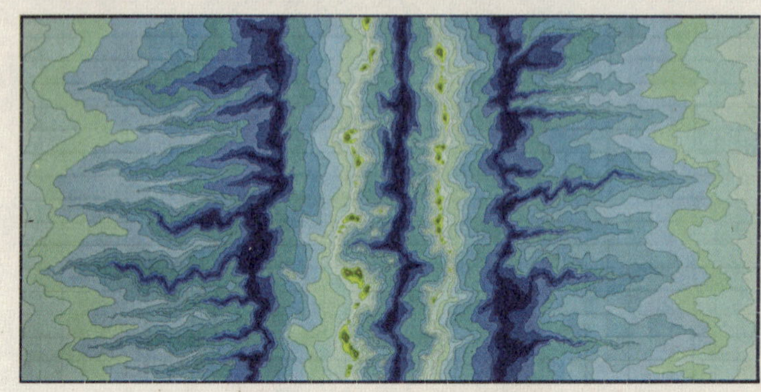

3.

Lordy Rodriguez earned a BFA from the School of Visual Arts in New York and an MFA from Stanford University in 2008. He lives and works in Palo Alto, California. He has had solo shows at the Hosfelt Gallery in San Francisco and at the Austin Museum of Art in Austin, Texas, both in 2008. His ink drawings use the language of cartography to describe abstract geological terrains or detailed maps with imaginary landmarks and pop-culture references, works in which he interrogates scale and mapmaking conventions.

1. **The Carolinas**
2004, ink on paper, 40 × 34 in (102 × 86 cm)

2. **America**
2002, ink on paper, 23 ¼ × 39 in (59 × 99 cm)

3. **Underwater Trenches**
2006, ink on paper, 36 × 72 in (91 × 183 cm)

4. **Volcano**
2006, ink on paper, 48 × 48 in (122 × 122 cm)

5. **Untitled**
2008, 12 ink drawings on paper, each 10 × 14 in (25 × 36 cm)

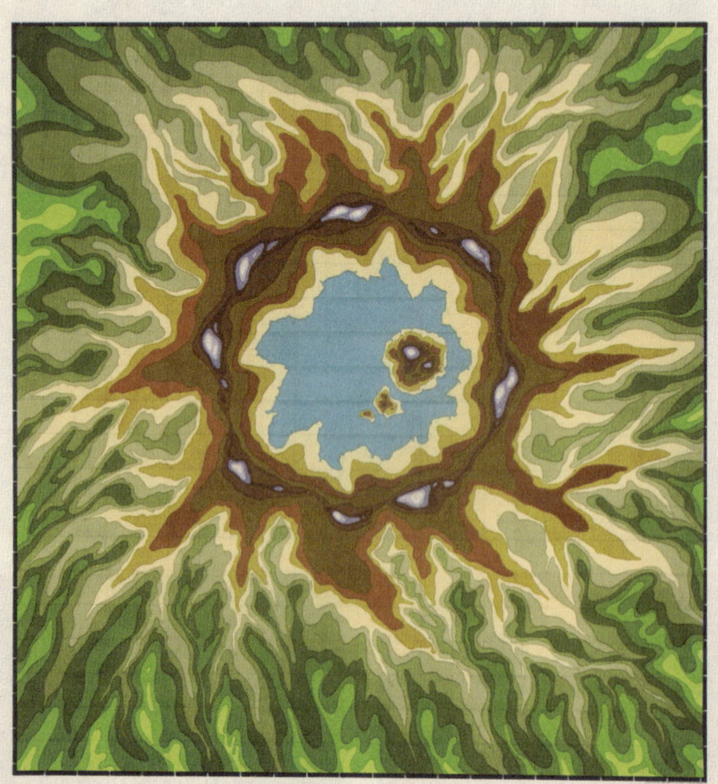

4.

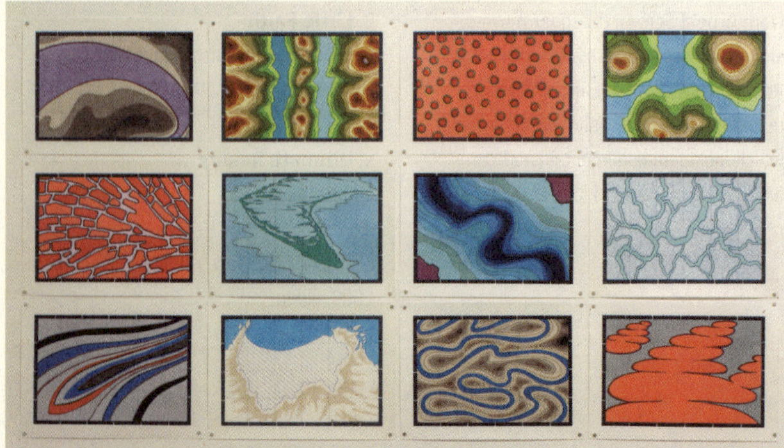

5.

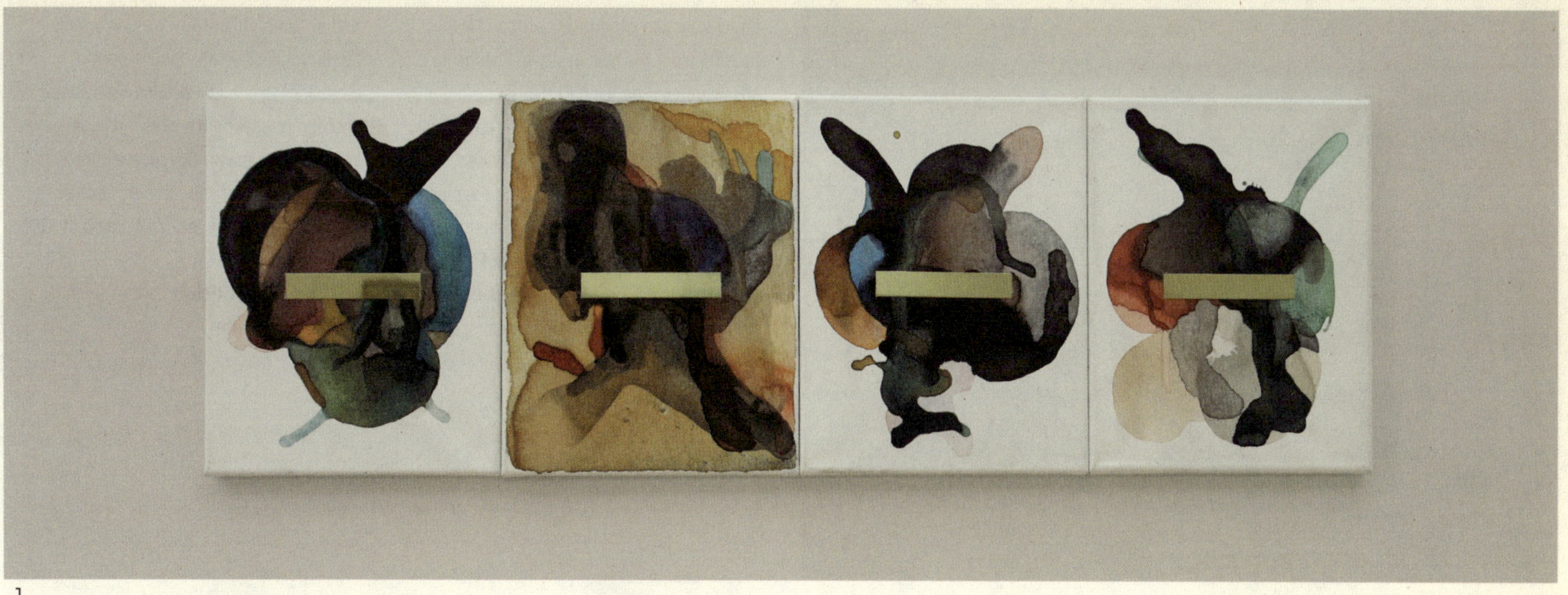

1.

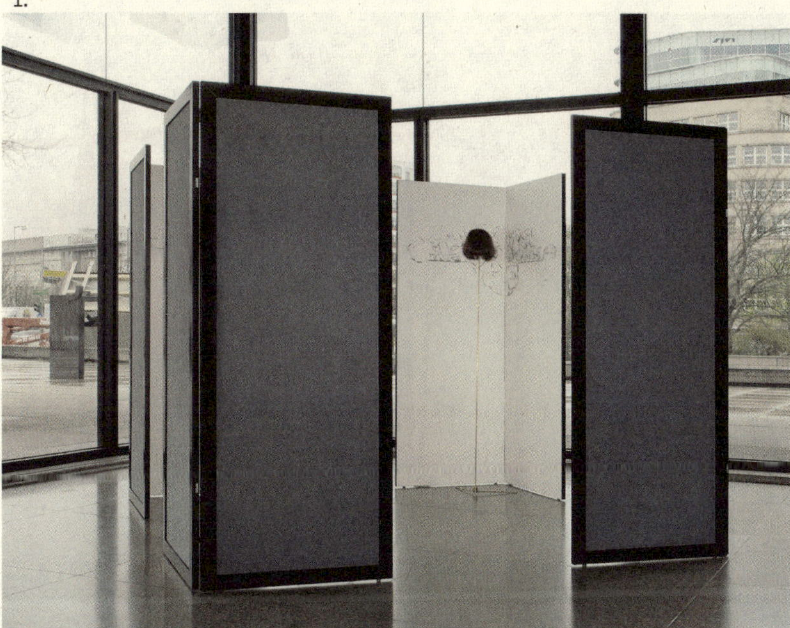

2.

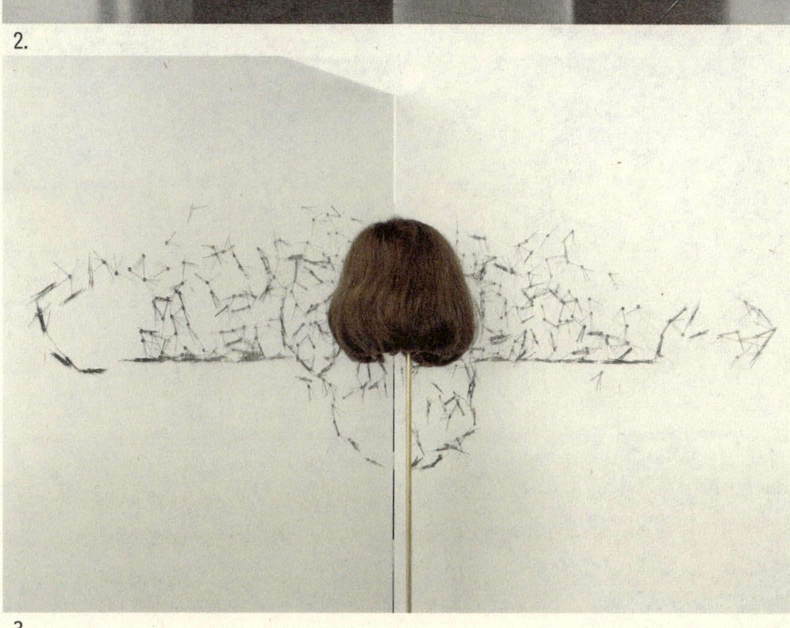

3.

Pamela Rosenkranz graduated from the Academy of Fine Arts in Bern, where she is based, and then from the Department of Comparative Literature at the University of Zurich. Her installations explore the institutional status of an artwork, how it comes to be recognized as an artwork, and the interaction between form and content. **Uncontent** (2008), included in Manifesta 7, comprises objects arranged within a circle of mirrors, which produces an infinite reflection: inside and outside become indistinguishable.

1. **Visions of the Argument**
2008, watercolor with brass on four canvases, 11 1/2 × 34 3/4 in (30 × 88 cm)

2 & 3. **Resisting the Present**
2008, Plexiglas, fabric, frames, wigs, magnets, and steel pins, dimensions variable

4. **Wie ein ziel** (Like a Goal)
2008, chair, latex, paint, textiles, and wood

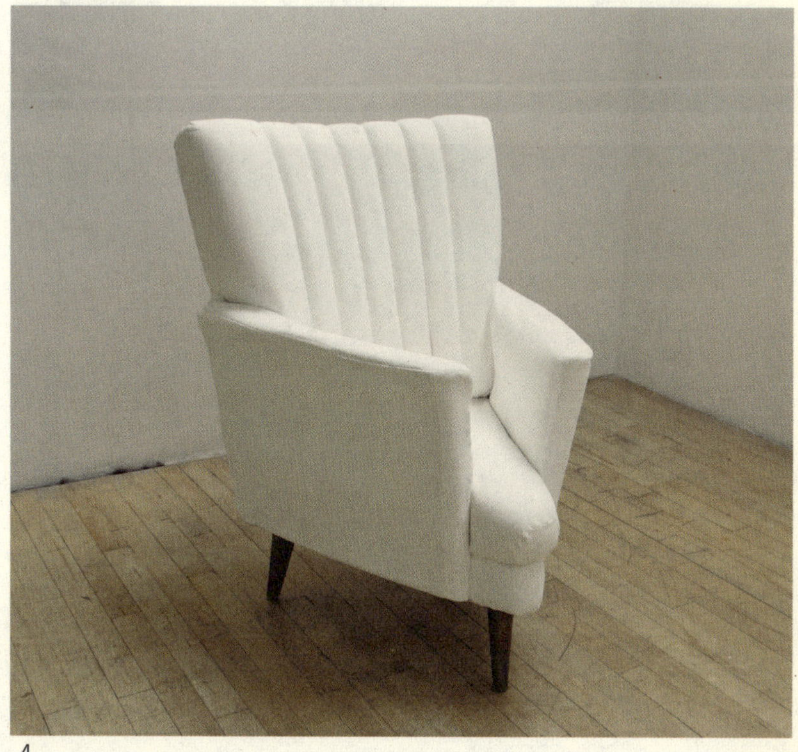

4.

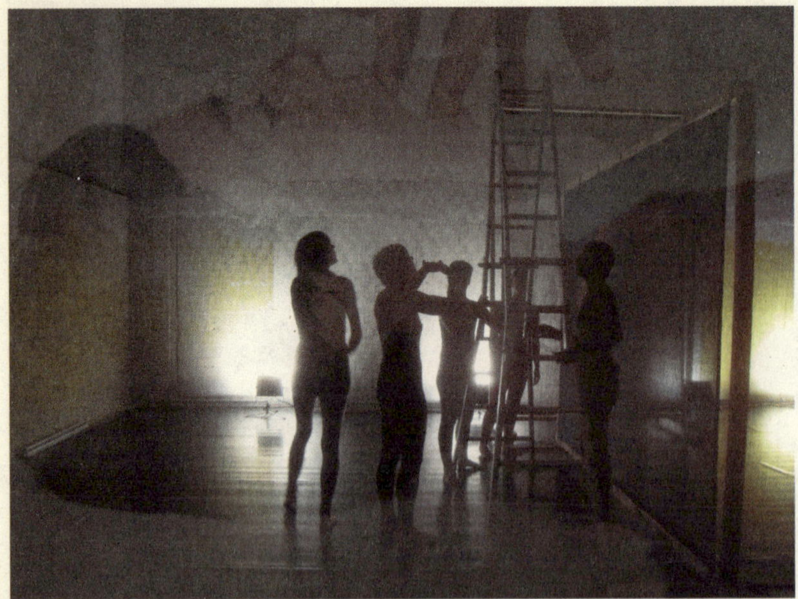
1.

Emily Roysdon graduated with an MFA in 2006 from the University of California, Los Angeles. She lives in New York and is an editor and cofounder of LTTR, a feminist and queer artist collective. Her video, photography, text, and performance pieces explore language, memory, and history. In **Untitled (David Wojnarowicz Project)** (2001-07), for example, she revisits Wojnarowicz's well-known series Arthur Rimbaud in New York, in which he photographed his lover wearing a mask of Rimbaud. Roysdon has instead photographed a figure wearing a Wojnarowicz mask. Roysdon explores the notion of identification in her piece on Wojnarowicz, a gay artist who died of AIDS.

1, 2, 3, 4 & 5. **Untitled**
2008, performance

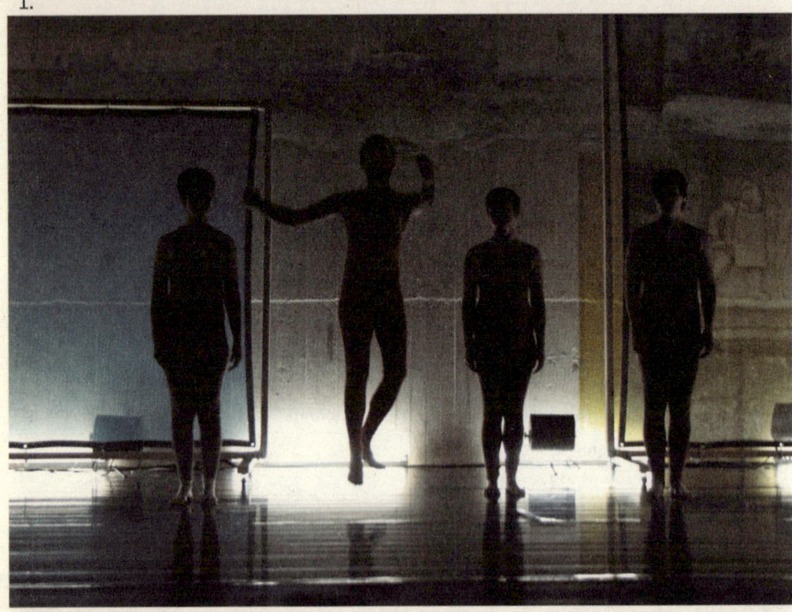
2.

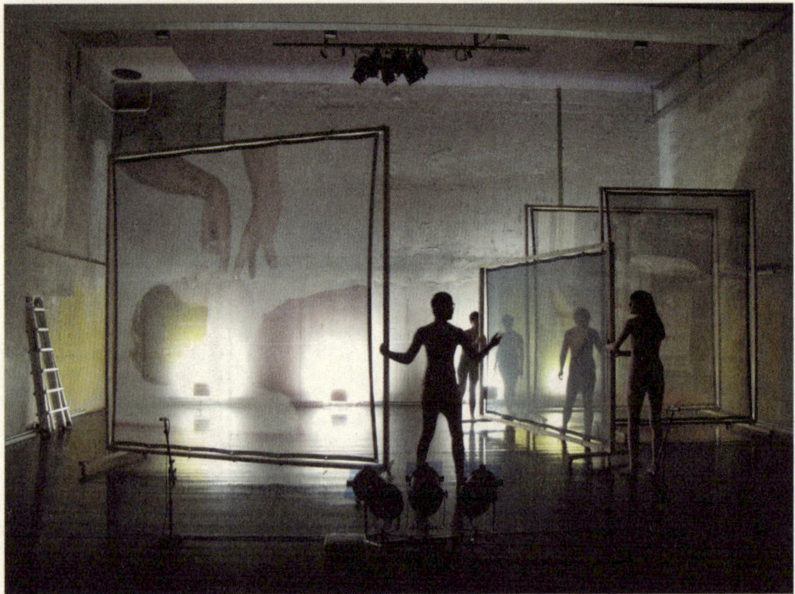
3.

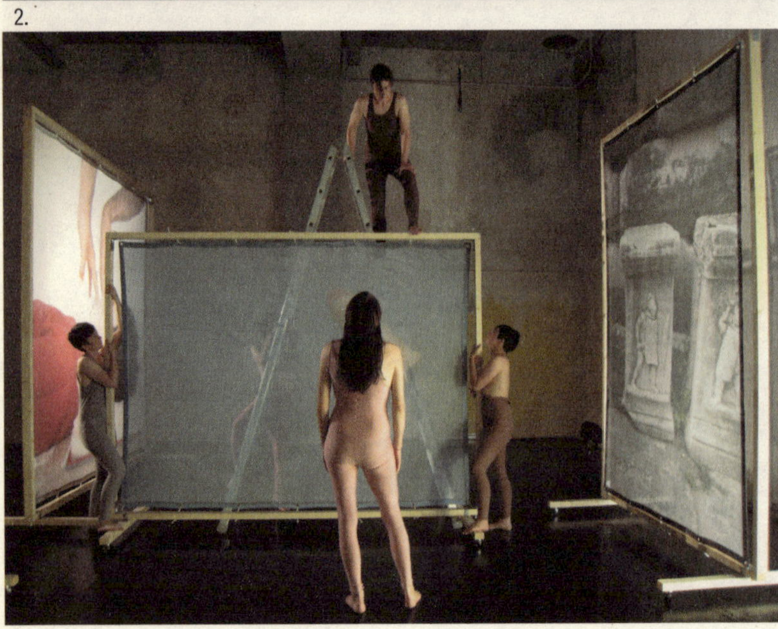
4.

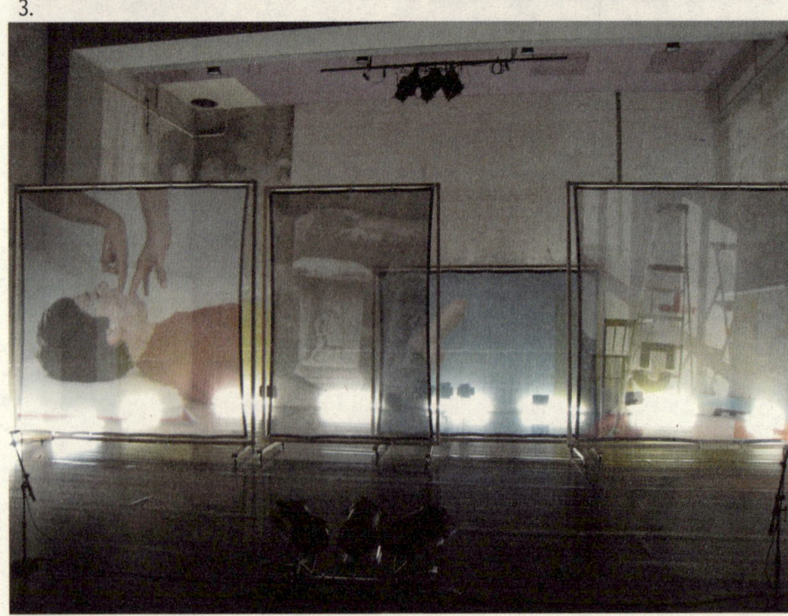
5.

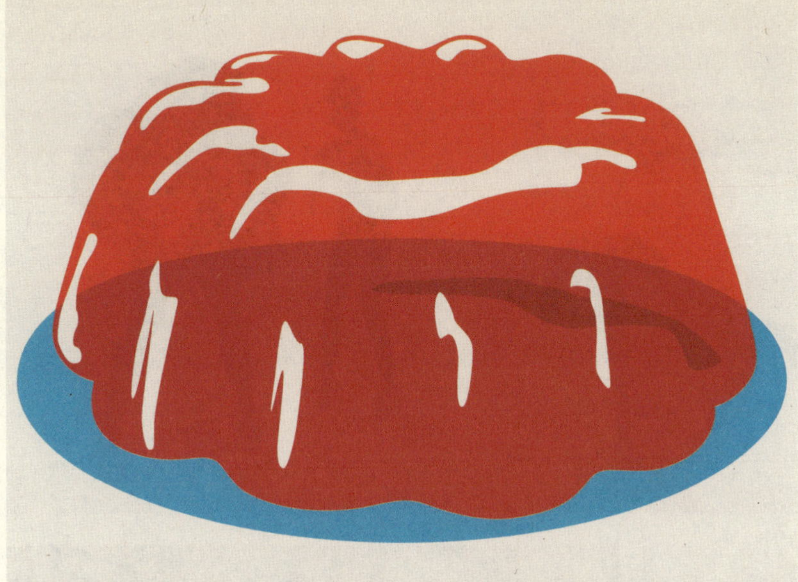

1.

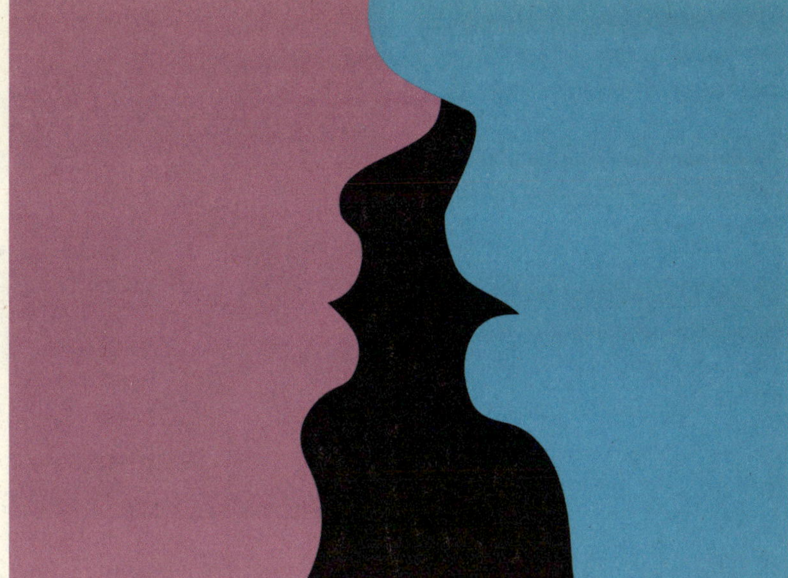

2.

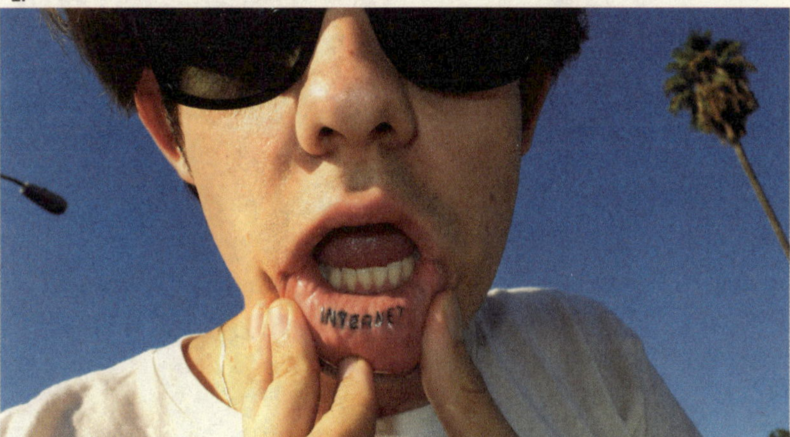

3.

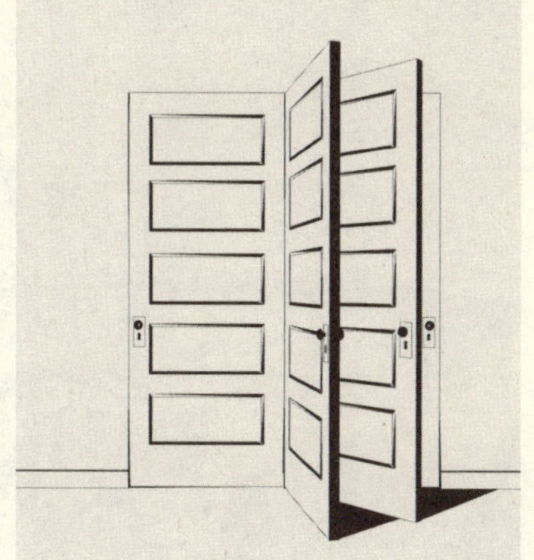

4.

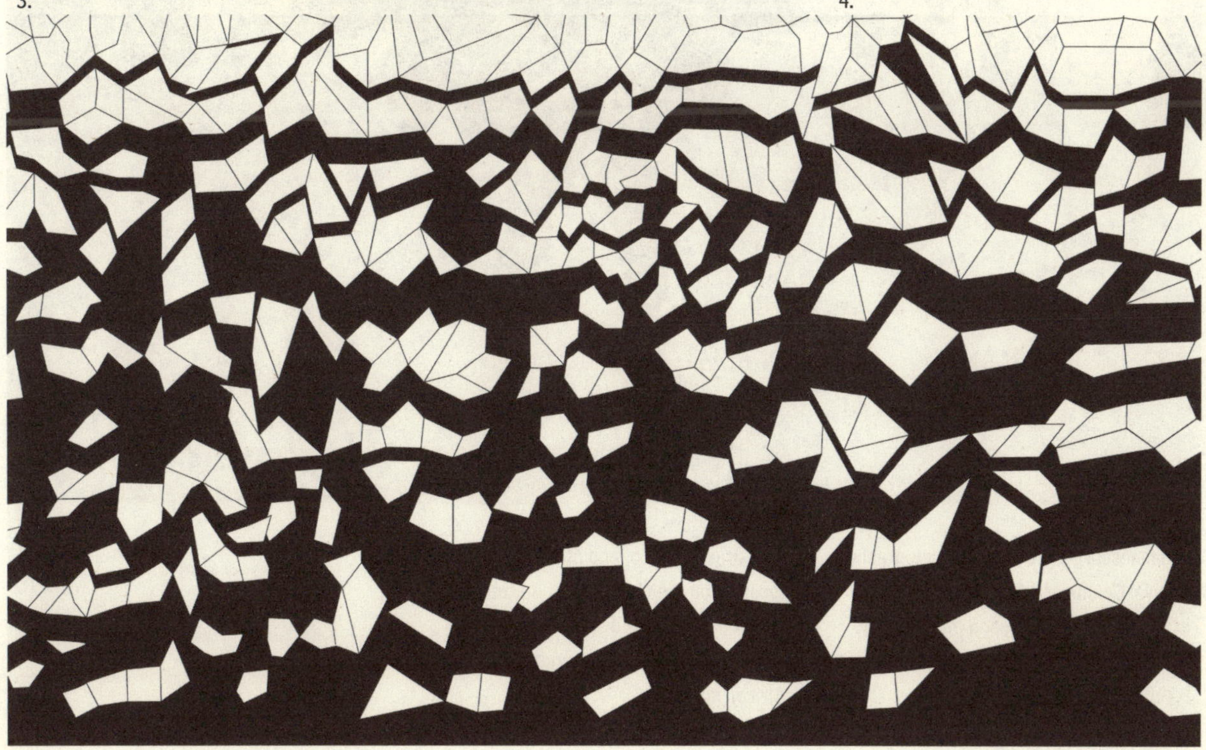

5.

Rafaël Rozendaal's playful, interactive Web-based projects often involve ordinary objects such as toilet paper, Jell-O, or a burning cigarette. "The Web is the most intimate platform for art there has ever been," says Rozendaal, who draws from Surrealism as well as the bright colors and animation references of Pop art.

1. **Jello Time .com**
2007, website, jellotime.com

2. **Much Better Than This .com**
2006, website, muchbetterthanthis.com

3. **Self-Portrait with Tattoo**
2006, digital image, dimensions variable

4. **Big Long Now .com**
2006, website, biglongnow.com

5. **Broken Self .com**
2007, website, brokenself.com

RUGA, ATHI-PATRA

b. 1984 Umtata, South Africa

1. Warm leatherette

2007, leatherette, lamé, butcher's hooks, and canola oil, dimensions variable

2. ...But don't worry you can suntan (for Katrina)

2008, performance

3. Even I Exist in Embo: Jaundiced tales of counterpenetration #5

2007, Lambda print, $15\frac{3}{4} \times 23\frac{1}{2}$ in (40 × 60 cm)

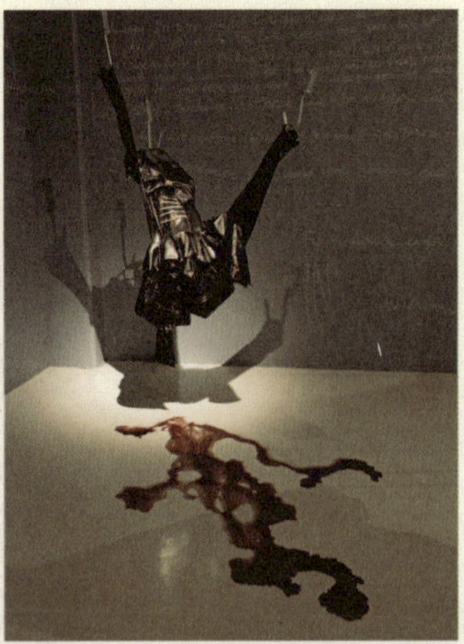

1.

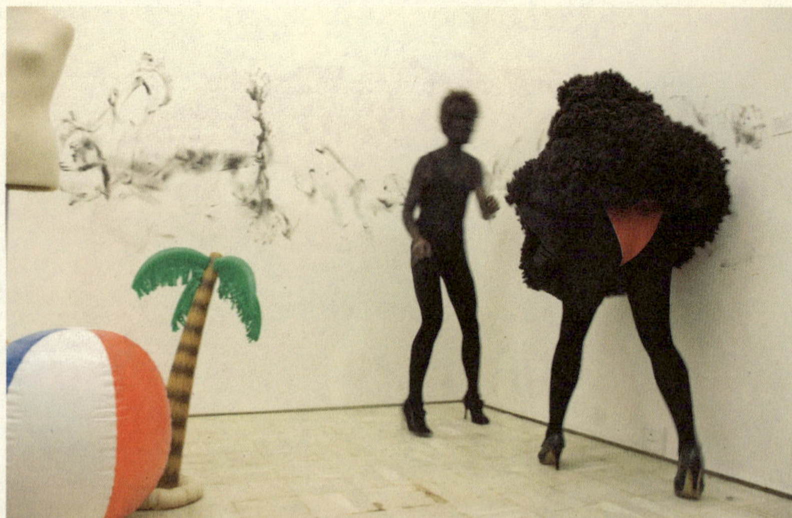

2.

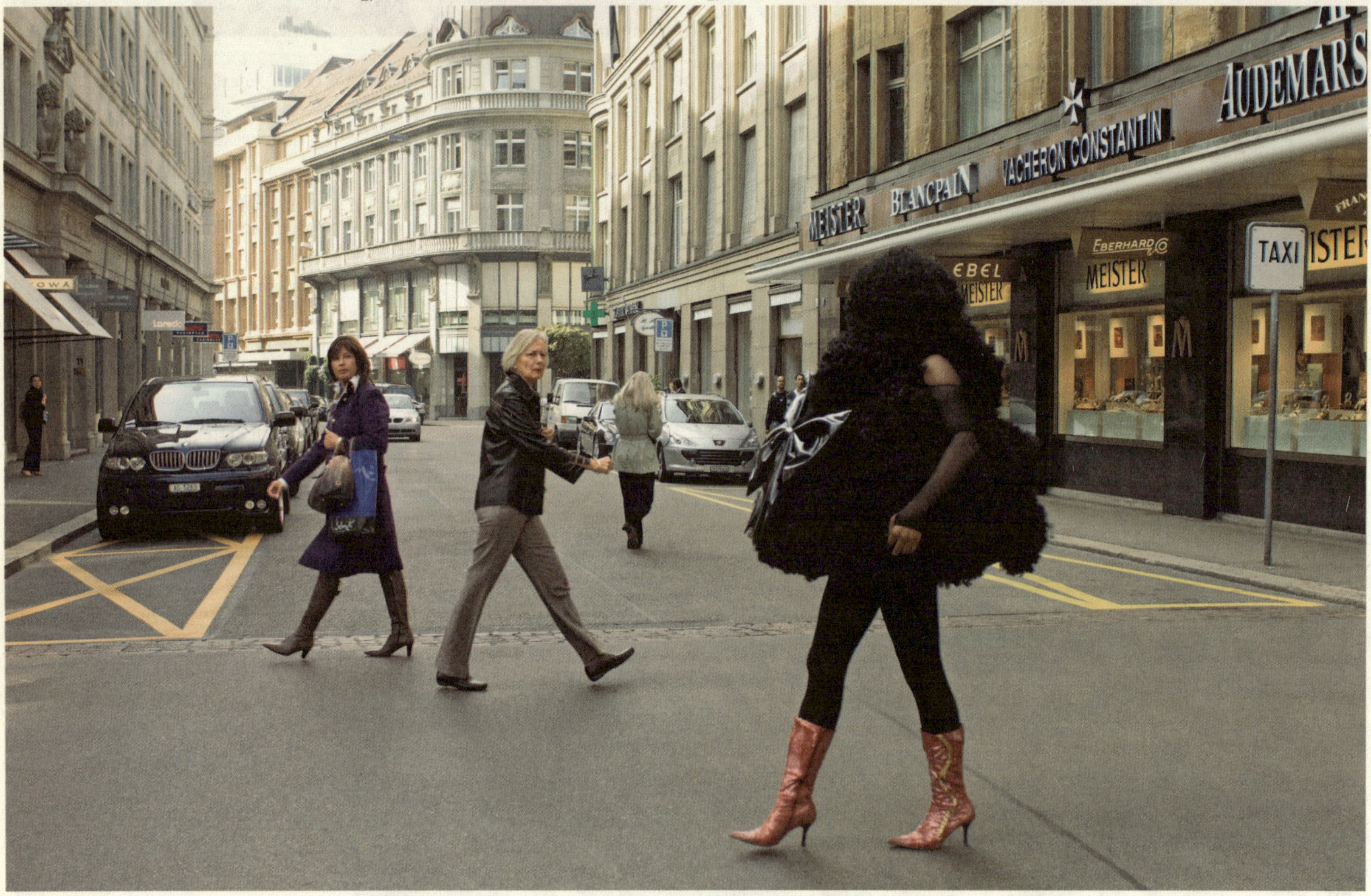

3.

Athi-Patra Ruga is an artist as well as a clothing designer with his own label, Just Nje/Amper Couture. He graduated from the Gordon Flack Davison Design Academy in Johannesburg, where he lives and works. His work was selected for the Dakar Biennial in 2008. The founder of Johannesburg's fashion and photography festival Confluence 4, Ruga also works in performance, video, and photography, exploring dress codes and the way fashion is utilized by people. His 2008 show "... of bugchasers and watussi faghags" at Art Extra in Johannesburg included tapestries, a video, and photographs focusing on the character of Beiruth, dressed in heels and spandex, who is pitted against historical South African imagery.

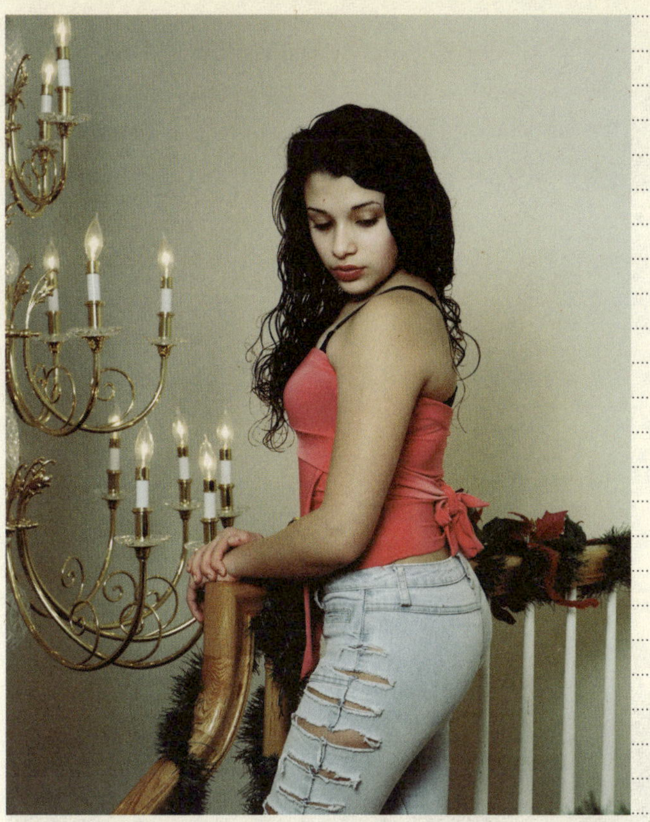

1.

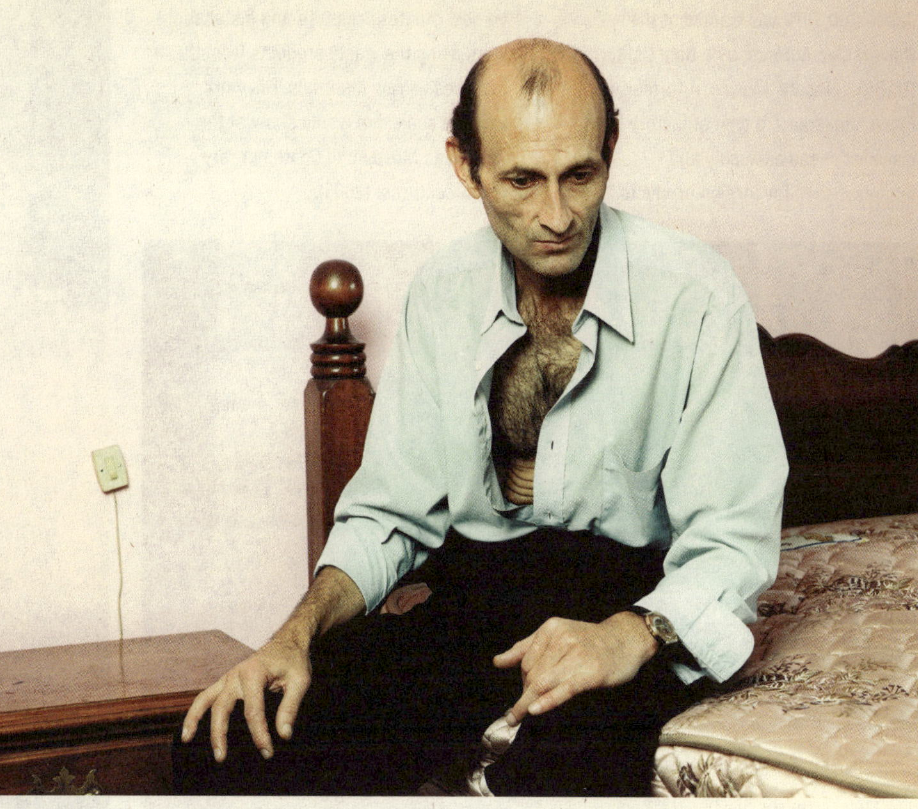

2.

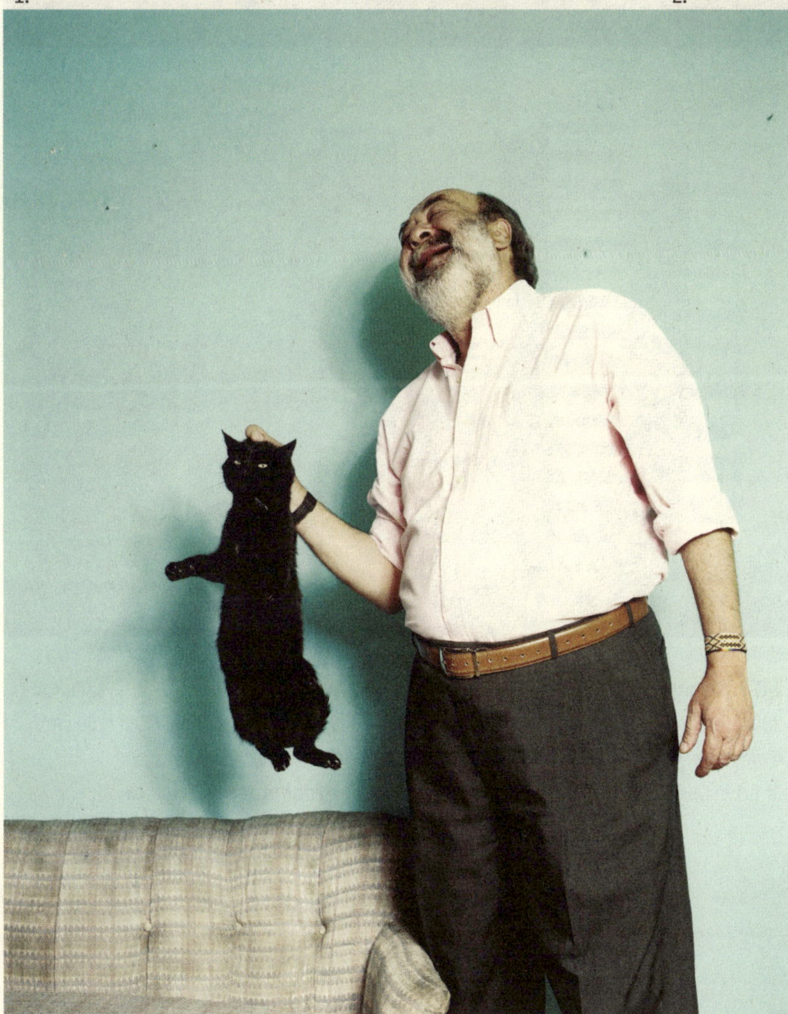

3.

Guadalupe Ruiz graduated in 2006 from the Hochschule für Gestaltung und Kunst in Zurich and currently lives and works in Geneva. Her photographs initially centered on psychologically charged portraits of her own family. Her range of subjects also includes portraits of sacred sites of indigenous people of Colombia, as well as sociologically inflected photographs of the interiors and private gardens of Colombians in six officially designated socioeconomic brackets.

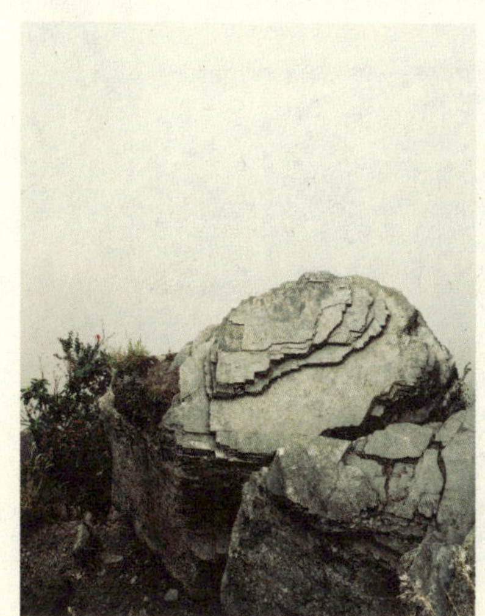

4.

1. **Chiken lips**
from the series **Hazardous reactions**
2006, color photograph, $35\frac{1}{2} \times 43\frac{3}{4}$ in
(90 × 111 cm)

2. **Gonzalo desgualetado**
from the series **La saga**
2006, color photograph, $21\frac{3}{4} \times 26\frac{3}{4}$ in
(55 × 68 cm)

3. **Everywhere I go III**
from the series **LatinoCall season 2**
2007, color photograph, $23\frac{3}{4} \times 19\frac{1}{2}$ in
(60 × 50 cm)

4. **Pico del Aguila**
from the series **La boca del viento**
2008, color photograph, $43\frac{3}{4} \times 35\frac{1}{2}$ in
(111 × 90 cm)

Jaime Ruiz Otis was trained at the Universidad Autónoma de Baja California (UABC) in Tecate, Mexico. A former worker in a maquiladora, a type of factory that provides cheap assembly and manufacturing for foreign products, he now creates sculpture and installation work using the waste products from these factories as raw materials. His work was the subject of a solo show at the San Diego Museum of Contemporary Art in California (2005).

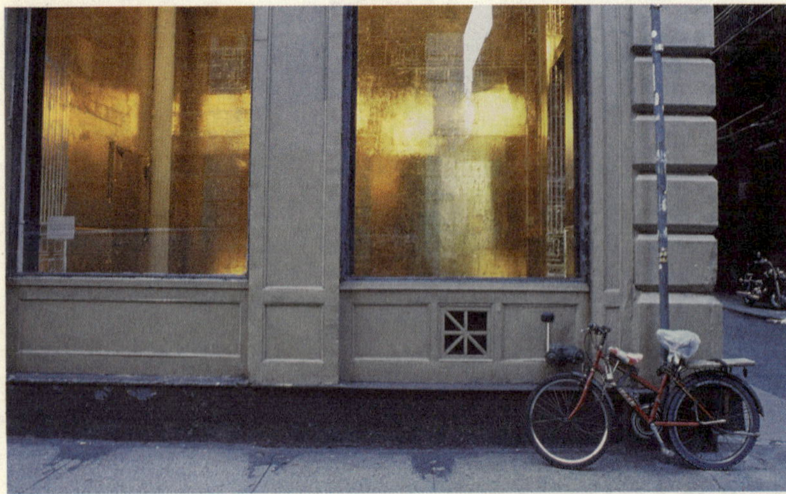

1.

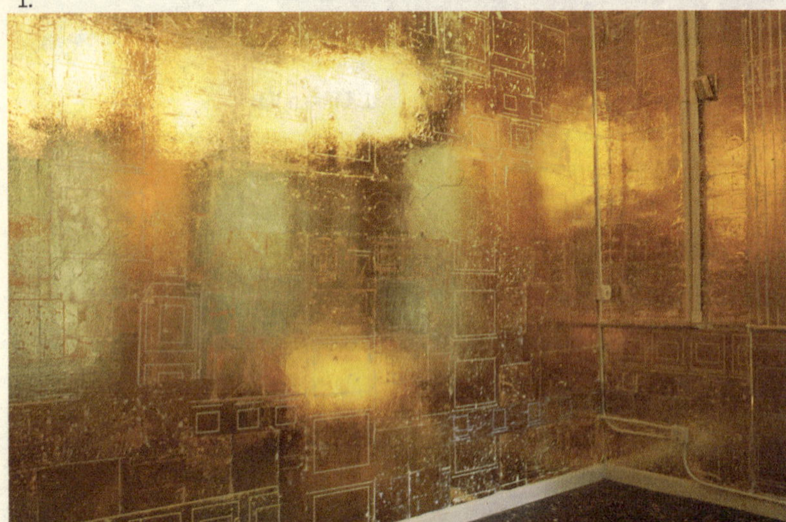

2.

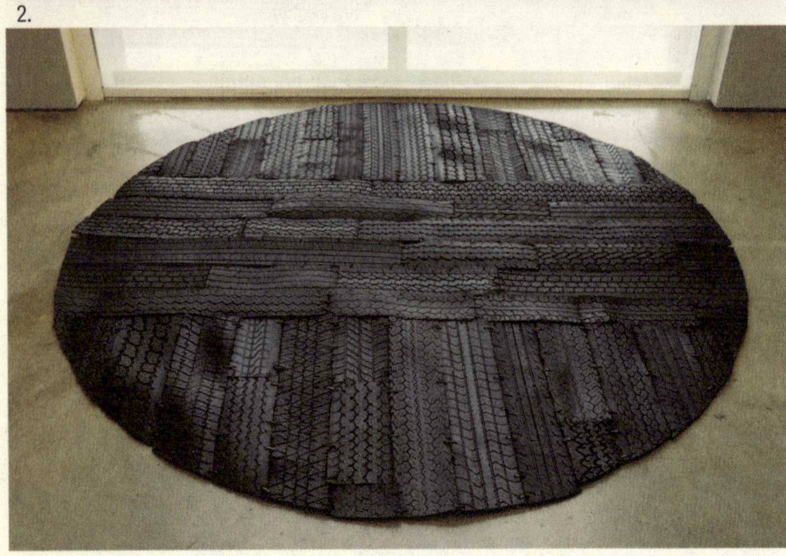

3.

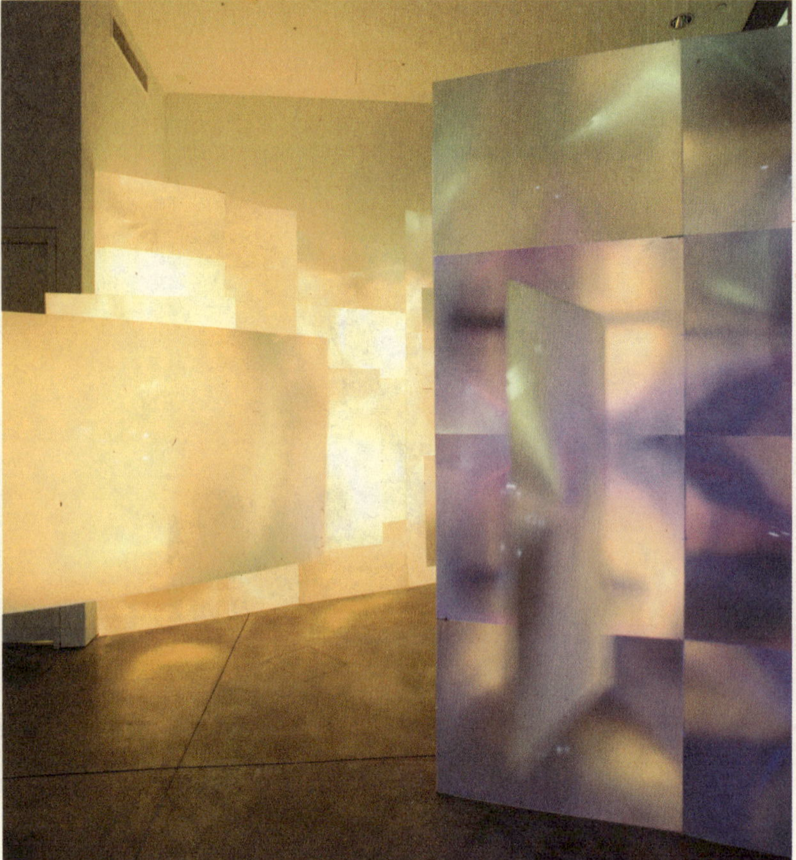

4.

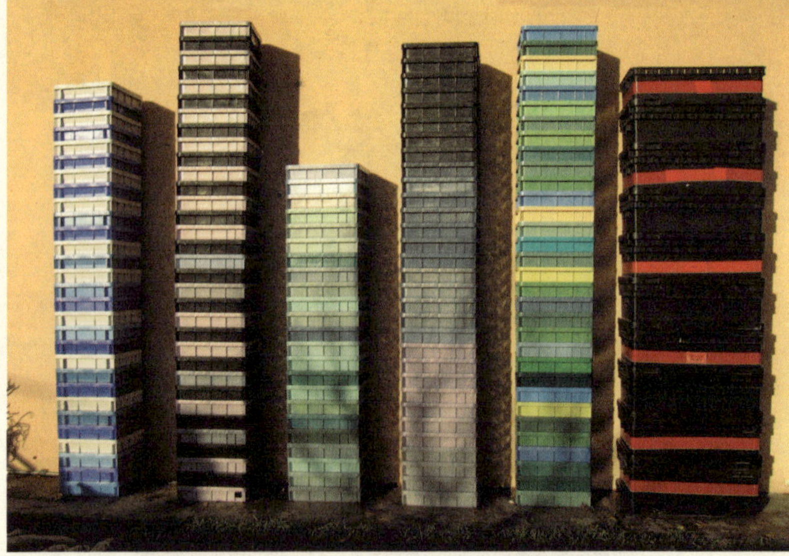

5.

1 & 2. Strange Kind Of Temple
2004, found industrial gold foil, dimensions variable, installation view at Art in General, New York

3. Tapte Radal
2000, tire tread, zip ties, 78 in (200 cm)

4. Introphotosensiproycta
2005, plasma TVs, magnifying acrylics, lightbulbs, and movement sensors, dimensions variable

5. Cajas de Lluvia
2007, reused plastic bins, fountain pump, and water, dimensions variable

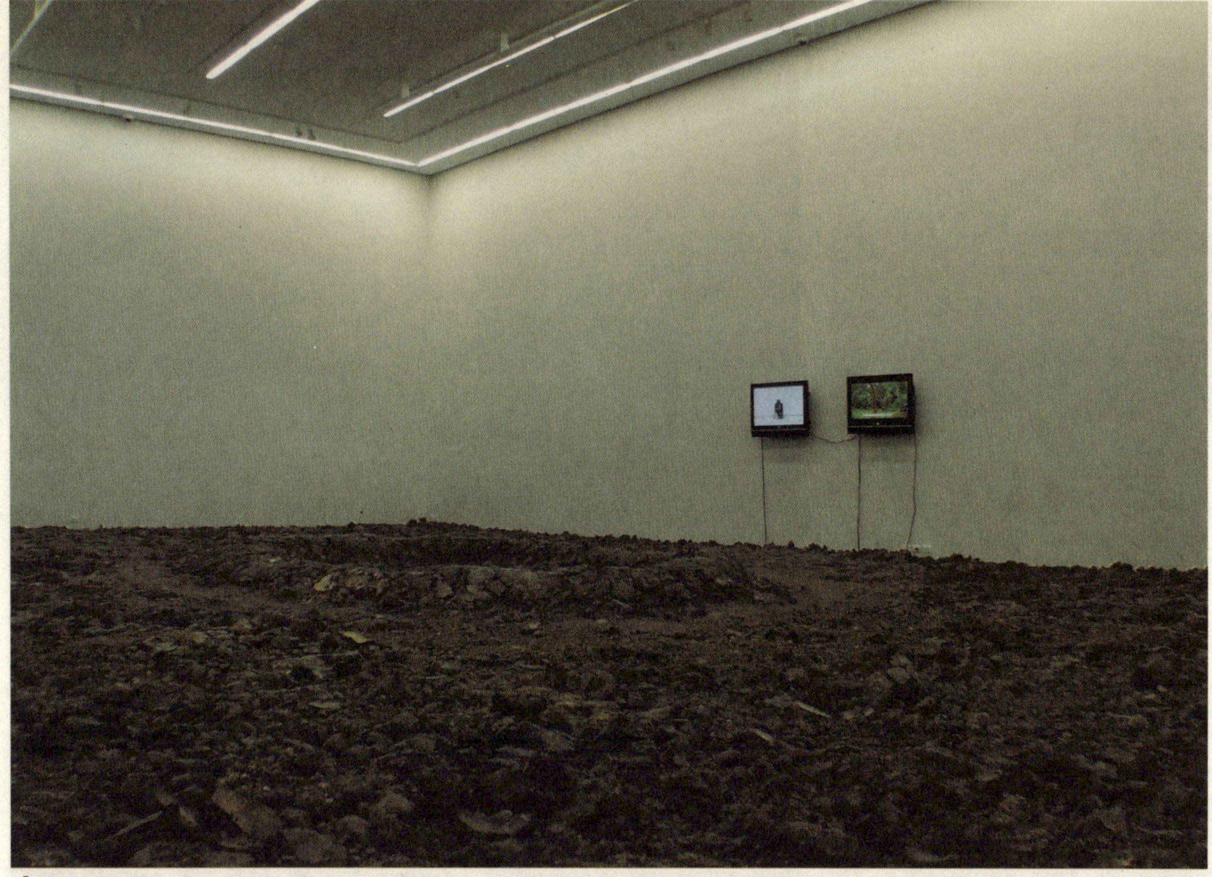

1.

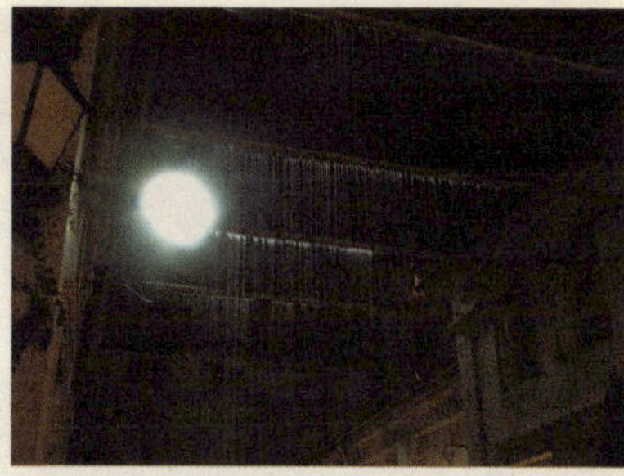

2.

Arin Rungjang graduated from Silpakorn University and the Ecole Nationale Superieure des Beaux-Arts in Paris. He lives in Bangkok. His installation and site-specific works are based on his interest in both conceptual art and spirituality. His ongoing piece **Collected Neons from Art Spaces** (2006-present) is a site-specific work in which he collects the neon tube lights from various well known museums and art institutions and resituates them in a different context within a gallery space, encouraging viewers to rethink where and how art is exhibited.

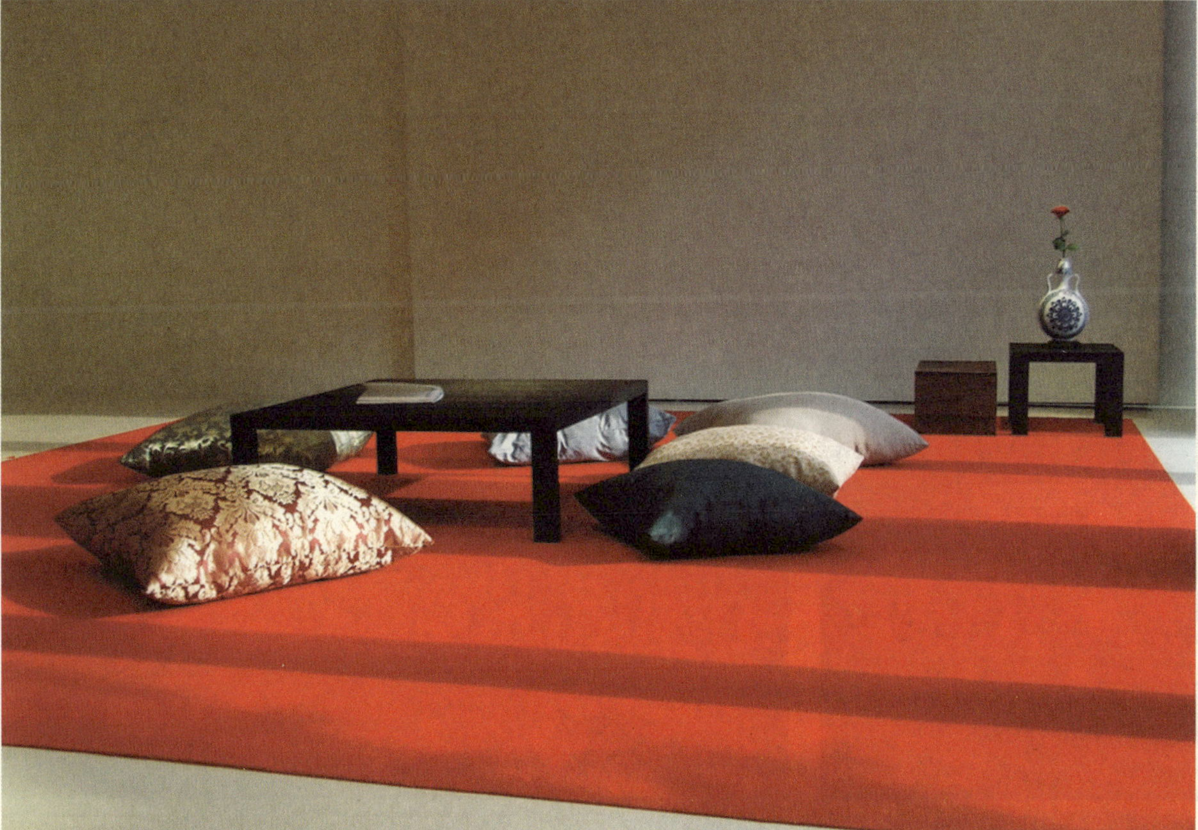

3.

1. **Never Congregate Never Disregard**
2007, mixed media, dimensions variable

2. **Duplicated Memorial [Big moon and waterfall]**
2006, light, water, and mixed media, dimensions variable

3. **In Defense of Lost Memories**
2008, mixed media installation, dimensions variable

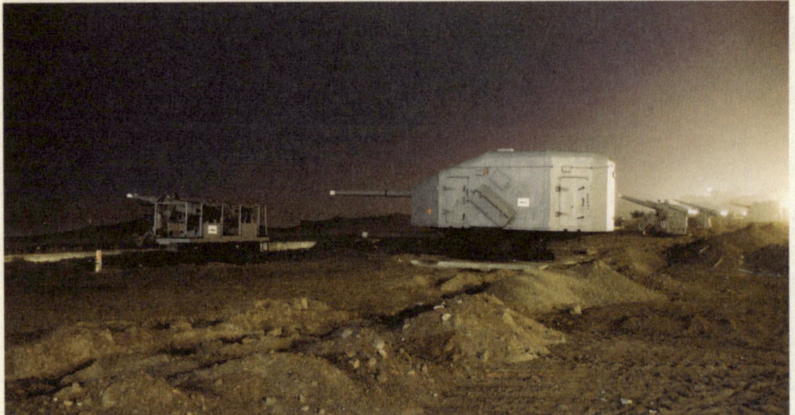
1.

Nicolás Rupcich lives and works in Santiago, Chile. His videos incorporate an absurd humor and an interest in the images and cameras that characterize city life. The protagonists of his work **Automatico/Automatic** (2006) are the cameras themselves: arranged in a circle in a forest, they are set up to take pictures of each other during the night, questioning the ease with which photographs can be made and put to use.

1. **War Scene**
2008, Lambda print, dimensions variable

2. **Stage**
2006, Lambda print, dimensions variable

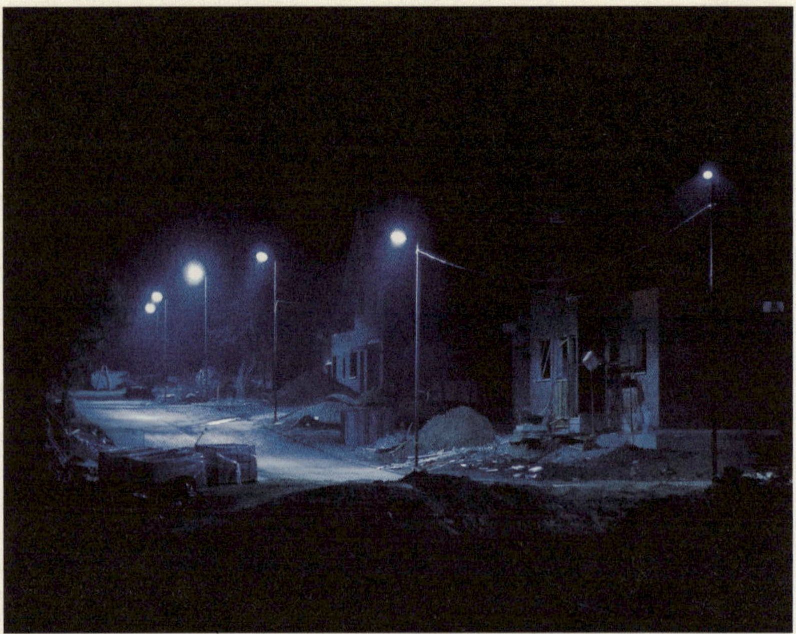
2.

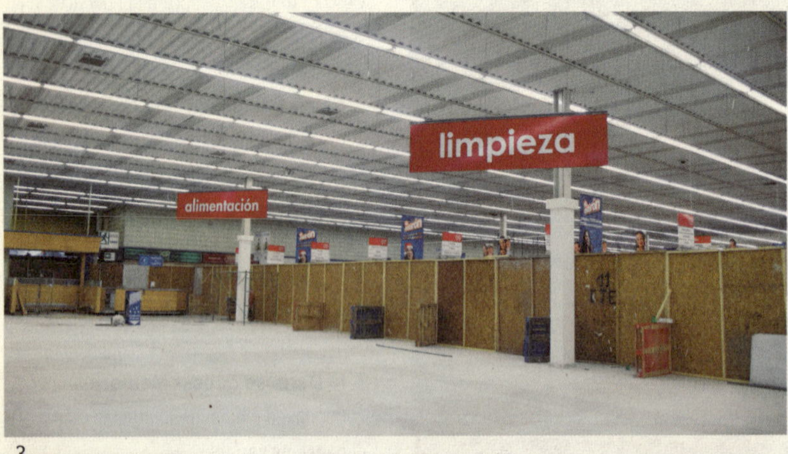

3.

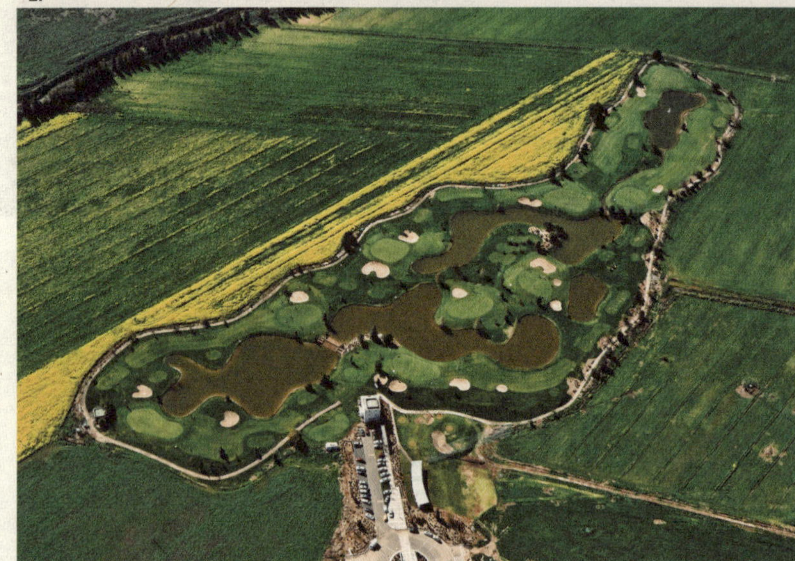
4.

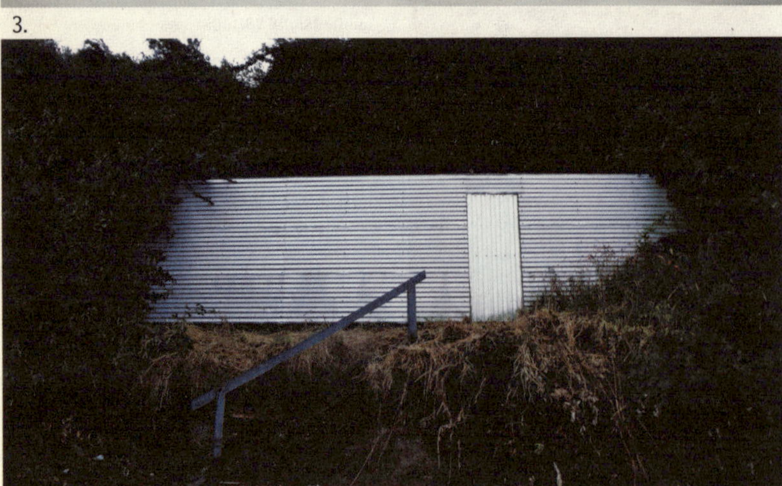
5.

6.

3. **Spatial Administration**
2007, Lambda print, dimensions variable

4. **Golf Court**
2008, Lambda print, dimensions variable

5. **Untitled**
2008, Lambda print, dimensions variable

6. **Untitled**
2008, Lambda print, dimensions variable

1. **Stripping**
2008, 340 pits, each 31 1/2 in (80 cm), total 32 3/4 × 164 ft (10 × 50 m)

2. **Untitled (White Glass)**
2008, glass, lacquer, 19 1/2 × 32 1/4 in (50 × 82 cm)

3. **Aussenportal**
2008, mortar, 47 1/4 × 84 1/2 × 13 3/4 in (120 × 215 × 35 cm)

4. **Untitled**
2008, salt, dimensions variable

5. **The Sound of Many Voices (in the Street Commanding Silence)** (detail)
2008, bituminous sheetings, 98 1/2 × 19 1/2 × 9 1/2 in (250 × 50 × 24 cm)

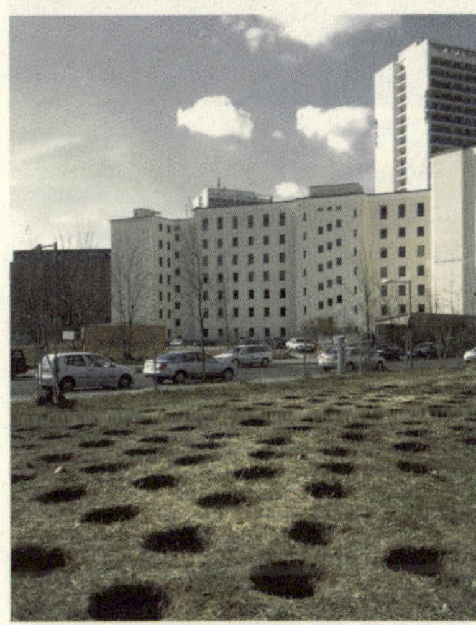
1.

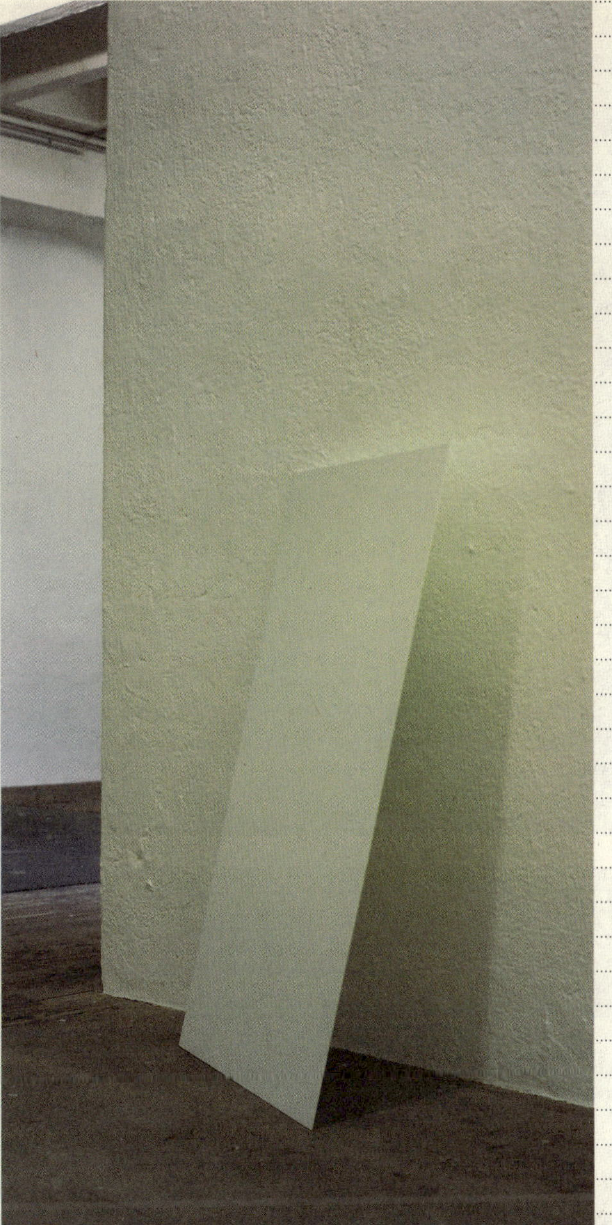
2.

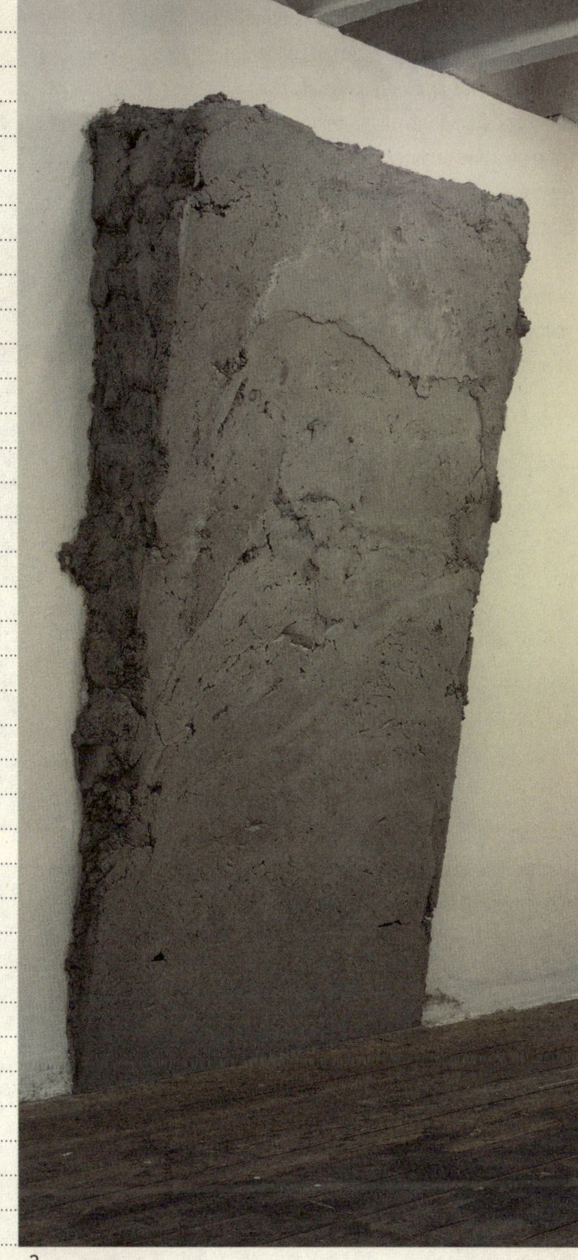
3.

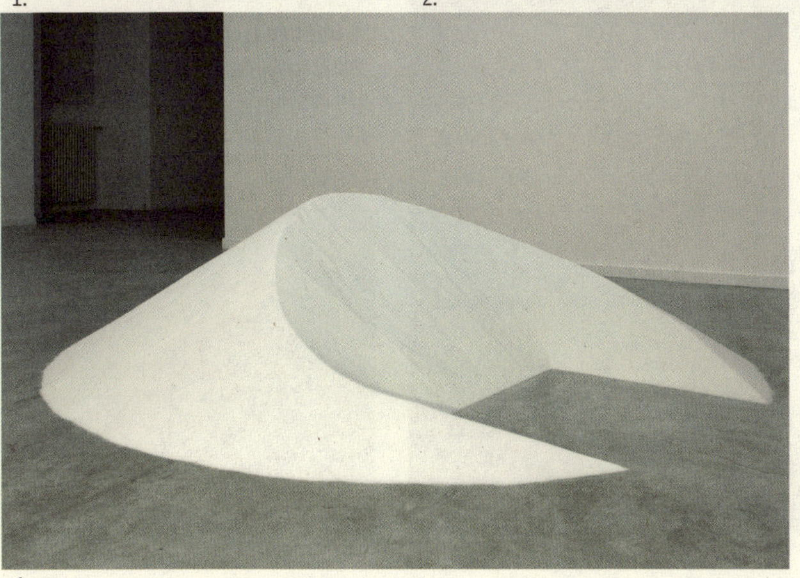
4.

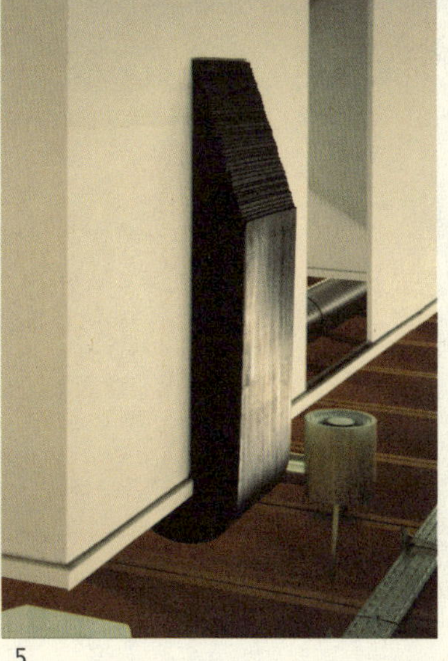
5.

Kilian Rüthemann graduated from the School of Art and Design in Basel. His sculptures and installations are made of common construction materials such as roofing tar, metal, and foam, and challenge viewers' assumptions about function and their potential. His work also draws on the traditions of Minimalist sculpture and the work of such artists as Wolfgang Laib or Joseph Beuys. Rüthemann piled salt along a wall, challenging the kinds of materials that are considered worthy of being an artwork and the notions of weight and gravity in sculpture.

James Ryan received an MA in painting from the Royal College of Art in London, where he lives and works. His abstract paintings stem from an interest in geometry and architectural techniques. He creates a three-dimensional space that suggests a man-made environment, as in **Untitled (yellow)** (2007), a two-dimensional painting in which planes of yellow and ocher create the perception of a three-dimensional structure.

1.

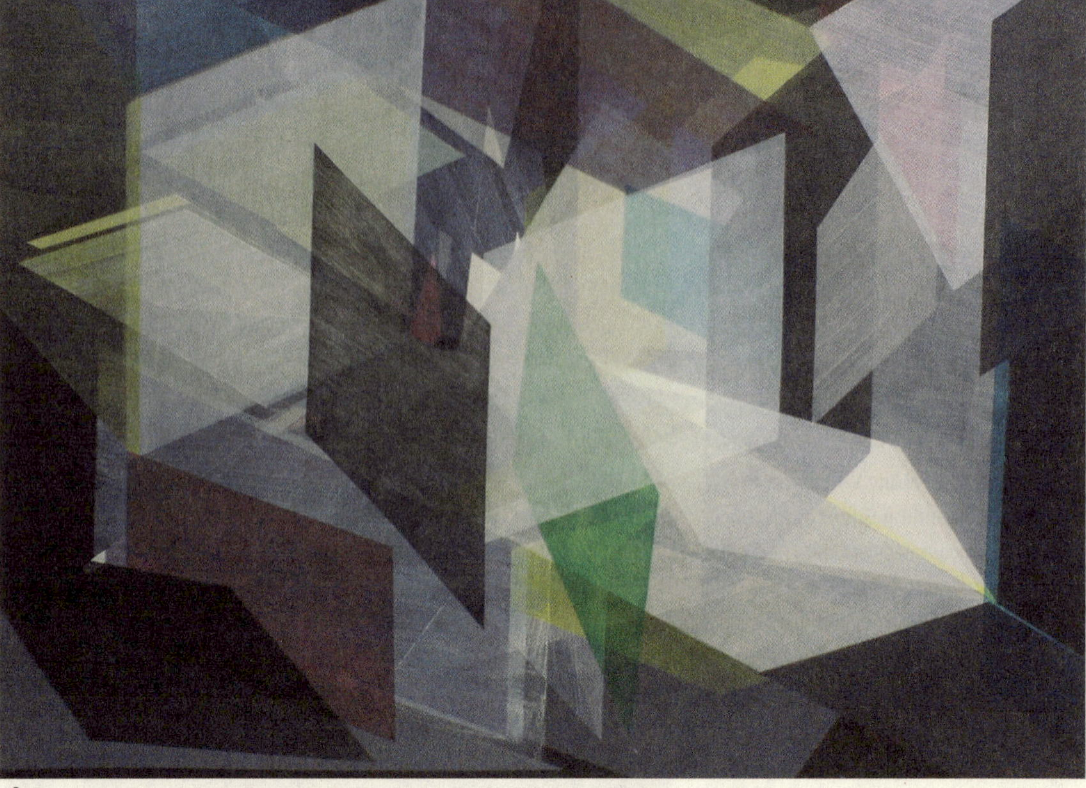

2.

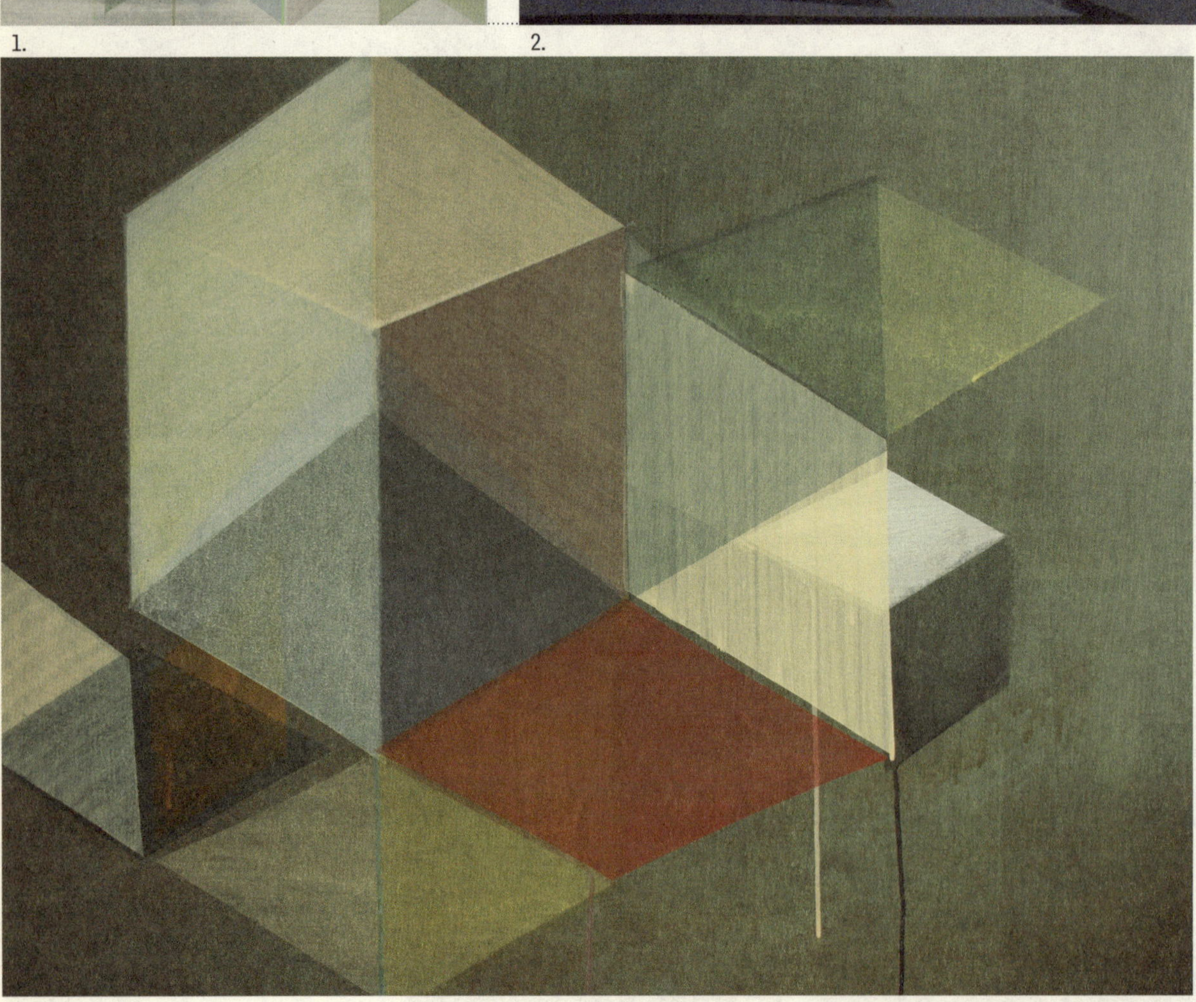

3.

1. **Isometric**
2008, acrylic on canvas, 24 × 30 in (61 × 76 cm)

2. **Untitled (structure)**
2006, acrylic on board, 29 ½ × 39 ½ in (75 × 100 cm)

3. **Cluster**
2007, acrylic on canvas, 29 ½ × 39 ½ in (75 × 100 cm)

4. **Untitled (yellow)**
2007, acrylic on canvas, 29 ½ × 29 ½ in (75 × 75 cm)

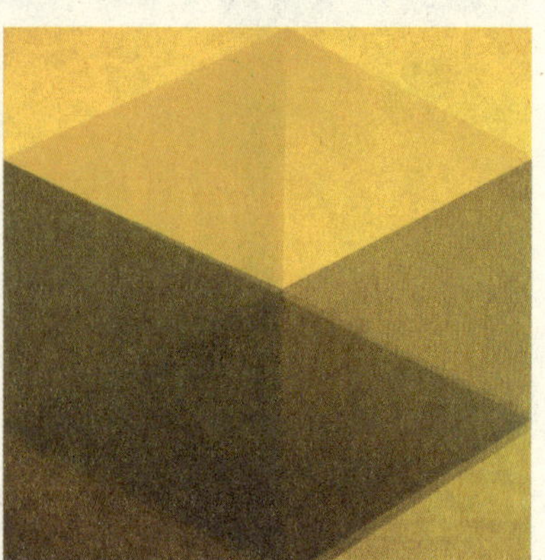

4.

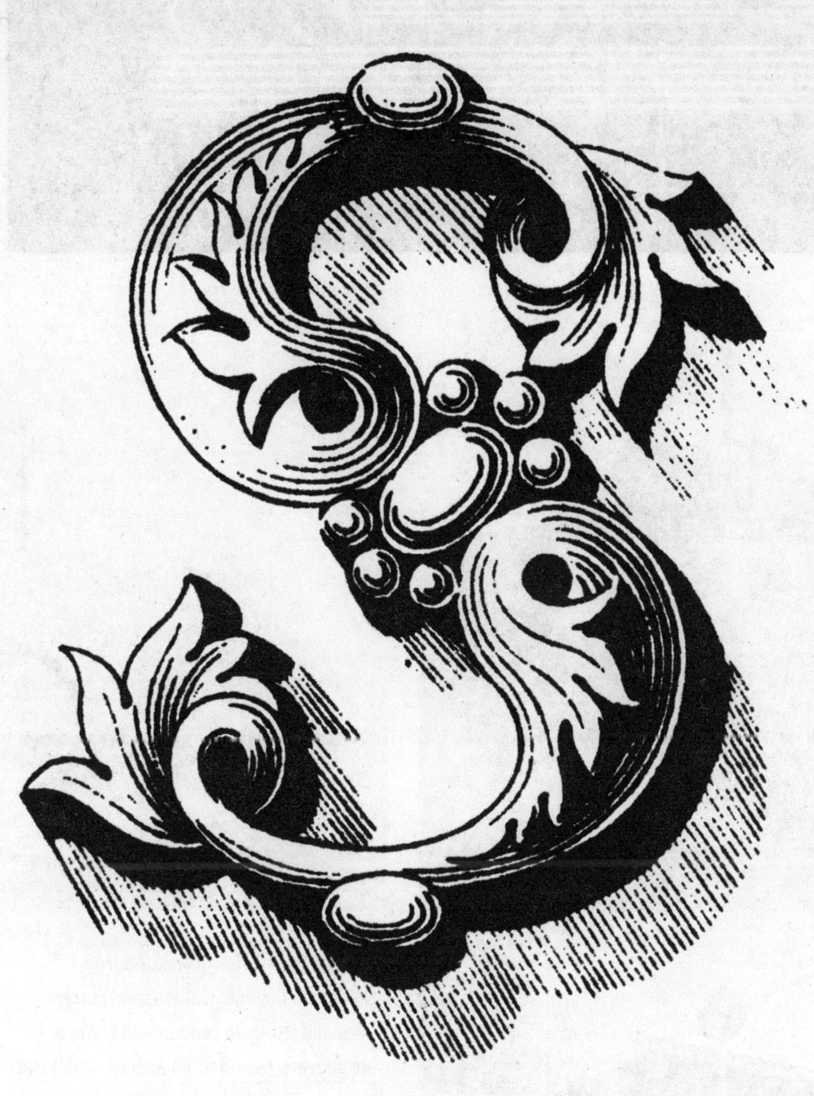

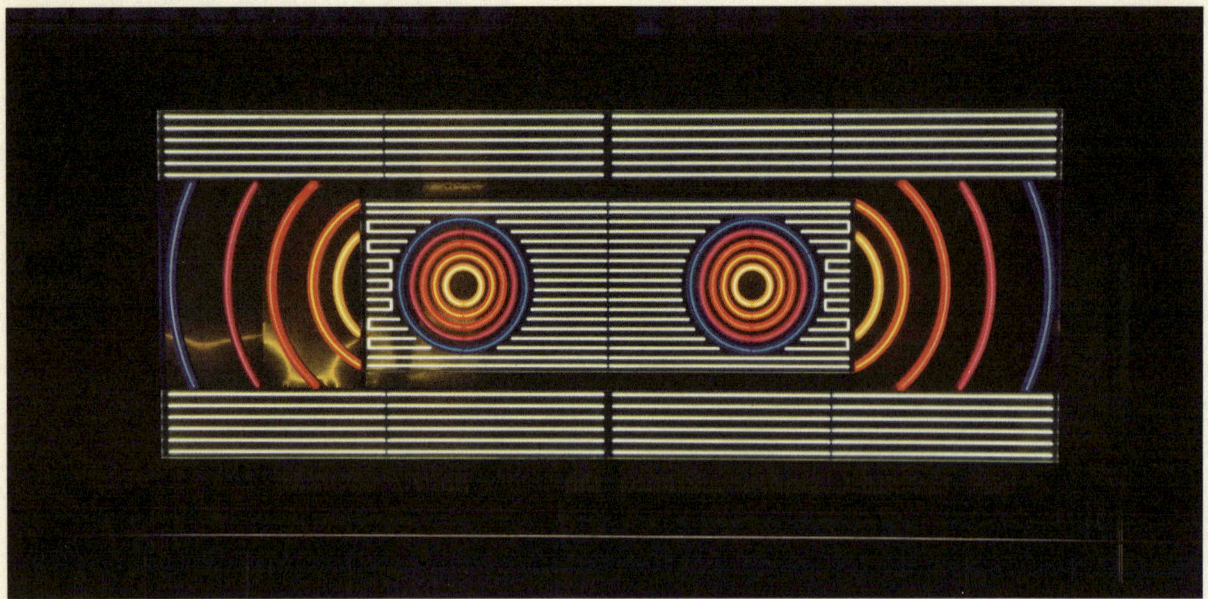

1.

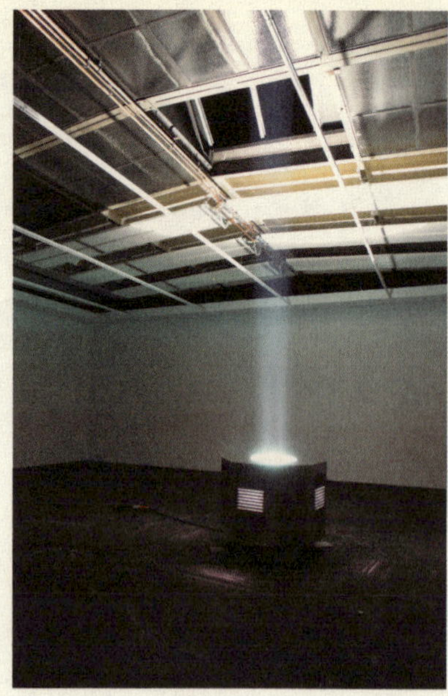

2.

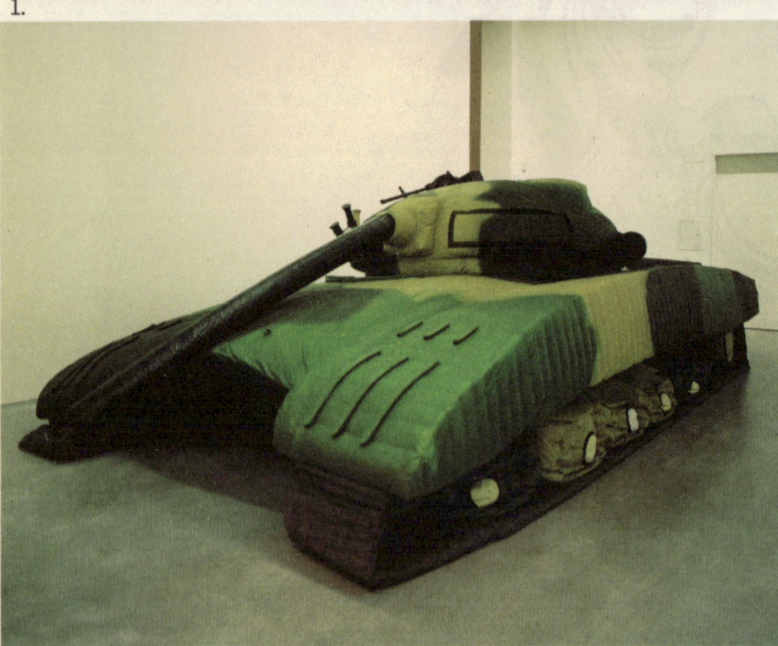

3.

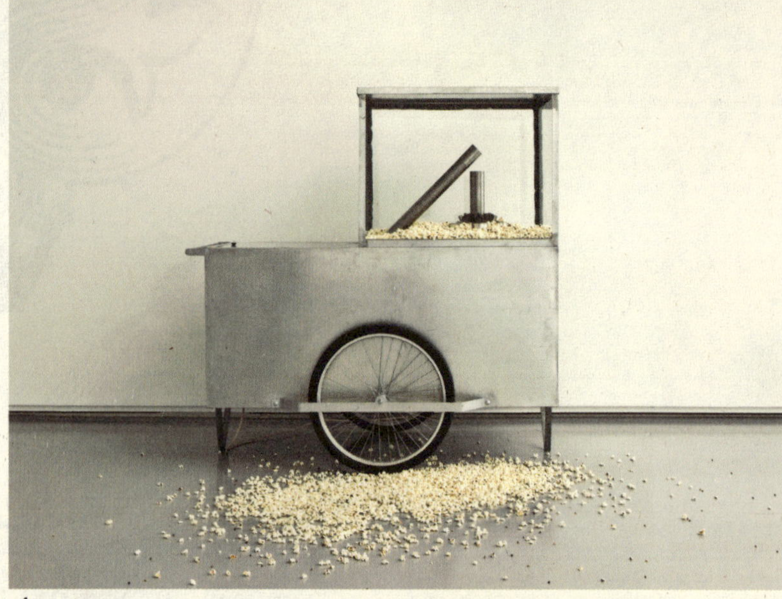

4.

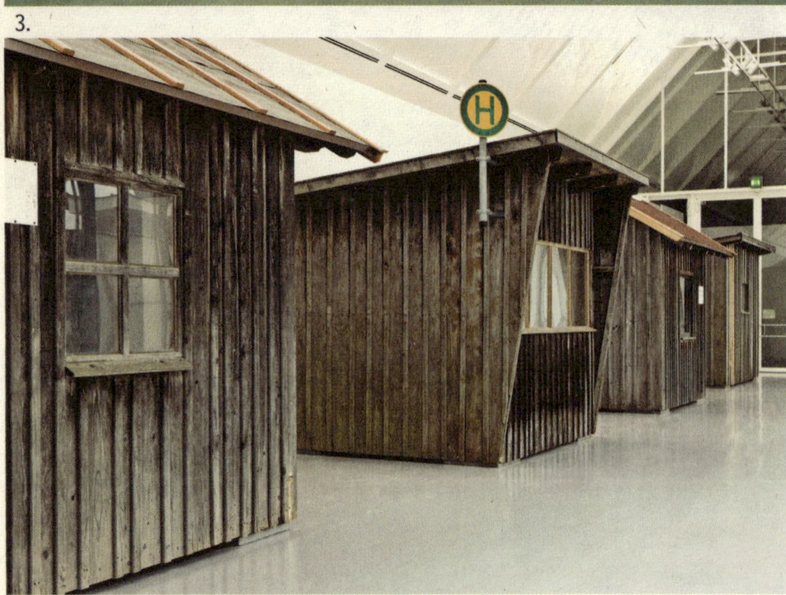

5.

Michael Sailstorfer graduated from Goldsmiths College, London, and currently lives and works in London and Munich. In his subversive and often absurd sculptural works – an old police car turned into a set of drums, for example – he dismantles and reconstructs everyday objects, transforming them in ways that interact with or comment on the exhibition space.

1. **Untitled (Junger Römer)**
2008, aluminum, neon, 118 × 315 × 11 ¾ in (300 × 800 × 30 cm)

2. **Unendliche Säule**
2006, searchlight, electric current, 33 ½ × 39 ¼ in (85 × 100 cm)

3. **T 72 (camouflage)**
2007, inflatable tank dummy, 4 air conveyors, Siemens control system, 98 ½ × 275 ½ × 106 ¼ in (250 × 700 × 270 cm)

4. **1:43 – 47, Frankfurt**
2008, iron, aluminum, electronic units, popcorn, 66 ½ × 66 ½ × 38 ¼ in (169 × 169 × 97 cm)

5. **Wohnen mit Verkehrsanbindung, Grosskatzbach**
2001-08, bus stop, bed, kitchen, table, chair, shelf, toilet, door, light, electric current, water, 100 ½ × 102 ¼ × 75 ½ in (255 × 260 × 192 cm)

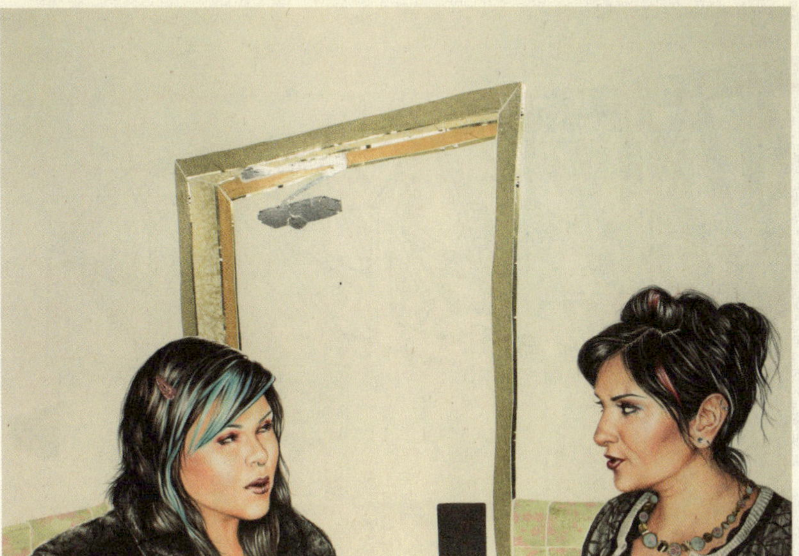

1.

Shizu Saldamando, a painter, graduated from UCLA and then earned an MFA from the California Institute of the Arts. She currently lives and works in Los Angeles. Her portraits of friends and members of her community play with questions of identity, exploring the hyphenated nationalities of many Americans, and the way consumer culture affects style. Her portraits document a world where identity is fluid, and Saldamando focuses on those changeable markers of affiliation.

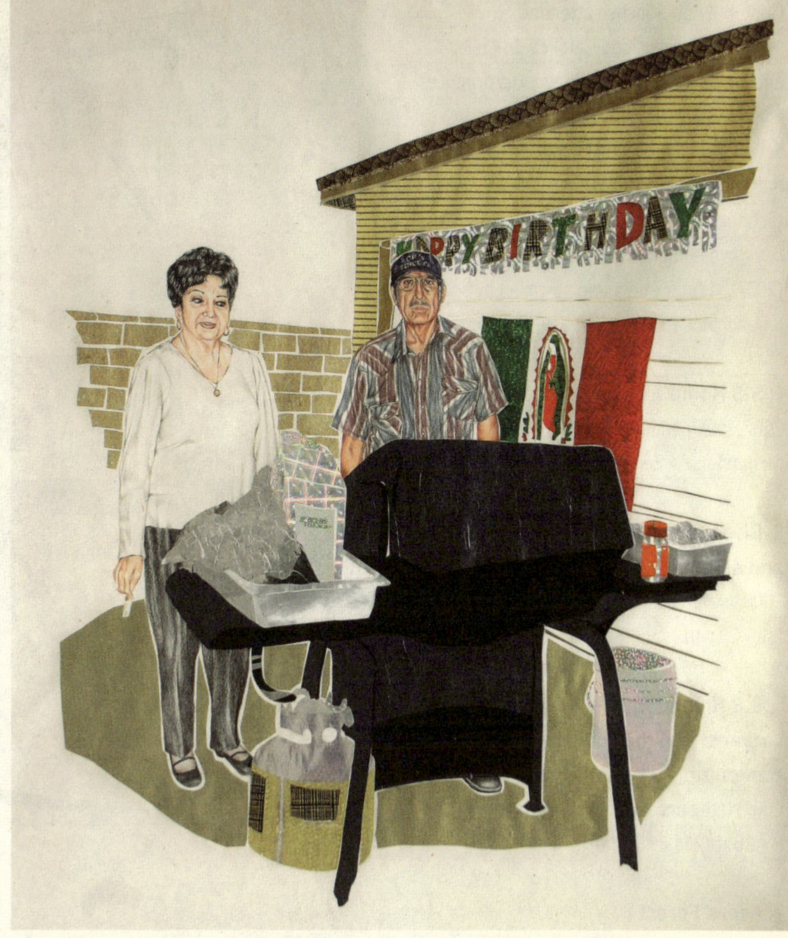

2.

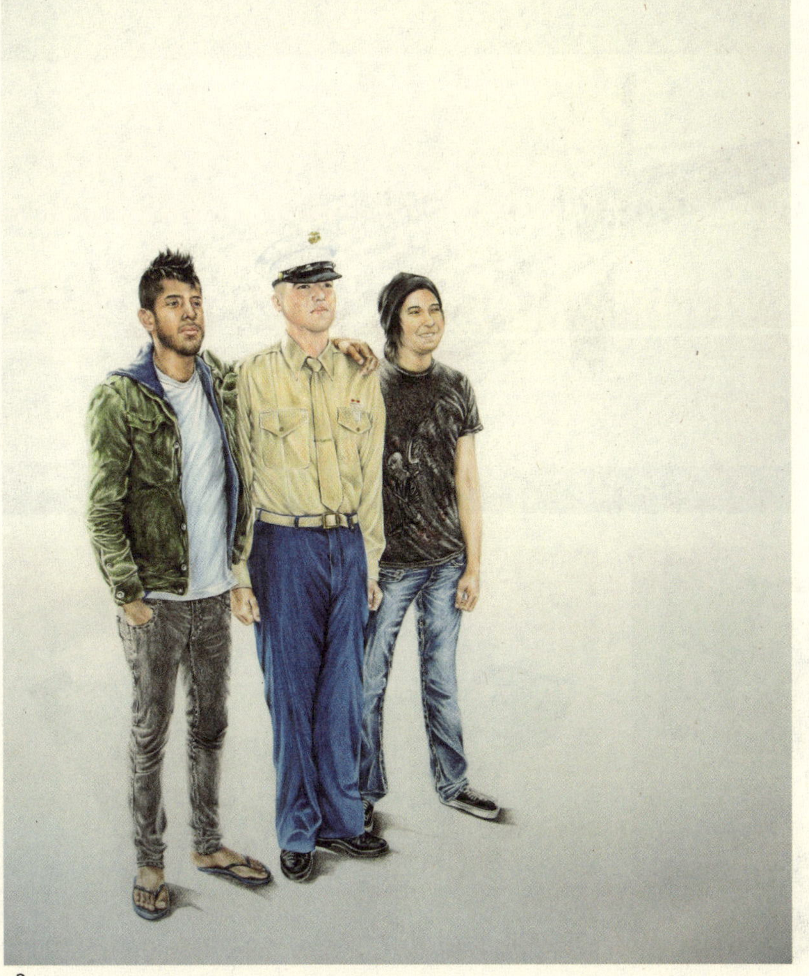

3.

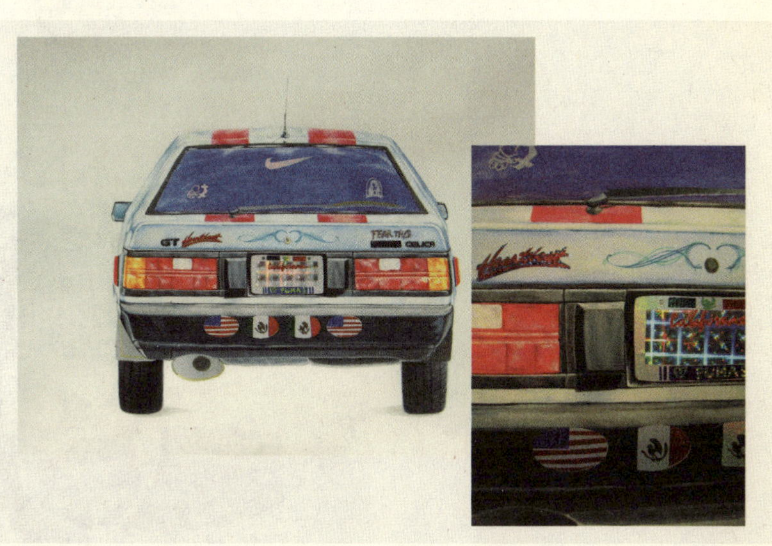

4.

1. Cindy and Asma in the Restroom
2007, colored pencil and collage (washi, origami, and prism paper) on paper, 32 × 44 in (81 × 112 cm)

2. Downey Happy Birthday
2007, colored pencil and collage (washi, origami, and prism paper) on paper, 50 × 40 in (127 × 102 cm)

3. Francisco's Graduation
2008, colored pencil on paper, 45 × 35 in (89 × 114 cm)

4. Notes on La Raza Cosmica Pt. 2
(detail inset)
2008, colored pencil and collage on paper, 35 × 45 in (89 × 114 cm)

Cristóbal Cea Sánchez attended Pontificia Universidad Católica de Chile, and currently lives in Santiago. His practice links painting, drawing, and installation with urban planning and design. He uses materials from watercolor to 3D modeling technologies to portray real and imagined city developments, including **WasteTopia** (2007), a futuristic home powered by a generator running on waste products.

1. **S.S Home / Gremlins on the Roof**
2007, latex, enamel, masking tape, and oil on plaster, 7 × 16 ft (213 × 488 cm)

2. **Given two Homes, a poop reservoir and an engine**
2008, watercolor on paper, 11 1/2 × 8 in (30 × 20 cm)

3. **S.S Neighborhood / Sustainable Lazyness and the concealed Generator**
2007, latex and enamel on plaster, 8 × 30 ft (244 × 488 cm)

4. **Fedex Forest**
2008, watercolor on paper, 5 × 5 in (13 × 13 cm)

5. **AdSense II**
2008, oil on canvas, 47 × 66 in (47 × 168 cm)

6. **Inverted Gothic**
2008, oil on canvas, 47 × 66 in (47 × 168 cm)

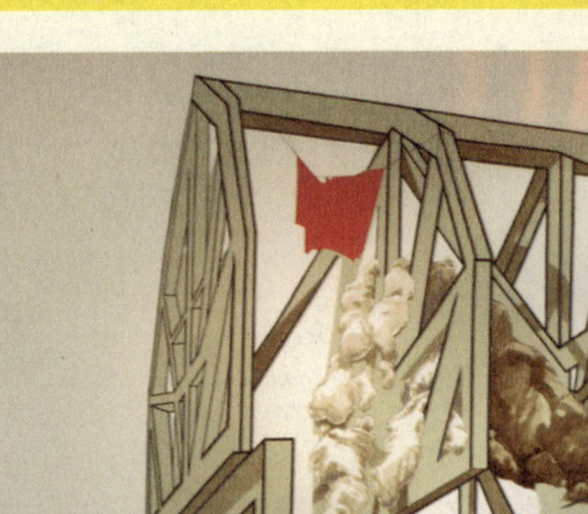

1.

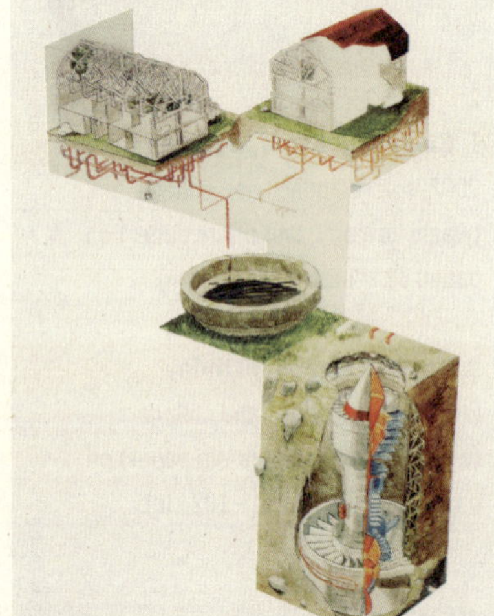

2.

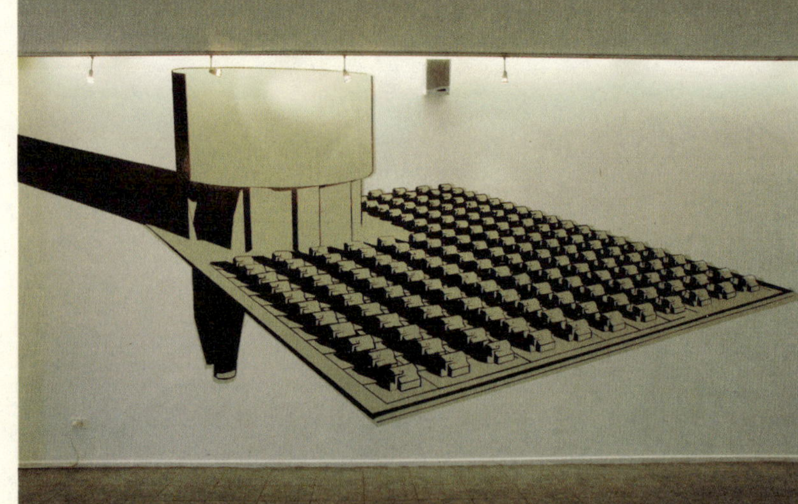

3.

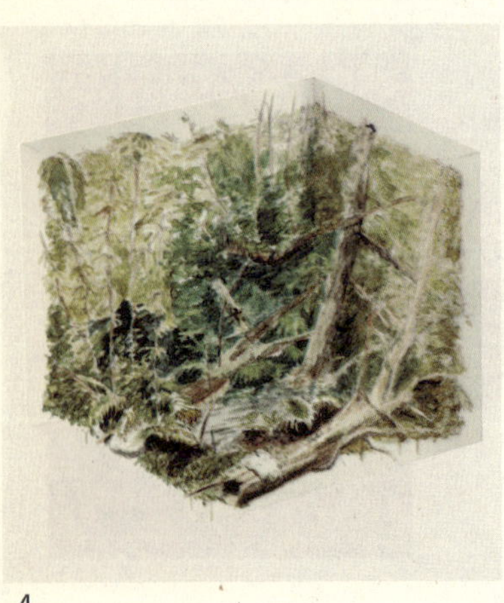

4.

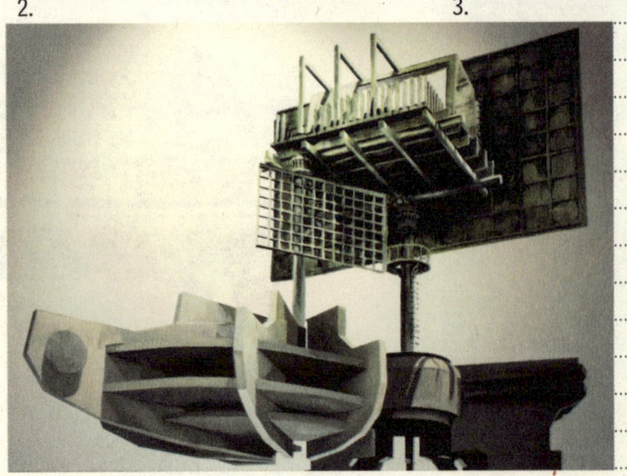

5.

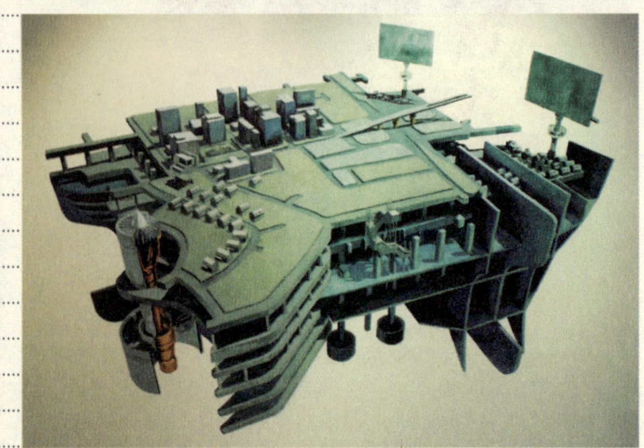

6.

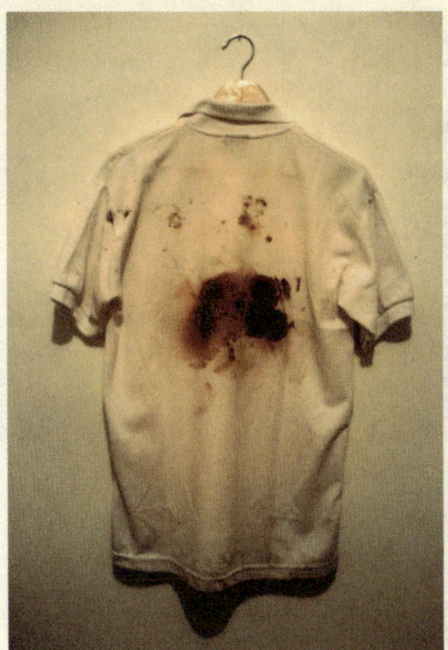
1.

Edwin Sanchez earned his BFA from the Universidad Jorge Tadeo Lozano in Bogotá, where he lives and works. His videos and performances, which incorporate other people and actions on city streets, explore the violence and crime encountered in urban centers. In **Knife Lesson** (2007), a thief gives a lesson on how best to stab someone. **Desired Objects** (2007) incorporates a series of appropriated color photographs of shoplifters taken by a shop owner who then displayed them near his cash machines as a warning to potential thieves.

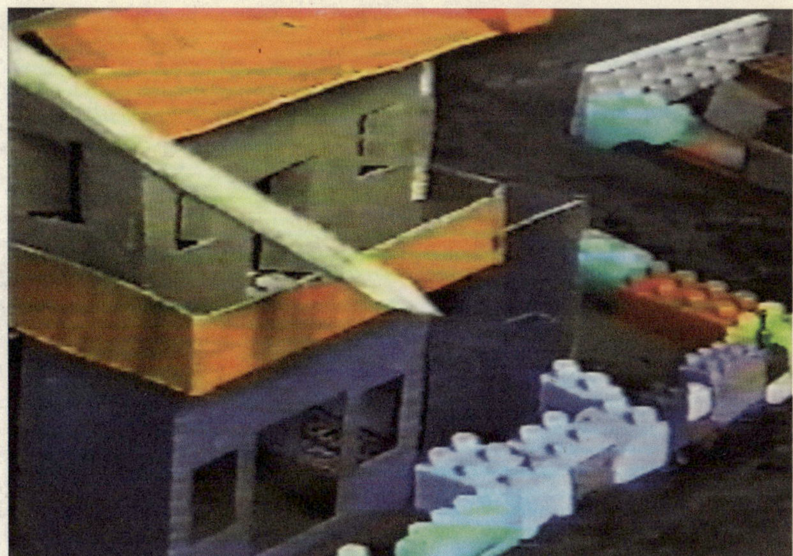
2.

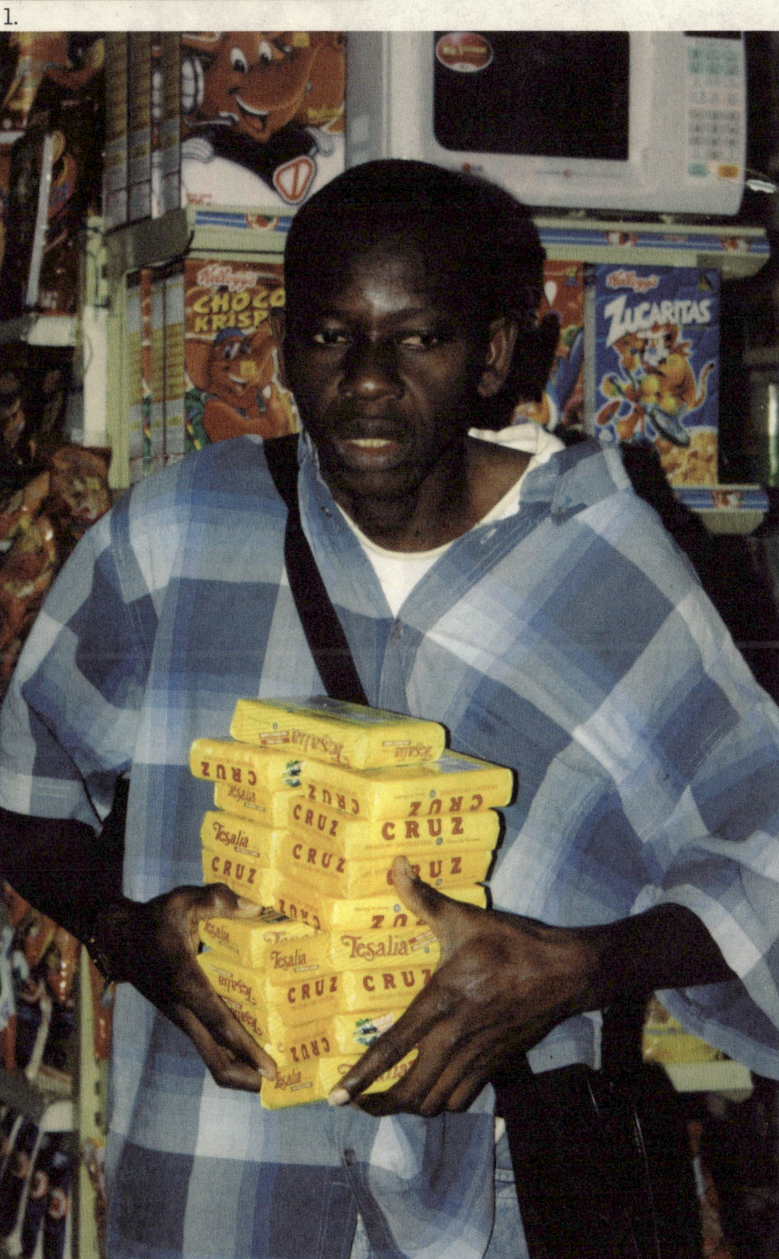

3.

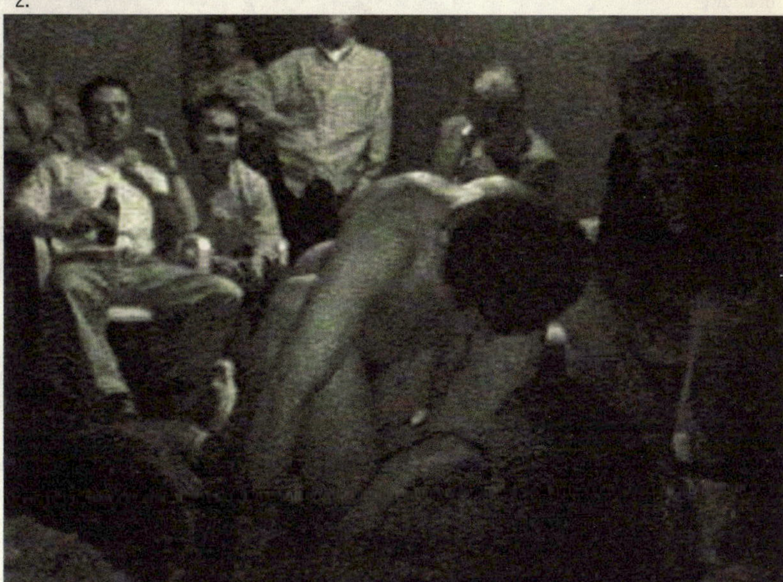
4.

1. Knife Sessions
2006-08, mixed media, dimensions variable

2. Intersections – trace
2008, video, 4 min 56 sec

3. Desired Objects (detail)
2007, photographic installation, dimensions variable

4. Zeus' Labyrinths
2004, video, 2 min 44 sec

5. Pleasure Museum
2006-present, mixed media, dimensions variable

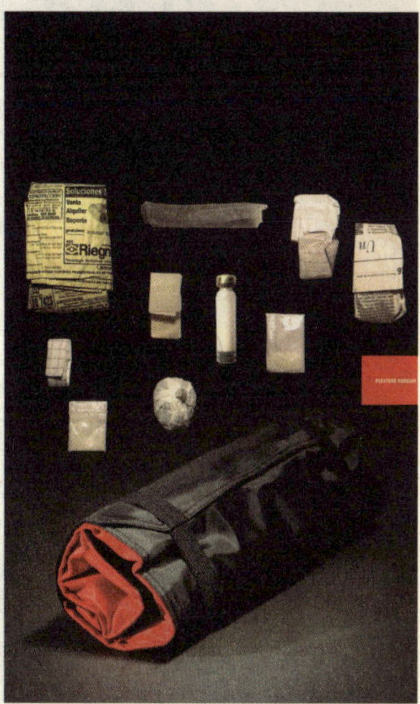
5.

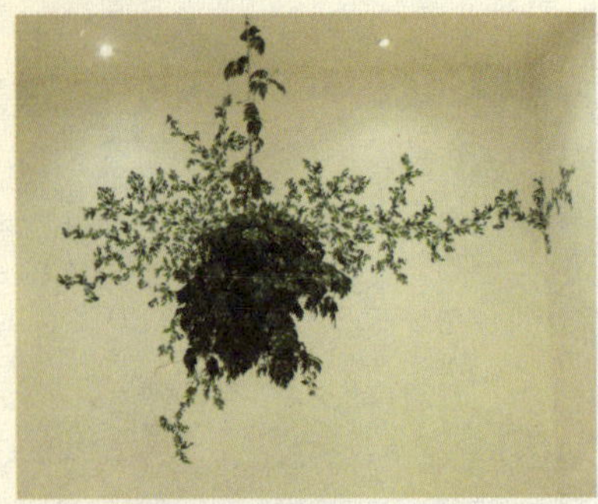

1.

Liliana Sanchez graduated in 2005 from the Universidad Nacional de Bogotá in Colombia. Her tactile drawings, photographs, and installations move between figuration and abstraction and are rooted in a sensory experience of nature.

1 & 2. **Out of Nature**
2008, serigraphy on fabric and plant, dimensions variable

3. **Cyclone** (detail)
2007, adhesive paper on acrylic, 59 × 59 in (150 × 150 cm)

4, 5 & 6. **Bucle**
2008, digital photographs, 39 ½ × 39 ½ in (100 × 100 cm), 30 ¼ × 60 in (77 × 152 cm)

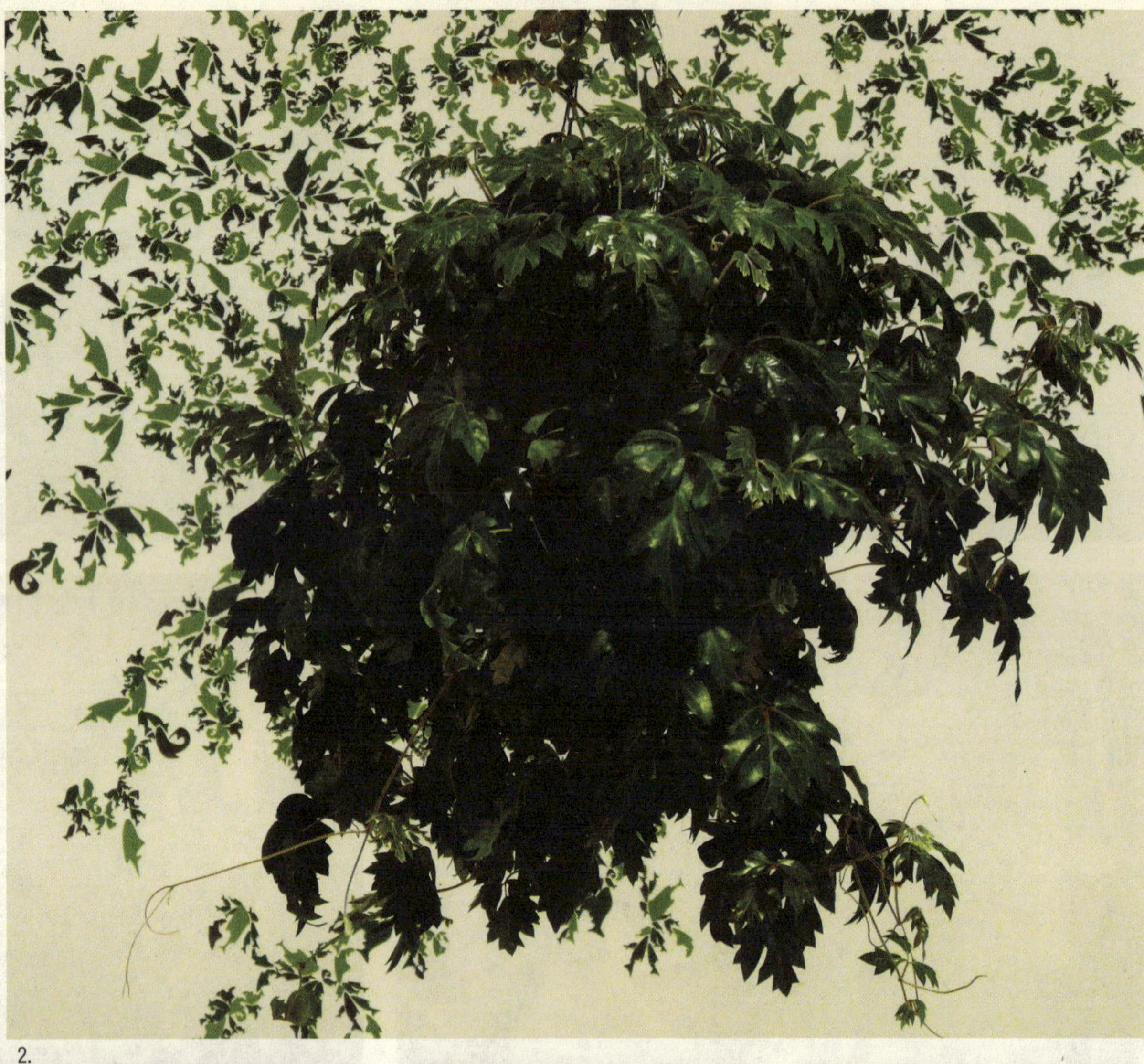

2.

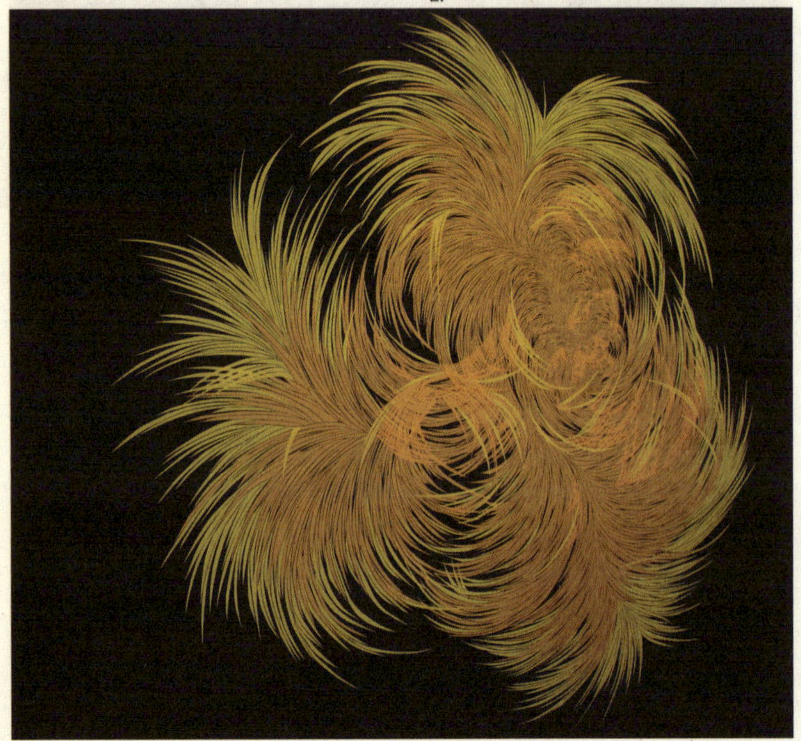

3.

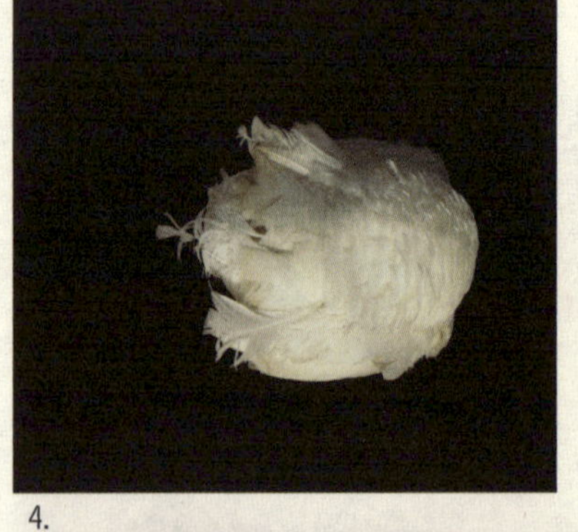

4.

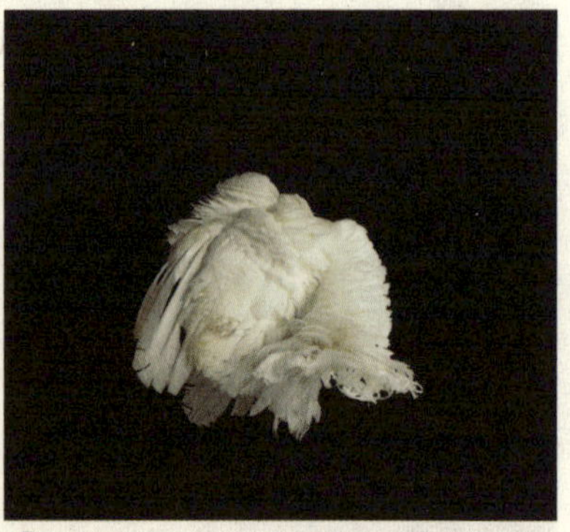

5.

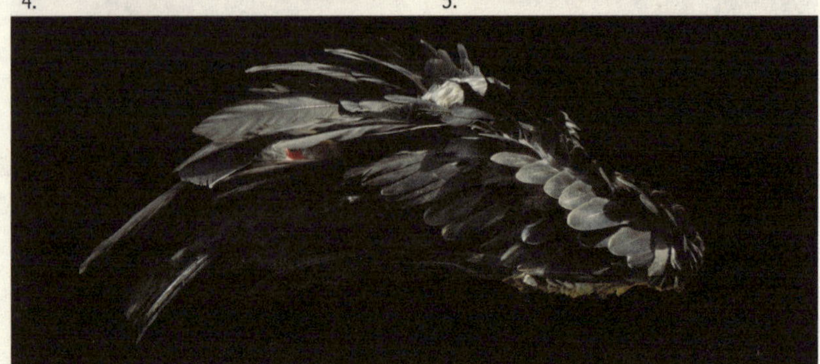

6.

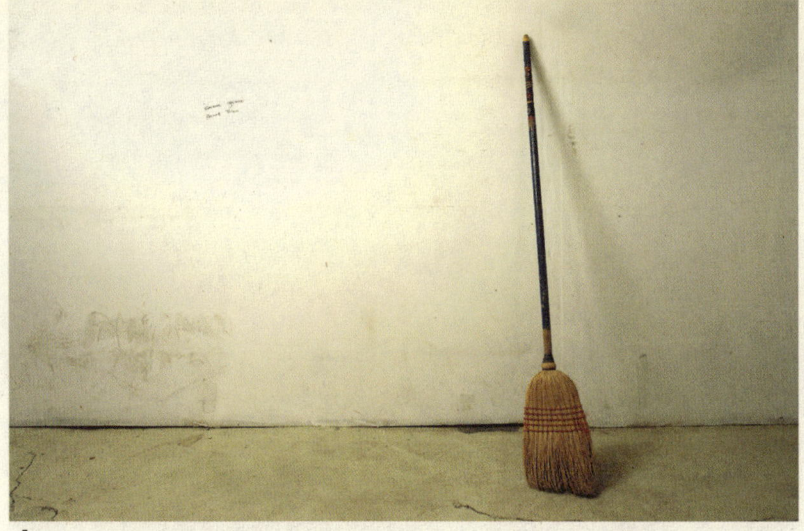

1.

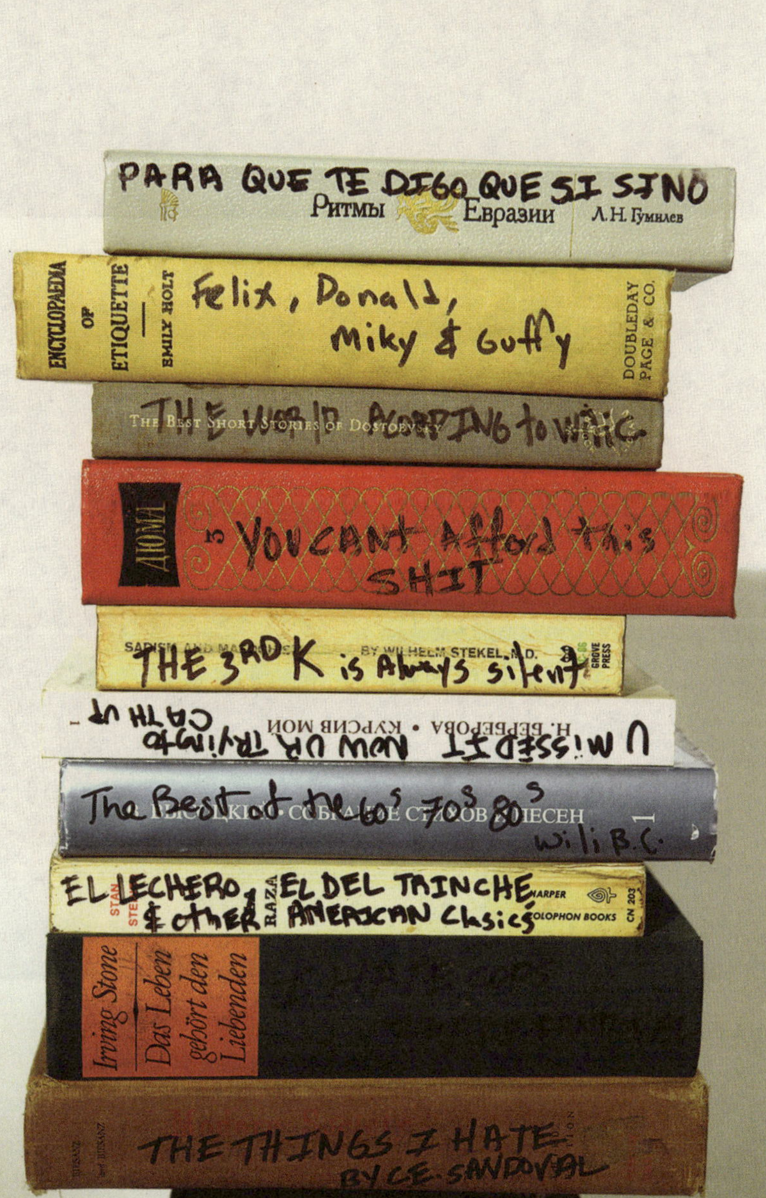

3.

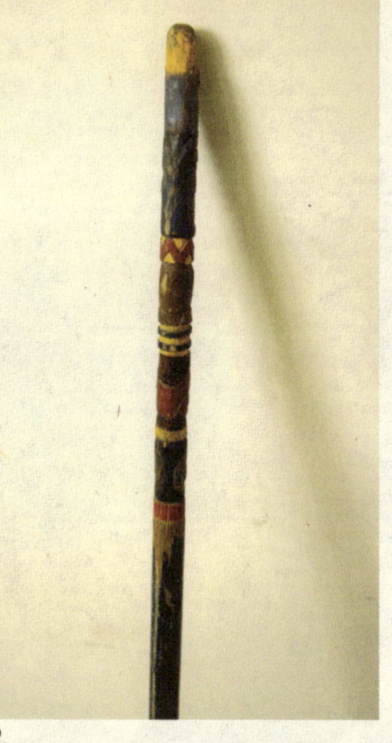

2.

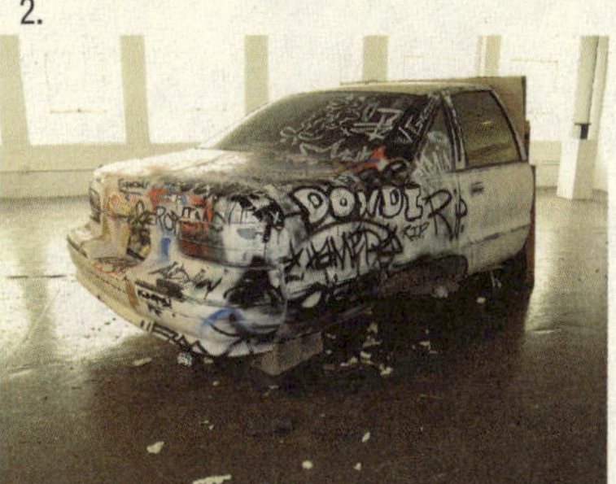

4.

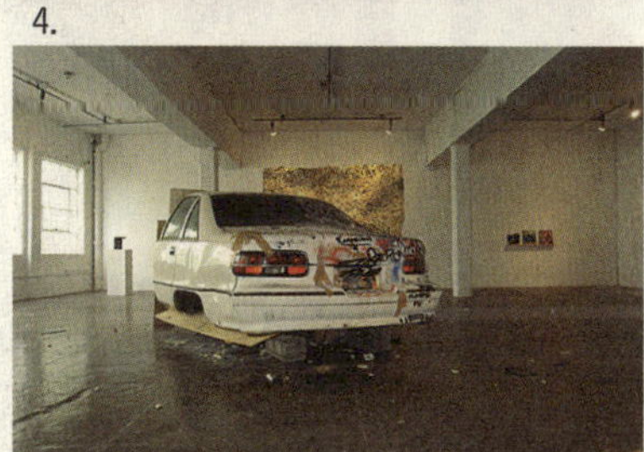

5.

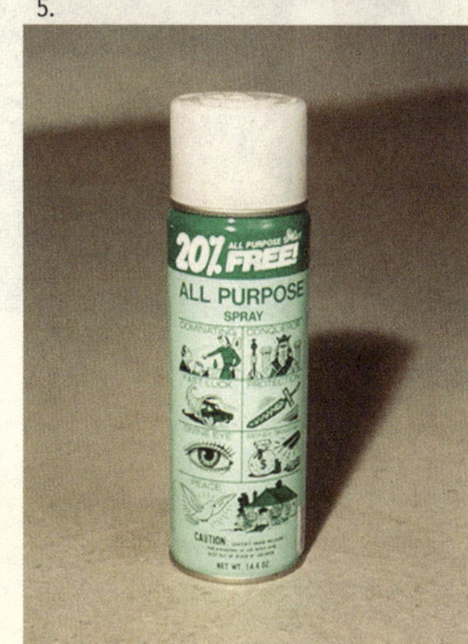

6.

Carlos E. Sandoval de Leon graduated with a MFA from Colombia University in 2008. In 2006 he exhibited in group shows at the Hudson Valley Center for Contemporary Art, New York, and at Ingalls & Associates, Miami. De Leon's installations center on found objects, which he decorates and camouflages in an effort to revitalize everyday commodities.

1 & 2. **Untitled (project broom, Carlisle Janitor broom with corn fill)**
1999-present, broom and Sharpie fine-point permanent marker, 56 × 11 in (242 × 28 cm)

3. **Untitled (el del trinche)**
2004, felt marker on found books

4 & 5. **Moby Dick (Tracy) (after ishmael, chico de cano y carl hampton)**
2008, sawed police car, custom felt interior, tinted windows, literature, beehive, and found pipe bomb, dimensions variable

6, 7, 8 & 9. **Untitled (praying at 1230 Fifth Avenue Between 103rd & 104th Street)**
2006, 12 oz aerosol spray

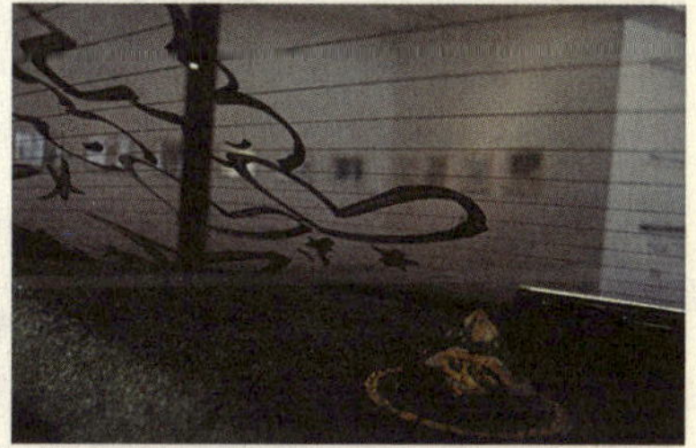

7.

8.

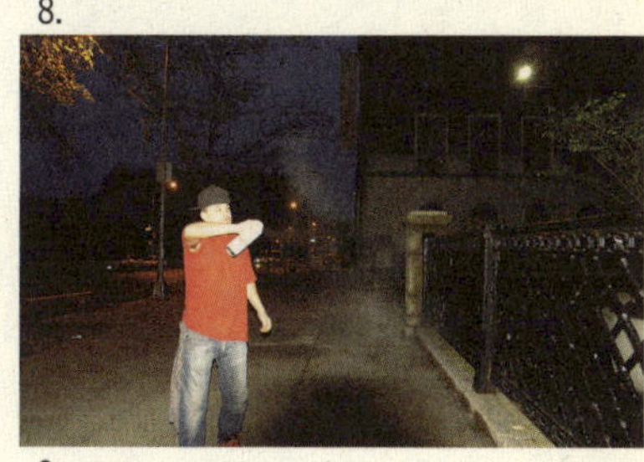

9.

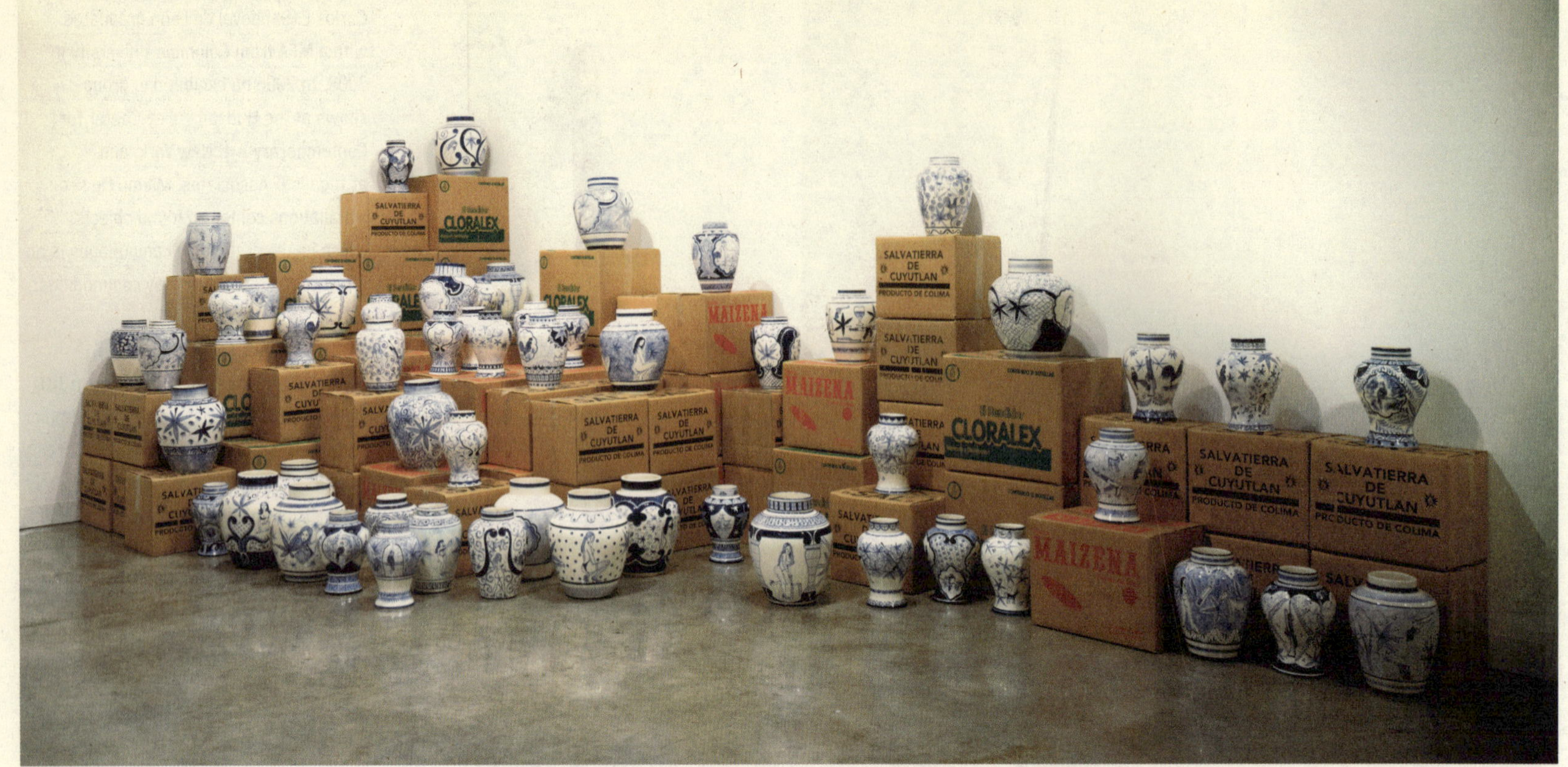

1.

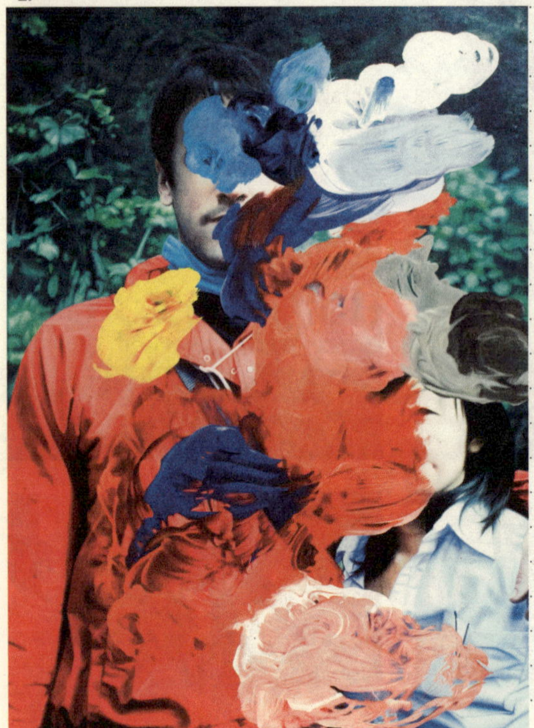

2.

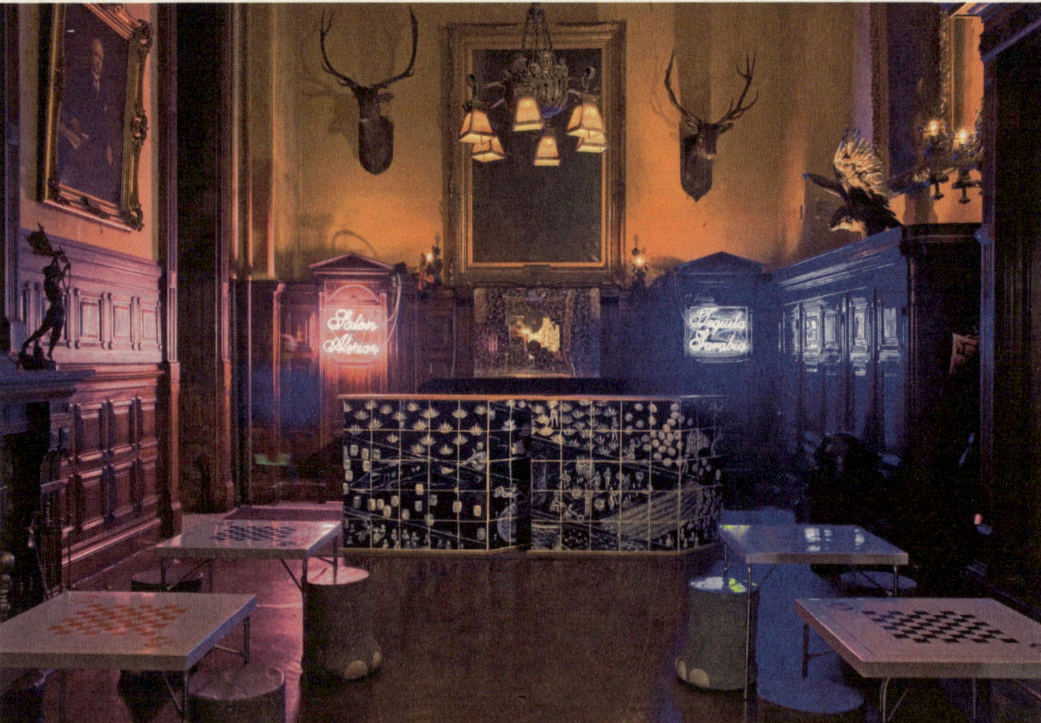

3.

Eduardo Sarabia earned a BFA from the Otis College of Art and Design in Los Angeles. He currently lives and works in Los Angeles, Guadalajara, and Berlin. His work, which was included in the 2008 Whitney Biennial, is comprised of ceramics, hand-woven textiles, and glassworks and is influenced by the black market and Mexican folklore. He creates fake evidence for his staged, fictional scenarios. For a 2006 exhibition at I-20 Gallery, for instance, he created materials confiscated at a fictional bust of an international ceramics smuggling ring.

1. A thin line between love and hate
2005, hand-painted ceramic vases with silkscreen boxes, dimensions variable

2. Tetris King and Queen of the Monarch Butterflies
2008, oil on canvas, 78 × 48 in (198 × 122 cm)

3. Salon Aleman at the Park Avenue Armory
2008, mixed media, dimensions variable, installation view at the Whitney Biennial

Aki Sasamoto graduated with an MFA from Columbia University in 2007, and currently lives and works in New York. She is a founding member of Culture Push, a group of artists who organize symposia, performances, and workshops. Her work in performance, sculpture, and dance focuses on everyday gestures.

Her performance **remembering/modifying/developing**, a musical belief-making system, was included in the Yokohama Triennial 2008. Her performance piece **feedback** involved Sasamoto and a participant eating pasta while listening to the radio and conversing with one another in the gallery space.

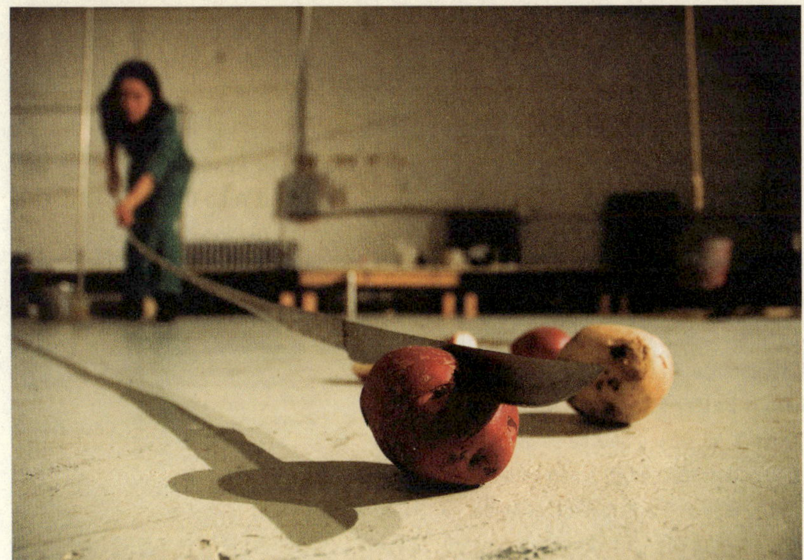

1.

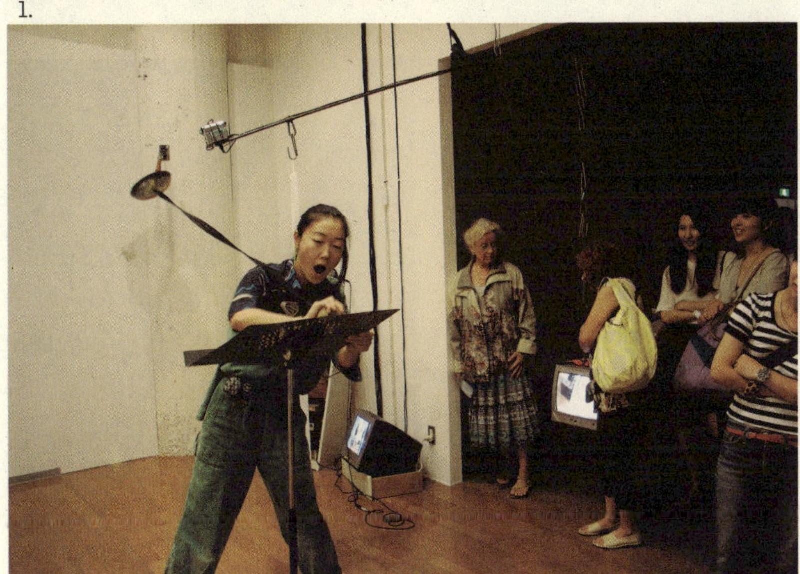

2.

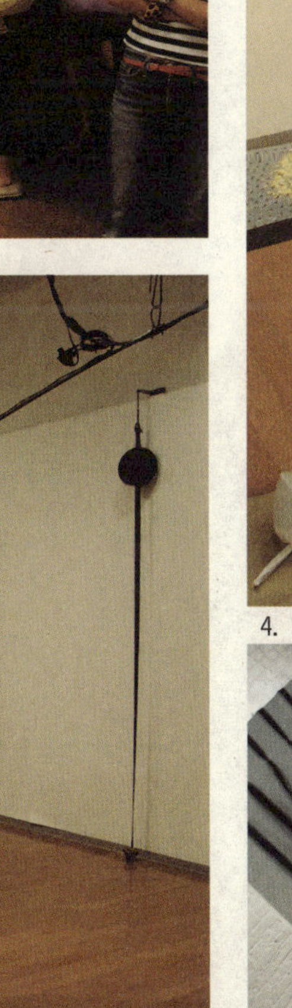

3.

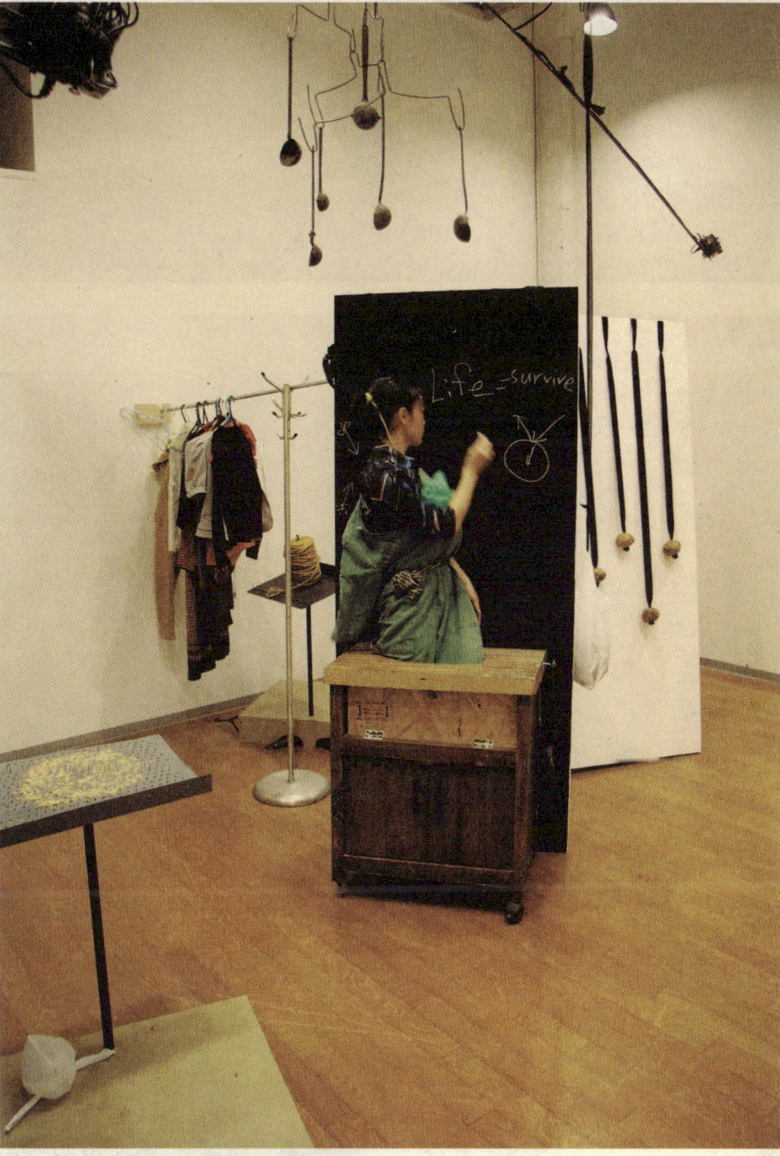

4.

5.

1. (The Long Utensil) in "cooking show"
2005, mixed media installation and performance

2 ,3, 4 & 5. remembering/modifying/developing
2007, mixed media installation and performance

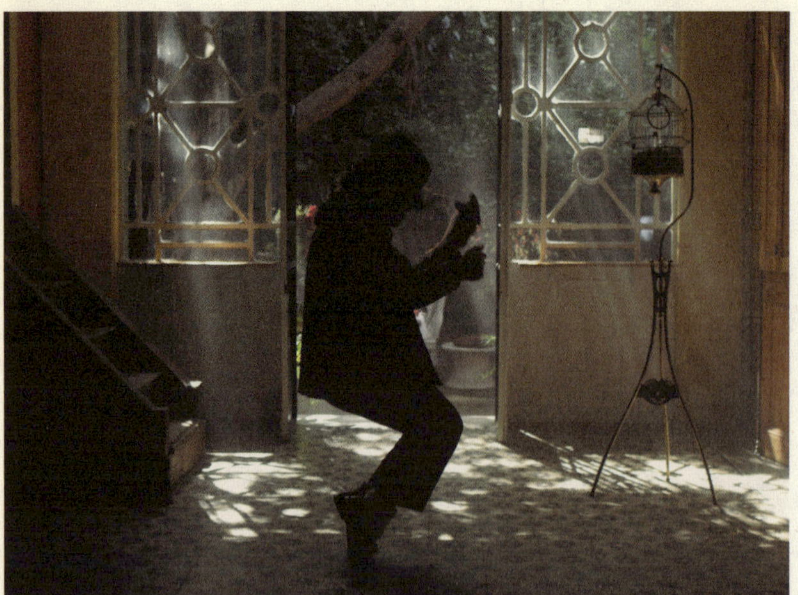
1.

Martín Sastre currently lives and works in Madrid. His videos, which often examine the impact of United States pop culture on the identities and self-images of South American artists, were included in the 2005 Venice Biennale. In **The Sastre Foundation for the Super Poor Art** he uses a farcical visual language to position himself as a Uruguayan artist negotiating for wider acceptance. In the 2008 video **Latins Do it Better (Madonna Meets Sor Kitty)**, he staked out the singer's house in London dressed as a nun with a Hello Kitty head and concluded that Madonna is herself a Latin artist.

1. **Freaky Birthday. (Michael Jackson Dancing)**
2006, video, 5 min

2. **Diana, The Rose Conspiracy. (Lady Di and Yoko Ono Nuns)**
2005, video, 20 min

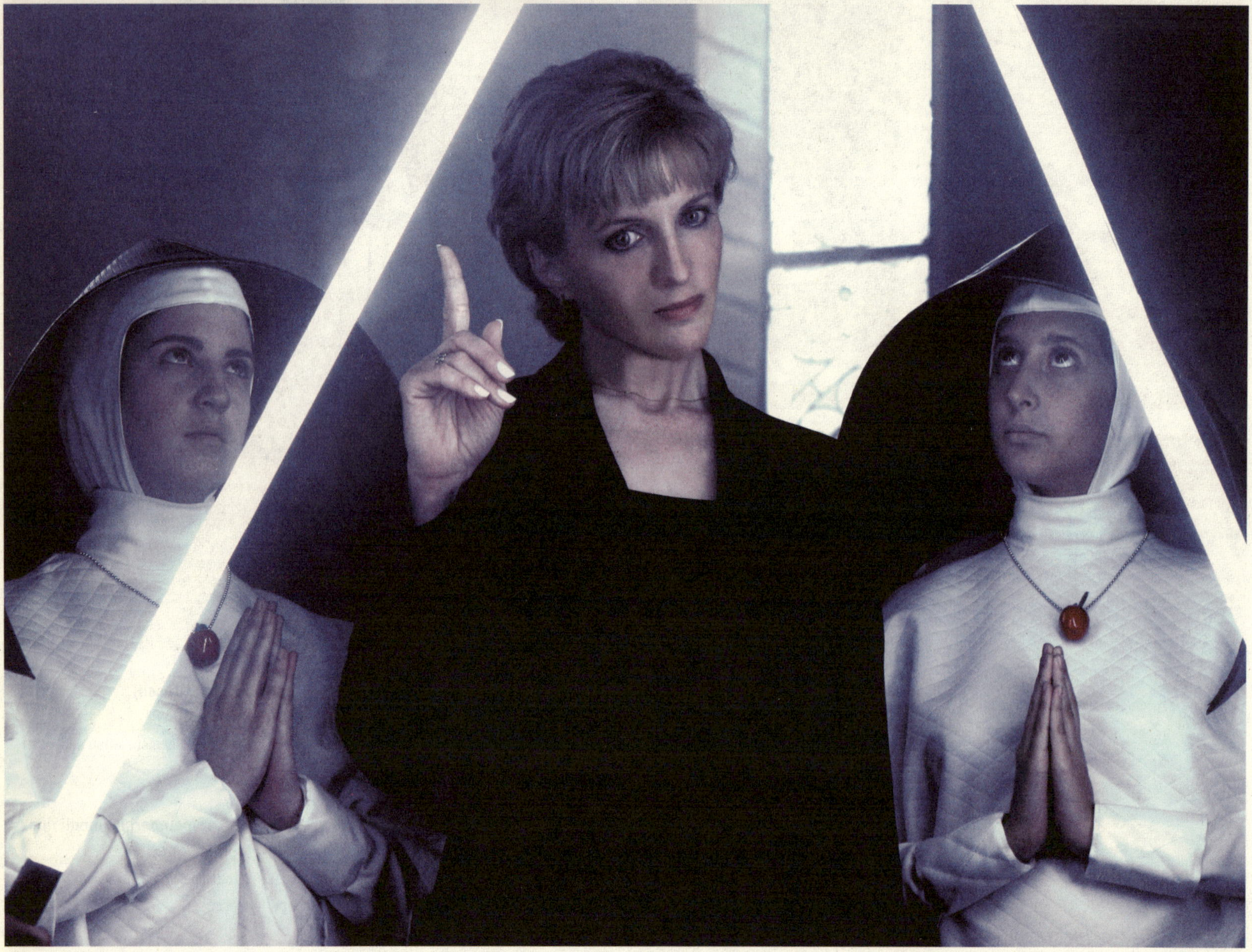

2.

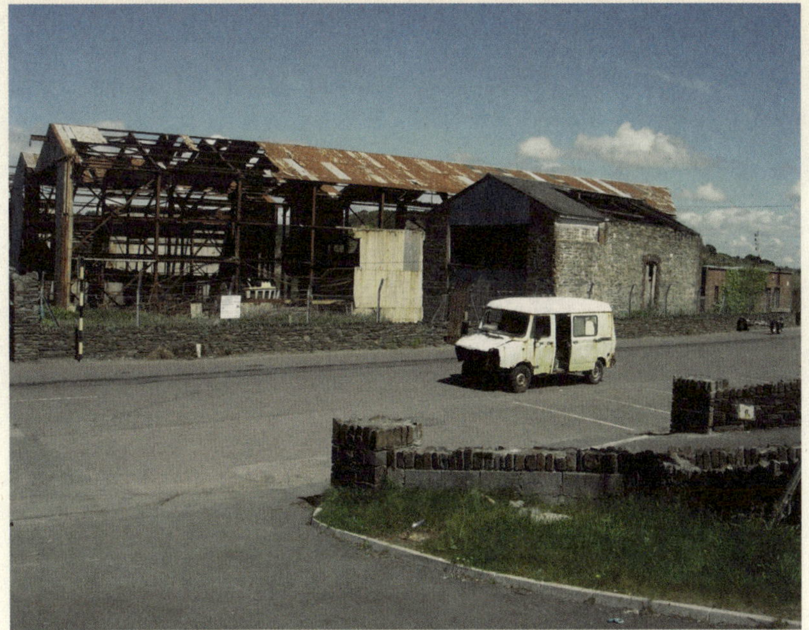

1.

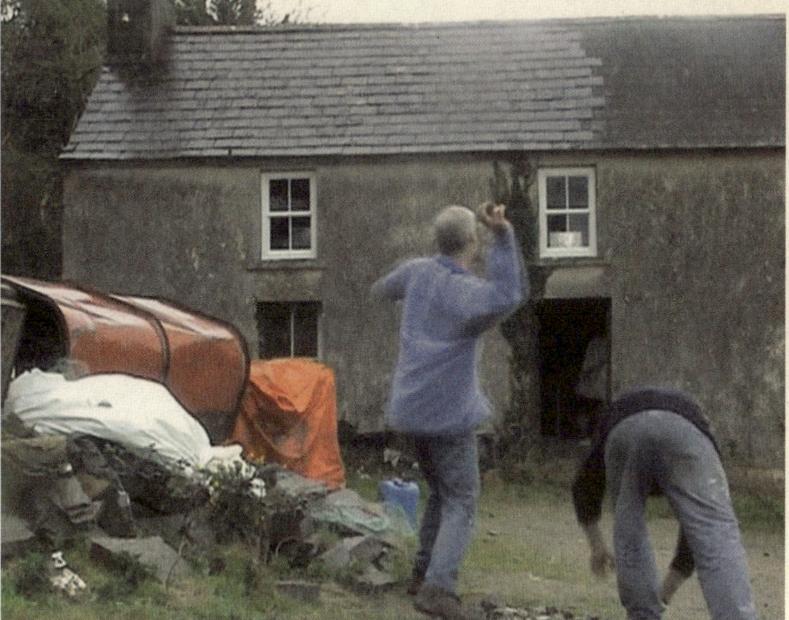

2.

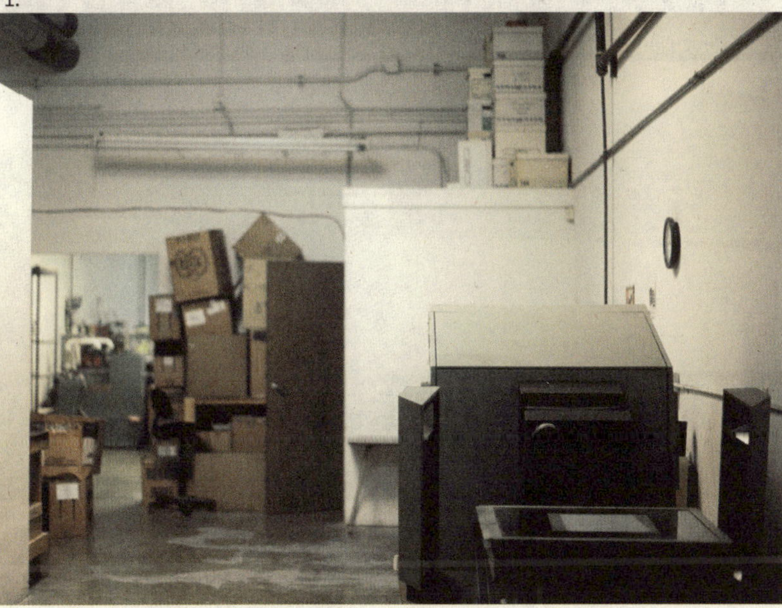

3.

Jorge Satorre graduated from the Universidad Autonoma Metropolitana, Azcapotzalco, Mexico. He lives and works in Paris. He worked as a magazine illustrator for several years but now produces drawings, videos, and performances. For **The Barry's Van Tour** (2007) Satorre restored an abandoned van, which had belonged to a fisherman, now deceased, on the island of Cork, Ireland, making drawings and videos throughout the process. He ultimately restored the van to its original spot, investigating the monumentality of the object and how his interventions were implicated, or not, in its status.

1. The Barry's Van Tour (making of)
2007, video, 13 min 33 sec

2. Windows Blowing Out
2005, video, 6 min 44 sec

3. National Balloon (detail)
2006, 46 pencil drawings on paper, each 8 1/4 × 12 in (21 × 30 cm); slide projection of 13 images, dimensions variable

4 & 5. My Dolmen
2007-08, 2 pencil drawings on paper, each 11 3/4 × 16 1/2 in (30 × 42 cm)

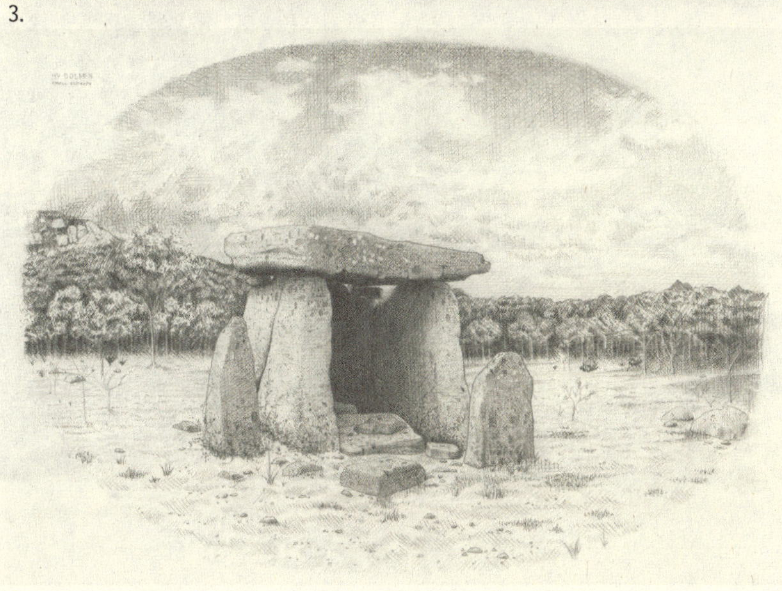

4.

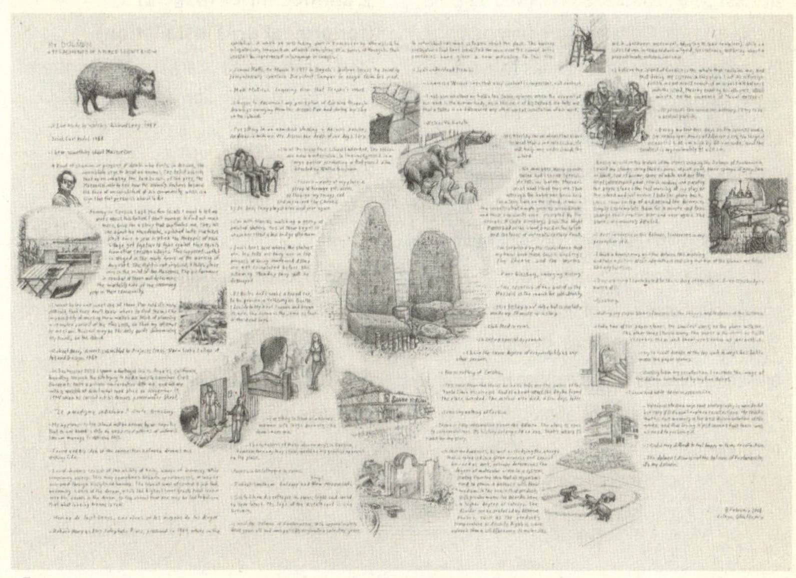

5.

1

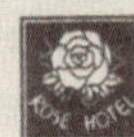

ROSE HOTEL
118 Surawongse Road.,Bangkok 10500 Thailand.
Tel : 266-8268-72 Fax : 266-8096

Dear stranger,

Hello again. I cannot remember when I last heard from you, or if I ever did, I have no idea. This time, I'm writing a letter here in this hotel room. To be more precise, I'm writing here in room number 205, which is located at the end of the 2nd floor hallway of the hotel. But actually, I'm writing this letter in a restaurant, in which the singer sings only sad songs. (Sadness seems to be very popular around here. But why would we need another's misery, beside our own? What is so comforting about sadness?) However, I will rewrite the letter on proper paper, eventually. By the way, I'm sorry for my hard-to-read hand writing. In this so-called computer age, I'm glad that I can even write at all. And do you know, sometimes I draw doodles?

I'm happy to tell you that I have stopped moving for a while now. I am still and static, just like the meaning of my name. I'm wondering where you are at the moment, because you did not tell me where you are headed. Is it far? At the farthest place I have been in my whole short life, there was nobody around to look at me. I thought I was free until I was simply asked to leave. And it was kind of weird, because there was no one around. Even though, I guess it is a little bit different from your place. I remember you said you needed to go there, to be there by yourself. By the way, do you still fear being stuck in Limbo? (Not limo. Yes, it is also kind of hard when you are struck in a limo, even worse if it is hijacked and moving fast with broken headlights.)

1.

Hello Stranger,

I am writing the text now. But you will read it later. Sorry, I know you are reading it "now", but

2.

y sounds, things seem real. ----- "Do you know which strait is the narrowest?" She ask

รู้ว่ามันจริงทั้งหมด ----- "คุณรู้มั้ยว่า ช่องแคบในทะเลที่แคบที่สุดในโลกอยู่ที่ไหน" เธอถามผม

3.

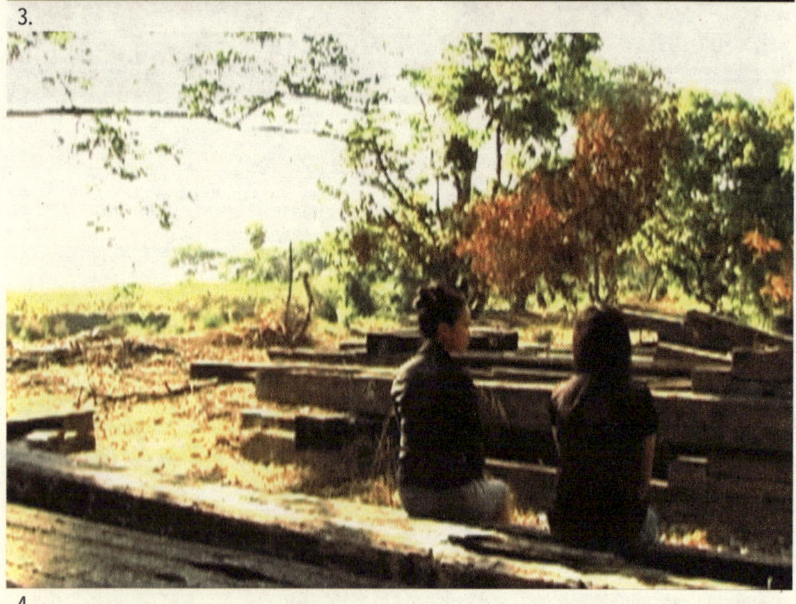

4.

In 2003 Sathit Sattarasart received a BFA in media art from Chulalongkorn University in Bangkok, where he continues to live and work. Sattarasart's art explores aspects of life in Bangkok's multicultural urban environment, but he deliberately constructs his use of documentary and text to avoid resemblance to representations of reality in mass media. Acutely aware of the communicative power of both images and language, Sathit plays their strengths and shortcomings off each other to trigger a series of oblique associations in his audience.

1. untitled letter (page 1) (for project drift installation)
2007, photocopies of artist's handwritten letter, 11 × 8 in (28 × 20 cm)

2. breeze
2006, video, 20 min

3. her eyes were rolling
2008, video, 2 min 30 sec

4. this construct can serve no purpose anymore
2008, video, 28 min

Deborah Satter lives and works in Los Angeles. Her ongoing project **MR. CALIFORNIA** was part of her MFA thesis project at the Art Center College of Design in LA. Beginning at the Camp Pendleton Marine Corps Base, Satter ultimately focused on one particular marine before and after his tour of duty in Iraq. Her chromogenic prints, Polaroids, and works in mixed media, as well as Super 8 film, explore the way masculine iconography in California is shaped by war and surfer culture.

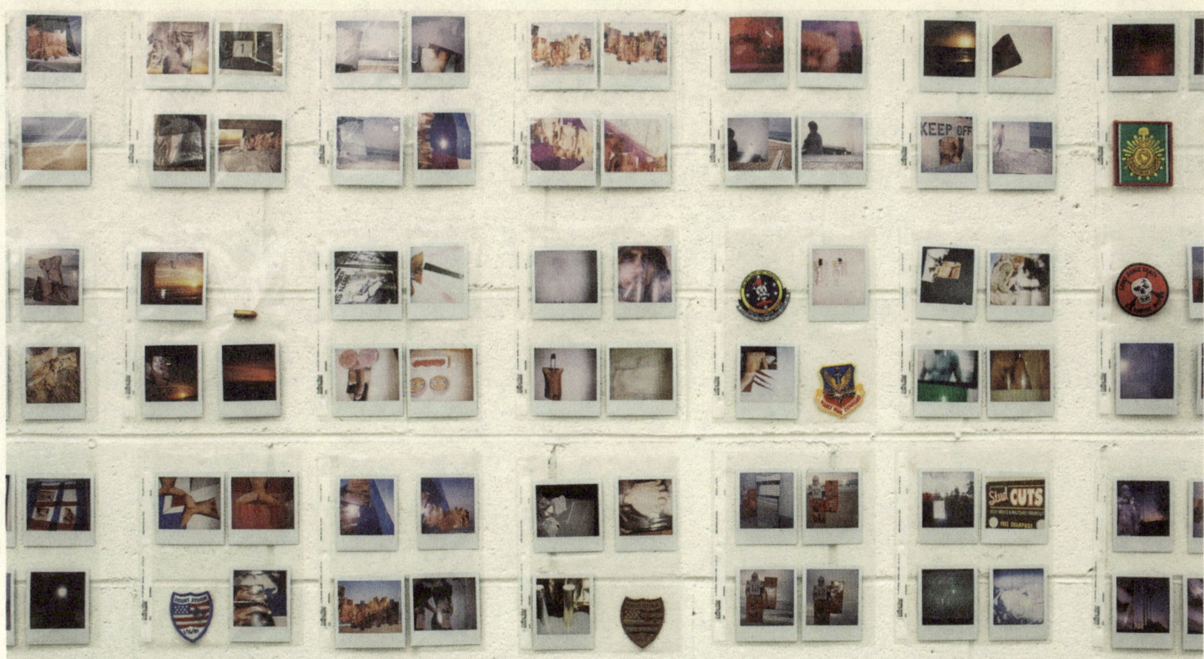

1.

1. Untitled (I) (detail)
2008, Polaroids, archival photo sleeves, patches, stickers, bullets, magnets, lapel pins, tape, and other mixed media, dimensions variable

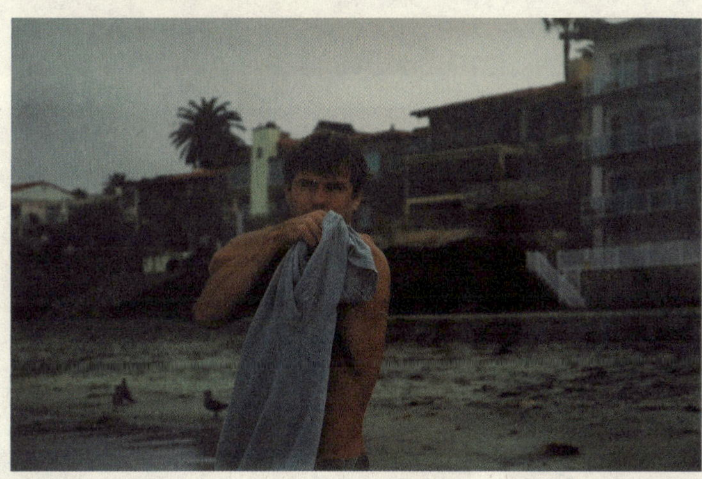

2.

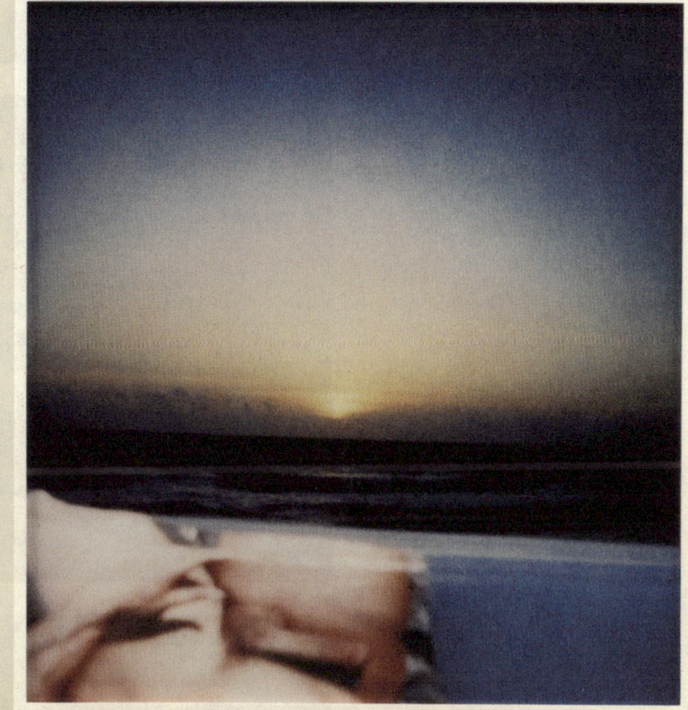

4.

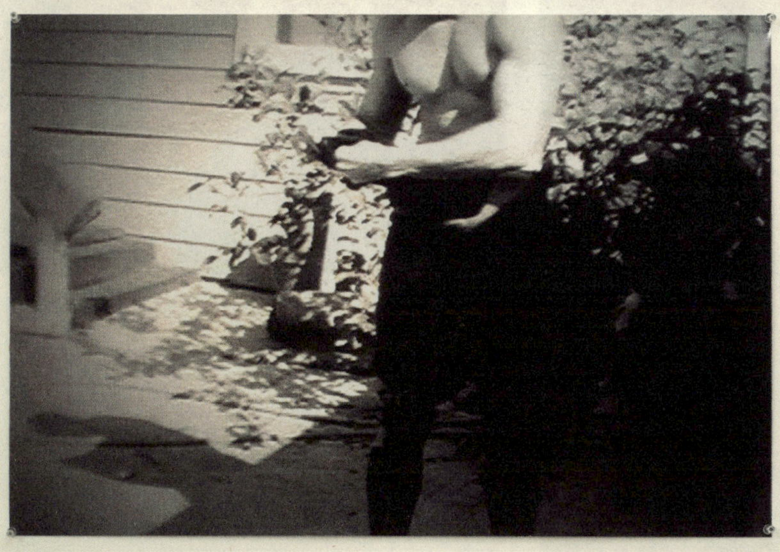

3.

2. Untitled
2008, unframed chromogenic print, 30 × 44 in (76 × 112 cm)

3. I'll blow everyone's brains out but not yours
2006-08, Super 8 film, 20 min 19 sec

4. Untitled
2008, enlarged Polaroid and framed chromogenic print, 30 × 29 in (76 × 74 cm)

Serban Savu graduated from the University of Art and Design in Cluj Napoca, Romania, and he currently lives and works in Cluj. His figurative oil paintings depict pedestrian situations, scenes located in his home country, in a neutral palette. His **Short Cut** (2007), for example, shows a figure in a yellow raincoat taking a shortcut near a canal, while **Modern Haircuts** (2007) is a view through a barbershop window.

1. **The Weekend**
2007, oil on canvas, 25 1/4 × 39 1/2 in (64 × 100 cm)

2. **I am a Voyeur**
2007, oil on canvas, 20 × 23 3/4 in (43 × 60 cm)

3. **About Love**
2007, oil on canvas, 20 × 23 3/4 in (43 × 60 cm)

4. **Hot Hours of the Afternoon**
2007, oil on canvas, 15 3/4 × 11 1/2 in (40 × 29 cm)

1.

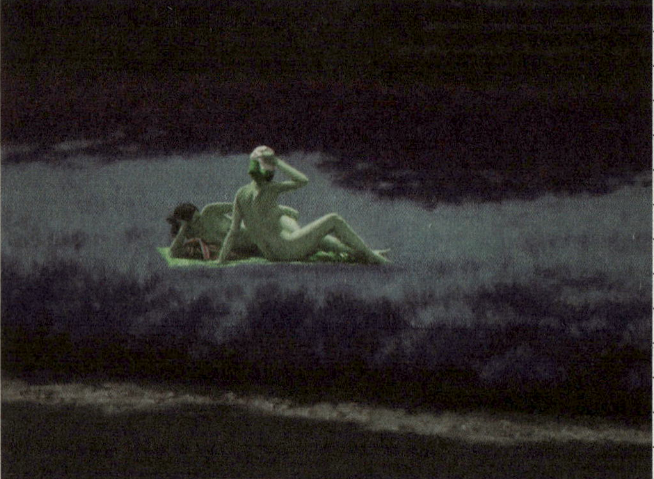

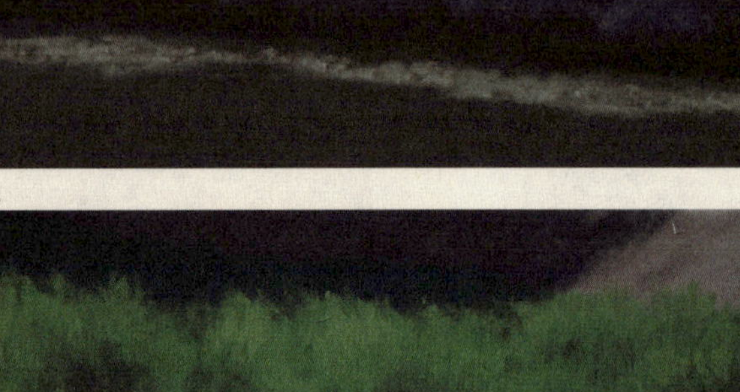

2.

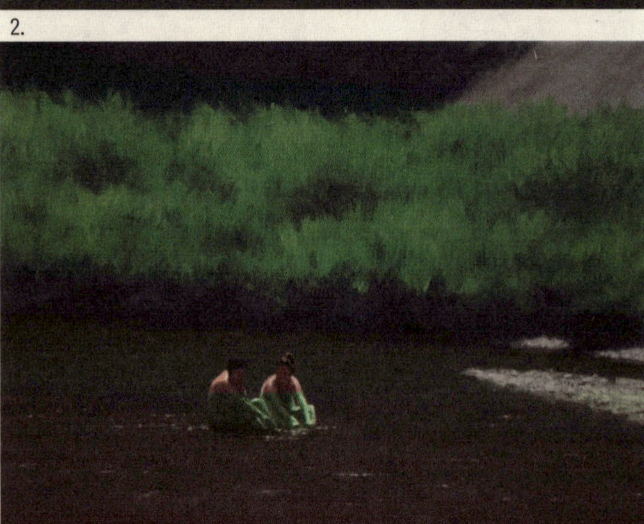

3.

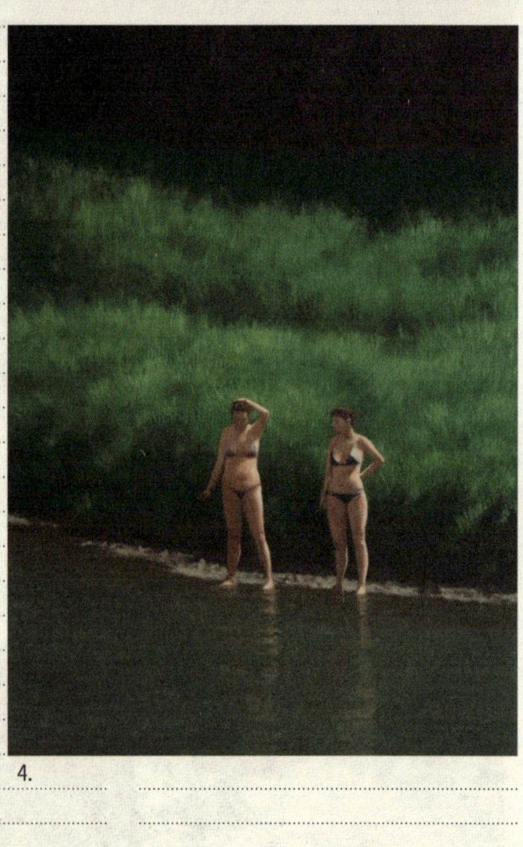

4.

Hiraki Sawa earned an MA in sculpture from the Slade School of Fine Art in London, where he currently lives and works. His video and animation work, set in whimsical domestic interiors, explores the concept of home and the interaction between public and private spheres.

1. **Migration**
2003, video, 7 min 10 sec

2 & 3. **Dwelling**
2002, video, 9 min 20 sec

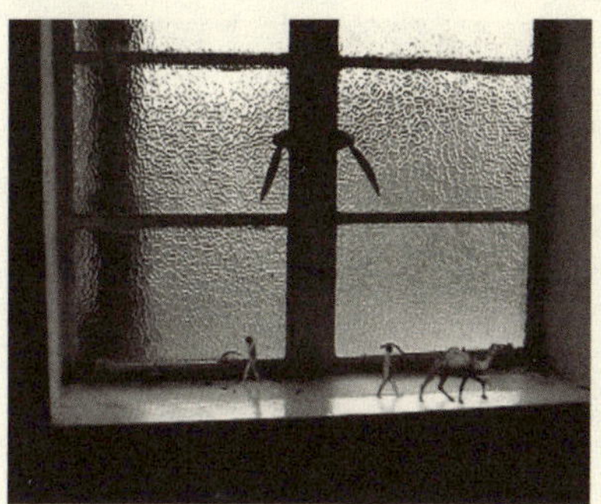
1.

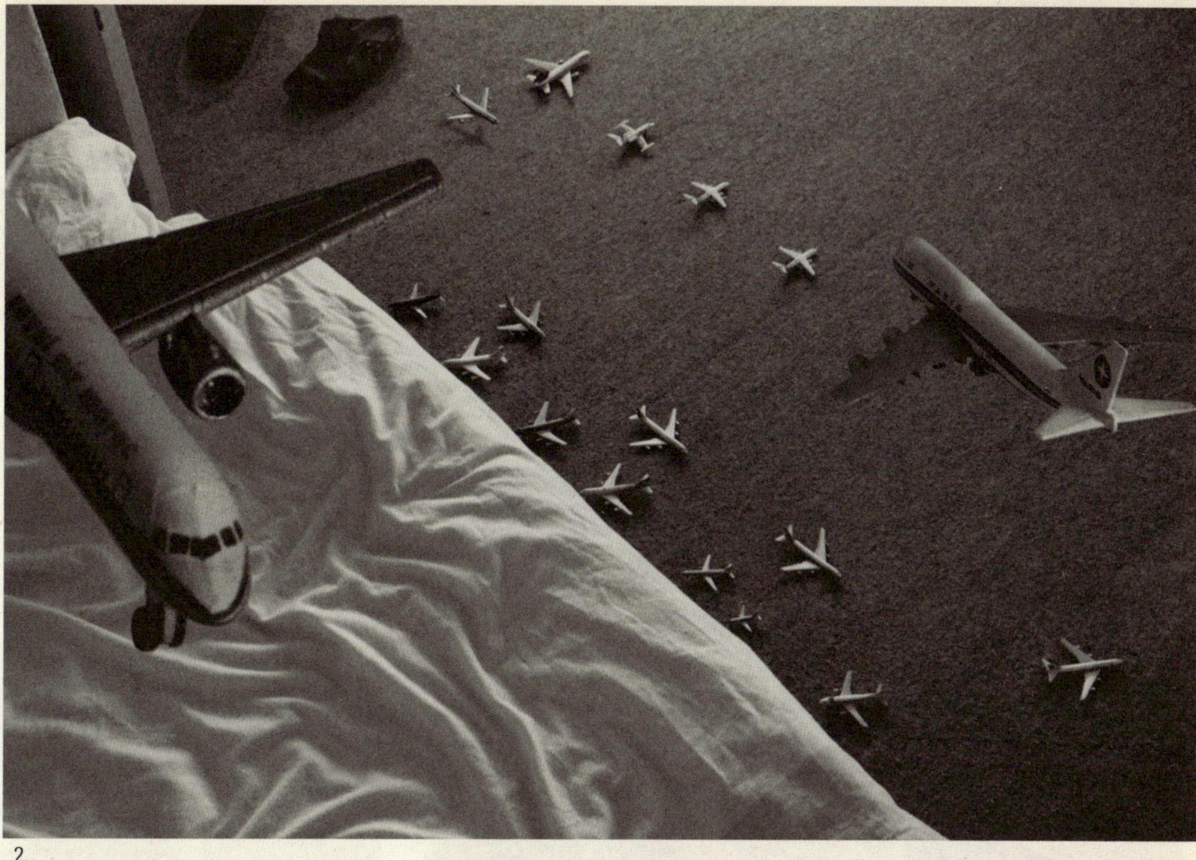
2.

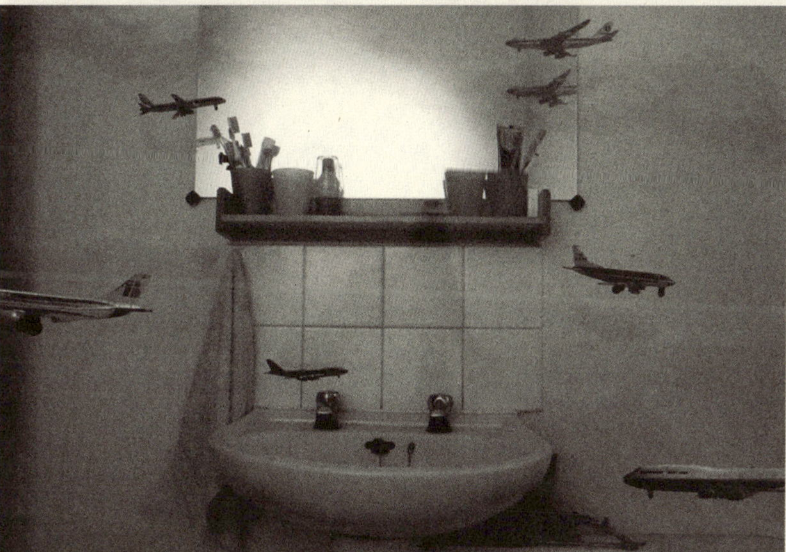
3.

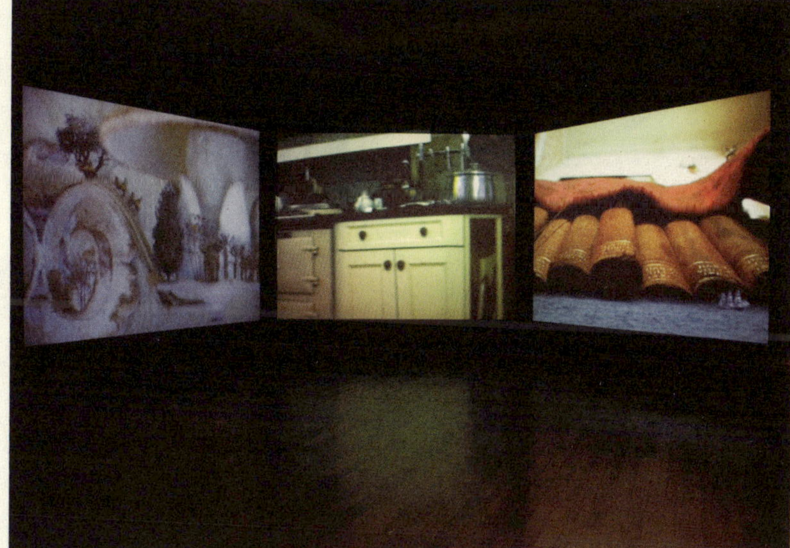
4.

4 & 5. **Going Places Sitting Down**
2004, 3-channel video, 8 min 40 sec

6. **Hidden Tree**
2007, video, 4 min 20 sec

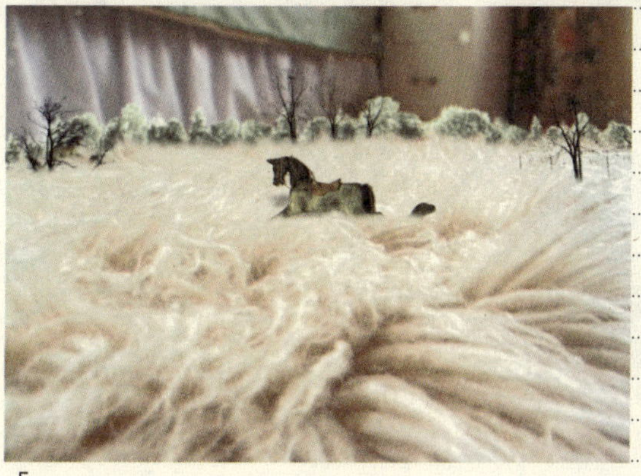
5.

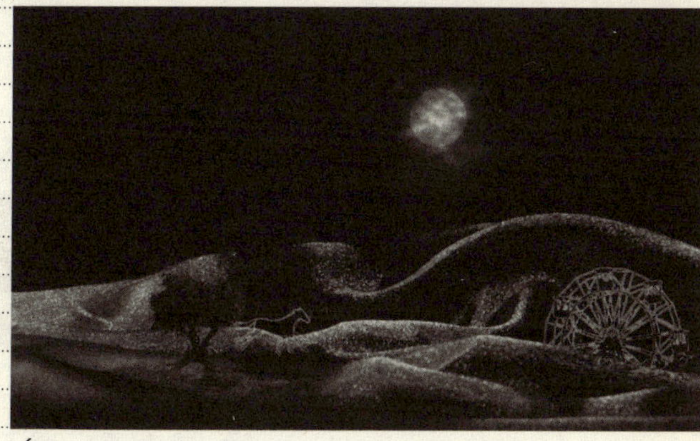
6.

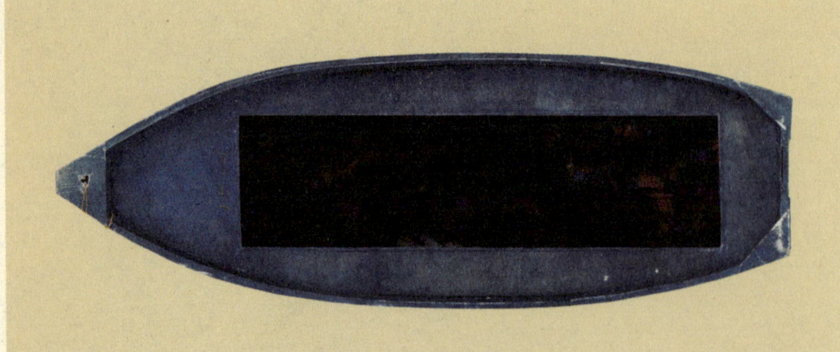

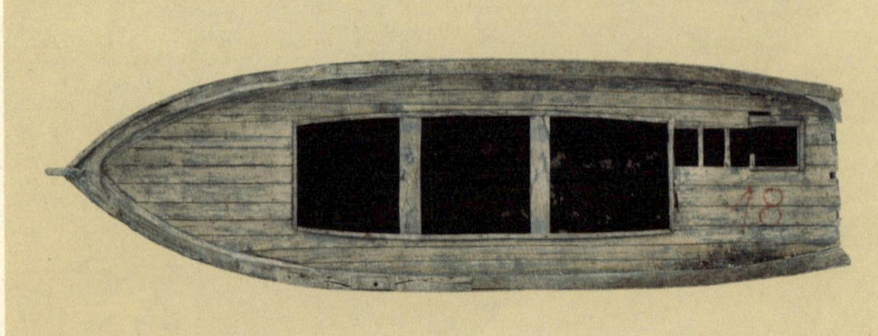

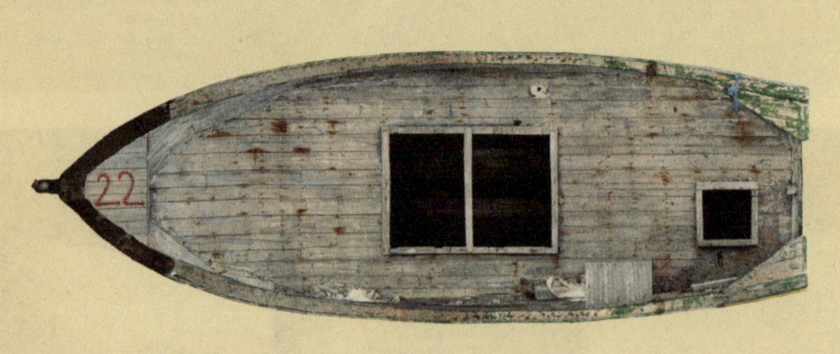

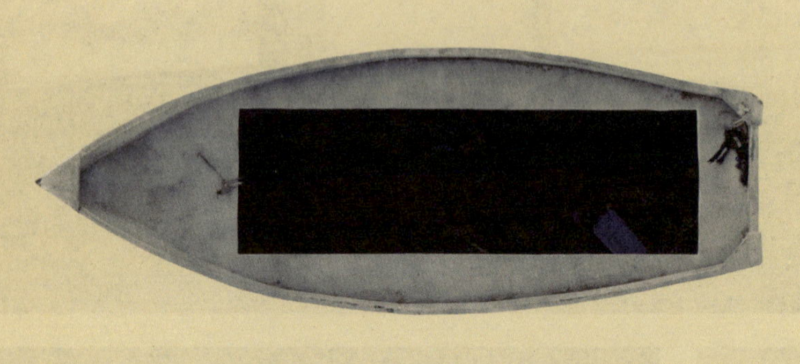

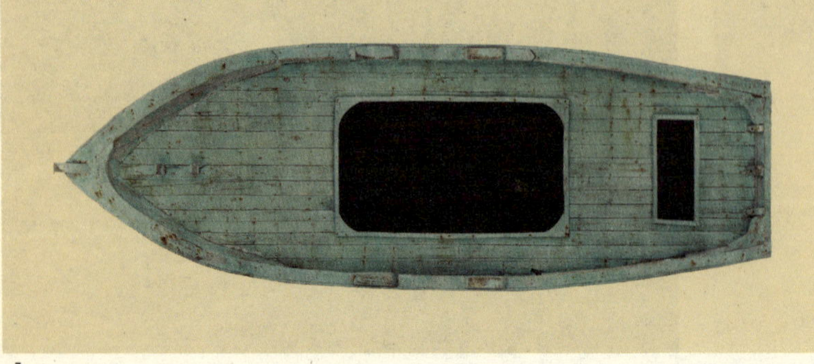

1.

Heiko Schafer studied at the Lette-Verein in Berlin. His conceptual photography often focuses on the way places are changed by human intervention and on political and historical movements, though figures are rarely present in his work. His 2008 work **Maritime Incidents** consists of bird's-eye-view photographs of African refugee boats captured by the coast guard near the coast of Sicily, combined with official informational text on illegal immigration across the Mediterranean Sea into Europe.

1. Maritime Incidents
2008, inkjet print, 45 3/4 × 23 in (116 × 58 cm)

2 & 3. Maritime Incidents
2008, paper and map

18	• • • approx. 24 Wooden fishing boat with inboard motor Propulsion: diesel. • • • •	15/10/2007 21:48 ZUL	5 miles South of Cava d'Aliga, Sicily, Italy	The migrants were intercepted by patrol boats of the Italian Coast Guard	The boat in which the migrants were transported was confiscated. All immigrants were brought to a refugee gathering area in Pozzallo and were taken care of by immigration Authorities •	32 Unknown Female(s) A M Male(s) 30A 2M	Italy

2.

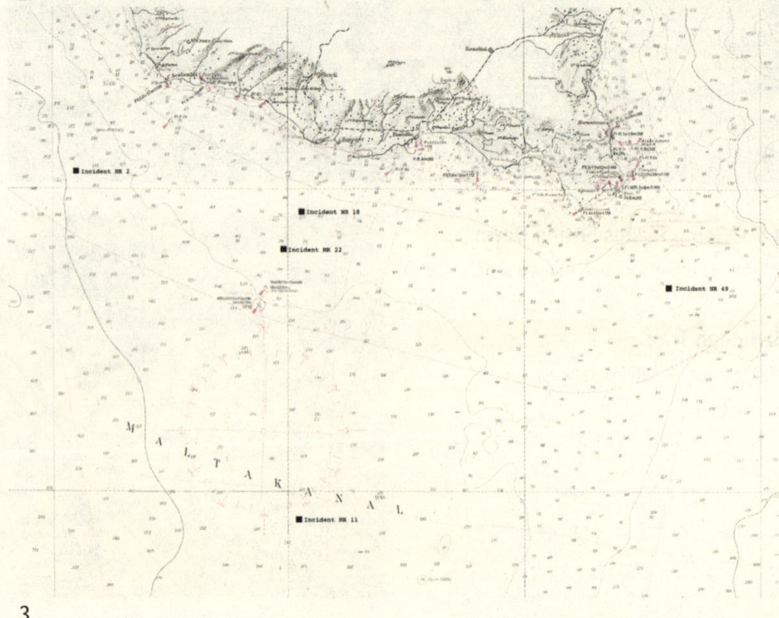

3.

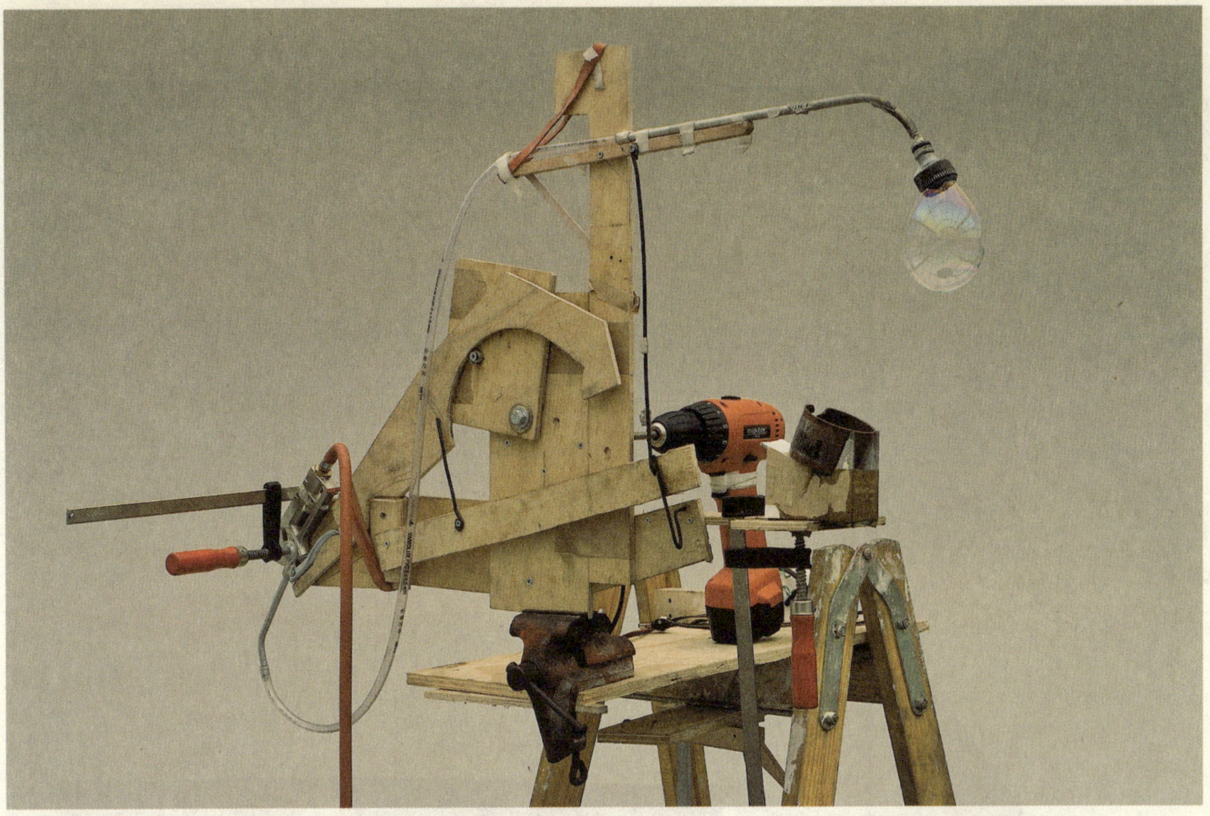

1.

Ariel Schlesinger graduated in 2003 from the Bezalel Academy for Art and Design in Jerusalem. He currently lives and works in Berlin. His installations use everyday objects, such as office supplies and materials from construction sites, while transforming their function. In his **L'Angoisse de la page blanche** (2008), two white pages move constantly toward each other while spinning on their own axes. In two untitled pieces from 2007 he burned parts of two worn-out Oriental carpets, drawing attention to the emptiness left by that "disaster."

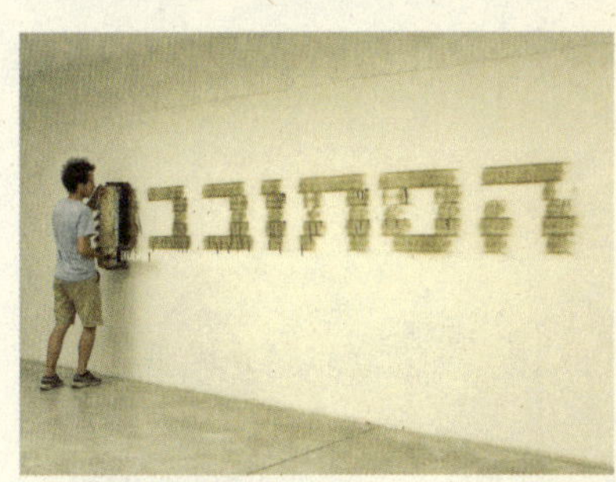

2.

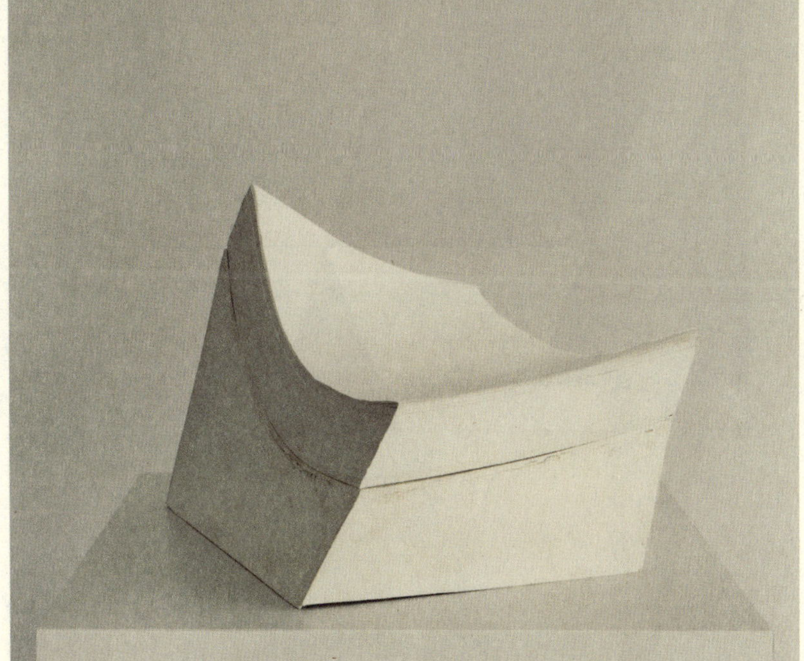

3.

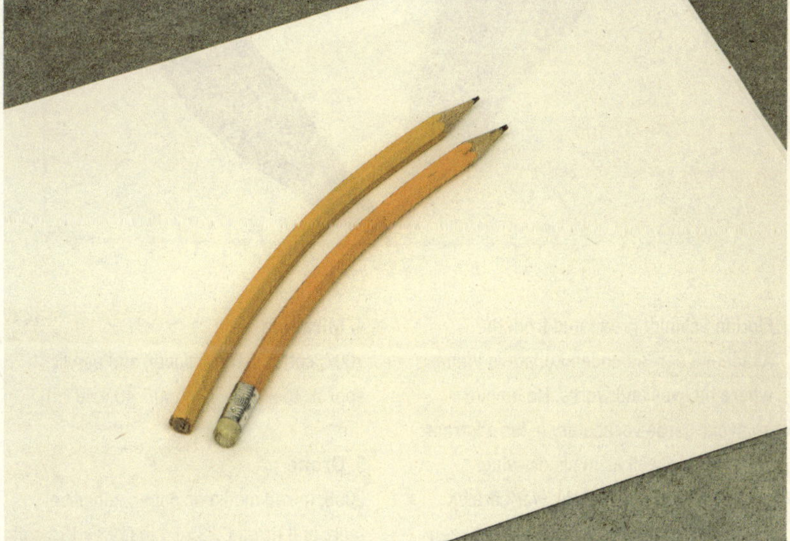

4.

1. Bubble Machine
2006, gas, soap bubble, ladder, electric drill, wood, stools, and high voltage transformer, 90 × 79 × 83 in (230 × 200 × 210 cm)

2. Graffiti Printer
2006, wood, cardboard, spray paint, punch cards, sensors, and batteries, 8 × 8 × 27 1/2 in (20 × 20 × 70 cm)

3. Untitled (paper stand)
2003, paper and wood, 12 × 8 1/2 × 8 in (30 × 21 × 20 cm)

4. Netally and I
2006, painted wood, aluminum rings, and rubber, 1/4 × 6 × 1 1/4 in (1 × 15 × 3 cm)

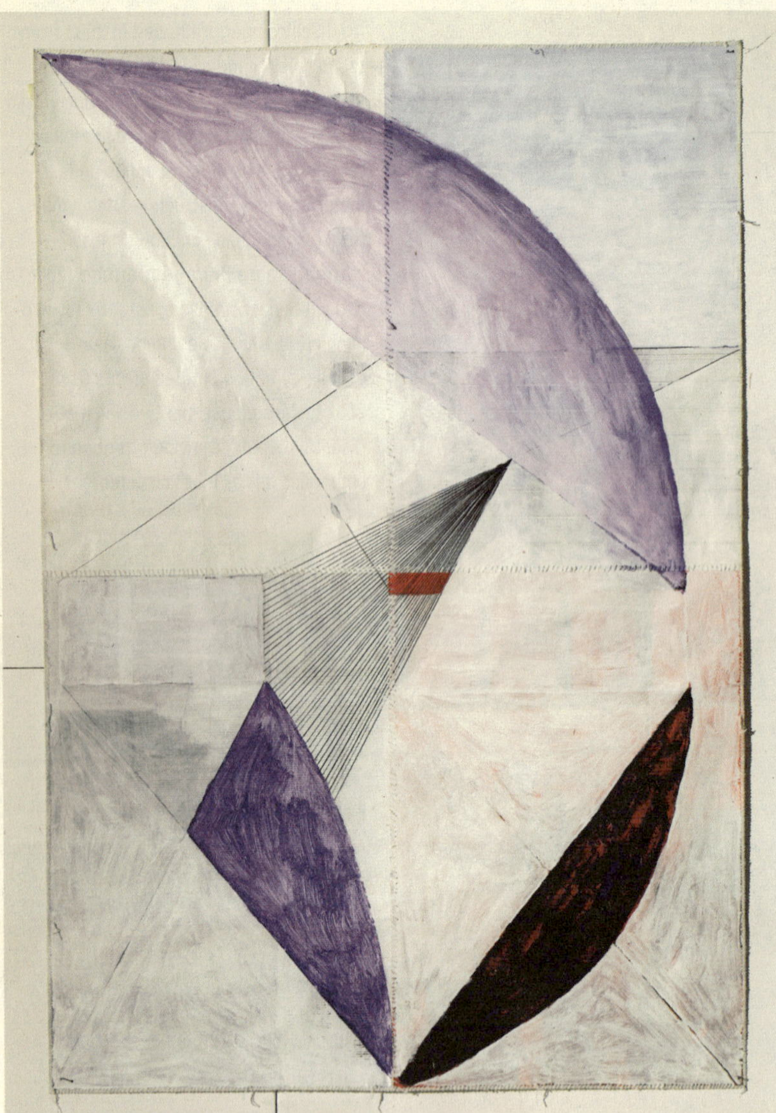

1.

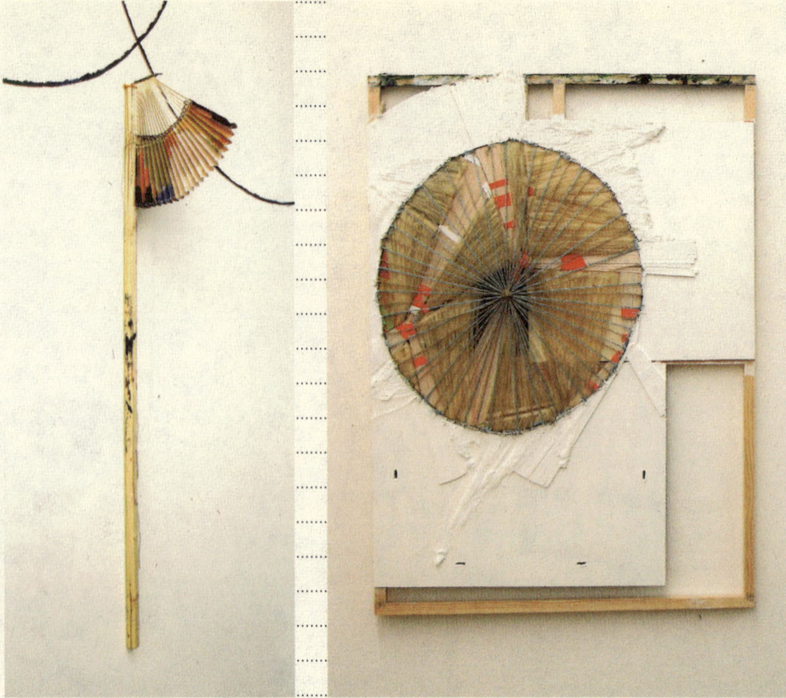

2. 3.

Florian Schmidt graduated from the Akademie der Bildenden Kunste in Vienna, where he lives and works. He employs an avant-garde vocabulary in his abstract paintings, as well as in his drawings and sculptural objects. His work draws broadly from art history, moving between abstraction and realism, geometric and organic shapes.

1. Anonyma
2008, lacquer, acrylic, and vinyl on paper, sewn thread, 78 × 54 in (198 × 138 cm)

2. Instrumenta
2007, wood, string, oil, and acrylic, $51\frac{1}{4} \times 1\frac{1}{4} \times 12\frac{1}{4}$ in (130 × 3 × 31 cm)

3. Varietät
2007, lacquer, string, wire, and wool on wood, $28\frac{1}{2}$ x $20\frac{1}{2}$ in (72 x 52 cm)

4. Mirabilia
2007, cotton, string, paper, and acrylic, approx 16 × 16 × 16 in (40 × 40 × 40 cm)

5. Drone
2008, mixed media on paper, adhesive tape, and thread, 78 × 54 in (198 × 138 cm)

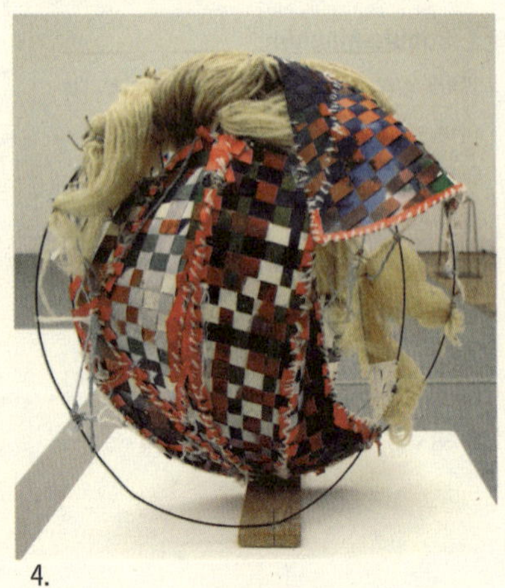

4.

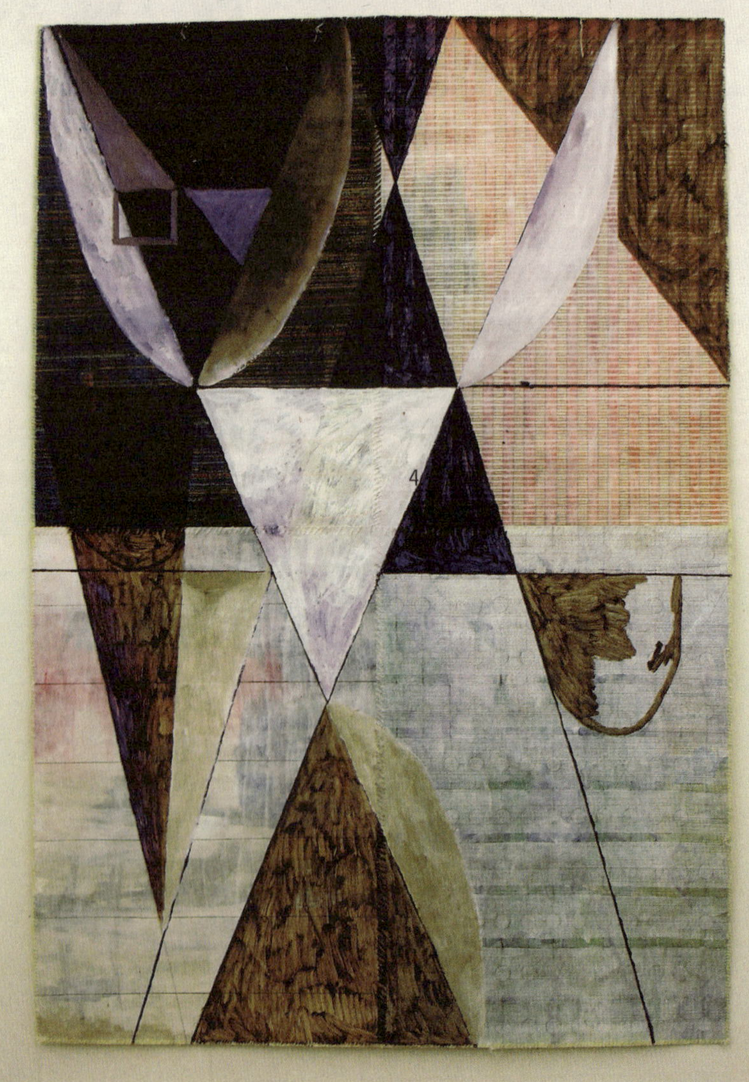

5.

Julia Schmidt earned a BA from the School of Art in Glasgow and lives and works in Germany. She was awarded the Villa Romana Prize from the Deutsche Guggenheim in 2008. Her installations often have a fragmentary quality; she incorporates the labor-intensive techniques of Old Master paintings, but draws on references from consumer culture or popular culture, as in her oil painting **Untitled (Crotch)** (2007), a close-up of an ornate chair and someone's crotch. As in **Untitled (Shellac)** (2007), her paintings may have familiar forms and motifs but no obvious narrative.

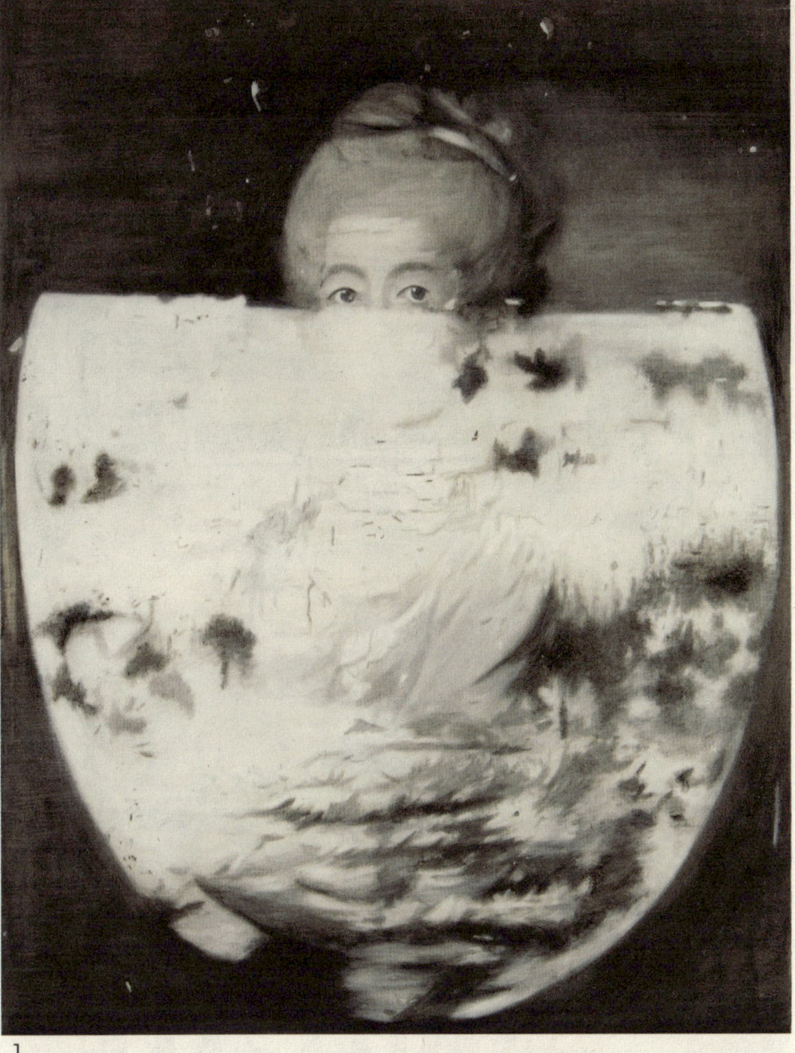

1.

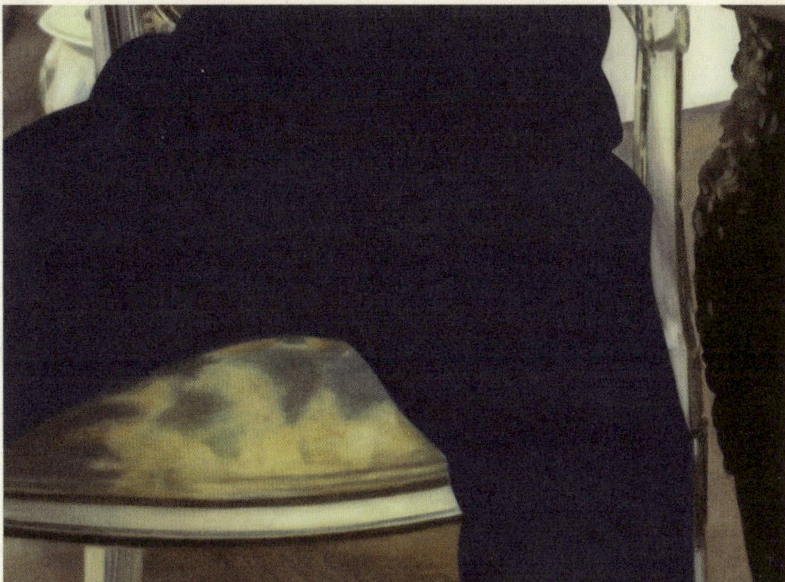

2.

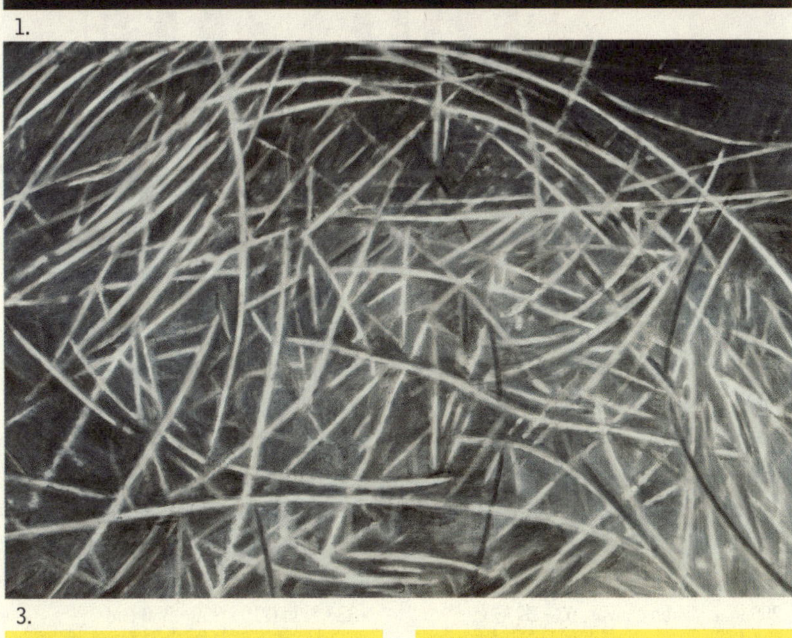

3.

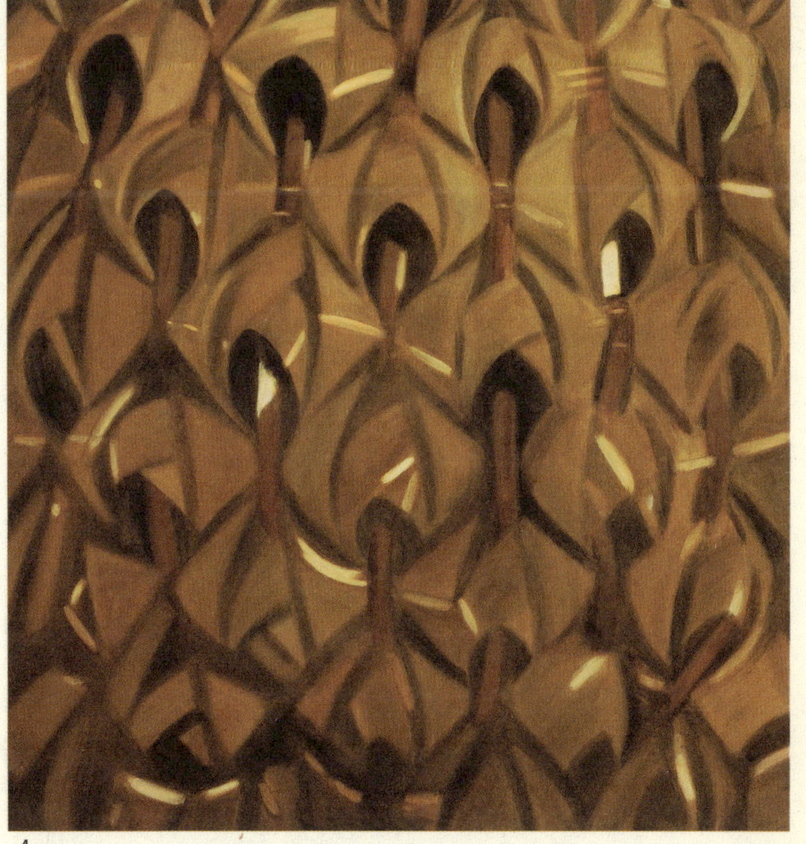

4.

1. **Untitled (Junge Frau mit Rosen)**
2006, oil on MDF, 27 ½ × 21 in (70 × 53 cm)

2. **Untitled (crotch)**
2007, oil on MDF, 42 × 59 in (107 × 150 cm)

3. **Untitled (bristles)**
2008, oil on MDF, 38 × 55 in (95 × 140 cm)

4. **Untitled (shellac)**
2007, oil on MDF, 31 ½ × 31 ½ in (80 × 80 cm)

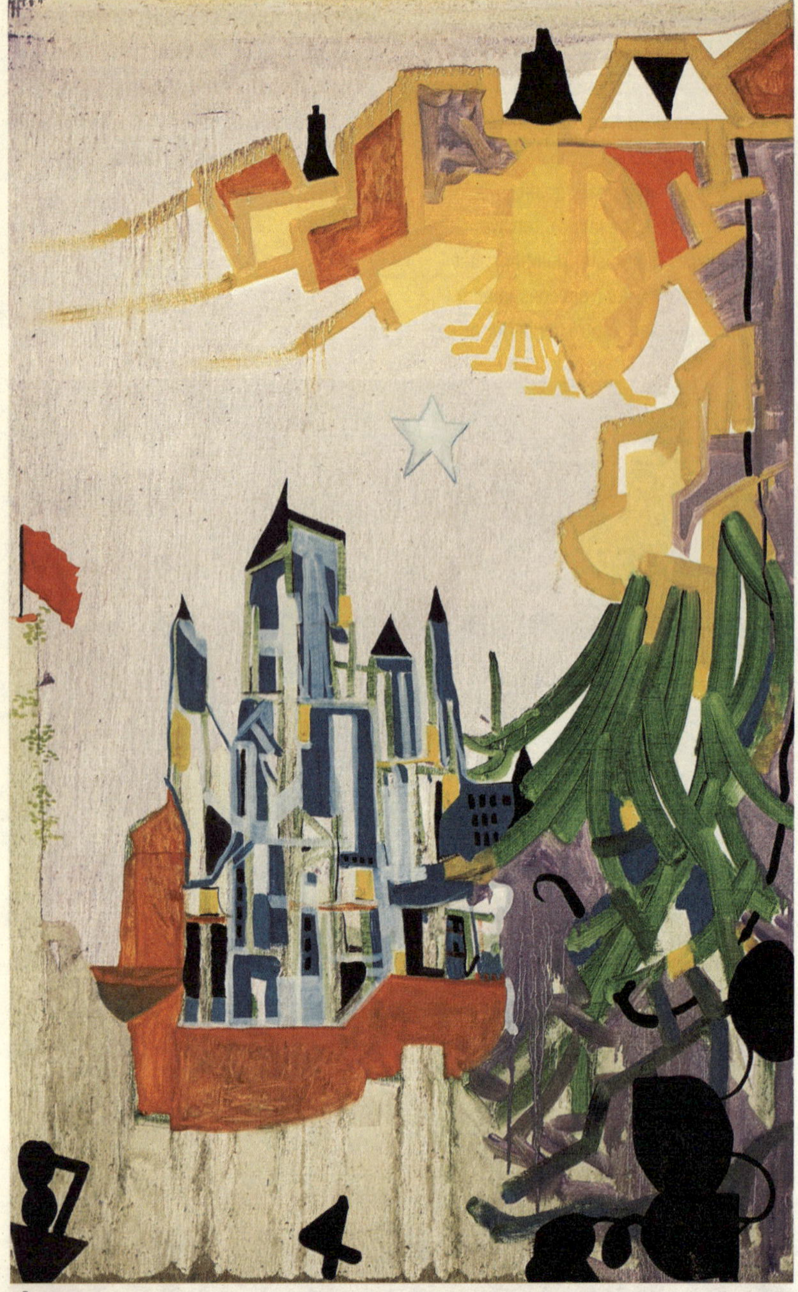

1.

2.

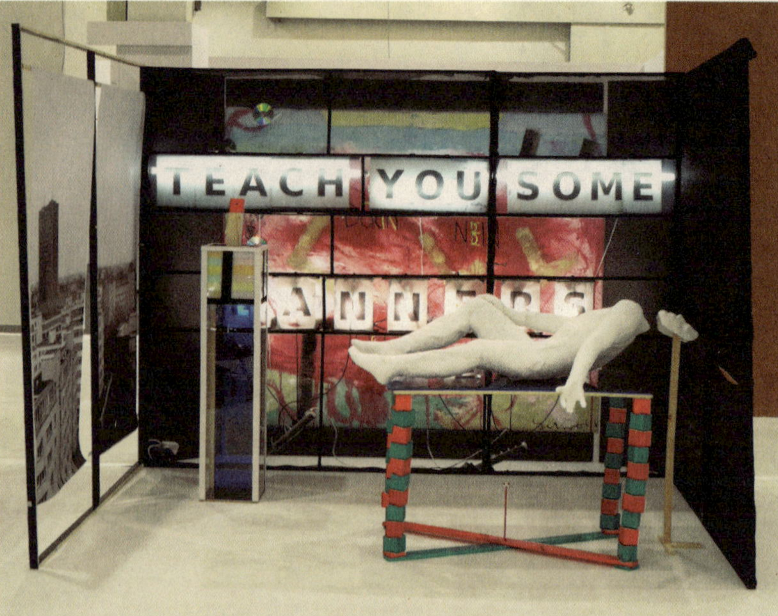

3.

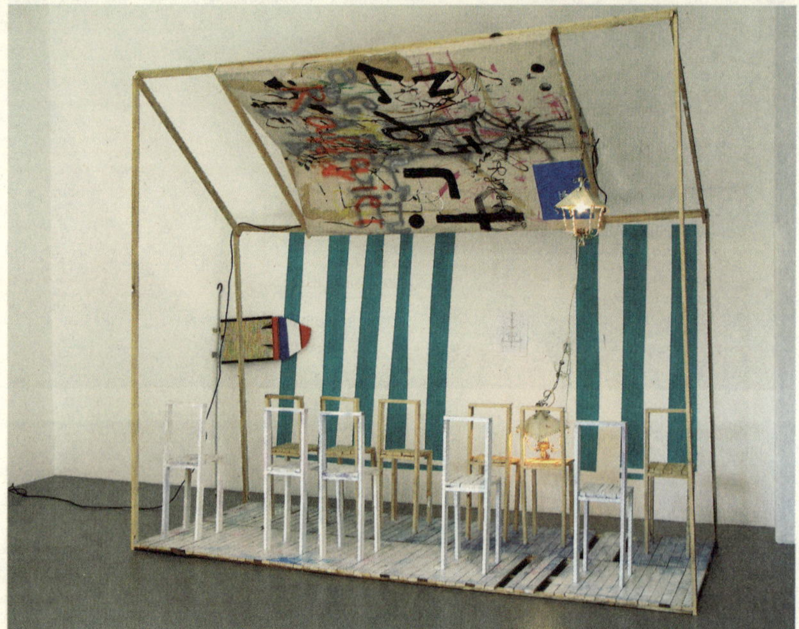

4.

Thomas Schroeren graduated from the Stadelschule in Frankfurt, Germany, and currently lives and works in Berlin. His installations and works in mixed media, made largely of found and everyday materials, draw on the idea of alternative lifestyles.

1. New City

2006, acrylic on canvas, 63 × $39\frac{1}{2}$ in (160 × 100 cm)

2. Kölner Dom

2007, mixed media, dimensions variable, installation view at Shapu Private Art Center/Courtyard Gallery, Beijing

3. Teach you some manners

2008, wood, glass, acrylic, foam, paint, varnish, plaster, shells, bitumen, fabric, paper, lightbulbs, and cable, $82\frac{3}{4}$ × $137\frac{3}{4}$ × $137\frac{3}{4}$ in (210 × 350 × 350 cm)

4. Guter böser Mayatempel

2007, wood, fabric, varnish, gouache, lanterns, paper print, 102 × 118 × 75 in (260 × 300 × 190 cm)

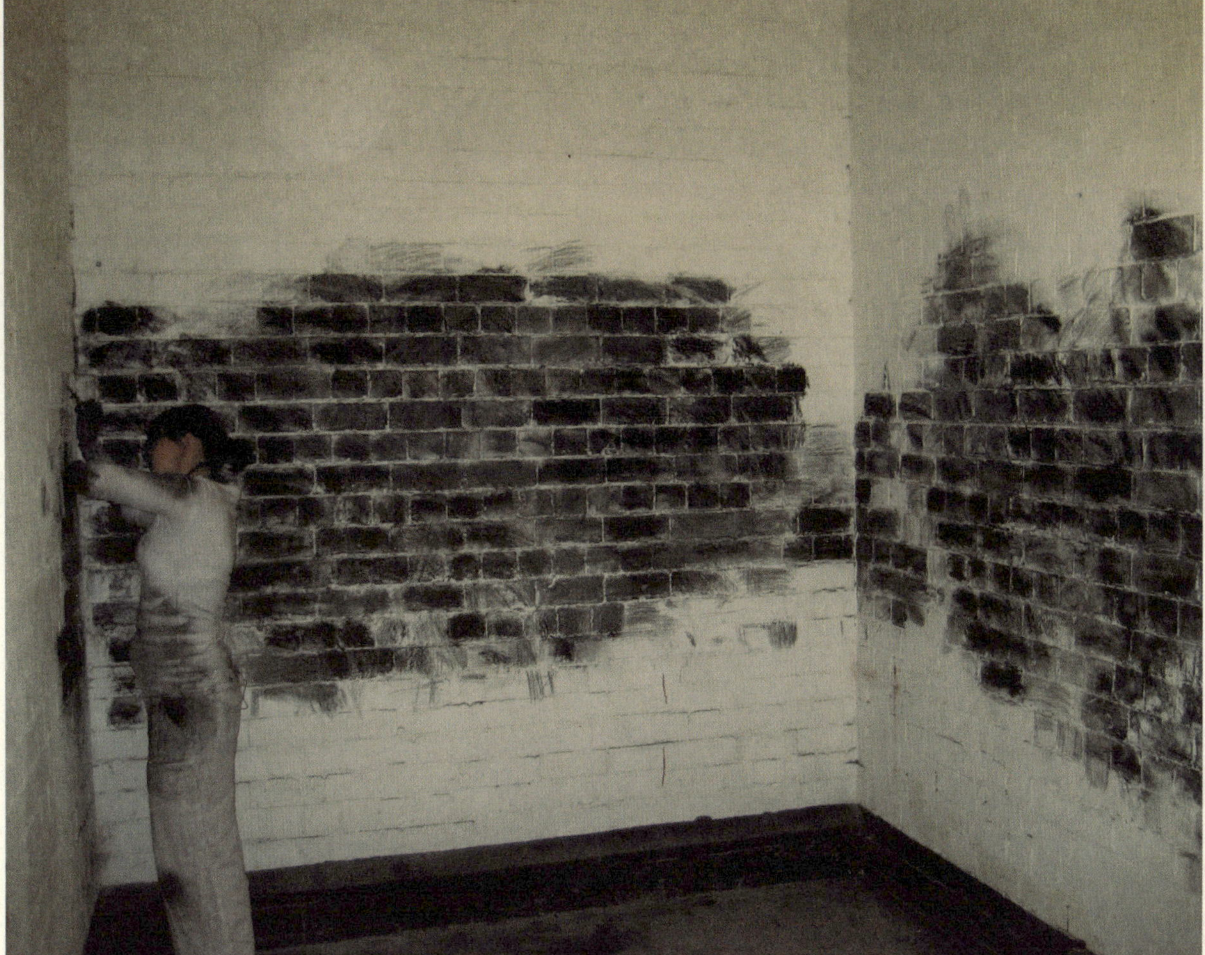

1.

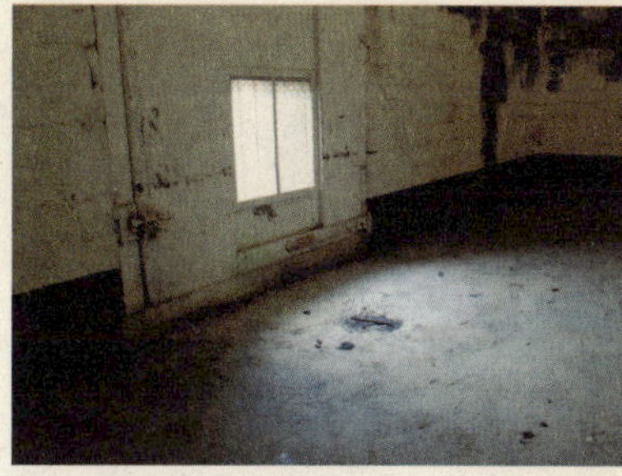

2.

Ruth Scott studied at the Norwich School of Art and Design, University of Sunderland, and later at Goldsmiths College, London. She has participated in group exhibitions in England and the United States. Scott employs a variety of media, including performance and video installation, always referencing drawing as a point of departure to sound out the boundaries between private and public space.

1, 2, 3 & 4. **Blacking**
2008, performance, graphite, and charcoal, 180 min

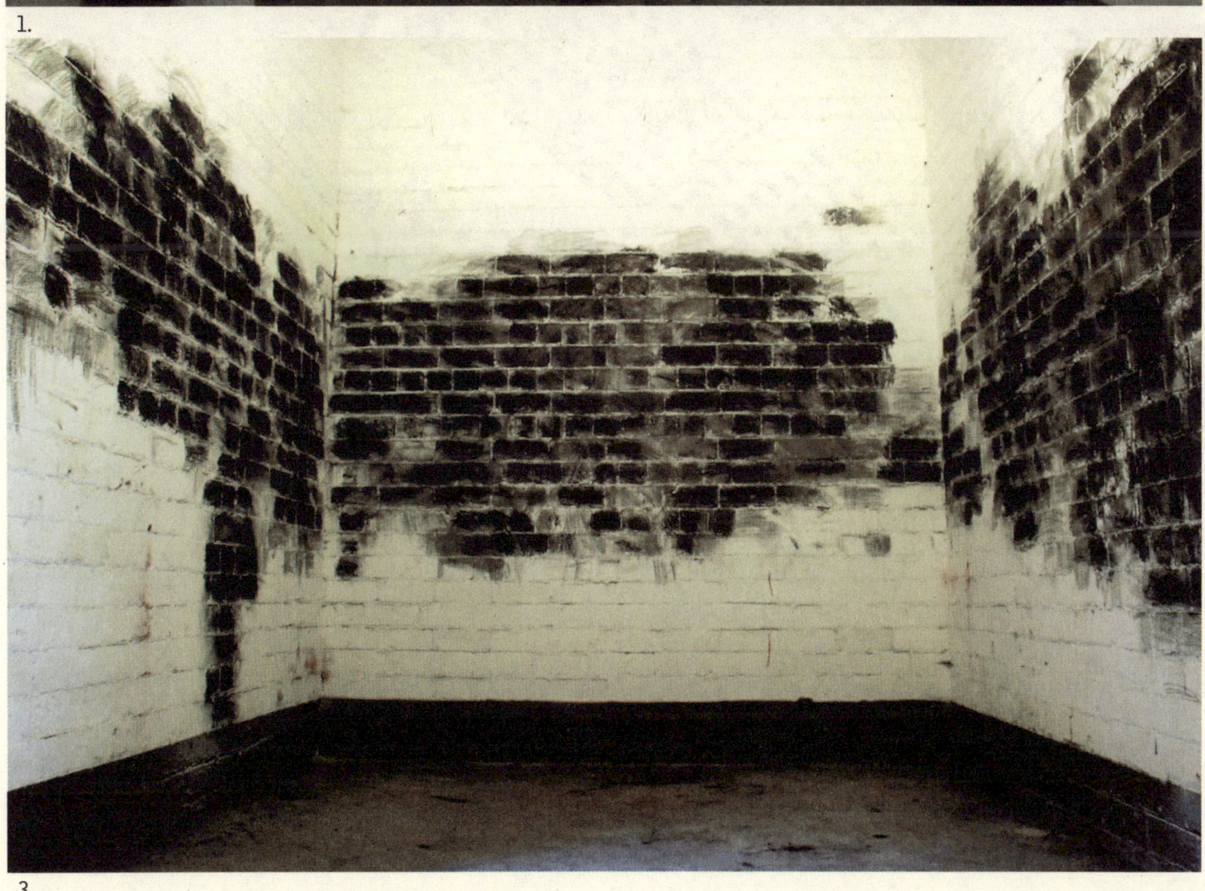

3.

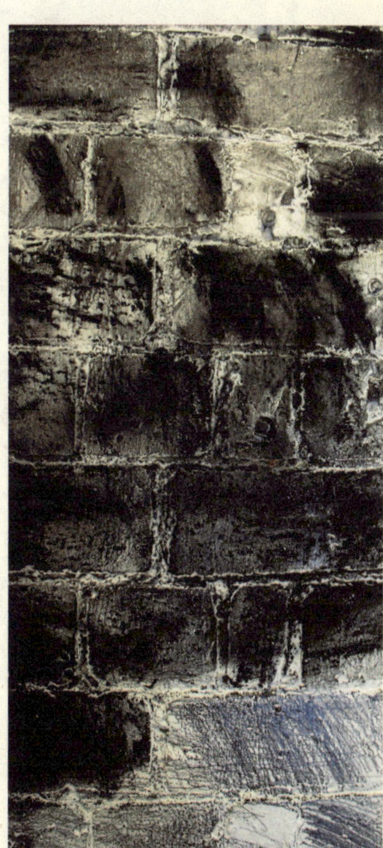

4.

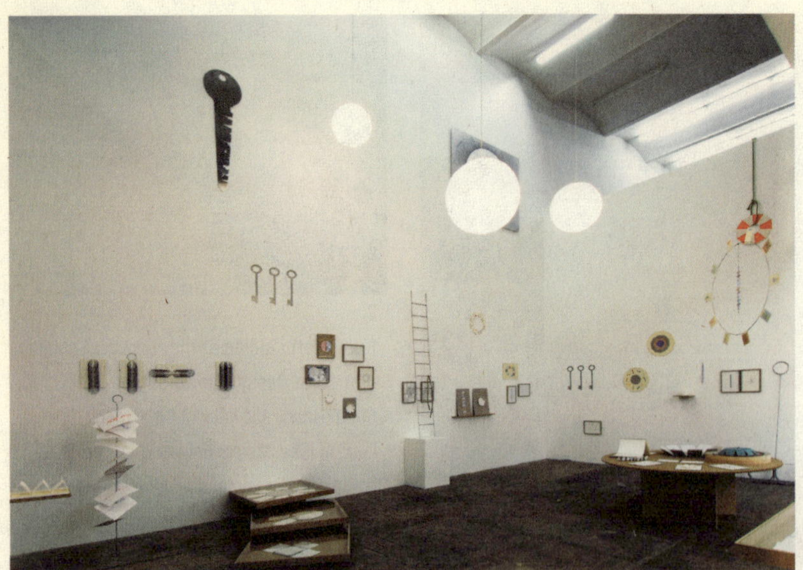

1.

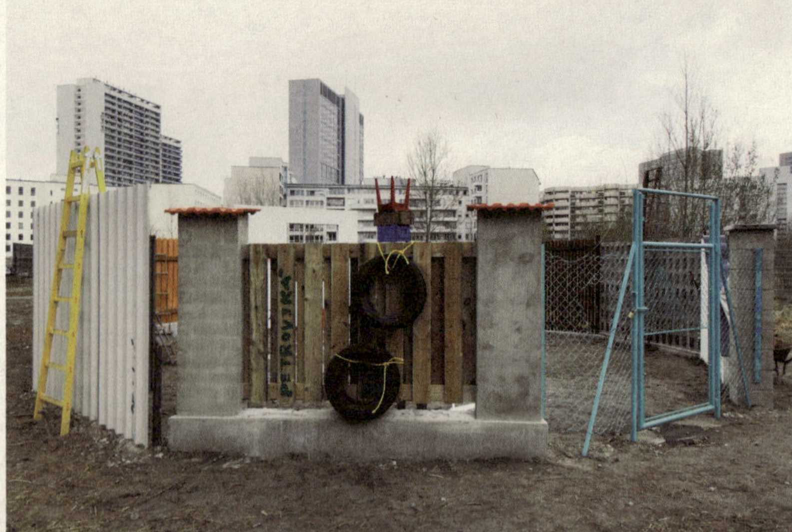

2.

3.

Kateřina Šedá lives and works in Brno and Prague, where she graduated from the Academy of Fine Arts. Her actions, drawings, installations, and videos are a response to the aftermath of communism and the introduction of a "free" market. Her art is rooted in her connection to her family members, namely her grandmother, and to her own community in Brno.

1 & 2. Over and Over

2008, drawings, models, and mixed media, dimensions variable, installation view at 5th Berlin Biennial

3. For Every Dog a Different Master

2007, social action, text, graphs, shirts, photographs, drawings, animation, and documentation, dimensions variable

1.

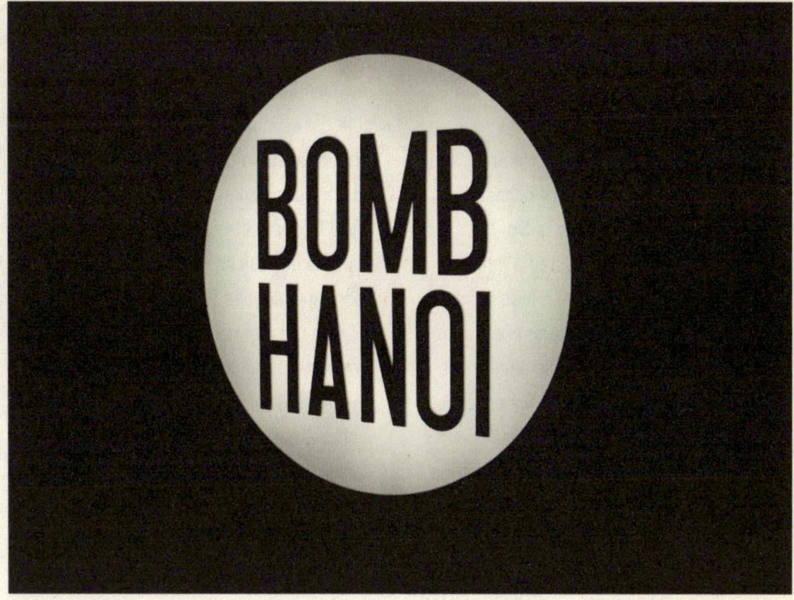

3.

Joaquin Segura works in performance and installation to push the limits of what is allowed and permitted in the name of art. An example of this is the video **Someone Else's Doc Martins**, in which the artist stops a stranger in the street and steals his shoes. Similarly, in **Hangover**, he drunkenly smashes his empty wine bottle over the head of the first passerby. Part agent provocateur, part urban anthropologist, Segura challenges boundaries in an effort to define them.

1 & 2. **Untitled (White Dove)**
2008, taxidermied dove, hand grenade, and safety pin, dimensions variable

3. **Untitled (Bomb Hanoi)**
2006, acrylic and steel, approx 59 × 59 × 8 in (150 × 150 × 20 cm)

4. **Untitled (Nitro-glycerine)**
2007, hand-woven wool tapestry, approx 79 × 118 in (200 × 300 cm)

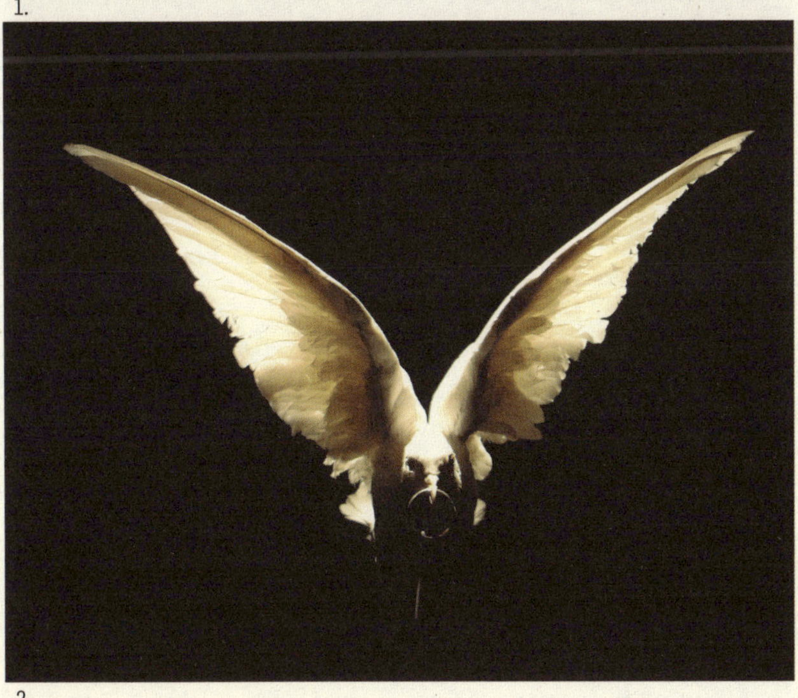
2.

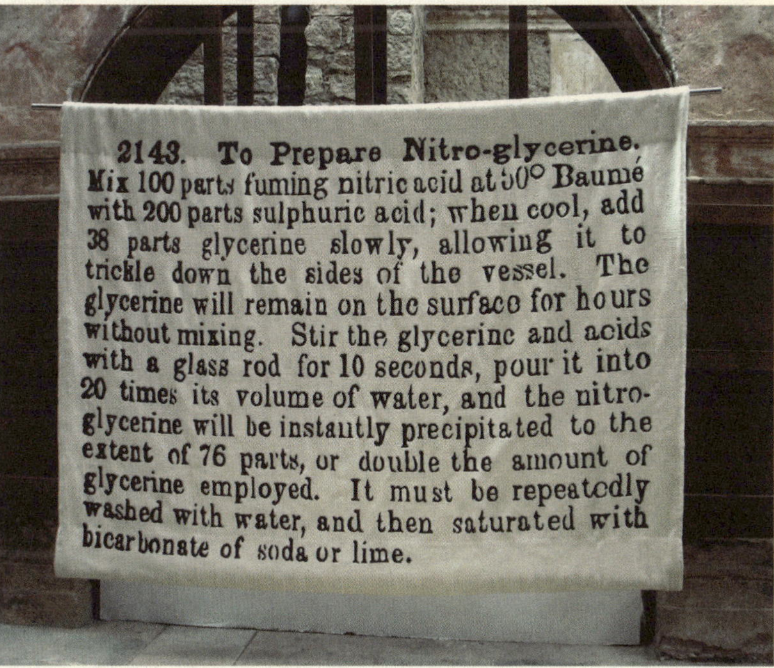

4.

Tino Sehgal creates what he calls "staged situations" – ephemeral, often interactive scenarios played out by a variety of collaborators, including dancers, academics, children, museum guards, and others. Though his works are occasionally playful – for his work **This Is So Contemporary** he instructed a number of museum guards at the German pavilion of the 2005 Venice Biennale to break into a choreographed dance while calling out "This is so contemporary!" – his practice is extremely rigorous, with Sehgal intimately involving himself in every stage of his work's production, exhibition, and distribution. No video or photographic documentation of his work exists, because he takes pains to ensure that whenever his "situations" are staged cameras are not permitted under any circumstances. Documentation of his work is therefore strictly verbal, and sales of his works are made only by way of an oral contract witnessed by a notary.

Sehgal has had solo exhibitions at venues around the world, including Fondazione Nicola Trussardi, Milan (2008), Magasin 3, Stockholm (2008), the CCA Wattis Institute for Contemporary Arts (2007-2008), and the Institute of Contemporary Arts, London (2007, 2006, 2005).

Sehgal's work is influenced by the two disparate academic disciplines in which he was trained: dance and political economy. In his work **This Situation** (2007), for instance, the performers strike choreographed poses lifted from a wide range of art historical sources but quickly break into wide-ranging dialogues (with each other as well as with the viewers of the piece) inspired by unattributed quotations that the performers recite from memory. Other works are more narrowly focused, and concerned with individual gestures or utterances. For his early work **Instead of Allowing Some Thing to Rise Up to Your Face Dancing Bruce and Dan and Other Things** (2000), Sehgal trains dancers to enact a series of movements taken from early video works by Dan Graham and Bruce Nauman while lying on the floor. In a similar move, his work **Kiss** (2002) consists of rotating pairs of dancers who bring kisses from famous works of art to life, from Auguste Rodin to Jeff Koons. In **This Is New** (2003) Sehgal instructs museum staff members to choose a headline from the day's newspaper that they will recite to museum-goers as they buy tickets, check their coats, or otherwise engage with aspects of the museum's operations where one would not expect to be ambushed by art. Here, as in all of Sehgal's work, the barriers between art and life begin to blur.

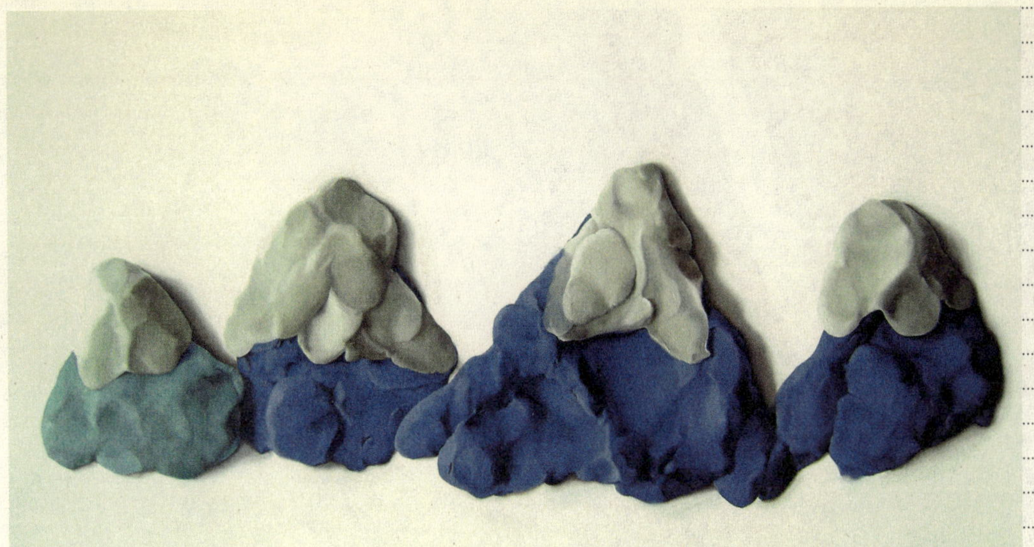

1.

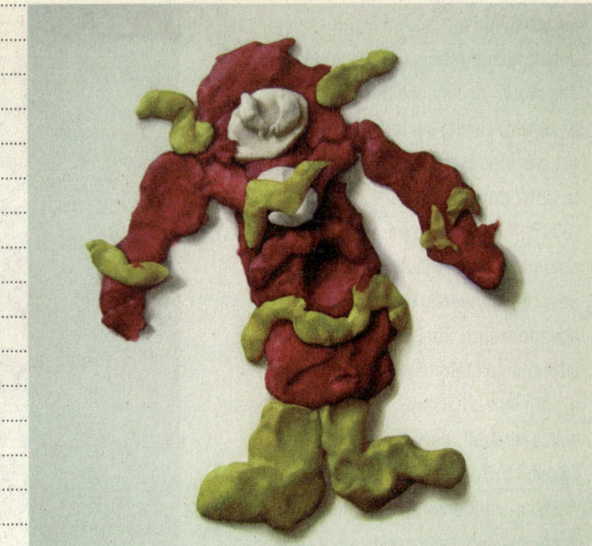

2.

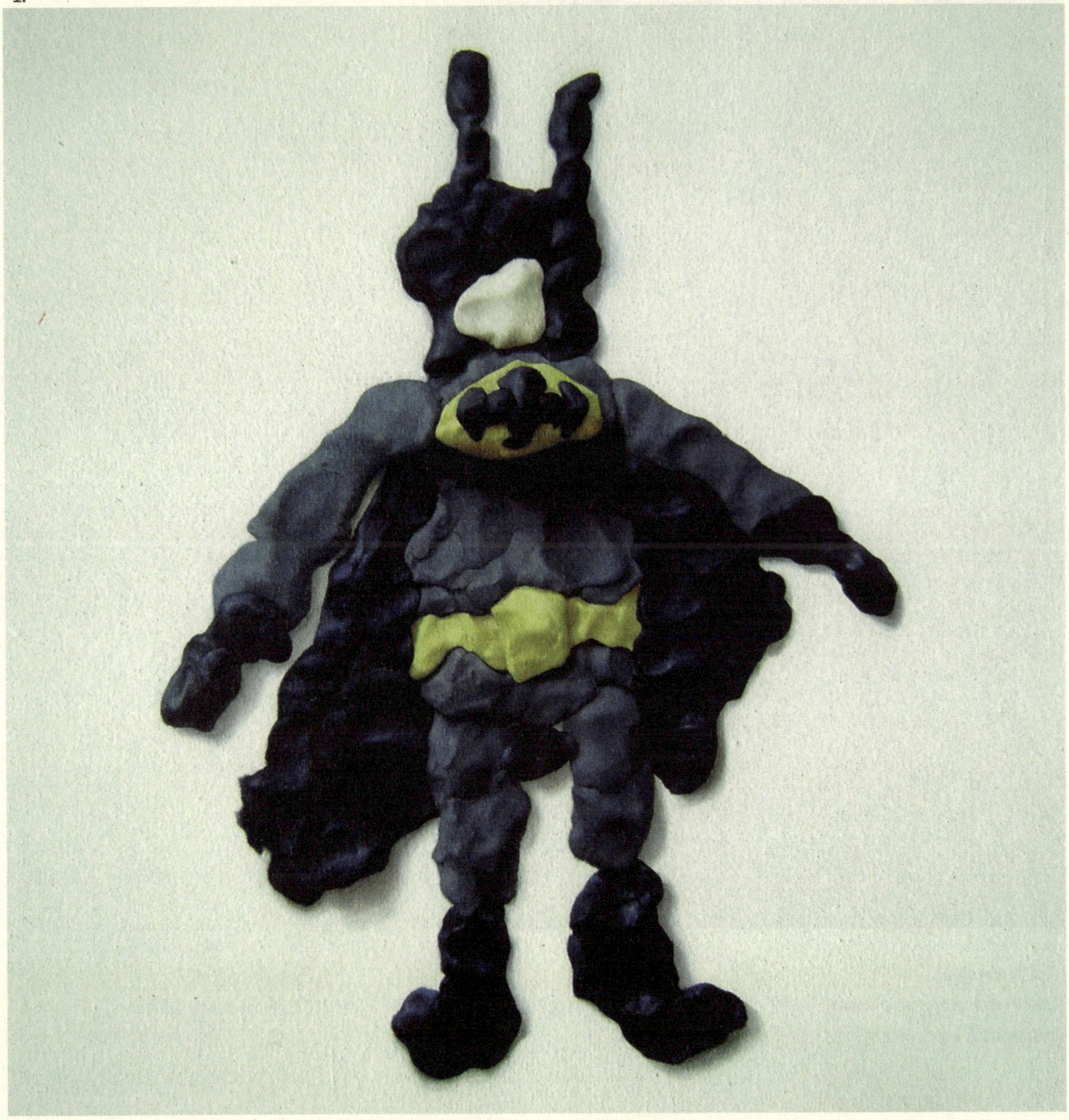

3.

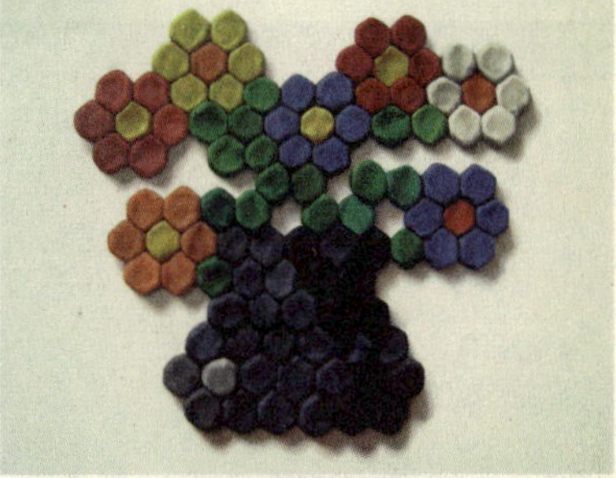

4.

Pablo Serra graduated from the University of Chile School of Art in Santiago, where he currently lives and works. In his oil paintings, he experiments with the medium of painting itself, attempting, as he has written, to "achieve a materiality in painting that conceals the painter." His 2008 series **The World Needs a Hero** consists of paintings of superheroes based on models made by his five-year-old nephew.

1. **Cordillera (mountain chain)**
2008, oil on canvas, 19 3/4 × 35 1/2 in (50 × 90 cm)

2. **Flash**
2008, oil on canvas, 23 3/4 × 23 3/4 in (60 × 60 cm)

3. **Batman**
2008, oil on canvas, 23 3/4 × 23 3/4 in (60 × 60 cm)

4. **Still life (flowerpot)**
2008, oil on canvas, 35 1/2 × 35 1/2 in (90 × 90 cm)

Lerato Shadi graduated from Johannesburg University in 2006 and lives and works in Johannesburg. Her often physically taxing performance and video art includes **Hema (Six hours of out-breath captured in 792 balloons)** (2007), footage of a performance staged by the artist at the offices of the advertising agency Ogilvy in Johannesburg. There, she spent six hours sitting on a staircase, exhaling every breath into a balloon, so that the staircase was eventually covered with nearly 800 colorful balloons. The piece relates to the modern work environment, in which such basic physical needs as breathing are taken for granted.

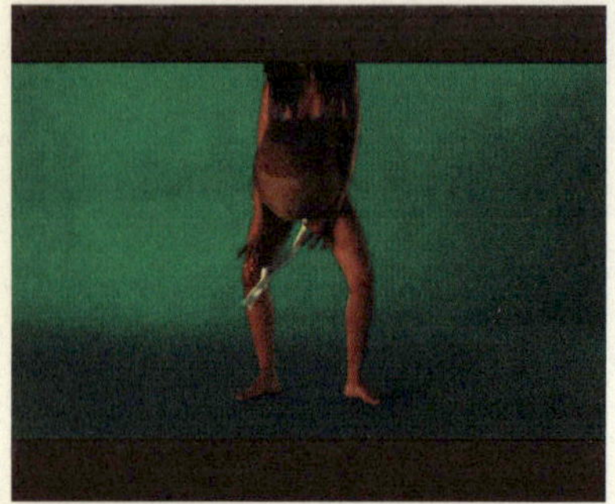

1.

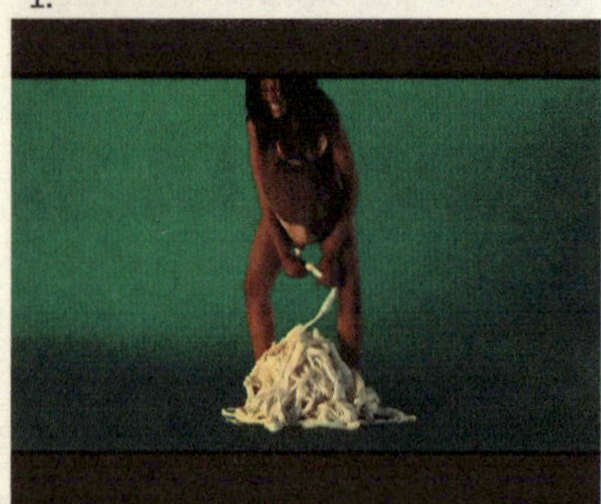

2.

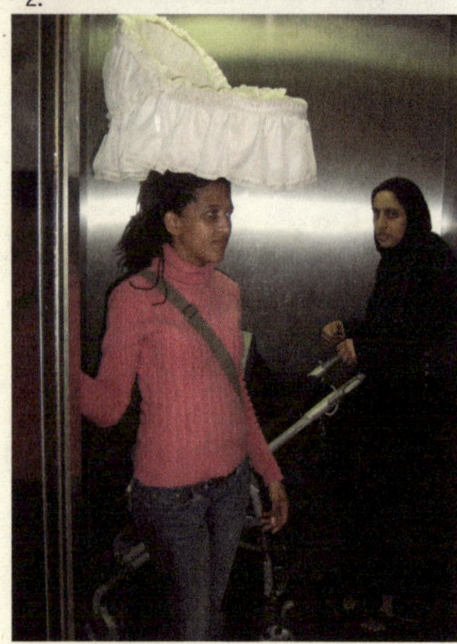

3.

4.

1 & 2. **Ableleng**
2007, video projection and wool installation, 4 min 59 sec

3. **My precious**
2006, performance, 120 min

4. **Exposed pupa**
2007, performance, 180 min

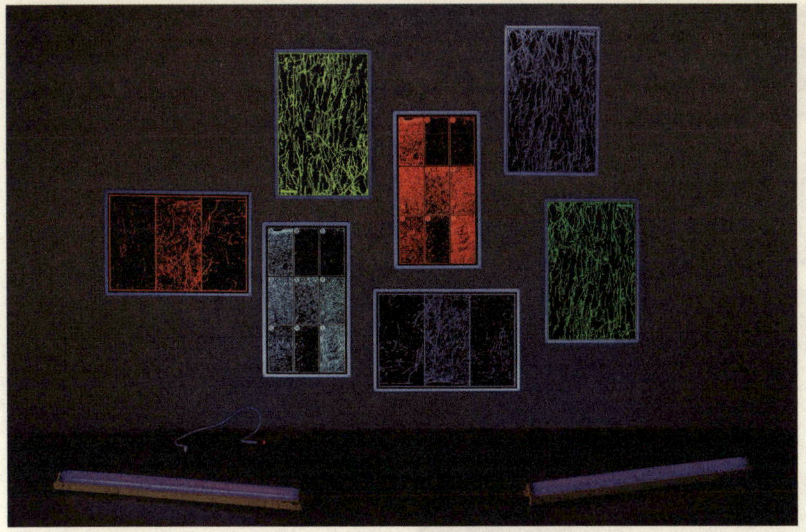

1.

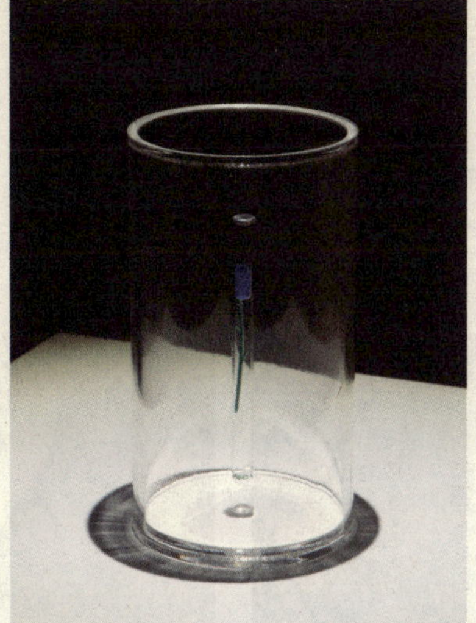

2.

Jeremy Shaw graduated from the Emily Carr Institute in Vancouver, where he lives and works. Shaw is a photographer, a video and installation artist, and a musician who records under the name Circlesquare. His works draw on his interest in youth subcultures and representations of sublime experiences. **Best Minds Part One** (2007) is comprised of two looped video projections showing a group of kids dancing violently, slowed down and accompanied by Shaw's melancholic score.

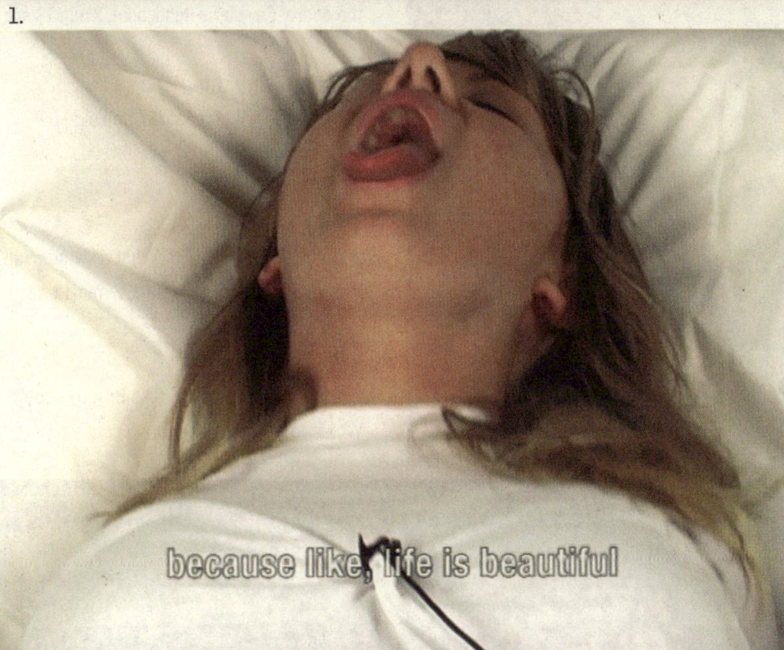

3.

4.

5.

1. Representative Measurements of Altered States (To Aid in Further Alterations)
2008, installation of silkscreen posters and UV lights, dimensions variable

2. Convenient Duality (Love Rose in Blue)
2008, readymade glass tube with synthetic flower in Plexiglas case, 5½ × 3 × 3 in (14 × 8 × 8 cm)

3 & 4. DMT
2004, 8-channel video installation

5. Single Hit of White Acid
2006, archival chromogenic print, 42 × 42 in (107 × 107 cm)

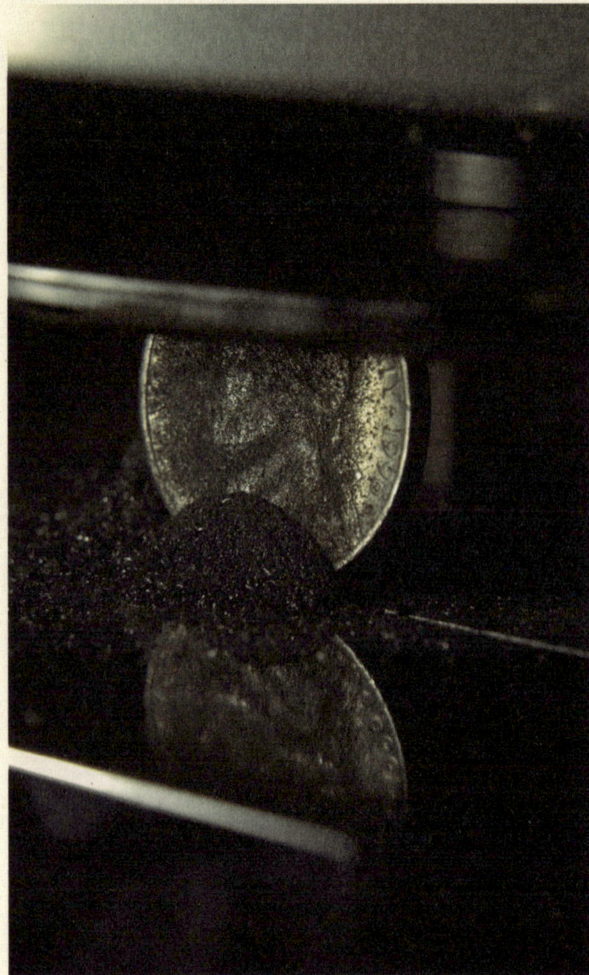

1.

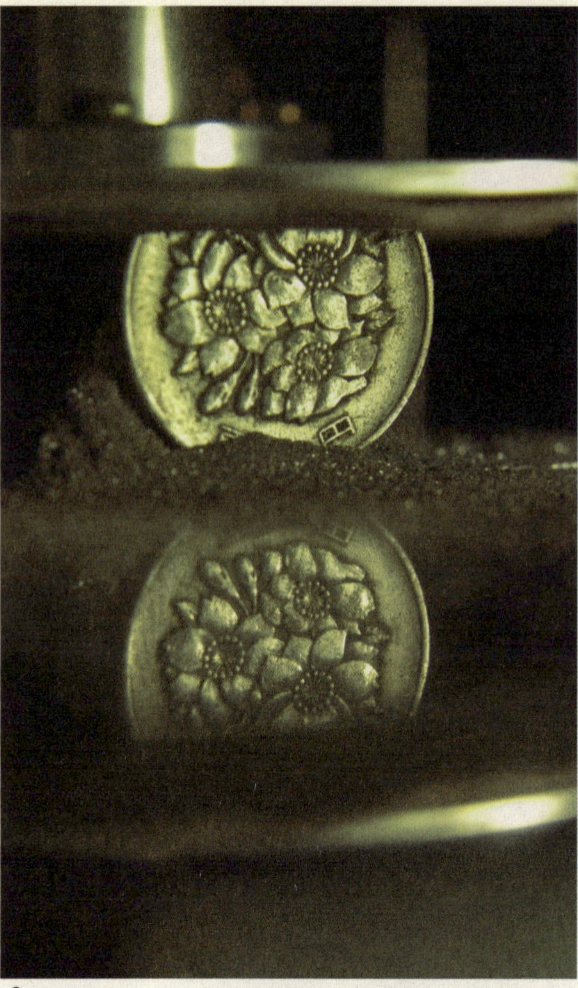

2.

Shin's art relies on his grinding machine, which he uses to pulverize a variety of objects, from high-tech gadgets like an iPod and a Sony Portable PlayStation to toys and coins. On the surface, this process (which the artist documents on video) seems little more than a boyish amusement. But the sameness of the dust that accumulates at the bottom of the screen by the end of each video reminds viewers of their own bodies' ultimate fate, and the process of destruction is tinged with melancholy.

1. **Coin Face**
2007, video with sound (intermezzo from the opera Cavalleria Rusticana), 3 min 13 sec

2. **Coin Living thing**
2007, video with sound (Swan Lake, by Tchaikovsky), 2 min 52 sec

3. **Astro Boy**
2006, video with sound (What a Wonderful World, by Louis Armstrong), 2 min 12 sec

4. **Alarm Clock**
2006, video with sound (Old Boy, by Yeong-Wook Jo), 4 min 12 sec

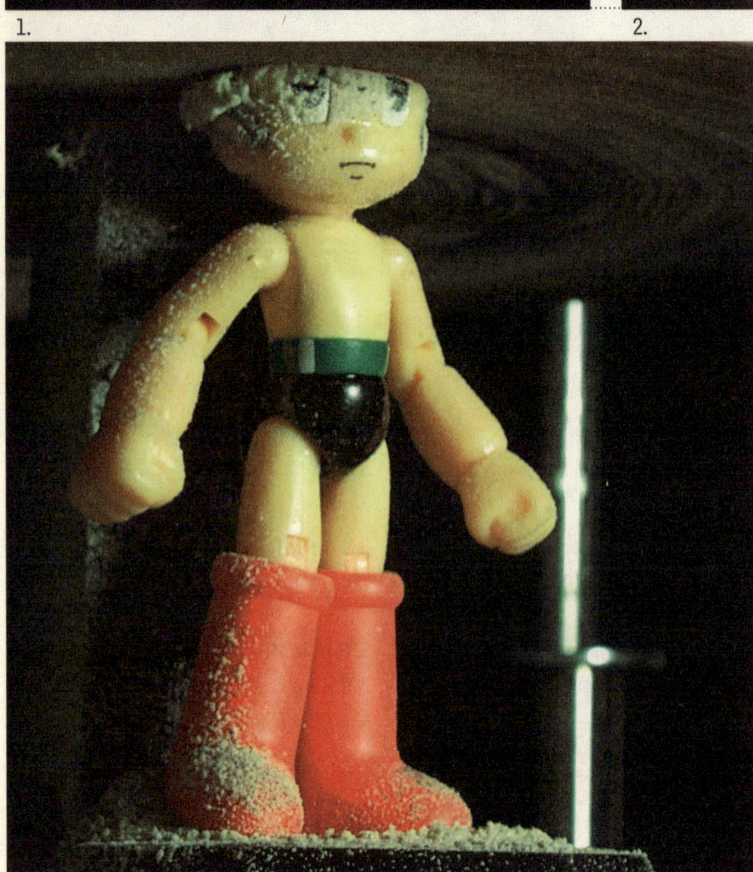

3.

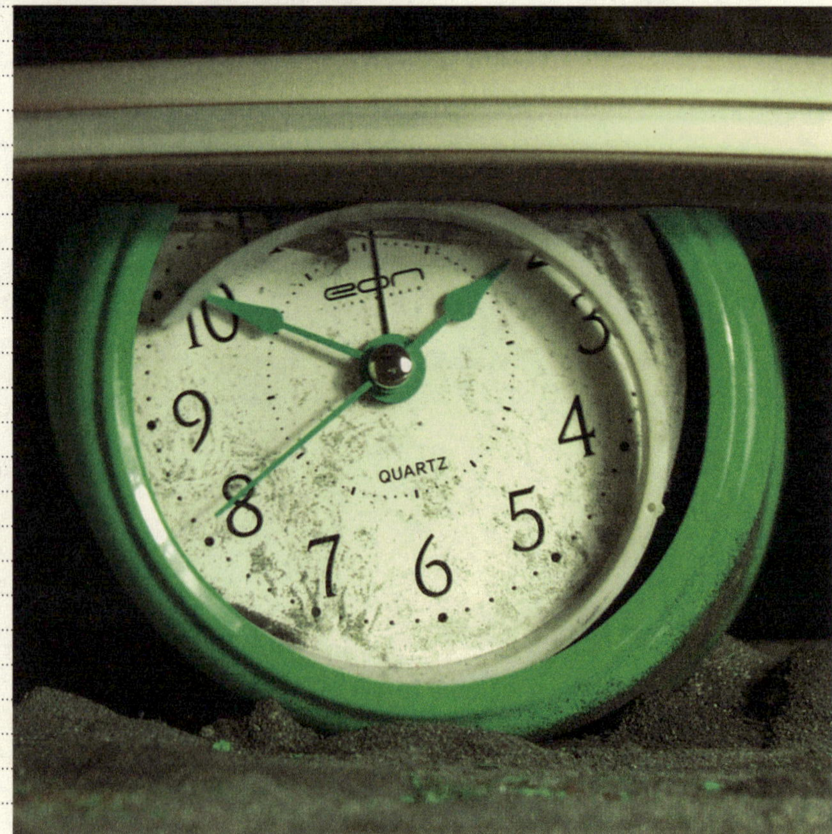

4.

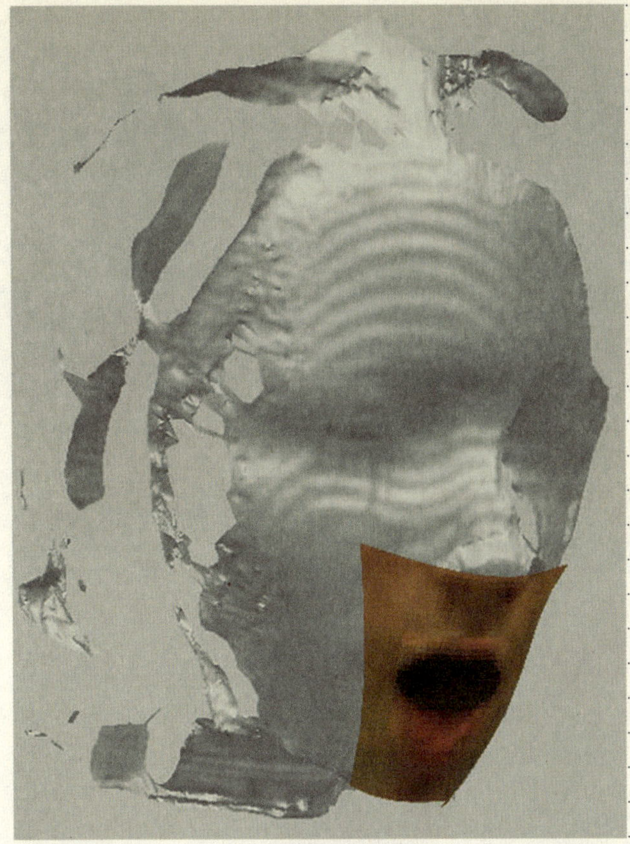

1.

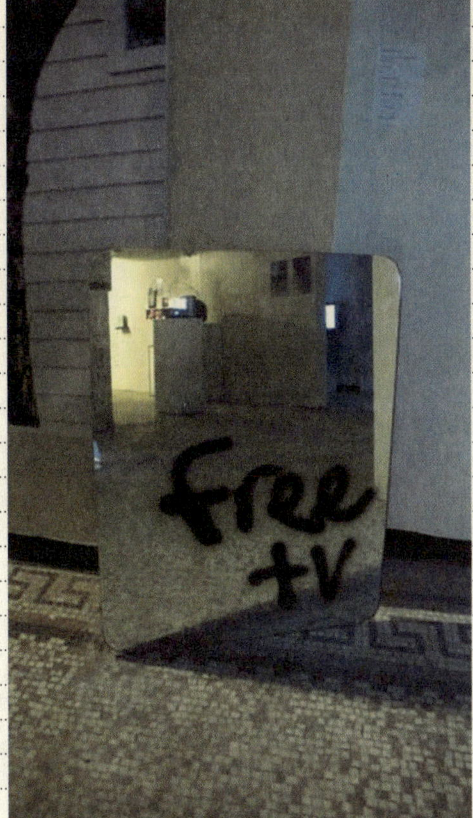

2.

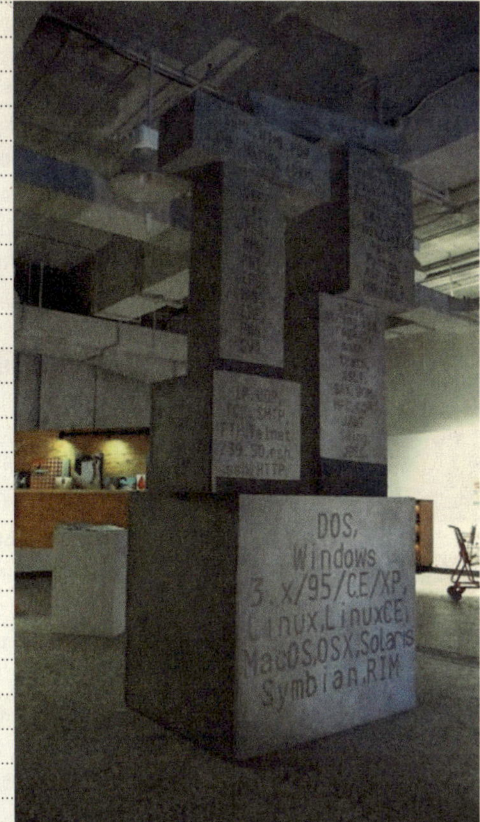

3.

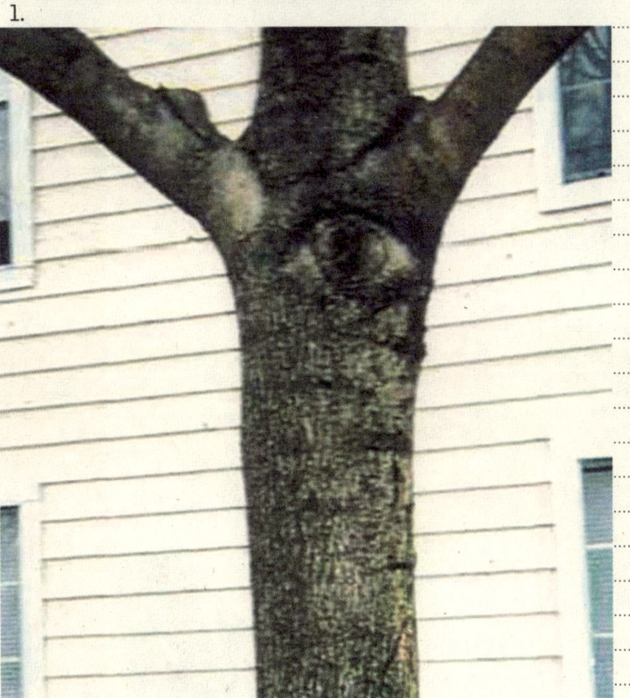

4.

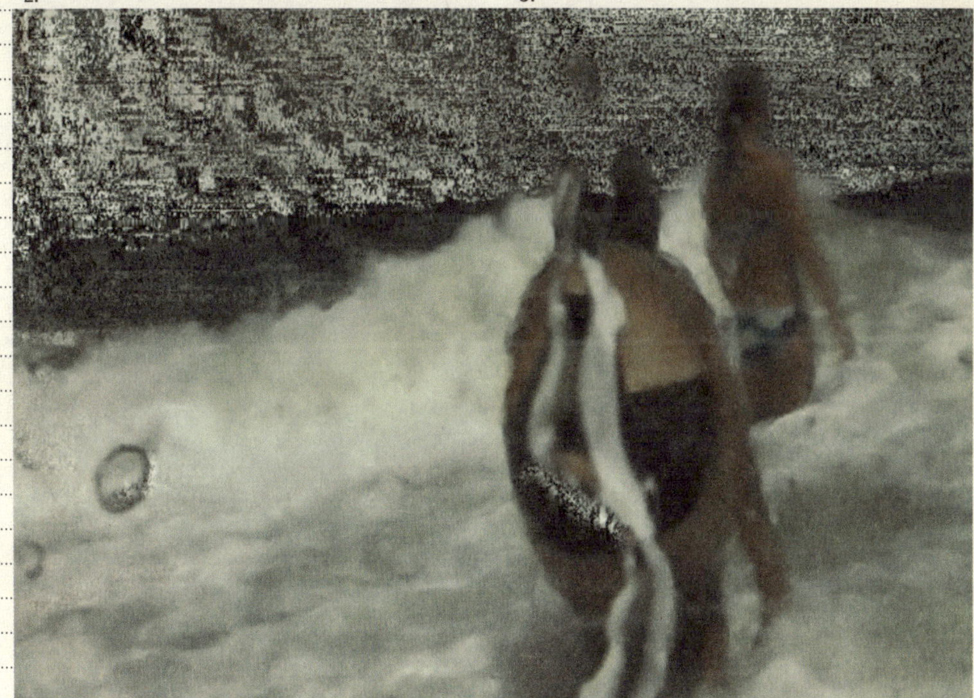

5.

Hayley Silverman graduated in 2008 from the Maryland Institute College of Art with a BFA in interdisciplinary sculptural studies, and she lives and works in New York City and Baltimore. She produces videos, installations, photographs, and works like **The Everything** (2008), a larger-than-life-size sculpture of stacked gray blocks inscribed with computer-related text such as "Python" and "ASP, PHP."

1. **Untitled**
2007, digital print

2. **Free TV**
2008, spray paint and mirror, 60 × 42 in (152 × 107 cm)

3. **The Everything**
2008, luan, wood, foam, spackle, and paint, 25 × 6 × 6 ft (8 × 2 × 2 m)

4. **11:11**
2008, found digital print, 5 × 2 ½ ft (152 × 79 cm)

5. **Wading**
2008, video, 23 sec

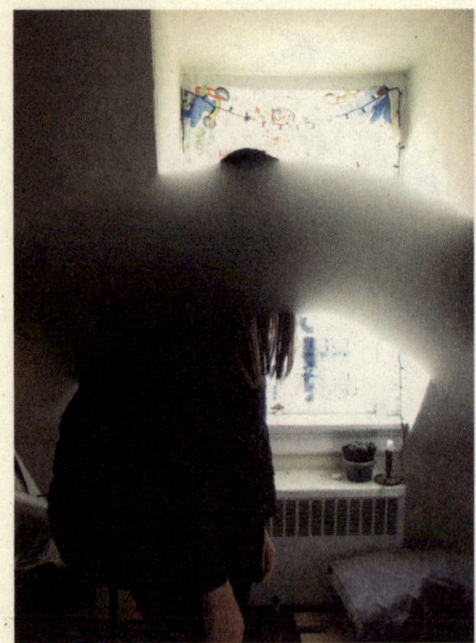

1.

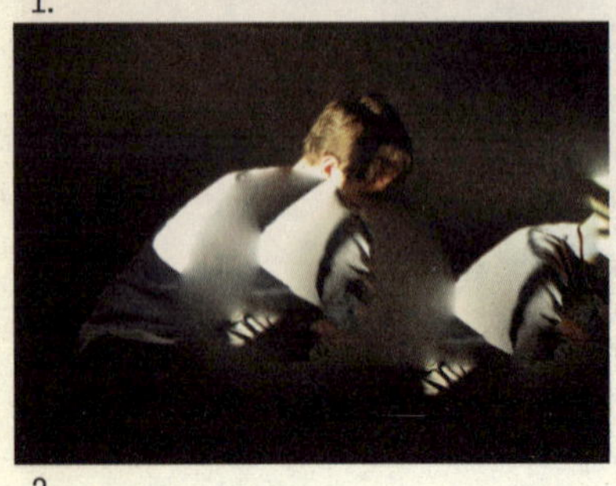

2.

William Simpson is a student at the Cooper Union in New York and lives and works in Brooklyn. His colored-pencil drawings are playful and capture an unmediated, almost childlike spontaneity. His work explores the influence of technology; his series of drawings, **Auras and Auroras** (2008) refers to and incorporates found Internet photographs.

1. **Untitled**
from the series **You Are Healed**
2008, archival inkjet print, 19 × 13 in (48 × 33 cm)

2. **Brothers 2**
from the series **You Are Healed**
2008, archival inkjet print, 13 × 19 in (33 × 48 cm)

3. **Heads**
2007, graphite, colored pencil, and monoprint, 18 × 17 in (45 × 48 cm)

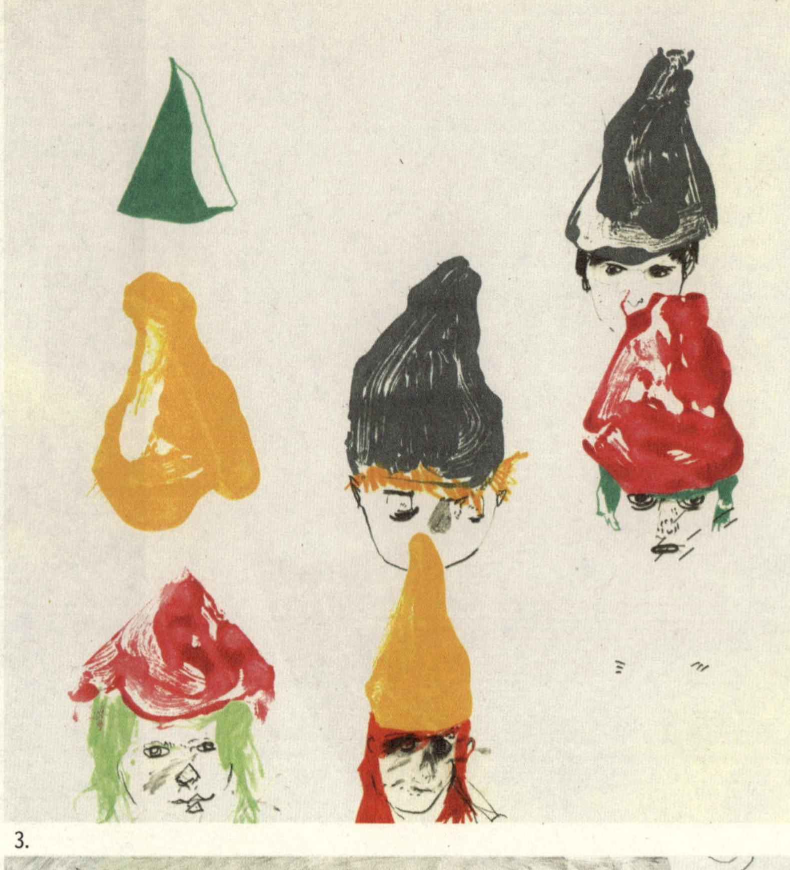

3.

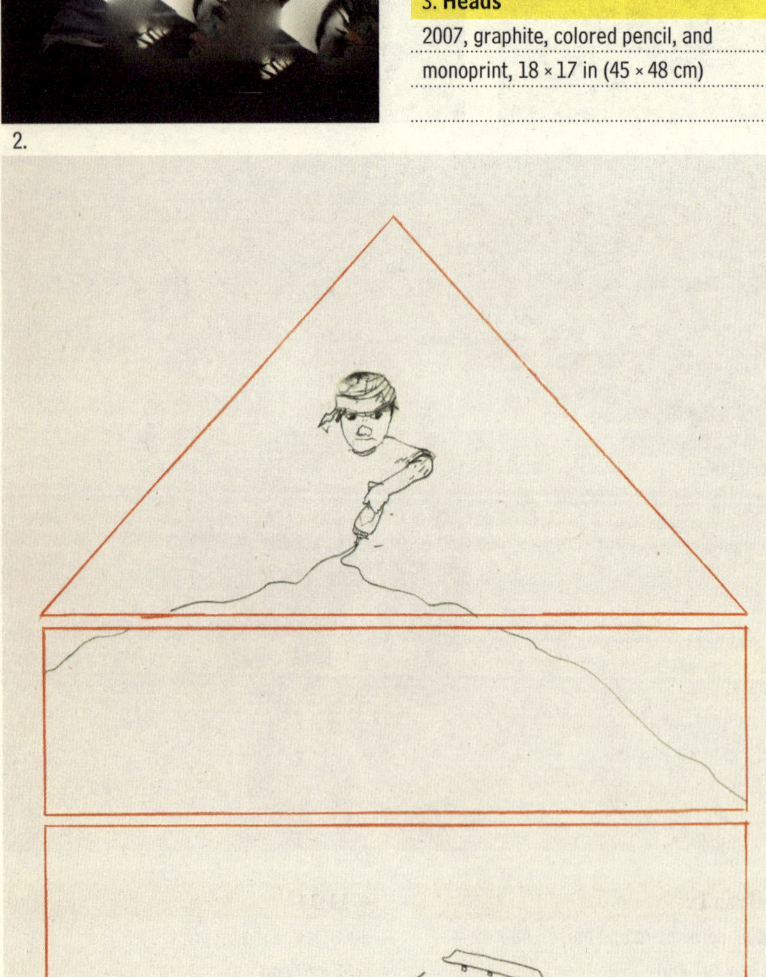

4.

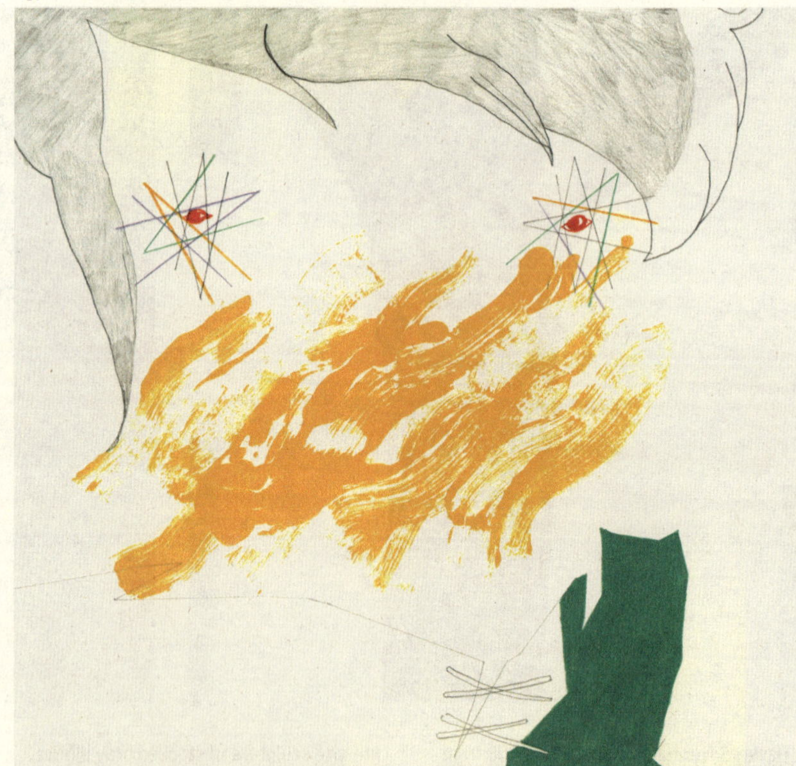

5.

4. **Sequence**
2008, graphite and colored pencil, 26 × 18 in (66 × 45 cm)

5. **Link**
2007, graphite, colored pencil, and monoprint, 18 × 17 in (45 1/2 × 43 cm)

Alexandre Singh attended the Ruskin School of Fine Art and Drawing in Oxford, UK, and graduated in 2005 from the School of Visual Arts in New York. He lives and works in Brooklyn. Singh's videos, installations, and collages combine consumer items and construction materials, referencing popular culture and commercialism. His collage **Adi Dassler** (2007) was a portrait of the founder of Adidas, and his video **Marque of the Third Stripe** (2007) alluded to the three stripes that signal the Adidas brand.

1. **Hello Meth Lab in the Sun**
with Jonah Freeman and Justin Lowe
2008, mixed media, dimensions variable, installation view at Ballroom, Marfa, Texas

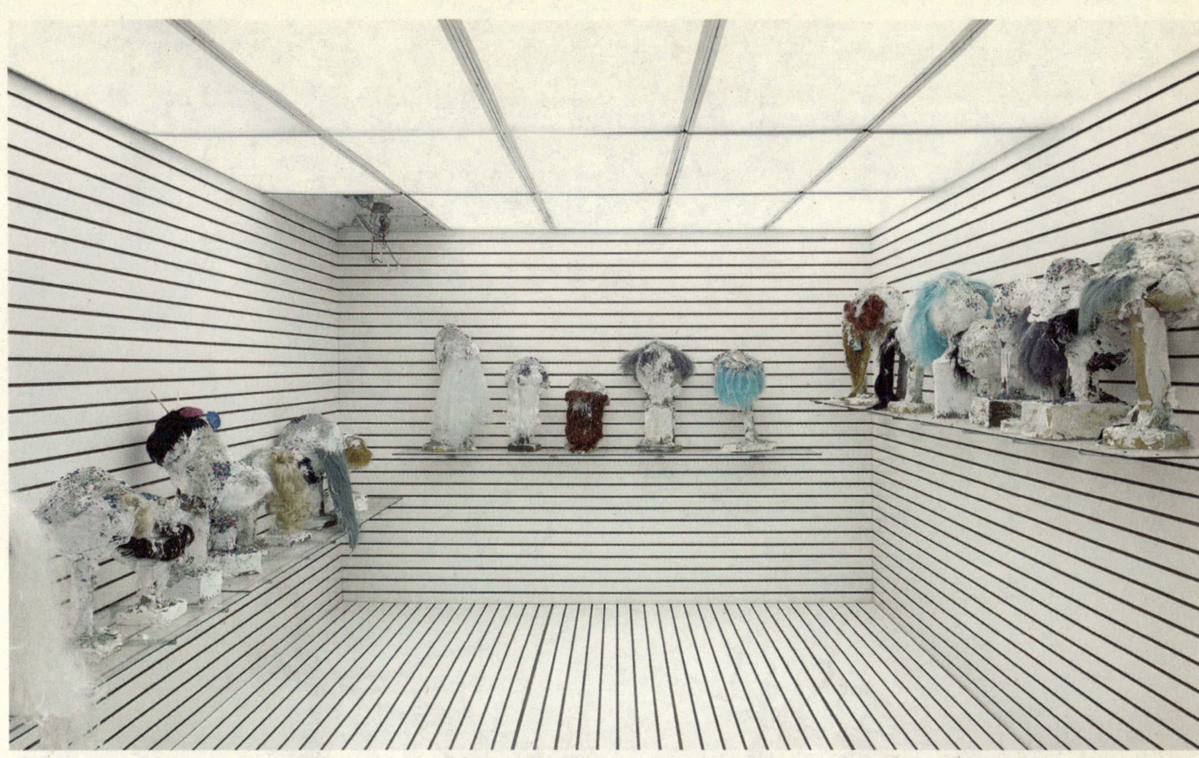

1.

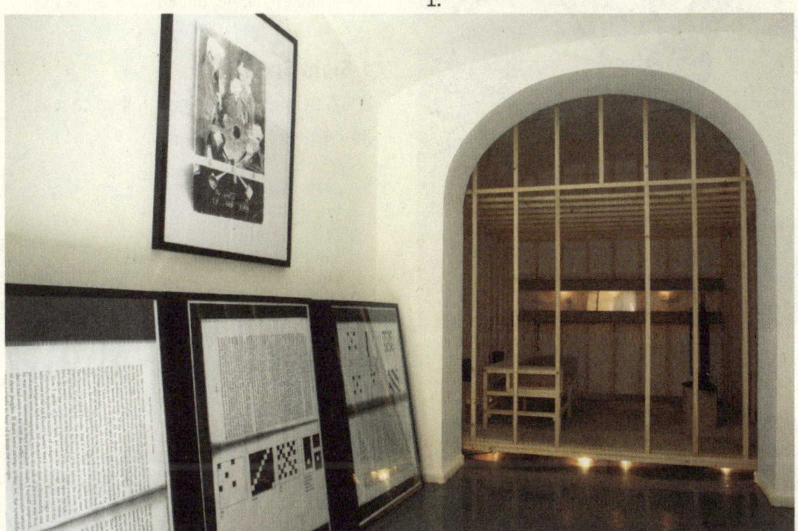

2.

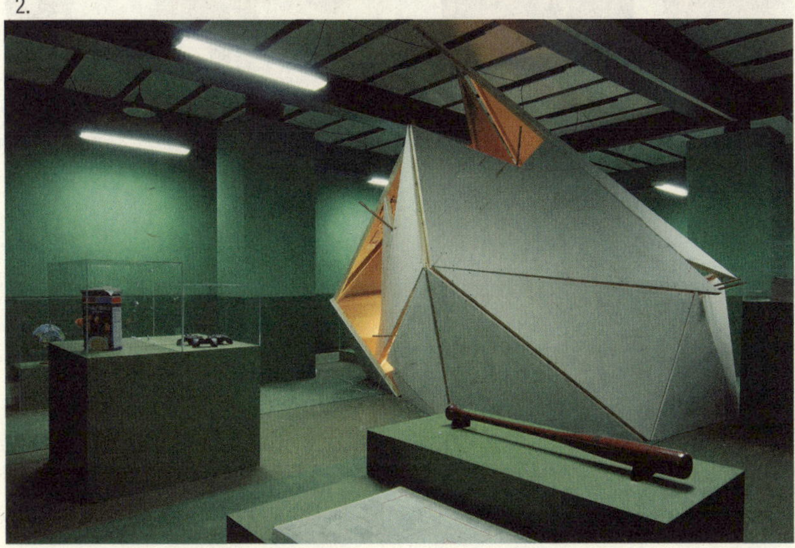

3.

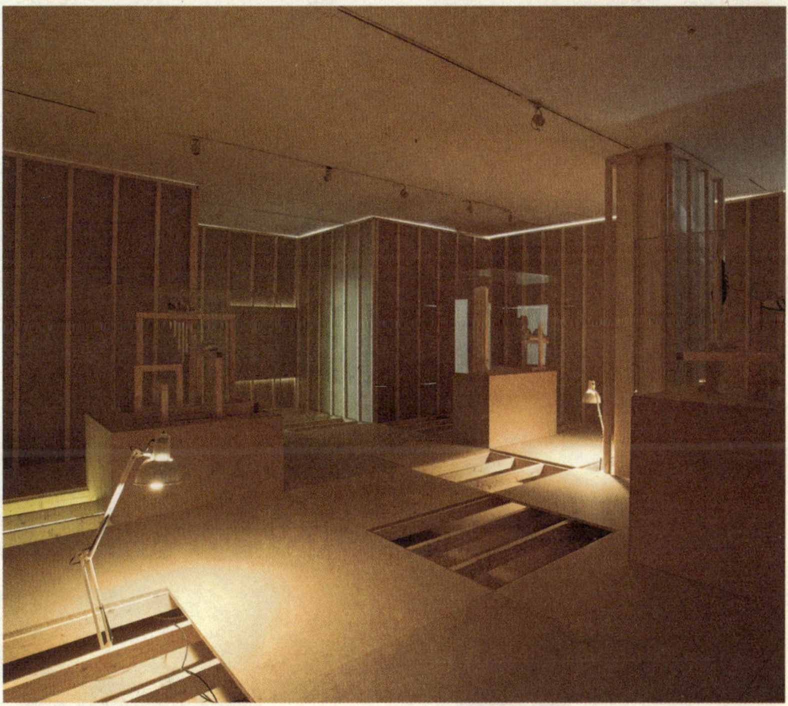

4.

2. **The Marque of the Third Stripe**
2008, 17 framed prints, each 59 × 39 $\frac{1}{2}$ in (150 × 100 cm), with wood, chipboard, lights, Mac mini, LCD screen, speakers, vitrine, Adidas shoes, and smoke machine, dimensions variable, installation view at Monitor Gallery, Rome

3. **Unclehead**
with Rita Sobral Campos
2008, mixed media, dimensions variable, installation view at Museu EDP, Lisbon

4. **The Marque of the Third Stripe**
2008, wood, chipboard, lights, vitrines, and Adidas shoes, dimensions variable, installation view at Royal College of Art, London

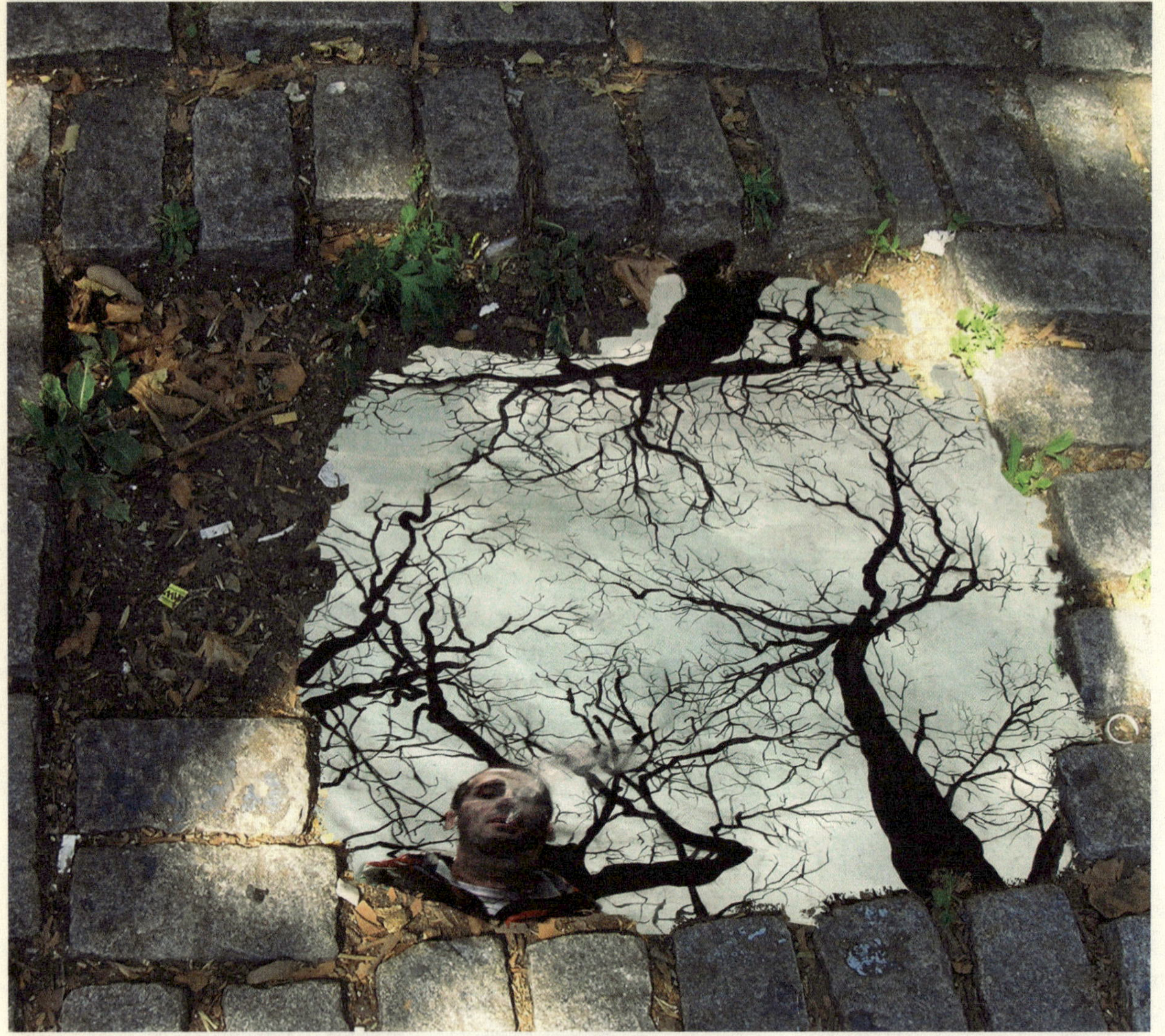

1.

Sumakshi Singh earned an MFA from the School of the Art Institute of Chicago and completed a residency at the Skowhegan School of Painting and Sculpture in Maine. She lives and works in Chicago. In her sculptures and installations, she creates unexpected interventions in the existing space: colorful caves or nests that seem to have grown from the floors or walls. For **Crack** (2004), she layered paint to mimic a crack in the gallery wall.

1. Interlude – (oasis)
2006, clear resin, dimensions variable

2. Micro Intervention Urban Fungus
2003-04, acrylic on polymer clay, copper wire, altered walls, moss, nails, and tinted Vaseline, 1 1/2 × 3/4 in (4 × 2 cm)

3. Mapping the Studio
2008, mixed media, dimensions variable

4. Sight Specific
2007, acrylic on aluminum foil on canvas, 34 × 4 1/2 ft (10.3 × 1.4 m)

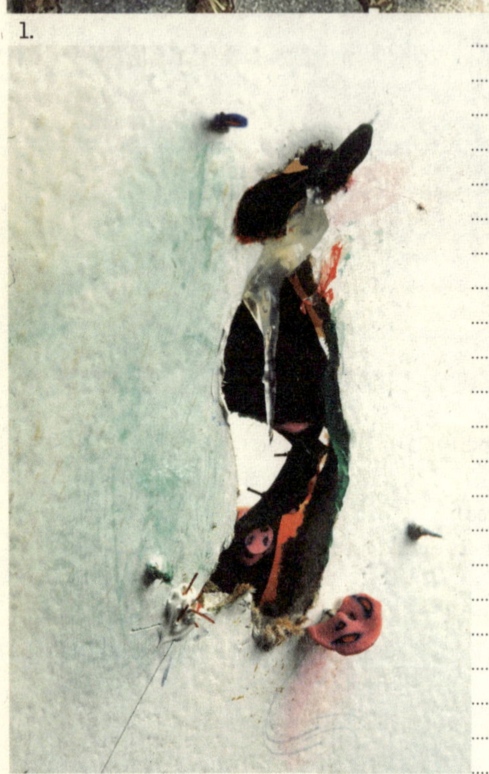

2.

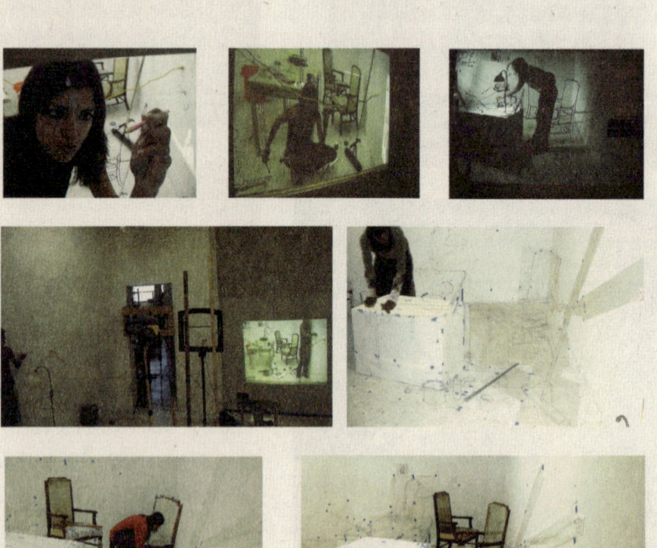

3.

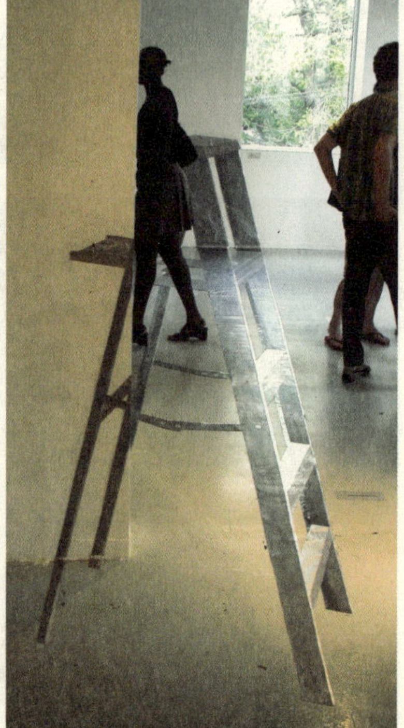

4.

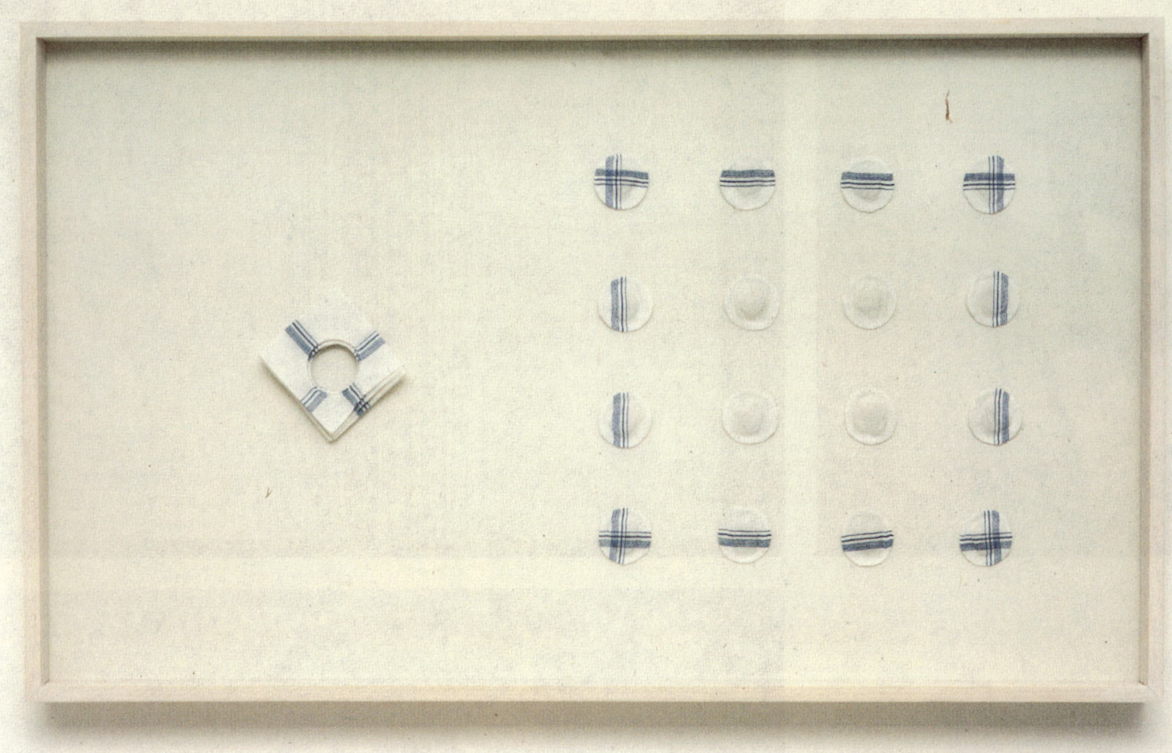

1.

Daniel Sinsel received an MA in painting in 2004 from the Royal College of Art in London, where he lives. His work, which combines conventions of painting with three-dimensional found objects, references the stylistic traditions of the German Bauhaus, but Sinsel is also known for his experimentation with materials: **Apfelstrudel** (2006) features chestnut shells and felt half-moons that have been sewn onto a tea towel. In the 2007 oil painting **Young Woman with Chocolate**, a chocolate bar and paper cone are depicted floating in a deep-black background near a portrait bust of a young woman decorated with an orange ribbon.

1. Taschentuchravioliunterhose
2006, vintage handkerchiefs, cashmere, and custom-made tray frame, 20 × 24 × 3 ½ in (51 × 61 × 9 cm)

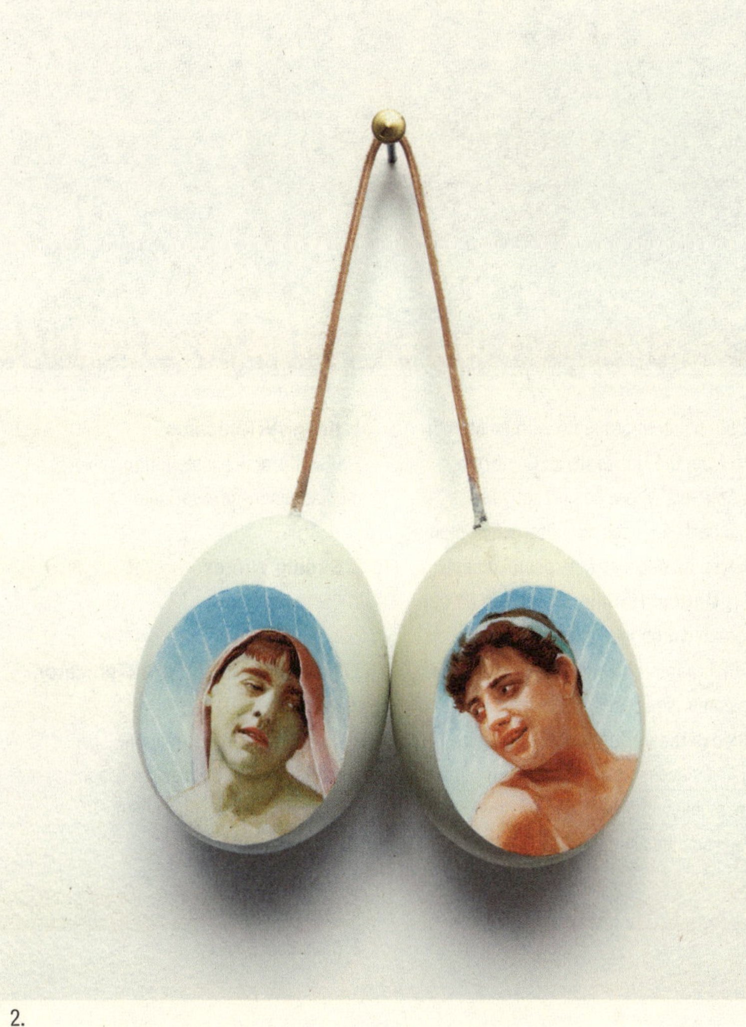

2.

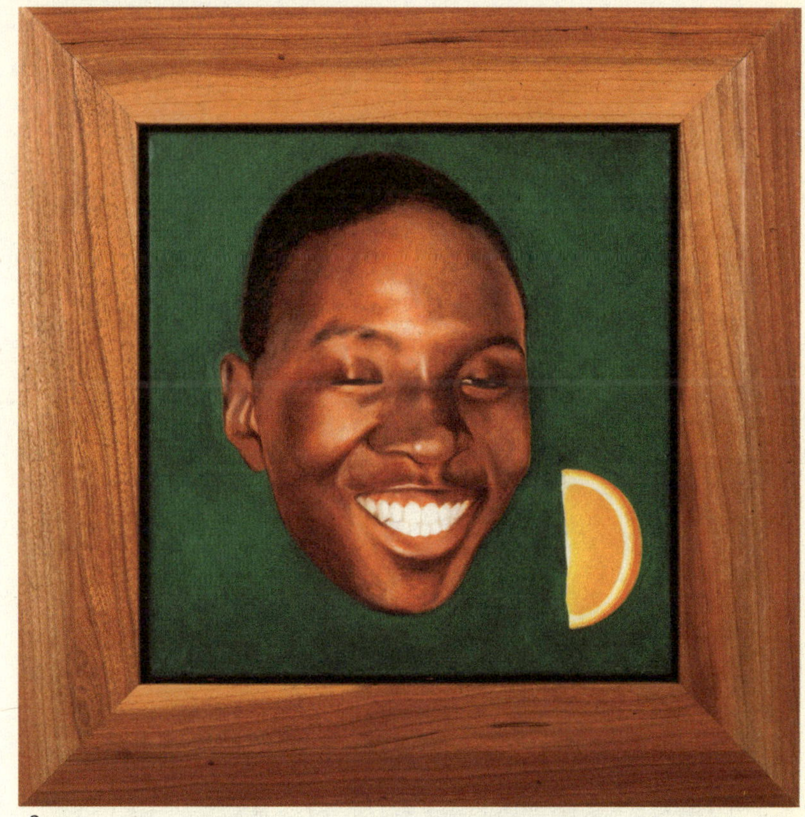

3.

2. Untitled (double eggs)
2004, oil on plaster, eggshell, and leather, 4 ¾ × 3 ¼ × 1 ¾ in (12 × 8 × 4 cm)

3. Untitled
2005, oil on linen, frame, 11 ¾ × 11 ¾ (30 × 30 cm)

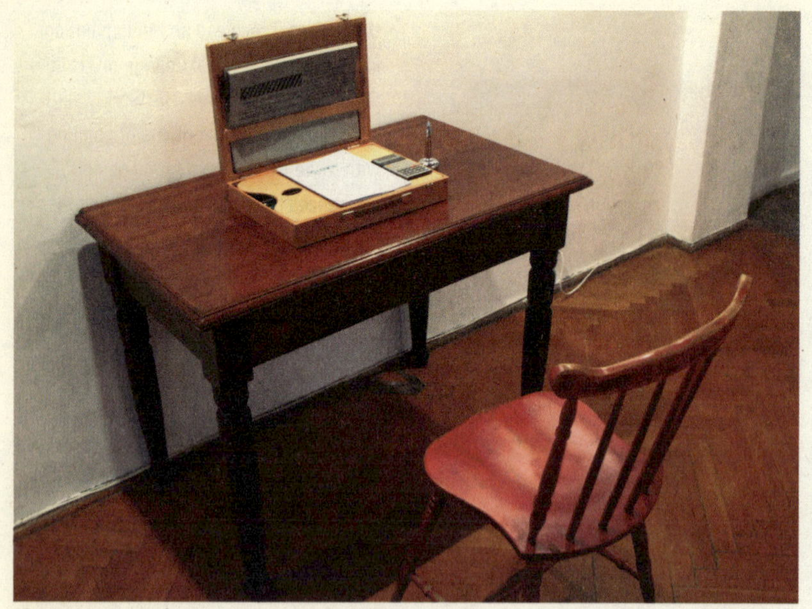

1.

2.

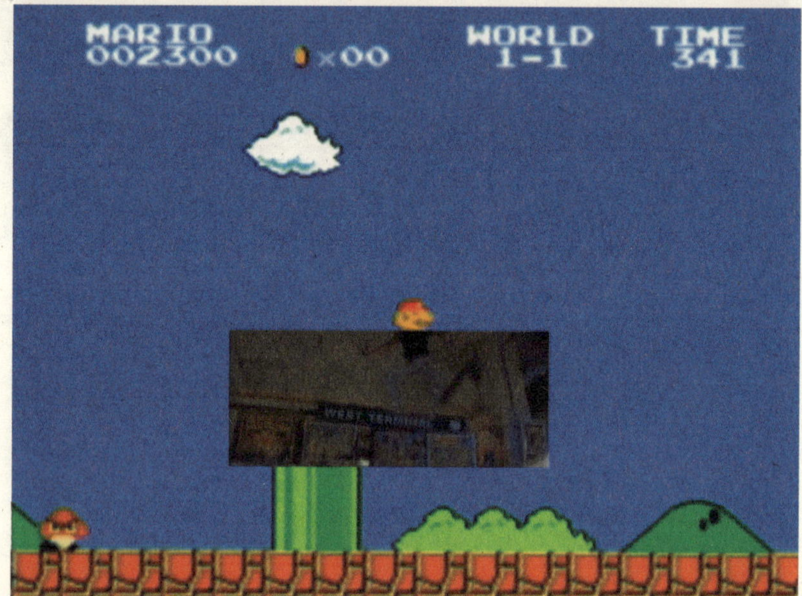

4.

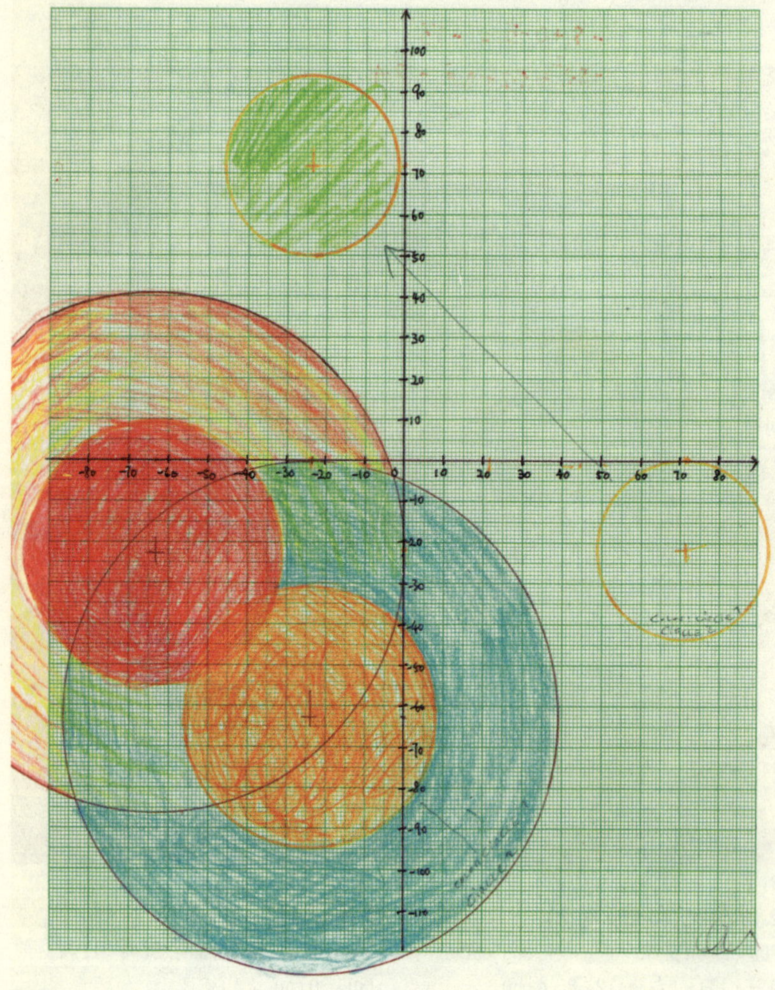

3.

Eric Siu plans to graduate with an MFA in 2010 from the University of California, Los Angeles, where he currently lives. In his performances and interactive-media projects, he deconstructs digital images. In his **Optical Handlers – eeyee** (2008), he created a goggle device that splits vision into four channels. The installation was comprised of the performance, a video of the performance, one set of goggles viewers could try, and four small screens allowing the public to view what the person was seeing.

1. **the grARTphicator**
2008, interactive installation, mixed media, dimensions variable

2. **Sliding Whites**
2005, video, 9 min

3. **grARTph** from **the grARTphicator**, (detail)
2008, interactive installation, audience invited to draw on graph paper with equations they are given, dimensions variable

4. **Super Cop World**
2005, video, 5 min

Jiří Skála studied at the Prague Academy of Fine Arts and lives and works in Prague. He is cofounder of the Etc. Gallery in Prague. His installations, performances, and videos often involve participants in gamelike interactions and draw on his interest in communication. **Handwriting Exchange**, for example, is an ongoing work in which Skála and strangers become acquainted through a three-month process of learning how to copy each other's handwriting.

1. **Mikrofiltration**
with Marek Ther
2001, performance and mixed media installation, dimensions variable

2. **Exchange of Handwriting**
2006, performance

3. **Helvetica Concentrated**
with Angela Detanico and Rafael Lain
2003, computer font

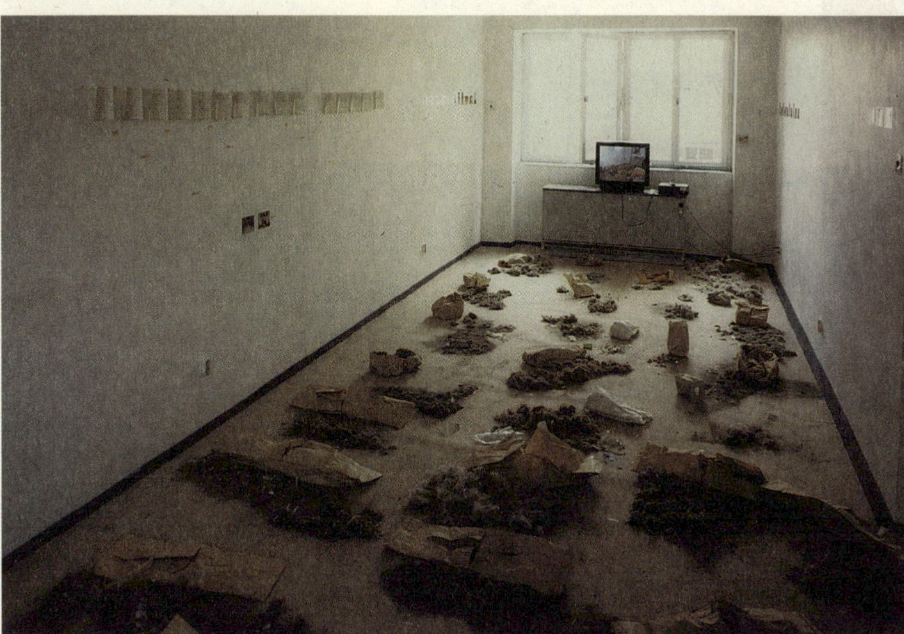

1.

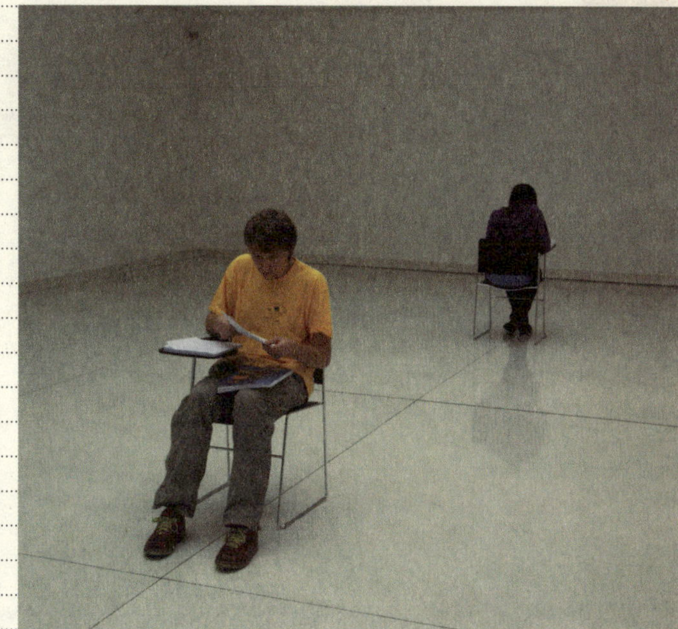

2.

3.

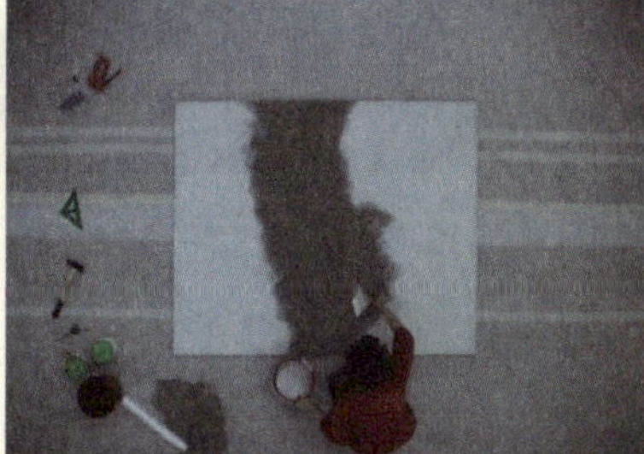

4.

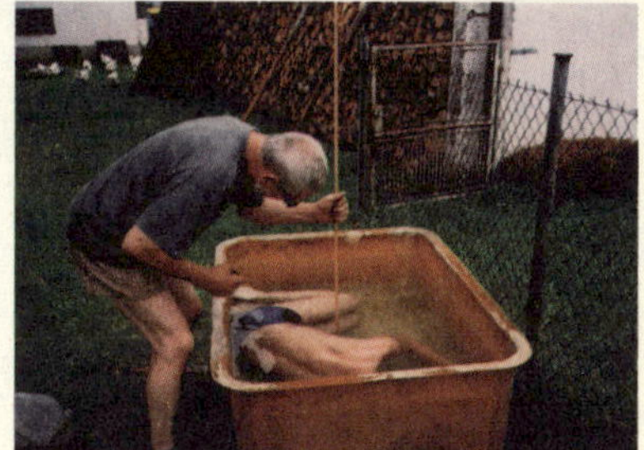

5.

4. **Local Stigma**
2004, video installation

5. **Every Volumes of Every Members of my Family**
2002, digital photograph

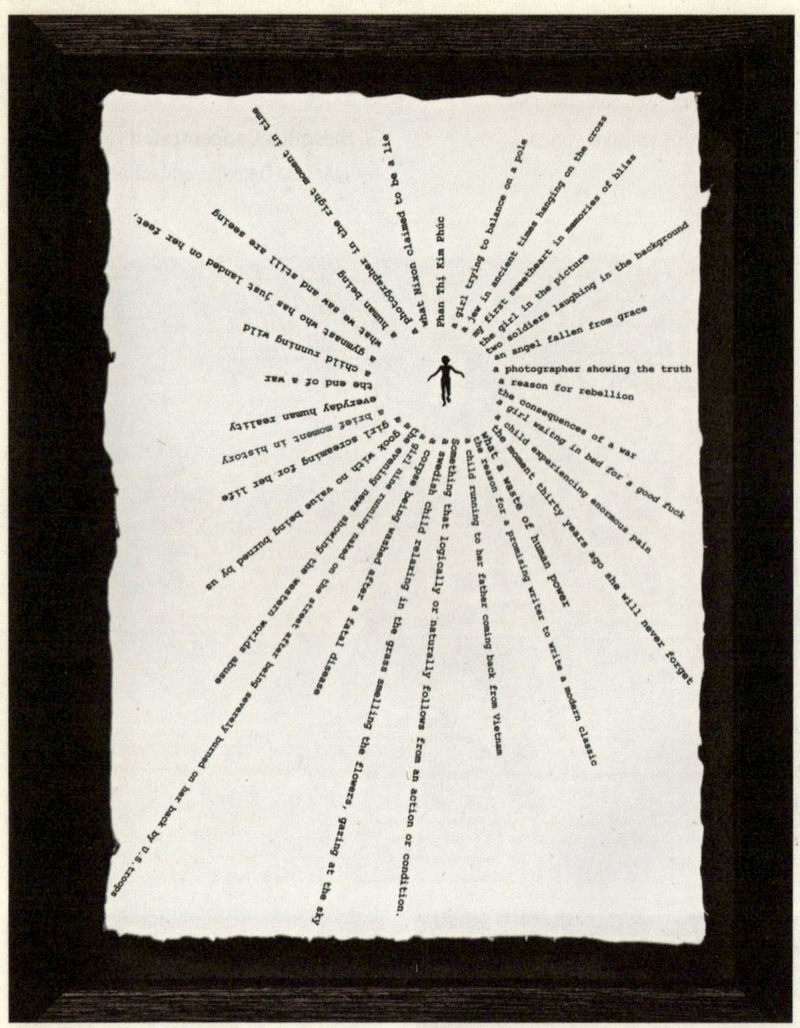

1.

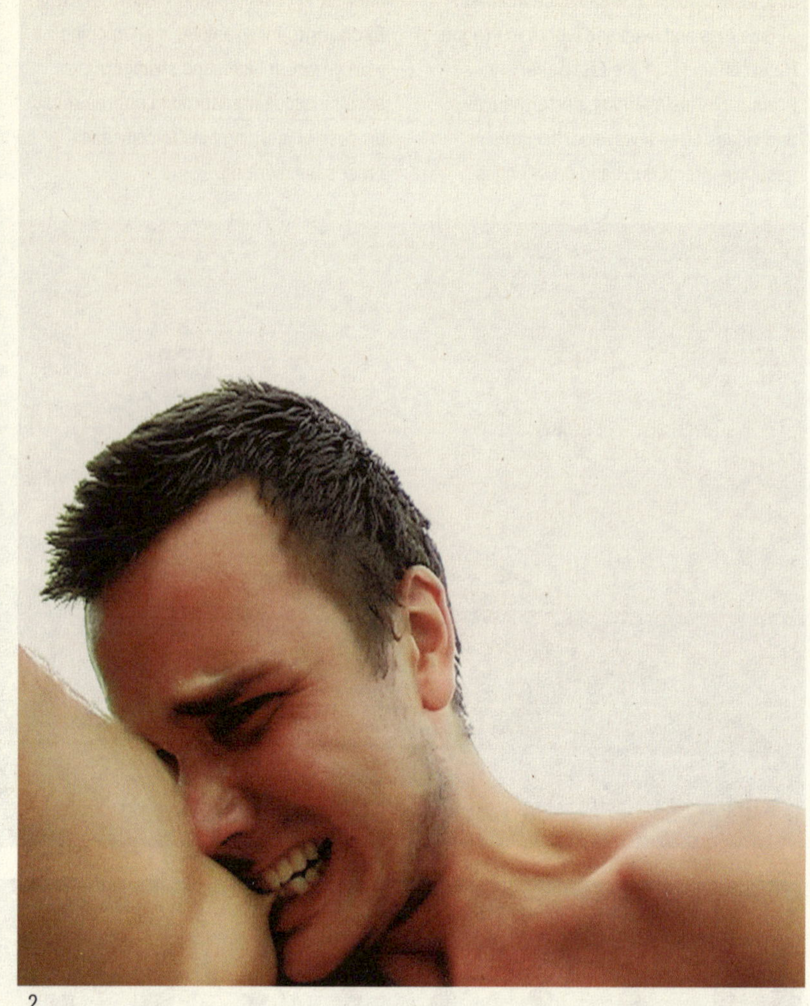

2.

Kristian Skylstad graduated from the Academy of Fine Arts, Oslo, where he lives and works. He runs two art spaces in Oslo, Galuzin and TAFKAG. His photographs, performances, and videos deal with the construction of masculine identity. His video **Love Me So** (2007) shows the artist, intoxicated and smoking a cigarette while he dances in a hotel room, playing with the idea of the disillusioned, self-destructive artist.

1. The Girl in The Picture
2008, inkjet print on rice paper with reflex-free and polarized glass, 9 ½ × 14 in (24 × 36 cm)

2. Deathication
2007, video, 10 min 41 sec

3. How To Disappear Completely
2007, mixed media, dimensions variable, installation view

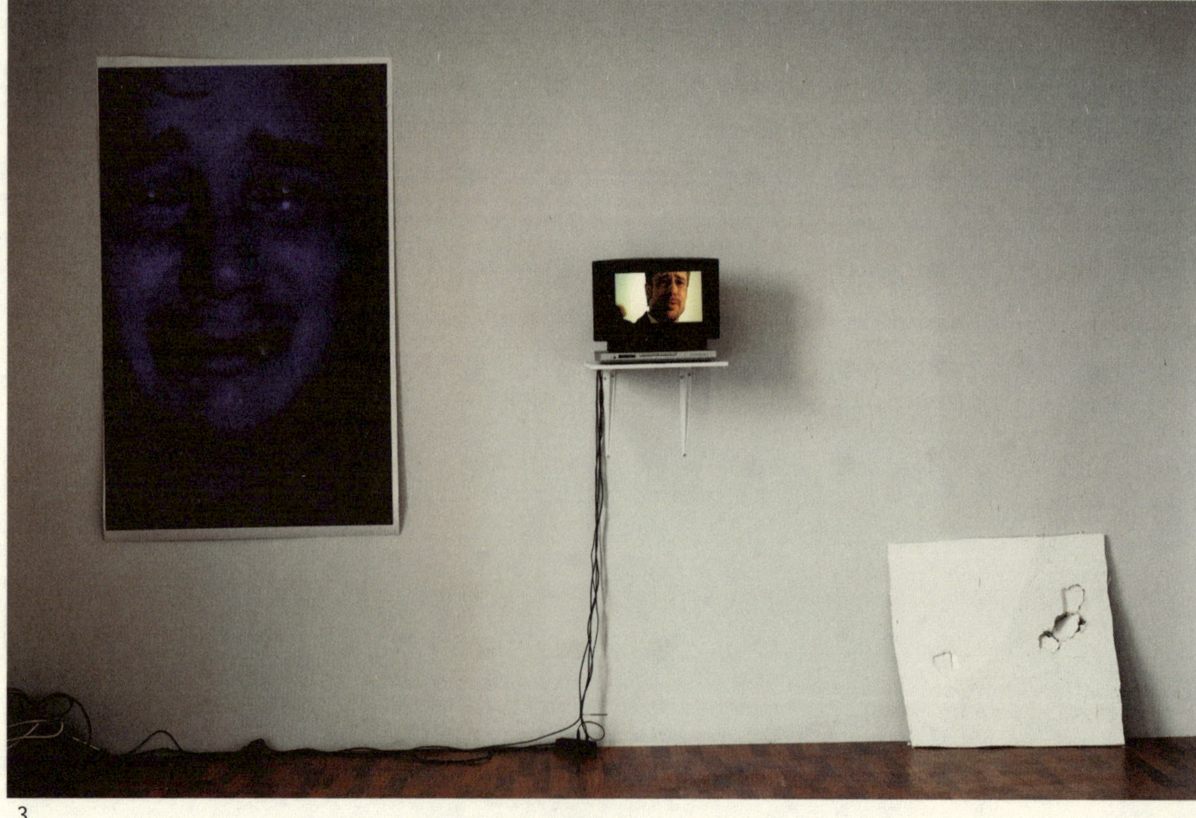

3.

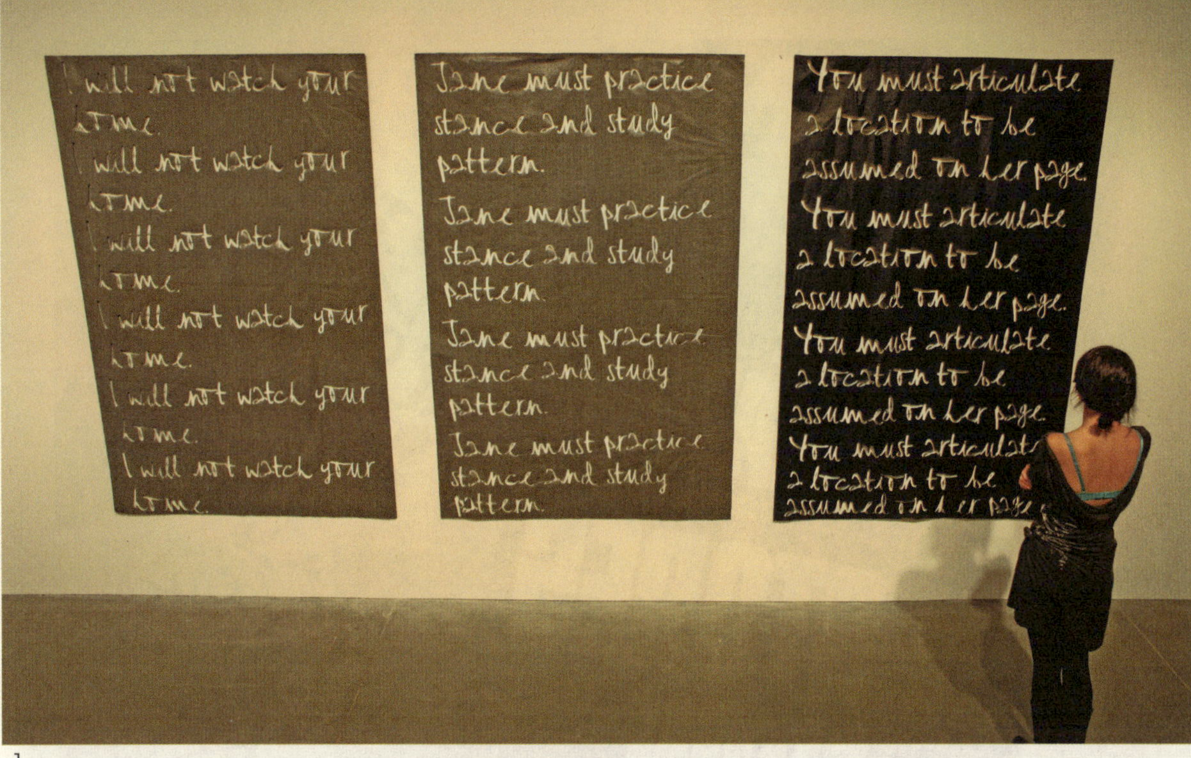

1.

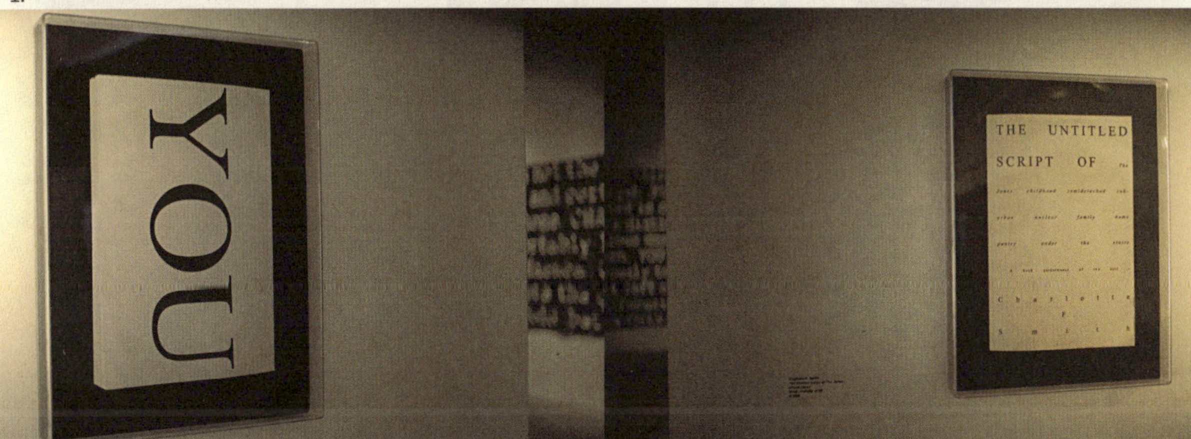

2.

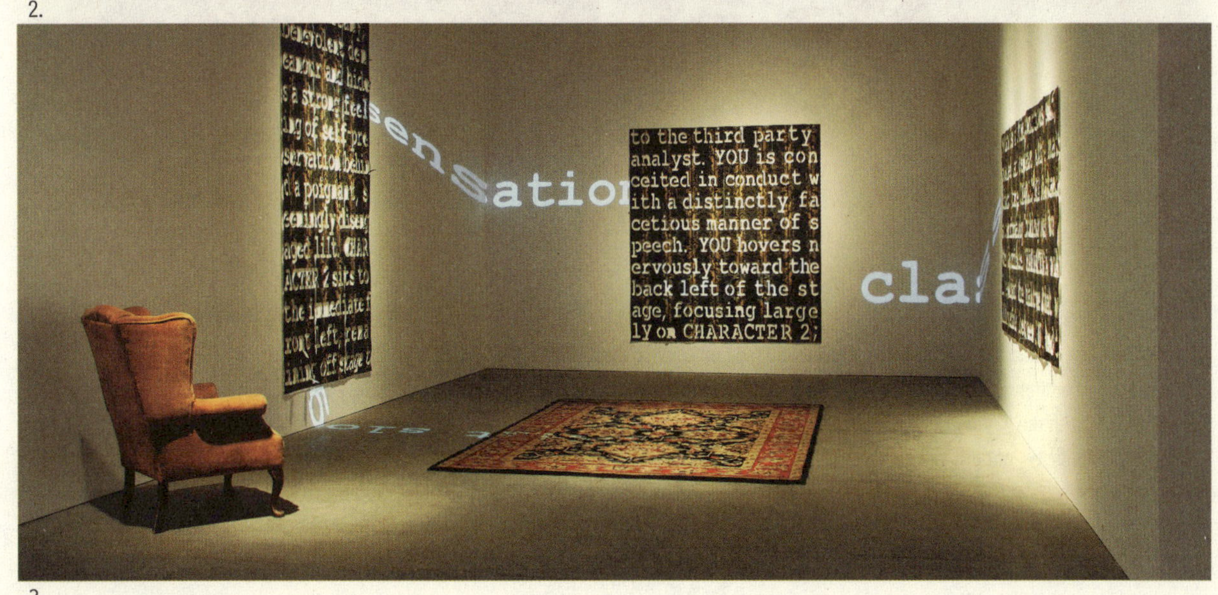

3.

Charlotte Smith graduated with an MFA in 2008 from the University of California Los Angeles. She currently lives and works in Culver City, California. Her work incorporates wallpaper, book projects, and video projections to explore language and concepts of place. Her paintings incorporate experimental texts and fragmented writing techniques. She is a member of [insertspace], a curatorial group in Birmingham, UK, that facilitates art projects in public sites.

1. (left) **I will not watch your home;** (center) **Jane must practice stance and study pattern;** (right) **You must articulate a location to be assumed on her page**
2008, black-ink carbon paper and steel pins, 3 parts, each 6 ¾ × 15 ft (2 × 5 m)

2. **The Untitled script of the Janes' childhood semidetached suburban nuclear family home pantry under the stairs**
2008, framed book, 6 × 9 in (15 × 23 cm)

3. **The Untitled installation of the script of the Janes' childhood semidetached suburban nuclear family home pantry under the stairs**
2008, wallpaper, carpet, and 3-channel video projection, dimensions variable

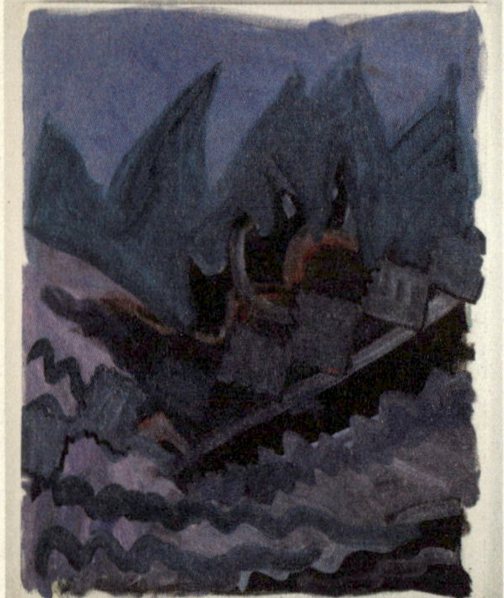

1.

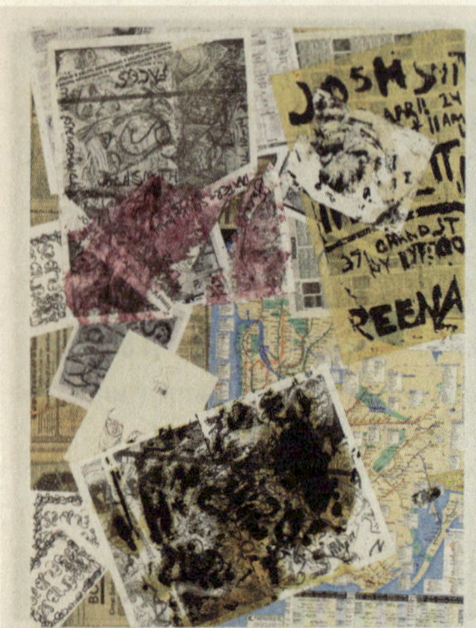

2.

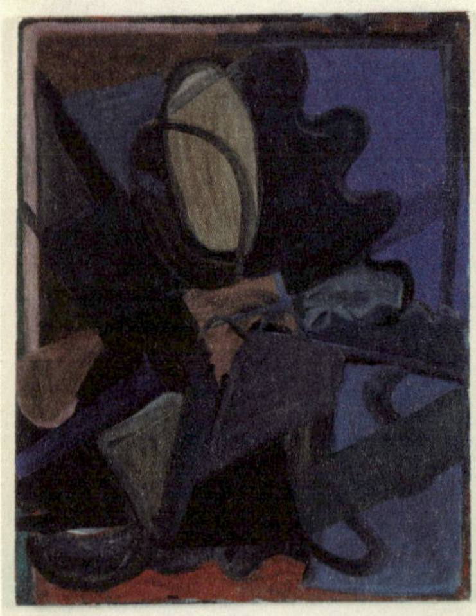

3.

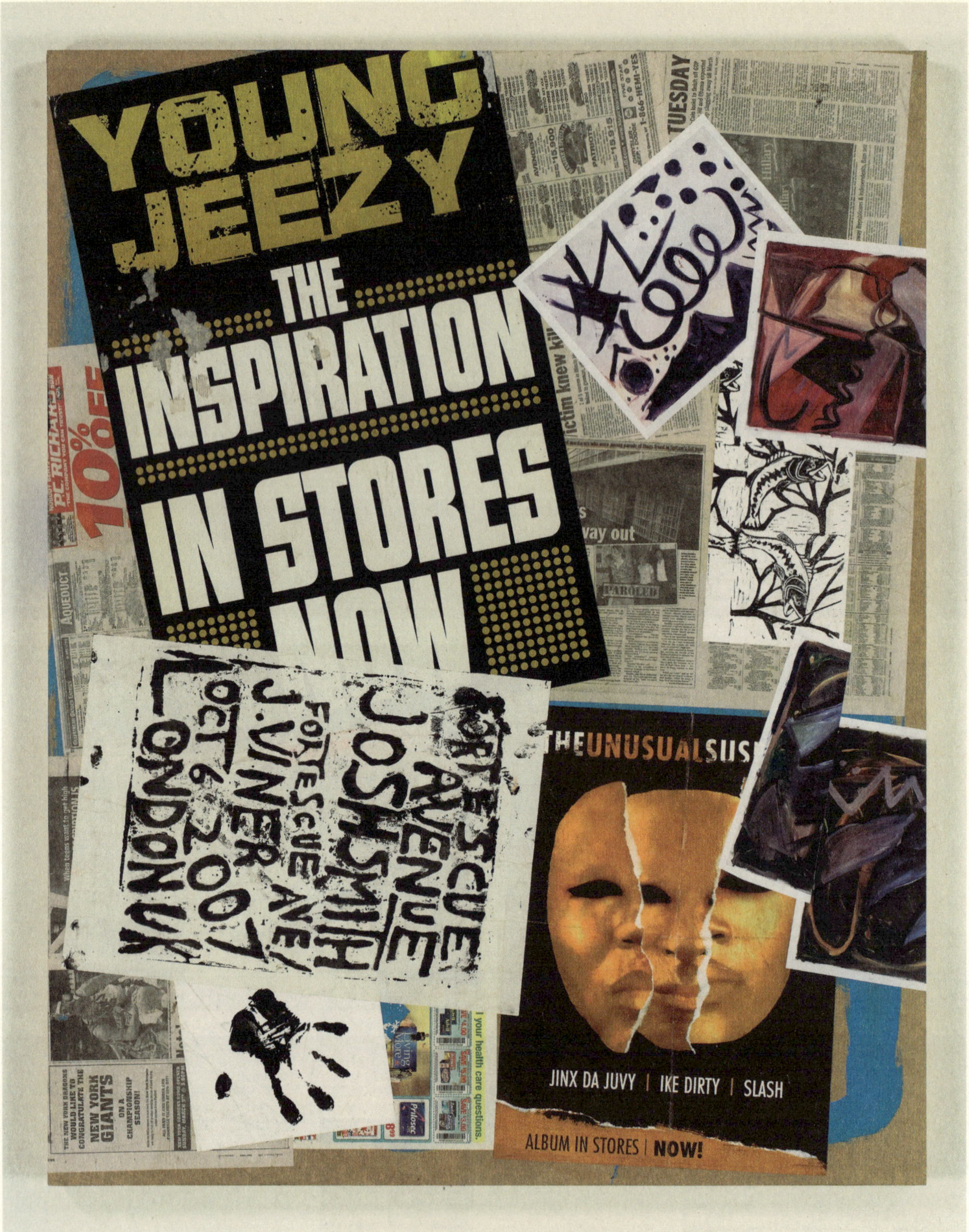

4.

Josh Smith lives and works in New York. He earned a BFA from the University of Tennessee, Knoxville, in 1998. His early works were expressionist, gestural paintings embedded with the letters of his own name. In more recent paintings and prints, this signature is less obvious, but Smith still seems to be playing with the cliches and archetypes of abstract art, wrestling with the history of painting and the "authenticity" of both artist and artwork.

1. **Untitled (JS0503)**
2008, oil on canvas, 60 × 48 in (152 × 122 cm)

2. **Untitled (JSC07346)**
2007, mixed media on panel, 48 × 36 in (122 × 91 cm)

3. **Untitled (JS0757)**
2007, oil on canvas, 60 × 48 in (152 × 122 cm)

4. **Untitled (JSC08060)**
2008, mixed media on panel, 60 × 48 in (152 × 122 cm)

Matthew Smith graduated with an MA from St. Martins College in London, where he lives and works. He has had solo exhibitions at White Columns in New York and at STORE gallery in London. He explores conventions of Conceptual art in his installations, which incorporate such functional objects as shelving, record jackets, and duvets, challenging accepted notions of how those objects are used.

1. **Untitled**
2008, laminated chipboard, wooden spoon, and silicon, $16\frac{1}{2} \times 13\frac{1}{2} \times 12$ in (42 × 34 × 30 cm)

2. **Typical Affair**
2006, shelving, record sleeve, paint, and tape, $39\frac{1}{2} \times 29\frac{1}{2} \times 9\frac{1}{2}$ in (100 × 75 × 24 cm)

3. (left) **Duvet with Stand No. 5**; (right) **Duvet with Stand No. 6**
2007, feather duvet with wooden stand, $55\frac{1}{4} \times 25\frac{3}{4} \times 25\frac{3}{4}$ in (140 × 65 × 65 cm) and $31\frac{1}{2} \times 31\frac{1}{2} \times 23\frac{3}{4}$ in (80 × 80 × 60 cm)

4. **Design For A Window**
2007, towels, $39\frac{1}{2} \times 27\frac{1}{2}$ in (100 × 70 cm)

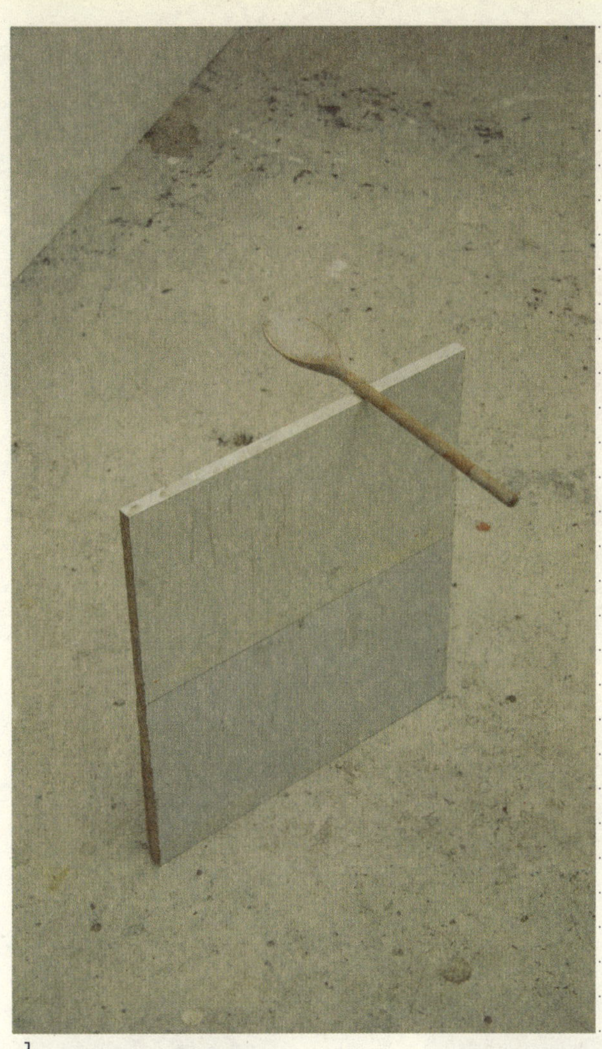
1.

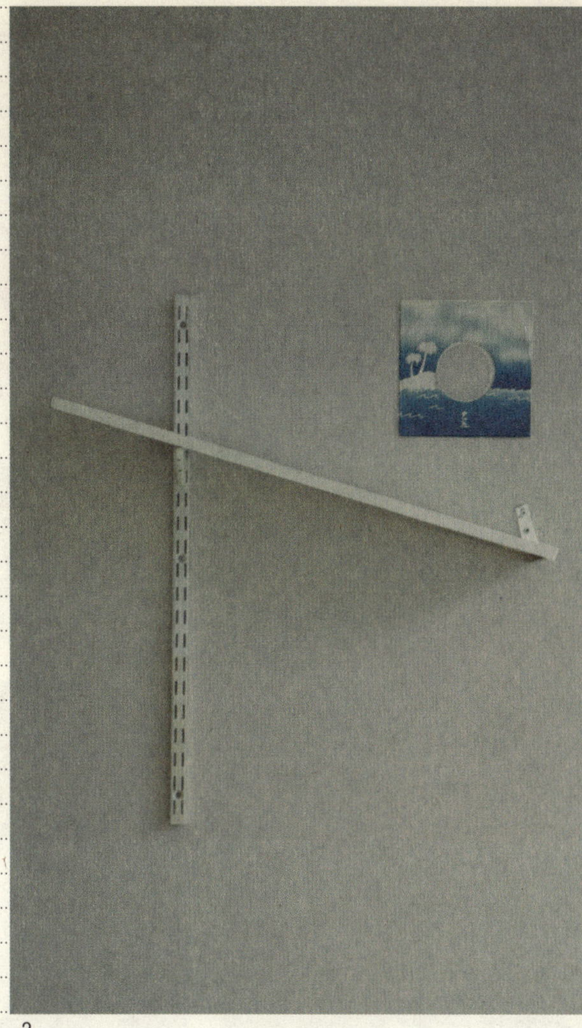
2.

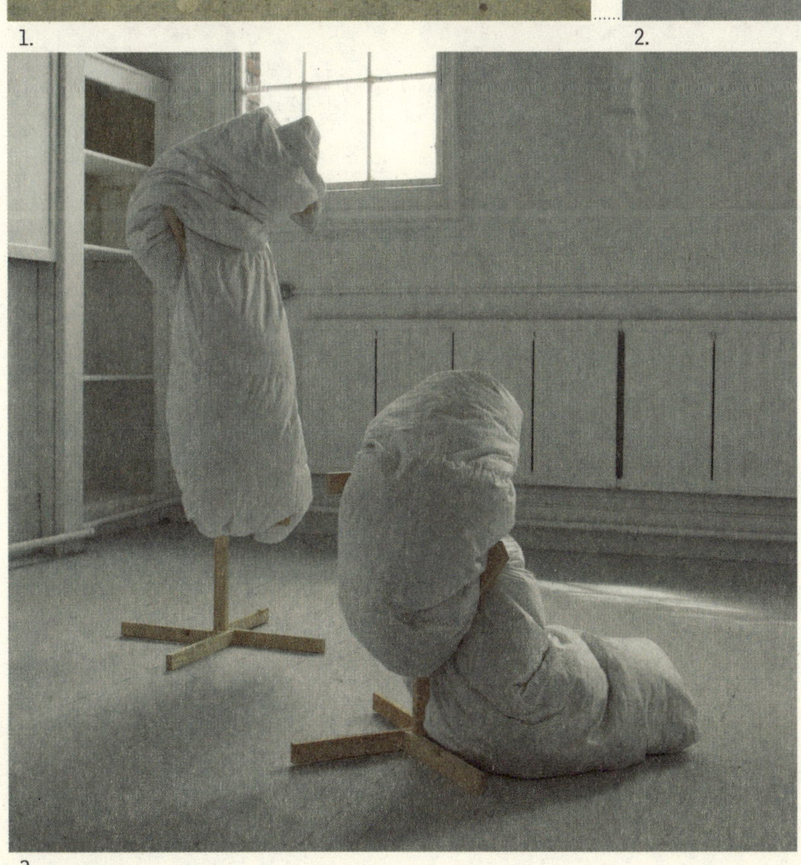
3.

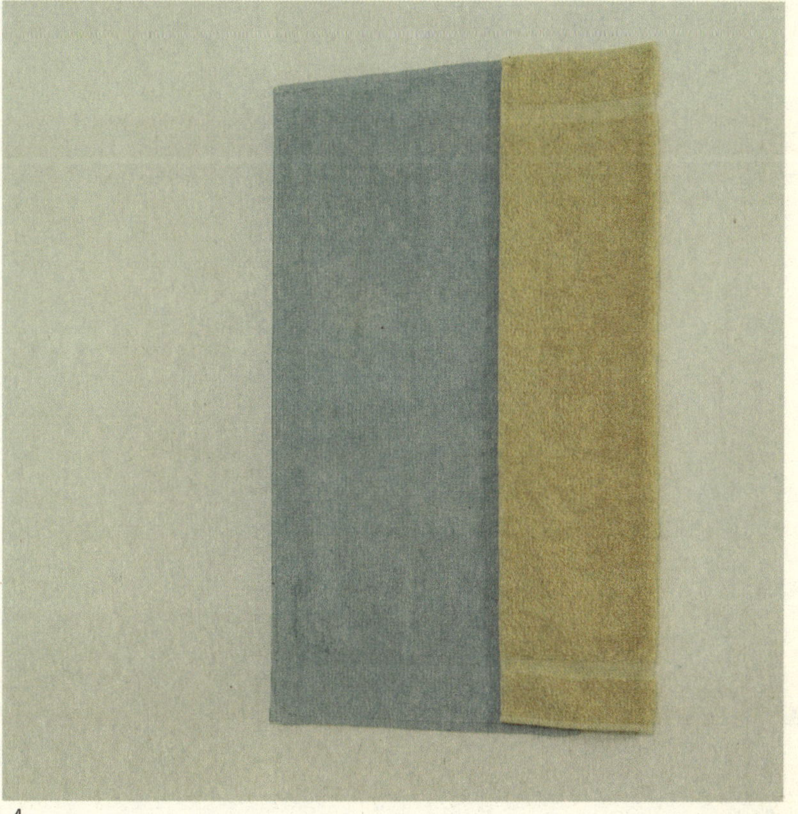
4.

Mark Soo lives in Vancouver, where he graduated from the Emily Carr Institute of Art and Design in 2001. His concept-driven artworks challenge social and civic boundaries. In **Monochrome Sunset (English Bay – Oppenheimer Park),** Soo illuminates the image of a sunset with a sodium light used in Vancouver to discourage drug use, drawing parallels between the acceptable euphoria experienced through watching a beautiful sunset and the drug-induced, chemical high, while simultaneously referencing promotional material produced by the local tourist board.

1. **Monochrome Sunset (English Bay – Oppenheimer Park)**
2006, Duratrans and Duraclear on Plexiglas, aluminum frame, low-pressure sodium streetlights and lamps, blue window film, approx 56 × 108 in (142 × 274 cm)

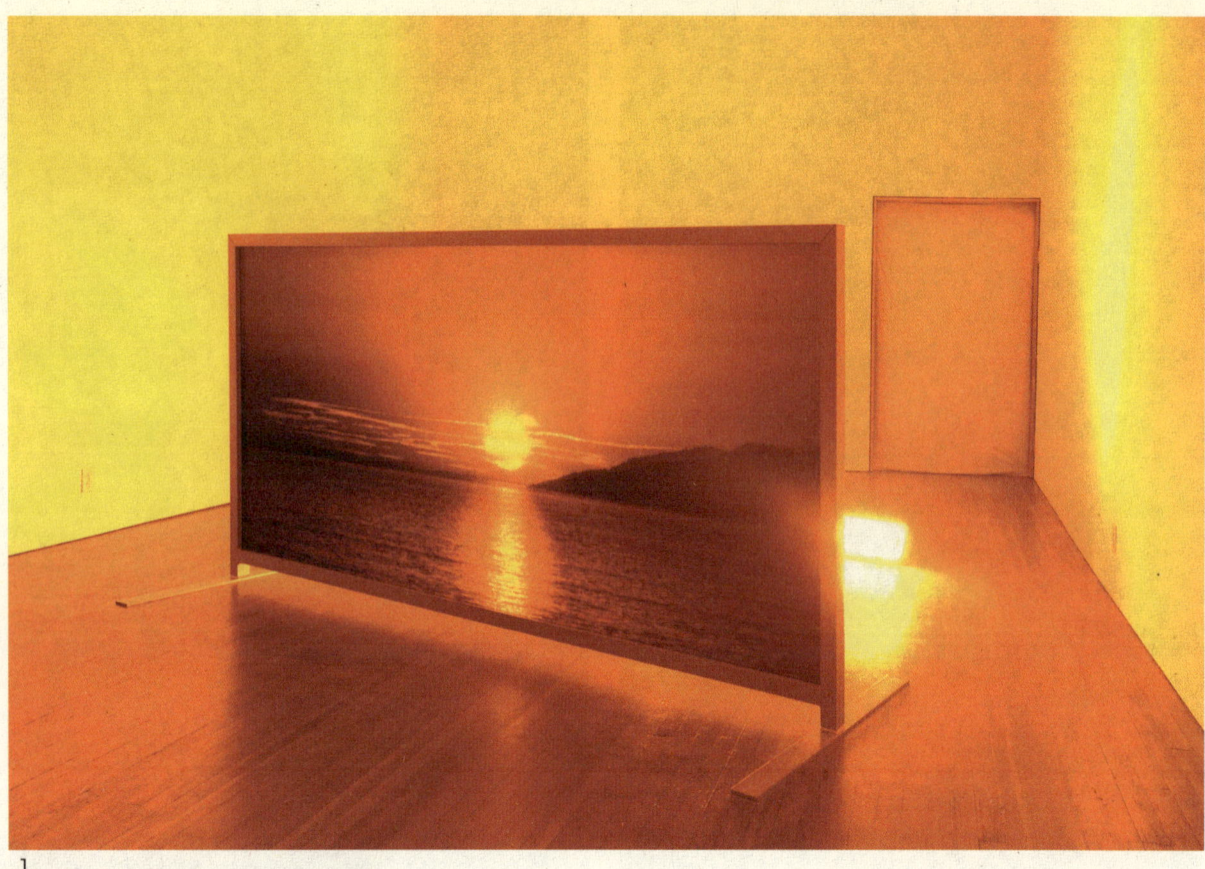

1.

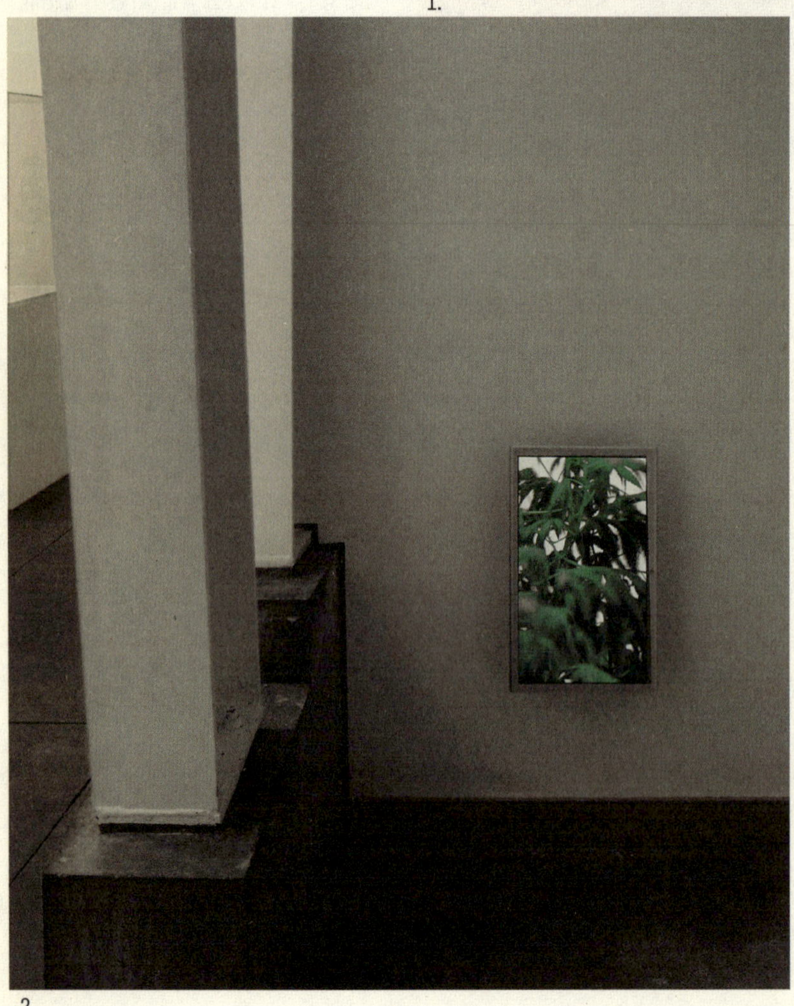

2.

3.

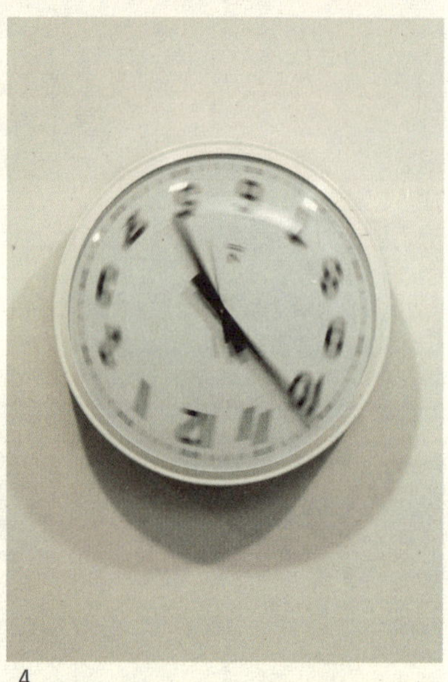

4.

2. **Sweet Life**
2008, video, 1 min 13 sec

3 & 4. **Untitled**
2008, aluminum, glass, mylar, wood, clock, and motor, 17 × 17 × 8 in (43 × 43 × 20 cm)

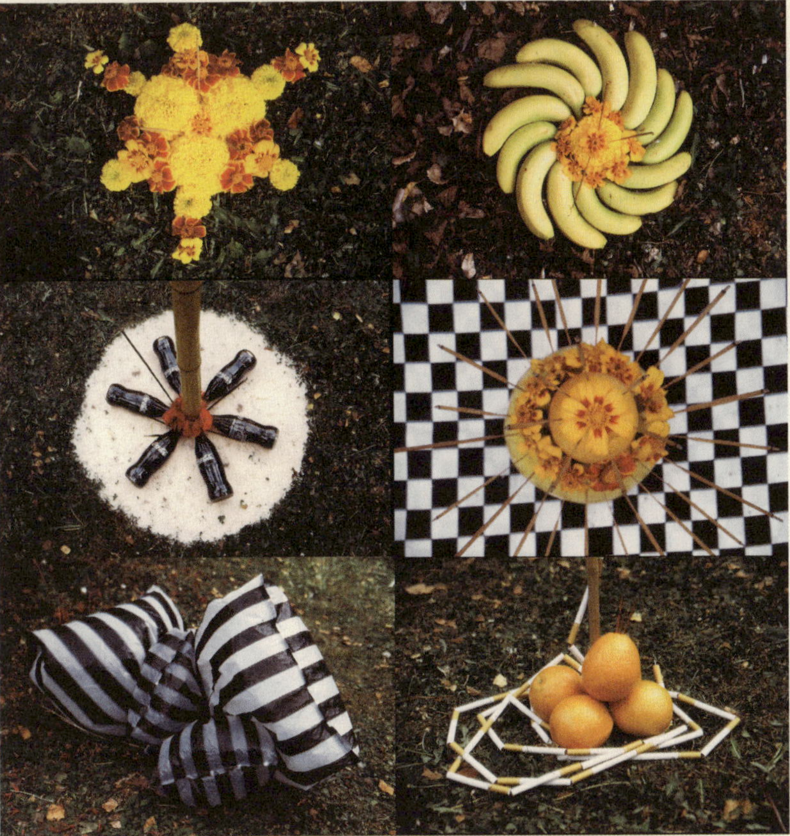

1.

Sriwhana Spong graduated from the Elam School of Fine Arts in Auckland, where she lives and works. Her films and videos have a nostalgic aesthetic that is also suggested by her sound tracks, comprised of music from other eras. Her films and videos, including **7 Days** (2007), have incorporated Balinese garden shrines, which she has reproduced using everyday materials such as cigarettes and Coke bottles.

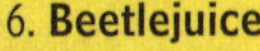

1. **Muttnick**
2005, Super 8 film, 3 min 48 sec

2. **Chatter**
2008, vinyl records and chalk, dimensions variable

3. **Untitled**
2007, lac necklace, pigment, mirror, bells, bobby pins, cigarette, and tobacco string

4. **Symphonic Variations & You Are Older Than Me and I am Younger Than You**
2008, glass beads, nylon, and Coke bottles

5. **Umbrella**
2007, lac and pigment, dimensions variable

6. **Beetlejuice**
2007, Super 8 film, 6 min 21 sec

7. **Candlestick Park**
2006, Super 8 film, 6 min 34 sec

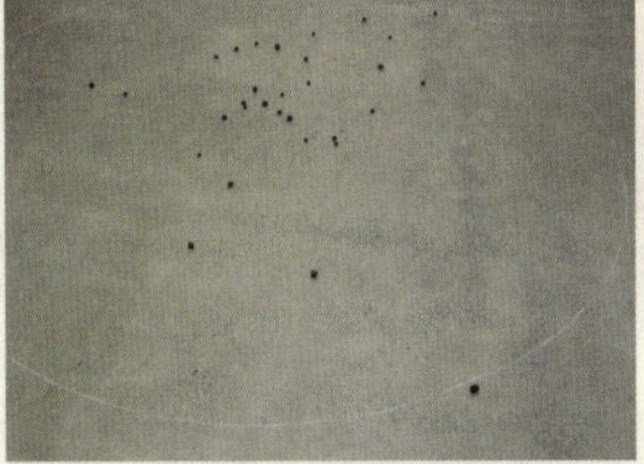

2.

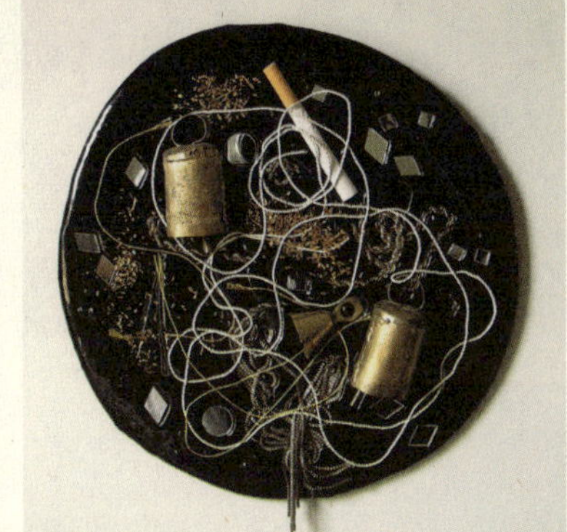

3.

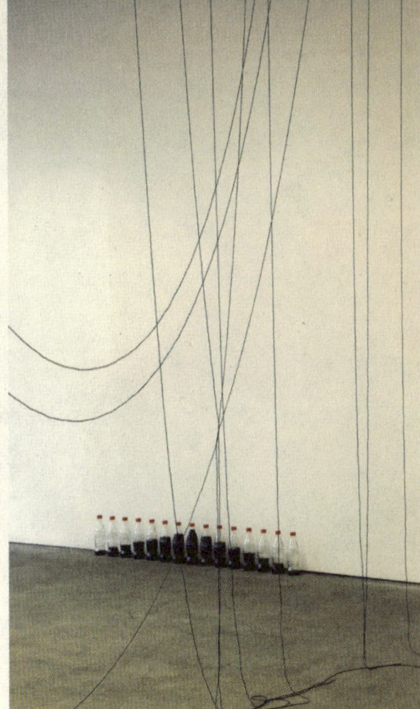

4.

5.

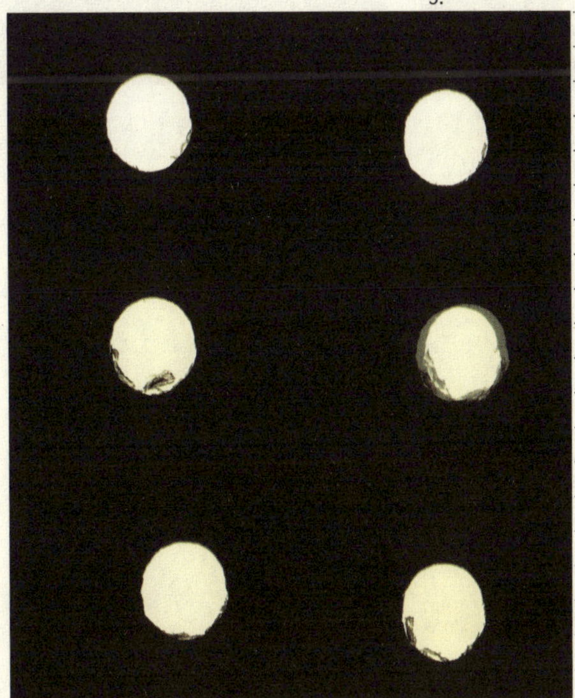

6.

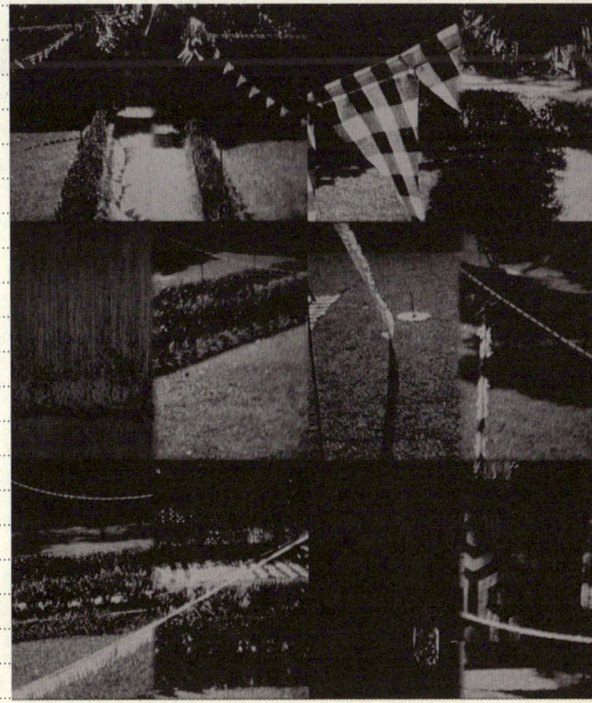

7.

STRICKER, MONIKA

b. 1978 Düsseldorf, Germany

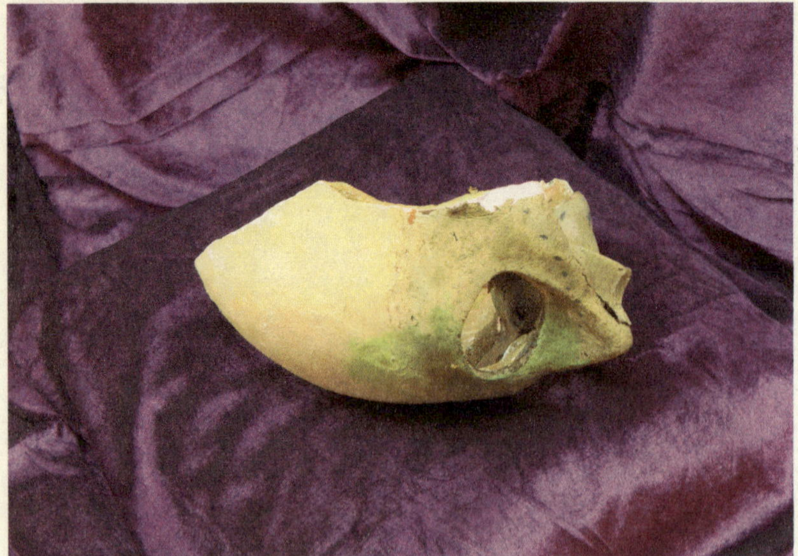

1.

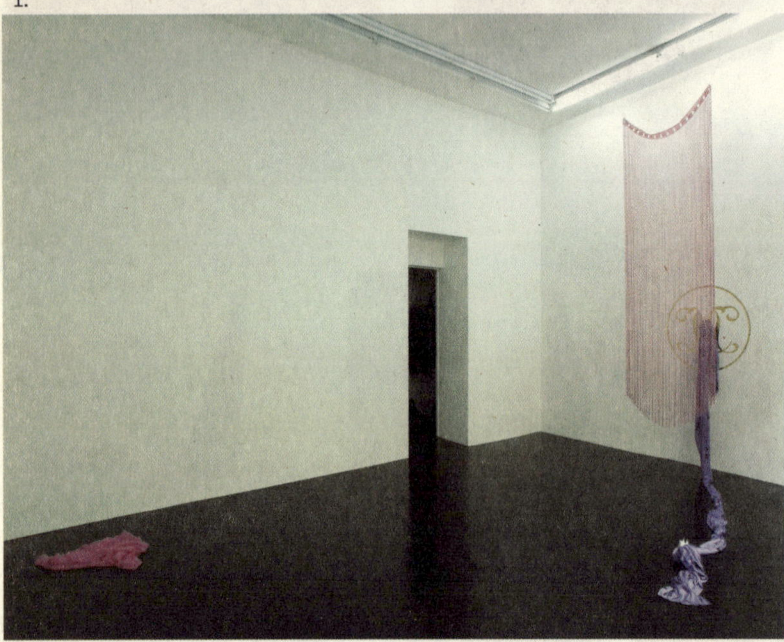

2.

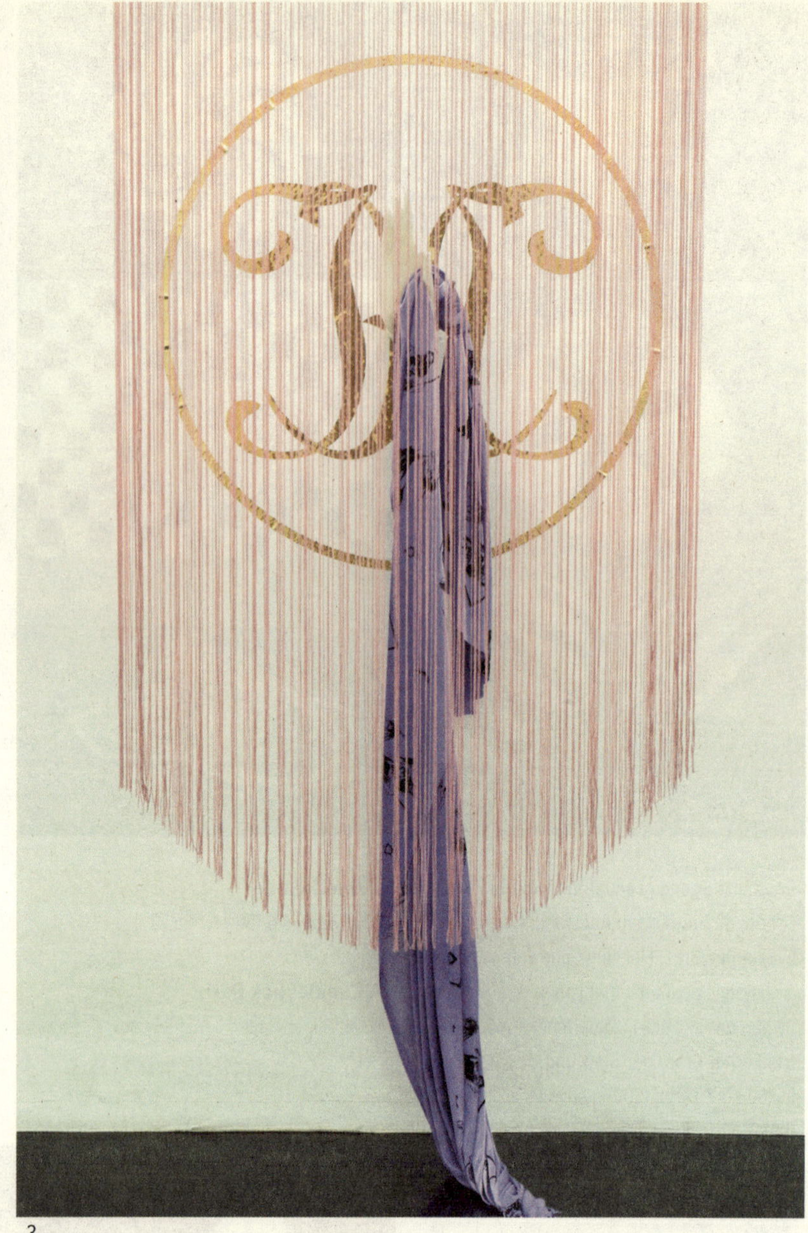

3.

Monika Stricker graduated in 2005 from the Kunstakademie Düsseldorf, where she currently lives and works. Her tactile sculptures, including her installation **Wisteria** (2008) at the Clages Gallery in Cologne, incorporate feminine references: silky fabrics, clutched by a female mannequin's hand, and a curtain of knotted pink nylon. Playing with the stereotypical representation of female hysteria, she makes ironic reference to feminine interiors, namely those of the "Desperate Housewives" who live on Wisteria Lane.

1. **Theatrical Property** (detail)
2007, masks, velvet, embroidery, jewelry, and print, dimensions variable

2 & 3. **Wisteria**
2008, fabric, marble hands, artificial fingernails, curtain, and golden vinyl, dimensions variable

4. **Katalysator**
2008, incense holder (designed by Harry Allen) and paint, 11 3/4 × 6 × 8 in (30 × 15 × 20 cm)

5. **Hook**
2008, Backnobber massage tool and acrylic glass, 23 3/4 × 11 1/2 × 2 1/4 in (60 × 29 × 6 cm)

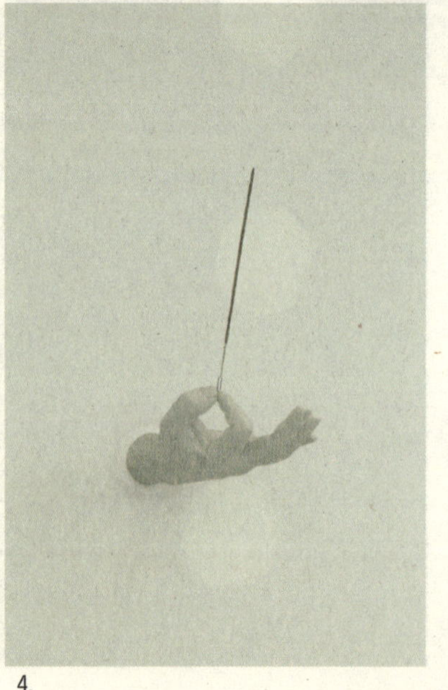

4.

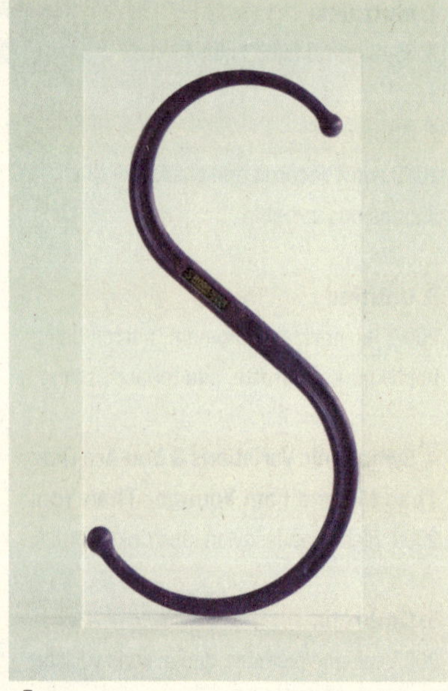

5.

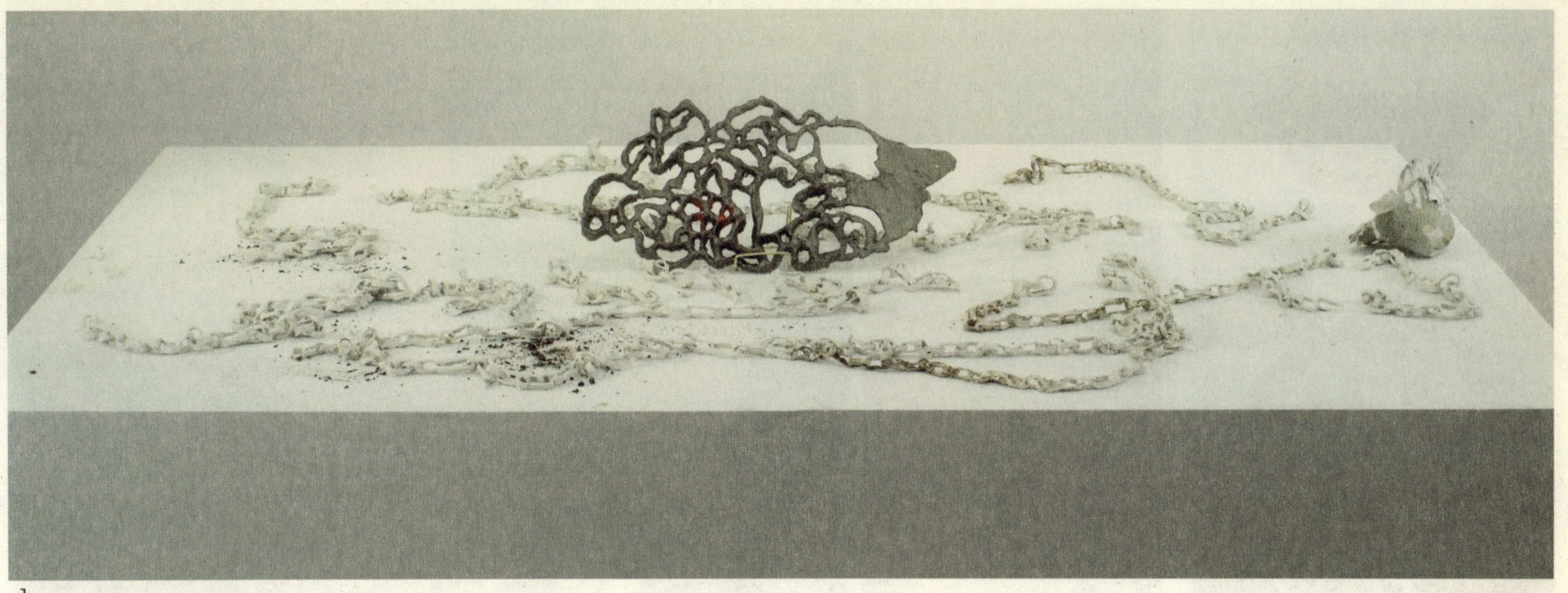

1.

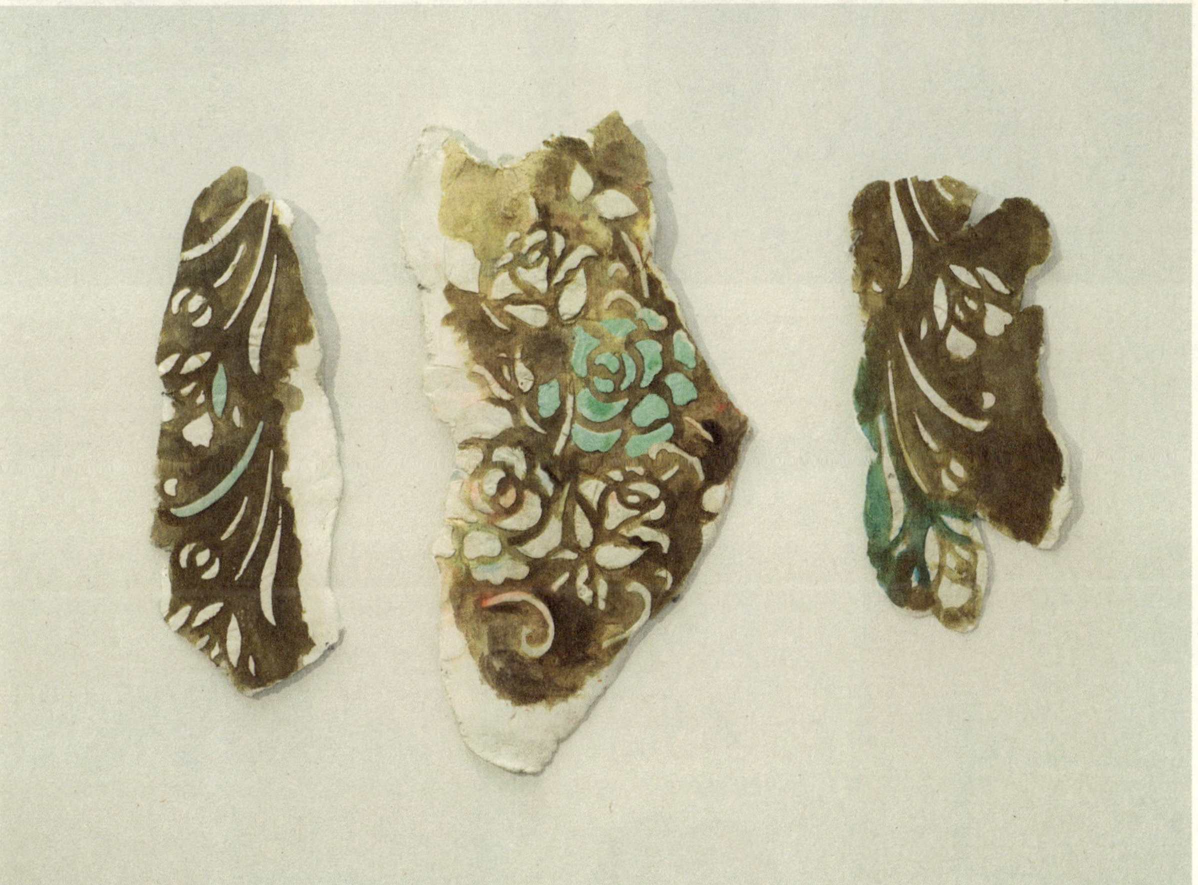

2.

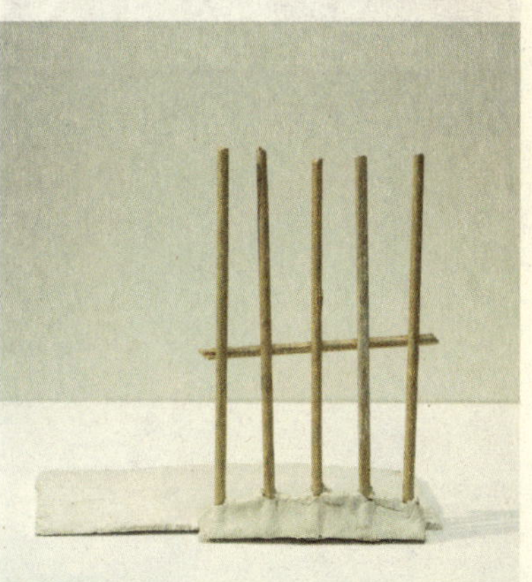

3.

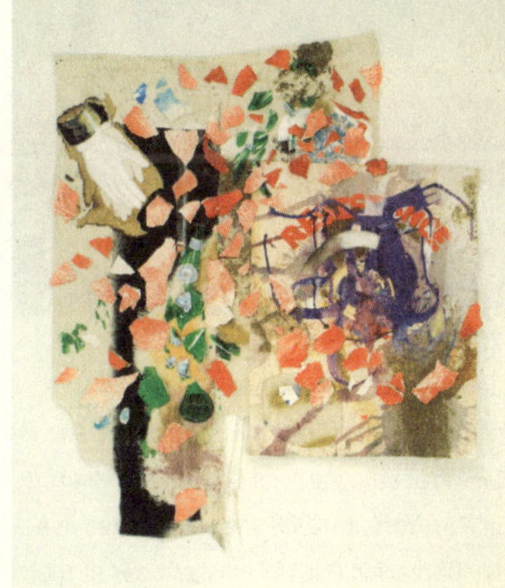

4.

Kianja Strobert earned a BFA from the School of the Art Institute of Chicago and an MFA from Yale University. She lives and works in Brooklyn. Her sculptures and works on paper explore the boundary between art and decoration. Strobert also works with the division between abstraction and figuration, seen in early large-scale metallic and black and white paintings as well as in a series of untitled floral watercolor paintings and ceramics from 2007.

1. Untitled
2007, raw clay, sugar, and dirt, dimensions variable

2. Chinoiserie Plate
2007, raw clay and paint, 3 parts: 9 ½ × 3 ½ in (24 × 9 cm); 11 ¾ × 6 in (30 × 15 cm); 8 × 4 in (20 × 10 cm)

3. Prison
2007, raw clay and wood, 5 ¼ × 4 ½ in (13 × 11 cm)

4. Untitled
2007, mixed media on canvas, 39 ½ × 37 in (100 × 94 cm)

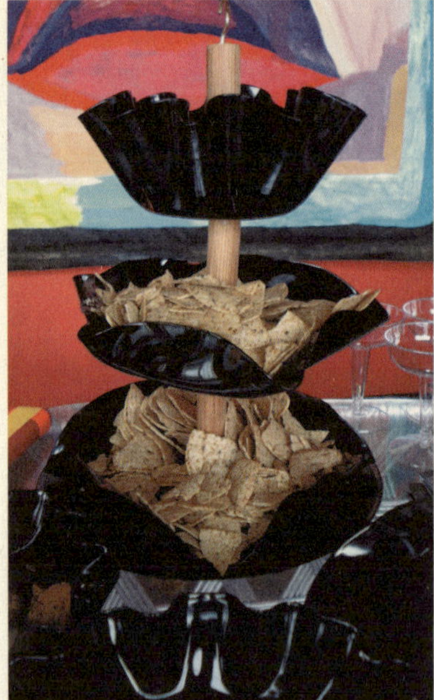

1.

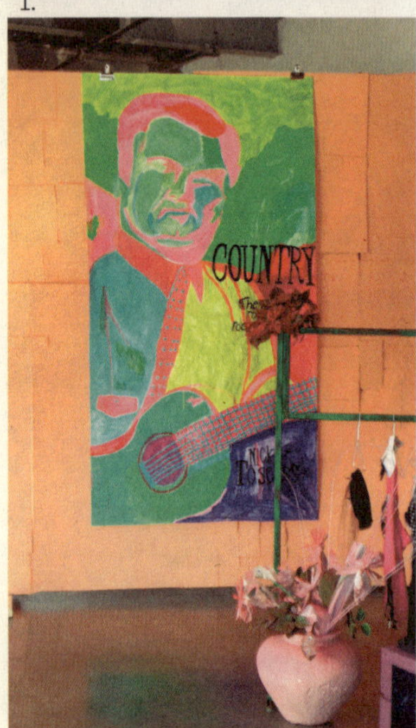

2.

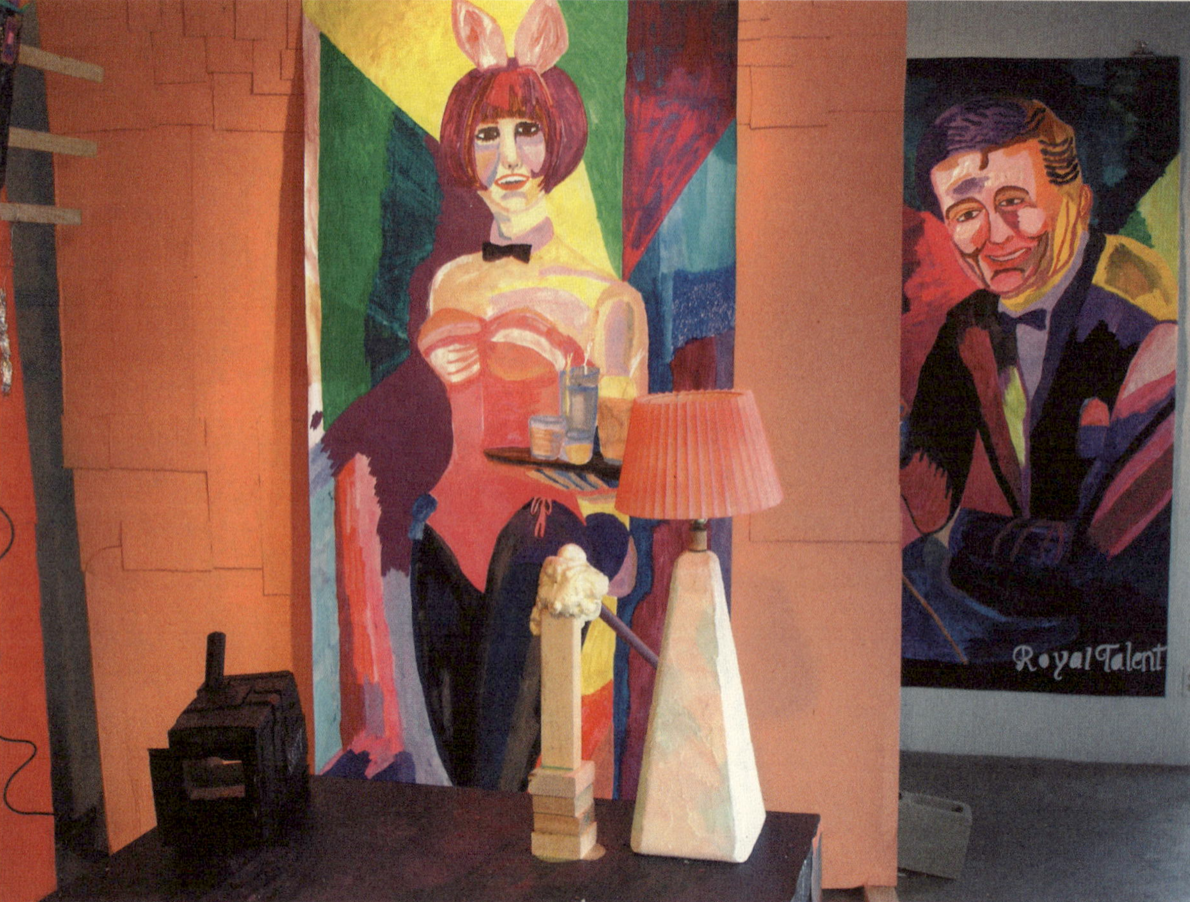

3.

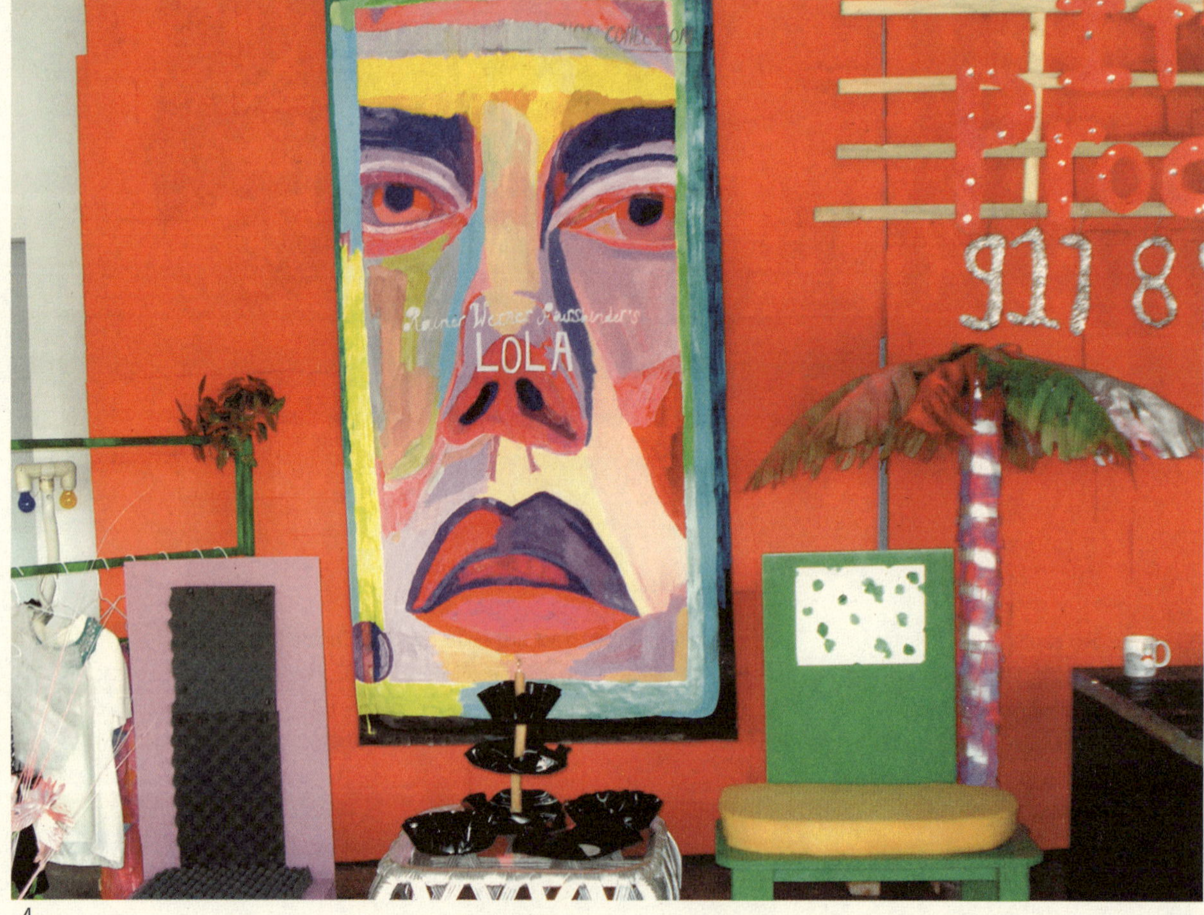

4.

Jennifer Sullivan earned a BFA in sculpture from Pratt in Brooklyn and an MFA from the Parsons School of Design in New York. In 2008 she participated in a My Barbarian PoLAAT master class at the New Museum in New York. She currently lives and works in Brooklyn. Her videos, performances, paintings, and sculptures include gouache, ink, and collage on paper, and paintings of scenes from such classic films as Klute and Pickpocket.

1, 2, 3 & 4. **It's a Process TV Studio**
2008, mixed media, dimensions variable

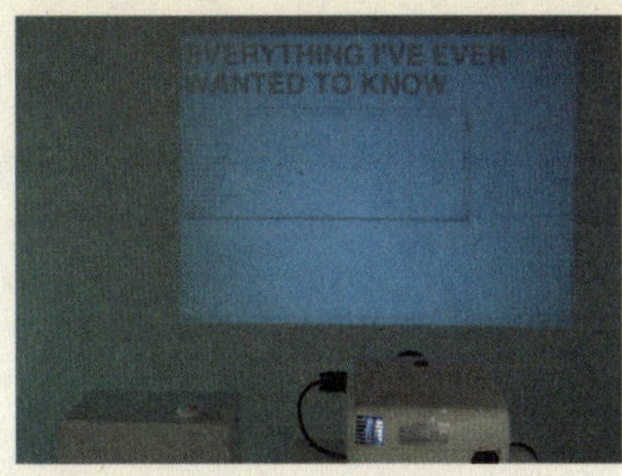

1.

Martine Syms lives and works in Chicago. She incorporates autobiographical elements into her digital work, in which she reorganizes found images, texts, and footage to alter their original meaning.

1 & 2. **Everything I've Ever Wanted to Know**
2007, HTML

3. **Untitled (Noah)**
2008, video, 18 × 24 in (46 × 61 cm)

EVERYTHING I'VE EVER WANTED TO KNOW

2.

Where did you come up with that?

You're not artistic and you have no integrity.

3.

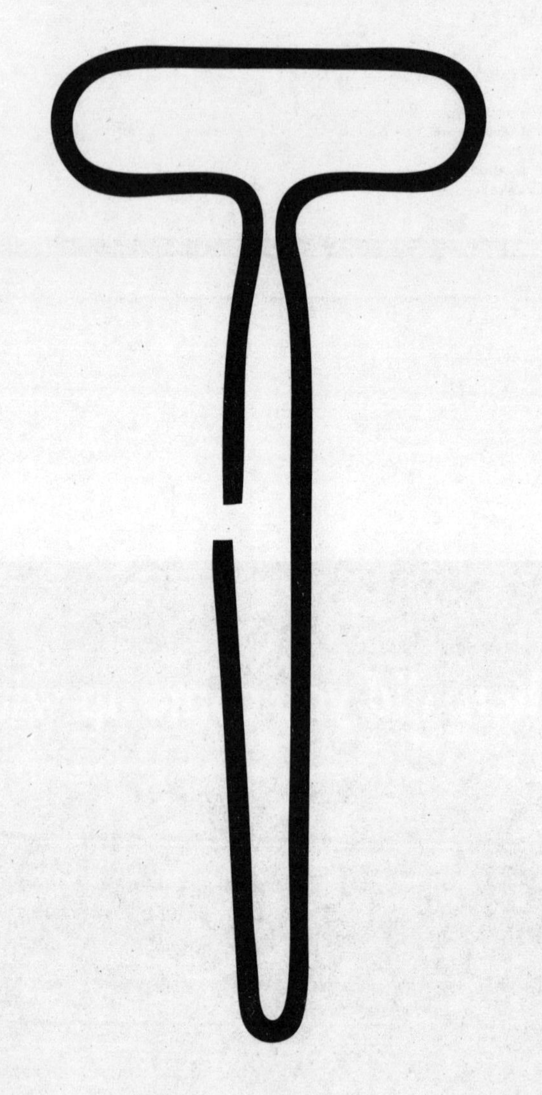

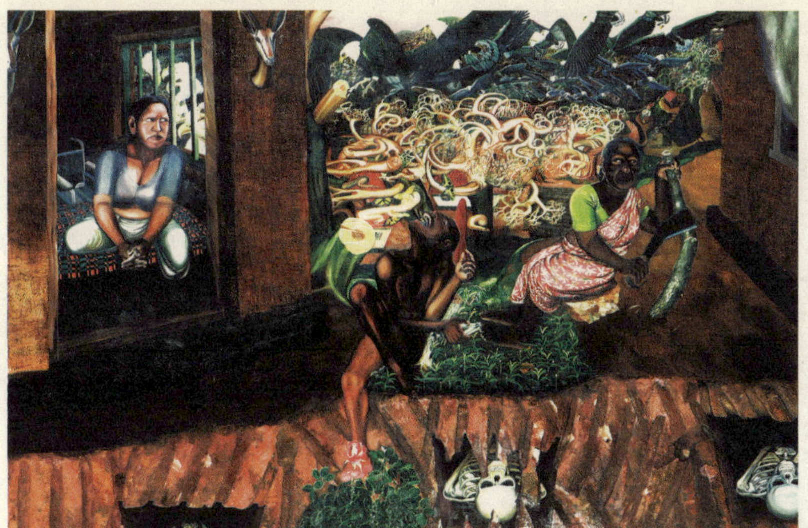

Ratheesh T. received his BFA in painting from the College of Fine Arts in Trivandrum and was invited to the UK on a Royal Over-Seas League Scholarship in 2004. His lush, multivalent paintings are constructed from dense narrative ecologies that are tinged with magic realism. Thematically, his work explores the intersections of the rural and the urban, the natural and the man-made, and the secular and the sacred. He currently lives and works in Trivandrum, Kerala, India.

1. Eagles
2006, oil on canvas, 66 × 108 in
(168 × 275 cm)

2. Colorless Gods
2007, oil on canvas, 108 × 66 in
(275 × 168 cm)

3. My Village
2004, oil on canvas, $41\frac{1}{2} \times 75\frac{1}{4}$ in
(105 × 191 cm)

4. Thicket
2007, oil on canvas, 78 × 120 in
(199 × 304 cm)

5. Motherland
2007, oil on canvas, 72 × 84 in
(183 × 214 cm)

1.

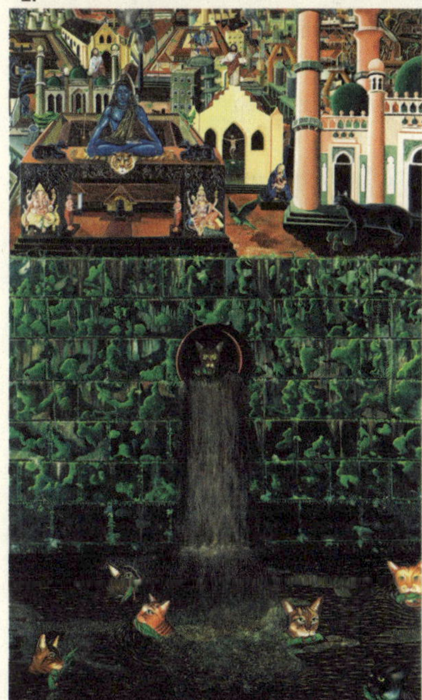

2.

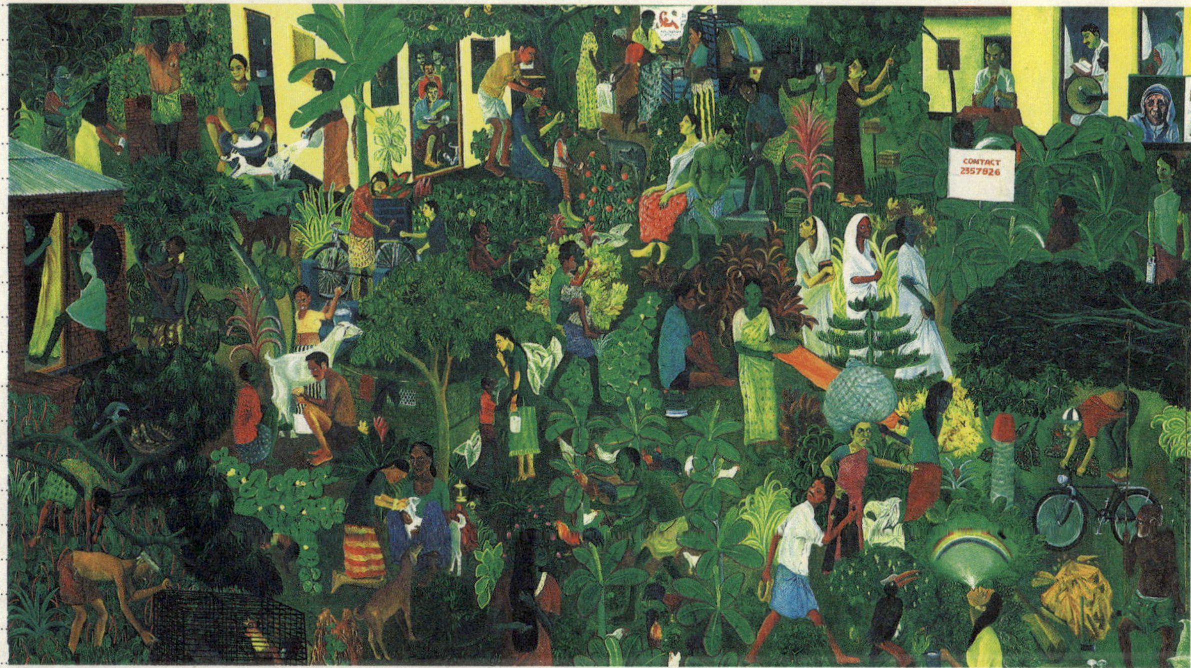

3.

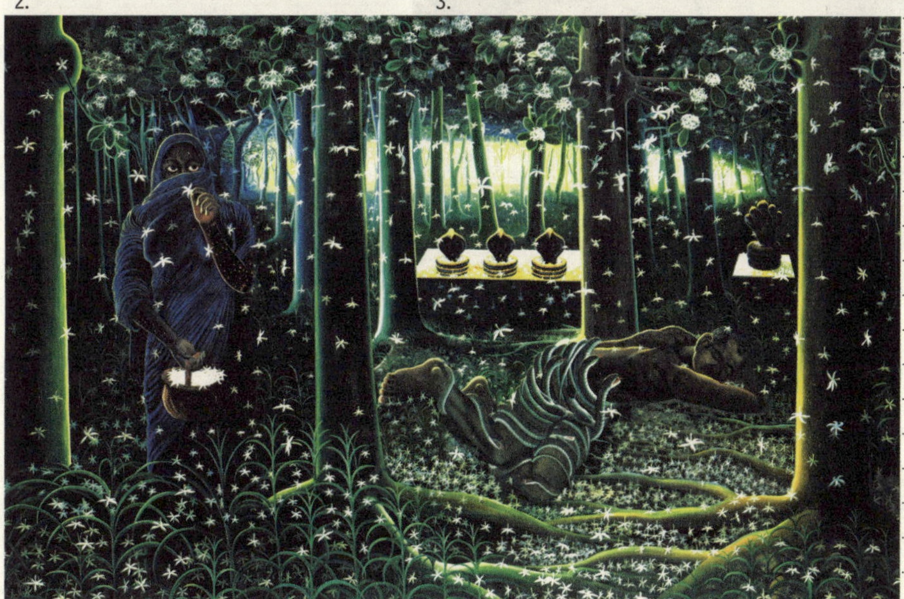

4.

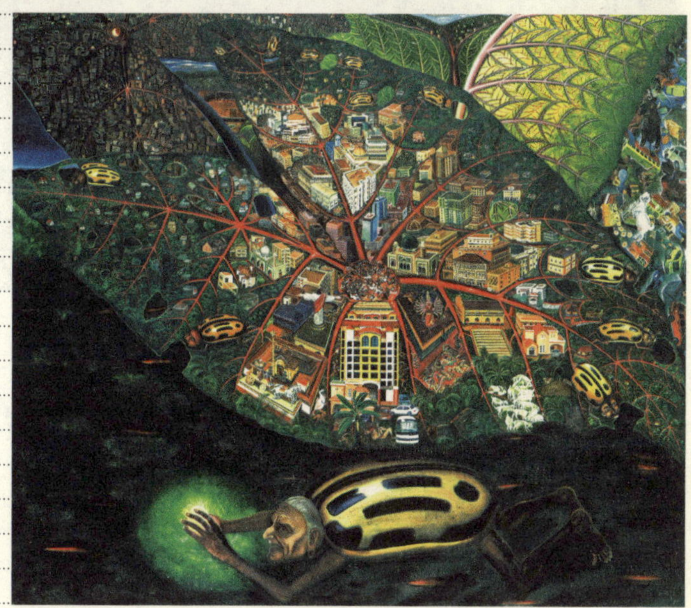

5.

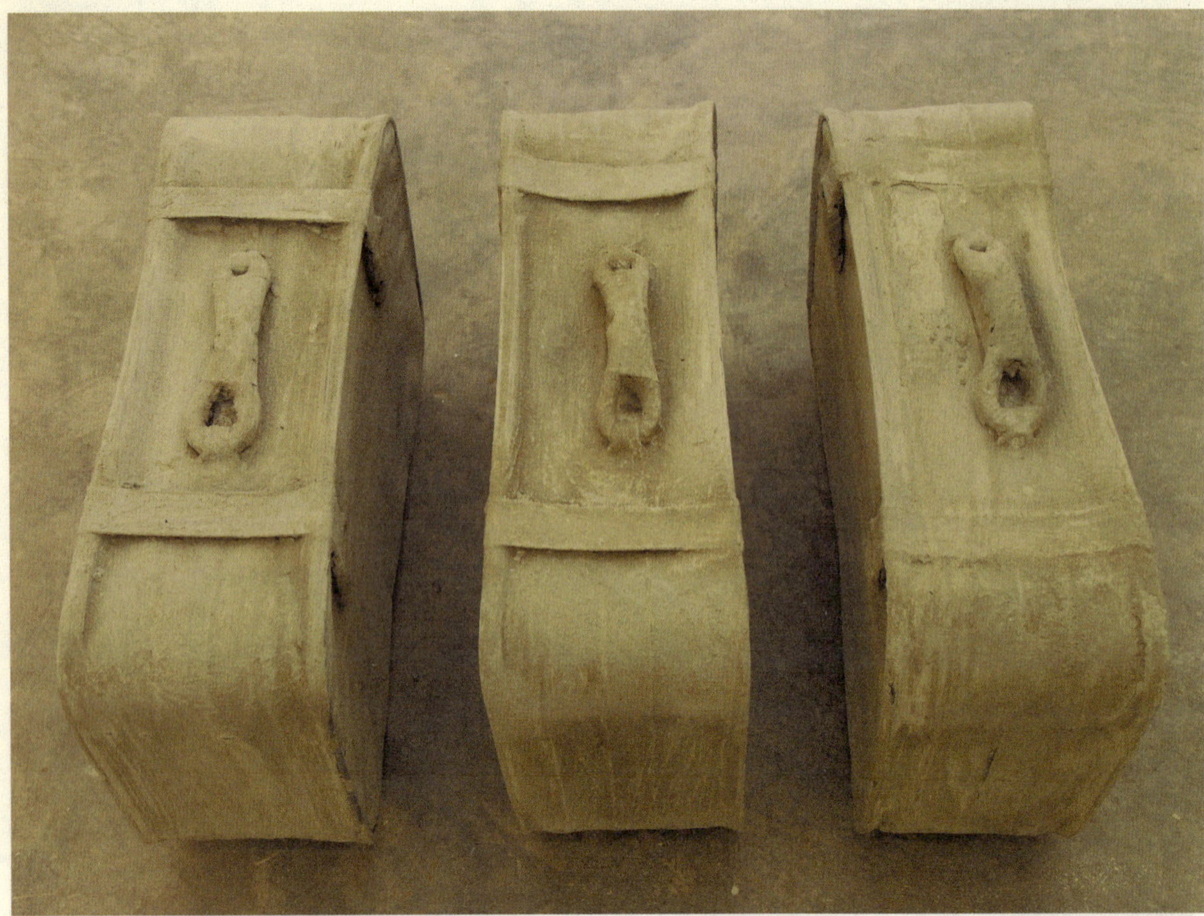
1.

Rayyane Tabet studied architecture and urban planning at the American University of Beirut and earned a BA in architecture from the Cooper Union in New York, where he lives and works. He is a founding partner of Ballman Tabet, an art and architecture partnership in New York. His drawings and installations, which draw on his memories of spaces and objects from his childhood in Beirut, include **Fossils** (2006), an installation of cement suitcases. The artwork references his memory of having a suitcase packed by the side of his bed in case he and his family had to flee.

1. **Machines of War, Fossils**
2006, concrete-covered suitcases, dimensions variable

2. **The Trans-Arabian Pipeline, Km. 1121 – Km. 1213**
2007, table, videos, models, drawings, photographs, documents, and text, 42 × 360 in (107 × 914 cm)

3. **Machines of War, String Duet**
2005, mattress, cotton strings, nails, and neon light, dimensions variable

4. **The Trans-Arabian Pipeline, After the Flood: Reversing the Trans-Arabian Pipeline**
2008, digital collage, 24 × 144 in (61 × 366 cm)

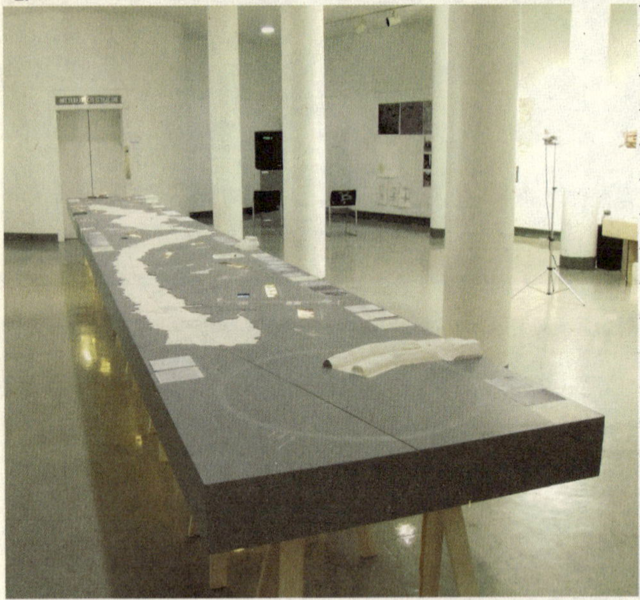
2.

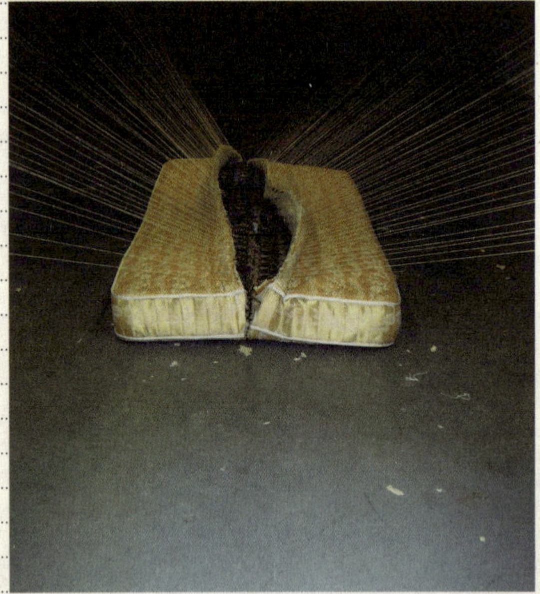
3.

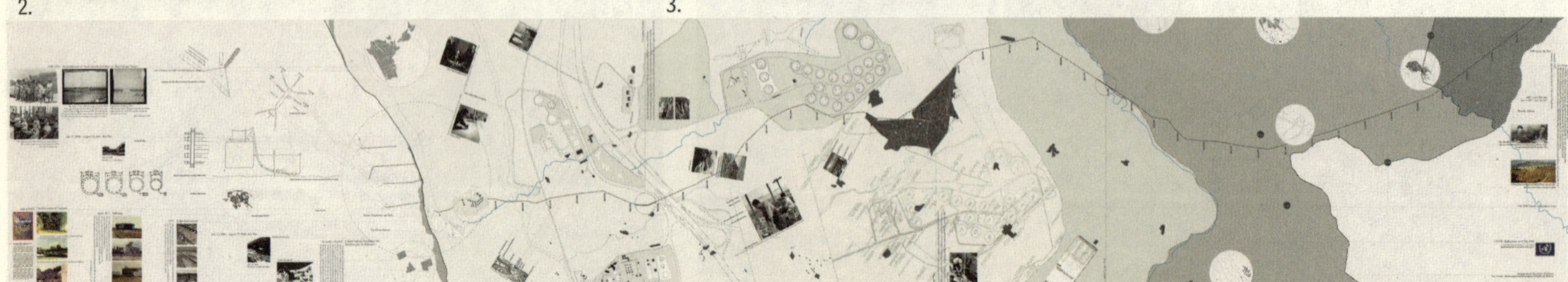
4.

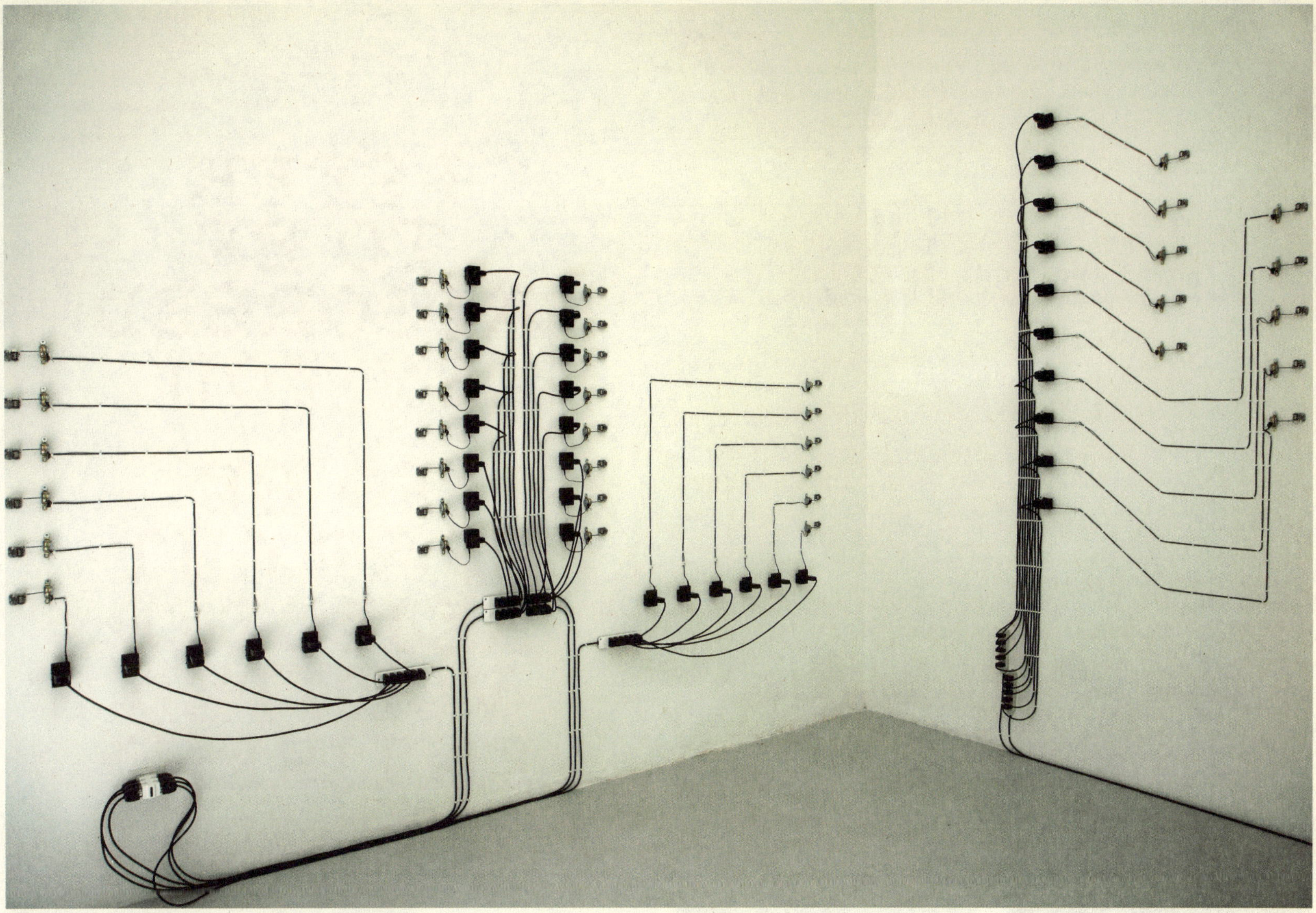

1.

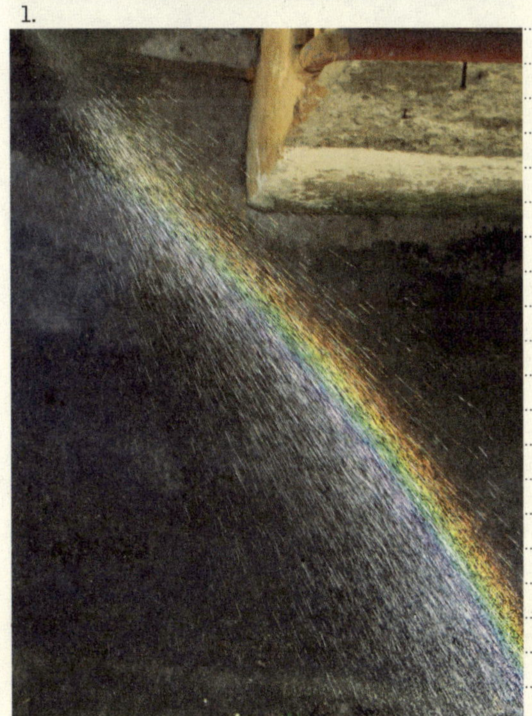

2.

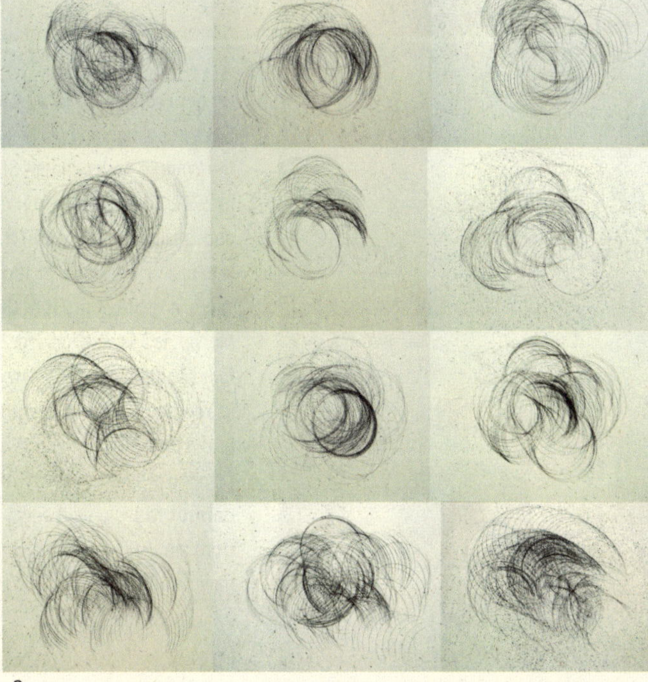

3.

Alberto Tadiello lives and works in Venice. His installations transform ordinary objects and mechanisms, confounding their original function. In **Pws 1200IPC KH3116** (2008) he bolted circular saws into the gallery wall and connected them to cables that oscillated rapidly when the saw was turned on.

1. EPROM
2008, music boxes, electric motors, transformers, and cables, dimensions variable

2. 40/42°
2007, hydraulic material, water, dimensions variable

3. Untitled
2008, ink on paper, 12 parts, each 32 × 40 in (82 × 102 cm)

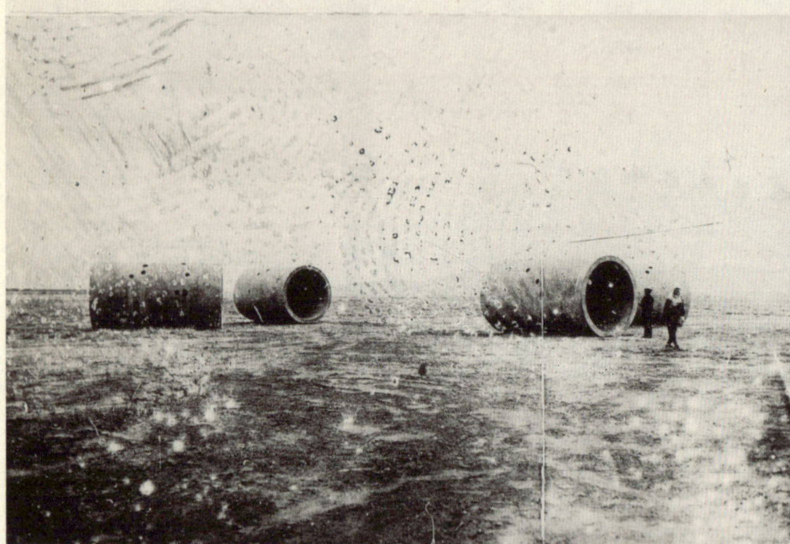

1.

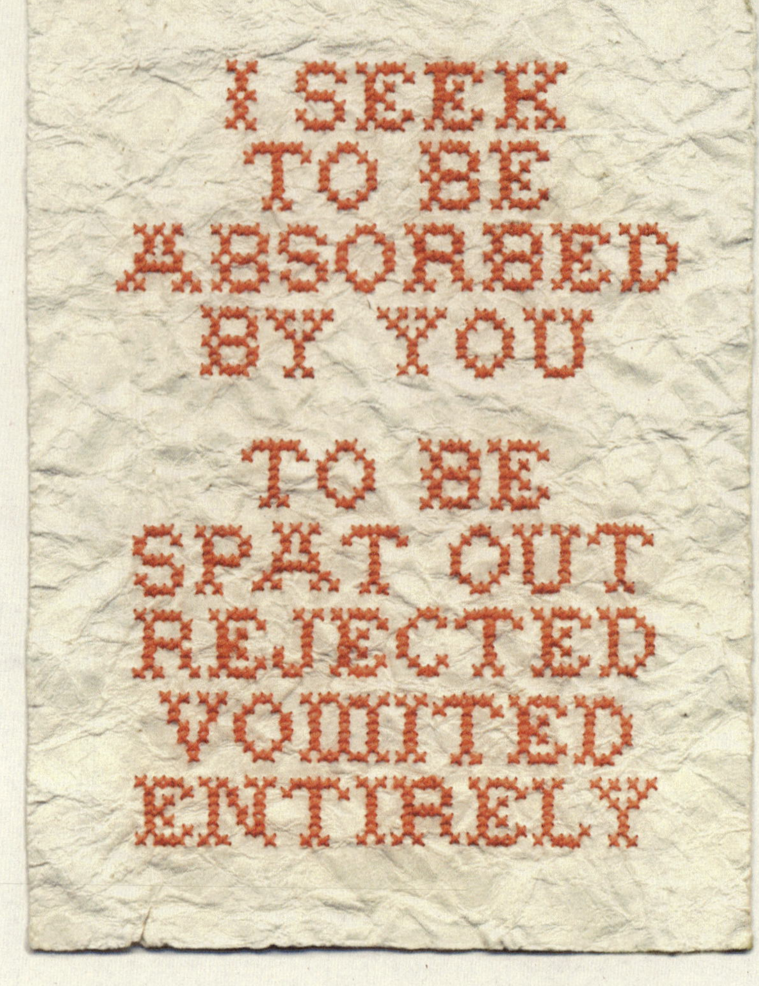

2.

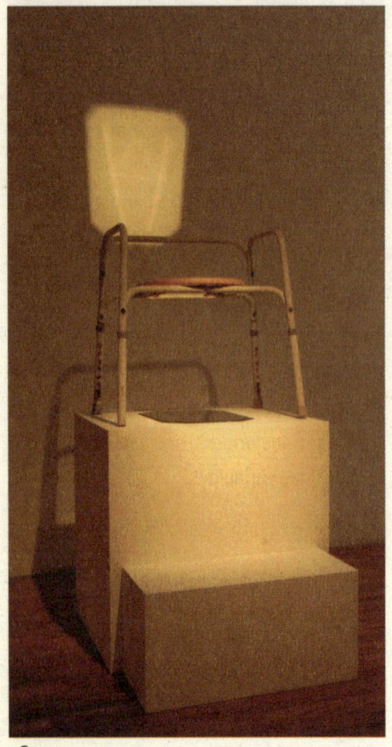

3.

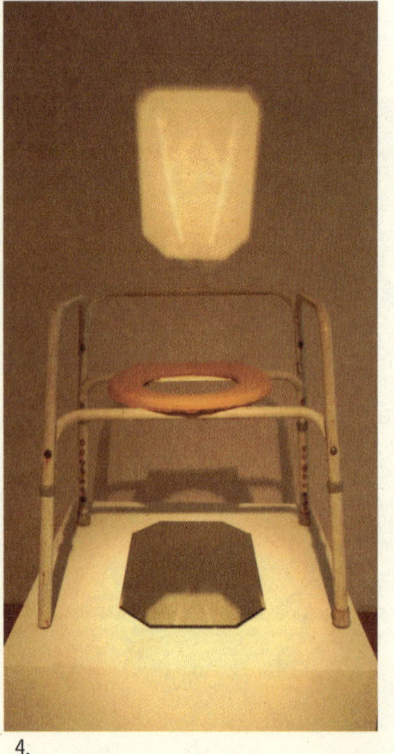

4.

Ginger Brooks Takahashi earned a BA from Oberlin College and participated in the Whitney Independent Study Program in 2007. She lives and works in Brooklyn and is a cofounder of **LTTR**, a queer and feminist art journal. For the year 2008-09, she is a resident artist at the Smack Mellon gallery in Brooklyn. She often focuses on queer, feminist, and social issues and politics in her artwork. On view at the New Museum in 2008, Takahashi's ongoing project **an army of lovers cannot fail** is a quilt sewn by participants from the many different spaces, art galleries, bookstores, and parties at which it has been installed.

1. **How did she find herself here? Nancy Holt, 1973-76**
2008, projection of 40 text and image slides, and installation with seating, dimensions variable

2. **Untitled**
from the series **Our Nature is Our Virtue**
2006-07, cotton thread on paper, 7 1/2 × 5 3/4 in (19 × 15 cm)

3 & 4. **Genital Portraits $25/per sitting**
2008, mirror, leather-covered toilet seat, pedestals, and found color pencil drawings on paper, dimensions variable

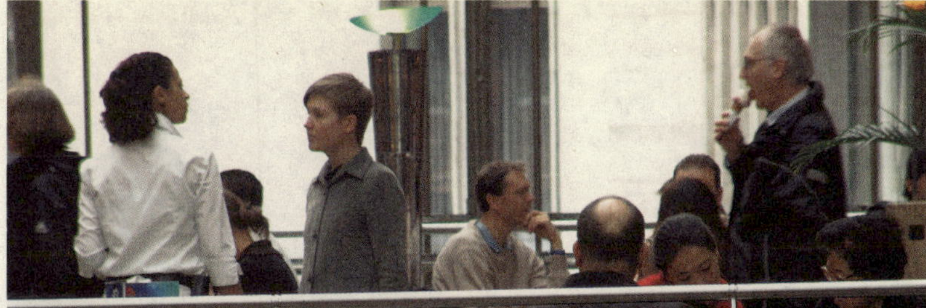
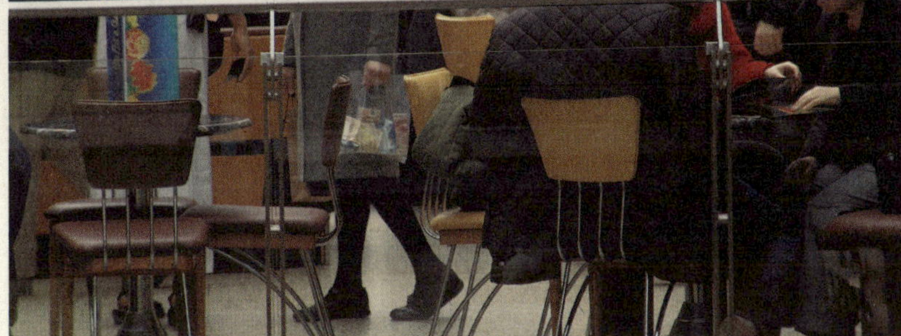

1.

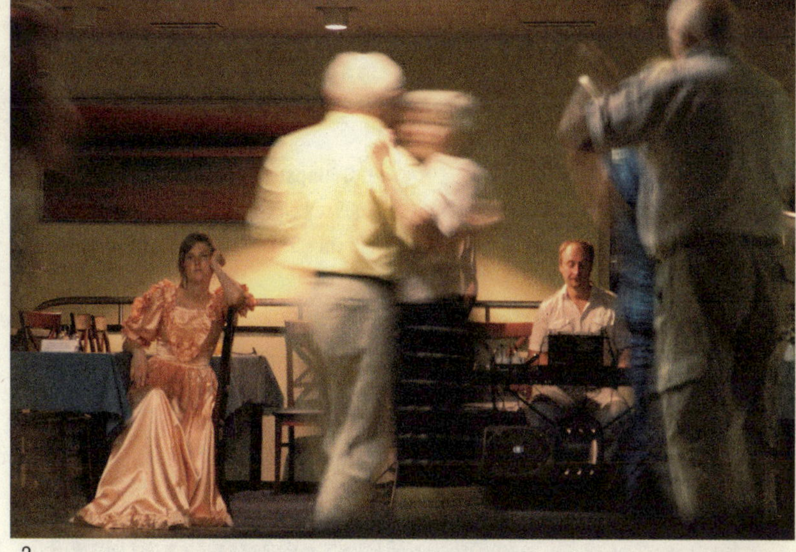

2.

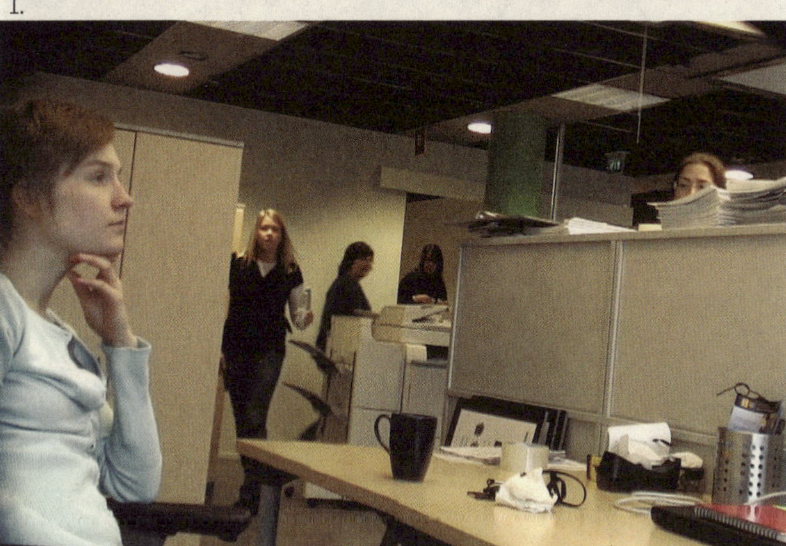

3.

4.

Pilvi Takala graduated from the Academy of Fine Arts, Helsinki, and lives and works in Amsterdam. For her video works and photographs she sets up events that explore the value systems of communities and the shared but unwritten rules they follow. Her video **The Trainee**, for example, is based on a one-month period during which a marketing trainee seems to threaten the rules of the workplace when she simply sits at her desk thinking all day. The video examines the way her colleagues begin to react to her odd behavior. **The Switch** explores the reactions of men in a Turkish coffee house to the unexpected presence of women.

1. Bag Lady
2006, 3-projector slide show, photographs, and text, 6 min

2. Wallflower
2006, posters and 2-channel video, 6 min 15 sec and 4 min 20 sec

3. The Trainee, "Working at Deloitte for a month"
2008, PowerPoint presentation

4. The Announcer
2007, video, 5 min 40 sec

5. Easy Rider
2005, video, 4 min 25 sec

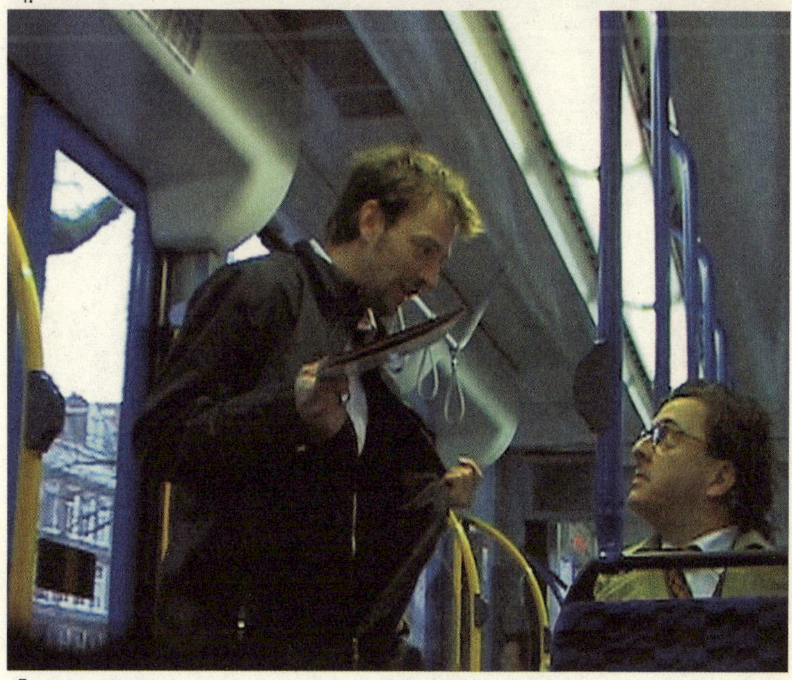

5.

Thakol Khaosa-ad graduated with a BFA from Bangkok's Silpakorn University in 1999. His oil paintings have snapshotlike compositions and sometimes employ techniques like cropping and unfocused blurriness, clues that Thakol takes his subjects from photographs and mass media. Looking, selecting, cutting, and adding are all stages in his process, and the resulting canvases function as a diaristic record of his gaze and imagination.

1. Collapse

2005, oil on canvas, 17 ¾ × 22 ½ in (45 cm × 57 cm)

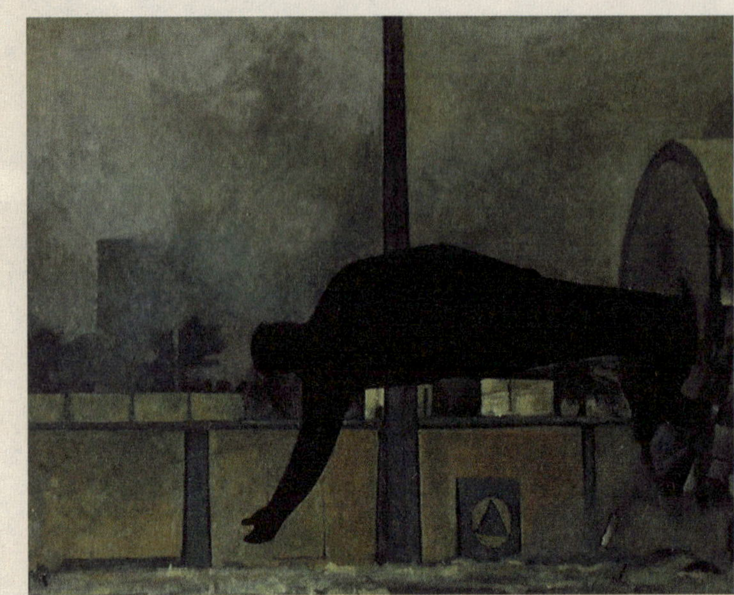

1.

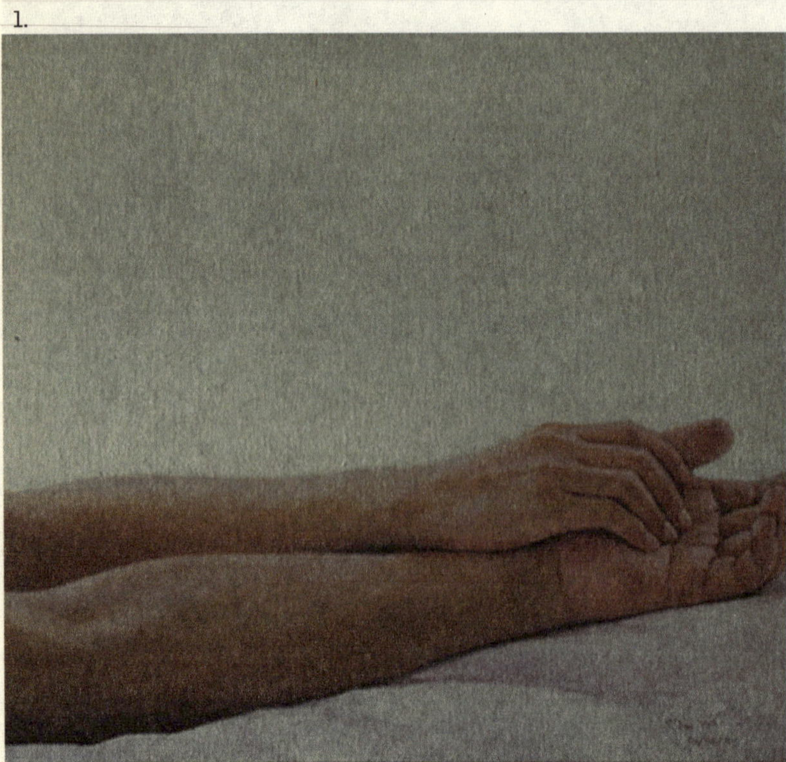

2.

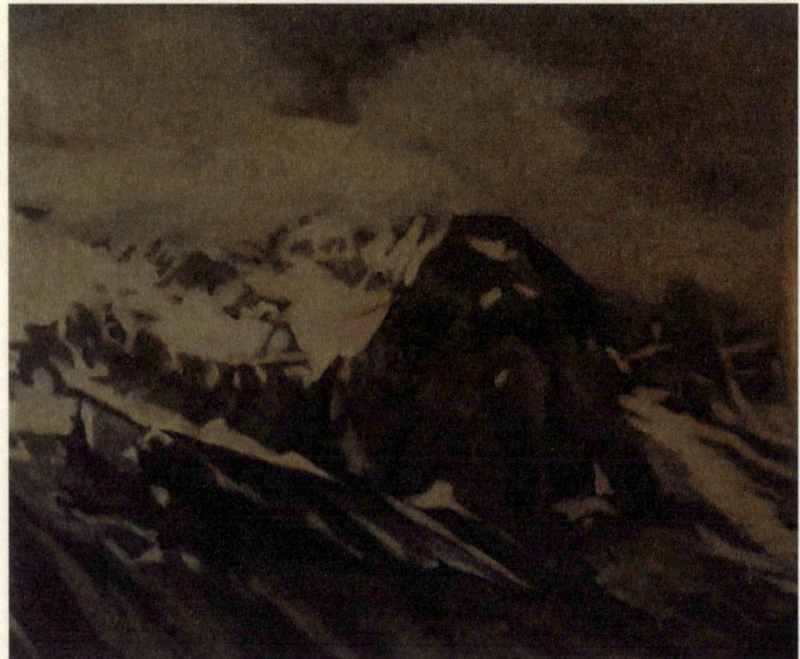

3.

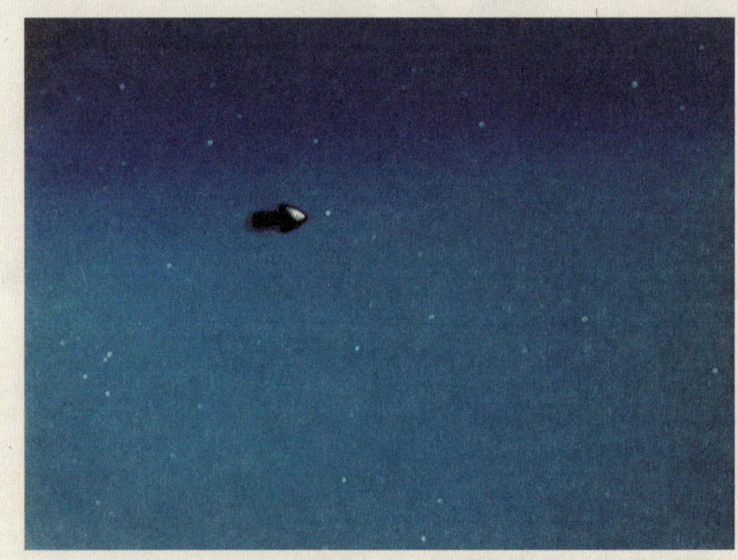

4.

2. Between

2006, oil on canvas, 13 ¾ × 15 ½ in (35 cm × 40 cm)

3. Untitled

2008, oil on canvas, 15 × 19 in (38 cm × 48 cm)

4. Curser

2008, oil on canvas, 16 × 21 ½ in (41 cm × 55 cm)

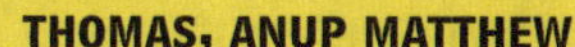

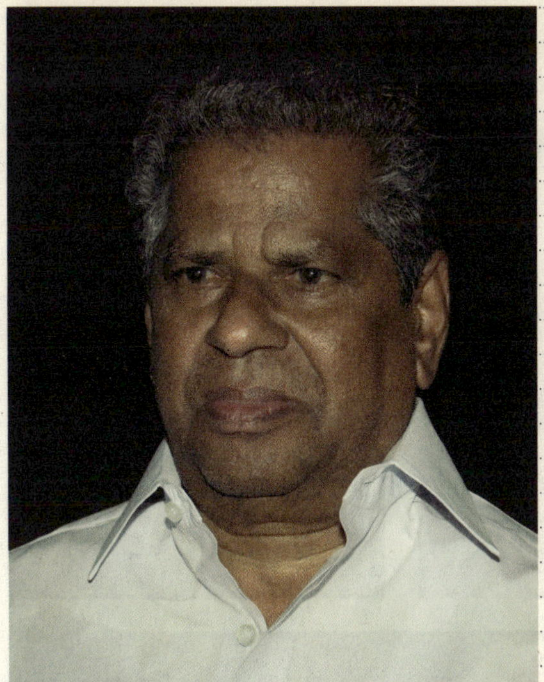

1.

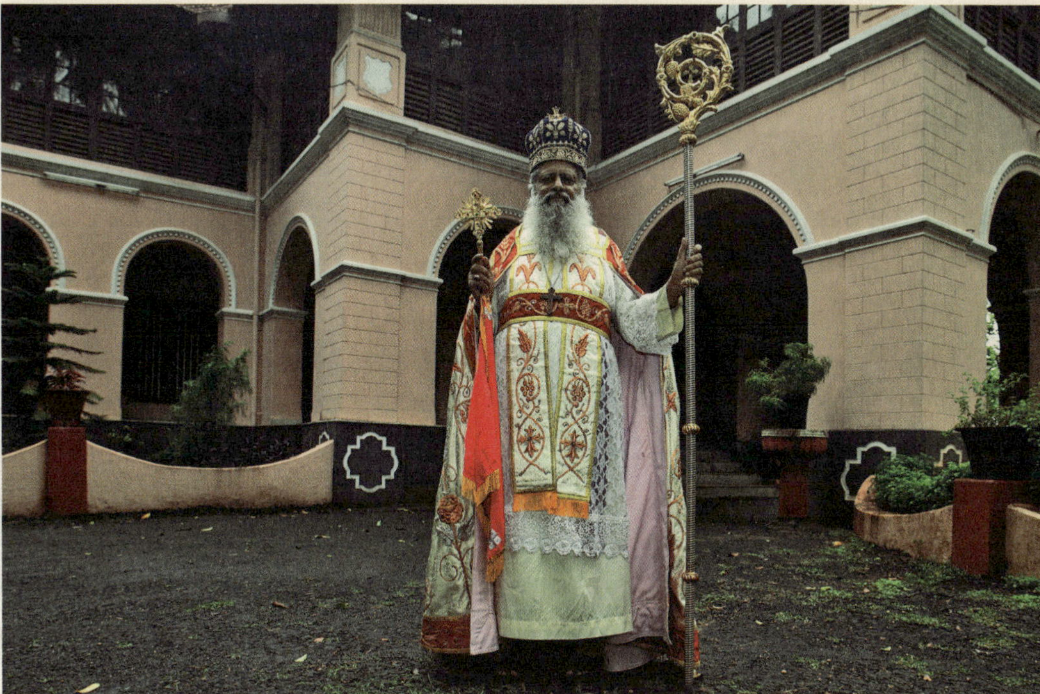

2.

3.

Anup Matthew Thomas graduated from the Srishti School of Art, Design, and Technology in Bangalore. He lives and works in India and the UK. Thomas's serial color photographs are visually seductive and critical of his subjects. His portraits of various rule-makers and law-enforcers, including **Cabinet** (2007) contain an implicit critique of the power structure in India.

1. **Cabinet (T U Kuruvilla, Minister for Public Works)**
2007, digital slide show

2. **Metropolitan (His Grace Dr. Mar Aprem Metropolitan, Chaldean Syrian Church of the East)**
2006, archival inkjet print on Hahnemühle photo rag paper, 44 × 66 in (117 × 168 cm)

3. **NCA Library**
2006, digital slide show

4. **Light Life**
2005, digital slide show

5. **Ambassadors**
2007, digital print

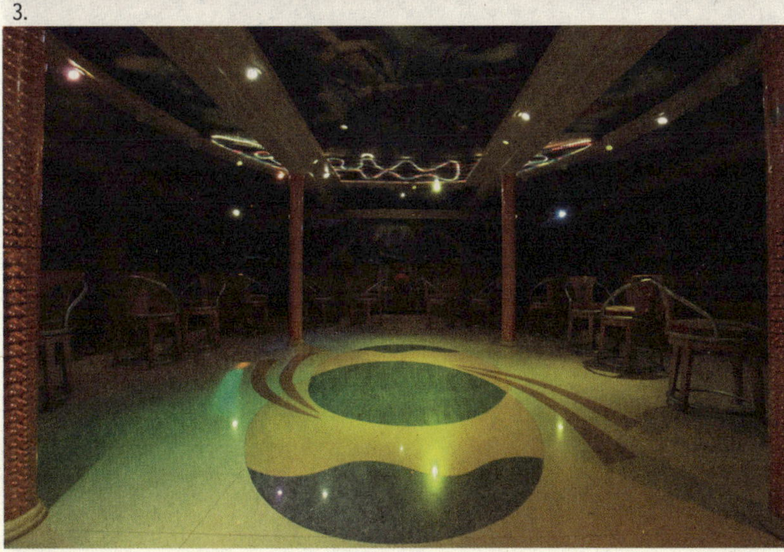

4.

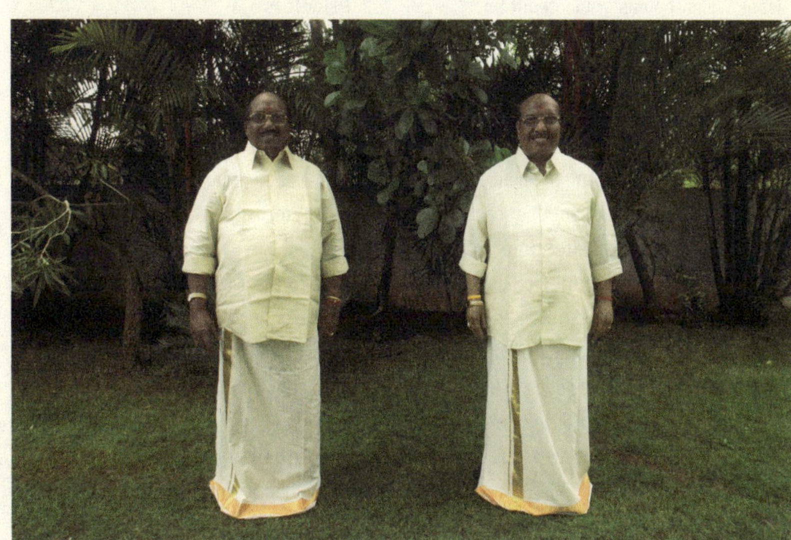

5.

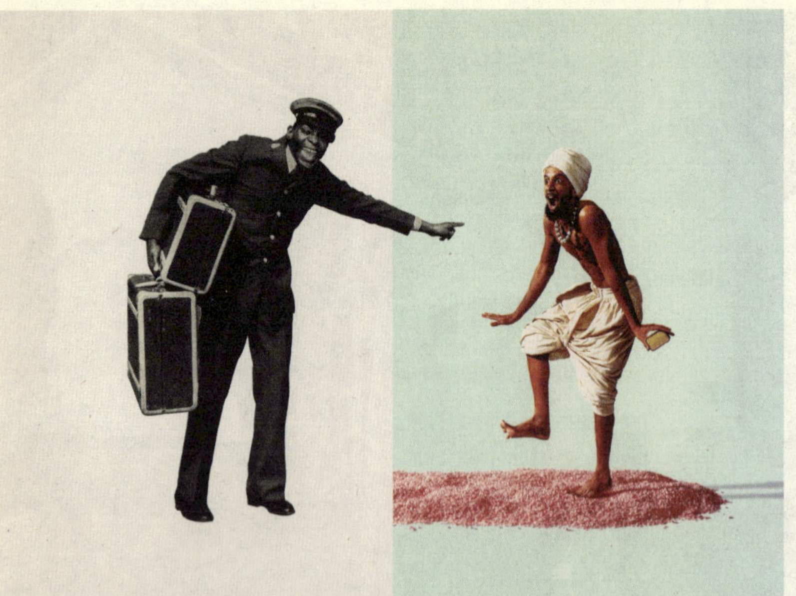

1.

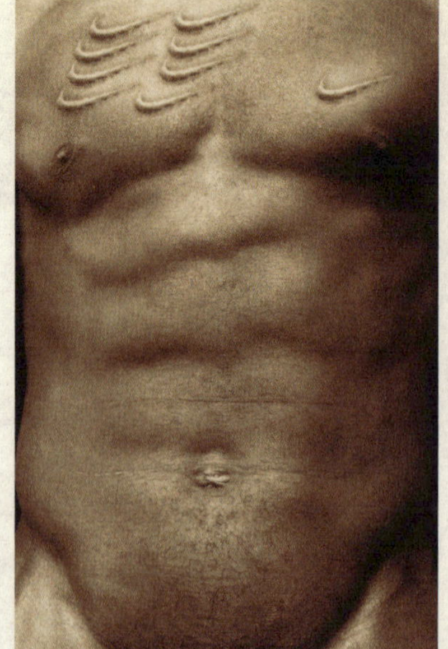

3.

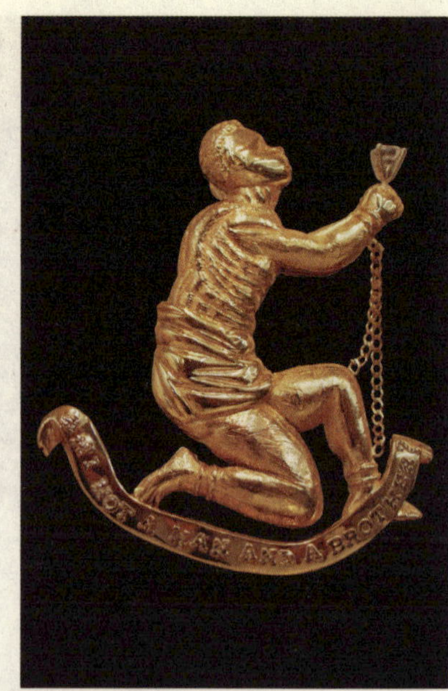

4.

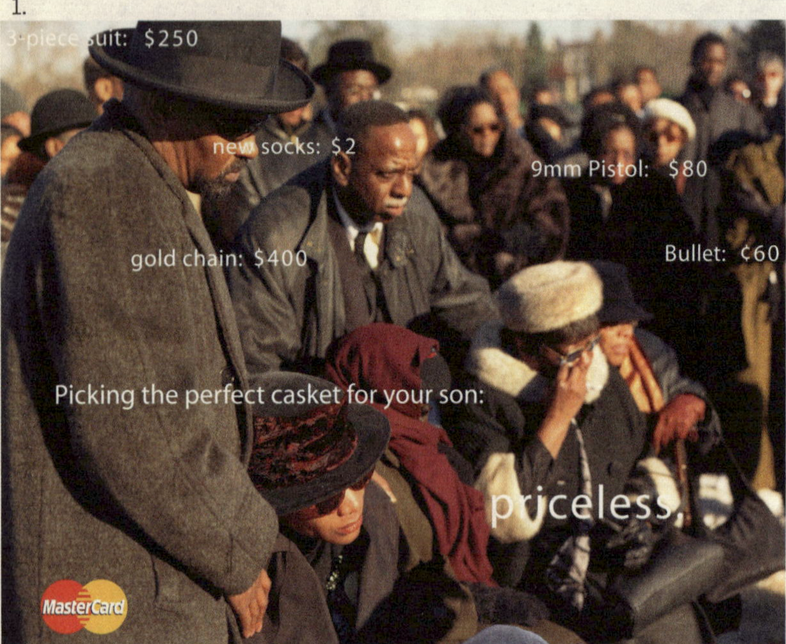

2.

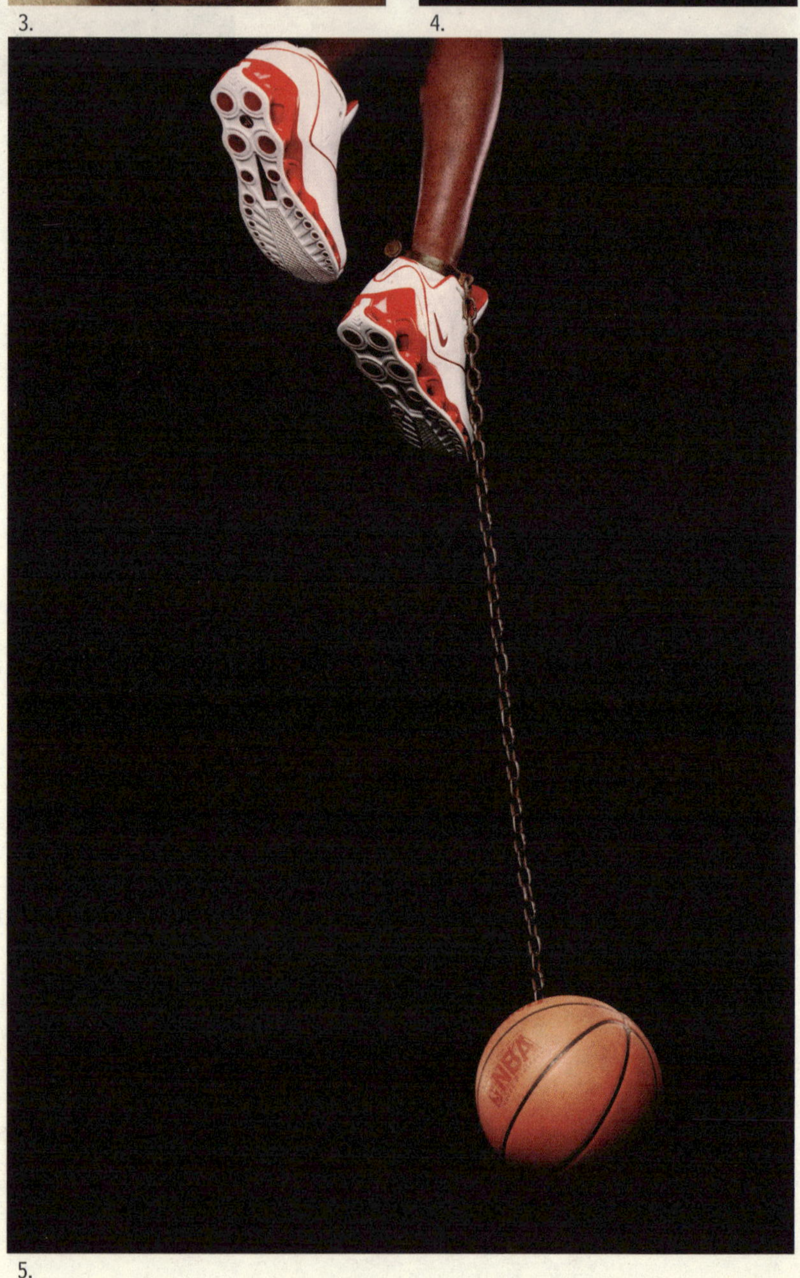

5.

Hank Willis Thomas graduated from the California College of the Arts with an MA in visual criticism and an MFA in photography. His photo-based work has tackled such issues as the commodification of black male identity and the media representations of African-Americans. His series **Unbranded: Reflections in Black by Corporate America** uses print ads to reveal the visual strategies of ad campaigns and the cultural stereotypes on which they are based (as seen in his Afro-American Express Card, for example).

1. **Now that's funny**
2008, lightjet print, 20 × 30 in (51 × 76 cm)

2. **Priceless**
2004, Lambda print, 71 × 90 in (180 × 229 cm)

3. **Scarred Chest**
2003, Lambda print, 30 × 20 in (76 × 51 cm)

4. **Ode to the CMB, Am I Not a Man and a Brother?**
2006-07, 24K gold and cubic zirconium, 5 × 3 in (13 × 8 cm)

5. **Basketball and Chain**
2003, Lambda print, 30 × 20 in (76 × 51 cm)

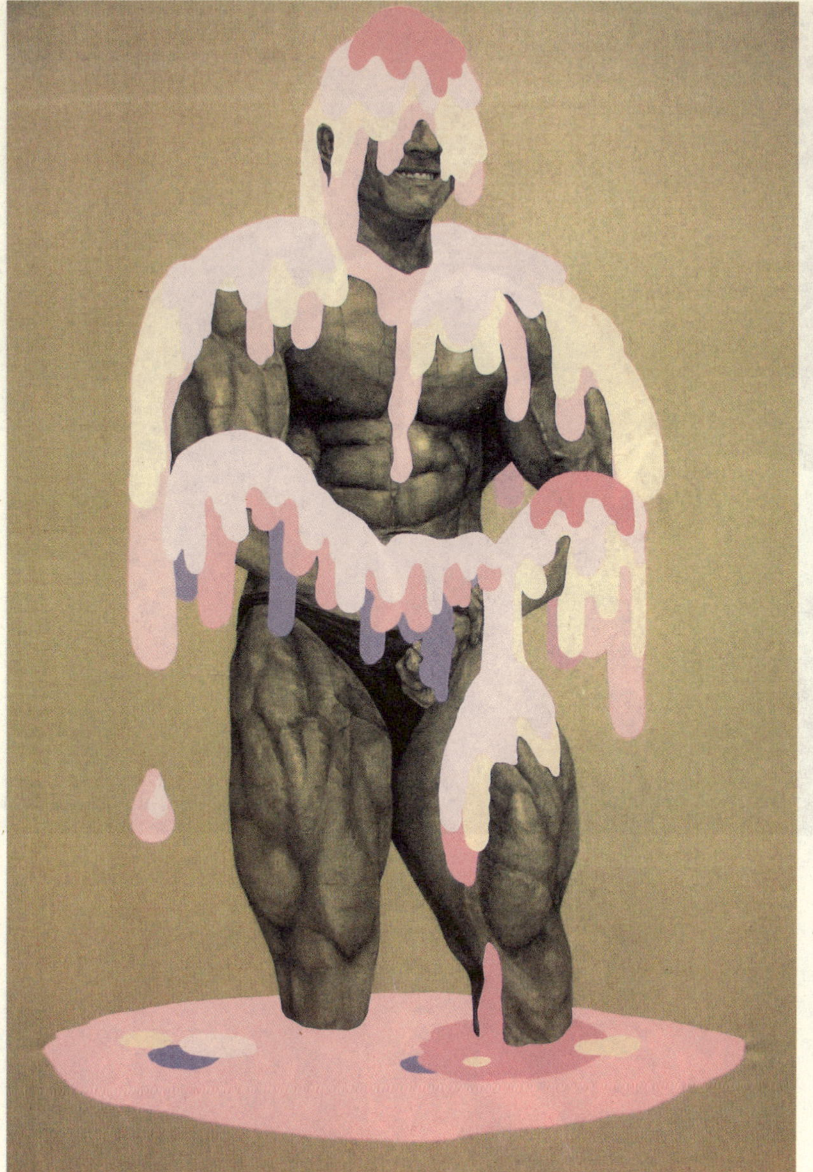

1.

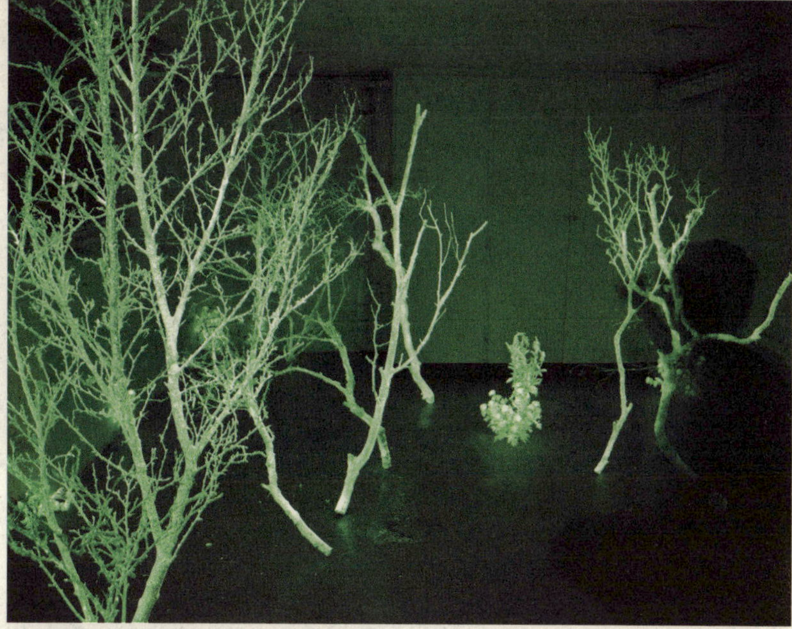

2.

3.

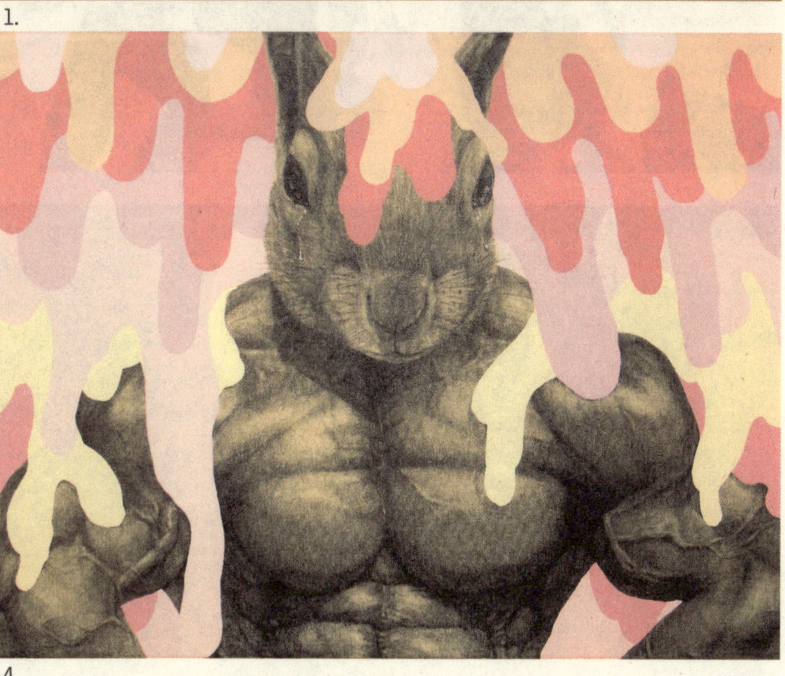

4.

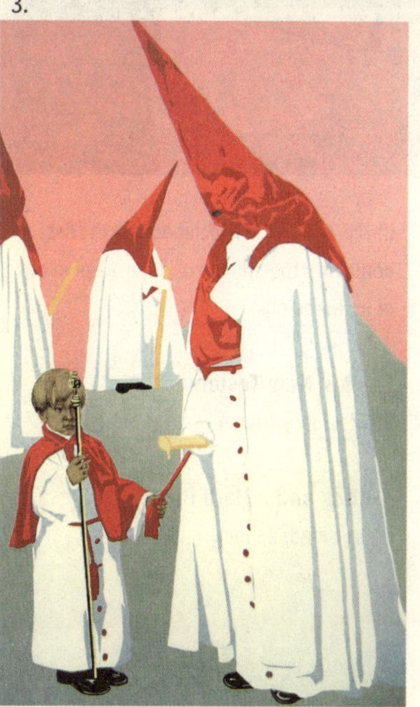

5.

Gudmundur Thoroddsen, who lives and works in Reykjavik, graduated with a BA in fine arts from the Iceland Academy of the Arts in 2003 and studied film theory at the University of Iceland in 2006. His painting-drawing hybrids, including his sugary, sweet-looking **Ice-Cream Land**, mix pencil drawings with poured pastel-colored acrylic paints and, with irony, take aim at consumer society and pop culture.

1. **Muscly man**
2007, acrylic and pencil on canvas,
90 ½ × 59 in (230 × 150 cm)

2. **Undergarden**
2008, plants, trees, and glow paint,
dimensions variable

3. **Blob Squirrel**
2008, acrylic and pencil on canvas,
25 ½ × 17 ¾ in (65 × 45 cm)

4. **Muscle Squirrel**
2006, acrylic and pencil on canvas,
25 ½ × 33 ½ in (65 × 85 cm)

5. **Easterbunny**
2004, acrylic and pencil on canvas,
90 ½ × 59 in (230 × 150 cm)

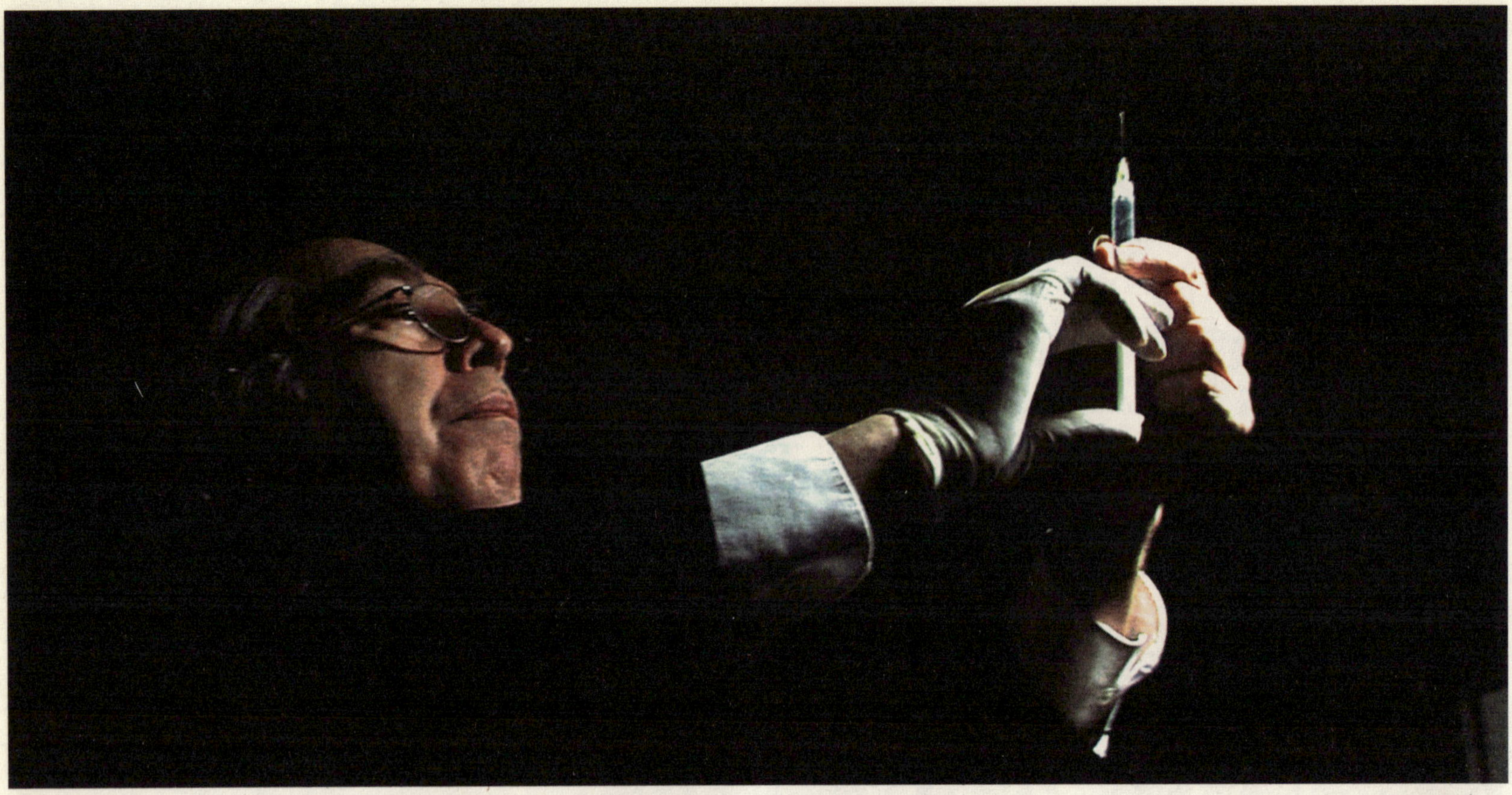

1.

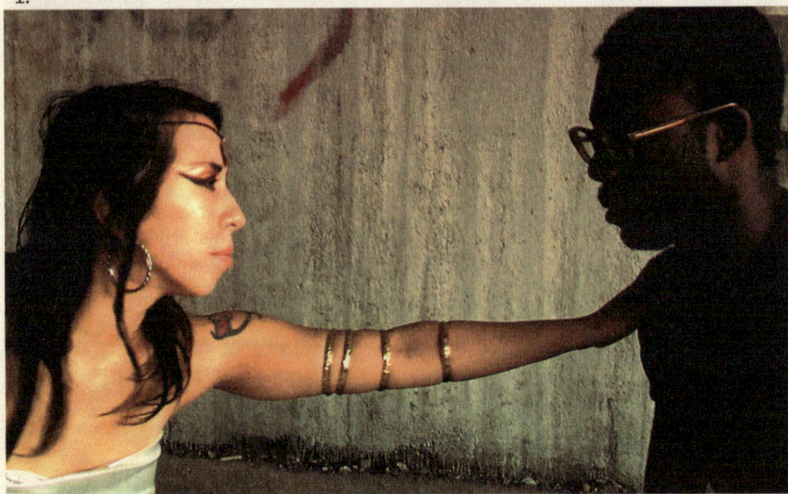

2.

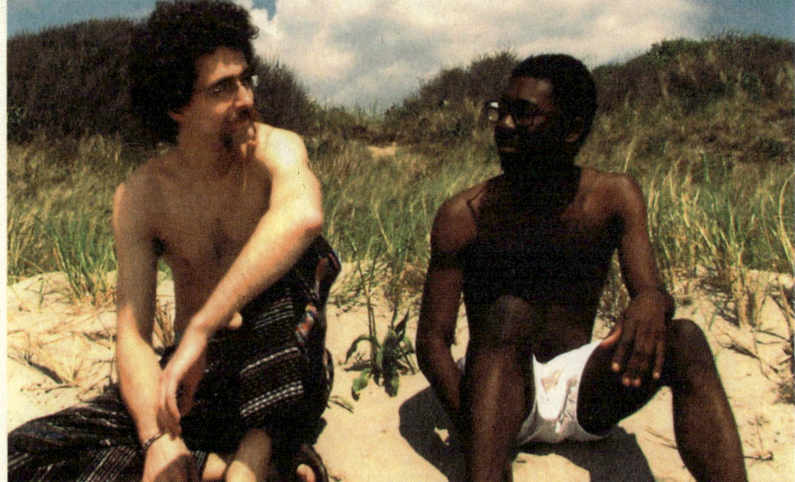

3.

Joshua Thorson completed an MFA at Bard College and currently lives and works in Brooklyn. His 2008 film **UFO Days**, screened in The Museum of Modern Art's series "CELLuloid: Cell Phone-Made Documentaries" and at New York's CRG Gallery, is about a police officer who is zapped by a UFO in Elmwood, Wisconsin; the town celebrates the event thirty years later with UFO Days festival. He also curated the exhibition "Perspectacle" at Mix NYC, which included works that dealt with the subject of queerness in all of its meanings.

1, 2 & 3. **New Testament**

2007, video, 20 min

4. **Rock and a Hard Place**

2006, video, 23 min

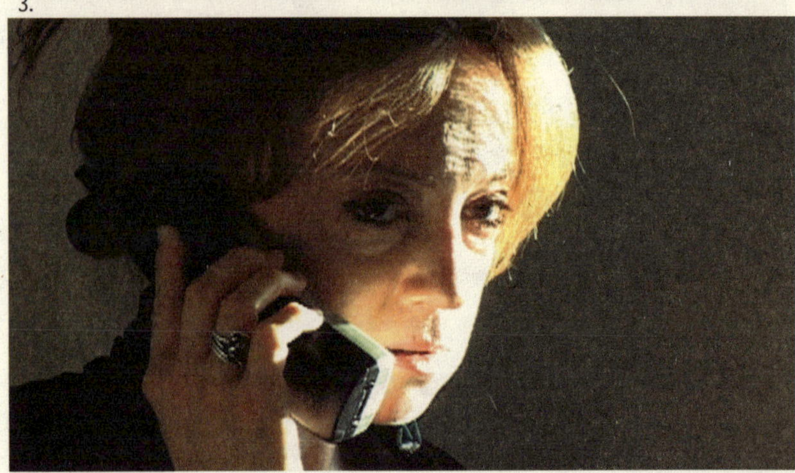

4.

Isaac Tin Wei Lin lives and works in Philadelphia. He attended the Rhode Island School of Design, and then the California College of the Arts, where he earned an MFA in drawing and painting. His work consists of frequently whimsical calligraphic paintings, sculptures, and photo-based drawings.

1. **Night Sun**
2005, ink and spray paint on paper, 84 × 60 in (214 × 152 cm)

2. **Haunted**
2008, found cardboard boxes and acrylic paint, 4 × 4 × 20 ft (122 × 122 × 610 cm)

3. **Lunch Party**
2006, ink on photograph, 12 × 18 in (31 × 46 cm)

4. **Law and Order**
2007, ink on paper, 108 × 120 in (274 × 305 cm)

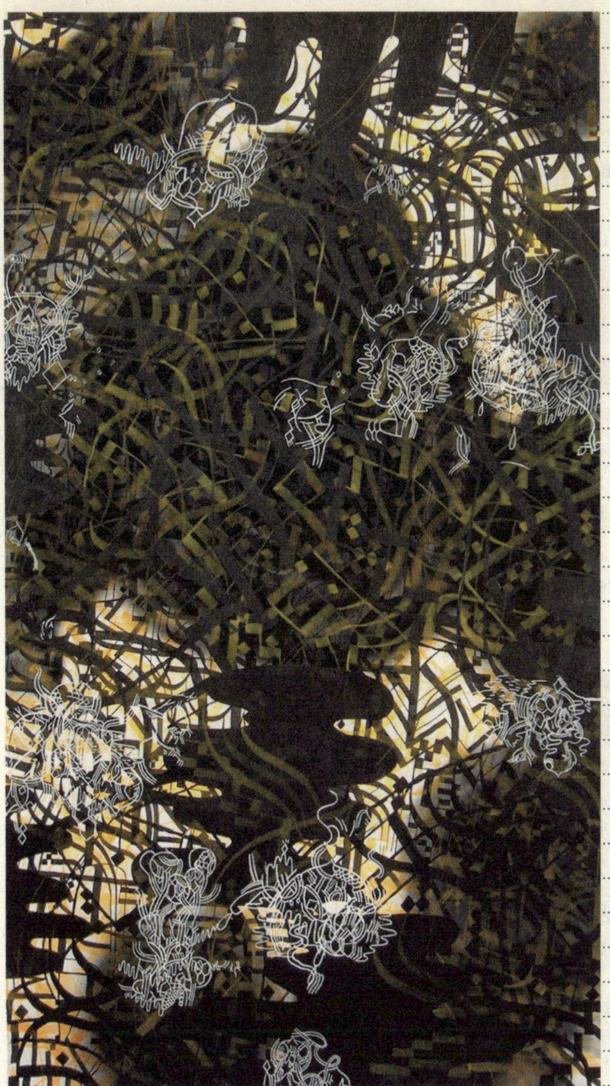

1.

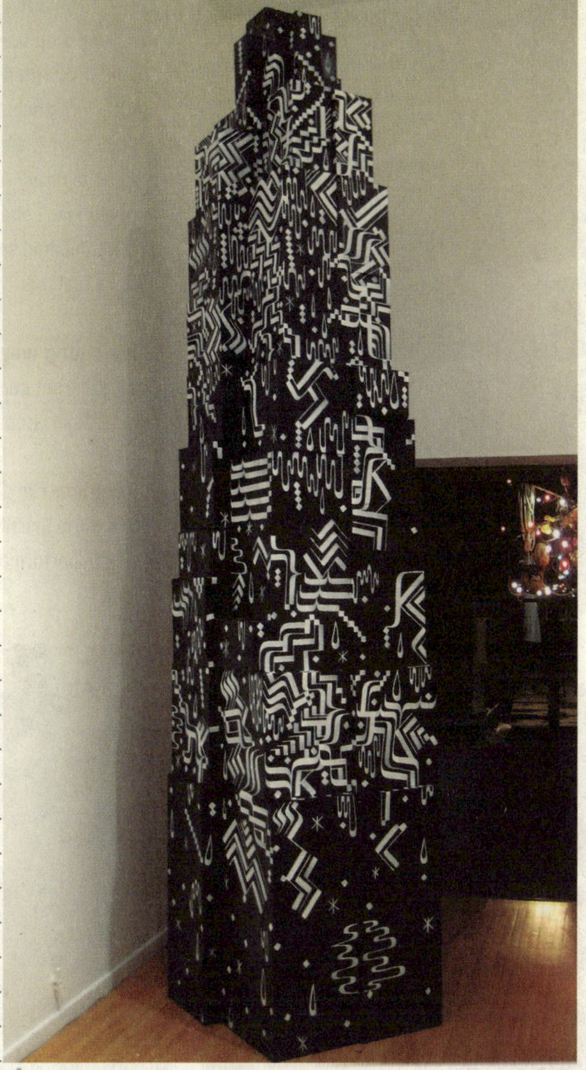

2.

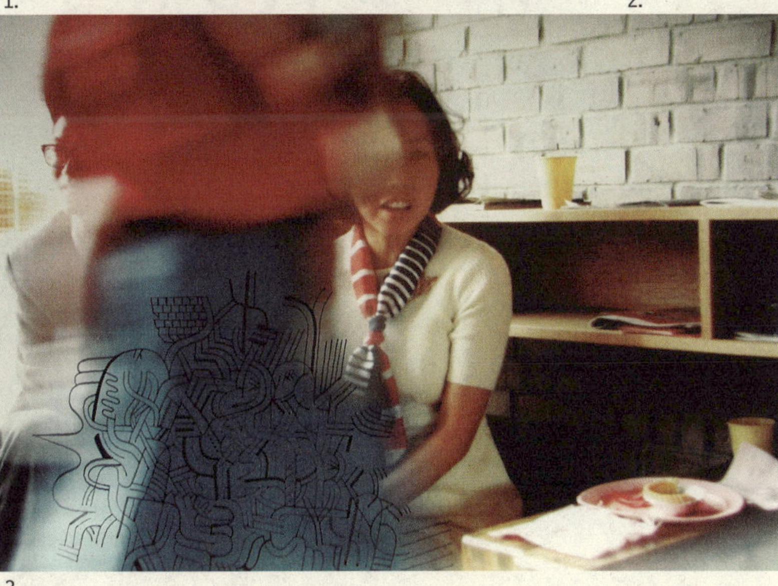

3.

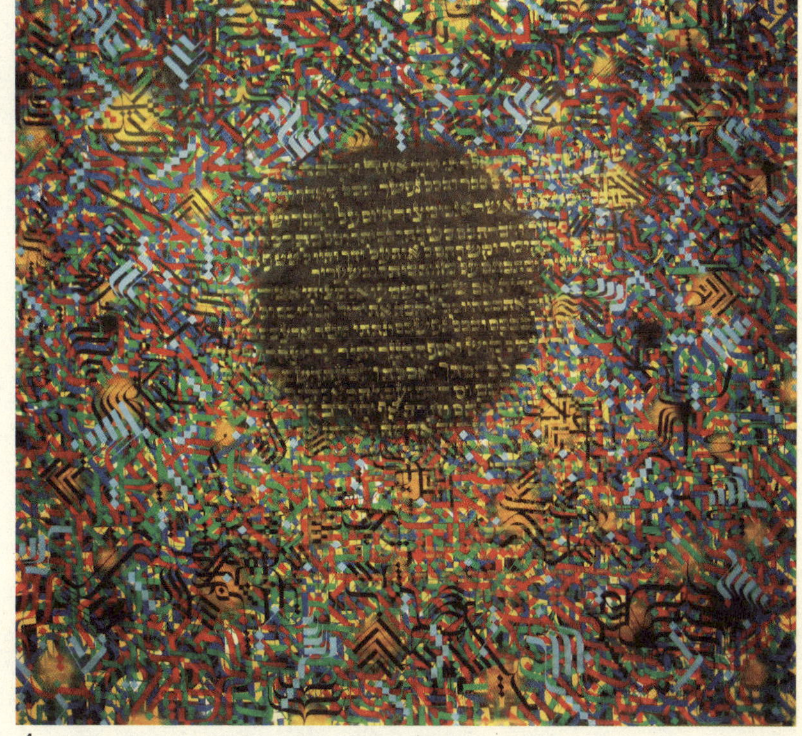

4.

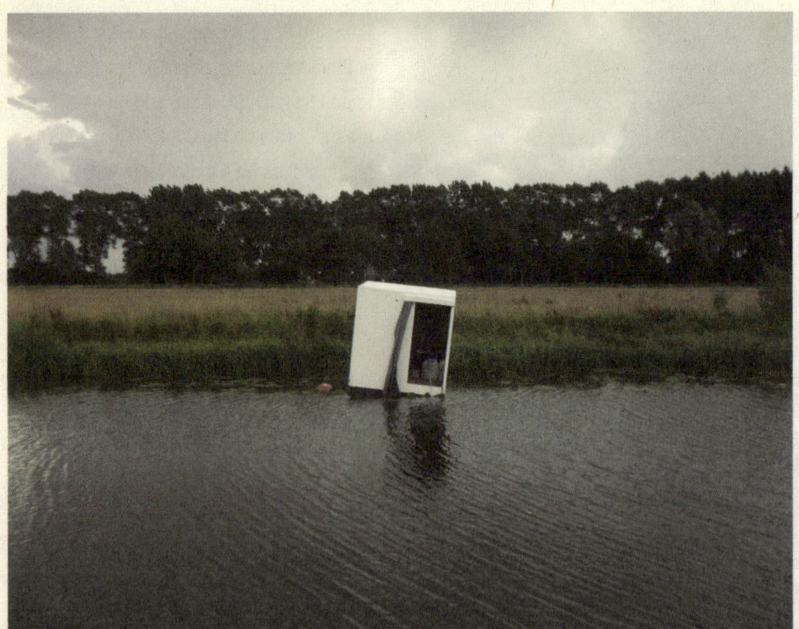
1.

Adrien Tirtiaux lives and works in Vienna, where he graduated from the Academy of Fine Arts with a degree in sculpture and performance. His work was included in Manifesta 7, the European Biennial of Contemporary Art, where his "spatial interventions" altered the appearance of the exhibition space according to social situations.

1. It's a long way to the sea
2006, itinerant performance, performance view at Sign, Groningen, Netherlands

2. Requiem für die Sofiensäle
with Kathrin Schaller
2004-05, performance at Sofiensäle, Vienna

3. Copenhagen rainbow
2007, social intervention at Israelplads, Copenhagen

4. After the snow
2007, framework, pedestal, and flyers, dimensions variable, installation view

5. Auprès de mon arbre
2007, wall paint, wood, mirrors, and framed photograph, dimensions variable

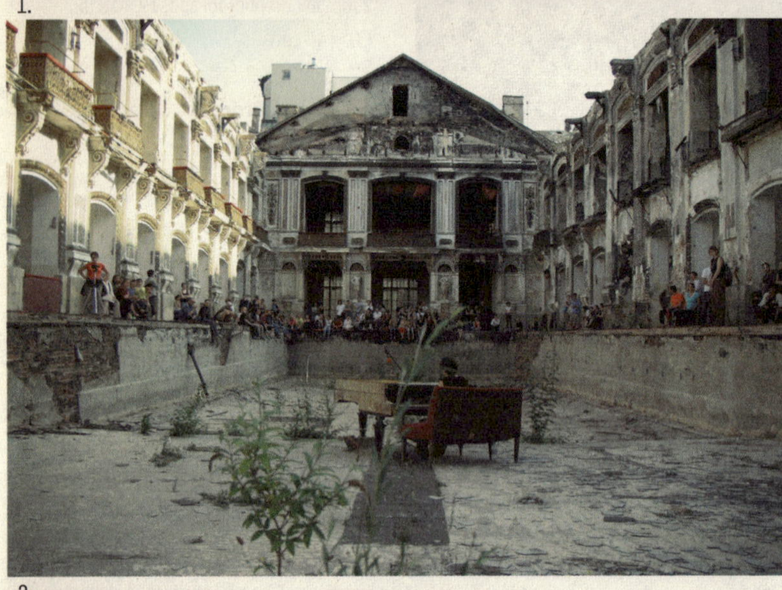
2.

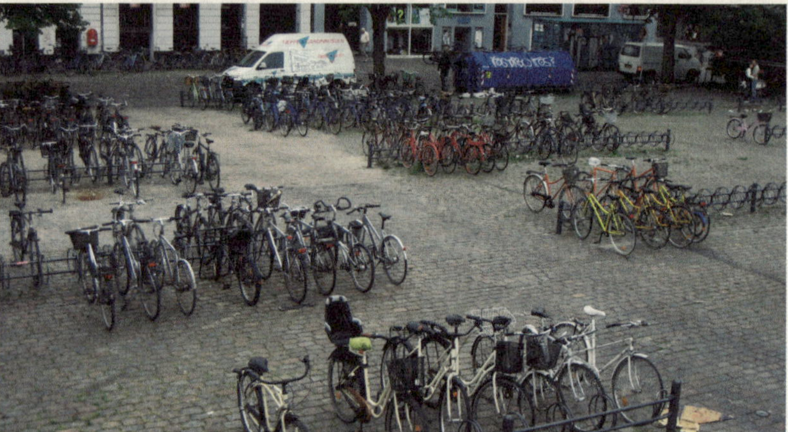
3.

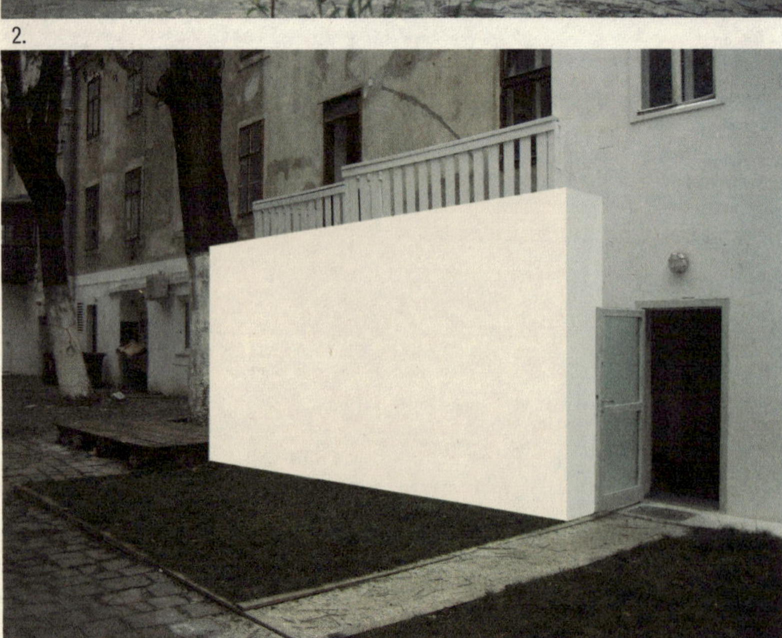
4.

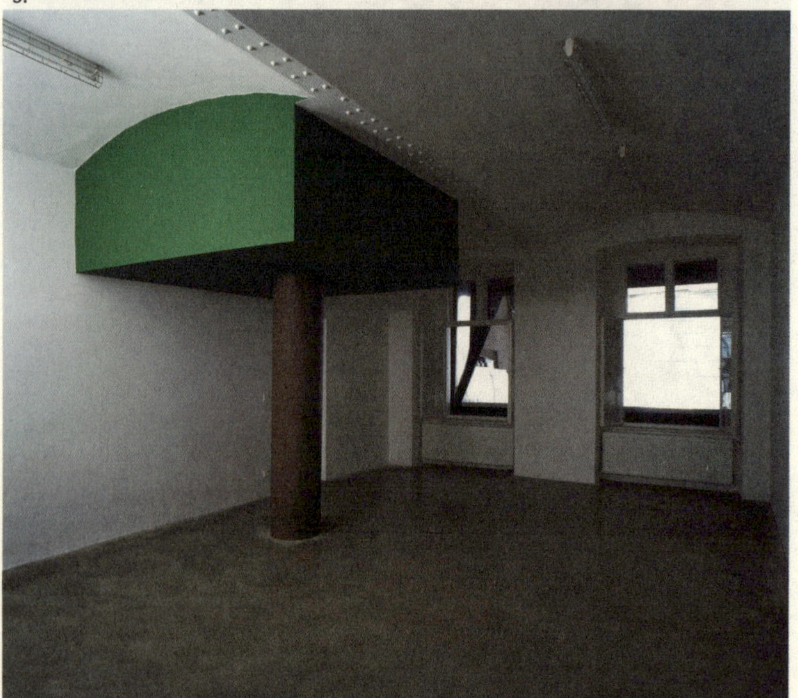
5.

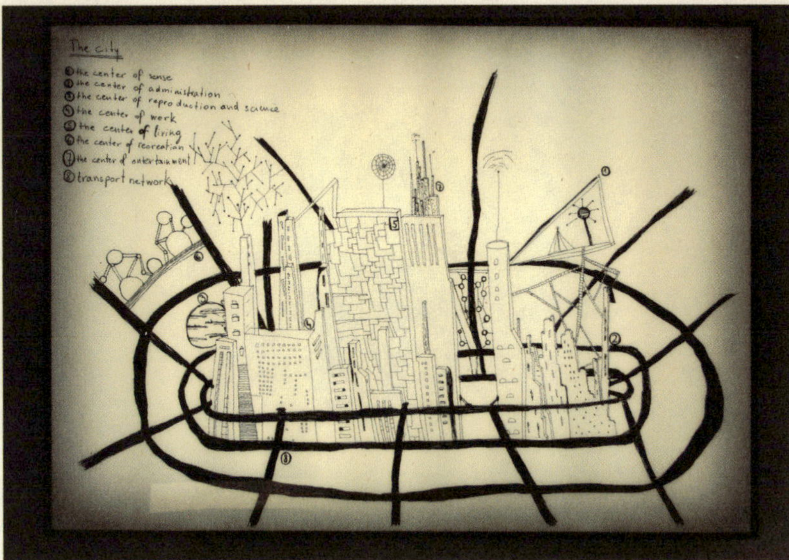

1.

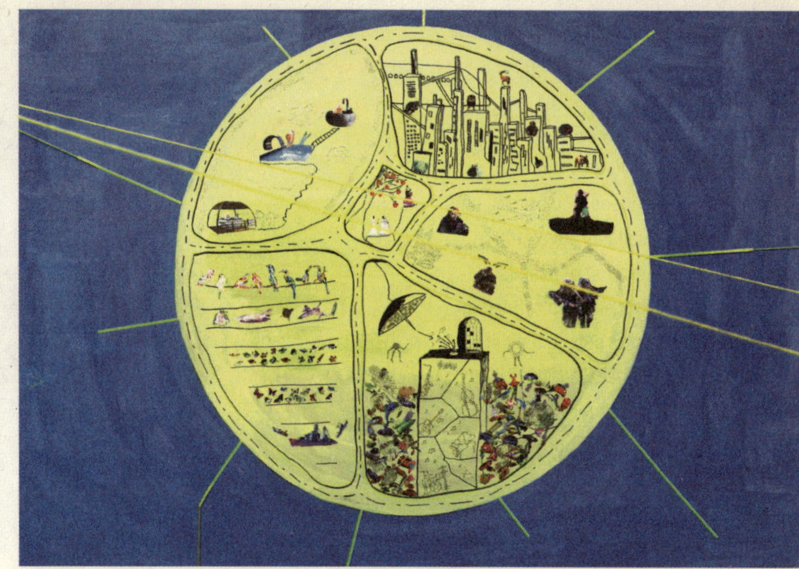

2.

Magda Tóthová graduated from the Universität für Angewandte Kunst in Vienna, where she currently lives and works. Her videos and installations explore her relationship to communism. In her 2003 video **Lenin and the Maiden**, for example, she caresses a statue of Lenin, transforming him over the course of the video into an object of affection. Her 2006 textile installation **Gust of Wind** incorporates a pleated white skirt that references Marilyn Monroe's garment famously blown upward by a gust of wind, but with the underwear revealed beneath covered with Lenin medals, suggesting the government's influence over the most private of realms.

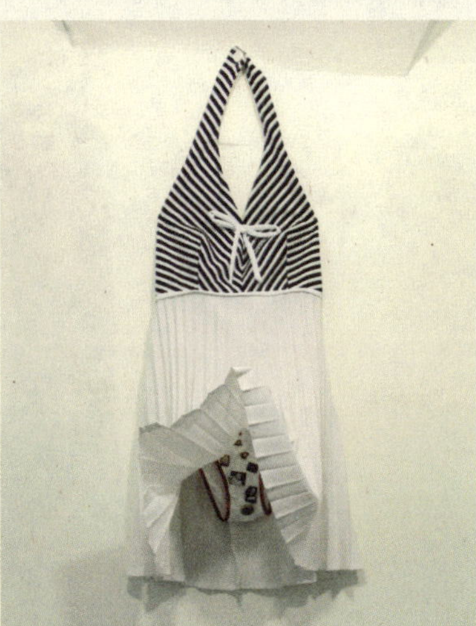

3.

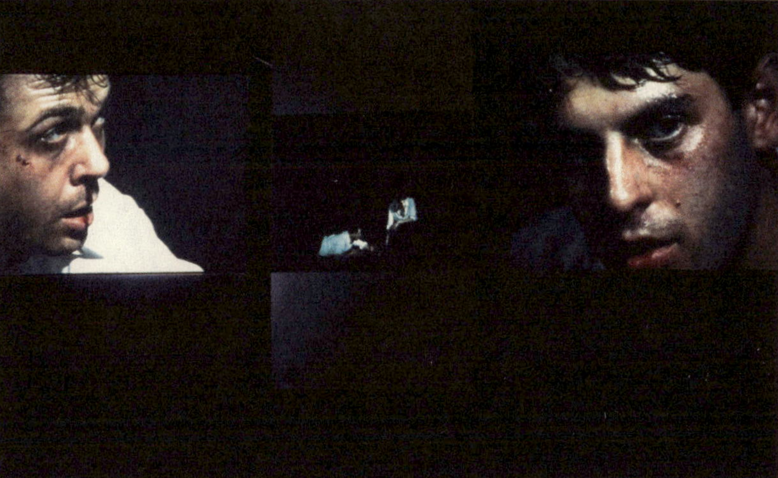

4.

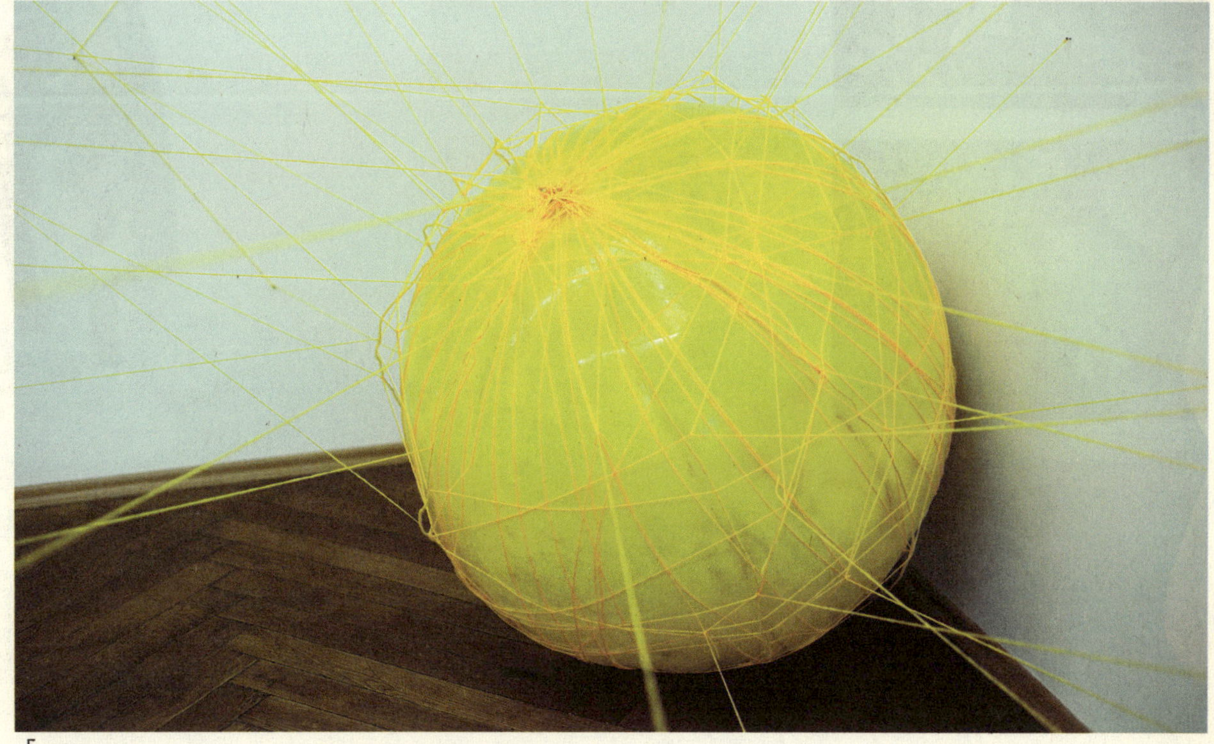

5.

1. **La Preda/The Prey/The City**
2007, light box, $49\frac{1}{4} \times 71$ in (125 × 180 cm)

2. **Global player long before Christ**
2006, collage on wood, acrylic, and stickers, 46 × 67 in (117 × 170 cm)

3. **Windstoss**
2006, fabric and badges, $31\frac{1}{2}$ in (80 cm)

4. **Fightforms**
2005, 3-channel video projection, 7 min

5. **Global player long before Christ/The Sun**
2006, balloon, wool, and wire, diameter approx 59 in (150 cm)

Ryan Trecartin graduated from the Rhode Island School of Design in 2004. He lives and works in New Orleans. His film **A Family Finds Entertainment** was shown in the 2006 Whitney Biennial. He structures his videos, sculptures, and performances as collaborative efforts, enlisting the cooperation of friends to produce work that ends up reflecting the concerns of young people amidst digital culture. **I-BE AREA** (2007) is a feature-length film that includes a cast of dozens and incorporates complex narratives exploring such themes as cloning, adoption, and virtual identity.

1 & 2. **I-BE AREA**
2007, video, color, sound, 1 hr 48 min

3. **A Family Finds Entertainment**
2004, video, 41 min 12 sec

4. **The Traveling Blonde Monster**
2006, mixed media, 72 × 42 × 3 in
(183 × 107 × 8 cm)

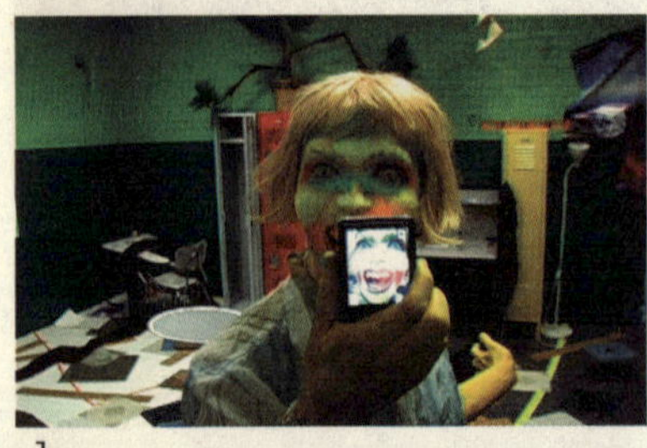
1.

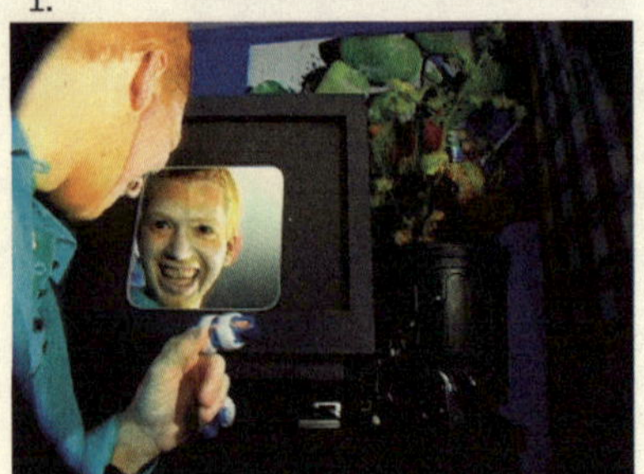
2.

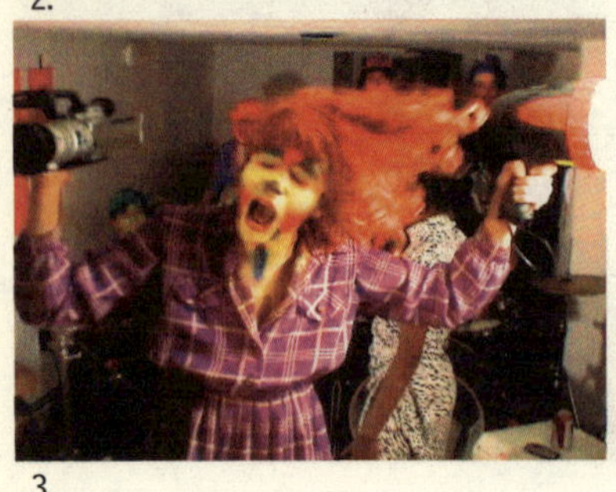
3.

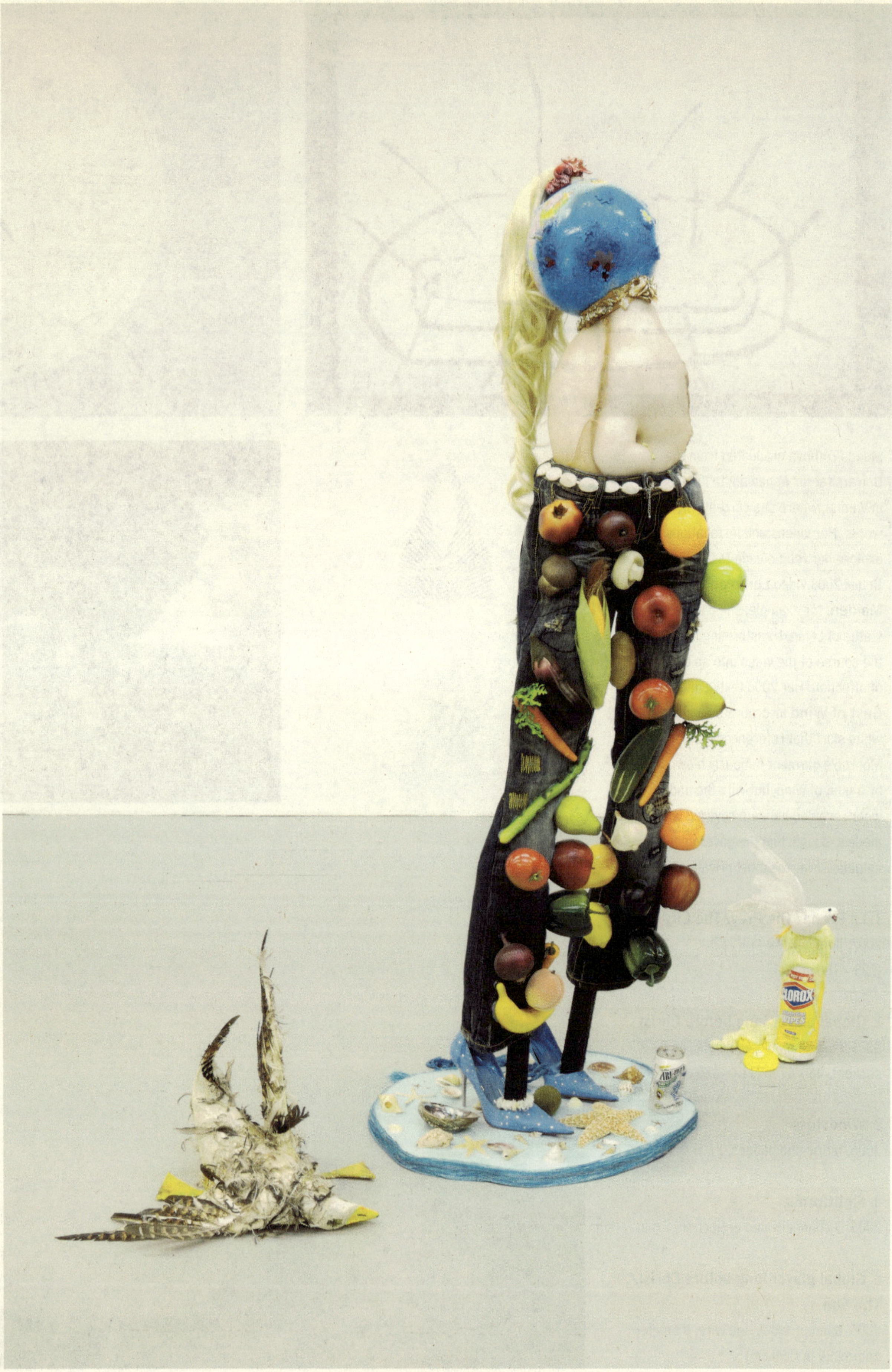

4.

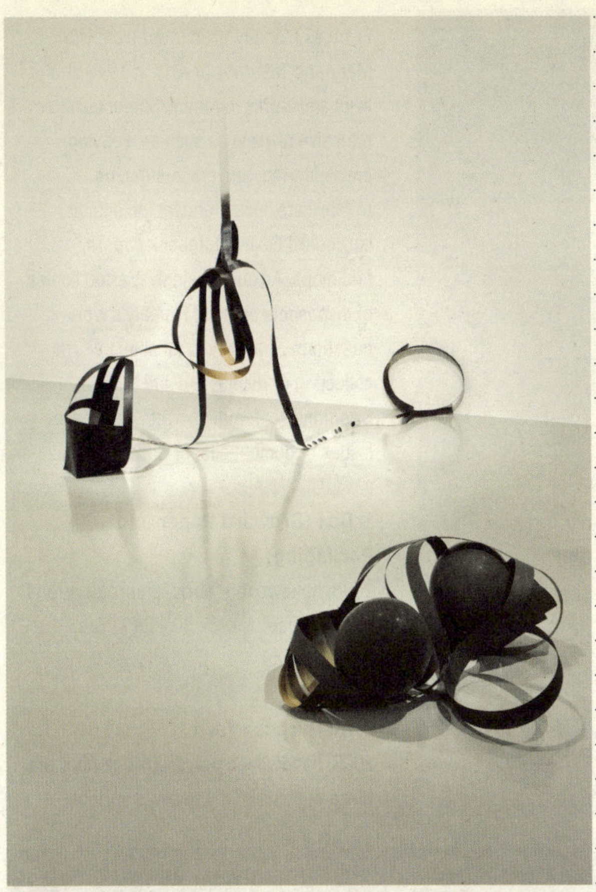
1.

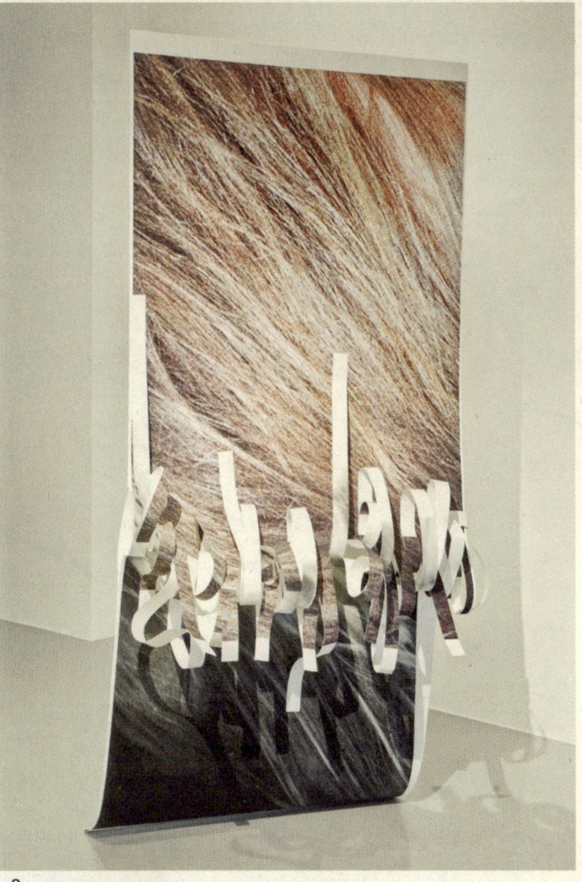
2.

Luca Trevisani lives and works in Berlin and Bologna. His installations, including one that combined two differently colored gases in a transparent tube, explore what he has called "ideas of togetherness, unity, and community." Other installations have suggested pairings of objects, for example, fans with photographs of soap bubbles, that evoke questions about the nature of symmetry and associations between different objects.

1. Soap bubble's skin
2008, balsa wood, paint, glue, prints on paper, PVC, and balloons, dimensions variable

2. Untitled
2008, digital print and pencil on paper, and double adhesive tape, 96 1/2 × 45 1/2 × 35 1/2 in (245 × 116 × 90 cm)

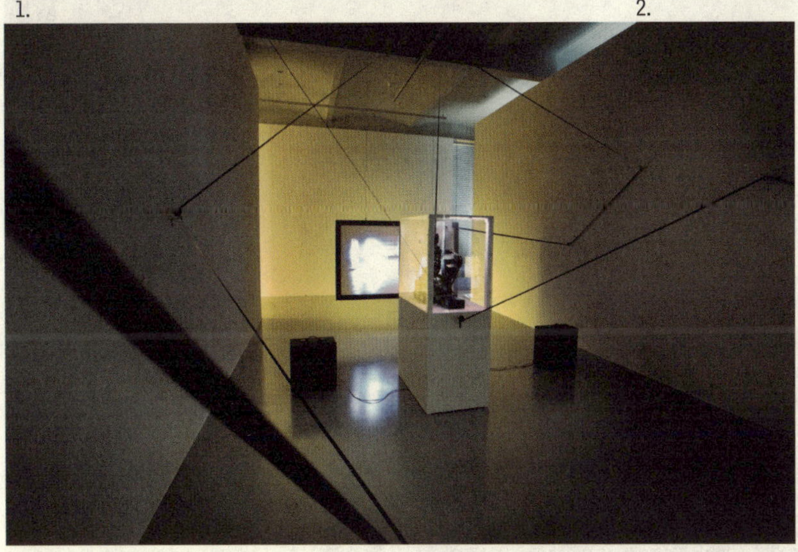
3.

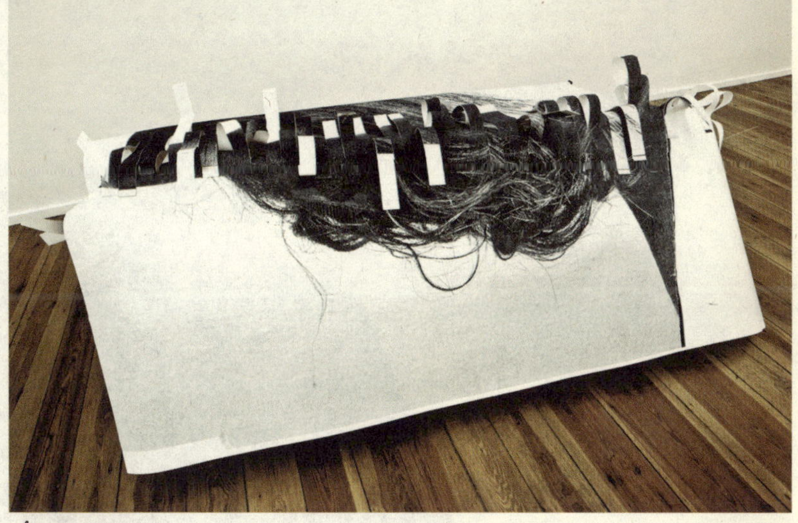
4.

3. Platinoiridio, version 1 of 2
2007-08, video, dimensions variable

4. Untitled
2008, digital print and pencil on paper, double adhesive foil, and metal rack, 35 1/2 × 94 1/2 × 45 1/4 in (90 × 240 × 115 cm)

5. Boundaries Are Boneless
2008, mixed media, dimensions variable

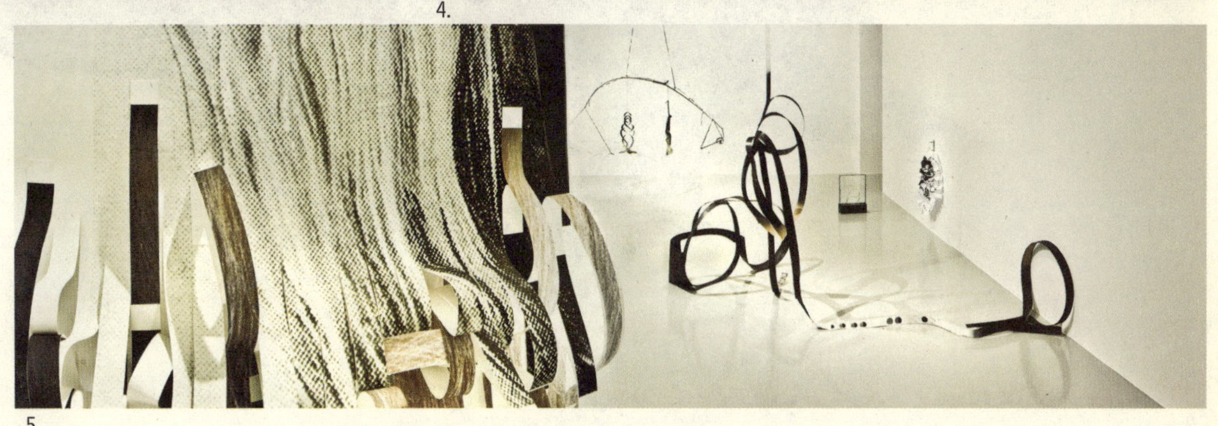
5.

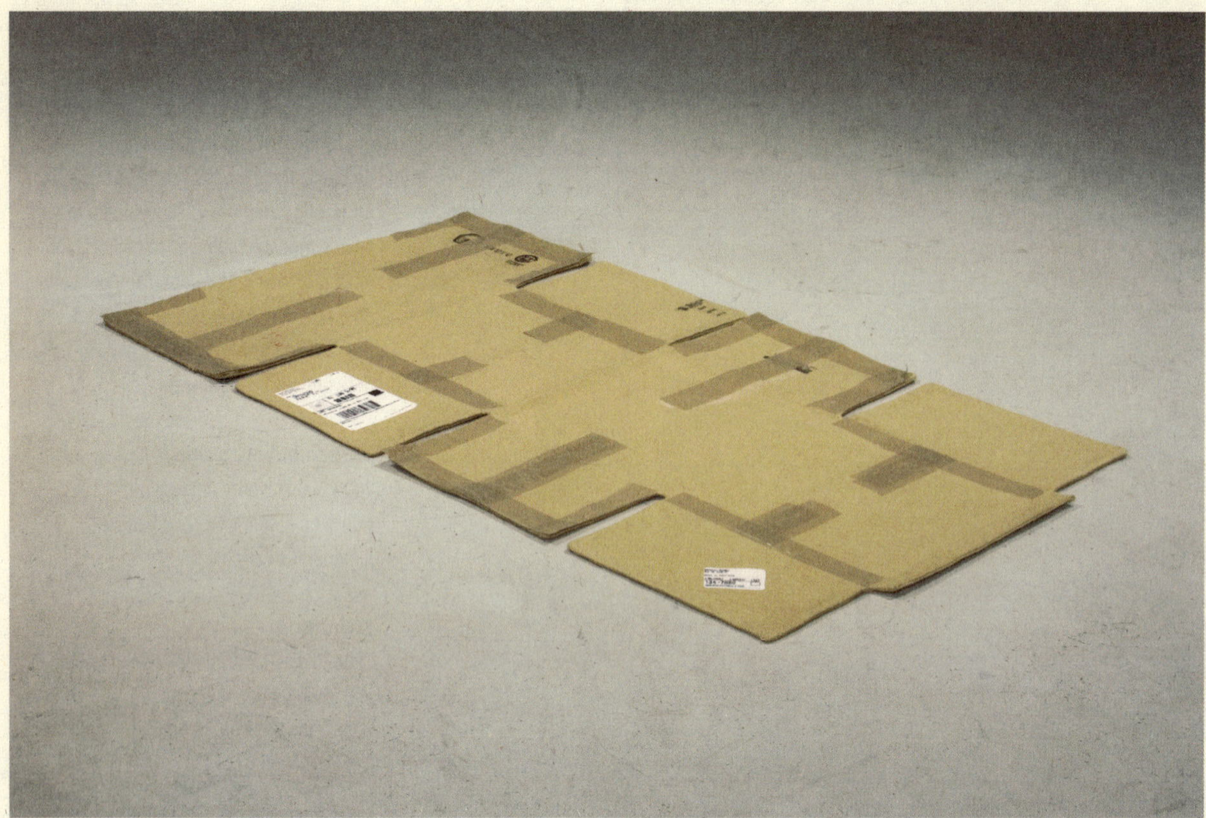

1.

Frances Trombly graduated from the Maryland Institute of Arts in 1998 and lives and works in Miami. She uses labor-intensive processes such as weaving, embroidering, and cross-stitching to fabricate such mundane objects as cardboard boxes, notebook papers, and mops. As painstakingly crafted copies of disposable objects, Trombly's work questions what makes an object worth collecting or displaying, and her traditionally "female" crafts reference issues of domestic labor and feminism.

1. **Box (Broward Paper and Packaging)**

2008, handwoven fabric, embroidery, and packing tape, approx 50 × 24 ½ in (127 × 62 cm)

2. **All Purpose Tarp**

2008, handwoven polypropylene fiber and three pedestals, dimensions variable

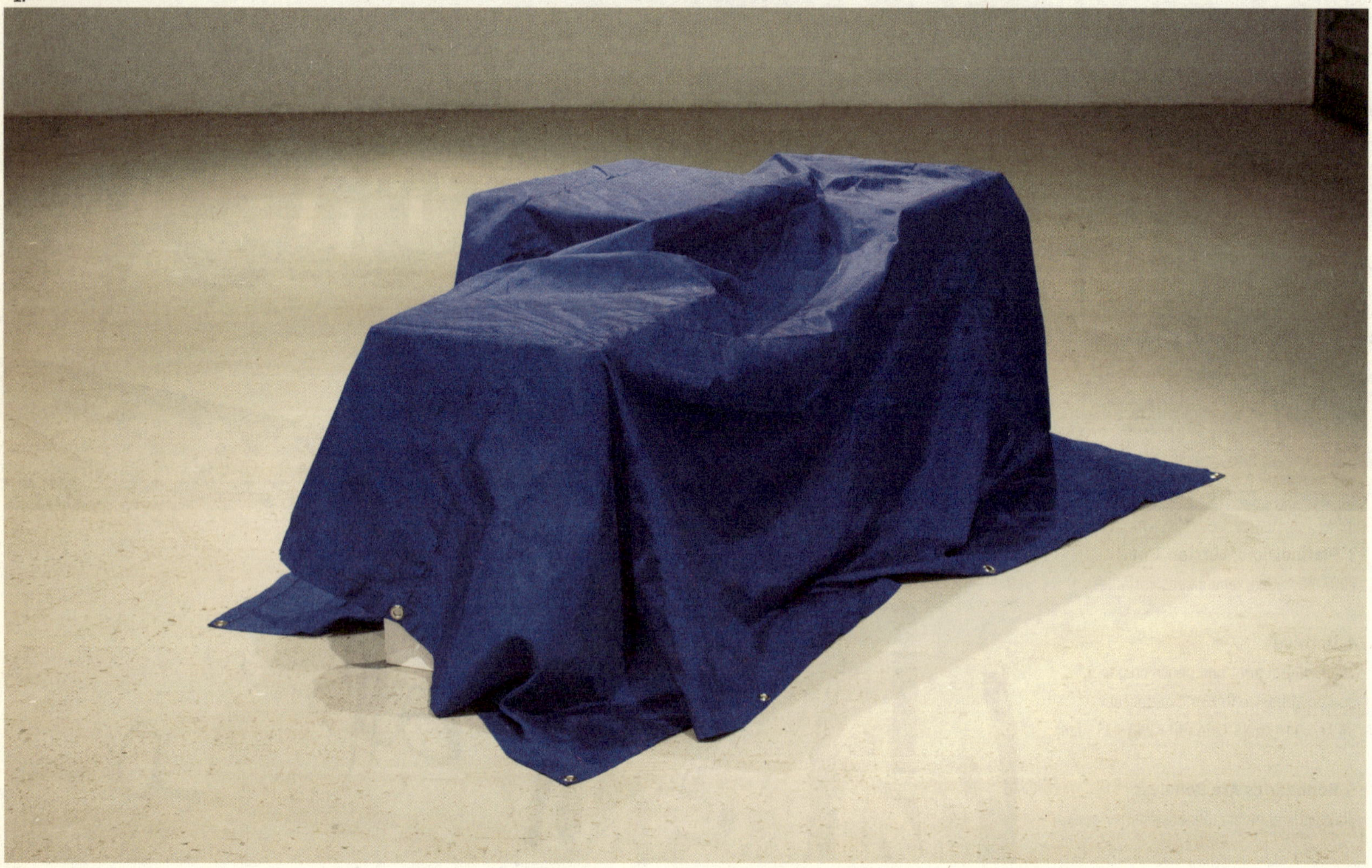

2.

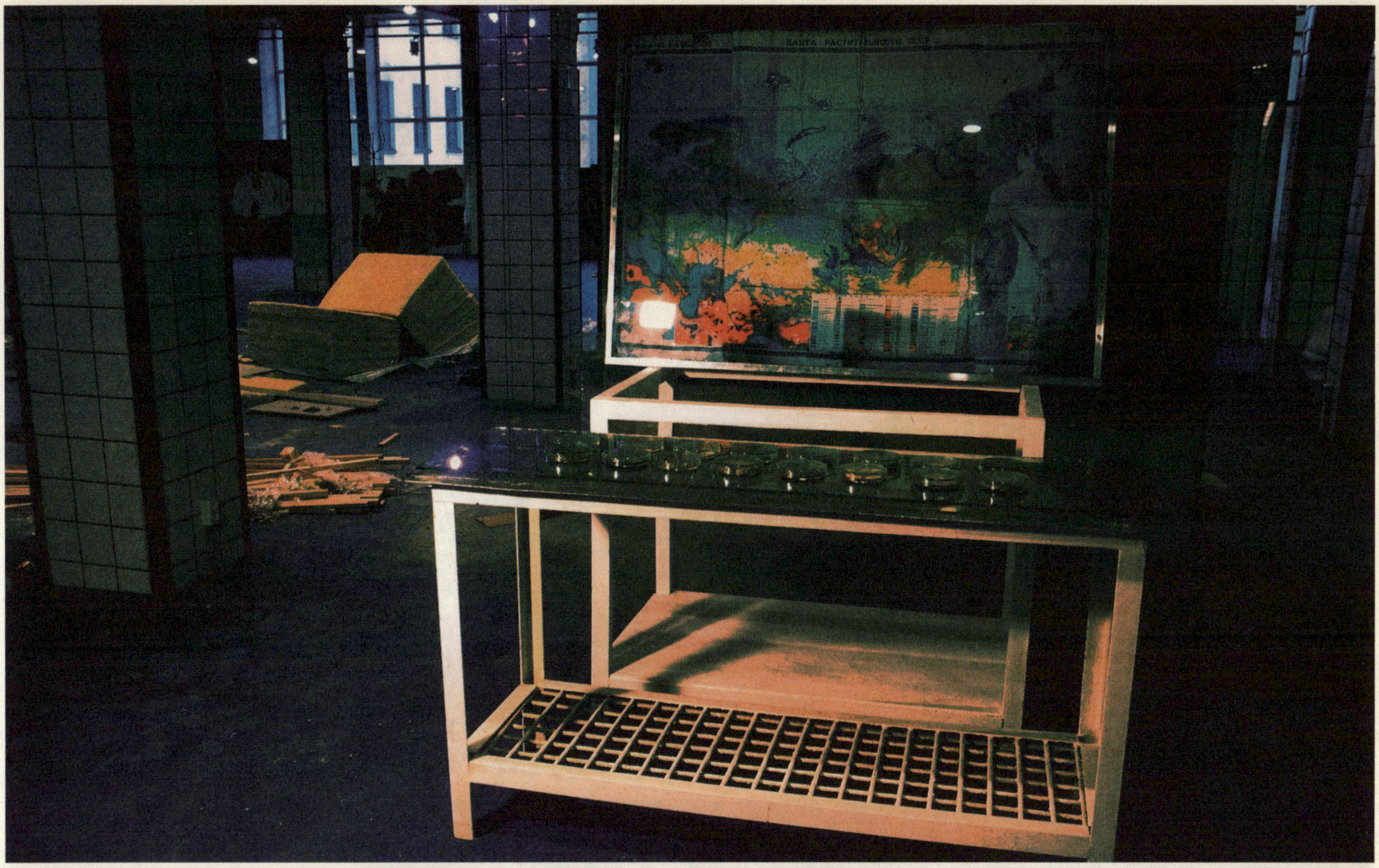

1.

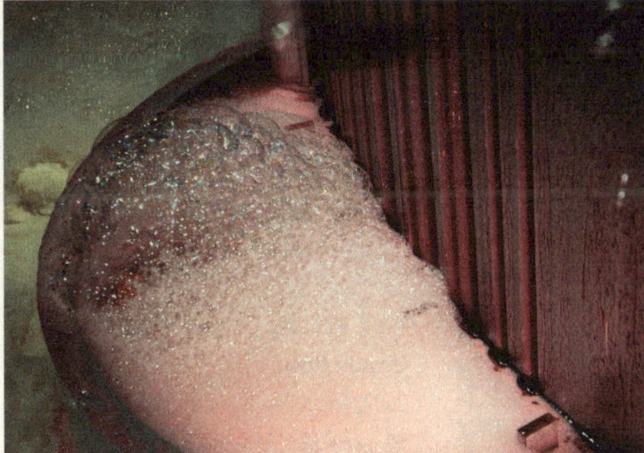

2.

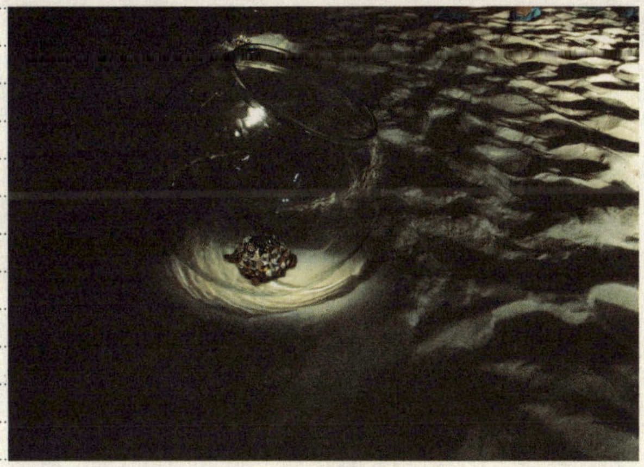

3.

Ilya Trushevsky studied at the St.Petersburg State University of Technology and Design and at the Institute of Contemporary Art in Moscow. He lives and works in Moscow and St. Petersburg. His video installations often play with the idea of illusion: for his 2004-06 video installation **Map of the World**, he used a computer to project flies onto a map of the world, which gradually covered the outlines of the countries, then the countries themselves, as a metaphor for time, and the eventual dissolution of political boundaries and power structures.

1. **Maps** (detail)
2008, print copy of map, 3 videos, pumps, black liquid, petri dishes, nutrient medium, and different kinds of mold, dimensions variable

2 & 3. **Sweet** (detail)
2008, bubbles and foam machines, fountain, fairy, pumps, sugar, salt, live tortoises, Swarovski crystals, and stroboscopes, dimensions variable

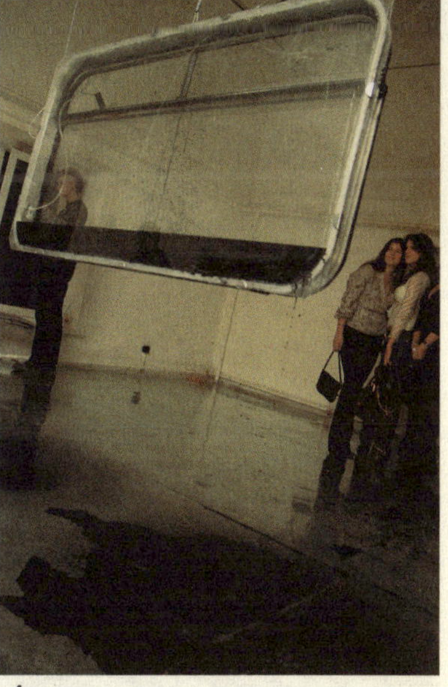

4.

4. **Metro** (detail)
2007, real metro wagon details, black liquid, pumps, electric system, plasma screens, 4 videos, and metal, dimensions variable

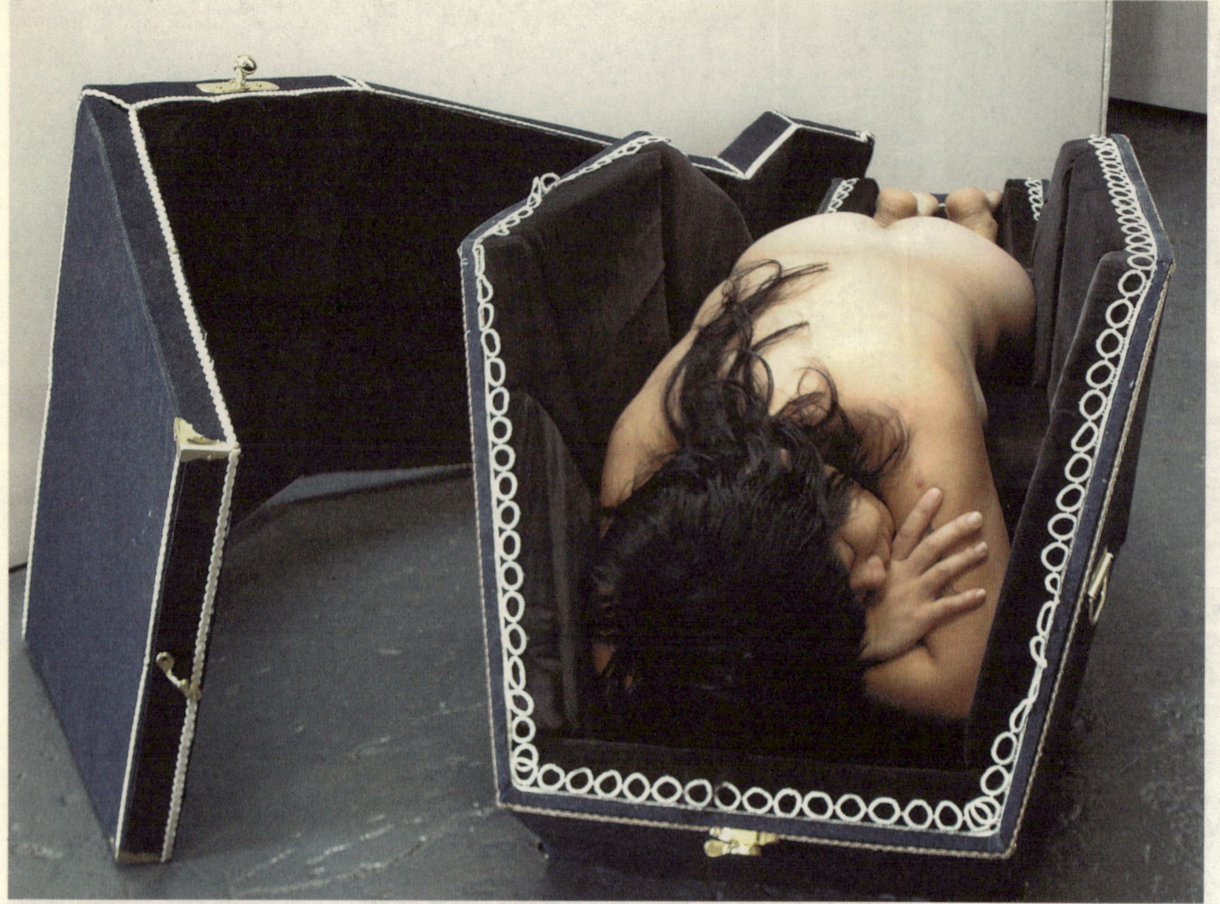

1.

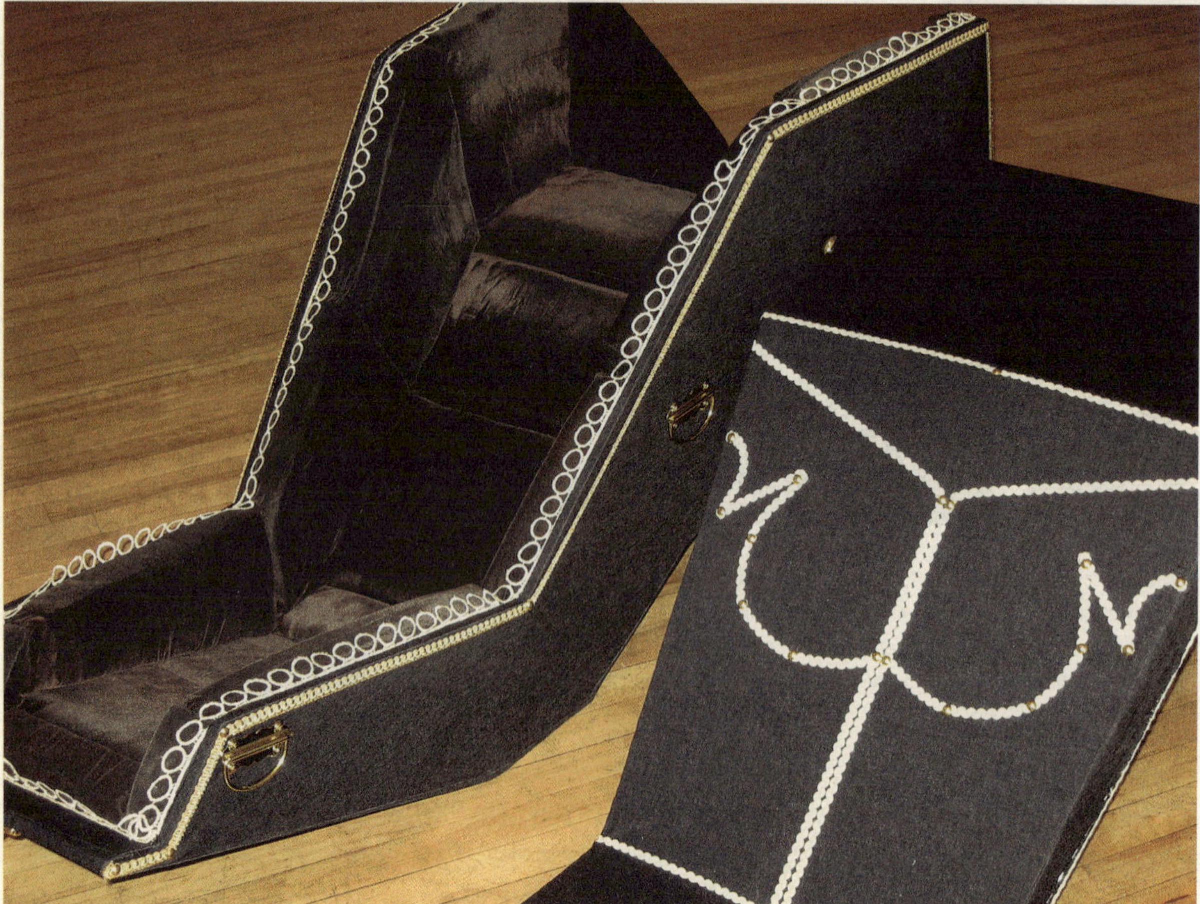

2.

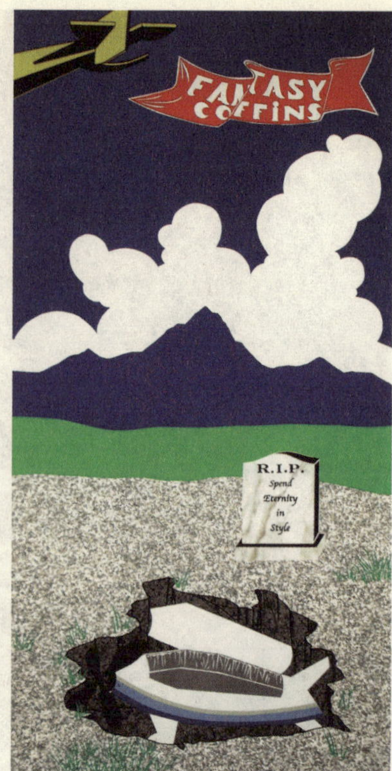

3.

Lan Tuazon participated in the Whitney Independent Study Program in 2003 and lives and works in New York. Her installations explore the way subjectivity is negotiated and represented, investigating the idea of ownership, exchange, and the gaze. In her **free portraits** series (2005), for example, she made three portraits of her subject: a frontal photograph, which the subject kept, a photograph of the subject with his or her back facing the camera, and an item from the scene, which she remade as a figurative sculpture.

1 & 2. **Fantasy Coffins, Bury Me Upside Down**
2007, wood, fabric, foam, and metal, 25 × 27 × 72 in (64 × 69 × 183 cm)

3. **Adverts: Fantasy Coffins**
2007, adhesive vinyl, 24 × 40 in (61 × 102 cm)

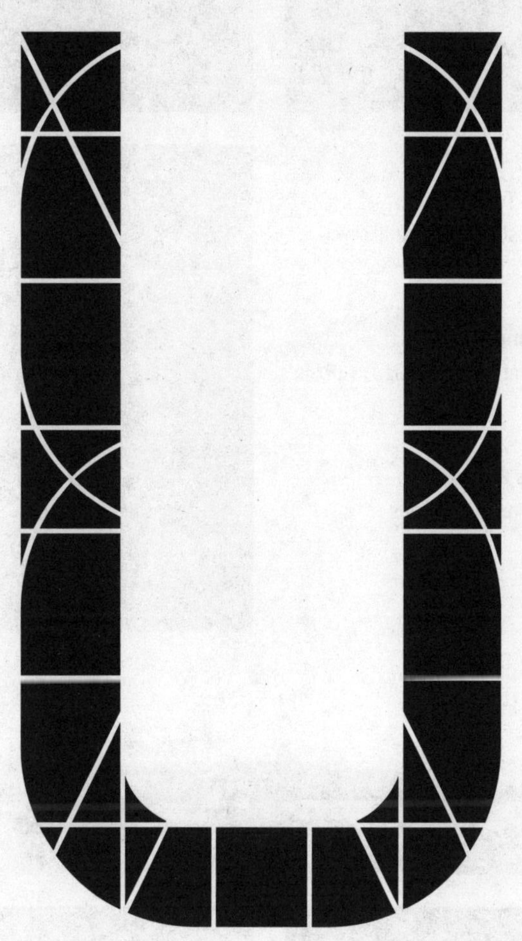

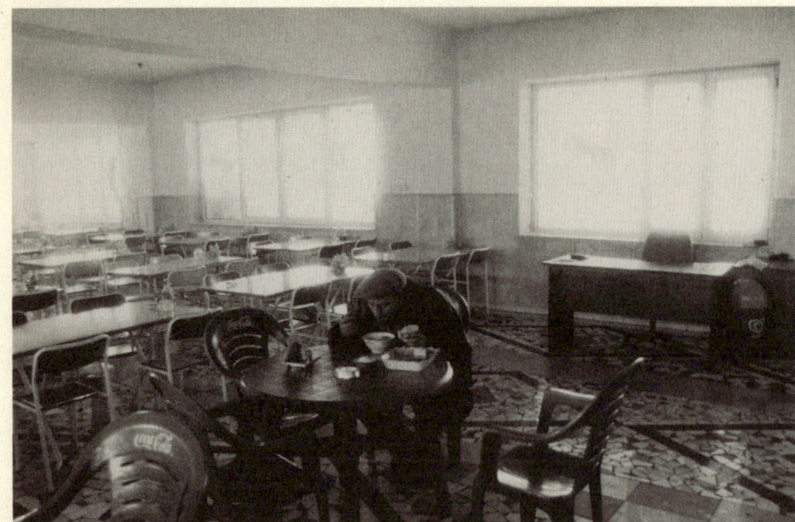

1.

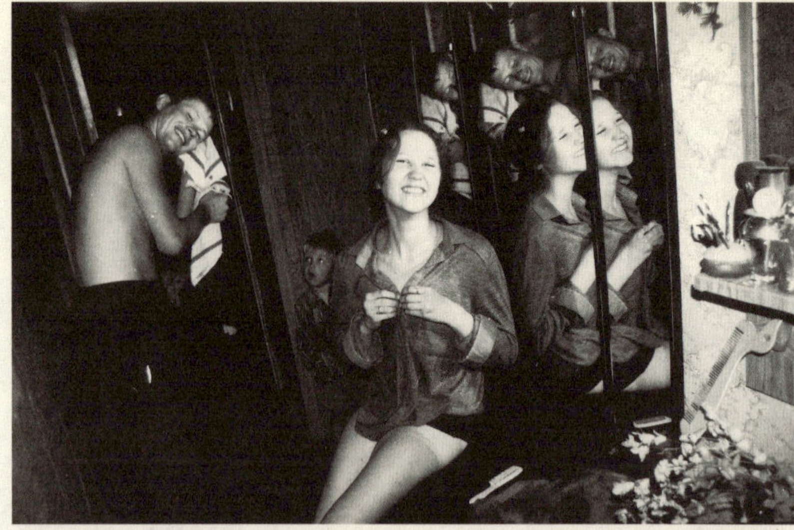

2.

Alexander Ugay lives and works in Almaty, Kazakhstan. He graduated from the State University of Kirgizia in Low in 2002 and is a member of artist group Bronepoezd ("Armored Train" in Russian). His work was included in the Moscow Biennial in 2007. The photographs in his series **Workers 24 Hours** were taken in the former Soviet factories of the Republic of Kazakhstan and reference the portraits of workers taken by August Sander. Recent photographs have focused on the devastated natural landscape surrounding Lake Aral.

1 & 2. **We are from Texas**
2002-05, gelatin silver prints, dimensions variable

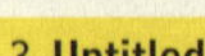

3. **Untitled**
from the series **Two Banks**
2006, 1 of 7 artist-printed gelatin silver prints, dimensions variable

4. **Paradise Landscapes**
2004, digital print on canvas, 31 1/2 × 197 in (80 × 500 cm)

5 & 6. **Workers 24 Hours**
2008, digital color photographs

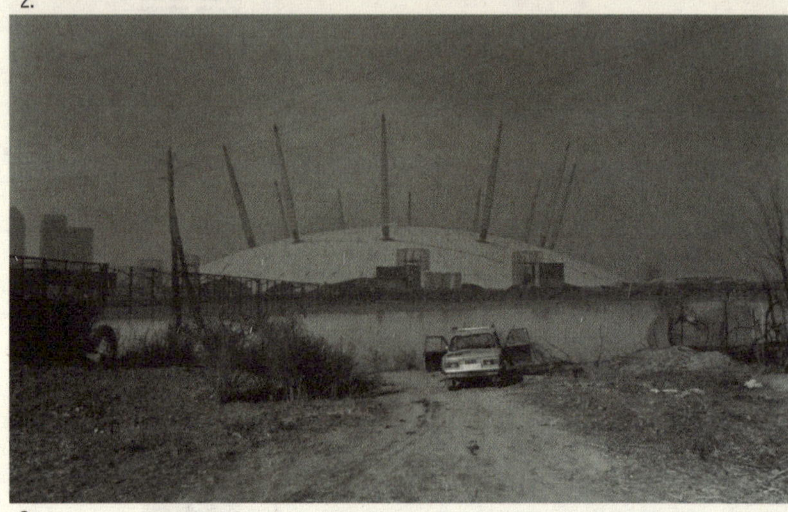

3.

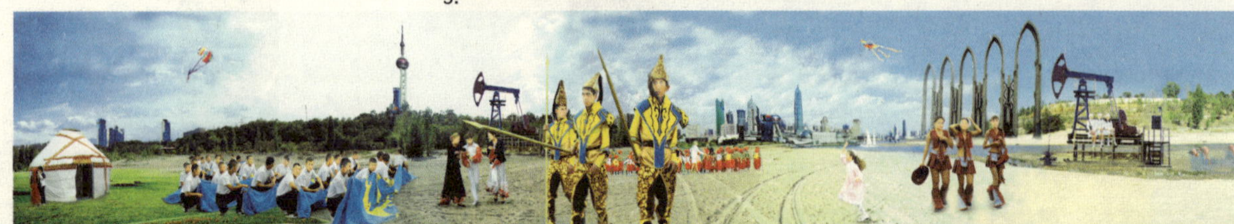

4.

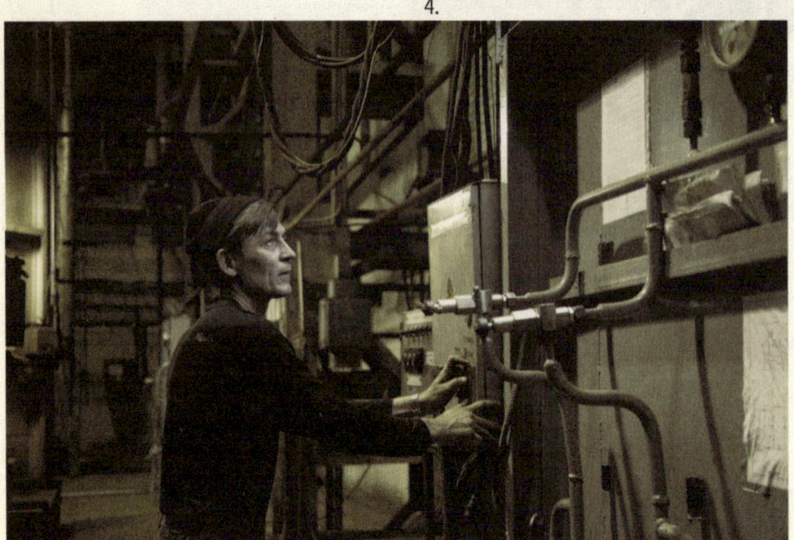

5.

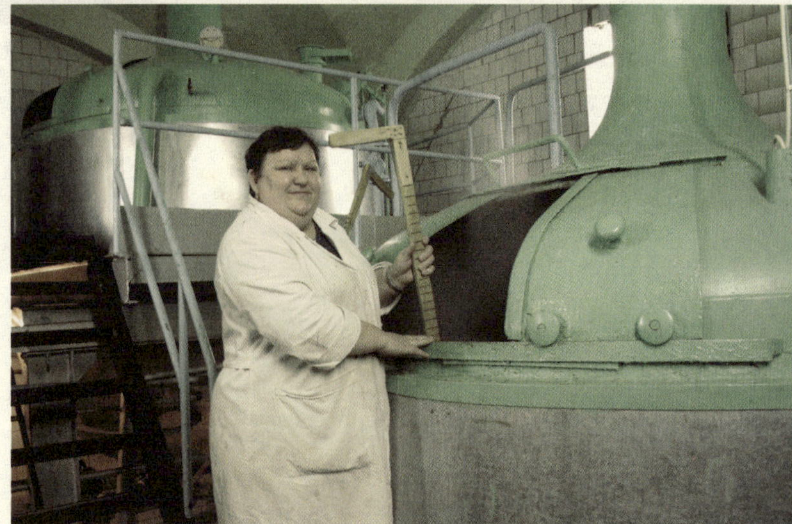

6.

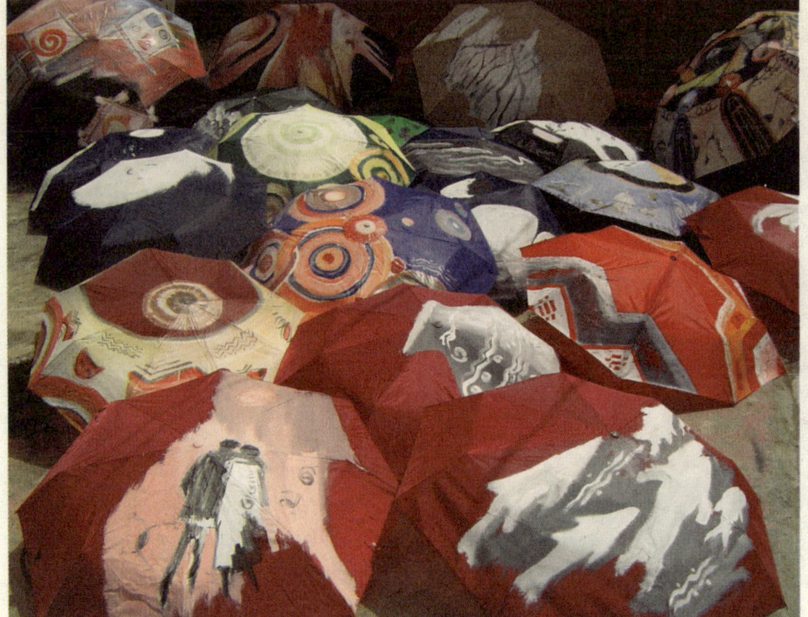

1.

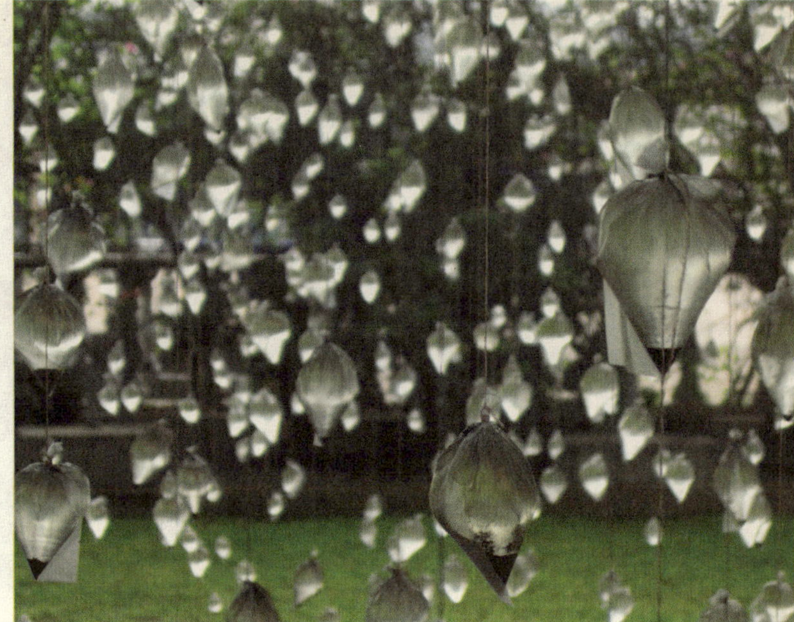

2.

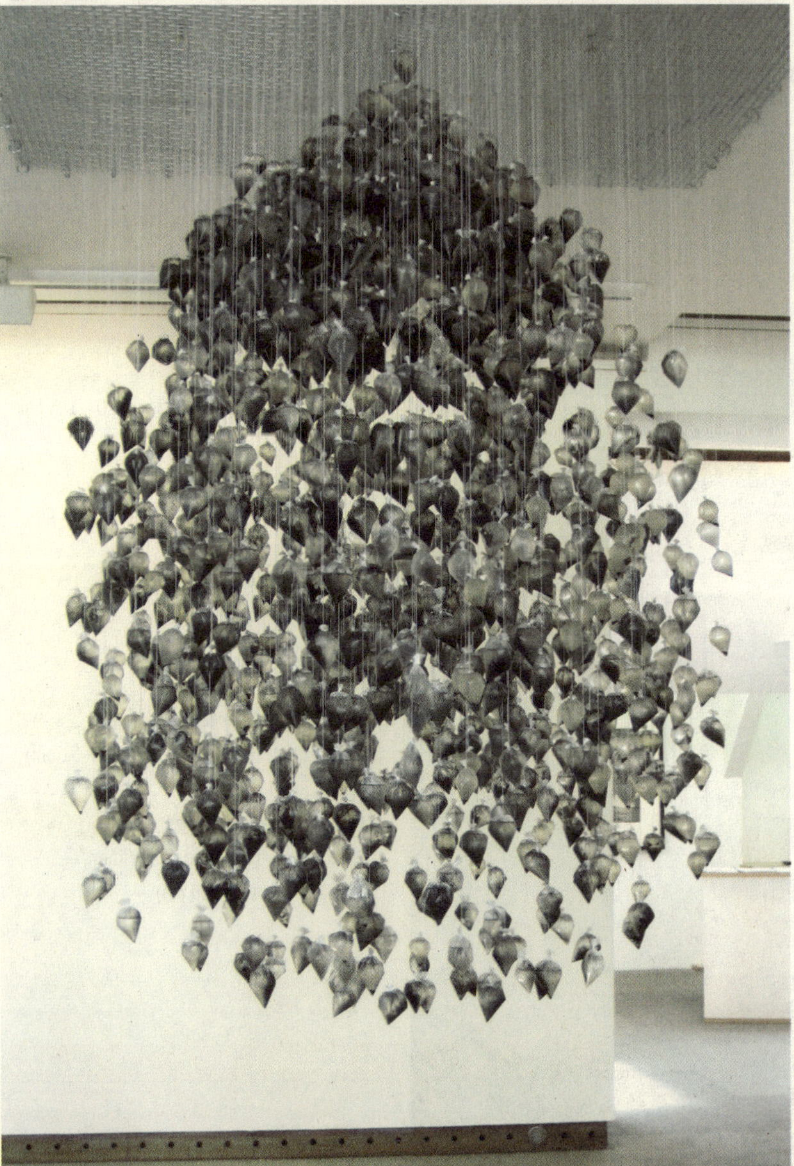

3.

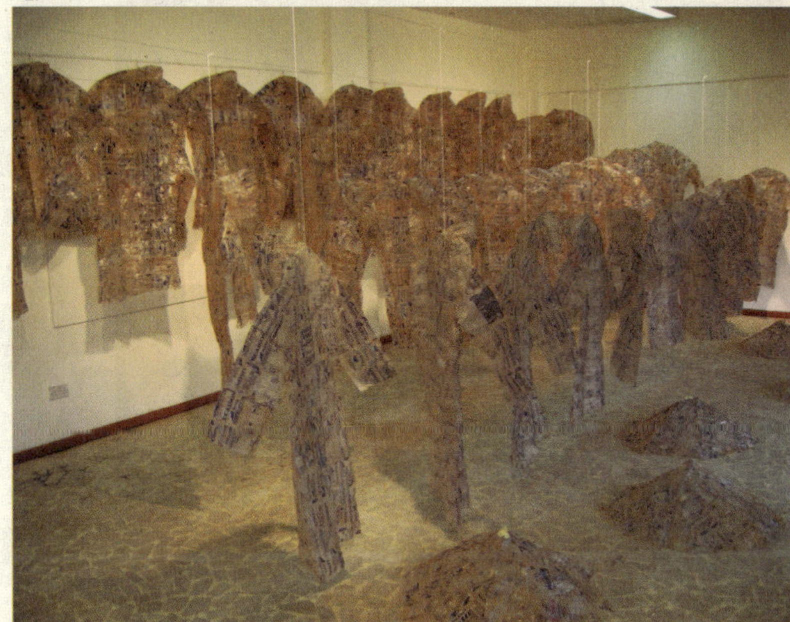

4.

Bright Ugochukwu Eke received his MFA from the University of Nigeria, Nsukka. His conceptually inflected installations utilize materials such as water, zinc roofing sheets, bottles, thread, and sand to address issues of environmental degradation, particularly as it affects his native Nigeria. His work has been included in the Trans Cape Contemporary African Art Exhibition (2007), South Africa, and in the Dak'Art Biennial (2006), where he was awarded the Djerassi Resident Artist Prize.

1. **Natural Connections**
2008, mixed media, dimensions variable

2. **Acid Rain**
2005, water, ammonium chloride, cellophane bags, and threads, dimensions variable

3. **Water Drop**
2008, water, charcoal, cellophane bags, and thread, dimensions variable

4. **Shields**
2006-08, plastic sachets and water, dimensions variable

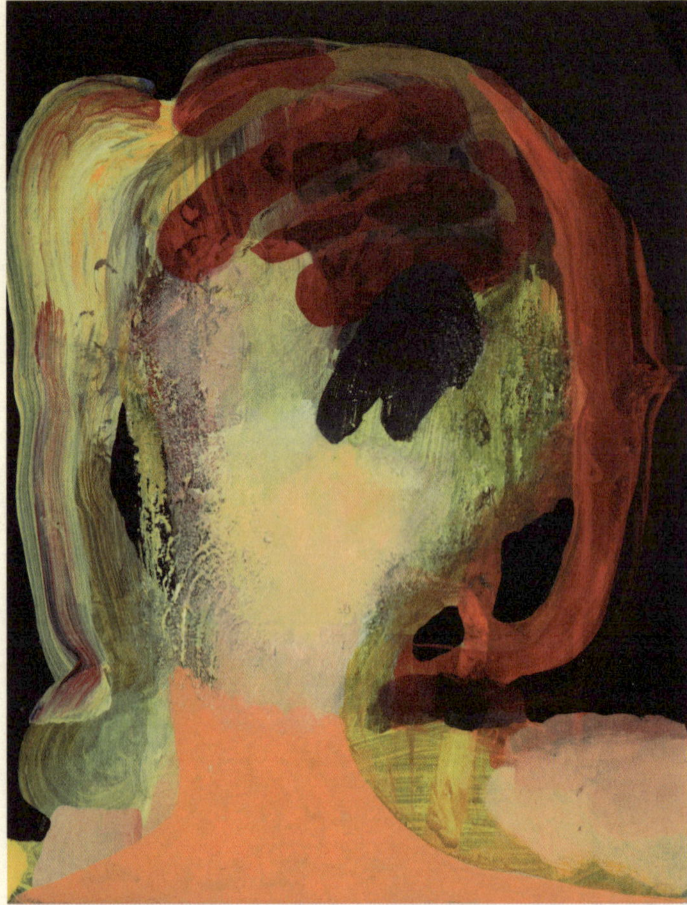
1.

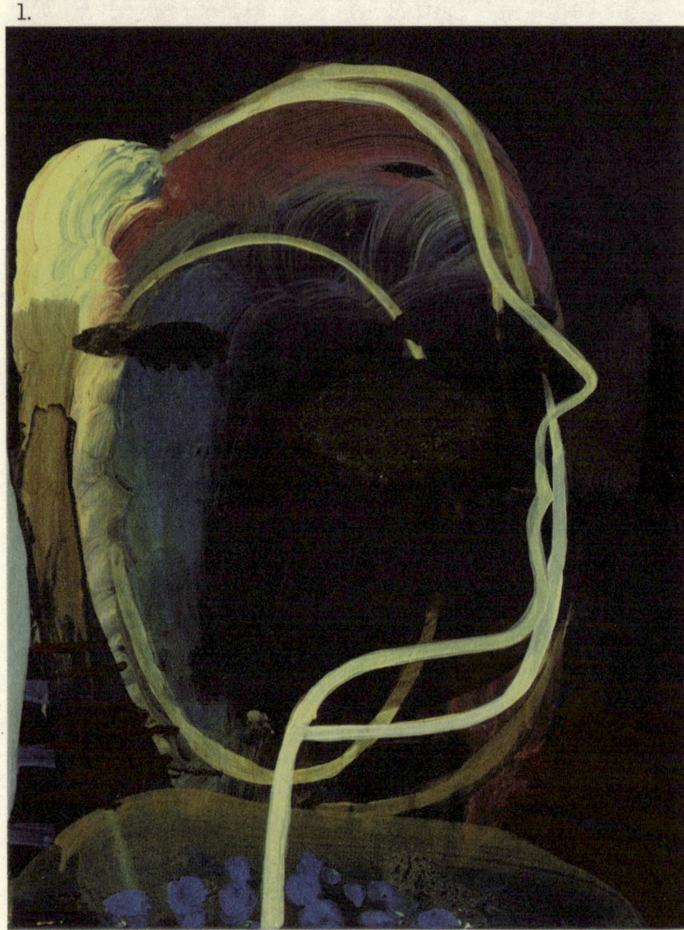
2.

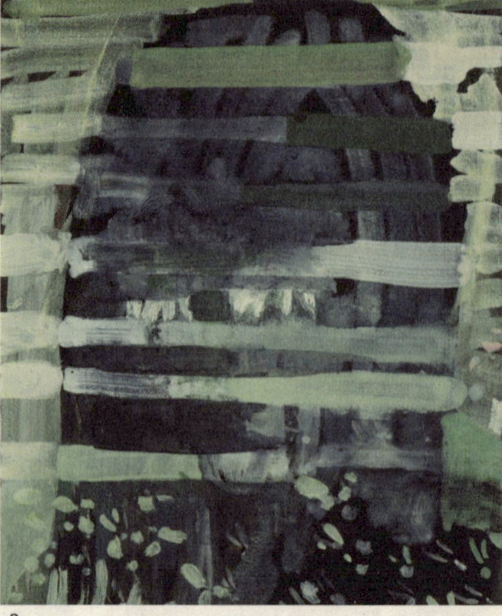
3.

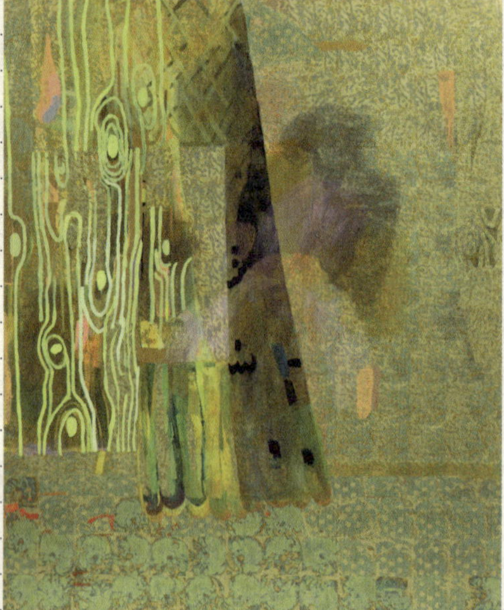
4.

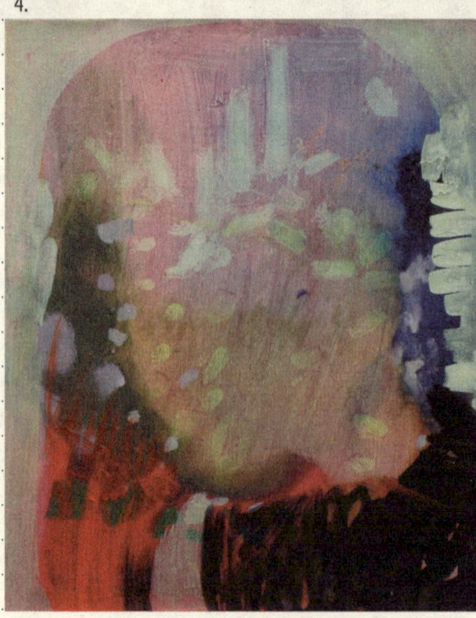
5.

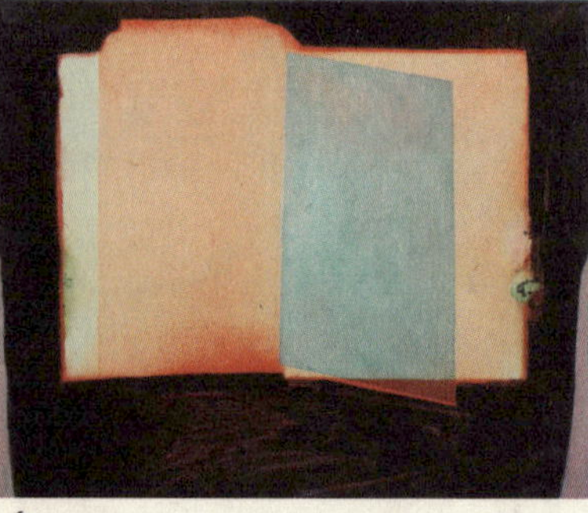
6.

Phoebe Unwin graduated from the Slade School of Fine Art in London, where she lives and works. Unwin's paintings, worked out in drawing books before they are transferred to canvas, shift between figuration and abstraction. Recurring motifs include sunglasses, modernist geometrical forms, and portraiture. Her work moves between explosive abstract motifs and a dark psychological space. **Turn to Pastel** (2008) shows a woman painting, her arm a nearly abstract bright pink "L" and her black hair rendered as a series of rough short brushstrokes.

1. **Hair from Behind**
2008, gloss paint and acrylic on linen, 20 × 16 in (51 × 40.5 cm)

2. **Gold**
2008, oil on linen, 87 × 72 in (220 × 185 cm)

3. **Small Green Head**
2008, oil on linen, 20 × 16 in (51 × 41 cm)

4. **Head Frame**
2008, gloss paint and acrylic on linen, 20 × 16 in (51 × 41 cm)

5. **Untitled (Portrait)**
2008, oil on linen, 24 × 20 in (61 × 51 cm)

6. **Covers and Insides**
2008, spray paint and oil on linen, 20 × 23 ½ in (51 × 60 cm)

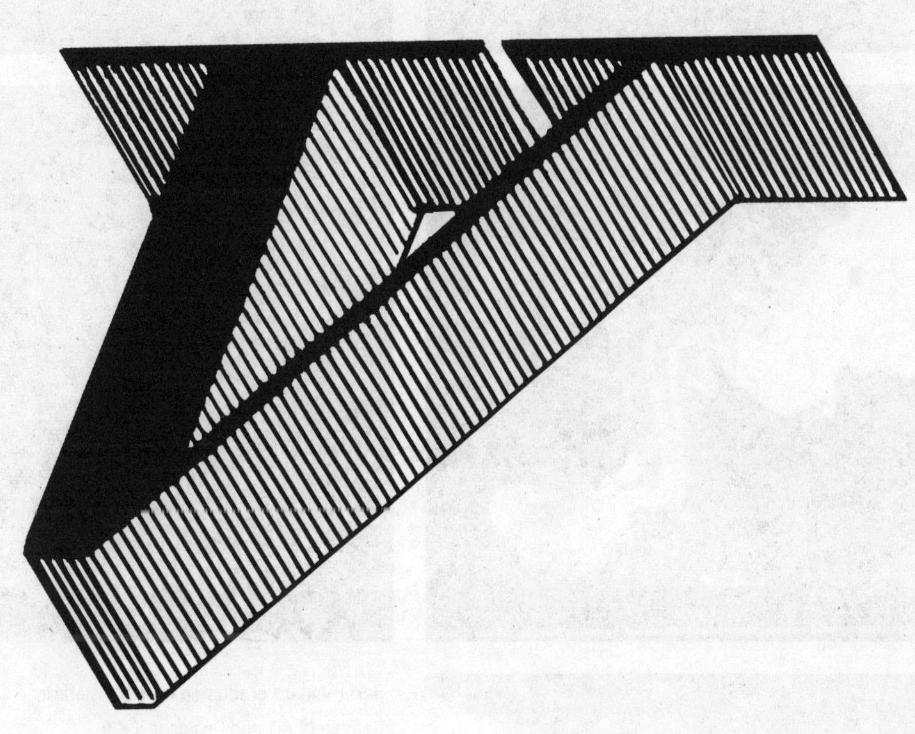

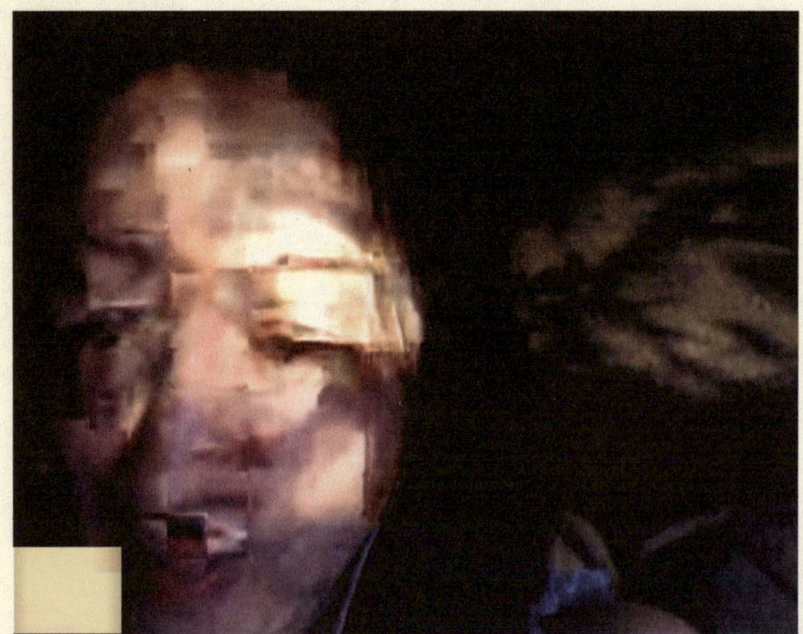
1.

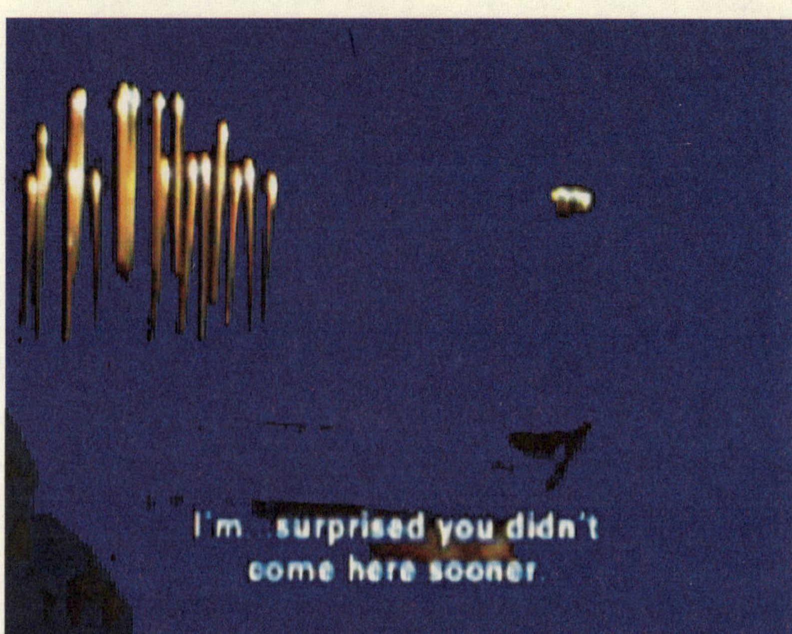

2.

3.

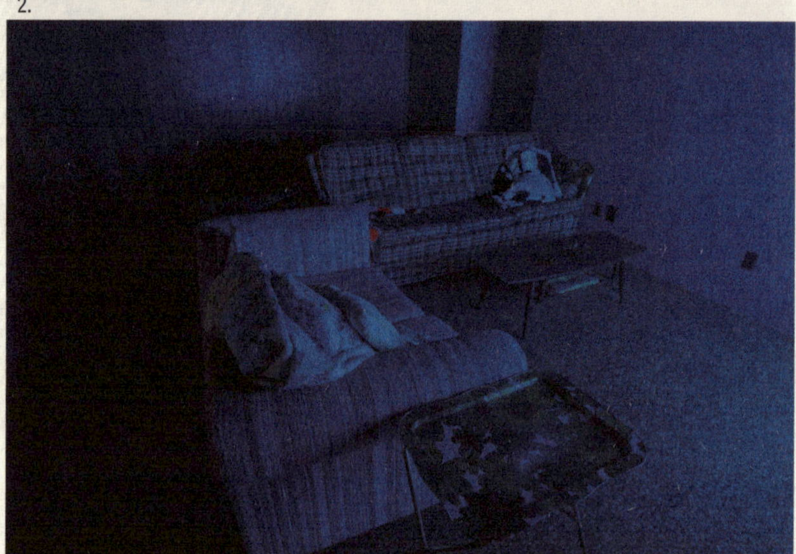
4.

5.

Jaret Vadera graduated from the Ontario College of Art and Design in 1999 and plans to complete her MFA at Yale University in 2009. Her work, in which found photographs are blurred and partially concealed with acrylic paint, explores the way the mind processes fragmented or ambiguous data. Other works, such as **1982 (Blade Runner)**, slow and fragment video clips, altering their reading.

1. **Andrea**
2005, digital print from screen capture of Skype conversation, 31 × 42 in (79 × 107 cm)

2, 4 & 5. **1982 (Blade Runner)**
2005, video of manipulated footage from the film Blade Runner, 3 min; video projector, and screen, projected at 36 × 48 in screen (91 × 122 cm)

3. **Untitled**
2008, digital print on backlight film, 16 × 22 in (41 × 56 cm)

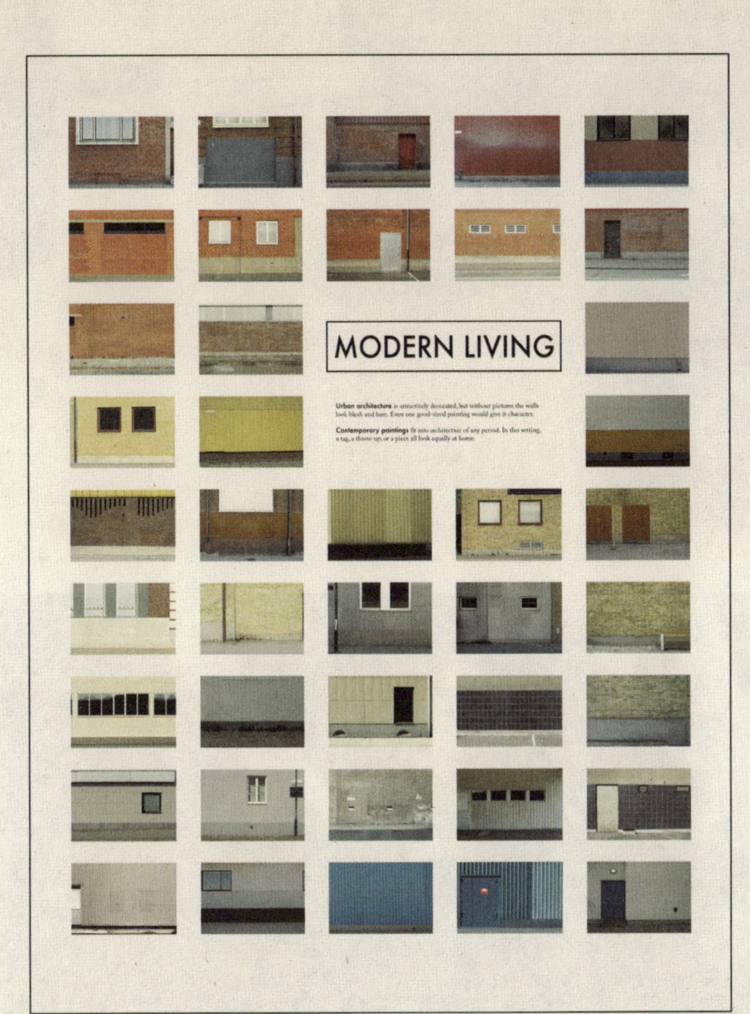

1.

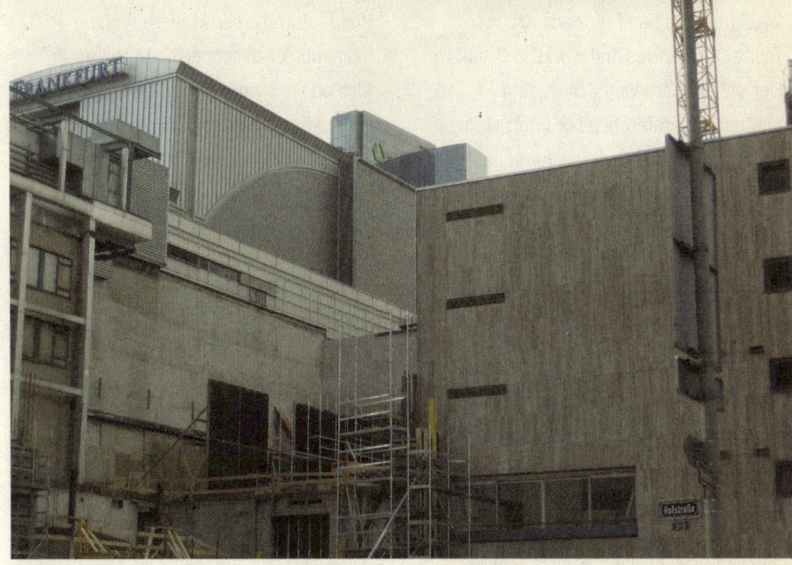

2.

Fredrik Vaerslev photographs a house or apartment, commissions a painting of that property, then photographs the painting in the house or apartment itself according to the homeowners' wishes. The artworks provoke a dialogue between interior and exterior, and between artist and subject.

1. **Modern Living** (detail)
2006, poster, 39 ½ × 27 ½ in (100 × 70 cm)

2. **Untitled**
from the series **My Architecture**
2008-present, digital image

3. **Property Paintings (vol. 1 of 12) Anne Britt**
with Shwan Dler Oaradaki
2007-09, Lightjet print, 30 × 34 ½ in (78 × 88 cm)

4. **Property Paintings (vol. 5 of 12) Stale Bernadette & Vanessa**
with Shwan Dler Oaradaki
2007-09, Lightjet print, 31 ½ × 34 ½ in (80 × 88 cm)

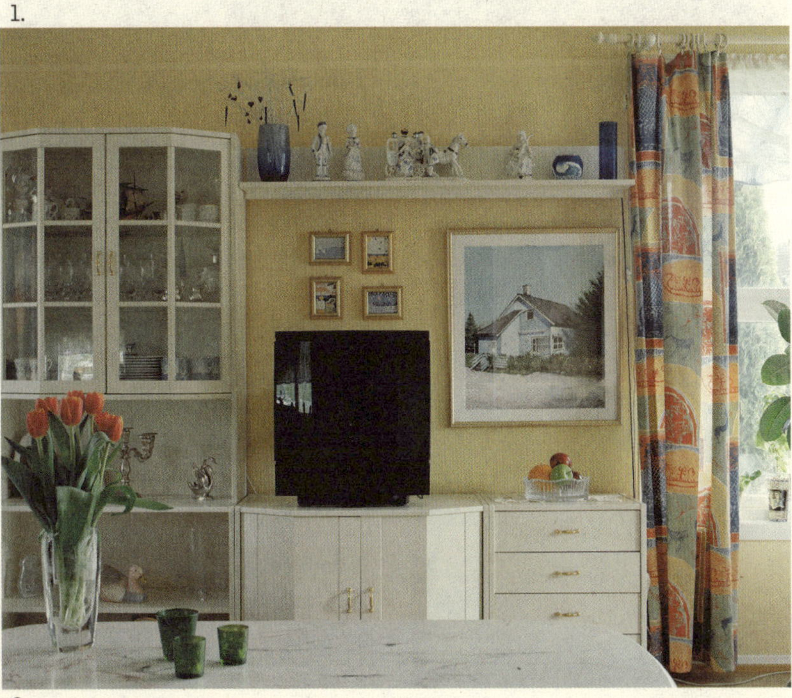

3.

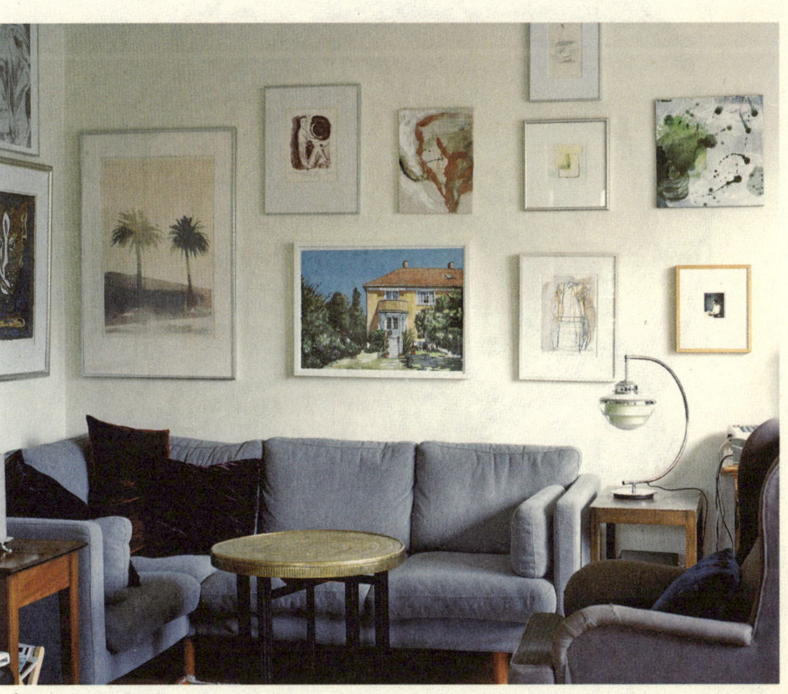

4.

J. Parker Valentine received her MFA in 2007 from the San Francisco Art Institute. She lives and works in Brooklyn. Her gestural drawings, films, and photographs reference her interest in mythology, filtered through personal experience. In a 2008 exhibition at the Lisa Cooley Gallery in New York, Valentine showed an untitled 16 mm film that featured a series of symbolic moments, each connected to the earth. Also on view were several intimate, enigmatic photographs and curtainlike sculptures that framed the doors and windows of the gallery, transforming sunshine into dim light.

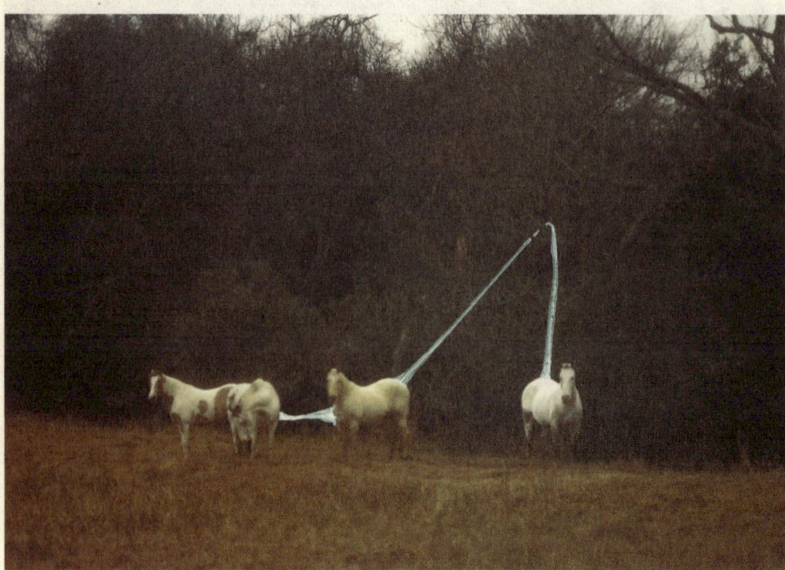

1.

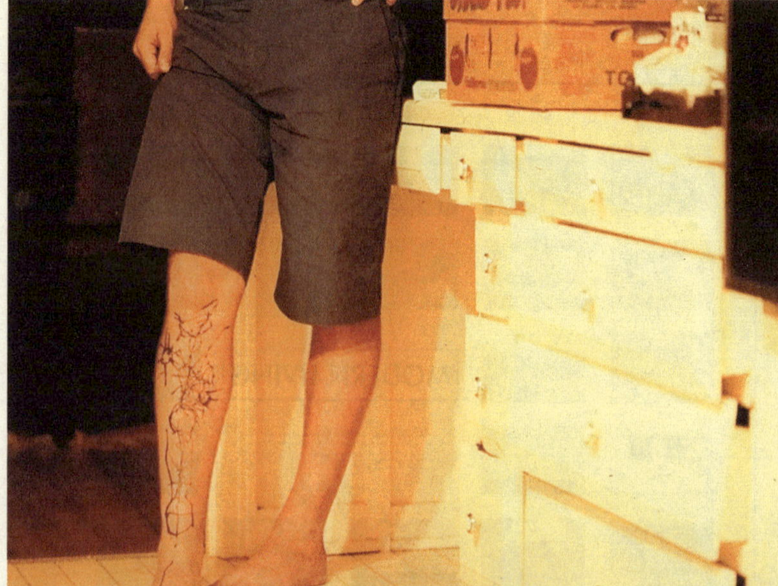

3.

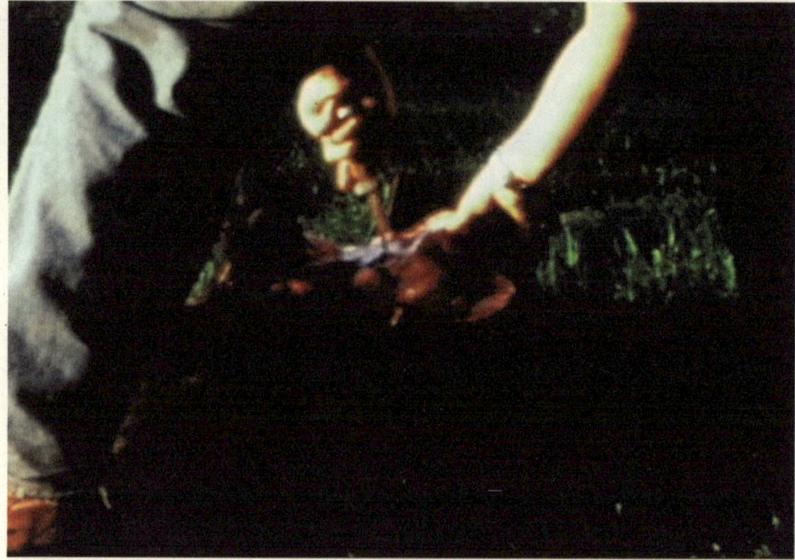

4.

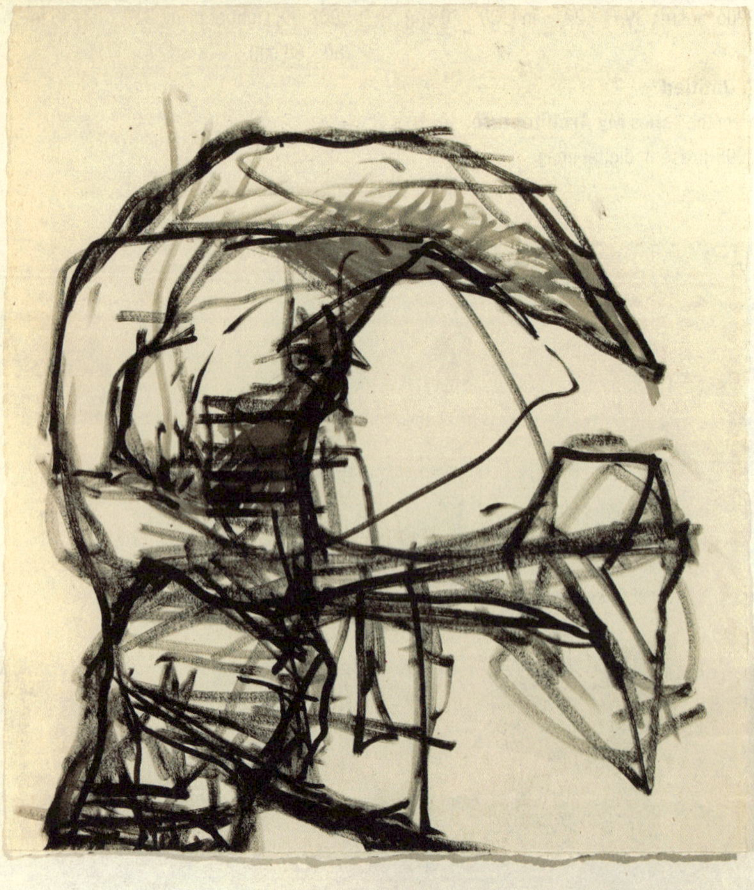

2.

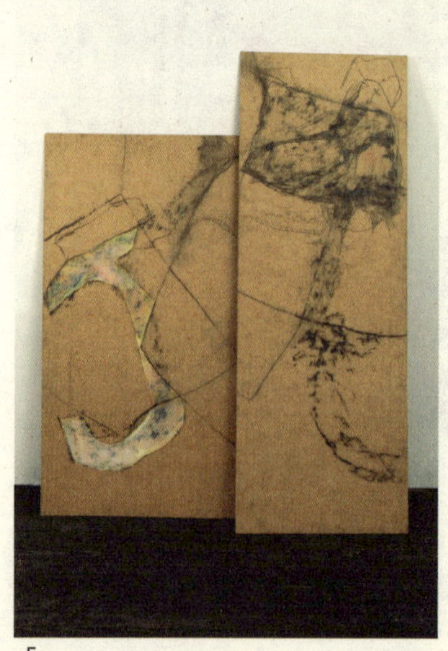

5.

1. Untitled
2008, ink on unique photograph, 4 × 6 in (10 × 15 cm)

2. Untitled
2008, ink on paper, 29 × 27 in (74 × 69 cm)

3. Untitled
2008, unique color photograph, 5 × 7 in (13 × 18 cm)

4. Untitled
2005-08, 16 mm film projection, 1 min

5. Untitled
2008, graphite and oil pastel on MDF, 57 ½ × 43 × 7 in (146 × 109 × 18 cm)

Guido Van Der Werve completed a residency in 2006 at the Rijksakademie in Amsterdam, where he lives and works. He had a solo exhibition at the Hayward Gallery in London in 2008. Wieland studied classical music and piano, and his melancholic, performance-based short films often create imaginary realities that revolve around music and the notion of time. Among his videos is one of the artist trudging before an icebreaker in the Gulf of Finland, accompanied by classical piano played by Van Der Werve himself.

1. **I smile at the world and the world smiles back**
2002, photograph mounted on aluminum, 28 3/4 × 19 3/4 in (73 × 50 cm)

2. **Nummer negen: The day I didn't turn with the world**
2007, time-lapse photography, 9 min

3. **I don't want to get involved in this, I don't want to be part of this, talk me out of it**
2005, 35 mm film, 11 min 46 sec

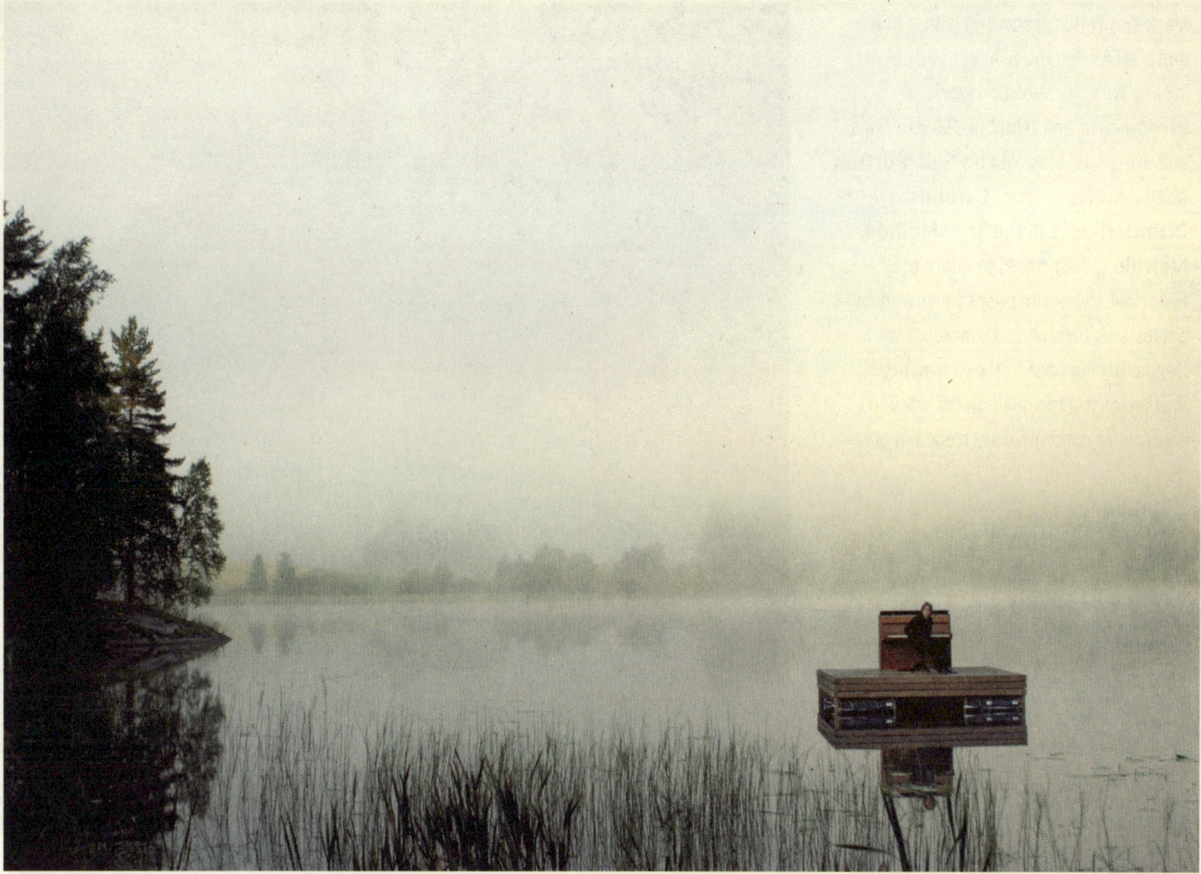

1.

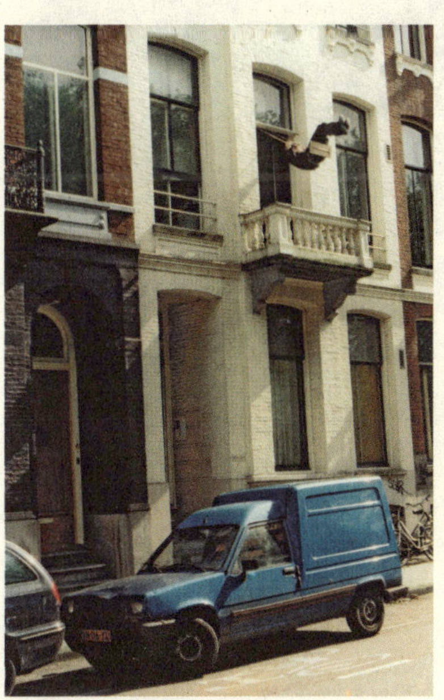

2.

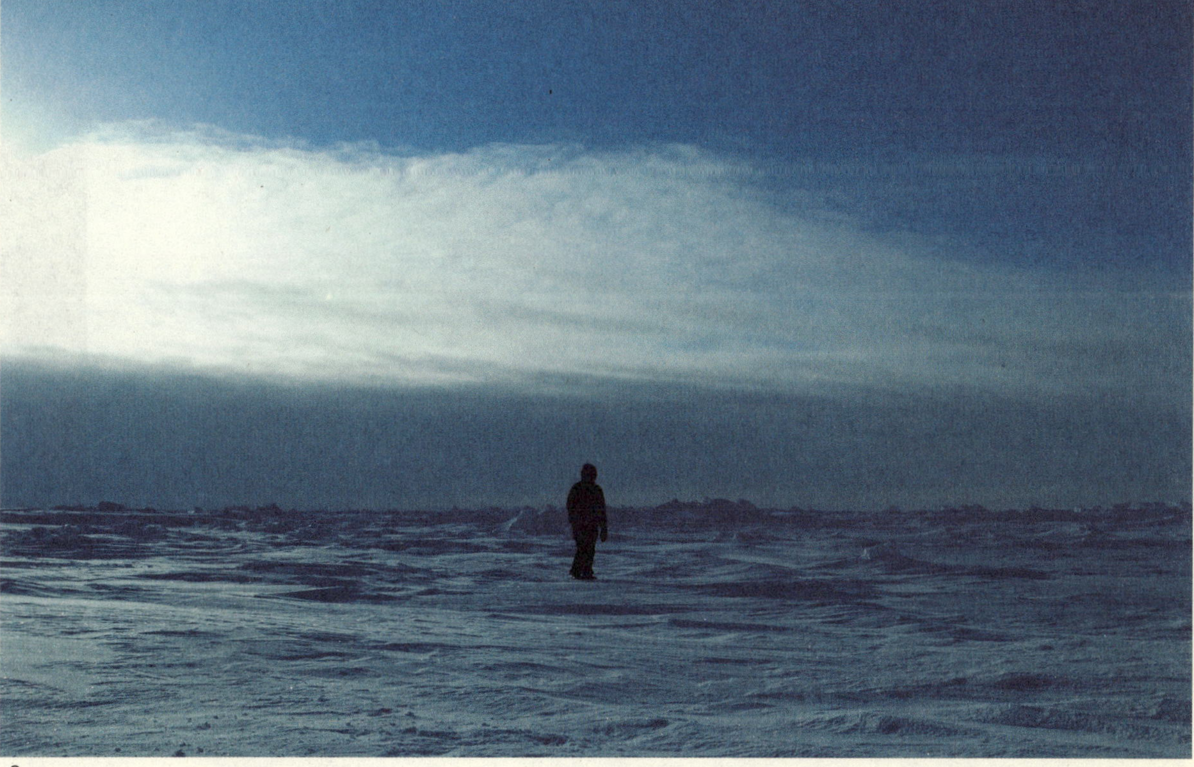

3.

VAN YETTER, MARK

b. 1978 East Stroudsburg, Pennsylvania, USA

Mark Van Yetter graduated with a BFA and a MFA from the School of Visual Arts in New York. He lives and works in Pennsylvania and Istanbul. His paintings and drawings, including his **Self-Portrait** (2006) and his abstract **Careful Disorderliness is the True Method, Melville** (2008), seem to quote art historical styles and poses borrowed from painters as diverse as Delacroix and Degas. Arcing back to these traditions, Van Yetter tries to position his work in contrast to contemporary trends in art.

1. **Untitled**
2008, oil on wood, 19 1/4 × 28 3/4 in (49 × 73 cm)

2. **Untitled**
2007, watercolor on paper, 22 1/4 × 29 1/2 in (57 × 75 cm)

3. **Self-Portrait**
2006, oil on wood, 19 1/4 × 13 in (49 × 33 cm)

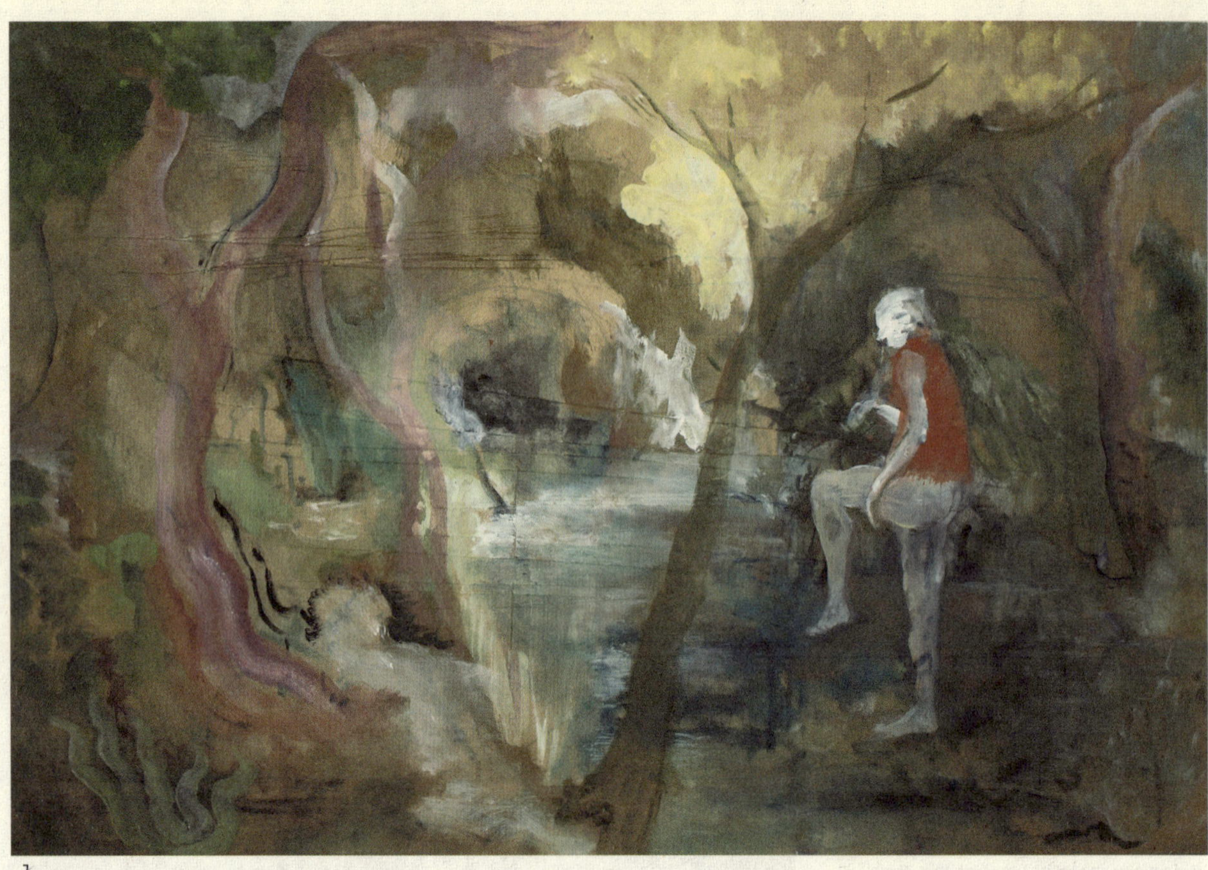

1.

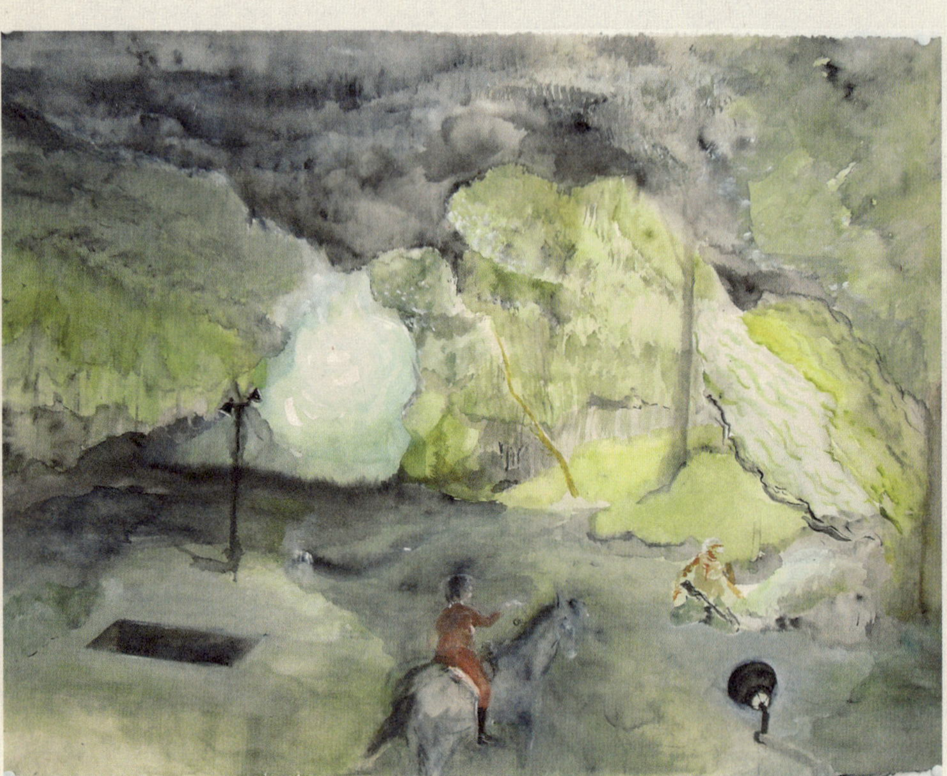

2.

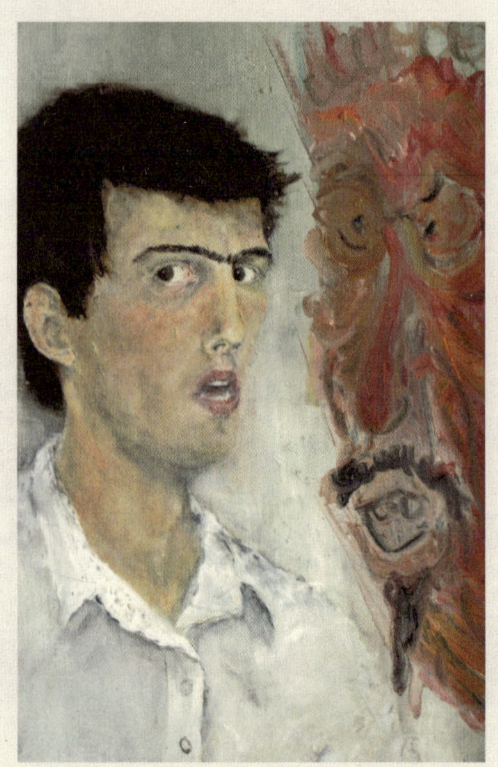

3.

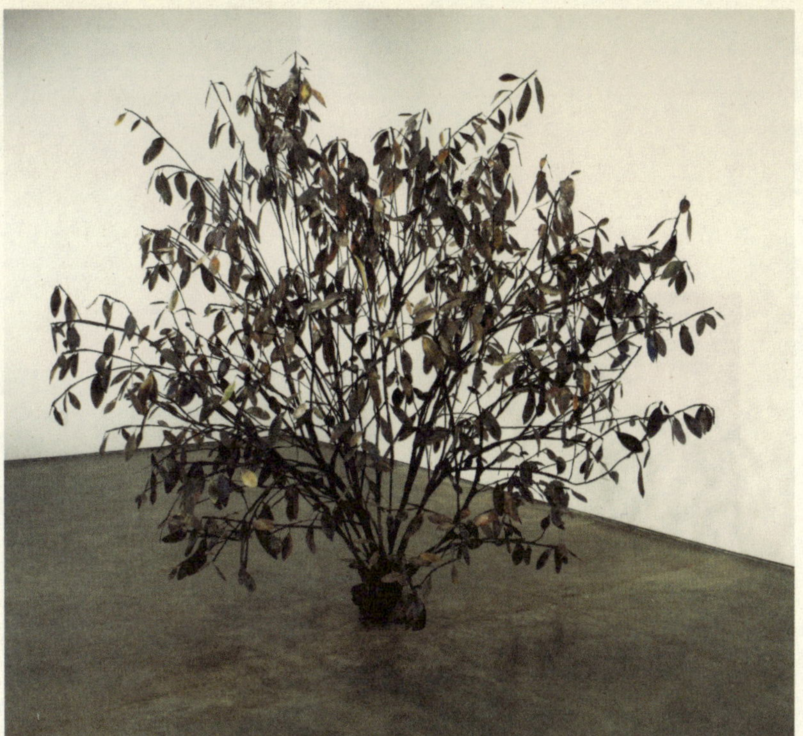

1.

Johannes VanDerBeek graduated with a BFA in 2004 from Cooper Union in New York, where he currently lives and works. His sculptures and works on paper are based on his observations and transformations of familiar objects. **Bush** (2007), for example, is a life-sized bush with leaves made out of wax, each being a semi-translucent painting of outer space.

Ruins (2007) is a large-scale sculptural ruin made of pages from Life, National Geographic, and Time magazines.

1 & 2. **Bush**
2007, wax, metal, wood, and pigment, 89 × 89 × 89 in (226 × 226 × 226 cm)

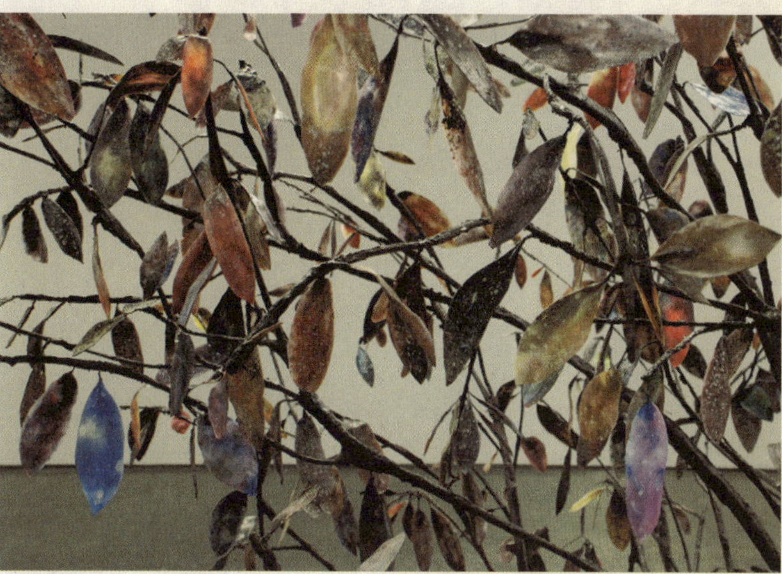

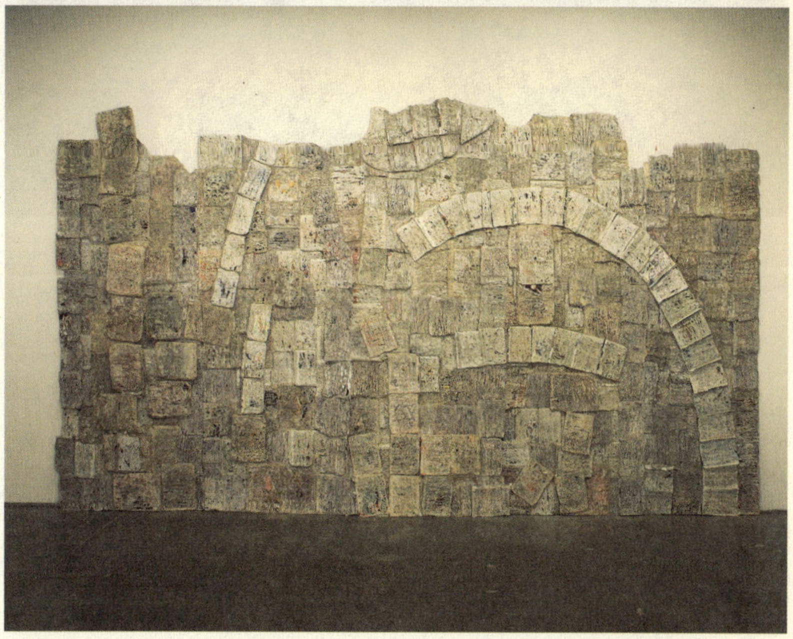

2.

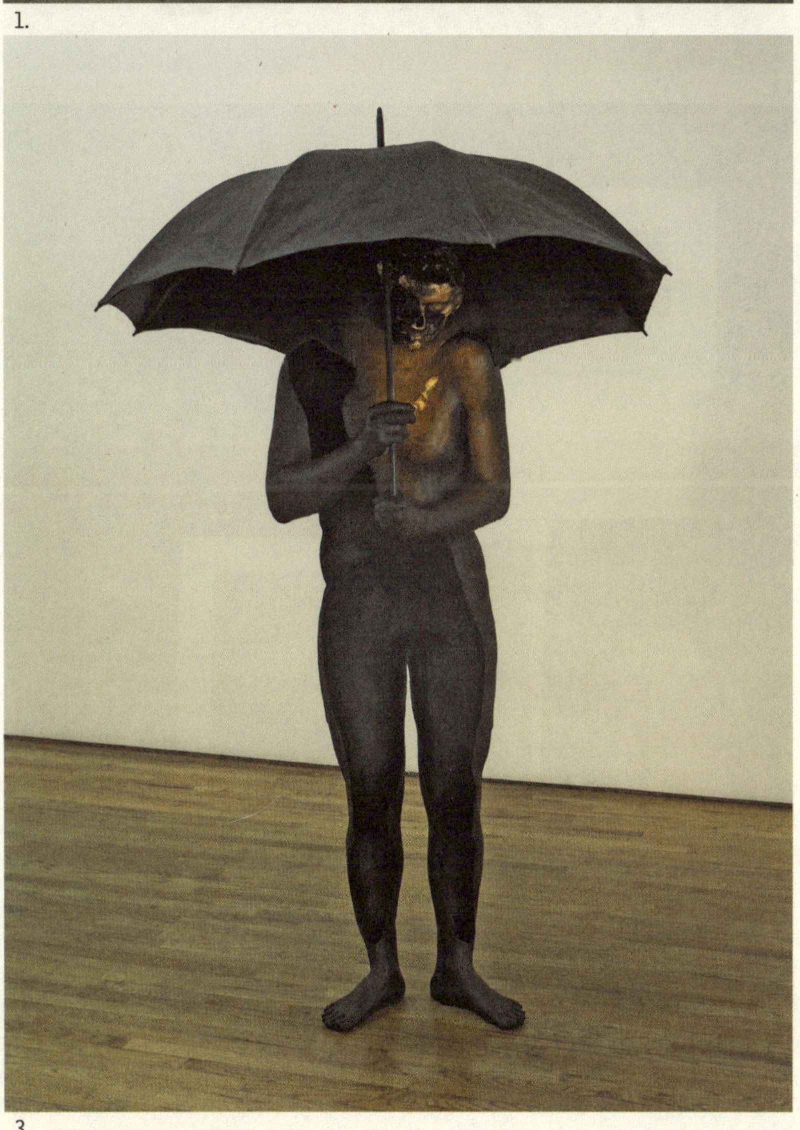

3.

4.

3. **Seeing A Man Stand Under An Umbrella From A Distance**
2007, fiberglass, HydroCal, umbrella, and acrylic paint, 79 × 44 1/2 × 43 in (201 × 113 × 109 cm)

4. **Ruins**
2007, Life, Time, and National Geographic magazines, wood and glue, 113 × 200 in (287 × 508 cm)

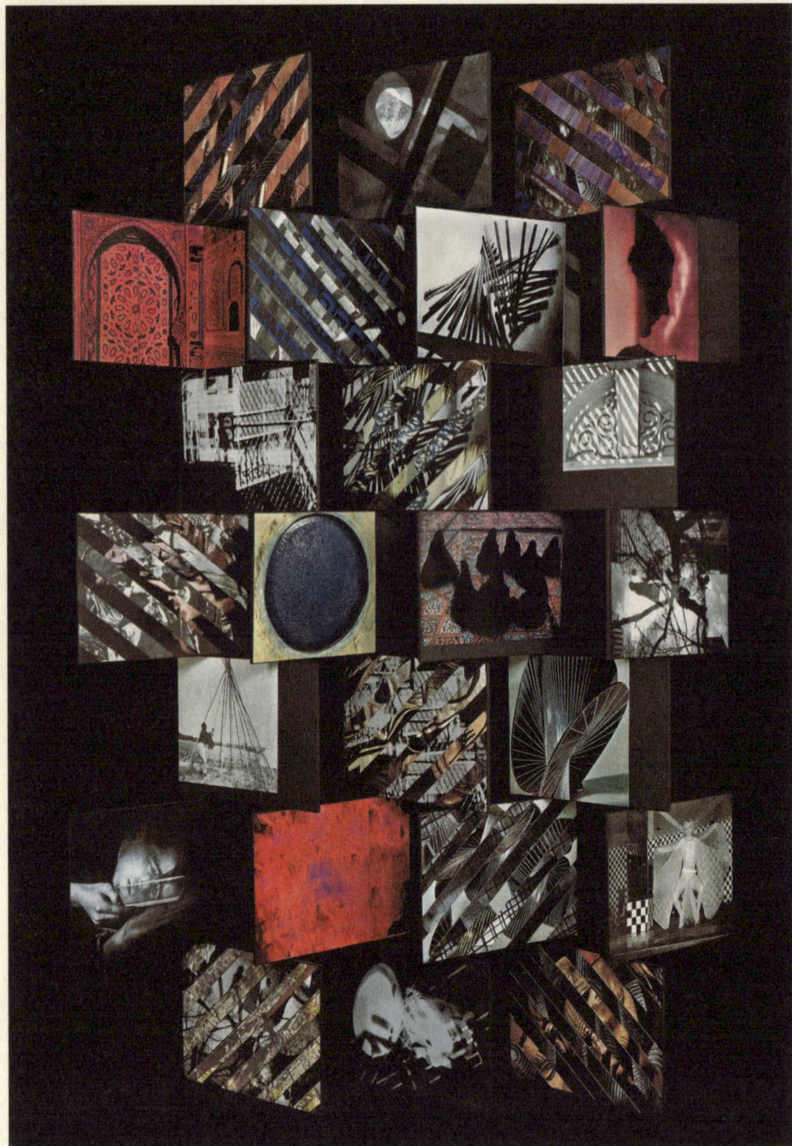

1.

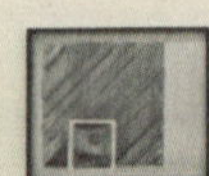
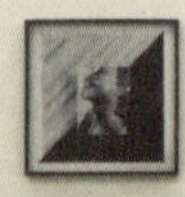
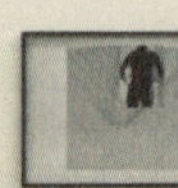
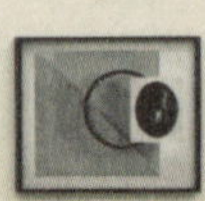
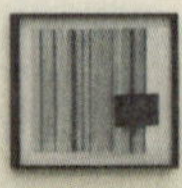
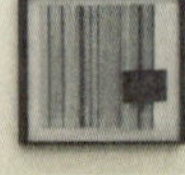

2.

3.

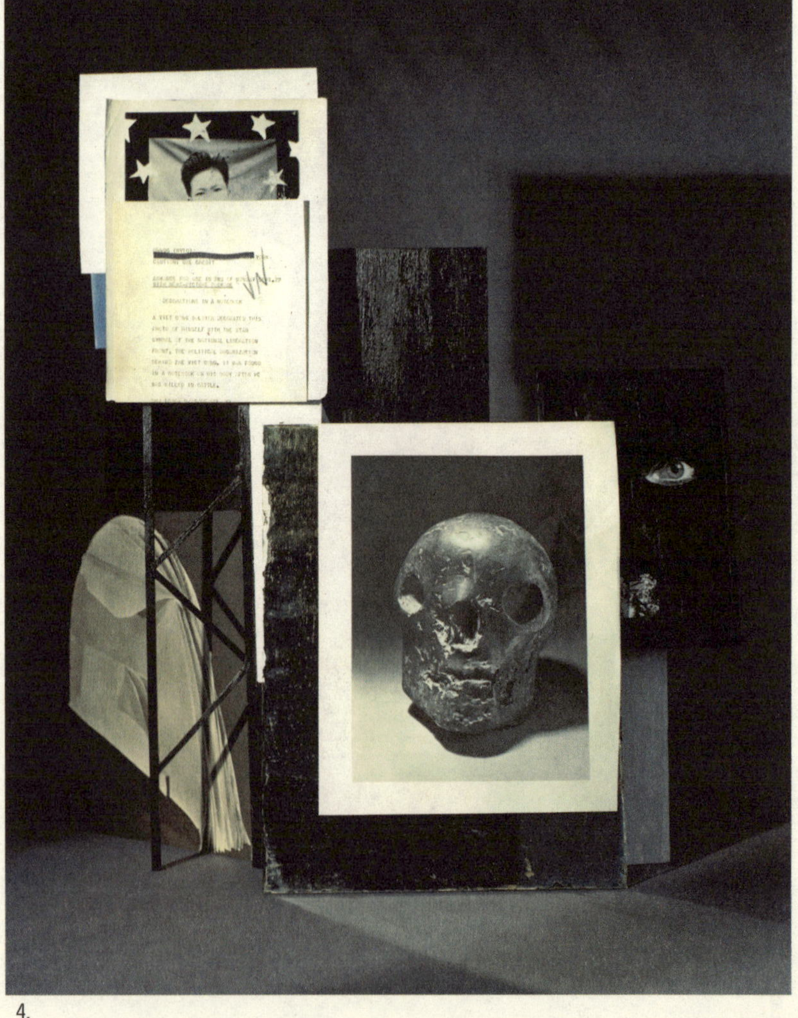

4.

Sara VanDerBeek was educated at Cooper Union in New York. Her photographs often depict collections of images arranged on and around sculptural environments of her own design. Her aesthetic is influenced by early Surrealist photography and European modernism, as well as the work of her father, experimental filmmaker Stan VanDerBeek, who died in 1984. Her work has been included in shows at the Hirshhorn Museum in Washington, D.C. (2008), and the Whitney Museum in New York (2008). She is the cofounder of Guild and Greyshkul Gallery in New York.

1. The Principle of Superimposition 2
2008, digital chromogenic print, 64 ½ × 44 ½ in (164 × 113 cm)

2. Four Photographers
2006, 6 digital chromogenic prints, each approx 18 × 21 in (46 × 53 cm)

3. Mrs. Washington's Bedroom
2006, digital chromogenic print, 20 × 24 in (51 × 61 cm)

4. Decorations in a Notebook
2006, digital chromogenic print, 24 × 20 in (61 × 51 cm)

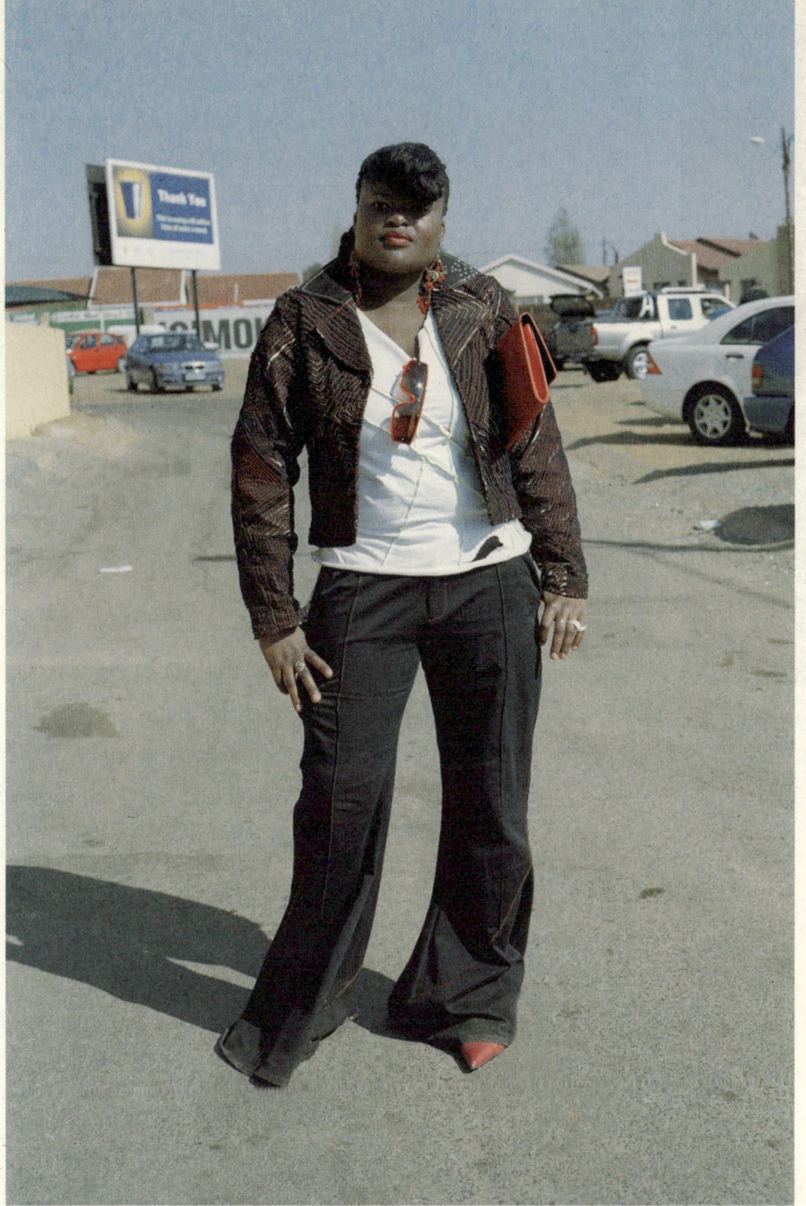

1.

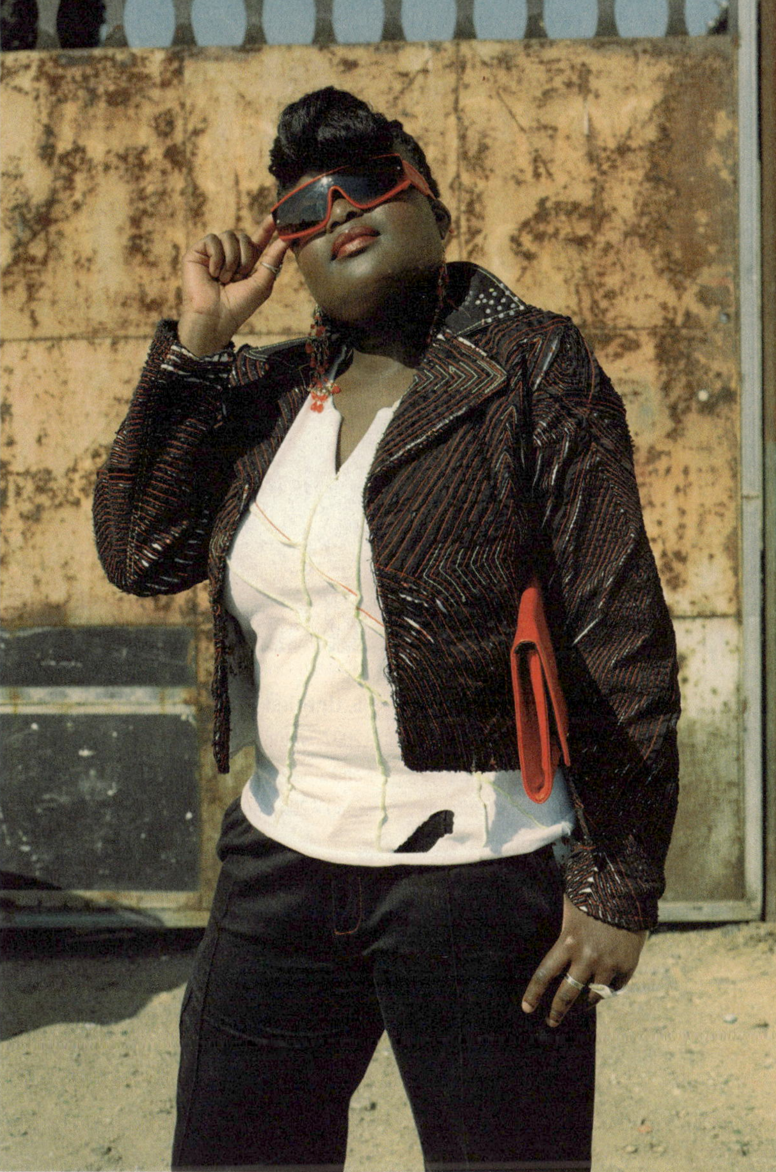

2.

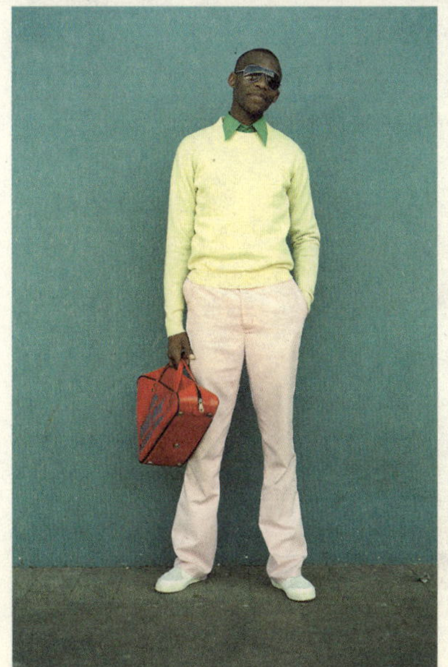

3.

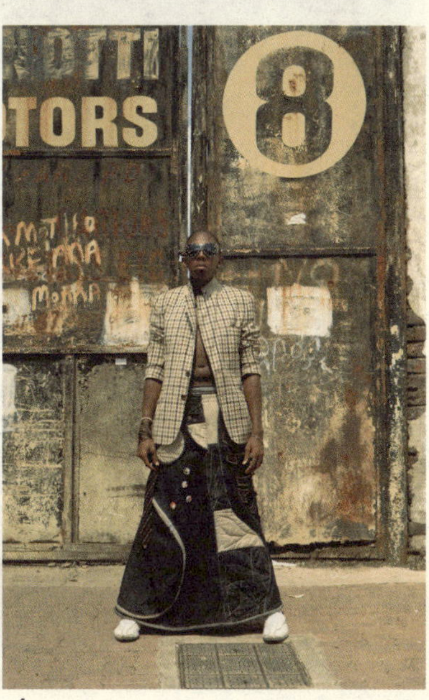

4.

Nontsikeleo Veleko graduated from the Market Photography Workshop in 2004 and currently lives and works in Johannesburg. She won the Standard Bank Young Artist of the Year Award in 2008 for her series **Wonderland.** Her color portraits and photographs document the fluid fashions and styles of South Africa, exploring the ways her subjects use fashion to construct and deconstruct their identities.

1 & 2. **Thobeka I**
2003-06, color photographs on cotton rag paper, dimensions variable

3. **Thabo II**
2003-06, color photograph on cotton rag paper, dimensions variable

4. **Sibu IV**
2003-06, color photograph on cotton rag paper, dimensions variable

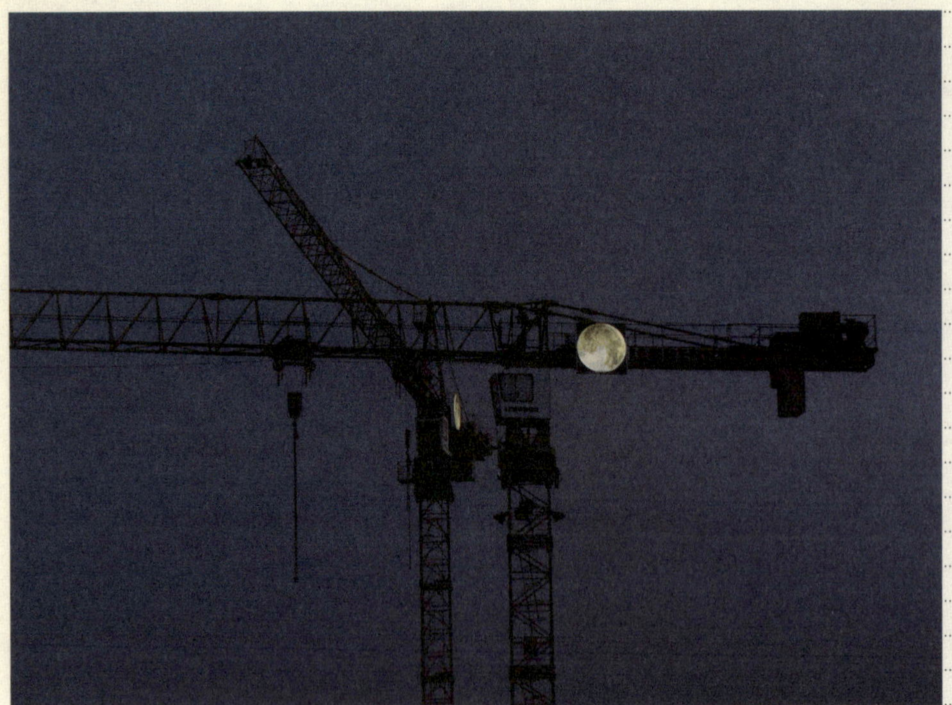

1.

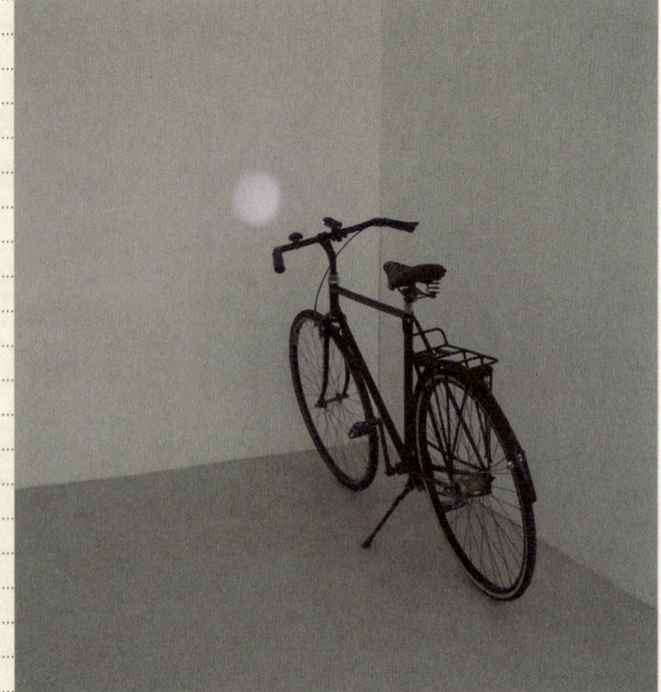

2.

Johannes Vogl studied at the Academy of Fine Arts in Karlsruhe, Germany, and at the Academy of Fine Arts in Vienna, and is based in Berlin and Vienna. His sculptures and installations are social critiques in which he plays with the functionality of familiar things. In **Gold Inoculation**, a machine shoots pieces of gold into the gallery wall, referring to nineteenth-century mine owners who would shoot gold nuggets into the walls of depleted mines to trick buyers into buying them.

1. **Fünf Monde** (Five Moons)
2007-08, light boxes on construction cranes, each 59 × 59 × 10 in (200 × 200 × 25 cm)

2. **Kleiner Mond** (Small Moon)
2006, bicycle and LED lamp, 71 × 27 ½ × 39 ½ in (180 × 70 × 100 cm)

3. **Watching the waves**
2005, steel, electronic equipment, drums, fish, and mixed media, 78 ¾ × 59 × 118 in (200 × 150 × 300 cm)

4. **Marmeladenbrot** (Jam Bread)
2006, screw clamp, motor, battery, bread, jam, and mixer, 12 × 6 × 4 in (30 × 15 × 10 cm)

5. **Untitled (A week of rain)**
2007, water, glass, copper, infusion sets, and steel, 137 ¾ × 59 × 15 ¾ in (350 × 200 × 40 cm)

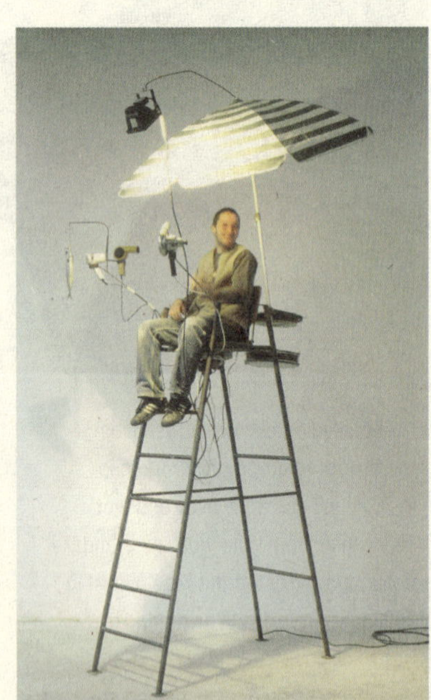

3.

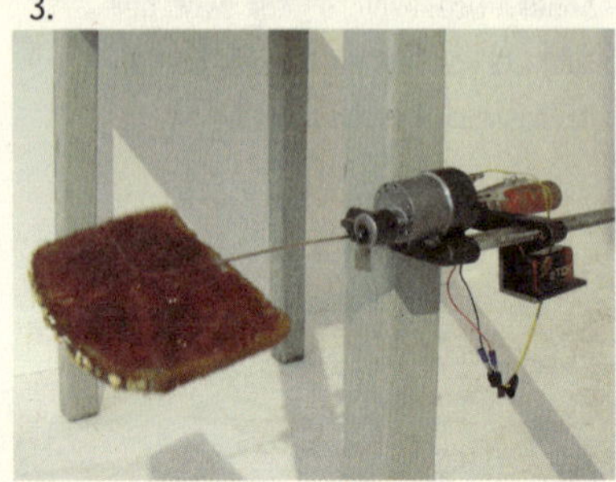

4.

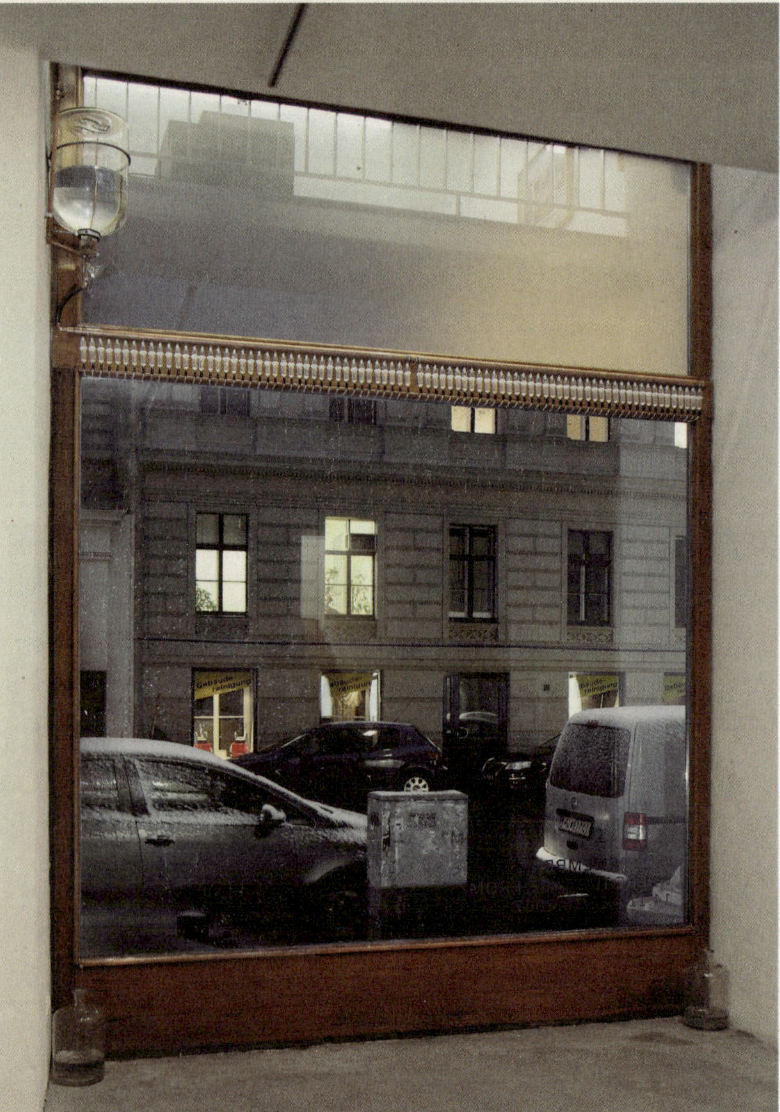

5.

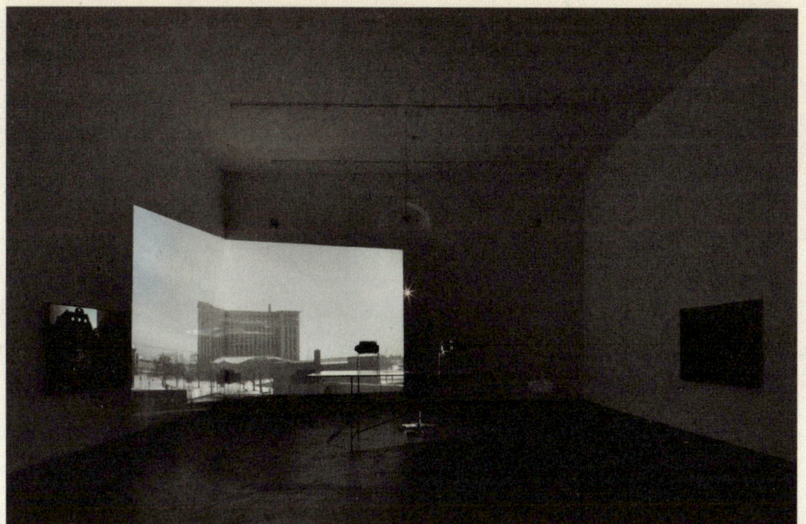

1.

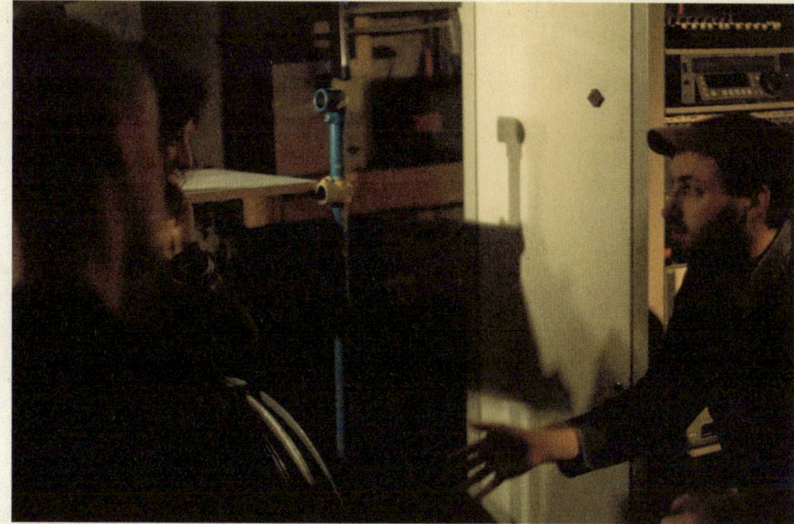

2.

3.

Tris Vonna-Michell studied at the Falmouth College of Art and the Glasgow School of Art. He is a performance artist and storyteller whose meandering narratives, such as **Down the Rabbit Hole** (2006-07), incorporate slide projectors, scattered photocopies, personal correspondence, and other ephemera. The work narrates the tale of a feigned amnesia trek around Europe in search of an avant-garde poet and musician named Henri Chopin. His work is not fixed or permanent; accompanied by an egg timer that is meant to dictate their length, his stories are told in dimly lit rooms in which the audience may become part of the structure of the performance.

1. Seizure

2004-08, installation, dimensions variable, installation view at Kunsthalle Zürich (2008)

2. ICA 60

2008, performance at the ICA, London

3. Studio A

2008, mixed media installation at 5th Berlin Biennial, KW Institute for Contemporary Art

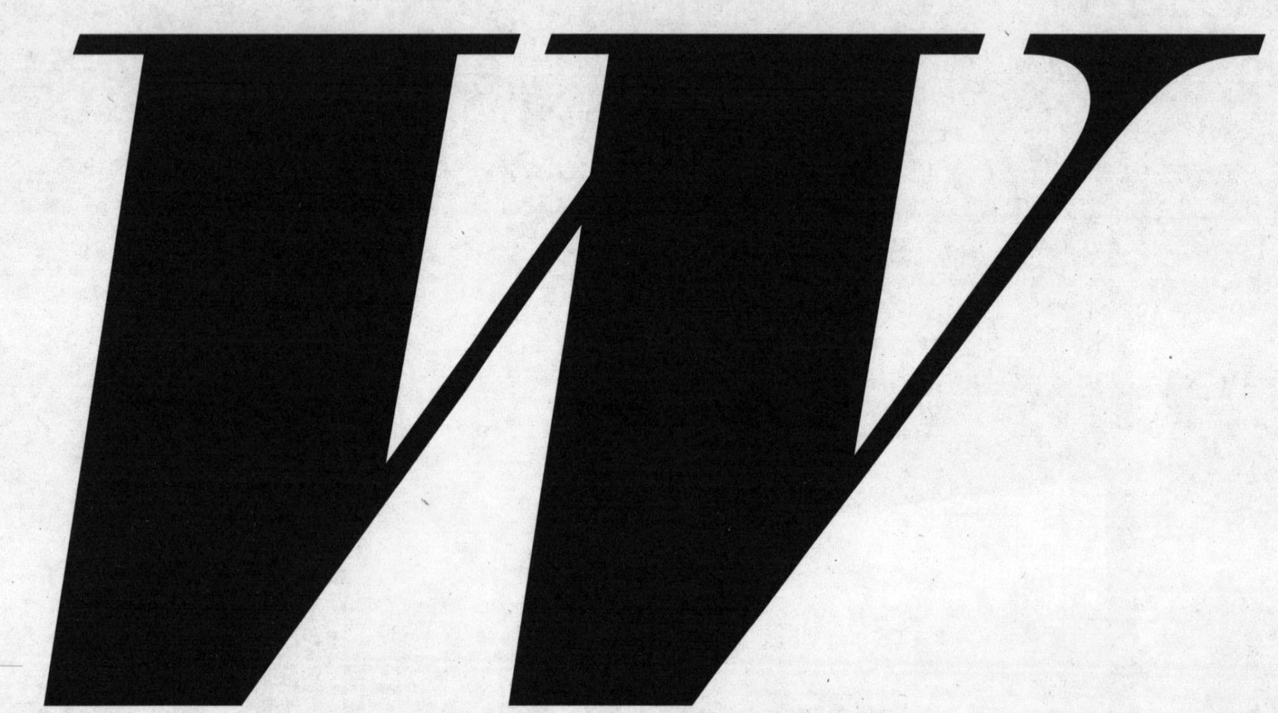

Richard T. Walker graduated from Goldsmiths College, London, with an MA in fine art in 2005. He incorporates spoken dialogue, original musical compositions, and text into his photographs and video work to investigate the relationship between language and the environment.

1. Repeated achievement
2008, archival inkjet print, $39\frac{3}{4} \times 60$ in (101×152 cm)

2. Successive inconceivable events
2005, video, 6 min 18 sec

3. Keep trying
2006, archival inkjet print, $19\frac{1}{2} \times 27\frac{1}{2}$ in (50×70 cm)

4. Sometimes i like you more than other times
2008, 2-channel video and 2 monitors, 9 min 26 sec

5. I'll be lost when i find you
2006, 5 or 6 channel video, 8 min 21 sec

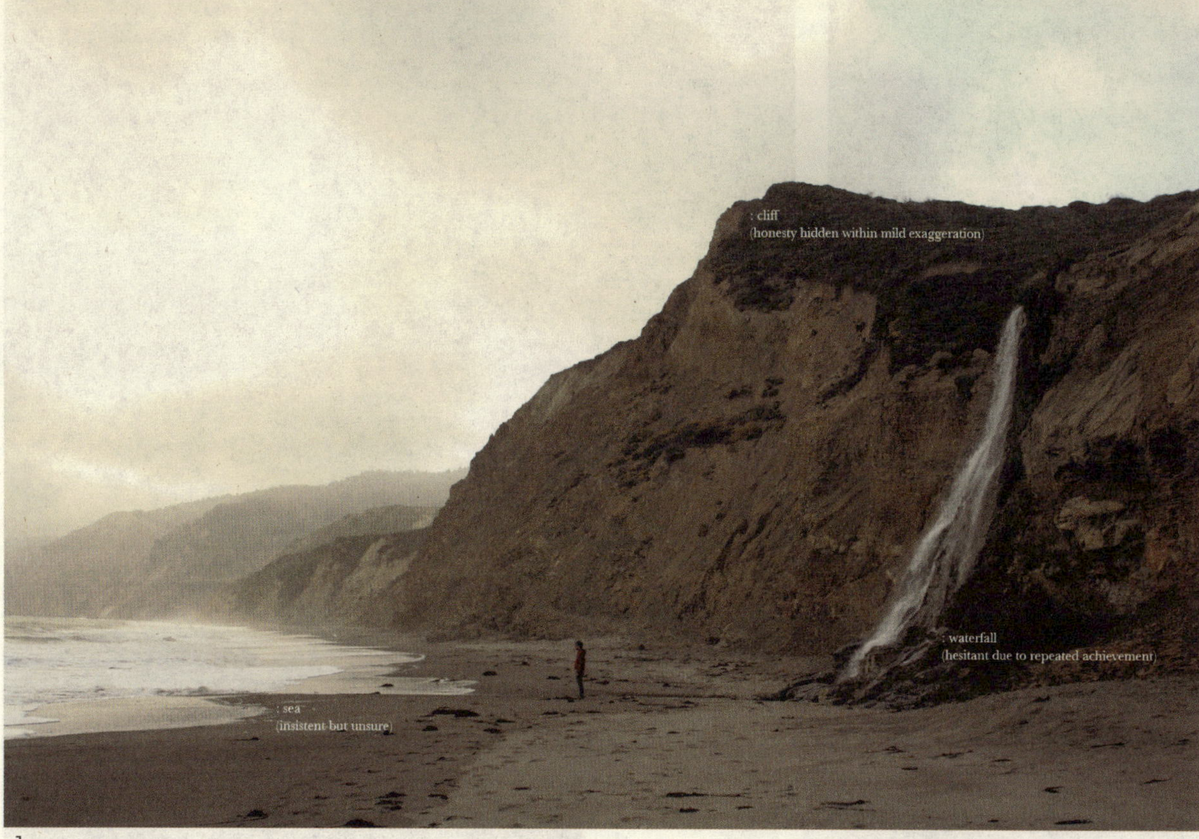

1.

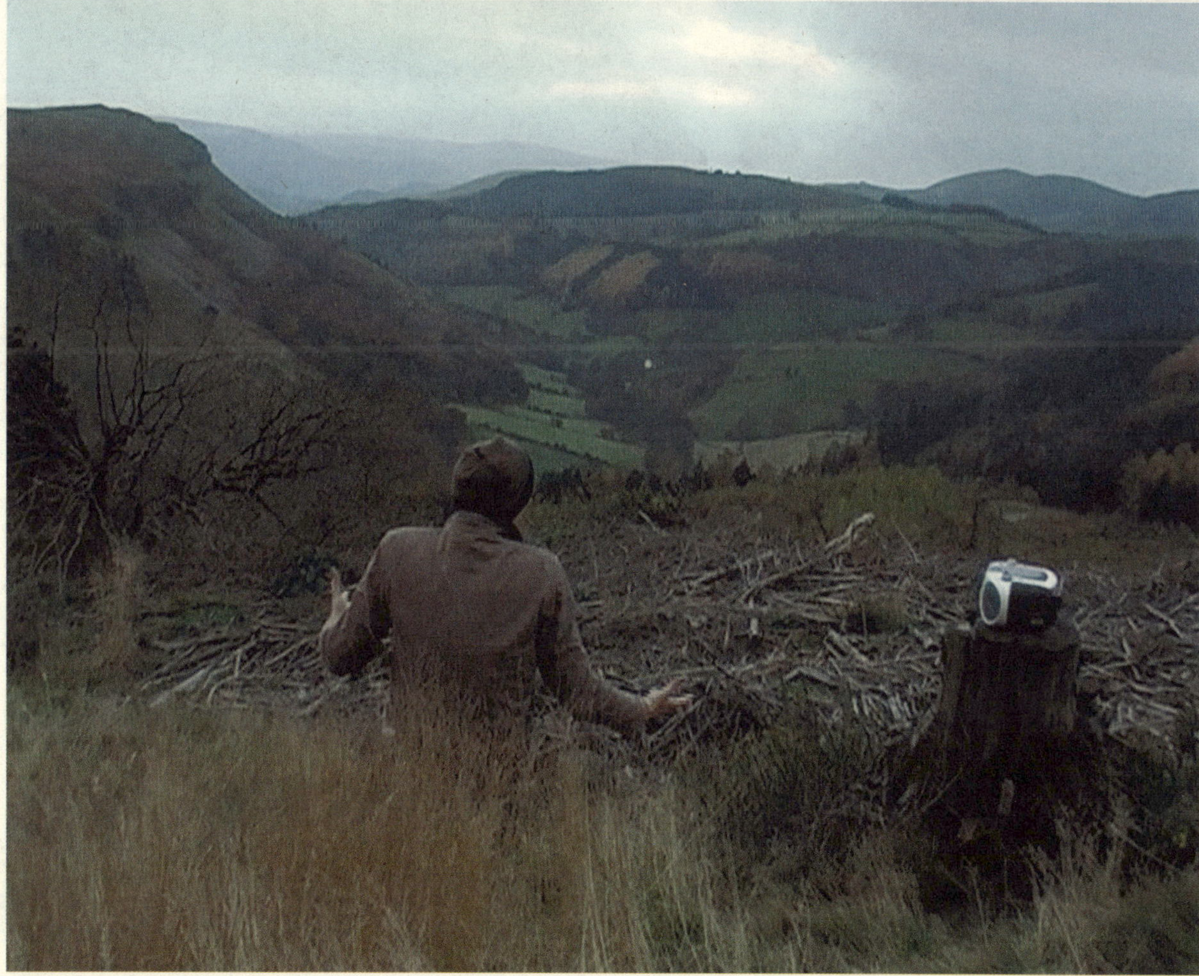

2.

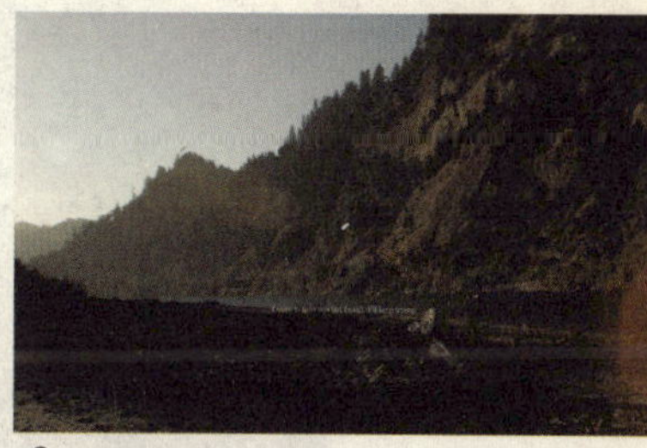

3.

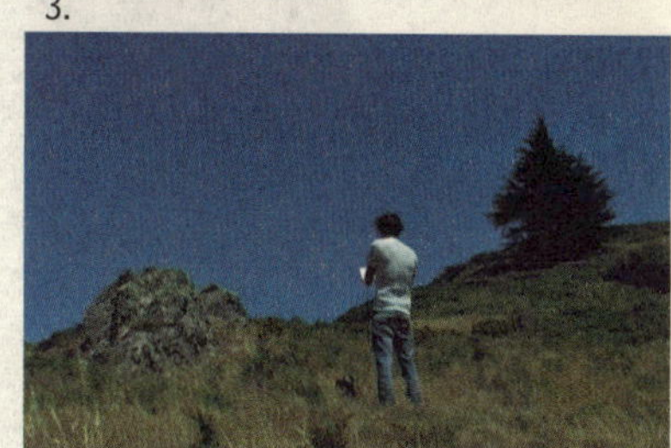

4.

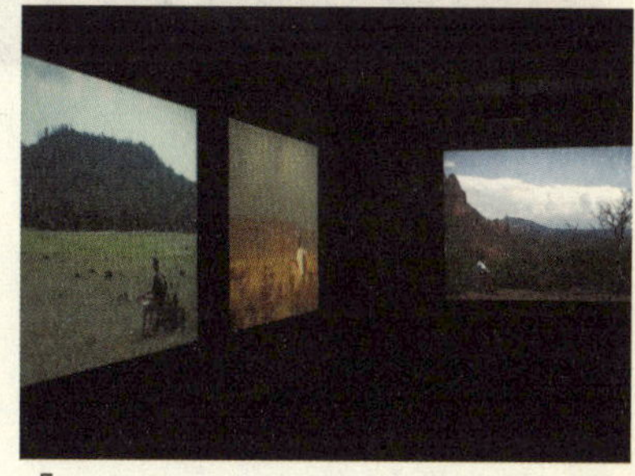

5.

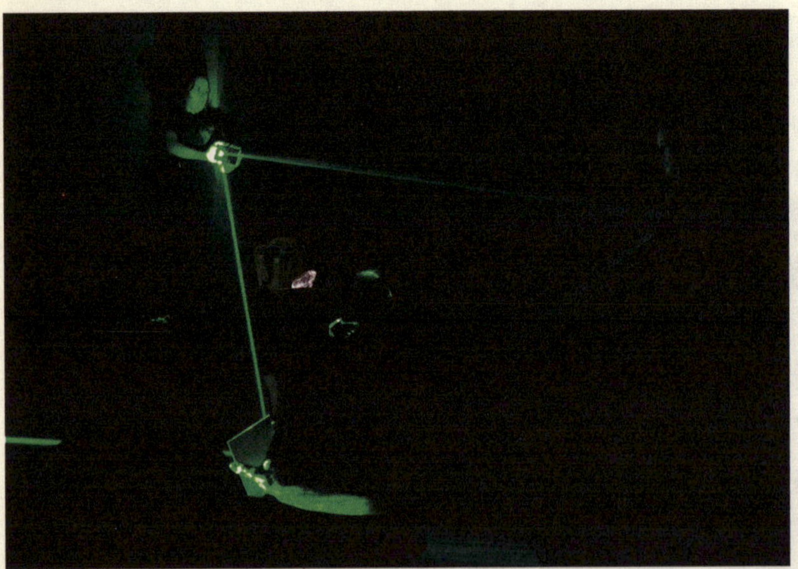

1.

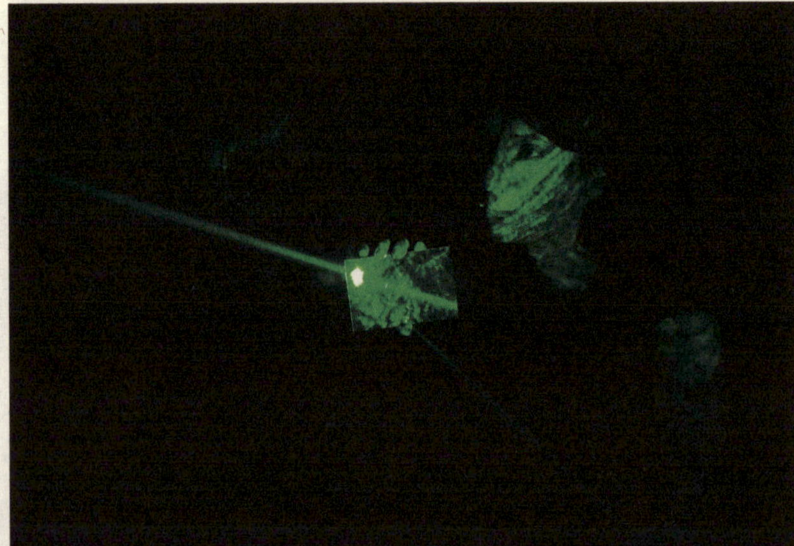

2.

3.

Emily Wardill graduated in 2000 with a BA from St. Martin's College in London, where she currently lives and works. A video and performance artist, she received the first Follow Fluxus – After Fluxus scholarship from the NKV and State Capital of Wiesbaden. Her films, which combine the documentary and the surreal, are concerned with strategies of communication. Her 2007 film **Ben**, for example, references two case studies on the nature of hallucination and paranoia.

1 & 2. **The Diamond (Descartes Daughter)**
2008, 16 mm film, 10 min

3. **Sick Serena and Dregs and Wreck and Wreck**
2008, 16 mm film, 12 min

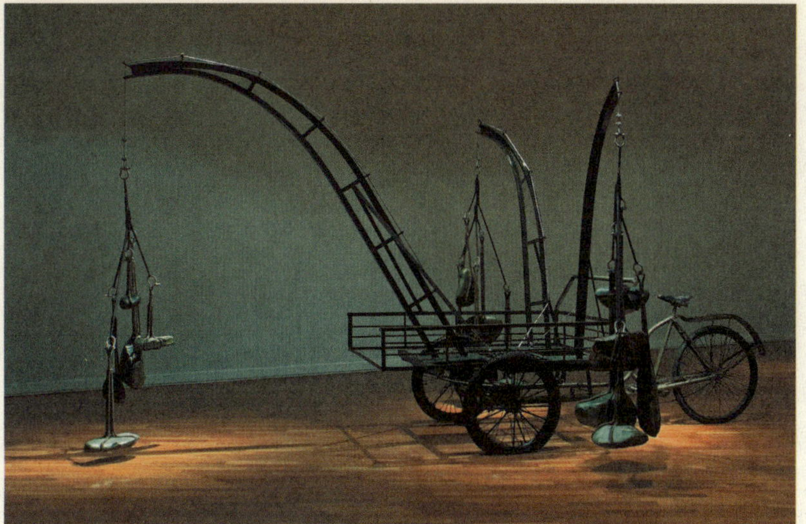

1.

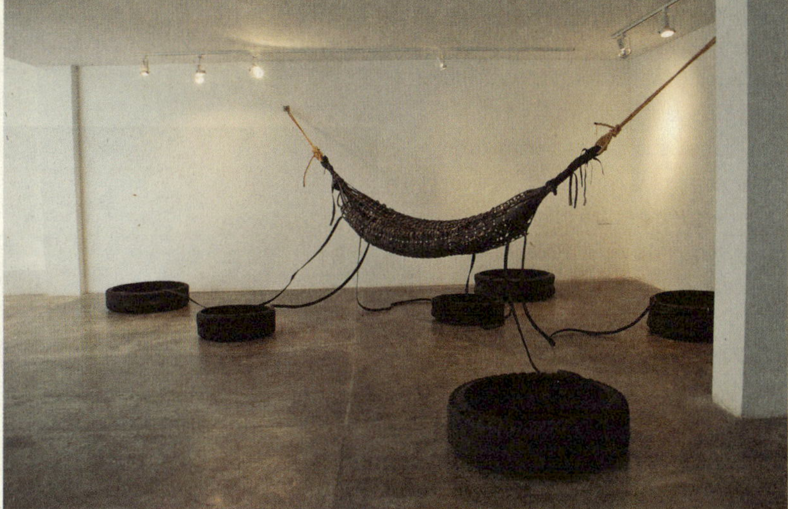

2.

Ishmael Randall-Weeks graduated in 2000 with a BA from Bard College and lives and works in Lima, Peru. He uses discarded materials in his sculptures, including the wood of trees that have been cut down near construction sites, boat parts, inner tubes, and old chairs, to create seemingly functional objects that reflect personal narratives. **Nomad** (2007) for instance, is a portable shelter made of a recycled tricycle cart, recycled cooking oil cans, a bed, a water tank, and a car battery, among other materials. **Hammock** (2008) is constructed from recycled tires, ropes, and hooks.

1. **Balances/Tensiones**
2006, tricycle, river rocks, forged construction steel, steel, and cables, approx 7½ × 14¼ × 9½ ft (2 × 4 × 3 m)

2. **Hammock**
2008, old tires, rope, and rivets, dimensions variable

3. **Progreso**
2006, old tires, inner tubes, rubber hosing, fishnets, steel, and sand, approx 52 × 337 × 131½ in (132 × 856 × 334 cm)

4. **Untitled (Drawing table)**
2008, old architect's drawing table, lamp, and collage of maps, 39½ × 59 × 34½ in (100 × 150 × 90 cm)

5. **Campamento #5**
2003-06, 3 years of newspapers (one brick per day), notebook with clippings, lamp, netting with newspaper dates, and steel, approx 7 × 11¾ × 10 ft (217 × 363 × 306 cm)

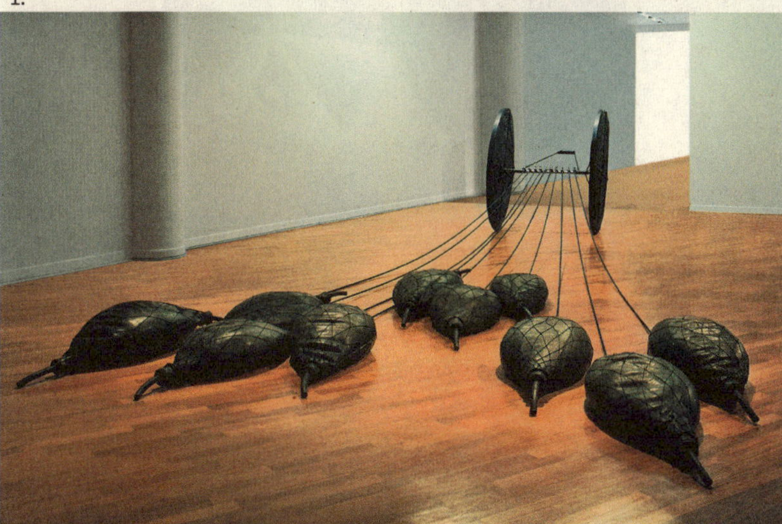

3.

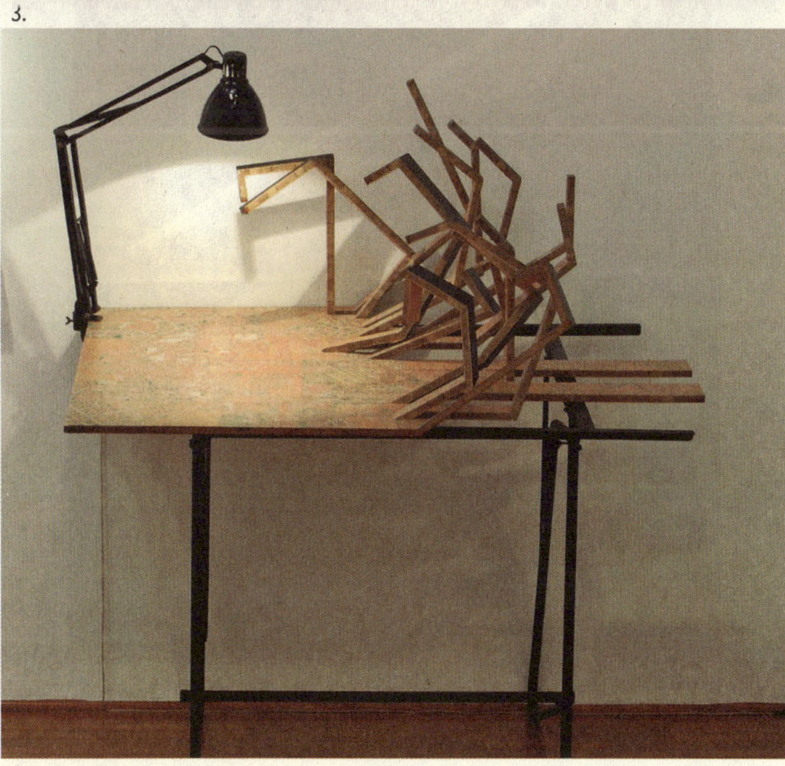

4.

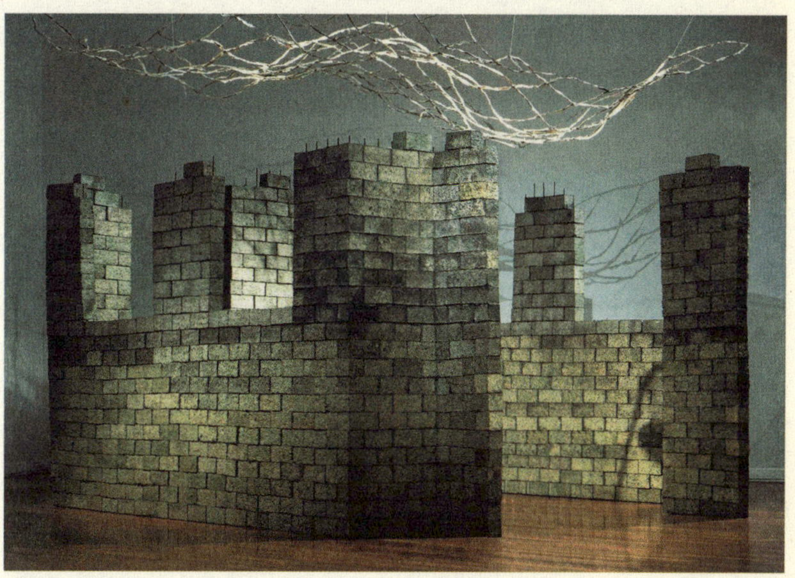

5.

Garth Weiser graduated in 2005 from Columbia University in New York, where he currently lives and works. Weiser often begins his paintings by making a three-dimensional structure as a sketch from which to paint, or draws on his memories of those structures. His paintings explore the nature of perception, using scale and perspective to disrupt visual expectations.

1. **877-394-4448**
2008, acrylic and gouache on canvas, 93 × 83 in (236 × 211 cm)

2. **Cannondale**
2008, acrylic and gouache on canvas, 90 × 85 in (229 × 216 cm)

3. **TV Keith**
2008, acrylic and gouache on canvas, 93 × 83 in (236 × 211 cm)

4. **Gran Turismo**
2008, acrylic and gouache on canvas, 93 × 83 in (236 × 211 cm)

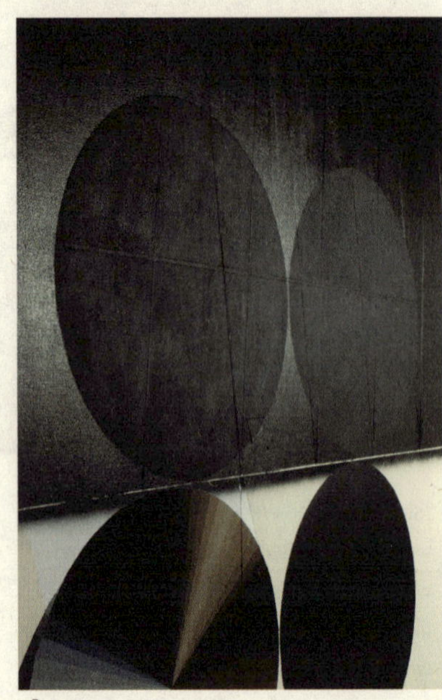

1.

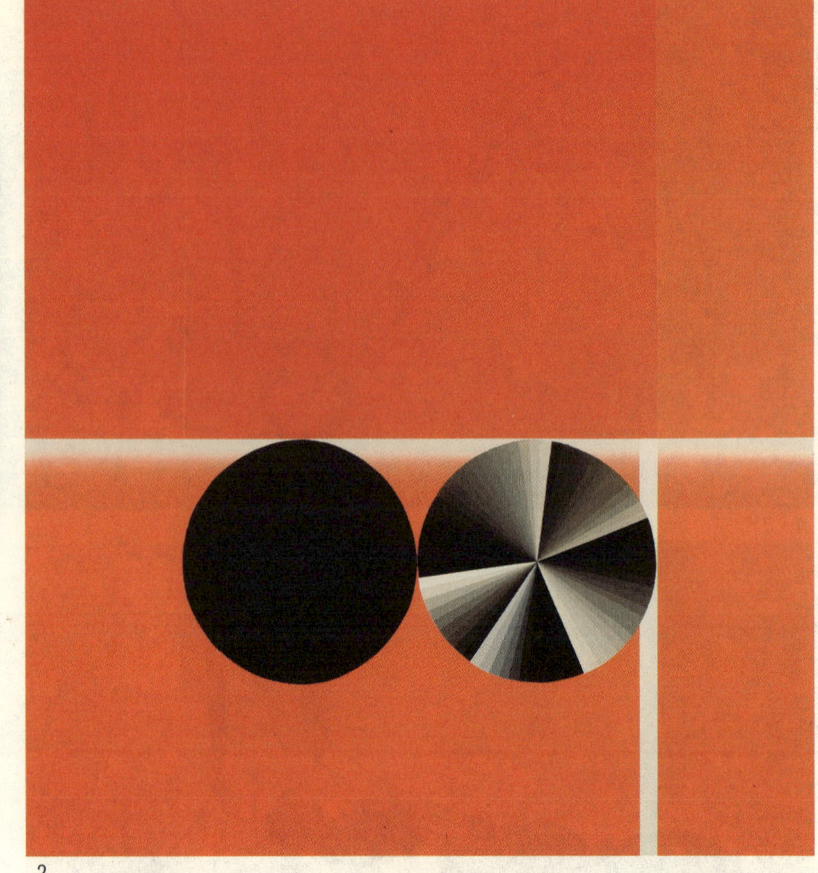

2.

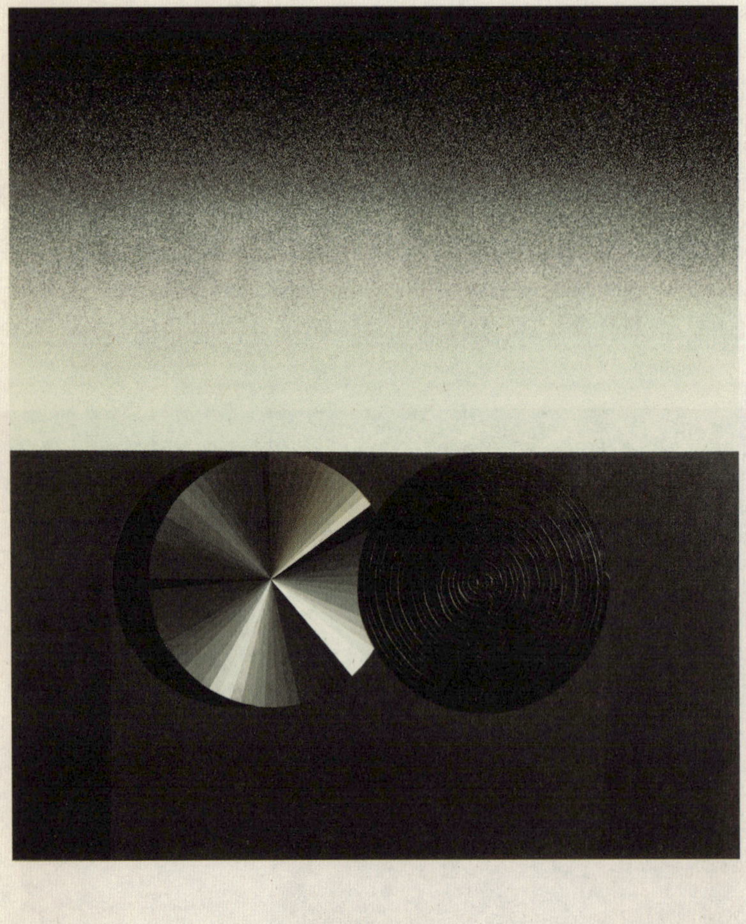

3.

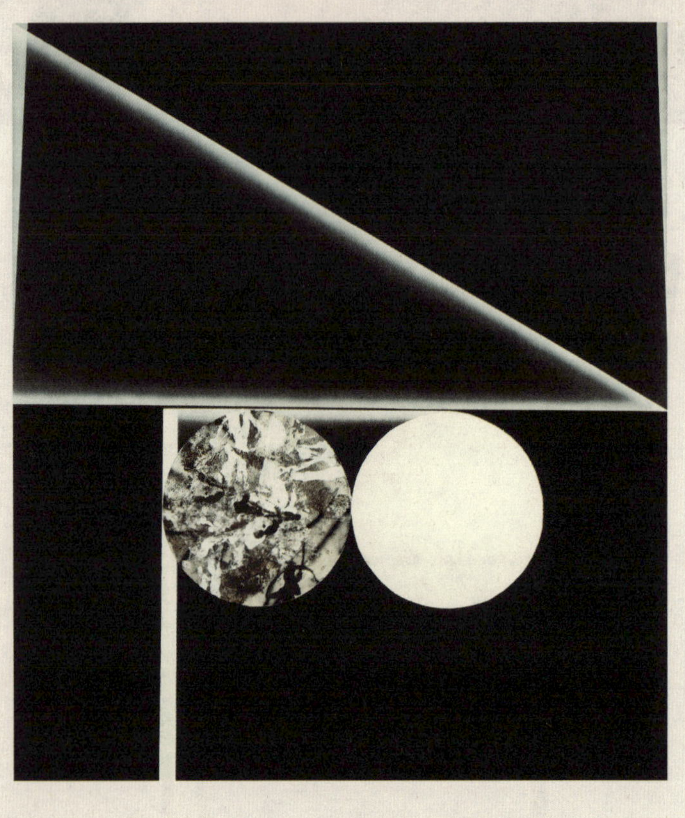

4.

Andro Wekua graduated in 1999 from the Visual Art School in Basel and currently lives and works in Zurich. His paintings and works on paper, which incorporate collage, pencil, and pen on photocopies, refer to the displacement of refugees, including his own memories growing up in war-torn Georgia. In 2007 he had a solo exhibition at Museum Boijmans in Rotterdam.

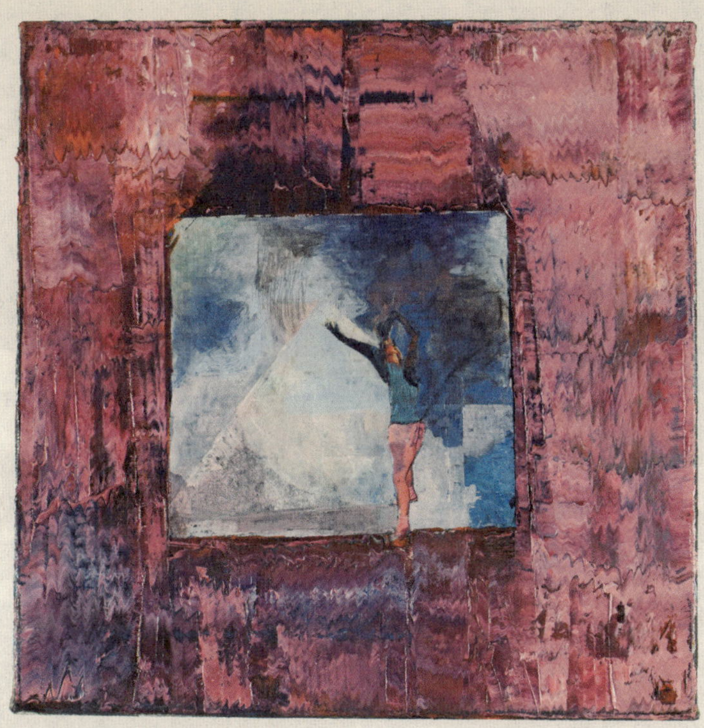

1.

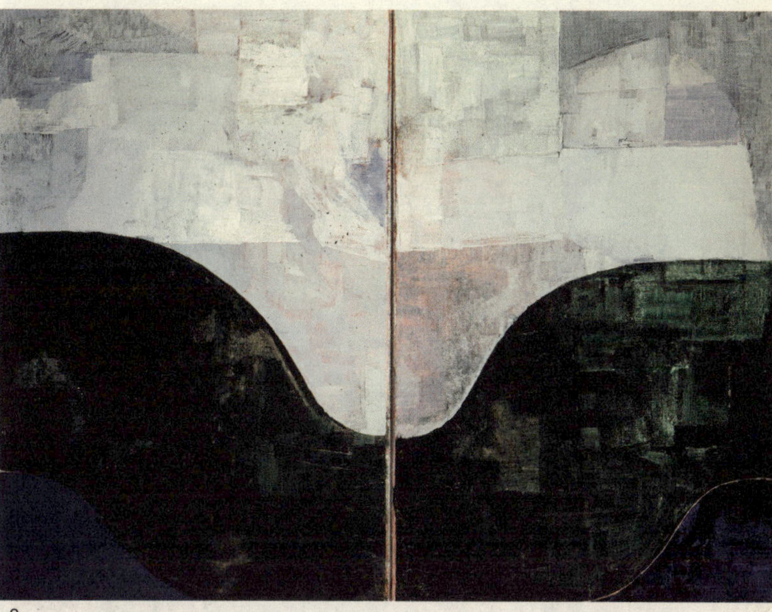

2.

1. My space, your show
2008, oil on canvas in frame, 17 × 17 in (44 × 44 cm)

2. Hier
2005, oil on canvas in frame, 2 parts, each $24\frac{1}{2} \times 32\frac{3}{4}$ (62 × 82 cm)

3. Wait to Wait
2006, wax figure, lacquered aluminum chair, uncolored and colored glass, bricks, motor, 4 collages, and felt pen and pencil on paper, $78\frac{3}{4} \times 82\frac{3}{4} \times 118$ in (200 × 210 × 300 cm)

4. Painted
2006, oil on canvas, $27\frac{1}{2} \times 23\frac{3}{4}$ in (70 × 60 cm)

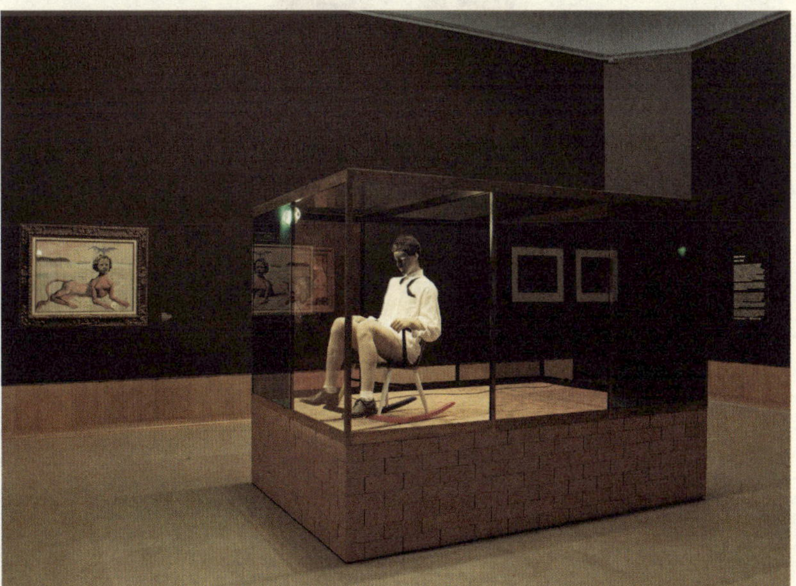

3.

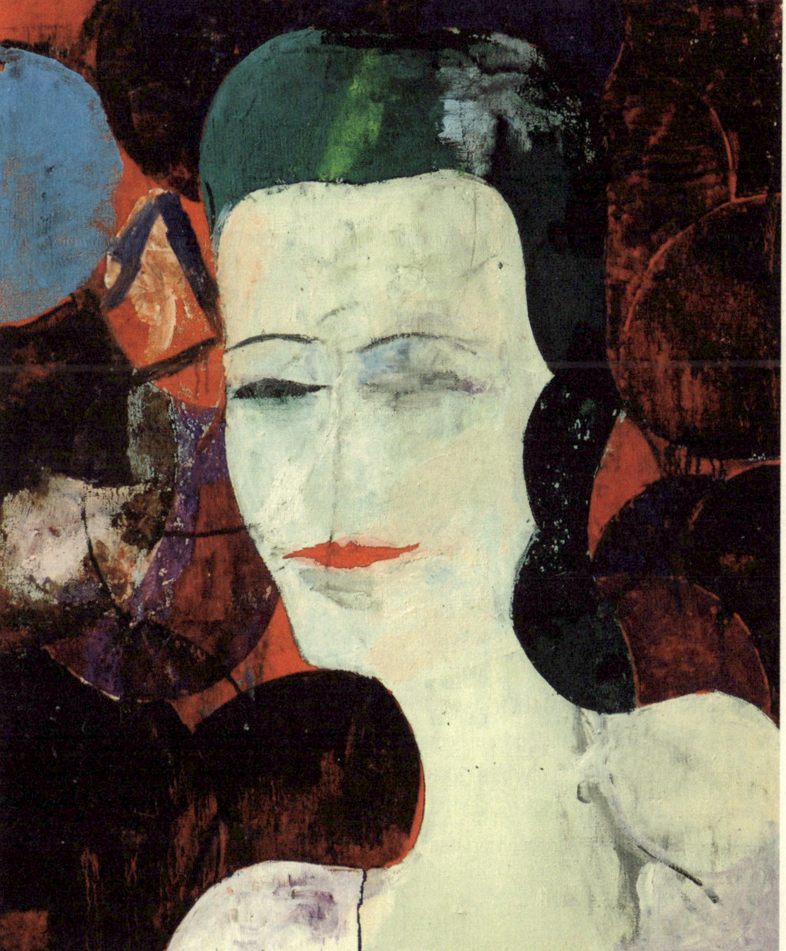

4.

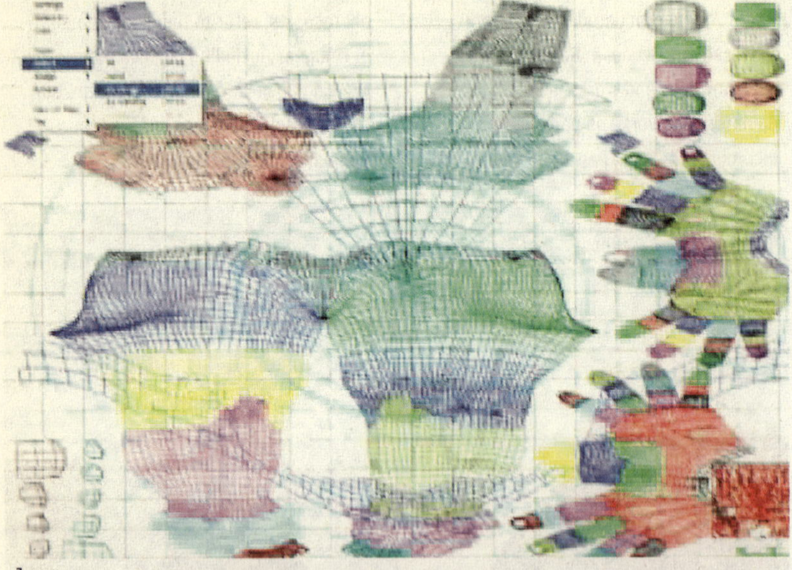
1.

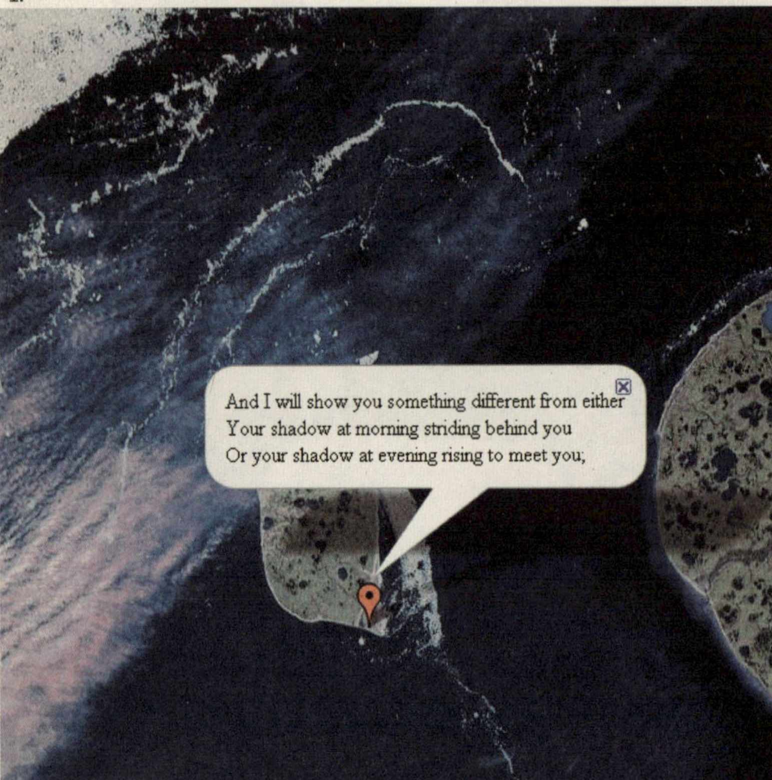

2.

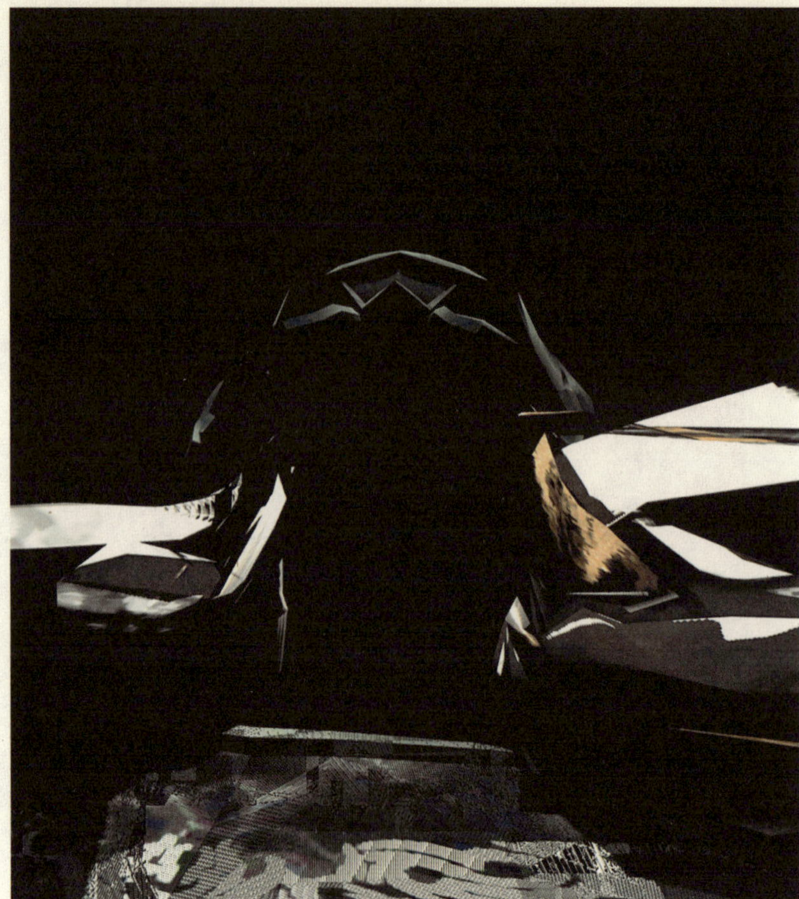
3.

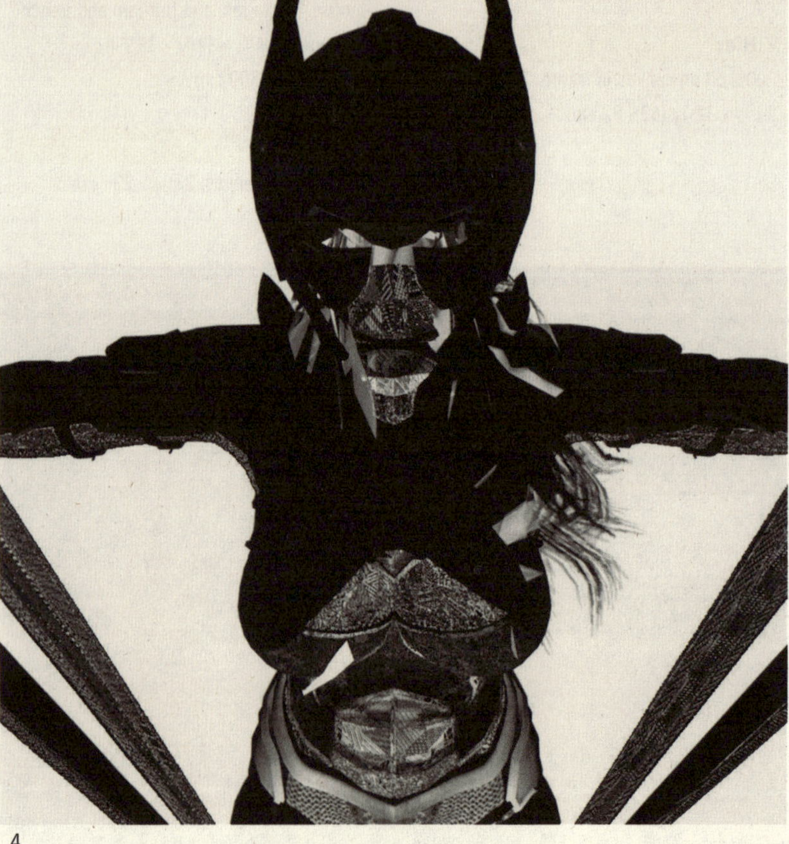
4.

James Whipple is currently a student at Parsons School of Design in New York. His video installation **Cave FX** (2006) is comprised of collected video footage of caves from sources ranging from home movies to virtual spaces. **Eye White** (2008), a video with sound, is a video tutorial on "skinning" a 3-D model, appropriated from YouTube.

1. **Eye White**
2008, video, 1 min 23 sec

2. **The Waste Land**
2006, modified Google Maps embed (browser-based)

3 & 4. **Female Armor**
2008, video, 12 min

1.

2.

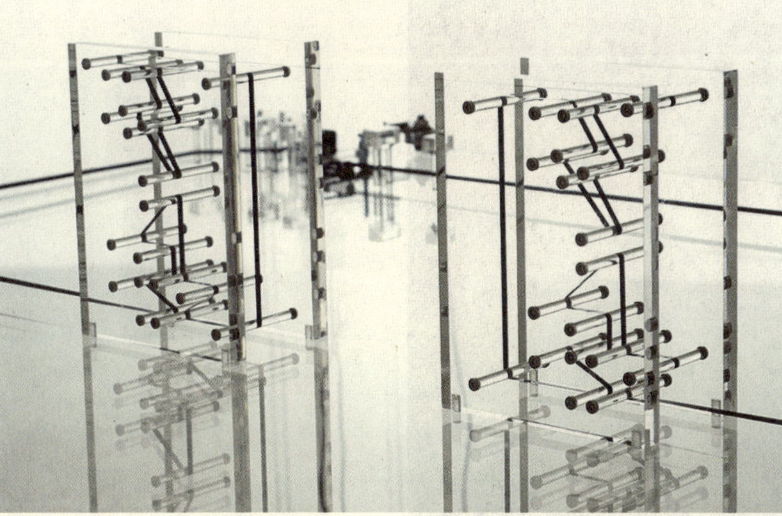

3.

4.

Joe Winter graduated with an MFA from the University of California, San Diego. He is an artist in residence at Eyebeam in New York City, where he lives and works. His installations include **Xerox Astronomy and the Nebulous Object-Image Archive** (2008), which reimagines the office photocopier as a scientific instrument for observing the cosmos, mixing technology with handmade practices. **One Ship Encounters a Series of Notable Exceptions** (2006) is a body of sculpture in which loops of cassette tape are moved through a transparent Plexiglas armature to create three-dimensional line-drawn scenes of a ship's encounters with various obstacles.

1 & 2. **Printershake/Earthquake**
2008, inkjet print, 11 × 8 1/2 in (28 × 22 cm)

3. **One ship struck by lightning, twice**
2006, acrylic, audiocassette tape, kinetics, and sound, 40 × 40 × 36 in (102 × 102 × 91 cm)

4. **Fantasie No. 1 for Mobile Pianos**
2005, mixed media, kinetic sound, and video installation, dimensions variable

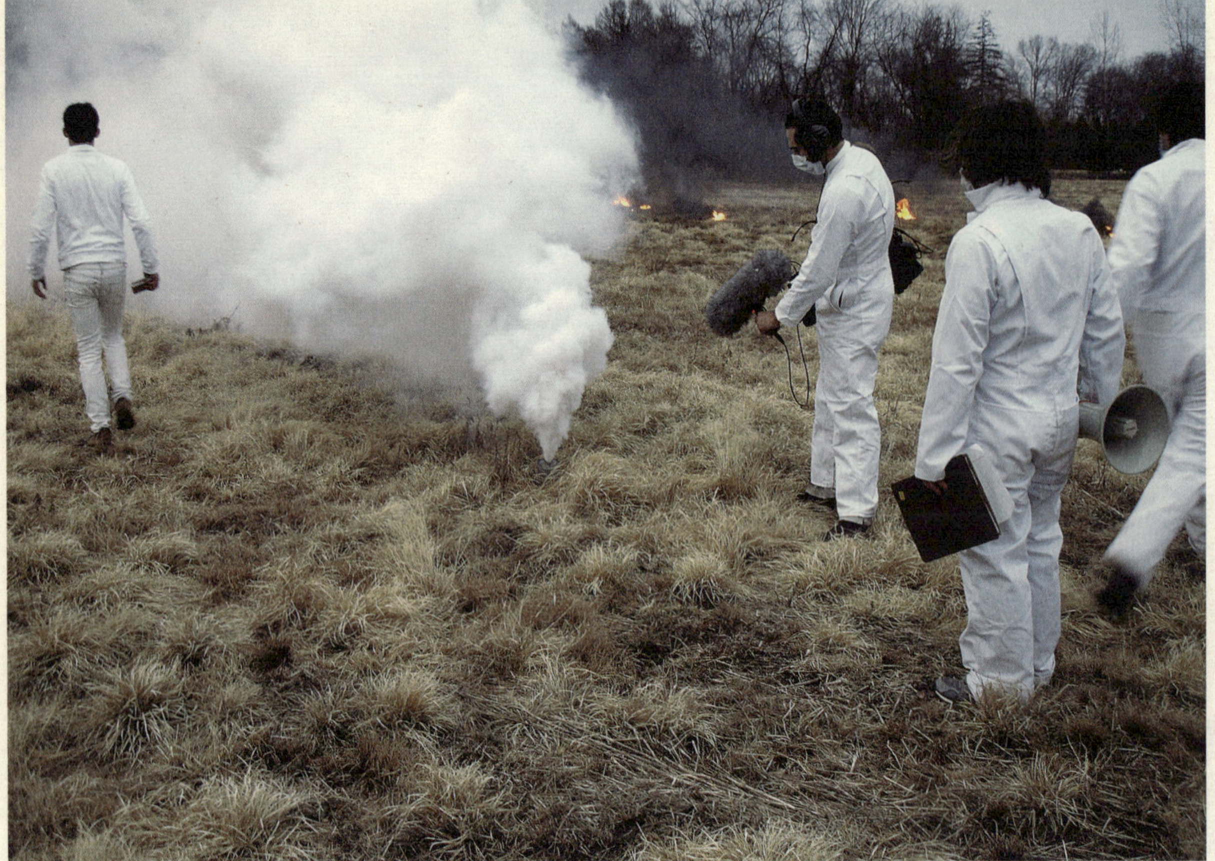

1.

2.

Jordan Wolfson attended the Rhode Island School of Design and the Konstfack College of Arts & Crafts in Stockholm. He lives and works in New York and Berlin. His sound work **Optical Sound**, in which crow calls were broadcast from speakers, was commissioned for the 2006 Whitney Biennial and installed on the roof of the museum. Wolfson had a solo exhibition in the fall of 2008 at the Swiss Institute in New York, which featured **untitled false document**, a three-minute, 16 mm film on identity and expression.

1. **Landscape for Fire**
2007, video, 7 min

2. **Nostalgia is Fear**
2004, car, artificial snow, artificial snowfall machine, and mix CD, dimensions variable

3. **I'm sorry but I don't want to be an Emperor...**
2005, 16 mm film, black and white, silent, 2 min 37 sec

4. **Neverland**
2001, video, 4 min

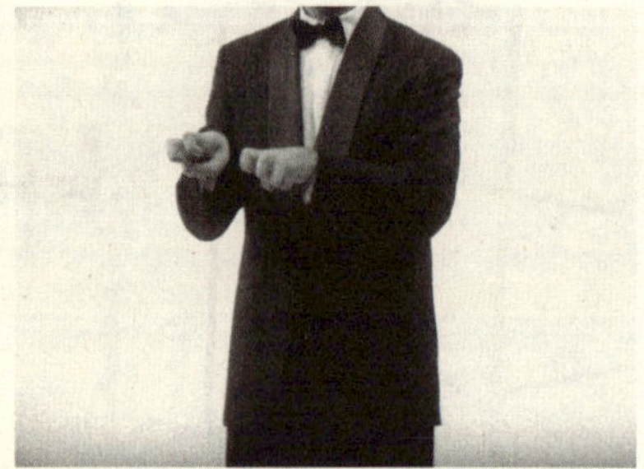

3.

4.

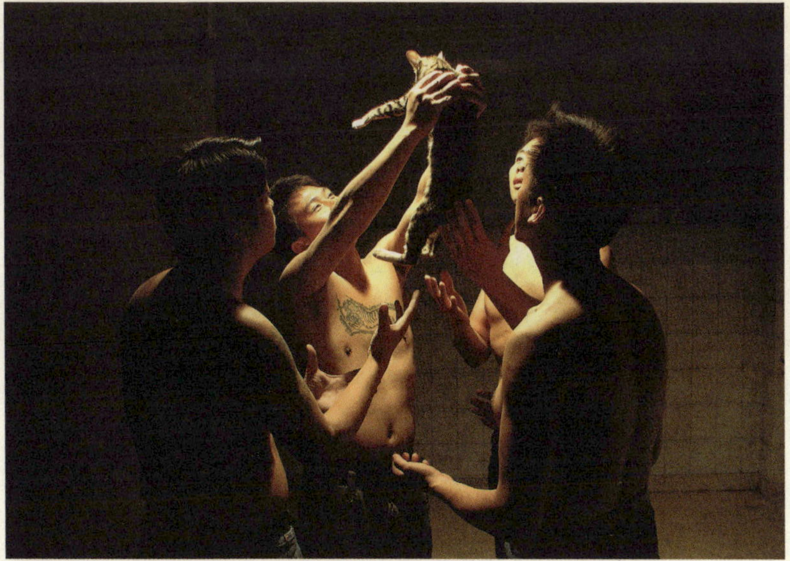

1.

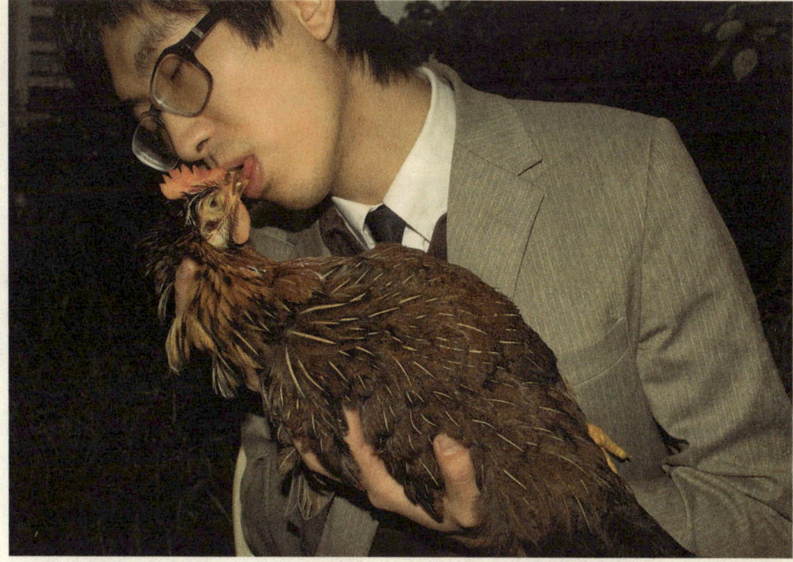

2.

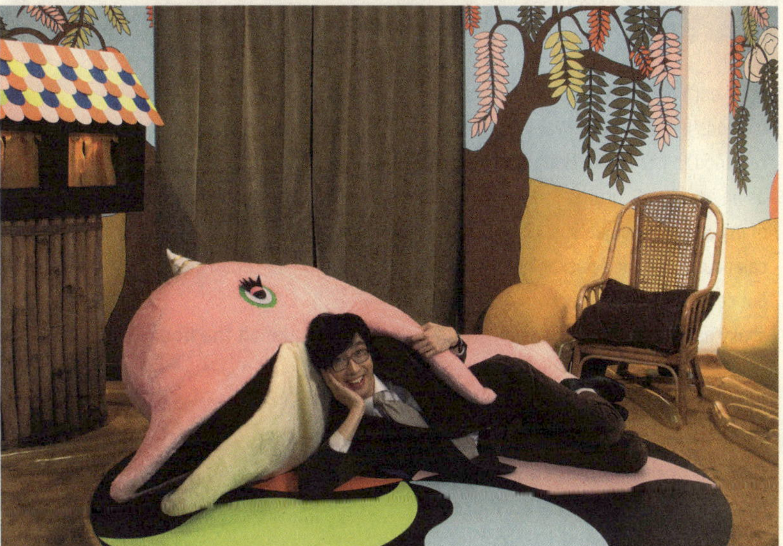

3.

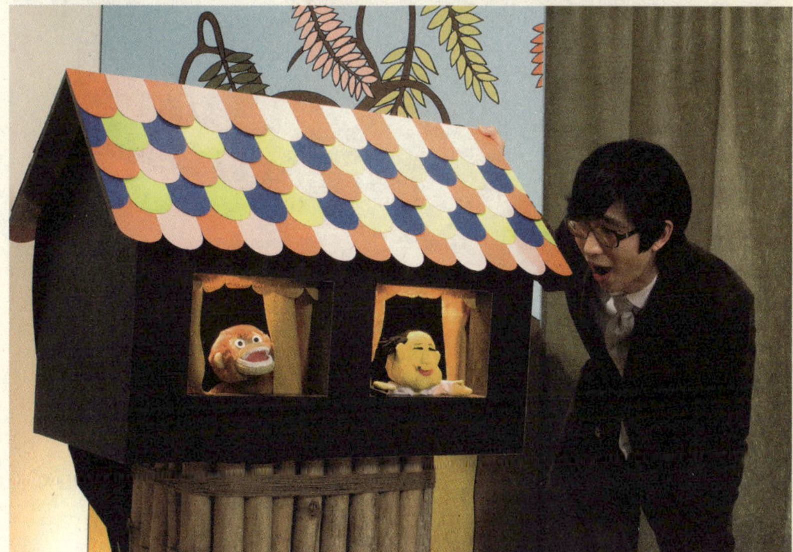

4.

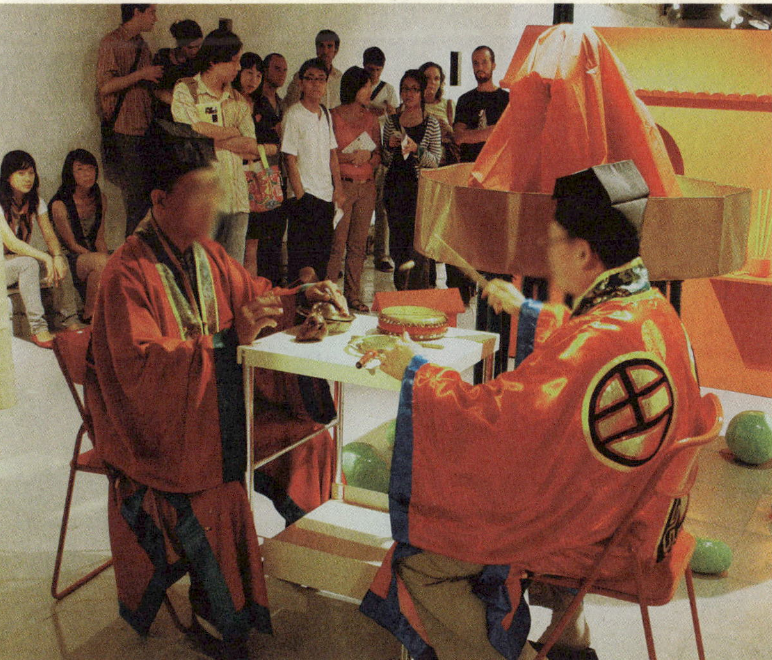

5.

Adrian Wong left a graduate program in psychology at Stanford to earn an MFA in sculpture from Yale University. He currently lives and works in Hong Kong, and his work revolves around his rediscovery of cultural ties to that city. His recent installation and performance work reimagines the 1960s Hong Kong television show Birthday Party and explores themes of memory and subjectivity.

1. **Hak Seh Wuih Tuhng Mau Jai** (Triads with Kitten)
2007, video, 3 min 20 sec

2. **Sak Gai** (Chicken Kiss)
2007, digital print, 24 × 36 in (61 × 91 cm)

3 & 4. **Sang Yat Fai Lok**
2008, wood, formica, carpeting, foam, felt, balloons, and dried fish, approx 16 1/2 × 16 1/2 × 13 ft (5 × 5 × 4 m)

5. **Bless All Ye Who Enter Here**
2007, pine, bamboo, epoxy, latex, incense, tea, and Taoist exorcist performance, 39 1/2 × 39 1/2 × 10 ft (12 × 12 × 3 m)

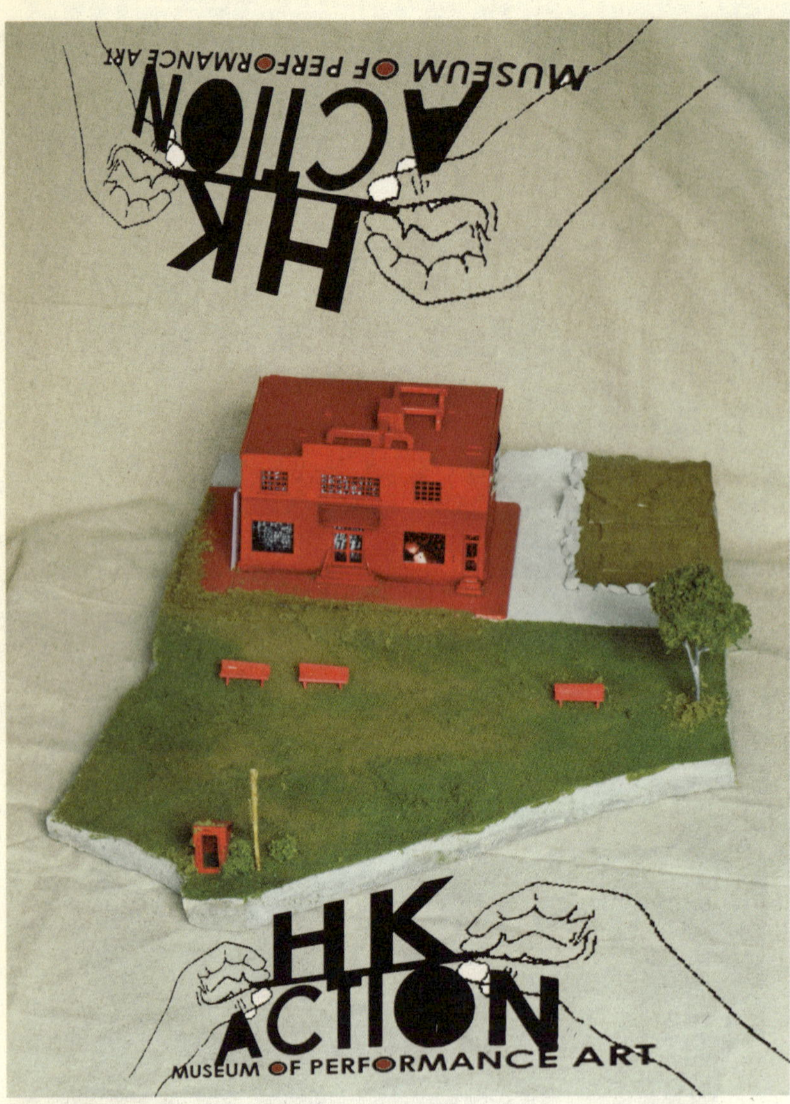

1.

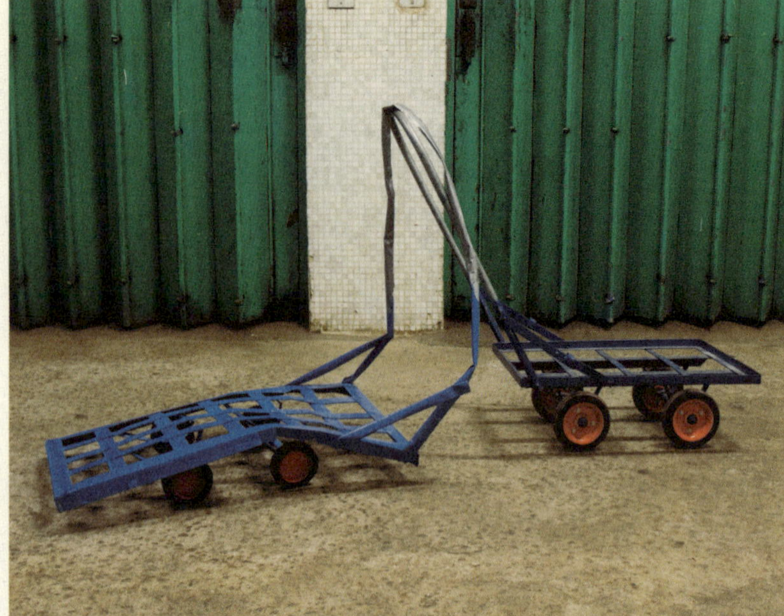
2.

After earning an MA from the University of Leeds in 2005, Doris Wai-yin Wong returned to her native Hong Kong to work as an artist and curator. She makes copies of mass-market objects, such as books, calendars, and food packaging. Washed-out colors, simplified backgrounds, and shaky handwriting give works an overtly handmade look, foregrounding issues of reproduction, uniqueness, and value.

1. If you got $, build HK a museum – HK Action Performance Art Museum
2007, poster and model, dimensions variable

2. Workshop
2008, mixed media, dimensions variable

3. Tribute to "Inside Looking Out – For the male artists along my way"
2008, video, 2 min 24 min

4. Remake all the books I read in UK (detail)
2005, acrylic on paper, dimensions variable

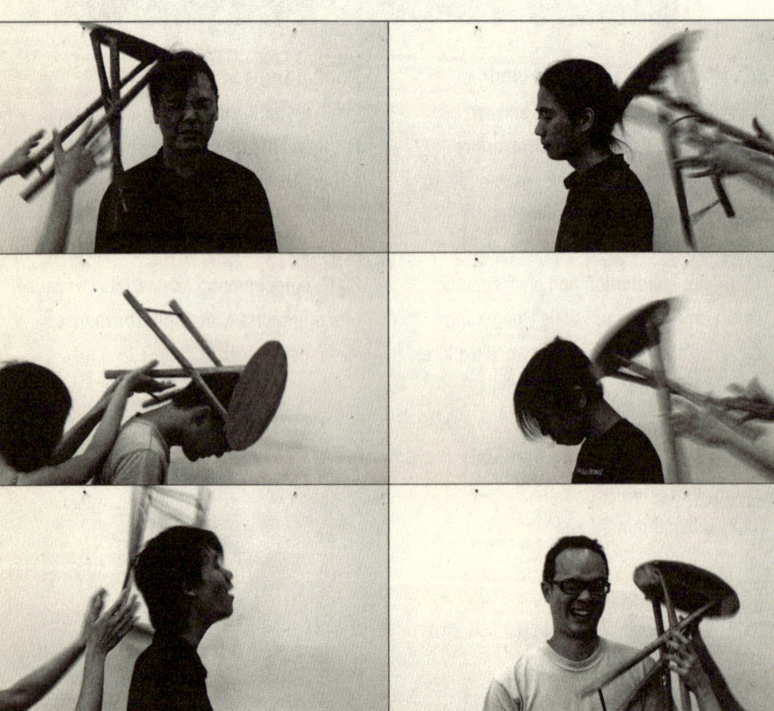
3.

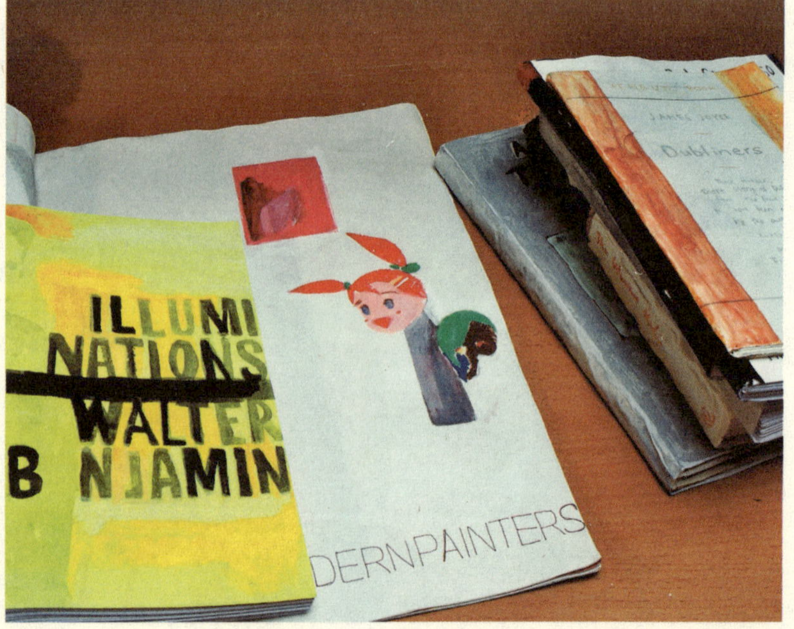

4.

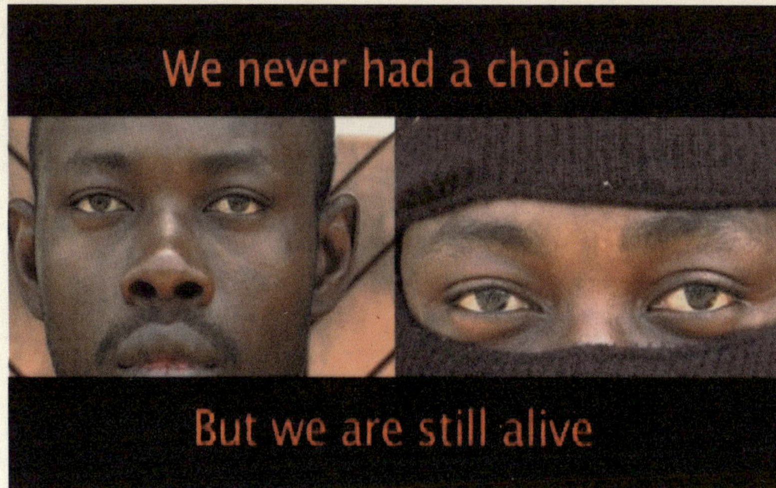

1.

2.

3.

4.

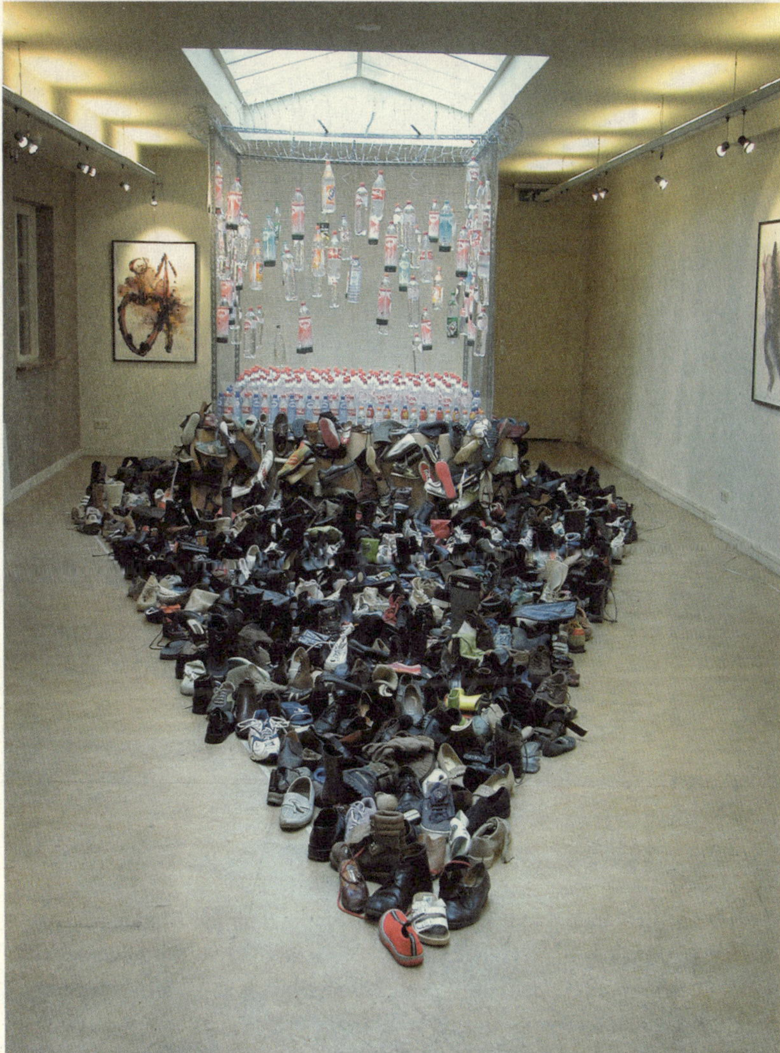

5.

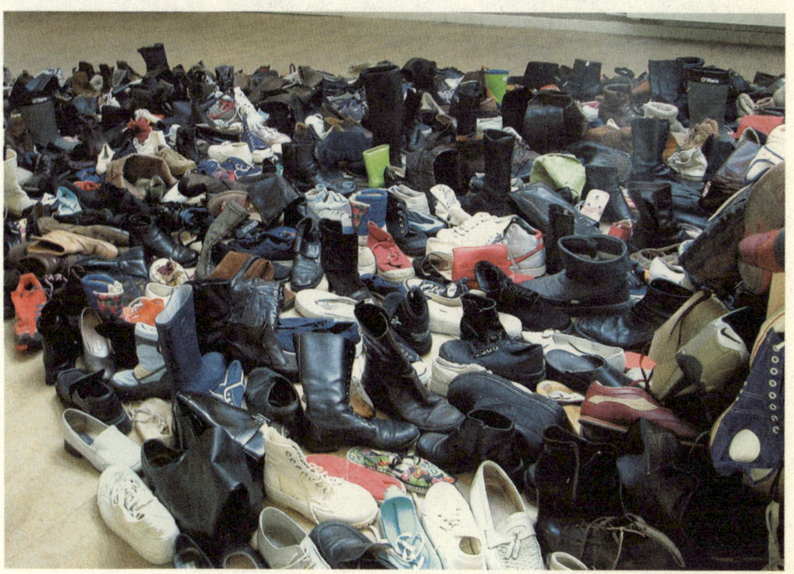

6.

1. Africa Best Deal I

2007, video, 4 min 31 sec

2, 3 & 4. **La Liste est Longue**

2006-07, video, 2 min 26 sec

5 & 6. **Sur le Chemin de L'immigration**

2006, mixed media, $19\frac{1}{2} \times 8\frac{1}{4} \times 9\frac{3}{4}$ ft (6 × 3 × 3 m)

Guy Wouete trained in multimedia research and creation at the Conservatoire des Arts et Métiers Multimedias in Bamako, Mali, and won the 8th Dak'art Biennial's Cultures France Award in Dakar, Senegal, in 2008. A self-taught artist, he works in a variety of mediums, including painting, video, drawing, and photography.

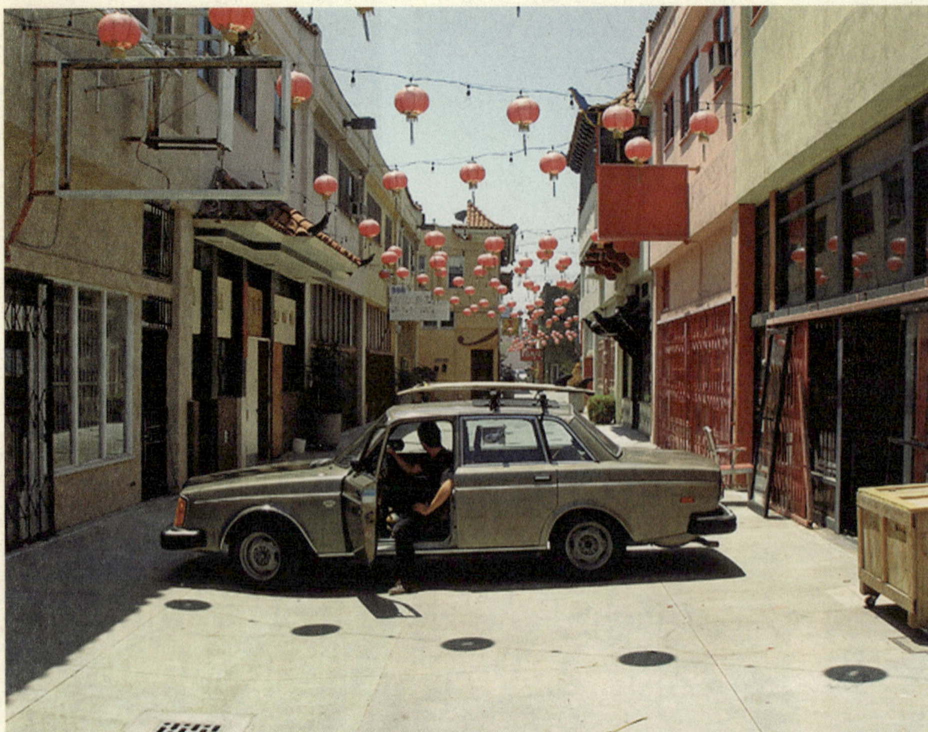

1.

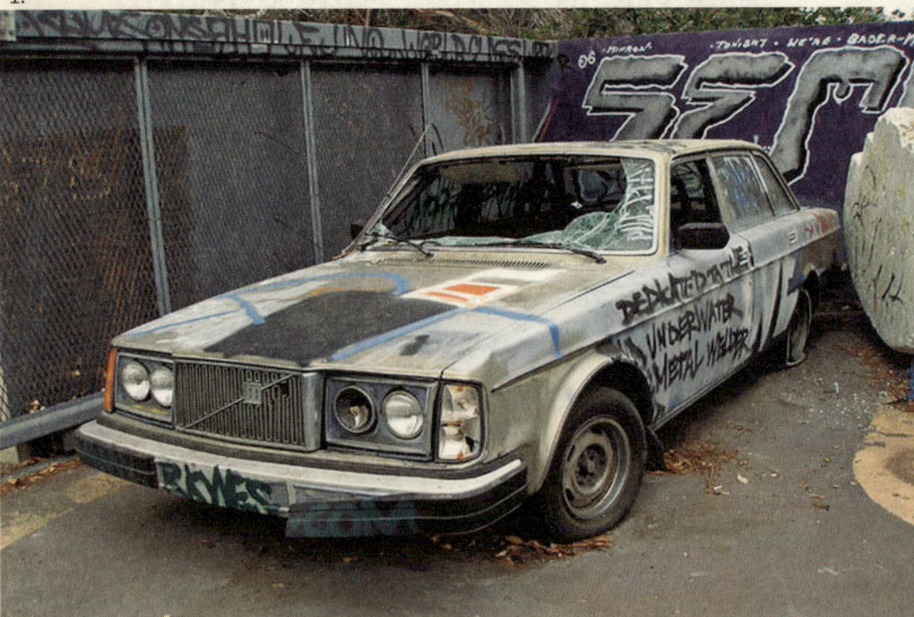

2.

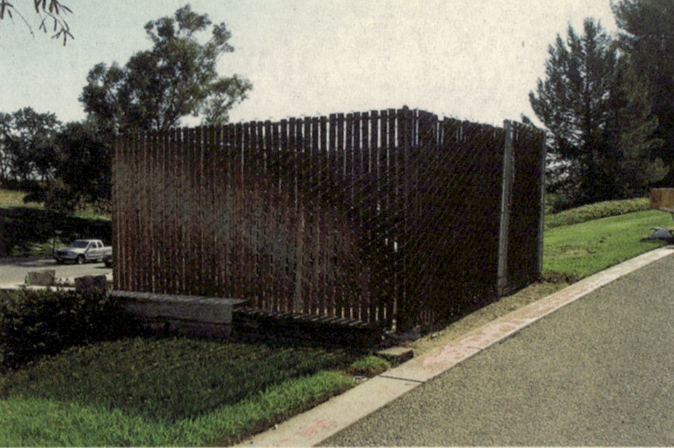

3.

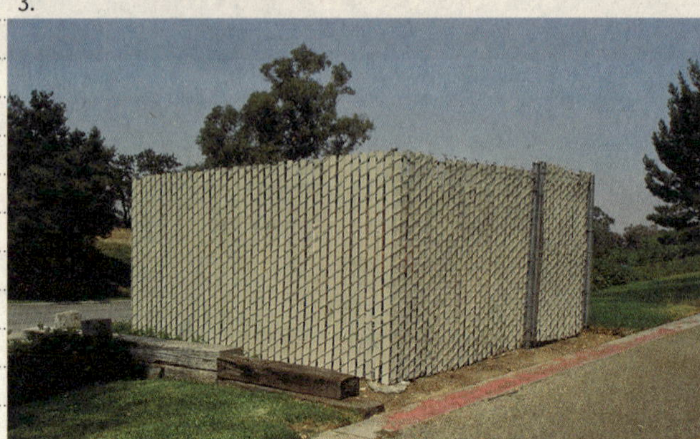

4.

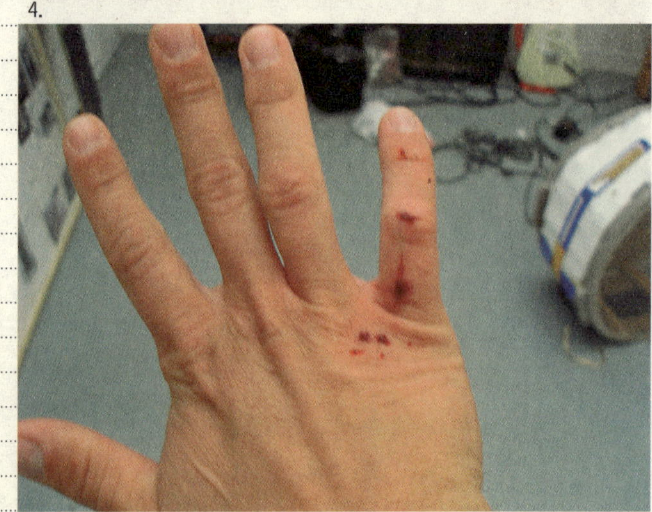

5.

Aaron Wrinkle graduated with an MFA from the California Institute of the Arts in 2008 and currently lives and works in Los Angeles. His paintings, photographs, billboards, and sculptures engage with the politics of art history, frequently incorporating the exhibiting art institution itself. His work questions the sorting and ranking of objects that are exhibited in museums and galleries.

1. **Me Partially Inside Restored 1977 264 GL 4 Door Sedan Volvo After Driving it Outside of Telic Arts Exchange, Chinatown, Los Angeles**
2008, digital photograph, 35 × 45 in (89 × 114 cm)

2. **1977 264 GL 4 Door Sedan Volvo Previously Owned By Douglas Huebler, Before Restoration, Vandalized from 1995-2008, Traded for House Painting and General Labor by Darcy Huebler and Luciano Perna**
2008, digital photograph, 35 × 45 in (89 × 114 cm)

3. **Water Main Fencing at California Institute of the Arts Before Restoration**
2008, digital photograph, 40 × 30 in (102 × 76 cm)

4. **Proposal for Restoration as Minimalism #1, Restored Water Main Fencing at California Institute of the Arts**
2008, digital photograph, 40 × 30 in (102 × 76 cm)

5. **Studio Photograph of Hand After Being Bit by Raymond Pettibon's Dog in the Art Publication Afterall's Office, California Institute of the Arts**
2008, digital photograph, 35 × 45 in (89 × 114 cm)

Wu Chi-Tsung attended Taipei National University of the Arts and continues to live in Taipei. He works with photography and video as both medium and subject, emphasizing the process of image-making over specific content. Choosing simple subject matter, such as raindrops or wire netting, and modifying elements of the technical process (camera shutter speeds, the focus on a projector), he calls attention to media's effect on our perceptions of the world.

1. **Wire**
2004, mixed media, dimensions variable

2. **Wire III**
2007, mixed media, dimensions variable

3. **Self-Portrait**
2004, color print, 60 × 40 in (152 × 102 cm)

4. **Dust**
2006, installation, HD camera and projector, dimensions variable

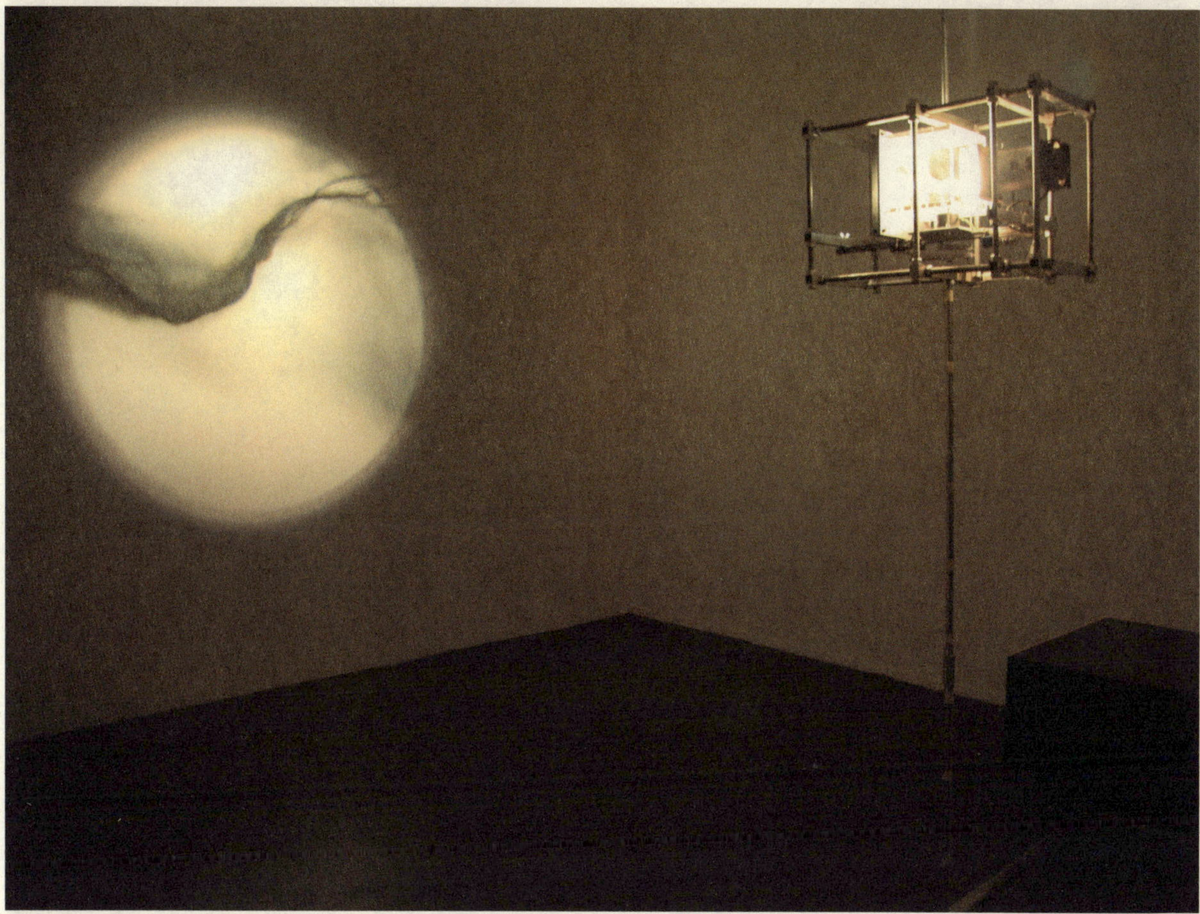

1.

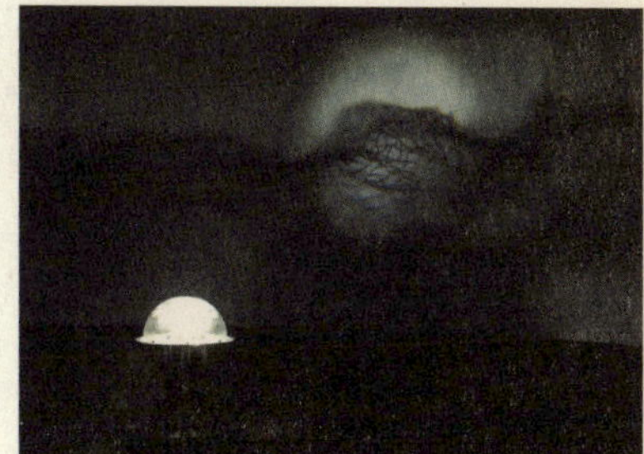

2.

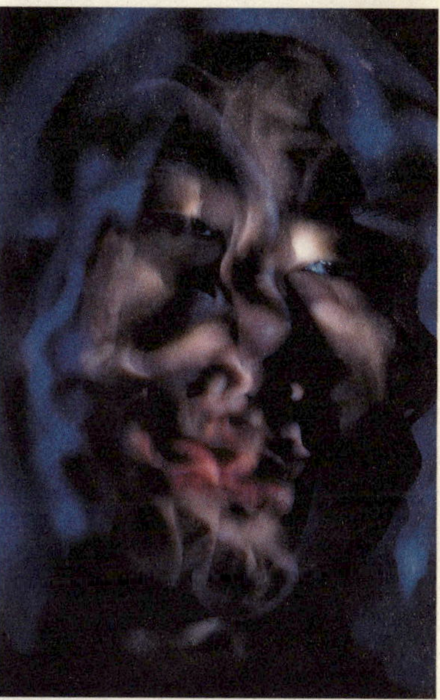

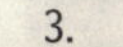

3.

4.

Wu Ingrid Tsang received a MFA from the University of California, Los Angeles in 2007. He currently lives in New York and Los Angeles. He is a cofounder of the performance troupe Marriage and works primarily with voice as his medium. In his ongoing work **Untitled (Phonos)** (2004–present), two paper cones face each other, both hanging from the ceiling, and an audio loop posits the voice as a sculptural medium and a metaphor.

1. **Lamento della Drag**
2008, performance, 15 min, performance view at REDCAT Studio Series, Los Angeles

2. **Someone Else's Song**
2005-07, performance series

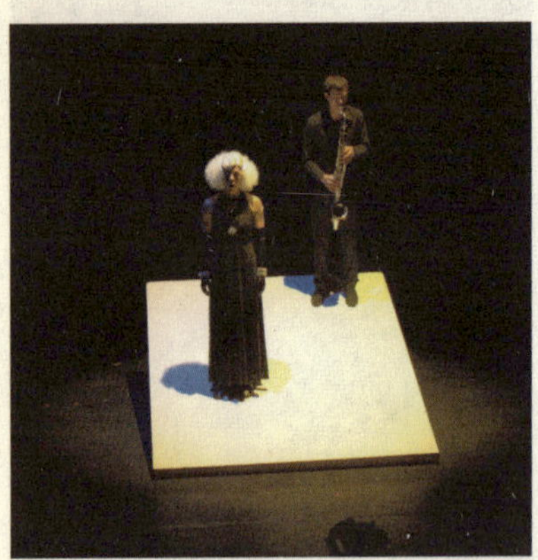

1.

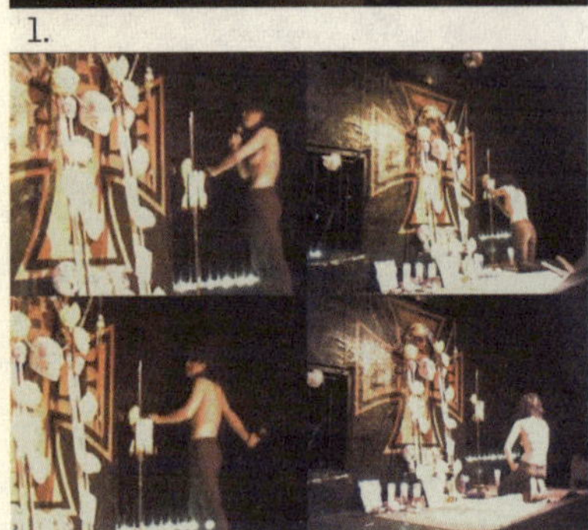

2.

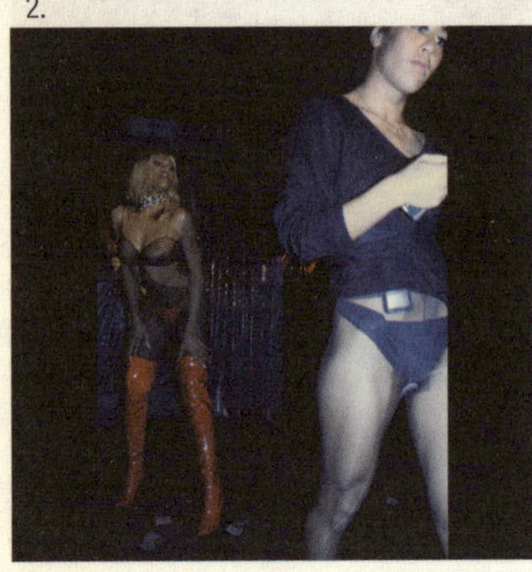

3.

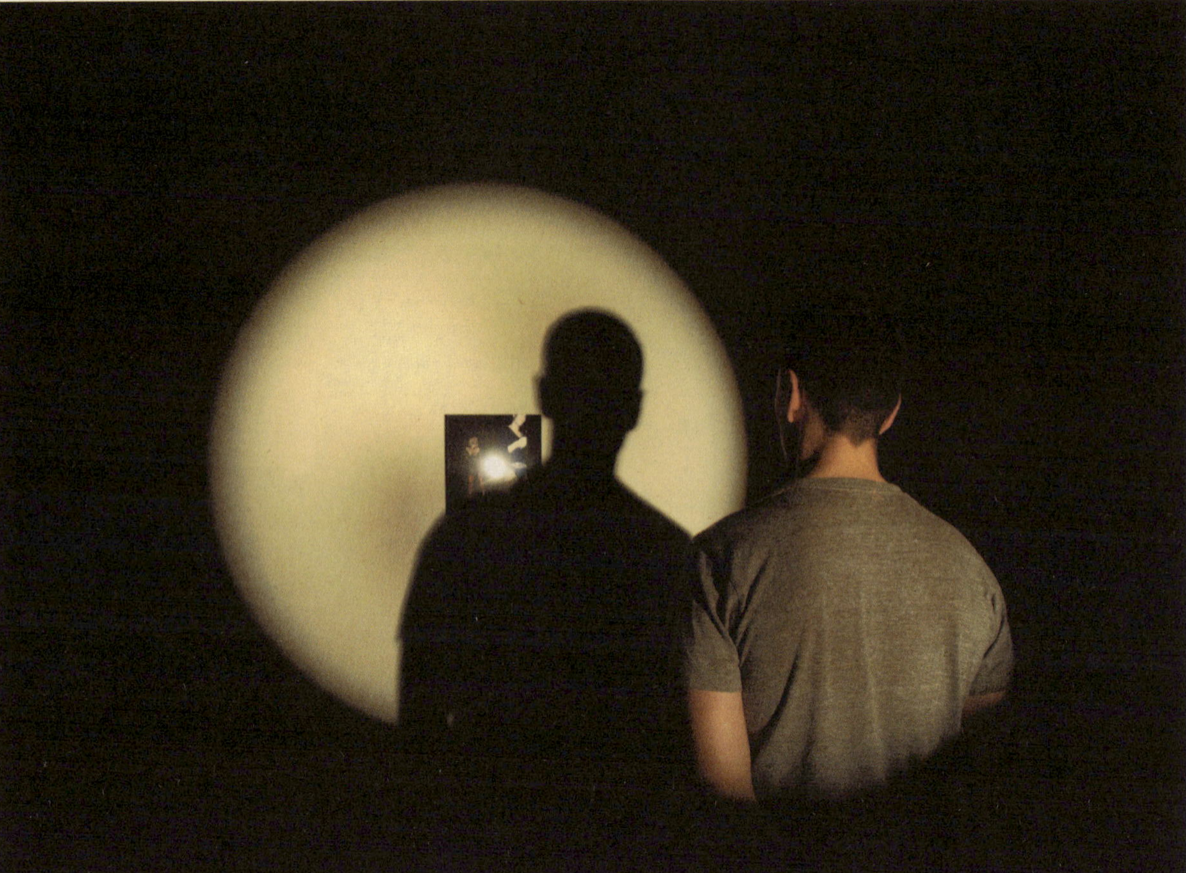

4.

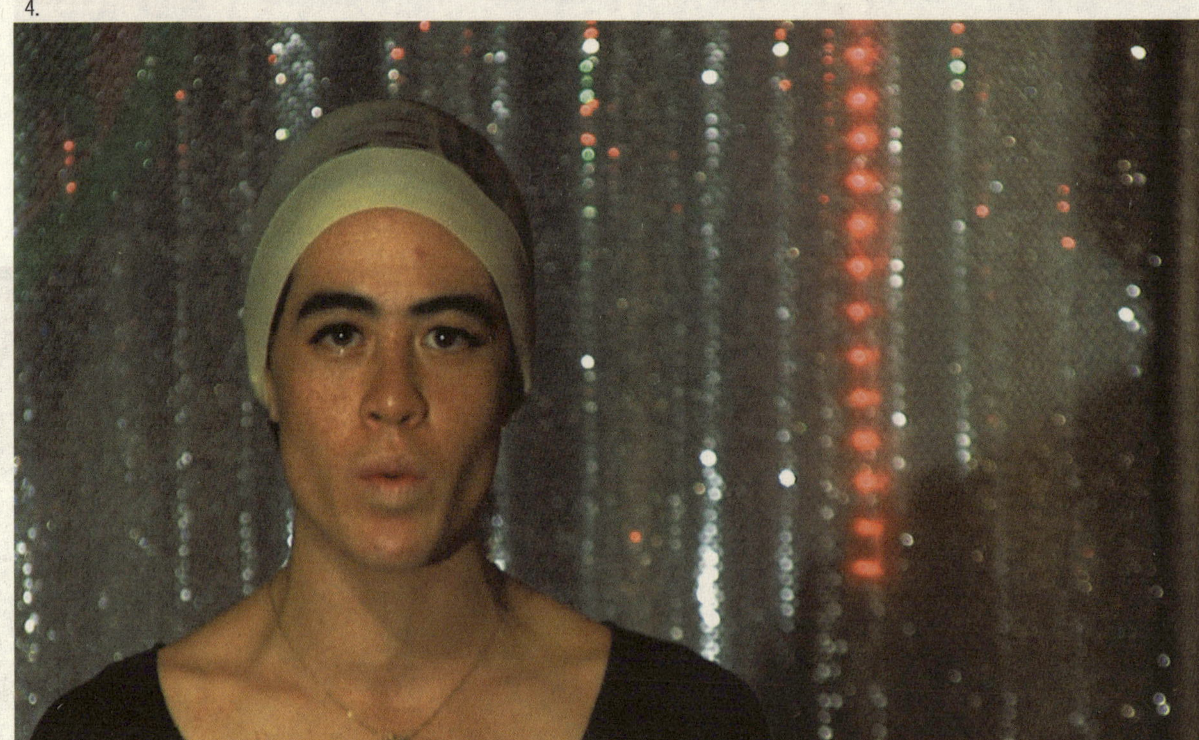

5.

3. **The Shape of a Right Statement II**
2008, Plexi-mounted digital chromogenic print and spotlight, dimensions variable

4. **The Shape of a Right Statement II**
2008, Plexi-mounted digital chromogenic print and spotlight, dimensions variable

5. **The Shape of a Right Statement I**
2008, video, 5 min 15 sec

Gesche Wuerfel graduated in 2006 with an MA in photography and urban cultures from Goldsmiths College in London, where she lives and works. Her chromogenic prints explore places in transition and the relationship people have with their environments. The serial nature and fixation on abandoned places in her work references the work of Bernd and Hilla Becher. Wuerfel's series **Go For Gold!** (2008) investigates the way preparations for the Olympic Games in London in 2012 are affecting people who live in the East End of the city during a transitional period for the cityscape.

1. **Hockey 3**
2007, digital chromogenic print on aluminum, 20 × 20 in (51 × 51 cm)

2. **Service Area 4**
2007, digital chromogenic print on aluminum, 20 × 20 in (51 × 51 cm)

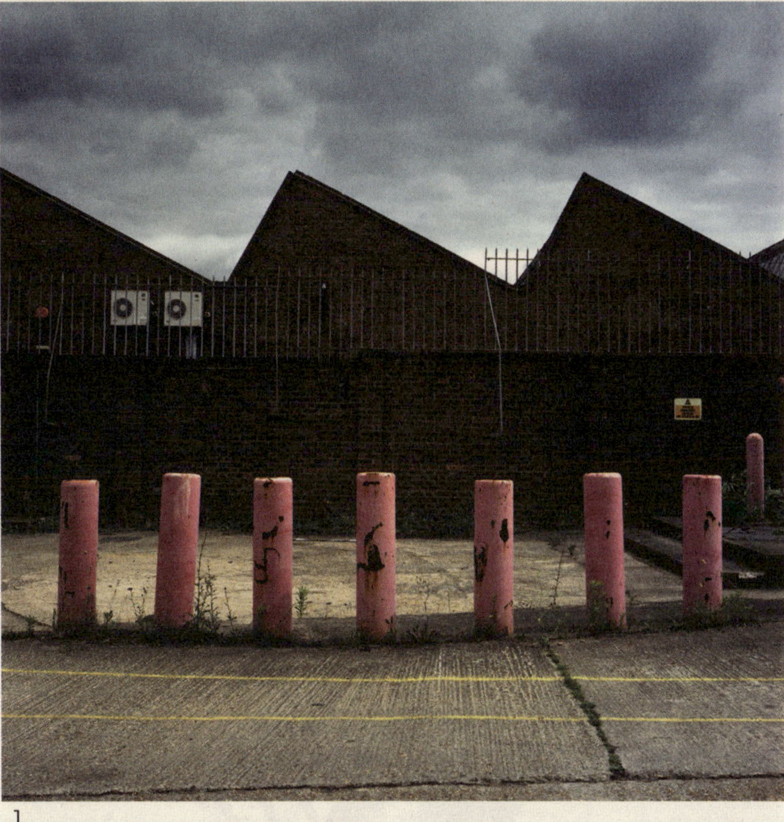

1.

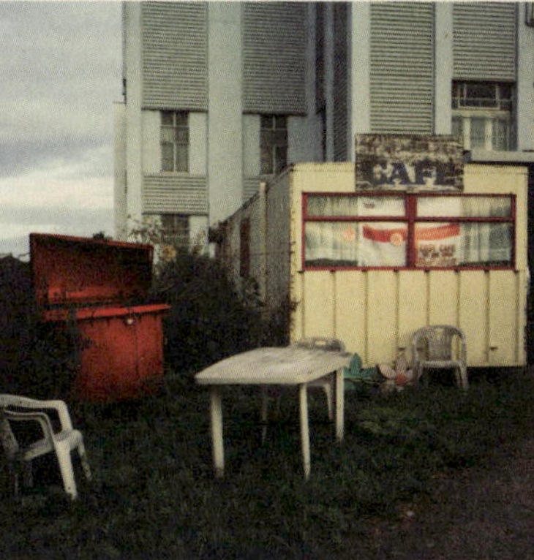

2.

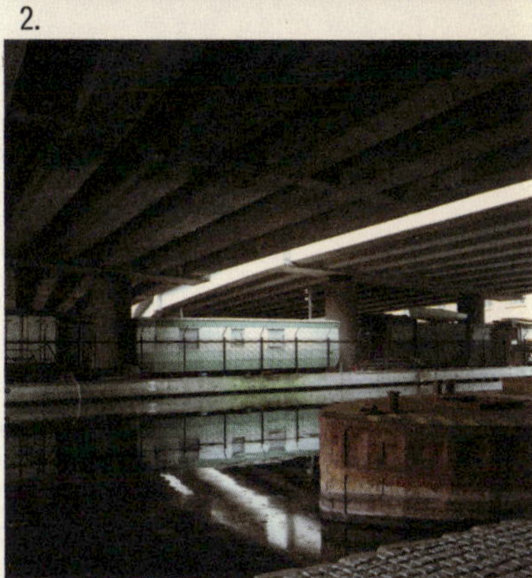

3.

4.

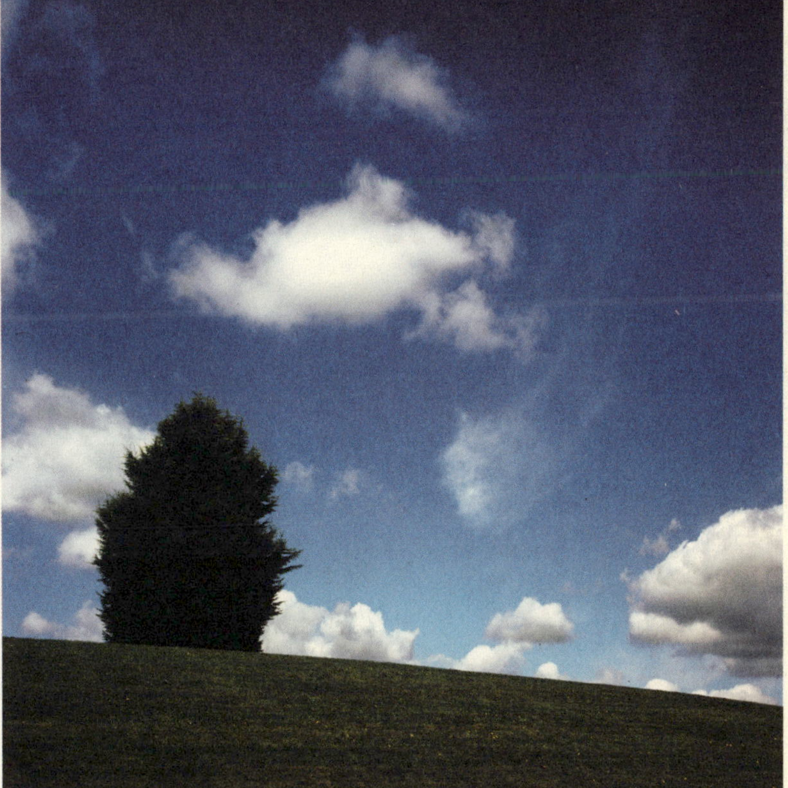

5.

3. **N 51o32.896 / W 000o01.564**
2008, digital chromogenic print on aluminum, 20 × 20 in (51 × 51 cm)

4. **N 51o31.552 / W 000o00.375**
2007, digital chromogenic print on aluminum, 20 × 20 in (51 × 51 cm)

5. **N 51o44.583 / W 000o00.599**
2007, digital chromogenic print on aluminum, 20 × 20 in (51 × 51 cm)

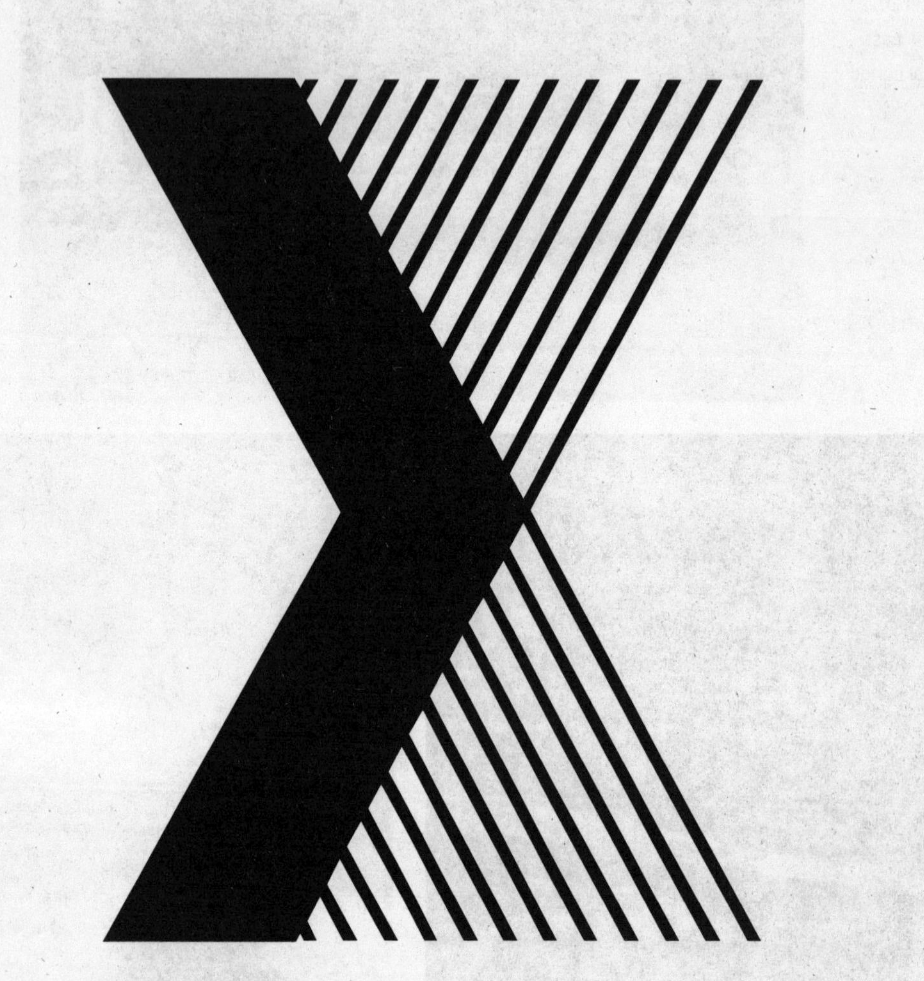

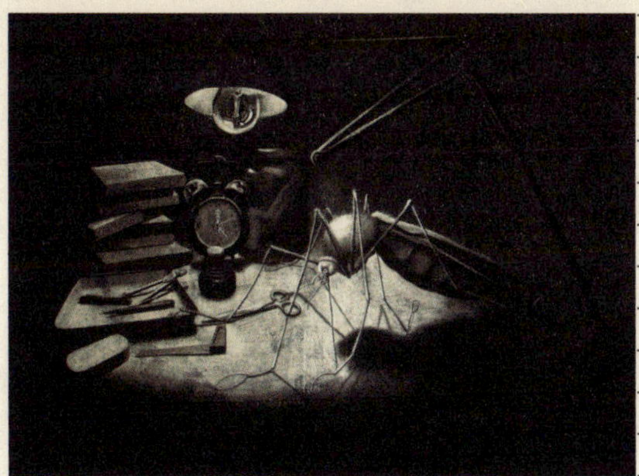
1.

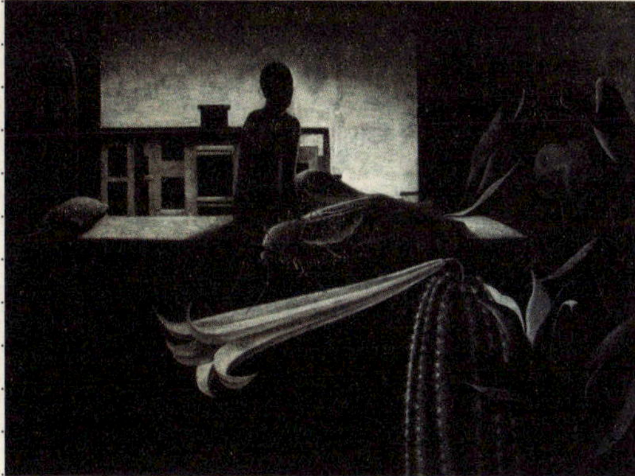
2.

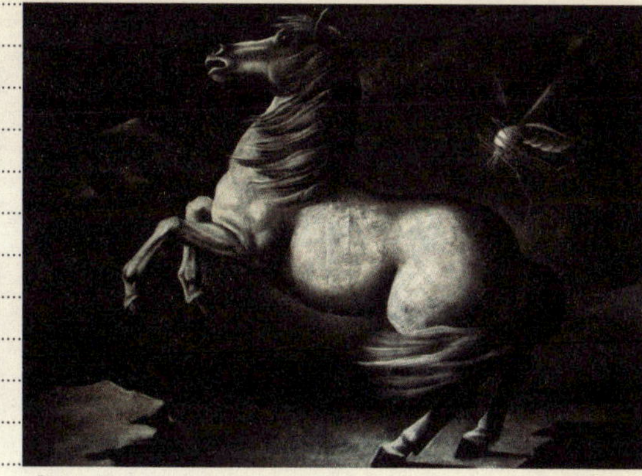
3.

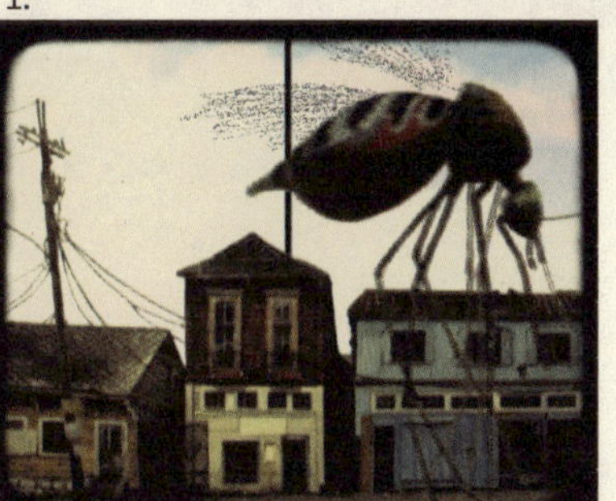
4.

Xun Sun graduated from the printmaking department of the China Academy of Fine Arts. His black and white murals were shown in a solo exhibition, "The New China," at the Hammer Museum in Los Angeles in 2008, and he has a solo exhibition in 2009 at the Drawing Center in New York. He started his own animation studio, Pi, in 2006, and he is known for animations that combine political cartoons with academic painting.

1, 2 & 3. **21G**
2007-08, oil, pencil, and pastel on canvas in frame, 3 of 50 parts, each 58 1/4 × 74 in (148 × 188 cm); video, 30 min

4. **Requiem**
2007, animation, 7 min 21 sec

5, 6, 7 & 8. **Lie**
2006, animation, 7 min 20 sec

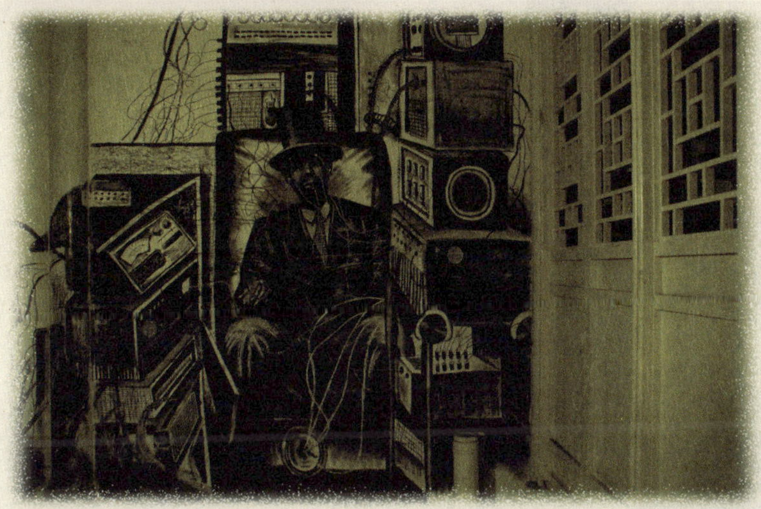
5.

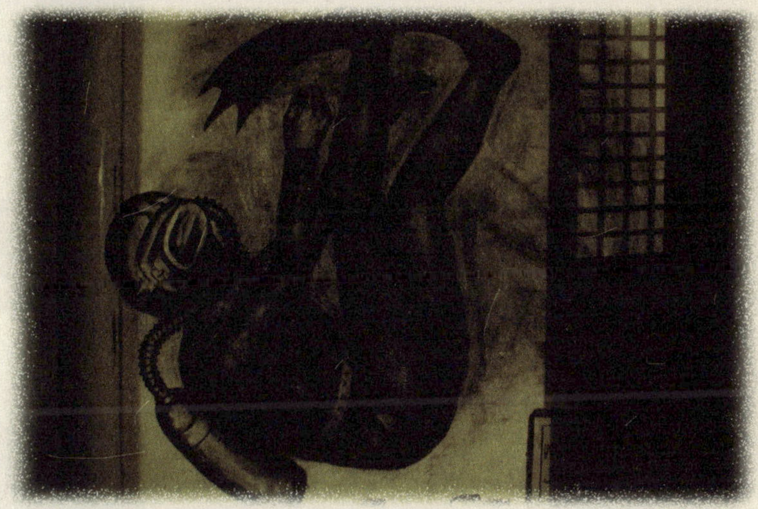
6.

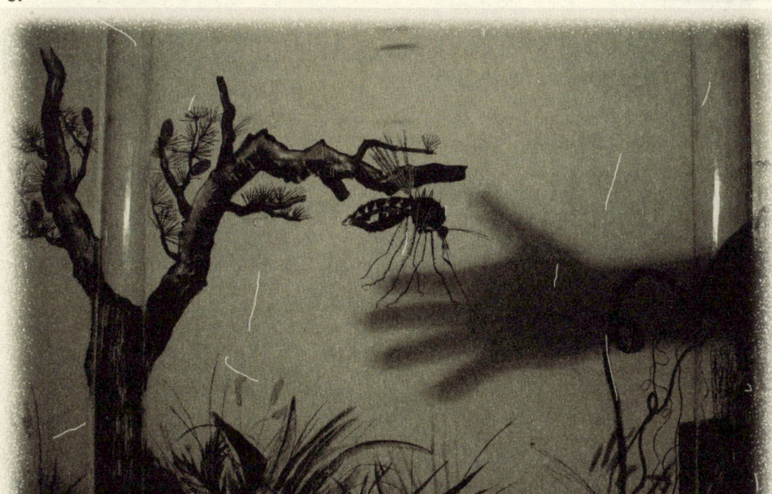
7.

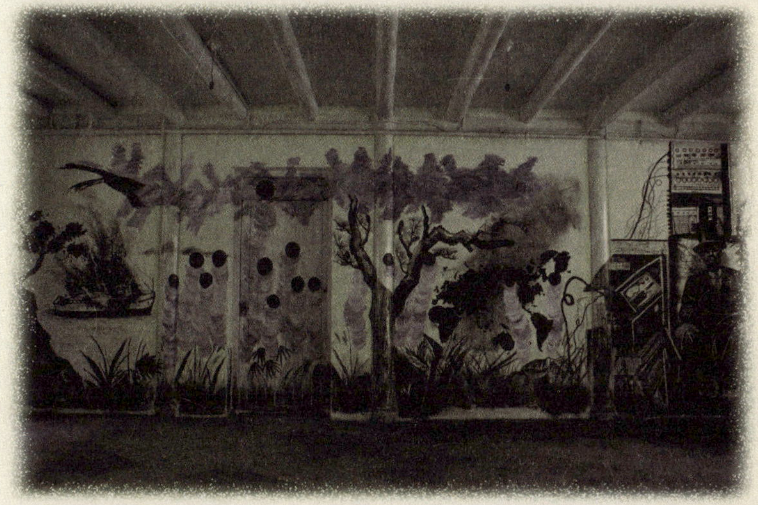
8.

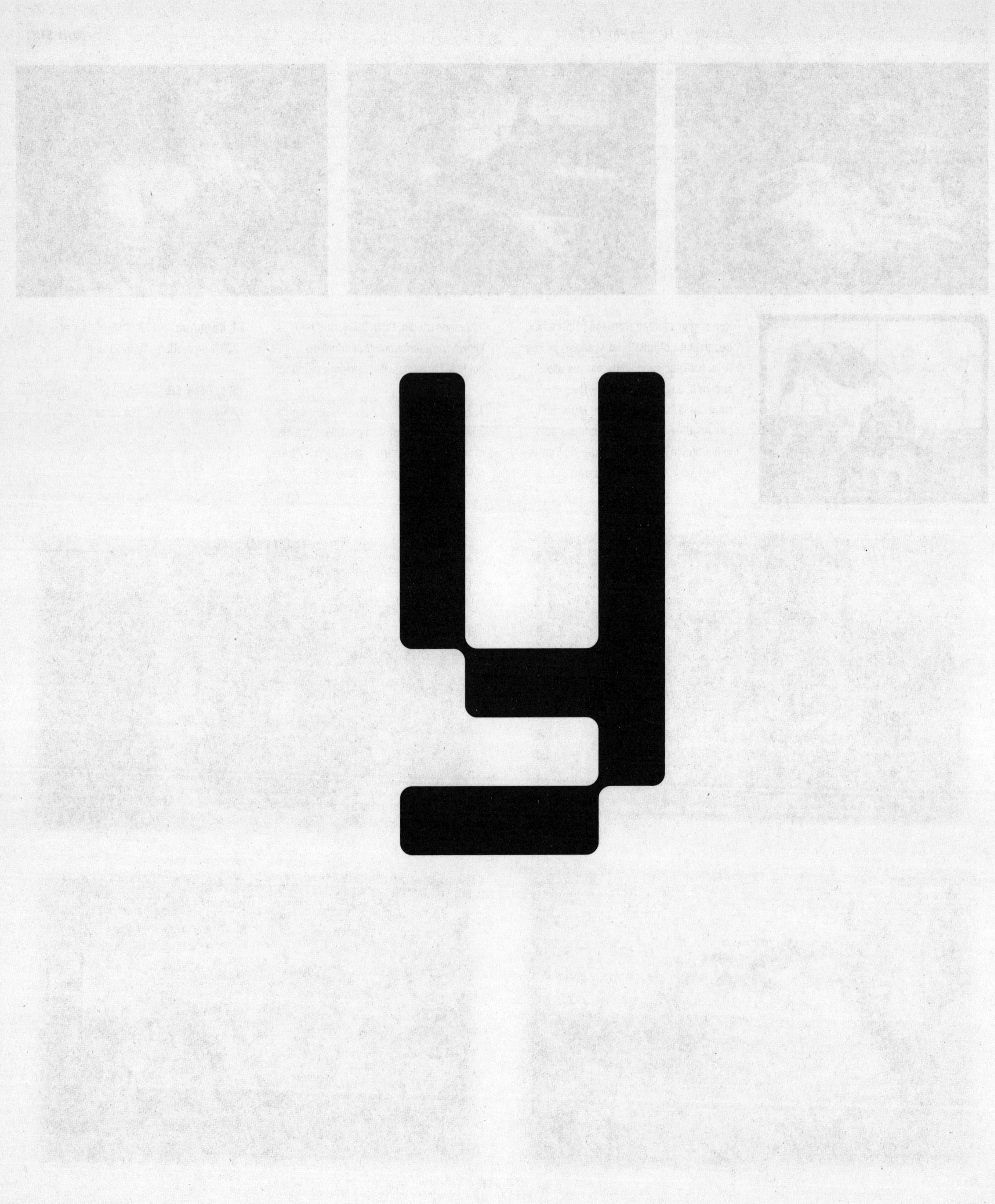

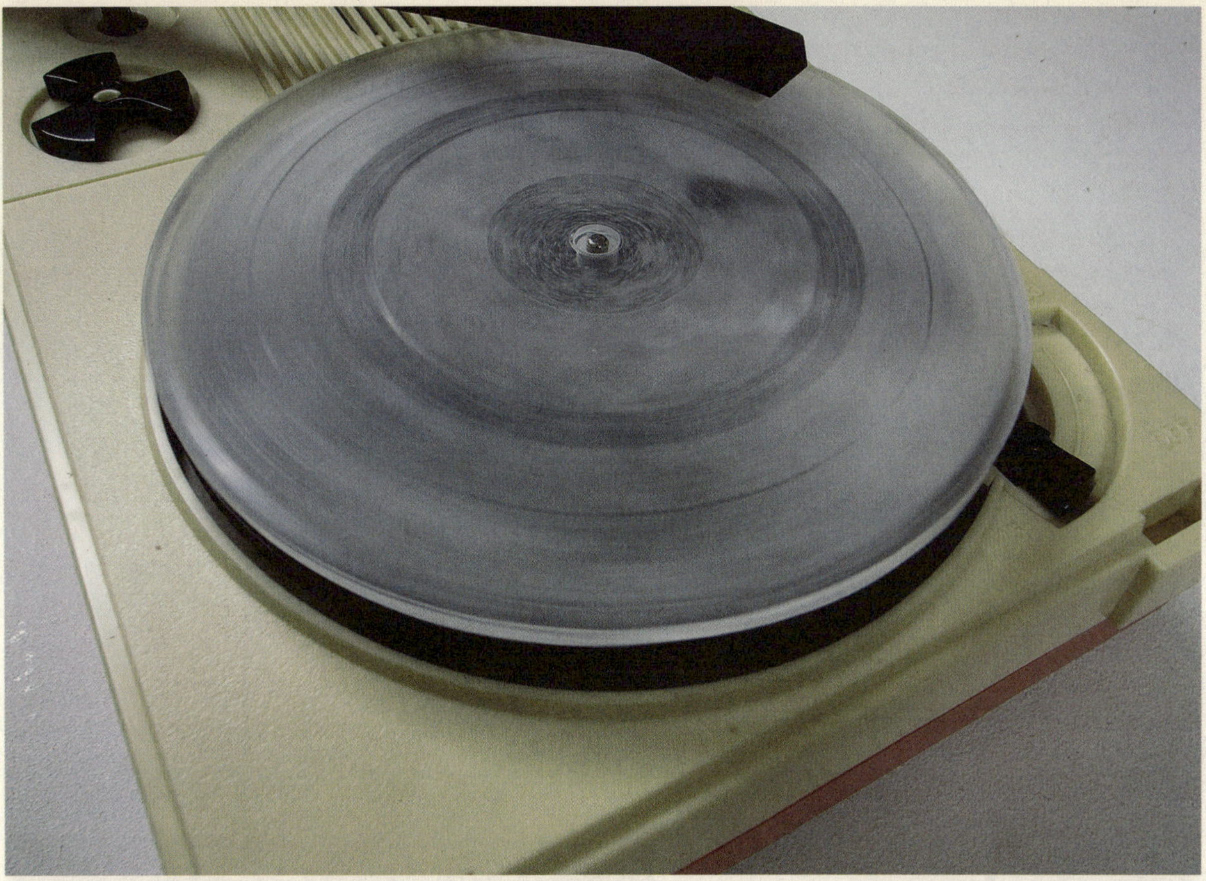

1.

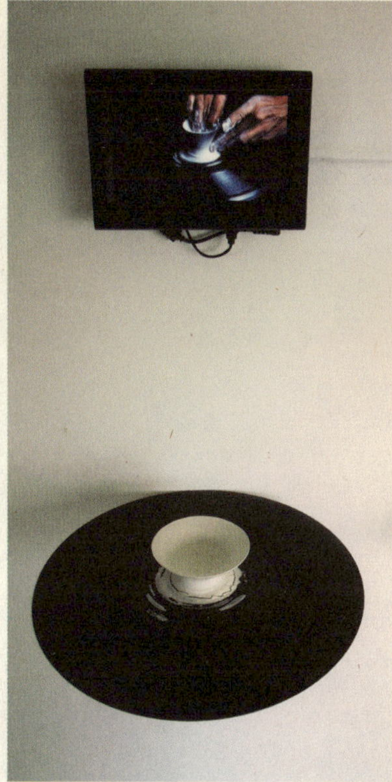

2.

Lyota Yagi graduated from Kyoto University of Art and Design and lives and works in Kyoto. His sound pieces and installations have included records custom made out of ice that melt as they are played on a portable record player. Yagi has also created an umbrella that plays the sound of falling rain. He uses common devices as records or MP3 players and then reworks their functions, contrasting technology with the ephemerality of music

1. Vinyl
2005, record made of ice, record player, and refrigerator

2. Portamento
2006, porcelain clay, record, record player, and video

3. Warp
2007, projector, digital video shot from a car, and pedestal turning at a velocity equal to, and in the opposite direction of, the moving image

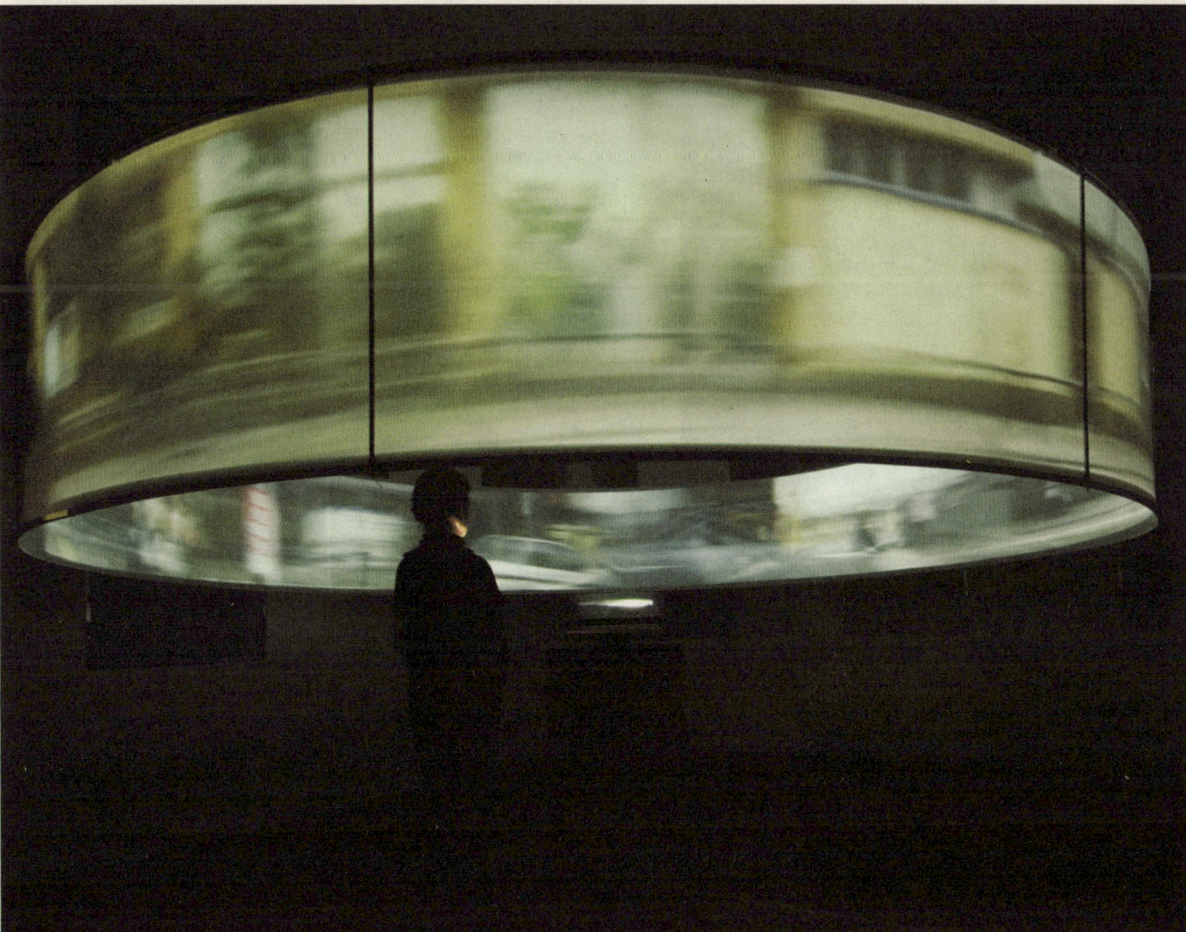

3.

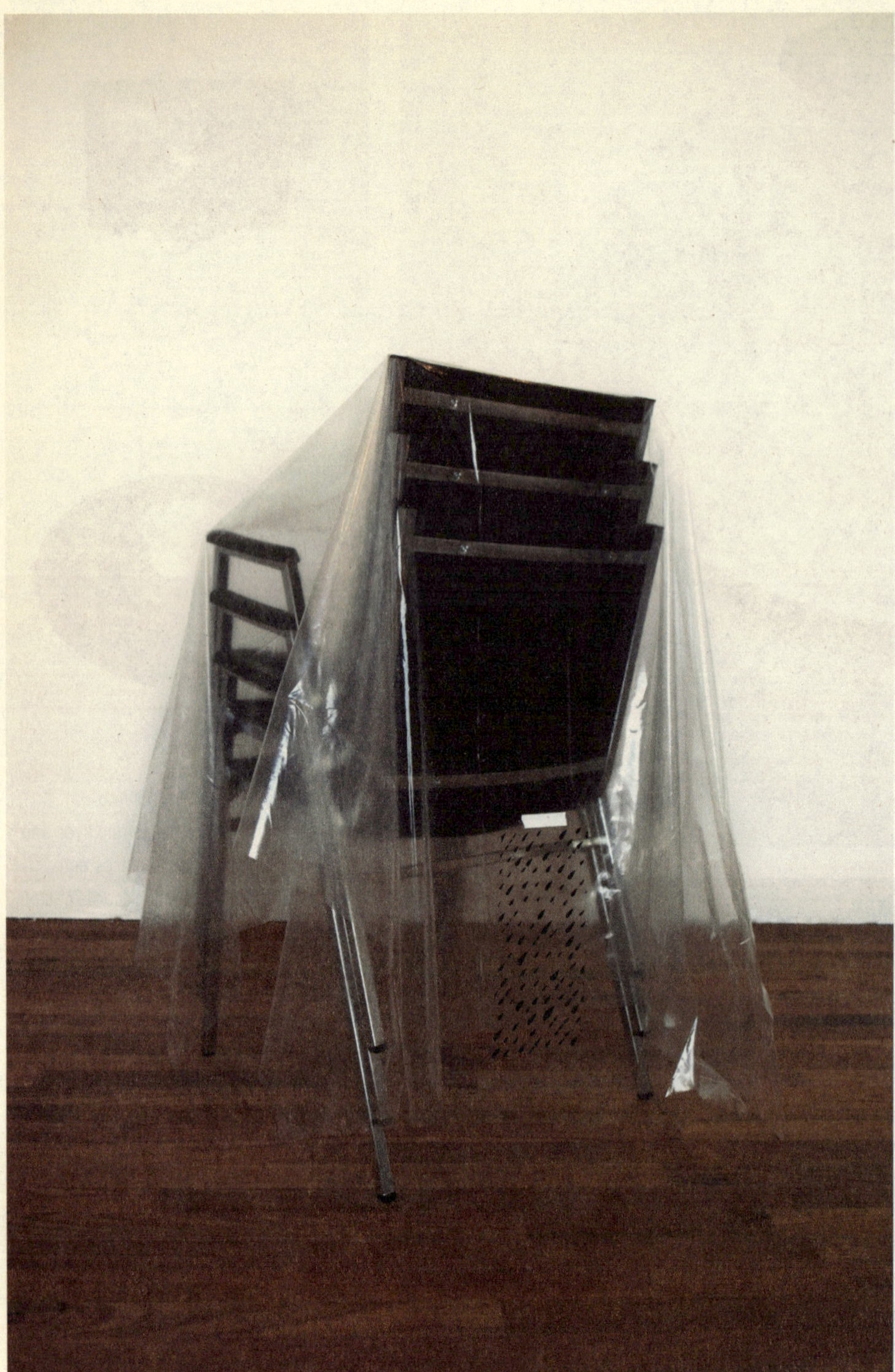

1.

2.

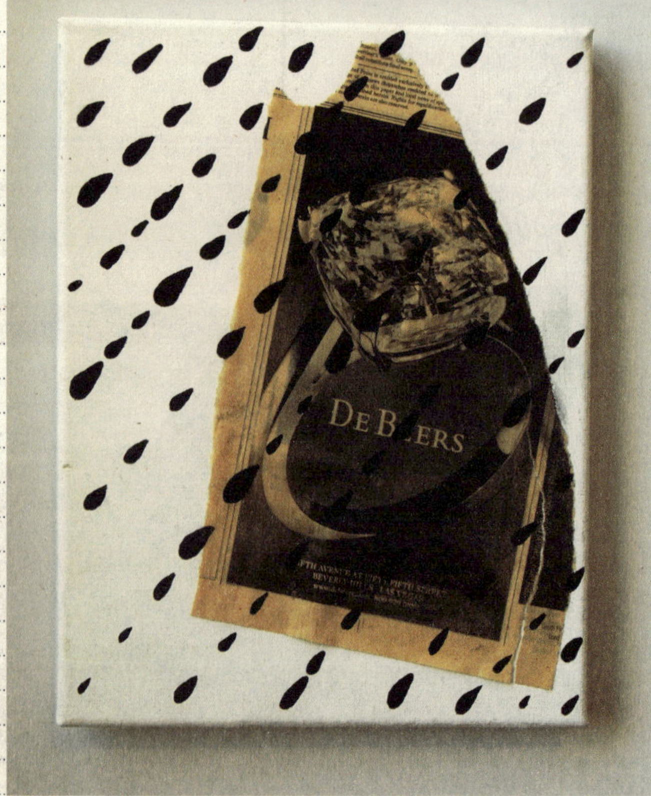

3.

Amy Yao obtained an MFA in sculpture from Yale University in 2007 and lives in New York. Her works cycle through a set of materials and motifs that include slim slats of wood, Plexiglas, ripped newsprint,and horsehair, to name a few. Empty space and transparent layers encourage the viewer to examine the works from a variety of angles. The resulting installations read like anagrams, strings of elements that shift relative to each other.

1. **Untitled**
2008, global stack chairs, plastic drop cloth, and paint on acetate, dimensions variable

2. **Untitled**
2008, glass, hair, and gouache on wooden dowel, dimensions variable

3. **DeBeers Tears**
2008, acrylic on canvas and newspaper, 12 × 8 in (31 × 20 cm)

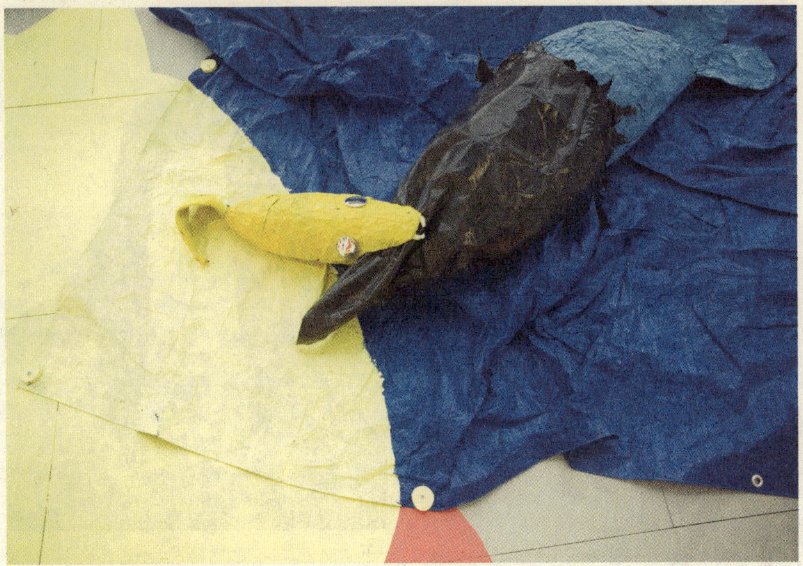

1.

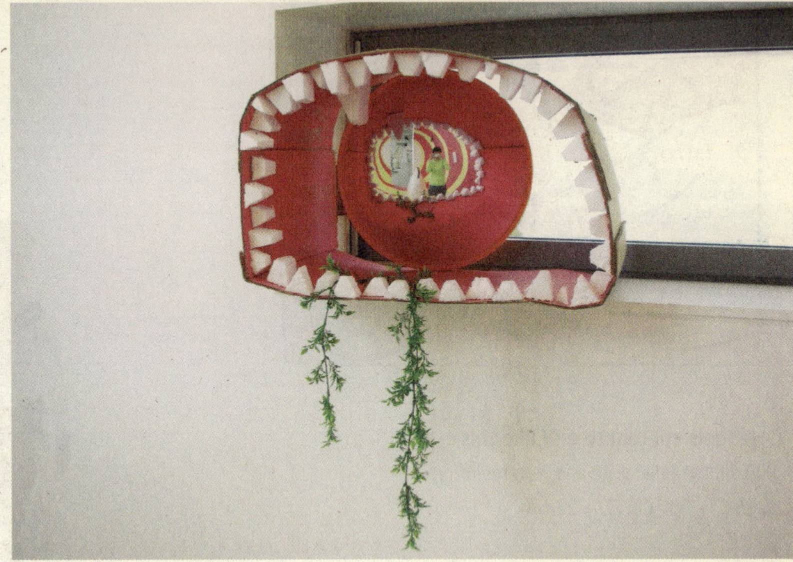

2.

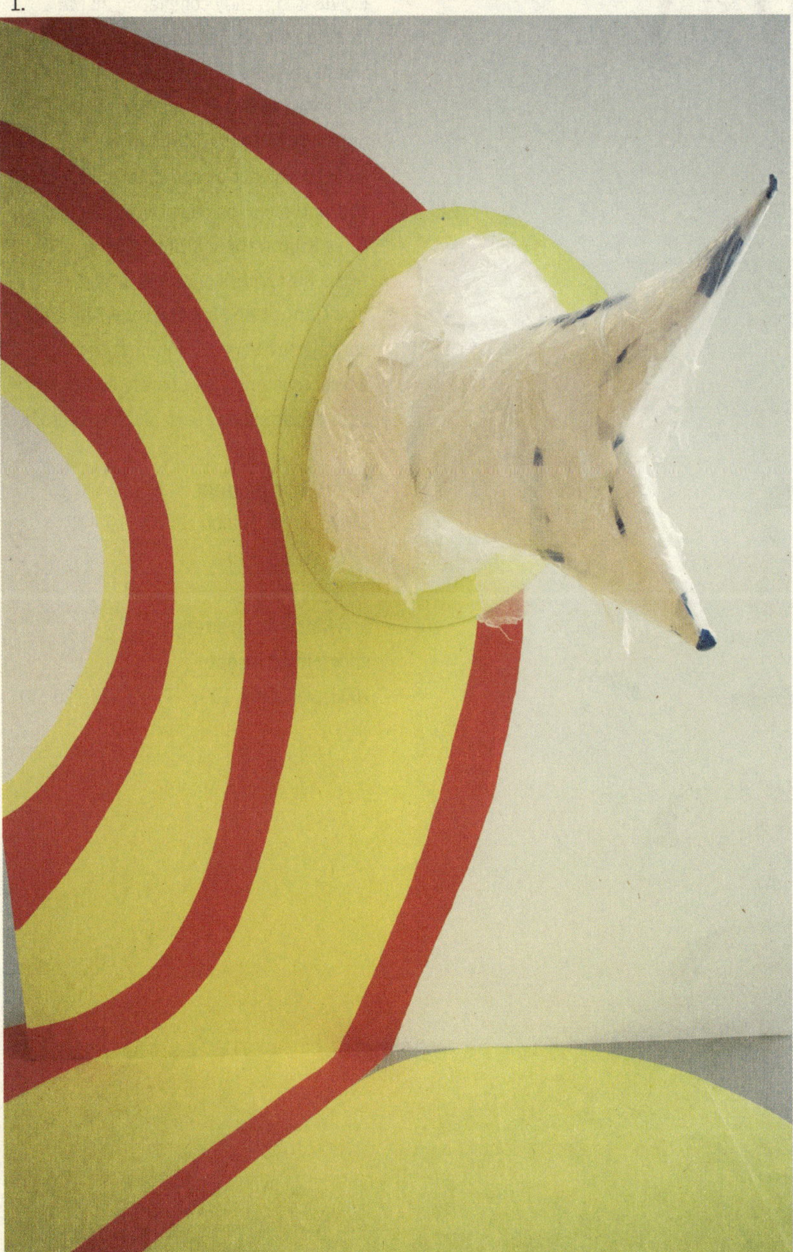

3.

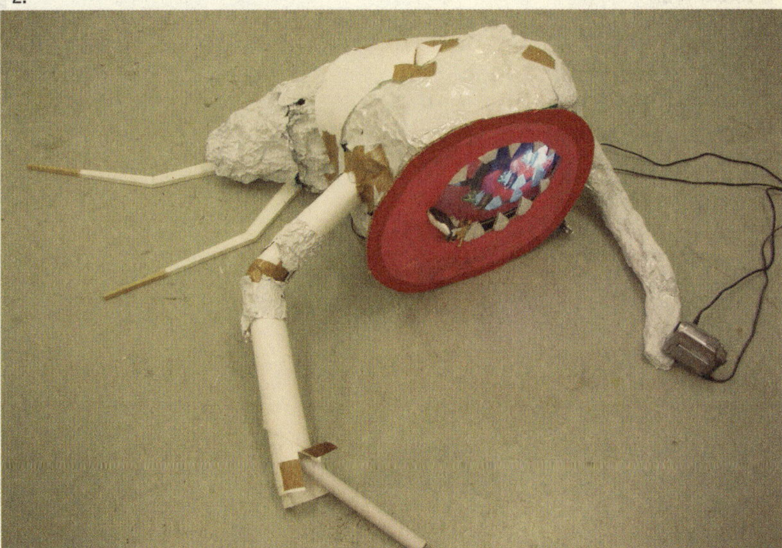

4.

Yohei Yashi earned a BA in fine art from Nottingham Trent University and an MFA from Goldsmiths College, London. She lives and works in London. A musician and vocalist with the band Woman as well as an installation artist, she employs cameras and TV monitors in her installations and sculptures to create fictional spaces combined with childlike contraptions. **Untitled (a mouse)** (2006) includes a TV monitor showing a plastic mouse and surrounded by blue, black, and green garbage bags.

1, 2 & 3. **Untitled (a whale)** (detail)
2007, TV monitor, video camera, and other mixed media, dimensions variable

4. **Mr. Demanding**
2007, TV monitor, video camera, and other mixed media, dimensions variable

5. **Untitled (a mouse)**
2006, TV monitor, spy camera, and other mixed media, dimensions variable

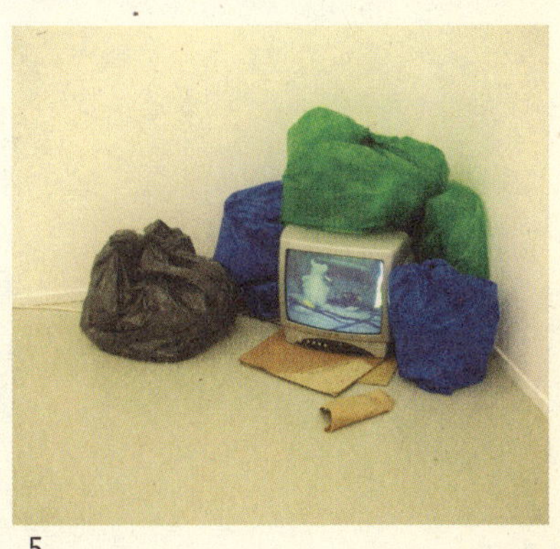

5.

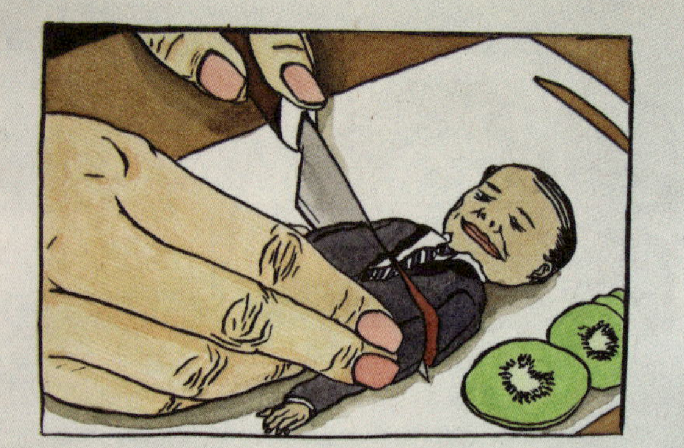

1.

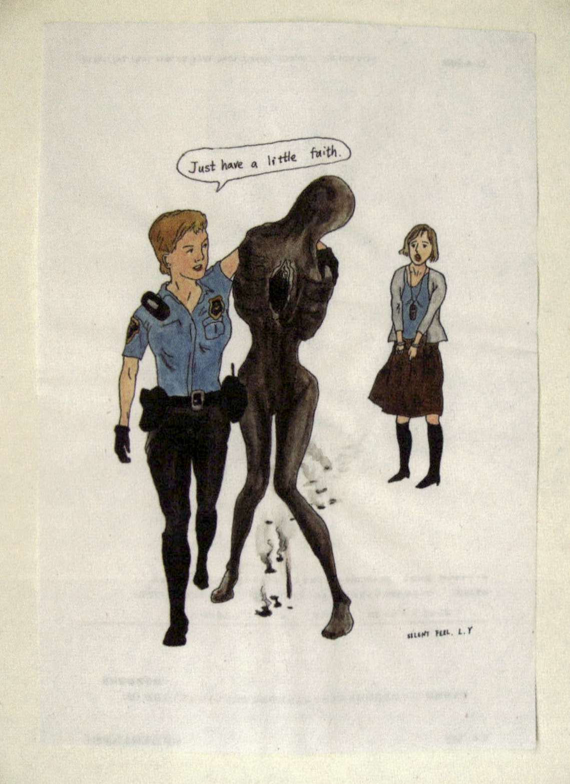

2.

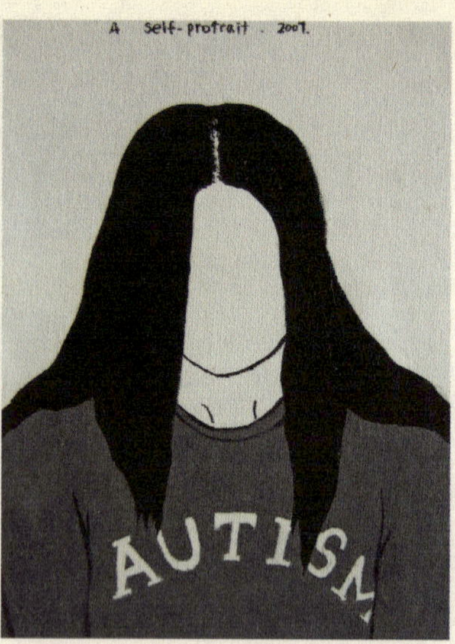

3.

1. He feels content to end like this
2008, lithographic print and watercolor on paper, $6\frac{1}{2} \times 8\frac{3}{4}$ in (17 × 22 cm)

2. Silent feel
2007, pen and watercolor on paper, $11\frac{3}{4} \times 8\frac{1}{4}$ in (30 × 21 cm)

3. Self-portrait (Autism)
2007, mixed media and oil on canvas, 8 × 6 in (20 × 15 cm)

Liu Yin is currently completing an MA from the Guangzhou Academy of Fine Arts, where she also earned a BA. She lives and works in Guangzhou. Her childlike drawings and watercolors draw on personal stories and themes. Her pen and watercolor on paper works include **Boys Killing their Mums** (2007), which twists the Chinese one-child policy. **You Cannot be Happy Every Day** (2007) portrays two very discontented birds in a tree, countering the Chinese tradition of birds representing peace and happiness.

4. You boring guys
2007, pen and oil on canvas, 10 × 12 in (25 × 31 cm)

5. A kind of extremely short-lived insect
2008, monoprint, $10\frac{1}{2} \times 7\frac{1}{2}$ in (27 × 20 cm)

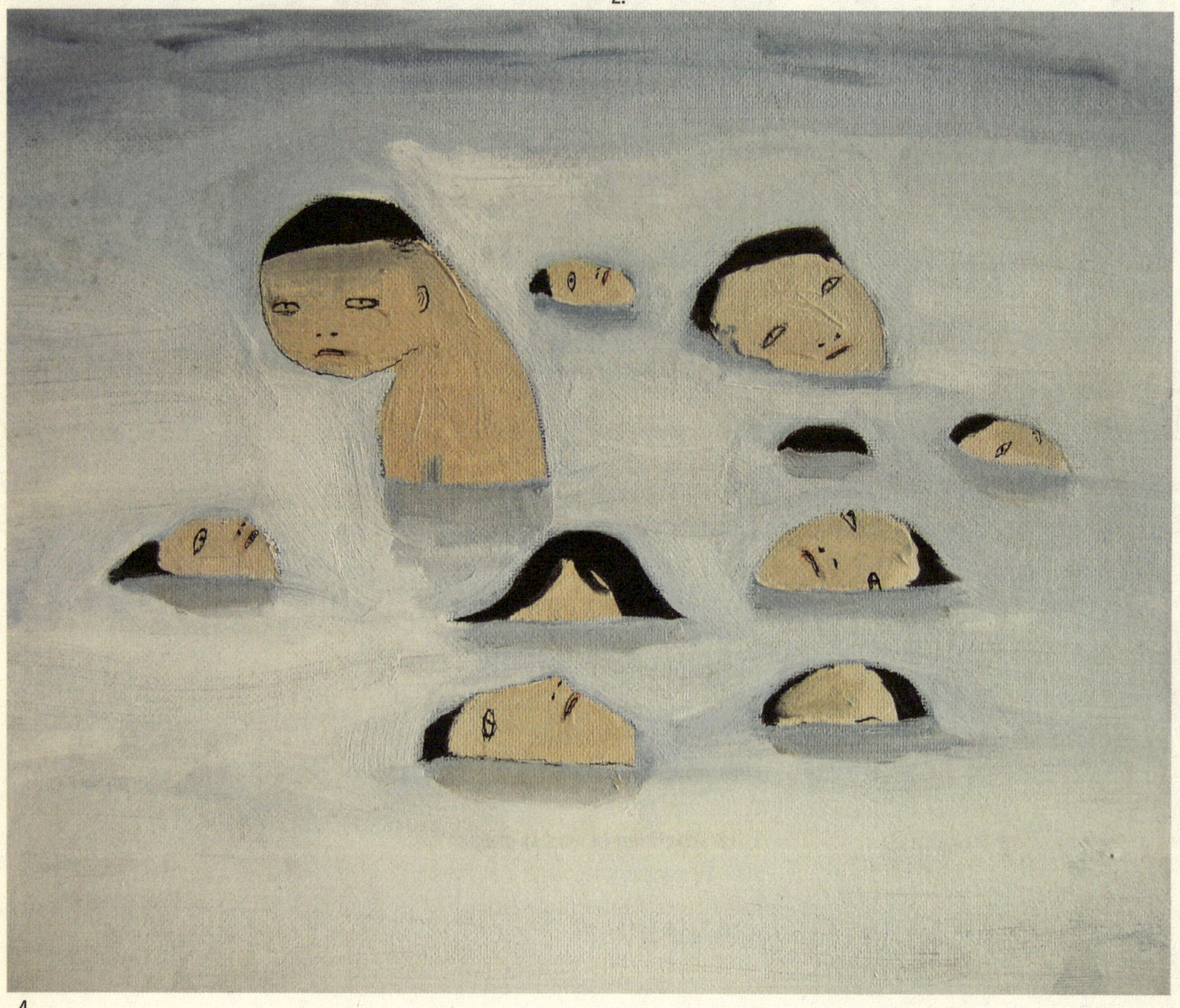

4.

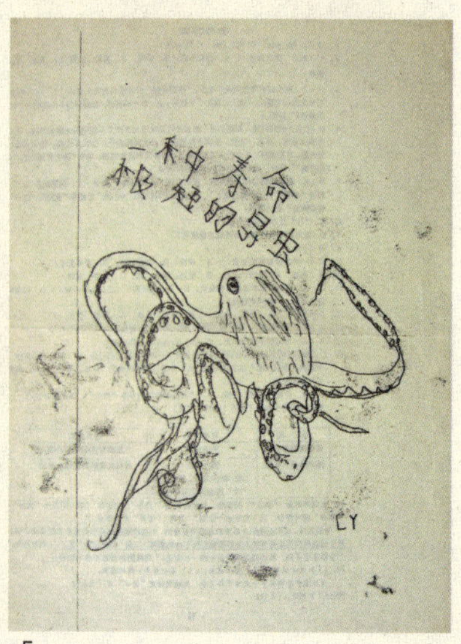

5.

Brenna Youngblood graduated with an MFA from the University of California, Los Angeles, where she lives and works. In her collages, drawn from her own archive of photographs, she layers fragments of photographs with paint and other materials. Her works reference distressed interiors as well as repressed historical narratives. Made in a muted palette, her collages blur the boundaries between painting and photography.

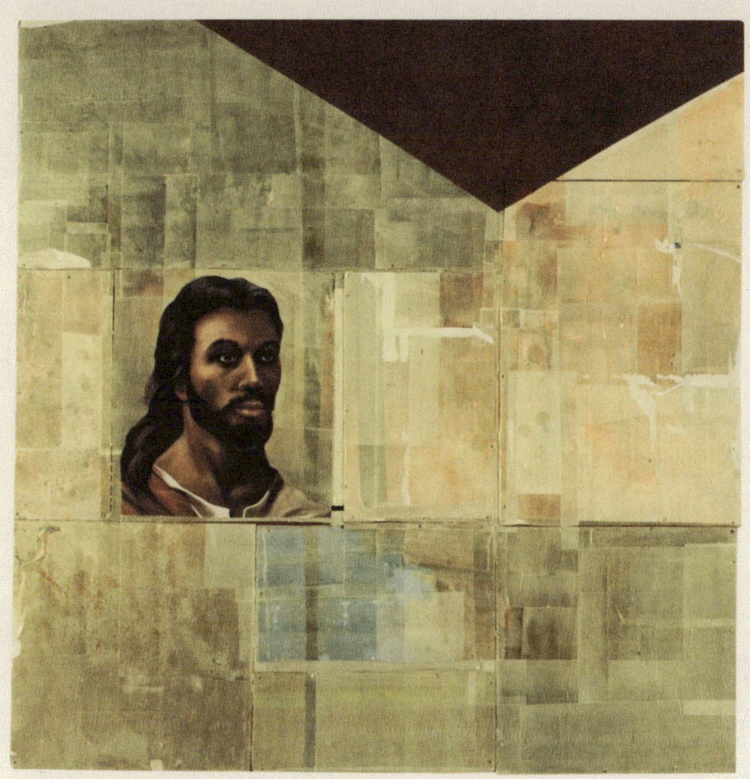

1.

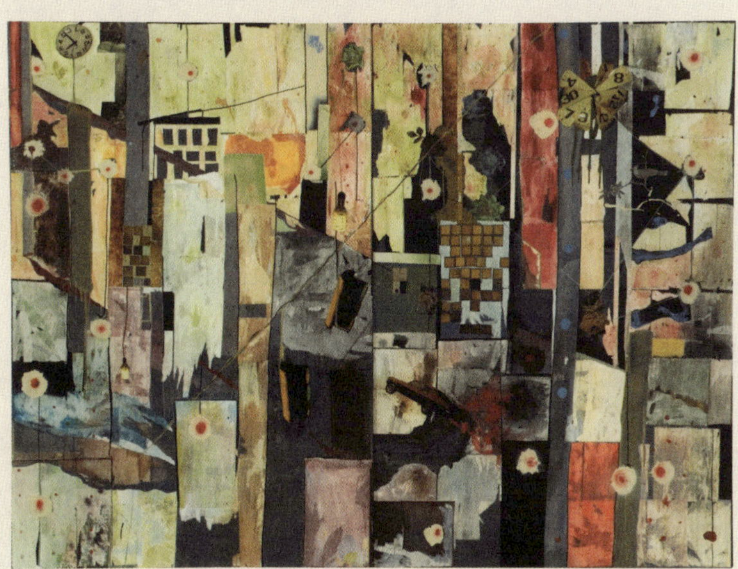

3.

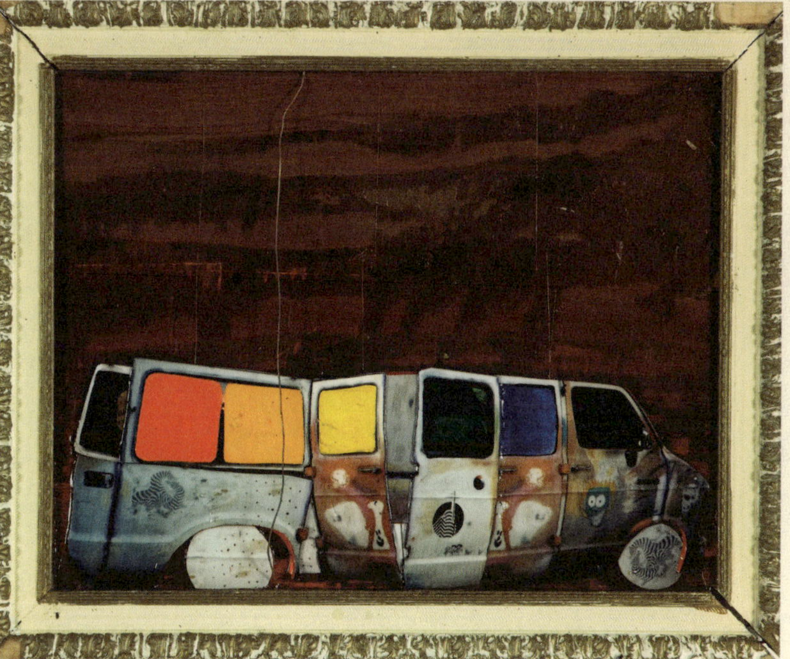

2.

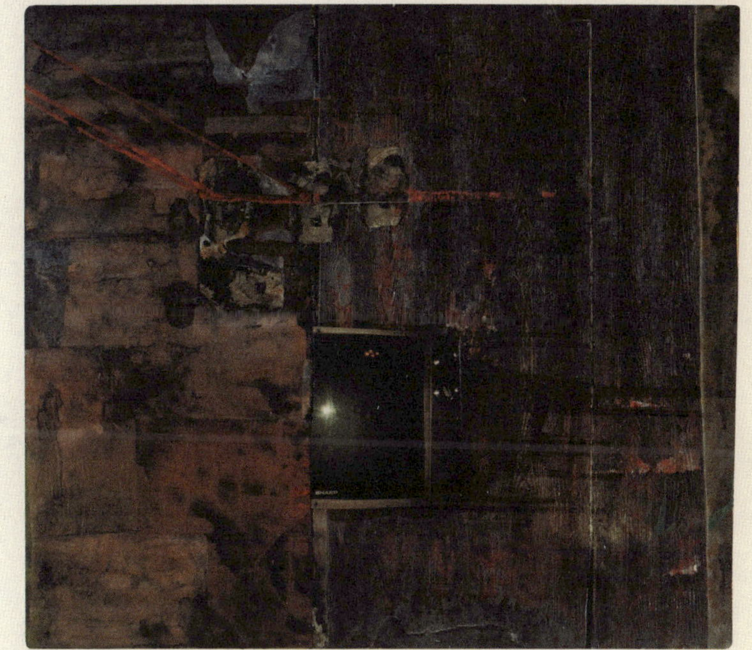

4.

1. Jesus and Sacagawea
2007, color photographs, acrylic paint, spray paint, and collage on panel, 72 × 72 in (185 × 183 cm)

2. Color Checker
2007, color photographs, acrylic paint, spray paint, and collage on panel with found frame, 15 × 19 in (38 × 48 cm)

3. The Leaving
2006, color photographs, acrylic paint, and spray paint on panel, 2 panels, each 71 × 96 in (180 × 244 cm)

4. As the World Turns
2008, color photographs, acrylic paint, spray paint, and collage on panel, 48 × 55 ½ × 1 ½ in (122 × 141 × 4 cm)

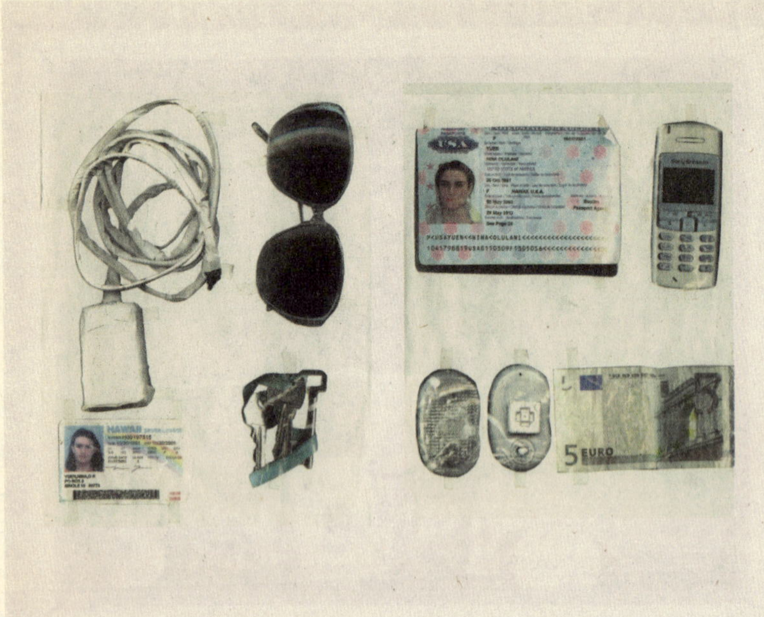

1.

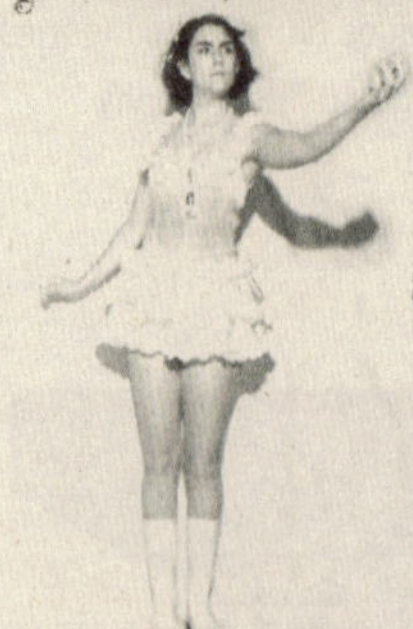

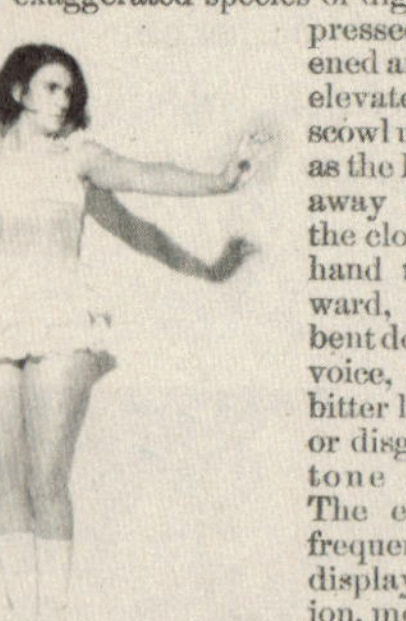

2.

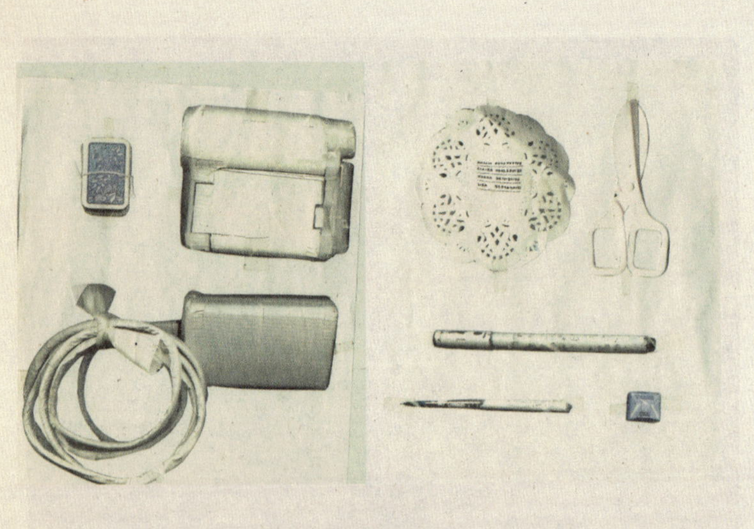

3.

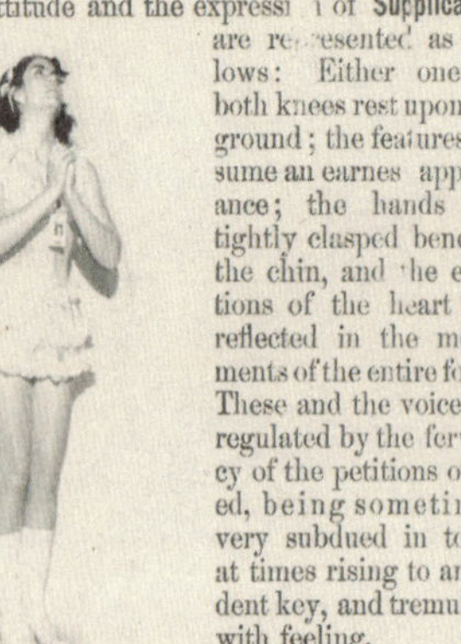

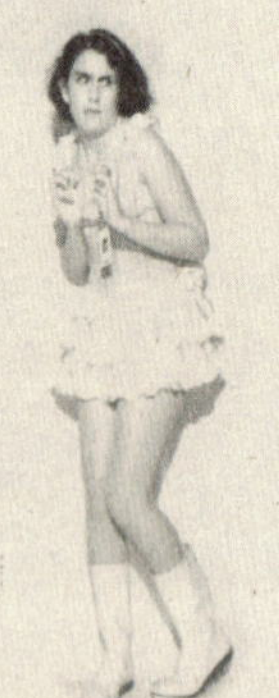

4.

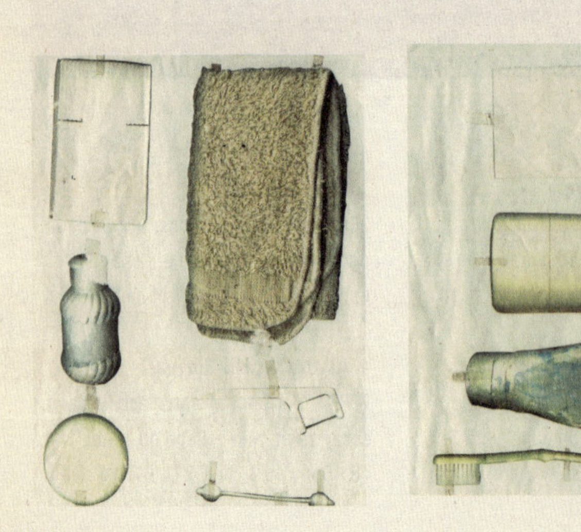

5.

Nina Yuen earned a BA from Harvard University and is currently a fellow at the Rijksakademie in Amsterdam. In her films, Yuen creates false memories and personas. For each film, she lives for at least a week in a constructed environment, following the conventions and dress codes of her created identity. Yuen frequently works with filmmaker Sung Kim, creating films that explore the complexity of identity and the frailty of relationships.

1. Work
2006, cutouts on paper, 8 1⁄2 × 11 in (22 × 28 cm)

2. Earnestness
2007, video still, 8 1⁄2 × 11 in (22 × 28 cm)

3. Play
2006, cutouts on paper, 8 1⁄2 × 11 in (22 × 28 cm)

4. Supplication
2007, video still, 8 1⁄2 × 11 in (22 × 28 cm)

5. Clean
2006, cutouts on paper, 8 1⁄2 × 11 in (22 × 28 cm)

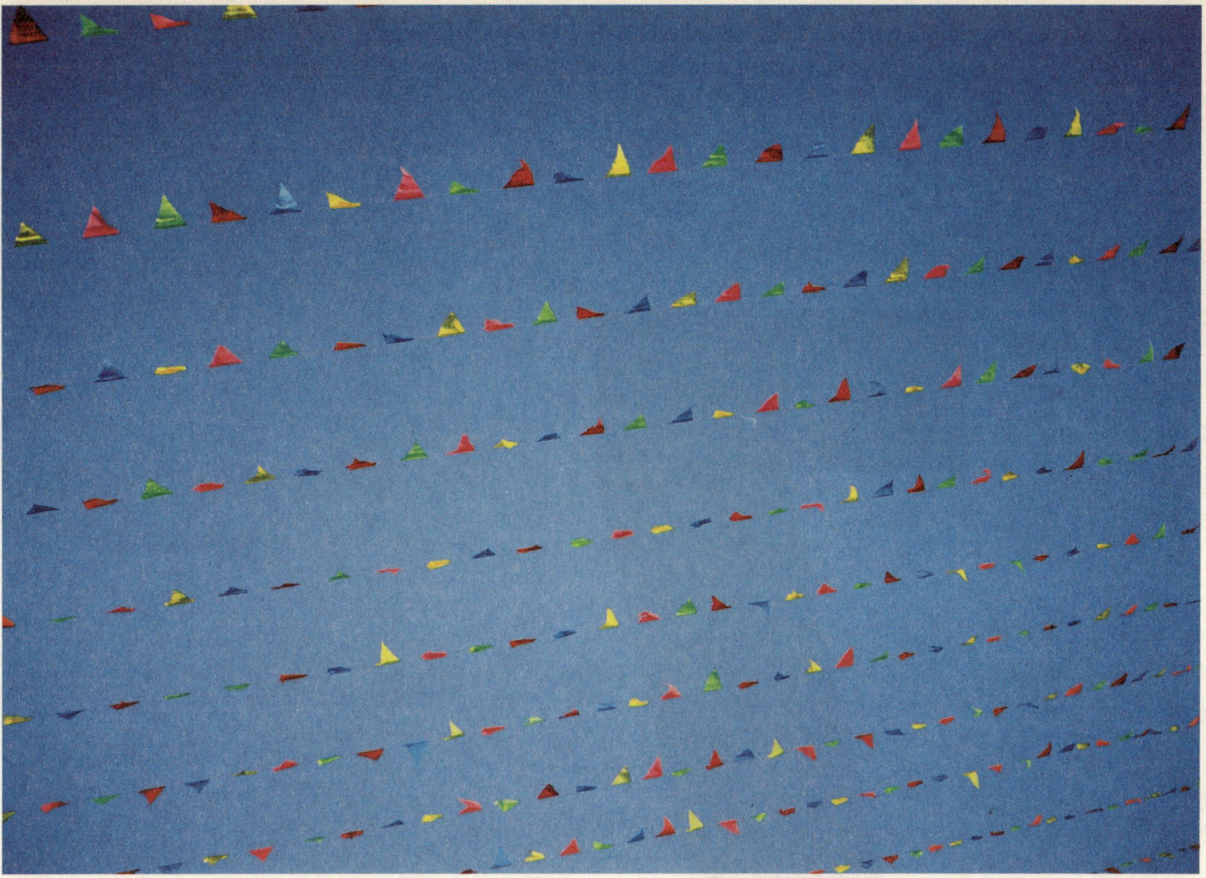
1.

Chu Yun lives in Beijing, and currently works in Shenzhen and Beijing. His installation **Who Has Stolen Our Bodies II** (2003) is made up of different colored partially used bars of soap. **Constellation** (2006), an installation involving blinking lights and improperly working pieces of electronic equipment (a fax machine and a washing machine among them), disrupts the traditional usefulness of the appliances by incorporating them into the artwork.

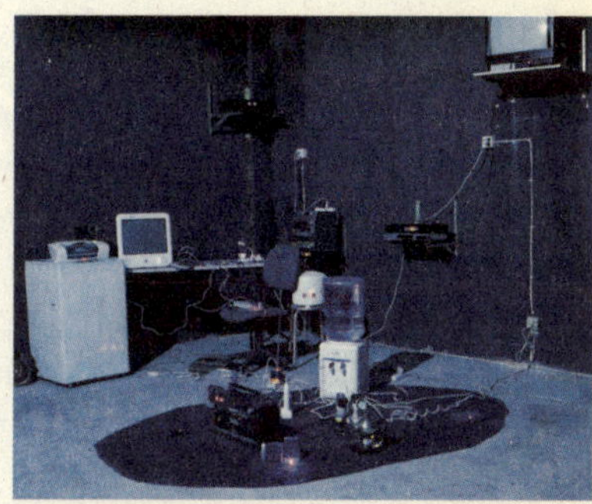
3.

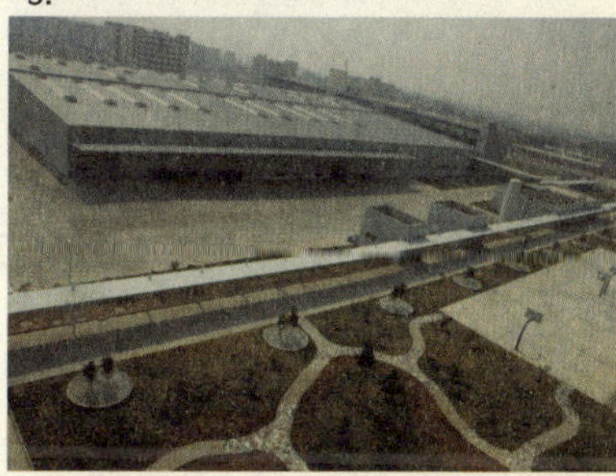
4.

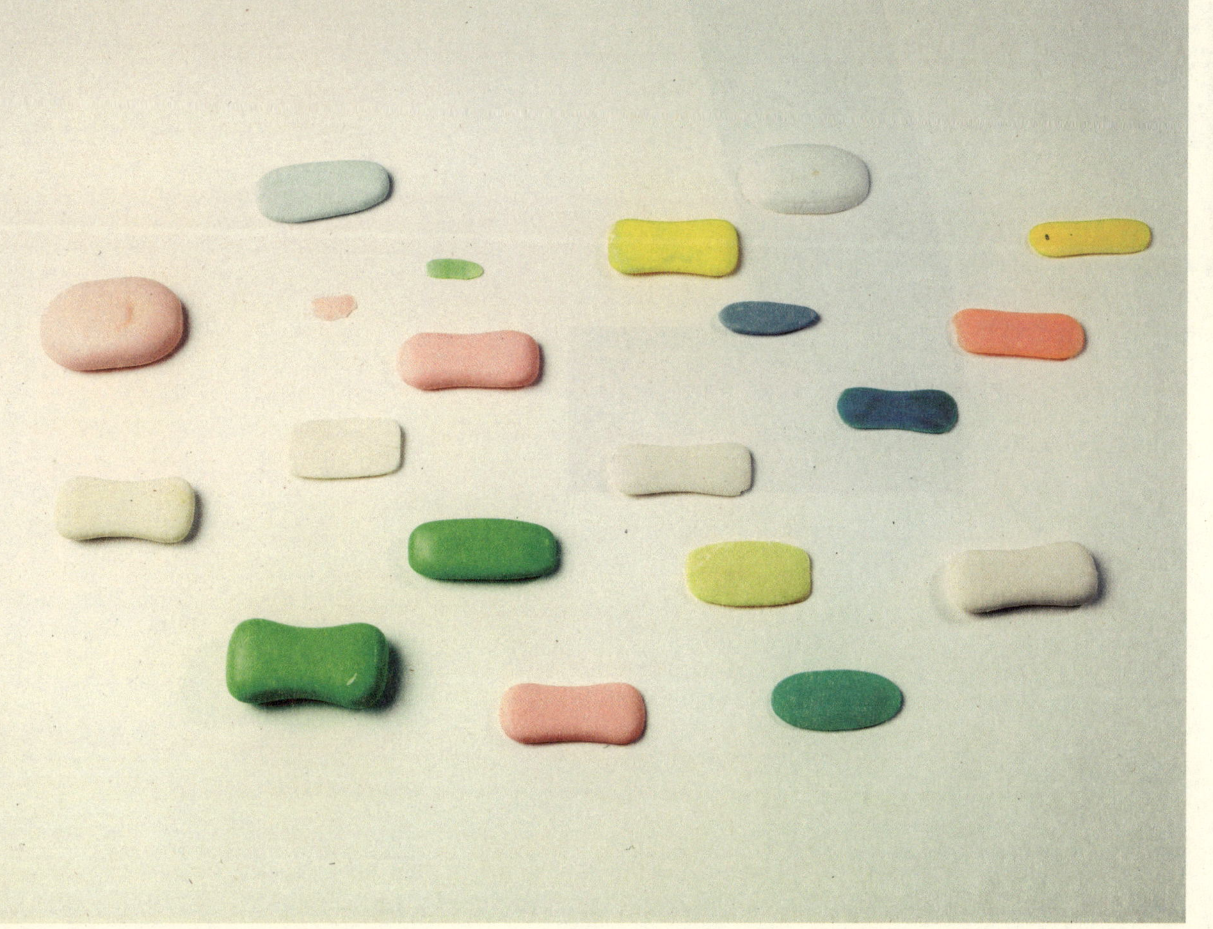
2.

1. **Unspeakable Happiness II**
2003, colored flags, dimensions variable

2. **Who Has Stolen Our Bodies II**
2003, soap, dimensions variable

3. **Constellation II**
2006, electrical appliances, dimensions variable

4. **Love**
2005, oaks, dimensions variable

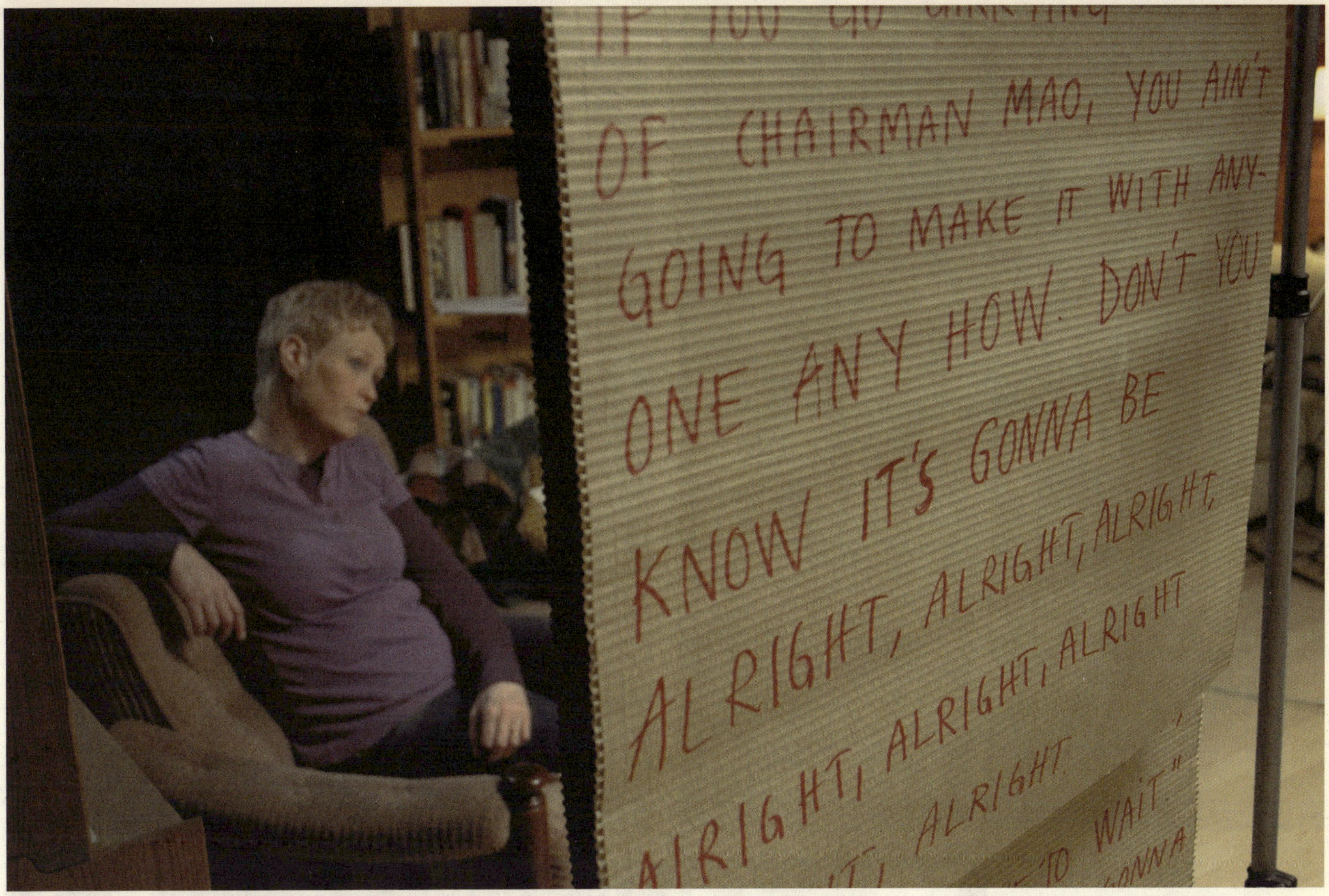

1.

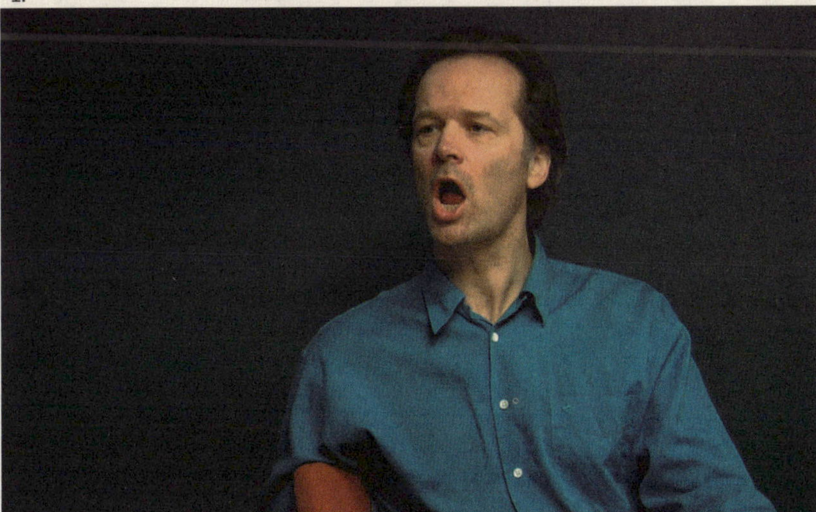

2.

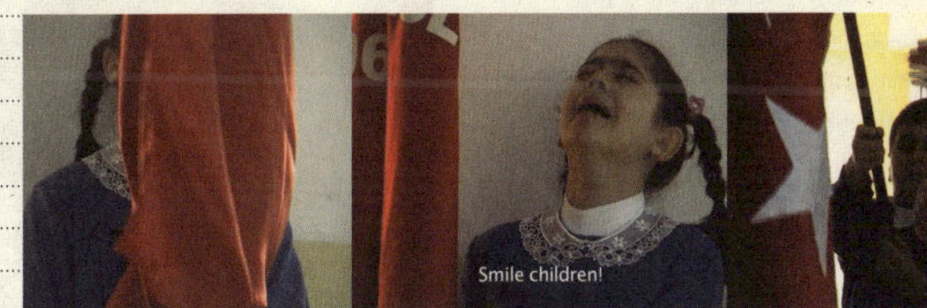

3.

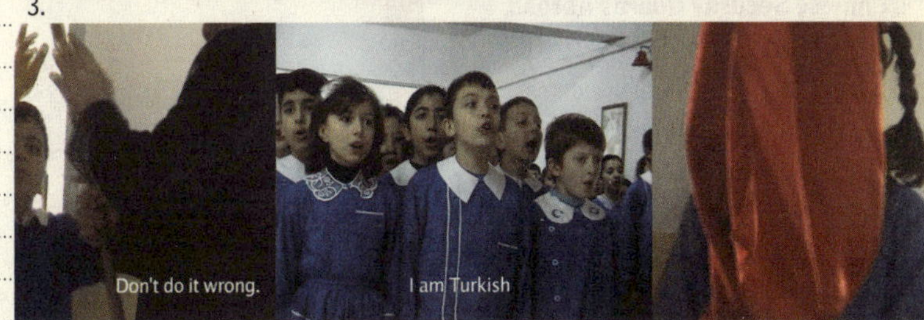

4.

Katarina Zdjelar graduated from the University of Arts in Belgrade and received an MFA from the Piet Zwart Institute of the Willem de Kooning Academie in Rotterdam, The Netherlands, where she lives and works. Her audiovisual works focus on the performative powers of speech. Her 2007 piece **A Girl, the Sun, and an Airplane Airplane** focused on the loss of language; she invited people from post-Communist Albania to pronounce words in Russian that are being replaced by other international languages. Her sound piece **Say gh Say ch** (2007) records the attempts of a couple from different backgrounds to pronounce typical sounds of the other's language.

1 & 2. **Everything is Gonna Be**
2008, video, 3 min 35 sec

3 & 4. **Don't Do It Wrong**
2007, video, 10 min 13 sec

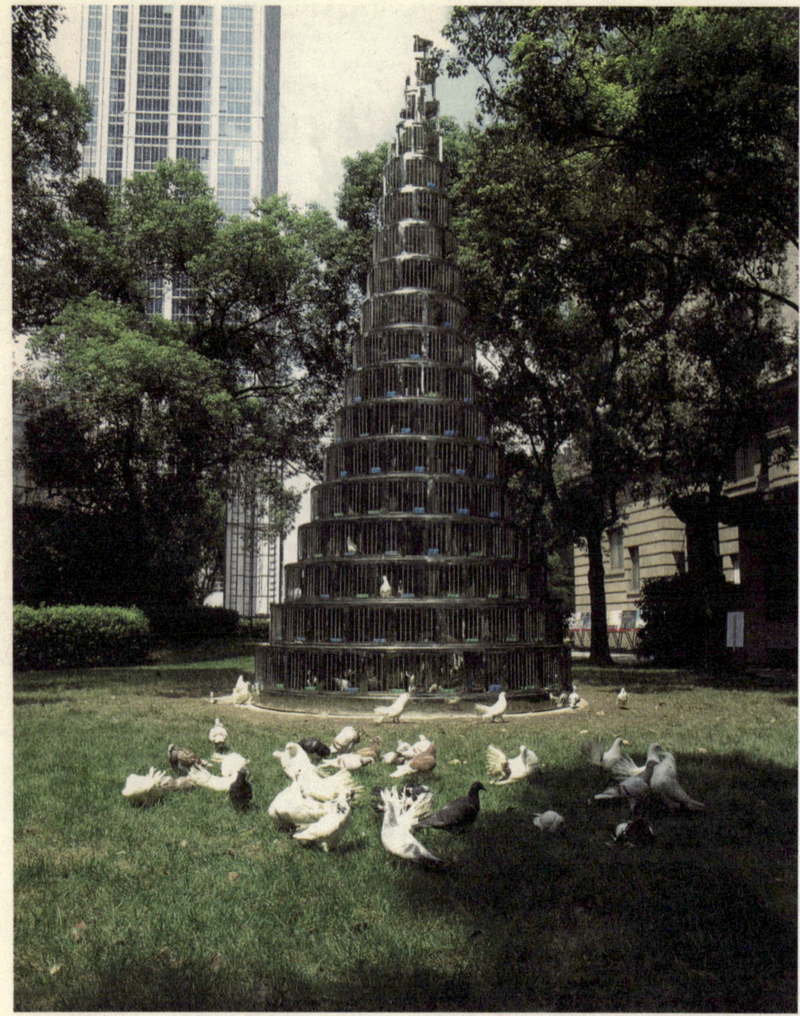

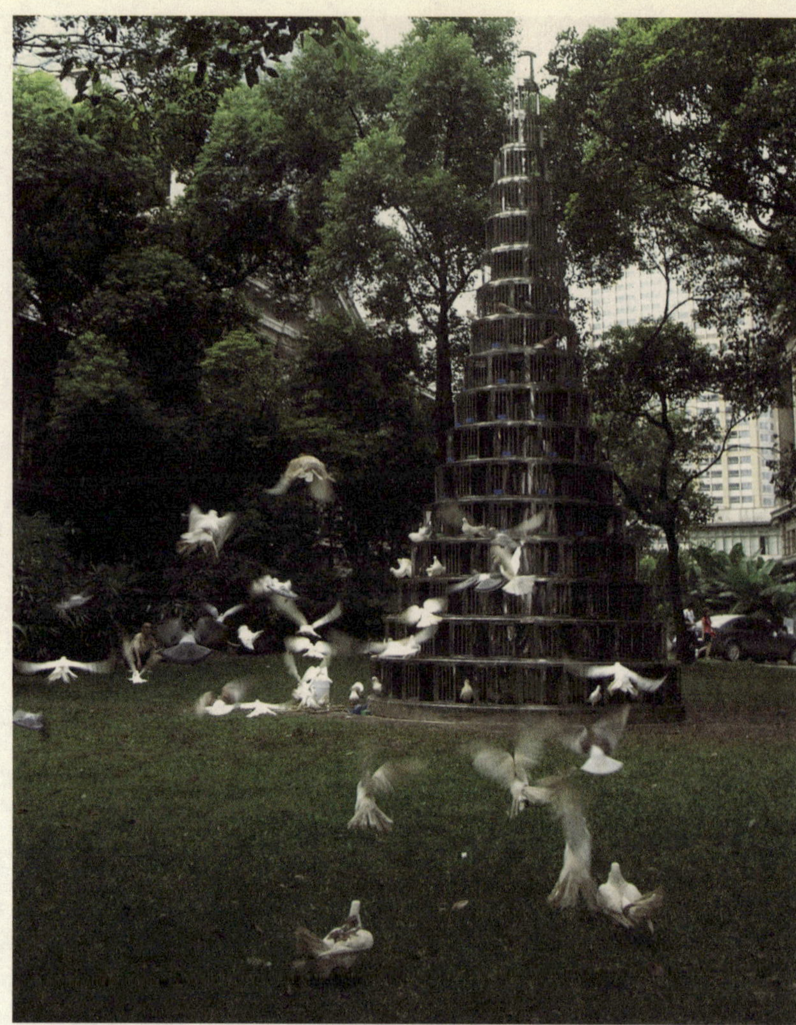

1.

Zhang Qing attended the Changzhou Institute of Technology, and since graduating has exhibited his work across China and in Germany. He works in video, installation, and performance to illuminate the contrast between the individual and society. In the **Football Field** series, a team plays a full-scale match in the confines of a small apartment, while in **Chinese Security Guards Abroad**, Qing sends Chinese guards to watch over entrances at different locations across the world. In 2004, Qing was nominated for a Contemporary Chinese Art Award.

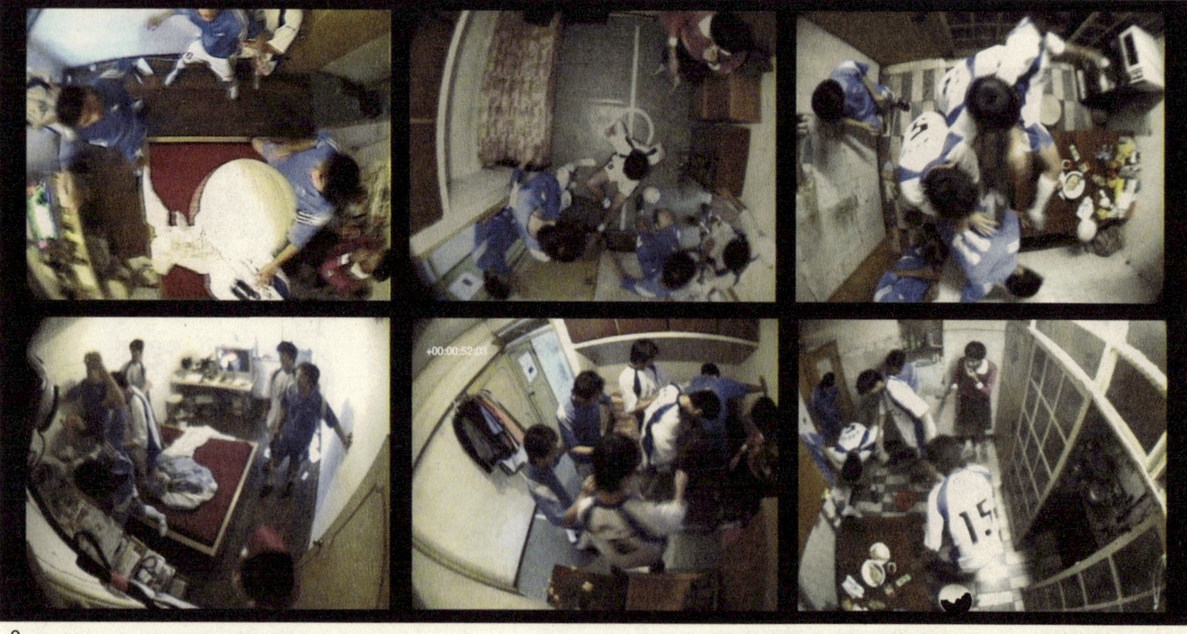

2.

1. Babel

2008, installation, stainless steel and pigeons, 289 × 136 in (735 × 346 cm)

2. Football Field No. 603

2006, 6-channel video

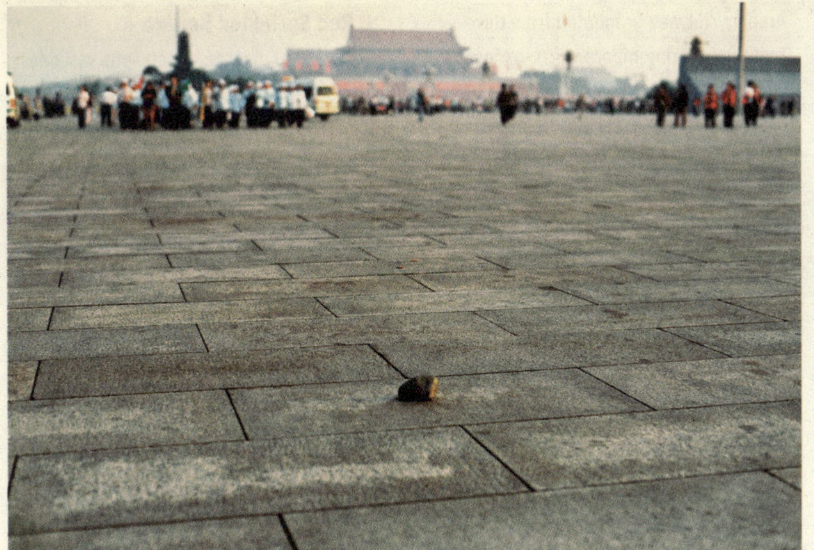
1.

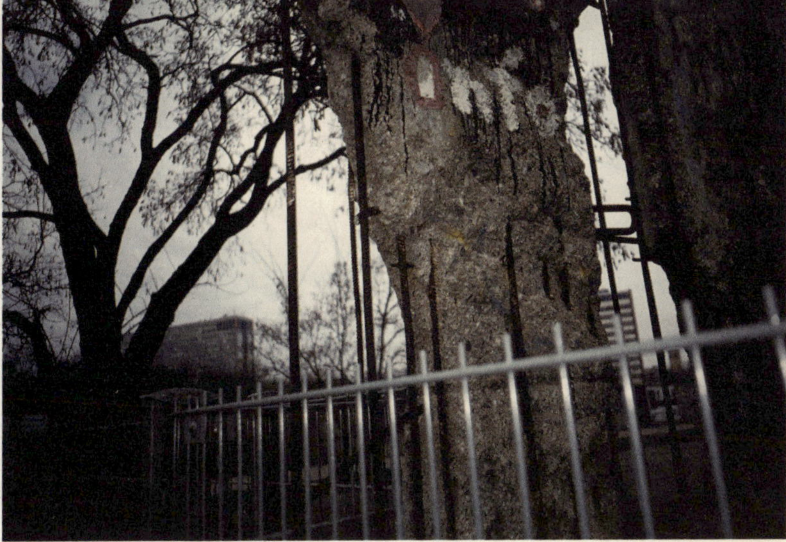
2.

Zhao Zhao graduated from the Xinjiang Academy of Fine Arts and lives and works in Beijing. His videos, performance works, and sculptures engage with politics and recent history and art history. In **Needle,** (2008), a project he estimates will take six years, the artist grinds a needle using a steel bar sawn from the Berlin Wall. **Euro** (2008) is a set of eight euro coins made of lead sheath taken from Anselm Kiefer's artwork Volkzahlung 1991.

1. **Cobblestone**
2007, color photograph, 31 ½ × 47 ¼ in (80 × 120 cm)

2. **Needle**
2008-present, ongoing performance in Berlin and Beijing

3 & 4. **On Tianshan**
2007, color photograph, 71 × 98 in (180 × 250 cm)

5. **Hair**
2007-08, artist's hair, dimensions variable

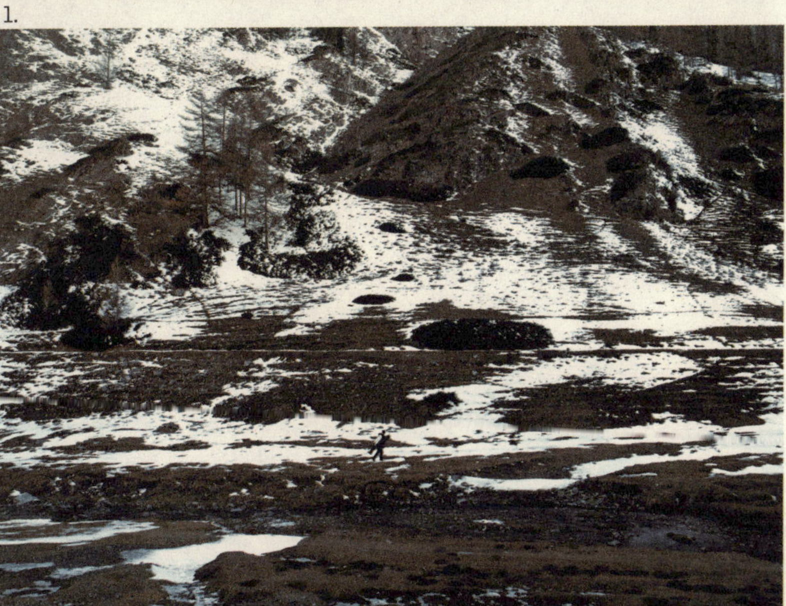
3.

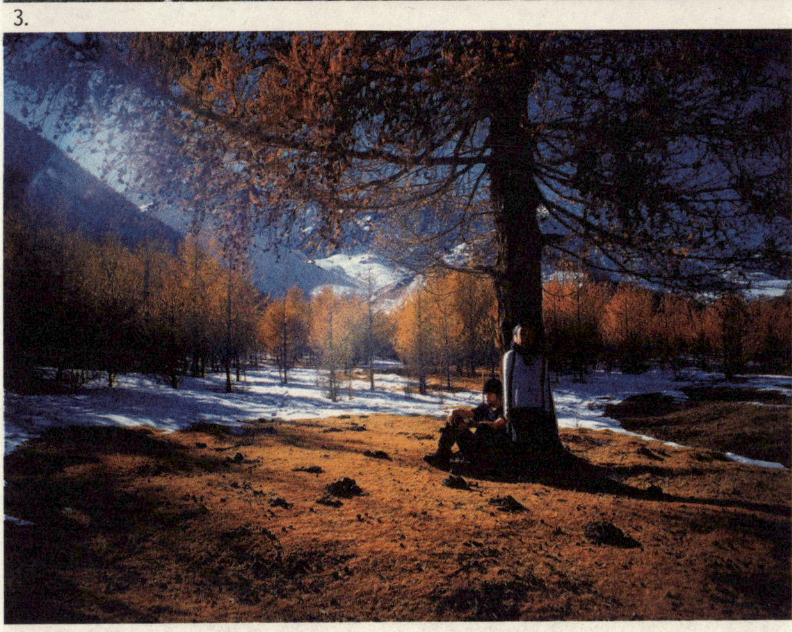
4.

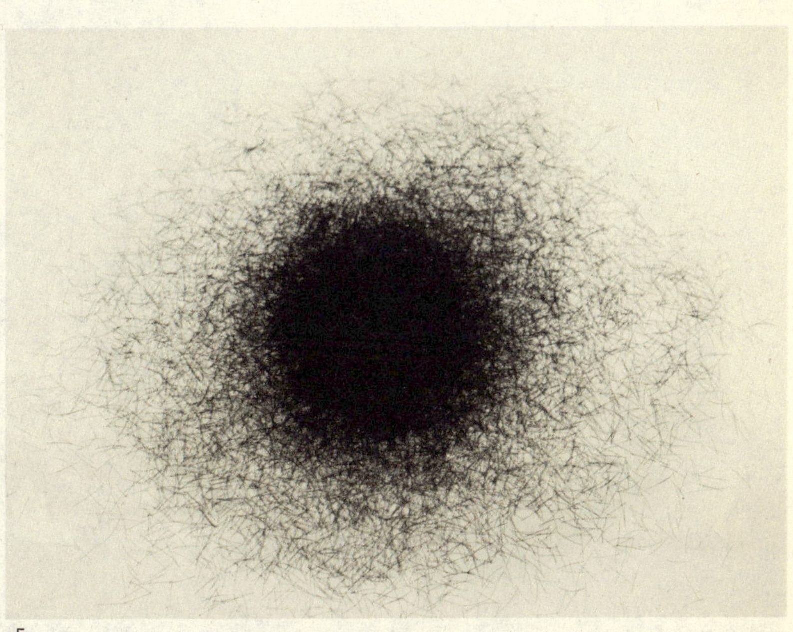
5.

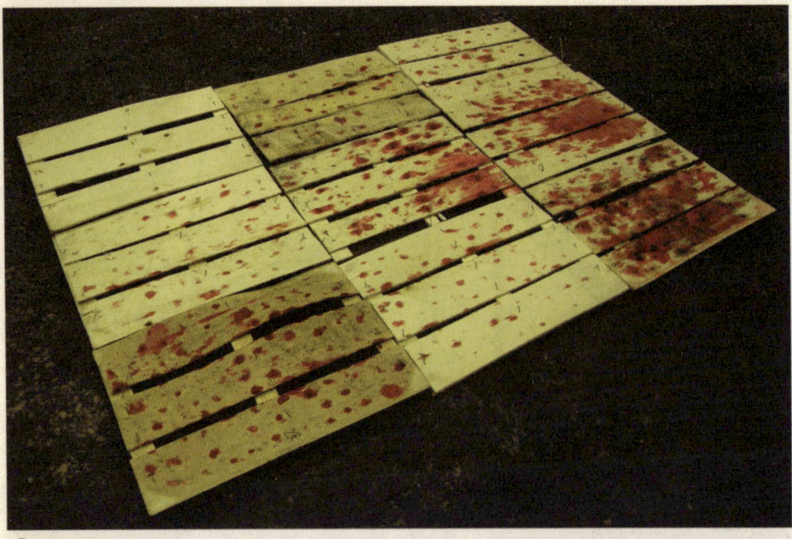
1.

Arseniy Zhilyaev graduated from the Institute of Contemporary Art in Moscow, where he currently lives and works. His drawings, paintings, sculptures, and installations incorporate principles of geometry and the symbiotic relationship between space and social interactions.

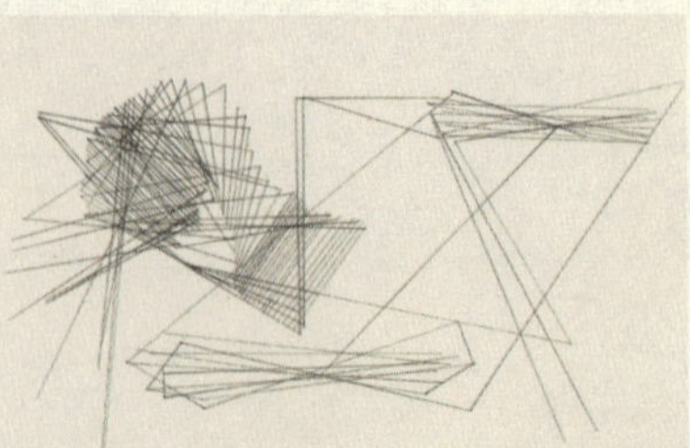
2.

1. **Red Sprinkled Square**
2007, found objects, dimensions variable

2. **Untitled**
from the series **Labour Movement**
2006, pencil on paper, 6 × 8 1/4 in
(15 × 21 cm)

3. **Longing for Impossible**
2007, found objects, table, wooden boxes, and drawings, dimensions variable

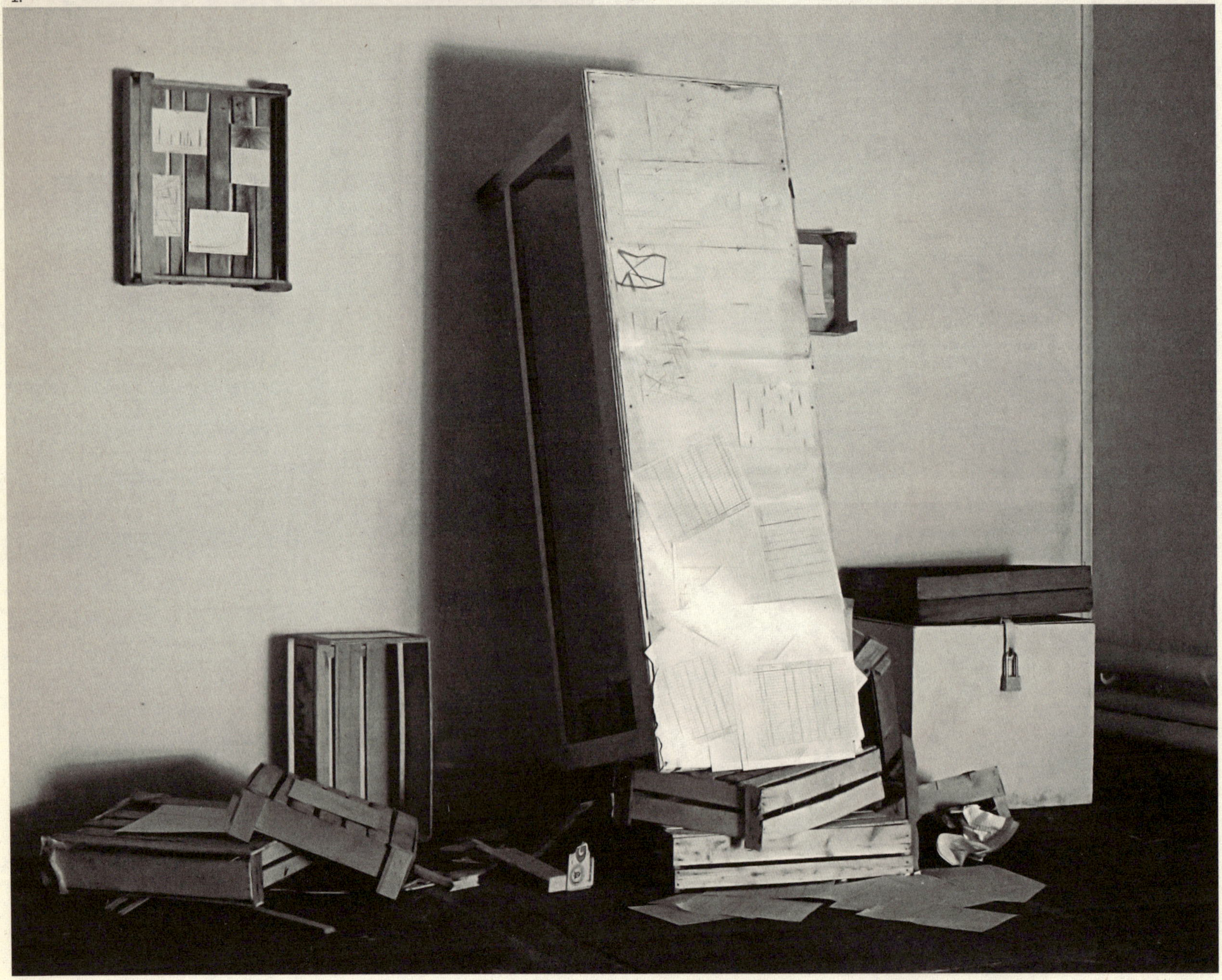

3.

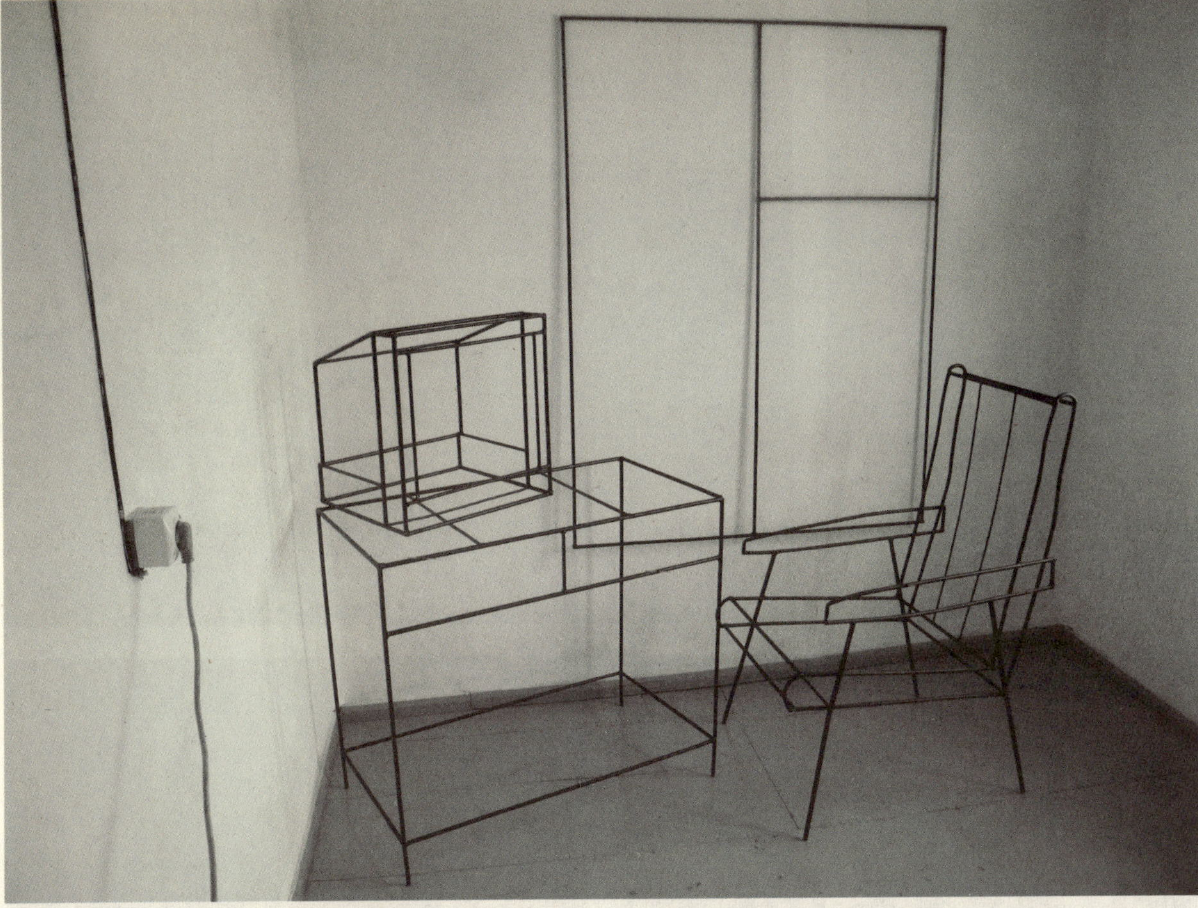
1.

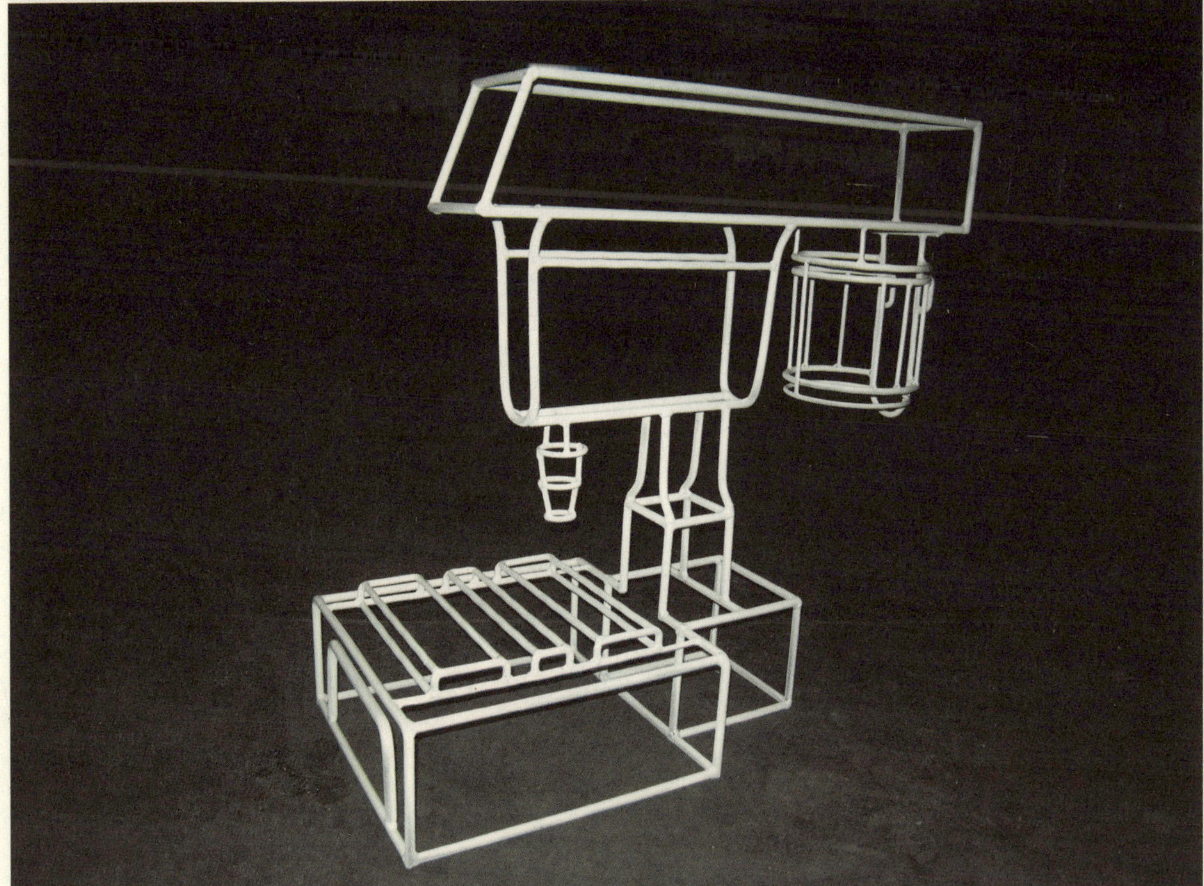
2.

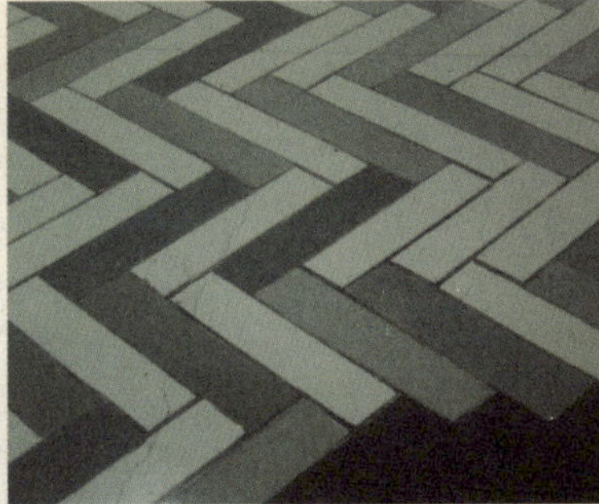
3.

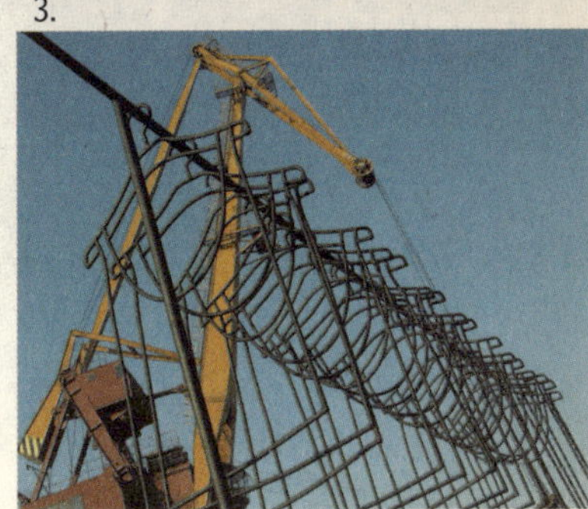
4.

Anya Zholud's paintings and sculptures focus on everyday items, including furniture, clothing, kitchen utensils, and teapots. Her installation **Things for Love** (2007) features paintings and sculptures of teapots, milk jugs, colanders, and an abacus, among other things. **Scheme of the Space** (2007) is a metal installation of the schematic outlines of a table and chair with a computer and a window.

1. **Scheme of the space**
2007, metal, 78 ¾ × 78 ¾ × 59 in (200 × 200 × 150 cm)

2. **Machine**
2008, metal, 27 ½ × 15 ¾ × 23 ½ in (70 × 40 × 60 cm)

3. **Museum of me** (detail)
2007, concrete and oil, 32 ½ × 32 ½ ft (10 × 10 m)

4. **Light Industry** (detail)
2008, metal, 51 × 78 ¾ in (130 × 200 cm)

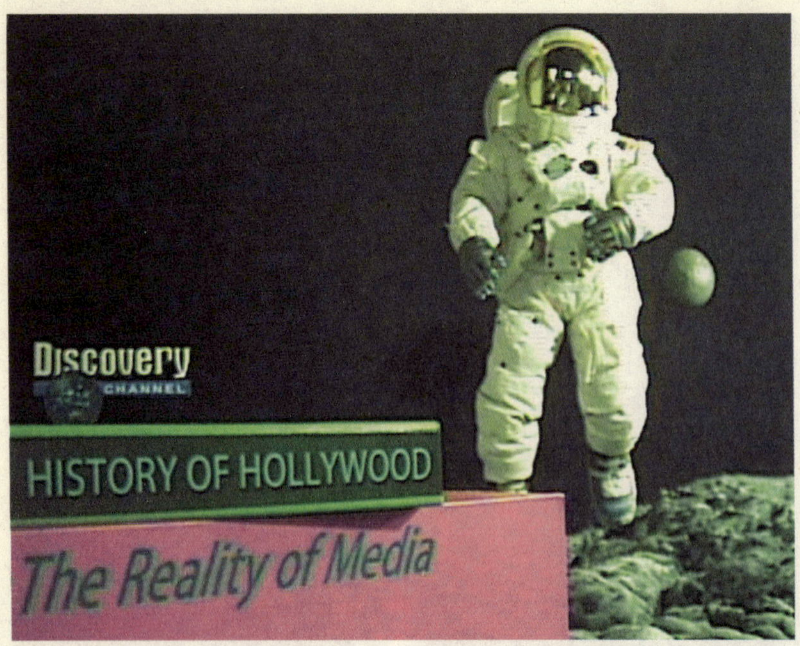

1.

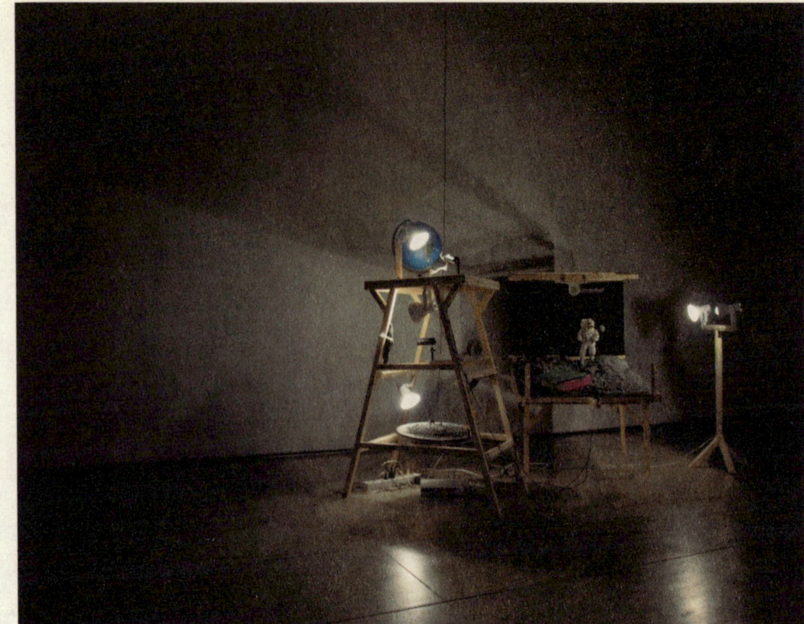

2.

Kijong Zin graduated from Kyungwan University in Korea and lives and works in Seoul. His video installations and photographs draw on television channels like CNN and the Discovery Channel, using fabricated imagery to explore the social implications of digital technology.

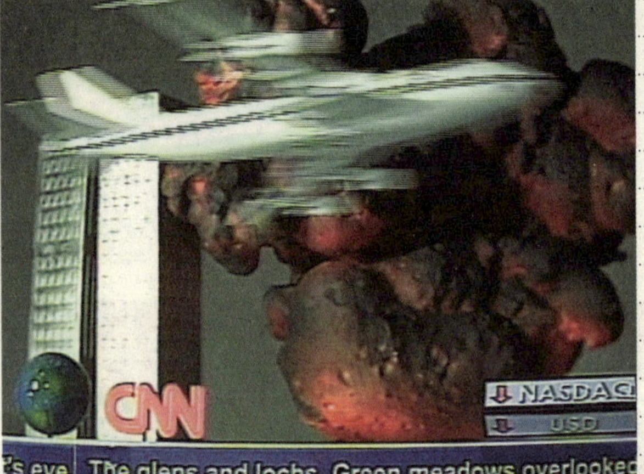

3.

4.

5.

6.

1 & 2. Discovery
2007, 4-channel real-time video, CCTV camera, and LCD monitor, dimensions variable

3 & 4. CNN
2007, 4-channel real-time video, CCTV camera, and LCD monitor, dimensions variable

5. Asian Tiger
2007, color photograph on super glossy paper, 26 × 39 $\frac{1}{2}$ in (66 × 100 cm)

6. National Geographic
2007, 4-channel real-time video, CCTV camera, and LCD monitor, dimensions variable

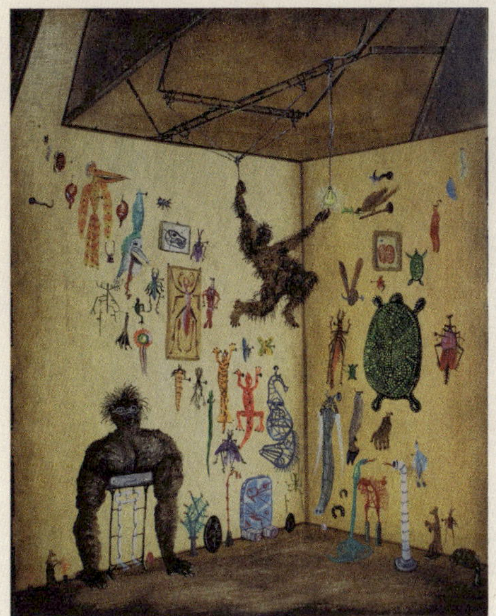
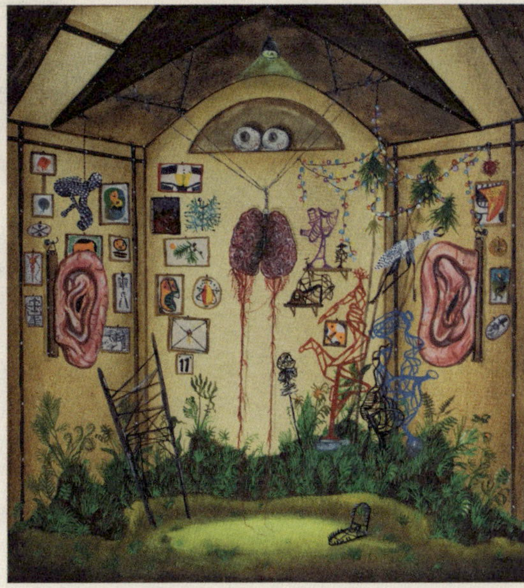
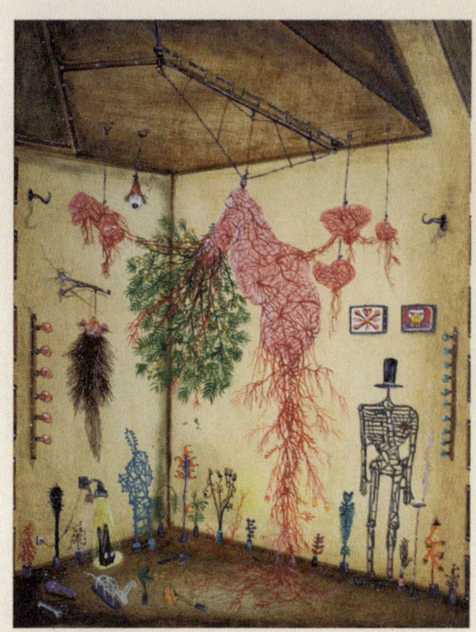

1.

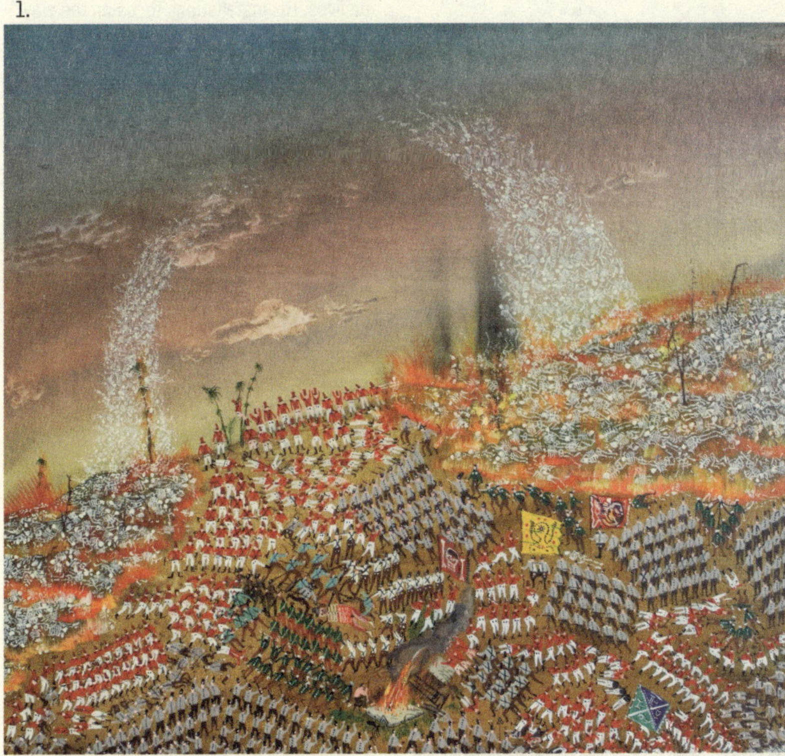

2.

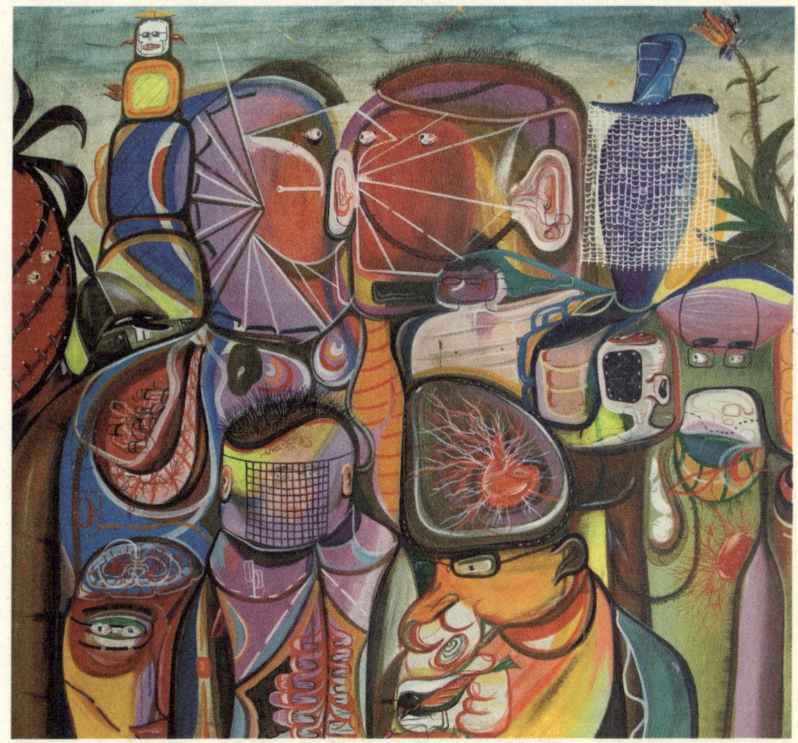

3.

Jakub Julian Ziolkowski studied at the Jan Matejko Academy of Fine Arts in Kraków, where he lives and works. His oil paintings, which reference Philip Guston as well as modernist abstraction, are both irreverent and graphically sophisticated. A familiar cast of characters populates his paintings, including plants, skeletons, viscera, serpents, and other creatures, many of which are seen in an untitled three-panel 2008 oil-on-board painting, and in his 2008 painting **Sculpture**.

1. Untitled
2008, oil on board, 3 panels: 12 3/4 × 10 in (33 × 26 cm); 12 1/2 × 11 3/4 in (32 × 30 cm); and 12 1/2 × 9 3/4 in (32 × 25 cm)

2. Rainbow
2008, oil on canvas, 22 1/2 × 25 1/2 in (58 × 65 cm)

3. My Friends
2008, oil on canvas, 51 × 55 in (130 × 140 cm)

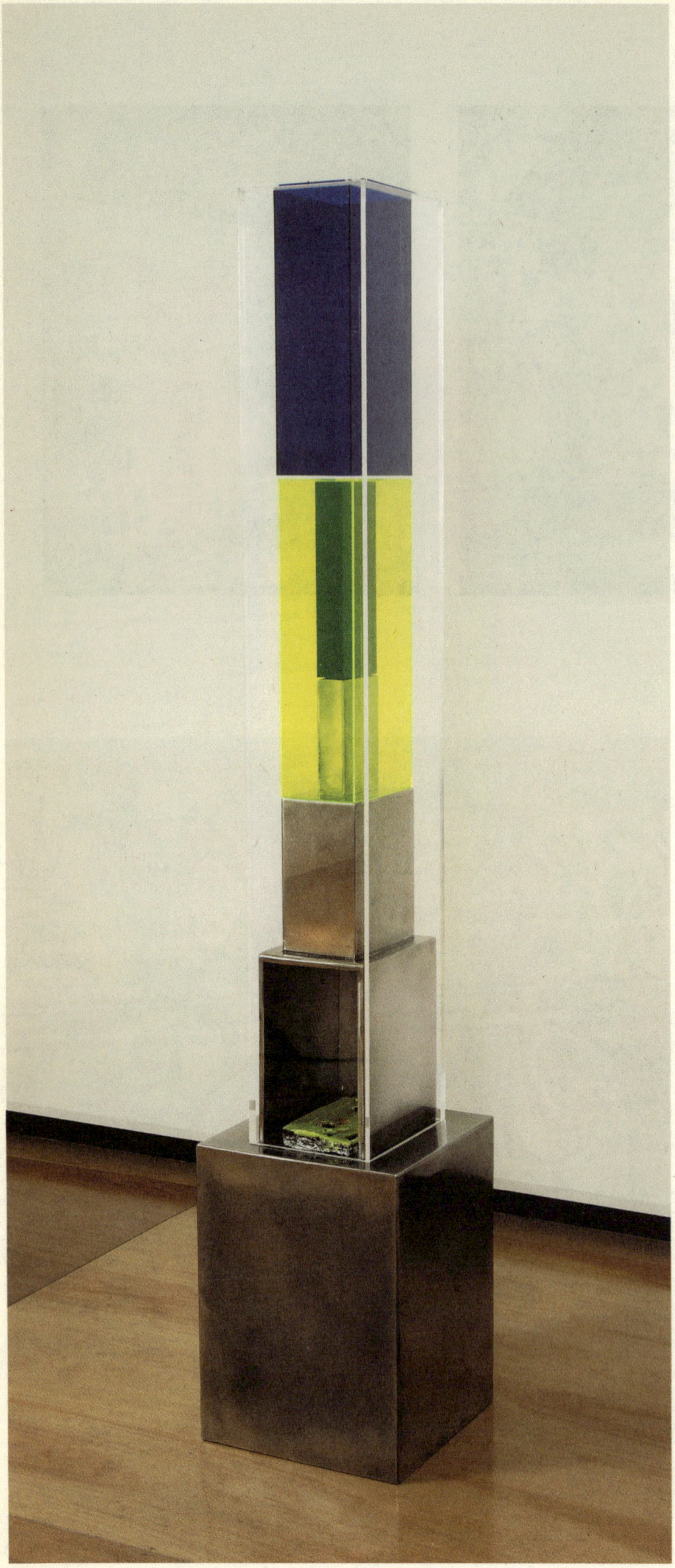

1.

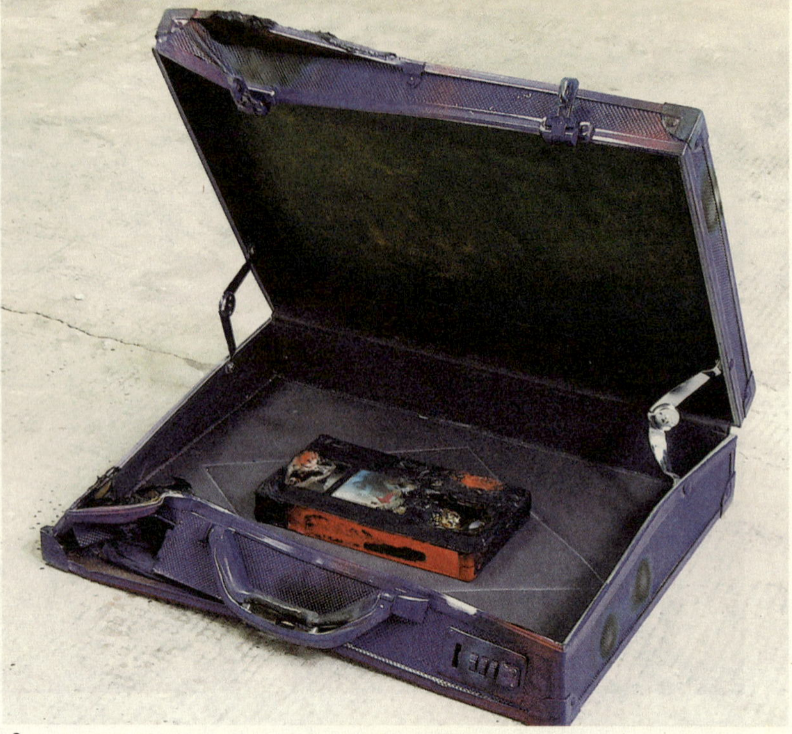

2.

3.

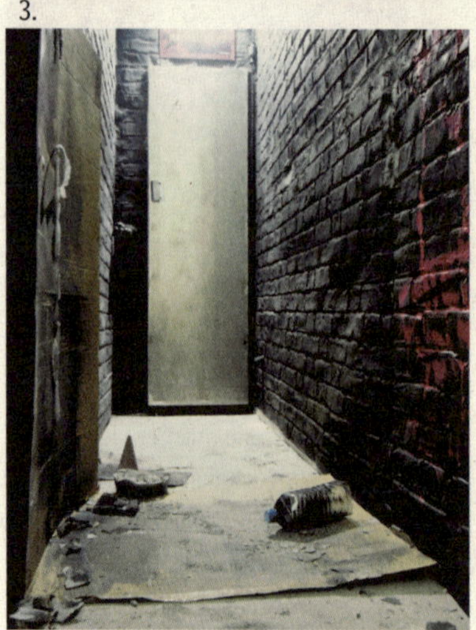

4.

Maximilian Zentz Zlomovitz attended the Universität der Künste in Berlin, where he lives. His installations focus on the way objects relate to one another in a particular space and scenarios and objects become signifiers of a person's world. In his exhibition "Waiting for Maleism", he displayed a range of objects commonly associated with men. In **Relaxx** (2008) he laid red plastic flooring down, marking out a domestic space, on which he installed an office chair, a yoga mat, and a fire extinguisher, signifiers of a male identity that the artist sees trapped in stereotype.

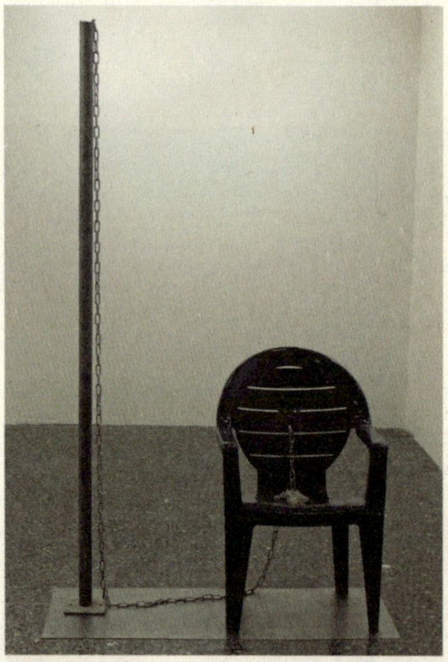

1. Express
2008, steel, acrylic glass, and wax,
67 × 11 3/4 × 11 3/4 in (170 cm × 30 × 30 cm)

2. Channel
2008, metal and plastic,
78 3/4 × 27 1/2 × 11 3/4 in (200 × 70 × 30 cm)

3. Chinese Restaurant
2006, steel, paint, cement, wood, aluminum, plastic, cardboard, paper, acrylic, graphite, shellac, pigments, and lightbulb, dimensions variable

4. metavideo
2007, aluminum suitcase, plastic, and spray paint, 11 × 18 × 16 in (28 × 45 × 41 cm)

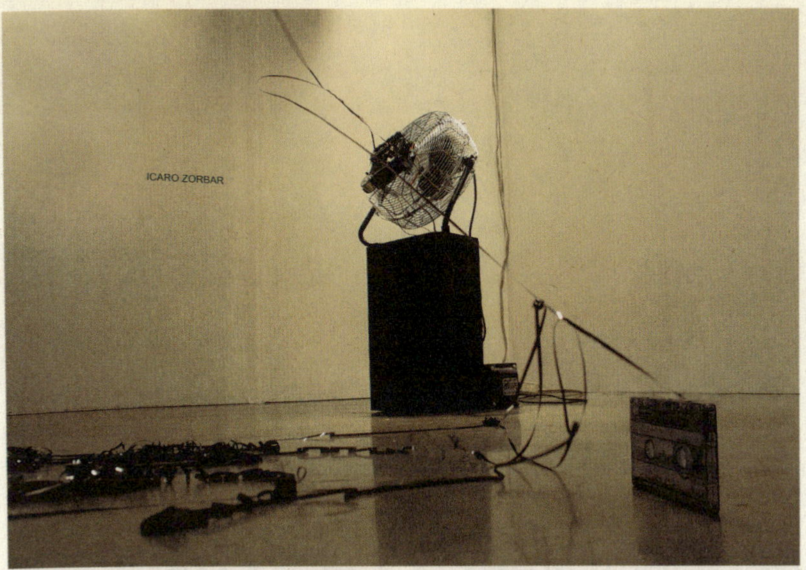

1.

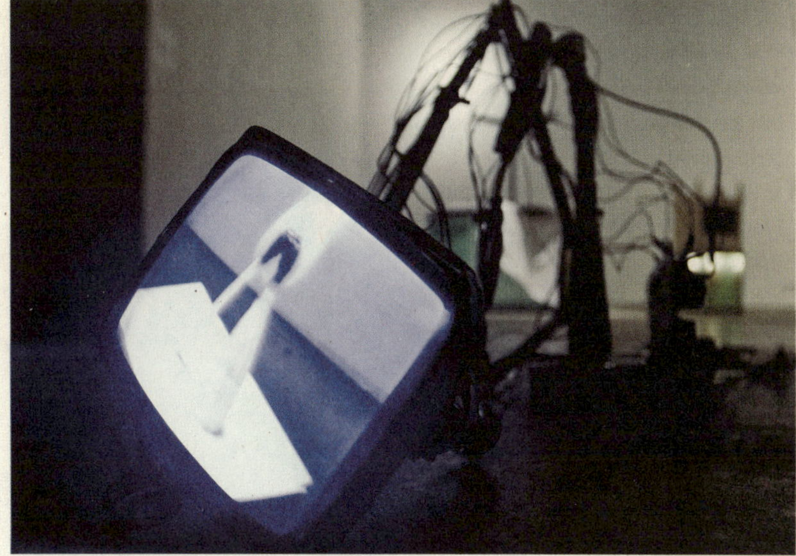

2.

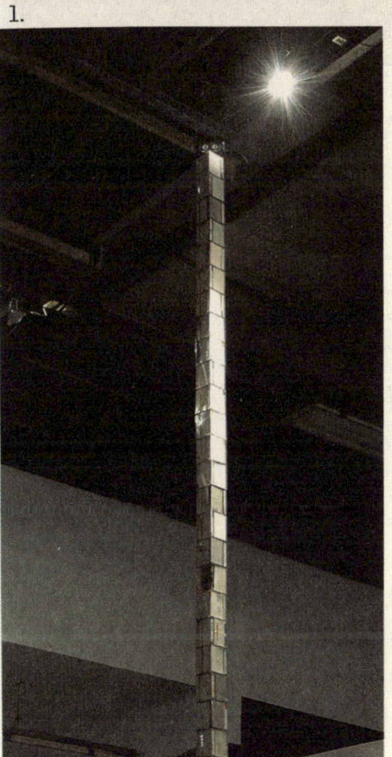

3.

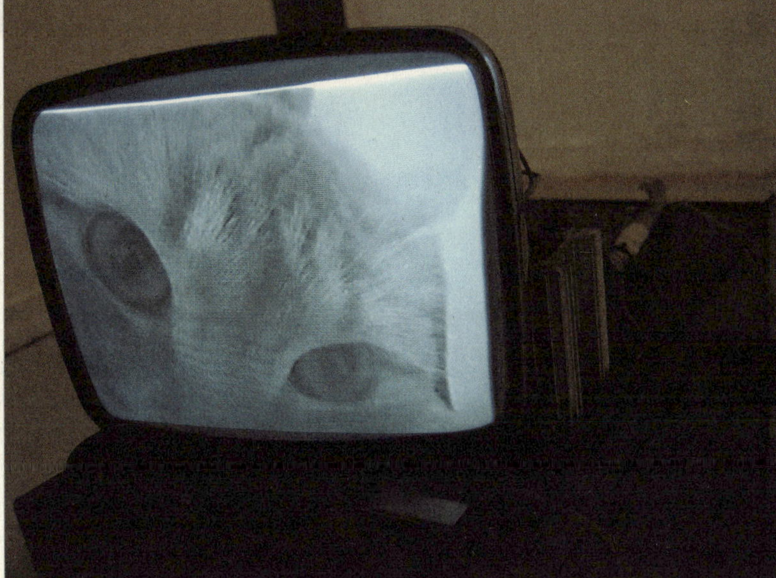

4.

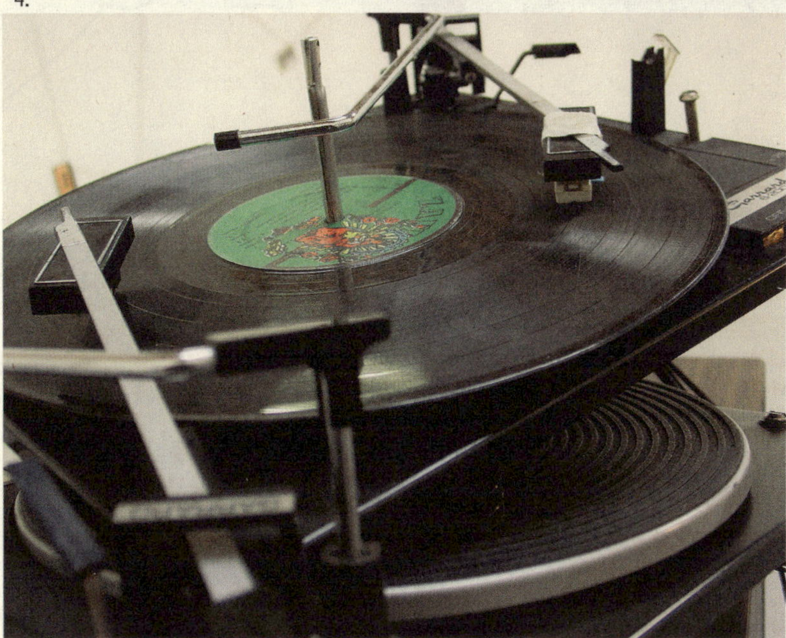

5.

Icaro Zorbar lives and works in Bogotá, Colombia. He holds an MFA from the Universidad Nacional de Colombia. He incorporates various machines, such as tape recorders, fans, record players, and music boxes, into his installations, working with what he calls "disillusionment in the face of technological reality."

1. ventila dor
2007, speaker, ventilator, tape player, and audiocassette, 47 × 24 × 60 in (119 × 61 × 152 cm)

2. te extraño: los solistas/i miss you: the soloists
2008, metallic structures, black and white monitors, and video, dimensions variable

3. nadie/nobody
2005, Walkman, broken audiocassettes, and audiocassette cases, dimensions variable

4. nuestra mascota/our pet
2005, television, 8 × 8 × 10 in (20 × 20 × 25 cm); video, 2 min

5. poco a poco/little by little
2006, 2 turntables, record, and amplifiers, 43 × 27 × 17 in (109 × 68 × 43 cm)

Damon Zucconi lives and works in New York. He graduated in 2007 with a BFA in interdisciplinary sculpture from the Maryland Institute College of Art. His installations, performances, and Web projects, such as **Flags Tethered to the Edge of the Frame** (2008), in which sheets of blue, yellow, and red flags appear to wave in a breeze, combining into different colors as they overlap, explore the various and unexpected ways of producing visual information.

1. **/ **
2008, altered found poster,
dimensions variable

2. **SEASON FOUR**
2008, digital image

3. **Attributing Value (Refractions) (from Bruce Nauman – 100 Live, 100 Die)**
2006-07, video

4. **The Arpa Network, Dec 1969; 4 Nodes**
2006, oil and enamel on panel,
33 ½ × 28 in (85 × 71 cm)

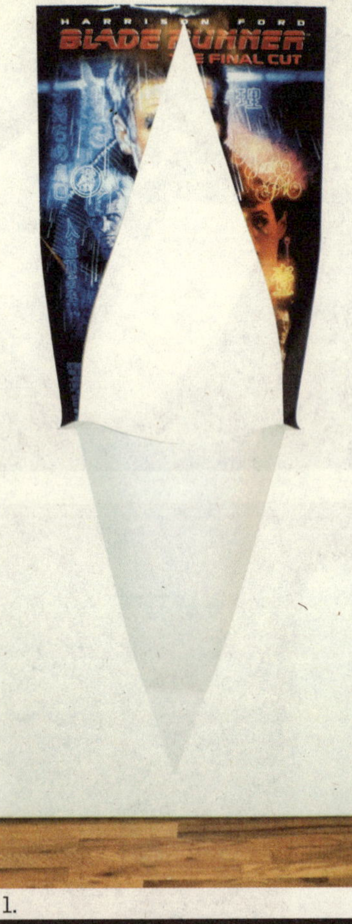

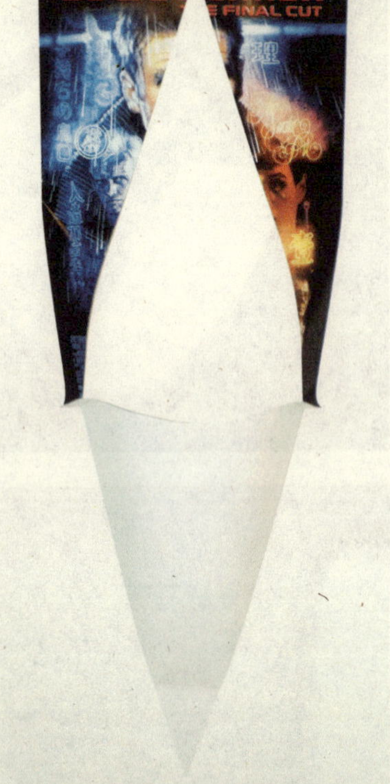

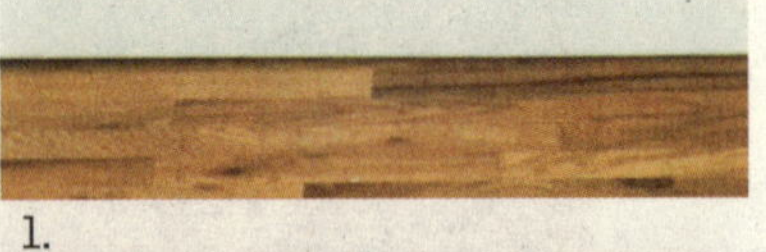

1.

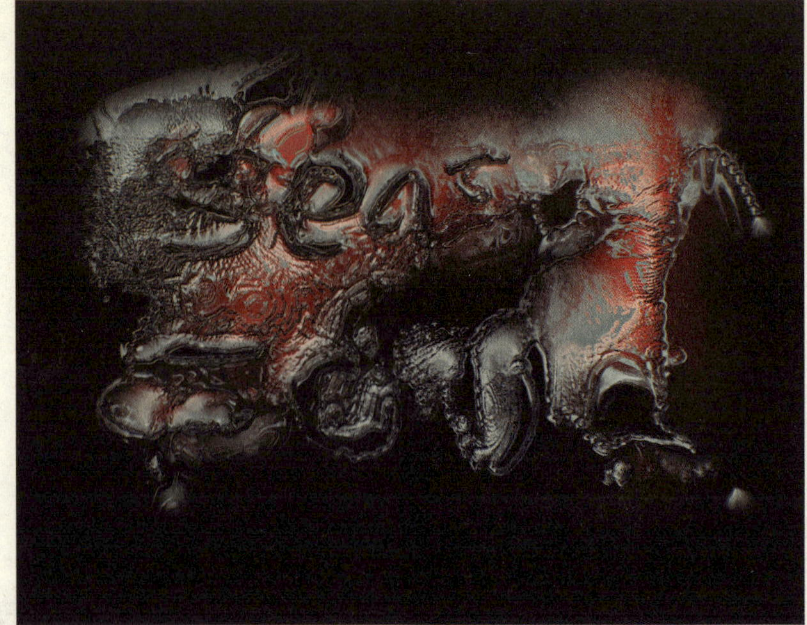

2.

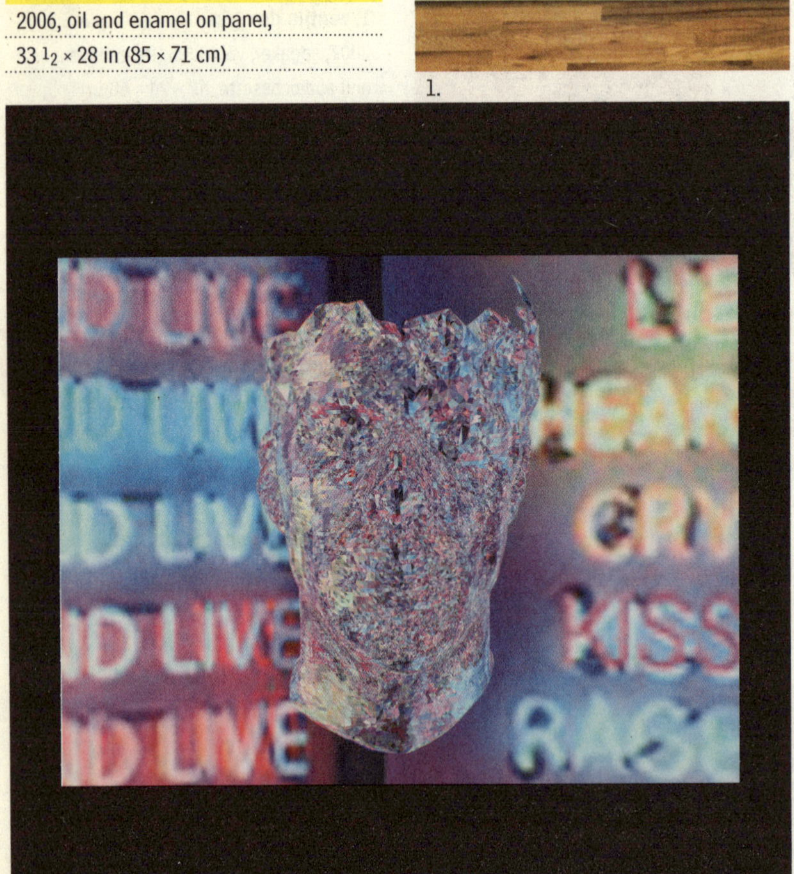

3.

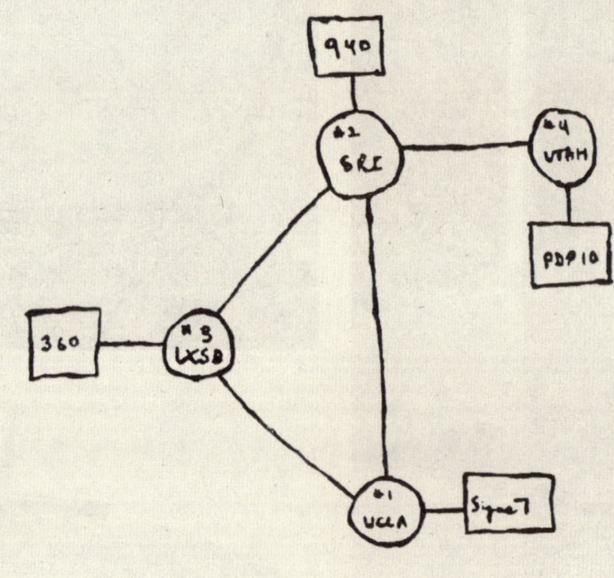

4.